U.S. Inflation Rate Since
1955 (rate of change for
CPI and PPI)

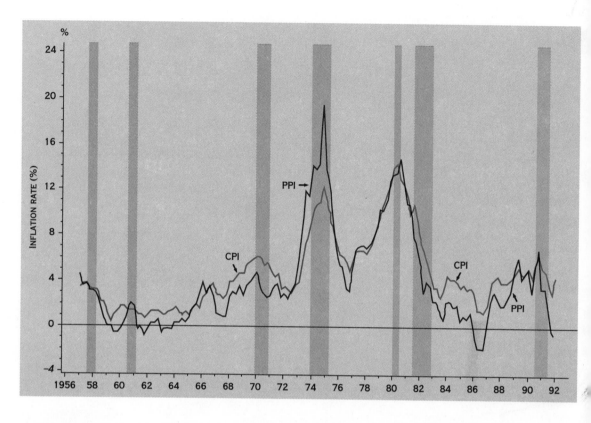

U.S. Deficits in Trade,
Goods and Services, and
Current Accounts,
1982–1991

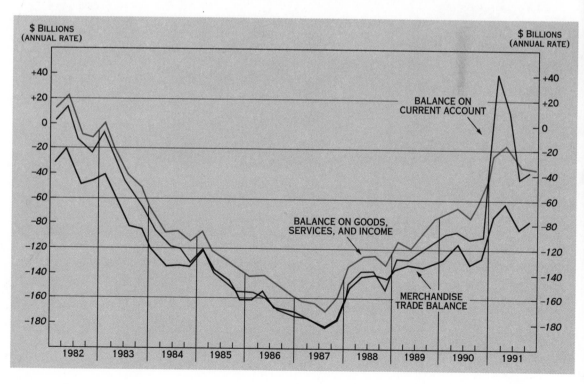

PRINCIPLES
OF ECONOMICS

JAMES F. RAGAN, JR.
KANSAS STATE UNIVERSITY

LLOYD B. THOMAS, JR.
KANSAS STATE UNIVERSITY

THE DRYDEN PRESS

HARCOURT BRACE JOVANOVICH COLLEGE PUBLISHERS

FORT WORTH   PHILADELPHIA   SAN DIEGO   NEW YORK   ORLANDO   AUSTIN   SAN ANTONIO
TORONTO   MONTREAL   LONDON   SYDNEY   TOKYO

EDITOR IN CHIEF	ROBERT A. PAWLIK
ACQUISITIONS EDITOR	RICK HAMMONDS
DEVELOPMENTAL EDITOR	RUTH ROMINGER
PROJECT EDITOR	JON GREGORY
ASSISTANT PROJECT EDITOR	MATT BALL
PRODUCTION MANAGER	ALISON HOWELL
DESIGNER	LINDA WOOTON MILLER
PHOTO/PERMISSIONS EDITOR	SHIRLEY WEBSTER, VAN STRENGTH
COPY EDITOR	LEON UNRUH

Cover collage: Copyright © 1992 Rick Smith Illustration

Copyright © 1993 by Harcourt Brace Jovanovich, Inc.

All rights reserved. No part of this publication may be reproduced or transmitted in any form or by any means, electronic or mechanical, including photocopy, recording, or any information storage and retrieval system, without permission in writing from the publisher.

Requests for permission to make copies of any part of the work should be mailed to: Permissions Department, Harcourt Brace Jovanovich, Publishers, 8th Floor, Orlando, Florida 32887

Permissions acknowledgments and photo credits appear on pages 1125-1126, which constitute a continuation of the copyright page.

Address for Editorial Correspondence
The Dryden Press, 301 Commerce Street, Suite 3700, Fort Worth, TX 76102

Address for Orders
The Dryden Press, 6277 Sea Harbor Drive, Orlando, FL 32887
1-800-782-4479, or 1-800-433-0001 (in Florida)

ISBN: 0-03-096632-9

Library of Congress Catalogue Number: 92-081302

Printed in the United States of America

3 4 5 6 069 9 8 7 6 5 4 3 2 1

The Dryden Press
Harcourt Brace Jovanovich

FOR MY WIFE, GAIL, WHOM I GREATLY LOVE AND ADMIRE,
AND FOR MY PARENTS, HELEN AND JIM, WHO PROVIDED
SUPPORT, LOVE, AND ENCOURAGEMENT.

JAMES F. RAGAN, JR.

———

FOR SALLY—WHOSE LOVE, ABSOLUTE GENEROSITY, AND
INDOMITABLE SPIRIT SUSTAINED THE INSPIRATION THAT
MADE THIS BOOK POSSIBLE.

LLOYD B. THOMAS, JR.

JAMES F. RAGAN, JR., is Professor of Economics and Department Head at Kansas State University. Prior to joining the faculty there, he worked as a research economist for the Federal Reserve Bank of New York. He has also been a visiting scholar at the Federal Reserve Bank of Kansas City and a visiting associate professor at Washington University. He earned a B.A. in economics from the University of Missouri in 1971 and a Ph.D. in economics from Washington University (St. Louis) in 1975.

Professor Ragan has published in such journals as *Review of Economics and Statistics, Economic Inquiry, Journal of Human Resources,* and *Southern Economic Journal.* He has presented papers before numerous groups, including the National Commission on Youth, the Conference on U.S. Productive Capacity, the National Commission for Employment Policy, and the American Enterprise Institute Conference on Legal Minimum Wages. His work has been cited in such publications as *The Wall Street Journal, Business Week,* and *U.S. News & World Report.*

Professor Ragan's special interests lie in labor economics, microeconomics, and public policy. He has taught principles of economics on a regular basis since 1977.

LLOYD B. THOMAS, JR., is Professor of Economics at Kansas State University. He earned a B.A. and an M.A. in economics from the University of Missouri in 1963 and 1964 and a Ph.D. from Northwestern University in 1970.

Professor Thomas has conducted extensive research within his academic interests—primarily the areas of macroeconomic policy and international finance—and has published in numerous economic journals. He is the author of a best-selling textbook entitled *Money, Banking, and Economic Activity* (Prentice-Hall, 1986), now in its third edition.

Recognized as an excellent teacher, Professor Thomas continues to make undergraduate instruction in principles of economics, money and banking, and intermediate economic theory an important focus of his professional career. He teaches graduate courses primarily in the areas of monetary theory and policy.

Professor Thomas has taught at Florida State University, Northwestern University, the University of California at Berkeley, the University of Delaware, and the University of Idaho.

The Dryden Press Series in Economics

KENNETT AND LIEBERMAN
The Road to Capitalism: The Economic Transformation of Eastern Europe and the Former Soviet Union

KIDWELL, PETERSON, AND BLACKWELL
Financial Institutions, Markets, and Money
Fifth Edition

KOHN
Money, Banking, and Financial Markets
Second Edition

KREININ
International Economics: A Policy Approach
Sixth Edition

LANDSBURG
Price Theory and Applications
Second Edition

LINK, MILLER, AND BERGMAN
EconoGraph II: Interactive Software for Principles of Economics

LOTT AND RAY
Applied Econometrics with Data Sets

NICHOLSON
Intermediate Microeconomics and Its Application
Fifth Edition

NICHOLSON
Microeconomic Theory: Basic Principles and Extensions
Fifth Edition

ORMISTON
Intermediate Microeconomics

OSER AND BRUE
The Evolution of Economic Thought
Fourth Edition

PUTH
American Economic History
Third Edition

RAGAN AND THOMAS
Principles of Economics
Second Edition (Also available in micro and macro paperbacks)

RAMANATHAN
Introductory Econometrics with Applications
Second Edition

RUKSTAD
Corporate Decision Making in the World Economy: Company Case Studies

RUKSTAD
Macroeconomic Decision Making in the World Economy: Text and Cases
Third Edition

SAMUELSON AND MARKS
Managerial Economics

SCARTH
Macroeconomics: An Introduction to Advanced Methods
Second Edition

SMITH AND SPUDECK
Interest Rates: Principles and Applications

THOMAS
Economics: Principles and Applications
(Also available in micro and macro paperbacks)

WACHTEL
Labor and the Economy
Third Edition

WALTON AND ROCKOFF
History of the American Economy
Sixth Edition

WELCH AND WELCH
Economics: Theory and Practice
Fourth Edition

YARBROUGH AND YARBROUGH
The World Economy: Trade and Finance
Second Edition

ZIMBALIST, SHERMAN, AND BROWN
Comparing Economic Systems: A Political-Economic Approach
Second Edition

THE HBJ COLLEGE OUTLINE SERIES

EMERY
Intermediate Microeconomics

EMERY
Principles of Economics: Macroeconomics

EMERY
Principles of Economics: Microeconomics

Preface

Economics is not totally foreign to beginning students. Everyone who has struggled with a budget, followed a political campaign, or read the headlines on unemployment, the federal budget deficit, or poverty has acquired some familiarity with economic issues. What is typically missing is an economic way of thinking—a framework for organizing thoughts, analyzing economic events, and evaluating economic policies. Economic literacy is important because economic issues facing governments and individuals shape the future of the nation and affect the well-being of its citizens. For these reasons and others, it is essential that economics be made accessible to everyone. Students may open a textbook, but how far they read depends on what is in the book and how it is presented.

In this book, we have attempted to convey both the importance of economics and our enthusiasm for the subject. We do not expect students to read economics for the joy of understanding. Rather, our philosophy is that we must first convince students that what they are reading is relevant. Toward that end, at the start of each chapter we raise critical policy issues and pose key questions to which students can relate. To sustain interest throughout the chapter, we include many examples and applications and provide historical background on the variables at issue—so they become more than abstract theoretical concepts. Economic theory is never presented for its own sake; there is always a payoff. Theory is integrated with empirical evidence, and the implications of the theory are clearly spelled out. Our goal is to have students develop a feel for the way economic principles relate to the real world around them.

A recent trend in principles textbooks is to provide broad coverage of many technical concepts at the frontiers of economics. Although this approach may excite instructors, too often students receive an extensive but shallow background in economics or become familiar with the latest theories without developing a solid background in basic economic analysis. We have rejected this approach and instead emphasize the fundamental concepts of economics (supply and demand, the gains from trade, opportunity cost, and so forth), ensuring that students acquire sufficient background in the fundamentals before moving on to more advanced topics.

This approach also permits us to devote considerable attention to important contemporary policy issues. Entire chapters are devoted to budget deficits, alternative viewpoints on monetary and fiscal policies, the consequences of inflation and unemployment, externalities and the environment, and discrimination and differences in labor market outcomes. Although this latter subject can be omitted in the event of time constraints, our experience indicates that students respond enthusiastically to this material. The topics—pay differentials, affirmative action, and comparable worth—underscore this book's commitment to important real-world issues and policies.

Traditionally, international issues are relegated to the back of the book. Given an increasingly interrelated global economy, this approach is no longer defensible. Agricultural problems cannot be discussed intelligently without considering protectionism and exchange rates. Market structure and antitrust policy cannot be studied as if competition came only from domestic sources. Similarly, analyses of monetary and fiscal policy, interest rates, budget deficits, and numerous other topics require an understanding of the interrelationships among national economies.

For this reason, gains from trade, trade restrictions, and related concepts are introduced at the beginning of the book. This allows us to integrate global issues with what are customarily considered domestic topics. By the time the student encounters the more technical concepts of international economics near the end of the book, he or she has already gained a familiarity with and an appreciation of international economics.

The organization of this book does not differ dramatically from that of most principles texts. For those adopting a paperback split, however, one difference should be noted—this text contains an unusually comprehensive set of core chapters common to both *Principles of Macroeconomics* and *Principles of Microeconomics*. This feature is designed to give instructors greater flexibility in topic selection.

Typically, macro splits do not contain information on elasticity (Chapter 5), despite the fact that many instructors would like to acquaint their students with at least the price elasticity of demand. Similarly, most macro splits omit the chapter on businesses (Chapter 6) even though many of its topics—the stock market, the present value concept, and balance sheets—are relevant to macroeconomics. The final core chapter (Chapter 7), on government, treats such topics as the rationale for government intervention, the principles of taxation, and public choice. In many texts, these topics are covered in several macro chapters and are ignored in the micro split, or they are covered in a public-finance section of microeconomics and ignored in the macro split. Because these subjects are appropriate for both macro-economics and microeconomics, we include them in the core so that all instructors have the option of including them in either course. At the same time, we recognize that not all instructors wish to cover these topics. Accordingly, the core chapters following supply and demand (Chapter 4) are structured so that they are not prerequisites for later chapters. Any or all of these chapters may be deleted without loss of continuity.

LEARNING AIDS

Among the pedagogical features of this book are the **Exhibits** (boxed inserts) interspersed throughout the chapters. These exhibits perform a variety of functions—illustrating real-life economic events, assessing current or proposed policies, and providing background on great economists. Through exhibits, students learn about the effect of macroeconomic conditions on presidential elections, the implications of the falling dollar of 1992 for European unification, the impact of agricultural supply restrictions on the rural Missouri economy, and whether pollution is more severe in capitalistic economies. Exhibits are written in a lively fashion to be both educational and entertaining.

To promote student involvement, we include the **Your Turn** feature, in which the student is quizzed on a subject just presented. (Answers to these quizzes appear at the end of the chapter.) These quizzes not only get students actively involved in economics, they also provide immediate feedback on how well the student has mastered such important concepts as factors shifting supply and demand curves, construction of price indexes, determinants of exchange rates, calculation of unemployment rates, and so forth.

To assist the student in learning the economist's vocabulary, **key terms** appear in boldface print when first introduced, and most are defined in the margins. These definitions are arranged alphabetically in a **glossary** at the end of the book for easy student access. Other important concepts (not quite key terms) are emphasized in italics.

At the end of each chapter, a summary organizes and highlights the important points of the preceeding pages. This is followed by a list of the chapter's key terms (arranged in order of presentation), and by study questions and problems. The questions are designed to test comprehension and ability to apply the concepts and principles of the chapter. Following answers to the **Your Turn** quizzes, most chapters conclude with a set of carefully selected references.

Figures and tables are used liberally to facilitate analysis, to illustrate concepts, and to give the student a feel for the variables under discussion. The figures are accompanied by captions that convey the message in a way that independently reinforces the text discussion.

NEW TO THE SECOND EDITION

This second edition of *Principles of Economics* represents a major overhaul of the first edition. While reviewers of our first edition were enthusiastic about its merits, there were suggestions for improvement—as is the case with any first edition. This new edition includes several totally new chapters as well as many new **Exhibits** and **Your Turns**. It adds **Part Openers** that preceed and overview the material to be presented in each section of the text. Every chapter has been revised with care.

An important feature of this second edition is the free **Study Guide** that is bound into the book. Our publisher convinced us that because many students around the country have felt shortchanged when purchasing increasingly expensive textbooks, and because the marginal cost of printing a study guide is surprisingly low, the study guide could be bound in and included with the text without either increasing its price or reducing its quality. This text—with study guide—is being marketed at the same price as major competing texts that do *not* include the study guides. We are banking on a solid student response to the increase in the value of this package. This study guide, written by Roger Trenary (recipient of numerous teaching awards at Kansas State University), has been painstakingly edited and improved with the help of Ragan and Thomas.

Among the new topics covered in this second edition are free-trade agreements (including the North American Free Trade Agreement hammered out in August 1992), the theory of managed trade, and recent developments in GATT and in the European Community. The transition of former Soviet republics and Eastern Europe from command economies toward capitalism, and the challenges posed by this transition, are carefully examined; and international topics in general are given increased emphasis.

The macroeconomics portion of this text has been reorganized and improved. A totally new chapter (Chapter 8) opens the macro section with an overview of the business cycle and an introduction to such key concepts as actual and potential GDP, the natural unemployment rate, and the measurement of inflation and unemployment. It is followed by a new chapter analyzing the consequences of inflation and unemployment. After this motivation, we proceed to national income accounting and then to the basic aggregate supply-aggregate demand model. Treatment of the AS-AD model has been enhanced through improved analysis of the slopes and shifting of the curves and more thorough treatment of the distinction between the short-run and long-run aggregate supply curves. Differing viewpoints of the various schools of thought are analyzed in the context of this framework.

In the microeconomics portion, the sections on industrial organization, regulation, and labor markets have been updated to reflect recent developments and policy changes. The chapter on the environment contains an expanded discussion of the work of Ronald Coase and the importance of property rights in dealing with externalities. It also examines recent changes in environmental policy, such as the trading of sulphur dioxide credits on the Chicago Board of Trade, effective in 1993. And through new case studies, students learn of economic transitions in agriculture, movements into and out of poverty, the success and failure of individual businesses, and other real-world adjustments that are missing from texts that are content to focus on abstract identities.

Because the exhibits in the first edition were popular, numerous new exhibits have been added to the second edition—on such timely topics as the recent proposals for expanded individual retirement accounts, the relationship between central bank independence and macroeconomic performance, proposed legislation to control budget deficits, and the debate on whether business executives are overpaid. And, because the **Your Turn** feature was so well received by adopters of the first edition, we have made even greater use of this feature in the second edition. Lastly, we have bolstered the public-choice coverage of this text by adding a new section in Chapter 7 as well as by including several new exhibits with a public-choice flavor in other chapters.

ANCILLARY PACKAGE

Principles of Economics is supported by the following supplementary materials:

STUDY GUIDE   Bound with the text and included at no extra charge, the *Study Guide* summarizes and outlines each chapter of the text and offers "hints and help" to the reader. This is followed by objective questions (fill-in-the-blank, true-false, multiple-choice); graphical and numerical problems; and answers to all questions and problems. The *Study Guide* has been carefully revised in this edition.

TESTBANKS   *Testbank A* contains approximately 2,400 multiple-choice questions, the majority of which are new to this edition. Professors Ragan and Thomas have developed more than 1,200 new questions to go with the best questions from the original version (written by John Sondey of South Dakota State University and Roger Trenary). To assist the instructor in creating exams, questions are coded according to the following categories: definition or fact, simple analysis, and complex interpretation. *Testbank B*, written by Steve Huenneke of Minot State University and Steve Peterson of the University of Idaho, also contains more than 2,000 coded questions, all new to this edition.

The ExaMaster testing system for both testbanks allows instructors to create customized tests by selecting any mixture of questions available, adding new questions, editing questions, and preparing scrambled versions of a test. All graphics are printed out, along with appropriate test items (no cutting and pasting required). Testbanks are available on computer disk for both the IBM system (5¼″ and 3½″disks) and Apple computers, and are also available in paperback.

INSTRUCTOR'S MANUAL   Prepared by Ragan and Thomas, the *Instructor's Manual* contains chapter outlines, ideas for lectures, answers to end-of-chapter questions in the text, and transparency masters. The *Instructor's Manual* is also available on computer disk, which allows instructors to add notes, edit the material, and prepare outlines or class handouts.

ACETATE TRANSPARENCIES   More than 100 four-color transparencies are available for overhead projectors. The transparencies feature key figures and tables from the text.

ELECTRONIC TRANSPARENCIES   Menu-driven, DOS-based presentation software illustrates more than 150 figures from the book. Particular topics are *easy* to access (by chapter and figure number).

COMPUTER SIMULATION PACKAGE   *ECO-Talk* computer simulation, developed by Michael Claudon (Middlebury College) and Kipley Olson (Apple Computer), consists of ten macro models and ten micro models designed to help students master concepts through simulation, practice with graphics, and quizzes on the models.

VIDEO PACKAGE   Milton Friedman's *Free to Choose* is available on videotape for those adopting *Principles of Economics*.

Acknowledgments

We have found that a project of this magnitude is truly a team effort. We are indebted to many individuals, and credit must be shared with all of them. We benefited enormously from working with the able team at HBJ. Among those deserving special thanks for major contributions are Rick Hammonds (acquisitions editor), Ruth Rominger (developmental editor), Linda Miller (designer), Ted Barnett (marketing), and Jon Gregory (project editor), who meticulously guided production through its numerous stages. Leon Unruh helped with outstanding copyediting. Contributing with permissions and photo research were Van Strength and Shirley Webster, respectively. Alison Howell (production manager) helped maintain the work pace during a demanding schedule.

We also benefited from the comments of many of our colleagues who offered suggestions in their areas of expertise. These include: Art Barnaby, Mike Babcock, Doug Beech, Arlo Biere, Bernt Bratsberg, Patrick Gormely, David Hula, Wayne Nafziger, Michael Oldfather, Ed Olson, Bryan Schurle, and Jeff Williams. We are especially indebted to Roger Trenary who, in addition to writing the *Study Guide*, provided a first-rate review of the entire manuscript. Patrick Gormely and John Knudsen (University of Idaho) contributed immeasurably to the project through Chapters 39 and 40, respectively. Bill Reece (University of West Virginia) helped greatly with the new public-choice discussion in Chapter 7. Stuart Dorsey (Baker University), Jon Miller (University of Idaho), Carol Tremblay (Oregon State University), and Roger Adkins, Wendell Sweetser, and Allen Wilkins of Marshall

University also contributed through constructive suggestions in specific sections of the text.

Manuscript reviewers played a special role, providing an objective assessment of our material and making constructive suggestions. We extend our appreciation to Jack E. Adams, University of Arkansas; Paul Barkley, Washington State University; George S. Bohler, Florida Junior College at Jacksonville; Thomas Bonsor, Eastern Washington University; Michael Brusin, College of San Mateo; Linda Carr, Livingston University; Bobby N. Corcoran, Middle Tennessee State University; Albert B. Culver, California State University-Chico; Vernon Dobis, Moorhead State University; Michael G. Ellis, New Mexico State University; John L. Fizel, Pennsylvania State University (Behrend College); J. P. Gilbert, MiraCosta College; Richard B. Hansen, University of Northern Iowa; Charles Hawkins, Lamar University; Janice Holtkamp, Iowa State University; R. Bradley Hoppes, Southwest Missouri State University; Jane Horvath, University of Hartford; David Hula, Kansas State University; Walter Johnson, University of Missouri at Columbia; Robert Keller, Colorado State University; Kathy Kemper, Everman, Texas; Norman L. Knaub, Penn State—Altoona; Susan N. Koenigsberg, San Francisco State University; Michael Kupilik, University of Montana; Robert Ley, Bemidji State University; Stephen E. Lile, Western Kentucky University; Charles Link, University of Delaware; Devinder M. Malhotra, University of Akron; Henry N. McCarl, University of Alabama at Birmingham; Barbara Morgan, San Francisco State University; Glenn Perrone, Pace University; Louis F. Pisciottoli, California State University at Fresno; George M. Radakovic, Indiana University of Pennsylvania; Jerry Riddle, Central Virginia Community College; Janet Rives, University of Northern Iowa; Keith Rowley, Baylor University; Lynda Rush, California State Polytechnic University at Pomona; Peter Schwartz, University of North Carolina-Charlotte; John Scoggins, California State University-Long Beach; Lee Spector, Ball State University; Ed Stuart, Northeastern Illinois University; James L. Swofford, University of South Alabama; Tom TenHoeve, Iowa State University; Victor Tremblay, Oregon State University; Roger Trenary, Kansas State University; Arthur L. Welsh, Pennsylvania State University; William J. Zahka, Widener University; and Armand Zottola, Central Connecticut State University.

Elizabeth Thomas contributed importantly to the clarity of exposition by making perceptive suggestions on numerous chapters of the text and study guide. We are indebted to Karen Gillespie and Susan Koch for typing and other help in manuscript preparation. Sunil Bhatnagar, Charles Kulp, and Weixin Shi provided able and valuable assistance in gathering data and constructing numerous computer-drawn graphs. Anthony Barilla and Kevin Boyd made constructive suggestions on the Testbanks and Study Guide, and Ray Kowalczewski provided research assistance for Chapter 35. We are grateful to many students, both graduate and undergraduate, who made constructive suggestions that improved this final product.

Finally, we acknowledge the support of our families. In addition to our wives, we are indebted to our parents for their years of support, their love, and their confidence in us. Our children—Elizabeth Thomas and Emily, Patrick, and Laura Ragan—have also sacrificed so that this book could be written. They, too, have our gratitude.

READER SUGGESTIONS

As we learned throughout the review process, the comments of others can strengthen a book. Accordingly, we encourage readers to share their thoughts and insights with us. Please write us in care of Harcourt Brace Jovanovich College Publishers, 301 Commerce Street, Suite 3700, Fort Worth, Texas 76102.

James F. Ragan, Jr.
Lloyd B. Thomas, Jr.

Brief Contents

Contents

3 The Price System 63

4 Supply and Demand 81

5 Demand and Supply Elasticities 107

6   Business Firms in the American Economy **135**

7   Government in the Economy—Spending and Taxation **163**

14   The Model of Aggregate Supply and Aggregate Demand 341

PART III

Banking, Monetary Policy, Interest Rates, and Economic Activity

397

15   Money, Banking, and the Creation of Bank Deposits 369

PART V

The National Debt,
Economic Growth,
and Productivity

521

**Consumer and
Business Behavior**

579

PART VII

Market Structure
and Government
Intervention

639

28 Industrial Organization and Antitrust Policy 725

29 Regulation 751

The Distribution
of Income
775

33 Interest, Rent, and Profit 859

34 Poverty and the Distribution of Income 881

The World Economy

971

I

The Basics

PART I OF *PRINCIPLES OF ECONOMICS* PROVIDES THE FOUNDATION FOR ECONOMIC ANALYSIS. IT SHOWS HOW ECONOMISTS APPROACH ISSUES— THE ASSUMPTIONS ECONOMISTS MAKE AND THE TECHNIQUES THEY USE TO DERIVE THEIR RESULTS. PART I ALSO ILLUSTRATES THE VALUE OF ECONOMIC MODELS WHEN USED PROPERLY. ■ THE EARLY, CORE CHAPTERS PROVIDE BACKGROUND ON THE PRIMARY ECONOMIC DECISION MAKERS— FIRMS, CONSUMERS, AND GOVERNMENT. FIRMS BUY LABOR (AND OTHER INPUTS) FROM CONSUMERS IN ORDER TO PRODUCE OUTPUT. CONSUMERS SELL LABOR IN ORDER TO EARN INCOME TO BUY THE GOODS THEY DESIRE. BOTH THE BUYING AND SELLING OF LABOR AND THE BUYING AND SELLING OF OUTPUT TAKE PLACE IN *MARKETS*. MARKETS PLAY AN INTEGRAL ROLE IN ECONOMIC ANALYSIS. UNDER CERTAIN IDEAL CONDITIONS, MARKETS LEAD TO SOCIALLY OPTIMAL OUTCOMES. BUT WHEN THESE CONDITIONS ARE NOT SATISFIED, GOVERNMENT INTERVENTION IN THE ECONOMY, IN PRINCIPLE, MAY LEAD TO BETTER OUTCOMES. AFTER EXAMINING THE OPERATION OF MARKETS IN THE ABSENCE OF GOVERNMENT INTERVENTION, PART I ANALYZES THE RATIONALE FOR GOVERNMENT INVOLVEMENT IN THE ECONOMY, THE LIMITATIONS OF GOVERNMENT, AND THE GROWTH OF GOVERNMENT. ■ BECAUSE NOT ALL MARKETS ARE DOMESTIC, THE SUBJECT OF INTERNATIONAL TRADE IS ALSO INTRODUCED. REASONS FOR TRADE ARE PRESENTED ALONG WITH INFORMATION ON THE VOLUME OF TRADE. WITH THE BACKGROUND PROVIDED IN PART I, THE READER IS EQUIPPED FOR A DETAILED STUDY OF EITHER MACROECONOMICS OR MICROECONOMICS.

Economics and Economic Thinking

ECONOMICS CAN BE UNDERSTOOD IN TERMS OF THE QUESTIONS IT ASKS AND THE APPROACH IT USES TO ANSWER THESE QUESTIONS. ECONOMIC ISSUES ABOUND. WHY DO WOMEN GENERALLY EARN LESS THAN MEN? HOW SUCCESSFUL ARE GOVERNMENT PROGRAMS DESIGNED TO AID THE NEEDY? SHOULD THE GOVERNMENT'S BUDGET BE BALANCED? HOW DOES TRADE AFFECT A NATION'S STANDARD OF LIVING?

ON A PERSONAL LEVEL, YOU MAKE ECONOMIC DECISIONS THROUGHOUT LIFE. IS COLLEGE A GOOD INVESTMENT? COMPARED TO A STATE UNIVERSITY, IS A DEGREE FROM AN EXPENSIVE PRIVATE COLLEGE WORTH THE ADDED EXPENSE? WHICH JOB SHOULD YOU TAKE? HOW CAN YOU BEST SPEND YOUR INCOME? SHOULD YOU BUY OR RENT A HOUSE?

IF YOU ENTER BUSINESS YOU CONFRONT NUMEROUS ECONOMIC DECISIONS—INCLUDING WHAT TO PRODUCE, HOW TO PRODUCE, AND IN WHAT QUANTITIES. IN POLITICS YOU FACE DIFFERENT ECONOMIC ISSUES. GIVEN ITS LIMITED ABILITY TO RESPOND TO SOCIETAL WANTS, HOW MUCH SHOULD A NATION SPEND ON DEFENSE, ON CARE FOR THE ELDERLY, ON ENVIRONMENTAL CLEANUP? EVEN AS A VOTER, YOU EVALUATE CANDIDATES PARTLY ON THE BASIS OF THEIR ECONOMIC VIEWS. OPINION POLLS CONSISTENTLY RANK ECONOMIC PROBLEMS—SUCH AS UNEMPLOYMENT, INFLATION, AND THE DEFICIT—HIGH ON THE LIST OF PUBLIC CONCERNS.

NO ONE ESCAPES THE FORCES OF ECONOMICS; WE MUST DEAL WITH THEM, INTELLIGENTLY OR OTHERWISE. ACCORDINGLY, IT IS

> Economics is the academic discipline most discussed by the general public. It is also one of the least understood.[1]
>
> [1]James B. Ramsey, *Economic Forecasting—Models or Markets?* (London: The Institute of Economic Affairs, 1977), p. 11.

important to build an understanding of economics. The principal goal of this book is to help build that understanding. With discipline and effort, one soon develops an inventory of economic facts and principles. More importantly, one develops an economic way of thinking. A word of caution: Resist the temptation to dismiss economic theory. As the great English economist John Maynard Keynes observed, those who disdain economic theory "are usually the slaves of some defunct economist."

Resources and Output

RESOURCES
Inputs (land, capital, and labor) used to produce goods and services.

LAND
A country's natural resources.

CAPITAL
Output such as machines, tools, and structures used to produce goods and services.

LABOR
The physical and mental abilities of workers.

ENTREPRENEUR
An individual who organizes resources for production, introduces new products or techniques of production, and reaps the rewards/bears the consequences of such endeavors.

Now that a sample of economic issues has been presented, the more basic question becomes: What is economics? However, before answering the question in detail, it is appropriate to introduce a few terms.

Each country has certain finite **resources**, which economists generally divide into three categories: land, capital, and labor. *Land* is a general term encompassing more than a country's soil. **Land** includes all natural resources—timber, minerals, rivers, and the like. **Capital** refers to goods produced in an economy that are, in turn, used to produce other goods and services. This book constitutes capital. So do a sports arena, an oil refinery, and a calculator.

Labor consists of the physical and mental abilities of workers—the production potential of miners, secretaries, accountants, and all others willing to contribute to output. Perhaps the best measure of labor is the quantity and composition of a country's labor force. Labor consists of more than the number of people available for work; it also encompasses the skills of workers. Those with more education or experience can generally produce more output than workers with fewer skills. Table 1.1 lists certain resources available to the United States in a recent year.

Sometimes *entrepreneurship* is considered a fourth resource category, although it is commonly viewed as a special type of labor. The hallmarks of an **entrepreneur** are innovation and risk taking. An entrepreneur organizes resources for production, attempting to take advantage of what is viewed as an opportunity. An entrepreneur may introduce a new product or attempt a new technique of production. When successful, an entrepreneur may reap substantial financial rewards—but success is by no means guaranteed. Those who introduce the wrong product—the

SELECTED U.S. RESOURCES		
LAND	**CAPITAL**	**LABOR**
3.6 million square miles of surface, including: 483 million acres of commercial timberland 472 billion short tons of proven coal reserves 152 million metric tons of proven sulphur reserves 920 million troy ounces of proven silver reserves	3.9 million miles of highway 4.2 million commercial buildings 4.7 million farm tractors 667 thousand grain combines 111 nuclear reactors	127 million people in the labor force; among those 25–64 years old, 85% have completed at least 4 years of high school, 26% at least 4 years of college.

SOURCES: U.S. Departments of Agriculture, Commerce, Energy, Interior, and Labor.

TABLE 1.1

EXHIBIT
1 . 1

The Sweet Smell of Success— Entrepreneurs with a Vision

Ray Kroc sold restaurant supplies until age 58, when he discovered a tiny restaurant in California where customers lined up for inexpensive hamburgers and french fries. Near the restaurant rose a pair of golden arches, a distinctive sign chosen by the restaurant's owners, Dick and Mac McDonald. Kroc had a vision that fast food was the wave of the future and that investors would be willing to pay for the opportunity to own their own McDonald's restaurant. In 1955, Kroc purchased franchise rights to the restaurant and later, despite exorbitant interest rates, he purchased the entire company.

Those wishing to operate a McDonald's franchise were forced to keep restaurants immaculately clean and to buy potatoes, cooking oil, and other products from common suppliers, a practice that maintained uniform quality across restaurants and kept costs low. Only those who ran a successful first franchise were permitted to operate a second McDonald's restaurant. Recognizing the importance of new products, Kroc also solicited ideas from franchisees, whose suggestions included the Big Mac and the Egg McMuffin. By the time he died in 1981, Kroc had built the world's largest and most profitable food service company.

Scott Olson found a different path to success—on roller skates. As a 19-year-old hockey player, Olson designed a pair of in-line skates, skates with a single line of wheels. Because of the skates' speed and maneuverability, they were a big hit not just with off-season hockey players but with recreational skaters as well. Initially building skates in his basement, he started the company Rollerblade in 1981 when demand for his skates soared. Ten years later, as sales of Rollerblade skates reached $100 million per year, Olson completed the sale of his company.

Not content with one successful venture, Olson founded a new company, Innovative Sports Systems, which produces skates whose wheels can be placed in the traditional two-by-two pattern or switched to the newer in-line style. If Olson's SwitchIt skates prove to be popular, he will be rewarded once again for his vision as an entrepreneur.

SOURCES: Adapted from Eugene Carlson, "McDonald's Kroc Bloomed Late but Brilliantly," *The Wall Street Journal*, May 23, 1989, p. B2, and Lois Therrien, "Rollerblade is Skating in Heavier Traffic," *Business Week*, June 24, 1991, pp. 114–115.

proverbial lead balloon—can expect to lose money on their venture. Exhibit 1.1 provides information on some recent entrepreneurs.

Economic resources are sometimes called *factors of production* in order to emphasize their role in producing goods and services:

$$\text{resources} \xrightarrow{\text{production}} \text{goods and services}$$

The distinction between goods and services is based on whether the *output*—what is produced—is tangible or intangible. Clothes, sporting goods, beverages, and other tangible products are termed *goods*. Examples of *services* include haircuts, income tax preparation, and computer repair.

ECONOMIC GOOD
A good that is scarce. At a price of zero the amount of the good desired exceeds the quantity available.

FREE GOOD
A good that is not scarce.

Sometimes the term "good" is used loosely to include both goods and services. For example, the expression **economic good** refers to any product that is *scarce*. That is, at a price of zero (if the good were free) the amount desired would exceed the quantity available. In contrast, a **free good** is any product so abundant that even at a zero price the amount available would fully satisfy all wants. Within a desert, sand is likely to be a free good. On many mountain ranges snow is a free good, although not always. If snowfall is insufficient for good skiing, the amount freely available may fall short of the amount desired. Ski resorts frequently pay for the creation of artificial snow.

At some colleges baseball games are free goods. Despite free admission, more seats are available than spectators. Of course, conditions can change. When a team contends for a national championship, interest in the game may swell so dramatically that some fans must be turned away. In that event, the college baseball game is no longer a free good—*even when no admission is charged.* Available seating is now insufficient to permit all who want to watch the game to see it—seats are scarce. For this reason the game becomes an economic good.

Economics as a Study of Scarcity and Choice

Naturally, we want more from life than baseball. In fact, human wants are seemingly unlimited. Although we may initially ask only for life's necessities, once they are within reach we tend to crave richer foods, more stylish clothing, larger homes, and assorted luxuries. Even then our wish list continues to grow. No matter how affluent the individual, invariably something else is desired.

SCARCITY OF RESOURCES
Insufficient resources are available to produce all goods and services desired by consumers.

While desires appear endless, economic resources are **scarce**—finite. Therein lies the rub. No society has sufficient resources to satisfy all human wants. *Because resources are limited, the amount of output that can be produced is also limited.*

Contrary to the Michelob slogan, and the illusion created by other advertisers, it is not true that we "can have it all." Instead, we must choose among competing options. *What* will be produced? Which wants will be met, and which will go unsatisfied? Should society build more shelter for the homeless and fewer roads and parks? Should we allocate fewer resources to consumer goods (such as VCRs) and transfer additional resources to the production of business computers and other forms of capital? Which do we prefer—more steel or cleaner air, additional organ transplants or better prenatal care?

In addition to determining what goods and services are produced, there is the question of *how*. Which production technique do we use? Should we generate electricity with coal, natural gas, or nuclear power? How do we grow our crops? For example, should we economize on labor, making farming more capital-intensive?

Moreover, there are allocation decisions. How are the goods and services to be distributed? *Who* are fed, and *who* go hungry? *Who* receive heart transplants? *Who* drive Mercedes, *who* get the Chevrolets, and *who* must walk? Such issues are at the heart of **economics**.

ECONOMICS
The study of how scarce resources are allocated among competing uses.

Scarcity limits options and forces choice. In a world without scarcity there would be no economic goods, only free goods. No one would need to do without. But that world—the Michelob world—is not where you were born. Here on earth society is forced to choose among competing options—and so are you. Conse-

OPPORTUNITY COST
The best alternative to the option chosen.

quently, such choices carry a cost: forgone opportunities, what we sacrifice as the consequence of our decisions. This is the essence of **opportunity cost**.

What would you do if you skipped your next class—earn money by working? Share a Coke with a friend? Sleep? What is your best alternative? Whatever it is, that is the opportunity cost of attending class. You may want both a mountain bike and stereo speakers, but you cannot afford both. The opportunity cost of the mountain bike is the speakers; the opportunity cost of the speakers is the bike.

So it is for society. Selecting one option requires forgoing another—perhaps not eliminating a program entirely, but at least reducing its size. If society chooses to reduce pollution by slicing student financial aid, the opportunity cost of a cleaner environment is fewer students receiving a college education. Similarly, if the government decides to lay claim to a greater percentage of the nation's output, the cost is a reduced share of output for the private, nongovernment sector. The opportunity cost of an aircraft carrier, for example, may be additional housing and consumer goods.

According to government statistics, over 30 million people in the United States live in *poverty*: they possess insufficient purchasing power to maintain what the government considers an adequate standard of living. Can poverty be reduced? Certainly. But at what cost? What is society willing to sacrifice to remove another million people from the poverty rolls? Choices are not always easy, but must be made.

Poverty

ARE POVERTY AND SCARCITY THE SAME CONCEPT? ASSUME THE GOVERNMENT WAGED A SUCCESSFUL WAR ON POVERTY, WIPING OUT POVERTY IN THIS COUNTRY. WOULD THAT ELIMINATE SCARCITY?

YOUR TURN

Economic Thinking

Despite differences in the questions they pose, economists share a common approach to problems—an economic way of thinking—based on certain principles. The first such principle has just been articulated: *Scarcity forces choice*. Other economic principles involve the ways in which decision makers behave and the processes through which choices are made. Finally, economic thinking starts with the status quo and considers the consequences of change. When you understand these basic economic principles—when you understand how economists think—then the arguments of economists are easier to follow and the subject of economics is easier to master.

RATIONAL BEHAVIOR

A basic tenet of economic thinking is that decision makers behave *rationally*. In other words, decision makers establish a particular goal or objective and then choose purposefully in an attempt to achieve that goal. For consumers, the assumed goal is to maximize happiness or well-being—what economists call *utility*. Here **rational behavior** simply means making choices that the consumer believes maximize utility. For example, if a consumer prefers brand X to brand Y and both are the same price, the consumer does not choose brand Y.

Rational behavior does not mean consumers never make what, in retrospect, was a bad decision. A consumer may try *new and improved* brand Y, only to discover that it too falls short of brand X. Such experimentation is not irrational. What is irrational is to continue purchasing brand Y after determining that brand X is the better buy (provides more utility for the money).

Producers are also presumed to behave purposefully. Economists assume that the goal of every producer is to maximize *profit*: the difference between income earned from selling a product and the cost incurred in producing it. For instance, when a farmer sells a crop for $50,000 that cost $48,000 to produce, the farmer earns $2,000 profit. An implication of profit maximization is that a producer uses the fewest resources necessary to produce the output. Using more resources than necessary increases production costs and reduces profit.

DECISION MAKING—A MATTER OF COSTS AND BENEFITS

Economic thinking also involves assumptions about how decisions are made. Economists assume that decision makers are guided by the perceived costs and benefits of an action. For example, when it comes to seat belts, economists assume that consumers *buckle up* if the perceived benefit (reduced risk of injury) outweighs the cost (time spent buckling and unbuckling). On the other hand, if the cost is viewed as greater than the benefit, seat belts will not be used.

Because costs and benefits differ among individuals, decisions also differ, but in a predictable manner. Consider the traveler who can either leave the airport immediately by taxi or wait for a bus that, after numerous stops, reaches the same destination. Which does the traveler choose? The answer, of course, depends on how the benefits of the taxi (including time saved) stack up against the costs (for example, higher fare). Not everyone reaches the same conclusion. A lawyer who charges clients $200 per hour likely places a higher value on time savings than does a poor student. Therefore, the lawyer is more likely to choose the taxi than is the student.

Given this view of the decision-making process, a change in costs or benefits affects outcomes—again in a predictable manner. If taxi fares decrease and bus fares stay the same, one expects the number of travelers choosing taxi service to increase. Similarly, if the government increases the costs of not wearing a seat belt—by imposing stiff fines on beltless drivers—one expects more drivers to buckle up. What emerges is the view that decision makers respond to incentives. As the benefits of an action increase or its costs decrease, that action becomes more likely. This

Responding to Incentives

YOUR TURN

(A) EVEN SUCH ADDICTIVE BEHAVIOR AS CIGARETTE SMOKING IS AMENABLE TO ECONOMIC INCENTIVES. CITE AT LEAST ONE POLICY THAT HAS REDUCED OR COULD REDUCE CIGARETTE SMOKING IN THE UNITED STATES. (B) INCENTIVES ALSO AFFECT CAREER DECISIONS. EXPLAIN HOW INCENTIVES CAN BE USED TO CONVINCE MORE PEOPLE TO ENTER THE NURSING PROFESSION.

framework gives economists a powerful tool for analyzing human behavior and for predicting consequences of programs that alter costs or benefits.

MARGINAL ANALYSIS

MARGINAL ANALYSIS
An examination of what occurs when current conditions change.

Economic thinking often involves **marginal analysis**—considering the effects of change. For example, one relies on marginal analysis when deciding to spend six hours this week studying economics rather than five hours. One simply determines that the benefits of the additional hour (greater understanding of economics and possibly a higher grade) exceed the costs (less leisure, less sleep, or perhaps a lower grade in another course). Had one reached a different conclusion, the extra time would not be allotted to economics.

Similarly, producers make marginal calculations. For example, a farmer may ask: How much more corn can I grow if I apply additional fertilizer? How much will the additional fertilizer increase my costs of production? Will the additional fertilizer increase or decrease my profit? In each case the farmer considers the consequences of changing current operations.

Marginal analysis is also appropriate for assessing government policy. Before a government raises tax rates, it is useful to know how the change will affect the economy. Similarly, if a government is concerned about poverty, it can make more-enlightened decisions when it knows how changes in various government programs are likely to alter poverty. Because decision making frequently deals with change, marginal analysis plays a central role in economic thinking.

Methodology

In addition to a common way of thinking, economists share a common methodology. In the tradition of Sherlock Holmes, economists approach problems scientifically.

How did Holmes solve a mystery? Relying on his keen sense of observation, he began by gathering important facts. Holmes then tied these facts together to form a coherent **theory**, thereby attempting to explain their underlying relationships. His next step was to test the theory. This testing involved examining one or more of the theory's **hypotheses** to determine their consistency with the evidence.

THEORY
A formulation of underlying relationships in an attempt to explain certain phenomena.

HYPOTHESIS
A proposition concerning a particular relationship or event—often part of a theory.

For example, in one of his celebrated cases, Sherlock Holmes sought to identify the thief of a jeweled crown—the so-called beryl coronet. After gathering bits of relevant evidence, Holmes theorized that the culprit was one Sir George Burnwell. A basic hypothesis of this theory was that the soles of Sir George's shoes would match tracks found in the snow at the scene of the crime. If the shoes did not fit, Holmes would be forced to reject the theory, or at least reformulate it to explain why the soles of the shoes did not match the tracks. On the other hand, a finding that the shoes did match would support the theory but not prove it, since alternative theories might also be consistent with the evidence. (The soles of other shoes might also match the impressions left in the snow.)[2]

---

[2]For a solution to the mystery, see A. Conan Doyle, *The Adventures of Sherlock Holmes* (New York: A&W Visual Library, 1975), pp. 261–288.

INFLATION RATE
The rate at which a nation's average prices rise over time.

Good theories make the world appear elementary: they ignore less important bits of information and focus on central relationships. Theories abstract and simplify. They do not attempt to explain every thought in a villain's mind nor every action—only the major events and relationships. Theories are built on a set of assumptions (for example, assumptions about the motives of the people involved). From these assumptions various conclusions are derived. Theories are then judged in terms of the quality of these conclusions—that is, in terms of the ability to explain and predict.

Interestingly, criminologists are not alone in using the **scientific method**: developing theories, gathering evidence (data), and determining whether the theories are consistent with the evidence. Theories also play a major role in economics: helping us learn cause-and-effect relationships and understand our complex world. For example, economists are interested in knowing why prices rise. The rate at which a nation's average prices rise is termed the **inflation rate**.

The inflation rate fluctuates over time. In the United States, prices rose an average of 13.5 percent in 1980 but only 1.9 percent in 1986 (Figure 1.1). With millions of goods and tens of millions of consumers, how can we ever hope to uncover the determinants of inflation? Obviously, we must simplify the task and concentrate on the key factors. In other words, we need a theory of inflation.

Actually, several theories have been advanced. Among them, one holds that inflation is a monetary phenomenon—the result of too much money chasing too

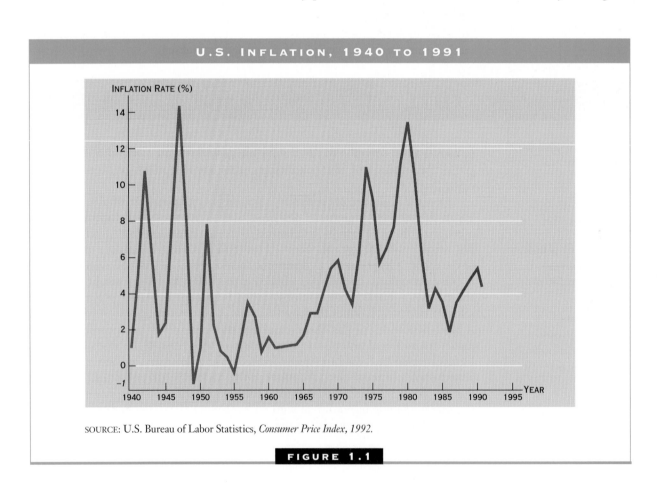

SOURCE: U.S. Bureau of Labor Statistics, *Consumer Price Index, 1992.*

FIGURE 1.1

MODEL

A formal presentation of a theory, often mathematical or graphical.

few goods. According to this theory, inflation is directly related to growth in the money supply: the faster government prints money, the faster prices rise. Alternative theories of inflation stress the role of other (nonmonetary) factors.

Theories are sometimes presented in terms of graphical or mathematical **models**. For example, Figure 1.2 presents a monetary model of inflation, according to which each 1 percent increase in growth in the money supply leads to a 1 percent increase in inflation. (For a review on interpreting graphs, see Appendix 1A at the end of this chapter.)

Given competing theories of inflation, which are credible and which are not? How are theories evaluated? As a starting point, an acceptable theory must be consistent with available evidence. Recall the scientific method, whereby theories are subjected to possible refutation. The monetary theory predicts that an increase in the growth of money is followed by an increase in the inflation rate. Is it? If not, we must either abandon the theory or reformulate it so that it is consistent with the evidence—and then test the new version.

What if two or more theories are consistent with the same data? Which theory is best? Because the answer is not always clear, economists often rely on statistics to help choose among competing theories. Assume the reason you are interested in a theory of inflation is so that you can forecast future inflation. One approach is to choose the theory with the smallest forecast error—the theory that, on average, comes closest to predicting the actual rate of inflation.

Assume that on average the monetary theory is off, in one direction or the other, by 10 percent, whereas all competing theories are off by at least 20 percent. Using the preceding decision rule, the monetary theory is selected for forecasting.

A MONETARY MODEL OF INFLATION

The monetary theory of inflation stresses the link between growth in money supply and rate of inflation. According to this monetary model of inflation, a 3 percent growth in money supply is associated with zero inflation. Each additional 1 percent growth in money supply leads to a 1 percent increase in inflation. When money supply grows at a 9 percent rate, inflation is 6 percent.

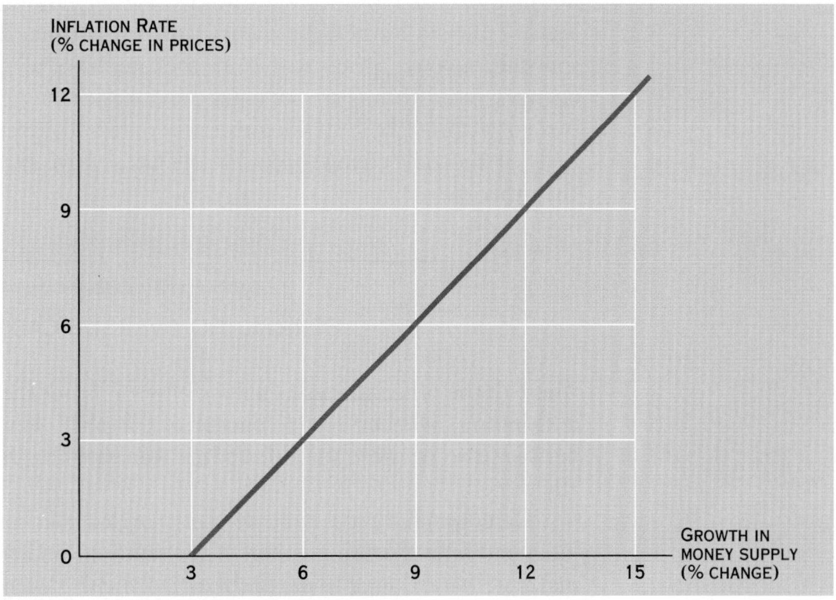

FIGURE 1.2

No theory permits perfect forecasting at all times. Despite this, as long as one theory forecasts better than others, it remains the best choice for forecasting.

Hazards to Clear Thinking

Economic theory helps one analyze and predict. By increasing knowledge of how the world works, it aids policymakers in formulating beneficial programs and in avoiding costly mistakes. But like any tool, economic theory must be used with care. Consider three of the most common stumbling blocks for would-be economists: the other-things-equal assumption, causality, and the fallacy of composition.

OTHER THINGS EQUAL

OTHER THINGS (BEING) EQUAL
A condition in which only the specific variables under consideration change; all other variables remain constant.

Generally, economic theories are built on the assumption of **other things (being) equal**: all variables are assumed to remain unchanged except those variables specifically under consideration. For example, ski-lift operators may have developed a theory that, other things (being) equal, consumers will purchase more ski-lift tickets if their price is reduced. Assume the price of ski-lift tickets decreases from one year to the next, yet consumers purchase *fewer* tickets. Should the ski-lift operators discard their theory?

Think carefully. The number of tickets purchased depends on factors other than ticket price. Perhaps snowfall was considerably lighter the second year, so that there were fewer days to ski. In that event, the change in the number of tickets purchased reflected changes in both snowfall and ticket price. After all, the theory does not predict that a lower price will increase the number of tickets purchased regardless of snowfall. Rather, the theory claims that other things (being) equal, including snowfall, a lower price will spur the purchase of additional tickets. If snowfall changes, other things are *not* equal and a basic assumption of the theory is violated. A theory cannot be tested legitimately unless its assumptions are satisfied. Accordingly, if snowfall changes, ski-lift operators have no legitimate basis for rejecting their theory.

CORRELATION VERSUS CAUSATION

Abuse of the other-things-equal assumption is not the only hurdle to clear economic thinking; another is the concept of causality. Having uncovered a relationship between two or more variables, some read into this relationship more than is actually there.

Demographic data indicate that married men consistently have lower unemployment rates than single men of the same age and education. Does this mean that marriage *causes* lower unemployment in men? Put another way, is a lower unemployment rate the direct consequence of being married? One could argue that the responsibilities of marriage cause workers to search harder for jobs and to hold on to jobs that single men might walk away from. In that event, marriage would indeed lead to a lower unemployment rate. But this is not the only feasible explanation for the statistical correlation (or association) between marriage and unemployment.

An alternative view is that married men and single men tend to differ in characteristics other than marriage. According to this scenario, unemployment differences result from these differences, not from marriage. Some men have poor health; others are emotionally unstable, irresponsible, and poorly adjusted. Such men are less likely to be married and more likely to be unemployed. The same characteristics that *turn off* women also *turn off* employers. If true, the difference in unemployment rates between married men and single men has nothing to do with marriage per se but instead is the consequence of poor health or personality quirks. Marital status and unemployment are correlated, but marital status has no impact on unemployment. We leave it to the reader to evaluate this theory. (It made little sense to the authors when they were single, but has become more appealing with time and family.)

The game of football can also help differentiate between correlation and causation. Each January the champions of the American Football Conference (AFC) and the National Football Conference (NFC) meet in the Super Bowl. A simplistic theory holds that a win by the NFC team causes the stock market to rise, whereas a win by the AFC team causes the stock market to fall.[3] What do the data show? Through 1991, 25 Super Bowl games had been played. For 22 of the 25 years the data actually support the theory—that is, the stock market advanced when the NFC team won and retreated when the AFC team won (Table 1.2, page 14). Undeniably, stock prices have been highly correlated with the outcome of the Super Bowl, but does anyone really believe that the Super Bowl *caused* the stock market to advance or decline? Sometimes two variables are correlated by chance: the fact that one event follows another does not necessarily mean that the first event caused the second.

THE FALLACY OF COMPOSITION

FALLACY OF COMPOSITION

Falsely concluding that what is true for the individual must be true for the group.

It is tempting to conclude that what is true for the individual is also true for the group. After all, the group simply consists of the individuals in it. But if this is your reasoning, you are guilty of the **fallacy of composition**. As an individual you may speak louder so others can hear you better. Does it therefore follow that when everyone in a room talks louder they can all be heard better? To the contrary, it is likely that each speaker simply drowns out the others. What is true for you as an individual, acting alone, does not hold true when everyone in the group does the same thing.

As a further example, consider an individual wheat farmer. The more wheat harvested by an individual farmer in a given year the larger the farmer's income. It does not follow, however, that aggregate income of wheat farmers increases whenever aggregate wheat production increases. An individual farmer produces such a

---

[3]More precisely, the theory categorizes teams in terms of their original football conference. This means that the Pittsburgh Steelers and the Indianapolis (formerly Baltimore) Colts are classified as members of the NFC even though the teams have since moved to the AFC.

IS THE SUPER BOWL RESPONSIBLE FOR SWINGS IN THE STOCK MARKET?

YEAR	WINNING TEAM	ORIGINAL CONFERENCE	PERCENTAGE CHANGE IN STOCK MARKET*
1967	Green Bay Packers	NFC	15.2
1968	Green Bay Packers	NFC	4.3
1969	New York Jets	AFC	−15.2
1970	Kansas City Chiefs	AFC	4.8
1971	Baltimore Colts	NFC**	6.1
1972	Dallas Cowboys	NFC	14.6
1973	Miami Dolphins	AFC	−16.6
1974	Miami Dolphins	AFC	−27.6
1975	Pittsburgh Steelers	NFC**	38.3
1976	Pittsburgh Steelers	NFC**	17.9
1977	Oakland Raiders	AFC	−17.3
1978	Dallas Cowboys	NFC	−3.1
1979	Pittsburgh Steelers	NFC**	4.2
1980	Pittsburgh Steelers	NFC**	14.9
1981	Oakland Raiders	AFC	−9.2
1982	San Francisco 49ers	NFC	19.6
1983	Washington Redskins	NFC	20.3
1984	Los Angeles Raiders	AFC	−3.7
1985	San Francisco 49ers	NFC	27.7
1986	Chicago Bears	NFC	22.6
1987	New York Giants	NFC	2.3
1988	Washington Redskins	NFC	11.8
1989	San Francisco 49ers	NFC	27.0
1990	San Francisco 49ers	NFC	−4.3
1991	New York Giants	NFC	20.3

* From end of prior year as measured by the Dow-Jones Industrial Average.
** Now members of AFC.
According to a naive theory (first offered by a stockbroker), the stock market advances when a team from the (original) National Football Conference wins the Super Bowl and declines when a team from the American Football Conference wins. Although this theory enjoys an admirable track record, its success is attributable to chance.
SOURCE: Adapted from Manufacturers Hanover Corporation, *Financial Digest* (January 16, 1987), p. 1. Updated by authors.

TABLE 1.2

miniscule share of the total wheat crop that the price of wheat received by the farmer can be taken as given. When the farmer produces twice as much wheat, the farmer's income from wheat doubles. But this is not true for wheat farmers as a group. Doubling the aggregate wheat crop causes wheat prices to plummet (unless the government intervenes to stabilize prices). If prices fall sufficiently, total income of wheat farmers may drop despite the higher volume of output.

Why Do Economists Disagree?

If economists are careful to avoid such pitfalls as the ones just discussed, then why do they disagree so often? According to an old saying, if all economists were placed end to end they still would not reach a conclusion. Actually, economists agree more than is commonly believed. According to one poll, 97 percent of economists agree that restricting trade between countries "reduces general economic welfare." And 98 percent conclude that limiting the ability of landlords to raise rents "reduces the quantity and quality of housing available."[4]

Disagreements, where they occur, sometimes arise because data fail to demonstrate convincingly the superiority of one theory. One data set may suggest that theory X is better, whereas other evidence favors theory Y. In such cases, disagreements among economists are not surprising. Fortunately, additional research sometimes leads to a consensus.

Differences also exist in the area of forecasts. A forecast can be thought of as a conditional statement: if event A occurs, event B will follow. Economic forecasts, however, often diverge because of differences in assumptions—for example, about whether or not event A will even occur. Two economists may agree that if the money supply grows 9 percent this year then prices will rise about 6 percent next year. Nonetheless, their predictions about inflation may differ markedly because one economist believes the money supply will grow 9 percent, whereas the other economist expects a much slower growth. Even a good model cannot forecast accurately when the assumptions on which it is based do not hold.

Certain disagreements among economists are attributable to differences in ideology. Some economists, like some noneconomists, are liberal; other economists are conservative. Liberals tend to have greater confidence than conservatives in the ability of government to solve problems. Therefore, it should come as no surprise that liberals tend to favor heavier doses of government intervention. If you hear two economists debate a proposal to scale back the size of government, realize that their differences arise not because economists cannot agree on how much government is optimal, but because conservatives and liberals cannot agree.

NORMATIVE VERSUS POSITIVE ECONOMICS

NORMATIVE ECONOMICS
Deals with value judgments.

Statements in **normative economics** cannot be tested—cannot be shown to be true or false. Instead, they reflect value judgments—subjective preferences of an individual. Because normative statements cannot be tested, they are not scientific. Examples of normative statements include: *spending on national defense should be decreased* and *lotteries are a good way for a state to raise revenues.*

POSITIVE ECONOMICS
Involves statements based on fact.

In contrast, statements in **positive economics** deal with facts. Such statements are either true or false. In principle they can be tested and, if not supported by the evidence, rejected. Factual statements about the past and predictions about the future both fall within the realm of positive economics. Examples include: *the share of government spending devoted to national defense has fallen since President Reagan left office*, and *a Texas lottery, if enacted, would generate at least $100 million a year in revenue for the state.* Note that the second statement makes no claim about whether or not Texas should have a lottery, only about what would occur if there were a lottery.

Economists, of course, sometimes make normative statements. If you are chairman of the Council of Economic Advisors, you cannot very well turn down the

---

[4]J. R. Kearl, C. L. Pope, G. C. Whiting, and L. T. Wimmer, "What Economists Think," *American Economic Review* (May 1979), p. 30.

president's request that you develop a set of policy recommendations. If Dan Rather, with the cameras rolling, asks for an assessment of a tax proposal, he is likely to receive an opinion. Most economics, however, deals with positive economics—as does this book. This is where economists make their greatest contribution. By formulating and testing theories, economists provide valuable information to individuals, businesses, unions, politicians, and other interested groups. But once the facts are on the table, economists can no better determine optimal policy than informed noneconomists can.

Consider the case of unemployment insurance, a program in which workers who lose their jobs may qualify for weekly unemployment insurance (UI) benefits while they are out of work. Economic research has uncovered certain findings such as:

1. For many workers UI benefits replace more than one-half their lost wages.
2. Unemployed workers spend less time looking for a job if they are receiving UI benefits.
3. On average, the higher weekly UI benefits are, the longer a person remains unemployed.
4. The UI system causes employers to lay off more workers than they otherwise would.

These findings do not indicate whether the UI program is good or bad; they do not tell policymakers whether UI laws should be amended, repealed, or left intact. What economic research does is heighten political awareness of the consequences of UI laws. Armed with such information, legislators frequently adjust previously enacted laws. As one economist observed:

> The congressional staff personnel I interviewed, none of whom had formal training in economics, indicated that economic research provided part of the impetus for changing the UI program.[5]

Macroeconomics Versus Microeconomics

MACROECONOMICS
The study of the aggregate economy.

MICROECONOMICS
The study of the individual units that comprise the economy.

GROSS DOMESTIC PRODUCT (GDP)
A measure of the total output of the economy.

Economics consists of two main branches: **macroeconomics** and **microeconomics**. Macroeconomics studies the big picture, the economy as a whole. Microeconomics focuses on smaller economic units, including consumers and business firms. If macroeconomics is the forest, microeconomics is the trees.

Consider production. Macroeconomics is concerned with aggregate output of the entire economy—what economists call **gross domestic product (GDP)**. How fast is GDP growing? What can society do to promote more rapid growth in the future? If growth turns negative, so that less output is being produced this year than last year, what can be done to soften the blow and alleviate economic hardship? In contrast, microeconomics examines the amount of output produced by

[5]Daniel Hamermesh, "The Interaction Between Research and Policy: the Case of Unemployment Insurance," *American Economic Review* (May 1982), p. 240.

individual industries and by the companies within those industries. It also addresses the question of whether the price and the volume of an industry's output depend on the number of business firms producing that product. In other words, what difference does it make whether a single company or 1,000 companies produce the product?

Output often flows across a country's borders. *Exports* are goods produced in one country but sold elsewhere. *Imports* are goods brought in from other countries. Macroeconomists compare the volume of exports and imports (Figure 1.3) and monitor how differences in the size of these flows affect the value of the U.S. dollar relative to foreign currencies. Of late, macroeconomists are examining why U.S. imports are so much greater than U.S. exports and analyzing the effect this has on the overall economy. Microeconomists focus on how trade restrictions affect particular groups and industries. For example, how do trade barriers affect employment of textile workers, income of farmers, or the standard of living of the average consumer? Similarly, in other fields of economics, macroeconomists study aggregate conditions while microeconomists focus on individual components.

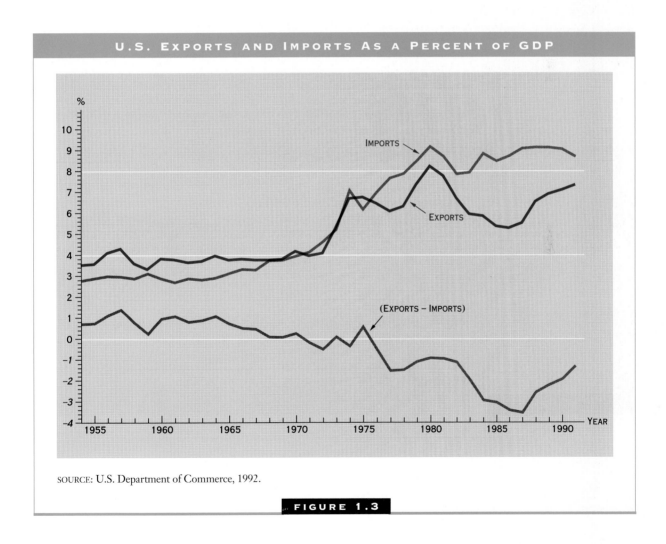

U.S. EXPORTS AND IMPORTS AS A PERCENT OF GDP

SOURCE: U.S. Department of Commerce, 1992.

FIGURE 1.3

E
X
H
I
B
I
T

1 . 2

It is no secret that forecasts of the economy are fallible. As a nonexperimental social science, economics cannot achieve the degree of precision that physicists attain in measuring the speed of light or even the lower degree achieved by meteorologists in predicting tomorrow's precipitation. It is less widely understood that, despite several notable mistakes, economic forecasters have been able to predict some, though not all, important economic variables better than simple rules of thumb and that their accuracy seems to have increased over time.

A long period of time is required to assess whether forecasting accuracy has changed. The longest documented history of economic forecasts with which I am familiar is the real output [real GDP] forecasts issued each November by the University of Michigan.[6] The accompanying chart displays these forecasts along with the actual GDP results since 1952. The forecasting errors made since 1969 are smaller on average than those made before, even though the changes in real GDP growth have been greater. Improved forecast accuracy has also been found by Mervin Daub for forecasts of real GDP in Canada and by Sir Terence Burns for two-year-ahead forecasts of both real growth and inflation rates in Britain.

A cynic might say that these errors are still too large, but an absolute standard is inappropriate for evaluating forecasts because levels of uncertainty vary over time. Small errors—more than half of which are less than one percentage point—are not a sign of great skill if other forecasts are even more accurate. The "huge" errors (more than a percentage point) made by the University of Michigan forecasters and shown in the chart (the recessions of 1974 and 1982 and the early recoveries in 1955 and 1959) might constitute brilliant forecasts if everyone else were even farther off the mark. The point is that without any sensible absolute standard, forecast evaluation must be taken as relative. If no superior record can be established, describing these errors as too large simply expresses the wish that the future should be less uncertain.

[6]*Real GDP* measures output growth net of inflation—that is, after adjusting for price changes. See note below.

NOTE: Until 1991, *Gross National Product (GNP)* was used in place of GDP. The two measures of output are highly similar (see the macroeconomics component of text for a comparison). Strictly speaking, the data in this chart refer to GNP rather than to GDP.

SOURCE: Stephen K. McNees, "The Accuracy Keeps Improving," *The New York Times*, January 10, 1988, p. F2. Copyright © 1988 by The New York Times Company. Reprinted by permission. Updated with GDP data from the U.S. Department of Commerce and forecasts from the Research Seminar in Quantitative Economics (RSQE) of the University of Michigan.

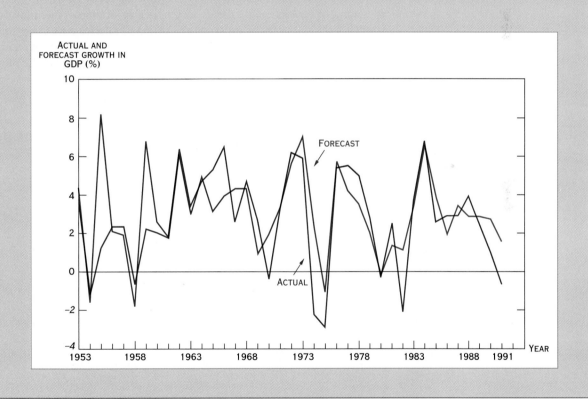

ACTUAL AND
FORECAST GROWTH IN
GDP (%)

FORECAST

ACTUAL

YEAR

What Do Economists Do?

Economists hold a variety of jobs. For example, macroeconomists may be employed to forecast economic activity over the coming year, to predict the effects of higher oil prices, to analyze the economic impact of tax reform. Some microeconomists forecast sales and profits for the company employing them. Others work for government agencies (for example, advising a state commission on the rate a public utility should be allowed to charge for electricity). Still others work as consultants (for example, helping a jury assess the economic loss a worker may have experienced from an injury or providing and interpreting evidence at a wage discrimination trial).

As Table 1.3 indicates, almost two-thirds of economists are employed in business and industry, working for such large corporations as General Electric and Citibank or for small businesses. Unlike many social sciences, economics offers substantial employment opportunities outside of teaching. Nevertheless, colleges and universities are the second-largest employer of economists, followed by the federal government. As might be expected, salaries vary by sector of employment (as well as by educational level and years of experience). Although salaries have risen since 1988, today's relative salaries are not substantially different from the pattern reported in Table 1.3. According to these numbers, the federal government pays the most, while the military and two-year colleges offer the lowest compensation.

DISTRIBUTION OF ECONOMISTS BY EMPLOYER AND SALARY, 1988

EMPLOYER	PERCENT EMPLOYED BY	AVERAGE ANNUAL SALARY
Business and industry	64.0	$34,900
4-year colleges and universities	16.3	45,000
2-year colleges	2.7	31,000
Nonprofit organizations	2.3	38,200
Federal government	7.8	47,400
Military	0.2	17,900
State and local government	5.2	38,000
Other*	1.5	33,600

* Includes those not reporting type of employer.
SOURCES: Employment data for 1988 came from the National Science Foundation, *U.S. Scientists and Engineers: 1988* (NSF 90–314). Salary figures for 1988 are authors' estimates based on 1986 salary figures from *U.S. Scientists and Engineers: 1986* (NSF 87–322) adjusted for average wage gains between 1986 and 1988.

TABLE 1.3

Summary

1. Economic resources consist of land, capital, and labor. Because these resources are limited, what society can produce is also limited; there are insufficient resources to satisfy all human wants.

2. Given resource scarcity, society must choose among alternatives: what to produce, how to produce it, and for whom. These issues are at the heart of economics.

3. When we choose one course we must forgo another. The opportunity cost of an action is what we give up to pursue our decision—that is, the best alternative to the choice we make.

4. Economists assume that economic decision makers behave rationally, that they choose purposefully in an attempt to achieve a given objective. For consumers the assumed goal is utility maximization; for producers it is profit maximization. In making choices, decision makers are assumed to compare the costs and benefits of a given action.

5. Marginal analysis is the study of change. In approaching economic problems, economists rely heavily on marginal analysis. Economic thinking also involves the principles of scarcity and choice, rational behavior, and the weighing of costs and benefits.

6. Economists construct theories to explain economic behavior and to predict economic events. A theory does not replicate the world precisely; instead, it simplifies, focusing on the most important relationships. A model is a formal version of a theory, often presented in mathematical or graphical terms.

7. Economics relies on the scientific approach. After a theory is formulated, evidence is gathered to determine whether it is consistent with the theory. If not, the theory must be revised or rejected.

8. To interpret evidence correctly, one must avoid certain pitfalls. Remember that:
   a. A theory cannot be tested when its "other-things-equal" assumption is violated.
   b. Correlation does not imply causation.
   c. What is true for the individual is not necessarily true for the group.

9. Statements in normative economics reflect value judgments; statements in positive economics deal with facts. Only issues in positive economics can be tested. Therefore, only positive economics is scientific.

10. Economics consists of two main branches. Macroeconomics focuses on the aggregate economy, analyzing such issues as inflation and the overall growth rate of the economy. Microeconomics focuses on smaller units of the economy, such as individual business firms and consumers.

Key Terms

resources	theory
land	hypothesis
capital	inflation rate
labor	scientific method
entrepreneur	model
economic good	other things (being) equal
free good	fallacy of composition
scarcity of resources	normative economics
economics	positive economics
opportunity cost	macroeconomics
rational behavior	microeconomics
marginal analysis	gross domestic product (GDP)

1. Which of the following are scarce economic resources?
   a. a bank teller
   b. fertilizer
   c. air
   d. a baseball game
   e. an ax
   f. a library
   g. a telephone
   h. a lake
   i. an ice cream cone

2. Are the following arguments legitimate? If not, indicate the source of the error.
   a. Because I washed my car yesterday, it rained today.
   b. If I leave the concert 10 minutes before it ends, I can avoid the traffic. If the entire audience leaves 10 minutes early, we can all avoid the traffic.
   c. Teenage Mutant Ninja Turtles were the top-selling toy in 1990. Two years later, despite a drop in price, consumers purchased fewer Teenage Mutant Ninja Turtles. This proves consumers are insensitive to price.
   d. A former coach of the Boston Celtics used to light a cigar in the closing minutes of a game if his team was well ahead. After the cigar was lit, the Celtics always won. Lighting the cigar assured victory.
   e. With record output this year, farmers are assured their highest income ever.

3. An agronomist developed a new strain of corn. To test his claim that its yield exceeds that of an older strain, he conducted the following experiment. He planted the new corn in rich soil, fertilized liberally, and watered as needed. He planted the older corn in heavy, clay soil, which he neither watered nor fertilized. The yield for his new strain of corn was 20 percent higher. Has the agronomist demonstrated that the new corn has a higher yield? Explain.

4. Environmentalists want to preserve the old-growth forests of the Pacific Northwest, home of the endangered spotted owl.
   a. What is the opportunity cost of preserving these forests?
   b. What is the opportunity cost of harvesting the trees of the forest?
   c. Is a decision to reduce the number of acres being preserved an example of marginal analysis?

5. (a) Assume the stock you purchase in a company later becomes worthless. Does this imply that your initial purchase was irrational? Explain. (b) Assume an insurance agent offers you the opportunity to purchase either $20,000 or $30,000 of life insurance. The two policies are identical except for the level of coverage. If both cost $200 per year, is it rational to purchase the $20,000 policy? Explain.

6. "Economics cannot be scientific as long as economists have differing views of what is good and bad." Do you agree? Why or why not?

7. Which of the following are statements in normative economics? Which are statements in positive economics?
   a. The president's economic policies make good sense.
   b. Unemployment is a more serious problem than inflation.
   c. The United States exported a larger share of its output last year than did Canada.
   d. Other things equal, if the price of housing falls more people will buy houses.
   e. There are more farmers in the United States today than 100 years ago.
   f. Poverty in the United States should be reduced.
   g. Inflation next year will be higher in Italy than in Spain.

8. (a) Does the economic cost of attending college include more than tuition and other direct expenses? What else might a student forgo? (b) Tuition and fees at a state university are $4,000 per year. If Amy starts college this year she must quit her $35,000-per-year job as a computer programmer. If Sam starts he loses the $12,000 he would earn as

a farm worker. From an economic perspective, is the cost of attending college the same for Amy as for Sam?

9. "Economic forecasts are rarely on target. Therefore, economists should stop forecasting." Do you agree? Defend your answer. Why do businesses and governments pay for forecasts that might be wrong?

10. Indicate whether the following topics are considered part of *macroeconomics* or *microeconomics*.
    a. the inflation rate
    b. the price of candy bars
    c. a country's unemployment rate
    d. the difference in unemployment rates of college graduates and high-school dropouts
    e. the difference in GDP this year versus last year
    f. the number of Nintendo games produced in a year

YOUR TURN
Answers

Poverty

POVERTY AND SCARCITY ARE DIFFERENT CONCEPTS. SCARCITY EXISTS BECAUSE THERE ARE INSUFFICIENT RESOURCES TO SATISFY ALL HUMAN WANTS. EVEN IF POVERTY WERE ELIMINATED, SCARCITY WOULD REMAIN. ALTHOUGH EVERYONE MIGHT BE GUARANTEED A MINIMALLY ACCEPTABLE STANDARD OF LIVING, SOCIETY STILL WOULD HAVE INADEQUATE RESOURCES TO PRODUCE EVERYTHING DESIRED.

Responding to Incentives

(A) ANYTHING THAT REDUCES THE PERCEIVED BENEFITS OF SMOKING OR INCREASES ITS PERCEIVED COSTS CAN BE EXPECTED TO REDUCE THE LEVEL OF SMOKING. THE SURGEON GENERAL HAS ATTEMPTED TO ALTER PERCEIVED COSTS THROUGH PUBLIC ANNOUNCEMENTS THAT CIGARETTE SMOKING HARMS THE HEALTH OF SMOKERS, THEIR FAMILIES, AND EVEN BABIES BORN TO PREGNANT SMOKERS. FEDERAL AND STATE GOVERNMENTS HAVE INCREASED THE COST OF SMOKING BY SUBJECTING CIGARETTES TO FEDERAL AND STATE TAXES. EVEN EMPLOYERS HAVE ALTERED INCENTIVES BY PAYING EMPLOYEES TO STOP SMOKING AND BY FORCING THOSE WHO DO SMOKE TO LEAVE THE WORKPLACE BEFORE "LIGHTING UP." (B) MORE PEOPLE WILL ENTER THE NURSING PROFESSION IF THE BENEFITS OF BECOMING A NURSE INCREASE (FOR EXAMPLE, BECAUSE OF HIGHER PAY FOR NURSES) OR IF THE COSTS OF BECOMING A NURSE DECREASE (FOR EXAMPLE, BECAUSE OF SCHOLARSHIPS).

Selected References

Becker, Gary S. *The Economic Approach to Human Behavior* (Chicago: University of Chicago Press, 1976), Chapter 1.

Boulding, Kenneth E. *Economics as a Science* (New York: McGraw-Hill, 1970).

Friedman, Milton. *Essays in Positive Economics* (Chicago: University of Chicago Press, 1953).

Fuchs, Victor. *Who Shall Live?* (New York: Basic Books, 1974).

Robinson, Joan V. *Introduction to the Theory of Employment*, 2d ed. (London: Macmillan, 1969), Chapter 13.

Use of Graphs in Economics— a Picture is Worth a Thousand Words

I

NTERPRETING GRAPHS IS ESSENTIAL TO THE PROCESS OF LEARNING ECONOMICS. BECAUSE MODERN ECONOMICS IS A QUANTITATIVE DISCIPLINE, MUCH OF ECONOMIC ANALYSIS INVOLVES EXAMINING RELATIONSHIPS AMONG VARIABLES. A GRAPH CAN BE DEFINED AS A VISUAL MECHANISM FOR ILLUSTRATING THE QUANTITATIVE RELATIONSHIP BETWEEN TWO VARIABLES. THIS BOOK CONTAINS HUNDREDS OF GRAPHS, AND FACILITY IN INTERPRETING THE GRAPHS INEVITABLY BENEFITS YOUR PROGRESS IN THIS COURSE. BEYOND THAT, YOU WILL ENCOUNTER A MULTITUDE OF GRAPHS IN OTHER COLLEGE COURSES, IN YOUR PROFESSIONAL CAREER, AND DURING YOUR LEISURE AS YOU READ JOURNALS AND NEWSPAPERS.

GRAPHS ARE OFTEN MORE EFFICIENT THAN WORDS OR TABLES IN THAT THEY DISPLAY A RELATIVELY LARGE AMOUNT OF DATA WITH PRECISION AND OFTEN MORE EASILY FACILITATE INTERPRETATION OF THE DATA. A GOOD GRAPH ILLUMINATES KEY FACTS AND CASTS IMPORTANT RELATIONSHIPS INTO SHARP RELIEF. THUS, A GOOD GRAPH IS AN EXCELLENT LEARNING DEVICE; A BAD GRAPH CONFUSES AND MISLEADS.

IN APPENDIX 1A WE OUTLINE CERTAIN KEY ASPECTS OF GRAPHS AS THEY PERTAIN TO ECONOMICS AND COVER TWO TYPES OF GRAPHS COMMONLY USED IN ECONOMICS. IN ADDITION, WE OFFER SOME TIPS FOR GETTING THE MOST FROM GRAPHS AND WE CAUTION AGAINST CERTAIN IMPORTANT PITFALLS IN INTERPRETING THEM.

TWO TYPES OF GRAPHS PERVADE ECONOMIC ANALYSIS IN GENERAL AND THIS BOOK IN PARTICULAR: TWO-VARIABLE GRAPHS AND TIME-SERIES GRAPHS. YOU WILL UNDOUBTEDLY RECOGNIZE BOTH TYPES OF GRAPHS FROM PREVIOUS WORK IN HIGH SCHOOL OR COLLEGE—ESPECIALLY IN MATHEMATICS, PHYSICAL SCIENCES, AND SOCIAL SCIENCES.

Two-Variable Graphs

As its name implies, a two-variable graph illustrates the relationship between two variables. Frequently one variable (**dependent variable**) moves *in response to* or *because of* changes in another variable (**independent variable**).

DEPENDENT VARIABLE
Variable whose behavior depends upon, or moves in response to, some other variable (independent variable).

INDEPENDENT VARIABLE
Variable that causes or influences the behavior of some other variable (dependent variable).

The horizontal axis of a graph is the *x-axis*; the vertical axis is the *y-axis*. These axes meet perpendicularly at the **origin**. In mathematics, convention displays the independent variable on the horizontal axis (*x*-axis) and the dependent variable on the vertical axis (*y*-axis). (Economists occasionally ignore this convention, thereby confusing students.)

ORIGIN
The point where the two axes of a graph meet. At the origin, both variables equal zero.

To illustrate construction of a typical two-variable graph in economics, consider the data in Table 1A.1, which indicate the relationship between income and consumption spending for different families.

Figure 1A.1 graphically illustrates the consumption-function data given in Table 1A.1—the relationship between family income and family consumption spending. Family income, the independent variable, is measured along the *x*-axis. Family consumption, the dependent variable, is measured along the *y*-axis. Changes in family income induce changes in family expenditures on consumer goods. Each point (*A, B, C, D, E, F*) on the graph depicts one income-consumption observation given in Table 1A.1. Joining these points by a straight line forms the consumption function. Point A ($4,000) is the *y-intercept*—the magnitude of *y* (consumption) when *x* (family income) is zero.[1]

Occasionally in economics the axes for the dependent and independent variables are reversed. An example is the *demand curve*—the relationship between the price of a good and the quantity consumers would like to purchase. A hypothetical demand curve for grapefruit is shown in Figure 1A.2. In the case of a demand curve, quantity demanded of an item depends upon its price. The price, shown on the *vertical axis*, is the independent variable. Quantity demanded is shown on the horizontal axis. Changes in price bring about changes in quantity demanded (dependent variable).

In some instances a relationship may be depicted wherein it is unclear which variable is the independent variable and which is the dependent variable. Many variables in economics are *interdependent*—causation goes both ways. For example, a strong economy might lead to rising stock prices, but a rising stock market might also stimulate economic activity. Two variables may affect, and be affected by, each other. A graph or diagram may illustrate a relationship between two variables without implying any direction of causation.

MOVEMENT ALONG A RELATIONSHIP VERSUS SHIFT IN THE RELATIONSHIP

It is important to recognize that a two-variable diagram in economics is constructed under the assumption of *ceteris paribus*—other things (being) equal. For

FAMILY INCOME AND CONSUMPTION PATTERNS	
FAMILY INCOME	**FAMILY CONSUMPTION**
0	$ 4,000
$10,000	$12,000
$20,000	$20,000
$30,000	$28,000
$40,000	$36,000
$50,000	$44,000

TABLE 1A.1

[1] A straight line can be described by the equation $y = a + bx$, where *y* is the dependent variable, *x* is the independent variable, *b* is the slope, and *a* is the *y*-intercept (the magnitude of *y* when *x* is zero). The data in Table 1A.1 and Figure 1A.1 may be expressed in equation form as $y = \$4,000 + 0.8x$, where *y* is family consumption and *x* is family income.

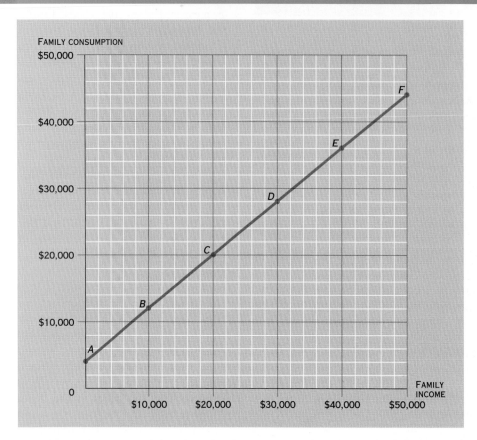

Family consumption expenditures depend on family income. The consumption function graph indicates the nature of this relationship. For example, as family income rises from $20,000 to $30,000, family consumption increases from $20,000 to $28,000 (points C and D).

SOURCE: Table 1A.1 (hypothetical data).

FIGURE 1A.1

example, consider the consumption function in Figure 1A.1. The figure shows the relationship between family income and family consumption, *assuming that all other factors besides family income that influence family consumption remain unchanged*. If any of these other factors change, the entire relationship between family income and family consumption changes. The relationship *shifts*. As an example, family consumption is influenced by attitudes toward thrift and by several other factors in addition to family income. Assume that when families become more concerned about their future well-being, they become more thrifty. Such families spend less on consumer goods

at each income level in order to save and provide for the future. Accordingly, the entire income-consumption relationship in Figure 1A.1 shifts downward.

Consider also Figure 1A.2. In reality, many factors besides the price of grapefruit influence the quantity of grapefruit demanded. The nation's population and level of per-capita income are obvious examples. The demand curve for grapefruit in Figure 1A.2 is constructed under the assumption that population and per-capita income remain constant. However, assume that both per-capita income and population increase in the next year. Accordingly, the position of the demand curve in Figure 1A.2 shifts

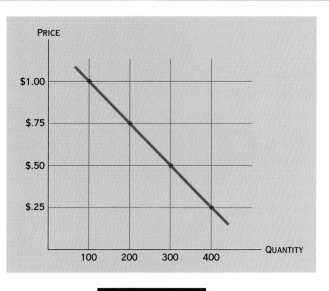

The demand curve for grapefruit shows the quantity of grapefruit that consumers would purchase at each price. In this instance, the independent variable (price) is measured along the vertical axis, whereas the dependent variable (quantity demanded) is measured along the horizontal axis. If the price of grapefruit were to fall from $1 to 50¢, quantity demanded would increase from 100 to 300.

FIGURE 1A.2

rightward or upward. In other words, more grapefruit are demanded at each and every price level.

POSITIVE AND NEGATIVE RELATIONSHIPS IN TWO-VARIABLE GRAPHS

Economic relationships are typically either positive or negative in nature. When an increase in one variable is associated with an increase in the other, the variables are said to be *positively* or *directly* related. An example is the consumption function in Figure 1A.1. An increase in family income gives rise to an increase in family consumption; thus family consumption is directly or positively related to family income. When an increase in one variable is associated with a decrease in the other variable, the variables are *negatively* or *inversely* related. An example is the demand curve in Figure 1A.2. An increase in the price of grapefruit leads to a decrease in the quantity demanded; thus price and quantity demanded are negatively or inversely related.

A substantial part of economics concerns the discovery of independent variables that cause fluctuations in key dependent variables. For example, economists attempt to find the determinants of birthrates, immigration patterns, exchange-rate movements, and housing starts. In fact, economists usually go beyond simply finding the appropriate independent variable(s) to explain key phenomena; they also attempt to pin down the approximate quantitative nature of the relationship. This brings us to the important concept of the *slope* of a graph.

THE SLOPE OF A GRAPH

A graph may be either linear (straight-line) or nonlinear (curvilinear). In either case, the slope provides quantitative information about the nature of the relationship. Slope shows *how much* one variable changes in response to a one-unit change in the other variable. Specifically, slope is the ratio of the vertical change to the horizontal change on the graph.

$$\text{slope} = \frac{\text{rise}}{\text{run}} = \frac{\Delta y}{\Delta x} \quad \text{where } \Delta \text{ means } \textit{change in}$$

$$\frac{\Delta y}{\Delta x} = \frac{y_2 - y_1}{x_2 - x_1}$$

Slope indicates the change in *y* (vertical axis) divided by the change in *x* (horizontal axis).

The ratio of the vertical change to the corresponding horizontal change as we move left to right along the line (that is, the ratio of the *rise* to the *run*).

SLOPE OF A LINEAR RELATIONSHIP

The consumption-function example illustrates slope in a linear relationship, such as Figure 1A.3, where the slope is constant at all points along the line. To measure slope in this instance, simply choose any two points along the line, measure the rise and the run, and compute their ratio. In Figure 1A.3 we see that as family income increases from $10,000 to $20,000, family consumption increases from $12,000 to $20,000. Hence, the *rise* or increase in consumption (ΔC) = $8,000 and the *run* or increase in income (ΔY) = $10,000. The slope = $\Delta C / \Delta Y$ = $8,000/$10,000 = 0.80. Each one-dollar increase in income induces the family to increase consumption by 80 cents. Note that the slope is positive in this example because the variables are directly or positively related.

Slope may be positive, negative, zero, or infinite; Figure 1A.4 provides examples of each. Remembering that slope = rise/run or $\Delta y / \Delta x$, you can confirm each slope category shown in Figure 1A.4 (page 29). In (A) the two variables vary directly or positively; hence, an increase in x gives rise to an increase in y. Because Δy and Δx are both positive as you move left to right along the line, so too is their ratio (the slope). In Figure 1A.4(B) the variables are negatively

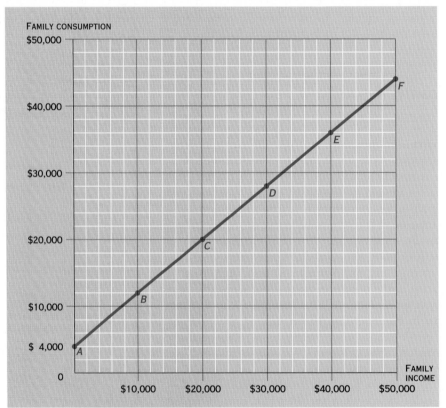

SLOPE OF LINEAR CONSUMPTION FUNCTION

The slope of a linear relationship is the same at all points along the line. This consumption function exhibits a slope of 0.80. Each time income increases by $10,000 (the *run*), consumption increases by $8,000 (the *rise*).

FIGURE 1A.3

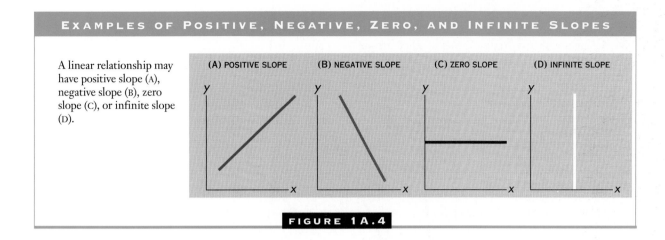

A linear relationship may have positive slope (A), negative slope (B), zero slope (C), or infinite slope (D).

(A) POSITIVE SLOPE

(B) NEGATIVE SLOPE

(C) ZERO SLOPE

(D) INFINITE SLOPE

FIGURE 1A.4

or inversely related; hence, an increase in x leads to a decrease in y. Because Δy and Δx are of opposite signs, their ratio (slope) is negative. In Figure 1A.4(C), y is constant irrespective of x; hence, whenever x changes y remains unchanged. The slope is $\Delta y/\Delta x = 0/\Delta x$ = zero. In Figure 1A.4(D) x never changes—Δx is always zero. Therefore, the slope of the line is $\Delta y/\Delta x = \Delta y/0$, which is undefined or infinity. You encounter each of these four relationships in the study of economics.

A RAY THROUGH THE ORIGIN

There is a straight line of special significance in economics that has a y-intercept of zero. This line is termed a "ray through the origin" or simply a "ray." Figure 1A.5 illustrates four rays of differing slopes.

RAY
A straight line of any slope that emanates from the origin. A straight line with a y-intercept of zero.

Given the grid on which the four *rays* of Figure 1A.5 are drawn, you can confirm the slope of each ray. Of particular significance in economics is the ray of slope = 1. Because this line has a slope of one and passes through the origin, it depicts the set of points at which x and y are equal. The ray of slope = 1 is a 45-degree line emanating from the origin. Any point lying above this ray indicates that y exceeds x; any point lying below the ray indicates that y is less than x. Any point on the 45-degree line indicates that y

and x are equal. Accordingly, the ray of slope = 1 is commonly used in graphs as a guideline or line of equality of the two variables.

45-DEGREE LINE
A ray with slope of (positive) one. It indicates points where the two variables have equal values if both variables are measured in the same units.

SLOPE OF A NONLINEAR RELATIONSHIP

Calculating the slope of a curvilinear relationship (a curved line) is more complex. The slope of such a relationship, unlike a linear one, changes as you move along the curve. This is illustrated in Figure 1A.6 (page 30).

To measure the slope of a curve at some particular point, construct a straight-line *tangent* to the curve at that point. A tangent is the unique line that *touches but does not intersect* the curve. Then measure the slope of the straight-line tangent by calculating the rise/run of the tangent. In Figure 1A.6, the line drawn tangent to the curve at point A exhibits a rise/run of 3/2 or 1.5; the slope of the curve at point A is therefore 1.5. At points B and D, the tangents are horizontal; therefore, the slope of the curve is zero at each of these points.[2] Can you confirm that the slope of the curve at point C is negative 1?

[2]Whenever a curve changes from a positive to a negative slope or vice versa, it must experience a zero slope. Whenever a curve experiences a *maximum* or *minimum*, its slope at such points is zero.

A ray is a straight line that begins at the origin. It may have any slope. Of special usefulness in economics is the 45-degree line—a ray with slope of plus 1. This line marks off all points at which the variables on the x- and y-axes have the same values (assuming both variables are measured in the same units). The 45-degree line is often used as a guideline or reference line.

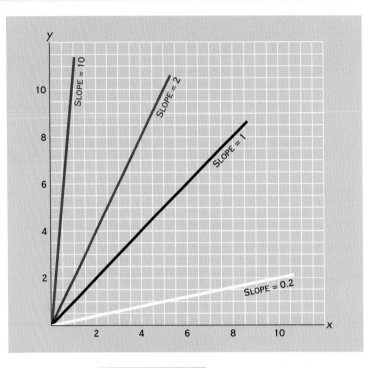

FIGURE 1A.5

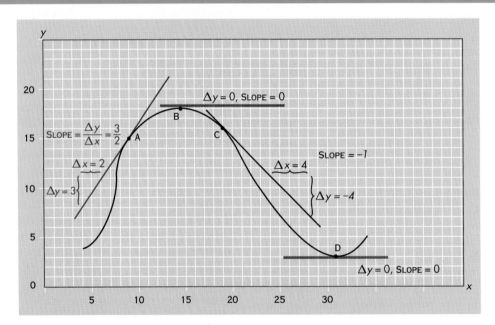

The slope of a curve changes as you move along the curve. At any point on the curve, the slope of the curve is the slope of the *tangent* drawn to the curve at that point. Hence, the slope of Figure 1A.6 at point A is the slope of the line drawn tangent at point A. Note that this slope is rise/run or $\Delta y/\Delta x$ or $3/2 = 1.5$.

FIGURE 1A.6

WHAT TO DO WHEN YOU SEE A TWO-VARIABLE GRAPH

When you encounter a two-variable graph in economics, it is important to adopt an active mode of thinking. When you do, the graph substantially facilitates your understanding of the material under discussion. Try proceeding in the following manner:

1. Immediately look at the variables given on the horizontal and vertical axes and briefly consider the nature of the relationship portrayed. Is the relationship positive (direct) or negative (inverse)? Is it linear or nonlinear?

2. Consider the probable causation involved, if any. Using intuition, does it seem plausible that
   a. the variable on the horizontal axis influences the variable on the vertical axis?
   b. the variable on the vertical axis influences the variable on the horizontal axis?
   c. causation is running both ways—the variables are interdependent?
   d. there is no causation involved—the variables are related only by chance?

3. Think about the *slope* of the graph. What is the *economic interpretation* of this slope?

4. Put the graph into words that explain precisely what the graph tells you.

5. Remember that a two-variable graph, like an economic model, *abstracts from reality*—it isolates the relationship between two variables *while all other factors are conceptually held constant*. Can you think of one such factor that, if changed, would alter the entire *position* of the relationship depicted in the graph?

Time-Series Graphs

A time-series graph simply plots the behavior of an important variable over time. Units of time (for example, years or months) are shown on the horizontal axis; the other variable is shown on the vertical

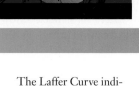

Analyzing a Graph: The Laffer Curve

GIVEN THE GRAPH IN FIGURE 1A.7, KNOWN AS A LAFFER CURVE, RESPOND IN WRITING TO THE PRECEDING FIVE SUGGESTIONS.

THE LAFFER CURVE

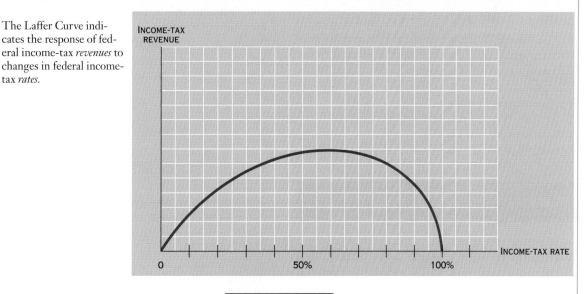

The Laffer Curve indicates the response of federal income-tax *revenues* to changes in federal income-tax *rates*.

FIGURE 1A.7

A time-series graph portrays the behavior of a particular variable over a period of time. Figure 1A.8 shows the fluctuations in the American unemployment rate since 1900.

SOURCE: U.S. Department of Labor, 1992.

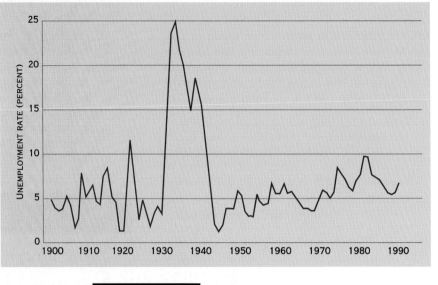

FIGURE 1A.8

axis. Figure 1A.8 is an example of a time-series graph, illustrating the course of the nation's annual unemployment rate from 1900 to 1991.

Time-series graphs are very informative because they efficiently convey historical information about a particular variable. In Figure 1A.8, the behavior of the U.S. unemployment rate since 1900 tells us a lot about our economic history. Note, for example, what happened to the unemployment rate in the 1930s. This period, the Great Depression, was a time of severe economic hardship.

TIME-SERIES GRAPH
Shows how a particular variable changes over time.

Pitfalls in Interpreting Graphs

When properly used, a graph is an efficient and effective means of conveying information. However, graphs can be used to distort facts and sometimes even to consciously misinform.[3] Candidates for political office, advertisers, and others have been known to deliberately mislead by manipulating graphs. Moreover, researchers may inadvertently mislead themselves as well as their readers by the faulty construction of a graph.

Because it is essential to be able to interpret correctly the information conveyed in a graph, we now warn readers of certain perils involved in reading graphs.

STEEPNESS OF A GRAPH AND CHOICE OF UNITS

The appearance of a graph may be altered dramatically at the discretion of the person constructing the graph by simply changing the units on the axes. For

[3]For more on this, see Darrell Huff and Irving Geis, *How to Lie with Statistics* (New York: Norton, 1954).

this reason, the apparent steepness of the rise or fall of a graphical relationship is not always a reliable indicator of the strength of the relationship between the two variables. Consider the factual information provided in Table 1A.2.

Table 1A.2 gives the level of the nation's consumer price index (CPI) and the nation's real output (real GDP) during each year from 1981 to 1991. The CPI measures changes in the general level of prices, whereas real GDP measures the value of the nation's annual output adjusted for changes in the price level. Growth in real GDP is highly desirable because it normally indicates there are more jobs and income available. On the other hand, rising prices are undesirable because they imply that each dollar of income purchases fewer goods and services. People love higher incomes and hate higher prices.

In the 1992 presidential campaign, the Democrats and Bill Clinton were running against the Republicans and incumbent President George Bush. Bush had been vice-president during the 1981–88 period in the Reagan Administration. Then Bush was elected president in 1988. As the incumbent president, Bush had a strong incentive to portray a "glowing" picture of the nation's economic performance during the previous several years. The Democratic challengers had a natural incentive to portray this economic performance as "less than glowing." Here's how the Republican and Democratic campaign staffs might hypothetically have portrayed the identical data from Table 1A.2 to support their own agendas (Figure 1A.9).

The Bush campaign graphs, *at first glance*, appear to demonstrate outstanding economic performance—a quite modest increase in prices and a robust expansion (except for the 1982 and 1991 recessions) in the nation's output. The Clinton graphs appear to show just the opposite results—a sharp increase in the consumer price index and rather anemic growth in real GDP. Neither side cheated or fudged the data in Table 1A.2. All each side did was construct the scales on the vertical axes of the two graphs in a manner conducive to convincing naive or unsophisticated viewers about the validity of the case they were attempting to portray. The moral: Look carefully at the gradation on the axes before drawing inferences about the magnitude of the change of a variable over time or about the strength of the relationship between two variables.

INTERPRETING GROWTH TRENDS

Aggregative economic data are frequently characterized by growth over time. For example, the nation's population, price level, and level of real output or GDP all rise persistently over time. To obtain a useful perspective on time-series data over time, it is frequently helpful to look at a particular variable *relative to some other key relevant variable* in the economy. Instead of looking at the level of wages over time, economists typically look at *real* wages (wages adjusted for changes in the price level). Instead of looking at real income in India, economists frequently look at real income *per capita*. Instead of looking at growth in the national debt, economists often look at growth in the debt *relative to the nation's GDP*.

Figure 1A.10 is a time-series graph that shows American defense spending since 1960, together with the percentage of the nation's gross income (GDP) spent on defense in the same period. An alarmist might use the top portion of the figure to emphasize the apparent *runaway growth* in defense spending. Indeed, defense spending increased by

BEHAVIOR OF CPI AND REAL GDP, 1981–1991		
YEAR	CPI	REAL GDP ($ BILLIONS)
1981	90.9	$3,843
1982	96.5	3,760
1983	99.6	3,907
1984	103.9	4,149
1985	107.6	4,280
1986	109.6	4,405
1987	113.6	4,540
1988	118.3	4,719
1989	124.0	4,837
1990	130.7	4,885
1991	136.2	4,850

SOURCE: *Economic Indicators*, U.S. Government Printing Office, 1992.

TABLE 1A.2

REPUBLICAN PORTRAYAL (BUSH)

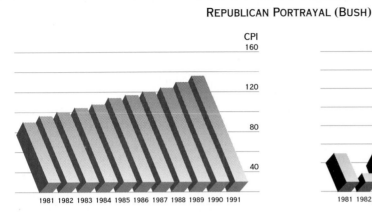

DEMOCRATIC PORTRAYAL (CLINTON)

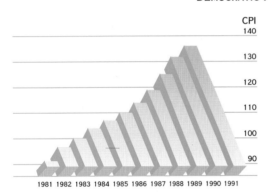

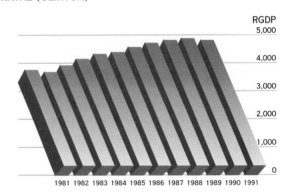

By changing the units along the vertical axis of a graph, the *apparent* relationship may be altered dramatically. The Bush graphs *seem* to indicate a relatively stable price level performance (CPI) and a strong economic growth performance (RGDP). The Clinton graphs *seem* to show the opposite. Actually, both candidates' graphs depict the same information (that is, the data of Table 1A.2). In interpreting a graph, always carefully note the gradation of the units along the axes.

SOURCE: Table 1A.2.

FIGURE 1A.9

more than 500 percent during 1960–1991. However, this analysis neglects to mention that the nation's output (GDP) increased even faster during the same period. As a result, the fraction of the nation's output allocated to defense was lower in the early 1990s than in the 1960s, as indicated in the lower portion of Figure 1A.10.

One can frequently obtain a better perspective on the growth of a time-series variable by viewing its growth relative to a key macroeconomic indicator—dividing it by the nation's GDP or the price level, for

example. Be careful in interpreting the meaning of a graph that merely plots the growth in the dollar value of a variable over time.

DISTORTION OF TREND BY CHOICE OF THE TIME PERIOD

Those who use data must constantly be wary of the potential distortion of the trend of time-series data by the selection of the starting point or ending point

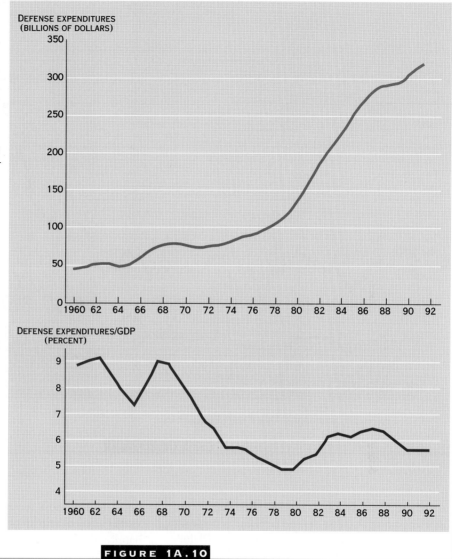

The top figure indicates that defense expenditures have increased dramatically since 1960. However, the bottom figure shows that defense expenditures have declined as a proportion of our nation's gross domestic product (GDP). It is often useful to view the magnitude of variables in relation to broad macroeconomic indicators.

SOURCE: *Economic Report of the President, 1992.*

DEFENSE EXPENDITURES (BILLIONS OF DOLLARS)

DEFENSE EXPENDITURES/GDP (PERCENT)

FIGURE 1A.10

in the series. The Democratic Party's supporters of 1992, in attempting to convince viewers of the *sluggish performance* of the U.S. economy during *recent years*, could begin the GDP graph at the point representing the previous peak or high point of the business cycle. A Bush supporter could best make the case for *robust growth* by beginning the GDP series at the low point of the business cycle (1982).

Assume someone wants to make the case that common stocks are a poor investment. U.S. stock-market performance during the past 25 years is shown in Figure 1A.11. On October 19, 1987, the Dow-Jones Industrials Average plummeted by a record-setting 509 points. One could begin the graph shortly prior to the crash and bring it up to the present. This graph would indicate a relatively modest performance of stock prices since mid-1987. Such a graph would be misleading because the Dow-Jones Industrials Average increased by more than 1500 points from 1982 until the 1987 crash. If one starts the graph in the early 1980s, the stock market's performance appears quite impressive for the decade in

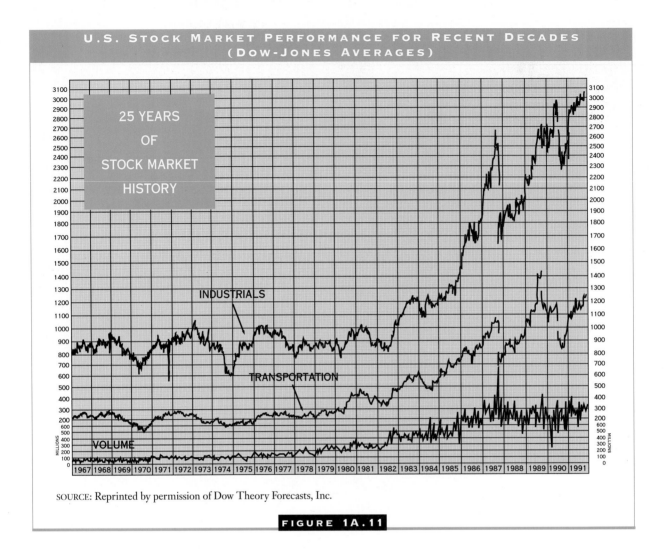

25 YEARS
OF
STOCK MARKET
HISTORY

INDUSTRIALS

TRANSPORTATION

VOLUME

SOURCE: Reprinted by permission of Dow Theory Forecasts, Inc.

FIGURE 1A.11

spite of the *Great Meltdown* of 1987. But that choice of starting point also distorts the facts and is misleading because the stock market did rather poorly during 1967–1982. In fact, the Dow-Jones Industrials Average of stock prices was actually lower in 1982 than in late 1965—17 years earlier.

To present time-series data objectively, it is usually best to show a long time span and to update the series to the most recent observations. In this way viewers may obtain an objective view of what actually happened. Portrayal of time-series data for a brief time span removes the data from historical context and runs the risk of misleading the viewer.

Analyzing a Graph: The Laffer Curve

1. THE LAFFER CURVE RELATES INCOME-TAX RATES AND INCOME-TAX REVENUES. THE RELATIONSHIP IS NONLINEAR. AT TAX RATES FROM ZERO TO ABOUT 60 PERCENT, THE RELATIONSHIP IS DIRECT OR POSITIVE. AT TAX RATES ABOVE 60 PERCENT, THE RELATIONSHIP IS INVERSE OR NEGATIVE.

2. THE INCOME-TAX RATE IS THE INDEPENDENT VARIABLE AND INCOME-TAX REVENUE, THAT IS, INCOME-TAX RECEIPTS, IS THE DEPENDENT VARIABLE. THE DIRECTION OF CAUSATION RUNS FROM THE INCOME-TAX RATE TO THE INCOME-TAX REVENUE. CHANGES IN INCOME-TAX RATES GIVE RISE TO CHANGES IN INCOME-TAX REVENUE.

3. THE SLOPE REVEALS THE ADDITIONAL TAX REVENUE (POSITIVE OR NEGATIVE) PER UNIT INCREASE IN THE INCOME-TAX RATE.

4. THE GRAPH TELLS US THAT WITH ZERO OR 100 PERCENT INCOME-TAX RATES, THERE IS NO INCOME-TAX REVENUE. AS THE INCOME-TAX RATE INCREASES FROM ZERO TO ABOUT 60 PERCENT, INCOME-TAX REVENUES INCREASE. HOWEVER, AS THE INCOME-TAX RATE RISES FROM 60 PERCENT TO 100 PERCENT, INCOME-TAX REVENUES DECLINE. MAXIMUM INCOME-TAX REVENUES ARE GENERATED WHEN THE INCOME-TAX RATE IS ABOUT 60 PERCENT.

5. THE LAFFER CURVE IS DRAWN FOR A GIVEN POINT OF TIME AND THEREFORE A GIVEN SIZE OF ECONOMY—A GIVEN NATIONAL INCOME OR GROSS DOMESTIC PRODUCT. IF THE NATION'S INCOME RISES, THE LAFFER CURVE MOVES UPWARD. HOWEVER, ZERO AND 100 PERCENT INCOME TAX RATES ALWAYS YIELD ZERO INCOME TAX REVENUE. SO THE LAFFER CURVE IS LIKELY TO GRADUALLY BOW INCREASINGLY UPWARD OVER TIME AS THE ECONOMY GROWS.

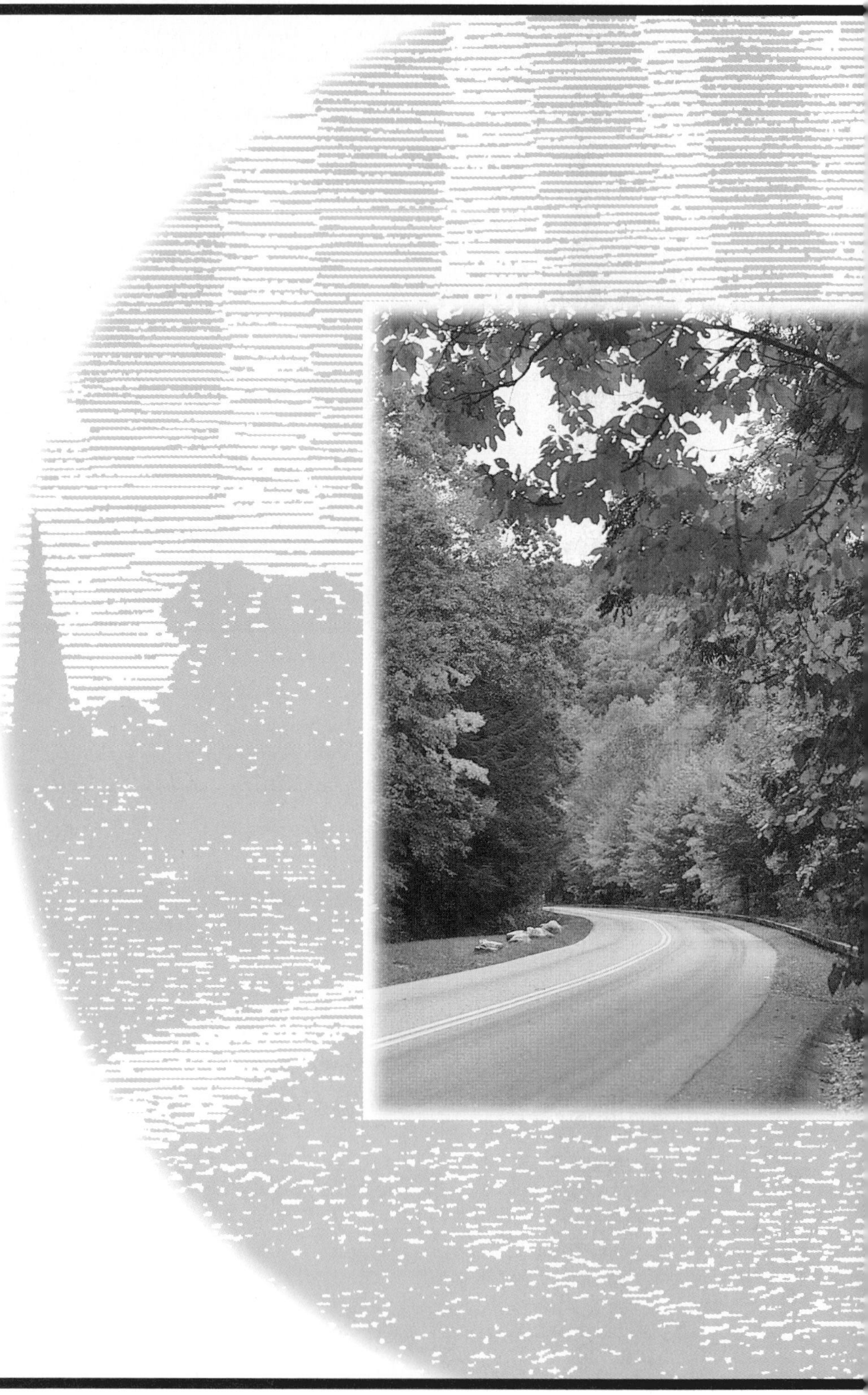

The Economic Decisions Facing a Country

AS YOU LEARNED IN CHAPTER 1, ALL COUNTRIES MUST CONFRONT THE FUNDAMENTAL ECONOMIC PROBLEM OF SCARCITY. LACKING SUFFICIENT RESOURCES TO SATISFY ALL WANTS, NATIONS MUST DECIDE WHAT GOODS TO PRODUCE, HOW TO PRODUCE THEM, AND FOR WHOM. HISTORICALLY, DIFFERENT COUNTRIES HAVE RELIED ON DIFFERENT *ECONOMIC SYSTEMS* TO ANSWER THESE QUESTIONS.

THROUGHOUT MUCH OF THIS CENTURY, ECONOMIC DECISIONS IN THE SOVIET UNION AND MUCH OF EASTERN EUROPE WERE MADE BY GOVERNMENT PLANNERS. BUT AS DISSATISFACTION WITH CENTRAL PLANNING INTENSIFIED, THE SOVIET SYSTEM COLLAPSED AND THE FORMER SOVIET REPUBLICS AND EASTERN EUROPEAN NATIONS BEGAN MOVING AWAY FROM A COMMAND ECONOMY AND IN THE DIRECTION OF CAPITALISM. DIFFERENT COUNTRIES ARE TRAVELING BY DIFFERENT ROUTES AND AT DIFFERENT SPEEDS, AND THE DEGREE TO WHICH THEY ULTIMATELY EMBRACE MARKETS AND PRIVATE PROPERTY REMAINS TO BE SEEN. BUT BECAUSE ALL ROADS FROM A COMMAND ECONOMY TO CAPITALISM ARE UNTRAVELED, THE RIDE PROMISES TO BE BUMPY.

CHAPTER 2 FIRST DEVELOPS A MODEL TO ANALYZE THE ECONOMIC DECISIONS FACING EACH COUNTRY AND THEN CONSIDERS HOW DIFFERENT ECONOMIC SYSTEMS MAKE THESE DECISIONS—FOCUSING ON THE ECONOMIES OF THE UNITED STATES AND EASTERN EUROPE AND THE PAST ECONOMIC SYSTEM OF THE SOVIET UNION. FINALLY, THE CHAPTER EXTENDS THE DISCUSSION TO INCLUDE TRADE

The restructuring of Eastern Europe is the great economic experiment of our time. Despite past experimentation, there is still no successful example of the transformation of a command system into a market economy.[1]

[1]Gary Jefferson and Peter Petri, "From Marx to Markets," *Challenge*, September/October 1990, p. 4.

between countries. All countries, regardless of their economic systems, engage in trade. What are the reasons for trade, and what are the consequences? Does trade benefit both trading partners or just one?

The Production Possibilities Curve

**PRODUCTION
POSSIBILITIES
CURVE**

A line revealing the maximum combinations of two goods that can be produced with a given quantity of resources, assuming that technology is fixed.

TECHNOLOGY

The body of knowledge encompassing techniques for transforming resources into output.

In Chapter 1 you learned that models play an important role in economics. One of the most basic of economic models is the **production possibilities curve**. Underlying this model are the assumptions that the quantity of resources is fixed, the resources can be used to produce either of two goods, and the country's **technology** or technical expertise is constant. Under these conditions, the production possibilities curve indicates the maximum combinations of the two goods that can be produced with available resources. Figure 2.1 depicts a hypothetical production possibilities curve for tractors and corn. According to Figure 2.1, the hypothetical country can produce 50 tractors (if it devotes all its resources to this activity), 4 million bushels of corn (if it produces only corn), or intermediate combinations of tractors and corn (if it divides resources between these two products).

Note that the production possibilities curve is not perfectly realistic; the assumption that a country produces only corn and tractors is, of course, simplistic. Nevertheless, recall that abstraction and simplicity are the hallmarks of a model. A model is judged on how well it explains and predicts—and on such criteria the production possibilities curve must be judged a success. The production possibilities curve demonstrates such concepts as scarcity, efficient production, trade-offs, opportunity cost, the law of increasing costs, and economic growth.

SCARCITY

The production possibilities curve is the boundary between feasible outcomes and nonfeasible outcomes. No matter how resources are used, the hypothetical country cannot reach point W (Figure 2.1). If the country produces 3 million bushels of corn, its remaining resources are insufficient to produce 35 tractors. Given the country's limited resources, point W and all other points that lie beyond the production possibilities curve are unattainable. *Because of scarcity, a country is limited to points on or below its production possibilities curve.*

EFFICIENT PRODUCTION

**INEFFICIENT
PRODUCTION**

Producing less than maximum output; occurs when resources are left idle or used ineffectively.

Although points below the production possibilities curve are feasible (Figure 2.1), they are in some sense unattractive. In particular, the points signify **inefficient production**. Production is said to be *efficient* when a country achieves maximum output from its resources. Clearly, point Z is inefficient. If the country decides to produce 2 million bushels of corn, it can also produce 35 tractors. To produce only 20 tractors—which is what the country does when it operates at point Z—means that the country is not achieving maximum output from its resources. Either it has

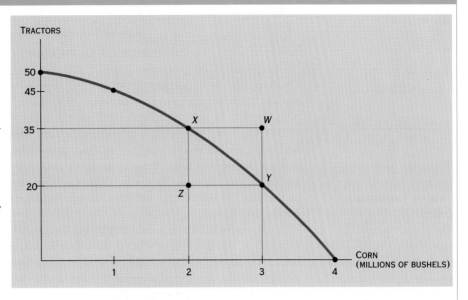

The production possibilities curve depicted shows the various combinations of tractors and corn that can be produced—assuming quantity of resources remains fixed and technology is constant. The country is limited to points *on* the curve (for example, *X* and *Y*) or points *below* the curve (for example, *Z*). Points *beyond* the production possibilities curve (for example, *W*) are unattainable.

FIGURE 2.1

EFFICIENT PRODUCTION
Achieving maximum feasible output from a given amount of resources.

idle resources (for example, unemployed workers and closed plants) or it is not putting its resources to their best use (for example, farmers produce tractors while transportation workers grow corn). Only points on the production possibilities curve signify **efficient production**. Thus, *the production possibilities curve consists of all combinations of output that are both feasible and produced efficiently.*

TRADE-OFFS

If production is efficient, the only way a country can produce more of one good is to give up some of the other good. Efficient production means operating on the production possibilities curve—that is, gaining maximum output from a country's resources. Therefore, the only way a country can produce more of one good is to devote additional resources to that good. But this means that resources must be diverted from the other good and, in the process, production of the other good must fall. In other words, the country faces a trade-off: additional corn means fewer tractors and, conversely, more tractors mean less corn.

OPPORTUNITY COST

The cost of additional corn is the number of tractors sacrificed to produce that corn (Figure 2.1). Consider what happens as the hypothetical country moves from point *X* on the production possibilities curve to point *Y*. Production of corn rises from 2 million bushels to 3 million while production of tractors falls from 35 units to 20 units. Therefore, the opportunity cost of the additional 1 million bushels of corn is 15 tractors.

THE LAW OF INCREASING COSTS

Observe that the opportunity cost of 1 million bushels of corn depends on a country's location along its production possibilities curve. Starting at the upper-left corner (Figure 2.1), the cost of moving from no corn to 1 million bushels is 5 tractors (50 − 45). Once the country produces the first million bushels, the cost of a second million is 10 tractors (45 − 35) and, as we have just seen, the cost of a third million bushels is higher yet—15 tractors. In other words, the cost of producing additional corn rises as the country devotes additional resources to the production of this good. These events reflect a proposition in economics known as the **law of increasing costs**.

LAW OF INCREASING COSTS

The hypothesis that the opportunity cost of a good rises as the quantity of the good produced increases.

The law of increasing costs holds that the opportunity cost of a good increases as more of the good is produced. In other words, a country must give up ever-increasing amounts of one good to achieve a given increase in the other good. Diagrammatically, the law of increasing costs implies that the production possibilities curve assumes a *bowed* shape—that is, the curve becomes steeper as the country moves down the curve.

The law of increasing costs can be explained in terms of specialization of resources. In general, resources are not perfectly adaptable to the production of both goods. As a country increases its production of one good, it must divert resources from the production of the other good. At first the cost of doing so is relatively minor. For example, when a country produces relatively little corn, the only resources employed in this activity are resources that are very proficient at producing corn—prime farmland, experienced farmers, and agricultural equipment. However, as a country increases production of corn, it must employ resources that are relatively less suited for growing corn. Ultimately, a country must transfer to farming those resources most suitable for producing tractors—industrial sites, skilled transportation workers, and manufacturing equipment. As resources that are less and less proficient at producing corn are transferred to this activity, the number of tractors given up to produce an additional 1 million bushels of corn rises. In other words, the opportunity cost of producing corn rises.

Nevertheless, production is not always subject to increasing costs. When resources are perfectly adaptable, production is characterized by *constant costs*. For example, assume resources are equally adept at producing tables and chairs. As Figure 2.2 illustrates, the production possibilities curve in this case is a straight line. The cost of producing another table is always two chairs—regardless of how many tables are produced. Because the opportunity cost does not change, the slope of the production possibilities curve is constant.

Empirical evidence indicates that increasing costs, rather than constant costs, are the norm. Therefore, production possibilities curves are traditionally drawn with a bowed shape.

SHIFTING THE PRODUCTION POSSIBILITIES CURVE

The production possibilities curve is drawn on the assumption that resources are fixed and technology is constant. But what happens when we relax these assump-

When resources are equally proficient at producing tables and chairs, the opportunity cost of each table is the same (regardless of the number produced). In this rendition the opportunity cost of one table is two chairs. Because the opportunity cost is constant, the production possibilities curve is a straight line.

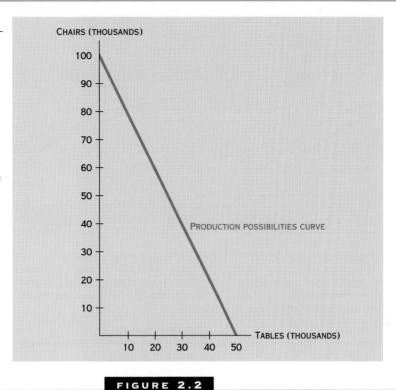

FIGURE 2.2

tions? If a country's resources or technology changes, so must its production possibilities curve. Because the amount of output a country can produce is limited by its resources, an increase in resources shifts the production possibilities curve outward. With additional resources a country can produce previously unattainable levels of output, as is illustrated in Figure 2.3(A) [page 44].

A country's potential output is similarly constrained by available technology. If technological progress occurs, allowing a country to gain additional output from its resources, the result is again an increase (outward shift) in the production possibilities curve. That is, if technological advances increase productivity of resources by 10 percent, it is possible to increase output by 10 percent [Figure 2.3(A)].

In reality, technological progress tends to occur unevenly across sectors, so that gains from technology are similarly spread unevenly. Figure 2.3(B) illustrates a case where technological progress occurs in the production of corn (due, for example, to the development of a new high-yielding strain of corn). As a result, if the hypothetical country devotes all its resources to the production of corn, it can now produce 5 million bushels of corn, rather than 4 million. However, the new strain of corn does not increase the number of tractors that can be produced with a given amount of resources. Consequently, if the country chooses to produce only tractors, it is still limited to 50 tractors. Therefore, the production possibilities curve rotates outward, remaining anchored at point *A*.

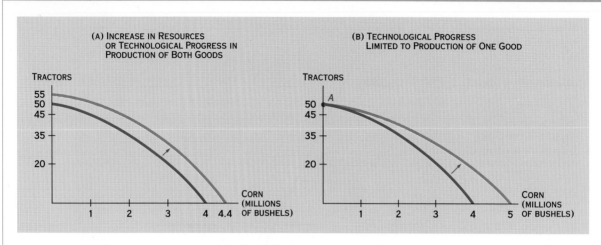

A production possibilities curve shifts rightward when a country acquires additional resources or when technological progress allows a country to obtain increased output from existing resources (A). The special situation in which technological progress is limited to the production of corn is depicted in (B). Both the initial production possibilities curve and the new production possibilities curve share the common end point *A*, reflecting the fact that when resources are used solely to produce tractors the country does not benefit from the technological advance.

FIGURE 2.3

Technological Advances in Tractor Production

ASSUME TECHNOLOGICAL PROGRESS OCCURS ONLY IN THE PRODUCTION OF TRACTORS. (A) DRAW A NEW PRODUCTION POSSIBILITIES CURVE, INDICATING HOW IT DIFFERS FROM THE ORIGINAL PRODUCTION POSSIBILITIES CURVE OF FIGURE 2.3. (B) WHEN A COUNTRY INITIALLY PRODUCES BOTH CORN AND TRACTORS, DOES A TECHNOLOGICAL ADVANCE IN TRACTOR PRODUCTION PERMIT IT TO PRODUCE MORE TRACTORS *AND MORE CORN*? EXPLAIN.

ECONOMIC GROWTH

ECONOMIC GROWTH
The ability of a country to produce greater levels of output—represented by an outward shift of its production possibilities curve.

An outward shift in the production possibilities curve represents **economic growth**, the ability of a country to increase its output. Because countries can raise their standards of living through economic growth, not surprisingly they sometimes attempt to accelerate growth. But how can countries accomplish this?

The production possibilities model indicates that growth occurs when a country increases its resources or develops new technologies. Therefore, economic growth depends on the rate at which a country acquires additional resources and the speed of its technological progress. Both factors, in turn, depend on a country's current production decisions—that is, on how it uses its resources in the present period.

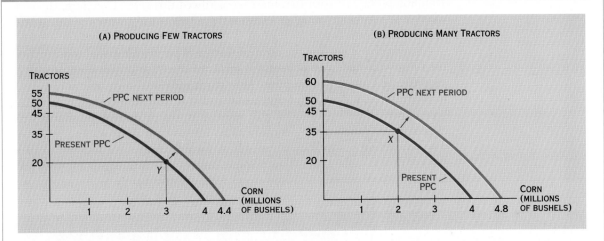

By producing tractors this period, a country increases its available capital next period, thereby spurring economic growth. When only a few tractors are produced, economic growth is modest (A). An increase in the production of tractors causes more rapid economic growth (B).

FIGURE 2.4

CAPITAL GOODS
Output used to produce other goods.

CONSUMER GOODS
Output consumed directly rather than used to produce other goods.

At this point in our discussion it is important to distinguish between *capital goods* and *consumer goods*. **Capital goods** are goods built in order to produce other goods and services. That is, capital goods—including factories, tools, and other equipment—contribute to *future* consumption. In contrast, **consumer goods**—such as food and clothing—are consumed directly. If a country is willing to defer consumption—to produce more capital goods and fewer consumer goods—it can accelerate economic growth. This important principle is illustrated in Figure 2.4.

Because tractors represent a capital good and corn a consumer good, the mix of tractors and corn produced during this period influences production possibilities in the future (Figure 2.4). By increasing tractor production, a country adds to its stock of capital and therefore to its ability to produce additional output next period. For example, if a country operates at point *Y*, producing 20 tractors this year, its production possibilities curve expands only slightly (A). On the other hand, if it operates at point *X*, producing 35 tractors in the present year, its production possibilities curve shifts farther outward next period (B). In summary, *by increasing the ratio of capital goods to consumer goods a country accelerates economic growth.*

Economic growth also depends on the pace of technological progress, something that society can influence. Because technological progress derives from research and development, *an increase in the amount of resources committed to research and development permits more rapid economic growth.*

OPTIMAL COMBINATION OF OUTPUT

What quantities of tractors and corn should society produce? Would it be better off operating at point *X* on its production possibilities curve or at point *Y* (Figure 2.4)?

Although point X permits more rapid economic growth, such growth carries a cost. In particular, the cost of operating at point X rather than at point Y is the additional 1 million bushels of corn that must be sacrificed this year. Therefore, the issue is whether society places a higher value on the additional 15 tractors or the additional million bushels of corn.

Alternatively, because the additional tractors permit additional consumption in the future, the issue can be recast in terms of the trade-off between present consumption and future consumption. How much additional corn must society receive in the future to induce it to forgo consumption of 1 million bushels of corn in the present period? As important as this question is, the production possibilities curve cannot provide the answer—it contains no information about societal preferences. The production possibilities curve indicates which choices are available to society, but not how to make them. This is something society must decide for itself and, as Exhibit 2.1 reveals, such decisions are sometimes difficult.

Alternative Economic Systems

Each society must decide which combination of goods to produce—that is, where to operate on its production possibilities curve. In the process, it must choose how to produce such goods. When a country fails to use its resources efficiently, it is forced to a point beneath the production possibilities curve. Finally, each country must decide how to allocate these goods to the various members of its society—that is, who gets the output after it is produced.

The way a society answers these questions depends on the **economic system** adopted by that country. Although there are different ways to categorize economic systems, one convention, at least for modern economies, is to define economic systems in terms of who owns the country's resources and how economic decisions are made. On this basis, two fundamental economic systems emerge: pure capitalism and the command economy.[2]

Pure capitalism is characterized by private ownership of resources and by reliance on **markets**, in which buyers and sellers come together and determine what quantities of goods and resources are sold and at what price. Here no central authority oversees production and consumption. Rather, economic decisions are coordinated by the actions of large numbers of consumers and producers, each operating in his or her own self-interest. Because property is privately owned, it can be used in whatever manner its owner chooses.

At the opposite extreme, a **command economy** is an economic system in which resources are publicly (collectively) owned and where central authorities (government agencies) dictate how such resources are used. In particular, the questions of *what*, *how*, and *for whom* are answered through government planning. Production takes place in government-owned companies whose output decisions are determined as part of the government's central economic plan. Companies are

ECONOMIC SYSTEM
An institutional arrangement for determining what goods are produced, how they are produced, and for whom.

PURE CAPITALISM
An economic system in which property is privately owned and markets rather than central authorities coordinate economic decisions.

MARKET
A mechanism through which buyers and sellers are brought together for the purpose of exchanging some good or resource.

COMMAND ECONOMY
An economic system in which property is publicly owned and central authorities coordinate economic decisions.

---

[2]Certain less developed countries rely on economic systems that emphasize tradition or heredity. Accordingly, when dealing with such countries it is often necessary to categorize economic systems using an alternative, more elaborate approach.

EXHIBIT
2 . 1

Trade-Off Between Jobs and Fish

Until it closed, a paper mill in Mechanic Falls, Maine, was the town's largest employer. Although the plant closing initially brought despair to the town's residents, the mood brightened after an employer was found who was willing to purchase and reopen the paper mill. But before the deal could be consummated, the prospective owner needed to obtain a waste-discharge license—and that proved to be a major obstacle.

The State Department of Environmental Protection and various private environmental groups opposed issuing a license on the grounds that the water discharged from the mill would warm the Little Androscoggin River, thereby reducing the river's population of brook trout. If the water discharges went unchecked, some claimed that all the trout would die. An alternative favored by environmentalists was to force the company to cool the water to its original temperature before returning it to the river, a costly procedure. If forced to do this, the would-be employer vowed that the mill would remain closed.

Other options included forcing the company to cool the water but not to the river's initial temperature. Less stringent cooling requirements would ease the financial burden on the company, allowing it to reopen the mill. As allowable water temperatures rose, the company would expand production, adding more and more jobs—but losses to the trout population would also mount. The production possibilities curve depicted illustrates the various options. Not surprisingly, different groups had different opinions regarding the optimal point on the production possibilities curve. Most town residents favored a point close to *A*; most environmental groups proposed operating near point *B*.

SOURCE: Adapted from *The New York Times*, "120 Jobs May Rest on Effect on Fish," February 15, 1987, p. 15.

MIXED ECONOMY
An economic system that mixes pure capitalism and a command economy. Some resources are owned privately, others publicly. Some economic decisions are made in markets, others by central authorities.

assigned specific output goals and allocated a certain quantity of resources with which to carry out the goals. The output is then distributed in accordance with government objectives.

Both purely capitalistic and command economies are theoretical extremes, unobserved in reality. All modern economies are classified as **mixed economies**; they contain elements of both economic systems, differing only in terms of the extent to which resources are privately owned and the role accorded to markets. For example, even though the economy of the United States is highly capitalistic, some resources are publicly owned (national parks, highways, public schools). Similarly, despite heavy reliance on markets, the U.S. government makes certain economic decisions (determining the amount of resources devoted to national defense and ordering companies to reduce pollution). On the other hand, even the pre-reform Soviet system—which approximated a command economy—contained traces of capitalism. Consider that Soviet farmers, although they spent most of their time producing for the state, were given small plots of land and permitted to sell the produce from that land in markets.

Because modern economic systems are hybrids of pure capitalism and a command economy, it is important to understand how economic decisions are made under each of these theoretical systems. Among other things, an appreciation of pure capitalism is essential for an understanding of the U.S. economy. And until one comprehends the enormity of the problems confronting a command economy, it is difficult to appreciate the pressures for economic reform in the Soviet Union and Eastern Europe or the challenges posed by that reform. For this reason, we first consider how pure capitalism and a command economy answer the basic questions of *what*, *how*, and *for whom*, and then study the economic transition under way in the former Soviet republics and Eastern Europe—a move away from a command economy and toward capitalism.

HOW CAPITALISTIC ECONOMIES ANSWER THE BASIC ECONOMIC QUESTIONS

CONSUMER SOVEREIGNTY
The principle that consumers, through spending decisions, determine how much of each good is produced.

A purely capitalistic system operates on the principle of **consumer sovereignty**: consumers determine which goods are produced and in what quantities. Consumers reveal preferences through their spending; in a sense, they vote with their dollars. Because companies are in business to make profit, they pay attention to what consumers want—to how they vote.

You see this happening frequently in the United States. When U.S. consumers decide they want more poultry and less beef, producers duly respond, raising more chickens and turkeys while reducing herd size. Similarly, when—in the face of rising energy rates—consumers indicate they want houses that are more energy-efficient, builders construct such houses. The actual mechanism through which consumer preferences are revealed and output levels are determined is explained more fully in Chapters 3 and 4. But this much should be clear: in capitalistic economies, when it comes to determining what is produced, the consumer is king.

Although determining how to produce is the responsibility of individual firms, the market provides signals—rewarding firms that choose the best production techniques and penalizing those that do not. To maximize profit, a company must select the technique that minimizes the costs of producing a given output. Companies that waste resources or that use them inefficiently inflate costs and sacrifice profit. Companies that fail to cover costs lose money—the market's way of indicating that better alternatives exist for the resources. Thus capitalism promotes efficient production.

In a capitalistic economy, the distribution of output is based on the distribution of income. Those whose labor is valued highly or who own large quantities of property are able to purchase more goods and services than those receiving lower wages and owning less property. It all boils down to this: those willing and able to pay the market price obtain the output; those without sufficient income leave the market empty-handed. Because resources are distributed unevenly and because market prices for labor and other resources vary greatly, the distribution of goods and services in a capitalistic economy is also highly uneven. In capitalistic-oriented countries, such as the United States, some dine on caviar and pheasant while others scavenge for scraps.

HOW COMMAND ECONOMIES ANSWER THE BASIC ECONOMIC QUESTIONS

In a command economy, government agencies (central planners) replace the market as arbiter of economic decisions. The government decides which goods are produced, which state companies produce them, which production techniques are used, and how the output is distributed.

Those who favor this type of economic system argue that a command economy overcomes various deficiencies of a capitalistic economy. For example, central planners can ensure that everyone, even those unable to contribute to production, are provided adequate food and shelter. Central planners can also guarantee that goods vital to the nation, including national defense, are adequately provided.[3] In Chapter 3, where the capitalistic system is discussed in greater detail, we illustrate how private markets sometimes fail to produce as much of certain goods as society desires and how at other times they produce output in socially unacceptable ways. For example, market producers may use heavily polluting fuels because of their lower cost even though society prefers that producers use more-expensive but cleaner fuels.

However, even supporters of a command economy concede it is fraught with problems. For example, if the government does not arrange to have enough or the right size of bolts produced, companies that require bolts as an input cannot meet their production goals. In an effort to avoid such problems, the government must fashion a detailed economic plan that coordinates the production activities of all firms. With hundreds of thousands of companies and products, however, such coordination is difficult to achieve—mistakes are inevitable. For example, due to a lack of communication, Soviet repair crews undertook extensive rehabilitation and remodeling of apartment complexes just months before they were scheduled to be torn down. Similarly, Soviet planners erred in deciding where to locate facilities by building factories in remote regions, far from workers and raw materials, and by constructing hydroelectric dams in regions that already had ample electricity.[4]

Another problem of command economies involves stipulating how production is to occur. Because central authorities are far removed from actual production sites, they are often less informed than plant managers and therefore may assign production techniques that fail to minimize costs. Inefficiencies arise for other reasons as well. Because managers and workers receive a bonus if their company meets its production goals, they have an incentive to request more resources from the

---

[3]For a further discussion of the strengths of a command economy, see E. Wayne Nafziger, *The Economics of Developing Countries*, 2nd Ed. (Englewood Cliffs, N.J.: Prentice Hall, 1990), pp. 425–426.

[4]These and other examples of problems confronting Soviet planners are found in Robert G. Kaiser, *Russia* (New York: Simon & Schuster, 1976), Chapter 9.

state than they actually need. From their perspective, it is better to be on the safe side and be able to handle any emergency that may arise. But excess resources assigned to one enterprise are unavailable elsewhere, which reduces the amount of output the country can produce.

Indicative of such waste, some Soviet collective farms were given so much fertilizer that it lay unused in ever-growing hills. Other collective farms burned fertilizer to conceal from central authorities the fact that their allocation was more than they could use. At the same time, other farms were left without adequate fertilizer—since available stocks were fully distributed (the cupboard was bare).

Quality and variety of output also suffer in a command economy. Because state enterprises are not motivated by profit, there is little incentive to produce goods of the type and quality demanded by consumers. When a factory is ordered to produce 100,000 pairs of shoes, it is easier to meet this goal—thereby earning bonuses for the manager and workers—if the factory produces identical, low-quality shoes than if it sets rigorous quality-control standards and introduces a variety of styles and colors.

Compared to capitalism, command economies foster a more equal distribution of output, but the process by which output is distributed is more complex. While capitalism relies on the price system to allocate—those who can pay the market price receive the goods—prices do not serve the same allocative function in a command economy, where prices are administered by the state and often bear scant relationship to the value consumers attach to additional units of a good. Frequently the amount consumers want to buy at the government-determined price exceeds the amount produced. Therefore, the government must resort to measures other than price rationing to distribute output.

Among such measures, the Soviet Union relied on queues. People lined up to buy a product, and when available stocks were depleted those still in line were turned away. It was estimated that Soviet families typically spent from 20 to 40 hours each week standing in line. In fact the appearance of a long line often attract-

ed passing shoppers, who asked what was for sale only after securing a place in line. For other products there was a waiting list. For example, Soviet automobiles were so scarce that consumers were forced to pay cash *up front*, forfeit choice of color, and still wait years for delivery. Families fortunate enough to obtain cars went to great lengths to protect them. Given shortages of auto parts, it was common for owners to lock windshield wipers and other removable parts inside their cars after parking them.

THE ROAD TOWARD CAPITALISM

Aware of the problems inherent in command economies, the Soviet Union in the late 1980s began moving to a more capitalistic system. The economic reforms instituted under Mikhail Gorbachev's *perestroika* (restructuring) program loosened the reins of Soviet central planners. In some cases, managers began making their own production decisions, choosing which companies to buy inputs from, and even negotiating over input prices. The role of incentives was also strengthened, with workers' pay rising with increased output or cost savings and falling when quality was substandard. Starting in 1987, Soviet citizens were permitted to become entrepreneurs, setting up their own small-scale businesses; yet attitudes toward entrepreneurs have evolved slowly. After years of propaganda denouncing entrepreneurship, many former Soviet citizens find it difficult to accept the notion that successful entrepreneurs are entitled to profits (see Exhibit 2.2, page 52).

One of the most fundamental steps in economic reform took place in the early 1990s, when the Soviet Union and much of Eastern Europe began transferring ownership of property from the state to private citizens. Although other countries had *privatized* various enterprises, the transfer of ownership from the public sector to the private sector had not previously been attempted on such a massive scale. Czechoslovakia accepted the challenge in January 1991 when the government began auctioning thousands of state-owned stores to its citizens. Months later, the Solidarity-led government of Poland adopted a different tack—*giving* away state property. Under the Polish plan, all adult citizens were given equal shares in each of a set of mutual funds that, in turn, own the majority stake in hundreds of Polish companies (see Exhibit 2.3, page 53).

Hungary, already a step closer to capitalism than many of its Eastern European neighbors by virtue of its close and lengthy ties with foreign companies, adopted a strategy of selling state property to foreign as well as Hungarian investors. By 1996, if all goes according to plan, the majority of state assets will be in the hands of private investors.

Following the lead of Eastern Europe, the Soviet Union announced plans in the summer of 1991 to relinquish control of most of its large enterprises by the end of 1995. Although the Soviet directive lost its force when the Soviet republics gained autonomy, the individual republics have shown that they are at least as committed to privatization as was the Soviet Union.

At the same time that the former Soviet republics and Eastern Europe are turning more and more resources over to the private sector, they are proceeding, at different rates, to increase the role of markets. Prices of an increased number of goods and resources are being set in the marketplace rather than in government ministries; stock markets are being created; competition from abroad is being

Don't Shoot the Entrepreneurs, Comrade—It's Bad for Business

En route from Camp David to the White House in George Bush's Marine helicopter last June, Mikhail Gorbachev peered out the window and pointed to the green ribbon of Maryland suburbs below. How, Gorbachev asked, do people buy those houses? Raising his voice above the roar of Marine One, Bush explained that a prospective buyer could read newspaper advertisements to find a home. More likely, he would ask a real-estate agent to find a seller. Gorbachev jerked his head upward and waved his arms in amazement. "In my country," he declared, "such an agent would be shot."

Entrepreneurship has traditionally been risky business, especially in the Soviet Union and parts of Eastern Europe, where the role of the entrepreneur is often not appreciated. Entrepreneurs are in business to make profit. Those who succeed in providing a valuable product or service receive their profit, while those who fail suffer a loss. Because entrepreneurship introduces another source of income (profit and loss), it exacerbates income inequality. Although entrepreneurs are generally admired in capitalistic countries for creating something of value, they have been vilified in predominantly command economies for contributing to unequal incomes. As one writer explains, resentment of those who prosper still runs deep in the former Soviet republics and Eastern Europe.

Egalitarianism remains embedded in the Soviet and East European psyche and is the core of many of the practical difficulties in implementing the transition to capitalism. Symptoms can be seen in the public's reactions to the so-called "cooperatives"—that is, privately run businesses—in the Soviet Union. Successful cooperatives are widely resented. Even though a cooperative is providing a needed good or service, one that cannot be obtained elsewhere at any price, many Soviet citizens are angry that the owner of the cooperative is making money. Sometimes the resentment turns to violence.

Soviet citizens have been taught from their earliest years that "profits" come from exploitation, when one person has the economic upper hand over another. The source of the resentment lies ultimately in the assumption that equality is a morally desirable state in itself.

If equality is a moral ideal, then any specific instance of inequality is morally suspect. If one person has a Mercedes when his neighbors still have to take the bus, then he is behaving "wrongly"—in violation of a moral ideal—no matter how he got the money to buy it. It doesn't make any difference if he runs a cooperative that makes an honest ruble by providing value for money.

Until such attitudes change, entrepreneurship is unlikely to flourish in the former Soviet republics or throughout Eastern Europe.

SOURCES: Kenneth Walsh, "The True Believer," *U.S. News and World Report,* July 1, 1991, p. 24, and Charles Murray, "The Pursuit of Happiness on the Road to Democracy," *The American Enterprise,* January/February 1991, p. 41. Reprinted by permission.

EXHIBIT

2.2

E
X
H
I
B
I
T

2 . 3

Poland plans to make every citizen a shareholder in an ambitious plan to turn this once-communist nation into a capitalist one practically overnight. Under the plan, the government would transfer majority ownership in 400 state enterprises to a group of stock funds to be created and run by Western investment managers. All of Poland's 27 million adults would receive vouchers giving them stakes in these "National Wealth Management Funds"—the equivalent of American-style stock mutual funds. Polish citizens would own shares in the funds, and the funds in turn would hold the shares of the newly private companies. Employees in the state enterprises also would receive shares directly.

Western analysts praised the plan as a sign that Warsaw remained committed to moving rapidly toward a market economy. "The plan is fair—everybody gets a stake—and it's fast," said David Lipton, an adviser to the Polish government and an economist at the World Institute for Development Economics, a research organization in Washington. Others added that the plan could serve as a model for other formerly communist nations of Eastern Europe, which face the problem of how to expand private enterprise quickly, fairly, and without inviting domination by foreign investors.

Czechoslovakia has begun making smaller companies private and has announced plans to sell 50 larger companies. Hungary, which has encouraged foreign investment, has set up a State Property Agency to handle the sales. And Germany has handed over much of the property once held by the East German state to a large holding company, which is selling assets.

The Polish government, aided by Western consultants, has worked on its plan for nearly two years. The government says it hopes to privatize nearly half the nation's 7,000 state-owned enterprises in about three years.

SOURCE: *The Kansas City Star*, "Poland Weighs Giving Stakes in Businesses to All Adult Citizens," June 28, 1991, p. A-1. Reprinted by permission.

encouraged through a relaxation of import and export controls; and unprofitable enterprises are being allowed to close.

As unemployment rises and as economies face the adjustment problems associated with creating the legal and financial infrastructure required of market-based economies, there will be calls to slow the pace of economic reform and even to reverse direction. As Hungary's finance minister observed: "The most difficult thing is to persuade the public that for the short term they will have to suffer a lot of disadvantages that will turn to advantages in the long term and will produce greater benefits."[5] Indeed, although the former Soviet republics and Eastern Europe will ultimately achieve a higher output once economic reforms are completed (due to greater efficiencies of a capitalistic-oriented system), output dropped

---

[5]*The Kansas City Star*, "Economic Change is Painful, Eastern Europeans Discover," July 7, 1991, p. A-12.

sharply during the early stages of reform; and economists at the World Bank predict that output per capita in these countries may not return to 1989 levels until 1996 or later. But if the countries stay the course, and the promised economic reforms are carried out, we will have witnessed one of the most exciting and profound economic experiments in recent history.

Trade

INTERNATIONAL TRADE
The exchange of goods or resources between countries.

Regardless of the economic system chosen, each country must decide how to use its resources. In the absence of **international trade**, each country is limited to points on its production possibilities curve. But what if two countries trade? Is it possible for each country to increase the amount of output available to its citizens? Can trade push a country beyond its production possibilities curve?

WHY COUNTRIES TRADE

Some consider trade to be a **zero-sum** game. According to this view, trade cannot create value: if one party benefits from trade, the other party must lose. In fact, the amount the first party gains must coincide exactly with the amount the second party loses.

SPECIALIZATION
An arrangement in which persons or countries concentrate on the production of a limited number of goods or activities, rather than becoming self-sufficient.

This view is incorrect. Trade is often a **positive-sum** game in which both parties gain. For example, both the butcher and the baker may benefit when one trades meat to the other for bread. Although both parties may be able to bake bread and butcher meat, there are reasons for each to **specialize** in the production of just one good: one party may have a natural gift for baking bread, the other for butchering meat. In addition, by specializing in one line of work, each trader gains the experience necessary to become highly proficient in that work. Finally, with specialization there is no unnecessary duplication of capital—it is not necessary for each party to have an oven and a meat grinder. Instead, each obtains specialized equipment for just one line of work—which may reduce the butcher's cost of preparing a pound of meat and the baker's cost of producing a loaf of bread.

For the preceding reasons, the total amounts of bread and meat produced may be greater when each party specializes in a single line of production. For example, rather than each producing ten pounds of meat and ten loaves of bread per hour, through specialization the butcher may be able to produce thirty pounds of meat and the baker thirty loaves of bread. In that event, the total amounts of bread and meat both increase (Table 2.1). With greater output to divide, it is possible for both parties to increase their consumption. *Specialization and trade increase total output and therefore permit a higher standard of living.*

The same logic applies to specialization and trade by countries. Under certain conditions trade increases total output, allowing citizens of each country to increase their average level of consumption. In particular, trade benefits both countries if the opportunity costs of the goods they trade differ by country.

Consider the following hypothetical example. Assume each unit of a resource in the United States can produce either two hams or six bottles of vodka, regardless of the quantities of each already produced. In this event, the opportunity cost of two hams is six bottles of vodka. Equivalently, the opportunity cost of one ham is

| SPECIALIZATION MAY INCREASE THE OUTPUT OF BOTH GOODS | | | | |

SPECIALIZATION MAY INCREASE THE OUTPUT OF BOTH GOODS

	AMOUNT OF MEAT AND BREAD PRODUCED IN ONE HOUR			
	(A) WITHOUT SPECIALIZATION		(B) WITH SPECIALIZATION	
	MEAT*	BREAD**	MEAT*	BREAD**
Worker 1	10	10	30	0
Worker 2	10	10	0	30
Total	20	20	30	30

*Pounds.
**Loaves.

TABLE 2.1

COMPARATIVE ADVANTAGE

The ability of one country to produce a particular good at a lower opportunity cost than a second country.

three bottles of vodka. Assume further that each resource in Russia can produce either one ham or five bottles of vodka. Comparing the two countries, it is apparent that the opportunity cost of ham is lower in the United States—the United States must sacrifice three bottles of vodka for each ham whereas Russia must sacrifice five. Because of the lower opportunity cost, the United States is said to have a **comparative advantage** in the production of ham.

Because the United States is relatively more proficient at producing ham, both the United States and Russia can benefit when the United States specializes in the production of ham and Russia in the production of vodka. The United States can trade some of the additional ham produced as a result of specialization to Russia for some of the additional vodka produced there. Under these conditions, both the United States and Russia realize greater output than when each country is self-sufficient in the production of the two goods.

To extend the example one step further, assume the two countries agree that the United States will export one ham for every four bottles of vodka imported from Russia. In that event, the United States is better off importing vodka than producing it. By trading with Russia, the United States obtains four bottles of vodka for each ham—one more bottle than it would receive if the vodka were produced in the United States (Table 2.2). Russia also gains, since the cost of a ham

HOW TRADE BENEFITS BOTH THE UNITED STATES AND RUSSIA

COUNTRY	THE OPPORTUNITY COST OF 1 HAM	
	(A) WITHOUT TRADE	(B) WITH TRADE
United States	3 bottles of vodka	4 bottles of vodka
Russia	5 bottles of vodka	4 bottles of vodka

If the United States produces 1 less ham it has sufficient resources to produce an additional 3 bottles of vodka. Alternatively, the U.S. can produce the ham and trade it to Russia for 4 bottles of vodka. Because the United States receives 1 extra bottle of vodka for each ham exported to Russia, trade benefits the United States. From the Russian perspective, trade lowers the cost of a ham from 5 bottles of vodka (if produced in Russia) to 4 bottles (if imported from the United States). Thus, trade is also advantageous to Russia.

TABLE 2.2

imported from the United States (four bottles of vodka) is less than the cost of a ham produced in Russia (five bottles of vodka).

In conclusion, trade permits each country to specialize in the production of goods for which it is relatively more proficient—that is, goods for which it has a comparative advantage. By producing goods in countries where the opportunity cost is lower and then trading the goods, both countries gain additional output. Thus trade creates value—output combinations not possible when a country is self-sufficient become possible when a country trades. In graphical terms, trade allows a country to move beyond its production possibilities curve.

YOUR TURN

How Trade Allows a Country to Move Beyond Its Production Possibilities Curve

ASSUME THE UNITED STATES HAS 1 MILLION UNITS OF A RESOURCE AND THAT EACH UNIT CAN PRODUCE EITHER TWO HAMS OR SIX BOTTLES OF VODKA. (A) IF THE UNITED STATES USES ALL ITS RESOURCES TO PRODUCE HAM, HOW MUCH HAM CAN IT PRODUCE? (B) IF THE UNITED STATES USES ONE-HALF ITS RESOURCES TO PRODUCE HAM AND ONE-HALF TO PRODUCE VODKA, HOW MUCH OF EACH GOOD CAN IT PRODUCE? (C) DRAW THE APPROPRIATE PRODUCTION POSSIBILITIES CURVE. (D) RUSSIA AGREES TO TRADE FOUR BOTTLES OF VODKA FOR EACH HAM THE UNITED STATES EXPORTS. AS A RESULT, THE UNITED STATES DECIDES TO PRODUCE ONLY HAM. IF THE UNITED STATES KEEPS ONE-HALF THE HAM IT PRODUCES AND TRADES THE OTHER ONE-HALF TO RUSSIA, HOW MUCH VODKA WILL THE UNITED STATES RECEIVE? (E) ADD ONE POINT TO THE DIAGRAM DRAWN IN (C) TO REPRESENT THE COMBINATION OF HAM AND VODKA AVAILABLE TO THE UNITED STATES AFTER TRADE. IS THIS COMBINATION OF HAM AND VODKA ATTAINABLE WITHOUT TRADE?

TRANSACTION COSTS REDUCE THE GAINS FROM TRADE

TRANSACTION COSTS
The costs associated with the exchange of a good or resource.

For expediency, the preceding discussion ignored **transaction costs**—the costs associated with exchange. But, as you know, the exchange of goods often consumes resources. For example, when a homeowner hires a real-estate agent to advertise and show the home, appraise its market value, handle the necessary paperwork, and otherwise assist in the sale of the home, the agent collects a fee for services rendered. On the sale of a $100,000 home, the agent may collect $6,000 or, in some markets, even more. This fee drives a wedge between the price paid by the buyer ($100,000) and the price received by the seller ($94,000).

Similarly, the exchange of goods and resources between countries often involves transaction costs. Businesses may need to establish foreign offices for making contacts with other countries, hire lawyers to negotiate contracts, and employ lobbyists to fight such impediments to trade as **import quotas**—limits on the quantity of a good that may be imported into a country. Transaction costs also include transportation costs (for example, the costs of shipping a good from one country to another). Where transaction costs are substantial, they often prevent countries from trading with each other. And where trade does occur, transaction costs reduce the gains from such trade. Therefore, anything that facilitates trade—from a reduction in transportation costs to the elimination of quotas—tends to magnify the volume of trade and the benefits derived from such trade.

IMPORT QUOTA
A restriction limiting the amount of a foreign good that may enter a country legally.

VOLUME OF TRADE

Despite the existence of transaction costs, countries still find trade advantageous. Currently, international trade exceeds $3 trillion per year. Table 2.3 lists volume of trade for selected countries, including the United States, the world's largest trading country (as measured by volume of imports). Much of the United States' trade is with adjacent countries (Canada and Mexico) and with Japan. Trade with Russia and other former Soviet republics is extremely modest.

Germany, on the other hand, trades more with the former Soviet republics than with Canada and Mexico combined, thereby underscoring the importance of transportation costs. Because transportation costs tend to rise with distance (other things equal), a country is more likely to trade with neighboring countries than with more distant countries. Of course, the magnitude of output is also important. The economies of some countries are so huge—including those of the United States, Germany, and Japan—that they export enormous volumes of output even to distant countries.

LOOKING AHEAD

Although various components of international trade are discussed in subsequent chapters, the more subtle points are deferred to Part X (on world economy), after you have acquired the tools and background necessary for a more careful consideration of these issues. The next task is to attain a deeper understanding of how markets work or, in some cases, why markets fail. This is the focus of Chapter 3.

1991 TRADE VOLUME FOR SELECTED COUNTRIES (BILLIONS OF U.S. DOLLARS)

COUNTRY	TOTAL IMPORTS	IMPORTS FROM				
		U.S.	CANADA	MEXICO	JAPAN	USSR*
U.S.	488	—	91	31	92	1
Canada	118	75	—	2	9	**
Japan	236	54	8	2	—	3
Germany	389	25	3	1	24	9
U.K.	210	24	3	**	12	2

*Soviet Union prior to its breakup, former Soviet republics following breakup.
**Less than $0.5 billion.
SOURCE: Organization for Economic Cooperation and Development, *Monthly Statistics of Foreign Trade* (Paris, June 1992).

TABLE 2.3

Summary

1. A production possibilities curve portrays the combinations of output that can be produced with a given technology and fixed resources, assuming the resources are used effi-

ciently. When a country fails to put its resources to their best use, or leaves them unused, it fails to reach its production possibilities curve.

2. When a country is *on* its production possibilities curve, the only way it can produce more of one good is to divert resources from the production of a second good. The amount of the second good sacrificed indicates the opportunity cost involved.

3. The law of increasing costs predicts that the opportunity cost of a good rises as output of the good increases. The principle is based on the argument that, as more and more of one good is produced, it is necessary to use resources less and less suited for production of that good. Where the law of increasing costs holds, the production possibilities curve is bowed.

4. When a country's stock of resources increases or when technological progress occurs, the country's production possibilities curve shifts outward, denoting economic growth. To spur economic growth a country can produce relatively more capital goods, and relatively fewer consumer goods, or increase the amount of resources devoted to research and development.

5. Different societies choose different economic systems for deciding what is produced, how it is produced, and for whom. Pure capitalism rests on private ownership of resources and use of markets. At the opposite extreme, a command economy is one where resources are publicly owned and decisions are made by central authorities. All modern economic systems are, to varying degrees, mixes of pure capitalism and a command economy. For that reason they are called mixed economies.

6. Capitalism is guided by consumer sovereignty—firms produce the combinations of goods demanded by consumers. To maximize profit, firms are induced to produce such goods at the lowest possible cost. Under capitalism, output is distributed on the basis of ability to pay.

7. In a command economy, central planners develop an elaborate scheme to determine what is produced. These central planners next assign production goals to companies and allocate resources. Finally, the government determines how output is distributed.

8. The former Soviet republics and Eastern Europe are in the process of moving to more capitalistic-oriented economies. The transition, while painful, should ultimately lead to higher levels of output.

9. Through specialization and trade it is possible to increase the amount of output produced and therefore to raise standards of living. When trading, countries and individuals should specialize in the production of goods for which they enjoy a comparative advantage—that is, goods they can produce at a lower opportunity cost.

10. Transaction costs reduce the gains from trade and, when large enough, prevent two potential traders from making an exchange. An increase in the amount of resources required to effect an exchange reduces the incentive to trade.

11. International trade currently exceeds $3 trillion per year. The United States alone imports about $500 billion annually. Because exchange costs tend to increase with distance, most countries conduct a disproportionate amount of trade with neighboring countries.

Key Terms

production possibilities curve	efficient production
technology	law of increasing costs
inefficient production	economic growth

capital goods
consumer goods
economic system
pure capitalism
market
command economy
mixed economy
consumer sovereignty

international trade
zero-sum game
positive-sum game
specialization
comparative advantage
transaction costs
import quota

Study Questions and Problems

1. For each of the following, explain whether the production possibilities curve shifts outward, shifts inward, or remains unchanged:
   a. average educational attainment of the population increases by one year
   b. due to war, one-third of a country's capital is destroyed
   c. the government decides to reduce spending on defense and instead to devote more resources to public housing
   d. because of a declining birthrate, a country's working-age population shrinks

2. For each of the following, indicate whether output increases or decreases. If output rises, specify whether the rise is due to greater efficiency in the economy or to economic growth.
   a. a previously idle automobile plant is back in operation
   b. a government pays farmers to idle cropland—that is, to remove land from production
   c. a new technique is discovered for converting industrial waste into energy
   d. an experienced builder temporarily employed as a cashier finds a construction job; a cashier temporarily working on a construction crew finds employment as a cashier

3. (a) Assume U.S. consumers want to buy more red convertibles than are currently available in dealer showrooms. How would you expect this situation to affect production of red convertibles? Why? (b) Would you expect the same response in a command economy? Explain.

4. Economists argue that production tends to be more efficient in capitalistic economies than in command economies. Analyze this argument.

5. In Mexico each unit of a resource can produce either one professional computer (with business and scientific applications) or three computer-game systems. Mexico has 100,000 units of this resource.
   a. Draw Mexico's production possibilities curve.
   b. What is the opportunity cost of one professional computer?
   c. Is the production of professional computers subject to constant or increasing costs?
   d. Which of the two goods being produced is considered a capital good?
   e. In the absence of trade, should Mexico increase production of professional computers or computer-game systems if it desires more rapid economic growth?

6. In Japan each unit of a resource can produce either two professional computers or eight computer-game systems.
   a. Based on the figures for Japan and Mexico (see problem 5), which country enjoys a comparative advantage in the production of professional computers?
   b. To increase world output, which country should specialize in the production of professional computers?
   c. Which country should export computer-game systems?

7. Tom can paint one window frame or two walls in one hour. In the same time, Sally can paint either two window frames or three walls.

a. For whom is the opportunity cost of painting window frames lower?

b. If Tom and Sally desire to minimize the time spent painting, who should specialize in painting window frames and who should specialize in painting walls?

8. Indicate whether each of the following increases or decreases the volume of world trade:

a. a decline in the price of oil reduces transportation costs between countries

b. the development of a new telecommunications system reduces the cost of obtaining information about both the availability of foreign goods and foreign interest in the goods produced in a country

c. a country levies a tax on all imported goods

d. a new law requires companies to obtain permits to export their products and to hire additional staff to complete necessary paperwork

9. Assume that the New York Yankees have two outstanding first basemen but only mediocre catchers. Assume further that the Los Angeles Dodgers have two outstanding catchers but only mediocre first basemen. If the Yankees trade one outstanding first baseman to the Dodgers for one outstanding catcher, is the trade more likely to be a zero-sum game or a positive-sum game? Explain.

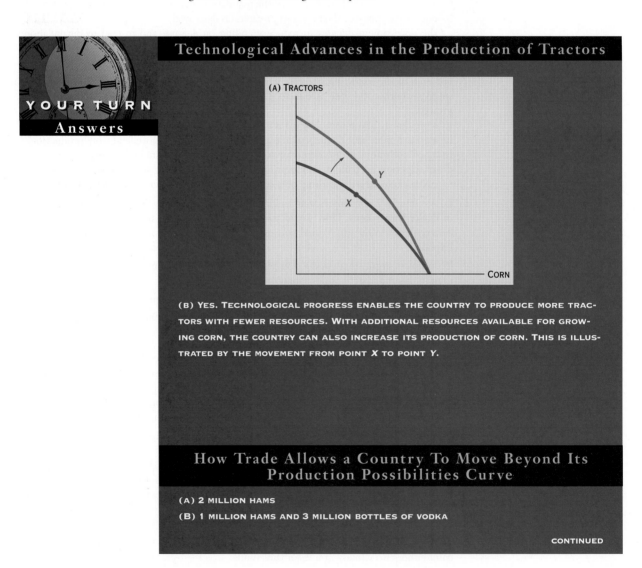

Technological Advances in the Production of Tractors

(A) TRACTORS

Y

X

CORN

(B) YES. TECHNOLOGICAL PROGRESS ENABLES THE COUNTRY TO PRODUCE MORE TRACTORS WITH FEWER RESOURCES. WITH ADDITIONAL RESOURCES AVAILABLE FOR GROWING CORN, THE COUNTRY CAN ALSO INCREASE ITS PRODUCTION OF CORN. THIS IS ILLUSTRATED BY THE MOVEMENT FROM POINT X TO POINT Y.

How Trade Allows a Country To Move Beyond Its Production Possibilities Curve

(A) 2 MILLION HAMS

(B) 1 MILLION HAMS AND 3 MILLION BOTTLES OF VODKA

CONTINUED

How Trade Allows a Country To Move Beyond Its Production Possibilities Curve

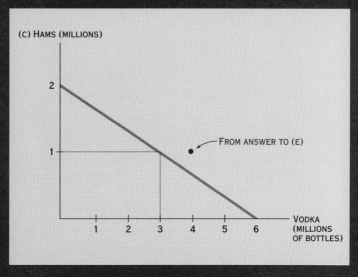

(D) 4 MILLION BOTTLES

(E) NO. WITHOUT TRADE IT IS NOT POSSIBLE TO OBTAIN BOTH 1 MILLION HAMS AND 4 MILLION BOTTLES OF VODKA.

Selected References

Blinder, Alan. *Hard Heads, Soft Hearts* (Reading, Mass.: Addison-Wesley, 1987). Incorporates such concepts as scarcity, efficiency, trade-offs, and opportunity cost into a discussion of economic policy.

Bredenkamp, Hugh. "Reforming the Soviet Economy," *Finance and Development*, June 1991, pp. 18–21. Analyzes the source of Soviet economic problems and prospects for reform.

Challenge, September/October 1990, pp. 4–16. Contains a set of essays on economic reform in the Soviet Union and Eastern Europe.

"A Survey of World Trade," *The Economist*, September 22, 1990, pp. 5–40. Discusses world trade policy.

"Business in Eastern Europe," *The Economist*, September 21, 1991, pp. 3–30. Examines the problems countries encounter as they move to a more capitalistic economic system.

The Journal of Economic Perspectives, Fall 1991. Contains papers from a conference on the economic transition in the former Soviet Union and Eastern Europe.

Kornai, Janos. *The Road to a Free Economy*, (New York: Norton, 1990). Presents a plan for Hungary's transition to a capitalistic-oriented economy.

Lipton, David, and Jeffrey Sachs, "Privatization in Eastern Europe: The Case of Poland," *Brookings Papers on Economic Activity* (1990:2), pp. 293–341. Discusses reasons for and challenges associated with transferring state-owned property to private citizens, with special emphasis on Poland.

U.S. International Trade Commission, *International Economic Review* (monthly government publication). Contains trade data and summaries of current U.S. trade developments.

3

The Price System

CHAPTER 2 INTRODUCED THE CONCEPT OF MARKETS, NOTING THEIR CRUCIAL ROLE IN SUCH LARGELY CAPITALISTIC COUNTRIES AS THE UNITED STATES. EVEN THE FORMER SOVIET REPUBLICS AND COUNTRIES THAT IN THE PAST HAVE RELIED HEAVILY ON GOVERNMENT PLANNING ARE REDISCOVERING THE VIRTUES OF MARKETS. ACCORDINGLY, IT IS IMPORTANT TO TAKE A CLOSER LOOK AT MARKETS, EXAMINING BOTH HOW THEY WORK AND WHY MARKET OUTCOMES ARE SOMETIMES DEEMED UNACCEPTABLE AND ARE THEREFORE MODIFIED BY GOVERNMENT.

> Prices are to guide and direct the economic activities of the people. Prices are to tell them what to do.[1]

[1]Benjamin M. Anderson, *Economics and the Public Welfare* (New York: Van Nostrand, 1949), p. 550.

The Participants

We begin with a discussion of the major participants in the economy: consumers, firms, and government.

CONSUMERS

Consumers earn income from their labor and from the property they own. For example, an employed person who also leases land to others receives both wage income and rental income. With their incomes, consumers buy various goods and services. Table 3.1 presents the spending pattern of urban consumers in the United States. Notice that, on average, housing is the largest expenditure. Altogether, housing, food, and clothing constitute about two-thirds of the spending of the typical urban consumer.

The term *household* is sometimes used in place of consumer, especially when economic decisions are made within a family setting. Clearly, some economic decisions—for example, whether both husband and wife should work and where to vacation—are based on the input of more than one individual. As previously observed, consumers are generally assumed to maximize their well-being or what economists dub "utility."

SPENDING PATTERN OF U.S. CONSUMERS*		
CATEGORY		**PERCENT OF SPENDING**
Food and beverages		17.7
food at home	10.1	
food away from home	6.1	
alcoholic beverages	1.5	
Housing		41.4
shelter	27.7	
fuel and other utilities	7.3	
household furnishings and operation	6.4	
Apparel		6.1
Transportation		17.8
Medical care		6.4
Entertainment		4.3
Other goods and services		6.3
tobacco	1.5	
personal care	1.2	
personal and educational expenses	3.6	
TOTAL		100.0

* Average for urban consumers (excludes rural consumers).
SOURCE: U.S. Department of Labor, Bureau of Labor Statistics, *Relative Importance of Components in the Consumer Price Indexes*, 1991.

TABLE 3.1

FIRMS

Firms or businesses are the unit of production. They hire workers and pay for the use of various property owned by consumers. Firms use these resources to produce the goods and services consumers buy.

Firms come in all sizes, from a company run and operated by one individual to such multinational giants as Toyota and Exxon. Although firms operate in all industries, Table 3.2 demonstrates that the industries with the most firms are the service sector (which includes hospitals, automobile repair, legal services, and so forth) and retail trade (which includes restaurants, grocery stores, department stores, and other shopping outlets). Altogether, the U.S. economy has approximately 18 million firms.

Regardless of size and the industry in which they operate, all firms share a common feature—the pursuit of profit.[2] Indeed, economists generally assume that profit maximization is the single goal of firms.

GOVERNMENT

The term **government** is used broadly to include all government and quasi-government bodies at the federal, state, and local levels. Although the local sector has

DISTRIBUTION OF FIRMS BY INDUSTRY	
INDUSTRY	**NUMBER OF FIRMS (THOUSANDS)**
Agriculture, forestry, fishing*	627
Mining	261
Construction	2,069
Manufacturing	689
Transportation, public utilities	826
Wholesale trade	676
Retail trade	2,789
Finance, insurance, real estate	2,574
Services	7,388
Miscellaneous	452
TOTAL	18,351

* Excludes farm proprietorships.
SOURCE: U.S. Department of Commerce, *Statistical Abstract of the United States, 1991*, Table 861.

TABLE 3.2

[2]Public schools, churches, and other not-for-profit institutions employ resources and produce goods and services; however, because they lack the profit motive, they are not classified as firms.

GOVERNMENT STATISTICS BY TYPE OF GOVERNMENT, 1991*			
TYPE OF GOVERNMENT	NUMBER OF GOVERNMENT UNITS	MILLIONS OF EMPLOYEES	SPENDING (BILLIONS OF DOLLARS)
Federal	1	3.0	$1,320
State and Local	83,236	15.4	742
state	50	4.3	N/A**
local	83,186	11.1	N/A**
TOTAL	83,237	18.4	$2,062

* Data on number of government units are for 1987.
** N/A = Not available.
SOURCES: U.S. Department of Commerce, *Census of Governments, 1987*, vol. 1, No. 1; *Survey of Current Business* (1992); U.S. Department of Labor, *Employment and Earnings* (1992).

TABLE 3.3

the largest number of government units and the most employees, spending is greatest at the federal level (see Table 3.3). American government agencies include the Federal Reserve System (which oversees the nation's money supply), the Postal Service, the Internal Revenue Service, state highway patrols, mayoral offices, various regulatory commissions, and many more. Unlike consumers and firms, government is not assumed to have a single, overriding goal or even to behave consistently. Government agencies may have conflicting agendas, and government officials may be motivated by private as well as public interests.

In a purely capitalistic economy, the government is limited to such activities as law enforcement. Individual consumers and firms are left to buy and sell as they see fit in the marketplace. In reality, government involvement is more extensive—as governments of all countries restrict, to varying degrees, the activities of both firms and consumers. Reasons for government involvement are addressed at the end of the chapter. Until then we ignore the role of government in order to concentrate on the interplay between firms and consumers in unrestricted markets.

Two Types of Markets

PRODUCT MARKET
A market in which a particular good or service is bought and sold.

RESOURCE (FACTOR) MARKET
A market in which a particular resource (factor of production) is bought and sold.

Markets can be divided into two categories: *product markets* and *resource* (or *factor*) *markets*. The difference relates to what is bought and sold. In **product markets** goods and services are exchanged; in **resource markets** the focus is on labor and other factors of production. Regardless of the type of market, buyers and sellers make contact, reach terms on the amount of an item to be exchanged, and agree on a price.

The Role of Money

BARTER

A system of exchange whereby goods and services are traded directly without the use of money.

Prices are usually stated in monetary terms. For example, a plumber might charge $100 to fix a leaky faucet. In this case the plumber performs a service and, in return, receives a certain amount of money ($100). An alternative method of exchange is **barter**, in which goods or services are traded without the use of money. For example, a nearsighted plumber might repair a faucet in return for a new pair of eyeglasses.

Although money is not necessary for exchange, it greatly facilitates exchange. Think of the difficulties involved in a barter economy. A plumber who wants glasses must first locate an optician with a leaky faucet. To eat, the plumber must find a farmer or grocer in need of plumbing services. The time spent searching for parties with whom to trade may well exceed the time spent plumbing. With money, exchanges are so much simpler. The plumber sells his or her services to whoever needs them and uses the money earned from this work to buy eyeglasses, food, or whatever else is desired. Simply put, money eliminates the need to find someone who has what you want and who also wants something you have. As a consequence, money reduces the transaction costs of exchange.

Governments issue the coins and currency we commonly associate with money, but it is important to realize that money is created even in the absence of government. In primitive economies, shells, stones, and sundry other goods have served as money. In modern economies, most money consists of checking accounts, which are issued not by governments but by private financial institutions. The main requirement is that the good serving as money, whatever it is, be generally accepted as a means of payment—a person accepting a good as money must be confident that this good will, in turn, be accepted by others. In prisoner-of-war camps during World War II, cigarettes became the accepted medium of exchange and therefore functioned as money (see Exhibit 3.1, page 68).

The Circular Flow of Income

The interplay between the type of markets (product and resource), the market participants (consumers and firms), and the terms of exchange (money for goods or resources) is illustrated with a model known as the **circular flow of income** (see Figure 3.1, page 70). Consumers sell their resources to firms and, in return, receive income payments (wages, rent, interest, and profit). These transactions take place in resource markets, which are depicted in the lower half of the diagram. Firms then combine these resources to produce goods and services, which they sell to consumers. Transactions in product markets are depicted in the upper half of the diagram. Note that firms and consumers participate in both resource and product markets, but in different capacities. In resource markets firms are on the buying (demand) side, whereas consumers are on the selling (supply) side. In product markets the roles are reversed.

E
X
H
I
B
I
T

3 . 1

The economy of a prisoner-of-war camp is typically very simple. There is no production of marketable goods and services and no buying and selling of resources. The principal economic activity is consumption. Still, economic decisions must be made, the paramount issue involving how to divide consumption among the prisoners.

During World War II, prisoners received weekly rations from their captors and various goods from the Red Cross. Although these were distributed equally, the values of the goods differed from prisoner to prisoner. Some smoked cigarettes, others did not. Some preferred tea, others coffee. Such differences in preferences meant that prisoners could increase their well-being (utility) by trading among themselves.

Trade initially consisted of barter; but over time markets became increasingly sophisticated, with cigarettes emerging as the medium of exchange. One former prisoner of war recounts these developments:

> Very soon after capture people realized that it was both undesirable and unnecessary, in view of the limited size and the equality of supplies, to give away or to accept gifts of cigarettes or food. "Goodwill" developed into trading as a more equitable means of maximizing individual satisfaction.
>
> We reached a transit camp in Italy about a fortnight after capture and received one-quarter of a Red Cross food parcel each a week later. At once exchanges, already established, multiplied in volume. Starting with simple direct barter, such as a nonsmoker giving a smoker friend his cigarette issue in exchange for a chocolate ration, more complex exchanges soon became an accepted custom. Stories circulated of a padre who started off round the camp with a tin of cheese and five cigarettes and returned to his bed with a complete parcel in addition to his original cheese and cigarettes; the market was not yet perfect. Within a week or two, as the volume of trade grew, rough scales of exchange values came into existence. Sikhs, who had at first exchanged tinned beef for practically any other foodstuff, began to insist on jam and margarine. It was realized that a tin of jam was worth one-half pound of margarine plus something else, that a cigarette issue was worth several chocolate issues, and a tin of diced carrots was worth practically nothing.

The outer arrows in Figure 3.1 represent the flow of resources and products; the inner arrows depict monetary flows. Note the circular nature of these flows. Money flows from firms to consumers (in resource markets) and then back to firms (in product markets). In each case these monetary flows are balanced by flows of resources or products in the opposite direction.

As a model, the circular flow diagram simplifies reality. For example, it considers only markets for *final products*—the goods and services purchased by consumers.

In this camp we did not visit other bungalows very much and prices varied from place to place; hence the germ of truth in the story of the itinerant priest. By the end of a month, when we reached our permanent camp, there was a lively trade in all commodities and their relative values were well known, and expressed not in terms of one another—one didn't quote bully [canned corned beef] in terms of sugar—but in terms of cigarettes. The cigarette became the standard of value. In the permanent camp people started by wandering through the bungalows calling their offers— "cheese for seven" (cigarettes)—and the hours after parcel issue were bedlam. The inconvenience of this system soon led to its replacement by an Exchange and Mart notice board in every bungalow, where under the headings "name," "room number," "wanted" and "offered," sales and wants were advertised. When a deal went through, it was crossed off the board. The public and semipermanent records of transactions led to cigarette prices being well known and thus tending to equality throughout the camp, although there were always opportunities for an astute trader to

make a profit from arbitrage. With this development everyone, including nonsmokers was willing to sell for cigarettes, using them to buy at another time and place. Cigarettes became the normal currency, though, of course, barter was never extinguished. . . .

The permanent camps in Germany saw the highest level of commercial organization. In addition to the Exchange and Mart notice boards, a shop was organized as a public utility, controlled by representatives of the Senior British Officer, on a no profit basis. People left their surplus clothing, toilet requisites, and food there until they were sold at a fixed price in cigarettes. Only sales in cigarettes were accepted—there was no barter— and there was no haggling. For food at least there were standard prices. . . . Thus the cigarette attained its fullest currency status, and the market was almost completely unified.

SOURCE: R. A. Radford, "The Economic Organisation of a P.O.W. Camp," *Economica* (November 1945), pp. 189–201. Reprinted by permission of Basil Blackwell, publisher, and the author.

But sometimes firms sell their output to other firms, as when steel companies sell steel sheeting to appliance makers. These transactions—the buying and selling of *intermediate products*—do not directly appear in the circular flow diagram.

The circular flow diagram also ignores taxes and saving, which represent *leakages* of income from the system. Because income that consumers save or pay in taxes is not available for consumption, the flow of output from firms to consumers is reduced. (Such complications are addressed later in the text.) But even if the circular flow model does not perfectly mirror reality, it is still useful in illustrating the interdependence of product and resource markets, the relationships between firms and consumers, and the role of money.

The lower half of the circular flow diagram depicts resource markets. Resources flow from consumers to firms, and in this way generate a reciprocal flow of income to consumers. In product markets (upper half of diagram), goods and services flow from firms to consumers, whereas money (consumer spending) flows in the opposite direction.

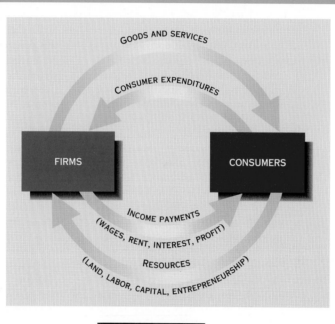

FIGURE 3.1

The Price System

Although the circular flow diagram provides an overview of capitalistic economies, it does not address a fundamental question: How do they work? With potentially millions of firms and consumers, each acting in their own self-interest, how is anything accomplished? In the absence of central authorities to guide the economy, what prevents the economy from grinding to a halt? What mechanism organizes production, links decisions of producers and consumers in a mutually consistent manner, and brings order rather than chaos to the economy?

In a capitalistic economy, economic activities are coordinated through the price system. In product markets, prices signal consumer preferences. In resource markets, prices indicate relative scarcity, telling firms which resources to buy and how to combine them.

PRICE SYSTEM

A mechanism for coordinating economic decisions in which prices are determined in markets and used to allocate resources and output.

The key to the **price system** is the adjustment of prices and the response triggered by that adjustment. When consumers want more of a good than firms are willing to sell, their competition for this good forces up price (more on this in Chapter 4). This induces firms to produce more of the good since, other things equal, a higher price indicates an opportunity for increased profits. Conversely, if consumers want less than firms wish to sell, firms are forced to lower price. This, in turn, provides a signal to reduce production of the good.

Prices send similar signals in resource markets. Prices tell resource owners where to employ their resources—namely, in those activities where the returns are the greatest. Prices also tell firms how to combine resources. For example, if the price of labor rises while the price of computers falls, this alerts producers that they can lower production costs by using additional computers and fewer workers. Similarly, skyrocketing oil prices send a signal to switch to energy-saving techniques of production.

In summary, in a capitalistic economy prices convey information about the value of resources and output. The pattern of product and resource prices tells firms what to produce and how. Similarly, the pattern shapes the decisions of consumers concerning their supply of resources and their purchases of goods and services. Whenever conditions change—on either the buying or selling side of the market—prices also change, thereby sending new information to firms and consumers. In the process, the price system coordinates economic activity, distributing resources where they are valued most highly, and linking the decisions of firms and consumers.

YOUR TURN

SUPPOSE CONSUMERS WANT ADDITIONAL STRAWBERRIES. (A) HOW ARE THESE PREFERENCES CONVEYED TO PRODUCERS? (B) WHY DO FIRMS HAVE AN INCENTIVE TO PRODUCE ADDITIONAL STRAWBERRIES? (C) IF STRAWBERRY PRODUCERS NEED ADDITIONAL STRAWBERRY PICKERS, HOW CAN THEY INDUCE ADDITIONAL INDIVIDUALS TO PICK STRAWBERRIES?

The Invisible Hand

Adam Smith, the eighteenth-century economist, described the price system as an "invisible hand" guiding economic decision makers. Recognizing that consumers and firms tend to act in their own self-interest, he addressed an important social issue: Will the price system lead to socially optimal outcomes? It is not obvious that what is in the interest of private parties—consumers and firms—is also in the best interest of society. But Smith argued that, in the presence of competition among both firms and consumers, the price system guides private parties to do what is best for society.

Smith explains this argument in a famous passage from his book, *The Wealth of Nations*:

> Every individual necessarily labours to render the annual revenue of the society as great as he can. He generally, indeed, neither intends to promote the public interest, nor knows how much he is promoting it. By . . . directing that industry in such a manner as its produce may be of the greatest value, he intends only his own gain, and he is in this, as in many other cases, led by an *invisible hand* to promote an end which was no part of his intention. Nor is it always the worse for the society that it

ADAM SMITH

Adam Smith is widely recognized as the founder of economics. Although much of Smith's work built upon the ideas of others, he expanded their arguments and integrated various strands of thought, blending theory with empirical observation.

Born in Scotland in 1723, Smith was educated at the University of Glasgow and later studied, at his own direction, at Oxford University. Upon completing his studies, he accepted a position at the University of Glasgow, initially as professor of logic and later as professor of moral philosophy, the discipline from which economics evolved. After publishing *The Theory of Moral Sentiment* in 1759, Smith was heralded as one of the prominent philosophers of his time. Although a popular and provocative lecturer, Smith left the university to become the highly paid tutor for a young duke. It was during his service as tutor in France that Smith began work on *The Wealth of Nations*, which, though it had limited impact in its first few years, is now regarded as one of the greatest treatises ever written in political economy.

In the book, Smith preached a *laissez-faire* or "hands-off" approach by the government. He argued that government involvement should be limited to those activities that promote the public good and that cannot be adequately provided by the market (for example, maintaining law and

Adam Smith

order, preserving national defense, and providing public education).

Smith's views were a sharp attack on the prevailing *mercantilist* philosophy, which favored massive government intervention as a means to increase a nation's wealth. Because mercantilists believed that a nation's wealth was a function of its gold and silver, they favored policies to promote exports and restrict imports, arguing that the gold and silver accumulated as a result of exports would benefit the entire country. Smith rejected this argument, pointing out that it is capital, rather than gold and silver, that increases a country's productive capacity.

Smith also presented a labor theory of value, which held that the value of all output was ultimately derived from labor—an argument later picked up and expanded upon by Karl Marx. Another theme of *The Wealth of Nations* was that output could be expanded through the division of labor, whereby individual workers specialize in narrowly defined activities. Before he died in 1790, Adam Smith had received worldwide acclaim; *The Wealth of Nations* was in its fifth edition and had been translated into French, Spanish, Italian, German, and Danish.[3]

[3]For a more detailed analysis of the life and influence of Adam Smith, see Robert L. Heilbroner, *The Worldly Philosophers*, 6th ed. (New York: Simon & Schuster, 1986), Chapter 3.

was no part of it. By pursuing his own interest he frequently promotes that of the society more effectually than when he really intends to promote it.[4]

The convergence of private and public interests can be illustrated with several examples. A firm minimizes the costs of producing a given output so that it may maximize its profits. But minimizing costs also benefits society because, when firms produce efficiently, society obtains the greatest output possible from its limited resources. Profit maximization also forces firms to produce those goods valued most highly by consumers. Again, there is harmony of public and private interests. Similarly, individuals toil so that they may increase their consumption. But through their labor they also benefit others by expanding the amount of output available for society. In summary, Smith argued that private parties are motivated by self-interest and that, through an invisible hand, pursuit of self-interest promotes the public good. The biography on page 72 provides additional background on the famous economist and his views.

Limitations of the Price System

The preceding discussion has painted a highly favorable picture of the price system. Individuals and firms are free to pursue the activities of their choice and yet, in so doing, they advance the interests of society. The price system leads to efficient production, so that society gains the maximum possible output from its resources. Moreover, resources are allocated across industries in just the right mix. Firms produce neither more nor less of a good than society wants. Thanks to an *invisible hand*, society receives the optimal amount of each good.

The preceding story is, however, incomplete. Despite its strengths, the price system has certain limitations, as Smith himself was aware. Indeed, it is because of these limitations that no country relies exclusively on capitalism to make its economic decisions.

COMPETITION

It is the price system *plus competition* that leads to harmony of public and private interests. In the absence of competition, the invisible hand fails. Take away competition, and firms are free to thwart the signals of the price system.

For example, high prices are a signal to increase production of a good—and when firms compete against one another, that is exactly what happens. But Adam Smith warned that rather than compete against one another, producers would often attempt to limit competition—to work together to keep production artificially low and prices artificially high:

> People of the same trade seldom meet together, even for merriment and diversion, but the conversation ends in a conspiracy against the public, or in some contrivance to raise prices.[5]

---

[4]Adam Smith, *An Inquiry into the Nature and Causes of the Wealth of Nations* (New York: Random House, 1937), p. 423 [originally published in 1776].

[5]Same as 4, p. 128.

Clearly in cases where firms raise prices and restrict output, they do not serve the interests of society.

Similarly, buyers of a resource (for example, hospitals) might conspire to limit their use of a resource (for example, nurses) in order to keep down the price of this resource. Although this may benefit resource buyers, it harms society by leading to an underuse of the resource (society has too few nurses).

In conclusion, competition in both product markets and resource markets is essential if the price system is to promote the interests of society. But competition may not be the natural outcome of unrestricted markets. Instead, individual groups of buyers or sellers may succeed in restraining competition for their own personal gain, in which event the price system fails to deliver socially optimal outcomes. In such cases, government intervention may be necessary to keep competition strong and to keep the price system functioning properly.

MARKET FAILURE

MARKET FAILURE
A situation in which unrestricted markets produce either more or less of a good than is socially optimal.

Even when markets are competitive, the price system may still fail to produce the socially optimal amount of a good—a phenomenon known as **market failure**. Markets fail in two principal areas: provision of *public goods* and production in the presence of *externalities*.

PUBLIC GOODS   A public good is one that is consumed collectively. Once produced, a public good is available to all consumers, including those who do not pay for it. Examples include national defense and the judicial system. Because individuals derive benefits from a public good whether or not they pay for it, they have no incentive to spend their income on public goods. Therefore, the price system cannot be counted on to provide sufficient quantities of public goods. Instead, the government must ensure the adequate provision of national defense, the judicial system, and other public goods.

EXTERNALITIES   Externalities (sometimes known as *spillover effects*) refer to the side effects of an economic activity; they arise when the production or consumption of a good affects others not in the market. As an example, consider pollution—an externality associated with the production of certain goods. Pollution imposes costs on society above and beyond those incurred by firms. Such costs include health problems, damage to wildlife, and loss of recreational facilities. Because firms do not bear these costs, they have an incentive to use production methods that pollute the environment, despite the harm done to society. The price system breaks down because it allows those imposing costs on others to escape the consequences of their actions. When externalities exist, government intervention may improve market outcomes (for example, by forcing firms to reduce pollution).

INCOME INEQUALITY

Under the price system, the distribution of income is based on consumers' command over resources and the market value of those resources. Consumers without

Is Bill Cosby Worth More Than Children's Hospital?

EXHIBIT 3.2

Bill Cosby earned $55 million in 1990 and an estimated $58 million in 1991.[6] This is more than the entire budget for some hospitals and school districts. Indeed, based on workers' average pay in 1990, Cosby's salary was equivalent to the earnings of 1,291 physicians, 2,888 licensed practical nurses, 2,738 elementary-school teachers, or 5,588 child-care workers. Although some wince at the idea of paying such staggering sums of money to select individuals while others go malnourished, the price system does not recognize hunger.

In economies that rely on the price system, an individual's income depends on the market's valuation of his or her services. When an individual produces highly valued services, that individual will be compensated commensurately. This is the case with Bill Cosby, who provides entertainment for millions of viewers, advertising revenues for his network, ticket sales for movie theaters, and book sales for publishers. Given the strong demand for his services, the price system rewards the talented entertainer with an eight-figure income. As shocking as it may be, the answer to the question posed above is: Yes, from the market's perspective, Bill Cosby is worth more than the entire staff of Children's Hospital.

[6]Peter Newcomb and Christopher Palmeri, "What's Not to Love?" *Forbes*, September 30, 1991, p. 113.

property and without labor to sell receive no income. Consumers with great wealth or with highly valued skills earn high incomes. Witness the lofty salary of Bill Cosby and other top entertainers (see Exhibit 3.2).

If society seeks some minimum standard of living for all its citizens, government intervention is necessary to achieve this goal. For example, the government may wish to tax those with high incomes to provide support for the poor, in the process creating a more equal distribution of income. Although there can be disagreement over how much *equity* or equality the government should attempt to achieve, the price system disregards equity entirely, focusing instead on *efficiency*—resource owners are rewarded on the basis of how much they contribute to output, not on the basis of how much they need. Therefore, when equity is a consideration, distribution of income under the price system is unacceptable.

ECONOMIC INSTABILITY

Capitalistic economies are generally viewed as inherently unstable. During some periods, unemployment rises to socially unacceptable levels. During other periods, capitalistic economies overheat, leading to inflationary pressures. If the government can promote greater economic stability, it may be able to reduce unemployment and mitigate inflationary pressures. This is a major issue of macroeconomics.

CONCLUSION

Despite its strengths, the price system has certain major limitations. It works well only when markets are competitive, and even then it fails to produce the socially optimal amount of output in the presence of public goods or externalities. The price system also results in a highly unequal distribution of income, failing to guarantee a basic standard of living for all consumers. Finally, economies that rely on the price system are characterized by considerable economic instability. For such reasons, governments have seen fit to modify market outcomes—to redirect the invisible hand. Although such intervention offers the potential to benefit society, it is important to recognize that government policy is not made by a benign, all-knowing god but by politicians. If they succumb to pressures from special-interest groups, government intervention may actually harm society. Therefore, despite weaknesses of the price system, one should not conclude that government always leads to socially preferable outcomes. The extent of government, its rationale, and the process of collective decision making are addressed in Chapter 7. However, before taking up these issues, it is essential to develop a deeper understanding of the process through which prices are determined. With this in mind, Chapter 4 introduces the economist's most important tools: supply and demand.

Summary

1. Consumers earn income by providing resources to firms. Firms earn profit by combining those resources to produce goods and services. Economists generally assume that consumers attempt to maximize utility and that firms attempt to maximize profits.

2. Consumers and firms interact in both resource and product markets. As the circular flow diagram illustrates, firms buy resources from consumers and consumers buy goods and services from firms.

3. In a monetary economy resource owners receive money for the resources they supply, whereas firms receive money for the goods and services they sell. Compared to barter, the use of money reduces transaction costs, thereby facilitating exchange. Money is any item generally accepted as a means of payment, not just coins and currency.

4. In a capitalistic economy the price system coordinates economic activity, reconciling the decisions of buyers and sellers. Product prices reveal consumer preferences; resource prices indicate the relative scarcity of resources.

5. Higher product prices send a signal to increase production, lower prices to decrease production. In resource markets a higher price tells firms to economize on the use of a resource, a lower price to use the input more intensively.

6. Under certain conditions the price system operates as an invisible hand promoting public well-being. When these conditions are satisfied, individual firms and consumers, acting in their own self-interest, pursue policies that are also in the best interest of society. The price system, while preserving personal freedom, directs firms to produce the socially optimal amount of each good and to produce it efficiently (at minimum cost).

7. To work well, the price system requires competition in both product markets and resource markets. When competition is lacking, government intervention may be necessary to promote a competitive environment.

8. Because consumers have no incentive to spend their income voluntarily on public goods (such as national defense), the price system fails to provide adequate quantities of public goods—even when markets are competitive. Nor are market outcomes likely to be optimal in the presence of externalities, such as pollution. Because of such instances of market failure, government intervention may advance the interests of society.

9. Yet another source of dissatisfaction with the price system is the distribution of income. The price system rewards consumers on the basis of how much they contribute to output, not on the basis of need. Those without property and without labor to sell receive no income. If society values equity, it will modify the distribution of income generated by the price system.

10. The price system is also characterized by economic instability. Because of this, government intervention may offer the potential to reduce unemployment and to mitigate inflationary pressures.

Key Terms

consumer
firm
government
product market
resource market

barter
circular flow of income
price system
market failure

Study Questions and Problems

1. (a) What is the difference between a product market and a resource market? (b) Provide an example of something sold in a product market and something sold in a resource market.

2. What advantage does a monetary economy have over a barter economy? If money is not necessary for trade, why was it created?

3. In the circular flow diagram, what is the relationship between firms and consumers?

4. What message is the price system sending to college students when the starting salary of engineers rises and the starting salary of mathematicians falls? Assuming that students are motivated in part by income, how would you expect this change in salaries to affect the pattern of college majors?

5. Assume the price of whole wheat bread increases. In the absence of other changes, how does this affect the profitability of baking and selling whole wheat bread? What signal does this send to bakers?

6. It is not from the benevolence of the butcher, the brewer, or the baker, that we expect our dinner, but from their regard to their own interest. We address ourselves, not to their humanity but to their self-love.[7]

   What does Adam Smith mean by this passage? What motivates the butcher—self-interest or public interest? Who benefits from the butcher's work?

7. A former executive at General Motors once proclaimed: "What is good for General Motors is good for the country."[8] (a) Under what conditions would this be true? (b) Suppose General Motors conspires with Ford and Chrysler to drive up the price of automobiles. Would this be good for the country?

8. Is the price system consistent with the philosophy: "From each according to his abilities; to each according to his needs"? Explain.

9. Provide three reasons why government intervention might be socially desirable.

---

[7]Same as 4, p. 14.
[8]Charles E. Wilson, appearance before a Congressional committee, 1952.

YOUR TURN
Answers

(A) THROUGH HIGHER STRAWBERRY PRICES. (B) OTHER THINGS EQUAL, A HIGHER PRICE FOR STRAWBERRIES INCREASES THE PROFITS FROM GROWING STRAWBERRIES. (C) BY OFFERING A HIGHER WAGE TO STRAWBERRY PICKERS—THAT IS, BY INCREASING THE PRICE FOR THIS RESOURCE.

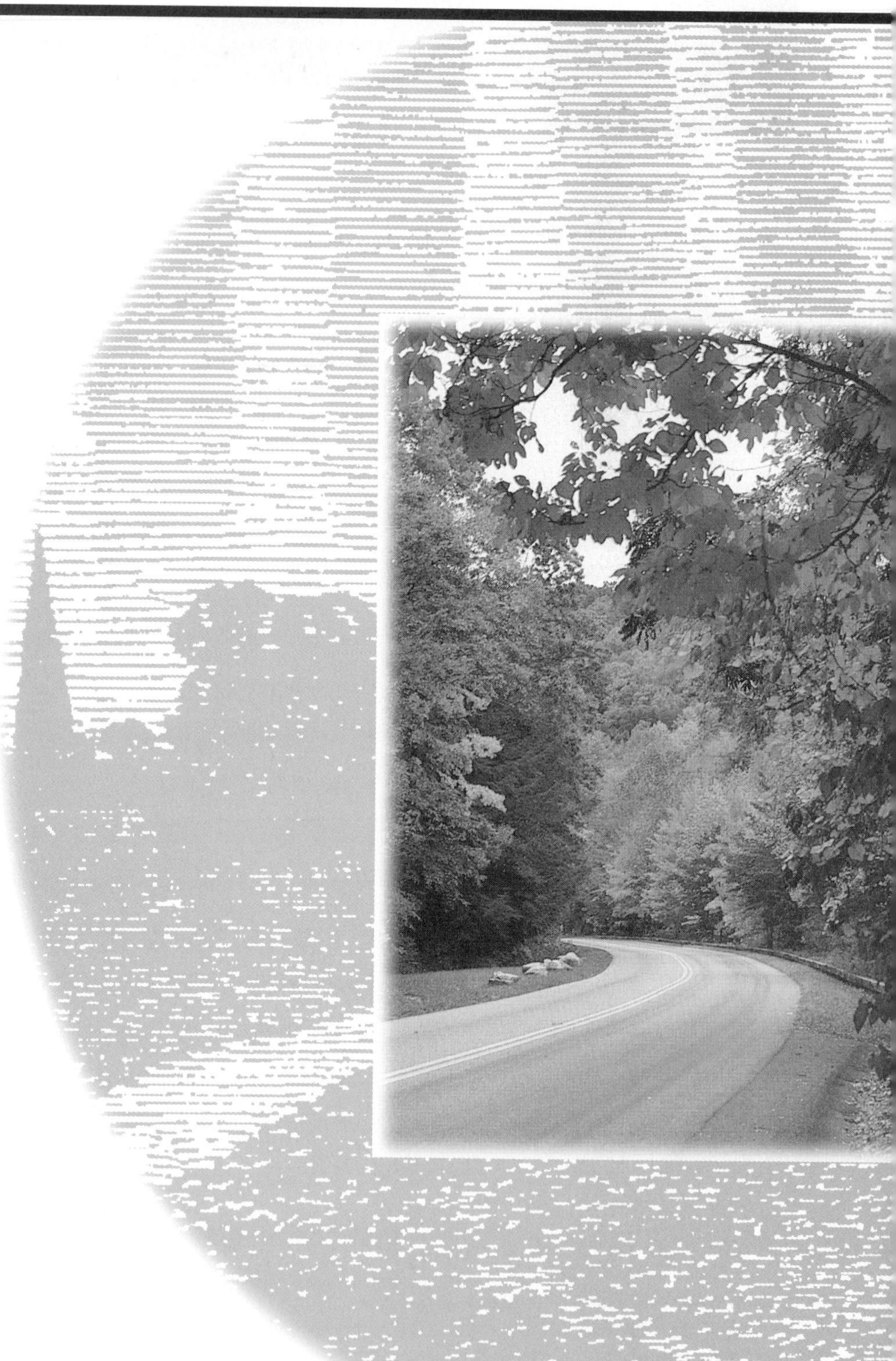

4

Supply and Demand

WHY DOES A 1952 MICKEY MANTLE BASEBALL CARD SELL FOR $50,000 OR A 1909 HONUS WAGNER CARD FOR $451,000? WHY HAVE PRICES FOR BASEBALL CARDS RISEN MORE RAPIDLY OF LATE THAN PRICES FOR STAMPS, DOLLS, AND OTHER COLLECTIBLES? THE ANSWER IN EACH CASE IS THE SAME: SUPPLY AND DEMAND. THE PRICE OF BASEBALL CARDS DEPENDS ON HOW STRONGLY BUYERS WANT THE CARDS AND ON HOW WILLING COLLECTORS, CARD STORES, AND DEALERS ARE TO SELL THEIR CARDS.

RECENTLY DEMAND HAS EXPLODED AS MORE PEOPLE STARTED COLLECTING CARDS AND AS INVESTORS BECAME CONVINCED THAT THE CARDS THEY PURCHASED TODAY COULD BE SOLD AT VASTLY INFLATED PRICES IN THE FUTURE. AS BUYERS COMPETED FOR AVAILABLE CARDS,

THEY DROVE PRICES HIGHER. OF COURSE, THERE IS NO GUARANTEE THAT PRICES WILL CONTINUE THEIR RECENT RISE. IF CARD COLLECTING TURNS OUT TO BE A FAD, PRICES MAY TUMBLE IN THE FUTURE.

THE PRICE OF BASEBALL CARDS ALSO DEPENDS ON THEIR SUPPLY. ONE REASON A ROOKIE MICKEY MANTLE CARD SELLS FOR $50,000 IS THAT IT WAS ISSUED LATE IN 1952 AND THEREFORE FEWER CARDS WERE PRINTED OF MANTLE THAT YEAR THAN OF OTHER PLAYERS.

SUPPLY AND DEMAND ARE EQUALLY IMPORTANT IN DETERMINING THE PRICES OF OTHER GOODS. ACCORDINGLY, IT IS IMPORTANT TO UNDERSTAND WHICH FACTORS DETERMINE THE AMOUNT OF A GOOD BUYERS WANT TO PURCHASE AND THE AMOUNT

In what has amounted to an explosion of value, [baseball] cards bought for mere pennies as part of bubble-gum packs just a few years ago have skyrocketed in price, with the rookie cards of some superstars now selling for more than $100 and even those of common players commanding prices many times their original cost.

Industry estimates indicate there are now about 1 million serious collectors, and more than 100 card shows and fairs every *week*. From a handful no more than five years ago, there are now more than 3,500 retail card stores and more than 10,000 dealers.

As unabashed investors have joined hobbyists in fueling the boom, the market for baseball cards has begun to take on the trappings of Wall Street.[1]

[1]Robert McG. Thomas, Jr., "Investors Hope a Rich Future Is in the Cards," *The New York Times*, April 10, 1988, pp. 19–20. Copyright © 1988 by The New York Times Company. Reprinted by permission.

sellers wish to provide. Under what conditions are the desires of buyers and sellers compatible? What happens when they are not?

Sometimes markets are not allowed to operate freely: governments set minimum legal prices for some goods, maximum legal prices for others. What are the immediate effects of price controls, and how do market participants respond? Chapter 4 provides answers to these questions, answers that allow you to begin mastering the basic tools of the economics trade: supply and demand. We begin with a discussion of demand.

Demand

As Chapter 3 explained, consumers are on the buying side of product markets. Given their limited incomes, consumers must decide how much of each good they would like to buy. These decisions are based on various factors, including the good's price.

The Law of Demand

The price of a good influences the amount consumers want to buy. High prices discourage consumption, which may be one reason you are driving that clunker instead of a sporty BMW. In contrast, low prices spur additional purchases. This explains why businesses sometimes put their merchandise *on sale*—they have found that customers buy greater quantities once the price is reduced. Such observations lead to an economic principle known as the **law of demand**:

OTHER THINGS (BEING) EQUAL, WHEN THE PRICE OF A GOOD RISES THE QUANTITY DEMANDED FALLS; WHEN THE PRICE FALLS THE QUANTITY DEMANDED RISES.

QUANTITY DEMANDED
The amount of a good consumers choose to buy at a particular price.

While the law of demand has an intuitive appeal, economists offer two explanations for the inverse relationship between price and **quantity demanded**. The first explanation rests on substitutability. A BMW and a Chevrolet are substitutes—both provide transportation. Likewise, butter and margarine are substitutes. As the price of a good falls, it becomes cheaper relative to its substitutes. The lower price induces some consumers to buy more of that good and less of the substitutes. Accordingly, consumption patterns change.

If the price of imported vehicles falls relative to the price of domestic vehicles, imports can be expected to carve out a larger share of the market. Or consider a price cut by Apple Computer. At a lower relative price, an Apple is more attractive than before. The price cut may be sufficient to convince some consumers to buy an Apple rather than an IBM or other substitute. Of course, the reverse holds for higher prices. If Apple raises prices, it loses potential customers to competing brands.

In addition to the substitution effect, there is a secondary reason for predicting a negative relation between price and quantity demanded. For any given income, a lower price increases consumer purchasing power: less income is now required to buy a given bundle of goods. As a result, consumers can increase consumption of various goods, including the good whose price has fallen. Conversely, a higher price

DEMAND SCHEDULE

A table showing the relationship between the price of a good and the quantity demanded per period of time, other things equal.

DEMAND CURVE

A diagram showing the relationship between the price of a good and the quantity demanded per period of time, other things equal.

reduces consumer purchasing power, which can be expected to reduce the quantity demanded of many goods.

Consider a specific example. Suppose the **demand schedule** in Figure 4.1 represents the demand for fish in Harbortown.[2] Consistent with the law of demand, the quantity demanded rises as price falls. For example, when the price of fish decreases from $5.00 to $4.50 per pound, the quantity demanded rises from 6 million pounds to 8 million pounds per month. The **demand curve** is obtained by plotting the points of the demand schedule. Notice that the demand curve is expressed in terms of a specific period of time, in this case, a month. To say that consumers want 8 million pounds of fish is vague. Is this the quantity demanded per week, per month, per year, or some other period of time? We must specify.

For simplicity we present a straight-line (linear) demand curve (Figure 4.1). But often demand curves are actually *curved*. If you become a corporate economist, one of your responsibilities may be to estimate the shape of the demand curves for your company's products.

Shifts in the Demand Curve

The amount of a good that consumers stand ready to buy depends on more than the price of that good. Other relevant factors include income, prices of other goods,

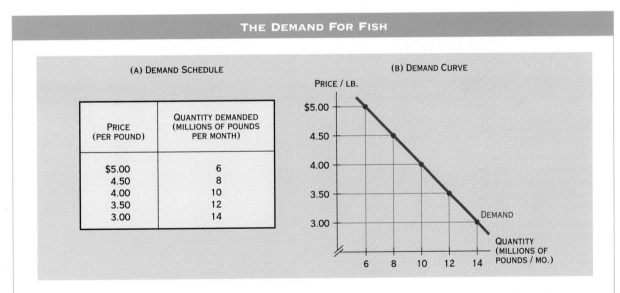

THE DEMAND FOR FISH

(A) DEMAND SCHEDULE

PRICE (PER POUND)	QUANTITY DEMANDED (MILLIONS OF POUNDS PER MONTH)
$5.00	6
4.50	8
4.00	10
3.50	12
3.00	14

(B) DEMAND CURVE

Demand can be represented either in tabular form (A) or graphically (B). Either way, demand is the relationship between price and quantity demanded (other things equal). According to the law of demand, *quantity demanded is inversely related to price*—the demand curve slopes downward.

FIGURE 4.1

---

[2]Actually, separate demand curves could be drawn for cod, perch, salmon, and the like. To keep the discussion general, we do not specify the type of fish.

number of potential buyers, tastes, and expectations. The demand curve is drawn on the assumption that *other things are equal*. This assumption allows us to isolate the relationship between price and the quantity demanded. That is, it indicates the effect of a price change provided that income, expectations, and all the other relevant factors affecting demand remain constant. Whenever one of these other variables changes, the result is a new demand curve—**a shift in demand**. We now discuss the major causes of such shifts.

INCOME

Generally, an increase in income increases demand for a good—shifts the demand curve rightward. With a higher income, consumers can afford to buy more of the good. Sometimes, however, consumption falls in response to a higher income. For example, as incomes rise consumers may decrease consumption of inexpensive foods (perhaps day-old bread, TV dinners, and generic brands) while expanding consumption of preferred foods (perhaps fresh bread, restaurant meals, and deli products). These responses are illustrated in Figure 4.2. An increase in income bolsters demand for **normal goods** (for example, fresh bread) while reducing demand for **inferior goods** (for example, day-old bread). A decrease in income has the opposite effect.

NORMAL GOOD
A good for which demand increases in response to a higher income.

INFERIOR GOOD
A good for which demand falls in response to a higher income.

PRICES OF SUBSTITUTES

In satisfying their wants, consumers can generally substitute one good for another—fish for meat, apples for pears, sweaters for jackets. Given such options, the

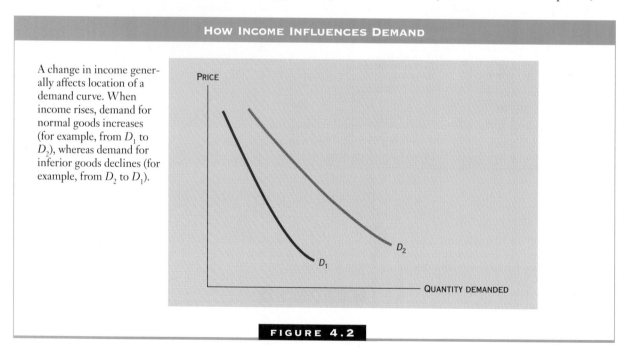

HOW INCOME INFLUENCES DEMAND

A change in income generally affects location of a demand curve. When income rises, demand for normal goods increases (for example, from D_1 to D_2), whereas demand for inferior goods declines (for example, from D_2 to D_1).

PRICE

D_2

D_1

QUANTITY DEMANDED

FIGURE 4.2

SUBSTITUTE GOODS
Goods that are substitutable in consumption. Two goods are substitutes when an increase in the price of one good increases demand for the other.

demand for a good depends on the prices of **substitute goods**. For example, when the price of beef rises, consumers can be expected to eat less beef and more fish. In other words, a higher price for beef increases the demand for fish (Figure 4.3A). In contrast, when the price of beef falls, consumers want to buy less fish. As consumers increase their purchases of beef, the demand for fish decreases (shifts leftward).

PRICES OF COMPLEMENTS

COMPLEMENTARY GOODS
Goods that are consumed together. Two goods are complements when an increase in the price of one good reduces demand for the other.

Complementary goods are goods that tend to be used together—for example, automobiles and gasoline, cameras and film, computer hardware and software. Because complements are used in tandem, a change in the price of one good alters demand for the other. But whereas an increase in the price of a substitute shifts demand outward, an increase in the price of a complement shifts demand inward (see Figure 4.3B). When the price of tennis balls skyrockets, one expects consumers to demand fewer tennis racquets. Some continue to play tennis but less frequently, prolonging the life of their racquets. Others decide that tennis is now too expensive and turn to jogging, swimming, or other sports. Some may even give up exercise altogether (switching from court time to television time). A reduction in the price of tennis balls should have the opposite effect—encouraging more tennis and, in the process, increasing demand for tennis racquets.

A CHANGE IN THE PRICE OF ONE GOOD MAY AFFECT DEMAND FOR ANOTHER

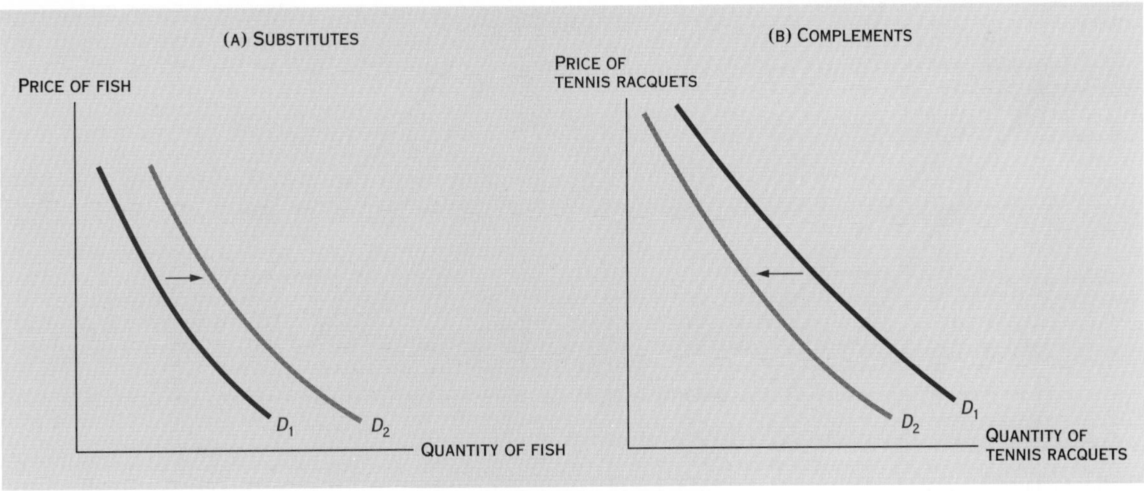

(A) SUBSTITUTES — PRICE OF FISH — D_1 — D_2 — QUANTITY OF FISH

(B) COMPLEMENTS — PRICE OF TENNIS RACQUETS — D_2 — D_1 — QUANTITY OF TENNIS RACQUETS

An increase in the price of beef (a substitute) shifts demand for fish outward (A). In contrast, when tennis balls increase in price, tennis becomes less popular, which dampens demand for tennis racquets (B).

FIGURE 4.3

NUMBER OF POTENTIAL BUYERS

Another variable affecting demand is the number of consumers in the market. If a state were to lower the legal driving age, demand for automobiles would likely increase. Some who previously could not legally drive in the state would take advantage of the law and visit an automobile dealer. States also regulate alcoholic beverages, with many states raising the legal drinking age in recent years. Although liquor laws are frequently broken, they do have an impact. These laws make it more difficult for minors to obtain alcohol and they introduce a new deterrent (penalties if caught). This is enough to influence the behavior of some young people, thereby reducing demand for alcohol.

TASTES

Demand also depends on the tastes or preferences of consumers. A recent government report, criticized by ranchers, advises U.S. consumers to reduce the amount of red meat in their diet. Some research links high consumption of red meat to heart disease, strokes, and colon cancer. At the same time, many nutritionists have begun emphasizing the benefits of fish, fruit, and vegetables. Such reports can be expected to alter consumer buying patterns, augmenting the demand for fish while depressing the demand for red meat (see Figure 4.4).

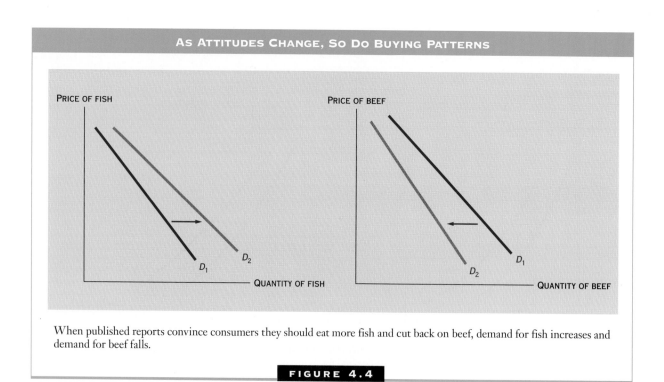

AS ATTITUDES CHANGE, SO DO BUYING PATTERNS

When published reports convince consumers they should eat more fish and cut back on beef, demand for fish increases and demand for beef falls.

FIGURE 4.4

EXPECTATIONS OF CONSUMERS

A belief that market conditions will change in the future can influence demand today. How do consumers react when they hear that stores may run out of bathroom tissue, that coffee prices will soon jump, or that production of their favorite beverage is being discontinued? Many try to beat the price hike or empty shelves by stocking up on the item now—buying more in the current period than they otherwise would. The result is an increase in current demand.

Distinguishing Between Changes in Demand and Changes in the Quantity Demanded

Because the events described in Figures 4.5(A) and (B) clearly differ, they must be given different names, so we can distinguish between them without confusion. The names economists have chosen to denote Figures 4.5(A) and (B), respectively, are **a change in demand** and **a change in quantity demanded**.

A SHIFT IN DEMAND VERSUS A MOVEMENT ALONG A DEMAND CURVE

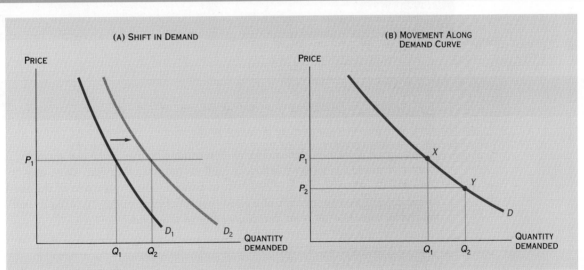

A shift in demand (A) occurs when some determinant of demand changes, other than a good's own price. An increase in demand means that at each price (for example, P_1) a greater quantity is now demanded (Q_2 rather than Q_1). A movement along a demand curve (B) occurs in response to a change in the price of the good. When price falls from P_1 to P_2, the quantity demanded increases from Q_1 to Q_2.

FIGURE 4.5

The expression "a change in demand" refers to a *shift in the demand curve*—the relationship between price and quantity demanded has been modified. At any given price, the quantity demanded is now different: it is higher if demand increases, lower if demand falls (see Figure 4.5A). *Again*, the major reasons for a change in demand: a change in income, different expectations, and so on.

Note carefully that a change in the good's own price does *not* cause a change in demand. When the price of a good changes, the quantity demanded either rises (if price falls) or falls (if price rises). But the demand curve does not shift. Instead, a change in a good's own price can be represented as a *movement along the demand curve* (see Figure 4.5B). There has been a change in quantity demanded, but not a change in demand.

This is an important point, one you are expected to master: *A change in a good's own price leads to a movement along a given demand curve (a change in quantity demanded); a change in any other variable relevant to consumers results in a new demand curve (a change in demand).*

Recognizing Shifts in Demand

YOUR TURN

HOW, IF AT ALL, DO THE FOLLOWING FACTORS AFFECT THE DEMAND FOR CASSETTE PLAYERS?

(A) THE PRICE OF CASSETTES FALLS.

(B) THE PRICE OF COMPACT DISC PLAYERS FALLS.

(C) THE PRICE OF CASSETTE PLAYERS FALLS.

(D) THE COUNTRY'S POPULATION INCREASES.

(E) CONSUMERS DECIDE TO SPEND MORE TIME WATCHING MUSIC VIDEOS AND LESS TIME LISTENING TO CASSETTES.

Supply

Despite its importance, demand alone determines neither price nor quantity purchased. A market must have sellers as well as buyers; otherwise, there can be no transactions. Accordingly, it is essential to consider the supply side of the market. What determines the amount of a good that sellers are willing to bring to market? Several factors are important, including price of the good.

The Law of Supply

QUANTITY SUPPLIED
The amount of a good firms choose to sell at a particular price.

The **law of supply** predicts a positive relationship between price and the **quantity supplied**:

OTHER THINGS (BEING) EQUAL, A HIGHER PRICE FOR A GOOD INCREASES THE QUANTITY SUPPLIED; A LOWER PRICE REDUCES THE QUANTITY SUPPLIED.

Price is an inducement, the carrot that prompts sellers to bring a good to market. As price rises, the incentive to sell intensifies. Not only do existing firms want to provide more of the good, but new firms may also be drawn into the market now that the reward for selling the product has been sweetened.

When the price of fish rises, additional resources are drawn into fishing. Boats and equipment that were idle at low prices are called into service. Vessels ordinarily used for other purposes (sightseeing or recreation) may be converted to fishing boats. Crews put in more hours, fishing some waters more intensively as well as traveling farther out to sea. New fishing operations may be started because of more favorable market conditions. All these responses contribute to a greater quantity supplied.

A higher price achieves similar results on land. When the price of corn rises, other things equal, farmers grow more corn. Some land is switched from less profitable crops to production of corn. Low-grade land that previously was idle is planted with corn. Not only does acreage increase, but so does yield per acre—due to more intensive use of fertilizer, pesticides, and irrigation.[3]

As is true for demand curves, supply curves are drawn on the assumption that other things are equal—that the other factors influencing supply do not change. Under these conditions, there is a unique functional relationship between price and the quantity supplied. That relationship can be expressed in terms of either a **supply schedule** or a **supply curve**. A hypothetical supply schedule and the corresponding supply curve are presented in Figure 4.6.

SUPPLY SCHEDULE
A table showing the relationship between the price of a good and the quantity supplied per period of time, other things equal.

SUPPLY CURVE
A diagram showing the relationship between the price of a good and the quantity supplied per period of time, other things equal.

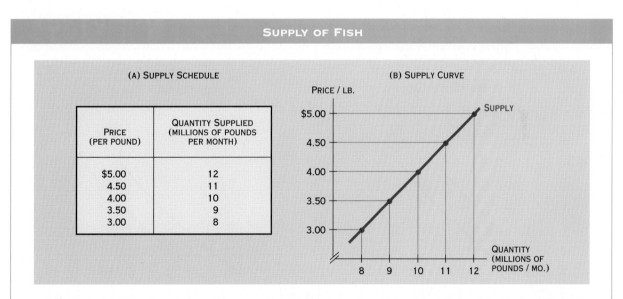

SUPPLY OF FISH

(A) SUPPLY SCHEDULE

PRICE (PER POUND)	QUANTITY SUPPLIED (MILLIONS OF POUNDS PER MONTH)
$5.00	12
4.50	11
4.00	10
3.50	9
3.00	8

(B) SUPPLY CURVE

The supply schedule (A) and supply curve (B) indicate that the quantity of fish supplied is a positive function of price (other things equal). This is consistent with the law of supply.

FIGURE 4.6

[3]For corn and other crops, empirical studies estimate that the increase in yield per acre has a greater effect on output than does the increase in acreage.

Analogous to the case of demand, a change in price leads to a *movement along the supply curve*. For example, in Figure 4.6, raising the price of fish from $3.00/pound to $3.50/pound increases the quantity of fish supplied from 8 million pounds to 9 million pounds per month. A change in the value of any other determinant of supply (besides the good's own price) results in a new supply curve: *a shift in supply*. When the supply curve shifts leftward, supply has decreased—at each price a lower quantity is now brought to market. When the supply curve shifts rightward, supply has increased. This is illustrated in Figure 4.7.

Shifts in Supply

The major forces responsible for changes in supply are costs of production, prices of other goods, and expectations.

COSTS OF PRODUCTION

Whereas a higher price increases the reward for production, higher costs reduce the incentive to produce. The result is a decrease in supply. Conversely, developments that make production less costly increase supply. Costs may change for several reasons, notably *a change in input prices, taxes*, and *technological change*.

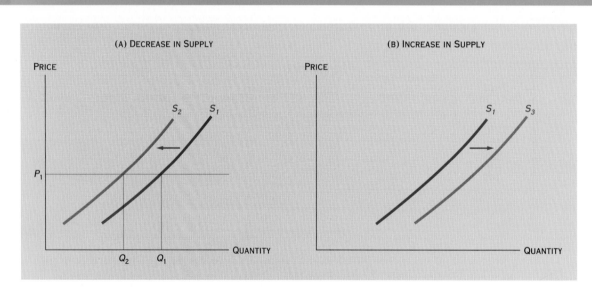

SHIFTS IN SUPPLY

(A) DECREASE IN SUPPLY

(B) INCREASE IN SUPPLY

Supply decreases when costs of production rise (for example, because of higher input prices), when prices of other goods (the firm could produce) increase, or when producers anticipate higher prices. At any given price (for example, P_1) a smaller quantity is now supplied (Q_2 rather than Q_1). In contrast, supply increases (B) when production costs fall, when prices of other goods decline, or when producers anticipate lower prices.

FIGURE 4.7

Higher input prices add to the costs of production. Assume the prices of fuel and boats rise, so that it costs more to catch fish. Some who fish may decide to leave the sea now that fishing is less lucrative. Others remain, but fish less. At each price suppliers are willing to sell fewer fish now that costs have increased. As this example illustrates, higher input prices reduce supply.

The imposition of a tax on output (or an increase in an existing tax) likewise adds to production costs.[4] Again the result is a leftward shift in the supply curve—the tax reduces the quantity that producers are willing to supply at each price.

Production costs, when they change, do not always head skyward. Sometimes they fall. When this happens the result is an increase in supply. Supply increases when input prices are reduced, when taxes on producers are lowered, or when costs otherwise decline. Technological advance provides an example of how production costs can fall, even if input prices and taxes do not. Technological advances have increased agricultural yields per acre, lowered the cost of radios, and permitted computers to be manufactured more cheaply. The result: greater supplies of food, radios, and computers.

PRICES OF OTHER GOODS THE FIRM COULD PRODUCE

Resources often can be diverted from the production of one good to another. For example, land may be suitable for growing both corn and wheat. For that reason, the supply of corn depends on the price of wheat. An increase in the price of wheat makes growing corn less attractive (the opportunity cost rises). As some land is switched from production of corn to wheat, the supply of corn falls (the supply curve shifts leftward). Conversely, more corn is grown when the price of wheat falls (the supply curve of corn shifts rightward).

EXPECTATIONS OF PRODUCERS

Expectations may affect producers as well as consumers, supply as well as demand. For some goods the expectation of higher prices provides producers with an incentive to reduce supply in the present period, deferring sales to the future. For example, oil producers may withhold oil from the market in the current period in anticipation of sharply higher prices in subsequent months. So for any given price, the amount supplied in the current period declines. Or suppose oil prices are expected to fall. Producers may want to increase supply now, before conditions deteriorate.

For other goods supply is independent of price expectations. An anticipated increase in the price of haircuts is unlikely to affect the current supply of haircuts. The central difference between oil and haircuts is that oil is storable, haircuts are not.[5] Oil not sold today can be sold later. In contrast, haircuts cannot be inventoried. Sales not made this period may be lost forever.

---

[4]Taxes are discussed more fully in Chapter 5.

[5]Because of the *storable* nature of oil, it is important to distinguish between *production* of oil and *supply* of oil. The expectation of higher oil prices induces producers to cut back current supply—to reduce the amount they are willing to sell this period at any given price. But current production does not necessarily decline. It may even increase as oil producers build up inventories.

A New Number One Crop?

E
X
H
I
B
I
T

4 . 1

The National Organization for the Reform of Marijuana Laws (NORML) claims that during the 1980s marijuana became the largest revenue-producing crop in the United States. Officials at the U.S. Department of Agriculture insist that corn remains king. Because marijuana growers are understandably reluctant to report their harvests, the debate is not likely to be resolved. But even if marijuana is only the second- or third-largest crop, it is clearly big business. Does our discussion of supply hold for illegal goods such as marijuana? Yes, the same forces operate.

Consider the law of supply as applied to marijuana. In response to a higher price, existing growers raise larger crops. Some take less profitable crops out of production in order to grow more marijuana; previously idle land is planted; and indoor cultivation expands. Lured by high potential profits, new producers enter the market—some consumers may even decide to grow their own and become sellers. A higher price for marijuana leads to a greater quantity supplied.

A change in costs of production also has the predicted effect: a shift in supply. Because of heightened concern over controlled substance abuse, the government expanded eradication programs, in which marijuana fields are sighted by air and then destroyed, and more aggressively pursued prosecutions. Such actions caused suppliers to spend more on security in order to avoid detection and to switch to more elaborate and expensive means of transportation. Both actions drove up the costs of marijuana production. As a consequence, the supply of marijuana decreased. How did this reduction in supply affect the price of marijuana? Read on.

The Interaction of Supply and Demand

Thus far we have dealt separately with demand and supply; it is now time to bring the two together and explain how prices are determined. We restrict our analysis to competitive markets, which contain a large number of buyers and sellers, none large enough to influence price. In such markets firms compete against each other for customers, and consumers compete for the available output. (For now we ignore government intervention, but consider the effect of government price controls later in the chapter.)

For a given price, the demand curve reveals the quantity demanded, the supply curve the quantity supplied. Neither curve, by itself, sheds any light on the price that will prevail. But bring supply and demand together and it is a different matter, as can be seen with the aid of the supply and demand schedules for fish given in Table 4.1.

Consider a price of $3.00/lb. At this price the quantity demanded (14 million pounds) exceeds the quantity supplied (8 million pounds)—there is an excess

SHORTAGE

The amount by which quantity demanded exceeds quantity supplied at a given price.

demand, or **shortage**, of 6 million pounds. This situation cannot persist. Rivalry among consumers will push up prices. Rather than accept less than they want, some fish-hungry consumers will offer sellers a higher price. Those who fish, finding that they can sell their product at a higher price, are only too happy to raise their prices. Higher prices reduce the shortage for two reasons: consumers reduce the amount of fish they want to buy while suppliers increase the amount they are willing to sell. At a price of $3.50/lb, the shortage shrinks to 3 million pounds. But as long as a shortage exists, upward pressure on prices will continue.

Now consider a price of $5.00/lb. At this price the quantity supplied (12 million pounds) exceeds the quantity demanded (6 million pounds). The market is characterized by an excess supply, or a **surplus**, of 6 million pounds. Such conditions cannot persist over time. Unable to sell as much as they would like, some who fish will cut prices in order to spur sales. (Would you want to be stuck with a load of smelly fish?) As prices fall, consumers will want to buy more fish; producers will want to sell less. Both forces cause the surplus to dwindle. The market will exert downward pressure on prices until the surplus is eliminated.

SURPLUS

The amount by which quantity supplied exceeds quantity demanded at a given price.

Equilibrium

EQUILIBRIUM PRICE

The price for which the quantity demanded equals the quantity supplied.

EQUILIBRIUM

A state of balance; a market is in equilibrium when the quantity demanded equals the quantity supplied.

Having peeked at Table 4.1, you realize that a price exists ($4.00) for which there is neither a shortage of fish nor a surplus. This is the **equilibrium price**. At this price the amount consumers choose to buy coincides exactly with the amount producers choose to sell. The market is in **equilibrium**, a state of balance. Producers have no incentive to lower prices; they are selling all they want at this price. Nor do consumers have any reason to bid up prices; at the equilibrium price they are consuming the amount desired. As long as supply and demand remain unchanged, there is no reason for price to move away from the equilibrium price.

Equilibrium can also be depicted graphically as the intersection of the supply and demand curves. In Figure 4.8 (page 94), the equilibrium price is $4.00 and the equilibrium quantity is 10 million pounds per month.

DEMAND AND SUPPLY OF FISH			
PRICE PER POUND	QUANTITY DEMANDED $(Q^D)^*$	QUANTITY SUPPLIED $(Q^S)^*$	$(Q^D - Q^S)^*$
$5.00	6	12	−6 } surplus
4.50	8	11	−3
4.00	10	10	0 equilibrium
3.50	12	9	3 } shortage
3.00	14	8	6

* Millions of pounds per month.

TABLE 4.1

Equilibrium occurs where supply and demand curves intersect. Here the equilibrium price is $4 and the equilibrium quantity is 10 million pounds per month. At any higher price (for example, $5) there is a surplus, which exerts downward pressure on price. When the price is below $4, the resulting shortage causes the price to increase.

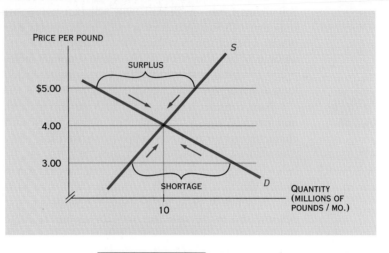

FIGURE 4.8

Disequilibrium

DISEQUILIBRIUM PRICE
Any price for which the quantity demanded differs from the quantity supplied.

DISEQUILIBRIUM
A state of imbalance; a market is in disequilibrium when the quantity demanded does not coincide with the quantity supplied.

Any price for which quantity demanded and quantity supplied differ is called a **disequilibrium price**. In unrestricted, competitive markets, disequilibrium prices cannot be maintained. Whenever the actual price exceeds the equilibrium price it falls, as producers attempt to unload unwanted surpluses. In contrast, whenever the actual price is below the equilibrium price, consumers respond to the shortage by bidding up the price.

As demand or supply changes, what previously was an equilibrium price becomes a **disequilibrium** price, and the market moves to its new equilibrium. How rapidly prices adjust depends on the market. In some markets price changes are almost instantaneous. For example, on the Minneapolis Grain Exchange, grain prices respond immediately to changes in buying or selling plans. In other markets adjustments may be more sluggish and, as we see later, the government sometimes impedes a market's movement to equilibrium.

Changes in the Equilibrium Price

Equilibrium corresponds to the intersection of supply and demand curves. Both supply and demand are crucial (see Exhibit 4.2); if either changes, the result is a new equilibrium. We now consider, in turn, a shift in demand, a shift in supply, and a shift in both demand and supply curves.

E
X
H
I
B
I
T

4 . 2

Marshall and the Two Blades of a Pair of Scissors

Early economists debated the relative importance of supply and demand in determining market price. Emphasizing costs of production, classical economists (such as David Ricardo) gave top billing to supply. A later school of thought, marginalism, focused on consumer utility or demand. According to the marginalist view, the price of a good is determined by the utility or satisfaction to consumers of an additional unit of that good. Alfred Marshall resolved the controversy by explaining that price depends critically on both supply and demand. In a famous passage comparing supply and demand to the two blades of a pair of scissors, Marshall writes:

> We might as reasonably dispute whether it is the upper or under blade of a pair of scissors that cuts a piece of paper, as whether value is governed by utility [demand] or cost of production [supply].

Another contribution of Marshall was explaining consumer responsiveness to price changes. Marshall presented certain principles that indicate why price changes have a disproportionately large effect on the quantity demanded of some goods but relatively little effect on the quantity demanded of others.[6]

Marshall was born in London in 1842. Despite pressure from his father to enter the ministry, Marshall studied mathematics and later turned to economics. He taught at Cambridge and Bristol, where he shaped the thinking of the next generation of English economists.

Though a gifted mathematician, Marshall attempted to keep economics comprehensible to the lay audience. He argued that "when a great many symbols have to be used, they become very laborious to any one but the writer himself." Marshall's highly influential book, *Principles of Economics*, went through eight editions before his death in 1924. It is still being sold today.

[6] The technical term for this "responsiveness" is the *price elasticity of demand*. This concept is discussed in Chapter 5. Marshall's work was not restricted to consumer goods. Extending his analysis to the demand for labor, Marshall also examined the responsiveness of employers to changes in the price of labor (the wage rate).

A CHANGE IN DEMAND

Earlier we explained why demand might change. Let us now consider the consequences of such change. As Figure 4.9 illustrates (page 96), an increase in demand leads to an increase in both equilibrium price and quantity. As demand increases from D_1 to D_2, the equilibrium price rises from P_1 to P_2 and the equilibrium quantity from Q_1 to Q_2. Analysis of a decrease in demand is symmetric: when demand falls, so do equilibrium price and quantity.

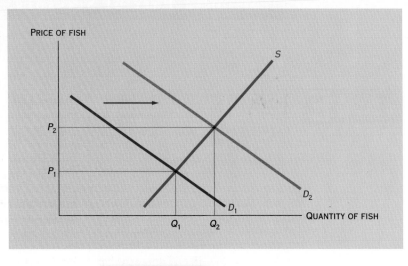

An increase in the demand for fish (perhaps the consequence of favorable reports on the health benefits of fish) increases the equilibrium price and quantity of fish.

FIGURE 4.9

A CHANGE IN SUPPLY

Like an increase in demand, a greater supply also puts upward pressure on quantity (Figure 4.10). The difference is that a greater supply depresses price. Given an increase in supply from S_1 to S_2, the equilibrium price falls from P_1 to P_2 while the

An increase in the supply of fish (for example, because of lower fishing costs) increases the equilibrium quantity of fish but reduces the equilibrium price.

PRICE OF FISH

S_1

S_2

P_1

P_2

D

QUANTITY OF FISH

Q_1 Q_2

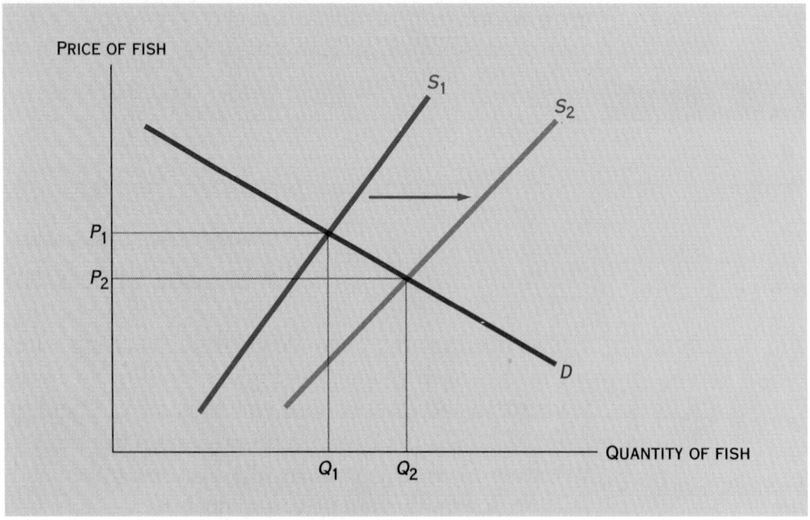

FIGURE 4.10

equilibrium quantity rises from Q_1 to Q_2. A decrease in supply has the opposite effect: the equilibrium price rises and the equilibrium quantity falls.

A CHANGE IN BOTH DEMAND AND SUPPLY

Now that you see the effect of a change in demand or supply, let's muddy the waters. Assume both the demand and supply curves shift. What happens to equilibrium price and quantity? For example, suppose the demand for fish and the supply of fish both increase. In that event, the new equilibrium quantity is higher—increases in demand and supply both exert upward pressure on quantity. But what happens to price? The answer is not obvious, since an increase in demand tends to raise price, whereas an increase in supply has the opposite effect.

Whether price rises, falls, or remains unchanged depends on the magnitude of the shift in demand relative to the shift in supply. This is shown in Figure 4.11. When supply increases to S_2, price is higher at the new equilibrium. When the supply curve shifts all the way to S_4(C), the new equilibrium price is lower. Finally, when supply increases to S_3 (so that at P_1 supply and demand shift by the same horizontal amount), the equilibrium price does not change. In analogous fashion, when demand and supply both decline, the equilibrium quantity falls; however, barring information on the extent to which demand and supply have changed, the effect on price is ambiguous.

When demand and supply curves shift in opposite directions, the effect on price is clear, but the effect on quantity is indeterminate. A simultaneous increase

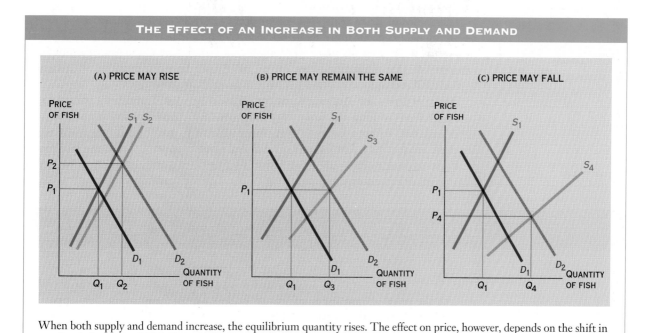

THE EFFECT OF AN INCREASE IN BOTH SUPPLY AND DEMAND

(A) PRICE MAY RISE (B) PRICE MAY REMAIN THE SAME (C) PRICE MAY FALL

When both supply and demand increase, the equilibrium quantity rises. The effect on price, however, depends on the shift in supply relative to the shift in demand. The equilibrium price may rise (A), remain unchanged (B), or fall (C).

FIGURE 4.11

in demand and decrease in supply raise the equilibrium price. A reduction in demand coupled with growth in supply pushes the equilibrium price lower. Whether quantity rises, falls, or remains unchanged depends on the relative shifts of the demand and supply curves.

Applying Supply and Demand Analysis to Automobile Export Restrictions

YOUR TURN

AS A RESULT OF INTENSE PRESSURE FROM CONGRESS, JAPAN AGREED TO LIMIT THE NUMBER OF AUTOMOBILES SHIPPED TO THE UNITED STATES. (A) HOW HAS THIS "VOLUNTARY EXPORT RESTRICTION" AFFECTED THE SUPPLY OF AUTOMOBILES IMPORTED BY THE UNITED STATES AND THE PRICE PAID BY U.S. CONSUMERS FOR IMPORTED AUTOMOBILES? (B) HOW AND WHY DOES A CHANGE IN THE PRICE OF IMPORTED AUTOMOBILES AFFECT THE DEMAND FOR DOMESTIC AUTOMOBILES (THAT IS, AUTOMOBILES PRODUCED IN THE UNITED STATES)? (C) GIVEN YOUR ANSWERS TO (A) AND (B), HOW HAVE VOLUNTARY EXPORT RESTRICTIONS AFFECTED THE PRICE OF DOMESTIC AUTOMOBILES?

Price Controls

So far we have assumed that markets operate free of government intervention. But sometimes governments erect barriers that may prevent equilibrium from being attained. A primary example is *price controls*, which may take the form of either a **price ceiling** or a **price floor**. A price ceiling refers to the maximum legal price at which a good may be sold. A price floor is the minimum legal price.

PRICE CEILING
The maximum legal price that may be charged for a good.

PRICE FLOOR
The minimum legal price that must be paid for a good.

Examples of price controls abound. Rent controls place a lid on rents, usury laws provide a cap on interest rates (the price paid for borrowing money). Federal minimum wage laws mandate that employers covered by these laws cannot hire labor at less than a specified rate of pay ($4.25 per hour in early 1993). In many agricultural markets, price supports place a lower limit on prices.

Price controls are often imposed for political reasons. Sometimes buyers pressure politicians to limit the price they must pay (as in the case of rent controls). In other instances sellers convince government officials to guarantee a minimum price for their product (as in the case of agricultural price supports). Given the frequency with which price controls are imposed, it is important to examine their impact. We begin with price ceilings.

Price Ceilings

Assume the government sets a maximum legal price for some good. To be specific, assume the price of gasoline is subject to an upper limit (as was true during part of the 1970s). What is the impact of this government decree? The answer depends on whether the maximum price is set above or below the equilibrium price:

A PRICE CEILING SET ABOVE THE EQUILIBRIUM PRICE HAS NO IMPACT. A PRICE CEILING SET BELOW THE EQUILIBRIUM PRICE TENDS TO CREATE A SHORTAGE.

These two statements can be visualized with the aid of Figure 4.12. Assume the government establishes a maximum legal price of P_1. Despite this action, motorists find it unnecessary to pay a price this high. Any station owner attempting to extract the maximum legal price from consumers loses customers to companies charging a lower price. Thus a maximum price set above the equilibrium price does not prevent the equilibrium price from being attained. Although the government rules out prices above P_1, these prices would not have prevailed even in the absence of a price ceiling.

On a more whimsical note, consider a proposal made in the late 1970s, when resentment toward OPEC was high: a bushel of wheat should sell for more than a barrel of oil. ("You can't eat oil.") At the time, oil was trading for about $30 per barrel and wheat at about $4 per bushel. Suppose the U.S. government, taking the recommendation seriously, sternly announced that it would not tolerate a price of wheat in excess of $30 per bushel. Would this pronouncement affect either the price or the quantity of wheat sold? Obviously not. Even without this "protection," no buyer would be foolish enough to pay more than dictated by the market—let alone $30 per bushel. All the government would be doing in this case is forbidding prices that the market had already ruled out.

Figure 4.12 also illustrates what happens when a price ceiling is set below the equilibrium price. A maximum price of P_2, if effectively enforced, creates a shortage of $Q_2 - Q_1$. Although the low price is considered attractive to consumers, producers are unwilling to supply more than Q_1 to the market.

In an unrestricted market, price rations out of the market those unwilling or unable to pay the equilibrium price. With price constrained below the equilibrium level, this rationing function is thwarted. Buyers unwilling to pay the equilibrium price remain in the market. How then will the available output be allocated? Given excess demand, who will leave the market satisfied and who will leave frustrated?

When price is frozen below the equilibrium level, the primary methods of allocating goods are *first-come first-served*, *government mandate*, and *sellers' choice*. In some situations the last may be first, but not when it comes to shortages. If there is

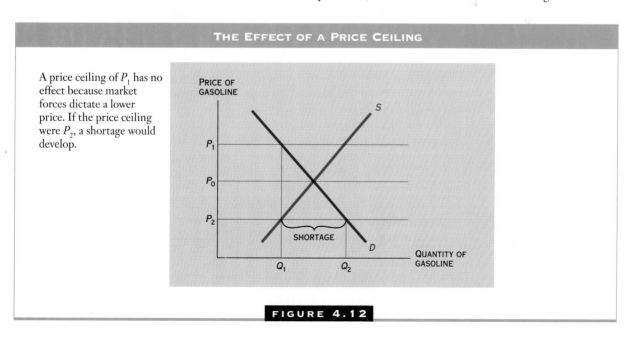

THE EFFECT OF A PRICE CEILING

A price ceiling of P_1 has no effect because market forces dictate a lower price. If the price ceiling were P_2, a shortage would develop.

PRICE OF GASOLINE

P_1

P_0

P_2

SHORTAGE

Q_1 Q_2

QUANTITY OF GASOLINE

S

D

FIGURE 4.12

not enough gasoline to go around at the price ceiling, one method of distributing the quantity available is on the basis of who is first in line at the pump. When the pumps run dry, those still in line are out of luck.

Alternatively, the government could decide which consumers receive how much. Under the Carter Administration, the government considered methods of allocating gasoline in the event of a severe shortage. For example, each driver might be permitted to purchase a specified number of gallons of gasoline per week. This is the approach commonly adopted during wartime. Not only is money required to purchase a product, but the consumer must also have a *ration ticket*, which conveys the right to buy a good.

Another option is to allow sellers to decide who can buy the good and who cannot. Under such circumstances the owner of a gasoline station is likely to give top priority to employees, friends, and regular customers. (If so, the owner may be surprised to discover how many friends he or she has.) Alternatively, given excess demand at the legal price, the owner might refuse to sell to members of a particular race, nationality, or sex. In other words, a price ceiling creates an environment conducive to discrimination.

Regardless of the nonprice method of allocation, many consumers will be thwarted in their attempts to purchase the product. Some may be willing to offer suppliers a little extra—either directly in the form of a price above the legal ceiling or indirectly by providing the seller with something else of value. In fact, when gasoline shortages developed in California during the "oil crisis," the press reported instances of service station attendants being offered personal favors in return for the opportunity to purchase gasoline. At the same time that some consumers are willing to pay more than the legal price rather than do without, suppliers have an incentive to sell at a price in excess of the price ceiling, thereby earning extra profits.[7] It should therefore come as no surprise that exchanges sometimes occur illegally in what is known as the **black market**.

Nonprice rationing occasionally crops up in markets that are not regulated by the government. For instance, recently a builder in California completed a subdivision and then offered all the houses for sale at a specified price. So many people wanted to purchase his houses that the builder resorted to a lottery to determine the lucky buyers. What this indicates is that the builder set the price too low: he could have sold all the houses at a higher price and therefore earned greater profits. Although the builder did not know the equilibrium or market-clearing price, he could have discovered it. Had he auctioned the houses, each would have sold to the buyer willing to pay the highest price.

Universities sometimes set prices for athletic events at levels that do not yield maximum profits. For example, every football game at the University of Nebraska is a sellout, and fans must be turned away. The university could generate additional revenues by raising ticket prices, but profit maximization is not a goal of universities. Still, economic forces do play a role. Universities generally find tickets for those contributing to their athletic programs (sellers' choice).

Price ceilings can do more than create allocation problems. Consider the case of rent controls, which keep the price of rental housing below market levels.

BLACK MARKET
A market in which goods are bought and sold at prices above the legal maximum.

---

[7]Note that a price ceiling could actually lead to a *higher* price than would occur in an unregulated market. In the extreme case, when controls effectively limit the quantity supplied to Q_1 (Figure 4.12), firms may be able to sell (illegally) their output for as much as P_1. Further note that when sellers differ in terms of their inclination to obey the law, a price floor is more likely to drive law-abiding suppliers from the market. Suppliers unwilling to charge more than the legal price earn less than those willing to break the law.

Although often supported as a way to protect low-income tenants, the negative repercussions of rent controls abound. Housing quality declines. Owners have little incentive to maintain housing, let alone make improvements, since the cost cannot be passed on to consumers through higher rents. By accelerating the rate at which housing deteriorates, controls reduce the stock of housing in the long run, exacerbating the shortage. Rent-controlled housing becomes difficult to find, so consumers are forced to spend more time searching for it, lower their standards (accept lower-quality housing or housing in a nonpreferred location), and often make side payments, effectively raising the price above the legal maximum. Market values for rent-controlled housing plunge, which lowers the amount cities collect in real-estate taxes. Sometimes property values become negative, as costs exceed rental income, inducing landlords to abandon their property.

Price Floors

Rather than set a maximum legal price, sometimes a government mandates a minimum price. As was the case for price ceilings, the ultimate impact depends on the level of the price floor relative to the equilibrium price:

A PRICE FLOOR SET BELOW THE EQUILIBRIUM PRICE HAS NO IMPACT. A PRICE FLOOR SET ABOVE THE EQUILIBRIUM PRICE TENDS TO CREATE A SURPLUS.

Consider the market for sugar depicted in Figure 4.13. When the price floor (P_1) is set below the equilibrium price (P_0), neither price nor quantity is affected. Because suppliers can sell their output at a price in excess of P_1, the price floor does not hinder attainment of equilibrium.

This is not the case when the minimum legal price exceeds the equilibrium price. A price floor of P_2 creates a surplus of $Q_2 - Q_1$. Producers want to sell more

THE EFFECT OF A PRICE FLOOR

A price floor of P_1 rules out all lower prices. However, because the equilibrium price is higher than P_1, the price floor has no effect. A price floor of P_2, which lies above the equilibrium price, tends to create a surplus.

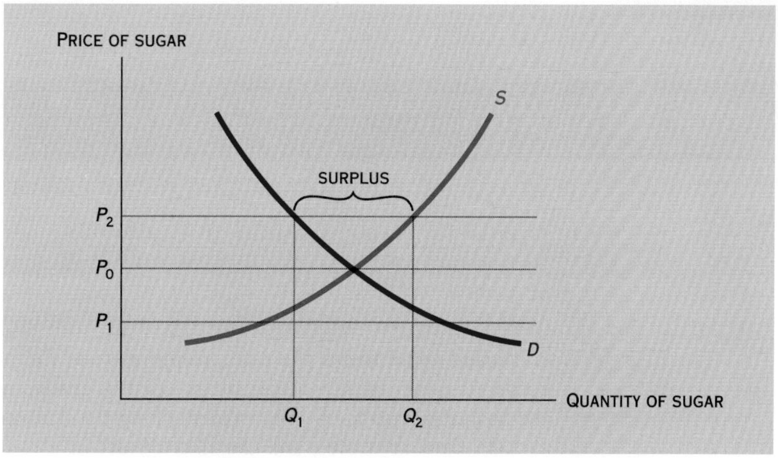

FIGURE 4.13

than the equilibrium quantity; consumers want to buy less. Unless the government buys the surplus, producers have an incentive to shave the price. Extra income can be earned by those willing to violate the law or clever enough to get around it (see Exhibit 4.3).

A Sweet Deal

E X H I B I T

4 . 3

In 1982, the federal government established price supports for sugar. Recently, while raw (unrefined) sugar was selling for as little as 3 cents per pound in world markets, the U.S. government enforced a minimum price of 22 cents per pound for sugar produced in the United States. To prevent buyers from switching to foreign-produced sugar, the government restricted sugar imports.

The cost advantage of up to 19 cents per pound for imports tempted more than a few producers to smuggle sugar into the United States. One of the favorite scams was to take advantage of a loophole in the law. In essence, raw sugar could be purchased legally at low prices in foreign markets and then brought into the United States for refining, provided that the refined sugar was sold outside the United States. Customs officials and agents for the Justice Department discov-ered that the volume of refined sugar leaving the United States was much less than the volume of raw sugar entering the country. The difference, estimated to be as much as 1 million tons since 1982, was being sold illegally in the United States at premium prices. Some companies allegedly filed false shipping documents, claiming they were exporting their refined sugar, while they were actually selling it in the United States. More than a dozen companies were indicted on charges of smuggling and falsifying documents.

Smuggling was not the only tactic for obtaining cheap sugar—potential profits spur creativity. Some U.S. companies actually imported candy, melted it down, and then extracted the sugar! Whenever a law sets prices at artificial levels, it creates incentives to violate the law—either in letter or in spirit.

Summary

1. According to the law of demand, the quantity demanded is inversely related to price—demand curves slope downward. A lower price induces consumers to buy relatively more of a good and less of substitutes. In addition, a lower price increases consumers' purchasing power, enabling them to buy more of the good.

2. A demand curve shows the relationship between the price of a good and the amount consumers want to buy, other things equal. A change in the price leads to a change in the quantity demanded—a movement along the demand curve. A change in any other variable (income, tastes, and the like) results in a change in demand—a shift of the demand curve.

3. A higher income boosts demand for normal goods but dampens demand for inferior goods. A lower income has the opposite effect.

4. A change in the price of one good may affect demand for another. If two goods are substitutes, a rise in the price of one increases demand for the other. In the case of complements, a higher price for one good reduces demand for the other.

5. Demand also depends on the number of potential buyers, tastes, and expectations.

6. The law of supply states that, other things equal, the quantity supplied is a positive function of price—supply curves slope upward.

7. Changes in costs of production, prices of other goods, and expectations lead to a change in supply—a shift of the supply curve.

8. Equilibrium occurs when the quantity demanded equals the quantity supplied. When price is above the equilibrium price, a surplus results, putting downward pressure on price. When price is below the equilibrium price, a shortage develops, putting upward pressure on price. A change in demand or supply results in a new equilibrium.

9. A price ceiling set below the equilibrium price tends to create a shortage. In response, a black market is likely to emerge. When price is not allowed to ration the available quantity, alternative methods of allocation must be used—for example, first-come first-served, government mandate, or sellers' choice. A price ceiling set above the equilibrium price has no impact.

10. A price floor set above the equilibrium price tends to create a surplus. Given excess supply, the price floor may be difficult to maintain. A price floor set below the equilibrium price has no impact.

Key Terms

law of demand	supply schedule
quantity demanded	supply curve
demand schedule	a shift in supply
demand curve	shortage
a shift in demand	surplus
normal good	equilibrium price
inferior good	equilibrium
substitute good	disequilibrium price
complementary good	disequilibrium
a change in demand	price ceiling
a change in quantity demanded	price floor
law of supply	black market
quantity supplied	

Study Questions and Problems

1. (a) Why do demand curves slope downward? (b) Why do supply curves slope upward?

2. (a) List several factors that would be expected to increase the demand for turkey. (b) List several factors that would be expected to increase the supply of turkey.

3. Would an increase in the price of hamburgers change the supply of hamburgers? Would it change the quantity supplied? Explain.

4. The following graph depicts the demand for and supply of VCR tape rentals in Pleasantville:

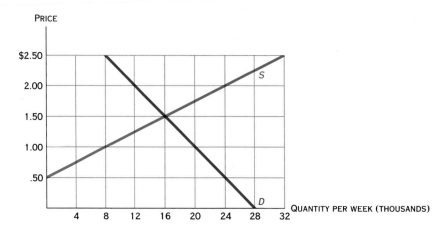

a. At which price is the quantity demanded equal to 8,000 tapes per week?
b. At which price is the quantity supplied equal to 8,000 tapes per week?
c. What is the equilibrium price for renting a tape? What is the equilibrium quantity?
d. If the rental price is $2 per tape, what is the quantity demanded? How many tapes are supplied at this price?
e. Will a price of $2 per tape lead to a shortage or a surplus of tapes?
f. At which price is there a shortage of 12,000 tapes per week?

5. Explain how each of the following affects the equilibrium price and the equilibrium quantity of trucking services. In each case, indicate whether the changes are due to a shift in the demand for trucking services or a shift in supply.
a. The tax on diesel fuel is raised.
b. Insurance rates for truckers are reduced.
c. The number of households seeking to move furniture and other possessions increases.
d. The price for shipping freight by rail (an alternative mode of transportation) is reduced.
e. The speed limit for trucks is increased, reducing the time required to make deliveries.
f. Engineers discover ways to increase the gas mileage of trucks without increasing the price of trucks.

6. Assume that a freeze damages this year's crop of oranges.
a. What effect does this have on the supply of oranges and on the price of oranges?
b. How does this change in the price of oranges affect the demand for apples?
c. Given your answer to (b), how does the price of apples change, other things equal?

7. In 1991, the Nissan Motor Company announced that it was developing a catalytic converter that could be manufactured without platinum. At the time, a major portion of the world's platinum output was used in the manufacture of catalytic converters.
a. How would Nissan's new catalytic converters affect the demand for platinum?
b. Assume that new platinum deposits are discovered. How would this affect the supply of platinum?
c. How would the shifts in supply and demand just discussed affect the equilibrium price of platinum?
d. How would these changes in supply and demand affect the equilibrium output of platinum? Explain.

8. Assume the quantity of houses demanded exceeds the quantity supplied. In the absence of price controls, how would you expect prices to adjust? As housing prices change, what happens to the quantity demanded and to the quantity supplied?

9. The government's price-support program guarantees farmers a minimum price per bushel of wheat.
   a. What impact does this program have when the minimum price is set below the equilibrium price of wheat?
   b. What impact does this program have when the minimum price is set above the equilibrium price of wheat?

10. Assume the equilibrium price of pens is higher in 1994 than in 1993, and the equilibrium price of pencils is lower. If the government imposed a price ceiling that prevented prices from rising in 1994, what impact would this have on the market for pens and on the market for pencils? Explain.

11. Can you spot the flaw in the following argument?

    An increase in the demand for pretzels increases their price. Consumers respond to a higher price by reducing the number of pretzels they buy. Therefore, an increase in the demand for pretzels results in consumers buying fewer pretzels.

    What mistake does the author make?

YOUR TURN
Answers

Recognizing Shifts in Demand

(A) A LOWER PRICE FOR CASSETTES, A COMPLEMENT, *INCREASES* THE DEMAND FOR CASSETTE PLAYERS. (B) A LOWER PRICE FOR COMPACT DISC PLAYERS, A SUBSTITUTE, *DECREASES* THE DEMAND FOR CASSETTE PLAYERS. (C) A LOWER PRICE FOR CASSETTE PLAYERS HAS *NO EFFECT* ON THE DEMAND FOR CASSETTE PLAYERS; IT SIMPLY INCREASES THE QUANTITY DEMANDED (A MOVEMENT ALONG THE DEMAND CURVE). (D) A GREATER POPULATION CAN BE EXPECTED TO *INCREASE* THE DEMAND FOR CASSETTE PLAYERS. (E) A CHANGE IN TASTES THAT MAKES LISTENING TO CASSETTES LESS FASHIONABLE *DECREASES* THE DEMAND FOR CASSETTE PLAYERS.

Applying Supply and Demand Analysis to Automobile Export Restrictions

(A) RESTRICTIONS ON THE NUMBER OF AUTOMOBILES ALLOWED TO ENTER THE UNITED STATES REDUCE THE SUPPLY OF IMPORTED AUTOMOBILES AND INCREASE THEIR PRICE. (B) A HIGHER PRICE FOR IMPORTED AUTOMOBILES INCREASES DEMAND FOR DOMESTIC AUTOMOBILES, SINCE THEY ARE SUBSTITUTES. (C) VOLUNTARY EXPORT RESTRICTIONS HAVE INCREASED THE PRICE OF DOMESTIC AUTOMOBILES. (ACCORDING TO SOME STUDIES, THESE RESTRICTIONS HAVE RAISED THE PRICE OF DOMESTIC AUTOMOBILES BY MORE THAN $600 PER VEHICLE.)

Selected References

The Margin. A magazine published by the University of Colorado that applies supply and demand analysis to current policy issues.

Marshall, Alfred. *Principles of Economics*, 8th ed. (London: Macmillan, 1920). A text first published 100 years ago that even today offers insights into the operation of markets.

Schuettinger, Robert, and Eamonn Butler. *Forty Centuries of Wage and Price Controls* (Washington, D.C.: The Heritage Foundation, 1979). A historical perspective on the problems associated with price controls.

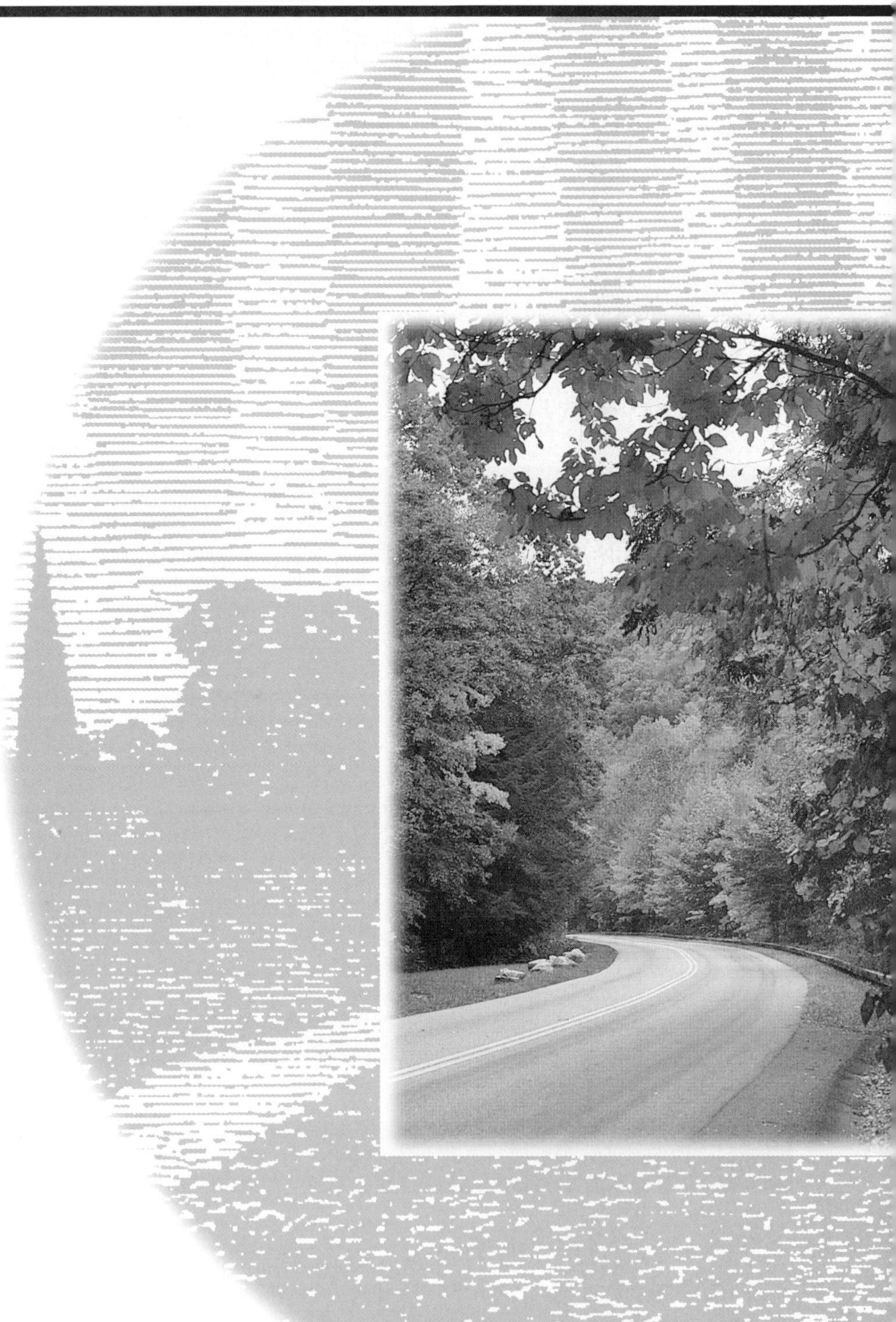

Demand and Supply Elasticities

DEMAND CURVES SLOPE DOWNWARD; SUPPLY CURVES SLOPE UPWARD. SO SAY THE LAWS OF DEMAND AND SUPPLY. WHILE THIS INFORMATION MAY BE USEFUL, IT IS OFTEN OF LIMITED VALUE. MORE IMPORTANT IS KNOWING THE *SENSITIVITY* OF QUANTITY DEMANDED (OR SUPPLIED) TO A CHANGE IN PRICE. BY *HOW MUCH* WILL QUANTITY CHANGE?

IT MATTERS A GREAT DEAL TO AT&T WHETHER DEMAND FOR ITS LONG-DISTANCE TELEPHONE SERVICE LOOKS LIKE D_1 OR D_2 IN FIGURE 5.1(A). IN BOTH CASES A LOWER PRICE INCREASES CONSUMER WILLINGNESS TO "REACH OUT AND TOUCH SOMEONE." BUT THERE IS MORE REACHING OUT AND TOUCHING WITH D_2 THAN WITH D_1.

PUBLIC POLICY IS ALSO INFLUENCED BY THE PERCEIVED RESPONSIVENESS OF CONSUMERS. FOR EXAMPLE, IN THE LATE 1970S MANY IN CONGRESS ADVOCATED A TAX ON OIL IN ORDER TO REDUCE U.S. DEPENDENCE ON FOREIGN SUPPLIES. THEY ARGUED THAT, BY RAISING PRICES, THE TAX WOULD MAKE CONSUMERS CONSIDERABLY MORE FRUGAL IN THEIR USE OF GASOLINE, HEATING OIL, AND OTHER PETROLEUM PRODUCTS. CRITICS OF THE PROPOSED TAX COUNTERED THAT CONSUMERS WERE NOT VERY RESPONSIVE TO PRICES OF SUCH PRODUCTS AND, CONSEQUENTLY, CONSUMPTION WOULD SCARCELY BE AFFECTED. TO HELP RESOLVE THIS DEBATE, WHAT WAS NEEDED WAS INFORMATION ON CONSUMER RESPONSIVENESS TO ENERGY PRICES. RECENT ECONOMIC STUDIES HAVE ATTEMPTED TO MEET THIS NEED.

Consumer responses to the energy price increases of the 1970s convinced the general public of what economists had long preached: "Price matters." However, neither economists nor the public have been very satisfied with the answers to the more difficult question: "But by how much?"[1]

[1]Foreword to Douglas Bohi, *Analyzing Demand Behavior: A Study of Energy Elasticities* (Baltimore: The Johns Hopkins University Press, 1981).

Producer responsiveness is also crucial. At the same time that Congress was debating the merits of an energy tax, it was grappling with the issue of whether the price of natural gas should be set by the market or by the government.[2] Some in Congress (especially conservatives and members from gas-producing states) argued that the volume of natural gas supplied was highly sensitive to price. Compared to the case of a government-enforced price ceiling, the price of natural gas would, they asserted, be slightly higher in an unrestricted market but production would be greatly expanded. Shortages would be eliminated and, with greater availability of natural gas, our dependence on imported oil would diminish.

Others saw things differently, contending that the price of natural gas would soar in the absence of price controls, with little additional production. At issue was whether the supply of natural gas was more closely approximated by S_1 or S_2 in Figure 5.1 (B). If Congress is to fashion a sensible energy policy, it must know how consumers and producers respond to prices—it needs to know *the price elasticities of demand and supply*.

Knowledge of these elasticities is important for other reasons. Suppose a tax is levied on producers. To what extent will the tax be absorbed by producers, and to what extent will it be passed on to consumers in the form of higher prices? The

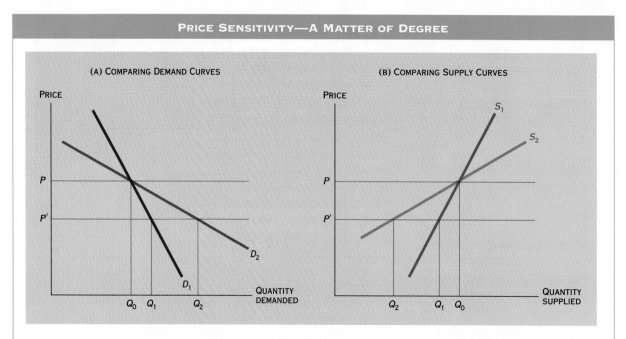

PRICE SENSITIVITY—A MATTER OF DEGREE

(A) COMPARING DEMAND CURVES

(B) COMPARING SUPPLY CURVES

Demand curve D_2 is more sensitive to price changes than is demand curve D_1. That is, for a given change in price, the change in quantity demanded is greater for D_2 than for D_1. For example, when price falls from P to P', quantity demanded increases from Q_0 to Q_2 if demand is D_2, but from Q_0 to Q_1 (a much smaller increase) if demand is D_1. Similarly, S_2 is more sensitive to price changes than is S_1.

FIGURE 5.1

[2]Congress initially chose to regulate the price of natural gas but began phasing out price controls in 1978.

answer depends on the price elasticities of demand and supply. Or consider a university's decision to raise ticket prices for its varsity basketball games. Will higher prices increase or decrease basketball revenues? The price elasticity of demand holds the key.

Among the other issues considered are how the quantity demanded of one good responds to a change in the price of a second good (*the cross elasticity of demand*) and how quantity demanded varies with income (*the income elasticity of demand*). For example, how much business can MCI be expected to lose if AT&T's long-distance rates are reduced? As incomes rise, how much more will consumers spend on long-distance telephone calls?

Chapter 5 presents the various demand elasticities just introduced and then analyzes the elasticity of supply. In the process it provides estimates of the elasticities for various goods, discusses the determinants of these elasticities, and explains the relevance of these numbers to consumers, businesses, and governments.

Price Elasticity of Demand

Elasticity is a measure of responsiveness. Assume the price of a good rises by 10 percent. Other things equal, the quantity demanded should fall. But by how much—1 percent, 10 percent, 100 percent . . . ? The answer is given by the **price elasticity of demand**:

$$E_d = \frac{\text{percentage change in quantity demanded}}{\text{percentage change in price}}$$

Strictly speaking, the numbers generated by this formula are negative, since price and quantity demanded move in opposite directions. By convention the negative sign is dropped.

If a 10 percent change in price leads to a 1 percent change in quantity demanded, the price elasticity of demand is 0.1 ($E_d = 1\% \div 10\%$). But if the quantity demanded changes by 100 percent, the elasticity is 10 ($E_d = 100\% \div 10\%$). Alternatively, if the elasticity is known, information about a price change permits a prediction of how much quantity demanded will change:

$$\text{percentage change in quantity demanded} = \frac{\text{percentage change in quantity demanded}}{\text{percentage change in price}} \times \text{percentage change in price}$$

$$= E_d \times \text{percentage change in price}$$

For example, if the price elasticity of demand for soft drinks is 0.5, we can predict that, other things equal, a 10 percent increase in the price of soft drinks will reduce the quantity demanded by 5 percent (that is, 0.5 × 10%).

The Midpoint Formula

Consider the demand curve for Charlie's Deluxe Hamburgers given in Figure 5.2 (page 110). At a price of $1.80, 1,200 burgers are demanded each week. But if the

Price elasticity of demand between points A and B is calculated on the basis of average price ($2.00) and average quantity demanded (1,000). The percentage change in price is 20 percent [($2.20 − $1.80)/$2.00 = .20]; the percentage change in quantity demanded is 40 percent [(1,200 − 800)/1,000 = .40]. Consequently, E_d = 40/20 = 2.0.

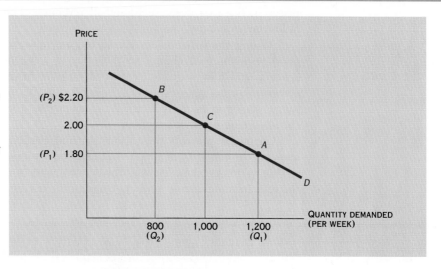

FIGURE 5.2

price rises to $2.20, consumers will want to buy only 800 burgers. Given these figures, what is the price elasticity of demand? To answer this we must compute the percentage change in both price and quantity demanded and then plug these numbers into the elasticity formula. But first we must agree on some terminology. How do we define "percentage change"?

Suppose we take P_1 = $1.80 and Q_1 = 1,200 as our reference point (point A on the demand curve in Figure 5.2). Then an increase in the price of hamburgers from $1.80 to $2.20 constitutes a price change of 22 percent:

$$\frac{P_2 - P_1}{P_1} = \frac{\$2.20 - \$1.80}{\$1.80} = .22 \text{ or } 22\%$$

Similarly, a reduction in the number of hamburgers purchased from 1,200 to 800 constitutes a change in the quantity demanded of 33 percent:

$$\frac{Q_1 - Q_2}{Q_1} = \frac{1,200 - 800}{1,200} = .33 \text{ or } 33\%$$

Based on these numbers, the elasticity of demand between points A and B is E_d = 33/22 = 1.5.

Someone else could just as easily take P_2 = $2.20 and Q_2 = 800 as the reference point and compute the elasticity by considering a movement from point B to point A on the demand curve in Figure 5.2. In that event, the change in price is 18 percent [($2.20 − $1.80)/$2.20 = .18] and the change in quantity demanded is 50 percent [(1,200 − 800)/800 = .50]. According to these numbers, the elasticity of demand is E_d = 50/18 = 2.8, which differs from the prior calculation (E_d = 1.5).

A definition should be consistent. Different people working with the same numbers should not obtain different answers. To avoid this possibility, our definition requires greater precision: we must specify a reference point. But should it be point A or point B? The convention adopted by economists is to use neither endpoint, but instead to use the midpoint (point C in Figure 5.2): the average of the two prices and the average of the two quantities.[3] The price elasticity of demand is then defined as:

$$E_d = \frac{\text{change in quantity demanded}}{\text{average quantity demanded}} \div \frac{\text{change in price}}{\text{average price}}$$

Return now to our example. Given an average price of $2.00 and an average quantity demanded of 1,000, the percentage change in price is 20 percent [($2.20 − $1.80)/$2.00 = .20] and the percentage change in quantity demanded is 40 percent [(1,200 − 800)/1,000 = .40]. Therefore, the price elasticity of demand over this range of the demand curve is 2.0.

Determining the Price Elasticity of Demand

TO HELP RAISE MONEY FOR A LOCAL CHARITY, YOU AGREE TO PRODUCE AND SELL A CALENDAR. BASED ON PRELIMINARY ANALYSIS, YOU ESTIMATE THAT 900 CALENDARS WILL BE SOLD THIS YEAR IF THE PRICE IS $5, BUT ONLY 700 CALENDARS IF THE PRICE IS $7. GIVEN THESE FIGURES, COMPUTE (A) THE CHANGE IN QUANTITY DEMANDED, AVERAGE QUANTITY DEMANDED, CHANGE IN PRICE, AVERAGE PRICE, AND (B) THE PRICE ELASTICITY OF DEMAND.

Categorizing Elasticities

ELASTIC DEMAND
Demand is elastic when $E_d > 1$.

INELASTIC DEMAND
Demand is inelastic when $E_d < 1$.

UNIT ELASTIC DEMAND
Demand is unit elastic when $E_d = 1$.

Economists often label demand for a good on the basis of its price elasticity. When $E_d > 1$, demand is said to be **elastic**. With an elastic demand curve, the change in quantity demanded is greater, *in percentage terms*, than the change in price. For example, demand for Charlie's Deluxe Hamburgers is elastic. A 20 percent change in price generated a 40 percent change in quantity demanded.

When $E_d < 1$, demand is termed **inelastic**—meaning that each 1 percent change in price leads to a change in quantity demanded of less than 1 percent. A third possibility is that $E_d = 1$, in which case demand is classified as **unit elastic**. In such cases, price and quantity demanded change by equal percentages. For example, a 10 percent increase in the price of a good reduces quantity demanded by 10 percent.

---

[3]The average price is defined as $(P_1 + P_2)/2$, the average quantity demanded is $(Q_1 + Q_2)/2$. In this example, the average price is ($1.80 + $2.20)/2 = $2.00; the average quantity demanded is (1,200 + 800)/2 = 1,000.

Different segments of a demand curve often have different elasticities. For example, in the five segments of this demand curve, price elasticity of demand ranges from 9.0 to 0.11. (Can you verify these numbers?)

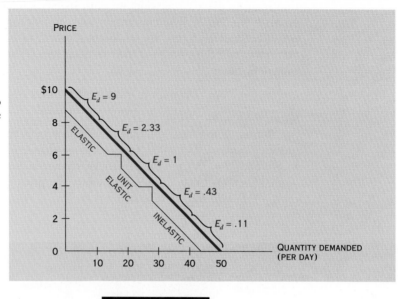

FIGURE 5.3

The same good may have an elastic demand for some set of prices, yet be inelastic over a different price range. This is illustrated in Figure 5.3. Over the five segments for which the elasticity is calculated, the price elasticity of demand ranges from 9 to 0.11. As the figure indicates, for *linear* (straight-line) demand curves the price elasticity of demand becomes smaller as you move down the demand curve. This is also true for demand curves that are nearly linear.[4] The only exceptions are depicted in Figure 5.4, which illustrates linear demand curves that do not slope downward.

Although most demand curves have negative slopes, in extreme cases the law of demand may be violated. Figure 5.4(A) presents the case where demand is **perfectly inelastic** ($E_d = 0$). Assume you are being held hostage in some foreign country.

PERFECTLY INELASTIC DEMAND
A demand that is totally unresponsive to price—represented by a vertical demand curve.

---

[4]For some nonlinear demand curves, E_d does not fall as you move down the curve. In fact, for the non-linear curve depicted (a rectangular hyperbola), demand at every segment is unit elastic.

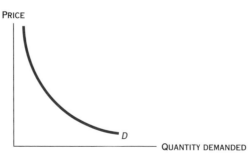

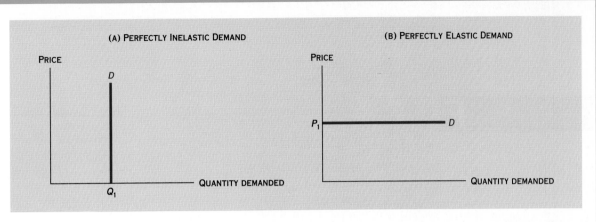

In (A) consumers want to purchase Q_1, regardless of price. Because the percentage change in quantity demanded (the numerator of the elasticity formula) is always zero, $E_d = 0$. At the opposite extreme (B), quantity demanded is so responsive to price that consumers purchase all that is offered at price P_1, but purchase nothing when price rises above P_1.

FIGURE 5.4

Your demand for airline tickets out of this foreign country may look like Figure 5.4(A)—assuming the tickets convey safe passage. If the price per ticket is $10,000, you want to buy one ticket. If the price is reduced to $10, you still want one ticket only. Even at this bargain price you are not likely to want to return to this country anytime soon. (And a round-trip ticket is out of the question.) Thus quantity demanded is not responsive to price, and demand is perfectly inelastic.

The demand curve in Figure 5.4(B) is **perfectly elastic**. Consumers are so responsive to price (E_d is so high) that they buy as much as they can at P_1, but nothing at prices above P_1. As discussed later in the text, the demand curve facing the typical wheat farmer is perfectly elastic. At the market price, buyers purchase as much wheat as the farmer wants to sell, but they buy nothing from the farmer if he or she attempts to charge more than the market price.

PERFECTLY ELASTIC DEMAND
A demand that is infinitely responsive to price—represented by a horizontal demand curve.

Elasticity and Total Revenue

TOTAL REVENUE
The price of a good times the quantity sold (TR = $P \times Q$).

More than just a formula, elasticity of demand has a variety of applications. One is revealing the effect of a change in price on *total revenue*. **Total revenue** is defined as total spending on a good: the product of price times quantity sold. Equivalently, from the buyers' perspective, total spending is price times quantity purchased.

A change in price has two effects on total revenue. A higher price means that each unit sold now contributes more to total revenue. On the other hand, given a downward-sloping demand curve, fewer units are sold at the higher price. Whether total revenue rises or falls (or remains unchanged) depends on which effect is

Elasticity Versus Slope

From a casual inspection of Figures 5.5(A) and (B), you might be tempted to conclude that D_2 is more elastic than D_1. Don't. Even though the slopes differ, over each price range the elasticities are identical. Both curves depict the same relationship between price of milk and quantity demanded. The only difference is that quantity is measured in gallons for (A) and in quarts for (B).

That slope and elasticity of demand are different concepts can also be driven home by computing elasticity at different places along a linear demand curve. Although the slope is the same everywhere, elasticity varies from one segment of the curve to another (as shown in Figure 5.3). Whereas slope is based on absolute changes in price and quantity, elasticity is based on relative changes.[5]

[5]Slope of a demand curve is defined as $\Delta P/\Delta Q$ where Δ is the symbol for *change in*. Elasticity is:

$$\frac{\Delta Q/Q}{\Delta P/P} = \frac{\Delta Q}{\Delta P} \times \frac{P}{Q} = \frac{P}{Q} \div \text{slope}$$

DIFFERENT SLOPES, SAME ELASTICITY

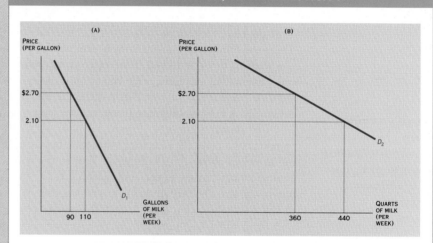

Although D_2 initially may appear more elastic than D_1, any difference is illusory. D_1 has a steeper slope because its quantity is measured in gallons rather than quarts. When price falls from \$2.70/gallon to \$2.10/gallon (a 25 percent drop), the quantity demanded increases from 90 gallons to 110 gallons or, equivalently, from 360 quarts to 440 quarts. Whether measured in gallons or quarts, the quantity demanded rises by 20 percent. In either case, $E_d = 0.80$.

FIGURE 5.5

stronger: the increase in revenue per unit (price) or the decrease in the volume of sales. This, in turn, hinges on the price elasticity of demand.

The relationship among elasticity, price, and total revenue is presented in Table 5.1. When demand is elastic, cutting price raises total revenue and increasing price lowers total revenue. Quantity demanded is so responsive to price that, when price changes, the volume of sales changes by a relatively larger amount, causing price and total revenue to move in opposite directions. In other words, the change in revenue per unit is swamped by a relatively greater change in the number of units sold. When demand is inelastic, the percentage change in price exceeds the percentage change in quantity demanded. Therefore, price and total revenue move in the same direction. Finally, for unit elastic demand, changes in price and quantity demanded offset one another. Whether price rises or falls, total revenue remains the same.

The role played by elasticity can also be illustrated diagrammatically. Because total revenue is the product of price and quantity purchased, it can be represented as an area beneath the demand curve, with sides corresponding to price and quantity demanded. Consider the demand curve in Figure 5.6 (page 116, reproduced from Figure 5.3). In (A), for P_1 = $6 total revenue is given by the rectangle $0P_1AQ_1$ = $120, and for P_2 = $8 the total revenue rectangle is $0P_2BQ_2$ = $80. Because $E_d > 1$, raising price diminishes total revenue (in this case by $40). When $E_d < 1$, case (B), a price hike raises total revenue. Finally, when $E_d = 1$, case (C), a price change has no impact on total revenue.

The preceding discussion has important implications. For example, assume a university wishes to maximize the total revenue generated by its varsity basketball program. Further assume that basketball games are not sellouts.[6] Should the university raise or lower the price of tickets? A lower price translates into greater ticket sales, a higher price into fewer sales. The crucial question is how responsive fans are to ticket price. In other words, what is the price elasticity of demand? If the university is operating on an inelastic portion of its demand curve, revenue is enhanced by raising price. In contrast, if demand is elastic the solution is to lower price. The

ELASTICITY OF DEMAND AND THE RELATIONSHIP BETWEEN PRICE AND TOTAL REVENUE

CATEGORY OF DEMAND	RELATIVE CHANGE IN PRICE (P) AND QUANTITY DEMANDED (Q^d)	EFFECT ON TOTAL REVENUE
Elastic ($E_d > 1$)	% change in Q^d > % change in P	$\downarrow P (\uparrow Q^d) \rightarrow \uparrow$ TR $\uparrow P (\downarrow Q^d) \rightarrow \downarrow$ TR
Inelastic ($E_d < 1$)	% change in Q^d < % change in P	$\downarrow P (\uparrow Q^d) \rightarrow \downarrow$ TR $\uparrow P (\downarrow Q^d) \rightarrow \uparrow$ TR
Unit elastic ($E_d = 1$)	% change in Q^d = % change in P	$\downarrow P (\uparrow Q^d) \rightarrow$ TR does not change $\uparrow P (\downarrow Q^d) \rightarrow$ TR does not change

TABLE 5.1

---

[6]If every game sold out and patrons were turned away, the university should clearly raise price. The university would make more money filling an arena and charging a high price than filling an arena and charging a low price.

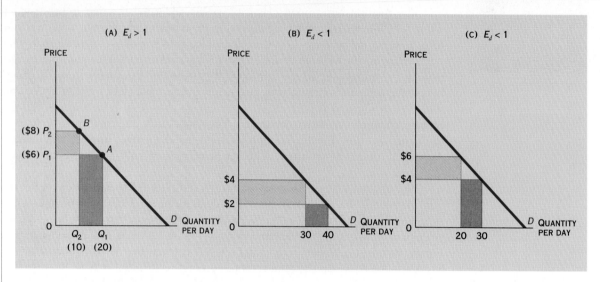

A price increase has a twofold effect on total revenue. (1) The gain in revenue resulting from a higher revenue per unit is shown by the color-shaded area. (2) The loss associated with reduced purchases is shown by the gray-shaded area. When $E_d > 1$, (A), revenue loss exceeds revenue gain—a higher price lowers total revenue. When $E_d < 1$, (B), revenue gain exceeds revenue loss—a higher price increases total revenue. When $E_d = 1$, (C), the shaded areas are equal—implying that total revenue does not change.

FIGURE 5.6

same reasoning can be applied to other issues confronting the university—for example, setting rates for parking permits and dormitory rooms.

Concern about total revenue extends beyond a university's borders. Now that the U.S. airline industry is deregulated, carriers have the ability to set airline fares. The general tendency has been for fares to drop following deregulation, reflecting the belief that demand for air travel tends to be elastic. Although this may be true for households, there is evidence that demand by business travelers is inelastic. In that event, the ticket price that maximizes total revenue in the business segment of the market exceeds the price that maximizes total revenue in the nonbusiness segment.

Accordingly, airlines have an incentive to charge a higher price for business travel than for personal travel. To a considerable extent, airlines have been able to do exactly that. Households generally are better able to plan in advance when they want to fly. Vacation dates, holidays, the school calendar, and other occasions that may call for travel are often known well ahead of time. Business travel, in contrast, is more likely to be in response to short-term developments. Airlines generally offer deep discounts for reservations booked in advance, say 30 days before the start of travel. Because households are more likely to meet these purchase deadlines, the result is a lower fare, on average, for these customers than for business travelers.

YOUR TURN

Maximizing Total Revenue

IN THE PREVIOUS YOUR TURN IT IS ASSUMED THAT YOU ARE PRINTING AND SELLING A CALENDAR. SUPPOSE A LOCAL BUSINESS AGREES TO PAY THE COSTS OF PRODUCTION, SO THAT ALL RECEIPTS FROM SALES OF THE CALENDAR GO TO CHARITY. BASED ON THE INFORMATION CONTAINED IN THE PREVIOUS YOUR TURN AND ASSUMING YOU WISH TO MAXIMIZE THE FUNDS RAISED FOR CHARITY, SHOULD YOU CHARGE A PRICE OF $5 OR $7 PER CALENDAR? WHY?

EXHIBIT 5.2

Elasticities and Revenues For TV Sports

Is the demand for TV sports entertainment inelastic? For some sports the evidence suggests that it is.

The National Collegiate Athletic Association (NCAA) long held exclusive control over TV contracts for college football. When the U.S. Supreme Court eliminated this monopoly power in 1984, the result was an explosion of televised football games. With more games broadcast, TV networks were willing to pay less per game. For example, when UCLA played Nebraska several years ago, the schools collected half of what they would have received under the old NCAA contract. The athletic director for the University of Nebraska estimated that TV revenues at his institution would plunge 40 percent. An NCAA official predicted that the loss at most schools would be at least 50 percent. More games on the tube meant lower total revenues—demand was inelastic.

Aware of what had happened in football, the National Basketball Association (NBA) adopted a different strategy, permitting fewer games to be televised. This increased the price networks were willing to pay per game and the total broadcast revenue collected by the NBA. As one reporter observed:

> Cutting the NBA's exposure has boosted the value of commercial time. As a result, the league will show a 16% increase in TV revenues this year while airing half as many games.

SOURCES: Adapted from "It Finally Happened: Too Much College Football on TV," *Business Week*, October 8, 1984, pp. 71 and 75; Brent Wellington, "Why Basketball Is Having a Championship Season," *Business Week*, March 4, 1985, pp. 75–76.

What Determines E_d?

Price elasticity of demand depends on several factors. The following four are generally considered to be the most important.

AVAILABILITY OF SUBSTITUTES

When good substitutes are readily available, consumers tend to be sensitive to price changes—E_d tends to be high. For example, there are numerous brands of tissue (Kleenex, Puffs, Scotts, and so on). Each brand is generally considered a good substitute for the others. In addition, other products can readily be substituted for tissue (for example, handkerchiefs, cotton balls for removing makeup). Accordingly, the demand for any given brand of tissue can be expected to be highly elastic.

When substitution possibilities are limited—as is the case for gasoline—E_d tends to be low. This does not imply, however, that elasticity of demand at Bob's Texaco station is low. If Bob raises the price of gasoline relative to that of competitors, he is likely to lose a substantial share of business. While there are few good substitutes for gasoline in general, many substitutes exist for Bob's Texaco gasoline—Kim's Texaco, Gabriel's Shell, Kathy's Exxon. As a general rule: the more narrowly defined a good, the more substitutes exist and therefore the more elastic is demand.

DEGREE OF NECESSITY

Goods viewed as necessities tend to have a low price elasticity of demand. We would find it difficult to get by without food, heating fuel in the winter,[7] or essential medical care.[8] As such, elasticity of demand for these goods and services is low: consumers are relatively insensitive to price. This is not the case for vacations, restaurant meals, or various luxuries: consumers can survive without them. Because of this low degree of necessity, E_d is high.

SHARE OF BUDGET SPENT ON THE GOOD

Typically, *the less of a consumer's budget devoted to a good, the less elastic is demand.* Because the average consumer spends such a minuscule portion of income on toothpicks, a price hike of, say, 20 percent is likely to have little effect on the quantity demanded. The budget can easily be stretched to accommodate spending a few cents more on toothpicks. Compare that to a 20 percent increase in the price of a new car. Given an average sticker price of nearly $20,000, that translates into an increase of several thousand dollars—which is not so easy to work into the budget. For that reason, big-ticket items, such as cars, tend to have a relatively high elasticity of demand.

---

[7]Those living in Miami or Honolulu may ignore this argument.

[8]The emphasis is on *essential*. Certain medical treatment (for example, elective cosmetic surgery) is difficult to call necessary. Demand for medical care tends to be more price elastic the less *necessary* it is. Consistent with this proposition, two economists found that the demand for physician house calls is more elastic than the demand for physician office visits, which in turn is more elastic than the demand for hospital admissions. See Charles E. Phelps and Joseph P. Newhouse, *Coinsurance and the Demand for Medical Services* (Santa Monica, Calif.: Rand Corp., October 1974), Table 12, cited in Robert Helms, "Contemporary Health Policy: Dealing with the Cost of Care," in William Fellner, ed., *Contemporary Economic Problems* (Washington, D.C.: American Enterprise Institute, 1978), p. 344.

TIME PERIOD

A longer time period allows for greater responsiveness on the part of consumers and, consequently, leads to a greater elasticity of demand. Consider the demand for gasoline. If the price of gasoline jumps, as it has when OPEC exerts its economic muscle, consumers initially make few adjustments. In the months immediately following a price hike, consumers may cut back on pleasure driving, combine trips, and do more carpooling, but these adjustments make only a modest dent in gasoline consumption. As time passes, however, consumers adapt their behavior in more fundamental ways. Cars wear out and are replaced with vehicles boasting better gas mileage. Greater use is made of nontraditional vehicles (for example, cars and trucks powered by compressed natural gas). Alternative energy sources such as gasohol (which is made from corn-based ethanol) are substituted for gasoline. As households move, they are more likely to locate close to work or to rail and subway stops. Public transportation is substituted for private automobile use. Accordingly, demand for gasoline can be expected to be more elastic in the long run (after consumers have had a chance to complete their adjustments) than in the short run. As the estimates of Table 5.2 indicate, price elasticity of demand is indeed greater in the long run (for gasoline as well as other products).[9]

ESTIMATED PRICE ELASTICITIES OF DEMAND FOR THE UNITED STATES

	ELASTICITY	
GOOD	SHORT RUN	LONG RUN
Owner-occupied housing	0.04	1.22
Medical care and hospital insurance	0.31	0.92
Shoe repair	1.31	1.81
China and glassware	1.54	2.55
Flowers and plants	0.82	2.65
Radio and TV repair	0.47	3.84
Motion pictures	0.87	3.67
Theater and opera	0.18	0.31
Commuter rail travel	0.72	0.91
Intercity rail travel	1.42	3.19
Foreign travel	0.14	1.77
Residential natural gas	0.1	0.5
Gasoline	0.2	0.7

SOURCES: Adapted from H. S. Houthakker and L. D. Taylor, *Consumer Demand in the United States: Analysis and Projections* (Cambridge: Harvard University Press, 1970), Table 4.2; (for natural gas and gasoline) Douglas R. Bohi, *Analyzing Demand Behavior* (Baltimore: The Johns Hopkins University Press, 1981), Table 7.1. Reprinted by permission.

TABLE 5.2

[9]The estimates of Table 5.2 are based on observed prices (that is, the segment of the demand curve that, given the past history of prices, is most relevant). For a different range of prices, different estimates of E_d can be expected. For example, if we were to move up the demand curve to uncharted areas of higher prices, E_d for gasoline might be considerably higher than the values given in Table 5.2.

YOUR TURN

Altering E_d Through Trade Policy

SUPPOSE CONGRESS PREVENTS FOREIGN COMPANIES FROM SELLING AUTOMOBILES IN THE UNITED STATES. HOW WOULD THIS AFFECT THE ELASTICITY OF DEMAND FOR FORDS IN THE UNITED STATES? WHY?

Other Elasticities of Demand

Quantity demanded depends on a good's own price but on other factors too—for example, on income and prices of other goods.[10] A key issue concerns the degree of responsiveness of demand to these other variables. This responsiveness is measured by the following two elasticities.

THE INCOME ELASTICITY OF DEMAND

What happens when income rises? For **normal goods** demand increases—so that at any given price a higher quantity is now demanded. For **inferior goods** demand falls—consumers reduce purchases of inferior goods by substituting preferred goods (which they are now better able to afford). In addition to the question of whether demand rises or falls, there is also the question of the magnitude of any change. Both issues can be addressed with a concept known as the **income elasticity of demand**. Holding price constant, the income elasticity of demand is given by the following formula:

$$E_d^y = \frac{\text{percentage change in quantity demanded}}{\text{percentage change in income}}$$

The income elasticity of demand is positive for a normal good, negative for an inferior good.[11]

Normal goods are often subclassified in terms of their income elasticity of demand. According to a commonly adopted convention, **luxuries** are defined as goods whose income elasticity of demand exceeds 1. Examples include cars, food away from home, and books. **Necessities** are normal goods for which $E_d^y < 1$. Examples are food, electricity, and cigarettes. According to this conventional definition, necessity does not mean "required for survival." Consumers could extinguish their cigarette habit without life going up in smoke. Even so, economists classify cigarettes as necessities because of their low income elasticity of demand.

Perhaps a more intuitive way to distinguish between necessities and luxuries is in terms of how consumption patterns change with income. When income doubles

LUXURY
A good for which the income elasticity of demand is greater than 1.

NECESSITY
A good for which the income elasticity of demand is greater than 0 but less than 1.

---

[10]Recall from Chapter 4 that when any of these other relevant factors change the result is a shift in the demand curve and consequently, for any given price, a change in the quantity demanded.

[11]The negative sign is not dropped for income elasticity of demand (as it is for price elasticity of demand). This is so we can distinguish between normal goods ($E_d^y > 0$) and inferior goods ($E_d^y < 0$).

CLASSIFICATION OF GOODS BASED ON INCOME ELASTICITY OF DEMAND		
TYPE OF GOOD	INCOME ELASTICITY	EFFECT OF A 10% GAIN IN INCOME
Normal	Positive	Quantity demanded rises
Luxury	Greater than 1	Quantity demanded rises in excess of 10%
Necessity	Less than 1	Quantity demanded rises by under 10%
Inferior	Negative	Quantity demanded falls

TABLE 5.3

consumers can buy twice as much of each good, but there is evidence that they do not. Instead, consumers spend more than twice as much on entertainment (for example) but less than twice as much on food. Necessities are the first priority. When income is low, necessities absorb a large share of the budget. As income rises consumers spend a few more dollars on necessities, but *as a percentage of the budget* expenditures on necessities fall (see Table 5.3). With a higher income consumers can devote a growing share of their income to other, less essential goods. It is these goods that economists dub "luxuries."

In forecasting consumer demand, many companies rely on estimates of income elasticity. Such estimates help the Coca-Cola Company, for example, gauge the likely effects of growing income on demand for its beverages. Or consider an investor who anticipates rapid income growth in the economy. Given this bullish outlook, the investor may want to purchase stock in growth industries—those likely to experience the most rapid advance in sales. Which industries are these? Income elasticities of demand provide important clues.

The Income Elasticity of Demand for Gasoline

YOUR TURN

ACCORDING TO THE U.S. BUREAU OF LABOR STATISTICS, CONSUMERS WHOSE INCOME IS $24,000 PER YEAR PURCHASE TWICE AS MUCH GASOLINE AS CONSUMERS WHOSE INCOME IS $6,000 PER YEAR. WHAT DOES THIS SUGGEST ABOUT THE INCOME ELASTICITY OF DEMAND? IS GASOLINE AN INFERIOR GOOD, A NECESSITY, OR A LUXURY?

THE CROSS ELASTICITY OF DEMAND

Suppose the Anheuser-Busch Company lowers the price of its Busch beer. Will this cannibalize sales of Budweiser (also produced by Anheuser-Busch)? Despite possibly higher revenue from the sales of Busch beer (if $E_d > 1$), a lower price might reduce overall company revenue by heavily tapping into sales of Budweiser. How sensitive is quantity demanded of one good (Budweiser) to price of a second good (Busch)? The answer is provided by the **cross elasticity of demand**:

$$E_{1,2} = \frac{\text{percentage change in quantity demanded of good 1}}{\text{percentage change in price of good 2}}$$

SUBSTITUTE GOODS
Goods for which the cross elasticity of demand is positive.

COMPLEMENTARY GOODS
Goods for which the cross elasticity of demand is negative.

INDEPENDENT GOODS
Goods for which the cross elasticity of demand is zero.

The value of the cross elasticity indicates the relationship between two goods. When the cross elasticity is positive, the goods are **substitute goods** (for example, Budweiser and Busch). When the price of one good falls, consumers buy relatively more of it at the expense of the second (substitute) good. That is, quantity demanded of the second good falls. When the cross elasticity is negative, the goods are **complementary goods** (for example, cameras and film). Consumers want more, not only of the good whose price has fallen, but also of the second (complementary) good. Finally, when the cross elasticity equals zero, the goods are **independent goods** (for example, pencils and automobiles). The quantity demanded of one good does not depend on the price of the other. Exhibits 5.3 and 5.4 illustrate the relevance of cross elasticities to producers and jurists.

It Only Hurts When You Drink

EXHIBIT 5.3

Several years ago, the federal excise tax on distilled spirits was raised by $2/gallon, leading to an increase in the price of hard liquor. The tax on beer and wine was not raised. How would the price increase for hard liquor affect demand for beer and wine? Liquor producers and distributors were thirsty for an answer.

Estimated cross elasticities are close to zero, indicating that the demands for beer and wine are each insensitive to the price of spirits.[12] Anheuser-Busch

need not schedule an extra production shift. Liquor stores need not stock up on wine. A higher price for spirits will have little if any effect on the demand for beer and wine.

spirits leads consumers to switch to beer. A second study estimates that a 10 percent change in the price of spirits affects demand for beer and wine each by less than 1 percent. See James Johnson and Ernest Oksanen, "Estimation of Demand for Alcoholic Beverages in Canada . . ." *Review of Economics and Statistics* (February 1977), pp. 113–117; Kenneth Clements and Lester Johnson, "The Demand for Beer, Wine, and Spirits: A Systemwide Analysis," *Journal of Business* (July 1983), Table 8.

[12]One study estimates that the demand for wine is independent of the price of spirits (the cross elasticity of demand is zero). Nor does it find evidence that a higher price for

Elasticity of Supply

Elasticity of supply is, in many ways, analogous to (price) elasticity of demand. The central difference is that, whereas elasticity of demand considers the percentage change in quantity *demanded*, **elasticity of supply** focuses on quantity *supplied*. Thus, the formula for the elasticity of supply is:

$$E_s = \frac{\text{percentage change in quantity supplied}}{\text{percentage change in price}}$$

Cross Elasticities in the Courtroom

EXHIBIT 5.4

Economists and producers are not the only parties concerned with how changes in the price of one good affect demand for another. Cross elasticities have played major roles in the courtroom. Two of the more famous cases involve Du Pont and the Brown Shoe Company.

U.S. antitrust laws are designed to prevent a company from dominating the market it serves. In an attempt to enforce these laws aggressively, in 1947 the U.S. Department of Justice brought suit against Du Pont charging the company with "conspiracy to monopolize interstate commerce in cellophane." As evidence, the Justice Department presented figures showing that almost 75 percent of the cellophane sold in the United States was produced by Du Pont.

Du Pont countered that the relevant market included Pliofilm™, aluminum foil, waxed paper, and other flexible wrapping materials. With less than 20 percent of this broader market, Du Pont contended that it faced considerable competition. To prove its case, Du Pont presented evidence that the cross elasticity of demand between cellophane and other packaging materials was positive and high.

Accepting these cross-elasticity figures, the U.S. Supreme Court ruled in favor of Du Pont:

If a slight decrease in the price of cellophane causes a considerable number of customers of other flexible wrappings to switch to cellophane, it would be an indication that a high cross-elasticity of demand exists between them; that the products compete in the same market. The court below upheld that the "[g]reat sensitivity of customers in the flexible packaging markets to price or quality changes" prevented Du Pont from possessing monopoly control over price. . . . The record sustains these findings. . . .

In the Brown Shoe Case (1962), the U.S. Department of Justice sued to prevent the Brown Shoe Company from acquiring the Kinney Shoe Company. The government claimed that if the merger were allowed it would seriously lessen competition in the shoe industry. Not so, claimed lawyers for Brown; the two companies compete in separate markets. To support their claim, Brown's lawyers presented evidence that the Brown Shoe Company produced a higher-grade, higher-price shoe than Kinney. But the Department of Justice refuted this argument by demonstrating that the cross elasticity of demand between the two brands of shoes was significantly greater than zero. This implied that the two brands were close substitutes and therefore were being sold in the *same* market. Accepting these cross-elasticity figures, the court denied the merger.

SOURCE: Adapted from United States v. E. I. Du Pont de Nemours and Company, 351 U.S. 377 (1956); United States v. Brown Shoe Company, 370 U.S. 294 (1962).

Certain terminology also carries over from our discussion of elasticity of demand. For example:

supply is *elastic* when $E_s > 1$
supply is *inelastic* when $E_s < 1$
supply is *unit elastic* when $E_s = 1$

**PERFECTLY INELASTIC
SUPPLY**
A supply that is totally unresponsive to price—repre-
sented by a vertical supply
curve.

**PERFECTLY ELASTIC
SUPPLY**
A supply that is infinitely
responsive to price—represented by a horizontal supply curve.

MARKET PERIOD
A period of time during
which the quantity supplied
cannot be changed—repre-
sented by a perfectly inelastic supply curve.

SHORT RUN
A period of time during
which at least one input is
fixed.

A vertical supply curve is said to be **perfectly inelastic,** a horizontal supply curve **perfectly elastic.**

The main determinant of E_s is the time period. *The longer the time period, the more elastic supply is.* Based on the time dimension, supply decisions can be studied in three different periods: the market period, the short run, and the long run.

The **market period** can be thought of as a time period so short that the quantity supplied cannot be changed—that is, supply is perfectly inelastic (see Figure 5.7A). Consider the supply of apples. In the market period, the apples have already been picked. The growers take their crops to market, selling them for whatever they can get. Although a high price is obviously preferred, growers do not hold back apples even when the price is low—rotten apples have no value.

Next consider a one-year period, which in this example can be considered the **short run.**[13] Over this period, apple growers are responsive to price (see Figure 5.7B). When price is high, producers may use more water, fertilizer, and fungicides in order to increase the quantity of marketable apples. Even hard-to-reach apples will be picked. Still, the number of apples is limited by the number of fruit-bearing trees. In the short run, quantity supplied can be changed, but responsiveness is limited because some of the inputs necessary for production (for example, trees) cannot be changed.

Over a longer period of time, quantity supplied is even more responsive to price, since new orchards can be planted (see Figure 5.7C). In the **long run,** no inputs are fixed, not even the number of fruit-bearing trees. Given differences in ability of producers to respond to price changes, a given change in demand will

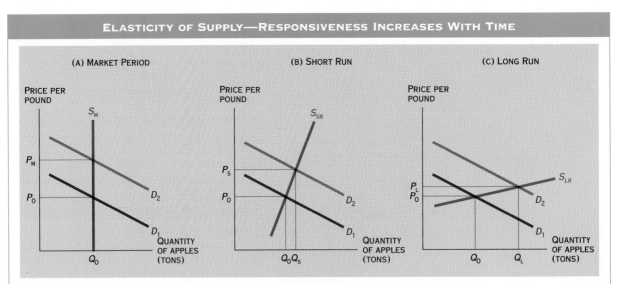

ELASTICITY OF SUPPLY—RESPONSIVENESS INCREASES WITH TIME

Elasticity of supply is greater in the long run (C) than in the short run (B). In the market period (A), $E_s = 0$. Consequently, a given increase in demand elicits a greater response from producers the longer they have to adjust to the change in demand.

FIGURE 5.7

---

[13] The calendar provides no simple rule for distinguishing among time periods. A given length of time (say one year) might be considered the short run in one industry but the long run in a second industry.

ESTIMATED PRICE ELASTICITIES OF SUPPLY FOR THE UNITED STATES

GOOD	ELASTICITY	
	SHORT RUN*	LONG RUN
Aggregate farm output**	0.25	1.79
Livestock	0.38	2.90
Crops	0.17	1.56
Individual crops:		
Green lima beans	0.10	1.7
Cabbage	0.36	1.2
Carrots	0.14	1.0
Cucumbers	0.29	2.2
Lettuce	0.03	0.16
Onions	0.34	1.0
Green peas	0.31	4.4
Green peppers	0.07	0.26
Tomatoes	0.16	0.90
Watermelons	0.23	0.48

*Short run is defined as two years by Tweeten (top three lines), one year by Nerlove and Addison (individual crops).
**Weighted average of crops and livestock.
SOURCES: Data from Luther G. Tweeten, *Foundations of Farm Policy* (Lincoln: University of Nebraska Press, 1979), Table 9.5; Marc Nerlove and William Addison, "Statistical Estimation of Long-Run Elasticities of Supply and Demand," *Journal of Farm Economics* (November 1958), Table 3.

TABLE 5.4

LONG RUN
A period of time long enough to change the quantities of all inputs.

have the greatest effect on quantity supplied in the long run and the smallest effect (no change) in the market period.

Empirically, how responsive is quantity supplied to price? Table 5.4 presents estimates for various agricultural products. According to this table, the supplies of livestock and most crops are highly inelastic in the short run but generally elastic in the long run.

Tax Incidence

TAX INCIDENCE
The distribution of the tax burden—that is, who ultimately pays the tax.

Governments tax the sales of many items. One reason—especially with regard to *sin taxes*—is to discourage activities (such as smoking, drinking, and gambling) that some legislators consider unhealthy or of questionable morality. A second reason for such taxes is to raise revenue for the government. Sometimes producers are forced to absorb the bulk of any tax. In other cases they are able to pass on most of the tax to consumers in the form of higher prices. How the tax burden is shared between producers and consumers—the **tax incidence**—depends on the price elasticities of demand and supply.

THE ROLE OF ELASTICITIES

Suppose the government levies a fixed tax on each unit of output sold, say, $.50 per pack of cigarettes. (A constant per-unit tax is called a *unit* or *specific* tax.) Assuming the tax is collected from producers, the tax can be viewed as increasing the cost of production, which shifts the supply curve up and to the left (the supply curve shifts by a vertical amount equal to the tax). If, in the absence of any tax, producers are willing to supply Q_1 cigarettes at $1.00 per pack, they are now willing to supply this same quantity only if they receive $1.50 per pack (see Figure 5.8). The extra $.50

THE INCIDENCE OF A TAX DEPENDS ON THE PRICE ELASTICITY OF DEMAND

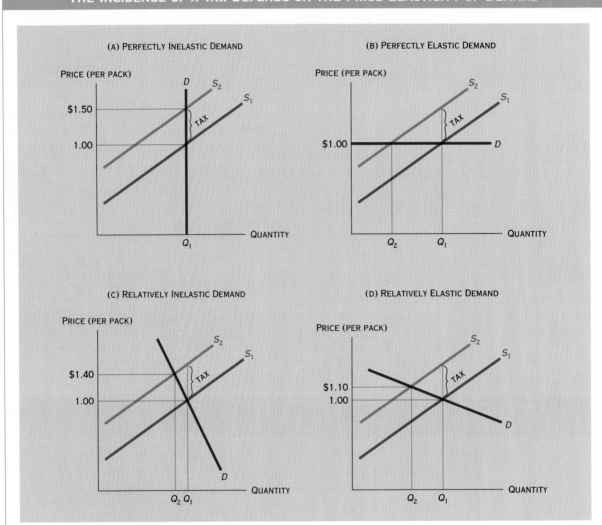

The less sensitive quantity demanded is to price, the more of a tax producers pass on to consumers. In (A) the entire tax is passed on—price increases by the full amount of the tax ($.50). In (B) none of the tax is passed on. In (C) consumers bear more of the tax than do consumers in (D)—$.40 versus $.10—because demand is relatively more inelastic in (C) than in (D).

FIGURE 5.8

just compensates producers for the tax they must pay—that is, the $1.50 price is equivalent to $1.00 per pack net of taxes.

It does not follow, however, that a $.50 tax raises the price of cigarettes by $.50. Unless demand for cigarettes is perfectly inelastic (Figure 5.8A), the new equilibrium price is less than $1.50 per pack. In the limiting case of a perfectly elastic demand curve (Figure 5.8B), price does not rise at all. Given a downward-sloping demand curve (Figure 5.8C and D), price rises—but by an amount less than the tax. How much price rises depends on the price elasticity of demand. The higher the elasticity of demand, the smaller the price increase induced by the tax. In other words: *given supply, the more elastic demand is, the less of a tax is passed on to consumers.* On the other hand, a higher elasticity of demand leads to a greater change in quantity.

Tax incidence also hinges on elasticity of supply. As illustrated in Figure 5.9, the higher the elasticity of supply, the larger the price increase resulting from a tax. That is: *given demand, the more elastic supply is, the more of a tax is shouldered by consumers.*

Because demand and supply elasticities vary from one good to another, the effect of a tax similarly varies. This suggests, depending on the goal of the tax, that some goods may be better candidates for taxation than others. If the goal is to generate tax receipts for the government, a tax is more effective the lower the price elasticity of demand. With a high elasticity, quantity demanded falls more precipitously and, since the government receives tax revenues only on units actually sold, tax receipts suffer. Lawmakers may find the cigarette tax an appealing vehicle for

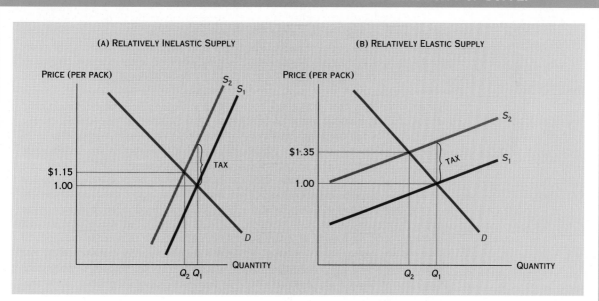

THE INCIDENCE OF A TAX DEPENDS ON THE PRICE ELASTICITY OF SUPPLY

The more elastic supply is, the more of a tax producers pass on to consumers. Accordingly, price rises by a greater amount in (B), where supply is relatively more elastic.

FIGURE 5.9

raising government revenues precisely because the elasticity of demand for cigarettes is so low. On the other hand, if the reason for taxing cigarettes is to reduce consumption, the low elasticity of demand implies that the tax will not be very successful. The lower the price elasticity of demand, the more effective a tax is at raising government revenue; the less effective it is at curtailing consumption.

Obtaining Reliable Estimates of Elasticity[14]

Before moving on to Chapter 6, it is necessary to underscore the importance of obtaining accurate information on supply and demand. Because elasticities are computed from supply and demand curves, any errors made in estimating these curves lead to corresponding errors in the elasticity calculations. Exhibit 5.5

Identifying Demand—Price/Quantity Combinations Do Not a Demand Curve Make

To estimate the price elasticity of demand, it is necessary to have information about the demand curve. How can that information be obtained?

One possibility is to gather data on various price/quantity combinations. For example, a company may observe that when it charges a price of P_1 consumers purchase the quantity Q_1. Suppose the company raises price to P_2 and, at the higher price, finds that consumers buy only Q_2. The company might be tempted to infer that its demand curve intersects these two points (A and B in Figure 5.10). But this would be a valid conclusion only if all the other variables affecting demand remained unchanged.

Another possibility is that, in addition to price changing between the two periods, the demand curve also shifted. This would happen, for instance, if income or population changed or if prices of substitutes or complements were different in the two periods. For such reasons, the demand curve in the first period may actually be given by D_1, the demand curve in the second period by D_2. The company could make a serious mistake by inferring that D_{false} is its demand curve. By so doing it would be underestimating the sensitivity of quantity demanded to price—that is, the company would be underestimating the price elasticity of demand. In that event the company would lose more customers than anticipated each time it raised price.

To estimate actual demand curves, such as D_1 and D_2, the researcher must account for changes in any variable that causes the demand curve to shift (for example, changes in income or population). Fortunately, there are statistical procedures that do this, that net out the effects of shifts in demand. Although such procedures are outside the scope of this course, it is important to realize that the different price/quantity combinations observed in actual experience do not necessarily lie on the same demand curve.

EXHIBIT 5.5

---

[14]Some instructors may wish to delete this section due to the technical nature of the material.

When demand curves shift over time, observed price/quantity combinations such as (P_1/Q_1) and (P_2/Q_2) do not identify a demand curve. To estimate actual demand curves (D_1 and D_2), one must know how other variables (for example, income and population) changed between the two periods.

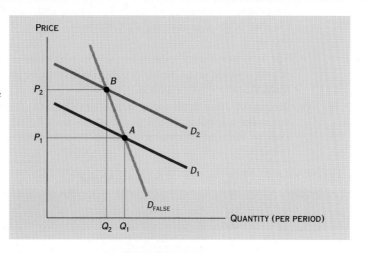

FIGURE 5.10

discusses one of the more common errors made when estimating demand curves. Remember: elasticity estimates are only as reliable as the supply and demand curves on which they are based.

Summary

1. Price elasticity of demand measures responsiveness of quantity demanded to price. In particular, price elasticity of demand is defined as the percentage change in quantity demanded divided by the percentage change in price. Percentages are calculated using average price and average quantity.

2. Price elasticity of demand generally varies from one segment of a demand curve to another. For linear (or nearly linear) demand curves, elasticity becomes progressively smaller as one moves down the demand curve.

3. When demand is elastic ($E_d > 1$), price and total revenue move in opposite directions. When demand is inelastic ($E_d < 1$), price and total revenue are positively related. When demand is unit elastic ($E_d = 1$), total revenue is unaffected by price.

4. Price elasticity of demand tends to be lower when good substitutes are not readily available, when the good is considered a necessity, and when the share of the budget spent on this good is small. Elasticity is also lower the less time consumers have to adjust to a price change—that is, the shorter the time period.

5. The income elasticity of demand measures the percentage change in quantity demanded divided by the percentage change in income. The income elasticity of demand is positive for normal goods and negative for inferior goods. Within the class of normal goods, the income elasticity is greater than one for luxuries, less than one for necessities. The income elasticity of demand enables us to predict how consumption patterns will respond to a change in income, and hence to long-term economic growth.

6. The cross elasticity of demand measures, in percentage terms, how the quantity demanded of one good responds to a change in the price of a second good. For substitutes the cross elasticity is positive, for complements it is negative, and for independent goods it is zero.

7. Elasticity of supply is defined as the percentage change in quantity supplied divided by the percentage change in price. The longer producers have to adjust to price changes, the greater the elasticity of supply is. Consequently, supply is more elastic in the long run than in the short run and, in turn, more elastic in the short run than in the market period.

8. The incidence of a tax depends on the price elasticities of both supply and demand. More of a tax is passed on to consumers (and less is borne by producers) the less elastic demand is and the more elastic supply is.

9. Because of shifts in demand, various price/quantity combinations observed in actual experience may not lie on the same demand curve. Failure to account for shifts in demand leads to incorrect inferences about the true relationship between price and quantity demanded.

Key Terms

price elasticity of demand	cross elasticity of demand
elastic demand	substitute goods
inelastic demand	complementary goods
unit elastic demand	independent goods
perfectly inelastic demand	elasticity of supply
perfectly elastic demand	perfectly inelastic supply
total revenue	perfectly elastic supply
normal goods	market period
inferior goods	short run
income elasticity of demand	long run
luxuries	tax incidence
necessities	

Study Questions and Problems

1. Economists from the University of Chicago estimate that the short-run price elasticity of demand for cigarettes is 0.4. (a) Based on this figure, how much does a 10 percent hike in the price of cigarettes curtail the quantity demanded? (b) How large a price hike is required to achieve a 10 percent reduction in quantity demanded?

2. For consumers in general, the short-run price elasticity of demand for cigarettes is 0.4, but for teenagers (who are less likely than adults to be addicted to nicotine) the elasticity is estimated to be 1.2.
   a. Based on these numbers, how would you characterize the overall demand for cigarettes (elastic, inelastic, or unit elastic)? How would you characterize the demand for cigarettes by teenagers?
   b. Would raising the tax on cigarettes reduce quantity demanded by a larger percentage for teenagers or for adults?

3. An elected representative from California spoke out against increasing the tax on oil producers, arguing that any higher tax "will end up on the backs of consumers. You can't sock it to the big oil companies . . . they'll just pass [all of it] along to the consumers." (a) What was the representative implying about the price elasticity of

demand for oil? (b) Does available evidence support his claim? (c) If the representative were correct and if a new tax were imposed, how much less oil would be demanded?

4. Which of the following products has the lowest price elasticity of demand? For which product would you expect price elasticity to be highest? Why?
   a. food
   b. dairy products
   c. yogurt
   d. peach yogurt

5. Consider the following demand schedule for movie tickets:

PRICE PER MOVIE TICKET	QUANTITY DEMANDED (TICKETS PER YEAR)
$9	6
7	10
5	14
3	18

What is the price elasticity of demand between:
   a. $P = \$9$ and $P = \$7$
   b. $P = \$7$ and $P = \$5$
   c. $P = \$5$ and $P = \$3$

6. (a) Suppose a friend spends $50 per month on jeans, regardless of the price of jeans. What is her price elasticity of demand for jeans? (b) A second friend spends more on jeans when the price is low, while reducing spending when the price is high. Is her demand for jeans elastic or inelastic?

7. (a) Provide examples of several goods that you expect to have an inelastic demand. For each good, explain why you think demand is inelastic. (b) Provide examples of several goods that you expect to have an elastic demand. For each good, explain why you think demand is elastic.

8. The following editorial recently appeared in a collegiate newspaper:

> Residence hall occupancy is at its lowest rate ever. . . . What everyone on campus didn't know was that [the department of] housing is once again discussing raising the rates to stay in residence halls. Simple rules of supply and demand discredit the reasoning behind consideration of raising housing fees. When demand is down, producers lower prices to attract customers.

Evaluate this editorial. Would raising housing rates be a sign that university officials do not understand economics? Would "lower[ing] prices to attract customers" generate more housing revenue for the university? On what does the answer depend?

9. Several years ago, a Chicago commuter railroad reduced fares by 40 percent. According to *The Wall Street Journal*, ridership increased by 50 percent. Assume the increase in railroad travel was the direct response by riders to the fare cut—that is, assume that the lower fare caused quantity demanded to increase by 50 percent. (a) In that event, what is the price elasticity of demand? (b) If the 50 percent increase in ridership was the short-run response, would you predict a relatively larger or smaller response in the long run?

10. Suppose the demand for grapes increases. Will the resulting change in price be greatest in the market period, the short run, or the long run? What about the change in the quantity actually sold?

11. Consider the following quotation from *The Wall Street Journal*:

> To U.S. farmers this year, a bountiful harvest is not something to rejoice over. So the news last week that the Agriculture Department is predicting a mammoth fall crop exceeding previous expectations was a shock to this farmland hamlet.

What is the problem? Why would higher output levels diminish farm revenue? What can we infer about the price elasticity of demand for agricultural products?

12. (a) Would you expect the income elasticity of demand to be higher for basic telephone service or for ocean cruises? Why? (b) Bookstores report that purchases of Bibles pick up when income levels fall. ("When times are good, people play; when times are bad, people pray.") What can we infer about the income elasticity of demand for Bibles?

13. Elasticities can also be computed for the labor market. The price elasticity of the demand for labor is defined as the percentage change in the quantity of labor demanded divided by the percentage change in the price of labor (the wage rate). (a) In recent years, workers at various companies have accepted pay cuts in an effort to expand employment. This strategy has been more successful in some companies than in others. Discuss the role of the price elasticity of demand for labor in determining the effect of a pay cut on the level of employment. (b) Will an increase in the minimum wage have a greater effect on employment if demand for labor is elastic or inelastic?

14. The short-run cross elasticity of demand for residential electricity with respect to a change in the price of natural gas is estimated to be 0. The long-run cross elasticity is put at 0.5.[15] (a) Based on these numbers, are electricity and natural gas substitutes, complements, or independent in the long run? (b) What about the short run? (c) Why is the relationship between these two goods different in the short run than in the long run?

15. Assume a state currently taxes gasoline at the rate of 20 cents per gallon. A state legislator claims that doubling the tax, to 40 cents per gallon, would double gasoline tax receipts for the state. Do you agree? Why or why not?

16. A *subsidy* can be viewed as a negative tax. Rather than taxing a producer (and increasing costs), the government may provide financial support through a subsidy, thereby lowering costs of production. Suppose the government subsidizes production of cheese. (a) How will this affect the price of cheese? (b) Will the magnitude of any price change depend on the price elasticity of demand? Explain.

17. Assume more people attend concerts this year than last year, despite higher prices. Does this imply that the demand for concerts is upward sloping? Explain.

18. Reread question 9 in light of the arguments appearing in Exhibit 5.5. (a) Can we be confident that the increase in ridership was completely attributable to the fare cut? Explain. (b) If some other factor were involved, would the elasticity computed in 9(a) be accurate? (c) Why might it be important to obtain an accurate estimate of the elasticity of demand for railroad travel?

YOUR TURN
Answers

Determining the Price Elasticity of Demand

(A) 200, 800, $2.00, $6.00. (B) 0.75.

[15]T. R. Lakshmanan and William Anderson, "Residential Energy Demand in the United States," *Regional Science & Urban Economics* (August 1980), pp. 383 and 385.

Maximizing Total Revenue

A PRICE OF $7 RAISES $4,900 FOR THE CHARITY, COMPARED TO ONLY $4,500 WHEN THE PRICE IS $5. THE HIGHER PRICE RAISES MORE REVENUE BECAUSE E_d < 1.

Altering E_d Through Trade Policy

THE ELASTICITY OF DEMAND FOR FORDS WOULD FALL (BECOME LESS ELASTIC) BECAUSE OF A REDUCED AVAILABILITY OF SUBSTITUTES (FOREIGN AUTOMOBILES). ALTHOUGH A HIGHER PRICE STILL REDUCES THE NUMBER OF FORDS CONSUMERS CHOOSE TO BUY, THE QUANTITY DEMANDED FALLS BY A LESSER AMOUNT BECAUSE CONSUMERS ARE DENIED THE CHANCE TO SUBSTITUTE FOREIGN AUTOMOBILES FOR FORDS.

The Income Elasticity of Demand for Gasoline

BECAUSE THOSE WITH FOUR TIMES AS MUCH INCOME PURCHASE ONLY TWO TIMES AS MUCH GASOLINE, THE INFERENCE IS THAT QUANTITY DEMANDED RISES ABOUT HALF AS FAST AS INCOME. IN OTHER WORDS, AS INCOME RISES, THE PERCENTAGE OF THE BUDGET SPENT ON GASOLINE FALLS. THIS MEANS THAT GASOLINE IS CLASSIFIED AS A *NECESSITY*.

THE AMERICAN SYSTEM
OF FREE ENTERPRISE . . .
GIVES EVERY ONE OF US
GREAT OPPORTUNITY, IF
ONLY WE SEIZE IT
WITH BOTH HANDS.

—AL CAPONE, 1929

6

Business Firms in the American Economy

BUSINESS FIRMS ARE WHERE THE ACTION IS IN THE U.S. ECONOMY. FIRMS PRODUCE ALMOST ALL OUR GOODS AND SERVICES, HIRE MOST OF OUR WORKERS, AND OWN A LARGE PORTION OF THE NATION'S WEALTH. THEIR DECISIONS ABOUT INVESTMENT, POLLUTION CONTROL, AND OUTPUT INFLUENCE OUR CURRENT AND FUTURE QUALITY OF LIFE. IN CHAPTER 6, WE DISCUSS THE VARIOUS FORMS OF BUSINESS ORGANIZATION (THAT IS, PROPRIETORSHIPS, PARTNERSHIPS, AND CORPORATIONS) AND LOOK AT THE DISTRIBUTION OF AMERICA'S BUSINESS ACTIVITY ACROSS THE DIFFERENT FORMS AND SIZES OF BUSINESS FIRMS. IN ADDITION, THE CAUSES AND POSSIBLE CONSEQUENCES OF THE CORPORATION TAKEOVER MOVEMENT OF THE PAST DECADE ARE ANALYZED. WE THEN LOOK AT THE TYPES OF SECURITIES ISSUED BY FIRMS AND PROVIDE A FRAMEWORK FOR UNDERSTANDING THE FORCES THAT PRODUCE FLUCTUATIONS IN STOCK AND BOND PRICES. FINALLY, WE OVERVIEW CERTAIN BASIC ELEMENTS OF BUSINESS-FIRM ACCOUNTING BY ANALYZING THE NATURE OF THE BALANCE SHEET AND INCOME STATEMENT.

Size Characteristics of American Firms

The American business sector consists of millions of very small firms that control only a minor portion of the nation's productive capacity, many intermediate-size firms, and a few hundred huge corporations that have great economic power, as indicated by their assets, sales, and employment figures. There are more than 18 million firms in America. The largest 500 of these firms—less than one-hundredth of 1 percent of all firms—receive annual revenues that are nearly half as large as the nation's GDP. The sales of General Motors Corporation—the nation's largest firm, with annual revenues in excess of $120 billion—exceed the gross domestic product of such nations as Denmark, Greece, and Austria. The combined annual receipts of America's five largest firms exceed the combined gross domestic products of Egypt, Switzerland, Norway, Portugal, and New Zealand.

America's 25 largest industrial corporations, ranked by annual sales, are listed in Table 6.1. No doubt you are familiar with most of these giant firms.

THE 25 LARGEST U.S. INDUSTRIAL CORPORATIONS, 1991
(RANKED BY ANNUAL SALES)

RANK 1991	RANK 1990	COMPANY	1991 SALES ($ BILLIONS)
1	1	General Motors (Detroit)	123.8
2	2	Exxon (Irving, Texas)	103.2
3	3	Ford Motor (Dearborn, Mich.)	89.0
4	4	IBM (Armonk, New York)	64.8
5	6	General Electric (Fairfield, Conn.)	60.2
6	5	Mobil (Fairfax, Virginia)	56.9
7	7	Philip Morris (New York)	48.1
8	9	E.I. Du Pont De Nemours (Wilmington, Del.)	38.0
9	8	Texaco (White Plains, New York)	37.6
10	10	Chevron (San Francisco)	36.8
11	11	Chrysler (Highland Park, Mich.)	29.4
12	13	Boeing (Seattle)	29.3
13	15	Proctor and Gamble (Cincinnati)	27.4
14	12	Amoco (Chicago)	25.6
15	14	Shell Oil (Houston)	22.2
16	17	United Technologies (Hartford, Conn.)	21.3
17	23	Pepsico (Purchase, N.Y.)	19.8
18	20	Eastman Kodak (Rochester, N.Y.)	19.6
19	25	ConAgra (Omaha, Nebraska)	19.5
20	18	Dow Chemical (Midland, Michigan)	19.3
21	24	McDonnell Douglas (St. Louis)	18.7
22	22	Xerox (Stamford, Conn.)	17.8
23	21	Atlantic Richfield (Los Angeles)	17.7
24	19	USX (Pittsburgh)	17.2
25	28	RJR Nabisco Holdings (New York)	15.0

SOURCE: *Fortune*, April 24, 1992. Reprinted by permission of *Fortune 500*. © 1992 by Time Inc.

TABLE 6.1

At the other end of the spectrum are millions of small firms with a tiny share of the nation's total receipts. The smallest 80 percent of American firms produce only about 10 percent of the nation's output. Small firms tend to be relatively risky and short-lived, exhibiting an average lifetime of roughly five years. Table 6.2 indicates the number of firms and total receipts of firms arranged according to industry.

Approximately one-half of all firms are located in the broadly classified industries of agriculture and services. Such firms tend to be small—the family farm, the shoe repair shop, the barbershop. Firms in these sectors constitute approximately one-half of all firms, but account for only about 10 percent of the receipts of all firms. Although roughly 12 percent of all firms are in agriculture, they account for only about 2 percent of total receipts of firms. On the other hand, the 3 percent of firms engaged in manufacturing receive approximately 30 percent of total receipts. Manufacturing firms tend to be large, agricultural and service firms small.

Failures of Business Firms

Figure 6.1 (page 138) indicates the failure rate of American business firms from 1970 to 1989. In the 1980s less than 1 percent of the nation's firms failed each year. Note the rather dramatic increase during the 1980s. This is due partly to a liberalization of bankruptcy laws, which has enticed more firms to declare bankruptcy. In addition, the 1980s witnessed periods of hardship for certain sectors of the economy such as agriculture, real estate, and petroleum. Severe problems in these sectors have ripple effects—spilling over and dragging down businesses in other sectors.

DISTRIBUTION OF FIRMS AND RECEIPTS BY INDUSTRY*

INDUSTRY	NUMBER OF FIRMS (MILLIONS)	RECEIPTS OF FIRMS ($ BILLIONS)
Agriculture, forestry, fisheries	2.4	177
Mining	0.3	108
Construction	2.1	558
Manufacturing	0.7	2,998
Transportation, public utilities	0.8	786
Wholesale and retail trade	3.5	2,978
Finance, insurance, real estate	2.6	1,754
Services	7.4	916
TOTAL	19.8	10,275

*This table (unlike Table 6.3) includes some 1.8 million farm proprietorships.
SOURCE: *Statistical Abstract of the United States*, 1991. Figures are based on income-tax returns filed with the Internal Revenue Service.

TABLE 6.2

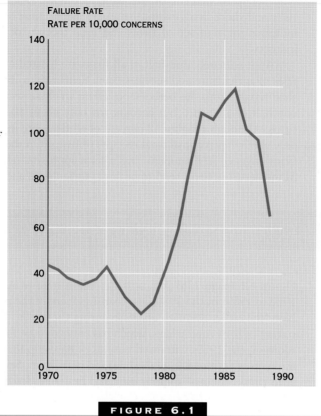

In the 1970s, less than 1 percent of America's business firms failed each year. This failure rate increased sharply in the 1980s because of distress in the agriculture and oil sectors and because of the liberalization of bankruptcy laws.

SOURCE: *Statistical Abstract of the United States*, 1991.

FIGURE 6.1

Although tens of thousands of firms go under each year, the number of firms in existence continues to increase significantly.

Forms of Business Enterprise

The three primary forms of business organization are the proprietorship, the partnership, and the corporation. The relative numbers of these three forms of business enterprise among the 20 million American firms, along with their shares of total sales in America, are illustrated in Figure 6.2. The key point is that proprietorships and partnerships are extremely numerous but contribute only a small portion of total national output. Proprietorships, for example, make up 71 percent of all firms but receive only 6 percent of all sales. Corporations constitute one-fifth of all firms but reap 90 percent of total sales. America's business is distributed very unevenly among firms.

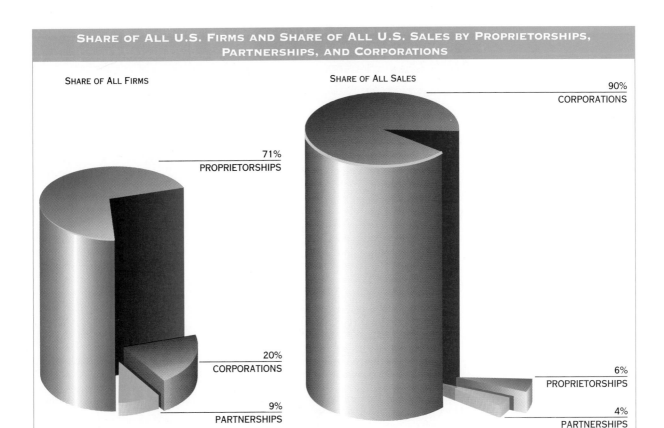

SHARE OF ALL U.S. FIRMS AND SHARE OF ALL U.S. SALES BY PROPRIETORSHIPS, PARTNERSHIPS, AND CORPORATIONS

SHARE OF ALL FIRMS

71%
PROPRIETORSHIPS

20%
CORPORATIONS

9%
PARTNERSHIPS

SHARE OF ALL SALES

90%
CORPORATIONS

6%
PROPRIETORSHIPS

4%
PARTNERSHIPS

Proprietorships and partnerships constitute 80 percent of all firms but conduct only 10 percent of the nation's business. Corporations constitute 20 percent of all business firms but reap 90 percent of total sales.

SOURCE: *Statistical Abstract of the United States*, 1991.

FIGURE 6.2

Table 6.3 (page 140) provides a more detailed breakdown of the number of firms in each organizational category by revenue and average size (farm proprietorships are not included). Note that the average corporation is more than 10 times larger than the average partnership and more than 50 times larger than the average nonfarm proprietorship. More than 75 percent of all firms (all three classifications combined) have annual revenues of less than $100,000. Less than 4 percent of all firms have annual sales in excess of $1 million. Even within the corporate category, less than 20 percent of firms exceed the $1 million sales level. The point is that while almost all of America's large firms are corporations, many corporations are surprisingly small.

PROPRIETORSHIP

A firm owned by a single individual who has unlimited liability for the firm's debts.

PROPRIETORSHIPS

The most prevalent form of business organization, and the form involving the fewest legal complications, is the individual **(sole) proprietorship**. In a proprietorship, the firm is owned by a single individual. Many people dream of owning and

	NUMBER OF FIRMS	TOTAL REVENUE ($ BILLIONS)	AVERAGE SIZE (REVENUES)
Nonfarm proprietorships			
Revenues under $100,000	11,715,000	$ 198	$ 16,901
Revenues of $100,000–$1,000,000	1,334,000	320	239,880
Revenues of $1,000,000 and above	43,000	93	2,163,000
All nonfarm proprietorships	13,091,000	$ 611	$ 46,673
Partnerships			
Revenues under $100,000	1,317,000	$ 12	$ 9,112
Revenues of $100,000–$1,000,000	285,000	74	259,649
Revenues of $1,000,000 and above	44,000	326	7,409,100
All partnerships	1,648,000	$ 412	$ 249,390
Corporations			
Revenues under $100,000	1,424,000	$ 42	$ 29,494
Revenues of $100,000–$1,000,000	1,582,000	576	364,096
Revenues of $1,000,000 and above	605,000	8,568	14,161,983
All corporations	3,612,000	$9,185	$ 2,542,912

*This table excludes the nation's approximately 2 million farm proprietorships, as does Table 3.2 in Chapter 3.

SOURCE: *Statistical Abstract of the United States*, 1991, Table Number 860. Figures based on returns filed with the Internal Revenue Service.

TABLE 6.3

running their own business; proprietors have total control over their businesses. No stockholders or partners must be consulted when a proprietor wishes to change marketing strategy, hire new workers, or alter the nature of the business in a minor or major way. Proprietorships are especially prevalent in farming, construction, and wholesale and retail trade. Think of the small businesses in your hometown—drugstores, dry cleaners, restaurants, service stations. Most are likely to be proprietorships. Roughly 85 percent of all farming operations are organized as proprietorships.

The ease of establishing a proprietorship—basically just hang out your shingle and announce you are in business—helps explain its popularity. The total discretion the owner exerts over the business and the possibility of earning healthy financial rewards via wise decisions and hard work are very appealing. In fact, many proprietors continue in business even though they could earn more working for someone else. A proprietor's income is taxed by the Internal Revenue Service as personal income.

There are two significant drawbacks to the proprietorship form of business organization. First, proprietors are personally liable for all debts of the firm. This means the owner's home, car, and other personal belongings may legally be confiscated to cover the firm's liabilities in the event of extreme financial problems incurred by the firm. Second, it is difficult to raise large amounts of financial support with a proprietorship. For this reason, proprietorships are limited to small-capitalized types of enterprises. You do not see this form of business organization in such large-scale industries as steel and automobiles.

PARTNERSHIPS

PARTNERSHIP

An unincorporated firm with two or more owners who have unlimited liability for the firm's debts.

The **partnership** is more complex than the proprietorship, but closer in its legal nature to the proprietorship than to the corporation. In a partnership, two or more individuals agree to own and operate a business. Each partner agrees to contribute a specified portion of the resources—labor and financial capital—to the firm and agrees to receive (or absorb) a certain portion of the profits (or losses). The partnership is a common type of business organization in such areas as law, medicine, accounting services, and investment banking in states whose laws prevent professional groups in these fields from forming corporations. Partnerships are typically larger than proprietorships but smaller than corporations. However, some of the larger partnerships are vastly more powerful—both in size and influence—than are millions of the nation's smaller corporations.

A partnership can bring together the financial resources and expertise of several individuals. This mix allows the firm to be larger and more efficient than would be possible in a proprietorship. For example, partners in a large accounting firm, law firm, or medical practice can specialize in a particular area of expertise. When one needs considerable financial resources—say $1 million—to start up a firm, most individuals must find partners in order to get started. Like the proprietorship, the partnership's income is taxed as personal income.

The partnership form of organization has certain severe drawbacks. Like the proprietor, each partner is personally liable for the debts of the firm. Also, partnerships are usually unable to raise huge amounts of financial capital. Perhaps the most troublesome aspect of the partnership, however, is the problem of decision making. In this regard, the partnership may be the least efficient form of business organization. The corporation selects officers who make key decisions; the sole proprietor makes decisions unilaterally. In a partnership, it is often necessary for each partner to agree before the firm can implement important decisions. This often causes problems.[1]

A partnership has been likened to a marriage arrangement entered into chiefly for the financial benefit of the participants—there is likely to be undue haggling over the terms. Further, the death or departure of one partner may result in the dissolution of the firm. In that event, remaining partners must commence a renegotiation of the terms of the new partnership. Moreover, a partner leaving the firm

---

[1]Remember that each partner is personally accountable for the liabilities of the firm, including those resulting from unwise actions by the other partners. The more wealthy partners therefore have a natural incentive to pursue more conservative or risk-averse business policies than the less affluent partners. The wealthy partners have more to lose.

may experience difficulties or delays in obtaining financial settlement: a new partner must be found or remaining partners must be willing to buy out the departing partner.

CORPORATIONS

CORPORATION

A firm that takes the form of an independent legal entity with ownership divided into shares and each owner's liability limited to his or her investment in the firm.

A **corporation** is a more complex form of business organization than either the proprietorship or the partnership. The key legal distinction is that a corporation is treated as a fictitious individual, separate and distinct from its actual owners. As a result of this distinction, the owners have *limited liability*—their personal assets are not at risk in the event of financial disaster of the corporation. On the other hand, this form of organization leads to *double taxation*. First, the corporation's profits are taxed by the federal government via the corporate income tax. Second, the dividend income paid from after-tax profits by the corporation to its individual owners (stockholders) is taxed via the individual income tax.[2]

A corporation is formed when a state's corporation commissioner approves legal papers specifying the general nature of the activities in which the firm seeks to engage. Corporations are owned by stockholders. **Common stock** consists of certificates that signify ownership. This stock is issued in the form of *shares* to its owners in exchange for cash. Each share of common stock entitles its owner to one vote. A large corporation may have perhaps 400 million shares of stock outstanding, a single individual owning perhaps 10 shares or 40 million shares. A *board of directors* of the corporation, elected by its stockholders, selects the top management and oversees the general activities of the firm.

COMMON STOCK

A certificate of partial ownership of a corporation that gives its holder a vote in the selection of the firm's directors and a residual claim on the assets and profits of the firm.

The corporate form of business has major advantages not available to proprietorships and partnerships. As indicated, the owners (stockholders) have limited liability in the event of adverse circumstances of the firm. When you purchase 10 shares of common stock in IBM Corporation, you become one of its owners. In the event of insolvency of the firm, the most you can lose is the amount you paid for your 10 shares. Laws prohibit the corporation's creditors from coming after your personal assets. Also, unlike partnerships and proprietorships, which typically terminate with the death of an owner, the corporation potentially has eternal life. Such considerations explain why the corporation is a superior business organization when it comes to raising large amounts of financial resources. Millions of individual investors all around the world are willing to purchase shares in corporations because they stand to participate in the success of the firms and yet cannot conceivably lose any more than the value of the shares they own. Also, because of their continuity, corporations normally find it easier to borrow large amounts of funds than do partnerships and proprietorships.

The drawbacks to the corporate form of business organization include the possibility of conflicting goals of owners and management, the double taxation of

---

[2]Income earned by corporations that pay no dividends but reinvest all profits in the corporation is not subject to double taxation. See Chapter 7 for a discussion of the corporate income tax and the individual income tax.

income, and the cost and difficulty of forming a corporation. State laws differ somewhat in this area, but services of attorneys and substantial fees are normally involved. These costs rule out consideration of the corporate form of business for millions of small or temporary business ventures. (See Table 6.4.)

Ownership versus Control in Corporate America

Corporations are run by hired managers—a president, vice presidents, a board of directors, and others. Legally these executives are the employees of the owners of such firms—the stockholders. This arrangement has the pragmatic advantage of avoiding the indecision and haggling over day-to-day operations typical of partnerships. However, many observers are increasingly concerned over the separation of *ownership* and *control* in corporate America. These critics charge that the managers tend to look after their own interests instead of those of the owners of the corporation.

ADVANTAGES AND DISADVANTAGES OF THE THREE PRIMARY TYPES OF BUSINESS ORGANIZATIONS		
TYPE OF FIRM	**ADVANTAGES**	**DISADVANTAGES**
Proprietorship	1. Firm is easy to set up 2. Decision making is simple; owner has total control 3. Income is taxed only once—as personal income	1. Owner has unlimited personal liability for obligations of the firm 2. Difficulty in raising financial capital
Partnership	1. Firm is easy to set up 2. Access to more financial capital than proprietorship 3. Some specialization is possible; more management skills available 4. Income is taxed only once	1. Decision-making problems 2. Unlimited liability for partners 3. Legal complications when any change in ownership occurs
Corporation	1. Limited liability of owners for obligations of firm 2. Access to large blocks of financial capital via issuing stocks and bonds 3. Firm can hire professional management and replace management when necessary 4. Firm potentially has eternal life as distinguished from owners' lives	1. Double taxation of income of firm 2. Possibility of conflicting goals of owners and management 3. More costly to establish than proprietorship or partnership

TABLE 6.4

Stockholders' (owners') interests are best served when the firm maximizes profits. Maximum profits keep the price of stock as high as possible, thereby maximizing the wealth of the individual shareholders. Management, however, may be more interested in maximizing its own power, income, and job security. In pursuit of these goals, management has an incentive to expand the firm beyond the size that maximizes shareholder wealth. The *power* of management is related to the amount of resources under its control—the size of its *empire*. Payment of profits to stockholders reduces resources in the hands of management. Moreover, the compensation of management seems related to the *size* or *growth* of the firm rather than to its efficiency or current profitability. Management may therefore have a further incentive to maximize the *size* of the firm rather than remain *lean and mean* in order to maximize profits. When this is true, management may use current profits to build unnecessary facilities or to acquire new divisions rather than to pay out dividends to the stockholders.

The Corporate Takeover Movement

The bulk of the shares of common stock of many large American corporations are owned by a large number of relatively small shareholders. Managers of corporations are technically agents of their stockholders. In principle, when stockholders are dissatisfied with management's performance, they can replace them with a new team. In practice, however, stockholders frequently have neither sufficient knowledge of the firm's day-to-day operations nor the initiative to oust ineffective management. Many individuals hold shares of stock in five, ten, or thirty different corporations. When these stockholders are unhappy with a firm's performance, they can attend stockholders' meetings, voice their views, and attempt to elect a new board of directors. However, it is usually less frustrating to just sell the shares and invest in companies with more satisfactory management.

When such stockholder dissatisfaction becomes widespread, the price of the stock drops significantly below the value of the assets of the firm. Investor-entrepreneurs are likely to see this discrepancy and to implement a *takeover bid*, which may be waged by an individual, a group, or most commonly, another corporation. This investor-entrepreneur *(raider)* buys up shares of stock in the company by making a *tender offer* to shareholders (that is, an offer to purchase the shares at a premium to the current market price of the shares). In this way the raider attempts to gain voting control of the *target firm*. Management may be replaced and peripheral or unimportant divisions may be sold off in order to help pay for the acquisition or make the business more profitable.

CORPORATE MERGERS IN AMERICA

Historically, merger movements in America have come in great waves. Surges of merger activity occurred in the 1890s, 1920s, 1960s, and in the past decade. In earlier periods mergers were almost always *friendly*, both firms favoring the merger.

HOSTILE TAKEOVER
A merger accomplished by purchasing controlling interest directly from the stockholders of the target firm, against the wishes of its management.

The distinguishing aspect of the recent merger movement is the **hostile takeover**—acquisitions in which the purchasing company (raider) bypasses the target company's management and purchases controlling interest in the company directly from its stockholders.

In such industries as airlines, takeovers have resulted in consolidation within the industry—fewer firms in operation. Many takeovers result in divestment (selling off) of peripheral operations and a focusing of efforts on the largest or most profitable divisions. Such *spin-offs* often increase efficiency by allowing management to concentrate efforts on a limited range of operations. However, other mergers are motivated by diversification—purchasing businesses unrelated to mainline operations.

In terms of the number and magnitude of transactions, the merger movement of the 1980s exceeded those of the past. Annual transactions involved in mergers averaged more than $100 billion throughout the 1980s, with the figure approaching $200 billion per year in the second half of the decade. Of the hundred largest mergers in American history, fewer than 10 percent occurred prior to the 1980s. In the past two or three years, corporate takeover activity has subsided.

CAUSES OF THE RECENT TAKEOVER MOVEMENT

Several factors joined to explain the *merger mania* of the 1980s. An easing of enforcement of antitrust statutes occurred as a more tolerant attitude toward merger activity became prevalent. The globalization of markets and the increasing U.S. market penetration by large foreign firms has led to the view that larger and more efficient American firms are required to compete with foreign giants. Larger firms often benefit from *economies of scale*—efficiencies attributable to larger size—that allow them to produce goods and services at lower cost than smaller firms.

In addition, a dynamic world economy, advances in technology, or changes in market conditions sometimes require a major restructuring of corporate assets and activities. It is often easier for new management, with its fresh viewpoint and lack of ties with current employees or the community, to come in and implement difficult but essential changes. Innovations in financing tactics have made possible many mergers that formerly would not have been feasible.

Finally, the stock market price of a company's shares is sometimes low relative to the replacement costs of the plant, equipment, and other resources owned by the firm. It is frequently much cheaper to purchase an existing operation than to build from scratch. This is especially true when stock prices are depressed. As stock prices reached high levels in the early 1990s, the incentive for hostile takeovers declined.

CONSEQUENCES OF THE TAKEOVER MOVEMENT

Many economists have a *laissez-faire* philosophy about the corporate takeover phenomenon. They believe takeovers usually benefit both stockholders and society. Other economists, however, are more skeptical about the consequences. They believe that not all the effects are beneficial and that the adverse consequences of corporate takeovers have been underestimated.

POSITIVE ARGUMENTS   The view is commonly expressed that the ever-present possibility of a corporate takeover serves the purpose of motivating existing management to do its utmost to serve stockholders by maximizing efficiency and profitability. When management is incompetent, lazy, or pursues objectives at odds with the goals of stockholders, the price of the company's stock is likely to reflect this fact. In this event both the stockholders and society at large suffer. Stockholders are cheated because the stock's price is lower than it should be; society loses because the presence of inefficiency implies that the nation is operating below its production possibilities curve.

When management does its job properly, this is reflected in the price of the company's stock. In principle, there is no incentive for corporate raiders to attempt a takeover. Hence, the possibility of a corporate takeover is viewed as a beneficial mechanism that forces management to behave itself, work hard, and look after the interests of its stockholders.

Wall Street evidently believes acquisitions are beneficial: stock prices of acquired firms typically rise by about 30 percent as the result of a takeover. It is estimated that gains to shareholders of acquired companies averaged about $35 billion annually during the decade ending in 1989. To place this figure in perspective, it is equivalent to about one-half of total cash dividends paid out annually by corporations.

Acquired firms may grow to become more profitable as new management directs operations toward areas more compatible with consumer demand. New management is believed more likely to shut down unprofitable and inefficient operations and to sell off peripheral divisions to more specialized firms. In the American steel and textile industries, hostile takeovers have facilitated important wage concessions needed in order to compete with less-expensive imports. In the oil industry, takeovers have held down what many observers believe to be a propensity of management to invest excessive resources in exploration. *Bust-up takeovers* of conglomerate firms have led to the sale of peripheral divisions to specialized firms better equipped to operate them.

NEGATIVE ARGUMENTS   Critics of the takeover movement believe that the constant threat of takeover makes it harder for management to take the *long view*. In other words, management is forced to attempt to keep *current* profits high in order to maximize the price of the company's stock and to minimize the company's vulnerability to raiders. Corporate investment projects are allegedly biased by the threat of takeover toward those with immediate and obvious payoffs, and away from research and development and projects yielding long-term benefits. Longer-term investments often result in new technologies that raise living standards.

In addition, the takeover movement may have adverse side effects on the nation's financial structure and macroeconomy. Firms typically finance acquisitions by borrowing (that is, by issuing new debt). The money raised by borrowing is used to acquire the stock of the company being purchased. The corporate takeover movement, by increasing the debt of many firms, has increased the vulnerability of firms to financial problems in the event of a severe business downturn. This is because the firms are obligated to continue paying interest on their debt (debt service) at a time when their sales and revenues are declining.

On the human level, takeovers can result in wrenching changes in the lives of employees, managers, customers, and suppliers of the firm. Takeovers can result in layoffs, pay cuts, and plant closings. Entire communities are sometimes devastated. Of course, supporters of the takeover movement point out that these transitional costs are simply manifestations of changing technology and changing markets in a dynamic economy.

DEFENSIVE PLOYS TO AVOID A TAKEOVER

The defensive tactics employed by management of target firms to avoid hostile takeovers are often destructive and costly to both stockholders and society at large. A firm may sell off desirable assets to obtain funds with which to purchase its own shares on the market, thereby making them unavailable to raiders. Even worse, a firm may sell off its *crown jewels*—the firm's most attractive assets—in a destructive effort to reduce potential raiders' interest in attempting a takeover. A firm may repurchase stock from hostile raiders at a price significantly higher than the market price to get them to drop the takeover effort—a form of bribery dubbed *greenmail*. Firms may also issue *poison pills* to deter raiders—rights granted existing shareholders to purchase additional stock (usually at half price) in the event of a hostile takeover bid. These *pills* greatly raise the takeover cost, thus *poisoning* the firm to hostile raiders. In an environment of widespread takeovers, corporate management's attention is partially diverted from the socially desirable goal of producing to the wasteful task of fending off raiders.

Supporters of the takeover movement acknowledge the detrimental effects of these defensive tactics. However, they view these tactics as evidence of management's contempt for stockholders. The sooner such deceitful management is ousted, the better!

Corporations—The Financial Side

CORPORATE SECURITIES

Corporations require outside funds in order to finance plant construction, equipment purchases, and inventories of goods. Corporations raise funds by issuing equities and debt instruments. Equities are ownership claims consisting of *common stock* and *preferred stock*. On balance, corporations are net debtors or deficit-spending units. Forms of corporate debt include bonds, bank loans, and *commercial paper*— short-term IOUs issued in large denominations by large corporations of impeccable financial reputation. Of special interest are three important instruments of equity and debt finance—common stocks, preferred stocks, and bonds.

COMMON STOCK **Common stock** represents claims of ownership in the corporation. Holders of common stock own a pro-rata part of the firm, the portion of each stockholder being the number of shares owned relative to the total number of shares of common stock outstanding. Generally, the stockholders share in the firm's annual profits. Each corporation's board of directors meets periodically and declares a **dividend**—a payout based on the firm's recent and prospective future profits.[3] Dividends are typically paid quarterly, though in some cases they are paid less frequently. Dividends are a form of income that stockholders receive on a regular basis. In addition, shareholders may eventually benefit from selling their shares at a higher price than they originally paid for them. Such income is known as **capital gains**. Once issued, many common stocks are traded on organized exchanges such as the New York Stock Exchange or the American Stock Exchange, or through an informal over-the-counter (OTC) network of dealers. The prices of thousands of these stocks are quoted daily in major newspapers (see Exhibit 6.1). Other companies are privately owned (that is, the shares of their stock are not available for purchase by the public). Prices of such stock are not made public information.

PREFERRED STOCK **Preferred stock** represents a hybrid sort of claim that involves payment of a relatively high dividend but carries no voting rights and no prospects of participating in the long-term growth of the firm via capital gains. Consider Du Pont Corporation. Owners of Du Pont preferred stock receive $3.50 per share each year as long as the firm earns enough to pay this dividend. Du Pont cannot legally pay dividends on its common stock until dividends on its preferred stock are paid in full. Owners of Du Pont preferred stock are *preferred* stockholders in the sense that they have prior claim (over common stockholders) on the firm's profits and assets. To the investor, this makes the preferred stock less risky than the common stock. On the other hand, preferred stockholders do not benefit from the long-term growth in the firm's profits, whereas common stockholders do (via increased dividends and capital appreciation). Preferred stock is a more conservative investment than common stock.

CORPORATE BOND

An IOU or evidence of debt issued by a corporation that carries a specified schedule of interest payments to be made to the bondholder (lender) and a date for redemption of the principal face value.

BONDS Bonds are a distinctly different animal than common and preferred stocks. **Bonds** are *debts* of corporations—a type of long-term IOU issued by corporations. Unlike stockholders, bondholders do not own a piece of the firm; they are creditors and receive *interest payments* instead of dividends. Semi-annual interest payments continue until the bond matures, at which time the original *principal* is repaid to the bondholder. Bonds are typically sold in $1,000 denominations. Consider Texaco 8⅞ bonds due in the year 2005. This bond is a contractual agreement to pay the bondholder 8⅞ dollars per 100-dollar face amount ($88.75 per $1,000 denomination) each year and also to pay back the $1,000 original principal at maturity in the year 2005. A corporation is obligated to pay the interest and principal as scheduled, or the firm may be declared bankrupt. Bondholders are legally entitled to the full amount they are owed before stockholders receive a penny.

STOCKS AND BONDS AS INFLATION HEDGES

From the investor's viewpoint, bonds are less risky than preferred stock, which is in turn less risky than common stock. However, there is another important consideration—inflation. The tendency for the U.S. price level to rise persistently over time

---

[3]Some firms pay out the bulk of their annual profits in dividends. Others, especially rapidly growing firms, pay little or no dividend. They choose instead to plow back most or all of the profits into the firm for financing expansion or research and development.

implies that bondholders are usually paid off (at maturity) in dollars with considerably less purchasing power than the dollars initially lent to the firm. In contrast, common stock prices have a strong tendency to rise sufficiently in the long run to keep pace with increases in the nation's price level. During this century, while the American price level has increased by roughly 900 percent, common stocks have increased considerably more. Common stock has been a good hedge against inflation when viewed from the perspective of several decades. This is because stock prices follow corporation profits, which tend to increase over time in line with the price level. But consider the investor who purchases bonds—the Texaco 8⅞s of 2005. This investor will receive exactly $1,000 per bond when they mature in the year 2005, no matter how high the U.S. price level has risen by that year. Hence, unless the annual interest payment is commensurately high, bonds tend to be a poor long-term investment in an era of high inflation.[4]

Discounting Expected Future Returns to Compute Present Value

We now present a general approach to understanding how the market places a specific price on any particular stock, bond, or other financial asset. This framework helps one understand intuitively why stocks and bonds fluctuate in price. Consider Equation 6.1.

$$\text{PV (or price)} = \frac{R_1}{1 + i} + \frac{R_2}{(1 + i)^2} + \frac{R_3}{(1 + i)^3} + \cdots + \frac{R_n}{(1 + i)^n} \quad \textbf{(6.1)}$$

In Equation 6.1, PV represents the present value (or price) of the asset; $R_1, R_2, \ldots, R_n$ indicate the annual returns (flows of income) currently expected from the asset in years $1, 2, \ldots, n$; i represents the interest rate used to discount these expected future returns (discussed later).

Every financial asset holds the promise of yielding a stream of returns in future years $(R_1, R_2, \ldots, R_n)$. For some securities the promise may involve only one return to be received in one year (R_1) or perhaps in 40 years (R_{40}).[5] Most bonds promise a finite series of annual returns, involving constant payments for 10, 20, or 30 years. Common stocks, preferred stocks, and some rare types of bonds issued in foreign countries potentially involve an infinite number of annual returns—they are expected to yield returns *in perpetuity* or as long as the corporation is in existence.

---

[4]Actually, the market price (and hence yield) of existing bonds fluctuates to compensate potential new investors for the expected depreciation in the real value of the principal due to expected inflation. If the outlook for inflation worsens, the current market price of the Texaco 8⅞s of 2005 (and all other existing bonds) will decline sufficiently to entice investors to be willing to buy and hold the bonds. In 1981, with inflation in double-digit territory, the price of high-quality bonds fell dramatically. Bond prices fell so low that astute investors were able to lock in 12–15 percent yields. In principle, bonds are a good inflation hedge if yields are high enough. Historically, bonds generally have not been a good hedge against inflation when viewed from the perspective of several decades. Returns from common stocks have significantly exceeded returns from bonds over the long haul.

[5]Examples of securities promising a single lump-sum payment of principal in one year and in 40 years, respectively, are a one-year U.S. Treasury bill (issued by the U.S. government) and a 40-year zero-coupon bond (issued by corporations and other entities). A zero-coupon bond is a long-term bond that pays no annual interest but instead pays a specific sum of money (usually in thousand-dollar denominations) at some distant future date. It sells at a price considerably below its future face value.

Buying Common Stocks

C onsidering that nearly 50 million Americans own common stocks, two things are apparent. First, you don't have to be rich to buy stocks. Second, owning stocks is appealing to many people. When you buy shares of stock, you purchase a share of the company's profits or losses in the future. You own a piece of the company and directly participate in the future success or failure of the firm.

Suppose you are considering the purchase of a few shares of International Business Machines (IBM). To find its current price and other relevant information, turn to the financial pages of any major newspaper. On Friday, April 3, 1992, *The Wall Street Journal* revealed the following data on IBM's stock, together with corresponding information on thousands of other stocks for the previous day's trading activity (April 2 1992).

Reading from the left, the first two columns reveal the highest and lowest price at which IBM traded in the previous 52 weeks. IBM ranged from a high of $114¾ ($114.75) to a low of $82¾ per share. The stock pays a dividend of $4.84 per share each year ($1.21 quarterly), which represents a yield of 5.9 percent per year based on IBM's most recent price ($82¼). The price-earnings ratio (PE) of 12 indicates that the stock is selling at a price that is 12 times the company's annual earnings or profits per share. The next column indicates the number of shares traded that day, in hundreds of shares. Shares traded on April 2, 1992, totaled 2,072,800. The next three columns reveal the highest, lowest, and closing prices of the stock for the most recent trading day (April 2, 1992). IBM traded as high as $83½, as low as $81⅞ (a

EXHIBIT 6.1

| 52 Weeks | | | | | Yld | Vol | | | Net |
Hi	Lo	Stock	Sym	Div	%	PE	100s	Hi	Lo	Close	Chg
9⅜	3	Intlake	IK	...		17	29	5⅞	5¾	5¾	...
29⅝	20	IntAlum	IAL	1.00	4.5	93	4	22½	22⅜	22⅜	...
▼114¾	82¾	IBM	IBM	4.84	5.9	12	20728	83½	81⅞	82¼	- ⅝

For common stocks, expected returns consist of annual dividends and perhaps some appreciation in the price of the stock (capital gains). For bonds, returns consist of fixed annual interest payments. For common stocks there is considerable uncertainty about future returns (*R*s) because firms have no legal obligation to pay any specific dividend and because the financial condition of the corporation can change considerably over time. For bonds the *R*s are subject to less uncertainty because the corporation issuing the bonds enters a contractual agreement with the bondholder to pay a specific stream of *R*s over time. Hence, in the case of common stocks, market participants revise the expected stream of *R*s on a daily basis. This is not generally the case with bondholders, although this does occur when financial problems of the corporation increase sufficiently to evoke the possibility of default.

52 Weeks Hi	Lo	Stock	Sym	Div	Yld %	PE	Vol 100s	Hi	Lo	Close	Net Chg
108	75	IntFlavor	IFF	2.72	2.6	24	316	105¼	104⅜	105¼	+ ⅝
34¾	6⅞	IntGameTech	IGT		...	51	4509	34⅛	31¾	31¾	-2¼
31½	23⅞	IntMultfood	IMC	.80	3.0	13	189	26⅞	26⅝	26¾	– ¼
78½	59⅛	IntPaper	IP	1.68	2.3	20	2449	73⅞	72⅞	73⅛	– ⅝

new low for the year), and closed the day at \$82¼, for a loss on the day of ⅝ of a dollar or 62.5 cents per share (final column).

To determine whether IBM is currently a sound stock to purchase, you would be well advised to gain as much information and insight as possible about the company's prospects for the next few years. The price of any company's stock is closely related to the outlook for current and future profits. If profits expand sharply over the years, the price of the stock will probably do so also. The moderate price / earnings ratio (PE) of IBM indicates that the consensus of investors is that IBM will experience moderate but not sensational growth. More glamorous, rapid-growth stocks often sell at PE ratios of 30 or 40 while stocks with less attractive growth prospects may sell at PE ratios of 5 or 10.

This does not mean that IBM is a poor stock to buy. Each stock's price already reflects the marketplace's opinion of the company's prospects. If you are smarter, more perceptive, or more diligent than other investors, you may be able to select stocks that outperform broad market averages. Although a few have been able to do this on a consistent basis, it is extremely difficult. Again, this is because the market tends to be *efficient*—it already reflects all readily available information about each company's future prospects.

SOURCE: Data on IBM's stock from *The Wall Street Journal*, April 3, 1992. Reprinted by permission of *The Wall Street Journal*. © 1992, Dow Jones & Company, Inc. All rights reserved.

PRESENT VALUE
The value now of one or a series of payments to be received in the future; often referred to as the *discounted present value* of future payments.

To find the **present value** (today's value, or PV) of a return (R) expected to be received *in the future*, one must *discount* that return. The present value of a promise to receive one dollar in the future is less than one dollar. If you have one dollar today you can invest the dollar at interest in a risk-free asset, such as a savings account, and accumulate more than a dollar in the future. The rate of discount—the interest rate—is indicated by i in the denominator of Equation 6.1. The present value of each expected future return ($R_1, R_2, \ldots, R_n$) is less than its face value by an amount that depends on the level of the interest rate and the number of years in the future that the return will be received.

Figure 6.3 (page 152) summarizes the relationship between the present value of one dollar, the number of years in the future that the dollar will be received, and the interest rate used to discount the future return.

The value today (present value) of the promise of $1 in the future declines as the length of time before that dollar is to be received increases. This present value also declines as the interest rate used to discount the future return rises.

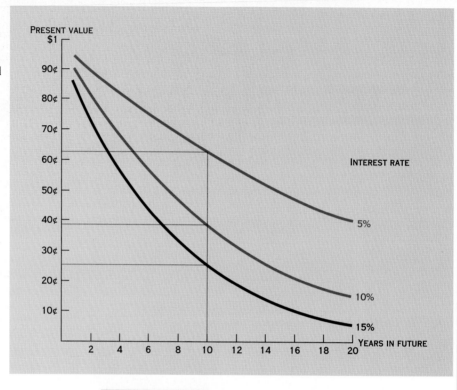

FIGURE 6.3

What is the present value of the promise to receive one dollar in ten years when the rate of discount is 5 percent? Answer: $1/(1.05)^{10} = 61¢$. What is the present value of the promise to receive $1 in 20 years when the rate of discount is 15 percent? Answer: $1/(1.15)^{20} = 6¢$! Note that the present value of $1 tails off rapidly as you increase the length of time into the future that it is to be received. This is especially true when the interest rate is high. The present value of $1 to be received in ten years falls from 61¢ to 39¢ to 25¢ as the discount rate increases from 5 percent to 10 percent to 15 percent, respectively.

The current price of a share of IBM stock is the sum of the present values of the unlimited number of future annual returns expected from each share of stock. In reality, because the present value tails off rapidly with time into the future, the price of IBM stock is dominated by the returns expected in the next five or ten years.

You now have the tools with which to understand why the prices of individual stocks and the stock market in general fluctuate significantly over time. As new information becomes available each day, market participants revise their estimates for the Rs of Equation 6.1. In addition, interest rates fluctuate over time. An increase in interest rates, unless accompanied by a compensating increase in the Rs expected from stocks, depresses stock market prices. For bonds an increase in interest rates unambiguously decreases bond prices because the Rs are fixed by contractual arrangement and do not fluctuate once the bond is issued. A decline in interest rates unambiguously increases bond prices. A decline in interest rates also increases stock prices unless the same forces that depress interest rates also depress the returns (Rs) expected from stocks commensurately.[6]

Behavior of Stock Prices in Recent Decades

Figure 6.4 illustrates the behavior of the Standard & Poors 500, a broad index of common-stock prices, over the 1954–1991 period. Figure 6.4 also indicates the behavior of the price-earnings ratio for the basket of stocks in the S & P index.

Figure 6.4 reveals that although the stock market was basically flat during 1965–1982, the period after 1982 witnessed a strong bull market. From the 1982 lows to the 1992 highs, the Standard and Poors index increased by about 230 percent or approximately 14 percent per year. Using the framework of Equation 6.1, it is clear that this bull market was driven by persistent upward revisions in the returns expected (Rs) and by a sustained decline in interest rates (i). The Reagan and Bush Administrations' policies were perceived by market participants as bullish for stocks. Income-tax rates (individual and corporate) were slashed significantly; inflation was brought down sharply below the rates experienced in the 1970s; deregulatory measures were implemented; and corporate profits increased strongly after 1982. The economic expansion that began in late 1982 lasted for nearly eight years.

Note in Figure 6.4 that the price-earnings ratio of stocks increased significantly in the 1980s: market participants were willing to pay more and more for each dollar of current profits earned by corporations. This willingness can be explained partly by the persistent upward revisions of the prospective returns (Rs) expected from stocks owing to the gradually improving perception of the U.S. economic environment, and partly by the sustained decline in interest rates in the U.S. economy. Since stocks compete with bonds and other interest-bearing instruments for investor attention, a decline in interest rates makes stocks more attractive. Investors are willing to pay more (higher share prices) for each dollar of current profits because bonds become less desirable when interest rates decline.

Note the "Crash of '87" in Figure 6.4. On October 19, 1987, stock prices plunged by about 20 percent! This episode illustrates that herd psychology can be a powerful force and that people can lose an awful lot of money in a very short period of time. Nevertheless, stocks were an excellent investment in the decade of the 1980s. However, resist thinking that stocks will necessarily be a good investment during the next decade. Before aggressively converting your life's savings into shares of common stocks, ponder the experience of the 1970s (Figure 6.4). In that

---

[6]In recessions, interest rates typically fall. Other things equal, this causes stock prices to go up. However, recessions are associated with a significant drop in corporation profits. Hence, the Rs of Equation 6.1 are revised downward. Because recessions result in a decrease in both the numerator and denominator of Equation 6.1, the net effect on stock prices is ambiguous. Severe recessions usually cause a decline in the stock market because corporation profits (and the Rs of Equation 6.1) drop sharply.

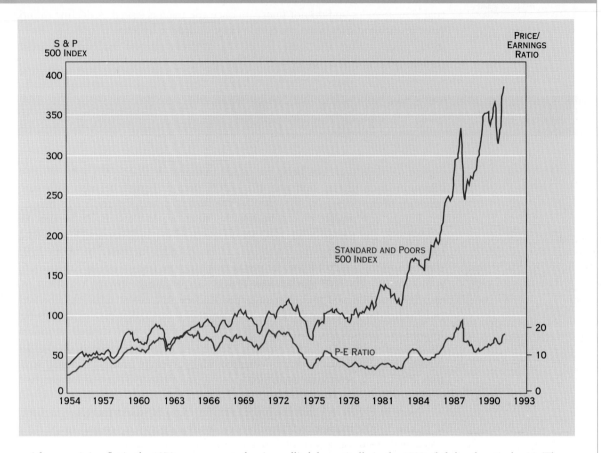

After remaining flat in the 1970s, common stock prices rallied dramatically in the 1980s (left-hand vertical axis). The price/earnings ratio is measured on the right-hand vertical axis.

SOURCE: Citibank Economic Database, 1992.

FIGURE 6.4

decade, stock prices remained flat while the American price level doubled. Each dollar invested in stocks in 1970 was worth fifty cents a decade later. Or, for an even more sobering admonishment, study the period 1929–1933. Common stocks lost about 90 percent of their value in the Great Depression. Nevertheless, when viewed with the perspective of several decades, common stocks have consistently outperformed such alternatives as bonds, bank certificates of deposits, and other debt instruments.

YOUR TURN

ASSUME **OPEC** (ORGANIZATION OF PETROLEUM EXPORTING COUNTRIES) ANNOUNCES AN AGREEMENT TO REDUCE OUTPUT OF OIL SHARPLY, LEADING TO EXPECTATIONS OF CONSIDERABLY HIGHER OIL PRICES. ANALYZE, VIA THE FRAMEWORK OF EQUATION 6.1, THE PROBABLE EFFECT OF THIS *ANNOUNCEMENT* ON (A) THE PRICE OF COMMON STOCK OF OIL COMPANIES AND (B) THE DOW JONES (AND OTHER) STOCK MARKET AVERAGES.

The economic status of any firm is summarized in two key documents—the balance sheet and the income statement. Both documents provide important information about the financial condition of the firm. Financial analysts and stock-market investment advisors scrutinize both documents with care.

THE BALANCE SHEET

BALANCE SHEET

A financial report listing a firm's assets and liabilities at a moment in time.

ASSETS

Items that the firm owns and claims that the firm has upon entities external to the firm.

LIABILITIES

Debts of the firm or claims that outsiders have on the firm.

The firm's **balance sheet** is a statement of its assets and liabilities at a given point in time. The firm's **assets** consist of items that the firm owns and of claims that the firm has against outside entities. Its **liabilities** are claims that outside entities have against resources of the firm (that is, what the firm *owes*). It is essential to recognize that the balance sheet is a snapshot—it looks at the *stock* of assets and liabilities *at a given point in time*. The balance sheet changes from day to day as the value of assets and liabilities fluctuate.

THE BALANCE SHEET SUMMARIZES THE CURRENT FINANCIAL POSITION OF A FIRM BY COMPARING ITS ASSETS AND ITS LIABILITIES.

Consider the hypothetical balance sheet of the fictitious company, California Computer Corporation.

■ BALANCE SHEET—CALIFORNIA COMPUTER CORPORATION (DECEMBER 31, 1992)

ASSETS		LIABILITIES	
Cash	$ 1,000,000	Accounts payable	$ 5,000,000
Accounts receivable	$ 4,000,000	Short-term bank loans	$ 3,000,000
Inventory	$ 6,000,000	Long-term debts (mortgages and bonds)	$ 15,000,000
Real estate, plant, and equipment	$ 20,000,000		
Total assets	$ 31,000,000	Total liabilities	$ 23,000,000
		Net worth	$ 8,000,000

Assets of California Computer include cash on hand (chiefly checking and savings accounts); accounts receivable (monies owed the firm by its customers); inventories of computers and other items; and the firm's real estate, plant, and equipment. California Computer's assets sum to $31 million. Its liabilities consist of accounts payable (monies owed by California Computer to its suppliers and others), bank loans, and long-term debt such as bonds issued and mortgages on its buildings. Total liabilities sum to $23 million.

NET WORTH
The difference between a firm's assets and its liabilities: net worth is the residual equity or claim of the owners of the firm.

Total assets of any solvent firm (that is, any firm that is not bankrupt) exceed total liabilities. For California Computer, total assets exceed total liabilities by $8 million. This difference, known as **net worth**, is the owners' equity in the business or the owners' claim against the assets of the firm. The $8 million net worth of California Computer means that if the firm were to cease operations, sell off all its assets at full value, and pay off its liabilities, it would still have $8 million. These funds would accrue to the owners of the firm.

ACCOUNTING IDENTITIES

1. NET WORTH = TOTAL ASSETS − TOTAL LIABILITIES
2. TOTAL ASSETS = TOTAL LIABILITIES + NET WORTH

The first accounting identity is simply a definition; the second identity follows from the definition of net worth (1). Because net worth is the difference between total assets and total liabilities, it follows logically that total assets are equal to total liabilities plus net worth. For solvent firms, net worth is positive—total assets exceed total liabilities. When net worth is negative, the firm is technically bankrupt—liabilities exceed assets.

As a firm grows over time, the entries on its balance sheet increase. As the firm becomes larger, it normally requires additional plant and equipment and a larger stock of inventories. Moreover, as the firm does business with more customers, its cash requirements and accounts receivable typically expand.

From the second identity (2), we know that the firm's liabilities or net worth, or both, must grow as its assets increase. A firm's profits may be either paid out in dividends or retained by the firm. If the firm is highly profitable, it can finance much of its growth via *retained earnings* (that is, by plowing profits back into the business). To the extent that the firm does this, its assets expand without a compensating increase in its liabilities. And, therefore, the firm's net worth increases, together with the owners' stake in the firm. If the firm does not earn and retain sufficient profits to finance expansion, it must seek outside financing. The firm may issue new equity shares—ownership claims—by taking in new partners (if it is a partnership) or new shareholders (if it is a corporation). Or, the firm can issue debt (that is, borrow funds from banks or issue new bonds to obtain financial capital).

THE INCOME STATEMENT

INCOME STATEMENT
A financial report showing the revenues, costs, and profits from the firm's activities over a specified period of time.

As time goes by, California Computer Corporation is productively engaged in the enterprise of manufacturing and selling computers. To know the firm's flow of income over one year or one quarter, we consult the firm's **income statement**, or its statement of profit or loss.

The income statement for a specified interval shows the firm's revenues from sales during that period, the expenses of the firm, and its net income—the profits remaining after expenses are deducted from sales.

■ INCOME STATEMENT—CALIFORNIA COMPUTER CORPORATION
(JANUARY 1, 1993—DECEMBER 31, 1993)

Total sales		$8,000,000
Less		
Materials	$2,000,000	
Labor costs	$3,000,000	
Depreciation	$1,000,000	
Miscellaneous costs	$ 500,000	
Total cost of goods sold	$6,500,000	$6,500,000
Gross profit		$1,500,000
Less: sales and administrative costs		100,000
Net operating profit		$1,400,000
Less: state and local taxes and interest expense		200,000
Net income before federal income taxes		$1,200,000
Less: corporate income tax		400,000
Net income after taxes		$ 800,000
Less: dividends paid on common stock		$ 200,000
Addition to retained earnings		$ 600,000

To begin with, focus on the column of items farthest right and ignore the individual items contributing to the cost of goods sold. Total sales receipts of California Computer were $8 million in 1993. Deducting the cost of goods sold of $6.5 million, we calculate a gross profit of $1.5 million. When we subtract sales and administrative costs, interest expense on the firm's debts, and state and local taxes, we obtain net income before federal taxes of $1,200,000. After paying $400,000 in corporate income taxes to the Internal Revenue Service, California Computer Corporation earned $800,000 in 1993. One-fourth of these profits were paid out in dividends to the owners of common stock in California Computer. The remaining $600,000 (retained earnings) were plowed back into the firm. The 1993 profitability of the firm raised its net worth by $600,000.[7]

Turning briefly to the individual costs of goods sold, the materials, labor, and miscellaneous costs of producing computers are obvious; only depreciation requires elaboration. Firms require the use of capital goods—equipment, plants, trucks, and so forth—to produce their output. These capital goods do not last forever; they have a finite lifetime, wearing out gradually. The accounting charge for the annual cost of such capital assets as equipment and buildings is known as **depreciation**. Rather than attributing all this cost to the year in which the capital goods are installed, accountants reduce or depreciate the value of the assets over a period of time estimated to reflect their lifetime. For example, if a new building costing $10

---

[7]Of course, the net worth of the firm during 1993 may have increased by more than $600,000 or may even have decreased. The values of individual assets and liabilities fluctuate throughout the year, producing changes in net worth. Given the 1993 retained earnings of $600,000, we *can* state that the net worth of California Computer is higher at the end of 1993 by $600,000 than it would have been if it had no retained earnings in 1993.

million is erected in 1993 and is expected to have a useful life of 20 years, the firm might claim a depreciation cost of $500,000 annually for 20 consecutive years. This depreciation cost, like other costs, may be deducted from the firm's revenues for purposes of figuring its taxable income.

Summary

1. The magnitude of business activity is distributed highly unevenly across American business firms. The smallest 80 percent of the nation's 18 million firms produce only 10 percent of output. The largest 1 percent of American firms produce more than one-half our output.

2. The three forms of business enterprise are the individual proprietorship, the partnership, and the corporation. Eighty percent of America's firms are proprietorships and partnerships, but they collectively account for only 10 percent of the nation's sales.

3. A sole proprietorship is a nonincorporated business owned by one person. Easy to set up, its decision making is simple and its income is taxed once by the IRS—as personal income of the owner. Drawbacks include the unlimited personal financial liability of the owner and the difficulty of raising large amounts of funds from outside sources.

4. A partnership is an unincorporated business owned by two or more persons, each of whom has a financial interest in the business. Its advantages and disadvantages are similar to those of the proprietorship. However, decision making is more cumbersome because of the need for all partners to agree on policy decisions.

5. A corporation is a business that is legally incorporated under state laws. Chief advantages include the limited liability of its owners for the debts of the corporation and the superior access to large blocks of financial capital. Drawbacks include the costs of setting up the corporation, the double taxation of its income by the federal government, and the difficulties caused by conflicting goals of management and owners (stockholders).

6. When a corporation is poorly managed, the price of its stock declines relative to the true value of its assets. This, in turn, makes the company attractive to corporate *raiders*—firms that purchase a majority share of the company's stock and take over operations of the firm. A *market for corporate control* emerged with the hostile takeover movement of the 1980s. During 1985–1990, roughly ten corporate mergers were announced each day, on average.

7. Some economists applaud the corporate takeover movement, viewing the potential threat of takeover as a beneficial mechanism forcing corporate management to work hard to look after the interests of the stockholders. Other economists are more reserved. They worry that the takeover movement induces firms to place excessive emphasis on short-term profits at the expense of long-run considerations. Also, by stimulating an increase in corporate indebtedness, the takeover movement probably has increased the fragility of America's financial structure.

8. To obtain funds above and beyond those generated internally, firms issue equities and debt instruments. Common stocks are equities—claims of ownership in the form of shares. Stockholders receive dividends and the possibility of capital gains—appreciation in the market price of the shares. Debt instruments issued by firms include bonds. A corporate bond is a contractual agreement by the firm to pay interest to the lender on

the principal at a specified rate for a specified period and to return the principal at maturity. The bondholder has no ownership claim on the firm, but has a prior claim on the firm's assets above stockholders in the event of financial problems.

9. The present value of any asset—a stock, bond, factory, apartment building—is the sum of the discounted stream of future returns currently anticipated from the asset. In the case of common stocks and many other assets, these future returns are not known with certainty. To discount these future returns, the interest rate is used. An increase in interest rate, unless offset by a corresponding increase in expected returns, inevitably reduces the present value (and price) of the asset.

10. A steady upward revision in the market's perception of the future returns expected from stocks, combined with a major decline in interest rates, generated a bull market in stocks after 1982. From the low of 1982 to the high of 1992, market averages nearly quadrupled. Common stocks outperformed bonds in the 1980s and in the long period since 1900.

11. A firm's balance sheet is a snapshot, at a given point of time, of its assets (what it owns) and its liabilities (what it owes). The amount by which assets exceed liabilities is the net worth of the firm: it is the owners' equity in the firm.

12. A firm's income statement details its receipts, expenses, and profits for a given period of time such as a quarter or a year.

Key Terms

(sole) proprietorship
partnership
corporation
common stock
hostile takeover
preferred stock
corporate bond

present value
balance sheet
assets
liabilities
net worth
income statement

Study Questions and Problems

1. Assume that after you graduate from college you go into business and establish a prosperous computer software firm. After five years of growth you begin to consider the possibility of incorporating the firm. What considerations will influence your decision?

2. What are the advantages of a partnership over an individual proprietorship? What are the disadvantages?

3. What is the basis for the view that conflicting goals of corporate stockholders and management cause problems for stockholders as well as for society at large? What sort of mechanisms exist to inhibit these conflicting goals?

4. What is your position on the merits of the corporate takeover movement of the past decade? Defend your position analytically.

5. Assume you inherit $100,000 and are considering the purchase of common stocks, preferred stocks, and corporation bonds. How would you allocate the $100,000 among these three forms of investment? Defend the answer in the context of your personal investment objectives.

6. Why do you suppose that common stocks outperformed corporate bonds in the 1980s? In the period since 1900? In what kind of an environment would you expect bonds to outperform stocks?

7. Write down an expression (formula) that allows you to calculate the present value or price of the following:
   a. a bond that pays $80 a year (per $1,000 denomination) each year until maturity (four years from now), if interest rates are currently 9 percent.
   b. a zero coupon bond that makes a single payment of $1,000 in 1999, if interest rates are currently 7 percent.
   c. a promise to receive $100 in one year, if interest rates are currently 6 percent.

8. Look in *The Wall Street Journal*, Standard and Poor's *The Outlook* (or other financial publication) and examine the overall behavior of stock market prices during the past year. In terms of the present value formula presented in this chapter, explain the cause of this fluctuation in stock prices.

9. Using rough estimates or even guesses, prepare a balance sheet of your *family*. Based on your family's assets and liabilities, what is the size of the family's net worth? How has this net worth changed in the past year?

YOUR TURN
Answers

(A) STOCK PRICES OF OIL COMPANIES ARE LIKELY TO RISE. HIGHER OIL PRICES WILL SHARPLY EXPAND THE REVENUES OF OIL COMPANIES IN THE FUTURE. THIS UPWARD REVISION OF FUTURE RS (IN THE MINDS OF INVESTORS) IS IMMEDIATELY REFLECTED IN THE HIGHER STOCK PRICES OF OIL COMPANIES—AS SOON AS OPEC MAKES ITS ANNOUNCEMENT. (B) IN SPITE OF HIGHER STOCK PRICES FOR OIL COMPANIES, THE OVERALL STOCK MARKET IS LIKELY TO DROP FOR AT LEAST TWO REASONS. FIRST, THE INCREASE IN OIL PRICES WILL INCREASE PRODUCTION COSTS FOR MILLIONS OF FIRMS. ENERGY PRICES, FERTILIZER PRICES, AND OTHER PRICES WILL INCREASE, PUTTING PRESSURE ON PROFITS OF NONOIL-PRODUCING FIRMS. SECOND, THE INFLATIONARY EFFECT OF THE OIL PRICE INCREASE IS LIKELY TO LEAD TO RESTRICTIVE POLICIES IMPLEMENTED BY THE GOVERNMENT IN AN ATTEMPT TO LIMIT INFLATION. BOTH THESE FACTORS WILL LEAD MARKET PARTICIPANTS TO REVISE DOWNWARD THE FUTURE RETURNS EXPECTED FROM STOCKS (THAT IS, THE RS OF EQUATION 6.1). THE STOCK MARKET IS LIKELY TO PLUNGE THE MOMENT THE ANNOUNCEMENT IS MADE BY OPEC.

Selected References

Demsetz, Harold, Mark Hirschey, and Michael Jensen. "The Market for Corporate Control," *American Economic Review*, May 1986, pp. 313–329. These three articles analyze the economic aspects of the corporate takeover movement.

Rohatyn, Felix G. "Takeover Mania," *Challenge*, May/June 1986, pp. 30–34. This article presents the case against a government laissez-faire policy toward corporate takeovers.

Symposium on Takeovers. *The Journal of Economic Perspectives*, Winter 1988, pp. 3–82. A series of excellent articles on the corporate takeover movement by leading experts in the field.

TAXES, AFTER ALL,
ARE THE DUES
THAT WE PAY FOR
THE PRIVILEGE OF
MEMBERSHIP IN AN
ORGANIZED SOCIETY.

—FRANKLIN D. ROOSEVELT

7

Government in the Economy—
Spending and Taxation

WE LIVE IN A *MIXED ECONOMY*. THE PRIVATE MARKETS AND THE GOVERNMENT SHARE IN ANSWERING SUCH FUNDAMENTAL QUESTIONS AS *WHAT* WILL BE PRODUCED AND *FOR WHOM* IT WILL BE PRODUCED. ONE CANNOT ASSESS THE ROLE OF GOVERNMENT BY MEANS OF A SIMPLE NUMBER. HOWEVER, A CRUDE INDICATOR OF THE SCOPE OF GOVERNMENT ACTIVITY IN THE UNITED STATES IS THAT ABOUT 80 PERCENT OF THE GOODS AND SERVICES WE ENJOY ARE PROVIDED BY PRIVATE MARKETS, WHEREAS 20 PERCENT ARE PROVIDED TO US COLLECTIVELY BY FEDERAL, STATE, AND LOCAL GOVERNMENTS.

There are several reasons why societies deem it appropriate for governments to intervene in the economy. First, people benefit when markets are highly competitive. Governments seek to promote competition by enacting and enforcing antitrust laws, by prohibiting discrimination, and by other measures. Where competition is inherently impractical for technical reasons, governments impose regulations on producers in order to protect the public. Examples include regulations placed on utilities and local telephone services. Second, governments implement macroeconomic stabilization policies in an attempt to avoid the extremes of rampant inflation and economic depression. These stabilization policies, known as fiscal policy and monetary policy, are analyzed in detail in Parts II and III of this text. Third, governments deliberately intervene to modify the distribution of national income and wealth. This intervention is intended to moderate the extremes of poverty and affluence in society. Other important reasons for governmental economic activity include correcting for misallocation of the nation's resources resulting from external (or spillover) effects, and stepping in to provide public goods.

CORRECTING FOR MISALLOCATION OF RESOURCES DUE TO EXTERNALITIES (OR SPILLOVER EFFECTS)

The production of private goods and services often leads to *externalities*, or *spillover effects*, in which the costs incurred by producers or the benefits received by consumers differ significantly from the total costs of producing or total benefits of consuming when the whole of society is considered. Externalities arise when the actions of producers and consumers affect *third parties*—people other than producers and consumers involved in the transactions. Spillover or external effects may be either positive or negative—they may be beneficial or detrimental.

NEGATIVE EXTERNALITIES

Uncompensated costs imposed on third parties as a result of consumption or production by other individuals or firms.

NEGATIVE EXTERNALITIES Negative externalities occur when producers or consumers impose costs on third parties not involved in the production or consumption of a good. For example, a firm burning coal to produce electricity may effectively ignore spillover costs (acid rain, air pollution, greenhouse effects) in a free, unfettered market. In this case, the cost of producing electricity from society's viewpoint exceeds the costs shouldered by the producer. When negative externalities exist, *market failure* occurs in the sense that signals are given to produce a socially excessive output of goods whose production yields such external effects.

Recall from Chapter 4 that the costs of producing a good influence the position of the supply curve for the good. An increase in the cost of producing a good—higher material prices, higher wages—shifts the supply curve to the left. When external costs are ignored, supply curves of goods whose production results in negative externalities lie farther to the right than when firms pay the *full* cost of production. Therefore the market price is lower, and the quantity produced and exchanged is larger than is socially desirable. This principle is illustrated in Figure 7.1.

When polluting firms are allowed to ignore the negative externalities they impose on society, the supply curve of the product (S_1) reflects only the private costs of producing. Given the demand curve for the product (D), the market price is P_1 and the quantity exchanged is Q_1. If the firms were fully charged for these spillover costs, the supply curve would shift leftward to S_2, reflecting the true cost of production from society's viewpoint. As a result of the higher cost of production, market price would rise to P_2 and quantity of output produced and exchanged would fall to Q_2. This represents the optimum output from society's viewpoint.

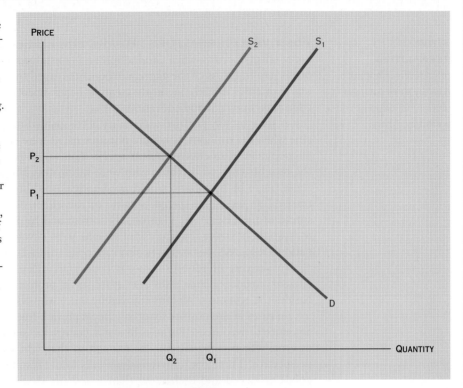

FIGURE 7.1

In the absence of government intervention, the supply curve of the product (electricity, steel, plutonium) whose production yields negative external effects is S_1. Given the demand curve (D), the market price is P_1 and the quantity produced and exchanged is Q_1. If a government forces a firm to pay the full costs by imposing a per-unit tax on a product equal to the per-unit spillover costs to society, the supply curve shifts leftward to S_2. This drives up the price to P_2 and reduces the quantity exchanged to Q_2. Because the cost of production in this scenario reflects the full cost to society, the reduced output (Q_2) is optimal from society's viewpoint. The moral: free markets fail by giving us too much of those goods whose production involves negative externalities and therefore too little of everything else.[1]

There are several ways that governments can deal with the problem of negative externalities. As suggested, governments can impose a tax on production in order to drive up the price and reduce output. Also, governments can require firms to install pollution abatement equipment, regulate firms' output or shut them down, or sell

---

[1]A less obvious application of market failure resulting from negative externalities is that of oil-tanker spills. Although such *spills* are described as "accidents," their frequency may be attributed to the fact that only a portion of the costs involved are borne by those responsible for the spills. Hence, from society's viewpoint, inadequate precautions are taken. If the oil companies were charged the full cost of such spills, their occurrence would be extremely rare. (Oil companies would take measures to ensure that tanker captains are not intoxicated while on duty.)

pollution rights. As to selling rights, polluting firms would be required to purchase the right to pollute, and the proceeds could, in principle, be used to reimburse those harmed by the pollution.

POSITIVE EXTERNALITIES

Benefits received but not paid for by third parties as a result of production or consumption by others.

POSITIVE EXTERNALITIES **Positive externalities** occur when positive third-party effects occur—when production and consumption of a good confer benefits on society in excess of the aggregate benefits reaped by the consumers of the product. Examples include medical research, other scientific research on the cutting edge of technology, and education.

A substantially positive externality accompanied development of the polio vaccine when the millions who were not vaccinated were spared the disease. Similarly, development of an effective AIDS vaccination would benefit society far in excess of the benefits enjoyed by those who were vaccinated. Millions of persons (including those yet to be born) who would not be vaccinated but who otherwise would contract AIDS would be spared because of the effect of the vaccine in slowing the spread of the disease. In addition, all current and future medical insurance premiums would be lower if a successful vaccine were developed. Thus, the share of the nation's resources devoted to health care costs would be reduced.

In the case of education, positive external effects occur because an informed citizenry reduces crime rates and other social problems, and yields other benefits besides the economic benefits enjoyed by those who obtain the education.

In cases where positive external effects prevail, free markets allocate suboptimal amounts of resources. Because demand curves for such products ignore positive external effects, they are not far enough to the right when viewed from society's perspective. Therefore, unfettered markets would result in a lower quantity of such goods produced and exchanged than is socially desirable. Consequently, governments might justifiably intervene through subsidies for medical and scientific research, provision of public schools, and other mechanisms for stimulating output of goods with positive external effects.

PROVIDING PUBLIC GOODS

PUBLIC GOOD

A good or service that cannot be provided for one person without being made available to others, and once provided for one person can be provided for others at no additional cost.

A second example of market failure that necessitates government intervention in the economy involves a unique product known as a public good. A **public good** has two special characteristics. First, it cannot be withheld from those who do not pay for it (it lacks the *excludability* characteristic possessed by a private good). Second, once produced, the cost of providing the good or service to an extra user is negligible or zero. Examples of a public good include national defense, lighthouses, and the national weather bureau. Because of its unique characteristics, a public good is provided collectively to society rather than privately to individuals.

Consider national defense. A defense system benefits me whether I help pay for it or not. It is inherently impossible to deny me the benefits of the system once it is in place. In contrast, if I refuse to pay for a Big Mac or a haircut (private goods), I am effectively barred from obtaining the good or service. Further in contrast to the hamburger or haircut, it costs nothing to provide the services of national defense, lighthouses, and the weather bureau to me (an extra user).

Public goods must be provided collectively via governments or they are unlikely to be available—or will be available in inadequate quantity. Assume a large river valley has been plagued by periodic flooding and a private contractor is considering building a dam at a cost of $100 million. The contractor attempts to sell *subscriptions* to each of the several thousand inhabitants of the valley. Because each inhabitant knows that he or she will benefit from the dam irrespective of whether a subscription is purchased, there is an incentive to hold back and depend on the generosity of neighbors. This *free-rider* problem makes it unlikely that the project will ever get off the ground. Thus a government steps in, builds the dam, and uses its taxing authority to pay for the project.

Star Wars: A Public or Private Good?

IN ORDER TO HOLD DOWN GROWTH OF THE NATIONAL DEBT, ASSUME THE GOVERNMENT DECIDES TO MARKET THE SDI SYSTEM ("STAR WARS") PRIVATELY BY USING A PRIVATE FIRM TO SELL SUBSCRIPTIONS TO THE AMERICAN PEOPLE. ESTIMATED COST OF THE PROJECT OVER THE NEXT DECADE IS $900 BILLION (APPROXIMATELY $3,600 PER AMERICAN, OR $12,000 PER HOUSEHOLD). ANALYZE THE VIABILITY OF THE PROPOSAL.

Note that many goods and services provided by governments do not strictly meet the criteria for public goods. For example, education is not a public good in the sense we have defined the concept; in principle, it can be withheld from nonpayers. Also, the cost of educating an additional person is certainly not zero. A system of private education coexists with our public system. The public education concept is usually defended on the basis of positive external effects and other grounds—not because it is a public good in the technical sense. Police protection comes very close to being a pure public good. It is extremely difficult to exclude me from the benefits of police protection (lower crime rates) if I refuse to help pay for it. In addition, the cost of protecting an additional individual is small. And what about snow removal from public streets provided by local governments?

Many goods and services provided by governments are *quasi-public goods*, having some (but not all) of the characteristics of pure public goods as we have defined them. Consider public libraries, tennis courts, golf courses, swimming pools, and roads.

Public Choice Theory

We have so far discussed the role of government from an idealistic viewpoint. That is, we have shown how government intervention in the economy, *in principle*, can benefit society. In this chapter and elsewhere in the book, we argue that governments, among many other things: (1) promote competition and regulate monopoly to help consumers, (2) pursue monetary and fiscal policies to stabilize the economy, (3) redistribute income to alleviate poverty, (4) correct for problems associated with externalities, and (5) provide public goods that markets undersupply.

Does this public interest theory of government help us understand governments as they actually function? The actions of governments do not always achieve such lofty goals. In later chapters, when we discuss such topics as agriculture, international trade, regulation, and budget deficits, we will see that governments frequently pursue policies that have the effect of shifting income from consumers (including poor and middle-income consumers) to wealthy producers; shielding existing producers from competition and promoting inefficient production (both at the expense of consumers); and implementing policies that have effects opposite to stated objectives.

Thus, when governments step in to correct a problem, the results typically are not straightforward improvements in efficiency and equity enjoyed by a well-served and satisfied public. In most cases, we see substantial departures of results from the stated good intentions. Of course, our standard for judging government actions, like our standard for markets, is not perfection. But the record of government performance seems particularly bleak. Is this an accident or is there something systematic about government that leads to our disappointment? Can economic analysis help us understand why government is so often disappointing? It is this issue that is at the heart of **public choice analysis**.

PUBLIC CHOICE ANALYSIS

The application of basic economic principles to analyze government decision making.

Many analysts claim that public choice theory helps us explain and understand the actual, as opposed to the ideal, behavior of government. Public choice analysts assume that government actions, like market actions, are the results of individual choice behavior. They argue that the only important differences between the public choices indicated by government actions and the private choices seen elsewhere in the economy result from differing institutional constraints facing individual decision makers. In private markets individuals face constraints created by prices and technology, and in politics they face constraints created by a political system that combines diverse views to arrive at political outcomes. An individual generally can choose what to have for lunch today, but the same individual cannot choose the kind of lunch to be served in the cafeteria of the local public school. He or she can choose to run for school board, or to vote for this candidate or that, or to lobby the local school authorities, or to take other political actions, but the choice itself is out of reach of the individual. The constraints on public choices are fundamentally different than the constraints on private choices, while the individuals making the choices are the same. Public choice analysis—the use of economic analysis to understand the effects of political constraints on individual behavior in public matters—helps us to understand the frequently perverse behavior of government.

Although many of the central insights of public choice theory were well known in the eighteenth and nineteenth centuries (discussed in such important works as Adam Smith's *The Wealth of Nations*), these ideas have been most effectively rehabilitated in recent decades by Professors James Buchanan and Gordon Tullock and their students, colleagues, and other followers. Buchanan describes public choice theory in the following way:

> Public choice theory has been the avenue through which a romantic and illusory set of notions about the workings of governments and the behavior of persons who govern has been replaced by a set of notions that embody more skepticism about what governments can do and what governors will do, notions that are surely more consistent with the political reality that we may all observe about us.[2]

Buchanan labels this revised view of government "politics without romance."

---

[2]James Buchanan, "Politics without Romance: A Sketch of Positive Public Choice Theory and Its Normative Implications." Reprinted in James M. Buchanan and Robert D. Tollison, eds., *The Theory of Public Choice—II* (Ann Arbor: University of Michigan Press, 1984), p. 11.

THE FOUNDATIONS OF PUBLIC CHOICE THEORY

Buchanan, who received the 1986 Nobel Prize in economics for this work, argues that public choice theory rests on three assumptions. The first is "methodological individualism," the idea that political action is ultimately the result of individual choices. Second is the assumption of "economic man," the idea that individuals pursue a policy of self-interest in both private and public actions (although self-interest need not be the only motivation). Finally, he views "politics as exchange," which means that in politics, as in private markets, we engage in exchange to further our interests. Buchanan's main inference from these assumptions is his "theory of constitutions," which attempts to understand the particular set of political constraints we observe and to derive better constraints. Thus, Buchanan focuses on the political choice process rather than the outcomes or government actions that come out of the process.

Others have been more concerned with the outcomes. The unhappy implication of the above assumptions is that individual actions in the political sphere are often designed to harm the many to serve the few or to harm the poor to serve the wealthy. Mancur Olson explains how political choices will systematically favor policies that bring concentrated benefits to small groups at the expense of large but widely dispersed costs imposed on the many.[3] The individuals making up small groups tend to have greater incentives to take forceful political action than do the individuals making up large groups. Members of large groups are unwilling to devote much effort to political endeavors because individually they face small gains or losses. The issue is left to the small group with large individual stakes. What's worse, members of the small, concentrated *special-interest group* have powerful incentives to devote resources to learning about the issues affecting them, while members of the large, diffuse group (having little at stake) remain ignorant of the issues. Most consumers and taxpayers never know what hit them.

RENT SEEKING

In one of the major branches of public choice analysis, Gordon Tullock and others have intensively studied the pursuit of government actions on grants that convey excessive profits, a process known as *rent seeking*. Examples of rent seeking include lobbying Congress to limit sugar imports, thereby doubling the price of candy and other sweets, and bribing a local official to award a contract to your firm rather than to a competitor. Two negative consequences emerge from this process. The first is the more visible harm to consumers who have to pay excessive prices resulting from the government action. The second is more subtle and probably more harmful. This is the wasteful use of society's resources either to acquire the government grant or to protect oneself against its acquisition by others. Tullock describes a country beset by pervasive rent seeking:

> First there was a very large number of economic institutions which promoted inefficiency—government-sponsored monopoly, for example. Numerous and detailed

---

[3]Mancur Olson, *The Logic of Collective Action* (Cambridge, Mass.: Harvard University Press, 1965); *The Rise and Decline of Nations* (New Haven: Yale University Press, 1982).

regulations which not only created monopolies but sharply reduced efficiency were also very common. Second, the principal economic activity of the more intelligent and better-educated citizens was not actually producing things but attempting to achieve returns of one sort or another or at least to avoid exploitation by achieving the favor and special consideration of the government. It was obvious that this activity, although personally profitable, was socially unproductive.[4]

These rent-seeking activities impede the economic growth of the nation and adversely affect the distribution of income.

CONCLUSION

Public choice theory has two important implications. First, it provides a convincing example of the power of economic analysis to help us understand human behavior and the world we observe. Second, it helps us avoid romantic, wishful notions of using government to solve our economic problems. It forces us to examine government as it actually is.

The Growth, Size, and Allocation of Government Spending

GROWTH IN GOVERNMENT

Although we live in a predominantly capitalistic economy in which the bulk of our needs are satisfied by private enterprise, government has grown enormously in size and scope during the past 100 years. This growth has occurred in virtually all industrial nations. At the beginning of the twentieth century in the United States, combined government expenditures (federal, state, and local) amounted to roughly 8 percent of our gross domestic product. No federal income tax existed before 1913. Revenues from taxes on tobacco and liquor, and tariffs on imports sufficed to balance the federal budget. By 1993, combined government expenditures amounted to approximately 36 percent of our GDP. How can we explain this enormous expansion of government? Several factors have contributed.

THE URBANIZATION MOVEMENT Demand for goods and services (schools, roads, parks, and so forth) provided by governments has grown faster than the nation's collective income. The movement from a predominantly rural society in which people are relatively self-sufficient to an urban society in which people are highly specialized and interdependent has crucial implications. For example, such a transformation greatly impacts the need for public facilities: streets, transportation, police and fire protection, sanitation.

---

[4]Gordon Tullock, "The Backward Society: Static Inefficiency, Rent Seeking, and the Rule of Law," in James M. Buchanan and Robert D. Tollison, eds., *The Theory of Public Choice—II* (Ann Arbor: University of Michigan Press, 1984), p. 224.

A farmer in the last century may have drawn his water from his well, fed his garbage to his pigs, and protected his family with his rifle. His grandson in the city would be ill-advised to try to provide these services for himself.[5]

WAR AND DEFENSE   Prior to World War II, we did not maintain a huge and expensive military operation in times of peace. We did not maintain military bases and armed forces throughout the world. Nor did we maintain a great and permanent arsenal of enormously expensive weapons. The escalation of the Cold War (1945–1950) increased the share of government expenditures on defense. In the 1980s, defense spending constituted about 25 percent of federal government expenditures and 6 percent of the nation's gross domestic product. Largely because of the demise of the Soviet Union as a military threat, these ratios are on a declining trajectory.

EGALITARIANISM AND INCOME SECURITY   Government has increasingly provided for those adversely affected by the force of economic events as well as for those unable to provide for themselves because of infirmities. In earlier times, each family cared for its aged, infirm, and handicapped. Those without families lived on pittances in a state of squalor. As life expectancy lengthened, family ties weakened, and average living standards increased, public support programs proliferated—including welfare payments, unemployment benefits, Social Security, and agricultural subsidies. Increasingly, the masses of middle-class Americans have voted themselves more generous medical, retirement, and income support programs. Expanded spending on such income security programs is the primary source of increase in the share of GDP spent by government in the past 30 years.

GOVERNMENT EXPENDITURES—PURCHASES AND TRANSFERS

Government expenditures consist of two principal categories: *government purchases of goods and services* and *government transfer payments*. Government purchases involve the costs of such finished goods as computers, tanks, and desks as well as the costs of such government employees as supreme court justices, highway patrol officers, high-school teachers, postal workers, and grounds keepers. These **government purchases** are *exhaustive* in that they consume or preempt economic resources—such resources are thus diverted from private use for use in providing public goods and services.

GOVERNMENT PURCHASES
Federal, state, and local government spending on final goods and services, including costs of hiring government employees but excluding government transfer payments.

GOVERNMENT TRANSFER PAYMENTS
Government payments for which no good or service is currently rendered to the government.

Government transfer payments involve government payments to individuals or firms for which no concurrent good or service is provided to the government in exchange. Examples include Social Security benefits, welfare payments, unemployment compensation, veterans' benefits, and interest paid on federal debt. Government transfer payments differ from government purchases in that transfers are *nonexhaustive*. Transfers do not consume economic resources or reallocate them away from private use. The system of taxes and transfer payments merely transfers income—and claims to real resources—within the private sector of the economy.

Figure 7.2 indicates the pattern of total federal, state, and local government expenditures—government purchases and transfer payments—relative to GDP

[5]Otto Eckstein, *Public Finance*, (Englewood Cliffs, N.J.: Prentice-Hall, 1964) p. 4.

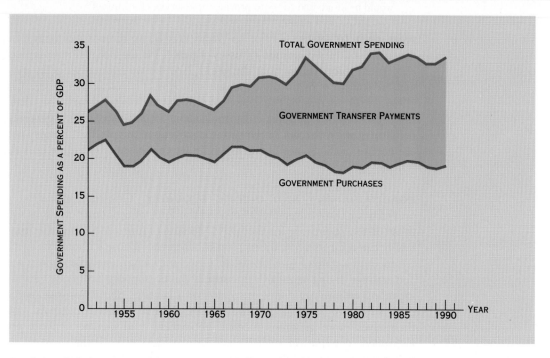

Purchases of goods and services by federal, state, and local governments have continued to absorb about 20 percent of GDP since 1960. The explosive growth of transfer payments accounts for the rising path of total government spending relative to GDP.

SOURCE: *Economic Report of the President*, 1992.

FIGURE 7.2

since 1955. Note that although the ratio of total government spending to GDP has risen, this is accounted for almost entirely by the growth of transfer payments. Government purchases have continued to absorb approximately 20 percent of GDP since 1960.[6] Transfer payments have risen from roughly 6 percent to 16 percent of GDP in the same period.

MEASURING THE RELATIVE SIZE OF GOVERNMENT

Which is the better measure of the size of government—total spending (including transfer payments) or government purchases only? The answer depends on one's reason for asking the question. If one is trying to measure the portion of the nation's output absorbed or consumed by government, one looks at government purchases, which indicate the amount of economic resources removed from the private sector in order to satisfy the desire for goods provided by government. In this

[6]The ratio of government purchases/GDP increased sharply from 1900–1960. This increase was due chiefly to greater urbanization and resulting growth in demand for public goods, and the emergence of the American defense establishment following World War II.

case government transfers are omitted because such funds are collected from the private sector and are paid back to the private sector, thus remaining available to satisfy private wants.

Nevertheless, total government spending (purchases plus transfers) is in many ways the superior measure of the magnitude of government. It is true that transfer payments do not consume real resources. However, the government determines to whom these resources are available via its system of taxes and transfers. Total expenditures (including transfers) indicate the share of the economy for which government decision making replaces private-market decision making. Assuming the norm of balanced budgets in the long run, total expenditures also indicate the fraction of the nation's GDP that must be paid in taxes to operate the government. By these standards, government has continued to expand steadily relative to GDP.

Although government spending in the United States has grown relative to GDP, in many nations government spending is considerably larger than in the United States. Figure 7.3 indicates the ratio of government expenditures to GDP in a sample of nations. A clear pattern exists for countries that are highly developed economically: they exhibit relatively large government sectors.

GOVERNMENT SPENDING—WHERE DOES IT GO?

Figure 7.4 (page 174) illustrates the allocation of federal expenditures and combined state- and local-government expenditures among alternative uses.

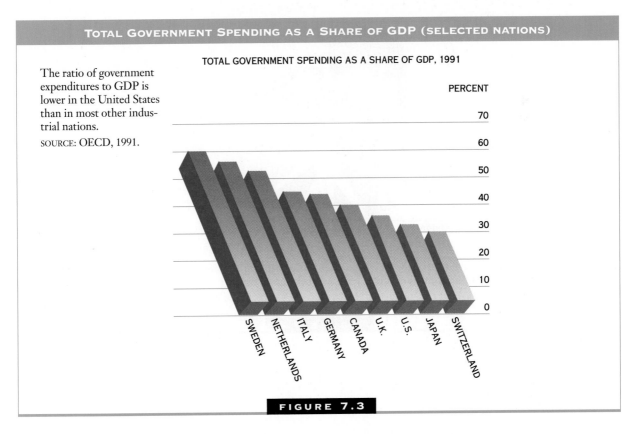

TOTAL GOVERNMENT SPENDING AS A SHARE OF GDP (SELECTED NATIONS)

TOTAL GOVERNMENT SPENDING AS A SHARE OF GDP, 1991

The ratio of government expenditures to GDP is lower in the United States than in most other industrial nations.

SOURCE: OECD, 1991.

FIGURE 7.3

FEDERAL GOVERNMENT

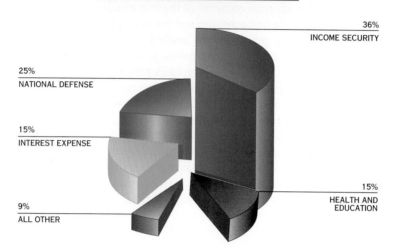

36%
INCOME SECURITY

25%
NATIONAL DEFENSE

15%
INTEREST EXPENSE

15%
HEALTH AND
EDUCATION

9%
ALL OTHER

STATE AND LOCAL
GOVERNMENTS

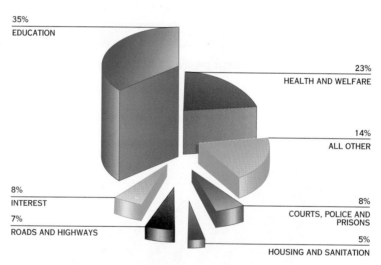

35%
EDUCATION

23%
HEALTH AND WELFARE

14%
ALL OTHER

8%
INTEREST

7%
ROADS AND HIGHWAYS

8%
COURTS, POLICE AND
PRISONS

5%
HOUSING AND SANITATION

Federal government expenditures are chiefly for income security and national defense; most of state/local government spending is for education and health and welfare.

SOURCE: U.S. Department of Commerce, *Survey of Current Business*, 1992, and *Economic Report of the President*, 1992.

FIGURE 7.4

The largest components of federal expenditures are economic security (Social Security, farm subsidies), national defense, and health and education programs. However, interest expense (debt service) has been the fastest-growing expenditure during the past 15 years. This growth is attributable to the string of huge federal budget deficits that has quadrupled our national debt since 1980. A larger stock of debt (given the level of interest rates) necessitates larger annual interest expense for the debtor (the federal government).

The largest single expenditure for state and local governments is education. Other uses of state/local funds, in order of magnitude, include health and welfare, roads and highways, and courts, police, and prisons.

Paying for Government Expenditures— Taxation

In principle, governments have access to three potential sources of funds to pay for their expenditures: printing money, borrowing from private individuals and firms, and levying taxes. Because only the federal government has the authority to print money, the first source is not open to state and local governments. Furthermore, national governments that have resorted to printing money to finance major expenditures have unleashed enormous inflationary forces.[7] Hence, the first source is not really a viable or responsible means for financing government. The second source— borrowing—is prohibited by statute for most state and local governments, except in the case of financing such capital expenditures as schools and roads. The heavy resort to borrowing by the federal government has serious adverse consequences, which are analyzed in Chapter 21.

That leaves taxation as the most prudent source of revenues for all levels of government. In the balance of this chapter, we analyze the various aspects of taxation, including the major types of taxes used to finance federal, state, and local government in the United States. We also analyze the two most significant pieces of federal income-tax legislation enacted in recent decades.

THE FUNCTION OF TAXES

One might view the purpose of taxes in two ways. The obvious function is to provide revenues with which to pay for goods and services provided by government. An alternative and more sophisticated way of viewing taxes is to regard them as a vehicle for releasing such real resources as steel, lumber, and workers from the production of private goods so they may be used to produce such government goods and services as schools, highways, missiles, and postal services. Taxes serve this function by depressing demand for (and therefore output of) private goods and services. For example, income taxes depress private consumption expenditures and output. Sales taxes perform a similar role. Property taxes motivate the building of

---

[7]Severe inflation, known as hyperinflation, was experienced by several European nations in the early 1920s and again in the late 1940s as a result of printing money to finance war. In 1923, several trillion German marks were required to purchase what one mark purchased in 1913. On this, see Exhibit 15.1.

less elaborate houses; they also reduce spendable income, thereby restraining consumption.

PROGRESSIVE, PROPORTIONAL, AND REGRESSIVE TAXES

Various types of taxes may be classified by how total tax liability varies with level of income.

PROGRESSIVE TAX
The fraction of income paid in tax rises as income rises.

1. A **progressive tax** is one in which the percentage of income paid in taxes rises with the level of income. A person who earns twice as much income pays more than twice as much tax. A familiar example is the federal income tax (as well as the state income tax), with its pattern of percentage tax brackets rising with income.

PROPORTIONAL TAX
The fraction of income paid in tax remains constant at all income levels.

2. A **proportional tax** is one in which the percentage of income paid in taxes is the same for all income levels. A person who earns twice as much income pays exactly twice as much tax. Although examples are not easy to find, certain taxes come close to being proportional within fairly broad ranges of income (though not for all ranges of income).

REGRESSIVE TAX
The fraction of income paid in tax declines as income rises.

3. A **regressive tax** is one in which the percentage of income paid in taxes declines as income rises. Those with high incomes yield a smaller fraction of their income to the government than those with lower incomes. A classic example is the *poll tax*, in which each individual is charged a flat fee (perhaps $2) in order to vote. This tax was outlawed in 1973 by the 24th Amendment to the U.S. Constitution.

The concepts of progressive, proportional, and regressive taxes are illustrated schematically in Figure 7.5.

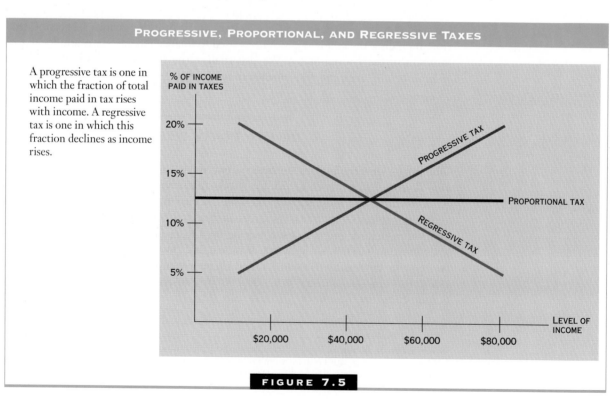

PROGRESSIVE, PROPORTIONAL, AND REGRESSIVE TAXES

A progressive tax is one in which the fraction of total income paid in tax rises with income. A regressive tax is one in which this fraction declines as income rises.

FIGURE 7.5

SHIFTING AND INCIDENCE OF TAXES

TAX INCIDENCE
The distribution of the tax burden—that is, who ultimately pays the tax.

As you think of various types of taxes, ask yourself whether each type appears to be progressive, proportional, or regressive. In certain cases the answer is more complex than meets the eye; this is because the tax is not always borne by the entity that actually remits the tax to the government. The **incidence** of a tax refers to the resting place of the tax—who actually absorbs or bears the burden of the tax. In many cases taxes are *shifted* to second parties through higher prices, increased rents, lower wages, and the like. For example, apartment owners may shift all or part of an increase in property taxes to tenants by raising rents. Excise taxes levied on the sale of cigarettes may be partially shifted to consumers through higher prices. Although economists agree that the burden of the corporate income tax is shared by the public (via higher prices), by the owners of the corporation (via lower after-tax profits), and by the employees of the corporation (via lower wages and fringe benefits), they disagree on how this burden is distributed among the three.

CONCEPTS OF EQUITY OR FAIRNESS

Issues of equity fall into the domain of *normative economics*. Reasonable individuals often differ in their interpretation of what is equitable or fair. In the area of taxation there are two broad, generally accepted norms of equity. It is widely agreed that our system of taxation should conform to the norms of horizontal and vertical equity. **Horizontal equity** means that those with equal ability to pay taxes should be treated equally (that is, they should pay the same amount of taxes). **Vertical equity** refers to the principle that those of unequal ability should be treated unequally. Specifically, those with greater ability to pay should pay a larger absolute (and perhaps relative) amount of taxes.

When society perceives that widespread violations of the principles of horizontal and vertical equity exist in the tax code, taxpayer morale and compliance is likely to deteriorate. Certain federal tax reforms in recent years were implemented to remedy perceived gross violations of these principles.

The Federal Tax System

The sources of funds used to finance the federal government are illustrated in Figure 7.6.

Unlike earlier decades, the 1980s and 1990s became the era of huge federal budget deficits, when more than one-sixth of the funds expended by the federal government were obtained through borrowing. Of the remaining funds expended, more than 90 percent were obtained through three taxes—the individual income tax, the payroll tax, and the corporate income tax.

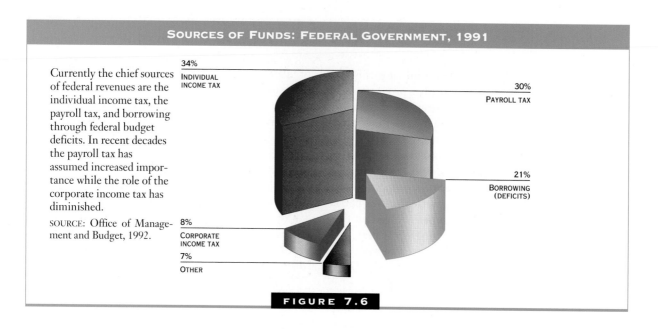

Currently the chief sources of federal revenues are the individual income tax, the payroll tax, and borrowing through federal budget deficits. In recent decades the payroll tax has assumed increased importance while the role of the corporate income tax has diminished.

SOURCE: Office of Management and Budget, 1992.

34%
INDIVIDUAL INCOME TAX

30%
PAYROLL TAX

21%
BORROWING (DEFICITS)

8%
CORPORATE INCOME TAX

7%
OTHER

FIGURE 7.6

INDIVIDUAL INCOME TAX

Everyone is familiar with the **federal individual income tax**; it is the chief source of revenue for the U.S. Treasury. Given the perspective of U.S. history, however, it is a fairly recent source of revenue. The federal income tax was established in 1913 by the 16th Amendment to the U.S. Constitution, but was a minor source of federal revenue until the 1940s. Income tax rates were raised to extremely high levels during World War II, the top rate set at 91 percent. Tax rates have been lowered several times since then, including two major cuts in the 1980s. Today the top rate is 31 percent.

Each year April 15 is a day of reckoning, as more than 110 million taxpayers are required to file a tax return and to settle up with the Internal Revenue Service. However, April 15 is fairly painless for most taxpayers because most have paid the bulk of their income taxes through regular *withholding* from paychecks during the calendar year. Employers are required to withhold funds from paychecks and to forward the proceeds, together with payroll tax receipts, to the IRS. The majority of taxpayers deliberately arrange to have their employer *overwithhold*, thus assuring a rebate from the IRS after the annual tax return is filed.

To illustrate the nature of the individual income tax, consider Table 7.1, which applies to a married couple with two children filing a joint income tax return in April 1992 (for calendar year 1991).

In figuring tax liability, individuals and couples first calculate **adjusted gross income**. This is computed by adding total wage or salary income, dividends and interest earned, and other forms of income, then subtracting certain allowable **adjustments** including alimony paid, moving expenses, and contributions to retirement plans. **Taxable income** is then calculated by subtracting exemptions and deductions from adjusted gross income. The allowance for *personal exemptions* was $2,150 per person in 1991. Thus a family of four would have had $8,600 in

FEDERAL INCOME TAX FOR FAMILY OF FOUR, 1991*				
ADJUSTED GROSS INCOME	TAXABLE INCOME	PERSONAL INCOME TAX	AVERAGE TAX RATE (%)	MARGINAL TAX RATE (%)
$ 10,000	$ 0	$ 0	0	0
20,000	5,700	855	4.3	15
30,000	15,700	2,355	7.9	15
40,000	25,700	3,855	9.6	15
60,000	45,700	8,376	14.0	28
100,000	85,700	19,682	19.7	31
1,000,000	985,700	298,682	29.9	31

*Assumes family uses standard deduction ($5,700 in 1991) rather than itemizing. The personal exemption was $2,150 in 1991. Both the personal exemption and the standard deduction are indexed to increase each year in line with the nation's consumer price index.

TABLE 7.1

exemptions. In specifying total *deductions*, taxpayers have the option of *itemizing* various allowable deductions such as interest paid on a mortgage and charitable contributions, or accepting a *standard deduction*. In Table 7.1 we assume the family opts for the $5,700 standard deduction. Because of exemptions and deductions, the first $14,300 of adjusted gross income is shielded from income taxes for this family.[8]

We observe first that the personal income tax is progressive. This is indicated by the fact that the **average tax rate**—the fraction of income paid in taxes—rises with income.

AVERAGE TAX RATE
The percentage of total income paid in taxes.

$$\text{average tax rate (ATR)} = \frac{\text{tax paid}}{\text{income}}$$

According to the fourth column of Table 7.1, a family earning $20,000 pays 4.3 percent of this to the IRS, whereas a family earning $40,000 pays 9.6 percent and a family earning $100,000 pays 19.7 percent. A doubling of income more than doubles tax liability, implying that the tax is progressive.

The last column of Table 7.1 indicates the **marginal tax rate**—the percentage of any *increment* of income that must be paid in taxes.

MARGINAL TAX RATE
The percentage of an *additional* dollar of income paid in taxes.

$$\text{marginal tax rate (MTR)} = \frac{\text{increment in taxes paid}}{\text{increment of income}}$$

For taxable income, the personal income tax code currently has three marginal tax brackets. For joint returns, the first $34,000 of taxable income is subject to a marginal tax rate of 15 percent. Taxable income between $34,000 and $82,150 is

[8]Actually, Table 7.1 neglects two details of the tax law and therefore may be slightly in error in some instances, although the basic conclusions are unaltered. First, the maximum tax rate for income earned in the form of long-term capital gains is 28 percent rather than 31 percent. Second, the total amount allowable as a deduction for personal exemptions in computing taxable income is reduced by 2 percent for each $2,500 by which the taxpayer's adjusted gross income exceeds $150,000. Thus, the personal exemption is totally phased out when family income reaches $275,000.

taxed at 28 percent. Taxable income in excess of $82,150 is taxed at 31 percent.[9] This tax structure is simpler than the structure that prevailed before the Tax Reform Act of 1986. Prior to that legislation, there were 14 marginal tax brackets, ranging from a low of 11 percent to a high of 50 percent.

The marginal tax rate is an important concept in economic analysis. Because it indicates the percentage of any *addition* to income that must be given up in taxes, the marginal tax rate is believed to influence incentives to work, invest, and take risks in order to earn extra income. One of the cornerstones of the Reagan Administration's policies in the 1980s was to reduce marginal tax rates in order to stimulate such incentives, thereby seeking to ignite an expansion in the nation's output and standard of living.

PROGRESSIVITY OF THE PERSONAL INCOME TAX   Two factors account for the progressive nature of the federal income tax (as illustrated in Table 7.1). The first several thousand dollars of adjusted gross income is not subject to any tax at all because of exemptions and deductions. A family of four taking the standard deduction owes no tax on the first $14,300 of income.[10] This is true whether the family earned a total of $20,000 or $100,000. Hence, a smaller percentage of a lower-income family's earnings are subject to the income tax. Moreover, the marginal tax rate is higher for upper-income families. These factors explain the progressive nature of the tax and the fact that the average tax rate converges toward, but never reaches, the marginal rate as income rises.

In reality the individual income tax is not as progressive as Table 7.1 suggests. Although the table assumes taxpayers choose the $5,700 standard deduction, many higher-income individuals itemize deductions (many of which are called "loopholes" by critics), taking advantage of many features that open a large gap between total income earned and taxable income.

In addition, the degree of progressivity of the income tax has been significantly reduced in recent decades. A series of tax reductions since the 1950s has reduced rates for all income levels, but especially for the upper brackets.[11] Prior to the income-tax cuts of the 1980s, upper-income individuals increasingly arranged their financial affairs so as to avoid taxes legally by using more of the generous array of deductions and credits.

As a result of the decline in progressivity of the individual income tax and the sharply expanded role of the payroll tax, the overall American tax system today (including all types of taxes) is roughly proportional or perhaps slightly progressive. A 1985 study, which employed relatively progressive assumptions about the incidence of various taxes, indicated that the richest 10 percent of Americans yielded

---

[9]These threshold income levels ($34,000 and $82,150 for joint returns) at which one jumps to higher marginal tax brackets are indexed to the consumer price index. Hence, if by the year 1999 the consumer price index has increased by 30 percent, these two thresholds will be 30 percent higher. Also, the allowance for the personal exemption ($2,150 in 1991) and the standard deduction ($5,700 in 1991 for joint returns) will increase over time in line with the consumer price index. Such indexation is designed to prevent *bracket creep*, the process by which inflation formerly bumped taxpayers into higher marginal tax brackets, thereby causing the percentage of income paid in taxes to rise over time as the price level increased.

[10]Each member receives a $2,150 exemption, and the standard deduction is $5,700 for the family. Hence, exemptions and deductions total $14,300 in 1991 (more in later years).

[11]The top bracket, for example, dropped from 91 percent in the early 1950s to 31 percent today. Middle- and lower-income bracket rates have not dropped as much, absolutely or relatively.

25.3 percent of their income in taxes, whereas the poorest 10 percent paid 21.9 percent.[12] The corresponding ratios for 1966 were estimated at 30.1 percent and 16.8 percent, respectively.

The Flat Tax: Is It Proportional?

SUPPOSE THAT OUR CURRENT INCOME TAX SYSTEM IS EXCHANGED FOR ONE IN WHICH ALL TAXABLE INCOME IS TAXED AT A FLAT RATE OF 20 PERCENT, BUT THAT DEDUCTIONS AND EXEMPTIONS ARE RETAINED. SUPPOSE, FOR A JOINT RETURN, THE STANDARD DEDUCTION IS $6,000 AND THE EXEMPTION IS $2,500 PER PERSON. ASSUMING A FAMILY OF FOUR FILING A JOINT RETURN, CONSTRUCT A TABLE WITH COLUMNS INDICATING GROSS INCOME, TAXABLE INCOME, TAX LIABILITY AND THE AVERAGE TAX RATE FOR GROSS INCOME LEVELS OF $20,000, $50,000, AND $100,000. IS THIS TAX REGRESSIVE, PROPORTIONAL, OR PROGRESSIVE? EXPLAIN.

TAX LOOPHOLES What are these *loopholes* that reduce the progressivity of the income tax and also produce numerous violations of the principles of horizontal and vertical equity? Although the Tax Reform Act of 1986 reduced the length of the list somewhat, many loopholes remain firmly entrenched in the law.

1. *Nontaxability of Interest on Municipal Bonds* Income received in the form of interest on bonds issued by municipalities and other political subdivisions (for example, water districts) is not taxable by the federal government. By the same token, state governments do not tax interest earned on U.S. government securities. If an individual invests $1 million in municipal bonds yielding 6 percent, the $60,000 annual stream of interest income is not subject to federal income taxation. This special treatment is defended on the basis of encouraging local communities to issue bonds to finance schools, roads, sewers, and the like. The tax-free nature of the bonds makes it possible for communities to borrow at lower interest rates, and thus enjoy lower local taxes. Critics charge that this subsidy creates inequities and is inefficient, costing the government much more in lost revenues than is saved by cities. The difference is a windfall tax break for affluent Americans.

2. *Preferential Treatment of Homeowners* Homeowners have access to two major deductions not available to renters: property taxes and interest on home mortgages. Consider two families with identical incomes and circumstances, except that one rents and the other owns. The renter pays considerably more income taxes, a violation of the principle of horizontal equity. Also, because homeowners have higher incomes on average than renters, this circumstance reduces the progressivity of the income tax.

3. *Other Loopholes* Many fringe benefits are not taxable by the IRS. Suppose California pays its new English professors $25,000 per year and throws in $5,000 worth of insurance premiums covering medical, dental, and life insurance. Suppose Colorado pays its new English professors $30,000 but

[12]See Joseph Pechman, *Who Paid the Taxes, 1966–85?* (Washington, D.C.: The Brookings Institution, 1985). Results such as these depend upon certain assumptions regarding tax incidence and are therefore somewhat controversial. When Pechman uses less-progressive assumptions about tax incidence, the overall tax system actually appears slightly regressive.

provides no such fringe benefits. Although the two teachers are compensated equally, the Colorado teacher pays tax on $5,000 of additional income. Some argue that fringe benefits are a form of income and should be treated as such.

Another loophole deals with tax treatment of funds contributed to certain retirement programs. Many professionals and self-employed individuals establish retirement accounts and contribute large chunks of current income to the accounts each year. Income contributed to such accounts is not subject to taxation until it is withdrawn at retirement. Meanwhile, income otherwise taxable is compounding over the years in the retirement account of the contributor. Typically, upper-bracket individuals avail themselves of these attractive retirement programs; lower-bracket taxpayers find it difficult to do so.[13] This circumstance diminishes the progressivity of the individual income tax.

One could go on at length detailing the inequities and loopholes in the income tax. Yet in spite of loopholes, the general perception seems to prevail that the income tax is the *best* or *fairest* form of tax. Perhaps for this reason the personal income tax is becoming an increasingly important source of state tax revenue. Only seven states currently have no income tax: Alaska, Florida, Nevada, South Dakota, Texas, Washington, and Wyoming.

PAYROLL TAX

In 1935, in the depths of the Great Depression, Congress enacted the Social Security Act—thus creating a compulsory social insurance system for workers and self-employed persons. Employees are entitled to receive retirement benefits (up to a ceiling level) based on previous earnings and independent of need. The **payroll tax** may be viewed as the compulsory premium paid to cover this *old-age* insurance, as well as disability insurance and Medicare benefits.

In 1992, each individual contributed 6.2 percent of the first $55,500 of wage and salary income for Social Security and an additional 1.45 percent of the first $130,200 of such income for Medicare. Employers are required to match these payments. The tax bases ($55,500 and $130,200) are indexed to rise with the price level over time.

The payroll tax is easily the most rapidly growing source of federal government revenue: the share of federal revenues provided by the payroll tax has doubled since 1960. The maximum annual contribution (employee plus employer) has increased from $348 in 1965 to more than $10,000 today, and continues to increase each year. Today the payroll tax generates almost as much revenue as the individual income tax.

The payroll tax is regressive. This is partly due to the fact that only the first $55,500 of wage and salary income is subject to the Social Security tax (and the first

---

[13]The Economic Recovery Tax Act of 1981 (ERTA) authorized establishment of individual retirement accounts (IRAs) for virtually all workers. Contributions are deductible from federal income taxes, but the maximum annual contribution is rather low relative to some of the programs used by upper-bracket taxpayers. The Tax Reform Act of 1986 restricted deductibility of IRA contributions to those earning less than $50,000 annually. This act also reduced the maximum deductible contributions allowable for other retirement programs.

$130,200 is subject to the Medicare tax). Income in excess of these thresholds is exempt from payroll taxes. In addition, wealthy individuals typically receive a larger portion of their total income from sources other than wages and salaries than do low-income recipients. Hence, a smaller fraction of the total income of the wealthy is subject to the payroll tax than is the case for lower-income recipients.

CORPORATE INCOME TAX

In 1950 the corporate income tax was second only to the individual income tax as a source of revenue for the federal government, accounting for about one-fourth of federal revenues. Because of liberalized depreciation allowances, expanded deductions, and tax credits—and especially because of the rapidly increasing role of payroll taxes—its relative importance declined sharply between the 1950s and the 1980s. By 1986, the corporate income tax contributed less than 10 percent of federal revenues. However, the Tax Reform Act of 1986 put a stop to this declining trend by eliminating certain deductions and tax credits and slowing depreciation allowances. On balance, the Tax Reform Act shifted roughly $120 billion in taxes from individuals to corporations over a five-year period ending in 1992.

The **corporate income tax** is levied on profits, not on gross corporate income. All costs—such as wages and interest expense—are deductible from gross income before arriving at taxable income (that is, profits). The corporate income-tax code applies a progressive or graduated tax-rate scale on profits of each corporation up to $100,000 and a flat ceiling of 34 percent against all profits above $100,000.[14] The tax therefore *appears* to be progressive overall, though basically proportional for large corporations earning more than $100,000. However, some economists believe that the corporate income tax is largely shifted forward onto consumers in the form of higher prices. This issue is controversial among economists, and extremely difficult to resolve. If the corporate income tax were fully shifted onto consumers through higher prices, it would be a regressive tax like the sales tax.

Quite a few economists oppose the corporate income tax on the ground that it represents *double taxation* of corporate profits. Taxes are first levied on corporate profits and then levied, via the individual income tax, on dividends paid to stockholders. This double taxation is alleged to impair investment spending, long-term growth of productivity, and growth of living standards. Such critics advocate abolishing the corporate income tax and collecting the revenues via the individual income tax at the time profits are paid to the owners (that is, the shareholders).

Advocates of the corporate income tax argue that its abolition would reduce federal revenues and necessitate increases in other taxes. Further, they believe the tax is progressive. If so, its elimination would further reduce the progressivity of the overall tax system.

---

[14]The existing top rate was reduced from 46 percent to 34 percent by the Tax Reform Act of 1986. However, the act also sharply reduced deductions and credits available to corporations. The net effect of the legislation was to raise significantly the taxes corporations actually pay.

E
X
H
I
B
I
T

7 . 1

The Social Security System— Will You Ever Receive Benefits?

In 1983, the Social Security system was essentially transformed from a pay-as-you-go system to one that is funded. Prior to 1983, the contributions for social insurance were directly transferred from workers to retirees. The monthly Social Security check your grandparents received came *not* from funds they paid in earlier but from the payroll taxes your parents were paying each month. The trust fund picked up any annual surplus of payroll taxes in excess of benefits paid out, and it made good on any deficit. But the size of the Social Security trust fund was relatively small, amounting typically to less than one year's outlays.

This system worked fine as long as we had stable population, wage, and salary growth without major demographic changes. Given these favorable conditions, an expanding volume of payroll tax receipts can adequately fund an expanding pool of retirees. However, departure from these conditions may impair the actuarial soundness of the system and precipitate a crisis of confidence in its long-term viability. The soundness of the Social Security system was called into question in the late 1970s because of a slowdown in population growth, important emerging changes in the age structure of the population, and a slowdown of real wage and salary growth.

For many years the average expected life of Americans has been rising. In addition, the U.S. birth rate increased sharply during the baby-boom years of 1946–1964. Given the typical retirement age of roughly 65 years, these factors assure a surge of retirees coming on stream after 2010. Moreover, the percentage of the population above age 65 is expected to double between 1990 and 2030. Because the birth rate declined significantly after 1964, the number of young workers entering the labor force began declining in the early 1980s. In earlier years there were about five current workers paying into the system for each retiree drawing benefits. That ratio is now slightly above 3:1, and is projected to decline to 2:1 by the year 2030.

Viewed from the perspective of the late 1970s, other factors also contributed

State and Local Government Finance

State and local governments rely heavily on sales and property taxes and on grants from the federal government. However, state and local government tax receipts traditionally have been insufficient to cover expenditures. A major portion of the shortfall has been covered by federal transfers or grants to state and local governments. Typically, the federal government allocates grants to the states and the states award grants to local governments. These grants may be restricted, *earmarked* for specific uses, or may be unrestricted, *block* grants. Since the late 1960s, an increasing portion of these transfers has been unrestricted. In the past ten years, the portion of state and local government revenues provided by grants has been

to an impending Social Security crisis. Real wages, which had grown steadily for generations, expanded more slowly after the 1960s. Congress liberalized benefits and expanded coverage to include a larger percentage of the population. This confluence of events made it readily apparent by the late 1970s that the system was in trouble.

In 1983, President Ronald Reagan appointed a bipartisan commission headed by Alan Greenspan (now chief of the Federal Reserve System). After studying the problem, the commission recommended a series of measures designed to increase revenues and reduce benefits. Congress immediately enacted these reforms into law.

As a result of these changes and the fact that the baby boomers are moving into their years of maximum earnings, today the trust fund is increasing rapidly and government actuaries expect it to reach the enormous sum of $12 trillion ($12,000 billion) by 2020. This means the fund would expand from about 3 percent of GDP in 1990 to about 30 percent of GDP in 2020. However, the fund is then expected to decline rapidly—as the masses of baby boomers retire—and be in the red by the year 2050.

The problem Social Security faces in the next decade or two is keeping Congress' hands off the nest egg. The surplus in Social Security is mixed in with general government revenues and expenditures in calculating the reported federal budget deficit. Because of the buildup of the trust fund, the reported budget deficit will be significantly reduced or eliminated in the next decade. This circumstance will surely tempt politicians to reduce taxes or expand programs. Such action would be utterly irresponsible, because all the surplus funds (and possibly more) will be needed to keep the Social Security system afloat in the second quarter of the next century. To protect the system, Social Security should be taken totally off budget as soon as possible.

declining. Lower levels of government increasingly have been required to call upon their own financial resources.

The sources of funds for all state and local governments combined are given in Figure 7.7 (page 186).

SALES TAX AND EXCISE TAX

The **sales tax** is a key source of revenue for most states, accounting for about one-third of the aggregate revenue of the 50 state governments. States typically levy a 4–7 percent charge on the value of sales, collectable from the merchants.[15] Some

---

[15]Five states have no general sales tax. These states are Alaska, Delaware, Montana, New Hampshire, and Oregon.

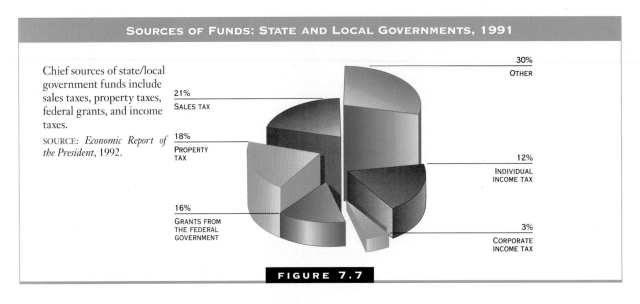

SOURCES OF FUNDS: STATE AND LOCAL GOVERNMENTS, 1991

Chief sources of state/local government funds include sales taxes, property taxes, federal grants, and income taxes.

SOURCE: *Economic Report of the President*, 1992.

30%
OTHER

21%
SALES TAX

18%
PROPERTY TAX

16%
GRANTS FROM THE FEDERAL GOVERNMENT

12%
INDIVIDUAL INCOME TAX

3%
CORPORATE INCOME TAX

FIGURE 7.7

states exempt food from the sales tax. A few states exempt certain other items, such as medical supplies. The sales tax is attractive to states because of its high yield and relatively low collection costs. Although the tax is levied on the seller, much of it is frequently shifted to the consumer.

The sales tax is regressive because it applies to expenditures but not to saving. On average, people with high incomes save a larger fraction of their incomes than do people with low incomes. Because a larger fraction of the low-income individual's income is spent, it is therefore subject to the sales tax. This principle is illustrated in Table 7.2.

The table assumes a 4 percent sales tax, and also assumes that expenditures rise less than proportionally with income. A family with $10,000 income is assumed to spend the entire income. Hence, the family pays $400 in sales taxes, or 4 percent of its income. A family with $20,000 income saves $2,000 and spends $18,000; it therefore pays $720 of sales taxes, or 3.6 percent of its income. As income rises, the percent of income spent declines. Hence, if a $100,000 income earner spends $50,000 annually, she pays $2,000 in sales taxes, or only 2 percent of income.[16] The

REGRESSIVITY OF A 4 PERCENT GENERAL SALES TAX

INCOME	SPENDING	TAX PAID	TAX PAID ÷ INCOME
$ 10,000	$10,000	$ 400	4.0%
20,000	18,000	720	3.6%
40,000	30,000	1,200	3.0%
100,000	50,000	2,000	2.0%

TABLE 7.2

[16]Table 7.2 assumes all expenditures are subject to the sales tax. In most states, certain items (food, rent, medical expenses) are exempt from the sales tax. To the extent that lower-income families spend a larger proportion of their income on these exempted items than higher-income families, this example (Table 7.2) exaggerates the actual degree of regressivity of the sales tax.

sales tax is made less regressive by exempting food, since low-income families spend a relatively large portion of their income on food.

The **excise tax** is quite similar to the sales tax, except that it applies to a much narrower range of items. The federal government levies an excise tax on tobacco, liquor, gasoline, tires, and long-distance telephone calls. States also levy excise taxes—typically on liquor, gasoline, cigarettes, and certain luxury items. The excise tax tends to be regressive for the same reason that the sales tax is regressive—the poor spend a larger fraction of their income on items subject to the tax than do the rich.

PROPERTY TAX

The chief source of revenue for local governments is the **property tax**, which is levied on the assessed value of homes, office buildings, and such other business and personal property as cars, boats, and land. Nonprofit organizations, such as colleges and churches, usually are exempt from the tax. Local governments calculate the appropriate tax *rate* on property by first establishing the *assessed value* on each piece of property. The tax rate is then set at a level that, given the aggregate assessed value of the community, yields the desired amount of tax receipts.

The property tax is controversial. Most economists believe it is regressive for the same basic reason that the sales tax and excise tax are regressive: poor families pay a larger fraction of their income for housing than do the affluent. Given that the property tax is proportional to the assessed value of the property, the fraction of income paid in the form of property taxes typically declines as income rises.

There are additional shortcomings associated with the property tax. Because it is an expensive undertaking, local communities do not have the resources to reassess values frequently. Because of rising property values caused by the inflation of recent decades, an older home may be assessed at 30 percent of current market value whereas a new home may be assessed at full value. Two homes of equal market value may therefore be subject to grossly different property taxes.

With the decay and declining property values of parts of America's inner cities, property tax *rates* may have to be raised to offset the decline in assessed valuation. Yet such measures can be self-defeating, as businesses and individuals are driven to relocate elsewhere. Meanwhile, in the burgeoning suburbs, rising home values and new home construction provide abundant tax receipts, and sometimes even permit reductions in property tax rates. Because school financing by local communities traditionally has been accomplished predominantly via property tax revenues, inner-city youths are likely to receive reduced educational facilities and opportunities. For this reason, the constitutionality of financing public education primarily through the property tax has been challenged in several states.

Important Tax Legislation of the Past 15 Years

Two of the most important pieces of federal tax legislation of the past 40 years have been enacted in the last 15 years. These include the Economic Recovery Tax Act of

1981 (ERTA) and the Tax Reform Act of 1986. These two acts were designed with different objectives in mind.

THE ECONOMIC RECOVERY TAX ACT OF 1981

This legislation, the cornerstone of Reaganomics or supply-side economics, implemented consecutive income-tax cuts in the summers of 1981, 1982, and 1983. The prime objective of this legislation was to get *marginal* income-tax rates down in order to promote incentives to work, produce, and earn income. The three consecutive tax reductions reduced income-tax rates on average by about 25 percent. The top marginal rate was brought down from 70 percent to 50 percent. In addition, tax breaks were targeted at corporations to stimulate investment, and tax incentives were given to promote saving by the masses of Americans. A rather large tax deduction was granted two-earner households in an effort to increase willingness of both members to seek employment, thereby stimulating national output. Unfortunately, this legislation was unaccompanied by spending cuts or other tax hikes to offset the income-tax cuts. Therefore, ERTA is responsible for ushering in the era of huge federal budget deficits, which continue to this day. The main goal of this legislation was to stimulate economic growth. It was not designed with fairness and economic efficiency as paramount considerations.

THE TAX REFORM ACT OF 1986

The idea behind this legislation was to improve the fairness and efficiency of the federal tax system and to reduce further marginal income-tax rates without aggravating the federal budget deficit. It was designed to be "revenue neutral." The object was to broaden the **tax base**—the total income subject to the income tax—and use the proceeds to finance a cut in *tax rates*. In this legislation, tax rates were cut across the board, the top bracket being reduced from 50 percent to 28 percent. In order to broaden the tax base, many deductions (or "loopholes") were eliminated.

The Tax Reform Act contributed to improved economic efficiency in several ways. First, by reducing marginal tax rates, the incentive to search for deductions or cheat on taxes is reduced. Demand for the services of tax lawyers and accountants and time spent arranging financial affairs to minimize the tax bite are all reduced, improving the nation's resource allocation. Activities that are based solely on tax considerations are *inefficient*—they result in misallocation of the nation's resources. For example, if large tax breaks are given for investing in apartment buildings, an excessive number of such buildings will be erected—with high vacancy rates. From society's viewpoint, this is inefficient—it is a waste of scarce resources. By reducing tax breaks for such activities, the act contributed to an improvement in the nation's resource allocation.

Many believe the Tax Reform Act also contributed favorably to the equity aspects of the tax system. The act eliminated many loopholes that allowed the wealthy to avoid taxes. It also sharply increased the magnitude of the personal exemption and standard deduction. This resulted in 5 million low-income earners being taken off the tax rolls. These measures helped move the after-tax income distribution slightly in the direction of greater equality. Unfortunately, in its zeal to improve equity and efficiency, the Tax Reform Act neglected considerations of long-term economic growth. Favorable treatment of capital gains was eliminated. Over a five-year period, about $120 billion of taxes were transferred from individuals to corporations, which undertake the bulk of the nation's investment. And several of the features of the 1981 tax legislation (ERTA) that promoted saving and investment were repealed. Because the Tax Reform Act on balance produced adverse implications for economic growth, new proposals to promote saving and investment are likely to be forthcoming as Congress attempts to deal with the poor growth performance of the U.S. economy vis à vis Japan, Germany, and other emerging economic powers.

Summary

1. Government intervenes in the economy in order to promote competition, to implement policies that stabilize the macroeconomy, and to modify the distribution of income and wealth. In addition, the government steps in to provide public goods and sometimes intervenes to correct misallocations of resources associated with positive and negative externalities.

2. Public choice analysis involves the application of economic principles to help understand the outcome of the political process. This analysis helps us to understand why stated *good* intentions often end up leading to *perverse* results, that is, why government policies sometimes end up being harmful.

3. Government has become more pervasive in the sense that the ratio of government spending (and taxes) to our gross domestic product has gradually increased over the years. Among the sources of this government growth are the urbanization movement (especially 1900–1950) and the growth of the defense establishment (especially 1940–1965). Also contributing to the expanded role of government since the 1950s is the growth of income-security programs, the dominant source of government growth during the past 30 years.

4. Government purchases of goods and services are exhaustive—they consume scarce economic resources. Government transfer payments are nonexhaustive—they transfer income within the private sector of the economy but do not consume resources or divert them to the production of government goods and services. In the past 30 years, government purchases have expanded in line with GDP; government transfers have expanded much faster than GDP.

5. Federal government expenditures are primarily for economic security, national defense, health and education, and interest on federal debt. State and local government expenditures are mainly for education, health and welfare, police and fire protection, and roads and highways.

6. The real function of taxes is to limit the use of economic resources—lumber, labor, steel—in the production of private goods and services so that the resources may be used for public goods and services.

7. Taxes are classified as progressive, proportional, or regressive—depending on whether the percentage of income paid in taxes rises, remains constant, or declines as the level of income rises. Examples of progressive taxes are income and inheritance taxes. Examples of regressive taxes are payroll, sales, and excise taxes.

8. In terms of the volume of tax receipts, the most significant tax is the individual income

tax. Individuals compute their annual tax liability by first calculating adjusted gross income (adding all forms of income and adjusting the total for certain allowances). They then compute taxable income by subtracting from adjusted gross income their exemptions and deductions. The individual income tax is progressive chiefly because the ratio of taxable income to total income tends to rise as income rises (that is, high-income earners find that exemptions and deductions shield a smaller percentage of their total income than is true for low-income earners). Also, the marginal tax rate is higher for higher taxable income levels than for lower levels. The degree of progressivity of the individual income tax has decreased in recent decades.

9. Certain loopholes exist that allow many taxpayers to reduce their tax liability legally. Examples include the nontaxability of interest income earned on municipal bonds, availability of deductible retirement contributions, and deductibility of property taxes and mortgage interest payments.

10. These loopholes sometimes create gross violations of the norms of horizontal and vertical equity. Horizontal equity is the notion that those of equal financial means should contribute equally to the financing of government. Vertical equity is the notion that those of greater financial resources should contribute more in taxes than those of lesser financial means.

11. Major federal tax legislation was enacted in the Economic Recovery Tax Act of 1981 (ERTA) and the Tax Reform Act of 1986. While ERTA was aimed chiefly at stimulating economic growth, the Tax Reform Act was primarily concerned with improving the fairness and efficiency of our federal tax system.

Key Terms

negative externalities
positive externalities
public good
public choice analysis
government purchases
government transfer payments

progressive tax
proportional tax
regressive tax
tax incidence
average tax rate
marginal tax rate

Study Questions and Problems

1. Explain carefully why it is true that even a conservative economist—who seeks to minimize governmental intervention in economic affairs—might support a large tax on the production of electricity via nuclear power.

2. What is the economic rationale for a large government subsidy for research on the AIDS virus?

3. Explain the meaning of a pure public good. Discuss why each of the following can or cannot be classified as a pure public good:
   a. the public library in your hometown
   b. the national weather bureau
   c. the federal interstate highway system
   d. a municipal airport
   e. a municipal rose garden

  f. computer software, such as Wordperfect™

  g. municipal street snow removal

 4. Explain whether the following government expenditures are exhaustive or nonexhaustive:

  a. police protection

  b. veterans' benefits

  c. salaries for high-school teachers

  d. food stamps

  e. national defense

  f. postal service

  g. interest on federal debt

 5. Explain whether the following taxes or license fees are progressive or regressive:

  a. a $1 per barrel federal excise tax on beer

  b. a $25 hunting license

  c. the federal individual income tax

  d. the federal payroll tax

 6. What might be done (via tax law) to make the federal income tax more progressive? Less progressive?

 7. Some economists believe the corporate income tax is regressive. How can this be true? Explain.

 8. An industrial firm in your town routinely dumps toxic waste into the river instead of disposing of it in a manner that causes no negative externality. Relative to proper disposal, how does this practice affect the firm's cost of production? The price of its product? The amount of output it produces? What sort of regulations, if any, do you favor imposing on the firm?

 9. How might public choice analysis explain the following political phenomena?

  a. Congress places quotas on imported cars.

  b. Huge budget deficits occur year after year.

 10. Concerning the individual income tax:

  a. explain the difference between average and marginal tax rates.

  b. if the marginal tax rate is higher than the average tax rate, is the tax progressive?

YOUR TURN
Answers

Star Wars: A Public or Private Good?

CLEARLY, THE PROJECT WILL STALL BECAUSE OF THE *FREE-RIDER* PROBLEM. NO INDIVIDUAL CAN BE EXCLUDED FROM THE BENEFITS OF THE SDI SYSTEM ONCE IT IS OPERATIONAL. FEW INDIVIDUALS WOULD PURCHASE SUBSCRIPTIONS, ESPECIALLY IN VIEW OF THE EXORBITANT COST. THIS IS A PURE PUBLIC GOOD, AND MUST BE PROVIDED COLLECTIVELY OR NOT AT ALL.

The Flat Tax: Is It Proportional?

GROSS INCOME	TAXABLE INCOME	TAX LIABILITY	TAX LIABILITY/INCOME
$ 20,000	$ 4,000	$ 800	4.0%
$ 50,000	$ 34,000	$ 6,800	13.6%
$ 100,000	$ 84,000	$ 16,800	16.8%

THIS SCHEME IS PROGRESSIVE AS INDICATED IN COLUMN FOUR. AS INCOME RISES, THE PERCENTAGE OF INCOME PAID IN TAXES INCREASES. THE FIRST $16,000 OF INCOME IS

SHIELDED FROM TAXES BY THE STANDARD DEDUCTION ($6,000) AND THE FOUR EXEMP-
TIONS ($10,000). THESE EXEMPTIONS AND DEDUCTIONS CONSTITUTE A SMALLER PER-
CENTAGE OF GROSS INCOME FOR HIGH-INCOME FAMILIES THAN FOR LOWER-INCOME FAM-
ILIES. THEREFORE, EVEN THOUGH THE MARGINAL TAX RATE IS 20 PERCENT AT ALL
TAXABLE INCOME LEVELS, THIS SCHEME IS PROGRESSIVE.

Selected References

Aaron, Henry J., and Harvey Galper. *Assessing Tax Reform* (Washington, D.C.: The Brookings Institution, 1985). This book analyzes various tax reform proposals in the light of
basic principles of public finance.

Buchanan, James. "The Constitution of Economic Policy," *American Economic Review* (June
1987), pp. 243–250. The Nobel Prize lecture of Buchanan.

Buchanan, James, and Gordon Tullock. *The Calculus of Consent* (Ann Arbor: University of
Michigan Press, 1962). Classic treatise by two noted public choice economists.

Hyman, David N. *Public Finance*, 3rd edition (Chicago: Dryden Press, 1990). This is a comprehensive intermediate-level textbook on government finance.

Johnson, David B. *Public Choice: An Introduction to the New Political Economy*. (Mountain View,
Calif.: Mayfield Publishing Co., 1991). Introductory textbook on public choice theory.

Pechman, Joseph A. *Who Paid the Taxes, 1966–85?* (Washington, D.C.: The Brookings Institution, 1985). A work that analyzes the distribution of the burden of taxes by income
class.

Rosen, Harvey S. *Public Finance*, 2nd edition (Homewood, Illinois: Richard D. Irwin, 1988).
This public finance text includes a lucid analysis of all aspects of the Social Security
system.

11

IN PART I, WE DEVELOPED A SET OF ANALYTICAL TOOLS AND CONCEPTS THAT WILL BE INVALUABLE IN THE REMAINDER OF THE COURSE. WE STUDIED SUCH ISSUES AS THE RATIONALE FOR GOVERNMENT INTERVENTION IN THE ECONOMY, HOW SUPPLY AND DEMAND DETERMINE PRICES OF INDIVID- UAL GOODS, AND HOW MARKETS ALLOCATE ECONOMIC RESOURCES AMONG ALTERNATIVE USES. THE LATTER SUBJECTS FALL WITHIN THE DOMAIN OF MICROECONOMICS. WE NOW EMBARK ON THE STUDY OF *MACROECONOM- ICS*, THE STUDY OF THE ECONOMY AS A WHOLE. IN PART II, WE BEGIN BY SKETCH- ING THE NATURE OF THE BUSINESS CYCLE AND LOOKING INTO THE MEANING AND MEASUREMENT OF SUCH KEY MACROECO- NOMIC CONCEPTS AS OUTPUT, UNEM- PLOYMENT, AND INFLATION. THESE CON- CEPTS PLAY A MAJOR ROLE THROUGHOUT THE REMAINDER OF THE BOOK. ■ THE EARLY PORTIONS OF PART II (CHAPTERS 8–10) INTRODUCE THE MAJOR MACRO- ECONOMIC CONCEPTS, ANALYZE THE CON- SEQUENCES OF UNEMPLOYMENT AND INFLATION, AND SKETCH THE PRINCIPLES AND PROCEDURES USED TO MEASURE THE VALUE OF THE NATION'S OUTPUT. THE LATTER CHAPTERS OF PART II (CHAPTERS 11–14) DEVELOP A FRAMEWORK OF ANALY- SIS THAT WILL ALLOW YOU TO UNDERSTAND THE FACTORS THAT PRODUCE FLUCTUA- TIONS IN ECONOMIC ACTIVITY, INFLATION, AND OTHER IMPOR- TANT MACROECO- NOMIC PHENOMENA. IN MASTERING THIS FRAMEWORK, YOU WILL COME TO UNDERSTAND THE RATIONALE FOR IMPLEMENTING GOVERN- MENT POLICIES INTENDED TO INFLUENCE THE NEAR-TERM COURSE OF THE NATION'S ECONOMIC ACTIVITY.

Macroeconomy, National Income Determination, and Fiscal Policy

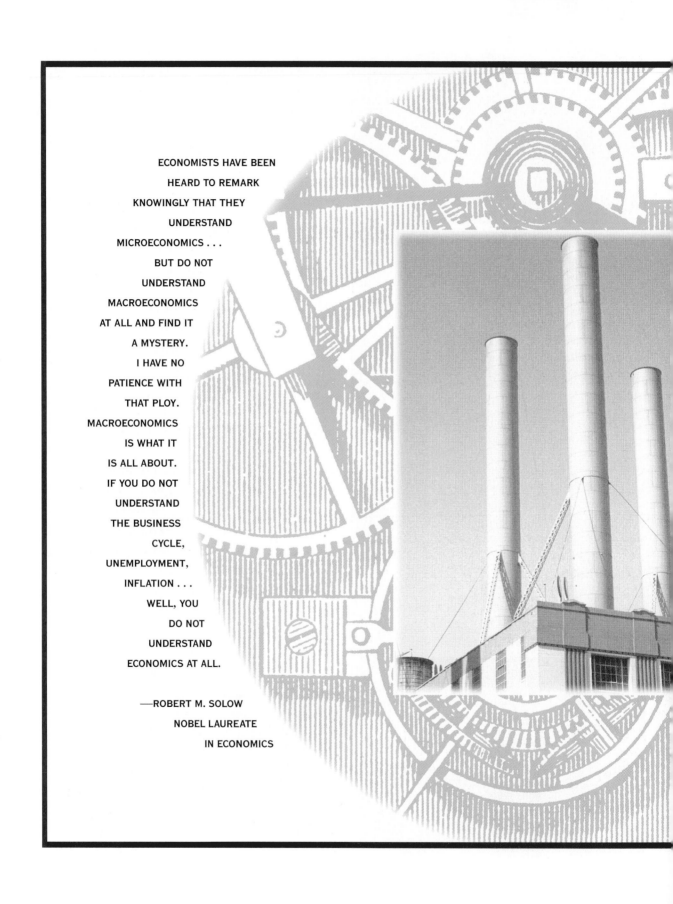

ECONOMISTS HAVE BEEN
HEARD TO REMARK
KNOWINGLY THAT THEY
UNDERSTAND
MICROECONOMICS . . .
BUT DO NOT
UNDERSTAND
MACROECONOMICS
AT ALL AND FIND IT
A MYSTERY.
I HAVE NO
PATIENCE WITH
THAT PLOY.
MACROECONOMICS
IS WHAT IT
IS ALL ABOUT.
IF YOU DO NOT
UNDERSTAND
THE BUSINESS
CYCLE,
UNEMPLOYMENT,
INFLATION . . .
WELL, YOU
DO NOT
UNDERSTAND
ECONOMICS AT ALL.

—ROBERT M. SOLOW
NOBEL LAUREATE
IN ECONOMICS

Introduction to Macroeconomics: Fundamental Concepts

WITH THIS CHAPTER, WE BEGIN OUR ANALYSIS OF MACROECONOMICS—THE STUDY OF THE BEHAVIOR OF THE OVERALL ECONOMY. DERIVED FROM THE GREEK LANGUAGE, "MACRO" MEANS "LARGE," IN CONTRAST TO "MICRO," WHICH MEANS "SMALL." IN MACROECONOMICS, WE STUDY THE BROAD ECONOMIC VARIABLES THAT INDICATE THE OVERALL PERFORMANCE OF THE NATION'S ECONOMY. WE LOOK BEYOND THE DETAILS OF THE PRICES OF INDIVIDUAL GOODS, MARKET STRUCTURES, AND RESOURCE ALLOCATION STUDIED IN MICROECONOMICS AND FOCUS ON SUCH AGGREGATIVE ECONOMIC VARIABLES AS GROSS DOMESTIC PRODUCT (GDP), UNEMPLOYMENT, AND INFLATION.

IN THIS CHAPTER, WE OUTLINE SOME OF THE KEY MACROECONOMIC CONCEPTS THAT PLAY A MAJOR ROLE IN LATER CHAPTERS. WE SKETCH THE NATURE OF THE BUSINESS CYCLE AND DISCUSS THE MEASUREMENT OF UNEMPLOYMENT AND INFLATION. WE PROVIDE THE INITIAL FOUNDATION FOR LEARNING ABOUT SUCH THINGS AS THE DETERMINATION OF THE NATION'S OUTPUT AND INCOME AND THE CAUSES AND CONSEQUENCES OF INFLATION AND UNEMPLOYMENT AS WELL AS THE ROLE OF GOVERNMENT POLICIES AIMED AT CONTROLLING THESE PHENOMENA.

Macroeconomics
The study of the aggregate economy.

BUSINESS CYCLE

A pattern of irregular but repeated expansion and contraction of real output.

NOMINAL GDP

The value of all final goods and services produced by a nation in a given year, measured in prices prevailing in that year.

REAL GDP

GDP adjusted for inflation; the value of gross domestic product in constant or base-year prices.

Historically, all industrial nations have experienced periodic fluctuations in economic activity known as **business cycles**. The business cycle refers to the recurring pattern of expansion and contraction of an economy's output. An economy's output is measured by gross domestic product (GDP).

It is essential at the outset to distinguish between **nominal GDP** and **real GDP**. GDP may be defined as the dollar value of all final goods and services produced by a nation in a given year. The nation's gross domestic product is measured each year in prices prevailing in that year. This is known as *nominal GDP* or actual GDP. If prices rise in a particular year, nominal GDP will increase even if the physical quantity of goods and services produced remains constant. In order to ascertain the extent to which a nation's actual production of goods and services increases or decreases relative to a previous year, it is necessary to adjust the nominal GDP for inflation. The adjusted value is known as *real GDP*, or GDP expressed in constant dollars, that is, in prices of some earlier base or reference year.

Suppose nominal GDP rises by 7 percent in 1994 but the price level rises 4 percent. Then real GDP increases by only 3 percent. If nominal GDP increases by 4 percent while prices rise 5 percent, real GDP declines. For many purposes, real GDP is a more useful measure than is nominal GDP. For example, employment and unemployment are more closely linked to real GDP than to nominal GDP. The business cycle concerns the ups and downs of real GDP.

The business cycle consists of four phases: the expansion, the peak, the contraction, and the trough. In the *expansion* phase, the nation's output or real GDP increases, together with employment and business profits. The nation's unemployment rate typically declines. Eventually, the expansion comes to an end at the *peak* of the business cycle, when output and employment reach their highest levels of the cycle. This is followed by a period of *contraction* of output and employment. In this phase, output, employment, and profits decline. Unemployment rises.

RECESSION

A period of time in which a nation's real output declines for at least two consecutive quarters (six months).

DEPRESSION

A very severe and prolonged economic downturn.

If real GDP (output) decreases for at least two consecutive quarters, that is, for at least six months, the contraction is typically classified as a **recession**. Sometimes, if the contraction is extremely severe and prolonged, it is considered to be a **depression**, though there is no clear-cut criterion for distinguishing a depression from a recession.[1] At the end of the contraction, the economy reaches the *trough*—the low point of the business cycle. The trough is followed by a period of economic expansion, and the cycle repeats itself. These cycles are irregular in severity and in length.

The "average" business cycle lasts for about five years, but some have lasted nearly a decade and others lasted for only two or three years. The nature of the business cycle is illustrated schematically in Figure 8.1 (page 198).

---

[1] An unemployed worker once distinguished a depression from a recession as follows: "A recession is when other people are out of work. A depression is when I am out of work."

Economic Activity During Recession

The economy is generally considered to be in recession when real GDP declines for at least two consecutive quarters. But additional insight into the damage done by economic downturns can be gained by looking at several other key indicators of economic activity. In the table below, we indicate the duration of each of the eight recessions that have occurred in the United States since 1950. In addition, the percentage decline in real GDP, industrial production, and business profits from the peak of the cycle to the trough is indicated, together with the maximum unemployment rate reached during each downturn.

Note that both industrial production and business profits are more volatile over the course of the business cycle than is real GDP. Industrial production declines by a relatively larger amount than real GDP during recessions chiefly because it omits the huge, stable service sector, which is included in GDP. Profits drop sharply in recession because wage costs and other costs fail to decline commensurately with sales in the short run. Of course, during the ensuing economic expansion phase of the cycle, industrial production and business profits increase considerably faster than real GDP.

The two most severe recessions of the past 40 years were the 1973–1975 and 1981–1982 downturns. These were the two longest recessions of the post-World War II era, each lasting 16 months. The nation's unemployment rate reached higher levels in these recessions than in any others. Also, the percentage declines in industrial production, real GDP, and profits were relatively severe. Based on the indicators in the table, the 1990–1991 recession was relatively mild.

DURATION AND SEVERITY OF POST–1950 RECESSIONS

CYCLE PEAK	CYCLE TROUGH	DURATION (MONTHS)	% DECLINE IN REAL GDP	% DECLINE IN INDUSTRIAL PRODUCTION	HIGHEST UNEMPLOYMENT RATE (%)	% DECLINE IN PRE-TAX PROFIT
July 1953	May 1954	10	-3.2	-9.4	6.1	-24
Aug 1957	Apr 1958	8	-3.3	-13.5	7.5	-27
Apr 1960	Feb 1961	10	-1.2	-8.6	7.1	-18
Dec 1969	Nov 1970	11	-1.0	-6.8	6.1	-20
Nov 1973	Mar 1975	16	-4.9	-15.3	9.0	-24
Jan 1980	July 1980	6	-2.3	-8.6	7.8	-18
July 1981	Nov 1982	16	-3.0	-12.3	10.8	-31
July 1990	May 1991	10	-1.0	-5.1	6.9	-12
Average		11	-2.5	-10.0	7.7	-22

SOURCE: Data from Citibank Economic Database.
Note: Dating of the most recent trough (May 1991) is tentative.

EXHIBIT

8.1   TABLE 8.1

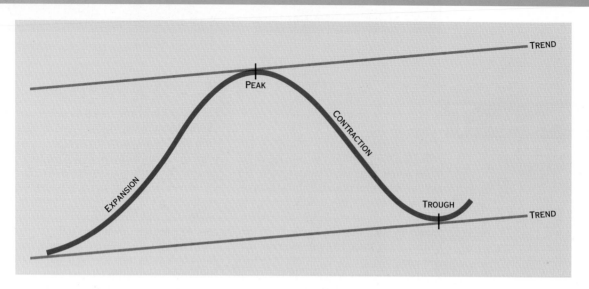

THE PHASES OF THE BUSINESS CYCLE (BEHAVIOR OF REAL GDP)

Economic activity goes through cyclical episodes of expansion and contraction. Between 1950 and 1992, the nation experienced eight such business cycles—an average of one complete cycle every five years.

FIGURE 8.1

MONETARY POLICY

The use of certain tools by the Federal Reserve System to alter the availability of credit, the level of interest rates, and the supply of money in order to influence economic activity.

FEDERAL RESERVE SYSTEM

The central bank of the United States; the organization responsible for conducting monetary policy by influencing the supply of money and credit and the level of interest rates.

FISCAL POLICY

The deliberate manipulation of federal expenditures and taxes for the purpose of influencing economic activity.

STABILIZATION POLICIES

In an effort to "tame the business cycle" or at least to combat the extremes of severe inflation on the one hand and deep recession and high unemployment on the other, government authorities sometimes implement *stabilization policies*. Such policies are aimed at stabilizing economic activity, that is, preventing large, undesired fluctuations in output, employment, and the price level. Stabilization policies consist of monetary policy and fiscal policy.

Monetary policy involves the use of certain tools to influence the availability of credit, the level of interest rates, and the amount of *money* in the economy (checking accounts and currency) in order to provide economic stimulus or restraint as deemed appropriate. Monetary policy is conducted by the central bank, known in the United States as the **Federal Reserve System**. For example, during the period of recession and stagnation of 1990–1992, the Federal Reserve pushed down interest rates and made loans more easily available to the public through financial institutions in an effort to boost economic activity.

Fiscal policy involves changing federal government expenditures or taxes for the purpose of influencing economic activity. When the economy is very weak, appropriate fiscal policy measures might include tax reductions and/or increased government spending to stimulate economic activity. In the 1990s, however, use of fiscal policy to stimulate economic activity is constrained by the existence of massive federal *budget deficits*, that is, the shortfall of federal tax revenues relative to federal expenditures. Stimulative fiscal actions—tax cuts or expenditure hikes—involve larger budget deficits. Because many observers feel that these deficits are already dangerously large in the 1990s, the use of stimulative fiscal actions may be inhibited in the next few years by the fear of aggravating the deficit problem.

In the next several chapters, we will look in depth at the details of monetary and fiscal policies, including the method by which these instruments influence economic activity. There is disagreement among economists over the relative merits of monetary and fiscal policy as well as the wisdom of attempting to use these instruments to stabilize economic activity over the course of the business cycle.

Unemployment and the Goal of Full Employment

High employment of workers is one of the nation's paramount macroeconomic objectives. High employment leads to a high level of national output. Jobs provide individuals and families with incomes. Moreover, jobs give people a sense of fulfillment—a sense of importance, well-being, and solidarity with society. Involuntary unemployment breeds alienation. Since the Great Depression of the 1930s, a major objective of macroeconomic policy has been to establish and maintain a high level of employment. This is perhaps the most important thing government can do to help all Americans enjoy a reasonably prosperous and fulfilling life.

As illustrated in Figure 8.2 (page 200), unemployment is a worldwide problem. Some countries (Japan, Sweden) have had more success than the United States in achieving low unemployment. Other nations (France, England) have had considerably less success recently than the United States.

Measuring Unemployment in the United States

LABOR FORCE
Those individuals 16 years of age and over who are counted as either employed or unemployed.

UNEMPLOYMENT RATE
Percentage of the labor force that is unemployed, that is, out of work and looking for work.

To estimate the nation's unemployment rate, the Bureau of Labor Statistics (BLS) of the U.S. Department of Labor samples 60,000 households each month. Each member of the family age 16 or older is asked whether he or she has a job. If so, the person is counted by the government as *employed*. If not employed, the person is then asked whether he or she looked for work in the last month. If the person did, then he or she is counted as *unemployed*. If not, the person is considered *not in the labor force*. The **labor force** is made up of all those who have been classified as employed plus those who have been classified as unemployed. The labor force excludes those persons who are neither working nor looking for work.

labor force = those classified as employed + those classified as unemployed

The findings of the BLS 60,000-household survey are then extrapolated in order to estimate the overall U.S. unemployment rate. If the estimates for the labor force and the number unemployed are 125,000,000 and 7,500,000, respectively, the nation's unemployment rate is estimated to be

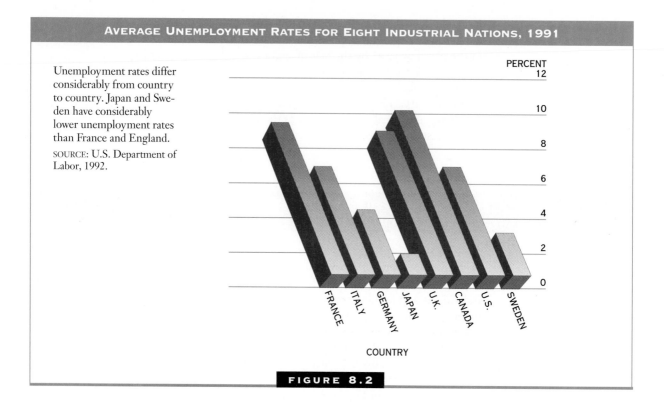

Unemployment rates differ considerably from country to country. Japan and Sweden have considerably lower unemployment rates than France and England.

SOURCE: U.S. Department of Labor, 1992.

PERCENT

FRANCE   ITALY   GERMANY   JAPAN   U.K.   CANADA   U.S.   SWEDEN

COUNTRY

FIGURE 8.2

$$\text{unemployment rate} = \frac{\text{number unemployed}}{\text{number in labor force}} \times 100$$

$$U = \frac{7.5 \text{ million}}{125 \text{ million}} \times 100 = 6.0 \text{ percent}$$

The historical pattern of the U.S. unemployment rate since 1900 is depicted in Figure 8.3.

The preceding equation for measuring the unemployment rate, however, tends to understate the severity of the unemployment problem for two reasons.[2] First, anyone who is employed even for a few hours each week is counted as being employed. Many such people may be *underemployed* in the sense that they would prefer full-time work but are unable to find it. At the bottom of the 1991 recession, when 8.5 million Americans were officially listed as unemployed, another 5.6 million were reported as working part time "for economic reasons" (involuntarily working part time). Second, workers may become discouraged about job prospects after a period of unsuccessful job search and stop looking for work. Such *discouraged workers* are not counted as part of the labor force and therefore do not show

---

[2]Partially offsetting this bias, however, is the fact that the following *are* counted as unemployed: people who register for work in order to qualify for welfare but who really do not want work and persons who do not find work because they have set unrealistic demands in terms of salary or other aspects of the job (such as hours of work).

up in the unemployment statistics. The understatement of unemployment because of discouraged workers is especially significant in periods of economic recession when unemployment is high and job prospects are bleak. In such circumstances, many people may stop actively searching for work. These discouraged workers, who are not counted as being officially unemployed, are known as the *hidden unemployed*. At the bottom of the 1991 recession it was estimated that 1 million workers wanted jobs but were not looking because they thought none were available.

This line of argument suggests that when unemployment is rising during an economic downturn, the increase in the reported unemployment rate *understates* the additional hardship felt by individuals and families. However, there is a mitigating consideration. Many of those who become officially (or hidden) unemployed during hard times are *secondary workers* in a family—workers in households in which two or more members are labor force participants. If the primary family breadwinner remains fully employed but a spouse or teenage son or daughter becomes unemployed (officially or hidden), one could argue that things are not as bad as they sound.

LABOR FORCE PARTICIPATION RATE

The percentage of the working-age population that is in the labor force.

An important labor-market concept is the **labor force participation rate** (LFPR)—the fraction of the population age 16 and above officially in the labor force. Among the 191 million working-age (16 and older) civilians in 1992, roughly 127 million were in the labor force. Hence, the LFPR of 16-and-over civilians was roughly 66 percent. This is the primary measure of the LFPR. One could compute the labor force participation rate for such other subsets of the population as teenagers, blacks, women, men over age 60, and so forth. A demographic phenomenon with important economic implications is the fact that the LFPR of women in the United States has trended strongly upward from 20 percent in 1900 to more than 55 percent today.

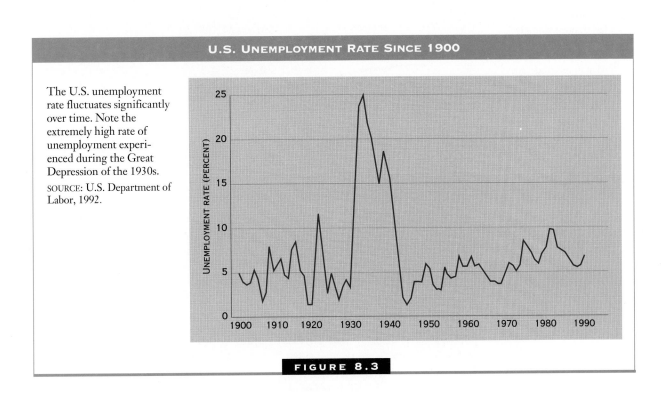

U.S. UNEMPLOYMENT RATE SINCE 1900

The U.S. unemployment rate fluctuates significantly over time. Note the extremely high rate of unemployment experienced during the Great Depression of the 1930s.

SOURCE: U.S. Department of Labor, 1992.

FIGURE 8.3

$$\text{labor force participation rate (LFPR)} = \frac{\text{labor force}}{\text{population}} \times 100$$

Labor force participation rates for men, women, and all civilians for the 1950–1991 period are illustrated in Figure 8.4.

Calculating Labor Market Statistics for Medicine Bow

THE TOWN OF MEDICINE BOW HAS 500 WORKING-AGE MEN AND 500 WORKING-AGE WOMEN. OF THE 400 MEN IN THE LABOR FORCE, 18 ARE UNEMPLOYED. THIS COMPARES TO A FEMALE LABOR FORCE OF 300 AND FEMALE UNEMPLOYMENT OF 24.

A. HOW MANY PEOPLE IN MEDICINE BOW ARE IN THE LABOR FORCE, AND HOW MANY ARE UNEMPLOYED?

B. COMPUTE THE OVERALL LABOR FORCE PARTICIPATION RATE FOR THE TOWN OF MEDICINE BOW AND THE SEPARATE LABOR FORCE PARTICIPATION RATES OF THE TOWN'S MEN AND WOMEN.

C. WHAT IS THE TOWN'S UNEMPLOYMENT RATE? WHAT ARE THE UNEMPLOYMENT RATES OF THE MEDICINE BOW MEN AND WOMEN?

LABOR FORCE PARTICIPATION RATES, 1950–1991

While the labor force participation rate of females has trended strongly upward, the LFPR of males has declined somewhat in recent decades. Overall, the nation's civilian LFPR has increased significantly since the mid-1960s.

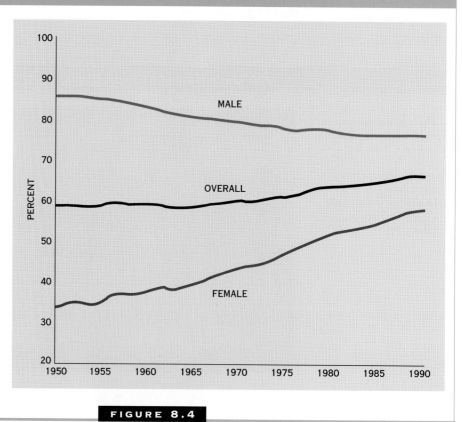

FIGURE 8.4

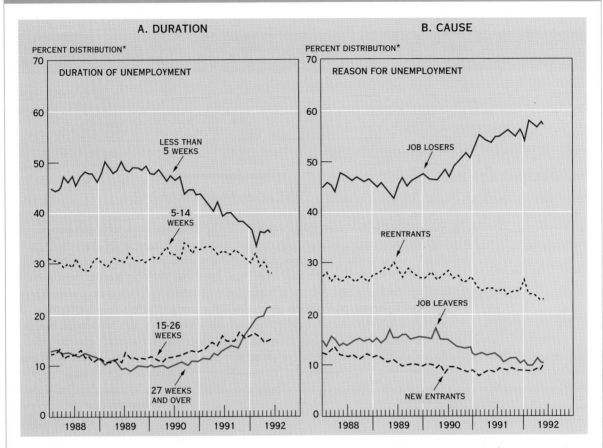

A large portion of the unemployed have been out of work for a fairly brief period. This portion increases during economic expansion and declines in recession (A). About half of the unemployed are job losers, that is, fired or laid off. The remainder of the unemployed left work voluntarily or were entering or reentering the labor force (B). The portion of the unemployed who lose their job increases during periods of recession.

FIGURE 8.5

CHARACTERISTICS OF UNEMPLOYMENT: DURATION AND CAUSE

Figure 8.5 indicates certain important characteristics of unemployment. Figure 8.5(A) shows the distribution of the unemployment by duration of unemployment. Typically, more than 40 percent of total unemployment involves people out of work for less than five weeks; less than 15 percent of the unemployed remain out of work for more than 27 weeks. Note that during the 1990–1991 recession, the percentage of the unemployed who were out of work less than five weeks declined while the share who were out of work for longer periods increased. In recessions, the incidence of longer-term unemployment always increases.

Figure 8.5(B) shows the proportion of the unemployed who lost jobs (were fired or laid off), voluntarily left jobs, reentered the labor force after a period of absence, or entered the labor force for the first time. About half the unemployed lost their jobs, 10–15 percent quit, and 35–40 percent were reentering or initially entering the labor force. The proportion of the unemployed who are job losers rises in recession (1990–1991) and declines during economic expansion.

Categories of Unemployment

For conceptual purposes it is useful to classify unemployment into three categories: frictional, structural, and cyclical or deficient-demand unemployment.

FRICTIONAL UNEMPLOYMENT

FRICTIONAL UNEMPLOYMENT
Unemployment due to normal job search by individuals who have quit their jobs, are initially entering the labor force, or are reentering the labor force.

Given the method for measuring the U.S. unemployment rate, it is inevitable that a significant number of normally employed people happen to be between jobs for a brief period at the time of the survey. One worker may have quit a job to look for another. A second worker may have been fired one week before the survey and may end up finding a new job three weeks later. Another individual may be seeking initial employment one month after graduating from high school or college. In a dynamic labor market, it is inevitable on any given day that a substantial number of viable workers are gainfully involved in the labor-market search process. Such individuals who are temporarily *in the pipeline* are considered to be **frictionally unemployed**. While the volume of frictional unemployment fluctuates with the state of the economy, demographic factors, and other considerations, perhaps 2 to 4 percent of the labor force is frictionally unemployed at a given point of time.

Workers differ in background, skill, and other characteristics. Jobs differ in terms of working conditions, required skills, concentration and effort required, and the like. It therefore takes time to line up the right workers in the right jobs. It is often rational for a worker to remain unemployed for several weeks, even though job offers are being received, in order to find a better job. Only in a totalitarian society or one in which workers are never willing to leave a job to seek a better alternative would one observe little or no frictional unemployment. Frictional unemployment is a normal manifestation of a healthy, vibrant labor market.

STRUCTURAL UNEMPLOYMENT

STRUCTURAL UNEMPLOYMENT
The portion of unemployment accounted for by those out of work for long periods because their job skills do not match those required for available jobs; often caused by structural changes in the economy.

Structural unemployment results from important changes in the structure of the economy and other factors that create a mismatch between job skills sought by employers and job skills possessed by unemployed individuals. Unlike frictional unemployment, structural unemployment constitutes a serious national problem. In the case of structural unemployment, lots of job vacancies coexist for long periods with lots of unemployed workers. The vacancies perhaps call for skills in accounting, engineering, or the use of computers and other high-tech equipment. The unemployed workers may be trained in fields of low demand or, more likely, possess few marketable skills because they never attended college or even dropped out of high school. The latter individuals frequently do not possess the technical skills required by employers in a modern society. On average, the level of skills sought by employers with vacant jobs significantly exceeds the skills possessed by the structurally unemployed.

A continuing pool of structural unemployment persists because of continuing changes in technology, changes in the structure of government and private expenditures, and other factors. The supply of workers with particular skills adapts to an increase in demand with a significant time lag. In the 1950s the coal mining industry introduced automated mining equipment at the same time that millions of American households converted their home heating systems from coal to natural gas or oil. Demand for coal miners dropped sharply, and large pockets of structural unemployment cropped up in Appalachia and other U.S. coal mining regions. Many of these workers were 40–60 years of age and found it quite difficult to retool, move to a new region or city, and find alternative work. In the mid-1980s, while the U.S. service sector was booming, special circumstances created problems in many portions of the agricultural and manufacturing sectors. In particular, an unusually strong dollar in foreign-exchange markets during 1983–1985 put American industries subject to foreign competition at a disadvantage. Thousands of blue-collar workers in the steel, textile, automobile, and other industries lost their jobs.

More recently, the removal of the Soviet Union as a military threat and the need to redirect resources to attack other national problems and hold down the budget deficit has resulted in cutbacks in defense expenditures and closing of military bases in the United States. This results in structural unemployment in industries serving national defense and in communities in which bases have been closed.

Even in a booming economy, a residue of structural unemployment persists. To attack this problem, incentive programs and microeconomic policies to improve job training and labor mobility have been tried from time to time. In general, a massive upgrading of the education and job-skill levels of the bottom one-third of youngsters coming through our school systems would be required to substantially reduce structural unemployment. Barring such a Herculean achievement, it is difficult to be optimistic about solving the problem of structural unemployment. Stimulative monetary and fiscal policies are relatively inefficient means of attacking the problem, though a vibrant economy is essential if the massive uplifting of education, job skills, and training are to have a chance to succeed in sharply reducing structural unemployment.

CYCLICAL UNEMPLOYMENT

CYCLICAL UNEMPLOYMENT
Unemployment attributable to weak aggregate demand; the difference between the actual unemployment rate and the rate associated with full employment.

Cyclical unemployment—the component of unemployment most sensitive to the business cycle—occurs when the economy is operating at an output level below its potential. Cyclical unemployment is sometimes called "deficient-demand" unemployment because it typically is associated with levels of aggregate spending (aggregate demand) too low to call forth a high level of output and employment. When economic activity is far below capacity levels, demand for labor is low and millions of normally employed and productive individuals are involuntarily out of work for a sustained period. As the economy picks up strength, these people are put back to work. At the peak of the business cycle the economy typically approaches *full employment*, a condition in which cyclical unemployment is eliminated. In today's economy, full employment is probably consistent with a reported unemployment rate of 5 to 5.5 percent. Cyclical unemployment is the type of unemployment most potentially amenable to eradication through stimulative monetary and fiscal policy measures.

THE RESPONSE OF UNEMPLOYMENT TO ECONOMIC ACTIVITY

Care should be taken not to overstate the distinction among frictional, structural, and cyclical unemployment. All three types of unemployment may respond to the overall state of the economy. When economic activity strengthens materially, cyclical unemployment declines as firms step up production and hire additional workers. But frictional and structural unemployment are also likely to decline somewhat. The number and quality of job vacancies increase, thereby reducing average search time required by many individuals to find the desired job. This reduces the amount of frictional unemployment. A stronger economy is also likely to reduce structural unemployment, as firms are more likely to hire workers with marginal skills and train them for productive work. During the economic booms associated with World War II and the Korean War, the U.S. unemployment rate fell below 3 percent. At the end of the long economic expansion of the 1960s, when the U.S. economy was clearly in a state of excessively stimulated activity, the unemployment rate averaged 3.5 percent over a two-year period. Most economists believe that, under similar conditions today, this unemployment rate would be higher than in the late 1960s.

The Full-Employment Unemployment Rate—The Natural Rate of Unemployment

Because of the existence of frictional and structural unemployment, *full employment* does not imply a zero unemployment rate. In fact, the lowest unemployment rate achieved for a single year in the past 40 years is 3.5 percent (1969). In the five most recent business cycles, the low point on the unemployment cycle—which occurs near the peak of the business cycle—has yielded an average unemployment rate of 5.2 percent. Most economists today believe that efforts to push the reported unemployment rate below 5 percent through stimulative monetary and fiscal policies would unleash powerful forces that would accelerate the inflation rate in labor and product markets.

NATURAL RATE OF UNEMPLOYMENT

The minimum sustainable unemployment rate below which inflation tends to accelerate; the percentage of the labor force either frictionally or structurally unemployed.

The **natural unemployment rate** is the lowest unemployment rate that can be sustained without igniting an acceleration in the existing rate of inflation. We might regard it as the unemployment rate that would exist when cyclical unemployment is eliminated, leaving only the core of frictional and structural unemployment. Since *potential GDP* is the highest output that the nation can produce without triggering an acceleration in the inflation rate, the natural unemployment rate may also be considered the unemployment rate that would prevail when actual GDP is just equal to potential GDP.

Some economists dislike the connotation of the term "natural unemployment rate" because this rate fluctuates over time and because there is nothing "natural" or good about a situation in which millions of individuals remain involuntarily out of work as a result of structural unemployment. Such economists have suggested an alternative, though cumbersome, term—NAIRU (nonaccelerating inflation rate of unemployment)—since the natural unemployment rate is defined as the lowest unemployment rate that can be sustained without setting off an acceleration of inflation.

At the NAIRU or natural unemployment rate, wages and prices may be rising but the inflation rates are *stable*, neither accelerating nor decelerating. Labor markets are in a state of balance, with expectations of inflation fully adapted to the existing rate of inflation. At the natural unemployment rate, there is neither excessive nor deficient demand for labor. Because the term "natural unemployment rate" has been widely accepted in economics literature, we use it in this book.

FLUCTUATIONS IN THE NATURAL UNEMPLOYMENT RATE

The natural unemployment rate fluctuates over time, and there is a strong consensus that it increased significantly between the early 1960s and the early 1980s. Several factors contributed to this phenomenon. Most importantly, the percentage of the U.S. labor force made up of young workers (under age 25) increased steadily in this period because of the *baby boom* of 1946–1964. The baby boom produced a sustained increase in the number of 18-year-olds coming into the labor force after 1963. Young workers on average exhibit weaker job attachment and higher labor-market turnover than older workers. Hence, frictional unemployment rates are higher for younger workers. Structural unemployment also is relatively high among young workers because of their limited job skills. The influx of young workers into the labor force from the mid-1960s to the early 1980s pulled up the nation's frictional and structural unemployment rates. The natural unemployment rate increased.

In the same period a major and sustained increase in the labor force participation rate of women took place. In the past, women, like young workers, exhibited higher labor market turnover and higher frictional unemployment rates than men. The increasing proportion of the labor force composed of women contributed to the increase in the frictional and natural unemployment rates. In addition, the nation generally liberalized its provision of benefits for unemployed workers. This reduced the personal financial hardship of being unemployed and allowed individuals to be more deliberate in their job search. The lengthening of average search time raises the frictional and the natural rates of unemployment. The natural unemployment rate increased in the 1970s, reaching a peak in the early 1980s.

Since the early 1980s, at least one of these factors has worked in reverse, *lowering* the natural unemployment rate. Because the American birthrate dropped after 1964, the number of youths graduating from high school and entering the labor force began to decline around 1982. This factor and the gradual aging of the baby boomers pulled down the natural unemployment rate after the early 1980s.

While the labor force participation rate of females may continue to increase, it seems likely that the *rate of increase* may slow down. Furthermore, the skill levels of women are increasing and female turnover rates are declining. It seems likely, therefore, that the natural unemployment rate will remain considerably lower than that of the early 1980s for several more years until the *echo baby boomers*—the children of the baby boomers—begin entering the labor force in large numbers in the late 1990s. Many economists estimate that the natural unemployment rate today is in the 5 to 5.5 percent range—compared to 6 percent or higher a decade ago.

GOVERNMENT POLICIES TO REDUCE THE NATURAL RATE OF UNEMPLOYMENT

If output could be boosted above *potential* GDP by reducing unemployment below the natural unemployment rate, gains would accrue to society in terms of higher incomes and living standards. Offsetting this gain, however, would be an unacceptable acceleration of inflation and other problems. No one, therefore, advocates deliberate use of monetary and fiscal policy to push the unemployment rate below the natural rate. However, if the *natural unemployment rate itself* could be reduced through policy measures, we could aim for higher living standards and lower unemployment rates without experiencing the scourge of accelerating inflation.

Microeconomic programs with incentives to improve the functioning of labor markets have been suggested. Labor-market information services with computerized job lists and training opportunities might reduce frictional and structural unemployment. Some have advocated public service employment—the government serving as an *employer of last resort*. A less radical proposal would have the government simply remove some of the obstacles that its own institutions and laws have created. For example, the Social Security, welfare, and disability insurance programs could be altered to increase incentives to work and earn income. The system of unemployment insurance could be redesigned along the same lines. Finally, a reduction in the level of the minimum wage could remove an obstacle that blocks employment prospects for many unskilled young individuals. Experience and labor market research, however, suggests that the potential for policy-induced reductions in the natural unemployment rate is not dramatic.

Inflation: Its Meaning and Measurement

INFLATION

A persistent and sustained increase in the general level of prices; a persistent decline in the value of the monetary unit (for example, the dollar).

Policymakers are concerned not only about unemployment, but also about inflation. **Inflation** refers to a sustained, continuing increase in the general level of prices. Equivalently, it can be viewed as a sustained, continuing decrease in the purchasing power of a domestic currency such as the dollar, mark, or yen. When there is inflation the value of a currency in terms of the goods and services it buys persistently declines. Seven percent annual inflation sustained for a decade, for example, doubles the price level and cuts the purchasing power of a dollar in half.

Inflation has been a major problem, periodically afflicting market economies throughout history. In the United States, inflation was relatively subdued for the first 20 years following the end of World War II. It began to accelerate in the late 1960s and became a very serious problem in the 1970s, reaching double-digit rates by the end of the decade. While the inflation rate has declined considerably since the early 1980s, it remains a concern for those who conduct the nation's monetary and fiscal policies.

MEASURING INFLATION

PRICE INDEX
A weighted average of the prices of goods and services expressed in relation to a base year value of 100.

To measure inflation, economists use a **price index**. A price index is a measure of the average level of prices in a given year *relative* to the average level of prices in a particular year, called the **base year**. The price index is therefore designed to show the *change* in the general level of prices since the base year. The current value of a price index is calculated by comparing the cost of buying a particular bundle of goods in the current year with the cost of buying exactly that same bundle of goods in the base year. For example, the price index for 1993 using 1982 as the base year is calculated as follows:

$$P_{1993} = \frac{\Sigma(P_i^{1993} \times Q_i^{1982})}{\Sigma(P_i^{1982} \times Q_i^{1982})} \times 100 \qquad (8.1)$$

In Equation 8.1, P_i indicates the price of good i and Q_i indicates the quantity purchased of good i in the year indicated in the superscript. P_i times Q_i indicates expenditures on good i. Hence, the denominator of the equation represents the sum of expenditures on the items in the market basket in 1982, the base year. The numerator indicates what it costs in 1993 to purchase the same market basket of goods that was purchased in 1982. Both the numerator and denominator are expressed as a flow of expenditures per year. Therefore, the ratio of the two expressions is a pure number, devoid of units. This ratio is multiplied by 100 to create an index number of convenient magnitude. Thus, if the flow of expenditures on the basket of goods in 1982 was $8,000 and the expenditures required in 1993 to purchase that same basket is $16,000, our price index for 1993 is 200. This is shown as follows:

$$P_{1993} = \frac{\$16,000/year}{\$8,000/year} \times 100 = 200$$

This index number of 200 indicates that the cost of purchasing the market basket has doubled since the base year of 1982, when the index value was established at 100. Alternatively, we may say that the level of prices has increased by 100 percent since the year 1982. If this price index were a precise measure of purchasing power change, one would need $200 in 1993 to be as well off as one would have been in 1982 with $100. Note that a price index does *not* indicate the absolute *level* of prices; it indicates the *change* in the price level since the base year.

In the United States there are three major indexes of prices: the **consumer price index (CPI)**, the **producer price index (PPI)**, and the **GDP deflator**

CONSUMER PRICE INDEX
The most widely quoted index of U.S. prices; based on the market basket of goods and services purchased by a typical household.

CONSUMER PRICE INDEX (CPI) This index number is possibly the most widely quoted economic statistic in the world. The consumer price index, sometimes called the "cost-of-living" index, seeks to measure the change in the cost of the basket of goods and services purchased by the typical urban American consumer. To construct the CPI, the Bureau of Labor Statistics employs about 250 agents to collect price information from 19,000 retail stores and 57,000 homeowners and tenants in 85 cities each month. Approximately 125,000 individual price quotations are obtained each month. The CPI is based on prices of food, clothing, housing, transportation, fuel, medical expenses, and other items purchased for day-to-day living. The base year of the CPI is the average of 1982–1984 (1982–1984 = 100). The behavior of the CPI during 1960–1991 is illustrated in Figure 8.6 (page 210).

Consumer prices have risen more than four fold since 1960; a dollar today buys less than a quarter did in 1960.

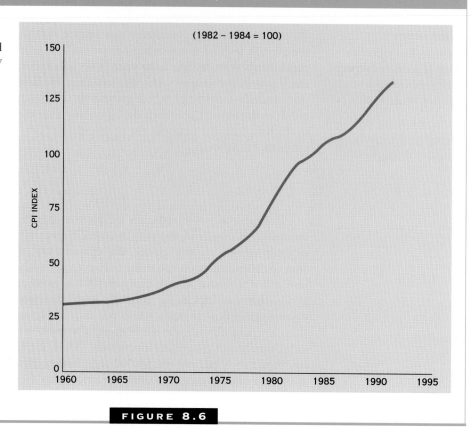

(1982 – 1984 = 100)

FIGURE 8.6

PRODUCER PRICE INDEX

A price index based on a large sample of materials and goods purchased by firms; formerly known as the wholesale price index.

PRODUCER PRICE INDEX (PPI) This index, also computed by the Bureau of Labor Statistics, differs fundamentally from the CPI. It does not include services. The PPI focuses on prices paid by firms for their inputs, rather than on prices paid by households. The PPI, which replaced the old Wholesale Price Index in 1978, measures prices at an early stage of the distribution system. The sample of goods involves 2,800 items, including raw materials and intermediate products such as glass and steel. Published price data and data obtained with questionnaires sent to producers are used. The PPI is a relatively sensitive price index, moving rapidly in response to changes in supply and demand for the goods that constitute the index. The PPI often signals changes in inflationary pressures before the CPI. This follows from the fact that higher costs to producers (as measured by the PPI) often lead to higher prices paid by households (as measured by the CPI). The base year for the PPI is 1982 (1982 = 100).

GDP DEFLATOR

A weighted average of prices of all final goods and services produced in the economy.

GDP DEFLATOR Although it receives less publicity than the CPI and PPI, this index is often preferred by professional economists. The U.S. Department of Commerce computes the GDP deflator in order to ascertain changes in the price level of goods and services entering the GDP. This index differs from the CPI in that it excludes import prices and interest rates and encompasses a broader group of goods and services. Although the CPI and PPI are published monthly, the GDP deflator is available only on a quarterly basis. A subindex of the GDP deflator, the personal consumption expenditures (PCE) deflator, is sometimes considered superior to the CPI by professional economists because of its method of construction.

Calculating Your Personal Price Index

ASSUME THAT YOU ENTERED COLLEGE THREE YEARS AGO AND THAT SELECTED ITEMS IN YOUR ANNUAL BUDGET HAVE INCREASED IN PRICE AS FOLLOWS SINCE YOU MATRICULATED:

A. APARTMENT RENT: $250 TO $275
B. SOFT DRINKS: $0.50 TO $0.75
C. TUITION: $4,000 TO $5,000
D. GAS FOR CAR: $0.90 TO $1.20

ASSUME FURTHER THAT IN YOUR FIRST YEAR OF COLLEGE YOU PAID RENT 12 TIMES ANNUALLY, CONSUMED 600 SOFT DRINKS, PAID TUITION ONCE ANNUALLY, AND PURCHASED 1,000 GALLONS OF GAS. USING ONLY THESE FOUR ITEMS AS YOUR MARKET BASKET, CALCULATE YOUR CURRENT PRICE INDEX RELATIVE TO THE BASE YEAR (YOUR FIRST YEAR OF COLLEGE). WHAT IS THE PERCENTAGE INCREASE IN YOUR PRICE INDEX SINCE THE BASE YEAR?

SHORTCOMINGS IN OUR PRICE INDEXES

The price indexes (particularly the CPI) are of more than casual interest to millions of Americans. In fact, a significant portion of the population is directly affected by the price indexes because of the widespread use of escalator clauses. In recent years, almost 10 million American workers had contracts calling for wage hikes tied explicitly to the CPI. About 6 million military and civil-service retirees and about 40 million Social Security recipients receive benefits indexed to the CPI. Even the fate of 20 million schoolchildren who eat subsidized hot lunches depends on the reported CPI because of escalator clauses in funding provisions.

It is therefore clearly important that our price indexes be valid indicators of changes in the level of prices. However, for several reasons our price indexes tend to *overstate* the true rate of inflation. That is, it is widely believed that our price indexes exhibit *upward bias*. Given the number of people with a strong vested interest in the reported price indexes, it is not surprising that political considerations have sometimes delayed implementation of measures required to correct obvious flaws in these measures of inflation.

There are two major sources of bias in the popular price indexes. The first concerns the evolving *quality* of goods and services produced. The price indexes are intended to measure the change over time in the cost of purchasing a given market basket of goods and services. However, the quality of those goods changes over time and, for the most part, is gradually improving. Think back 15–20 years to

The Economics of Presidential Elections

Conventional wisdom holds that the state of the economy at presidential election time is of crucial importance in determining the outcome of the election. Whether the incumbent party is returned to presidential office seems to a large extent a pocketbook issue. Incumbent presidential candidates are almost always reelected when the economy is *on their side* on election day. Pollster George Gallup once claimed that there is no way an incumbent president can lose if both peace and prosperity prevail. When an incumbent president does not seek reelection, the prospects of the incumbent party's candidate are believed strongly influenced by prevailing economic conditions. Especially important indicators of voter sentiment are thought to be the unemployment rate, the inflation rate, and the level of interest rates—especially the home mortgage rate. The recent growth rate of the economy also seems important, presumably because it yields insight into the economic outlook for the near-term.

Table 8.2 provides indicators of economic conditions at the time of the eleven presidential elections dating back to 1948.

Note that incumbent presidents (indicated by asterisk) sought reelection seven times during the 40-year interval. On the five occasions that an incumbent was successful the economy was solid. On the two occasions that an incumbent lost (Gerald Ford in 1976 and Jimmy Carter in 1980) economic conditions were poor.

items that your family presently purchases—cars, tires, and shirts, for example. Cars in those days got about 15 miles per gallon and tires lasted about 25,000 miles. Today you can get 30–50 miles per gallon in many automobiles, and tires are typically good for 40,000–50,000 miles. Twenty years ago one had to spend 10 minutes ironing a shirt. Today we have no-iron shirts. And although today we have to spend considerably more for cars, tires, and shirts than we did in the past, we generally get a more desirable product. Part of what shows up as an increase in price then is actually payment for the increase in quality of the product. The price indexes, by inadequately addressing this consideration, tend to overstate the true price increases.[3]

The second major source of bias springs from the use of a *prior year's* consumption pattern in determining the *weights* of various products in the current price index. Note in Equation 8.1 that the price index for 1993 is built on the assumption that consumers still purchase the same quantities of each item they purchased in 1982. The index shows the change in the flow of expenditures required in 1993 to purchase the same quantities of each item purchased in 1982. In reality—since we

---

[3]Only in the case of automobiles does the BLS adequately allow for quality change. Each year the BLS sends a team of analysts to Detroit. As innovative and quality-improving features are added to new models, the BLS adjusts the price accordingly before entering it into the CPI. Hence, if a new car costs an additional $500 to produce this year because of installation of air bags, $500 is deducted from the final price before entering it into the CPI. To use this procedure on thousands of individual products would be prohibitively expensive.

For example, both inflation and unemployment rates were higher in 1976 than in the six previous election years. In 1980, inflation was out of control and interest rates were high; 1980 was a recession year in which real output was on the decline. Ronald Reagan defeated incumbent President Jimmy Carter in a landslide.

Economists have turned the intuition that Americans vote their pocketbooks into equations used to predict the winners of presidential elections. Perhaps the best-known prognosticator is Ray Fair of Yale University. Professor Fair uses a simple model to explain voter behavior. The model includes the inflation rate for the two years before the election and the growth rate of real per-capita income for the six months before the election. The model also spots an incumbent-party candidate 4 percentage points. Arguably simplistic and naive, Fair's model correctly predicted sixteen of the nineteen presidential elections before the 1992 presidential campaign, including President Bush's 1988 victory over Michael Dukakis. Before you use Fair's model as the basis for a wager, however, it is wise to acknowledge an alternative formula that also has proved amazingly accurate: If the American League wins the World Series in October of an election year, the Republicans win the White House.

know that demand curves are almost universally downward-sloping—consumers change the relative quantities of the various goods and services purchased in response to price changes. In 1993, consumers will expand purchases of items whose prices have fallen since 1982—such as PCs, VCRs, and tape players—and restrict purchases of items whose prices have risen sharply. The index therefore puts too much weight on items that have risen in price and too little weight on items that have declined in price. Hence, the reported price index overstates the increase in the *cost of living*.[4] Anyone whose income keeps pace with the reported CPI is actually coming out ahead, even if the quality of goods and services is constant over time. Both the CPI and PPI employ prior-year weights and therefore are subject to this *substitution bias*.

The upshot of these shortcomings in our price indexes is that perhaps the first percentage point or so of inflation reported each year may be written off as merely reflecting upward bias in the price index. Reported inflation above that amount is likely to be the real stuff.

---

[4]The reported CPI accurately reports changes in the cost of living in this regard only for the individuals who never change their buying patterns in response to changes in relative prices among goods and services. That is, it is accurate only for those individuals whose demand curves for all items in the market basket are perfectly inelastic.

ELECTION-YEAR ECONOMIES, 1948–1988

ELECTION YEAR	CANDIDATE/(PARTY) (WINNER LISTED FIRST)	ECONOMIC INDICATOR**			
		UNEMPLOYMENT RATE (%)	INFLATION RATE (%)	INTEREST RATE (%)	GROWTH RATE (%)
1988	George Bush (R) Michael Dukakis (D)	5.6	4.1	10.0	2.7
1984	Ronald Reagan* (R) Walter Mondale (D)	7.5	4.3	13.0	4.0
1980	Ronald Reagan (R) Jimmy Carter* (D)	7.7	12.9	11.1	−4.6
1976	Jimmy Carter (D) Gerald Ford* (R)	7.8	5.7	7.0	1.7
1972	Richard Nixon* (R) George McGovern (D)	5.6	2.9	5.3	6.0
1968	Richard Nixon (R) Hubert Humphrey (D)	3.5	4.5	6.5	5.0
1964	Lyndon Johnson* (D) Barry Goldwater (R)	5.0	1.0	4.5	3.7
1960	John Kennedy (D) Richard Nixon (R)	5.6	1.4	4.8	−0.4
1956	Dwight Eisenhower* (R) Adlai Stevenson (D)	4.1	2.2	3.8	1.1
1952	Dwight Eisenhower (R) Adlai Stevenson (D)	3.4	3.1	3.0	1.3
1948	Harry Truman* (D) Thomas Dewey (R)	3.9	8.9	2.0	5.4

*Incumbent candidate.
**Variables are defined as follows: unemployment rate is for August of election year; inflation is rate of increase in consumer price index for the 12-month period ending August of election year; interest rate is prime loan rate for August of election year; growth rate is annual growth rate in real GDP for six-month period ending third quarter of election year.
Source: Adapted and updated from *Citibank Economic Database*, 1992.

TABLE 8.2

Summary

1. Industrial nations experience patterns of repeated expansion and contraction of economic activity known as business cycles. The four phases of the business cycle are expansion, peak, contraction, and trough. Though highly variable in length and amplitude, business cycles last about five years on average.

2. Governments use measures known as stabilization policies in an effort to avoid extreme swings of economic activity. Such policies include monetary policy and fiscal policy. Monetary policy involves measures that influence the level of interest rates, availability of credit, and the supply of money. Fiscal policy involves changes in tax rates and government expenditures. Both monetary and fiscal policy are used to influence aggregate spending, output, employment, and prices.

3. The nation's labor force officially consists of those who are employed plus those not working but searching for employment. The U.S. Department of Labor counts as unemployed those who are out of work but seeking employment. The nation's official unemployment rate is the ratio of the number unemployed to the number in the labor force (times 100).

4. The labor force participation rate is the percentage of the population above age 16 in the labor force. The overall U.S. labor force participation rate has increased steadily in the past 30 years because of increasing labor force participation rates of women.

5. Unemployment may be categorized as frictional, structural, or cyclical. Frictional unemployment consists of those temporarily in the job-search process on the day the unemployment survey is taken. Much of the frictional unemployment is voluntary. Structural unemployment is a more serious situation in which millions of job vacancies coexist with millions of involuntarily unemployed workers because the skills sought by the employers differ from the skills possessed by the unemployed. Cyclical unemployment occurs when the nation's output is below potential GDP and normally employed workers are thrown out of work.

6. The natural unemployment rate is the minimum unemployment rate that could be sustained without inducing an increase in the nation's inflation rate. It is considered to be the unemployment rate prevailing when actual and potential GDP are equal and when only frictional and structural unemployment exist. The natural unemployment rate fluctuates over time because of fluctuations in the percentage of the labor force frictionally and structurally unemployed. The natural unemployment rate increased from the mid-1960s until the early 1980s and has declined somewhat since.

7. All market-oriented economies have been plagued periodically by inflation. Inflation has become more persistent and severe after World War II and was especially virulent in the 1970s.

8. To measure inflation we use a price index—an index of the cost of purchasing a market basket of goods relative to the cost of buying that basket in some base year. In the United States the three main price indexes are the consumer price index (CPI), the producer price index (PPI), and the GDP deflator.

9. These price indexes are important to Americans because of considerable use of escalator clauses in wage and salary adjustments and retirement benefits. It is believed that the indexes are subject to a slight upward bias—they tend to overstate the magnitude of inflation.

Key Terms

macroeconomics
business cycle
nominal GDP
real GDP
recession
depression
monetary policy
Federal Reserve System
fiscal policy
labor force
unemployment rate

labor force participation rate
frictional unemployment
structural unemployment
cyclical unemployment
natural unemployment rate
inflation
price index
consumer price index (CPI)
producer price index (PPI)
GDP deflator

1. Explain the difference between nominal GDP and real GDP. If you are trying to compare the economic performance of Japan and the United States over the past ten years, which GDP measure would you use?

2. List the four phases of the business cycle. How does the unemployment rate typically change over the business cycle? How do business profits change?

3. Define stabilization policy and explain the difference between monetary policy and fiscal policy.

4. Explain how the U.S. unemployment rate is measured. What shortcomings do you see in this procedure? Can you think of a better method for measuring the unemployment rate?

5. Define the following terms:
   a. underemployment
   b. discouraged worker
   c. hidden unemployment
   d. secondary worker
   e. labor force participation rate

6. Why do most economists believe that in today's economy it would be unwise to try to push the unemployment rate below 5 percent with stimulative macroeconomic policies?

7. Assume you have been appointed chair of the President's Council of Economic Advisors. What programs would you recommend to the president in order to attack the problem of structural unemployment? Explain.

8. List and define the three types of unemployment. Which is the most amenable to change by monetary and fiscal policies?

9. What factors have caused the natural unemployment rate to decline since the early 1980s? Explain.

10. Explain the impact on the natural unemployment rate of the following events:
    a. The government extends the duration of unemployment benefits from six months to one year.
    b. Congress passes a strong education bill, and a larger portion of youngsters complete high school and college.
    c. "Echo baby boomers" flood the labor market around the turn of the century.

11. By using the current prices of a half-dozen major items in your personal budget, together with the prices of these items and quantities five years ago (if you aren't sure, estimate them or look them up in Bureau of Labor Statistics, *Monthly Labor Review*), compute your personal price index today relative to the base year of five years ago. How do you interpret this number?

12. Explain why the CPI is said to overstate the increase in the cost of living in the United States.

Calculating Labor Market Statistics for Medicine Bow

YOUR TURN
Answers

A. THE LABOR FORCE CONSISTS OF 700 PEOPLE (400 MEN AND 300 WOMEN). THE NUMBER OF PEOPLE UNEMPLOYED IS 42 (18 MEN AND 24 WOMEN).

B. THE LABOR FORCE PARTICIPATION RATE IS THE PERCENTAGE OF THE WORKING-AGE POPULATION IN THE LABOR FORCE. IT IS CALCULATED AS 100 TIMES THE RATIO OF

THE LABOR FORCE TO THE WORKING-AGE POPULATION, OR 100 × 700/1,000 = 70 PERCENT. THE LFPR FOR MEN IS 80 PERCENT. THE LFPR FOR WOMEN IS 60 PERCENT.

C. THE UNEMPLOYMENT RATE IS THE PERCENTAGE OF THE LABOR FORCE UNEMPLOYED. IT MAY BE CALCULATED BY TAKING 100 TIMES THE RATIO OF THE NUMBER UNEMPLOYED TO THE LABOR FORCE. THE TOWN'S UNEMPLOYMENT RATE IS 100 × 42/700 = 6 PERCENT. THE MALE UNEMPLOYMENT RATE IS 100 × 18/400 = 4.5 PERCENT. THE FEMALE UNEMPLOYMENT RATE IS 100 × 24/300 = 8 PERCENT.

Calculating Your Personal Price Index

THE CURRENT PRICE INDEX IS CALCULATED AS FOLLOWS. TAKE THE EXPENDITURES NEEDED TODAY TO PURCHASE THE MARKET BASKET CONSUMED IN THE BASE YEAR, DIVIDE BY THE EXPENDITURES REQUIRED IN THE BASE YEAR TO BUY THE SAME BASKET, AND MULTIPLY THE ANSWER BY 100. EXPENDITURES IN THE BASE YEAR TO PURCHASE THE FOUR ITEMS WERE $250 (12) + $0.50 (600) + $4,000 (1) + $0.90 (1,000) = $8,200. THE CURRENT COST OF BUYING THE SAME BASKET IS $275 (12) + $0.75 (600) + $5,000 (1) + $1.20 (1,000) = $9,950. HENCE

$$\text{PRICE INDEX} = \frac{\$9,950}{\$8,200} \times 100 = 121.3$$

THE PERCENTAGE INCREASE IN THE PRICE LEVEL SINCE MATRICULATION IS ESTIMATED TO BE 21.3 PERCENT.

Selected References

Baily, Martin N., and Arthur M. Okun (eds.). *The Battle Against Unemployment and Inflation*, 3rd ed. (New York: Norton, 1982). This series of articles analyzes the relationship of monetary and fiscal policies to unemployment.

Ehrenberg, Ronald G., and Robert S. Smith. *Modern Labor Economics*, 4th ed. (New York: Harper Collins, 1991). This popular labor economics textbook goes into greater depth on the issues surveyed in this chapter.

Gordon, Robert J. "The Consumer Price Index: Measuring Inflation and Causing It," *The Public Interest*, Spring 1981, pp. 112–134. This article points out flaws in our chief measure of prices (some of which have now been corrected).

Triplett, Jack E. "The Measurement of Inflation: A Survey of Research on the Accuracy of Price Indexes," in Paul H. Earl (ed.), *Analysis of Inflation* (Lexington, MA: Lexington Books, 1975). Chapter 2 summarizes economists' studies of our price indexes.

WHEN MORE AND MORE
PEOPLE ARE THROWN OUT
OF WORK, UNEMPLOYMENT
RESULTS.

—CALVIN COOLIDGE

Unemployment and Inflation: Their Consequences

IN THE LAST CHAPTER, WE INTRODUCED TWO KEY CONCEPTS OF MACROECONOMICS: UNEMPLOYMENT AND INFLATION. WE BRIEFLY DISCUSSED THE MEANING OF UNEMPLOYMENT AND INFLATION AND ANALYZED IN SOME DEPTH THE WAY THAT EACH IS MEASURED IN THE UNITED STATES. IN THIS CHAPTER, WE EXPLORE THE *CONSEQUENCES* OF BOTH UNEMPLOYMENT AND INFLATION.

IN THE LAST CHAPTER, WE ALSO SKETCHED THE NATURE OF THE BUSINESS CYCLE. WHEN ECONOMIC ACTIVITY IS VERY STRONG AND THE ECONOMY IS NEAR THE PEAK OF THE BUSINESS CYCLE, THE DEMAND FOR GOODS AND SERVICES IS TYPICALLY ROBUST. BECAUSE FIRMS ARE PRODUCING A HIGH LEVEL OF OUTPUT, DEMAND FOR LABOR IS HIGH. THE NATION'S UNEMPLOYMENT RATE IS LOW. IN SUCH CIRCUMSTANCES, THE PROSPECTS FOR INCREASED INFLATION ARE ENHANCED. THE MAIN DANGER ENCOUNTERED BY THE ECONOMY IS INFLATION.

ON THE OTHER HAND, WHEN ECONOMIC ACTIVITY IS WEAK AND THE ECONOMY IS NEAR THE CYCLICAL TROUGH, THE DEMAND FOR GOODS AND SERVICES IS TYPICALLY SOFT. BECAUSE THE NATION'S OUTPUT AND SALES ARE DOWN, DEMAND FOR LABOR IS LOW. THE NATION'S UNEMPLOYMENT RATE IS RELATIVELY HIGH. IN SUCH CONDITIONS, THE UPWARD PRESSURES ON PRICES TEND TO BE MINIMAL. INFLATION IS SUBDUED. THE CHIEF RISK IS EXCESSIVE UNEMPLOYMENT RATHER THAN RISING INFLATION.

THOSE IN CHARGE OF THE NATION'S MONETARY AND FISCAL POLICIES, IN DECIDING ON THE APPROPRIATE POLICIES TO IMPLEMENT AT ANY POINT IN TIME, MUST ASSESS THE RISKS OF ESCALATING inflation and higher unemployment. In addition, it is essential that they thoroughly understand the nature and consequences of both unemployment and inflation. In this chapter we present in some detail the consequences of unemployment as well as the effects of inflation.

Consequences of Unemployment

Several adverse effects occur when unemployment increases significantly. Perhaps the most straightforward economic consequence of unemployment is the resulting sacrifice of aggregate output and income in the nation. In addition, the *distribution of the impact* of unemployment is highly uneven—it falls disproportionately on such disadvantaged groups as ethnic minorities, unskilled workers, youth, and the lower economic classes. Moreover, a rise in unemployment triggers an increase in social problems such as delinquency, alcoholism, and mental debilitation; reduces government tax revenues and thereby impairs the provision of public goods such as streets and roads, educational facilities, and other infrastructure; and probably has negative implications for the economy's long-run growth. The consequences of unemployment are pervasive and long-lasting in nature.

LOSS OF OUTPUT AND INCOME

An increase in unemployment above the natural rate moves us farther below society's production possibilities curve. An increase in unemployment shrinks the nation's output and income, thereby reducing the standard of living of the nation as a whole. There is simply less income to be distributed within the nation because fewer people are working and producing output. The relationship between the U.S. unemployment rate and this loss of output at any time is quantified in what has become known as *Okun's law*.

Arthur Okun, as chairman of the President's Council of Economic Advisors in the 1960s, was concerned about the national sacrifice or waste associated with the operation of the economy at an output level significantly below the full-employment level. He was concerned about the costs of a slack or underused economy. To understand these costs, consider Figure 9.1, which illustrates the path of actual and potential GDP since the early 1960s.

POTENTIAL GDP
The hypothetical output level produced under conditions of full employment—when only frictional and structural unemployment exist.

Potential GDP may be defined as the hypothetical level of output or GDP that would be produced if the unemployment rate were maintained at the natural rate of unemployment—the unemployment rate that prevails when all cyclical unemployment is eliminated, leaving only the core of frictional and structural unemployment.

Potential GDP typically increases over time because of growth of the labor force and growth of productivity—output per worker. Since the early 1960s, the labor force has grown because of both an increasing population and a rising labor force participation rate. Productivity rises over time because of the development of new technologies, growth of capital goods per worker, and improved skills and education on the part of the work force.

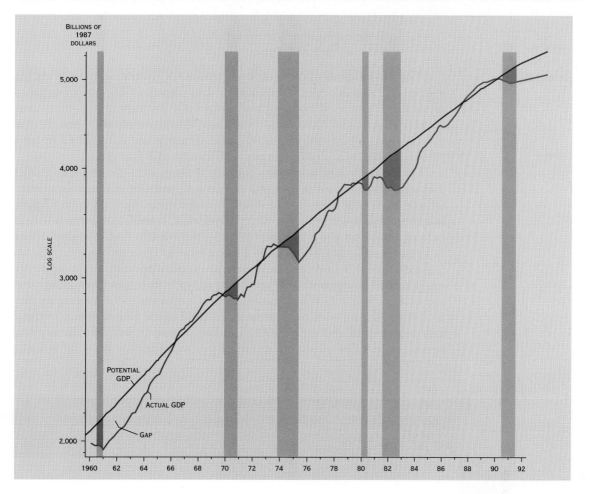

The output gap is the difference between potential GDP and actual GDP. This output gap increases during recessions (shaded areas). A crucial economic consequence of unemployment in excess of the natural rate is the resulting loss of output and income.

FIGURE 9.1

OUTPUT GAP

The magnitude by which actual GDP falls short of potential GDP.

Actual GDP may deviate from potential GDP to the extent that the actual unemployment rate differs from the economy's natural unemployment rate. Occasionally, when the economy is near the peak of the business cycle, the actual unemployment rate falls below the natural rate of unemployment and actual GDP moves above potential GDP (1967–1969, 1973, and 1988–1989 in Figure 9.1). More commonly, the unemployment rate exceeds the natural rate. In this event, an **output gap** exists, equal to the shortfall of actual GDP relative to potential GDP.

In Figure 9.1, shaded areas indicate periods of economic contraction, that is, periods when real GDP is declining. Unshaded areas indicate periods of economic expansion. Most of the time—even when output is expanding—an output gap has

OKUN'S LAW
Rule of thumb that indicates
that each 1 percent of unemployment above the natural
rate is associated with a 2.5
percent gap between actual
and potential GDP.

existed, as actual GDP has fallen short of potential GDP. **Okun's law**, which estimates the relationship between the nation's unemployment rate and this loss of
output, may be expressed in equation form:

$$\left(\frac{\text{Potential GDP} - \text{Actual GDP}}{\text{Actual GDP}}\right) \times 100 = 2.5\,(U - 5.5\%) \qquad (9.1)$$

The left-hand side of the equation expresses the dollar magnitude of the output
gap or GDP gap—the gap between actual and potential GDP—as a percentage of
actual GDP. Hence, if potential and actual GDP are running at annual rates of
$6,400 billion and $6,200 billion, respectively, the output gap is 3.2 percent of actual GDP, that is, $200 billion/$6,200 billion. If actual and potential GDP are each
running at rates of $6,200 billion per year, there is no output gap.

On the right-hand side of the equation, U represents the unemployment rate.
The expression states that each one percentage point that the unemployment rate
exceeds the natural unemployment rate (assumed in the equation to be 5.5 percent)
is associated with a 2.5 percent output gap. Hence, if the unemployment rate is 7.5
percent, the output gap is 5 percent. That is, the loss of output (the gap) is running
at 5 percent of actual GDP. If (as in a severe recession year such as 1982) the unemployment rate is 9.5 percent, the economy is operating with a 10 percent output
gap. In the $3,000 billion (GDP) economy of 1982, the output gap was running at a
rate of about $300 billion per year, or a loss of output and income averaging roughly
$1,200 per year for each man, woman, and child in the United States. In the slug-
gish economy of the early 1990s, the loss of output was considerably smaller
because the unemployment rate was much lower than in the 1981–1982 recession.

ASSUME THE ECONOMY TURNS WEAK IN 1995, AND THE UNEMPLOYMENT RATE
INCREASES TO 8 PERCENT. USING OKUN'S LAW AS EXPRESSED IN EQUATION 9.1, CAL-
CULATE THE 1995 LOSS OF OUTPUT IF ACTUAL GDP IN 1995 IS $6,800 BILLION.

YOUR TURN

DISTRIBUTION OF THE IMPACT OF INCREASED UNEMPLOYMENT

If, when the unemployment rate rises from 5.5 percent to 7.5 percent, each American loses 5 percent of annual income, the financial burden of the increased unemployment is shared equally. But this is hardly what happens. Instead, the burden
falls predominantly upon a small segment of society, those thrown out of work and
their families.

A large portion of the unemployed are low-income, unskilled workers heavily
composed of minority groups and young workers. A rule of thumb is that the
unemployment rate of blacks is double that of whites. Hence, a 1 percentage point
increase in the white unemployment rate in an economic downturn is likely to be
accompanied by a 2 percentage point increase in unemployment of black workers.
Unemployment rates of teenagers are several times that of white workers over age
20. Unemployment rates of black teenagers fluctuate within a range of roughly
25–50 percent, depending on the state of the economy.

Table 9.1 gives the unemployment rate of selected groups at two points of time: June 1990 and November 1982. The 1982 date represents a time of very depressed economic activity: the trough of the most severe recession of the past 50 years. The 1990 date represents the peak of the ensuing, long economic expansion that followed the 1981–1982 recession. Note the differential impact of the decline in unemployment across groups in 1990 relative to the depressed year of 1982. While the white unemployment rate was about 5 percentage points higher in 1982 than in 1990, the unemployment rate of blacks was 8 percentage points higher. The unemployment rate of black teenagers was nearly 15 percentage points higher. Clearly, the ranks of the unemployed are drawn disproportionately from disadvantaged groups in time of economic weakness. Conversely, such disadvantaged groups benefit strongly from an increase in economic activity and the resulting reduction in the nation's unemployment rate.

OTHER CONSEQUENCES OF UNEMPLOYMENT

Sociologists have established that crime rates, juvenile delinquency, and alcoholism are linked to the unemployment rate (see Exhibit 9.1). So are the incidence of mental health problems, suicide, and other social maladies.

Returning to economic considerations, when unemployment is high and output is depressed, less revenue flows into state and local government treasuries. After a fairly short time, deterioration can usually be found in the quality of such public services as streets, parks, libraries, schools, and university classrooms.

Finally, in addition to shrinking the nation's *current* standard of living, severe unemployment may have longer-run effects on the economy's productive capacity—and therefore on the future path of potential GDP and future living standards. In periods of economic weakness, business profits fall disproportionately, and investment expenditures on new plant and equipment and research and development are scaled back.[1] In such an environment, firms scramble to survive and are forced to abandon potential investment projects whose payoffs are not immediate.

UNEMPLOYMENT RATES (%) FOR VARIOUS GROUPS

GROUP	NOVEMBER 1982	JUNE 1990	DIFFERENCE
White workers, total	9.6	4.5	5.1
Black workers, total	18.7	10.7	8.0
White teenagers	21.3	12.5	8.8
Black teenagers	46.0	31.2	14.8
White males over age 20	9.0	4.1	4.9
Black males over age 20	17.6	9.7	7.9
Overall unemployment rate	10.7	5.3	5.4

SOURCE: Bureau of Labor Statistics, *Monthly Labor Review*.

TABLE 9.1

[1]In the last eight recessions, the average decline in real GDP has been 2.5 percent (peak to trough). The average decline in business pretax profits has been 22 percent. See Exhibit 8.1 in the last chapter (page 201).

The Human Tragedy of Unemployment

I n discussing unemployment it is essential to keep in mind that the consequences go far beyond the purely economic effects. In our culture, an individual's perception of personal worth and self-esteem is tied to working—maintaining a job. Social scientists believe that next to the death of one's spouse or being sent to jail, involuntary loss of one's job is among the most traumatic and stressful experiences of life. If society cares about the individuals that constitute the society, then full employment is a desirable goal for social as well as economic reasons.

A leading U.S. student of the personal consequences of unemployment has estimated that a 1 percentage point increase in the nation's unemployment rate sustained over a 6-year period leads to an additional[2]

- 920 suicides
- 648 homicides
- 495 deaths from cirrhosis of the liver
- 20,240 fatal heart attacks or strokes
- 37,000 total premature deaths
- 3,340 admissions to state prisons
- 4,227 admissions to mental hospitals

The dimensions of the personal consequences of unemployment may be glimpsed through the following personal recollection from the 1930s and the photograph from the 1980s.

Hell yes. Everybody was a criminal. You stole, you cheated through. You were getting by, survival. Stole clothes off lines, stole milk off back porches, you stole bread. I remember going through Tucumcari, New Mexico, on a freight. We made a brief stop. There was a grocery store, a supermarket kind of thing for those days. I beat it off the train and came back with rolls and crackers. This guy is standing in the window shaking his fist at you.

It wasn't a big thing, but it created a coyote mentality. You were a predator. You had to be. The coyote is crafty. He can be fantastically courageous and a coward at the same time. He'll run, but when he's cornered, he'll fight. I grew up where they were hated, 'cause they'd kill sheep. They'll kill a calf, get in the chicken pen. They're mean. But how else does a coyote stay alive? He's not as powerful as a wolf. He has a small body. He's in such bad condition, a dog can run him down. He's not like a fox. A coyote is nature's victim as well as man's. We were coyotes in the Thirties, the jobless.[3]

[2]Harvey Brenner, "Estimating the Social Costs of National Economic Policy: Implications for Mental and Physical Health, and Criminal Aggression," study prepared for the Joint Economic Committee, U.S. Congress (Washington, D.C., October 1976).

[3]Studs Terkel, *Hard Times* (New York: Pantheon Books, 1970), page 34.

EXHIBIT 9.1

The nation's future capital stock is therefore lower than it would have been if the economic weakness and unemployment could have been avoided.

Furthermore, by depriving young individuals of an early opportunity to gain job skills and a decent livelihood, attitudes and motivation levels may be adversely

Eating from a McDonald's dumpster—the 1980s

affected. All of this means that the *future level of potential GDP* may decline as a result of a high current level of unemployment.

Consequences of Inflation

The consequences of inflation are inherently more difficult to analyze than the consequences of unemployment. Clearly, an increase in unemployment shrinks the "size of the pie," impacts most heavily on the lower economic classes, and results in impairment of state and local government services.

The consequences of inflation are much more difficult to pin down with precision. In large part, this is because the consequences of inflation depend upon the extent to which inflation fools people, that is, the extent to which inflation is anticipated. Unanticipated inflation generally has more damaging consequences than inflation that is accurately anticipated.

Furthermore, the consequences of inflation change over time. Society's institutions adapt to continuing inflation. This adaptation, in turn, alters the consequences of inflation. The consequences of inflation in the 1990s are therefore likely to be quite different from the consequences of inflation in the 1950s or 1960s.

For example, conventional wisdom in the 1950s and 1960s held that inflation redistributed income and wealth from the elderly to the younger members of the population. Many of the elderly, being retired, were living off of nonwage income that was relatively fixed and independent of the current inflation rate. Hence, inflation reduced the living standards of the elderly. However, because of a host of institutional changes triggered by the high inflation of the 1970s, the impact of inflation on the well-being of the elderly has been radically altered.

Statutory interest rate ceilings that formerly limited the interest rate payable by depository institutions on savings and time deposits were abolished in the 1980s.

Since a disproportionate amount of these deposits are owned by the elderly—who live off of savings rather than current wages—the sharp upsurge of interest rates in the 1980s had favorable implications for the well-being of older people. In 1972, Social Security benefits were indexed to increase in lockstep with the consumer price index. As a result of these and other changes, it is not clear in the 1990s that the elderly are hurt by inflation.

There are three general consequences of inflation that we will explore in the remainder of this chapter: the effect on the distribution of the nation's income and wealth, the effect on long-term economic growth, and the effect on the use of the nation's resources, that is, on economic efficiency. We will emerge with the view that the adverse implications of inflation are severe and that every effort should be made to keep inflation in check.

IMPACT ON THE DISTRIBUTION OF INCOME AND WEALTH

Inflation brings about a rather arbitrary redistribution of the nation's income and wealth. These redistributive effects depend largely on whether inflation is accurately anticipated and the extent to which society's institutions are adapted to deal with inflation.

REAL INTEREST RATE
The difference between the actual (nominal) interest rate and the rate of inflation.

For example, the consequences of inflation for creditors and debtors depend on the behavior of *real* interest rates. The **real interest rate** is the difference between the actual or nominal interest rate and the inflation rate. If the actual interest rate is 8 percent while inflation is 4 percent, the real interest rate is 4 percent. If the actual interest rate is 5 percent while inflation is running at 7 percent, the real interest rate is negative 2 percent.

If the nominal interest rate adjusts sufficiently to maintain the real rate constant during an episode of escalating inflation, the creditor-debtor relationship is unaltered by inflation. There are no redistributive effects between lenders and borrowers in this event. However, if the real interest rate is induced to change by a change in the inflation rate, important redistributive effects will occur. Consider the following three potential scenarios, in which inflation escalates from an annual rate of 2 percent to 10 percent.

| | SCENARIO A | | SCENARIO B | | SCENARIO C | |
	PERIOD 1	PERIOD 2	PERIOD 1	PERIOD 2	PERIOD 1	PERIOD 2
Inflation rate	2%	10%	2%	10%	2%	10%
Nominal interest rate	5%	8%	5%	13%	5%	18%
Real interest rate	+3%	−2%	+3%	+3%	+3%	+8%

In the first scenario, the actual interest rate rises only from 5 percent to 8 percent, so the *real* interest rate declines from 3 percent to *negative* 2 percent. This might happen if the public is fooled by the inflation. It could also happen if the Federal Reserve aggressively pursues actions to hold down interest rates or if various institutional or legal barriers such as statutory interest ceilings prevent interest rates from rising in line with inflation.

Because the real interest rate declines in this scenario, income and wealth are redistributed from lenders to borrowers, that is, from creditors to debtors. Debtors reap a windfall gain as inflation reduces the real value of the principal borrowed and the interest rate is not sufficiently high to compensate lenders for this. The debtors' gains are the creditors' losses. This scenario typically prevails during periods of severe and rising inflation.

But who are the creditors and who are the debtors? In the aggregate, households are net creditors while firms and the government are net debtors. In the early 1990s, the total amount of debt outstanding was in the neighborhood of $12,000 billion, or $12 trillion. When intrasector debts are netted out, businesses and governments owed about $3,000 billion to households. We can therefore state that for each 1 percent that the real interest rate declines because of inflation (as in Scenario A), about $120 billion is redistributed from creditors to debtors annually, including a *net* redistribution of roughly $30 billion from American households to firms and the government.

Of course, important redistributive effects occur *within* the household sector itself, depending on the arrangement of each household's assets and liabilities. For example, the 30-year-old couple that takes out a low-interest, fixed-rate, long-term mortgage on a new home benefits at the expense of the retired person who deposits funds in a savings account in the local savings and loan institution that pays interest at a rate below the inflation rate.

Scenario A tends to occur when inflation is on the upswing. Expectations do not adjust instantaneously to the course of actual inflation. Interest rates therefore may not rise point for point with inflation. Thus the 1965–1980 period, in which inflation kept ratcheting higher and higher, was a period of low or negative real interest rates. In this period the elderly, being major creditors or lenders, were severely affected by inflation (Social Security benefits were not indexed to the CPI until 1972, either). People age 25–50, being debtors on balance, benefitted from the experience. In this period, the new family home became an investment that permitted millions of families to accumulate significant wealth. Keep in mind, however, that much of this wealth came at the expense of those who provided the funds for the mortgage—those who deposited funds in savings accounts in banks and savings and loan associations!

In Scenario B, inflation has a neutral effect on creditor-debtor relationships. The real interest rate remains constant as inflation accelerates. This scenario will occur if three conditions exist: inflation is accurately anticipated, the Federal Reserve permits interest rates to move freely in line with changes in inflation expectations, and other regulations that inhibit interest rate movements are nonexistent.

In Scenario C, real interest rates are very high. This scenario occurs when inflation is running *below* the level anticipated by the public or if the Fed is pursuing extremely restrictive monetary policies. This scenario occurred in the United States during 1981–1985, as the inflation rate came down much faster than expected from more than 12 percent to less than 4 percent in the span of a couple of years. Real interest rates were also very high in the 1930s, when the country experienced severe *deflation*. Although nominal interest rates were low in the 1930s, real rates were high because of falling prices.

In Scenario C, creditors benefit at the expense of debtors because of the abnormally high level of real interest rates available. Households, particularly elderly individuals living off the proceeds of savings, benefit at the expense of firms and the government. Debtors come under increased financial stress. Farm foreclosures, business bankruptcies, and home repossessions escalate as a result of the high real interest rates.

If inflation is accurately predicted in advance and if society's institutions have been adapted to the phenomenon of inflation, its redistributive consequences will

Does Inflation Reduce Your Family's Living Standard?

E X H I B I T

9 . 2

Inflation of the magnitude experienced in this country in the past 30 years may have adverse consequences for the long-run growth of living standards. However, many individuals naively and incorrectly jump to the conclusion that the following statement is valid:

> "In 1992, because the CPI increased by 4 percent, every American was robbed of 4 percent of his or her living standard."

This statement is fallacious because increases in prices of goods and services systematically increase the *incomes* of those who own the resources with which the goods and services are produced.

Higher wheat prices raise the income of wheat farmers. Higher automobile prices increase the gross receipts of the automobile manufacturers, providing the wherewithal to grant pay hikes to auto workers and executives. Higher prices charged for such services as haircuts, medical care, legal and accounting services directly increase the incomes of barbers, doctors, lawyers, and accountants. An increase in the price level increases the tax revenue of each state (as well as the federal government) because the states rely on income and sales tax receipts, both of which are boosted when prices go up. Hence, everyone who works for a state (or the federal) government is much more likely to receive pay hikes when prices are rising than in a zero-inflation environment.

A person agreeing with the earlier quotation forgets that if we take away inflation of prices, we also take away the major source of the increase in income of the people. If the nation had experienced zero inflation in 1992 rather than 4 percent, then the increase in wages and salaries, on the average, would have been lower by about 4 percent. Collectively, if the price level doubles, income also doubles. Therefore, it is not true that the "average" person is made worse off by inflation.

This is not to say that *no one* is made worse off because of inflation. Millions of individuals are hurt financially because of inflation's redistributive effects, while millions of others benefit from inflation. The outcome for each individual depends on the source of one's income, together with the nature and amount of one's assets and liabilities and the behavior of the *real* (inflation-adjusted) interest rate during the inflation. A good exercise for you to undertake would be to attempt to calculate whether your family would have been better off in the past four years if the country had averaged zero inflation rather than the 4 or 5 percent actually experienced. Warning: this is a very difficult exercise, which may explain why so many individuals fall into the trap of agreeing with the above quotation.

be minimized. **Indexation** refers to the use of escalator clauses that explicitly tie certain payments such as wage rates and Social Security payments to the nation's price index. When widespread escalator clauses protect workers, retirees, and owners of financial assets from the potential ravages of inflation, fewer people are hurt by inflation. Conversely, there are fewer windfall benefits to be reaped by the beneficiaries of inflation. This explains why many nations move toward more comprehensive indexation of wages, salaries, and various financial contracts and instruments when severe inflation appears.

IMPACT ON LONG-TERM ECONOMIC GROWTH

John Maynard Keynes, perhaps the greatest economist in the world in the first half of this century, used to argue that a little bit of inflation was a good thing for the economy. Keynes believed that mild inflation redistributed income and wealth from the "idle" classes (the retired) to the "active" classes (younger people) and tended to ensure a healthy level of business profits. Strong profits were believed to have beneficial implications for new investment in plant, equipment, and technology. In this way, long-term economic growth would be bolstered by an environment of modest inflation. Today, there is a strong consensus among economists that inflation is harmful. This does not imply that Keynes was wrong. The consequences of inflation in recent decades are likely to be quite different from those in an earlier era.

Keynes believed that inflation stimulated long-term growth. Apparently, he assumed that Scenario A always prevails during inflation. Business firms, being debtors, benefit in this scenario. Since people are fooled by inflation in this scenario, real interest rates decline and wages rise more slowly than prices. Income is redistributed from both lenders and workers to the firms. Business profits thus rise, yielding favorable implications for investment and long-term economic growth.

The first problem with Keynes' analysis is the assumption that inflation necessarily reduces real interest rates and real wages, thereby redistributing wealth and income in favor of firms. This is typically the case with unanticipated inflation. In the inflationary era of the past 50 years, however, the share of national income made up by profits has *declined* somewhat. The wage share has gone up. Once inflation becomes entrenched, and once society's laws and institutions have been adapted to it, Scenarios B and C are as likely to prevail during inflation as Scenario A.

Several other negative consequences for long-term growth are produced by inflation. First, higher inflation rates typically result in *more variable* inflation. This means that when inflation is high, it becomes more difficult to predict the future price level. Since the expected profitability of an investment project depends on the expected future price level in the economy, risk-averse firms tend to shy away from investment projects that have long-term expected payoffs. In other words, investment projects become more of a gamble in a high-inflation environment and firms tend to shrink their planning horizon. They invest only in projects with quick paybacks. This bias caused by inflation against *longer-term* investment projects, which often are the ones that introduce technological change, has unfavorable implications for long-term economic growth.[4]

Inflation may impair growth in other ways. Inflation tends to drive funds away from bonds and stocks in favor of such inflation hedges as real estate, gold and silver, antiques, and works of art. Hence, insufficient funds may be available for investment in plant and equipment. Economic growth may also suffer if inflation ends up reducing the saving propensity of the population. Finally, countries with strong inflation propensities tend to become trapped in a syndrome known as *stop-go macroeconomic policies*. The economy is alternatively subjected to *stop* policies—restrictive measures to hold down inflation—and *go* measures—stimulative policies to get the economy moving again after the stop policies raise unemployment to intolerable levels. Such inconsistent policies add to the environment of instability and uncertainty that breeds low levels of investment and growth.

IMPACT ON THE NATION'S RESOURCE ALLOCATION

When inflation is severe, individuals and firms are induced to behave in ways that, although advantageous from *their* points of view, are highly inefficient from *society's* viewpoint. As a result of such inefficient behavior, the nation's standard of living is reduced.

Inflation imposes a tax on money balances because such balances depreciate in value each year by an amount proportional to the inflation rate. Therefore, when inflation is severe, people respond by seeking to hold a smaller portion of their wealth in the form of money. But this requires more financial transactions, more trips to the bank, and more time generally spent on personal financial affairs. In the case of relatively severe inflation, time is spent marking up prices, reprinting catalogues and menus, and so forth. Time available for productive activities is reduced, to the detriment of the nation. Such costs have been dubbed the *shoe-leather* costs of inflation. Similarly, inflation diverts managerial talent away from the task of producing goods and services to the socially nonproductive task of dealing with the uncertainties of inflation. Time spent on hedging activities in the futures markets and foreign exchange markets exemplifies socially inefficient activities that would be minimized in a low-inflation environment.

---

[4]Prior to the 1980s, our tax system, in conjunction with inflation, created a bias against investment and growth. Depreciation allowances, which provide tax deductions for expenditures associated with real investment in plant, equipment and technology, were based on *historic or actual* costs rather than *replacement* costs. With these replacement costs escalating rapidly with inflation, firms could not recover sufficient tax savings to finance a major portion of replacement costs when it came time to replace worn-out or obsolete machinery. Moreover, inflation combined with the tax code tended to overstate business profits for income tax purposes, causing firms to pay taxes on *fictitious* profits. These burdens on the firm meant that inflation created a bias against investment in plant, equipment, and technology. However, because changes in the tax laws in the 1980s reduced or eliminated these biases against firms, future inflation may not have the same adverse consequences for investment and growth as was the case in the past.

Other examples of socially inefficient behavior can be found in financial and labor markets. Long-term contracts become too risky for all parties. Hence, contracts are shortened, thereby requiring more time and other resources spent in frequent contract renegotiations. In financial markets, long-term bonds are risky both to issuers and to potential buyers. If inflation turns out to exceed expectations, the lenders lose. If inflation turns out to be less severe than expected, the issuers of the securities—firms and the government—lose. As a result of the risks perceived by both debtors and creditors, activity in long-term bond markets dries up in periods of severe inflation. An increasing portion of the transfer of funds from creditors to debtors is conducted in short-term financial markets. This implies more time devoted to financial affairs and more frequent refinancing decisions by firms and governments and more frequent personal investment decisions by households.

The same principle applies to labor markets. Shorter contracts induced by the uncertainties of inflation imply more human resources allocated to negotiating wages and salaries and fewer resources allocated to producing goods and services. These efficiency losses depend on the severity of inflation. When inflation is held to low levels like those experienced in recent decades in Japan and Switzerland, such losses are probably inconsequential. In times of double-digit inflation, such losses become quite significant.

Summary

1. An increase in unemployment leads to a loss of output and income in the nation. The magnitude of this loss is estimated by Okun's law, which states that each 1 percent of unemployment in excess of the natural rate results in a loss of national output equivalent to 2.5 percent of actual GDP.

2. The costs of unemployment are not shared equally. Instead, these costs are chiefly borne by minority groups, youth, unskilled workers, and the lower economic classes. Also, increased unemployment leads to an increase in such social problems as crime, alcohol and drug abuse, and delinquency.

3. An increase in unemployment, by depriving state and local governments of tax revenues, results in impairment of the services provided by these units of government.

4. A stagnant economy and high unemployment, by impairing investment spending and depriving workers of an opportunity to gain work skills and habits, hurts the long-run growth of potential output and living standards.

5. Inflation brings about an arbitrary redistribution of the nation's income and wealth. High inflation typically redistributes income and wealth from creditors to debtors. Some individuals benefit from inflation. Others are hurt by inflation.

6. High inflation tends to reduce the share of national output devoted to investment in plant and equipment and new technology, thereby reducing long-term economic growth.

7. Inflation creates incentives for individuals and firms to engage in certain activities that are inefficient from society's point of view. Such activities move the economy farther below the production possibilities curve and reduce national output and living standards.

Key Terms

potential GDP   real interest rate
output gap   indexation
Okun's law

Study Questions and Problems

1. Using Okun's law as expressed in Equation 9.1, and using the current U.S. unemployment rate, estimate the current per capita loss of output and income in the nation if the U.S. population is currently 255 million.

2. Suppose the U.S. economy slips into a recession next year. Which groups in society would be most hurt by this development? Explain.

3. Analyze the longer-run impact of high unemployment on the nation's standard of living.

4. "While the chief effect of increased unemployment is to reduce the size of the pie, the main consequence of inflation is to redistribute the pie." Analyze.

5. Analyze the effect of high inflation on the long-run growth of living standards.

6. Why might real interest rates decline during a period of rising inflation? What are the implications of a decline in real interest rates for the distribution of income and wealth?

7. From your *personal* vantage point, do you prefer a very high or a very low real interest rate over the next decade? Explain.

8. Why do economists claim that the consequences of inflation depend on the extent to which inflation is accurately anticipated by the people?

9. Economists claim that in periods of high inflation, people are induced to pursue activities that are inefficient or wasteful from *society's* point of view. Can you give a couple of examples?

YOUR TURN
Answers

IF WE PLUG THE 8 PERCENT UNEMPLOYMENT RATE INTO THE RIGHT-HAND SIDE OF EQUATION 9.1, WE CALCULATE THAT THE OUTPUT GAP IS 6.25 PERCENT OF ACTUAL OUTPUT [2.5 (U − 5.5%) = 2.5 (2.5%) = 6.25%]. TAKING THIS PERCENTAGE OUTPUT GAP TIMES THE ACTUAL GDP OF $6,800 BILLION PER YEAR YIELDS AN ANNUAL OUTPUT LOSS OF $425 BILLION.

Selected References

Baily, Martin N., and Arthur M. Okun (eds.). *The Battle Against Unemployment and Inflation*, 3rd ed. (New York: Norton, 1982). This series of articles analyzes the relationship of monetary and fiscal policies to unemployment.

Feldstein, Martin S. "Inflation and the American Economy," *The Public Interest*, March 1982, pp. 63–76. A lucid analysis of inflation's consequences.

Fischer, Stanley, and Franco Modigliani. "Towards an Understanding of the Real Effects and Costs of Inflation," *Weltwirtschaftliches Archiv*, 1978, pp. 810–833. Examines the economic effects of inflation.

Hall, Robert E. (ed.). *Inflation: Causes and Effects* (Chicago: University of Chicago Press, 1982). These twelve articles by eminent economists explore various aspects of inflation.

Solow, Robert. "The Intelligent Citizen's Guide to Inflation," *The Public Interest*, Winter 1975, pp. 30–66. Excellent analysis of the effects of inflation, written for the layperson.

GET YOUR FACTS FIRST,
THEN YOU CAN DISTORT
THEM AS YOU PLEASE.

—MARK TWAIN

Measuring the Macroeconomy

IN ORDER TO GAUGE THE OVERALL PERFORMANCE OF THE ECONOMY, WE NEED MEASURES OF ITS AGGREGATE OUTPUT AND INCOME. IN THE ABSENCE OF SUCH MEASURES, IT WOULD BE IMPOSSIBLE TO ASCERTAIN, FOR EXAMPLE, THE APPROXIMATE LEVEL OF INCOME OF THE NATION IN 1993 RELATIVE TO 1960 OR SOME OTHER YEAR. IT WOULD ALSO BE IMPOSSIBLE TO JUDGE THE SIZE OR GROWTH PERFORMANCE OF THE UNITED STATES ECONOMY RELATIVE TO JAPAN, ITALY, OR GERMANY.[1]

BUSINESSES REQUIRE VALID MEASURES OF THE ECONOMY'S OUTPUT PERFORMANCE AS WELL AS FORECASTS OF EXPECTED PERFORMANCE IN ORDER TO FORMULATE CRUCIAL DECISIONS REGARDING PRODUCTION, EMPLOYMENT, INVENTORIES, AND EXPENDITURES ON NEW PLANT AND EQUIPMENT AND ON RESEARCH AND DEVELOPMENT.

ECONOMISTS HAVE A SPECIAL NEED FOR RELIABLE DATA ON NATIONAL OUTPUT AND INCOME, AND ON THE VARIOUS ELEMENTS CONTRIBUTING TO OUTPUT AND INCOME. TO STUDY THE EFFECTS OF MACROECONOMIC POLICIES AND THE INFLUENCE OF MYRIAD OTHER EVENTS ON NATIONAL PERFORMANCE,

---

[1]Even if each country has perfect data indicating the aggregate value of its output, it is difficult to compare the size of the various national economies because each country has its own currency. How many U.S. dollars are equivalent to one German mark or one British pound? One is tempted to use the current exchange rate. Suppose the U.S.–British exchange rate is two dollars to the pound, with U.S. output measured at $6,000 billion per year and British output at £600 billion per year. Since one pound is twice as valuable as the dollar (given the exchange rate), one is tempted to state that the value of U.S. output is five times greater than the value of British output. However, such a calculation is subject to a wide margin of error because there is no assurance that the purchasing power of two dollars in the United States conforms to the purchasing power of one pound in England. Exchange rates often fail to reflect accurately differences in the domestic purchasing power of the two currencies.

reasonably accurate data on the overall economy's production and its major components are essential.

In the next several chapters, many new terms are introduced and new concepts developed. Your comprehension of macroeconomic principles is closely related to how well you master the new terms and concepts. Before turning to the nuts and bolts of measuring the nation's macroeconomy, let us sketch the nature of two essential categories of economic variables—stocks and flows.

Economic Variables—Stocks and Flows

Most of the key variables in macroeconomics are *stock* variables or *flow* variables. A *stock variable* is one that is measured as an amount *at a given point of time*. Hence, one might state that on January 1, 1993, the U.S. population consisted of a stock of 254 million people. A lake is a stock of water; a shoe store's inventories consist of a stock of shoes or their dollar value. The U.S. capital stock consists of all its capital goods—plants, equipment, structures—at a given point of time. The U.S. money stock (the total of checking accounts and currency in the country, known as M-1) amounted to $992 billion on September 21, 1992.

Net worth or wealth is a stock variable because it is derived by subtracting the value of the stock of liabilities (debts) from the value of the stock of assets. If your family currently has total assets (home, cars, furniture, savings) of $100,000 and total liabilities (mortgage, consumer loans) of $60,000, your family's net worth is $40,000. The magnitude of your family's net worth changes every month as the value of assets and liabilities fluctuates, and as the monthly flow of saving (dissaving) adds to (subtracts from) family wealth.

Flow variables are measured as rates *per unit of time*. Hence, investment spending is expressed as the rate of spending on new plant and equipment per year. Population growth is the rate of change of the stock of population—the annual flow of births and net immigration minus deaths in the nation. Exports are the annual flow of products sold abroad. Expenditures are a flow of purchases per year. Family income is a flow of earnings expressed as a monthly rate or annual rate.

In economics, as in nature, stocks and flows interact and influence each other. Rainfall and the rate of evaporation (flows) influence the stock of water in a lake. Likewise, the flow of investment spending influences the nation's stock of capital. The stock of money in the economy influences the flow of expenditures on goods and services. Your family's stock of wealth or net worth influences its annual flow of expenditures. The nation's birthrate (flow) influences the population (stock), and the size of the population influences the flow of births as well as the birthrate. For example, because of China's enormous population, the government has imposed rigid sanctions limiting the number of children each woman is allowed to bear.

Whenever you come across a new variable or new concept in economics, it is an excellent idea instinctively to ask yourself: Is this a flow variable? A stock variable? Neither one? If you do this and also add the new terms to your list of economics terms (in your notebook), you will be a step ahead of the game!

National Income Accounting

NATIONAL INCOME ACCOUNTING

The set of rules and procedures used to measure the total flow of output produced by a nation, together with the income generated by this production.

National income accounting is the study of the procedures for measuring the aggregate output and income of a nation, together with the components of this output and income. It is concerned with such *flow* variables as gross domestic product (GDP), investment, government purchases, net exports, wages and salaries, and profits. Although very crude attempts to measure the national output of England were initiated 300 years ago, only in the post-World War II era have economists and international organizations implemented relatively serious attempts to measure systematically an economy's total output together with its components.

The acknowledged pioneer in the development of national income accounting is Simon Kuznets, recipient of the 1971 Nobel Prize in economics. Kuznets developed many of the concepts for measuring the macroeconomy that have been used by industrial nations in the past 50 years. In 1984, British economist Sir Richard Stone was awarded the Nobel Prize for his leadership in a United Nations program in which standardized procedures for national income accounting were developed and instituted. Today, more than 100 nations use these standardized procedures.

GROSS DOMESTIC PRODUCT (GDP)

The aggregate money value of all final goods and services produced by the economy in a given period, typically one year.

In this chapter we sketch the elements of national income accounting and examine alternative methods of estimating **gross domestic product (GDP)**—the dollar value of a nation's production of final goods and services in a given year. GDP is the most popular measure of a nation's annual output; per capita GDP—that is, GDP divided by the population—is a commonly used indicator of the standard of living of the people of a nation. We survey the components of GDP and discuss the corrections that must be made to reported GDP in order to assess the changes in a nation's material progress over time. We also explore the shortcomings of GDP as a measure of the well-being of a nation and discuss an experimental alternative measure.

GDP and the Circular Flow of Income

To understand the basic relationships among the flows of output, income, and expenditures in the macroeconomy, consider first a simplified economy with no government sector and no foreign trade. In other words, assume initially there are no taxes, there is no government spending, and the nation is totally isolated from all other nations. Figure 10.1 indicates the flow of income and output in such an idealized economy.

In this scheme we lump all producing units into the category "Firms" and the spending units into the category "Households." Most members of society play a dual role in this system. In their role at the firms, they are employed, produce goods and services, and earn income. In their role as "Households," they spend the bulk of their incomes on the same goods and services they collectively produce at the "Firms."

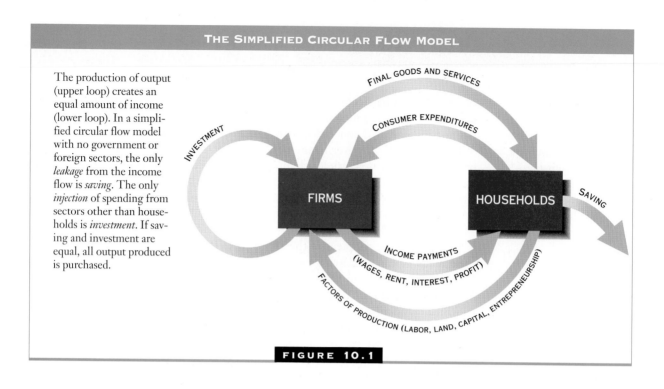

The production of output (upper loop) creates an equal amount of income (lower loop). In a simplified circular flow model with no government or foreign sectors, the only *leakage* from the income flow is *saving*. The only *injection* of spending from sectors other than households is *investment*. If saving and investment are equal, all output produced is purchased.

FIGURE 10.1

INTERMEDIATE GOOD
A good that is used as an input in producing other goods and services.

Firms purchase inputs in the form of labor, land, capital, and entrepreneurship —known as *factors of production*—from the households, paying out wages, rent, interest, and profits in return. The firms then use these resources, along with other materials and intermediate goods they purchase from each other, to produce final goods and services. **Intermediate goods and services** are those used in the production of other goods and services. For example, leather is an intermediate good used in the production of shoes and baseball gloves. Steel is an intermediate good used to produce buildings and cars. These final goods and services (gross domestic product) are then sold back to the households via the top loop of Figure 10.1.

A fundamental lesson of the *circular flow model* is that the production by firms of a certain value of goods and services (upper loop) creates a precisely equivalent flow of income for the factors of production (lower loop). Every dollar of output produced creates one dollar of income earned by the factors of production.

Another fundamental lesson of the circular flow model is that the income earned by the households (lower loop) provides the means by which households finance the purchases of the goods and services (upper loop) they collectively produce by supplying the factors of production to the firms.

Any event that causes a reduction in the production of goods and services produces an equivalent reduction of the income of the population. Any factor that causes a reduction of expenditures leads to a reduction of output and income. Figure 10.1 illustrates the interdependence between production decisions and expenditure decisions in a market economy.

The model depicted in Figure 10.1 ignores the government sector and foreign trade. There are no taxes, government services, exports or imports. If the only goods produced were *consumer goods* and if the households spent their entire income on these consumer items, the upper flow of expenditures would always be precisely equal to the upper flow of output (GDP). Since the production of GDP always produces an equivalent flow of income, a zero-saving society would return 100 percent of its income to the spending stream. Whatever output firms collectively produce would always be sold to the households. There would never be any problems associated with insufficient or excessive spending relative to the volume of goods and services available.

However, even in the context of the simplified circular flow model of Figure 10.1, not all final output is in the form of consumer goods. A portion of output consists of *investment goods*—tools and machines that firms produce to facilitate production of goods and services. Also, households save part of their income. Therefore, not all the income paid to the households (lower loop) is returned to the spending stream by households (upper loop). Some of the income *leaks* from the circular flow in the form of saving. On the other hand, not all the expenditures of this simple model originate in the household sector. Firms purchase some of the final goods and services that are produced; these are the investment goods noted in Figure 10.1.

In this two-sector model of consumption and investment, there is no assurance that output and expenditures will always balance. When—given current levels of output—the withdrawal of funds by households from the flow of spending (saving) exceeds the injection of spending on final goods by firms (investment), firms will not sell all their current output. The nation's inventories rise, signaling firms to cut the level of output and to lay off workers. When—given current levels of output— investment spending added to the expenditure flow by firms exceeds the withdrawal from the flow in the form of saving, firms will sell more than their current output. In this case inventories decline, signaling firms to expand production and employment. In this simple model *and in the real world*, fluctuations in saving and investment decisions result in fluctuations in national output and employment.

Approaches to Measuring GDP

In the simplified circular flow model illustrated in Figure 10.1, we assumed there was no government or foreign sector. We now move to a more realistic depiction, in which we acknowledge the existence of government spending and taxes, together with exports and imports. This more realistic circular flow model is presented in Figure 10.2.

Firms produce output (GDP), thereby creating an equal amount of income paid out to households in the process. There are now three *leakages* from this income stream that limit the amount of household spending on GDP. First, part of the income is saved. Second, part of it is taxed away. Third, part of the income is spent on imported goods. These three *leakages* from the flow indicate that perhaps only two-thirds of the income generated in the production of GDP is returned to the stream by households. On the other hand, there are three sources of demand for American output coming from parties other than American households. Firms purchase part of the output in the form of new plants and equipment (investment). The government (federal, state, local) purchases part of it. And foreigners purchase part (exports). All output is sold when the three leakages from the income flow (saving, taxes, imports) are precisely balanced by the three nonhousehold sources of spending (investment, government purchases, exports).

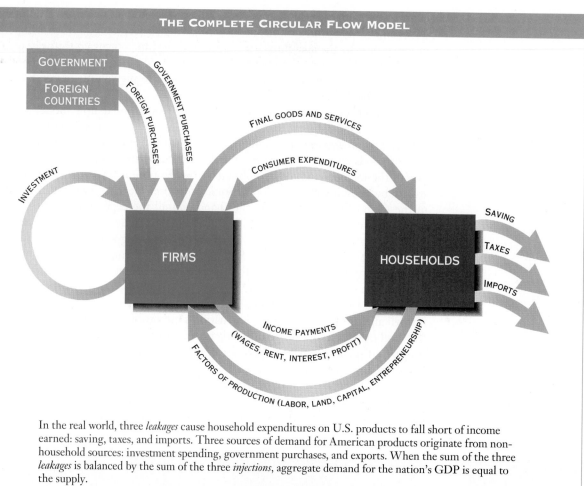

THE COMPLETE CIRCULAR FLOW MODEL

GOVERNMENT

FOREIGN COUNTRIES

FOREIGN PURCHASES

GOVERNMENT PURCHASES

INVESTMENT

FINAL GOODS AND SERVICES

CONSUMER EXPENDITURES

FIRMS

HOUSEHOLDS

SAVING

TAXES

IMPORTS

INCOME PAYMENTS
(WAGES, RENT, INTEREST, PROFIT)

FACTORS OF PRODUCTION (LABOR, LAND, CAPITAL, ENTREPRENEURSHIP)

In the real world, three *leakages* cause household expenditures on U.S. products to fall short of income earned: saving, taxes, and imports. Three sources of demand for American products originate from non-household sources: investment spending, government purchases, and exports. When the sum of the three *leakages* is balanced by the sum of the three *injections*, aggregate demand for the nation's GDP is equal to the supply.

FIGURE 10.2

There are two basic approaches to measuring a nation's output of goods and services (GDP): the *flow-of-output approach* (measuring the top loop of Figure 10.2) and the *flow-of-income approach* (measuring the bottom loop). Barring measurement error, the two approaches yield identical results. This follows from the previously mentioned principle that every dollar of output produced creates one dollar of income earned.

FLOW-OF-OUTPUT APPROACH

The flow-of-output approach seeks to sum the output of all newly produced final goods and services in a given year. *Final goods and services* are those not used in the production of other goods and services. In computing GDP, sales of new autos and new houses are included, but the steel sold (an intermediate good) to the automaker and to the building contractor are *not* included. To do so would mean *double counting* (that is, counting the production of steel once as it rolls out of the steel mill and once again as it becomes part of the value of the auto or house).

GDP or GNP?

EXHIBIT 10.1

For 50 years, the most popular measure of the output of the U.S. economy was **GNP**, or **gross national product**. However, the U.S. Department of Commerce announced in late 1991 that it was replacing GNP with a concept less familiar to Americans but more popular with the rest of the world: **GDP**, or **gross domestic product**.

The distinction between GNP and GDP is a minute one, and the two numbers move in an almost identical pattern much of the time. While GNP measures all output produced by workers and capital supplied by U.S. residents or corporations regardless of location, GDP tallies up the output produced by all workers and firms located within the United States, irrespective of nationality or national ownership. Thus, the share of output generated by American capital that is used to produce the Big Macs sold by McDonald's in Moscow—measured by profits—are included in GNP but not in GDP. Profits earned by Japanese capital on cars produced in Tennessee by Japanese-owned Toyota are excluded from GNP but included in GDP.

In making the switch, the U.S. government sought to obtain a better measure of U.S. production. The shortcomings in the traditional GNP measure became apparent in 1990 after Iraq invaded Kuwait and the world price of oil soared. These events triggered a sharp drop in the U.S. index of consumer confidence, which contributed to the 1990–1991 recession in the United States. However, the gross national product (GNP) figures obscured the actual depth of the downturn because of the temporary surge of profits earned abroad by U.S. oil companies in response to the spike in oil prices. GDP figures are unaffected by profits earned abroad by American firms. In early 1991, when oil prices came back down, the decline in these profits made it appear that the U.S. economy continued to shrink. In the second quarter of 1991, while real GNP declined at a rate of 0.5 percent per year, real GDP increased somewhat.

Most economists welcome the replacement of GNP with GDP. In addition to being less susceptible to distortion by such transitory events as changing oil prices and exchange rates, use of the GDP measure facilitates international comparisons of economic performance. European nations have employed the GDP yardstick for the better part of 40 years.

Since the objective is to measure output in the *current* year, transactions involving used items are not counted. Hence, purchases of used houses or used cars have no impact on GDP. Similarly, sales of such assets as land, stocks, and bonds are not included because they do not represent current production.

In the flow-of-output approach to GDP accounting, four categories of goods and services are included: consumption expenditures (C), investment spending (I), government purchases (G), and net exports or exports minus imports ($X - M$). The various subcategories of these major components, along with their 1991 magnitudes, are given in Table 10.1 (page 242). Consumption is the largest expenditure category, constituting two-thirds of the nation's GDP. The second largest category is government purchases of goods and services (19 percent of GDP), followed by

GROSS DOMESTIC PRODUCT VIA SUM OF OUTPUT PRODUCED, 1991 ($ BILLIONS)		
	AMOUNT	**% OF GDP**
I *Consumption*	$3,889	(68.5)
Durable goods	445	
Nondurable goods	1,252	
Services	2,192	
II *Gross private domestic investment*	$ 727	(13)
Fixed investment		
Nonresidential structures	175	
Producers' durable equipment	376	
Residential structures	195	
Change in inventories	−19	
III *Government purchases of goods and services*	$1,088	(19)
Federal	445	
State and local	642	
IV *Net exports of goods and services*	−$ 31	(−0.5)
Exports	591	
Imports	622	
Gross Domestic Product =	$5,673	(100)

SOURCE: Department of Commerce, *Survey of Current Business*, 1992.

TABLE 10.1

gross private domestic investment (13 percent of GDP). Typically, exports and imports are about equal in size, thereby canceling each other's impact on GDP. In the early 1990s, however, the U.S. trade deficit implied that net exports contributed negatively to our GDP—we purchased more of foreign nations' output than they did of ours. We turn now to a more detailed look at each component of GDP.

CONSUMPTION EXPENDITURES (C)
Household expenditures on all goods and services except housing; consists of household expenditures on durable goods, nondurables, and services.

CONSUMPTION (C) Consumption—variously known as "consumer expenditures" and "personal consumption expenditures"—includes such durable goods as automobiles, refrigerators, and VCRs; such nondurables as food, clothing, and tennis balls; and such services as medical care, haircuts, and educational expenditures. Consumer services are both the largest and fastest growing component of personal consumption expenditures. This is because in an affluent nation such as the United States, most individuals have satisfied their rudimentary needs for basic food, shelter, and clothing. As income rises, an increasing portion of expenditures tends to be allocated to such consumer services as entertainment, travel, health services, and education.[2]

---

[2]Economists use the concept of *income elasticity of demand* to measure the responsiveness of demand for various goods and services to a change in income. Income elasticity of demand is the percentage change in purchases of a product divided by the percentage change in income that initiated the change in purchases. A 10 percent increase in income may result in a 15 percent increase in expenditures on travel but only a 2 percent increase in spending on food. In this case the income elasticity of demand for travel and food are 1.5 and 0.2, respectively. In general, income elasticity of demand for consumer services is higher than for other components of consumer expenditures. See Chapter 5 for an in-depth discussion of income elasticity of demand.

Consumer goods and services are not used to produce other goods and services but are directly used by households either immediately (food, entertainment) or gradually (clothing, ballpoint pens). Consumption spending is closely linked to national **disposable income**—household income available after taxes.

GROSS INVESTMENT (*I*)
The total value of all investment goods produced in the economy during a specific time period, normally one year.

NET INVESTMENT
The net addition to the nation's capital stock in a given period; gross investment minus depreciation.

GROSS PRIVATE DOMESTIC INVESTMENT (*I*) In an earlier chapter we defined investment as expenditures on capital goods—goods used to produce other goods and services. Investment involves expenditures that replace or add to the nation's stock of capital. **Gross investment** refers to *total* expenditures on investment goods, including those that replace worn-out or obsolete machinery and other capital. **Net investment** refers to the *net addition* to the nation's total stock of capital in a given period of time.

The difference between gross investment and net investment is known as depreciation, capital consumption, or replacement investment. In any given year, a large portion of gross investment involves replacing worn-out and obsolete capital goods. Net investment is nearly always positive (gross investment > depreciation) in the United States. However, on rare occasions gross investment is insufficient to offset depreciation, the total capital stock declines, and net investment is negative. An example of this rarity occurred in 1933. Table 10.2 shows the magnitude of the components of gross and net investment in 1929 and in several subsequent years. As indicated in Table 10.1, gross investment may be divided into fixed investment and inventory investment. *Fixed investment* includes spending on nonresidential structures, producers' durable equipment, and residential structures. (The relative magnitudes of these components for 1991 are shown in Table 10.1.)

The classification of new homes (residential structures) as investment rather than consumption is one of many rather arbitrary close calls that must be made in national income accounting. A home is a very long-lived asset that provides a flow of benefits to its occupants. However, the same could be said of a new set of encyclopedias or a new stereo receiver, both of which are classified as consumer goods in the national income accounts.

Inventory investment, which can be either positive or negative, is defined as the net change in national aggregate business inventories in a given year. The change in inventories serves as a balancing item in the national income accounts. GDP is

GROSS AND NET INVESTMENT EXPENDITURES FOR SELECTED YEARS ($ BILLIONS)

COMPONENT OF INVESTMENT	1929	1933	1965	1991
Producers' durable equipment	$ 5.6	$1.5	$ 46.4	$376
New construction	8.9	1.5	57.2	370
Change in inventories	1.7	−1.6	9.9	−19
Gross private domestic investment	16.2	1.4	113.5	727
Depreciation	7.9	7.0	56.0	623
Net private domestic investment	8.3	−5.6	57.5	104

TABLE 10.2

intended to measure *output*, but does so by summing final *sales*, which are more accessible. When inventories rise in a given year, output necessarily exceeds sales; tallying up sales results in an understatement of output unless we add the increase in inventories to total sales. When inventories fall in a given year, the implication is that sales exceed output. Adding the (negative) change in inventories to sales provides an accurate measure of current output or GDP.

GOVERNMENT PURCHASES (G)

The value of goods and services purchased by all levels of government—federal, state, and local—in a given period; total government expenditures minus government transfer payments.

GOVERNMENT PURCHASES OF GOODS AND SERVICES (G) Our measure of GDP must come to grips with the huge amount of goods and services the nation *collectively* provides through government.

Government output, unlike the other components of GDP, is not sold in private markets. Therefore, national income accountants are faced with a conceptual problem in placing a dollar value on government output. What is the value of the annual services provided by upgrading the interstate highway system? The services provided by a public high-school algebra teacher? A highway patrolman? The accountants simply assume that the value of government goods and services is measured by their cost (for example, the salary of the teacher or the expenditures on the interstate highways).

The most straightforward way to estimate **government purchases** is to add the total expenditures of all three levels of government (federal, state, local) on goods and services and salaries of government employees. For example, the federal government spends on aircraft carriers and on salaries of postal workers, the federal judiciary, and members of Congress. State governments spend on roads, bridges, and salaries of university football coaches and professors. Local governments spend on libraries, fire engines, and salaries for police officers and high-school teachers.

It is important to understand that government purchases as measured in the national income accounts are considerably smaller than total government spending. As indicated in Chapter 7, a sizable portion of government's budget is in the form of transfer payments, which are not included in the GDP computation. **Government transfer payments** are government payments for which no concurrent goods or services are rendered. Coupled with taxes, they rearrange purchasing power in the private sector of the economy. Examples of government transfer payments include unemployment benefits, Social Security payments, interest on the national debt, subsidies to agriculture, and veterans' benefits. These payments do not represent expenditures for goods and services, which is what GDP attempts to measure. Adding transfer payments to GDP computation would make the national income accounts guilty of double counting, since most of the income received by recipients of transfer payments shows up in purchases of consumer goods.

GOVERNMENT TRANSFER PAYMENTS

Expenditures by government for which no goods or services are concurrently received by the government.

A significant part of government purchases that shows up in GDP is in reality investment expenditures. Federal spending on interstate highways or new airport safety equipment, state spending on new prison facilities or new university libraries, and local spending on new elementary schools all are forms of investment expenditures—spending on goods that increase the productivity of society and yield a long-lasting flow of benefits to the constituents of the nation. Since the national income accounts designate *investment* (gross private domestic investment) to include only *private* forms of investment spending, government investment expenditures are included with other forms of government purchases. If the federal government were to count separately its operating and investment expenditures, total investment in the United States would appear higher.

NET EXPORTS OF GOODS AND SERVICES (*X* — *M*) If we attempt to tally American GDP by summing consumption, investment, and government expenditures, we would be off the mark. GDP is a measure of *output* produced in this country, and a significant amount of our *purchases* are produced abroad (Japanese automobiles, French wine). We must subtract such expenditures on imports to arrive at domestic output (GDP). On the other hand, some of what we produce is sold beyond our borders (exports), and the value of these transactions must be added to domestic sales (*C, I, G*). This reasoning indicates that we should add net exports (*X* — *M*) to *C, I,* and *G* in order to arrive at U.S. GDP.

Table 10.1 indicates that, for 1991, net exports amounted to a negative $31 billion, or about −0.5 percent of our GDP. That is, the total flow of U.S. purchases exceeded production of GDP by $31 billion. By running substantial trade deficits in the past decade, we have in a sense been living *beyond our means*, enjoying more goods and services each year than we produce domestically, and financing the difference (the trade deficit) by borrowing from other nations. Prior to the 1980s, the United States was a persistent net exporter, selling more goods and services to the rest of the world than we purchased from them. In those years our total output of GDP exceeded the sum of consumption, investment, and government purchases.

BEHAVIOR OF THE FOUR SHARES OF GDP (*C, I, G, X* — *M*) Figure 10.3 (page 246) illustrates the behavior since the 1940s of each of the four shares of GDP (*C, I, G, X* — *M*) expressed as a percentage of the total GDP. One is struck by the relatively high degree of stability of each of the four shares.[3] For example, consumption has hovered around 65 percent of GDP and government purchases around 20 percent of GDP.[4] Investment expenditures exhibit the most short-range variability of the components, but the long-term trend in the ratio of the share of investment to GDP has been flat. Note that the U.S. trade balance has been negative since 1983. This swing from a positive to a negative trade balance reversed a long history of American trade surpluses.

FLOW-OF-INCOME APPROACH

Concerning Figure 10.2, we stated that the production by firms of any given magnitude of GDP (top loop) creates a precisely equivalent flow of income (bottom loop). Therefore, another way to tally the nation's GDP is to sum all the incomes

---

[3]Note in Figure 10.3 that much of the instability in these ratios occurred in the first five years depicted (1946–1951). World War II had recently ended (1945). During that war many consumer goods were not available. Therefore, immediately after the war a temporary surge of spending on such items as refrigerators and washing machines occurred. By 1951 or so, this splurge was over. Similarly, the abnormally large net export surplus in the early postwar years resulted from a surge of American supplies ordered by war-ravaged European nations.

[4]How does one square this little-known fact with the well-known fact that government budgets have outpaced GDP? The answer lies in the fact that government transfer payments, which are not included in GDP, or in our *G* of Figure 10.3, have been the source of the growth of government budgets relative to GDP. Government purchases of goods and services have *not* grown faster than GDP since the early 1950s.

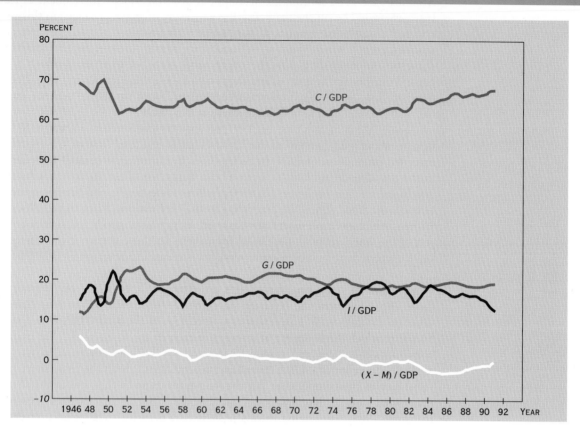

With the exception of the early postwar period (1946–1952), the shares of GDP constituted by the four components have remained rather stable. Investment spending is the most volatile component of GDP.

SOURCE: National Income Accounts, *Citibank Economic Database*, 1992.

FIGURE 10.3

earned in the economy. Consider the income earned in the production of a new Buick that sells for $20,000. Assume the following incomes are generated:

Wages of General Motors' employees	$10,000
Interest paid to GM bondholders	1,000
Rent paid on buildings	1,000
Profits of GM stockholders	2,000

However, this totals only $14,000. The remaining $6,000 consists of materials that General Motors purchases from its suppliers (glass, steel, tires, engines, and so on). These materials are *intermediate goods*.

General Motors, in purchasing $6,000 of materials and fashioning them into a final good worth $20,000, has contributed $14,000 of value to the product. This is known as **value added**—the difference between the sales price of a good and the cost of intermediate goods used to produce it.

Tracing this $6,000 back to the producers of these materials, we find that the $6,000 is accounted for by wages, interest, rent, profits *and* the purchases of materials from other firms.

The following accounting identity applies to each firm in the U.S. economy:

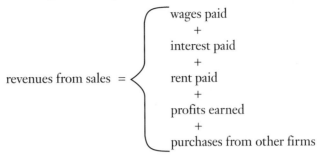

$$\text{revenues from sales} = \begin{cases} \text{wages paid} \\ + \\ \text{interest paid} \\ + \\ \text{rent paid} \\ + \\ \text{profits earned} \\ + \\ \text{purchases from other firms} \end{cases}$$

This accounting identity follows from the definition of profits as a residual item—sales revenues minus all costs of production. If we apply this identity to all firms in the nation and subtract "purchases from other firms" from both sides of the equation, we obtain

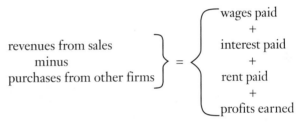

$$\left. \begin{array}{c} \text{revenues from sales} \\ \text{minus} \\ \text{purchases from other firms} \end{array} \right\} = \begin{cases} \text{wages paid} \\ + \\ \text{interest paid} \\ + \\ \text{rent paid} \\ + \\ \text{profits earned} \end{cases}$$

The left-hand side of the equation is total sales minus purchases of intermediate goods. For the aggregate economy, this is equivalent to the sum of *values added* and also is the definition of GDP. Hence, the accounting identity for the entire U.S. economy is

$$\text{GDP} = \text{wages} + \text{interest} + \text{rent} + \text{profits}$$

which provides accountants a second method for computing GDP.

Table 10.3 provides the steps involved in calculating GDP with the flow-of-income approach. The components are discussed in turn.

COMPENSATION OF EMPLOYEES This item, which constitutes about 60 percent of GDP, includes wages and salaries paid by firms and government to employees. It also includes such fringe benefits paid by employers as pension contributions, health insurance, and Social Security contributions. Since these supplementary payments are part of the cost to firms of employing labor, they are treated as wage and salary payments.

NET INTEREST This item includes interest payments paid by businesses to lenders. When you purchase a bond issued by a utility company, the interest payments you receive are included. Interest paid by government is a government transfer payment, and is not included.

RENTAL INCOME This item is the payment to property owners for the use of their resources. For example, house and apartment rents received by landlords are included.

GROSS DOMESTIC PRODUCT VIA SUM OF INCOME GENERATED, 1991

ITEM	AMOUNT ($ BILLIONS)
Compensation of employees	$3,388
+	
Net interest	480
+	
Rental income	42
+	
Proprietors' income	380
+	
Corporate profits	252
equals	
National income (NI)	4,542
+	
Indirect business taxes and miscellaneous items	507
equals	
Net domestic product (NDP)	5,049
+	
Depreciation	623
equals	
Gross Domestic Product (GDP)	5,673

SOURCE: Department of Commerce, *Survey of Current Business*, 1992.

TABLE 10.3

PROPRIETORS' INCOME Proprietors' income consists of net income earned by businesses that are not incorporated—the net income of partnerships and proprietorships.

CORPORATE PROFITS This item refers to the net income of corporations. It can be divided into three components: dividends paid to stockholders, retained earnings, and corporate income taxes.

All five items—compensation of employees, net interest, rental income, proprietor's income, corporate profits—are forms of income. Do these items add up to GDP? Unfortunately, no—economic life is not quite so simple. Two nonincome items must be added to the five forms of income in order to arrive at GDP: depreciation and indirect business taxes.

DEPRECIATION
The value of the nation's capital equipment that is used up in a given period, normally one year; indicates how much investment is needed to keep the nation's capital stock intact.

DEPRECIATION Most machines and equipment survive well beyond the accounting period in which they are purchased. If all the cost of buying machines and equipment is allocated to the year in which a machine is purchased, profits for that period are severely understated. And profits of future years are overstated. To avoid this, firms allocate the cost of equipment over a period of several years. The annual estimate of the amount of capital used up or consumed in each year is known as **depreciation**. Depreciation is an accounting mechanism that provides a more stable and accurate statement of profits in a given year. Table 10.3 reflects that in 1991 a huge charge of $623 billion was made against GDP for depreciation. This may be regarded as a portion of business receipts not available to pay out as income.

INDIRECT BUSINESS TAXES The government imposes taxes on certain products, which firms treat as costs of production and add to the prices of their products. These *indirect business taxes* include license fees, customs duties, federal excise taxes, business property taxes, and sales taxes. This flow of indirect taxes does not create income for the nation, and must therefore be added to the five forms of income, along with depreciation, in order to arrive at GDP.

Other National Accounts

In addition to GDP, there are several other measures of the nation's output and income that are essential to our study of macroeconomics. The output and income measures that separate GDP and disposable income—the income available to households after taxes—are briefly outlined.

NET DOMESTIC PRODUCT (NDP)
Gross domestic product minus a depreciation allowance for the value of capital goods wearing out during the period.

NET DOMESTIC PRODUCT (NDP) Although gross domestic product (GDP) is predominantly used to indicate the size of a nation's economy, **net domestic product (NDP)** is actually a better measure. GDP includes the production of output required to replace worn-out equipment. If we subtract this depreciation or replacement investment from GDP, we obtain a measure of the net output available to society. If GDP in 1993 is $6,500 billion and if $500 billion of that output represents production of capital goods to replace those worn out, the actual amount of new goods and services available is $6,000 billion. This concept—gross domestic product minus depreciation or capital consumption—is known as net domestic product (NDP). NDP represents the value of new goods and services available to an economy in a given year.

If NDP is conceptually a more appropriate measure of an economy's performance, why is GDP the more popular concept? The answer lies in the difficulty in estimating depreciation or capital consumption. It is much easier to compute GDP than NDP. The two concepts are closely related, with NDP typically amounting to 90 percent of GDP.

NATIONAL INCOME (NY)
The aggregate income received by the resource owners of land, labor, capital, and entrepreneurship; equal to GDP minus the sum of depreciation and indirect business taxes.

NATIONAL INCOME (NY) When computing GDP and NDP, the prices paid by buyers of final goods and services are used. Encompassed in these prices are a variety of indirect taxes (as noted earlier). For example, a new automobile costing $15,000 may include in its price a $300 federal excise tax and a $600 state sales tax. These taxes are known as indirect taxes because they are not levied directly on incomes. We pay them indirectly by purchasing products on which such taxes are levied. These taxes produce revenues for governments but do not generate income for individuals. If we deduct these indirect taxes from NDP, we obtain the total payment of income to the factors of production—land, labor, capital, entrepreneurs. These payments are known as **national income (NY)**.

PERSONAL INCOME (PY) A portion of national income is not received as income by persons. For example, only part of corporate profits are paid out (as dividends) to persons; some are paid to the U.S. Treasury (via corporate income tax), some are retained by the firm. Also, corporations pay contributions to the Social

Security system for their workers. On the other hand, recall that government transfer payments are not included in GDP. However, they do lead to personal income. Given these considerations, to get from national income (NY) to *personal income* (**PY**) we subtract retained corporate profits, corporate income taxes, and Social Security contributions made by firms, and add government transfer payments.

DISPOSABLE INCOME (y_d) Income in the hands of individuals after deducting income taxes; income available to households to spend and save.

DISPOSABLE INCOME (y_d) Not all of personal income is available to households for spending and saving. Individuals face federal, state, and sometimes local income taxes. Deducting these items from personal income yields **disposable income** (y_d)—personal income available after income taxes.

Figure 10.4 illustrates the relationship among the five alternative measures of the nation's income. Among these measures, the two that we frequently single out in macroeconomic models are gross domestic product and disposable income.

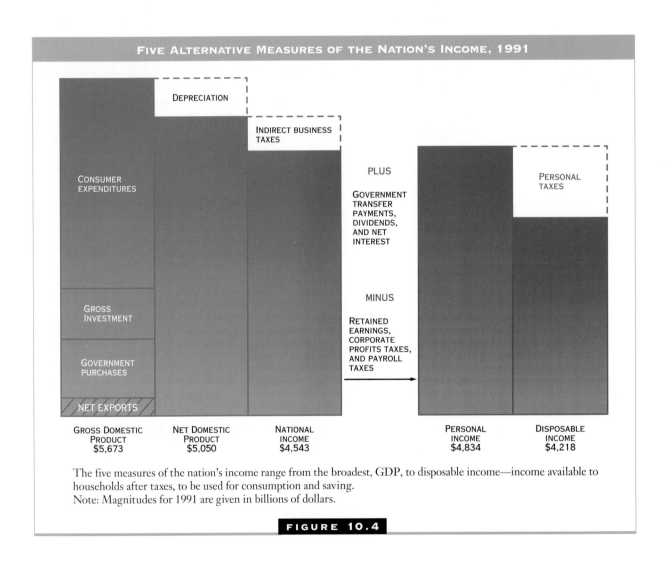

FIVE ALTERNATIVE MEASURES OF THE NATION'S INCOME, 1991

| GROSS DOMESTIC PRODUCT $5,673 | NET DOMESTIC PRODUCT $5,050 | NATIONAL INCOME $4,543 | PERSONAL INCOME $4,834 | DISPOSABLE INCOME $4,218 |

The five measures of the nation's income range from the broadest, GDP, to disposable income—income available to households after taxes, to be used for consumption and saving.
Note: Magnitudes for 1991 are given in billions of dollars.

FIGURE 10.4

If you are 18–22 years old, the U.S. gross domestic product has more than quadrupled during your lifetime. Table 10.4 indicates that between 1972 and 1991, *nominal GDP* increased from a little more than $1,200 billion to around $5,700 billion. However, this by no means indicates that the real output and real income of the nation increased by a similar factor. When the prices of goods and services double over a period of years, nominal GDP doubles even when the actual amount of goods and services produced and sold remains unchanged. Nominal GDP in any given year is reported in prices prevailing in that year. Since the price level typically rises over time, nominal GDP increases more rapidly than real GDP. This is illustrated in Figure 10.5 (page 252), which shows the behavior of nominal and real GDP since 1947.

Table 10.4 shows that while nominal GDP increased by almost 400 percent during 1972–1991, real GDP increased by less than 60 percent. The price level increased by approximately 200 percent, that is, it roughly tripled. Thus, in this

NOMINAL GDP, REAL GDP, AND THE GDP DEFLATOR, 1929 AND 1970–1991 ($ BILLIONS)			
YEAR	NOMINAL GDP	GDP DEFLATOR	REAL GDP (1987 DOLLARS)
1929	103.9	12.3	846.7
...	...	...	...
1970	1,010.7	35.1	2,875.8
1971	1,097.2	37.0	2,965.1
1972	1,207.0	38.8	3,107.1
1973	1,349.6	41.3	3,268.6
1974	1,458.6	44.9	3,248.1
1975	1,585.9	49.2	3,221.7
1976	1,768.4	52.3	3,380.8
1977	1,974.1	55.9	3,533.2
1978	2,232.7	60.3	3,703.5
1979	2,488.6	65.5	3,796.8
1980	2,708.0	71.7	3,776.3
1981	3,030.6	78.9	3,843.1
1982	3,149.6	83.8	3,760.3
1983	3,405.0	87.2	3,906.6
1984	3,777.2	91.0	4,148.5
1985	4,038.7	94.4	4,279.8
1986	4,268.6	96.9	4,404.5
1987	4,539.9	100.0	4,539.9
1988	4,900.4	103.9	4,718.6
1989	5,244.0	108.4	4,836.9
1990	5,513.8	112.9	4,884.9
1991	5,672.6	117.0	4,848.8

SOURCE: Data from *Citibank Economic Database*, 1992.

TABLE 10.4

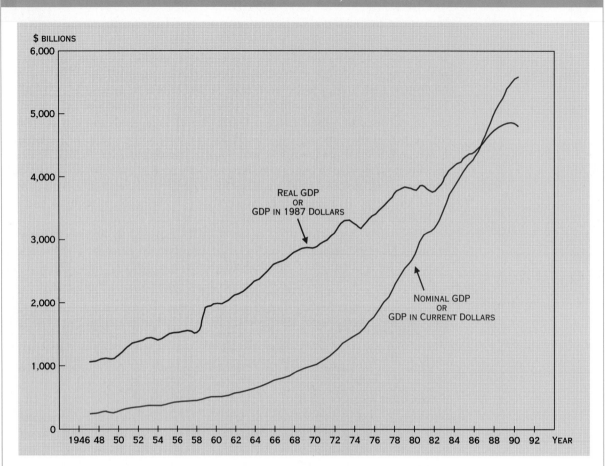

If the level of prices rises over time, nominal GDP or GDP in current dollars rises faster than the real GDP or GDP in constant (base-year) dollars. Because 1987 is the base year used for the price index (GDP deflator), nominal and real GDP are equal in 1987.

SOURCE: National Income Accounts, *Citibank Economic Database*, 1992.

FIGURE 10.5

GDP DEFLATOR

A price index constructed by taking a weighted average of prices of all goods and services that enter into the nation's gross domestic product; it reveals the change since the base year in the cost of purchasing the items that constitute the nation's GDP.

particular period, most of the reported increase in GDP was attributable to higher prices, not greater real output of goods and services.

To determine what actually happened to real output of goods and services over a period of years, we must adjust the nominal GDP to compensate for changes in the price level. Constructed for this purpose, the **GDP deflator**, a price index, is a weighted average of the prices of all final goods and services that enter into GDP.[5] The index is set relative to the prices that existed in a base year, when its starting value is taken as 100. Currently, the GDP deflator is based on the reference year

[5]By *a weighted average* we mean that all the prices that enter into the GDP deflator are not counted equally in calculating the index. If consumers spend 10 times as much on hamburger as they spend on butter, the price of hamburger is given 10 times the importance (*weight*) as the price of butter.

$1987 = 100.[6]$ If, in the current year, the GDP deflator is 135, the implication is that the average price of goods and services in the nation's GDP has risen 35 percent since 1987. 1992 real GDP is calculated using the following expression:

$$1992 \text{ real GDP} = \frac{1992 \text{ nominal GDP}}{\text{GDP deflator for } 1992} \times 100$$

Real GDP is sometimes called GDP in "constant" dollars as opposed to GDP in "current" dollars (nominal GDP).

YOUR TURN

ASSUME THE (NOMINAL) GDP FOR 1993 IS $6,140 BILLION AND THE GDP DEFLATOR IS 124 (1987 = 100). CALCULATE REAL GDP FOR 1993.

Limitations of GDP Accounting

Economists who work with macroeconomic data make no pretense that GDP provides an accurate indicator of the overall well-being of American society. There is no claim that GDP, income, or wealth reflects in any way a nation's collective spiritual, emotional, or overall condition. What GDP attempts to measure is the state of the nation's *material* well-being. However, even this narrower economic measure of the nation's pulse is very difficult to capture.

WHY GDP IS A FLAWED MEASURE OF ACTUAL OUTPUT

There are two major reasons why GDP is an imperfect measure of the nation's output and income.

NEGLECT OF NONMARKET ACTIVITY The valuable services of the spouse who chauffeurs the children, cleans the home, prepares the meals, and so on, is *not* included in the nation's GDP. If the spouse tires of this role, takes a "real" job, and hires someone to perform the domestic services, not only is his or her income included in GDP, but so is the income paid to the hired domestic help. If two spouses are bored cleaning their own homes and hire each other to clean each other's home at $5,000 apiece annually, the nation's GDP rises $10,000 per year! Clearly this points to a problem in national income accounting—in general, *only market transactions are counted*. If no dollars are actually paid out, the activity is not included in GDP.

---

[6]Note in Figure 10.5 that nominal and real GDP are equal in 1987. This indicates that 1987 is the base year.

If you repair your own plumbing, rake your own leaves, or construct an addition to your home by the sweat of your brow, this productive activity is neglected in national income accounting. Because do-it-yourself activities are not counted, the measured GDP tends to understate the nation's true output. The only nonmarket activities included in GDP are the estimated value of food produced and consumed on the farm, the estimated fair market rental value of homes occupied by owners, and the estimated value of goods and services produced by government. Since nations differ radically in the proportion of total economic activity conducted in the marketplace, official GDP data distort the true differences in output, income, and living standards among nations.

THE UNDERGROUND ECONOMY Economists are convinced that a significant portion of output of final goods and services is conducted in the "subterranean economy," and therefore never shows up in the GDP figures. Part of this output consists of such illegal activities as the cocaine trade, prostitution, and loan-sharking. For obvious reasons such transactions go unreported. Perhaps an even larger portion of the *underground economy* emanates from unreported legal activity, unreported so that income may be hidden from the Internal Revenue Service. Hence, some waiters and cab drivers fail to report all income earned. Some merchants do not enter all sales into the cash register. And some plumbers have been known to quote two prices for their services—$40/hour if you pay by check, $35/hour if you pay in cash.

Over the years a gradual increase in marginal tax rates faced by Americans increased the incentive to hide income (these rates were reduced in the 1980s). Some economists believe the increase in the amount of currency relative to checking accounts since 1960 indicates a relative growth of the underground economy.[7] The size of this underground economy is variously estimated at 5–20 percent of GDP. There seems to be disagreement over the issues of how fast the underground economy is growing and how fast the American ethic of voluntary income-tax compliance is eroding. But there is agreement that measured GDP would be at least $300 billion greater than the currently stated figure if all output of final goods and services were reported.

<hr />

WHY GDP IS A FLAWED MEASURE OF WELL-BEING

We have indicated that GDP understates actual output of the United States because it fails to include output not sold in markets and omits output sold in the underground economy. Several additional considerations suggest that GDP is a poor measure of the *well-being* or welfare of the nation. Even if GDP were corrected to measure output accurately, it would be a flawed *measure of economic welfare*.

NEGLECT OF LEISURE TIME As citizens of a nation become wealthier, they often increase their leisure time; they opt for more *psychic income* from recreation, entertainment, and travel. For a family earning $60,000 annually, an extra thousand

---

[7]In 1960 the ratio of currency to checking accounts in banks was about 25 percent. The ratio has increased to about 40 percent today.

dollars of income may appear less inviting than a week in the mountains. As evidence of this, the length of the average American workweek has gradually declined from more than 50 hours in 1900 to around 35 hours in 1992. Hence, measured GDP has grown more slowly than would have been the case if we had maintained the 50-hour work ethic. Since the populace voluntarily opted for the additional leisure, we are clearly better off—but the increased well-being is not included in the GDP figures. This factor tends to make the growth of reported GDP understate the growth in well-being of the nation.

"BADS" AS WELL AS "GOODS" ARE COUNTED IN GDP The 1986 Chernobyl nuclear disaster in the Soviet Union clearly made that nation worse off. Hundreds of people were immediately killed or incapacitated. The longevity of thousands more was threatened by extensive exposure to radiation. A considerable geographic area was rendered uninhabitable for generations. Yet the reported Soviet GDP was probably stimulated because of the accident, as major expenditures were required to clean up the area and to provide medical care and housing for those impaired by the accident.[8]

Similar analyses apply to such American natural disasters as Hurricane Andrew of 1992, the San Francisco earthquakes of 1906 and 1989, the Mount Saint Helens volcanic eruption of 1980, and numerous less-massive natural disasters. Wars are a powerful example of the principle. Clearly, World War II imposed great economic hardship on the nation's people as breadwinners were killed and wounded, income taxes were raised sharply, and production of such durable goods as cars and refrigerators was suspended in order to devote resources to production of military goods. Yet American involvement in the war stimulated a major boost in reported GDP. Suppose, today, we could reach agreement with all nations to cut armaments production by 50 percent. Clearly we would be better off. The federal deficit would decline, taxes could be reduced, and we could enjoy more "goods" in place of the "bads" (bombs and missiles). Nevertheless, the reported GDP would decline temporarily.

NEGLECTS ENVIRONMENTAL DAMAGE AND OTHER ADVERSE EFFECTS OF PRODUCTION The output of the steel and chemical industries is counted in GDP in the form of final sales of cars and fertilizer. However, in producing steel and chemicals, *negative externalities* occur. Air and water in the vicinity of the steel and chemical plants may become contaminated. Since this pollution is undeniably detrimental to the country's well-being, its negative value should in principle be added to gross domestic product, thus reducing the reported GDP. However, no such correction is made, and therefore reported GDP overstates true GDP. Other similar shortcomings of reported GDP are commonplace. GDP counts output of services in the form of air transportation but not the noise pollution imposed upon residential areas surrounding airports, the market value of cigarettes produced but not the agony suffered by those who contract lung cancer, the value of liquor sold but not the enormous losses suffered by families of individuals killed by drunken drivers, the value of output produced in Los Angeles but not the inconveniences of urban congestion endured by those who reside there.

---

[8]Of course, the shut-down of the plant resulted in reduced output of electric power, no doubt temporarily offsetting some of the induced output created by the disaster. But part of the plant was reopened after a surprisingly brief shutdown.

CORRECTING GDP—A MEASURE OF NET ECONOMIC WELFARE (NEW)

Professors William Nordhaus and James Tobin of Yale University have attempted to construct an improved measure of the nation's well-being that reflects the disenchantment with mere material goods and services. They have adjusted the reported GDP figures to deal with some of the shortcomings just discussed. For example, Nordhaus and Tobin add to the Commerce Department's GDP figures their estimated value of increased leisure time and of goods and services not transacted in formal markets. They deduct expenditures on bombs and missiles and the estimated value of the costs associated with commuting, urban congestion, and environmental degradation.

The result of their efforts is the measure of *net economic welfare (NEW)*, which has increased more slowly over the past 50 years than has GDP. American society may choose, through the political process, to implement policies that reduce GDP in order to increase NEW. Government prohibition of strip-mining coal and careful limitation of timber cutting and oil drilling on government-owned land are examples. Similarly, the government imposes emission standards on new automobiles and coal-fired power plants. Can you think of additional examples?

Summary

1. National income accounting encompasses the procedures for measuring the nation's aggregate output and income, along with its components. Such data are needed to analyze and describe the economy's performance and to study the influence of various economic events and macroeconomic policies on the nation's economic activity.

2. Macroeconomic variables may be classified as stock variables and flow variables. Stock variables are measured at a given point of time and are expressed in units of quantity or dollar value. Examples include the population, the money supply, and the capital stock. Flow variables are measured as a rate per unit of time. Examples include investment, exports, consumption, profits, and income.

3. Gross domestic product (GDP), the most popular measure of the nation's output, is defined as the dollar value of a nation's production of final goods and services in a given year. A closely related concept, net domestic product (NDP), is constructed by deducting the amount of capital consumed or worn out from GDP. NDP is thus a measure of the net output available to society. Although NDP is conceptually a superior indicator, GDP is predominantly used because it is difficult to estimate the amount of capital worn out in a given year.

4. The circular flow model illustrates the interdependent nature of production decisions and expenditure decisions. Firms hire factors of production from households and produce final goods and services (GDP). In producing this GDP, firms pay out incomes to the households, allowing them to purchase the output they collectively helped to produce.

5. Two methods of measuring the nation's GDP are the flow-of-output approach and the flow-of-income approach. The former approach sums the sales of consumer goods, gross private domestic investment, government purchases of goods and services, and net exports. Since GDP seeks to measure *output*, and since *sales* do not always coincide with output in any given accounting period, the change in business inventories is added and

counted as a component of gross private domestic investment. The flow-of-income approach to computing GDP totals the wages and salaries, rents, interest, and profits to arrive at national income. GDP is then obtained by adding indirect business taxes, miscellaneous items, and depreciation to national income.

6. GDP is reported each year in current dollars. Because the price level typically rises over time, the growth of this reported or *nominal GDP* overstates the growth of actual output or *real GDP*. To compute real GDP, we use a special index of prices known as the *GDP deflator* to adjust the nominal GDP for changes in the price level. Real GDP is the appropriate variable to consider when seeking to determine the change in the nation's output or standard of living.

7. There are several imperfections in national income accounting that render reported measures of the nation's output somewhat flawed indicators of our well-being. GDP ignores the growth of leisure time and fails to record output not sold in organized markets, thus understating our well-being. On the other hand, GDP neglects environmental damage and other adverse side effects associated with producing the nation's GDP. Moreover, GDP counts the production of such "bads" as nuclear missiles and expenditures to repair damages associated with nuclear and natural disasters on the same basis as the production of "goods." An experimental measure that seeks to correct these flaws is known as net economic welfare (NEW).

Key Terms

national income accounting
gross domestic product (GDP)
intermediate good
consumption expenditures (C)
gross investment
net investment
government purchases (G)

government transfer payments
depreciation
net domestic product (NDP)
national income (NY)
disposable income (Y_d)
GDP deflator

Study Questions and Problems

1. Explain why measures of aggregate output and income are essential to businesses and economists.

2. At the beginning of the year, Joe Jogger buys 10 pairs of red sneakers on sale. Joe wears out and throws away a new pair about every four months. The number of pairs of red sneakers Joe has in his closet on any given day is what sort of variable? What sort of variable is the rate at which Joe wears out his sneakers? Is there a relationship between the variables?

3. Explain the difference between stock variables and flow variables. Give one example of a flow variable and one example of a stock variable in nature and in economics that is not mentioned in this chapter.

4. Imagine you are starting a business that makes a special kind of T-shirt. What are the *factors of production* you would need? What *intermediate goods*? Describe what your *final goods* might look like.

5. Why are intermediate goods not included in calculating GDP?

6. Which of the following are included in GDP?
   a. raw steel
   b. purchase of a new washing machine
   c. purchase of a used house
   d. sale of Ford automobiles to Japan
   e. purchase of 100 shares of Ford Motor stock
   f. Social Security payments
   g. salary of a university professor
   h. interest payments on the national debt

7. In 1990 nominal GDP was $5,514 billion, the GDP deflator was 112.9 and the base year for the deflator was 1987 (1987 = 100). If both real and nominal GDP in 1987 were $4,540 billion, how much had real GDP grown by 1990?

8. Analyze the basic principles illustrated in the circular flow-of-income model.

9. In the flow-of-output approach to GDP, we attempt to measure *output* by totaling *sales* of consumption, investment, government, and net export goods. Explain why the adjustment for the change in the nation's inventories makes this procedure a conceptually valid one.

10. In the flow-of-income approach to GDP, why do we add indirect business taxes and depreciation on top of employee compensation, interest, rents, and profits to arrive at GDP?

11. Discuss the shortcomings of U.S. reported GDP as an indicator of the nation's economic performance. In view of these shortcomings, do you believe that reported GDP overstates or understates the conceptually ideal measure of GDP as a measure of the well-being of the nation?

REAL GDP IN 1993 = $\dfrac{\$6{,}140 \text{ BILLION}}{124}$ × 100 = $4,952 BILLION

YOUR TURN
Answers

Selected References

Challenge Magazine, November/December 1979, contains two excellent articles on the underground economy: Edgar L. Feige, "How Big Is the Irregular Economy?" and Peter M. Gutmann, "Statistical Illusions, Mistaken Policies."

Kuznets, Simon. *Modern Economic Growth* (New Haven, Conn.: Yale University Press, 1966). Chapter 1 is devoted to national income accounting.

Nordhaus, William, and James Tobin. "Is Growth Obsolete?" *Fiftieth Anniversary Colloquium V* (National Bureau of Economic Research, Columbia Press, 1972). Discusses the construction of the measure of net economic welfare (NEW).

Sommers, Albert T. *The U.S. Economy Demystified* (Lexington, Mass.: Lexington Books, 1988, revised edition). Chapter 2 presents a clear discussion of national income accounting.

U.S. Department of Commerce. *Survey of Current Business.* Reports the national income data. See especially each July issue.

YOU CAN MAKE EVEN A
PARROT INTO A LEARNED
ECONOMIST—ALL IT
MUST LEARN ARE THE
TWO WORDS "SUPPLY"
AND "DEMAND."

—ANONYMOUS

The Aggregate Supply–Aggregate Demand Model of Macroeconomics: Introduction

IN THE PAST THREE CHAPTERS, WE HAVE INTRODUCED SUCH MACROECONOMIC CONCEPTS AS GROSS DOMESTIC PRODUCT (GDP), BUSINESS CYCLES, UNEMPLOYMENT, RECESSION, AND INFLATION. IN ORDER TO UNDERSTAND IMPORTANT MACROECONOMIC PHENOMENA, WE NEED A BASIC FRAMEWORK OF ANALYSIS. THE MODEL OF AGGREGATE SUPPLY AND AGGREGATE DEMAND PROVIDES IMPORTANT INSIGHT INTO MANY KEY MACROECONOMIC DEVELOPMENTS. THE AGGREGATE SUPPLY–AGGREGATE DEMAND MODEL IS SKETCHED IN THIS CHAPTER AND DEVELOPED MORE THOROUGHLY IN THE NEXT SEVERAL CHAPTERS. ONCE THIS BASIC FRAMEWORK IS MASTERED, IT WILL BE MUCH EASIER TO UNDERSTAND THE CAUSES OF SUCH CRUCIAL PHENOMENA AS BUSINESS CYCLES, INFLATION, AND UNEMPLOYMENT. IN THIS CHAPTER, WE PRESENT THE BASIC MODEL OF AGGREGATE SUPPLY AND AGGREGATE DEMAND. WE THEN BREATHE LIFE INTO THE MODEL BY REVIEWING THE MACROECONOMIC HISTORY OF THE UNITED STATES IN THE PAST 30 YEARS IN THE CONTEXT OF THE AGGREGATE SUPPLY–AGGREGATE DEMAND MODEL.

The Basic Aggregate
Supply–Aggregate Demand Model

The basic aggregate supply–aggregate demand framework is illustrated in Figure 11.1.

AGGREGATE DEMAND CURVE

Recall from Chapter 4 the definition of a demand curve for a specific good or service. The demand curve for steak is the relationship between the price of steak and the quantity consumers wish to purchase—*other factors remaining constant*. If other factors relevant to demand for steak do not remain constant, the entire position of the demand curve for steak shifts rightward or leftward. For example, if income rises, the demand curve for steak shifts rightward.

In a somewhat analogous fashion, the nation's **aggregate demand curve** is defined as the relationship between the nation's price level and the amount of *real output* (goods and services) demanded—*other factors remaining constant*. If factors relevant to demand for real output other than the price level do not remain constant, the entire position of the aggregate demand curve shifts. For example, if the stock market rises sharply, people feel wealthier and increase major purchases, shifting the aggregate demand curve rightward.

AGGREGATE DEMAND CURVE

The aggregate demand curve shows the quantity of the nation's output demanded at each possible price level.

AGGREGATE DEMAND AND SUPPLY CURVES

The nation's aggregate demand and aggregate supply curves jointly determine the price level and the level of real output.

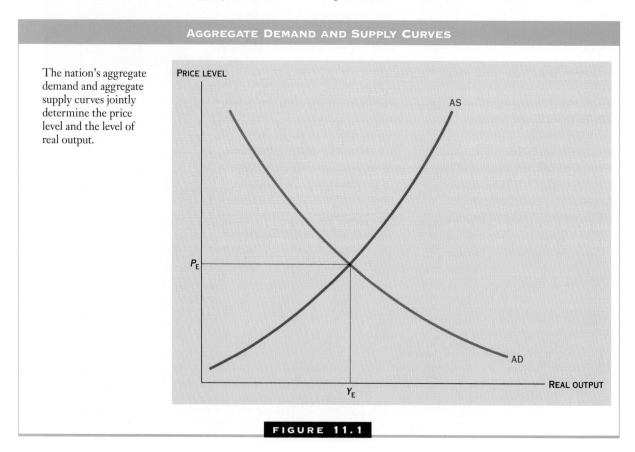

FIGURE 11.1

The fundamental explanation of the downward slope of the aggregate demand curve differs from the explanation of the shape of the demand curve for a specific product. If the price of steak falls, people substitute steak for hamburger and chicken, increasing the quantity of steak demanded. In the aggregate demand-curve formulation, the nation's *price level*—the average price of all goods and services—occupies the vertical axis. A decline in the price level indicates that prices of goods and services *on average or in general* are reduced. Hence, there is no substitution effect.

Several factors account for the downward slope of the aggregate demand curve. If the price level falls while the amount of personal money balances (checking accounts and currency holdings), savings accounts, bonds, and other financial assets remains constant, the real purchasing power of this financial wealth increases. This *wealth effect* stimulates buying of goods and services. Moreover, a decline in American prices makes domestic goods more attractive to foreigners, and demand for American exports rises. Similarly, some American demand for imported goods is redirected toward domestically produced goods because of the decline in domestic prices. For these reasons, the aggregate demand (AD) curve in Figure 11.1 is downward sloping.

AGGREGATE SUPPLY CURVE

AGGREGATE SUPPLY CURVE

The aggregate supply curve shows the quantity of the nation's output supplied at each possible price level.

The **aggregate supply curve** is defined as the relationship between the nation's price level and the amount of output firms desire to produce—*other factors remaining constant*. As shown in Figure 11.1, the typical aggregate supply (AS) curve slopes upward. As prices rise, more output is produced—*other factors remaining constant*. An in-depth analysis of the aggregate supply curve is given in Chapter 14. For now, we explain the positive slope by the fact that profits tend to rise when prices rise—at least in the short run—and by the fact that increased profits motivate firms to step up production.

The profit earned by producing one unit of output is simply the difference between the price of the good and the cost of producing it. The cost of producing a good depends on input costs—wage rates, raw material prices, factory/building rents, and so forth. These input costs tend to remain fixed for considerable periods of time, but not indefinitely. Workers and firms often enter into contracts that fix wages for from one to three years. Even in the absence of such contracts, wages and salaries typically are adjusted once each year. The same scenario frequently holds for raw materials, as firms contract with suppliers to purchase the materials at fixed prices for a specified period.

As the price level rises, prices of at least some inputs remain fixed for significant periods of time. For this reason, *profit margins*—profits per unit of output—increase and firms expand output. Similarly, when the price level falls, certain costs initially fail to decline, profit margins decline, and firms reduce output. The sluggishness of input prices accounts for the positive slope of the aggregate supply curve.[1]

---

[1] It is useful to distinguish between a short-run and a long-run aggregate supply curve. In the short run, many input costs remain fixed as the price level rises. Firms respond to increased profit margins by sharply stepping up output. In the long run, wages and other input prices have ample time to adjust to the higher price level. In the long run, profit margins are not greatly stimulated by higher output prices and output is therefore less responsive to changes in the price level. The long-run aggregate supply curve is steeper than the short-run curve.

PRODUCTIVITY
The amount of output produced per unit of input.

As is the case with the supply curve for an individual product, changes in factors that influence production (other than price) shift the entire position of the aggregate supply curve. An example is growth of **productivity**, which is defined as output per unit of input (such as one hour of work). Technological progress stimulates productivity, shifts the aggregate supply curve rightward, and allows more output to be produced at each price level.

EQUILIBRIUM

In Figure 11.1, the aggregate demand (AD) and aggregate supply (AS) curves intersect to determine the nation's equilibrium price level (P_E) and real output—the level of real goods and services produced and exchanged (Y_E). In Figure 11.1, any price level above P_E causes an excess of aggregate production over aggregate sales (AS > AD), which leads to an undesired buildup of inventories and induces firms to reduce prices. A decline in prices discourages production and encourages buying—a process that continues until the price level returns to P_E.

If the price level is less than P_E, aggregate demand exceeds aggregate supply. This condition leads to an unintended decrease in the nation's inventories, and many buyers cannot obtain the goods and services they desire. Accordingly, the signal is given to raise prices, which encourages production and inhibits purchases—a process that continues until equilibrium returns at the price level of P_E and the output level of Y_E.

CHANGES IN THE NATION'S PRICE LEVEL AND REAL OUTPUT

In any economy, real output and the price level constantly undergo change. These changes are attributable to frequent shifts in the aggregate supply and aggregate demand curves illustrated in Figure 11.1. Certain of these changes are at least partially predictable, and others are not. In Figure 11.1, we see that factors that raise aggregate demand (shifting the aggregate demand curve rightward) tend to raise the price level and the amount of real output produced and exchanged. A decrease in aggregate demand tends to reduce the level of prices and real output. Factors that increase aggregate supply (shifting AS rightward) reduce the price level and raise real output. A decrease in aggregate supply raises the price level and reduces real output.

Inflation is defined as a sustained or persistent increase in the level of prices. We see from the framework of Figure 11.1 that inflation may be caused by persistent increases in the aggregate demand curve, persistent decreases in the aggregate supply curve, or some combination of the two. Historically, the predominant source of inflation in all nations has been persistent increases in aggregate demand, fueled by rising government expenditures and excessive growth in the nation's money supply.

FACTORS SHIFTING AGGREGATE DEMAND AND AGGREGATE SUPPLY

Components of aggregate demand include consumer spending, investment expenditures, government purchases, and net foreign demand for domestic products (that is, foreign demand for U.S. exports minus American demand for imports). The components of aggregate demand shift for various reasons. Consumption may increase because of an improved economic outlook, higher wealth owing to higher stock and bond prices, or an income-tax reduction that increases take-home pay. Investment expenditures for new plant and equipment and housing may increase because of a decline in interest rates, an increase in the utilization rate of existing plant capacity, new tax incentives, or an improved economic outlook. Government spending rises when federal, state, or local governments authorize higher outlays. Export demand may rise when foreign nations become more affluent, when trade barriers are removed, or when exchange-rate movements make prices of American goods and services (measured in yen, marks, francs, and so forth) lower to foreign buyers.

Several considerations influence the position of the aggregate supply curve. For example, the growth of American technology gradually shifts the aggregate supply curve rightward (increases aggregate supply) over time, as do growth in the labor force and increases in the amount of capital goods per worker. On the other hand, increases in input costs in the production process—such as higher wages, higher raw-material prices, higher oil and energy prices—shift the curve leftward.

YOUR TURN

IN 1989 CONGRESS RAISED THE LEVEL OF THE MINIMUM WAGE FROM $3.35 TO $4.25 PER HOUR OVER THE NEXT TWO YEARS. USING THE AGGREGATE SUPPLY–AGGREGATE DEMAND FRAMEWORK, ANALYZE THE EFFECT OF THIS LEGISLATION UPON THE NATION'S PRICE LEVEL AND REAL OUTPUT.

STABILIZATION POLICIES—MONETARY AND FISCAL POLICIES

U.S. officials attempt to stabilize output at levels corresponding to reasonably low unemployment rates without triggering inflationary pressures. Such measures are known as *stabilization policies*, which consist of monetary and fiscal policy. *Monetary policy*—conducted by the Federal Reserve System—aims at bringing about deliberate changes in interest rates, credit availability, and the supply of money (checking accounts and currency) in order to influence aggregate expenditures. (We analyze this process in Part III.) *Fiscal policy* involves deliberate changes in the federal government's flow of expenditures and tax receipts in order to influence aggregate spending and overall performance of the economy. (Chapters 13, 14, and 21 address issues of fiscal policy.)

Both monetary and fiscal policies influence key macroeconomic variables, primarily by influencing the position of the aggregate demand curve.[2] For example,

---

[2]Fiscal policy, such as investment tax credits and other tax devices, may provide incentives to install new capital goods, thus enhancing production capability and ultimately shifting the aggregate supply curve rightward. Monetary policy, by influencing interest rates and investment spending for new plant and equipment, affects the position of the aggregate supply curve in the long run. Also, the *mix* of monetary and fiscal policies likely influences the composition of current output between consumption goods and investment goods, thereby influencing aggregate supply. Although we ignore these considerations here, we return to them in Part V.

when output is low and unemployment is high, stimulative policies may be necessary. In this case, the Federal Reserve works to push down interest rates and increase the supply of money and credit, thereby increasing investment and consumption spending, and shifting the aggregate demand curve rightward. This results in higher real output, and the price level tends to rise. The federal government may also implement stimulative fiscal policy by reducing taxes (thus increasing consumption) or by increasing federal expenditures, which shifts the aggregate demand curve rightward.

To illustrate the general task of stabilization policy, consider the situation depicted in Figure 11.2, which depicts aggregate supply and aggregate demand curves with price level on the vertical axis and real output on the horizontal axis. Assume initially that the economy is at A, the intersection of AD_1 and AS_1. The price level is P_1 and real output is Y_1.

Corresponding to each level of real output is a specific magnitude of employment and unemployment. In Figure 11.2 the level of output Y_1 is far below capacity.

STIMULATIVE MONETARY AND FISCAL POLICIES

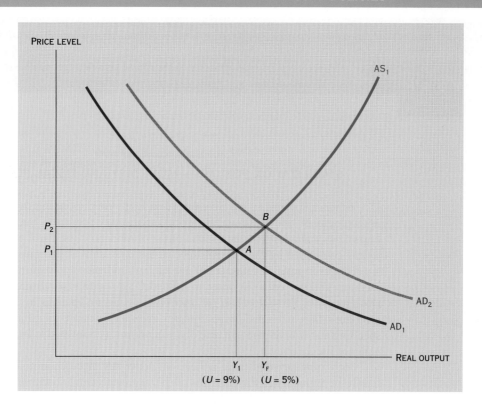

Monetary and fiscal policy work principally by shifting the aggregate demand curve. If the economy is initially at A, output is depressed and the unemployment rate is high. By boosting aggregate demand from AD_1 to AD_2, stimulative monetary and fiscal policies could in principle move us to B, raising real output to Y_F and reducing the unemployment rate.

FIGURE 11.2

POTENTIAL OUTPUT
The output level (real GDP) that would be produced if the actual unemployment rate were equal to the natural unemployment rate, that is, if the economy were at full employment.

Hence, employment is rather low and the unemployment rate is high—9 percent in this example. Figure 11.2 indicates that the level of output associated with full employment is Y_F. This full-employment output level is known as **potential output** or **potential GDP**. In this case real output must be considerably larger than the current production level of Y_1 in order to generate enough jobs so that the actual unemployment rate is reduced to the natural unemployment rate—the lowest rate that can be sustained without igniting an acceleration of inflation. Although economists inevitably disagree about the precise unemployment rate under such conditions, for illustrative purposes assume this natural unemployment rate, or full-employment unemployment rate, is 5 percent.

In this situation, officials in charge of monetary and fiscal policies may in principle attempt to stimulate economic activity by shifting the aggregate demand curve rightward from AD_1 to AD_2. Ideally the output target (Y_F) would be hit and the unemployment rate reduced to the desired level of 5 percent.

Alternatively, picture an aggregate demand curve (AD_3) rightward of AD_2 in Figure 11.2 that intersects AS_1 at a point northeast of point B, yielding a real output level in excess of our full-employment output level Y_F. Such a situation is undesirable in the sense that the economy is attempting to produce an output level in excess of that which would occur at full employment, that is, when unemployment is 5 percent. Severe inflation would ensue, and restrictive monetary and fiscal policies would be called for in order to return the aggregate demand curve to AD_2.

Although this conduct of stabilization policy may seem straightforward, policymakers face fundamental difficulties in the real world. For example, there is uncertainty about the position and slope of the aggregate demand and aggregate supply curves. Also, policymakers cannot know the precise nature of the nonpolicy factors currently shifting the AS and AD curves. Finally, there is disagreement about the level of real output that yields full employment. Hence, it is much more difficult to hit point B with real output at Y_F than one might assume from an analysis of Figure 11.2; real output may end up significantly below (or above) the Y_F magnitude because of the uncertainties involved. In fact, many economists believe the task so formidable and the potential errors so large that policymakers should not even make the attempt. In Parts III and IV we discuss in greater detail how monetary and fiscal policies are conducted in the United States and address the issue of whether deliberate efforts to conduct active stabilization policies are beneficial to the nation's economic health.

Post-1960 U.S. Macroeconomic History

Figure 11.3 illustrates real GDP for the period 1960–1991, along with *potential GDP*. The latter concept refers to the amount of real output the economy hypothetically produces under conditions of full employment—when the economy steams along at near-capacity production levels and unemployment exhibits a relatively low rate of perhaps 5 percent. Potential GDP rises over time as the work force expands and as labor productivity (output per worker) increases. The gap between actual GDP and potential GDP is an indicator of the output performance of the

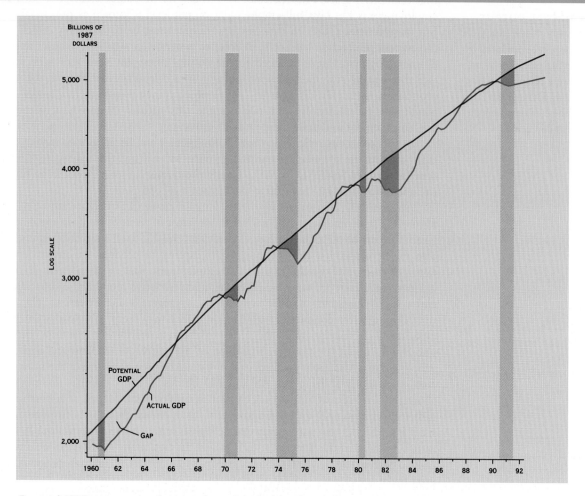

Potential GDP rises over time because of growth in the labor force and increases in output per worker (productivity). Actual GDP fluctuates about the potential trend because of changes in aggregate demand and supply. The United States experienced six recessions (shaded areas) between 1960 and 1992.

SOURCE: Federal Reserve System, 1992.

FIGURE 11.3

economy. The larger the gap, the greater the loss of output because of an underused or slack economy. And the nation's unemployment rate varies directly with the magnitude of this gap.

In Figure 11.3, the shaded areas indicate periods of *recession*—periods in which real GDP is declining. In the period 1960–1992, the nation experienced six recessions. Unshaded areas represent periods of economic expansion—periods of uninterrupted growth of real GDP. Much of the post-1960 U.S. macroeconomic history is told by this figure, together with the simple macroeconomic framework presented in Figures 11.1 and 11.2. The following outline highlights certain key developments of the 1960s, 1970s, 1980s, and early 1990s.

THE 1960s

When John F. Kennedy was inaugurated president in January 1961, the U.S. economy was in a recession. The nation's unemployment rate hovered around 7 percent, considerably higher than the natural unemployment rate at the time. As shown in Figure 11.3, a significant gap existed between actual and potential output. Furthermore, the Soviet Union had recently launched the satellite Sputnik, and fears abounded that our adversary might be overtaking the United States technologically and gaining economically. Inflation in the United States had been rather subdued for several years, and the new administration felt the time was right to pursue policies designed to stimulate expansion of output and employment. Income-tax cuts were implemented in the early 1960s, shifting the aggregate demand curve rightward. The U.S. economy responded with rapid growth of real output, and the unemployment rate dropped below 5 percent by spring 1965. At that point things looked good. The stock market moved to an all-time high, with the Dow Jones Industrials Average reaching 1,000 in late 1965. Moreover, inflation remained at low and tolerable levels.

In late 1965, U.S. politicians made an ill-fated decision to escalate expenditures for the Vietnam War sharply without providing for a tax hike or a reduction in nonmilitary spending. The economy was already operating near capacity in 1965 (actual GDP close to potential GDP). Given the intention to raise military spending, a clear need existed to depress consumer spending (through a tax increase) or nonmilitary government spending to avoid excessive aggregate demand. Because no such compensating actions were taken, the aggregate demand curve shifted rightward, output escalated sharply, and the unemployment rate dropped below 4 percent by early 1966. This excessively stimulative fiscal policy resulted in an overheated economy, and the inflation rate increased sharply.[3]

Richard M. Nixon was inaugurated president in January 1969, inheriting an environment of high inflation and very low unemployment (3.4 percent). The inflation rate, approximately 5 percent, seemed outrageous and intolerable at the time. A mild recession (1969–1970) slowed the inflation rate somewhat, but not as much as most economists expected.

---

[3]This policy error was attributable to political factors, not to any poor state of economic art or faulty economic advice. President Lyndon B. Johnson was warned in the fall of 1965 by his economic advisors that a tax increase was needed to compensate for expanded military spending and to avoid an overheated and inflationary economy. With congressional elections on the horizon (November 1966), LBJ decided to wait until January 1967 to request the income-tax hike. Congress delayed action until July 1968, when a temporary 10 percent surtax was imposed. This measure proved too little too late. Furthermore, Federal Reserve monetary policy was relatively stimulative in 1967 and 1968, negating the effects of the temporary tax hike.

Unlike the record of most earlier business cycles, inflation continued at a rather high rate even in the first year of the ensuing recovery (1971). Although the early part of the expansion phase is the period in which inflation normally reaches a cyclical low, it appeared that inflation had become so entrenched in the system that it was sustained not on the basis of exuberant economic activity, but merely on the basis of powerful *inflationary expectations*. Workers were demanding and firms were granting large wage hikes on the basis that the price level was expected to rise significantly in the foreseeable future. The Nixon Administration, which had previously espoused nonintervention by the government in marketplace decision making, turned 180 degrees, opting for a comprehensive *wage-price freeze*.

On August 15, 1971, an across-the-board freeze on wages and prices was imposed. The economics of this measure are illustrated in Figure 11.4. When the freeze was imposed, the aggregate supply (AS_1) and aggregate demand (AD_1) curves intersected to yield a price level of P_1 and a real output level of Y_1. Note that there is no tendency for the price level to rise above P_1 as long as AD_1 does not shift rightward or AS_1 shift leftward. Unfortunately, in the year following imposition of the freeze (1972), the aggregate demand curve shifted sharply rightward (AD_2 in Figure 11.4). In 1972, the money supply increased by more than 9 percent and fiscal policy also became more stimulative. Cynics suggest this occurred because the Nixon Administration desired to stimulate the economy and push the unemployment rate down before the November 1972 election.[4] Economic policy is sometimes intertwined with politics.

In any event, with the price level frozen at P_1, aggregate demand for goods and services (Y_2) exceeded aggregate supply (Y_1), inventories began to disappear from merchants' shelves, and buyers became frustrated. Even though reported inflation was dead in the water because of controls, the equilibrium price level P_2 was significantly higher than the actual level P_1 and prices rose quickly as soon as the controls were dismantled in 1973. The controls merely disguised and postponed inflation![5]

In 1973 and 1974, the U.S. economy was humbled by the simultaneous existence of double-digit inflation and the severe contraction of economic activity. Inflation increased from 3.5 percent in 1972 to 12.3 percent in 1974; the unemployment rate escalated from 4.8 percent in August 1973 to more than 8 percent throughout 1975. A new term, stagflation (stagnation plus inflation), appeared in the economics jargon to describe this *worst-of-all-worlds* macroeconomic debacle.

STAGFLATION
A situation in which sluggish or declining output is accompanied by strong inflation.

[4]Nixon lost the 1960 election to Kennedy by a mere 150,000 votes. As President Dwight Eisenhower's vice president for the period 1953–1960, he had the bad fortune to preside over a recession during the 1960 election. About 1 million voters lost their jobs in the months preceding the 1960 election, and it is likely that this cost Nixon the election. Voters thrown out of work rarely vote for the incumbent party. Thus Nixon had every reason to desire a strong economy as the November 1972 election approached.

[5]One can make a case in favor of such controls when a psychological shock is needed to bring down inflationary expectations honed by years of high inflation. Entrenched inflationary expectations can lead to large wage hikes even in the absence of high demand. If so, the aggregate supply curve persistently shifts leftward even in the face of a slack economy, leading to higher prices and lower output. By announcing controls, the government attempts to provide the shock that eliminates inflationary expectations and halts the leftward shift of the aggregate supply curve. This was the major rationale for the imposition of controls in 1971.

Part of the inflationary jump during the period 1973–1974 can be attributed to the rapid, predictable movement of the actual price level to the equilibrium price level upon the termination of wage–price controls in 1973 (movement from P_1 to P_2 in Figure 11.4). However, much of the problem was attributable to a series of adverse supply shocks, a phenomenon we now analyze.

ECONOMICS OF SUPPLY SHOCKS

In early 1973, the Organization of Petroleum Exporting Countries (OPEC) reduced oil production, resulting in a 400 percent increase in the price of crude oil. This dramatic increase in the price of a crucial input meant that the real output producers were willing to supply at each and every price level was reduced. Alternatively stated, the price level required to call forth the supply of any given real-output level increased in the face of this *supply shock*. The implications of an adverse supply shock are illustrated in Figure 11.5, where the OPEC oil-price hike shifted the aggregate supply curve from AS_1 to AS_2. Given the aggregate demand curve

IMPACT OF PRICE FREEZE AND EXPANSION OF AGGREGATE DEMAND

In August 1971, a comprehensive freeze of wages and prices was imposed on the U.S. economy. At the time the freeze was implemented, aggregate demand and supply were AD_1 and AS_1. After the freeze was imposed, monetary and fiscal policies turned stimulative, shifting aggregate demand to AD_2. While the *equilibrium* price level increased from P_1 to P_2, actual prices were not allowed to increase. This created a shortage of goods and services. People attempted to purchase Y_2 units of output, but only Y_1 units were available.

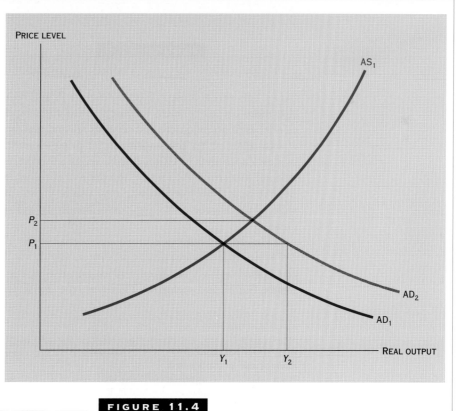

FIGURE 11.4

An adverse supply shock shifts the nation's aggregate supply curve leftward (decreases aggregate supply). This phenomenon causes *stagflation*—rising prices and falling output. The price level is boosted from P_1 to P_2 and real output falls from Y_1 to Y_2.

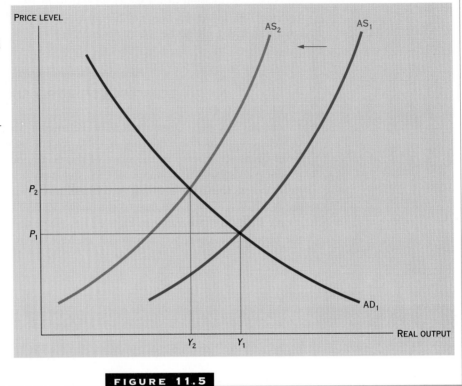

FIGURE 11.5

(AD_1), this shock drove the price level to P_2 and reduced real output to Y_2. Given that more had to be spent to purchase the higher-priced oil and related products, purchases of nonoil goods and services fell and real output declined.[6]

In addition to the enormous oil-price increase during 1973–1974, adverse worldwide weather in 1974 caused a severe shortfall in the production of basic agricultural foodstuffs. As a result, the price of corn, wheat, and soybeans doubled during one year. This phenomenon may also be viewed as contributing to the leftward shift of the aggregate supply curve, breathing additional life into the stagflation curse.

The delayed response of two *devaluations* of the U.S. dollar (late 1971 and early 1973) also may be viewed as an adverse supply shock. The markdown of the value of the dollar vis-à-vis other currencies meant that the dollar was worth fewer yen, marks, francs, and so forth.[7] Therefore, the dollar price of goods imported by the

---

[6]In this analysis we assume that the aggregate demand curve remained unchanged in the face of the oil shock (that is, that monetary and fiscal policymakers did not respond to the shock by aggressively tightening or easing their policies).

[7]Until March 1973, exchange rates were held constant for long periods of time—changing very infrequently. The U.S. dollar was devalued in 1934, 1971, and 1973. Such devaluations involved significant, one-shot markdowns of the value of the dollar in terms of the number of units of foreign currency per dollar. Since 1973, exchange rates have been allowed to float—changing each day in response to the market forces of supply and demand.

United States tended to rise in proportion to the magnitude of the devaluations (approximately 16 percent). To the extent that such higher-priced imports consisted of raw materials and other inputs in the production process, the aggregate supply curve shifted leftward in response to the devaluations.

Because inflation and unemployment are both undesirable, monetary and fiscal policymakers are placed in a *no-win* situation when adverse supply shocks occur. The dilemma is illustrated in Figure 11.6.

Assume we begin at *A*, the intersection of AS_1 and AD_1, and the price level is P_1 while output is Y_1. The series of supply shocks shifts aggregate supply from AS_1 to AS_2, moving us from *A* to *B*, and the price level rises to P_2 while real output falls to Y_2. Assume further that U.S. officials declare inflation *public enemy number one*. By pursuing highly restrictive monetary and fiscal policies, aggregate demand can be reduced from AD_1 to AD_2, moving us to intersection *C*, the price level at the preshock level P_1. Thus inflation is prevented. Note, however, that now the real output level is Y_3, a low level corresponding to a very high unemployment rate. Inflation is prevented—but at the cost of a significant contraction in output and employment.

At the other extreme, assume the monetary and fiscal authorities are determined to prevent the supply shocks from reducing output below the initial level Y_1.

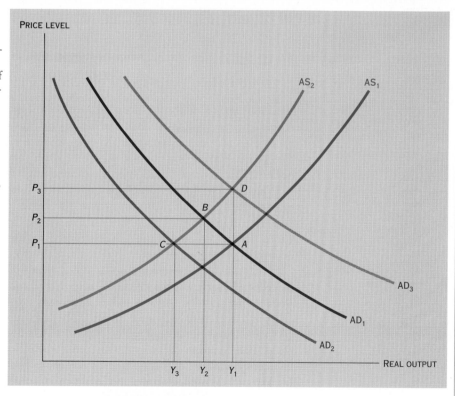

POLICY RESPONSES TO ADVERSE SUPPLY SHOCK

An adverse supply shock that shifts aggregate supply from AS_1 to AS_2 simultaneously raises the price level and reduces output. If those responsible for monetary and fiscal policy attempt to prevent output from falling, they must boost aggregate demand, exacerbating the increase in prices. If they are determined to prevent inflation, they must reduce aggregate demand. But this causes a larger reduction in output and employment. In either case, monetary and fiscal policymakers are likely to be criticized. However, the real culprit is the supply shock itself, which necessarily increases prices, unemployment, or both.

FIGURE 11.6

They could implement highly stimulative measures, thereby shifting aggregate demand from AD_1 to AD_3. Given the aggregate supply curve AS_2, we move to D (in Figure 11.6), where output level remains at Y_1 but the price level balloons to P_3—inflation jumps to extremely high rates for a couple of years as the equilibrium price level increases from P_1 to P_3.

Monetary and fiscal policies that leave the aggregate demand curve anywhere between AD_2 and AD_3 inevitably lead to higher prices *and* lower output (higher unemployment) than existed prior to the adverse supply shocks. And monetary and fiscal authorities almost always are accused of *causing* inflation or unemployment—or perhaps both! Nevertheless, as we plainly see from Figure 11.6, the source of the problems are the supply shocks that produced the leftward shift in the aggregate supply curve. The lesson in this analysis is that monetary and fiscal policy, no matter how competently executed, cannot prevent a negative supply shock from wreaking increased economic hardship.

The U.S. responded to the supply shocks by pursuing an intermediate policy—allowing aggregate demand to be sufficiently high to permit a sharp increase in prices, but not high enough to prevent the severe recession of 1974–1975. Real output declined by about 5 percent and the unemployment rate reached 9 percent in May 1975, as the economy entered the recovery phase. Meanwhile, the inflation rate averaged 11 percent per year throughout a recession that was then the most severe since the Great Depression of the 1930s.

As the oil shock of 1973–1974 began to wear off, U.S. inflation slowed from the double-digit rates of 1973 and 1974 to around 6 percent in 1976. The economy emerged from recession in early 1975 and entered an expansion that would last almost five years (Review Figure 11.3).

THE 1980s

The 1980s opened with the shortest recession followed by the briefest recovery on record. The recession lasted only the first six months of 1980; the ensuing recovery lasted only one year. A second OPEC oil-price hike in 1979 again doubled the price of crude oil. This shock, coupled with very strong aggregate demand conditions in the late 1970s, boosted inflation back to double-digit levels in 1979 and 1980.

The election of 1980, which elevated Ronald Reagan to the presidency, may be regarded partly as a mandate for a return to better economic times—especially a mandate to tame the inflation dragon. An average inflation rate of 7 percent per year in the 1970s doubled the U.S. price level within a single decade. In addition, the growth of real output and living standards slowed to a trickle in the 1970s.

The monetary authorities, under the leadership of Paul Volcker (chairman of the Federal Reserve Board), cracked down on inflation with a vengeance in the early 1980s. Aggregate demand was reduced through a policy of restricted credit availability and extremely high interest rates. The brief recovery from mid-1980 to mid-1981 ended, and the economy descended into the most severe recession since the 1930s. The economists' long-absent term *depression* returned to network news as the unemployment rate soared to 10.8 percent in late 1982 and business bankruptcies, automobile repossessions, and home and farm foreclosures increased dramatically. The nation paid a large price for a successful battle against inflation.

The inflation rate decreased much faster than even the Reagan Administration had hoped, declining from an annual rate of more than 14 percent in the first half of 1980 to less than 4 percent by the end of 1982. Moreover, the inflation rate remained much lower throughout the 1980s than the severe rates experienced during the 1970s.

During the period 1983–1989, the unemployment rate descended slowly from more than 10 percent to around 5 percent as the economy staged a prolonged expansion phase following the 1981–1982 recession. To the surprise of many, the inflation rate continued to decline for several years during this recovery, reaching roughly 1 percent in 1986. This atypical phenomenon—declining inflation several years into economic recovery—can be explained using our aggregate demand–aggregate supply framework.

The 1980s witnessed an interesting reversal of certain adverse supply shocks of the 1970s. First, the U.S. dollar rose strongly on foreign-exchange markets between 1980 and 1985. This appreciation of the dollar reduced the cost of goods imported into the United States and imposed great wage–price discipline on American industries exposed to foreign competition, especially the manufacturing sector. Second, shortly after the point at which the dollar stopped rising (early 1985), the price of crude oil collapsed, falling by more than 50 percent in less than one year. And bumper agricultural output helped hold down the price of such basic foodstuffs as wheat and corn.

In short, many observers believe the Reagan Administration had the *good fortune* to preside over a series of favorable supply shocks that reversed the *bad luck* of the Nixon, Ford, and Carter Administrations of the 1970s. The aggregate supply curve shifted rightward, conferring the benefits of higher output and lower prices.

To a significant extent, however, the strong dollar can be attributed to the policies implemented in the 1980s by the Reagan Administration. Any *consequences* of the strong dollar, such as lowering the price of imports and thereby lowering the rate of inflation, are thus attributable to the Administration's policies.[8] But the drop in oil prices in the mid-1980s was primarily attributable to the severe worldwide slump of 1981–1983, together with energy conservation measures implemented in the 1970s in response to the first oil shock. In addition, the favorable worldwide crop production was clearly a fortuitous event.

Critics of the Reagan Administration's policies tend to use terms such as "luck" to describe the coexistence of economic expansion and declining inflation. However, supporters point out that one cannot quarrel with success and, furthermore, that a good bit of the so-called "luck" can be accounted for by the new policies implemented by the Reagan Administration. We now turn to these new policies, known as *supply-side economics*.

---

[8]Likewise, the enormous U.S. international trade deficits of the 1980s are also largely attributable to the strong dollar. When the U.S. dollar is expensive to foreigners, so are our export products. On the other hand, foreign products look cheap to Americans as the dollar buys more yen, marks, francs, and so forth. Hence, as a result of the strong dollar, U.S. imports soared and exports stagnated during 1983–1987. Because the dollar declined for several years beginning in early 1985, our trade deficit began to decline in the late 1980s. Today, the trade deficit is much smaller than in 1987.

Reaganomics—The *Supply-Side Revolution*

The anemic growth of U.S. productivity and living standards in the 1970s, coupled with unacceptably high rates of inflation, created an intellectual environment conducive to new ideas in macroeconomic theory and innovations in macroeconomic policy. The thesis of *supply-side economics*—the catchphrase of Reagan economic philosophy—was that the supply side of the economy had for too long been neglected. Future policy should focus on expanding productive capacity and incentives to work and produce rather than focusing on measures that merely expand aggregate demand for goods and services. Government policy should be more concerned with the aggregate supply curve and less concerned with manipulating the aggregate demand curve.

**SUPPLY-SIDE
ECONOMICS**
Measures designed to shift the nation's aggregate supply curve rightward, thereby stimulating economic activity without raising prices.

Figure 11.7 indicates the intended rationale of **supply-side economics**—to implement measures that persistently shift the aggregate supply curve rightward. If successful, supply-side measures shift the aggregate supply curve from AS_1 to AS_2, moving the economy from A to B. This move involves an increase in real output, thus raising employment and lowering the unemployment rate. Moreover, the price level declines from P_1 to P_2, thus providing additional leeway for monetary and fiscal authorities to stimulate aggregate demand without igniting inflation. No person of sound mind can quarrel with the *objective* of supply-side economics!

THE INTENT OF *SUPPLY-SIDE* ECONOMICS

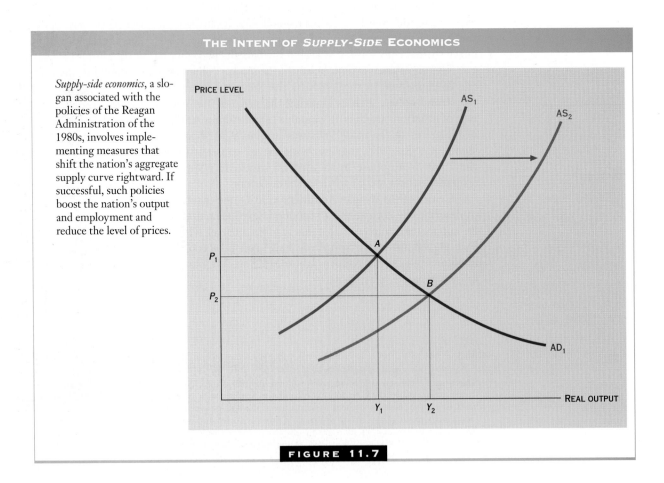

Supply-side economics, a slogan associated with the policies of the Reagan Administration of the 1980s, involves implementing measures that shift the nation's aggregate supply curve rightward. If successful, such policies boost the nation's output and employment and reduce the level of prices.

FIGURE 11.7

Recall from the discussion of production-possibilities curves in Chapter 2 that nations that devote a larger share of current output to investment in plant, equipment, and technology experience a more rapid outward shift in the curve over time. Because saving and investment promote economic growth, a fundamental objective of supply-side economics must be to stimulate the share of income saved and the share of output allocated to investment goods. This farsighted objective requires reducing the public's consumption propensities and enhancing saving habits. It requires reducing the share of output sold to consumers and to the government and increasing the share devoted to productive investment in plant, equipment, and technology.[9]

In the early 1980s, the Reagan Administration implemented federal tax legislation intended to promote investment incentives. By reducing the corporate income-tax rate, the Administration intended to free up funds with which to finance investment in new plant and equipment. Inasmuch as severe inflation is itself a likely detriment to long-range planning and investment, the Administration's success in bringing down inflation in the 1980s must be counted a positive factor in the investment and aggregate supply equations. Moreover, the Administration's continuation of a movement—initiated in the Carter Administration—toward less governmental involvement in regulating private enterprise may have contributed to increased efficiency and growth.

On the saving front, individual taxpayers who established IRAs (individual retirement accounts) were given a major tax break that encouraged them to save more in order to set aside funds for establishing and maintaining an IRA. By reducing marginal income-tax rates for millions of individuals and firms, the Administration hoped to stimulate incentives to work and produce as well as to save and invest.

Unfortunately, a major negative consequence of the tax cuts of the early 1980s was a string of annual budget deficits of unprecedented size—$150 billion to $250 billion per year. This huge increase in government dissaving more than offset any increase in private saving available, and the domestic pool of funds for investment spending dwindled. For this and other reasons, interest rates were exceptionally high during the first half of the 1980s, and America became dependent on foreign funds to finance domestic investment and budget deficits.

Critics of the Reagan Administration's supply-side policies point out that productivity growth was not significantly higher during the 1980s than during the dismal performance of the 1970s. Nor did the saving and investment rates respond positively to the policies implemented in the early 1980s. In fact, most measures of the private saving rates of Americans declined significantly in the 1980s. We will have more to say about supply-side economics in Chapter 14.

THE 1990s

President George Bush took office in January 1989, during the seventh year of economic expansion following the severe 1981–1982 recession. Some key economic

---

[9]Actually, increased government expenditures on capital goods are quite consistent with an enlightened supply-side philosophy. Government expenditures on such things as highways, bridges, research laboratories, and high schools are likely to have the same favorable impact on the nation's productive capacity as are private investment expenditures.

A Brief History of Individual Retirement Accounts (IRAs)

EXHIBIT 11.1

Individual Retirement Accounts (IRAs) are tax-deductible, self-managed retirement programs available to millions of households. Made attractive to the masses of Americans by the Economic Recovery Tax Act of 1981 (ERTA), IRAs are aimed at addressing the shortfall of saving and investment that economists believe has contributed to the relatively slow rate of long-term economic growth in the United States in recent decades. The rationale for the program is to boost the incentive to save. This, in turn, should lead to lower interest rates and larger levels of investment spending on plant, equipment and new technologies. The American saving rate is lower than that of our major competitors—particularly Japan.

In the 1981 legislation, all individuals with wage and salary income were authorized to contribute up to $2,000 annually to an IRA and to deduct the contribution each year from taxable income. This meant that an individual in a 30 percent marginal tax bracket could reduce federal tax liability by $600 each year by making the $2,000 IRA contribution. Couples filing joint returns (in the event each individual earned at least $2,000 annually) were allowed to contribute and deduct up to $4,000 to an IRA. In addition, income earned in the IRA account compounds tax free over the years until it is withdrawn at retirement. Hence, the IRA legislation provided strong incentives for each household to save a portion of income and use it to contribute to an IRA in order to reduce income-tax liability.

Figure 11.8 indicates that the number of tax returns claiming an IRA deduction increased dramatically from 1981 to 1985, when more than 16 million American taxpayers took IRA deductions. Because of the surging federal budget deficit and the resulting need to boost tax revenues, 1986 legislation sharply reduced the number of taxpayers eligible for IRAs. Individuals with incomes in excess of $35,000 (couples filing joint returns with incomes above $50,000) who were participants in employer-sponsored retirement plans or tax-sheltered annuities were barred from deducting IRA contributions from taxable income. As the figure indicates, the number of taxpaying units contributing to an IRA dropped sharply to 5.2 million by 1990.

New IRA proposals keep popping up in Congress. In August 1992, the Senate Finance Committee recommended new IRA legislation even more generous than the original 1981 program. In this proposal, all wage and salary earners would again be authorized to contribute to an IRA and deduct up to $2,000 initially (this figure was to be indexed to rise over time with the price level). Furthermore, this proposed IRA account could be raided without penalty if the funds withdrawn were used to finance a first-time home purchase or certain educational and medical expenses. While this proposed legislation did not become law, it is likely that you will be hearing more

indicators were favorable. For example, the unemployment rate stood at 5.4 percent and the inflation rate (consumer price index) was running at an annual rate of 4.5 percent. The stock market was close to a record high.

about IRAs. Because the IRA is widely perceived as a middle-class tax break, and because politicians like to curry favor with the middle class, it is a good bet that new IRA proposals will be forthcoming in the near future.

To an economist, the crucial issue about IRA legislation is the following: To what extent do IRA tax breaks result in *additional* saving on the part of American households, and to what extent do the IRA contributions merely represent a re-channeling of existing saving from other outlets to the IRA. Only if IRAs result in a powerful boost in household saving rates can IRA tax deductions be considered sound economic policy.

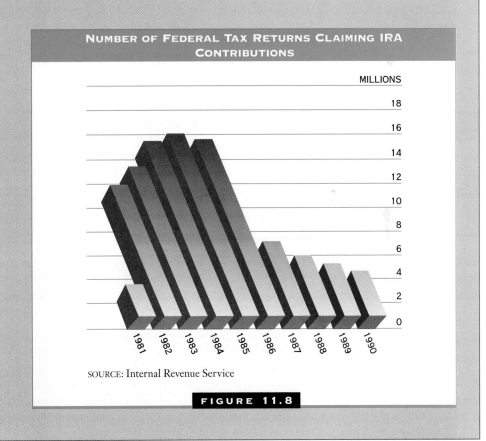

NUMBER OF FEDERAL TAX RETURNS CLAIMING IRA CONTRIBUTIONS

SOURCE: Internal Revenue Service

FIGURE 11.8

On the other hand, the economy was plagued with some deep-seated and serious problems. The "twin deficits"—the federal budget deficit and the international trade deficit—were large and persistent. The budget deficit appeared to be particularly intractable because our elected officials were reluctant to face the wrath of voters who might be angered by tax hikes or program cutbacks required to bring down the deficit. Debt burdens of individuals and firms were unusually large by conventional criteria. The continuing problems of low saving and investment rates and anemic growth in productivity and living standards persisted, thus clouding the longer-range outlook for the U.S. economy.

In July 1990, the long economic expansion ended and the economy entered a recession. Unlike the three previous recessions, which were triggered primarily by restrictive Federal Reserve actions intended to stem surging inflation, the 1990–1991 recession was caused by a decline in consumer and business confidence. This shifted the nation's aggregate demand curve downward (leftward), producing a contraction in output. The decline in consumer and business confidence may have been induced by the crisis in the Persian Gulf as Saddam Hussein invaded Kuwait, continuing problems in the U.S. banking industry, the paralysis of government in dealing with the budget deficit, and the decline in real estate prices in many parts of the country. Millions of Americans became apprehensive about their job security.

The American economy typically expands at relatively rapid rates in the first two years of economic recovery following a recession. However, in the second half of 1991 and most of 1992, output increased at an unusually slow rate—a rate insufficient to significantly push down the nation's unemployment rate. In the presidential campaign of 1992, a debate took place about what to do about the economy. George Bush favored selected fiscal measures such as reduced capital gains taxes and tax credits for new home buyers. Successful candidate Bill Clinton advocated targeted government investment in infrastructure. Some economists favored broad income tax cuts to boost spending. However, with the federal deficit projected to exceed \$350 billion in 1992, many economists were reluctant to advocate fiscal stimulus. The Federal Reserve implemented a series of measures to provide stimulus and interest rates declined sharply in late 1991 and in 1992.

President Clinton took office in January 1993 in an economy characterized by low inflation, low interest rates, moderately high unemployment, and a troublesome legacy of low productivity and output growth.

Summary

1. The intersection of the nation's aggregate demand and aggregate supply curves determines the price level and level of output of real goods and services.

2. An increase in aggregate demand causes higher real output and a higher price level. An increase in aggregate supply raises real output and reduces the price level.

3. Aggregate demand consists of four components: consumer demand, investment demand, government purchases of goods and services, and net foreign demand for U.S. goods and services. These components of demand shift in ways not always predictable, causing fluctuations in the nation's output and price level.

4. The U.S. economy of the 1960s can be divided into two periods. The 1961–1965 era witnessed rapid growth without inflation, the stock market moving to record highs in late 1965. The 1966–1969 period witnessed an economy overstimulated with expenditures

associated with escalation of U.S. involvement in Vietnam. Inflation increased and unemployment declined to unsustainably low levels. The decade ended in recession.

5. The U.S. economy of the 1970s was plagued by a series of supply shocks that shifted the aggregate supply curve leftward. These supply shocks included dramatic increases in the price of oil, adverse weather conditions in 1974, and two devaluations of the U.S. dollar. Largely because of the supply shocks, the 1970s was a decade of stagflation—persistent coexistence of inflation and economic stagnation with accompanying heavy unemployment and poor growth in productivity.

6. At the beginning of the 1980s, inflation was running at double-digit rates. A very severe recession (1981–1982) drove down inflation to the 4 percent range.

7. A series of favorable supply shocks aided the economy during the period 1982–1986. The phenomenal appreciation in the U.S. dollar during 1982–1985 and the collapse of oil prices in 1986 shifted the aggregate supply curve rightward, partially reversing the bad fortune of the 1970s. These favorable supply shocks explain why the U.S. inflation rate continued to drift down from approximately 4 percent at the end of 1982 to approximately zero in mid-1986, even though the economy was in a period of economic expansion.

8. The early 1990s was a period of relatively weak economic activity. A recession triggered by declining consumer and business confidence began in July 1990, and the economy was plagued by stagnation as the presidential election of 1992 approached.

9. *Supply-side economics*, the economic slogan of the Reagan Administration of the 1980s, involves implementation of policies intended to shift the nation's aggregate supply curve rightward. Although no one disputes the merits of this intent, there is considerable doubt whether this maneuver was effectively carried out in the 1980s.

YOUR TURN
Answers

THIS LEGISLATION RAISES THE WAGES OF MILLIONS OF THE NATION'S UNSKILLED WORKERS. THIS INCREASE IN THE COST OF A MAJOR INPUT (LABOR) SHIFTS THE NATION'S AGGREGATE SUPPLY CURVE LEFTWARD—A DECREASE IN AGGREGATE SUPPLY. ALSO, THE LEGISLATION INCREASES AGGREGATE INCOME, SHIFTING THE AGGREGATE DEMAND CURVE RIGHTWARD OR UPWARD. CLEARLY, THE NATION'S PRICE LEVEL IS INCREASED BY THIS LEGISLATION. THE EFFECT ON REAL OUTPUT DEPENDS ON THE SLOPES OF THE NATION'S AS AND AD CURVES AND THE MAGNITUDES OF THE SHIFTS IN THESE TWO CURVES IN RESPONSE TO THE LEGISLATION. DEPENDING ON THESE CONDITIONS, OUTPUT COULD BE EITHER INCREASED OR DECREASED BY THE LEGISLATION.

Key Terms

aggregate demand curve
aggregate supply curve
productivity

potential output (or potential GDP)
stagflation
supply-side economics

1. Explain the fundamental difference between a demand curve for a specific good and an aggregate demand curve.

2. Why does a decrease in the nation's price level result in an increase in quantity of output demanded? A decrease in quantity supplied?

3. Explain the influence of the following upon the *position* of the nation's aggregate demand curve:
   a. a sharp decline in the stock market
   b. a 20 percent decline in the value of the U.S. dollar in foreign-exchange markets
   c. a decrease in income tax rates
   d. a sharp increase in interest rates
   e. an increase in the supply of money (currency holdings and checking accounts)

4. Explain the impact of the following upon the *position* of the aggregate supply curve:
   a. the price of oil falls by 50 percent
   b. workers accept a 10 percent wage cut
   c. the price level rises 20 percent
   d. the amount of capital per worker declines
   e. technological breakthroughs boost labor productivity

5. Using the aggregate supply–aggregate demand diagram, explain the forces that prevail when the economy is temporarily out of equilibrium.

6. Assume the equilibrium real-output level is currently above the output level needed to generate full employment. What are the consequences, and what monetary and fiscal policies are called for to correct the situation?

7. Assume the government raises income tax rates sharply. Explain, using the aggregate demand–aggregate supply framework, what happens to the size of the gap between actual GDP and potential GDP.

8. Using the aggregate supply–aggregate demand framework, analyze the events of the 1970s that caused stagflation.

9. Explain what happens when aggregate demand is stimulated while rigid wage–price controls are in place.

10. Explain the dilemma in which those in charge of monetary and fiscal policies are placed when a major adverse supply shock occurs.

11. Using the basic macroeconomic framework of this chapter, explain how it was possible for aggregate demand to increase significantly during 1983–1986 while the inflation rate continued to decline.

12. Analyze the rationale underlying *supply-side* economics. What supply-side policies were implemented in the 1980s? What policies, if any, were counterproductive? Explain.

Blinder, Alan S. *Economic Policy and the Great Stagflation* (New York: Academic Press, 1981). This work outlines the supply shocks of the 1970s.

Economic Report of the President (Washington, D.C.: published annually). This report discusses contemporary macroeconomic events and conditions.

MY PROBLEM LIES IN
RECONCILING MY GROSS
HABITS WITH MY NET
INCOME.

—ERROL FLYNN

Aggregate Demand—
The Building Blocks

AS DISCUSSED IN CHAPTER 11, THE NATION'S PRICE LEVEL AND LEVEL OF REAL OUTPUT ARE JOINTLY DETERMINED BY AGGREGATE SUPPLY AND AGGREGATE DEMAND. THESE AGGREGATE SUPPLY AND AGGREGATE DEMAND CURVES FREQUENTLY SHIFT, INITIATING CHANGES IN OUTPUT AND EMPLOYMENT ON THE ONE HAND AND CHANGES IN THE PRICE LEVEL ON THE OTHER.

IN THE PAST 50 YEARS, THE TYPICAL MACROECONOMIC PATTERN HAS BEEN ONE OF RISING OUTPUT COMBINED WITH RISING PRICES. IN TERMS OF FIGURE 11.1, THIS IMPLIES THAT A RIGHTWARD-SHIFTING AGGREGATE DEMAND CURVE HAS INITIATED CHANGES IN REAL OUTPUT AND IN THE PRICE LEVEL. IN THE LONG RUN, THE AGGREGATE SUPPLY CURVE GRADUALLY SHIFTS RIGHTWARD AS THE POPULATION, LABOR FORCE, AND OUTPUT PER WORKER ALL INCREASE. THE GROWTH OF PRODUCTIVITY, WHICH GRADUALLY SHIFTS THE AGGREGATE SUPPLY CURVE RIGHTWARD, IS THE PREDOMINANT SOURCE OF GROWTH OF LIVING STANDARDS OVER THE LONG RUN. BUT THE FACT THAT THE PRICE LEVEL HAS INCREASED MORE THAN 500 PERCENT SINCE THE END OF WORLD WAR II IMPLIES THAT THE RIGHTWARD SHIFT OF AGGREGATE DEMAND HAS OUTPACED THE RIGHTWARD SHIFT OF THE AGGREGATE SUPPLY CURVE.

Short-run business cycle phenomena are caused primarily by changes in aggregate demand. In the expansion phase of the business cycle the aggregate demand curve shifts rightward, which leads to expanding real output, declining unemployment, and a rising price level. A contraction of aggregate demand typically leads to recession, in which output declines and the price level falls or at least increases at a slower-than-normal pace.

Aggregate demand is so important in macroeconomics that this chapter is devoted exclusively to the elements that make up aggregate demand.

Aggregate Demand—The Components

In order to focus in detail on the elements underlying the aggregate demand curve, in this chapter and in Chapter 13 we largely ignore the upward-sloping aggregate supply curve of Figure 11.1. In essence, we are temporarily assuming that the aggregate supply curve is horizontal, as illustrated in Figure 12.1. Note in this case that a rightward or leftward shift of the aggregate demand curve of any magnitude

THE AGGREGATE SUPPLY-AGGREGATE DEMAND MODEL WHEN THE AS CURVE IS HORIZONTAL

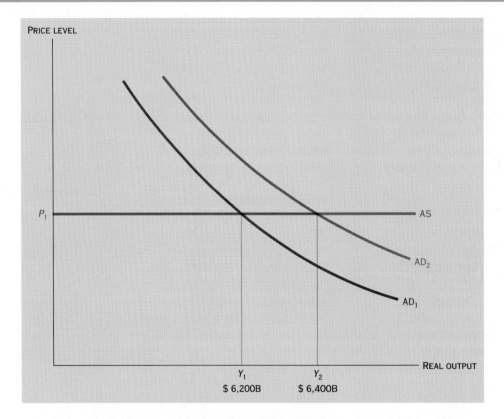

If the nation's AS curve were horizontal, any shift in the AD curve (AD_1 to AD_2) would result in a precisely equivalent change in equilibrium output ($Y_2 - Y_1$).

FIGURE 12.1

would lead to a precisely equal change in the nation's real output. For example, if the nation's aggregate demand curve shifts rightward by $200 billion ($AD_1$ to AD_2 in Figure 12.1), then the increase in equilibrium output ($Y_2 - Y_1$) would be precisely $200 billion. The nation's price level would remain unchanged.

After completing Chapters 12 and 13, you will have a clear understanding of the forces that govern the nation's aggregate demand curve. This knowledge, in turn, provides the basis for understanding the role of monetary and fiscal policy in the American economy. In Chapter 14, we will return to the complete macroeconomic model with upward-sloping aggregate supply curve.

As discussed in Chapters 10 and 11, aggregate demand consists of four components: *consumer demand* (*C*), *investment demand* (*I*), *government purchases* (*G*), and *net exports* (*X* − *M*) of U.S. goods and services. An increase in any of these factors results in a rightward shift of the aggregate demand curve, leading to greater real output. A contraction in any of these four components leads to a downward (leftward) shift in aggregate demand, resulting in lower levels of output and employment.

The relative shares of our nation's aggregate demand (and gross domestic product) contributed by the four components of demand are illustrated in Figure 12.2 (page 288). Consumption spending (*C*) makes up about two-thirds of total expenditures (aggregate demand) and consists of spending on durable goods, nondurables, and services. Government purchases of goods and services by all levels of government (*G*) accounts for about one-fifth of total spending.[1] Investment spending (*I*), which is composed chiefly of expenditures for producers' durable goods and structures (residential and nonresidential), accounts for slightly less than government purchases. The final component of aggregate demand is net exports (*X* − *M*). Foreign purchases of American goods and services (*X*) is a direct source of demand for U.S. output. On the other hand, American demand for foreign goods and services (*M*) represents income earned by Americans that is siphoned off from the domestic expenditure scene. Since U.S. imports have exceeded exports in recent years, the *open economy* or international sector has been a net *negative* source of demand for American goods and services. In other words, we spend more on foreign goods than foreigners spend on ours. Hence, in Figure 12.2, *C* + *I* + *G* accounts for 101 percent of aggregate demand for U.S. goods and services. The trade deficit accounts for a negative 1 percent.

Consumer Demand (*C*)

Inasmuch as consumer spending constitutes the major portion of aggregate demand, economists have devoted an enormous amount of research effort toward understanding consumer behavior. The relationship between consumption and disposable income (personal income after taxes) is one of the cornerstones of

---

[1]Remember that government purchases do not include all government expenditures. Some government expenditures are in the form of transfer payments such as unemployment compensation, Social Security benefits, and interest on the federal debt. Such transfer payments do not of themselves constitute demand for goods and services. However, such transfers directly place incomes into people's pockets, and this leads to private expenditures, mainly in the form of consumption.

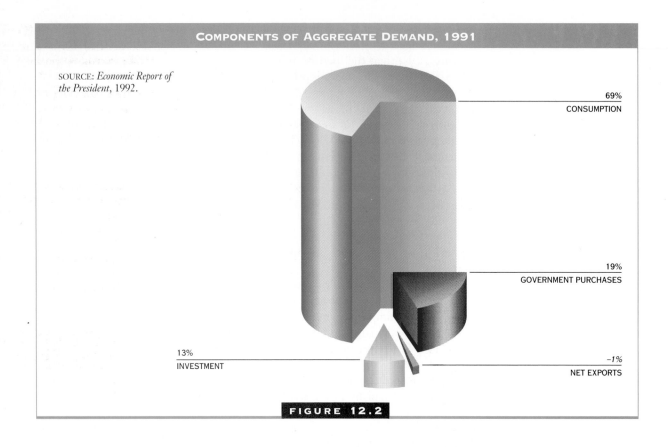

SOURCE: *Economic Report of the President*, 1992.

69%
CONSUMPTION

19%
GOVERNMENT PURCHASES

13%
INVESTMENT

−1%
NET EXPORTS

FIGURE 12.2

macroeconomic analysis. This relationship forms the basis of a multiplier effect by which changes in investment spending and other components of aggregate spending lead to amplified changes in the nation's equilibrium level of output and income.

THE CONSUMPTION FUNCTION

DISPOSABLE INCOME
Personal income available for spending; the difference between personal income and income taxes.

Intuition and plain common sense tell you that a major factor influencing your spending is your income, or more specifically, your **disposable income (Y_d)**—personal income available to spend after taxes. The same is true for the nation's aggregate consumption expenditures, which depend importantly on aggregate disposable income. The historical relationship between aggregate disposable income and aggregate consumption expenditures in the United States is illustrated in Figure 12.3. Note the extremely strong correlation between consumer spending and disposable income. But remember that correlation does not necessarily imply causation. From Figure 12.3, we can infer that at least one of the following is true:

a. Disposable income strongly influences consumption.

b. Consumption strongly influences disposable income.

c. Some third factor simultaneously accounts for the behavior of both disposable income and consumption; their high correlation therefore does not indicate any causal association between the two.

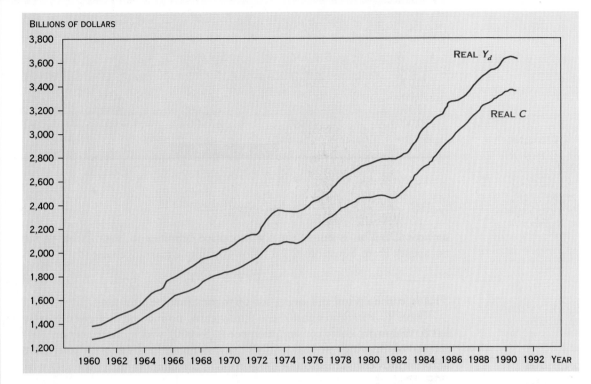

Aggregate consumption expenditures and aggregate disposable income are highly correlated over time. Economists believe that much of this correlation reflects the influence of disposable income upon consumption spending.

SOURCE: U.S. Department of Commerce, 1992.

FIGURE 12.3

CONSUMPTION FUNCTION

The relationship between consumer expenditures and disposable income, holding all other determinants of consumer spending constant.

SAVING

The difference between disposable income and consumption expenditures.

John Maynard Keynes, the great British economist of the first half of this century, believed that the first explanation is correct. Keynes argued that a "fundamental psychological law" exists whereby consumers consistently respond to any increase in disposable income by spending a major portion of the extra income. This relationship between disposable income and consumption expenditures is known as the **consumption function** or the *propensity-to-consume relationship*. Keynes integrated the consumption function into macroeconomic analysis. His framework implies that shifts in any of the components of aggregate demand lead to an amplified change in the nation's output and income (that is, a *multiplier effect*).

Assume the consumption-income relationship indicated in Table 12.1 applies to a typical American family.

In relating the information in Table 12.1, consider the following identity:

$$S \equiv Y_d - C \tag{12.1}$$

Saving is defined as disposable income (Y_d) minus expenditures on goods and

RELATIONSHIP BETWEEN FAMILY DISPOSABLE INCOME AND FAMILY CONSUMPTION				
Y_d	C	S	MPC	MPS
$ 0	$ 4,000	$-4,000	—	—
10,000	12,000	-2,000	0.80	0.20
20,000	20,000	0	0.80	0.20
30,000	28,000	+2,000	0.80	0.20
40,000	36,000	+4,000	0.80	0.20
50,000	44,000	+6,000	0.80	0.20

TABLE 12.1

services (C). This is simply the commonplace definition of saving (that is, income not spent). From Equation 12.1 it follows by simple rearrangement that

$$C + S \equiv Y_d \qquad (12.2)$$

That is, consumption and saving add up to total income after taxes.

Table 12.1 indicates that if the family earns no income in a given year, it still has certain unavoidable consumption needs ($4,000), which can be met only by borrowing or drawing on the family's past savings. This factor is referred to as **autonomous consumption** or the portion of consumption that depends on factors other than income.

Note that if family income were $10,000 the family's expenditures would be $12,000. In addition to its autonomous consumption of $4,000, the family spends 80 percent of additional income as income rises from zero. This factor is referred to as *induced consumption* or additional consumption triggered by the rise in disposable income. Keynes labeled this crucial concept the **marginal propensity to consume (MPC)**. In Table 12.1:

$$\text{MPC} = \frac{\text{change in consumption}}{\text{change in disposable income}} \quad \text{or} \quad \frac{\Delta C}{\Delta Y_d} = \frac{\$ 8,000}{\$10,000} = 0.80$$

According to Keynes' *fundamental psychological law*, the size of the MPC is somewhere between 0 and 1. We have adopted this assumption in our example:

$$0 < \text{MPC} < 1$$

When disposable income changes, people change expenditures in the same direction—but not by the full change in income.

In Table 12.1 we observe that as income rises in increments of $10,000, expenditures respond in increments of $8,000. In our example the family responds to increases in its income by spending 80 percent of the increase. That is, the MPC is 0.80.

Since the family responds to rising income by spending 80 percent of any increase, it is by definition saving the remaining 20 percent of the increase. The fraction of additional income saved is known as the **marginal propensity to save (MPS)**. In Table 12.1

AUTONOMOUS CONSUMPTION

The portion of consumption that is independent of disposable income; consumer expenditures that would occur in the event that disposable income were zero.

MARGINAL PROPENSITY TO CONSUME (MPC)

The ratio of the change in consumption to the change in disposable income that induces the change in consumption; the slope of the consumption function.

MARGINAL PROPENSITY TO SAVE (MPS)

The ratio of the change in saving to the change in disposable income that induces the change in saving; the slope of the saving function.

$$\text{MPS} = \frac{\text{change in saving}}{\text{change in disposable income}} \quad \text{or} \quad \frac{\Delta S}{\Delta Y_d} = \frac{\$\,2,000}{\$10,000} = 0.20$$

Saving rises $2,000 each time disposable income rises $10,000. Given Equation 12.2, it follows that

$$\Delta C + \Delta S \equiv \Delta Y_d \tag{12.3}$$

and

$$\frac{\Delta C}{\Delta Y_d} + \frac{\Delta S}{\Delta Y_d} \equiv 1 \tag{12.4}$$

That is, $\text{MPC} + \text{MPS} \equiv 1$.

Equation 12.3 states that by definition any change in disposable income is allocated to a change in spending (ΔC) and to a change in saving (ΔS). If in Equation 12.4 we then divide Equation 12.3 by ΔY_d, we obtain the proposition that the marginal propensity to consume and the marginal propensity to save must total exactly 1. Hence, if you know the MPC you can immediately calculate the MPS. If you know the MPS you can immediately calculate the MPC.

The information provided in Table 12.1 can be expressed algebraically by the following equations:

$$C = \$4,000 + 0.80\,Y_d$$
$$S = -\$4,000 + 0.20\,Y_d$$

That is, the family depicted in Table 12.1 spends $4,000 plus 80 percent of disposable income; it saves a negative *$4,000* plus 20 percent of disposable income. The same information is conveyed graphically in Figure 12.4 (page 292).

The family consumption function (C–C) and **saving function** (S–S) are plotted directly from the information given in Table 12.1, and from the consumption and saving equations. When disposable income (Y_d) is zero, consumption is $4,000 and saving is minus *$4,000*. The family is forced to borrow or withdraw from past savings $4,000 to finance this subsistence level of consumption.

As income rises to $20,000, expenditures also reach $20,000 and saving rises to zero (from a negative amount). The income level at which saving is zero is known as the **break-even level**, indicated in Figure 12.4 by the income at which the consumption line crosses the 45-degree line. The break-even level is also the income level at which the saving line crosses the horizontal axis, indicating a zero level of saving. At income levels above $20,000, consumption falls short of income (the C–C line lies below the 45-degree line) and saving breaks into positive territory.

What meaning can we attach to the slopes of the consumption and saving functions? Regarding the consumption function:

$$\text{slope} = \frac{\text{rise}}{\text{run}} = \frac{\Delta C}{\Delta Y_d} = \frac{+\$16,000}{+\$20,000} = 0.80.$$

Regarding the saving function:

$$\text{slope} = \frac{\text{rise}}{\text{run}} = \frac{\Delta S}{\Delta Y_d} = \frac{+\$\,4,000}{+\$20,000} = 0.20.$$

BREAK-EVEN INCOME LEVEL
Income level at which consumption equals income; income level at which saving is zero.

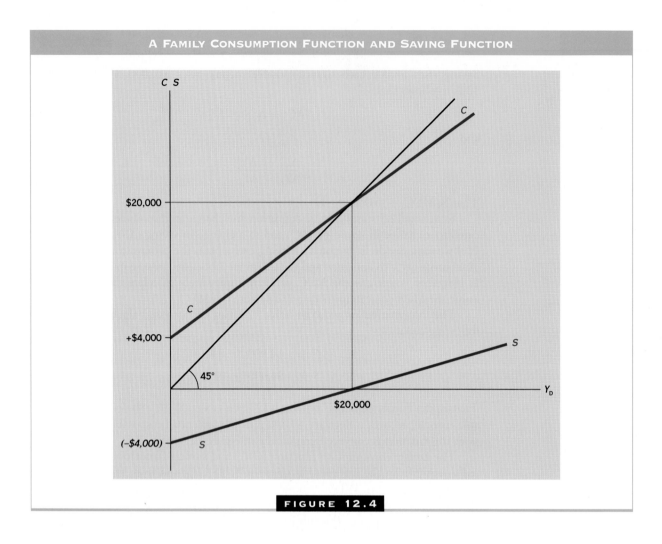

FIGURE 12.4

The slope of the consumption function is the MPC (0.80 in our example). The slope of the saving function is the MPS (0.20 in our example). Clearly, 0.80 + 0.20 = 1. This confirms Equation 12.4.[2]

At this point you should recognize the key implication of this analysis for aggregate demand: Any factor that changes disposable income also induces a change in consumption in the same direction. For example, an income-tax cut that raises Y_d also leads to a rightward movement along the consumption function, such as that in Figure 12.4. This movement, in turn, produces a rightward shift of the AD schedule of Figure 12.1. A tax hike, by reducing disposable income and inducing a contraction of consumption along the consumption function, shifts the AD schedule leftward. This shift leads to a decline in economic activity. The consumption function provides the intellectual basis for the use of discretionary fiscal policy to influence economic activity.

---

[2]Question: What do you obtain when you geometrically add together the consumption line (C–C) and the saving line (S–S) of Figure 12.4? You obtain the 45-degree line that begins at the origin of the figure. Can you explain why? Since a 45-degree line bisects the right angle at which the vertical axis meets the horizontal axis, it delineates all points of equality of the variables on the two axes. Because $C + S$ must total Y_d by definition, C–C plus S–S must add up to the 45-degree line.

YOUR TURN

ASSUME THAT YOUR PERSONAL CONSUMPTION FUNCTION CAN BE DESCRIBED BY THE
EQUATION $C = \$2,000 + .90\,Y_d$:

A. CONSTRUCT A TABLE (LIKE TABLE 12.1) THAT INDICATES YOUR C, S, MPC, AND
MPS AT VARIOUS Y_d LEVELS FROM 0 TO $50,000.

B. WHAT IS YOUR BREAK-EVEN LEVEL OF DISPOSABLE INCOME?

C. WHAT IS YOUR AUTONOMOUS CONSUMPTION?

D. IF YOUR DISPOSABLE INCOME WERE $100,000, HOW MUCH WOULD YOU SAVE?

OTHER FACTORS THAT INFLUENCE CONSUMER SPENDING

We have discussed two general categories of consumption: an *autonomous* portion that occurs independently of disposable income and an *induced* portion that responds to changes in Y_d. Analytically, we may treat changes in Y_d as moving us *along* a given consumption schedule (for example, line C–C in Figure 12.4). Changes in other factors influencing consumption are treated as *shifting the entire position* of the consumption function.[3] Several factors other than Y_d influence consumer spending and therefore shift the C–C line of Figure 12.4.

WEALTH   Consumers spend not only on the basis of current income (Y_d), but also on the basis of their stock of wealth or net worth (that is, the net value of their assets minus their liabilities). Consider two families each earning $40,000 annually. Assume one family owns a home and $400,000 worth of stocks, bonds, and savings accounts. Assume the second family rents a home and owns $20,000 worth of financial assets. Quite likely the first family annually spends more on consumer goods than does the second family. In terms of Figure 12.5 (page 294), the wealthy family's consumption schedule (C_w–C_w) lies vertically above that of the poorer family (C_p–C_p). In the figure, the wealthier family spends $35,000 of the $40,000 disposable income, saving $5,000; the poorer family spends $28,000, saving $12,000.

In the context of the overall economy, changes in stock market prices, prices of other financial assets, and real estate values can initiate important changes in wealth, thereby shifting the nation's consumption function. When the U.S. stock market crashed in October 1987, more than $1,000 billion of financial wealth dissolved. Many economists anticipated a resulting downward shift in the nation's consumption function and a decline in aggregate demand for goods and services (see Exhibit 12.1, page 296).

EXPECTED FUTURE Y_d   Spending patterns are influenced not only by current and recent disposable income but also by disposable income expected in the future. A just-graduated physician and a veteran college English professor may each earn $30,000 annually. Very likely, however, the physician will spend more than the professor because the physician's expected future income is much higher than the

---

[3]Recall the concept of a demand curve from Chapter 4. Now consider the demand curve for Coca-Cola. A change in the price of Coke moves you along the demand curve for Coke; a change in other factors relevant to the demand for Coke (price of Pepsi, income, population, and so on) shifts the entire position of the demand curve for Coke. Similarly with the consumption function. A change in disposable income moves us along the consumption function; a change in other factors influencing consumption shifts the entire position of the consumption function.

Consumption depends not only on disposable income but also on wealth. Families with greater wealth tend to consume more at each level of disposable income than do families with less wealth. An increase in wealth shifts the consumption function upward.

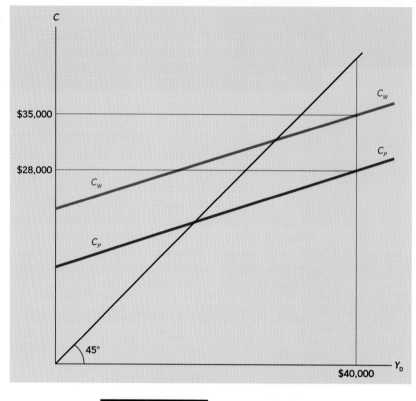

FIGURE 12.5

professor's. This insight has important macroeconomic implications. Suppose a recession emerges. Consumers may not cut back spending in line with the decline in disposable income because the setback is expected to be temporary. Moreover, federal tax changes implemented to influence aggregate consumption and aggregate demand must be perceived as permanent in order to be fully effective.[4] Hence, a temporary tax hike implemented in 1968 for the purpose of slowing consumption and aggregate demand had little effect on consumers. The tax increase was announced as a temporary, one-shot affair; consumers simply paid the taxes out of savings instead of restraining consumption.

THE GENERAL PRICE LEVEL When the price level declines, the real value of such financial assets as money and government bonds rises. Consumers are thus

---

[4]Economist Milton Friedman was awarded the 1976 Nobel Prize in Economics for several path-breaking studies. One of the most significant was *A Theory of the Consumption Function*. In this work Friedman formalized the relationship between consumption and *permanent income*, a measure of average expected future income. Because Friedman believes that consumers spend on the basis of permanent income instead of current income, income-tax changes do not appreciably influence consumer spending if they are perceived as temporary. Friedman's work represents an important refinement of Keynes' theory, which treats consumption simply as a function of *current income.*

better off, and the consumption function shifts upward. On the other hand, if the price level were to double, the real value of these financial assets would be cut in half. Consumers would feel poorer and the consumption function would shift downward. This phenomenon, known as the **wealth effect**, helps account for the downward slope of the aggregate demand curve of Figure 12.1.

WEALTH EFFECT
The effect that a change in the nation's price level exerts on consumption, aggregate demand, and equilibrium output by changing the real value of such financial assets as money, savings accounts, and government bonds held by individuals.

THE EXPECTED FUTURE INFLATION RATE Consumer behavior may be influenced by changes in the outlook for inflation. Suppose people expect the inflation rate to rise to 8 percent next year from a current rate of 4 percent. Some consumers may step up buying to beat the anticipated price hikes. If so, the consumption function may shift upward.[5] On the other hand, other consumers may feel more insecure about the future because of higher expected inflation. Such consumers are likely to step up their saving rates (that is, their consumption functions shift downward). Because different consumers react differently to changes in expected future inflation, it is difficult to predict the effect of changes in expected inflation upon the consumption function. In this area, as in other areas of economics, human behavior is connected with psychology.

STOCK OF DURABLE GOODS OWNED BY HOUSEHOLDS When consumers are well stocked with state-of-the-art automobiles, VCRs, refrigerators, and vacuum cleaners, there is clearly little need to purchase durable goods. On the other hand, if the bulk of these durable goods owned by consumers are obsolete or in a run-down state, there is great scope for massive purchases of such items. This factor helps explain the enormous consumption boom immediately following the end of World War II. Automobiles, refrigerators, and many other durable goods were not produced during the war (1942–1945). Consumption simply exploded after the war as people rushed out to purchase newly available cars, washing machines, and other durables.

Investment Expenditures

Investment demand—spending on producers' durable equipment and various types of building structures—is the most volatile component of aggregate demand. The categories of investment are reviewed in Table 12.2 (page 296). Gross investment or total spending on investment goods is predominantly made up of producers' durable equipment such as machines and tools, nonresidential structures such as factories and commercial buildings, and residential structures such as houses and apartment buildings.

---

[5]Is it rational in general to buy goods now in order to beat expected price hikes? This depends on whether the real interest rate you can earn on your savings is positive. Suppose a new Ford costs $15,000 this year and you expect next year's model to increase 6 percent to $15,900. If you can earn more than 6 percent on a savings account or one-year certificate of deposit, you will accumulate sufficient funds to afford the higher price a year from now. Hence, there is no reason to run out and buy the car just to beat the price hike. During the 1980s, the interest rate available to consumers exceeded the inflation rate by a significant margin. In the early 1990s, this was not always the case.

The Great Crash of 1987—
What Were the Consequences?

On Black Monday, October 19, 1987, the stock market crashed. The Dow Jones Industrials lost 508 points, or 23 percent of its total value in a single day. Descriptions of the atmosphere on Wall Street ranged from "hysteria" to "panic." A few days later, a crazed Miami speculator walked into a Merrill-Lynch office and gunned down his broker and everyone else in sight. Several suicides were linked to the collapse. Stock market crashes are the stuff of personal tragedy.

What are the consequences of a stock market crash for the macroeconomy? Most economists agree that the net effect is contractionary (that is, aggregate demand and economic activity are induced to fall). Following the *crash of '87*, economic prognosticators immediately revised their forecasts downward. However, no one can confidently predict how powerfully a stock market crash spills over to pull down the real economy, because the responses of people that produce the real economic effects are intimately connected with psychology.

Thomas Juster, an economist with the University of Michigan's highly regarded *Survey of Consumer Confidence*, believes that a stock market crash has two effects on consumers. First, there is a direct wealth effect. More than 50 million American households own shares of stock directly, in their personal portfolios of common stock and mutual funds. For many more individuals, stocks are an important component of retirement or pension programs. On Black Monday, Americans lost $500 billion of this paper wealth. It simply evaporated in the stock market *meltdown of '87*. Because consumer spending—especially on expensive durable goods—depends on wealth or net worth as well as on disposable income, aggregate consumption is likely to decline when the stock market drops. A rule of thumb derived from empirical research on consumer behavior is that the drop in consumption is likely to amount to 2 or 3 percent of the contraction in paper wealth. Inasmuch as stock values declined roughly $1,200 billion in the last five months of 1987, this wealth effect suggested a downward shift of the consumption function of perhaps $24 billion to $36 billion for 1988.

Second, according to Juster, even the majority of Americans who do not own stock are likely to become more conservative in their spending propensities. A

GROSS INVESTMENT SPENDING BY COMPONENT, 1991 (IN BILLIONS)	
Producers' durable equipment	$376
Nonresidential structures	175
Residential structures	195
Change in inventories	−19
Gross investment	$727 billion

SOURCE: U.S. Department of Commerce, *Survey of Current Business*, 1992.

TABLE 12.2

stock market crash, which they (and everyone else) fail to comprehend, tends to create anxiety about job stability and prospects for future income and living standards. An instinctive reaction is to postpone purchases of such big-ticket items as cars, houses, and furniture until the outlook clears.

Similarly, business firms that invest in plant and equipment and research and development are likely to become more cautious after a stock market crash. Investment spending is closely related to the outlook for the future. Historically, the stock market has been a leading indicator of economic activity. Thus, a crash in stock values is likely to be interpreted by business executives as a signal that less prosperous times may well lie ahead. Investment and research expenditures tend to be scaled back or postponed. For these reasons, most economists recognized that the *Great Crash of 1987* significantly raised the prospects for a contraction in aggregate demand and a recession in 1988.

As it turned out, a recession did *not* occur in 1988. A possible explanation lies in compensating measures implemented by the Federal Reserve to bolster the economy. Sensing that the stock market crash might spill over and pull down the economy, the Fed quickly put into place policies to boost aggregate demand. Also, American exports began to increase strongly in 1988 in response to the sustained decline in the international value of the dollar that began in 1985. These two considerations may have offset the effects of the crash in stock prices and prevented an economic downturn.

Conceptually, it is useful to distinguish between *gross* investment and *net* investment. *Gross investment* is total spending on investment goods, including expenditures required to replace worn-out and obsolete equipment and structures. *Net investment* is the *net addition* to the nation's stock of capital goods in a given period, such as one year. Net investment is therefore the difference between gross investment and depreciation. Suppose that next year gross investment spending is $800 billion, while depreciation or replacement investment is $600 billion. Then net investment is $200 billion, and the nation's capital stock increases by $200 billion.

Over time, as output grows, the capital stock required to produce this larger output increases. Hence, net investment is almost always positive (that is, gross investment almost always exceeds depreciation).

net investment   = gross investment minus depreciation

gross investment = net investment plus depreciation or replacement investment

INVESTMENT SPENDING—THE ROLE OF INTEREST RATES

Investment goods are those produced for the purpose of facilitating production of other goods and services. Investment goods normally have a relatively long lifetime: a new lathe may last 30 years, a tractor 20 years, an apartment building 60 years. The bulk of investment expenditures are financed with borrowed money. Firms with substantial internal funds on hand have alternatives to using the funds for investment projects. For example, they can place the funds in such financial assets as bonds and earn the going interest rate. The opportunity cost of investing in new plant and equipment or apartment buildings is the current interest rate. Entrepreneurs invest only in those potential projects for which the expected rate of return on the investment exceeds the interest rate. Given the array of returns expected from various potential investment projects in the nation, this implies that a decline in the level of interest rates brings more investment projects into the realm of feasibility—that is, more investment projects appear profitable and are undertaken. The relationship between the interest rate and total investment spending is illustrated in Figure 12.6. This is known as the investment demand curve.

The investment demand curve indicates an inverse relationship between the interest rate and investment spending, *all other factors remaining constant.* A new investment project expected to yield 7.5 percent annually (on the funds invested) will be built if interest rates are 6 percent, but not if they are 8 percent. Federal Reserve monetary policy, by influencing the level of U.S. interest rates, is capable of moving us along this demand curve, thereby altering the level of investment spending.

However, there are many other factors besides interest rates that strongly influence investment spending. Changes in these factors may be viewed as *shifting the position* of the investment demand curve of Figure 12.6. The position of the curve is believed to be quite volatile.

OTHER FACTORS THAT INFLUENCE INVESTMENT SPENDING

Among the factors that affect investment decisions and shift the investment demand curve are changes in business confidence, changes in the capacity utilization rate of existing plant and equipment and expected future growth of aggregate demand, changes in income-tax provisions, and changes in stock market prices.

BUSINESS CONFIDENCE   Investment spending is inherently a forward-looking activity. It is risky to borrow large sums of money to build a new factory or install new equipment. In doing so, one is *betting the business* on the future. When the outlook for the future of the economy worsens, returns expected from investment pro-

Given other considerations, a decline in interest rates stimulates investment expenditures because it increases the number of potential projects that appear profitable.

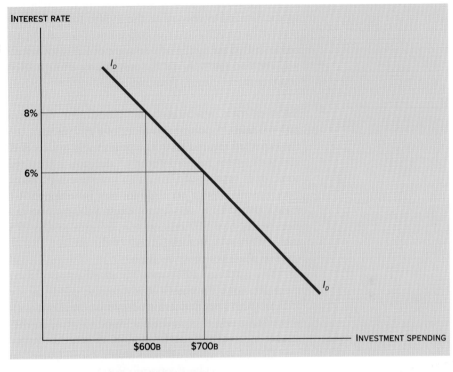

FIGURE 12.6

jects are revised downward. The investment demand curve illustrated in Figure 12.6 shifts leftward, and less investment spending is forthcoming at each and every interest rate. When the economic outlook improves, businesses revise expected returns upward, the investment demand schedule shifts rightward, and a larger magnitude of investment occurs at each and every interest rate. Keynes argued that investment depends upon the "animal spirits" of businesses. Translated, this suggests that business confidence is volatile, and returns expected from potential investment projects can be revised considerably and in a relatively brief time period. That is, the investment demand curve shifts about, bringing sharp fluctuations in actual investment spending (review Figure 10.3).

CAPACITY UTILIZATION RATE AND EXPECTED FUTURE GROWTH OF DEMAND When firms are currently operating their existing plant at 80 or 90 percent of capacity and are anticipating healthy future demand growth for their product, they must expand or modernize their production facilities to meet the expected future market. Here the investment demand curve lies far to the right. On the other hand, when the existing plant is producing only at 60 percent of capacity because of limited sales and when the outlook for sales growth is modest or bleak, the investment demand curve is low or far to the left. Thus we can state that, *given* *other factors*, the higher the economy's current capacity utilization rate, the farther to the right is the investment demand curve. The greater the expected future sales growth, *given other factors*, the farther to the right is the investment demand curve. In the Great Depression of the 1930s, many firms were operating at less than 50 percent of capacity and the outlook was dismal. As a result, the investment demand curve shifted far to the left. In spite of fairly low interest rates, investment spending was anemic; many firms did not spend enough even to replace worn-out capital equipment.

INCOME-TAX PROVISIONS Investment decisions are typically made on a rational basis. A potential builder of a new factory or apartment building calculates the expected returns from the project and evaluates the findings in view of the risk and the current rate of interest. A decision is then made. Government tax policy is sometimes capable of tilting this investment decision. From time to time the U.S. government allows a *tax credit* for new investment. A 10 percent *investment tax credit* means that if IBM decides to invest $100 million in new equipment, the corporation would owe $10 million less in taxes to the IRS. Because the government is essentially paying for 10 percent of the project, this is likely to have a positive influence on the investment decision.

The nature of *depreciation tax allowances* also has an important impact on investment decisions. Purchases of investment goods are a cost of doing business and the IRS provides a tax deduction (depreciation allowance) for such expenditures. A firm that installs new equipment is allowed to write off the cost of the equipment against taxable income *over a period of years*. When this depreciation policy is liberal—firms are allowed to write off investment expenditures quickly—potential projects are more attractive. The Economic Recovery Tax Act of 1981 (ERTA) generally liberalized depreciation allowances, thus tending to stimulate investment. However, more recent legislation removed some of the incentives supplied by ERTA by slowing down depreciation allowances.

THE LEVEL OF STOCK MARKET PRICES Firms may finance new investment projects by issuing debt (selling bonds or borrowing from banks) or by issuing equity shares (that is, shares of stock). When stock prices are high, firms find it attractive to obtain funds by issuing new shares of stock. When stock prices are depressed, firms are reluctant to issue new shares. To do so dilutes the portion of the company owned by existing shareholders without obtaining a price commensurate with management's perception of the true worth of the company. Hence, when the stock market is depressed, the investment demand curve of Figure 12.6 is farther to the left than when stock prices are booming.

Equilibrium Output in a Simple Economy with No Government or International Trade

Imagine a primitive nation with no government sector (no taxes or government spending) and no foreign trade. Let this simple, closed economy be known as

Primitavia. Remember the two types of goods produced—consumer goods and investment goods. Although this two-sector economy is in an infant stage of development, its people are like modern-day Americans in that they obey Keynes' "fundamental psychological law." Further, they have a marginal propensity to consume of 0.60, so that each dollar increase in income leads to an increase in consumer spending of 60 cents. Investment spending depends on such factors as business confidence and interest rates, and is assumed to be independent of the level of output and income.

Before analyzing equilibrium output in Primitavia, consider the circular flow of income and expenditures in this two-sector economy illustrated in Figure 12.7. Remember that every dollar's worth of output produced (upper flow) creates a dollar of income earned (lower flow). In Primitavia, since there are no taxes, every dollar of output creates a dollar of disposable income—income available to spend. Of course, a portion of this flow of income is withdrawn from the flow by households. This is saving, and is the only *leakage* from the circular flow. The larger portion of income is returned to the spending stream by households in the form of consumer spending. Investment is shown as an injection of spending into the flow by firms, although households actually also contribute to investment by spending on housing. You should observe that only when the withdrawal from the flow in the form of saving is precisely matched by investment do aggregate expenditures ($C + I$) precisely match aggregate output.

The expenditure schedule for Primitavia (that is, the relationship between output and income on the one hand and consumption and investment spending on the other hand) is given in Table 12.3 (page 302).

CIRCULAR FLOW OF INCOME IN PRIMITAVIA

In a primitive two-sector economy, the only *leakage* from the circular flow is saving. The only *injection*, or nonhousehold form of spending, is investment spending. If saving equals investment, then expenditures equal output.

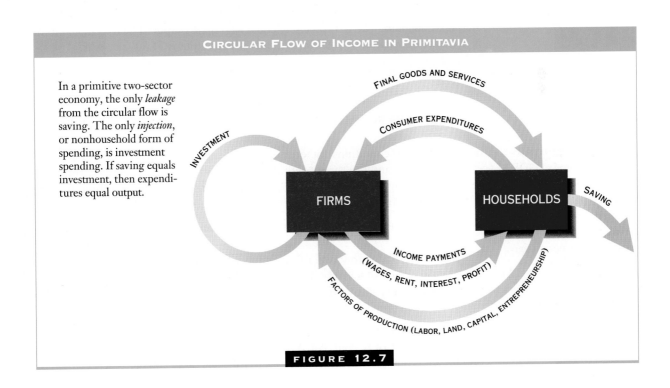

FINAL GOODS AND SERVICES

CONSUMER EXPENDITURES

INVESTMENT

FIRMS

HOUSEHOLDS

SAVING

INCOME PAYMENTS
(WAGES, RENT, INTEREST, PROFIT)

FACTORS OF PRODUCTION (LABOR, LAND, CAPITAL, ENTREPRENEURSHIP)

FIGURE 12.7

EXPENDITURES SCHEDULE FOR PRIMITAVIA

OUTPUT AND INCOME (Y)	CONSUMPTION (C)	SAVING (S)	INVESTMENT (I)	AGGREGATE EXPENDITURES (C + I)	RELATIONSHIP OF SALES TO OUTPUT	INVOLUNTARY CHANGE IN INVENTORIES	OUTPUT DECISION
$1,200	$ 920	$280	$400	$1,320	Sales > output	—	Increase
1,300	980	320	400	1,380	Sales > output	—	Increase
1,400	1,040	360	400	1,440	Sales > output	—	Increase
1,500	1,100	400	400	1,500	Sales = output	0	Maintain
1,600	1,160	440	400	1,560	Sales < output	+	Decrease
1,700	1,220	480	400	1,620	Sales < output	+	Decrease

TABLE 12.3

Table 12.3 indicates that when output of $1,200 per year is produced, consumers spend $920 per year. Because investment spending is $400, aggregate expenditures (C + I) total $1,320; firms sell more than current output and the nation's aggregate inventories decline involuntarily. This gives a clear signal to firms to step up their level of production.

Suppose firms respond by increasing output to $1,700 per year. Consumers now spend $1,220 and firms spend $400 on investment goods. Aggregate expenditures (total sales) are thus $1,620 per year. In this instance firms are producing more than they can sell; the nation's inventories rise involuntarily and firms are given the signal to curtail production. Output accordingly falls to a lower level.

Note in Table 12.3 that only when output of $1,500 per year is produced does aggregate spending (C + I) precisely equal aggregate output. The overall economy is in a state of balance, or equilibrium, only when output is $1,500 per year.

CONDITIONS FOR MACROEQUILIBRIUM IN THE TWO-SECTOR MODEL

EQUILIBRIUM OUTPUT
The unique level of GDP at which aggregate demand equals output; the only output level at which there is no involuntary change in inventories, hence no signal to change production.

There are three conditions for **equilibrium output** in Primitavia's simple, two-sector economy, and the three conditions are equivalent (that is, they are three different ways of saying the same thing). If any one condition is met, all three are met. If any one condition is not met, none is met.

1. $Y = C + I$. Aggregate expenditures or sales (C + I) equals aggregate output (Y).
2. $S = I$. The withdrawal of funds from the circular flow (saving) is precisely matched by the injection of funds (investment).
3. Involuntary change in inventories = 0. There is no involuntary change in the economy's aggregate stock of inventories.

Note in Table 12.3 that all three conditions are met when Primitavia produces an annual output of $1,500. All three conditions are violated at all other levels of output. Thus output in Primitavia settles to the level of $1,500 per year.

GRAPHIC ILLUSTRATION OF EQUILIBRIUM OUTPUT

Figure 12.8 illustrates in diagrammatic form the same information given in Table 12.3. Aggregate output and income is indicated on the horizontal axis and aggregate expenditures $(C + I)$ on the vertical axis. This framework is called the *income–expenditure diagram* or the *45-degree diagram*. The aggregate expenditures line $(C + I)$ is an upward-sloping function of output and income because the marginal propensity to consume is positive. Any increase in output pulls up consumption and, hence, aggregate spending $(C + I)$.

A 45-degree line starting from the origin of Figure 12.8 is drawn to serve as a guideline that delineates equal magnitudes on the two axes. Since equilibrium requires that aggregate spending (measured on the vertical axis) just precisely equals aggregate output (measured on the horizontal axis), equilibrium must occur at the point where the aggregate expenditures line $(C + I)$ intersects the 45-degree line. This occurs in Figure 12.8 when Primitavia produces $1,500 of output per year. If its firms produce less than $1,500, note that the aggregate spending line lies above the 45-degree guideline. In this event sales exceed output, the nation's inventories decline, and firms step up output. If output exceeds $1,500 per year, the aggregate spending line lies below the 45-degree line. In this event output exceeds aggregate

DETERMINATION OF EQUILIBRIUM OUTPUT

The equilibrium level of output is the unique level at which the expenditures line $(C + I)$ crosses the 45-degree line. Only at this output level are expenditures precisely equal to output.

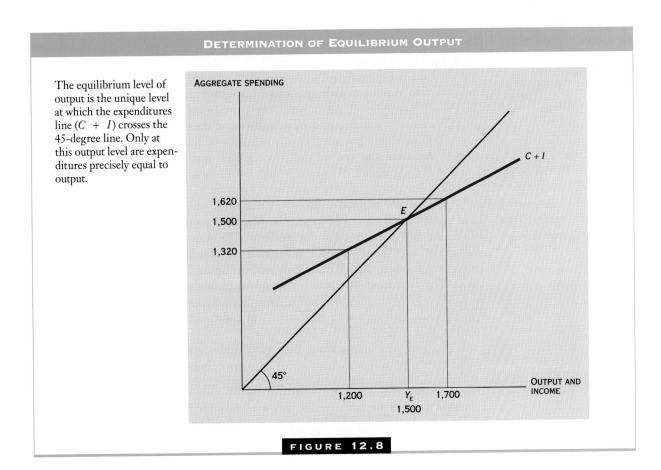

FIGURE 12.8

sales, the nation's inventories rise, and firms curtail output. Only at point E, with output at $1,500, are output and sales in perfect harmony, with no signal given to change the level of production. This is equilibrium.[6]

The Multiplier—Black Magic or Simple Logic?

Assume Primitavia is an agrarian society—the bulk of its people depend on agriculture and fishing for their livelihood. Further assume that breakthroughs in agricultural and fishing technology occur. Ladders are invented to assist in picking fruit from the trees and fishing nets are developed to increase the take from the seas. The producers in Primitavia—the farmers and fishermen—decide to take advantage of these new inventions, and increase their annual investment spending from $400 to $440. Assuming Primitavia initially has some idle resources—labor and materials—the expansion of investment expenditures causes equilibrium output to increase by some multiple (larger than one) of the initial shift in spending (investment) that touches off the expansion process. This expansion of equilibrium output in Primitavia is illustrated in Figure 12.9.

Initially the economy is in equilibrium at Y_{E_1}, with output running at $1,500 per year. The intersection of the aggregate expenditures line ($C + I_1$) and the 45-degree guideline is at point A in Figure 12.9. The expansion of investment spending means that the aggregate spending line shifts upward to $C + I_2$, a vertical shift of $40. Starting at point A with output of $1,500, demand and sales expand by $40 to $1,540. This is shown in the figure as the move from A to B. The expansion of sales initially causes inventories to decline by $40, and thus induces firms to step up output by $40 to $1,540 per year. This is indicated by the move from B to C in the figure. If this were the end of the process, the **multiplier** would be exactly one because the expansion of output would be precisely equal to the initial shift in spending that touched off the expansion of output.

However, the consumption function and the marginal propensity to consume now enter the picture. The expansion of output from $1,500 to $1,540 places an additional $40 of income into the pockets of the workers and the owners of firms. Given the MPC of 0.60, these individuals respond by increasing expenditures on consumer goods by $24. This is indicated in Figure 12.9 by the movement from C to D. The expansion of consumer spending causes output of consumer goods to expand by $24 ($D$ to E in the figure). This, in turn, puts additional income into people's pockets and induces a further rise of consumer spending of MPC $\times \Delta Y = 0.60 \times \$24 = \$14.40$ (E to F in the figure).

This two-way interactional process of additional consumer spending calling forth extra output that induces added consumer spending continues, theoretically,

MULTIPLIER

The ratio of the change in equilibrium output to the original change in spending (C, I, G, or net exports) that caused the change in output.

---

[6]To keep Figure 12.8 as simple as possible, the consumption, investment, and saving lines are not in the figure. If they were, the upward-sloping saving schedule would intersect the horizontal investment line at the output level of $1,500. At output levels above $1,500, saving exceeds investment (withdrawal from the flow of income exceeds the injection of investment). At output levels below $1,500, investment exceeds saving. In a two-sector model, $C + I$ always intersects the 45-degree line at the same output level where the saving and investment schedules intersect.

An increase in investment expenditures, by inducing additional output and therefore placing added income in people's pockets, pulls up consumption. The result is that the increase in equilibrium output $(Y_{E_2} - Y_{E_1})$ is a *multiple* of the initial increase in investment spending.

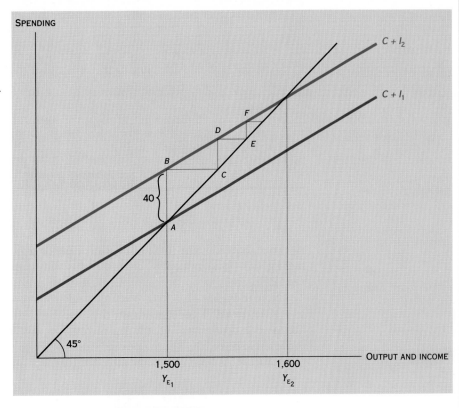

FIGURE 12.9

through an infinite number of steps. In the limit, as indicated in Figure 12.9, output reaches the new equilibrium level of $1,600 per year. An expansion of investment expenditures of $40 per year pulls up equilibrium output by $100, which is 2.5 times the magnitude of the increase of investment spending. Hence, we know the multiplier is 2.5.

$$\text{multiplier} = \frac{\text{change in equilibrium output}}{\text{initial shift in spending that initiates change in output}}$$

$$\text{multiplier} = \frac{\$100 \text{ per year}}{\$40 \text{ per year}} = 2.5$$

Table 12.4 traces the multiplier process through a period of *rounds*. In the first round investment spending rises by $40 per year and firms respond by raising GDP by $40 per year. The income created by this additional GDP feeds back in the second round to pull up consumer spending by $24 per year. Firms react by stepping up production of consumer goods by $24 per year and the cumulative increase in GDP at this point is $64 per year. The two-way interaction between output growth and consumer spending continues until output has ultimately expanded by $100. Of

		EXPANSION OF OUTPUT ASSOCIATED WITH SUSTAINED INCREASE IN INVESTMENT SPENDING OF 40 DOLLARS PER YEAR		
ROUND	ΔI	ΔC	$\Delta GDP \equiv \Delta Y_d$	CUMULATIVE ΔGDP
1	+40		+40.0	+ 40.0
2		+24.0	+24.0	+ 64.0
3		+14.4	+14.4	+ 78.4
4		+ 8.64	+ 8.64	+ 87.04
5		+ 5.18	+ 5.18	+ 92.22
.		.	.	.
.		.	.	.
		.	.	
		$\Sigma = +60$	$\Sigma = +100$	+100.00

TABLE 12.4

this total, $60 is in the form of consumer goods and $40 is in the form of investment goods—ladders and fishing nets. This multiplier process is illustrated in Figure 12.10.

Note in Figure 12.10 that nothing is said about the amount of time that elapses in a given *round*. This depends on the time lag involved in output responding to increased expenditures and the lag involved in consumers responding to income growth. However, the figure does indicate that more than 90 percent of the multiplier process has been completed after five (of the infinite number of) *rounds*.

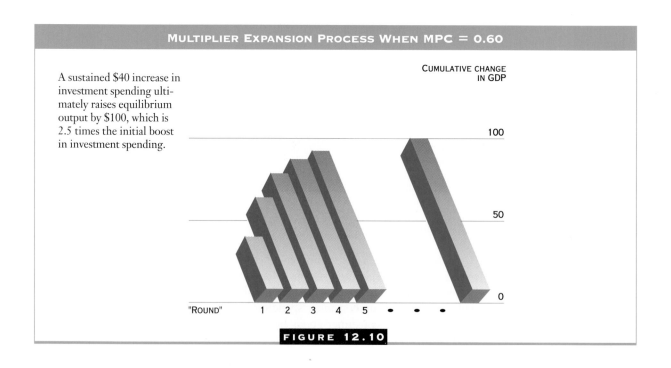

MULTIPLIER EXPANSION PROCESS WHEN MPC = 0.60

A sustained $40 increase in investment spending ultimately raises equilibrium output by $100, which is 2.5 times the initial boost in investment spending.

CUMULATIVE CHANGE IN GDP

100

50

0

"ROUND"   1   2   3   4   5   •   •   •

FIGURE 12.10

THE MULTIPLIER AS THE SUM OF AN INFINITE GEOMETRIC SERIES

In Table 12.4, the ΔC and ΔGDP columns contain a series of numbers related to each other by a common factor, 0.6, which is the MPC. You may recall from high-school algebra that such a series of numbers is known as an *infinite geometric progression*. The formula for the sum of such a series of numbers is the initial number in the series times $1/(1 - r)$, where r is the ratio that relates the numbers (0.6 in Table 12.4). Hence, the sum of the ΔC column is $24 \times 1/(1 - .60) = 60$ and the sum of the ΔGDP column is $40 \times 1/(1 - .60) = 100$. Because this ratio that relates the consecutive numbers in the column is in fact the MPC, the multiplier for the GDP column is $1 \div (1 - MPC)$:

$$\text{multiplier} = \frac{1}{1 - \text{MPC}}$$

Because $MPC + MPS \equiv 1$ and $1 - MPC \equiv MPS$, we can also write the expression for the multiplier as follows:

$$\text{multiplier} = \frac{1}{\text{MPS}}$$

The size of this simple multiplier depends strictly on the size of the MPC and its close relative, the MPS. The larger the MPC (smaller the MPS) the larger the multiplier, as indicated in Table 12.5.

The intuitive explanation underlying the positive relationship between the magnitude of the MPC and the magnitude of the multiplier is quite straightforward. A large MPC indicates that any initial shift in spending, by pulling up output and income, induces a large expansion in consumer spending. Total spending and output are therefore pulled up quite substantially after a series of *rounds*. At the other extreme, an MPC of zero indicates that any initial shift in spending, by pulling up output and income, induces no expansion in consumer spending. In this event the change in equilibrium output is identical to the initial shift in spending, and the multiplier equals one.

RELATIONSHIP BETWEEN MPC, MPS, AND THE SIMPLE MULTIPLIER

MPC	MPS	SIMPLE MULTIPLIER
0	1.0	1.0
0.4	0.6	1.67
0.5	0.5	2.0
0.6	0.4	2.50
0.7	0.3	3.33
0.8	0.2	5.0
0.9	0.1	10.0
0.99	0.01	100.0

TABLE 12.5

WHY THE REAL-WORLD MULTIPLIER IS SMALLER THAN THE SIMPLE MULTIPLIER

Economic studies estimate that the MPC in the United States is in the 0.8 to 0.9 range. Table 12.5 indicates that this puts the simple multiplier in the range of 5 to 10. An increase in investment spending of $10 billion—caused by lower interest rates or tax changes favorable to business—is thus predicted to lead to an expansion in GDP of $50 billion to $100 billion. In reality the true multiplier is only about 2, even though the MPC is in the 0.8 to 0.9 range. Three factors *water down* the actual expansion in the nation's real GDP associated with any given increase in spending.

INCOME TAXES All modern societies have income taxes. As GDP begins to expand because of a shift in spending, part of the extra GDP is skimmed off in the form of taxes. An increase in GDP does not lead to an equivalent increase in disposable income. If the typical American is in a 25 percent marginal tax bracket (federal, state, and local income taxes combined), a $1 increase in gross income yields only a 75-cent increase in disposable income. Given an MPC of 0.8, the individual returns only 60 cents of the extra dollar in gross income to the spending stream (0.8×75 cents). The effective MPC out of GDP is reduced by the existence of income taxes, and the true multiplier is reduced considerably relative to a society with no income taxes. By reducing the swings in GDP associated with shifts in spending, income taxes act as an **automatic stabilizer** or *built-in stabilizer*.[7] As GDP rises, so do taxes paid (the government budget deficit declines)—which holds back expenditures and limits the expansion. As GDP declines in recession, taxes paid drop off—which prevents disposable income from declining as much as GDP and thereby supports aggregate spending—and the government budget deficit expands, providing spending support to a depressed economy.

EFFECTS ON INVESTMENT SPENDING Assume consumer spending or government spending shifts upward, touching off an expansion in GDP. The rising GDP is likely to induce an increase in the desire to borrow. Given the amount of funds available in the economy, this means that interest rates will go up. The interest rate–investment demand relationship of Figure 12.6 indicates that higher interest rates lead to lower investment expenditures, a phenomenon known as **crowding out**. The initial expansion of consumption or government spending, by driving up GDP and interest rates, may crowd out some investment spending. If so, part of the extra GDP (in the form of government goods and consumer goods) is offset by the reduced output of investment goods. In this event the true multiplier is not as large as the simple multiplier.

AUTOMATIC STABILIZER OR BUILT-IN STABILIZER A feature of the economy that acts automatically to inhibit economic fluctuations without discretionary policy changes being implemented.

CROWDING-OUT EFFECT The tendency for an expansionary fiscal policy to induce an offsetting reduction in investment expenditures by raising interest rates.

---

[7]Adding income taxes (assume a marginal tax rate of t) into the model changes the multiplier expression to $m = \dfrac{1}{1 - \text{MPC}(1 - t)}$. When MPC is 0.8 and t is .25, the multiplier is $\dfrac{1}{1 - .8(.75)} = \dfrac{1}{.40} = 2.5$.

By assuming a marginal income-tax rate of 25 percent in this instance, the multiplier is halved (from 5 to 2.5). The higher the marginal tax rate, the smaller the multiplier. One beneficial side effect of the increase in U.S. marginal income-tax rates during this century has been the reduction in the size of the multiplier. Shifts in expenditures now give rise to less volatile changes in output because the multiplier is smaller than in earlier times.

CROWDING-IN EFFECT
The tendency for an expansionary fiscal policy to induce an *increase* in investment spending by stimulating sales growth and utilization rate of existing plant and equipment.

In reality, however, things are not quite so simple. Figure 12.6 indicates the relationship between interest rates and investment spending when *all other factors that influence investment are held constant.* As GDP increases in response to the initial increase in spending, the business outlook tends to improve and the utilization rate of existing plant capacity increases. These factors shift the investment demand curve of Figure 12.6 to the right. It is possible, therefore, that investment spending may increase *in spite of* higher interest rates. Instead of crowding out, we may get **crowding in**—a favorable response of investment spending to the initial shift in spending. The actual outcome produced by an initial shift in spending depends on the state of the economy at the time the economic stimulus occurs and the steepness of the investment demand curve of Figure 12.6. At any rate, the true multiplier is likely to differ from the simple multiplier as a result of induced effects on investment spending.

PRICE LEVEL EFFECTS   Equilibrium output in the income–expenditure or 45-degree-diagram framework is related to the aggregate supply–aggregate demand model in Figure 12.11 (page 310). The income–expenditure framework in the top portion of the figure neglects price–level considerations. Instead, the framework assumes that the relevant portion of the nation's aggregate supply curve is horizontal, so that the increased demand for goods and services is fully reflected in additional real output rather than partially reflected in higher prices. In Figure 12.11, when investment spending increases, the expenditure line shifts upward, touching off a multiple expansion of output and income from Y_{E1} to Y_{E2}. In the bottom portion of the figure, the aggregate demand curve shifts horizontally by the same magnitude, $Y_{E2} - Y_{E1}$. Thus, if the nation's aggregate supply curve were horizontal or flat (AS_{flat}), equilibrium output would increase from Y_{E1} to Y_{E2} in the lower portion of Figure 12.11. However, the aggregate supply curve normally slopes upward, as indicated by AS_{normal}. In the figure, equilibrium output actually rises only from Y_{E1} to Y_{E3}. Part of the increase in expenditures is manifested in higher prices rather than in higher real output.

The extent to which the initial increase in spending is dissipated in higher prices instead of greater real output depends on the state of the economy at the time the stimulus occurs. When the economy is initially operating far below capacity with considerable unemployment, the aggregate supply curve is quite flat and almost all the increased spending results in increased real output. When the economy is initially operating fairly close to full capacity, the aggregate supply curve is quite steep. In this event much of the increase in spending is reflected in higher prices.

Summary

1. In the context of the aggregate supply–aggregate demand framework, business cycle phenomena are accounted for largely by a shifting aggregate demand curve. Aggregate demand shifts upward to account for cyclical upswings and downward to account for periods of declining economic activity. The chief long-run source of increasing living standards is a rightward-shifting aggregate supply curve stemming from growth in productivity. However, over the long term the aggregate demand curve has shifted rightward at a faster rate than the aggregate supply curve. As a result, the U.S. price level has persistently risen along with real output.

An upward shift of the expenditures line $(C + I)$ in the top portion of Figure 12.11 raises equilibrium output from Y_{E1} to Y_{E2} and shifts the aggregate demand curve in the bottom portion of Figure 12.11 by the same horizontal distance $(Y_{E2} - Y_{E1})$. When the nation's aggregate supply curve is not horizontal, some portion of the added expenditures is manifested in higher prices rather than higher real output. Given the upward-sloping aggregate supply curve in the bottom figure, real output increases only to Y_{E3}, not to Y_{E2} as the simple multiplier predicts.

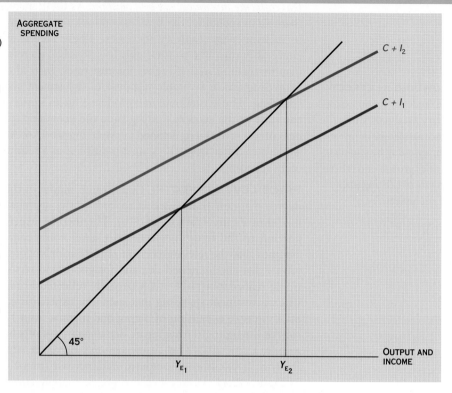

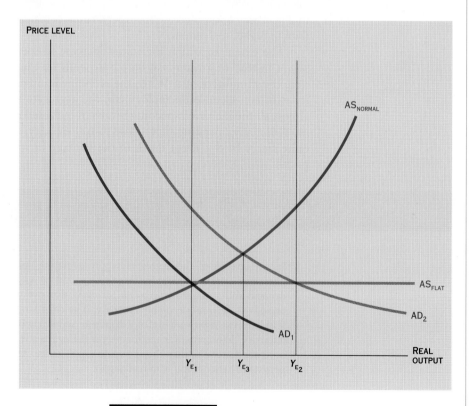

FIGURE 12.11

2. Aggregate demand for U.S. goods and services consists of four components: consumption, investment, government purchases, and net U.S. exports. The largest component is consumption expenditures; the smallest is net exports, which has been negative in recent years.

3. Factors that influence consumption spending include disposable income, wealth, expected future income, the general price level, expected future inflation, and the nation's stock of durable goods owned by households.

4. A cornerstone of macroeconomics is the consumption function or the propensity-to-consume relationship—the relationship between disposable income and consumer spending when all other factors are held constant. Keynes postulated the existence of a "fundamental psychological law," whereby consumers consistently respond to any change in income by changing expenditures by a stable fraction of the change in income. This fraction is known as the marginal propensity to consume. Keynes' hypothesis has been borne out by extensive statistical analysis over the years.

5. Conceptually there are two components of consumer spending: autonomous consumption and induced consumption. Induced consumption is the portion dependent upon disposable income, depicted as a movement along the consumption function. Autonomous consumption is the portion of consumption attributable to factors other than income, depicted as the intercept of the consumption function on the vertical axis. Changes in autonomous consumption are caused by changes in wealth, expected future income, expected inflation, and other factors. These factors shift the entire position of the consumption function.

6. Saving, which is income not consumed, is also depicted graphically as a function of disposable income. The amount of saving at any income level is depicted as the vertical distance between the 45-degree line and the consumption function. The *break-even* level of income is that level at which saving is zero and the consumption line intersects the 45-degree line. At income levels below the break-even level, saving is negative. At higher income levels, saving is positive.

7. The slope of the consumption function is $\Delta C/\Delta Y_d$, the marginal propensity to consume (MPC). The slope of the saving schedule is $\Delta S/\Delta Y_d$, the marginal propensity to save (MPS). The MPC and the MPS must add up to one. When one geometrically adds the consumption function and the saving function, one always obtains a 45-degree line that begins at the origin.

8. Investment spending consists almost entirely of expenditures on producers' durable goods and structures, both residential and nonresidential. Since investment goods are typically long-lived and quite expensive, the bulk of investment is financed by borrowing. Therefore, the interest rate is a key determinant of the magnitude of investment spending. The investment demand schedule relates the volume of investment spending to the interest rate, all other factors (being) held constant.

9. Several other factors influence investment spending, and changes in these factors may be viewed as shifting the position of the investment demand curve. Factors that shift the investment demand curve include changes in business confidence, changes in the utilization rate of existing plant capacity, changes in expected future sales growth, changes in income-tax provisions, and changes in the level of stock market prices.

10. Equilibrium output occurs at the output level where aggregate spending equals output and income. In a simple two-sector economy (consumption and investment) with no government and no foreign trade, this is also the output level at which saving and investment are equal and where no involuntary change in inventories occurs. At equilibrium output the aggregate expenditures schedule ($C + I$) intersects the 45-degree guideline.

11. The multiplier is defined as the ratio of the change in the nation's equilibrium output to the initial shift in spending that initiates the change in the nation's output. The magnitude of this multiplier depends on the magnitude of the MPC. If the MPC is zero, the

multiplier is one because the initial shift in spending induces no additional response on the part of consumers. If the MPC is positive, the multiplier is larger than one. The larger the MPC, the larger the multiplier.

12. The actual, real-world multiplier is considerably smaller than the simple multiplier because income taxes reduce the effective MPC out of GDP and because part of the expenditure increase typically shows up in higher prices instead of higher real output. In addition, the initial increase in spending—by raising GDP and interest rates—may crowd out some investment spending.

Key Terms

disposable income (Y_d)
consumption function
saving
autonomous consumption
marginal propensity to
  consume (MPC)
marginal propensity to
  save (MPS)

break-even income level
wealth effect
equilibrium output
multiplier
automatic stabilizer
crowding-out effect
crowding-in effect

Study Questions and Problems

1. Name the four components of aggregate demand and list them in descending order of magnitude (largest to smallest).

2. Explain why part of total government expenditures is not included as a component of aggregate demand under the *government* category (G).

3. What is a consumption function? Construct a table and a graph that illustrate your probable income-consumption relationship under various hypothetical incomes ranging from zero to $20,000. What sorts of factors would cause this consumption function to shift upward?

4. Define the marginal propensity to consume and the marginal propensity to save. In your consumption function (question 3), calculate your MPC and MPS in the income range $10,000–$20,000.

5. Explain why the MPC and the MPS must always add up to precisely one.

6. Draw a diagram illustrating the investment demand curve. Label the axes. Explain why the curve is downward sloping. What factors would shift this investment demand curve leftward? Explain.

7. Given other factors, explain the consequences of the following events for the position of the nation's investment demand curve:
   a. depreciation schedules are lengthened (that is, annual deductions are reduced)
   b. the nation's capacity utilization rate declines sharply
   c. expected future sales growth is revised upward
   d. the interest rate rises sharply
   e. the stock market crashes

8. In a two-sector economy (consumption and investment), explain the conditions for macroequilibrium. Why are these conditions equivalent?

9. Assume a simple two-sector economy with autonomous consumption spending of $1,000 billion, an MPC of 0.80, and investment spending of $400 billion. Construct an expenditure table (such as Table 12.3) and indicate the equilibrium level of output. Construct a 45-degree diagram or income-expenditure diagram (see Figure 12.8) and indicate the equilibrium output level.

10. Assuming an MPC of 0.75 and an expansion in investment spending of $100 billion per year, trace the multiplier process on equilibrium output. What percent of the increase in equilibrium output occurs in the first five *rounds*?

11. Explain why a smaller MPS implies a larger multiplier.

12. Explain why our simple multiplier—that is, $\frac{1}{\text{MPS}}$ or $1/(1 - \text{MPC})$—is considerably larger than the true multiplier in the United States economy today.

YOUR TURN
Answers

A.	Y_d	C	S	MPC	MPS
	$ 0	$ 2,000	$-2,000	0.90	0.10
	10,000	11,000	-1,000	0.90	0.10
	20,000	20,000	0	0.90	0.10
	30,000	29,000	+1,000	0.90	0.10
	40,000	38,000	+2,000	0.90	0.10
	50,000	47,000	+3,000	0.90	0.10

B. $20,000.

C. $2,000.

D. $8,000 BECAUSE C = $2,000 + 0.90

   ($100,000) = $92,000.

   ALTERNATIVELY, S = -$2,000 + 0.10

   ($100,000) = $8,000.

Selected References

Dillard, Dudley. *The Economics of John Maynard Keynes* (Englewood Cliffs, N.J.: Prentice-Hall, 1948). This is a clear *translation* of the framework presented in Keynes' 1936 book, *The General Theory of Employment, Interest, and Money*.

Hall, Robert E., and John B. Taylor. *Macroeconomics: Theory, Performance, and Policy*, 3rd. ed. (New York: Norton, 1991). Chapter 6 gives a clear discussion of consumption behavior and the multiplier.

Keynes, John Maynard. *The General Theory of Employment, Interest, and Money* (New York: Harcourt Brace, 1936). This is Keynes' classic work, but it is very heavy reading. Dillard's translation is recommended.

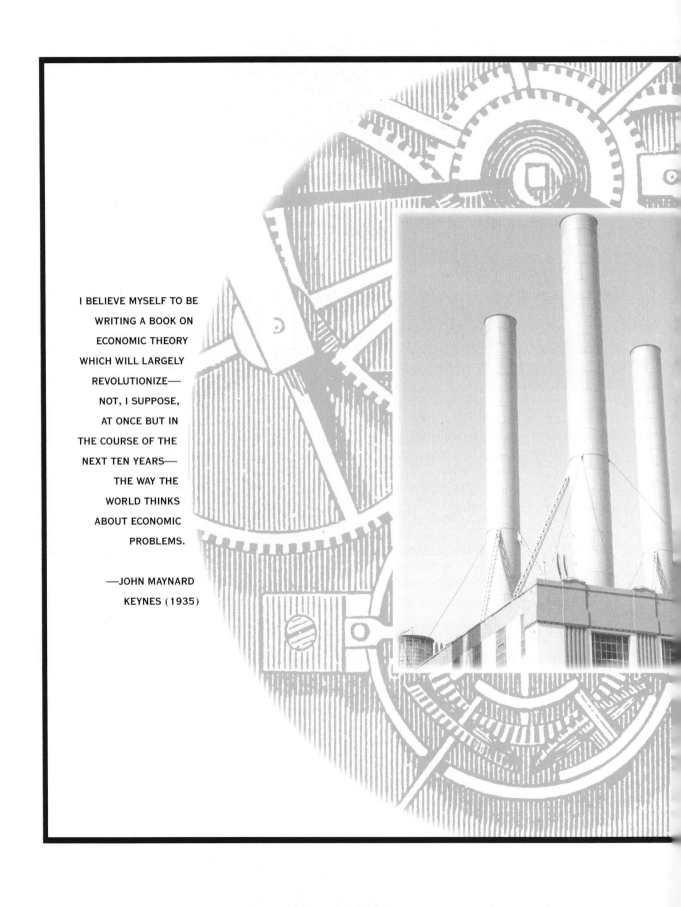

I BELIEVE MYSELF TO BE
WRITING A BOOK ON
ECONOMIC THEORY
WHICH WILL LARGELY
REVOLUTIONIZE—
NOT, I SUPPOSE,
AT ONCE BUT IN
THE COURSE OF THE
NEXT TEN YEARS—
THE WAY THE
WORLD THINKS
ABOUT ECONOMIC
PROBLEMS.

—JOHN MAYNARD
KEYNES (1935)

13

Macroeconomic Equilibrium in Models with Government and International Sectors

CHAPTER 12 EXAMINED THE FACTORS THAT DRIVE CONSUMPTION AND INVESTMENT SPENDING. YOU LEARNED THAT THE NATION'S OUTPUT GRAVITATES TO THE LEVEL AT WHICH AGGREGATE EXPENDITURES AND OUTPUT ARE IN A STATE OF BALANCE. IN THE SIMPLIFIED TWO-SECTOR (CONSUMPTION AND INVESTMENT) WORLD OF CHAPTER 12, THIS OCCURS AT THE UNIQUE OUTPUT LEVEL AT WHICH $C + I$ SPENDING EQUALS GDP, OR S EQUALS I. YOU ALSO LEARNED THAT ANY SHIFT IN EXPENDITURES INITIATES A CHANGE IN EQUILIBRIUM OUTPUT THAT IS SOME MULTIPLE OF THE INITIAL SHIFT IN SPENDING. THE SIZE OF THIS MULTIPLIER VARIES DIRECTLY WITH THE MAGNITUDE OF THE MARGINAL PROPENSITY TO CONSUME (MPC).

IN THIS CHAPTER WE BRING GOVERNMENT SPENDING AND TAXATION AS WELL AS INTER-NATIONAL TRADE INTO THE MODEL AND CONSIDER EQUILIBRIUM OUTPUT IN THE CONTEXT OF THIS MORE REALISTIC FRAMEWORK. WE THEN LOOK AT THE CONNECTION BETWEEN THE LEVEL OF OUTPUT AND THE NATION'S EMPLOYMENT LEVEL, AND DEMONSTRATE THAT THE ECONOMY MAY SETTLE AT AN EQUILIBRIUM OUTPUT LEVEL EITHER ABOVE OR BELOW THE UNIQUE OUTPUT LEVEL THAT LEADS TO FULL EMPLOYMENT. POTENTIAL MEASURES DESIGNED TO MOVE EQUILIBRIUM OUTPUT TO THE FULL-EMPLOYMENT OUTPUT LEVEL ARE ALSO ANALYZED. FURTHER, IN THE ABSENCE OF SUCH DISCRETIONARY POLICY ACTIONS, WE ASSESS THE EFFECTIVENESS OF THE ECONOMY'S SELF-CORRECTIVE MECHANISMS THAT MAY OPERATE EVENTUALLY TO MOVE THE NATION'S EQUILIBRIUM OUTPUT TOWARD THE FULL-EMPLOYMENT OUTPUT LEVEL.

To move closer to reality we now introduce the government sector—expenditures and taxation—as well as international trade into our model.

Government purchases (G) are an important source of demand for goods and services. On the other hand, income taxes (T) represent a withdrawal of funds from the circular flow model. An increase in government purchases is stimulative, that is, it expands equilibrium output. An increase in income taxes in contractionary, that is, it reduces equilibrium output.

Until now we have purposely neglected the role of international considerations in our analyses. American exports (X) constitute a source of expenditures or demand for U.S. goods and services. On the other hand, American purchases of imports (M) represent a leakage from the circular flow of income. This suggests that net U.S. exports ($X–M$) should be included—together with C, I, and G—in our expenditures schedule. In our complete model, therefore, expenditures consist of $C + I + G + (X–M)$. For example, a $10 billion expansion in U.S. exports has the same stimulative effect on U.S. gross domestic product (GDP) as does a $10 billion increase in investment or government purchases.

International trade has become increasingly important in recent decades as the value of imports and exports increased relative to our GDP. The economic fortunes of nations have become increasingly intertwined. An expansion of income in Europe, for example, boosts American exports (X), triggering a multiple expansion of American GDP. An increase in America's income level stimulates the Mexican, Japanese, European, and many other economies as we purchase more of their products.

Consider the circular flow of income in this four-sector economy depicted in Figure 13.1. Firms produce the nation's GDP (top flow), which creates an equal amount of income (lower loop). This income is paid out to the households, which return most of the income to the spending stream through consumption expenditures (upper flow). However, income taxes (T) and imports (M) as well as saving represent withdrawals of income from the flow (right side of figure). These *leakages* limit consumption spending on American goods and services out of gross income. Clearly, consumption expenditures are not sufficient to buy back all the output (GDP) produced. However, injections to the expenditure stream from nonhousehold sectors include federal, state, and local government purchases of goods and services (G) and exports (X) as well as investment expenditures (I).[1]

EQUILIBRIUM CONDITIONS IN THE FOUR-SECTOR MODEL

In this complete four-sector model of the demand side of the economy, output gravitates to an equilibrium level at which aggregate spending—$C + I + G + (X–M)$—just precisely exhausts aggregate output or GDP.

---

[1]Technically, since housing is counted as investment in the national income accounts, part of investment spending is provided by households. We ignore this consideration in Figure 13.1 by making the simplifying assumption that investment spending is initiated strictly by *firms*.

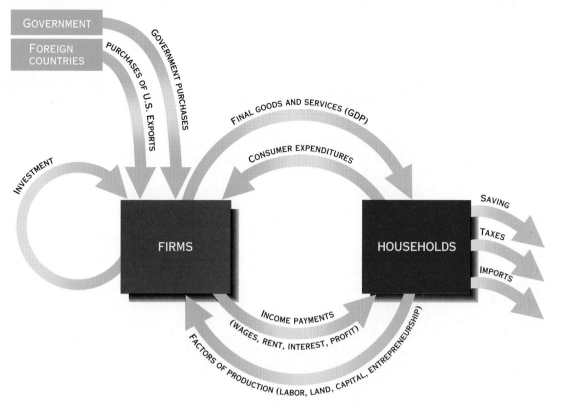

CIRCULAR FLOW OF INCOME IN MODEL WITH GOVERNMENT SECTOR AND INTERNATIONAL TRADE

GOVERNMENT

FOREIGN COUNTRIES

PURCHASES OF U.S. EXPORTS

GOVERNMENT PURCHASES

FINAL GOODS AND SERVICES (GDP)

CONSUMER EXPENDITURES

INVESTMENT

FIRMS

HOUSEHOLDS

SAVING

TAXES

IMPORTS

INCOME PAYMENTS
(WAGES, RENT, INTEREST, PROFIT)

FACTORS OF PRODUCTION (LABOR, LAND, CAPITAL, ENTREPRENEURSHIP)

When we add the government sector and international trade to our simplified circular flow model, there are three *leakages*—saving, taxes, and imports. There are three *injections* to the flow—investment, government purchases, and exports. Equilibrium occurs at the output level at which the $S + T + M$ leakages are balanced by the $I + G + X$ injections.

FIGURE 13.1

$$\text{GDP or } Y = C + I + G + (X{-}M) \qquad\qquad \textbf{13.1}$$

Another way to define this equilibrium condition is to state that the withdrawal of income by households from this circular flow $(S + T + M)$ is precisely balanced by the injections of spending into the flow by entities other than households $(I + G + X)$.

$$S + T + M = I + G + X \qquad\qquad \textbf{13.2}$$

In either case, there is no involuntary change in the nation's inventories, and firms therefore continue to produce the same level of GDP until this equilibrium is disturbed by some change in spending.

$$\text{Involuntary change in inventories } = 0 \qquad\qquad \textbf{13.3}$$

In equilibrium, the nation's aggregate stock of inventories does not change *involuntarily*. This does not rule out the possibility that firms may *deliberately* alter inventory levels. For example, if aggregate demand and sales are expected to rise strongly, firms are likely to increase inventories *voluntarily* in order to accommodate the expected growth of demand. In equilibrium, there can be no *involuntary* change in inventories stemming from an unexpected discrepancy between output and sales.

These three equations (and corresponding statements) are alternative ways of saying the same thing. In equilibrium, all three conditions are satisfied. When the economy is out of equilibrium, none of the conditions is satisfied.

Table 13.1 indicates a hypothetical schedule of output and expenditures in a four-sector model with consumption, investment, government purchases, and international trade. Equilibrium occurs at the output level at which aggregate spending—$C + I + G + (X–M)$—precisely equals output. In Table 13.1, this occurs when output is $5,000 billion. At output levels below $5,000 billion, aggregate spending exceeds output, inventories decline involuntarily, and firms are signaled to raise output. At output levels above $5,000 billion, aggregate expenditures and sales—$C + I + G + (X–M)$—fall short of output, the nation's inventories rise involuntarily, and firms are signaled to cut back production. Hence, output of $5,000 billion is **equilibrium output** for this economy—the output level at which aggregate production and sales are in a state of balance.

EQUILIBRIUM OUTPUT
The level of GDP at which aggregate demand is equal to GDP; the level of output toward which the economy tends to settle.

The information in Table 13.1 is illustrated in the context of our 45-degree diagram (income–expenditure diagram) by Figure 13.2, in which equilibrium output occurs where the $C + I + G + (X–M)$ line intersects the 45-degree line. This is the output level at which aggregate expenditures precisely equal output. Inventories remain at the current, desired level, and no signal is given to deviate from current output of $5,000 billion. At output levels above $5,000 billion, note that the $C + I + G + (X–M)$ line is below the 45-degree line, implying sales fall short of output and inventories rise involuntarily. This output is unsustainable; firms will cut back. At output levels below $5,000 billion, the $C + I + G + (X–M)$ line lies above the 45-degree line. Sales—$C + I + G + (X–M)$—exceed output, causing an undesired reduction of aggregate inventories. Firms are signaled to step up output. As in the simple two-sector model of Chapter 12, equilibrium output occurs at the output level at which aggregate expenditures equal output. The only difference is that we now include government purchases (G) and net exports ($X–M$) among the components of aggregate expenditures.

OUTPUT AND EXPENDITURES SCHEDULE IN MODEL WITH GOVERNMENT AND INTERNATIONAL SECTORS ($ BILLIONS PER YEAR)

OUTPUT (Y)	C	I	G	(X–M)	AGGREGATE EXPENDITURES	INVOLUNTARY CHANGE IN INVENTORIES	OUTPUT
3,000	2,200	600	1,100	−100	3,800	−	rises
4,000	2,800	600	1,100	−100	4,400	−	rises
Y_E = 5,000	3,400	600	1,100	−100	5,000	0	remains unchanged
6,000	4,000	600	1,100	−100	5,600	+	falls
7,000	4,600	600	1,100	−100	6,200	+	falls

TABLE 13.1

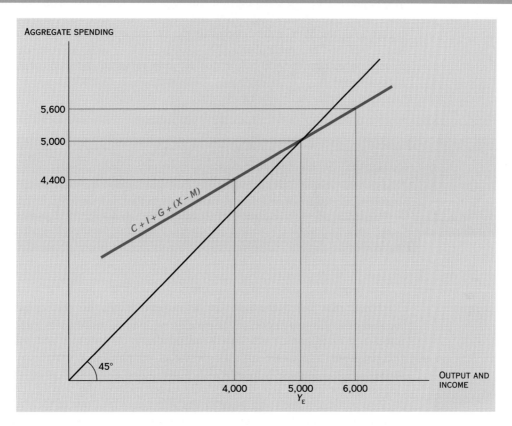

In the four-sector model with government expenditures and international trade, equilibrium occurs at the output level (Y_E) at which the expenditures line, $C + I + G + (X–M)$ intersects the 45-degree line.

FIGURE 13.2

THE MULTIPLIER AGAIN

A shift in any of the components of aggregate spending shifts the aggregate expenditures line, $C + I + G + (X–M)$, and results in a change in equilibrium output that is a multiple of the shift in spending. The magnitude of this multiplier depends on the slope of the $C + I + G + (X–M)$ line. If we make the simplifying assumption that I, G, and $(X–M)$ are determined by factors other than domestic output and income, that is, that they are independent of U.S. GDP, then the magnitude of this multiplier depends on the slope of the consumption function (the MPC). In this event, the slope of the expenditures line is the same as the slope of the consumption function, and our multiplier is the same as the simple multiplier of Chapter 12.

If shown separately in Figure 13.2, the investment expenditures (I) line, the government purchases (G) line, and the net exports $(X–M)$ line would all be horizontal in this case, not varying with the level of output. Thus, when we add I, G, and $(X–M)$ spending to the consumption spending line, our aggregate spending line is parallel to the consumption line and vertically above it by the amount of $I + G + (X–M)$ spending. Given the data of Table 13.1 and the construction of Figure 13.2, the MPC is 0.60. Accordingly, the slope of the $C + I + G + (X–M)$ line is 0.60 and the multiplier is 2.5—that is, $1/(1 – .60)$. An increase in government expenditures of $400 billion, for example, raises equilibrium output by $1,000 billion.

European Recession and United States Output

YOUR TURN

SUPPOSE THAT EUROPEAN NATIONS SLIP INTO RECESSION AND THAT EUROPEAN DEMAND FOR U.S. EXPORT PRODUCTS THEREFORE DROPS BY $4 BILLION. ASSUMING THAT THE MARGINAL PROPENSITY TO CONSUME IN THE UNITED STATES IS 0.80, COMPUTE THE IMPACT OF THE EUROPEAN RECESSION ON EQUILIBRIUM OUTPUT IN THE UNITED STATES.

Note that we have not yet mentioned taxes in the context of this income–expenditures model. Analytically we may consider two types of taxes: lump-sum taxes, which are levied independently of income, and income taxes. Income taxes complicate matters somewhat by driving a wedge between gross income (Y) and disposable income (Y_d). A one-dollar increase in gross income raises disposable income by less than a dollar. This reduces the size of the multiplier because it reduces the magnitude of the effective MPC out of GDP. The model with an income tax present is treated in the appendix to this chapter. Here we deal with the simpler concept of lump-sum taxes.

Assume lump-sum taxes are reduced by $100 billion—that is, government reduces taxes by $100 billion through means other than reducing income-tax *rates*. What is the effect on equilibrium output? Return to your multiplier intuition.

$$\text{shift in expenditures} \times \text{multiplier} = \text{change in } Y_E$$

Since the MPC is 0.60, the lump-sum tax cut shifts the consumption function vertically upward by $60 billion. That is, because taxes are reduced by $100 billion, each and every output (GDP) level is associated with $100 billion more of disposable income and $60 billion more of consumer spending than is the case prior to the tax cut. Both the consumption function and the $C + I + G + (X–M)$ schedule shift upward by $60 billion. As a result, we compute the change in Y_E to be $60 billion $\times$ 2.5 = $150 billion. Equilibrium output and income rise by $150 billion as a result of the tax cut.

Alternatively, suppose government raises *transfer payments* (unemployment benefits, Social Security payments, and the like) by $100 billion. The analysis is quite similar. These transfers represent a dollar-for-dollar increase in disposable income. People increase consumption expenditures by the MPC times the change in transfers. Hence, the aggregate expenditures line shifts up by $60 billion and equilibrium output increases by $150 billion. A transfer payment is simply a negative lump-sum tax. An increase in transfer payments has the same effect as an identical cut in taxes.

Each level of output (and income) is associated with a specific magnitude of employment—and a specific unemployment rate. An upward shift in aggregate expenditures raises the nation's output and employment levels and reduces its unemployment rate. A downward shift in aggregate spending initiates a contraction in the nation's output and employment and leads to an increase in its unemployment rate.

Given the size of the nation's labor force, it follows that there is some output level that just suffices to generate full employment. We call this Y_F, the *full-employment level of output*. Output levels below Y_F result in a loss of output, income, and job opportunities for individuals seeking employment. Output levels above Y_F result in labor shortages in specific markets, bottlenecks and shortages in some product markets, and substantial inflationary pressures in labor and product markets.

RECESSIONARY GAP

RECESSIONARY GAP
The amount by which equilibrium GDP falls short of the full-employment GDP level; the amount of additional output required to generate full employment.

Keynes, writing in the 1930s, parted company with mainstream economists of his day. He asserted that the economy is likely at times to settle and remain at an equilibrium output level below the level required to yield full employment. In the 1930s, with the world economy mired in the Great Depression, Keynes understandably neglected the case in which equilibrium output exceeds the full-employment output level, Y_F. Instead, he focused attention on the issue of *underemployment equilibrium*—the prospect of an economy stuck in an equilibrium in which substantial involuntary unemployment persists. This case, known as a **recessionary gap**, is illustrated in Figure 13.3 (page 322).

The economy gravitates toward an output level of $6,200 billion per year, the equilibrium level of output (Y_E) in Figure 13.3. However, an output level of $6,400 billion is needed to generate full employment of the nation's labor force. The *recessionary gap* is the amount by which equilibrium (actual) output falls short of full-employment output. When a recessionary gap prevails in the economy, the unemployment rate is higher than the rate associated with full employment.[2]

If the nation's firms were to produce an output level of Y_F in the presence of a recessionary gap, aggregate spending, $C + I + G + (X–M)$, would be insufficient to purchase the output. Note in the top portion of Figure 13.3 that at output level Y_F, expenditures—$C + I + G + (X–M)$—fall short of the 45-degree line. Expenditures fall short of output, inventories rise involuntarily, and firms reduce output. There is not enough demand in the economy to justify producing a full-employment output level. The economy settles in at an *underemployment equilibrium*. In Figure 13.3, the magnitude of this recessionary gap is $200 billion.

---

[2]Note that the existence of a recessionary gap does not imply that the economy is in recession—a period of falling real output. It merely implies that the output is below the full employment level. Output may be rising in the recovery phase of the business cycle and a large recessionary gap may exist because output is still a long way below the Y_F level. Such was the case in 1992, for example.

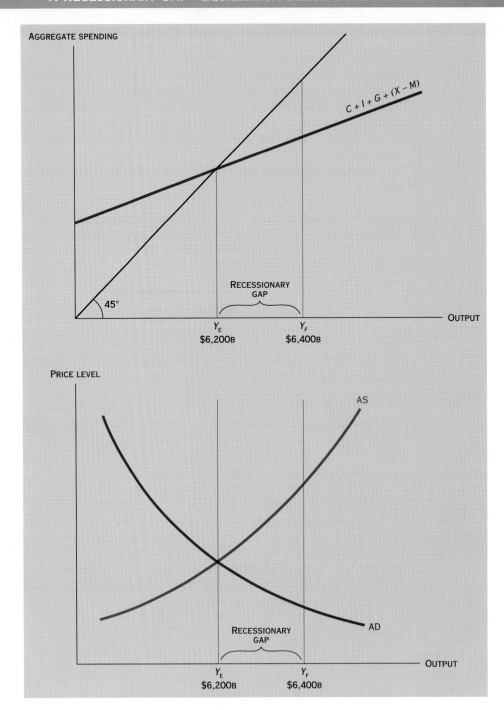

A recessionary gap occurs when equilibrium output (Y_E) is less than the full-employment output level (Y_F). This gap is defined as the amount of additional output required to generate full employment—$200 billion per year in this example.

FIGURE 13.3

Most of the time the U.S. economy operates with some recessionary gap. This is illustrated in Figure 13.4, which shows actual and potential GDP for the period since 1960.

Potential GDP is defined as the hypothetical output level that would be produced if the economy were maintained at full employment. Potential GDP rises over time because the labor force and output per worker (productivity) increase over time. The distance between potential GDP and actual GDP when potential GDP exceeds actual GDP may be viewed as the magnitude of the recessionary gap. This gap reached its largest level in the recession year 1982, when it stood at roughly $300 billion. In 1992, the recessionary gap was approximately $250 billion.

POTENTIAL AND ACTUAL GDP SINCE 1960

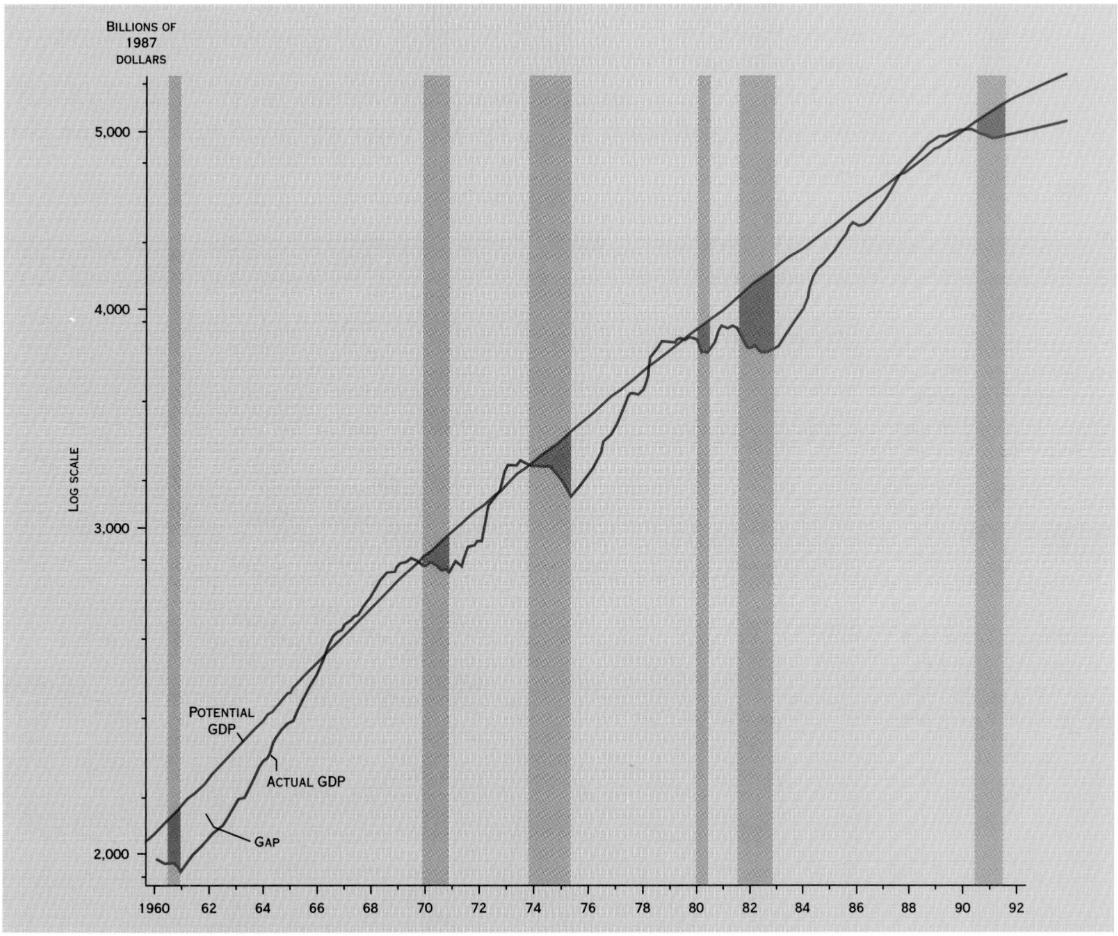

When actual GDP is below potential GDP, a recessionary gap exists. The largest gaps occur at the troughs (low points) of business recessions. The largest recessionary gap existed in the 1982 recession.

SOURCE: Federal Reserve System, 1992.

FIGURE 13.4

Economists of Keynes' era argued that Y_E in Figure 13.3 could not really be considered an *equilibrium state*, because forces that would push Y_E rightward until it coincided with Y_F would automatically be unleashed. This alleged mechanism involved falling wages and prices and their influence through the *wealth effect* on spending and output. In particular, with output below Y_F, involuntary unemployment exists. Given competitive markets, this excess supply of labor should lead to declining wages and prices. Now recall our discussion in Chapter 12 about the role of changes in wealth shifting the consumption function and aggregate demand for goods and services. Keynes' contemporaries argued that falling prices—by raising the real value of people's checking accounts, savings accounts, and government bonds—would induce an upward shift in the consumption function. Therefore, the expenditures line, $C + I + G + (X–M)$, would shift upward. This mechanism is illustrated in Figure 13.5.

In Figure 13.5, aggregate spending is initially $C_1 + I + G + (X–M)$ and output is in equilibrium at Y_{E1}. Because wages and prices in competitive markets

HOW THE WEALTH EFFECT AUTOMATICALLY CORRECTS A RECESSIONARY GAP

With output at Y_{E1}, a large recessionary gap prevails and considerable unemployment exists. If wages and prices decline in response to the unemployment, real wealth is stimulated. This boosts consumption and therefore shifts the expenditures line upward. In principle, this mechanism continues to operate until output is boosted to Y_{E4}, the full-employment level of output.

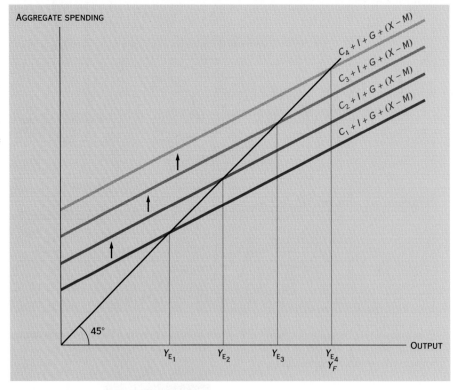

FIGURE 13.5

should decline when involuntary unemployment prevails, the initial output of Y_{E_1} is associated with falling prices. This leads, via the wealth effect, to an upward shift in consumption spending. Hence, aggregate expenditures shift upward to $C_2 + I + G + (X–M)$ and output is boosted to Y_{E_2}. However, since Y_{E_2} is also below Y_F, the price level continues to decline. The wealth effect continues to boost consumption spending and aggregate demand until output reaches Y_{E_4}, the state of full employment. In this view the only true equilibrium output is Y_{E_4}, the full-employment level.[3] In this view there is no such thing as an underemployment equilibrium, and no need for government to intervene with its stabilization tools of monetary and fiscal policy to boost aggregate spending. The economy contains a neat **self-correcting mechanism**, and a *laissez-faire* philosophy on the part of government is appropriate.

One did not have to possess an intellect as brilliant as Keynes' to observe in the 1930s that something was wrong with this analysis. Although output and employment remained at unusually low levels during the 1930s in nations throughout the world, the system did not correct itself. It was boosted out of its doldrums at the end of the decade only by the stimulus of government expenditures associated with the onset of World War II.

Certainly in today's economy a major problem with the self-correcting mechanism hypothesis lies in the assumption that the level of wages and prices always declines when output is below the full-employment level. It is not unusual in depressed times to find specific examples of declining commodity prices. Prices of certain manufactured goods sometimes decline in periods of steep recession. Wages and salaries in isolated sectors have been known to take a hit. However, the overall level of wages and prices exhibits considerable resistance to downward pressure. Even in 1982, when the U.S. unemployment rate pushed above 10 percent—the highest level since the 1930s—the general level of wages and prices continued to increase. The same situation prevailed in the summer of 1992, when the unemployment rate hovered around 7.5 percent. In fact, in *none* of the past six recessions did the level of wages or prices decrease. Resistance to downward wage and price movements stems from written contracts, labor unions, minimum-wage laws, federal price supports, and noncompetitive economic behavior by firms. Also, some economists believe that an *implicit contract* (or *understanding*) exists between firms and workers that prevents wages and salaries from being cut in periods of temporarily depressed economic activity.[4]

If one assumes that wages and prices do not decline when output is below Y_F, the initial aggregate demand schedule of Figure 13.5, $C_1 + I + G + (X–M)$, is not induced to shift upward—because the wealth effect via falling prices is nonexistent. Left to its own devices, the economy is stuck at output Y_{E_1} indefinitely. For this reason, Keynes called for active intervention on the part of government to

[3]An equilibrium is a state of balance in which there is no tendency toward change. At any output level below Y_F there is a tendency for output to change, *in this view*, because falling wages and prices, through wealth effects on consumption, shift up the aggregate expenditures schedule. In this event, Y_{E_1}, Y_{E_2}, and Y_{E_3} are not true equilibrium states. The only true equilibrium is Y_{E_4} or Y_F.

[4]Arthur M. Okun has outlined this latter hypothesis in depth in *Prices and Quantities: A Macroeconomic Analysis* (Washington, D.C.: The Brookings Institution, 1981). In Okun's analysis, the implicit contract is based on long-term considerations and loyalty between employers and employees. In the implicit contract, firms forgo cutting wages in hard times in return for an understanding that workers stay with the firm in good times when new job opportunities develop.

SELF-CORRECTING MECHANISM

The forces in the economy that tend to push equilibrium output toward the full-employment output level in the absence of government implementation of monetary and fiscal policies.

JOHN MAYNARD KEYNES

(1883–1946)

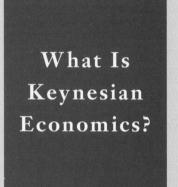

What Is Keynesian Economics?

You have perhaps encountered the term "Keynesian" (pronounced "caynsian") in connection with readings or discussions about economics. John Maynard Keynes, an Englishman, was probably the world's most eminent and influential economist in the period spanning the two world wars (roughly 1915–1945). Keynes focused his analytical mind and brilliant pen on the crucial macroeconomic issues of his time.

Keynes' early writings were often polemical in nature, attacking contemporary politicians, important economic policy decisions, and conventional modes of thinking. For example, his *Economic Consequences of the Peace* (1919) exposed the folly of attempting to extract massive reparations payments from (the vanquished) Germany after World War I. *The Economic Consequences of Mr. Churchill* (1925) attacked Winston Churchill's decision to return England to the gold standard in 1925 at the exchange rate that existed prior to World War I. Because the level of prices in England had increased more rapidly than in most other countries, this decision required England to deflate her domestic price level sharply in order to be competitive in international markets. To deflate domestic prices, the British government imposed an era of tight money and austere budgetary policies. While the United States and other industrial nations prospered during 1925–1929, the unemployment rate in England never fell below 10 percent.

Keynes' most influential work was *The General Theory of Employment, Interest, and Money*, published in 1936. For years Keynes had been deeply bothered by the failure of the conventional economic analysis of the times to explain adequately the events of the Great Depression of the 1930s. The prevailing view held that economic downturns were self-correcting and did not require macroeconomic intervention on the part of government. Indeed, such efforts by the government were viewed as detrimental and inappropriate. Hence, a philosophy of *laissez-faire* ("let do" or "leave it alone") described the contemporary view of the proper role of government in macroeconomic life.

Keynes believed that changes in aggregate demand precipitated by private agents (principally consumption and investment spending) could lead to excessive or inadequate aggregate expenditures in the economy. In particular, such behavior could lead to a downward shift in aggregate spending (in both the 45-degree and aggregate demand–aggregate supply frameworks). This would result in depressed economic activity and distress for workers and firms. In the absence of government intervention, the AD curve could intersect the AS curve at a level of real output far below the level required to generate full employment of the work force. Further, the economy could remain stuck at such a suboptimal output level for an indefinite or at least intolerable period of time.

Keynes therefore advocated aggressive action by the central government to attempt to stabilize output at a level sufficient to generate high levels of employment and prosperity. In particular, he advocated fiscal policy measures to shift the expenditures line and AD curve upward in the 1930s. Keynes felt this could be done most effectively by increasing government expenditures or by reducing taxes to boost consumption spending. He published an *open letter* to President Franklin D. Roosevelt in *The New York Times* in 1934. In this letter Keynes proposed ways the government could shift the AD curve upward, thus lifting the economy out of the Great Depression.

During the 1950s and 1960s, a debate took place between Keynesians (followers of Keynes) and monetarists (Milton Friedman and his disciples) over the relative strength of fiscal policy and monetary policy. Keynesians typically argued that changes in taxes and government expenditures exert a more powerful and predictable effect on economic activity than do changes in the supply of money. Monetarists typically argued that changes in money are more powerfully and predictably linked to subsequent changes in economic activity than are fiscal policy measures. It is worth noting that Keynes (who died in 1946)

believed that both monetary and fiscal policy were potent weapons in normal economic times. However, in a period of depression such as the 1930s, Keynes believed that monetary policy was ineffective and that stimulative fiscal actions were required to boost aggregate spending and economic activity.

By the 1970s, an element of consensus that both monetary and fiscal policy were powerful instruments of macroeconomic policy prevailed in the economics profession. The debate turned to the propriety of efforts to *employ* monetary and fiscal policies *actively* to stabilize economic activity. *Keynesian economics* has come to signify a philosophy of *activism* on the part of government in the macroeconomy. Keynesian economists generally advocate active use of both monetary and fiscal policy to attempt to stabilize the level of real output at levels sufficient to generate relatively high levels of output and employment but not so high as to lead to severe inflation.

Monetarists and other critics of Keynesians are very skeptical of the use of active monetary and fiscal policy to *fine tune* the economy. This skepticism is based on both technical factors and the belief that political considerations are likely to influence macroeconomic policy-making. These critics of Keynesian economics typically prefer a steady policy of modest growth in the money supply irrespective of the contemporary economic situation. They believe, in the long run, such a modest policy will outperform the activist prescription advocated by Keynesian economists. We analyze this debate in some depth in Chapter 20.

Some writers have depicted Keynes as anticapitalistic, perhaps even socialist. This portrayal is inaccurate. Keynes believed that the capitalistic system is the most desirable form of economic organization. In order for capitalism to operate properly, however, Keynes believed, occasional active intervention by government in the macroeconomy is necessary. On a personal level, Keynes benefitted considerably from the capitalistic system. He was never a man lacking in self-assurance. In the prime of his life, Keynes spent the first 20 minutes each morning in bed planning his day's speculations in the foreign-exchange and commodities markets. Though he suffered an early, severe setback in the post-World War I deflation, Keynes recovered his losses and ultimately amassed a fortune for his own portfolio and that of his academic affiliation—King's College, Cambridge.

boost aggregate demand and help the economy out of its stagnation. This can be done, in principle, by implementing stimulative monetary and fiscal policies. Although Keynes felt in the 1930s that stimulative fiscal policies were more effective, today most economists believe that stimulative monetary policy is equally effective (see Exhibit 13.1).

REMOVING RECESSIONARY GAP THROUGH STIMULATIVE MACROPOLICIES

Assume output (Y_E) is currently $6,300 billion and Y_F is $6,500 billion. A recessionary gap of $200 billion initially exists, as illustrated in Figure 13.6. To boost equilibrium output from $6,300 billion to $6,500 billion and to remove the recessionary gap, we must consider the basic multiplier intuition.

$$\text{initial shift in spending} \times \text{multiplier} = \text{change in } Y_E$$

BOOSTING AGGREGATE EXPENDITURES TO REMOVE RECESSIONARY GAP

To eliminate the recessionary gap of $200 billion associated with the expenditures line, $(C + I + G + X - M)_1$, macroeconomic stimulus can be implemented. Stimulative monetary and fiscal policies can boost C, I, or G and in principle raise the expenditures line to $(C + I + G + X - M)_2$. This boosts Y_E to Y_F, removing the recessionary gap.

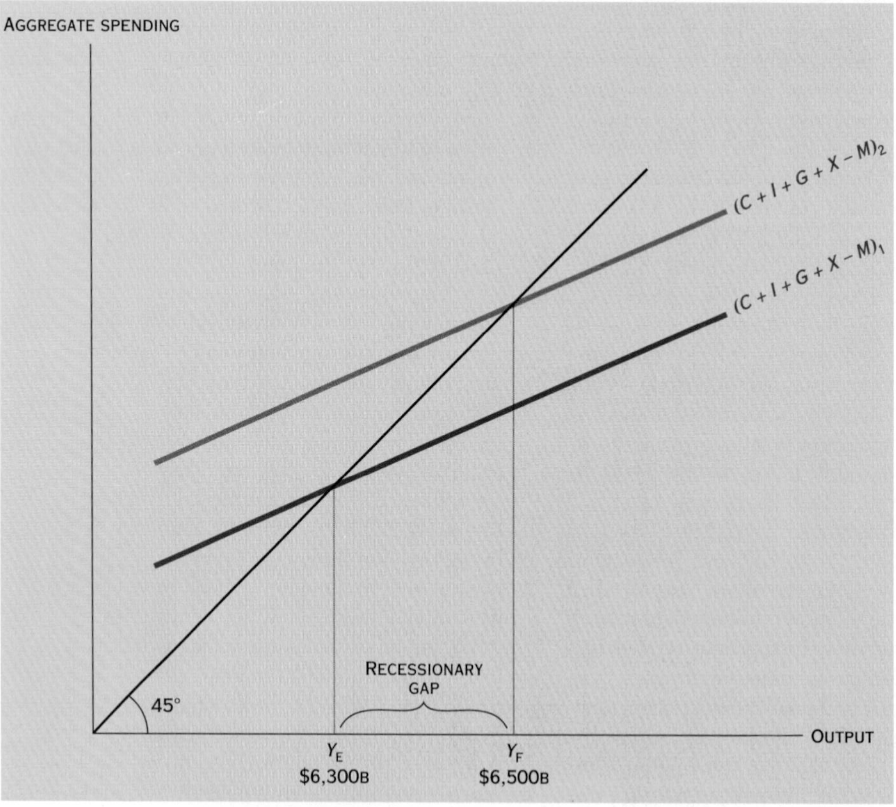

FIGURE 13.6

Assume the MPC is 0.75, so the multiplier is 4. The desired change in Y_E is $200 billion—the magnitude of the recessionary gap. Hence, we can write

$$\text{necessary shift in spending} \times 4 = \$200 \text{ billion}$$
$$\text{necessary shift in spending} = \$50 \text{ billion}$$

To remove the recessionary gap totally and bring the economy to full employment, macroeconomic policy must shift the aggregate expenditures line, $C + I + G + (X–M)$, upward (vertically) by $50 billion. By pulling up consumer expenditures, this initial shift touches off a multiplier effect and raises equilibrium output by $200 billion.

To shift the aggregate expenditures schedule upward by $50 billion, stimulative monetary and fiscal policies can be employed. Stimulative monetary policies, by bringing down interest rates and increasing the supply of money, boost investment spending and (perhaps) also consumption spending. Stimulative fiscal policy involves an increase in government purchases, a cut in taxes, an increase in government transfer payments—or some combination of these measures.

Removing a Recessionary Gap

YOUR TURN

ASSUME A RECESSIONARY GAP OF $270 BILLION EXISTS AND THE ECONOMY'S MARGINAL PROPENSITY TO CONSUME IS 0.90. TO ELIMINATE THE GAP THROUGH THREE ALTERNATIVE PROCEDURES, CALCULATE THE

A. NECESSARY INCREASE IN G

B. NECESSARY CUT IN LUMP-SUM TAXES, T

C. NECESSARY INCREASE IN TRANSFER PAYMENTS

INFLATIONARY GAP

INFLATIONARY GAP
The amount by which equilibrium GDP exceeds the full-employment GDP level; occurs when aggregate expenditures exceed the capacity to produce goods and services.

An **inflationary gap** occurs when there are excessive aggregate expenditures for goods and services. Firms, individuals, and government are collectively attempting to purchase more goods and services than the economy can produce without overstimulating the economy and igniting an acceleration in the inflation rate. This situation is illustrated in Figure 13.7 (page 330). In the event firms produce full-employment output, aggregate spending, $C + I + G + (X–M)$, exceeds output. In other words, equilibrium output exceeds the full-employment output level, and the difference is known as the inflationary gap.

Historically, inflationary gaps are the typical state of affairs in time of war. They sometimes also occur in peacetime. In wartime, government expenditures on the military effort are rapidly increased without commensurate increases in taxes to force down consumption spending. As a result, aggregate spending becomes excessive and a period of inflation ensues. Examples in the American experience include World Wars I and II and the Korean and Vietnam wars. In addition, inflationary gaps tend to occur in peacetime when the economy is near the peak of the business cycle. Review Figure 13.4. Those periods in which actual GDP exceeds potential

An inflatory gap exists when equilibrium output (Y_E) exceeds the full-employment output level (Y_F). There is too much spending. If firms actually produce an output of Y_F, expenditures, $C + I + G + (X–M)$, exceed output. This results in inflation.

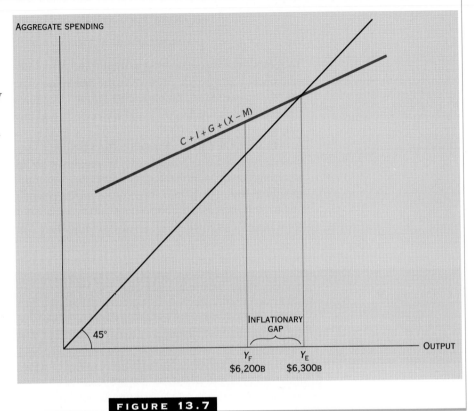

FIGURE 13.7

GDP (1966–1969, 1973, and 1988–1989) are periods in which an inflationary gap prevails.

INFLATIONARY GAP—THE SELF-CORRECTING MECHANISM

In Figure 13.8 we illustrate the automatic *self-correcting mechanism* that tends to remove an inflationary gap without any policy actions taken by government. In the figure, the economy is initially operating with aggregate expenditures of $C_1 + I + G + (X–M)$ and output at Y_{E1}. The magnitude of the inflationary gap is initially $Y_{E1} - Y_F$. This inflationary gap will self-destruct or automatically eliminate itself. As prices rise, the real value of the money, government bonds, and savings accounts held by individuals is reduced. Hence, the *real wealth* of individuals is reduced, resulting in a downward shift of the aggregate consumption function. In Figure 13.8, suppose the aggregate expenditures line initially shifts downward to $C_2 + I + G + (X–M)$, reducing equilibrium output to Y_{E2}. Because a (smaller) inflationary gap of $Y_{E2} - Y_F$ still exists, inflationary pressure continues, further reducing real wealth in the hands of private individuals. Accordingly, consumption spending and aggregate spending continue to shift downward in real terms, further reducing

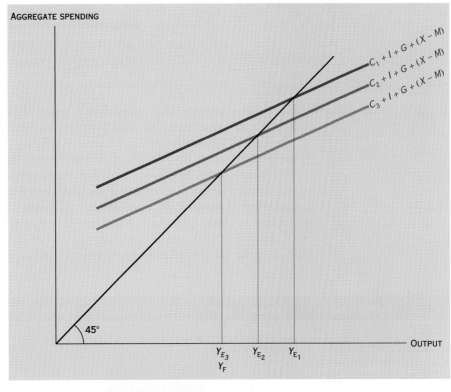

With output initially at Y_{E_1}, an inflationary gap of $Y_{E_1} - Y_F$ exists. In this event, the price level rises, thus reducing real wealth of private citizens. This mechanism, which shifts the expenditures line downward, continues until output is reduced to Y_{E_3} and the inflationary gap is eliminated.

AGGREGATE SPENDING

$C_1 + I + G + (X - M)$

$C_2 + I + G + (X - M)$

$C_3 + I + G + (X - M)$

45°

OUTPUT

Y_{E_3} Y_{E_2} Y_{E_1}

Y_F

FIGURE 13.8

equilibrium output and lessening the inflationary pressures. Finally, when aggregate demand has shifted downward to $C_3 + I + G + (X–M)$, equilibrium output is reduced to Y_{E_3}. At that point the inflationary gap is eliminated through the automatic correcting force of the wealth effect. Barring outside factors that would continue to shift aggregate demand upward (such as rapidly increasing government spending or money supply), inflation experiences a natural death.

ASYMMETRY IN THE SELF-CORRECTING MECHANISMS

There is a fundamental asymmetry in the way our economy handles inflationary and recessionary gaps. An inflationary gap inevitably results in inflation, thereby reducing real aggregate expenditures through the wealth effect and thus self-destructing. A recessionary gap also corrects itself when it results in a falling level of prices. However, modern economies have strong institutional features that prevent the general price level from declining during normal periods of recession. Therefore, the recessionary gaps are not self-correcting in contemporary macroeconomic circumstances. Keynesian economists believe in such instances government should move in aggressively with stimulative monetary and fiscal policies to boost the economy to a higher level of activity.

NIPPING AN INFLATIONARY GAP THROUGH MONETARY AND FISCAL RESTRAINT

The fact that an inflationary gap eventually disappears of its own accord does not mean that macroeconomic policy should ignore the opportunity to fight existing inflation or offset incipient inflationary pressures through monetary and fiscal restraint. As we documented in Chapter 9, inflation is highly undesirable: it arbitrarily redistributes the nation's income and wealth, and thereby creates tension and distrust in society. In addition, inflation impairs the economy's long-term growth and induces various activities that are inefficient from society's viewpoint. Every effort should be made by those in charge of monetary and fiscal policy to keep inflation in check. Consider the situation illustrated in Figure 13.9.

In Figure 13.9, assume the marginal propensity to consume (MPC) and the slope of the initial aggregate expenditures line $(C + I + G + X - M)_1$ are both

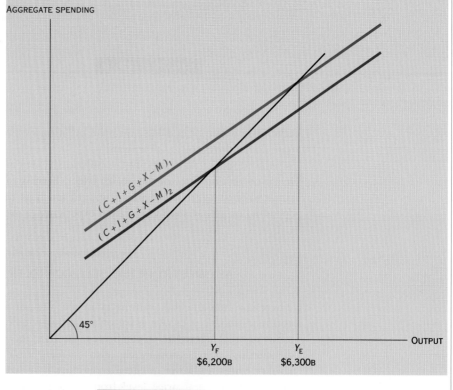

REMOVING INFLATIONARY GAP THROUGH MACROECONOMIC POLICY RESTRAINT

Equilibrium output (Y_E) exceeds the full-employment output level (Y_F). Aggregate expenditures— $(C + I + G + X - M)_1$—are too high relative to the economy's productive capacity (Y_F). Monetary and fiscal policy restraint may be used to shift the expenditures schedule downward to $(C + I + G + X - M)_2$ and eliminate the inflationary gap.

FIGURE 13.9

0.80. Equilibrium output is $6,300 billion and Y_F is $6,200 billion. An inflationary gap of $100 billion prevails. To remove the inflationary gap, the aggregate expenditures line must be shifted downward from $(C + I + G + X–M)_1$ to $(C + I + G + X–M)_2$. This can be done by reducing any of four components of demand—C, I, G, or X–M. Because we know that the MPC is 0.80, the multiplier is 5. Hence:

$$\text{needed shift in spending} \times \text{multiplier} = \text{needed change in } Y_E$$

$$\text{needed shift in spending} \times 5 = -\$100 \text{ billion}$$

$$\text{needed shift in spending} = -\$20 \text{ billion}$$

A downward shift of the aggregate expenditures schedule of $20 billion is required to eliminate the inflationary gap. This can be done by reducing government purchases by $20 billion, raising taxes or reducing transfer payments sufficiently to shift consumption downward by $20 billion, tightening monetary policy and raising interest rates sufficiently to snuff out $20 billion of investment spending—or some combination of these measures.

Summary

1. In the four-sector economy with consumption, investment, government, and international sectors, macroequilibrium from the demand side of the economy occurs at the unique output level where aggregate expenditures, $C + I + G + (X–M)$, equal output. Alternatively stated, equilibrium occurs were $S + T + M$ leakages from the circular income flow are precisely balanced by $I + G + X$ expenditures and where there is no involuntary change in the nation's stock of inventories.

2. Each output level in the economy is associated with a specific magnitude of employment and unemployment. Producing a larger output level induces an expansion of employment and a drop in the nation's unemployment rate. There is a unique output level (Y_F) that just suffices to create full employment.

3. If output settles below the level needed to generate full employment, a recessionary gap exists. If wages and prices are downwardly flexible in response to involuntary unemployment and excess plant capacity, the recessionary gap automatically corrects itself. The mechanism involved is that wages and prices decline in response to the involuntary unemployment, triggering a positive wealth effect on consumer demand that raises aggregate expenditures and output until Y_F is reached. If wages and prices are downwardly inflexible, the recessionary gap may persist unless aggregate spending is boosted by stimulative monetary and/or fiscal measures.

4. If equilibrium output exceeds the full-employment level, an inflationary gap exists. In this situation the levels of wages and prices rise persistently. This reduces the real wealth of households, shifting the consumption function and the aggregate expenditures schedule downward. This process continues until the inflationary gap is eliminated.

5. Since wages and prices exhibit greater upward than downward flexibility, inflationary gaps and recessionary gaps are asymmetrical in their self-correcting mechanisms. Left to its own devices, an inflationary gap will self-destruct. This need not be the case with a recessionary gap.

6. Macroeconomic policies to combat a recessionary gap include stimulative monetary policy to reduce interest rates and boost investment spending and stimulative fiscal policy in

the form of tax cuts to boost consumption spending or increases in government expenditures. Policies designed to eliminate an inflationary gap include restrictive monetary policy to drive up interest rates and reduce investment spending and contractionary fiscal policy in the form of higher taxes to cut consumption spending and cuts in government expenditures.

7. Keynesian economists typically advocate active implementation of monetary and fiscal policies to attempt to stabilize output at a level near Y_F. For both political and technical reasons, critics of Keynesians are skeptical of this activist philosophy. These critics tend to advocate a more modest approach on the part of macroeconomic policymakers that calls for stable policies which are not substantially altered in an effort to influence macroeconomic activity.

Key Terms

equilibrium output
recessionary gap
self-correcting mechanism

Keynesian economics
inflationary gap

Study Questions and Problems

1. Analyze the three conditions for equilibrium output in the four-sector economy. Explain why these three conditions are equivalent.

2. Assume actual output initially exceeds equilibrium output. Explain the mechanism by which output is induced to return to equilibrium. Illustrate with a 45-degree diagram.

3. Assume the MPC is 0.80 and equilibrium output is currently $6,000 billion. Assume government purchases rise by $40 billion. Using a simple 45-degree diagram, analyze the effect on equilibrium output. Conduct the same analysis for the case in which lump-sum taxes are increased by $40 billion. In this analysis, what is the net effect of a combined increase in government purchases and lump-sum taxes of $40 billion each?

4. Explain the meaning of an *inflationary gap* and a *recessionary gap*. Analyze the mechanism by which these gaps are alleged to be *self-correcting*. Why might it be true that an inflationary gap may have a more effective automatic self-correction mechanism than a recessionary gap?

5. Assume a recessionary gap of $100 billion currently prevails and the economy's MPC is 0.75. How large an increase in government purchases would eliminate the gap? How large a cut in lump-sum taxes? How large an increase in government transfer payments?

6. What is the general attitude of Keynesian economists regarding the government's responsibility for the level of output and employment in the economy? On what bases can one oppose this Keynesian viewpoint? Analyze.

7. Assume the government wishes to eliminate an inflationary gap of $100 billion through fiscal policy measures. If the multiplier is 2, how much must the government cut its purchases? By how much must it raise (lump-sum) taxes to eliminate the gap? By how much must the government reduce transfer payments to eliminate the gap?

European Recession and United States Output

GIVEN THE MPC IN THE UNITED STATES OF 0.80, THE MULTIPLIER IS 5. THE DOWN-WARD SHIFT IN FOREIGN DEMAND FOR U.S. EXPORTS OF $4 BILLION INITIATES THE MULTIPLIER PROCESS AND DECREASES U.S. EQUILIBRIUM OUTPUT BY $20 BILLION.

$$\text{SHIFT IN SPENDING} \quad \times \quad \text{MULTIPLIER} \quad = \quad \Delta Y_E$$
$$(-\$4 \text{ BILLION}) \quad \times \quad 5 \quad = \quad -\$20 \text{ BILLION}$$

Removing a Recessionary Gap

BECAUSE THE MPC IS GIVEN TO BE 0.90, THE SIMPLE MULTIPLIER IS 10. HENCE, THE EXPENDITURES LINE $C + I + G + (X-M)$ MUST BE SHIFTED UPWARD BY $27 BILLION IN ORDER TO INCREASE EQUILIBRIUM OUTPUT BY $270 BILLION. THIS CAN BE DONE BY:

A. INCREASING G BY $27 BILLION

B. REDUCING LUMP-SUM TAXES BY $30 BILLION, WHICH INCREASES DISPOSABLE INCOME BY $30 BILLION AND SHIFTS THE CONSUMPTION AND AGGREGATE EXPENDITURES SCHEDULES UPWARD BY $27 BILLION

C. RAISING GOVERNMENT TRANSFERS BY $30 BILLION, WHICH OPERATES IN THE IDENTICAL FASHION OF A LUMP-SUM TAX CUT OF $30 BILLION, SHIFTING THE EXPENDITURES LINE $C + I + G + (X-M)$ UPWARD BY $27 BILLION.

Selected References

Economic Report of the President. (Washington, D.C.: published annually). Discusses contemporary macroeconomic events and policies.

Glahe, Fred R. *Macroeconomics: Theory and Policy*, 4th ed. (San Diego: Harcourt Brace Jovanovich, 1989). An intermediate macroeconomics text that analyzes these issues in depth.

Miller, Roger L. *The Economics of Macro Issues* (St. Paul: West Publishing Company, 1992). Discusses certain issues presented in this chapter.

Elementary Mathematics of Income Determination in Model with Government Sector and Income Tax

With just a little elementary algebra we can learn a lot of elementary macroeconomics in a few pages. We begin with the condition for macroequilibrium in the economy with a government sector:

$$Y = C + I + G \qquad \text{(13A.1)}$$

In equilibrium, aggregate spending $(C + I + G)$ equals output or GDP (Y).[5] We write general equations for consumption, investment, and government purchases as follows:

$$C = a + bY_d \qquad \text{(13A.2)}$$

$$I = I_0 \qquad \text{(13A.3)}$$

$$G = G_0 \qquad \text{(13A.4)}$$

Equation 13A.2, the consumption function, states that consumer spending has two components: an exogenous or autonomous portion (a) that depends on factors other than disposable income and a portion induced by disposable income. In the equation, b is the marginal propensity to consume (MPC) and bY_d indicates the magnitude of induced consumption (that is, the consumption that depends on the level of Y_d).

---

[5]For the sake of simplicity of notation, we have omitted the international sector (exports and imports) from the presentation in this appendix. The same principles and conclusions hold when the international sector is included.

Equations 13A.3 and 13A.4 indicate that investment and government purchases are *exogenous* (that is, they are not dependent on income or output but are determined by factors outside the model). Such exogenous factors may include interest rates, business confidence, or political considerations. Diagrammatically, we may depict the three equations in terms of our income–expenditure or 45-degree diagram (see Figure 13A.1).

In an economy with no taxes, output and gross income and disposable income are identical. However, in an economy with taxes, disposable income differs from output and gross income as follows:

$$Y_d = Y - T \qquad \text{(13A.5)}$$

In Equation 13A.5, T represents the dollar amount of taxes collected, Y is gross output and income, and Y_d is disposable income. Assuming we have an income tax that skims off a fixed proportion (t) of gross income, the taxes collected (T) are tY and

$$Y_d = Y - tY = Y(1 - t) \qquad \text{(13A.6)}$$

We can now restate the consumption function equation (13A.2) as follows:

$$C = a + bY(1 - t) \qquad \text{(13A.7)}$$

We are now in a position to solve for equilibrium output by substituting into Equation 13A.1:

$$Y = a + bY(1 - t) + I_0 + G_0$$

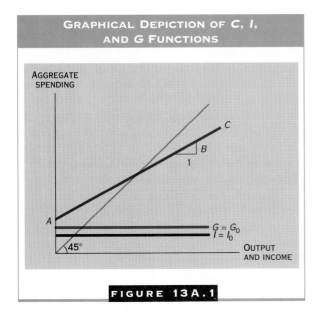

GRAPHICAL DEPICTION OF C, I, AND G FUNCTIONS

AGGREGATE SPENDING

C

B

1

A

$G = G_0$
$I = I_0$

45°

OUTPUT AND INCOME

FIGURE 13A.1

Solving, we obtain

$$Y - bY(1 - t) = a + I_0 + G_0 \quad \text{(13A.8)}$$

$$Y = \frac{a + I_0 + G_0}{1 - b(1 - t)} \quad \text{(13A.9)}$$

$$= \frac{1}{1 - b(1 - t)} (a + I_0 + G_0) \quad \text{(13A.10)}$$

The expenditure shifts that can touch off the multiplier process in Equation 13A.10 are changes in autonomous consumption (Δa), changes in investment (ΔI), and changes in government purchases (ΔG). The multiplier is now $\frac{1}{1 - b(1 - t)}$. Note that for the special case in which there is no income tax (that is, $t = 0$) the multiplier reduces to the simple multiplier employed in Chapters 12 and 13 $\left(\frac{1}{1 - \text{MPC}}\right)$, that is, $\frac{1}{1 - b}$.

Equation 13A.10 tells us that equilibrium output depends on five factors: autonomous consumption (a), autonomous investment (I_0), autonomous government expenditures (G_0), the MPC (b), and the existing income-tax rate (t). Now let's breathe life into the model by making some reasonable assumptions about the magnitudes of these key parameters. Solving for the nation's equilibrium level of output, assume

$$a = \$400 \text{ billion}$$

$$I_0 = \$600 \text{ billion}$$

$$G_0 = \$1,000 \text{ billion}$$

$$b = 0.75$$

$$t = 0.20$$

Given these assumptions, Equation 13A.9 tells us that

$$Y = \frac{\$400b + \$600b + \$1,000b}{1 - .75(.80)} = \$5,000 \text{ billion}$$

Equilibrium output in these conditions is $5,000 billion per year. The graphical depiction of aggregate expenditures and equilibrium output in this example is given by Figure 13A.2.

In this model with income taxes, the multiplier differs from our simple multiplier:

$$\text{multiplier} = \frac{\text{change in } Y}{\text{initial shift in spending}}$$

$$= \frac{1}{1 - \text{MPC}(1 - t)}$$

In our simple model with no income tax ($t = 0$), the multiplier depended only on the MPC. In the presence of an income tax, the multiplier depends on the level of the tax rate (t) as well as the magnitude of the MPC (b). The income tax, by creating a wedge between Y and Y_d, reduces the effective MPC out of GDP. As GDP rises, Y_d rises by a lesser amount.

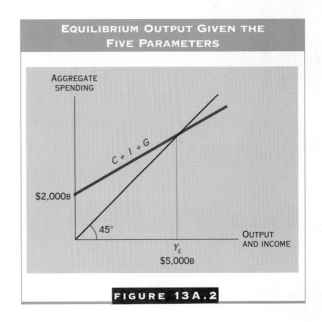

EQUILIBRIUM OUTPUT GIVEN THE FIVE PARAMETERS

AGGREGATE SPENDING

$C + I + G$

$2,000B

45°

Y_E
$5,000B

OUTPUT AND INCOME

FIGURE 13A.2

THE MPC, INCOME-TAX RATE, AND THE MULTIPLIER			
MPC	SIMPLE MULTIPLIER $t = 0$	MULTIPLIER WHEN $t = 0.20$	MULTIPLIER WHEN $t = 0.50$
0.5	2	1.67	1.33
0.6	2.5	1.92	1.43
0.75	4	2.50	1.60
0.8	5	2.78	1.67
0.9	10	3.57	1.82

TABLE 13A.1

Hence, income taxes restrain consumption out of GDP and reduce the size of the multiplier. The higher the level of the income-tax rate the larger the wedge, and given the MPC out of disposable income, the smaller the magnitude of the multiplier. This is illustrated in Table 13A.1, which uses this multiplier formula under alternative income-tax rates to compute the size of the multiplier.

Note that for any given MPC, an increase in the income-tax rate reduces the size of the multiplier. In the U.S. economy, with the MPC believed to be in the 0.80–0.90 range, the existence of an income tax brings down the multiplier by a very substantial amount. For this reason our tax system serves as an *automatic stabilizer* or *built-in stabilizer*. Any swings in Y_E caused by shifts in C, I, G and $(X–M)$ spending are reduced or moderated in the presence of an income tax. In fact, the higher the income-tax rate the greater the power of this stabilizing effect.

In our model, when the MPC is given, the multiplier process can be touched off by any one of four factors: a change in autonomous consumption (shift in consumption function), a change in investment spending, a change in government expenditures, or a change in t (the income-tax rate). A change in autonomous consumption, investment spending, or government spending shifts the $C + I + G$ line of Figure 13A.2, changing equilibrium output by the multiplier effect. A change in the income-tax rate (t) alters the *slope* of the $C + I + G$ line and changes the size of the multiplier, thereby changing equilibrium output. We examine these factors in turn.

Beginning with our initial assumed parameters and Y_E of $5,000 billion, assume that the stock market crashes, shifting the consumption function downward by $40 billion. In terms of equation 13A.10, a has decreased by $40 billion. Our multiplier formulation indicates that

$$\Delta Y_E = \text{shift in spending} \times \text{multiplier}$$

$$\Delta Y_E = -\$40 \text{ billion} \times 2.5 = -\$100 \text{ billion}$$

Equilibrium output falls by $100 billion. Using similar analysis, if government spending rises by $80 billion, equilibrium output expands by $200 billion. If investment spending rises by $20 billion, equilibrium output expands by $50 billion.

Finally, beginning with an equilibrium output of $5,000 billion, assume the income-tax rate (t) increases from 20 percent to 25 percent. We calculate from Equation 13A.10 that the multiplier is reduced from 2.50 to 2.285. If we multiply this by total autonomous expenditures ($a + I_0 + G_0$) of $2,000 billion, the new equilibrium output is calculated to be $4,570 billion.

Economists have noted that economic fluctuations in the United States have been milder after 1945 than in the prewar era. This condition is illustrated in Figure 13A.3, which indicates the annual percentage change in real output in the pre- and post-1945 eras.

Several factors may have contributed to the comparatively stable economy of modern times. Monetary and fiscal policymakers may have become more adept at implementing countercyclical policies to stabilize the economy. Such institutional changes as bank deposit insurance and unemployment insurance have surely contributed to economic stability by smoothing the *ripple effects* associated with economic downturns. Because of such changes, economic agents that precipitate shifts in consumption and investment spending may behave in a less volatile manner in the modern era. However, many economists would emphasize an alternative explanation: income-tax rates were much lower in the earlier peri-

od. Following World War II, the income-tax system emerged as a powerful automatic stabilizer. No one likes high income-tax rates. They may have adverse incentive effects or supply-side effects that slow the long-term growth trend of potential GDP, a consideration we ignore in this model. However, on the demand side of the economy, high income-tax rates do have at least one favorable side effect. They serve as a shock absorber by acting to inhibit changes in economic activity initiated by shifts in C, I, G, or $(X–M)$ spending. Given the fact that higher income-tax rates reduce the size of the economy's multiplier and given that income taxes were lower before World War II, one would expect to observe a more stable economic environment afterward.

Question: What are the implications of the income-tax cuts associated with the 1981 Economic Recovery Tax Act and the 1986 Tax Reform Act for future economic stability?

ANNUAL FLUCTUATIONS IN REAL OUTPUT

Fluctuations in economic activity have been milder in the post-World War II era than in earlier times.

SOURCE: *Historical Statistics of the Unites States* and *Economic Report of the President*, 1992.

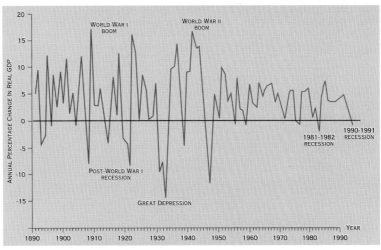

FIGURE 13A.3

E
X
H
I
B
I
T

13A.1

I DO BELIEVE IN SUPPLY-
SIDE ECONOMICS.

—RONALD REAGAN

WAITING FOR SUPPLY-
SIDE ECONOMICS
TO WORK IS LIKE
LEAVING THE
LANDING LIGHTS
ON FOR AMELIA
EARHART.

—WALTER HELLER

The Model of Aggregate Supply and Aggregate Demand

CHAPTER 11 INTRODUCED THE SIMPLE AGGREGATE SUPPLY—AGGREGATE DEMAND MODEL AND SURVEYED THE U.S. ECONOMIC HISTORY OF RECENT DECADES USING THAT MODEL AS A BASIC FRAME-WORK. CHAPTERS 12 AND 13 ANALYZED THE COMPONENTS OF AGGREGATE DEMAND AND THE MECHANISM THROUGH WHICH INITIAL SHIFTS IN ANY OF THE COMPONENTS OF AD RESULT IN A MAGNIFIED CHANGE IN THE NATION'S EQUILIBRIUM LEVEL OF OUT-PUT AND INCOME. THESE CHAPTERS ADDED TO THE ANALYTICAL FRAMEWORK THAT IS ESSENTIAL FOR UNDERSTANDING HOW MONE-TARY AND FISCAL POLICIES INFLUENCE ECONOMIC ACTIV-ITY.

IN CHAPTER 14, WE PROBE MORE DEEPLY INTO THE AGGREGATE SUPPLY—AGGRE-GATE DEMAND MODEL BY ANA-LYZING MORE CAREFULLY THE NATURE OF THE AGGREGATE SUPPLY AND AGGREGATE DEMAND CURVES. AS WE SHALL DISCOVER, THE SHAPES OF THE AS AND AD CURVES HAVE IMPORTANT IMPLICATIONS FOR MANY MACROECONOMIC ISSUES. MANY OF THE DISAGREE-MENTS AMONG MACROECONO-MISTS SPRING FROM THE DIF-FERENT THEORETICAL SPECTACLES THROUGH WHICH THEY VIEW THE AS AND AD CURVES. IN THIS CHAPTER WE EMPHASIZE THE NATION'S AGGREGATE SUPPLY CURVE AND CONCLUDE THE CHAPTER WITH AN ANALYSIS OF SUPPLY-SIDE ECONOMICS.

Figure 14.1 illustrates the AS–AD model. The equilibrium price level (P_E) and real output level (Y_E) are determined by the intersection of the AS and AD curves. Shifts in the AS and AD curves result in changes in the level of output and employment as well as changes in the nation's price level.[1]

The AD curve gradually shifts rightward in the long run because of population growth, rising wealth, increasing government expenditures, and growth in the nation's money supply. In the short run, the AD curve may shift rightward or leftward owing to changes in consumer and business confidence, changes in wealth resulting from changes in the stock market or home prices, changes in interest rates, changes in income abroad, changes in exchange rates, changes in monetary and fiscal policy in the United States, and other factors.

The AS curve tends to shift rightward in the long run because of an expanding labor force and productivity growth stemming from new technologies and increasing capital per worker. In the short run, the AS curve may shift rightward or leftward as a result of changing wages and other input prices, changing weather conditions, changing expectations, and other factors.

YOUR TURN

ANALYZE THE IMPACT OF EACH OF THE FOLLOWING EVENTS ON THE POSITION OF THE AGGREGATE DEMAND CURVE, THE POSITION OF THE AGGREGATE SUPPLY CURVE, THE NATION'S PRICE LEVEL, AND THE LEVEL OF REAL OUTPUT:

A. CONSUMER CONFIDENCE IMPROVES SHARPLY

B. THE FEDERAL RESERVE PUSHES UP INTEREST RATES

C. OIL PRICES FALL

D. THE DOLLAR FALLS SHARPLY IN FOREIGN EXCHANGE MARKETS

The Aggregate Demand Curve

It is essential to recognize that the aggregate demand curve of Figure 14.1 is a fundamentally different animal than the demand curve for a single product that we developed in Chapter 4. One cannot derive the nation's AD curve by summing up all of the demand curves for individual goods and services. In drawing up a demand curve for steak, we hold constant the prices of all other goods. A decrease in the price of steak thus causes consumers to purchase more steak relative to chicken, hamburger, fish, and other goods that are substitutes for steak. When the *price level* of the nation declines, there is no substitution effect because the *overall* price level is depicted on the vertical axis and the quantity of *aggregate* output demanded is depicted on the horizontal axis.

Also, when we draw up a demand curve for an individual good, we hold income constant. A decrease in the price of steak effectively increases the *real* income of each consumer, thus increasing quantity demanded of steak through the income

---

[1]Review the first 4 pages of Chapter 11, particularly the section entitled "Factors Shifting Aggregate Demand and Supply."

Aggregate supply and aggregate demand determine the equilibrium level of prices and output of goods and services (real GDP). Shifts in the AS and AD curves initiate changes in output, employment, and the price level.

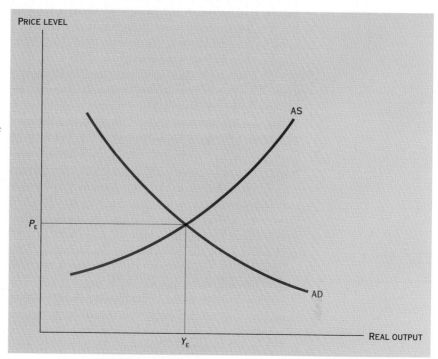

FIGURE 14.1

effect. In drawing up the nation's aggregate demand curve, income cannot realistically be considered constant as the price level changes. As we emphasized in Chapter 9, a change in the nation's price level changes the nominal or actual income level of the nation. If the nation's price level were to drop 20 percent, nominal income would also decline 20 percent and the level of real income would remain constant. We therefore cannot appeal to the income effect to help explain the downward slope of the nation's aggregate demand curve.

Therefore, in explaining the downward-sloping nature of the nation's aggregate demand curve, we must look for reasons other than those that explain the nature of the demand curve for an individual good or service. In searching for the explanation, it is useful to remember that aggregate demand for goods and services consists of four components: consumption demand (C), investment demand (I), government demand (G), and net exports ($X–M$). Let's see how each of these components of demand may be influenced by changes in the nation's price level.

A decline in the nation's price level induces a comparable decline in nominal income and therefore does not increase *real income*. Therefore, there is no income effect involved in explaining the shape of the aggregate demand curve. However, the lower level of prices does exert a positive *wealth effect*, as indicated earlier. By raising the real purchasing power of such forms of financial wealth held by individuals as money (checking accounts and currency), savings accounts, and government bonds, the decline in the price level exerts a positive effect on consumer spending (C), the largest component of aggregate demand. This wealth effect constituted the explanation that classical economists (pre-1930) relied on to explain the downward-sloping aggregate demand curve.

In addition, a decline in the price level tends to reduce the level of interest rates. This occurs because lower prices reduce the amount of money that individuals and firms need to hold to finance expenditures (lower prices mean that less money is required to purchase things). Given the *supply* of money in the nation, this reduction in *demand for money* induces a decline in the level of interest rates. This, in turn, boosts expenditures on such interest-sensitive items as plant and equipment, housing, automobiles, and certain other consumer durable goods.

Third, a decline in the price level may influence the real quantity of goods and services purchased by government to some extent. For example, if a government contract is written in terms of a given level of nominal expenditures, a lower price level implies that such an authorization would purchase a larger number of goods and services for the government. For example, if your state legislature authorizes $6 million for the purchase of books for a university library, a lower price level makes possible the acquisition of a larger number of books. On the other hand, if Congress authorizes the Pentagon to purchase 400 tanks, a decline in prices would have no effect on real output purchased by government—the government still gets 400 tanks.

A fourth reason that the nation's AD curve slopes downward involves international trade. A lower American price level, assuming that exchange rates do not move to negate the effect fully, would result in a net increase in expenditures on American goods through export and import activity. Lower U.S. prices imply greater foreign purchases of U.S. exports, so exports (X) would increase. Further, lower U.S. prices imply a decrease in American demand for imported goods and services (M). Americans increasingly purchase U.S. goods in place of those formerly purchased abroad. Hence, a lower U.S. price level positively influences the net U.S. trade balance (X–M) and results in an increase in quantity of U.S. output demanded.

The Aggregate Supply Curve

Like the AD curve, the nation's aggregate supply curve is a fundamentally different beast than the supply curve for a single good. When we draw a supply curve for wheat, we hold constant the price of goods that are substitutes from producers' viewpoints (corn, soybeans, and so forth). An increase in the price of wheat induces farmers to switch land from corn and soybeans into wheat production. In an aggregate supply curve, we are interested in the response of aggregate output to the nation's overall price level. There is no substitution of one product for another by producers in response to a higher general price level. The nation's AS curve cannot be derived by adding up all of the supply curves for the individual goods and services that constitute GDP.

The explanation for the upward-sloping aggregate supply curve lies in the fact that as the nation's price level increases, some input prices do not increase. In this event, an increase in the price level raises profit margins of firms and induces them to step up output.

The profit earned by producing one unit of output is simply the difference between the price of the good and the cost of producing it. The cost of producing a good depends, among other things, on the price of inputs—wage rates, raw material prices, factory or building rents, and so forth. These input prices tend to remain fixed for considerable periods but not indefinitely. Workers and firms often enter into contracts that fix wages and salaries for one to three years. Even in the absence of contracts, wages and salaries are typically changed once a year or less frequently. The same situation often holds for raw materials, as firms contract with suppliers to purchase the materials at fixed prices for a specified period.

As the price level rises, prices of some inputs remain fixed for significant periods of time. For this reason, *profit margins*—profits per unit of output—increase and firms expand output. Similarly, when the price level falls, certain costs initially fail to decline, profit margins fall and firms reduce output. The sluggishness of input prices accounts for the positive slope of the aggregate supply curve.

The slope of the AS curve is likely to vary with the level of economic activity. When output is quite low relative to the economy's potential output, the AS curve is likely to be relatively flat. There are lots of well-qualified idle workers available, firms are operating their plants at a low rate of utilization, and materials are plentiful. For these reasons, firms are willing to step up output significantly without requiring much inducement in the form of higher prices of their products.

On the other hand, suppose output is initially much closer to capacity levels. To expand output in this event, significantly higher output prices are required. Costs of production begin to rise sharply with expanded production because firms may be forced to hire less-productive workers as the pool of available workers declines. Firms may also have to bring on line less efficient plant and equipment. Some firms may have to add shifts and pay an overtime premium to workers. The extra cost of producing extra output rises significantly as the nation approaches capacity output, and significantly higher output prices are therefore required to induce firms to increase production. The nation's AS curve is therefore relatively steep if the economy is operating close to full-employment levels of output.

VIEWPOINTS ON THE AGGREGATE SUPPLY CURVE

It is important to distinguish between the short-run aggregate supply curve and the long-run aggregate supply curve. The long run is defined as a period long enough that all input prices are able to adjust completely to changes in output prices (the general price level). In the long run, expectations are fully adjusted to the existing price level and no one is fooled by changes in the price level. Economists agree that in long-run equilibrium, because all input prices are fully adjusted to the nation's price level, the long-run aggregate supply curve is vertical. Higher output prices do not increase profit margins in this instance and therefore do not evoke additional output of goods and services.

In the short run, higher output prices result in higher profit margins for firms to the extent that input prices do not adjust immediately and fully to the higher price level. Hence, higher output prices induce an increase in the quantity of output produced. The short-run aggregate supply curve is therefore typically drawn as upward sloping, as in Figure 14.1.

Macroeconomists differ in their views of the shape of the short-run aggregate supply curve. In addition, they disagree about the time period involved in the "long run," and therefore about the merits of applying short-run analysis to macroeconomic issues. If the "short run" becomes extremely short, it virtually disappears and becomes irrelevant. Long-run analysis becomes the appropriate framework. If the "long run" constitutes a *very* long period of time, and if the "short run" extends for a lengthy period, short-run analysis becomes increasingly appropriate.

MAINSTREAM VIEWS   Mainstream economists view the aggregate supply curve as being relatively flat for extended periods of time. Due to "stickiness," wages and other input prices move with considerable inertia. Wages, rents, utility prices, and certain other input prices often remain constant for considerable periods of time—sometimes for five years or more. Unlike prices in the stock market and commodity markets, which change instantaneously to clear these markets continuously, these input prices are sticky. Wages and rents may be set contractually and come up for renegotiation annually or perhaps every three years. Manufacturing firms have been known to write contracts with suppliers that permit access to certain raw materials at fixed prices for five years or more. Utility rates are regulated by utility commissions and are commonly held constant for several years at a time. In other words, many input prices are revised periodically only after existing contracts and other arrangements expire. These input prices are therefore independent of short-run changes in the nation's overall price level.

If input prices are quite sticky, the nation's short-run aggregate supply curve may be relatively flat. Relatively small increases in the price level raise profit margins significantly and induce increases in production. In this event, changes in the aggregate demand curve exert significant effects on real output, as indicated in Figure 14.2(A). Stimulative monetary and fiscal policies, by shifting the nation's aggregate demand curve rightward, have a large positive impact on output in the short run, while exerting only a minor upward effect on the nation's price level. An increase in aggregate demand from AD_1 to AD_2 increases output from Y_1 to Y_2, while increasing the price level only from P_1 to P_2. In this mainstream view, there is considerable potential for effective use of monetary and fiscal policies to boost output and employment in the event output is below the full-employment level.

NEOCLASSICAL VIEWS   Modern neoclassical economists believe that markets clear very rapidly, that is, that input prices are highly flexible. Economic agents are said to take all available information into account in their behavior. These agents, in the neoclassical view, understand the forces that cause changes in the nation's price level. Resource owners (workers, suppliers of raw materials, and so on) are unlikely to be systematically fooled by higher output prices. Therefore, input prices are likely to rise almost concurrently and fully with output prices.

In this case, the nation's aggregate supply curve is quite steep or vertical, even in the short run. Higher output prices do not provide much stimulus to profitability, and firms therefore do not respond to higher output prices by increasing production significantly. The short-run aggregate supply curve is quite steep in this

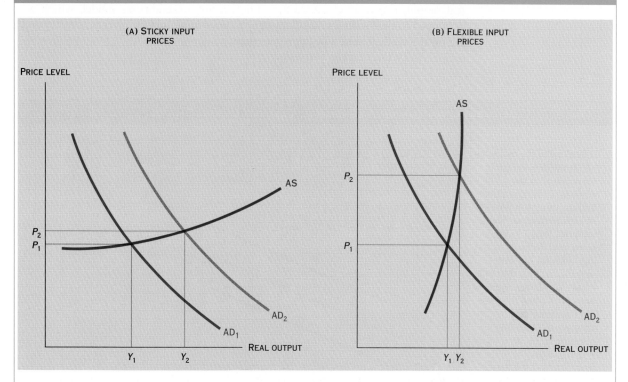

If the short-run AS curve is relatively flat, stimulative macroeconomic policies boost output considerably and the price level slightly (A). If the short-run AS curve is relatively steep, most of the stimulus is manifested in higher prices (B). Economists disagree about the shape of the nation's short-run AS curve.

FIGURE 14.2

case, and in the extreme case of continuous market clearing the AS curve is vertical. Shifts in the nation's aggregate demand curve lead to large changes in the price level and little or no change in the equilibrium level of output. Monetary and fiscal policy are ineffective in this event and should be abandoned. In Figure 14.2(B), the increase in AD results chiefly in higher prices rather than in additional output.

Economists who hold this view—a minority of economists—are sometimes known as economists of the "rational expectations macroeconomics" or "new classical macroeconomics" school. We shall have more to say about this viewpoint in Chapter 20, when we analyze the alternative viewpoints of macroeconomic analysis.

RELATIONSHIP BETWEEN THE INCOME-EXPENDITURES MODEL
AND THE AGGREGATE DEMAND CURVE

It is important to understand the relationship between the income-expenditures model (45-degree model) of Chapter 13 and the aggregate demand curve of the

AS–AD model of this chapter. Figure 14.3 helps explain the relationship. The figure indicates that although the horizontal axes of both models measure the nation's real output, the vertical axes differ. The income-expenditures model, which was developed to deal with a noninflationary environment, places aggregate real spending on the vertical axis. The aggregate demand curve of the AS–AD model uses the nation's price level on the vertical axis.

EXPLANATION OF AGGREGATE DEMAND CURVE SHAPE

The slope of the nation's aggregate demand curve (B) depends on the response of consumption and the other components of expenditures to changing price levels. As the price level declines (B), the expenditures line shifts upward (A). This shift indicates that a larger output is demanded when the price level declines. The stronger the spending response $(C + I + G + X–M)$ to a decline in the price level (A), the flatter the aggregate demand curve in (B).

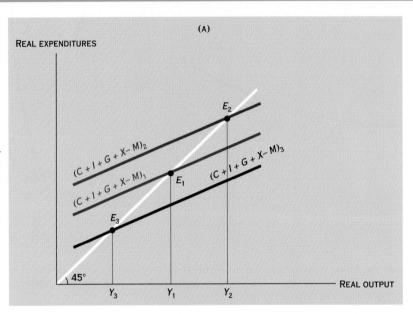

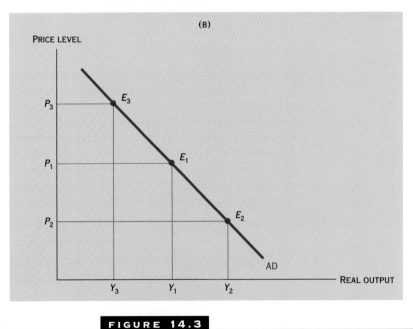

FIGURE 14.3

Assume that aggregate expenditures are initially $(C + I + G + X–M)_1$, in part (A) of Figure 14.3, with the economy in equilibrium at E_1. The nation's output is Y_1, with the price level at P_1 in part (B). To understand the linkage, suppose the nation's price level is lower—say P_2. What happens to the aggregate expenditures line (A) and, hence, to real output demanded? Since the real value of money, savings accounts, and government bonds is enhanced, this positive *wealth effect* stimulates consumption. By the same token, investment spending, government purchases, and net exports are likely to strengthen via the channels discussed earlier. The expenditures schedule is thereby boosted to $(C + I + G + X–M)_2$. The new equilibrium is E_2 in (A), with output at Y_2. Accordingly, in (B), we indicate the lower price level of P_2 is associated with output demanded of Y_2.

On the other hand, suppose the nation's price level is much higher—say P_3. The decline in the four components of aggregate demand reduces the nation's expenditures schedule (A) to $(C + I + G + X–M)_3$. Output demanded declines to Y_3, and (B) indicates that a price level of P_3 is consistent with output demanded of Y_3. The economy settles at E_3 in the figure.

Because consumption makes up roughly two-thirds of aggregate spending, the strength of the wealth effect is an important issue in macroeconomics. If the wealth effect is quite strong, the AD curve tends to be relatively flat. Small declines in the price level would trigger relatively strong wealth effects and substantially increase output demanded. On the other hand, if the wealth effect is quite weak, a relatively large decline in the price level is required to induce a significant boost in expenditures. The AD curve would be relatively steep.

As a general proposition, **Keynesians** tend to be skeptical of the strength of the wealth effect and the price-level effects on the other components of expenditures. They believe the AD curve is relatively steep. In addition, they believe in sticky wages; Keynesians are wary of the proposition that prices are flexible on the downside. **Monetarists** typically believe the wealth effect is powerful and therefore the AD curve is relatively flat. In addition, monetarists have more faith in the existence of downward price flexibility. These issues have important implications for the efficacy of the economy's *self-correcting mechanism* and, hence, for the need for active use of monetary and fiscal policies to stabilize economic activity at output levels near full employment.

KEYNESIANS

School of economics characterized by advocacy of active use of monetary and fiscal policies to combat cyclical fluctuations. Keynesians are skeptical of the effectiveness of the economy's self-correcting mechanism.

MONETARISTS

School of economics characterized by skepticism of government ability to conduct effective countercyclical stabilization policies. Monetarists prefer to strengthen and place more emphasis on the economy's self-correcting mechanism.

THE ECONOMY'S SELF-CORRECTING MECHANISM ONCE AGAIN

In Chapter 13 we illustrated the economy's self-correcting mechanism via the income-expenditures framework. A decline in the nation's price level in response to a large *recessionary gap* boosts real consumption and aggregate expenditures, pushing the economy back in the direction of full employment. An *inflationary gap*, in which equilibrium output exceeds the full-employment output level, unleashes the opposite forces. Rising prices, by reducing real wealth, continue to exert a contractionary influence on real spending and output until the inflationary gap is eliminated. We illustrate these principles in the context of the more complete aggregate demand–aggregate supply framework in Figure 14.4 (page 350).

In Figure 14.4(A), assume the economy is initially at A, the intersection of AD and AS_1. The recessionary gap is equal to $Y_F – Y_1$. If wages and materials' prices decline in response to the unemployment and idle capacity, the aggregate supply curve shifts rightward. Why? Recall from Chapter 11 that reduced prices of inputs to the production process (oil, land, lumber, labor, and so forth) shift the aggregate supply curve rightward. As the aggregate supply curve shifts to AS_2, the economy moves to B, with output boosted to Y_2. Because a (smaller) gap still exists, the process continues until the aggregate supply curve shifts to AS_3. The economy moves to C and full employment is automatically restored, assuming wages and prices decline whenever excessive unemployment exists and assuming declining prices trigger positive effects on C, I, G, and $X–M$.

In Figure 14.4(B), the economy is initially at D, the intersection of AD and AS_4. Output is at Y_4, and an inflationary gap of $Y_4 - Y_F$ prevails. Equilibrium output exceeds the full-employment output level; the economy is overheated. Wages and prices are rising rapidly. As wages and materials' prices escalate, the nation's aggregate supply curve shifts leftward (decrease in aggregate supply). The economy initially moves to point E in (B), with output at Y_5. Because some inflationary gap still exists, however, the mechanism of increasing wages and materials' prices continues until the aggregate supply schedule shifts to AS_6. At this point (F), actual output has been reduced to the full-employment output level (Y_F) and the inflationary gap has self-destructed.

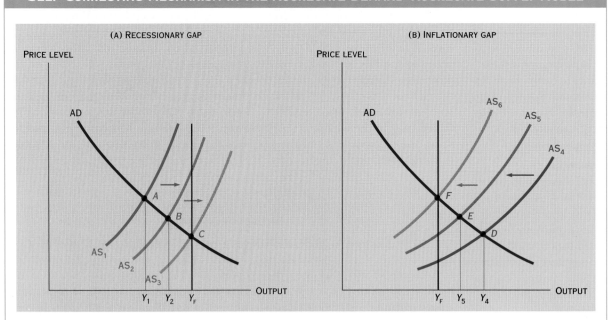

SELF-CORRECTING MECHANISM IN THE AGGREGATE DEMAND–AGGREGATE SUPPLY MODEL

In (A) the economy is initially at A, with a recessionary gap present. To the extent that wages and materials' prices decline, the aggregate supply curve shifts rightward, and this process continues until the gap has been eliminated. In (B) the economy is initially at D. An inflationary gap prevails. Wages and materials' prices increase, shifting the aggregate supply curve leftward until the gap is eliminated.

FIGURE 14.4

KEYNESIANS, MONETARISTS, AND THE SELF-CORRECTING MECHANISMS

Keynesian and monetarist views on the reliability of the self-correcting mechanism, and therefore on the need for active stabilization policies, depend on the perceived nature of the nation's aggregate demand curve as well as on the extent of price level flexibility in the economy. Consider the economy's self-correcting mechanism for a recessionary gap in the presence of two alternative aggregate demand curves. Figure 14.5 illustrates the mechanism for the correction of the gap given Keynesian and monetarist perceptions of the nature of the nation's aggregate demand curve.

The Keynesian view of the aggregate demand curve (AD_k) is given in Figure 14.5(A). Because Keynesians believe the wealth effect is weak, they view the aggregate demand curve as quite steep. With the economy initially at the intersection of the aggregate demand curve and AS_1, a recessionary gap exists $(Y_F - Y_1)$. As

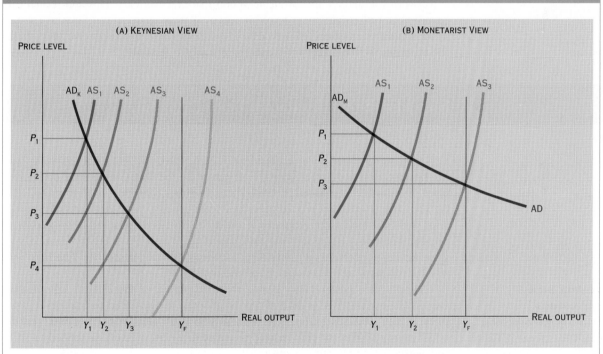

SELF-CORRECTING MECHANISM UNDER KEYNESIAN AND MONETARIST PERCEPTIONS OF THE AGGREGATE DEMAND CURVE

As indicated in (A), Keynesians view the aggregate demand curve as steep because the wealth effect is weak. In this case a major decline in wages and other input prices is required to shift the aggregate supply curve sufficiently rightward to return the economy to full employment. Monetarists believe the wealth effect is strong and the aggregate demand curve is relatively flat (B). A relatively modest decline in input prices suffices to bring the economy to full employment.

FIGURE 14.5

falling wages and other input prices shift the AS curve rightward, the demand and output responses are relatively meager. In the figure, the price level must fall all the way to P_4 to boost the economy to full employment. Such a steep decline in prices might be unsettling to normal economic relationships. For example, debtors would suffer considerable stress in paying off debts fixed in nominal dollars. Since Keynesians are also skeptical of the actual flexibility of wages and prices on the downside, they reject reliance upon the self-correcting mechanism. In the words of Nobel Laureate James Tobin, the wealth effect "is a pretty weak reed on which to pin hopes for self-adjustment of the economy."[2]

Because Keynesians are skeptical both of the power of wealth effects and of the existence of downward price flexibility, they advocate active use of government's monetary and fiscal policy tools to boost aggregate demand when large recessionary gaps prevail.

Monetarists view the aggregate demand curve as relatively flat, as indicated by AD_m in Figure 14.5(B). A decline in the price level from P_1 to P_3 would boost the economy to full employment, because the wealth effect is viewed as powerful. Coupled with the view that wages and prices are highly responsive to market forces of supply and demand and a skeptical view of the ability of government to conduct effective stabilization policies, monetarists reject the Keynesian prescription for active government intervention in the macroeconomy. They believe that the natural forces of the market are sufficient to eliminate recessionary gaps and return the economy to full-employment levels of output. Rather than calling for active stabilization policies, monetarists advocate measures to assure competitive markets in the economy so that prices and wages maintain high flexibility.

Supply-Side Economics

When Ronald Reagan became president in early 1981, the American economy was not healthy. Successful restriction of oil output by the OPEC cartel had driven the price of oil to $35 per barrel in 1980, about 14 times the price that had prevailed a decade earlier. Inflation was running at an annual rate of 12 percent and interest rates were sky high. The economy of the 1970s had been plagued by *stagflation*—the combination of stagnant output and rising prices. Productivity growth was slow, raising concerns about long-term increases in living standards. The time was ripe for innovations in economic ideas and policies.

Supply-side economics became the catchphrase of the Reagan Administration in the early 1980s, as several supply-siders were appointed to high-level positions in the Administration. The idea was to deemphasize policies intended to boost aggregate demand and instead to concentrate on measures intended to shift the aggregate supply curve rightward by stimulating the desire to work, produce,

SUPPLY-SIDE ECONOMICS
School of economics that emphasizes the importance of promoting policies to shift the aggregate supply curve rightward by implementing measures that boost the incentive to work, produce, save, and invest.

[2]James Tobin, "Keynesian Economics and Its Renaissance," in David A. Reese (ed.), *The Legacy of Keynes* (San Francisco: Harper and Row, 1987), p. 116.

save, and invest. Figure 14.6 illustrates the case for supply-side policies rather than traditional demand-side policies in order to boost output.

Ever since Keynes' pathbreaking analysis of the 1930s, macroeconomic policy had concentrated on aggregate demand. With the economy initially at A in Figure 14.6(A) and a recessionary gap present, stimulative monetary and fiscal policies are capable of boosting aggregate demand from AD_1 to AD_2. This raises output from Y_1 to Y_2, but unfortunately also pushes up the price level unless the nation's AS curve is perfectly flat or horizontal. Supply-side economics (B) concentrates on the aggregate supply curve. If this curve can be shifted rightward from AS_1 to AS_2 through government policies, we can achieve higher output without higher prices. In fact, as indicated in (B), the price level would decline from P_1 to P_2. Such a decline would allow room for some expansion in aggregate demand, yielding even more output without pushing prices above the original P_1 level—in principle.

Clearly, there is much to be gained from a successful supply-side program. In this sense we are all supply-siders. Thoughtful liberals and conservatives, Democrats and Republicans alike, favor supply-side economics, although many would prefer to call it by another name. The main point of contention is whether the Reagan Administration's policies of the 1980s in fact represented an efficient and effective set of supply-side measures. What measures does an ideal supply-side program include?

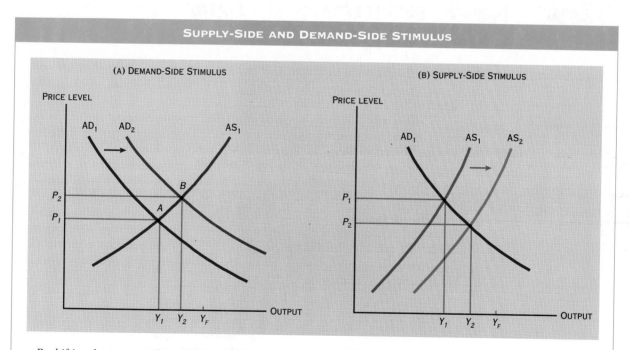

SUPPLY-SIDE AND DEMAND-SIDE STIMULUS

(A) DEMAND-SIDE STIMULUS

(B) SUPPLY-SIDE STIMULUS

By shifting the aggregate demand curve rightward, traditional demand stimulus boosts real output and increases the price level (A). By shifting the aggregate supply curve rightward, successful supply-side policies boost output but *lower* the price level (B).

FIGURE 14.6

WHAT SHIFTS THE AGGREGATE SUPPLY CURVE RIGHTWARD?

Recall the sorts of factors that shift the nation's aggregate supply curve rightward, increasing the total output that firms willingly produce at each and every price level:

1. a decrease in wages and salaries
2. a decrease in the prices of other inputs—land, capital, materials
3. an increase in the nation's labor supply and work effort
4. an increase in the nation's capital stock
5. an increase in technology, which raises productivity

Supply-side economics, to be successful, must involve policies that implement changes in some of these five measures in order to promote a sustained and persistent rightward shifting of the nation's aggregate supply curve. Other than by promoting free international trade and competitive labor and product markets, there is little government potential for bringing about items 1 and 2. Indeed, no one advocates general measures to reduce wages and salaries. Supply-side economics must therefore focus on increasing the nation's labor force and work effort, boosting the stock of capital by promoting investment spending, and fostering technological change by boosting research and development efforts in private corporations and university and government laboratories. These are the arenas in which supply-side economics must work—stimulating the search for new technologies and increasing the incentives to work, produce, save, and invest.

To a large extent supply-side economics has two components: increasing the incentive to work and increasing the share of output allocated to investment in new plant, equipment, and technology. The latter objective is illustrated in Figure 14.7.

When supply-side measures successfully increase the share of the nation's output devoted to investment goods at the expense of consumption goods and government goods, we move from *A* to *B* on the production possibilities curve. This boosts the speed with which the curve shifts outward over time (that is, it increases the rate of economic growth).[3] Also, when the incentive to work is stimulated, thus increasing the size of the nation's labor force and the effort expended per worker, the nation's production possibilities curve shifts rightward more rapidly. Given that these are the fundamental objectives of any viable supply-side economics program, was the Reagan Administration program efficiently designed to promote these objectives? What measures might future administrations implement to yield a more effective supply-side program?

---

[3]In Chapter 10 we noted that some government purchases are actually investment goods such as bridges, university buildings, laboratories, and computers. From a supply-side viewpoint, little or nothing is to be gained by curtailing these investment-type government purchases in favor of more private investment spending. The benefits are yielded by reallocating from government noncapital-type expenditures and consumption expenditures to investment expenditures public or private.

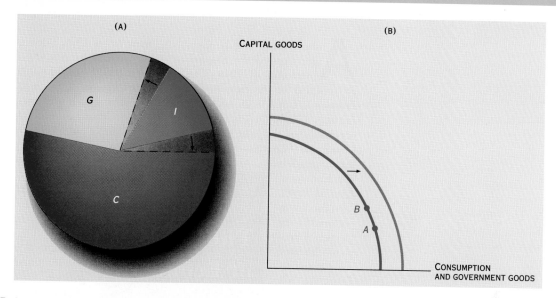

By increasing the share of current output in the form of new plant and equipment (I) and by reducing the share in the form of consumer and government goods (A), we move from A to B on the nation's production possibilities curve (B). This causes the curve to shift outward over time at a faster rate and the size of the pie (A) grows more rapidly. Concurrently, the nation's aggregate supply curve shifts rightward more rapidly.

FIGURE 14.7

THE REAGAN SUPPLY-SIDE PROGRAM

The first Reagan Administration (1981–1985) put in place a series of initiatives that were intended to shift the nation's AS curve rightward. The legacy of high inflation inherited from the 1970s was attacked through highly restrictive Federal Reserve monetary actions in the early 1980s. Because rapid inflation is believed to be detrimental to investment and economic growth, a successful attack on inflation was viewed by many as an essential prerequisite to the supply-side program. Inflation came down much more rapidly in the early 1980s than even the Administration had thought feasible. Government regulations, viewed as diverting resources from productive activities and limiting the ability of firms to use resources efficiently, were reduced. Several key measures were implemented in the major tax legislation of the early 1980s, the Economic Recovery Tax Act (ERTA) of 1981.

ERTA reduced individual income-tax rates by a total of 25 percent in three stages from 1981 to 1983. When one includes federal and state income taxes and the Social Security payroll tax, the marginal tax rate faced by most individuals—especially those with high incomes—had increased considerably between the 1930s and 1980. The rationale in the 1981 legislation for the large reduction in these rates

After World War II, Congress passed the Employment Act of 1946. This act provided for the creation of a President's Council of Economic Advisors (CEA). In addition, the act established the Joint Economic Committee of Congress and required that the president submit an annual *Economic Report*. This document, prepared by the Council of Economic Advisors, analyzes and defends the administration's economic policies. It also provides a gold mine of statistical information on the economy.

The stated purpose of the CEA is to gather data and make economic forecasts; educate the president, Congress, and the public on economics matters; and formulate an economic program to achieve the goals set forth in the Employment Act of 1946. These goals call for policies to promote employment and price-level stability. The Employment Act charged the executive branch with responsibility for fulfilling the goals of the act. In providing for the creation of the Council of Economic Advisors, Congress acknowledged the link between economic analysis and the nation's economic policy. The chairmanship of the CEA is a Cabinet-level position.

The head of the CEA typically reflects the economic philosophy and political viewpoints of the president. Heads of the CEA in Democratic administrations (Kennedy, Johnson, Carter) in recent decades typically have been Keynesian, favoring active use of government's monetary and fiscal policy tools to maintain high levels of output and employment. Heads of the CEA in Republican administrations tend to

was the desire to boost incentives to work and earn income. High marginal tax rates had particularly impaired work incentives for affluent two-earner households. By 1980, marginal tax rates of such households had frequently reached 50 percent or higher. By providing an additional exemption for such households and sharply lowering marginal rates, ERTA sought to induce *both* members of potential two-earner families to enter the work force rather than for one to remain home and pursue household activities.

Also, the individual income tax was indexed to prevent inflation from gradually kicking people into higher and higher marginal income-tax brackets. The 1970s was a decade of significant **bracket creep**, as rising wages and salaries—even when they merely kept pace with inflation—moved individuals into higher brackets in the progressive federal tax table. This meant that taxpayers whose gross earnings just

BRACKET CREEP
The tendency for inflation to push individuals automatically into higher marginal- and average-tax rates in an unindexed income-tax system.

be more conservative, favoring less intervention by government. Murray Weidenbaum, Martin Feldstein, and Beryl Sprinkle served as CEA heads during Ronald Reagan's presidency (1981–1988). Weidenbaum and Feldstein were important architects of the Administration's supply-side program. When large deficits emerged, Feldstein clashed publicly with Administration officials and returned to his teaching position at Harvard in 1984. He was replaced by Sprinkle, a University of Chicago-trained economist noted for his monetarist views.

When President George Bush assumed office in 1989, he appointed Michael Boskin of Stanford University to be head of the CEA. Boskin, the son of a self-employed contractor, grew up in Los Angeles. He attended the University of California at Berkeley, where his senior thesis explored the effects of taxes on work incentives of low-income residents of Oakland, a community adjacent to Berkeley. Boskin's study was published in the *National Tax Journal*, and the Berkeley economics department awarded him the Chancellor's Cup as the most outstanding graduate of the class of 1967. Boskin stayed on at Berkeley for his Ph.D. His dissertation examined the effects of income maintenance programs (welfare) on the size of the labor force.

Boskin is considered a *mainstream conservative*. He is an eclectic economist, accepting portions of various schools of thought. Boskin regards the nation's budget deficit as a serious problem and favors a *flexible freeze* on government spending rather than a tax hike as the preferred solution. In the flexible freeze, real (inflation-adjusted) government spending is not allowed to increase, though some government programs may increase at the expense of others. Over time, the real growth of economic activity gradually increases real revenues and eliminates the deficit.

Boskin considers himself a moderate supply-sider. He believes that incentives are very important and accepts the general philosophy of supply-side economics outlined in this chapter. For example, Boskin favors keeping marginal income-tax rates low and advocates favorable tax treatment of capital gains. He rejects some of the more extreme supply-side positions discussed later in this chapter. In fact, Boskin once wrote a book critical of some aspects of the Reagan Administration's supply-side program.

INDIVIDUAL RETIREMENT ACCOUNT (IRA)
Voluntary, tax-deductible, self-managed retirement savings program first authorized by legislation in the early 1980s to promote the incentive to save.

kept pace with inflation found that their take-home pay (disposable income) did not. Tens of millions of Americans suffered a decline in their real disposable income during the 1970s because of the effects of *bracket creep* in an era of high inflation. *Indexation of income taxes* put an end to this mechanism by automatically triggering a reduction in marginal income-tax rates each year by an amount sufficient to prevent bracket creep.

In an effort to boost the incentive to save and thereby reduce the share of output allocated to consumption and free up funds to finance the needed increase in the investment share of output, ERTA established a new voluntary retirement program featuring tax-deductible contributions by individuals. **Individual retirement accounts (IRAs)** were established. Every individual earning $2,000 or more annually in wage or salary income was allowed to make a tax-deductible contribution to a self-managed retirement plan of up to $2,000 per year. For an individual in a 25 percent marginal income-tax bracket, tax liability was reduced $500 annually if the individual made the maximum contribution. The idea was to reward people for saving more (consuming less). Also, by reducing marginal income-tax rates and bringing down inflation dramatically, the Reagan Administration raised the effective after-tax rate of return accruing to those who save.

To promote advances in technology, tax credits for research and development expenditures were granted. In an effort to stimulate investment spending, the corporation income tax was reduced, depreciation allowances were speeded up, and the capital-gains tax was reduced. The lower capital-gains tax was defended on the grounds of stimulating venture capital in risky areas in which the frontiers of technology are being challenged. When such companies hit paydirt, their stockholders were to be accorded preferential tax treatment in that their capital gains would be taxed at lower rates than such other forms of income as wages and salaries. Supply-siders believe that favorable capital gains treatment helps direct funds into areas of high risk that have considerable promise for yielding technological advances.[4]

Most economists see considerable merit in the concept of supply-side economics. Reduction of marginal tax rates is likely to exert a positive effect on work incentives, particularly in two-earner households. Efforts to boost the share of output allocated to investment are widely commended as necessary to speed the growth of capital per worker and thereby boost productivity of labor. Economists believe that technological change is a key element yielding a rightward-shifting aggregate supply curve and economic growth. Mainstream economists who count themselves as moderate supply-siders include the head of President George Bush's Council of Economic Advisors (CEA), Michael Boskin, and former CEA head Martin Feldstein, who was an architect of the supply-side legislation of the early 1980s.

CONTROVERSIAL PROPOSITIONS OF EXTREME SUPPLY-SIDERS

In their zeal to promote supply-side economics, however, some supply-siders took extreme positions that undermined the credibility of the overall program. While perhaps no individual simultaneously espoused all these controversial viewpoints, all of them were put forward at various times in the effort to move the major tax cuts proposed by supply-siders into legislation, which culminated in the enactment of the 1981 tax reduction legislation.

Viewed from the perspective of a moderate supply-sider, three extreme propositions stand out:[5] (1) Large tax cuts do *not* lead to enlarged budget deficits. (2) Larger deficits *do* result, but their potential adverse consequences are neutralized by an offsetting increase in saving in the private sector of the economy. (3) Because of additional supply-side stimulus, restrictive monetary policy can knock out inflation without reducing output or increasing unemployment.

---

[4]Preferential tax treatment of capital gains existed far before the 1981 ERTA, although that legislation further reduced the capital-gains tax. The Tax Reform Act of 1986 terminated this preferential treatment, at least temporarily. During 1988–1992, President George Bush persistently indicated his desire to reestablish favorable tax treatment of capital gains.

[5]This discussion draws on the evaluation of supply-side economics by Martin Feldstein, head of the first Reagan Administration's Council of Economic Advisors. See Feldstein, "Supply-Side Economics: Old Truths and New Claims," *American Economic Review*, May 1986, pp. 26–30.

TAX CUTS AND BUDGET DEFICITS   The proposed supply-side tax cuts of the early 1980s were quite large. Most economists were wary because they thought such cuts would cause unprecedented budget deficits. Some, nevertheless, defended the tax cuts as a mechanism for pressuring government to reduce expenditures or at least to hold the line on new programs. They saw the consequences of deficits as a reasonable price to pay for slowing the growth in government spending relative to GDP. But a radical fringe of the supply-side movement denied that the deficit would increase even if government failed to cut back expenditures. They argued that the incentive effects stimulated by the reduced tax rates would unleash such a torrent of economic activity that the federal government would collect as much or more revenue in spite of significantly lower tax rates. Arthur B. Laffer was the leader of this movement, and the *Laffer Curve* in Figure 14.8 illustrates this idea.

Laffer correctly reasoned that with income-tax rates of zero and 100 percent the government would reap no income-tax receipts. With a zero tax rate, lots of income would be earned but it would not be taxed. With a 100 percent tax rate, there would be no reason to work and earn income, at least in the *above-ground* economy. Hence, no income-tax receipts would accrue to the Treasury. Because the actual income-tax rate is between zero and 100 percent and since a large amount of income-tax receipts are actually received by the Internal Revenue Service, the curve in Figure 14.8 must begin at the origin, rise to a certain point (M), and then decline to meet the horizontal axis at the 100 percent tax rate. All of this seems agreeable enough.

The controversial issue is: At what point on the Laffer Curve is the economy operating? Laffer asserted that the U.S. economy was by 1981 at some point (L) to the right of the point of maximum revenue (M). In Laffer's view, the income-tax rate by 1981 (l) exceeded the rate (m) that would maximize federal tax revenue. It follows, in this view, that a cut in income-tax rates would stimulate revenues and

---

THE LAFFER CURVE

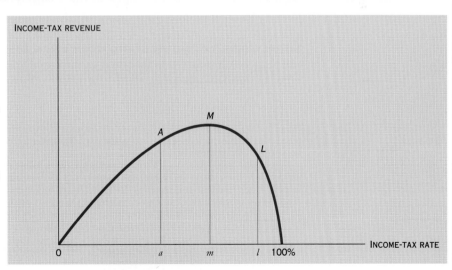

As income-tax rates increase from zero to 100 percent, tax revenues increase to point M and then decline. Laffer argued that the economy was at L in 1981, at tax rate l above tax rate m, which maximizes tax revenue. If this were true, a tax cut would increase revenue. In reality, the economy was at A with income-tax rate a. The tax cut reduced revenue and ushered in large deficits—as most economists believed it would.

FIGURE 14.8

---

therefore actually *reduce* the deficit. Very few economists agreed with this proposition.[6] Most felt the economy was at a point like *A*, to the left of the revenue-maximizing income-tax rate. Most economists correctly predicted that a tax cut would reduce federal tax revenues and enlarge the deficit.

BUDGET DEFICITS AND PRIVATE SAVING The economy's total saving consists of private saving (by individuals and firms) and government saving or dissaving (budget surplus or deficit). A large pool of total saving is essential if a nation is to finance a healthy level of investment spending without borrowing from other nations. Opponents of the 1981 tax cuts feared that the resulting budget deficit would result in a decline in the nation's gross pool of saving, produce an increase in interest rates, and result in either an increase in borrowing from the rest of the world or a contraction in domestic investment expenditures. Both increased foreign indebtedness and reduced investment are viewed as undesirable. The latter result—the *crowding out* of investment—is diametrically opposed to the goal of supply-side economics.

To refute the proposition that larger deficits would reduce the gross pool of domestic saving, a group of bright young economists trotted out an old doctrine known as the **Ricardian equivalence theorem**. This theorem postulates that under certain highly restrictive conditions, an increase in government budget deficits induces an offsetting boost in private saving, thus leaving gross saving unaltered. Individuals—aware of the increased burdens that deficits may place on their descendants—increase their saving rates so as to leave a larger inheritance with which their heirs can cover this future burden.

While Ricardo acknowledged that real-world people do not really behave that way, it seems that some of today's economists believe otherwise. Hence, the proposition is seriously advanced that larger deficits do not raise interest rates, crowd out investment, or lead to increased borrowing from abroad.[7] Contrary to the predictions of this remarkable viewpoint, the increased federal deficits of the 1980s were not accompanied by an increase in private saving rates. Instead, saving rates decreased to alarmingly low levels. Moreover, an enormous increase in American borrowing from abroad took place in the 1980s. The investment share of GDP failed to increase in spite of a series of investment incentives implemented in 1981.

SUPPLY-SIDE ECONOMICS AND COST-FREE DISINFLATION In early 1981, the Reagan Administration inherited an intolerably high rate of inflation. The first order of business was to disinflate—to reduce inflation from double-digit rates to

RICARDIAN EQUIVALENCE THEOREM Hypothesis that increased federal budget deficits induce an equivalent increase in private saving, thus leaving the gross pool of saving (government plus private) unaltered. If valid, most of the alleged adverse consequences of budget deficits are nonexistent.

---

[6]Note that this issue hinges on the concept of elasticity. It is true that $R = B \times r$, where R represents income-tax revenue, B represents the tax base (income subject to the tax), and r represents the income-tax rate. If a 25 percent reduction in r leads to an increase in B of 25 percent or more, R does not decline and the deficit does not increase. Economists believe that a reduction in r boosts B somewhat by inducing people to work longer and harder and by providing fewer incentives to seek tax deductions and hide income in the underground economy. In the U.S. economy of the 1980s, however, few economists expected the relative increase in B to be as large as the relative cut in r. If they were correct, a reduction in r would lead to less R. This is what happened when income-tax rates were reduced in the early 1980s.

[7]On this issue, key papers include Robert Barro, "Are Government Bonds Net Wealth?" *Journal of Political Economy*, November/December 1974, pp. 1095–1117, and Paul Evans, "Do Large Deficits Produce High Interest Rates?" *American Economic Review*, March 1985, pp. 68–87. For a critical view of the proposition, see Robert J. Gordon, *Macroeconomics* (Glenview, Ill.: Scott Foresman, 1990) 5th ed., pp. 415–416.

much lower, acceptable levels. Clearly, in the short run, this would require restrictive monetary policies to slow down aggregate demand. In the conventional view of economists, such restrictive measures inevitably lead to a transition period of at least a year or two of higher unemployment and financial distress for many individuals and firms.

A few extreme supply-siders denied that any hardship would be involved. True, the aggregate demand curve would shift downward as monetary policy became more restrictive. But the supply-side tax cuts would quickly shift the aggregate supply curve rightward, neutralizing the contractionary effects on output exerted by the decline in aggregate demand. Hence, in this view, inflation could be knocked out of the system without accompanying hardship in the form of reduced output and higher unemployment.

Moderate supply-siders and other mainstream economists doubted this proposition because supply-side measures require considerable time to develop. It takes time to plan new investment projects in response to new investment incentives, for example. And it takes time to build the investment projects after the plans are completed. It seems reasonable to assume that the nation's aggregate supply curve would slowly shift rightward in response to new incentives, taking years to reach maximum effect. On the other hand, restrictive monetary policy operates quickly to shift the aggregate demand curve downward. The overwhelming consensus among economists is that there is no way to knock out a powerfully entrenched inflation without paying for it with a transition period of hard times. This consensus view turned out to be correct. The 1981–1982 recession turned out to be the most severe since the 1930s. Output declined sharply and the unemployment rate soared above 10 percent in 1982. Not until the second half of 1985 did the unemployment rate fall to 7 percent.

A CRITIQUE OF THE 1980s SUPPLY-SIDE PROGRAM

Looking back, it seems clear that the Reagan Administration's supply-side program was not as successful as many supply-siders predicted. Certainly many good things happened in the 1980s. Inflation was reduced dramatically. The stock market more than tripled from its depressed values of 1982. One of the longest cyclical expansions in history commenced at the end of 1982 and continued until mid-1990. However, other indicators reveal little reason for cheer. Budget deficits soared and the national debt tripled in eight years. The United States went from the world's largest international creditor nation in 1980 to the largest debtor nation by 1988. The nation's private saving rate declined to an all-time low. The bottom line is that productivity growth failed to recover from its lethargic performance of the 1970s. The real wage of the average worker actually declined during the 1980s.[8] With the aid of several years' hindsight, it is not difficult to pinpoint shortcomings in the Reagan Administration's supply-side program. Many of these shortcomings were

---

[8]The standard of living of the average American family did not decline in the 1980s. The increasing labor force participation rate of women more than offset the decline in real wages per worker. As a result, the average level of family real income increased by about 1 percent per year in the 1980s.

immediately anticipated by mainstream economists when the proposed program was unveiled at the beginning of 1981.

THE SUPPLY-SIDE EFFECTS WERE EXAGGERATED A consensus has developed that the likely supply-side responses were overstated. Research by Michael Boskin suggested that a 10 percent increase in the real after-tax yield from saving would boost actual saving by 2–4 percent. The Reagan program, by sharply reducing inflation, reducing marginal income-tax rates, and authorizing IRAs, did significantly boost the real after-tax returns from saving. However, aggregate private saving did not respond. While this by no means constitutes sufficient proof, it suggests that Boskin's estimates may have been too optimistic. Also, the labor force response to the reduction in marginal rates was weaker than expected. According to Charles Schultze, CEA head in the Carter Administration, "There's nothing wrong with supply-side economics that division by 10 couldn't cure." Schultze was suggesting that some supply-siders were grossly overstating the likely response of saving and work effort to the supply-side incentives. Clearly, the passage of ERTA was well timed to cushion the severe recession of the early 1980s. However, many economists believe the boost to the economy came principally from simple old Keynesian forces. That is, they believe that the demand-side effects of ERTA were stronger than its supply-side effects.

LARGE DEFICITS NEGATED THE FAVORABLE ASPECTS OF THE PROGRAM The consensus view of economists is that both monetary and fiscal policies strongly influence aggregate demand. The enlarged deficits resulting from the 1981 tax cuts represent powerful demand stimulus from fiscal policy. To prevent excessive aggregate demand in the face of this large increase in deficits, monetary policy had to be maintained in a relatively restrictive posture. This *mix of policies*—a stimulative fiscal policy accompanied by a restrictive monetary policy—is precisely the opposite prescription of the mix that one would propose if the objective is to increase the share of output devoted to investment goods and thereby shift the aggregate supply curve rightward. This perverse mix means that interest rates will be higher than would be the case if the mix were tilted toward more restrictive fiscal and more stimulative monetary policies. Since investment spending is more sensitive to interest rates than is consumption, the Reagan Administration's mix of policies was a prescription for a high-consumption, low-investment economy. Many economists regard the perverse mix of monetary and fiscal policies associated with the enlarged deficits of the 1980s as the fly in the ointment that neutralized the many favorable aspects of the supply-side program.

SUPPLY-SIDE PROGRAMS INCREASE INEQUALITY OF INCOME DISTRIBUTION Cynics have sometimes labeled supply-side economic programs "trickle-down" economics. This term suggests that if a lot of money is thrown at the rich, some of it will "trickle down" to the poor. This criticism is perhaps unfair, given the objective of the supply-side program. Supply-side policies almost inevitably increase the inequality of the nation's income distribution because such policies are designed to promote incentives by rewarding those who achieve financial success. Furthermore, on balance, wealthy people receive the capital gains and dividends, own the corporations, and make the decisions to invest. And wealthier individuals tend to have higher marginal propensities to save than the less affluent. For these reasons the supply-side tax breaks are necessarily targeted toward those in the upper-income brackets if they are to achieve the goals of supply-side economics.

This is a good example of trade-offs in economics. To promote more rapid economic growth, one might have to pursue measures that sacrifice other objectives—in this case a more equal distribution of the nation's income. Those who place higher priority on the goal of reduced inequality than on economic growth naturally tend to view supply-side economics in a negative light.

Summary

1. The nation's aggregate demand curve slopes downward. A decrease in the nation's price level stimulates each of the four components of aggregate demand: consumption, investment, government purchases, and net exports. Hence, a lower price level results in greater real output demanded.

2. The aggregate supply curve slopes upward. An increase in the price level stimulates production in the short run because certain input prices lag behind output prices, stimulating profits margins and output decisions.

3. Changes in the nation's output and price level are triggered by shifting AS and AD curves.

4. Economists agree that the long-run aggregate supply curve is vertical. They disagree about the shape of the nation's short-run AS curve. Mainstream economists believe it is relatively flat. In this case, changes in aggregate demand that result from monetary and fiscal policies are capable of producing important changes in output and employment. Neoclassical economists or new classical macroeconomists believe the short-run AS curve is quite steep. In this case, monetary and fiscal policies chiefly influence the nation's price level rather than real output and employment.

5. A decline in the nation's price level increases the real value of such financial assets as money, savings accounts, and government bonds. This boosts the wealth of individuals and tends to boost consumer expenditures. The other components of AD also respond positively to a lower price level.

6. Keynesian economists believe that the wealth effect and the other price level effects are relatively weak. They believe the nation's aggregate demand curve is steep. Therefore, a major price level decline would be required to move the economy to full employment. Monetarists view the aggregate demand curve as being relatively flat because they think the wealth effect and the other price-level effects on expenditures are strong.

7. In the context of the aggregate supply–aggregate demand model, one can view the economy's self-correcting mechanism as operating by shifting the aggregate supply curve. Assuming perfectly flexible prices, existence of a recessionary gap implies falling wages and prices of other inputs. This shifts the aggregate supply curve rightward, and the process continues until the full-employment output is restored. An inflationary gap also tends to self-destruct because rising prices shift the aggregate supply curve leftward until output is lowered to the full-employment output level.

8. Because Keynesians are skeptical of the strength of wealth effects and the existence of downward wage and price flexibility in today's economy, they are unwilling to rely upon the self-correcting mechanism to alleviate recessionary gaps. Instead, they prescribe stimulative monetary and fiscal policies. Monetarists, believing more strongly in the wealth effect and downward flexibility of prices and wages, prefer a government policy of nonintervention in the economy.

9. A viable supply-side economics program consists of a set of measures to boost the nation's aggregate supply schedule by stimulating incentives to work and produce, to speed the rate of technological innovation, and to boost the share of the nation's output allocated to investment goods.

10. The Reagan Administration's supply-side program of the 1980s consisted of steep cuts in marginal income-tax rates to promote incentives to work and earn income and a series of measures to boost saving and investment. Many such measures were implemented with the enactment of the Economic Recovery Tax Act (ERTA) in 1981.

11. Some zealous supply-siders overstated the case for the supply-side tax cuts. Dubious propositions advanced by supporters of the tax cuts included the arguments that revenues would not decline and the deficit would not increase with the tax cut, that the deficit would increase but would be benign because it would stimulate a comparable increase in private saving, and that the favorable supply-side effect of the tax cut would permit a restrictive monetary policy to bring down inflation without adverse effects on output and employment.

12. Critics of the Reagan supply-side program charge that the effects of lower tax rates on incentives to work and save were overstated by supply-siders, that the ensuing large budget deficits counteracted the favorable effects of the program, and that the supply-side program increased income inequality in America.

Key Terms

Keynesians
monetarists
supply-side economics

bracket creep
individual retirement accounts
Ricardian equivalence theorem

Study Questions and Problems

1. Why does the aggregate demand curve slope downward? Suppose the U.S. price level increases. Explain the impact on each of the four components of aggregate expenditures (C, I, G, and X–M).

2. What is the distinction between the long-run aggregate supply curve and the short-run AS curve? Which curve is likely to be steeper? Explain why.

3. Explain, using diagrams, how the shape of the nation's short-run AS curve has implications for the effectiveness of monetary and fiscal policies.

4. Explain the mechanism by which the aggregate supply curve is induced to shift in such a manner that an inflationary gap is automatically eliminated.

5. Analyze the different viewpoints of monetarists and Keynesians toward reliance on the economy's self-correcting mechanism when output is significantly below full-employment levels.

6. Explain the basic goals of supply-side economics.

7. Why is it almost inevitable that any successful supply-side program increases income inequality? How could one minimize that tendency? Explain.

8. Why is a policy of promoting saving an integral part of any successful supply-side program? What actually happened to the nation's saving rate in the 1980s?

9. Explain the connection, if any, between the *mix* of monetary and fiscal policies and the shares of the nation's output allocated to consumption and investment goods.

10. Draw a Laffer Curve and label the axes. Do you think the nation's average income-tax rate today is above or below the rate that maximizes total income tax revenue? Defend your answer.

11. Suppose you could rewrite the Reagan Administration's supply-side program with the aid of hindsight. How would your program differ from the one implemented in the Economic Recovery Tax Act of 1981? Rationalize your program.

YOUR TURN
Answers

A. THE IMPROVEMENT IN CONSUMER CONFIDENCE SHIFTS THE CONSUMPTION FUNCTION AND THE AGGREGATE DEMAND CURVE UPWARD. THIS BOOSTS REAL OUTPUT AND RAISES THE PRICE LEVEL.

B. THE INCREASE IN INTEREST RATES REDUCES INVESTMENT EXPENDITURES ON PLANT, EQUIPMENT, AND HOUSING. THIS SHIFTS THE AGGREGATE DEMAND CURVE LEFTWARD OR DOWNWARD, REDUCING OUTPUT AND THE PRICE LEVEL.

C. THE DECLINE IN THE PRICE OF OIL, AN IMPORTANT INPUT, SHIFTS THE AGGREGATE SUPPLY CURVE RIGHTWARD. THIS BOOSTS OUTPUT AND REDUCES THE NATION'S PRICE LEVEL.

D. THE FALLING DOLLAR STIMULATES AGGREGATE DEMAND FOR U.S. GOODS AND SERVICES BY MAKING AMERICAN PRODUCTS CHEAPER IN FOREIGN MARKETS AND MAKING FOREIGN PRODUCTS MORE EXPENSIVE IN THE UNITED STATES. THIS RIGHTWARD SHIFT IN THE AGGREGATE DEMAND CURVE BOOSTS U.S. OUTPUT AND THE PRICE LEVEL. TO THE EXTENT THAT THE U.S. IMPORTS INPUTS SUCH AS RAW MATERIALS, THE FALL IN THE DOLLAR MAY ALSO RAISE INPUT PRICES, THEREBY SHIFTING THE AGGREGATE SUPPLY CURVE LEFTWARD. THIS EFFECT IS LIKELY TO BE MUCH LESS POWERFUL THAN THE AGGREGATE DEMAND EFFECT.

Selected References

Boskin, Michael J. "Tax Policy and Economic Growth: Lessons from the 1980s." *The Journal of Economic Perspectives*, Fall 1988, pp. 71–97. An evaluation of major tax legislation of the 1980s by the head of President George Bush's Council of Economic Advisors.

Bosworth, Barry P. *Tax Incentives and Economic Growth* (Washington, D.C.: The Brookings Institution, 1984). A critical review of the Reagan supply-side program.

Feldstein, Martin. "Supply-Side Economics: Old Truths and New Claims," *American Economic Review*, May 1986, pp. 26–30. A critique by a moderate supply-side economist.

Hailstones, Thomas J. *Viewpoints on Supply-Side Economics* (Reston, Va.: Reston Publishing Co., 1982). A discussion of all aspects of supply-side economics by economists of all persuasions.

Lindsey, Lawrence B. *The Growth Experiment* (New York: Basic Books, 1990). A sympathetic postmortem on the Reagan Administration's experiment with supply-side economics, written for the lay public in nontechnical terms.

Reese, David A. (ed.). *The Legacy of Keynes* (San Francisco: Harper and Row, 1987). A retrospective on Keynesian economics by supporters and critics, including Nobel Laureates James Tobin and James Buchanan.

III

Banking, Monetary Policy, Interest Rates, and Economic Activity

ECONOMISTS BELIEVE THAT CHANGES IN THE QUANTITY OF *MONEY* IN THE ECONOMY—THE AMOUNT OF CHECKING ACCOUNTS AND CURRENCY—HAVE AN IMPORTANT IMPACT ON SUCH KEY VARIABLES AS AGGREGATE SPENDING, OUTPUT, THE NATION'S PRICE LEVEL, AND THE RATE OF UNEMPLOYMENT. IN THIS SECTION OF THE TEXT, WE EXPLORE IN SOME DEPTH THE ROLE THAT THE SUPPLY OF MONEY PLAYS IN AN ECONOMY. ■ SINCE THE QUANTITY OF MONEY AND THE LEVEL OF INTEREST RATES ARE INTIMATELY TIED UP WITH THE LENDING ACTIVITIES OF PRIVATE BANKS, WE BEGIN THIS SECTION OF THE BOOK WITH AN ANALYSIS OF COMMERCIAL BANKING. WE ARE PARTICULARLY INTERESTED IN THE MECHANISM THROUGH WHICH PRIVATE BANKS INFLUENCE THE CREATION OF DEMAND DEPOSITS, WHICH CONSTITUTE THE MAJOR PORTION OF OUR MONEY. WE THEN EXAMINE THE NATURE AND FUNCTIONS OF OUR CENTRAL BANK, KNOWN AS THE FEDERAL RESERVE SYSTEM ("THE FED"). IN PARTICULAR, WE EMPHASIZE THE TOOLS OR INSTRUMENTS THAT THE FED USES TO INFLUENCE BANK LENDING, THE LEVEL OF INTEREST RATES, AND THE SUPPLY OF MONEY. ■ IN CHAPTER 17 WE PRESENT AN IN-DEPTH ANALYSIS OF ONE OF THE KEY VARIABLES IN MACROECONOMICS—THE INTEREST RATE. YOU WILL EMERGE WITH A SOLID FEEL FOR THE FACTORS THAT INFLUENCE THE LEVEL OF INTEREST RATES, INCLUDING THE ROLE PLAYED BY THE FED IN THE DETERMINATION OF INTEREST RATES. THE FINAL CHAPTER OF THIS SECTION OUTLINES THE *TRANSMISSION MECHANISM* OF MONETARY POLICY, THAT IS, THE AVENUES THROUGH WHICH FEDERAL RESERVE ACTIONS ULTIMATELY INFLUENCE ECONOMIC ACTIVITY. IT EXAMINES IN DETAIL THE NATURE OF *VELOCITY*, THE LINK THAT CONNECTS THE MONEY SUPPLY TO THE NATION'S GDP.

A BANK IS A PLACE THAT
WILL LEND YOU MONEY
IF YOU CAN PROVE
YOU DON'T NEED IT.

—BOB HOPE

Money, Banking, and the Creation of Bank Deposits

THE SUBJECT OF MONEY IS INHERENTLY INTERESTING TO MOST PEOPLE. AS THE ADAGE STATES, "MONEY MAKES THE WORLD GO 'ROUND." ALTHOUGH PHILOSOPHICAL TYPES MAY BE CRITICAL OF THE MOTIVE, THE PRINCIPAL DRIVING FORCE PROPELLING THE MAJORITY OF STUDENTS TO ENROLL IN COLLEGE (AND TAKE THIS COURSE) IS INTIMATELY RELATED TO MONEY. MONEY IS WHAT WE USE TO PAY FOR GOODS AND SERVICES. THE COLLEGE EDUCATION PROVIDES THE JOB THAT YIELDS THE INCOME THAT PUTS MONEY IN THE BANK AND ALLOWS US TO PAY FOR THE THINGS WE DESIRE.

IN THIS CHAPTER WE STUDY THE NATURE OF MONEY, SKETCH HOW BANKS OPERATE, AND OUTLINE THE ROLE OF OUR FINANCIAL INSTITUTIONS IN THE CREATION OF MONEY. CHAPTER 16 ANALYZES THE NATURE OF OUR CENTRAL BANK—THE FEDERAL RESERVE SYSTEM (THE "FED")—AND THE TOOLS THE FED USES TO CONTROL THE SUPPLY OF MONEY AND INFLUENCE THE LEVEL OF INTEREST RATES AND THE AVAILABILITY OF CREDIT. CHAPTER 17 ANALYZES INTEREST RATES, A KEY VARIABLE IN THE LINKAGE BETWEEN FEDERAL RESERVE POLICY ACTIONS AND ECONOMIC ACTIVITY. CHAPTER 18 ANALYZES THE LINK BETWEEN MONEY AND THE ECONOMY AND OUTLINES ALTERNATIVE VIEWPOINTS ABOUT THE ROLE THAT THE SUPPLY OF MONEY PLAYS IN THE NATION'S ECONOMY.

Definition of Money

MONEY

Anything widely accepted as payment for goods and services; any generally accepted medium of exchange.

Money is usually defined as the stock of those items that have a unique characteristic—widespread acceptability for the purpose of making payment. Such items as tobacco, gold, and woodpecker scalps served this function in more primitive times. Today, currency and coins are widely used to make payment. In fact, the government has designated these items to be *legal tender*, which simply means that no seller can refuse to accept currency and coins as payment for goods and services. However, a substance does not have to be legal tender to be money. Checking accounts in various financial institutions are widely used to make payment and are therefore considered money. Indeed, these checking accounts make up the bulk of our money supply even though they are not classified as legal tender.

Hence, our most widely quoted and popular measure of the supply of money consists of demand deposits and other checkable deposits in financial institutions and currency and coins in the hands of the public. This is known as **M-1**, or the *narrow* measure of money.

$$\text{M-1} = DDO + C^P$$

M-1

Demand deposits and other checkable accounts plus currency and coins in the hands of the public; the narrow medium of exchange or *transactions* measure of money.

C^P designates currency and coins available for immediate spending, held by the public—individuals and nonfinancial firms. C^P does not include currency and coin currently held by financial institutions, the U.S. Treasury, or the Federal Reserve System. The *DDO* component of M-1 consists of demand deposits and other checkable accounts, including NOW (negotiable order of withdrawal) accounts and ATS (automatic transfer service) accounts. NOW and ATS are essentially interest-bearing checking accounts in financial institutions (commercial banks, savings and loan associations, mutual savings banks, and credit unions).

MONEY VERSUS INCOME AND WEALTH

The term *money* is used loosely and often incorrectly in everyday conversation. Hence, we hear that engineers and accountants earn "good money" upon graduation and that baseball star Ryne Sandberg and Electronic Data Systems founder Ross Perot "have a lot of money." Correct terminology would state that engineers and accountants earn a substantial *income* and that Sandberg and Perot have amassed considerable *wealth* as a result of years of very high income, wise investing, and business acumen.

It is essential to avoid the imprecise use of such key terms as income, wealth, and money. Income is a *flow* of dollars earned per unit of time. A recent college graduate, for example, may earn an income of $25,000 per year. Wealth is a *stock* concept, measured in dollars at a given point of time. Before he divided his fortune with his children a few years ago, Sam Walton's wealth was estimated at $12 billion ($12,000 million). The wealth of an individual includes the stock of such financial assets as currency, checking accounts, savings accounts, stocks and bonds owned by the individual, as well as the value of such other assets as houses, cars, furniture, and jewelry. Wealth is accumulated over time by saving and through appreciation in value of existing assets. The wealth or net worth of the average American family is somewhat less than $100,000. Money is also a stock concept, but one that is much narrower in scope than is wealth. That is, money is only a small portion of the total stock of wealth. The narrow measure of money (M-1) constitutes only about 2 percent of total wealth.

Functions of Money

Money serves several crucial functions in a society, and the importance of these functions becomes quite apparent when one considers the alternative to a monetary economy (that is, a barter economy). A barter economy is one in which market participants exchange goods and services for other goods and services rather than for money. In a monetary economy, money serves three functions—a medium of exchange, a unit of account, and a store of value.

MEDIUM OF EXCHANGE Money serves as a *medium of exchange* or a physical means of payment. One gives up a $10 bill for a box-seat ticket to a major-league baseball game. Consider the complexity of life without money—a farmer would have to trade perhaps three bushels of wheat for the baseball ticket. If the baseball club was not interested in wheat, the farmer would have to first find a third party wishing to buy wheat who offered a product acceptable to the baseball club. For exchange to take place in a barter economy a *coincidence of wants* must exist—both parties to the transaction must desire the goods offered by the other party. One does not have to be especially imaginative to see the inefficient state of affairs today if we were to revert to a barter system.

Indeed, it is difficult to imagine a society ever achieving a level of prosperity comparable to that enjoyed by modern industrial countries in the presence of a barter system. Vast amounts of time would be expended in the process of exchange, leaving less time for productive work and the enjoyment of leisure. Introduce money in the form of the $5 bill, the $20 gold piece, or the woodpecker scalp, and you eliminate the exchange prerequisite of a coincidence of wants. In a money economy, each person exchanges his or her product or labor for dollars and directly uses these dollars to purchase goods and services.

UNIT OF ACCOUNT The American dollar, Italian lira, and German mark (and other currencies) serve as measuring sticks or standards of value by which we judge the material worth of apples, shoes, or a ticket to a symphony orchestra performance. In the United States, the dollar serves as a yardstick or common denominator by which we compare the relative value of thousands of goods and services. Most of us have a firm impression of the approximate value in dollars of the hundreds of items we frequently purchase, such as hamburgers, movie tickets, telephone services, and haircuts. In a barter economy, without money serving as the *unit of account*, no common denominator or yardstick would exist. Each product would be potentially exchangeable for every other product, and we would therefore

In approximately a dozen episodes in documented history, inflation became so severe that the store-of-value and medium-of-exchange functions of money totally broke down. In these episodes, known as *hyperinflation*, the monetary system collapsed. People refused to accept the currency and ultimately a new currency had to be issued.

In each instance of hyperinflation, an enormous increase in the quantity of money in circulation accompanied the acceleration of inflation. All of these episodes occurred in periods of great political upheaval—revolution or all-out war—in which the survival of the existing government was in jeopardy. These governments were either unable or unwilling to finance themselves by taxation or by borrowing from private firms and individuals. Instead, they simply printed currency.

When the inflationary process becomes sufficiently extreme that people rush to spend the currency quickly, hyperinflation may ensue. The desire to get rid of money before it loses its value shifts the nation's aggregate demand curve rightward and only accelerates the speed of the inflation. One hears stories of German children in the early 1920s waiting outside the factory gates on payday. When their parents handed them their pay, the children raced to the store as quickly as possible to spend the money before prices doubled again. Ultimately, merchants and others refused to accept the currency.

Hyperinflation creates grotesque examples of income redistribution. Note in Table 15.1 the German inflation of the 1920s. Suppose a German worker took out a valuable life insurance policy on himself, equivalent to ten years of current income, in November 1922. Suppose the worker died one year later. The policy would be worthless. His family would not bother to collect the proceeds because they would not even pay for a postage stamp.

Could hyperinflation happen in the United States? The evidence indicates

have to become acquainted with a vastly larger number of rates of exchange or prices in order to survive the rigors of economic life. Instead of apples having one price (for example, 49 cents per pound) as is the case in a money economy, apples would have a different price for each of the thousands of other goods and services (one haircut per five pounds of apples, one gallon of gas per two pounds of apples, and so forth).[1] One can see that economic life is greatly simplified when money is introduced to serve the function of the unit of account.

STORE OF VALUE All of us make expenditures that do not synchronize precisely with our receipt of income. We may deposit a paycheck or other source of funds on

---

[1]The formula in statistics for the number of different combinations of *n* items taken 2 at a time is $n(n-1)/2$. In a barter economy with 1,000 items, because each good potentially can be traded for each other good, there would exist $1,000(999)/2 = 499,500$ different prices. In a money economy, there would exist only 1,000 prices, each one expressed in dollars—the unit of account or standard of value.

that it is extremely unlikely, barring a civil war or overthrow of the U.S. government. Many countries have experienced inflation rates of 50 or 100 percent per year for many years without crossing the threshold that touches off the mad scramble of hyperinflation. Alternatively stated, no country's monetary system has ever collapsed without prolonged abuse as witnessed by years of inflation at rates in excess of 100 percent per annum. Nevertheless, these episodes serve as a reminder of what can happen if a government abandons all semblance of responsibility in its conduct of government finance.

FOUR EPISODES OF HYPERINFLATION		
COUNTRY	APPROXIMATE PERIOD	RATIO OF PRICE LEVEL (ENDING MONTH TO BEGINNING MONTH)
Germany	August 1922–November 1923	1.02×10^{10}
Greece	November 1943–November 1944	4.70×10^{8}
Hungary	August 1945–July 1946	3.81×10^{27}
Russia	December 1921–January 1924	1.24×10^{5}

SOURCE: Adapted from Phillip Cagan, "The Monetary Dynamics of Hyperinflation," in Milton Friedman (ed.), *Studies in the Quantity Theory of Money* (Chicago: University of Chicago Press, 1956), p. 26.

TABLE 15.1

the first of the month, but gradually spend the funds throughout the month. Similarly, we may hold back some funds earned earlier in the year to be spent at Christmas or during a vacation. By holding money (primarily in checking accounts), we store purchasing power through time. This *store of value* allows us to finance a flow of expenditures not synchronized with the receipt of funds. But money is not the only medium in which purchasing power may be stored. One may hold common stocks, gold, bonds, real property, and the like. Money, however, has the advantage that it is perfectly *liquid*—that is, it is immediately available to spend. Various assets differ in their **liquidity**, or ease with which they may be converted to money. Savings accounts are very liquid because it is easy and almost costless to convert these accounts to checking accounts (M-1). On the other hand, real estate and common stocks are relatively *illiquid*—significant costs are incurred when these assets are sold.

If the price level is stable over time, money serves as a satisfactory vehicle for storing value. If prices are rising rapidly, money functions poorly and people

LIQUIDITY
The ease and willingness with which one may convert an asset into money when one needs cash. Savings accounts are highly liquid; land is not.

attempt to reduce the use of money as a means of storing value. In those historical instances when inflation has become extremely severe, the breakdown of the store-of-value function of money has also led to a collapse of its medium-of-exchange function. People simply refused to accept money because they had lost confidence in its store-of-value function. Accordingly, the process of exchange degenerated into a system of barter (see Exhibit 15.1).

BROADER MEASURES OF MONEY (M-2, M-3, L)

The definition of money is arbitrary. Moreover, the boundary that separates a specific measure of money and its close substitutes is not perfectly distinct. Economists who emphasize the medium-of-exchange function of money prefer the narrow

MONETARY AGGREGATES AND COMPONENTS ($ BILLIONS, APRIL 1992)	
Currency	272
Demand deposits	310
Other checkable deposits*	357
M-1	**939**
M-1 plus Overnight RPs issued by commercial banks 　plus overnight Eurodollar deposits Money market mutual fund shares (general purpose) Savings deposits at all depository institutions Small time deposits at all depository institutions** Money market deposit accounts (MMDAs)	
M-2	**3,474**
M-2 plus Large time deposits at all depository institutions*** Term RPs Term Eurodollar deposits Money market mutual fund shares (institutions)	
M-3	**4,190**
M-3 plus Banker's acceptances Commercial paper Savings bonds Short-term Treasury securities	
L	**5,032**

*Includes NOW, ATS, and credit-union share-draft balances and demand deposits at thrift institutions.
**Time deposits issued in denominations of less than $100,000.
***Time deposits issued in denominations of $100,000 or more.
SOURCE: *Federal Reserve Bulletin*, 1992.

TABLE 15.2

(M-1) measure of money. M-1 includes only those items used to finance transactions—hence, it is sometimes referred to as the *transactions* measure of money. However, other economists prefer alternative, broader measures of money—measures that include other highly liquid financial assets besides the ones actually used to make payment. Such economists sometimes emphasize the store-of-value function of money. More importantly, they stress that the purpose of defining and controlling the money supply is to allow monetary policy the opportunity to contribute to the stability of economic activity by controlling the quantity of money. Therefore, the *best* measure of money is the one most closely connected with economic activity.

The preceding discussion suggests that selecting the assets to be included in our definition of money becomes an empirical issue. After all, there exists a multitude of highly liquid instruments that, though not directly usable to finance transactions, are easily converted to transactions money (M-1). Of all the potential candidates for our measure of the money supply, we should focus on the one most intimately associated with aggregate spending and economic activity. Although there is currently no consensus on which measure is the best, the Federal Reserve regularly reports four separate measures of money: M-1, M-2, M-3, and L. The items included in each measure are given in Table 15.2.

It is beyond the scope of this economics course to define all the various items (in the table) that go into the various broader measures of money (that is, M-2, M-3, and L). The main point is that these items consists of highly liquid *near-monies* that are close substitutes for M-1 because of the ease with which they may be converted to the medium-of-exchange form of money, M-1. These various measures of the money supply are frequently referred to as the **monetary aggregates**. Their growth and relative magnitudes are illustrated in Figure 15.1 (page 376). The chief measure of money is M-1, and that is the measure we use throughout this book.

MONETARY AGGREGATES
The various measures of the nation's money supply, including M-1, M-2, M-3, and L.

The Evolution of Money

In ancient civilizations, certain substances that were esteemed and available in convenient sizes emerged naturally as money and became widely acceptable as a means of payment. Because of their ornamental qualities and divisibility into convenient sizes, such metallic substances as bronze, silver, and gold became common forms of money thousands of years ago.

Early monies were **full-bodied** or **commodity monies**. Their value was the same whether used in exchange for goods and services (as money) or for nonmoney purposes (as a commodity). Natural economic forces of supply and demand ensured this equality of value. If a gold coin were worth more in its money use than in its commodity use, industrial users would discontinue using metallic gold and sell the metal for use as coins. This reduced the industrial supply of gold, driving up its price for nonmoney uses. At the same time, the quantity of gold used as money increased, driving down the purchasing power of each coin. If gold was worth more as a commodity than its monetary value, gold was withdrawn from monetary circulation, melted down, and used for industrial purposes. This mechanism ensured that the value of gold as money never deviated markedly from its value as a commodity.

FULL-BODIED MONEY
A form of money whose value in exchange (as money) is equivalent to its value as a commodity.

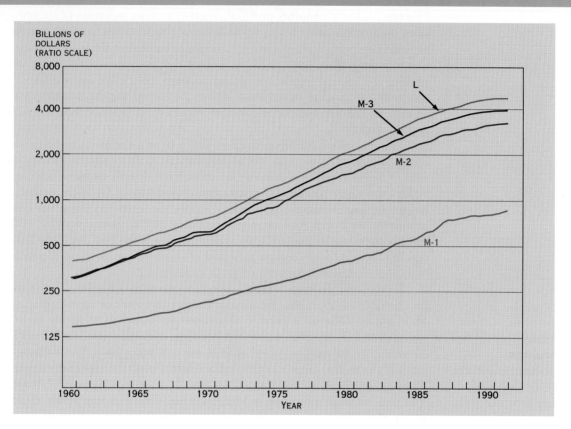

M-1, M-2, M-3, and L are the nation's monetary aggregates. M-1, the narrow measure, consists of checking accounts in financial institutions and currency in the hands of the nonbank public. The other monetary aggregates include M-1 plus various other highly liquid substitutes for M-1.

SOURCE: Federal Reserve System, 1992.

FIGURE 15.1

FIAT MONEY

Money that attains its value by government decree; it has little value as a commodity. All U.S. currency and coins today are fiat money.

Today, all our currency and coins are **fiat** or **fiduciary monies**. They derive their value from government decree rather than from the material of which they are composed. Their value in exchange considerably exceeds their value as a commodity. A $20 bill contains only about two cents worth of paper, printing inks, and other materials. A quarter contains perhaps five cents worth of nickel and copper. An advantage of fiat money over full-bodied money is that it costs the government much less to produce—fewer of the nation's resources are used to produce the money, freeing the resources for other uses. Our 1993 money supply (M-1) of approximately $1,000 billion would cost roughly $1,000 billion to produce if it were a full-bodied or commodity money. It actually costs a tiny fraction of that to produce our fiat money.

The disadvantage of fiat money is the tendency for those in control (the government) sometimes to issue too much. When this happens, we get inflation—the persistent decline in the value of the dollar. Some politicians and a few economists are so concerned about the prospects for the potential overissue of money that they advocate a return to the *gold standard*—an old-fashioned system of full-bodied money.

GOLDSMITHS—A FORERUNNER OF MODERN FRACTIONAL RESERVE BANKING

Our modern fractional-reserve banking system has its roots in the *goldsmiths* who operated hundreds of years ago. These craftsmen, who were in the business of molding gold into fine ornamental objects for merchants and aristocrats, possessed secure storage facilities for their gold. Wealthy individuals and merchants in possession of gold coins and bullion therefore were attracted to the goldsmiths as a safe means of storing gold. The goldsmiths provided these storage services for a modest fee, issuing a receipt to the owner in exchange for the gold. These receipts, or *gold certificates*, were *as good as gold* because they entitled the bearer to a specific amount of gold on demand. Inevitably, the receipts became widely acceptable as a medium of exchange and began to circulate as money. What seller would refuse payment in gold certificates if these certificates were redeemable in gold upon demand?

At first this system involved the creation of no new money. The goldsmiths were mere warehouses for gold, issuing receipts for gold deposits and maintaining the metal as 100 percent backing behind the receipts. Soon, however, the goldsmiths noted that withdrawals of gold on a given day were only a small fraction of total gold deposits. Furthermore, on a typical day new gold deposits were roughly equivalent to withdrawals. The goldsmiths saw an opportunity for earning handsome profits without undue risk. Why not make loans to local merchants or other reputable borrowers and earn interest income by doing so? Soon the goldsmiths were granting loans by issuing new gold certificates or by lending out some of the gold deposited by other individuals.

Although this procedure was probably illegal, the goldsmiths were engaging in money creation! Whenever they granted new loans, the volume of the medium of exchange increased—the currency component (C^P) of the money supply increased. Of course, the goldsmiths no longer maintained 100 percent gold backing behind the paper currency in circulation. You will soon note the analogy to our modern banking system, the main difference being that the process is now perfectly legal!

Commercial Banking and the Supply of Money

The largest portion of our money (M-1) today consists of *checking accounts*—demand deposits and other accounts in *banks* on which checks may be written in order to make payments. We use the term "banks" broadly, to include not only commercial banks but also savings and loan associations, mutual savings banks, and credit unions.[2] These latter three institutions are sometimes known as *thrift institutions*.

---

[2]Because of deregulation of the financial system in the 1980s, these various institutions have become more homogeneous in nature—more similar in the activities they are allowed to pursue. Earlier regulations limited the banking activities of the nonbank financial institutions (savings and loan associations, mutual savings banks, and credit unions) and ensured the uniqueness of commercial banks in various traditional activities. Although many specific regulations still exist constraining the activities of banks and nonbank financial institutions alike, these institutions today compete against one another on a much more level playing field.

Changes in the volume of these checking accounts (hence, the money supply) in the nation are intimately connected with activities of these banks. Therefore, it is essential that we learn about the nature of banks and their role in the money-creation process.

THE BANK BALANCE SHEET

BANK BALANCE SHEET
A statement of a bank's assets, liabilities, and capital accounts (or net worth).

BANK ASSETS
Items a bank owns.

BANK LIABILITIES
Items a bank owes; the debts of the bank.

CAPITAL ACCOUNTS
The difference between a bank's assets and its liabilities; indicates owners' equity stake in the bank.

The most efficient way to begin our analysis of banking is to study the **bank balance sheet**—the statement of the bank's assets and liabilities at a given point in time. The hypothetical balance sheet of a representative American bank lists only the major categories; some details are deliberately omitted so that we can focus on the big picture. Such a balance sheet is shown below.

A balance sheet is a statement of assets and liabilities of a corporation, individual, or other entity *at a given point in time*. **Bank assets** are indications of what the bank *owns* or of claims that the bank has on outside entities. **Bank liabilities** are indications of what the bank *owes* or of claims that outsiders have on the bank. Fundamental accounting identities that always hold true include:

$$\text{net worth} = \text{assets} - \text{liabilities} \qquad (15.1)$$

or

$$\text{assets} = \text{liabilities} + \text{net worth} \qquad (15.2)$$

Because net worth at any point in time is defined as the difference between assets and liabilities (Equation 15.1), it follows that assets are identically equal to liabilities plus net worth (Equation 15.2). In banking, the terms "capital" or **capital accounts** are usually employed in place of "net worth." In other words, *capital accounts* is synonymous with the *net worth* of the bank.

BANK ASSETS Bank assets include cash, deposits maintained at the Federal Reserve System, earning assets (loans and securities), and such other assets as data

REPRESENTATIVE BANK

ASSETS		LIABILITIES	
Cash	$1 million	Demand deposits and NOW and ATS accounts	$50 million
Deposits at Federal Reserve	4.1m		
Loans	80m	Time and savings accounts	75m
Securities	50m		
		Other liabilities	10m
Other assets	8.9m	Total liabilities	135m
		Capital accounts	9m
Total assets	$144m	Total liabilities and capital	$144m

Cash holdings of a financial institution plus its deposit at the Federal Reserve.

REQUIRED RESERVES

The minimum amount of reserves a financial institution is required to hold based on the institution's deposit liabilities and the percentage reserve requirement set by the Fed.

RESERVE REQUIREMENT

The percentage of a bank's deposit liabilities that by law it must hold in reserves—in cash or deposits with the Federal Reserve.

EXCESS RESERVES

The amount by which the reserves of a financial institution exceed its required reserves.

processing equipment, computers, and buildings. All banks are required to hold **reserves**, defined as cash on hand and deposits at the Federal Reserve. The dollar amount of reserves that each bank must maintain is known as **required reserves**. Required reserves are calculated by using the Fed's **reserve requirement** or required-reserve ratio, the minimum legally allowable ratio of reserves to a bank's demand deposits and other checkable accounts.[3]

Assume the reserve requirement applicable to demand deposits and other checkable accounts is 10 percent. In the case of our Representative Bank, the dollar amount of required reserves is calculated as $10\% \times \$50$ million = $5 million. Note that the $50 million total to which the 10 percent reserve requirement applies is the sum of the bank's demand deposits, NOW, and ATS accounts.

Actual reserves, indicated on the asset side of the bank's balance sheet, are $5.1 million ($1 million cash plus $4.1 million in deposits at the Fed). The bank therefore has **excess reserves**—reserves in excess of the required amount—of $0.1 million.

Because banks are in business to earn profits, and because reserves yield no interest income, banks typically keep only a minimal amount of excess reserves. The great bulk of bank assets are interest-earning assets (that is, loans and securities).[4] Banks would carry an even larger portion of assets in the form of interest-earning assets were it not for the constraints on bank activities posed by the existence of reserve requirements.

Reserve requirements may be regarded as a form of tax levied on banks, which forces them to maintain a larger percentage of their assets in the form of idle, non-interest-earning assets (reserves) than they would voluntarily maintain. As we shall discover, the existence of reserve requirements enhances the Federal Reserve's ability to achieve broad control over the banking system's lending and investing activities and the nation's supply of money. These reserve requirements may therefore be viewed as socially desirable, inasmuch as they facilitate the government's constitutional mandate of regulating the creation of money.

BANK LIABILITIES AND CAPITAL ACCOUNTS A crucial category of bank liabilities involves checking or *transactions accounts*—demand deposits and other checkable deposits. These accounts are important because they constitute the major portion of our money supply (M-1) and exert an important influence upon economic activity. Time and savings deposits consist of various types of interest-bearing noncheckable bank deposits, including passbook savings accounts, small certificates of deposits (CDs), and large-denomination CDs (negotiable CDs). Some of these deposits—though not included in the nation's narrow (M-1) measure of money—are included in the broader measures (M-2 and M-3 and L), as reflected in Table 15.2. Other liabilities consist of other claims by outsiders upon the bank—for example, debts incurred by the bank in borrowing funds from the Federal Reserve and alternative sources, and bills payable.

The capital account or the net worth of the Representative Bank is $9 million, or 6.25 percent of the value of its total assets (or total liabilities plus capital). This

---

[3]Actually a second set of reserve requirements (much lower) is sometimes levied on certain types of bank time deposits. In the interest of simplicity, we ignore this consideration here.

[4]These loans are diversified and include business, real-estate, consumer, and agricultural loans. The securities banks purchase are predominantly bonds issued by municipalities and bonds and short-term obligations issued by the U.S. government.

capital account may be viewed as the bank owners' equity in the business and derives from personal funds invested in the bank by its owners plus profits plowed back into the bank over the years. The capital account may be regarded as a *cushion* that protects the bank owners and large depositors from the possibility of **insolvency** (most depositors are protected by federal insurance of $100,000 maximum per depositor).

BANK INSOLVENCY
Condition in which value of bank liabilities exceeds value of assets, that is, capital accounts are negative.

Banks need this cushion of protection. Given a bank's deposits and other liabilities, the value of its assets fluctuates continuously as security prices change and some borrowers default on loans. If the value of assets drops below the value of liabilities at any point in time, the bank is technically insolvent and may be closed or merged with another bank. This involves a change of ownership and management together with a total loss of investment and equity to the original owners. Given other factors, the larger the bank's *capital accounts ratio* (capital accounts/total assets), the lower its exposure to risk of insolvency.

THE TRADE-OFF BETWEEN BANK SAFETY AND PROFITABILITY

In view of the preceding considerations, bank management is torn between conflicting objectives. On the one hand, management must prudently limit the risk of insolvency by maintaining a reasonably healthy capital accounts cushion and by allocating its assets prudently.[5] On the other hand, management strives to earn a high rate of return on the owners' investment dollar. To earn higher rates of return, management must seek higher-yielding (hence often riskier) securities and loans. Moreover, the bank must not maintain an excessive ratio of capital accounts to total assets. Given the rate of return earned on the bank's assets, the rate of return on the owner's equity (or capital) declines as the capital accounts ratio rises.[6] Balancing this inherent trade-off between safety and profitability is a constant challenge to bank management. With the aid of hindsight, it is clear that many banks were not sufficiently prudent in the 1980s. Bank failures soared.

WHY DO BANKS FAIL?

A bank becomes insolvent when the value of its assets declines sharply, dissolving the net worth or capital accounts—the residual that remains when liabilities are subtracted from assets. This almost always occurs when loans become *bad loans* as a

---

[5]Extensive regulations prohibit banks from investing in such risky securities as common stocks, gold, real estate, and corporation bonds. Banks are basically confined to purchasing municipal and U.S. government securities and making loans.

[6]Assume our Representative Bank typically earns annual profits equal to 1 percent of its total assets (1% × $144 million = $1.44 million). If it maintains a capital account cushion of 10 percent of total assets ($14.4 million), its rate of return on equity for the owners is 10 percent per year (that is, $1.44 million/$14.4 million). If it operates on a 5 percent capital/total assets ratio ($7.2 million of capital), the bank owners reap a return of 20 percent per annum (that is, $1.44 million/$7.2 million). In reducing its capital accounts ratio, bank management earns a greater rate of return but increases the risk of insolvency.

result of changes in market conditions. In the 1980s, a classic squeeze on farm income imposed by rising costs and falling agricultural prices coupled with unusually high interest rates made it impossible for many farmers to meet interest payments on their loans. Even though the banks may have been able to repossess farmers' property (pledged as loan collateral), plummeting farm-land values frequently meant that the collateral was worth less than the amount owed the bank.

Similarly, the sharp decline of oil prices in the mid-1980s caused widespread defaults on loans in the oil patch. In addition, many larger U.S. banks had huge outstanding loans to such developing nations as Brazil, Argentina, and Mexico. Raw materials prices of products produced and exported by these nations plummeted during the severe 1981–1982 worldwide recession and remained depressed for several years thereafter. This made it quite difficult for these nations to generate revenues with which to meet their debt-service payments. The viability of many of these loans remains fragile even today.

Figure 15.2 illustrates the number of bank failures each year since 1960, clearly indicating the severe deterioration since 1980. Largely because of the depressed conditions in the agriculture and energy sectors, together with falling real estate prices in some regions, more U.S. banks failed each year between 1982 and 1991 than in any year since the 1930s. Even in the early 1990s, the American banking system remained in a less-than-robust state of financial health. The Federal Deposit Insurance Corporation's (FDIC's) list of "problem banks"—those whose financial condition warrants concern and rather close surveillance by the regulatory authorities—remained lengthy. The number of banks gaining notoriety by making the list increased from less than 400 in the mid-1970s to more than 1,500 by 1990. By 1992, however, the financial condition of U.S. banks was clearly improving.

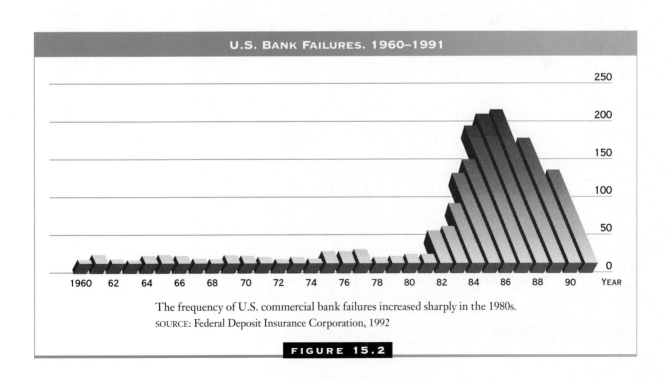

U.S. BANK FAILURES. 1960–1991

The frequency of U.S. commercial bank failures increased sharply in the 1980s.
SOURCE: Federal Deposit Insurance Corporation, 1992

FIGURE 15.2

The American savings and loan (S&L) debacle of the late 1980s and early 1990s represents the biggest financial disaster since the Great Depression of the 1930s. An enormous shakeout in the industry eliminated about one-third of the nation's S&Ls by 1992. The government agency that insured the deposits in S&Ls, the Federal Savings and Loan Insurance Corporation (FSLIC), went bankrupt because it had nowhere near enough financial resources to make good on the liabilities of the insolvent S&Ls. In 1989, a huge federal bailout was put in place, a bailout that is expected to cost taxpayers about $500 billion over the next 30 years.

Who's to blame? There are plenty of culprits. Congress, several recent presidential administrations, the regulatory authorities, the accounting firms that audit the S&Ls, and management of the S&Ls all contributed to the mess that burst into the national spotlight in the late 1980s.

Born in the Great Depression as a mechanism for encouraging home ownership for the masses of Americans, the S&L concept was flawed from the beginning. These institutions were to issue *short-term* savings deposits and use the funds to provide *20- and 30-year* mortgages at interest rates fixed over the life of the loans. This system was a disaster waiting to happen. If interest rates ever increased sharply, the cost of obtaining funds for an S&L would rise above the average yield on its portfolio of fixed-rate mortgages, which changes only slowly over time. This, of course, is a prescription for losing money. If sustained for a long period, it is a ticket to insolvency for the S&Ls—including those that are managed quite prudently.

After 45 years of stability and prosperity in the S&L industry, all hell broke loose in the late 1970s. U.S. inflation escalated into double-digit range. To bring down inflation, the Federal Reserve pushed interest rates to extremely high levels. Because the yields paid to S&L customers were limited by government regulations, they became unattractive relative to yields available elsewhere. The institutions faced the prospect of massive *disintermediation*—withdrawal of funds by depositors. This would have forced S&Ls to sell off bundles of mortgages and other assets at prices sharply below their original cost, quickly bankrupting a large percentage of the nation's S&Ls.

To avoid this, the S&Ls convinced Congress to pass the Depository Institutions Deregulation Act of 1980, which phased out the ceilings on interest rates payable to depositors. This measure slowed the demise of the S&Ls but did not solve the basic problem. As long as the average cost of obtaining funds exceeded the average interest rate earned on their portfolio of mortgages, the S&Ls operated in the red. In 1981 and 1982 alone, industry losses totaled about $11 billion, and about 500 S&Ls became insolvent.

In 1981, S&Ls were first permitted to issue adjustable-rate mortgages (ARMs). ARMs were designed to protect the S&Ls by shifting the risk of rising interest rates onto the homebuyer. With an ARM, automatic increases in the interest rate on outstanding mortgages are triggered when interest rates rise in financial markets. While increasing reliance on ARMs promised eventually to help stabilize the S&L industry, the instrument provided little relief in the

1980s. The fundamental problem was that the S&Ls were locked into previously issued long-term fixed-rate mortgages for years to come.

In an additional effort to allow the S&Ls to compete on a level playing field, Congress passed the infamous Garn-St. Germain Act in 1982. This Act permitted S&Ls to enter such new activities as making loans to businesses and consumers. The idea seemed sensible—allowing the S&Ls to diversify their assets in order to provide greater long-term stability to the industry.

Although these laws designed to help the S&Ls augured well for the long term, they came too late. Like drought-stricken farmers praying for rain, the S&Ls were praying for a drop in interest rates. Unfortunately, these rates remained abnormally high throughout the first half of the 1980s, partly because of the burgeoning federal budget deficit. Finally, when interest rates came down sharply, the other shoe fell. The price of oil collapsed. Oil-producing states were hit hard. The problem in Texas is illustrative of oil-producing states. Plummeting oil prices hammered the Texas economy and brought down the real estate industry, to which S&Ls had loaned heavily. In Houston and other Texas cities, prices of homes and commercial real estate collapsed. This bankrupted hundreds of Texas S&Ls.

As more and more S&Ls become insolvent, the FSLIC became aware of the enormity of the crisis. It did not have nearly enough resources to cover the losses of the insolvent S&Ls in the event they were closed down. The regulatory authorities then made a disastrous decision to liberalize accounting procedures to disguise the insolvencies, hoping to buy time for an industry recovery that might return bankrupt institutions to solvency.

While the 1982 Garn-St. Germain Act sensibly allowed the S&Ls to diversify assets somewhat, several states went overboard. Texas, California, and Florida, for example, authorized state-chartered S&Ls to engage in almost any lending practices they desired. These institutions began committing funds to windmill farms, racetracks, junk bonds, and large real estate ventures of dubious merit. The deregulation of both interest rates payable by S&Ls and their allowable activities greatly increased the opportunities for risky business. Because deposits were insured, funds flowed to the S&Ls paying the highest interest rates (and taking the biggest risks with the funds attracted). Speculative activity increased and fraudulent behavior became commonplace.

Common sense dictates that if the S&Ls are to be authorized to take more risk with their depositors' money while the government insures the depositors, increased surveillance over S&L activities is required. Unfortunately, the regulatory authorities were pitifully understaffed during the period in which the crisis was developing.

Especially imprudent was the policy of permitting *insolvent* S&Ls to continue operations unchecked. Because potential returns typically increase with an increase in risk, these institutions had a powerful incentive to take increased risk in a desperate attempt to pull themselves out of insolvency. Because no individual owner's wealth was at stake (the firm already being insolvent), the S&Ls faced

E
X
H
I
B
I
T

essentially a "heads I win, tails the government loses" proposition. The insolvent S&Ls took bigger and bigger risks and went further and further into the red, at the taxpayers' eventual expense, as speculative activity became increasingly rampant. Our government engaged in a cover-up, and not until after the 1988 election did it get serious about closing bankrupt S&Ls and leveling with the American people about the magnitude of the losses to the taxpayers.

In early 1989, President George Bush unveiled a plan designed to put the S&L disaster behind us eventually. The government is to spend hundreds of billions of dollars over the next 30 years to merge or close hundreds of insolvent S&Ls. The program also calls for stricter accounting practices and higher capital requirements for S&Ls to cushion against potential recurrence of such crises. Further, the power of the FDIC was expanded, including the absorption of the devastated FSLIC.

The S&L fiasco is the ultimate example of Murphy's Law. To reach the magnitude of disaster that it became, a series of things had to go wrong. Unfortunately, everything that possibly could go wrong did go wrong! Unhappily, this episode did nothing to reverse the downward spiral in Americans' confidence in their government.

15.2 (CONT.)

How Financial Institutions Create Money

One of the most unfathomable topics in economics for those who have not formally studied the subject is the question of how money comes into existence and what makes the quantity of money fluctuate. Who controls the money supply? What role do banks play in this process? Why is M-1 today approximately five times larger than it was two decades ago? As we will learn in this chapter and in Chapter 16, the keys to these questions are locked up in the fact that the bulk of our money supply consists *not* of physical substances like paper currency and metallic coins but rather of checking accounts, which are simply entries on the ledgers of banks. We also learn that, while banks collectively create money through their lending and investing activities, the Federal Reserve System maintains a rather firm grip on the ability of banks to engage in these money-creating activities. Clearly, the Fed is responsible for the *trend* behavior in the supply of money, though perhaps not for the weekly gyrations.

As you know from personal experience, checking accounts—demand deposits and other checkable accounts—serve as our primary means of payment. You probably pay your apartment rent or dorm fee and most other large payments by transferring funds from your checking account to that of the payee. Checks are the instruments used to bring about these transfers of funds. However, the actual payments consist of the transfer of deposit accounts—the bookkeeping entries. Although numerous smaller purchases are conducted by the payment of currency and coins, well over 90 percent of the *total dollar value* of transactions in the United States is made through the transfer of demand deposits in financial intermediaries.

Within our holdings of money ($DDO + C^P$) and other liquid assets, the public determines the portion held as currency (C^P). If you have $600 in your checking account or passbook savings account, you are free to withdraw whatever portion of the $600 you desire to hold as currency. Hence, the currency portion (C^P) of the money supply is determined by the public within the constraints of its deposit balances. Banks respond passively to the wishes of the public in granting currency.

Paradoxically, however, even though C^P passively adapts to the public's needs, the total money supply ($DDO + C^P$) does not. Although short-run variations in M-1 are influenced by actions of banks and the public, the basic trend behavior of the money supply is determined by the Federal Reserve System. A goal of Chapter 16 is to outline the tools used by the Fed to achieve this control over the money supply. In the remainder of this chapter, we analyze the important role of banks in creating money in a system of **fractional reserve banking**—a system in which banks maintain only a rather small proportion of deposit liabilities in the form of reserves (cash and deposits at the Federal Reserve).

FRACTIONAL RESERVE BANKING
A system in which banks hold reserves equivalent to only a rather small fraction of deposit liabilities.

THE SIMPLE MECHANICS OF MONEY CREATION

Whenever banks make new loans or purchase securities, new money is created. We illustrate this with the device of the *T-account*, which is simply a statement of the *change in the balance sheet* associated with a given event.

BANK LENDING AND DEPOSIT CREATION Suppose your Hometown Bank lends a local hardware store $100,000 to expand its inventories of products. The bank's T-account indicates the following:

HOMETOWN BANK

ASSETS	LIABILITIES
Loans + $100,000	Demand deposits + $100,000

The bank makes the funds available to the hardware store by increasing the store's demand deposit account.[7] No exchange of physical currency or coins takes place. The bank has created new money (DDO) simply by adding an entry to its books stating that the checking account of the borrower is being increased by $100,000. The compensating item on the asset side (balance sheets must always balance!) is the increase in loans.

---

[7]Of course, the borrower may demand the funds in currency. This would be highly unusual but would not alter our conclusion that new loans create new money. Remember that M-1 = $DDO + C^P$. If the loan is requested in currency, C^P rises by $100,000 but DDO does not change. While sitting in the bank, the currency does not count as part of C^P or M-1. When outside the bank in the hands of the public, it does.

Of course, the local merchant who borrowed the $100,000 is not going to leave the funds sitting in a checking account. Instead, assume the funds are for use in purchasing supplies from firms that do not bank at Hometown Bank. In that event, the final state of the T-accounts associated with the loan is as follows:

HOMETOWN BANK			OTHER BANKS	
ASSETS	LIABILITIES		ASSETS	LIABILITIES
Loans + $100,000			Deposits at Fed + $100,000	DDO + $100,000
Deposits at Fed − $100,000				

The hardware store owner wrote checks amounting to $100,000 to suppliers for the purchase of hardware. These checks were deposited in various other banks, which sent the checks to the Federal Reserve. Why the Fed? Because the Fed serves as a clearing agent for checks involving banks in different cities. Remember that each bank maintains accounts, known as reserves, at the Fed. In this example, the Fed clears the checks by reducing (debiting) the reserve account of Hometown Bank and adding to (crediting) the reserve account of the various other banks. The Fed then returns the checks to Hometown Bank so that it becomes aware they were written. The transactions are completed when Hometown Bank reduces the hardware store's checking account by $100,000. This negates the initial demand deposit entry created on Hometown Bank's balance sheet when the loan was granted.

Note in the preceding T-account that Hometown Bank ends up with the same amount of deposits it had before the $100,000 loan was granted. So is the money supply back to its initial pre-loan level? No—the money supply remains higher by $100,000 as long as the loan remains outstanding. The $100,000 increase in money, initially created by Hometown Bank, remains in the banking system in accounts at various other banks. The basic principle is simple: Whenever bank lending rises, bank deposits and the supply of money increase. On the other hand: When bank lending is reduced, deposits are extinguished and the supply of money falls. People write checks to banks, reducing the amount of *DDO* and the supply of money.

BANK SECURITY PURCHASES AND DEPOSIT CREATION Money also is created whenever banks purchase securities. Assume Metro Bank buys $400,000 worth of U.S. government securities from various securities dealers. The relevant T-accounts are as follows:

METRO BANK			VARIOUS SECURITIES DEALERS' BANKS	
ASSETS	LIABILITIES		ASSETS	LIABILITIES
U.S. securities + $400,000			Deposits at Fed + $400,000	DDO + $400,000 (of securities dealers)
Deposits at Fed − $400,000				

As in the Hometown Bank example, bank deposits at the Fed are involved when Metro Bank pays for its securities by writing checks on its Federal Reserve account in the amount of $400,000. These checks, when deposited by the various securities dealers in commercial banks, result in $400,000 of new demand deposits (and money) in the United States. The dealers' banks increase the dealers' checking accounts and send the checks to the Federal Reserve. The Fed completes the transaction by reducing Metro Bank's reserve account and increasing the securities dealers' banks' reserve accounts by $400,000. The money supply is increased for as long as the securities held by banks are increased.

The key to understanding why the money supply rises when banks buy securities from the public (or dealers) is that banks use their Federal Reserve accounts (which are not part of the money supply) to pay for the securities. As soon as these checks are deposited into checking accounts by the public (or dealers), *DDO* and the money supply immediately increase. On the other hand, when banks sell securities to the public (or dealers), the money supply declines as checks are written to the banks by the public (or dealers) to pay for these securities. The public uses checking accounts to pay for these securities, and the supply of money falls.

At this point you may view this system of money creation as potentially chaotic and uncontrollable. Inasmuch as banks can always increase profits by expanding loans and purchasing securities, aren't they likely to engage in more of such activities than is consistent with the national interest? Aren't they likely to tend toward creating *too much* money? The answer is no—at least not as long as the Federal Reserve has its eye on the situation and its hands on the wheel.

Recall—both in the loan and security examples—that the initial bank involved lost reserves when it acquired earning assets. Hometown Bank, in expanding loans by $100,000, lost deposits at the Fed (reserves) of $100,000. Metro Bank, in buying $400,000 of securities, paid for them by giving up $400,000 of reserves. Whenever individual banks acquire loans and securities, they lose reserves on a dollar-for-dollar basis. Therefore, such acquisition by any given bank can occur only if the bank has reserves it can afford to lose (that is, excess reserves).[8] Once banks use up their excess reserves, expansion of bank lending and investing activities comes to a screeching halt. Because the Fed exerts a firm grip over the amount of reserves and excess reserves in the American banking system through techniques to be discussed in Chapter 16, it has ultimate control over aggregate bank lending and investing, and hence, the money-creation process.

MULTIPLE EXPANSION OF BANK DEPOSITS

A *fractional-reserve banking system* is one in which banks are required to maintain reserves that are only a fraction of deposit liabilities. The amount of bank deposits is a rather sizable multiple of the amount of reserves (cash and deposits at the Federal Reserve System) maintained by the banks. Each additional dollar of reserves that enters the banking system results in an expansion of several dollars in the

---

[8]If the Metro Bank had only $100,000 in excess reserves prior to purchasing $400,000 in securities, it would have become deficient in reserves by $300,000. Banks have no choice but to abide by the Fed's reserve requirements since the regulatory authorities have the ultimate power to deny FDIC insurance. Such denial would inflict a severe, if not fatal, wound upon the bank.

amount of deposits in the system (and in M-1, M-2, and the other monetary aggregates). Although any one bank can contribute to the deposit expansion process only by the amount of its excess reserves, the *banking system* (all banks combined) can create an amount of new deposits that is a *multiple* of any initial excess reserves in the banking system.

New reserves come into the banking system from several sources. We will learn in Chapter 16 that the Federal Reserve System, through deliberate measures, is easily capable of dominating the aggregate amount of reserves. The public, by withdrawing or depositing currency in banks, also initiates fluctuations in reserves. Regardless of the source of the change in reserves in the banking system, the deposit expansion process is fundamentally the same.

Assume the reserve requirement applicable to all demand deposits is 10 percent and that initially the banking system has no excess reserves (that is, it is fully *loaned up*). Now assume a customer of Bank A deposits $1 million of currency in a checking account. The immediate effect on Bank A's T-account is as follows:

BANK A

Cash + $1 million	DDO + $1 million

The bank gains $1 million of liabilities in the form of demand deposits and $1 million of assets in the form of cash. Because the bank is only required to maintain 10 percent reserve backing on demand deposits, its required reserves increase by $0.1 million (or $100,000). However, because its reserves increased by a full $1 million, it initially finds itself with $0.9 million ($900,000) of excess reserves. To earn additional profits, Bank A has an incentive to trade its excess reserves for earning assets (remember, reserves pay no interest). Suppose the bank uses its excess reserves to expand its loans by $0.9 million.

BANK A (STEPS)

1. Cash	+ $1 m	DDO +	$1 m
2. Loans	+ $0.9m	DDO +	$0.9m
3. Deposits at Fed	– $0.9m	DDO –	$0.9m

BANK A (NET FINAL EFFECT)

Cash	+ $1 m	DDO +	$1 m
Deposits at Fed	– $0.9m		
Addendum: reserves	**+ $0.1m**		
Loans	+ $0.9m		

In the left-hand T-account, Bank A receives the original $1 million cash deposit in step 1. In step 2 the bank creates new deposits of $0.9 million in making a loan to a local farmer to purchase equipment. In step 3 the farmer writes checks for the equipment totalling $0.9 million, and the funds are cleared out of Bank A. The net effect on Bank A of all three steps is indicated in the right-hand net T-account. Deposits in the bank are increased by $1 million (the original cash deposit). Reserves are increased by $100,000, which is sufficient to support the additional deposits, given the 10 percent reserve requirement. The remaining $900,000 of reserves initially deposited in Bank A were loaned out, and thus have left Bank A.

Now suppose the farm implement dealers bank with Bank B. After the farmer presents his checks to the implement dealers and the checks clear, Bank B's T-account is indicated in step 1.

BANK B (STEPS)		BANK B (NET FINAL EFFECT)	
1. Deposits at Fed + $0.9m	*DDO* + $0.9m (implement dealers)	Deposit at Fed + $0.09m **Addendum: reserves + $0.09m**	*DDO* + $0.9m
2. U.S. Securities + $810,000 Deposits at Fed − *$810,000*		U.S. Securities + $0.81m	

In step 1 the implement dealers deposit the checks and the bank increases the checking accounts accordingly. The Fed also increases (credits) Bank B's reserve account. Bank B is now in a position quite similar to that initially experienced by Bank A. Bank B's reserves have increased by $900,000, but its required reserves have increased by only $90,000 (that is, 10% × $900,000). Bank B finds itself with $810,000 of excess reserves. Suppose Bank B trades those excess reserves for earning assets by purchasing $810,000 of U.S. government securities from various dealers.

Step 2 indicates the acquisition of securities by Bank B. The bank pays for the securities by writing a check on its Federal Reserve account and the Fed *collects* from Bank B by decreasing its Federal Reserve checking account. The net final effect on Bank B, shown in the right-hand T-account, indicates that its demand deposit liabilities increased by $0.9 million ($900,000), its reserves increased by $0.09 million ($90,000), and its earning assets in the form of securities increased by $0.81 million ($810,000).

Bank B, in purchasing government securities, wrote checks on its Fed account and gave the checks to various securities dealers who bank with Bank C. When the checks are deposited and cleared, Bank C's T-account is as follows:

BANK C	
1. Deposits at Fed + $810,000	*DDO* + $810,000 (securities dealers)

Bank C increases the checking accounts of the securities dealers by $810,000 and sends the checks to the Fed, which credits Bank C's reserve account by $810,000. Bank C is now in the same position in which Bank A and Bank B earlier found themselves—with excess reserves. Because Bank C's actual reserves increased by $810,000 while required reserves expanded only by $81,000, its excess reserves have increased by $729,000. Bank C therefore trades these excess reserves for earning assets (loans and/or securities), and a fourth bank (Bank D) enters the picture.

Assuming each bank trades all its excess reserves for earning assets, the final disposition of the original reserves of $1 million injected into the banks via the initial deposit of currency is illustrated in Table 15.3. Also illustrated is the expansion of demand deposits in each bank in the chain.

The $1 million of new reserves, initially deposited in Bank A in the form of currency, is now scattered throughout the banking system. Each bank maintains just enough additional reserves to support its increased deposits. Given the reserve requirement of 10 percent, each bank maintains reserves in the amount of one-tenth its increased deposits. Each bank, in the process of ridding itself of excess reserves by adding to its holdings of loans and/or securities, creates new deposits that eventually reside elsewhere in the chain of banks.

Note that the final, total expansion of deposits in the banking system amounts to $10 million, or ten times the initial deposit of $1 million of reserves. This follows from the fact that the **simple deposit expansion multiplier** is the reciprocal of the reserve-requirement percentage:

SIMPLE DEPOSIT EXPANSION MULTIPLIER
The maximum expansion of demand deposits per unit of additional reserves; the reciprocal of the reserve requirement for *DDO*.

$$\text{simple deposit expansion multiplier} = \frac{1}{\%RR_{DDO}} = \frac{1}{10\%} = 10$$

Actually, we may view the expansion of deposits as consisting of two parts: the $1 million deposit directly established by the original deposit of cash and the additional $9 million of *derived deposits* induced by bank lending and investing activities. This critical, induced portion is indicated by the following formula:

$$\text{induced change in deposits} = \text{initial change in excess reserves} \times \text{simple deposit expansion multiplier}$$

$$\text{induced change in deposits} = \$0.9 \text{ million} \times 10$$

$$\text{induced change in deposits} = \$9 \text{ million}$$

FINAL DISPOSITION OF RESERVES AND DEPOSIT CREATION RESULTING FROM $1,000,000 CASH DEPOSIT*		
BANK	**RESERVES***	**DEPOSITS**
A	+ $ 100,000	+ $ 1,000,000
B	+ 90,000	+ 900,000
C	+ 81,000	+ 810,000
D	+ 72,900	+ 729,000
.	.	.
.	.	.
.	.	.
Banking System	+ $1,000,000	+ $10,000,000

*Reserve requirement is assumed to be 10 percent.

TABLE 15.3

In the example, the initial change in excess reserves induced by the $1 million cash deposit into Bank A is $900,000. The simple deposit expansion multiplier, the reciprocal of the reserve-requirement percentage, is ten. Hence, the induced expansion of deposits is $9 million.[9]

The key to understanding the deposit expansion process lies in grasping that although each *individual bank* loses reserves on a dollar-for-dollar basis when it grants loans or purchases securities, these reserves are not lost to the *banking system*—they remain in the banks. Bank A, in lending or investing, loses reserves that flow into Bank B. An *individual bank* may easily rid itself of excess reserves of $1 million by lending or investing $1 million. But the only way the entire *banking system* can rid itself of $1 million of excess reserves is to create enough new deposits so that all excess reserves become required reserves. If the reserve requirement is 20 percent, demand deposits must expand by $5 million before required reserves can rise by $1 million and all excess reserves can be exhausted. If the reserve requirement is 10 percent, excess reserves are exhausted when deposits have expanded by $10 million.

YOUR TURN

SUPPOSE, IN RUMMAGING THROUGH YOUR ATTIC, YOU COME ACROSS AN OLD SHOE BOX CONTAINING $100,000 OF CURRENCY. SUPPOSE THAT THE PERCENTAGE RESERVE REQUIREMENT FOR ALL BANKS IS 20 PERCENT. IF YOU DEPOSIT YOUR NEWLY FOUND TREASURE IN YOUR CHECKING ACCOUNT, CALCULATE:

A. THE MAXIMUM AMOUNT YOUR BANK CAN INCREASE ITS LOANS OR SECURITY HOLD-INGS

B. THE MAXIMUM AMOUNT THE BANKING *SYSTEM* CAN EXPAND DEPOSITS

C. THE INCREASE IN THE NATION'S MONEY SUPPLY AFTER THE BANKING SYSTEM HAS USED UP ALL EXCESS RESERVES CREATED BY YOUR DEPOSIT

REAL-WORLD DEPOSIT MULTIPLIER VERSUS SIMPLE DEPOSIT MULTIPLIER

In the real world, the expansion of deposits in response to new reserves in the banking system is not as large as predicted by the simple deposit expansion multiplier. The simple multiplier overstates the true expansion multiplier. One reason is that banks do not actually attempt to maintain zero excess reserves. For precautionary reasons banks hold some excess reserves and, as the deposit expansion process unfolds, banks deliberately add to their excess reserves. Because they do not really rid themselves of all excess reserves, the banking system does not create as many deposits as the simple multiplier formula predicts. Also, as the expansion of

---

[9]The total change in M-1 induced by the $1 million cash deposit is $9 million. Demand deposits increased by $10 million ($1 million direct and $9 million induced). However, C^P decreased by $1 million when the cash was deposited in the bank. Hence, M-1 ultimately increased by $9 million.

deposits takes place, the public is likely to hold some of this added financial wealth in the form of currency. To the extent that currency is withdrawn from banks during the deposit expansion process, bank reserves decline somewhat. This decline means that fewer deposits can be supported than is the case if the public failed to increase currency holdings during the deposit expansion process (as the simple deposit expansion multiplier assumes).

A LOOK AHEAD

You now have the tools with which to understand how banks create money as a side effect of their efforts to earn profits by purchasing securities and making loans. In Chapter 16 you will learn how the Fed maintains control over these banking activities and, hence, over the nation's supply of money.

Summary

1. Money is commonly defined as the stock of those items widely used to make payment. In the United States the most prevalent measure is M-1, the *transactions* or *narrow* measure of the money supply. M-1 consists of checking accounts in financial institutions plus currency and coins held by individuals and firms.

2. The supply of money is an important concept because its magnitude influences such key macroeconomic variables as GDP, employment, and the level of prices. The Federal Reserve is capable of controlling the money supply within reasonable bounds.

3. Money serves the functions of medium of exchange, unit of account, and store of value.

4. As primitive societies evolved from barter to money economies, early monies were full bodied. This meant that the substance was worth roughly the same amount whether used as a material or as money. Gold coins at the turn of the century were full bodied. Today all of our money is fiduciary or fiat money. The value of this money as a substance is considerably less than its value as money (that is, its value in purchasing goods and services).

5. Today the bulk of our money supply consists of checking accounts in depository institutions or *banks*. The lending and investing activities of these banks create deposits and therefore intimately influence the nation's supply of money.

6. Bank assets include reserves (cash and deposits at the Fed), earning assets (loans and securities), and such other assets as equipment and buildings. Bank liabilities include transactions accounts (demand deposits and other checkable deposits), time deposits (savings accounts, CDs, negotiable CDs), and other liabilities (borrowings and bills payable).

7. Capital accounts are simply a residual item equivalent to total assets minus total liabilities. Capital accounts are the bank owners' equity in the bank. The capital account may be regarded as a cushion that protects the bank from possible insolvency owing to a potential contraction in the value of assets. A bank is technically insolvent at any time

the value of its assets drops below the value of liabilities (that is, when its capital accounts or net worth becomes negative).

8. More banks failed in the past decade than in any period since the Great Depression of the 1930s. The causes may be found in the depressed agriculture, real estate, and energy sectors and in the problem loans to less-developed countries. Banks were forced to write off bad loans, formally acknowledging that they would not be repaid. Hence, the value of bank assets declined without a corresponding decline in bank liabilities.

9. Banks create new money when they grant new loans and purchase additional securities (that is, when they expand their earning assets). Such acquisition of earning assets is constrained by the existence of reserve requirements. Reserve requirements mandate that banks maintain at least some minimum percentage of their transactions-accounts liabilities in the form of reserves. Reserves consist of cash in banks and deposits at the Fed. Since reserves pay no interest, banks have an incentive to maintain few, if any, excess reserves (that is, reserves in excess of required reserves).

10. When new reserves enter the banking system, the amount of demand deposits in the system ultimately expands by a multiple of the new reserves. This happens because, in order for all the new reserves to become required reserves, deposits must expand by a multiple $(1/\%RR_{DDO})$ of the new reserves. Banks have an incentive to keep expanding loans and investments (thus creating deposits) until they use up excess reserves. Given a 10 percent reserve requirement, demand deposits must expand by $50 million in order to exhaust $5 million of new reserves.

Key Terms

money	capital accounts
M-1	reserves
liquidity	required reserves
monetary aggregates	reserve requirement
full-bodied/commodity money	excess reserves
fiat/fiduciary money	bank insolvency
bank balance sheet	fractional reserve banking
bank assets	simple deposit expansion multiplier
bank liabilities	

Study Questions and Problems

1. Distinguish among the terms "money," "income," and "wealth." Is money a form of income? Is money a form of wealth?

2. Explain the contribution to society that money makes by analyzing the major problems that would exist if we were to revert suddenly to a system of barter.

3. What are the advantages and disadvantages of replacing our fiduciary money system with one of full-bodied money?

4. Explain the meaning of a bank's capital accounts. What is meant by bank insolvency? Why have so many banks become insolvent in recent years?

5. Define the following terms: "reserves," "required reserves," "excess reserves." Assuming a 15 percent reserve requirement and a $6 million deposit of coins by Scrooge McDuck into his checking account, calculate the initial change in his bank's:
    a. reserves
    b. required reserves
    c. excess reserves

6. Is money created directly when you
    a. deposit $10,000 cash in your checking account?
    b. borrow $10,000 from your bank?

    Explain each answer.

7. If additional loans and securities owned by banks mean more profits for banks, and if banks create money when they make loans and buy securities, why don't banks engage in much more lending, investing, and money creation than they do?

8. Explain why the U.S. money supply falls when Hometown Bank sells $600,000 in securities to dealers.

9. "Even though any individual bank can lend or invest only the amount of initial excess reserves it possesses, the aggregate banking system can lend or invest a rather large *multiple* of its initial excess reserves." Is this statement true? If so, can you resolve the apparent paradox?

10. Assume the reserve requirement is 25 percent and that $10 million of currency found in a cave is deposited into a Bank A checking account. Compute:
    a. the maximum expansion of loans and securities by Bank A.
    b. the maximum expansion of the amount of demand deposits in the banking system.

YOUR TURN
Answers

A. YOUR BANK IS REQUIRED TO KEEP 20 PERCENT OF YOUR $100,000 DEPOSIT ON HAND IN THE FORM OF RESERVES. IT CAN LEND OUT OR BUY SECURITIES WITH THE REMAINING $80,000.

B. THE BANKING SYSTEM CAN EXPAND DEPOSITS BY A MULTIPLE OF THE INITIAL EXCESS RESERVES OF $80,000 CREATED BY YOUR DEPOSIT. THIS MULTIPLE IS THE RECIPROCAL OF THE RESERVE REQUIREMENT, THAT IS, $1/20\%$, OR 5. HENCE, THE MAXIMUM EXPANSION OF DEPOSITS IS 5 TIMES $80,000 OR $400,000 ON TOP OF THE INITIAL DEPOSIT OF $100,000.

C. TOTAL DEPOSITS INCREASE BY $500,000 IF WE COUNT THE INITIAL DEPOSIT OF $100,000 AS WELL AS THE $400,000 OF INDUCED DEPOSITS RESULTING FROM THE BANKING SYSTEM EXHAUSTING ALL OF THE EXCESS RESERVES THAT ARE CREATED BY YOUR INITIAL DEPOSIT. HOWEVER, CURRENCY HOLDINGS (C^P) DECLINE BY $100,000 WHEN YOU MAKE THE DEPOSIT BECAUSE, EVEN THOUGH IT WAS HIDDEN IN YOUR ATTIC, THE CASH WAS COUNTED (AS C^P) IN THE NATION'S MONEY SUPPLY. ONCE THE CURRENCY IS DEPOSITED INTO THE BANK, IT NO LONGER COUNTS AS C^P. HENCE, *DDO* INCREASES $500,000, C^P DECREASES $100,000 AND THE MONEY SUPPLY (M-1) INCREASES $400,000.

Selected References

Hutchinson, Harry D. *Money, Banking, and the United States Economy*, 7th ed. (Englewood Cliffs, N.J.: Prentice-Hall, 1992). Excellent treatment of commercial banking and money creation.

Mishkin, Frederic. *Money, Banking, and Financial Markets*, 3rd ed. (Boston: Little, Brown & Co., 1992). Discusses bank creation of money.

Pierce, James L. *The Future of Banking* (New Haven: Yale University Press, 1991). A systematic framework for understanding the problems of the banking industry.

Thomas, Lloyd B. *Money, Banking, and Economic Activity*, 3rd ed. (Englewood Cliffs, N.J.: Prentice-Hall, 1986). A clear discussion of the nature and functions of money in Chapters 1 and 2.

THERE HAVE BEEN
THREE GREAT INVENTIONS
SINCE THE BEGINNING
OF TIME: FIRE, THE WHEEL,
AND CENTRAL BANKING.

—WILL ROGERS

The Federal Reserve System and Its Conduct of Monetary Policy

EVERY MAJOR NATION HAS A CENTRAL BANK—AN ORGANIZATION WHOSE CHIEF FUNCTION IS TO SET THE TONE FOR THE NATION'S FINANCIAL POLICIES, INTEREST RATES, AND AVAILABILITY OF MONEY AND CREDIT. THE U.S. CENTRAL BANK IS THE FEDERAL RESERVE SYSTEM, POPULARLY KNOWN AS *THE FED*. THE FED WAS ESTABLISHED WHEN PRESIDENT WOODROW WILSON SIGNED THE FEDERAL RESERVE ACT INTO LAW IN 1913. HOWEVER, CENTRAL BANKS HAVE EXISTED IN OTHER NATIONS FOR HUNDREDS OF YEARS. THE BANK OF ENGLAND, FOR EXAMPLE, WAS ESTABLISHED IN 1694. OTHER PROMINENT CENTRAL BANKS INCLUDE THE BANK OF JAPAN, THE BANQUE DE FRANCE, AND THE DEUTSCHE BUNDESBANK.

THE FEDERAL RESERVE SYSTEM WAS ESTABLISHED AS AN INDEPENDENT AGENCY OF GOVERNMENT IN RESPONSE TO A SERIES OF BANKING PANICS IN THE LATE NINETEENTH AND EARLY TWENTIETH CENTURIES. RECALL FROM CHAPTER 15 THAT BANKS MAINTAIN ON HAND A RATHER SMALL FRACTION OF THEIR ASSETS IN THE FORM OF CASH. SUCH A SYSTEM IS INHERENTLY UNSTABLE IN THE EVENT OF PANIC. IN THE EARLY BANKING PANICS, THE RUSH BY DEPOSITORS TO WITHDRAW CURRENCY FORCED THOUSANDS OF BANKS TO SUSPEND PAYMENTS. WHAT WAS SEVERELY NEEDED WAS AN AGENCY TO PROVIDE LIQUIDITY (THAT IS, CASH) TO THE BANKING SYSTEM IN THE EVENT OF DISTRESS. THIS WAS THE MAJOR MOTIVATING FORCE UNDERLYING THE ESTABLISHMENT OF A CENTRAL BANK IN THIS COUNTRY. AS WE DOCUMENT IN THIS CHAPTER, HOWEVER, THE CONTEMPORARY ROLE OF A CENTRAL BANK GOES FAR BEYOND THIS IMPORTANT ORIGINAL FUNCTION.

OVERVIEW

FEDERAL RESERVE SYSTEM (THE FED)
The central bank of the United States; the organization responsible for conducting monetary policy by influencing the supply of money and credit and the level of interest rates.

Today the **Federal Reserve System** performs several important functions, the most important of which is to conduct monetary policy—a subject that we carefully survey in this chapter.

SUPERVISING AND REGULATING BANKS The Fed is one of three federal agencies that determine regulations governing banks and supervise their operations. As discussed in Chapter 15, the Fed sets reserve requirements for banks and establishes guidelines for banks' capital accounts. The Fed also enforces liquidity standards that require banks to keep at least some minimal portion of their assets above and beyond their required reserves in highly liquid form (that is, in assets easily and quickly convertible to cash). Other agencies participating in bank supervision and regulatory functions are the Comptroller of the Currency, the Federal Deposit Insurance Corporation, and individual state banking agencies.

OPERATING A CHECK-COLLECTION SYSTEM Many out-of-town checks are processed by the Fed. Processing is facilitated by the fact that all banks and thrift institutions maintain deposit accounts at the Fed. The Fed clears checks by making simple bookkeeping entries. Banks in which checks are deposited have their Fed accounts increased (credited); banks on which checks are written have their accounts reduced (debited) by the amount in question.

CENTRAL BANK
Official agency that oversees the banking system and is responsible for the conduct of monetary policy.

ISSUING CURRENCY Today all the paper currency is placed into circulation by the Fed. Look at a $1 bill (or any other denomination bill) and note the inscription "Federal Reserve Note." All coins are issued by the Treasury. The Fed and the Treasury put currency and coins into circulation in response to the amount requested by the public, as manifested by deposits and withdrawals of currency and coins from banks and other financial institutions.

SERVING AS BANKER'S BANK AND FISCAL AGENT FOR THE U.S. TREASURY The Fed provides banking services to private banks and thrift institutions. These private financial institutions maintain accounts at the Fed just as people have checking accounts at private banks. The U.S. Treasury also maintains a checking account at the Fed, conducting enormous transactions through that account each day.

CONDUCTING THE NATION'S MONETARY POLICY This is perhaps the most important and most challenging function of the Fed. In this function the Fed attempts to influence such key variables as GDP growth, the unemployment rate, and the nation's inflation rate by using certain tools of monetary policy.

The rather complex structure of the Federal Reserve System is outlined in Figure 16.1. Major players in this scheme include the Board of Governors, the Federal Open Market Committee, the Federal Reserve Banks, and the member banks.

The U.S. central banking system is unique in that we have twelve separate Federal Reserve Districts, each district having a Federal Reserve Bank. There are also 25 branches associated with these twelve Fed banks. This system was conceived as a political compromise between populists who voiced strong distrust of "big bankers" and concentration of financial power in the hands of a few, and those who favored

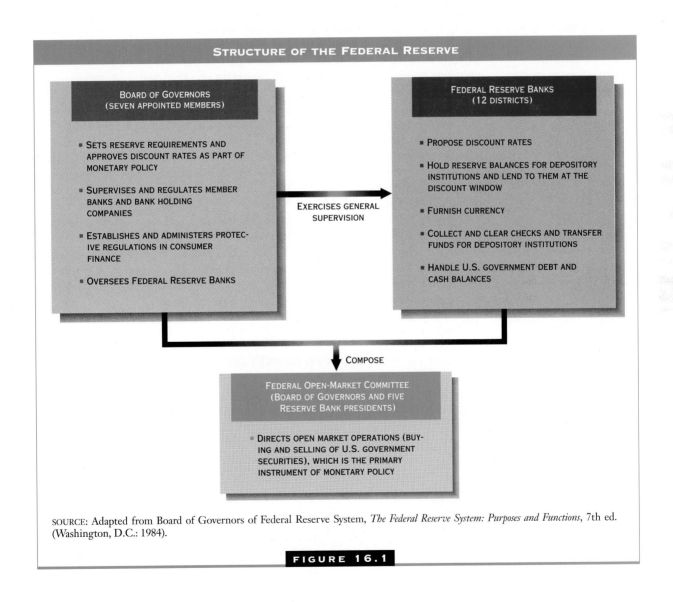

STRUCTURE OF THE FEDERAL RESERVE

BOARD OF GOVERNORS
(SEVEN APPOINTED MEMBERS)

- SETS RESERVE REQUIREMENTS AND APPROVES DISCOUNT RATES AS PART OF MONETARY POLICY
- SUPERVISES AND REGULATES MEMBER BANKS AND BANK HOLDING COMPANIES
- ESTABLISHES AND ADMINISTERS PROTEC-IVE REGULATIONS IN CONSUMER FINANCE
- OVERSEES FEDERAL RESERVE BANKS

EXERCISES GENERAL SUPERVISION

FEDERAL RESERVE BANKS
(12 DISTRICTS)

- PROPOSE DISCOUNT RATES
- HOLD RESERVE BALANCES FOR DEPOSITORY INSTITUTIONS AND LEND TO THEM AT THE DISCOUNT WINDOW
- FURNISH CURRENCY
- COLLECT AND CLEAR CHECKS AND TRANSFER FUNDS FOR DEPOSITORY INSTITUTIONS
- HANDLE U.S. GOVERNMENT DEBT AND CASH BALANCES

COMPOSE

FEDERAL OPEN-MARKET COMMITTEE
(BOARD OF GOVERNORS AND FIVE RESERVE BANK PRESIDENTS)

- DIRECTS OPEN MARKET OPERATIONS (BUY-ING AND SELLING OF U.S. GOVERNMENT SECURITIES), WHICH IS THE PRIMARY INSTRUMENT OF MONETARY POLICY

SOURCE: Adapted from Board of Governors of Federal Reserve System, *The Federal Reserve System: Purposes and Functions*, 7th ed. (Washington, D.C.: 1984).

FIGURE 16.1

the traditional model of a single central bank. The populists favored as many as 50 separate central banks, each with autonomy to conduct policies deemed appropriate for its geographical region. The compromise resulted in twelve regional banks that initially had considerable autonomy over setting policies. However, the decision-making power has since shifted to the central unit—the *Board of Governors* in Washington. Today the twelve regional (district) banks are little more than branches, with the power residing in Washington.

BOARD OF GOVERNORS

BOARD OF GOVERNORS (OF THE FEDERAL RESERVE SYSTEM)
Key seven-person board that dominates the decision-making process in conducting monetary policy.

This seven-person **Board of Governors** is the nucleus of the Federal Reserve System. Each member is appointed by the president of the United States for a 14-year term. The terms are staggered so that one appointment expires every two years. This staggering was arranged to prevent a president from *stacking* the board with individuals sympathetic to the incumbent party's political interests. Normally a president makes two appointments in one term of office and four appointments in a two-term presidency.[1]

One member of the Board of Governors is designated by the president to serve as chairperson for a four-year term. This appointment is renewable within the 14-year term on the Board of Governors. The chairperson of the Board of Governors—through public statements, international diplomacy, and ability to influence views and votes of other board members—holds a position of considerable power. In fact, it is often asserted that the chairperson of the Federal Reserve Board is the second most powerful individual in America!

DISCOUNT RATE
The interest rate charged on loans to financial institutions made by the Federal Reserve.

The Board of Governors dominates the conduct of U.S. monetary policy. It sets the level of reserve requirements and the **discount rate**—the interest rate charged by the Fed on loans it makes to banks and thrift institutions. Also, the Board constitutes the majority of the **Federal Open Market Committee (FOMC)**, which establishes the overall tone of monetary policy and wields the most important instrument of policy—*open market operations*.

FEDERAL OPEN MARKET COMMITTEE (FOMC)
The committee responsible for determining the basic thrust of monetary policy and conducting open market operations; consists of the seven members of the Board of Governors and five of the twelve Federal Reserve Bank presidents.

FEDERAL OPEN MARKET COMMITTEE (FOMC)

The Federal Open Market Committee meets in Washington, D.C., approximately every six weeks to formulate the nation's monetary policy. The FOMC consists of the seven members of the Board of Governors and five of the twelve district Federal

---

[1]Exceptions occur in the case of death or resignation from the board. Such resignations have become more frequent in recent years. When John LaWare was appointed on August 15, 1988, he became the seventh member of the (then) existing board to have been appointed by then-President Ronald Reagan. In his first three years in office (January 1989–January 1992) President George Bush made three appointments.

ALAN GREENSPAN

CHAIRMAN OF THE FEDERAL
RESERVE BOARD OF
GOVERNORS, 1987–

Reserve Bank presidents. Actually, each of the twelve Fed Bank presidents, accompanied by a key research staff member, attends the FOMC meetings and voices opinions on the appropriate thrust of policy. However, only five are permitted to vote on policy decisions. The New York Fed Bank president is a permanent voting member of the FOMC. The remaining eleven presidents serve on an alternating basis, four at a time.

In the FOMC meetings, current trends in inflation, unemployment, exchange rates, and other key data are reviewed. In the light of current and expected developments, members of the FOMC express their opinions concerning implementation of appropriate policies. After extended discussion, and when a near consensus appears imminent, a policy statement known as an *FOMC directive* is written. Members of the FOMC then formally vote on whether to implement the directive. This directive—usually stated in terms of the desired thrust of interest rates, credit availability, and behavior of the monetary aggregates (M-1, M-2, and so forth)—forms the operational basis of policy. That is, the FOMC directive establishes the degree of monetary stimulus or restraint to be implemented.

THE DISTRICT FEDERAL RESERVE BANKS

Nominally, each of the twelve district Federal Reserve Banks is *owned* by the *member banks* within the district. Each member bank buys shares of stock in the district Fed and receives a modest annual dividend on those shares. However, this *ownership* of the Fed by private commercial banks does not carry implications of *control* in any meaningful sense. Indeed, if it did, the potential conflict of interest could easily result in implementation of policies contrary to the public interest.

Each of the twelve district Federal Reserve Banks is governed by a nine-person board of directors. The directors consist of three bankers, three individuals from the nonbank business community, and three individuals from other occupations. The district boards elect the presidents of the individual Federal Reserve Banks. As mentioned, the presidents sit on the important FOMC. One can visualize the potential influence of private bankers on Fed policy through their presence on the board of directors of the Federal Reserve Banks. This potential conflict of interest has resulted in occasional proposals to disenfranchise the Fed Bank presidents from voting privileges on the FOMC. Supporters of the status quo argue that the three-tier background requirement of the composition of the board of directors provides a sufficient safeguard.

Figure 16.2 illustrates the boundaries of the twelve Federal Reserve districts, together with the cities in which the twelve district banks and their branches are located.

MEMBER BANKS

Of the 12,000 commercial banks in the United States, approximately 5,000 are members of the Federal Reserve System. All *national banks*—those chartered by the

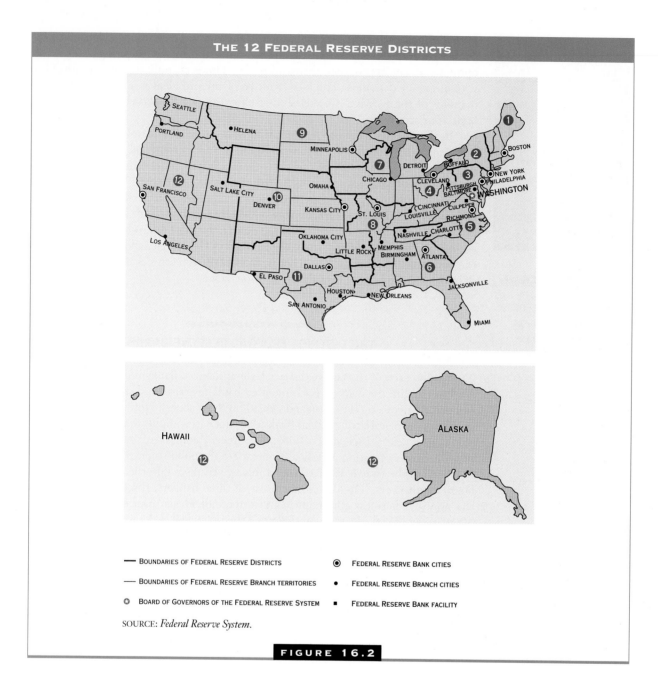

- ─── BOUNDARIES OF FEDERAL RESERVE DISTRICTS
- ─── BOUNDARIES OF FEDERAL RESERVE BRANCH TERRITORIES
- ⊙ BOARD OF GOVERNORS OF THE FEDERAL RESERVE SYSTEM

- ◉ FEDERAL RESERVE BANK CITIES
- ● FEDERAL RESERVE BRANCH CITIES
- ■ FEDERAL RESERVE BANK FACILITY

SOURCE: *Federal Reserve System.*

FIGURE 16.2

U.S. Comptroller of the Currency—are required to be members. Banks chartered by the individual states (*state banks*) are *not* required to be members, and less than 15 percent have chosen to join. The member banks technically own the Fed, as noted, and share certain of the costs and benefits that come with membership. However, both the costs and benefits of membership were reduced significantly in the 1980s when federal legislation subjected all banks (and thrift institutions) to a uniform set of *reserve requirements* and simultaneously gave them all access to borrowing privileges at the Fed.[2]

THE INDEPENDENT STATUS OF THE FED

When the Fed was established, there was a deliberate intent to minimize exposure of the organization to political pressures from both the executive and legislative branches of government. The fear that the conduct of monetary policy might be swayed by politically motivated desires of incumbents is responsible for the long and staggered appointments of members of the Board of Governors, and for prohibition of reappointment to the board for more than one full term. Even more critical in maintaining the political independence of the Fed, in the view of many observers, is the fact that it is set up to be independent of the purse strings of Congress. Unlike other government agencies, the Fed does not receive funding from Congress. By virtue of its huge portfolio of securities, the Fed earns revenues of more than $15 billion annually. Operating expenses in 1992 were less than $2 billion. The Fed simply uses whatever funds it needs to run its operations appropriately and turns the remainder of its revenues over to the U.S. Treasury.

There are pros and cons to the independent status of the Fed. The major advantage is that the Fed can potentially ignore short-term political needs of incumbent politicians seeking reelection. It can afford to take the *long view*, which is essential to prudent economic management and to a stable macroeconomic and financial environment. In particular, the existing arrangement reduces the prospects for a *political business cycle*, in which the economy is alternately subjected to monetary stimulus in the year prior to elections and monetary restraint to control inflation immediately thereafter.

A potential serious disadvantage of the Fed's independence is that monetary policy can sometimes operate at cross purposes with other aspects of economic policy. Coordination of monetary and fiscal policies is essential to a smooth-running economy. Critics of the existing system charge that the Fed is not subject to appropriate constraints. Some suggest that the Fed should be made part of the Treasury Department, thus coming under the purview of the executive branch and the president. The voters would then evaluate the conduct of monetary policy through the political process. In the event of monetary policy negligence, voters could "throw the rascals out." Opponents of this viewpoint believe that monetary policy is too arcane a subject to be comprehended by the electorate and therefore the democratic

---

[2]Recall from Chapter 15 the notion that reserve requirements are essentially a *tax* that forces banks to hold more noninterest-bearing funds than they would otherwise prefer. Prior to the 1980s, nonmember banks were subject to more lenient reserve requirements (set by their state banking authority) than member banks. This was the major cost of membership—forgoing a chance to earn bigger profits. The benefits of membership included access to the Fed's discount window, check-clearing services, other services, and perhaps a slight prestige factor. The Depository Institutions Deregulation and Monetary Control Act of 1980 (DIDMCA) imposed a uniform set of reserve requirements on *all* depository institutions (member and nonmember) and gave borrowing privileges at the Fed to all institutions.

E
X
H
I
B
I
T

16 . 1

A major argument in favor of an independent central bank is that such an arrangement is likely to be more conducive to achieving a relatively stable price level over a period of years. If a central bank is subservient to the executive or legislative branch of government, the conduct of monetary policy may sometimes be dictated by the short-term political needs of incumbent politicians rather than by legitimate long-run objectives such as price level stability. Monetary policy affects output and unemployment more quickly than the inflation rate. Politicians may therefore be motivated to boost economic activity as elections approach, even though such actions may require a post-election recession to bring down the inflation that results from excessive stimulation.

A recent study discovered a significant negative correlation between the degree of independence of central banks around the world and the average magnitude of inflation over a lengthy period. Professor Alberto Alesina of Harvard University ranked the degree of independence of the central banks of industrial nations. He ranked central banks from 1 (least independent) to 4 (most independent). These rankings were derived on the basis of such criteria as the presence of government officials on the board of directors of the central bank; the extent of informal contacts between officials in the executive branch and the central bank; and the formal relationship between the central bank and the government, for example, the extent to which the central bank is required to help finance budget deficits.

We have updated the Alesina study by computing the average inflation rate (consumer price index) during the 1971–1990 period for each of the 17 countries whose central bank is ranked by Alesina. The findings are indicated in Figure 16.3.

Countries with highly independent central banks exhibited relatively low inflation rates from 1971 to 1990. For example, the two countries judged to have the most independent central banks—West Germany and Switzerland—set the world standard for achieving low inflation. Countries with central banks that were ranked among the *least* independent exhibited considerably higher rates of inflation. For example, Spain and Italy exhibited inflation rates three times higher than those of Switzerland and West Germany.

Were the low inflation rates experienced purchased at the cost of relatively high unemployment rates? The answer is generally no. Such low-inflation nations as Japan, Switzerland, and Germany averaged lower unemployment rates over the 20-year period than did high-inflation countries like England and Italy.

The implication: The United States might be well served if Congress doesn't mess with the Fed's independence.

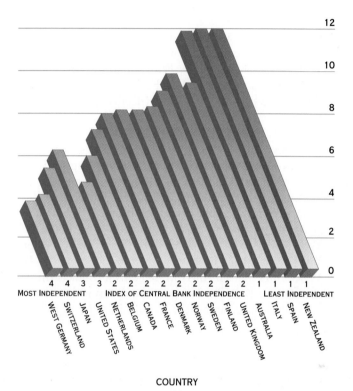

AVERAGE
INFLATION
RATE (%)

| 4 | 4 | 3 | 3 | 2 | 2 | 2 | 2 | 2 | 2 | 2 | 2 | 2 | 1 | 1 | 1 | 1 |

MOST INDEPENDENT   INDEX OF CENTRAL BANK INDEPENDENCE   LEAST INDEPENDENT

WEST GERMANY, SWITZERLAND, JAPAN, UNITED STATES, NETHERLANDS, BELGIUM, CANADA, FRANCE, DENMARK, NORWAY, SWEDEN, FINLAND, UNITED KINGDOM, AUSTRALIA, ITALY, SPAIN, NEW ZEALAND

COUNTRY

SOURCE: Rankings of independence of central banks are taken from Alberto Alesina, "Politics and Business Cycles in Industral Democracies," *Economic Policy*, April 1989, p. 81. Inflation rates are computed from data from Federal Reserve Bank of St. Louis.

FIGURE 16.3

mechanism would fail to function properly. Furthermore, such individuals are fearful of entrusting the monetary reins to politicians. As evidence of the abdication of responsibility by politicians, they point to the huge budget deficits of the past decade.

All this notwithstanding, we must be careful not to overstate the extent of the Fed's independence from the political mechanism. Its independence is fragile—the freedom to conduct short-range monetary policy, not the freedom to pursue actions deemed by objective observers to be contrary to the interests of the nation. The Congress originally created the Federal Reserve System and could potentially modify, emasculate, or even abolish the Fed. The Fed, acutely aware of the fragility of its independence, is eager to preserve it. Toward that end the Fed is in frequent communication with both the White House and Congress in order to assure a smooth coordination between monetary policy and other facets of national economic policy.

BALANCE SHEET OF THE FEDERAL RESERVE SYSTEM

Consider briefly a simplified balance sheet of the Federal Reserve Banks (all twelve District Banks combined). Understanding the Fed's balance sheet is essential to a clear understanding of the Fed's functions, how it finances itself, and how it conducts monetary policy. The Fed's assets and liabilities as of May 29, 1992, are shown in Table 16.1; some lesser details of the balance sheet are intentionally omitted, however, so we are not overwhelmed.

FEDERAL RESERVE ASSETS The Fed's asset holdings include coins, loans to banks and other financial institutions, holdings of U.S. government securities, and such other assets as buildings, furniture, automobiles, and computers. Coins are Treasury-minted metallic currency held at Federal Reserve banks for the purpose of supplying the public's coin needs on request. When individuals and firms need coins, they withdraw them from their accounts in banks and thrift institutions. When these institutions run low, they request a shipment of coins from the Fed and pay for them by having their balances at the Fed marked down (reduced). When the Fed itself runs low on coins it contacts the Treasury, which sends a shipment to the Fed. The Fed pays the Treasury by marking up (increasing) the Treasury's deposit account at the Fed (liability side of Fed's balance sheet).

FEDERAL RESERVE SYSTEM BALANCE SHEET, MAY 29, 1992 ($ BILLIONS)			
ASSETS		**LIABILITIES**	
Coins	$ 0.49	Federal Reserve Notes	$289.68
Loans to financial institutions	0.15	Deposits of financial institutions	23.50
Government securities	276.80	Deposits of U.S. Treasury	5.58
Other assets	54.85	Other liabilities	6.91
		Capital accounts	6.62
Total assets	$332.29	*Total liabilities and capital accounts*	$332.29

SOURCE: *Federal Reserve Bulletin*, August 1992.

TABLE 16.1

DISCOUNTS AND ADVANCES
Loans to banks and other depository institutions by the Federal Reserve.

Loans to financial institutions by the Fed—known in the financial market jargon as **discounts and advances**—are made in response to requests by the banks and other financial institutions. These loan requests are initiated in order to meet unanticipated reserve deficiencies. Suppose a bank, at the end of the day, calculates its reserves to be $18 million and its required reserves to be $18.2 million. It can avoid the potential reserve deficiency by calling the Fed and requesting a short-term loan of $200,000. The change in the Fed's balance sheet associated with this transaction is simply:

FED

ASSETS	LIABILITIES
Loans + $200,000	Deposits of banks + $200,000

For our purposes, the most important Federal Reserve asset is also its largest—holdings of U.S. government securities. The Fed—unlike any individual, firm, or government agency—has *unlimited* capacity to purchase securities at its own discretion. The Fed pays for such purchases by simply marking up (increasing) the deposit account of the seller's bank at the Fed. In other words, *the Fed pays for its security purchases by creating new reserves in the banking system.* Suppose the Fed purchases $750 million of U.S. government bonds from private citizens. The T-account (Fed's balance sheet change) is simply:

FED

ASSETS	LIABILITIES
U.S. government securities + $750 million	Deposits of banks + $750 million

The $750 million of reserves created by the transaction show up on the liability side of the Fed's balance sheet. The Fed does not buy securities for the same reason that private citizens, banks, and others do (that is, to earn interest or profits). The Fed buys (or sells) securities solely with the intent of providing the amount of reserves in the U.S. banking system deemed appropriate to provide the desired financial climate in the nation. However, a pleasant side effect of the Fed's huge security portfolio is that it provides the Fed with handsome annual revenues of $15–$25 billion, depending on the level of interest rates.

FEDERAL RESERVE LIABILITIES Liabilities of the Fed include the paper currency outstanding that it has issued (Federal Reserve Notes); deposits of banks, other financial institutions, and the U.S. Treasury at the Fed; and other liabilities such as bills payable.

All paper currency is presently issued in the form of Federal Reserve Notes (formerly the Treasury issued paper currency as well). Federal Reserve Notes make up the bulk of the C^P portion of the money supply (remember that M-1 = DDO + C^P). Treasury coins constitute only a tiny portion of C^P. The Fed issues new currency passively in response to public demand. As the public demands additional currency from banks, the banks wire the Fed and request currency. The Fed issues new paper currency, sends it to the banks by armored truck, and the liability item *Federal Reserve Notes* increases accordingly.

The other chief liabilities of the Fed are the deposits maintained there by depository institutions (banks and thrift institutions) and the U.S. Treasury. The Fed serves as a bank for private banks and the Treasury in the same sense as private commercial banks serve as banks for individuals and firms. Banks and the Treasury maintain checking accounts at the Fed, and these accounts are actively used to make payments.

The Fed's capital accounts represent *shares* in the Federal Reserve owned by banks, together with certain other accounts. In a real sense, however, the Fed is owned by all the people, not just by the banks.

Tools of Federal Reserve Policy

The ultimate goal of monetary policy is to provide a stable financial environment and to move the economy closer to such macroeconomic objectives as price level stability, low unemployment, and perhaps a stable exchange rate in international markets. To achieve these goals the Fed employs certain instruments or tools of policy. These tools include open market operations, discount rate policy, and changes in reserve requirements. We now sketch the mechanism by which each of these tools influences interest rates, credit availability, and the nation's money supply.

OPEN MARKET OPERATIONS

Whenever the Fed purchases anything from private individuals, firms, or banks, it creates new reserves in the banking system on a dollar-for-dollar basis. To illustrate, assume the Fed purchases a new fleet of cars for official business purposes. Assume the Fed issues a check drawn on itself to General Motors corporation for $900,000. General Motors deposits the check in its commercial bank account in Detroit. The U.S. money supply immediately rises by $900,000. More important, however, is the impact on *reserves*. The Detroit bank sends the check to the Fed, which pays off the bank by marking up its deposit account at the Fed by $900,000. This is a pure bookkeeping entry, with no exchange of physical units of money involved. Because these bank deposit accounts at the Fed count as reserves, total reserves in the banking system have expanded by $900,000.

A similar result would occur if the Fed purchased ballpoint pens, candy bars, common stocks, corporation bonds, or pork-bellies futures. No matter what the Fed buys, it pays for its purchase by creating new reserves (that is, deposits of private banks at the Federal Reserve). For purposes of controlling total reserves in the banking system, the Fed has chosen to focus its activities on the market for U.S. government securities. The market in which existing government securities are

OPEN MARKET OPERATIONS
Buying and selling of U.S. government securities by the Fed with a view toward influencing monetary and credit conditions.

traded is sometimes referred to as the "open market." Hence the term **open market operations**. The government securities market is an extremely active and well-developed financial market. Thousands of banks and thrift institutions are in the market regularly, along with such other institutions as money market mutual funds, pension funds, nonfinancial corporations, and wealthy individuals.

Thirty-eight firms have been authorized by the Federal Reserve to serve as primary dealers in government securities, having special privileges to bid in Treasury auctions and conduct business with the Fed. These dealers hold inventories of government securities and stand ready to buy or sell upon request. Because the government securities market is so highly developed and efficient, it makes sense that the Fed conduct its policy almost exclusively by buying and selling in this market.

Suppose total reserves in the banking system are $40 billion and the Fed desires an expansion to $41 billion in order to increase the availability of money and credit and drive down interest rates. The Fed simply contacts the thirty-eight dealers and arranges to purchase $1 billion from the dealer offering the most competitive quotation (lowest price and highest yield). The Fed issues a check to the dealer for $1 billion, and the relevant T-accounts are as follows:

FED		DEALER'S BANK	
ASSETS	**LIABILITIES**	**ASSETS**	**LIABILITIES**
U.S. securities + $1 billion	Deposit of dealer's bank + $1 billion	Deposits at Fed + $1 billion	*DDO* (dealer) + $1 billion

As soon as the dealer deposits the check, the money supply (M-1) increases by $1 billion. The dealer's bank then forwards the check to the Fed, which pays the dealer's bank by adding $1 billion to the bank's account at the Fed. Bank reserves in the system have thus increased by $1 billion. Because the bulk of these new reserves are *excess reserves*, a multiple expansion of deposits (and money) is touched off as banks expand their holdings of securities and loans.

When the Fed wishes to implement a restrictive monetary policy, it contacts the dealers and arranges to sell securities. The dealers write checks to the Fed. Demand deposits and the money supply fall. The Fed collects on the checks by deducting (reducing) the reserve accounts of the dealers' banks. Hence, bank reserves decline dollar-for-dollar with the magnitude of the Fed's portfolio of securities.

The open market operations tool gives the Federal Reserve fingertip control over aggregate reserves in the banking system.[3] This ability to fine-tune reserves is the chief advantage of this tool, which is the bread-and-butter instrument of Fed

---

[3]A major part of the Fed's open market operations is conducted for *defensive purposes*—to defend bank reserves from undesired short-term changes emanating from a variety of factors. When private citizens withdraw currency from banks to finance vacations, reserves fall (remember that a bank's reserves include cash on hand as well as deposits at the Fed). The Fed purchases securities to replenish the reserves. When the U.S. Treasury writes checks on its Fed account to pay government employees, this action pumps reserves into banks. The Fed sells securities in the open market to offset this factor and to maintain its grip over total reserves. Each year the Fed buys and sells hundreds of billions of dollars worth of government securities to defend total reserves—to maintain the status quo.

policy. Although the Fed can accurately control aggregate bank reserves, its control over the supply of money (M-1, M-2, and so forth) is much less precise. This imprecision is attributable to the fact that the multiplier linking reserves to the money stock fluctuates in a way that is not easily predictable.

YOUR TURN

SUPPOSE THE U.S. ECONOMY IS ON THE VERGE OF EXCESSIVE DEMAND STIMULUS, WITH THE UNEMPLOYMENT RATE AT A TEN-YEAR LOW AND INFLATION BEGINNING TO AC-CELERATE. EXPLAIN IN DETAIL HOW THE FEDERAL RESERVE COULD USE ITS CHIEF POLICY TOOL—OPEN MARKET OPERATIONS—IN AN EFFORT TO SLOW DOWN AGGREGATE SPENDING.

DISCOUNT POLICY

All banks and other depository institutions are granted the privilege of occasionally borrowing at the Federal Reserve for the purpose of covering short-run reserve deficiencies. In financial jargon, this facility is known as the *discount window*. The Federal Reserve establishes the *rules of the game* or criteria for legitimate use of the discount window and sets its interest rate, known as the *discount rate*. Although the Fed changes the discount rate periodically, the criteria for borrowing remain fixed. Financial institutions are permitted to borrow to meet unanticipated reserve deficiencies resulting from unexpected losses of reserves. However, it is not considered legitimate to borrow for *profit*—to turn around and use the proceeds from the discount window to make new loans or to purchase securities.

For analytical purposes we can separate the consequences of a change in the Federal Reserve discount rate into two effects: a mechanical effect and a psychological or announcement effect.

MECHANICAL EFFECT OF DISCOUNT RATE CHANGE Assume the Fed raises its discount rate. All banks currently borrowing at the Fed experience an immediate increase in their cost of funds. Some of these banks decide to pay off their loans from the Fed quickly, and some sell off certain short-term securities to obtain funds to do so. Some banks also raise the loan rates they charge their customers, encouraging them to repay the loans quickly. These actions indicate that interest rates tend to rise. As banks repay the discount window, bank reserves and the money supply tend to decline. Hence, an increase in the Fed's discount rate leads to monetary restriction—higher interest rates and a lower money supply. By the same token, a reduction in the Federal Reserve discount rate tends to lead to monetary expansion and to a decline in interest rates.

The association between the discount rate and other short-term interest rates is fairly strong, as illustrated in Figure 16.4. Part of this strong statistical relationship between the discount rate and other interest rates is attributable to the fact that a change in the discount rate precipitates a sympathetic move in other rates, as just indicated. However, a good part of the association is explained by the fact that the Fed often changes its discount rate to keep it in line with other rates in the economy. Hence, if short-term interest rates rise sharply, the Fed is likely to raise its discount rate.

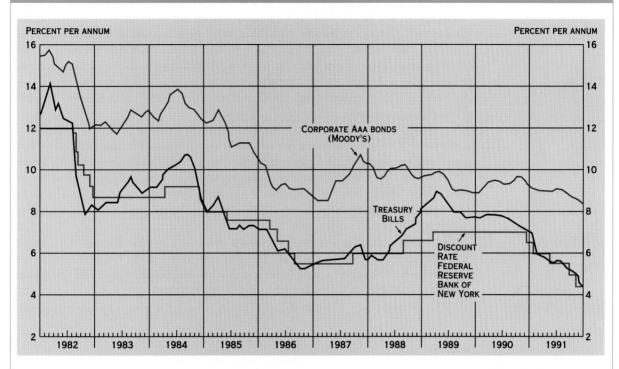

PERCENT PER ANNUM

PERCENT PER ANNUM

CORPORATE AAA BONDS
(MOODY'S)

TREASURY
BILLS

DISCOUNT
RATE
FEDERAL
RESERVE
BANK OF
NEW YORK

1982 1983 1984 1985 1986 1987 1988 1989 1990 1991

The Federal Reserve discount rate is closely correlated with other interest rates in the economy. This is partly because of the influence the discount rate has on other interest rates. Also, it reflects the fact that the Fed tends to change the discount rate to keep it in reasonably close alignment with other interest rates.

SOURCE: Council of Economic Advisors, 1992.

FIGURE 16.4

ANNOUNCEMENT EFFECT OF DISCOUNT RATE CHANGE If a change in the Fed's discount rate catches the financial markets by surprise, a fairly strong *announcement effect* occurs. Suppose the Fed unexpectedly jumps its discount rate from 4 percent to 5 percent. Economic agents are almost sure to interpret this discount-rate hike as a signal that the Fed is moving toward a more restrictive monetary policy. One can expect the Fed to follow up the discount-rate hike with restrictive open market operations—sales of securities by the Fed to drain reserves from the system. Bankers and others are given the signal that interest rates will soon move higher and credit availability will become more restrictive in the weeks ahead.

To prepare for this more stringent financial climate, bank management is likely to become more conservative in its lending and investing policies. Bankers may examine loan applications more carefully and raise loan rates across the board. If the Fed thinks the banks are becoming too lax or accommodative in their lending practices, a good way to rein them in is to post a sharp increase in the discount rate. Because financial markets dislike monetary restriction, the announcement of the discount-rate hike is likely to set off an immediate drop in stock and bond prices.

If the Fed fears an undesired recession is imminent and believes that commercial-bank lending policies should be loosened, it might shock the markets with a sharp drop in the discount rate. Bankers and others would immediately infer that monetary stimulus is on the way. This move would create anticipation of lower interest rates and more liberal provision of reserves by the Fed to the banking system. Hence, bankers are likely to become more accommodative of loan requests. Loan rates and yields in the market are likely to decline. The money supply will increase as banks expand loans. Stock and bond prices may rise when the discount-rate cut is announced.

Frequently, however, a change in the Fed's discount rate has little or no announcement effect because bankers and other financial market participants have seen the discount-rate change coming. As noted, the discount rate is usually kept in fairly close alignment with certain short-term yields, such as those on government securities. When this differential becomes fairly large, it is a pretty good bet that the Fed will restore the normal relationship by changing its discount rate. Most changes in the Fed's discount rate do not catch agents in financial markets by surprise. A recent exception was the sharp reduction in the discount rate in late December 1991, from 4.5 percent to 3.5 percent. While many financial market participants had expected a half-point cut in the discount rate, the full percentage point reduction caught the financial markets by surprise.

CHANGES IN RESERVE REQUIREMENTS

RESERVE REQUIREMENTS
The percentage of deposits that financial institutions are required by the Fed to hold in the form of reserves—cash and deposits at the Fed.

Within broad ranges set by law, the Fed is authorized to change the **reserve requirements** applicable to all banks and thrift institutions. This is potentially an extremely powerful tool of policy, and it is not used frequently. Furthermore, the tool is redundant in the sense that the open market operations tool provides sufficient ammunition for the Fed to achieve its policy objectives. Unlike other tools of policy, a change in reserve requirements does not operate by changing reserves in the banking system. Instead, it alters the multiplier linking reserves to the money supply.

Recall from the analysis in Chapter 15 that the relationship between reserves and aggregate deposits in the banking system is given by the following formula:

$$\text{demand deposits} = \text{reserves} \times \text{deposit multiplier}$$

Whereas open market operations and changes in the discount rate derive their impact principally by altering reserves in the system, a change in reserve requirements leaves reserves unchanged but alters the deposit multiplier linking reserves to deposits. A cut in reserve requirements, by initially freeing up excess reserves and causing an expansion of bank lending and security purchases, increases the deposit multiplier and the supply of money. An increase in reserve requirements forces banks to reduce loans and security holdings, thus reducing deposits and the supply of money. The amount of deposits that can be supported by the existing stock of reserves decreases. In other words, the deposit multiplier decreases when reserve requirements are raised.

We illustrate the potential power of the reserve requirement tool by examining its effect on the aggregate balance sheet of *all* banks. Assume initially the reserve requirement is 10 percent, applicable to *DDO*—demand deposits and other checkable deposits. The initial balance sheet of the aggregate banking system is as follows:

ALL BANKS ($ BILLIONS)

ASSETS		LIABILITIES	
Reserves (cash and deposits at Fed)	$ 40	*DDO*	$400
Loans and securities	$360	Other liabilities and capital	$200
Other assets	$200		

Given the 10 percent reserve requirement, the banking system is fully extended: there are just enough reserves ($40 billion) to support existing deposits ($400 billion). In other words, there are no excess reserves in the aggregate banking system.

Now assume the Fed reduces the reserve requirement for *DDO* to 8 percent. Required reserves in the banking system immediately drop from $40 billion to $32 billion. Actual reserves are unaffected, remaining at $40 billion. The system suddenly finds itself with $8 billion of excess reserves.

Individual banks, in order to increase profits, use their excess reserves to expand loans and security holdings. This, in turn, creates new deposits (and money) in the banking system. This process of deposit expansion continues until the system runs out of excess reserves. Given the 8 percent reserve requirement, excess reserves are exhausted when banks have collectively expanded their loans and investments by $100 billion, driving *DDO* up by $100 billion to a level of $500 billion. At the end of the expansion process the aggregate balance sheet is as follows:

ALL BANKS ($ BILLIONS)

ASSETS		LIABILITIES	
Reserves (cash and deposits at Fed)	$ 40	*DDO*	$500
Loans and securities	$460	Other liabilities and capital	$200
Other assets	$200		

This result can be confirmed by a calculation using our simple deposit formulation:

initial change in excess reserves × deposit multiplier =

ultimate change in deposits

$8 billion × (1/.08) = $100 billion

The reduction in reserve requirements releases $8 billion of excess reserves. The deposit multiplier, which is the reciprocal of the percentage reserve requirement (.08), is now 12.5. We confirm that *DDO* (and M-1) ultimately expands by $100 billion as a result of the reduction in reserve requirements.

As you can see, this tool is quite powerful. In fact, it is too blunt to be used as a day-to-day tool of policy. Instead, the Fed conducts its monetary policy primarily with the other two instruments and leaves reserve requirements unaltered for years at a time. In the severe 1974–1975 recession, however, the Fed reduced reserve requirements three times in an effort to provide a strong dose of monetary stimulus. More recently, in an effort to spur banks into a more aggressive lending policy to combat a sluggish economy, the Fed cut the basic reserve requirement from 12 percent to 10 percent in April 1992.

Intermediate Targets of Monetary Policy

The Fed manipulates its instruments—open market operations, the discount rate, and reserve requirements—in order to influence ultimately the unemployment rate or the rate of inflation. For example, the Fed purchases securities in the open market when it seeks to drive down the unemployment rate. In order for the Fed security purchases to reduce unemployment, they must first expand bank reserves, touch off an expansion of bank lending and investing activities, reduce interest rates and increase the supply of money, and lead to an expansion of aggregate demand for goods and services. All this causes firms to step up production and hire more workers. This chain of influence of Federal Reserve policy is illustrated schematically in Table 16.2.

Although the Fed's ultimate goal is to influence output, employment, and prices, the Fed cannot use these variables to guide its day-to-day and week-to-week decisions. The reason is that moving through the sequence illustrated in Table 16.2 takes time. For example, it may take six to 12 months for Federal Reserve open market security purchases to be reflected in a decline in the nation's unemployment rate. Furthermore, there is no hard-and-fast linkage between Fed security holdings

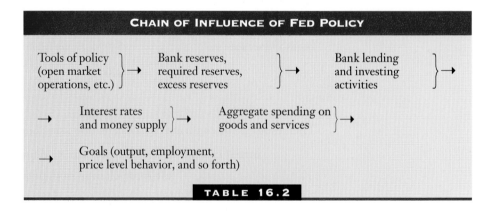

CHAIN OF INFLUENCE OF FED POLICY

Tools of policy (open market operations, etc.) → Bank reserves, required reserves, excess reserves → Bank lending and investing activities →

→ Interest rates and money supply → Aggregate spending on goods and services →

→ Goals (output, employment, price level behavior, and so forth)

TABLE 16.2

and the unemployment rate. This absence of a rigid link is due to the fact that many other factors besides the Fed security portfolio influence reserves, interest rates, the money stock, aggregate demand, and unemployment.

For these reasons the Fed conducts monetary policy by setting shorter-term objectives known as **intermediate targets**. An intermediate target variable is one that is closely connected with the ultimate goal (for example, the unemployment rate) but that the Fed can influence more quickly and accurately than the ultimate goal. Any of the variables of Table 16.2 positioned between the tools of policy and the goals are potential intermediate targets of monetary policy. For example, the Fed might set target levels for M-1 or Treasury bill yields that it feels are consistent with achieving the desired unemployment-rate goal. The Fed then aggressively uses its tools in an effort to hit the intermediate targets. If, as the year progresses, new information becomes available indicating that the initial target magnitude is inconsistent with the goal, the Fed revises the target level. Also, in light of developments in the economy, the Fed may modify its goals and adjust its intermediate target objectives.

INTERMEDIATE TARGET
A variable (such as the money supply or interest rates) the Fed attempts to control in the short run in order to influence such ultimate objectives as unemployment and inflation rates.

CRITERIA FOR AN IDEAL INTERMEDIATE TARGET

To be a viable intermediate target of monetary policy, a variable must have a powerful effect on the economy. It must be strongly linked to aggregate spending and the nation's GDP. If it is not, the Fed is wasting its time in controlling the variable. Further, the Fed must be capable of *dominating*, or at least strongly *influencing*, the behavior of the variable. Finally, a reasonably frequent and accurate measurement of the variable must be possible. If, for example, a variable is measured only once per month, it is not an ideal target; daily or weekly readings more effectively enable the Fed to monitor and control the target variable.

Disagreement exists among professional economists and among individual members of the Federal Open Market Committee regarding which variable is the best monetary policy target. This is primarily attributable to differences of opinion about which monetary variables are most closely linked to aggregate demand and GDP. Some economists, known as *monetarists*, believe that the money supply measures (M-1, M-2, and so on) are the preferred intermediate targets. Such economists believe that the link between the money supply and GDP is very strong. *Keynesian economists* believe that interest rates exert stronger influence on spending decisions and GDP than do M-1 and M-2. Such individuals prefer an interest-rate target. If the goal of policy is to slow down aggregate spending and reduce the inflation rate, monetarists might recommend slowing the annual growth of M-1 from, say, 6 percent to 4 percent. Keynesians might advocate raising short-term interest rates, for example, from 7 percent to 9 percent.

EVOLUTION OF THE FED'S TARGETING POLICY

During World War II and for several years thereafter, the Fed adopted a strategy of strict targeting of interest rates. To help hold down interest expense for the U.S.

Treasury in a period of extremely rapid growth of government debt, the Fed agreed to hold interest rates at very low levels. This agreement between the Treasury and the Fed required that the Fed directly intervene in the open market to prevent long-term bond yields from exceeding 2.5 percent. Treasury bill yields were to be kept at or below three-eighths of 1 percent! This agreement implied that whenever yields threatened to move above these targets, the Fed was obligated to purchase securities aggressively in the open market. This pumped reserves into the banking system, expanded bank lending and investing activities, and held down the level of interest rates. This single-minded effort to prevent interest rates from rising is referred to as *pegging interest rates*.

The Fed policy of rigidly pegging yields—which was conducted from 1942 to 1951—is today regarded by most economists as unwise and counterproductive. The implications of the policy are illustrated in Figure 16.5. In the figure, the supply and demand for loanable funds interact to determine the interest rate. For example,

THE FED'S POLICY OF RIGIDLY PEGGING INTEREST RATES

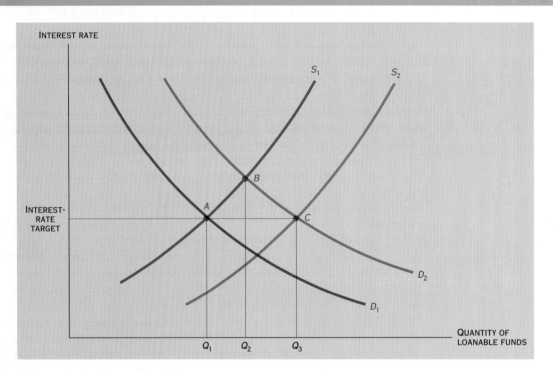

A Federal Reserve target regime of pegging interest rates is a procyclical policy—it destabilizes the economy. When economic activity is expanding, the demand for funds rises, tending to increase interest rates. To prevent this and remain on its interest-rate target, the Fed must increase the supply of funds (and money) at a time when the economy is already gaining momentum. In periods of economic weakness, demand for funds declines, tending to pull down interest rates. To stay on its interest-rate target, the Fed must tighten its policy and reduce the supply of funds available.

FIGURE 16.5

the Fed can influence the supply curve of funds available, shifting it rightward when it purchases securities in the open market. The demand for funds shifts about in response to changes in economic activity and other phenomena. As an example, the demand curve shifts rightward (increases) when GDP rises sharply.

When the demand curve is quite stable, the Fed can peg interest rates without causing great volatility in the quantity of funds and the supply of money. Unfortunately, this is not always the case. When the economy picks up steam, the demand for funds shifts rightward as people seek to borrow more funds and to hold more transactions accounts to finance purchases of the enlarged output. With the economy initially at point A in Figure 16.5—with the interest rate on target—suppose the economy strengthens. Then demand for funds shifts to D_2. To prevent the economy from moving to point B—with interest rates exceeding the target—the Fed must shift the supply curve of funds to S_2. To do this, the Fed purchases securities in the open market, triggering an expansion in bank lending. We end up at point C, with the interest rate remaining on target but the quantity of funds expanding to Q_3.

This illustrates an important principle: A policy of strict interest-rate pegging is a **procyclical policy**—stimulating the economy when it is already strong and restricting the economy when it is weak. This is precisely what happened during World War II. Although the economy was already booming because of sharply escalated military spending, the Fed's successful efforts to hold down interest rates resulted in M-1 growth that averaged more than 20 percent per year from 1942 to 1945. When price controls were lifted in 1945, a period of severe inflation ensued.

After the inflationary implications of the policy became clear, the Fed reached an *accord* with the Treasury in 1951, freeing itself to abandon its strict interest-rate pegging regime. Nevertheless, Fed policy in much of the period since the early 1950s, though not going to the extreme of *pegging* interest rates, may be described as attempting to *smooth* the short-run fluctuations in interest rates, that is, dampen interest-rate fluctuations.

Periods of increasing *demand* for funds have often been accommodated by Fed actions to increase the *supply* of funds in order to resist upward pressure on interest rates. Growth rates of bank reserves and the money supply have frequently been more rapid in periods of strong economic activity than in periods of recession. This was especially true in the 1950s and 1960s.

By the early 1970s, many academic economists and financial market practitioners had become convinced that the growth rate of the money supply was a crucial determinant of economic activity in general and inflation in particular. For the first time in peacetime American history, inflation reached double-digit levels in 1973 and 1974. Largely because of these developments, Congress passed legislation in 1975 requiring the Fed to adopt and publicly announce target ranges each year for intended money growth (M-1, M-2, and so on) for the forthcoming year.

In actuality, the money supply has frequently departed from its specified range. This is partially attributable to the difficulty of controlling the short-run movements in the money supply. But mostly it is because of the fact that, as a particular year unfolds, unforeseen developments occur that convince the Fed that the original target is not appropriate. The experience of 1986 is a good example. As the year unfolded, the economy weakened and inflation came down significantly. In many quarters talk of *deflation* replaced fears of inflation. To avert recession, the Fed

EXHIBIT

16 . 2

How Strictly Should the Fed Adhere to Its Money Growth Targets?

Each year, the Federal Reserve announces its intended target range for the growth rate of certain monetary aggregates for the forthcoming year. The table below indicates these target ranges for M-1, M-2, and M-3 for each year during 1980–1991, together with the actual outcome.

Several points indicated in the table are worthy of note. First, the target ranges for the growth of monetary aggregates have been wide, typically three or four percentage points in latitude. This is intended to provide the Fed considerable discretion as economic conditions change.

Second, after grossly exceeding its M-1 target range in 1985 and 1986, the Fed stopped specifying target ranges for this variable. The link between M-1 and economic activity had become so unstable and unreliable after the early 1980s that the Fed finally refused to be committed to specific M-1 growth rate targets.

Finally, note that the Fed often fails to stay within its monetary growth target range. M-1 growth remained within its specified range in only one of seven years. M-2 and M-3 growth remained within the specified range in seven and eight of

the 12 years, respectively. Critics of the Fed argue that these deviations erode the credibility of the Federal Reserve in the battle against inflation. Supporters argue that the Fed needs considerable discretion to deviate from the target range to compensate for unforeseen disturbances in the economy.

Monetarists and Keynesians disagree about the extent to which the Fed should stick to such targets once they are announced. Monetarists believe that the growth rate of the monetary aggregates is the dominant factor determining the growth rate of nominal GDP, real output, and the price level. In fact, monetarists argue that much of the past instability in economic activity is attributable to instability in the growth of monetary aggregates. In the view of monetarists, the Fed should announce relatively low annual growth rates for the monetary aggregates and adhere rigorously to these targets. Milton Friedman even argues that the Board of Governors should announce such targets each year and be required to offer their resignations in the event the targets are missed.

Keynesians do not believe any rigid link exists between growth of the monetary aggregates and growth of nominal

implemented a stimulative policy of open market security purchases and pushed money supply growth sharply above the target range it had announced at the beginning of the year.

THE MONEY SUPPLY TARGETING EXPERIMENT, 1979–1982

Although the Fed began announcing money growth targets in 1975, it also specified certain interest-rate targets. When the interest-rate and money-growth targets

GDP. They view this link as being highly elastic, changing with interest rates and other economic conditions. Keynesians would allow the Fed maximum leeway to depart from the announced target range. Keynesians praise the Fed's massive acceleration of the growth rate of M-1 above its target range in 1985 and 1986. In the Keynesian view, this aggressive flexibility on the part of the Fed spared the nation an economic contraction in 1986.

FEDERAL RESERVE GROWTH RATE TARGETS FOR MONETARY AGGREGATES AND ACTUAL OUTCOMES, 1980–1991 (PERCENT PER YEAR)						
	M-1		**M-2**		**M-3**	
YEAR	**TARGET**	**OUTCOME**	**TARGET**	**OUTCOME**	**TARGET**	**OUTCOME**
1980	4.0–6.5	7.4	6.0– 9.0	8.9	6.5–9.5	9.5
1981	3.5–6.0	2.5	6.0– 9.0	9.3	6.5–9.5	12.3
1982	2.5–5.5	8.8	6.0– 9.0	9.1	6.5–9.5	9.9
1983	4.0–8.0	10.4	7.0–10.0	12.2	6.5–9.5	9.8
1984	4.0–8.0	5.4	6.0– 9.0	8.0	6.0–9.0	10.7
1985	4.0–7.0	12.0	6.0– 9.0	8.7	6.0–9.5	7.6
1986	3.0–8.0	15.5	6.0– 9.0	9.2	6.0–9.0	9.0
1987	*	6.3	5.5– 8.5	4.3	5.5–8.5	5.8
1988	*	4.2	4.0– 8.0	5.2	4.0–8.0	6.3
1989	*	0.6	3.0– 7.0	4.7	3.5–7.5	3.6
1990	*	4.2	3.0– 7.0	3.9	1.0–5.0	1.8
1991	*	7.8	2.5– 6.5	3.1	1.0–5.0	1.3

SOURCE: Federal Reserve System.

*The Federal Reserve has not specified targets for M-1 growth since 1986.

TABLE 16.3

came into conflict, the Fed typically opted for interest rates, allowing money growth to deviate from the target range. This priority changed in late 1979, when the Fed elevated money growth to its number one priority. This became known as the "monetarist experiment."[4]

In the late 1970s, the U.S. economy experienced a sustained recovery from the 1973–1975 recession. Output expanded rapidly and the inflation rate escalated from less than 6 percent in 1976 to more than 10 percent in 1979. The U.S. dollar fell

---

[4]Many monetarists do not consider this episode a "monetarist experiment" because a tenet of monetarism was violated—that the growth rate of money should be quite modest and stable.

sharply in foreign-exchange markets in 1979 as speculators pointed to rapid U.S. money growth as evidence of our lack of resolve to contain inflation.

In October 1979, only two months after Paul Volcker was appointed chairman of the Fed's Board of Governors, a new policy was announced. Targets would no longer be set for interest rates. Instead, interest rates would be permitted to rise to whatever level was consistent with the Fed's (reduced) money growth targets. No longer would the Fed provide funds to the market through open market security purchases to hold down the upward pressure on interest rates when the demand for funds was rising. The Fed stuck religiously to this policy for almost three years. Interest rates reached unprecedented levels. For example, the prime loan rate went above 20 percent in 1980 and again in 1981.

This *monetarist regime* had both good and bad consequences. On the positive side, inflation was rather quickly brought under control. Also, the long and dramatic foreign-exchange market slide of the dollar was halted and replaced with a five-and-a-half-year rally that continued until 1985. On the negative side, the nation sustained two back-to-back recessions during 1980–1982, separated by the briefest recovery phase on record. The magnitude of financial distress—as indicated by farm foreclosures, business failures, and loan defaults in general—reached extremely high levels. And the unemployment rate was unusually high in the early 1980s.

Partly because of these adverse events of the early 1980s and partly because there was reason to expect that the link between money and economic activity would remain rather uncertain for several years as the American financial system was deregulated, the Fed abandoned strict monetary targeting in August 1982. Since 1986, the Fed has even refused to specify a target range for the growth of M-1, although it continues to set target ranges for M-2 and M-3. Public pressure for the Fed to stick to money growth targets seems to vary with the magnitude of contemporary inflation. In the early 1990s, inflationary pressures have been mild.

Summary

1. A central bank is an agency or organization that establishes the overall financial policy in the nation. This agency influences the nation's interest rates, availability of credit, and supply of money. The American central bank, in existence approximately 80 years, is known as the Federal Reserve System (or the Fed).

2. Functions of the Federal Reserve System—in addition to conducting monetary policy—include supervision and regulation of banks and thrift institutions, issuing paper currency, processing checks, serving as a banker's bank, and serving as a bank for the U.S. Treasury.

3. The Fed is deliberately set up to be independent of both the executive and legislative branches of government. It is unique in that it entails twelve separate banks. At an earlier time these individual Fed banks possessed considerable autonomy. Today, power is centralized in the Board of Governors in Washington, D.C.

4. The Board of Governors consists of a seven-person committee, each member appointed by the president for a fourteen-year term. The terms are staggered so that one appointment expires every two years. One member of the board is designated by the president to serve as chairperson. The board sets reserve requirements, determines the discount rate, and comprises the majority of the voting members of the Federal Open Market Committee (FOMC).

5. The FOMC consists of the seven members of the Board of Governors and the twelve presidents of the individual Federal Reserve Banks. Only five of these presidents are voting members of the FOMC at any given time. The FOMC meets in Washington about eight times annually and also meets on short notice by special telephone hookup. The FOMC decides upon the thrust of monetary policy in the light of contemporary economic developments and policy goals.

6. The chief Federal Reserve assets are its holdings of U.S. government securities and loans to financial institutions. Important liabilities include paper currency it issues (Federal Reserve Notes) and deposits held by banks and thrift institutions at the Fed. The U.S. Treasury also keeps a checking account at the Fed and uses this account to pay for government purchases and for salaries of government employees.

7. Whenever the Fed purchases goods, services, or securities from nongovernment entities, it makes payment by marking up (increasing) some depository institution's deposit account at the Fed (that is, it makes payment by creating new reserves).

8. Reserves play a crucial role in determining the availability of credit and the supply of money in the economy. The Fed has fingertip control over the total amount of reserves in the banking system because it has *total* control over its portfolio of government securities. Each dollar of securities the Fed purchases from private entities creates one dollar of new reserves in the banks. Each dollar of securities the Fed sells extinguishes one dollar of reserves. Changes in aggregate reserves touch off a multiple expansion or contraction of deposits (and money) in the U.S. economy. The size of the actual deposit expansion multiplier varies considerably over time. Therefore, the Fed's control over total deposits and the money supply is much less precise than its control over reserves.

9. To implement an expansionary monetary policy, the Fed may purchase securities in the open market, reduce the discount rate, and reduce the level of reserve requirements. To pursue monetary restriction the Fed may sell securities from its portfolio, raise the discount rate, and raise the reserve requirement.

10. Because it takes considerable time for the Fed's tools to impinge upon the goals of policy and because the relationship between the tools and the goals is rather uncertain, the Fed employs a system of intermediate targets. An intermediate target is a variable that strongly influences aggregate spending and policy goals and that the Fed can control more sensitively in a given week or month than such goals as unemployment or inflation. Prominent candidates for intermediate targets include the level of interest rates and the growth rate of the money supply.

11. Monetarists advocate selection of the money supply as the Fed's intermediate target. Monetarists believe the Fed can accurately control the money supply and that it is closely linked to aggregate spending. Keynesians typically prefer an interest-rate target because they believe expenditures are more closely linked to interest rates than to the money supply.

Key Terms

central bank
Federal Reserve System
    (the Fed)
Board of Governors (of the
    Federal Reserve System)
discount rate
Federal Open Market
    Committee (FOMC)

discounts and advances
open market operations
reserve requirements
intermediate target
procyclical policy

1. What are the chief functions of our central bank, the Federal Reserve System?

2. What features give the Federal Reserve independence from the executive and legislative branches of government? Is this independence desirable? Analyze.

3. What is the largest asset category of the Federal Reserve? Why is this an asset?

4. List the two largest liabilities of the Fed. Explain why these items are liabilities of the Fed.

5. Suppose the Federal Reserve System were to sell off $600,000 worth of used office equipment to private citizens. Explain why both the money supply and bank reserves would decline by $600,000 as a direct result.

6. Explain how the Fed tool of open market operations gives the Fed *fingertip control* over aggregate bank reserves in the United States.

7. Suppose the Fed were to reduce sharply its discount rate from 5 percent to 3 percent, catching the financial community by surprise. Explain the consequences of this measure for:
   a. reserves
   b. the money supply
   c. interest rates

8. Two alternative means of providing stimulus to a depressed economy are for the Fed to purchase securities in the open market and for the Fed to reduce reserve requirements applicable to banks and thrift institutions. Analyze the differences in how these two instruments derive their monetary stimulus.

9. Outline the three monetary policy instruments the Fed can use if its objective is to cool off an economy suffering from excessive demand for goods and services.

10. Define the meaning of an intermediate target of monetary policy. What characteristics should a particular variable possess to be considered a potential intermediate target of monetary policy?

11. Suppose the Fed is rigidly targeting short-term interest rates and the economy unexpectedly slides into a severe recession. What would the Fed be forced to do to remain on its target? How would you characterize this policy? Explain.

12. What is the basis for disagreement between monetarists and Keynesians regarding the appropriate variable for the Fed to select as its intermediate monetary policy target?

YOUR TURN
Answers

TO IMPLEMENT MONETARY RESTRAINT, THE FED WOULD SELL SECURITIES IN THE OPEN MARKET. THE BUYERS OF THESE SECURITIES WOULD PAY THE FED WITH CHECKS WRITTEN ON BANK CHECKING ACCOUNTS IN PRIVATE BANKS. THE FED, IN COLLECTING PAYMENT, DEBITS THE RESERVE ACCOUNTS (DEPOSITS AT THE FED) OF THE BANKS ON WHICH THESE CHECKS ARE WRITTEN. THIS MEANS, FOR EXAMPLE, IF THE FED SELLS $800 MILLION OF GOVERNMENT SECURITIES, AGGREGATE BANK RESERVES DECREASE BY $800 MILLION. THIS DECLINE IN AGGREGATE RESERVES IN THE NATION FORCES BANKS TO REDUCE THEIR LOANS AND/OR SELL OFF SECURITIES. THESE ACTIONS BY BANKS RESULT IN A LOWER U.S. MONEY SUPPLY AND A HIGHER LEVEL OF INTEREST RATES. THIS IS CONSISTENT WITH THE FED'S OBJECTIVE OF RESTRAINING AGGREGATE SPENDING ON GOODS AND SERVICES.

Selected References

Board of Governors of the Federal Reserve System. *Annual Report.* In addition to providing a wealth of statistical information, this annual document overviews financial markets and monetary policy in the most recent year and publishes the Directives of the FOMC meetings during the year.

Board of Governors of the Federal Reserve System. *The Federal Reserve System: Purposes and Functions,* 7th ed. (Washington, D.C.: Board of Governors, 1984). This primer, free from any district Fed bank, surveys the structure and functions of the Fed. See especially Chapters 1, 2, 7.

Friedman, Milton. "The Case for Overhauling the Federal Reserve," *Challenge Magazine,* July/August 1985. Friedman critiques the independent structure of the Federal Reserve.

Thomas, Lloyd B. *Money, Banking, and Economic Activity,* 3rd ed. (Englewood Cliffs, N.J.: Prentice-Hall, 1986). Gives in-depth coverage of Federal Reserve policy.

Wilcox, James A. *Current Readings on Money, Banking, and Financial Markets* (Boston: Little, Brown & Co., published annually). This reader contains a series of timely articles on financial markets, banking, and monetary policy.

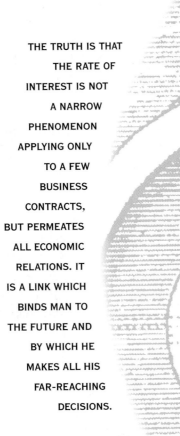

THE TRUTH IS THAT
THE RATE OF
INTEREST IS NOT
A NARROW
PHENOMENON
APPLYING ONLY
TO A FEW
BUSINESS
CONTRACTS,
BUT PERMEATES
ALL ECONOMIC
RELATIONS. IT
IS A LINK WHICH
BINDS MAN TO
THE FUTURE AND
BY WHICH HE
MAKES ALL HIS
FAR-REACHING
DECISIONS.

—IRVING FISHER, 1907

Interest Rates

FEW VARIABLES HAVE A GREATER BEARING ON THE STATE OF YOUR MATERIAL WELL-BEING THAN INTEREST RATES. THE INCOME YOU EARN FROM SAVINGS ACCOUNTS, THE MORTGAGE PAYMENT ON YOUR HOME, YOUR AUTOMOBILE LOAN PAYMENTS, AND CREDIT CARD CHARGES ALL AFFECT YOUR STANDARD OF LIVING. IN A LESS DIRECT SENSE, BY INFLUENCING FOREIGN EXCHANGE RATES, INTEREST RATES EVEN EXERT A MAJOR IMPACT ON THE COST OF IMPORTED VCRS AND AUTOMOBILES AND ON THE COST OF TRIPS TO EUROPE.

FOR MANY BUSINESSES, INTEREST COSTS REPRESENT AN IMPORTANT COMPONENT OF TOTAL COSTS. EXAMPLES INCLUDE AIRLINES (NEW AIRCRAFT ARE PURCHASED WITH BORROWED FUNDS), AGRICULTURE (SPRING PLANTING IS FINANCED WITH BANK LOANS), RETAILING (INVENTORIES ARE FINANCED BY BORROWING), AND CONSTRUCTION (NEW HOMES AND COMMERCIAL BUILDINGS ARE FINANCED THROUGH CONSTRUCTION LOANS). MANY BUSINESSES ARE AFFECTED BY THE INFLUENCE OF INTEREST RATES ON THE DEMAND FOR THEIR PRODUCTS. FOR EXAMPLE, RISING INTEREST RATES REDUCE THE DEMAND FOR NEW HOMES BY RAISING MONTHLY MORTGAGE PAYMENTS FOR PROSPECTIVE BUYERS. RISING INTEREST RATES ALSO REDUCE THE DEMAND FOR NEW CAPITAL GOODS SUCH AS TRACTORS AND FACTORIES AS WELL AS CONSUMER DURABLE GOODS SUCH AS CARS AND TELEVISION SETS. INDUSTRIES NEGATIVELY AFFECTED BY RISING INTEREST RATES ARE KNOWN AS *INTEREST-SENSITIVE INDUSTRIES.*

Interest rates also perform important functions from the perspective of society at large. Interest rates influence decisions to save and to invest in plant and equipment, thereby helping determine the growth in the nation's standard of living over time. Moreover, interest rates (or yields on various assets) provide signals that direct the flow of capital both internationally and domestically to the areas of greatest need. For example, when interest rates (properly adjusted for risk) are higher in the United States than in Japan, funds tend to flow from Japan to the United States, thus helping finance profitable U.S. ventures. When interest rates (adjusted for risk) are higher for farm loans than for business loans, this indicates a greater need for the direction of funds to agriculture. By providing signals that indicate where the usefulness of funds is greatest, interest rates help allocate credit in a socially desirable way.

In Chapter 17 we consider the meaning of interest rates and study the distinction between nominal (actual) and real (inflation-adjusted) interest rates. We develop a simple but useful framework that allows you to understand the forces that cause interest rates to fluctuate considerably over time. For example, the framework enables you to understand why interest rates almost always rise in inflationary times and fall during periods of declining inflation. The analytical framework also gives you an intuitive feel for the role played by other important factors—such as large federal budget deficits, the Federal Reserve System, and the natural influence of the business cycle—in interest-rate determination.

The Meaning of Interest Rates

INTEREST RATE
The price paid per dollar borrowed per year, expressed as a percentage (for example, 8 percent).

The **interest rate** may be defined as the price for the use of credit or the price for the use of loanable funds. It is sometimes referred to as the time value of money. Even in a world of zero inflation, you can expect to receive a positive interest rate for the temporary use of your funds. This is because of the human trait of *time preference*. Both you and the borrower prefer present consumption over future consumption. By using your funds, the borrower can advance consumption from the future to the present; the borrower can enjoy the goods and services *now*. This is worth something, and the borrower is willing to pay (interest) for it. In other words, you charge interest to compensate for postponing your consumption.

In addition, capital is productive. Society can step up its total output and standard of living in the future by abstaining from current consumption—by currently producing more capital goods and fewer consumer goods. The act of saving (refraining from consuming) is the essential economic mechanism for freeing up resources for the production of capital goods. An entrepreneur is willing to pay you a positive interest rate for the use of your funds because capital is productive. The entrepreneur uses your funds to purchase capital goods and earns a positive rate of return by doing so.

Hence, because of time preference and productivity of capital, interest rates would be positive even in a hypothetical world of zero inflation. Such an interest rate would fluctuate over time and normally would be rather low—perhaps in the 2 to 3 percent range. In the real world of positive inflation rates, interest rates are significantly higher and fluctuate in a much broader range.

WHICH INTEREST RATE?

In the U.S. economy there are literally thousands of different interest rates or yields. Securities, loans, savings accounts, and other interest-bearing instruments differ in safety, tax considerations, maturity, marketability, and other characteristics that create a difference in the supply–demand environment and, hence, in the yield. However, all these various interest rates typically move in tandem, driven by similar supply and demand considerations. Many of these yields are essentially determined in auction markets and, like the price of wheat, fluctuate every hour of the trading day. A few, such as the interest rates charged by banks to borrowers, are set at a fixed level for weeks or months at a time and are changed only periodically. Even these interest rates, however, are ultimately governed by underlying market forces. A few of the more visible and commonly quoted interest rates are singled out for special mention.

PRIME LOAN RATE

A benchmark bank loan rate that is widely publicized and used as a standard by which other bank loan rates are set.

PRIME LOAN RATE The **prime loan rate** (the prime) is a benchmark interest rate that major banks use to set their loan rates for various customers. A well-established small business borrowing $40,000 might be charged two percentage points above the prime rate, whereas a middle-income household seeking a home improvement loan may have to pay four percentage points above the prime. The prime rate is sometimes defined as the rate banks charge their biggest and best corporate customers. However, this is not strictly correct, since some large corporations frequently obtain multimillion dollar loans *below* the prime loan rate (that is, at a discount from the prime rate). The prime loan rate is adjusted periodically by banks in response to changes in the cost of funds to banks—that is, to movements in short-term interest rates in the U.S. economy. The behavior of the prime rate in recent years is illustrated in Figure 17.1.

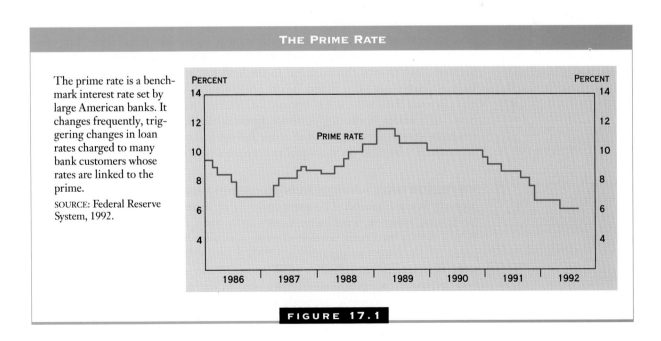

THE PRIME RATE

The prime rate is a benchmark interest rate set by large American banks. It changes frequently, triggering changes in loan rates charged to many bank customers whose rates are linked to the prime.

SOURCE: Federal Reserve System, 1992.

FIGURE 17.1

TREASURY BILL YIELD   This is the interest rate or yield available on short-term U.S. government securities. These securities are perhaps the safest of any in the U.S. economy. This follows from the fact that the U.S. government has constitutional authority to raise taxes or print money, if need be, to honor its obligations. There is virtually no chance that the U.S. government will default on its debt obligations. The **Treasury bill yield** is therefore often quoted as a sort of standard, minimal yield among securities. Recent behavior of the Treasury bill yield is illustrated in Figure 17.2, alongside other yields or interest rates.

DISCOUNT RATE   This is the interest rate charged by the Federal Reserve System to financial institutions that borrow on a very short-term basis from the Fed. This rate typically remains fixed at a given level for several weeks or months before being changed. The Fed periodically adjusts the **discount rate** in order to implement a change in monetary policy or simply to keep its loan rate in line with other changing rates in the economy. The discount rate is frequently lower than many other interest rates and yields in the economy. Its recent pattern is illustrated in Figure 17.2.

FEDERAL FUNDS RATE   This is the interest rate involved in the trading of short-term funds between depository institutions such as commercial banks. Such institutions are required to maintain reserve deposits at the Federal Reserve, as noted in Chapter 15. The dollar amount of required reserves is calculated by multiplying the percentage reserve requirement times the checking account liabilities of the bank or thrift institution. The **federal funds market** is the market in which institutions with excess reserves lend these Federal Reserve deposits to institutions that are deficient, usually on a one-day basis. The **federal funds rate**, a sensitive barometer of conditions in financial markets, is commonly cited in the financial press.

CORPORATE BOND YIELD   Businesses that need funds for such long-term projects as building factories or purchasing capital equipment often issue long-term bonds. A *bond* is a debt instrument or IOU that makes a series of annual interest payments and returns the principal to the lender at maturity, which is often 10 to 30 years after the bond is issued. There are thousands of corporate bonds outstanding. *Corporate bond yields* differ because of differing maturities and because of perceived differences in the financial condition of various corporations. These bond yields are quoted daily in *The Wall Street Journal* and in the financial pages of many newspapers. The yield on high-quality corporate bonds is illustrated in Figure 17.2.

MORTGAGE RATE   A mortgage is a long-term loan secured by a lien on the real property being financed. The great majority of American homes are financed by mortgages, either at fixed-interest rates or at rates that vary over time. During 1975–1985, an increasing portion of mortgages were ARMs—adjustable rate mortgages. The interest rate payable on ARMs is linked by formula to certain interest rates and changes periodically. However, fixed-rate mortgages have returned to favor in recent years as households have been willing to pay a premium to eliminate the risk of higher monthly mortgage payments. The *mortgage rate* is crucial to millions of Americans, because the mortgage payment is typically the dominant expenditure item in the family budget.

TREASURY BILL YIELD
The yield on safe, short-term government securities known as Treasury bills.

DISCOUNT RATE
The interest rate charged by the Fed on loans to banks and other depository institutions.

FEDERAL FUNDS MARKET
Market in which banks trade their excess reserve deposits (at the Fed) on a one-day basis.

FEDERAL FUNDS RATE
The interest rate on loans made among financial institutions in the federal funds market.

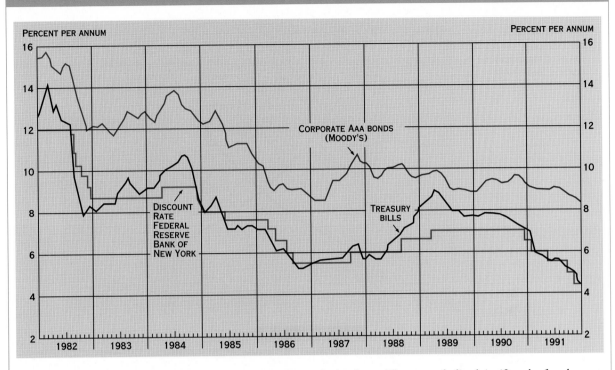

Interest rates fluctuate considerably over time in response to market forces. These rates declined significantly after the early 1980s.

SOURCE: Council of Economic Advisors, 1992.

FIGURE 17.2

The Loanable Funds Model of Interest Rates

As we stated, an interest rate is a price—the price for the use of funds. Interest rates, much like the price of wheat and lemons, are determined in the marketplace by the impersonal forces of supply and demand. The model we use to understand the forces governing interest rates employs the *supply of loanable funds* and the *demand for loanable funds*—hence its name, the **loanable funds model** of interest rates. This model is illustrated in Figure 17.3 (page 430).

LOANABLE FUNDS MODEL
A framework that explains interest rate determination via the supply and demand for loanable funds.

THE SUPPLY OF LOANABLE FUNDS

Lenders are willing to make their funds available at a price—the rate of interest. The supply of loanable funds originates from millions of individual savers, thousands of firms, and other entities that find themselves in a *surplus position*. These surplus units have more funds available than their current expenditures. They serve

The interest rate is determined by the market forces of supply and demand for loanable funds.

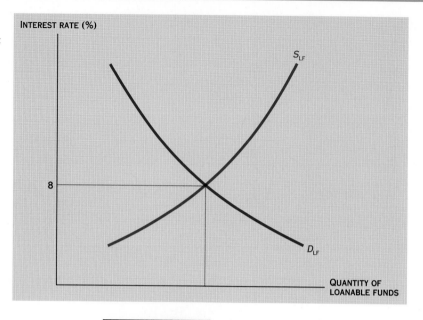

FIGURE 17.3

their own needs, as well as society's, by lending their funds at interest. Note that this supply curve (like most) is upward sloping. This slope indicates that potential lenders must be compensated with a higher interest rate in order to coax from them a larger amount of funds. Potential lenders have other options besides lending. They may purchase real estate, play the stock market, or blow the funds on consumer goods or vacations. The level of the interest rate influences the attractiveness of lending relative to using the funds for these alternative activities. A higher interest rate makes lending more attractive, thus inducing an increase in the quantity of loanable funds supplied in the market.

Of course, a variety of other factors besides the interest rate influences the willingness of potential lenders to supply funds to the market. Attitudes toward thrift, the need to acquire a nest egg to finance retirement or a college education, the perceived risk involved in the loan, tax considerations, and a hundred other factors influence the supply of loanable funds. These factors, as they change over time, shift the entire position of the supply curve of Figure 17.3. For example, the introduction of special tax incentives for establishing *Individual Retirement Accounts* (IRAs) in the 1980s may have stimulated the willingness of Americans to save and thereby may have shifted the supply of loanable funds to the right (remember, this is an *increase* in the supply of loanable funds). Also, because different age groups in society exhibit different saving patterns, a change in the age structure of the population normally shifts the supply curve.[1] The Federal Reserve System, by using its

---

[1] On balance, older people in their retirement years are dissavers. They tend to spend more than current income, drawing on past savings earned during their working years. When the proportion of the population in retirement rises, this tends to pull down the nation's saving rate and shift the supply of loanable funds leftward.

tools of monetary policy discussed in Chapter 16, can also shift the supply curve rightward or leftward. For example, suppose the Fed desires to increase the supply of funds in order to push down interest rates and stimulate economic activity. In this event, the Fed purchases government securities in the open market. This pumps reserves into the banking system and touches off an expansion in bank lending. This action shifts the supply curve of loanable funds rightward.

THE DEMAND FOR LOANABLE FUNDS

The demand for loanable funds originates from *deficit-spending units* in society—individuals, firms, or governments that spend more than current income and finance the difference by borrowing. Typically included in this group are millions of individuals, the majority of business firms, the federal government, and many local units of government.[2] The demand curve for loanable funds is downward sloping because a lower interest rate makes it more attractive (or less painful) to borrow. Potential borrowers often have alternatives to borrowing. Usually, these alternatives involve liquidating other assets such as securities or savings accounts to obtain funds or postponing the purchase of the new house, automobile, or TV. An increase in interest rates makes these alternatives more attractive and eliminates some of the potential borrowers from the loanable funds market.

Like the supply curve, the demand curve for loanable funds is constructed under the assumption that all other factors affecting borrowing except the interest rate are held constant. That is, the demand curve for loanable funds isolates the relationship between the interest rate and the quantity of loanable funds demanded. In reality, as these other factors change over time, the entire position of the demand curve shifts. For example, an increase in federal budget deficits or an increase in the general willingness of Americans to incur debt because of a change in attitudes increases borrowing at each and every rate of interest. This shows up as a rightward shift in the demand for loanable funds (an *increase* in demand). The Tax Reform Act of 1986 eliminated the federal income-tax deductibility of interest expense incurred from consumer borrowing. This act, by making borrowing less attractive, shifted the demand curve leftward (*decrease* in demand).

How Changes in Supply and Demand Affect Interest Rates

The equilibrium rate of interest is determined by the intersection of the supply and demand curves for loanable funds. In Figure 17.3 this intersection occurs at an interest rate of 8 percent. In financial markets, actual interest rates adjust rapidly toward equilibrium. The supply and demand curves for loanable funds shift frequently in response to a multitude of different events, thus bringing about frequent

---

[2]Most households, firms, and units of government simultaneously engage in lending *and* borrowing. If you have a mortgage on your house and a savings account, you are a borrower (through your mortgage) and a lender (through your savings account) simultaneously. In the aggregate, on balance, households are net-surplus units or lenders. Firms and governments on balance are net-deficit-spending units or borrowers.

changes in the interest rates observed. Review Figures 17.1 and 17.2, and note the considerable fluctuation in the level of interest rates over time.

Note that each of the four interest-rate series depicted in Figures 17.1 and 17.2 shows considerable variability over time. Any event that increases the demand for loanable funds (shifts D_{LF} rightward) or reduces the supply of loanable funds (shifts S_{LF} leftward) results in higher interest rates. Any factor that decreases the demand for loanable funds or increases the supply of loanable funds results in lower interest rates. The underlying analysis for interest-rate changes is illustrated in Figure 17.4.

In Figure 17.4(A), suppose we begin initially with S_{LF}^1, D_{LF}^1, *the equilibrium* at A, and an interest rate of 8 percent. When individuals become less thrifty and go on a consumption binge, the supply curve shifts leftward to S_{LF}^2. The new supply–demand intersection occurs at B, and the interest rate rises to 10 percent.

In Figure 17.4(B), suppose we begin initially at C, with a supply and demand for loanable funds of S_{LF}^1 and D_{LF}^1, and an initial interest rate of 8 percent. Suppose further that businesses become more pessimistic about the outlook for future sales and reduce borrowing to finance inventories and expansion of facilities. This shifts down the demand for loanable funds from D_{LF}^1 to D_{LF}^2. As indicated in (B), the intersection of supply and demand moves from C to D, and the interest rate declines to 6 percent.

Another example or two may help reinforce your understanding of the mechanics of interest-rate determination. Suppose that the federal budget deficit rises sharply because of increased government expenditures. Because the government must finance this deficit, the demand curve for loanable funds shifts rightward, pulling up the level of interest rates. Suppose further that the public becomes

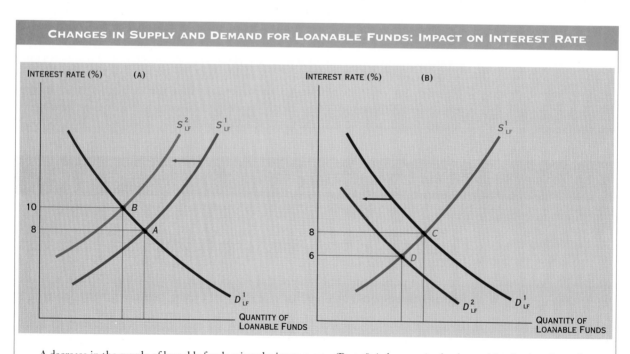

CHANGES IN SUPPLY AND DEMAND FOR LOANABLE FUNDS: IMPACT ON INTEREST RATE

A decrease in the supply of loanable funds raises the interest rate. (Part *A*) A decrease in the demand for funds reduces the interest rate (Part *B*).

FIGURE 17.4

concerned about the financial condition of the Social Security system and increases its propensity to save in order to provide for retirement. This change in behavior shifts the supply curve for funds rightward (increase in supply), resulting in a reduction of interest rates.

YOUR TURN

SUPPOSE XYZ CORPORATION, A HIGHLY RESPECTED AND PREVIOUSLY STABLE MANUFAC- TURING FIRM, STUNS FINANCIAL MARKETS BY ANNOUNCING A HUGE OPERATING LOSS IN THE CURRENT YEAR. ANALYZE, BY USING SUPPLY AND DEMAND ANALYSIS, THE EFFECT OF THIS ANNOUNCEMENT ON THE YIELD OF XYZ CORPORATE BONDS CURRENTLY BEING ISSUED.

The Role of Expected Inflation in Interest-Rate Behavior

The rate of inflation that the public expects to prevail in the future exerts an important effect on the current level of interest rates. The public's expectation of inflation tends to be strongly influenced by recent inflation and by other factors that affect the outlook. When inflation has been high during recent times, people tend to expect it to remain high. As a result, interest rates are usually very high in periods of severe and sustained inflation and relatively low in periods of subdued inflation. Our simple loanable funds model in Figure 17.5 may be used to demonstrate why interest rates tend to vary with the rate of inflation expected to prevail.

IMPACT OF AN INCREASE IN EXPECTED INFLATION ON INTEREST RATES

An increase in the rate of inflation expected by the public reduces the supply of loanable funds, increases the demand, and raises interest rates.

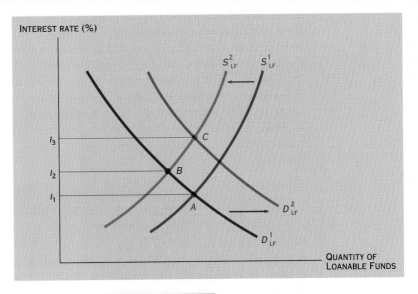

FIGURE 17.5

Suppose initially we are in a period of relatively low inflation. Expected inflation is currently quite low, and the supply and demand curves for loanable funds are represented by S_{LF}^1 and D_{LF}^1. The equilibrium is at A and the interest rate is i_1 (relatively low). Suppose further that some event occurs that causes the public to raise its perception of the inflation rate likely to prevail during the next several years. This event might be a major hike in oil prices, initiation of military hostilities, a large increase in the money supply, a sharp fall in the foreign-exchange market value of the dollar, or any of several other events. Whatever the cause, when expected inflation rises, both the supply and demand for loanable funds shift, bringing about a new and higher level of interest rates.

Because people believe inflation will be higher, they are less willing than before to loan funds at any given interest rate. This follows directly from the fact that the real value of the principal lent out will diminish more rapidly if inflation is severe. Lenders will be repaid in dollars with lower purchasing power. Lending is therefore less profitable. In terms of Figure 17.5, this implies that the supply curve shifts leftward (a *decrease* in supply) to S_{LF}^2. In the figure, this decrease in the supply of funds moves the equilibrium to B and raises the interest rate to i_2.

However, the story is not over. For the same reason that the supply of loanable funds shrinks, the demand for loanable funds increases. Potential borrowers—encouraged by the fact that higher inflation reduces the real burden of their debt (principal incurred)—want to borrow *more* at each and every interest rate. The demand for funds shifts rightward (*increase* in demand) to D_{LF}^2.

The increased demand for funds, in conjunction with the decreased supply, moves the equilibrium to C in Figure 17.5. Hence, the increase in expected inflation pulls up the interest rate from i_1 to i_3.

This tendency of expected inflation—through the forces of the marketplace—to influence interest rates strongly is known as the **Fisher Effect**. Irving Fisher, the great American economist of the early twentieth century, analyzed in depth the role of inflation in financial markets. Fisher hypothesized that the level of interest rates should move approximately on a one-for-one basis with the magnitude of expected inflation. As a result, if correctly anticipated, actual inflation should have a neutral impact on the distribution of wealth between borrowers and lenders. That is, the interest rate should rise just enough to compensate the lender for the damage done to the real value of the principal by inflation. Inflation would be *neutralized* by the increase in interest rates. Fisher's efforts were acknowledged by later students of the subject who dubbed his theory the "Fisher Hypothesis."

Does the principle illustrated in Figure 17.5 really work in practice? Yes, provided that interest rates are allowed to be determined by market forces rather than being set by administrative decree or by regulation or law. We offer two pieces of evidence that the Fisher Effect works in practice: evidence from the U.S. economy and evidence from a cross section of nations.

FISHER EFFECT
The effect that higher expected inflation has in inducing higher interest rates.

U.S. EVIDENCE ON THE FISHER EFFECT

Figure 17.2 and Figure 17.7 (page 437) indicate that U.S. interest rates were very high in 1982 and were considerably lower from 1983 to 1992. The 1978–1982 period was one of rampant inflation and therefore *expected* inflation was also very high. As inflation expectations increased in the late 1970s and early 1980s in response to a dramatic increase in world oil prices and rapidly escalating wage and price level increases, the supply curve of loanable funds shifted leftward, the demand curve shifted rightward, and interest rates escalated dramatically. The Treasury bill yield reached 15 percent in 1981 (Figure 17.7).

As inflation subsided after 1981, the public gradually became convinced that the days of severe inflation were over, at least for a while. Because of this decline in expected inflation, the willingness to lend increased (S_{LF} shifted rightward), the desire to borrow decreased (D_{LF} shifted leftward), and interest rates came down.

Studies indicate that financial markets have become more sensitive to inflation in recent decades. Prior to World War II, interest rates often failed to rise during periods of inflation. After World War II and especially in the late 1960s, expected inflation began to exert a strong influence on the behavior of borrowers and lenders. Following about 15 years of very subdued inflation, prices began to increase rapidly after the mid-1960s. With some time lag, interest rates began to rise in response. The 1965–1982 period, an era of rather volatile inflation behavior, witnessed a high degree of interest-rate responsiveness to the state of expected inflation.

Although interest rates have been responsive to inflation in the past 30 or 40 years, interest rates have not increased sufficiently on average to fully preserve neutrality between debtors and creditors in periods of high inflation. That is, on average, debtors have benefitted during periods of severe inflation.[3]

INTERNATIONAL EVIDENCE ON THE FISHER EFFECT

A second way to conduct a crude test of the Fisher Hypothesis that interest rates are strongly influenced by expected inflation is to compare interest rates in nations experiencing considerably different rates of inflation. If the Fisher Effect is working, countries experiencing high rates of inflation should exhibit high interest rates. Note the evidence in Figure 17.6.

The pattern illustrated in Figure 17.6 is consistent with Fisher's Hypothesis. Nations that have experienced relatively severe inflation (Italy, England) typically have exhibited relatively high interest rates. Such nations as Japan, Switzerland, and Germany—which have been able to keep inflation in check—have experienced relatively low interest rates. This strong positive association between inflation rates and interest rates among a cross section of nations is no coincidence. The forces of supply and demand really work!

Other Factors That Influence Interest Rates

In addition to expected inflation, many other factors influence the level of interest rates by influencing the supply and/or demand for loanable funds. Among the most

---

[3]Much sophisticated research has been conducted on measuring the strength of the Fisher Effect. The consensus in the literature seems to be that although interest rates definitely rise with expected inflation, they do not rise sufficiently to preserve neutrality. Typical estimates for the period since 1960 suggest that changes in interest rates usually amount to 60–80 percent of changes in expected inflation. The Fisher Hypothesis in its strong form suggests that the response should be a full 100 percent.

The level of interest rates is strongly affected by expected inflation. Nations with high inflation tend to have high interest rates. Nations with low inflation typically have low interest rates.

*Inflation rate is average rate of increase in consumer prices from 1975 to 1989. Interest rate is average short-term interest rate on three-month Treasury bills or three-month interbank loans from 1975 to 1989.

SOURCE: Fashioned from data obtained from the Federal Reserve Bank of St. Louis and *The Federal Reserve Bulletin*, 1992.

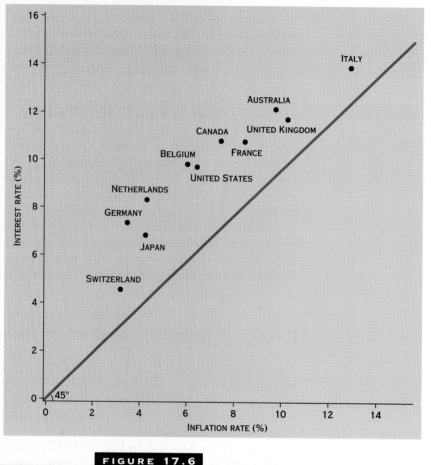

FIGURE 17.6

important factors thought to influence interest rates are the business cycle, the size of the federal budget deficit, and the Federal Reserve System.

THE ROLE OF THE BUSINESS CYCLE

Interest rates typically exhibit a pronounced cyclical pattern, rising during the expansion phase of the business cycle and falling in recessions. This pattern is primarily attributable to the behavior of private credit demands over the course of the business cycle.

In the expansion phase of the business cycle, unemployment declines and job stability and consumer confidence improve. Consumers are more inclined to purchase such *big-ticket* items as cars and stereo equipment, which tend to be financed largely by borrowing. Moreover, businesses become more optimistic as sales and

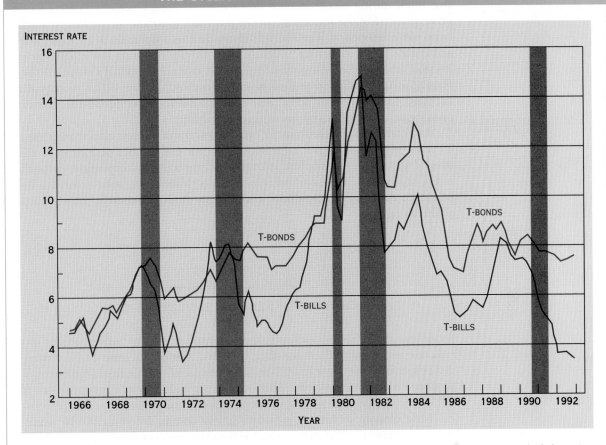

Interest rates fluctuate systematically over the course of the business cycle. They decline during recessions (shaded areas) and increase during the expansion phase of the cycle, especially in the late stages.

*Shaded areas are periods of recession; unshaded areas are periods of cyclical expansion.

SOURCE: Data obtained from the Federal Reserve System, 1992.

FIGURE 17.7

profits rise. These firms expand borrowing to finance purchases of additional plant and equipment and to build up inventories to meet the expected increase in sales. Thus the demand for funds shifts rightward, tending to pull up interest rates.

As the economy gains strength, two other factors often contribute to additional upward pressure on interest rates. The actual inflation rate and therefore expected inflation are usually rising as the economy approaches the peak of the cycle. This increase in expected inflation boosts interest rates through the Fisher Effect. In addition, the Federal Reserve, fearing an acceleration of inflation, is likely to tighten credit and reduce the supply of funds in this phase of the business cycle.

In periods of recession, firms cut output and lay off workers. Unemployment rises and profits fall. Both consumer and business confidence tend to deteriorate in this environment. Demand for funds to finance consumer durable goods and business investment declines. This downward shift in the demand curve for loanable funds during recession pulls down interest rates. Once the Federal Reserve becomes aware of the seriousness of the recession, it is likely to implement a stimulative monetary policy. The Fed is likely to purchase securities in the open market and reduce its discount rate. These actions by the Fed shift the supply curve of loanable funds rightward, giving the interest rate an additional downward thrust. Finally, as the trough of the recession approaches, the rate of inflation typically declines. The decline in actual and expected inflation reinforces the downward pressure on interest rates by way of the Fisher Effect.

In Figure 17.7 we illustrate the cyclical pattern of interest rates during the past 25 years. Note that interest rates declined in each of the five periods of recession (shaded areas). Interest rates tended to rise during economic expansion, particularly in the later phases of the cyclical upswing. It is clear that in order to forecast interest rates accurately, one must be able to forecast the business cycle. This has proven a difficult task.

THE ROLE OF FEDERAL BUDGET DEFICITS

Intuitively it may seem apparent that an increase in federal budget deficits should raise interest rates. Indeed, we have indicated that an increase in borrowing by deficit spenders directly shifts the demand curve for loanable funds rightward. This tends to raise the interest rate. Moreover, larger budget deficits might arouse fears of higher inflation, thus pulling up interest rates through the Fisher Effect.

Most economists agree that budget deficits do raise interest rates. However, we must point out that there is disagreement in the profession on this issue. There is surprisingly little empirical evidence, at least prior to the 1980s, that past U.S. budget deficits increased interest rates. Economists who do not believe that budget deficits significantly raise interest rates have advanced two reasons to support their conclusion. One concerns the worldwide scope of the *capital market* or market for loanable funds. The other concerns the alleged tendency of larger budget deficits to stimulate the propensity of individuals to save.

The first reason for doubting that U.S. budget deficits substantially affect interest rates is that the size of these deficits, though enormous in an absolute sense, is rather small relative to the total pool of available funds in the world. Financial markets in various nations have become increasingly integrated in recent decades so that these markets are now almost worldwide in scope. As interest rates in the United States begin to rise in response to large federal borrowing demands, the quantity of funds available to meet the demands increases sharply as institutions in foreign nations lend their money in the United States. This sensitive supply response tends to limit the upward pressure on American interest rates.[4]

---

[4]Note that this is really a hypothesis about the elasticity or responsiveness of the supply curve for loanable funds. Specifically, the hypothesis is that this supply curve is very flat—the quantity of funds supplied is highly responsive to the interest rate. A small increase in the U.S. interest rate allegedly induces a large increase in the quantity of funds supplied since funds are drawn to the United States from all around the world. If this is true, larger deficits would have a modest (though positive) effect on interest rates.

The second reason that some economists deny that large deficits affect U.S. interest rates involves the alleged relationship between larger deficits and saving behavior of individuals. Suppose the public is *future oriented* and perceives that larger budget deficits today imply higher taxes or a lower standard of living in the future. This perception may be caused by the view that taxes will have to be raised later to pay interest on the enlarged debt or by the view that the deficits hinder the future prosperity of the economy. To protect themselves (or their heirs) from the future belt-tightening, the public allegedly steps up its current saving rate. If so, the supply curve of loanable funds shifts rightward, perhaps sufficiently to neutralize the direct effect on interest rates of the government's increase in demand for funds with which to finance the deficit. Interest rates might not be affected by deficits in this analysis.

Supporters of this second position point out that it is consistent with rational behavior. That is, since larger deficits today imply greater future interest expenditures by government to finance the larger debt and therefore higher future tax rates, it makes sense for perceptive individuals to increase their saving rate today. Critics of this view regard it as a bit unrealistic. Have any of your friends raised their saving rate because of the increased deficits of the past decade? Those who are dubious of this position point out that almost all measures of private saving rates have *declined* in the past ten years—the same period in which the large federal deficits emerged in the U.S. economy. Professional financial market participants believe almost uniformly that larger actual deficits or expected future deficits significantly raise interest rates. Academic economists are divided in their opinion. Ultimately the issue will be resolved by empirical investigation. As of the early 1990s, the empirical evidence on the role of deficits is mixed.[5]

THE ROLE OF THE FEDERAL RESERVE SYSTEM

The Federal Reserve System is capable of exerting a major impact upon the level of interest rates by influencing the supply of loanable funds available in the market. When the Fed desires lower interest rates and easier credit conditions, it pursues actions to provide an increase in the funds available in financial institutions (primarily banks) for loans to the public. The supply curve for loanable funds shifts rightward and interest rates decline. When the Fed is in a restrictive mood, it takes actions which reduce the amount of funds that financial institutions have available to loan out. The supply curve of loanable funds decreases (shifts leftward), and interest rates rise.

During the 1940s, the Fed overwhelmed the other forces influencing interest rates and forced these rates down to abnormally low levels in order to assist the Treasury in financing the war. However, such a herculean effort by the Fed to dictate interest rates may have adverse side effects on the economy and may not be in

[5]Paul Evans, in a series of papers, has advanced the view that larger deficits and expected future deficits are neutralized by an induced increase in saving, and therefore do not affect interest rates. See, for example, "Do Large Deficits Produce Higher Interest Rates?" *American Economic Review*, March 1985, pp. 68–87. For a contrary view, see Lloyd B. Thomas and Ali Abderrezak, "Anticipated Future Budget Deficits and the Term Structure of Interest Rates," *Southern Economic Journal*, July 1988, pp. 150–161.

the nation's interest. For example, if the Fed attempts to hold down interest rates during a period of rising inflation, the Fed is likely to exacerbate the inflation.

The Federal Reserve has the tools with which to bring about major changes in interest rates if it desires to do so. However, there is sometimes a tendency among the lay public and the financial press to attribute to the Fed changes in interest rates that are actually caused principally by such other factors as changes in inflationary expectations and changes in cyclical conditions in the economy. Note the dramatic upswing in interest rates from 1977 to 1981 (Figure 17.7). This episode may best be described *not* as resulting from aggressive efforts by the Fed to reduce the supply of funds and push up interest rates but rather by the Fed passively allowing interest rates to rise in response to escalating inflationary expectations. The Fed could perhaps have prevented this increase in interest rates by aggressively pumping funds into banks. The Fed chose not to do so because it wanted to choke off the inflation that had been escalating in the 1970s.

By the same token, the major decline in interest rates after 1981 was not principally caused by more stimulative policies implemented by the Federal Reserve. Rather, this decline in interest rates is best viewed as the response of financial markets first to the severe recession of 1981–1982 and somewhat later to the gradual decline in expected inflation. Certainly the Fed was quite willing to see interest rates come down after the early 1980s. But it would *not* be correct to suppose that the big drop in yields during these years was *caused* by the Fed aggressively increasing the supply of funds available.

When the economic environment is one of substantial inflation and the public is highly sensitized to the inflation, the Fed may find it difficult or impossible to use stimulative monetary actions to bring down long-term interest rates such as those on mortgages and bonds. Suppose that the Fed aggressively pumps funds into the banks in a period in which inflation is relatively high. If the public is convinced that rapid expansion of the supply of loanable funds and the supply of money will result in higher inflation, the announcement that the Fed is stepping up the growth of loanable funds may itself alter the expected rate of inflation. In that event, the announcement of the move to a more stimulative policy by the Fed may, through the Fisher Effect, actually *boost* long-term interest rates. Thus, the role of the Fed in interest-rate behavior is a complex one in an era in which people are highly sensitized to inflation.

Real versus Nominal Interest Rates

REAL INTEREST RATE
The nominal (actual) interest rate minus the expected rate of inflation; the real cost to the borrower (and return to the lender) in terms of goods and services.

In economic analysis it is crucial to distinguish between the *real* interest rate and the *nominal* (actual) interest rate. The **real interest rate** is the rate that would prevail in a hypothetical world of zero permanent inflation. But the world we live in is a world of varying and almost always positive rates of inflation. To calculate the real interest rate, we subtract the expected rate of inflation from the *nominal (actual)* interest rate. If a student loan is granted at 8 percent and expected inflation is 5 percent per annum, the real interest rate on the loan is 3 percent. If the 30-year mortgage on your home is at 10 percent interest and you expect inflation to average 6 percent per year during the next 30 years, the real mortgage rate is 4 percent. By engaging in this transaction, the lender earns and the borrower pays 4 percent per year after allowing for inflation.

The real interest rate is difficult to calculate in many instances because of the problem in estimating the expected rate of inflation. Most of us are fairly confident that inflation in the next six months or year will not differ radically from its recent behavior. In addition, there are survey opinion polls of professional economists and the general public regarding short-run inflation expectations. Therefore, reliable estimates of short-term real interest rates can be calculated. However, no one can feel confident about forecasting the average inflation rate over a long period such as a decade.[6] There are simply too many factors that can influence inflation in future years that cannot be anticipated. Such factors include future oil prices, agricultural conditions, military and political developments, economic policies, and many others. Therefore, long-term real interest rates are inherently difficult to measure.

The fundamental forces underlying the level of the real rate of interest are the thriftiness of the populace and the productivity of capital, although other factors temporarily influence real rates. When people become more thrifty, the supply of loanable funds increases and the real interest rate falls. When the rate of return expected on real economic investment (productivity of capital) rises, the demand for funds rises and the real rate of interest rises. It is the level of the *real* interest rate, not the actual or nominal interest rate, that governs most important economic decisions. The flow of financial capital (loanable funds) among nations, the decision to invest in new plant and equipment, and the redistributive effects of inflation between borrowers and lenders are strongly influenced by the real rate of interest (see Exhibit 17.1).

As an indication of the general behavior of real interest rates in the past 25 years, we have computed the real prime-loan rate and the real yield on U.S. Treasury bills. These real interest rates are illustrated in Figure 17.8, which indicates that real yields were generally positive (although low) until around 1973, swung into very low or negative territory during the remainder of the 1970s, and moved up sharply to very high levels in the 1980s, particularly in the 1980–1985 period. These high real interest rates had important consequences for the U.S. economy. Lenders benefitted handsomely from the situation, whereas debtors were burned, sometimes to the point of insolvency. A massive flow of foreign funds poured into the U.S. financial markets, attracted by the high real yields on bonds and other assets. The great demand for the U.S. dollar (to finance acquisition of these assets) drove up the foreign-exchange market value of the dollar to the point that many American industries became subject to intense foreign competition.[7] A rapidly escalating U.S. international trade deficit was experienced in the 1982–1987 period,

---

[6]Inflation during the 1970s was much higher than anyone would have predicted at the beginning of the decade. And the Federal Reserve's policy of disinflation implemented in 1980 brought down the inflation rate in the early 1980s much faster than even the most ardent supporters of the policy had hoped or predicted.

[7]Suppose the dollar rises from 120 yen to 150 yen because of the increased demand for high-yielding American financial assets. The cost of the dollar, and therefore the cost of U.S. goods and services, rises 25 percent as viewed by the Japanese. Correspondingly, the cost to Americans of the yen and Japanese products falls sharply. This places the American manufacturing sector under increased competitive pressures.

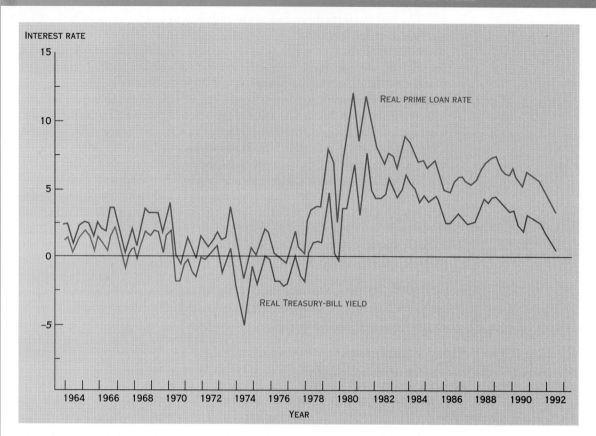

Real (inflation-adjusted) interest rates declined (and often became negative) in the 1970s but then increased to unusually high levels in the early 1980s. In recent years, real interest rates have declined significantly.

*Real rates are calculated using Federal Reserve data for prime loan rate and Treasury bill yield, and assuming expected inflation for each period is equal to the actual inflation rate in the most recent six months.

FIGURE 17.8

partly in response to high American real interest rates and associated inflows of loanable funds from abroad.

In the sluggish U.S. economy of the early 1990s, the real interest rate declined significantly. In fact, the real Treasury bill yield approached zero in the autumn of 1992. This decline in real rates eased the burden of debt. By the same token, millions of American households watched their interest income dwindle as short-term interest rates plunged to levels not witnessed for 30 years. The U.S. dollar depreciated to new lows against several foreign currencies, providing a competitive advantage to U.S. export industries.

EXPLANATION FOR THE HIGH REAL INTEREST RATES IN THE 1980S

There are several alternative hypotheses seeking to explain the remarkably high real interest rates that prevailed in the 1980s. Some analysts emphasize the

The extent to which the Fisher Effect is operable—the extent to which interest rates adjust to the ongoing rate of inflation—has powerful implications for the distribution of income in the nation and the well-being of various sectors of the economy. Consider the following three scenarios involving the relationship between inflation and the interest rate.

In Scenario A, interest rates are not sufficiently high to compensate for inflation. The real interest rate is *negative*. Debtors benefit at the expense of lenders, as inflation rapidly reduces the real value of the principal and the interest rate fails to compensate for this. Debtor groups in society generally include the government, business firms, farmers, and middle-aged people. Lenders generally include the household sector and elderly individuals. Many individuals, however, are net debtors. In fact, the classic beneficiary of Scenario A is the family of the 40-year-old breadwinner with a home financed by a $100,000 mortgage. The value of the home rises each year by an amount in excess of the interest payable on the mortgage (which is tax deductible). The real net worth of the family rises at the expense of the individuals (lenders) who placed funds in the savings institution that granted the mortgage. This scenario occurred in the 1970s as the U.S. inflation rate kept ratcheting higher, and as interest-rate ceilings and the Federal Reserve tended to inhibit rising interest rates.

Scenario B is the normal state of affairs. It occurs when financial markets are free, expectations are accurately formed, and the Fisher Effect is fully working. The interest rate is roughly three percentage points above the inflation rate, so the real interest rate is positive but rather low. There are no major redistributive effects between borrowers and lenders in this scenario in which the Fisher Effect is working to perfection.

In Scenario C, the interest rate is exceptionally high in relation to the ongoing inflation rate. Real interest rates are very high. This situation occurred in the 1980–1985 period (see Figure 17.8). It also occurred in the 1930s, when interest rates were fairly low but the inflation rate was *negative*. This scenario reverses the consequences of Scenario A. Income is redistributed from debtors to lenders. The government loses and bondholders benefit. The business sector in general comes under pressure, as this sector is a net debtor on balance. Many small businesses fail. Farm foreclosures soar as the burdens of debt become overwhelming. Bank failures increase as a rising percentage of bank loans become *bad loans*. Elderly individuals as a group fare well in this scenario, as do others who lend money.

If Scenario B always prevailed, the financial markets would neutralize many damaging consequences of changes in the price level. Unfortunately, this is not always the case. The economy often takes the shape of Scenario A or C.

	SCENARIO A(%)	SCENARIO B(%)	SCENARIO C(%)
Interest rate	10	8	12
Inflation rate	13	5	4
Real interest rate	−3	+3	+8

EXHIBIT

17.1

improved U.S. business climate resulting from major tax reductions for the corporate sector in the early 1980s, the general movement toward dismantling government regulations, and perhaps a perceived probusiness attitude on the part of the Reagan and Bush Administrations. Such developments tend to increase the returns expected from investment in plant and equipment—that is, increase the expected productivity of capital. This stimulates the demand for loanable funds and raises real interest rates. The strong stock-market performance of the 1980s is consistent with this view.

A less assuring explanation for the high real interest rates of the 1980s is that huge actual and prospective federal budget deficits forced up actual and real rates to abnormal levels.[8] Another explanation, applicable only to the *early* 1980s, is that the Federal Reserve System overreacted to the severe inflation of the 1979–1981 period and pursued a highly restrictive monetary policy. This policy allegedly maintained actual and real interest rates at abnormally high levels in the early 1980s. It seems plausible that more than one factor contributed to the unreal level of real interest rates in the 1980s.

An interesting alternative explanation is that, on deeper analysis, real interest rates actually were not high at all. If one allows for the fact that interest paid is often tax deductible and interest earned is taxable, interest rates in the 1980s do not seem unreasonable. Suppose you pay 10 percent for your bank loan while inflation is running at 4 percent and your combined federal-state-local income-tax bracket is 40 percent. If we ignore taxes, we compute the real interest rate as 6 percent—historically a very high rate. However, your *after-tax* real rate is only 2 percent.[9] If one adds tax considerations to the analysis, real interest rates in the 1980s seem reasonable. The actual mystery in this view is not why real rates were so high in the 1980s, but rather why they were so *low* in earlier years and in the early 1990s.

Summary

1. An interest rate is the price of loanable funds. There are many different interest rates or yields in the economy because of differences in the characteristics of various types of loans.

2. Interest rates are determined in competitive markets by the impersonal forces of supply and demand. An increase in demand for or a decrease in supply of loanable funds raises

---

[8]Some seat-of-the-pants support for this view comes from the observation that interest rates fell sharply on the announcement in late 1985 that the Gramm-Rudman-Hollings Act (deficit-reduction legislation) had become law.

[9]Because you are in a 40 percent income-tax bracket and because interest expense is tax deductible, you are paying only 60 percent of the interest. The government pays the rest. Hence, your after-tax *nominal* interest rate is 6 percent (.60 × 10 percent). Deducting the 4 percent inflation from this figure, we obtain an after-tax *real* interest rate of 2 percent.

interest rates. An increase in supply of or a decrease in demand for loanable funds reduces interest rates. The demand and supply curves for loanable funds are continually shifting about, causing frequent changes in interest rates.

3. When actual and expected inflation escalate, the supply of loanable funds decreases and the demand increases, thus raising interest rates. Hence, when inflation is rampant, interest rates are typically high. This compensates lenders for depreciation of the real principal because of inflation. The Fisher Effect in its strong form asserts that interest rates should rise sufficiently during inflation to preserve neutrality between lenders and borrowers. However, studies indicate that in most episodes of severe inflation borrowers benefit because interest rates fail to increase sufficiently to protect lenders fully.

4. Interest rates exhibit a strong procyclical tendency, rising in business expansions to a peak in the boom phase of the cycle and declining in recessions. This procyclical behavior of interest rates can be attributed primarily to fluctuations in the demand for loanable funds by households and businesses over the course of the business cycle.

5. The Federal Reserve System, by manipulating the supply of loanable funds, is capable of exerting a major impact on the level of interest rates. However, most major swings in interest rates historically were not initiated by deliberate Fed actions, but were attributable to cyclical factors and major swings in expected inflation.

6. Large federal budget deficits increase the demand for loanable funds and therefore raise interest rates unless the supply of loanable funds also increases. Some economists believe that the general populace responds to larger budget deficits by raising their current saving rate, thereby shifting the supply of loanable funds rightward and neutralizing the impact of the deficits on interest rates. Also, world financial markets have become more integrated in recent years. As U.S. interest rates begin to rise, foreign funds are attracted to the United States. Since the size of U.S. budget deficits is rather small relative to this worldwide pool of funds, the impact of deficits on U.S. interest rates may not be as large as is commonly believed.

7. Because many important economic decisions are governed by *real* interest rates, it is important to distinguish between *real* and *nominal* (actual) interest rates. The real interest rate is the rate computed after deducting the expected inflation rate from the actual interest rate. Real interest rates swung from very low levels in the 1970s to high levels in the 1980s. This major swing may be attributable to an increase in the expected productivity of capital, increased federal budget deficits, or more restrictive Federal Reserve policy. Alternatively, one could argue that real interest rates were not very high in the 1980s considering the income-tax treatment of interest income and interest expense. In this view, the real question is why real rates were so low prior to the 1980s and in the 1990s.

Key Terms

interest rate
prime loan rate
Treasury bill yield
discount rate
federal funds market

federal funds rate
loanable funds model
Fisher Effect
real interest rate

Study Questions and Problems

1. Assume interest rates rise sharply next year. What impact would this have on you personally? What are the implications for the U.S. economy?

2. Distinguish between the real interest rate and the nominal interest rate. How do the concepts of time preference and productivity of capital enter into the determination of the real interest rate?

3. Note from Figure 17.2 that the Treasury bill yield is typically lower than the corporate bond yield. Can you explain why?

4. Explain why the supply curve of Figure 17.3 is upward sloping. What factors shift the supply curve leftward? If Americans change from an *enjoy-now* to a *plan-for-the-future* society, what happens to the supply curve? To interest rates?

5. Explain why the demand curve of Figure 17.3 is downward sloping. List three factors that would shift this demand curve rightward.

6. Explain the reasoning that lies behind the Fisher Effect. Using the tools of supply and demand, explain how a sharp decline in expected inflation would bring about a decline in interest rates.

7. Assume the economy slides into a period of severe recession. Explain by using supply-and-demand analysis what would happen to interest rates.

8. Why do you suppose interest rates were so high in 1981? Why did they drop so much from 1982 to 1987 (see Figure 17.7)?

9. Analyze the impact of increased budget deficits on the level of interest rates.

10. Obtain data from the most recent *Federal Reserve Bulletin* on the recent prime loan rate, Treasury bill yield, and the recent trend rate of inflation. From this data compute the real prime loan rate and the real Treasury bill yield. How do your figures compare to the real prime rate in 1988–1989 (see Figure 17.8)? What do you think accounts for the change in these real rates?

11. How might it be that the announcement of a large increase in the U.S. money supply would lead to an *increase* in actual interest rates on long-term bonds and mortgages?

YOUR TURN
Answers

THE ANNOUNCEMENT MAKES LENDERS LESS WILLING TO PURCHASE BONDS OF XYZ CORPORATION. THE SUPPLY CURVE OF LOANABLE FUNDS TO THIS FIRM SHIFTS LEFTWARD, RAISING THE YIELD ON XYZ BONDS. AN INCREASE IN THE PERCEIVED DEFAULT RISK ON A PARTICULAR BOND ALWAYS RAISES THE YIELD ON THE BOND (REDUCES THE BOND'S PRICE) BY REDUCING WILLINGNESS OF LENDERS TO PURCHASE IT. THE YIELD RISES SUFFICIENTLY TO COMPENSATE LENDERS FOR THE RISK INVOLVED IN HOLDING THE BOND.

Selected References

Fisher, Irving. *The Theory of Interest* (New York: Macmillan, 1930). This is the classic treatment of the role of expected inflation in interest-rate determination.

Summers, Lawrence H. "The Nonadjustment of Nominal Interest Rates: A Study of the Fisher Effect," in James Tobin, ed., *Macroeconomics, Prices, and Quantities* (Washington, D.C.: The Brookings Institution, 1983), pp. 201–241. This is a comprehensive and technical study of the Fisher Effect during the past 100 years.

Thomas, Lloyd B. *Money, Banking, and Economic Activity*, 3rd ed. (Englewood Cliffs, N.J.: Prentice-Hall, 1986). Chapters 5 and 6 cover interest rates in depth.

Van Horne, James C. *Financial Markets: Rates and Flows*, 3rd ed. (Englewood Cliffs, N.J.: Prentice-Hall, 1990). This work is the most comprehensive analysis of all aspects of interest rates available today. Chapter 4 summarizes much of the empirical literature on the Fisher Effect.

THE GREAT DEPRESSION
IN THE UNITED STATES,
FAR FROM BEING A
SIGN OF INHERENT
INSTABILITY OF
THE PRIVATE
ENTERPRISE SYSTEM,
IS A TESTAMENT
TO HOW MUCH
HARM CAN
BE DONE BY
THE MISTAKES
OF A FEW MEN
WHEN THEY
WIELD VAST
POWER OVER
THE MONETARY
SYSTEM OF A
COUNTRY.

—MILTON FRIEDMAN
NOBEL LAUREATE
IN ECONOMICS

18

The Impact of the Fed and the Money Supply on Economic Activity

IN CHAPTERS 16 AND 17 WE DEMONSTRATED THAT THE FEDERAL RESERVE SYSTEM, THROUGH ITS INSTRUMENTS OF MONETARY POLICY, IS CAPABLE OF EXERTING APPRECIABLE INFLUENCE UPON THE SUPPLY OF MONEY AND THE LEVEL OF INTEREST RATES. IN CHAPTER 18 WE EXPLORE THE TRANSMISSION MECHANISM OF MONETARY POLICY—THE CHANNELS THROUGH WHICH MONETARY POLICY INFLUENCES ECONOMIC ACTIVITY. WE ALSO EXPLORE DIFFERENT VIEWPOINTS ABOUT THE IMPACT OF CHANGES IN THE MONEY SUPPLY UPON ECONOMIC ACTIVITY. WE NOTE THAT ALTHOUGH THERE EXIST DIFFERENCES OF OPINION AMONG ECONOMISTS ABOUT THE TRANSMISSION MECHANISM AND OTHER ASPECTS OF MONETARY POLICY, THERE IS A CLEAR CONSENSUS THAT MONETARY POLICY IS A POTENT TOOL. ALMOST ALL ECONOMISTS AGREE THAT FEDERAL RESERVE ACTIONS HAVE AN IMPORTANT IMPACT UPON ECONOMIC ACTIVITY THROUGH THEIR EFFECT UPON AGGREGATE DEMAND FOR GOODS AND SERVICES.

HOW DOES MONETARY POLICY INFLUENCE THE ECONOMY?

There are three alternative channels through which Federal Reserve monetary policy may influence the economy: the interest-rate, portfolio-adjustment, and wealth channels.

INTEREST-RATE CHANNEL Federal Reserve monetary policy can influence economic activity through its impact on interest rates and thereby through its effects upon interest-sensitive domestic components of aggregate expenditures as well as through net exports of goods and services. Investment expenditures on plant, equipment, inventories and housing are thought to be sensitive to the level of interest rates. In addition, such other components of spending as consumption and local government expenditures can be influenced somewhat by interest rates. When the Fed is pursuing a stimulative monetary policy, it purchases securities in the open market. This action pumps reserves into the banking system, increases the supply of loanable funds as well as the money supply, and lowers the level of interest rates. The decrease in interest rates, after some time, results in increased home-building activity; increased expenditures on plant, equipment, and inventories; and perhaps some stimulus to consumption and local government spending. This is the channel traditionally emphasized by Keynesian economists.

In addition, the decline in U.S. interest rates initiated by the Fed is likely to trigger a depreciation of the U.S. dollar in the foreign exchange market as foreign demand for U.S. bonds and other dollar-denominated financial assets declines. If the dollar falls from 130 yen to 120 yen, the price of U.S. goods declines in Japanese markets. U.S. exports to Japan increase. By the same token, the depreciation of the dollar implies that the U.S. price of an imported Toyota automobile or Sony VCR increases. Americans therefore buy fewer Japanese and more American products. In this way, lower U.S. interest rates increase demand for U.S. goods and services. The net export position of the United States improves.

PORTFOLIO-ADJUSTMENT CHANNEL The second avenue through which Fed policy and the money supply can influence economic activity is by upsetting the *portfolio equilibrium* of the public. In this mechanism people hold a balanced portfolio of money, financial assets such as bonds and stocks, and real assets such as houses and cars. When the Fed increases the supply of money, a disequilibrium is created in which people are holding more money than desired relative to bonds, stocks, cars, and houses. To restore equilibrium, the public spends these excess money balances. This spending stimulates the bond and stock markets as well as the automobile and housing industries. When holdings of such nonmoney assets as bonds and durable goods reach the desired relationship to the enhanced supply of money, the adjustment process is complete and the economy reaches a new equilibrium. In this channel an increased supply of money directly stimulates spending, independently of any effect on interest rates. This portfolio-adjustment channel is emphasized by monetarists.

WEALTH CHANNEL The third way in which Federal Reserve monetary policy may influence economic activity is by altering the net worth or wealth of the private sector of the economy, thereby stimulating consumption spending, the largest component of aggregate demand. In this mechanism an increase in the supply of money reduces interest rates and elevates stock and bond prices. More than 50 million American households own stocks, either directly or through retirement fund holdings. The net worth of millions of individuals rises, resulting in an increase in expenditures on new cars and other durable consumer goods.

THE LINK BETWEEN MONEY AND ECONOMIC ACTIVITY— THE EQUATION OF EXCHANGE

An efficient means of analyzing the influence of the supply of money (hence the Federal Reserve System) on the economy is by the famous **equation of exchange**, expressed in Equation 18.1.

$$MV \equiv \Sigma P_i Y_i \qquad (18.1)$$

EQUATION OF EXCHANGE
Equation which sets forth the relationship between the supply of money, velocity, the price level, and real output; $MV \equiv PY$.

VELOCITY
The number of times annually that an *average dollar* is spent on final goods and services; the ratio of the nominal GDP to the money supply.

In the equation, M represents the supply of money (most commonly the M-1 version) and V represents the **velocity** of money or the turnover rate of money in purchasing newly produced goods and services (that is, GDP). On the right-hand side, P_i represents the price of individual good or service i and Y_i represents the annual number of units of good or service i purchased. Clearly then, $P_i Y_i$ indicates annual expenditures on item i (say, eggs). If we sum such expenditures on all of the goods and services that enter into the nation's gross domestic product, we arrive at spending on GDP (that is, $\Sigma P_i Y_i$).

Frequently the equation of exchange is presented in slightly altered form

$$MV \equiv PY \qquad (18.2)$$

where Y represents the quantity of the nation's output of goods and services or an index of such output and P represents the average price at which the output is purchased or an index of such prices.

The right-hand side of Equations 18.1 and 18.2 indicates the annual expenditures on newly produced goods and services (GDP) and is sometimes termed the "goods side" of the equation of exchange. The left-hand side, known as the "money side," states that the supply of money times its velocity is also a way of defining expenditures on newly produced goods and services (that is, GDP). This is true by virtue of the fact that velocity is defined as the ratio of GDP to the stock of money:

$$V \equiv \frac{\Sigma P_i Y_i}{M} \equiv \frac{PY}{M} \equiv \frac{\text{GDP}}{M}$$

Since V is defined strictly in terms of the other three variables in the equation of exchange, the equation is an *identity* or *tautology*—true by definition. Everyone agrees with the equation of exchange. It must be true; it cannot be falsified. If M is $900 billion and GDP is $5,400 billion per year, then V is 6/year. If M is $900 billion and GDP is $6,300 billion per year, then V is 7/year. The equation of exchange is a simple identity that states that GDP expenditures viewed from the *money side* precisely equal GDP expenditures viewed from the *goods side*.

Because the equation of exchange is an identity or tautology, one is tempted to ask, "How can it be of any use?" Its value lies in illuminating the key role played by the velocity of money. Look again at Equations 18.1 and 18.2. Note that velocity can be viewed as a multiplier that links the stock of money to the premier measure of the nation's economic activity—GDP. Suppose the money supply rises. Then one of two things (or a little of each) *must* happen: velocity must decline or GDP ($\Sigma P_i Y_i$ or PY) must rise.

If velocity remains constant in the face of an increase in M engineered by the Fed, GDP spending must increase in proportion to M—a 7 percent increase in M causes a 7 percent increase in GDP spending. On the other hand, if velocity fluctuates in a wild and unpredictable manner, one cannot predict with any confidence the effect that a 7 percent increase in M would have on the nation's GDP. The equation throws into clear relief the crucial role of the velocity of money.

Also, one can analyze the role of *fiscal policy* (changes in government taxation, expenditures, and transfers) upon GDP expenditures in the context of the equation. A stimulative fiscal policy involves increased government spending or transfer payments or a reduction in taxes in the context of a situation in which the money supply remains constant. Since M is held constant, a stimulative fiscal policy must boost velocity if it is to stimulate GDP expenditures. Likewise, a restrictive fiscal policy must reduce velocity in order to reduce GDP expenditures. Again, the crucial importance of understanding the nature of velocity is evident.

MONETARIST AND KEYNESIAN VIEWS OF VELOCITY

As a general principle, economists of monetarist persuasion (Milton Friedman, Allan Meltzer, Karl Brunner, William Poole, and Beryl Sprinkle) believe that velocity is a stable and well-behaved variable that tends to move in steady, rather predictable trends and is independent of the supply of money. Changes in the supply of money therefore have a predictable and powerful impact on aggregate spending and GDP. Monetarists believe that fiscal policy measures exert little impact on velocity and therefore are incapable of having much impact on aggregate spending and GDP. Monetarists simply believe that monetary policy is a substantially more powerful tool than fiscal policy.

Keynesian economists (Paul Samuelson, James Tobin, Lawrence Summers, Robert Eisner, and Alan Blinder) believe that the money supply exerts an important impact on aggregate spending, but they tend to be quite skeptical about the alleged stability and predictability of velocity. Therefore, if the supply of money increases by 7 percent, the impact on aggregate spending and GDP is thought to be uncertain. Aggregate spending and GDP may rise 12 percent or perhaps only 2 percent. Stimulative fiscal measures, in the view of Keynesians, boost the velocity of money and produce a strong increase in expenditures and GDP, even when the supply of money is held constant. In short, Keynesians view the velocity of money as rather unstable, elastic in response to fiscal policy measures, and extremely difficult to predict. To Keynesians, fiscal policy is at least as powerful as monetary policy.

For you to draw your own conclusions about velocity and find your own position along the Keynesian-monetarist spectrum of viewpoints, we must explore the nature of the velocity beast and its close relative—money demand—in some depth.

The Nature of Velocity and Money Demand

There are several alternative measures of velocity—one for each measure of the supply of money. Hence we can designate $V_1 = \dfrac{GDP}{M\text{-}1}$, $V_2 = \dfrac{GDP}{M\text{-}2}$, $V_3 = \dfrac{GDP}{M\text{-}3}$. Each measure of velocity is a multiplier that links a particular measure of money to GDP expenditures.

The velocity of M-1 and M-2 over a long span of years preceding 1960 is illustrated in Figure 18.1. In Figure 18.2 (page 454), we illustrate the velocity of M-1 in the past 30 years.

Velocity is intimately tied to the amount of money people find it desirable to hold relative to expenditures. Most individuals and firms have several forms in which their wealth is held. They may hold wealth in money, bonds, stocks, real estate, works of art, certificates of deposits, gold coins, and in many other media. Individuals, within the limits of their own wealth, have the discretion to determine

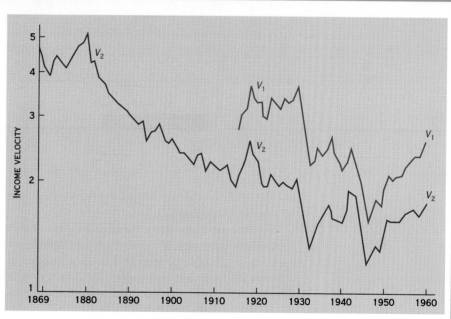

TWO MEASURES OF VELOCITY*

The velocity of money trended downward from the 1870s until the mid-1940s. After the 1940s, velocity persistently trended upward (until the 1980s).

$^*V_1 = \dfrac{GDP}{M\text{-}1}$ $V_2 = \dfrac{GDP}{M\text{-}2}$

SOURCE: *A Monetary History of the United States, 1867–1960,* by Milton Friedman and Anna Jacobson Schwartz (copyright 1963 by National Bureau of Economic Research), published by Princeton University Press: chart 57 (top), p. 640, in adapted form. Reprinted with permission of Princeton University Press.

FIGURE 18.1

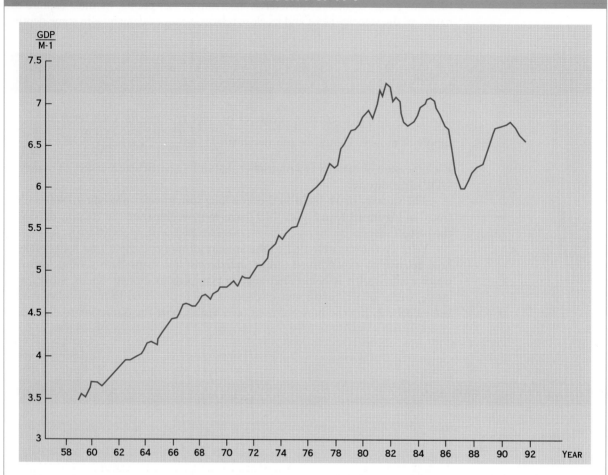

In the 1960s and 1970s, velocity of M-1 persistently increased. Since 1980, M-1 velocity has become more unstable.
SOURCE: Data from Federal Reserve System, 1992.

FIGURE 18.2

how they allocate this wealth among the various forms, including money balances (M-1 or M-2, for example).

Holding wealth in the form of money has both advantages and disadvantages. The primary advantage is convenience and *liquidity*—wealth held in money form is immediately available to spend.[1] The disadvantage of holding money involves the forfeiture of the return one might have obtained from interest on bonds, dividends from stocks, or appreciation from real estate or gold. In other words, the cost of

---

[1]A related point is that money has perfect stability of nominal (though not real) value. If one holds $1,000 in money, it will still be $1,000 a year from now. If one holds $1,000 in common stock or real estate, it is likely to amount to less or more than $1,000 a year from now. This absence of fluctuation of nominal value contributes to the desirability of holding money, at least in noninflationary times.

holding money is an *opportunity cost*—the return one forgoes by holding wealth in the form of money, which traditionally has paid no interest.[2]

━━━━━━━━

THE DEMAND FOR MONEY

TRANSACTIONS DEMAND FOR MONEY
Money held to finance a stream of expenditures that does not coincide precisely in time with the receipt of funds such as paychecks.

The motives for holding money (*demand for money*) may be divided into three categories: the **transactions motive**, the *precautionary motive*, and the *speculative motive*. People and firms hold money to finance anticipated expenditures (transactions motive), to provide a prudent safety net to protect against unforeseen expenses or loss of income (precautionary motive), and to take advantage of a good investment opportunity in the event it should arise (speculative motive).

Economists concur that the predominant reason for holding money is the transactions motive—the motive we emphasize in our analysis. Money balances (demand deposits and currency) must be maintained in order to finance a pattern of expenditures that is not synchronized precisely over time with the receipt of income. People are typically paid on a monthly, biweekly, or weekly basis but spend funds almost daily. Money must be held to finance expenditures that come later in the week or month. In Figure 18.3 (page 456), we illustrate the behavior of a typical worker's money balances over time.

Assume the worker earns $2,000 (take-home pay) at the beginning of each month and spends the entire income each month. Assume for simplicity that the worker holds no precautionary or speculative money balances and thus ends each month with zero holdings of money. The worker deposits $2,000 in the bank on the first of the month and spends the funds at a constant rate until the money balances are exhausted on the last day of the month. Then another paycheck of $2,000 is received and the cycle repeats itself.

We can compute this worker's average demand for money and velocity of money. Money demand, or the average stock of money maintained, is approximately $1,000 because the worker starts the month with $2,000, ends with zero, and spends the funds at a constant rate. The *transactions velocity* of this worker's money may be computed as follows:

$$\text{velocity} = \frac{\text{annual expenditures}}{\text{average money holdings}} = \frac{\$24{,}000/\text{year}}{\$1{,}000} = 24/\text{year}$$

The transactions velocity of this worker's money balances is 24 times per year.[3] In other words, if average money holdings of $1,000 must finance annual expenditures

────────

[2]In the past, money paid no interest. Currency obviously does not pay interest, and legislation enacted in the 1930s prohibited interest payments on checking accounts. Since 1980, federal legislation has allowed banks to pay interest on certain types of checking accounts, and an increasing portion of such accounts now pay interest. One might characterize the opportunity cost of holding money today as the *difference* between the interest paid on money and the returns available on other (nonmoney) assets.

[3]Note that our measure of velocity in this example differs slightly from that employed in Equations 18.1 and 18.2 and Figures 18.1 and 18.2. In the numerator of this example we use *total expenditures* or *transactions*, not just expenditures for newly produced goods and services (GDP). GDP does not include purchases of used items or financial transactions in stocks, bonds, and the like. Our measure of velocity (known as *transactions velocity*) of the typical worker is therefore considerably larger than V (GDP velocity) of Equations 18.1 and 18.2 because total transactions are considerably larger than GDP. However, the basic principles governing the behavior of the two measures of velocity are the same.

People hold money in order to finance expenditures that do not coincide precisely with the timing of income received. The less frequently one is paid, the more money one must hold on average, given the amount of annual expenditures.

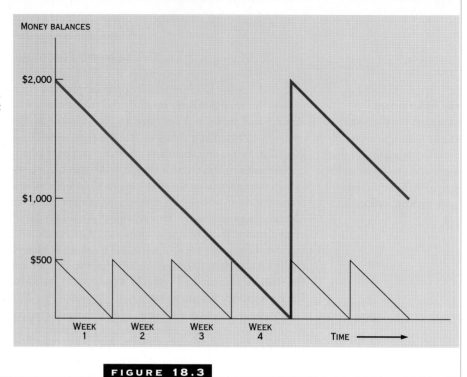

FIGURE 18.3

of $24,000, the turnover rate or number of times the average dollar must be spent is 24 times per year. Another way to state the same proposition is to say that the worker holds sufficient money on average to finance 1/24 of a year's expenditures or a little more than 15 days' worth of expenditures.

Suppose the worker's employer switches to a weekly pay period, paying out $500 the first of each week (assume a 28-day month with precisely four weeks for simplicity). This money balance pattern is also shown in Figure 18.3 (black lines). The worker begins each week with $500 and spends the funds at a constant rate, exhausting the funds at the end of each week. Average money balances are now only $250, and transactions velocity increases to 96/year.

$$\text{velocity} = \frac{\text{annual expenditures}}{\text{average money holdings}} = \frac{\$24,000/\text{year}}{\$250} = 96/\text{year}$$

The move to a weekly pay period increases the efficiency of the payments system by increasing the degree of synchronization between receipt and expenditure of funds, thus reducing money demand. This raises the velocity of money. Anything that improves this synchronization and reduces money demand pulls up the velocity of money. Anything that permits the financing of annual expenditures without holding as much money on average results in an increase in the velocity of money. Hence, increasing use of charge accounts and credit cards and a movement toward more frequent pay periods have worked to increase the nation's velocity of money since the 1940s, as indicated in Figures 18.1 and 18.2.

YOUR TURN

Calculating Velocity

SUPPOSE U.S. GROSS DOMESTIC PRODUCT (GDP) IS $6,000 BILLION PER YEAR, WHILE M-1 AND M-2 ARE $1,000 BILLION AND $3,000 BILLION, RESPECTIVELY. CALCULATE THE INCOME VELOCITY OF M-1 AND M-2 (THAT IS, THE GDP VELOCITY). ALSO, CALCULATE THE NUMBER OF DAYS' WORTH OF GDP EXPENDITURES COLLECTIVELY HELD IN THE FORM OF M-1 ON AVERAGE.

DETERMINANTS OF MONEY DEMAND AND VELOCITY

In our analysis of the typical worker we have emphasized the transactions motive for money demand and the role of institutional factors such as frequency of pay periods. A more complete analysis of the determinants of money demand and velocity includes the following factors: institutional factors underlying the payments process, *financial technology* and the availability of substitutes for money, the level of interest rates, and the degree of economic uncertainty.

INSTITUTIONAL FACTORS AND THE PAYMENTS PROCESS As indicated in the preceding analysis, more frequent pay periods reduce the average money balances one needs to maintain throughout the month, thus raising velocity. Increasing usage of charge accounts and credit cards has a similar impact because it increases the degree of synchronization between receipt and expenditures of funds. If one is paid on the first of the month and uses a credit card to finance most expenditures, one needs to hold very little M-1 except on the date when the credit card bill comes due. If the credit card bill comes due around payday, one holds very little money on average and velocity is quite high. The increasing use of credit cards since World War II has contributed to the rising trend of velocity illustrated in Figure 18.2.

FINANCIAL TECHNOLOGY AND SUBSTITUTES FOR MONEY The emergence of a large array of satisfactory substitutes for demand deposits has also contributed to the uptrend in velocity. Passbook savings accounts, bank certificates of deposit (CDs), U.S. government securities, **money market mutual fund** shares (MMMFs), and other instruments designed for firms and other large-deposit customers allow firms and individuals to economize on relatively unattractive demand deposits as a means of storing wealth over time.[4] We characterize these various money-economizing devices under the category of *financial technology*.

INTEREST RATES Interest rates clearly influence money demand and velocity. When interest rates are high, the opportunity cost of holding money is high and individuals and firms scramble to convert demand deposits into such interest-yielding alternatives as CDs, MMMF shares, and securities. Velocity increases. When

MONEY MARKET MUTUAL FUNDS (MMMFs)
Institutions that pool funds of thousands of individuals to buy large blocks of safe, interest-bearing assets. These accounts ("shares") are checkable and pay a yield that floats with yields in the market.

---

[4]Two techniques that allow firms and other entities with substantial funds to hold less money on average are *sweep accounts* and *repurchase agreements*. In a sweep arrangement, the bank's computer automatically *sweeps* checking account funds into interest-bearing savings accounts each day. A repurchase agreement specifies that the bank sell securities to a customer in exchange for checking account funds at the close of business each day. The next morning when the bank opens, it *repurchases* these securities by replenishing the funds (with interest) in the checking account.

EXHIBIT 18.1

Money Market Mutual Funds and the Velocity of M-1

An excellent example of the way that financial innovations influence money demand and velocity is the emergence of *money market mutual funds* (*MMMFs*) in the U.S. economy in the late 1970s.

MMMFs issue *shares* that are actually interest-bearing deposits with limited check-writing privileges. Most MMMFs authorize checks to be written in amounts of not less than $250 or $500. A minimum initial deposit of anywhere from $1,000 to $20,000 is normally required to open an MMMF account. MMMFs pool the savings of thousands of individuals and invest the funds in large blocks of safe, short-term securities issued by the U.S. government, large banks, and nonfinancial corporations of high credit standing. The MMMFs pay interest on the shares at a rate that floats daily in line with the yield earned on the portfolio of short-term securities.

These MMMFs are attractive to individual savers because of their competitive yield and check-writing features. Unlike savings accounts in banks and thrift institutions, MMMF shares are not insured. However, they are considered quite safe because the MMMF portfolio of assets consists of relatively safe investments.

In the late 1970s, when interest rates soared at a time that banks and thrift institutions were subject to ceilings on

---

interest rates are low, the incentive to economize on money is reduced and people hold more money balances relative to expenditures. Velocity falls. Interest rates exhibit a pronounced *procyclical* pattern, rising during the expansion phase of the business cycle and declining in recessions. Since velocity and interest rates are directly related, velocity also exhibits a procyclical pattern—rising during business expansions and declining (or at least rising more slowly than its long-term trend) in periods of recession.

ECONOMIC UNCERTAINTY The degree of economic uncertainty or the extent of confidence in the economic future influences the amount of wealth individuals and firms seek to hold in liquid form, thus influencing velocity. When there is great uncertainty or lack of confidence in the future, people seek to hold fewer common stocks, bonds, and other nonmoney assets; they prefer to hold the most conservative of assets—money. Velocity declines. As one perceives the future more clearly and confidence improves, one is willing to take more risks—getting out of money in favor of the stock market, bonds, and real estate. Velocity of money thus rises. This uncertainty factor helps to explain why velocity is often low in periods of economic depression and war. In this connection, note in Figure 18.1 the sharp drop in velocity during the early 1930s and again during World War II (1941–1945.)

rates payable on savings and time deposits, MMMFs became extremely popular. Total assets of MMMFs soared from $4 billion at the beginning of 1978 to $230 billion by the end of 1982. A significant portion of these funds was transferred from bank demand deposits to MMMF shares. This reduced the propensity to hold bank demand deposits and rapidly pulled up the velocity of M-1—GDP/(M-1)—during the late 1970s (review Figure 18.2). MMMF shares are included in M-2 but not in M-1.

By the mid-1980s, ceiling interest rates payable by banks and thrift institutions were phased out. These institutions are now allowed to pay competitive interest rates. Recently, therefore, there is less tendency to switch funds from banks and savings and loan institutions to MMMFs in times of soaring interest rates. Nevertheless, MMMF shares remain a very attractive, liquid saving instrument for millions of individuals in our deregulated financial environment. In late 1992, Americans held more than $500 billion in some 650 MMMFs. The current yields payable, along with total assets and average maturity of assets, are quoted regularly in the financial pages of major American newspapers.

Economic Uncertainty and Velocity

YOUR TURN

SUPPOSE IBM AND GENERAL MOTORS STUN AMERICA BY ANNOUNCING WITHIN THE SAME MONTH THAT THEY ARE FILING FOR CHAPTER 11 (BANKRUPTCY) PROTECTION. ANALYZE THE IMPACT OF THESE ANNOUNCEMENTS ON THE VELOCITY OF M-1 AND M-2.

ACCOUNTING FOR THE MAJOR CHANGES IN VELOCITY

Given our analysis thus far, we can broadly account for the long-term swings in velocity illustrated in Figures 18.1 and 18.2. On balance, velocity trended downward between 1880 and 1945 and increased afterward until the 1980s. In the quarter century following the American Civil War, the U.S. price level declined and interest rates remained relatively low. In such an environment, money is the favored medium for storing wealth. Banking flourished without significant inroads from such nonbank competitors as savings associations and credit unions. Few substitutes for money were available. Velocity drifted downward. During the 1930s and

1940s, velocity was given an additional powerful downward thrust by the uncertainties of depression and war and by the prevalence of extremely low and falling interest rates.[5]

In the period following World War II, a variety of events conspired to account for the prolonged upward movement in velocity. Savings and loan associations and credit unions spread rapidly throughout the nation, giving millions of individuals an alternative to holding funds in bank demand deposits. New financial instruments (Treasury bills, money market mutual fund shares, sweep accounts, repurchase agreements, and others) came on stream to give individuals and firms viable alternatives to holding deposits. These developments, coupled with the fact that interest rates trended upward from the 1940s until the early 1980s, resulted in steady increases in the opportunity cost of holding money. Hence, the demand for money steadily declined relative to income. Velocity increased. Charge accounts and credit cards became increasingly prevalent, improving the synchronization process just outlined. The early postwar successes in confining recessions to mild downturns and avoiding depression-magnitude catastrophes gradually raised confidence that a repeat of the experience of the 1930s was not in the cards. The growth of velocity from 1945–1981 was remarkably persistent (Figures 18.1 and 18.2).

Since 1981, velocity has deviated from its sustained post-World War II uptrend (review Figure 18.2). Significant declines in velocity occurred in the 1981–1982 and 1990–1991 recessions and in 1986. The first decline might be attributed to the severe 1981–1982 recession (the deepest since the 1930s). This recession produced a decline in interest rates and an increase in economic uncertainty. The unprecedented 9 percent 1986 contraction in velocity is largely attributable to the sharp decline in interest rates in that year. Individuals apparently decided to park lots of funds in bank checking deposits, especially in interest-bearing *other checkable deposits* (included in M-1). This decision was apparently made as a result of the sharp decline in the yield advantage of securities, CDs, and other instruments relative to the yields on NOW and ATS accounts.[6]

The Crude Quantity Theory of Money and Modern Monetarism

Monetarists emphasize the dominant role of the transactions demand for money; they are dubious about the relative importance (or even the existence) of other motives for holding money. Therefore, monetarists stress the first two factors on our list of determinants of money demand and velocity. Because these institutional

---

[5]Primarily because of aggressive efforts by the Federal Reserve to minimize borrowing costs for the U.S. Treasury, short-term yields were maintained at less than 1 percent during the 1940s. Clearly, in those years, people weren't sacrificing much income by stashing large amounts of wealth in checking accounts.

[6]These interest-bearing *other checkable accounts* first became available nationwide with the 1980 passage of the Depository Institutions Deregulation and Monetary Control Act. Since they are included in M-1, one would expect some initial increase in demand for M-1 and decline in velocity as the public became accustomed to these deposits in the 1980s. Since the interest rates payable on these insured NOW and ATS accounts are more sluggish than those in the financial markets, these accounts become more attractive in a period of sharply declining yields.

factors underlying the payments process and the state of financial technology evolve only slowly and smoothly over time, monetarists believe velocity is stable in the short run and is not influenced by the supply of money.

THE OLD-FASHIONED QUANTITY THEORY OF MONEY

Early forerunners of today's monetarists took the preceding notions to an extreme, arguing that one could regard velocity as constant in the short run, it being determined by the slowly evolving factors underlying the synchronization between receipts and expenditures. These *crude quantity theorists* also believed that the normal level of output was the full-employment level. Any deviations from a full-employment output were thought to set in motion a powerful corrective mechanism returning output to the full-employment level, as we outlined in Chapters 13 and 14. These beliefs are summarized in Equation 18.3, in which bars (overbars) above variables indicate the variables are fixed or constant in the short run.

$$M\overline{V} = P\overline{Y} \tag{18.3}$$

If one takes velocity (V) and real output (Y) as constant in Equation 18.3, as early forerunners of today's monetarists did, it is clear that the level of prices (P) varies in exact proportion to the supply of money (M): a 12 percent increase in M causes a 12 percent increase in P. In this framework a necessary and sufficient cause of inflation is growth in the stock of money. This proposition, known as the **crude quantity theory of money**, denies any role for such nonmonetary factors as oil prices or wage behavior in the inflation process. The proposition also denies a role for excessively stimulative fiscal policies—government spending hikes and tax cuts—in the inflation process.

CRUDE QUANTITY THEORY

The proposition that velocity is constant in the short run and that aggregate demand (*PY*) and the price level vary proportionally with the money supply.

A simple test of the crude quantity theory is provided in Figure 18.4, which illustrates the relationship between money growth and inflation in recent years in a cross section of nations. The crude quantity theory implies that the points should cluster along the 45-degree line, the inflation rate being equal to the growth rate of money. Although this prediction cannot be confirmed, it is true that countries with high money growth (Italy, Spain) experienced rapid inflation, whereas the countries that held down money growth (Japan, Switzerland) experienced relatively modest inflation.

In Figure 18.5, we further test the crude quantity theory by examining the relationship between U.S. money growth and inflation in various decades. Again, a positive relationship exists between money growth and inflation, but it is a loose one. While average annual money growth accelerated from 6.5 percent in the 1970s to 7.5 percent in the 1980s, the average inflation rate (CPI) slowed from 7.4 percent in the 1970s to 5.1 percent in the 1980s. The inflation rate in the 1940s was only about one-half the growth rate of the money supply, whereas the inflation rate exceeded the money growth rate in the 1970s. Clearly, money growth fails to tell the whole story in accounting for inflation. (Note that many points in Figures 18.4 and 18.5 fall significantly off of the 45-degree line, in contrast to the predictions of the crude quantity theory.)

There is little dispute that runaway money growth is the dominant culprit in accounting for the instances of extreme inflation in the past, such as the episodes

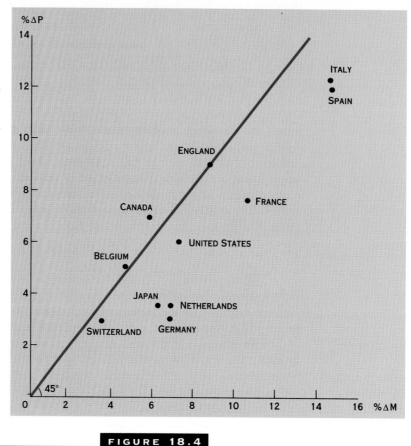

On average, nations with rapid money growth exhibit severe inflation, whereas nations with low money growth experience relatively modest inflation. However, the relationship between money growth and inflation is much looser than implied by the crude quantity theory.

*%ΔM indicates average annual growth of money supply during 1975–1990; %ΔP indicates average annual inflation rate (consumer price index) during 1975–1990.

SOURCE: Data from Federal Reserve Bank of St. Louis, 1992.

FIGURE 18.4

experienced by eastern European nations immediately following World Wars I and II (see Exhibit 15.1, page 372). However, many economists tend to be eclectic in their approach to inflation, arguing that such phenomena as higher oil prices, wage hikes, increases in import costs, and other factors on the cost side often initiate the rather mild episodes experienced in the United States in the past 40 years.

Furthermore, such critics of the quantity theory argue that aggregate demand (*MV*) is not driven solely by the money supply. Stimulative fiscal policy, as well as monetary policy, may give rise to excessive aggregate demand for goods and services, which is the fundamental cause of inflation. Critics of the crude quantity theory (and critics of modern monetarism) believe that velocity is highly elastic, capable of increasing significantly when nonmoney factors favor an expansion of economic activity. Suppose firms wish to expand spending on inventories or plant while the Fed is holding back on the money supply. These firms may approach financial institutions for loans. The banks may have no excess funds on hand because of tight Fed policies. However, the institutions can normally obtain the funds by either liquidating securities or issuing large blocks of negotiable CDs to corporate lenders. In utilizing these channels, the banks are tapping idle money

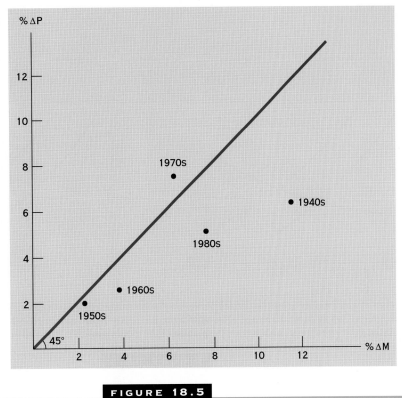

Although the link between U.S. money growth and inflation is a positive one, it is a rather loose relationship.

*Each point depicts average money growth rate (M − 1) and average inflation rate (consumer price index) in the decade.

SOURCE: Data from *Citibank Economic Database*, 1992.

FIGURE 18.5

balances and transferring the funds to active spenders. Alternatively, the firms may bypass the financial institutions and issue bonds or short-term IOUs known as *commercial paper* directly to the public. Although such actions do not change the supply of money, they do stimulate the velocity of money and facilitate an increase in spending by transferring money balances from inactive money holders to active money holders—those who wish to spend on goods and services. Hence, aggregate spending (*MV*) rises in spite of a constant money supply.[7] Velocity of money is boosted.

Many economists are critical of the assumption that the normal state of affairs is one of full employment. The impact of an increase in the money supply upon the price level surely depends on the state of the economy at the time the monetary stimulus is applied. These ideas are illustrated in Figure 18.6.

---

[7]This analysis helps explain why velocity exhibits a distinct procyclical pattern. In a period of strong economic expansion, banks sell securities and certificates of deposit to obtain funds with which to meet burgeoning loan demand. Velocity rises as funds are transferred (via the banks) from savers to active spenders. In periods of recession, such activities cease as loan demand drops off. Velocity falls or returns to its long-term trend dictated by the evolution of the payments process and the state of financial technology.

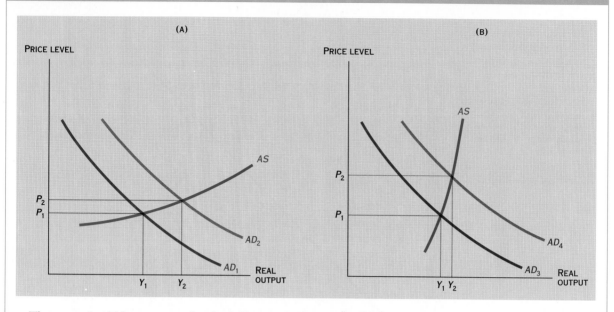

The manner in which money growth is divided between inflation and output growth depends on the steepness of the nation's aggregate supply curve. If the aggregate supply curve is relatively flat, money growth is reflected mainly in output growth. If the aggregate supply curve is quite steep, most of the money growth is reflected in higher prices.

FIGURE 18.6

In Figure 18.6(A), the stimulative monetary policy occurs when the economy has a significant pool of unemployment and unused plant capacity. The aggregate supply curve is relatively flat, indicating that extra output can be called forth without necessitating sharply higher prices. The stimulative policy shifts the aggregate demand curve from AD_1 to AD_2, causing a slight increase in the nation's price level (P_1 to P_2) and a significant expansion in real output (Y_1 to Y_2). In terms of the *equation of exchange*, a 10 percent increase in M gives rise to perhaps an 8 percent increase in Y and a 2 percent increase in P.

In Figure 18.6(B), the stimulus occurs in the context of an economy already functioning close to full capacity. The relevant portion of the aggregate supply curve is steeply rising, indicating that additional output is forthcoming only at sharply higher levels of prices. The stimulative monetary policy shifts the aggregate demand curve from AD_3 to AD_4, causing a sharp increase in the price level and only a modest increase in real output. A 10 percent increase in M results in perhaps a 2 percent increase in Y and an 8 percent increase in P.

The illustrations in Figure 18.6(A) and (B) indicate that stimulative monetary policies, by increasing aggregate demand for goods and services, normally increase *both* real output *and* the level of prices. The distribution of this mix of output growth and inflation depends upon the state of the economy when the stimulus is applied. Only when the aggregate supply curve is vertical is *all* the demand stimulus reflected in higher prices.

THE MODERN QUANTITY THEORY—MONETARISM

The problems with the crude quantity theory lie in the assumptions that V and Y may be regarded as constant in the short run. Figures 18.1 and 18.2 illustrate clearly that velocity has exhibited considerable variability over time. Therefore, aggregate spending (MV) does not move in proportion to M. Furthermore, output (Y) is not always pumping at full capacity. When the economy is operating at less than full capacity, a 10 percent increase in spending (MV) does not result in a 10 percent rise in prices; some of the increased spending is reflected in larger output (Y).

Modern monetarists as well as nonmonetarists reject the crude quantity theory of money because its assumptions caricature the true nature of velocity and real output. But again, it is acknowledged that the theory is not far off the mark in explaining the role of money in the extreme pathological episodes of runaway inflation.

MONETARISM
The viewpoint that monetary instability is the dominant cause of output fluctuations and that money supply growth is the dominant cause of inflation.

THE MONETARIST VIEW OF VELOCITY Modern **monetarists** reject the notion that velocity is constant; they argue that it is stable and predictable. The hypothesis of stable velocity follows from the monetarist view that people hold money only to finance expenditures. The timing of these expenditures does not mesh perfectly with the receipt of income. The amount of money people must hold relative to expenditures, in the monetarist view, evolves slowly over time as the state of financial technology and other institutional factors underlying the synchronization between receipts and expenditures slowly change. Modern monetarists acknowledge that major changes in interest rates and uncertainty can alter money demand and velocity, but they tend to deemphasize these factors.

Hence, monetarists argue that the multiplier linking money and GDP—velocity—is more stable and predictable than our expenditures multiplier of Chapter 12, the multiplier linking changes in government or investment expenditures to the change in GDP. Monetarists therefore believe that monetary policy is a more reliable and powerful instrument than fiscal policy.

In contrast to monetarists, nonmonetarists emphasize the sensitivity of money demand and velocity to interest rates and economic uncertainty. Since it is difficult to forecast interest rates, nonmonetarists believe that changes in velocity seldom can be predicted accurately. Keynesian economists believe that the expenditures multiplier is more stable than the velocity of money. It follows then that Keynesians place more faith in the power of fiscal policy than in monetary policy.

THE MONETARIST VIEW OF INFLATION Monetarists typically argue that the root cause of inflation can always be found in excessive growth of the nation's supply of money. The strong statistical association between money growth and inflation, such as that illustrated in Figures 18.4 and 18.5, is often presented by monetarists as evidence that inflation is a monetary phenomenon. Critics charge that the strong positive correlation between money growth and inflation, while undeniable, is sometimes misleading and is misinterpreted by monetarists. Correlation does not imply causation.

Using our aggregate demand–aggregate supply framework, assume prices of imported raw materials rise, or oil prices increase, or Congress raises the level of the minimum wage. Any such event gives rise to a leftward shift (decrease) in the nation's aggregate supply curve. In Figure 18.7, AS_1 shifts to AS_2. If the Fed does not respond, the aggregate demand curve remains at AD_1 and we move from point A to point B. Real output declines from Y_1 to Y_2 and the price level rises from P_1 to P_2. If the Fed is concerned about the decline in output and employment, it may pursue a stimulative policy of increasing the money supply to counteract the decline in economic activity. If so, the aggregate demand curve shifts from AD_1 to AD_2. Real output is returned to its original Y_1 level, but the price level is boosted to P_3 as we move to point C in the illustration. During this event, inflation occurs as the level of prices rises from P_1 to P_3.

After the fact, we note in Figure 18.7 that both the money supply and the price level increased. But was the money growth the *root cause* of the inflation? Monetarists, since they believe that the fundamental responsibility of the Federal Reserve is to ensure price level stability, would respond in the affirmative. But many economists would disagree, citing factors that shifted the aggregate supply curve as the fundamental sources of the inflation. If the aggregate supply curve had not shifted in the first place—because of higher import prices, higher oil prices, or higher wages—no inflation would have occurred. Those who place high priority on high output and employment performance argue that the adverse supply shock is what forced the Fed to increase the supply of money to avert recession. Critics of monetarism argue that monetarists tend to forget the complex interaction between aggregate supply forces and monetary policy that contributes to the powerful correlation between money growth and inflation we observe when we analyze graphs such as Figures 18.4 and 18.5.

STIMULATIVE MONETARY POLICY RESPONSE TO AN ADVERSE SUPPLY SHOCK

An aggregate supply shock such as an oil price hike shifts the nation's aggregate supply curve leftward. This raises the price level and reduces output. If the Fed wishes to prevent a decline in output, it must increase the money supply to boost the aggregate demand curve. In this situation, what then is the cause of the inflation? Economists differ in their interpretation of the causes of inflation.

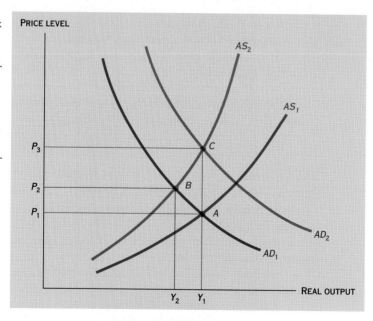

FIGURE 18.7

MILTON FRIEDMAN
(B. 1912)

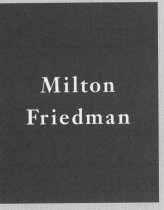

Milton Friedman

Ask any economist who the world's foremost monetarist is and the response is almost sure to be Milton Friedman. The recipient of the 1976 Nobel Prize in economics, Friedman is clearly one of the most influential economists of this century.

Friedman is well known to the public for his tenacious defense of free markets. His best-selling book, *Free to Choose* (written with his wife, Rose Director Friedman), was developed into a television series with the same title. The theme of the book and TV series concerns the merits of a free-market economy with minimal government regulation and intervention in promoting individual initiative, prosperity, and economic growth. For many years Friedman delved into major contemporary issues in his regular column in *Newsweek*. Unlike those of many famous economists, his writings have had a significant effect on laymen, as well as on students and professional economists.

Friedman has made major contributions to the economics literature in many areas. One of his most outstanding contributions is his monumental book, *A Monetary History of the United States (1867–1960)*, written with Anna J. Schwartz in 1963. This book contains a treasure of data and information for students of monetary economics. Covering almost a century of history, it traces the relationship between the rate of change in the supply of money and changes in economic activity. The thesis of the book is that many major U.S. economic fluctuations—periods of severe inflation and deep recession—were caused by prior changes in the nation's money supply. Especially provocative is the chapter titled "The Great Contraction, 1929–33." In this chapter Friedman marshals evidence in support of his hypothesis that America's Great Depression was caused primarily by a series of mistakes made by the Federal Reserve System.

One of Friedman's more contested positions is his view that the Federal Reserve should give up efforts to stabilize the economy by discretionary monetary policy measures and instead simply increase the money supply at a slow, constant rate each year. He advocated this position in his book, *A Program for Monetary Stability*, written more than 40 years ago, and has never wavered.

Although undoubtedly a controversial figure, Friedman is enormously respected by economists of all ideological stripes. Many consider him to be the most creative economist of their lifetime. Friedman retired from the University of Chicago more than a decade ago, following nearly 30 years of service to that institution. He continues to encourage and stimulate the younger generation of economists from his current base at Stanford University's Hoover Institution.

THE MONETARIST VIEW OF DISCRETIONARY MONETARY POLICY Partly because they believe that monetary policy is an extremely potent tool, monetarists favor removing the Federal Reserve's power to conduct discretionary stabilization policies. Many monetarists are convinced the political and technical obstacles that confront the Fed's objective of conducting policies designed to smooth the swings in economic activity successfully are very formidable. These monetarists advocate that the Fed abandon its discretionary monetary policy and adopt a *constant monetary growth rule*. In this rule the money supply grows at some specific slow and steady rate, *irrespective of contemporary economic conditions*.

Inasmuch as they believe that velocity moves in a stable and consistent pattern, monetarists are confident that slow and stable money growth leads to a rather steady expansion of aggregate spending (*MV*) and GDP. Although the money growth rule may not lead to the elimination of the business cycle, monetarists believe that it would lead to the elimination of future episodes of double-digit inflation and severe recession. And that, they point out, is a better economic performance than the Fed has delivered in the past.

The majority of economists today do *not* favor implementation of the constant money growth proposal; they favor continuation of discretionary monetary policy. These critics of monetarism admit that the Fed has made many serious mistakes in the past. However, they believe that the Fed has learned from these mistakes. In the current state of the art, they believe the Fed is today capable of outperforming a constant money growth rule. We analyze the *rules-versus-discretion debate* in some depth in Chapter 20.

Summary

1. Monetary policy and the supply of money can influence economic activity by altering the level of interest rates, by creating a disequilibrium in portfolio holdings of money relative to other financial and nonfinancial assets, and by altering stock and bond prices and the wealth of private citizens and firms. Economists disagree about the relative importance of these three channels of influence.

2. An effective mechanism for highlighting the role of money is the *equation of exchange*. This equation, an identity, states that the money supply times velocity is precisely equal to aggregate demand for GDP, which is also equivalent to the number of units of final output purchased times the average price of these final goods and services. The *equation of exchange* states that if aggregate demand is to rise, either the money supply or its velocity (or both) must rise.

3. Old-fashioned or *crude* quantity theorists asserted that both velocity (V) and real output (Y) are constant in the short run and therefore the price level (P) varies exactly in proportion to the supply of money (M). A 15 percent increase in M causes a 15 percent increase in P. In this theory the one and only cause of inflation is excessive money supply growth.

4. Modern monetarists as well as nonmonetarists reject the crude quantity theory as too rigid. They believe that money growth can influence real output as well as prices in the short run. Furthermore, monetarists reject the notion of a constant velocity in favor of a stable and predictable velocity. They believe that velocity, which is the multiplier linking the money supply to GDP spending, is more stable and predictable than the Keynesian multiplier, which links changes in government and investment spending to GDP spending.

5. Nonmonetarists regard velocity as a flexible and elastic variable whose behavior is extremely difficult to predict in advance. Hence, the link between the money supply and

the economy is alleged to be weak and highly uncertain. Fiscal policy is thought to be just as powerful as monetary policy.

6. Real-world data indicate a positive statistical association between money growth and inflation, both for a cross section of nations in a uniform time interval and for the United States in different decades. Monetarists and nonmonetarists disagree over the underlying causal role of money in this statistical association.

7. Money growth is more likely to result in inflation if it occurs while the economy is close to full employment than if the economy contains considerable *slack*. This is because the nation's aggregate supply curve becomes increasingly steep as output approaches the full-employment level.

8. Monetarists believe that fiscal policy has little effect on aggregate demand and output, since it allegedly does not significantly affect velocity. Keynesians believe fiscal policy alters velocity, thereby strongly influencing aggregate demand and output.

9. Monetarists favor abolishing monetary policy discretion. They believe that a rule in which money growth is fixed at a modest, constant rate of increase provides a more stable, healthy economic environment than the Fed can deliver through efforts to stabilize the economy through discretionary policies. Keynesians disagree, asserting that monetary discretion can surely outperform any predetermined constant money growth rule.

Key Terms

equation of exchange
velocity (*V*)
transactions demand for money
liquidity

money market mutual funds (MMMFs)
crude quantity theory
monetarism

Study Questions and Problems

1. Assume the Fed decides to implement a restrictive monetary policy and conducts a policy of open market sales of securities, thereby reducing the supply of money. Analyze three different channels through which this restrictive policy might achieve its objective of restraining aggregate demand for goods and services.

2. Using a rough estimate of your annual expenditures and your average M-1 holdings, compute the transactions velocity of your money. Why is this so much higher than the recent level of *income* velocity in the United States illustrated in Figure 18.2 (between 6.0 and 7.0)?

3. In your own words explain why the *equation of exchange* is an identity rather than a theory that one could potentially test in order to ascertain its truth or falsity.

4. Assume GDP is currently $6,650 billion per year and the supply of money is $950 billion. What is the velocity of money? The nation collectively holds enough money to finance how many days' worth of GDP expenditures?

5. What is the chief advantage of holding money as a means of storing wealth over time? What is the chief disadvantage?

6. Analyze as many factors as you can think of that would make the velocity of money decline.

7. Explain why velocity systematically tends to increase in periods of robust economic expansion.

8. Outline the differences of opinion between monetarists and Keynesians regarding the nature and behavior of velocity.

9. What is the effect on velocity if the following occurs?
   a. Congress outlaws the use of credit cards.
   b. Banks begin to pay interest on all demand deposits.
   c. Great uncertainty is created as the chairman of the Federal Reserve Board resigns.

10. Suppose M increases 8 percent in the next year while V remains constant. Outline the consequences for inflation and real output growth if the economy were initially operating with
   a. 11 percent unemployment
   b. 5 percent unemployment

11. What differences in views distinguish modern monetarists from their forerunners, the crude quantity theorists?

YOUR TURN
Answers

Calculating Velocity

THE INCOME OR GDP VELOCITY IS DEFINED AS THE RATIO OF GDP TO THE MONEY SUPPLY (M-1 OR M-2). BECAUSE M-1 IS $1,000 BILLION, ITS INCOME VELOCITY IS $6,000 BILLION PER YEAR / $1,000 BILLION = 6 PER YEAR. BECAUSE M-2 IS $3,000 BILLION, ITS INCOME VELOCITY IS $6,000 BILLION PER YEAR / $3,000 BILLION = 2 PER YEAR. BECAUSE AVERAGE MONEY BALANCES (M-1) ARE ONE-SIXTH OF ANNUAL GDP EXPENDITURES, U.S. INDIVIDUALS AND FIRMS HOLD SUFFICIENT M-1 ON AVERAGE TO FINANCE 365/6 OR ABOUT 61 DAYS OF GDP EXPENDITURES.

Economic Uncertainty and Velocity

THESE ANNOUNCEMENTS WOULD SEND A SHOCK WAVE THROUGH AMERICA, CAUSING MILLIONS OF INDIVIDUALS AND FIRMS TO DUMP STOCKS AND CORPORATE BONDS IN FAVOR OF SUCH SAFE HOLDINGS AS CHECKING ACCOUNTS, SAVINGS ACCOUNTS, AND MONEY MARKET MUTUAL FUND SHARES. THIS INCREASE IN THE PREFERENCE TO HOLD M-1 AND M-2 MEANS THAT THE VELOCITY OF THESE MONETARY AGGREGATES WOULD DECLINE.

Selected References

Friedman, Milton. "Money: Quantity Theory," *International Encyclopedia of the Social Sciences* (New York: Macmillan Company and Free Press, 1968), pp. 432–447. A lucid exposition by the world's most eminent monetarist.

Mayer, Thomas. *The Structure of Monetarism* (New York: Norton, 1978). Delves into some of the broader, philosophical aspects of monetarism.

Modigliani, Franco, and Thomas Mayer. "The Monetarist Controversy Revisited" and "Response," *Contemporary Policy Issues*, October 1988, pp. 3–24. A critique of modern monetarism (by Modigliani) and a rebuttal by a monetarist (Mayer).

Thomas, Lloyd B. *Money, Banking, and Economic Activity*, 3rd ed. (Englewood Cliffs, N.J.: Prentice-Hall, 1986). Chapters 15–17 provide in-depth coverage of demand for money and velocity.

I V

Inflation, Unemployment and Economic Policies

ECONOMISTS ARE OFTEN CONFRONTED WITH *TRADE-OFFS*—THE NOTION THAT IMPROVEMENT IN ONE AREA SOMETIMES LEADS TO DETERIORATION IN ANOTHER. ONE OF THE POTENTIAL TRADE-OFFS THAT ECONOMISTS HAVE BEEN CONCERNED WITH IS ILLUSTRATED BY THE PHILLIPS CURVE—A GRAPH DEPICTING AN INVERSE RELATIONSHIP BETWEEN THE RATE OF UNEMPLOYMENT AND THE RATE OF INFLATION IN THE NATION. IN THE OPENING CHAPTER, WE EXAMINE THE NATURE OF THE PHILLIPS CURVE IN SOME DEPTH AND LOOK AT THE ALTERNATIVE VIEWS ECONOMISTS HAVE ABOUT THE RELATIONSHIP BETWEEN INFLATION AND UNEMPLOYMENT. THIS CHAPTER ALSO EMPLOYS THE ANALYTICAL FRAMEWORK DEVELOPED IN PART II TO ANALYZE THE *CAUSES* OF INFLATION, TOGETHER WITH THE HISTORY OF INFLATION AND THE NATURE OF INFLATION IN CONTEMPORARY AMERICA. ■ THE ECONOMICS PROFESSION IS SPLINTERED OVER THE WISDOM OF HAVING THE GOVERNMENT AND THE FEDERAL RESERVE ATTEMPT TO CONDUCT DISCRETIONARY FISCAL AND MONETARY POLICIES FOR THE PURPOSE OF STABILIZING ECONOMIC ACTIVITY NEAR FULL EMPLOYMENT. CHAPTER 20 ANALYZES THE DIFFERENT VIEWPOINTS IN THAT CONTROVERSY. WE WILL LEARN THE BASES FOR THE FUNDAMENTAL DISAGREEMENT AMONG ECONOMISTS OVER THE NATURE AND SEVERITY OF THE OBSTACLES THAT CONFRONT POLICYMAKERS WHO ATTEMPT TO STABILIZE OUR ECONOMY BY PREVENTING COSTLY ECONOMIC DOWNTURNS AND EPISODES OF SEVERE INFLATION.

IN NO PERIOD IN THE PAST
FORTY YEARS HAS THE
AMERICAN ECONOMY
BEEN FREE OF EXCESSIVE
UNEMPLOYMENT AND
INFLATION TENDENCIES
SIMULTANEOUSLY.
NOR HAS ANY OTHER
INDUSTRIAL NATION
FOUND THE HAPPY
COMBINATION. HITTING
THE DUAL TARGET
OF HIGH UTILIZATION
AND ESSENTIAL PRICE
STABILITY REMAINS THE
MOST SERIOUS UNSOLVED
PROBLEM OF STABILIZATION
POLICY THROUGHOUT THE
WESTERN WORLD.

—ARTHUR OKUN

19

Inflation and the Phillips Curve

IN CHAPTER 8, WE SKETCHED THE NATURE AND MEASUREMENT OF UNEMPLOYMENT IN THE UNITED STATES. WE ANALYZED THREE CATEGORIES OF UNEMPLOYMENT: FRICTIONAL, STRUCTURAL, AND CYCLICAL UNEMPLOYMENT. WE DEFINED THE CONCEPT OF THE NATURAL UNEMPLOYMENT RATE: THE RATE THAT PREVAILS WHEN THE ECONOMY IS PRODUCING AT A SUFFICIENTLY HIGH LEVEL OF OUTPUT THAT ALL CYCLICAL UNEMPLOYMENT IS ELIMINATED, LEAVING ONLY THE CORE OF FRICTIONAL AND STRUCTURAL UNEMPLOYMENT. WE ALSO OUTLINED THE MEANING OF INFLATION AND DEMONSTRATED HOW THE NATION'S PRICE INDEXES ARE CONSTRUCTED.

IN CHAPTER 9, WE ANALYZED IN SOME DEPTH THE *CONSE-QUENCES* OF UNEMPLOYMENT AND INFLATION. ARMED WITH THE ANALYTICAL TOOLS DEVELOPED IN PARTS II AND III OF THIS TEXT, WE ARE NOW PREPARED TO PROBE MORE DEEPLY INTO THE NATURE OF THE TWIN PROBLEMS OF UNEMPLOYMENT AND INFLATION. IN THIS CHAPTER, WE ARE ESPECIALLY INTERESTED IN THE NATURE OF THE RELATIONSHIP BETWEEN THE NATION'S UNEMPLOYMENT AND INFLATION RATES. ALSO, WE BRIEFLY ANALYZE THE CAUSES OF INFLATION. FINALLY, WE EXAMINE THE NATURE OF THE PRICE LEVEL AND INFLATION IN TODAY'S ECONOMY VIS-À-VIS THE ECONOMY OF THE PRE-WORLD WAR II ERA.

The Phillips Curve—the Trade-off between Inflation and Unemployment

PHILLIPS CURVE

A graph illustrating the relationship between the unemployment rate and the rate of inflation.

Both unemployment and inflation are undesirable. Unhappily, much evidence from the past indicates the existence of a short-run conflict between the goal of creating full employment and the goal of maintaining price-level stability. Ideally, one hopes that monetary and fiscal policies can be adjusted to push the unemployment rate to a very low level without touching off any inflation. Unfortunately, the evidence suggests that this may not be possible. Early studies provided evidence that seems to indicate that inflationary forces begin to set in when the economy is well short of full employment—before actual GDP reaches potential GDP. Furthermore, this evidence indicated that the inflation rate accelerates as the unemployment rate declines. Statistical evidence of the apparent *trade-off* between inflation and unemployment was discovered by British economist A. W. Phillips. The hypothesis of the existence of a trade-off between inflation and unemployment is known as the **Phillips Curve**.

Phillips actually studied the relationship in England between the unemployment rate and the inflation rate of *wages*. Over a long period of British history he observed a pattern of points such as those illustrated in Figure 19.1. In the figure,

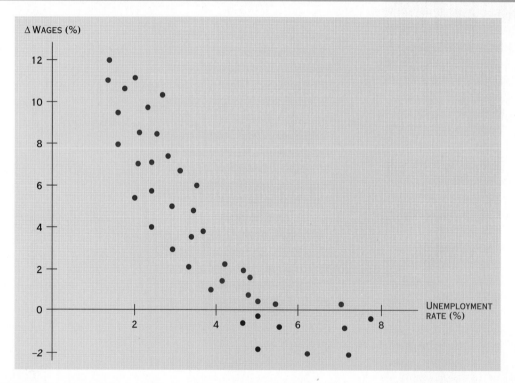

RATE OF CHANGE IN WAGES AND UNEMPLOYMENT RATES IN ENGLAND FOR VARIOUS YEARS

A. W. Phillips discovered that, in England, wages increased rapidly in years when the nation's unemployment rate was low. Wages increased more slowly or even declined in years when the unemployment rate was high. This statistical relationship formed the basis of what came to be called the "Phillips Curve."

FIGURE 19.1

each point represents the actual unemployment rate and the average percentage wage hike in England for a particular year. Phillips was struck by the powerful tendency for wages to rise rapidly in years of low unemployment and for wages to rise more slowly in years of high unemployment. In years of extremely high unemployment, the rate of change in wages was typically *negative*—the level of wages actually *declined*.

Phillips did not offer any explanation or hypothesis to account for the powerful statistical relationship. However, subsequent economists did so, and we turn to the theoretical underpinnings of the Phillips Curve momentarily.

Since wages make up the major portion of production costs, the rate of wage increase and the rate of inflation are highly correlated. Large wage hikes lead to large price hikes; modest wage increases are typically associated with modest inflation. Because the rate of inflation is of more interest to economists than the rate of wage increase, the Phillips Curve was reformulated with the inflation rate on the vertical axis. Such a Phillips Curve, as conventionally drawn, is shown in Figure 19.2.

In Figure 19.2, note again that the rate of *inflation* is indicated along the vertical axis. This conventional Phillips Curve indicates the terms of the hypothesized trade-off between inflation and unemployment. Low unemployment is alleged to be associated with relatively high inflation; high unemployment tends on average to be associated with low inflation.

The terms of the trade-off are indicated by the *slope* of the Phillips Curve. The slope in Figure 19.2 shows the extra inflation incurred when the unemployment

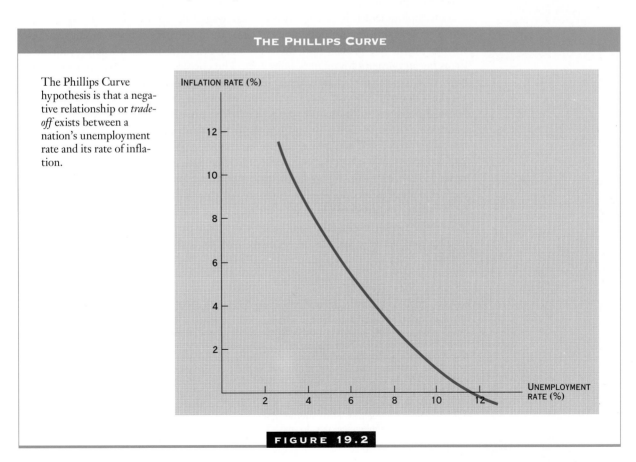

THE PHILLIPS CURVE

The Phillips Curve hypothesis is that a negative relationship or *trade-off* exists between a nation's unemployment rate and its rate of inflation.

FIGURE 19.2

rate is reduced by one percentage point. Alternatively stated, the slope indicates the reduction in inflation obtained when the unemployment rate rises by one percentage point. As traditionally drawn, the Phillips Curve is relatively flat at high unemployment rates and becomes steeper as unemployment declines. As unemployment declines, the terms of the trade-off worsen as larger increases in inflation are required to obtain equal successive reductions in unemployment.[1]

Theoretical Intuition Underlying the Phillips Curve

How can we rationalize the alleged existence of a Phillips Curve—the existence of a trade-off between inflation and unemployment—as depicted in Figure 19.2? There are several potential explanations that appear intuitively plausible: a theory of wage behavior based on labor–management bargaining, a structural explanation, and an aggregate demand–aggregate supply explanation.

BARGAINING HYPOTHESIS

Suppose average wage hikes in the nation are determined through bargaining between representatives of labor and management. When the economy is booming and unemployment is low, one expects large wage hikes to be forthcoming on average. The bargaining advantage goes to labor in this situation because sales are very strong, profits are robust, and there are very few alternative workers available to firms because unemployment is quite low. The cost to firms of a strike is extremely high in this scenario. Large wage hikes tend to emerge in such circumstances. Workers demand big pay hikes and firms are willing to grant such wage increases because market conditions are such that firms can shift the increased costs onto consumers through higher prices. On the other hand, when unemployment is high, the tables are turned and management has the upper hand in the negotiations. Sales and profits are down, alternative workers may be available to firms, and the cost of a strike is relatively low. Firms know that significant price hikes cannot be made to stick in a sluggish economic environment, so they adopt a hard-nosed approach in negotiations and tend to grant very meager wage hikes. Because average price-level inflation is closely connected to average wage increases in the nation, this reasoning implies that inflation and unemployment rates are inversely related.

---

[1] When unemployment is relatively high, economic stimulus is relatively efficient in the sense that unemployment can be reduced considerably without inducing much additional inflation. Millions of highly qualified and normally employed workers are available. The Phillips Curve is relatively flat. When the unemployment rate is relatively low, economic stimulus runs into diminishing returns in producing further reductions in unemployment. The pool of highly qualified workers is diminished, and a larger portion of the remaining unemployment consists of the core elements of frictional and structural unemployment. This means that more macroeconomic stimulus is required to reduce unemployment from 6 percent to 5 percent than from 10 percent to 9 percent. Hence, more additional inflation is generated in reducing unemployment from 6 percent to 5 percent. Economic stimulus becomes less efficient as the unemployment rate declines. Hence, more additional inflation is generated per unit reduction in unemployment as the unemployment rate declines. The Phillips Curve becomes steeper.

Assume initially we are far to the right on the Phillips Curve of Figure 19.2. Unemployment is high and almost all sectors of the economy exhibit excess productive capacity. There is very little pressure for price increases in any of the industries, and the nation's inflation rate is therefore low. As the economy expands and unemployment declines, the pace of expansion is not uniform across all sectors of the economy. A few sectors hit full capacity and begin to experience rapid price increases even when the nation's unemployment rate is still at, say, 7 or 8 percent. As the expansion proceeds and unemployment declines below 7 percent, more and more sectors reach full capacity. They run into *production bottlenecks*, or inability to expand output, and sharp price increases occur. Finally, when unemployment is reduced to perhaps 4 or 5 percent, prices are rising in almost all sectors of the economy. Since the proportion of the nation's industries or sectors experiencing these inflationary pressures increases as the unemployment rate falls, this reasoning indicates the existence of a Phillips Curve—a negative relationship between inflation and unemployment.

A GENERAL AGGREGATE SUPPLY–AGGREGATE DEMAND EXPLANATION

The nation's aggregate supply and aggregate demand curves are continually shifting about in response to a variety of forces. Over time, both the AS and the AD curve are normally shifting rightward (an *increase* in aggregate supply and aggregate demand). The AS curve drifts rightward over time because of increases in the quantity of such resources as labor and capital and because of improvements in technology. The amount of output that firms collectively produce at each and every price level increases with labor force, capital stock, and technological growth. Aggregate demand also increases over time because of such factors as increases in household and government expenditures and growth in the nation's money supply. In a typical year, the rightward shift of the aggregate demand curve dominates that of the aggregate supply curve. If the *AD* curve exhibits greater variability than the *AS* curve, history generates a pattern of inflation and unemployment rates that cluster along a negatively sloped Phillips Curve. Consider the analysis depicted in Figure 19.3 (page 478).

From an initial equilibrium at A, suppose aggregate supply increases from AS_1 to AS_2 in a one-year period. This moves us to B in Figure 19.3. However, suppose that aggregate demand also increases (shifts rightward) in the same year by a relatively large amount to AD_2, moving the equilibrium to C. The move from A to C implies higher equilibrium levels of prices and real output. As the price level moves from P_1 to P_2, we experience inflation. The *rate* of inflation is directly linked to the *magnitude* of the change in the equilibrium price level—to the size of the difference between P_1 and P_2. This situation yields a certain inflation rate and a certain unemployment rate—one point along a Phillips Curve.

Now, to demonstrate how this framework can generate a trade-off between inflation and unemployment (a Phillips Curve shaped like that of Figure 19.2), suppose hypothetically that aggregate demand had shifted by a different amount than from AD_1 to AD_2. First, suppose AD had shifted farther to the right than AD_2. Suppose AD had shifted to AD_3 (dashed line in Figure 19.3). In this event, the new

The greater the rightward shift of the aggregate demand curve, the more rapid the increase in price level and the greater the new level of output (lower the unemployment rate). A downward-sloping Phillips Curve is generated when shifts in the nation's aggregate supply curve are dominated by shifts in the aggregate demand curve.

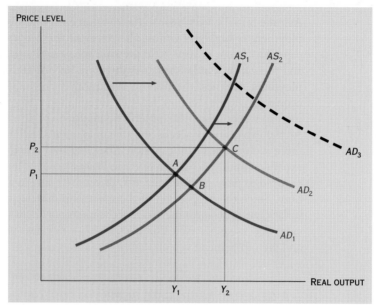

FIGURE 19.3

equilibrium price level and output level would have exceeded P_2 and Y_2, respectively. This implies that inflation would have been more severe and the unemployment rate would have been lower (since real output would have increased by a larger amount) than was the case when aggregate demand shifted from AD_1 to AD_2. We would have moved up and to the left along a Phillips Curve. Alternatively, suppose aggregate demand had shifted up by a *lesser* amount than indicated by the move from AD_1 to AD_2. Then both output growth and price-level inflation would have proceeded more slowly. The slower output growth (accompanied by lower inflation) would have resulted in a higher unemployment rate. We would have moved downward and rightward along a Phillips Curve.

We can see that a world in which aggregate demand consistently shifts by a larger (though varying) magnitude than does aggregate supply generates a series of unemployment rate and inflation rate observations that would trace out a negative relationship between inflation and unemployment—a Phillips Curve of the nature illustrated in Figure 19.2.[2]

---

[2]On the other hand, in those (less-common) episodes in which the magnitude of aggregate supply shifts are dominating the shifts of the aggregate demand curve, economic events will trace out points that fall along an upward-sloping Phillips Curve. The negative supply shocks triggered by the OPEC oil cartel in 1973 and 1974 (coupled with the worldwide drought of 1974) resulted in a large leftward shift in the nation's aggregate supply curve. Even though aggregate demand increased somewhat, it was swamped by the leftward-shifting AS curve. This implies the phenomenon of *stagflation*, that is, the simultaneous existence of higher inflation and falling output (higher unemployment). In the 1973–1975 period, the United States experienced both rapidly increasing inflation and a sharp increase in the unemployment rate. Note the pattern of inflation and unemployment in these years (Figure 19.4). Both unemployment and inflation were higher in 1975 than in 1973.

SUPPOSE, OVER A TWO-YEAR PERIOD, THAT OIL PRICES FALL DRAMATICALLY AND THE WORLD IS BLESSED WITH UNUSUALLY BOUNTIFUL AGRICULTURAL HARVESTS. SUPPOSE, IN THE SAME PERIOD, AGGREGATE DEMAND INCREASES VERY MODESTLY. ANALYZE THE CHANGES IN THE UNEMPLOYMENT AND INFLATION RATES THAT WOULD BE TRACED OUT IN THIS SCENARIO. WOULD THE OBSERVATIONS APPEAR TO FALL ALONG A NEGATIVELY OR POSITIVELY SLOPED PHILLIPS CURVE IN THIS PERIOD?

The Shifting Phillips Curve

The conception of the Phillips Curve as a stable and predictable inverse relationship between inflation and unemployment reached its high point in the late 1960s. After that, it collapsed. Figure 19.4 depicts the *actual combinations* of inflation and

U.S. INFLATION AND UNEMPLOYMENT RATES, 1963–1991

In the 1960s, a stable Phillips Curve prevailed. After the 1960s, the relationship between inflation and unemployment became unstable. One explanation is that the Phillips Curve exists, but shifts right and left in response to such events as changes in expected inflation and changes in composition of the labor force.

SOURCE: *Economic Report of the President*, 1992.

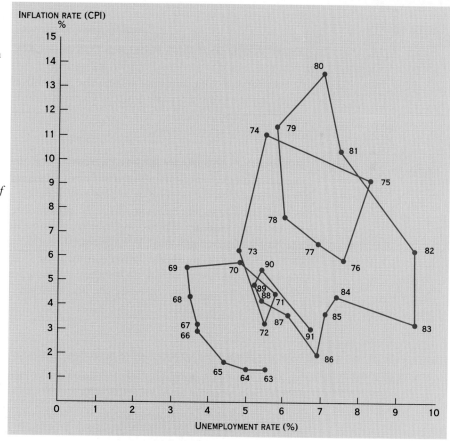

FIGURE 19.4

unemployment prevailing each year since 1963. In the 1960s, inflation and unemployment rates clustered along a well-defined Phillips Curve (shown in the lower left segment of the figure). However, since the 1960s, the points no longer fall along a single, stable Phillips Curve. Rather, there appear to be a *family* of Phillips Curves, each pertaining to a rather brief interval of time. In this family of Phillips Curves one observes separate, negatively sloped segments for the 1960s, 1976–1979, 1980–1982, and 1986–1989.

One way to interpret the pattern of points in Figure 19.4 is to think of the Phillips Curve being derived based on "other things equal," just like a demand curve. As we change the amount of demand stimulus in the economy—*holding constant all other factors that influence inflation and unemployment*—we trace out a stable Phillips Curve. But there are many factors in the economic environment besides the magnitude of demand stimulus that influence unemployment and inflation. Examples include demographic factors, technological change, supply shocks, and changes in expected inflation. As these factors change over time, the *entire position* of the trade-off changes—the Phillips Curve shifts. A trade-off between inflation and unemployment still exists, in this view, but its position is unstable and shifts up or down periodically. Although few economists recognized in the 1950s or 1960s that it might happen, the Phillips Curve shifted sharply rightward in the 1970s and early 1980s. Since the early 1980s, happily, it has shifted back to the left.

RIGHTWARD-SHIFTING PHILLIPS CURVE—LATE 1960S TO EARLY 1980S

At least three factors combined during the period from roughly 1969 through 1982 to worsen the position of the Phillips Curve, to shift it rightward. As a result, the nation's ***discomfort index***—the sum of the unemployment rate and the inflation rate—increased in this period.[3]

RISING INFLATIONARY EXPECTATIONS   For any given amount of macroeconomic stimulus (hence, unemployment rate), wage and salary hikes are likely to be closely related to the outlook for inflation. If inflation is expected to be severe, average wage and salary increases are large. If inflation is expected to be subdued, these increases are modest. All this implies that an increase in expected inflation shifts the Phillips Curve rightward. Without question this happened in the 1970s and the early 1980s. Years of rising inflation commencing in the mid-1960s convinced people by the beginning of the 1970s that inflation was going to be around for a while—that we would not soon see the low inflation rates of the early 1960s. Note

---

[3]The term *discomfort index* was popularized in the mid-1980s by the Reagan Administration for the purpose of calling attention to the improvement in U.S. macroeconomic conditions in President Reagan's tenure. In 1980, the year before the Reagan Administration took office, the unemployment and inflation rates stood at 7.1 percent and 12.4 percent, respectively. This yielded a discomfort index of 19.5. In 1988, the last year of the Reagan Administration, the unemployment and inflation rates were 5.5 percent and 4.1 percent, respectively, yielding a discomfort index of 9.6 percent, roughly half of the 1980 index. In 1991, the unemployment and inflation rates were 6.7 percent and 3.0 percent, so the discomfort index was 9.7 percent. What was it last year? Check the *Federal Reserve Bulletin* or most recent *Economic Report of the President* to find the data.

in Figure 19.4 that the cluster of unemployment–inflation points for the 1970s lies rightward of the points for the 1960s. In the late 1970s, inflation again accelerated, this time reaching double-digit levels. This further ratcheted inflationary expectations upward. This ratcheting shifted the Phillips Curve rightward again in the early 1980s, as indicated by the points for 1980–1982. Many economists agree that the chief factor accounting for the rightward shift of the Phillips Curve from the 1960s to the early 1980s was the significant increase in inflationary expectations.

DEMOGRAPHIC CHANGES We have already outlined the consequences of the substantial influx into the labor force of women and teenagers in the late 1960s and 1970s for the nation's frictional and overall unemployment rates. From the perspective of the Phillips Curve, these demographic changes imply that the unemployment rate associated with each and every magnitude of economic stimulus (and hence, inflation) increased between the 1960s and the early 1980s. Stated alternatively, given the increase in frictional unemployment associated with the change in labor force composition, the amount of economic stimulus (hence inflation) required to achieve any given unemployment rate increased. This means the Phillips Curve shifted rightward.

LIBERALIZATION OF UNEMPLOYMENT BENEFITS On average, unemployment benefits were made more generous after the 1960s. This generosity increases frictional unemployment by increasing the incentive to quit an unsatisfactory job and to take more time in the job-search process. This implies, again, that achieving any given unemployment rate requires a more stimulated economy and, hence, more inflation. Thus, the move toward more liberal unemployment benefits predictably shifted the Phillips Curve rightward. The magnitude of the shift was probably relatively modest, however.

THE 1980s—A LEFTWARD-SHIFTING PHILLIPS CURVE

Two of the three factors that conspired to shift the Phillips Curve rightward during the 1970s worked in reverse to shift the Phillips Curve leftward after 1982. As a result, we enjoyed a more favorable combination of unemployment and inflation in the 1986–1992 period than we had experienced in almost 20 years. The factors responsible for the leftward-shifting Phillips Curve were the changing age composition of the labor force and the reduction of inflationary expectations resulting from the successful battle against inflation during the early 1980s.

Because the U.S. birthrate declined significantly after the early 1960s, the number of youths coming into the labor force declined in the 1980s. Also, the *baby boomers* were aging in the 1980s. Many were entering middle age, a period in which labor market turnover rates are low. These factors reduced frictional unemployment and pulled down the overall unemployment rate associated with any given amount of economic stimulus and inflation. The surprisingly rapid reduction of inflation during 1981–1983, coupled with the maintenance of very modest inflation for several years thereafter, convinced people that severe inflation was gone for the foreseeable future. The gradual winding down of inflationary expectations in the 1980s resulted in a leftward-shifting Phillips Curve. Hence, the long business cycle expansion of 1982–1990 resulted in a sustained reduction of unemployment without reigniting severe inflation because the Phillips Curve was gradually shifting leftward.

Is the Phillips Curve Really a Menu of Policy Choices?

As noted earlier, both theoretical intuition and observation from history suggest that a robust economy tends to exhibit relatively low unemployment and high inflation, whereas a *soft* economy typically results in higher unemployment and lower inflation. That is, both history and intuition suggest the existence of a downward-sloping Phillips Curve. Within broad limits, government can manipulate its monetary and fiscal policy tools to provide any desired magnitude of macroeconomic stimulus. One's first instinct might be to regard the Phillips Curve as a menu of policy choices—that is, that the government may choose to operate at any point along the Curve. Most economists today believe that such a conception of the Phillips Curve is incorrect. The reasoning is subtle, and involves the effect of changes in actual inflation upon expected inflation and, hence, on the *position* of the Phillips Curve. Consider the analysis in Figure 19.5.

If the government regards the Phillips Curve as a long-run menu of the various attainable combinations of unemployment and inflation, policymakers might attempt to move us from *A* to *B* in Figure 19.5. That is, government could attempt to trade off an increase in inflation in exchange for a reduction in unemployment. To bring about this change, the government would implement stimulative monetary and fiscal policies. At first, as inflation begins to rise, workers are fooled by the inflation and real wages decline. Business profits expand and firms step up output and employment.[4] Therefore, unemployment declines and the move from *A* to *B* in Figure 19.5 is achieved successfully in the short run.

However, in the long run, expectations of inflation adjust to the ongoing rate of inflation. As soon as workers become aware that their wages have fallen relative to the price level, they demand *catch-up* compensation. When this happens, firms' profits, output, and employment revert to the normal levels and the unemployment rate returns to the normal level, U_N. Hence, we would move from *B* to *C* in Figure 19.5.

When the government notes that its attempts to reduce unemployment have been frustrated, it could further boost economic activity in an attempt to push the unemployment rate below U_N. As inflation again accelerates (to perhaps 9 percent), workers are fooled again. Output, profits, and employment rise and unemployment declines again—temporarily. We move from *C* to *D*, again experiencing a *short-run* trade-off between inflation and unemployment. Once the inflation becomes fully

---

[4]Those frictionally unemployed workers in the process of job search might mistake the new higher *nominal* wage and salary offers as being higher *real* offers. If so, they would tend to accept employment more quickly. Frictional (and total) unemployment therefore declines when inflation exceeds expected inflation.

Many economists believe that in the long run—a time period sufficiently long to permit expectations of inflation to adapt fully to existing inflation—there is no trade-off between inflation and unemployment. In other words, economists believe that the long-run Phillips Curve is vertical, consisting of points such as *ACE*.

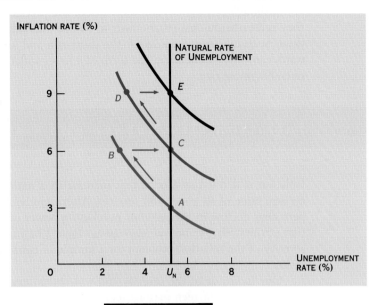

FIGURE 19.5

NATURAL UNEMPLOYMENT RATE HYPOTHESIS

View that there is no long-run trade-off between inflation and unemployment; that the nation's long-run Phillips Curve is a vertical line at the natural rate of unemployment.

anticipated, however, profits, output, and employment return to normal levels and we move to point *E* in Figure 19.5. Hence, the long-run Phillips Curve consists of points such as *ACE* in the figure. That is, the long-run Phillips Curve is a vertical line at the economy's natural, or NAIRU, unemployment rate. This view is known as the **natural unemployment rate hypothesis**.

In the long run, expectations of inflation catch up with actual inflation. There is no *labor fooling* in the long run. Since efforts to move along a perceived short-run Phillips Curve to reduce unemployment raise inflation and thereby raise *expected* inflation, the position of the short-run Phillips Curve shifts rightward as we move from *A* to *B*. Policy efforts to exploit a short-run Phillips Curve systematically produce a shift in the Phillips Curve. In this analysis, the only way to keep the unemployment rate below U_N is to attempt to fool workers permanently by always keeping actual inflation above expected inflation. But this requires a disastrous policy of continual escalation of the inflation rate. We would soon have runaway inflation. In terms of Figure 19.5, point *A* is clearly preferable to point *E*. The clear implication is that government should not attempt to reduce the unemployment rate below the natural rate through stimulative macroeconomic policies.

The problem, of course, is that the precise level of the natural unemployment rate is unknown. Furthermore, it fluctuates over time. Economists disagree about the level of the natural rate, liberals tending to believe it is relatively low and conservatives estimating it to be relatively high. The natural rate increased during the period from the mid-1960s to the early 1980s and has declined since then. In spite of the lack of consensus among economists about the precise magnitude of the natural unemployment rate, it is agreed that the further the nation's unemployment rate declines below 6 percent, the greater the chances of running into accelerating inflation.

Although economists are uncertain of the precise natural unemployment rate, they agree unanimously that efforts to reduce the natural rate itself would be beneficial. Such measures would shift the short-run and long-run Phillips Curves leftward, conferring benefits in the form of a lower inflation rate associated with each unemployment rate.

Inflation: Its Nature and Causes

Inflation is defined as a persistent increase in a nation's general price level—the average price of all goods and services. Alternatively, inflation may be defined as a persistent decline in the value or purchasing power of a nation's unit of currency, that is, the dollar, franc, ruble, or peso. Table 19.1 indicates the pervasiveness and severity of the inflation problem for a sample of thirteen nations in the 1970s and 1980s.

One indicator of the severity and widespread existence of inflation is the fact that five of the thirteen nations represented in the table experienced double-digit annual inflation (or more) throughout the 1970s and 1980s. In the 1970s, prices throughout the world were ravaged by a severe drought, a dramatic increase in oil prices, and excessive economic stimulus in many countries toward the end of the decade. Most industrial nations reacted to the severe and accelerating inflation of

AVERAGE ANNUAL INFLATION RATE (CONSUMER PRICES)		
COUNTRY	1970S	1980S
Argentina	119%	355%
Brazil	35	211
Israel	42	88
Mexico	17	65
Italy	14	10
Spain	15	9.3
United Kingdom	13	6.7
France	9.3	6.7
Canada	7.6	6.2
United States	7.5	5.0
Switzerland	5.0	3.4
West Germany	4.9	2.8
Japan	8.8	2.3

SOURCE: *Citibank Economic Database* and Federal Reserve Bank of St. Louis.

TABLE 19.1

the late 1970s by implementing monetary policy restraint in the first half of the decade of the 1980s. For this reason, coupled with the decline in world oil prices, almost all industrial nations witnessed a slowdown in inflation during the 1980s. However, such nations as Argentina, Brazil, Israel, and Mexico experienced a dramatic acceleration in inflation in the 1980s.

Inflation has been an almost intractable problem in the United States for the past 30 years. It has persisted at significant levels during periods of recession as well as prosperity. As we approach the mid-1990s, some economists believe that we are embarking on an era of extremely low inflation not witnessed since the early 1960s. However, the experience of the past 30 years suggests that low inflation may be difficult to sustain. Economists and politicians have been unable to devise a lasting cure for inflation in the context of a society in which both prosperity and economic freedom (in the sense of minimal government involvement in private wage and price decision making) are paramount national objectives.

CAUSES OF INFLATION

In principle, inflation may originate from aggregate demand forces or from cost or aggregate supply forces. In reality, the preponderant source of inflation throughout history has been excessive growth in aggregate demand for goods and services relative to expansion in a nation's capacity to produce.

DEMAND–PULL INFLATION We illustrate this type of inflation in Figure 19.6. In the figure, the initial equilibrium price level (P_1) is indicated by the intersection

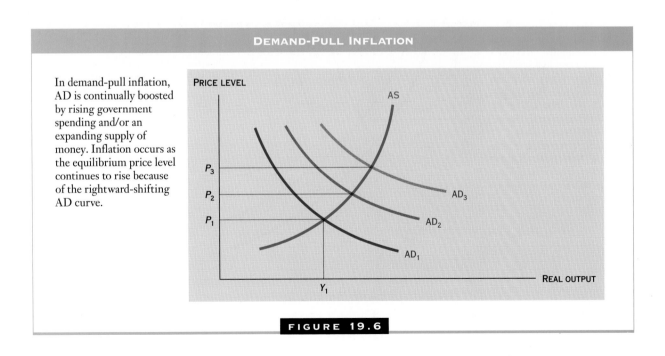

DEMAND-PULL INFLATION

In demand-pull inflation, AD is continually boosted by rising government spending and/or an expanding supply of money. Inflation occurs as the equilibrium price level continues to rise because of the rightward-shifting AD curve.

FIGURE 19.6

of the nation's aggregate supply and aggregate demand curves. Initially, the price level is P_1 and the output level is Y_1. Continuing expansion in government spending and the money supply boost the aggregate demand curve to AD_2, AD_3, and so forth. This pulls the price level up to P_2, P_3, and so forth.

In time of war, **demand–pull inflation** almost always occurs. Political expediency leads to increasing government military expenditures without commensurate tax hikes. Rather than requiring that the bonds issued to finance the additional expenditures be absorbed by the private sector of the economy, the central bank often facilitates the wartime finance by purchasing a signficant portion of the newly issued debt. This results in rapid expansion of the nation's money supply. The rapid growth of money and government expenditures boost aggregate demand, thereby fueling inflation.

Demand–pull inflation tends to be a chronic problem in nations with fragile political structures, because such countries frequently resort to inflationary means of financing government. It is almost inherent in Brazil, Argentina, Mexico, and many other countries. And the industrial nations are not immune to recurring bouts with the disease.

COST–PUSH INFLATION If the fundamental source of rising prices originates in the cost or supply side of the economy rather than from excessive growth of aggregate expenditures, the inflation is known as **cost–push inflation**. In Figure 19.7, we illustrate this problem with our familiar AS–AD framework.

DEMAND–PULL INFLATION
Inflation caused by rightward-shifting AD curve, usually triggered by increasing money supply and government expenditures.

COST–PUSH INFLATION
Inflation caused by leftward-shifting AS curve, usually triggered by wage hikes or price increases of other inputs (such as oil) that are caused by factors other than excess demand for these inputs.

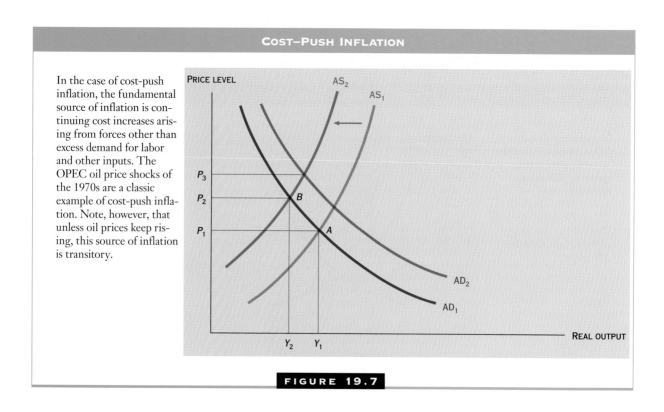

COST–PUSH INFLATION

In the case of cost-push inflation, the fundamental source of inflation is continuing cost increases arising from forces other than excess demand for labor and other inputs. The OPEC oil price shocks of the 1970s are a classic example of cost-push inflation. Note, however, that unless oil prices keep rising, this source of inflation is transitory.

FIGURE 19.7

In the figure, the initial equilibrium is at A, the intersection of AS_1 and AD_1. Initially, the price level is P_1, and output is Y_1. Now, suppose that a worldwide drought occurs, driving up prices of basic foodstuffs. Or suppose that world oil prices rise dramatically because of supply cutbacks engineered by the OPEC cartel. Or, suppose that Congress increases the minimum wage 30 percent. Each of these forces would shift the nation's aggregate supply curve leftward, moving the economy to point B and raising the price level to P_2 in the figure. In the new equilibrium, prices will have increased and output will have fallen. This combination of rising prices and falling output is known as **stagflation**. This phenomenon characterized much of the 1970s in the industrial nations.

STAGFLATION
Combination of rising prices and stagnant or declining aggregate output (rising unemployment).

Since the government may be committed to high levels of output and employment, it may implement stimulative monetary and fiscal measures to boost the economy. If so, the aggregate demand curve would be shifted rightward to AD_2. This boosts output above the depressed level of Y_2, but aggravates the inflation problem by driving the equilibrium price level to P_3.

Since both aggregate supply and aggregate demand forces have contributed to inflation in this instance, there may be room for disagreement about the nature of this inflation. However, the initial impetus for the inflation was the negative supply shock that shifted the aggregate supply curve leftward. Hence, most economists would label it an example of cost–push inflation.

Since cost–push inflation can be sustained only by a *continuing* leftward shift in the aggregate supply curve, and since it seems unlikely that a continuing or steady stream of such events is likely to occur, most economists would list this type of inflation as a secondary type, dominated in frequency and severity by the traditional demand–pull type of inflation.

The Nature and History of U.S. Inflation

Figure 19.8 (page 488) illustrates the history of the U.S. price level from the beginning of the republic about 220 years ago to the present. The figure depicts the wholesale price index, the forerunner of our producer price index. The consumer price index has exhibited a very similar pattern.

The most striking aspect of Figure 19.8 is the difference in price-level behavior after World War II relative to that in the nation's first 170 years. Although the early period was subject to periodic bursts of inflation, these episodes were followed by falling prices, that is, **deflation**. The price level kept returning to its *normal* or standard level. After World War II, these episodes of deflation have disappeared from the American scene.[5] The level of prices has followed a one-way street—upward.

DEFLATION
Period of time in which the nation's price level declines; period in which the value of the unit of currency rises.

---

[5]One need not look with regret at this departure of deflation from the American scene. These periods of falling prices were typically hard times, with heavy unemployment, financial distress, and widespread foreclosures on farms and other enterprises. A primary concern in the U.S. presidential election of 1896 was the issue of halting the twenty-year deflation of prices that was bankrupting thousands of enterprises. Though it may sound strange, *deflation* is in many ways a much more damaging phenomenon than *inflation*.

PRICE-LEVEL BEHAVIOR BEFORE WORLD WAR II

The basic early pattern was one of severe wartime inflation followed by a major postwar contraction of economic activity and deflation of prices. Hence, the general level of prices was approximately the same in 1800, 1875, 1925, and 1945. Emerging prominently in Figure 19.8 are the sharp price-level increases during the Revolutionary War, the War of 1812, the Civil War, and the two world wars. These are classic examples of demand–pull inflation, in which aggregate demand increases much faster than the nation's capacity to produce goods and services.

Political considerations and the urgency of war are such that wars are seldom financed fully by tax increases. The resulting government deficit is financed by issuing bonds to the public and to the central bank. Central bank purchasing of government debt is essentially equivalent to printing currency to finance war. Governments fail to force down other public and private forms of expenditures sufficiently to compensate for the expansion of military expenditures. Aggregate

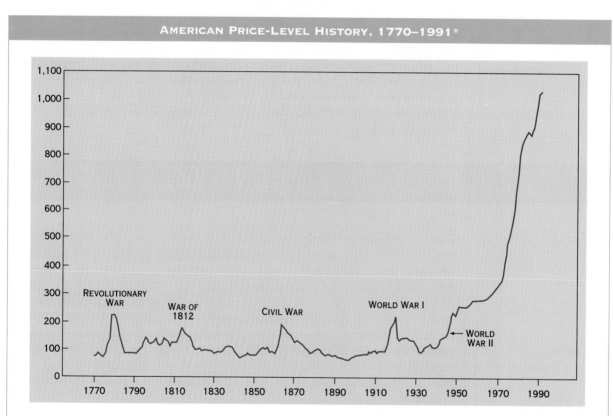

AMERICAN PRICE-LEVEL HISTORY, 1770–1991*

Before 1940, periods of rising prices (inflation) were followed by episodes of falling prices (deflation). Hence, there was no long-term upward trend in the American price level during the period 1770–1940. Since 1940, the U.S. economy has developed a bias toward inflation; periods of deflation have disappeared from the American experience.

*Wholesale price index, 1910–1914 = 100.

SOURCE: Data from *Historical Statistics of the United States*, 1992, and *Economic Report of the President*, 1992

FIGURE 19.8

demand becomes excessive, as illustrated in the AS–AD framework of Figure 19.6. The result is demand–pull inflation.

At the end of each war prior to World War II, a sharp cutback in government expenditures on military procurement occurred while large numbers of men released from the armed forces entered the civilian labor force. The sharp reduction in aggregate demand resulted in severe cuts in output and employment. The wartime boom was inevitably followed by a postwar deflationary bust in which profits declined precipitously, unemployment increased, and widespread financial distress prevailed.

One should remember that activist monetary and fiscal policies to combat heavy unemployment are a phenomenon of the past 60 years or less. In the earlier period, one may characterize the government's role in the macroeconomy as one of *laissez-faire*. There was no attempt to use monetary and fiscal policies to boost economic activity during the postwar contractions that occurred before World War II. Furthermore, there was limited *scope* for doing so, since the Federal Reserve System was not established until 1913. And many institutional features of the economy that today limit downward flexibility of wages and prices did not come on stream until during or after the depression of the 1930s. The severe business-cycle contractions that prevailed before World War II were thus characterized by sharp declines in wages and prices.

POST-WORLD WAR II PRICE-LEVEL BEHAVIOR

Before the Second World War, the American price level exhibited a symmetrical pattern. Price-level increases and decreases occurred with equal frequency. (You may be surprised to learn that the price level was higher in 1780 and 1810 than in 1935.) Inflation was always followed by deflation, leaving the long-term trend of prices roughly unchanged. This symmetry has given way in recent decades to considerable *downward inflexibility* of wages and prices. A glance at Figure 19.8 confirms the one-way nature of price-level changes in the past 40 or 50 years. The most recent year in which the consumer price index declined for the year as a whole was 1955.[6]

In Figure 19.9, we examine the most recent 35 year period in more detail by illustrating two measures of *inflation*—the rates of change in the consumer price index and the producer price index. Clearly evident in the figure are the experience of relatively stable prices (low inflation) between 1958 and 1965, the acceleration of inflation from 1965 to 1970 (the Vietnam War years), the two episodes of double-digit inflation (peaking in 1974 and 1980), and the period of moderately low inflation since the early 1980s.

---

[6]The powerful upward momentum of the price level is indicated by the fact that during about 200 consecutive months from 1965 until 1982, the CPI did not decline for even a *single month*, even though the 17-year interval encompassed four recessions. During the 1950–1990 period, the CPI declined in less than 2 percent of the months. The PPI tells a similar though somewhat less severe story.

CAUSES OF THE CHANGE IN PRICE-LEVEL BEHAVIOR SINCE THE 1930S

In Figure 19.9 shaded areas represent periods of business recession and unshaded areas periods of economic expansion. An important point to note is that post-World War II recessions have stemmed inflation only in the sense that the *inflation rate* was induced to fall. The price *level* continued to rise but at a slower rate. This contrasts with the pre-1940 experience, in which inflation rates became *negative* (price level *fell*) during severe recessions. Note in the figure that even at the ebb of the inflation cycle following the two most severe postwar recessions (1973–1975 and 1981–1982), the CPI inflation rate was proceeding at more than 2 percent per

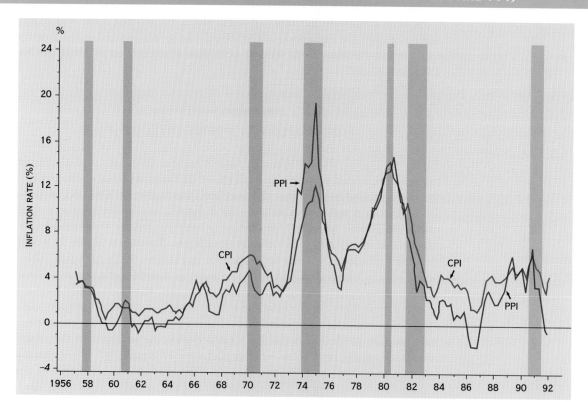

Two measures of inflation are the annual rate of increase in the consumer price index (CPI) and in the producer price index (PPI). Inflation was subdued in the early 1960s, accelerated during the Vietnam War (1965–1970), and reached rates over 10 percent per year in both 1974 and 1980 following major increases in oil prices. Inflation came down dramatically in the early 1980s, and remained in the vicinity of 4 percent per year in the past decade.

*Points plotted are twelve-month moving average rates of inflation. Shaded areas depict business recessions.

SOURCE: Data from *Citibank Economic Database*, 1992.

FIGURE 19.9

year. Economists believe that several factors have increased the inertia in the inflation process, making the price level less downwardly flexible since the 1930s.

ROLE OF GOVERNMENT IN THE ECONOMY As a result of the severe economic hardship experienced during the 1930s, the philosophy toward government responsibility for the overall performance of the economy underwent a transformation. Instrumental in this change in thinking was the development by Keynes of a new framework of macroeconomic analysis. This framework was generally interpreted as implying that deliberate use of monetary and fiscal policies for purposes of contributing to economic stability was both feasible and appropriate. A *laissez-faire* philosophy toward the macroeconomy was alleged to be inappropriate. This emerging belief that government should take responsibility for the state of economic prosperity was embodied in the Employment Act of 1946. The act mandates that the federal government implement its monetary and fiscal policies in such a manner as to contribute toward "maximum production, employment, and purchasing power."

The *technical feasibility* of achieving greater economic stability improved dramatically in the first two or three decades after the Great Depression of the 1930s. This was partially the result of the government's new activist philosophy toward minimizing the severity of economic setbacks through the use of stimulative monetary and fiscal policies.[7]

AUTOMATIC STABILIZER
Features in the economy that work automatically (without requiring discretionary measures) to stabilize economic activity or inhibit economic fluctuations.

Even more important was the increasing strength of the **automatic** (or built-in) **stabilizers** associated with the federal budget. The ratios of taxes to GDP and of government expenditures to GDP increased from less than 10 percent in the 1920s to more than 25 percent by the 1960s. As GDP falls in recession, tax receipts automatically decline and transfer payments rise. This stimulates aggregate demand and output, cushioning the economic contraction. With the growth of the government budget relative to GDP, these automatic stabilizers became more powerful; they absorbed a larger portion of any potential decline in GDP during recessions.[8]

Because of the increased power of the automatic stabilizers, the willingness to implement monetary and fiscal policies to stabilize the economy, and the reduced volatility in the spending patterns of individuals and firms that these developments induced, the stability of aggregate demand for goods and services has increased significantly since World War II. The average duration of recessions has been cut in half, and periods of expansion have lasted twice as long. The economy has operated much closer to capacity on average. Fluctuations of output about the long-term growth trend have diminished. (Review Figure 13.A3, page 339.)

---

[7]Prior to World War I, the United States was on the gold standard. This prevented implementation of stimulative monetary policy measures, even if they were deemed to be desirable, because the money supply was rigidly tied to the U.S. gold stock. Even though the gold standard was abandoned in 1914, the Federal Reserve's modern philosophy of implementing discretionary monetary policies to combat cyclical instability did not evolve until the 1950s.

[8]It has been estimated that the portion of any potential decline in GDP during recessions absorbed by the automatic stabilizers increased from about 6 percent in 1932 to more than 35 percent by the mid-1970s. See Robert J. Gordon, "Postwar Macroeconomics: The Evolution of Events and Ideas," in Martin Feldstein (ed.), *The American Economy in Transition* (Chicago: University of Chicago Press, 1980).

The relative mildness of the first few postwar recessions, coupled with increasing public awareness of the government's commitment to high employment, strengthened the emerging perception that severe economic downturns like the 1930s depression could be avoided in the future. A potent side effect of this growing perception was an increase in the inflationary propensity of the economic system. The growing awareness that depressions could be avoided increased the resolve of workers toward resisting wage cuts and reduced the vigor with which firms pursued wage cuts in recessions. Hence, the post-World War II American economy has exhibited increasingly *sticky wages and prices*—a reduction in the extent to which wages and prices fall in response to excess capacity and unemployment.

These tendencies have probably been reinforced by the use of measures to reduce the financial hardship of the unemployed. Increased availability of unemployment benefits and other government transfer payments may have caused workers to become less willing to accept pay cuts and more willing to become unemployed. As a result, a much more severe economic contraction would be needed to bring about a reduction in the price level today than would have been required in the 1870s or 1930s, for example.

THE LABOR MOVEMENT AND INSTITUTIONAL CHANGES The great hardship suffered by workers in the 1930s stimulated the American unionization movement. The Wagner Act of 1935 guaranteed the right of workers to organize, and the proportion of the U.S. labor force belonging to unions increased from 6 percent in 1933 to more than 30 percent in the 1950s (though it has declined considerably in recent decades). Because union wages are less likely to decline in time of weak economic activity than are nonunion wages, greater unionization probably contributed to increased wage rigidity until the 1980s, when the trend toward lower unionization accelerated.

Other institutional changes, many of which were initiated in the 1930s, have contributed to the decreased downward flexibility of prices and have increased the inflation tendency of the system. Federal insurance of bank deposits—implemented in 1934 with the creation of the Federal Deposit Insurance Corporation—was without question a socially beneficial change. However, an important side effect of FDIC insurance has been the virtual elimination of the bank runs and contraction of deposits that contributed to falling prices in pre-1934 cyclical downturns. Minimum-wage laws, first implemented in the Fair Labor Standards Act of 1938, produce an obvious obstacle to downward wage and price flexibility. Also, as noted earlier, unemployment insurance and other measures that reduce the personal cost of being unemployed probably have reduced the willingness of workers to accept lower wages, which previously contributed to downward wage and price flexibility.

Summary

1. The Phillips Curve is a figure depicting an inverse relationship between a nation's unemployment and inflation rates. High unemployment is depicted as being compatible with

low inflation; lower unemployment leads to higher inflation, in the view of the Phillips Curve.

2. Theoretical underpinnings for the existence of a Phillips Curve include the labor–management bargaining hypothesis of wage behavior, a structural explanation, and a general aggregate supply–aggregate demand explanation.

3. The relationship between unemployment and inflation appeared to be quite stable in the 1960s. However, the Phillips Curve has become unstable since then. The short-run Phillips Curve shifts in response to such forces as changing inflationary expectations and changing age and sex composition of the nation's labor force. The Phillips Curve shifted persistently rightward from the late 1960s until the early 1980s. Since then, fortunately, it has shifted leftward.

4. Economists today do not typically view the Phillips Curve as a long-run menu of policy options. The government may not be able to exploit a perceived trade-off between inflation and unemployment in the long run. For example, the use of stimulative monetary and fiscal policies for the purpose of moving northwesterly along a perceived Phillips Curve will temporarily reduce unemployment and increase inflation. However, the Phillips Curve will shift rightward as soon as inflation expectations adjust to the new, higher actual rate of inflation. In the view of the widely accepted *natural unemployment rate hypothesis*, the nation's long-run Phillips Curve is a vertical line at the natural rate of unemployment.

5. Prior to World War II, inflation and deflation occurred with equal frequency. Wartime inflation was always followed by a postwar period of falling prices. As a result, the U.S. price level was approximately the same in 1945 as in 1800.

6. Since 1945, the U.S. economy has no longer experienced the old-fashioned episodes of deflation (falling prices). The U.S. price level today is more than five times higher than in 1945. In the modern economy, prices rise even during periods of recession, albeit more slowly than during expansion.

7. Several factors account for this decrease in downward wage and price-level flexibility and for the increased inertia in the inflation process. These factors include the increased power of the automatic stabilizers associated with the federal budget, the more active role of government (especially the Federal Reserve) toward conducting stabilization policy, the perception on the part of the public that the government is committed to avoiding severe economic downturns, and such institutional changes as minimum-wage legislation, the introduction of unemployment insurance, and the federal insurance of bank deposits. All these changes came during or after the Great Depression of the 1930s.

Key Terms

Phillips Curve
discomfort index
natural unemployment rate
   hypothesis
demand–pull inflation

cost–push inflation
stagflation
deflation
automatic stabilizer

1. Define a Phillips Curve. Draw the curve and carefully label the axes. What is the economic meaning of the *slope* of this curve at any point?

2. Analyze two intuitively plausible explanations for the existence of a negative or inverse relationship between the nation's unemployment and inflation rates.

3. Explain carefully how the following events would alter the position of (shift) the nation's short-run Phillips Curve:
   a. the labor force participation rate of women declines
   b. Congress abolishes the minimum wage
   c. eligiblity requirements for receiving unemployment benefits are eased

4. If the data from history seem to confirm the existence of a downward-sloping Phillips Curve, why do many economists believe the government is incapable of "buying" a lasting reduction in unemployment by accepting higher inflation?

5. Why do you suppose that some countries have much higher rates of inflation than others (review Table 19.1)?

6. Analyze the distinction between demand–pull and cost–push inflation.

7. Explain why a changing role of government in macroeconomic life since the 1930s may have imparted a predisposition toward inflation in the economy in recent decades, as compared to the earlier era.

8. Using the AS–AD framework of analysis, demonstrate why a government commitment to high levels of output and employment may lead to severe inflation if the economy receives a series of supply shocks such as OPEC oil price hikes.

9. The sluggish U.S. economy of 1990, 1991, and 1992 helped push the inflation rate to the lowest level in nearly 30 years. Explain how this development presented an enhanced opportunity (in the form of a favorable short-run Phillips Curve) to the national administration in office in 1993.

YOUR TURN
Answers

BOTH THE REDUCTION IN OIL PRICES AND THE BOUNTIFUL HARVESTS WORK TO SHIFT THE NATION'S AGGREGATE SUPPLY CURVE SHARPLY RIGHTWARD. WITH THE MODEST INCREASE IN AGGREGATE DEMAND, WE END UP WITH A REDUCTION IN INFLATION (AND PERHAPS EVEN A DECLINE IN THE PRICE LEVEL) AND A SIGNIFICANT INCREASE IN OUTPUT. HENCE, UNEMPLOYMENT AND INFLATION BOTH DECLINE. THESE OBSERVATIONS TRACE OUT POINTS THAT APPEAR TO FALL ALONG A *POSITIVELY* SLOPED PHILLIPS CURVE.

Selected References

Baily, Martin N., and Arthur M. Okun (eds.). *The Battle Against Unemployment and Inflation*, 3rd ed. (New York: Norton, 1982). This series of articles analyzes the relationship of monetary and fiscal policies to unemployment.

Blinder, Alan. *Hard Heads, Soft Hearts* (New York: Addison-Wesley, 1987). Chapters 2 and 3 provide a readable discussion of inflation, unemployment, and stabilization policy.

Friedman, Milton. "The Role of Monetary Policy," *American Economic Review*, March 1968, pp. 1–17. This article presents the natural unemployment rate hypothesis and foresees the demise of the notion of a stable Phillips Curve.

Garfinkel, Michelle R. "What is an Acceptable Rate of Inflation?—A Review of Issues," St. Louis Federal Reserve Bank *Review*, July/August 1989, pp. 3–15. This article analyzes the costs and benefits of attempting to eliminate modest rates of inflation such as those of the past decade.

Hall, Robert E. (ed.). *Inflation: Causes and Effects* (Chicago: University of Chicago Press, 1982). These twelve articles by eminent economists explore various aspects of inflation.

UNFORTUNATELY,
POLICYMAKERS CANNOT
ACT AS IF THE ECONOMY
IS AN AUTOMOBILE THAT
CAN QUICKLY BE STEERED
BACK AND FORTH.
RATHER, THE PROCEDURE
OF CHANGING AGGREGATE
DEMAND IS MUCH CLOSER
TO THAT OF A CAPTAIN
NAVIGATING A GIANT
SUPER-TANKER.
EVEN IF HE GIVES A
SIGNAL FOR A HARD TURN,
IT TAKES A MILE BEFORE
HE CAN SEE A CHANGE,
AND TEN MILES BEFORE THE
SHIP MAKES THE TURN.

—ROBERT J. GORDON

Alternative Viewpoints on the Conduct of Stabilization Policies

ONE OF THE MOST CONTROVERSIAL ISSUES IN CONTEMPORARY MACROECONOMICS CONCERNS THE QUESTION OF HOW MONETARY AND FISCAL POLICIES SHOULD BE CONDUCTED TO CONTRIBUTE BEST TO A HEALTHY AND PROSPEROUS ECONOMY. MACROECONOMIC ISSUES OF THIS KIND TEND TO BE EXTREMELY DIFFICULT TO RESOLVE THROUGH SCIENTIFIC INQUIRY. IT IS RELATIVELY EASY TO SPECIFY THE NECESSARY CONDITIONS FOR MONETARY OR FISCAL POLICY TO EXERT A POWERFUL AND PREDICTABLE EFFECT ON THE ECONOMY. BUT WHETHER THESE CONDITIONS ACTUALLY PREVAIL IN THE REAL WORLD IS AMAZINGLY DIFFICULT TO DISENTANGLE, EVEN IN A WORLD OF MASSIVE DATA BASES, HIGH-SPEED COMPUTERS, AND LARGE MACROECONOMIC MODELS. FURTHERMORE, THE STRUCTURE OF THE ECONOMY CHANGES OVER TIME. UNLIKE PHYSICS AND CHEMISTRY, FUNDAMENTAL RELATIONSHIPS IN ECONOMICS CHANGE. FOR EXAMPLE, THE RELATIONSHIP BETWEEN THE MONEY SUPPLY AND ECONOMIC ACTIVITY WAS ALTERED BY THE DEREGULATION OF THE FINANCIAL SYSTEM IN THE 1980S.

VIEWPOINTS OF ECONOMISTS ON THE APPROPRIATE ROLE OF GOVERNMENT IN CONDUCTING POLICIES TO STABILIZE THE ECONOMY HAVE CHANGED SIGNIFICANTLY IN THE PAST CENTURY. TO UNDERSTAND AND APPRECIATE THE DEVELOPMENT OF MACROECONOMIC POLICY, ONE MUST GO BACK ABOUT ONE HUNDRED YEARS.

IN THE NINETEENTH CENTURY AND THE FIRST THIRD OF THE TWENTIETH CENTURY, CLASSICAL ECONOMICS HELD SWAY. CLASSICAL DOCTRINE ESPOUSED A *LAISSEZ-FAIRE* PHILOSOPHY TOWARD MACROECONOMIC INTERVENTION ON the part of government, stressing the *automatic correction mechanism* outlined in Chapters 13 and 14.

The Great Depression of the 1930s resulted in the demise of classical economics. Because of the depression and a new theoretical framework supplied in Keynes' 1936 *The General Theory of Employment, Interest, and Money*, a new consensus prevailed from roughly the 1940s through the 1960s. This consensus held that Keynesian economics—the active use of monetary policy and fiscal policy to keep economic activity at robust but noninflationary levels—was fundamentally appropriate. This Keynesian viewpoint was challenged modestly in the 1950s and 1960s and severely in the 1970s by the monetarists, led by Milton Friedman and other economists at the University of Chicago. Monetarists believe that monetary policy is much more powerful than fiscal policy but cannot be implemented successfully to stabilize economic activity. Monetarists believe that it is inappropriate for the Federal Reserve to use discretionary monetary policy. They believe the Fed should simply increase the money supply at some modest, fixed rate each year, irrespective of current economic conditions.

A fourth framework, which emerged in the 1970s, is rational expectations macroeconomics (REM), or the new classical macroeconomics. Developed by Robert Lucas (University of Chicago), Robert Barro (Harvard University), and Thomas Sargent and Neil Wallace (University of Minnesota), this school mounts an even stronger rejection of Keynesian economics. Emphasizing the role of expectations and the efficient, market-clearing mechanisms of classical economics, REM proponents argue that systematic, discretionary monetary and fiscal policies are likely to have little or no impact on such key variables as output, employment, and unemployment.

In Chapter 20 we survey the four basic schools of thinking about the appropriate strategy for implementation of monetary and fiscal policies. It would be an exaggeration to say that orthodox thinking has come full circle from classical economics to Keynesianism to monetarism to the new classical economics during this century. Nevertheless, the predominant mode of thinking has evolved dramatically since the 1920s. Most economists today remain Keynesian in the sense that they favor active use of monetary and fiscal policies to combat major economic fluctuations. However, both monetarists and proponents of REM have posed serious challenges to this viewpoint in the past 25 years.

Classical Economics and Macroeconomic Policy

CLASSICAL ECONOMICS
Viewpoint that dominated economic thinking before Keynes. It held that market prices would quickly adjust to boost the economy out of recession, and therefore government intervention in the macroeconomy was unnecessary.

Classical economists (the generations that preceded Keynes' analysis in the 1930s) emphasized the natural tendency of the economy to reach equilibrium at a full-employment level of output. When aggregate demand is insufficient initially to buy back a full-employment level of output, interest rates, wages, and prices decline. These changes boost aggregate demand and raise output. As long as output is below full-employment levels, these mechanisms continue in operation, boosting economic activity. There is no such thing as an equilibrium (resting place) below full-employment output levels, in the classical view. The only true equilibrium is said to be at full employment.

SAY'S LAW
The view that production creates its own demand because it generates an equivalent amount of income with which the output may be purchased.

The cornerstone of classical economics was **Say's law**, which states that the production of goods and services creates the necessary and sufficient means with which to purchase everything produced. In simplified language, "Supply creates its own demand." The implication is that when a full-employment level of output is produced, all of it is purchased. In a barter economy one cannot quarrel with Say's law. A farmer exchanges wheat for lumber and clothing. The production (supply) of wheat is the direct source of the demand for lumber and clothing. Supply of goods and services in general gives rise to an equivalent demand for other goods and services.

In a money economy it is not so obvious that Say's law is necessarily valid. The farmer's wheat is exchanged for *money*, but not all receipts are necessarily exchanged for goods and services. The act of saving—the withdrawal of income from the expenditure stream—potentially causes complications in the analysis. Unless the saving is counterbalanced by an equivalent amount of investment spending when output is at full employment, aggregate spending may be insufficient to buy back all the output produced.

THE CLASSICAL ADJUSTMENT MECHANISM

In the classical view, the interest rate adjusts to equate saving and investment intentions, as illustrated in Figure 20.1.

In classical economics the interest rate is viewed as the reward for saving, or the opportunity cost of consuming. People make choices regarding *present* consumption versus *future* consumption. Individuals have a positive *time preference*; they prefer to consume *now* rather than later. The higher the rate of interest, the more wealth one accumulates for future consumption by abstaining from consumption now (that is, by saving).[1] In this view, an increase in interest rates—by increasing the opportunity cost of current consumption—stimulates saving. Hence, our saving curve in Figure 20.1 is an upward-sloping function of the interest rate. Classical economists believed (as do modern economists—see Chapter 12) that investment spending is also related to the interest rate in the manner illustrated in Figure 20.1. Hence, in the classical scheme of things, the interest rate adjusts to bring saving and investment decisions into equilibrium. In classical thinking, when aggregate demand is insufficient to buy back all the full-employment output, intended saving exceeds intended investment. In terms of Figure 20.1, this implies that the interest rate (i_2) exceeds the equilibrium interest rate (i_E) and must therefore decline. The decline in interest rates, by stimulating investment and retarding saving (boosting consumption), works to remedy the shortfall of aggregate demand.

---

[1]Suppose a rational individual is deciding whether to spend $1,000 now on a vacation or save the funds for retirement in 40 years. At a 2 percent real interest rate, the $1,000 would grow to $2,208 in inflation-adjusted terms in 40 years. At a 5 percent rate, the funds would grow to $7,040 in real terms in 40 years. You can see intuitively how an increase in real interest rates raises the opportunity cost of current consumption and therefore works to overcome the natural preference to *enjoy now*. Each dollar set aside today in *depriving yourself* buys more goods and services in the future. As interest rates increase, this margin of future buying power over present buying power escalates dramatically.

In classical economics, the interest rate adjusts to equate intentions to save and invest. For example, if intended saving initially exceeds intended investment, the interest rate falls. This boosts investment and reduces saving until equilibrium is restored.

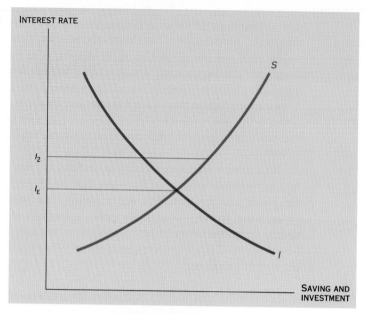

FIGURE 20.1

Also, in the classical view, free and competitive market forces ensure that wages and prices fall when output is initially below full-employment levels. Involuntary unemployment implies that the quantity of labor supplied exceeds the quantity demanded at the existing wage rate. Wages (and therefore prices) allegedly decline whenever less than full employment prevails. Declining prices trigger an increase in the real value of money balances, savings accounts, and government bonds held by individuals and firms. This boost in real wealth induces an increase in expenditures on goods and services. Given flexible prices, this *wealth effect* (as outlined in Chapters 13 and 14) works to stimulate economic activity until full employment is reached.

This classical view implies that there is no need for active government intervention in the macroeconomy. Free and competitive markets suffice to keep the economy hovering near full employment and always give the economy a corrective boost when it temporarily drops below full employment. The appropriate role of government in the economy is a very limited one, in this view, and does not include active attempts to use monetary and fiscal policy to influence economic activity. A philosophy of *laissez-faire* permeated the thinking of the classical economists: government should keep its hands off the macroeconomy.

The Keynesian Revolution

It is no coincidence that the seeds of the Keynesian revolution were planted in the 1930s with the publication of Keynes' pathbreaking *General Theory* in 1936. The decade was not kind to classical economics. Real GDP fell by 30 percent in the United States from 1929 to 1933 and did not return to 1929 levels until 1939. Unemployment soared to 25 percent and remained above 10 percent throughout the 1930s. The classical self-correcting mechanism did not appear to be working. In *General Theory*, Keynes presented an alternative set of analytical tools for understanding the macroeconomy.

Keynes emphasized that saving and investment decisions are made by different sets of people. Furthermore, he believed that these decisions were not effectively brought into balance by changes in the interest rate. In Keynes' framework the crucial determinant of saving is *not* the interest rate, but rather the level of disposable income (recall the consumption function and saving function of Chapter 12). Also, Keynes felt that investment spending was relatively insensitive to changes in the interest rate and depended largely on the highly variable "animal spirits" of businesses. Finally, Keynes argued that technical factors at times might prevent the interest rate from falling enough to bring saving and investment into equilibrium. For all these reasons, Keynes rejected the classical view of the interest rate as the equilibrator of saving and investment decisions, as portrayed in Figure 20.1. When, at current output levels, saving exceeds investment, these variables are brought into equilibrium through a contraction in output and income instead of a decline in interest rates.

Furthermore, Keynes questioned the classical assumption of highly flexible wages and prices. He did not quarrel with the proposition that wages and prices rise in periods of excess demand for labor, goods, and services. But he believed that certain impediments inhibited the downward flexibility of wages and prices in periods of weak demand or excess supply. He believed that the structure of the economy could not be described adequately by the idealized supply and demand model of perfectly competitive markets. Unions, monopolistic and oligopolistic industries, minimum-wage laws, government price supports, and other institutional factors render the classical assumption of downwardly flexible wages and prices unrealistic. When wages and prices are inflexible in the downward direction, the classical self-correcting mechanism fails to lift the economy out of depression. Keynes attacked those who advocated reliance on the economy's self-corrective mechanism through his famous dictum: "In the long run, we're all dead."

Inasmuch as Keynes believed the self-correcting mechanism does not work on the downside, he called for aggressive government intervention to boost aggregate demand when the economy is weak.[2] Given the disastrous experience of the 1930s, economists throughout the free world became convinced that Keynes was fundamentally correct. To maintain prosperity, the capitalistic system required occasional intervention by government to give the economy a "shot in the arm."

In the Employment Act of 1946, the U.S. government officially acknowledged a commitment to promote a prosperous and strong economy—implicitly by using its tools of monetary and fiscal policy when needed. The **Keynesian** prescription was adopted not only by Keynes' homeland (England) and the United States, but by all industrialized nations. By the late 1940s, classical economics had been thoroughly overturned by the new Keynesian orthodoxy. This Keynesian prescription for

KEYNESIANS
Economists who, like Keynes, believe that a capitalistic economy does not tend automatically toward a full-employment equilibrium; hence, activist monetary and fiscal policies are advocated.

---

[2]Keynes' framework of analysis in principle applies equally to the reverse case in which an inflationary gap exists—the case in which aggregate demand is excessive at full-employment output. Such a situation calls for implementation of contractionary or restrictive monetary and fiscal policies. Because Keynes developed his framework in the midst of the Great Depression, he naturally emphasized the recessionary gap situation.

active implementation of monetary and fiscal policies to stabilize economic activity went relatively unchallenged for three decades after Keynes' book appeared in 1936.

Today, the economics profession is divided, with many economists unwilling to be labeled "Keynesian." Keynesian economics reached its high tide of popularity in the mid-1960s. A picture of Keynes appeared on the cover of *Time* magazine in 1965, a year that represents a sort of watershed in macroeconomic thinking. It came *after* the Keynesian-inspired tax cuts of the early 1960s gave a much-needed boost to economic activity and *before* the escalation of the Vietnam War (1966–1968) ushered in fifteen years of economic nightmares in the United States.

THE MONETARIST CRITIQUE OF KEYNESIAN ECONOMICS

In the early days of their debates (1950s and 1960s), Keynesians and monetarists clashed over the issue of whether monetary policy or fiscal policy was the more powerful and effective instrument of policy. Keynesians—armed with the consumption function, multiplier, and other analytical tools introduced in Keynes' 1936 work—argued that fiscal policy was the more powerful. **Monetarists**— emphasizing the stability of money demand and velocity as well as the crowding-out hypothesis—were convinced that monetary policy was the more powerful. In fact, some monetarists claimed that fiscal policy was *totally* ineffective. By the 1970s, a consensus had been reached in the profession that *both* monetary and fiscal policy were quite potent.

MONETARISTS
Economists who share the view that money exerts a dominant effect on economic activity and that a capitalistic economy has an effective self-regulating mechanism. Activist policies are thought to hinder these corrective mechanisms and to destabilize economic activity, and are therefore rejected.

More recently the debate turned to the issue of whether policy makers are capable of implementing these powerful tools to contribute to a more stable business cycle. Keynesians argue in the affirmative, advocating policy activism to attempt to stabilize the economy at a high level of output and employment. Monetarists dissent from this view, arguing that efforts to implement discretionary policies to stabilize economic activity are likely only to make things worse.

In the unqualified simple diagrams used in introductory economics (Figure 20.2), the case for active government intervention to stabilize economic activity at high output levels appears to be incontrovertible and noncontroversial at first glance.

Given the aggregate supply and aggregate demand curves, the economy settles to an output level of Y_E, well short of full-employment output (Y_F). A recessionary gap ($Y_F - Y_E$) exists. The natural inclination of Keynesian-trained economists is for the government to "go for it"—to use monetary and fiscal policy measures to boost aggregate demand and move the equilibrium output toward Y_F.

In the real world, things are not nearly so simple. Critics of policy activism point out that such diagrams are quite nice for pedagogical purposes in the classroom, but in the real world we really *don't know* the positions of the aggregate demand and aggregate supply curves; these positions are subject to considerable uncertainty. Also, there is disagreement about the *slopes* of these curves. If the aggregate supply curve is relatively steep, as monetarists tend to believe, stimulus to aggregate demand results in considerable inflation. Furthermore, there is much uncertainty about the *dynamics* of the system—how rapidly the aggregate demand and aggregate supply schedules shift over time and how fast output and the price level change in response to such shifts. Many economists believe that monetary and

In the context of a simple diagram, the case for stimulative policies appears quite strong when equilibrium output is significantly below full-employment output. In the real world of uncertainty about the positions, slopes, and dynamics of the aggregate supply and aggregate demand curves, the case for policy activism is not so unambiguous.

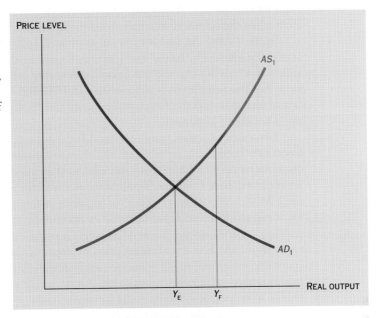

PRICE LEVEL

AS_1

AD_1

REAL OUTPUT

Y_E Y_F

FIGURE 20.2

fiscal policies influence the economy with a rather significant and variable time lag. This simply means that economists are not sure exactly *when* monetary and fiscal policy measures are reflected in changes in output, employment, and inflation.

Finally, there is even disagreement among economists as to what output level constitutes *full employment*. As noted in Chapter 8, the natural unemployment rate fluctuates over time and is subject to uncertainty. This is another way of saying that the full-employment output level of the economy is not known.[3]

Given these uncertainties about the positions, slopes, and dynamics of the aggregate supply and demand curves, and the uncertainty about the full-employment output level, monetarists stress the fact that mistakes are inevitable when using discretionary policies. The larger and more frequent such mistakes are, the less attractive is the case for using discretionary policies. This is particularly true if the economy's self-correcting mechanism is operable. Why employ uncertain policy measures if the economy inherently stabilizes at output levels near full employment when left to its own devices?

Monetarists can point to numerous serious mistakes in the conduct of Federal Reserve monetary policy. Numerous gross errors were made in the 1930s. The Fed sharply raised its discount rate in 1931 while output, income, and the price level were declining and the unemployment rate was above 10 percent. The Fed sat back

[3]In the spring of 1989, the U.S. unemployment rate dropped to 5 percent, its lowest level in 15 years. Some economists proclaimed that full employment was at hand. Others argued that we should aim for a 4.5 percent rate.

and watched the collapse of the banking system as the public panicked and withdrew currency from banks, thereby precipitating a multiple contraction of bank deposits and money. Moreover, the Fed raised reserve requirements in 1937 and 1938 while the economy was still mired in depression.

In the 1940s, the Fed became an engine of inflation as it held interest rates at artificially low levels. In the late 1960s and again in the late 1970s, the Fed was too stimulative, paving the way for episodes of severe inflation. In retrospect, it seems clear that the Fed hit the brake too hard in 1981 and 1982, helping to account for a severe recession and the first instance since the 1930s in which the unemployment rate went above 10 percent.

Advocates of activist monetary and fiscal policies cannot deny that errors have frequently been made in the past. But they point out that this does *not* imply that discretionary policies have done more harm than good. In numerous instances, policy measures have been beneficial. Some point to the increase in economic stability since World War II as evidence of superior macroeconomic policies in the past forty years. (However, other factors may account for this improvement in economic stability.)[4] Furthermore, the Fed has surely learned from its mistakes. No one today can imagine the Fed repeating its gross mistakes of the 1930s. The improvement in economic information and economic analysis as well as the experience gained from past mistakes convince activists that discretionary policies on balance will contribute to economic stability in the future.

Nevertheless, the monetarist critics of activist policies have, at the least, done the world a favor by emphasizing how complicated the economy is and by outlining the obstacles to conducting successful discretionary stabilization policies. Lags are a serious problem. There is considerable uncertainty in the various links through which changes in policy ultimately influence economic activity. Things are not at all simple. Policymakers have every reason to be humble in view of their record.

The Monetarist Position

Monetarists usually assert that the Federal Reserve, on balance, actually contributed to the *instability* of the economy in the past. Furthermore, monetarists believe that discretionary monetary policy is likely to continue to destabilize economic activity. This is thought to be true partly because of political forces and partly because the Fed has demonstrated an annoying propensity to become sidetracked from its true objective by various *pseudo-objectives* such as attempting to hold down nominal interest rates to assist the government in financing its debt or attempting to influence foreign-exchange rates or stock market fluctuations.

---

[4]Because income-tax rates have been much higher in the postwar period, the size of the effective marginal propensity to consume out of GDP and the size of the income multiplier have decreased sharply (see Chapter 13A, p. 339). Therefore, exogenous shifts in investment, net exports, and other components of aggregate demand give rise to smaller fluctuations in economic activity. The *automatic stability* or *built-in stability* of the economy has increased. This factor, rather than the use of successful monetary and fiscal policy, probably accounts for most of the improvement in economic stability in the second half of the twentieth century. See Robert J. Gordon, "Evolution in Postwar Macroeconomics," in Martin S. Feldstein (ed.), *The American Economy in Transition* (Chicago: University of Chicago Press, 1980).

Monetarists also believe that the Fed is incapable of contributing to economic stability even if it casts aside all political considerations and focuses all attention on the one valid objective of monetary policy—stabilizing aggregate demand for goods and services. This skeptical viewpoint is based on forecasting inadequacies and the uncertainties about the positions, slopes, and dynamics of the aggregate supply and demand curves (as noted earlier). In the current state of the art, in the view of monetarists, the Fed is simply incapable of consistently putting in place policies that contribute to economic stability.

To obtain an understanding of the procedures recommended by monetarists, we return to the equation of exchange, $MV \equiv PY$. Recall that M represents the money supply and V (velocity) indicates the turnover rate of the money supply in purchasing newly produced goods and services (GDP). MV thus represents spending on final goods and services (GDP). On the right side, P is the average price of the individual goods and services entering into GDP and Y is the real quantity of GDP produced. Hence, PY is a measure of nominal GDP. The equation of exchange states that spending on GDP from the *money* side (MV) is identically equal to GDP spending viewed from the *goods* side (PY).

The equation of exchange describes the relationship among the money supply, velocity, and GDP expenditures at a given point in time, such as 1993. If we convert the equation to its dynamic form to relate the *growth rates over time* of these variables, we obtain the following:

$$\%\Delta M + \%\Delta V = \%\Delta P + \%\Delta Y \qquad (20.1)$$

In this expression the growth rate of money plus the growth rate of velocity is the growth rate of GDP expenditures, which in turn is equivalent to the growth rate of the price level (the inflation rate) plus the growth rate of real output. If the supply of money grows 8 percent in one year and velocity increases 2 percent, nominal GDP rises at a 10 percent annual rate. The inflation rate ($\%\Delta P$) and the real-output growth rate ($\%\Delta Y$) must therefore sum to 10 percent. If $\%\Delta P$ is 5 percent, $\%\Delta Y$ is also 5 percent. If $\%\Delta P$ is 8 percent, $\%\Delta Y$ must be 2 percent.

THE CONSTANT MONEY-GROWTH RULE

The goal of monetary policy, in principle, should be to ensure that aggregate expenditures ($\%\Delta M + \%\Delta V$) expand at a rate that allows real output to grow over time at a rate comparable to the growth of potential real GDP without igniting inflationary pressures. Most monetarist economists are convinced that the political and technical obstacles confronting the Fed's efforts to conduct policies that successfully smooth the swings in economic activity are very severe. These economists advocate that the Fed abandon its discretionary monetary policy and adopt a rule in which the money supply grows at some slow and steady rate *irrespective of contemporary economic conditions*. But how fast should the supply of money grow in this automatic scheme? We can shed some light on that issue by examining the variables in Equation 20.1.

Ideally, a worthy goal is to aim for zero inflation in the long run ($\%\Delta P = 0$). Real output growth ($\%\Delta Y$) can expand in the long run only as fast as the sum of labor-force growth and labor productivity growth—roughly 3 percent per year. Hence, the desired growth rate of nominal GDP expenditures is approximately 3 percent per year. To arrive at the appropriate rule for constant money growth ($\%\Delta M$), one must forecast (or guess) the trend growth rate of velocity ($\%\Delta V$). If the best forecast for velocity trend is zero growth, the appropriate money growth rule is 3 percent per year. If one expects a rising trend for velocity, the money growth rule is established at a somewhat slower rate.

THE LAGS OF POLICY   The existence of monetary policy lags is instrumental in the monetarist view that the fixed money-growth rule is superior to the conventional activist or discretionary policy. The monetarist viewpoint is illustrated through the hypothetical cyclical output behavior indicated in Figure 20.3. With the aid of hindsight in this hypothetical scheme, we note that output peaked at time t_0 and that the economy then began to slide into recession. Ideally, a stimulative monetary policy is immediately implemented at that point (if not earlier) to cushion the downturn. However, given the lags in publication of data and the imperfections of and conflicting stories told by the various business cycle indicators, those in charge of policy are not aware of the economic downturn until t_1. This passage of time ($t_0 - t_1$) is known as the **recognition lag**.

In any bureaucratic organization, further time elapses between the recognition of need for action and the implementation of corrective action. This period

RECOGNITION LAG

The period that elapses between the point at which a change in policy is needed and when the need is recognized by policymakers.

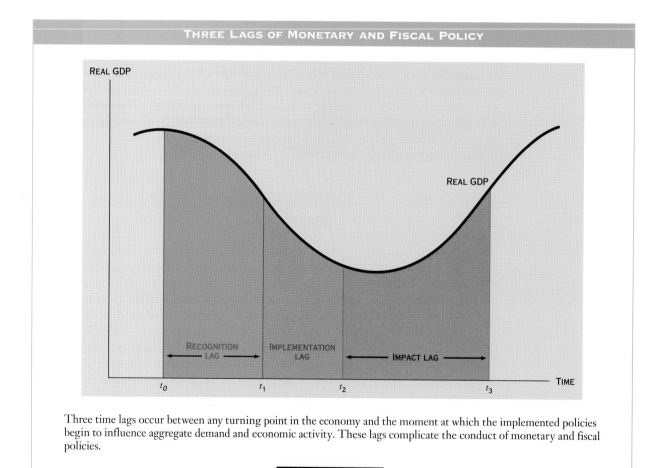

THREE LAGS OF MONETARY AND FISCAL POLICY

Three time lags occur between any turning point in the economy and the moment at which the implemented policies begin to influence aggregate demand and economic activity. These lags complicate the conduct of monetary and fiscal policies.

FIGURE 20.3

IMPLEMENTATION LAG
The period that elapses
between the point at which a
need for policy change is
recognized and when the
change in policy is implemented.

$(t_1 - t_2)$ is known as the **implementation lag**. In the case of discretionary *fiscal policy*, the implementation lag can be long and detrimental because legislated changes in tax rates and expenditures require congressional action. Such action is heavily influenced by the prevailing political winds and other impediments. In the case of monetary policy, the implementation lag tends to be brief because the Federal Open Market Committee conducts regularly scheduled meetings every six weeks in Washington and is equipped (by telephonic hookup) to conduct emergency meetings if necessary. The FOMC has authority to order immediate changes in monetary policy.

Finally, at time t_2, stimulative policies are put in place. The Fed may reduce its discount rate and pump reserves into the banking system through open market purchases of securities. However, considerable time passes $(t_2 - t_3)$ before the stimulative measures begin to influence spending, GDP, and employment strongly. This **impact lag** of monetary policy is believed to be rather long and variable.[5] The economic stimulus—which ideally would have occurred at time t_0—does not occur until time t_3, at a time when the economy has already bottomed out and is recovering strongly on its own. The emerging stimulus, by contributing to an overheated economy and its associated inflationary pressures, may do more harm than good.

IMPACT LAG
The period that elapses
between the point at which a
new policy is implemented
and when the policy begins
to influence economic activity.

Monetarists argue, in terms of the dynamic equation of exchange, that velocity growth behaves in a smooth, predictable pattern. Hence, slow and steady growth in M yields slow and steady growth in aggregate spending ($\%\Delta M + \%\Delta V$), the desired norm. By doing this, the *constant (fixed) money-growth rule* avoids the extremes of severe inflation (such as the 1970s) and depressions (such as 1929–1933). No one claims that the money growth rule is Utopian, that it prevents periods of inflation and recession.[6] Monetarists admit that unexpected movements in velocity are bound to give rise to occasional bouts of mild inflation and recession. Allegedly, however, we would experience a more satisfactory economic performance than the Fed has delivered in the 80 years of its existence.

THE ACTIVIST CRITIQUE OF THE MONETARIST POSITION

Advocates of activist monetary and fiscal policies believe that the monetarists overstate both the power of the automatic corrective mechanisms in the economy and the stability and predictability of velocity. Such economists view velocity as a flexible variable, increasing in cyclical recoveries, declining in recessions, and fluctuating sharply in response to changes in institutional factors, expectations, interest rates, and uncertainty. Therefore, the link between the money supply and economic activity is believed to be a loose and uncertain one. If one cannot predict the future behavior of velocity within reasonable bounds, one cannot specify in advance the appropriate growth rate of money for the constant money-growth rule.

---

[5]Milton Friedman once estimated the impact lag of monetary policy to be anywhere from six to eighteen months. More recently, Robert Gordon has estimated the mean lag to be nine months.

[6]Monetarists frequently assert that the Fed has a natural tendency to be too stimulative. Political forces may dictate this bias, since stimulative policies tend to influence output and employment more quickly than they influence inflation. Congress often pressures the Fed to pursue stimulative policies to get the economy moving in election years (every other year). A constant money-growth rule would tend to make the Fed immune to such pressures, as suggested in Exhibit 20.1 (pages 508–509).

E
X
H
I
B
I
T

20.1

When the Federal Reserve System was founded many decades ago, its framers were wary of the possibility of political considerations creeping in to influence Fed policy. Numerous safeguards were implemented with a view toward minimizing the exposure of the institution to political pressures. Governors were to have one nonrenewable fourteen-year term. Appointment dates were staggered so that one governor's term expired every two years. Hence, a one-term U.S. president normally would appoint only two of the seven members of the Board of Governors, and thus be unable to *stack* the board for political purposes. Most importantly, the Fed has its own financial resources, mainly in the form of large annual interest income from its huge portfolio of securities. Unlike government agencies that must request operating budgets from Congress each year, the

Fed is financially independent. This enables the Fed to be objective in its decision making, because it reduces the feasibility of retribution by Congress for unpopular policy actions the Fed believes are needed for the nation's long-term economic health.

In spite of the safeguards, the Fed is by no means immune to outside political considerations. Some economists speak of a "political business cycle" in which the Fed is alleged to have a propensity for stimulating economic activity in (especially presidential) election years and then moving to compensate by tightening credit once the election is past. The evidence seems mixed. President Richard Nixon sought reelection in 1972. As the election approached, with wage and price controls in place, Fed policy turned quite stimulative. This, coupled with a severe oil price shock a few months later, boost-

These policy activists (including most Keynesians) believe the Fed should maintain a discretionary policy so that it can respond to these surprise changes in velocity by aggressively altering the growth rate of money. In 1986, for example, the velocity of money (GDP/M-1) declined by about 9 percent. The Fed, by rapidly expanding the supply of money (M-1 increased 16 percent in 1986), prevented a potential contraction in aggregate demand (*MV*), saving the nation from a recession. In a constant money-growth rule regime, the Fed is handcuffed and unable to respond to such swings in money demand and velocity.

On average, a philosophical difference exists between monetarists and non-monetarists concerning the relative magnitude of the costs of inflation and unemployment. Monetarists tend to be politically conservative and regard inflation as *public enemy number one*. Keynesians (the activists) are on the liberal side of the spectrum, typically regarding unemployment as a more serious social disease than inflation. Activists typically prefer a high-pressure economy and are willing to accept the risk of higher inflation as a price for maintaining low rates of unemployment.

Critics of the constant money-growth rule cannot deny that the Fed has made some major policy mistakes. However, they believe that the Fed has learned from these errors. The state of the art of central banking has surely improved. Advocates

ed U.S. inflation into the double-digit range in 1973. In 1980, however, as President Jimmy Carter ran for reelection against Ronald Reagan, the Fed clamped down in an effort to contain inflation that was already rampant. Interest rates increased dramatically.

In the year leading up to the 1992 presidential election, the Fed pursued extraordinarily stimulative measures. The Fed reduced its discount rate to the lowest level in almost 30 years and aggressively expanded bank reserves. The basic reserve requirement was reduced from 12% to 10% in April 1992. While some may suspect that the Fed was bending to the pressure exerted by the incumbent politicians, others point out that the economy was mired in a drawn-out period of stagnation and argue that the extraordinary stimulus was necessary to counteract not only a stagnant economy, but

also an apparent decrease in the willingness of banks to make normal loans to businesses and other borrowers.

An advantage of a constant money-growth rule is that the Fed would be unable to play politics with the U.S. economy. The Fed could stare down any politician looking for election-year economic stimulus by simply observing that it had no choice—it was following the constant money-growth rule. To the extent that the *political business cycle* really exists and damages the U.S. economy in the long run, the case for handcuffing the Fed with the constant money-growth rule emerges strongly. However, the evidence on the existence of a *political business cycle* is inconclusive. Furthermore, advocates of the *status quo* point out that there are many offsetting benefits of preserving the authority of the Fed to conduct discretionary monetary policy.

of activist Federal Reserve monetary policy are convinced that the Fed of the 1990s can significantly outperform a rigid constant money-growth rule.

Rational Expectations Macroeconomics (REM)—The New Classical Macroeconomics

By combining the flexible price, market-clearing tenets of classical economics with some fairly strong assumptions about the way people form expectations, the new classical macroeconomics school arrives at some rather startling conclusions about macroeconomic policy.

Like monetarists, proponents of **rational expectations macroeconomics (REM)** believe the economy contains an inherent self-correcting mechanism. This mechanism is thought to bring equilibrium output back to the natural level—the level corresponding to the natural unemployment rate. Like monetarists, proponents of REM stress the possibility of instability created by efforts to conduct active monetary and fiscal policies in an attempt to smooth economic fluctuations.

ROBERT J. BARRO,
HARVARD UNIVERSITY

—A LEADING PROPONENT
OF RATIONAL EXPECTATIONS
MACROECONOMICS

RATIONAL
EXPECTATIONS
MACROECONOMICS
(REM) OR NEW
CLASSICAL
MACROECONOMICS
Modern school of econo-
mists that emphasizes the
effectiveness of market
forces pushing the economy
toward full employment and
views discretionary stabilization policies as being
ineffective.

Unlike monetarism, REM implies that *systematic* and *predictable* changes in the money supply have *no impact* on real output and unemployment. Hence, proponents of REM arrive at the same conclusion as monetarists—government should not attempt to implement countercyclical monetary and fiscal policies—although by a totally different route.

Let us examine the assumptions underlying REM so we understand the basis for the startling conclusion that discretionary monetary and fiscal policies are useless—even harmful—and should be abandoned.

ASSUMPTIONS OF REM

As the term implies, the key ingredient in REM is the assumption that individuals and firms form expectations *rationally*. Expectations are said to be rational if economic agents take into account all relevant, available information and use this information *efficiently* in formulating expectations. This by no means implies that economic agents have perfect foresight, anticipating the future with perfect accuracy. Forecasts are frequently incorrect. But REM assumes that economic agents do not make *systematic* mistakes in forecasting future economic phenomena. For example, people do not consistently overestimate or underestimate future inflation. Forecast errors are *random*—sometimes too high, sometimes too low—because people quickly learn from mistakes and try not to repeat them.

This assumption is in contrast with much earlier work in economics, which held that expectations are *adaptive*: they change gradually over time in response to recent phenomena. Given adaptive expectations, economic agents tend persistently to underestimate inflation while it is accelerating and overestimate it while it is slowing down.

Proponents of REM believe that individuals and firms are quite sophisticated in economic matters, that they understand the fundamental workings of the economy. For example, individuals and firms are well aware of the linkage between money supply growth, inflation, and interest rates. They are aware of the tendency for a *political business cycle*—the tendency for the economy to be well stimulated in election years. And they are aware of the threshold unemployment and inflation rates that trigger corrective efforts by the Federal Reserve System. Basically, these economic agents are assumed to be as smart and perceptive as the best economic analysts.

Suppose the inflation rate has been declining in recent years from 6 percent to 4 percent to 2 percent currently. In adaptive expectations, agents sluggishly revise their forecasts of future inflation downward in response to the recent decline in actual inflation. If rational expectations prevail, economic agents focus attention on the behavior of the factors that state-of-the-art economic models include as determinants of future inflation—changes in oil prices, the money supply, the U.S. exchange rate with other nations, and so forth. If these factors on balance indicate that inflation will accelerate, agents revise their inflationary expectations upward in spite of the fact that the recent trend of inflation has been downward.

In addition, proponents of REM believe that the competitive model of supply and demand accurately describes most of our product and resource markets. Prices of goods, services, and labor (wages) change quickly in response to shifts in supply and demand curves. Economic agents quickly process new information into supply and demand curves, and prices and wages respond quickly to the information. Markets continuously clear and are in equilibrium.

IMPLICATIONS OF REM FOR MACROECONOMIC POLICY

As indicated, REM has crucial implications for the effectiveness of countercyclical monetary and fiscal policies. We illustrate this point in Figure 20.4.

Given the aggregate supply (AS_1) and aggregate demand (AD_1) curves of Figure 20.4, assume the economy currently is at A, with equilibrium output (Y_{E1}) significantly below Y_F. A recessionary gap prevails. The natural inclination of a Keynesian is to implement stimulative monetary and fiscal policies to shift the aggregate demand curve rightward from AD_1 to AD_2, raising output toward the full-employment level. A monetarist—skeptical of the motives of government officials and cognizant of uncertainty, forecasting difficulties, and policy lags—counsels the Fed and Congress to restrain themselves and leave the macroeconomy to its own devices. An advocate of REM argues that stimulative monetary and fiscal policies are ineffective and inappropriate for an entirely different reason. Actions of the public taken in response to the (correct) anticipation of implementation of stimulative policies nullify the real effects of the policies, rendering them ineffective in boosting output and employment.

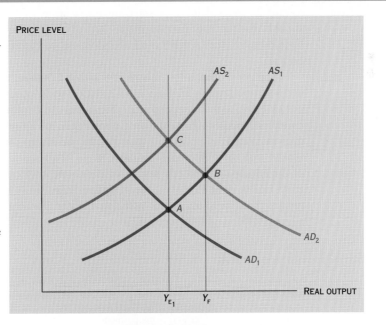

IMPACT OF ANTICIPATED POLICIES ON ECONOMIC ACTIVITY

With the economy initially in equilibrium at A (output of Y_{E1}), a recessionary gap exists. Conventional analysis indicates that stimulative monetary and fiscal policies—by boosting aggregate demand—move the economy to B and generate full employment. However, when workers and firms anticipate the policy stimulus, they raise wages and other input prices. This shifts the aggregate supply curve leftward. The equilibrium moves from A to C, and the effect of policy stimulus on output and employment is nullified.

FIGURE 20.4

Based on experience, the public comes to expect the government to implement stimulative macroeconomic measures to boost the economy whenever a large output gap develops. As soon as such policy is announced through a tax cut, boost in money supply growth, or whatever, firms raise prices and workers push for larger wage hikes. Firms generally grant the wage increases, both firms and workers believing that these price and wage hikes will be *ratified* or *validated* by the stimulative macropolicies. These price and wage hikes shift the nation's aggregate supply schedule leftward to AS_2, nullifying all or much of the potential impact of the stimulative policy upon real output and employment. Instead of moving from *A* to *B* in Figure 20.4, we move from *A* to *C*. Since the aggregate supply curve shifted leftward, much of the additional demand imparted by monetary and/or fiscal stimulus is simply dissipated in higher prices.[7]

If workers and firms formulate expectations rationally, and if wages and prices adapt immediately to changes in expectations, predictable monetary and fiscal policies are totally ineffective in stimulating output and employment. Only *unanticipated* or *surprise* policies have an impact.

> *Policy Ineffectiveness Theorem:* Anticipated changes in the money supply and/or fiscal policy have no effect on real variables such as output, income, and employment; they affect only the price level. In the REM framework, only *unanticipated* or *surprise* policies influence output and employment.

POLICY INEFFECTIVENESS THEOREM
Proposition advocated by proponents of REM that only *surprise* or *unanticipated* policies have an effect on such real economic variables as output and employment.

The **policy ineffectiveness theorem**, if valid, yields both good news and bad news. The bad news is that discretionary monetary and fiscal policies are useless for purposes of assisting the economy out of a recession. The only effective discretionary policies are the unexpected ones, and the public quickly catches on to the government's game of trying to stimulate the economy whenever it is down. Since government policy is incapable of fooling the people consistently for constructive purposes, government should give up the game. Besides, in the view of REM proponents, the economy corrects itself, the unemployment rate gravitating quickly toward its natural level. A startling implication of REM is that the government should rescind the Employment Act of 1946, the Humphrey-Hawkins Full-Employment Act of 1978, and abandon use of discretionary monetary and fiscal policies.

The good news implied by REM is that a *credible*, preannounced anti-inflationary macropolicy can lead us out of inflation without any accompanying loss of output or increase in unemployment. Suppose, while inflation has been running at an annual 10 percent rate, the Fed announces its intention to slow annual money growth from 10 percent to 2 percent. To the extent that economic agents are convinced that the Fed means business, wage hikes are dramatically curtailed because of the anticipated severely restricted economic environment. The aggregate supply curve shifts rightward, or at least dramatically slows its leftward movement. This means that the output loss associated with eliminating inflation by restricting aggregate demand is reduced. Under strong assumptions about totally credible anti-

---

[7]It has been suggested that well-intentioned countercyclical policies might even systematically *destabilize* economic activity. Suppose the government systematically grants large investment tax credits in recessions to boost investment and later removes the credits when the economy is strong. As the economy starts into recession, firms postpone investment projects as they wait for the credits to be granted. This slows investment spending in the recession, causing the downturn to be deeper than it would otherwise be.

inflation measures, rational expectations, and instantaneous market clearing in labor and product markets, inflation may be eliminated without any cost in the form of a temporary rise in unemployment.

PHILLIPS CURVE IMPLICATIONS OF REM

The preceding analysis is explained in the context of a Phillips Curve framework in Figure 20.5. Recall from Chapter 19 that most economists believe stimulative macropolicies can boost us from *A* to *B* in the *short run*, buying at least a temporary reduction in unemployment by accepting a higher rate of inflation. The boost in inflation tends initially to fool workers, depress real wages, and boost profits, output, and employment. Hence, the stimulative macropolicies reduce unemployment in the short run, until people's expectations adjust to the new level of inflation.

Not true in a world of rational expectations! Agents observe the stimulative macropolicies as they are implemented and immediately revise their inflation expectations upward. Wage inflation is boosted immediately—as soon as the policy is announced. Because the workers are not fooled by the stimulative policies, real wages do not decline, profits do not increase, and neither do output and employment. Unemployment remains at the same level (U_N in Figure 20.5), and we move from *A* to *C* rather than from *A* to *B*. The stimulative policy, since it was immediately diagnosed and acted upon by firms and individuals, had no effect on such real

REM AND THE VERTICAL SHORT-RUN PHILLIPS CURVE

Conventional analysis indicates that a short-run trade-off between inflation and unemployment exists. By boosting aggregate demand, monetary and fiscal policy can fool workers, reduce real wages (by boosting inflation), and reduce unemployment for a time. In a rational-expectations world, people learn to anticipate such stimulative policies whenever the economy is depressed. Workers are not fooled, the boost in inflation does not reduce real wages, and unemployment does not decline. In a REM world, the short-run Phillips Curve is vertical. Policy is ineffective.

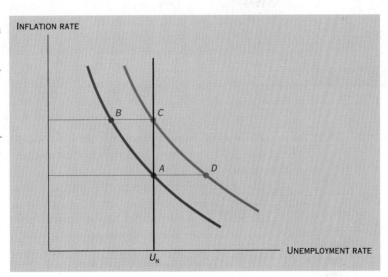

FIGURE 20.5

EXHIBIT

20.2

Some economists touted the Fed's efforts to bring down inflation in the early 1980s as constituting a good laboratory experiment for testing the validity of REM. By the time President Jimmy Carter appointed Paul Volcker to chair the Board of Governors in August 1979, inflation was running at double-digit rates. This inflation (based on the CPI) had escalated from less than 7 percent in 1977 to more than 13 percent by early fall 1979. This acceleration in inflation, coupled with an apparent lack of confidence around the world in the U.S. government's resolve to fight it, resulted in a persistent decline in the value of the dollar in foreign-exchange markets. In October 1979, under the leadership of Volcker, the Fed announced a dramatic change in the manner it would conduct monetary policy.

Instead of attempting to hit established targets for short-term interest rates, the Fed announced it would instead seek to hit money-growth targets, which would be set at much more modest growth rates than actual recent money-growth rates. This implied that the Fed would no longer purchase securities and pump reserves into the banking system to hold down interest rates during periods in which the rates were under upward pressure. Interest rates would be permitted to rise dramatically, if need be, in order to equilibrate surging credit demands with the modest growth in funds available, as consistent with the Fed's modest money-growth target.

The Fed was in essence telling the world of its new resolve to conquer inflation irrespective of the short-range consequences for financial markets and economic activity. The Fed was announcing a change of regime from one of short-run accommodation of credit demands to one of strict monetarism—strict adherence to modest money growth.

This change of regime was deliberately implemented with a view toward bringing down the public's expectations of inflation in order to allow the Fed to fight inflation with minimum damage to U.S. output and employment. The Fed's implementation of this policy is itself tes-

variables as output, employment, and unemployment, even in the short run. Only when individuals and firms are *surprised* by monetary and fiscal policies do these policies generate real effects.

By the same token, conventional analysis indicates that to get out of an entrenched inflation environment we must endure a transition period of higher unemployment. As macropolicies become highly restrictive, inflation slows down, wage deceleration lags behind, and real wages initially rise. Hence, profits decline and firms reduce output and employment. Unemployment rises at first, and we move from C to D in Figure 20.5. Inflation comes down, but at a cost of a transition period of higher unemployment.

In the extreme REM view, we can get out of the inflation without cost. The announcement of the credible restrictive policy itself reduces expected inflation and immediately slows wage inflation in line with actual inflation. Therefore, real wages

timony to the increased influence of REM.

According to critics of REM, this episode clearly constitutes an anticipated tightening of monetary policy, since it was announced publicly and had a major impact on the outlook for inflation. The strong form of REM predicts that expected changes in policy only influence price-level behavior, not such real economic variables as output and employment. According to REM, the short-run Phillips Curve is vertical and inflation should have come down without an increase in unemployment. REM states that the unemployment rate is not influenced by anticipated changes in policy.

As predicted by REM, inflation came down sharply—much more sharply in fact than most economists or the Reagan Administration thought possible. But output went into a slump and the unemployment rate surged above 10 percent in 1982, reaching its highest level since the 1930s. Critics of REM claim this episode shows the folly of the theory. A severe tightening of monetary policy

announced clearly in advance, contrary to the predictions of REM, threw 6 million people out of work. Clearly, the short-run Phillips Curve is not vertical!

Supporters of REM believe this episode does not tarnish the credibility of their theory. After decades of alleged Federal Reserve deceit and unreliability, the institution's credibility was said to be at a low point by 1979. The public simply did not believe the Fed when it announced its commitment to reduce money growth sharply. In order for the Fed to make its commitment to eradicate inflation truly credible to the American populace, according to many advocates of REM, the Fed would probably have to abandon discretionary monetary policy. This could be accomplished only by returning to a gold standard or yielding to a constant money-growth rule, as advocated by Milton Friedman and other monetarists.

do not rise during the period of disinflation. There is no reduction in profits, output, and employment. Unemployment does not rise, and we move from C to A in Figure 20.5, rather than from C to D. Presto! The inflation is reduced without cost.

In the REM world, even the short-run Phillips Curve is vertical. There exists no trade-off between inflation and unemployment, even in the short run. Both the long-run and short-run Phillips Curves are vertical lines.

Like the monetarist world, the rational expectations world tends to paint the government as the villain, the cause of most of the economy's problems. Since the economy allegedly has inherent correction mechanisms and since *anticipated policy change* is nullified by actions of the public, the government should not intervene in the macroeconomy. Indeed, any failure of the economy to adjust its output to the natural level is attributable to government measures that have created rigidities. These measures include minimum wage legislation, farm price supports, and other

EXHIBIT

20.3

Rational Expectations and the Change in Price-Level Behavior After World War II

Prior to World War II, periods of deflation (falling prices) alternated with periods of inflation, with the result that prices were no higher on average in the 1900–1930 era than in the 1770–1800 era. There was no net inflation in America over the sweep of history until World War II. Today, however, the price level is at least four times higher than it was in 1950 (review Figure 19.8 on page 000). Downward price-level flexibility has disappeared from the American scene. Why?

There are plenty of potential explanations. Some economists claim that the economy has become less competitive—that unions have become stronger and industries more concentrated. Others attribute the disappearance of downward price flexibility to the increasing strength of the nation's built-in stabilizers. As the size of the government sector (and the level of tax rates) has increased relative to the economy, this has imparted a high degree of inertia to aggregate demand. For this reason, we no longer experience the severe cyclical contractions that formerly led to deflation. The increased stability of the U.S. economy allegedly accounts for the radical change in price-level behavior.

While certain of the preceding hypotheses may in fact contribute to the explanation, proponents of REM emphasize another consideration that seems highly plausible—the commitment of the U.S. government to the maintenance of a high level of prosperity in general and output and employment in particular. In acknowledgement of the Keynesian revolution, Congress passed the Employment

measures that provide barriers to competition, and failure to use antitrust statutes to break up monopolies. In the view of REM, government policies should be aimed at promoting competitive markets instead of meddling in the macroeconomy.

While Keynesians tend to paint the government as the *good guy*, riding in to eradicate recessions caused by the inherent instabilities of a capitalistic, free-market economy, REM proponents tend to view government as the *villain* that interferes with the natural tendency of a market economy's *invisible hand* to yield optimal results. REM, or the new classical macroeconomics, seeks to turn Keynesian economics on its head!

CRITIQUE OF NEW CLASSICAL MACROECONOMICS (REM)

REM has made a considerable impact on the economics profession in the relatively short period of the past 20 years. Nevertheless, only a small minority of economists believe the doctrine is valid in its strong form that implies macropolicy is largely ineffective. Many believe that REM overstates the economics acumen and awareness of individual firms, workers, and consumers. Do they really comprehend the

Act of 1946. This law mandated that the government implement stimulative monetary and fiscal policies, if necessary, to keep the economy strong. As time progressed, workers and firms learned to anticipate the use of stimulative policies whenever the economy weakened significantly. In earlier times, macroeconomic weakness in the economy often portended great personal hardship for workers and financial disaster for firms. As the economy weakened, wages and prices declined abruptly as workers and firms scrambled to survive.

If allowing the economy to remain depressed is against the law, workers and firms are basically insured against widespread unemployment and widespread loss of sales. The downside risk is largely eliminated, or at least severely reduced.

In that event, there is no reason for workers to accept wage cuts and firms to reduce prices in periods in which the economy is temporarily weak. Macroeconomic stimulus can be counted on to bring the economy back up to snuff.

A side effect of the Keynesian revolution is the elimination of the symmetrical price-level behavior that existed before World War II. In the view of REM, only the abandonment of discretionary macroeconomic policies would bring back the noninflationary long-term environment of the olden days. Some supporters of REM suggest that we should abolish the Employment Act and the Humphrey-Hawkins Act, leaving the economy to its self-correcting devices.

workings of the economy? Do they really understand monetary and fiscal policy and pay close attention to those who implement such policies?

It seems unlikely that individuals and firms are rational in the sense defined by REM. Although it is true that the assumption that expectations are strictly *adaptive* seems naive, given the uncertainty about future events it seems likely that past events do play a significant role. Our expectation about inflation next year is conditioned by current and recent inflation as well as by new developments that macroeconomic models indicate are important determinants of inflation. Studies demonstrate that inflation expectations are sluggish. They exhibit considerable inertia, not changing radically in response to current swings in oil prices, money growth, and other factors that a sophisticated macroeconomic model might predict would bring about a change in the inflation rate. When inflation was ratcheting upward between 1965 and 1980, inflation expectations consistently lagged behind actual inflation. As the actual inflation rate came down in the early 1980s, expectations again lagged behind.[8]

---

[8]See M. A. Akhtar, A. Stephen Englander, and Cornelis A. Los, "Surveys of Expectations: Forward or Backward Looking?" *Quarterly Review* (Federal Reserve Bank of New York, Winter 1983–1984), pp. 63–66.

Moreover, contracts and other impediments prevent wages from adapting quickly to changes in expected inflation. Three-year labor contracts for workers written in 1980 and 1981 prevented wage hikes from slowing down in the next two or three years in line with the reduction in actual and expected inflation. What *appeared* to be rational when the contracts were written no longer appeared rational a year or two later. Numerous studies of the nature of expectations have been conducted. Only a few demonstrate rationality on the part of economic agents. Several studies of the policy ineffectiveness hypothesis demonstrate that anticipated changes as well as unanticipated changes in aggregate demand strongly affect output and employment. The prediction of REM that actual unemployment rates should cluster closely around the natural unemployment rate with random departures from the natural rate is not supported by the facts.

Nevertheless, rational expectations theory is probably here to stay as an integral element of macroeconomic analysis. The unsatisfactory performance of the U.S. economy since the mid-1960s, the disenchantment with Keynesian economics, and the reduced appeal of monetarism since 1980 have opened the door for alternative approaches to macroeconomics. Though few economists take REM seriously in its extreme version, most agree that it contains an important kernel of truth. As people systematically come to expect a policy change, they take actions that diminish the policy's impact on such real economic variables as output and employment. At the very least, REM has provided an alternative mode of analysis that has stimulated thinking among economists about aggregate supply as well as aggregate demand. REM has elevated the role of expectations to center stage in the analysis of macroeconomic policy. (See Exhibit 20.3).

Summary

1. Economists strongly disagree over the issue of the propriety of government efforts to intervene actively in the macroeconomy to attempt to reduce the fluctuations of output and income inherent in a free-market economy. Keynesians favor such efforts; monetarists and rational expectations macroeconomists do not.

2. The classical economists who preceded Keynes' pathbreaking *General Theory* of 1936 emphasized the tendency of the economy to gravitate strongly toward a full-employment level of output. Key elements in the framework of classical economics were the role of the interest rate in equilibrating saving and investment decisions and the role of wage and price-level flexibility in generating an automatic corrective mechanism in the macroeconomy.

3. In his attack on classical thinking, Keynes introduced a whole new kit of analytical tools. Keynes was especially critical of the assumption of downward wage and price flexibility and the assumption that the interest rate would adjust to bring saving and investment into equilibrium at full employment. In Keynes' view, the economy could settle at an equilibrium far short of full employment. Therefore, Keynes felt that government should intervene actively with stimulative policy measures when the economy was depressed. In Keynes' view, a *laissez-faire* philosophy was inappropriate.

4. Keynesian economics held center stage from the late 1930s through the late 1960s. Monetarism gradually made some inroads in the 1950s and 1960s, and became a powerful

force in the 1970s as inflation accelerated throughout the world. Its influence diminished somewhat in the 1980s and 1990s as the link between the various money supply measures and GDP loosened.

5. Monetarists emphasize the political and technical obstacles that make it difficult to conduct successful discretionary macroeconomic policies. Technical obstacles include uncertainty about the nature of the aggregate supply and aggregate demand schedules, the natural unemployment rate, and the lags of policy. Monetarists believe that well-intentioned Fed policies have done more harm than good and are likely to continue to do harm. Monetarists recommend that the Fed abandon discretionary policies and implement a constant money-growth rule. In such a regime, the Fed simply increases the money supply at some modest but constant rate, irrespective of contemporary economic conditions.

6. Rational expectations macroeconomics (REM) or the new classical macroeconomics is critical of policy activism for different reasons. Once it becomes understood that the government systematically implements stimulative policies whenever the economy weakens, workers and firms take actions that partially or totally nullify the effects of the policies on output and employment. In the view of REM, only unanticipated or surprise policies have real effects. Since the government cannot systematically fool the people for socially beneficial purposes, it should abandon discretionary monetary and fiscal policies.

7. Today the economics profession is splintered on the issue of macroeconomic policy. While some economists fit squarely in the Keynesian, monetarist, or REM camps, many economists are eclectic in these matters. Bits and pieces of each of the three camps' viewpoints seem sensible to many economists. Most economists still favor policy activism, but there seems to be a consensus that fine-tuning is inappropriate. The powerful instruments of monetary and fiscal policy should be adjusted only in response to major swings in aggregate demand, aggregate supply, output growth, and inflation.

Key Terms

classical economics
Say's law
Keynesians
monetarists
recognition lag
implementation lag

impact lag
rational expectations
   macroeconomics (REM) or
   new classical macroeconomics
policy ineffectiveness theorem

Study Questions and Problems

1. Explain the logic of the classical view that the only true equilibrium output is a full-employment level of output.

2. Assume you are debating against the proposition that government should adopt a *laissez-faire* philosophy toward the macroeconomy. What elements of the classical model would you attack? Explain why.

3. Analyze the factors that make the successful conduct of activist monetary and fiscal policies more difficult than it appears at first glance.

4. Assume the Federal Reserve decides to abandon discretionary policies in favor of a constant money-growth rule. You are hired by the Fed as a consultant to determine how fast the money supply should grow in this new regime. How would you go about arriving at a decision?

5. Do you think a constant money-growth rule would outperform monetary discretion over the next five years? Defend your answer.

6. "The Keynesian prescription for activist macroeconomic policies to stabilize output at high levels, while effective at first, has met with inevitable failure and should now be abandoned." What is the intellectual basis for this statement?

7. In what ways are monetarism and rational expectations macroeconomics (REM) similar? In what ways do they differ?

8. "Policymakers cannot even exploit a *short-run* Phillips Curve, much less a *long-run* trade-off." What is the logic of this argument? Do you agree or disagree?

Selected References

Barro, Robert J. *Macroeconomics*, 3rd edition, (New York: Wiley and Sons, 1990). An intermediate macroeconomic text by a leading proponent of rational expectations macroeconomics.

Begg, David. *The Rational Expectations Revolution in Macroeconomics* (Baltimore: The Johns Hopkins University Press, 1982). A complete and somewhat technical exposition of rational expectations macroeconomics.

Forman, Leonard. "Rational Expectations and the Real World," *Challenge Magazine*, November/December 1980. A critique of rational expectations macroeconomics.

Gordon, Robert J. "Evolution in Postwar Macroeconomics," in Martin S. Feldstein (ed.), *The American Economy in Transition* (Chicago: University of Chicago Press, 1980). An excellent review of the evolution of macroeconomic thinking in the past 50 years.

Maddock, Rodney, and Michael Carter. "A Child's Guide to Rational Expectations," *The Journal of Economic Literature*, March 1982, pp. 39–51. A worthwhile survey of the issues involved in rational expectations macroeconomics.

V

The National Debt, Economic Growth, and Productivity

ONE OF THE CRUCIAL ISSUES FACING AMERICA INVOLVES THE LARGE BUDGET DEFICITS THAT NOW SEEM TO BE ALMOST INTRACTABLY BUILT INTO OUR ECONOMY. CHAPTER 21 INTRODUCES THE MEANING AND MEASUREMENT OF BUDGET DEFICITS AND THE NATIONAL DEBT. AFTER DISPOSING OF SOME OF THE BOGUS ARGUMENTS ABOUT THE DANGERS OF LARGE BUDGET DEFICITS, THE CHAPTER ANALYZES SOME OF THE VALID CONCERNS ABOUT LARGE AND PERSISTENT BUDGET DEFICITS. ■ MUCH OF THE MATERIAL PRESENTED IN THE PAST THREE SECTIONS OF THIS BOOK DEALS WITH THE BEHAVIOR OF OUTPUT AND INCOME IN THE CONTEXT OF A PARTICULAR POTENTIAL OUTPUT LEVEL OR A PARTICULAR CAPACITY TO PRODUCE GOODS AND SERVICES. A SEPARATE BUT EXTREMELY CRITICAL ISSUE THAT HAS BEEN DEEMPHASIZED UNTIL NOW IS THE ISSUE OF THE GROWTH OF LIVING STANDARDS OVER THE LONG RUN. THIS IS THE ISSUE OF *ECONOMIC GROWTH*— THE EXPANSION OVER TIME IN A NATION'S CAPACITY TO PRODUCE GOODS AND SERVICES. IN THE LONG RUN, THE ONLY WAY A NATION CAN ACHIEVE RISING LIVING STANDARDS IS FOR THE AVERAGE WORKER TO BECOME MORE PRODUCTIVE, THAT IS, TO INCREASE OUTPUT PRODUCED PER YEAR. CHAPTER 21 ANALYZES THE PRINCIPLES OF LONG-RUN ECONOMIC GROWTH AND DISCUSSES SOME OF THE POSSIBLE EXPLANATIONS FOR THE SLOWDOWN IN OUR PRODUCTIVITY GROWTH SINCE THE EARLY 1970S. FINALLY, THE CHAPTER DISCUSSES POLICIES TO STIMULATE GROWTH OF LIVING STANDARDS AND LOOKS AT THE OUTLOOK FOR PRODUCTIVITY GROWTH TO YEAR 2000.

LARGE BUDGET DEFICITS
WILL BLEED THE
COUNTRY SLOWLY.

—ROBERT M. SOLOW,
NOBEL LAUREATE
IN ECONOMICS

The Economics of Federal Budget Deficits and the National Debt

ONE OF THE MOST PROMINENT MACROECONOMIC ISSUES FACING THE UNITED STATES SINCE THE EARLY 1980S INVOLVES THE ECONOMIC CONSEQUENCES OF LARGE FEDERAL BUDGET DEFICITS AND THE BURGEONING STOCK OF GOVERNMENT DEBT. COMMENCING WITH THE SUBSTANTIAL INCOME-TAX REDUCTIONS AND NATIONAL DEFENSE BUILDUP OF THE EARLY 1980S, ANNUAL BUDGET DEFICITS OF UNPRECEDENTED MAGNITUDE HAVE BECOME PART OF THE NATIONAL ECONOMIC LANDSCAPE. THE ANNUAL FEDERAL BUDGET DEFICIT IS THE AMOUNT BY WHICH ANNUAL FEDERAL GOVERNMENT EXPENDITURES EXCEED ANNUAL TAX REVENUES. THE PATTERN OF FEDERAL GOVERNMENT EXPENDITURES, TAX RECEIPTS, AND DEFICITS DURING THE PAST FORTY YEARS IS ILLUSTRATED IN FIGURE 21.1.

THE FIGURE INDICATES THAT WHILE BUDGET DEFICITS WERE SMALL AND TRANSITORY IN THE 1950S AND 1960S, THEY HAVE BECOME LARGE AND PERMANENT IN THE PAST FIFTEEN TO TWENTY YEARS. BUDGET DEFICITS HAVE OCCURRED IN EVERY YEAR SINCE 1969. THE MAGNITUDE OF THE ANNUAL DEFICIT INCREASED SHARPLY DURING RONALD REAGAN'S PRESIDENCY IN THE 1980S. THE NATIONAL DEBT—THE CUMULATIVE SUM OF PAST DEFICITS—ROUGHLY TRIPLED DURING REAGAN'S TWO TERMS IN office (January 1981 to January 1989). This national debt in 1993 was approximately five times as large as in 1980. In other words, the national debt has increased four times as much in the past 15 years as it did in the previous 200 years of this nation! Clearly, this represents a radical change in the way our government conducts its financial affairs. The consequences of this change in federal budgetary policy deserve careful scrutiny.

Growing public awareness of the potential dangers inherent in huge budget deficits resulted in various congressional efforts to control these deficits with special legislation in the past ten years. In the mid-1980s, federal legislation (the Gramm-Rudman-Hollings Act) was enacted. This mandated a gradual phaseout of the budget deficit over several years. Though successful in limiting the red ink for a couple of years, this arrangement collapsed in the late 1980s. More recently, Congress, by requiring that *new* (additional) expenditures be matched by new revenues, tried to prevent the annual deficit from spiraling even further out of control. To date, however, these efforts have not been successful. The deficits in the early 1990s are even larger than the Reagan deficits of the 1980s. For a variety of reasons, it is

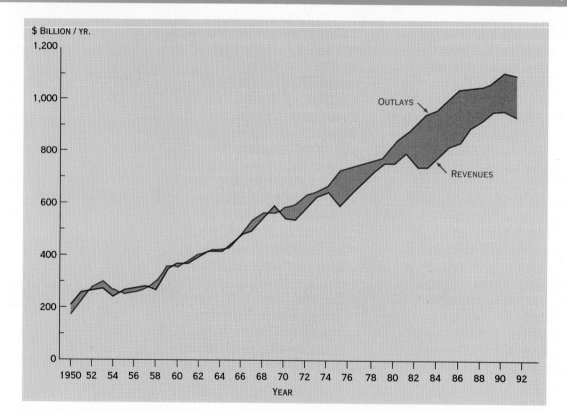

Before the 1970s, federal expenditures were closely aligned with federal revenues. Beginning in the 1980s, huge deficits have been a persistent feature of American government finance.

SOURCE: *Economic Report of the President*, 1992.

FIGURE 21.1

difficult to visualize a return to balanced budgets or even to modest deficits like those of the 1960s and 1970s in the foreseeable future.

The Consequences of Deficits

Everyone has heard acquaintances speak of the federal government's fiscal management in terms of gloom and doom. And aspiring politicians seeking to unseat incumbents rail against deficits by invoking images of a bankrupt federal Treasury and unconscionable burdens placed upon the backs of our grandchildren. As we shall learn in Chapter 21, the issues are far more complex than indicated by everyday discussions of politicians and the public.

Large budget deficits may have both short-term and long-term consequences. These deficits have private consequences (to you personally) and social consequences (to the nation as a whole). Some of the short-term consequences probably have affected you personally, though you may have not been aware that these effects are related to the deficits. The availability of a student loan, the monthly payments on an auto loan, the cost of an imported VCR and the cost of a summer vacation in Europe are all influenced by federal budget policy. In some instances, summer job prospects may even be influenced by large budget deficits. Not all of these short-term consequences are adverse. You may have benefited in certain ways from the large deficits.

In this chapter we explore the facts and principles concerning federal budget deficits and the national debt. Perspectives on the magnitude of deficits and the debt are obtained by comparing their size and growth to other relevant variables in the economy. We put to rest some commonly expressed fallacious views about the national debt sometimes expressed by the person on the street. Legitimate concerns about the potential adverse effects of large deficits are carefully analyzed. Conceptual measurement problems associated with deficits and the debt are discussed so that one may achieve a realistic view of the magnitude of deficits and the stock of debt. You will emerge from this chapter with a much clearer perspective on the economics of large budget deficits and rapidly escalating national debt.

The Economics of the National Debt

THE MEANING AND MAGNITUDE OF FEDERAL BUDGET DEFICITS AND THE NATIONAL DEBT

BUDGET DEFICIT
The shortfall of federal receipts relative to expenditures, measured at an annual rate.

The amount by which annual federal tax receipts exceed annual federal expenditures is the **budget surplus** or **budget deficit** (if negative). This surplus or deficit is a *flow* variable, measured per unit of time (usually one year). The government finances budget deficits by selling bonds and shorter-term securities to American individuals and firms, foreigners, U.S. government agencies, and the Federal

NATIONAL DEBT
The total stock of bonds and other federal government IOUs outstanding; the sum of past federal budget deficits minus the sum of past surpluses.

Reserve System. The sum total of these bonds and other securities outstanding at a given point of time is the government debt or **national debt**. This is a *stock* of financial claims against the federal government. When the government runs a surplus in its budget, some debt is retired—the national debt decreases. When budget deficits are experienced, the federal government issues new securities—the national debt increases.

Because the federal budget has been in surplus only one year since 1960, the national debt has increased persistently in recent decades. The growth of the total federal debt—the *gross national debt*—including that portion held by government agencies (about 25 percent of the gross debt) is illustrated in Figure 21.2 for the period 1900–1992. For many purposes the *net* debt is a superior measure. The *net national debt* excludes that portion held by government agencies, thereby measuring the net indebtedness of the federal government to private American firms and

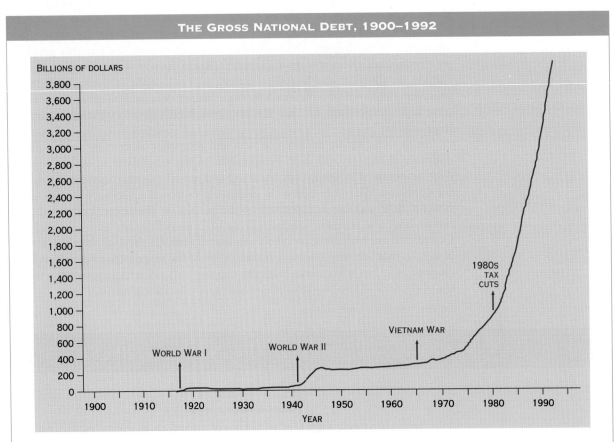

THE GROSS NATIONAL DEBT, 1900–1992

Except during wars, the national debt grew very slowly until the 1970s. Since then it has increased rapidly. The national debt tripled in the 1980s.

SOURCE: Data from *Economic Report of the President*, 1992, and *Historical Statistics of the United States*, 1992.

FIGURE 21.2

individuals, foreigners, and the Federal Reserve System. The gross debt and the net debt exhibit the same general pattern of growth.

The most striking aspect of Figure 21.2 is the dramatic increase in the national debt since the mid-1970s, especially since 1980. Prior to the 1980s, the great bulk of the debt was incurred during wars and periods of depression or recession. Note the increases in the debt during World War I and World War II. All nations have typically found it impractical to raise taxes precipitously enough in wartime to match increased military expenditures. Hence, they experience large budget deficits and an escalation of the national debt. In cyclical downturns like the 1930s, 1974–1975, and 1981–1982, the debt almost inevitably increases rapidly because the depressed economic activity automatically increases the budget deficit. This is primarily due to the induced slowdown in tax receipts of the U.S. Treasury, although expenditures for unemployment benefits and other assistance programs are also stimulated in recessions.

In 1992 the gross national debt passed $4,000 billion, or $4 trillion. The *net* debt came to about $3,000 billion, or $3 trillion. These figures may seem more meaningful when we calculate that in 1992 the gross debt and net debt amounted to approximately $16,000 and $12,000, respectively, for every man, woman, and child in the United States. As we discuss later in the chapter, this recent unprecedented rate of growth of the national debt, together with the prospect of further rapid growth to come, is cause for serious concern to most professional economists.

MEASURES OF THE RELATIVE GROWTH OF THE NATIONAL DEBT

It seems reasonable to assume that just as a growing economy is capable of supporting prudent growth in such private forms of debt as mortgage debt, corporate debt, and consumer debt, it is also capable of supporting a moderate or reasonable rate of growth of government debt. Government debt expanded more slowly than private forms of debt from the late-1940s through the mid-1970s. More recently, however, federal government debt has grown more rapidly than mortgage debt, corporate debt, and consumer debt.[1]

The slow growth of government debt in the first twenty-five years after World War II ensured an ample supply of available funds with which to finance the postwar boom in private construction activity as well as strong expansion in consumer spending and corporate investment spending. From the late-1940s to the mid-1970s, government debt expanded at less than half the growth rate of private forms of debt. In this period (in which the ratio of government debt to GDP was steadily falling), most economists found it difficult to get excited about any alleged deleterious effects of deficit spending or arguments about imposing a burden on future generations. More recently, however, this viewpoint has changed because of the explosive escalation of government debt.

---

[1] The average annual growth rate of U.S. government debt during 1950–1991 was 6.7 percent. The average annual growth rates of mortgage debt and consumer debt during the same interval were 10.3 percent and 9.2 percent, respectively. However, the growth rate of the government debt during the more recent end of the interval, 1975–1991, accelerated to 12.5 percent per annum!

E
X
H
I
B
I
T

21 . 1

Figure 21.3 illustrates who owns the national debt—the bonds and other securities issued to finance budget deficits over the years. The debt is distributed among the American private sector (banks, other corporations, and individuals), the government sector (federal agencies, state and local governments, and the Federal Reserve), and foreign holders.

One of the largest holders of government debt is the U.S. government itself; the Federal Reserve System and federal agencies hold almost one-third of the total debt. As indicated in our discussion of monetary policy (Chapter 16), the Fed buys and sells government securities (components of the national debt) in order to implement open market operations, its chief policy tool. In 1992 the Fed's total portfolio of government debt amounted to almost $300 billion, or about 8 percent of the total national debt. Since the Fed turns back about 90 percent of its total revenues (predominantly interest earned on government bonds) to the U.S. Treasury, the portion of the debt sold to the Fed is almost without interest cost to the Treasury.

Other government agencies also purchase government bonds. The Social Security Administration, for example, maintains a trust fund to cover any monthly shortfall between current payroll tax receipts and current retirement benefits. This trust fund consists primarily of government bonds. Altogether, government agencies besides the Federal Reserve own about one-fourth of the national debt.

Approximately 10 percent of the federal debt is owned by state and local government units. State and local governments normally exhibit budget surpluses and invest those funds predominantly in safe U.S. government bonds.

American individuals *directly* own about 7 percent of the federal debt in the form of U.S. Savings Bonds and other types of government securities. Figure 21.3 indicates that almost 40 percent of the national debt is held by banks and such other financial and nonfinancial firms as money market mutual funds, insurance companies, and other entities with idle funds to invest. Because this wealth is ultimately owned by the individual Americans who have invested in money market mutual funds, purchased insurance, and own stock in American firms, U.S. households directly or indirectly own a large share of the debt.

Foreign investors including individuals, banks, corporations, and governments own about 13 percent of the U.S. national debt. These foreign buyers are attracted to our government debt because of its attractive yield, perceived safety, and because of the widespread acceptabil-

A FALLACIOUS VIEW OF THE NATIONAL DEBT

At this point we pause to examine a fallacious argument sometimes expressed by uninformed observers of American budgetary policy. Consider the following statement:

ity of dollar-denominated assets in international commerce. The portion of our national debt that is *externally* held has increased from less than 3 percent in the 1950s to around 13 percent today.

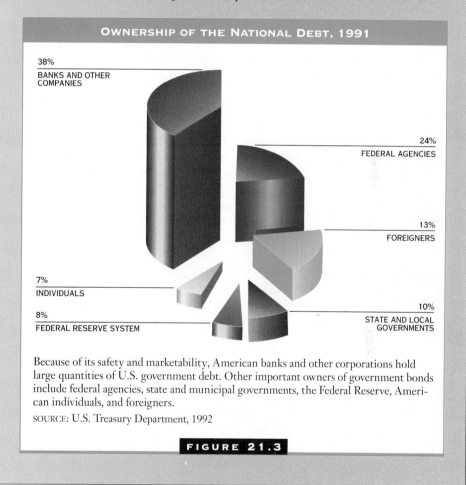

OWNERSHIP OF THE NATIONAL DEBT, 1991

38%
BANKS AND OTHER COMPANIES

24%
FEDERAL AGENCIES

13%
FOREIGNERS

7%
INDIVIDUALS

8%
FEDERAL RESERVE SYSTEM

10%
STATE AND LOCAL GOVERNMENTS

Because of its safety and marketability, American banks and other corporations hold large quantities of U.S. government debt. Other important owners of government bonds include federal agencies, state and municipal governments, the Federal Reserve, American individuals, and foreigners.

SOURCE: U.S. Treasury Department, 1992

FIGURE 21.3

Like all debts, the national debt must eventually be paid off. We are placing an unfair burden on future generations by forcing them to tighten their belts and sacrifice in order to pay off debts incurred by the present generation.

The fallacy lies in the assumption that the national debt must be paid off at some future date. *The national debt never will be paid off—any more than debt incurred by*

General Motors, AT&T, or the aggregate of American consumers or mortgagors (home buyers) will ever be extinguished.

Although the federal government pays off each individual holder of government debt when the securities mature, it does so on balance by *rolling over* or *refinancing* the debt—by issuing new securities.[2]

The process is precisely the same as that followed by the aggregate of American corporations and individuals. Each debt is honored as it comes due at maturity. However, on balance, the funds that pay off maturing debt come from issuing new debt. Hence, the total debt of GM, AT&T, and most other stable American corporations shows a sustained uptrend over time. Likewise, while each individual consumer debt and home mortgage is eventually repaid or extinguished (barring personal bankruptcy), the total magnitude of consumer debt and mortgage debt expands over time in any prosperous, growing economy. Willingness to incur debt, if done in a conservative and prudent manner, is an essential element in the economic process. Modern industrial societies would never have reached their current state of affluence in the absence of the willingness of firms and individuals to borrow.

U.S. government debt is a highly safe and desirable investment outlet for thousands of banks and other financial and nonfinancial firms, and for millions of individual savers. Because the U.S. Treasury has the constitutional authority to tax or even print money to honor its debt obligations, securities issued by the U.S. government are the safest investments in the world. The Treasury has no difficulty finding lenders—buyers of its securities—though one cannot deny that at times the cost to the Treasury of doing so (interest rate offered) is quite high.

When one acknowledges that the national debt need not and will not ever be repaid or extinguished, a totally different perception of the *burden* of this debt emerges. Our grandchildren (or theirs) need not tighten their belts to the tune of $16,000 or more per person and pay off the debt resulting from our extravagance. Any *intergenerational burden* of the debt is *not* attributable to the necessity of paying off or even reducing the magnitude of the national debt.

INTERGENERATIONAL BURDEN

The costs imposed by the current generation upon future generations by bequeathing an inadequate capital stock.

Economists believe that any **intergenerational burdens**—burdens imposed by one generation upon another—are attributable to the quality and quantity of the physical and human capital stock passed on to the next generation. A legitimate concern is that large budget deficits and the escalating national debt may ultimately *crowd out* or displace private investment in plant, equipment, and technology. Unless the deficits are attributable to growth of government *capital expenditures*—projects such as schools, scientific research laboratories, and infrastructure—these deficits may lead to a reduced rate of growth of the national's capital stock. We return to this argument later in the chapter.

It is incorrect to start with the assumption that future generations will have to tighten their belts, reduce consumption, and use the proceeds to extinguish the debt they have inherited. However, interest must be paid to those who lend to the government—those bondholders and other owners of the stock of government debt. To obtain funds with which to pay this interest, the government must either issue additional debt or obtain funds through tax receipts. As we shall establish in

---

[2]The Treasury is heavily involved in financing activities every week. This process involves refinancing debt currently maturing as well as issuing additional debt to finance current budget deficits. About half the marketable debt matures every 24 months. Treasury issue of new debt frequently amounts to $10 billion to $20 billion each week.

this chapter, when the government adopts a passive attitude of habitually stepping up its borrowing to meet growing interest expense on a rapidly expanding debt, severe inflation may ultimately occur. Hence, to be prudent, the government must meet growing interest costs on the national debt through increased tax revenues.

A SECOND FALLACY: INTEREST PAYMENTS ARE A DRAIN OF RESOURCES

This brings us to a second bogus argument associated with the national debt, expressed in the following hypothetical plea:

> Interest payments on the national debt represent a drain on the nation's limited economic resources. It is a pure waste of our real resources to use them just to pay interest on the debt.

This argument is fallacious because interest payments on the debt—to the extent that the debt is domestically held—do not represent a use of economic resources at all. It is true that if our debt is held by foreigners, we *will* suffer a loss of resources. That is, we *will* have to give up American goods and services as they exchange their interest coupons, either now or later, for American computers, wheat, and high-tech equipment. In this event, fewer of America's resources would be available for domestic use. However, only about 13 percent of the total U.S. government debt is owned by foreigners.

In the case of domestically held debt, interest payments on the debt involve a *transfer of income* from American taxpayers to American bondholders of the same generation. Hypothetically, if each individual in the U.S. holds an equal share of the bonds and also is in the same tax bracket, one could view this process as one in which each individual is simply taking dollars out of one pocket and putting them back into another pocket. However, taxpayers and bondholders are different entities. A large national debt therefore inevitably involves income redistribution effects. But domestically held debt does not involve any using up of the nation's real economic resources.

INDICATORS OF THE MAGNITUDE OF THE DEBT BURDEN

If funds to service the debt are to be obtained through tax revenues, it is true, given other factors, that *the larger the debt, the higher the tax rates required to service the debt.* The higher taxes largely represent income transfers to domestic holders of U.S. government debt, so there is no net loss of resources to the nation overall. However, if the increased tax rates required to service the enlarged debt (fund the interest payments) produce a reduction in the incentive to work, save, or invest in real capital goods, then economic growth and the future standard of living will be reduced relative to that which would prevail if the debt were lower.

Also, given the political realities that limit government spending, more government dollars spent on interest payments are likely to mean fewer government dollars spent on education, health care, and other government services. Increased interest expenditures are likely to result in a reduction in other forms of government spending.

Some perspective into the probable quantitative importance of these considerations may be obtained by observing the trends of the ratios of government debt/GDP and interest payments/GDP. In Figure 21.4 we illustrate the ratio of the gross national debt to GDP since 1939. Given a set of tax *rates*, federal tax *receipts* rise at least proportionally with the growth of GDP. Therefore, unless interest rates increase, *tax rates* do not have to be raised over time to meet interest payments on the national debt as long as the debt grows no more rapidly than GDP. Figure 21.4 indicates that, after reaching a peak of more than 100 percent at the end of World War II, the ratio of the debt to GDP persistently declined until the mid-1970s. The government debt was growing much more slowly than economic activity in general. Any burdens or economic consequences of the debt were declining during this era, and economists often were impatient with those who spent time worrying about the debt. Note, however, that the debt/GDP ratio began increasing in the early

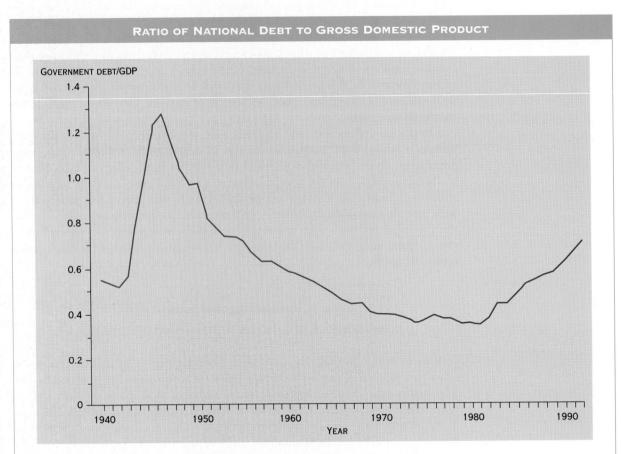

RATIO OF NATIONAL DEBT TO GROSS DOMESTIC PRODUCT

GOVERNMENT DEBT/GDP

YEAR

The size of the national debt relative to a nation's gross domestic product may be viewed as an indicator of the nation's capacity to handle the debt. The ratio of the national debt to GDP continually declined from the end of World War II (1945) until the mid-1970s. In the past 15 years, the ratio has been increasing.

SOURCE: Data from *Economic Report of the President*, 1992.

FIGURE 21.4

1980s. The debt has been growing considerably faster than GDP since 1980. The ratio today is back to its level of the 1950s, and is increasing rapidly.

An even better indicator of potential problems associated with the national debt is the ratio of the cost of *servicing* the debt to GDP. This ratio of government interest expenditures to GDP for the 1940–1991 period is illustrated in Figure 21.5.

The percentage of GDP that must be taken in taxes to meet the interest payments on the national debt declined steadily from almost 2 percent in 1946 to about 1.2 percent during the 1960s. That is, the transfer of income from taxpayers to bondholders amounted to only about 1 percent of the nation's GDP during the 1960s. This ratio increased dramatically after the mid-1970s to more than 3 percent in the mid-1980s, and has been higher in recent years than at any time since World War I. The portion of the federal government budget spent on debt service—interest—has increased sharply, as indicated in Figure 21.6 (page 534).

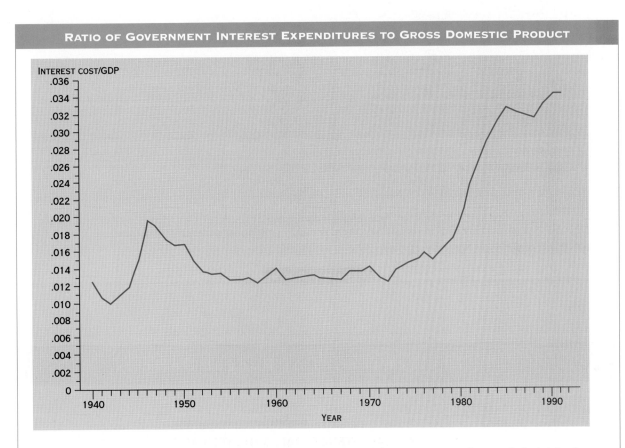

RATIO OF GOVERNMENT INTEREST EXPENDITURES TO GROSS DOMESTIC PRODUCT

The ratio of government interest expenditures to GDP is an indicator of the income tax rate that must be levied simply to service the debt. This ratio declined from the mid-1940s to the 1960s, when it hovered around 1 percent. Since the early 1970s, the ratio has increased sharply. In the early 1990s, the ratio exceeds 3 percent.

SOURCE: Data from *Economic Report of the President*, 1992.

FIGURE 21.5

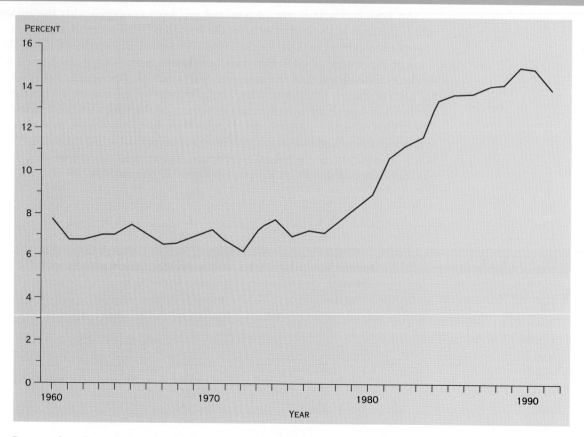

Because of rapidly escalating debt, the share of the federal budget required to meet interest payments has increased sharply in the past 15 years. Interest expenditures have been the most rapidly growing component of federal spending.

SOURCE: Data from *Economic Report of the President*, 1992.

FIGURE 21.6

The Economics of Budget Deficits

ACTUAL, STRUCTURAL, AND CYCLICAL BUDGET DEFICITS

The existing budget deficit may be divided into a *cyclical* or *induced* portion and a *structural* or *high-employment* portion. It is quite useful to distinguish between the cyclical and structural portions of the existing deficit.

total budget deficit = cyclical deficit + structural deficit

The portion of the actual deficit attributable to a shortfall of actual GDP relative to full-employment GDP.

The **cyclical deficit** is the portion of the deficit attributable to the shortfall of actual GDP from potential GDP. That is, the cyclical deficit is attributable to the effect of economic slack (depressed economic activity) upon federal expenditures and receipts. It has been estimated that for each $100 billion that actual GDP falls short of potential GDP, the budget is induced to swing into the direction of deficit (or increased deficit) by about $30 billion. Hence, if our $6,000 billion (GDP) economy is operating 5 percent below potential GDP, we have a cyclical or induced deficit of approximately $90 billion.[3] Economic recessions thus automatically lead to significantly larger budget deficits even in the absence of any changes in tax rates or spending decisions. Budget deficits are reduced automatically during periods of economic recovery unless legislated tax cuts are implemented or government programs are expanded.

STRUCTURAL DEFICIT OR HIGH-EMPLOYMENT DEFICIT

The deficit that would prevail under conditions of full employment; depends on legislated programs and tax rates, not on economic activity.

The **structural deficit** (or surplus), sometimes referred to as the **high-employment deficit** (or surplus), indicates the size of the deficit or surplus that would *hypothetically* exist if the economy were operating at a high level of output and employment. This high level of output and employment is commonly taken to be that which would prevail if the unemployment rate were at the economy's *natural unemployment rate*, an unemployment rate of perhaps 5 or 5.5 percent. The structural deficit (or surplus) is attributable to the level and structure of taxes and government appropriations and is not altered, for example, as aggregate demand and GDP increase during the expansion phase of the business cycle. Since the cyclical effect of economic activity on the federal budget is removed, any changes in the structural budget deficit or surplus reflect changes in tax legislation or changes in government expenditures. Changes in the structural deficit thus indicate *discretionary changes in fiscal policy*—changes in tax and expenditure decisions.

In Figure 21.7 (page 536) the horizontal axis measures the economy's current utilization rate—the ratio of actual GDP to potential GDP—which increases as we move *right to left*. The vertical axis measures the budget deficit or surplus. For any given legislated budget—legislated government expenditures and existing federal tax code—the figure indicates the responsiveness of the federal deficit to the state of the economy. For example, if Budget *A* is in place and actual GDP is 95 percent of potential, the budget deficit is $60 billion. If the economy were at full employment (actual GDP/potential GDP being 100 percent) with Budget *A* in place, a surplus of $30 billion would exist. The structural deficit associated with Budget *A* is a negative $30 billion—a structural budget *surplus* of $30 billion. In this circumstance, with the economy actually operating at point *E* in the figure, the actual budget deficit of $60 billion can be decomposed into a cyclical deficit of $90 billion and a structural surplus of $30 billion.

Note that, for any given legislated budget, the intersection of the budget line with the vertical axis indicates the size of the structural deficit or surplus. In Figure 21.7, Budget *A* exhibits a structural budget *surplus* of $30 billion and Budget *B* a structural *deficit* of approximately $40 billion. Budget *C* exhibits a structural deficit of about $105 billion, and Budget *D* a structural deficit of $150 billion.

---

[3]Five percent of $6,000 billion indicates an output shortfall of $300 billion. Since each $100 billion of output loss raises the budget deficit by $30 billion, we compute a cyclical or induced deficit of $90 billion.

The slope of the budget line in Figure 21.7 indicates the magnitude of the *automatic stabilizing effect* of the federal budget. As actual GDP moves farther below potential GDP (left to right on the horizontal axis), the budget moves in the direction of increasingly large deficits. This is entirely because of the cyclical component of the budget deficit. A decrease in GDP induces a contraction of federal tax receipts and an increase in federal transfer payments in the form of income-support programs.

The concept of the structural deficit or surplus allows us to compare the magnitude of fiscal stimulus among alternative budgets. The actual budget deficit does not permit such comparisons, because the actual budget deficit or surplus depends on both the existing tax and expenditure structure *and* the current state of the economy. Budget *B* in Figure 21.7 is more stimulative than Budget *A*, since Budget *B* involves a larger deficit at each and every level of economic activity. By the same token, Budget *D* is more stimulative than Budgets *A*, *B*, and *C*. A convenient benchmark for gauging the macroeconomic posture of federal budget policy from year to year is the change in the structural deficit. When the structural deficit is reduced in

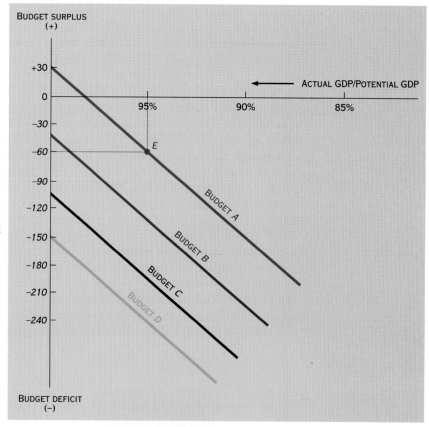

THE TOTAL BUDGET DEFICIT (WITH STRUCTURAL AND CYCLICAL PORTIONS)

The actual budget deficit (or surplus) consists of a structural portion and a cyclical portion. The structural deficit is indicated by the intersection of the existing budget line with the vertical axis (that is, the deficit that would occur if GDP were 100 percent of potential GDP). The cyclical portion depends on the state of the economy. For any given legislated budget, the cyclical deficit increases as the gap between actual and potential GDP widens (that is, as we move rightward along the horizontal axis).

FIGURE 21.7

a given year, budgetary policy is becoming more contractionary or restrictive. Clearly, if Budgets *A*, *B*, *C*, and *D* occur in chronological order, federal budget policy or fiscal policy is becoming increasingly stimulative.

Economists are more concerned about possible adverse effects of long-lasting structural budget deficits than cyclical deficits. In fact, cyclical deficits are almost uniformly viewed as being beneficial, since they provide support to a depressed economy. When, for example, the economy moves into a period of recession because of a decrease in consumer and business confidence, the deficit increases as federal tax receipts automatically decline and transfer payments increase in the form of unemployment and public-assistance benefits. All this puts more cash into the hands of private citizens and firms, thereby providing support to aggregate demand and economic activity. When the economy is booming, the deficit shrinks as tax receipts surge and transfers decline. This inhibits aggregate demand for goods and services. Some economic studies suggest that this automatic stabilizing effect of the budget prevents perhaps 35–40 percent of the fluctuations in GDP that would occur if the budget were not structured to serve this stabilizing function.[4]

If one were to attempt to prevent cyclical deficits from occurring, one would have to raise tax rates and reduce government expenditures during periods of depressed economic activity. This would further depress the economy. In a booming economy, if the actual budget were in surplus, a policy of insisting on an annually balanced budget would require a tax cut or expenditure increase, thus creating excessive economic stimulus and exacerbating inflationary pressures. Rigid adherence to a philosophy of annually balancing the budget would require the use of perverse fiscal policies that would lead to an amplification of economic fluctuations. Thus, no economist would advocate a philosophy calling for a rigid policy of balancing the budget each year.

YOUR TURN

THE PRESIDENTIAL CAMPAIGN OF 1932 BETWEEN HERBERT HOOVER AND FRANKLIN D. ROOSEVELT WAS WAGED DURING THE DEPTHS OF THE GREAT DEPRESSION. BOTH CANDIDATES ADVOCATED FISCAL MEASURES TO ATTEMPT TO REDUCE THE BUDGET DEFICIT— TAX HIKES AND/OR EXPENDITURE REDUCTIONS. EVALUATE THE SOUNDNESS OF THESE PROPOSALS.

LARGE STRUCTURAL DEFICITS OF THE PAST DECADE

As the U.S. economy recovered from the severe 1981–1982 recession, the overall deficit failed to come down between 1982 and 1986 (although it did come down temporarily between 1987 and 1989 before increasing to new record highs in the early 1990s). Even though the *cyclical* deficit decreased sharply because of economic expansion, a steadily increasing *structural* component of the deficit counteracted the declining cyclical deficit and prevented the overall deficit from coming down. This is indicated in Figure 21.8 as well as Table 21.1.

---

[4]See Robert J. Gordon, *Macroeconomics* (Boston: Little, Brown & Co., 1978), p. 494.

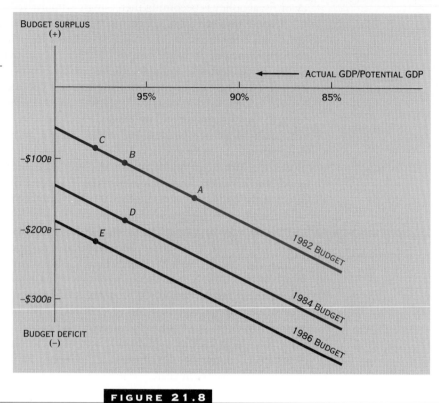

Because of tax reductions and spending increases, the budget line shifted downward during the economic recovery of 1982–1986. Even though the cyclical deficit declined dramatically in the recovery, the expanding structural deficit prevented a major decline in the actual deficit.

FIGURE 21.8

In Figure 21.8, the budget line shifted downward over time as a result of discretionary increases in government expenditures and decreases in income tax rates. Although the economy staged a strong recovery after 1982, the actual deficit failed to come down. Instead of moving from *A* to *B* to *C*, as would have occurred if tax rates and expenditure authorizations had remained unaltered, the economy actually moved from *A* to *D* to *E*. The structural deficit increased rapidly enough to overwhelm the declining cyclical component of the deficit. Fiscal policy was becoming increasingly stimulative during this period as the structural deficit increased from $49 billion in 1982 to $185 billion in 1986 (Table 21.1).

Remember that a cyclical deficit can be eliminated by economic expansion during the recovery phase of the business cycle. A structural deficit cannot be outgrown. It can be reduced only through tax hikes or expenditure cuts. Table 21.1 indicates that annual structural deficits in the range of $150 billion to $200 billion were built into our federal budget in the late 1980s and early 1990s.

Remember also that *the correct measure of the posture or thrust of fiscal policy is the structural deficit, not the cyclical deficit or actual deficit.*

To illustrate changes in U.S. government budgetary posture since the mid-1950s, we show the actual quarterly behavior of the structural budget deficit or surplus relative to GDP in Figure 21.9 (page 540). A cursory glance at the figure indicates several key facts. First, the structural budget exhibited a *surplus*, on

FEDERAL BUDGET DEFICITS: STRUCTURAL AND CYCLICAL COMPONENTS (BILLIONS OF DOLLARS)

FISCAL YEAR	REPORTED DEFICIT	STRUCTURAL DEFICIT	CYCLICAL DEFICIT
1980	$ 74 billion	$ 48 billion	$ 26 billion
1981	79	43	36
1982	128	49	79
1983	208	108	100
1984	185	134	51
1985	212	177	35
1986	221	185	36
1987	150	120	30
1988	155	158	(−3)*
1989	154	148	6
1990	221	150	71
1991	269	172	97
1992	352**	191**	161**

*Indicates a *surplus.*
**Indicates CBO projections for 1992, made in January 1992.
SOURCE: Congressional Budget Office, 1992.

TABLE 21.1

balance, between 1955 and 1962. In the next decade the structural budget was in deficit by an average magnitude of perhaps 1 percent of GDP. This swing toward fiscal stimulus was initiated by tax cuts in the early 1960s and by escalation of both domestic social programs and military spending associated with Vietnam between 1965 and 1968. De-escalation of the Vietnam War and a tax hike in the late 1960s reduced the relative size of the structural deficit for a few years. However, the structural deficit increased after 1974 to about 2 percent of GDP between 1975 and 1980 and ballooned to more than 4 percent of GDP during the mid-1980s. It has declined to around 3 percent of GDP in the early 1990s.

The unprecedented peacetime structural budget deficits that commenced in the early 1980s are attributable largely to the generous income-tax cuts of the first Reagan Administration, along with the escalation of defense expenditures unaccompanied by significant cuts in nondefense spending. Unlike large structural deficits of the past, which occurred *temporarily* under the emergency conditions of wartime finance, the deficits of the 1980s and 1990s have occurred in time of peace and have proven to be more intractable. This is why interest on the part of economists, news commentators, and the general public in the venerable issues of deficit finance and debt burdens has staged a resurgence in the past decade.

MEASUREMENT AND CONCEPTUAL PROBLEMS IN INTERPRETING BUDGET DEFICITS

In addition to the need to adjust the deficit to allow for cyclical conditions, several other considerations complicate any analysis of budget deficits and debt burdens.

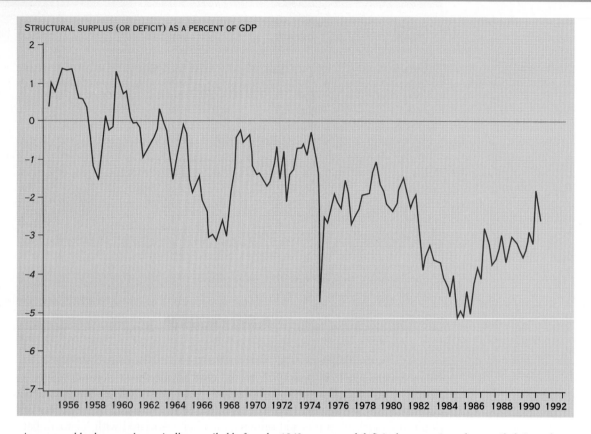

STRUCTURAL SURPLUS (OR DEFICIT) AS A PERCENT OF GDP

A structural budget *surplus* typically prevailed before the 1960s; structural deficits have consistently prevailed since then. These structural deficits increased sharply in the 1980s, reaching more than 4 percent of GDP by the mid-1980s. The structural deficit/GDP ratio has declined somewhat in recent years, to around 3 percent of GDP.

*These figures are actually deficits cyclically adjusted to the *midpoint* of cyclical expansions and not to the *peaks* of expansions. They therefore overstate somewhat the high-employment deficit magnitudes.

SOURCE: Data from *Survey of Current Business*, 1992.

FIGURE 21.9

The net result of all of these considerations is to reduce somewhat the perceived size and adverse consequences of the deficits of the past decade.

OFF-BUDGET ACTIVITIES Borrowings of certain government agencies to finance services provided to the public are listed as *off-budget activities* and are not included in official budget deficits. One could argue that such off-budget deficits, amounting to perhaps $20 billion annually, should be reported as budget deficits. This consideration suggests that reported deficits *understate* the true deficits.

STATE AND LOCAL GOVERNMENT SURPLUSES In the past decade, state and local governments have collectively exhibited net surpluses averaging $20 billion to $40 billion per annum. At the same time, federal grants to state and local governments have typically amounted to $120 billion to $150 billion per year. One could view part of the federal deficit as the source of state/local surpluses. The net deficit of *all* levels of government—federal, state, and local—is smaller than the federal deficit.

ABSENCE OF FEDERAL GOVERNMENT CAPITAL BUDGET American business firms and most state and local governments compile a separate *capital budget* and *operating budget* to emphasize the distinct difference between borrowing to fund such capital projects as schools and bridges that yield a flow of benefits far into the future and borrowing to meet current operating costs. The federal government does not do this. One could argue that federal expenditures on buildings, dams, highways, education facilities, and so forth should be included in a separate capital budget, thus making the reported budget deficit $20 billion to $30 billion smaller in the early 1990s.

INFLATION ACCOUNTING FOR INTEREST PAYMENTS Assume the net government debt is $3,000 billion, the average interest rate paid for debt service is currently 7 percent, and inflation is 4 percent. Seven percent interest on a $3,000 billion debt implies annual interest expense of $210 billion. All this interest is reported as current government spending and thus contributes, dollar-for-dollar, to the reported budget deficit. However, since 4 percent inflation implies that the real value of the stock of debt decreases $120 billion during the year, one may conceptually regard $120 billion of the interest paid as simply compensation paid to the lender for the reduction in the real value of the debt. The government gains $120 billion in real terms because of the reduction in real value of its debt liability. In other words, one could argue that only the *real* interest expense—$90 billion— should be included in the reported budget deficit. The net cost to the government is $90 billion, not $210 billion. The other $120 billion is compensation paid by the government for the $120 billion *balance sheet* gain shifted from private individuals and firms to the government. If inflation is relatively severe, this consideration suggests that the actual deficit considerably exceeds the **real deficit**, which is calculated by subtracting from the reported deficit this balance-sheet gain experienced by the government.[5]

REAL DEFICIT
The actual deficit adjusted for the net balance sheet gain experienced by government because of inflation; actual deficit minus the inflation rate times the net federal debt outstanding.

THE MIX OF MONETARY AND FISCAL POLICY

Because both monetary and fiscal policy strongly affect aggregate demand and GDP, any desired level of nominal GDP can in principle be attained through various combinations of monetary and fiscal stimuli. That is, a given level of GDP can be achieved by powerful fiscal stimulus coupled with rigid monetary restraint, by powerful monetary stimulus coupled with severe fiscal restraint, and by various

---

[5]See Robert Eisner, *How Real Is The Deficit?* (New York: The Free Press, 1986). Eisner emphasizes the distinction between the reported deficit and the real deficit. The real deficit may be defined as the difference between the reported deficit and the reduction in the real value of the existing stock of government debt in a given year because of inflation. Eisner marshals support for the hypothesis that the real deficit is the superior measure.

other combinations of monetary and fiscal policies. Although the *level* of GDP can in principle be achieved with various combinations of monetary and fiscal policies, the *composition* of that output is likely to depend on the *mix* of monetary and fiscal policies.

Many economists believe that in the first half of the 1980s a combination of strong fiscal stimulus coupled with monetary restraint produced economic distortions that impaired several sectors of the U.S. economy. One might describe the situation through the analogy of driving a car with one foot on the accelerator (fiscal stimulus) and one foot on the brake (monetary restraint). The car (economy) may continue to lurch forward, but the process is hard on the engine (economic growth and certain sectors of the economy).

Increasing structural budget deficits coupled with monetary restraint in the early 1980s placed upward pressure on real (inflation-adjusted) interest rates in the United States. This created a large demand on the part of foreigners for high-yielding U.S. financial assets. This *capital inflow* drove up the value of the U.S. dollar in foreign-exchange markets to levels that made it difficult for American industries exposed to foreign competition to compete in world markets. U.S. exports stagnated and imports increased dramatically. Our international trade deficit increased from about $30 billion in 1981 to $140 billion in 1985, and remained above $100 billion throughout the 1980s. Many economists believe that the dollar was significantly overvalued (in the sense of putting American firms at a competitive disadvantage) during much of this period, causing considerable hardship for such U.S. industries as textiles, agriculture, lumber, electronics, automobiles, and shoes.[6]

A combination of less fiscal stimulus (smaller budget deficits) and more monetary stimulus may have resulted in the same level of aggregate demand and GDP but in a stronger performance by American export- and import-competing industries. The U.S. manufacturing sector would have been stronger and perhaps the service sector would have been weaker in this scenario.

Moreover, the fiscal/monetary imbalance in the early 1980s, by driving up real interest rates, reduced the fortunes of interest-sensitive industries relative to other sectors. Hence, construction activity and investment in plant and equipment may have been stronger had the mix of policy included less fiscal stimulus and more stimulative monetary policy. In other words, the mix of policy may have tilted the mix of output toward less investment and more consumption than would have prevailed in the presence of a more balanced mix of policies. The mix of monetary/fiscal policies pursued in the 1980s seems to have been counterproductive to the stated Reagan Administration objectives of stimulating investment and long-term economic growth.

Legitimate Concerns about the Spiraling Debt

There are two potential long-range consequences of the federal budget policy conducted during the past decade that are a continuing source of concern to thoughtful observers of the American economic and political scene. Both of these potential

---

[6]Martin Feldstein, head of President Ronald Reagan's Council of Economic Advisors from 1982 to 1984, frequently espoused this viewpoint.

consequences—impaired investment spending and severe inflation—have been discussed earlier and are now addressed in greater depth.

THE ISSUE OF CROWDING OUT AND GROWTH OF LIVING STANDARDS

As mentioned, because the stock of government debt grew much more slowly than privately issued debt in the first twenty years after World War II, there was room for vast expansion of construction activity and healthy expansion of private investment in plant and equipment. The federal government was not competing in the capital markets against private firms and individuals for the limited pool of funds available, and interest rates were relatively low.

Beginning with the growth of social programs and the escalation of the U.S. involvement in the Vietnam War in the 1960s, federal deficit spending increased in magnitude. These deficits escalated dramatically in the early 1980s. Real interest rates rose to unusually high levels in the 1980s. Those who believe in the **crowding-out** hypothesis assert that these high real-interest rates were attributable in large part to the massive budget deficits that tended to displace private borrowers in the marketplace and impair expenditures on the crucial category of plant, equipment, and research and development. If valid, this hypothesis implies that large budget deficits impose a burden on future generations in the form of a reduced capital stock inherited by them.[7]

CROWDING OUT
The adverse effect of increased deficits on investment spending owing to the negative effect of higher interest rates associated with the larger deficits.

There is reason to believe that larger budget deficits exert upward pressure on the level of interest rates. Increased budget deficits mean increased demand for loanable funds that, unless offset by an equivalent increase in the supply of funds available, must pull up interest rates.[8] If investment spending is sensitive to the interest rate, budget deficits may result in a lower capital stock passed on to future generations, and hence a reduced future standard of living. This is the sense in which our extravagance today may come at the expense of our grandchildren.

However, it is not clear that deficit spending inevitably reduces current investment spending and the future capital stock. In assessing this issue, one should take into account the circumstances in which the budget deficits are incurred. One should also distinguish between structural deficits—those caused by changes in tax rates or planned expenditures—and cyclical deficits. If increasing deficits are caused

---

[7]Again, it is important to specify the types of government expenditures leading to rapid growth in the debt. If the debt grows to finance expansion of transfer payments and military spending, the capital stock bequeathed to future generations will likely be reduced. If the public debt is incurred to build highways, dams, universities, and high-tech facilities, the expanding debt may actually be increasing the stock of capital available to future generations.

[8]Actually, economic studies frequently have been unable to discern any positive relationship between budget deficits and interest rates in the American data prior to the 1980s. This seems rather surprising. Two explanations have been advanced. The first is that there *is* a causal relationship, but the magnitude of federal deficits prior to the 1980s was so small relative to the economy that the statistical studies were unable to uncover the relationship. The second explanation, known as the *Ricardian-equivalence theorem*, asserts that budget deficits trigger an increase in the supply of savings, which neutralizes the impact of government deficits on interest rates. The alleged mechanism is that the budget deficits trigger a perception on the part of the public that future tax rates must rise and the standard of living must fall. To cushion this expected effect, the public steps up its current rate of saving. The increase in supply of funds owing to the increase in saving offsets the increase in demand for funds owing to the enlarged deficit, and the increase in budget deficits is alleged to have no impact on interest rates. See Chapter 17 for more on this issue.

EXHIBIT

21.2

Public-choice economists argue that large budget deficits are a natural outcome of the pattern of incentives facing the individuals serving in Congress. Politicians find it highly desirable to spend money to please the various constituents back home. But rising government expenditures must be financed in some way. People do not like taxes. Borrowing to fund growing expenditures represents an alternative to higher taxes. Budget deficits are less visible to voters than taxes because much of the costs of deficits are borne *in the future*. Politicians can conceal the full cost of government expenditures from the public by incurring new debt rather than raising taxes to pay for growth of government. The costs of deficit finance—higher future taxes and/or lower future living standards—are not fully recognized by the electorate.

An apt analogy that indicates why we have large federal budget deficits is the following: Suppose 535 ministers gathering at an annual convention go out to a large restaurant together for their evening meal. As they scan the menu, they agree to divide the tab at the end of the evening equally. Each individual is to pay 1/535 of the total tab. Each individual is allowed to order separately. In this situation, there is virtually no incentive for any individual to be conservative in ordering, since each additional dollar of food and drink ordered by an individual increases his or her bill by only one-fifth of a penny. Individuals who normally are teetotallers order drinks. People experiment with exotic, expensive dishes. Health buffs order cheesecake desserts, and the total tab per person may end up three times as high as if the individuals were billed separately.

Congressional decision making functions in a similar fashion. Each of our representatives has a strong incentive to push for new "pork barrel" projects for the home district, because the extra cost to the district is quite small compared to the additional benefits to the district provided by the project. At the margin, a $20 million highway project for the local region appears to the local constituents to be almost "free." Even if the benefits flowing from the project are perceived to total only $1 million, there is incentive to go for it. Public-choice economists like Nobel Laureate James Buchanan point out that the resulting budget deficits are a predictable outcome of our system of political incentives. Viewed from this perspective, special legislation may be

CROWDING IN
The favorable effect of increased deficits upon investment spending owing to the stimulative effect of larger deficits upon aggregate demand, output, and the utilization rate of capital equipment.

by the automatic influence of depressed economic activity upon the federal budget, it is unlikely that crowding out of investment will occur. In fact, since the budget deficit in this case tends to cushion the drop in economic activity, the increased deficit may have a favorable effect on investment.

Even if the larger deficit is *structural* in nature, one must be cautious in advancing the crowding-out hypothesis. If such stimulative budgetary policy is conducted at a time of depressed economic activity, we may get **crowding in**—a *positive* response of investment spending to increased structural deficits. The stimulative fiscal policy may encourage investment spending. Investment in plant and equipment may be stimulated because of the beneficial effect of the increased deficit upon output, employment, and the utilization rate of plant and equipment. Though

required to control federal budget deficits.

One simple approach involves a constitutional amendment mandating balanced budgets. One drawback of this would be that this would require tax increases in the midst of economic downturns, since the deficit automatically increases as the economy weakens. A more enlightened law would mandate a balanced *structural* budget, thus allowing expanding cyclical deficits in recessions. The movement toward the constitutional amendment gained momentum in the 1970s and 1980s when thirty-two of the required thirty-four states passed resolutions calling for a constitutional convention that would mandate a balanced federal budget. The movement recently has lost momentum, however.

Public-choice economists have made other proposals to control the deficit. Some favor giving the president a *line-item veto*, that is, authority to veto or reduce expenditures on specific items in an appropriations bill without being forced to reject the entire bill. Perhaps the most effective proposal yet offered would be to link congressional salaries to the magnitude of the deficit. Suppose congressional salaries were automatically reduced by 20 percent for each one percentage point that the ratio of the structural deficit to GDP exceeds some arbitrary level, say 2 percent. In this scheme, if the ratio of the structural deficit to GDP reached 4 percent, congressional salaries would be slashed 40 percent. No doubt, this mechanism would eliminate any prospect for the runaway budget deficit scenario outlined on the next page.

JAMES BUCHANAN

interest rates are probably higher than they would otherwise be as a result of the larger deficit, the expected rate of return from investment spending is also higher because of the beneficial effect of the deficit upon economic activity. Hence, firms may step up investment spending in spite of higher interest rates.

When the government runs large deficits in years of very strong economic activity, conditions are most conducive to crowding out. In this instance, sustained federal pressures on credit markets and interest rates are likely to tilt the mix of output away from private investment in plant and equipment. Only when the government deficit spending is used primarily to fund scientific research or highly productive public capital projects can we be optimistic in this instance about the impact of deficit spending upon the total capital stock and standards of living in the future.

The abrupt shift in federal budget posture in the past ten to fifteen years to one of structural deficits of unprecedented magnitudes stimulated visions of a potentially nightmarish Latin American-type scenario in which the deficits feed upon themselves, thus degenerating into a vicious cycle of escalating growth. The fundamental requirement for this scenario to occur is for the ratio of annual government budget deficits to the nation's GDP to exceed the growth rate of real GDP. If this situation occurs and remains in place, the ultimate outcome is likely to be one of severe inflation created by the government as a means of alleviating the pressures caused by the debt explosion.

To illustrate the mechanism proposed in the preceding discussion, assume the stock of the national debt held by the public is currently $3,000 billion. Assume further that the budget deficit is running at a rate of $300 billion annually and the average interest rate the government is paying to service the debt is 8 percent. This means that, in the current year, $240 billion is being paid to the bondholders in the form of interest by the U.S. Treasury. Since the current deficit is $300 billion in this example, the national debt a year hence will be $3,300 billion and annual interest costs will rise to $264 billion if interest rates remain at 8 percent. This means that, given no changes in taxes or expenditures, the deficit will expand next year to $324 billion. The debt will therefore grow the following year to $3,624 billion and interest costs will balloon to $290 billion ($3,624 × 8 percent).

Note in the preceding scenario that the interest-service portion of government expenditures grows from $240 billion to $290 billion in two years, a growth rate of about 10 percent per year. Unless GDP grows at an exceptionally rapid rate or interest rates fall, the ratio of interest expense to GDP will continue to rise. Because interest payments on the accumulated stock of government debt are a significant component of government spending, a high level of deficits incurred *now* builds in high future costs and makes it more difficult for *future* budget makers to control deficits. Between 1980 and 1991, interest payments on the national debt were the most rapidly growing portion of the federal budget (review Figure 21.6).

Large budget deficits, once established, become increasingly difficult to control because of the escalating locked-in component of interest expenditures.

To avoid this disastrous debt explosion scenario, it is not necessary to balance the budget, that is, to eliminate deficits *totally*. What *is* required is to bring the deficit down sufficiently that the deficit/GDP ratio is below the trend rate of the nation's real GDP growth. Potential U.S. GDP growth for the next several years is estimated to be approximately 2.5 percent per year. Budget deficits of the magnitude of those experienced in the early 1990s exceed 2.5 percent of GDP and therefore leave the debt explosion issue very much alive.

In this scenario, the longer the political process delays taking measures to halt the explosion of deficits, debt, and interest payments, the greater will be the magnitude of tax hikes and austerity programs required to reverse the process. At some point, responsible judgment will likely give way to expediency and the government may give in to the temptation to use inflation to extricate itself from the vicious circle of increasing debt and interest payments. That is, the government may, in effect, repudiate its interest payments obligation by paying in depreciated dollars.

This process commences when the Federal Reserve System purchases large amounts of government debt rather than insisting that it be predominantly absorbed in the private marketplace. This method of government finance is virtually identical in its effects to a procedure of simply printing currency to finance government expenditures.[9] Either procedure results in rapid growth of the money supply and aggregate demand and the resulting diminution in the value of the currency—inflation.

Not only is the procedure of repudiation highly irresponsible in that it violates the trust of those who voluntarily loaned money to their government, but it also unleashes all the adverse effects associated with inflation that we studied in Chapter 9. The history of nations that have abandoned all semblance of budgetary prudence is a history of inflation.

Summary

1. The national debt is the sum of past deficits. It consists of a stock of long-term and short-term securities held by American firms and individuals, foreigners, government agencies, and the Federal Reserve System. Since budget deficits have been exceptionally large in the last decade, the debt has increased at a very rapid rate. Its magnitude reached $4,000 billion or $16,000 per person in 1992.

2. Over the entire period since the end of World War II, the national debt has grown more slowly than GDP and also more slowly than such private forms of debt as mortgage debt, consumer debt, and business indebtedness at banks. However, since the mid-1970s the government debt has increased more rapidly than these other variables. This has stimulated renewed interest in the economic consequences of deficits and the national debt.

3. It is a fallacy to assume that our debt places a burden on future generations because it ultimately must be paid off. While individual components of the debt are repaid at maturity, the government is continually involved in refinancing the debt. A growing economy is capable of supporting a growing volume of debt, both public and private. The national debt will never be retired or paid off. The same is true of business debt, consumer debt, and mortgage debt.

4. It is a fallacy to assume that interest payments on a domestically held debt represent a use of American resources. Such payments do not use up resources but do redistribute U.S. income and wealth. However, given other factors such as the level of GDP, a larger debt implies that tax rates must be higher in order to service the debt without displacing other forms of government spending. These higher tax rates could reduce incentives to work, save, or invest, thus possibly reducing future standards of living. Also, if the debt is held by foreigners, American resources are given up when foreigners cash in their interest checks for American-made merchandise.

5. The actual budget deficit conceptually may be divided into a cyclical component and a structural component. The cyclical component is caused by the feedback of economic activity on federal tax receipts and expenditures. The structural component is the portion

---

[9]When the Treasury finances expenditures by selling bonds to the public, the reduced checking accounts (money balances) of the bond buyers neutralize the increased money balances placed into the hands of the recipients of government expenditures. The money supply does not change. When the Treasury finances expenditures by selling bonds to the Federal Reserve System, no funds are withdrawn from the checking accounts of private citizens to offset the funds pumped in when the Treasury issues checks to pay for its expenditures. The money supply rises. Regulations prohibit the Fed from purchasing *newly issued* government debt. However, the Fed could circumvent the intent of this regulation by purchasing large quantities of already outstanding bonds at the same time that the government issues a large amount of new debt.

that would exist in the event the economy were operating at a high level of output and employment. Discretionary changes in fiscal policy—changes in tax rates or expenditures—produce shifts in the structural deficit.

6. Interpretation of federal budget deficits is clouded because of failure to include off-budget activities and state and local government surpluses, and because of absence of capital budgeting and inflation accounting for interest payments.

7. Economists are more concerned about large, long-lasting structural deficits than about cyclical deficits because structural deficits are more likely to crowd out investment and result in a lower future capital stock. The magnitude of structural deficits increased during the 1980s because of large tax cuts and defense expenditure growth. A large structural deficit persists today.

8. The *mix* of monetary and fiscal policies has important implications for the composition of current output as it pertains to the consumption–investment mix and the prosperity of industries exposed to foreign competition relative to purely domestic sectors.

9. There are two important potential adverse consequences of large budget deficits and burgeoning stock of debt. First, business spending on plant and equipment may be reduced. If so, the capital stock inherited by future generations is reduced, thus lowering their standard of living. This is the sense in which our deficit spending may impose an *intergenerational burden*. Whether or not crowding out of private investment occurs is a complicated issue, hinging on the circumstances in which budget deficits occur. The second potential consequence of large deficits and increasing debt is the development of a vicious circle of expanding interest payments, deficits, and debt. If deficits exceed a certain threshold relative to GDP, this debt explosion may occur. If so, the only feasible way for the government to relieve the burden of the exploding interest expense is through inflation. In practice, this occurs when the Federal Reserve heavily *monetizes* the debt—the Treasury borrows heavily from the Fed rather than from the public. If this happens, inflation arrives with a vengeance.

Key Terms

budget surplus
budget deficit
national debt
intergenerational burden
cyclical deficit

structural deficit or
   high-employment deficit
real deficit
crowding out
crowding in

Study Questions and Problems

1. Explain the relationship between budget deficits and the national debt.

2. Explain the effects that burgeoning deficits of the 1980s had on firms that rely heavily on exporting for business.

3. Itemize several short-term consequences for America of the large budget deficits of the past 15 years.

4. What causes the federal deficit to respond to changes in economic activity? Which part of the deficit acts as an automatic stabilizer? Explain.

5. Should we set a timetable to pay off the national debt by a certain year—for example, by the year 2010? Explain why or why not.

6. Discuss the various indicators of the relative size or *burden* of our national debt. Which do you believe is the most important indicator? Explain.

7. Why is it sometimes asserted that large budget deficits lead to a situation in which federal interest expenditures displace other forms of government expenditures?

8. Differentiate between the actual budget deficit and the structural deficit. Under what conditions are the two measures identical?

9. Evaluate the hypothesis that federal budget deficits crowd out private investment expenditures. Why is the hypothesis highly debatable? Under what circumstances is the hypothesis most likely to be valid?

10. Why might increased structural deficits *crowd in* investment during a severe recession?

11. Explain three considerations that suggest our reported deficits may understate or overstate the deficit.

12. Why might a very complacent attitude on the part of Congress and the president ultimately result in severe inflation?

YOUR TURN
Answers

ANY EFFORTS TO BALANCE THE BUDGET DURING A DEPRESSION WOULD ONLY EXACERBATE THE STATE OF THE ECONOMY. TO BALANCE THE BUDGET OR REDUCE THE DEFICIT, TAX HIKES AND EXPENDITURE CUTS ARE NECESSARY. BUT BOTH THESE MEASURES REDUCE AGGREGATE DEMAND AND THE LEVEL OF ECONOMIC ACTIVITY. IN OTHER WORDS, THE STRUCTURAL DEFICIT IS BEING REDUCED (FISCAL POLICY BECOMES MORE RESTRICTIVE) WHEN ECONOMIC ACTIVITY IS WEAK. STRUCTURAL BUDGET DEFICITS SHOULD BE REDUCED DURING PERIODS OF ROBUST ECONOMIC ACTIVITY, NOT DURING PERIODS OF WEAKNESS.

Selected References

Congressional Budget Office. *The Economic and Budget Outlook: Fiscal Years 1993–1997*, (Washington, D.C.: 1992). This annual document details the budget and projects future outlays, receipts, and deficits.

Eisner, Robert. *How Real Is the Federal Deficit?* (New York: The Free Press, 1986). In this provocative work, Eisner presents the case for a new measure of federal deficits, one that takes account of inflation and other economic phenomena.

Heilbroner, Robert and Peter Bernstein, *The Debt and the Deficit* (New York: W. W. Norton, 1989). A very readable analysis of the consequences of budget deficits, written for the layperson.

Rock, James M. (ed.). *Debt and the Twin Deficits*, (Mountain View, Cal.: Bristlecone Books, 1991). Excellent collection of articles on the consequences of budget deficits, written by distinguished economists.

Schultze, Charles L., "Of Wolves, Termites, and Pussycats, or Why We Should Worry about the Budget Deficit." *The Brookings Review*, Summer 1989, pp. 26–33. This article examines the case for reducing the federal budget deficit.

U.S. Treasury. *Treasury Bulletin*. This quarterly publication provides a wealth of data on all aspects of the national debt and government financing activities.

Yellen, Janet L., "Symposium on the Budget Deficit." *Journal of Economic Perspectives*, Spring 1989, pp. 17–21. This article summarizes viewpoints on the consequences of budget deficits.

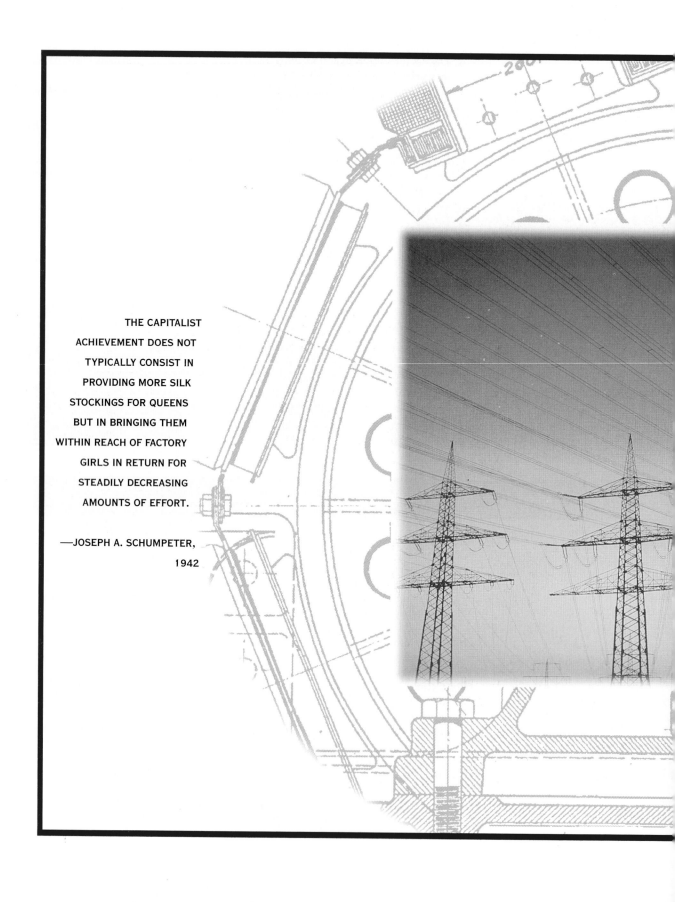

THE CAPITALIST
ACHIEVEMENT DOES NOT
TYPICALLY CONSIST IN
PROVIDING MORE SILK
STOCKINGS FOR QUEENS
BUT IN BRINGING THEM
WITHIN REACH OF FACTORY
GIRLS IN RETURN FOR
STEADILY DECREASING
AMOUNTS OF EFFORT.

—JOSEPH A. SCHUMPETER,
1942

Economic Growth and Productivity Behavior in Industrial Nations

ON AVERAGE, MEMBERS OF YOUR GENERATION ARE CONSIDERABLY RICHER IN TERMS OF MATERIAL POSSESSIONS AND LIVING STANDARDS THAN YOUR GRANDPARENTS WERE WHEN THEY WERE THE SAME AGE. FURTHERMORE, YOUR GRANDCHILDREN ARE LIKELY TO BE MORE AFFLUENT THAN YOU. REAL OUTPUT AND INCOME PER PERSON IN THE UNITED STATES TODAY IS AT LEAST SIX TIMES THE LEVEL OF 100 YEARS AGO. MOREOVER, GROWTH IN PER-CAPITA INCOME IS NOT UNIQUE TO THE UNITED STATES. IT HAS OCCURRED IN ALL OF THE INDUSTRIALIZED NATIONS DURING THE PAST 150 TO 200 YEARS.

IN CHAPTER 22 WE FOCUS ON THE LONG-RUN GROWTH IN OUTPUT, INCOME, AND LIVING STANDARDS IN INDUSTRIAL NATIONS. CHAPTER 39 ANALYZES THE GROWTH CHALLENGES OF LESS DEVELOPED COUNTRIES (LDCS)—NATIONS IN WHICH THREE-FOURTHS OF THE EARTH'S INHABITANTS DWELL. PER-CAPITA INCOME IN LDCS IS TYPICALLY LESS THAN ONE-TENTH THAT OF SUCH INDUSTRIAL NATIONS AS FRANCE, JAPAN, AND THE UNITED STATES.

ECONOMIC GROWTH
Long-run expansion in an economy's capacity to produce goods and services. Implies a sustained rightward shifting of a nation's production possibilities curve and aggregate supply curve.

To an economist, **economic growth** indicates the gradual long-run expansion of a nation's capacity to produce goods and services. Economic growth concerns the slope of the *potential GDP* line—the growth of GDP under conditions in which the unemployment rate is maintained at the natural rate of unemployment. Economic growth means that the nation's production possibilities curve and aggregate supply curve are shifting rightward over time. Economic growth is not concerned with short-run business cycle conditions; it deals with the longer-term trend of economic progress.

Analysts sometimes use the term "economic growth" rather loosely to describe expansion of actual output and income in a short-run context. For example, a newspaper might state that "economic growth is expected to be 3 percent next year," indicating that real GDP is expected to rise 3 percent in the next year. Such "growth" can occur even in the absence of a rightward shift of the production possibilities curve or aggregate supply curve as the economy advances in the recovery phase of the business cycle. In this instance, we might be simply increasing output within the context of a given capacity because the aggregate demand curve shifts upward during economic recovery.

In Parts II and III of this text, we discussed the use of government's monetary and fiscal policy tools to boost economic activity when it is sluggish and when the unemployment rate significantly exceeds the economy's natural rate of unemployment. Such stabilization policies essentially increase short-run output and income within the context of a given capacity to produce goods and services. These stabilization policies, when successful, clearly benefit society by stimulating output and income in the short run. However, they do not constitute an important source of rising living standards from one generation to the next. In that sense, they pale in significance when compared to the true source of economic progress—the long-run expansion of the average worker's capacity to produce goods and services.

MEASURES OF ECONOMIC GROWTH

Two measures of economic growth are commonly used. The first is the rate of growth of *real GDP*—the output of goods and services of the nation—over a period of years. The second measure is the growth rate of *per-capita real GDP*. Recall that production of output creates an equal amount of income in the nation as a whole. This is the central importance of output or GDP—it is our collective source of income.

Depending on the nature of one's interest in economic growth, one might prefer to focus on the growth rate of real GDP or on the growth rate of *per-capita* real GDP. If one is interested in a nation's potential *economic power* and the growth thereof, real GDP and its growth are the relevant variables. China's real GDP clearly exceeds that of Switzerland. Furthermore, China's real GDP is growing faster than Switzerland's. Hence, China probably has more economic power than Switzerland.

On the other hand, if one's interest is to examine the *well-being of the average inhabitant* of a country and its rate of change, real output per capita and its growth rate are the relevant indicators. Real output (or income) per capita is known as the **standard of living**. Even though China is potentially more powerful than Switzerland (the Chinese economy is larger), Switzerland has a much higher standard of living. Switzerland produces roughly one-fourth as much output as China with less than 1 percent of China's population. The average Swiss citizen has far more material possessions than her Chinese counterpart. In this chapter our primary focus is on growth of living standards—output per capita.

STANDARD OF LIVING
The average output or real income per person; annual output divided by the population.

Table 22.1 indicates the growth of real output and per-capita real output for the United States over the past 60 years. Over the 60-year period, real output increased at an average annual rate of 2.9 percent. Because the population increased at an average rate of 1.2 percent per year, the standard of living (per-capita output) grew at an average annual rate of 1.7 percent. This performance implies that living standards double in 41 years.

The growth rate of per-capita real income is not a perfect measure of the rate of improvement in welfare. It ignores such important considerations as changes in leisure time and other indicators of change in quality of life (for example, changes in environmental pollution) and also ignores the distribution of income across the population. Clearly, it makes a difference whether the fruits of economic progress are widely shared by the people or are captured by a tiny minority of the population. Nevertheless, the growth rate of real output (and income) per capita provides a reasonable approximation of the improvement in living standards. Economists place considerable stock in this variable.

In this chapter we concentrate on the principles of long-term economic growth—the gradual rightward shifting of production possibilities curves and aggregate supply curves over time. We especially emphasize **productivity growth** of labor—the expansion of output per hour of work. Productivity growth is the predominant source of rising living standards that commenced roughly 200 years ago and has continued to the present. After surveying productivity growth in various

PRODUCTIVITY GROWTH
Expansion of output and real income per hour of work; the main source of rising living standards.

U.S. REAL GDP AND PER-CAPITA REAL GDP, 1929–1990

YEAR	GDP (BILLIONS OF 1987 DOLLARS)	POPULATION (MILLIONS)	PER-CAPITA GDP (1987 DOLLARS)
1929	847	122	6,943
1933	595	126	4,722
1940	922	132	6,985
1950	1,437	152	9,454
1960	1,973	181	10,900
1970	2,876	205	14,029
1980	3,776	228	16,561
1990	4,885	252	19,385

SOURCE: *Economic Report of the President*, 1992.

TABLE 22.1

countries, we explore the fundamental determinants of productivity growth and assess the probable causes of the slowdown of American productivity growth in the past 20 years. The chapter concludes by analyzing certain proposals designed to boost America's sagging productivity growth.

PRODUCTIVITY GROWTH AND GROWTH IN LIVING STANDARDS

Technically, one must distinguish between growth in productivity (output per *hour of work*) and growth in living standards (output per *capita*). If the length of the workweek and the fraction of the total population employed were to remain constant over time, growth in living standards would proceed at precisely the same rate as the growth of productivity. Since the length of the workweek and the fraction of the total population working both fluctuate over time, the growth rate of output per worker (per-capita income) typically differs somewhat from the growth rate of productivity.

Over relatively brief intervals of time, it is not unusual for growth of per-capita income to outpace productivity growth. This occurs when the percentage of the population employed rises, as in the 1970s when the baby boomers (born between 1946 and 1963) flooded into the work force and as the labor force participation rate of women increased.

In the United States the length of the workweek has been gradually declining for decades. This decline has been offset by the increasing labor force participation rate. But there are obvious limits to the growth of the labor force participation rate attributable to changes in the age structure of the population and other factors that influence the fraction of the population working or seeking employment. For all intents and purposes, these factors are of relatively minor importance in the long run, leaving the growth rate of productivity as the overwhelmingly predominant source of growth in living standards. The growth rate of productivity is one of the most crucial variables in economic analysis.

IMPORTANCE OF ECONOMIC GROWTH

In the short-run context of a single year, economic growth means relatively little to the material well-being of the average individual. In the long run—say over a 25-, 50-, or 100-year period—the rate of growth makes a tremendous difference. Relatively small annual increases in output per capita, when compounded for 50 or 100 years, add up to surprisingly large increases in living standards. The immense difference in living standards that exists today between LDCs such as Nigeria and Ethiopia and developed nations such as France and Germany can be explained by the 2 percent annual growth differential in favor of Germany and France sustained over 150 years. If Nigeria and Germany start with identical per-capita incomes and Germany grows 2 percent per year for 150 years while Nigeria remains stagnant, the standard of living in Germany at the end of the period is 19.5 times that of Nigeria!

Per-capita U.S. GDP in 1990, measured in 1987 dollars, was roughly $20,000. Suppose you plan to retire in the year 2040. If per-capita output growth averages 2 percent per year over the 1990–2040 period, GDP per capita in 2040 will be somewhat more than $53,000 (in dollars of 1987 purchasing power). If 3 percent annual growth could be achieved, GDP per capita would exceed $87,000 when you retire (in 1987 dollars). Clearly, small differences in growth rates make big differences in living standards over the long haul.

YOUR TURN

ASSUME, HYPOTHETICALLY, THAT PER-CAPITA OUTPUT IN MODERNIA GROWS STEADILY AT 1.5 PERCENT ANNUALLY WHILE THAT IN LAGGARDIA REMAINS CONSTANT. IF THE COUNTRIES INITIALLY HAD IDENTICAL LIVING STANDARDS, HOW MUCH RICHER WOULD MODERNIANS BE (THAN LAGGARDIANS) AFTER 50 YEARS? 100 YEARS? 200 YEARS? HINT: USE A CALCULATOR WITH A Y^x KEY, WHERE $Y = 1.015$ AND X IS THE NUMBER OF YEARS.

Fostering productivity growth is crucial to America for many reasons. Obviously, more rapid growth means more material possessions for Americans. But there are more important, substantive considerations. America's international position of economic superiority is dwindling and the vast gulf that once separated our living standards from our nearest competitors' is gone. More rapid growth would help fortify our position of world leadership. Economic growth can provide the basis for freeing up more leisure time, a healthier workplace, a safer environment, and a more adequate provision of education and health-care services to all Americans. As Nobel Laureate Robert Solow observed, "Redistributing income is *not* something Americans are very good at." Realistically, strong economic growth is essential if we are to come to grips with the compelling problems of poverty, education, and adequate health care for our people as we enter the twenty-first century.

ECONOMIC GROWTH IN HISTORICAL PERSPECTIVE

Given the long scope of human history, economic growth is a recent phenomenon. Until 200 years ago, the human condition was characterized by almost universal poverty, hunger, disease, and periodic plagues—an existence of misery and brief life expectancy. Living standards in Europe at the time European settlers began to arrive on American soil were roughly the same as those that prevailed 1,500 years earlier. Century after century went by without any significant change in living standards. The experience of low and basically unchanging living standards endured in the twentieth century by such LDCs as Ethiopia and Nigeria are much closer to the norm of historical experience than are the modern growth miracles of the United States, Japan, and western European nations.

Significant, sustained increases in living standards commenced with the industrial revolution in England at the beginning of the eighteenth century and spread to Europe and the United States somewhat later. Modern economic growth is attributable to **industrialization**—the application of machinery and technology to the production process. The increasing reliance upon automation in place of animal sources of power and unskilled labor-intensive processes steadily pulled up output per worker and living standards in the past 150–200 years.

INDUSTRIALIZATION
Movement toward widespread application of technology and capital goods in production processes.

E
X
H
I
B
I
T

22.1

Although we should perhaps not take the results very seriously, let us conduct a provocative experiment in the hypothetical economics of growth. Given the 1991 actual GDP size (gross domestic product in 1988 American dollars) of various nations and given the actual growth rate of real GDP experienced by each nation over the 20-year period ending in 1991, what will be the magnitudes of these economies in the years 2010 and 2040 if these growth rates continue? The information is provided in Table 22.2.

In the unlikely event that the growth rates of the past 20 years continued for several decades, some interesting changes in the international power structure would emerge in the next 50 years. Japan—with roughly one-half the population and two-fifths the output of the United States in 1991—would overtake us by the year 2040. China (the People's Republic)—seventh on our short list in 1991 with an output less than 15 percent

of America's—would surpass the stronger European economies well before 2010 and would overtake the United States by the year 2040. Such is the power of compound interest! England— the predominant world power of the nineteenth century and roughly at parity with Italy and France in 1991—would continue her long pattern of decline and slide to last place on the list by the year 2040.

Before you lose any sleep over these projections, read the section on the convergence of living standards. It is unlikely that past growth rates generated by Japan and China can continue for a long period. Nevertheless, the Japanese growth rate continued to exceed 4.5 percent per year in the 1987–1991 period. China, which experienced a phenomenal growth rate in excess of 9 percent annually during 1980–1988, slowed to "only" 5 percent per year during 1989–1991.

International Level and Growth of Living Standards Since 1870

Productivity growth in nations that today are industrialized has resulted in an enormous increase in the standard of living over the past one or two centuries. In the sample of 16 nations for which reliable output and income data going back more than a century are available, the average standard of living increased by a factor of more than eight between 1870 and 1990.

In the United States the level of affluence has expanded somewhat faster than this average. American productivity (output per work hour) increased thirteen-fold between 1870 and 1990 (slightly more than 2 percent per year). Given the significant reduction in the average length of the workweek, the standard of living of the

COUNTRY	1991 GDP IN BILLIONS OF 1988 DOLLARS	GROWTH RATE (%) 1971–1991	PROJECTED REAL GDP (IN 1988 U.S. DOLLARS)	
			YEAR 2010	YEAR 2040
United States	4,953	2.5	7,918	16,608
France	823	2.8	1,390	3,184
Italy	792	3.0	1,388	3,370
Great Britain	776	2.1	1,152	2,148
Germany	973	2.5	1,555	3,263
Canada	488	3.6	955	2,760
Japan	2,024	4.4	4,587	16,693
China	634	7.0	2,293	17,454

SOURCES: 1991 GDP in 1988 U.S. dollars computed by taking 1988 data from *Statistical Abstract of the United States*, 1991, and compounding it via real GDP growth rates provided in *Economic Report of the President*, 1992. The last two columns are calculated by extrapolating 1991 real GDP in 1988 U.S. dollars at 1971–1991 growth rates ahead to the years 2010 and 2040.

TABLE 22.2

average American increased somewhat more slowly. In 1990 it was roughly nine times higher than that of our 1870 counterpart.[1]

TENDENCY FOR LIVING STANDARDS TO CONVERGE

All industrial countries have experienced sustained growth in productivity and income per capita. In addition, both productivity levels and living standards have clearly tended to *converge*. Today's industrial nations that exhibited relatively low productivity levels and living standards in the nineteenth century have systematically tended to grow faster than nations that were relatively affluent. In Table 22.3 we list the sixteen nations for which output per capita data are available for 1870 and 1979. These countries are ranked according to the 1870 level of output per capita, from low (Japan) to high (Australia).

The data in Table 22.3 reveal the existence of a strong negative relationship between the *level* of the early (1870) standard of living and the subsequent *rate of growth*. Countries relatively poor in 1870 have consistently grown faster than those that were relatively rich. In other words, there is a tendency for living standards to converge. Japan, Finland, and Sweden, the poorest countries in 1870, have exhibited

---

[1]These observations are based on data on pages 8 and 212 of Angus Maddison, *Phases of Capitalist Development* (Oxford: Oxford University Press, 1982), updated by authors.

				AVERAGE GROWTH
COUNTRY	1870 GDP/CAPITA*	1979 GDP/CAPITA*	RATIO 1979 TO 1870	PER YEAR (%) (PER-CAPITA OUTPUT)
Japan	251	4,419	17.6	2.66
Finland	384	4,287	11.2	2.24
Sweden	415	4,908	11.8	2.29
Norway	489	4,760	9.7	2.11
Germany	535	4,946	9.2	2.06
Denmark	572	4,483	7.8	1.91
Austria	573	4,255	7.4	1.86
Italy	593	3,577	6.0	1.66
Canada	619	5,361	8.6	2.00
France	627	4,981	7.9	1.92
United States	764	6,055	7.9	1.92
Switzerland	786	4,491	5.7	1.61
Netherlands	831	4,396	5.3	1.54
Belgium	925	4,986	5.4	1.56
Great Britain	972	3,981	4.1	1.30
Australia	1,393	4,466	3.2	1.07
Mean	671	4,647	6.9	1.79

PER-CAPITA OUTPUT LEVELS AND GROWTH RATES IN INDUSTRIAL NATIONS, 1870–1979

* Figures are in 1970 U.S. dollars.
SOURCE: Angus Maddison, *Phases of Capitalist Development* (Oxford: Oxford University Press, 1982), p. 8. Reprinted by permission of the publisher.

TABLE 22.3

the fastest growth rates. Australia and Great Britain, the two richest in 1870, have experienced the lowest rates of advance.

The American standard of living in 1870 was more than three times that of Japan. By 1979, the U.S. margin of superiority over Japan was only 37 percent. The range between the richest and poorest of the sixteen countries has narrowed dramatically. In 1870 the richest nation (Australia) had a standard of living roughly 5.5 times that of the poorest (Japan). By 1979 the ratio of the richest standard of living (the United States) to the poorest (Italy) was less than two-to-one.

The **convergence principle** is illustrated in Figure 22.1. Clearly, the figure indicates that countries that were rich in 1870 have grown more slowly than countries that were relatively poor.[2] Why is this true? What explanation lies behind the convergence phenomenon?

CONVERGENCE PRINCIPLE

Tendency of industrial nations with relatively low living standards to grow more rapidly than more affluent nations, thereby reducing the gap in living standards.

[2]Modern evidence supporting the convergence hypothesis is yielded by the recent growth performance of the newly industrialized nations of the Pacific Rim, such as Korea, Singapore, Taiwan, and Malaysia. In the past two decades these emerging economies have been experiencing growth rates of per-capita output at least *twice* those exhibited by the United States and European countries. Japan dramatically narrowed its gap with the United States in the 1950s and 1960s with phenomenal growth rates in excess of 10 percent per year.

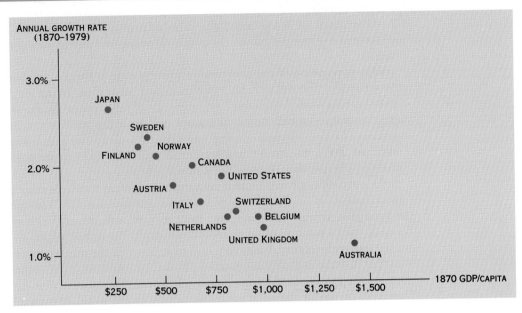

In the long run, a tendency exists for living standards to converge. Industrial nations with low living standards tend to grow more rapidly than nations with high living standards. This fact is attributable to poorer industrial nations implementing the technologies of wealthier countries.

SOURCE: Table 22.3.

FIGURE 22.1

WHAT EXPLAINS THE TENDENCY OF LIVING STANDARDS TO CONVERGE?

All reasonably developed nations stand to benefit from shared information. European nations benefit from advances in American computer technology; America benefits from advances in Japanese robotic technology. Although economists have not pinpointed all the factors that account for the tendency of living standards of industrialized nations to converge, there is a consensus that the international diffusion of technological advances is at the heart of the phenomenon.[3] Today these technological improvements spread from country to country much more rapidly than in the past.

Improved communications among countries enable new technology to spread across borders more rapidly. Widespread and technically rigorous education levels permit nations to obtain technological knowhow and train the work force to implement new production procedures. Although the technologically poor nations have

---

[3]See William J. Baumol, "Productivity Growth, Convergence, and Welfare," *American Economic Review*, December 1986, pp. 1072–1085.

much to learn and benefit handsomely from the technologically advanced nations, the reverse flow of information and corresponding benefits are meager. This fundamental asymmetry in the spread of technology across nations does much to explain the convergence of living standards. The relatively poor among the industrial nations tend to close the gap on the rich by learning and implementing their technologies.

One implication of the convergence phenomenon is that one nation need not perceive other countries as rivals in technological innovation. In the long run, each nation benefits from the scientific achievements of other countries. Factors encouraging innovation in one nation ultimately pull up living standards in many other countries. Competitiveness among countries is a short-run phenomenon. Each individual in the advanced nations eventually benefits from technological breakthroughs, whether they occur at home or abroad.

One should not conclude that convergence of living standards among industrialized nations is an inevitable, preordained phenomenon. At one time people believed that Argentina was destined to be an economic power. Moreover, nations can fall from a position of preeminence. Spain was the richest nation in the world in the sixteenth century. England was a great power in the nineteenth century, but note her position in the rankings today (Table 22.2). And don't forget the decline of the Roman Empire in the fifth century. It is foolish to assume that America will *necessarily* be one of the great economic powers of the world 100 years from now, irrespective of how we manage our economic affairs in the interim.

THE CONVERGENCE PHENOMENON AND LESS DEVELOPED NATIONS (LDCS)

In Chapter 39 we analyze the problems of less developed nations (LDCs) in some depth. A huge chasm exists between the affluence level of the industrial nations just discussed and the LDCs. Furthermore, in many cases the convergence phenomenon is nonexistent. The chasm has been widening instead of narrowing.

In LDCs the education level of the population is quite low. A severe shortage of engineers, scientists, and technicians prevails. Advanced technological developments benefitting the industrial nations are often not feasible to implement in the LDCs. Even more fundamentally, most LDCs concentrate production in agriculture and raw materials. The absence of a substantial manufacturing base reduces the feasibility of imitating the sophisticated technological breakthroughs that have lifted living standards in industrial nations. LDCs do benefit from the technology of advanced nations, especially in agriculture. But the scope for widespread diffusion of the technological breakthroughs of the advanced nations to the LDCs is inherently limited.

The Sources of Economic Growth

Societies increase their output and income in two fundamental ways—by increasing their inputs of such resources as labor, capital, and land and by increasing the productivity of these inputs. It is useful to focus on the following expression:

$$\text{total output} = \text{worker hours} \times \text{labor productivity}$$

The nation's aggregate output (GDP) is viewed as the product of labor input (expressed in hours of work) and the productivity of labor (measured as output per worker per hour).

In a hypothetical economy with one million workers, each working 2,000 hours per year (a 50-week, 40-hour per week pattern), total hours worked per year are 2 billion. If average productivity (average real output per hour of work) is $10, the real output or GDP of this society is $20 billion per year.

In this framework it is clear that output can be increased only by an increase in hours worked, an increase in labor productivity, or some combination of the two. What determines the number of hours worked? This depends upon the working-age population, the labor force participation rate (the fraction of the working-age population actually in the labor force), and the average length of the workweek. Productivity of labor depends chiefly upon the level of technology, the amount of capital available for each worker, and the level of education, training, and skills of the work force. These factors that determine real output of a nation are summarized in Figure 22.2.

In the United States, real output has grown over the years partly because of an increase in labor input but chiefly because of growth of productivity of labor. Total hours worked have increased markedly over the long haul as the massive increase in employment has overwhelmed the effect of a declining workweek. One of the most respected students of economic growth is Edward F. Denison. In a careful empirical study, Denison found that for the 1929–1982 period in the United States, an increase in the quantity of labor accounted for about one-third of the increase in real output and income, whereas the increase in labor productivity accounted for about two-thirds of the growth. Denison further analyzed the sources of the increase in labor productivity during the period. His findings are reported in Table 22.4.

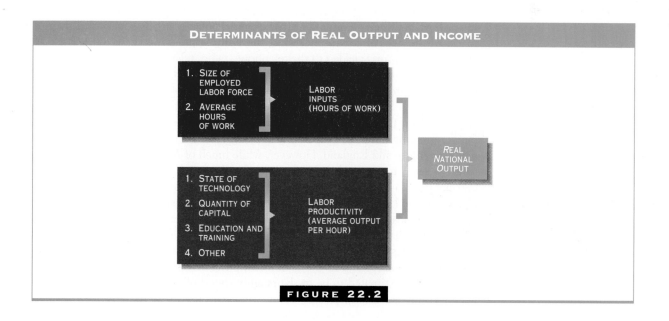

DETERMINANTS OF REAL OUTPUT AND INCOME

1. SIZE OF EMPLOYED LABOR FORCE
2. AVERAGE HOURS OF WORK

LABOR INPUTS (HOURS OF WORK)

1. STATE OF TECHNOLOGY
2. QUANTITY OF CAPITAL
3. EDUCATION AND TRAINING
4. OTHER

LABOR PRODUCTIVITY (AVERAGE OUTPUT PER HOUR)

REAL NATIONAL OUTPUT

FIGURE 22.2

ACCOUNTING FOR U.S. PRODUCTIVITY GROWTH, 1929–1982	
1. Technological advance	40%
2. Quantity of capital	28
3. Education and training	21
4. Other factors	11
	100%

SOURCE: Edward F. Denison, *Trends in American Economic Growth*, 1929–1982 (Washington, D.C.: The Brookings Institution, 1985), p. 30.

TABLE 22.4

TECHNOLOGICAL CHANGE

INVENTION

The discovery of new knowledge.

INNOVATION

The application of new technical knowledge to such economic processes as production and distribution.

At a given point of time, a society has a certain stock of knowledge pertaining to the production of goods and services. Discovery of new knowledge leads to technological change. Development of this technical knowledge consists of **invention** and **innovation**. Invention is the discovery of new knowledge. Innovation is the development of methods for applying this knowledge to economic processes. The development and implementation of technical knowledge are the leading sources of productivity growth. Denison estimated that these factors accounted for 40 percent of productivity growth between 1929 and 1982.

In American economic history, numerous examples remind us of the role of technological change in lifting our productivity and living standards. In the field of agriculture, animal sources of power were replaced by machines powered by fossil fuels. Development of fertilizers, hybrid seeds, and irrigation technology have also contributed to the tremendous increase in agricultural productivity. This productivity growth is reflected in the fact that the percentage of the American population engaged in agriculture has declined from 70 percent in 1840 to 2 percent today. In transportation, railroads replaced animals, sailing vessels were rendered obsolete by steamships, and then automobiles, trucks, and airplanes largely superseded the railroads. In the field of communications, the Pony Express was replaced by the telegraph, which in turn yielded to the telephone, radio, television, and fax machines.

Research and development (R and D) expenditures are an indicator of the resources devoted by a nation to the growth of technology. In the 1985–1990 period, the United States allocated 2.8 percent of its GDP to R and D expenditures of all kinds. This figure is comparable to the R and D share of national output in such rapidly growing nations as Japan and Germany, and it exceeds the R and D effort made by France and England. However, while much of American R and D expenditure is related to national defense, virtually all of such expenditures in Japan and Germany go to *civilian* R and D spending—the type most conducive to productivity growth and rising living standards. Ironically, in demanding at the end of World War II that Japan abandon all efforts to reestablish military preeminence, the United States may have helped assure the dramatic economic resurgence of Japan.

Economists believe that the returns to research and development are quite high, both to society and to the firm making the investment. Such returns to society have been estimated to be in the neighborhood of 30 percent. So why don't we get more private R and D? There are two reasons. First, the expected returns, though large, are highly *uncertain*. Risk-averse firms tend to shy away from heavy R and D spending. Second, great uncertainty exists about the feasibility of the inventor preventing imitation by rivals. Hence, the returns to *society* may be significantly higher than returns to *individual firms* making the breakthroughs.

Research and development expenditures have large positive externalities or spillover effects—they ultimately provide benefits to society far in excess of the benefits captured by the individuals consuming goods directly resulting from R and D efforts. Recall our discussion in Chapter 7 in which we noted that free markets do not allocate adequate resources to endeavors in which positive spillovers exist. For this reason government intervention is appropriate. Accordingly, government laboratories conduct R and D activities, and the government sometimes subsidizes private research and development spending.

THE CAPITAL STOCK

Figure 22.3 (page 564)

CAPITAL DEEPENING
Expansion in the average amount of capital goods per worker. An important source of productivity growth.

Workers become more productive when equipped with a larger capital stock—more plant, machinery, and tools. Net investment results in growth of the nation's capital stock. Over the long run America's capital stock has grown faster than its labor force, resulting in an increase in capital per worker. This process, known as **capital deepening**, is a prime source of rising labor productivity and living standards. In the past 100 years the American ratio of capital stock to labor has increased by a factor of about three. Denison estimates that this growth of real capital accounts for 28 percent of the increase in labor productivity in America between 1929 and 1982.

The saving-investment process is the mechanism that provides for growth of the capital stock over time. If our objective is to boost the growth rate of labor productivity, we must save and invest a larger portion of our current incomes. That is, we must produce *fewer* sports cars, yachts, and TV sets and *more* machine tools, tractors, and blast furnaces.

The fraction of U.S. gross domestic product allocated to investment goods has been lower than that of most other industrial nations. Partly for this reason and partly because of the demographically induced spurt of labor-force growth from 1965 to 1982, the U.S. capital/labor ratio slowed its rate of growth significantly and even declined for several years after 1965. At the same time, our productivity growth also slowed appreciably. It is unlikely that this timing reflects mere coincidence.

Figure 22.3 (page 564) illustrates the fraction of output allocated to investment goods and the growth rate of productivity in the manufacturing sector for a sample of eight industrial nations during the 1960–1983 period. Note that the positive relationship is fairly strong. Japan, which devoted the largest share of output to capital goods, also experienced the most rapid productivity growth rate. The United States and England, which had the weakest investment performance, ranked poorly in terms of productivity growth.

HUMAN CAPITAL—THE EDUCATION, TRAINING, AND SKILLS OF THE WORK FORCE

HUMAN CAPITAL
The stock of knowledge and skills possessed by the population.

Human capital refers to the collection of skills and knowledge embodied in the hands and minds of workers. A nation's growth rate is influenced significantly by

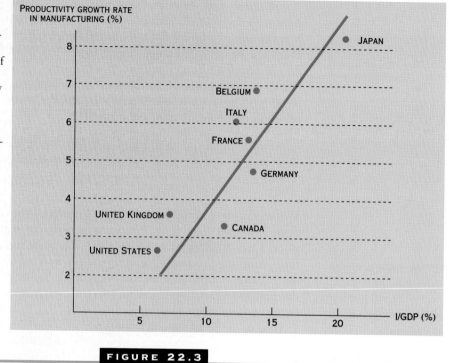

THE INVESTMENT/GDP RATIO AND THE ANNUAL PRODUCTIVITY GROWTH RATE IN MANUFACTURING FOR INDUSTRIAL NATIONS, 1960–1983

A significant positive relationship exists between the fraction of output allocated to investment goods and productivity growth of nations. Countries that invest heavily tend to grow rapidly.

SOURCE: Manufacturing productivity growth rates from Bureau of Labor Statistics, *Monthly Labor Review*, 1984. Investment-to-GDP ratios from Lawrence Summers and Chris Carroll, "Why is U.S. National Saving So Low?" *Brookings Papers on Economic Activity*, 1987:2.

FIGURE 22.3

the rate at which it invests in this human capital through formal education, vocational education, and on-the-job training. In the United States, our stock of human capital has increased over the years. In 1870, 2 percent of our 18-year-olds were high-school graduates; today more than 75 percent are. In 1950, 8 percent of the work force were college graduates; today more than 20 percent have completed college. Denison estimated that one-fifth of the productivity growth in the 1929–1982 period was attributable to improvements in human capital.

The United States has plenty of room for improvement in the area of human capital. The American school system falls woefully short of the Japanese system in the crucial areas of mathematics and science. Scholastic Aptitude Test (SAT) scores of American high-school students declined for 20 consecutive years before hitting bottom in the mid-1980s. Millions of American high-school graduates are ill-equipped to perform work other than menial chores. To assure continuance of our position of economic and political preeminence, major changes are needed now and in the future.

OTHER FACTORS INFLUENCING PRODUCTIVITY

Productivity is also influenced by a multitude of additional factors that are difficult to quantify. Attitudes and motivation of workers play a role. Improved resource allocation, which has helped boost productivity over the years, has come from several sources. A major source was the large transfer of workers out of agriculture into the manufacturing sector. Because productivity levels are higher in manufacturing, this transfer pulled up the overall productivity of the labor force. Other positive factors were the movement over the years since 1930 toward freer international trade, which stimulated efficiency, and the decline in discrimination in hiring practices. Negative factors influencing productivity include work stoppages, expenditures necessitated to combat dishonesty and crime, and government regulations that inhibit production.

The Slowdown in American Productivity Growth

In recent decades, American productivity growth has lagged behind that of many of our competitors. The average annual productivity growth in the manufacturing sector for a sample of industrial nations in the 1960–1990 period is indicated in Figure 22.4. Productivity growth in the manufacturing sector exceeds that of the agricultural and service sectors. Since 1960, Japan's manufacturing sector productivity

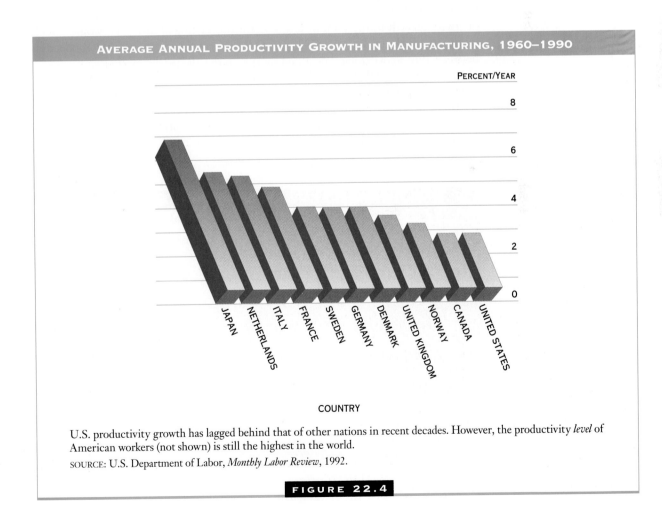

AVERAGE ANNUAL PRODUCTIVITY GROWTH IN MANUFACTURING, 1960–1990

PERCENT/YEAR

COUNTRY

U.S. productivity growth has lagged behind that of other nations in recent decades. However, the productivity *level* of American workers (not shown) is still the highest in the world.

SOURCE: U.S. Department of Labor, *Monthly Labor Review*, 1992.

FIGURE 22.4

growth has averaged nearly 7 percent per year (though it slowed to around 4 percent per year in the last decade). The corresponding rates for France, Germany, England, and the other industrial nations have also topped that of the United States over the 30-year period.

Part of this relatively poor U.S. productivity performance may be simply a manifestation of the convergence principle already discussed. Keep in mind that these figures indicate the *change* in productivity, not the *level*. By latest count the U.S. economy is still the most productive in the world. We produce about 25 percent more output per worker than Japan, for example.

Nevertheless, there is reason for concern. The United States has experienced a severe slowdown in productivity growth since the mid-1960s. Although the slowdown has hit all industrial nations, it has hit the United States harder. In certain sectors, such as steel and automobile manufacturing, our productivity *levels* have been surpassed by other countries. To the extent that productivity growth is influenced by government policy measures of all stripes and colors, it seems essential to bear in mind these productivity implications in designing such government policies.

Table 22.5 details the U.S. productivity performance since World War II. Two measures of productivity growth are given: the total business sector (the broader measure) and the nonfarm business sector. The key points may be summarized briefly. The 1947–1965 period was a *golden age* of productivity growth, with productivity growth in the total business sector proceeding at rates that would double living standards in less than 22 years. Productivity growth slowed moderately between 1965 and 1973 and declined sharply in the 1973–1991 period.

Additional detail is provided in the last three rows of Table 22.5. We focus on the productivity growth experience by decades but have adjusted slightly the period starting and ending points to capture cyclical peak-to-peak results in order to minimize the potentially distorting effects of cyclical fluctuations on longer-term productivity growth comparisons.[4] The key observation here is that both measures of

TRENDS IN AMERICAN PRODUCTIVITY GROWTH (AVERAGE ANNUAL GROWTH RATES)

	SECTOR	
PERIOD	**ALL BUSINESS (%)**	**NONFARM BUSINESS (%)**
1947–1965	3.34	2.77
1965–1973	2.58	2.31
1973–1991	0.86	0.68
1960:1–1969:3	2.82	2.47
1969:3–1979:4	1.27	1.12
1979:4–1990:2	1.07	0.85
1947–1991	2.12	1.75

SOURCE: U.S. Department of Labor, Bureau of Labor Statistics, 1992.

TABLE 22.5

[4]On the cyclical behavior of productivity growth, see Exhibit 22.2.

productivity indicate that productivity growth plunged in the 1970s and remained depressed more recently.

The post-World War II performance of productivity in the total business sector (the broadest productivity measure) is illustrated in Figure 22.5. The figure reveals that productivity growth slowed dramatically in the 1970s. The performance deteriorated further in the 1980s in spite of a series of measures intended to boost saving, investment, and productivity.

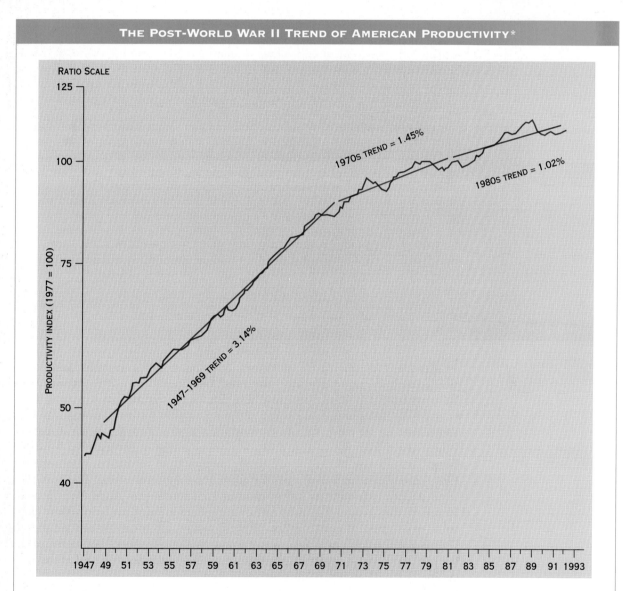

THE POST-WORLD WAR II TREND OF AMERICAN PRODUCTIVITY*

American productivity growth was very strong from the late 1940s through the mid-1960s. It slowed dramatically in the 1970s and deteriorated even further in the 1980s—in spite of a series of policy measures designed to stimulate growth.

*Series illustrated is productivity in the all-business sector.
SOURCE: U.S. Department of Labor, *Monthly Labor Review*, 1992.

FIGURE 22.5

If we remove the growth trend from the labor productivity data, we find that productivity exhibits a regular and largely predictable pattern over the course of the business cycle. Productivity rises during the expansion phase of the business cycle and declines during recessions.

In looking at productivity growth over time intervals, such as a five- or ten-year period, it is essential to be aware of the cyclical characteristics of productivity. Otherwise one is likely to miscalculate the *trend growth* of productivity, which is the item of crucial importance. Suppose one is interested in the rate of growth of productivity in the decade of the 1970s. One can simply look at the productivity *level* at the beginning and end of the decade and compute its annual *growth rate*. But this procedure yields an incorrect estimate of the trend growth of productivity. January 1970 happened to fall in the middle of a national recession. December 1979 came at a cyclical peak. By mixing cyclical effects with the growth trend, one *overestimates* the trend growth of productivity in the 1970s. To calculate trend productivity growth accurately, it is essential to begin and end the sample period at comparable points of the business cycle.

Labor productivity typically rises strongly in the early phases of the business cycle expansion and increases more slowly in the second half of the expansion. In the early phases of business downturns (recessions), productivity growth becomes negative as the *level* of productivity declines. In the second half of the downturn, the productivity level tends to flatten before expanding rapidly again when recovery ensues.

In recessions, as declining aggregate demand induces firms to reduce output,

Reactions to this severe slowdown have been highly variable. Some have recoiled with alarm, experiencing visions of America as a second-rate power 50 or 100 years from now. These pessimists fear that for the first time in American history our living standards could begin declining so that future generations will be poorer than we are today. Others express little concern about the recent slowdown. When viewed from the vantage point of a longer period of history, they point out, things don't look so bleak. For one thing, the growth of productivity from the late 1940s through the mid-1960s was far above the long-term norm. The post-1965 trend doesn't look quite as bad when compared to the pre-World War II trend. Moreover, they believe that many factors ganged up to cause the productivity slowdown of the past 20 years. Several of these factors are reversible and are already changing with implications for a better productivity performance between now and the year 2000. These optimists, therefore, project an imminent reversal of the sluggish productivity growth of the past two decades.

Part of the explanation for the differing reactions to the post-1965 slowdown in productivity growth lies in the fact that there is no consensus in the economics profession as to its cause. A host of factors that might reasonably be linked with the slowdown have occurred, but economists disagree upon the weights to be assigned these factors.

firms are reluctant initially to reduce employment in proportion to the contraction in output. Uncertain of the eventual depth and duration of the downturn and mindful of the costs of rehiring and retraining workers when prosperity returns, firms react cautiously. Because firms reduce employment by a relatively lesser amount than they reduce output, labor productivity (output per worker hour) declines as a matter of arithmetic. As the recession continues and deepens, firms are forced by financial pressures to lay off more workers. In this latter phase of the downturn, employment declines roughly in step with output. This yields a flat pattern for productivity—approximately zero productivity growth.

As the recession gives way to economic recovery, firms again proceed with caution. As output starts to pick up, firms are conservative about taking on new workers. Instead, existing employees are used more fully. Output is boosted much faster than employment, and productivity increases at a rapid pace. As the recovery continues and economic activity becomes more robust, firms begin adding aggressively to their payrolls. This slows the growth of productivity after the first year or two of recovery. Nevertheless, productivity still expands nicely during the middle portion of recovery. In the latter stages of the expansion phase of the cycle, productivity growth tapers off. Firms may hire workers of lower quality as the pool of unemployed workers approaches depletion. In addition, utilization rates of the economy's productive capacity may rise above optimal levels, reducing efficiency of workers.

CAUSES OF THE PRODUCTIVITY SLOWDOWN

As mentioned, there is disagreement about the causes of the American productivity slowdown. Productivity is difficult to measure and students of the subject use different methodologies. Some economists might delete some of the factors on our list and add others. However, most of the following considerations would appear on any list compiled by leading scholars in the field. The factors are *not* intended to be ranked in order of importance.

CHANGES IN THE COMPOSITION OF THE LABOR FORCE Because of the U.S. baby boom of 1946–1963, a large influx of young workers into the labor force occurred during the period from the mid-1960s until the early 1980s. In addition, a steady increase in the labor force participation rate of women took place. Having had less experience on the job, these youthful workers and newly working women exhibited lower productivity *levels* than the work force as a whole. Hence, the gradual increase in the proportion of the labor force composed of youthful workers and women tended to slow the trend growth of productivity. In addition, the rapid growth in the sheer number of workers coming on stream held down the growth of capital per worker, thus inhibiting productivity growth. Although this explanation rings true for the period from the mid-1960s until around 1982, the demographics indicate a *decrease* in the influx of young workers into the labor force during the period from 1982 until the mid-1990s. Hence, this explanation fails to account for the continued weak productivity performance after 1982.

INCREASING GOVERNMENT REGULATIONS During the 1970s, an increase in governmental regulation of American business occurred. Firms were required to invest substantial sums in safety and pollution-abatement equipment. The speed limit on highways was reduced to 55 miles per hour. Resources were spent in order to comply with affirmative action guidelines. While many of these regulations undoubtedly contributed to an improved quality of life, they diverted time and effort from other productive activities and diverted corporation funds from investment in plant and equipment and research and development. The regulations therefore contributed to the productivity slowdown.

A POOR INVESTMENT AND SAVING PERFORMANCE As noted earlier, net investment results in growth in the nation's capital stock. Over the long run America's capital stock has grown faster than its labor force, thus resulting in more capital per worker. This capital deepening has been a prime source of rising labor productivity and living standards. Investment spending tends to embody new technology. Obsolete equipment is replaced, raising output per worker. A worker using a jackhammer can remove old pavement faster than one with a pick. A worker using a backhoe can move more dirt than one using a shovel. A secretary using a word processor can type a manuscript more efficiently than one using a typewriter. Included among the many factors that have contributed to the relatively poor investment performance of the past 25 years are a declining saving rate of the American people, an unstable macroeconomic environment, the adverse effect of inflation on the financial condition of firms, and the large structural budget deficits of the past decade.

MACROECONOMIC CONDITIONS The 1965–1982 period was one of considerable instability in the American economy. The 17-year period included two separate bouts with double-digit inflation, the two most severe recessions since the Great Depression of the 1930s, the Vietnam War, and an experiment with wage–price controls. No one can be certain of the precise effect of the macroeconomic environment on long-term economic growth, but it seems likely that it plays a significant role. Recessions impair productivity growth by reducing corporate profits and investment spending. Inflation reduces productivity growth in the long run by shortening the planning horizons of firms and by diverting funds from research and development and projects with long-term payoffs embodying technological change to speculative hedges and investment projects with quick payoffs. During most of this period (until the tax-law changes of the early 1980s), economists believe that inflation created a negative bias against investment spending through the tax system. Again, however, this explanation fails to account for the continued sluggish productivity growth since 1982.

A SLOWDOWN IN RESEARCH AND DEVELOPMENT SPENDING Technological change has been the most important factor contributing to rising productivity and living standards over the long run. New technology leads to innovation, which raises output produced per worker. Research and development expenditures lead to technical change, innovation, and economic growth. The share of U.S. gross domestic product allocated to research and development expenditures fell by 25 percent between 1965 and 1978, from 2.8 percent to 2.1 percent of GDP. This decline in R and D spending was attributable partly to a cutback in federal support and partly to a decline in spending by business in response to the economic instability of the 1970s. In the 1980s, research and development spending returned to its earlier and larger share of GDP. Given the lags between R and D spending and productivity growth, we were probably still feeling the adverse effects of the 1965–1978 slowdown in the past decade.

SUPPLY SHOCKS OF THE 1970S In 1974 and again in 1979–1980, the Organization of Petroleum Exporting Countries (OPEC) posted dramatic increases in the price of oil. Energy prices soared. Capital goods are energy-intensive; they use a lot of energy. The sharp increase in the cost of energy rendered a significant portion of the nation's capital stock obsolete. Many older and relatively inefficient capital goods such as generators, furnaces, and gas-guzzling trucks were retired from service. The oil shocks exerted an effect almost like a nuclear exchange, immobilizing a portion of our capital stock. The decline in the capital/labor ratio induced by the energy shocks naturally exerted a contractionary influence on productivity. An increase in energy prices induces firms to use more workers per unit of capital in production processes because labor is less energy-intensive. This signal slows down the capital deepening process and exerts a drag on labor productivity. Once again, however, this factor cannot help explain the continued stagnation of productivity in the past decade. Oil prices, both in absolute and real terms, are much lower today than in 1980.

SHIFT TO A SERVICE ECONOMY In recent decades a significant shift in the composition of American output has occurred toward services and away from manufacturing and agriculture. Americans are spending a smaller fraction of their incomes on food and manufactured items. They are spending an increasing portion on services—education, medical care, legal services, entertainment, financial advice, beauty salon services, and restaurant meals. In general, productivity levels in services have significantly lagged behind those in manufacturing and agriculture. Services, on average, tend to be labor-intensive; they cannot be put on an assembly line and standardized. For this reason, productivity in services is inherently lower than that of manufacturing. Some economists argue that the United States and other industrial economies are becoming increasingly service oriented and that overall productivity growth must therefore inevitably slow down.[5]

---

[5]However, development of the service sector may raise productivity in manufacturing and agriculture. Computer consultants may lead to more efficient inventory management of firms. Accounting firms may free up time for taxpaying firms and individuals, leading to productive effort. If the growth of the service sector reflects primarily a decision by agricultural and manufacturing firms to hire services formerly accomplished internally, it is not clear that the rise of the service sector inevitably leads to a decline in the nation's overall productivity.

To the extent that the preceding factors account for the slowdown in productivity growth in the past two decades, there is some reason to be hopeful about productivity growth resuming a more robust path in the next decade. Several of the negative factors are reversible and are now moving in a manner conducive to an improved productivity performance in the years ahead. For example, the baby boomers are moving into middle age—typically years of high productivity—in large numbers. The average woman in today's labor force has more longevity and higher productivity than her counterpart of 20 years ago. The macroeconomy has been considerably more stable and has exhibited lower inflation in the past decade than in the 1965–1982 period. Oil prices have declined dramatically in real terms relative to the early 1980s. Government regulations were eased during the Reagan Administrations of the 1980s, though some of these were reinstituted during President Bush's tenure. These indicators generally bode well for productivity growth.

On the other hand, American saving rates are the lowest in the industrialized world. We allocate a much lower share of our nation's annual output to investment than do such nations as Japan and Germany. Our huge federal budget deficit continues to be an obstacle to long-run economic growth. Though U.S. nonmilitary research and development expenditures have increased in the past decade, we allocate a smaller share of our annual output to this important category than many other nations. We cannot afford to be complacent about our productivity performance. The demise of the Soviet Union as a military threat and the resulting "peace dividend" provide an unprecedented opportunity to get the American productivity performance back on track in the longer term. It is crucial that American economic policies be designed with this long-term consideration foremost in mind.

Policies to Boost Economic Growth

The unsatisfactory performance of American productivity growth during the past quarter century naturally has stimulated interest in measures that might boost the rate of growth of American living standards. Indeed, to a significant extent, the *Reagan Revolution* of the 1980s involved this issue. As is commonly the case, economists disagree about the most fruitful measures for stimulating productivity and long-term economic growth.

A widely accepted viewpoint held by economists of all persuasions is that, other things equal, a larger capital stock implies more output per worker and higher living standards. If we produce more investment goods and fewer consumer and government goods, the nation's capital stock will grow more rapidly and so will productivity and living standards. In other words, a movement from *A* to *B* along America's production possibilities curve in Figure 22.6 increases the speed with which the curve shifts outward over time.

Economists disagree about the appropriate mechanisms for bringing about the movement from *A* to *B* in Figure 22.6, as well as about other measures for enhancing economic growth.

The location of the 1999 production possibilities curve (PPC) depends upon the portion of output we allocated to investment goods in earlier years. A higher-investment economy implies more rapid economic growth (a more rapidly shifting production possibilities curve).

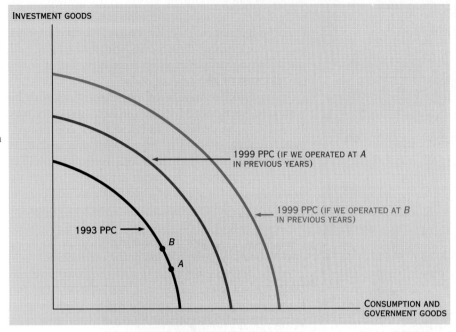

INVESTMENT GOODS

1999 PPC (IF WE OPERATED AT *A* IN PREVIOUS YEARS)

1999 PPC (IF WE OPERATED AT *B* IN PREVIOUS YEARS)

1993 PPC

B

A

CONSUMPTION AND GOVERNMENT GOODS

FIGURE 22.6

KEYNESIAN VIEWS

Keynesians advocate the active use of both monetary and fiscal policies to keep the economy strong, with actual GDP hovering close to potential GDP, to keep the unemployment rate close to the natural rate. During recessions, investment declines by a relatively larger amount than do other components of output. As a result, we experience a significant slowdown in the growth of the nation's capital stock. After the recession ends, the capital stock per worker is lower than would have been the case in the event the recession had been avoided. Furthermore, research and development expenditures tend to be scaled back during severe economic downturns. Keynesians support the aggressive use of both monetary and fiscal policies to minimize the frequency, duration, and depth of economic downturns.

Keynesians are quite critical of the *mix* of monetary and fiscal policies in the 1980s. In principle, a given level of aggregate demand and output can be obtained with various mixes of monetary and fiscal stimuli. A stimulative monetary policy (rapid money supply growth) could be combined with restrictive fiscal policy (a budget surplus or high-employment surplus) to produce a desired level of output. The same current output could be obtained via a tighter monetary policy combined with a more stimulative fiscal policy.

KEYNESIAN ECONOMISTS
JAMES TOBIN OF YALE
UNIVERSITY (TOP) AND
ROBERT SOLOW OF
THE MASSACHUSETTS
INSTITUTE OF TECHNOL-
OGY, BOTH NOBEL LAU-
REATES IN ECONOMICS,
WERE CRITICAL OF THE
MIX OF POLICIES IMPLE-
MENTED IN THE 1980S.

The mix of monetary and fiscal policies is likely to influence the *composition* of current output—the share of output consisting of investment goods versus consumption and government goods. With the defense buildup and the tax cuts of the early 1980s, the Reagan Administration implemented a stimulative fiscal policy (large budget deficits) and the Federal Reserve responded with tight money. Keynesians argue that this tight money/stimulative fiscal policy mix is precisely the opposite of the correct prescription if the objective of policy is to boost the share of output allocated to investment goods.

The evidence now in on our experiment with huge deficits seems consistent with this Keynesian view. In the first five years following the U.S. recession of 1973–1975, the shares of American GDP constituted by consumption and investment (producers' durable equipment) averaged 62.9 percent and 7.45 percent, respectively. In this period, deficits were quite small. In the five years following the 1981–1982 recession (in which structural budget deficits increased), the corresponding ratios averaged 65.7 percent and 7.04 percent, respectively. In the period of escalating deficits, the share of national output constituted by consumption increased sharply. The share constituted by investment declined somewhat, even though several specific tax measures aimed at boosting saving and investment were implemented in tax legislation in the early 1980s.[6]

The large budget deficits and the restrictive monetary policies of the early 1980s pushed interest rates (and real interest rates) to very high levels. An increase in interest rates moves us upward and leftward along our investment demand schedule of Chapter 12 (Figure 12.6 on page 299), reducing investment spending. Although other measures to stimulate investment spending were implemented under the Reagan economic program, Keynesians regard the perverse mix of monetary and fiscal policies as the major factor that prevented the desired increase in the share of output going to investment (the move from *A* to *B* in Figure 22.6).

Some Keynesians favor a national sales tax or some other form of consumption tax as a means of discouraging consumption spending and reducing the federal budget deficit. To the extent that the resulting increase in the nation's aggregate saving rate (private plus government) resulted in lower interest rates and greater investment spending, the enactment of a consumption tax would tend to promote the desired reallocation of current output from consumer goods to capital goods.

THE SUPPLY-SIDE POSITION

Supply-siders emphasize the disincentive effects of high tax rates. In this view, taxes were too high in America prior to the 1980s. The high tax rates stifled the incentive to save, invest, and work. Progressive income taxes, higher Social Security taxes, and inflation combined to boost millions of middle-income Americans into high tax brackets. When one includes federal income taxes, payroll taxes, and state

---

[6]The figures indicate that we financed this consumption boom during the 1983–1987 period largely by running large international trade deficits and borrowing from abroad. Our trade position (exports minus imports) moved from an average *surplus* of 0.7 percent of GDP between 1975 and 1979 to a *deficit* of 1.8 percent of GDP between 1983 and 1987. Hence, we financed the increase in the consumption share of output primarily not by reducing the investment share but by increasingly buying more foreign goods than the amount of good we sold abroad. We financed the increasing consumption share partially by crowding out investment, but mainly by crowding out net exports of goods and services.

income taxes, the typical American worker earning $28,000 annually was yielding thirty to forty cents of each additional dollar of income to the government by 1980. Higher-bracket individuals were yielding even more. Such rates, in the view of supply-siders, create serious adverse supply-side effects.

In the inflationary environment of the 1970s, taxes on capital gains and interest income depressed the effective rate of return on investment. Inflation and the existing income-tax code combined to impair the financial condition of many firms and to create a bias against investment in plant and equipment. Furthermore, existing tax loopholes encouraged socially wasteful diversion of funds into luxury condominiums, hobby farms, and purebred horses—diverting these funds from more socially useful investment.

The centerpiece of supply-side economics was the substantial reduction in income-tax rates implemented under the Economic Recovery Tax Act of 1981. This law, by reducing the tax due on each extra dollar of income earned, stimulated the incentive to earn income—to work and invest.

Supply-siders advocated removing the bias against saving and investment by reforming capital-gains taxes and depreciation allowances, by eliminating the tax deductibility of consumer interest expense, and by indexing the income tax to prevent inflation from pushing taxpayers into higher brackets. Except for the capital gains tax proposal, all these proposals are currently embedded in the nation's tax law. However, the Tax Reform Act of 1986 took back some of the investment incentives implemented in the Economic Recovery Tax Act of 1981. In addition to these fiscal measures, supply-siders pushed for a streamlining of environmental restrictions and an easing of other forms of government regulation thought to inhibit productivity.

But what was the supply-siders' response to the charge made by contemporary critics that the large income-tax cut would increase the federal budget deficit and interest rates and therefore interfere with the goal of boosting investment? Some supply-siders believed that the tax cut would force government to reduce expenditures, thereby averting significantly larger deficits. Most were aware that the deficit would increase but felt that the beneficial effects of lower tax rates would outweigh any detrimental effects of larger deficits. A few extreme supply-siders took refuge in the Laffer Curve proposition that the deficit would not increase because the reduction in income-tax rates would unleash a substantial increase in effort, output, and taxable income. This proposition, held by few economists in 1980, was rejected by events of the 1980s—the emergence of the huge budget deficits.

Some say that supply-side economics in general has been discredited by the events of the past decade. Others argue that it was not really given a chance—that tax rates were not significantly reduced on balance or that tight Federal Reserve policy counteracted the beneficial effects of the supply-side measures. At any rate, the fact remains that American productivity growth failed to improve in the past decade over its dismal performance in the 1970s. Productivity growth remains a major challenge for policymakers.

Summary

1. The two primary measures of economic growth are the rates of increase in real output (real GDP) and per-capita real output. Real output of a nation is an indicator of the

economic power of the nation; per-capita output indicates the well-being or standard of living of the people.

2. Economic growth involves increases in the economy's productive capacity over time. Economic growth implies that the nation's production possibilities curve and its aggregate supply curve are shifting outward over time.

3. The standard of living is measured by output per capita. Labor productivity refers to output per hour of work. If the length of the average workweek and the fraction of the population working both remain constant over time, the growth rates of productivity and living standards are identical. In recent decades, output per capita (the average standard of living) has grown somewhat faster than productivity because the fraction of the population working has trended upward. In the long run, the overwhelming source of rising living standards is growth in productivity.

4. The enormous chasm between living standards of affluent nations such as the United States and Japan and impoverished countries such as Ethiopia and Nigeria can be explained by the miracle of compound interest over a period of a century or two. If two countries start with identical living standards and one experiences 2 percent annual growth in per-capita output for 150 years and the other stagnates (zero growth), the country experiencing growth achieves a standard of living 20 times as high as the stagnant country.

5. Economic growth is a comparatively recent phenomenon, encompassing only the last two or three centuries. Prior to the Industrial Revolution, living standards were relatively unchanged for thousands of years.

6. Living standards of industrial nations have a tendency to converge over time. That is, industrial nations with low levels of per-capita output and income tend to grow faster than those with high levels. This phenomenon is chiefly due to the international diffusion of technological change. Less-affluent industrialized nations adopt the sophisticated technologies developed by the most advanced of the industrial nations. In general, however, less developed nations find it quite difficult to benefit from this international diffusion of technology. The immense gulf between living standards in LDCs and industrial nations has been *widening* over time.

7. Growth of total output can be decomposed into a portion attributable to growth of labor inputs and a portion attributable to growth of productivity of labor. Over a period encompassing most of this century, roughly one-third of the increase in output has been attributable to increases in labor inputs. About two-thirds of the growth is accounted for by rising labor productivity. The three most critical factors accounting for increases in labor productivity have been technological advances, increases in the quantity of capital goods, and improved education and skills embodied in the work force.

8. The period from the end of World War II until the mid-1960s was one of rapid growth in productivity and living standards. The industrialized nations experienced a slowdown in productivity growth after the mid-1960s, and the U.S. slowdown was especially severe. Some of the factors contributing to this productivity slowdown have been a rather anemic saving and investment pattern, government regulations that diverted resources from investment in new plant and equipment, unstable macroeconomic conditions, a slowdown in research and development efforts, the supply shocks of the 1970s, and changes in the composition of the labor force. Moreover, the trend toward a service economy has slowed productivity growth because productivity in the service sector tends to be lower than that in manufacturing and agriculture.

9. With the exception of the increasing role of services, the forces that have slowed American productivity growth appear to be potentially reversible. In fact, several of the forces that reduced productivity growth between 1965 and 1982 are now working to boost productivity growth. These include a more stable macroeconomic environment, some improvement in research and development spending, a significant decline in real oil and

energy prices, a decrease in government regulations, and favorable changes in the composition of the labor force. The continuing weakness in private saving and investment patterns together with the large federal budget deficits remain as negative forces working to inhibit productivity growth.

10. Policies designed to stimulate productivity growth must recognize the fundamental importance of technological change, capital deepening, and human capital in the growth process. In this vein, measures that encourage research and development spending, stimulate saving and investment, and encourage investment in education and training (human capital) are appropriate.

Key Terms

economic growth
standard of living
productivity growth
industrialization
convergence principle

invention
innovation
capital deepening
human capital

Study Questions and Problems

1. In what sense is the growth rate of a nation's real GDP a good measure of the nation's economic progress? Per-capita real GDP?

2. Define the term *productivity growth*. Define the term *standard-of-living growth*. Is it possible for growth in productivity to exceed growth in living standards? For growth in living standards to exceed growth in productivity? Explain.

3. Explain why the process of industrialization results in a major increase in living standards.

4. Explain the meaning of the convergence principle in living standards. What accounts for its existence? If the principle is valid, what does it imply about the relative growth rates to be experienced by England and the United States in the next decade?

5. Explain carefully why the *mix* of monetary and fiscal policies may have important implications for the long-term growth in living standards.

6. Suppose, after graduation, that your income rises in line with the growth in living standards during the ensuing 30 years. How much more affluent will you be after 30 years if living standards grow at 3 percent annually than if they remain constant? *Hint*: Using the calculator's y^x key, y is 1.03 and x is 30.

7. What are the three chief factors accounting for growth in labor productivity? Explain in your own words why each of these factors lifts productivity and living standards.

8. Do you feel that we should be concerned about the American productivity slowdown of the past 25 years? Why?

9. Assume you are chairperson of the President's Council of Economic Advisors and the president charges you with developing a plan to boost America's productivity growth significantly. What would be the key ingredients of your plan? Explain and defend.

10. Explain why productivity of labor fluctuates over the course of the business cycle.

AFTER 50 YEARS, MODERNIANS WOULD BE 2.10 TIMES AS AFFLUENT AS LAGGARDIANS.
AFTER 100 YEARS, MODERNIANS WOULD BE 4.43 TIMES RICHER. AFTER 200 YEARS
THEY WOULD BE 19.64 TIMES RICHER THAN LAGGARDIANS.

YOUR TURN
Answers

Selected References

Baumol, William J. "Productivity Growth, Convergence, and Welfare," *American Economic Review*, December 1986, pp. 1072–1085. This article outlines the basis for the convergence hypothesis and presents evidence in support of the hypothesis. For an exchange of views on this issue, see the December 1988 issue of the *American Economic Review*.

Baumol, William J., Sue Anne Batey Blackman, and Edward N. Wolff, *Productivity and American Leadership* (Cambridge, Mass.: MIT Press, 1989). An excellent source on the issue of the U.S. productivity problem.

Denison, Edward F. *Trends in American Economic Growth, 1929–82* (Washington, D.C.: The Brookings Institution, 1985). This quantitative study details the determinants of economic growth and analyzes the slowdown since 1973.

Kendrick, John (ed.). *International Comparisons of Productivity and Causes of the Slowdown* (Cambridge, Mass.: Ballinger Publishing Company, 1984). Several economists analyze causes of productivity growth and its slowdown in the United States and in other nations.

Maddison, Angus. *Phases of Capitalist Development* (Oxford, England: Oxford University Press, 1982). This work contains a wealth of information on the history of growth in living standards over many countries.

Seidman, Laurence S. *Saving for America's Future* (New York: M.E. Sharpe, Inc: 1990). This book analyzes the essential role of saving in the economic growth process and examines policies to increase American saving and investment.

"Symposium on the Slowdown in Productivity Growth." *The Journal of Economic Perspectives*, Fall 1988, pp. 3–97. This is an excellent and timely collection of articles by such outstanding economists as Stanley Fischer, Zvi Griliches, Dale Jorgenson, Mancur Olson, and Michael Boskin.

VI

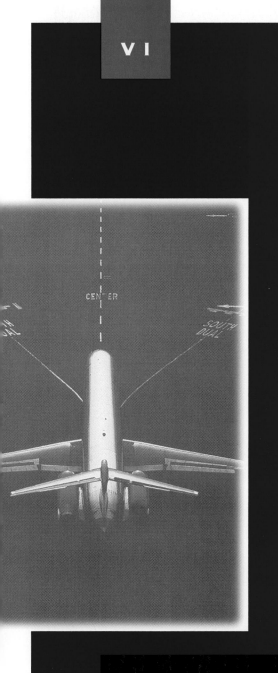

Consumer and Business Behavior

PART VI BEGINS THE FORMAL TREATMENT OF MICRO-

ECONOMICS. IN THIS SECTION, WE TAKE A CLOSER

LOOK AT BOTH CONSUMERS AND PRODUCERS.

CONSUMER BEHAVIOR IS EXAMINED WITHIN

THE CONTEXT OF *UTILITY THEORY*, IN WHICH

CONSUMERS ARE ASSUMED TO MAXIMIZE

THEIR WELL-BEING (OR *UTILITY*). THIS

MODEL PROVIDES IMPORTANT INSIGHTS

INTO PRICES, THE LAW OF DEMAND, AND

CONSUMER BUYING PATTERNS. ■ NEXT,

THE FIRM'S PRODUCTION DECISIONS

ARE ANALYZED IN EACH OF TWO TIME

PERIODS—THE SHORT RUN, WHEN THE

FIRM IS CONSTRAINED BY SOME INPUT (FOR

EXAMPLE, A FIXED PLANT SIZE), AND THE

LONG RUN, WHEN THE FIRM HAS SUF-

FICIENT TIME TO ALTER

ALL INPUTS. AS PRO-

DUCTION CHANGES, SO DO THE COSTS OF

PRODUCTION. THE ANALYSIS OF THESE COSTS

PROVIDES THE BASIS FOR PART VII OF THE TEXT.

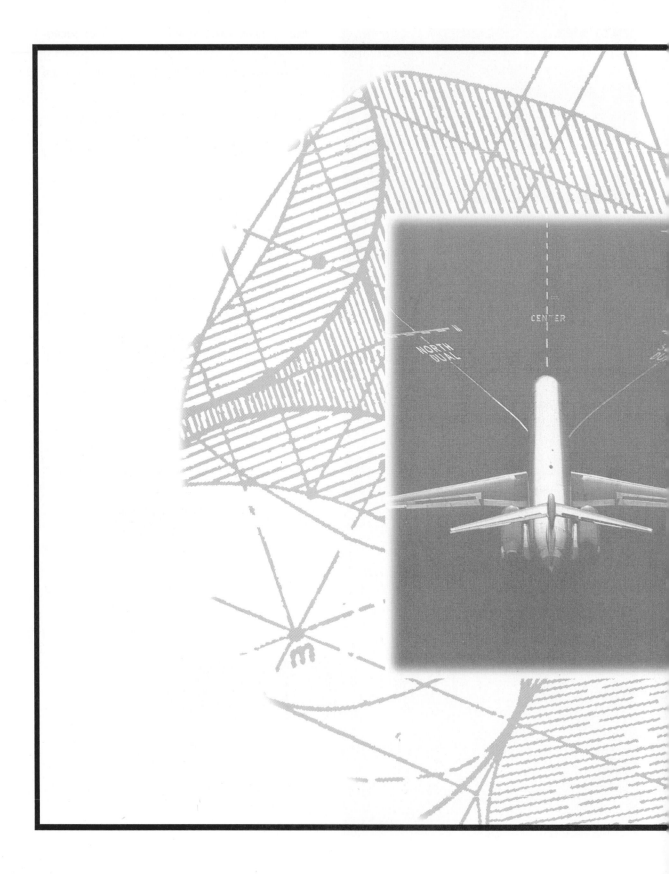

Demand and Utility

WHY, ASKED ADAM SMITH, IS THE PRICE OF WATER LOW, THE PRICE OF DIAMONDS HIGH? SHOULD NOT WATER, WHICH IS NECESSARY FOR LIFE, BE VALUED MORE HIGH-LY THAN DIAMONDS, WHICH WE COULD EASILY SURVIVE WITHOUT? THIS *PARADOX OF VALUE* CAN BE RESOLVED WITH MARGINAL UTILITY THE-ORY, THE FOCUS OF THIS CHAPTER.

WE WOULD NOT DEVOTE ALMOST A CHAPTER TO MAR-GINAL UTILITY THEORY IF THAT WERE ITS SOLE CONTRI-BUTION. IT IS NOT. THE THEO-RY PROVIDES A DEEPER UNDERSTANDING OF DEMAND, INCLUDING ADDED INSIGHT INTO THE LAW OF DEMAND. IT PRESENTS A METHOD FOR ALLOCATING INCOME SO AS TO MAXIMIZE A CONSUMER'S LEVEL OF SATISFACTION. IT EXPLAINS WHY A COMMUNITY CONCERNED ABOUT CRIME MAY NONETHELESS REFUSE TO HIRE ADDITIONAL POLICE.

CHAPTER 23 ALSO SHOWS HOW TO DERIVE A MARKET DEMAND CURVE FROM THE DEMAND CURVES OF INDIVID-UAL CONSUMERS, HOW TO VALUE THE BENEFITS TO CON-SUMERS OF BEING ABLE TO PURCHASE A GOOD, AND HOW RESEARCH USING RATS SUP-PORTS DEMAND THEORY.

Nothing is more useful than water: but it will pur-chase scarce any thing; scarce any thing can be had in exchange for it. A dia-mond, on the contrary, has scarce any value in use; but a very great quantity of other goods may frequently be had in exchange for it.[1]

[1]Adam Smith, *The Wealth of Nations* (New York: Random House, 1937), p. 28. (Originally published in 1776.)

Marginal Utility Theory

MEASURING UTILITY

The theory of marginal utility rests upon certain assumptions. The first is that consumers maximize their well-being, what economists call **utility**. A second and less defensible assumption is that utility can be measured. Not only must a person be able to indicate which of two goods is preferred, but the intensity of preference must also be quantifiable. It is not enough that a person prefers Pepsi to Coke. The person must also indicate by how much—for example, a glass of Pepsi yields ten units of utility, a glass of Coke eight.

The founders of marginal utility theory believed that a utility-measuring device would be developed one day. Perhaps it will. Imagine being plugged into a machine that senses the pleasures you experience. A needle swings farther to the right the greater the pleasure. Mom's homemade apple pie kicks the needle well to the right of center; dorm food barely budges the needle. Such a device could open up a whole new world of advertising. Pepsi might adopt the slogan "more utility per glass." But, while such developments may lie ahead, utility meters remain, at present, only a dream.

If the assumption that utility can be measured is currently unrealistic, then why not abandon marginal utility theory? Quite simply because marginal utility provides some important insights. After sketching this theory, we consider some of its applications.

TWO MEASURES OF UTILITY—TOTAL AND MARGINAL

TOTAL UTILITY
The total amount of satisfaction received from all the units consumed of a good.

MARGINAL UTILITY
The extra satisfaction (change in total utility) from consuming one more unit of a good.

Consumption of a good generates utility. If more than one unit is consumed, it is important to distinguish between total utility and marginal utility. **Total utility** measures the cumulative satisfaction received from *all* units of a good that are consumed. It is obtained by summing the utilities generated by each unit of the good. That is, you add the utility of the first unit consumed, the utility of the second unit, and so on. In contrast, **marginal utility** of a good simply measures the satisfaction provided by the *last* unit consumed.

Which concept is more appropriate? That depends on the question being asked. If the question is whether a pizza or a dish of ice cream is more satisfying, the issue revolves around which provides more *total* utility. If you choose ice cream, you may then face the decision of whether you want two scoops or three. Now the emphasis is on *marginal* utility. How much extra utility would a third scoop of ice cream provide?

Marginal utility and total utility schedules are related, as the following example illustrates. Suppose you spend an afternoon at the student union. While there you consider drinking some Coke. Columns (A) and (B) of Table 23.1 present a hypothetical total utility schedule that measures the satisfaction you derive from various quantities of Coke. A single Coke provides 20 units of utility, two Cokes provide 32 units, and so on. From the total utility schedule, you can compute the marginal utility of any given Coke. For example, the marginal utility of the third Coke is 5—drinking three Cokes rather than two increases total utility by 5 units (from 32 to 37). The marginal utility numbers are given in column (C) of Table 23.1 and presented graphically in Figure 23.1 (page 584). Observe that these numbers become smaller as the quantity of Cokes consumed increases. That first Coke tastes great. But additional Cokes are less satisfying. As you drink more and more, your thirst subsides and you start to fill up. You may even tire of the taste. Thus, while *total* utility increases with consumption, *marginal* utility declines.

LAW OF DIMINISHING MARGINAL UTILITY
The proposition that marginal utility of a good eventually declines as consumption of the good increases.

Declining marginal utility is not something unique to Coke; it is so common that economists have developed a name for it: **the law of diminishing marginal utility**. Formally, the law of diminishing marginal utility can be stated as follows: Beyond some point, the more units of a good consumed the less utility an additional unit provides.[2] This law or hypothesis is the centerpiece of marginal utility theory.

Although the numbers in Table 23.1 are all positive, it is possible that marginal utility could eventually become zero—further consumption would not alter total utility. For example, if the student union provides unlimited free Coke refills on "student appreciation day," there is still a limit to how many glasses you want to drink. You can be expected to stop at the point at which further consumption provides no further utility. The fact that some students walk away from cups still half full indicates they have reached the point where marginal utility is zero.

Negative marginal utilities may also occur, when consumption is pushed too far. Take dinner at Grandma's. She does something special to cauliflower that only she can do. As you say to yourself, "If I eat another bite of this I'll get sick," Grandma empties the bowl on your plate. "I made this cauliflower just for you," she says; so you choke it down despite its negative marginal utility.

TOTAL AND MARGINAL UTILITY OF COKES

(A) QUANTITY	(B) TOTAL UTILITY	(C) MARGINAL UTILITY
0	0	
1	20	20
2	32	12
3	37	5
4	40	3

Although drinking additional Cokes increases total utility, the marginal utility of successive Cokes diminishes.

TABLE 23.1

[2]The law of diminishing marginal utility does not rule out the possibility that marginal utility might initially increase before starting its decline, but only the declining segment of the marginal utility schedule is relevant. As long as marginal utility is increasing, it is always worthwhile to consume the next unit of the good. That is, consumption will continue until after marginal utility has started to decline.

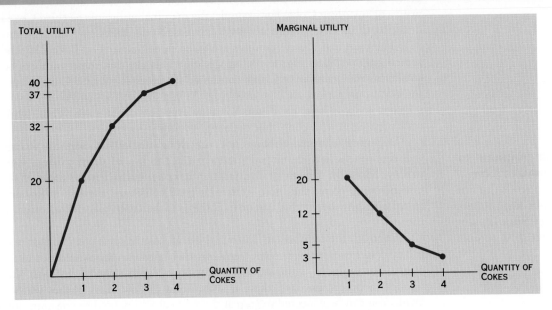

These figures (drawn from Table 23.1) demonstrate that the marginal utility of successive Cokes diminishes.

FIGURE 23.1

CONSUMER EQUILIBRIUM

CONSUMER EQUILIBRIUM
A situation in which the consumer is obtaining the maximum total utility consistent with a given income (budget); a consumer is in equilibrium when marginal utility per dollar is the same for each good and all income is spent.

Marginal utility theory can also be used to solve allocation problems. Because of scarcity you must choose among competing bundles of goods, but which bundle should you choose? That is, how should you spend your income?

To keep matters simple, we initially consider two goods and assume the law of diminishing marginal utility holds for each. Later we extend the analysis to include additional goods. The model assumes that the consumer has a fixed income or budget to spend on these goods. Furthermore, this income is not large enough to satisfy all wants.[3] The consumer also faces fixed prices. Under these conditions, how should the income be spent in order to maximize utility? *Total utility is maximized when the marginal utility per dollar of each good is equal and all income is spent.* When these requirements are satisfied, the consumer is said to be in *equilibrium.*

To illustrate **consumer equilibrium**, consider the following example. You arrive at the student union with $4 in your pocket, planning to spend this money on drink and song. Cokes are $1.00 each and the jukebox is $.50 per selection. Table 23.2 presents utility schedules for Cokes and records—total utility, marginal utility, and marginal utility per dollar—which is simply the ratio of the marginal utility of a good to the price of the good. From these schedules it is clear that both

[3]Without this budget constraint, the solution to our problem would be trivial: consume as much as you want—that is, consume each good up to the point where marginal utility is zero.

UTILITY SCHEDULES FOR COKES AND RECORDS

COKES

QUANTITY	TOTAL UTILITY (TU)	MARGINAL UTILITY (MU)	MU/P*
1	20	20	20
2	32	12	12
3	37	5	5
4	40	3	3

RECORDS

QUANTITY	TOTAL UTILITY (TU)	MARGINAL UTILITY (MU)	MU/P**
1	9	9	18
2	17	8	16
3	24	7	14
4	30	6	12
5	35	5	10
6	39	4	8

*The price per Coke is assumed to be $1.00.
**The price per record is assumed to be $.50.

TABLE 23.2

goods satisfy the law of diminishing marginal utility. Assuming these utility schedules reflect your preferences, how should you spend your money?

The first purchase should be a Coke. It provides more utility per dollar, more bang per buck, than does a record. After that, head for the jukebox (as Table 23.3, page 586, demonstrates). The marginal utility per dollar of the first record (18) exceeds the marginal utility per dollar of the second Coke (12). Note that the emphasis is on marginal utility *per dollar*. To be sure, the second Coke has a higher marginal utility than the first record. But, while the Coke costs twice as much, it fails to deliver twice the satisfaction. It is not presently a *good buy*. In making purchases, consumers consider price as well as utility. We recognize this by dividing marginal utility of a good by its price to obtain marginal utility per dollar.

After playing the first record, you play a second and a third—marginal utility per dollar is higher for these records than for the second Coke. At this point you have $1.50 left. How should you spend it? Marginal utility per dollar of the second Coke is identical to that of the fourth record, so you are indifferent to which good you buy. In fact, you have just enough money to buy both. Which is purchased first does not matter.

This situation corresponds to consumer equilibrium. You have spent your entire budget, and the marginal utility per dollar of the last Coke is identical to the marginal utility per dollar of the last record. To convince yourself further that utility is maximized by purchasing two Cokes and playing four records, consider any other combination of purchases costing $4 or less. All have lower total utility.

For example, if you were to buy three Cokes, you could afford to play only two records. Although the extra Coke would provide 5 more units of utility, forgoing

SEQUENCE OF PURCHASES	REASON FOR PURCHASE
First purchase: Coke	MU/P of first Coke (20) is greater than MU/P of first record (18).
Second purchase: Record	MU/P of first record (18) is greater than MU/P of second Coke (12).
Third purchase: Record	MU/P of second record (16) is greater than MU/P of second Coke (12).
Fourth purchase: Record	MU/P of third record (14) is greater than MU/P of second Coke (12).
Fifth purchase: Either*	MU/P of fourth record (12) equals MU/P of second Coke (12).

Based on information in Table 23.2, Table 23.3 indicates how you should spend your income in order to maximize total utility. Consumer equilibrium is reached with the purchase of two Cokes and the playing of four records.

*If you buy a Coke here, your sixth and final purchase will be a record. If you play a record, your final purchase will be a Coke.

TABLE 23.3

the third and fourth records would reduce total utility by a greater amount—by 13 units (7 + 6). Drinking three Cokes would therefore reduce total utility by 8 units (13 − 5). Nor would you maximize utility if you were to drink only one Coke. Although you could now afford to play records five and six, the extra utility derived from hearing them (9 units) is less than the utility you would lose by forgoing the second Coke (12 units).

Given the utility schedules of Table 23.2, total utility is maximized only with two Cokes and four records, the combination for which the marginal utility of the last dollar spent on each is equal.[4] This condition can be restated algebraically as

$$\frac{MU_{Coke}}{P_{Coke}} = \frac{MU_{record}}{P_{record}}$$

where P denotes price.

What if we consider more than two goods? In that case our condition for consumer equilibrium generalizes. When a consumer purchases n goods, the following equality must hold:

$$\frac{MU_1}{P_1} = \frac{MU_2}{P_2} = \ldots = \frac{MU_n}{P_n}$$

---

[4]The astute reader may observe that in some cases strict equality of ratios may not be possible. For instance, what if you had decided to spend one more dollar at the student union? Regardless of whether you purchase an extra Coke or play two more records, the marginal utility of the last dollar spent on Coke will not equal the marginal utility of the last dollar spent on records. What should you do? In this case play two more records, since marginal utility of those two records (9) exceeds marginal utility of another Coke (5). More generally, total utility is maximized if (a) buying one more unit of a good (for example, Coke) does not increase total utility, (b) buying one less unit of the good does not increase total utility, and (c) the entire income is spent. Given $5, these three requirements are satisfied with the purchase of two Cokes and six records.

FROM MARGINAL UTILITY TO DEMAND

Demand curves can be derived directly from a consumer's marginal utility schedules. To illustrate, we return to the student union and consider the effects of a price change. Suppose the price of Coke is reduced to $.50. At this price buying two Cokes and playing four records no longer maximizes your total utility. The marginal utility per dollar of the second Coke does not equal the marginal utility per dollar of the fourth record. Nor is the budget being fully spent. To achieve consumer equilibrium, you must buy three Cokes and play five records. When you do this, your budget is fully spent, and the marginal utility per dollar is the same for the last Coke and the last record.[5] Total utility is therefore maximized.

We have just plotted two points on your demand curve. At a price of $1.00 you demand two Cokes; at a price of $.50 you demand three Cokes. In a similar fashion, by considering other prices we could finish tracing your demand curve (see Figure 23.2).

The link between marginal utility and demand can also be thought of in less technical terms. Because the marginal utility of the first Coke is high, you are prepared to buy it even at a relatively high price. But successive Cokes provide less and less additional utility. Therefore, you are willing to buy them only at lower prices. The lower the marginal utility of an additional Coke, the less you are willing to pay for it. Because of diminishing marginal utility, consumers are willing to buy more of a good only if its price is reduced—demand curves are downward sloping.

PLOTTING A DEMAND CURVE FROM MARGINAL UTILITY SCHEDULES

Because of the law of diminishing marginal utility, you are willing to consume more of a good only if its price is reduced. This demand curve is based on the utility schedules of Table 23.2.

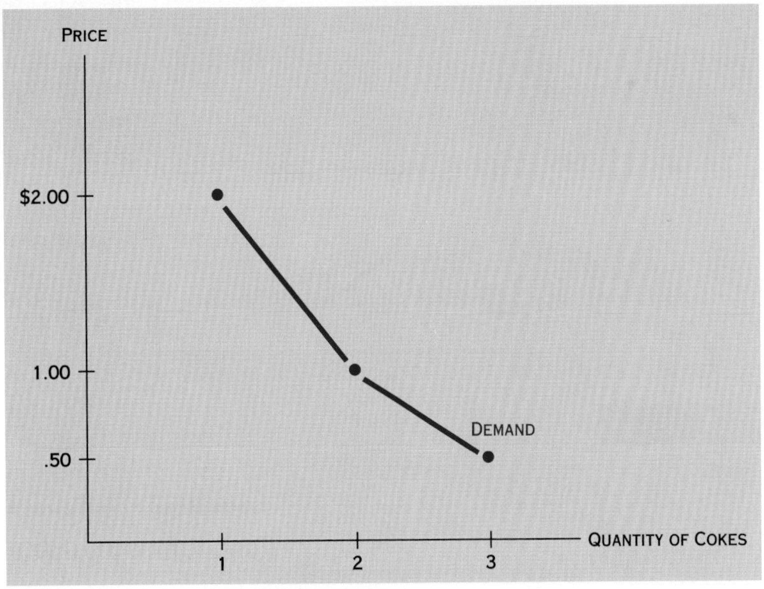

FIGURE 23.2

[5]For each good, $MU/P = 5/.50 = 10$.

Consumer Surplus[6]

CONSUMER SURPLUS
The difference between the maximum amount a consumer is willing to pay for a given quantity of a good and the amount actually paid.

Another implication of diminishing marginal utility is that the total benefit a consumer derives from consuming a good generally exceeds the amount the consumer spends on that good. That is, the consumer reaps a surplus or net benefit from the purchase of the good. Formally, this added value is known as **consumer surplus**

To illustrate, assume the price of a Coke is $.50. If you are willing to pay a maximum of $2.00 for the first Coke, up to $1.00 for the second, and up to $.50 for the third, the total value to you of three Cokes is $3.50 ($2.00 + $1.00 + $.50). Yet, at a price of $.50, the cost of three Cokes is only $1.50. You enjoy a consumer surplus of $2.00 ($3.50 − $1.50).

Consumer surplus can also be depicted diagramatically, as in the following figure:

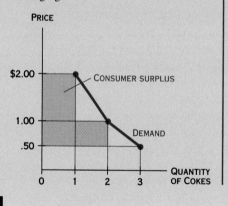

Because the demand curve indicates a consumer's willingness to pay, consumer surplus is represented by the shaded area beneath the demand curve and above the market price. At a price of $.50, consumer surplus is $2.00, consisting of $1.50 from the first Coke and $.50 from the second.

Under certain circumstances consumer surplus can be used to evaluate various projects or goods. For example, suppose the university, as a show of appreciation, wants either to give a free concert or to provide five-cent Cokes during finals week. Which gesture would have a greater value to students? Consumer surplus provides one possible framework for answering this question. Suppose each student's consumer surplus can be estimated for both the free concert and the five-cent Cokes. By adding the consumer surplus of each student, we can estimate the aggregate consumer surplus of the free concert and the five-cent Cokes. Whichever option has the higher consumer surplus can be taken to be the one the students value more highly.

[6]This exhibit may be omitted without loss of continuity to the chapter.

EXHIBIT 23.1

IRRATIONAL BEHAVIOR

Consumers are not always rational; sometimes they react impulsively, failing to consider the consequences of their actions. For example, they may buy certain eye-appealing food while shopping because they are tired or hungry, even though it is not a good buy. Is this sufficient reason to reject marginal utility theory? No, the theory can still be useful despite an occasional irrational act.

First, the model indicates the optimal choice, providing a standard with which to judge the actual choice. Second, because most people act rationally most of the time, the model predicts which combination of goods a consumer will actually purchase. Finally, at the aggregate level the model predicts consumption patterns of the general population. Although a few people may act irrationally at any point in time, their actions are outweighed by the majority of people who are rational. For example, even when a few people violate the law of demand, as long as most people behave rationally the aggregate demand curve for a good slopes downward.

RESOLVING THE PARADOX OF VALUE

Early economists puzzled over the relationship between price and value. Why should the price of diamonds exceed the price of water? Isn't water more valuable? Shouldn't it therefore command a higher price? Equipped with an understanding of marginal utility theory, we can explain why diamonds have a higher price than water and why early economists were confused about the matter. (You have an opportunity to understand something that Adam Smith, one of the greatest economists of all time, did not fully comprehend!)

The key to the puzzle is scarcity and how it affects marginal utility. Water is cheap because it is so abundant. Another gallon provides little additional utility. Therefore, consumers are willing to pay very little for the extra water. In contrast to water, the supply of diamonds is extremely limited. Because the value or utility of an additional diamond is high, consumers are prepared to pay a high price for it. Of course, the degree of scarcity may change over time and, as it does, so will marginal utility of an additional unit. Other things equal, the scarcer a good becomes, the higher its marginal utility and therefore its market price.

Recently, California experienced its worst drought in more than 50 years. Lakes dried up; crops withered and died. The lack of water prompted cities to ration water and impose stiff fines on those who exceeded their allotment. In San Francisco, customers who repeatedly violated water limits had their water shut off. In Santa Barbara, water sprinklers were banned, prompting some home owners to paint their parched lawns green. In this setting the marginal utility of additional water soared, and so did the price consumers were willing to pay for it.

Early economists stumbled over the concept of value because they failed to distinguish marginal utility from total utility. Yes, water is essential to life. Yes, it has a high total value or total utility. But, contrary to their thinking, this does not imply that water should have a high market value. *Price depends on marginal utility, not on total utility*. Because water is so plentiful it has a low marginal utility, and consequently a low price, even though its total utility is high. Although the solution to the puzzle may appear obvious today, early economists can hardly be faulted for not thinking in terms of marginal utility. Marginal utility theory was not developed until the nineteenth century (see Exhibit 23.2) (page 590).

OTHER APPLICATIONS OF MARGINAL UTILITY THEORY

Marginal utility theory helped reformulate economic thinking. Its centerpiece, marginal analysis, has been extended to other areas of economics, including pro-

EXHIBIT

23.2

The Founders of Marginal Utility Theory

Although Adam Smith posed the water–diamond paradox, neither he nor his contemporaries satisfactorily resolved this paradox. Not until the *marginal revolution* of the late nineteenth century did economists have a model able to explain why luxuries could command a higher price than necessities. Although the seeds of marginal utility theory can be found in earlier writings, credit for developing this theory is attributed to three economists—William Stanley Jevons, Carl Menger, and Lèon Walras. Working independently of one another—Jevons in England, Menger in Austria, and Walras in Switzerland—the three economists published separate books between 1871 and 1874 that laid out the elements of marginal utility theory.

In a sharp break from the prevailing line of thought, the three economists argued that value and price depend on marginal utility to the consumer, not on the cost of producing a good or on the amount of labor.[7] This argument was used, especially by Menger's followers, to attack the works of Karl Marx, which are based on a labor theory of value. Despite the importance to economics of marginal analysis and utility, economists did not generally recognize the significance of marginal utility theory until the twentieth century.

[7]Were the marginalists right or were their contemporaries? For a resolution of this debate, return to Chapter 4, Exhibit 2.

duction and labor markets. Although we cover these topics later, before leaving marginal utility theory we consider a few of its other applications.

Marginal utility theory can explain what might appear to be the irrational voting behavior of a community. Suppose a community is very concerned about crime. Does this imply that it will want to expand its police department? Are voters likely to pass a proposal to hire additional police officers? Not necessarily. Although the total utility of police protection may be high, the marginal utility of a little more protection may be low. Citizens may feel that the money to hire additional police could be better spent filling potholes or providing new parks. Or they may prefer lower taxes, accepting less police protection in the process. There is nothing inconsistent about thinking that police protection is the most important service the government can provide and yet voting not to spend more on this service. When citizens vote on a proposal, they are voting on its marginal utility, not its total utility.

The same logic applies to various organizations. A zoo may consider its big cat exhibit to be its prize attraction, yet there is nothing inconsistent about trading one of its cats for monkeys or exotic birds. The marginal utility of an improved monkey exhibit may be high; the loss of a big cat may reduce utility very little.

Marginal utility theory was even behind Mayor Edward Koch's plan to conserve water in New York City. The city's houses and apartment buildings do not have water meters. Therefore the price that a homeowner pays for additional water—to water a lawn or fill a swimming pool—is zero. Because additional water is free to the consumer, the consumer uses water up to the point where its marginal utility is zero. As long as the marginal utility of an additional gallon is positive, it is used. But while additional water is free to the consumer, it costs the city money.

The mayor proposed requiring owners of all residences to install water meters by 1996. Once water usage can be measured, it will be possible to charge customers directly on the basis of their usage. When forced to pay for extra water, consumers will refrain from using water that has low marginal utility. Studies suggested that installing and using meters would curtail water consumption by at least 15 percent.[8]

YOUR TURN

ACCORDING TO A CALIFORNIA PHYSICIST, HIGH TEMPERATURES AND HIGH ATMOSPHERIC PRESSURE ON URANUS AND NEPTUNE MAY HAVE TRANSFORMED THEIR INDIGENOUS CARBON INTO DIAMONDS. SUPPOSE HE IS CORRECT. IF THESE DIAMONDS ARE MINED AND TRANSPORTED TO EARTH, THEN (FOR RESIDENTS OF EARTH): (A) HOW WILL THE TOTAL UTILITY OF DIAMONDS CHANGE? (B) WILL THE MARGINAL UTILITY OF DIAMONDS RISE, FALL, OR REMAIN UNCHANGED? (C) HOW WILL THE PRICE OF DIAMONDS BE AFFECTED?

The Law of Demand— An Alternative Explanation[9]

Some students are uneasy about using marginal utility to explain the law of demand. Although a theory should be judged primarily in terms of its ability to predict and explain, the assumption that utility can be measured is admittedly unrealistic. For those troubled by this assumption, an alternative explanation of the inverse relationship between price and quantity demanded involves using income and substitution effects.

THE INCOME AND SUBSTITUTION EFFECTS OF A PRICE CHANGE

INCOME EFFECT
The change in quantity demanded of a good that results from a change in purchasing power (when the price of the good changes).

A price change is likely to affect quantity demanded for two reasons: it alters consumers' purchasing power and it changes the attractiveness of this good relative to its substitutes. For example, assume the price of a good is reduced and the prices of all other goods are unchanged. Because of the lower price of this good, you can now buy a given bundle of goods with less income than before. With the income that remains you can make additional purchases of various goods including, if you wish, the good whose price has been reduced. For example, if the price of Pepsi-Cola falls, you may spend part of the additional income to buy another quart or six-pack of Pepsi. This change in quantity demanded resulting from a higher effective income (or purchasing power) is called the **income effect**.

[8]See *The New York Times*, "Mayor Koch Says Meters in Homes Will Save Water," January 12, 1986, p. 6E.
[9]Some instructors may wish to delete this section, which contains technical material.

A price change may also affect quantity demanded by changing *relative prices*—that is, the price of one good compared to another. If the price of Pepsi falls and the prices of other beverages remain unchanged, Pepsi becomes a better buy than it was before the price cut. This induces many consumers to change their spending patterns—to buy more Pepsi and less of other beverages. This is exactly what happened several years ago. In an effort to increase sales volume in supermarkets, Pepsi aggressively reduced its price. As a result, it won a bigger share of soft-drink sales, overtaking Coke in many stores. The increased quantity demanded resulting from a lower relative price is termed the **substitution effect**.

SUBSTITUTION EFFECT
The change in quantity demanded of a good that results from a change in the price of the good relative to its substitutes.

FROM INCOME AND SUBSTITUTION EFFECTS TO A DEMAND CURVE

As you may recall from earlier chapters, consumers respond to higher incomes by increasing purchases of normal goods and by decreasing purchases of inferior goods. This means that the income effect is positive for normal goods but negative for inferior goods. These income effects have implications for the shape of demand curves.

For normal goods the income effect reinforces the substitution effect. Suppose the price of a good falls. Consumers buy more of the good while cutting back on substitute products (the substitution effect). In addition, the lower price results in greater purchasing power, which again increases quantity demanded (the income effect). In other words, both substitution and income effects lead to an inverse relationship between price and quantity demanded. Therefore, demand curves for normal goods must slope downward.

For inferior goods matters are more complicated, because income and substitution effects tug in opposite directions. A lower price still induces a consumer to buy relatively more of a good (the substitution effect) and it still increases the consumer's effective income. But a consumer reacts to an increase in income by demanding *less* of an inferior good. Thus, while the substitution effect leads to an increase in the quantity demanded, the income effect leads to a reduction in the quantity demanded.

As long as the substitution effect is stronger than the income effect, the demand curve of an inferior good slopes downward. If the income effect outweighs the substitution effect, however, a lower price leads to a *lower* quantity demanded—the demand curve of the inferior good slopes upward! Although this theoretical possibility cannot be dismissed, empirical research has failed to uncover a convincing, real-world example of an upward-sloping demand curve. Therefore, demand curves apparently slope downward—even for inferior goods.[10] Although most research on demand curves has dealt with human consumption, some innovative studies find that demand curves slope downward even for animal consumers (see Exhibit 23.3, page 594).

---

[10]Economists have looked far and wide for an exception to the law of demand—that is, for a good whose demand curve slopes upward. Some claim that potatoes in nineteenth-century Ireland may have been such a good, but most economists find this argument unconvincing. See Gerald Dwyer, Jr., and Cotton Lindsay, "Robert Giffen and the Irish Potato," *American Economic Review* (March 1984), pp. 188–192.

From Individual Demand to Market Demand

MARKET DEMAND CURVE

A curve showing the relationship between the price of a good and the total quantity demanded by all consumers in the market (per period of time); obtained by summing the demand curves of individual consumers.

Both marginal utility theory and income and substitution effects explain why the quantity demanded by an individual consumer can be expected to be inversely related to price. In turn, when individual demand curves slope downward, so does the **market demand curve**. To obtain aggregate or market demand for a good, we simply add the demand of all individuals in the market. This procedure is illustrated in Figure 23.3 and the corresponding Table 23.4 (page 594). For simplicity we assume the market contains only two consumers, you and a friend. But the same technique can be applied to any market, regardless of the number of consumers.

Market demand for a good is obtained by adding, at each price, the quantity demanded by all consumers in the market. For example, if the price is $2 you want to buy one unit, your friend none; total quantity demanded is therefore one unit. If price falls to $1, your quantity demanded rises to two, your friend's to one; altogether three units are demanded. At a price of $.50, you each want three units; so the aggregate quantity demanded is six units.

Although marginal utility theory provides information about individual and market demand, it focuses exclusively on the buying side of the market. Because supply is as important as demand in determining price and quantity, we present a detailed analysis of production in Chapter 24.

MARKET DEMAND—THE SUM OF INDIVIDUAL DEMAND CURVES

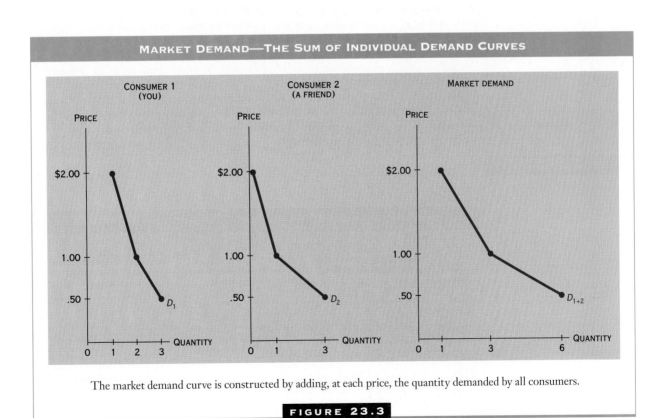

The market demand curve is constructed by adding, at each price, the quantity demanded by all consumers.

FIGURE 23.3

Oh Rats! Testing Consumer Demand Theory Inside a Cage

Scientists study animals to determine whether their behavior is consistent with that of humans. Often behavioral patterns are found to apply across species. Is this true for economic behavior? In a rather unusual experiment, this question was addressed by economists working in collaboration with psychologists and biologists. At issue: Is the behavior of animals consistent with consumer demand theory?

Male rats were placed in experimental chambers, each containing two levers.[11] Depressing the first lever would release one liquid (for example, root beer); depressing the second lever would release a different liquid (such as cherry cola). Food and water were always available, so the rats did not need to consume either flavored beverage to satisfy their hunger or thirst. Experiments were conducted to answer two questions: (1) Is the rats' behavior consistent with the substitution effect? (2) Are demand curves of rats downward sloping?

Each rat was given an "income" of so many lever presses per day (for example,

300). Once the income was used up, the lights above the levers were turned off for the remainder of the day. The next morning the lights were turned back on, signaling that additional income (lever presses) had been provided. The amount of fluid released by a lever could be adjusted, which corresponded to a change in price. For example, doubling the amount of root beer released by a lever would be equivalent to a 50 percent reduction in the price of root beer. By changing the amount of a fluid released, the researchers could determine the response of the animals to a change in price.

DERIVING MARKET DEMAND FOR A TWO-CONSUMER MARKET

(1) PRICE	(2) QUANTITY DEMANDED BY CONSUMER 1 (YOU)	(3) QUANTITY DEMANDED BY CONSUMER 2 (A FRIEND)	(4) QUANTITY DEMANDED BY ALL CONSUMERS (YOU AND YOUR FRIEND)
$2.00	1	0	1
1.00	2	1	3
.50	3	3	6

The market demand schedule indicates the total quantity demanded at each price (column 4). Total quantity demanded is obtained by adding, at each price, the quantities demanded by all consumers in the market (columns 2 and 3).

TABLE 23.4

In the first experiment, the price of, say, root beer was lowered while the price of cherry cola was raised. At the same time, income was adjusted to guarantee that our animal consumer could still purchase the original combination of beverages. For example, if a rat initially purchased 12 milliliters of root beer per day and 3 milliliters of cherry cola, he would be given sufficient income still to be able to purchase these quantities. Of course, economic theory predicts that the consumption pattern will change. According to the substitution effect, a lower relative price for root beer should lead consumers to purchase more root beer and less cherry cola. In fact, for all rats the predicted response prevailed.

Confirmation of the substitution effect does not, however, guarantee that demand curves will slope downward. If a particular beverage is an inferior good and if the income effect is stronger than the substitution effect, then the demand curve will slope upward. To determine the actual shape of rats' demand curves, a second experiment was conducted. The price of one beverage was changed while holding constant income and the price of the other good. By repeating this experiment, researchers were able to plot a rat's demand curve. For every rat considered and every beverage, the quantity consumed was inversely related to price. As predicted by the law of demand, the demand curves were downward sloping.

[11]Rats are not the only animals used in such experiments. See, for example, Raymond Battalio, John Kagel, Howard Rachlin, and Leonard Green, "Commodity-Choice Behavior with Pigeons as Subjects," *Journal of Political Economy* (February 1981), pp. 67–91.

SOURCE: Adapted from John Kagel, Raymond Battalio, Howard Rachlin, and Leonard Green, "Demand Curves for Animal Consumers," *Quarterly Journal of Economics* (February 1981), pp. 1–15.

Summary

1. Total utility denotes a consumer's total level of satisfaction. Marginal utility refers to the change in total utility associated with a one-unit change in consumption.

2. According to the law of diminishing marginal utility, as consumption increases, marginal utility eventually declines. Because of the law of diminishing marginal utility, demand curves slope downward.

3. Consumer equilibrium occurs when the consumer spends the entire budget and the marginal utility per dollar is the same for each good consumed. At consumer equilibrium total utility is maximized.

4. Price depends on marginal utility of a good, not on total utility. This explains why many goods necessary for survival (including water) have lower prices than many nonessential

goods (such as diamonds). Although the total utility of water is high, its marginal utility is low.

5. A price change for a good triggers both substitution and income effects. According to the substitution effect, consumers want to buy more of a good when its relative price is reduced. A lower price also increases effective income. The change in quantity demanded due to this change in effective income is called the income effect.

6. For normal goods demand curves must be downward sloping. For inferior goods demand curves slope downward when the substitution effect outweighs the income effect. Available evidence indicates that for all known inferior goods the substitution effect is more powerful than the income effect. Therefore, demand curves evidently slope downward even for inferior goods.

7. Market demand is obtained by adding the demand of all individual consumers in the market. Market demand indicates the total quantity demanded by consumers at each price.

Key Terms

paradox of value (diamond–
   water paradox)
utility
total utility
marginal utility
law of diminishing marginal
   utility

consumer equilibrium
consumer surplus
income effect
substitution effect
market demand curve

Study Questions and Problems

1. According to a scientist at Cornell University, abundant energy reserves, in the form of methane gas, lie beneath the earth's crust. If the scientist is correct, how will extraction of these reserves affect total and marginal utilities of energy products (for example, heating and air conditioning)?

2. A market has three consumers: Rafael, Shawna, and Maurice. The following table presents their demand schedules. Based on these schedules, construct the market demand schedule.

PRICE	QUANTITY DEMANDED BY RAFAEL	QUANTITY DEMANDED BY SHAWNA	QUANTITY DEMANDED BY MAURICE
$4	1	0	1
3	2	1	3
2	3	2	5
1	4	3	7

3. Jennifer enjoys bowling and miniature golf. The extent of her enjoyment is revealed by the following utility schedules.

Compute Jennifer's marginal utility schedule for each activity.

GAMES OF BOWLING	TOTAL UTILITY	GAMES OF MINIATURE GOLF	TOTAL UTILITY
1	8	1	12
2	12	2	20
3	15	3	24
4	17	4	26

4. Refer to the utility schedules of question 3. (a) Assume initially that the price for both bowling and miniature golf is $2 per game. Given a budget of $6, how many games of each should Jennifer play? (b) Now suppose the price per game of bowling is $1, half the price of miniature golf. With a $6 budget, how many games of each would maximize Jennifer's utility? Justify your answers. (c) Based on the above information, plot Jennifer's demand for bowling.

5. (This problem is based on Exhibit 23.1.) (a) From your answer to question 4, compute Jennifer's consumer surplus from bowling when the price is $1 per game. (b) Which has a higher consumer surplus, water or diamonds? (c) How would the consumer surplus of water change if water were a free good?

6. Suppose the price of movie tickets rises. (a) According to the substitution effect, how are consumers likely to respond? (b) How will the income effect influence quantity demanded? On what does your answer depend?

YOUR TURN
Answers

(A) AN INCREASE IN THE QUANTITY OF DIAMONDS WOULD INCREASE THE TOTAL UTILITY OF DIAMONDS. (B) BECAUSE DIAMONDS WOULD BE LESS SCARCE, THE MARGINAL UTILITY OF AN ADDITIONAL DIAMOND WOULD BE LOWER. (C) ACCORDINGLY, THE PRICE CONSUMERS WOULD BE WILLING TO PAY WOULD ALSO FALL.

Indifference Curve Analysis

As noted in the foregoing chapter, marginal utility theory rests on the assumption that utility (or satisfaction) can be quantified. For example, in Table 23.2 it was assumed that one Coke provides 20 units of utility, two Cokes 32 units of utility. The theory developed in this appendix is based on a more realistic assumption—that an individual can indicate which of two bundles, if either, is preferred. The level of utility need not be quantified. Because this assumption is less restrictive, many prefer this theory to that of marginal utility. As was true for marginal utility theory, the theory presented can be used to indicate which combination of goods maximizes a consumer's utility and to explain why demand curves slope downward. We demonstrate both points immediately after introducing the key components of the theory—indifference curves and budget lines.

INDIFFERENCE CURVES

Consider two bundles of goods, A and B. Given your preferences, there are three distinct possibilities: bundle A is preferred, bundle B is preferred, or bundles A and B are valued equally (you are indifferent between the two bundles). An **indifference curve** consists of all combinations of goods that you value equally.

INDIFFERENCE CURVE
A curve depicting all combinations of two goods among which an individual is indifferent—that is, all combinations that have the same total utility.

As an example of an indifference curve, consider Figure 23A.1, which we will assume depicts your preferences toward pizza and ice cream. Each point on the indifference curve represents the same value or utility. Although bundle A contains more pizza, bundle B contains more ice cream. The extra ice cream in bundle B just compensates for the loss of three slices of pizza. In other words, four slices of pizza and two scoops of ice cream generate the same utility as seven slices of pizza and one scoop of ice cream.

CHARACTERISTICS OF INDIFFERENCE CURVES

DOWNWARD SLOPE As long as both goods generate utility, indifference curves must have a negative slope. An increase in the amount of one good must be offset by a decrease in the amount of the second good in order to keep the level of satisfaction the same. If you receive more pizza without forgoing any ice cream your utility increases, implying that you are no longer on the same indifference curve.

This indifference curve depicts all combinations of pizza and ice cream that have the same total utility.

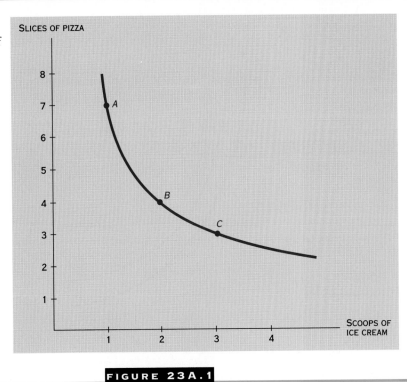

FIGURE 23A.1

CONVEX SHAPE The indifference curve in Figure 23A.1 is drawn with a *convex* shape, meaning that it bows toward the origin. In other words, the slope of the indifference curve becomes flatter as you move down the curve.[12] Your willingness to substitute pizza for ice cream depends on how much of each you currently have. Another scoop of ice cream has greater value the less ice cream you already have. Likewise, another piece of pizza has less value the more pizza you have. If you are at point *A* on the indifference curve, you are willing to trade three pieces of pizza for another scoop of ice cream. But if you are at point *B*, with less pizza and more ice cream, you are willing to give up only one piece of pizza for another scoop. It is because of this dimin-

ished willingness to part with pizza that the indifference curve is convex.

BIGGER BUNDLES MEAN MORE UTILITY Using a different combination of goods we can now trace a new indifference curve. Suppose you begin with five pieces of pizza and three scoops of ice cream, and list all other combinations that you consider equally attractive. All these points must lie on another indifference curve. This indifference curve (along with two others) appears in Figure 23A.2 (page 600). A graph containing multiple indifference curves is called an **indifference map**.

INDIFFERENCE MAP
A set of indifference curves.

Note that indifference curves with larger bundles of goods lie farther up and to the right than do indifference curves with smaller bundles. What does this say about the utility of the respective indifference curves? Assuming that you place a positive value on additional units of each good, bigger bundles of

---

[12]The slope of the indifference curve is called the *marginal rate of substitution* because it indicates the rate at which the consumer is willing to substitute one good (in this case, pizza) for the other (ice cream). The fact that the indifference curve becomes flatter as you move down the curve implies that there is a diminishing marginal rate of substitution between the two goods.

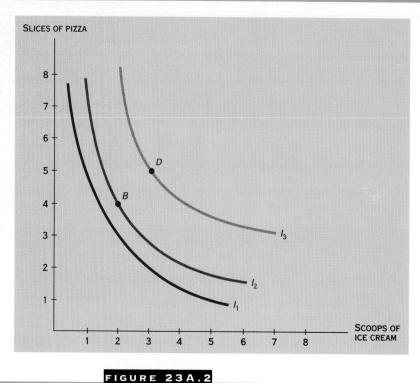

An indifference map is a set of indifference curves.

FIGURE 23A.2

goods generate higher levels of utility. Five pieces of pizza and three scoops of ice cream (point D on indifference curve I_3) provide more satisfaction than four pieces of pizza and two scoops of ice cream (point B on indifference curve I_2). This implies that points on indifference curve I_3 are associated with higher utility than points on I_2. More generally, movements to the northeast on the indifference map correspond to increases in utility.

INDIFFERENCE CURVES DO NOT INTERSECT
Assuming that more of a good is preferred to less, indifference curves cannot cross. Thus, the situation portrayed in Figure 23A.3 cannot exist. According to this figure, the consumer is indifferent to points A and B (because they lie on the same indifference curve) and also indifferent to points A and C. It therefore follows that the consumer must be indifferent to points B and C. But this cannot be. Point B is associated with the same amount of ice cream and more pizza. Therefore, point B is preferred to point C. Allowing indifference curves to intersect violates

the assumption that the consumer wants more of each good.

THE BUDGET LINE

In the quest for higher utility, the consumer faces a constraint—a limited budget or income. The consumer does not have sufficient funds to purchase all combinations of the two goods. The limits imposed by the budget are revealed through the consumer's **budget line**. A budget line incorporates information on both the available funds to spend and the price of each good. We illustrate this by continuing our example.

BUDGET LINE
A line indicating all combinations of two goods that can be purchased with an income, given the price of each good.

Suppose you have $4 to spend on pizza and ice cream. Further suppose that you must pay $.50 for

Indifference curves cannot intersect; that would violate the assumption that the consumer wants more of each good. The curves portrayed here indicate that the consumer is indifferent to points *A* and *B* and also indifferent to points *A* and *C*. This implies that the consumer is indifferent to points *B* and *C*—which is impossible. Because point *B* corresponds to more pizza than point *C* and the same amount of ice cream, *B* is preferred.

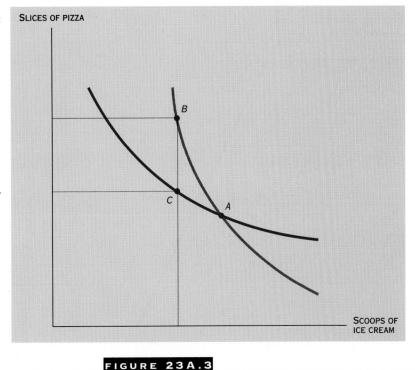

SLICES OF PIZZA

SCOOPS OF ICE CREAM

FIGURE 23A.3

each slice of pizza and $1.00 for each scoop of ice cream. Figure 23A.4 (page 602) illustrates your budget line. If you devote your entire budget to pizza, you can purchase eight pieces (point *X*). At the other extreme, by forgoing pizza entirely, you can purchase four scoops of ice cream (point *Y*). Alternatively, you could purchase various combinations of both pizza and ice cream. For example, if you buy four slices of pizza, you still have enough income to buy two scoops of ice cream (point *Z*).

Because a budget line is derived from a given income and given prices, any change in income or prices leads to a new budget line. For example, a reduction in the price of ice cream increases the amount of ice cream that can be bought with a given income.

CONSUMER EQUILIBRIUM

Bringing together the indifference map and the budget line, we have yet another example of scarcity and

choice. In this case the issue is: Given a limited income, what combination of goods should you buy to maximize total utility? This can be visualized in terms of Figure 23A.5 (page 602), which plots Figures 23A.2 and 23A.4 on the same graph.

As noted earlier, higher indifference curves correspond to higher levels of utility. As such, you prefer points on I_3 to points on I_2, which in turn are preferred to points on I_1. Unfortunately, every combination of goods shown on I_3 costs more than $4; therefore, they are unattainable. Only points on or below the budget line satisfy the requirement that you spend no more than $4.

Given this budget constraint, utility is maximized at point *B*, where indifference curve I_2 is tangent to (just touches) the budget line. Any other combination of goods that satisfies the budget constraint (for example, point *E*) lies on a lower indifference curve, indicating a lower level of utility. Therefore, **consumer equilibrium** occurs at point *B*. To maximize your utility, you should buy four slices of pizza and two scoops of ice cream.

The budget line runs from point X to point Y. It indicates which combinations of pizza and ice cream can be purchased with a given income—in this case $4.

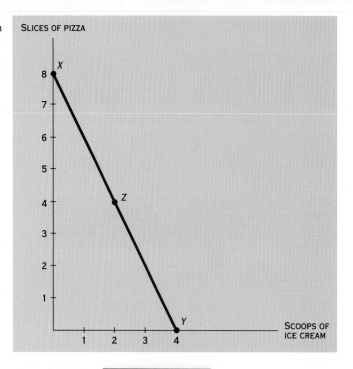

FIGURE 23A.4

Consumer equilibrium occurs at point B, where the indifference curve I_2 is tangent to the budget line. Although point D would yield higher utility, it lies beyond the budget line. Point E satisfies the budget constraint but is on a lower indifference curve than I_2, and therefore yields less utility than point B.

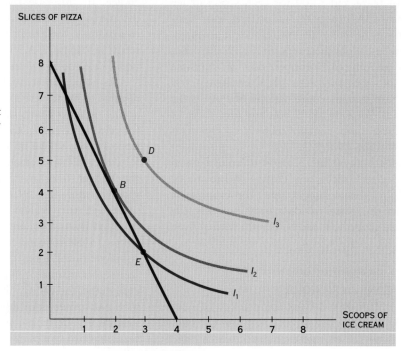

FIGURE 23A.5

YOUR TURN

(A) ASSUME YOU HAVE $4 IN INCOME. IF PIZZA IS PRICED AT $.50 PER SLICE AND ICE CREAM AT $.50 PER SCOOP, DRAW YOUR BUDGET LINE. TO YOUR DIAGRAM ADD THE BUDGET LINE OF FIGURE 23A.4. WHAT CAN YOU CONCLUDE ABOUT THE EFFECT OF A PRICE REDUCTION ON THE BUDGET LINE, OTHER THINGS EQUAL? HOW WOULD A PRICE INCREASE AFFECT THE BUDGET LINE? (B) ASSUME PIZZA IS PRICED AT $.50 PER SLICE AND ICE CREAM AT $1.00 PER SCOOP. WHAT WILL THE BUDGET LINE LOOK LIKE IF YOUR INCOME IS $3? NOW DRAW BUDGET LINES ASSOCIATED WITH INCOMES OF $4 AND $5. WHAT CAN YOU CONCLUDE ABOUT THE EFFECT OF A HIGHER INCOME, ASSUMING THAT PRICES DO NOT CHANGE?

CONSUMER EQUILIBRIUM

A situation in which the consumer obtains the maximum total utility consistent with the consumer's budget; occurs where the consumer's indifference curve is tangent to the budget line.

DERIVING DEMAND FROM INDIFFERENCE CURVES

Indifference curve analysis can also be used to derive a consumer's demand curve. To illustrate, consider

the effect of changing the price of ice cream. Assuming income and the price of pizza remain unchanged, how will a change in the price of ice cream alter consumer equilibrium? Answer this question and you have your demand curve for ice cream.

Assume the price of ice cream falls to $.50 per scoop. This rotates the budget line—as Figure 23A.6 illustrates—so that consumer equilibrium no longer occurs at point B. Given the lower price of ice cream, it is now possible to reach a higher indifference curve, I_3. In particular, the new consumer equilibrium occurs at point D, where I_3 is tangent to the new

---

THE EFFECT OF A CHANGE IN PRICE

When the price of ice cream falls, the budget constraint rotates outward—enabling you to reach a higher indifference curve. Point D represents the new consumer equilibrium.

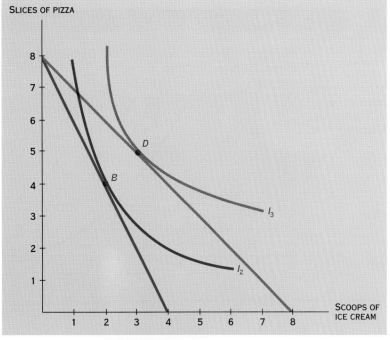

FIGURE 23A.6

budget line. You now maximize utility by buying five slices of pizza and three scoops of ice cream.

This experiment provides us with a second point on your demand curve (Figure 23A.7). When ice cream is $1.00 a scoop you demand two scoops. But at a price of $.50 you demand three scoops. Your demand curve slopes downward. By repeating this experiment (using other budget lines and other indifference curves from your indifference map), you can obtain other points on your demand curve.

Summary

1. Indifference curve analysis can be used in place of marginal utility theory. Both indicate the combination of goods that maximizes a consumer's utility, and both can be used to derive demand curves. An advantage of indifference curve analysis is that it is applicable even when utility cannot be measured.

2. An indifference curve comprises all combinations of two goods among which an individual is indifferent. Assuming that the consumer wants more of each good, indifference curves slope downward and are convex, becoming flatter as you move down the curve. Higher indifference curves mean a higher utility level. Indifference curves do not intersect.

3. A budget line consists of all combinations of the two goods that can be purchased with a specified income. The budget line is determined by the level of income and the prices of the two goods.

4. Consumer equilibrium occurs where the budget line is tangent to an indifference curve. It indicates the combination of goods that maximizes utility subject to the budget constraint. Any other combination of goods satisfying the budget constraint provides less utility; any combination providing more utility violates the budget constraint.

5. A consumer's demand curve can be obtained by varying the price of the good while holding constant income and the price of the other good. A change in the price leads to a new budget line and therefore to a new consumer equilibrium. By finding the quantity demanded at each price, we can construct the consumer's demand curve.

Key Terms

indifference curve   budget line
indifference map   consumer equilibrium

THE DEMAND CURVE FOR ICE CREAM

As the price of ice cream falls from $1.00 per scoop to $.50, the quantity of ice cream demanded rises from two scoops to three scoops. (The numbers are from Figure 23A.6.)

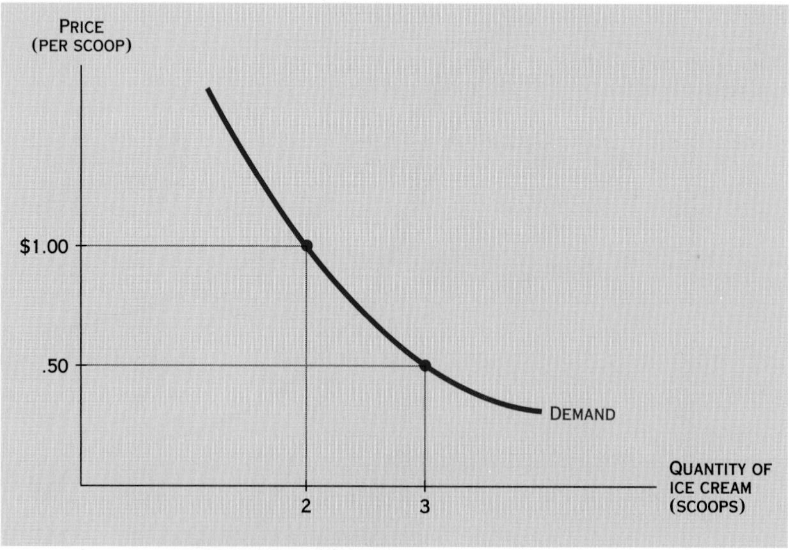

FIGURE 23A.7

1. You have $100 to spend on movies and compact discs. Movies are priced at $5, compact discs at $20.
   (a) Draw your budget line, labeling the axes of your diagram.

(b) The price of compact discs falls to $10. On the same diagram draw your new budget line. Be sure to indicate which is the new budget line.
(c) Not only does the price of compact discs fall to $10, but the price of movies is reduced to $2.50. Draw and label this third budget line.

2. In Figure 23A.6 a lower price for ice cream led to an increase in the desired quantity of *pizza*. Why would you buy more pizza when its price was not reduced?

YOUR TURN
Answers

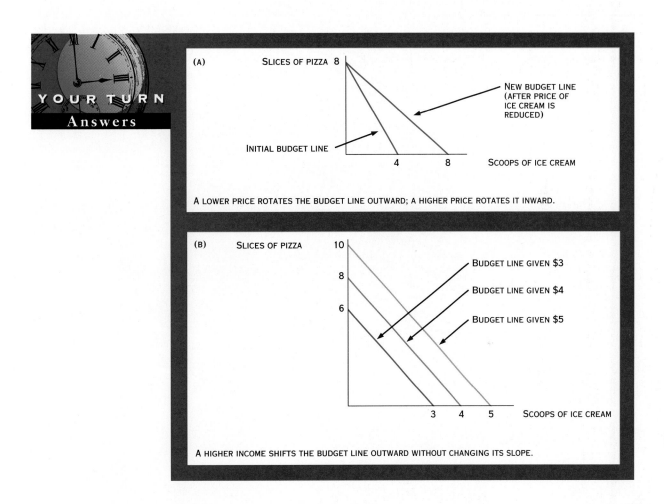

(A)

SLICES OF PIZZA 8

NEW BUDGET LINE (AFTER PRICE OF ICE CREAM IS REDUCED)

INITIAL BUDGET LINE

4   8   SCOOPS OF ICE CREAM

A LOWER PRICE ROTATES THE BUDGET LINE OUTWARD; A HIGHER PRICE ROTATES IT INWARD.

(B)

SLICES OF PIZZA   10

8

6

BUDGET LINE GIVEN $3

BUDGET LINE GIVEN $4

BUDGET LINE GIVEN $5

3   4   5   SCOOPS OF ICE CREAM

A HIGHER INCOME SHIFTS THE BUDGET LINE OUTWARD WITHOUT CHANGING ITS SLOPE.

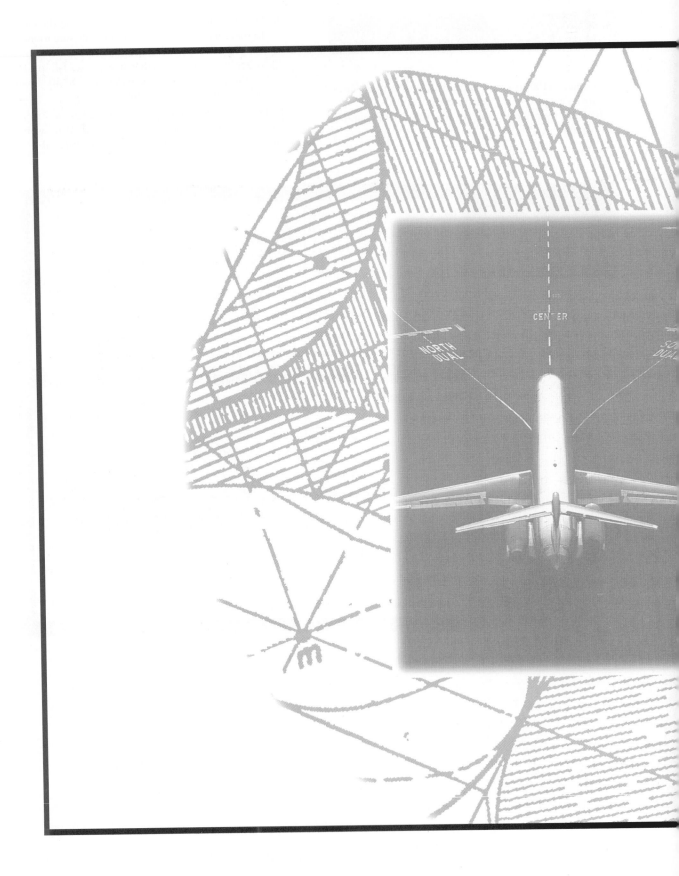

Costs and Production

KEVIN OLSON, THE OWNER OF A WISCONSIN DAIRY FARM, AND IBM ARE BOTH IN BUSINESS TO MAKE MONEY. THE GIANT COMPUTER MAKER HAS BEEN MORE SUCCESSFUL IN RECENT YEARS, WITH ANNUAL PROFITS RUNNING IN THE BILLIONS OF DOLLARS.[2] KEVIN HAS NEVER EARNED MORE THAN $30,000 FROM HIS DAIRY OPERATIONS, AND LAST YEAR HE LOST MONEY. STILL, THERE ARE SIMILARITIES BETWEEN KEVIN'S COMPANY AND IBM. BOTH MAKE PRODUCTION DECISIONS, BOTH ARE CONCERNED ABOUT COSTS, AND BOTH ARE WEIGHING THE CONSEQUENCES OF EXPANDING OPERATIONS.

CHAPTER 24 STUDIES THESE KINDS OF GENERAL BUSINESS DECISIONS AND CONCERNS. AS SUCH IT FOCUSES ON THE PRODUCTION SIDE OF THE MARKET, UNLIKE CHAPTER 23, WHICH DEALT WITH THE BUYING SIDE. OBVIOUSLY, CONSUMERS ARE IMPORTANT. IBM WOULD NOT PRODUCE COMPUTERS AND OLSON WOULD NOT PRODUCE DAIRY PRODUCTS UNLESS THERE WAS SUFFICIENT DEMAND FOR THEIR PRODUCTS. IN SUBSEQUENT CHAPTERS DEMAND REEMERGES AS A MAJOR FORCE, INFLUENCING PRICE, PRODUCTION, AND PROFITS. BUT FIRST A DETAILED UNDERSTANDING OF PRODUCTION IS ESSENTIAL.

[2]According to accountants, IBM has averaged almost $5 billion per year in profits over the past ten years, despite a bad year in 1992.

> We are not interested in size for size's sake. What is important is the size of the profits.[1]

[1]Frank Lorenzo, chairman of Texas Air, commenting on his company's acquisition of Eastern Airlines and People Express; *The New York Times*, September 21, 1986, p. 20F.

MAXIMIZING PROFITS

To understand and predict the production decisions of a firm, we first must agree on what motivates the firm. What is the target a business aims at when making decisions? We assume that the goal of business firms, from Olson's dairy to IBM, is to maximize profits.

Admittedly, there are exceptions to this rule. The owner of a company may hire her incompetent son as vice president, knowing that profits will suffer as a consequence. Because of prejudice, white workers may be hired even though more-qualified blacks are available at the same wage rate. In such cases the owner sacrifices profits for other considerations.

Why then do we assume profit-maximizing behavior? First of all, for most firms this is a reasonable assumption. Companies are in business primarily to make money, and generally they pursue policies designed to make as much as possible. Second, profit maximization is a simple assumption on which powerful models can be built. More complex behavior could be assumed, but that would lead to more complicated, less manageable models. Models are judged primarily in terms of how well they explain and predict. On that score, models based on the profit-maximization assumption perform well. They do a good job of explaining business behavior; their hypotheses generally are supported by available evidence. In essence, the assumption of profit maximization simplifies without detracting from models' ability to explain economic decisions and relationships.

Profit for a firm is defined as follows:

$$\text{profit} = \text{total revenue} - \text{total cost}$$

Profit may be either positive or negative. A positive profit indicates that the total revenue accruing to the firm from production exceeds the total cost of production. A negative profit, known as a *loss*, occurs when revenues fall short of production costs. If total revenue and total cost are equal, profit is zero.

Measuring revenue is usually straightforward. Total revenue is simply the average price per unit times the number of units sold:

$$\text{total revenue} = \text{price} \times \text{quantity}$$

To measure total cost requires an added step: we must first determine what constitute costs of production.

ECONOMIC COSTS AND ECONOMIC PROFIT

EXPLICIT COSTS
Direct payments made to others for the resources they own.

Economists define the total cost of production as the sum of explicit and implicit costs. **Explicit costs** arise when a firm makes payments to others. Examples are the wages paid to workers, the cost of electricity purchased from a utility, and the rental charges on equipment leased from an office supply store. The firm receives

IMPLICIT COSTS
The opportunity costs of using resources already owned by the firm.

ECONOMIC PROFIT
Total revenue minus the total cost of production (implicit as well as explicit).

resources from others and, in return, makes a direct or explicit payment for those resources. **Implicit costs** are the opportunity costs of using resources the firm already owns. Even though no payment is made to others, there is a cost to using your own resources: you sacrifice the income that could have been earned from alternative uses of these resources.

Economic profit is the difference between total revenue and total cost, as defined by economists. It is obtained by subtracting all costs, explicit and implicit, from a company's total revenue.

To illustrate the concept of economic profit, and the importance of implicit costs, consider the dairy barn that Kevin Olson could rent to others for $10,000 per year. If he decides instead to use the barn himself, he must forgo that $10,000. Although no money actually changes hands, using his own barn implicitly costs Olson $10,000. (If you like, think of Olson as renting the building to himself.) Suppose Olson uses this building to generate $100,000 in total revenue. In addition to the implicit rent, he incurs $90,000 in explicit costs. Has Olson earned any economic profit from his dairy operations? Clearly not. Once implicit costs are included, total cost equals total revenue (see Table 24.1a). Even though total revenue exceeds payments to others, Olson is no better off producing than had he decided not to produce and, instead, rented the barn to someone else. Production has added nothing to profit.

As important as implicit rents are to Olson, other implicit costs are just as relevant to other producers, including salaries forgone by the owner and depreciation of company equipment. Consider Sam, the owner/manager of a local grocery store. Because he owns the business, Sam decided not to pay himself a salary, despite the fact that he could earn $30,000 per year at Winn-Dixie. Last year the store generated $150,000 in total revenue and $125,000 in explicit costs. Sam claims that his store earned $25,000 in profits. Do you agree?

The $25,000 figure is inflated because Sam has ignored the implicit cost of managing his store. By working for himself, Sam sacrificed the $30,000 he could have earned elsewhere. Rather than working for free, Sam has an imputed salary of $30,000. Once we add this to the explicit costs of operating the store, we see that the total cost amounted to $155,000. The store actually lost $5,000 (see Table 24.1b). Financially, Sam would have been better off working for Winn-Dixie.

TWO EXAMPLES OF ECONOMIC PROFIT		
(a) Olson's Dairy Farm		
Total revenue		$100,000
Total cost		100,000
Explicit (payments to others)	$90,000	
Implicit (rent on barn)	10,000	
Profit (total revenue – total cost)		$0
(b) Sam's Grocery Store		
Total revenue		$150,000
Total cost		155,000
Explicit	$125,000	
Implicit (forgone salary)	30,000	
Profit		*–$5,000*

TABLE 24.1

Depreciation refers to the decline in an asset's value due to wear and tear or to obsolescence. Suppose a company owns a machine whose market value at the start of the year is $1,000. After the firm operates the machine for a year, its value falls to $700. The machine has depreciated by $300. This is the cost of using the machine, even though the company already owns it.

To compute economic profit it is necessary to consider all costs of production, implicit as well as explicit. Not only must we count direct payments made to others, we must also include implicit rent, imputed salary, depreciation, and any other costs of using a firm's own resources.

ECONOMIC VERSUS ACCOUNTING PROFITS

Accountants have their own definition of profit. Whereas the economist includes all costs of production, both explicit and implicit, the accountant either ignores implicit costs or measures them differently. For example, an accountant does not include Sam's forgone salary of $30,000 as a cost. Because no money was ever paid, the value of Sam's services does not appear in the accountant's ledger. As a result, **accounting profit** differs from economic profit.

ACCOUNTING PROFIT
Total revenue minus accounting costs. (Because accountants and economists measure costs differently, accounting profit differs from economic profit.)

Depreciation is another area of disagreement. Accountants use generally accepted accounting practices to compute depreciation. One such practice is *straight-line depreciation*, which assumes that an asset declines in value by a constant amount each year. Suppose a machine is purchased for $1,000, lasts five years, and has no scrap value at the end of the period. Then straight-line depreciation is $1,000/5 or $200 per year. In contrast, the economist emphasizes the change in market value. If the machine has a market value of $700 after one year, the economist measures depreciation in the first year as $1,000 − $700 = $300.

That accountants treat implicit costs differently than economists is no indictment of the accounting profession. It merely underscores the fact that economic profits and accounting profits are different concepts with different roles to play. The accountant is concerned with keeping an accurate record of transactions to satisfy the demands of investors and to comply with government regulations, including the payment of taxes. Such records are also used to spot embezzlement and other misappropriations.

Accounting costs are often less subjective and easier to measure than economic costs. Take depreciation. The accountant merely plugs information on historical costs and asset life into a formula. The economist must estimate the market value of a machine after it has been in use, which is not always an easy task.

Despite such problems, economic profit remains the appropriate concept for measuring the economic success of a firm. To the extent that accounting profit ignores implicit costs, it may overstate true profitability—recall Sam the grocer. Economic profit tells the owners of a firm whether they could benefit from reallocating their resources—working for others or renting out the company's property. A negative economic profit (economic loss) indicates that a firm is not earning enough to cover its opportunity costs; the firm's resources would receive a higher return if employed elsewhere. Unless conditions are expected to improve sufficiently, the owners would be better off discontinuing production and selling assets or reemploying them in alternative, more profitable lines of business.

In contrast, a positive or **pure economic profit** is a sign of success. It tells the firm not to take its resources out of the industry. Even a zero economic profit—what economists call **normal profit**—is acceptable, being just enough to keep the firm in business. It signifies that the firm could not benefit from reallocating resources. Total revenue is high enough to reimburse the owners for all explicit costs and to compensate them fully for use of their own resources. Although a pure economic profit obviously is preferred, a firm earning a zero economic profit has no incentive to discontinue production. Because production decisions are based on economic profit rather than accounting profit, unless otherwise stated "profit" in this book means economic profit.

- When total revenue exceeds total cost (explicit plus implicit), a firm is said to earn pure economic profit.
- When total revenue equals total cost, a firm is earning a normal profit.
- When total revenue is less than total cost, a firm is suffering an economic loss.

THE ALLOCATIVE FUNCTION OF PROFITS

Why did the U.S. oil industry grow so rapidly in the 1970s? Why did the automotive industry expand early this century while the horse and buggy industry contracted? Why have so many farmers left agriculture? The answers lie in the high economic profits of the former industries (oil and automobiles) and the losses of the latter industries.

In addition to measuring the economic success of an individual firm, economic profits allocate resources throughout the economy. Resources flow out of sectors suffering losses and into sectors earning profits. If firms in an industry are losing money, this is a signal that the resources owned by these firms are not employed in the activity where they are valued most highly. The fact that returns to these resources fall shy of their opportunity costs indicates that higher returns are available in other industries. To take advantage of these higher returns, owners pull their resources out of the unprofitable industry. As a consequence, production in the industry shrinks. Some firms scale back operations; others leave the industry altogether.

In contrast, pure economic profits pull resources into an industry. With the added resources, output expands as new firms enter the industry and existing firms increase production. Only when firms in an industry are earning normal or zero economic profits is there no incentive to reallocate resources. With normal profits there is no reason for additional resources to flow into the industry nor for existing resources to leave.

Two Time Periods: the Short Run and the Long Run

Business has been so poor lately that Sam contemplates leaving the grocery business. In the meantime he faces a more pressing issue: Should he lay off some of his employees? Down the road, the owners of Stephensons' Orchards are weighing whether to apply more fertilizer and fungicides to the trees this year and whether to plant additional orchards (even though the trees would not bear fruit for at least several years). The Hues Paint Company is deciding how many workers to hire this month and whether building a larger factory makes economic sense.

Decisions, decisions. Businesses make them every day. Some pertain to current operations—the volume of grocery business this period, the number of apples grown, the quantity of paint produced. Other decisions center on the future ability of a company to produce. Should the company remain in business and, if so, what scale of operations is most appropriate?

Based on the time dimension, economists partition business decisions into two categories: the short run and the long run. The distinction is based on the ability to vary quantities of *inputs*—the resources used in production. The **short run** is defined as a period of time so short that the quantities of some inputs cannot be changed (for example, the size of a building or the number of fruit-bearing trees). In the **long run**, in contrast, a firm has sufficient time to vary the quantities of all inputs. New factories can be built, new orchards can be planted, stores can change size or even go out of business. Because the time needed to change all inputs varies from industry to industry, what constitutes the long run also varies. It takes years before utilities can build new power plants, but neighborhood lemonade stands may be able to increase all inputs within hours.

In the following sections we examine the firm's operations, first in the short run and then in the long run. To keep matters simple, we assume the firm uses only two inputs in production—capital and labor.[3] The amount of capital is assumed to be fixed in the short run—only labor can be varied. In the long run, however, the amounts of both inputs can be changed.

SHORT RUN
A period of time so short that the quantities of some inputs cannot be changed.

LONG RUN
A period of time long enough to change the quantities of all inputs.

Production in the Short Run

THE PRODUCTION FUNCTION

With additional quantities of inputs, the firm can alter the level of output or *total product* it produces. The technical relationship between the amount of inputs a firm uses and the maximum producible output is known as the firm's **production function**

A production function is simply a device for converting information about input usage into information about potential output. You might think of it as a computer that has been programmed by a production engineer. You ask the computer to determine the maximum output that can be produced with a given quantity of inputs, and the computer flashes the answer on the screen. An assumption underlying production functions is that the level of technology is fixed. If technological advances make it possible to squeeze more output from a given quantity of inputs, the result is a new production function—the computer must be reprogrammed.

PRODUCTION FUNCTION
A relationship indicating the maximum amount of output that can be produced per period with various quantities of inputs and a given technology.

---

[3]The case where a firm uses more than two inputs is examined in Chapter 31.

THE SHORT-RUN PRODUCTION FUNCTION OF THE HUES PAINT COMPANY			
(A) LABOR	(B) TOTAL PRODUCT*	(C) MARGINAL PRODUCT*	(D) AVERAGE PRODUCT*
0	0		
1	100	100	100
2	220	120	110
3	330	110	110
4	420	90	105
5	480	60	96
6	510	30	85

*Gallons per week.
The production function shows the relationship between units of labor and total product. Based on the production function, marginal product and average product can be calculated.

TABLE 24.2

A short-run production function for the Hues Paint Company is presented in Table 24.2 (A) and (B). In the short run, labor is the only variable input. Therefore, the short-run production function is simply the relationship between labor and total product, given a fixed amount of capital.

AVERAGE PRODUCT AND MARGINAL PRODUCT

AVERAGE PRODUCT OF LABOR
Total product divided by the quantity of labor, holding capital constant.

MARGINAL PRODUCT OF LABOR
The increase in output associated with a one-unit increase in labor, holding capital constant.

At the Hues Paint Company labor is essential for production; without labor paint cannot be produced. With a single worker, 100 gallons can be produced per week. With two workers, output rises to 220 gallons per week. Thus with two workers average **product of labor**, the average output per worker, is 220/2 = 110 gallons.

Another concept, even more important than average product, is the **marginal product of labor**. Defined as the change in total product divided by the change in labor, marginal product measures the increase in output attributable to the hiring of an additional unit of labor. When the firm increases labor from one worker to two, total product rises from 100 to 220 gallons, an increase of 120. Therefore, marginal product of the second worker is 120 gallons. For each worker Table 24.2 reveals total product, marginal product, and average product. Total product and marginal product are also graphed in Figure 24.1 (page 614).

THE LAW OF DIMINISHING RETURNS

How does marginal product change as the amount of labor increases? According to the **law of diminishing returns**, marginal product of labor ultimately declines. Eventually, each extra unit of labor increases total product by less than the preceding unit. Formally, the law of diminishing returns can be stated as follows:

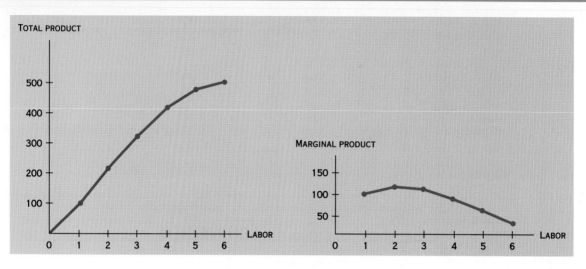

*The figures are taken from Table 24.2.

FIGURE 24.1

When at least one input is fixed, increases in the variable input beyond some point lead to increasingly smaller additions to output.

Note that the law of diminishing returns assumes that some input is fixed. In our discussion we are assuming that the amount of capital cannot be changed. Accordingly, the law of diminishing returns is a short-run proposition; it does not apply to the long run.

The notion of diminishing returns is intuitive. Assume you have a fixed plant size and a fixed number of machines. If you keep adding workers, the number of machines per worker declines. Workers must share machines to a greater extent and eventually may have to wait for an available machine. In addition, because the most important jobs are completed first, as more and more workers are hired they are assigned to less-important work. In this environment, employing additional labor increases output by relatively smaller and smaller amounts. Marginal product declines. Eventually, marginal product may even turn negative. (At some point, given the fixed plant size, workers start to get in each other's way.)

Or consider the case of agriculture, where land can be considered fixed. Does output double every time a farmer doubles the labor input? Certainly not. When labor doubles, the amount of land per worker is cut in half. Ultimately, working on smaller plots of land takes its toll. At some stage total product increases more slowly than labor. The same reasoning applies to other variable inputs. Farmers can increase their crop yields through irrigation, but as additional water is applied, the gains from further application of water decline (see Exhibit 24.1).

The law of diminishing returns does not rule out the possibility that marginal product may initially rise before turning downward. In fact, this is what occurs in

T hose who have witnessed parched fields realize the importance of water to farming. Even today states battle over water rights. But precisely how do yields respond to applications of water? How much additional corn (or wheat or cotton) can a farmer anticipate from additional irrigation? This is an issue of no small importance to farmers.

To learn the answer, economists, working with agronomists, have estimated agricultural production functions. Because weather conditions vary across and even within states, separate production functions must be estimated for different regions. The following is a segment of a production function for Colby, Kansas, based on data for 1971. It shows the relationship between irrigation water, measured in inches per acre, and corn yield, measured in pounds per acre.[4]

As these figures indicate, water greatly affects corn yields. An irrigation of 23 inches of water maximizes the yield per acre. Until that point is reached, additional water increases the output of corn. Notice that over this range each additional inch of water has a smaller impact than prior doses. In other words, water is important, but there are diminishing returns to irrigation.

[4]The yield per acre also depends on the amount of fertilizer. The production function presented here is based on an application of 180 pounds of nitrogen per acre.

SOURCE: Adapted from Roger W. Hexem and Earl O. Heady, *Water Production Functions for Irrigated Agriculture* (Ames, Iowa: Iowa State University Press, 1978), p. 79, equation 6.1.

EXHIBIT 24.1

INCHES OF WATER	POUNDS OF CORN	MARGINAL PRODUCT OF WATER
6	5,746	
7	6,107	361
8	6,445	338
9	6,761	316
10	7,055	294
.	.	.
.	.	.
.	.	.
23	8,871	7
24	8,856	-15

Table 24.2. Marginal product of the second worker exceeds that of the first worker. Diminishing returns do not set in until three workers are employed.

Why the delay? Why doesn't marginal product decline at the outset? Some machines or operations run more smoothly with two workers than with one. Consider a large factory with a single worker. That worker must run back and forth across the floor to operate all machines and perform all jobs. The factory was not designed for such an arrangement. With one worker, labor is *spread too thin*. When a second worker is added, output more than doubles. The additional worker permits division of labor, with each worker specializing in certain tasks (see Exhibit 24.2). The workers can devote a larger share of their time to production and waste less time moving from one job to another.

Marginal product may continue to increase for a while but ultimately, as more and more labor pours into the factory, the gains from further division of labor evaporate. The plant becomes crowded, the amount of equipment per worker shrinks, and as a consequence marginal product falls. The law of diminishing returns does not predict exactly when marginal product will peak, only that marginal product will turn lower at some point and thereafter continue its descent.

Costs in the Short Run

FIXED COSTS AND VARIABLE COSTS

Higher levels of output require greater amounts of inputs. Therefore, as production expands, total costs increase. In the short run these costs can be divided into two categories—fixed costs and variable costs.

FIXED COSTS
Costs that are independent of the level of production.

Fixed costs do not fluctuate with the level of output. They reflect payments to fixed inputs and must be paid regardless of how much, if anything, is produced. Property taxes and fire insurance are examples. So is the salary of a security guard hired to keep people out of a building at night. If the company president draws a fixed salary, independent of the company's operations, this too is a fixed cost.

VARIABLE COSTS
Costs that increase as the level of production rises.

Variable costs depend on the level of production. If production is to increase, companies must use additional variable inputs—for example, additional electricity, raw materials, and hourly production workers. Therefore, spending on variable inputs must rise.[5]

The **total cost** of production is the sum of total fixed cost plus total variable cost:

$$\text{total cost} = \text{total fixed cost} + \text{total variable cost}$$
$$(\text{TC} = \text{TFC} + \text{TVC})$$

Figure 24.2 illustrates the relationship among these three terms. Because total variable cost depends on the level of production, so does total cost.

PER-UNIT COSTS

Costs of production can alternatively be presented on an average or per-unit basis. Because most of the analysis in subsequent chapters relies on an understanding of unit costs, it is necessary to introduce the following terms.

---

[5]We assume that the firm faces a fixed price for each input. The possibility that an input price depends on the quantity of inputs used is explored in Chapter 31.

Adam Smith on the Division of Labor

Adam Smith considered the division of labor so important that this was the first topic addressed in *The Wealth of Nations*. In a classic passage, Smith recounts the manufacture of pins in eighteenth-century England:

> One man draws out the wire, another straights it, a third cuts it, a fourth points it, a fifth grinds it at the top for receiving the head; to make the head requires two or three distinct operations; to put it on, is a peculiar business, to whiten the pins is another; it is even a trade by itself to put them into the paper; and the important business of making a pin is, in this manner, divided into about eighteen distinct operations, which, in some manufactories, are all performed by

distinct hands, though in others the same man will sometimes perform two or three of them.

According to Smith, one pin factory employing ten workers in distinct jobs produced 48,000 pins per day, an average of 4,800 pins per worker. In contrast, Smith claims that a single worker forced to perform each and every task in that factory could produce no more than 20 pins per day. Because of increased specialization of labor, an increase in the number of workers initially leads to a more than commensurate increase in output.

SOURCE: Adam Smith, *The Wealth of Nations*. New York: Random House, 1937 (originally published in 1776), pp. 3–5.

E X H I B I T

24 . 2

THE TOTAL COST OF PRODUCTION

At each level of output (such as q_1), total cost is the sum of total variable cost and total fixed cost.

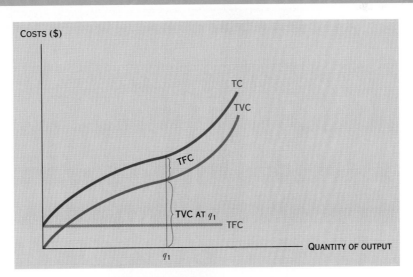

FIGURE 24.2

Average fixed cost is total fixed cost divided by the quantity of output produced:

$$AFC = \frac{TFC}{q}$$

Average variable cost is total variable cost divided by the quantity of output:

$$AVC = \frac{TVC}{q}$$

Average total cost is total cost divided by the quantity of output:

$$ATC = \frac{TC}{q}$$

Equivalently, average total cost can be rewritten as $ATC = AFC + AVC$.

MARGINAL COST

Our analysis requires one final measure of cost, in many ways the most important.

Marginal cost is the change in total cost divided by the change in output:

$$MC = \frac{\Delta TC}{\Delta q}$$

Marginal cost is generally computed by considering a one-unit change in output ($\Delta q = 1$). That is, *marginal cost measures the increase in total cost associated with the production of an additional unit of output.* Because only variable costs change with output (remember, fixed costs are fixed), marginal cost can be expressed alternatively as the change in total variable cost divided by the change in output:

$$MC = \frac{\Delta TVC}{\Delta q}$$

COST SCHEDULES FOR A HYPOTHETICAL FIRM

q	TFC	TVC	TC	AFC*	AVC*	ATC*	MC
0	$120	$ 0	$120				
1	120	50	170	$120	$50	$170	$ 50
2	120	84	204	60	42	102	34
3	120	108	228	40	36	76	24
4	120	127	247	30	32	62	19
5	120	150	270	24	30	54	23
6	120	180	300	20	30	50	30
7	120	218	338	17	31	48	38
8	120	266	386	15	33	48	48
9	120	325	445	13	36	49	59
10	120	400	520	12	40	52	75
11	120	495	615	11	45	56	95
12	120	612	732	10	51	61	117

*Amounts are rounded to the nearest dollar.

TABLE 24.3

TYING COSTS TOGETHER

Table 24.3 presents the cost schedules for a hypothetical firm. Note that average fixed cost declines as the quantity of output increases. This reflects the fact that total fixed cost does not vary with output. Thus, for the firm in question, average fixed cost can be expressed as: AFC = $120/q$. As total fixed cost is *spread* over a larger quantity of output, the fixed cost per unit declines.

In contrast, Table 24.3 reveals that average variable cost, average total cost, and marginal cost initially decline but then turn higher. This reflects the fact that marginal productivity of labor initially rises and then, when diminishing returns set in, marginal product falls. Productivity and costs are inversely related, as Figure 24.3

MARGINAL COST IS INVERSELY RELATED TO THE MARGINAL PRODUCT OF LABOR

Until E^* employees are hired, the marginal product of labor is rising. This means that additional workers are adding more to output than are previously hired workers, which causes the marginal cost of output to fall. When the marginal product reaches a maximum (at E^*), marginal cost is at a minimum (at q^*). Beyond E^*, diminishing returns set in. As the marginal product of labor falls, increasing quantities of labor are required to produce each additional unit of output, which means that marginal cost must be rising.

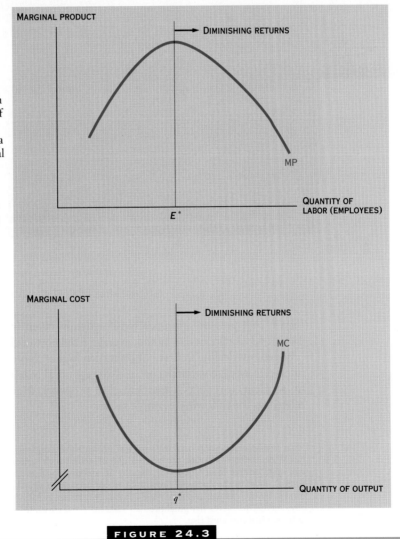

FIGURE 24.3

illustrates. *Whenever marginal product of labor rises, the marginal cost of output falls. Whenever marginal product falls, marginal cost rises.*

To understand why this is so, consider what happens when the marginal product of labor is rising. When this occurs, output is increasing more rapidly than labor. As output per worker expands, the amount of labor required to produce an additional unit of output falls. Therefore, the cost of producing an additional unit of output (marginal cost) must also fall.

On the other hand, falling marginal productivity implies that each additional unit of labor is adding less to output than previous units. Because the contributions of additional labor are becoming smaller and smaller, the firm requires an ever-increasing amount of labor to produce a given increase in output. These growing labor requirements mean that the marginal cost of output is rising. For example, when the marginal product of labor is cut in half, a firm needs twice as much labor as before to produce one more unit of output—marginal cost doubles.[6]

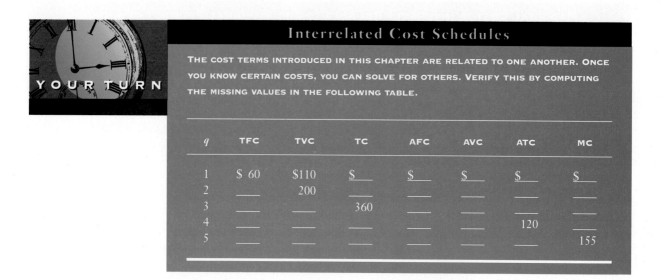

Interrelated Cost Schedules

YOUR TURN

THE COST TERMS INTRODUCED IN THIS CHAPTER ARE RELATED TO ONE ANOTHER. ONCE YOU KNOW CERTAIN COSTS, YOU CAN SOLVE FOR OTHERS. VERIFY THIS BY COMPUTING THE MISSING VALUES IN THE FOLLOWING TABLE.

q	TFC	TVC	TC	AFC	AVC	ATC	MC
1	$ 60	$110	$ ___	$ ___	$ ___	$ ___	$ ___
2	___	200	___	___	___	___	___
3	___	___	360	___	___	___	___
4	___	___	___	___	___	120	___
5	___	___	___	___	___	___	155

SHORT-RUN COST CURVES

Figure 24.4 presents graphically information taken from the last four columns of Table 24.3. As previously noted, average fixed cost declines as output increases. The other curves decline at first but then turn higher. Note that the marginal cost curve intersects average variable cost and average total cost at their lowest points. This is no accident; it reflects a mathematical property. Marginal and average values are related, as the following example shows.

---

[6]The inverse relationship between marginal product and marginal cost can also be shown algebraically. Let W denote the wage rate, the cost per unit of labor, which is assumed to be constant. If the firm hires one more unit of labor, total cost rises by an amount equal to the wage rate and output rises by an amount equal to the marginal product of labor. Because marginal cost is the change in total cost (W) divided by the change in output (MP), it can be written as MC = W/MP. From this equation, it is obvious that whenever marginal product rises marginal cost must fall, and whenever marginal product falls marginal cost must rise.

Consider a basketball star who scores 20 points in the first game of the season. Assuming the player nets an additional 10 points in the second game, the player's average falls to 15 points per game (see Table 24.4, page 622). If fewer than 15 points are scored in the third game, the average falls again; if more than 15 points are scored, the average rises. More generally, whenever the marginal value (in this case, points scored in the most recent game) is below the previous average, the average must fall; whenever the marginal value is above the previous average, the average must rise. Finally, whenever the marginal value coincides with the previous average, the average remains unchanged.

Because this marginal/average relationship is universal, it also applies to costs. Consider the relationship between marginal cost and average cost (that is, ATC). Whenever marginal cost is below average cost, average cost must be falling. Whenever marginal cost is above average cost, average cost must be rising. Finally, whenever marginal cost equals average cost, average cost is neither rising nor falling— average cost has reached its minimum value but has not yet started to rise. Graphically, this means that *the marginal cost curve intersects the average cost curve at its minimum value* (see Figure 24.4). The same logic applies to average variable cost. The marginal cost curve intersects the AVC curve where AVC is at its minimum.

AVERAGE AND MARGINAL COST CURVES*

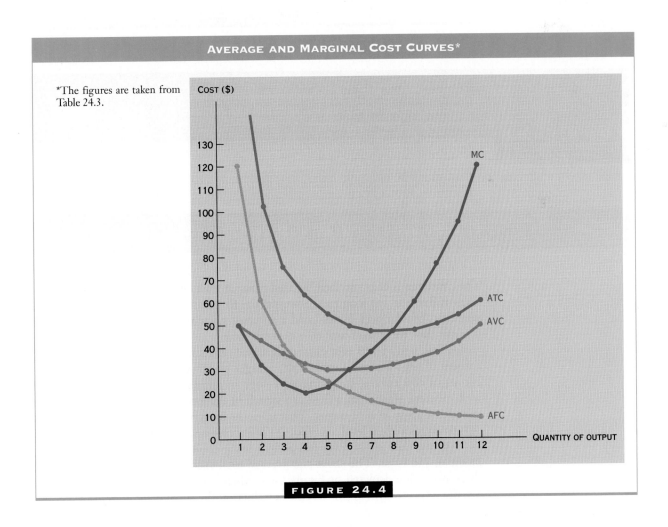

*The figures are taken from Table 24.3.

FIGURE 24.4

THE RELATIONSHIP BETWEEN MARGINAL VALUE AND AVERAGE—AN EXAMPLE			
GAME	**MARGINAL VALUE***	**AVERAGE**	**COMMENT**
1	20	20	
2	10	15	
3	(a) < 15	< 15	Marginal value less than average pulls down average.
	(b) > 15	> 15	Marginal value greater than average pulls up average.
	(c) 15	15	Marginal value equal to average keeps average unchanged.

*Marginal value refers to points scored in the most recent game—that is, the increase in total points for the season resulting from the play of one more game.

TABLE 24.4

The Relationship between AVC and ATC Curves

WHY DOES THE VERTICAL DISTANCE BETWEEN THE AVC AND ATC CURVES BECOME SMALLER AS OUTPUT INCREASES?

YOUR TURN

Costs in the Long Run

The short run is characterized by fixed costs: at least one input—for example, plant size—is fixed. In the long run, however, the firm has sufficient time to change the quantities of all inputs. It can build a different plant, either larger or smaller. *In the long run there are no fixed costs; all costs are variable.*

A firm's short-run cost curves are based on its fixed inputs. With a different amount of fixed inputs—for example, a larger plant—the firm would have a different set of cost curves. By taking advantage of different cost structures associated with different plant sizes, a firm can switch in the long run to a plant that is more suited to a given level of output. That is, in the long run a firm can move to a plant that produces a given level of output at the lowest possible cost.

Assume that in the long run a firm has a choice of three plant sizes: small, medium, and large. The short-run average total cost curves associated with these three plants are depicted in Figure 24.5, where they are labeled $SRAC_s$, $SRAC_m$, $SRAC_p$, respectively. For low levels of production the small plant is appropriate. For

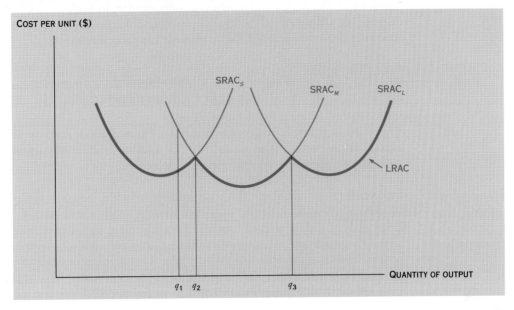

The long-run average cost curve consists of segments from short-run average cost curves, each corresponding to a different plant size.

FIGURE 24.5

example, q_1 output can be produced more economically with the small plant than with the medium plant—at q_1 the $SRAC_s$ curve is below $SRAC_m$. For output levels between q_2 and q_3, average (total) cost is lower with the medium plant than with either the small or the large plant. Therefore, over this range the company must use the medium plant if it is to minimize its production costs. If business continues to grow, at some stage even the medium plant will become uneconomical. For output beyond q_3, costs are lowest with the large plant.

Each plant size is appropriate over a different range of production. Which plant the firm should select in the long run therefore depends on the expected level of production. Based on the three short-run average cost curves in Figure 24.5, it is possible to construct the firm's **long-run average cost curve**. The long-run average cost curve (LRAC) indicates the least costly way to produce a given level of output once the firm has time to alter all inputs, including plant size. In Figure 24.5, the long-run average cost curve is represented by the heavy color line. Why don't we distinguish between average total cost and average variable cost in the long run? There is no need—all costs are variable in the long run.

Generally, a firm has available more than three plant sizes in the long run. When it does, the LRAC curve contains segments from more than three short-run average total cost curves. In the limit, a different plant size—and a different short-run cost curve—may exist for each level of output. Figure 24.6 (page 624) depicts a long-run average cost curve comprised of an infinite number of short-run cost curves, each tangent to the long-run cost curve at a single point.

LONG-RUN AVERAGE COST CURVE

A curve revealing the lowest cost per unit at which a firm can produce each level of output, given sufficient time to change all inputs.

The long-run average cost curve in Figure 24.6 is smoother than the corresponding curve in Figure 24.5, reflecting the fact that minor adjustments in plant size are possible. Still, the shapes are broadly similar. In both cases LRAC initially declines but ultimately, as the level of production increases, the curve turns higher. Are other shapes possible? What determines the particular shape?

THE SCALE OF OPERATIONS

The shape of a firm's long-run average cost curve depends on how average costs change as production is expanded. As the level of production increases, average costs may decrease, remain constant, or increase.

ECONOMIES OF SCALE
A situation in which long-run average cost declines as the firm increases its level of output.

ECONOMIES OF SCALE With **economies of scale**, long-run average cost falls as output rises—the firm's long-run average cost curve slopes downward. Economies of scale arise for a number of reasons. First, a greater scale of operations allows for greater specialization. As additional workers are hired, work can be divided into smaller, more narrowly defined jobs. This division of labor allows workers to master one job, rather than attempting to perform many. This is the idea behind Henry Ford's assembly line, which greatly reduced the cost of producing automobiles.

Specialization extends to nonlabor inputs as well. A precision metal-cutting machine or an advanced computer system may not be worth the cost to a company

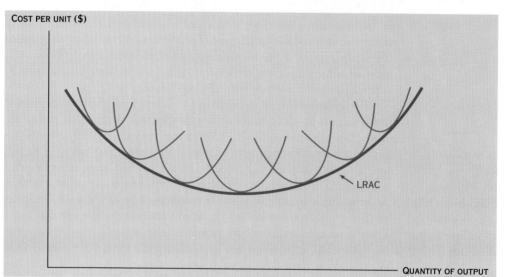

THE LRAC CURVE WHEN INFINITESIMAL CHANGES IN PLANT SIZE ARE POSSIBLE

COST PER UNIT ($)

LRAC

QUANTITY OF OUTPUT

This smooth long-run average cost curve consists of points from an infinite number of short-run average cost curves, some of which are illustrated.

FIGURE 24.6

producing low levels of output because the machines cannot be fully utilized; they will stand idle much of the time. Therefore, at low levels of output the company may settle for machines that are less suited to the tasks at hand. But as production expands, companies can take advantage of the more specialized equipment. Moreover, machines that can handle twice the load typically cost less than twice as much as the smaller machines. So by moving to larger, more sophisticated machines a company may be able to cut costs per unit.

Average cost may fall for other reasons. The costs of designing a car are independent of the number produced. Design costs per vehicle therefore decline as more vehicles are produced. This gives General Motors a cost advantage over smaller automakers. Likewise, any given level of advertising costs General Motors less per vehicle. For such reasons, one might anticipate that the automotive industry is characterized by economies of scale. Available evidence supports this contention. General Motors and Chrysler have been found to enjoy significant economies of scale and, with a different product mix, so would Ford.[7]

CONSTANT RETURNS TO SCALE

A situation in which long-run average cost does not change with the level of output.

CONSTANT RETURNS TO SCALE Beyond some point, further reductions in long-run average cost may not be possible. Economies of scale may ultimately give way to **constant returns to scale**. Constant returns to scale are characterized by a flat LRAC curve. If output doubles, total cost also doubles. Therefore, cost per unit of output remains unchanged.

For example, a study of the electricity industry found that, as of 1970, the average cost of producing electricity declined until 20 billion kilowatt hours per year of electricity were produced. Beyond that point, the average cost was the same whether a company produced 20 billion kilowatt hours, 30 billion, or more. Despite differing firm sizes, most electricity in the United States is generated by companies experiencing constant returns to scale.[8] Thus, with constant returns to scale, firms of different sizes can coexist, each experiencing similar unit costs.

MINIMUM EFFICIENT SCALE

The level of output at which economies of scale end.

The level of output at which economies of scale disappear is called **minimum efficient scale**. Figure 24.7 (page 626) depicts the case of a firm that experiences economies of scale until output reaches q_1 and constant returns to scale beyond that point. Accordingly, q_1 is the firm's minimum efficient scale.

The prevalence of economies of scale differs by industry. Consequently, minimum efficient scale also differs. Table 24.5 (page 626) reports estimates of minimum efficient scale for selected industries. According to these estimates, economies of scale are more important in the cigarette and paint industries than in the shoe and fabric industries. Therefore, technological considerations suggest that the cigarette and paint industries will have fewer firms.

DISECONOMIES OF SCALE A firm may become too big, too unwieldy. Long-run average cost may rise as production expands. In that event, a firm is experiencing **diseconomies of scale**. Steven Jobs, who founded both the Apple Computer Company and NeXT, is familiar with this concept:[9]

DISECONOMIES OF SCALE

A situation in which long-run average cost rises with the level of output.

[7]Ann Friedlaender, Clifford Winston, and Kung Wang, "Costs, Technology, and Productivity in the U.S. Automobile Industry," *Bell Journal of Economics* (Spring 1986), pp. 1–20.

[8]Laurits Christensen and William Greene, "Economies of Scale in U.S. Electric Power Generation," *Journal of Political Economy* (August 1976), pp. 655–676.

[9]Deborah Wise and Catherine Harris, "Apple's New Crusade," *Business Week*, November 26, 1984, p. 156.

When you start growing [too big], you start adding middle management like crazy. . . . People in the middle have no understanding of the business, and because of that, they screw up communications. To them, it's just a job. The corporation ends up with mediocre people that form a layer of concrete.

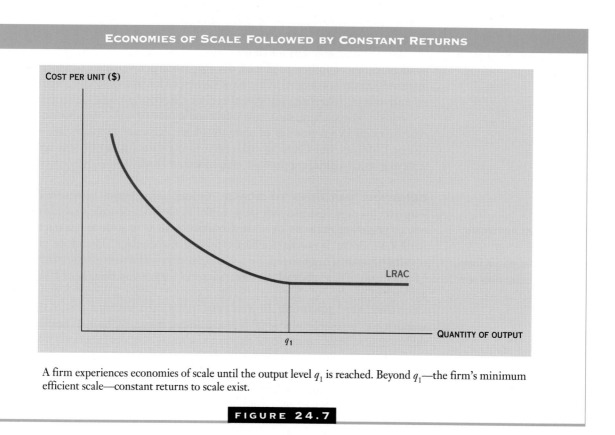

ECONOMIES OF SCALE FOLLOWED BY CONSTANT RETURNS

A firm experiences economies of scale until the output level q_1 is reached. Beyond q_1—the firm's minimum efficient scale—constant returns to scale exist.

FIGURE 24.7

MINIMUM EFFICIENT SCALE AS A PERCENT OF INDUSTRY OUTPUT

INDUSTRY	FIRM OUTPUT AS A PERCENT OF INDUSTRY OUTPUT*
Shoes	1
Fabrics	1
Cement	2
Ordinary steel	3
Petroleum refining	4–6
Glass bottles	4–6
Cigarettes	6–12
Paints	14

*For firm operating at minimum efficient scale.

SOURCE: Adapted from William G. Shepherd, *The Economics of Industrial Organization*, 3rd ed. (Englewood Cliffs, N.J.: Prentice-Hall, 1990), p. 230.

TABLE 24.5

Large companies may find it difficult to motivate workers or to control and coordinate operations. They may become too bureaucratic, bogged down in red tape. As a company grows, it may add extra layers of management that contribute little to output. Those at the top may become so insulated from operations that they find it difficult to assimilate information and respond to problems. As the company grows, total costs outpace output—average cost rises.

Note that diseconomies of scale are not the same thing as diminishing returns. The law of diminishing returns was invoked to explain the shape of *short-run* cost curves, whereas diseconomies of scale refer to the shape of *long-run* cost curves. The law of diminishing returns requires at least one input to be fixed. In contrast, diseconomies of scale explain why average cost may rise even as the firm increases the quantities of all inputs. Although diminishing returns must occur in the short run, a firm may never experience diseconomies of scale. Its short-run average cost curves must turn up; its long-run average cost curve need not.

Some industries have LRAC curves like the one depicted in Figure 24.7. But even here one must be careful not to assume that diseconomies of scale could never arise. It is possible that, if firms push production to higher levels than they have yet experienced, LRAC might eventually turn up. Without evidence on what happens to costs at production levels not yet experienced, one cannot know whether or not diseconomies will ultimately appear.

In more competitive industries, characterized by a large number of small producers, the data indicate that diseconomies of scale do arise. This is why no firm grows large enough to take a big share of the market. This is also why the model of perfect competition (the focus of Chapter 25) is based on U-shaped long-run average cost curves.

SHIFTING THE COST CURVES

The cost curves of this chapter are drawn on a number of assumptions, the most important being that input prices and the state of technology are constant. For different input prices or a different technology, the result would be a different set of short-run, and therefore long-run, cost curves.

Lower input prices drive down the cost of producing any given level of output, thereby shifting down the cost curves. Conversely, higher input prices, by raising the cost of production, shift cost curves higher. As with lower input prices, technological advances also reduce the cost of production. In addition, technological advances may alter the shape of the LRAC curve, prolonging the range over which economies of scale exist (see Figure 24.8, page 628). As a result, optimal firm size may increase, as it has in the beer industry (see Exhibit 24.3, page 629).

When the Past Does Not Matter— The Case of Sunk Costs

SUNK COST
A cost that has already been incurred and cannot be recovered.

As you will learn in Chapter 25, all costs are not equally important. At any point in time, the only costs relevant for current decisions are costs not yet incurred—that is, costs over which a person has some control. The rational person should ignore **sunk costs**, costs incurred in the past that are not affected by what happens now or in the future.

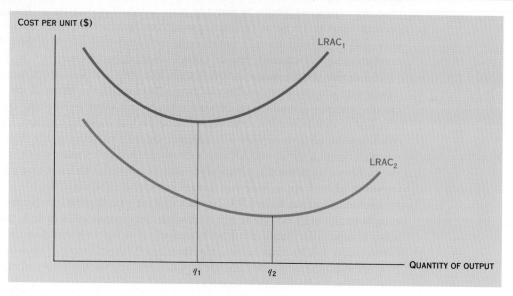

Technological advance shifts cost curves lower and may raise minimum efficient scale—in this case from q_1 to q_2.

FIGURE 24.8

Suppose you paid $20 apiece for some Christmas trees, planning to sell them for $40. 'Twas the night before Christmas and all through the lot stood many a tree not yet bought. A bearded gentleman approaches, offering $5 for a tree. Should you refuse to sell on the grounds that you will lose $15 on the transaction? No, the cost of the tree is a *sunk* cost; it is no longer relevant. In retrospect, you wish you had not bought so many trees, but you cannot roll back time. In a couple of hours the trees will have no value. Take whatever you can get for the tree.

Or consider another example. Suppose you paid $5,000 for a machine that will last two years. It has no resale value—perhaps it would cost more to move and reassemble than it is worth. After you purchased the machine the business climate worsened. The machine no longer looks like a good buy. If used it will contribute $6,000 to revenues over the next two years and $4,000 to variable costs. But the total cost of buying and using the machine ($5,000 + $4,000) will exceed total revenue.

Does it make sense to operate the machine in the short run? The decision is not whether or not to buy the machine—it already has been purchased. At issue is whether or not to operate the machine. Because the machine will contribute more to revenue than to variable costs, it should be used. In the short run the cost of acquiring the machine is a sunk cost and therefore can be ignored. This is not the case, however, in the long run. The cost of buying and using a yet unpurchased machine would exceed the revenues generated by that machine. Therefore, the current machine will not be replaced once it wears out.

EXHIBIT 24.3

Growing Economies of Scale— The Case of Beer

The number of independent breweries in the United States declined from 369 in 1950 to just over 30 today. At the same time, average output per brewery skyrocketed. Why has the industry moved to fewer but larger companies? One of the main reasons has been technological advancement, which has increased the range over which economies of scale hold. As a consequence, brewers that expanded have been able to drive down their cost per unit. Those that did not grow faced higher unit costs, which ultimately drove them from the industry.

Economies of scale grew for several reasons. First, more advanced equipment was developed, with subsequent cost savings. For example, high-speed canning lines handle 2,000 cans per minute, more than six times the volume handled by older equipment. To keep these modern lines running, a plant must produce at least 2.2 million barrels per year. Other innovations reduced the cost of building large plants and allowed breweries to take advantage of greater automation. Another breakthrough came in the area of water treatment. Because water quality

and taste vary by region, breweries initially could not produce the same, homogeneous beer in different parts of the country. But with advances in water treatment, breweries were able to operate multiple plants. Because beer is a heavy, high-cost product to ship, the opening of additional plants closer to major markets reduced shipping costs. Large brewers also have been able to take advantage of national advertising campaigns, which can reduce the cost per consumer of delivering a message.

For such reasons, economies of scale in the beer industry have grown over time. According to one study, minimum efficient scale increased from 4 million barrels in 1960 to 8 million barrels in 1970 and 18 million barrels in 1978.

SOURCES: Adapted from Victor J. Tremblay, "Scale Economies, Technological Change, and Firm Cost Asymmetries in the U.S. Brewing Industry," *Quarterly Review of Economics and Business* (Summer 1987), pp. 71–86; Charles Keithahan, "The Brewing Industry," Staff Report of the Bureau of Economics, Washington, U.S. Federal Trade Commission, December 1978.

Summary

1. Economic models generally assume that the goal of firms is to maximize profit. Economic profit is the difference between total revenue and the explicit and implicit costs of production.

2. Explicit costs refer to actual payments to resource owners outside the firm. Implicit costs are the opportunity costs of using the firm's own resources.

3. Positive or pure economic profits pull resources into an industry; economic losses cause resource owners to move resources out of the industry. An economic loss indicates that the firm is better off selling its resources or employing them in another business. If total revenue equals total cost, the firm is receiving a normal profit; it is earning enough to cover all explicit and implicit costs but nothing extra.

4. In the short run at least one input is fixed; therefore, the firm incurs fixed costs. In the long run all inputs and therefore all costs are variable.

5. A production function shows the relationship between a firm's inputs and the maximum producible output. Marginal product refers to the change in output associated with a one-unit increase in the variable input. According to the law of diminishing returns, when at least one input is fixed, increasing the variable input ultimately causes its marginal product to fall.

6. Because of declining marginal productivity, average and marginal cost curves must eventually rise in the short run. Marginal cost intersects the average variable cost and average total cost curves at their minimum value.

7. Each plant size has associated with it a different set of short-run cost curves. By changing plant size, a company can alter average cost in the long run. The long-run average cost curve, which consists of segments of short-run cost curves, indicates the least costly way to produce a given level of output once the firm has had time to alter all inputs, including plant size.

8. When a firm enjoys economies of scale, its long-run average cost curve slopes downward. Over any output range for which the firm experiences constant returns to scale, its long-run average cost curve is flat—average cost is constant. If the firm encounters diseconomies of scale, its long-run average cost curve rises.

9. In different industries, firms have different-shaped long-run average cost curves. In competitive industries, characterized by a large number of small firms, long-run average cost curves are U-shaped. They decline at first, but beyond some level of output they turn higher.

10. Higher input prices shift cost curves higher. Lower input prices or technological advances shift cost curves lower.

11. Costs incurred in the past that cannot be recovered are called sunk costs. The only costs relevant for current decisions are costs not yet incurred. Sunk costs should be ignored.

Key Terms

explicit costs
implicit costs
economic profit
accounting profit
pure economic profit
normal profit
short run
long run
production function
average product of labor
marginal product of labor
law of diminishing returns
fixed costs

variable costs
total cost
average fixed cost
average variable cost
average total cost
marginal cost
long-run average cost curve
economies of scale
constant returns to scale
minimum efficient scale
diseconomies of scale
sunk costs

1. Indicate whether each of the following is an implicit cost or an explicit cost:
   a. payments to AT&T for long-distance telephone service
   b. depreciation on company-owned machinery
   c. interest payments a company does not have to make because the owner loans money to the company *interest-free*
   d. the secretaries' salaries
   e. the lease payments forgone by a service station that decides to operate its tow truck instead of renting it out
   f. insurance payments on the company car

2. a. Construct the marginal product schedule for the following production function:

LABOR	TOTAL PRODUCT
0	0
1	3
2	8
3	15
4	21
5	25
6	26
7	24

   b. Graph the total product and marginal product curves.
   c. When does the firm first experience diminishing returns to labor?

3. a. Some companies offer a policy of lifetime employment, in which workers draw salaries regardless of current production schedules. Do these salaries constitute a fixed cost or a variable cost?
   b. In the textile industry many employees are paid on the *piece-work system*. If workers receive $2 per garment and no further compensation, are their labor costs classified as fixed or variable?

4. Basketball star Michael Jordan endorses products for more than one dozen companies, including Nike Shoes and General Mills ("Better eat your Wheaties"). But when the Coca-Cola Company decided in 1991 not to renew Jordan's contract, an industry analyst offered the following explanation: "It's the law of diminishing returns." (a) If Jordan's endorsements lead to additional sales for a company, in what sense might endorsements of additional products lead to diminishing returns? (b) If Jordan's endorsements are characterized by diminishing returns, does this imply that his endorsement of another product would have no impact on sales of the product? Explain.

5. Suppose a company experiences economies of scale for the first 100 units produced each period and constant returns to scale thereafter. (a) Draw its long-run average cost curve. (b) If the average cost of producing 101 units of output is $3, what is the total cost of producing 101 units? The total cost of producing 102 units? The marginal cost of increasing production to 102 units? (c) Over the range of constant returns to scale, how do marginal cost and average cost compare?

WAGONS PRODUCED	TOTAL COST
0	$ 30
1	60
2	80
3	90
4	110
5	150

6. The Little Red Wagon Company has the following cost schedule:
   a. Construct the schedules for total fixed cost, total variable cost, average fixed cost, average variable cost, average total cost, and marginal cost.
   b. Graph the average variable cost, average total cost, and marginal cost curves.

7. "If the law of diminishing returns did not hold, the world's entire food supply could be grown in a single flower pot." Explain this argument. (The amount of land can be considered fixed. Analyze what happens as more and more labor is applied.)

8. The price of oil fell by more than 50 percent in 1986, causing many oil companies to incur losses. These companies had to decide which wells, if any, to shut down. (a) In making their decisions, should the oil companies consider the past costs of drilling for oil? (b) Should drilling costs be considered when deciding whether or not to drill new oil wells?

9. Only medium-size companies in a given industry are earning pure economic profit. Both small and large companies are losing money. (a) What does this say about the long-run average cost curves of firms in this industry? (b) What long-run response is appropriate for firms that wish to remain in the industry?

10. The average research and development outlay for a new drug approved in the 1980s was $231 million. The marginal manufacturing cost for a typical prescription, however, is just a few dollars.[10]
    a. In light of the research and development costs required to bring a new drug to market, how is long-run average cost likely to change as production of a drug increases from 50,000 to 60,000 prescriptions per year?
    b. Over this range of output, is production characterized by economies of scale, diseconomies of scale, or constant returns to scale?
    c. Given your answers to parts (a) and (b), is the marginal cost of producing 50,000 prescriptions per year greater than, less than, or equal to the average cost of production?

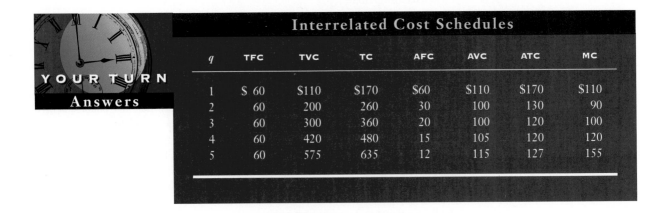

Interrelated Cost Schedules

YOUR TURN
Answers

q	TFC	TVC	TC	AFC	AVC	ATC	MC
1	$ 60	$110	$170	$60	$110	$170	$110
2	60	200	260	30	100	130	90
3	60	300	360	20	100	120	100
4	60	420	480	15	105	120	120
5	60	575	635	12	115	127	155

The Relationship between AVC and ATC Curves

AT EACH LEVEL OF OUTPUT, ATC = AVC + AFC. GRAPHICALLY, THIS MEANS THAT THE HEIGHT OF THE ATC CURVE EXCEEDS THE HEIGHT OF THE AVC CURVE BY AN AMOUNT EQUAL TO AFC. AS OUTPUT INCREASES, AFC BECOMES SMALLER (FOR EXAMPLE, $AFC_2 < AFC_1$). AS AFC'S CONTRIBUTION TO ATC DIMINISHES, THE VERTICAL DISTANCE BETWEEN AVC AND ATC DECREASES.

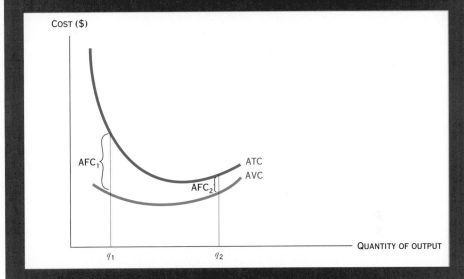

[10]Thomas Stewart, "Brainpower," *Fortune*, June 3, 1991, p. 56.

The Optimal Combination
of Variable Inputs

Companies often hire more than one input. In the long run the firm hires both labor and capital. Even in the short run a firm may hire multiple inputs—for example, skilled labor and unskilled labor. Appendix 24A presents a method for determining the optimal input mix when the firm buys two separate inputs and input prices are fixed—that is, independent of the amount the firm buys. A more general approach is presented in Chapter 31, which allows for both the possibility that the firm hires more than two inputs and the possibility that the price of an input changes as the firm purchases additional quantities of the input.

Isoquants

Assume that a firm uses two inputs. To be specific, let us call these inputs capital and labor (but the analysis is the same no matter what name we give the inputs). Generally, a given level of output can be produced in a number of different ways. For example, a company may be able to substitute computers or robots (capital) for workers. By using more capital, the firm can produce the same output with fewer hours of labor. Alternatively, by expanding labor the company can cut back on capital.

The relationship between output and potential combinations of inputs can be depicted graphically by an **isoquant**. An isoquant shows all possible combinations of labor and capital that can produce a given level of output, assuming the inputs are used efficiently. (Efficiency, in this context, means that the firm is operating on its production function—that is, obtaining the maximum output from its inputs.)

ISOQUANT
A curve depicting the various input combinations that are capable of producing a given level of output when used efficiently.

In Figure 24A.1, isoquant $q_1 = 10$ illustrates the various methods of producing 10 units of output. Isoquant $q_2 = 20$ shows how 20 units of output can be produced. Note that q_2 lies beyond q_1, indicating that the firm needs a larger quantity of inputs to produce 20 units of output than to produce 10. In turn, 30 units of output require an even greater amount of inputs, which is why q_3 is the highest of the three isoquants.

As was true with indifference curves, isoquants generally have a convex shape—the slope flattens as you move down the curve. This reflects a diminishing ability to substitute labor for capital. When a firm is producing output with a relatively high mix of capital, it is easy to substitute labor for capital. But as the amount of capital is reduced, substitution of labor for capital becomes more difficult—the amount of labor required to replace a unit of capital increases.[11]

---

[11]On a technical note, the slope of the isoquant reflects the marginal product of labor divided by the marginal product of capital (slope $= -MP_l/MP_k$). Because movements down the isoquant signify an increase in labor and a decrease in capital, they imply that the marginal product of labor is falling relative to the marginal product of capital. That is, the slope of the isoquant becomes flatter as the firm moves down the curve.

The Isocost Line

In producing any given level of output, a firm has a choice of options. Which combination of inputs should it select? The answer depends on the price of capital and the price of labor. To see this, we introduce the **isocost line**. An isocost line shows the various input combinations that can be purchased with a given sum of money. The equation for an isocost line is as follows:

$$(P_l \times L) + (P_k \times K) = \text{total cost}$$

ISOCOST LINE
A line showing all the combinations of capital and labor that can be purchased with a given amount of money.

Suppose a company contemplates spending $100 on inputs. If the price of labor is $5 per unit and the price of capital is $10, the company's isocost line is:

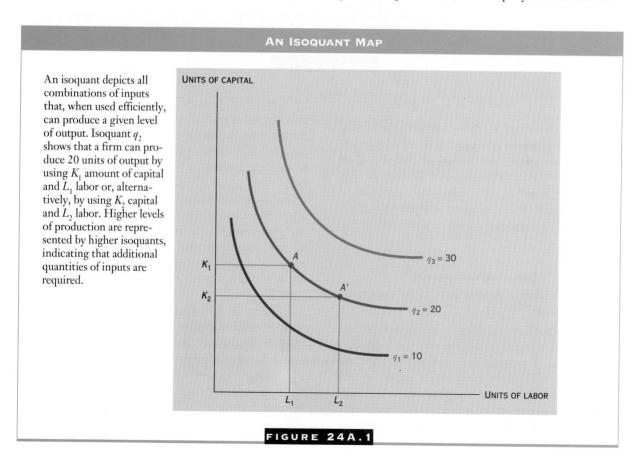

AN ISOQUANT MAP

An isoquant depicts all combinations of inputs that, when used efficiently, can produce a given level of output. Isoquant q_2 shows that a firm can produce 20 units of output by using K_1 amount of capital and L_1 labor or, alternatively, by using K_2 capital and L_2 labor. Higher levels of production are represented by higher isoquants, indicating that additional quantities of inputs are required.

FIGURE 24A.1

An isocost line illustrates all possible combinations of inputs that can be purchased with a given sum of money. For example, points X, Y, and Z lie on the $100 isocost line.

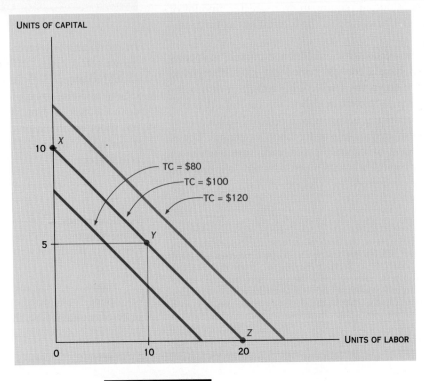

UNITS OF CAPITAL

TC = $80
TC = $100
TC = $120

UNITS OF LABOR

FIGURE 24A.2

$$(\$5 \times L) + (\$10 \times K) = \$100$$

This line is illustrated in Figure 24A.2. As this figure shows, with $100 the company can buy 20 units of labor and no capital, or 10 units of capital and no labor, or various combinations of both labor and capital (for example, 10 units of labor and 5 units of capital). Also illustrated in Figure 24A.2 are the isocost lines associated with expenditures of $80 and $120.

THE LEAST-COST COMBINATION OF INPUTS

Let us return to the question posed earlier: Which combination of inputs should the firm use to produce a given level of output? For example, suppose the company plans to produce 20 units of output. Which combination of labor and capital allows the firm to produce this output at the lowest possible cost? The answer is found in Figure 24A.3, which presents the isoquant and isocost lines on the same diagram.

Total cost is minimized at point A, where the isoquant is tangent to the $100 isocost line. This corresponds to the purchase of 6 units of capital and 8 units of labor. Note that this is the lowest isocost line to reach the isoquant. The firm cannot produce 20 units of output if it spends less than $100 on inputs. Other input combinations (including B and C) also allow the firm to produce 20 units of output, but such combinations lie on a higher isocost line—that is, they cost more than $100. *To minimize the cost of producing a given level of output, the firm must operate on the lowest isocost line consistent with that level of production.*

When relative input prices change, so does the optimal combination of inputs. A decline in the price of labor relative to capital induces the firm to substitute labor for capital; this is illustrated in Figure 24A.4 (page 638). As the relative price of labor falls, the isocost line becomes flatter. This leads to a new tangency, at point A'. In other words, firms change their technique of production in response to changing input prices. When the relative price of labor

The least costly way to produce 20 units of output is with 6 units of capital and 8 units of labor. This result is given by point *A*, where the isoquant is tangent to the $100 isocost line. Input combinations *B* and *C* are inferior because they produce the same output at a higher cost.

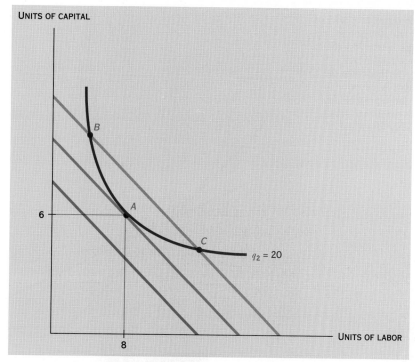

UNITS OF CAPITAL

$q_2 = 20$

UNITS OF LABOR

FIGURE 24A.3

falls, the firm substitutes labor for capital; when the relative price of capital falls, capital is substituted for labor.

Summary

1. An isoquant indicates the alternative methods of producing a given level of output. Assuming that inputs are used efficiently, it shows all input combinations capable of producing a particular level of output. Higher levels of output can be represented by higher isoquants.

2. Isoquants generally have a convex shape, reflecting the fact that the less you have of one input the more difficult it is to substitute that input for a second input.

3. An isocost line shows the various input combinations that can be purchased with a given amount of money.

4. The optimal input combination is given by the tangency of the isoquant with an isocost line. This represents the least costly way to produce the given level of output.

5. A change in relative input prices shifts the slope of the isocost lines. This leads to a new tangency with the isoquant and therefore a new least-cost combination of inputs. The company uses more of the input whose relative price has fallen and less of the input whose relative price has risen.

Key Terms

isoquant   isocost line

Study Question

Assume a company faces a price of $10 per hour for both capital and labor. (a) Draw an isocost line corre-

When the relative price of labor falls, the isocost lines become flatter. As a result, the new tangency A' occurs farther down the isoquant. A reduction in the relative price of labor causes the firm to substitute labor for capital.

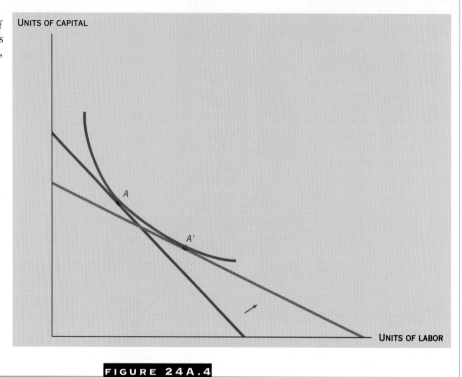

FIGURE 24A.4

sponding to expenditures of $200. (b) Draw an isoquant that is tangent to this line. (c) Now assume the price of labor rises to $20 per hour. Draw the new isocost line associated with expenditures of $200. (d) Can the company still reach the isoquant drawn in part (b)?

MARKETS DIFFER IN SUCH DIMENSIONS AS NUMBER OF SELLERS, TYPE OF PRODUCT, AND ABILITY OF FIRMS TO RAISE PRICE. BASED ON SUCH CHARAC- TERISTICS, ECONOMISTS PARTITION PRODUCT MARKETS INTO FOUR CATEGORIES: PERFECT COMPETITION, MONOPOLISTIC COMPETITION, OLIGOPOLY, AND MONOPOLY. PART VII EXAM- INES PRODUCTION DECISIONS IN EACH OF THESE FOUR TYPES OF MARKETS AND EX- PLORES THE ROLE OF MARKET STRUCTURE ON SUCH OUTCOMES AS LEVEL OF OUTPUT, PRICE, PROFIT POTENTIAL, RESOURCE ALLOCATION, AND RATE OF TECHNOLOGI- CAL ADVANCE. ■ TO ASSESS EMPIRI- CALLY THE EXTENT OF COMPETITION WITHIN SPECIFIC INDUSTRIES, ECONO- MISTS RELY ON THE *MARKET CONCENTRA- TION RATIO* AND THE *HERFINDAHL INDEX*. THESE MEASURES ARE DISCUSSED IN CHAPTER 28, ALONG WITH GOVERNMENT (ANTITRUST) POLICY DESIGNED TO SHAPE MARKET STRUCTURE AND INFLU- ENCE THE BEHAVIOR OF FIRMS. GOV- ERNMENT INFLUENCE ALSO EXTENDS TO VARIOUS MARKETS THROUGH REGULA- TIONS THAT RESTRICT PRICE, LIMIT THE NUMBER OF FIRMS THAT MAY SELL A PRODUCT, MANDATE MINIMUM LEVELS OF SAFETY, DISALLOW CERTAIN TYPES OF PRODUCTION, AND IMPOSE OTHER CON- STRAINTS. AFTER EX- AMINING MARKETS IN THE ABSENCE OF GOV- ERNMENT INTERVEN- TION AND SIZING UP THE STRENGTHS AND WEAKNESSES OF VARIOUS MARKET STRUCTURES (CHAPTERS 25–27), PART VII CLOSES WITH A FORMAL TREATMENT OF GOVERNMENT ANTITRUST POLICY AND REGULATION (CHAPTERS 28 AND 29).

Market Structure and Government Intervention

Perfect Competition

DOES THE NUMBER OF PRODUCERS IN A MARKET MATTER? DOES IT MAKE ANY DIFFERENCE WHETHER A TOWN IS SERVED BY ONE GROCERY STORE OR BY MANY? ADAM SMITH ARGUED THAT COMPETITION BENEFITS SOCIETY AND THAT COMPETITION IS GREATER WHERE THERE ARE MANY PRODUCERS. MOST ECONOMISTS AGREE WITH SMITH THAT COMPETITION GENERALLY LOWERS PRICE, AND THEY CITE OTHER POTENTIAL ADVANTAGES, INCLUDING THE WAY RESOURCES ARE DISTRIBUTED ACROSS INDUSTRIES. YET, UNDER CERTAIN CONDITIONS, UNBRIDLED COMPETITION MAY BE UNDESIRABLE.

HOW DO MARKETS DIFFER, AND WHY ARE THESE DIFFERENCES IMPORTANT TO SOCIETY? SHOULD WE PROMOTE A CERTAIN TYPE OF MARKET? AFTER AN OVERVIEW OF THE DIFFERENT MARKET STRUCTURES, CHAPTER 25 FOCUSES ON ADAM SMITH'S IDEAL— PERFECT COMPETITION. ALTERNATIVE TYPES OF MARKETS ARE EXAMINED IN SUBSEQUENT CHAPTERS.

If [production] is divided between two different grocers, their competition will tend to make both of them sell cheaper, than if it were in the hands of one only; and if it were divided among twenty, their competition would be just so much the greater, and the chance of their combining together, in order to raise the price, just so much the less.[1]

[1]Adam Smith, *The Wealth of Nations* (New York: Random House, 1937), p. 342. [Originally published in 1776.]

The Structure of Markets

Although all firms sell a product, they do not all sell in similar types of markets. Agricultural markets, for example, differ from apparel markets. Buyers of wheat pay the same price for a given grade of wheat, no matter who produced it. Wheat from Gormely's farm is indistinguishable from wheat grown by thousands of other farmers. In contrast, different brands of jeans are not viewed as identical. Consumers are willing to pay more for designer jeans than for basic jeans. Therefore, although Gormely cannot influence the price of his wheat, Calvin Klein has some control over the price of his jeans.

Different yet is the market for electricity. In most communities the market contains only one seller of electricity: you either buy electricity from the local utility or you do without. Unlike producers of wheat or jeans, the utility company does not face competition from other firms in the market—there are no other firms. Some barrier, in this case a government license, prevents competing firms from entering the market.

Given such differences in the structure of markets, no single model can be expected to explain adequately the outcomes in all markets. Instead, different models are appropriate for different types of markets. Although real-world markets sometimes defy easy classification, economists recognize four basic **market structures**: perfect competition, monopoly, monopolistic competition, and oligopoly. Markets are categorized on the basis of various characteristics, the most important of which are now discussed (and summarized in Table 25.1).

MARKET STRUCTURE
The distinguishing characteristics of a market, including number of firms, the similarity of the products they sell, and the ease with which new firms can enter the market.

NUMBER OF SELLERS

Perfect competition and monopolistic competition are each characterized by a large number of sellers. In contrast, oligopoly has a small number of sellers; monopoly has but one.

A COMPARISON OF THE FOUR MARKET STRUCTURES

MARKET STRUCTURE	NUMBER OF FIRMS	TYPE OF PRODUCT	ENTRY INTO INDUSTRY	FIRM'S INFLUENCE OVER PRICE	EXAMPLES
Perfect competition	Many	Homogeneous (identical)	Easy	None	Many agricultural markets*
Monopolistic competition	Many	Differentiated	Easy	Moderate	Clothing, restaurants, dry cleaners
Oligopoly	Few	Homogeneous or differentiated	Difficult	Moderate or substantial	Autos, steel, infant formula
Monopoly	One	Unique	Difficult or impossible	Substantial*	Local utilities

*In the absence of government regulation.

TABLE 25.1

TYPE OF PRODUCT

In perfectly competitive markets all firms produce a homogeneous (identical) product. Monopolistic competition, on the other hand, is noted for product differentiation—consumers view each firm's product as distinct. Although other firms in the monopolistically competitive market produce close substitutes, none produces the exact same product. In the case of oligopoly, products may be either homogeneous (as with steel) or differentiated (as with autos). Steel is steel, no matter who produces it, but a Chevrolet is not the same as a Ford. Finally, because the monopolist is the only producer in the market, its product is unique.

ENTRY INTO THE INDUSTRY

Producers find some markets easier to enter than others. Almost anyone can grow vegetables. The main requirements are soil and seeds. By comparison, the auto industry is much harder to crack. To start an auto company requires technical knowledge and perhaps billions of dollars. Even then it is a risky proposition, as John DeLorean discovered. In addition to financial and technical barriers, entry may be limited by government policy, including patents, or by inaccessible resources. If potential companies can be denied access to the raw materials needed for production, they can be kept out of a market.

Both perfect competition and monopolistic competition are characterized by **free entry**; new firms find it easy to set up shop and start producing. This is not the case with oligopoly or monopoly. There, considerable barriers to entry greet would-be producers. In fact, it is because of these barriers that oligopoly has only a few producers and monopoly has only one.

Although much is made of barriers to entry, it should be observed that barriers to exit sometimes occur. This means that firms attempting to leave an industry face obstacles—for example, laws restricting plant closings. Another example comes from the state of Rhode Island, which in 1982 adopted a plan designed to slow the exodus of land from agriculture. Farmers signing up for this program promised that their land would never be developed. These agreements restricted land use not only for those signing the contract but for all future owners of the land. Perfect competition requires complete mobility of resources and thus **free exit** as well as free entry.

FIRM'S INFLUENCE OVER PRICE

A perfectly competitive firm has no control over the price of its product. Because the market contains many other producers of the same product, the individual firm has no market power. In all other market structures, producers have the potential to influence price.

Unless restricted by the government, a monopolist can set any price it wishes. Its only constraint is the demand for its product—a higher price reduces the amount consumers want to buy. Even a monopolistically competitive firm has some limited market power, despite the fact that it must compete with numerous other firms in its market. Because each firm produces a product slightly different from that of its competitors, a firm can raise price without losing all its customers.

The extent to which an oligopolist can influence price depends on whether or not the oligopolist "combines together" with other oligopolists in the industry. Sometimes oligopolists form a *cartel*, an organization designed to raise price and profits for members of the cartel. Perhaps the most famous cartel is OPEC, which in its first ten years succeeded in raising the price of oil from less than $3 per barrel to about $34 per barrel. In other oligopolistic industries, such as steel, producers do not band together. Instead, they actively compete against one another. This limits the ability of steel companies to influence price.

EXAMPLES

The preceding theoretical considerations provide a basis for categorizing markets. Sometimes a particular designation is arbitrary—real-world markets do not always neatly fit into a given category. Nonetheless, economists generally agree on most classifications.

Most public utilities are monopolies—the government usually allows only one natural gas company to serve a community, only one electric company, and only one sewage treatment company. Polaroid is an example of a monopoly that is not a utility. Because of the patents it holds, Polaroid is the only company that sells a camera with self-developing film. Examples of oligopolistic industries are aluminum, tires, and autos. Much of the manufacturing sector is oligopolistic. Most retail markets are characterized by monopolistic competition, including grocery stores, florist shops, and restaurants. Many agricultural markets come closest to the perfectly competitive framework. This is not always the case though. For many years the state of New York limited entry into the dairy market, permitting the emergence of an oligopolistic milk cartel (see Exhibit 25.1).

IMPLICATIONS OF MARKET STRUCTURE

Economists have developed theories for each market structure. These theories indicate that different market structures have different implications concerning industry output, price, and profit potential. Market structure also influences the flow of resources into an industry, the level of advertising, and perhaps other factors as well. Some economists argue, for example, that the rate of technological innovation depends on market structure.

The remainder of this chapter is devoted to perfect competition. Monopoly (in Chapter 26) and monopolistic competition and oligopoly (in Chapter 27) follow. Although Chapters 25, 26, and 27 analyze markets in the absence of government intervention, subsequent chapters introduce government regulation and antitrust policy.

Restricting Entry and the Price of Milk in New York City

With almost 8 million people, New York City has a lot of milk drinkers, but until recently only five dairies were licensed to distribute milk in the city. A 1937 state law authorized entry restrictions "to prevent destructive competition"—a euphemism for maintaining high prices and guaranteeing profits for existing producers. The five dairies took full advantage of the law. Repeatedly, they were found guilty of price fixing and dividing up markets (agreeing not to compete for each other's customers). Milk prices in New York were among the highest in the country and dramatically higher than in neighboring New Jersey.

In 1985, barriers to entry were eased in Staten Island. Then in 1987, a federal judge ruled the state licensing law unconstitutional. This opened the milk spigots of other dairies. With additional milk flowing to the market, the price of milk in New York City fell by about $.50 per gallon. Do barriers to entry affect price? Clearly they do.

SOURCES: Adapted from William Greer, "Is Albany Helping Maintain the Sellers' Market in Milk?" *The New York Times*, February 23, 1986, p. 7E; Mark Uhlig, "Milk Regulations Are a Hot Potato," *The New York Times*, January 18, 1987, p. 6E.

Perfect Competition

Competition has many meanings. You and other students compete for parking spaces; workers compete for jobs; companies compete for customers. **Perfect competition** has a more specific meaning. It refers to a particular market arrangement in which individual firms have no control over the price of the product they sell. For a market to be perfectly competitive, the following conditions must hold:

1. The product market contains *a large number of buyers and sellers*, none of whom has a significant share of the market. Each of the market participants is too small to affect market supply or demand appreciably.

2. The firms all sell an *identical (homogeneous) product*.

3. The industry is characterized by *free entry* and *free exit*. No barriers prevent firms or resources from entering the industry or from leaving it.

4. Buyers and sellers have *perfect information* about price and other conditions in the market.

PRICE TAKER
An economic unit that has no control over price. The perfectly competitive firm is a price taker in the product market.

Together, these four conditions imply that the perfectly competitive firm is a **price taker**—it has no control over output price. The firm can sell as much as it wants at the market price, but if it attempts to charge a higher price it will find no buyers. There are a large number of other producers selling the identical product. Moreover, buyers know the price each seller is asking. In this environment, no buyer is willing to pay a firm more than the lowest price available elsewhere. Any firm attempting to charge more than its competitors will find no takers. At the same time, the perfectly competitive firm has no reason to offer its product for less than the prevailing market price. It can sell as much as it chooses at this price; to sell for less would mean forgoing profits. Graphically, the demand curve facing a perfectly competitive firm is perfectly elastic (see Figure 25.1).

The model of perfect competition rests on a number of rigorous assumptions. Doesn't this limit the usefulness of the model? Why study it? First of all, some markets closely approximate perfect competition. This is certainly true for many agricultural products (see Exhibit 25.2). Some economists go further, arguing that the predictions of this model are widely confirmed, even in markets that are not perfectly competitive. For example, Milton Friedman writes:

> [A]s I have studied economic activities in the United States, I have become increasingly impressed with how wide is the range of problems and industries for which it is appropriate to treat the economy as if it were competitive.[2]

Even though all the conditions for perfect competition may not be satisfied, this still may be the most appropriate framework for analysis.

The model of perfect competition also provides a standard for comparison. For example, monopolists often are accused of charging high prices. But what does "high" mean? A relevant interpretation is given by comparing price under monopoly with price under perfect competition. Because perfect competition is in some sense *ideal*, it is the logical basis for comparison. It may even serve as a target for government policy.

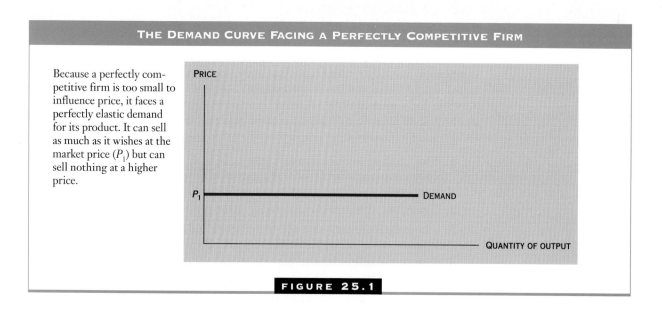

THE DEMAND CURVE FACING A PERFECTLY COMPETITIVE FIRM

Because a perfectly competitive firm is too small to influence price, it faces a perfectly elastic demand for its product. It can sell as much as it wishes at the market price (P_1) but can sell nothing at a higher price.

FIGURE 25.1

---

[2]Milton Friedman, *Capitalism and Freedom* (Chicago: University of Chicago Press, 1962), p. 120.

The Individual Farmer
as a Price Taker

According to the 1987 Census of Agriculture, 352,000 U.S. farms raised wheat. Harvesting 55.9 million acres, they produced 2.1 billion bushels. Worldwide, wheat production totaled 18.5 billion bushels. An even larger number of farms produced corn, soybeans, and hay (see Table 25.2). The number of farms has shrunk slightly since the census but remains high.

Admittedly, the large farms produce much of the output, but even they account for a small share of the market. In 1987, the 65,000 largest U.S. farms harvested only 20 percent of U.S. cropland. Even the largest farm was too small to affect supply appreciably.

A second requirement of perfect competition is that firms produce a homogeneous output. Again, this condition is satisfied. For each grade and variety of wheat, each farm's output is identical. Buyers do not care where the wheat comes from.

The assumptions about entry/exit and perfect information also hold, at least approximately. Every year new farmers start growing wheat, while others reemploy the land in other crops or leave farming altogether. No significant barriers obstruct movement into or out of this industry. Finally, information about markets is widely available. Buyers and sellers know crop estimates, level of sales, and related facts. At any time, farmers know what they can sell their wheat for.

The end result is that individual wheat farmers are price takers. None is large enough or powerful enough to influence the price of wheat.

NUMBER OF U.S. FARMS AND PRODUCTION BY CROP, 1987

CROP	NUMBER OF FARMS SELLING (IN THOUSANDS)	ACRES HARVESTED (IN MILLIONS)	UNITS OF OUTPUT (IN MILLIONS)
Corn	627	65.5	7,218 bushels
Wheat	352	55.9	2,108 bushels
Soybeans	442	57.2	1,938 bushels
Hay	995	60.1	147 tons

SOURCES: U.S. Department of Commerce, *1987 Census of Agriculture, United States Summary*, Table 1, and (for acres and units of output) U.S. Department of Agriculture, *Agricultural Statistics: 1990*, Table 553.

TABLE 25.2

EXHIBIT 25.2

Production in the Short Run

How much output should a perfectly competitive firm produce? We tackle this issue first in the short run and then in the long run. In the short run at least one input (for example, plant size) is fixed. The production decision therefore centers on the most profitable level of output given the constraint of the fixed inputs. In the long run the firm has greater flexibility; because no inputs are fixed, it can switch to a larger plant or a smaller plant. This gives the firm a greater opportunity to affect its average costs. Long-run adjustments in output are also greater at the industry level. An industry can expand in the long run as new firms enter or shrink as existing firms leave.

Although long-run adjustments are addressed shortly, the present section focuses on the short run. We begin by examining the conditions for profit maximization. What level of output maximizes short-run profits for a perfectly competitive firm? Two equivalent approaches are presented. The first focuses on total revenue and total costs; the second centers on price and marginal cost.

PROFIT MAXIMIZATION—COMPARING TOTAL REVENUE AND TOTAL COST

Because profit is defined as total revenue minus total cost, a straightforward approach to profit maximization is to (1) compute total revenue and total cost for each potential level of output; (2) subtract total cost from total revenue, yielding the profit possible at the various levels of output; and (3) select that level of output for which profit is greatest.

To illustrate this approach we use the cost schedules from Table 24.3. The total variable cost and total cost schedules are reproduced in Table 25.3. Total fixed cost for the firm is $120, the difference between total cost and total variable cost. To save space the schedule for total fixed cost is omitted from Table 25.3.

Total revenue is the product of price times quantity. Therefore, the total revenue that this firm can earn from production depends on the output price. Column 4 presents the total revenue schedule for a price of $60. If the firm sells one unit of output it receives $60; if it sells two units it receives $120, and so on. Column 5 indicates the profit (or loss) that can be earned at various levels of output. It is simply the difference between total revenue (column 4) and total cost (column 3). For example, if the firm produces two units of output it receives $120 in total revenue but incurs $204 in costs. The result is a loss of $84.

Given a price of $60, how much output should the firm produce? From column 5, we see that the maximum profit possible is $95. This is the amount that is earned if the firm produces nine units of output. For any other level of output, profit is less than $95. Figure 25.2 (page 650) illustrates the situation diagramatically. The difference between total revenue and total cost is greatest for nine units of output; therefore, to maximize profit the firm must produce nine units of output.

The preceding analysis is based on a price of $60. With a different price, total revenue for the firm also differs. Column 6 presents the firm's total revenue schedule when the price is $40 (TR = $40 × q). An examination of column 7, listing

	COSTS		PRICE = $60		PRICE = $40		PRICE = $20	
(1) q	(2) TVC	(3) TC	(4) TR	(5) PROFIT	(6) TR	(7) PROFIT	(8) TR	(9) PROFIT
0	$ 0	$120	$ 0	–$120	$ 0	–$120	$ 0	–$120
1	50	170	60	– 110	40	– 130	20	– 150
2	84	204	120	– 84	80	– 124	40	– 164
3	108	228	180	– 48	120	– 108	60	– 168
4	127	247	240	– 7	160	– 87	80	– 167
5	150	270	300	30	200	– 70	100	– 170
6	180	300	360	60	240	– 60	120	– 180
7	218	338	420	82	280	– 58	140	– 198
8	266	386	480	94	320	– 66	160	– 226
9	325	445	540	95	360	– 85	180	– 265
10	400	520	600	80	400	– 120	200	– 320
11	495	615	660	45	440	– 175	220	– 395
12	612	732	720	– 12	480	– 252	240	– 492

If a firm produces, it should choose that level of output for which TR – TC is greatest. This corresponds to 9 units when P = $60 and 7 units when P = $40. If P = $20, the firm shuts down, since TR < TVC for all output.

TABLE 25.3

profits, reveals that all the numbers are negative. At a price of $40 the firm cannot earn a profit, no matter how much it produces.

Does this mean that the firm should produce nothing? That is, should the firm **shut down**? Clearly not. If it ceases operations in the current period, it loses $120, the fixed costs of production. If, instead, it produces seven units of output, it can cut its loss to $58. No one is in business to lose money, but sometimes there is no alternative. In such cases the best option is to minimize loss. Given a price of $40, losses are minimized at an output level of seven units.

Suppose the price falls to $20. The total revenue and profit schedules based on a price of $20 are given in columns 8 and 9. Once again the firm is destined to lose money. This should come as no surprise. If the firm cannot make a profit when the price is $40, it cannot do so at a price of $20. What is different about these two cases is that, given a price of $20, production simply exacerbates the firm's loss. The minimum possible loss, $120, occurs when the firm produces nothing. Given a price of $20, the firm should shut down.

SHUTTING DOWN
Temporarily halting operations; producing no output in the current period. This limits the firm's loss to its fixed costs.

Minimizing Losses—A Graphical Account

(A) ON THE SAME DIAGRAM, GRAPH THE TOTAL COST CURVE OF TABLE 25.3 AND THE TOTAL REVENUE CURVE WHEN PRICE = $40. FOR WHICH LEVEL OF OUTPUT IS THE VERTICAL DISTANCE BETWEEN THE TWO CURVES MINIMIZED? (B) ON ANOTHER DIAGRAM, GRAPH THE TOTAL COST CURVE AND THE TOTAL REVENUE CURVE WHEN PRICE = $20. FOR WHICH LEVEL OF OUTPUT ARE THE TWO CURVES CLOSEST?

YOUR TURN

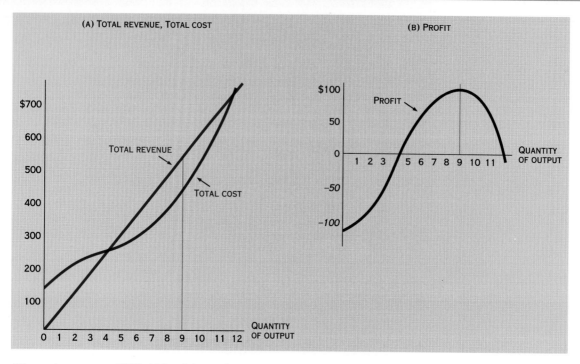

The total cost curve of Table 25.3 and the total revenue curve (given a price of $60) are depicted in (A). For each quantity of output, profit is equal to the vertical distance between these two curves (TR − TC). Profit is also depicted separately in (B). To maximize profit the firm must produce nine units of output.

FIGURE 25.2

SHUTTING DOWN—THE GENERAL RULE The preceding example demonstrates two points. (1) Sometimes a firm should produce in the short run even though it loses money. (2) At some sufficiently low price the firm is better off shutting down. But exactly when should a firm produce, and under what conditions does it make sense to halt operations? *The firm should produce in the short run if total revenue from production exceeds total variable cost. If total revenue is below total variable cost at all levels of output, the firm should shut down.*

In the short run, fixed costs are sunk costs: regardless of whether or not the firm produces, they cannot be avoided. As such they are irrelevant for decisions in the short run. The firm has control only over its variable costs. Therefore, in deciding whether or not to produce in the short run, the firm compares total revenue with total variable cost (not total cost).

If the firm does not produce it loses an amount equal to its fixed costs. If production can trim these losses, or eliminate them, it should be undertaken. This occurs when production contributes more to revenues than it adds to costs—that is, when total revenue exceeds total variable cost. On the other hand, production makes no sense if it adds to a firm's losses—which is what happens when total revenue is less than total variable cost. Therefore, a necessary condition for production is:

$$TR \geq TVC$$

In our foregoing example, this condition was satisfied given a price of $60 or $40. It was not satisfied for a price of $20, which is why the firm shut down in the final case.

The preceding analysis explains why businesses sometimes operate despite losing money. It is not that those running a company are unaware of the losses, which in some instances may be quite heavy (see Exhibit 25.3). Rather, they have reached the conclusion that, regardless of the level of output, their company will lose money in the current period. They continue to produce because they believe losses would be even greater if they shut down.

A RESTATEMENT   The preceding analysis can be summarized as follows. Firms make two types of production decisions. The first concerns whether or not to produce. The second centers on the level of output once the decision has been made to

Despite Losses, USAir Keeps Flying

Although the airline industry is not perfectly competitive, the shut-down rule applies to its firms, as to firms in all industries. Regardless of market structure, a firm should operate in the short run whenever total revenue covers total variable cost—even if the firm suffers heavy losses. USAir clearly understands this rule.

The first quarter of 1991 is one that USAir would prefer to forget. Already in the midst of an economic downturn, the United States launched its war with Iraq. The combination of a weak economy and increased fears of terrorism reduced total revenue for USAir, while soaring fuel prices, triggered by the Middle East conflict, raised operating costs. As a consequence, USAir lost $169 million during the first three months of 1991.[3]

Given this unfavorable climate, did it make sense to keep the planes flying, or would USAir have been better off canceling all flights until conditions improved? Airline analysts agree that the decision to continue flying was the correct one. Because of the tremendous fixed costs of operating a major airline, USAir would have incurred substantially greater losses had it shut down.

Business later improved when the war ended, fuel costs dropped, and the economy rebounded. But USAir wisely decided to keep flying and not to wait for this turnaround. Even during the lean months, ticket revenues exceeded the variable costs of operating the airline.

[3]These are estimates of accounting profits provided by the company. But economic profits, properly defined, were also negative during this period.

EXHIBIT 25.3

produce. The profit-maximizing firm is guided by two principles: (1) *produce only if TR ≥ TVC* and (2) *if production is to occur, choose that level of output for which TR − TC is greatest.*

PROFIT MAXIMIZATION—COMPARING MARGINAL REVENUE AND MARGINAL COST

Rather than implement the preceding approach, economists generally rely on a second, equivalent method for determining the profit-maximizing level of output. Whereas the previous approach emphasized total cost and total revenue, the alternative focuses on marginal cost and marginal revenue.

MARGINAL REVENUE
The increase in total revenue associated with a one-unit increase in output.

MARGINAL REVENUE **Marginal revenue** measures the increase in total revenue that the firm receives from selling one more unit of output. In the model of perfect competition (and only in perfect competition), marginal revenue coincides with price. Because the perfectly competitive firm is a price taker, each additional unit sold adds to total revenue an amount equal to its price. This is illustrated in Figure 25.3(A). Given a perfectly elastic demand curve at price P_1, the firm receives an additional P_1 in revenue for each additional unit of output it sells ($MR = P_1$). Thus, the firm's marginal revenue curve (MR_1) is a horizontal line drawn at the price P_1.

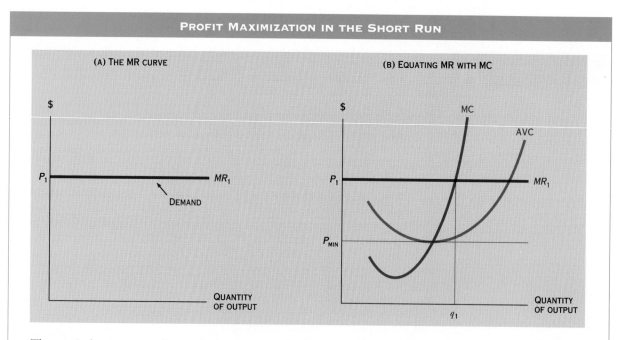

PROFIT MAXIMIZATION IN THE SHORT RUN

(A) THE MR CURVE

(B) EQUATING MR WITH MC

The marginal revenue curve for a perfectly competitive firm lies along its demand curve (A). Because the firm receives a price of P_1 for each unit sold, marginal revenue of each additional unit is P_1. Given a price of P_1, the firm produces q_1 output—which is determined by the intersection of the marginal revenue and marginal cost curves (B). The firm produces in the short run because $P_1 ≥ AVC$. If price were less than P_{min}, the firm would shut down.

FIGURE 25.3

SOURCE: Reprinted by permission of NEA, Inc.

MR = MC If the firm produces, it maximizes profit by producing up to the point where marginal revenue equals marginal cost (MR = MC). This is given by the intersection of the marginal revenue and marginal cost curves. In Figure 25.3(B) this occurs at output level q_1. At output levels below q_1, marginal revenue is greater than marginal cost. This means that another unit of output contributes more to revenue than to cost—it adds to a firm's profit or decreases its loss. As long as marginal revenue exceeds marginal cost, the firm continues to expand its output. Therefore, production continues until point q_1.[4]

Why doesn't the firm produce more than q_1 output? If it did, the additional output would cost more to produce than it generated in revenue (MC > MR). Because this would reduce the firm's profits or increase its losses, the firm does not produce beyond q_1. The profit-maximizing firm produces only to the point where MR = MC.

P ≥ AVC The preceding was based on the assumption that the firm does in fact choose to produce in the current period. But as you recall, unless the firm receives a sufficiently high price for its output it shuts down. Therefore, before deciding how much to produce, the firm must first decide whether or not to produce. That decision is based on the relationship between price and average variable cost.

We previously showed that the firm will produce only when:

$$TR \geq TVC$$

Because TR = $P \times q$ and TVC = AVC $\times q$, this requirement can be restated as:

$$P \times q \geq AVC \times q$$

Dividing both sides by q yields the following equivalent expression:

$$P \geq AVC$$

---

[4]When dealing with whole units of output, there is often no level of output for which marginal revenue equals marginal cost. In such a case, the firm should produce the highest level of output for which marginal revenue exceeds marginal cost. For example, in Figure 25.3(B), if q_1 = 10.5 machines, the firm should produce 10 machines.

The profit-maximizing firm produces only when $P \geq$ AVC. If for all levels of output $P <$ AVC, the firm shuts down.

In terms of Figure 25.3(B), the firm produces only when it receives a price of P_{min} or higher, where P_{min} is given by the minimum value of the average variable cost curve. For $P \geq P_{min}$ there is some level of output for which $P \geq$ AVC. But for $P < P_{min}$ price is less than average variable cost for all levels of output, so the firm shuts down. Because $P_1 > P_{min}$, the firm in Figure 25.3(B) produces in the short run.

SHORT-RUN PROFIT OR LOSS Profit for the firm can be computed with the aid of the ATC curve. Total profit is profit per unit times the number of units sold: $(P - ATC) \times q$.[5] When price is greater than average total cost, the firm earns an economic profit; when price is less than average total cost, the firm incurs a loss. Both possibilities are depicted in Figure 25.4. The firm in (A) produces q_1 output, earning a profit of $P_1 - ATC_1$ on each unit sold. Total profit is $(P_1 - ATC_1) \times q_1$, which is represented by the shaded area in Figure 25.4(A).

In Figure 25.4(B) the firm is suffering a loss. Given a price of P_2 the firm produces q_2 amount of output (where $MR_2 = MC$). At this level of output, price is less than average total cost ($P_2 < ATC_2$). Nonetheless, the firm produces because price exceeds average variable cost. Although the firm is not recovering all its costs, the price is more than high enough to cover variable costs.

Normal Profit

YOUR TURN

ILLUSTRATE DIAGRAMMATICALLY THE SITUATION WHERE A PROFIT-MAXIMIZING FIRM EARNS A NORMAL PROFIT (THAT IS, ECONOMIC PROFIT EQUALS ZERO). AT THE PROFIT-MAXIMIZING LEVEL OF OUTPUT, HOW DO THE VALUES OF AVERAGE TOTAL COST AND PRICE COMPARE?

SUMMARY To maximize profit the firm must satisfy two requirements: (1) *produce only if* $P \geq AVC$ and (2) *if production occurs, produce up to the point where* $MR = MC$. When the firm does produce, it earns a profit when $P >$ ATC but suffers a loss when $P <$ ATC.

OUR EXAMPLE REVISITED

Our earlier example helped illustrate the first approach to profit maximization (comparing total revenue and total cost). Let us return to that example, but this time applying the rules of the second approach ($MR = MC$, $P \geq$ AVC). Instead of examining the firm's TVC and TC schedules (as we did in Table 25.3), we look

---

[5]To see that this is equivalent to our definition, note that:

$$\text{profit} = TR - TC$$
$$= P \times q - ATC \times q$$
$$= (P - ATC) \times q$$

A firm earns a profit if $P > \text{ATC}$ but suffers a loss if $P < \text{ATC}$. At a price of P_1 the firm earns a profit of $(P_1 - \text{ATC}_1) \times q_1$, represented by the shaded area in (A). At a price of P_2 the firm suffers a loss of $(\text{ATC}_2 - P_2) \times q_2$, represented by the shaded area in (B).

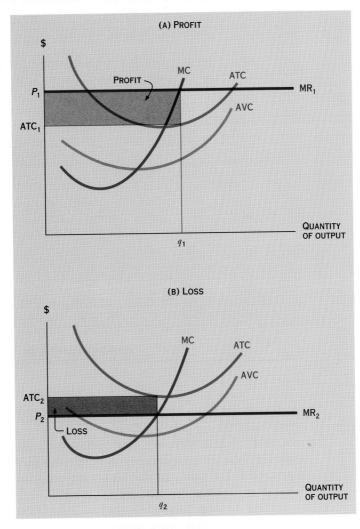

FIGURE 25.4

at the firm's cost data from a different perspective. Table 25.4 (page 656), presents three cost schedules: average variable cost, average total cost, and marginal cost—all consistent with the cost schedules of Table 25.3.

Let us determine the profit-maximizing level of output for each of three prices. Assume initially that the price is $60. Then marginal revenue for each level of output is $60 (see column 5). Marginal revenue exceeds marginal cost for the ninth unit of output ($60 > $59) but not for the tenth unit ($60 < $75). Therefore, if the firm produces it should produce nine units of output. But is the firm better off shutting down? Because price exceeds average variable cost at nine units of output ($60 > $36.11), the firm determines that production should proceed. Given a price of $60, the firm produces nine units of output in order to maximize profit.

FINDING THE PROFIT-MAXIMIZING LEVEL OF OUTPUT BY COMPARING MR AND MC

	COSTS			PRICE = $60		PRICE = $40		PRICE = $20	
(1) q	(2) AVC*	(3) ATC*	(4) MC	(5) MR	(6) PROFIT	(7) MR	(8) PROFIT	(9) MR	(10) PROFIT
0					−$120		−$120		−$120
1	$50.00	$170.00	$ 50	$60	− 110	$40	− 130	$20	− 150
2	42.00	102.00	34	60	− 84	40	− 124	20	− 164
3	36.00	76.00	24	60	− 48	40	− 108	20	− 168
4	31.75	61.75	19	60	− 7	40	− 87	20	− 167
5	30.00	54.00	23	60	30	40	− 70	20	− 170
6	30.00	50.00	30	60	60	40	− 60	20	− 180
7	31.14	48.29	38	60	82	40	− 58	20	− 198
8	33.25	48.25	48	60	94	40	− 66	20	− 226
9	36.11	49.44	59	60	95	40	− 85	20	− 265
10	40.00	52.00	75	60	80	40	− 120	20	− 320
11	45.00	55.91	95	60	45	40	− 175	20	− 395
12	51.00	61.00	117	60	− 12	40	− 252	20	− 492

*Numbers are rounded to nearest cent.
To maximize profit, the firm should produce when P = $60 or P = $40 (since P > AVC) but not when P = $20 (since P < AVC). Once it decides to produce, the firm compares MR and MC. The profit-maximizing level of output is 9 when P = $60 and 7 when P = $40.

TABLE 25.4

The actual level of profits can be computed by plugging the appropriate value of ATC into the formula: profit = $(P − ATC) \times q$. For example, if six units are sold, ATC = $50; therefore, total profit equals ($60 − $50) × 6 = $60. Column 6 of Table 25.4 presents the profit schedule for different levels of output given a price of $60. It confirms that profits are maximized at an output of nine units. Given P = $60, the firm can earn $95 in profit.

When the price falls to $40, the firm reduces output to seven units. This is the last level of output for which marginal revenue ($40) exceeds marginal cost. Moreover, at seven units of output, price ($40) exceeds average variable cost ($31.14), indicating that production should occur. Even though the firm is losing money (see column 8), this is better than shutting down—in which case losses would swell to $120.

Finally, consider a price of $20. Although marginal revenue is greater than marginal cost for the fourth unit of output, the firm should not produce. If it does, price is less than average variable cost. This tells the firm that its best option is to shut down, thereby limiting its loss to $120.

An examination of Tables 25.3 and 25.4 reveals that, as advertised, the two approaches to profit maximization yield identical answers. Whether you rely on the total approach (comparing TR and TC) or the marginal approach (comparing MR and MC), you reach the same conclusion concerning the amount of output a firm should produce and the amount of profit it earns.

THE SHORT-RUN SUPPLY CURVE OF A PERFECTLY COMPETITIVE FIRM

Thus far the discussion has focused on the production decisions of a perfectly competitive firm, where price plays a central role in the analysis. Price for the individual firm is given—the firm is a price taker. But how is that price determined? To obtain the answer it is necessary to derive the short-run supply curve, first for the individual firm and then for the industry in which the firm is selling.

The firm's short-run supply curve is derived from its marginal cost curve. To be explicit: *the firm's short-run supply curve is given by the segment of its marginal cost curve that lies above average variable cost.* This is illustrated in Figure 25.5.

As previously indicated, production occurs only when $P \geq P_{min}$, where P_{min} equals the minimum value of average variable cost. At P_{min} the firm is indifferent between producing q_{min} and shutting down. In either case, its loss equals its fixed costs. For prices above P_{min} the firm supplies output, and the marginal cost curve indicates how much (since the firm produces to the point where $P = $ MC). For example, when $P = P_1$ the firm supplies q_1 output. When $P = P_2$, output falls to q_2. In other words, the marginal cost curve above minimum average variable cost reveals the relationship between price and quantity supplied. Therefore, this segment of the marginal cost curve must be the firm's short-run supply curve.

THE INDUSTRY'S SHORT-RUN SUPPLY CURVE

A curve indicating the relationship between the price of a good and the amount supplied by the industry in the short run. (In the short run the number of firms in the industry is fixed.)

THE INDUSTRY'S SHORT-RUN SUPPLY CURVE

The industry's short-run supply curve is derived from the short-run supply curves of firms currently in the industry. Because the number of firms is fixed in the short run, industry output can be increased only by increasing the output of existing firms. The industry supply curve indicates the aggregate quantity supplied,

THE FIRM'S SHORT-RUN SUPPLY CURVE

The firm's short-run supply curve—represented by the heavy line—consists of the segment of the firm's marginal cost curve that lies above average variable cost.

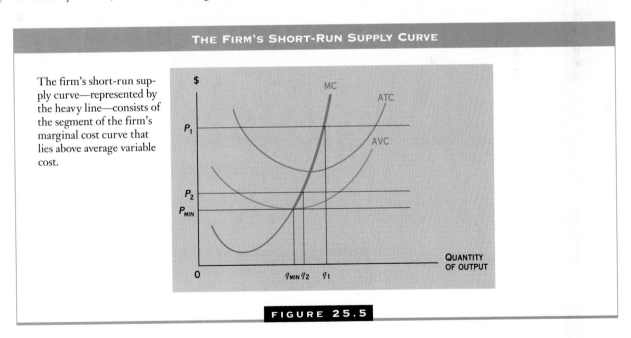

FIGURE 25.5

at each price, by all firms in the industry. When input prices do not change as the industry expands, the short-run supply curve for the industry is obtained by adding (horizontally) the short-run supply curves of each firm in the industry. This is illustrated in Figure 25.6.

Even though competitive industries have many firms, for simplicity we demonstrate this technique for an industry with two firms. The same process applies, however, regardless of the number of firms in the industry. At a price of $3 Firm 1 supplies 15 units of output and Firm 2 supplies 20 units. The total amount supplied by this industry for $P = \$3$ is $15 + 20 = 35$ units of output. When price rises to $5 the two firms supply, respectively, 25 and 30 units of output. Altogether, 55 units are supplied by the industry.

In the event that all firms in the industry have identical cost curves, deriving the industry's short-run supply curve is even simpler. For example, if the industry contained 1,000 firms all similar to Firm 1, each would supply 25 units when the price was $5. Therefore, the quantity supplied by the industry at this price would be $1,000 \times 25 = 25,000$. More generally, the amount supplied by the industry at any price would simply be 1,000 times the amount supplied by Firm 1.

The aggregation procedure just discussed is based on the assumption that input prices remain constant as the industry expands. Later in the chapter we explain why input prices might change. When input prices do change, derivation of the supply curve becomes more complicated.[6]

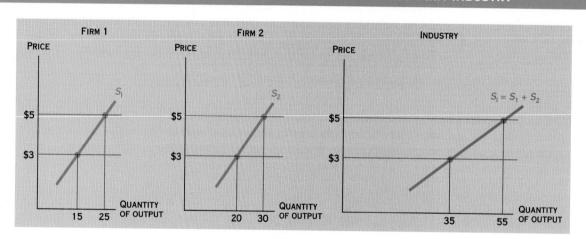

DERIVING THE SHORT-RUN SUPPLY CURVE FOR A TWO-FIRM INDUSTRY

When input prices remain constant, the short-run supply curve for an industry is obtained by adding, at each price, the quantity supplied by all firms in the industry. For example, at $P = \$3$ Firm 1 supplies 15 units of output and Firm 2 supplies 20 units. Therefore, the quantity supplied by this two-firm industry is $15 + 20 = 35$. Other points can be obtained in similar fashion.

FIGURE 25.6

---

[6]When input prices increase as the industry expands, the short-run supply curve of the industry is steeper than when input prices remain constant. With higher input prices, cost curves for firms in the industry shift upward. In response, firms scale back the amount of output they are willing to sell. Therefore, although higher output prices still induce firms to increase the quantity supplied, firms increase quantity by a lesser amount when input prices also rise.

SHORT-RUN EQUILIBRIUM FOR THE INDUSTRY

Given the industry's supply curve, we are now in a position to describe short-run equilibrium for the industry and, in the process, explain how price is determined for the perfectly competitive firm. In addition to industry supply, it is necessary to introduce industry demand, which consists of the demand by all buyers of the industry's product.

Figure 25.7(B) presents the short-run supply and demand curves for a perfectly competitive industry. Equilibrium price and quantity for the industry are determined by the intersection of these two curves. The equilibrium price, $5, is then taken as given by all firms in the industry. Figure 25.7(A) depicts the situation for an individual perfectly competitive firm. Note that although price depends on aggregate supply of the industry, the firm represents such a minuscule part of the industry that it has no perceptible impact on price, no matter how much it supplies. It is for this reason that the perfectly competitive firm is considered a price taker. In this example the firm produces 25 units of output, given by the intersection of the price (or marginal revenue) curve and the marginal cost curve.

Long-Run Equilibrium in Perfect Competition

Short-run equilibrium, both for the firm and the industry, are depicted in Figure 25.7. But how can we characterize long-run equilibrium? In the long run all inputs are variable. Firms can build larger plants, in response to profit opportunities, or switch to smaller plants. Even the number of firms in the industry may change in

SHORT-RUN EQUILIBRIUM FOR A PERFECTLY COMPETITIVE INDUSTRY AND ONE OF ITS FIRMS

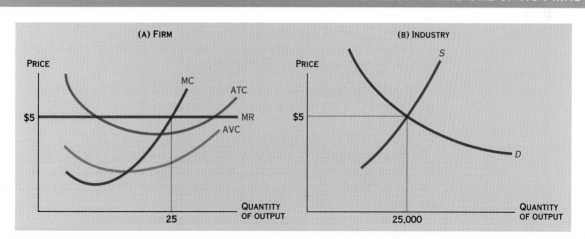

The equilibrium price and quantity are determined by the intersection of industry supply and demand curves. The equilibrium price, $5, is taken as given by the individual firm. To maximize profits, the firm produces 25 units of output.

FIGURE 25.7

the long run. Profits lure new firms to the industry and losses cause some existing firms to leave the industry, because their resources can earn more elsewhere. For these reasons short-run equilibrium may not correspond to long-run equilibrium. In the long run, industry output may expand or contract, depending on whether firms are earning profits or losing money in the short run.

Equilibrium refers to a state of balance. In long-run equilibrium the firm has no incentive to change its operations: it is producing the desired amount of output and its plant is just the right size. The desired amount of output, of course, is the amount that maximizes profits. In the long run, profits are maximized when marginal revenue or, equivalently, price equals long-run marginal cost. The logic is similar to that applied in our short-run analysis. The only difference is that in the long run all inputs are variable, so that when the firm increases its output it also increases plant size. In the short run, of course, plant size is fixed.

Long-run equilibrium requires that the firm produce its output at the lowest possible long-run cost. The firm must not be able to produce the same level of output more cheaply by switching to a different plant size. This means that the firm must be operating on its long-run average cost curve. Thus, in long-run equilibrium firms produce the profit-maximizing level of output with the optimal plant size.

Another condition for long-run equilibrium is that firms earn zero economic profits (that is, normal profits). In other words, price must equal average total cost. To see why, suppose instead that firms in the industry were earning positive economic profits. Because entry into a perfectly competitive industry is easy, new firms would be moving into the industry to take advantage of profits there. Alternatively, if firms were suffering losses, some would be leaving the industry and reemploying their resources elsewhere, in order to earn higher returns.

An industry cannot be in a state of balance if firms are still in the process of moving into or out of the industry. Long-run equilibrium requires that all adjustments be completed, that the industry be at rest. As long as economic profits are positive or negative, the industry is not at rest. Firms are either entering the industry (when profits are positive) or leaving the industry (when profits are negative). Only when economic profits equal zero is there no incentive for additional entry or exit. Therefore, only when economic profits equal zero can an industry be in long-run equilibrium.

> Long-run equilibrium requires that (1) firms maximize profits ($P = \text{LRMC}$) and (2) firms earn normal profits ($P = \text{LRAC}$).

Figure 25.8 depicts long-run equilibrium for the firm. The firm, facing a price of P_1, produces q_1 output. The firm is maximizing profits ($P = \text{LRMC}$) and earning normal profits ($P = \text{LRAC}$). These two conditions, in turn, imply that $\text{LRMC} = \text{LRAC}$. (When $P = \text{LRMC}$ and $P = \text{LRAC}$, then $\text{LRMC} = \text{LRAC}$.) As Chapter 24 explained, marginal cost and average cost are equal at only one point— where average cost is at a minimum (point E in Figure 25.8). Thus *long-run equilibrium implies that the firm must be producing at the minimum point of its long-run average cost curve.*

Because the firm is producing q_1 with the optimal plant size, point E is also the minimum point on the firm's short-run average cost curve. Consequently, at point E short-run marginal cost equals short-run average cost ($\text{SRMC} = \text{SRAC}$). Putting everything together, in long-run equilibrium the following equality holds:

$$P = \text{LRMC} = \text{LRAC} = \text{SRAC} = \text{SRMC}$$

An implication of the preceding analysis is that perfect competition forces firms to produce at the lowest possible average cost in the long run. Firms that do not have the optimal plant size cannot survive in the long run. Nor can firms that operate their plants at the wrong level, producing either too much or too little. To remain in business in the long run, a firm must earn at least normal profits. In perfect competition this occurs only when the firm produces efficiently—that is, at the lowest possible average cost. Firms that are not efficient cannot compete with those that are, and ultimately are driven from the industry.

LONG-RUN SUPPLY FOR THE INDUSTRY

Long-run equilibrium for the firm is represented in Figure 25.8, but how can we illustrate long-run equilibrium at the industry level? Equilibrium, whether short-run or long-run, requires that industry demand equal industry supply. The only difference between the short run and the long run is that entry and exit of firms affects industry supply in the long run.

Different perfectly competitive industries have different **industry long-run supply curves**. The shape depends on what happens to input prices (and therefore cost curves) as new firms enter the industry. In **constant-cost industries**, input prices remain constant as the industry expands; in **increasing-cost industries**, input prices increase; and in **decreasing-cost industries**, input prices decrease. The following sections derive the long-run supply curve and describe long-run equilibrium for all three cases.

CONSTANT-COST INDUSTRIES Assume an industry is initially in long-run equilibrium (illustrated at point A in Figure 25.9, page 662). At the equilibrium price (P_1) the firm produces q_1 output and the industry produces Q_1. Now assume

THE INDUSTRY'S LONG-RUN SUPPLY CURVE
A curve indicating the relationship between the price of a good and the amount supplied by the industry after the entry of new firms to the industry or the exit of existing firms.

CONSTANT-COST INDUSTRY
An industry in which input prices (and therefore cost curves) remain unchanged as the industry expands.

INCREASING-COST INDUSTRY
An industry in which input prices increase as the industry expands.

DECREASING-COST INDUSTRY
An industry in which input prices decrease as the industry expands.

LONG-RUN EQUILIBRIUM FOR A PERFECTLY COMPETITIVE FIRM

Long-run equilibrium occurs at point E. The firm is maximizing profits (P = LRMC) and earning normal profits (P = LRAC). Together, these two conditions imply that the firm must be operating at the minimum point of its long-run average cost curve. At this point, short-run marginal cost also equals short-run average cost.

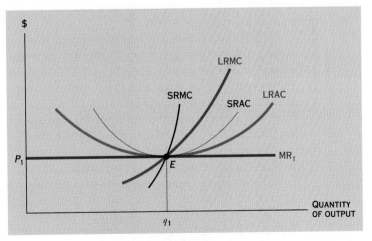

FIGURE 25.8

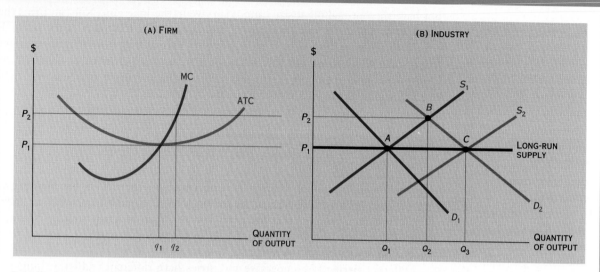

Initially the industry is in equilibrium at point A, producing Q_1 output and selling it at price P_1. At this price the firm sells q_1 output, earning normal profits. If industry demand increases to D_2, price rises to P_2 in the short run and industry output rises to Q_2 as individual firms increase output to q_2. Firms are now earning economic profits ($P > ATC$), which attracts additional firms to the industry. Their entry leads to a new short-run supply curve, S_2, and a new long-run equilibrium, point C. At P_1 the firm once again produces q_1 output; however, because of the additional firms, industry output rises to Q_3.

FIGURE 25.9

further that demand for the industry's product increases, perhaps because of an increase in population or a change in tastes. Let us work through what happens, first in the short run and then in the long run. Let S_1 denote the initial short-run supply curve, based on the number of firms in the industry prior to the increase in demand. Once demand increases, the industry moves from point A on the short-run supply curve to point B. Price rises from P_1 to P_2, and industry output expands to Q_2. At the higher price, existing firms increase production in the short run to q_2 in order to maximize profits.

The situation just outlined corresponds to short-run equilibrium, but does it represent long-run equilibrium? Obviously not. At q_2, firms in the industry are earning economic profits, since $P_2 > ATC$. In response, new firms are drawn into the industry. With additional firms, industry output expands. This expansion is represented by a rightward shift in the short-run supply curve. Firms continue to enter the industry, and the supply curve continues to shift rightward, until profits are eliminated. This occurs at point C, where the short-run supply curve is S_2.

Because of the entry of new firms, the initial equilibrium price, P_1, is restored in the long run. Firms once again produce q_1 output, earning normal profits. There is no incentive for additional firms to enter the industry or for existing firms to leave. Point C therefore corresponds to long-run equilibrium.

The line running through point A (the initial equilibrium) and point C (the final equilibrium) is the industry's long-run supply curve. *For a perfectly competitive constant-cost industry, long-run supply is perfectly elastic.* An increase in demand leads to an increase in output but in the long run has no effect on price. P_1 is the only price consistent with long-run equilibrium, since it is the only price for which firms earn a normal profit.

What if, instead of increasing, demand shifts to the left? If demand falls, long-run equilibrium is once again established through a change in the number of firms in the industry, only now it is the exodus of firms that brings the industry back into equilibrium. Suppose the industry is initially at point C in Figure 25.9. If demand falls from D_2 to D_1, price initially falls below P_1, leading to short-run losses. Some firms leave the industry and, as they do, the short-run supply curve shifts leftward, raising price. This process continues until price returns to P_1. The new long-run equilibrium corresponds to a smaller number of firms, each producing q_1 output. As with an increase in demand, quantity changes in the long run but not price.

A key assumption of this analysis is that the firm's cost structure remains constant as the industry expands or contracts. Whether an industry contains 1,000 firms or 10,000, the firm's cost curves are the same. It is because of this assumption that the industry is labeled a constant-cost industry. This assumption does not always hold, however, and in such cases the story has a different ending. To understand this, read on.

INCREASING-COST INDUSTRIES As an industry expands it requires larger quantities of inputs—additional labor, raw materials, machinery, and so forth. In constant-cost industries input prices remain fixed even as the industry purchases increasing amounts of inputs. Generally, however, an expansion of industry output drives up input prices. For example, an increase in the demand for wheat may raise the price of land, as wheat farmers bid away land from competing uses, or may increase the cost of irrigation, as farmers are forced to use more arid land. In such cases, the cost curves of wheat farmers shift upward as the industry expands.

Figure 25.10 (page 664) illustrates long-run equilibrium for an increasing-cost industry. Initially the industry is in equilibrium at point A. Once again assume that demand for the industry's product increases, raising price in the short run to P_2. Because firms earn profits at this price new firms enter the industry, shifting the industry supply curve rightward. This is where the similarity with constant-cost industries ends. As the increasing-cost industry expands, its firms' cost curves shift upward. Profits are squeezed from two directions: price falls (as industry supply increases) and average cost rises (because of higher input prices).

This process continues until once again price equals average cost ($P_3 = \text{ATC}_2$ in Figure 25.10A). Note that the price associated with the final equilibrium (P_3) exceeds the price at the initial equilibrium (P_1). This implies that an increased quantity is available in the long run only at a higher price. *The long-run supply curve of an increasing-cost industry slopes upward.* Available evidence indicates that most industries fall into the increasing-cost category—that is, most industries have upward-sloping supply curves in the long run as well as the short run.

DECREASING-COST INDUSTRIES A third possibility exists, although it is rare in practice. As an industry expands, its firms may face *lower* input prices. For example, as the personal computer industry expands, its firms buy more and more microchips. This could lead to lower chip prices, perhaps because of economies of scale in the microchip industry. In such an event, firms in the personal computer industry find that their cost curves shift lower as their industry expands. If average cost falls, the only way economic profits can be eliminated is if price falls below its initial level (see Figure 25.11, page 664). In that case, an increase in demand for the

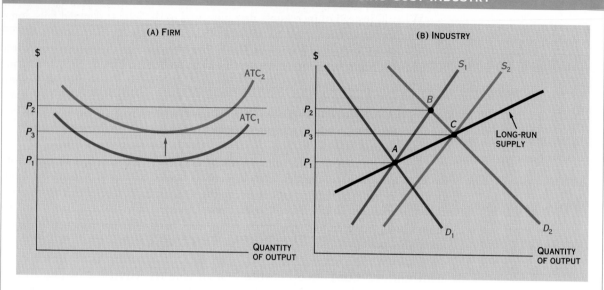

An increase in industry demand raises price in the short run from P_1 to P_2. As new firms enter the industry, supply increases from S_1 to S_2. The expansion of industry output shifts the firm's average cost curve from ATC_1 to ATC_2. Because of higher unit costs, additional output will be supplied in the long run only at a price above the initial equilibrium price (that is, $P_3 > P_1$). The long-run supply curve in an increasing-cost industry is upward sloping.

FIGURE 25.10

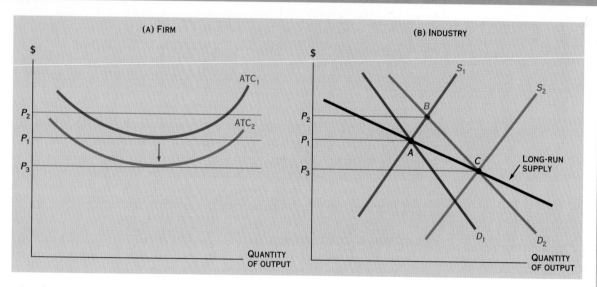

In a decreasing-cost industry, higher demand means a higher price in the short run (P_2) but a lower price in the long run (P_3). As the industry expands, cost curves for the firm shift lower, enabling the firm to earn normal profits while selling at a lower price.

FIGURE 25.11

industry's product leads not only to increased output in the long run but also to a lower price. *The long-run supply curve of a decreasing-cost industry is downward sloping.*

An Evaluation of Perfect Competition

Now that the mechanics of perfect competition have been studied, it is time to assess this market structure. In what ways is perfect competition the best of all possible worlds? In what ways does it fall short of the ideal? Certain government policies (for example, antitrust laws) are predicated on the belief that society benefits when markets are made more competitive. What is the basis of this contention?

IN PRAISE OF PERFECT COMPETITION

PRODUCTIVE EFFICIENCY One virtue of perfect competition is that it leads to output being produced in the long run at the lowest possible cost. Resources are being used efficiently. Firms cannot lower average cost of production by building a different plant size or operating their plant at a different level of output. To survive in the long run, firms must produce at the minimum point of their long-run average cost curves. This condition, known as **productive efficiency**, guarantees that an industry's output cannot be produced at a lower cost.

Not only is production efficient under perfect competition, but consumers pay a price just high enough to cover those costs. The requirement that firms earn only normal profits in the long run means that the market price is the minimum price producers require to supply that level of output. Price is inflated by neither unnecessary costs nor excess profits. It is in this sense that price is kept to a minimum.

EFFICIENT ALLOCATION OF RESOURCES Production may be efficient in the sense that average costs are minimized, but that by itself does not assure maximum consumer satisfaction. Firms may be producing the wrong mix of goods. For example, a country may be producing both barley and corn at their minimum average cost, but if it produces more barley than desired and not enough corn, then the economy is in some sense inefficient. In particular, it is inefficient in the way it allocates resources among its industries. It is overallocating resources to the production of barley—that is, funneling too many resources into this industry—and underallocating resources to the production of corn.

The price consumers are willing to pay for another unit of a good measures the value consumers place on that unit. Stated differently, price reflects the marginal benefit derived from a good. Marginal cost, on the other hand, measures the cost of producing another unit of the good. Think of it as the opportunity cost of the resources used to produce the additional output.

When price exceeds marginal cost, the value consumers place on an additional unit exceeds the cost of producing it. Therefore, consumers benefit from its production. But when price is less than marginal cost, the extra output should not be produced. The value consumers place on this additional output falls short of the

PRODUCTIVE EFFICIENCY
An industry's output is produced at the lowest cost possible.

cost of producing it. In other words, the resources required to produce the additional output are valued more highly in another industry. Thus, consumers benefit from additional production of a good when $P > MC$ and are made worse off when $P < MC$.

The ideal situation is for production to proceed up to the point where $P = MC$. The last unit produced would have a value that just matched the cost of producing it. When this occurs resources are said to be allocated efficiently. Resources cannot be redistributed among industries without reducing consumer satisfaction. Because price equals marginal cost under perfect competition, resources are allocated efficiently when all industries are perfectly competitive.

Efficient allocation of resources occurs when $P = MC$ in each industry.

OTHER CONSIDERATIONS Apart from reasons of efficiency, some individuals favor perfect competition because it is consistent with maximum individual freedom. Decisions are made by individual consumers and producers, not dictated by some third party. There is no need for outside intervention. Individuals acting in their self-interest promote the public interest. For those who distrust government bureaucrats and dictators, this is an appealing arrangement. To quote Adam Smith:

> The statesman who should attempt to direct private people in what manner they ought to employ their capitals, would not only load himself with a most unnecessary attention, but assume an authority which could safely be trusted to no one and would be dangerous in the hands of a man who had folly and presumption enough to fancy himself fit to exercise it.[7]

There are no economic power brokers in the world of perfect competition. No individual consumer or business is powerful enough to rig the market, to pursue policies that economically harm other parties. Not only are resources allocated efficiently, some people consider the way they are allocated to be a virtue itself. Be that as it may, conditions exist in the real world that make perfect competition less than perfect.

SOME POSSIBLE DRAWBACKS TO PERFECT COMPETITION

Although perfect competition has some advantages, it may be impossible or undesirable for several reasons.

ECONOMIES OF SCALE Perfect competition requires a particular technology, one in which economies of scale disappear when firm size is small. Costs of production are minimized when there are a large number of small firms each operating at the minimum point of its long-run average cost curve. Suppose, however, that an industry is characterized by extensive economies of scale. We cited several examples of such industries in Chapter 24 (for example, automobiles, utilities, and breweries). In such industries costs of production are minimized when an industry contains very few firms, each operating a large plant. We return to this issue in Chapters 26 and 27. The point of the present discussion is this: when extensive economies of

---

[7]Same as 1, p. 423.

scale exist, it is neither efficient nor desirable for an industry to have a large number of small firms, as perfect competition requires.

EXTERNALITIES A stated advantage of perfect competition is that it leads to efficient allocation of resources. This is true, however, only when private producers pay the full cost of their production. When there are externalities—for example, pollution—resources are not allocated efficiently under perfect competition.

It is useful to distinguish between the private cost of production and the social cost. The *private cost* includes only those costs paid by the producer; the *social cost* adds to this figure any additional costs borne by society. Assume that production in an industry creates pollution that causes $1 billion worth of damage to the environment. This $1 billion is included in the social cost of production but excluded from the private cost, because firms do not actually pay these pollution costs.

For resources to be allocated efficiently from the perspective of society, price should equal marginal social cost—that is, the relevant marginal cost concept includes the added cost to society of the additional pollution. Under perfect competition, however, producers consider only the costs that they themselves must pay. Therefore, production occurs at the point where price equals marginal private cost. When marginal private cost and marginal social cost diverge, perfect competition leads to an allocation of resources that is inefficient from the perspective of society. This issue is addressed in Chapter 35, along with ways to correct this misallocation.

OTHER CONSIDERATIONS Some individuals criticize perfect competition on other grounds, including equity, innovation, and variety of products. Even if perfect competition would lead to efficient production and efficient allocation of resources among industries, some would not embrace it.

Perfect competition maximizes satisfaction of consumers subject to a given distribution of resources among members of society. Some individuals are wealthy; others are poor. If you do not like the initial distribution of resources, you will not like the distribution of products under perfect competition. Some critics are willing to sacrifice a certain amount of efficiency for greater equity—that is, for a more equal distribution of output among the populace. They consider perfect competition less than perfect because it does not conform to their notion of the ideal distribution of output.

Others contend that perfect competition may not be the optimal market structure for innovation. Why should a perfectly competitive firm invest in research and development if other firms, which do not bear these costs, can quickly adopt any new technology? Unless a firm can gain an edge over its competitors, it has little incentive to develop a new technology. Concentrated industries (that is, those dominated by a few large firms) may prove more conducive to innovation because barriers to entry deny new firms access to the company's technology. Moreover, large noncompetitive firms may have more money to invest in research and development than small competitive firms. Therefore, some economists suggest that technological progress is likely to occur more rapidly when product markets are not perfectly competitive. We return to this argument in Chapter 27.

Finally, some believe that a world of perfect competition would be rather bland. Perfect competition does not allow for product differentiation among producers. Do we really want a world where all department stores stock the same merchandise, where clothing of one manufacturer is indistinguishable from clothing of other manufacturers, where all colas taste the same? Some would be willing to trade a little efficiency for product variety and greater consumer choice.

Before perfect competition can be fully evaluated vis-à-vis other market structures, we must examine these other market structures in more detail. That is the goal of the next two chapters.

Summary

1. Markets differ from one another in terms of number of firms, ease of entry, type of product (homogeneous or differentiated), and ability of the firm to influence price. Economists recognize four market structures: perfect competition, monopoly, monopolistic competition, and oligopoly. An industry's price, level of output, potential for profits, and related matters all depend on its market structure.

2. Perfect competition requires a large number of buyers and sellers of a homogeneous product, free entry and exit, and perfect information. Under these conditions the firm is a price taker—that is, demand for the firm's product is perfectly elastic. Because of this, the marginal revenue from selling an additional unit of output equals the price.

3. To maximize profits in the short run a perfectly competitive firm must satisfy two conditions. (1) Produce only when $TR \geq TVC$ or, equivalently, $P \geq AVC$. If this condition is not satisfied, the firm should shut down. (2) Produce that level of output for which $TR - TC$ is greatest. This means producing to the point where $MR = MC$.

4. The short-run supply curve of a perfectly competitive firm consists of that segment of its marginal cost curve that lies above average variable cost. For any given price, the marginal cost curve above average variable cost indicates the quantity of output the firm supplies to maximize profits. The industry's short-run supply curve is obtained by adding (horizontally) the short-run supply curves of all firms in the industry.

5. Short-run equilibrium for the industry requires that demand for the industry's product equal industry supply. Once the industry's price is determined, it is taken as given by individual firms in the industry.

6. Long-run equilibrium in perfect competition requires that firms maximize profits ($P = LRMC$) and that firms earn only normal profits ($P = LRAC$). These conditions are satisfied only when the firm produces at the minimum point of its long-run average cost curve. To survive in the long run, a perfectly competitive firm must produce efficiently—it must have the optimal plant size and operate this plant at the level that minimizes average cost.

7. The number of firms in an industry is fixed in the short run but may change in the long run. New firms enter an industry if it is profitable; some existing firms leave if the industry is losing money. Because of this, supply in the long run differs from supply in the short run.

8. The shape of the long-run supply curve depends on what happens to input prices as the industry expands. In constant-cost industries, long-run supply is perfectly elastic. Because input prices (and therefore cost curves) remain constant, there is no pressure in the long run for the output price to rise or fall. In increasing-cost industries, higher input prices lead to a higher output price and therefore to an upward-sloping supply curve in the long run. In decreasing-cost industries, lower input prices result in a downward-sloping supply curve.

9. Perfect competition has several appealing characteristics. Because of productive efficiency, an industry's output is produced at the lowest possible cost. Assuming that there are

no externalities, resources are also allocated efficiently across industries. Under these conditions, consumer satisfaction is maximized. Perfect competition is also consistent with maximum freedom of individuals.

10. Perfect competition is neither possible nor desirable when an industry has extensive economies of scale. In such a situation efficient production requires that an industry have a small number of firms, large in size, rather than many small firms. When private costs of production differ from social costs, resources are not allocated efficiently under perfect competition. Some people believe that perfect competition has other shortcomings: the distribution of output may be highly unequal, technological advances may not be as rapid as possible, and the choice of products may be limited.

Key Terms

market structure
free entry
free exit
perfect competition
price taker
shutting down
marginal revenue
the firm's short-run
   supply curve

the industry's short-run supply curve
the industry's long-run supply curve
constant-cost industry
increasing-cost industry
decreasing-cost industry
productive efficiency
efficient allocation of resources

Study Questions and Problems

1. (a) Some industries produce a homogeneous product, others a differentiated product. Explain the difference between these two types of products.
   (b) A large city may have hundreds of gasoline stations. Are they perfect substitutes for one another? What type of market structure best describes the retail gasoline market in Los Angeles? Why?

2. If no industry fully satisfies the assumptions of perfect competition, is there any reason to study this market structure? Defend your answer.

3. A perfectly competitive firm has fixed costs of $60 and the variable costs given in the following table:

q	1	2	3	4	5
TVC	$110	$200	$300	$420	$575

(These numbers come from the first Your Turn section of Chapter 24.) How many units of output should the firm produce in the short run if (a) $P = \$95$, (b) $P = \$105$, (c) $P = \$115$, (d) $P = \$125$? In each case, how much profit would be earned?

4. (a) Draw the short-run supply curve for the firm described in question 3. (b) Assume the industry contains 10,000 firms all identical to this firm. Draw the short-run supply curve for the industry.

5. Assume a perfectly competitive firm is producing ten units of output. The marginal cost of the tenth unit is $50; the price is $40. If the firm wishes to maximize profit, should it increase production, decrease production, or leave production unchanged? Why?

6. New Store has the following total revenue and total cost schedules:

q	TR	TC
0	$ 0	$ 100
1	200	350
2	400	500
3	600	630
4	800	850
5	1,000	1,100

a. What is the marginal revenue of the second unit of output? What is the marginal cost of the second unit of output?
b. Which market structure best characterizes New Store's product market? On what basis did you reach your conclusion?
c. How many units of output should New Store produce in order to maximize profit? Show how you derived your answer.
d. Given your answer in (c), how much profit (or loss) does New Store make?
e. At the profit-maximizing level of output, what is the average profit or loss per unit of output?

7. Why does long-run equilibrium for a perfectly competitive firm occur at the minimum point of its LRAC curve?

8. As the trucking industry expands, it requires additional motor fuel. More fuel can be supplied only when the petroleum industry operates high-cost oil wells, which drives up the price of fuel. (a) Under these conditions would the trucking industry be characterized as a constant-cost, an increasing-cost, or a decreasing-cost industry? (b) Suppose demand for trucking increases. How does this affect the price of trucking services in the long run?

9. Assume the price of shirts is $20 and the price of pants is $30. The marginal cost of producing each is $25. Are resources being allocated efficiently? Which industry, if either, should receive additional resources? (Assume there are no externalities.)

10. For many industries Congress has erected barriers that restrict access of foreign producers to U.S. markets, thereby limiting foreign competition. How are such restrictions on the supply of foreign producers likely to affect the prices paid by U.S. consumers?

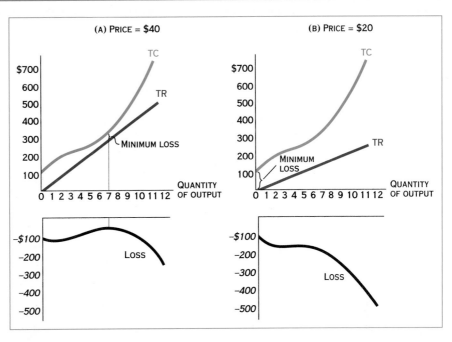

Answers to Your Turn

(A) Minimum loss (TC − TR) is at $q = 7$. (B) Minimum loss is at $q = 0$.

(A) PRICE = $40

(B) PRICE = $20

NORMAL PROFIT

Answers to Your Turn

Profit maximization requires $P = MC$; normal profit requires $P = ATC$. Both conditions are satisfied only when price intersects the ATC curve at its minimum value.

Monopoly

MONOPOLY AND PERFECT COMPETITION ARE POLAR EXTREMES. UNDER PERFECT COMPETITION THERE ARE A LARGE NUMBER OF PRODUCERS, NONE POWERFUL ENOUGH TO INFLUENCE PRICE. WITH MONOPOLY THERE IS BUT ONE SELLER OF A PRODUCT. YOU EITHER BUY FROM THAT SELLER OR DO WITHOUT. AS THE EXCLUSIVE SELLER OF A PRODUCT, THE MONOPOLIST HAS THE POTENTIAL TO DICTATE PRICE. ALTHOUGH THIS POTENTIAL IS SOMETIMES CONSTRAINED BY THE GOVERNMENT (SEE CHAPTER 29), THE UNREGULATED MONOPOLIST CAN CHARGE ANY PRICE IT CHOOSES.

CHAPTER 26 ANALYZES MONOPOLY IN THE ABSENCE OF GOVERNMENT REGULATION. HOW DO MONOPOLISTS DETERMINE WHICH PRICE TO CHARGE? DOES MONOPOLY GUARANTEE PROFITS? WHY DO MONOPOLISTS HAVE A BAD IMAGE? TO WHAT EXTENT IS IT DESERVED?

The monopolists, by keeping the market constantly understocked, by never fully supplying the effectual demand, sell their commodities much above the natural price, and raise their emoluments [profits].[1]

[1]Adam Smith, *The Wealth of Nations* (New York: Random House, 1937), p. 61. [Originally published in 1776.]

The Meaning of Monopoly

MONOPOLY

An industry with only one seller. There are no good substitutes for the product of the monopolist.

Monopoly is derived from two Greek words: *mono* (single) and *polein* (to sell). A monopolist then is the only seller of a product that has no close substitutes. Because no other firm sells a similar product, the industry comprises a single producer, the monopolist. Unlike the case of perfect competition, there is no need to distinguish between the firm and the industry. With monopoly, the firm *is* the industry!

Given this definition, monopoly might appear easy to identify. In reality, the issue of what constitutes monopoly is more complex. Whether a market contains more than one seller depends on how you define the market. If only one bus company carries passengers between St. Louis and Chicago, is it a monopolist? In the narrow sense it is—it is the only company providing bus service over this route. On the other hand, if the market is defined more broadly as the market for transportation, the bus company ceases to be a monopolist. It competes with airlines, automobiles, and the railroad.

The issue is whether other forms of transportation are a good substitute for bus travel. Substitutability is a matter of degree. Because of this, some prefer to also think of monopoly as a matter of degree. Any firm that faces a downward-sloping demand curve has some **monopoly power**. The greater the firm's influence over price, the greater its monopoly power.

MONOPOLY POWER

The ability of a firm to influence output price by changing the amount it sells. Any firm facing a downward-sloping demand curve has some monopoly power.

The preceding discussion suggests a certain arbitrariness in classifying a company as a monopolist. Despite this, such classifications are important because monopoly is often prohibited by law (see Chapter 28). Although no clear-cut procedures exist to identify monopoly, economic tools are available to make the government's job more manageable. Some of these tools are discussed later, but you are already familiar with one—the cross elasticity of demand. Evidence that two goods have high, positive cross elasticities has been accepted by courts as proof that two goods are close substitutes (Exhibit 5.4). If a good has a close substitute, its producer is not a monopolist.

Maintaining Monopoly through Barriers to Entry

The economic behavior of a monopolist is examined shortly, but first a preliminary question must be addressed. How can a firm maintain its monopoly position? In other words, why don't competing firms enter the industry? Although various reasons can be offered, depending on the particular industry, the major explanations are control of strategic raw materials, economies of scale, and assorted government restrictions.

CONTROL OF AN ESSENTIAL RAW MATERIAL

One way to assure monopoly status is to deny other producers access to a resource essential for the production of a good. It is difficult to produce polished diamonds unless you first possess raw diamonds. By controlling an estimated 80 percent of the world's raw diamonds, the DeBeers Company of South Africa has gone a long way toward establishing a diamond monopoly. And until the U.S. government intervened in the 1940s, Alcoa was able to maintain a virtual monopoly in the aluminum industry. A key to this dominance was Alcoa's control of almost all the known bauxite, an ore necessary for the production of aluminum.

ECONOMIES OF SCALE

Assume an industry experiences economies of scale over the entire range of production. Under these circumstances, a monopoly is likely to evolve. As a company becomes larger, its average cost of production falls. The largest company in the industry can produce output at a lower average cost than all other firms. Because of this cost advantage, it can profitably sell its output at a price below what other companies require to stay in business. As these other companies experience losses year after year, they ultimately leave the industry. Unable to duplicate the low costs of the monopolist, new firms are unlikely to enter. Under these circumstances, the monopoly may be maintained indefinitely.

PATENTS AND COPYRIGHTS

PATENT

An exclusive right, granted by the government, to market a product or process for 17 years.

Government protection provides an additional source of monopoly. When the government issues a **patent**, it grants its holder the exclusive right to market a product or process for 17 years (longer if the patent is renewed). The purpose of a patent is to encourage research and development, which ultimately may benefit millions in society. The Burroughs–Wellcome Company spent tens of millions of dollars developing a drug (AZT) to impede the AIDS virus and to prolong the lives of its victims. The Upjohn Company made a similar investment developing Minoxidil, which promotes hair growth in some balding men. Without the prospect of being able to recoup investment costs—which the patent provides—drug companies would have little incentive to undertake costly research.

Patents helped launch Xerox and other high-tech companies. Today patents motivate companies to design new computer hardware and software. Of course, some research would be undertaken even without this form of monopoly protection. Dan Bricklin invented *VisiCalc*, the computer spreadsheet, without bothering to file for a patent. Today he regrets his inaction. With a patent he would have earned not only the admiration of computer users but also millions of dollars.

As Bricklin's achievements demonstrate, technological progress occurs even in the absence of patents. But advances would come at a much slower pace. Without patents, competitors could copy a company's product at will. The rewards for innovation would quickly disappear, as other firms began selling similar products. Realizing this, a company would have less incentive to invest in research and development—let someone else make the heavy investment. The present system was created to dispel this attitude and, instead, to promote innovation by granting the inventor exclusive rights to a product over the life of the patent. Of course, patent

E
X
H
I
B
I
T

26.1

Companies are sometimes tempted to copy a patented product or process, hoping to tap into a monopolist's profits. The penalty for those that succumb can be stiff. Recently, a judge ruled that Smith International had infringed on a patent granted the Hughes Tool Company. The patented product was a rubber seal used in drilling for oil. Smith International was ordered to pay Hughes $227 million, thereby wiping out one-half of Smith's net worth.

Exxon, Kodak, and Ford were other losers. Exxon reached an $86 million settlement with Lubrizol Corp. after Lubrizol charged the giant oil company with violating its patents for motor-oil additives. Kodak was forced out of the instant-camera business and in 1991 agreed to pay Polaroid $925 million for infringing on its patents. And Ford was forced to pay $10 million to Robert Kearns for violating the inventor's patents on windshield wipers. Although obtaining a patent may take years and may cost thousands of dollars, such patent holders as Kearns and Polaroid consider the investment well worth the cost.

SOURCES: Adapted from Clemens P. Work, "Inventors' Just Rewards," *U.S. News & World Report*, March 3, 1986, p. 43; Paula Dwyer, "The Battle Raging Over 'Intellectual Property,'" *Business Week*, May 22, 1989, p. 82; Joseph White, "Ford to Pay $10.2 Million to Inventor," *The Wall Street Journal*, November 15, 1990, p. A4; and *The Wall Street Journal*, "Kodak to Pay Polaroid $925 Million to Settle Suit," July 16, 1991, p. A5.

COPYRIGHT

An exclusive right, granted by the government, to publish, copy, or sell a piece of music, art, or literature.

rights must be enforced if they are to have any value. As Exhibit 26.1 demonstrates, those who violate patents do so at their own peril.

A **copyright** grants the holder exclusive rights to literary and artistic works. Composers copyright songs, authors copyright books, studios copyright movies. Similar to patents, though easier to obtain, copyrights are designed to protect the property of authors and artists and, in so doing, to encourage creativity.

LICENSING AND OTHER GOVERNMENT RESTRICTIONS

Government sponsorship of monopolies is not limited to patents and copyrights. Congress has given exclusive rights to deliver first-class mail to the U.S. Postal Service, thereby creating a postal monopoly. Other activities, from selling drugs to operating a television station, require the approval of federal agencies. When only one company is granted permission to engage in an activity, at least in a certain region of the country, a monopoly is born. State and local governments also create monopolies. For example, a city may grant a company exclusive rights to sell cable television service or to operate a racetrack.

The Basic Model of Monopoly

PRICE AND MARGINAL REVENUE FOR THE MONOPOLIST

Because of barriers such as those just described, a monopolist is the sole source of a product, the only producer in an industry. Therefore, demand for the monopolist's product coincides with demand for the industry's product. Industry demand curves are downward sloping and, accordingly, the monopolist must lower price if additional units are to be purchased. Later we consider the case where the monopolist can sell its good to different consumers at different prices. But for now, assume that all output is sold at the same price.

In order to sell additional output, a monopolist must lower price—not just on the last unit sold but on all preceding units as well. Because of this, for all output beyond the first unit *marginal revenue is less than price.* This is illustrated in Table 26.1.

If the monopolist sets the price at $18, a single unit is purchased. To sell two units the monopolist must lower the price to $16. The marginal revenue of the second unit is $14 (that is, $32 − $18). Thus, the marginal revenue from selling the second unit is $2 less than the price received. (The reason, of course, is that the monopolist must cut the price of the first unit by $2). As Table 26.1 shows, for all units after the first, marginal revenue is less than price.

DEMAND, MARGINAL REVENUE, AND TOTAL REVENUE FOR A MONOPOLIST

PRICE	QUANTITY	TOTAL REVENUE	MARGINAL REVENUE
$20	0	$ 0	
18	1	18	$18
16	2	32	14
14	3	42	10
12	4	48	6
10	5	50	2
8	6	48	− 2
6	7	42	− 6
4	8	32	−10
2	9	18	−14

The monopolist must lower price in order to sell additional output. Because price must be reduced for all units, not just the last unit sold, marginal revenue is less than price for all output beyond the first unit.

TABLE 26.1

The demand and marginal revenue schedules of Table 26.1 are portrayed graphically in Figure 26.1.[2] Because marginal revenue is less than price, the marginal revenue curve lies below the demand curve. The demand and marginal revenue curves of the monopolist lie in stark contrast to those of the perfectly competitive firm. Whereas the competitive firm faces perfectly elastic demand and marginal revenue curves, the demand and marginal revenue curves of the monopolist are downward sloping.

MARGINAL REVENUE, TOTAL REVENUE, AND ELASTICITY OF DEMAND

Figure 26.1 also illustrates the relationship among marginal revenue, total revenue, and the elasticity of demand (E_d). As you may recall from Chapter 5, total revenue reaches a maximum where $E_d = 1$. (This occurs at the midpoint of a linear demand curve.) When $E_d > 1$, total revenue can be increased by reducing price. When $E_d < 1$, total revenue can be increased by raising price. Because marginal revenue is derived from total revenue, it is similarly linked to the elasticity of demand.

What does this tell us about the price a monopolist would like to charge? The answer is that a monopolist would not want to operate on the inelastic segment of its demand curve. For example, the firm in Figure 26.1 would not want to set a price of $6. Because demand is inelastic at $6, the firm could increase total revenue by raising price and reducing output. A lower output would also reduce any variable costs of production. Therefore, when a firm is on the inelastic range of its demand curve, it can increase profits simply by raising price.

The same conclusion can be reached by examining marginal revenue. When demand is inelastic marginal revenue is negative. The last unit sold *reduces* total revenue. The firm can earn additional profits by restricting output and raising price. Exactly which price the monopolist should charge depends on the costs of production (as we see in the next section). But even without considering costs, we can conclude that the monopolist does not want to be on the inelastic segment of its demand curve.

YOUR TURN

IF THERE WERE NO COSTS OF PRODUCTION, WE COULD SKIP THE NEXT SECTION. THE FIRM WOULD CONCENTRATE EXCLUSIVELY ON TOTAL REVENUE. (IF TC = 0, PROFIT = TR − 0.) ASSUMING PRODUCTION IS COSTLESS, HOW MUCH OUTPUT SHOULD THE FIRM IN TABLE 26.1 PRODUCE IN ORDER TO MAXIMIZE PROFITS? WHAT PRICE SHOULD IT CHARGE? HOW MUCH PROFIT WILL THE FIRM EARN?

PROFIT MAXIMIZATION IN THE SHORT RUN

The general rules for profit maximization are the same for all firms regardless of their market structure. *If a monopolist produces, it should produce to the point where*

[2]Notice that the marginal revenue curve is twice as steep as the demand curve. This is true for all linear (straight-line) demand curves.

When demand is elastic, a lower price increases total revenue (that is, MR > 0). When demand is inelastic, a lower price decreases total revenue (MR < 0). Total revenue is maximized when the elasticity of demand equals one.

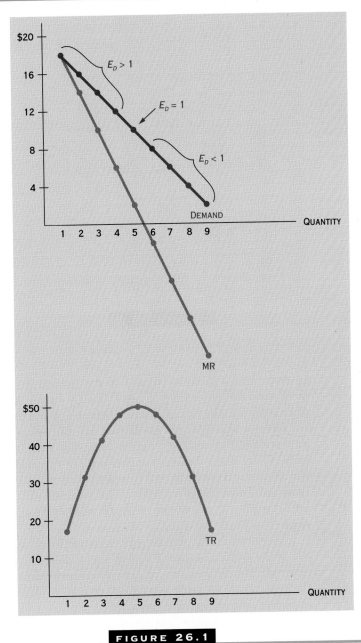

FIGURE 26.1

marginal revenue equals marginal cost. Until that point is reached, additional output adds more to revenue than to costs and thus increases profits.

Profit maximization for a monopolist is illustrated in Figure 26.2 (page 680). The monopolist produces Q_1 output, given by the intersection of the marginal revenue and marginal cost curves. But what price does the monopolist charge? To maximize profit the monopolist chooses the highest price *consistent with the sale of*

To maximize profit the monopolist produces Q_1 output, represented by the intersection of the marginal revenue and the marginal cost curves. The monopolist sells this output for P_1, which is the vertical distance between Q_1 and the demand curve. Profit is represented by the shaded area.

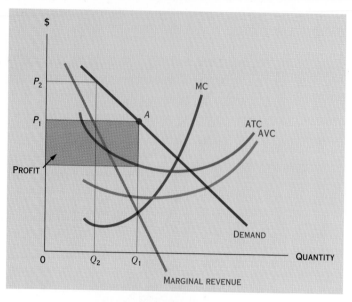

FIGURE 26.2

Q_1 *units.* This is given by point A on the demand curve, which lies directly above Q_1. Consumers are willing to pay P_1 for Q_1 output, but not a penny more. Thus price is equal to the vertical distance between Q_1 and the demand curve.

Observe that P_1 is not the highest possible price. The monopolist could have set a price of P_2 and sold Q_2 output. Why didn't the monopolist charge the higher price? Quite simply because a higher price in this case would have reduced profits. For all output between Q_2 and Q_1 marginal revenue exceeds marginal cost. Each of these units contributes to profits. Therefore, the firm should not stop producing until it reaches an output rate of Q_1. *The monopolist does not charge the highest price that anyone would be willing to pay.*

Also observe that, unlike perfect competition, price does not equal marginal cost at the profit-maximizing level of output. Because price is greater than marginal revenue for the monopolist, price is also greater than marginal cost. MR = MC is the general rule for profit maximization; P = MC is a special case that holds only in perfect competition.

Profit maximization can also be illustrated with a numerical example. Table 26.2 replicates the demand and revenue schedules of Table 26.1. Because a profit-maximizing monopolist would not produce where MR < 0, the inelastic portion of the demand schedule is deleted. Also appearing in Table 26.2 are the total cost, marginal cost, and profit schedules of the monopolist. From the table we see that the third unit of output is the last unit for which MR > MC. Therefore, to maximize profit the monopolist produces three units of output, sets a price of $14 (from column 2), and earns a profit of $10.

PROFIT MAXIMIZATION FOR A MONOPOLIST

(1) QUANTITY	(2) PRICE	(3) TOTAL REVENUE	(4) MARGINAL REVENUE	(5) TOTAL COST	(6) MARGINAL COST	(7) PROFIT
1	$18	$18	$18	$20	$ 8	$– 2
2	16	32	14	24	4	8
3	14	42	10	32	8	10
4	12	48	6	44	12	4
5	10	50	2	60	16	–10

The monopolist maximizes profit by producing three units and selling each for $14.

TABLE 26.2

MINIMIZING SHORT-RUN LOSSES

Monopoly does not guarantee profits. If demand for a product is weak, total cost may exceed total revenue at all levels of output. A patented technique for turning gold into lead is unlikely to earn its inventor any profits. In a similar vein, although a bus company may have exclusive rights to transport passengers between two towns, if demand for bus service is sluggish the company may lose money.

When profits are unattainable, the short-run goal of the monopolist is to minimize losses. The same rules apply as in perfect competition. The monopolist produces in the short run provided that $P \geq \text{AVC}$. This is illustrated in Figure 26.3 (page 682), where losses are minimized at Q_1 output. Although price falls short of average total cost, price does exceed average variable cost. The monopolist loses less money than if it produced no output.

On the other hand, in situations where $P < \text{AVC}$, production only adds to losses. Accordingly, the monopolist's best option is to shut down. *If* P < *AVC the monopolist does not produce in the short run.*

LONG RUN FOR THE MONOPOLIST

The monopolist has greater flexibility in the long run. Given time the monopolist can alter plant size to take advantage of possible cost savings. But when losses persist—regardless of plant size—the monopolist leaves the industry in the long run. Like other firms, the monopolist seeks the maximum return on its resources. When higher returns are available elsewhere, the monopolist transfers its resources to other industries.

Although losses are not consistent with long-run equilibrium, profits are. In the case of perfect competition, the entry of new firms into the industry ultimately eliminates economic profits. With monopoly, however, barriers to entry shield the

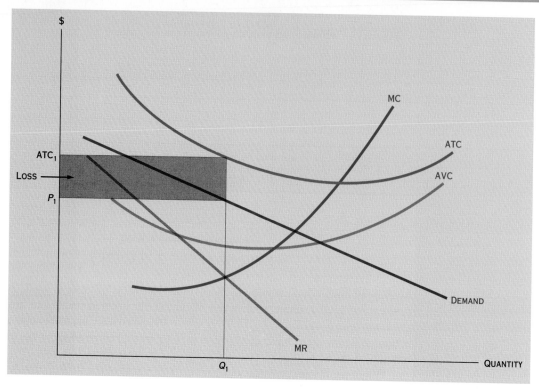

The monopolist minimizes short-run losses by producing Q_1 output. Because price exceeds average variable cost, the monopolist loses less money than by shutting down.

FIGURE 26.3

monopolist from competitors. As a result, the monopolist may be able to enjoy economic profits even in the long run.

CONCERN ABOUT THE LONG RUN MAY CONSTRAIN THE MONOPOLIST IN THE SHORT RUN

Although barriers to entry protect the monopolist, that protection is not always complete. In some cases barriers can be overcome. Firms may locate alternative sources of a crucial raw material or develop a new, competing technology. Often the government intervenes. For example, the government ended Alcoa's virtual monopoly of the aluminum industry by building integrated aluminum plants during World War II and then selling them to Reynolds Metals and Kaiser Aluminum. In addition, the government has split up some companies, such as Standard Oil and AT&T, while forcing others to sell plants to rival firms.

For such reasons a monopolist may worry that its industry will eventually evolve into a different market structure. Even if the monopolist can maintain its barriers to entry, it may fear other government action. For example, in the past the oil industry has been slapped with price controls and a *windfall* or *excess-profits* tax.

Such concerns may force the monopolist to alter its behavior. If its goal is to maximize profit over the long run, the monopolist may choose to sell more output to the public and charge a lower price than the model of short-run profit maximization suggests. Lower short-run profits have two advantages: (1) they reduce the incentive of other firms to attempt entry into the monopolist's industry, and (2) they make government intervention less likely. In both cases the result may be to prolong the period over which economic profits are earned. In summary, when a monopolist feels threatened by potential rivals or by adverse government actions, it may sacrifice short-run profits in order to earn greater profits over the long run.

Price Discrimination

The basic model of monopoly must also be modified when the monopolist is able to charge different prices to different customers. Until now we have assumed that the monopolist sets a single price, but clearly this is not always the case. Universities typically charge students a lower price for football tickets than they charge the general public. They also reduce the price of education for certain students by offering scholarships. Some pharmacies and restaurants offer senior-citizen discounts. Movie theatres generally set lower ticket prices for children than for adults. Railroads charge different customers different rates depending on what is shipped. Producers sometimes sell their products for less in foreign markets than at home, a practice known as *dumping*.[3]

PRICE DISCRIMINATION
The practice of selling a good at different prices that are not attributable to differences in cost.

Price discrimination occurs when a company charges different prices to different buyers and when these price differences are not caused by differences in cost. Note the second requirement. A person lodging at the San Francisco Hilton pays more than someone staying at the Hilton in Little Rock, Arkansas, but this is not price discrimination. The San Francisco Hilton cost more per room to build. In addition, wages, taxes, and other operating costs are higher in San Francisco. Nor does AT&T discriminate against citizens of Los Angeles when it charges them more to call New York than it charges residents of Philadelphia. Transmission costs increase with distance. In contrast, the practice of charging young moviegoers less than adults does constitute price discrimination, since it costs no more to show a movie to adults.

The primary motive for price discrimination is to increase profits. Consider an orthodontist whose services are demanded by two new patients. Suppose one patient is prepared to pay $4,000 to have his teeth straightened but the other will go no higher than $3,000. If the orthodontist sets a common price of $4,000, she earns $4,000 in fees from the first patient and nothing from the second. If she charges both $3,000, she earns a total of $6,000. But she can do better than that. By charging the first patient $4,000 and the second $3,000, she earns a total of $7,000. The orthodontist may not know exactly what each patient is prepared to pay but, by gathering information on where the patients (or their parents) are employed, where

---

[3]Dumping is discussed in Chapter 37.

they live, whether they are covered by dental insurance, and so forth, she can usually differentiate among clients on the basis of ability to pay.[4]

Not all businesses charge different prices. Before a company can engage in price discrimination, three conditions must hold:

1. The company must have some monopoly power and therefore face a downward-sloping demand curve.
2. The company must be able to segment buyers into different markets having different elasticities of demand.
3. The company must be able to prevent the resale of its product.

The first condition is obvious. Only companies with a downward-sloping demand curve have the ability to influence price. The second condition is more subtle. To maximize profit the firm must equate marginal revenue and marginal cost in each market. When elasticity of demand differs across markets, the price at which MR = MC also differs. This is illustrated in Figure 26.4 where, for

PRICE DISCRIMINATION—THE EFFECT OF ELASTICITY OF DEMAND

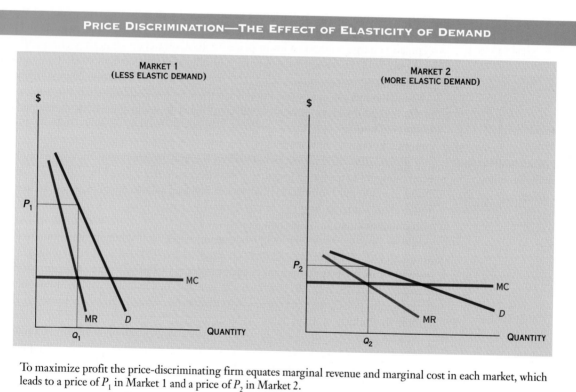

To maximize profit the price-discriminating firm equates marginal revenue and marginal cost in each market, which leads to a price of P_1 in Market 1 and a price of P_2 in Market 2.

FIGURE 26.4

[4]This practice is by no means limited to orthodontists. A noted psychologist acknowledged charging patients anywhere from $5 per hour to $100. "Everybody should pay, but nobody can pay more than he can afford." [Cited in James Koch, *Industrial Organization and Prices*, 2nd ed. (Englewood Cliffs, N.J.: Prentice-Hall, 1980), p. 394.] Even unions discriminate. Construction unions often charge lower rates for residential work than for industrial projects. When Chrysler was experiencing financial difficulties, the United Automobile Workers Union charged it less (in wage rates) than it charged GM and Ford.

simplicity, marginal cost is assumed to be constant. The company charges a higher price in the market where demand is less elastic because consumers there are less responsive to higher prices.

Not only must a company be able to sell in two or more markets, it must be able to prevent the resale of its product across markets. Why doesn't Sony charge men more than women (or bankers more than clerks)? If it attempted to do so, men would ask their wives or girlfriends to make the purchase for them, thereby avoiding the high-price market. More generally, secondary markets would crop up—low-price buyers would purchase a good from the company and then resell that good in the high-price market for less than the company was asking. Some companies have considered drastic measures to prevent the resale of their product. Rohm & Haas provides a classic example (see Exhibit 26.2).

Unlike Rohm & Haas, the orthodontist does not have to worry about the resale of her product—orthodontic services cannot be transferred from one patient to another. Nor do movie theatres need to be concerned about children selling their tickets to adults. Adults are admitted only if they have an adult ticket, which is distinguishable from a child's ticket.

No Arsenic, Please

The Rohm & Haas Company sold a plastic, methyl metacrylate, that was a key ingredient in the manufacture of dentures. Dental laboratories were charged $45 per pound. This compound also had a less glamorous use as an industrial plastic. Because other industrial materials were close substitutes, Rohm & Haas set a price of only $.85 per pound for its industrial users.

When dental labs learned of the price differential, some began purchasing the material from industrial buyers. Determined to halt this practice, Rohm & Haas contemplated ways to keep the markets separate. One proposal was to add poison to the industrial plastic. The company reasoned that the Food and Drug Administration (FDA) would never allow dental labs to manufacture dentures with tainted materials. This plan was detailed in company correspondence:

> A millionth of one percent of arsenic or lead might cause them [the FDA] to confiscate every bootleg unit in the country. There ought to be a trace of something that would make them rear up.

Although Rohm & Haas rejected this proposal, it did leak stories that the industrial plastic had been contaminated.

SOURCES: Adapted from Corwin D. Edwards, *Economic and Political Aspects of International Cartels*, U.S. Senate, Subcommittee on War Mobilization of the Committee on Military Affairs, 78th Congress, Second Session (1944), p. 19, cited in Douglas F. Greer, *Industrial Organization and Public Policy*, 3rd ed. (New York: Macmillan, 1992), p. 438.

EXHIBIT 26.2

Although price discrimination increases profits for producers, it has a mixed effect on consumers. Some buyers are forced to pay more as a result of price discrimination. On the other hand, many buyers in the low-price market would be forced to forgo consumption if the producer sold to everyone at the same price. Without price discrimination, fewer children would attend the movies and fewer low-income individuals could afford orthodontic treatment.

An Evaluation of Monopoly

Let's face it: monopolists have a bad image. Consumers complain of shabby treatment at the hands of monopolies, and governments are often eager to break up monopolies (as we learn in Chapter 28). These negative connotations are sometimes deserved, but they are not the entire story. Let's assess monopoly, first dwelling on its vices and then considering possible redeeming features. To keep things simple, we consider a monopolist not engaged in price discrimination.

THE EVILS OF MONOPOLY

RESTRICTING OUTPUT AND RAISING PRICE A major criticism of monopoly is that it leads to a higher price than does perfect competition and to a lower output. Thus consumers are harmed on two fronts. To illustrate this argument, consider an industry that is initially perfectly competitive. Now assume that someone buys all existing plants, in the process becoming a monopolist. For the moment, assume that the cost of producing a given level of output is the same under monopoly as it was under perfect competition, so that the marginal cost curve of the monopolist is identical to the industry supply curve under perfect competition. (The monopolist's marginal cost curve and the supply curve under perfect competition are both obtained by summing the marginal cost curves of all plants in the industry.)

The consequences of transforming the industry from perfect competition to monopoly are illustrated in Figure 26.5. Under perfect competition Q_c output is produced and sold at a price of P_c, given by the intersection of the industry supply and demand curves. In contrast, the monopolist equates marginal revenue and marginal cost. Thus, the monopolist restricts output to Q_m while raising price to P_m.

On theoretical grounds then, monopolists can be expected to inflate price in order to increase profits. But do monopolists really behave in this fashion? As Exhibit 26.3 (page 688) indicates, available evidence supports the theory of monopoly. Indeed, the effect of monopoly on price and profits is sometimes dramatic.

INEFFICIENT ALLOCATION OF RESOURCES In the absence of externalities, perfect competition leads to efficient allocation of resources. Resources flow into an industry until the value to consumers of another unit of output (price) equals the cost of producing another unit (marginal cost). In contrast, *monopoly is characterized by an underallocation of resources to the industry.*

This situation is illustrated in Figure 26.5. At Q_m price exceeds marginal cost—the value of another unit is greater than the cost of producing it. Society would like

A perfectly competitive industry produces Q_c output, because at this level industry demand equals industry supply. The competitive price is P_c. In contrast, the monopolist produces Q_m, determined by the intersection of marginal revenue and marginal cost. By limiting output to Q_m, the monopolist can raise the price to P_m.

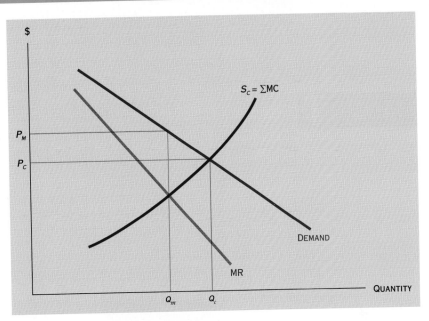

FIGURE 26.5

additional resources to flow into this industry. But the monopolist restricts the flow of resources into the industry in order to limit output. These resources are diverted instead to other industries for the production of output that has a lower value to consumers.

This misallocation of resources reduces the welfare of society. But by how much is society harmed? Economic studies place this welfare loss at roughly 1 percent of the nation's output.[5] These low estimates have led some observers to suggest that monopoly may not be so bad after all. Some have even questioned the value of regulating monopoly and enforcing antitrust (antimonopoly) laws. Might these resources be better employed elsewhere?[6]

Before giving up the fight against monopoly, we must be confident that we are measuring the full costs of monopoly. Today most economists believe that monopoly imposes other costs on society in addition to the direct costs stemming from output restrictions.

MONOPOLY RENT SEEKING AND REGULATION   To the extent that a monopoly generates profits—or what are often called "monopoly rents"—it is a valuable

[5]The initial study was by Arnold Harberger, "Monopoly and Resource Allocation," *American Economic Review* (May 1954), pp. 77–87. See also F. M. Scherer and David Ross, *Industrial Market Structure and Economic Performance*, 3rd ed. (Boston: Houghton Mifflin, 1990), p. 667; Paul D. Scanlon, "FTC and Phase II: The McGovern Papers," *Antitrust Law and Economics Review* (Spring 1972), pp. 33–36.

[6]George Stigler quipped that if the cost of monopoly were as low as some suggest, "economists might serve a more useful purpose if they fought fires or termites instead of monopoly." See G. Stigler, "The Statistics of Monopoly and Merger," *Journal of Political Economy* (February 1956), p. 34.

EXHIBIT

26.3

Tungsten carbide is a hard metal with important industrial applications. It was available in the 1920s for about $50 per pound until General Electric and the Krupp Company of Germany established a world monopoly giving General Electric exclusive rights to the U.S. market. During the time that General Electric monopolized the U.S. market, the price of tungsten carbide fluctuated between $225 and $453 per pound. In 1942, the U.S. government, relying on antitrust laws, broke up this monopoly. With other producers in the market, the price of tungsten carbide fell below $45 per pound and remained there. Thus, the price under monopoly was approximately five to ten times greater than the price charged in the face of competition.

In the early 1970s, when Bausch & Lomb possessed monopoly power in the soft contact-lens market, it produced these contact lenses at a cost of less than $5 per pair and sold them for more than $60. When competitors eventually broke into the market, the price fell sharply.

Burroughs–Wellcome spent $80 million researching and developing a drug (AZT) to treat the AIDS virus. In 1987, the Food and Drug Administration approved the drug for distribution in the United States. This gave Burroughs–Wellcome exclusive rights to the only drug known to help victims of AIDS. For a one-year supply of the drug, the company initially set a rather healthy price of $8,300 wholesale ($10,000 retail). At that price, revenues in the first year alone were estimated to be $250 million—more than triple the research and development costs. When asked why such a high price was chosen, the company president responded that "the efficacy and speed of introduction of competitive products are unknown." In other words, convinced that competition ultimately would drive down the price, the company wanted to earn as much as possible before those competitive pressures materialized.

SOURCES: Adapted from Walter Adams, "Public Policy in a Free Enterprise Economy," in Walter Adams, ed., *The Structure of American Industry*, 5th ed. (New York: Macmillan, 1977), p. 485 [cited in Edwin Mansfield, 6th ed., *Economics* (New York: Norton, 1989), p. 503]; William G. Shepherd, *The Economics of Industrial Organization*, 3rd ed. (New York: Prentice-Hall, 1990), p. 106; Marilyn Chase, "AIDS Drug Comes to a Worried Market," *The Wall Street Journal*, March 23, 1987, p. 6.

asset to its owner.[7] Companies are therefore willing to devote resources in an attempt to secure this asset. For example, companies competing for a cable television franchise may hire lawyers and lobbyists in an effort to win the franchise or even bribe public officials. From the perspective of society, resources used in the pursuit of monopoly power are wasted—they produce no socially valuable output. The social cost of **rent-seeking** activities is the value of the output these resources could have created had they been used in other activities.

RENT SEEKING
The use of scarce resources in an attempt to secure a monopoly and therefore earn monopoly profits.

[7] See Gordon Tullock, "The Welfare Costs of Tariffs, Monopolies, and Theft," *Western Economic Journal* (June 1967), pp. 224–232.

The value of monopoly rents appears to be high. One study estimated that they amounted to more than 7 percent of national output in India and about 15 percent in Turkey.[8] Given rents of this magnitude, one would expect rent seeking to attract considerable resources (although reliable estimates are not yet available).

The social costs of monopoly also include the costs of preventing and controlling monopolies. Resources used in fighting monopoly are being diverted from the production of goods and services. Thus, in assessing monopoly the costs of rent seeking and regulation must be added to the costs of restricting output.

TECHNOLOGICAL PROGRESS   Some economists argue that monopolists may be slow to innovate, denying society the benefits of new technologies and slowing economic growth. Rather than push hard to introduce new technologies, monopolists may pursue a more leisurely pace. In the view of Sir John Hicks, "The best of all monopoly profits is a quiet life."[9] Such tendencies may be offset by other forces, however, as we see shortly.

INCOME DISTRIBUTION   At the same time that monopolists reduce the size of the economic pie through inefficiency, they take a large slice for themselves. That is, monopolists increase their share of income at the expense of others. Surely some monopolists are noble; some may be sweet, loving grandmothers. But it is difficult to argue that monopolists as a class are more deserving than nonmonopolists. Accordingly, some attack monopoly for contributing to an "unfair distribution of income."

Although fairness is in the eyes of the beholder, we can say something objective about the distribution of income. Because monopoly creates wealth for those who hold it, there is a tendency for monopoly to make the distribution of income more unequal. According to one study, the wealthiest 0.27 percent of families in the United States own 18.5 percent of the country's assets. If all monopoly power were eliminated, the wealth of these super-rich would fall to 13 percent or less of assets.[10] To those who value an egalitarian distribution of income, monopoly moves us in the wrong direction.

POTENTIAL ADVANTAGES OF MONOPOLY

The case against monopoly having been presented, can anything be said in defense of monopoly? Monopoly has two potential advantages, both related to costs. Under certain circumstances monopoly may (a) reduce current costs of production and (b) promote more rapid technological progress, thereby reducing costs in the future.

NATURAL MONOPOLIES   Earlier we examined the consequences of transforming a competitive industry into a monopoly. We showed that *if the total cost of*

---

[8]Anne O. Krueger, "The Political Economy of the Rent-Seeking Sector," *American Economic Review* (June 1974), pp. 291–303.

[9]John Hicks, "Annual Survey of Economic Theory: The Theory of Monopoly," *Econometrica* (January 1935), p. 8.

[10]William S. Comanor and Robert H. Smiley, "Monopoly and the Distribution of Wealth," *Quarterly Journal of Economics* (May 1975), pp. 191–193.

producing a given level of output is the same under perfect competition and monopoly, price is higher under monopoly and output is lower. We now relax this assumption and consider the case where the cost of production is lower with monopoly.

Certain monopolies arise because of economies of scale; these are called **natural monopolies**. In a natural monopoly the average cost of production declines throughout the relevant range of production. Therefore, a given level of output can be produced at the least cost when there is only one producer in the industry. This is illustrated in Figure 26.6. A single firm can produce 100 units at an average cost of $10, leading to a total cost of $1,000. With two firms each producing 50 units, total cost rises to $1,500. With four firms producing 25 units apiece, total cost climbs to $2,000. Other options are similarly inferior to monopoly. If output is to be produced with the fewest resources, there can be only one firm in the industry.

Although costs are minimized with one producer, restricting output to a single firm has an ambiguous effect on price. To remain in business, a company must charge a price that covers costs. If the industry were composed of two or more smaller firms, they would have higher average costs than the monopolist and therefore require a higher price to stay in business. In other words, the monopolist's lower costs permit it to charge a lower price. On the other hand, there is no guarantee that the monopolist will actually charge less—at least voluntarily. This is why governments often regulate natural monopolies. The government may attempt to take advantage of economies of scale by allowing only one producer while, at the same time, trying to protect the public by restricting the ability of the monopolist to raise price. The reasons for regulating natural monopolies, and the problems posed by regulation, are analyzed in Chapter 29.

TECHNOLOGICAL INNOVATION Monopoly power may promote investment in research and development, thereby spurring technological advances. As previously mentioned, this is the rationale for patents. The incentive to innovate depends on the expected financial returns. When these returns must be shared with other producers, the incentive to innovate is blunted.

NATURAL MONOPOLY
An industry characterized by extensive economies of scale. The total cost of producing a given output is minimized when only one firm is in the industry.

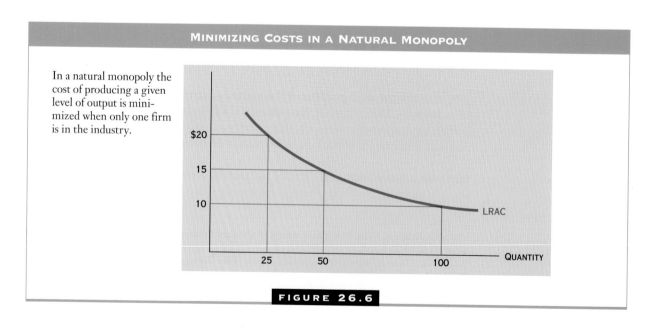

MINIMIZING COSTS IN A NATURAL MONOPOLY

In a natural monopoly the cost of producing a given level of output is minimized when only one firm is in the industry.

FIGURE 26.6

There may be a second, related reason for protecting the monopolist.[11] If other producers were allowed to enter the market once they "stole" a monopolist's invention, they would have an incentive to devote resources to the theft of this invention. At the same time, the monopolist would invest resources to protect its invention. The resources devoted both to theft and to its prevention are socially unproductive, adding nothing to output. Patents and other forms of monopoly protection free up resources to produce output valued by society.

Has monopoly had the predicted effect? Do innovations occur more rapidly in the presence of monopoly power? We examine the evidence in Chapter 27 after presenting the models of monopolistic competition and oligopoly.

Summary

1. A monopolist is the only seller of a product that has no close substitutes. Other firms are kept out of the industry through barriers to entry. The major barriers are control of an essential raw material, economies of scale, and government protection, including patents, copyrights, and licenses.

2. As the only producer in the industry, the monopolist faces a downward-sloping demand curve. To sell additional output, the monopolist must lower price on each unit sold. Because of this, the marginal revenue from additional output is less than price.

3. The monopolist does not want to operate on the inelastic segment of the demand curve, since marginal revenue is negative there. When demand is inelastic, the monopolist can increase profit by restricting output and raising price.

4. To maximize profits in the short run, the monopolist produces where marginal revenue equals marginal cost, provided that price is at least as high as average variable cost. If price is less than average variable cost, the monopolist shuts down to minimize losses.

5. Once the level of output is determined, the monopolist sets the highest price consistent with the sale of this output. Although higher prices could be charged, the monopolist would not be able to sell the profit-maximizing level of output at these higher prices.

6. Because of barriers to entry, a monopolist may be able to earn positive economic profits in the long run. Unless the monopolist can earn at least normal profits, it will leave the industry.

7. Price discrimination occurs when different buyers are charged different prices not resulting from differences in cost. This practice allows the monopolist to increase profits. Price discrimination is possible only if the monopolist can segment buyers into different markets and prevent the resale of its product.

8. Compared to perfect competition, monopoly leads to a higher price and reduced output in the industry. Because the monopolist restricts the flow of resources into the industry, monopoly leads to an inefficient allocation of resources. Other social costs of monopoly include the costs of monopoly rent seeking and regulation. Monopoly has also been criticized for making the distribution of income more unequal.

9. In certain circumstances monopoly may have beneficial effects. In a natural monopoly the costs of producing a given output are minimized when only one firm is in the industry. Monopoly protection (for example, patents) may also accelerate technological innovation.

---

[11]This argument comes from Richard A. Posner, "The Social Costs of Monopoly and Regulation," *Journal of Political Economy* (August 1975), p. 825.

monopoly

monopoly power

patent

copyright

price discrimination

rent seeking

natural monopoly

1. Explain why you agree or disagree with the following statements:
   a. "The price of monopoly is upon every occasion the highest which can be got."—Adam Smith
   b. To maximize profit, the monopolist should equate price with marginal cost.
   c. The monopolist may be able to earn positive profit in the long run.
   d. Even a monopolist may lose money.
   e. If marginal revenue declines as output increases, total revenue must also decline.

2. In what sense is the New York Yankees ball club a monopoly? The ability of the ball club to raise ticket prices is tempered by the availability of alternative activities. In the broad sense, there are substitutes for Yankees ball games. List some of these substitutes.

3. Why does the marginal revenue curve of the monopolist slope downward?

4. Consider the monopolist whose demand schedule is:

P	$9	$8	$7	$6	$5	$4	$3
Q	0	1	2	3	4	5	6

   Assume each and every unit costs $5 to produce—the total cost of one unit is $5, the total cost of two units is $10, and so on.
   a. Construct the monopolist's marginal revenue schedule.
   b. Compute its marginal cost schedule.
   c. Assuming that the goal of the monopolist is to maximize profits, how much output should it produce?
   d. What price should it charge?
   e. How much profit will it earn?

5. In each case indicate whether the monopolist should increase or decrease production in order to maximize profits. Explain your reasoning.
   a. The elasticity of demand is 0.50.
   b. Marginal revenue of an additional unit exceeds marginal cost.
   c. The monopolist is producing at the point where its demand curve intersects its marginal cost curve.

6. In *Welfare and Competition*, Tibor Scitovsky claims that the monopolist "may regard his immunity from competition as precarious or be afraid of unfavorable publicity and public censure." What does Scitovsky mean? Isn't a monopolist immune from competition and therefore free to do anything it pleases?

7. Which of the following constitute price discrimination?
   a. selling lobsters at a lower price in Maine than in Colorado
   b. giving employees a 25 percent discount on all items purchased from the store
   c. charging children less than adults for a luncheon buffet
   d. charging business executives more to fly on an airplane than vacationers
   e. selling a Japanese good at a higher price in Japan than in the United States
   f. selling a Japanese good for less in Japan than in the United States
8. Economists argue that monopoly causes misallocation of resources. Explain this argument.
9. According to the consulting firm Booz–Allen & Hamilton, the average price of hospital care is 30 percent higher in communities served by two hospitals than in one-hospital communities.[12] How can this finding be explained? Doesn't competition lead to *lower* prices?

TO MAXIMIZE PROFITS THE FIRM SHOULD PRODUCE FIVE UNITS OF OUTPUT, SELLING EACH FOR $10 AND EARNING $50 IN PROFITS.

YOUR TURN
Answers

[12]Cited in Ron Winslow, "Rival Operations," *The Wall Street Journal*, June 6, 1990, pp. A1 and A6.

Monopolistic Competition and Oligopoly

THE WORLD IS FILLED WITH COMPANIES LIKE MCDON-ALD'S. FACING STIFF COMPE-TITION FROM BURGER KING, WENDY'S, AND OTHER FAST-FOOD RESTAURANTS, MCDON-ALD'S CAN HARDLY BE CHAR-ACTERIZED AS A MONOPOLIST. YET IT IS NOT A PERFECTLY COMPETITIVE FIRM EITHER; IT SELLS A PRODUCT THAT DIF-FERS SLIGHTLY FROM THAT OF ITS COMPETITORS. THIS GIVES MCDONALD'S SOME INFLU-ENCE OVER THE PRICE OF ITS BURGERS AND FRIES. AS WITH MOST FIRMS IN THE REAL WORLD, MCDONALD'S FALLS SOMEWHERE BETWEEN PER-FECT COMPETITION AND MONOPOLY.

UNTIL ABOUT 60 YEARS AGO MOST ECONOMISTS WERE CONTENT WITH JUST TWO MODELS OF MARKET STRUC-TURE: PERFECT COMPETITION AND MONOPOLY. EVEN TODAY SOME ECONOMISTS ARGUE THAT OTHER MODELS ARE INCOMPLETE, LESS POWER-FUL, OR EVEN UNNECESSARY. FOR EXAMPLE, THEY CONCEDE THAT THE FAST-FOOD INDUS-TRY DOES NOT SATISFY ALL THE REQUIREMENTS OF PER-FECT COMPETITION BUT ARGUE THAT THIS MODEL NONETHELESS DOES A GOOD JOB OF EXPLAINING PRICE AND OUTPUT IN THIS MARKET.

MOST ECONOMISTS, HOWEV-ER, BELIEVE THAT MODELS OF INTERMEDIATE MARKET STRUCTURES HELP US BET-TER UNDERSTAND HOW REAL-WORLD MARKETS OPERATE. THEY POINT OUT THAT CER-TAIN FACTS ARE INCONSIS-TENT WITH THE MODEL OF PERFECT COMPETITION. FOR EXAMPLE, THE PERFECTLY COMPETITIVE FIRM WOULD NEVER ADVERTISE, SINCE IT CANNOT INFLUENCE THE PRICE OF ITS PRODUCT. YET MCDONALD'S SPENDS MORE

Both monopolistic and competitive forces combine in the determination of most prices, and therefore a hybrid theory affords a more illuminating approach to the study of the price system than does a theory of perfected competition, supplemented by a theory of monopoly.[1]

[1]Edward H. Chamberlin, *The Theory of Monopolistic Competition* (Cambridge, Mass.: Harvard University Press, 1933), preface.

than $200 million a year on television commercials, trying to convince consumers to frequent its restaurants.

Chapter 27 considers models that fall in between perfect competition and monopoly, focusing on the market structures known as *monopolistic competition* and *oligopoly*. Similar to monopolies, both oligopolistic and monopolistically competitive firms have some control over the price of their product. But unlike monopolies, they must share the market with other firms. Monopolistically competitive industries consist of a large number of small firms; oligopolistic markets are dominated by a few large firms. We begin with a discussion of monopolistic competition.

Monopolistic Competition

The theory of monopolistic competition is credited to independent work by Edward Chamberlin of Harvard University and to influential British economist Joan Robinson (see biography on page 697).[2] This theory, argues Robinson, is an attempt at greater realism. Traditionally, when economists observed some real-world phenomenon that was

> inconsistent with the assumptions of perfect competition, they were inclined to look for some complicated explanation of it, before the simple explanation occurred to them that the real world did not fulfill the assumptions of perfect competition.[3]

To Robinson and Chamberlin a more reasonable approach was to formulate a new theory, which was consistent with the facts.

The theory of **monopolistic competition** rests upon three assumptions: product differentiation, a large number of sellers, and free entry and exit.

MONOPOLISTIC COMPETITION
A market structure characterized by a large number of firms selling distinct (differentiated) products and in which entry into and exit from the industry is easy.

PRODUCT DIFFERENTIATION In monopolistically competitive markets each firm produces a product that, while highly similar to those of other firms, is viewed by consumers as distinct. That is, the products of the various firms are close but not perfect substitutes. The Nashville phone directory lists more than 100 different new-car dealers. All sell cars, but all dealers are not the same. They differ in location, size, reputation, quality of service, friendliness, and makes of automobiles. Their products are therefore distinct.

Product differences may be real or imagined. What is important is that consumers believe that such differences exist. Even when two goods are identical, as long as a consumer views one as superior, he or she is willing to pay a higher price for that good. Accordingly, producers have an incentive to distinguish their product, to make it appear more attractive than others on the market.

The aspirin industry provides a classic example of **product differentiation**. Inherently all brands of aspirin are indistinguishable: they all contain the same chemical compound. Yet the price of aspirin varies widely, with Bayer aspirin typically selling for several times as much as lesser-known brands. Much of this is due

---

[2]Chamberlin, *The Theory of Monopolistic Competition*; Joan Robinson, *The Economics of Imperfect Competition* (London: Macmillan, 1933).
[3]Robinson, same as 2, p. 4.

JOAN V. ROBINSON

(1903–1983)

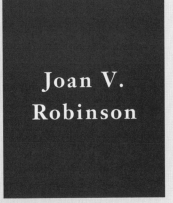

Joan V. Robinson

The accomplishments of Joan V. Robinson extended well beyond the theory of monopolistic competition. A gifted and prolific writer, Robinson made important contributions in such diverse fields as growth theory, international trade, economic philosophy, and Keynesian macroeconomics. Indeed, she is credited with helping Keynes formulate the ideas behind his *General Theory*.

Robinson was critical of *laissez-faire* economics lambasting the marginal productivity theory of distribution. At the same time, she defended Marxian economics. Although much of her work was outside of mainstream economics, she was widely respected by economists of all persuasions. One economist, writing before Robinson's death, claimed:

She is the only great economist that has ever lived who is not a man. She is also the only great living economist who has not been awarded the Nobel prize. These two are the great scandals of the economics profession.[4]

Except for a spell in India, Joan Robinson spent most of her career on the faculty of Cambridge University in England. She continued writing after her retirement in 1971, publishing an introductory economics text at the age of 70.

[4]Thanos Skouras, "The Economics of Joan Robinson," in J. R. Shackleton and Gareth Locksley, *Twelve Contemporary Economists* (London: Macmillan, 1981), pp. 216–217.

to advertising. Bayer has convinced many consumers that it is the Cadillac of the aspirin industry, somehow more effective than other brands. A positive image can be worth more than any real difference.

Admittedly, all brands of aspirin are not identical in every dimension. Subtle differences exist in terms of freshness, child-proof containers, tamper-proof packaging, liquid or tablet or capsule form, flavoring, and buffering. But actual differences are less than commonly perceived. Aspirin makers have been extremely effective in differentiating their products. Sometimes this differentiation has bordered on the deceptive. For a long time Anacin advertised that it contained the ingredient most recommended by doctors without revealing the ingredient: aspirin. In its commercials Excedrin boasted that it contained two ingredients, failing to name either: aspirin and caffeine. Whatever it takes, aspirin makers want you to believe that what they are selling is superior to other products on the market.

NUMBER OF SELLERS A monopolistically competitive market contains enough sellers that the actions of each can be considered independent. Not only are there too many firms to collude (to coordinate their decisions), but each firm constitutes such a small share of the market that its behavior has only a negligible effect on others in the market. Consequently, each firm can assume that rivals will ignore its actions. This means, for example, that monopolistically competitive firms set their prices in isolation, without fear that others will follow their lead.

Not all industries satisfy this requirement. As one of this country's Big Three automobile producers, General Motors is aware that its competitors are watching closely. Any price change it announces is likely to influence Ford and Chrysler. If it offers rebates or discount financing, its rivals are likely to follow suit. The automobile manufacturing industry simply does not have enough sellers to be monopolistically competitive. Instead it is oligopolistic.

In contrast, there are sufficient retail car dealers in Nashville for the assumption of independence to be defensible. A dealer can discount its car prices or improve service without worrying how its competitors will respond. Likewise, there are so many shoe stores, dry cleaners, and video shops in urban areas that such markets are considered monopolistically competitive.

FREE ENTRY AND EXIT The final requirement is that producers must be free to move resources into or out of the industry. Unlike the monopolist, firms in a monopolistically competitive market are not sheltered from competition. When the market is profitable, new firms enter; when conditions sour, firms pull out. For example, when car sales plummeted in the early 1990s, more than 1,000 U.S. dealerships went out of business. When car sales later improved, numerous new dealerships were formed.

MONOPOLY AND COMPETITION—A BIT OF EACH

The similarities to perfect competition are obvious. Both monopolistically and perfectly competitive industries are characterized by a large number of firms and by free entry and exit. But unlike perfect competition, each monopolistically competitive firm sells a distinct product. This is where the monopoly element appears. Because no other firm sells exactly the same product, a monopolistically competitive firm has some control over its price—its demand curve slopes downward.

A monopolistically competitive firm can raise its price without losing all its customers. Some shoppers will continue to buy from the firm—despite its higher price—because they believe it offers a superior product, or they trust the manager, or they find the store conveniently located. Brand loyalty often plays a role. Whatever the reason, some customers will stick with a company even if it raises its price relative to that of its competitors. In contrast, a perfectly competitive firm attempting to charge more than competitors ends up with no customers.

Although product differentiation gives the firm some discretion over price, the presence of close substitutes limits the firm's ability to raise price. With similar products on the market, consumers are highly sensitive to price. A car dealer that raises its prices by 10 percent can expect to lose considerably more than 10 percent of its customers. In other words, demand for the firm's product, though not perfectly elastic, is highly elastic.

The demand curve facing a monopolistically competitive firm is illustrated in Figure 27.1. Note that, similar to a monopolist, the firm also has a downward-sloping marginal revenue curve. As you learned in Chapter 26, a downward-sloping demand curve implies that the firm must lower price to sell additional output, meaning that marginal revenue declines with output.

EQUILIBRIUM IN THE SHORT RUN

The rules for short-run profit maximization are the same for the monopolistically competitive firm as for the monopolist. Production continues to the point where marginal revenue equals marginal cost. The firm then sells this level of output for the highest price possible given its demand curve. If price exceeds average total cost, the firm earns a profit; if price falls short of average total cost, the firm suffers a loss; if price equals average cost, the firm earns a normal profit. All three cases are illustrated in Figure 27.2 (page 700). For simplicity, the average variable cost curve has been omitted from the diagram, but $P \geq AVC$ remains a condition for production.

LONG-RUN EQUILIBRIUM

The monopolistically competitive firm does not accept losses in the long run and, unlike the monopolist, cannot earn long-run profits either. Only normal profits are possible in the long run. To understand why this must be true, assume that firms are enjoying short-run profits. Because entry is easy, new firms will be drawn into

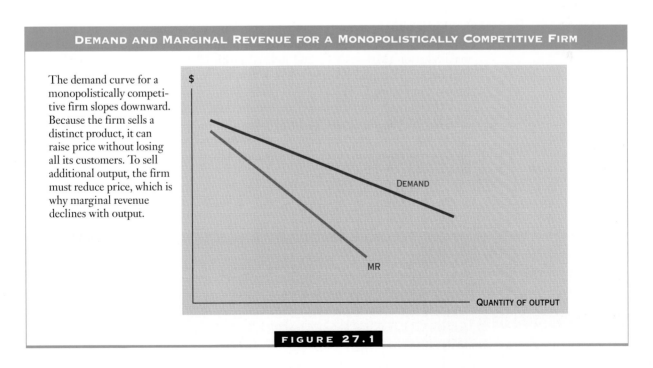

DEMAND AND MARGINAL REVENUE FOR A MONOPOLISTICALLY COMPETITIVE FIRM

The demand curve for a monopolistically competitive firm slopes downward. Because the firm sells a distinct product, it can raise price without losing all its customers. To sell additional output, the firm must reduce price, which is why marginal revenue declines with output.

$

DEMAND

MR

QUANTITY OF OUTPUT

FIGURE 27.1

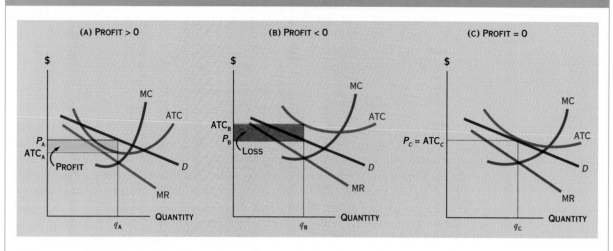

(A) PROFIT > 0

(B) PROFIT < 0

(C) PROFIT = 0

The monopolistically competitive firm produces where marginal revenue equals marginal cost. The firm sells this level of output at the price dictated by its demand curve. If $P > $ ATC, the firm earns a profit in the short run (A). If $P < $ ATC, the firm suffers a loss (B). If $P = $ ATC, the firm breaks even (C).

FIGURE 27.2

the industry. As the number of competitors increases, each firm's share of the market dwindles: new firms take away some of the existing firms' customers. For example, with more car dealers in a city, existing dealers can expect to sell fewer cars, other things equal. This is represented by a leftward shift in the firm's demand curve.

Entry into the industry continues and demand continues to fall until profits are eliminated. Thus, long-run equilibrium is characterized by two conditions: profit maximization (MR = MC) and normal profit ($P = $ LRAC). The second condition occurs when the demand curve is tangent to the long-run average cost curve (point X in Figure 27.3).

Alternatively, if the industry is characterized by short-run losses, equilibrium is achieved by the departure of firms from the industry. As some firms pull out, remaining firms gain customers—their demand curves shift rightward. This process continues until normal profits are established. Only then is the industry in long-run equilibrium.

YOUR TURN

Equilibrium for the Monopolistically Competitive Firm

A MONOPOLISTICALLY COMPETITIVE FIRM PRODUCES 100 UNITS OF OUTPUT PER PERIOD, SELLING EACH FOR $75. MARGINAL REVENUE AND MARGINAL COST OF THE ONE-HUN-DREDTH UNIT ARE EACH $50. AVERAGE TOTAL COST IS $60. (A) DOES THIS SITUATION CORRESPOND TO SHORT-RUN EQUILIBRIUM? WHY OR WHY NOT? (B) DOES THIS SITUA-TION CORRESPOND TO LONG-RUN EQUILIBRIUM? EXPLAIN.

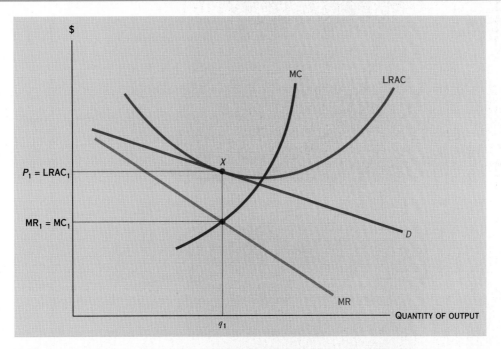

Long-run equilibrium requires the firm to maximize profits (MR = MC) and to earn only normal profits (P = LRAC). Here, both conditions are satisfied.

FIGURE 27.3

EVALUATING MONOPOLISTIC COMPETITION

Perfect competition was praised for efficiently allocating resources to those sectors where they are valued most highly and for producing an industry's output at the lowest possible cost. Monopolistic competition falls short of the perfectly competitive ideal, yet few economists are alarmed by this. In fact, in some industries the advantages of monopolistic competition may outweigh the disadvantages. At issue are the costs and benefits of product differentiation. We begin with the costs.

Resources are not allocated efficiently under monopolistic competition. As illustrated in Figure 27.3, price exceeds marginal cost—the value to consumers of another unit of output is greater than the marginal cost of producing it. From the perspective of society, not enough output is being produced.

Nor is industry output being produced efficiently, that is, at the minimum possible cost. Long-run equilibrium for the firm occurs where demand is tangent to the long-run average cost curve. Because the firm's demand curve is downward sloping, this tangency can occur only on the declining segment of the average cost curve, not where average cost is at a minimum. This is illustrated in Figure 27.4 (page 702). The firm produces q_1 output at an average cost of $LRAC_1$. Had the firm produced q_2 output instead, the average cost would have been only $LRAC_2$.

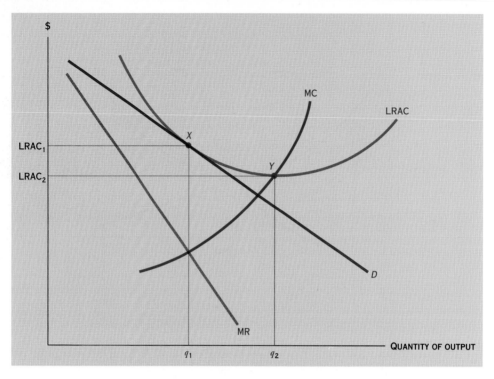

The monopolistically competitive firm does not minimize the average cost of production. It operates at point X on its LRAC curve; average cost is minimized at point Y.

FIGURE 27.4

Another way to describe the situation is to say that monopolistically competitive firms have *excess capacity*—they are underutilizing their resources. By producing more output, monopolistically competitive firms could drive down unit costs. In a sense, the monopolistically competitive industry is populated with too many firms. With fewer firms, each producing a greater output, average cost could be reduced and prices to consumers would fall.

But do we really want fewer firms? A large number of restaurants provides greater variety of food and atmosphere. Having many brands of clothing permits consumers to satisfy their individual tastes. Remember too that monopolistically competitive firms differ in quality and service. With fewer dry cleaners you may be forced to accept shirts that are too starchy or poorly pressed. With fewer car dealers you may be unable to find one that gives you the level of service you desire.

The existence of extra firms also saves consumers time. If a community has fewer grocery stores, each serving more people, consumers on average must travel farther to do their shopping. Average travel time to restaurants, dry cleaners, and similar establishments also increases. Given the value of consumers' time, as well as the value they place on choice and variety, monopolistic competition does not appear so bad after all. Whether it is as desirable as perfect competition, with its lower prices but homogeneous output, depends on how the benefits of product differentiation stack up against the costs. On this issue, opinions vary.

NONPRICE COMPETITION

Monopolistically competitive firms are always introducing "new and improved" products in an effort to win additional customers. The debate over the benefits of product differentiation deals largely with the extent to which "new and improved" really is better.

Although the monopolistically competitive firm earns only normal profits in the long run, the short run is another story. By increasing demand for its products, a firm may be able to create short-run profits. These profits ultimately disappear as competitors imitate successful products; by then, however, the firm may have another new product to dazzle the public.

Monopolistically competitive firms can increase demand for their products through various forms of **nonprice competition**, including product development, packaging, and advertising. Product development refers to the creation and introduction of a distinct product, either totally new or in a different form. Examples include liquid soap, chicken nuggets, Velcro balls and mitts, and disposable diapers. Such products are often the outgrowth of research and development. Product development can also take the form of a new or improved service.

Even if the basic product remains unchanged, companies can often increase market share by repackaging an item. Cosmetic companies discovered that the same lipstick they had been selling for years became a big hit once it was placed in see-through tubes. Motts boosted its sales by bringing out applesauce in single-serving containers. So strong was the demand for convenience that consumers gobbled up the newly packaged applesauce even though a six-pack of single-serving containers was priced 35 percent higher than a jar containing the same volume of applesauce. And sales of Hot Tamales, Jelly Jos, and Mike and Ike candies jumped 25 percent after their manufacturer replaced their stodgy black and white boxes with colorful designs featuring animated grapes and other modern characters.

Companies can sometimes spur demand without changing either the basic product or the way it is packaged. A successful advertising campaign may convince consumers that a product is better, or at least more alluring. Often ads do little more than create an image or make better use of an established image. The Morris-the-Cat commercials were so successful for 9-Lives that the brand became the leading seller of canned cat food. Sales of dry and semimoist 9-Lives, which consumers did not associate with Morris the Cat, remained sluggish. The company, however, found an easy way to change that. It added a picture of finicky Morris to its packages of dry and semimoist cat food. Within four months, sales of these two items doubled.[5,6]

---

[5]Some economists prefer to classify the pet-food industry as oligopolistic rather than as monopolistically competitive. The following chapter considers the procedures economists use in an effort to categorize industries by market structure.

[6]The previous two paragraphs incorporate examples from Philip Gutis, "What's New in Food Packaging," *The New York Times*, June 8, 1986, and Alecia Swasy, "Sales Lost Their Vim? Try Repackaging," *The Wall Street Journal*, October 11, 1989, p. B1.

Nonprice Competition in the Video Industry

If you want to watch *Batman* on your home videocassette recorder, nearly every video store has a copy for rent. But if your taste runs to stomach-turning cult movies such as *Horrors of the Black Museum* or *Blood Feast*, Video Vault in Alexandria, Va., has them to go. "Guaranteed Worst Movies in Town" is Video Vault's slogan. Owner Jim McCabe notes proudly that his inventory of film turkeys on video also includes *Scum of the Earth*, *Kill Baby Kill* and several copies of *Plan 9 From Outer Space*, which, he adds, "is considered the worst movie of all time."

Stocking hard-to-find cult movie classics is Video Vault's way of attracting attention in the maturing and overcrowded retail video industry. Growth in the rental business has slowed, but many single- and dual-outlet video retailers are finding new ways to attract customers. Other profit-making ideas from the video independents include home delivery of video rentals, mail-order sales and rentals, wide-ranging inventories, and attention-getting promotions to lure customers to the store.

"The days of opening a store, putting posters in the windows and having the customers flock in are gone," says Lou Berg, owner of Audio-Video Plus in Houston. A firm believer that video shopping should be fun, Mr. Berg makes his two Houston outlets attractions in themselves. An inflated gorilla hanging from an Empire State Building replica over the front door announced the arrival of *King Kong* on video. A costumed Ninja Turtle greeted kiddies one weekend. When a *Star Trek* video was released, Mr. Berg built a replica of the *Starship Enterprise's* bridge and took pictures of customers sitting in Captain Kirk's chair.

In New York, Michael Becker plays to the ethnic, cosmopolitan life style of Manhattan's Upper East Side by stocking some 1,200 foreign films, as well as the usual assortment of American movies. Since returning videos is an annoyance, Mr. Becker's Video Room uses bicycle messengers to pick up and deliver videos from apartment house doormen. His bike crew, weaving through Manhattan traffic, makes as many as 600 deliveries on a busy Saturday.

Salzer's Video in Ventura, Calif., is next to a Highway 101 exit ramp that's used by 42,000 cars on an average day. Location isn't Mr. Salzer's only weapon. He spent $12,000 on a sort of video automatic teller machine tied to his store's computer. It allows customers both to return and to rent videos after business hours. Playing the fast-food and merchandising angles, Mr. Salzer stocks beer, wine, ice cream, potato chips, T-shirts and posters, in addition to 20,000 video titles. "A lot of people think we're crazy, but we're looking at a real high profit margin."

Mail order is getting attention from video retailers. In Alexandria, Mr. McCabe's Video Vault started renting cult movies by mail this spring. Mr. McCabe says word of his service has spread through underground horror genre magazines such as *Gore Gazette* and *Psychotronic Video*. "I've got members in 35 states," he says, "and they definitely aren't renting *Ferris Bueller's Day Off*."

SOURCE: Eugene Carlson, "Video Stores Try Sharper Focus in Market Glut," *The Wall Street Journal*, July 2, 1990, p. B1. Reprinted by permission.

EXHIBIT

27.1

THE EFFECTS OF ADVERTISING

The goal of advertising is to increase demand, thereby boosting revenue for the firm. By creating a favorable image or name (face) recognition, advertising can sell anything from cat food to designer jeans. But advertising is also an expense. As illustrated in Figure 27.5, advertising shifts the firm's cost curves upward.

This does *not* mean, however, that the average cost of the firm's product is higher if it advertises. Because advertising increases the amount the firm can sell, it causes the firm to move down its average cost curve. To the extent the firm enjoys economies of scale, advertising could boost sales sufficiently so that average cost is actually lower in the presence of advertising. In Figure 27.5, if advertising increases output from q_1 to q_3, average cost falls from ATC_1 to ATC_3. Of course, if output rises only to q_2, average cost climbs to ATC_2. The effect of advertising on the firm's average cost is therefore ambiguous. In summary, advertising generates benefits for the firm, including increased product demand and possibly a lower average cost. When the benefits of advertising exceed the costs, the firm finds it profitable to advertise.

Even when the firm benefits from advertising, it is not clear that society does. Do the millions of dollars spent on 9-Lives commercials really benefit consumers?

ADVERTISING CAN ALTER A FIRM'S AVERAGE COST

Advertising shifts the firm's average cost curve upward but increases the amount of the product the firm can sell. If advertising increases sales volume from q_1 to q_3, average cost falls, despite the costs of advertising. However, if output increases only to q_2, average cost rises.

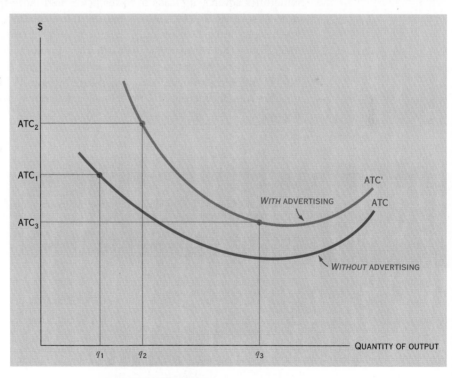

FIGURE 27.5

They do not improve the product, and it is questionable whether they provide any useful information. To take a more dramatic case, consider advertisements for cigarettes. They were considered so harmful to society that in 1971 the U.S. government banned cigarette ads on television and imposed restrictions on printed ads. Other advertisements have been criticized as misleading. For such reasons, some individuals want the government to place further restrictions on advertisements and, in the process, to lessen firms' ability to differentiate their products.

Advertising also has its defenders. At its best, advertising informs. Consumers learn of competing products and the advantages of each. Advertising can also convey valuable information about price—for example, letting consumers know that a discount store sells the same drug as a pharmacy but at half the price. This information saves consumers time and money.

A much-cited study compared the price of eyeglasses in states that permitted advertising and states where advertising was restricted. The study found that the price of eyeglasses was at least 25 percent higher in states that restricted advertising. Prohibition of advertising increased the monopoly power of established companies, making it harder for new firms to break into the market.[7]

Sometimes professional groups condemn advertising as unethical or demeaning. The real reason may be economic. State bar associations prohibited advertising by lawyers until 1977, when the U.S. Supreme Court ruled these bans unconstitutional. Taking advantage of the opportunity to advertise, lawyers began aggressively competing for clients and, as they did, the price of many legal services fell by 50 percent or more.

As the preceding discussion demonstrates, the effects of advertising are mixed. Sometimes advertising leads to lower prices and more-informed decisions by consumers. At other times it conveys no useful information and may even mislead. It is for this reason that an overall assessment of advertising is so difficult. This also underscores the controversy over whether product differentiation, which often relies heavily on advertising, benefits society. Perhaps the merits of advertising and product differentiation are best judged case by case. Whatever the merits, advertising and product differentiation often play a key role in the final market structure—oligopoly.

Advertising and Elasticity of Demand

IN ADDITION TO INCREASING DEMAND FOR A FIRM'S PRODUCT, ADVERTISING MAY INCREASE BRAND LOYALTY. HOW DOES GREATER LOYALTY BY CONSUMERS AFFECT PRICE ELASTICITY OF DEMAND?

---

[7]Lee Benham, "The Effect of Advertising on the Price of Eyeglasses," *Journal of Law and Economics* (October 1972), pp. 337–352.

Oligopoly

OLIGOPOLY

OLIGOPOLY
A market structure in which a small number of firms dominates the industry; other firms are kept out through barriers to entry.

The central difference between monopolistic competition and **oligopoly** pertains to the number of firms in the industry and their relative size. In oligopoly a few large firms dominate the market. For example, in the United States the four largest makers of infant formula produce more than 95 percent of the industry's output; the four largest aircraft companies account for three-fourths of the domestically produced aircraft.

BARRIERS TO ENTRY

In contrast to monopolistic competition, firms find entry into oligopolistic markets difficult. Barriers exist for basically the same reasons they do in monopoly. The number of companies having access to a critical raw material may be small. The government may permit only a limited number of producers in a community. For example, it may grant only two cable television franchises or may license only a handful of radio stations. Alternatively, economies of scale may provide cost advantages for large, established firms. It has been estimated, for example, that to minimize the average cost of production the locomotive industry can have no more than four producers, the cigarette industry no more than seven.[8]

MUTUAL INTERDEPENDENCE

Because an oligopolistic industry has relatively few firms, the assumption of the monopolistically competitive model—that rivals ignore a firm's decisions—is no longer tenable. A firm realizes that once it accounts for a significant share of the market, its actions are likely to influence others in the market. Accordingly, each firm takes into account the anticipated response of rivals when formulating its own strategy. This relationship among firms in the industry is known as **mutual interdependence**.

MUTUAL

INTERDEPENDENCE
An interrelationship among producers. Firms, aware that their actions affect others in the industry, make decisions only after taking into account how rivals are likely to respond.

To the steelmaker USX, mutual interdependence means looking beyond its own factory gates. If it accepts a strike, rather than accede to union demands, it may be unable to meet customer orders. In that event, other steel companies will increase production in order to sell to present USX customers. USX is aware of this and knows that some of these lost customers may never come back. It also realizes that price cutting after the strike ends may be an ineffective way to rebuild business. Other steel companies, wanting to hold on to their customers, are likely to cut their prices as well. Therefore, before taking any action USX must carefully consider

[8]Louis Esposito, Norman Noel, and Francis Esposito, "Dissolution and Scale Economies: Additional Estimates and Analysis," *Antitrust and Law Review* (Fall 1971), Table 1.

how its decisions will affect rival steel producers and, in turn, how their responses will affect USX.

Similarly, General Motors is aware that any increase in Ford's share of the U.S. automotive market comes partially at GM's expense. Therefore, General Motors closely monitors activity at Ford. When the aerodynamic styling of Ford's Taurus and other cars became a big hit, General Motors accelerated plans to redesign its own cars.

TYPE OF PRODUCT

Firms in an oligopolistic industry may produce either homogeneous or differentiated products. The output of the steel and the aluminum industries is usually considered homogeneous—uniform across producers. Differentiated oligopolies include the automobile, aircraft, and mainframe computer industries.

NONPRICE COMPETITION

When the products of different firms are distinct, an oligopolistic firm has an incentive to make its product stand out. Therefore, as with monopolistic competition, advertising is common. For example, Proctor & Gamble and Philip Morris each spend more than $2 billion annually on advertising.

Nonprice competition is generally viewed by companies as preferable to price cutting. If Proctor & Gamble lowers the price on Tide, other detergent makers can quickly match the decrease, maintaining their share of the market. The end result may be lower not higher profits at Proctor & Gamble. But if Proctor & Gamble can run an effective advertising campaign—convincing consumers that Tide really is better than other detergents—the competitors may be unable to prevent Tide from taking away customers.

Product development has a similar advantage over price cutting. Even when a successful new product is ultimately imitated by competitors, it may take years before they can bring their versions to market. In the meantime, the oligopolist introducing the new product may be able to earn substantial profits.

This is what Apple Computer did when it introduced its Macintosh personal computer with desktop publishing capability. The product enjoyed enviable success and was largely responsible for Apple's rebound. While earnings at IBM fell, earnings at Apple soared, and within two years the value of Apple's stock had increased sixfold.

As might be expected, competitors took notice. To quote one publication:

> The Macintosh won't be unique for long. Graphics options for the IBM PC are improving fast, and dozens of companies are finding ways to adapt PCs for desktop publishing. . . . The competition has its eye on other Macintosh features too.[9]

In summary, although competitors can quickly and easily match a price reduction, responding to a successful advertising campaign or to a new product is more

---

[9]Katherine Hafner and Geoff Lewis, "Apple's Comeback," *Business Week*, January 19, 1987, p. 86.

difficult and takes longer. Therefore, where products are distinct, oligopolists typically rely on nonprice competition as a means to improve their position in the market.

PRICE STABILITY

If oligopolistic firms compete primarily through nonprice competition, rather than by adjusting price, one would predict that such industries will be characterized by considerable price stability. There is evidence that in many oligopolistic industries prices are stable over long periods of time. One study found that prices in the steel and chemicals industries remain unchanged on average for more than twelve months at a time.[10] Even more dramatic is the case of sulphur. From 1926 to 1938 its price was frozen at $18 per ton. Compared to more competitive markets, oligopolistic prices tend to be sticky.

Formal Models of Oligopoly

Fifty years ago the economist Paul Sweezy observed that:

> Oligopoly is probably the typical case throughout a large part of the modern economy, and yet the theory of oligopoly can scarcely be said to be in a very advanced state, consisting as it does of special cases which allow of little generalization.[11]

Despite the emergence since then of new theories of oligopoly, this view remains largely true today.

Unlike other market structures, there is no universal theory of oligopoly. Instead, the theory of oligopoly consists of a large number of different models, each a special case that holds only under certain restrictive conditions. Before a model can be formulated, various assumptions must be made. In the case of oligopoly, the number of potential assumptions is enormous. How do other firms in the industry react when one firm adjusts its price? Do they maintain their present prices, match the first firm's price change, or adopt some different strategy? Do firms cooperate with each other—that is, collude—or do they regard each other as adversaries? Is there one firm that is the first to change prices, a price leader?

Different assumptions lead to different models. While one model may appear most appropriate for a particular oligopolistic industry, a different model may be superior for a second industry. No model is consistent with the behavior of every oligopolistic industry. Time constraints prevent a discussion of all models of oligopoly, but the present section discusses some of the most famous models, starting with Sweezy's kinked demand curve.

---

[10]Dennis W. Carlton, "The Rigidity of Prices," *American Economic Review* (September 1986), pp. 637–658.
[11]Paul Sweezy, "Demand Under Conditions of Oligopoly," *Journal of Political Economy* (August 1939), p. 568.

KINKED DEMAND CURVE
The demand curve facing an oligopolist if rivals in the industry match the firm's price reductions but ignore its price increases.

The **kinked demand curve** model was posed as a potential explanation of price stability under oligopoly. Its central premise is that "rivals react differently according to whether a price change is upward or downward."[12]

Consider an industry in which firms sell differentiated products and do not collude. Assume one of the oligopolists is currently selling q_1 output at a price of P_1. How much, it wonders, can it sell if it adopts a new price? In other words, what does its demand curve look like? The answer clearly depends on how its rivals react.

If rivals ignore the price change, the firm's demand curve will be highly elastic. Because products in the industry are close substitutes, the firm stands to win many new customers if it lowers its price and lose many customers if it raises price. On the other hand, if rivals match any price change demand will be much less elastic. A lower price will increase sales somewhat as consumers buy more of the industry's product, but the firm cannot expect to take customers away from its competitors, because they are similarly reducing their prices. Thus the firm faces two potential demand curves, which are labeled D_{ignore} and D_{match} in Figure 27.6(A).

DERIVATION OF THE KINKED DEMAND CURVE AND THE CORRESPONDING MARGINAL REVENUE CURVE

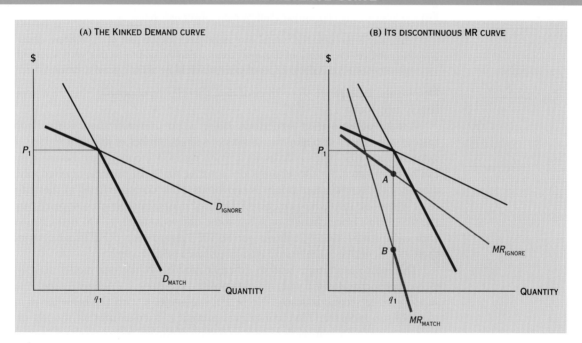

According to the kinked demand curve model, a firm assumes that rivals ignore a price increase but match a price cut. The result is a kinked demand curve (depicted by the heavy line), which consists of segments of D_{ignore} (for $P > P_1$) and D_{match} (for $P < P_1$). The marginal revenue curve associated with the kinked demand curve is discontinuous, jumping from point A to point B.

FIGURE 27.6

[12]Same as 11, p. 568.

Which demand curve is relevant? According to this model, the firm's demand curve consists of segments of each. If the firm lowers its price it expects others to follow suit, in order to retain their customers. Thus for prices below P_1, D_{match} is the appropriate demand curve. But if the firm raises its price it expects rivals to do nothing since, by keeping their prices unchanged, they pick up many of the firm's customers. Accordingly, for prices above P_1, D_{ignore} is relevant. The firm's complete demand curve is represented by the heavy color line in Figure 27.6(A), with a kink at P_1.

Corresponding to the demand curves D_{ignore} and D_{match}, respectively, are the marginal revenue curves MR_{ignore} and MR_{match}. These are added to the model in Figure 27.6(B). Each marginal revenue curve is applicable over the price range where its demand curve is applicable. Thus, MR_{ignore} comes into play for prices above P_1, and MR_{match} comes into play for prices below P_1. The relevant section of each marginal revenue curve is depicted by a heavy color line. Notice that at q_1, where the kink occurs, marginal revenue jumps from point A to point B. That is, the marginal revenue curve associated with a kinked demand curve has a gap or vertical break in it. This has important implications.

The kinked demand curve and its corresponding marginal revenue curve are reproduced in Figure 27.7. Assume the firm initially faces the marginal cost curve MC_1. To maximize profit, it produces q_1 output and charges a price of P_1. (The firm would not produce less than q_1, because MR > MC here, nor more than q_1,

PRICE RIGIDITY—THE HALLMARK OF A KINKED DEMAND CURVE

A shift in costs (for example, from MC_1 to MC_2) does not affect price or output as long as the marginal cost curve intersects the marginal revenue curve where it is discontinuous (between points A and B).

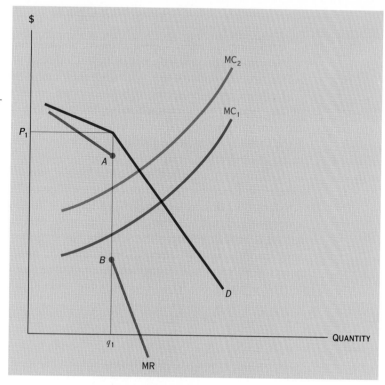

FIGURE 27.7

because that would lead to MC > MR.) Now assume that the marginal cost curve shifts upward to MC_2, perhaps as a result of higher wage rates. Profits are still maximized at an output of q_1 and a price of P_1. In fact, for any marginal cost curve that intersects the marginal revenue curve at its vertical break, P_1 remains the optimal price for the firm. This model thus explains why prices of oligopolistic firms are so inflexible. Given a kinked demand curve, prices remain rigid for a wide range of costs.

Despite the insights of this model, the kinked demand curve has been highly criticized. First, it is not a complete model. It explains why a price, once established, is likely to persist over time. But it does not explain how that price was initially obtained. Second, some empirical work suggests that prices are frequently no more rigid in oligopolistic industries than in monopolistic industries, despite the fact that monopolists do not have kinked demand curves.[13] This suggests that price rigidity is often caused by some factor other than a kinked demand curve. Most economists conclude that the kinked demand curve model remains a special case, relevant for no more than a small number of oligopolistic industries.

The limited applicability of the kinked demand curve is actually not surprising once you realize that there are other, equally defensible ways to model the behavior of rival firms. For example, *game theory* provides an alternative approach (see Exhibit 27.2). In addition, the kinked demand curve is limited to those cases where firms in an industry are adversaries. In many industries firms work together as partners, rather than as rivals. In such instances the appropriate model must be built upon the assumption of collusion.

COLLUSION

The preceding discussion was based on the assumption that firms do not coordinate their activities—that they do not collude. Collusion is tempting, however, because it offers firms an opportunity to increase their prices and profits.

Collusion may be secret or public, formal or implied. Sometimes producers band together to form a **cartel**, an organization that determines how much output each firm will produce and either explicitly or implicitly determines price. The goal of the cartel is to increase profits in the industry and to apportion these profits among the individual firms.

CARTEL

An organization of producers that determines price and output for its members in order to increase their profits.

Collusion is generally illegal in the United States, but that does not prevent its occurrence. Each year the Justice Department prosecutes companies for conspiring to fix prices or restrict output. One of the most famous cases involved the electric equipment industry. In the 1950s, the major suppliers of electrical equipment devised a number of ingenious schemes for rigging the market. For government contracts, bids were coordinated to assure each company a specified share of the market. For example, it was agreed ahead of time that General Electric would submit the winning bid 40.3 percent of the time. Other firms would intentionally

---

[13]George Stigler, "The Kinky Oligopoly Demand Curve and Rigid Prices," *Journal of Political Economy* (October 1947), pp. 432–449; "The Literature of Economics: The Case of the Kinked Oligopoly Demand Curve," *Economic Inquiry* (April 1978), pp. 185–204.

Game Theory

Although **game theory** can be highly mathematical—depending on the number of *players* in the game and on their strategies—we illustrate this theory with a simple two-player game. The players are two oligopolists—Jones and Johnson. The strategy in this game concerns price.

Suppose production costs have just increased. Each company must decide whether to maintain its price at $10 or to raise it to $12. If both companies raise price, each will earn $1,000 in profits (see Table 27.1). If one company raises price to $12 and the other keeps price at $10, the low-price company will see its profits rise to $1,200, and the high-price company—losing many of its customers—will see its profits fall to $400. Finally, if both companies keep the price at $10, each will earn $600.

What should Jones do? Assuming that Jones and Johnson do not communicate with each other, the solution is for Jones to charge a price of $10. No matter which price Johnson sets, Jones will earn $200 more by charging $10 rather than $12. Johnson has a similar payoff table and, for the same reason, can also be expected to charge $10.

From the perspective of the individual firm it is rational to maintain the price at $10. Yet Jones and Johnson would each be better off if they *both* raised the price to $12. In that event, profits of each would climb from $600 to $1,000. The problem is that neither believes the other will charge $12. Each firm, aware of the other's situation, expects its rival to charge $10. If only Jones and Johnson could coordinate their activities—could work together for a common end—they would each agree to charge $12. This example underscores the incentive that firms have to collude and provides another perspective on price stability in the absence of collusion.

PAYOFF TABLE (PROFITS) FOR JONES

		JOHNSON	
		P = $12	*P* = $10
JONES	*P* = $12	$1,000	$400
	P = $10	$1,200	$600

The profit that Jones earns depends on the price each firm charges. If Johnson sets a price of $12, Jones can earn $1,000 by also charging $12 or $1,200 by charging $10. If Johnson's price is $10, Jones can earn $400 by charging $12 or $600 by charging $10.

TABLE 27.1

E X H I B I T

2 7 . 2

quote the government higher prices, assuring General Electric the work no matter what price it charged. Other approaches were also adopted:

> A "phases of the moon" system was used to allocate low-bidding privileges in the high voltage switchgear field, with a new seller assuming low-bidding priority every two weeks. The designated bidder subtracted a specified percentage margin from the book price to capture orders during its phase, while others added various margins to the book price. The result was an ostensibly random pattern of quotations, conveying the impression of independent behavior.[14]

Although this conspiracy was uncovered, and the guilty parties punished, other conspiracies go undetected.

It must also be remembered that collusive arrangements are legal in many countries; sometimes they even enjoy government protection. When a few countries are the major suppliers of a commodity, they often band together to form *international commodity agreements* whose purpose is to maintain high prices for the commodity and high revenues for the producing countries. Among the commodities that have been covered by such agreements are bauxite, tin, rubber, and tea. Because such commodities are traded in international markets, consumers cannot escape the effects of collusion even when firms in their own country do not participate.

Some collusion is more subtle than cartels or agreements to fix market share. Often companies are aware of common goals (for example, high prices) and informally work together to achieve these goals. They may refrain from such competitive practices as advertising and posting prices, and each may agree not to precipitate a price war. Executives who violate the implicit code of behavior may be brought back in line through arm twisting or intimidation by other members of the industry. Sometimes companies have an understanding that they will not *raid* the others' customers, in essence making customers captives of their present supplier. Informal agreements such as these are often referred to as **gentlemen's agreements**.

Although less structured than cartels and the like, informal agreements may nonetheless be effective. A case in point is the famous "Gary dinners," hosted by Judge Elbert Gary, chairman of the board at U.S. Steel, and attended by executives of all major steel companies:

> Judge Gary once explained that the "close communication and contact" developed at these dinners generated such mutual "respect and affectionate regard" among steel industry leaders that all considered the obligation to cooperate and avoid destructive competition "more binding . . . than any written or verbal contract."[15]

Whatever its form, collusion is designed to increase industry profits. In fact, in the limiting case the colluding partners act as a monopolist operating more than one plant.[16] The industry marginal cost curve is obtained by summing the marginal cost curves of the individual firms. The group then decides to produce that level of output for which industry marginal revenue equals industry marginal cost and to charge that price given by the industry demand curve. The difficult part in this

GENTLEMEN'S AGREEMENT
An informal understanding among members of a group to pursue practices that are in the best interests of the group.

---

[14]F. M. Scherer and David Ross, *Industrial Market Structure and Economic Performance*, 3rd ed. (Boston: Houghton Mifflin, 1990), p. 237.
[15]Same as 14, pp. 235–236.
[16]This case was discussed in Chapter 26, p. 686.

arrangement is agreeing on how to distribute industry profits. For example, if individual firms are to be assigned a certain share of the market, each firm will lobby for a large share. Ultimately however, the firms must reach a consensus if the cartel is to survive.

Survival is by no means assured. The success and longevity of a collusive agreement hinges on a variety of factors, including number of firms, heterogeneity of products, and antitrust laws.

NUMBER OF FIRMS   The more firms in the industry the more likely it is that at least one of them will not go along with the agreement. By operating outside a cartel—undercutting its price—a rogue firm stands to pick up much of the cartel's business, perhaps causing the cartel to unravel. Even when all firms agree to collude, cheating may still occur. The more firms there are in an industry, the more difficult it is to spot cheating and identify the guilty party.

An individual firm has an incentive to shave its price secretly since, by so doing, it can increase greatly the amount of output it sells. It will gain customers at the expense of firms adhering to the cartel price. Once secret discounting begins, it has the potential to spread throughout the industry, undermining the agreement among producers. For example, cheating threatened to rip OPEC apart, as the following passage indicates:

> Ali Khalifa al Sabah, oil minister of Kuwait, warned that a "significant drop" in oil prices would inevitably result if other OPEC members continued hidden discounting and other violations of OPEC agreements. Without naming any countries, but obviously with Iran, Libya, Nigeria, and Venezuela in mind, Sheik Ali said that "individual interests have dominated collective interests inside OPEC. . . . We cannot continue to sacrifice if other members continue to violate the resolutions."[17]

PRODUCT HETEROGENEITY   Collusion is more difficult when products in the industry are distinct, rather than identical. With identical products, firms decide on a single common price. But when products are distinct, firms must agree on an entire set of prices. For example, if Ford and General Motors were to collude, they would have to come to terms on the prices each charges. They might agree that Ford should charge more for its Taurus than General Motors charges for its Chevrolet Lumina, but settling on the size of that premium would be difficult. General Motors would favor a large premium, in order to make the Lumina a better buy; Ford would push for a more modest premium.

LEGAL BARRIERS   Collusion in the United States is also hindered by antitrust laws. Ford and General Motors cannot legally coordinate pricing decisions or otherwise conspire to raise their collective profits. As the electric equipment conspiracy demonstrates, laws are sometimes broken; but legal restrictions and the penalties imposed on guilty parties raise the cost of colluding and reduce its occurrence.

OTHER CONCERNS   Even where legal, collusive arrangements typically have been short lived. Problems mount over time. To the extent collusion succeeds in raising price and profits, it increases the incentive of new firms to enter the industry. Although entry into oligopolistic markets is not easy, barriers can sometimes

---

[17]Youssef Ibrahim, "OPEC Confronts Deep Split in Ranks," *The Wall Street Journal*, October 21, 1982, p. 37.

be overcome. When new firms gain access to the market, existing firms lose customers and see profits fall. If the new firms do not participate in the collusion, they can force existing firms to abandon their arrangements, or at least modify them.

In addition, demand for an industry's product is more elastic in the long run than in the short run. Consumers' ability to substitute increases with time. Therefore, other things equal, if firms maintain an artificially high price they can anticipate losing more and more business as time passes. For such reasons, even successful cartels generally see their power erode over time (see Exhibit 27.3).

The Decline of OPEC?

The Organization of Petroleum Exporting Countries (OPEC) is considered one of the most successful cartels in history, yet not even it is immune to economic forces. Members of OPEC realized that, as a united front, they wielded tremendous economic power; they were producing most of the world's oil, and beneath their soil lay most of the known oil reserves. In 1973, they shocked the world by raising the price of oil from approximately $2.50 per barrel to $10 and making this price stick. Within ten years oil was selling for $34 per barrel, and OPEC had created hundreds of billions of dollars in new wealth for its members.

History teaches us that the very success of cartels often leads to their own undoing. A high price deters consumption and, at the same time, encourages greater production. Between 1979 and 1985, oil consumption in the United States fell from 37 quads (quadrillion British thermal units) to 30 quads. Worldwide, oil consumption declined by about 20 percent. Meanwhile, spurred by the high price of oil, non-OPEC countries increased drilling and exploration. Major discoveries in the North Sea, Alaska, and Mexico provided new sources of oil. In this environment, OPEC was forced to cut back its own production in order to prop up prices. Daily production by OPEC nations fell from 31 million barrels in 1979 to 16 million in 1985. With the cutback, OPEC's share of the market fell to 30 percent and oil revenues sagged. Saudi Arabia, which had absorbed much of the decline in production, watched its oil revenues plunge from $113 billion in 1981 to $16 billion five years later.

OPEC realized that under a strategy of enforcing high prices its share of the market would continue to decline. Therefore, in late 1985 it adopted a new approach—it would maintain its "fair share" of the market. Unfortunately for OPEC, that meant accepting a much lower price. It could have a high price or high output, but not both. Although oil prices have spiked up occasionally since 1985, these higher prices have been the result of such crises as Iraq's invasion of Kuwait and not a consequence of OPEC's might. OPEC may not be through as a cartel, but many analysts contend that its best days are history. They predict that OPEC will never again enjoy the high measure of success that it did in the late 1970s.

EXHIBIT 27.3

Although collusion is generally illegal in the United States, companies have been able to skirt antitrust laws through the practice of **price leadership**—firms in an industry follow the lead of a particular company, the price leader. When it raises price, so do they; when it lowers price, they quickly follow suit. Even though representatives of the individual companies may never make contact with one another, the result is common prices.

Sometimes companies follow the lead of the largest firm in the industry, especially when that firm dominates the market (as does IBM in the mainframe computer market). At other times companies follow the low-cost firm, realizing that it is in their best interests to avoid a price war. If they attempted to charge less than the firm with the lowest average cost, it could retaliate by driving the price down to a level where only it enjoyed profits. To avoid this situation, other firms let the low-cost firm set the price and they follow suit. Finally, the price leader may be a *barometric firm*—that is, the first to realize that industry demand or costs have changed. If other firms recognize the barometric firm's ability to detect changing market conditions quickly, they may follow any price change it initiates.

Among the price leaders in U.S. industries have been Alcoa (aluminum), Du Pont (nylon), American Can and Continental Can (tin cans), and American Tobacco and R. J. Reynolds (cigarettes). As the latter two industries indicate, price leadership sometimes rotates from one company to another. In the ready-to-eat cereal industry, Quaker Oats has emerged as a price leader, as the following passage demonstrates:

> Prices of breakfast cereals are going up about 4 percent, or 12 cents on a $3 box. Quaker Oats Co. kicked off this year's round of increases: "We felt it necessary to do it now to maintain our [profit] margins in the face of rising costs," a Quaker spokesman said. [Within two weeks General Mills and Kellogg, which account for two-thirds of the market, announced similar price hikes.][18]

An Evaluation of Oligopoly

In many respects oligopoly possesses the same advantages and disadvantages as monopoly. Because of economies of scale, costs may be minimized when an industry contains only a few producers. On the negative side, consumers are likely to face a price in excess of average total cost inasmuch as barriers to entry permit economic profits even in the long run. In addition, oligopoly leads to an inefficient allocation of resources—the value of another unit of the oligopolist's product exceeds the marginal cost of producing it.[19]

---

[18]Richard Gibson, "U.S. Cereal Makers Milk Price Increases an Average of 4%," *The Wall Street Journal*, September 26, 1991, p. B4.

[19]Because the oligopolist's demand curve is downward sloping, price exceeds marginal revenue. Given that marginal revenue equals marginal cost in equilibrium, price must therefore exceed marginal cost.

OLIGOPOLY AND TECHNOLOGICAL CHANGE

The assessment of oligopoly also hinges on the relationship between market structure and technological progress.[20] Some economists have argued that, compared to more competitive markets, oligopoly facilitates the introduction of new technology, thereby fostering economic growth. According to John Kenneth Galbraith: "A benign Providence . . . has made the modern industry of a few large firms an almost perfect instrument for inducing technical change."[21] Prior to Galbraith, Joseph Schumpeter extolled the virtues of large firms and monopoly power.[22]

**SCHUMPETER–
GALBRAITH
HYPOTHESIS**
The claim that innovation occurs more rapidly when firms are large in size and comprise a substantial share of the market.

According to the **Schumpeter–Galbraith Hypothesis**, innovation frequently requires massive investment and perhaps a large research and development staff. Xerox spent more than $16 million creating its 914 copy machine, and RCA poured $65 million into the development of its color television. Individuals and small companies do not have the resources necessary to undertake such investments. Beyond that, companies operating in a competitive environment do not have as strong an incentive to undertake research and development since their rewards for innovation quickly disappear as competitors flood the market with imitations of the new product. In contrast, barriers to entry provide the oligopolist with some protection and may permit it to earn economic profits on the new product even in the long run. According to this scenario, large oligopolistic firms have a greater ability and a greater incentive to innovate than do small competitive firms.

Not everyone subscribes to the Schumpeter–Galbraith view that big is better. Some contend that the bureaucracies of large firms stifle creativity and that oligopolistic firms often become complacent. Consistent with this latter view, studies of the major inventions since 1880 reveal that most were attributable to individuals or small businesses.[23] Less than one-third were the outgrowth of research and development by corporate giants.

But inventions are only the first stage of creating a useful product. Typically, inventions must be developed and refined before they are marketable. Because this can be an expensive, time-consuming process, it is here that the corporate resources often prove valuable. For example, although Kodachrome film was invented outside of the Kodak laboratories, it required an additional ten years of research—financed by Kodak—before this invention was ready to market. Thus, while large oligopolies are not generally the *source* of new ideas, they often play a key role in turning these ideas into finished products.

Highlighting the importance of size, statistics reveal that large firms contribute disproportionately to research and development in the United States. Manufacturing companies with 10,000 or more employees spend about five times as much per employee on research and development as do smaller companies. Most small companies do not even engage in formal research and development. Thus size appears important for technological growth, but only to a point. In general, the very largest

---

[20]This section draws heavily from Scherer and Ross, same as 14, pp. 613–660.

[21]J. K. Galbraith, *American Capitalism: The Concept of Countervailing Power* (Boston: Houghton Mifflin, 1952), p. 91.

[22]Joseph Schumpeter, *Capitalism, Socialism, and Democracy* (New York: Harper & Row, 1942).

[23]John Jewkes, David Sawers, and Richard Stillerman, *The Sources of Invention* (New York: St. Martin's Press, 1959); Daniel Hamberg, "Invention in the Industrial Research Laboratory," *Journal of Political Economy* (April 1963), pp. 95–115.

firms spend no more on research and development per employee than slightly smaller firms, nor do they receive a proportionately greater share of patents.

These results are broadly supportive of the Schumpeter–Galbraith view, as are findings that productivity growth tends to be greater in oligopolistic industries than in more competitive industries.[24] Even so, economists continue to debate the importance of market structure. A leading authority on the subject finds evidence that industries classified as oligopolies have been blessed with greater opportunities for advancement. He concludes that these industries would have experienced above-average technological growth regardless of market structure. In other words, he questions whether an oligopolistic market structure actually *causes* the more rapid rates of innovation that have been observed.[25]

Others concede that oligopoly facilitates technological progress in some industries but argue that the optimal amount of market power varies from industry to industry. In their view, a mix of competitive and oligopolistic industries is more conducive to technological growth than having all industries oligopolistic (or all industries competitive). In summary, there is no consensus over the extent to which oligopoly promotes technological growth. The Schumpeter–Galbraith view may have merit, but how much is unclear.

Looking Ahead

This completes our formal presentation of market structure. In Chapter 28, we examine how market structure in the United States has changed over time. Is the economy becoming less competitive, as some have suggested? What role has the government played in shaping American industry and, in turn, how has government policy changed over time? Drawing on the analysis common to recent chapters, we study the actual structure of American business.

Summary

1. Most industries in the real world fall somewhere between perfect competition and monopoly. The theories of monopolistic competition and oligopoly were formulated in an attempt to help explain behavior in these intermediate market structures.

2. Monopolistically competitive markets contain many firms, acting independently of one another, selling differentiated products. Entry to and exit from the industry is relatively easy. Because no other firm sells exactly the same product, a monopolistically competitive firm has some discretion over the price it charges.

---

[24]Douglas Greer and Stephen Rhoades, "Concentration and Productivity Changes in the Long and Short Run," *Southern Economic Journal* (October 1976), pp. 1,031–1,044; Louis Amato, J. Michael Ryan, and Ronald Wilder, "Market Structure and Dynamic Performance in U.S. Manufacturing," *Southern Economic Journal* (April 1981), pp. 1,105–1,110.

[25]F. M. Scherer, "Market Structure and the Employment of Scientists and Engineers," *American Economic Review* (June 1967), pp. 524–531.

3. Assuming that price covers average variable cost, the monopolistically competitive firm maximizes profit in the short run by producing where marginal revenue equals marginal cost. For long-run equilibrium a second condition must also hold: price equals average total cost. That is, monopolistically competitive firms earn only normal profit in the long run.

4. A feature of monopolistic competition is nonprice competition, designed to increase demand for the firm's product. In addition to product development and packaging, nonprice competition includes advertising. Advertising increases a firm's total cost but, given economies of scale, it may boost sales sufficiently to reduce average cost. Although some advertising harms society—for example, by misleading consumers—studies show that where advertising increases competition it can lead to lower prices.

5. Under monopolistic competition resources are not allocated efficiently (price does not equal marginal cost), nor is the average cost of production minimized. If the industry contained fewer firms, each producing a larger output, average cost would be lower. On the other hand, the wide range of products under monopolistic competition provides consumers greater choice, and the presence of numerous firms saves consumers time.

6. Oligopoly is characterized by mutual interdependence. Because a few large firms dominate the market, each is aware that its actions affect rivals.

7. Where oligopolistic products are distinct, competition is more likely to consist of product development or advertising than price cutting, since the former is more difficult to respond to. This preference for nonprice competition is one reason prices tend to be more stable under oligopoly than in more competitive market structures.

8. The kinked demand curve offers a second explanation for price stability. According to this model, rivals match a price cut but ignore a price increase. Because neither response is what the firm wants, it is reluctant to alter price in either direction.

9. Although the kinked demand curve model assumes that firms are adversaries, firms have a strong incentive to collude. By working together against consumers, rather than against one another, firms can increase their profits. Collusion is generally against the law in the United States but is condoned and even promoted in many countries. Even where illegal, it sometimes still occurs.

10. Collusion can take many forms, from price fixing to allocating market shares to gentlemen's agreements. An organization of producers that sets price or output is called a cartel. Collusive agreements are more likely to be successful when the industry contains very few firms and when they produce a homogeneous product.

11. Some oligopolies are characterized by price leadership. Whenever a particular firm raises or lowers price, other firms follow suit.

12. Resources are allocated inefficiently under oligopoly, and price may exceed average total cost even in the long run (because of barriers to entry). On the other hand, where economies of scale are important, oligopoly may be the market structure that minimizes the average cost of production.

13. Some economists, including Schumpeter and Galbraith, argue that oligopoly promotes technological progress. According to this view, large oligopolistic firms have both a greater capacity to finance research and development and a greater incentive than do small competitive firms. The evidence is mixed. Although oligopoly does not lead to a greater number of inventions, in some industries it helps develop the inventions, turning ideas into finished products. Large firms do carry out a disproportionate amount of research and development. But while oligopolies typically invest heavily in research and development, spurring technological progress, the exact contribution of market structure is unclear. Some economists believe that investment in research and development depends primarily on factors other than market structure.

monopolistic competition
product differentiation
nonprice competition
oligopoly
mutual interdependence
kinked demand curve

game theory
cartel
gentlemen's agreement
price leadership
Schumpeter–Galbraith Hypothesis

Study Questions and Problems

1. Describe the demand curve of a monopolistically competitive producer. Why does it assume this particular shape?

2. Does the monopolistically competitive firm operate at the minimum point of its average total cost curve? Defend your answer.

3. In a recent year, forty-eight new cold and cough remedies were brought to market. That same year, makers of cold and cough remedies spent $360 million to advertise their products. (a) What were the advertising objectives of these companies? (b) Do you think the addition of another forty-eight cold and cough remedies benefits consumers? Defend your view.

4. The retailer Merry-Go-Round has developed a reputation for being the first to spot a fashion trend and the first to get the product to market. Among its fashion hits were prewashed jeans with bleached-out patterns, pants made from parachute cloth, and cotton doctors' pants in bold prints. In each case, after seeing how strong sales were for Merry-Go-Round, competitors began selling their own versions of the fashionable clothing. (a) How did Merry-Go-Round's introduction of trendy clothing affect its profits in the short run? (b) How did the eventual stiff competition from other retailers affect long-run profits from the sale of the new fashion? (c) In light of what happens to profits in the long run, does Merry-Go-Round have any incentive to introduce new fashions in the future? Explain.

5. (a) Advertising has been criticized as wasteful to society or even worse. Explain why. (b) Now discuss some of the ways society may benefit from advertising.

6. (a) In what ways is monopolistic competition similar to perfect competition? In what ways is it different? (b) In what ways is monopolistic competition similar to oligopoly? In what ways is it different?

7. (a) What gives the kinked demand curve its kink? (b) If oligopolists are reluctant to change price, as the kinked demand curve model implies, does this mean that they do not compete against one another? Explain.

8. What is a *gentlemen's agreement*? How does it differ from a cartel?

9. According to the president of Delta Air Lines:

> When you've got somebody in your market, you cannot let them take all the traffic away. Unfortunately, it gets down to a question of who can bleed the most.[26]

---

[26]Bridget O'Brian, "'Chapter 11' Airlines, Struggling to Survive, May Depress Prices, Profits at Strong Carriers," *The Wall Street Journal*, July 9, 1991, p. C1.

(a) Given this philosophy, how is Delta likely to respond to a fare cut by a competing airline? (b) In deciding whether to reduce fares, does a competing airline consider Delta's likely response? Why is Delta's response relevant?

10. Compaq Computer Corp. slashed its suggested retail prices by as much as 34 percent. Toshiba quickly followed with its own round of cuts on selected models, as did IBM. Even scrappy Dell Computer Corp., already a low-price manufacturer, reduced systems by as much as $900.[27]

Is the reaction of these other computer makers consistent with (a) the kinked demand curve model and (b) price leadership? Which model do you feel is more appropriate for the personal computer industry? Why?

11. Analysts claim that consumer loyalty in the computer industry has eroded recently. Whereas consumers once had a strong preference for a particular brand of computer, consumers today are more interested in price. (a) How will this loss of brand loyalty affect elasticity of demand for IBM computers? (b) Is there anything IBM (and other computer makers) can do to restore brand loyalty? Explain.

12. Although collusion in the United States is generally illegal, agricultural *marketing orders* allow Sunkist and other fruit growers to form cartels. For some crops, boards limit the amount of output each producer in the United States can legally sell. (a) Discuss two factors that are likely to determine the success of these cartels. (b) If successful, how are the cartels likely to affect price and output?

13. Evaluate the following argument:

The design of a new, more advanced aircraft or a super train requires many tens of millions of dollars. Size is important. Therefore, if we want to spur technological growth in agriculture, we should replace small, family farms with large, corporate farms.

14. In 1991, Time Warner Inc. offered existing shareholders the right to buy additional shares of its stock. What made the offer so unusual was that shareholders who agreed to participate in the voluntary stock-purchase plan would not know the purchase price in advance. If 60 percent of shareholders participated (the minimum required for the plan to proceed), the price per share would be $63. But as the participation rate increased, so would the purchase price. If all shareholders participated, the share price would climb to $105. As some investors observed, Time Warner was setting up a classic *game theory* model (see Exhibit 27.2). (a) Who were the *players* in this game? (b) Shortly after Time Warner presented its plan, its stock was selling for approximately $90 per share. Based on this price, should a shareholder participate in this plan if she expects all other shareholders to participate? (c) Assuming a price of $90, should a shareholder participate if the expected participation rate is 60 percent? (d) Suppose a shareholder receives confidential information that several large pension funds, which collectively own one-third of Time Warner's stock, will not participate. How might this information affect the shareholder's strategy of whether or not to participate? [Note: In response to criticism by shareholders, Time Warner withdrew the aforementioned plan and instead offered shareholders the right to purchase additional stock at a predetermined price of $80 per share. At this price, holders of 98 percent of Time Warner stock participated in the stock-purchase plan.]

---

[27]Annetta Miller, "These Prices Are Insane," *Newsweek*, May 27, 1991, p. 43.

YOUR TURN
Answers

Equilibrium for the Monopolistically Competitive Firm

(A) YES. AT 100 UNITS OF OUTPUT, MARGINAL REVENUE EQUALS MARGINAL COST (MR = MC = $50), AND PRICE EXCEEDS AVERAGE VARIABLE COST. THEREFORE THE FIRM IS IN SHORT-RUN EQUILIBRIUM. (B) NO. BECAUSE PRICE EXCEEDS AVERAGE TOTAL COST, THE SITUATION DOES NOT CORRESPOND TO LONG-RUN EQUILIBRIUM. NEW FIRMS WILL ENTER THE INDUSTRY UNTIL ECONOMIC PROFITS ARE ELIMINATED.

Advertising and Elasticity of Demand

IF ADVERTISING INCREASES BRAND LOYALTY, CONSUMERS ARE LESS LIKELY TO SWITCH TO COMPETING BRANDS WHEN THE FIRM RAISES PRICE, MEANING THAT DEMAND FOR THE FIRM'S PRODUCT BECOMES *LESS* ELASTIC.

Selected References

Adams, Walter, ed. *The Structure of American Industry*, 8th ed. (New York: Macmillan, 1990).

Carlton, Dennis, and Jeffrey Perloff. *Modern Industrial Organization* (New York: Harper Collins, 1990).

Galbraith, J. K. *American Capitalism: The Concept of Countervailing Power* (Boston: Houghton Mifflin, 1952).

Scherer, F. M. *Innovation and Growth: Schumpeterian Perspectives* (Cambridge, Mass.: MIT Press, 1984).

Scherer, F. M. and David Ross. *Industrial Market Structure and Economic Performance*, 3rd ed. (Boston: Houghton Mifflin, 1990).

Industrial Organization and Antitrust Policy

IN THE MIDST OF THE COLA WARS OF THE 1980S, PEPSICO PETITIONED THE FEDERAL TRADE COMMISSION FOR PERMISSION TO ACQUIRE SEVEN-UP. SHORTLY THEREAFTER, THE COCA-COLA COMPANY ATTEMPTED TO PURCHASE DR PEPPER. THE FEDERAL TRADE COMMISSION REJECTED BOTH REQUESTS ON THE GROUND THAT THE ACQUISITIONS WOULD SERIOUSLY RESTRICT COMPETITION IN THE SOFT-DRINK INDUSTRY. A SUBSEQUENT MERGER OF SEVEN-UP AND DR PEPPER WAS ALLOWED.

AS CHAPTER 27 INDICATED, CONCENTRATING POWER IN THE HANDS OF A FEW LARGE COMPANIES MAY EITHER BENEFIT CONSUMERS OR HARM THEM. HOW DO GOVERNMENT AGENCIES, INCLUDING THE FEDERAL TRADE COMMISSION, DETERMINE WHICH MERGERS TO APPROVE AND WHICH TO OPPOSE? ALTHOUGH SOME SUBJECTIVITY IS INVOLVED, GOVERNMENT AGENCIES RELY HEAVILY ON THE TOOLS DISCUSSED IN THIS CHAPTER. THESE TOOLS ASSESS THE EXTENT OF COMPETITION WITHIN AN INDUSTRY AND MEASURE THE CHANGE IN COMPETITION IN THE EVENT OF A MERGER.

THEY ALSO ENABLE US TO TRACK CHANGES IN THE COMPETITIVENESS OF THE OVERALL ECONOMY. SOME INDIVIDUALS WORRY THAT MARKET POWER IS BECOMING CONCENTRATED IN THE HANDS OF A DWINDLING NUMBER OF COMPANIES. IS THERE ANY MERIT TO THIS ARGUMENT?

A COUNTRY'S INDUSTRIAL STRUCTURE DEPENDS ON POLITICAL AS WELL AS ECONOMIC CONSIDERATIONS. IN THE UNITED STATES, GOVERNMENT POLICY HAS EVOLVED OVER TIME THROUGH LEGISLATION, JUDICIAL RULINGS,

Antitrust enforcers have struggled for years—since the Sherman Act was passed in 1890—to define what constitutes an "unacceptably few" number of competitors.[1]

[1]Robert Pitofsky, "Coke and Pepsi Were Going Too Far," *The New York Times*, July 27, 1986, section 3, p. 2.

and enforcement activities of the executive branch. The second half of the chapter traces U.S. antitrust policy over the past century, highlighting major laws and court rulings, and discussing the conflicting approaches to big business that have characterized recent presidencies.

Assessing the Extent of Competition

Monopoly power, or the ability to influence price, varies from industry to industry. At the one extreme (perfect competition), firms have no influence over price. At the other extreme, a firm is the only seller of the product and can dictate any price it chooses. Most industries fall somewhere between these two extremes: firms have slight to moderate control over price, depending on such factors as number of firms in the industry and their relative size. The market power of producers tends to be greater when an industry contains a few large firms rather than many small firms.

Based on these observations, economists have devised a number of measures of monopoly power. Although none is perfect, each reveals valuable information about specific markets. These gauges enable us to compare the degree of competition across industries and to determine whether a given industry is becoming more competitive or less competitive over time. When used in conjunction with other data, the measures generally paint a fairly reliable picture of market power within an industry. The two most commonly used measures of monopoly power are the *market concentration ratio* and the *Herfindahl Index.*

The Market Concentration Ratio

A concentration ratio measures the share of the market accounted for by the largest firms in an industry. For example, the *four-firm concentration ratio* measures sales of the four largest firms in the industry as a percentage of total industry sales. Although one could just as easily compute concentration ratios for the five, eight, or ten largest firms in the industry, the four-firm concentration ratio is the one most widely used. Therefore, unless otherwise specified, **market concentration ratio** refers to the market share of the four largest firms.

MARKET CONCENTRATION RATIO
The percentage of industry sales attributable to the four largest firms in an industry.

Concentration ratios range in value from 0 to 100 percent. Highly competitive industries have very low concentration ratios, since the four largest firms produce only a small fraction of the industry's output. At the other extreme, industries containing no more than four firms have concentration ratios of 100 percent—four firms or fewer produce all the industry's output.

In general, the higher the concentration ratio the greater the monopoly power wielded by firms in the industry. Accordingly, concentration ratios provide evidence of market structure. Based on its concentration ratio of 69 percent, the U.S. tire industry is classified as oligopolistic—a few firms dominate the market. On the other hand, a concentration ratio of 6 percent reveals that the women's dress industry is highly competitive.

DEFINING THE PRODUCT MARKET

Although concentration ratios are easy to compute, they must be used with care. The first consideration involves defining the relevant product market. If a market is defined too broadly or too narrowly, the concentration ratio may be misleading. A case in point is the soft-drink industry.

In defending their proposed acquisitions, the managements of Pepsi and Coke argued that their beverages compete directly with juices, powdered drinks, teas, milk, and other beverages. Had the market been defined broadly to include all these drinks, the concentration ratio would have been very low even after the mergers. The implication—that considerable competition exists—would make it difficult for the government to reject the mergers.

The Federal Trade Commission, however, argued that the relevant market included only carbonated soft drinks. Coke and Pepsi controlled 68 percent of this narrowly defined market, and their combined market share would have swelled to 82 percent had the mergers actually taken place. Seen in this light, the market was dominated by two giants, and allowing them to gobble up their rivals would have seriously diluted competition. Once the market was narrowly defined, the decision to deny the mergers was easy.[2]

SHORTCOMINGS OF THE CONCENTRATION RATIO

Even if the product market is properly defined, the market concentration ratio suffers from several weaknesses. (a) It overlooks competition from imports, other industries, and prospective producers. (b) It focuses on national output, even though many markets are local or regional. (c) It ignores the distribution of sales among the top four producers.

OTHER SOURCES OF COMPETITION Concentration ratios measure producers' share of *domestically* produced output. By ignoring imports, they overstate the power of domestic producers. For example, even though the market concentration ratio in the U.S. automobile industry is 90 percent, U.S. producers are severely limited in their ability to control price. With imports recently accounting for more than 25 percent of the market, U.S. automobile makers face stiff competition from foreign producers.

Concentration ratios also overstate the power of companies that face competition from other industries. Despite the high concentration ratio in the soft-drink industry, Coca-Cola and PepsiCo find their ability to raise price limited by the presence of beverages from other industries. Similarly, the advertising rates charged by the major television networks (ABC, CBS, and NBC) are constrained by other communications industries. Although these three networks dominate the national television industry, advertisers have alternative avenues for reaching consumers—

---

[2]Although the issue of what constitutes the relevant market is not always clear-cut, another economic tool guides policymakers in this decision. The *cross elasticity of demand* indicates whether two goods are close substitutes. If they are, they are part of the same market. See Exhibit 5.4.

local television, cable, radio, newspapers, magazines, billboards, mail, and telephone. Monopoly power is influenced not just by the market structure within an industry but also by the degree of competition across industries.

In addition to actual competition from producers in other countries or industries, firms may also feel pressure from *potential* new rivals in the industry. In the absence of effective entry barriers, profits attract new firms to the industry. As in perfectly competitive markets, the increased supply reduces price and, in the long run, eliminates profits. Thus, even though an industry may have few firms at present, the ability of new firms to break into the market may undermine the market power of current producers. According to a new theory, competitive pressures depend more on resource mobility than on the number of firms in the industry (see Exhibit 28.1).

GEOGRAPHIC MARKETS Although concentration ratios may overstate market power for the preceding reasons, at other times they understate market power. Typically, concentration ratios are computed for the country at large. For national markets, such as breakfast cereals and cigarettes, this is the correct procedure. But where markets are local or regional, national concentration ratios underestimate the market power of producers. Even though individual producers may each claim only a small share of national sales, within their respective local markets each may have few if any rivals.

A good example of this is newspaper publishing. Despite a relatively low concentration ratio of 25 percent for the country as a whole, most cities contain only one or two daily newspapers. The potential for monopoly power is therefore great. Similarly, the four largest producers of ready-mixed concrete capture a combined 8 percent of the national market. But, because of high transportation costs, cement tends to be purchased locally, and that often means doing business with the only cement company around.

DISTRIBUTION OF MARKET SHARE A final criticism of concentration ratios is that they do not reveal how the market share is distributed among the four largest producers. Suppose industries X and Y have concentration ratios of 60 percent. The largest company in industry X controls 45 percent of the market and the next three companies each have a 5 percent share. In contrast, the four largest companies in industry Y each have a 15 percent share of the market. Are the two industries equally competitive?

Most economists would argue that industry X is less competitive. The largest firm sells nine times as much as its nearest rival, controlling almost one-half the market. As the dominant force in the industry, it is likely to wield considerable power. By way of comparison, the largest firm in industry Y must compete with three other firms just as large. Because market share is distributed more evenly, no firm has much influence over price.

NEED FOR SUPPLEMENTAL INFORMATION Because of the shortcomings just documented, the concentration ratio must be used with care. The implication is not that it has little value but that market power is multidimensional. No single instrument can adequately characterize the power of firms in an industry. Concentration ratios provide important insights into markets, but they must be supplemented with additional information. Industry analysts must also pay attention to imports, interindustry competition, barriers to entry, the geographic nature of markets, and the distribution of output among the largest producers. When used in conjunction

The Theory of Contestable Markets

A **contestable market** is one where resources can be moved into and out of an industry at little or no cost. All resources, including capital, are highly mobile. As an example, some point to the market for air travel. Airplanes and flight crews can easily be transferred from one route to another. Therefore, regardless of the number of airlines currently serving a city, the market for air travel to and from the city might be viewed as contestable.

An implication of this theory is that competition is based not on the number of producers currently in an industry but instead on the number of actual plus *potential* producers. A market may have a concentration ratio of 100 percent yet, if it is contestable, its producers earn only normal profits in the long run. If they attempted to charge a price in excess of average total cost, new firms would quickly enter the industry, charge a lower price, and take business away from existing producers. The presence of potential competition prevents existing firms from earning economic profits.

Although this theory is largely untested, it has been used to defend mergers in markets that already have high concentration ratios. For example, in 1986, TWA was allowed to merge with Ozark Airlines, its main rival in the St. Louis market. After the merger, TWA controlled 82 percent of the market. Those favoring the merger claimed that other airlines would invade the St. Louis market if TWA set excessive air fares. They also observed that TWA competes with other cities for connecting flights. If travel through St. Louis became more expensive, an increased number of flights would be booked through Kansas City, Chicago, or other cities (on other airlines). Accordingly, supporters of the merger argued that the St. Louis market would remain competitive despite TWA's high market share.

Opponents countered that although the theory of contestable markets is impeccable, it is not widely applicable to the real world and certainly not relevant in the airline industry.[3] They noted that TWA controls nearly three-fourths of the gates at St. Louis's Lambert Airport (other airlines have similar locks at other airports). Because this severely limits the number of flights other airlines can offer to and from St. Louis, many analysts believe that TWA is effectively shielded from competition—both from existing carriers and from potential rivals.

In conclusion, the theory of contestable markets awaits further scrutiny. But, to the extent it is relevant for certain markets, it provides another reason why concentration ratios should not be used blindly. If markets are contestable, current producers may have less influence over price than concentration ratios would suggest.

[3]See William G. Shepherd, "'Contestability' vs. Competition," *American Economic Review* (September 1984), pp. 572–587.

SOURCES: Adapted from William J. Baumol, John C. Panzar, and Robert D. Willig, *Contestable Markets and the Theory of Industry Structure* (San Diego: Harcourt Brace Jovanovich, 1982); Scott Kilman, "Growing Giants," *The Wall Street Journal*, July 20, 1987, p. 1; *The Kansas City Times*, "TWA Boosted '87 Fares in St. Louis by Twice U.S. Average, Report Says," September 21, 1988, p. D1.

EXHIBIT

28.1

with such data, the concentration ratio provides a good description of competitive pressures within an industry. It can help identify market structures and guide policymakers on the advisability of mergers.

The Herfindahl Index

HERFINDAHL INDEX
A measure of market concentration obtained by squaring the market share of each firm in the industry and then summing these numbers.

A competing gauge of industrial concentration is the **Herfindahl Index** (or, as it is sometimes called, the Herfindahl-Hirschman Index). The Herfindahl Index (HI) sums the market share of all firms in the industry, but only after the market shares have been squared. Thus, assuming there are n firms in the industry, the Herfindahl Index is computed as

$$ \text{HI} = \sum_{i=1}^{n} S_i^2 $$

where S_i^2 is the market share squared of firm i.

Under monopoly, the Herfindahl Index achieves its maximum possible value of $100^2 = 10,000$. Although the Herfindahl Index could theoretically approach zero, its lowest observed value is approximately 11. As with concentration ratios, higher numbers indicate greater concentration of power. In general, industries with higher concentration ratios have higher Herfindahl Indexes, but there are exceptions, as Table 28.1 illustrates.

The Herfindahl Index is subject to many of the same criticisms as the concentration ratio. It does, however, overcome one shortcoming—the failure of the concentration ratio to distinguish between industries dominated by a single firm and industries where the largest firms are approximately equal in size (and therefore more effective rivals). By squaring market shares, the Herfindahl Index assigns disproportionately high values to dominant firms. For example, one firm with a 45 percent market share contributes substantially more to the Herfindahl Index than three firms with 15 percent market shares. [$45^2 = 2,025 > 675 = 3 \times (15^2)$.] Thus, the Herfindahl Index effectively captures the market power of firms that dwarf their competitors.

In 1982, the Justice Department began emphasizing the Herfindahl Index rather than the concentration ratio. Under guidelines issued at that time, an industry is considered to be "unconcentrated" if its Herfindahl Index is less than 1,000, "moderately concentrated" if it has a value between 1,000 and 1,800, and "highly concentrated" if the value exceeds 1,800. Although the Justice Department considers other factors—including import competition and ease of entry into the industry—mergers are evaluated primarily in terms of their impact on the Herfindahl Index. In general, the Justice Department opposes mergers if they increase the index by more than 100 points in moderately concentrated industries or by more than 50 points in highly concentrated industries. Mergers are usually approved if the index rises by a lesser amount or if the industry remains unconcentrated despite the merger (see Table 28.2 page 732).

These Justice Department guidelines explain why certain mergers in the brewing industry were approved and others disallowed. Table 28.3 (page 732) presents the market shares of the major brewers in 1981. At that time the Herfindahl Index was just above 1,600, indicating a "moderately concentrated" industry. Heileman,

CONCENTRATION IN MANUFACTURING, SELECTED INDUSTRIES, 1987

INDUSTRY	NUMBER OF FIRMS	CONCENTRATION RATIO	HERFINDAHL INDEX
Chewing gum	8	96	ND
Cigarettes	9	92	ND
Motor vehicles	352	90	ND
Cereal breakfast foods	33	87	2,207
Greeting cards	147	85	2,830
Photographic equipment	717	77	2,241
Aircraft engines	372	77	2,201
Primary aluminum	34	74	1,934
Tires and innertubes	114	69	1,897
Soap and detergents	683	65	1,698
Prerecorded records and tapes	462	63	1,505
Cookies and crackers	316	58	1,278
Synthetic rubber	58	50	920
Farm machinery	1,576	45	802
Rubber and plastic footwear	54	39	688
Petroleum refining	200	32	435
Women's handbags	316	31	415
Newspapers	7,473	25	250
Bolts, nuts, washers	834	16	120
Sporting and athletic goods	1,708	13	94
Jewelry, precious metal	2,294	12	68
Ready-mixed concrete	3,749	8	25
Women's dresses	5,398	6	24
Special tools and dies	7,207	5	14
Wood pallets	1,678	4	13

Note: ND = not disclosed.

SOURCE: U.S. Bureau of the Census, *1987 Census of Manufactures, Concentration Ratios in Manufacturing* (1992).

TABLE 28.1

the fourth largest brewer, wanted to merge with Schlitz, the third largest. Had the merger been allowed, the market share at Heileman would have climbed to approximately 16 percent.

Defenders of the merger, while conceding that it would raise the concentration ratio and Herfindahl Index, argued that the merger would actually create greater competition in the industry. The two big brewers, Anheuser–Busch and Miller, shared 53 percent of the market, and their market share had been climbing over time. Some worried that the industry was evolving into a *duopoly* (two-firm industry) in which Anheuser–Busch and Miller, after squeezing out their competitors, would be free to inflate their prices. If a third large brewer could be created—for example, through the Heileman–Schlitz merger—it would slow the growth of these two giants. Furthermore, with a strong rival, Anheuser–Busch and Miller would have less discretion over price. In essence, supporters of the merger argued that an industry with three big companies is likely to be more competitive than an industry having just two.

Despite this argument, the Justice Department ruled against Heileman. The merger would have caused the Herfindahl Index to rise by 125 points in an industry

JUSTICE DEPARTMENT MERGER GUIDELINES

VALUE OF HERFINDAHL INDEX AFTER THE PROPOSED MERGER	INDUSTRY CLASSIFICATION	LIKELY RESPONSE OF JUSTICE DEPARTMENT*
< 1,000	Unconcentrated	Approve merger.
1,000–1,800	Moderately concentrated	Approve merger if Herfindahl Index increases by less than 100 points; oppose merger if Herfindahl Index increases by more than 100 points.
> 1,800	Highly concentrated	Approve merger if Herfindahl Index increases by less than 50 points; oppose merger if Herfindahl Index increases by more than 50 points.

*The 1992 guidelines formalize exceptions to these rules. In particular, mergers that increase the Herfindahl Index by more than the specified amount will be allowed if the firms proposing the merger can demonstrate that entry of competitors into the industry is easy or that prices will not rise as a consequence of the merger.

SOURCES: U.S. Department of Justice, *1982 Merger Guidelines; 1992 Merger Guidelines.*

TABLE 28.2

that was moderately concentrated.[4] Because this exceeded the allowable increase of 100 points, the Justice Department considered the merger to be anticompetitive. Although some have criticized this decision, pointing out that the combined share of Anheuser–Busch and Miller has continued to grow, the Herfindahl numbers explain the rationale for rejecting the merger.

MARKET SHARE BY BREWERY, 1981

COMPANY	PERCENT
Anheuser-Busch	30.4
Miller	22.5
Schlitz	8.0
Heileman	7.8
Pabst	7.5
Coors	7.4
Stroh	3.5
Others	12.9

SOURCE: *Brewers Digest*, February 1982. Reprinted by permission of Sichel Publishing Co. © 1982. All rights reserved.

TABLE 28.3

[4]The increase in the Herfindahl Index is given by the formula

$$\Delta HI = S_{a+b}^2 - S_a^2 - S_b^2$$

where S_a and S_b are the premerger market shares of firms a and b, and S_{a+b} is the combined postmerger share. In the case of Heileman and Schlitz, the increase would have been $15.8^2 - 8.0^2 - 7.8^2 = 124.8$.

They also explain why, the following year, Stroh was allowed to acquire Schlitz. Because Stroh was smaller than Heileman, the Stroh–Schlitz merger satisfied the Justice Department's guidelines—it added only 56 points to the Herfindahl Index.

Concentration Ratios and the Herfindahl Index

THE FOLLOWING TABLE DEPICTS THE MARKET SHARES IN INDUSTRIES A AND B:

FIRM	INDUSTRY A (%)	INDUSTRY B (%)
1	22	42
2	20	10
3	20	10
4	18	8
5	6	8
6	5	8
7	5	7
8	4	7
Total	100	100

(A) COMPUTE THE CONCENTRATION RATIO FOR EACH INDUSTRY. (B) COMPUTE THE HERFINDAHL INDEX. (C) ACCORDING TO THE CONCENTRATION RATIO, IS INDUSTRY A OR B MORE HIGHLY CONCENTRATED? (D) DO YOU OBTAIN SIMILAR RESULTS WITH THE HERFINDAHL INDEX? WHY OR WHY NOT?

Overall Concentration in the U.S. Economy

The preceding discussion has focused on concentration within specific industries, but how concentrated is the overall economy? Has it become more or less concentrated over time? Some who worry about the evils of market power—high prices, reduced output, inefficiency—claim that market power is becoming concentrated in the hands of fewer and fewer companies. They argue that big firms are gobbling up their smaller rivals and, as a consequence, the economy is becoming less competitive. It is easy to cite specific instances. For example, the concentration ratio for the brewing industry has soared from about 18 percent 40 years ago to more than 80 percent today. But is this representative of the economy at large? What do aggregate data reveal?

VALUE ADDED IN MANUFACTURING

Aggregate concentration can be measured in various ways. One approach is to measure the *value added* of the largest companies, where value added refers to a company's net contribution to output. (For example, if a company purchases materials for

$300 and turns them into a product selling for $400, it has contributed $100 to output.) As measured by value added, concentration within manufacturing has increased over time (see Table 28.4). In 1947, the 50 largest manufacturing companies contributed 17 percent of the value added in manufacturing. By 1987, the percentage had risen to 25 percent. Similarly, the share of value added by the 100 and 200 largest manufacturing companies also rose.

Of course, many large companies are *conglomerates*—firms that sell unrelated product lines. For example, General Electric operates in more than two dozen industries, including light bulbs, refrigerators, brokerage services, medical equipment, defense, and television broadcasting (it owns NBC). Even though conglomerates may be large in terms of total value added, when their production is spread out across many industries, they may have small market shares within individual industries. Indeed, the period from 1950 to 1975 was characterized by *diversification*—adding new product lines. In 1950 only 10 percent of the 200 largest manufacturing companies sold products in 10 or more different industries, but by 1975, the figure had more than quadrupled (see Table 28.5). To the extent companies diversify by transferring resources from traditional products to new lines of business, their mar-

SHARE OF VALUE ADDED BY THE LARGEST MANUFACTURING COMPANIES*

	YEAR				
	1947	1958	1967	1977	1987
50 largest companies	17	23	25	24	25
100 largest companies	23	30	33	33	33
200 largest companies	30	38	42	44	43

*Percentage of total value added in U.S. manufacturing accounted for by the largest manufacturing companies.

SOURCE: U.S. Bureau of the Census, *Census of Manufactures, Concentration Ratios in Manufacturing.*

TABLE 28.4

INCREASED DIVERSIFICATION IN MANUFACTURING, 1950–1975*

	1950	1975
Percentage of companies selling in 10 or more industries	9.5	45.0
Percentage of companies selling in 21 or more industries	1.0	11.0
Average number of product lines per company	4.8	10.9

*Diversification of the 200 largest U.S. manufacturing companies.

SOURCE: David J. Ravenscraft and F. M. Scherer, *Mergers, Sell-Offs, and Economic Efficiency* (Washington, D.C.: The Brookings Institution, 1987), pp. 30–31.

TABLE 28.5

ket shares in their traditional industries may actually shrink. Thus, the increase in value added by large companies is no indication that industries in general are becoming less competitive.

CONCENTRATION RATIOS IN MANUFACTURING

Most economists argue that concentration ratios provide a more accurate picture of market power than do data on aggregate value added. The distribution of concentration ratios reveals information about market structure at one point in time, and changes in that distribution indicate whether market power is increasing or decreasing.

There are different ways to extract information from concentration ratios. Perhaps the simplest is to look at the share of output (measured by value added) that is produced in concentrated industries. Although this share has risen over short periods of time, notably following World War II, any trend over an extended time frame appears to be toward reduced concentration. The percentage of industries having a concentration ratio of at least 50 percent is lower today than at the turn of the century (see Table 28.6).

An alternative approach is to examine the change in concentration in industries identified as oligopolistic. Between 1947 and 1967, concentration ratios increased in eight oligopolistic industries but declined in ten.[5] By this measure, oligopolistic industries did not become more concentrated even in the early postwar period. Average concentration ratios also fail to detect any clear trend. Average concentration for manufacturing was the same in 1982 as in 1954 (37 percent).[6] Because of

THE SHARE OF TOTAL VALUE ADDED PRODUCED BY CONCENTRATED INDUSTRIES (MANUFACTURING ONLY)*

PERIOD	PERCENT OF VALUE ADDED BY CONCENTRATED INDUSTRIES
1895–1904	32.9
1947	24.4
1954	29.9
1958	30.2
1963	33.1
1972	29.0
1982	25.2

*Concentration ratio ≥ 50 percent.

SOURCE: F. M. Scherer and David Ross, *Industrial Market Structure and Economic Performance*, 3rd ed., p. 84. Copyright © 1990 by Houghton Mifflin Company. Adapted with permission.

TABLE 28.6

[5]James V. Koch, *Industrial Organization and Prices*, 2nd ed. (Englewood Cliffs, N.J.: Prentice-Hall, 1980), p. 187.
[6]F. M. Scherer and David Ross, *Industrial Market Structure and Economic Performance*, 3rd ed. (Boston: Houghton Mifflin, 1990), p. 84.

statistics such as these, many industrial economists still agree with an assessment made more than 40 years ago:

> The extent of concentration shows no tendency to grow, and it may possibly be declining. Any tendency either way, if it does exist, must be at the pace of a glacial drift.[7]

CONCENTRATION IN THE AGGREGATE ECONOMY

The preceding discussion has centered on concentration in manufacturing. One reason for this focus is that manufacturing has traditionally been the largest sector of the U.S. economy. More important, statistics on concentration are more widely available for manufacturing industries than for nonmanufacturing industries.

Despite the shortcomings of nonmanufacturing data, William Shepherd has studied the market structure of the aggregate U.S. economy.[8] He concludes that: (a) most output is produced in "effectively competitive" industries (defined as those with concentration ratios below 40 percent, low entry barriers, and flexible pricing) and (b) the economy has become more competitive over time. Shepherd estimates that 77 percent of output was produced by effectively competitive industries in 1980, compared to 52 percent in 1939 (see Table 28.7). Among the explanations given for this increased competition are growth in imports, deregulation, and antitrust policy. To repeat an earlier caveat, confidence in this study must be tempered by data concerns. But at a minimum, this study reinforces the conclusion of the previously discussed manufacturing studies: *market concentration has not increased over time.*

THE STRUCTURE OF THE U.S. ECONOMY

TYPE OF INDUSTRY	PERCENT OF NATIONAL OUTPUT		
	1939	1958	1980
Monopoly	6.2	3.1	2.5
Oligopoly	41.4	40.6	20.8
Effectively competitive*	52.4	56.3	76.7
Total	100.0	100.0	100.0

*Concentration ratio < 40 percent, low entry barriers, and flexible pricing.

SOURCE: Adapted from William G. Shepherd, "Causes of Increased Competition in the U.S. Economy," *Review of Economics and Statistics* (November 1982), Table 2. Reprinted by permission of Elsevier Science Publishers B. V. (Amsterdam).

TABLE 28.7

[7]Morris Adelman, "The Measurement of Industrial Concentration," *Review of Economics and Statistics* (November 1951), p. 295.

[8]William G. Shepherd, "Causes of Increased Competition in the U.S. Economy, 1939–1980," *Review of Economics and Statistics* (November 1982), pp. 613–626.'

Antitrust

ANTITRUST POLICY
Government laws and procedures designed to shape market structure and influence the behavior of firms.

In addition to economic factors, such as economies of scale, concentration depends on government policy toward big business. The government can encourage big business, halt its spread, break up large companies, or force them to leave certain markets. The government also establishes the rules of the game, spelling out which business practices are acceptable and which are not. Government actions aimed at influencing the structure and conduct of business are referred to as **antitrust policy**.

Antitrust policy is neither static nor consistent. Behavior considered legitimate at one point in time is sometimes deemed inappropriate at some other point in time. Nor is there consistency across all segments of the economy. Various lines of business—including agriculture, banking, baseball, and newspaper publishing—are exempt from at least some antitrust provisions. Nor do antitrust laws currently apply to export associations or labor unions.[9]

Although the stated objective of antitrust laws is to channel market structure and firm behavior in competitive directions, these laws do not always promote competition or protect consumers from the abuses of business. In some instances antitrust policy actually results in *higher* prices. This reflects the fact that policy is influenced by political as well as economic considerations. In this section we review antitrust policy, summarize important laws and court rulings, discuss the major issues, and examine how antitrust policy in the United States has evolved over time.

Major Antitrust Legislation

TRUST
A combination of companies acting in concert in order to increase control of an industry.

PREDATORY PRICING
A practice whereby one or more firms temporarily reduce price in order to drive weaker firms from the industry and then raise price once these competitors have been eliminated.

Antitrust laws were motivated by developments in the late nineteenth century. Advances in mass production, communication, and finance contributed to growing economies of scale. At the same time, the railroad linked diverse regions of the country, enabling companies to expand their markets. In many industries companies discovered that they must grow to survive. Often this meant merging with other companies. Mergers were frequently accomplished by forming a **trust**, in which a board of trustees coordinated the activities of the individual companies. That is, the trust acted along the lines of a cartel.

Many trusts maintained monopoly or near-monopoly positions, doing whatever was necessary to eliminate competitors. For example, through its control of pipelines, Standard Oil was able to deny competitors access to crude oil. In addition, it required railroads to carry its oil at discount prices and even forced them to pay Standard Oil if they shipped competitors' oil. Through such practices, Standard Oil was able to capture 90 percent of the market.

Other trusts engaged in **predatory pricing**. They would sell a product below cost until weaker rivals, unable to withstand the mounting losses, were forced from the industry. Once the competitors were eliminated, the trust would then raise

---

[9]Initially the courts ruled that unions were covered by antitrust law. As a result, certain practices (for example, the union boycott) were declared illegal. Congress later exempted unions.

prices, often to exorbitant levels. The public, questioning both the tactics employed by trusts and the results, petitioned Congress for relief. The result was a series of antitrust laws (see Table 28.8).

THE SHERMAN ACT

The first antitrust law was the *Sherman Act*, enacted by Congress in 1890. Its key provisions are:

> *Section 1* Every contract, combination in the form of a trust or otherwise, or conspiracy, in restraint of trade or commerce among the several states, or with foreign nations, is hereby declared to be illegal. . . .
>
> *Section 2* Every person who shall monopolize, or attempt to monopolize, or combine or conspire with any other person or persons to monopolize any part of the trade or commerce among the several states, or with foreign nations, shall be deemed guilty of a misdemeanor.[10]

Although setting the tone of government policy, this law proved less effective than supporters envisioned. The main problem was lack of clarity; the language was general and often ambiguous. What constitutes a monopoly? Must a firm control the entire market? Is monopoly *per se* illegal or only monopoly achieved through illegal practices? Which practices are legal, and which are illegal? In an attempt to be more specific, Congress enacted additional legislation.

THE CLAYTON ACT

The *Clayton Act* of 1914 prohibits certain clearly defined business practices. It bans some, though not all, forms of *price discrimination*—selling goods to different buyers

SUMMARY OF MAJOR ANTITRUST LAWS	
LAW (DATE ENACTED)	**KEY PROVISIONS**
Sherman Act (1890)	Restricts interstate restraint of trade and attempts to monopolize.
Clayton Act (1914)	Outlaws tying contracts, interlocking directorates, and other specific business practices.
Federal Trade Commission Act (1914)	Created an agency (the FTC) to help enforce antitrust laws.
Robinson–Patman Act (1936)	Generally limits price concessions, especially to large buyers, if one or more competitors would be harmed.
Celler–Kefauver Act (1950)	Places restrictions on mergers (for example, by prohibiting companies from buying the assets of a rival if this reduces competition).

TABLE 28.8

[10]This was later changed to make violations felonies rather than misdemeanors.

at different prices not justified by cost differences. It also outlaws **tying contracts**, in which the sale of one good is conditional on the sale or purchase of a second good. This means, for instance, that General Motors (GM) could not require railroads hauling GM cars to purchase locomotives manufactured by GM.

The Clayton Act prevents companies from buying stock in other companies if the result is reduced competition. It also bans **interlocking directorates** between competing companies. If two companies compete in the same market, the same individual cannot serve on the board of directors of both companies.

THE FEDERAL TRADE COMMISSION ACT

The *Federal Trade Commission Act* is a companion to the Clayton Act. Enacted in 1914, it prohibits "unfair methods of competition in commerce." Its central feature, however, was the creation of the Federal Trade Commission (FTC), an agency to enforce both the Clayton and FTC Acts. The Commission can initiate lawsuits and issue *cease-and-desist orders*, directing companies to halt practices deemed by the FTC as violating antitrust laws. The Commission also conducts economic research on market structure.

As amended in 1938 by the *Wheeler–Lea Act*, the FTC also has authority to halt false or deceptive business practices. For example, in the absence of evidence to support its claim, Listerine mouthwash was ordered to stop advertising that it killed the germs causing sore throats. A bread company, advertising that it contained 400 percent more fiber than whole wheat bread, was ordered to disclose the source of its fiber—wood pulp.

THE ROBINSON–PATMAN ACT

The most controversial antitrust law is probably the *Robinson–Patman Act*. Enacted in 1936, this law amends the Clayton Act by further restricting price discrimination. Unless justified by differences in cost, charging competing companies different prices for "goods of like grade and quality" is generally prohibited if at least one competitor would be harmed.

The intent of the Robinson–Patman Act is to protect small retailers from chain stores that, because of their high-volume purchasing, were often able to buy goods at a lower price than the smaller companies. By passing these cost savings on to consumers in the form of lower prices, the chains were able to gain business at the expense of the small retailers. This law attempts to halt volume discounts and other preferential treatment, thereby shielding small companies from the competitive pressures of large companies. Where small companies are less efficient, this has the effect of fostering inefficiency and promoting higher prices. For this reason, economists generally are critical of the Robinson–Patman Act.

THE CELLER–KEFAUVER ACT

The Clayton Act was further strengthened through enactment of the *Celler–Kefauver Act* of 1950. This law adds several provisions designed to strengthen restrictions against mergers. Although the Clayton Act prohibits companies from acquiring stock in another company in order to reduce competition, companies discovered an alternative way to gain control of rival firms—buying their assets. The Celler–Kefauver Act closes this loophole.

Key Antitrust Rulings

Although Congress enacts the laws, it is the responsibility of the courts to interpret them. Given the vagueness of certain statutes, judicial rulings play a critical role in shaping antitrust policy. Some of the major antitrust cases are presented in the following pages (and summarized in Table 28.9).

PRICE FIXING

The courts have strongly opposed *price fixing*—agreements among companies to set prices—arguing that such behavior is in and of itself illegal. In the *Addyston Pipe Case* (1899), six producers of iron pipes were convicted of rigging prices. Although they claimed that their prices were fair and reasonable, the Supreme Court rejected this defense, ruling that the level at which prices were set was irrelevant. Price fixing was a violation of the Sherman Act.

The *Socony–Vacuum Case* (1940) reinforced the *Addyston* ruling. The Supreme Court held: "Any combination which tampers with price structures is engaged in unlawful activity." Conspiracies to fix prices are "illegal *per se*." The *per se* doctrine makes conviction relatively easy. Prosecutors need not consider motives or reasonableness of behavior, but only show that price fixing actually occurred.

SUMMARY OF MAJOR ANTITRUST CASES

RULING (DATE ISSUED)	KEY PROVISION
Addyston Pipe (1899), *Socony–Vacuum* (1940)	Ruled that price fixing is always illegal.
Standard Oil of New Jersey (1911)	Established the rule of reason, allowing "reasonable" monopolies.
Alcoa (1945)	Overturned the rule of reason, arguing that the Sherman Act forbids all monopolies.
Berkey Photo versus Eastman Kodak (1979)	Retreated from the Alcoa decision—a monopoly may be defensible if achieved because of lower costs.
Du Pont (1957)	Restricted vertical mergers.
Bethlehem Steel (1958)	Restricted horizontal mergers that impair competition.
Von's Grocery (1966)	Restricted horizontal mergers that contribute to a trend toward concentration.

TABLE 28.9

STANDARDS FOR MONOPOLY

The policies of the courts toward monopoly have been less consistent than their policies toward price fixing. A controversy continues even today over the appropriate standard for monopoly. Is monopoly *per se* illegal, or must a monopoly first engage in unacceptable behavior? One of the first cases to address this issue involved *Standard Oil of New Jersey*.

THE RULE OF REASON   In 1911, the Supreme Court found Standard Oil in violation of the Sherman Act. The Court ruled that (a) Standard Oil, with a 90 percent share of the petroleum market, could be considered a monopoly and (b) Standard Oil had achieved its monopoly position illegally, through

> acts and dealings wholly inconsistent with . . . advancing the development of business power by usual methods, but which, on the contrary, necessarily involved the intent to drive others from the field and to exclude them from their right to trade.

This second finding was critical because, according to the decision, monopoly *per se* is not illegal, only monopoly achieved through unreasonable business practices. This doctrine became known as the **rule of reason**. Because the Standard Oil trust achieved its dominance through unreasonable behavior, it was dissolved, leading to competition among the many companies that had comprised the trust.

> **RULE OF REASON**
> The doctrine that all monopolies are not illegal, only monopolies that have engaged in unreasonable behavior.

The rule of reason played a central role in the *U.S. Steel* ruling, issued in 1920. Although U.S. Steel controlled 52 percent of the market, the Supreme Court, noting that its market share had slipped, concluded that the company had not achieved monopoly status. Furthermore, even though the company may have enjoyed market power because of its large size, U.S. Steel had not abused that power. According to the court: "The law does not make mere size an offense or the existence of unexerted power an offense. It . . . requires overt acts."

In the wake of the rule of reason, cases involving monopolizing markets dwindled. Although market dominance was often easy to establish, prosecutors had a more difficult time proving that a company had obtained its monopoly position as the result of particular overt acts. The burden of prosecution eased, however, as the result of the **Alcoa Case** (1945).

THE ALCOA CASE   Alcoa held 90 percent of the market for aluminum ingots. In keeping with earlier court rulings, this was sufficient to classify the company as a monopoly under the Sherman Act. At issue was whether Alcoa violated section 2 of the Sherman Act. Had Alcoa attempted to monopolize the market? It had not engaged in price fixing, predatory pricing, or other unreasonable activities. Rather, its dominance stemmed primarily from its patents and its control over the key raw material, bauxite ore. Nonetheless, the New York Court of Appeals ruled against Alcoa.[11] In its decision, the Court declared:

> Having proved that Alcoa had a monopoly of the domestic ingot market the [government] had gone far enough. . . . Congress . . . did not condone "good trusts" and condemn "bad" ones; it forbade all.

With the *Alcoa* decision, the courts effectively overturned the rule of reason.

---

[11]The Supreme Court did not hear this case because four of its judges disqualified themselves on the ground they had been involved in earlier litigation of the case.

No longer must a prosecutor show that a company is a bad monopoly, having engaged in unreasonable acts. All that is required is proof that it is a monopoly. Whereas the rule of reason required evidence on *conduct* (overt acts), the *Alcoa Case* established a much weaker standard for conviction: evidence on market *structure* (a monopoly or near-monopoly position). As a result of this decision, prosecution of monopolies intensified.

REASSESSING THE ALCOA CASE Beginning in the mid-1970s, the courts appeared to retreat from the *Alcoa* decision and move closer to the rule of reason. For example, in *Berkey Photo versus Eastman Kodak* (1979) an appellate court ruled that "the mere possession of monopoly power does not ipso facto condemn a market participant"; behavior of the monopolist must also be considered.

In *Berkey* the court determined that Kodak's monopoly of the film and camera markets was defensible because it resulted from innovation, rather than improper behavior. The court ruled that the Sherman Act does not

> deprive the leading firm in an industry of the incentive to exert its best efforts. . . .
> If a firm that has engaged in the risks and expenses of research and development were required in all circumstances to share with its rivals the benefits of those endeavors, this incentive would very likely be vitiated.

Accordingly, the court's decision generally favored Kodak.

As the preceding discussion indicates, judicial standards are dynamic, evolving over time. Given changes in both public attitudes and composition of the courts, this is hardly surprising. Undoubtedly, the courts will continue to redefine standards. But such rulings, regardless of their nature, are unlikely to still the debate: Should antitrust policy be based on market conduct or on market structure?

MERGERS

HORIZONTAL MERGER
A merger between companies in the same market.

VERTICAL MERGER
A merger between a company supplying an input and a company buying it.

CONGLOMERATE MERGER
A merger between companies in unrelated markets.

A *merger*, or joining of two firms, can assume different forms. A **horizontal merger** occurs when the two firms are competitors, selling in the same market (for example, when one brewery purchases a second brewery). A **vertical merger** occurs when the output of one company is an input of the other company. An example is the acquisition of an auto parts company by an automobile manufacturer. Finally, a **conglomerate merger** involves companies in unrelated markets. For example, an automobile company might purchase a brewery.

The Clayton and Celler–Kefauver acts place restrictions on horizontal and vertical mergers but do little to block conglomerate mergers—which in recent decades have constituted the majority of all merger activity. The full impact of these laws can be assessed only by studying judicial decisions involving mergers. Based on such decisions, it is clear that horizontal and vertical mergers have been curtailed.

In 1957, the Supreme Court ruled that Du Pont's acquisition of stock in General Motors constituted a vertical merger. Noting that General Motors purchased two-thirds of its finishes from Du Pont and over one-half of its fabrics, the court concluded that the supplier/purchaser relationship between the two companies denied competitors access to a large part of the automotive market. Accordingly, Du Pont was ordered to sell its 23 percent interest in General Motors.

The following year a district court prevented a horizontal merger between *Bethlehem Steel* and Youngstown Steel. The merger would have created a company with a 21 percent share of the overall steel market and higher market shares for such product lines as cold-rolled steel. Even in the absence of the merger, the industry was highly concentrated. For such reasons the court concluded that the merger would have seriously impaired competition.

In 1966, the Supreme Court tightened the standards for horizontal mergers when it prevented *Von's Grocery* Company from acquiring Shopping Bag Food Stores, even though the two companies had a combined market share of only 7.5 percent of the Los Angeles market. The Supreme Court, however, was concerned about the growing concentration in this market. Between 1948 and 1958, the twenty largest grocery companies in Los Angeles had increased their share of the market from 44 percent to 57 percent. The court argued that if it permitted continued merger activity, the market

> would slowly but inevitably gravitate from a market of many small competitors to one dominated by one or a few giants, and competition would thereby be destroyed. Congress passed the Celler–Kefauver Act to prevent such a destruction of competition.

Accordingly, the merger was disallowed.

Enforcement

Antitrust policy does not end with judicial decisions; the final ingredient is enforcement. In the United States, enforcement is primarily the responsibility of two government agencies—the Federal Trade Commission (FTC) and the Antitrust Division of the Justice Department. The agencies can investigate the activities of firms, issue standards outlining acceptable and unacceptable behavior, and file suits to halt certain actions. In addition, the FTC can issue cease-and-desist orders if it believes a company is violating the law. The FTC's decisions, however, can be appealed through the courts. Finally, private parties can initiate suits seeking damages for antitrust violations by other firms, and for relief from further violations.

The aggressiveness of the antitrust agencies has varied over time depending, among other things, on the philosophy of the president and those serving on the agencies. Following a sluggish start, "trust busting" became a passion under Teddy Roosevelt. The passion soon cooled, only to be rekindled in the wake of the Great Depression, when public resentment toward big business intensified. The number of antitrust suits filed by the Justice Department soared, setting a record in the 1940s. After another lull, antitrust efforts picked up from 1968 to 1980. During this period the FTC and the Justice Department attacked numerous companies, including such giants as IBM, AT&T, Xerox, and the major cereal companies.

Under President Reagan (1981–1989), antitrust activity again ebbed. Suits against IBM and the cereal companies were dropped (see Exhibit 28.2, page 744). Standards for mergers were relaxed. The Justice Department began emphasizing the "efficiency-enhancing potential" of mergers, "which can increase the competitiveness of firms and result in lower prices to consumers."[12] It also promised to pay more attention to foreign competition, arguing that concentration poses less of a threat when U.S. producers compete with imports.

---

[12]Department of Justice, *1984 Merger Guidelines*. In *Federal Register* Vol. 49, No. 127, p. 26,834.

E
X
H
I
B
I
T

28.2

Concentration in the Cereal Industry

In 1972, the FTC launched an antitrust case against Kellogg, General Mills, and General Foods, which together held 80 percent of the ready-to-eat cereal market. The cornerstone of this suit was the theory of **shared monopoly**—the firms allegedly were acting as a monopolist attempting to maximize joint industry profits. Even though the FTC had uncovered no evidence of price fixing or of any conspiracy to limit competition, it asserted that the companies must be acting in concert. How else could their dominance be explained? Because economies of scale were relatively unimportant, the agency claimed that the industry would not have evolved naturally into its present, highly concentrated state.

The FTC suggested that the companies used heavy advertising and product proliferation to deny rivals entry into the market. In essence, they were charged with introducing enough products to fill available shelf space in grocery stores. The cereal makers countered that these practices were evidence of competition, not collusion. Companies introduced new brands to satisfy consumer wants and in an effort to win customers from rival producers.

The FTC dropped the case in 1982, amid criticism from the Reagan Administration that a novel theory (shared monopoly) should not serve as the basis for breaking up the cereal companies. Many in Congress were also unimpressed

with the FTC's case. A majority of senators and over 100 representatives sponsored a bill to prevent the FTC from proceeding with the case. The FTC has backed away from the theory of shared monopoly and is now concentrating on cases for which there is specific evidence of wrongdoing.

SOURCES: Adapted from Margaret Warner, "Ruling to Drop Suit Against Cereal Firms Deals Blow to 'Shared Monopoly' Theory," *The Wall Street Journal*, September 11, 1981. "FTC Drops 10-Year-Old Antitrust Suit Against the 3 Largest U.S. Cereal Makers," *The Wall Street Journal*, January 18, 1982, p. 4.

Reagan appointees applauded the court's decision in *Berkey Photo versus Eastman Kodak* and argued for a return to the rule of reason. In outlining administration policy, the chief of the Justice Department's Antitrust Division stated that antitrust prosecution requires evidence of serious business improprieties, that are intended to interfere with competitors, other than by improving the situations of one's consumers. A company that is large and has a large market share is free and should be free to go on competing aggressively, keeping its prices down and capturing an even larger market share if it can.[13]

The Reagan policy called for opposing mergers that would harm the public and prosecuting such illegal acts as price fixing. But large companies would no longer automatically be viewed with suspicion. Instead, the Reagan Administration often emphasized the **superiority hypothesis**: Companies with a large market share were successful, not because of monopoly power, but because of their superior performance.[14] That is, a favorable cost structure (lower cost curves) allowed highly efficient companies to grow more rapidly than their competitors and thus obtain a large share of the market.

Under the Bush Administration, the government adopted a generally tougher stance on antitrust enforcement. The FTC and the Justice Department opposed more mergers, sought stiffer penalties for antitrust violations, and openly challenged the superiority hypothesis. The one area where the Bush Administration looked favorably on size was in international markets. In such industries as banking, the United States, once the world leader, has become a smaller, less important world player. As foreign rivals expanded rapidly, restrictive antitrust policies limited the size of U.S. companies and made it more difficult for these companies to compete internationally. Concerned by such developments, the Bush Administration viewed large firm size as a way to increase U.S. competitiveness and expand exports in certain global markets and therefore as something that can be in the best interest of the country, despite increased concentration in domestic markets. Early evidence indicates that President Clinton will be at least as aggressive in enforcing antitrust policy as was Bush.

In the final analysis, antitrust enforcement remains an art. Although subject to the broad directives of Congress, antitrust agencies have considerable latitude over both the intensity and direction of their activities. From an economic perspective, these agencies should balance the benefits of concentration, including economies of scale, against the abuses of monopoly power. Because different people have different perceptions about the benefits and costs of big business, there is a range of opinion over what constitutes optimal policy. As new presidents are elected and new executive appointments made, one can be confident that antitrust enforcement will continue to change in the years ahead.

SUPERIORITY HYPOTHESIS
The claim that large oligopolistic producers captured sizable market shares due to their superior efficiency (lower cost curves).

Market Share and Profitability

THERE IS EVIDENCE THAT LARGE, OLIGOPOLISTIC FIRMS EARN A HIGHER RATE OF PROFIT THAN SMALL, COMPETITIVE FIRMS. THIS MAY BE BECAUSE OF MONOPOLY POWER OF THE LARGE FIRMS OR BECAUSE OF THEIR COST SUPERIORITY. (A) EXPLAIN THESE ALTERNATIVE VIEWS. (B) DO BOTH VIEWS PREDICT THAT PRICES WILL RISE AS LARGE FIRMS INCREASE THEIR MARKET SHARE? (C) WHICH VIEW IS MORE CRITICAL OF BIG BUSINESS?

[13]Robert Taylor, "Antitrust Enforcement Will Be More Selective," *The Wall Street Journal*, January 1, 1982, p. 6.
[14]The source of the superiority hypothesis is Harold Demsetz, "Industry Structure, Market Rivalry, and Public Policy," *Journal of Law and Economics* (April 1973), pp. 1–9.

Summary

1. Highly concentrated markets are difficult to evaluate. The domination by a few large firms may reflect favorable cost developments, either economies of scale or superior efficiency of the successful firms. Alternatively, concentration may result from the exploitation of monopoly power. In the latter case, the result is higher prices and reduced output. Concern over the abuse of monopoly power has led to antitrust policy— government actions aimed at influencing the structure and conduct of business.

2. There are various proxies for monopoly power, the two most popular being the market concentration ratio and the Herfindahl Index. The market concentration ratio measures the percentage of industry sales claimed by the four largest producers in the industry. The Herfindahl Index is obtained by summing the market share squared of each firm in the industry. For both measures, higher values indicate greater concentration of power.

3. Neither the market concentration ratio nor the Herfindahl Index provides a complete picture of monopoly power. Accordingly, each should be supplemented with information about competition from imports, other industries, and potential new rivals. In addition, markets must be properly defined if these measures are to provide reliable information.

4. Current antitrust policy emphasizes the Herfindahl Index. Mergers in concentrated industries generally are not allowed if they would increase the Herfindahl Index by more than a specified amount.

5. The share of value added by large manufacturing companies has increased over time. But because of diversification, the concentration of power within individual industries has not increased. That is, although the largest companies are producing a greater share of total manufacturing output, market concentration ratios have not trended upward. If anything, market concentration—both in manufacturing and for the overall economy— may be lower today than at the start of the century.

6. Concentration depends in part on government policy. This consists of antitrust legislation, court rulings, and enforcement by the two antitrust agencies—the Federal Trade Commission (FTC) and the Antitrust Division of the Justice Department.

7. National antitrust legislation began with the Sherman Act in 1890. Thereafter, laws were added to prohibit specific practices and make enforcement easier.

8. The courts are responsible for interpreting the legislation. Although the courts have consistently opposed certain practices (for example, price fixing), their policy toward monopoly has changed over time. Initially the courts adopted the "rule of reason," condemning only those monopolies that engaged in unreasonable behavior. The *Alcoa* decision changed the standard from behavior to market structure—monopoly, even if achieved as a result of reasonable behavior, was declared illegal. More recently the courts appear to have retreated from the *Alcoa* decision, adopting a more tolerant attitude toward monopoly power.

9. The FTC and the Justice Department enforce the antitrust laws—investigating the practices of firms, attempting to halt violations, and establishing merger guidelines. In addition, the FTC investigates fraudulent advertising and issues cease-and-desist orders.

10. Enforcement has fluctuated over time. Under the Reagan Administration, merger guidelines were relaxed and antitrust agencies became more tolerant of big business. But in the post-Reagan era, antitrust agencies are challenging more mergers and, with the exception of global markets, taking a more skeptical view of big business.

market concentration ratio
contestable market
Herfindahl Index
antitrust policy
trust
predatory pricing
tying contract
interlocking directorates

rule of reason
Alcoa Case
horizontal merger
vertical merger
conglomerate merger
shared monopoly
superiority hypothesis

Study Questions and Problems

1. Explain what effect, if any, the following actions have on the industry's market concentration ratio.
   a. In the face of falling demand for U.S. steel, the largest steel company in the United States purchases an oil company.
   b. A foreign automobile company starts manufacturing cars in the United States, rather than overseas, and becomes the fifth-largest automobile producer in the United States.
   c. Each of the aluminum companies loses 10 percent of its sales, as soft-drink companies switch from aluminum cans to bottles.
   d. The fourth-largest brewery sells one of its plants to the second-largest brewery.
   e. The fourth-largest brewery sells one of its plants to the tenth-largest brewery.

2. (a) What is monopoly power? (b) Explain why market concentration is not a perfect measure of this power.

3. Assume an industry consists of six firms. Sales figures for each are as follows:

FIRM NUMBER	ANNUAL SALES (MILLIONS OF UNITS)
1	100
2	80
3	80
4	60
5	40
6	40

   a. Compute the concentration ratio and the Herfindahl Index for this industry.
   b. How would a merger of the two smallest firms affect the concentration ratio and the Herfindahl Index?
   c. Would such a merger satisfy the guidelines of the Justice Department? Why or why not?

4. In 1987, Chrysler purchased American Motors Corporation (AMC). Prior to this purchase the market share of vehicles produced in the United States was as follows:

General Motors	55%
Ford	25%
Chrysler	14%
Honda	3%
American Motors	1%
Volkswagen	1%
Nissan	1%

    a. According to Justice Department guidelines, was this industry unconcentrated, moderately concentrated, or highly concentrated?

    b. Did the merger satisfy the Justice Department guidelines? Explain.

    c. Do you think the merger will decrease competitive pressures within the automotive industry? Explain.

    d. Would a merger of Chrysler and Honda have satisfied the merger guidelines?

5.   We should rethink our attitude toward profitable giants such as the International Business Machines Corporation. . . . We ought to think about how to get more I.B.M.s, instead of attacking the one we have.[15]

Do you agree with the preceding quotation? Explain the pros and cons of having industry giants such as IBM. What do you think our antitrust policy should be toward such giants?

6. Indicate whether each of the following constitutes a horizontal, vertical, or conglomerate merger.

    a. Harcourt Brace Jovanovich acquires another publishing company: Holt, Rinehart and Winston.

    b. General Cinema, which operates movie theaters, buys Harcourt Brace Jovanovich.

    c. Trans World Airlines purchases Ozark Airlines.

    d. Nabisco, which makes cookies and crackers, buys a flour mill.

    e. The tobacco company R. J. Reynolds acquires Nabisco.

    f. IBM buys stock in Intel, a computer-chip manufacturer.

7. Identify the law prohibiting

    a. tying contracts and interlocking directorates.

    b. "conspiracy in restraint of trade or commerce."

    c. purchase of a competitor's assets in order to gain control of the company.

    d. volume discounts on the purchase of "goods of like grade and quality."

8. Which court decision

    a. established the "rule of reason"?

    b. overturned the rule of reason, claiming that Congress outlawed even good monopolies?

    c. declared price fixing "illegal *per se*"?

    d. prevented the merger of two companies with a combined 7.5 percent share of the market out of concern that mergers would eventually reduce the competitiveness of this market?

9. How has antitrust policy changed over the past 25 years? Do you think that recent developments reflect a permanent change in government policy toward big business? Explain.

[15]Joseph Bower, "The Case for Building More I.B.M.s," *The New York Times*, February 16, 1986, p. 2F.

YOUR TURN
Answers

Concentration Ratios and the Herfindahl Index

(A) THE CONCENTRATION RATIO IS 80 PERCENT FOR INDUSTRY *A* AND 70 PERCENT FOR INDUSTRY *B*. (B) THE RESPECTIVE VALUES FOR THE HERFINDAHL INDEX ARE 1,710 AND 2,254. (C) INDUSTRY *A*. (D) NO. IN CONTRAST TO THE CONCENTRATION RATIO, THE HERFINDAHL INDEX INDICATES THAT INDUSTRY *B* IS MORE HIGHLY CONCENTRATED. THIS IS BECAUSE INDUSTRY *B* CONTAINS A FIRM WITH A VERY LARGE MARKET SHARE. THE HERFINDAHL INDEX (BECAUSE IT SQUARES MARKET SHARES) WEIGHTS THE INFLUENCE OF LARGE FIRMS MORE HEAVILY THAN DOES THE CONCENTRATION RATIO.

Market Share and Profitability

(A) ACCORDING TO THE MONOPOLY POWER VIEW, A HIGHLY CONCENTRATED MARKET GIVES FIRMS THE ABILITY TO RAISE PRICE AND EARN ECONOMIC PROFITS IN THE LONG RUN. IN CONTRAST, THE EFFICIENCY VIEW (SUPERIORITY HYPOTHESIS) ARGUES THAT A COMPANY WITH A HIGH MARKET SHARE CAN PRODUCE AT A LOWER COST PER UNIT THAN CAN SMALLER COMPANIES, ENABLING IT TO EARN A HIGHER RATE OF PROFIT. (B) NO. ONLY THE MONOPOLY POWER VIEW PREDICTS HIGHER PRICES (BECAUSE OF INCREASED MONOPOLY POWER). A COMPANY WITH SUPERIOR EFFICIENCY EARNS HIGH PROFITS BECAUSE OF ITS LOWER COSTS, NOT HIGHER PRICES. AN INCREASE IN ITS MARKET SHARE WILL NOT INCREASE PRICE. (C) THE MONOPOLY POWER VIEW.

Selected References

Carlton, Dennis W., and Jeffrey M. Perloff. *Modern Industrial Organization* (New York: Harper Collins, 1990).

Scherer, F. M. and David Ross. *Industrial Market Structure and Economic Performance*, 3rd ed. (Boston: Houghton Mifflin, 1990).

Shepherd, William G. *The Economics of Industrial Organization*, 3rd ed. (Englewood Cliffs, N.J.: Prentice-Hall, 1990).

Stelzer, Irwin M. *Selected Antitrust Cases: Landmark Decisions*, 7th ed. (Homewood, Ill.: Irwin, 1986).

Waldman, Don E. *The Economics of Antitrust* (Boston: Little, Brown & Co., 1986).

Regulation

NOT ONLY DOES GOVERNMENT INFLUENCE MARKET STRUCTURE THROUGH ANTITRUST POLICY, IT OVERSEES THE OPERATION OF VARIOUS MARKETS. THE FEDERAL GOVERNMENT DECIDES WHICH PRODUCTS AT&T MAY SELL AND HOW MUCH IT MAY CHARGE FOR LONG-DISTANCE CALLS. IT DETERMINES WHO MAY OPERATE TELEVISION AND RADIO STATIONS AND WHAT THEY MAY BROADCAST. FINANCIAL REGULATIONS LIMIT THE INVESTMENT ACTIVITIES OF BANKS, FORCE COMPANIES TO FOLLOW SPECIFIC ACCOUNTING RULES, AND PROHIBIT *INSIDE TRADING* OF STOCKS (TRADING BASED ON CONFIDENTIAL INFORMATION). VARIOUS GOVERNMENT AGENCIES LIMIT THE AMOUNT OF POLLUTION COMPANIES MAY GENERATE AND REQUIRE THEM TO PROVIDE A SAFE WORK ENVIRONMENT. STILL OTHER AGENCIES FORCE THE RECALL OF UNSAFE PRODUCTS, LIMIT THE USE OF FOOD ADDITIVES, AND PREVENT THE SALE OF NEW DRUGS PENDING GOVERNMENT APPROVAL.

ACCORDING TO THE CENTER FOR THE STUDY OF AMERICAN BUSINESS, THE FEDERAL GOVERNMENT OPERATES 53 SEPARATE REGULATORY AGENCIES WITH A COMBINED STAFF OF MORE THAN 120,000.[2] BEYOND THAT, INDIVIDUAL STATES AND CITIES HAVE THEIR OWN REGULATORY BODIES THAT DETERMINE HOW LAND SHALL BE USED (ZONING REGULATIONS), WHO SHALL BE ALLOWED TO CUT HAIR OR SELL EYEGLASSES (OCCUPATIONAL LICENSING), AND HOW MUCH UTILITIES MAY CHARGE FOR NATURAL GAS AND ELECTRICITY. SOME CITIES REGULATE LOCAL TRANSPORTATION, LIMITING THE NUMBER OF TAXIS ON CITY STREETS AND SETTING THEIR FARES.

> Regulation is a political instrument. It is adopted and administered in a political process to serve social and political purposes—in both the best and the worst sense of those terms.[1]
>
> [1]Alfred Kahn, *The Deregulation Experience* (Chicago: Harris Bank, 1990), p. 9.

[2]Melinda Warren and James Lis, *Regulatory Standstill: Analysis of the 1993 Federal Budget* (St. Louis: Washington University Center for the Study of American Business, 1992).

Regulation affects virtually every business and consumer in some form or another.

What are the reasons for regulation and what are its consequences? Does society in general benefit or merely special-interest groups? Although governmental regulations remain pervasive, they have eased in certain industries—notably transportation, communication, and finance. Entry restrictions have been relaxed, and firms have been given greater discretion over price and service. Has this *deregulation* of industry been a success or a failure? Chapter 29 explores these issues, following a brief survey of regulation in the United States.

The Evolution of Federal Regulation

The same distrust of big business that motivated antitrust laws also led to the creation of the Interstate Commerce Commission (ICC) in 1887. Consumers worried about the growing monopoly power of railroads and the effect on price. Competition by a large number of railroads was not practical. With duplicate trains, depots, and tracks, the costs of rail transportation would be unnecessarily high. Economic efficiency demanded that only a small number of railroads serve a region. But with little competition from other carriers, what was to prevent a railroad from charging exorbitant prices? The solution was to create a government agency (the ICC) that would control entry into the industry, thereby limiting the costs of transportation, and at the same time would cap the rates that railroads could charge their customers.

Unlike the railroad industry, trucking has the ingredients of a competitive industry. The market is capable of supporting a large number of trucking companies, and competition among these companies could be expected to keep trucking rates low. As the highway system developed, the trucking industry began taking business away from railroads. Even where railroads enjoyed a cost advantage, they were unable to match lower trucking rates, because rail charges were set by the ICC. For railroads to compete with trucking, either they had to be given the freedom to reduce their rates or truckers had to be prevented from undercutting the price of rail service. Congress chose the latter option, and in 1935 the trucking industry was brought under the jurisdiction of the ICC.

During the 1930s, regulation was similarly extended to other industries. The Civil Aeronautics Board (CAB) was created to regulate air travel and the Federal Communications Commission (FCC) to regulate the various means of communications—telephone, telegraph, and broadcasting. The Securities and Exchange Commission (SEC) was established to guarantee more accurate information on the value of stocks and other securities, to combat fraud and malpractice in the securities industry, and to regulate brokers and other securities dealers. The SEC was also empowered to set brokerage fees, although it has not done so since 1975. The number of federal regulatory agencies continued to grow through 1978, with the greatest growth occurring from 1969 through 1978.

In 1970, the Occupational Safety and Health Administration (OSHA) was created to reduce the incidence of death and injury in the workplace. This agency issues safety and health rules and inspects job sites for compliance. Employers are cited and fined for each violation, and ordered to take corrective action. For example, in 1991, the Citgo Petroleum Corporation was fined $6 million for an explosion at one of its Louisiana refineries and ordered to identify and control production processes involving hazardous materials. USX recently paid $3.5 million in fines for safety deficiencies and record-keeping violations at two Pennsylvania plants. USX also agreed to changes related to noise levels, operation of cranes, record keeping, and safety training.

In 1972, the push for increased safety reached the product market. The Consumer Product Safety Commission (CPSC) was established "to protect the public from unreasonable risks of injury associated with consumer products." The commission requires companies to report defects in their products and to correct them. It can also ban the sale of hazardous products.

The Environmental Protection Agency (EPA) was formed in 1970 to coordinate environmental policy. The agency seeks abatement of air and water pollution and the control of solid waste, pesticides, radiation, and toxic substances. It monitors activities affecting the environment, sets standards and enforces them, and engages in research. The responsibilities of the EPA and various other regulatory bodies are summarized in Table 29.1.

SELECTED FEDERAL REGULATORY AGENCIES

AGENCY	YEAR CREATED	PRINCIPAL FUNCTION
Interstate Commerce Commission (ICC)	1887	To regulate interstate ground transportation, including the railroad, trucking, bus, and water carrier industries.
Federal Energy Regulatory Commission (FERC)*	1920	To regulate water power and the interstate sale of electricity and natural gas.
Federal Communications Commission (FCC)	1934	To regulate interstate and foreign communications by radio, television, telephone, telegraph, and the like.
Securities and Exchange Commission (SEC)	1934	To regulate the markets for stocks and other securities and to protect investors by seeking full disclosure of pertinent information.
Civil Aeronautics Board (CAB)**	1938	To regulate the airline industry.
Environmental Protection Agency (EPA)	1970	To coordinate environmental policy, set pollution standards, and otherwise enforce environmental legislation.
Occupational Safety and Health Administration (OSHA)	1970	To promote the health and safety of workers by issuing and enforcing rules covering the workplace.
Consumer Product Safety Commission (CPSC)	1972	To reduce injuries to consumers from unsafe products.

*Formerly known as the Federal Power Commission.
**Abolished in 1984.
SOURCES: Adapted from Ronald Penoyer, *Directory of Federal Regulatory Agencies* (St. Louis: Center for the Study of American Business, 1982); Office of the Federal Register, *The United States Government Manual, 1992/93* (Washington, DC: U.S. Government Printing Office, 1992).

TABLE 29.1

THE CHANGING NATURE OF REGULATION

ECONOMIC REGULATION
The regulation of specific industries, designed to influence such outcomes as price, service, and number of producers in an industry.

SOCIAL REGULATION
Broad-based regulations designed to improve the environment and to enhance health and safety.

DEREGULATION
The removal of government regulations.

The focus of regulation has shifted over time. Early regulation tended to be industry-specific, directed, for example, at the railroad industry, the airline industry, or the securities industry. It was concerned primarily with setting price, controlling entry into the industry, and establishing service standards. Because this type of regulation focused on economic outcomes in the industry, it became known as **economic regulation**. In contrast, the new regulation of recent decades has been primarily **social regulation**. Concerned with the general well-being of society, social regulation attempts to improve the quality of the environment and to promote greater health and safety throughout the economy, for both workers and consumers. Social regulation is broader in scope than economic regulation, with regulatory bodies generally having jurisdiction over all industries.

As social regulation expanded, so did the costs of regulation. Between 1970 and 1980, the administrative costs of regulatory agencies increased by 120 percent in real terms—that is, after netting out for the effects of inflation. Staffing of federal regulatory agencies also soared, from 70,000 employees in 1970 to 122,000 in 1980.

The growth in regulatory budgets slowed in the 1980s, and the staffing actually declined (see Table 29.2). Although partially attributable to President Reagan, who campaigned against "regulatory excesses," the turnaround actually began prior to the Reagan presidency. Both Presidents Ford and Carter pushed regulatory reform. Indeed, most of the laws **deregulating** industry were passed during the Carter Administration. Foremost was the Airline Deregulation Act of 1978, which relaxed entry restrictions, allowed airlines to reduce fares, and led to the eventual elimination of the CAB. Two years later Congress extended deregulation to the trucking, railroad, and financial industries.[3]

	STAFFING AND ADMINISTRATIVE COSTS OF FEDERAL REGULATORY AGENCIES	
YEAR	**STAFFING (FULL-TIME POSITIONS)**	**ADMINISTRATIVE COSTS (MILLIONS OF 1993 DOLLARS)**
1970	69,946	$ 4,993
1980	121,706	10,930
1990	114,592	12,749
1993	126,501*	14,020*

*Estimated.
SOURCE: Melinda Warren and James Lis, *Regulatory Standstill: Analysis of the 1993 Federal Budget* (St. Louis: Washington University Center for the Study of American Business, 1992), Tables A.2 and A.3. Adapted with permission.

TABLE 29.2

---

[3] The specific laws achieving deregulation were the Motor Carrier Act, the Staggers Railway Act, and the Depository Institutions Deregulation and Monetary Control Act.

But whereas President Carter was committed to reducing *economic* regulation, President Reagan was equally intent on scaling back *social* regulation. Reagan sliced the budget at OSHA, arguing that many of the agency's regulations imposed costs on business without contributing to health or safety. By the end of his second term the number of OSHA inspectors had been cut by 30 percent. Similarly, the budget for the Consumer Product Safety Commission was lower in Reagan's final year in office than in Carter's final year. Although the budget of the EPA continued to grow, its rate of advance was more moderate during the Reagan Administration.

Social regulation has rebounded in the 1990s, in part because of the more favorable views of regulation by Presidents George Bush and Bill Clinton. Staffing of federal regulatory agencies has been restored to pre-Reagan levels, and many recent appointees are pursuing a more activist role for their agencies. One of the areas experiencing the fastest rate of regulatory growth is the environment. Although Bush may not be remembered as "the environmental president" he pledged to become, by the time he left office he had increased staffing at the EPA by 26 percent and had substantially boosted the agency's budget. And President Clinton is emphasizing the environment to an even greater extent than did Bush. As a result of these changes and others made over the preceding two decades, the share of regulatory budgets earmarked for the environment has increased from 15 percent in 1970 to almost 40 percent today (see Figure 29.1).

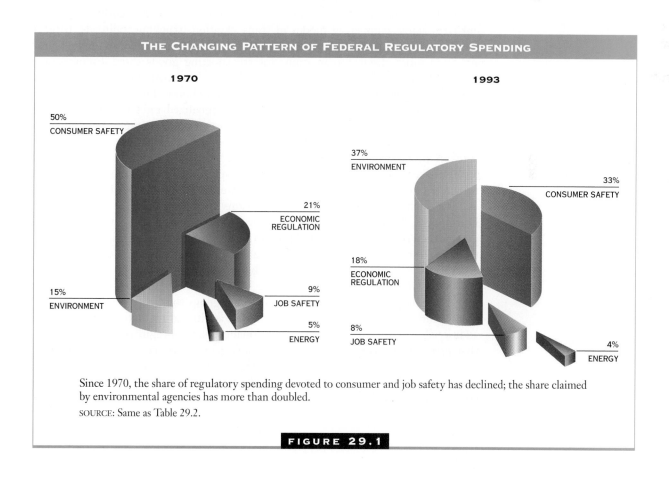

THE CHANGING PATTERN OF FEDERAL REGULATORY SPENDING

1970

50% CONSUMER SAFETY

21% ECONOMIC REGULATION

15% ENVIRONMENT

9% JOB SAFETY

5% ENERGY

1993

37% ENVIRONMENT

33% CONSUMER SAFETY

18% ECONOMIC REGULATION

8% JOB SAFETY

4% ENERGY

Since 1970, the share of regulatory spending devoted to consumer and job safety has declined; the share claimed by environmental agencies has more than doubled.

SOURCE: Same as Table 29.2.

FIGURE 29.1

The Costs and Benefits of Regulation

Left to their own, private markets may fail to allocate resources efficiently. In such cases, government regulation can increase the well-being of society. Even the harshest critics of regulation acknowledge the legitimate role of government. At issue is not the need for government regulation, but its scope.

Those seeking to reduce government's role attack regulations on two grounds: (a) regulations are sometimes extended to markets that would operate more efficiently unregulated and (b) in markets where intervention is appropriate, regulation is often excessive. Regulations impose costs on society. These consist of both the administrative costs of regulatory agencies, including staff salaries and overhead, and the costs of complying with the regulations. In addition to the extra paperwork, regulations force firms to add product features they would not otherwise provide (for example, catalytic converters on automobiles) and to alter production processes. For instance, coal-burning power plants must install stack scrubbers or otherwise reduce sulphur emissions from the coal. This raises the cost of electricity.

Costs rise even further because of the inefficient resource use mandated by various regulatory agencies. Prior to deregulation the ICC forced trucks to return empty on long hauls rather than picking up additional cargo. Moreover, by equalizing fares across competing modes of transportation (trucking, railroads, barges), the ICC removed the incentive to use the most efficient mode. For example, trucks are often more efficient than trains for transporting goods short distances, and trains are more efficient for long hauls. Ideally, these cost differences would be reflected in rate schedules, so that shippers would choose the least costly mode of transportation. The ICC, however, frequently equalized rates to guarantee each industry a share of both long-distance and short-distance markets. In some cases the ICC even subsidized trucking companies making long hauls so they could compete on routes where railroads were more efficient. As a result, transportation resources best suited for long-distance travel were often used for short hauls while resources best suited for short-distance travel were used for long hauls.

For such reasons government regulations increase the costs of production. During the 1970s, compliance costs were estimated to be about twenty times greater than administrative costs.[4] If that ratio still holds, then based on administrative costs of roughly $14 billion (see Table 29.2), the total cost of federal regulations is currently in the neighborhood of $294 billion per year.

From an economic perspective, the costs of regulation should be compared with the benefits. Further regulation is advantageous to society when the benefits from additional regulation exceed the costs of additional regulation. But when the additional benefits fall short of the additional costs, then regulation is excessive. In that case society would benefit from transferring resources from regulation to other activities—for example, producing greater output for consumers.

Some regulations pass the cost/benefit test; others do not. For example, one study found that mandated safety features on automobiles provided benefits in

---

[4]Murray Weidenbaum and Robert DeFina, *The Cost of Federal Regulation of Economic Activity* (Washington, D.C.: The American Enterprise Institute, May 1978), p. 2.

excess of costs but that regulations dealing with automobile emissions and fuel economy had costs that exceeded benefits.[5] Before assessing the impact of various regulations, it is important to understand their rationale. This will help you understand why certain regulations are socially desirable and why others are not.

YOUR TURN

NEW DRUGS CAN BE SOLD IN THE UNITED STATES ONLY IF THEY WIN THE APPROVAL OF THE FOOD AND DRUG ADMINISTRATION (FDA). HISTORICALLY, TO BE APPROVED THE DRUGS HAD TO BE THOROUGHLY TESTED IN CLINICAL TRIALS AND FOUND TO BE SAFE AND EFFECTIVE. RECENTLY HOWEVER, IN RESPONSE TO CRITICISM BY AIDS ACTIVIST GROUPS AND OTHERS, THE FDA HAS APPROVED THE SALE OF CERTAIN DRUGS BEFORE THE DRUGS WERE COMPLETELY TESTED. WHAT IS THE MAJOR BENEFIT OF THE FDA'S TRADITIONAL STANDARDS, BASED ON EXTENSIVE TREATMENT AND COMPELLING EVIDENCE THAT A DRUG IS SAFE AND EFFECTIVE? ON WHAT BASIS MIGHT THE TRADITIONAL APPROACH BE CRITICIZED?

Why Regulate?

There are two principal theories of regulation: the *public-interest theory* and the *special-interest theory*. The former argues that regulations arise because of the failure of private markets to generate socially optimal outcomes (in terms of price, costs, and output). Where market failure exists, regulations can improve the well-being of society. The special-interest theory paints a less favorable view of regulation. According to this theory, regulation is designed to protect special-interest groups at the expense of the general public. For example, regulators may restrict competition and raise price, enabling a regulated firm to earn higher profits but harming consumers.

The Public-Interest Theory of Regulation

PUBLIC-INTEREST THEORY OF REGULATION
The theory that regulation is a response to market failure and therefore designed to benefit society.

Adam Smith extolled the virtues of private markets, arguing that consumers and producers "promote the public interest" more effectively than any government. If this were always true, then government intervention could only harm the public interest. Smith's argument holds, however, only when certain ideal conditions prevail. When these conditions are not satisfied, market outcomes are not optimal. In such cases government may serve the public interest. Among the reasons for market failure, and therefore government regulation, are natural monopoly, externalities, and imperfect information.

---

[5]Robert W. Crandall, Howard Gruenspecht, Theodore Keeler, and Lester Lave, *Regulating the Automobile* (Washington, D.C.: The Brookings Institution, 1986).

NATURAL MONOPOLY

In a natural monopoly the average cost of production falls as the scale of operations increases (see Figure 29.2). In this situation competition is not efficient. The average cost of producing a given output is minimized when only one firm is in the industry. Therefore, by limiting production to a single firm the government minimizes costs of production. Society does not necessarily benefit, however, if the firm granted monopoly status is allowed to charge any price it wishes. Therefore, in the case of natural monopoly, regulation has a second function—to protect consumers from high prices.

EXTERNALITIES

Externalities arise when parties engaged in neither the production nor the consumption of a good are nonetheless affected by the good. For example, production may entail a side effect—pollution. The individual firm has no incentive to reduce pollution voluntarily. Expenditures on pollution control would put the firm at a competitive disadvantage—it would face higher costs than firms that did not control pollution. Therefore, if society wants less pollution, the government must step in and regulate industry. Regulation may assume a variety of forms, from direct controls requiring specific pollution-control equipment to taxation. These forms are examined in Chapter 35. Regardless of its form, however, regulation is necessary if society is to respond to externalities.

IMPERFECT INFORMATION

Consumers cannot choose wisely if they lack relevant information. Unaware of the dangers, they may consume unsafe drugs, buy defective products, and work with

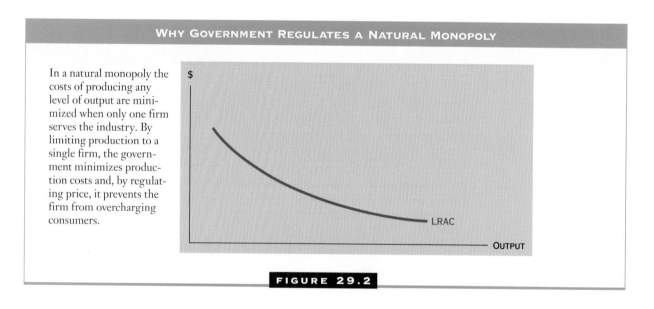

WHY GOVERNMENT REGULATES A NATURAL MONOPOLY

In a natural monopoly the costs of producing any level of output are minimized when only one firm serves the industry. By limiting production to a single firm, the government minimizes production costs and, by regulating price, it prevents the firm from overcharging consumers.

FIGURE 29.2

hazardous chemicals. Companies generally lack the incentive to voluntarily reveal shortcomings in their products. Worse than that, they may be able to boost sales by making false claims. Information is valuable and, accordingly, consumers are prepared to spend income on services such as *Consumer Reports*, which evaluate various products. But markets may fail to provide adequate information or to discipline unscrupulous producers adequately. In that event, government can benefit society by gathering and disseminating information pertinent to consumers and workers and by preventing companies from making false or deceptive claims. This is the rationale for warning labels on cigarettes, EPA mileage ratings on cars, and posted weight limits and safety instructions on ladders.

Some individuals argue that the government should do more than assure consumers of accurate information—that it should force unsafe products from the market and mandate minimum safety standards in the workplace. According to this argument, even when information is widely available, consumers lack the expertise to evaluate it. If consumers are not sophisticated enough to make intelligent decisions, the government should decide for them—for example, force them to buy products with extensive safety features.

Others dismiss this view, contending that once consumers have sufficient information they should be free to choose. By restricting consumer choice to safe products and safe workplaces, the government may actually reduce the well-being of its citizens. This argument is illustrated in Figure 29.3.

Safety features are costly to provide, both in products and in the workplace. As products are made safer, production costs rise, pushing up price (Figure 29.3A). A

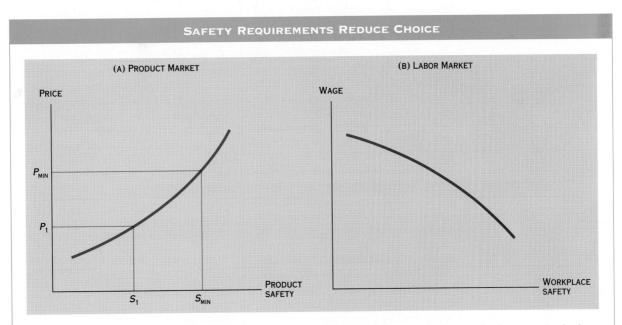

SAFETY REQUIREMENTS REDUCE CHOICE

(A) PRODUCT MARKET

PRICE

P_{MIN}

P_1

S_1 S_{MIN} PRODUCT SAFETY

(B) LABOR MARKET

WAGE

WORKPLACE SAFETY

There is a trade-off between product safety and price (A). As companies spend more on safety, production costs rise, leading to higher prices. If the government mandates S_{min} safety, consumers cannot buy products with less safety (for example, S_1) and a lower price (P_1), even if such products are preferred. In the workplace, added safety leads to lower wages (B). If the government mandates more safety than workers desire, they are forced to accept lower-paying, less-attractive jobs.

FIGURE 29.3

All-Terrain Vehicles

T he all-terrain vehicle (ATV) has a poor safety record. These three- and four-wheeled motorized bikes often overturn, leaving the driver vulnerable. From 1982 to 1987, ATVs were responsible for an average of 15 deaths and 5,000 injuries per month. Citing these statistics, various consumer groups and politicians argued that government intervention was necessary to protect consumers. Some wanted the Consumer Product Safety Commission to establish a minimum age for driving the ATV and to force manufacturers to refund the purchase price to previous buyers now concerned about the vehicle's safety. Others urged the CPSC to go further—to declare the ATV unsafe and ban its use.

At the other extreme, some objected to government intervention entirely. They noted that motorcycle accidents claim the lives of nearly 400 riders each month, yet the CPSC would not dream of banning their use. Why should ATVs be singled out? Besides, claimed supporters, ATVs are safe when operated properly; the fault lies with the rider. As evidence they cited statistics that many accidents occurred when riders were driving unfamiliar terrain at high speed, were riding double (contrary to manufacturers' directions), or were under the influence of alcohol. Almost one-third of the accidents involved people 14 years and younger, who often lack the experience to drive any vehicle safely. Even though the fault often lies with the rider, manufacturers were developing their own voluntary standards. For such reasons, many saw no need for government regulation.

After considering both sides of the debate, the government adopted an intermediate position. In 1988, the CPSC—working in conjunction with the Justice Department—reached a settlement with ATV manufacturers in which they agreed to halt all sales of three-wheeled ATVs, to sponsor training programs for new customers, to spend $8.5 million advertising the potential hazards of ATVs, and to stop marketing the ATV as a vehicle suitable for children. Under the agreement, companies are allowed to continue selling four-wheeled ATVs and are under no obligation to make refunds.

Although ATVs are still considered dangerous, the ATV-related injury rate has fallen since the CPSC settlement went into effect.

SOURCES: Adapted from Jeanne Saddler, "Consumer Safety Agency's Role Is Questioned," *The Wall Street Journal*, September 23, 1987, p. 64; Jeanne Saddler, "Pact of All-Terrain Vehicle Makers with U.S. Revised," *The Wall Street Journal*, March 15, 1988, p. 22; Barry Meier, "All-Terrain Vehicles: Still a Safety Hazard," *The New York Times*, December 30, 1989, p. 16; *The Manhattan Mercury*, "ATVs Called Kid Killers," March 1, 1990, p. B7.

EXHIBIT

29.1

product with S_1 safety sells for P_1, but with S_{min} safety, price rises to P_{min}. Similarly, wages depend on safety in the workplace. A competitive firm can afford to spend only so much per worker. The less it spends on safety, the more it has left for wages (Figure 29.3B). Consistent with this view, empirical studies find that, other things equal, riskier (less safe) jobs pay higher wages.[6]

Suppose the government imposes minimum product safety standards of S_{min} [see (A)]. Consumers must now pay at least P_{min} for this product. Consumers who do not feel the added safety is worth the higher price prefer a product with fewer safety features, but are denied the chance to buy it. Moreover, low-income consumers unable to pay P_{min} are squeezed from the market entirely. Likewise, minimum workplace standards keep workers from less-safe, higher-paying jobs even when workers believe the higher wage more than compensates for the added risk of injury. Therefore, according to this view, by restricting choice, safety regulations can reduce the satisfaction of workers and consumers.

To summarize, when markets fail to provide adequate information, government regulations can improve social well-being. There is a debate, however, over whether the government should merely provide information or whether it should force consumers to act according to what it perceives to be the consumers' best interests. Should individuals be free to accept known risks, or are some risks so great that the government should step in to protect individuals from their own voluntary decisions? Exhibit 29.1 provides a specific example around which to focus the debate: Should government regulate all-terrain vehicles?

The Special-Interest Theory of Regulation

SPECIAL-INTEREST THEORY OF REGULATION
The theory that regulation is designed to protect special-interest groups at the expense of the public.

The public-interest theory of regulation is grounded in the belief that regulation is an attempt to improve the general well-being of society. In contrast, the special-interest theory holds that regulation is designed to benefit certain segments of the economy at the expense of others—without improving the general well-being of society. According to this view: "As a rule, regulation is acquired by the industry and is designed and operated primarily for its benefit."[7]

Industry may receive direct benefits from the government, including tax breaks and subsidies, or indirect benefits, including reduced competition. For example, prior to deregulation the CAB protected existing airlines by refusing to allow a single new carrier to fly any of the major routes. In trucking, the ICC actually reduced the number of licensed carriers, despite continued growth in the volume of freight transported by truck.

Regulatory agencies can also legitimize otherwise illegal activities. Price fixing among private producers violates antitrust statutes, yet regulatory agencies can legally fix prices. In many instances these prices exceed the levels that would prevail in the absence of regulation. When regulatory agencies restrict competition and

---

[6]See Greg J. Duncan and Bertil Holmlund, "Was Adam Smith Right After All? Another Test of the Theory of Compensating Wage Differentials," *Journal of Labor Economics* (October 1983), pp. 366–379.

[7]George Stigler, "The Theory of Economic Regulation," *Bell Journal of Economics and Management Science* (Spring 1971), p. 3.

raise price, they achieve the same results as an industry cartel. It is no wonder then that producers rather than consumers often petition for regulation. Nor is it any surprise that many producers bitterly fight deregulation. Without government protection from competitors, profits of existing companies may fall and inefficient firms may be driven out of business.

CAPTURE HYPOTHESIS
The claim that regulators promote the interests of the industry they regulate rather than protecting the public.

Even if regulation is not initially for the benefit of industry, many economists believe that the regulators will soon be *captured* by industry. According to the **capture hypothesis**, regulators pursue policies to protect the industry's firms rather than to protect consumers. Regulators might advance the interests of industry for a variety of reasons. First, regulators may identify with and be sympathetic toward industry. Members of regulatory commissions often come from the industry they regulate. Furthermore, many return to that industry some time after leaving the commission (although federal regulators must wait one or more years before returning to the industry they regulated).

Even when regulators lack a pro-industry bias, they may find it difficult to restrain the firms they are charged with overseeing. Where they lack important information about a firm, they may mistakenly allow the firm to charge excessive rates. Alternatively, regulated firms may be able to sidestep any constraint. For instance, if price is capped, firms may reduce the quality and therefore the cost of providing their service. In other words, a commission may be outgunned or outflanked by firms in the industry.

Finally, regulatory commissions try to avoid driving firms out of business. By setting prices high enough to allow inefficient firms to earn normal profits, they guarantee that firms with lower unit costs will earn economic profits. To protect its firms, a regulatory commission may even limit competition from other industries. Recall how the ICC acquired jurisdiction over trucking and water transportation, limiting the ability of these industries to undersell railroads. Thus, instead of promoting competition, regulatory commissions sometimes squash it for the benefit of regulated firms.

Unions may also have a vested interest in regulation. Where existing firms are unionized, regulatory barriers prevent low-wage nonunion firms from entering the industry, taking business away from union firms, and therefore jobs away from union members. By propping up prices, regulation also limits competition among existing firms in the industry. Even if some other firm obtains a cost advantage through lower labor costs, it is not permitted to undercut the firm's price and take away its customers. By protecting a firm from its more efficient rivals, regulation lessens the firm's opposition to higher union wages.

At the same time, regulation increases the union's incentive to negotiate higher wages. Because the firm will not lose market share to its rivals, the union need not fear that higher wages will lead to massive job loss. Interpreted in this light, trucking and airline unions did not oppose deregulation out of fear that the public would be harmed. Instead, they sought to preserve their own highly paid jobs.

Similarly, various consumer groups find regulation advantageous. Even if most consumers are harmed, certain segments may benefit. For example, regulators sometimes establish "lifeline" programs, forcing companies to provide electricity or telephone service at less than cost to those with an income below some threshold. The regulators then allow the companies to make up these losses by charging other consumers higher rates. In this case the subsidized low-income users rally behind regulation. The special-interest theory of regulation also explains why small communities opposed deregulation of the airline industry. The CAB had forced airlines to retain unprofitable, low-traffic routes. The communities worried that they would lose air service if airlines were free to pull out.

Even the regulators have a vested interest in continued regulation. Not only are their jobs at stake, but their prestige, power, and chances for promotion depend on the size and growth of the regulatory agency. Regulatory growth is a form of empire building. In conclusion, according to the special-interest theory of regulation, regulation exists not because it is in the public interest, but because various groups promote regulation as a means of serving their own personal interests.

The Effects of Regulation

With these insights into the *why* of regulation, it is now appropriate to examine the consequences. Regulation has led to cleaner air, a safer workplace, and more-informed consumers. It has also increased the costs of production. Beyond these obvious effects, regulation has altered the price of output, quality of service, profits, productivity, and wages.

PRICE

Consistent with the capture hypothesis, regulatory agencies often set prices above the levels that would prevail in the absence of regulation. An FTC study found that taxi fares were 13–16 percent higher in cities that regulate taxis. In industries where price restrictions have been eliminated, prices have tended to fall immediately. Deregulation has led to lower rates for rail and trucking transportation, brokerage services, and air travel. Lower air fares alone are estimated to save consumers $6 billion per year.[8]

But whereas consumers in general pay lower fares as a result of airline deregulation, these savings are not spread uniformly across passengers. Air fares are roughly 10–30 percent higher in major airports dominated by a single carrier than in other airports.[9] This has led many analysts to conclude that the savings from deregulation would be even greater if airlines were not allowed to dominate particular airports (through mergers, control of gates, and other anticompetitive practices).

In addition to raising price directly (by establishing price floors above competitive levels), regulation sometimes inflates price indirectly by increasing costs of production. Economists at the Brookings Institution estimate that government-mandated safety features add more than $600 to the price of a new car and that

---

[8]Steven Morrison and Clifford Winston, *The Economic Effects of Airline Deregulation* (Washington, D.C.: The Brookings Institution, 1986), p. 33, and "The Dynamics of Airline Pricing and Competition," *American Economics Association Papers and Proceedings* (May 1990), p. 390.

[9]Gloria Hurdle et al., "Concentration, Potential Entry, and Performance in the Airline Industry," U.S. Department of Justice Discussion Paper, February 1988; Severin Borenstein, "Hubs and High Fares: Dominance and Market Power in the U.S. Airline Industry," *Rand Journal of Economics* (Autumn 1989); U.S. Department of Transportation, *Airline Competition Report*, 1990.

regulations on automobile emissions raise the cost of owning and operating a car by an additional $1,600.[10]

Where the industry is a natural monopoly, regulation may lower price, yet even this is unclear. A widely cited study of electrical utilities found no evidence that regulation had reduced the average price of electricity.[11] Either electric utilities have little long-run monopoly power or regulatory commissions have been ineffective in keeping down rates. Instances where regulation reduces price are rare; more commonly price rises.

SERVICE

The effect of regulation on service is mixed. When regulation creates a monopoly, it may lessen the level of service. Certainly it lessens consumer choice. Consumers dissatisfied with the services of the monopolist cannot switch to another producer in the industry. Second, if regulation forces a firm to accept a lower price than desired, the firm may try to offset the lower price by reducing service. Consistent with these arguments, customers in the railroad and trucking industries reported that service improved greatly following deregulation: "A corporate traffic manager compared negotiating for trucking service in the fall of 1981 to 'walking into a candy store.'"[12]

In other industries the situation is reversed: regulation leads to a greater level of service. For example, regulators sometimes force cable franchises to carry more television channels than the companies would like. Moreover, where regulation eliminates price competition, companies may switch to nonprice competition. This is what happened in the airline industry. When the CAB prevented airlines from reducing fares, they competed for passengers by spending more on meals, offering greater personal attention (more employees per passenger), allowing customers to cancel reservations without penalty, and maintaining flights with low-load factors (numerous empty seats).

In a very real sense, airlines provided too much service. Consumers placed a lower value on many services than it cost to provide them. That is, consumers preferred lower fares to the additional services. Accordingly, following deregulation consumers flocked to no-frills, low-fare airlines and booked seats on heavily discounted flights, despite numerous restrictions. The effect of deregulation on airline service is examined more fully in Exhibit 29.2. In summary, regulation may either increase or decrease service. Yet, to the extent that regulation prevents consumers from choosing the mix of services they desire, it is likely to reduce consumer well-being.

PROFITS

Regulation has an ambiguous effect on profits. Where regulation promotes a cartel by restricting entry and raising price, it may increase industry profits. On the other

---

[10]Same as 5, *Regulating the Automobile*.

[11]George Stigler and Claire Friedland, "What Can Regulators Regulate? The Case of Electricity," *Journal of Law and Economics* (October 1962), pp. 1–16.

[12]Martha Derthick and Paul J. Quirk, *The Politics of Deregulation* (Washington, D.C.: The Brookings Institution, 1985), p. 1.

Airline deregulation was opposed largely because of a concern that service would deteriorate. Some feared that service to small communities would be curtailed, while others worried that safety would suffer. Fortunately, neither of these predictions has come to pass.

With deregulation, airlines were free to add and drop routes. Where air traffic was low, major airlines did in fact halt service. But where major airlines pulled out, commuter airlines stepped in. The number of communities served actually increased under deregulation.

The other major concern was that airlines would skimp on safety. Critics of deregulation argued that high fares allowed airlines to devote more resources to safety and that, under deregulation, airlines would be forced to sacrifice safety in order to match competitors' lower fares. Although the Federal Aviation Administration (FAA) continues to monitor safety, airlines had traditionally exceeded FAA standards, meaning that they were legally free to reduce safety. Moreover, the FAA's budget was cut following deregulation, making it less likely that airlines violating FAA safety standards would be caught.

Despite such arguments, there is no evidence that airline safety has suffered following deregulation. A half-dozen studies of the issue find that regulation has had no effect on air safety. Indeed, both the overall accident rate and the accident rate involving fatalities have fallen since airlines were deregulated. According to these studies, market forces are sufficiently strong to prevent airlines from shortchanging safety. Airlines with subpar safety records face higher insurance rates and a loss of passengers.[13] Manufacturers of aircraft (for example, Boeing, McDonnell Douglas, and Lockheed) suffer large drops in the value of their stock whenever one of their planes is in an accident involving design flaws.

In summary, a strong safety record is vital to the commercial success of airlines and aircraft manufacturers. Safety is good business, even in unregulated skies.

Even though deregulation has not eliminated air travel to small communities or reduced safety, it has affected service. Airlines have cut back on certain amenities, including meals. With greater traffic, flight delays have become more common. But government must share the blame for these delays. The government has failed to expand runway capacity, to hire additional air traffic controllers, and to adjust landing fees to reduce congestion during peak travel hours. On the positive side, travelers have a greater number of flights from which to choose. They also have a greater variety of flights, ranging from no-frills to premium service. Finally, the percentage of passengers required to change airlines in order to complete a flight has declined, as has the percentage of passengers required to change planes.

[13]One study estimates that a fatal accident within the past six months costs an airline as many passengers as a $78 increase in fares. See Morrison and Winston, "Enhancing the Performance . . .," p. 67 (see Sources below).

SOURCES: Adapted from Steven Morrison and Clifford Winston, "Air Safety, Deregulation, and Public Policy," *Brookings Review* (Winter 1988), pp. 10–15; Morrison and Winston, "Enhancing the Performance of the Deregulated Air Transportation System," *Brookings Papers on Economic Activity: Microeconomics* (1989), pp. 61–123; Nancy Rose, "The Financial Influences on Airline Safety," in Leon Moses and Ian Savage, eds., *Transportation in an Age of Deregulation* (New York: Oxford University Press, 1989), pp. 93–114; Richard McKenzie, "Making Sense of the Airline Safety Debate," *Regulation* (Summer 1991), pp. 76–84; Richard McKenzie and Norman Womer, "The Impact of the Airline Deregulation Process on Air-Travel Safety," *Center for the Study of American Business* (September 1991).

EXHIBIT

29.2

hand, regulation imposes costs on firms and limits their ability to adjust price. The regulated price may be set either too low or too high to maximize profits.

In the airline industry, regulation apparently had an adverse effect on profits. According to one study, profits increased by at least $2.5 billion per year once the industry was deregulated.[14] Freed of government constraints, airlines have been able to switch to the more efficient hub-and-spoke system, in which travelers are routed through major airports (hubs). With improved scheduling, special fares, and increased flexibility, airlines have also been able to increase both the number of flights and the number of passengers per flight. Because of heavy fixed costs, the result is a lower cost per passenger.

Similarly, deregulation has increased profits in the railroad industry by about $3 billion per year. The Staggers Rail Act of 1980 eased government restrictions and gave railroads greater discretion over price. Although price has declined, so has average cost. Railroads have been able to reduce the fraction of time rail cars are empty and to otherwise improve efficiency. Labor productivity (ton-miles per employee) rose by 44 percent in the four years immediately following enactment of the Staggers Act.[15]

LABOR PRODUCTIVITY

The adverse effects of regulation on labor productivity (output per worker) are not specific to the railroad industry. To the extent funds are used to meet government regulations rather than to acquire capital, workers have less equipment to work with. Moreover, workers may be forced to spend time complying with regulations rather than producing output. Finally, regulations sometimes impede the introduction of new technology. It has been estimated that regulations have reduced the nation's productivity growth by 0.4 percent per year.[16]

UNION WAGES

Where regulation limits competition from low-wage firms, unions may be able to negotiate higher wages. Conversely, deregulation, by increasing competition, may erode union wages. There is some evidence that it has. Following deregulation new airlines were created and existing airlines expanded into new markets. Competition led to lower fares, especially in markets served by low-cost, nonunion airlines. Once one airline cut fares, others serving the same route were forced to follow suit to avoid losing passengers.

When two recessions hit during the early 1980s, several airlines were in serious financial trouble. To keep their companies afloat, unions at Braniff, Western, and

---

[14]Same as 8, *The Economic Effects of Airline Deregulation*, p. 40. Airline profits decreased in the early 1990s, but that primarily reflected such factors as a weak economy rather than deregulation.

[15]Clifford Winston et al., *The Economic Effects of Surface Freight Deregulation* (Washington, D.C.: The Brookings Institution, 1990), p. 5; *Economic Report of the President, 1986*, p. 164.

[16]Robert E. Litan and William D. Nordhaus, *Reforming Federal Regulation* (New Haven: Yale University Press, 1983), p. 33.

Pan Am agreed to wage cuts of approximately 10 percent. To remain competitive, other airlines demanded similar concessions. Virtually every union contract negotiated between 1981 and 1983 mandated pay cuts for airline employees.[17] Some contracts further reduced wages by introducing a *two-tiered wage structure*, in which new employees are paid substantially lower wages than current employees.

Although the wage cuts were partially attributable to the recessions, many analysts believe they would not have been possible without deregulation. Not only had regulation sheltered inefficient airlines from competition, it had also encouraged unions to resist concessions. Their jobs would be secure even if the company faltered. The CAB would find a healthy airline to acquire their company and would even force the new airline to recognize their seniority rights. Therefore, when the industry was regulated, unions had little reason to be conciliatory. Deregulation changed the bargaining climate, paving the way for concessions. This is true not only for the airline industry but also for trucking and railroads.

Regulating Natural Monopoly— A Closer Look

The analysis to this point has been rather broad in scope, discussing the various reasons for regulation and considering the consequences. We now take a more detailed look at the special case of natural monopoly, thereby gaining an appreciation of how regulatory commissions operate under natural monopoly and what potential problems they face. We also consider an alternative to regulation—public ownership.

THE ROLE OF A REGULATORY COMMISSION

The government frequently grants monopoly status to companies providing local telephone service, electricity, water, or natural gas. This avoids duplication of costs (unnecessary wiring, pipelines, and so forth) and allows the output to be produced at a lower cost than possible with multiple producers. This situation, natural monopoly, is depicted in Figure 29.4 (page 768). Because the demand curve intersects a declining average cost curve, the average cost of production is minimized when only one firm serves the market.

Typically, the government creates a regulatory commission to oversee the operation of natural monopolies. If left to itself, a monopolist would produce to the point where marginal revenue equals marginal cost, Q_m, and set a price of P_m. To protect the public interest, the regulatory commission limits the price that the monopolist may charge. But what price should the commission allow?

MARGINAL COST PRICING
A regulatory procedure intended to equate price with marginal cost, and thereby promote efficient allocation of resources.

MARGINAL COST PRICING If resources are to be allocated efficiently, production should continue to the point where price equals marginal cost (**marginal cost pricing**). This is given by the intersection of the demand and marginal cost curves

---

[17]Peter Cappelli, "Airlines," in David Lipsky and Clifford Donn, eds., *Collective Bargaining in American Industry* (Lexington, Mass.: Heath and Co., 1987), p. 160.

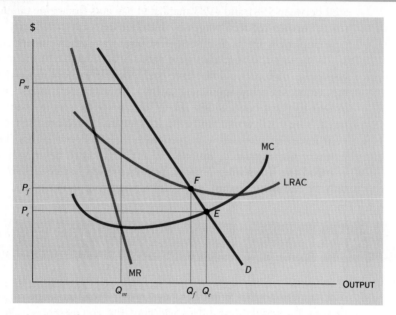

An unregulated monopolist sells Q_m output at a price of P_m in order to maximize profit. This is less output and a higher price than society desires. Efficient allocation of resources occurs at E, where marginal cost intersects the demand curve (the marginal cost of producing Q_e output corresponds to the price consumers are willing to pay). However, if the regulatory commission sets price at P_e, the firm will not produce in the long run because price is less than long-run average cost. To ensure long-run production while limiting the firm to normal profit, the regulatory commission may choose to equate price with long-run average cost (F). Confronted with a price of P_f, the firm will produce Q_f output.

FIGURE 29.4

(point E). But whereas P_e is necessary for efficient allocation, it is also impractical. At a price of P_e the firm would lose money, since price is below average cost. Therefore, if the regulatory commission were to set a price of P_e, in an attempt to achieve efficient allocation of resources, it would drive the firm out of business.

AVERAGE COST PRICING
A regulatory procedure intended to equate price with average cost, and thereby limit the firm to normal profits.

AVERAGE COST PRICING Rather than equate price with marginal cost, the commission may choose to set price equal to average cost (**average cost pricing**). This occurs where demand intersects the average cost curve (point F). By capping price at P_f, the commission limits the firm to normal profits. The firm earns enough to stay in business but nothing extra. Although P_f does not provide efficient allocation of resources, it is superior to the unregulated price of P_m. Consumers benefit from both a lower price and a higher level of output ($Q_f > Q_m$).

SUBSIDIES AND ACCESS FEES There are ways to keep the firm in business at a price below P_f, but they involve supplemental funding. For instance, the government could subsidize the firm, paying it an amount equal to its production losses. If the firm loses $1 million from production, the government would pay the firm $1 million to keep it operating. Indeed, by setting a price of P_e and coupling that with a subsidy, the government could induce the firm to produce Q_e output, thereby achieving efficient allocation of resources.

Alternatively, funds could be raised by charging consumers an *access fee* independent of their usage. For instance, telephone users are charged a monthly access fee for the privilege of making long-distance calls. This fee is above and beyond the payment for any calls actually made. The access fee allows the commission to set a lower price on the service provided (for example, long-distance calls). If price is set below average cost, the access fee can offset the loss the firm incurs in providing the service.

REGULATION IN PRACTICE

In theory, a regulatory commission may wish to equate price with marginal or average cost, but often the location of a firm's cost curves is unknown to the regulatory commission. How then does the commission set price? Two approaches are common: rate-of-return regulation and price-cap regulation.

RATE-OF-RETURN REGULATION
A form of regulation limiting a firm to a prescribed rate of return on its capital (rate base).

RATE BASE
The value of a firm's capital, as determined by a regulatory commission.

RATE OF RETURN
The annual return received on a firm's capital (or rate base) expressed as a percentage of the firm's capital.

RATE-OF-RETURN REGULATION Under rate-of-return regulation, the regulatory commission establishes (a) a **rate base** and (b) an allowable **rate of return**. The rate base measures the value of the firm's capital as determined by the regulatory commission. The rate of return is the percentage return the firm earns on its rate base. For example, a firm receiving $12 per year on each $100 of its rate base has a 12 percent rate of return.

The commission may not allow all of a company's capital to be included in its rate base. If the commission considers the cost of capital excessive, it may include only a fraction of the cost. If equipment is considered unnecessary, its cost may be excluded altogether. Once the commission establishes a rate base, it then calculates the price the firm must charge in order to earn the allowable rate of return. This is the price consumers pay. By adjusting the rate of return and therefore price, the commission determines how much profit the firm will be allowed to earn. Typically the commission seeks a "fair rate of return," designed to achieve normal profits.

The rate-of-return approach has been criticized for inflating costs. If the firm expects to earn normal profits, what incentive does it have to be efficient? If costs rise, the commission will increase price in order to maintain the allowable rate of return. Similarly, the firm has little incentive to introduce a new cost-saving technology. The commission will offset any reduction in costs by decreasing revenues.

Costs may be further inflated if the commission allows an excessive rate of return. If the rate of return includes an element of economic profit, then the firm has an incentive to acquire unnecessary capital. By increasing its rate base the firm can earn additional economic profits. As noted earlier, although the commission may not include all capital expenditures in the rate base, often a firm can rationalize unnecessary costs, especially if the commission has been *captured* by the firm. If regulated firms incur added costs, then the commission may be unable to suppress the firm's price effectively. This may explain why regulated utilities apparently charge as much for electricity as unregulated utilities.

PRICE-CAP REGULATION There is an alternative to rate-of-return regulation. Rather than adjust price to achieve a given rate of return, the commission could simply set a ceiling on the price a firm is allowed to charge. Such an approach—

Capping the Price of Long-Distance Telephone Service

In 1989, the FCC voted to abandon rate-of-return regulation in favor of a price cap on long-distance telephone service. At the time, AT&T had an allowable rate of return of just over 12 percent on equipment used for interstate calls. Under the FCC ruling, prices of long-distance telephone calls were initially capped at their December 1988 levels but are allowed to rise thereafter by 3 percent less than the annual inflation rate. For example, if inflation is 5 percent in a particular year, AT&T can raise prices by 2 percent.

The FCC estimates that adoption of the price cap will save consumers $900 million in the first four years alone. AT&T, which supported the change, is also expected to benefit because of cost savings. As a spokesman for AT&T acknowledged, "We'll have the incentive to really try to be more efficient." That greater efficiency, in turn, is expected to boost profits at AT&T.

Given the success of the AT&T price cap in lowering costs to consumers, in 1991 the FCC extended the price cap to the eight largest local telephone companies—GTE and the seven regional Bell companies. The FCC ruling limits the fees local telephone companies can charge for interstate services, such as connecting customers to long-distance companies. Unlike the AT&T price cap, the local telephone companies are required to share their profits with customers once profits exceed a certain level. According to FCC economists, the price cap on local telephone companies will initially save long-distance customers approximately $1 billion per year, with even greater savings in the long run.

SOURCES: Adapted from Mary Lu Carnevale and Janet Guyon, "FCC Alters Long-Distance Regulation of AT&T," *The Wall Street Journal*, March 17, 1989, p. A3; Janet Guyon, "FCC Hopes New Regulations Will Cut Phone Rates," *The Wall Street Journal*, August 6, 1987, p. 23; *The Kansas City Star*, "FCC to Set Price Caps for Phone Firms," September 20, 1990, p. A3.

PRICE-CAP REGULATION
A form of regulation limiting the price a firm may charge (but not limiting allowable profits).

price-cap regulation—ends the firm's willingness to incur unnecessary costs. With a price cap, the more a firm reduces the costs of producing a given output the greater the firm's profits. The challenge of price-cap regulation is to choose an initial price cap and a formula for adjusting the cap over time. Exhibit 29.3 indicates the approach recently adopted by the FCC.

Public Ownership

Rather than regulate firms, sometimes governments own and operate a business themselves. Examples of public (government) ownership at the federal level include the Postal Service, Tennessee Valley Authority, Amtrak, and the Government Printing Office. Locally, many governments provide water, trash collection, street repair, transportation, and a host of other services.

Through public ownership, the government can achieve the desired level of output and prevent private firms from inflating price. On the other hand, government ownership often leads to inefficiency. Because public firms are not in business to maximize profits, management has little incentive to minimize costs. Unlike the private sector, rewards to management are not based on its contribution to profits; political considerations may be more important than economics. For instance, where politicians determine the wages of public employees, they may be able to win the votes of public employees by paying high wages and preserving unnecessary

A Better Way to Collect Solid Waste

Solid waste can be collected either directly by the government (for example, through a city sanitation department) or by private refuse companies. In Canada the two approaches are equally common; in the United States the majority of municipalities rely on private firms. The presence of both arrangements in the same industry has provided economists an opportunity to assess the impact of public ownership. At least in this industry, public ownership is the inferior option.

A study of 132 Canadian municipalities found that, other things equal, the cost of collecting solid waste was 28 percent lower for private firms. A second study examined the consequences of privatization in Canada—replacing public trash collection with private trash collection in the same municipality. Both West Vancouver and Richmond converted from public collection of solid waste to private collection. The private firms served the same households and even used the same vehicles (purchased directly from the cities). The private firms improved service by removing restrictions on the number of cans allowed each household, yet still managed to reduce collection costs. Costs fell by 19 percent in West Vancouver and by 66 percent in Richmond.

Economists have reached similar conclusions in the United States. Public waste collection suffers from inferior management and lower labor productivity. One study of 1,377 U.S. communities concluded:

> Compared to private firms with contracts in cities of over 50,000, municipal [public] refuse-collection agencies in such cities have higher employee absentee rates (12 percent vs. 6.5 percent); employ larger crews (3.26 men vs. 2.15); serve fewer households per shift (632 vs. 686); spend more time servicing each household (4.35 man-hours per year vs. 2.37); and are less likely to utilize labor-incentive systems (80 percent vs. 89 percent).[18]

When it comes to collecting solid waste, private firms are more efficient than public agencies.

[18]E. S. Savas (see Sources below), p. 71.

SOURCES: Adapted from Glen Tickner and James C. McDavid, "Effects of Scale and Market Structure on the Costs of Residential Solid Waste Collection in Canadian Cities," *Public Finance Quarterly* (October 1986), pp. 371–393; J. C. McDavid, "The Canadian Experience with Privatizing Residential Solid Waste Collection Services," *Public Administration Review* (September 1985), pp. 602–608; E. S. Savas, "Policy Analysis for Local Government: Public Versus Private Refuse Collection," *Policy Analysis* (Winter 1977), pp. 49–74.

EXHIBIT

29.4

jobs. Consistent with this view, a large body of evidence indicates that, on average, federal employees earn more than comparable employees in the private sector.[19]

The Office of Management and Budget (OMB) estimates that the federal government could save billions of dollars annually by contracting out services such as data processing. According to the Government Accounting Office (GAO), federally operated hydroelectric power plants cost 20 percent more to operate than comparable plants in the private sector. Similarly, public trash collection is more costly than collection by private firms (see Exhibit 29.4). Such findings have sparked interest in **privatization**—turning selected government functions over to private firms. Where the result is lower costs, governments can ease budgetary pressures. In summary, even though regulation of private firms entails various difficulties, public ownership often fails to provide a superior alternative.

PRIVATIZATION
Transferring production of a good from the public sector to the private sector.

Summary

1. Government regulates business by imposing various rules on producers. *Economic regulation* refers to rules imposed on a specific industry—designed, for example, to limit entry into the industry, set price, and mandate various services. By contrast, *social regulation* cuts across industries. Its goal is to achieve certain results throughout the economy—a cleaner environment, safer products, and a workplace free of hazards.

2. Regulation has tended to expand since the creation of the Interstate Commerce Commission more than 100 years ago. At first the growth consisted of additional economic regulation, but more recently the emphasis has shifted to social regulation. Among the new agencies charged with social regulation are the Consumer Product Safety Commission, the Occupational Safety and Health Administration, and the Environmental Protection Agency. The growth of regulatory budgets slowed in the 1980s, and the number of federal regulators declined. This was caused both by economic deregulation and by the slowdown in social regulation accompanying the Reagan presidency. During the 1990s, social regulation has rebounded.

3. There are two competing explanations for regulation. According to the public-interest theory of regulation, government intervention is a response to market failure and therefore designed to benefit society. Reasons for market failure include natural monopoly, externalities, and imperfect information.

4. In contrast, the special-interest theory of regulation holds that regulation is designed to protect special-interest groups at the expense of the general public. For instance, regulation may shield existing producers from competition by restricting entry of new firms into an industry and by propping up price. Regulation may also benefit unions, certain consumer groups, and even the regulators themselves.

5. Regulation has achieved various benefits, from a cleaner environment to safer products. It has also imposed various costs on society. Resources must be transferred from production to administer regulations and to comply with them. Costs rise further when regulations prevent efficient allocation of resources—for example, when the ICC induced shippers to use high-cost modes of transportation. Regulations have also affected price, service, profits, labor productivity, and wages. To assess regulations accurately, one must compare their benefits with their costs.

---

[19]See Sharon P. Smith, *Equal Pay in Public Sector: Fact or Fantasy* (Princeton: Princeton University Press, 1977); Alan B. Krueger, "Are Public Sector Workers Paid More Than Their Alternative Wage?" in Richard Freeman and Casey Ichniowski, eds., *Public Sector Unionism* (Chicago: University of Chicago Press, 1987); Daniel Shapiro and Morton Stelcner, "Canadian Public–Private Sector Earnings Differentials, 1970–1980," *Industrial Relations* (Winter 1989), pp. 72–81; William Moore and John Raisian, "Government Wage Differentials Revisited," *Journal of Labor Research* (Winter 1991), pp. 23–25.

6. Government commissions frequently regulate utilities and other natural monopolies. The objective is to minimize costs of production and to keep price low for consumers. Unless a regulated monopolist receives other funds (for example, access fees or a government subsidy), it must be allowed to charge a price that covers average cost—otherwise it will not produce in the long run.

7. Under rate-of-return regulation, the commission sets a price that enables the company to earn an allowable rate of return on its rate base. Generally, the allowable rate of return is chosen with the intention of achieving normal profits. A drawback of rate-of-return regulation is that if the firm expects to receive normal profits, regardless of its production costs, it loses its incentive to minimize costs.

8. With price-cap regulation firms maintain their incentive to minimize costs, since lower costs mean higher profits. The difficulty here is choosing the initial price cap and setting a formula that will adjust it in the future.

9. Public ownership is an alternative to regulation of private firms. By directly producing a good, the government can determine price and output levels. A drawback to this approach is that government production is generally more costly than production by private firms.

Key Terms

economic regulation	marginal cost pricing
social regulation	average cost pricing
deregulation	rate-of-return regulation
public-interest theory of regulation	rate base
special-interest theory of regulation	rate of return
capture hypothesis	price-cap regulation
	privatization

Study Questions and Problems

1. What is the difference between economic regulation and social regulation? Provide an example of each.

2. Do you consider deregulation of the airline industry to be a success? Why or why not?

3. Under what circumstances does regulation benefit society?

4. Are there any industries where you think regulation is either excessive or inadequate? Support your view.

5. Recently, the National Transportation Safety Board considered new regulations for the fishing industry. These included formal training for both captains and crews, new safety requirements for vessels, and periodic inspection of vessels.
   a. Cite at least one benefit of such proposals.
   b. Many in the fishing industry opposed added safety requirements. What could account for their opposition?

6. Some who agree that regulation might, in theory, improve upon market outcomes argue that regulation, as actually practiced, fails to achieve socially optimal outcomes. In the words of one economist:

   The [relevant] comparison is not between imperfect markets and perfect regulation, but between imperfect markets and imperfect regulation.[20]

(a) Why might regulation fall short of the social ideal?

(b) If markets and regulation are both imperfect, how does one decide whether a particular regulation benefits society?

7. Some economists argue that certain public utility commissions have set rates of return so low that their utilities are unable to earn a normal profit. What effect would such a practice have on the price of utility services in the short run? How would this affect the ability of utilities to meet consumer needs in the long run? Explain your reasoning.

8. What is the objective of marginal cost pricing? Why might a regulatory commission decide not to equate price with marginal cost?

9. Explain why rate-of-return regulation may promote inefficient production. Does price-cap regulation suffer from the same drawback? Explain.

10. First-class mail is delivered by a publicly owned monopoly—the U.S. Postal Service. How might costs change if mail delivery were turned over to the private sector? Why?

YOUR TURN
Answers

THE MAJOR BENEFIT OF THE FDA'S TRADITIONAL, TOUGH STANDARDS IS TO KEEP UNSAFE DRUGS OFF THE MARKET AND PREVENT THEM FROM HARMING PATIENTS. TO BE ON THE SAFE SIDE, THE FDA TRADITIONALLY REQUIRED AN AVERAGE OF TEN YEARS OF TESTING AND REVIEW BEFORE A DRUG COULD BE APPROVED. IN THE MEANTIME, PATIENTS WHO WOULD HAVE BENEFITTED FROM TREATMENT WITH A DRUG ULTIMATELY FOUND TO BE SAFE AND EFFECTIVE WERE DENIED THE OPPORTUNITY TO RECEIVE THAT DRUG. IT WAS ON THIS BASIS THAT THE FDA WAS CRITICIZED. ACT–UP AND OTHER GROUPS WERE ESPECIALLY CRITICAL OF THE FDA FOR KEEPING NEW DRUGS FROM PATIENTS WHO SUFFERED FROM AIDS AND OTHER LIFE-THREATENING DISEASES. RESPONDING TO SUCH CONCERNS, IN 1991 THE FDA ANNOUNCED PLANS TO ELIMINATE FOUR YEARS OF TESTING AND REVIEW FOR DRUGS DESIGNED TO TREAT LIFE-THREATENING DISEASES.

Selected References

Kahn, Alfred. "I Would Do It Again," *Regulation* (No. 2, 1988), pp. 22–28.

Meier, Kenneth J. *Regulation* (New York: St. Martin's Press, 1985).

Moore, Thomas. "Unfinished Business in Motor Carrier Deregulation," *Regulation* (Summer 1991), pp. 49–57.

Morrison, Steven, and Clifford Winston. *The Economic Effects of Airline Deregulation* (Washington, D.C.: The Brookings Institution, 1986).

Morrison, Steven, and Clifford Winston. "Enhancing the Performance of the Deregulated Air Transportation System," *Brookings Papers on Economic Activity: Microeconomics* (1989), pp. 61–123.

Nowotny, Kenneth, et al. (eds.). *Public Utility Regulation* (Boston: Kluwer Academic Publishers, 1989).

Savas, E. S. *Privatization* (Chatham, N.J.: Chatham House Publishers, 1987).

Smith, Robert S. "Compensating Wage Differentials and Public Policy," *Industrial & Labor Relations Review* (April 1979), pp. 340–341.

Stigler, George. "The Theory of Economic Regulation," *Bell Journal of Economics and Management Science* (Spring 1971), pp. 3–21.

Weidenbaum, Murray L. *Business, Government, and the Public*, 4th ed. (Englewood Cliffs, N.J.: Prentice-Hall, 1990).

Winston, Clifford et al. *The Economic Effects of Surface Freight Deregulation* (Washington, D.C.: The Brookings Institution, 1990).

---

[20]John Wenders, "Commentary on Electric Utility Industry," in Kenneth Nowotny et al., eds., *Public Utility Regulation* (Boston: Kluwer Academic Publishers, 1989), p. 78.

VIII

PART VIII SHIFTS THE FOCUS FROM PRODUCT MAR-
KETS TO RESOURCE MARKETS. BECAUSE LABOR IS
THE MOST IMPORTANT FACTOR OF PRODUCTION
AND THE PRIMARY SOURCE OF INCOME, THE
NEXT THREE CHAPTERS ARE DEVOTED TO
UNDERSTANDING HOW LABOR MARKETS OPER-
ATE. FOLLOWING AN ANALYSIS OF COMPETI-
TIVE LABOR MARKETS, CHAPTER 30
EXPLORES WAGE DIFFERENTIALS AMONG
WORKERS AND THEN INTRODUCES UNIONS
INTO THE ANALYSIS. CHAPTER 31 PRESENTS
ALTERNATIVE MODELS OF THE LABOR MAR-
KET WHEN THE ASSUMPTION OF PERFECT
COMPETITION IS RELAXED. NEXT, CHAPTER
32 DELVES INTO DIFFERENCES IN LABOR
MARKET OUTCOMES BY GENDER, RACE,
AND ETHNICITY AND ASKS TO WHAT
EXTENT THESE DIFFERENCES ARISE FROM
DISCRIMINATION. THIS CHAPTER ALSO
EXAMINES SUCH GOVERNMENT POLICIES
AS EQUAL PAY, COMPARABLE WORTH, AND
AFFIRMATIVE ACTION. ■ CHAPTER 33
ANALYZES NONLABOR INCOME: INTEREST,
RENT, AND PROFIT. TOPICS INCLUDE THE
ROLE OF INTEREST RATES IN ALLOCATING
CAPITAL, THE IMPACT OF RENTS ON PRICE,
AND THE SOURCES OF PROFIT. FINALLY,
CHAPTER 34 STUDIES THE DISTRIBUTION
OF INCOME ACROSS FAMILIES, PAYING SPE-
CIAL ATTENTION TO THOSE WITH THE LEAST
INCOME. WHO ARE THE POOR, HOW HAVE
THEIR NUMBERS CHANGED OVER TIME, AND
TO WHAT EXTENT HAS
THIS BEEN THE
RESULT OF GOVERN-
MENT POLICY? AFTER
WORKING THROUGH PART VIII, THE READER
SHOULD EMERGE WITH A FIRM GRASP OF HOW
RESOURCE MARKETS OPERATE AND THEIR CONTRI-
BUTION TO PRODUCTION AND TO THE GENERATION
OF INCOME.

The Distribution of Income

HUMAN LABOR IS NOT
AN *END* BUT A MEANS.

—FREDERIC BASTIAT
(1801–1850), *SOPHISMES
ÉCONOMIQUES*

The Labor Market—Why Are My Wages So Low (High)?

IN A RECENT YEAR, SENIOR AIRLINE PILOTS PULLED DOWN $193,000 FROM THE FRIENDLY SKIES OF UNITED; MAJOR LEAGUE BASEBALL PLAYERS AVERAGED $1.1 MILLION; AND TOP EXECUTIVES RECEIVED COMPENSATION PACKAGES WORTH SEVERAL MILLION DOLLARS. IN CONTRAST, MANY COLLEGE STUDENTS TOIL FOR THE MINIMUM WAGE. EVEN FOR BROADLY DEFINED OCCUPATIONS, MAJOR WAGE DIFFERENCES EMERGE. MANAGERIAL AND PROFESSIONAL WORKERS EARN ALMOST FOUR TIMES AS MUCH AS PRIVATE HOUSEHOLD WORKERS (SEE TABLE 30.1). HOW ARE WAGES DETERMINED? WHAT ACCOUNTS FOR THE EXTREME VARIANCE IN EARNINGS?

ALTHOUGH THESE QUESTIONS MAY BE OF INTEREST IN THEIR OWN RIGHT, THERE ARE OTHER REASONS FOR STUDYING THE LABOR MARKET.

LABOR IS THE MOST IMPORTANT FACTOR OF PRODUCTION AND THE PRIMARY SOURCE OF INCOME. WAGES AND SALARIES ACCOUNT FOR APPROXIMATELY THREE-FOURTHS OF NATIONAL INCOME IN THE UNITED STATES. WITHOUT AN APPRECIATION OF THE LABOR MARKET, ONE CANNOT FULLY UNDERSTAND THE ECONOMY.

LABOR MARKETS DIFFER FROM OTHER FACTOR MARKETS IN TERMS OF THE PERSONAL RELATIONSHIPS INVOLVED. ANOTHER UNIQUE FEATURE IS THE TRADE UNION. HOW DO UNIONS AFFECT WAGES? WHAT ELSE DO UNIONS DO? DO THEY BENEFIT THE COUNTRY AT LARGE OR MERELY IMPROVE THE RELATIVE SITUATION OF UNION MEMBERS? THESE ARE SOME OF THE QUESTIONS ADDRESSED IN CHAPTER 30. AFTER A DISCUSSION OF WAGE DETERMINATION IN competitive labor markets, we consider reasons for wage differences across workers and then turn to the economic impacts of unions.

Chapters 31 and 32 extend our analysis of labor markets. In Chapter 31 we modify the competitive model of this chapter to consider the case of a company large enough to influence price, in either the product market or the labor market. We also address the situation in which a firm hires multiple inputs (for example, both skilled and unskilled labor). In Chapter 32 we examine the labor market success of different groups (including women and minorities) and consider reasons for these differences.

MEDIAN EARNINGS OF FULL-TIME WAGE AND SALARY WORKERS BY OCCUPATION, 1991

OCCUPATION	NUMBER OF WORKERS (IN THOUSANDS)	WEEKLY EARNINGS
Managerial and professional	23,109	$ 627
Engineers	1,838	835
Computer systems analysts	600	792
Elementary school teachers	1,344	537
Lawyers	370	1,008
Technical, sales, and administrative support	25,141	394
Health technicians	1,027	423
Sales	7,873	418
Secretaries	2,991	359
Bank tellers	318	281
Service occupations	8,908	280
Private household	306	164
Firefighting	197	616
Waiters and waitresses	518	218
Child-care workers	181	217
Precision production, craft, and repair	10,642	483
Automobile mechanics	619	385
Construction trades	3,365	483
Machinists	464	476
Operators, fabricators, and laborers	14,329	351
Textile sewing machine operators	604	215
Truck drivers, heavy	1,676	429
Rail transportation	112	773
Farming, forestry, and fishing	1,397	263
Farm managers	58	362
Farm workers	563	239
Forestry and logging	63	314
TOTAL	83,525	430

SOURCE: U.S. Bureau of Labor Statistics, *Employment and Earnings*, January 1992, pp. 223–227.

TABLE 30.1

The Model of Perfect Competition

According to the model of perfect competition, each firm buys too little labor to influence the price of labor (the wage rate). Nor can workers dictate how much they are paid. Instead, the price of labor is taken as given by individual firms and workers. The product market is likewise assumed to be competitive, which means the firm is a price taker there as well as in the labor market. Assuming the firm wishes to maximize profits, how much labor does it employ?

The Demand for Labor

THE FIRM'S DEMAND FOR LABOR

Suppose you operate a small clothing company while in school, perhaps employing needy students and professors. How many workers should you hire? To answer this question, you first need to know how much workers contribute to output—in this case, how many T-shirts they produce. Such information is contained in the production function depicted in columns (i) and (ii) of Table 30.2 (page 780). Based on this information, the first worker hired would produce 15 shirts per day, the second 12 shirts, and so forth. The additional output from hiring another unit of labor, which we previously defined as the *marginal product of labor*, is depicted in column (iii). Consistent with the law of diminishing returns, marginal product falls as additional labor is employed.[1]

MARGINAL REVENUE PRODUCT OF LABOR
The increase in total revenue to a firm resulting from the hiring of an additional unit of labor.

To convert labor's contribution from physical output (T-shirts) to dollars, we calculate the **marginal revenue product of labor**—the increase in revenue received by a firm as the result of hiring an additional unit of labor. When a firm sells its output in a competitive product market, marginal revenue product is simply equal to the marginal product of labor times output price.

Returning to our example, suppose each T-shirt sells for $10. Then the first unit of labor contributes $150 per day to revenue, $10 for each of the 15 shirts it produces. Accordingly, its marginal revenue product is $150. In turn, marginal revenue product of the second worker is $10 × 12 = $120. These and other values of marginal revenue product appear in column (iv) of Table 30.2.

Now that you know how much each additional unit of labor would generate in revenue, how many units should you hire? That depends on the price of labor.

---

[1]The law of diminishing returns does not rule out the possibility that marginal product may initially increase before declining, but we can safely ignore the range of increasing marginal product. If it is profitable to hire a given amount of labor, and the marginal product of an additional unit of labor is still higher, then it is even more profitable to hire that additional labor. In other words, a profit-maximizing firm would not stop hiring in the range where marginal product of labor is rising. We lose nothing essential, and gain simplicity, by assuming marginal product of labor declines from the outset.

DERIVING YOUR FIRM'S DEMAND FOR LABOR

(I) UNITS OF LABOR (WORKERS)	(II) TOTAL OUTPUT PER DAY (T-SHIRTS)	(III) MARGINAL PRODUCT OF LABOR	(IV) MARGINAL REVENUE PRODUCT
0	0	—	—
1	15	15	$150
2	27	12	120
3	36	9	90
4	43	7	70
5	48	5	50
6	51	3	30

Columns (i) and (ii) show the quantity of output that can be produced with various amounts of labor. Based on this information, the marginal product of labor, column (iii), can be computed. Marginal revenue product, column (iv), indicates how much additional revenue your company would receive from the hiring of an additional unit of labor. Given an output price of $10, marginal revenue product is equal to $10 times the marginal product of labor.

TABLE 30.2

Assume you must pay each worker a wage of $80 per day. Then, to maximize profits you should hire three workers. Each of the first three workers adds more to revenue than to costs, thereby bolstering profits. The same cannot be said for additional labor. Beyond the third worker additional labor would cost more than it contributed to revenue, which would eat into profits. This leads to the following hiring rule:

Hire additional labor as long as MRP > wage; do not hire when MRP < wage.

At a wage of $80, the third worker should be hired (MRP = $90 > wage) but not the fourth worker (MRP = $70 < wage).

What if you faced a wage of $50 per day? How many workers should you employ? Not only do the first three workers contribute to profits, but now so does the fourth (MRP = $70 > wage). Therefore, the fourth worker should also be hired. What about the fifth? Hiring the fifth worker would neither contribute to profits nor detract from them. The fifth worker would add the same amount to revenue as to costs—$50. For that reason, profits can be maximized by employing either four units of labor or five. The MRP numbers from Table 30.2 are duplicated in Figure 30.1(A).

Until now we have implicitly assumed that labor must be hired in whole units, but that is not always the case. Sometimes companies can hire fractional units of labor—for example, hire a worker for one-third or one-half of a day. When labor is perfectly divisible, MRP can be represented as a continuous line, as in Figure 30.1(B). Profits are maximized when the amount of labor hired is given by the intersection of the MRP curve and the wage. Given a wage of $80 and divisible labor, you should hire 3.5 units.

The labor demand curve of a firm is based on the MRP of labor. For a given wage, the MRP curve indicates the amount of labor a company should employ in order to maximize profits. But what determines the wage that must be paid? To

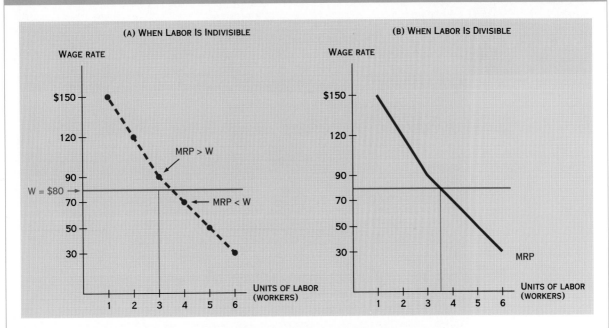

When labor must be hired in whole (indivisible) units (A), a company should employ the largest amount of labor for which MRP > W. Given a wage rate of $80 per day, 3 units of labor should be hired. When labor is divisible (B), a company should employ the amount of labor for which MRP = W. The MRP curve in (B) is constructed to intersect the points in (A). Given this curve and a wage of $80 per day, 3.5 units of labor will maximize profits.

FIGURE 30.1

learn this, we must go beyond your (hopefully lucrative) enterprise and consider the market demand for labor and the market supply of labor.

THE MARKET DEMAND FOR LABOR

MARKET DEMAND FOR LABOR
The relationship between the wage rate and the total amount of labor demanded by all firms in the labor market (other things equal).

DERIVED DEMAND
The demand for a resource; determined by (derived from) the demand for the product it produces.

Competitive labor markets are characterized by multiple buyers of labor. The **market demand for labor** is obtained by summing the labor demand (or MRP) curves of the individual firms in the market. The market demand curve indicates, for each wage, how much labor is demanded by all firms in a particular labor market. Because labor demand curves of individual firms are inversely related to wages, the market demand curve for labor must also slope downward.

Demand for labor is a **derived demand**—that is, it depends on the demand for the product it produces. Labor is employed not as an end, but as a means to produce something else. If demand for new housing increases, demand for construction workers likewise increases. If tax simplification reduces households' demand for tax assistance, demand for tax accountants falls.

THE BOND PAPER COMPANY SELLS ITS PAPER FOR $20 PER BOX. IT HAS NO INFLUENCE OVER EITHER THE PRICE OF PAPER OR THE WAGE IT MUST PAY ITS WORKERS. THE FOLLOWING TABLE SHOWS THE RELATIONSHIP BETWEEN LABOR AND OUTPUT.

EMPLOYEES	BOXES OF PAPER PER DAY
0	0
1	20
2	35
3	45
4	53
5	60
6	65

(A) WHAT IS THE MRP OF THE SECOND WORKER?

(B) HOW MANY EMPLOYEES SHOULD BE HIRED IF THE WAGE IS $210 PER DAY? (ASSUME WORKERS MUST BE PAID FOR A FULL DAY.)

(C) HOW MANY EMPLOYEES SHOULD BE HIRED IF THE WAGE IS $165 PER DAY?

(D) NOW SUPPOSE THAT BECAUSE OF INCREASED DEMAND FOR PAPER THE PRICE OF PAPER RISES TO $30 PER BOX. (I) HOW DOES THIS AFFECT THE FIRM'S LABOR DEMAND CURVE? WHY? (II) FACING A WAGE OF $165 PER DAY, HOW MANY WORKERS SHOULD THE COMPANY EMPLOY?

The Supply of Labor

LABOR SUPPLY OF AN INDIVIDUAL

SUBSTITUTION EFFECT (FOR LABOR)

The change in the amount of labor supplied that can be attributed to a change in the opportunity cost of leisure. By increasing the opportunity cost of leisure, a higher wage rate induces an individual to substitute work for leisure.

Consider the wage you were paid on your most recent job (or your current job). If that wage were increased, would you want to work more hours or less? Your response may differ from that of your classmates. The reason is that an increase in the wage rate has offsetting effects: the **substitution effect** and the **income effect**. Whether you choose to increase or decrease hours of work depends on which of these two effects is stronger. At a higher wage the reward for working increases. Put another way, you now sacrifice more for each hour you do not work. As the opportunity cost of not working (leisure) rises, you have an incentive to substitute work for leisure—to spend more time working and less time in leisure.

Although a higher wage encourages additional hours of labor through the substitution effect, the income effect works in the opposite direction. A given amount of work generates more income at a high wage than at a low wage. With the additional income, a consumer can afford more leisure. Assuming that leisure is a normal good, the increase in income (stemming from the higher wage) increases the demand for leisure. To obtain additional leisure, the consumer reduces hours of work.

**INCOME EFFECT
(FOR LABOR)**
The change in the amount of labor supplied that can be attributed to a change in income. A higher income increases the demand for leisure, reducing the hours of work.

If the substitution effect dominates, the labor supply curve has the traditional upward slope of most supply curves [Figure 30.2(A)]. If the income effect dominates, labor supply has a negative slope [Figure 30.2(B)], indicating that a higher wage rate *reduces* the amount of labor supplied. Finally, it is possible that an individual's labor supply curve is *backward bending* [Figure 30.2(C)]. In that event the individual responds differently to a wage change, depending on the level of the wage. Initially an increase in the wage rate brings forth additional labor, but beyond some point [W_0 in Figure 30.2(C)] a higher wage rate results in less labor being supplied. This occurs once the income effect outweighs the substitution effect.

Empirical studies have been performed separately for males and for females. They suggest that, overall, the substitution effect is stronger for females—higher wages induce women to work additional hours. The evidence is less clear for men. Although males appear less responsive to wages, studies suggest that for many groups of males the income effect dominates.

THE MARKET SUPPLY OF LABOR

**MARKET SUPPLY
OF LABOR**
The relationship between the wage rate and the total amount of labor supplied to the market (other things equal).

Although the labor supply curve for individuals can take different shapes, the **market supply of labor** is upward sloping. A higher wage in a labor market brings

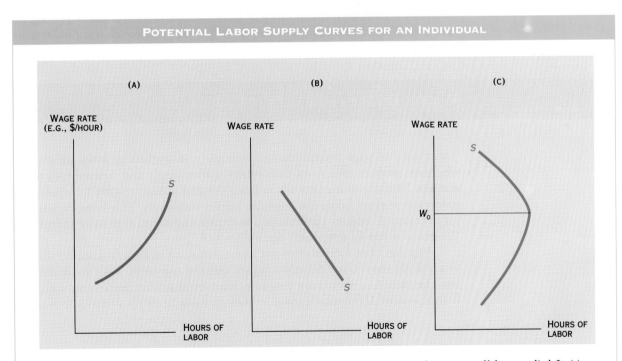

POTENTIAL LABOR SUPPLY CURVES FOR AN INDIVIDUAL

In (A) the substitution effect outweighs the income effect—a higher wage increases the amount of labor supplied. In (B) the income effect is stronger—a higher wage decreases the amount of labor supplied. In (C) the substitution effect dominates for wages below W_0, and the income effect dominates for all higher wages. The result is a backward-bending labor supply curve.

FIGURE 30.2

forth additional labor for two reasons. First, a higher wage rate can be expected to attract individuals who were not previously working. Now that the reward for work has increased, some people formerly out of the labor force will decide to enter this labor market. Second, some people working in other labor markets (for example, different occupations or industries) will switch to this labor market in response to the higher wage. In fact, empirical research indicates that workers are very responsive to wage differences across markets.[2]

Wage Determination

Wage rates are determined in competitive markets by the interaction of labor supply and demand. In Figure 30.3(A) the equilibrium wage rate is $80 per day. At higher wages the quantity of labor supplied would exceed the quantity demanded, driving down wage rates. At lower wages labor shortages would develop, causing firms to bid up wage rates.

Although labor supply is upward sloping for the market, this is not the case for individual firms in the market. Remember that the theory of competitive labor markets assumes that each firm is too small to influence the price of labor. For that reason labor supply to a firm can be represented as a horizontal line [Figure 30.3(B)]. The interpretation is that each firm pays the market-determined wage rate ($80/day), regardless of the quantity of labor it employs. Given this wage rate, the firm then hires labor up to the point where the wage rate equals marginal revenue product.

Wage Differentials

The theory of wage determination in competitive markets provides insight into why some workers earn more than others. Labor supply and demand vary across markets. Workers in markets where labor demand is high relative to supply earn more than workers facing less favorable market conditions. This helps explain why some groups of workers (for example, aerospace engineers) earn more than others (for example, fast-food workers). See Figure 30.4.

Why don't fast-food workers get jobs as aerospace engineers? Lacking the necessary skills, they do not directly compete with the engineers. They are in different labor markets. One should not conclude, however, that labor markets are completely independent. If the wage earned by aerospace engineers rises relative to wages in

---

[2]This responsiveness can be illustrated in terms of college decisions. Statistical analysis by Richard Freeman reveals that college enrollments can largely be explained by labor market conditions for college graduates:

> Over 95% of the variation in the fraction of young men in college over the 1951–74 period can be attributed to two simple measures of the economic incentive to enroll: the income of graduates relative to other workers and relative employment opportunities.

Freeman also finds students' choice of majors to be highly responsive to relative wages of occupations. See R. Freeman, *The Overeducated American* (New York: Academic Press, 1976), p. 53.

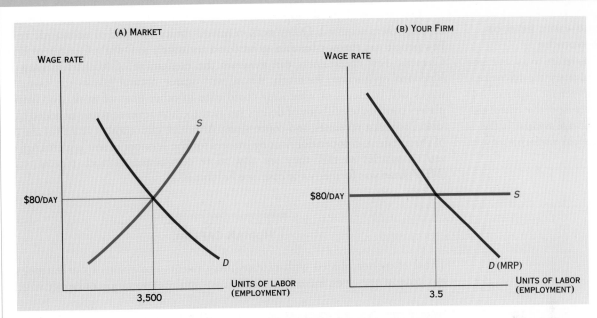

The equilibrium wage rate is determined by the intersection of market labor supply and demand curves. At this wage rate ($80/day), you employ 3.5 units of labor.

FIGURE 30.3

MARKET-BASED WAGE DIFFERENTIALS

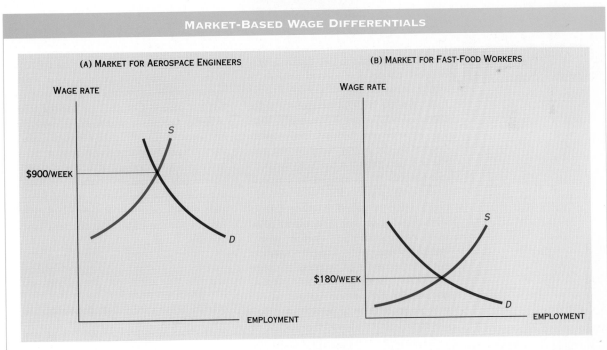

A relatively strong demand for and low supply of aerospace engineers leads to a high rate of pay; the opposite is true for fast-food workers.

FIGURE 30.4

other occupations, one would predict that more people will enter this line of work—that is, acquire the skills necessary to become aerospace engineers.

One reason then for wage inequality is skill differences. Some differences are innate, others acquired. Differences in innate ability can lead to **economic rents** Few people can throw a baseball as hard and accurately as Dwight Gooden or Roger Clemens. Few entertainers can generate the excitement of Michael Jackson and Madonna or Luciano Pavarotti. Those with scarce natural talents can command wages well in excess of what they could earn in other lines of work. Top baseball players contribute millions of dollars per year to their team in terms of added ticket sales, broadcast revenues, and concessions. Although club owners yearn for the days of cheap talent, competition among owners for the services of star athletes has driven up salaries so that they are now more commensurate with players' values (MRP) than was formerly the case (see Exhibit 30.1).

ECONOMIC RENT OF A WORKER

The return to a scarce natural talent: the difference between the wage received (because of that talent) and the wage available in the best alternative line of work.

HUMAN CAPITAL

Those of us not blessed with extraordinary talents can enhance our earnings by investing in ourselves, incurring present costs in the expectation of higher wages in

---

EXHIBIT 30.1

The Market for Professional Baseball Players

Increased competition for major league baseball players has caused salaries to soar, from an average of $45,000 in 1976 to $1,084,000 in 1992. The source of the increased competition? *Free agency.* Until 1977, professional baseball players were covered by the *reserve clause*, which gave the ball club exclusive rights to the player's services for as long as he stayed in baseball. A player either accepted the club's offer or found another line of work. In addition, the team owner could sell a player's contract, whether or not the player approved. This arrangement enabled the owner to suppress the player's salary.[3] Statistical analysis suggests that, under the reserve clause, salaries were no more than 20 percent of a player's contribution to team revenues.[4]

Beginning in 1977, ball players with at least six years of major league experi-ence were allowed to become free agents after their contracts expired. As a free agent a player can sell his services to the highest bidder. Competition for the top athletes has made hundreds of players millionaires. In 1992, the Chicago Cubs signed Ryne Sandberg to a four-year contract extension valued at $28.4 million. Apparently the owners of the Cubs were convinced that the talented second baseman would contribute at least $28.4 million to team revenues over the next four years.

[3]Formally, the owner had *monopsony* power. This model is developed in Chapter 31.

[4]Gerald Scully, "Pay and Performance in Major League Baseball," *American Economic Review* (December 1974), p. 929; *The Business of Major League Baseball* (Chicago: University of Chicago Press, 1989).

HUMAN CAPITAL
The knowledge and skills acquired by workers, principally through education and training.

the future. Examples of self-investment or **human capital** are schooling and training. Economic studies clearly show that workers with more human capital tend to earn higher wages than those with less human capital. Less clear are the reasons for this difference.

Human capital theory argues that these investments directly contribute to earnings by increasing a worker's skills. Workers with greater skills are worth more to a company (have a higher MRP) and consequently command higher wages. Critics of human capital theory offer alternative explanations for the positive association between education and earnings.

SCREENING HYPOTHESIS
The claim that employers make hiring decisions on the basis of a person's education but that education does not make a worker more productive.

The **screening (credentialism) hypothesis** asserts that education opens doors for those receiving it but does not increase their productivity. Even if this were true, it would not follow that education has no value. Individuals differ in terms of characteristics that appear to be correlated with education—ability, motivation, capacity to learn, and so forth. Even if education did not increase a worker's productivity, it could signal to employers that certain workers, by virtue of their higher education, are likely to have high ability and motivation. Thus, education could help sort employees, matching highly productive employees with companies that value high productivity the most. Such sorting would benefit society through a more efficient allocation of labor, as well as benefiting the individual through higher wages. Needless to say, the social benefits from education are higher if education does more than sort individuals. Human capital theorists claim that it does; supporters of the screening hypothesis are more skeptical.

Is education a good investment for an individual? As Figure 30.5 (page 790) illustrates, at each age earnings tend to be higher the more education a person has. By age 37 college graduates on average are earning almost twice as much as those who have not attended college. But weighing against these higher earnings are the costs of education. Tuition and fees typically run several thousand dollars per year at public universities and exceed $20,000 per year at some private colleges. In addition to direct costs—including tuition, fees, and books—education also entails the opportunity cost of forgone earnings. Suppose you earn $5,000 this year, working either part-time during the school year or in the summer. Had you not committed yourself to college, you probably could have earned a higher salary, perhaps $15,000. In that event you are implicitly sacrificing $10,000 this year to attend college—the difference between the $15,000 you could have earned and the $5,000 you did earn. This too is a cost of education.

There are other reasons for attending college besides higher earnings, but these nonfinancial considerations are difficult to measure. Therefore, we focus here on the financial benefits. Are the increased earnings you can expect to receive with a college degree sufficiently high to compensate you for the costs of your education? Although no guarantees are given, the available evidence indicates that for most individuals the expected returns from investing in college are high, at least as high as the returns from investing in stocks and other financial instruments. Education appears to be a good investment.

COMPENSATING WAGE DIFFERENTIALS

Differences in skills and education are not the only reasons for wage differentials; nonwage characteristics of the job can also be important. Jobs differ in various

MICHAEL EISNER

Over the past 30 years in the United States, the average pay of chief executive officers (CEOs) increased twice as fast as the average pay of factory workers. As a result, CEOs in large U.S. corporations now earn $2.5 million per year—more than eighty times as much as factory workers. In contrast, pay disparity between executives and factory workers is approximately 17 to 1 in Japan, 23 to 1 in Germany, and 35 to 1 in Britain.

Michael Eisner, chairman of the Walt Disney Company, earns more in one day than the average Disney employee makes in a year. Since assuming the helm of Disney in 1984, Eisner has averaged $11 million per year, including salary, bonuses, and long-term compensation. Is any executive worth that kind of money, or is this simply a situation of management rewarding itself to the detriment of shareholders? Consider, in turn, the arguments for and against the present system of compensating executives, and then decide for yourself which side has the more compelling case.

IN DEFENSE OF THE PRESENT SYSTEM—PAYING FOR PERFORMANCE Roy Disney, a major shareholder in the Walt Disney Company, is one of many who believe that executives such as Eisner are "worth every penny of what we're paying them. . . .

I would hate to think of where we would be without them." Under Eisner, the Walt Disney Company has refurbished its old theme parks and added new ones, produced a string of hit movies, expanded its retail presence, and successfully developed real estate. As a result, the value of Disney stock has increased sevenfold.

Analysts estimate that the most talented CEOs contribute millions of dollars to their companies, millions more than would be earned had their companies hired bosses with only average skills. As in the case of baseball, the superstars in the field tend to pull their own weight. Companies could hire less-talented personnel, but the lower labor costs would be offset by lower revenues.

Still, $11 million is a lot to pay an executive. Why couldn't Disney cut Eisner's pay from $11 million to $1 million, which is still a hefty sum? If it did that, the company would undoubtedly end up searching for a new CEO. Eisner has proven himself to be one of the best corporate leaders around. Other companies are interested in his talents and would be willing to compensate adequately for them, even if Disney were not. Actual or potential competition for Eisner forces Disney to pay him his lofty salary.

Admittedly, an executive's contributions cannot be measured perfectly.

COMPENSATING WAGE DIFFERENTIAL
The wage premium a worker receives for a job with undesirable characteristics, to compensate for those characteristics.

dimensions: safety, working conditions, job security, and the like. According to the **theory of compensating wage differentials**, a person requires extra compensation—a wage premium—to accept a job with unpleasant characteristics. In other words, jobs with undesirable features require higher wages to attract workers of a given skill level than do jobs with desirable features.

Sometimes companies make mistakes, paying bosses more than they are worth. But executives who do not *earn* their high salaries are not likely to keep drawing these salaries.

A SKEPTICAL VIEW—PAYING FOR MORE THAN PERFORMANCE The problem with the preceding arguments, say critics, is that they ignore the mechanism by which executive pay is set. The CEO's compensation is determined by a board of directors, many of whom were nominated by the very CEO whose pay they must now set. In light of the directors' own high compensation (on average, more than $32,000 per year for less than 100 hours of work), many people agree with the president of the United Shareholders Association: "Board members are dependent upon—and thus beholden to—the CEO for their positions, pay, and perks. What prevails is a you-scratch-my-back, I'll-scratch-yours system of corporate governance." To critics of the present compensation system, executive pay will remain excessive until boards can be made to represent the interests of shareholders, rather than the CEO.

In fact, boards are coming under increased pressure to justify executive pay levels. Institutional investors (pension funds, mutual funds, insurance compa-nies, and the like) now own the majority stake of many corporations. As their clout grows, these investors are demanding more information from the companies in which they invest, meeting with directors to discuss such issues as executive compensation, and voting against reelection of directors viewed as overly generous to the company's executives. Shareholder groups are also pressuring boards to seek advice from outside compensation experts before setting pay for top executives. Finally, in 1992, the Securities and Exchange Commission (SEC) granted shareholders the right to vote on nonbinding resolutions on executive compensation. Until that time, compensation was considered "ordinary business" of the company and was therefore exempt from direct shareholder input. As executive salaries outpace salaries in general, many who believe that corporate boards are not sufficiently independent of top management want shareholders to decide whether or not executives are overpaid.

SOURCES: Adapted from John Byrne, "What, Me Overpaid?" *Business Week*, May 4, 1992, pp. 142–148; "The Flap Over Executive Pay," *Business Week*, May 6, 1991, pp. 90–96; "Who Made the Most and Why," *Business Week*, May 2, 1988, p. 51; Robert Rankin, "Executives' Pay is 'Out of Control,'" *The Kansas City Star*, May 16, 1991, p. A10; Geoffry Colvin, "How to Pay the CEO Right," *Fortune*, April 6, 1992, pp. 60–69.

Empirical research provides some support for this theory. Industries with low job security (high layoff rates) pay more than industries offering greater security.[5] In addition, occupations with a high risk of death pay higher wages than "safe"

[5]See James Ragan and Sharon Smith, "The Impact of Differences in Turnover Rates on Male/Female Pay Differentials," *Journal of Human Resources* (Summer 1981), pp. 343–365.

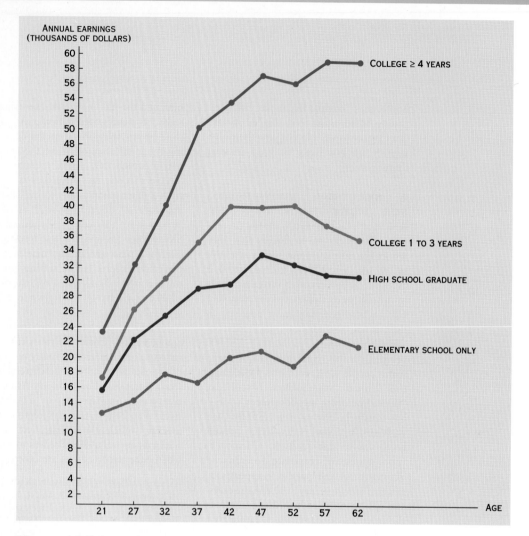

*Year-round, full-time workers.

SOURCE: U.S. Bureau of the Census, *Money Income of Households, Families, and Persons in the United States: 1990* (1991).

FIGURE 30.5

occupations.[6] An example of a job with a compensating wage differential is provided by *The Wall Street Journal* (October 10, 1983):

[6]See Robert Smith, "Compensating Wage Differentials and Public Policy: A Review," *Industrial and Labor Relations Review* (April 1979), pp. 339–352; Stuart Dorsey, "Employment Hazards and Fringe Benefits: Further Tests for Compensating Differentials," in John Worrall, ed., *Safety and the Work Force* (Ithaca, N.Y.: ILR Press, 1983); Ronald Meng, "Compensating Differences in the Canadian Labour Market," *Canadian Journal of Economics* (May 1989), pp. 413–424. According to this last study, each work fatality per 1,000 employees raises annual pay by $2,700 per worker. For a company with 1,000 employees this translates into an additional $2.7 million in wage costs.

Each day when Tom Geer goes to work, it's with the satisfying thought that he will labor for only 10 minutes and be paid for 12 hours. . . . The catch—and of course there has to be one—is the job site. Mr. Geer does his work deep inside a nuclear power plant [where radiation increases his risk of cancer].

MARKET IMPERFECTIONS AND DISCRIMINATION

Although wage differentials would arise even in perfectly competitive markets, market imperfections also contribute to wage disparity across individuals. If certain groups (for example, women or minorities) are barred from high-paying jobs, they will tend to earn lower wages. Other forms of discrimination may also affect wages, as we will see in Chapter 32. To the extent unions contribute to higher wages, those denied access to unions earn less than their union counterparts. Relative wages are also influenced by legislation (see Exhibit 30.3, page 792).

Labor Unions

4% of nothing is nothing. . . . We want 12%.
—placard of anonymous union worker on strike

The model of perfect competition in labor markets is not applicable when either buyers or sellers of labor control the price of labor. Monopoly power on the part of companies (monopsony) is discussed in Chapter 31. The balance of this chapter considers the opposite situation, where sellers of labor form a monopoly—a **union**.

In 1991, 17 million U.S. workers—15 percent of all employees outside agriculture—were members of labor unions. Wages of these workers were directly affected by their unions. Unions can even influence wages of nonunion workers. In addition to wages, unions affect employment, labor productivity, fringe benefits, and the level of output. For such reasons, our discussion of labor markets cannot be complete until we consider the roles of unions.

EARLY LABOR UNIONS

The earliest unions in the United States were formed in the 1790s, and consisted of workers from a common craft or trade. Among the first unions were those representing shoemakers in Philadelphia, carpenters in Boston, and printers in New York. The major objectives of these unions included raising wages and reducing the workday, which at the time was commonly 12 hours or longer.

Beginning in Philadelphia in 1827, various unions began forming citywide federations or associations of labor unions. A few years later, national federations were organized. Many of the early unions and their federations were short-lived. They often folded in response to economic downturns, which reduced the bargaining power of unions, or as the result of government intervention, which was decidedly hostile.

EXHIBIT

30.3

The Fair Labor Standards Act of 1938 established a minimum wage of $.25 per hour. This law has been amended numerous times, and in late 1992 the federal minimum wage stood at $4.25 per hour. The effects of a minimum wage depend on its level. If set below the market-determined wage, a minimum wage does not adversely affect employment (see Figure 30.6A). But if set above the competitive wage, employment falls (as illustrated in Figure 30.6B).

Because young workers are among the least skilled and experienced, one might predict that they would bear the brunt of any employment loss. Empirical research bears this out. After reviewing more than a dozen studies, a widely cited article concludes that each 10 percent increase in the minimum wage reduced teenage employment by between 1 and 3 percent.[7]

Workers losing their jobs obviously experience a reduction in income. On the other hand, low-productivity workers still employed after the minimum-wage hike see their hourly wages raised from W_1 to MIN. Whether their wage *income* (wage per hour times hours worked) rises or falls depends on how hours worked are affected. One study finds evidence that employers respond to a higher minimum wage by forcing teenagers out of full-time jobs and into part-time employment.[8] In some cases the result is lower income despite a higher hourly wage.

Even where income is raised, workers are not necessarily better off. Employers may respond to higher minimum wages by cutting other costs—for example, by reducing fringe benefits or providing less training. In the latter case, higher wages today may come at the expense of future wages. Because wages rise with human capital, any reduction in the acquisition of training can be expected to lead to slower wage growth in the future.[9]

[7]Charles Brown, Curtis Gilroy, and Andrew Kohen, "The Effect of the Minimum Wage on Employment and Unemployment," *Journal of Economic Literature* (June 1982), p. 508.

[8]Edward Gramlich, "Impact of Minimum Wages on Other Wages, Employment, and Family Incomes," *Brookings Papers on Economic Activity* (1976, 2), pp. 442–443.

[9]Support for this hypothesis is provided by Masanori Hashimoto, "Minimum Wage Effects on Training on the Job," *American Economic Review* (December 1982), pp. 1,070–1,087, and Linda Leighton and Jacob Mincer, "Effects of Minimum Wages on Human Capital Formation," in Simon Rottenberg, ed., *The Economics of Legal Minimum Wages* (Washington, D.C.: American Enterprise Institute, 1981), pp. 155–173.

In the early nineteenth century the courts considered unions "criminal conspiracies." Even after unions were declared legal in 1842, the courts regularly issued *injunctions*—restraining orders that prohibited unions from striking, picketing, and other activities. The courts ruled that such actions violated employers' rights. The Sherman Act of 1890, as interpreted by the courts, further limited union powers on the ground that efforts by unions to raise wages constituted "restraint of trade."

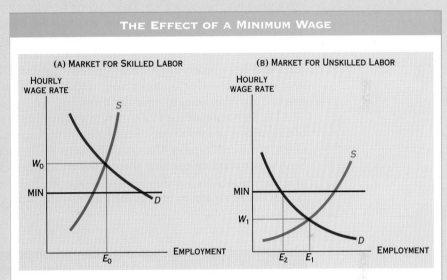

THE EFFECT OF A MINIMUM WAGE

(A) MARKET FOR SKILLED LABOR

HOURLY WAGE RATE

S

W_0

MIN

D

EMPLOYMENT

E_0

(B) MARKET FOR UNSKILLED LABOR

HOURLY WAGE RATE

S

MIN

W_1

D

EMPLOYMENT

E_2 E_1

Because the minimum wage is set below W_0, employment of skilled labor is unaffected (A). In contrast, the employment of unskilled workers falls (B). Because companies are forced to raise the hourly wage from W_1 to MIN, they reduce employment of unskilled labor from E_1 to E_2.

FIGURE 30.6

The courts even sanctioned *yellow-dog contracts*—agreements workers signed as a condition of employment whereby they promised not to join a union. Workers who then joined could be fired for breach of contract. More important, union organizers could be found guilty of inducing workers to violate their contracts. The yellow-dog contract enabled employers to obtain injunctions halting organization drives. Certainly the climate was not conducive to the growth of unionism.

MAJOR LABOR LEGISLATION

Political attitudes toward unions gradually changed, and by the early 1930s many in Congress had become convinced that government intervention was both excessive and biased. With the courts so heavily involved in labor-management relations, some complained of "government by injunction." Others argued that a government of, by, and for the people should welcome such democratic institutions as labor unions, rather than oppose them. Out of this new and more sympathetic environment came two important pieces of pro-union legislation.

The first was the *Norris–LaGuardia Act* of 1932, limiting the ability of courts to issue injunctions against unions and outlawing yellow-dog contracts (see Table 30.3). That was followed three years later by the *National Labor Relations Act (NLRA)*. Also known as the *Wagner Act*, the NLRA is considered so important to unions that it has been dubbed labor's Magna Carta. This law prohibits management from interfering with workers' rights to organize and forces management to bargain in "good faith" with unions representing a majority of their employees. The Wagner Act also created the *National Labor Relations Board (NLRB)*. This agency investigates unfair labor practices and, when deemed appropriate, issues cease-and-desist orders against management. The NLRB also has responsibility for *certifying* unions—that is, conducting elections to allow workers to choose which union, if any, they want to represent them.

The legislation of the 1930s marked a switch in government attitudes from one of obstructing unions to one of encouragement. Largely because of this legislation, union membership more than doubled between 1930 and 1940 (see Table 30.4). Sentiment toward unions later soured, however, in part because of the large number of strikes immediately following World War II. To balance the pro-union legislation of the 1930s and to protect the public, some parties advocated new legislation.

MAJOR LABOR LEGISLATION		
LAW	**DATE ENACTED**	**MAJOR PROVISIONS**
Norris–LaGuardia Act	1932	Limited injunctions against unions; prohibited yellow-dog contracts.
National Labor Relations Act (Wagner Act)	1935	Established the National Labor Relations Board to halt unfair labor practices by management and to conduct union representation elections; required companies to bargain with unions chosen by their workers.
Taft–Hartley Act	1947	Restricted unfair labor practices by unions; allowed states to prohibit union shops.
Landrum–Griffin Act	1959	Increased democracy within unions; restricted potential abuse by union officers.

TABLE 30.3

UNION MEMBERSHIP IN THE UNITED STATES, 1930–1991

| | UNION MEMBERSHIP | |
YEAR	NUMBER (IN THOUSANDS)	AS A PERCENTAGE OF NONAGRICULTURAL EMPLOYMENT
1930	3,401	11.6
1935	3,584	13.2
1940	8,717	26.9
1945	14,322	35.5
1950	14,267	31.5
1955	16,802	33.2
1960	17,049	31.4
1965	17,299	28.4
1970	19,381	27.3
1975	19,611	25.5
1980	20,095	22.2
1985	16,996	17.4
1990	16,740	15.2
1991	16,568	15.2

SOURCES: U.S. Bureau of Labor Statistics, *Handbook of Labor Statistics* (1980); *Earnings and Other Characteristics of Organized Workers* (1980); *Employment and Earnings*, January 1987 and 1992.

TABLE 30.4

CLOSED SHOP

A work arrangement that permits a company to hire only those workers who are currently members of a union.

UNION SHOP

A work arrangement that requires employees to join a union within a certain period of time after they are hired.

OPEN SHOP

A work arrangement in which employees cannot be compelled to join a union, even if one has been chosen to represent the company's work force.

RIGHT-TO-WORK LAWS

Legislation enacted by certain states to require open shops (that is, to outlaw compulsory union membership).

In this environment, and despite intense lobbying by unions, Congress passed the *Taft–Hartley Act* of 1947 (formally entitled the Labor–Management Relations Act).

Among its provisions, the Taft–Hartley Act permits the president to seek an injunction ordering union workers back to work during an 80-day "cooling off" period if the strike threatens the public health or safety. These injunctions have not always succeeded in getting union members back to work, as President Carter discovered during the 1977 coal strike. Whereas the Wagner Act prohibits unfair labor practices on the part of management, the Taft–Hartley Act proscribes unfair labor practices by unions. Unions are required to bargain in good faith, and procedures were established to allow workers to *decertify* (vote out) unions.

The Taft–Hartley Act also affects work arrangements. In a **closed shop**, companies cannot hire workers who do not already belong to the union representing its employees. In a **union shop**, companies face no restriction on who is hired, but new employees must join the union or forfeit their jobs. In an **open shop**, companies have discretion over who is hired, and individual workers choose whether or not to join a union, if one exists. The Taft–Hartley Act outlaws most closed shops and permits states to ban union shops. To date, approximately twenty states have **right-to-work laws** requiring open shops.

Responding to charges of corruption among union leaders, Congress passed the *Landrum–Griffin Act* in 1959 (formally known as the Labor–Management Reporting and Disclosure Act). Although expanding the list of unfair labor practices by unions, it was designed primarily to protect individual union members and increase union democracy. The Landrum–Griffin Act requires election of union officials by secret ballot, limits union loans to its officers, and places restrictions on union office-holding by ex-convicts.

Do Wage Concessions Really Save Jobs?

In difficult times unions occasionally accept wage cuts. Such "give backs" became increasingly common in the early 1980s, prompting unions to debate the wisdom of this practice. As one reporter observed:

> Many [union members] believe that past concessions haven't saved jobs and that calls for such aid have become merely a new management tactic to lower workers' wages rather than a way to keep companies afloat. . . . The workers here [at General Tire] note that about two dozen rubber industry facilities have closed nationwide in the past five years despite numerous concessions by [union] workers. And they say the fortunes of auto, steel, trucking and airline companies haven't improved with the help of wage cuts.[10]

What about it? If employment falls despite wage cuts, should we conclude that lower wage rates have no effect on union employment?

Clearly not. Given a downward-sloping labor demand curve, employment is higher with wage concessions than without. The problem faced by some unions is that labor demand has declined over time due to reduced product demand or, in some cases, to substitution of capital for labor. Given this decline in labor demand, employment may fall even if wage rates are reduced. This illustrated in Figure 30.7.

Assume labor demand falls from D_1 to D_2. If the wage rate remains at W_1, employment falls from E_1 to E_2. Wage concessions can limit, if not totally prevent, the loss of jobs. By accepting a cut in pay to W_2, the union can save $E_3 - E_2$ jobs. Wage rates do matter.

In some cases production remains unprofitable despite the concessions. But even here wage cuts reduce company losses. This may permit the company to stay in business longer (and workers to remain employed longer) even if the plant eventually closes. When it comes to employment, wage rates are important, although they are not the whole story.

[10]Robert Greenberger, "More Workers Resist Employers' Demands for Pay Concessions," *The Wall Street Journal*, October 13, 1982, pp. 1 and 16.

HARD TIMES FOR UNIONS

As Table 30.4 indicates, unionization rates have been declining since the mid-1950s. Unions have found it increasingly difficult to organize workers and in recent years have been winning less than one-half of all *representation elections*, in which workers decide whether or not to become affiliated with a union (see Table 30.5, page 798). At the same time, workers in many companies are voting out (decertifying) their unions. Increasingly, management is taking on unions and winning, replacing strikers with new employees. This practice appears to have gained momentum in the wake of President Reagan's 1981 decision to fire air traffic con-

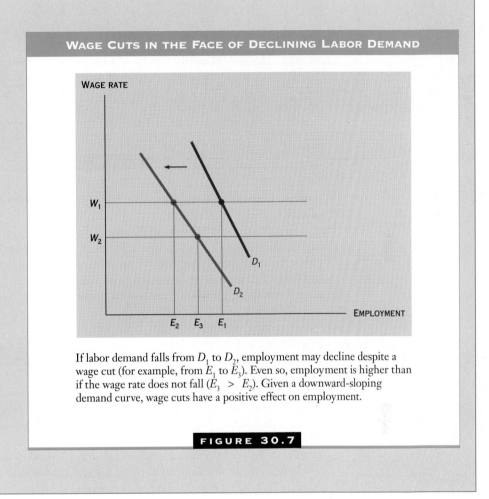

WAGE CUTS IN THE FACE OF DECLINING LABOR DEMAND

If labor demand falls from D_1 to D_2, employment may decline despite a wage cut (for example, from E_1 to E_3). Even so, employment is higher than if the wage rate does not fall ($E_3 > E_2$). Given a downward-sloping demand curve, wage cuts have a positive effect on employment.

FIGURE 30.7

trollers engaged in an illegal strike. Also tarnishing the image of unions have been the wage give backs in steel, copper, airlines, trucking, and other industries.

What accounts for the hard fortune of unions in recent years? First of all, attitudes have changed. Some analysts contend that unions' views are no longer representative of the general public. Legislation in recent years has generally not been pro-union, and the elections of Presidents Reagan and Bush did not help the union cause. Union leaders are especially critical of President Reagan's appointments to the NLRB, arguing that this body has adopted a pro-management bias. Management, in turn, has become more sophisticated and militant, hiring lawyers and other specialists to combat unions. This is especially true in industries facing stiff competition. Deregulation in the airline and trucking industries and increased

REPRESENTATION ELECTIONS AND DECERTIFICATION VOTES

FISCAL YEAR	REPRESENTATION ELECTIONS	PERCENT WON BY UNION	DECERTIFICATION VOTES	PERCENT LOST BY UNION
1955	4,372	66.4	157	65.0
1960	6,380	58.6	237	68.8
1965	7,576	60.8	200	64.0
1970	8,074	55.2	301	69.8
1975	8,577	48.2	516	73.4
1980	8,198	45.7	902	72.7
1985	4,614	42.4	865	75.6
1989	4,413	46.7	622	70.9

SOURCES: National Labor Relations Board, *Fifty-fourth Annual Report* (1991), and selected earlier annual reports.

TABLE 30.5

foreign competition in other sectors have put intense pressure on some companies to cut costs.

Shifts in the composition of employment have also hurt unions. Industries with high unionization (including manufacturing, construction, and transportation and public utilities) have experienced a decline in relative employment at the expense of industries having low unionization rates (including retail trade, finance, and services). Even if unionization rates had remained constant in each industry, aggregate unionization would have declined.

A related development has been women's increased share of employment. Women are less likely to join unions than are men. This appears to be caused in part by the different distribution across jobs—women tend to hold occupations and work in industries characterized by low unionization. Moreover, as discussed in Chapter 32, women tend to have a more intermittent history of work and are more likely to work part time. Support for unions tends to be greater among full-time workers and among those with a strong, continuous commitment to work. Because unions have been less successful in organizing women, the increased share of women in the labor market has accentuated the decline in unionization.

Aware of the problem, unions are intensifying efforts to organize women and workers in traditionally nonunion industries. Whether their efforts will succeed remains to be seen, but unions have made gains in at least one area. The share of government workers represented by unions is much higher today than 30 years ago.

THE AFL–CIO

Most large unions are affiliated with the AFL–CIO, an organization formed in 1955 by the merger of the American Federation of Labor (AFL) and the Congress of Industrial Organizations (CIO). The AFL, which dates back to 1886, was an association of national *craft* unions, representing workers with a common skill or craft. The CIO embodied an alternative approach to unionism—organizing workers along *industrial* lines, as when a single union represents all workers in the auto industry regardless of their skills or the nature of their jobs.

As separate entities, the AFL and CIO often engaged in representational fights, each side raiding the other for members. By merging, the two organizations ended their rivalry and created a unified front, which they hoped would be more effective in achieving common goals (for example, the defeat of antiunion legislation). Despite such hopes, the merger was unable to rekindle growth in unionization or to increase labor's might. In the final analysis, the success of a union depends on its ability to affect conditions in the labor market or to induce employers to make concessions, not on the size of the federation with which it is affiliated.

How Unions Raise Wages of Their Members

Unions have many goals, perhaps the foremost being higher wages for their members. Wages can be raised by (a) increasing the demand for union workers, (b) restricting labor supply, or (c) collective bargaining.

INCREASING THE DEMAND FOR UNION LABOR

Because the demand for labor is a derived demand, anything increasing demand for their employer's product raises demand for union workers. This, in turn, puts upward pressure on union wages and employment (see Figure 30.8). This is the rationale behind the *union-label* campaign. If a union can convince you to buy clothing manufactured by the International Ladies Garment Workers Union and to

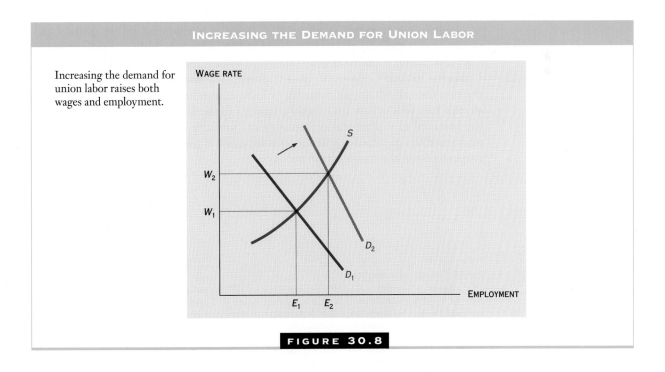

INCREASING THE DEMAND FOR UNION LABOR

Increasing the demand for union labor raises both wages and employment.

FIGURE 30.8

© 1985 Tribune Media Services, Inc.
All Rights Reserved

"We're from the Central Labor Union Council and we're doing a survey on union label purchases. Please unmake your bed for a sheet, blanket and pillowcase check, and remove your trousers for an underwear check."

SOURCE: *St. Louis Post Dispatch*. Reprinted by permission; Tribune Media Services.

shop at grocery stores employing union cashiers, it is increasing demand for union garment workers and cashiers.[11]

Legislation provides an alternative means for achieving union goals. Laws requiring that grain or oil be transported in U.S. ships and tankers benefit the U.S. maritime industry and its heavily unionized work force. The United Auto Workers Union has lobbied Congress to limit imports of automobiles into the United States. Because the overwhelming majority of U.S. autoworkers belong to the UAW, any shift of auto production from other countries to the United States offers the UAW the potential to expand union employment. Similarly, when the government gives preference to unionized construction companies, it tends to raise union wages and employment in the construction industry.[12]

---

[11]This may be a good time to ask your instructor to sing the ILGWU theme song: "Look for the Union Label." Then again, it may not.

[12]In addition to increasing demand for union labor by altering product demand, unions may be able to increase wages and employment of their members through *featherbedding*—a practice whereby companies are forced to pay for more labor than is necessary to produce a given amount of output. For example, union rules require theaters to employ a minimum number of union musicians at Broadway musicals, regardless of the number of musicians actually needed or used. Although only nine musicians performed at *The Best Little Whorehouse in Texas*, the union forced the producers to pay twenty-five musicians. In effect, featherbedding places a lower limit on both the wage of union workers and their employment.

RESTRICTING THE SUPPLY OF LABOR

Rather than altering the demand for labor, some unions pursue a strategy based on the supply of labor. If a union can restrict the number of people trained or certified for an occupation, it can raise wages in that occupation (see Figure 30.9). For example, some states require workers in certain occupations (including barbers and electricians) to obtain licenses before they may work in the state. Here, supply can be restricted by the licensing board, which may be influenced by the union. Alternatively, a craft union may be able to control supply by inducing employers to hire only workers who have completed an apprenticeship program operated by the union. Note that supply restrictions reduce employment, unlike programs that increase demand for union labor.

COLLECTIVE BARGAINING

COLLECTIVE BARGAINING

The process through which unions and management negotiate wages, fringe benefits, and nonmonetary terms of employment.

A third route to higher wages is **collective bargaining**, through which the union and management negotiate a contract. Management may agree to pay higher wages than it would like in order to avoid a strike. By withholding labor from the company, a union can generally impose costs on the company: lost sales and profits.[13] To avoid this and the ill will resulting from a strike, management may agree to pay higher wages than would prevail in the absence of the union (see Figure 30.10).

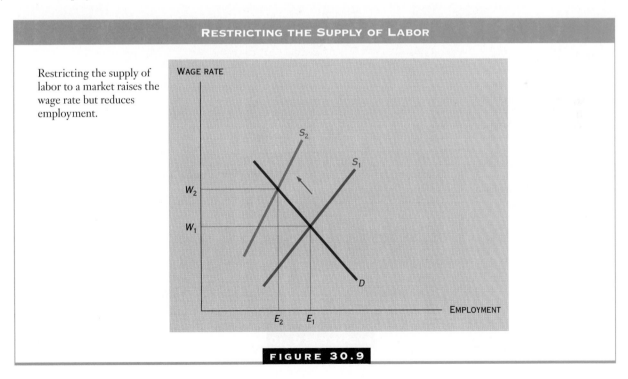

RESTRICTING THE SUPPLY OF LABOR

Restricting the supply of labor to a market raises the wage rate but reduces employment.

FIGURE 30.9

---

[13]Costs from a strike may extend to other parties as well. For example, a strike by steelworkers may curtail production of automobiles, leading to layoffs in the automobile industry.

Unlike the previous two cases, where unions achieved higher wages by shifting labor demand or labor supply, collective bargaining leads to an excess supply of labor for high-paying union jobs. For an example of how a union can create excess supply of labor, consider the sanitation workers union of New York City. In response to 100 job openings in the early 1970s, 63,147 people applied.[14]

The success of a strike cannot be guaranteed. A strike is most effective when it shuts down production. If a company continues to produce, the strike's cost to the company is reduced. A company may be able to continue operations by (a) replacing strikers with new employees (called "scabs" by the workers on strike), (b) shifting current, nonstriking employees (including supervisors) to the union jobs, or (c) substituting capital for labor. According to some analysts, companies are becoming better equipped to carry on production during a strike. For that reason, a strike puts less pressure on many companies today than it did 20 or 30 years ago (see Exhibit 30.5).

The cost of a strike to a company also depends on what is being produced. If a good can be inventoried (for example, steel and tires), the company can build up a large stockpile in anticipation of a strike. By drawing down inventories during a strike, the company may be able to maintain its revenues. In contrast, some goods and services (for example, newspapers and airplane travel) cannot be inventoried. Accordingly, a strike is likely to prove more costly to companies producing such items than to companies producing goods that can be inventoried.

NEGOTIATING HIGHER WAGES

In the absence of a union, competitive pressures dictate the wage W_1. However, through collective bargaining, the union may negotiate a higher wage, W_2. At W_2 there is excess supply of labor ($E_3 - E_2$). The higher wage reduces the quantity of labor demanded while simultaneously increasing the quantity supplied.

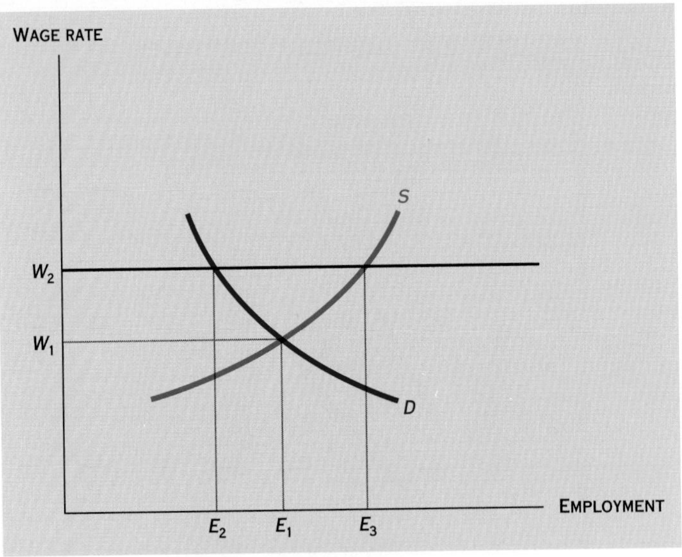

FIGURE 30.10

[14]This example was cited in Robert I. Lerman, "The Public Employment Bandwagon Takes the Wrong Road," *Challenge* (January/February 1975).

Are Strikes Becoming Less Effective?

EXHIBIT 30.5

When labor contracts with AT&T expired in 1992, analysts speculated about whether members of the Communications Workers of America and the International Brotherhood of Electrical Workers would go on strike. If union leaders did call a strike, most analysts thought the strike could last considerably longer than the 28-day strike in 1986. Management at AT&T pledged that it would meet a strike by having nonunion supervisors fill in for union workers, calling back retired workers, and hiring temporary replacements. The unions threatened to take business away from AT&T in the event of a strike by asking customers sympathetic to the union to switch to Sprint or MCI. But given AT&T's ability to continue operations during a strike, most analysts were convinced that the company could outwait the union. Accordingly, union officials chose not to strike and instead asked employees to stay on the job until a new contract was reached.

AT&T is not the only company to have gained the upper hand in negotiating with unions. *Newsweek* reported that nationwide, "companies are discovering that they can survive a strike by using their computers. And that is having a dramatic effect on labor–management relations. 'Automation has shifted the whole balance of power in favor of management,' says Professor Harley Shaiken, who has given the trend a name: telescabbing.

"Shaiken and others cite many recent examples of strikes that had negligible effects because of automation. A strike against Consolidated Edison Co., which ended after more than two months, went unnoticed by most New Yorkers because the electric system is highly automated. A major strike against several oil refineries had little impact because the pumps and valves are almost completely automated. And a strike at a jet-engine plant in Ohio didn't stop production because computers have simplified the work of highly skilled machinists so it now can be done by superiors and secretaries. Even in the steel industry, new processes make it possible to continue operating during a strike. A study by the Wharton School at the University of Pennsylvania found that many capital-intensive companies achieve 90 percent of usual production levels during a strike; most other firms manage 50 to 80 percent.

"Automation and computerization have other strike-breaking effects. Because of them, the ratio of workers to supervisors has dropped dramatically in the past 20 years: at AT&T, from 5 to 1 to 2 to 1, which is one reason why supervisors are able to handle the system during the strike."

SOURCES: John Brecher and Alexander Stille, "'Telescabbing': The New Union Buster," *Newsweek*, August 29, 1983, p. 53, reprinted by permission; *The Kansas City Star*, "AT&T Trying to Avert Strike by Two Unions," May 31, 1992, p. A3.

How Unions Affect Wages of Nonunion Workers

The effect of unions may spill over to the nonunion sector. Consider an industry with both union and nonunion companies. Suppose that managers of the nonunion companies wish to remain union-free. What can they do to lessen the likelihood that their employees will vote for union representation? They can reduce the incentive to unionize by paying wages higher than dictated by competitive labor markets. If union wages rise, nonunion companies may respond by raising wages of their employees too (although perhaps by a lesser amount). In that event, both union and nonunion employees in the industry benefit from higher union wages.

Other nonunion workers may not fare so well. In particular, the positive effect discussed in the preceding paragraph does not carry over to industries where employers do not feel threatened by potential unionization of their work forces. Collective bargaining raises wages in unionized companies (from W_1^U to W_2^U in Figure 30.11A), thus reducing union employment (from E_1^U to E_2^U). Some of the displaced workers ($E_1^U - E_2^U$) may flow over to nonunion markets—a low-paying nonunion job may be preferable to no job at all. This increase in labor supply to nonunion markets depresses wages there (from W_1^N to W_2^N). According to this scenario, higher union wages depress nonunion wages. In summary, some nonunion

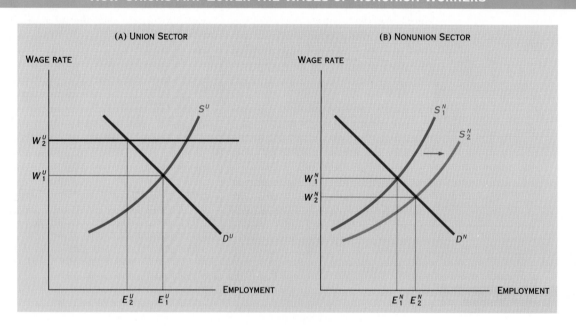

HOW UNIONS MAY LOWER THE WAGES OF NONUNION WORKERS

Higher wages in the union sector (A) reduce union employment (from E_1^U to E_2^U). When some workers unable to obtain union employment switch to the nonunion sector (B), labor supply in the nonunion sector increases. Assuming wages in the nonunion sector are determined by labor supply and demand, the result is lower wages for nonunion workers (W_2^N).

FIGURE 30.11

workers appear to have their wages raised because of unions (although not as high as union wages); others have their wages pulled down.

The Union Wage Premium

What is the relative wage premium associated with union membership—that is, how much more do union workers receive than comparable nonunion workers? That depends on the union and the time period. Some unions are more powerful than others; some time periods are more conducive to large union premiums than are other periods. If we consider the average premium in normal times, it appears that union employees receive wages about 15 percent higher than nonunion workers with similar skills and backgrounds.

As Table 30.6 illustrates, the net advantage of union membership varies by race and by gender. Because unions typically raise wages by a larger percentage for low-paid workers, blacks tend to benefit more from union membership than whites. For the same reason, one might also expect women to benefit more than men. But women are less likely to be members of powerful unions, so the effect of union membership by gender is mixed.

Nonwage Effects of Unions

The impact of unions extends well beyond wages; among its nonwage effects are higher fringe benefits. One economist estimated that whereas union wages are approximately 14.8 percent higher than nonunion wages, when fringe benefits are included the net advantage rises to 17.3 percent.[15]

ESTIMATED WAGE PREMIUM FROM UNION MEMBERSHIP BY YEAR AND RACE/GENDER*			
	1967	1973	1975
All workers	11.6	14.8	16.8
White men	9.6	15.5	16.3
Black men	21.5	22.5	22.5
White women	14.4	12.7	16.6
Black women	5.6	13.2	17.1

*The wage premium is an estimate of the percentage wage gain due to union membership.

SOURCE: Orley Ashenfelter, "Union Relative Wage Effects," in Richard Stone and William Peterson, eds., *Econometric Contributions to Public Policy* (New York: St. Martin's Press, 1979), Table 6, p. 33. © 1979 by St. Martin's Press, Incorporated.

TABLE 30.6

[15]Richard Freeman, "The Effect of Trade Unionism on Fringe Benefits," *Industrial and Labor Relations Review* (July 1981).

Through strikes and restrictive work practices (featherbedding), unions reduce output; but in other areas their effects are positive. By reducing sources of discontent, they may increase morale and, in turn, output per worker. By raising wages, unions may force management to run a tighter ship, to find ways to cut other costs. They may also foster a spirit of cooperation among workers. Under unionism, wages and job security depend more on seniority (that is, job tenure) than on performance of the individual. In this environment, workers are less likely to see each other as rivals and more likely to work together, to train and assist those needing help. Unions can also be a source of information to management, pointing out ways to improve operations within a company.[16] But, do these positive effects outweigh the negative effects? On that issue the evidence is mixed. In some industries unions raise the output per worker; in other industries the reverse is true.

Unions also affect the distribution of income. Although one may not applaud the wage gains achieved by baseball or pilots' unions, unions appear especially concerned about workers at the bottom of the income distribution. One result is less racial inequality of wages. Blacks are more likely to belong to unions than whites; they also enjoy a union wage premium at least as large as that received by whites (see Table 30.6). Together these statements imply that unions narrow the difference in pay between blacks and whites—in the absence of unions, the pay of blacks would be even further behind that of whites.

In addition, unions protect the rights of individual workers, reducing the ability of management to engage in capricious or discriminatory behavior. Unions demand that employees be treated fairly, with dignity, rather than as some impersonal resource to be used at the will of management. For some workers this is the most important reason to join a union.

Unions have also been a major force behind the enactment of important pieces of legislation, from the Civil Rights Act to laws on child labor, worker safety, and plant closings. Because these laws affect the entire work force—not just union members—some consider unions a voice for all workers. For such reasons, unions enjoy support even in the nonunion community.

Summary

1. According to the model of perfect competition, wages are determined by the intersection of market labor supply and demand. The firm's labor demand curve is based on the marginal revenue product of labor. A profit-maximizing firm should hire up to the point where the wage rate equals marginal revenue product.

2. Demand for labor is derived from product demand. When product demand increases (decreases), so does labor demand.

3. The number of hours an individual wants to work may vary positively or negatively with the wage rate, depending on whether the substitution effect or income effect dominates. But the amount of labor supplied to a market increases with the wage rate.

4. Wage rates vary greatly across individuals. One reason is differences in labor supply and demand. Wages tend to be higher for those with large amounts of human capital. Wage differences also arise because of economic rents, compensating wage differentials, labor market imperfections, and discrimination.

---

[16]These arguments on the positive effects of unions come from Richard Freeman and James Medoff, *What Do Unions Do?* (New York: Basic Books, 1984).

5. When set above the market rate of pay, a minimum wage reduces employment. Each 10 percent increase in the minimum wage reduces teenage employment by between 1 and 3 percent. Although minimum wages raise the income of some workers, others find their income reduced, because of either lost employment or a reduction in hours worked. To the extent employers respond to a higher minimum wage by providing less training to their employees, a minimum wage may result in slower wage growth.

6. Less than one in six U.S. workers belongs to a labor union. Unionization soared after the pro-union legislation of the 1930s but has been declining since the 1950s.

7. Unions can raise wages of their members by increasing demand for union workers, restricting labor supply, or engaging in collective bargaining.

8. Unions may increase or decrease wages of nonunion workers. Nonunion companies that worry about possible union organization may raise wages of their employees in an effort to keep them from voting for union representation. In contrast, when workers displaced by high union wages transfer to nonunion markets, increasing labor supply there, the result can be lower nonunion wages.

9. On average, union workers appear to earn about 15 percent more than comparable nonunion employees, but the size of this premium varies over time and across unions.

10. Unions raise fringe benefits, exert both positive and negative effects on output, and alter the distribution of income. Unions narrow differences in pay between black and white workers.

Key Terms

marginal revenue product of
  labor
market demand for labor
derived demand
substitution effect (for labor)
income effect (for labor)
market supply of labor
economic rent of a worker
human capital

screening hypothesis
compensating wage differential
union
closed shop
union shop
open shop
right-to-work laws
collective bargaining

Study Questions and Problems

1. Assume your firm faces the following production function:

NUMBER OF WORKERS	UNITS OF OUTPUT
0	0
1	50
2	90
3	120
4	145
5	165

Each unit of output sells for $2 regardless of the number of units sold.

   a. What is the marginal product of the third worker?

   b. What is the third worker's marginal revenue product?

   c. Assuming that your goal is to maximize profit, how many workers should you hire if the wage is $65 per worker?

   d. How many workers should you hire if the wage is $45 per worker?

2. In 1992, Madonna signed a $60 million contract with Time Warner. The contract covers Madonna's next seven albums and television, merchandising, and publishing rights. On what basis might the chairman of Time Warner explain his company's decision to pay the entertainer such a large sum of money?

3. Why don't all workers receive the same wage rate? Provide several explanations.

4. What is a backward-bending labor supply curve? Why does it bend backwards?

5. How does additional education affect the rate of pay a worker can expect to receive? Provide two alternative explanations for the relationship between education and earnings.

6. Economists argue that a higher minimum wage harms many of the workers it was designed to help—those with low skills and low income. Explain this argument.

7. Explain how government policy toward unions has changed over time. Has this had any impact on the success of unions?

8. (a) What do you consider to be the major contributions of unions? (b) Do unions have any adverse effects on the economy? Explain.

9. What is the difference between a craft union and an industrial union? Which category best describes the earliest U.S. unions?

10. Explain why a strike may impose greater costs on some companies than on others.

11. How has the rate of unionization changed in the United States over the past 40 years? What accounts for this change? Do you think the election of a democratic president in 1992 will reverse the decline in unionization?

12. Do unions raise or lower wages of nonunion workers? Explain.

YOUR TURN
Answers

(A) $300. (B) 2. (C) 3. (D) (I) THE LABOR DEMAND CURVE SHIFTS RIGHTWARD. OTHER THINGS EQUAL, A HIGHER OUTPUT PRICE INCREASES MRP. TO PROVE THIS, FIRST COMPUTE MRP WHEN THE PRICE IS $20 PER BOX. THEN CONSTRUCT THE NEW MRP SCHEDULE FOR A PRICE OF $30 PER BOX. (II) 5.

Selected References

Becker, Gary. *Human Capital* (New York: National Bureau of Economic Research, 1964). Shows that economic tools can be used to explain educational decisions and other choices made by individuals. One of many pathbreaking books that led to the 1992 Nobel Prize in economics for this University of Chicago economist.

Brown, Charles, Curtis Gilroy, and Andrew Kohen. "The Effect of the Minimum Wage on Employment and Unemployment," *Journal of Economic Literature* (June 1982), pp. 487–528. Surveys minimum wage research.

Ehrenberg, Ronald, and Robert Smith. *Modern Labor Economics*, 4th ed. (New York: Harper-Collins, 1991). A popular labor economics text.

Estey, Marten. *The Union*, 3rd ed. (New York: Harcourt Brace Jovanovich, 1981). Provides history and background on organized labor.

Freeman, Richard, and James Medoff. *What Do Unions Do?* (New York: Basic Books, 1984). Discusses the positive and negative effects of unions.

Hamermesh, Daniel, and Albert Rees. *The Economics of Work and Pay*, 5th ed. (New York: Harper and Row, 1993). Another widely used text on labor economics.

Kaufman, Bruce. *The Economics of Labor Markets* (Orlando: The Dryden Press, 1991). Provides thorough coverage of labor topics.

Killingsworth, Mark. *Labor Supply* (Cambridge, England: Cambridge University Press, 1983). Reviews studies on labor supply.

Marshall, F. Ray, and Vernon Briggs, Jr. *Labor Economics*, 6th ed. (Homewood, Ill.: Irwin, 1989). Discusses the history of the union movement and important labor legislation.

Rees, Albert. *The Economics of Trade Unions*, 3rd ed. (Chicago: University of Chicago Press, 1989). An extensive but nontechnical economic discussion of unions.

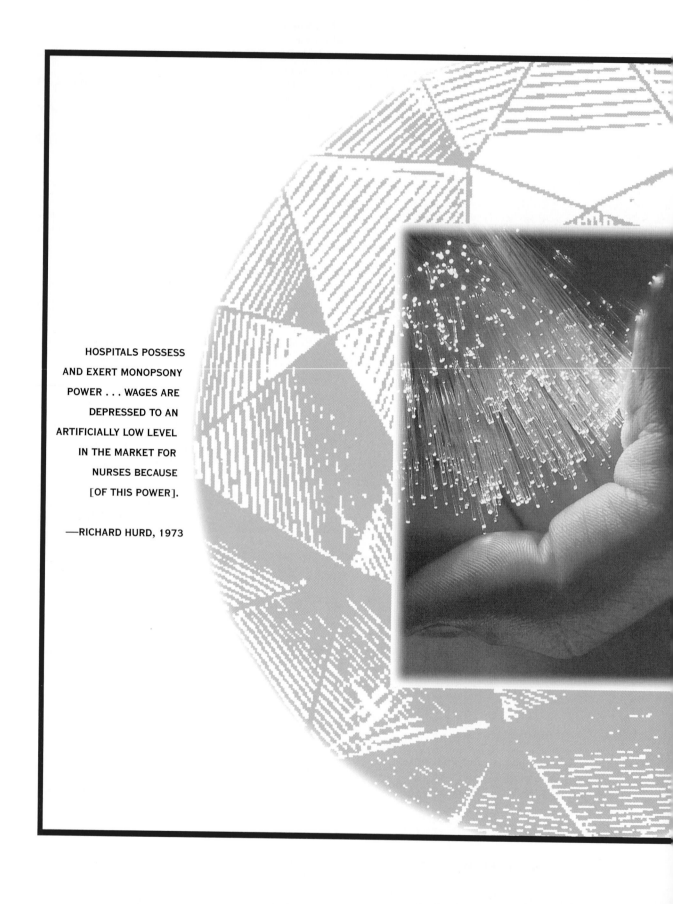

HOSPITALS POSSESS
AND EXERT MONOPSONY
POWER . . . WAGES ARE
DEPRESSED TO AN
ARTIFICIALLY LOW LEVEL
IN THE MARKET FOR
NURSES BECAUSE
[OF THIS POWER].

—RICHARD HURD, 1973

Alternative Models of the Factor Market[1]

FIRMS PARTICIPATE IN TWO TYPES OF MARKETS: PRODUCT MARKETS, WHERE THEY SELL THEIR OUTPUT, AND FACTOR MARKETS, WHERE THEY BUY THEIR INPUTS.

CHAPTER 30 SKETCHED THE THEORY OF WAGE DETERMINATION ON THE ASSUMPTION THAT THE FIRM WAS TOO SMALL TO INFLUENCE EITHER THE PRICE OF ITS OUTPUT OR THE PRICE OF ITS VARIABLE INPUT, LABOR. IN OTHER WORDS, THE MODEL ASSUMED THAT THE FIRM HIRED LABOR IN A PERFECTLY COMPETITIVE LABOR MARKET—PAYING THE MARKET WAGE—AND SOLD ITS OUTPUT IN A PERFECTLY COMPETITIVE PRODUCT MARKET. AS YOU KNOW, HOWEVER, NOT ALL PRODUCT MARKETS ARE (PERFECTLY) COMPETITIVE. WHERE FIRMS FACE DOWNWARD-SLOPING DEMAND CURVES, THEY CAN INFLUENCE PRODUCT PRICE. SIMILARLY, NOT ALL FACTOR MARKETS ARE COMPETITIVE. IN SOME LABOR MARKETS THE WAGE A COMPANY PAYS DEPENDS ON THE AMOUNT OF LABOR IT HIRES. IN SUCH MARKETS THE FIRM, THROUGH ITS HIRING DECISIONS, INFLUENCES THE WAGE IT MUST PAY.

CHAPTER 31 STUDIES HIRING DECISIONS OF FIRMS THAT OPERATE IN PRODUCT MARKETS OR FACTOR MARKETS THAT ARE NOT PERFECTLY COMPETITIVE. WE CONSIDER FIRST THE CASE WHERE FIRMS INFLUENCE WAGE RATES AND THEN THE CASE WHERE FIRMS HAVE CONTROL OVER THEIR PRODUCT PRICE. NEXT, WE EXTEND THE ANALYSIS TO CONSIDER THE SITUATION WHERE A COMPANY BUYS

---

[1]Chapter 31 is more technical than Chapter 30. Instructors who do not want to give their course a heavy theoretical emphasis can delete as much material as they choose from this chapter without creating gaps in later chapters.

more than one variable input. If a company is hiring several different types of labor or buying capital as well as labor, how should these inputs be combined? We tackle this issue first for the case where factor markets are competitive and then for the case where firms have some influence over the price they pay for their inputs.

The models of this chapter and the previous chapter are tied together by a common thread: demand for a factor is based on the marginal productivity of that factor. We wrap up our discussion by analyzing what marginal productivity theory does and does not say about the distribution of income.

Monopsony in the Labor Market

MONOPSONIST

The only buyer of a particular input.

MARGINAL FACTOR COST

The increase in the total cost of an input associated with using an additional unit of the input.

The model of perfect competition assumes that firms confront a given, market-determined wage—that is, firms are *wage takers*. But this assumption is not always reasonable. When a company is the only one hiring a particular type of labor, it can influence the price of labor. It has monopoly power on the buying side of the market. Such a company is called a **monopsonist**.

With only one firm in the labor market, the supply of labor to the firm is synonymous with the supply of labor to the market. Thus, a monopsonist confronts an upward-sloping labor supply curve (Figure 31.1). **Marginal factor cost (MFC)** measures the incremental cost of hiring an additional unit of the factor of production—in this case, labor. For example, suppose a company must pay each worker $90/day if it hires three workers but $100/day if it hires four. MFC of the fourth worker is $130—the wage of the fourth worker ($100) *plus* an additional $10 for each of the first three workers.[2] Because MFC exceeds the wage ($130 > $100), MFC lies above the labor supply curve.

HIRING DECISIONS UNDER MONOPSONY

As observed in the previous chapter, a worker's contribution to revenue is measured by the worker's marginal revenue product (MRP). To maximize profit the monopsonist hires labor up to the point where MRP = MFC. Until this point is reached additional labor adds more to revenue than to costs (MRP > MFC). Beyond this point the reverse is true (MRP < MFC). The monopsonist portrayed in Figure 31.1 hires E_1 workers and pays a wage of W_1. Note that the wage is not given by the height of the MFC curve at E_1. To maximize profits the monopsonist pays the lowest wage possible consistent with hiring E_1 workers. That wage, given by the point on the supply curve directly above E_1, is W_1.

---

[2]Alternatively, MFC can be computed directly as the change in total labor cost associated with hiring the fourth unit of labor. When four workers are employed instead of three, total labor cost rises from 3 × $90 = $270 to 4 × $100 = $400, a change of $130.

A monopsonist hires where MFC = MRP (E_1) and pays the lowest wage necessary (W_1) to obtain this amount of labor. In competitive labor markets, the intersection of market MRP and labor supply determines the wage rate (W_2) and employment (E_2). Compared to competitive labor markets, monopsony leads to a lower wage rate and lower employment.

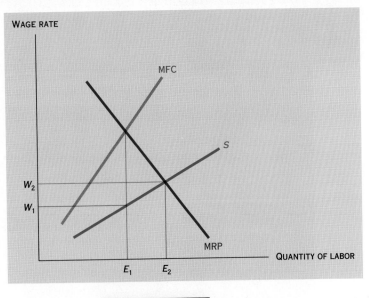

FIGURE 31.1

In competitive labor markets, wages and employment are determined by the intersection of market MRP and market labor supply. In terms of Figure 31.1, the competitive outcome would be W_2 and E_2. A comparison of competitive and monopsonistic outcomes illustrates how the monopsonist uses its monopoly power to curtail wages and employment.

As an example of monopsony, consider an isolated community with a single mining company. By deciding how many miners to employ (E_1), the company determines the wage rate (W_1). Other markets may be approximated by the model of monopsony, even when they contain more than one employer. The majority of registered nurses work in hospitals. If the hospitals act in concert, they may be able to suppress wages of RNs.[3]

HOW UNIONS AND MINIMUM WAGES ALTER HIRING DECISIONS

In the preceding discussion, we assumed that the monopsonist was free to choose the wage rate. However, unions or minimum-wage legislation may place a lower limit on wages. If that limit is above the wage the monopsonist would have chosen, wage rates rise. Based on our discussion of competitive markets, you might predict

[3]For evidence of this, see Richard Hurd, "Equilibrium Vacancies in a Labor Market Dominated by Non-Profit Firms: The 'Shortage' of Nurses," *Review of Economics and Statistics* (May 1973), pp. 234–240; Charles Link and J. H. Landon, "Monopsony and Union Power in the Market for Nurses," *Southern Economic Journal* (April 1975), pp. 649–659; Daniel Sullivan, "Monopsony Power in the Market for Nurses," *Journal of Law & Economics* (October 1989), pp. S135–S178.

THE MARGINAL REVENUE PRODUCT FOR A MONOPSONIST IS GIVEN BY THE FOLLOWING SCHEDULE:

NUMBER OF WORKERS	MRP
1	$8.00
2	7.50
3	7.00
4	6.50
5	6.00
6	5.50

THE MONOPSONIST FACES THE LABOR SUPPLY SCHEDULE PRESENTED BELOW:

NUMBER OF WORKERS	WAGE
1	$5.00
2	5.50
3	6.00
4	6.50
5	7.00
6	7.50

A. GIVEN THE LABOR SUPPLY SCHEDULE, CONSTRUCT THE MFC SCHEDULE OF THE MONOPSONIST.

B. WHAT LEVEL OF EMPLOYMENT SATISFIES THE MONOPSONIST'S RULE FOR PROFIT MAXIMIZATION?

C. GIVEN YOUR ANSWER TO B, WHAT WAGE WILL THE MONOPSONIST PAY IN ORDER TO MAXIMIZE PROFIT?

that higher wage rates reduce employment. Surprising as it may seem, in monopsonistic markets the employment effect of a higher wage rate may be either positive or negative, depending on how much the wage is raised.

A minimum wage, whether imposed by the government or a union, precludes wages below a certain level. Accordingly, it alters the shapes of the labor supply and MFC curves. To the left of E_2 in Figure 31.2, the supply and MFC curves become horizontal, with values equal to MIN. This reflects the fact that until the wage rate is raised above MIN, each additional unit of labor costs MIN. Beyond E_2 (where MIN intersects S), the original supply and MFC curves prevail.

Confronted with a wage rate of MIN, the monopsonist *increases* employment from E_1 to E_2. (The monopsonist would not hire less than E_2 because, for employ-

In the absence of wage constraints, a monopsonist pays W_1 and hires E_1 units of labor. When the monopsonist is forced to pay the wage MIN, employment rises to E_2 (because MFC is affected). At a still higher wage, MIN', employment falls below E_1.

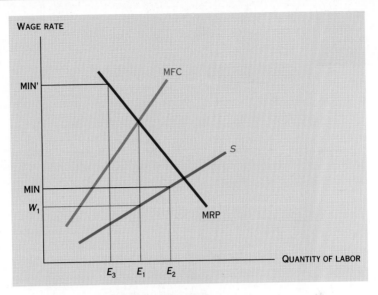

FIGURE 31.2

ment less than E_2, MRP > MFC.) Even under monopsony, if the minimum wage is set too high, employment falls. For example, a wage of MIN' reduces employment to E_3. For further analysis of the effects of a minimum wage, work through the Your Turn on page 816.

Although the model of monopsony indicates that a minimum wage may increase employment, economists discount this possibility on the ground that monopsony is rare. As predicted by the competitive theory of labor markets, empirical studies invariably find that a higher minimum wage reduces employment of low-productivity workers.

Factor Demand in Noncompetitive Product Markets

Let us drop the assumption that the firm is a monopsonist. Instead, assume that the firm is in a perfectly competitive labor market, paying a given wage regardless of the number of workers hired (that is, it faces a perfectly elastic labor supply curve). Assume, however, that the firm is selling its output in a noncompetitive product market and therefore must lower price in order to sell additional output.

Recall that **marginal revenue product** is the increase in revenue attributable to the hiring of an additional unit of labor. Equivalently, it is equal to the marginal product of the additional labor times the marginal revenue of the output (MR):

$$MRP = MP_l \times MR$$

If product markets are competitive (as we assumed in the previous chapter), the marginal revenue from selling an additional unit of output is simply the price

YOUR TURN

THE MRP AND LABOR SUPPLY SCHEDULES OF THE PRECEDING YOUR TURN ARE COMBINED BELOW:

NUMBER OF WORKERS	MRP	WAGE
1	$8.00	$5.00
2	7.50	5.50
3	7.00	6.00
4	6.50	6.50
5	6.00	7.00
6	5.50	7.50

AN ASSUMPTION OF THIS LABOR SUPPLY SCHEDULE IS THAT THE MONOPSONIST IS FREE TO SET ANY WAGE IT CHOOSES. BUT SUPPOSE THE MONOPSONIST IS NOW CONFRONTED WITH A MINIMUM WAGE OF $6.50.

A. CONSTRUCT THE MONOPSONIST'S NEW LABOR SUPPLY SCHEDULE, GIVEN THE CONSTRAINT THAT IT MUST PAY EACH WORKER A WAGE OF AT LEAST $6.50.

B. CONSTRUCT THE MFC SCHEDULE ASSOCIATED WITH THIS NEW LABOR SUPPLY SCHEDULE.

C. GIVEN A MINIMUM WAGE OF $6.50, WHAT LEVEL OF EMPLOYMENT SATISFIES THE MONOPSONIST'S RULE FOR PROFIT MAXIMIZATION?

D. GIVEN YOUR ANSWER TO C, WHAT WAGE MUST THE MONOPSONIST PAY IN ORDER TO MAXIMIZE PROFIT?

E. DOES THE MINIMUM WAGE CAUSE THE MONOPSONIST TO INCREASE OR DECREASE THE LEVEL OF EMPLOYMENT? (HOW DOES YOUR ANSWER TO C COMPARE TO YOUR ANSWER TO B IN THE PRECEDING YOUR TURN?)

received. Therefore, in competitive product markets MRP can be rewritten as $MP_l \times P$.

In contrast, in noncompetitive product markets $MR < P$, as we observed in Chapters 26 and 27. Multiplying both sides of the inequality by MP_l, we have:

$$MP_l \times MR < MP_l \times P$$

This has important implications. It says that marginal revenue product is lower for a firm with monopoly power than for an otherwise similar firm that sells in a perfectly competitive product market. This is illustrated in Figure 31.3. For a given marginal product schedule, MRP_c depicts the MRP curve when the output market is competitive ($MR = P$) and MRP_m shows the corresponding MRP curve when the firm has monopoly power ($MR < P$).[4]

---

[4]The marginal revenue product of a firm in a competitive product market—what we have labeled MRP_c—is sometimes called the *value of marginal product*.

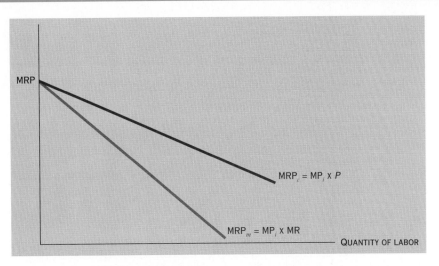

MRP$_c$ denotes the marginal revenue product curve of a competitive firm—one that faces a fixed output price. MRP$_m$ depicts the marginal revenue product curve of an otherwise identical firm that sells its output in a noncompetitive product market. Because the noncompetitive firm must lower price to sell additional output, the firm's marginal revenue is less than price. For this reason, the firm's marginal revenue product curve is steeper and lies leftward of the competitive firm's marginal revenue product curve.

FIGURE 31.3

Not only does MRP$_m$ lie leftward of MRP$_c$, it is also steeper (less elastic). For a firm selling in a competitive product market, MRP slopes downward for only one reason—as additional labor is hired the marginal product of labor declines. But for a firm selling in a noncompetitive product market, marginal revenue also declines—because the firm must lower price to sell the additional output. This further lessens labor's contribution to revenue, causing MRP to fall more precipitously than if the product market had been competitive.

The shape and location of a firm's MRP curve become important when considering how much labor the firm must hire in order to maximize profit. Assuming the firm faces a fixed wage rate, the firm should hire labor up to the point where:

$$MRP = W$$

Because MRP$_m$ < MRP$_c$, a monopolist (or any other firm able to influence product price) hires less labor than a perfectly competitive firm with the same marginal product schedule. This is illustrated in Figure 31.4 (page 818). A monopolist hires up to the point where MRP$_m$ = W; the competitive firm continues to hire until MRP$_c$ = W. In other words, *monopoly power in the product market leads to lower employment in the labor market.* This should come as no surprise. In comparing monopoly with perfect competition, we previously observed that the monopolist restricts output in order to drive up price and profit. Because the monopolist produces less output it hires less labor.

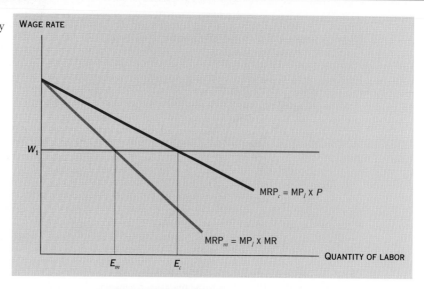

Given wage W_1, a perfectly competitive firm hires an amount of labor equal to E_c. A monopolist having the same MP_l schedule hires only E_m labor.

FIGURE 31.4

The General Rule For Hiring: MRP = MFC

We have addressed the firm's hiring decisions in different settings, based on whether product and labor markets are competitive or noncompetitive. As it turns out, there is a general rule that applies in each case—regardless of the type of market in which the firm operates: To maximize profit, a firm should hire up to the point where

$$MRP = MFC$$

The cost of hiring an additional unit of labor (marginal factor cost) should equal the revenue contributed by that unit (marginal revenue product). Even though this rule is perfectly general, the values of MRP and MFC depend on the nature of the product and labor markets.

The model of the preceding chapter was a special case in which both product and labor markets were competitive. Because the labor market was competitive, the wage rate did not change as the firm hired additional labor. Rather, the cost of another worker was simply the wage that must be paid to that worker:

$$MFC = W$$

Because the product market was competitive, the marginal revenue of additional output was equal to the output price and, consequently

$$MRP = MP_l \times P$$

As shown in this chapter, when a firm has monopoly power in the labor market

$$MFC > W$$

TABLE 31.1

HOW MONOPOLY POWER AFFECTS MRP, MFC, WAGE RATES, AND EMPLOYMENT		
	PERFECTLY COMPETITIVE PRODUCT MARKET	**NONCOMPETITIVE PRODUCT MARKET**
Perfectly competitive labor market	$MRP = MP_l \times P$ $MFC = W$	$MRP < MP_l \times P*$ $MFC = W$
Noncompetitive labor market (monopsony)	$MRP = MP_l \times P$ $MFC > W**$	$MRP < MP_l \times P*$ $MFC > W**$

*Compared to perfect competition in the product market, $MRP < MP_l \times P$ leads to reduced employment.
**Compared to perfect competition in the labor market, $MFC > W$ leads to reduced employment and a lower wage rate.

When monopoly power exists in the product market

$$MRP < MP_l \times P$$

In either case—whether monopoly arises in the labor market or the product market—the result is a lower level of employment (see Table 31.1). When monopoly power exists in the labor market, the wage rate is also reduced. In contrast, monopoly power in the product market has no effect on the wage a firm must pay.

Shifts In Labor Demand

A firm's labor demand curve is drawn on the basis of certain conditions. When these conditions change, so does the firm's labor demand curve.

PRODUCT DEMAND

As you learned in Chapter 30, demand for labor is a derived demand, based on demand for the product the firm is producing. When product demand increases, leading to higher levels of production, demand for labor also rises (shifts rightward). In technical terms: an increase in product demand increases marginal revenue and consequently MRP. Likewise, a decline in product demand lowers MRP.

MARGINAL PRODUCTIVITY OF LABOR

Companies respond to a change in labor productivity by buying either more or less labor, depending on whether marginal product rises or falls. Although workers can increase their productivity by investing in human capital, labor productivity also depends on factors over which the worker has no control. Workers generally interact with other inputs (for example, capital). A change in the quantity or quality of capital is likely to change the marginal product schedule of labor and, with it, the demand for labor. Whether labor demand falls or rises depends on whether capital and labor are **substitute inputs** or **complementary inputs**.

Assume a company increases its use of capital, perhaps because of technological advance raising the productivity of capital or perhaps because the price of capital has been reduced. If capital can be substituted for labor, the company may reduce its demand for labor. For example, increased use of industrial robots has reduced demand for welders and spray painters. Likewise, demand for farm labor has declined sharply in the United States as farmers substituted combines, mechanical cotton pickers, and other machinery for labor.

In other cases, capital and labor are complements. Here firms respond to increased capital usage by demanding more workers. For example, an increase in the number of computers can be expected to increase demand for computer programmers, data processors, and computer repair workers. An increase in commercial airplanes is likely to increase demand for pilots, flight attendants, and mechanics.

SUBSTITUTE INPUTS
Inputs that are substitutes in production: an increase in the price of one increases demand for the other.

COMPLEMENTARY INPUTS
Inputs that are complements in production: an increase in the price of one reduces demand for the other.

Multiple Inputs

We have been focusing on the demand for labor even though firms often hire other variable inputs. In the long run, when capital is variable, firms simultaneously adjust quantities of both capital and labor. Even in the short run a company may hire different types of labor (for example, skilled and unskilled). We now consider input demand when a firm hires more than one variable input. We address two questions: (a) What combination of inputs enables the firm to produce a given level of output at the lowest cost? (b) How much of each input should the firm hire in order to maximize profit? We take up these questions first for competitive and then for noncompetitive factor markets.

MINIMIZING COSTS WHEN FACTOR MARKETS ARE COMPETITIVE

The total cost of producing a given output is minimized when the marginal product of the last unit of each input hired is proportional to the input's price. If capital (k) and labor (l) are the inputs, the cost-minimizing rule is to hire inputs until

$$\frac{MP_k}{P_k} = \frac{MP_l}{P_l}$$

In other words, the marginal product per dollar is the same for each input. Alternatively, this expression can be rewritten as

$$\frac{MP_k}{MP_l} = \frac{P_k}{P_l}$$

Costs are minimized when the ratio of marginal products equals the ratio of input prices.

To understand why this condition minimizes the costs of producing a given level of output, consider what happens when the condition does not hold. In particular, suppose the firm chooses a combination of capital and labor for which $(MP_k/P_k) > (MP_l/P_l)$. This implies that the last dollar spent on capital contributes more to output than does the last dollar spent on labor. At the margin, capital has a bigger bang per buck than labor. This tells the firm that it should buy more capital and less labor. By substituting capital for labor, the firm can increase its output without spending any more on inputs. In a similar vein, if $(MP_l/P_l) > (MP_k/P_k)$, the firm can costlessly increase output by substituting labor for capital. Only when $(MP_k/P_k) = (MP_l/P_l)$ does the firm get the most output for its money. Only then is it purchasing the optimal mix of inputs.

The same logic applies when more than two inputs are used. Given inputs 1 through n, the firm should buy quantities of each so that

$$\frac{MP_1}{P_1} = \frac{MP_2}{P_2} = \ldots = \frac{MP_n}{P_n}$$

COST MINIMIZATION—AN APPLICATION[5] As farmers know, fertilizer can increase corn yields. Two fertilizers often applied are nitrogen and phosphorous. Their exact contribution to corn yields depends on how much of each is used and on soil conditions. In an experiment on Ida Silt loam in western Iowa, different amounts of these fertilizers were applied to different plots of land. Corn yields were then estimated as a function of the amounts of nitrogen and phosphorous applied. Table 31.2 lists some of the combinations of nitrogen and phosphorous that resulted in a yield of 130 bushels per acre.[6] Also presented in Table 31.2 is the ratio of the marginal products for each combination of fertilizer.

ALTERNATIVE WAYS TO PRODUCE CORN YIELDS OF 130 POUNDS PER ACRE

POUNDS OF NITROGEN	POUNDS OF PHOSPHOROUS	MP OF NITROGEN/ MP OF PHOSPHOROUS
186	228	5
190	211	2
195	207	13/9
207	195	1/2
215	193	1/5

SOURCE: Earl Heady, John Pesek, William Brown, and John Doll, "Crop Response Surfaces and Economic Optima in Fertilizer Use," Chapter 14, in Earl Heady and John Dillon, *Agricultural Production Functions* (Ames, Iowa: Iowa State University Press, 1961), Table 14.11. Reprinted by permission. © 1961 by Iowa State University Press.

TABLE 31.2

[5]This section is based on Earl Heady, John Pesek, William Brown, and John Doll, "Crop Response Surfaces and Economic Optima in Fertilizer Use," Chapter 14, in Earl Heady and John Dillon, *Agricultural Production Functions* (Ames, IA: Iowa State University Press, 1961).

[6]Nitrogen was applied in the form of ammonium nitrate and phosphorous in the form of triple superphosphate. Thus, the numbers in Table 31.2 measure the pounds of ammonium nitrate and triple superphosphate per acre.

Such information tells corn farmers in western Iowa how to achieve yields of 130 pounds per acre at the lowest possible cost. Cost minimization requires that marginal product ratios equal input price ratios. When nitrogen costs five times as much per pound as phosphorous, cost minimization requires that the marginal product of nitrogen be five times as great as the marginal product of phosphorous. This condition is met when the farmer applies 186 pounds of nitrogen per acre and 228 pounds of phosphorous (line 1, Table 31.2). When nitrogen costs twice as much as phosphorous, the least-cost combination is 190 pounds of nitrogen and 211 pounds of phosphorous (line 2). More generally, information on marginal products tells a producer how to vary input ratios in response to changing input prices.

MAXIMIZING PROFIT WHEN FACTOR MARKETS ARE COMPETITIVE

Maximizing profit requires not just producing a given output at the lowest possible cost; the firm must also choose the appropriate level of output. When a company produces too much output or too little output it does not maximize profits, even if that output is produced using the optimal combination of inputs.

We previously showed that the firm should hire labor until its MRP equals the price of labor. More generally, profit maximization requires that the MRP of each input equals the price of that input. When capital and labor are the inputs, the conditions for profit maximization are

$$MP_l \times MR = P_l$$
$$MP_k \times MR = P_k$$

where MR denotes the marginal revenue of output. These conditions can be rewritten as

$$\frac{MP_l}{P_l} = \frac{1}{MR}$$
$$\frac{MP_k}{P_k} = \frac{1}{MR}$$

For more than two inputs, the rule can be stated as

$$\frac{MP_1}{P_1} = \frac{MP_2}{P_2} = \ldots = \frac{MP_n}{P_n} = \frac{1}{MR}$$

As the preceding equations indicate, the conditions for profit maximization are stronger than the conditions for minimizing the costs of producing a given output. Not only must the marginal product of each input be proportional to the input price, but for each input the ratio of marginal product to input price must equal the reciprocal of the marginal revenue of output.

To understand the significance of this latter condition, assume that $MP_l/P_l = MP_k/P_k > 1/MR$. Although the firm is producing its output at the lowest possible cost (since $MP_l/P_l = MP_k/P_k$), it is not maximizing profit. In particular, the firm is producing too little output. The last units of labor and capital both contribute more to revenue than to costs ($MP_l \times MR > P_l$ and $MP_k \times MR > P_k$). Therefore, to maximize profits, the firm must hire more of both inputs and expand its production. Conversely, if $MP_l/P_l = MP_k/P_k < 1/MR$ the firm is producing too much output and, consequently, must reduce its use of labor and capital if it is to maximize profits.

Where product markets are competitive, the rule for profit maximization can be restated as

$$\frac{MP_1}{P_1} = \frac{MP_2}{P_2} = \ldots = \frac{MP_n}{P_n} = \frac{1}{P}$$

where P is the output price. Because marginal revenue equals price in competitive output markets, the reciprocal of marginal revenue equals the reciprocal of price.

Multiple Inputs

ASSUME YOU HIRE BOTH SKILLED AND UNSKILLED LABOR. THEIR MARGINAL PRODUCTS ARE THREE AND TWO, RESPECTIVELY. SKILLED LABOR COSTS $9 PER UNIT; UNSKILLED LABOR COSTS $6. YOUR OUTPUT SELLS IN A COMPETITIVE PRODUCT MARKET FOR A PRICE OF $2 PER UNIT. ARE YOU HIRING THE PROFIT-MAXIMIZING AMOUNTS OF LABOR? IF NOT, SHOULD YOU HIRE MORE OR LESS SKILLED LABOR? SHOULD YOU INCREASE OR DECREASE THE AMOUNT OF UNSKILLED LABOR? EXPLAIN YOUR ANSWERS.

PROFIT MAXIMIZATION—AN APPLICATION Let us return to the Iowa corn farmers who must determine how much nitrogen and phosphorous to apply to their fields. Because the price of corn is fixed for individual farmers, the rule for profit maximization can be expressed as follows:

$$\frac{MP_{nit}}{P_{nit}} = \frac{MP_{phos}}{P_{phos}} = \frac{1}{P_{corn}}$$

Optimal input use depends on the prices of both inputs and output. Suppose nitrogen costs $.18 per pound and phosphorous costs $.12 per pound. If corn sells for $2.00 per bushel, the condition for profit maximization is

$$\frac{MP_{nit}}{\$.18} = \frac{MP_{phos}}{\$.12} = \frac{1}{\$2.00}$$

The farmer should continue applying fertilizer until the marginal product of the last pound of nitrogen is 0.09 bushel of corn and the marginal product of the last pound of phosphorous is 0.06 bushel of corn. (These are the numbers for which the preceding equalities hold.) Based on estimated marginal product schedules, these conditions are satisfied when the farmer applies 185 pounds of nitrogen per acre and 190 pounds of phosphorous.[7]

---

[7]This example is taken from Heady, Pesek, Brown, and Doll, same as 5, Table 14.8.

More generally, when marginal product schedules are known, producers can adjust input usage until the conditions for profit maximization are met. The theory of optimal input use is not some idle theory. As the preceding application indicates, it helps farmers and other producers make important economic decisions.

HIRING MULTIPLE INPUTS IN NONCOMPETITIVE FACTOR MARKETS

In the case of monopsony, the price of an input no longer coincides with marginal factor cost. Therefore, the conditions for combining inputs must be modified. For example, when labor and capital are the variable inputs, the condition for minimizing the cost of a given output is

$$\frac{MP_l}{MFC_l} = \frac{MP_k}{MFC_k}$$

The requirement for maximizing profit can be expressed as

$$\frac{MP_l}{MFC_l} = \frac{MP_k}{MFC_k} = \frac{1}{MR}$$

The Marginal Productivity Theory of Income Distribution

The theory of factor pricing in competitive markets is called marginal productivity theory—to emphasize that the demand for a factor is based on its marginal product. However, this title is misleading in the sense that it gives top billing to demand. As you are aware, in competitive factor markets an input's price is determined by supply as well as demand. Marginal productivity theory tells firms how much labor to hire in order to maximize profits. Beyond that, it predicts how income will be distributed.

In competitive factor markets, profit maximization requires companies to hire labor up to the point where wage equals marginal revenue product. Because marginal productivity theory applies equally to nonlabor inputs, this proposition can be generalized: Each factor receives a payment equal to its marginal revenue product. Thus, according to the **marginal productivity theory of income distribution**, income payments are based on the contribution to revenue of the last unit of a factor hired. Inputs whose marginal contribution to revenue is high receive high incomes; those that contribute less are paid less. Although some find this conclusion reassuring, the marginal productivity theory of income distribution has been widely attacked. Two criticisms frequently are raised.

MARGINAL PRODUCTIVITY THEORY OF INCOME DISTRIBUTION
The theory that income is distributed to factors of production according to each factor's marginal revenue product. In particular, the theory predicts that each input will be paid an amount equal to its marginal revenue product.

"THE DISTRIBUTION OF INCOME IS NOT JUST"

Is it fair that some people live regally, simply because they inherited property? Should others be condemned to poverty because they were born without wealth and have few labor market skills? What about people unable to work because of their age or some physical or mental disability? Doesn't fundamental justice dictate that all individuals receive at least some minimal income regardless of how much they contribute to output?

Posing questions such as these, some critics attack marginal productivity theory because they don't like its conclusion about how income will be distributed. Some go so far as to say that this theory was created to rationalize the actual distribution of income in capitalistic societies. Such criticisms are invalid. Marginal productivity theory falls within the realm of positive economics. It predicts how income will be distributed but makes no claim that this distribution is best. One can accept marginal productivity theory without denying that the government has the legitimate right to alter the distribution of income through a system of taxes and transfers.

"LABOR MARKETS ARE NOT COMPETITIVE"

Marginal productivity theory predicts how factor payments will be determined in *competitive* factor markets. Some contend that, as elegant as it may be, this theory is irrelevant because factor markets frequently are not competitive. In monopsonistic markets, workers are paid a wage less than their marginal revenue product. At the same time, through policies such as featherbedding, some unions can force companies to pay their members a wage in excess of marginal revenue product. Clearly then, the prediction of marginal productivity theory—that wages equal marginal revenue product—is not always correct. Those who see abundant imperfections in the labor market will be more dubious about the applicability of this theory than those who see the labor market as basically competitive.

Granted that marginal productivity theory does not explain perfectly the distribution of income, most economists believe that it does a pretty fair job—especially in the long run, when competitive forces are at their strongest. Although some embrace alternative models (for example, Marxian economics),[8] most economists contend that marginal productivity theory provides the best framework currently available for explaining how factor incomes are determined.

This does not mean that noncompetitive forces should be ignored. Where appropriate, the competitive model should be modified. For example, in Chapter 32 we introduce discrimination into otherwise competitive labor markets. We analyze the impact of discrimination on pay and productivity and assess the extent to which pay differentials reflect differences in productivity and the extent to which they reflect traits unrelated to productivity. Our argument is not that competitive forces completely determine the distribution of income. It is that, in the opinion of most economists, one cannot satisfactorily explain factor payments without taking into account a factor's marginal productivity.

[8]This is discussed in Chapter 40.

Summary

1. According to marginal productivity theory, demand for a factor of production is based on that factor's marginal product. If the marginal product schedule increases or if output demand rises, demand for the factor increases.

2. To maximize profit a firm should hire labor, or any other factor, up to the point where marginal revenue product equals marginal factor cost.

3. In the case of monopsony there is only one buyer of labor. Therefore, that buyer can influence the price of labor. Compared to the case of perfect competition, monopsony leads both to lower employment and to lower wage rates.

4. Monopoly power in the product market has no effect on wage rates but does reduce employment. Because monopolists restrict industry output, they demand less labor.

5. In competitive labor markets the condition for profit maximization simplifies to $MRP = W$. Because of this, the marginal productivity theory of income distribution predicts that each factor will receive a payment equal to marginal revenue product. This theory makes no claim, however, that this distribution is just or somehow superior to alternative distributions of income.

6. If a firm hires multiple inputs, the total cost of producing a given output is minimized when the ratio of marginal product to marginal factor cost is the same for each input.

7. For a firm to maximize profit, the ratio of marginal product to marginal factor cost for each input should equal the reciprocal of the marginal revenue of output.

Key Terms

monopsonist
marginal factor cost (MFC)
marginal revenue product (MRP)
substitute inputs

complementary inputs
marginal productivity theory
  of income distribution

Study Questions and Problems

1. Draw the labor supply curve for (a) a firm in a perfectly competitive labor market and (b) a monopsonist. Why are the shapes different?

2. Explain how each of the following would affect demand for coal miners. Indicate whether the labor demand curve would increase, decrease, or remain unchanged.
   a. an increase in the demand for coal
   b. an increase in capital, when capital and labor are substitute inputs
   c. an increase in capital, when capital and labor are complementary inputs
   d. a decrease in the wage rate of coal miners

3. The daily labor supply and MRP schedules for Memorial Hospital are depicted below:
   a. What is the marginal factor cost of the second nurse? Does the second nurse contribute more to the hospital's revenues than to its costs?
   b. How many nurses should Memorial Hospital hire in order to maximize profits? What wage will it pay?
   c. Compare the MRP and the wage of a fifth nurse. Why doesn't the hospital hire five nurses?

NUMBER OF NURSES	MRP	WAGE
1	$70	$50
2	68	52
3	66	54
4	64	56
5	62	58
6	60	60

4. Assume nitrogen costs $.05 per pound and phosphorous costs $.10 per pound. Based on information in Table 31.2, what is the least costly way to produce 130 pounds of corn per acre?

5. Assume a company has no control over wage rates: it must pay $12 per hour for skilled labor and $9 per hour for unskilled labor. The marginal product of skilled labor is six and the marginal product of unskilled labor is three. Indicate whether the company is using the optimal input mix, relatively too much skilled labor (and not enough unskilled), or relatively too much unskilled labor (and not enough skilled). Explain how you reached your conclusion.

6. The Ace Card Company operates in perfectly competitive product and labor markets. It hires two types of workers—craftsmen and operatives. Currently, the marginal product of craftsmen is four and the marginal product of operatives is two. Output sells for $4 per unit.
   a. If the company must pay a wage rate of $16 for craftsmen and $8 for operatives, is the company hiring the profit-maximizing amounts of labor? (If not, should the company hire more or less of each?)
   b. Suppose the wage rate for craftsmen falls to $12 and the wage rate for operatives falls to $6. How should the company change the amounts of labor it uses?
   c. What can you conclude about the effect of lower input prices?

7. (a) Does the marginal productivity theory of income distribution claim that factor payments should be based on a factor's contribution to revenue? (b) If we agree that income should be based in part on need, must we reject marginal productivity theory as an explanation of how income is actually determined? Defend your answer.

8. *Bilateral monopoly* refers to the situation where a monopsonist bargains with a union. Here, there is only one buyer of labor, the company, and only one seller of labor, the union. In this setting, the union may be able to limit the ability of the monopsonist to depress wages and employment. That is, employment and wages may more closely approximate the perfectly competitive equilibrium if a monopsonist is restrained by a union. Present this argument in diagrammatic form. First show the labor market outcome for a monopsonist when the firm is not forced to negotiate with a union. Then indicate the union wage rate that would cause employment to rise to the level of a perfectly competitive labor market.

Monopsony

A.

NUMBER OF WORKERS	MFC
1	$ 5
2	6
3	7
4	8
5	9
6	10

B. MRP = MFC = $7 WHEN THREE WORKERS ARE HIRED.

C. WAGE = $6.00 (FROM THE LABOR SUPPLY SCHEDULE).

When a Monopsonist Confronts a Minimum Wage

A.

NUMBER OF WORKERS	WAGE
1	$6.50
2	6.50
3	6.50
4	6.50
5	7.00
6	7.50

B.

NUMBER OF WORKERS	MFC
1	$ 6.50
2	6.50
3	6.50
4	6.50
5	9.00
6	10.00

C. MRP = MFC = $6.50 WHEN FOUR WORKERS ARE HIRED.

D. WAGE = $6.50.

E. THE MINIMUM WAGE CAUSES THE MONOPSONIST TO *INCREASE* THE LEVEL EMPLOYMENT FROM THREE WORKERS (WHEN THERE WAS NO MINIMUM WAGE) TO FOUR WORKERS.

Multiple Inputs

NO. YOU SHOULD CUT BACK ON BOTH SKILLED AND UNSKILLED LABOR. THE LAST UNIT OF EACH CONTRIBUTES LESS TO REVENUE THAN IT COSTS. IN PARTICULAR, $MP_s \times P = 3 \times \$2 = \$6$, WHICH IS LESS THAN THE \$9 COST PER UNIT OF SKILLED LABOR. SIMILARLY, $MP_U \times P = 2 \times \$2 = \$4$, WHICH IS LESS THAN THE \$6 COST PER UNIT OF UNSKILLED LABOR. (ALTERNATIVELY, $MP_s/P_s = MP_U/P_U = 1/3 < 1/P = 1/2$.)

Discrimination and Differences in Labor Market Outcomes

LAST YEAR IN THE UNITED STATES ABOUT TWO-THIRDS OF ALL ADULTS WERE EITHER WORKING OR LOOKING FOR WORK. NOT ALL GROUPS FARED EQUALLY. THE UNEMPLOYMENT RATE OF BLACKS WAS MORE THAN DOUBLE THE UNEMPLOYMENT RATE OF WHITES. AMONG FULL-TIME EMPLOYEES, WOMEN EARNED ROUGHLY $8,000 LESS THAN MEN.

CHAPTER 32 HIGHLIGHTS DIFFERENCES IN LABOR MARKET SUCCESS BY RACE, ETHNICITY, AND GENDER, AND ANALYZES POSSIBLE REASONS FOR THESE DIFFERENCES. AFTER DEFINING CERTAIN ESSENTIAL TERMS, WE ASSESS THE DIVERGENT TRENDS IN MALE AND FEMALE LABOR SUPPLY. WE THEN EXAMINE DIFFERENCES IN PAY AND UNEMPLOYMENT ACROSS GROUPS.

Women's secondary status is at least as striking in the labor market as it is everywhere else. Every standard labor market statistic shows marked differentials on the average between men and women, in both the level of economic participation and the distribution of economic rewards.[1]

[1]Cynthia B. Lloyd and Beth Niemi, *The Economics of Sex Differentials* (New York: Columbia University Press, 1979), p. 1.

Labor Force Participation

MEASURING LABOR FORCE PARTICIPATION

LABOR FORCE
Those individuals who have a job or are looking for one; the number of people employed or unemployed.

The **labor force** comprises all individuals who either have a job or are actively searching for one. Those with jobs are classified as *employed*. Those without jobs but looking for work are counted as *unemployed*. Thus, the labor force consists of all individuals who are either employed or unemployed. Excluded from the labor force are individuals not interested in working as well as those who are interested but, convinced that suitable employment is presently unavailable, are not currently searching for work. A country's population is composed of two mutually exclusive groups: those in the labor force and those not in the labor force.[2] The preceding relationships are illustrated in Figure 32.1 for the population 16 and older.

LABOR FORCE PARTICIPATION RATE
Percentage of the population that is in the labor force:

$$\frac{\text{labor force}}{\text{population}} \times 100$$

One measure of a country's labor supply is its **labor force participation rate**—the percentage of the population that is in the labor force. Based on the numbers in Figure 32.1, the U.S. labor force participation rate for August 1992 can be computed as follows:

$$\frac{127.4 \text{ million}}{191.8 \text{ million}} \times 100 = 66.4 \text{ percent}$$

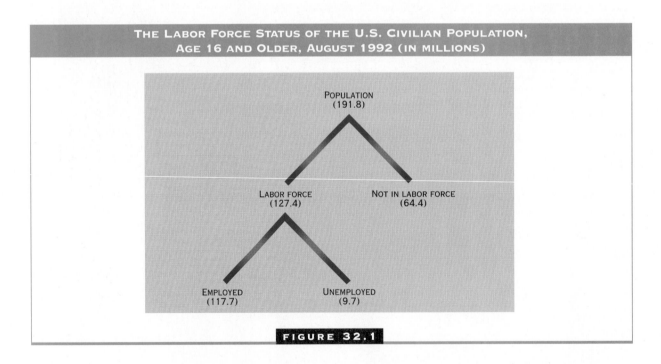

THE LABOR FORCE STATUS OF THE U.S. CIVILIAN POPULATION, AGE 16 AND OLDER, AUGUST 1992 (IN MILLIONS)

POPULATION (191.8)

LABOR FORCE (127.4)

NOT IN LABOR FORCE (64.4)

EMPLOYED (117.7)

UNEMPLOYED (9.7)

FIGURE 32.1

---

[2]Actually, there are two population and labor force series—one limited to civilians, the other including members of the armed forces. The numbers presented here refer to the more widely used civilian series.

LABOR FORCE PARTICIPATION BY GENDER

In addition to this country's aggregate labor force participation rate, the United States Department of Labor also publishes separate labor force participation series by gender. Females have a lower labor force participation rate than males, but this difference has been narrowing over time (see Table 32.1 and Figure 32.2, page 834). Labor force participation of males fell from 86 percent in 1900 to 74 percent in 1990. This primarily reflects the fact that men have been retiring earlier and living longer. Thus, the share of the male population 65 and older has risen over time and the labor force participation rate of this group, which was already low, has dropped sharply. Both effects have depressed the overall labor force participation rate of men.

Labor force participation of women has moved in the opposite direction. At the turn of the century, only one in five women was in the labor force. By 1980, the figure was one in two, and today a clear majority of women are either working or looking for work. Although labor force participation has increased for all groups of women, the fastest growth has been among married women.

This explosion in the labor supply of women has occurred worldwide, not just in the United States (see Table 32.2, page 835). It has accelerated economic growth and increased our standard of living. Many consider it to be "the most revolutionary change taking place in the labor market."[3]

LABOR FORCE PARTICIPATION RATES, 1900–1990*

YEAR	MALES	MALES, AGED 65 AND OLDER	FEMALES	MARRIED FEMALES
1900	85.7	63.1	20.0	5.6
1920	84.6	55.6	22.7	9.0
1930	82.1	54.0	23.6	11.7
1940	79.1	41.8	25.8	15.6
1950	81.6	41.4	29.9	23.0
1960	80.4	30.5	35.7	31.7
1970	76.6	24.8	41.4	40.2
1980	75.1	19.3	49.9	49.3
1990	74.4	17.6	56.8	N/A**

*Data for 1950 and later refer to the population 16 and older; earlier figures refer to 14 and older.
**N/A = not available.
SOURCES: U.S. Bureau of the Census, *Historical Statistics of the United States, Colonial Times to 1970* (1975); *1980 Census of the Population, General Social and Economic Characteristics, United States Summary* (1983); *1990 Census of Population and Housing*, CPH-L-80 (1992).

TABLE 32.1

---

[3]Ronald Ehrenberg and Robert Smith, *Modern Labor Economics*, 4th ed. (New York: HarperCollins, 1991), p. 175.

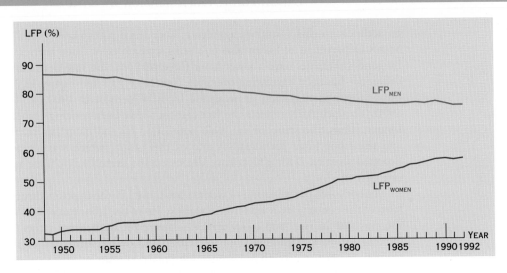

*Data for 1992 are for first eight months only.

SOURCE: U.S. Bureau of Labor Statistics.

FIGURE 32.2

WHY HAS FEMALE PARTICIPATION INCREASED?

Researchers have studied this phenomenon extensively and offered various explanations for it. Among the most frequently cited factors are lower birth rates, higher wages, the emergence of labor-saving devices, an improving job distribution, and a change in attitudes.[4]

The U.S. birthrate (births per population) has fallen throughout most of this century, especially over the past 40 years. According to a companion statistic, the *fertility rate*, the estimated births per female declined from 3.5 in the 1950s to 1.8 in the 1980s. Children, especially young children, inhibit labor force participation of women. Therefore, the reduction in number of children has opened the door for women to spend more time in the labor force.

The decision to work also depends on the compensation one receives. Research strongly indicates that higher wages attract additional women into the labor market. Since World War II, wages of women have been rising an average of 1.5 percent per year above and beyond the inflation rate. Responding to this growing compensation, more and more women are entering the job market and staying. According to two experts, the increased wages of women combined with their reduced fertility explain nearly 60 percent of the growth in female labor force participation since 1950.[5]

[4]These explanations are not totally independent. As wages of women have increased over time, the opportunity cost of withdrawing from the labor force to raise a family has increased. Therefore, higher wages have contributed to the decline in the birthrate.

[5]James P. Smith and Michael P. Ward, "Time-Series Growth in the Female Labor Force," *Journal of Labor Economics* (January 1985, Supplement), p. 89.

LABOR FORCE PARTICIPATION OF WOMEN BY COUNTRY				
	ALL WOMEN		MARRIED WOMEN	
COUNTRY	1960	1980	1960	1980
Australia	29.5	55.4	19.2	50.8
Britain	43.4	62.3	33.7	57.2
France	44.5	57.0	35.6	52.6
Germany	46.5	56.2	36.5	54.4
Israel	29.0	39.2	25.7	43.5
Italy	35.2	39.9	18.5	35.4
Japan	47.7	52.7	36.0	41.9
Spain	22.7	33.2	N/A	26.0
Sweden	51.0	76.9	43.1	75.6
USSR	77.4	88.2	N/A	N/A

N/A = not available.
SOURCE: Jacob Mincer, "Intercountry Comparison of Labor Force Trends and of Related Developments," *Journal of Labor Economics* (Chicago: University of Chicago Press, January 1985, Supplement), Table 1. Reprinted by permission.

TABLE 32.2

Other factors are also important, but their contributions are difficult to quantify. Attitudes concerning women in the workplace have progressed and job opportunities have improved. Some researchers emphasize the emergence of a large clerical sector early this century and, more recently, the rapid growth in service, retail trade, and other traditionally female jobs. Part-time employment has increased relative to full-time employment, making it easier for women to both work and meet other commitments. Microwaves, dishwashers, and other modern appliances allow work at home to be accomplished more quickly. Families also save time by eating out more frequently and making greater use of dry cleaning, day care, and other services. The result is more time available for work outside the home.

In summary, a rising wage has increased the incentive to work, while factors such as reduced fertility, time-saving innovations, and increased availability of part-time work have provided women with greater opportunities to work. The result has been a tendency to substitute work in the labor market for work at home. Because work at home is not counted as labor force activity, the switch from home to market has corresponded to an increase in the labor force participation of women.

YOUR TURN

Labor Force Participation

HOW WOULD EACH OF THE FOLLOWING AFFECT LABOR FORCE PARTICIPATION?

A. INCREASING THE FERTILITY RATE

B. REDUCING THE COST OF WORKING THROUGH SUBSIDIZED DAY CARE

C. POSTPONING ELIGIBILITY FOR SOCIAL SECURITY RETIREMENT BENEFITS (FOR EXAMPLE, FROM AGE 62 TO AGE 67)

D. INCREASING THE WAGES OF WOMEN

E. REDEFINING THE LABOR FORCE TO INCLUDE UNPAID HOMEMAKERS

The Lord spoke to Moses and said, Speak to the Israelites in these words: When a man makes a special vow to the Lord which requires your valuation of living persons, a male between twenty and sixty years old shall be valued at fifty silver shekels. . . . If it is a female, she shall be valued at thirty shekels.[6]

—Leviticus 27:1–4

Since the time of Moses, the economic plight of women has been inferior to that of men. One reason women tend to earn less than men is that they are more likely to work part-time or part-year. But even if we restrict ourselves to full-time year-round workers, annual data indicate that women are paid just over 70 percent as much as men. That is, they experience a **pay gap** of almost 30 percent. Data on weekly earnings tell a similar story [see Table 32.3, columns (A) and (B)]. The lower earnings of women depress their labor force participation, increase poverty among

PAY GAP

The difference in pay between two groups, traditionally specified in percentage terms.

	FEMALE EARNINGS AS A PERCENTAGE OF MALE EARNINGS, FULL-TIME EMPLOYEES		
YEAR	(A) ANNUAL EARNINGS	(B) WEEKLY EARNINGS	(C) HOURLY EARNINGS
1939	58.1	N/A	N/A
1960	60.8	N/A	N/A
1965	60.0	N/A	N/A
1967	57.8	62.4	68.8
1970	59.4	62.3	68.7
1975	58.8	62.0	67.7
1980	60.2	63.4	69.1
1981	59.2	64.6	70.4
1982	61.7	65.0	70.7
1983	63.6	65.6	71.3
1984	63.7	67.8	74.0
1985	64.6	68.2	74.2
1986	64.3	69.2	75.3
1987	65.0	70.0	76.3
1988	66.0	70.2	76.7
1989	68.5	70.1	76.3
1990	71.1	71.8	78.2
1991	N/A	74.0	80.3

N/A = not available.
SOURCES: Median annual earnings of year-round full-time employees are from the U.S. Bureau of Census; median weekly earnings of full-time employees are from the U.S. Bureau of Labor Statistics. Hourly earnings are computed by dividing the weekly earnings of full-time workers by their average weekly hours.

TABLE 32.3

[6]The full passage indicates that the higher "valuation" of males is based on their greater ability to pay (wages).

female-headed families, and raise concerns about equity. These pay differences demand an explanation.

After tackling the pay-gap issue, we analyze the data in Table 32.3, which suggest that the relative earnings of women have improved since the mid-1970s. Is this upturn transitory, or is it a sign of real progress by women?

WHY DO WOMEN EARN LESS THAN MEN?

HOURS WORKED   One reason women earn less than men is that they work fewer hours. Within the class of full-time employees—defined by the U.S. Department of Labor as those working 35 or more hours per week—men typically work an extra 3.5 to 4 hours per week. For example, in 1991, male full-time employees averaged 44.9 hours per week compared to 41.4 hours for female full-time employees. Part of the higher weekly pay of men is compensation for extra hours of work. In particular, for every additional $100 earned by a male, more than $20 is payment for the extra hours worked. When measured on an hourly basis, the earnings of women move closer to the earnings of men [see Table 32.3, column (C)].

HUMAN CAPITAL   Because of their higher labor force participation, men tend to have more years of experience than women. Not only do they have more total experience, they generally have greater experience on their present job. The typical man has spent five years with his current employer, the typical woman less than four years. Furthermore, on average men have completed twice as much job training as women.[7] Men also have slightly higher educational attainment. In 1990, 25 percent of men 25 and older had completed at least four years of college compared to 19 percent of women.

According to the theory of human capital, a worker's productivity and therefore earnings depend on the worker's human capital. Men, by virtue of their greater human capital, earn more than women. One commonly cited study found that differences in education, training, and other work history accounted for 40 percent of the pay gap between white men and women.[8] Other studies put the figure slightly lower. Altogether, differences in human capital and in hours worked appear to explain approximately one-half of the male/female pay gap.

OCCUPATION AND LEVEL OF WORK   As Table 32.4 (page 838) reflects, men and women are distributed unevenly across jobs. Women account for nearly 100 percent of all dental hygienists but just 10 percent of all dentists. They comprise 86 percent of the elementary school teachers but only 41 percent of college faculty. About 99 percent of secretaries are women, but less than 1 percent of automobile mechanics. The uneven job distribution is important because women tend to be concentrated in low-paying jobs, men in high-paying jobs.

---

[7]U.S. Bureau of Labor Statistics, "Employee Tenure and Occupational Mobility in the Early 1990s," USDL 92–386 (June 1992); Greg J. Duncan and Saul Hoffman, "On-the-Job Training and Earnings Differences by Race and Sex," *Review of Economics and Statistics* (November 1979), pp. 594–603.

[8]Mary Corcoran and Greg J. Duncan, "Work History, Labor Force Attachment, and Earnings Differences between Races and Sexes," *Journal of Human Resources* (Winter 1979), pp. 3–20.

OCCUPATION	PERCENT FEMALE
Dental hygienists	99.8
Secretaries	99.0
Receptionists	97.1
Child-care workers	96.0
Household cleaners and servants	95.8
Registered nurses	94.8
Dressmakers	93.3
Bank tellers	90.3
Telephone operators	89.2
Elementary school teachers	85.9
College and university teachers	40.8
Physicians	20.1
Dentists	10.1
Engineers	8.2
Airplane pilots and navigators	3.4
Heavy-truck drivers	2.5
Firefighters	1.4
Carpenters	1.3
Plumbers	1.0
Tool and die makers	0.8
Automobile mechanics	0.8
Brick and stone masons	0.2

SOURCE: U.S. Bureau of Labor Statistics, *Employment and Earnings* (January 1992), pp. 185–190.

TABLE 32.4

Not only is this true for broad occupational categories, it also holds for detailed classifications within an occupation. When accounting work is broken down into five levels, data indicate that 46 percent of entry-level accountants are women but only 5 percent of senior accountants (see Table 32.5). Similarly, women are largely concentrated at the bottom rungs of the attorney, personnel, and drafting positions. Even though *at each level* women earn 90–103 percent as much as men, within the broader occupational categories they earn substantially less—because of their unfavorable distribution within each occupation. A good part of the lower earnings of women can be attributed to the fact that women are concentrated in the low-paying occupations and, within a given occupation, in the lower positions.

This explanation is incomplete, however, because it begs the question of why women generally hold inferior jobs. On that topic a debate rages: to what extent is the different job distribution of men and women caused by discrimination, and to what extent does it reflect nondiscriminatory factors, such as differences in the preferences of men and women?

Even in a world without labor market discrimination, the distribution of jobs would differ. To begin with, culture and socialization each play a role. Surveys indicate that women place less emphasis on monetary rewards than do men and are more interested in nurturing and helping others. Consistent with these preferences, women are more likely to be in such fields as health care, social work, and primary

THE DISTRIBUTION OF WOMEN WITHIN FOUR OCCUPATIONAL CATEGORIES, 1981

OCCUPATION AND LEVEL	AVERAGE MONTHLY SALARY	FEMALE PAY AS A PERCENT OF MALE PAY	FEMALE WORKERS AS A PERCENT OF ALL WORKERS
Accountant I	$1,377	99	46
Accountant II	1,679	98	34
Accountant III	1,962	96	19
Accountant IV	2,402	95	11
Accountant V	2,928	90	5
All accountants		83	23
Attorney I	1,873	103	28
Attorney II	2,338	99	24
Attorney III	3,031	95	13
Attorney IV	3,738	94	9
All attorneys		78	15
Personnel I*	2,321	101	21
Personnel II*	2,933	94	10
Personnel III*	3,574	90	7
All personnel		87	13
Drafter I	923	103	34
Drafter II	1,075	101	26
Drafter III	1,301	96	18
Drafter IV	1,611	94	8
All drafters		82	13

*Director of personnel.
SOURCE: Adapted from Mark S. Sieling, "Staffing Patterns Prominent in Female–Male Earnings Gap," *Monthly Labor Review* (June 1984), pp. 29–33.

TABLE 32.5

education. In addition, women disproportionately choose fields requiring a lesser degree of mathematical ability (for example, the humanities rather than the physical sciences).[9]

Job choice is also influenced by family responsibilities, which have been shouldered disproportionately by women. Because of such responsibilities, women are more likely than men to place restrictions on hours of work and to limit themselves to jobs that are close to home. They are also less likely to relocate. Such restrictions limit the choice of jobs.[10]

[9]Thomas N. Daymont and Paul J. Andrisani, "Why Women Earn Less Than Men: The Case of Recent College Graduates," *Industrial Relations Research Association, Proceedings of the Thirty-Fifth Annual Meeting* (1983), pp. 429–430; Morton Paglin and Anthony Rufolo, "Heterogeneous Human Capital, Occupational Choice, and Male–Female Earnings Differences," *Journal of Labor Economics* (January 1990), pp. 123–144.
[10]Beth Niemi, "Geographic Immobility and Labor Force Mobility: A Study of Female Unemployment," in Cynthia B. Lloyd, ed., *Sex, Discrimination, and the Division of Labor* (New York: Columbia University Press, 1975), pp. 61–89.

Finally, according to human capital theory, women choose different jobs than men because of differences in their expected work lives. Individuals expecting to work a relatively short time find it unprofitable to incur the heavy investments necessary to enter certain occupations (for example, medicine, law, higher education). Instead, they choose occupations requiring less human capital. Similarly, those expecting to withdraw temporarily from the labor force have an incentive to avoid areas (such as engineering and the physical sciences) where one's skills quickly deteriorate upon withdrawal from the labor force. Rather, they gravitate toward fields subject to less obsolescence (for example, the fine arts and humanities).

Because women, on average, have shorter work lives than men and a greater tendency to withdraw from the labor force,[11] they choose different occupations than men—generally those requiring less human capital and having lower rates of obsolescence. Consistent with this view, studies show that occupational choice does depend on one's expected work life.[12] Taking this argument a step further, to the extent women have less human capital within a given occupation, they are more likely to be in the lower-level positions within that occupation. Thus, human capital theory offers an explanation for the inferior job distribution of women.

A competing school of thought argues that human capital is less important than discrimination in explaining occupational distribution. First of all, differences in human capital may themselves result from discrimination. For example, employers may train men for a certain position, but not women. Beyond that, doors are sometimes shut to women regardless of their human capital. Until 1967, when it was sued, Southern Bell Telephone Company had not permitted any woman to work as a switchman. Instead, women had been assigned to lower-paying occupations, such as telephone operator. Similarly, some banks have traditionally hired men and women for different jobs. A woman may be hired as a teller, whereas a man with similar education and experience is hired as a loan officer.

Other positions have requirements—often of questionable validity—that all applicants must be a certain minimum height or be able to lift a minimum weight. Because women are less likely to meet these requirements, many find their paths into these occupations blocked. To the extent women are denied access to certain higher-paying occupations, their job distribution is neither voluntary nor consistent with maximum earnings.

According to the **theory of occupational crowding**,[13] women are crowded into certain occupations, resulting in low wages there (see Figure 32.3A). In contrast, restricting the supply of labor into male-intensive occupations leads to high wages in those occupations (see Figure 32.3B). From an economic perspective, the optimal means of ending this type of discrimination is to break down barriers to entry, ensuring that women have the same access to jobs as do men. Some groups, however, advocate a different approach, **comparable worth**, which would force

THEORY OF OCCUPATIONAL CROWDING

A theory that the lower wages of women (or minority workers) result from their being denied entrance into certain high-paying occupations and, instead, their being crowded into other occupations, thereby depressing wages in those occupations.

COMPARABLE WORTH

A doctrine that each job has an intrinsic value, independent of labor supply and demand, and that jobs with similar intrinsic values have similar (comparable) worth.

---

[11]In 1950, the expected work life (number of years in the labor force) was 15 years for young women and 41 years for young men. By 1980, the difference had narrowed, but young men still could be expected to work 10 more years than young women (37 years versus 27). See Shirley Smith, "Revised Worklife Tables," *Monthly Labor Review* (August 1985), Table 3.

[12]Solomon Polachek, "Occupational Self-Selection: A Human Capital Approach to Sex Differences in Occupational Structure," *Review of Economics and Statistics* (February 1981), pp. 60–69; Arthur E. Blakemore and Stuart A. Low, "Sex Differences in Occupational Self-Selection: The Case of College Majors," *Review of Economics and Statistics* (February 1984), pp. 157–163.

[13]Barbara Bergmann, "Occupational Segregation, Wages and Profits When Employers Discriminate by Race or Sex," *Eastern Economic Journal* (April/July 1974), pp. 103–110.

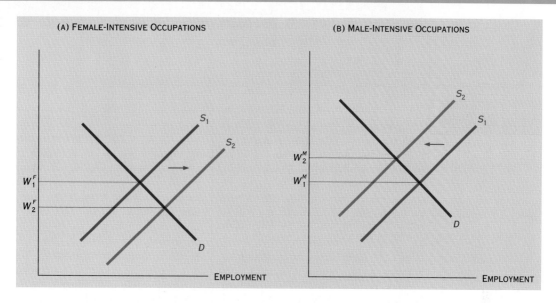

(A) FEMALE-INTENSIVE OCCUPATIONS

(B) MALE-INTENSIVE OCCUPATIONS

When women face obstacles that limit their access to certain occupations, they are crowded into the remaining occupations. This increased labor supply in female-intensive occupations depresses wages there (A). In contrast, wages increase in male-intensive occupations where labor supply is artificially restricted (B).

FIGURE 32.3

EMPLOYEE DISCRIMINATION

A preference of employees to work with members of the same group (for example, other males) and to avoid contact with different workers (for example, women).

CUSTOMER DISCRIMINATION

A preference of customers to be served by members of a particular group (for example, males).

companies to raise wages in female-intensive occupations, regardless of labor supply and demand (see Exhibit 32.1, page 832).

In addition to the discrimination of employers, women may be underrepresented in certain jobs because of the prejudices of employees or customers. According to the theory of **employee discrimination**, if males prefer working with or being supervised by other males, they will demand additional compensation if females are hired. To avoid the added costs of men and women working together, employers will maintain work forces segregated by gender.[14] **Customer discrimination** arises when consumers are not indifferent about who supplies a service. If consumers prefer male surgeons, male auto mechanics, and male pilots, women entering such occupations can expect less business and lower pay. In turn, women will be less likely to choose such lines of work.

To summarize, the occupational distribution of men and women is likely to differ both because of voluntary choice (for example, because of differences in expected work lives) and because of discrimination. Unfortunately, research to date does not permit us to estimate with any confidence the relative importance of these competing explanations. Although occupational differences contribute substantially to male/female differences in pay, debate continues on why such differences exist.

---

[14]See Gary Becker, *The Economics of Discrimination* (Chicago: University of Chicago Press, 1957). Although the evidence is limited, one study of young workers finds no sign of employee discrimination against women. See James Ragan and Carol Tremblay, "Testing for Employee Discrimination by Race and Sex," *Journal of Human Resources* (Winter 1988), pp. 123–137.

Comparable Worth

Jobs dominated by women pay less than jobs dominated by men. To some this is evidence that women's work is undervalued. The solution they propose is equal pay for *comparable worth*. Under such a system, jobs are evaluated in terms of such characteristics as skills, responsibility, mental demands, and working conditions. The number of points assigned to each category is then summed to determine a job's total score or evaluation. If librarians received the same score as electricians, their pay would be raised to equal that of electricians. Since most librarians are women and most electricians men, the net effect would be to narrow pay differences by gender. Recently, a number of city and state governments have switched to such point systems, and a major push is now under way to extend the comparable worth approach to other sectors of the economy, both government and private.

Opponents of comparable worth cite various criticisms. First, the approach is subjective. The characteristics chosen to evaluate jobs and the weights assigned to each are arbitrary. Beyond that, there is no objective way to compare these characteristics across jobs. Second, the comparable worth approach assumes there is an intrinsic value for each job, independent of market forces. The value of a librarian is assumed to be the same regardless of the number of librarians and regardless of society's demand for librarians. Because wages are set independently of labor supply and demand, the result will be too many people in some occupations and not enough in others. Having the wrong mix of workers will reduce the value of the country's output and lower the standard of living.

By changing the structure of wages across occupations, comparable worth sends the wrong signal to women. In recent years women have made great strides in penetrating many previously male-dominated fields. Between 1972 and 1991, the percentage of lawyers and

Occupational Distribution

YOUR TURN

SOME STATES HAVE ENACTED LAWS THAT "PROTECT" WOMEN BY KEEPING THEM OUT OF JOBS DEEMED "TOO STRENUOUS" OR "TOO DANGEROUS." HOW ARE SUCH LAWS LIKELY TO AFFECT THE EARNINGS OF WOMEN? WHY?

DISCRIMINATION WITHIN AN OCCUPATION Not only may discrimination lead to an uneven distribution of jobs among men and women, it may also result in lower pay for women *within a given occupation*. On this issue, the evidence is mixed. Within a given company, women doing the same job as men almost invariably receive the same pay. Indeed, the **Equal Pay Act of 1963** requires a company to establish "equal pay for equal work."

judges who are women increased from 4 percent to 19 percent, the percentage of engineers from 1 percent to 8 percent, the percentage of police and detectives from 3 percent to 14 percent, and the percentage of pharmacists from 13 percent to 37 percent. If the relative pay of librarians, secretaries, and other female-intensive occupations increases, the incentive for women to enter traditionally male occupations will be blunted. Occupational segregation will persist.

Finally, an increase in the pay of female-intensive jobs will cause employers to reduce employment there. Because most of the workers in these jobs are female, the brunt of the disemployment will be borne by females. Thus, a policy designed to help women will make many worse off.

Taking a different view, supporters of comparable worth contend that market forces are already constrained by unions, minimum-wage laws, and various institutional forces. Given existing market imperfections, they argue that the economy can accommodate the comparable worth system without drastic consequences. They also criticize market wages for failing to measure a worker's value accurately. Because of discrimination, workers (women) may be paid less than they contribute to output. Finally, some stress equity or fairness over efficiency. Even if comparable worth does create problems and reduce the value of output, they are willing to pay that price to create greater equality of pay by gender.

Ultimately, one's assessment of comparable worth depends on how much confidence one has in market forces and on how much weight one assigns to non-market considerations, such as equity. Most economists are critical of comparable worth, but many women's groups and unions embrace the concept.

On the other hand, there is evidence that compared to women in the same occupation, men are more likely to find employment in the higher-paying companies.[15] Again, the question is why. One view is that the higher-paying employers can have their pick of employees and, preferring men to women, they discriminate against women. Alternatively, it may be that men are disproportionately concentrated in higher-paying companies because they have more human capital than women and companies that pay the highest wages demand the most productive employees. There seems to be merit in both arguments.

Where does this leave us? Among full-time employees, women earn approximately 26 percent less per week than men. About half of this difference (13 percent of the 26 percent) apparently reflects differences in human capital and in hours

---

[15]Francine D. Blau, *Equal Pay in the Office* (Lexington, Mass.: Heath and Co., 1977).

worked. The other half is largely attributable to the fact that women are concentrated in low-paying occupations and, within an occupation, tend to work for low-paying companies. This inferior job distribution of women reflects both discrimination and differences in human capital, the contribution of each being difficult to measure.

IS THE PAY GAP NARROWING?

Whether measured on an annual, weekly, or hourly basis, since the mid-1970s the pay of women has increased faster than the pay of men. For example, weekly earnings of women as a percentage of men's earnings have increased from 62 percent to a record 74 percent. Will these gains be maintained or will they turn out to be transitory? Although only time will tell, several studies suggest that the higher relative pay of women is here to stay and that continued advances are likely in the future.[16]

These predictions are based primarily on changes in the relative human capital of men and women. From 1950 through the early 1970s, educational attainment of female workers relative to male workers declined. Moreover, most of the increased labor force participation of women resulted from the entry of inexperienced workers into the labor force rather than from greater work experience of women already in the labor force. In other words, the share of employed females with limited work experience increased. As a result, there was no increase in the average human capital of female workers relative to male workers.

More recently, the percentage of female employees with college degrees and the percentage with extensive experience have both increased. As differences in the human capital of men and women have narrowed, relative earnings of women have improved. The human capital gains of women are expected to continue and, if they do, further contraction of the male/female pay gap can be anticipated. According to one study:

> By the year 2000 a 40-year-old working woman will have 5.2 more years of work experience than her counterpart had in 1980. As a result . . . wages of working women will rise at least 15 percent faster than those of men [over this period.][17]

Continued occupational advances (caused in part by increased human capital) should also benefit women. As women gain greater access to higher-paying traditionally male occupations, one of the major sources of pay differences will diminish in importance.[18]

---

[16]James P. Smith and Michael P. Ward, *Women's Wages and Work in the Twentieth Century* (Santa Monica: The Rand Corporation, 1984); June O'Neill, "The Trend in the Male–Female Wage Gap in the United States," *Journal of Labor Economics* (January 1985, Supplement), pp. 91–116; Francine D. Blau, "Occupations and Earnings of Women Workers," in Karen S. Koziara et al., eds., *Working Women: Past, Present, Future* (Washington, D.C.: Bureau of National Affairs, 1987), pp. 37–68; June O'Neill, "Women and Wages," *The American Enterprise* (November/December 1990), pp. 25–33.

[17]Smith and Ward, same as 16.

[18]Judith Fields and Edward Wolff, "The Decline of Sex Segregation and the Wage Gap, 1970–80," *Journal of Human Resources* (Fall 1991), pp. 608–622.

Earnings vary by race as well as gender. Among year-round full-time workers, black and other nonwhite males earn approximately 25 percent less than white males; nonwhite females earn nearly 10 percent less than white females.

Many of the explanations cited for the lower pay of females also apply to our discussion of racial differences. For example, nonwhites generally have less human capital than whites. Among blacks—the largest racial minority in the United States—only 12 percent of those 25 and older have college degrees, compared to 22 percent of whites. Moreover, there is evidence, at least among older workers, that blacks have often received an inferior education. Among Southern schools in the 1920s the student/teacher ratio was 50 percent higher for blacks than for whites; the school year was 20 percent shorter; and funding per student was substantially lower.[19] Because the returns to education depend on the quality of education as well as on the quantity, blacks have been at a double disadvantage.

Blacks are six years younger on average than whites, and black males have a considerably lower rate of labor force participation than white males. For such reasons, blacks have less job experience than whites. They also have less job training. According to numerous studies, the lower human capital of blacks (as measured by education, experience, and training) accounts for most of their lower earnings.

The inferior job distribution of blacks also plays a role—blacks are concentrated in low-paying jobs. As with women, this appears to reflect both lower levels of human capital and discrimination. Some researchers also stress

> the enormous prelabor market disadvantage of blacks—the burden of coming from families and neighborhoods of low socioeconomic conditions which fail to provide the background resources [such as reading materials] that facilitate economic success.[20]

Although nonwhites continue to earn less than whites, their relative position has generally improved, despite some recent backtracking (see Figure 32.4, page 846). From 1955 through 1965, nonwhite males (in year-round full-time jobs) earned between 58 and 66 percent as much as white males. Beginning in 1975, the income ratio of nonwhite to white males has ranged from 72 to 79 percent. The gains of nonwhite women have been even more dramatic. In 1955, they earned just over half the income of white women. Since 1974, they have consistently earned at least 90 percent as much as white women.

These advances have not occurred evenly across age groups. The relative income of older blacks has improved very little. The bulk of the gains have accrued to young blacks, especially those with substantial education.[21] In other words, young blacks are getting off to a better start vis-à-vis whites than their parents did.

---

[19]David Card and Alan Krueger, "School Quality and Black-White Relative Earnings: A Direct Assessment," *Quarterly Journal of Economics* (February 1992), pp. 151–200.

[20]Richard Freeman, "Black Economic Progress after 1964: Who Has Gained and Why?" in Sherwin Rosen, ed., *Studies in Labor Markets* (Chicago: University of Chicago Press, 1981), p. 283.

[21]Same as 20, p. 254; James Smith and Finis Welch, "Black Economic Progress After Myrdal," *Journal of Economic Literature* (June 1989), pp. 533–539.

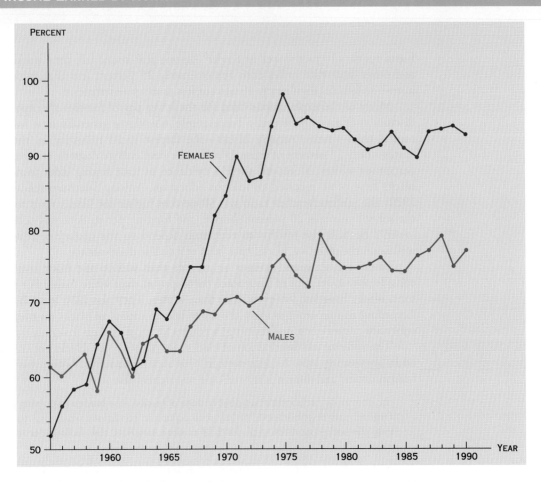

*Median income of year-round full-time workers.

SOURCE: Adapted from U.S. Bureau of the Census, *Current Population Reports*, Series P-60. Data for years after 1987 are not strictly comparable to prior data.

FIGURE 32.4

If this success can be maintained, then as today's young blacks age and as their parents retire, the overall ratio of black income to white income is likely to climb even higher. However, before we can predict the future, we must first understand the past. Why has the income of black workers risen faster than the income of white workers?

EXPLAINING THE INCREASED RELATIVE INCOME OF BLACKS

A major factor contributing to the income gains of blacks has been their overall increase in education. In 1960, median educational attainment of whites was three years greater than the educational attainment of blacks. Today whites enjoy an advantage of less than one year. As suggested earlier, advances have also been made in terms of quality of education. School segregation has declined, and racial differences in student/teacher ratios, length of school year, and funding per student have all narrowed. According to one study, improved school quality is responsible for 15–20 percent of the increased relative pay of blacks between 1960 and 1980.[22]

Migration patterns have also helped narrow the racial pay gap. As blacks moved from the low-wage South to the high-wage North and from lower-paying rural areas to the cities, the average pay of blacks increased. Migration over the period 1940–1970 is estimated to have raised the relative pay of blacks by 11–18 percent.[23]

Blacks have also benefited from increased government intervention in labor markets. In the 1960s, Congress enacted legislation outlawing racial discrimination and President Johnson signed an executive order calling for contractors to increase their hiring of minorities or risk losing government contracts (see Exhibit 32.2, page 848). Several studies provide evidence that these actions had a direct bearing on the economic progress of blacks, especially in the South where civil rights enforcement was targeted.[24]

"We don't discriminate on the basis of age, sex, religion, color or national origin—we just don't hire Scorpios."

SOURCE: From *The Wall Street Journal*—permission, Cartoon Features Syndicate.

Although progress has occurred, there is evidence that some of the reported advances are illusory. That is, blacks have not benefited nearly as much as statistics (such as those portrayed in Figure 32.4) suggest. During most of the period when

[22]Same as 19, p. 194.

[23]Smith and Welch, same as 21, Table 20.

[24]Same as 20, pp. 269–283; Jonathan Leonard, "The Impact of Affirmative Action on Employment," *Journal of Labor Economics* (October 1984), pp. 439–463; John Donohue III and James Heckman, "Continuous Versus Episodic Change: The Impact of Civil Rights Policy on the Economic Status of Blacks," *Journal of Economic Literature* (December 1991), pp. 1603–1643.

Three of the government's main weapons against discrimination are the *Equal Pay Act*, the *Civil Rights Act*, and *Executive Order 11246*. The Equal Pay Act of 1963 mandates "equal pay for equal work." While accepting pay differences based on skill, effort, responsibility, and working conditions, the law prohibits pay discrimination based on such factors as a worker's race or gender. Unfortunately, this law has not been especially effective. An employer can sidestep the equal-pay provisions by assigning blacks and whites to different jobs or by not hiring blacks at all. Unless blacks and whites perform the same job, the Equal Pay Act does not apply.

The **Civil Rights Act of 1964** is broader in scope and therefore more effective, banning discrimination in terms of both pay and employment. In particular, **title VII** makes it illegal

> to refuse to hire or to discharge any individual, or otherwise to discriminate against any individual with respect to his compensation, terms, conditions, or privileges of employment, because of such individual's race, color, religion, sex, or national origin.

Following a 1972 amendment, which strengthened the law and extended its coverage, the Civil Rights Act applies to private employers with fifteen or more workers, unions with fifteen or more members, employment agencies, nonreligious educational institutions, and state and local governments.

The *Equal Employment Opportunity Commission (EEOC)* administers both the Equal Pay Act and the Civil Rights Act. Although responsible for enforcement of these laws, its powers are limited. The commission cannot issue cease-and-desist orders, fine employers, or require that workers fired as the result of discrimination be reinstated. The EEOC typically seeks voluntary compliance and, if that fails, encourages individuals to file lawsuits. Until the Reagan presidency, it also emphasized class-action lawsuits against companies it believed to have exhibited a pattern of discrimination. Both AT&T and General Motors signed out-of-court settlements with the EEOC, each calling for the particular company to spend more than $40 million to hire, train, and promote women and minorities and, in the case of AT&T, to provide back pay for the injured parties.

In 1965, President Johnson signed Executive Order 11246, establishing the Office of Federal Contract Compliance Programs. This order requires all but the smallest companies doing business with the federal government to refrain from discrimination against women and minorities. Beyond that, these employers must statistically analyze their work forces and identify any areas where women or minorities are underrepresented. If significant underrepresentation does occur, the employer must file an **affirmative-action** plan that sets forth specific goals and timetables for increasing the employment of women or minorities. Companies that do not file affirmative-action plans or fail to meet their timetables can lose current government contracts and be barred from bidding on future contracts. At present, more than 30 million workers are covered by this executive order.

Affirmative Action
A policy designed to increase the representation of women or minorities (for example, to increase their relative employment).

EXHIBIT

32.2

the relative income of black workers was improving, labor force participation of blacks declined, both in absolute terms and relative to the labor force participation of whites. The blacks dropping out of the labor force were predominantly those with low skills and therefore low earnings. Had they remained in the labor force, the average income among black workers would have been lower. In other words, part of the reported increase in relative income of black workers is artificial, reflecting the fact that fewer low-skilled blacks are now included in the income statistics. Accordingly, statistics on the average income of black workers overstate the economic progress of blacks. On the other hand, there is evidence that the bulk of the reported gains is real.[25] Advances in education, migration, and a reduction in discrimination have unambiguously improved the relative income of blacks.

Pay Differences by Ethnicity

Recently, as more and better data have become available, economists have begun studying pay differences by ethnicity. A general theme of this research is that education explains a good portion of these differences in pay. On average, the lower a group's educational attainment the lower its earnings (see Table 32.6). This is true not only for broadly defined ethnic groups, such as Hispanics, but also for various subgroups. For example, Mexican Americans generally have less education than

RELATIVE PAY AND EDUCATION OF VARIOUS ETHNIC GROUPS (MALES ONLY)

ETHNIC GROUP	PAY AS A PERCENT OF PAY RECEIVED BY WHITES	YEARS OF EDUCATION AS A PERCENT OF EDUCATION OF WHITES
Hispanic		
Mexican	72	76
Puerto Rican	76	79
Cuban	89	91
Central and South American	83	95
Other Hispanic	87	89
Asian origin		
Filipino	74	95
Chinese	108	110
Japanese	106	107

SOURCES: Adapted from Cordelia Reimers, "Labor Market Discrimination Against Hispanic and Black Men," *Review of Economics and Statistics* (November 1983), Table 1; Barry Chiswick, "An Analysis of the Earnings and Employment of Asian–American Men," *Journal of Labor Economics* (April 1983), Table 1.

TABLE 32.6

[25]Charles Brown, "Black–White Earnings Ratios Since the Civil Rights Act of 1964: The Importance of Labor Market Dropouts," *Quarterly Journal of Economics* (February 1984), pp. 31–44; Wayne Vroman, "Black Men's Relative Earnings: Are the Gains Illusory?" *Industrial and Labor Relations Review* (October 1990), pp. 83–98.

Cuban Americans and earn correspondingly lower wages. Some groups—including Japanese, Chinese, and Jewish Americans—have more education than whites in general and earn higher salaries. This suggests that the inhibiting effects of discrimination can sometimes be offset through heavy investment in human capital.

Earnings also vary with fluency in English and, for immigrants, with length of time in the United States and place of education. The U.S. labor market places a lower value on foreign schooling, either because it is of a lower quality or because some of what is learned in other countries is not relevant in the United States. Similarly, those with language deficiencies are at a disadvantage compared to other immigrants and to native Americans.[26]

The Structure of Unemployment

UNEMPLOYMENT RATE
Percentage of the labor force unemployed:

$$\frac{\text{unemployment}}{\text{labor force}} \times 100$$

Another measure of labor market success, besides earnings, is the **unemployment rate**—the percentage of the labor force that is unemployed. As Table 32.7 indicates, unemployment is distributed unevenly across groups. The unemployment rate of blacks is more than double the unemployment rate of whites and about 25 percent higher than the unemployment rate of Hispanics. Unemployment differences also exist by gender, although the nature of the relationship is changing over time. Until recently the unemployment rate of women was appreciably higher than the unemployment rate of men, but in recent years it has dipped below the unemployment rate of men.

Some of the same factors contributing to differences in earnings also influence the structure of unemployment. Unemployment varies inversely with human capital. For instance, the unemployment rate for those with less than four years of high

UNEMPLOYMENT RATES BY RACE, HISPANIC ORIGIN, AND GENDER, 1992*	
White	6.5
Black	14.2
Hispanic origin	11.4
Male	7.9
Female	6.9

*Average for first eight months of the year.
SOURCE: U.S. Bureau of Labor Statistics, *Employment and Earnings*, 1992.

TABLE 32.7

[26]Walter McManus, William Gould, and Finis Welch, "Earnings of Hispanic Men: The Role of English Language Proficiency," *Journal of Labor Economics* (April 1983), pp. 101–130; Gilles Grenier. "The Effects of Language Characteristics on the Wages of Hispanic-American Males," *Journal of Human Resources* (Winter 1984), pp. 35–52; Sherrie Kossoudji, "English Language Ability and the Labor Market Opportunities of Hispanic and East Asian Immigrant Men," *Journal of Labor Economics* (April 1988), pp. 205–228; Barry Chiswick, "Speaking, Reading, and Earnings Among Low-skilled Immigrants," *Journal of Labor Economics* (April 1991), pp. 149–170.

school is almost five times greater than the unemployment rate for college graduates. Unemployment is also a function of occupation and industry (see Table 32.8). In addition, discrimination can increase a group's unemployment rate. Because human capital, the distribution of employment, and extent of discrimination vary by race, ethnicity, and gender, these factors contribute to differences in group unemployment rates.

Added insight into unemployment can be gained by examining frequency of unemployment (how often members of a group become unemployed) and duration of unemployment (how long the unemployment lasts). Blacks have a higher frequency of unemployment than whites, in part because of higher layoff rates (job loss). In addition, once unemployed, they tend to remain unemployed longer than whites. Thus, both frequency and duration of unemployment are unfavorable for blacks.

In turn, women have a higher frequency of unemployment than men. One reason is that women are more likely than men to move into and out of the labor force, in part because of their typically greater family responsibilities. Because entry into the labor force is often accompanied by unemployment (it takes time to find a job), women are more likely to become unemployed than men. On the other hand, women have shorter spells of unemployment. This shorter duration of unemployment partially offsets their greater frequency of unemployment.

UNEMPLOYMENT RATES BY OCCUPATION, INDUSTRY, AND EDUCATIONAL ATTAINMENT, 1991

Occupation	
Managerial and professional	2.8
Technical, sales, clerical	5.1
Service	7.5
Precision production	7.9
Operators, fabricators, laborers	10.5
Industry	
Mining	7.7
Construction	15.4
Manufacturing	7.2
Transportation and utilities	5.3
Wholesale and retail trade	7.6
Finance, insurance, real estate	4.0
Service industries	5.7
Agriculture	11.6
Government and self-employed	2.8
Educational attainment	
Less than 4 years of high school	13.7
High school: 4 years only	6.9
College: 1 to 3 years	5.4
4 years or more	3.0

SOURCES: Data on the unemployment rate by educational attainment are unpublished, obtained from the U.S. Bureau of Labor Statistics. Data on unemployment rates by occupation and industry come from *Employment and Earnings*, January 1992.

TABLE 32.8

During the late 1960s, the unemployment rate of women was more than 50 percent higher than the unemployment rate of men. Since that time, the unemployment rates of men and women have moved closer together. Indeed, recently the unemployment rate of women dipped below the unemployment rate of men (see Figure 32.5).

Several factors appear responsible for the improvement in the relative unemployment rate of women. First, male–female differences in total experience and tenure on current job have narrowed over time. As women acquire additional human capital and greater job seniority, they become relatively less vulnerable to layoffs. In addition, the growing labor force attachment of women implies fewer bouts of unemployment associated with entry into the labor market. In other words, in terms of experience, length of time on current job, and labor force attachment, men and women are becoming more and more alike. Affirmative action may have also benefited women by increasing demand for female workers relative to male workers. Exhibit 32.3 (page 853) addresses this issue.

Fluctuations in the pattern of unemployment also reflect changes in the strength of the economy. As the economy weakens and the overall unemployment rate rises, the *relative* unemployment of women falls. There are two reasons for this. To begin with, men tend to be concentrated in those sectors of the economy most sensitive to changes in economic activity. When the unemployment rate rises, it rises most dramatically in male-intensive industries, such as construction and manufacturing. (During the economic downturn of the early 1990s, 1.4 million jobs were eliminated in manufacturing, and the unemployment rate in construction

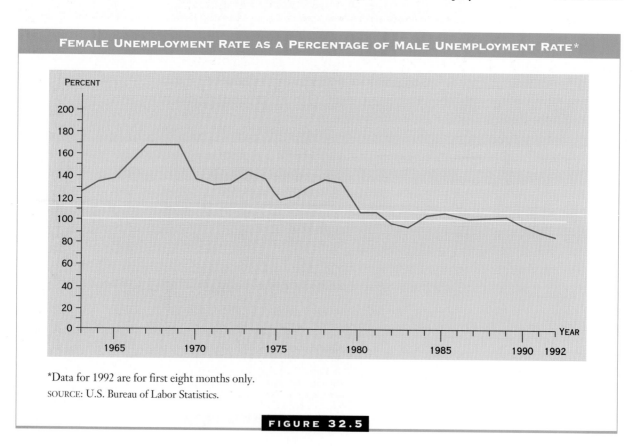

FEMALE UNEMPLOYMENT RATE AS A PERCENTAGE OF MALE UNEMPLOYMENT RATE*

*Data for 1992 are for first eight months only.

SOURCE: U.S. Bureau of Labor Statistics.

FIGURE 32.5

The Impact of Anti-Discrimination Policy

The government has adopted various measures to combat discrimination in the labor market (see Exhibit 32.2). For example, the Equal Pay Act requires that discriminating employers raise the pay of women to equal that of men performing the same work. By increasing the relative pay of women, this law induces employers to substitute male for female workers. The increased pay of women leads to lower female employment, as the figure on the bottom left illustrates.

Some of those losing jobs $(E_1 - E_2)$ wind up unemployed. (Others may withdraw from the labor force now that jobs are harder to find.) The net effect of higher pay for women is reduced employment and a higher rate of unemployment.

Other government policy is more benign toward women. For example, through affirmative-action plans, the government forces contractors to increase the ratio of female employment.

This can be represented as an increase in the demand for female workers. As indicated in the figure on the bottom right, females benefit from both higher wages and higher employment.

The impact on unemployment depends on what happens to female labor force participation. Higher wages coupled with increased job prospects are likely to draw additional women into the labor market. However, as long as labor force participation rises by a proportionately smaller amount than employment, the unemployment rate of women will fall.

In summary, government policies designed to raise wages of women adversely affect female employment unless the government simultaneously raises demand for female workers. Although the preceding analysis is presented in terms of female unemployment rates, it applies equally to the unemployment rates of minorities.

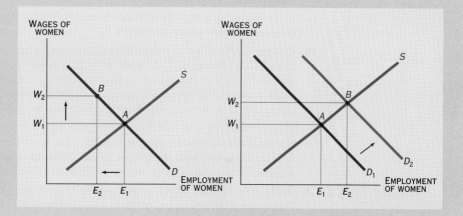

reached 17 percent.) In contrast, employment is much less sensitive to economic downturns in female-intensive sectors, such as retail trade and services. As a consequence, when the economy weakens, male job loss exceeds female job loss.

Beyond that, women who become unemployed during a downturn are more likely than men to drop out of the labor force and therefore not be counted as unemployed. Women are more likely to time labor force participation, working when jobs are easy to find and wages good and withdrawing when conditions deteriorate. For these reasons, during an economic downturn the unemployment rate of women rises more slowly than the unemployment rate of men. On the other hand, the unemployment rate of women falls more slowly during the ensuing recovery and expansion.

Although this concludes the discussion of labor markets, much of the material in this chapter is relevant to our analysis of income inequality and poverty. Individuals with low labor force participation and low wages have a disproportionate chance of being poor. We return to this topic in Chapter 34, but first concentrate on other factor payments: interest, rent, and profits.

Summary

1. Whether measured by labor force participation, wages, or unemployment, labor market outcomes vary by gender, race, and ethnicity. Chapter 32 helps explain the reasons behind these differences.

2. The labor force participation rate measures the percentage of the population either employed or looking for work. Although labor force participation remains higher for men, differences by gender have narrowed over time. Labor force participation of men has declined, largely because of lower labor market activity among elderly men. In contrast, labor force participation of women, especially married women, has climbed steadily throughout the century. Among the reasons are increased wages of women, lower fertility, labor-saving devices, and changes in attitudes.

3. Among full-time workers, women earn almost 30 percent less than men. This reflects the lower human capital of women, shorter workweeks, discrimination, and occupational distribution—women tend to be concentrated in low-paying occupations and, within an occupation, in low-paying companies.

4. Occupational differences reflect both discrimination and voluntary choice, the importance of each being hotly debated. According to human capital theory, differences in expected work lives lead women to choose different occupations than do men. But sometimes women settle for certain occupations not by choice but because they are denied entrance to other occupations. According to the theory of occupational crowding, women are channeled into traditionally female jobs, which drives down wages there.

5. Although the male/female pay gap remains wide, it has narrowed over the past 20 years. During that time frame, the relative human capital of women has risen and women have increased their penetration of certain traditionally male occupations.

6. Blacks earn less than whites, in part because of their lower average age and education, an inferior job distribution, and discrimination. Differences in human capital appear responsible for over half of the racial differences in pay.

7. Racial pay differences have narrowed over time, especially among women and young workers. Increases in the relative quantity and quality of education have played a role, as have migration, antidiscrimination laws, and affirmative action. Although real, the

improvement in the average income of black workers has been overstated because of the withdrawal from the labor force of many low-skilled blacks.

8. Ethnic differences in pay reflect many of the same factors that underlie pay differences by gender and race. In addition, language skills and, for immigrants, origin of education are relevant. Some groups with high education (Chinese, Japanese, and Jewish Americans) earn more than most white Americans; Hispanics earn less.

9. Differences in unemployment rates arise from such factors as human capital, sector of employment, and discrimination. The unemployment rate of blacks is more than double the unemployment rate of whites. For many years the unemployment rate of women exceeded that of men, but as women have gained experience and seniority their unemployment situation has improved. In recent years the unemployment rate of women has been comparable to or even lower than the unemployment rate of men. Because men are concentrated in cyclically sensitive industries, recessions raise the unemployment rate by a greater amount for men than for women.

Key Terms

labor force
labor force participation rate
(male/female) pay gap
theory of occupational
    crowding
comparable worth

employee discrimination
customer discrimination
Equal Pay Act of 1963
Civil Rights Act of 1964, title VII
affirmative action
unemployment rate

Study Questions and Problems

1. Pleasantville has a (working-age) population of 1,000. Currently, 540 residents are employed and 60 are unemployed.
   a. How large is the labor force in Pleasantville?
   b. Compute the town's labor force participation and unemployment rates.

2. The women's movement once adopted the slogan *59 cents* to highlight the fact that women earned 59 cents for every dollar received by male workers.
   a. Is this slogan still appropriate today or does it need to be updated? Explain.
   b. Why do women, on average, earn less than men?

3. If 45 percent of all workers are women, why aren't 45 percent of all plumbers, bankers, and corporate officers women?

4. (a) Why do blacks earn less than whites? (b) What forces might cause racial wage differentials to shrink in the future?

5. Why are blacks more likely to be unemployed than whites?

6. Differences between men and women in pay, labor force participation, and unemployment rates have all declined in recent years. How would you explain the narrowing of each?

7. Under the apartheid system in South Africa, workers are segregated along the lines of race. (a) How does denying blacks access to certain occupations affect wage rates in those occupations? Illustrate diagrammatically. (b) If blacks are crowded into the remaining occupations, how does this affect wage rates in the predominantly black occupations? (c)

If segregation is abolished and occupational distributions by race become more similar, how are relative wages of blacks likely to change?

8. In most universities, faculty in finance, computer science, and engineering earn substantially higher salaries than faculty in philosophy, modern languages, and education, even though faculty in the different fields have comparable amounts of education and comparable teaching responsibilities. Some universities, however, have adopted a policy of paying faculty in all departments the same salaries. Assess this policy. What are the economic consequences of eliminating pay differences by field? (*Hint*: see Exhibit 32.1.)

9. Michigan has a law that prohibits employers from discriminating on the basis of a person's weight. Arguing that obesity does not affect work performance, the National Association to Advance Fat Acceptance has lobbied for national legislation banning weight discrimination.

   a. If Congress enacted legislation requiring equal pay regardless of weight, how might this affect employment and unemployment of overweight workers?

   b. Would the law's impact be any different if an affirmative-action clause were added? Explain your answers. (*Hint*: read Exhibit 32.3).

Labor Force Participation

(A) DECREASE LABOR FORCE PARTICIPATION; (B), (C), (D), (E) INCREASE LABOR FORCE PARTICIPATION.

YOUR TURN
Answers

Occupational Distribution

THE PROTECTED JOBS TEND TO BE HIGHLY PAID. THE HIGH SALARIES MAY BE TO COMPENSATE WORKERS FOR STRENUOUS OR DANGEROUS WORK (THE THEORY OF COMPENSATING WAGE DIFFERENTIALS) OR THEY MAY RESULT FROM THE VERY RESTRICTIONS THAT LIMIT LABOR SUPPLY (THE THEORY OF OCCUPATIONAL CROWDING). THE "PROTECTIVE" LAWS MAY EVEN BE A SCREEN TO PRESERVE HIGHLY PAID JOBS FOR MEN (TO LEGALIZE DISCRIMINATION). IN ANY CASE, TO THE EXTENT WOMEN ARE DENIED ACCESS TO THESE HIGH-PAYING JOBS, THE SALARIES OF WOMEN ARE DEPRESSED.

Selected References

Borjas, George. *Friends or Strangers* (New York: Basic Books, 1990). Examines the effect of immigration on the U.S. economy.

Donohue, John, III, and James Heckman. "Continuous Versus Episodic Change: The Impact of Civil Rights Policy on the Economic Status of Blacks," *Journal of Economic Literature* (December 1991), pp. 1603–1643. Studies the decline of the racial pay gap, emphasizing the role of federal civil rights policy; contains extensive bibliography.

Fuchs, Victor. *Women's Quest for Economic Equality* (Cambridge, Mass.: Harvard University Press, 1988). Highly readable discussion of the economic situation of women.

Gunderson, Morley. "Male–Female Wage Differentials and Policy Responses," *Journal of Economic Literature* (March 1989), pp. 46–72. Discusses the male/female pay gap, equal pay, and comparable worth; contains extensive bibliography.

Hoffman, Emily, ed. *Essays on the Economics of Discrimination* (Kalamazoo, Mich.: W. E. Upjohn Institute, 1991). Contains a series of papers dealing with various dimensions of discrimination.

O'Neill, June. "Women and Wages," *The American Enterprise* (November/December 1990), pp. 25–33. A nontechnical discussion of the advances in the relative wages of white and black women and the reasons for these gains.

Strober, Myra. "Human Capital Theory: Implications for HR Managers," *Industrial Relations* (Spring 1990), pp. 214–239. Reviews competing theories of wage determination— including human capital theory, the screening hypothesis, and radical (Marxist) theory—in an effort to provide insights on pay differences by gender and by race.

IT IS A SOCIALIST IDEA
THAT MAKING PROFITS
IS A VICE; I CONSIDER
THE REAL VICE
IS MAKING LOSSES.

—SIR WINSTON CHURCHILL

Interest, Rent, and Profit

THE IDEA WAS SIMPLE—DIS-
COUNT RETAILING. STARTING
WITH A SINGLE STORE IN
ARKANSAS, SAM WALTON
BUILT ONE OF THE LARGEST
RETAILING EMPIRES IN THE
UNITED STATES—WAL-MART.
BECAUSE OF WAL-MART'S
SUCCESS, WALTON ACCUMU-
LATED MORE THAN $22 BIL-
LION IN WEALTH BEFORE HIS
DEATH IN 1992, MAKING WAL-
TON AND HIS CHILDREN THE
RICHEST FAMILY IN AMERICA.[1]
ALTHOUGH WALTON WORKED
HARD, HIS WEALTH WAS NOT
A TESTAMENT TO HIS RAW
LABOR. OTHERS WORK EQUAL-
LY HARD BUT WITHOUT WAL-
TON'S FINANCIAL SUCCESS.
RATHER, WALTON'S WEALTH
GREW OUT OF A DIFFERENT
SOURCE OF INCOME—PROFIT.

PREVIOUS CHAPTERS
FOCUSED ON LABOR INCOME,
AND RIGHTLY SO SINCE THE
BULK OF ALL INCOME CON-
SISTS OF WAGES. BUT AS
WALTON'S SUCCESS DEMON-
STRATES, WAGES ARE NOT
THE ONLY SOURCE OF
INCOME. CHAPTER 33 EXAM-
INES THREE OTHER TYPES OF
INCOME—INTEREST, RENT,
AND PROFIT.

---

[1] See *Forbes*, "The Forbes Four Hundred," October 21, 1991, pp. 150–151.

Interest

Each year millions of consumers borrow to finance purchases of automobiles, housing, clothes, and even college education. They are joined by various businesses that borrow funds to build new factories and purchase equipment. Even the federal government enters the credit market, borrowing to finance its budget deficit.

In each case, borrowers pay for the privilege of obtaining credit—that is, gaining access to lenders' funds. They agree not only to return the borrowed funds but also to pay interest on these funds. Their interest payments depend on both the volume of credit (amount borrowed) and the price of credit—the **interest rate**. For example, if you borrow $2,000 for one year at an interest rate of 10 percent, your interest payments are 10 percent of $2,000 (that is, $200). Equivalently, your lender receives $200 in interest income. More generally, **interest income** refers to the interest payments received by lenders for the use of their funds. Net interest income of U.S. lenders reached $450 billion in 1991 but moved lower in 1992 as interest rates fell.

INTEREST RATE
The price paid for the use of lenders' funds (expressed in percentage terms).

INTEREST INCOME
The payments received by lenders for the use of their funds (expressed in dollars).

The Market for Loanable Funds

LOANABLE FUNDS MODEL
A model that explains interest rates in terms of the demand for and supply of lenders' funds. According to this model, the interest rate is the price paid for the use of these funds.

According to the **loanable funds model**, interest rates are determined by the supply of and demand for credit. By saving part of their past income, millions of households accumulate surplus funds. Various businesses and state and local governments also acquire more funds than they presently need. These entities are willing to lend funds—at a price—to parties willing to pay for use of these **loanable funds**. The interest rate is the price borrowers pay for the use of lenders' funds. It is determined by the demand for and supply of loanable funds.

DEMAND FOR LOANABLE FUNDS

POSITIVE TIME PREFERENCE
A preference to consume now rather than wait.

The demand for loanable funds is the cumulative demand by consumers, businesses, and government. Consumers generally seek funds because of a **positive time preference**—they prefer consumption in the present to consumption in the future. Rather than wait until they have saved enough to purchase a new car, many consumers want to drive that new car today. They place such a premium on present consumption that they are willing to borrow, at a positive interest rate, to make that consumption possible.

The principal reason businesses borrow funds is because of the *productivity of capital*. Output could be produced with little or no capital. Crops could be grown without tractors; fish could be caught without nets; medicine could be practiced without hospitals. Why then do firms want capital? Simply put, capital permits higher levels of output. It increases the amount of corn produced, the number of fish caught, and the health of consumers.

ROUNDABOUT

PRODUCTION

The process of obtaining
capital and using it to produce consumer goods rather
than producing consumer
goods directly, without
capital.

Capital leads to **roundabout production**. Instead of producing consumer goods directly, resources are first used to create capital, which itself is a resource. Capital is then combined with other resources to produce the consumer goods. Thus, roundabout production entails using the output of some earlier time period, capital, to increase production in the present period.

When a firm lacks the desired amount of capital, it seeks additional capital, and the funds necessary to purchase this capital. Even though the firm must pay interest on any funds it borrows, the capital it obtains with these funds increases output and therefore revenue to the firm. As long as additional capital contributes more to revenue than to costs, a firm has an incentive to acquire the additional capital.

The productivity of capital also contributes to consumers' demand for funds. Education and other forms of *human capital* may contribute sufficiently to a person's future earnings so that he or she can enjoy a higher standard of living by borrowing funds to attend college, even though the funds must be paid back with interest.

The final entity seeking loanable funds is the government. By borrowing funds the government finances expenditures in excess of the revenues it receives from taxes, fees, and other sources. These expenditures may be either to acquire capital (for example, highways and bridges) or to increase present consumption by various citizens (for example, to buy food and medicine for low-income families).

The aggregate demand for loanable funds consists of the total demand by consumers, businesses, and government. The demand for loanable funds is downward sloping (see Figure 33.1). An increase in the interest rate raises the price of borrowed funds and therefore reduces the quantity demanded, both for present consumption and for investment (acquiring capital). A higher interest rate means that

THE MARKET FOR LOANABLE FUNDS

The equilibrium interest rate is determined by the supply of and demand for loanable funds. The demand for loanable funds slopes downward, reflecting the fact that borrowers want additional loanable funds when the price of these funds (the interest rate) falls. The supply of funds slopes upward, reflecting the fact that a higher interest rate induces lenders to part with a greater quantity of funds.

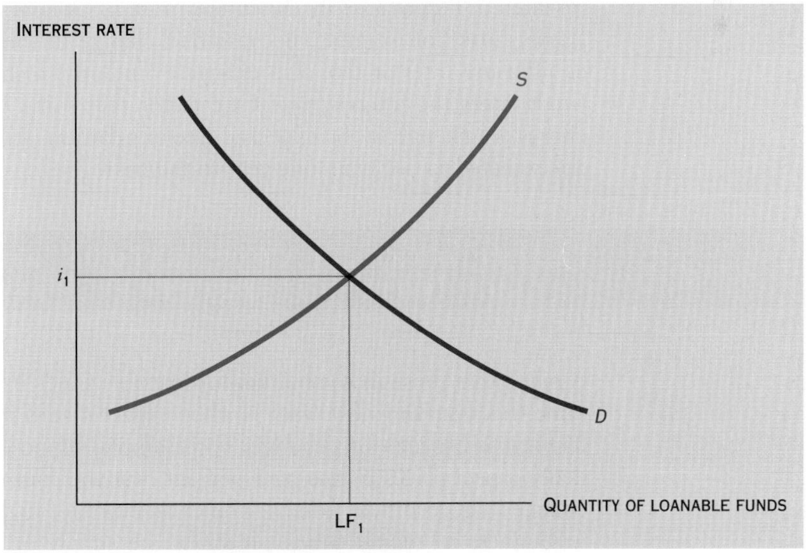

FIGURE 33.1

consumers must sacrifice more consumption in the future for each dollar they borrow. As present consumption becomes more expensive, consumers scale back current spending and consequently reduce the amount of funds they wish to borrow. Similarly, a higher interest rate raises the cost of acquiring capital with loanable funds. Because of the increased cost, businesses, consumers, and (to a lesser extent) government all seek fewer funds with which to purchase capital.

SUPPLY OF LOANABLE FUNDS

While some consumers, businesses, and governments seek to borrow loanable funds, other entities are willing to supply such funds. The amount of funds made available depends on the interest rate. Other things equal, lenders supply a greater quantity of loanable funds when the interest rate rises. That is, the supply of loanable funds is upward sloping.

Lenders have alternatives to loaning out their funds. Households with past savings can purchase more goods for themselves or can buy stocks, real estate, and other assets. Businesses with cash balances can acquire additional assets or even other companies. State and local governments with surpluses can increase spending or reduce taxes. The willingness of those with surplus funds to make these funds available to other entities depends on the price they receive for lending their funds. That price is the interest rate.

THE EQUILIBRIUM INTEREST RATE

As in other markets, the equilibrium price is determined by supply and demand. In the market for loanable funds, the equilibrium interest rate is given by the intersection of the demand for loanable funds and the supply of loanable funds. This is represented in Figure 33.1 by the interest rate i_1. Of course, if the demand for loanable funds shifts (for example, because of a change in the productivity of capital), the equilibrium interest rate also changes. Similarly, a shift in the supply of loanable funds alters the interest rate. One factor that shifts both the supply and demand curves is a change in the expected rate of inflation—that is, the rate at which prices are expected to rise from one year to the next.

Inflationary Expectations and Real versus Nominal Interest Rates

Assume that those in the market for loanable funds initially expect prices to be the same this year and next (that is, they expect a zero inflation rate). Consider what happens if expectations change. For example, suppose borrowers and lenders suddenly expect prices to rise by 5 percent over the coming year, perhaps because of a change in government policy. The expectation of higher inflation reduces lenders' willingness to supply funds—it shifts the supply of loanable funds leftward (see Figure 33.2). Equivalently stated, it raises the price (interest rate) lenders require to provide a given quantity of funds.

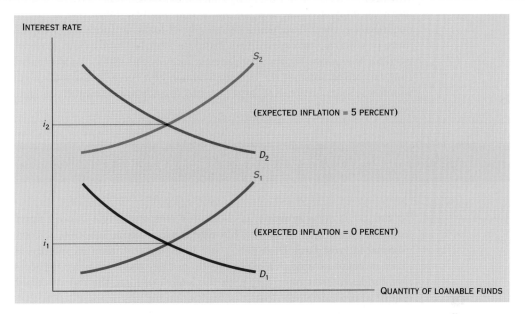

INTEREST RATE

S_2

(EXPECTED INFLATION = 5 PERCENT)

i_2

D_2

S_1

(EXPECTED INFLATION = 0 PERCENT)

i_1

D_1

QUANTITY OF LOANABLE FUNDS

An increase in expected inflation reduces the supply of loanable funds but increases the demand for loanable funds. Both effects put upward pressure on the interest rate. Here the interest rate rises from i_1 (when expected inflation is 0 percent) to i_2 (when expected inflation is 5 percent).

FIGURE 33.2

NOMINAL INTEREST RATE
The interest rate measured in actual dollars borrowers must pay.

REAL INTEREST RATE
The nominal interest rate minus the expected rate of inflation.

A higher expected inflation rate also increases the demand for loanable funds. For any given interest rate, borrowers seek more funds the greater the expected increase in prices. This reflects the fact that as prices rise borrowers can repay their loans with "cheaper" dollars. That is, a dollar received one year from now will buy less than a dollar buys today. The higher the inflation rate the greater the advantage from being able to buy now, before prices rise, and therefore the greater the incentive to obtain funds today. Because an increase in expected inflation reduces the supply of loanable funds while increasing demand for loanable funds, it raises the equilibrium interest rate. The new equilibrium interest rate in Figure 33.2 is i_2.

The actual interest rate borrowers pay lenders—the rate specified in the loan agreement—is called the **nominal interest rate**. The nominal interest rate indicates the number of dollars that must be paid in one year for every $100 borrowed today. As inflationary expectations rise, so does the nominal interest rate.

The nominal interest rate can be contrasted with the **real interest rate**. The real interest rate is defined as the nominal interest rate minus the expected inflation rate. It indicates how much borrowers must pay lenders above and beyond the expected inflation rate in order to gain access to their funds. If each 1 percent increase in expected inflation raises the nominal interest rate by 1 percent, as some economists believe, then the real rate of interest is independent of the expected rate of inflation.

The real rate of interest is not constant over time, as Figure 33.3 indicates. Changes in the supply of or demand for loanable funds can affect real as well as nominal interest rates. For instance, real interest rates rise if the population becomes less thrifty, reducing the supply of loanable funds, or if capital becomes more productive, increasing the demand for loanable funds. Both reasons have been cited for the unusually high real interest rates of the 1980s. An alternative explanation, favored by some, is the increased demand for funds by the federal government, which was forced to borrow large sums to finance the mammoth budget deficits of recent years.

The Structure of Interest Rates

To this point our discussion has been in terms of a single interest rate (actually a single real interest rate and, given expectations about inflation, a corresponding nominal interest rate). In reality, there is an array of different interest rates at any given moment in time. All borrowers do not pay the same price for access to loanable funds. Interest rates vary with the length of loan, the risk of default, and the cost of administering the loan.

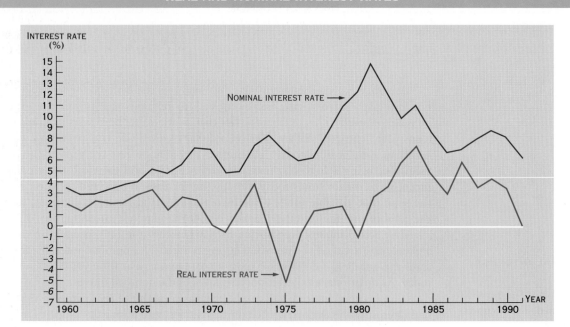

REAL AND NOMINAL INTEREST RATES*

*These are the interest rates paid by the U.S. government to borrow funds for one year. The nominal interest rate is the actual interest rate paid. The real interest rate is estimated by assuming that the expected inflation rate for the coming year equals the actual inflation rate for the prior year.

SOURCE: *Federal Reserve Bulletin*, 1992.

FIGURE 33.3

LENGTH OF LOAN

Interest rates typically differ, depending on how soon a loan must be repaid. One reason is that borrowers and lenders may expect conditions to change from one period to the next. For example, the interest rate on one-year loans might be expected to rise from 6 percent this year to 8 percent next year. Then, by making consecutive one-year loans, lenders could expect to earn an average of 7 percent over the two-year period. For this reason, they will not agree to a two-year loan that pays less than 7 percent. By the same token, because one-year loans are expected to become more expensive next year, borrowers are willing to pay a higher price to obtain funds for two years than for one year. More generally, expectations that short-term interest rates will rise in the future pull up long-term interest rates today.

Even when short-term interest rates are not expected to rise, long-term interest rates may exceed short-term rates. If lenders are reluctant to tie up their funds for an extended period of time, they will demand a premium (higher interest rate) on long-term loans. Consistent with this view, for about 80 percent of the period since 1950, long-term rates have exceeded short-term rates. In late 1992 the U.S. government was forced to pay an interest rate of more than 7.0 percent to borrow funds for 30 years, compared to a rate of less than 3.5 percent to borrow funds for one year. By historical standards this was an unusually high premium.

RISK OF DEFAULT

RISK OF DEFAULT
The probability that a borrower will fail to meet its interest obligations or repay the loan.

When a lender loans funds there is always a **risk of default**—the borrower may fail to pay interest or to repay the loan. In the 1980s, U.S. banks lost billions of dollars when Mexico and other debtor nations defaulted on their loans. Similarly, those who lent funds to the Washington Public Power Supply System (aptly nicknamed "Whoops") lost $2.25 billion plus interest when the utility halted construction of two nuclear power projects. Without revenues from the power plants, the utility was unable to meet its financial obligations.

Although lenders cannot eliminate the risk of default, they take this risk into account when making loans. Borrowers with a higher risk of default are charged higher interest rates to compensate lenders for the possible loss of their funds. For example, Chrysler recently paid an interest rate of 13 percent to borrow funds through 1997, almost double the rate paid by the U.S. government. This reflected lenders' convictions that Chrysler was much more likely to default than the U.S. government.

ADMINISTRATIVE COSTS

Lenders incur various loan-processing costs (for example, bookkeeping). These costs are often the same regardless of a loan's size. Consequently, administrative costs per dollar lent tend to fall as size of the loan increases. Because of this cost advantage, large loans typically carry a lower interest rate, other things equal, than small loans. In turn, the fact that large companies tend to borrow greater sums of money helps explain why they generally pay lower interest rates (for a given risk of default) than small companies and households.

Interest Rates and the Allocation of Capital

Although capital is productive, additional capital is not equally productive for every firm or project. An additional $100 million in capital may increase revenues by $15 million per year if used to open new Wal-Mart stores but by only $5 million per year if used to build another plant for Bethlehem Steel. Society benefits when resources, including capital, are allocated efficiently—when they are used in those sectors where they create the greatest value for society.

When interest rates are determined competitively—by the supply of and demand for funds—they allocate capital where it is most productive. If the market interest rate (adjusted for risk) is 10 percent, projects that return at least $10 per year on each $100 borrowed will be undertaken; projects with lower rates of return will not. In our example, Wal-Mart will borrow funds because it can use them profitably, but Bethlehem Steel will not. In summary, competitively determined interest rates allocate loanable funds and therefore capital to those firms and projects where they are valued most highly. On the other hand, when interest rates are set artificially, capital is not allocated efficiently (see Exhibit 33.1).

Rents

PURE ECONOMIC RENT
The payment for using a resource that is fixed in supply.

Noneconomists use the term "rent" to describe payments for the use of various property—a car leased from Avis, an apartment, even space on a billboard. To the economist, rent means something different. **Pure economic rent** is the payment to a resource that is fixed in supply—that is, a resource whose supply curve is perfectly inelastic. The classic example is land. Indeed, economists first studied economic rent in the context of rent on land. Today the term economic rent is used more broadly to include certain income payments to resources other than land.

To understand the concept of economic rent, it is helpful to consider the controversy that initially prompted economic analysis of rents. The discussion is then extended to cover rents to inputs other than land.

Land Rents

The price of grain—what the British call "corn"—rose sharply in early nineteenth-century Britain. This led to widespread economic hardship and to public indignation. Who was responsible? Noting that high land rents accompanied high corn prices, some blamed the landowners. Claiming that high rents caused high corn

Usury Laws

E X H I B I T

33 . 1

State governments sometimes attempt to "protect" borrowers through **usury laws**, which impose a ceiling on legal interest rates. When that ceiling is below market rates, interest rates can no longer perform their rationing function. In the following figure, the amount of funds demanded at the maximum legal interest rate is Q_2, but lenders are willing to supply only Q_1 funds.

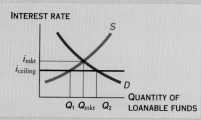

Usury Laws
Legislation that prohibits lenders from charging more than a specified interest rate on certain types of loans.

Because interest rates are not allowed to determine who obtains credit and who does not, banks and other lenders are forced to resort to various means of nonprice rationing. They make funds available only to their best customers and to those with the very best credit ratings—borrowers with the highest incomes (primarily white males) and the most collateral. These privileged borrowers benefit from usury laws because they are able to obtain funds at below-market interest rates. Other borrowers are squeezed from the market entirely, unable to obtain any funds at legal interest rates. Their only source of funds are *loan sharks*, who charge exorbitant interest rates, in part to compensate for the risk of being jailed or fined for violating usury laws. An irony of usury laws is that the very people they were intended to help—the poor and powerless—are the ones victimized by these laws.

Another consequence of usury laws is that lower-valued projects may be funded at the expense of higher-valued projects. For example, suppose Rachel is willing to pay an interest rate of 20 percent to borrow funds but Joe, an equal credit risk, is prepared to pay only 15 percent. If the maximum legal interest rate is 15 percent, lenders have no reason to prefer loaning funds to Rachel, even though she values the funds more highly. Given excess demand for credit, Rachel is just as likely to be squeezed from the market as Joe (and perhaps more likely if the lender considers gender when rationing funds).

Finally, it is worth emphasizing that usury laws, when effective, not only distort the distribution of credit, they also reduce the *volume* of credit. In the absence of the interest rate ceiling, the quantity of loanable funds would be Q_{mkt} rather than Q_1.

prices, they proposed limiting the amount of rent landowners could charge. Economist David Ricardo, however, argued that causation ran in the opposite direction: "Corn is not high [in price] because a rent is paid, but a rent is paid because corn is high."

Ricardo's analysis is presented in Figure 33.4, (page 868). Ricardo argued that the amount of land, or what he called "the original and indestructible powers of the

When the supply of land is fixed, the price of using land (rent) is determined by the demand for land. If demand is D_1, rent is P_1. If demand increases to D_2—because of a higher price for corn—rent rises to P_2. If demand for land decreases to D_3, rent is zero.

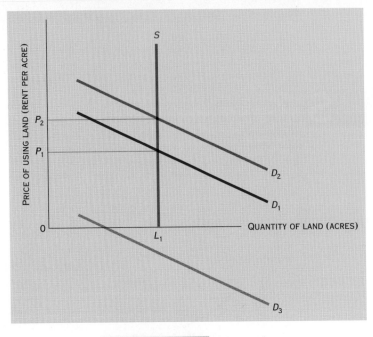

FIGURE 33.4

soil," is fixed, determined by nature. As such, the supply of land is perfectly inelastic. Changes in rent (the price of using land) are therefore completely determined by changes in the demand for land. If demand increases from D_1 to D_2, rent rises from P_1 to P_2. Similarly, a reduction in the demand for land lowers rents. If demand falls to D_3, land is no longer scarce and therefore landowners receive no rent. Because landowners gain nothing by leaving land idle, they rent their land at the market price whether that price is high, low, or even zero.

In modern terminology, the demand for land is a *derived demand*, determined by the demand for corn.[2] When the price of corn is high, demand for land is similarly high, leading to high rents. Although landowners benefit from high rents, they are in no way responsible for those high rents. High rents result from high corn prices.

Because high rents are the consequence of high corn prices, not the cause, forcing landowners to roll back rents would not reduce the price of corn. It would merely transfer income from landowners to tenants. The path to lower corn prices, claimed Ricardo, lay not in lower rents but in greater availability of corn. Accordingly, he and his followers fought to repeal the Corn Laws, which limited imports of food into Britain. In 1846, after a long struggle, the Corn Laws were rescinded. Corn imports increased, and the price of corn fell, as Ricardo had predicted.

[2]For a review of the concept "derived demand," see page 781.

Even though lower rents would not reduce the price of corn, they offered govern-ment an opportunity to raise tax revenues without reducing either the supply of land or the quantity of corn. When supply is upward sloping, a tax on any resource raises the price of that resource and reduces the quantity supplied [see Figure 33.5(A)]. With fewer resources employed, the country's output falls.

In contrast, when supply is perfectly inelastic, a tax affects neither price of the resource nor the quantity supplied. For example, in Figure 33.5(B), the tax reduces the after-tax return to landowners from P_1 to P_2, but landowners still supply L_1 units of land. Tenants continue to pay P_1 rent (since demand for land is not affected by the tax), but landowners must now remit $P_1 - P_2$ of this rent to the govern-ment. That is, the tax is borne entirely by landowners. Because the price of land does not change to tenants, the tax does not distort the allocation of resources. Farmers continue to use the same amount of land and to produce the same level of output. Thus, the tax raises revenue for the government without harming economic efficiency.

This is one reason various economists have found land taxes to be so appealing. Land taxes have also been supported by those who view rent as an *unearned surplus*.

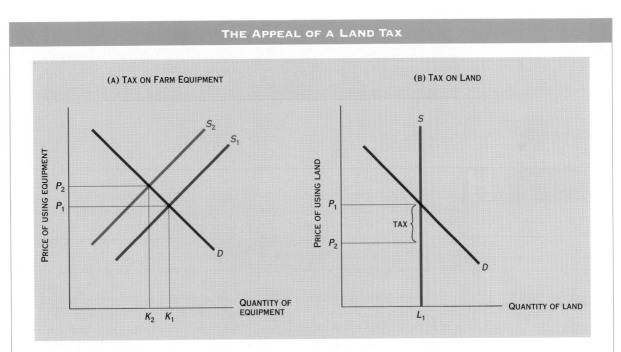

THE APPEAL OF A LAND TAX

(A) TAX ON FARM EQUIPMENT

(B) TAX ON LAND

In general, a tax levied on a resource raises the price of that resource and lowers the amount used by producers (A). On the other hand, if the supply of a resource is fixed, the tax neither raises the price of the resource nor curtails its use. Because the supply of land is perfectly inelastic, landowners cannot pass on any of the tax to users (B). The after-tax payment received by landowners decreases by the full amount of the tax, from P_1 to P_2. Because the price and quantity of land used are unaffected by the tax, the price and quantity of the output produced with land are similarly unaffected.

FIGURE 33.5

If demand for land increases, as one would expect in a growing economy, landowners receive higher rents even though they have done nothing to make their land more productive.

Ricardo predicted that, over time, competition for land would raise the share of income going to landowners. This bothered some political thinkers, who viewed landowners as no more deserving of rising income than tenants. Economist John Stuart Mill suggested that future increases in rent be taxed away from landowners. Henry George went further, proposing that all rent be expropriated from landowners—present rents as well as future increases in rent (see Exhibit 33.2).

Rents to Other Resources

ECONOMIC RENT
The premium received by a resource in excess of its opportunity cost.

Landowners are not alone in receiving a surplus—that is, a payment in excess of opportunity cost. Barry Larkin, Danny Tartabull, and other top sluggers receive $5 million per year to play baseball, considerably more than necessary to induce them to face opposing pitchers. This premium or additional income is as much a surplus as the payments to landowners. As such it can be considered an **economic rent**. More generally, any resource is said to receive an economic rent when it receives a

Henry George and the Single Tax

Henry George viewed land as a gift of nature. He believed that society in general contributed to the value of land and therefore society in general should share the rewards. This could be accomplished by taxing away the pure economic rent of land and using these proceeds for the public good.

George's proposal was known as the *single tax* because he believed this tax would raise so much revenue for the government that no other taxes would be needed. Under George's plan the government would not tax improvements to land (for example, from draining swamps or irrigating arid farm land). Nor would George tax capital, such as the buildings on land. His tax would be based solely on the rents land would command in the absence of all such improvements.

George sketched his theory in *Our Land and Land Policy* and developed it more fully in *Progress and Poverty*, a highly successful book published in 1879. Critics attacked his single tax on the grounds that it would not raise sufficient revenue for the government, that it would be difficult to administer, and that it would be unfair to the many landowners who had purchased land at high prices in the expectation of receiving high rents. His views proved popular with many voters, however, and he twice ran for mayor of New York City. He finished second in 1886 and died during the 1897 campaign.

EXHIBIT 33.2

payment in excess of its opportunity cost—that is, an income greater than required to keep the resource in its present employment.

The difference between economic rent and the previously defined pure economic rent is that opportunity cost is zero in the case of pure economic rent. When supply is perfectly inelastic, the entire payment to a resource owner constitutes economic rent. In contrast, when opportunity cost is positive, only a portion of the factor payment is economic rent. Thus, a pure economic rent is a special type of economic rent that arises when supply of a resource is perfectly inelastic.

Whenever input supply curves are upward sloping, all but the last unit supplied receive an economic rent. This is illustrated in Figure 33.6(B), which depicts supply and demand for librarians. If the wage is W_1, all librarians except the last receive a wage in excess of their opportunity cost—that is, all but the last librarian are willing to work for less than W_1. The aggregate economic rent received by all librarians can be represented by the area above the supply curve and below the market wage.

YOUR TURN

THE TOWN OF GULLIESVILLE HAS HIRED THREE DEPUTY SHERIFFS—JOHN, SUE, AND TERRY—AT A MARKET WAGE OF $18,000 PER YEAR. HAD JOHN NOT RECEIVED AN $18,000 OFFER, HE WOULD HAVE REFUSED THE JOB. SUE, ON THE OTHER HAND, WAS WILLING TO ACCEPT THE JOB PROVIDED THAT IT PAID AT LEAST $17,000 PER YEAR. TERRY, WHO HAS ALWAYS WANTED TO BE A DEPUTY SHERIFF, WOULD HAVE WORKED FOR A WAGE AS LOW AS $15,000 PER YEAR. WHAT IS THE ECONOMIC RENT OF (A) JOHN, (B) SUE, (C) TERRY, AND (D) THE DEPUTIES AS A GROUP?

ECONOMIC RENT

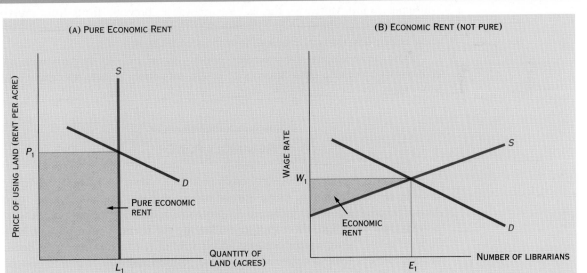

Economic rent is the difference between the payment received by a resource and the opportunity cost of that resource. When supply is perfectly inelastic (A), the resource has a zero opportunity cost and the entire payment is pure economic rent (shaded rectangle). When supply is upward sloping (B), the opportunity cost is greater than zero. For an individual librarian, economic rent is the difference between the actual payment (W_1) and the minimum payment he or she requires to work as a librarian (given by the supply curve). Aggregate economic rent of all librarians is depicted by the shaded triangle in (B).

FIGURE 33.6

Profit

ECONOMIC PROFIT
The residual that remains after all production costs, implicit as well as explicit, are subtracted from total revenue. This residual accrues to the firm.

By selling a product, a firm generates revenue. Out of this revenue the firm must pay for any resources it uses. That is, costs, both explicit and implicit, must be subtracted from total revenue. (Remember that the economist, unlike the accountant, subtracts implicit costs as well as direct payments to others.) The *residual*—what remains after paying for the use of resources—is the firm's **economic profit**. For this reason, the firm is sometimes called the *residual claimant*. When the firm can sell its output for more than the cost of production, it is rewarded with a positive residual—a profit. But when resource costs exceed total revenue, the firm bears the consequences: the residual is negative, and the firm suffers a loss.

The Sources of Profit

Why does a residual exist? Why do costs and revenues sometimes differ? To understand the origin of profit it is helpful first to examine the opposite situation—a world in which all firms earn zero economic profits (normal profits).

Assume markets are perfectly competitive, the future is known, and innovation is nonexistent. In such an environment there is no potential for profit. Lacking entry barriers, firms cannot earn monopoly profits. Nor do firms have the opportunity to gamble on the future—for example, to try to anticipate a change in consumer demand before other firms do. All firms know in advance which products consumers want. Moreover, the lack of innovation prevents firms from creating successful new products or introducing new techniques for cutting costs. Under these conditions, the opportunity for profit is nonexistent.

Profits arise because the preceding conditions fail to hold. In particular, most economists recognize three sources of profit: monopoly power, uncertainty, and innovation.

MONOPOLY POWER

Firms are not all price takers; many enjoy monopoly power—the ability to drive up price by restricting output. As we learned earlier, this may lead to economic profit. Although other firms are attracted to profitable industries, various barriers may prevent their entry into these industries. Among the barriers discussed in Chapter 26 were patents, government licenses, and control of crucial raw materials. Because of such barriers, firms are sheltered from competition and may be able to earn economic profits, even in the long run.

UNCERTAINTY

Firms must make decisions in an uncertain world. As such, they assume risks. They make subjective assessments about future markets, costs, government policy, even the weather. When these assessments prove correct, or when the firm is plain lucky—as when an unanticipated event boosts product demand—the firm is rewarded with profit. On the other hand, when fate is unkind, the firm incurs a loss. Viewed in this light, profit and loss are the fruit of decision making under uncertainty. For those who succeed—the ones with foresight or good fortune—the fruit is sweet; for others the taste is bitter.

Consider the uncertainty faced by automakers. What type of cars will consumers want in five years? What types of styling will appeal to them? How important will be size, safety, comfort, and miles per gallon? The answers depend on income levels, the price of gasoline, and consumer tastes. Although these are all unknowable, the lead time required to plan and design a new car forces automobile producers to make judgments about the future.

Sometimes those judgments will be wrong. Automobile companies may produce too many large cars, as happened after the oil crisis in the mid-1970s. Or they may produce cars that are too boxy, as General Motors did during part of the 1980s. Ford did a better job of anticipating consumer preferences. Its reward was to earn greater profits than General Motors. In turn, the owners of Ford (the shareholders) saw their stock climb 31 percent in the two years following Ford's introduction of its new line of vehicles. Over the same period, stock in General Motors dropped 13 percent in price.[3]

INNOVATION

Even in the absence of innovation, uncertainty would lead to profit and loss. Firms would still be forced to make assessments about future demand, government policy, and a host of other developments. The fact that firms can introduce new products and new methods of production creates added uncertainty. Will the new products catch on? Will new methods of production really cut costs? Depending on the answer, innovations may create either profit or loss.

In some cases the success of an innovation is stunning, and so are the rewards. Consider Bill Gates and Estée Lauder. Sensing an opportunity to write and sell computer software, Gates dropped out of school at age 19 to start his own company. That company, Microsoft, proved so successful that at age 31 Gates became the industry's first billionaire. Before Gates was even born, Lauder was peddling her skin cream to the beauty salons of New York City. The cream was so popular that department stores added her line of products. By the time she was 83, the daughter of Jewish immigrants had built a sales staff of several thousand workers and a personal fortune of $5.2 billion.[4]

Not all new products are a success. To the contrary, losses are more common—as most small companies fold within a few years after beginning operations. Innovation carries with it considerable risk. But for those who accept the risk and succeed, the rewards can be substantial. Ask Bill Gates.

---

[3]These figures, for the period 1986–1987, exclude dividend payments. If dividends are included, the value of Ford's stock increased by 41 percent while the value of GM's stock was virtually unchanged.

[4]*Fortune*, "The Billionaires," October 12, 1987, pp. 144–149; *Fortune*, "The Billionaires," September 9, 1991, pp. 53–64.

The Role of Profit

The role of profit is not always appreciated. Sometimes profit is attacked as undeserved, even harmful to the economy. Where profit results from entry restrictions, which shelter a firm from competition, the interests of society may indeed be harmed. But some criticize all profit. For instance, Karl Marx argued that profit results from the exploitation of labor. Such a view neglects the positive functions of profit. Most economists argue that profit, where it does not result from entry restrictions, serves three important functions: allocating resources, inducing efficient production, and encouraging innovation.

RESOURCE ALLOCATION

For the value of society's output to be maximized, resources must flow to those sectors where they are valued most highly. Profit and loss signal whether additional resources should enter an industry or present resources should leave. When firms in an industry are earning profit, this indicates that the value of resources employed there exceeds their opportunity cost. Society therefore benefits when additional resources are drawn into the industry. Conversely, when firms in an industry are losing money, the implication is that resources are valued more highly elsewhere and should therefore leave their present industry.

EFFICIENT PRODUCTION

If output is to be maximized, resources must also be used efficiently within an industry. Production that wastes resources reduces the amount of output available to society. Profit is the incentive for firms to use resources efficiently; loss is the penalty for wasting resources.

INNOVATION

Profit also spurs new ideas, new products, new production techniques. Without the opportunity for profit, entrepreneurs would have little reason to innovate and society would be the worse off, because innovation leads to faster economic growth and additional products for consumers. However, innovation does not guarantee perpetual profits. Harvard economist Joseph Schumpeter argued that competition would ultimately eliminate profit to the innovator, as other firms copied the new product or process. But one innovation would be followed by another and, where successful, the innovator would earn short-run profits. According to Schumpeter, it is the lure of profit, even temporary profit, that leads to innovation.[5]

---

[5]For further discussion of Schumpeter's theory, see Chapter 27 or refer directly to Joseph Schumpeter, *Capitalism, Socialism, and Democracy* (New York: Harper and Row, 1942).

The Functional Distribution of Income

How is a country's income divided? What are the shares going to wages, interest, rent, and profit? Government statistics are available (see Table 33.1), but it is important to realize that they are not based on economic definitions. For instance, statistics on profit pertain to accounting profit. Recall that accounting profit ignores certain implicit costs—for example, forgone salary and implicit rent on land owned by the company. To the extent certain costs are excluded, accounting profit overstates economic profit.

Government statistics on rent include payments for the use of capital as well as for the use of land. On the other hand, they exclude economic rent to labor. Income received by proprietorships (noncorporate businesses) includes both profit and the imputed salary of the proprietor. Despite the fact that government statistics do not mesh precisely with economic definitions, these statistics still provide useful information. Among the major conclusions that can be drawn are the following.

1. The share of income going to profits is less than commonly perceived. At present, corporate profits amount to less than 10 percent of the income in the United States (see Table 33.1).

2. The bulk of income consists of payments to labor. Measured narrowly as employee compensation, labor income accounted for 75 percent of total income in 1991. If proprietors' income is included, the figure climbs to 83 percent.

THE DISTRIBUTION OF INCOME IN THE UNITED STATES, 1900–1991

TIME PERIOD	COMPENSATION OF EMPLOYEES (%)	PROPRIETORS' INCOME (%)	NET RENTAL INCOME OF PERSONS* (%)	CORPORATE PROFITS (%)	NET INTEREST (%)	TOTAL (%)
1900–1909	55.0	23.7	6.8	5.5	9.0	100.0
1910–1919	53.6	23.8	9.1	5.4	8.1	100.0
1920–1929	60.8	17.5	7.8	6.2	7.7	100.0
1930	63.8	15.2	5.7	8.6	6.7	100.0
1940	65.6	15.8	3.4	11.1	4.1	100.0
1950	64.8	16.2	3.2	14.5	1.3	100.0
1960	69.8	12.3	3.6	11.6	2.7	100.0
1970	74.3	9.6	2.2	9.0	4.9	100.0
1980	74.4	8.2	0.3	8.0	9.1	100.0
1990	73.7	8.2	−0.3	8.1	10.3	100.0
1991	74.6	8.1	−0.2	7.6	9.9	100.0

*Gross rental income from land and capital minus depreciation of capital. Value is negative when depreciation exceeds gross rental income.

SOURCES: The top three lines are from Irving B. Kravis, "Income Distribution: Functional Share," from David L. Sills, ed., *International Encyclopedia of Social Sciences*, Vol. 7 (New York: Macmillan and Free Press, 1968), p. 134. Reprinted with permission of Macmillan Publishing Company. Copyright © 1968 by Crowell Collier and Macmillan, Inc. More recent data are from the U.S. Department of Commerce, *The National Income and Product Accounts of the United States, 1929–82* (1986) and *Survey of Current Business*, July 1992.

TABLE 33.1

3. Contrary to the prediction of Ricardo, rent's share of income has not increased over time. Over the past 80 years it has declined steadily—at least as measured by the government. In fact, gross rental income in recent years has failed to cover depreciation of rental property, causing net rental income to turn negative.

4. When measured by employee compensation, labor's share has increased from 55 percent at the start of the century to 75 percent today. On the other hand, if proprietors' income is attributed to labor, labor's share has been fairly stable. These divergent findings reflect the fact that proprietors' share of income has trended downward, offsetting the increase in employee compensation. The decline in proprietors' relative income is caused, in turn, by the changing nature of production. As economic activity has become increasingly organized by corporations, proprietorships have become less important.

5. Interest income rose during the 1980s. As previously discussed, interest rates were unusually high during this period. In addition, the level of borrowing rose as government and business increased their demand for funds.

Summary

1. Interest income refers to the payments borrowers make to lenders for the use of their funds. Consumers are willing to pay interest because of a positive time preference—they prefer present consumption to future consumption. Firms are willing to pay for the use of funds because they can be used to acquire capital, which permits an expansion of output. Firms have an incentive to acquire additional capital as long as it contributes more to revenue than to costs.

2. Interest income depends on the price charged for using funds (the interest rate) and the volume of funds loaned. According to the loanable funds model, these are determined by the demand for and supply of loanable funds.

3. The actual interest rate that borrowers pay lenders is called the nominal interest rate. The nominal interest rate fluctuates with the expected rate of inflation. Other things equal, a higher expected rate of inflation increases demand for loanable funds while reducing the supply. Both put upward pressure on the nominal interest rate.

4. The real interest rate is defined as the nominal interest rate minus the expected rate of inflation. Both nominal and real interest rates depend on length of the loan, risk of default, and cost of administering the loan.

5. When interest rates are determined competitively—by the supply of and demand for loanable funds—they allocate funds where they are valued most highly. But when interest rates are set artificially low, through usury laws, they are unable to allocate funds efficiently. Usury laws also reduce the volume of credit and the share received by those with low credit ratings.

6. Economic rent is the difference between the payment received by a resource and the opportunity cost of that resource. In the special case where supply of a resource is fixed, the entire payment constitutes rent. To signify this, the expression *pure economic rent* is used.

7. When supply is fixed, a tax on the resource is borne entirely by the resource owner. Because price does not rise to resource users, the quantity of the resource used does not change. As such, the tax has no adverse effect on the economy's output.

8. When resource supply is upward sloping, all but the last unit supplied receive a payment in excess of opportunity cost. Therefore, all but the last unit hired receive some economic rent.

9. Profit, as defined by economists, is the residual that accrues to a firm after all costs have been netted out (implicit as well as explicit). That residual may be either positive or negative. The opportunity for profit comes from several sources: monopoly power, uncertainty, and innovation.

10. Profit serves three important functions for the economy—it promotes efficient allocation of resources, efficient production, and innovation.

11. As measured by statistics of the U.S. government, employee compensation accounts for three-fourths of all income in the United States. If proprietors' income is included, labor's share exceeds 80 percent.

12. Employee compensation has been rising faster than income in general and, contrary to the predictions of Ricardo, rent's share of income has fallen.

Key Terms

interest rate
interest income
loanable funds model
loanable funds
positive time preference
roundabout production
nominal interest rate

real interest rate
risk of default
usury laws
pure economic rent
economic rent
economic profit

Study Questions and Problems

1. What happens to the equilibrium interest rate in each of the following cases and why?
   a. Consumers decide to save more of their income in order to support themselves better after they retire.
   b. Technological innovations increase the productivity of additional capital.
   c. Households decide that college education is no longer a good investment, and the percentage of the population wanting to attend college falls.
   d. States enact stricter usury laws, which reduce the rate of interest lenders may legally charge.

2. Why does the nominal interest rate differ from the real interest rate? Under what condition are the two interest rates the same?

3. Why do lenders charge different customers different interest rates? Is this practice justified?

4. Assume the government, concerned about a declining farm economy, induces lenders to make more funds available to agriculture than lenders would in the absence of government intervention. On what basis could this action be criticized?

5. The following table depicts the supply of mechanics to a community:

ANNUAL WAGE	QUANTITY SUPPLIED
$20,000	1
21,000	2
22,000	3
23,000	4

  a. If the market wage is $21,000 per year, how much economic rent does the first worker receive? How much does the second receive?

  b. If the market wage rises to $23,000, how much economic rent do the first and second workers now receive?

  c. What is the total economic rent of all four mechanics when the annual wage is $23,000?

6. Even though the opportunity cost of land *in the aggregate* is zero, individual parcels of land have alternatives uses [for example, agriculture, residential housing, or commercial development (including retail shopping and office use)].

  a. Draw the supply curve of land available for commercial use. Is it perfectly inelastic?

  b. Assume land is taxed only when used for commercial purposes. How will this tax affect the quantity of land used commercially? How will it affect the price tenants pay for use of this land? Explain your reasoning.

7. A seat on the New York Stock Exchange entitles its holder to earn income by buying and selling stocks for clients. The price of a seat fell from a record $1.1 million in 1987—before the stock market crash—to $400,000 in 1990. The number of seats on the Stock Exchange is fixed, and therefore did not change during this period. What accounted for the lower price? Illustrate this situation using supply and demand curves.

8. What does it mean to say that a firm is the "residual claimant"?

9. Why do economic profits exist? If firms are willing to accept normal profits, why do some receive positive economic profits?

10. Suppose the government taxed away all profits and reimbursed firms for any losses they incurred in production. What effect would this have on the economy?

11. How has labor's share of income in the United States changed this century? Does your answer depend on how "labor's share" is defined? Explain.

(A) $0, (B) $1,000, (C) $3,000, (D) $4,000.

YOUR TURN
Answers

Selected Reference

Blaug, Mark. *Economic Theory in Retrospect*, 4th ed. (London: Cambridge University Press, 1985). Provides a historical discussion of roundabout production, the Corn Laws, and the single tax.

YOU HAVE THE POOR
AMONG YOU ALWAYS.

—JOHN 12:8

Poverty and the Distribution of Income

THE UNITED STATES HAS ONE OF THE HIGHEST STANDARDS OF LIVING IN THE WORLD. IT ALSO HAS OVER 30 MILLION PEOPLE LIVING IN POVERTY. WHY DOES POVERTY EXIST IN A NATION AS AFFLUENT AS THE UNITED STATES? WHO ARE THE POOR, AND HOW HAVE THEIR NUMBERS CHANGED OVER TIME? IS THE NATION WINNING ITS SELF-PROCLAIMED "WAR ON POVERTY," OR IS IT ON THE VERGE OF SURRENDER? CHAPTER 34 STUDIES THE DISTRIBUTION OF INCOME IN THE UNITED STATES, PAYING SPECIAL ATTENTION TO THOSE AT THE BOTTOM. IT ALSO EXAMINES THE MAJOR GOVERNMENT PROGRAMS DESIGNED TO ALLEVIATE POVERTY.

The Distribution of Income

MEASURING INCOME INEQUALITY

Although median family income in the United States is approximately $35,000,[1] that income is distributed unevenly. Over 5 percent of families have an annual income of at least $100,000, but almost one family in ten has an income below $10,000 (see Table 34.1). Although these numbers are revealing, they do not readily lend themselves to analysis. As incomes have risen over time, have they risen more rapidly for those at the bottom of the income distribution or for those at the top? That is, has the distribution of income become more equal or less equal? To answer such questions, the distribution of income is generally presented in an alternative fashion.

One convention is to arrange families in order of income and then to divide them into five groups of equal size called *quintiles*. The first quintile consists of the 20 percent of families having the least amount of income in a year. The second quintile consists of the next 20 percent of families, arranged in order of income, and so forth. In 1990, families with incomes of $16,845 or less were assigned to the first quintile; families with incomes between $16,846 and $29,043 made it to the second quintile. The full distribution by quintile is presented in Table 34.2.

THE DISTRIBUTION OF FAMILY INCOME BY INCOME BRACKET, 1990*

FAMILY INCOME	PERCENT OF FAMILIES
Under $5,000	3.6
$ 5,000 to $ 9,999	5.8
$ 10,000 to $14,999	7.5
$ 15,000 to $24,999	16.4
$ 25,000 to $34,999	16.2
$ 35,000 to $49,999	20.0
$ 50,000 to $74,999	18.2
$ 75,000 to $99,999	6.9
$100,000 and over	5.4
Total	100.0
Median income	$35,353

* Before taxes.

SOURCE: U.S. Department of Commerce, *Current Population Reports*, Series P-60, No. 174 (1991), p. 199.

TABLE 34.1

---

[1]"Median" means midpoint. Half of all families have an income below the median income; half of all families have a higher income.

THE DISTRIBUTION OF FAMILY INCOME BY QUINTILE, 1990*				
QUINTILE	**INCOME**	**PERCENT OF FAMILIES**	**PERCENT OF INCOME**
First (bottom)	$16,845 or less	20	4.6
Second	$16,846 to $29,043	20	10.8
Third	$29,044 to $42,039	20	16.6
Fourth	$42,040 to $61,489	20	23.7
Fifth (top)	$61,490 or more	20	44.3
	Total	100	100.0

* Before taxes.
SOURCE: U.S. Department of Commerce, *Current Population Reports*, Series P-60, No. 174 (1991), pp. 58 and 202.

TABLE 34.2

Table 34.3 presents the *cumulative* distribution of income for families. It contains the same information as Table 34.2, but in a different format. The cumulative distribution indicates the percentage of income received by a given quintile or a lower quintile. For example, the first quintile received 4.6 percent of total income in 1990; the second quintile received 10.8 percent. Together they received 15.4 percent. Therefore, the cumulative percentage of income received by the bottom two quintiles was 15.4 percent. Similar calculations reveal the cumulative distribution of the bottom three and bottom four quintiles (32.0 percent and 55.7 percent, respectively).

Information about the cumulative distribution of income can be presented diagrammatically with a **Lorenz curve**. A Lorenz curve shows the relationship between percentage of families and percentage of income. For example, the Lorenz curve of Figure 34.1 (page 884) shows that in 1990 the bottom 40 percent of families, when arranged by income, received 15.4 percent of the nation's total income.

All Lorenz curves share a common feature. They start at the bottom left corner of the box (zero percent of families receive zero percent of income) and they end at the top right corner (100 percent of families receive 100 percent of income).

LORENZ CURVE

A diagram illustrating the cumulative distribution of income by families.

THE CUMULATIVE DISTRIBUTION OF FAMILY INCOME BY QUINTILE, 1990*				
QUINTILE	**INCOME**	**PERCENT OF FAMILIES**	**PERCENT OF INCOME**
First	$16,845 or less	20	4.6
Second or lower	$29,043 or less	40	15.4
Third or lower	$42,039 or less	60	32.0
Fourth or lower	$61,489 or less	80	55.7
Fifth or lower	All levels	100	100.0

*Before taxes.
SOURCE: Same as Table 34.2.

TABLE 34.3

The Lorenz curve graphs the cumulative distribution of income by families. The area between the Lorenz curve and the line of complete equality measures the degree of income inequality across families. The larger the area, the greater the inequality.

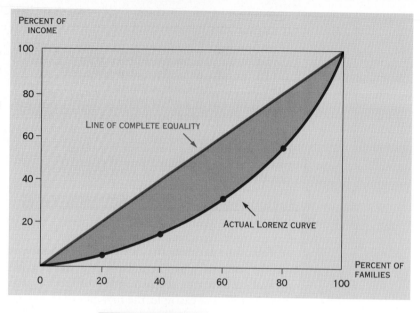

FIGURE 34.1

What is revealing is the path of the Lorenz curve between these two points. If the distribution of income were perfectly equal, the first 20 percent of families would receive 20 percent of income, the first 40 percent of families would receive 40 percent of income, and so on. Therefore, the Lorenz curve would be a diagonal line.

A comparison of the actual Lorenz curve with this hypothetical Lorenz curve reveals how much inequality exists within a country. The more evenly income is distributed, the closer the actual Lorenz curve is to the line of complete equality. Therefore, one measure of income inequality is the size of the area between these two curves (represented by the shaded area of Figure 34.1). A smaller area denotes less income inequality; a larger area, greater inequality.

YOUR TURN

SUPPOSE INCOME IS DISTRIBUTED AS UNEVENLY AS POSSIBLE—A SINGLE FAMILY RECEIVES A COUNTRY'S ENTIRE INCOME. (A) DRAW THE LORENZ CURVE ASSOCIATED WITH THIS DISTRIBUTION. (B) SHADE THE AREA BETWEEN THIS LORENZ CURVE AND THE LORENZ CURVE CORRESPONDING TO COMPLETE EQUALITY OF INCOME.

A DECLINE IN INCOME INEQUALITY

The Lorenz curve tracks changes in income inequality over time. When Lorenz curves are plotted for 1929 and 1990, the latter lies closer to the line of complete

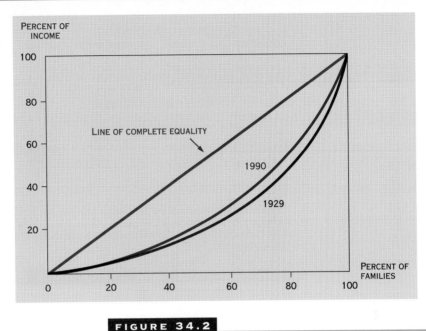

The Lorenz curve for 1990 lies closer to the line of complete equality than does the Lorenz curve for 1929. This implies that income was distributed more equally in 1990.

PERCENT OF INCOME

LINE OF COMPLETE EQUALITY

1990

1929

PERCENT OF FAMILIES

FIGURE 34.2

equality (see Figure 34.2). The implication is that income was distributed more evenly in 1990 than in 1929. Other indicators reinforce this conclusion. For example, the share of income received by families in the top quintile fell from 54 percent in 1929 to 44 percent in 1990, and the share received by the top 5 percent of families shrank from 30 percent to 17 percent (see Table 34.4, page 886).

What is not clear from Figure 34.2 is whether the transformation to a more equal distribution of income has been gradual and continuous. An inspection of data for intervening years reveals that this has not been the case. The distribution of income became more equal throughout the first half of this century and then changed very little over the next 30 years—the share of income received by the bottom quintile hovered around 5 percent while the share received by the top quintile remained at just over 40 percent. Since 1980, there has been a modest reversal of equality. For example, the share of income received by the upper quintile has risen to 44 percent, bolstering the popular view that the well-to-do have improved their relative situation of late. Yet, despite the relapse of recent years, the distribution of income remains more equal today than during the first half of this century.

INTERNATIONAL COMPARISONS

By constructing separate Lorenz curves for each country, it is possible to compare the distribution of income across countries. For example, Figure 34.3 (page 886) reveals that income is distributed more equally in Japan than in the United States

THE DISTRIBUTION OF FAMILY INCOME, VARIOUS YEARS*

QUINTILE	PERCENT OF INCOME					
	1929	1935–1936	1950	1965	1980	1990
First	}12.5**	4.1	4.5	5.2	5.2	4.6
Second		9.2	12.0	12.2	11.5	10.8
Third	13.8	14.1	17.4	17.8	17.5	16.6
Fourth	19.3	20.9	23.4	23.9	24.3	23.7
Fifth	54.4	51.7	42.7	40.9	41.6	44.3
Total	100.0	100.0	100.0	100.0	100.0	100.0
Top 5 percent	30.0	26.5	17.3	15.5	15.3	17.4

*Before taxes.
**Data unavailable separately for first and second quintiles; 12.5 for both quintiles together.
SOURCES: U.S. Department of Commerce, *Historical Statistics of the United States, Colonial Times to 1970*, Part 1 (1975), p. 301; *Current Population Reports*, Series P-60, No. 151 (1986), p. 37, and No. 174 (1991), p. 202.

TABLE 34.4

and, in turn, more equally in the United States than in Honduras. As a general rule, the distribution of income is more equal in industrialized countries (such as Japan and the United States) than in less developed countries (such as Honduras). The distribution is also more equal in centrally planned economies (for example, China

LORENZ CURVES BY COUNTRY

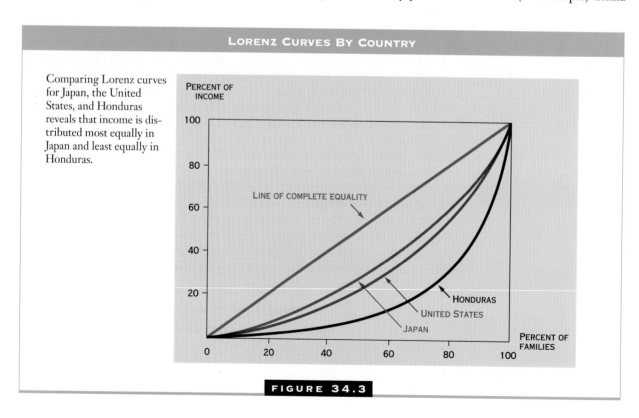

Comparing Lorenz curves for Japan, the United States, and Honduras reveals that income is distributed most equally in Japan and least equally in Honduras.

FIGURE 34.3

and the Soviet Union before its collapse) than in capitalistic countries.[2] Among the reasons for this, wealth is less concentrated in centrally planned economies and wage inequality is less severe.

Why Incomes Differ

Income inequality can be traced to differences in both wage income and nonwage income. First, wage rates differ. Among the reasons previously cited (in Chapters 30 and 32) are differences in age, human capital, discrimination, unions, and economic rents. Second, for any given wage rate, those who work more hours during the year receive higher wage incomes. Beyond that, families with multiple wage earners tend to earn more than families with a single wage earner.

Wealth is also distributed unevenly. In fact, the distribution of wealth is more unequal than the distribution of income. The wealthiest 3 percent of families hold 27 percent of the nation's wealth.[3] Because greater wealth leads to greater nonwage income—interest, rent, and profit—those with high concentrations of wealth can expect high incomes, even in the absence of work.

As uneven as the distribution of wealth currently is, it is actually more equal today than during the first half of the century. Indeed, the movement to greater equality of wealth contributed directly to greater equality of income. As the wealthy have seen their fortunes shrink, at least in relative terms, their income advantage over the rest of the population has narrowed. In some cases, fortunes have been wiped out, eliminating a family's once-healthy nonwage income (see Exhibit 34.1, page 888).

The Effect of Taxation and Transfers on the Distribution of Income

MEANS TEST
A requirement that a family's income not exceed a certain level; if it does the family is declared ineligible for that particular form of public assistance.

Our discussion of the distribution of income has dealt with income before taxes and before government transfer payments (Social Security, housing subsidies, and so on). As it turns out, the effect of taxation on the distribution of income is not terribly important. Low- and middle-income families pay about the same percentage of their income in taxes as do high-income families. As a consequence, the after-tax distribution of income is not substantially different from the before-tax distribution.[4]

Transfer payments are another story. Many transfer payments are **means-tested**: only families with incomes below a certain level qualify and, among those that

---

[2]See Margaret E. Grosh and E. Wayne Nafziger, "The Computation of World Income Distribution," *Economic Development and Cultural Change* (January 1986), pp. 347–359.

[3]U.S. Department of Commerce, *Household Wealth and Asset Ownership: 1988*, Series P-70, No. 22 (1991), p. 47.

[4]In technical terms the current tax system is approximately *proportional*. For evidence of this, see Joseph A. Pechman, *Who Paid the Taxes, 1966–85?* (Washington, D.C.: The Brookings Institution, 1985), especially pp. 4–5.

The Mighty Hath Fallen

E
X
H
I
B
I
T

34.1

Nelson Bunker Hunt was once the wealthiest person in the world, with an estimated fortune of $16 billion. At the time, he boasted that "a billion dollars isn't what it used to be." Since then, both his wealth and his attitude have changed.

Hunt lost billions of dollars speculating on commodities, including an unsuccessful attempt in 1979 to corner the market for silver. His losses mounted with the purchase of speculative oil and coal leases. Then, as the price of oil plunged in the 1980s, the value of his oil properties and real estate plummetted. Unable to meet financial commitments, Hunt defaulted on his loans and in 1988, after a court ordered him to pay damages

to a Peruvian silver company, Hunt filed for bankruptcy. After months of legal maneuvering, Hunt emerged from bankruptcy with only his cars, a house, and some personal possessions. Virtually all of the $16 billion fortune had been lost and, in the process, the distribution of wealth in the country had become a little more equal.

SOURCES: Adapted from John A. Jenkins, "The Hunt Brothers: Battling a Billion-Dollar Debt," *The New York Times Magazine* (September 27, 1987), p. 24; Wendy Zellner, "Well, Anyway You Can't Take It with You," *Business Week*, June 25, 1990, p. 68; Wendy Zellner, "Circling the Remains of the Hunt Fortune," *Business Week*, May 13, 1991, p. 42.

qualify, families with the lowest incomes receive the greatest aid. Therefore, these payments disproportionately benefit low-income families. If the value of transfer payments is included, the distribution of income becomes considerably more equal.[5] Figure 34.4 depicts the distribution of income both before and after adjusting for taxes and transfer payments. Almost all the change is due to the effect of transfer payments.

How Much Income Inequality Do We Want?

Few advocate complete equality of income. If everyone were guaranteed the same income, what incentive would a person have to work hard, to be diligent, to put in long hours? Why accept a job with a high risk of injury or poor working conditions? Why work at all? And why should entrepreneurs innovate if they do not receive any reward from the success of a new product or a new technique of production?

---

[5]According to one study, adjusting for taxes and transfers raised the share of income received by the bottom quintile from 5.4 percent to 12.5 percent in 1972; the share received by the top quintile fell from 41.4 percent to 33.3 percent. See Edgar K. Browning, "The Trend Toward Equality in the Distribution of Net Income," *Southern Economic Journal* (July 1976), p. 914. Other studies find a somewhat smaller effect but agree with the basic conclusion: transfers substantially reduce income inequality.

When taxes are subtracted from income and transfers are added, the distribution of income becomes more equal. Almost all the change results from the equalizing effects of transfer payments.

*1972 data derived from Edgar K. Browning, "The Trend Toward Equality in the Distribution of Net Income," *Southern Economic Journal* (July 1976), p. 914.

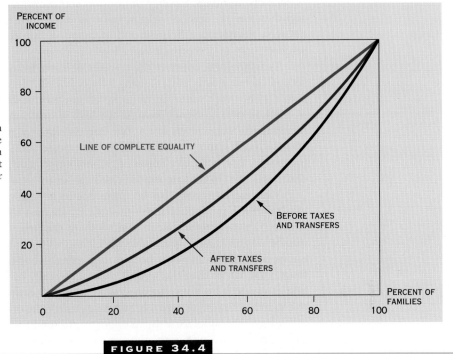

PERCENT OF INCOME

LINE OF COMPLETE EQUALITY

BEFORE TAXES AND TRANSFERS

AFTER TAXES AND TRANSFERS

PERCENT OF FAMILIES

FIGURE 34.4

Complete equality of income blunts or even eliminates the incentive to use resources efficiently. In turn, if resources remain idle or underused and if new technologies remain undeveloped, the result is a lower level of output. Although everyone gets an equal slice of the economic pie, that pie is likely to be quite skimpy. Equality has a cost.

Conversely, a pure market-based distribution of income—which rewards hard work, long hours, unpleasant employment, and innovation—encourages economic efficiency. By compensating resources on the basis of how much they contribute, such a system promotes maximum production. On the other hand, the resulting distribution of income is cold and impersonal. If rewards are based solely on one's contribution to output, those who do not contribute do not eat. Pity those unable to work—the young, the old, the ill, the physically impaired. Unless they have substantial nonwage income or someone to look after them, they may not survive.

Almost everyone agrees that such a distribution of income is intolerable and that those unable to make it on their own warrant public assistance. The thorny issues concern the magnitude of public support and its distribution. Who should receive assistance and how much? What form should the assistance take? How should the revenues necessary to fund this support be raised? As low-income families receive transfer payments, the distribution of income becomes more equal. How much equality do we want? These are all issues within the realm of *normative economics.*

To achieve greater equality, the government taxes income, transferring funds to the poor. But taxes reduce the effective reward for productive activities (work, innovation, and the like), thereby discouraging such activities among the general population. Similarly, transfer payments blunt work incentives of the poor. Because of such disincentives, a policy of taxation and transfers reduces economic efficiency and therefore the level of output. In other words, the government faces a trade-off between economic efficiency and equality of income: greater equality can be achieved only by accepting a lower level of output.

As an analogy, consider the transfer of water from one barrel, mostly full, to a second barrel, mostly empty, using a leaky bucket.[6] In the transfer, water that spills is lost. How much water (income) we choose to transfer likely depends on the size of the leak (the efficiency loss). If the leak is small, we may prefer large transfers, bringing the water levels in the two barrels close together. But if the leak is great, then so much water would be lost in the transfer that we may accept considerable inequality. The optimal amount of redistribution ultimately depends on (a) the size of the leak and (b) the importance one attaches to greater equality.

A distinction must also be made between *equality of outcomes* and *equality of opportunities*. Equal opportunity means that all start the race with an equal chance to win. Equal outcomes mean that all share the prize equally. Different outcomes may be viewed as more acceptable when they reflect differences in effort rather than unfair opportunity. If two people have equal labor-market skills but one works longer and harder than the second, should we really be bothered that income of the first is greater? Isn't income inequality more objectionable where it results from one individual starting with a big advantage over the other?

Those who emphasize equal opportunity tend to favor programs that give disadvantaged individuals a greater chance to succeed, as opposed to greater income per se. Such programs include breaking down entry barriers to certain occupations, facilitating worker mobility, attacking discrimination, bringing higher education within the reach of the poor, and providing good nutrition for children and expectant mothers.

Because views of equality vary across individuals, as does the emphasis placed on equality, there is no consensus concerning the proper role of government in the redistribution of income. Traditionally, however, the bulk of government support has been aimed at people near or below the *poverty line*. Before considering specific programs to alter the distribution of income, it is appropriate to take a look at the principal target of these programs—the poor.

Poverty

There are alternative views of poverty. Some define poverty in *relative* terms—for example, those in the bottom 20 percent of the income distribution or those whose income is less than 50 percent of the median income. The problem with such definitions is that they ignore changes in living standards caused by economic growth. Even if each family's purchasing power were to double, so that it could buy twice as much as before, poverty as just defined would not diminish. Indeed, if the poor

---

[6]This example comes from Arthur Okun, *Equality and Efficiency: The Big Tradeoff* (Washington, D.C.: The Brookings Institution, 1975).

were, by definition, those in the bottom quintile of the income distribution, the war on poverty would be doomed to failure. No matter how much income a country has or how it is divided, there must always be a bottom quintile.

Because of shortcomings in the concept of relative poverty, many prefer to define poverty in *absolute* terms—that is, in terms of how much income is required to maintain some minimum standard of living. According to this concept, one first determines how much income is required to buy basic goods and services. Those whose incomes fall below this level—the **poverty line**—are classified as poor. Note that when poverty is defined in absolute terms, the percentage of the population counted as poor may change over time even if the distribution of income remains constant. In particular, rising incomes tend to reduce poverty—other things equal—whereas falling incomes increase poverty.

POVERTY LINE
A level of income below which a family is classified as poor. The poverty line is based on the cost of those items deemed necessary to maintain a minimally acceptable standard of living.

The Official Poverty Line

The United States government relies on the concept of absolute poverty. It first began calculating poverty lines in 1964 based on estimates by the U.S. Department of Agriculture of the cost of an "economy food plan."[7] According to earlier research by the Department of Agriculture, families with three or more members spent an average of one-third of their income on food. Therefore, the poverty line for these families was set equal to three times the cost of the economy food plan. For smaller families the food budget was slightly less than one-third of income; therefore, a larger multiple was used. Because food budgets vary with family size, poverty lines also depend on family size. Poverty lines are updated each year to reflect changes in

POVERTY LINES BY FAMILY SIZE, 1990

NUMBER OF PERSONS IN FAMILY	POVERTY LINE
One	$ 6,652
Two	8,509
Three	10,419
Four	13,359
Five	15,792
Six	17,839
Seven	20,241
Eight	22,582
Nine or more	26,848

SOURCE: U.S. Department of Commerce, *Current Population Reports*, Series P-60, No. 175 (1991), p. 195.

TABLE 34.5

[7]The Department of Agriculture calculates the cost of four different food plans: economy, low-cost, moderate-cost, and liberal. The economy plan is the most basic—that is, least generous.

the cost of living as measured by the Consumer Price Index. The poverty lines for 1990 are presented in Table 34.5.[8]

Based on these figures, 33.6 million people in the United States were living in poverty, or about 13.5 percent of the population. Some argue, however, that the situation was actually worse—that government statistics understate poverty. They note that some individuals with incomes above the poverty line have high medical expenses, heavy debts, or other obligations that prevent them from achieving a minimally acceptable standard of living. If such individuals were counted as poor, the poverty rate would be substantially higher.

Others take the opposite position, contending that poverty is less severe than official figures indicate. One reason is that poverty statistics are based solely on money income. They exclude noncash government support—what are called **in-kind transfers**. Among the common in-kind transfers are food stamps, housing assistance, and free or subsidized medical care. If the value of in-kind transfers were counted as income, fewer families would have incomes below the poverty line. Also excluded from income is the rental value of owner-occupied housing. A family that owns its dwelling needs less income to achieve a given standard of living than a family that rents. Had imputed rents been counted as income for homeowners, poverty statistics would have declined further. In a recent experiment, the U.S. Department of Commerce computed poverty rates based on adjusted income—gross income minus taxes plus the value of in-kind transfers plus an imputed return on home equity. According to this alternative measure of income, the poverty rate in 1990 was less than officially estimated (9.8 percent rather than 13.5 percent).

What this points out is that any definition of poverty is arbitrary. How much poverty a country has depends on how one defines poverty. The official measure of poverty is used not because it is perfect but because some measure had to be chosen. Once a measure is selected, it can help identify the poor and track changes in their numbers over time. This may help the government fashion antipoverty programs and measure their success (or lack of success) in alleviating poverty.

IN-KIND TRANSFERS
Transfer payments that consist of goods and services rather than cash. Included are food, public housing, and medical care.

Who Are the Poor?

There is no simple profile of the poor. The poor are young and old, male and female, members of every race. They inhabit every state, live in cities and on farms. Yet, even though poverty permeates our entire society, it is not distributed evenly across groups.

As Table 34.6 indicates, blacks are three times as likely to be poor as whites, and poverty among Hispanics is almost as great as among blacks. Poverty is least likely in married-couple families and most likely in families without a husband present. Poverty is more common for children than for adults, as more than one-fifth of the population 14 and younger lives in poverty.

By contrast, the poverty rate among the elderly is *below* the national average. This is a relatively recent development (see Figure 34.5). In 1966, the poverty rate

---

[8]Actually, poverty lines (or what are sometimes called poverty indexes) also vary with the age of household head and location (urban or rural). The numbers in Table 34.5 are weighted averages.

THE DISTRIBUTION OF POVERTY, 1990

GROUP	PERCENT BELOW THE POVERTY LINE
All persons	13.5
White	10.7
Black	31.9
Hispanic	28.1
Age of person	
Under 15	21.4
15 to 24	16.1
25 to 44	10.4
45 to 54	7.8
55 to 59	9.0
60 to 64	10.3
65 and over	12.2
All families	10.7
Married-couple families	5.7
Male head, no wife	12.0
Female head, no husband	33.4
All unrelated individuals	20.7

SOURCE: U.S. Department of Commerce, *Current Population Reports*, Series P-60, No. 175 (1991), p. 15.

TABLE 34.6

POVERTY TRENDS FOR THE GENERAL POPULATION AND FOR THE POPULATION 65 AND OLDER*

*Poverty statistics for the elderly were not published for the period 1960–1965.
SOURCE: U.S. Department of Commerce, *Current Population Reports*, Series P-60.

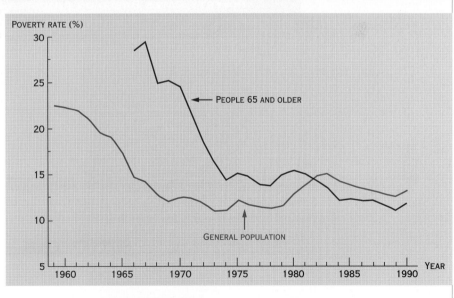

FIGURE 34.5

for those 65 and older was almost twice the national average. Since then, poverty has fallen faster for the elderly than for any other age group. This is attributable in part to increased social spending on the elderly. For instance, Social Security benefits have increased faster than wages over this period. Other forms of income, including pensions and interest, have also increased substantially. Because wealth is concentrated in the hands of the elderly,[9] they have been the principal beneficiaries of increased wealth in the economy.

If in-kind transfers are included, the relative gains of the elderly are even more dramatic—because in-kind transfers (notably medical care) are heavily skewed in favor of the aged. When poverty rates are based on adjusted income (income adjusted for taxes, in-kind transfers, and home ownership), the poverty rate among the elderly falls to 6 percent, compared to 15 percent for children (see Table 34.7). This is not to deny that many elderly live substandard lives. What it does indicate is that the elderly are no longer the most impoverished age group. That distinction now belongs to children.

Trends in Poverty

Between 1959 and 1969 the overall poverty rate fell from 22.4 percent to 12.1 percent (see Figure 34.5). This was due in part to a strengthening economy. As employment and wages increased, poverty eased. Transfer payments also increased rapidly during this period, and some analysts credit them with contributing to the decline in poverty.

After showing little movement during the 1970s, the poverty rate rebounded in the early 1980s as the economy experienced its most severe downturn since the Great Depression. Many workers lost their jobs or had their hours of work cut back,

POVERTY RATES BASED ON ADJUSTED INCOME, 1990*	
AGE GROUP	**PERCENT BELOW THE POVERTY LINE**
All persons	9.8
Under 18 years	14.9
18 to 24 years	13.6
25 to 44 years	8.1
45 to 64 years	6.0
65 years and older	6.2

* Adjusted income refers to total income minus taxes plus the value of transfer payments plus imputed return on equity in own home. For more detail see source.

SOURCE: U.S. Department of Commerce, *Current Population Reports*, Series P-60, No. 176-RD (1991), Table 2.

TABLE 34.7

[9]The median net worth in 1988 was $35,752 for all households but $73,471 for households whose head was 65 or older. See U.S. Department of Commerce, *Household Wealth*, p. 6.

pushing additional families below the poverty line. When the economy improved later in the decade, the rate of poverty lessened but stubbornly remained above the levels of the 1970s.

One reason for the lack of progress against poverty can be traced to the changing composition of families. The percentage of families headed by single females has increased substantially in recent years. As previously noted, this is the family arrangement with the highest incidence of poverty. Researchers have also found that wages of the least-skilled workers rose more slowly during the economic growth of the 1980s than during prior periods of growth. In part, this reflects a shift in labor demand in favor of more highly skilled workers. Because low-skilled workers benefited less from economic growth in the 1980s than in prior decades, fewer families were pulled out of poverty.[10]

Certain critics of government policy also point to the reorientation of federal spending by the Reagan Administration away from social programs and toward defense. Although defense spending was cut during the Bush Administration, little of the savings made its way to social programs. As seen by critics, the budget cutbacks in social programs allowed additional families to fall through the government's *safety net*.

DO TRANSFERS REDUCE POVERTY?

Not everyone accepts the preceding argument.[11] Some contend that transfer programs have actually promoted poverty by discouraging labor supply. Because the level of transfer payments is based on a family's income, individuals who work, and therefore earn wage income, are *rewarded* by having their transfer payments reduced or even eliminated. Once the lost transfer payments are factored in, work often loses its appeal. In extreme cases the government may reduce transfer payments on a dollar-for-dollar basis—an additional dollar of wage income leads to a one-dollar loss of transfer payments. In that event, additional work fails to increase income at all. Instead of encouraging individuals to work, gain experience, and ultimately pull themselves out of poverty, the government fosters reliance on transfer programs.

Critics of transfer programs also observe that until recently many states denied welfare payments to families as long as an able-bodied male was present. Such a provision encouraged the breakup of families, which in turn increased poverty. According to this view, the increase in the percentage of families headed by single females is, at least in part, the direct consequence of past transfer programs.

Even supporters of transfer payments concede that these programs have adverse incentives. What is at issue is the magnitude of these effects. Those favoring increased government support tend to downplay the disincentive effects, arguing that on balance transfer payments reduce poverty. Others disagree. Because

---

[10]Rebecca Blank, "Why Are Poverty Rates So High?" The Jerome Levy Economics Institute Conference on Poverty, 1991; Richard Freeman, *Working and Earning Under Different Rules: What the United States Can Learn from Labor Market Institutions in Other Developed Countries*, National Bureau of Economic Research, 1991; John Bound and George Johnson, "Changes in the Structure of Wages in the 1980s: An Evaluation of Alternative Explanations," *American Economic Review* (June 1992), pp. 371–392.

[11]See Lowell Gallaway and Richard Vedder, *Paying People to Be Poor*, National Center for Policy Analysis, Policy Report No. 121, February 1986; James Gwartney and Thomas S. McCaleb, "Have Antipoverty Programs Increased Poverty?" *Cato Journal* (Spring/Summer 1985), pp. 1–16.

there is no consensus on the impact of transfer programs, there is also no agreement on whether scaling back these programs has contributed to poverty. What is clear is that the downward trend in poverty had ended by the early 1970s. Although the poverty rate continues to fluctuate, it remains higher than 20 years ago.

CONFLICTING VIEWS OF POVERTY

See-saw, Margery Daw,
Jacky shall have a new master;
Jacky shall have but a penny a day,
Because he can't work any faster.

The success and even appropriateness of transfer programs depend on why people are poor. Does their poverty result from a lack of effort on their part—not working or not working any faster? If it does, concern about work disincentives is well placed. Alternatively, if poverty arises because of an inability to work, then disincentive effects are unimportant. Programs that provide income to individuals incapable of working unambiguously reduce poverty. The debate over how transfer payments affect poverty is thus colored by one's view of whether poverty is caused by inadequate effort or by factors beyond an individual's control.

The truth lies somewhere between these two extremes. Some poverty reflects the underutilization of labor market skills; other poverty is rooted in causes unrelated to labor markets—old age, illness, disability, and others. What this suggests is that different antipoverty programs may be appropriate for different families, depending on the family's situation. In particular, it may be appropriate to differentiate between families that can substantially contribute to their own support and those that cannot.

Recent government policy has moved in this direction. For instance, during the 1980s many states began requiring able-bodied adults to work in order to be eligible for transfer payments. Such a system, **workfare**, is designed not only to address work disincentives but to lay the groundwork for the working poor to pull themselves out of poverty. Those on workfare often receive remedial education, training, and child-care assistance. Once employed, they also gain valuable experience, working skills, and sometimes enhanced self-esteem. Such gains, it is hoped, will ultimately enable the person to become self-sufficient. To date, state workfare programs have met with mixed success. Not all participants find jobs, but for those who do, workfare can be the beginning of a new life (see Exhibit 34.2, page 898).

In 1988, Congress enacted legislation to implement workfare on a national basis by 1993. Single parents with children over the age of three are required to work or to participate in approved training and education programs in order to remain eligible for government support. In families with two parents, support is conditional on at least one parent searching for a job and, until one is found, spending a minimum of 16 hours per week performing some government or community service.

For those capable of working there is no doubt that work and job-market skills reduce one's chance of being poor. Among families where the household head works full time throughout the year, the poverty rate is less than 3 percent (see Table 34.8). The poverty rate is much higher when the household head works only part year and higher still when the head fails to work at all. Poverty is similarly related to education. Families whose head did not complete high school are ten

WORKFARE
A program in which low-income individuals receive government support in return for agreeing to work.

POVERTY RATES AMONG FAMILIES BY EMPLOYMENT STATUS AND EDUCATION OF HOUSEHOLD HEAD, 1990	
EMPLOYMENT STATUS OR EDUCATION*	POVERTY RATE (%)
Employment status in 1990	
Did not work	45.0
Worked part year	21.3
Worked year-round full time	2.9
Education	
Did not complete high school	21.8
Completed high school, no college	9.3
Completed some college, not a graduate	5.8
Completed college	2.2

*Employment series are for heads 16 and older; education series are for heads 25 and older.
SOURCE: U.S. Department of Commerce, *Current Population Reports*, Series P-60, No. 175 (1991), Tables 11 and 14.

TABLE 34.8

times as likely to be poor as families headed by a college graduate. The implication is that, for those who are employable, education, workfare, and other programs that enhance workers' skills may alleviate poverty.

IS POVERTY CHRONIC?

Employment or additional skills may be the ticket for some low-income families, but for others work is not an option. For them, escaping poverty is more difficult. Lacking the means to earn income, they tend to remain poor year after year. But how much poverty is long-term or chronic, and how much is transitory? If policy-makers want to combat poverty, they must understand its nature.

To shed light on this issue, one study tracked 5,000 families over a ten-year period.[12] It found that most poverty is transitory. Of those who were poor at some time during the ten years, most were poor two years or less. Poor law students became rich lawyers. Unemployed poor became employed nonpoor. Single adults (and their children) escaped poverty when they married or remarried. Yet, inter-spersed among the temporary poor was a small pool of chronic poor. About 2.6 percent of the people were poor in at least eight of the ten years.

Later studies reinforce these findings.[13] Consistent with the notion that much poverty is transitory, the Department of Commerce finds that more than 70 percent of the poor who work part year climb out of poverty as soon as they start working year-round full time. And most people who are poor exit poverty immediately

[12]Greg J. Duncan, et al., *Years of Poverty, Years of Plenty: The Changing Fortunes of American Workers and Families* (Ann Arbor, Mich.: Institute for Social Research, 1984).

[13]U.S. Department of Commerce, "The Revolving Door of Poverty," *Statistical Brief* SB-1-90, Bureau of the Census (1990); Randall Olsen, "Poverty Persistence," testimony before the Finance Committee of the U.S. Senate, March 8, 1991.

Cleveland Works

E
X
H
I
B
I
T

3 4 . 2

For 17 years, Donna Hayden was a social worker's nightmare. She drifted on and off welfare, had an abrasive personality and had been convicted of welfare fraud. At times desperate for food for the ten children she was raising, she would approach store managers, asking for work "so I could get something to eat so I wouldn't have to steal it out of his store," she says. Today, the 37-year-old Ms. Hayden is earning more than $30,000 a year working two jobs caring for the sick and the elderly. "The patients adore her," says a supervisor.

Ms. Hayden credits her dramatic turnaround to Cleveland Works, a not-for-profit agency pledged to the Sisyphean task of removing even the most entrenched from the welfare rolls. The comprehensive program doesn't come cheap: Funded with matching federal and local money, it costs about $6,000 per placement, or twice as much as other state programs. But at a time when government agencies are throwing their hands up at what many consider the insurmountable problems of those on welfare, Cleveland Works seems to work.

Five years after the program began, about 1,000 parents—or one-third of those involved in the program—have good paying jobs with medical benefits. And while other job-training programs handling less disadvantaged clients say 50 percent leave their jobs after only 90 days, Cleveland Works says more than 80 percent of its clients are still working a year later.

Unlike other programs that insist on trying to teach new skills, Cleveland Works tries to capitalize on a client's strengths: a thirty-words-a-minute typist is brought up to fifty and trained on computers. Most clients have a high-school education and the agency screens out those who aren't readily employable. Thanks to such on-site support services as day care and a legal clinic, and rigorous follow-up for at least a year, poor families can "go from hell to heaven," as founder and director David Roth puts it.

Ms. Hayden knew what hell was all about. One of thirteen children, Ms. Hayden left home when she was 11 years old and dropped out of school in the seventh grade. She had a baby at 16, another

upon becoming part of a married-couple family. On the other hand, the elderly who become poor generally lack the means to escape poverty, and many teenagers from poor families are still poor years later. This is especially true when the teenager comes from a family where the mother was a school dropout, the father was absent, or the teenager gave birth at an early age.

The picture that emerges is of two groups of poor. For the larger group, poverty is short-term. It often results from temporary illness, marital breakups, job loss, or other setbacks. For such individuals, transfer payments are a temporary crutch; they do not lead to long-term welfare dependency. At the same time, there is a small mass of chronic poor. For them, transfer payments provide more than temporary relief; they are a principal source of long-term income.

In conclusion, the poor are not a monolithic group. They differ in age, race, and family arrangement. Some are readily employable; others are not. Some remain poor briefly; others never escape poverty. There is no single cause of poverty and

at 17. By the time she came to Cleveland Works in 1987, she had six children [and was raising four nephews and nieces].

Pamela Williams, a former welfare recipient who runs Cleveland Work's orientation sessions, recalls her first meeting with Ms. Hayden. She was "basically very streetwise and had good people skills." She had clerical experience, had operated a switchboard and was certified to work with mentally ill patients. Ms. Williams concluded she had marketable skills but needed a lot of assistance. "I saw a lot of myself in her. She wasn't going to allow anything to stop her," she says.

Ms. Hayden along with about 200 clients received between 240 and 400 hours of training in language and math and interviewing and occupational skills. The program also provided her free furniture and lent her money when she needed it, which was always repaid. Ursula Hambrick, a workshop instructor and another ex-welfare recipient, worked on Ms. Hayden's appearance and speech. The instructor used videotaped interviews of her to help soften her crude manner and steer clear of slang. But even with all of the special training, Ms. Hayden couldn't find a job after nine interviews.

Finally, last year Ms. Hayden hit pay dirt with a full-time job at the Hospice of the Western Reserve. She bathes and takes care of other intimate needs of the dying. She recently celebrated her first year anniversary there with a 5 percent raise on her $324-a-week salary. A second job, helping an infirm elderly couple, pays $337.50 a week.

Ms. Hayden isn't home free, though. She hopes her husband soon will draw workers' compensation benefits for a disabling back injury. But because they owe the gas company $16,000 and the electric company around $5,000, they plan to file for personal bankruptcy. If they do, Cleveland Works attorneys say they'll handle the case.

SOURCE: Dorothy Gaiter, "Pygmalion Story," *The Wall Street Journal*, July 24, 1991, pp. A1, A4. Reprinted by permission.

therefore no single solution. It is for this reason that the government has a variety of programs to assist the poor.

Major Antipoverty Programs

Scores of government programs affect poverty, from tax laws that encourage business to expand hiring to college loans that enable students to increase their earnings power. Even general economic policy—including government spending, taxation, and monetary policy—impacts poverty by influencing the level of economic activity. In fact, some argue that a strong economy is the single most effective weapon against poverty.

Although programs such as those just cited may reduce poverty, the government's *war on poverty* has been waged primarily with (a) *employment and training programs* (designed to increase labor income of unemployed and low-skilled workers) and (b) *transfer programs* (designed to redistribute income from the population at large to those segments deemed to have special needs).

Employment and Training Programs

Government training programs are designed to impart valuable skills to workers so they may earn sufficient wage income to support themselves and their families. These programs have often failed to achieve their objectives. Many early programs were criticized as cost-ineffective, since only a small portion of program costs were devoted to training. Furthermore, the skills imparted to workers were not always the ones sought by employers. Many workers either failed to complete their training or failed to obtain jobs once the training was completed.

More recently, training programs have increased the percentage of funding devoted to training (rather than to administration, supplies, and so forth) and have attempted to work in conjunction with private employers. For example, the Job Training Partnership Act (JTPA) of 1982 established Private Industry Councils (PICs) through which representatives of the local business community attempt to identify the skills required in the local labor market. Although some fault the distribution of funds (states where workers already enjoy high wages receive more funding than low-wage states),[14] programs such as JTPA should enable the government to do a better job of matching worker skills to available jobs.

An alternative to training workers for jobs in the private sector is for the government itself to employ these workers through public employment programs. Such jobs are often criticized as "make-work." In other words, it is alleged that these workers are not producing valuable goods and services. There is also some question as to how many new jobs are created. When the federal government provided state and local governments with funds to create additional public-sector jobs, studies found that state and local governments used some of this funding to employ workers they would have hired anyway. Thus, there was only a modest expansion of public-sector jobs. Furthermore, some of those employed by the government would have been able to find jobs in the private sector, meaning that public-sector jobs were crowding out private-sector jobs. For such reasons, the government in recent years has shied away from public employment programs, emphasizing instead expanded employment in the private sector.

Transfer Programs

SOCIAL INSURANCE
Transfer programs based on some criteria other than income (for example, retirement or unemployment).

Government transfer programs fall into two categories—(a) **social insurance** and (b) **public assistance** or **welfare**. Social insurance programs are available to individuals regardless of their income. Examples are Social Security and unemployment

---

[14]See James F. Ragan and Daniel J. Slottje, "Problems with Allocating Federal Grants on the Basis of Unemployment Statistics," Research Paper No. 8713, Southern Methodist University, December 1987.

**PUBLIC
ASSISTANCE/WELFARE**
Transfer programs that are
means-tested—that is, available only to low-income
families.

insurance, which provide benefits to rich and poor alike. In contrast, welfare programs are means-tested—only low-income families qualify. As a result, the poor
receive a greater share of welfare payments than social insurance payments. In other
words, welfare programs are more effective at redistributing income to the poor.
The major transfer programs are listed in Table 34.9.

SOCIAL INSURANCE

SOCIAL SECURITY AND MEDICARE The single largest transfer program is
Old Age, Survivors, and Disability Insurance (OASDI) or, as it is commonly called,
Social Security. Established in 1935, Social Security has expanded greatly over time.
In 1994, an estimated 42 million beneficiaries will receive cash payments totalling
$318 billion, or roughly 5 percent of GDP. Beneficiaries include retired workers 62
and older; disabled workers; and spouses, children, and survivors of insured workers.

In 1965, the federal government increased its commitment to retired and disabled workers by creating *medicare*. Also included in the medicare program are victims of end-stage renal (kidney) disease. Medicare's main component, hospital
insurance, pays for care provided in hospitals and in various other health facilities.
In addition, those who qualify for medicare may purchase heavily subsidized health
insurance that pays most of the cost of physician services, laboratory fees, and medical equipment. Medicare is among the largest and most expensive of the transfer
programs providing in-kind benefits.

MAJOR TRANSFER PROGRAMS

PROGRAM	DATE ENACTED	EXPENDITURES (BILLIONS OF DOLLARS)	
		1991	1994*
Social insurance			
Cash benefits:			
Social Security (OASDI)	1935	$269	$318
Unemployment insurance (UI)	1935	27	27
In-kind benefits:			
Medicare	1965	104	143
Public assistance (welfare)			
Cash benefits:			
Aid to Families with Dependent Children (AFDC)	1935	24	30
Supplemental Security Income (SSI)	1972	16	24
In-kind benefits:			
Medicaid	1965	95	152
Food stamps, nutrition assistance	1964	28	35
Housing assistance	1937	17	24

*Estimated.
SOURCE: Executive Office of the President, *Budget of the United States Government, Fiscal Year 1993*.

TABLE 34.9

Both Social Security and medicare are financed by a payroll tax. In 1992, employers and employees each paid a Social Security tax of 6.2 percent of the worker's first $55,500 in wages and salaries and a medicare tax of 1.45 percent of the first $130,200 in wages and salaries. In other words, a worker earning $10,000 in 1992 paid $620 in Social Security taxes and an additional $145 in medicare taxes. A worker making $130,200 or more paid $5,329 in payroll taxes (6.2 percent of $55,500 plus 1.45 percent of $130,200). In each case the employer was required to match this tax. Thus, the combined employer-employee tax was as high as $10,658 for some workers.

Social Security benefits and taxes are determined by Congress. Currently, both monthly benefits and the tax base ($55,500 in 1992) are indexed to inflation—they rise in response to higher prices. But benefits and taxes can be changed at any time. When the postwar baby boom retires next century and the ratio of retirees to workers rises, it may be necessary to increase taxes further, to reduce benefits, or to adjust the system otherwise so that taxes will be sufficient to support benefits. Over the near term, however, Social Security is considered sound and, for many Americans, remains a major source of income (see Exhibit 7.1).

UNEMPLOYMENT INSURANCE   Unemployment insurance benefits are available to jobless workers who qualify for regular or extended unemployment insurance (UI) programs. Because these programs are administered by states, eligibility requirements and the level of benefits vary from state to state. Under the regular UI program, workers receive benefits for up to 26 weeks. Workers in states with high unemployment rates may also qualify for the extended UI program, which provides benefits for up to 13 additional weeks (39 weeks total). In addition, when the economy is weak, Congress often passes *emergency* measures further prolonging the period of support. In 1992, workers in high-unemployment states could draw UI benefits for up to 52 weeks. Regular and extended UI benefits are financed by a payroll tax levied on employers; emergency UI programs typically receive much of their funding from the federal government.

PUBLIC ASSISTANCE

AID TO FAMILIES WITH DEPENDENT CHILDREN   Through Aid to Families with Dependent Children (AFDC), federal, state, and local governments provide assistance to low-income families with children. Although the federal government pays for over half the cost of this program, individual states determine the level of benefits. For example, in 1992 the average monthly payment per family was $605 in California, but only $122 in Mississippi (see Table 34.10). Because the poor of the various states are treated differently, some have criticized AFDC as inequitable.

In the past, AFDC has also been criticized for encouraging family breakups. In some states the presence of an able-bodied male was sufficient to disqualify the family from AFDC. For a program that is supposed to help the children of low-income families, discouraging the father from living with them may actually worsen their plight. Recognizing this, Congress reformed the AFDC program in 1988 and now requires that states extend eligibility to two-parent families.

AVERAGE AFDC PAYMENT BY STATE, JUNE 1992	
STATE	**PAYMENT PER FAMILY**
Low-payment states	
Mississippi	$122
Alabama	140
Texas	162
Louisiana	167
High-payment states	
Connecticut	582
California	605
Hawaii	617
Alaska	815

SOURCE: U.S. Department of Health and Human Services, Office of Family Assistance, unpublished data, 1992.

TABLE 34.10

SUPPLEMENTAL SECURITY INCOME Low-income individuals who are aged, blind, or disabled may also qualify for cash assistance under Supplemental Security Income (SSI). The basic SSI program is paid for by the federal government out of general tax revenues; some states supplement these federal payments.

IN-KIND BENEFITS In addition to cash support, low-income families receive various types of noncash or in-kind benefits. In fact, the government spends over twice as much on in-kind transfers to the poor as on cash transfers. Among the major in-kind benefits are health care (medicaid), food (through food stamps, child nutrition programs, and the distribution of surplus foods), and housing assistance (including public housing and rent subsidies).

Negative Income Tax

NEGATIVE INCOME TAX
A program in which families with low incomes would receive a negative tax (that is, subsidy). The subsidy would be reduced as the family's income from other sources increased.

Some have proposed scrapping the myriad of public assistance programs and replacing them with a **negative income tax**—a single program for subsidizing low-income families. One version of the negative income tax, called the Family Assistance Plan, was endorsed by President Richard Nixon and passed the House of Representatives before being killed by the Senate. Presidents Ford and Carter later proposed their own variants of the negative income tax, again without success.

The program favored by these presidents is called a negative income tax because families with incomes below a certain level would receive a subsidy or *negative tax* from the federal government. For example, a family of four might be guaranteed a minimum income of $8,000 per year. If the family had no earned income, the government would provide the full $8,000. But if the family received income from other sources (for example, work), it would be viewed as less needy and therefore receive a lower level of support.

IMPLICIT TAX RATE
The amount by which the government reduces its subsidy in response to another dollar of earned income—that is, the change in subsidy divided by the change in earned income.

BREAK-EVEN INCOME
The level of income at which the government's subsidy disappears and beyond which the family must start paying income tax.

If the family earned $3,000 in wage income, the government might reduce the subsidy by $2,000. In that event the family would face an **implicit tax rate** of 2/3, meaning that the government reduces its subsidy by an amount equal to two-thirds the family's earned income.[15] Even though the family's wage income would rise from $0 to $3,000, its total income (earned income plus subsidy) would increase by only $1,000—from $8,000 to $9,000 (see Table 34.11).

Subsequent increases in income would further reduce the subsidy until it was eventually phased out. Beyond that point, the family would be required to start paying taxes—that is, its income would be subject to a positive tax rather than a negative tax. The point at which the negative income tax ends and a positive income tax begins is called the **break-even income**. Its value is given by the following formula:

$$\text{break-even income} = \frac{\text{guaranteed annual income}}{\text{implicit tax rate}}$$

In the preceding example, the break-even income would be $8,000/(2/3) = $12,000. Families with incomes below $12,000 would receive government assistance through the negative income tax; families with incomes above $12,000 would be taxpayers.

Those favoring a negative income tax argue that it would eliminate inequitable treatment of the poor by ensuring that income assistance is uniform across states. They also claim that it would be easier to administer than the present mix of programs. On the other hand, even supporters of a negative income tax concede that it probably would be more costly than current public assistance programs and that it would fail to eliminate the work disincentives plaguing these programs, although in many cases it would reduce existing disincentives.

Work disincentives arise for two reasons. First, a negative income tax reduces the cost of not working by guaranteeing some minimum income to those who do not work. Second, it reduces the effective benefit of work—wage income minus the implicit tax. Given an implicit tax rate of 2/3, a worker earning $4.50 per hour would actually net only $1.50 per hour once the lost subsidy is factored in. By

A HYPOTHETICAL NEGATIVE INCOME-TAX PLAN*			
EARNED INCOME	**SUBSIDY (NIT)**	**IMPLICIT TAX**	**TOTAL INCOME**
$ 0	$8,000	$ 0	$ 8,000
3,000	6,000	2,000	9,000
6,000	4,000	4,000	10,000
9,000	2,000	6,000	11,000
12,000	0	8,000	12,000

* Assumes a maximum subsidy of $8,000 and an implicit tax rate of two-thirds.

TABLE 34.11

---

[15]The term "benefit reduction rate" is sometimes used in place of "implicit tax rate."

reducing the effective rate of compensation, the negative income tax decreases the willingness of people to accept employment.

The work disincentive could be reduced by lowering the implicit tax rate. For example, cutting the implicit tax rate from 2/3 to 1/3 would effectively double the rate of compensation. Each hour worked would increase total income by $3.00 rather than by $1.50. This would encourage additional workers to accept employment, but it would also increase the number of families receiving a negative income tax. Given an implicit tax rate of 1/3, the break-even income would rise to $24,000. In other words, families whose income falls between $12,000 and $24,000—families whose need is less severe—would now be receiving government support. This could add considerably to the cost of the program. In fact, a major reason that Congress failed to enact a negative income-tax program was its belief that any negative income tax would either seriously discourage work or carry a high price tag. Neither option was considered attractive.

Although a negative income tax has not been implemented, dissatisfaction with welfare programs has prompted reforms at both the federal and state levels. The trend at present appears to be for the government to provide greater assistance in the form of day care, transportation, training, and health insurance but to expect greater work efforts from able-bodied adults who receive this assistance. Those capable of holding a job are now generally required either to look for work or to undergo the training and education that may lead to employment. If the number of poor with jobs can be increased, that would allow the government to concentrate on those individuals unable to support themselves.

Summary

1. Income is distributed unevenly in the United States. When arranged in order of income, the top 20 percent of families receive more than 40 percent of total income; the bottom 20 percent receive less than 5 percent.

2. One way to measure income inequality is with a Lorenz curve, which measures the cumulative distribution of income across families. The Lorenz curve indicates that the distribution of income is more equal now than it was during the first half of the century—despite an erosion in equality during the 1980s.

3. Income inequality is due to differences in both wage and nonwage income. Families that receive higher wage rates, work more hours, and have multiple wage earners tend to earn greater wage income than other families. Similarly, families with greater wealth tend to receive more nonwage income.

4. Taxes do not substantially alter the distribution of income, but transfer payments do. Because many transfer payments are geared to the low-income population, if the value of transfers is included the distribution of income becomes considerably more equal.

5. There is a trade-off between equality of income and economic efficiency. Programs designed to transfer income to the low-income population lead to lower levels of output. The issues of how much income equality a society should have and how best to achieve that equality fall within the realm of normative economics.

6. The U.S. government began calculating its official *poverty line* in 1964, based on the cost of food. Poverty lines are now updated annually based on increases in the general cost of living.

7. In the United States, approximately one person in seven lives below the poverty line. Although the rate of poverty declined sharply in the 1960s and stabilized in the 1970s, it increased during the early 1980s. Despite some later improvement, poverty remains more pervasive today than 25 years ago.

8. Poverty rates are higher than average for children, blacks, Hispanics, and female-headed households. They are lower than average for the elderly, the well educated, and families with a working head.

9. Some argue that greater transfer payments are needed to reduce poverty. In contrast, others claim that past transfer programs have contributed to poverty by reducing the incentive to work and by encouraging family breakups. Recent reforms have attempted to address these concerns by promoting work among the able-bodied poor (through workfare programs) and by extending eligibility to two-parent families.

10. Although some poverty is chronic, most poverty is short-lived. It results from temporary illness, marital breakups, job loss, or other setbacks. For such individuals, transfer payments do not lead to long-term welfare dependency.

11. The government's main weapons against poverty have been employment and training programs and transfer programs. Training programs are designed to impart valuable labor-market skills to workers so they may pull themselves out of poverty. In contrast, public employment programs directly create government jobs for the disadvantaged or unemployed worker. Because many question the value of public employment work, these programs have fallen out of favor in recent years.

12. Transfer programs provide either social insurance or public assistance. Social insurance programs include Social Security, medicare, and unemployment insurance. They provide payments, regardless of need, to persons who satisfy certain criteria (for example, retirement, disability, or unemployment). Public assistance or welfare programs provide benefits only to families below a certain income. Some public assistance programs provide cash (for example, AFDC and Supplemental Security Income); others provide in-kind (noncash) benefits (for example, food stamps, housing assistance, and medical care).

13. In place of public assistance programs, some advocate a negative income tax. This would provide a subsidy to low-income families, the value of which would be reduced as earned income increased. A negative income tax would be easier to administer than present programs and would eliminate the inequitable treatment of the poor across states. On the other hand, it would probably be costlier than present programs and would not eliminate work disincentives.

Key Terms

Lorenz curve	social insurance
means test	public assistance/welfare
poverty line	negative income tax
in-kind transfers	implicit tax rate
workfare	break-even income

Study Questions and Problems

1. The following table contains data on the distribution of income by race.

QUINTILE	PERCENT OF INCOME	
	WHITES	BLACKS
First	5.0	3.4
Second	11.0	8.8
Third	16.6	15.4
Fourth	23.4	25.1
Fifth	44.0	47.3
Total	100.0	100.0

   a. Construct the cumulative distribution of income for each race.
   b. Draw the corresponding Lorenz curves.
   c. For which group is income distributed more equally?

2. The United States has an estate tax but, because of a generous exemption, only large estates are subject to the tax. Thus, only the property of wealthy individuals is taxed before being transferred to heirs. How does this tax on inherited wealth affect the distribution of income? Why does it have this effect?

3. The United States is a rich country. Why doesn't the government guarantee everyone an income above the poverty line?

4. What is the difference between relative poverty and absolute poverty? On which is the government's poverty line based? How was the government's poverty line originally constructed?

5. Why do some claim that the government's count of poverty is too low? Why do others claim that it is too high?

6. How would more rapid economic growth affect poverty? Is growth by itself likely to eliminate poverty? Explain.

7. Why do you think poverty is more severe for blacks than for whites?

8. Many people view the elderly as more impoverished than the population in general. Was this image ever accurate? Is it accurate today? Compare poverty rates of the elderly and the rest of the population, both now and 25 years ago.

9. (a) Would free public housing reduce poverty, as measured by the government? Explain. (b) Would free day care and job training for the poor affect the rate of poverty? Why?

10. (a) What are the major social insurance programs? (b) What are the major public assistance programs? (c) Which programs are reserved exclusively for those with low income?

11. On what basis has the AFDC program been criticized?

12.

EARNED INCOME	NIT	IMPLICIT TAX	TOTAL INCOME
$ 0	$6,000	$ 0	$6,000
2,000	4,500	1,500	6,500
4,000	3,000	3,000	7,000
6,000	1,500	4,500	7,500
8,000	0	6,000	8,000

Based on the preceding table, find the values of the implicit tax rate, the guaranteed annual income, and the break-even income.

13. Consider a negative income tax with a guaranteed annual income of $6,000 and an implicit tax rate of 1/2.
    a. What would be the total income of a family that earned $8,000?
    b. What would be the break-even income?
    c. If the government cut the guaranteed annual income to $3,000, how would this alter the break-even income?

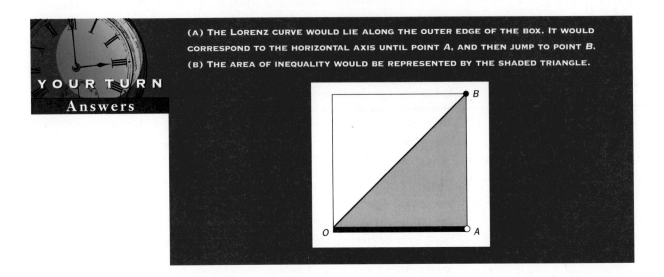

YOUR TURN
Answers

(A) THE LORENZ CURVE WOULD LIE ALONG THE OUTER EDGE OF THE BOX. IT WOULD CORRESPOND TO THE HORIZONTAL AXIS UNTIL POINT A, AND THEN JUMP TO POINT B.

(B) THE AREA OF INEQUALITY WOULD BE REPRESENTED BY THE SHADED TRIANGLE.

Selected References

Danziger, Sheldon, Robert Haveman, and Robert Plotnick. "How Income Transfers Affect Work, Savings and the Income Distribution," *Journal of Economic Literature* (September 1981), pp. 975–1,028. Analyzes the effects of transfer programs.

Duncan, Greg J., et al. *Years of Poverty, Years of Plenty: The Changing Fortunes of American Workers and Families* (Ann Arbor, Mich.: Institute for Social Research, 1984). Examines 5,000 families, tracking changes in income and poverty.

Executive Office of the President. *Budget of the United States Government, Fiscal Year 1993* (Washington, D.C.: Government Printing Office, 1992). Discusses transfer programs and their budgets.

Mishel, Lawrence, and David Frankel. *The State of Working America* (Armonk, N.Y.: M. E. Sharpe, Inc., 1991). Presents data on income, wages, wealth, and poverty in the United States and compares trends in the United States with those of other countries.

Murray, Charles. *Losing Ground* (New York: Basic Books, 1984). Studies poverty and the programs intended to reduce it.

Okun, Arthur. *Equality and Efficiency: The Big Tradeoff* (Washington, D.C.: The Brookings Institution, 1975). Discusses the conflicting goals of income equality and economic efficiency.

IX

Other Issues

PART IX APPLIES ECONOMIC PRINCIPLES TO TWO IMPORTANT AREAS OF POLICY: THE ENVIRONMENT AND AGRICULTURE. ENVIRONMENTAL ISSUES ARISE BECAUSE OF EXTERNALITIES, SUCH AS THE SULPHUR EMISSIONS OF A POWER PLANT THAT DESTROY FORESTS NOT OWNED BY THE PLANT. IN SUCH INSTANCES, MARKETS FAIL TO DELIVER SOCIALLY OPTIMAL OUTCOMES. HOW SHOULD SOCIETY RESPOND? HOW CLEAN SHOULD THE ENVIRONMENT BE, AND WHICH METHODS OF REDUCING POL-LUTION ARE MOST EFFICIENT? AFTER STUDYING THESE ISSUES, CHAPTER 35 ASKS WHETHER COUNTRIES ARE ON THE VERGE OF EXHAUSTING THEIR SUPPLIES OF NONRENEWABLE NATURAL RESOURCES. ■ CHAPTER 36 APPLIES SUPPLY AND DEMAND ANALYSIS, ELASTICITY, AND OTHER ECONOMIC TOOLS TO ANALYZE FINANCIAL PRESSURES IN AGRICULTURE, RESOURCE MOBILITY, AND THE MYRIAD OF GOVERNMENT FARM PROGRAMS. IT ALSO EXPLORES REASONS FOR GOVERNMENT INTER-VENTION IN AGRICULTURE, CRITICISMS OF U.S. FARM POLICY, AND ALTERNATIVES TO PRESENT POLICY.

Externalities, the Environment, and Nonrenewable Natural Resources

WHEN THE *EXXON VALDEZ* RAN AGROUND IN PRINCE WILLIAM SOUND, ALASKA, EXXON LOST NEARLY 11 MILLION GALLONS OF OIL; SOCIETY LOST A GOOD DEAL MORE. IN ADDITION TO THE WILDLIFE LOST TO THE OIL SPILL AND THE DAMAGE TO THE BEACHES, ALASKA'S FISHING INDUSTRY WAS DEVASTATED AND THE SUBSISTENCE LIFE-STYLE OF ALASKA NATIVES WAS PLACED IN JEOPARDY. AS THIS INCIDENT PAINFULLY ILLUSTRATES, THE IMPACTS OF SOME ECONOMIC ACTIVITIES, INCLUDING THE PRODUCTION AND TRANSPORTATION OF CRUDE OIL, EXTEND WELL BEYOND THE MARKETPLACE. WHERE THIS IS TRUE, PRIVATE MARKETS FAIL TO PRODUCE SOCIALLY OPTIMAL OUTCOMES.

CHAPTER 35 EXAMINES BOTH THE REASONS FOR THIS TYPE OF MARKET FAILURE AND THE PROPOSED SOLUTIONS, PAYING SPECIAL ATTENTION TO ENVIRONMENTAL ISSUES. HOW PURE AN ENVIRONMENT DOES SOCIETY WANT, AND HOW CAN IT BEST ACHIEVE THIS GOAL? AFTER ADDRESSING THIS ISSUE, THE CHAPTER TURNS TO ANOTHER ENVIRONMENTAL CONCERN: THE DEPLETION OF NONRENEWABLE NATURAL RESOURCES. ARE WE IN DANGER OF SOON RUNNING OUT OF OIL, NATURAL GAS, AND OTHER CRITICAL RAW MATERIALS?

The rocky banks on Latouche Island in Prince William Sound [Alaska] are blackened with oil. Dig down a few inches into the sand underlying the cobbles and your hand comes away covered in smelly, gummy crude.

Despite a $2.5 billion cleanup effort, remnants of the March 1989 Exxon Valdez oil spill still stain some of the beaches here, and many of the natives of the region are afraid to eat the food they hunt at traditional hunting grounds. What remains of the spill threatens what remains of their culture.[1]

[1]Allanna Sullivan, "Oil Spill Stains Alaska Natives' Life Style," *The Wall Street Journal*, September 5, 1991, p. A2.

Externalities arise when the actions of consumers or producers affect third parties—individuals who do not directly participate in the production or consumption of a particular good. The name "externality" was chosen because parties external to market transactions are affected by these transactions. Alternatively, externalities are often called *spillovers* to signify that the consequences of production or consumption "spill over" to affect third parties.

Externalities may be either positive (**external benefits**) or negative (**external costs**). For example, a private utility seeking to generate electricity may dam a river and, as a side effect, homeowners downstream may suffer less flood damage and farmers less crop damage. In that event, even though the utility was not motivated by an altruistic desire to help homeowners and farmers, these parties nonetheless benefit from the utility's decision to build a dam. Similarly, as a homeowner you benefit if your neighbors plant trees and flowers and otherwise beautify the neighborhood. In addition to any scenic benefits you enjoy, your property value appreciates as your neighborhood becomes more attractive.

Alternatively, if your neighbors start raising pigs, collecting junk cars, and hosting loud parties, their actions reduce the value of your property—that is, impose external costs on you. Other sources of external costs include buildings that block your view, barking dogs, toxic wastes, and cigarette smoke (see Exhibit 35.1).

Externalities are an example of market failure: the failure of free markets to allocate resources in a socially optimal manner. In particular, the tendency is for too many resources to be devoted to the production of goods associated with negative externalities and not enough resources devoted to the production of goods having positive externalities. The following section explains why externalities lead to market failure and why government intervention offers the potential to improve resource allocation.

POSITIVE EXTERNALITIES (EXTERNAL BENEFITS) Benefits received but not paid for by third parties as a result of others' production or consumption.

NEGATIVE EXTERNALITIES (EXTERNAL COSTS) Uncompensated costs imposed on third parties as a result of consumption or production by other individuals or firms.

Promoting Positive Externalities

Vaccines protect individuals from measles and other communicable diseases. As such, they benefit those receiving the vaccine. But they also benefit individuals who are not themselves inoculated. As additional people receive the vaccine, the likelihood diminishes that an unprotected individual will come into contact with someone carrying the disease.

The market demand for vaccinations is based on the **private benefits** of the vaccine—that is, the benefits to the individuals receiving it. In contrast, society's demand for vaccinations is determined by the **social benefits** of the vaccine, which include the benefits derived by those who are not inoculated as well as by those who are. Because the social benefits exceed the private benefits, society's demand for vaccinations lies to the right of the market demand (see Figure 35.1, page 914).

PRIVATE BENEFITS The benefits received by those consuming or producing a good.

SOCIAL BENEFITS Private benefits plus external benefits.

A Right to Smoke?

Smokers often argue that they have the right to smoke tobacco. Although smoking may shorten their lives, they contend that the decision is theirs to make. More and more, nonsmokers are contesting that claim, asserting instead that they have the right to a smoke-free environment. To quote the surgeon general: "The right of smokers to smoke ends where their behavior affects the health and well-being of others."

Does passive smoking—involuntarily inhaling others' smoke—harm nonsmokers? The National Academy of Sciences, the Department of Health and Human Services, and the Environmental Protection Agency all examined the evidence and, in separate reports, reached largely similar conclusions. Major findings of these reports include the following:

1. Passive smoking kills approximately 3,000 nonsmokers annually. Along with asbestos, involuntary smoking is the major cause of deaths from airborne pollution.

2. Passive smoking significantly increases the risks of asthma, bronchitis, and pneumonia in children and may stunt development of their lungs. Children who live with smokers are almost twice as likely to have health problems as children from households where no one smokes.

3. Smoke may irritate the eyes, nose, and throat of nonsmokers, causing headaches, sore throats, and other adverse reactions.

In addition, other studies conclude that employees who smoke inflict costs on their employers through increased absenteeism and higher insurance rates and that the taxes of nonsmokers help finance the medical treatment of smokers. For these reasons, smoking generates substantial external costs.

In the aftermath of these reports, nonsmokers have become more militant in their opposition to smoking, and governments and private companies have responded by imposing added restrictions on smokers. Smoking is now prohibited in most public buildings and many offices as well as on flights of six hours or less. Even in restaurants and other establishments that still allow smoking, nonsmokers have won nonsmoking sections. While the battle for control of the air continues, nonsmokers appear to be gaining ground. As their rights expand, the external costs of smoking will lessen.

SOURCES: Adapted from Charles LeMaistre, "Nobody Is Safe If a Smoker Is Around," *The New York Times*, January 4, 1987, p. 2F; *The Wall Street Journal*, "Parents' Cigarette Smoke Hurts Children, Study Says," June 16, 1991, p. B4; *The Kansas City Star*, "Secondhand Smoke Harms Thousands of Children, Study Charges," June 19, 1992, p. A2.

EXHIBIT 35.1

The equilibrium level of vaccinations is Q_{priv}, given by the intersection of market demand and supply. Q_{priv} is not socially optimal, however, inasmuch as private markets ignore external benefits. From the perspective of society, vaccinations should continue until Q_{soc}, which is where the benefit to society of another vaccination equals the cost of another vaccination. In other words, *when positive externalities*

The market demand for vaccinations, D_{priv}, is based on the private benefits accruing to those vaccinated. If left to the market, the number vaccinated is Q_{priv}, determined by the intersection of market demand and supply. Q_{priv} is less than the socially optimal number of vaccinations, Q_{soc}, because consumers ignore the external benefits accruing to those not vaccinated. To achieve the optimal number of vaccinations, the government offers a subsidy of $P_2 - P_3$ for each vaccination.

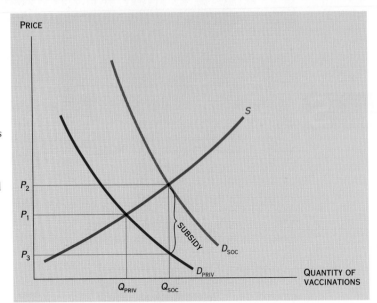

FIGURE 35.1

are present, markets lead to an underallocation of resources. Because private markets ignore external benefits, they produce less than the socially optimal level of output.

To correct for this underallocation of resources, the government could induce additional individuals to receive the vaccine. One way to accomplish this is to subsidize the vaccine, driving the price paid by consumers below the price received by producers. In particular, consumers would be willing to buy Q_{soc} vaccinations at a price of P_3 while producers would be willing to sell this quantity for a price of P_2. Both conditions can be satisfied if the government absorbs the difference between these two prices—for instance, by offering producers a supplemental payment of $P_2 - P_3$ per unit of vaccine. In summary, where positive externalities exist, subsidies offer a way to expand production and, in principle, to achieve the socially optimal level of output.

Responding to Negative Externalities

Where externalities are negative, markets lead to an overallocation of resources. Because markets ignore external costs, more output is produced than is socially optimal. As an illustration, consider a perfectly competitive industry whose firms dump raw sewage into a nearby river. To them, the river is a free good—a dumping ground they do not have to pay to use. But whereas disposal is costless to individual firms, it imposes significant costs on other members of society. It kills fish, causes health problems

PRIVATE COSTS

The costs incurred by those producing or consuming a good.

SOCIAL COSTS

Private costs plus external costs.

in humans, spoils recreational facilities along the river, and increases water purification costs for towns downstream that draw their drinking water from the river. Because of these external costs, the **private costs** of production—those actually incurred by the firms—are less than the **social costs** of production.

To maximize profit, each firm produces up to the point where the price it receives for its product equals the cost to the firm of producing another unit—that is, price equals marginal private cost (MPC). But when production is accompanied by external costs, as in our example, marginal social cost (MSC) is higher than marginal private cost. This implies that the cost to society of producing the last unit of output exceeds its value. In other words, given negative externalities each firm produces more than socially optimal. This is shown in Figure 35.2.

Figure 35.3 (page 916) illustrates negative externalities for the industry. S_{priv} is the supply curve for the industry in the absence of government intervention—obtained by aggregating the marginal cost curve of each firm (MPC). Given demand for the industry's product, market output is Q_{priv}. This is more than the socially optimal amount of output because it ignores the external costs of production. Instead, society seeks Q_{soc} output, given by the intersection of market demand and S_{soc}. It is here that price equals marginal social cost.

Note that the market price, P_{priv}, is too *low*. Because the market does not force firms to pay the full costs of production, they charge consumers an artificially low price. Had firms been required to pay the full social cost of production, the price would be P_{soc}. This is one instance where a low price is not socially beneficial: it contributes to excess consumption of this product at the expense of other products that do not have negative externalities.

One solution to this problem is to increase production costs to the firm. For example, the government could force or induce polluting firms to clean up the river or to dispose of their wastes in ways other than by dumping them into the river.

OVERPRODUCTION BY A POLLUTING FIRM

Because a firm does not pay external costs, these costs do not enter its production decision. Instead, a competitive firm produces up to the point where price equals marginal private cost, q_{priv}. From the perspective of society, all production costs should be considered, including external costs. Therefore, the socially optimal level of output for the firm is q_{soc}, where price equals marginal social cost.

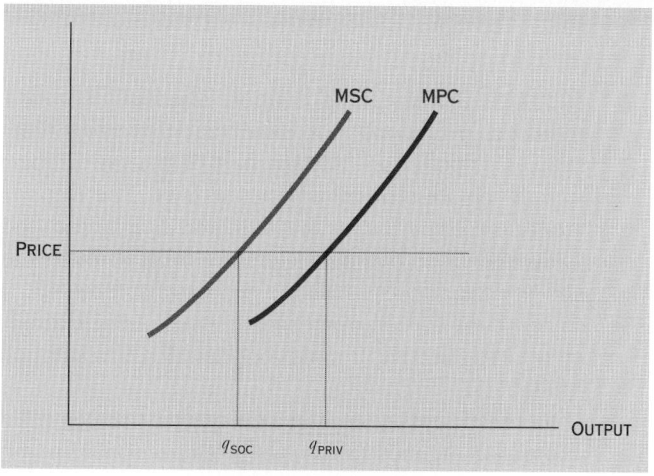

FIGURE 35.2

When firms pay only the private costs of production, industry supply is given by S_{priv}. In equilibrium, firms produce Q_{priv} output and charge price P_{priv}. From society's perspective, there is too much output and too low a price because external costs have been ignored. But when external costs are forced on producers—that is, when costs are internalized—then market supply is reduced to S_{soc} and excess production is eliminated.

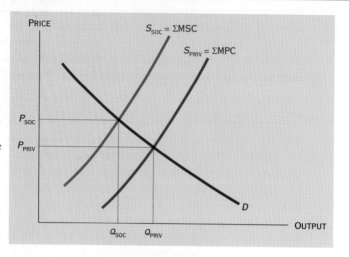

FIGURE 35.3

INTERNALIZE COSTS

To shift external costs from third parties back to those parties directly responsible for the costs.

Such actions would **internalize** the firms' pollution costs—that is, force the firms to absorb these costs rather than shift them on to third parties. As production costs increased, firms would raise price and consumers would reduce their consumption. If economic costs were fully internalized, price would rise to P_{soc} and the overallocation of resources to this industry would cease. Various proposals for internalizing costs are considered following a brief discussion of environmental problems.

The Environment

Although the foregoing example illustrates negative externalities by considering industrial pollution, it is important to realize that businesses are not the only sources of pollution. Almost half of the government facilities recently inspected were in violation of environmental laws. The Department of Defense alone generated more hazardous waste than the five largest chemical companies combined.[2] Consumers also pollute the environment through their garbage, fires, refrigerants, and sewage. Transportation, primarily automobile travel, is responsible for two-thirds of the carbon monoxide released in the United States. If environmental policy is to be effective, it must consider all sources of pollution, not just industrial pollution.

Statistics on environmental quality are compiled by the U.S. Environmental Protection Agency (EPA), the organization responsible for monitoring pollution

---

[2]Murray L. Weidenbaum, *Rendezvous with Reality: The American Economy After Reagan* (New York: Basic Books, 1988), p. 220.

As the preceding section explained, left to themselves markets fail to deal adequately with negative externalities such as pollution. Does this mean that pollution is inherently a more serious problem in capitalistic-oriented countries, such as the United States and Great Britain, than in command economies where the central authorities can direct state enterprises to use nonpolluting means of production? To the contrary, some of the most severe pollution in the world could be found in the Soviet Union prior to its breakup and in Eastern Europe, as the accompanying table indicates.

Although capitalistic firms have an incentive to maximize profit rather than to pursue social goals, state enterprises in command economies have their own objectives—to meet production targets. Historically, these production targets have played down environmental concerns for the sake of rapid economic growth. Command economies have not shown that they have an environmental record to be emulated. Conversely, capitalistic-oriented economies need not accept more pollution than society deems appropriate. As we will see later in the chapter, markets can be redirected to reduce pollution and to do so efficiently.

SULFUR DIOXIDE EMISSIONS PER PERSON (KILOGRAMS) AND PER DOLLAR GDP (GRAMS), 1988

	PER PERSON	PER DOLLAR GDP
East Germany*	317	31
Czechoslovakia	179	24
Bulgaria	115	21
Soviet Union**	65	10
United Kingdom	64	5
United States	84	4

*Prior to unification with West Germany.
**Data for the former Soviet Union are for 1987 and exclude nonstationary sources. As such, these estimates understate pollution in the former Soviet Union.
SOURCES: Worldwatch Institute, *State of the World, 1991*; U.S. Environmental Protection Agency, *National Air Quality and Emissions Trends Report, 1990*; U.S. Bureau of the Census, *Statistical Abstract of the United States, 1989*.

EXHIBIT

35.2

levels and enforcing the Clean Air Act, the Clean Water Act, and other environmental laws. EPA statistics paint a mixed picture of the environment. For example, a substantial number of citizens live in communities that are not in compliance with air quality standards (see Table 35.1, page 918). On the other hand, air quality

AIR POLLUTION STANDARDS AND COMPLIANCE*

POLLUTANT	STANDARD**		PERCENT OF POPULATION IN COUNTIES NOT IN COMPLIANCE	PERCENTAGE REDUCTION IN CONCENTRATION OF POLLUTANT, 1981–1990
Particulate matter (PM₁₀)	50	ug/m³	8	3***
Sulfur dioxide (SO₂)	0.03	ppm	1	24
Carbon monoxide (CO)	9	ppm	9	29
Nitrogen dioxide (NO₂)	0.053	ppm	3	8
Ozone (O₃)	0.12	ppm	26	10
Lead (Pb)	1.5	ug/m³	2	85

*Primary National Ambient Air Quality Standards.
**ug/m³ = micrograms per cubic meter
 ppm = parts per million
***Reduction for total suspended particulate over the period 1982–1990. Because of a change in sample filters, data for 1981 are not comparable.
SOURCE: U.S. Environmental Protection Agency, *National Air Quality and Emissions Trends Report, 1990* (1991).

TABLE 35.1

has generally improved since 1981. Perhaps most impressive, the average concentration of lead has fallen 85 percent. This is primarily because of the introduction of unleaded gasoline in 1975, a reduction in the lead content of leaded gasoline, and a requirement that new automobiles be equipped with catalytic converters. Significant gains have also been made in reducing levels of sulphur dioxide, a major cause of acid rain.

The pollutant most commonly in violation of air quality standards is ozone, the major component of what is commonly called "smog." In 1990, more than one-fourth of the population lived in counties that were not in compliance with ozone standards. The problem was especially severe in Los Angeles, where readings were more than twice the EPA standard.

Legislative Standards

Before placing too much emphasis on pollution levels or rates of compliance, it is important to ask how environmental standards are set. Under current policy, standards are often arbitrarily determined by Congress. For example, the current ozone standard is 0.12 parts per million, not to be exceeded for more than one hour per year. Prior to 1979, the standard was 0.08 parts per million; in 1971, the standard was even more stringent. The standard has been eased over time in part because of political pressure from cities not in compliance and in part because some recent scientific studies conclude that exposure to ozone at the rate of 0.30 parts per million, more than double the current standard, poses health problems only for those engaged in strenuous activities.[3] There is no compelling reason why the standard is 0.12 parts per million rather than 0.08 or 0.16; 0.12 is simply the figure chosen by Congress.

Along with air quality standards, Congress set a deadline for compliance with these standards. The initial deadline, stipulated by the Clean Air Act of 1970, was 1975. The deadline was later extended to 1987 and then 1988. When asked why the initial deadline of 1975 was selected, Senator Edmund Muskie, sponsor of the bill, admitted that the deadline was arbitrary, chosen without taking into account "economic and technological feasibility."[4] In that light, it is perhaps not surprising that the 1990 amendments to the Clean Air Act further extended the deadline. The ninety-six cities still in violation of the Clean Air Act were given up to 20 additional years to meet federal air quality standards. (The longest extension went to the cities with the dirtiest air.)

Cost–Benefit Analysis

Even though arbitrary standards do promote a cleaner environment, most economists criticize them as simplistic. Such standards may promote either too little environmental quality or too much.

How, you might ask, can the environment be too clean? The answer is that environmental purity carries a cost: resources used to reduce pollution are not available for other activities. If less were spent on environmental quality, the country could produce more cars, housing, and education. Alternatively, if additional resources were diverted to pollution control, we would have a cleaner environment but fewer other goods. In other words, the cost of a cleaner environment is the output that is sacrificed in order to achieve higher environmental standards. At present, environmental regulations reduce the nation's output by about 6 percent per year.[5]

How much pollution is optimal? Although there are different frameworks with which to address this question, most economists emphasize **cost–benefit analysis**, in which the costs to society of a cleaner environment are weighed against the benefits. The benefits include better health (for example, fewer illnesses and lower medical expenses), reduced crop damage, additional wildlife, and improved recreational facilities. As a general rule, the marginal benefits of pollution control decline as the level of pollution is reduced. When pollution is unchecked, even a slight improvement generates substantial benefits. But as pollution abatement continues, further gains in health, crop yield, wildlife population, and quality of recreational sites tend to taper off. This is illustrated in Figure 35.4 (page 920) by a declining marginal benefit curve.

COST–BENEFIT ANALYSIS
A framework for comparing the costs and benefits of a particular activity (for example, to determine the optimal level of that activity).

---

[3]Melinda Warren and Kenneth Chilton, *Clearing the Air: Regulating Ozone in the Public Interest* (St. Louis: Center for the Study of American Business, 1988), p. 1.

[4]Murray L. Weidenbaum, *Business, Government, and the Public*, 4th ed. (Englewood Cliffs, N.J.: Prentice-Hall, 1990), p. 90.

[5]Michael Hazilla and Raymond Kopp, "Social Cost of Environmental Quality Regulations: A General Equilibrium Analysis," *Journal of Political Economy* (August 1990), p. 867.

The marginal benefit of pollution control declines while the marginal cost increases. Pollution abatement should continue up to point Q^*, where the marginal cost of pollution control equals the marginal benefit.

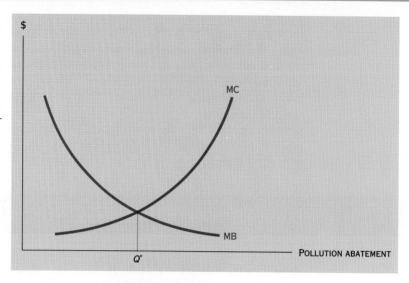

FIGURE 35.4

In contrast, the marginal cost of pollution abatement increases. Initial reductions in pollution are often easy, requiring only modest adjustments. But as firms tackle the more difficult pollution problems, further progress often requires installing costly equipment and altering production processes. As an example of how costs accelerate, consider the paper industry. The cost of eliminating 95 percent of the industry's water pollution was estimated to be $3 billion, compared to a cost of $7.8 billion to eliminate 98 percent of the pollution.[6] In other words, the cost of an incremental 3 percent improvement in water quality was more than the total cost of eliminating the first 95 percent of the pollution.

From an economic perspective, the optimal amount of pollution control is the amount for which the marginal cost of reducing pollution equals the marginal benefit. Until this point is reached (point Q^* in Figure 35.4), the benefits of additional pollution control exceed the added costs. Beyond this point further reductions in pollution cost more than they yield in benefits.

Environmentalists sometimes oppose cost–benefit analysis for fear that, once the costs of pollution abatement are recognized, environmental standards will be relaxed. But this will be true only if environmental standards are excessive to begin with. In many instances, cost–benefit analysis leads to tougher standards. For example, a cost–benefit study was responsible for the EPA reducing the allowable lead content in gasoline from 1.1 gram per gallon to 0.1 gram. According to this study, over the period 1985–1992, the lower lead content would yield $6.7 billion more in benefits than in costs.[7]

---

[6]Murray L. Weidenbaum, "Benefit–Cost Analysis of Government Regulation," *Toxic Substances Journal* (Autumn 1980), pp. 91–102.

[7]Ralph A. Luken, "Weighing the Benefits of Clean-up Rules Against Their Costs," *EPA Journal* (March 1988), pp. 9–12.

The primary difficulty in implementing cost–benefit analysis is obtaining reliable figures on costs and benefits. Alternative assumptions often yield conflicting estimates. With additional research, differences in estimates can sometimes be narrowed, but not eliminated. Accordingly, there may be different projections of the optimal amount of pollution. Thus, even with cost–benefit analysis some subjectivity is involved. Still, cost–benefit analysis provides useful information and a rational approach for formulating environmental policy. It is likely to achieve a higher level of social welfare than arbitrary standards, chosen without reference to economic costs and benefits.

YOUR TURN

Comparing the Costs and Benefits of Pollution Control

THE WIDGET INDUSTRY CURRENTLY GENERATES 6 TONS OF AIR POLLUTANTS PER MONTH. THE FOLLOWING TABLE DEPICTS THE TOTAL COSTS AND BENEFITS TO SOCIETY OF REDUCING POLLUTION TO LOWER LEVELS.

LEVEL OF POLLUTION (TONS/MO)	TOTAL BENEFIT OF REDUCING POLLUTION TO THIS LEVEL (MILLIONS OF $/MO)	TOTAL COST OF REDUCING POLLUTION TO THIS LEVEL (MILLIONS OF $/MO)
5	$15	$ 2
4	25	5
3	32	11
2	37	21
1	40	36
0	42	60

A. WHAT IS THE MARGINAL COST OF REDUCING POLLUTION FROM 5 TONS PER MONTH TO 4? WHAT IS THE MARGINAL BENEFIT? WHAT DOES THIS SAY ABOUT THE CURRENT LEVEL OF POLLUTION (6 TONS PER MONTH)?

B. CONGRESS IS CONSIDERING A LIMIT OF 2 TONS PER MONTH. WOULD THIS BE PREFERABLE TO THE CURRENT LEVEL OF POLLUTION? EXPLAIN.

C. FROM AN ECONOMIC PERSPECTIVE, WHAT IS THE OPTIMAL LEVEL OF POLLUTION? SHOW HOW YOU DERIVED THE ANSWER.

D. IF CONGRESS WISHED TO MAXIMIZE AIR QUALITY IN THIS INDUSTRY, HOW MUCH POLLUTION SHOULD IT ALLOW PER MONTH? WHY IS THIS NOT THE ECONOMICALLY OPTIMAL LEVEL OF POLLUTION?

Ways to Reduce Pollution

In addition to selecting acceptable levels of pollution, the government must also decide how to attack pollution. It can rely on voluntary compliance, require that firms take specific actions to eliminate pollution, tax either the pollution itself or the product that generates pollution, subsidize pollution-control equipment, or even sell firms the right to emit a limited amount of pollution. Because the costs and success of these different approaches often vary, it is important to examine the strengths and weaknesses of each.

VOLUNTARY COMPLIANCE

The government could appeal to the social conscience of individuals and firms, as it does when it asks them to prevent forest fires, to refrain from littering, and to dispose of chemicals responsibly. As long as the cost of compliance is low, compliance may be substantial. But as the cost rises, fewer and fewer parties are willing to contribute to a clean environment.

Firms that voluntarily use resources to reduce pollution increase their costs of production and earn lower profits than had they ignored pollution. In competitive industries, these lost profits are the difference between a firm remaining in business and closing its doors, because only firms that produce at the lowest possible cost can survive in the long run. In other words, firms that ignore pollution have lower costs and therefore can drive so-called "socially responsible" firms out of business. As an example of this, consider the economic demise of Larry Daniels (Exhibit 35.3).[8]

DIRECT REGULATION

Rather than rely on voluntary compliance, the government sometimes resorts to direct regulation—what is commonly referred to as "command and control." Firms and consumers are ordered to adhere to certain specific requirements. Those that do not are subject to fines and imprisonment. The government relies on direct regulation when it mandates that new cars must have catalytic converters and burn unleaded gasoline. Similarly, the government could attack the problem of contaminated fish by banning the use of chlordane or requiring that fish with high concentrations of the pesticide be removed from the market.

COST EFFECTIVE
Achieving a given objective (for example, the elimination of a certain volume of pollution) at the lowest cost possible.

The problem with direct regulation is that, in many cases, it is not **cost effective**. It prevents firms and consumers from achieving a given reduction in pollution using other, less costly techniques. For example, direct regulations often tie a firm to the best present technology even if superior technologies, which would permit the firm to reduce pollution more efficiently, become available in the future. Not only does this impose unnecessary costs on firms (once these technologies are available), it blunts the incentives of entrepreneurs to develop new technologies to deal with pollution.

At other times, the government fails even to take advantage of the best present technology. For example, the 1977 amendments to the Clean Air Act required power plants to install scrubbers on their new coal-powered boilers to remove from

---

[8]For further analysis of the limitations of voluntary compliance, see Jeffery Williams, "Social Traps and Incentives: Implications for Low-Input, Sustainable Agriculture," *Journal of Soil and Water Conservation* (January-February 1990), pp. 28–30.

E
X
H
I
B
I
T

35.3

Larry Daniels, a commercial fisherman in New Madrid, Missouri, had just come home with the day's catch when he got a letter from state health officials warning that many species of fish in the Mississippi and Missouri rivers were contaminated with chlordane, a toxic pesticide. Daniels promptly dumped his catch—350 pounds of carp, catfish, and drum—into a trash can. Then he closed his fish market and never reopened it. "I was not going to sell fish if it was hazardous to people, especially children. I just didn't want to contribute to any kid getting cancer down the road."

The highest level of chlordane was found in carp and catfish in the Mississippi at St. Louis. The fish there contained 1,389 parts of chlordane for each billion parts of fish. The U.S. Food and Drug Administration warns against eating fish containing chlordane at levels higher than 300 parts per billion. Chlordane is suspected of causing cancer; it is known to cause chronic liver damage and may damage the immune and nervous systems.

Four blocks from Daniels' closed fish market . . . Fred Moore is busy catching and selling fish. "I can't tell any difference in my business," he said. Don Whitehead, manager of the R & R Fish Market in St. Charles, said he sold catfish and buffalo from the nearby Missouri River, as well as fish from Kentucky. Customers don't ask whether the fish may be contaminated with chlordane, he said. "They aren't going to hurt you any worse than smoking cigarettes."

State officials say they are most concerned that some fishermen or market owners are mislabeling fish to circumvent the health advisory. "Everywhere you go, you now see signs saying 'Ohio River fish,'" Robinson said. "I don't believe it at all. The Ohio River is a long way away, and it's just not practical for most small merchants to bring in large shipments of fish from there." At a meeting in Charleston, Missouri, to explain the health advisory to commercial fishermen, Crellin said, he overheard a fisherman asking a friend how to spell "Kentucky" because he wanted to put that label on his fish.

Daniels, the fisherman in New Madrid, said his family had scraped by on food stamps until he found a job as a truck driver several weeks ago. He said he had no regrets about his decision. "A lot of guys around here are still fishing and selling them," he said. "It's just like selling marijuana to kids. There's a lot of people who do it, but that doesn't mean it's right. People can continue to eat the fish, but not from me, they won't."

SOURCE: Marjorie Mandel, "Contaminated Fish May Be Mislabelled," *St. Louis Post Dispatch*, May 3, 1987, pp. 1, 6. Reprinted by permission.

70 to 90 percent of the sulphur in the stack gas. This rule applied regardless of the sulphur content of the coal. The rule was inefficient because it precluded power plants from using alternatives that are less costly than scrubbing. In particular, for many utilities it would have been less costly to burn untreated low-sulphur coal or to burn moderate-sulphur coal whose sulphur content has been reduced through a washing process. Both methods would have eliminated *more* sulphur from the air

than scrubbing the gas of high-sulphur coal. Thus, the 1977 amendments increased the cost of generating electricity while sacrificing air quality.

Apparently, Congress was aware of the consequences of its actions but succumbed to political pressures. Had Congress allowed power plants to reduce sulphur emission by switching to low-sulphur coal (which is produced in the western United States), employment in eastern coal fields (whose coal has a high sulphur content) would have contracted. For that reason, representatives of the eastern coal-producing states opposed universal limits on sulphur emissions (for example, 1.2 pounds of sulphur per million BTUs of energy) and instead pushed through legislation that forced utilities to scrub all coal, even low-sulphur western coal.[9] In a concession to efficiency, the 1990 amendments to the Clean Air Act repealed the scrubbing requirement and allow firms to reduce sulphur emissions at the lowest cost possible.

EFFLUENT FEES

EFFLUENT FEE
A charge or tax levied on each unit of a pollutant emitted into the environment.

Because of the inefficiency of direct regulation, economists generally favor market-based strategies to reduce pollution. One of these is the **effluent fee**, which is a tax per unit of pollutant. By making pollution costly to the firm, the effluent fee gives the firm an incentive to curb its pollution. In particular, the firm will continue to eliminate pollution as long as this is less costly than paying the effluent fee. Unlike direct regulation, the effluent fee provides producers with an incentive to reduce pollution at the lowest possible cost—whether this entails installing specific pollution-control equipment, switching to a cleaner fuel, or recycling (see Exhibit 35.4). Thus, the effluent fee is cost effective.

One drawback of an effluent fee is that it requires continuous monitoring of pollution levels—to keep track of the amount of pollution emitted by each company so that taxes can be assessed. Monitoring is also required with direct regulation, to determine whether companies are complying with the law, but the government can get by with spot (random) monitoring. Because monitoring uses up resources, the added monitoring costs associated with an effluent fee increase the cost of this method of pollution control. But, as a practical matter, monitoring costs are often modest.

AN OUTPUT TAX

Instead of taxing pollution directly, an alternative is to tax the products responsible for that pollution. For example, if the production of steel contributes to air pollution, the government could levy a tax on each ton of steel produced. This would reduce the output of steel and, in turn, the amount of pollution generated by the steel industry.

An output tax has one advantage over an effluent fee. Because the tax is levied on production—rather than on the level of pollution—it does not require monitoring pollution. On the other hand, the output tax has a major drawback: it does not

---

[9]Lester B. Lave, "Coal and the Clean Air Act," in S. Fred Singer, ed., *Free Market Energy* (New York: Universe Books, 1984), pp. 181–185.

EXHIBIT
35.4

Turning Sludge into Dollars

Firms voluntarily recycle waste when it is profitable to do so. But when a cheaper alternative is available to the firm (for example, emitting waste into the environment), the firm has no incentive to recycle. The situation changes, however, if the firm is assessed a tax on its emissions. In particular, such a tax increases the benefits of recycling, since the recycled waste escapes taxation.

As the cost of waste disposal has increased, due in part to higher taxes, recycling has become more common. A chemical company that had been discharging 35,000 tons of fly ash each year located a company that was willing to use fly ash in the cement blocks it manufactured. In another instance, a timber company developed a procedure for converting its wastes into products such as vegetable wax. Finally, consider the chemical company that had been generating 1,000 cubic yards of calcium fluoride sludge each month. By combining this sludge with yet another waste product, the company was able to produce synthetic fluorspar, an input it previously had been purchasing from other companies.

In summary, whenever technologically feasible, companies have responded to higher disposal costs by recycling their waste products. They have done so not out of a sense of social responsibility but rather out of a more basic motive—making profits.

SOURCE: Adapted from Murray L. Weidenbaum, *Rendezvous with Reality: The American Economy After Reagan* (New York: Basic Books, 1988), p. 218.

reduce the amount of pollution per unit of output. For example, steel companies would have no incentive to burn low-sulphur coal, install scrubbers, or otherwise reduce the amount of pollution per ton of steel. Unlike an emission fee, an output tax does not reward companies for switching to a less-polluting technique of production. Therefore, for a given level of output, the amount of pollution is greater if an output tax is used rather than an effluent fee.

SUBSIDIZING POLLUTION CONTROL

In addition to reducing pollution through taxes, the government sometimes uses subsidies to encourage pollution abatement. By bearing part of the cost of pollution-control equipment, the government reduces the cost to firms of eliminating pollution. By itself, this is not likely to have much impact. If compliance remains voluntary, firms have no economic incentive to install pollution-control equipment, even if the government foots most of the bill. On the other hand, when firms are forced to curtail pollution (for example, as a result of direct regulation), subsidies reduce the costs to firms.

But this simply means that pollution-control costs are passed on to third parties—in this case, taxpayers. Therefore, those who create pollution do not bear the full consequences of their actions. In addition, to the extent subsidies keep the private cost of production below the social cost, firms continue to charge less than the socially optimal amount for their product and therefore consumers purchase more output than is socially optimal.

Another criticism of pollution-abatement subsidies concerns their cost effectiveness. By reducing the relative cost of pollution-control equipment, subsidies encourage firms to attack pollution by purchasing additional equipment, even though alternative approaches (for example, switching to a cleaner fuel) may have a lower social cost. In summary, pollution-control subsidies are criticized as inequitable (for shifting pollution costs to third parties), inefficient (in the sense of permitting excess production of the polluting product), and cost ineffective (for failing to reduce pollution at the lowest cost).

ASSIGNING PROPERTY RIGHTS

In attacking pollution, it is important to recognize why private markets fail to produce the socially optimal amount of pollution. Markets fail because property rights are not clearly defined or enforced. Do smokers have the right to exhale cigarette smoke into the air, or do nonsmokers have the right to a smoke-free environment? To whom do the nation's oceans and beaches belong—to swimmers and fishermen or to an oil company known to spill its cargo occasionally? Unless such issues are resolved, economic agents will continue to make conflicting claims on the environment.

On the other hand, if property rights were spelled out, the parties involved—those creating the pollution and those harmed by it—could sometimes reach their own solution (see Exhibit 35.5). Where that failed, the courts could assess damages against those who violate others' rights. For example, if swimmers owned the rights to a beach, a firm could not legally deposit its oil there unless it obtained permission of the swimmers. If the firm's oil washed up on the beach without their permission, the swimmers could sue for damages.

Although assigning property rights and seeking court enforcement is one remedy to the problem of pollution, this approach has problems of its own. The litigation process is costly and time-consuming. Beyond that, the burden of proof is on the plaintiff. For example, the swimmers must demonstrate that they were harmed by the pollution, provide evidence of the extent of their damages, and prove that the damages resulted from the acts of the defendant-firm. Even if the plaintiffs prevail, they may be unable to collect the full damages if the award exceeds the firm's ability to pay. For such reasons, many believe that lawsuits are not the most effective way to reduce pollution.

SELLING RIGHTS TO POLLUTE

Many economists favor a policy of selling firms the right to pollute. Although this is a controversial proposal, especially to those who view pollution as a moral rather

EXHIBIT

35.5

Correcting for Externalities in the Absence of Government Intervention—The Role of Bargaining and Property Rights

In 1991, Ronald Coase, professor emeritus of the University of Chicago, received the Nobel Prize in economics. In making the award, the Royal Swedish Academy of Sciences cited Coase's pathbreaking work on transaction costs and property rights. Coase showed that the market will lead to the optimal amount of pollution (or any other externality) provided that three conditions are satisfied:[10]

1. Property rights are clearly assigned.
2. The number of parties involved in the dispute is small.
3. The parties can negotiate at no cost.

As an illustration of Coase's argument, consider a firm that locates upstream from an outdoor resort. If the firm discharges its wastes into the river, the resort becomes less attractive and its business suffers. The owner of the resort understandably wants the firm to reduce its pollution. But suppose the firm has the right to use the river as a dumping grounds. What incentive does the firm have to reduce the amount of waste it sends downstream? The incentive comes in the form of the payment the resort is willing to make to induce the firm to cut back on its pollution. As long as the payment to the firm for reducing its pollution exceeds the cost to the firm of reducing pollution, the firm stands to gain from curbing its discharges into the river. The firm may recycle its wastes, ship them to an alternate disposal site, or simply reduce production. But whatever method is chosen, the two parties, by getting together and negotiating, are able to resolve the pollution problem.

Now suppose that rights to the river belong to the resort rather than to the firm. In this case, the firm must pay the resort to obtain permission to discharge its wastes into the river. How does this alternative assignment of property rights affect the outcome? In what many find to be a surprising result, Coase showed that the level of pollution will be identical to that which would prevail when the firm had property rights. Moreover, the method of reducing pollution will be the same regardless of which party is assigned rights to the river. Whichever party pays to reduce pollution will choose the least costly option available. Although the initial assignment of property rights determines who bears the costs, it has no impact on the level or method of pollution control.

As important as these findings are in dealing with pollution and other externalities, they depend critically on the assumptions underlying the analysis. When there are substantial costs associated with negotiations or when a large number of parties is involved, reaching an agreement may be difficult. For example, if the firm must satisfy hundreds of different landowners rather than a single resort, it is likely that one or more will balk at any proposed agreement. In such instances, government intervention is generally necessary to deal effectively with externalities. But even here, property rights remain an important consideration. Indeed, the EPA's current policy of allowing firms to buy and sell *rights to pollute* is based on the work of Ronald Coase and his insights concerning the role of property rights in achieving socially optimal outcomes.

[10]Ronald Coase, "The Problem of Social Cost," *Journal of Law and Economics* (October 1960), pp. 1–44.

POLLUTION RIGHT

A permit that entitles its
bearer to emit one unit of a
certain pollutant into the
environment.

**MARKET FOR
POLLUTION RIGHTS**

A market in which pollution
rights are bought and sold,
at prices determined by the
supply of and demand for
these permits.

than economic issue, economists defend this approach on various grounds. First, the government can limit pollution to what it considers the optimal level by selling only enough **pollution rights** to create this amount of pollution. Second, as with a pollution tax, selling rights to pollute would generate revenues for the government. These could be used for such projects as developing new pollution-control technologies and cleaning up the environment. Finally, if firms were required to buy a permit for each unit of pollution emitted, they would have an incentive to reduce pollution, because each unit eliminated voluntarily would mean one less permit to buy. Moreover, in eliminating that pollution, firms would be motivated to use the least costly approach available. Thus, a **market for pollution rights** would be cost effective.

Figure 35.5 illustrates how a market for pollution rights would work. The supply of pollution rights is perfectly inelastic, reflecting the fact that the government has decided to limit pollution to the level Q^*. The demand curve is downward sloping because firms respond to an increased price of pollution rights by reducing emissions—substituting pollution control for pollution rights. If the demand curve for pollution rights is given by D_1, the government sells pollution rights at a price of P_1 and collects $P_1 \times Q^*$ in revenues.

Over time, demand for pollution rights may increase as additional firms locate along the river. This raises the price of pollution rights, thereby generating more revenues for the government, but the level of pollution remains unchanged. Despite firms' greater desire to pollute, the quality of the environment does not deteriorate. Note that had firms been allowed to pollute at will, they would have created Q_1 pollution given the demand curve D_1 and Q_2 pollution given demand curve D_2. Thus a

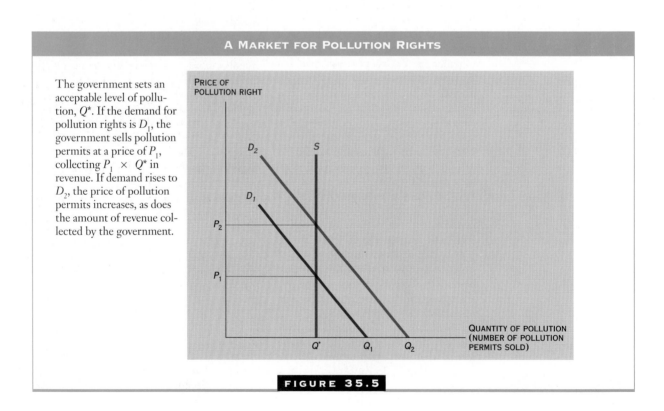

A MARKET FOR POLLUTION RIGHTS

The government sets an acceptable level of pollution, Q^*. If the demand for pollution rights is D_1, the government sells pollution permits at a price of P_1, collecting $P_1 \times Q^*$ in revenue. If demand rises to D_2, the price of pollution permits increases, as does the amount of revenue collected by the government.

FIGURE 35.5

market for pollution rights reduces pollution from the market level (Q_1 or Q_2) to that level determined to be socially acceptable (Q^*).

EMISSIONS TRADING Although currently there is no market for pollution rights—in which the government sells firms a license to pollute—the EPA has adopted several variations on this theme. Under its emissions trading program, companies that reduce pollution by more than the amount required earn emission reduction credits (ERCs), which may be used in certain circumstances to offset deficiencies in pollution control elsewhere. Two components of emissions trading are *offsets* and *bubbles*.

Offsets are used in areas of the country not yet in compliance with air-quality standards. New firms are allowed to enter the area, and existing firms to expand, provided that they can induce other firms in the area to reduce their pollution by an even larger amount. In other words, firms that need pollution credits (ERCs) can buy these credits from other firms that are willing, for a price, to *overcomply* with their own pollution standards. Offsets can also be used by a firm to increase pollution at one of its plants in exchange for tightening up pollution control at another plant. Thus, offsets allow continued economic growth in an area while, at the same time, improving air quality standards. This is more attractive than the alternative of banning all new sources of pollution, and thereby stifling economic growth.

Another virtue of offsets is that they take advantage of the fact that pollution control is less costly in some firms than in others. For example, according to one study the costs of eliminating an additional ton of hydrocarbons ranged from $41 at a gasoline terminal to $16,500 at a spray-painting operation.[11] By allowing more hydrocarbons to be released from spray painting—provided that fewer hydrocarbons are released from gas terminals—offsets reduce the costs of achieving a given level of pollution control. The major difference between a policy of offsets and the previously discussed market for pollution rights is that, with offsets, revenues from the sale of pollution rights accrue to the firm reducing pollution, rather than to the government.

Unlike offsets, which may be traded between firms, **bubbles** accommodate emissions trading within a single firm. When the Clean Air Act was initially enforced, emissions requirements were established for each source of pollution within a plant—that is, for every valve, smokestack, and other outlet for air pollution. A problem with this strategy was that it failed to account for the fact that reducing pollution was less costly at some ports than others. Therefore, the initial approach was not cost effective. Aware of this, in 1979 the EPA began implementing its bubble policy, under which a firm could create, subject to government approval, an imaginary bubble encompassing one or more of its plants.

Once a bubble is established, the firm sums emissions requirements for the individual sources of pollution to obtain a cumulative limit for the bubble. The firm is then allowed to exceed pollution standards at individual points provided that these excesses are offset at other points. In effect, the bubble permits the firm to spread pollution control across all sources in such a way that it can minimize the cost of achieving the specified level of pollution control.

In 1986, the EPA tightened its requirements for creating bubbles by mandating that the total emissions from a bubble be 20 percent below the sum of the limits for

OFFSETS
Reductions in pollution beyond the amount required of one firm (or plant) that are used to permit a second firm (or plant) in the same area to increase its pollution.

BUBBLE
An imaginary enclosure around one or more plants that becomes the basis for a firm's pollution-control requirements. In particular, a firm is allowed to exceed pollution-control standards at individual points in the bubble provided that these excesses are offset elsewhere within the same bubble.

[11]P. Ginberg and G. Schaumburg, *Economic Incentive Systems for the Control of Hydrocarbon Emissions from Stationary Sources*, Report to the Council on Environmental Quality, 1980.

the individual sources of pollution. For example, if a firm had ten sources of pollution, each permitted to discharge one ton of hydrocarbons, the total amount of hydrocarbons allowed under the new bubble policy would be eight tons. According to numerous economic studies, bubbles and other forms of emissions trading result in cost savings of at least 50 percent over the command-and-control approach of direct regulation.

The 1990 amendments to the Clean Air Act further expanded the use of pollution credits by establishing maximum levels of sulphur dioxide for individual utili-

The Advantages of a Bubble

A POWER PLANT OPERATES TWO BOILERS, THE SECOND OF WHICH HAS ADVANCED POLLUTION-CONTROL EQUIPMENT. THE FOLLOWING TABLE DEPICTS THE COSTS OF REDUCING POLLUTION TO SPECIFIED LEVELS FOR EACH OF THE BOILERS.

TONS OF POLLUTION PER MONTH	TOTAL COST OF REDUCING POLLUTION TO THIS LEVEL (MILLIONS OF DOLLARS)	
	BOILER 1	BOILER 2
10	$ 2	$ 1
9	5	2
8	11	3
7	16	4
6	22	5
5	29	8
4	37	14

A. ASSUME THE GOVERNMENT REQUIRES THAT EACH BOILER LIMIT ITS POLLUTION TO 8 TONS PER MONTH. WHAT IS THE TOTAL COST TO THE FIRM OF BRINGING BOTH ITS BOILERS INTO COMPLIANCE?

B. THE GOVERNMENT NOW AGREES TO CONSIDER BOTH BOILERS AS PART OF THE SAME BUBBLE. IF THE ALLOWABLE LEVEL OF POLLUTION FOR THIS BUBBLE IS 16 TONS PER MONTH, WHAT IS THE LEAST COSTLY WAY TO MEET THIS REQUIREMENT? HOW MUCH CAN THE FIRM SAVE EACH MONTH, COMPARED TO THE PREVIOUS LIMIT OF 8 TONS OF POLLUTION PER BOILER?

C. SUPPOSE THE GOVERNMENT, AS A CONDITION FOR BRINGING BOTH BOILERS UNDER THE SAME BUBBLE, DEMANDS THAT THE BUBBLE GENERATE NO MORE THAN 14 TONS OF POLLUTION PER MONTH. SHOULD THE FIRM ACCEPT THE GOVERNMENT'S OFFER, OR IS IT BETTER OFF UNDER THE OLD STANDARD THAT ALLOWED 8 TONS OF POLLUTION FROM EACH BOILER (16 TONS TOTAL)? EXPLAIN.

---

[12]Matthew Wald, "Electric Utility in Ohio to Buy Pollution Rights from Alcoa," *The New York Times*, July 1, 1992, p. C3.

ties (based on past emission rates) and allowing utilities that reduce pollution below their ceiling to earn credits that can be sold to other parties. One of the first trades under the 1990 amendments involved the sale of 25,000 tons of sulphur dioxide credits by an Indiana electric plant to Ohio Edison. According to Alcoa, co-owner of the plant, Ohio Edison will pay about $300 per ton over the five-year contract.[12] Although this particular deal was arranged by an investment banking company, sulphur dioxide credits are scheduled to begin trading on the Chicago Board of Trade in 1993. The EPA estimates that the 1990 amendments will reduce emissions of sulphur dioxide to roughly 60 percent of 1980 emission levels.

SUMMARY AND IMPLICATIONS

Table 35.2 summarizes certain alternative ways of reducing pollution. Of the various approaches, voluntary compliance is often the least effective. Those who take it upon themselves to reduce pollution incur greater costs than those who ignore the problem. This puts so-called "socially responsible" firms at a cost disadvantage; in competitive industries, they will be unable to compete in the long run with firms that ignore pollution.

Aware of the limits of voluntary compliance, the government relies heavily on direct regulation, whereby the government dictates exactly what firms and consumers must do to combat pollution. Where a particular pollutant is judged so harmful that its socially optimal level is zero, direct regulation is often the easiest way to halt emissions of this pollutant. Another advantage of direct regulation is that continuous monitoring of pollution levels is unnecessary. On the other hand, direct regulation suffers a number of major shortcomings. Foremost is the fact that it is not cost effective. Because of its rigid nature, firms and consumers are prevented from using less costly approaches to reduce pollution. Where direct regulation

SUMMARY OF ALTERNATIVE METHODS FOR REDUCING POLLUTION

PROGRAM	REQUIRES CONTINUOUS MONITORING	TENDS TO BE COST EFFECTIVE	GENERATES REVENUE FOR THE GOVERNMENT	COMMENT
Voluntary compliance	No	No	No	Generally ineffective.
Direct regulation	No	No	No	Politically popular.
Effluent fee	Yes	Yes	Yes	Provides a market incentive to reduce pollution.
Output tax	No	No	Yes	Does not reduce the amount of pollution per unit of output.
Pollution-control subsidy	No	No	No	Shifts pollution-control cost to third parties.
Market for pollution rights	Yes	Yes	Yes	Keeps pollution at socially acceptable levels regardless of the demand to pollute.

TABLE 35.2

mandates a specific technology, it also blunts the incentive to develop new technologies to deal with pollution. Finally, with direct regulation, firms have no incentive to reduce pollution beyond the level dictated by the government.

Sometimes the government couples direct regulation with pollution-control subsidies, so that firms will not have to bear the full cost of reducing pollution. But this merely shifts the cost from polluters to taxpayers. Subsidizing pollution-control equipment also tends to be cost ineffective because it discourages firms from using alternative approaches to pollution control (for example, burning cleaner fuels) even when they are less costly to society.

Economists generally favor a market-based approach to pollution control—for example, imposing effluent fees or instituting a market for pollution rights. An advantage of both effluent fees and pollution rights is that they provide an incentive to reduce pollution at the lowest cost possible. A drawback, usually minor, is that they require continuous monitoring of pollution levels. Although there is currently no formal market for pollution rights—in which the government sells a license to pollute—the EPA does allow emissions trading, which is the basic feature of the market for pollution rights.

An alternative to the effluent fee is a tax on the output of the polluting company. This leads to a reduction in output and therefore in pollution but, unlike the effluent fee, offers firms no incentive to reduce the amount of pollution per unit of output.

Some Complications

CROSS-MEDIA POLLUTION

It is entirely possible that somewhere in the country, toxic metals are being removed from the air, transferred to a waste water stream, removed again by water pollution controls, converted to a sludge, shipped to an incinerator and returned to the air.[13]

To be most effective, the government's attack on pollution must be integrated. Society gains little if pollution is simply transferred from one medium (for example, air) to another medium (water or land). We must concern ourselves with what happens to pollution after it is removed from a particular medium. It was this realization that led to the creation of the EPA in 1970. In justifying the new agency, President Nixon argued that

The environment must be perceived as a single interrelated system. . . . [We need to] examine interactions among forms of pollution and identify where on the ecological chain interdiction would be most appropriate.[14]

---

[13]Lee M. Thomas, former administrator of the EPA, quoted in *The New York Times*, "Some Solutions to Pollution Aren't the Final Word," May 11, 1986, p. 5E.

[14]Council on Environmental Quality, *Environmental Quality, 1985* (1986) (Washington, D.C.: Government Printing Office), p. 10.

But if the EPA was founded on the principle of integration, it has had limited success fostering that principle. The agency must administer a dozen separate laws, each addressing its own set of problems and espousing its own goals. Sometimes the requirements of one law are at cross purposes with a second law. Moreover, much pollution control remains within the province of states and local communities, which often vacillate in their approach to pollution control. The country has a long way to go before its environmental policy can be considered integrated and consistent.

THE INTERNATIONAL NATURE OF POLLUTION

As challenging as it is to develop an integrated national approach to pollution, devising an integrated global approach is even more difficult. Yet such an approach is important inasmuch as all countries share a common environment. Production or consumption in one country often creates pollution elsewhere. For example, winds blow sulphur dioxide from Mexican smelters into the United States, while different winds carry the sulphur dioxide emitted by U.S. utilities into Canada. In each case the resulting acid rain kills fish and destroys lakes and forests in the recipient country. Similarly, the chlorofluorocarbons (CFCs) and halons that countries pump into the air deplete the earth's protective ozone layer and intensify ultraviolet radiation, thereby increasing the risks of skin cancer and other health problems. Yet another concern is the *greenhouse effect*. The burning of fossil fuels has increased the concentration of carbon dioxide in the atmosphere, which is expected to increase global temperatures, alter rain patterns, and raise sea levels.

"Yes, we've Been Regulars since way back in 1988, when the "Greenhouse Effect" First Kicked in. How about you? This your First Trip to Alaska?..."

SOURCE: With permission of *The Minneapolis Star Tribune*.

Given the global nature of these problems, an effective response requires the concentrated actions of a significant number of nations. Fortunately, there are signs that some progress is being made. Since 1972, a number of world conferences have been called to deal specifically with environmental issues. More than 50 nations signed the Montreal Protocol, a 1987 treaty calling for countries to reduce emissions of CFCs to half their 1986 levels and to freeze consumption of halons. Three years later, almost 100 nations agreed to accelerate the phaseout of CFCs and to restrict sharply the use of other chlorine-based chemicals. Another treaty among the major industrial nations, including the United States, limits emissions of nitrogen oxide to their 1987 levels. Finally, the 1992 Earth Summit brought 178 nations together to discuss environmental issues and produced a commission to monitor compliance with international environmental agreements. At a minimum, there appears to be a heightened awareness of the fact that global problems require global solutions.

Nonrenewable Natural Resources

The availability of natural resources would be of interest even in the absence of environmental problems, but in fact the two are related. The greenhouse effect alluded to earlier is the direct consequence of burning fossil fuels. By replacing coal with natural gas and other cleaner sources of energy, less carbon dioxide would be emitted into the air, thereby lessening the damage. Similarly, substituting low-sulphur coal for high-sulphur coal would mitigate the problem of acid rain.

But if switching to cleaner sources of energy offers a way to curb pollution, it raises other concerns. Many sources of energy, including natural gas, are *nonrenewable*. In contrast to, say, timber—whose current supply can be replaced by planting new trees—once we exhaust the earth's supply of natural gas it is gone. Many nonenergy natural resources are also nonrenewable, from asbestos to zinc. This has created concern that the present generation is squandering the earth's natural resources, leaving behind a world in which future generations will have to worry not only about pollution but also about how to maintain consumption in the face of declining resources.

The "energy crisis" of the 1970s, and the country's newly discovered vulnerability to foreign supplies of energy, only intensified fears that the country was running out of resources. Reinforcing this view, the government ran "public-service" messages encouraging conservation, prohibited the use of natural gas for certain activities, and established programs to regulate the price and distribution of oil and natural gas. At the same time, some organizations were predicting that certain resources would soon be depleted. For example, in 1976 the American Electric Power Company ran advertisements claiming that in 12 years "America will be out of oil and gas."[15]

The predicted event did not materialize. In fact, in 1988 America had enough natural gas to last another 12 years—through the year 2000. This raises a number

---

[15]Arnold Hite, "Chicken Little Was Wrong About Oil, Too," *The Wall Street Journal*, February 3, 1988, p. 20.

of important issues. How were we able to postpone depletion of our stock of natural gas past 1988? Can we do it again in the year 2000? What led to the shortage of natural gas and other materials in the 1970s? Did the government's regulation of the oil and natural gas industries ameliorate the energy problem? How did government controls affect the country's dependence on foreign sources of energy?

Why the End Never Comes

EXPECTED LIFE (OF A RESOURCE)
Proven reserves divided by consumption.

PROVEN RESERVES
The amount of a natural resource that has been discovered and that producers are willing to extract given current costs and prices.

Periodically, statistics are compiled on the **expected life** of various resources. In 1976, such statistics placed the expected life of natural gas at 12 years. To see what these statistics do and do not mean, it is important to understand how they are constructed. The expected life of natural gas is based on its **proven reserves**, which in the United States amounted to 228 trillion cubic feet in 1976. U.S. consumption of natural gas that year amounted to 19.5 trillion cubic feet. Simple division reveals that if this rate of consumption were maintained, proven reserves would be depleted in 12 years.

But proven reserves do not include all of a resource that is locked in the earth. Rather, proven reserves refer to the quantity of a resource that has been discovered and that producers are willing to extract given current prices and technology. Extraction costs depend on the size of a deposit and its purity. They also vary with its location. A certain amount of a resource may lie near the earth's surface, easily accessible. Other deposits may be buried miles underground or beneath the ocean floor. In addition, it may be necessary to transport some deposits great distances across hostile terrain before reaching the market. For such reasons, some deposits are too costly to extract at present prices. These deposits are not counted as *proven reserves*.

As the price of a resource rises, and a larger quantity can be profitably extracted, proven reserves increase. (Oil that costs $25 per barrel to produce will not be part of proven reserves when the price is $20 per barrel but will be when the price is $30.) Proven reserves also expand when extraction costs decline (for example, because of a technological advance or government tax incentives). Finally, proven reserves increase as exploration leads to the discovery of new deposits of the reserve. In other words, proven reserves fluctuate over time.

Given this responsiveness in proven reserves, statistics on the expected life of various resources can be misleading. They should not be interpreted as indicating the date when the stock of a resource will be depleted. As a resource becomes more scarce, its price tends to rise. Not only does this directly increase proven reserves, it triggers additional exploration and provides added incentives to develop new, cost-saving technologies. These will further boost proven reserves. In fact, proven reserves often *increase* over time, as new reserves are added faster than current reserves are depleted.

There is a second reason why statistics on the expected life of a resource understate the actual remaining life, and that relates to demand. If the relative price of a resource rises, those using the resource will switch to substitutes. Other things equal, this will reduce consumption of the resource, slowing the rate at which it is depleted. In other words, as a resource becomes more scarce, the resulting higher price not only spurs exploration and production of the resource, it also curtails consumption. Both effects extend the resource's expected life. Because estimates of the expected life ignore the market responses of producers and consumers, they paint an unduly pessimistic picture of when, if ever, a given resource will be depleted. Accordingly, we can be quite confident that natural gas will be available well past the year 2000.

Explaining the Shortages of Raw Materials

The 1970s were a decade of shortages. The recession that began in late 1973 is frequently attributed to shortages of raw materials, which forced companies to curtail production and lay off employees. In addition, natural gas was in short supply throughout the decade, especially during the winter of 1976–1977. What accounted for these shortages? If prices adjust to reflect the relative scarcity of raw materials, as argued in the preceding section, then why were shortages not quickly eliminated?

The answer is that prices were *not* allowed to adjust. During much of this period the government artificially kept the prices of many raw materials below the market level, predictably creating a shortage (see Figure 35.6). From 1971 to 1974,

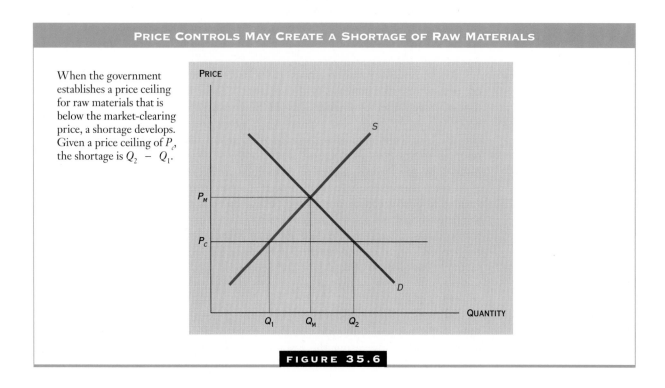

PRICE CONTROLS MAY CREATE A SHORTAGE OF RAW MATERIALS

When the government establishes a price ceiling for raw materials that is below the market-clearing price, a shortage develops. Given a price ceiling of P_c, the shortage is $Q_2 - Q_1$.

FIGURE 35.6

prices of goods and materials were subject to controls of various degree. During part of this period prices were frozen; at other times prices were allowed to rise, but only by a limited amount. As demand for raw materials increased because of a strengthening economy, pressure on prices mounted. Soon market prices were above controlled prices and, when that happened, firms were unable to obtain the quantities of raw materials they sought.

Price controls for natural gas have a much longer history. They were initiated in 1954 and continued until the Natural Gas Policy Act of 1978 phased out controls for most categories of natural gas. Controls for the remaining categories were eliminated by 1993 under the Natural Gas Wellhead Decontrol Act of 1989. Despite differences in the way controls on natural gas were set up, their effect was the same as for other products: *when controls keep a price below its market level, shortages develop.*

In the case of natural gas, shortages did not occur immediately. Given the heavy fixed costs of drilling for natural gas and the modest variable costs of operating existing wells, producers continued to sell large volumes of gas from existing wells, despite the imposition of controls. But controls did slow new drilling and exploration, threatening to create severe shortages in the future. Aware of this, the government attempted to fine-tune controls by allowing higher price ceilings on *new* wells (those drilled after a certain date) and on so-called "high-cost" wells. This mitigated some of the adverse effects on exploration and production, although it increased the complexity of price controls. For example, when the policy of partial decontrol of natural gas went into effect in 1979, there were 25 separate categories of natural gas, with different schedules for decontrol and with prices ranging from $.20 per million BTUs to $2.24.[16]

Despite such variations in the price-control program, its basic purpose was to keep the price of natural gas below its market-clearing level. As such, the shortages that developed were inevitable. The lesson of the shortages was not, as some inferred, that the country was running out of natural gas. Instead, the message was that when the price of natural gas (or any other good) is not allowed to rise to its market-clearing level, some consumers will be frustrated in their attempts to buy the good.

Price Controls and Imported Oil

Oil was also subject to price controls, but for the most part the country avoided oil shortages by increasing its imports from abroad. Thus the primary consequence of price controls on oil was to increase our dependence on foreign oil. To understand this, it is necessary to know how these controls were implemented.

The Energy Policy and Conservation Act of 1975 established price controls for domestically produced oil. Because only domestic oil was controlled, refiners that

---

[16]Murray L. Weidenbaum, *Business, Government, and the Public*, 3rd ed. (Englewood Cliffs, N.J.: Prentice-Hall, 1986), p. 120.

**ENTITLEMENT
PROGRAM**

A system for allocating oil
to U.S. refiners that consisted of entitlement fees (taxes)
on domestic oil and subsidies on imported oil. Once
the entitlement fees and
subsidies were taken into
account, all refiners faced
the same effective price for
their oil.

purchased foreign oil were forced to pay the higher world price. Unless something was done, this would put them at a cost disadvantage compared to refiners with access to domestic oil. To eliminate this distortion, the Energy Policy and Conservation Act also instituted an **entitlement program** designed to equalize the price of all oil sold in the United States. Refiners that wanted to buy price-controlled U.S. oil were first required to purchase entitlements from the government, giving them the authority to buy this oil. On the other hand, refiners that purchased the higher-priced imported oil were given a subsidy, financed by the entitlement fees. By adjusting entitlement fees and subsidies, the government established an effective common price for all domestic refiners, regardless of where they actually purchased their oil.

Because of the entitlement program, U.S. consumers were able to buy oil for less than the world price. This increased the quantity of oil demanded by U.S. consumers and reduced their incentive to conserve oil. At the same time, because U.S. producers were forced to accept less than the world price, they reduced the amount of oil they were willing to supply. Thus, the government's price-control program increased U.S. consumption of oil while simultaneously reducing U.S. production. Because the shortfall between domestic production and consumption is met through imports, the net effect of price controls on oil was to increase U.S. demand for imported oil, thereby increasing the country's vulnerability to OPEC.

Price controls on oil were abolished in 1981. The immediate effect was to allow the price of oil to rise in the United States, stimulating greater conservation by U.S. consumers and greater production and exploration by U.S. producers. These actions helped curb demand for imported oil and contributed to the pressure already being exerted on OPEC, as higher oil prices reduced worldwide consumption of oil and increased the supply of oil from non-OPEC countries. As the power of OPEC waned, oil prices plunged so that, despite the lifting of controls, oil prices in the United States dropped below their 1981 levels.

In summary, the history of price controls on oil and natural gas indicates that controls distort incentives for production and consumption. Controls either lead to shortages, as in the case of natural gas, or increase our dependence on foreign producers, as in the case of oil. Rather than being a solution to an "energy crisis," price controls prolong the crisis.

Summary

1. Externalities arise when the actions of producers or consumers affect third parties. Because markets ignore external benefits and costs, they fail to produce the socially optimal amount of output. Where externalities are positive, markets produce less output than socially desired; where externalities are negative, markets produce too much output.

2. In an attempt to move market output toward the socially optimal level, the government often subsidizes goods having external benefits while taxing goods having external costs. Taxes and other added costs are an attempt to internalize costs—to shift them back to those parties that create the external costs.

3. One of the major negative externalities is pollution. In an attempt to reduce pollution, the government has imposed various legislative standards for environmental quality. Although these standards reduce pollution, they are often arbitrary. As such, they may fail to achieve the optimal level of pollution.

4. From an economic perspective, society should continue to reduce pollution until the marginal cost of pollution control equals the marginal benefit. The cost of pollution control is measured in terms of the output that is given up in order to obtain a cleaner environment.

5. Voluntary compliance is generally not an effective way to reduce pollution because it imposes costs on those who clean up the environment. Accordingly, the government relies more heavily on the command-and-control approach of direct regulation, whereby firms and consumers must follow certain rigid requirements for reducing pollution. A drawback of direct regulation is that it prevents firms and consumers from using alternative, less costly techniques.

6. In place of direct regulation, economists generally prefer an effluent fee, which is a tax on each unit of pollution. The effluent fee provides firms and consumers an incentive to reduce pollution as efficiently as possible.

7. Alternatively, instead of taxing pollution, the government could tax the product that causes the pollution. The weakness of this approach is that firms and consumers have no incentive to reduce the amount of pollution per unit of output.

8. The government sometimes subsidizes the pollution-control equipment it requires firms to buy in order to ease the burden on these firms. But this merely transfers the cost of pollution control to the taxpayer and, by reducing the price firms charge, increases consumption of the polluting product. Finally, subsidies encourage firms to attack pollution by purchasing additional pollution-control equipment when alternative, more-efficient approaches are available.

9. Yet another approach is to establish a market for pollution rights, in which firms can buy the right to emit a certain level of pollution into the environment. Although the government does not presently sell pollution rights, it does allow firms that exceed pollution standards to sell pollution credits (which are, in effect, pollution rights) to other firms or to use these credits internally for offsetting pollution excesses elsewhere in the plant. An advantage of this approach is that it reduces pollution in those areas where it can be eliminated most efficiently.

10. Because the pollution removed from one medium is often deposited elsewhere, environmental policy must be integrated across the different media if it is to be truly effective. Given the global nature of many environmental problems, it is also desirable that environmental policy be integrated across countries.

11. Although many resources are nonrenewable, this does not imply that their supplies are fixed. *Proven reserves* of a resource—the amount producers are willing to extract— increase as the price of the resource rises, as extraction costs fall, and as new deposits are discovered. Accordingly, the proven reserves at a given point in time should not be interpreted as indicating when, if ever, a resource will be depleted. Indeed, proven reserves commonly rise over time, despite continued consumption.

12. Past shortages of natural gas in the United States were caused by price controls and were not a sign that natural gas would soon be depleted. Until 1981, price controls were also imposed on oil produced in the United States. These controls reduced domestic exploration and production of oil, blunted incentives to conserve oil, and consequently increased the country's demand for imported oil.

externalities
positive externalities/external
  benefits
negative externalities/external
  costs
private benefits
social benefits
private costs
social costs
internalize costs

cost–benefit analysis
cost effective
effluent fee
pollution rights
market for pollution rights
offsets
bubbles
expected life (of a resource)
proven reserves
entitlement program

Study Questions and Problems

1. (a) Demand for college education depends on the price of that education. Draw the market demand curve for college education. (b) Many scholars believe that a highly educated population benefits all of society (for example, by promoting medical advances and more rapid technological growth). Assuming this is true, draw society's demand curve for college education. (c) Based on the preceding demand curves, as well as on the supply curve, indicate the equilibrium level of college education and the socially optimal level. (d) What can the government do to foster the socially optimal level of education?

2. The country's air and water cannot be made too clean. We should demand that they be restored to their original, pristine state.

   Explain why you do or do not agree.

3. Why is government action generally necessary to reduce pollution? Why don't firms and consumers take it upon themselves to stop polluting?

4. Production of a good raises the concentration level of an airborne pollutant from 5 parts per million to 10 parts per million. An economic study estimates that the social costs and benefits of reducing pollution from current levels are as follows:

CONCENTRATION (PARTS PER MILLION)	TOTAL BENEFIT	TOTAL COST
9	$24,000	$ 10,000
8	44,000	25,000
7	60,000	45,000
6	72,000	70,000
5	80,000	100,000

a. A local politician argues that firms should be forced to restore air quality to its previous level (5 parts per million). Explain why you do or do not agree.

b. Assuming that the preceding estimates are correct, what is the socially optimal concentration of the pollutant? Explain.

c. Assume the benefits of reducing pollution are actually twice as great as estimated. How does this affect your conclusion about the optimal concentration of the pollutant?

d. If a new technology makes it less costly to remove the pollutant, how will this affect the optimal concentration of the pollutant?

5. Some of Vermont's landfills were leaking toxic substances, so the state recently passed a law requiring landfill operators to install liners to prevent leakage. The state also levied a new tax of $2.40 per cubic yard of trash deposited in any Vermont landfill.

a. The higher costs of operating landfills led to substantially higher prices for garbage pickup. Although some consumers and businesses protested, economists argued that the previous rates had been too low. In what sense is it possible to pay too little for a service?

b. How does raising the cost of using a landfill affect the incentive to recycle trash? Explain.

c. In another provision of the law, the government of Vermont agreed to subsidize recycling. On what economic grounds can this subsidy be criticized?

6. Copper smelters produce sulphur dioxide. To reduce emissions of this pollutant, the government could either tax firms on the volume of copper they produce or on their emissions of sulphur dioxide.

a. In what sense is the emissions tax preferable?

b. The copper tax has one modest advantage over the emissions tax. What is it?

7. Suppose the mayor of New York City receives five proposals for reducing carbon monoxide in the city: (i) appealing to residents of the city to curb unnecessary automobile use, (ii) imposing a tax of $5 per day on all vehicles operating in New York City, (iii) requiring meters on all vehicles in order to measure carbon monoxide emissions and then charging the owners an amount based on the level of emissions, (iv) banning the use of all cars and trucks every Monday, (v) subsidizing all train travel to and from the city and reducing subway fares in the city to $.10.

a. Which proposal is likely to be the least effective at reducing emissions of carbon monoxide?

b. Which proposal could be criticized for shifting to taxpayers the cost of controlling pollution?

c. Which proposal is an example of direct regulation?

d. Which proposal makes use of an effluent fee?

8. (a) What is an EPA *bubble*? (b) Why do economists prefer the bubble policy to the command-and-control approach of direct regulation?

9. The Bureau of Mines reports that world reserves of bauxite (aluminum ore) increased from 6 billion metric tons in 1965 to more than 20 billion metric tons today. How is this possible? Given the consumption of aluminum that occurred over this period, how could society end up with more of this exhaustible resource today than in 1965?

10. Explain how each of the following would affect proven reserves of the particular natural resource:

a. a *windfall-profits* tax on oil, which decreases the effective price that oil companies receive for selling a barrel of oil

b. a subsidy that suddenly makes it profitable to extract low-grade iron ore

c. the discovery of a major gold deposit in Alaska

d. a technological advance that lowers the cost of extracting diamonds

11. Suppose the government forces U.S. titanium producers to slash the price of their product.

a. How will this affect (i) domestic production of titanium and (ii) demand for imported titanium?

b. Assuming that the United States buys enough titanium to affect the world price, how will price controls on U.S. producers affect the world price of titanium?

YOUR TURN
Answers

Comparing the Costs and Benefits of Pollution Control

(A) MC = $3 MILLION; MB = $10 MILLION; THE CURRENT LEVEL OF POLLUTION IS HIGHER THAN SOCIALLY OPTIMAL. (B) YES. THE TOTAL BENEFIT OF REDUCING POLLUTION TO 2 TONS PER MONTH EXCEEDS THE COST OF DOING SO BY $16 MILLION ($37 MILLION MINUS $21 MILLION). (C) THE OPTIMAL LEVEL OF POLLUTION IS 3 TONS PER MONTH. AS POLLUTION IS BROUGHT DOWN TO THIS LEVEL, THE MARGINAL BENEFIT OF EACH REDUCTION IN POLLUTION EXCEEDS THE MARGINAL COST. BEYOND THIS POINT, THE REVERSE IS TRUE. (ALTERNATIVELY, 3 TONS OF POLLUTION OCCURS WHERE THE DIFFERENCE BETWEEN THE TOTAL BENEFITS OF REDUCING POLLUTION AND THE TOTAL COST IS MAXIMIZED: TB − TC = $21 MILLION.) (D) ZERO POLLUTION. THE MARGINAL COST OF REDUCING POLLUTION TO LESS THAN 3 TONS PER MONTH EXCEEDS THE MARGINAL BENEFIT.

The Advantage of a Bubble

(A) $14 MILLION (THAT IS, $11 MILLION PLUS $3 MILLION). (B) THE FIRM CAN REDUCE ITS POLLUTION-CONTROL EXPENDITURES TO $7 MILLION PER MONTH BY ALLOWING BOILER 1 TO EMIT 10 TONS OF POLLUTION WHILE LIMITING BOILER 2 TO 6 TONS OF POLLUTION. COMPARED TO THE PREVIOUS LIMIT (A), THIS RESULTS IN A COST SAVINGS OF $7 MILLION PER MONTH. (C) THE FIRM SHOULD ACCEPT THE GOVERNMENT'S OFFER. THE COST OF SATISFYING THE 14-TON LIMIT IS $13 MILLION ($5 MILLION FOR BOILER 1 AND $8 MILLION FOR BOILER 2). THIS IS $1 MILLION LESS THAN THE COST OF LIMITING POLLUTION EACH MONTH TO 8 TONS PER BOILER. EVEN THOUGH THE FIRM IS NOW PRODUCING 2 FEWER TONS OF POLLUTION EACH MONTH, IT IS ABLE TO REDUCE ITS POLLUTION-CONTROL EXPENDITURES BECAUSE IT NOW HAS DISCRETION OVER HOW IT REDUCES POLLUTION.

Selected References

Chilton, Kenneth, and Melinda Warren, eds. *Environmental Protection: Regulating for Results* (Boulder, Colo.: Westview Press, 1991). A book of readings on such issues as solid waste, global warming, and market-based remedies to pollution.

Council on Environmental Quality. *Environmental Quality* (Washington, D.C.: Government Printing Office). Discusses environmental legislation, cost-benefit analysis, and such environmental problems as acid rain and the greenhouse effect—the annual report of the President's Council on Environmental Quality.

Crandall, Robert. *Why Is the Cost of Environmental Regulation So High?* (St. Louis: Center for the Study of American Business, 1992). Analyzes the effect of environmental policy on the U.S. economy.

Hahn, Robert W., and Gordon L. Hester. "The Market for Bads: EPA's Experience with Emissions Trading," *Regulation* (Number 3/4, 1987), pp. 48–53. Analyzes the EPA's emissions trading program.

Resources for the Future. *Resources.* A free quarterly publication containing news and policy analysis of the environment and natural resources.

Singer, S. Fred, ed. *Free Market Energy* (New York: Universe Books, 1984). Examines U.S. energy policy and its alternatives.

U.S. Environmental Protection Agency. *EPA Journal* (Washington, D.C.: Government Printing Office). Bimonthly publication of the EPA. January/February 1991 issue discusses the 1990 amendments to the Clean Air Act.

U.S. Environmental Protection Agency. *National Air Quality and Emissions Trends Report* (Washington, D.C.: Government Printing Office). Details progress and problems in complying with air quality standards.

Economic Adjustment in Agriculture

THE FARM POPULATION CONTINUES TO DWINDLE AS FARMERS LEAVE THEIR LAND, EITHER FREELY FOR BETTER OPPORTUNITIES ELSEWHERE OR AS A RESULT OF FINANCIAL PRESSURES. THOSE PRESSURES WERE ESPECIALLY INTENSE DURING THE EARLY AND MID-1980s, WHEN FARMERS WERE BURDENED BY HEAVY DEBT AND LOW INCOME. WITH SO MANY FARMERS UNABLE TO REPAY THEIR LOANS, RURAL BANK FAILURES SOARED. FINANCIAL DISTRESS IN RURAL AMERICA REACHED ITS HIGHEST LEVEL SINCE THE GREAT DEPRESSION.

YET DESPITE THE RECENT HARDSHIP ENDURED BY A SUBSTANTIAL MINORITY OF FARMERS, THE ECONOMIC SITUATION OF THE AVERAGE FARMER HAS ACTUALLY IMPROVED THIS CENTURY. INDEED, DURING MUCH OF THE PRECEDING TWO DECADES THE AVERAGE INCOME OF FARM FAMILIES HAS BEEN AT LEAST AS HIGH AS THE AVERAGE INCOME OF NONFARM FAMILIES. RECENT POCKETS OF FINANCIAL DISTRESS IN AGRICULTURE HAVE COME IN THE FACE OF LONG-TERM PROGRESS, AT LEAST AS MEASURED ON A PER-FARM BASIS.

AFTER EXAMINING LONG-TERM TRENDS IN AGRICULTURE, INCLUDING CHANGES IN AGGREGATE FARM INCOME AND INCOME PER FARMER, CHAPTER 36 ADDRESSES THE RECENT FINANCIAL DISTRESS OF SOME OF THE NATION'S FARMERS. WE THEN CONSIDER THE RATIONALE FOR GOVERNMENT INVOLVEMENT, ANALYZE THE IMPACT OF CURRENT

The departure of families from the farm during the 1980s continued a trend. The difference was the terms under which they left. "If you look at the 1970s, people getting out then were selling their farms and retiring, or using profits to start up some other business. . . . The big difference was the people in the 1980s were evicted."[1]

[1]Darrell Hobbs, University of Missouri–Columbia, quoted in Matthew Schofield and Scott Canon, "Ex-farmers Adjust, Move on After Crisis," *The Kansas City Star*, August 11, 1991, p. A1.

farm programs—from propping up prices to subsidizing foreign sales of U.S. farm products—and discuss recent proposals to reduce the role of government in agriculture, now that average farm incomes have improved.

Why Study Agriculture?

Agriculture is a key sector of the United States economy. When defined broadly to include the production and sale of food and fiber, agriculture accounts for one-sixth of the country's output and provides employment for over 20 million workers. In terms of world trade, U.S. agriculture is even more important, helping to feed and clothe the world's population. For some commodities, including coarse grains and soybeans, the United States accounts for over half the world's exports. Because the United States sells more agricultural products to foreign countries than it imports, agriculture has helped to keep the country's trade deficit from becoming even larger.

Agricultural markets tend to be highly competitive. Most have a large number of producers, and entry into and exit from the industry is generally easy. In the case of major crops, including wheat and corn, hundreds of thousands of different farmers supply the market. For a given grade of product, output is homogeneous—buyers do not care from whom they purchase the product. Finally, information on price, supply, and other pertinent data is readily available to both buyers and sellers. Under such conditions, individual buyers and sellers are price takers. Although government intervention sometimes affects market supply or demand or impedes market adjustment, behavior of prices and incomes can be explained, especially over long periods, by the forces of supply and demand. As such, agriculture is an ideal setting to apply the tools learned earlier in the text—from shifts in supply and demand to price and income elasticities of demand.

Another reason for studying agriculture relates to the extensive government presence in what is inherently a competitive industry. On what basis can government intervention be defended? And what are the consequences of this intervention, in terms of both efficiency (producing output at the lowest cost possible) and equity (ameliorating the economic hardship of low-income farmers)? An analysis of government farm programs provides insights more generally into the nature and effects of government policy designed to alter market outcomes.

Trends in Agriculture

To examine developments in agriculture, it is necessary to consider both the aggregate income of all farmers and the average income per farmer. Largely because of changes in the farm population, the two series have moved in opposite directions. While aggregate income of farmers has decreased sharply, average income per farmer has drifted higher during much of the century.

Changes in Net Farm Income

NET FARM INCOME
The total revenue generated by a nation's farms minus farm production costs.

Net farm income is a measure of the aggregate income of all farmers. Defined as the total revenue from farming minus production costs, net farm income has fallen by more than 50 percent since 1945 after accounting for inflation (see Figure 36.1). As a percentage of national income, the decline has been even steeper—from 6.8 percent in 1945 to 1.0 percent in 1991.

Over the same period that net farm income has fallen, the relative price of farm products has also eroded. That is, the price of farm products has increased more slowly than prices in general (see Figure 36.2, page 948). Both developments can be explained in terms of supply and demand.

Central to this story is the dramatic growth in farm productivity. Higher-yielding crops have been continually introduced, along with more-effective herbicides and pesticides. Advances in machinery, livestock genetics, and farm management have further increased output per farmer. Since the end of World War II, output per hour of labor has increased by an average of 5.1 percent per year in agriculture, compared to only 1.8 percent per year in the nonfarm business sector.

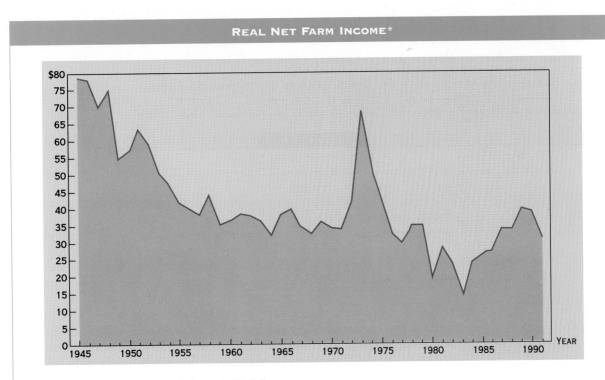

REAL NET FARM INCOME*

*Net farm income measured in billions of 1982 dollars.

SOURCES: U.S. Department of Agriculture, *National Financial Summary, 1990* (1991), Table 3; *Agricultural Outlook*, 1992, Table 29.

FIGURE 36.1

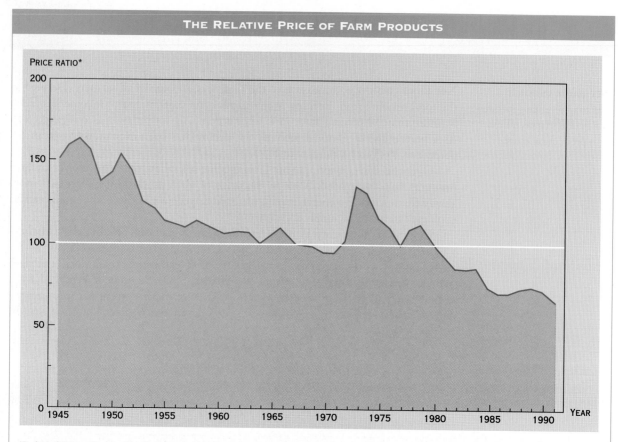

THE RELATIVE PRICE OF FARM PRODUCTS

PRICE RATIO*

YEAR

*Index of Prices Received by Farmers divided by the Consumer Price Index. The base year 1967 equals 100.

SOURCES: U.S. Department of Commerce, *Historical Statistics of the United States*, 1975, Table K 353; U.S. Department of Agriculture, *Agricultural Prices, Annual Summary*, various issues; U.S. Department of Labor, *Consumer Price Index*, 1992.

FIGURE 36.2

Because greater productivity permits greater output, the supply of agricultural products has grown rapidly.

At the same time, demand for agricultural products has increased only modestly. This is principally because of a low income elasticity of demand for food, estimated to be about 0.1 to 0.2.[2] That is, a 10 percent increase in income leads consumers to increase their food purchases by only 1 or 2 percent. Although consumers could buy 10 percent more of all goods, including food, they modify their spending patterns. As incomes rise, consumers devote relatively less of their budget to food and relatively more to the purchase of automobiles, stereo equipment, vacations, and other nonagricultural products. In other words, demand for agricultural products has increased more slowly than income; demand for nonagricultural products has increased more rapidly.

---

[2]See Charles Schultze, *The Distribution of Farm Subsidies: Who Gets the Benefits?* (Washington, D.C.: The Brookings Institution, 1971); P. S. George and G. A. King, *Consumer Demand for Food Commodities in the United States*, Giannini Foundation Monograph No. 26, University of California, Berkeley, 1971.

Although demand for farm products has increased over time, supply has grown even more rapidly, exerting downward pressure on the price of farm products.

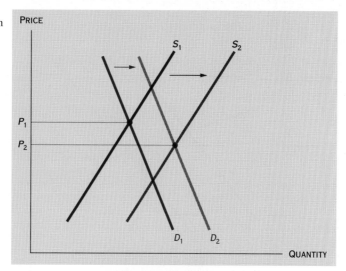

FIGURE 36.3

The uneven growth in supply and demand is illustrated in Figure 36.3. Because the supply of agricultural products has outstripped demand, the relative price of agricultural products has fallen over time. Accentuating this decline has been the low price elasticity of demand for agricultural products. If demand were elastic, an increase in supply would have only a modest effect on price. But because demand is inelastic, price must fall by a relatively large amount to restore equilibrium (see Figure 36.4, page 950). According to one widely cited study, the aggregate elasticity of demand for farm products has averaged 0.2 in the short run and 0.5 in the long run.[3] Other things equal, prices would have to fall by 5 percent in the short run (2 percent in the long run) just to increase quantity demanded by 1 percent.

The inelastic demand for farm products has, in turn, had adverse consequences for net farm income. Given an inelastic demand curve, a lower price reduces the total revenue from farm products (see Figure 36.5, page 951). Therefore, despite increasing output, farmers have received lower receipts for the sale of their output. Although productivity advances have helped to keep costs in check, they have not been sufficient to offset the decline in total revenues. As a consequence, net farm income has fallen over time.

In summary, the decline in net farm income can be explained as follows.

1. Supply has grown faster than demand, forcing down the relative price of farm products.

2. Because demand is inelastic, lower prices have resulted in lower revenues for farmers.

---

[3]Luther Tweeten, "Economic Instability in Agriculture: the Contributions of Prices, Government Programs and Exports," *American Journal of Agricultural Economics* (December 1983), Table 1.

Other things equal, increased supply reduces price by a relatively greater amount the less elastic is demand. For example, an increase in supply from S_1 to S_2 reduces price to P_E if demand is D_E; but given the relatively less elastic demand curve D_I, price plummets to P_I.

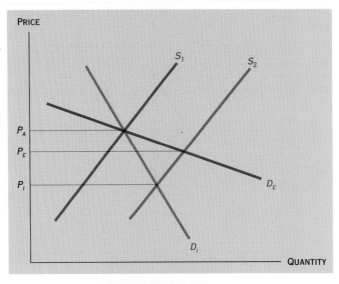

FIGURE 36.4

3. In the absence of cost savings to offset fully the lower total revenues, net farm income has fallen.

YOUR TURN

ALTHOUGH THE LONG-TERM TREND IS FOR VASTLY GREATER SUPPLY, SOMETIMES BAD WEATHER AND OTHER NATURAL DISASTERS REDUCE SUPPLY IN THE SHORT RUN. HOW WOULD A REDUCTION IN SUPPLY AFFECT PRICE AND TOTAL REVENUE OF FARMERS?

Leaving the Farm

Economic theory predicts adjustment: if resources earn less in an industry than they could elsewhere, the resource owners will transfer these resources to the industries offering higher returns. Given developments in agriculture—declining prices and shrinking net farm income—one would therefore predict that resources would leave agriculture.

As Table 36.1 illustrates, labor mobility in agriculture has been substantial. The farm population has declined from 30 million at the turn of the century to just under 5 million today. In percentage terms, the exodus from farming has been even more dramatic, with the share of the population engaged in farming falling from over 40 percent in 1900 to a current value of 2 percent. Land has also been withdrawn from agriculture, but on a more limited basis. Unless farmland is located close to urban areas or production facilities, it typically has a low opportunity cost.

Because demand is inelastic, a reduction in price from P_1 to P_2 lowers total revenue. In other words, the total revenue associated with P_2 (given by the rectangle $0P_2BQ_2$) is less than the total revenue associated with P_1 (given by rectangle $0P_1AQ_1$).

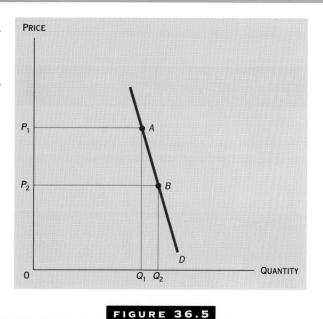

FIGURE 36.5

At the same time that the farm population has decreased, a growing share of the income received by farm families has come from *off-farm* sources (for example, wages from nonfarm employment or rent from nonfarm real estate). Indeed, off-farm income of farm operators now exceeds net farm income. In summary, many

		THE DWINDLING FARM POPULATION	

		THE U.S. FARM POPULATION*	
YEAR	**TOTAL (IN MILLIONS)**	**AS A PERCENT OF TOTAL POPULATION**	
1900	29.9	41.9	
1910	32.1	34.9	
1920	32.0	30.2	
1930	30.5	24.9	
1940	30.5	23.2	
1950	23.0	15.3	
1960	15.6	8.7	
1970	9.7	4.8	
1980	6.1	2.7	
1990	4.6	1.8	

*The definition of "farm" was changed in 1977, leading to a modest reduction in the size of the "farm population" after this date.
SOURCES: U.S. Department of Commerce, *Historical Statistics of the United States*, Part 2 (1975), p. 457; *Current Population Reports*, Series P-23 (1991).

TABLE 36.1

farmers have adjusted to the decline in net farm income by leaving agriculture entirely, and those who remain have reduced their reliance on farming as a source of income. This adjustment has been painful for some (see Exhibit 36.1), but it has alleviated financial pressures for those who remain in farming.

Changes in the Average Income of Farm Operators

Even though net farm income has decreased over the past 50 years, the farm population has declined even more dramatically, meaning that there are fewer farmers to

A Painful Exit from Farming

"We can't cut it in agriculture around here," Jerrold Taylor said. "That's become pretty clear." In 1975, Jerrold and Ann Taylor were worth—on paper, anyway—between $3 million and $4 million. But the Taylors, now both 47, and their neighbors fell like dominoes in the early 1980s. The Taylors liquidated their land and their business in 1989 to bring an end to their mounting debts.

The toll on the family has been more than just financial. Ann lost her 55-year-old brother to suicide. With his farm operation losing more and more money, Wallace Trump hanged himself rather than keep a morning appointment with his banker one Monday in June 1985. "He thought he was going to lose what he had worked his entire life for," Ann said. "We saw a lot of people going through that."

The Missouri Center for Health Statistics says that 375 Missouri farmers committed suicide from 1982 through 1990. Although farmers account for less than 3 percent of the state's population, they accounted for about 6 percent of the suicides.

Since 1989, Jerrold mostly has been unemployed. Their household income, mostly what Ann makes teaching music in the local schools and at home, is half what it was ten years ago. Jerrold picks up money through small business deals here and there. But he spends more of his time working to form a new economic base for Mercer County. His ideas are not particularly popular.

Small farmers and environmentalists attacked him when he worked, successfully, to bring a large, corporate hog operation to town. The farmers complained that they would be put out of business. Environmentalists worried about air and water contamination. The same concerns for a clean countryside surface in opposition to a proposed landfill. But to Jerrold Taylor, the choice is between new jobs or the death of their rural community. "We need to start over."

SOURCE: Scott Canon, "Talk Turns to Trash after Farm Failure," *The Kansas City Star*, August 11, 1991, p. A8. Reprinted by permission.

EXHIBIT 36.1

share in that income. In addition, off-farm income has grown substantially for farm operators. For these reasons, the decline in net farm income has not resulted in lower incomes on a per-farm basis. Indeed, in the 1970s, for the first time ever, the average income of farm families surpassed that of nonfarm families (see Figure 36.6). The situation was reversed in the early 1980s, as short-term financial pressures developed in agriculture. But by the latter half of the decade farmers were, on average, doing at least as well as their nonfarm counterparts. Given estimates that farmers earned only about 40 percent as much as nonfarmers during the 1930s, the economic plight of farmers has eased considerably.

If Figure 36.6 illustrates the general improvement in the average income of farmers, it also demonstrates the extreme variability of farm incomes. The movements in this series are caused almost entirely by fluctuations in the incomes of farmers rather than the incomes of nonfarmers. Because the 1970s were generally

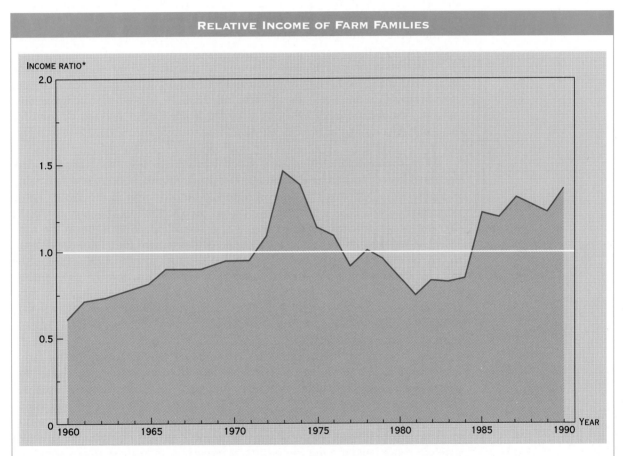

RELATIVE INCOME OF FARM FAMILIES

INCOME RATIO*

*Average income of farm-operator households divided by average income of all households.

NOTE: Income of farm-operator households equals net farm income plus off-farm income of farm-operator households adjusted for implicit costs. The series is constructed on the assumption that there is one farm-operator household per farm. Because a small percentage of farms contain more than a single household, the series is actually an upper estimate of the income of farm-operator households.

SOURCE: U.S. Department of Agriculture, *Farm Sector Review, 1987* (1989), Table 9, updated by authors.

FIGURE 36.6

prosperous years for agriculture and the early 1980s posed unusually severe financial pressures, it is useful to look more closely at developments during this period in order to see how rapidly conditions in agriculture can change.

Good Times, Bad Times

World demand for U.S. agricultural products soared during the 1970s for several reasons, including rapid income growth in developing countries and easy credit to finance purchases of farm products. In addition, the value of the dollar declined during the early 1970s, making imports from the United States less expensive. At the same time, the supply of food in other countries was adversely affected by a number of developments—from crop failures in the Soviet Union to the disappearance of anchovies off the coast of Peru. As a result, U.S. exports of farm products increased, both in total volume and as a share of world exports. After netting out for the effects of inflation, U.S. farm exports were almost three times greater in 1980 than in 1970.

This export boom triggered a run-up in the price of farmland. Given the increased demand for farm output, demand for land needed to produce this output also increased. Because real assets, including land, are viewed as a hedge against inflation, the inflationary environment of the 1970s further boosted demand for farmland. As a result, the price of farmland rose steadily during the 1970s (see Figure 36.7).

With the expectation that land prices would continue to rise, many farmers borrowed heavily to purchase additional farmland, despite high interest rates. But, as Figure 36.7 illustrates, the value of farmland headed south in the 1980s. Those same forces of supply and demand, which had been so kind to U.S. farmers in the previous decade, turned decidedly negative. A severe global recession in the early 1980s slowed demand for farm products, and debtor nations found it more difficult to buy on credit. Also, the dollar appreciated during the early 1980s, raising the price of imports from the United States. On top of this, foreign governments increased their subsidies to agriculture, thereby boosting foreign supply of farm products. Many nations that imported food during the 1970s became net exporters during the 1980s. As a result of these forces, U.S. exports of farm products declined during the early and mid-1980s.

With the export market shrinking and inflation subsiding, demand for farmland withered. Farmers who had borrowed heavily in expectation of rising land prices were squeezed by heavy debt and plunging land values. In many instances, farmers' equity turned negative—their liabilities exceeded the value of their assets. In other cases, equity remained positive but income, which had fallen as agricultural markets deteriorated, was now too low to meet interest obligations. Although financial conditions have since improved, as recently as 1986 about 16 percent of the nation's farmers were experiencing "financial stress" and hoping for either a strengthening in agricultural markets or increased government assistance.[4]

---

[4]This figure comes from U.S. Department of Agriculture, *Farm Sector Review, 1986*, p. 41. As defined by the Department of Agriculture, "financial distress" exists when a farmer's debt exceeds 40 percent of asset values and the farmer's income is insufficient to meet financial obligations.

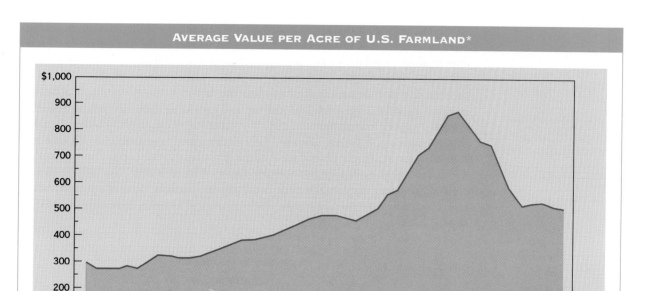

AVERAGE VALUE PER ACRE OF U.S. FARMLAND*

*In 1982 dollars.
SOURCE: U.S. Department of Agriculture, Economic Research Service.

FIGURE 36.7

Should Government Be in Agriculture?

Over the past 60 years, the government has funded dozens of programs designed to help farmers. Before examining the consequences of specific programs, it is appropriate first to ask why the government is so heavily involved in agriculture. Government intervention has been defended on various grounds; among the major arguments offered are the following.

REDUCTION OF RISK

Farming is characterized by a high degree of risk and uncertainty. Bad weather may wipe out a farmer's entire crop. On the other hand, universally favorable conditions may lead to bumper crops, which depress price and the aggregate income of farmers. Embargoes, trade disputes, and other political events may limit demand for U.S. farm products, while foreign subsidies swell world supply. Given inelastic product demand, such changes in market conditions are likely to lead to wide gyrations in the prices of farm products and the incomes of farmers. Some contend that price instability harms consumers, while income instability harms farmers. In their view, government intervention is necessary to smooth movements in prices and income.

Those critical of this argument counter that, even if stability is desired, government intervention is unnecessary. They point to the availability of private insurance against crop failure, futures markets to protect against a decline in product price, and other market instruments to reduce risk. Farmers' limited reliance on such market instruments is attributed to the fact that the government is heavily involved in stabilizing price and income and providing relief in the aftermath of natural disasters. For example, in 1988 the government provided $4 billion in aid to drought-stricken farmers, and in 1992 it provided assistance to Florida and Louisiana farmers after Hurricane Andrew hit. Clearly, the expectation of continued government assistance has reduced farmers' incentives to use crop insurance and other market instruments. But could private markets alone adequately reduce risk, or is some government intervention necessary? On this issue there is no consensus.

THE FAMILY FARM

Government intervention has also been defended as necessary to save *the family farm*. To quote one analyst:

> Farming occupies an honored place in our culture. Even big-city sophisticates who would sooner die than attend a Grange Hall dance find it reassuring to know that somewhere out there honest folk are working the earth much as it has been worked for centuries.[5]

Others trace reverence for the family farm to the view, held by Thomas Jefferson, that small-scale farming promotes democracy by instilling those very characteristics—independence, hard work, and a determination to succeed—that are the hallmarks of a democratic people.[6] Those who embrace such views find it tragic that families are driven from their farms despite their long hours and hard work. Some seek government protection of these individuals and preservation of their lifestyle.

Others argue that the government should support low-income farmers, just as it supports low-income nonfarmers, but reject pleas to save the family farm. They note that large corporate farms are generally more efficient than small family operations and, where that is true, saving the family farm is inefficient from an economic perspective—it leads to a higher cost of producing agricultural output. Why, they ask, should inefficient producers be sheltered from competition?

INCOME SUPPORT

Average income historically has been lower for those in farming although, as Figure 36.6 demonstrates, this is no longer always the case. But even when the average income of farmers is high, the distribution of income among farmers is highly

---

[5]Gregg Easterbrook, "Making Sense of Agriculture," *The Atlantic Monthly*, July 1985, p. 63.
[6]See Kenneth Deavors, "Rural Vision—Rural Reality," Benjamin H. Hubbard Memorial Lecture Series, University of Wisconsin–Madison, 1990.

unequal. Farm-operator households are three times as likely to have an annual income below $5,000 as are households in general.[7] For this reason, some favor government intervention in agriculture as a means of alleviating poverty.

The problem with this argument is that subsidizing an entire industry benefits *all* producers in the industry. In particular, subsidizing agriculture not only makes poor farmers less poor, it makes wealthy farmers more wealthy. It is difficult to defend on equity grounds a policy that indiscriminately increases incomes of all producers in an industry, regardless of their need.

EXTERNALITIES

Farming sometimes has adverse effects on the rest of society. Animal waste, fertilizer, and soil runoff contaminate water supplies while pesticides pose health risks in humans. Because of such externalities, government intervention can be justified as a means of protecting the public health and the environment. As a side effect, the government's presence may also alter income of farmers.

Government Farm Programs

COMMODITY CREDIT CORPORATION (CCC)
A government agency that purchases surplus commodities from farmers.

While debate continues over the proper scope of government intervention, one thing is clear: the government is heavily involved in agriculture. The government-run **Commodity Credit Corporation (CCC)** purchases surplus products from farmers, extends loans to farmers on highly favorable terms, and offers other assistance. Net outlays by the CCC have fluctuated between $6 billion and $26 billion per year since 1985. The total cost of government intervention is even greater when one considers the higher prices consumers pay as a result of this intervention.

Government involvement in agricultural markets can be traced back to the Great Depression, which hit the farm economy especially hard. Given the competitive nature of agriculture and the noncompetitive nature of many nonagricultural markets, prices of farm products fell more precipitously than those of nonfarm products. The government responded by buying surplus crops to prevent agricultural prices from declining further. Since then the government has experimented with a number of different farm programs. Most of them fall into one or more of the following categories: (a) price supports, (b) supply restrictions, (c) demand expansion, and (d) direct payments.

PRICE SUPPORT
A minimum price guaranteed by the government. The government preserves the minimum price by agreeing to buy any output offered at this price.

PRICE SUPPORTS

Price supports are designed to raise artificially the prices received by farmers. If the government views the equilibrium price as too low, it can set a price floor above

[7]Mary Ahearn and Hisham El-Osta, "Farm Wealth: Its Distribution and Comparison to the Wealth of U.S. Households," *Agricultural Income and Finance, Situation and Outlook Report*, June 1991.

this figure. The government supports (or maintains) the price floor by agreeing to buy any output offered at this price.

NONRECOURSE LOAN
A government loan that, at the farmer's discretion, may be either repaid or canceled. To cancel, the farmer transfers ownership of the commodity to the government, keeping whatever funds have been borrowed.

As a practical matter, price supports are often accomplished through the use of nonrecourse loans. The government, through the CCC, lends farmers money with the farm commodity serving as collateral. For example, the government might loan a farmer $3 per bushel of wheat. If the market price exceeds $3, the farmer can always sell his wheat and repay the loan. But if the price falls below $3, the farmer simply turns his wheat over to the government, and the loan is forgiven. This latter option, the nonrecourse feature of the loan, guarantees the wheat farmer a minimum of $3 per bushel of wheat.

Whenever price supports exceed the equilibrium level, they result in a surplus (see Figure 36.8). Consumers respond to the higher price by reducing their consumption, while farmers increase their production. To maintain the support price, the government is forced to buy the surplus. Although this may help farmers in the short run, it poses long-term problems. As surpluses mount over time, they become increasingly costly to store. And what is to become of these surpluses? If they are dumped on the market in the future, they will depress prices at that time—high prices in the present come at the expense of lower prices in the future. Price supports, by themselves, do not provide a lasting solution to farmers' problems.

SUPPLY RESTRICTIONS

Aware of this price-support dilemma, the government has designed a number of programs that reduce the supply of agricultural products. As Figure 36.9 illustrates,

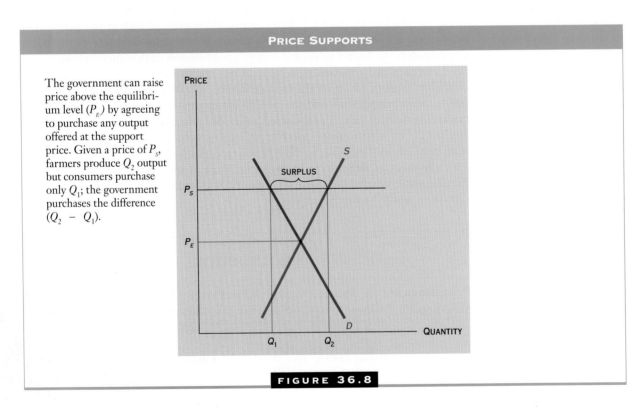

PRICE SUPPORTS

The government can raise price above the equilibrium level (P_E) by agreeing to purchase any output offered at the support price. Given a price of P_S, farmers produce Q_2 output but consumers purchase only Q_1; the government purchases the difference ($Q_2 - Q_1$).

FIGURE 36.8

a lower supply can increase price without contributing to a surplus. Supply restrictions have taken several forms. Under the *Acreage Reduction Program*, farmers must remove a certain amount of land from the production of a particular crop (for example, 20 percent) in order to qualify for the support price. At least part of this land must be "idled" (or "set aside"), and another portion of the land may have restrictions on its use. Other programs remove land from production for environmental reasons. For example, the *Conservation Reserve Program (CRP)* pays farmers to idle their highly erodible land, thereby reducing soil runoff and water pollution. The Agricultural Resources Conservation Program, of which the CRP is one component, is expected to enroll up to 60 million acres of environmentally sensitive land by 1995.

In 1983, the government experimented by making noncash payments to farmers who limited their planting of certain crops. Under the *Payment-in-Kind (PIK)* program, farmers who pulled some of their land from production were given some of the government's surplus crops. Farmers viewed the terms of payment as so attractive that nearly 80 million acres of cropland were idled that year. More cropland was taken out of production in the United States than was planted in western Europe![8]

Although removing land from production reduces output, it is important to realize that the reduction in output is often modest. Land differs in fertility. When farmers are paid to remove 20 percent of their land from production, they withdraw the 20 percent that is least productive. Moreover, now that they are devoting less land to production, they tend to use it more intensively. That is, on the acres planted they increase the amount of labor and farm machinery. As a consequence, despite a 20 percent reduction in acres planted, output falls by less than 20 percent.

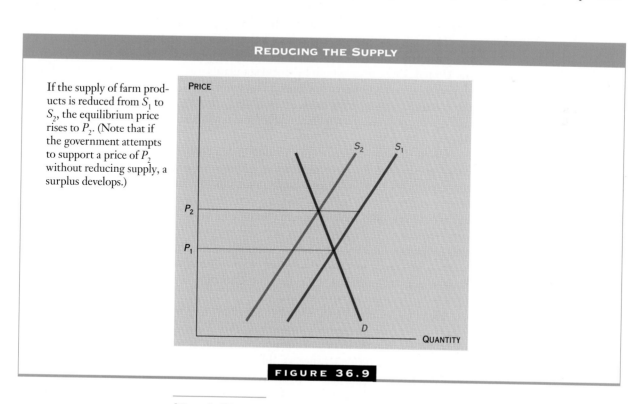

REDUCING THE SUPPLY

If the supply of farm products is reduced from S_1 to S_2, the equilibrium price rises to P_2. (Note that if the government attempts to support a price of P_2 without reducing supply, a surplus develops.)

FIGURE 36.9

[8]Council of Economic Advisers, *Economic Report of the President, 1987*, p. 149.

MARKETING ORDER
A directive, enforced by the Department of Agriculture, limiting the quantity of a product that each producer may sell on the market.

Some commodities are covered by **marketing orders**, which are more severe than land restrictions in the sense that they tell the farmer how much output may be sold rather than how much land may be used. In some years California lemon growers have been forced to watch more than half of their lemon crop rot because the Department of Agriculture, which enforces the marketing orders, would not allow them to sell additional lemons.

The preceding example illustrates one of the major criticisms of supply restrictions—they are inefficient. Either resources are left idle, instead of producing output, or output is produced but never brought to market. In either case society fails to take full advantage of its resources.

A second criticism of supply restrictions is that they often disrupt rural communities. If farmers plant fewer acres, they need less fertilizer, chemicals, machinery, and other resources. Those businesses that sell such products see their sales fall and, in turn, they lose money. Many who sell farm inputs are forced out of business, not only directly harming them but also weakening the communities they serve (see Exhibit 36.2). Therefore, although supply restrictions may benefit farmers, they harm other segments of the economy.

DEMAND EXPANSION

Unlike supply restrictions, policies that bolster demand for farm products increase both the equilibrium price and quantity. These programs therefore offer government a way to increase farm revenues without creating surpluses. Accordingly, such programs have been popular with politicians as well as farmers.

Through food stamps, the school lunch program, and assorted other measures, the government has boosted domestic demand for food; but, with consumption in the United States already high by world standards, such programs offer only a limited potential. An economist at Chase Econometrics once estimated that to eliminate the country's annual corn surplus, each man, woman, and child would have to eat an extra 1.5 pounds of corn flakes each day or drink an additional 50 gallons of corn whiskey each year.

Given that consumers in the United States cannot eat (much less drink) farmers to prosperity, the government has emphasized programs designed to increase the exports of farm products. Such programs include negotiating reductions in other countries' trade barriers, making loans to less-developed countries, and offering export subsidies that reduce the relative price of U.S. products in world markets. Sometimes the United States government buys directly from farmers and then sells to foreign countries at a lower price. For example, the federal government sold sugar to China for less than one-third of what it had paid U.S. sugar growers. And, because of grain subsidies, it has been widely observed that you can buy U.S. wheat for less in Moscow than in Kansas City.

Herein lies a major criticism of U.S. policy. Export programs cannot be judged simply in terms of the volume of food exports. When the United States pays three times the world price to export sugar, rice, butter, and other commodities, that policy can hardly be termed a success. The costs of export programs must be weighed against the benefits and, unfortunately, the costs often dominate.

Given the limited market for U.S. food, both domestically and internationally, some place more confidence in programs designed to stimulate nontraditional uses

E
X
H
I
B
I
T

36 . 2

The Fallout from Acreage Restrictions

Ike Cox thinks the government has gone too far in paying farmers not to grow. Government acreage cutbacks will cause Cox, co-owner of CTL Supply, to lose 25 percent of his grain-storage and seed business this year.

Cox and other small-town farm suppliers are not alone. Many of the nation's largest agribusiness companies—and even some farm groups—are reversing their positions on acreage set-asides, arguing that the United States quickly could become a second-rate agricultural power unless farmers are allowed to plant more to meet rising export demand.

The loss of status as the world's dominant grain exporter would send severe shocks through the U.S. economy. Midwestern cities would be hit especially hard because a large part of their economies are tied to farming and grain exports.

In Kansas City, a permanent decline in U.S. grain exports would slash business for the huge terminal elevators that dot the industrial district, reduce traffic on the railroads, and slow wheat trading at the Kansas City Board of Trade. Combine manufacturing in Independence, just now coming alive after a long shutdown, again could flounder. And the emergence of agricultural biotechnology companies in the Kansas City area could be nipped in the bud.

Farmers in Cox's territory, Harrison County, have flocked into the government's Conservation Reserve Program. For about $60 an acre per year from Uncle Sam, or $600 for the next ten years, growers in the county have agreed to plant native grass or trees on 58,000 acres. That's about 22 percent of Harrison County's cropland. So Harrison County farmers will need a lot less fertilizer, seed, and chemicals in the next decade. And they won't need nearly as much room to store their smaller harvests.

Unless farmers are encouraged to plant more acres, the rural economy may never recover from the farm crises of the mid-'80s, the critics say. That will permanently shrink the tax bases of the rural towns, and services will suffer. Cox points to a University of Missouri–Columbia study showing that the programs will cut $15 million a year out of the economy of northern Missouri because farmers will need fewer farm supplies. "Those dollars aren't going to be going through the economy here." Cox said, "It's going to hurt a lot more people than they think."

SOURCE: Dirck Steimel, "Dwindling Acres: Have We Gone Too Far?" *The Kansas City Star*, February 28, 1988, pp. 1–11J. Reprinted by permission; *The Kansas City Star*, © 1988.

of agricultural output. For example, the U.S. government sponsors research to develop nonfood products from corn and other crops and to spur demand for these products. Thanks to government support, billions of bushels of corn have been converted into the fuel "gasohol." Other uses for corn include disposable bottles, plastic sheeting, and even gas filters (see Exhibit 36.3, page 962). Similarly, sunflowers, once used mainly to produce bird food, are involved in the manufacture of fuel, fabric, and acoustical tile. Such nontraditional markets may offer farmers the opportunity to participate more fully in the country's economic growth.

EXHIBIT 36.3

Corn is replacing petroleum not just in gas tanks, but also in homes, factories, and other industrial applications. Already corn is used in the manufacture of adhesives, paper, deicing materials, and plastic bags. Scientists have discovered that products currently made from petroleum can alternatively be produced from corn starch. As technology improves, some scientists believe the United States may eventually produce all its plastics from corn. This would consume an extra 3 billion bushels of corn each year (about one-third the current U.S. corn crop), while saving a billion barrels of oil.

Because corn-based products are biodegradable, decomposing much more rapidly than petroleum-based products, this substitution would benefit the environment. Another obvious advantage to oil-importing countries, such as the United States, is that such developments would reduce dependence on foreign oil. For such reasons, research into the creation of new, agriculturally based products offers the possibility of not only helping farmers but benefiting society as well.

SOURCE: Adapted from Keith Schneider, "New Invention from the Cornfield," *The New York Times*, January 10, 1988, p. 36E; *The Kansas City Star*, "Corn Fiber Can Be Used to Make Paper," July 13, 1991, p. B2; Dirck Steimel, "Corn Farmers Join Battle of the Bags," *The Kansas City Star*, January 21, 1990, p. K1.

DIRECT PAYMENTS

TARGET PRICE
A minimum price guaranteed by the government. If the market price falls below the target price, the government reimburses farmers for the difference.

DEFICIENCY PAYMENT
A supplemental payment that farmers receive for each unit of output they produce, equal to the difference between the target price and the market price. If the market price exceeds the target price, there is no deficiency payment.

A drawback of the three preceding approaches—price supports, supply restrictions, and demand expansion—is that, in the process of aiding farmers, the government raises the price of agricultural products. Thus, farmers are helped at the expense of consumers. An alternative approach is for the government to make direct payments to farmers without raising prices. Under its **target price** program, the government guarantees farmers a minimum price for their product, a so-called "target price." But, unlike the price support program, the government does not promise to buy surplus commodities. Instead, farmers sell their commodities on the market, receiving supplemental government payments whenever the market price falls below the target price.

This program is illustrated in Figure 36.10. Given a target price of P_T, farmers produce Q_T output. But consumers are prepared to pay only P_M for this level of output, so the government makes up the difference. That is, for each unit sold, farmers receive a price of P_M from consumers and a **deficiency payment** of $P_T - P_M$ from the government. Total deficiency payments received by farmers amount to $(P_T - P_M) \times Q_T$, represented by the shaded area of Figure 36.10.

Deficiency payments depress the price consumers pay for farm products. In the absence of government intervention the price would have been P_E rather than P_M. It

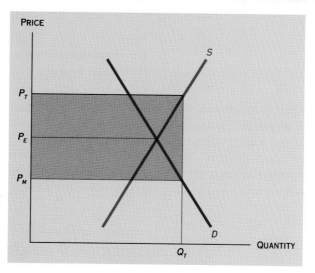

If the government sets a target price of P_T, farmers produce Q_T output. When the farmers bring this quantity to the market, they find that consumers are willing to pay only P_M. To supplement this low price, the government makes a deficiency payment of $P_T - P_M$ for each unit produced. Altogether, farmers receive deficiency payments of $(P_T - P_M) \times Q_T$, represented by the shaded area.

FIGURE 36.10

does not follow, however, that direct payments to farmers are socially beneficial. The funds needed to make these payments must be raised through taxes. Moreover, deficiency payments promote an overallocation of resources to agriculture. In terms of Figure 36.10, the last unit produced has a value of P_M (the price consumers are willing to pay for it), but the cost of producing that last unit is P_T. Thus, deficiency payments induce farmers to produce output whose value to society is less than the cost of producing it.

Under the 1990 Farm Bill, deficiency payments were eliminated for 15 percent of a farmer's cropland. The land still can be planted, but crops grown on it are not eligible for deficiency payments. The 15 percent provision was designed to reduce the cost to taxpayers and also to make farmers more responsive to market conditions when choosing which crop to plant on the last 15 percent of their land. (On land not eligible for deficiency payments, a farmer will compare the *market prices* of alternative crops rather than the artificial target prices.)

Criticisms of U.S. Farm Policy

U.S. agricultural programs have resulted in enormous budgetary costs, benefits that do not reach those most in need, huge surpluses of farm products, major trade disputes with other countries, and great harm to well-functioning international markets.[9]

---

[9]Council of Economic Advisers, *Economic Report of the President, 1987*, p. 147.

The government's farm policy has been criticized on several counts. Some argue that its costs outweigh benefits, others that it provides benefits to the wrong farmers. These and other criticisms are explored in the next few pages.

HIGH COSTS

Apart from administrative costs, the costs of farm programs include inefficient use of resources. These costs are ultimately borne by consumers (in the form of higher prices) and by taxpayers. According to a study by the U.S. Department of Agriculture, each dollar of cash income that the government transfers to farmers costs consumers and taxpayers as much as five dollars.[10] Because farmers gain less than the rest of society loses, farm programs reduce the average standard of living.

DISTRIBUTION OF BENEFITS

High costs, by themselves, do not imply that farm programs are inappropriate. Even though average income is reduced, these programs may effectively reduce poverty and narrow the distribution of income. If these are socially desirable goals, then farm programs may be an important element of the government's social policy.

But critics reject this argument, noting that farm programs are not an efficient way of reaching those in need. Because government support is based on the level of production, benefits go primarily to large farms. In recent years, farms with less than $20,000 in sales (generally run by part-time farmers) received an average of about $500 in direct government payments; farms with $40,000 to $99,999 in sales (mostly family farms) received just over $9,000. In contrast, farms with sales of $500,000 to $999,999 received farm subsidies exceeding $45,000 (see Table 36.2).

Because operators of large farms generally have higher incomes than those of small farms, and a lower incidence of poverty, output-based programs tend to provide the greatest assistance to those least in need. In some cases, large farms collect massive subsidies. For example, a California superfarm recently received $20 million in agricultural subsidies while an Illinois utility, which grew corn on the side, was paid more than $500,000. In light of such payments, it is difficult to defend current farm policy on distributional grounds. Nor can it be defended as a means to assist those suffering financial distress. Financial problems have been more common among small farms, yet they receive less support than large farms. In summary, whether need is defined in terms of income or financial distress, those receiving most of the government support are those least in need!

A GROWING ELASTICITY OF DEMAND

According to some studies, the price elasticity of demand for agricultural products has increased over time. This primarily reflects the increasingly global nature of

[10]Council of Economic Advisers, *Economic Report of the President, 1986*, p. 155.

AVERAGE DIRECT GOVERNMENT PAYMENT BY SIZE OF FARM OPERATION	
FARMS WITH SALES OF	**AVERAGE DIRECT GOVERNMENT PAYMENT***
Less than $20,000	$ 469
$ 20,000 to $ 39,999	3,887
$ 40,000 to $ 99,999	9,150
$ 100,000 to $249,999	21,262
$ 250,000 to $499,999	37,809
$ 500,000 to $999,999	45,172
$1,000,000 and over	42,787

*Average annual payment over the period 1987–1990.
SOURCE: U.S. Department of Agriculture, *National Financial Summary, 1990* (1991), Tables 30–33.

TABLE 36.2

agricultural markets and the fact that foreign demand is more elastic than domestic demand. As the share of agricultural output exported increases—as occurred during the 1970s and late 1980s—the average elasticity of demand for U.S. agricultural products increases.

Although aggregate demand for farm products remains inelastic, demand for some individual products has apparently become elastic. For example, over the period 1976–1982, the long-run elasticity of demand for soybeans was estimated to be 1.2.[11] In that event, restrictions limiting supply are likely to be inappropriate in the long run. For products whose demand is elastic, supply restrictions *depress* revenues of farmers.

GOVERNMENT PROGRAMS AS A COST OF PRODUCTION

Even where farm programs increase the revenues of farmers, they simultaneously inflate production costs. Programs that increase the income generated per acre of farmland increase demand for that land, driving up its price. In other words, the future value of government support becomes *capitalized* or built into the price of the land. Although this benefits those who own the land prior to the announcement of these programs, it does not help those who later buy or rent this land, since they must pay more to use the land. For such farmers, the benefits of farm programs are completely offset by higher land costs. Thus, government farm programs do not increase the profitability of farming; they merely increase the wealth of the initial land owners.

INSTABILITY

Another criticism of government policy is that, despite an apparent goal of stabilizing prices and incomes, the result may be greater instability. For example, some

[11]Same as 3.

point to trade embargoes, in which U.S. farm exports are withheld from foreign markets for political reasons. In addition to any short-term effect, this creates the impression that the United States is an unreliable supplier. Critics also note that farm policy is reversed over time and that, at any moment, policy is often inconsistent. For instance, agricultural research is supported in order to increase supply while acreage reserve programs and set-asides are implemented to reduce supply. Given such conflicting signals and uncertainty about what the government plans for the future, some view government as a source of instability.

Alternative Proposals

Given such criticisms, many favor less government intervention in agriculture and greater reliance on markets. Except for environmental issues, some see no compelling reason for the government's presence. To them, the issue is how to remove the government without further harming farmers. One proposal is to eliminate future subsidies while, at the same time, providing current farmers a one-time, lump-sum payment to compensate for the loss of future support. This would be less costly in the long run than present policy, would benefit consumers by reducing prices, and would eliminate overproduction in agriculture.

Others accept continued government involvement in agriculture, but argue that it should take a different form. Among the proposals currently debated are decoupling and targeting.

DECOUPLING

Under decoupling, payments to farmers would be independent of their level of production. For example, government support might consist of a fixed payment to all present farmers or a payment of so much per acre, regardless of how the land is used (even if it leaves agriculture). With government support no longer linked to production, farmers would have no incentive to produce more than the equilibrium quantity of output, thereby relieving the government of the commitment to buy surplus output. Moreover, because farmers would no longer receive prices in excess of market levels, resources would not be overallocated to agriculture. Those resources remaining in agriculture would be there because their value in agriculture exceeds their value in other industries.

TARGETING

Current farm policy is indiscriminate, providing support to all farmers regardless of their need. Some propose targeting assistance to certain categories of farmers—perhaps limiting support to impoverished farmers or small family farms. One proposal, offered by President Bush in 1992, would deny support to farmers whose off-farm income exceeds $100,000 per year. Although this could lower the cost to taxpayers by reducing the number of farmers eligible for support, it would still be inefficient in the sense that it subsidizes high-cost farmers. This latter effect could be mitigated by targeting aid to those farmers willing to leave agriculture. By subsidizing retraining and migration, the government could help those unable to earn an adequate living from farming to transfer to other industries. This would also lessen the hardship associated with resource adjustment from agriculture.

Summary

1. Agriculture is an essential industry, accounting for one-sixth of U.S. output. Because the United States exports more farm products than it imports, agriculture has prevented the trade deficit from becoming even larger.

2. Demand for farm products has grown slowly, because income elasticity of demand is low. At the same time, productivity advances have sparked rapid growth in the supply of farm products. Because of the more rapid growth in supply, the relative price of farm products has eroded over time.

3. Because aggregate demand for farm products is inelastic, the growth in supply has reduced total revenues from farming. Costs have not fallen commensurately and, as a result, net farm income has declined.

4. Despite the reduction in net farm income, a declining farm population has kept the average income of farmers from drifting lower. Increased income from off-farm activities has also helped farm households. In the 1970s, for the first time ever, average income of farm households exceeded average income of nonfarm households. Although this situation was reversed during the early 1980s, recent statistics suggest that average income of farm households is again at least as high as average income of nonfarm households.

5. The economic situation of farmers is much more volatile than that of the nonfarm population. With exports booming, farm incomes rose to record levels in the 1970s and the value of farmland soared. But as market conditions deteriorated, the 1980s brought lower incomes and new financial pressures. Farmers who borrowed heavily in anticipation of continued appreciation of land values were squeezed by declining land values and high interest obligations.

6. The government is heavily involved in agriculture. Through the Commodity Credit Corporation, it supports above-equilibrium prices for some products by purchasing surplus output. The government also restricts supply [for example, by paying farmers to take land out of production or, in extreme cases, by limiting the amount of output they can sell (through marketing orders)]. This raises the price received by farmers but disrupts rural communities and forces society to forgo output that could be produced.

7. Other government programs raise price by spurring demand for U.S. farm products, both here and abroad. In addition to increasing food consumption, the government promotes nonfood uses of agricultural products.

8. Target prices provide another form of government support. When the market price is less than the target price, the government reimburses farmers for the difference by making *deficiency payments*.

9. U.S. farm policy is criticized for raising taxes and inflating prices paid by consumers. And while farm programs provide some aid to low-income farmers, high-income farmers receive larger subsidies. Therefore, current policy is an inefficient way to reduce rural poverty and to narrow the distribution of income.

10. Some critical of current farm policy want to limit government support to certain groups of farmers (targeting) or make that support independent of the level of production (decoupling). The latter option has the advantage of eliminating the incentive to over-produce. Others seek the complete withdrawal of government from agriculture, perhaps after first compensating farmers for the loss of future subsidies.

Key Terms

net farm income

Commodity Credit Corporation (CCC)

price support

nonrecourse loan

marketing order

target price

deficiency payment

Study Questions and Problems

1. As incomes increase, does demand grow more rapidly for agricultural or nonagricultural products? Other things equal, how does this uneven growth in demand affect the relative price of agricultural products?

2. How does rapid technological growth in agriculture affect (a) the price consumers pay for food and (b) the total revenue derived from farming?

3. How could the government reduce its stockpile of surplus agricultural products? List three reasonable alternatives.

4. Describe each of the following programs: Acreage Reduction Program, Conservation Reserve Program, and Payment-in-Kind. What common element do the three programs share?

5. (a) What is a target price? (b) How does it differ from a support price? (c) How does it affect the amount of resources devoted to agriculture? Why?

6. Explain how each of the following programs affects the volume of agricultural output: (a) support prices, (b) supply restrictions, (c) demand expansion, and (d) target prices.

7. Other things equal, how is the volume of U.S. agricultural exports affected by each of the following factors?
   a. the value of the dollar
   b. income growth in developing countries
   c. agricultural subsidies of foreign governments
   d. export subsidies of the U.S. government
   e. crop failures overseas
   f. policies restricting U.S. farm output

8. According to a 1980 congressional study:

   Urban expansion is devouring farmland at a dangerous rate. . . . Between 9,000 and 14,000 acres of farmland are being converted daily to nonfarm uses.

The study recommended that farmland be protected and that development be discouraged. Suppose the study's recommendations were adopted (for example, through legislation penalizing the use of land for nonagricultural purposes).

    a. How would this legislation affect the distribution of resources between the agricultural and nonagricultural sectors?

    b. How would it affect the volume of farm output? How would it affect nonfarm output?

    c. What can we infer from the fact that urban users of land are prepared to pay a higher price than farmers?

    d. Do you think legislation discouraging the withdrawal of land from agriculture would benefit or harm society? Explain.

9. Comment on how supply restrictions affect the total revenue of farmers (a) if demand is elastic and (b) if demand is inelastic. For most agricultural products is demand elastic or inelastic?

10. There is a temptation to speak of "the farm problem" as if all farmers face the same problem. Why is this inappropriate? What insights do we gain by recognizing differences among farmers?

11. Do you think that current farm policy has generally benefited farmers? Why or why not?

A REDUCTION IN SUPPLY WOULD RAISE PRICE AND, GIVEN AN INELASTIC PRODUCT DEMAND, INCREASE TOTAL REVENUE OF FARMERS.

YOUR TURN

Answers

Selected References

Council of Economic Advisors. "Toward Agricultural Policy Reform," *Economic Report of the President, 1987*, Chapter 5. Examines the structure of farms and the rationale for government involvement in agriculture.

Cramer, Gail L., and Clarence W. Jensen. *Agricultural Economics and Agribusiness*, 5th ed. (New York: Wiley & Sons, 1991), Chapter 11. Analyzes proposals for increasing income of farmers.

Drabenstott, Mark, and Alan Barkema. "The Farm Economy Turns Down," *Federal Reserve Bank of Kansas City Economic Review* (First Quarter 1992), pp. 19–32. Analyzes recent developments in the farm economy and presents an outlook for future farm policy.

Gardner, Bruce. "Changing Economic Perspectives on the Farm Problem," *Journal of Economic Literature* (March 1992), pp. 62–101. Reviews economic analysis of the farm problem.

Moore, Thomas Gale. "Farm Policy: Justifications, Failures and the Need for Reform," *Federal Reserve Bank of St. Louis Review* (October 1987), pp. 5–12. Presents a critical analysis of farm policy and prospects for reform.

Penson, John B., Jr., Rulon D. Pope, and Michael L. Cook. *Introduction to Agricultural Economics* (Englewood Cliffs, N.J.: Prentice-Hall, 1986), Chapter 10. Studies farm policy and the importance of elasticities.

Robinson, Kenneth L. *Farm and Food Policies and Their Consequences* (Englewood Cliffs, N.J.: Prentice-Hall, 1989). Examines government farm policy.

U.S. Department of Agriculture, Economic Research Service. *Agricultural Outlook*. Monthly publication containing agricultural data and articles on farm policy. December 1990 issue discusses 1990 Farm Bill.

X

ALTHOUGH INTERNATIONAL EVENTS AND IMPLICA-
TIONS HAVE BEEN LIBERALLY WOVEN INTO THE
STORY TOLD THROUGHOUT THIS BOOK, THE
MAJOR PORTION OF THE PRECEDING SECTIONS
DEALS WITH THE ECONOMY OF A PARTICULAR
NATION. THIS SECTION IS DEVOTED *EXCLU-
SIVELY* TO THE ECONOMIC INTERACTION
AMONG NATIONS AND TO THE ECONOMIES
OF FOREIGN NATIONS. ■ THIS SECTION
BEGINS WITH A DISCUSSION OF TRADE
AMONG NATIONS—THE CAUSES AND CON-
SEQUENCES OF TRADE AND THE CONSE-
QUENCES OF TARIFFS, QUOTAS, AND
OTHER FORMS OF TRADE RESTRICTION.
CHAPTER 38 EXAMINES THE FINANCIAL
INTERACTIONS AMONG NATIONS. IN PAR-
TICULAR, THIS CHAPTER EXAMINES THE
CAUSES AND CONSEQUENCES OF CHANG-
ING EXCHANGE RATES AND LOOKS AT THE
BALANCE OF PAYMENTS OF A NATION.
CHAPTER 39 PROVIDES AN ANALYSIS OF
THE PROBLEMS CONFRONTED BY LESS-
DEVELOPED COUNTRIES (LDCS)—COUN-
TRIES IN WHICH ABOUT 75 PERCENT OF
THE EARTH'S INHABITANTS DWELL. ■
FINALLY, CHAPTER 40 ANALYZES THE
CAUSES OF THE REMARKABLE, RECENT
DEMISE IN CHINA, THE SOVIET UNION, AND
SEVERAL EASTERN EUROPEAN NATIONS OF
THE SOCIALIST OR PLANNED ECONOMY—A
SYSTEM THAT HAD RE-
MAINED IN PLACE FOR
MANY YEARS. THIS
CHAPTER ALSO EXAM-
INES THE PROBLEMS THESE NATIONS ARE
EXPERIENCING IN THEIR FLEDGLING EFFORTS TO
IMPROVE THEIR ECONOMIC LOT THROUGH THE
IMPLEMENTATION OF MARKET ECONOMIES.

The World Economy

International Trade

INTERNATIONAL TRADE TOUCHES ALL OUR LIVES. SOME, LIKE SHEILA JACKSON, BENEFIT FROM THE LOWER PRICES AND GREATER SELECTION MADE POSSIBLE BY TRADE. OTHERS, INCLUDING MARIA SANCHEZ, LOSE THEIR JOBS AS A RESULT OF TRADE, AS CONSUMERS SUBSTITUTE FOREIGN PRODUCTS FOR DOMESTIC PRODUCTS. ALTHOUGH SANCHEZ'S OPPOSITION TO IMPORTS IS UNDERSTANDABLE, IT IS IMPORTANT TO ASK HOW THE BENEFITS OF TRADE STACK UP AGAINST THE COSTS. IF BENEFITS DOMINATE, TRADE IS ADVANTAGEOUS TO SOCIETY; IF COSTS DOMINATE, TRADE IS HARMFUL.

BEFORE CONSIDERING WHY COUNTRIES TRADE OR, IN SOME CASES, WHY THEY ERECT BARRIERS TO IMPEDE TRADE, SOME BACKGROUND IS IN ORDER. HOW EXTENSIVE IS WORLD TRADE? WITH WHOM DOES THE UNITED STATES TRADE? AND WHAT DOES THE U.S. IMPORT AND EXPORT?

"There's nothing wrong with imports," said Sheila Jackson. "I buy American goods when they have a good price, but I've got three kids at home. I can't be wasting my money. These shoes came from Korea, and they didn't cost an arm and a leg."

Maria Sanchez has a different attitude. She lost her job of seven years when the Town and Country Shoe Factory recently closed its doors in Sedalia, Missouri. Some of the jobs were shifted to factories in Arkansas, but some were lost to producers overseas. Maria is still bitter. Although she has since found another job, the pay is lower. "You know, if they had kept foreign shoes out of the country, I might still have my old job."

INTERNATIONAL TRADE

World trade is dominated by large industrial nations. Of the $3.4 trillion exported in 1991, the eight largest trading nations accounted for nearly 60 percent of exports (see Table 37.1). Three countries alone—the United States, Germany, and Japan—were responsible for one-third of all trade. Because developing countries have lower levels of output, they generally play a much smaller role in world trade; yet even here there are exceptions. Hong Kong and Korea have grown so rapidly that, despite their developing status, each contributes between 2 and 3 percent of world trade.[1]

MERCHANDISE EXPORTS, 1991 (BY COUNTRY)

COUNTRY	EXPORTS		
	IN BILLIONS OF DOLLARS	AS PERCENT OF COUNTRY'S GDP	AS PERCENT OF WORLD EXPORTS
Industrial countries			
United States	$422	7.4	12.3
Germany	403	25.6	11.7
Japan	315	9.4	9.1
France	217	18.0	6.3
United Kingdom	185	18.2	5.4
Italy	169	14.7	4.9
Netherlands	134	46.5	3.9
Canada	127	21.4	3.7
Developing countries			
Hong Kong	99	N/A*	2.9
Korea	72	25.4	2.1
China, People's Republic	70	19.0	2.0
Malaysia	34	69.5**	1.0
Mexico	27	11.5**	0.8
South Africa	24	22.5	0.7

*N/A = not available.
**Figure is for 1990 for Malaysia and 1989 for Mexico.
SOURCE: International Monetary Fund, *International Financial Statistics* (August 1992). Reprinted by permission.

TABLE 37.1

[1]All the trade statistics of this chapter refer to *merchandise trade*—the exchange of *goods* between countries. An alternative way of measuring trade is to include the value of services as well as goods. Unfortunately, statistics on services are less readily available. Data on the volume of world trade are published only on a merchandise basis and, even in the United States, merchandise trade data are more detailed and more current than data that include services.

As Table 37.1 shows, countries vary greatly in terms of their share of output exported. The Netherlands exports almost 50 percent of its gross domestic product (GDP), and Malaysia exports about 70 percent. In contrast, the United States exports only 7 percent of its GDP to other countries.

Because the United States is a large, diverse country blessed with abundant natural resources, much of its trade is internal. Southern oil-producing states send heating oil to the North. Coastal states ship seafood inland. Agricultural states produce the food and fiber to feed and clothe urban residents. As a consequence of its diverse production, the United States relies less on international trade than most other countries. Yet despite exporting only a small portion of its output, the United States, because it produces more output than any other country, still accounts for 12 percent of world exports, more than any other country.

THE UNITED STATES PATTERN OF TRADE, 1991 (BY REGION AND COUNTRY)

REGION/ COUNTRIES	EXPORTS TO (BILLIONS OF DOLLARS)	IMPORTS FROM (BILLIONS OF DOLLARS)	TRADE SURPLUS (+) OR DEFICIT (−) (BILLIONS OF DOLLARS)
Western Europe	$118.7	$102.6	$16.1
European Community (EC)	103.2	86.5	16.7
United Kingdom	22.1	18.5	3.6
Germany	21.3	26.2	− 4.9
France	15.4	13.4	2.0
Netherlands	13.5	4.8	8.7
Eastern Europe	4.8	1.8	3.0
Commonwealth of Independent States	3.6	0.8	2.8
Western Hemisphere			
Canada	85.1	91.1	− 6.0
Mexico	33.3	31.2	2.1
Brazil	6.2	6.7	− 0.5
Venezuela	4.7	8.2	− 3.5
Asia			
Japan	48.1	91.6	−43.5
Korea	15.5	17.0	− 1.5
Taiwan	13.2	23.0	− 9.8
Singapore	8.8	10.0	− 1.2
Africa			
South Africa	2.1	1.7	0.4
Nigeria	0.8	5.4	− 4.6
Australia	8.4	4.0	4.4
OPEC	19.1	33.0	−13.9

SOURCE: U.S. Department of Commerce. *Survey of Current Business* (July 1992).

TABLE 37.2

TRADE BY THE UNITED STATES

TRADE DEFICIT
The amount by which a country's imports exceed its exports.

TRADE SURPLUS
The amount by which a country's exports exceed its imports.

As Table 37.2 illustrates, the United States trades with countries around the world. A large share of its exports go to its neighbors in North America, especially Canada, its top foreign buyer. Other major buyers of U.S. products are the large industrial nations, including Japan, the United Kingdom, and Germany. In turn, the United States tends to buy heavily from those countries that are its best customers. Lately, however, the United States has been buying more foreign products than it has been selling—that is, importing more than it exports (see Figure 37.1). The country's **trade deficit** hit a record $160 billion in 1987 before falling to $77 billion, or 1.4 percent of GDP, in 1991. Although the United States has a **trade surplus** with some countries, notably in Europe, this is more than offset by the trade deficit it is running with other countries.

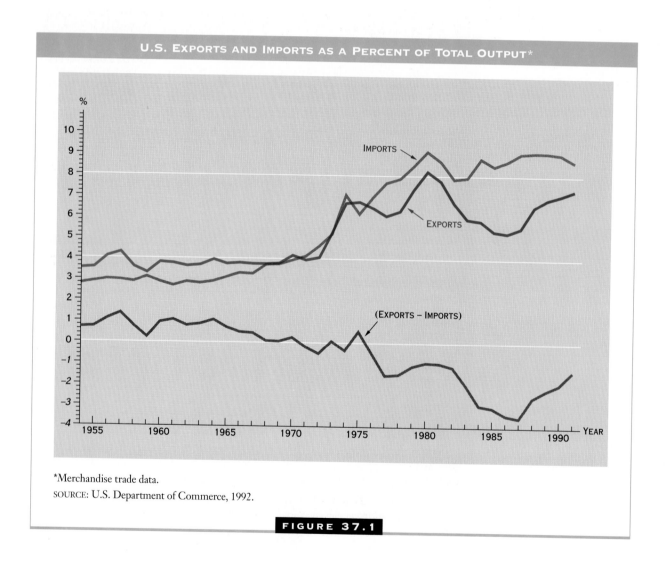

U.S. EXPORTS AND IMPORTS AS A PERCENT OF TOTAL OUTPUT*

*Merchandise trade data.

SOURCE: U.S. Department of Commerce, 1992.

FIGURE 37.1

Table 37.3 (page 978) shows the U.S. trade pattern in terms of the products exported and imported. The United States is a leading producer of capital goods. In recent years it has been exporting roughly $25–$30 billion each in aircraft and computers in addition to a large volume of other machinery. Another major source of exports is industrial materials and supplies, including coal, ores, and metal scrap. In many years the United States also exports large quantities of agricultural products, especially grains and soybeans; however, export volume varies considerably from year to year, depending on world supply and demand.

The United States is a major importer of petroleum and petroleum products, although petroleum's share of imports has fallen over the past dozen years. In 1980, approximately 30 percent of imports were petroleum; today the figure is closer to 10 percent. Other major imports include automobiles, telecommunications equipment, metals, textiles, clothing, and footwear.

Reasons For Trade

The preceding section documents the volume and pattern of international trade but does not address the fundamental question of why nations trade. Trade occurs so that nations may obtain goods not otherwise available or available domestically only at higher cost. In either case, trade permits the citizens of a country to increase their consumption and enjoy a higher standard of living.

ACCESS TO DIFFERENT GOODS AND RESOURCES

As rich and diverse as it is, the United States is incapable of producing certain goods and does a poor job of producing others. The United States simply does not have the right climate for growing bananas and coffee beans. Nor does it have rich deposits of every mineral. Among the minerals not currently produced in the United States are graphite, from which pencils, brake linings, and lubricants are made, and strontium, which is used in the manufacture of color television picture tubes, pigments, and ceramic magnets. Other strategic minerals, including bauxite and alumina (from which aluminum is manufactured), are produced domestically, but reserves are so low that imports are necessary unless the U.S. is prepared to scale back drastically its consumption of these minerals. Table 37.4 (page 978) highlights the U.S. import reliance on various minerals.

Most other countries are even more dependent on imports than is the United States. If each country were isolated and forced to make do with its natural mix of resources, standards of living would fall throughout the world, because consumption would be limited to those goods that could be produced within the country. U.S. citizens would be forced to give up their coffee, Ugandans their modern machinery. Trade makes such sacrifices unnecessary—it opens the door to products not otherwise available. By trading coffee beans and machinery, U.S. consumers can enjoy one of their favorite beverages; Ugandans can obtain modern equipment.

	EXPORTS		IMPORTS	
U.S. EXPORTS AND IMPORTS, 1991 (BY TYPE OF PRODUCT)				
PRODUCT	**IN BILLIONS OF DOLLARS**	**AS PERCENT OF EXPORTS**	**IN BILLIONS OF DOLLARS**	**AS PERCENT OF IMPORTS**
Food, feed, beverages	$ 35.7	8.4	$ 26.5	5.3
Industrial materials*	106.4	25.1	126.8	25.4
Petroleum	N/A**	N/A**	51.2	10.2
Capital goods***	167.0	39.5	120.7	24.1
Autos	40.0	9.5	84.9	17.0
Consumer goods***	45.9	10.9	108.0	21.6
Other	28.1	6.6	33.0	6.6
TOTAL	$423.1	100.0	$499.9	100.0

*Includes petroleum.
**N/A = not available.
***Excludes autos.
SOURCE: U.S. Department of Commerce, *Survey of Current Business* (July 1992).

TABLE 37.3

ABSOLUTE ADVANTAGE

Even when two countries are capable of producing the same products, trade may still be advantageous because of differences in resource endowments. Saudi Arabia

NET IMPORT RELIANCE OF THE UNITED STATES FOR SELECTED MINERALS			
MINERAL	**IMPORT RELIANCE***	**MINERAL**	**IMPORT RELIANCE***
Arsenic	100	Diamond	92
Columbium	100	Fluorspar	90
Graphite	100	Pt-group metals	88
Manganese	100	Tantalum	86
Mica	100	Cobalt	85
Strontium	100	Nickel	83
Thallium	100	Chromium	79
Bauxite and alumina	98	Tin	76
Gemstones	98	Tungsten	73

*Imports minus exports as a percentage of U.S. consumption (adjusted for changes in mineral stocks).
SOURCE: U.S. Bureau of Mines, *Mineral Commodity Summaries, 1991*, p. 3.

TABLE 37.4

and the United States can both produce oil and grain, but given Saudi Arabia's rich pools of easily accessible oil and its relatively barren soil, oil is less costly to produce in Saudia Arabia and grain is less costly to produce in the United States. Because of such cost differences, Saudi Arabia has found it profitable to export oil and import grain. Conversely, the United States has found that it benefits from trading grain for oil.

Similar cost differences exist for other products and other countries. Canada, blessed with natural resources, is a low-cost source of timber and many minerals. Japan, on the other hand, is poor in terms of natural resources but has an industrious, highly skilled work force. This permits it to produce electronic and other high-tech equipment at a lower cost than Canada. As a result, the two countries have discovered that each benefits if Canada trades natural resources to Japan for VCRs, cameras, and compact disc players.

An example will help illustrate the mutual gains from trade. To keep things simple, we limit the example to two countries and two goods and assume that labor is the only resource used in production. In the United States each worker can produce either 3 computers or 200 pairs of shoes per week. In Italy each worker can produce either 1 computer or 300 pairs of shoes per week.[2] According to these numbers, the United States can produce computers using less labor than Italy. (It takes a worker one-third of a week to produce a computer in the United States, compared to a full week in Italy.) Italy, on the other hand, can produce shoes using less labor than the United States. Because of these differences in resource costs, the United States is said to have an **absolute advantage** in the production of computers and Italy an absolute advantage in the production of shoes.

ABSOLUTE ADVANTAGE
The ability to produce a particular good using less resources than a second country (that is, a lower ratio of resources to output).

Given these differences in costs, both countries can gain from trade. To understand this, consider what happens when the United States transfers a worker from the shoe industry to the computer industry. Production of computers increases by 3 units, but 200 fewer pairs of shoes are produced (see Table 37.5, top line, page 980). Consider resource reallocation in the opposite direction in Italy. If one worker is switched from the computer industry to the shoe industry, Italy turns out 1 less computer but an additional 300 pairs of shoes. The bottom line of Table 37.5 indicates the net effect of this reallocation of labor within the two countries: the net production of computers in the two countries increases by 2 units; the net production of shoes rises by 100 pairs.

---

[2]This information can also be presented in tabular form:

COUNTRY	OUTPUT OF EACH WORKER (PER WEEK)		
	COMPUTERS	OR	PAIRS OF SHOES
United States	3		200
Italy	1		300

COUNTRY	CHANGE IN OUTPUT	
	COMPUTERS	PAIRS OF SHOES
United States	+ 3	− 200
Italy	− 1	+ 300
Net effect	+ 2	+ 100

By transferring one worker from the shoe industry to the computer industry, the United States produces 3 more computers but 200 fewer pairs of shoes. Italy transfers one worker from the computer industry to the shoe industry, producing 1 less computer but an additional 300 pairs of shoes. The net effect of this reallocation of resources is to produce 2 more computers and an additional 100 pairs of shoes.

TABLE 37.5

In other words, if Italy specializes in the production of shoes—producing more shoes than will be consumed in Italy—and the United States specializes in the production of computers, the two countries will end up with more computers *and* more shoes! By concentrating production in that country where production costs are lower (where absolute advantage exists), the two countries expand world output. In turn, if this extra output is divided between the two countries (more on this later), the average standard of living will rise in each country. Even though both countries can produce both goods, because costs differ there are economic reasons for specialization and trade.

COMPARATIVE ADVANTAGE

The preceding discussion assumed that each country enjoys an absolute advantage in the production of one good. But what if the same country can produce each good using less resources than the other country? Your initial response may be that, in such an instance, gains from trade would be impossible. Why would a country import a good that it could produce with less resources? But as David Ricardo demonstrated almost 180 years ago, specialization and trade may still be advantageous provided that opportunity costs differ by country.

To see this, we interchange two numbers from the preceding example. Suppose that each worker in the United States can produce either 3 computers or *300* pairs of shoes and that each worker in Italy can produce either 1 computer or *200* pairs of shoes. Based on these new numbers, the United States enjoys an absolute advantage in the production of both goods. Even so, both countries can benefit if the United States specializes in the production of computers, Italy specializes in the production of shoes, and the United States trades computers to Italy for shoes. We first show that this is true and then explain why.

Again the experiment consists of reallocating resources within the two countries. Let the United States move one worker from the production of shoes to computers while Italy moves two workers in the opposite direction, away from computers and into the shoe industry.[3] As Table 37.6 illustrates, production of computers rises by 3 units in the United States and falls by 2 units in Italy. Production of shoes falls by 300 pairs in the United States but rises by 400 pairs in Italy. Altogether, the two countries now have 1 extra computer and an additional 100 pairs of shoes. As in the first example, specialization and trade permit the two countries to expand their joint production and therefore to have a higher standard of living.

The reason that specialization and trade are mutually advantageous is that the *relative* cost of the two goods differs by country. The United States has a big absolute advantage in the production of computers—each worker produces 3 times as many computers in the United States as in Italy. In contrast, the absolute advantage in shoes is much smaller—each worker produces only 1.5 times as many shoes in the United States as in Italy. By specializing in computers, the United States can take advantage of its relatively larger absolute advantage in this industry.

This is perhaps easiest to understand by comparing the opportunity cost of computers in the two countries. In the United States the opportunity cost of 3 computers is 300 pairs of shoes or, equivalently, the opportunity cost of 1 computer is 100 pairs of shoes. Therefore, when measured by opportunity cost the cost of producing a computer is lower in the United States—the United States sacrifices only 100 pairs of shoes whereas Italy would have to sacrifice 200 pairs. Because the

GAINS FROM SPECIALIZATION AND TRADE—THE CASE OF COMPARATIVE ADVANTAGE		
	CHANGE IN OUTPUT	
COUNTRY	COMPUTERS	PAIRS OF SHOES
United States	+ 3	− 300
Italy	− 2	+ 400
Net effect	+ 1	+ 100

The United States transfers one worker from the shoe industry to the computer industry; Italy transfers two workers from the computer industry to the shoe industry. This reallocation leads to greater output of computers (because the increased production in the United States exceeds the loss in Italy) and greater output of shoes (because the increased production in Italy exceeds the loss in the United States).

TABLE 37.6

[3]A larger number of workers was transferred in Italy because workers are less productive there—that is, more workers are required to produce a given volume of output. The conclusion of this example—that specialization and trade permit greater output of both goods—does not hinge on twice as many workers being reallocated in Italy. To prove this to yourself, rework the example transferring 2 workers in the United States and 5 workers in Italy, or 3 workers in the United States and 5 in Italy.

COMPARATIVE ADVANTAGE

The ability to produce a particular good at a lower opportunity cost than a second country.

LAW OF COMPARATIVE ADVANTAGE

Total output is maximized when countries specialize in the production of those goods for which they have a comparative advantage.

opportunity cost of producing computers is lower in the United States, the United States is said to have a **comparative advantage** in the production of computers.

Conversely, the opportunity cost of producing shoes must be lower in Italy. If Italy sacrifices more shoes per computer, it must sacrifice fewer computers for a given quantity of shoes. For example, to produce 200 pairs of shoes Italy must forgo only 1 computer whereas the United States must give up 2 computers. Therefore, Italy has a comparative advantage in the production of shoes. Equivalently, the United States has a comparative *dis*advantage in the production of shoes.

To be advantageous, trade does not require that each country have an absolute advantage in the production of a different good. All that is necessary is that each country have a *comparative* advantage in the production of a different good. This proposition is known as the **law of comparative advantage**, and it explains why, in the preceding example, trade benefits both the United States and Italy, even though the United States has an absolute advantage in the production of both goods.

Equal Cost Ratios

IN THE UNITED STATES EACH WORKER CAN PRODUCE 3 COMPUTERS OR 300 PAIRS OF SHOES. IN ITALY THE CORRESPONDING NUMBERS ARE 2 COMPUTERS OR 200 PAIRS OF SHOES. (A) IN THE UNITED STATES WHAT IS THE OPPORTUNITY COST OF 1 COMPUTER? (B) IN ITALY WHAT IS THE OPPORTUNITY COST OF 1 COMPUTER? (C) UNDER THESE CONDITIONS IS TRADE ADVANTAGEOUS?

FROM PRODUCTION POSSIBILITIES TO TRADING POSSIBILITIES

The gains from specialization and trade can also be demonstrated diagrammatically with production possibilities curves. Accordingly, we recast the preceding example in terms of production possibilities curves. To do so, it is first necessary to specify how many workers each country has available for the production of computers or shoes. Let us assume arbitrarily that the United States has 1,000 workers available and Italy has 1,200.

Based on the preceding assumptions, the production possibilities curves for the two countries are presented in Figure 37.2. The United States can produce 3,000 computers and no shoes, 300,000 pairs of shoes and no computers, or such intermediate combinations of the two goods as 2,000 computers and 100,000 pairs of shoes. Because of lower output per worker in Italy, the potential output is lower there than in the United States, despite Italy's greater number of workers in these two industries.

In the absence of trade, each country is constrained to its production possibilities curve. But, as previously indicated, specialization and trade offer the two countries the potential to increase the amount of output available to their citizens. That is, world output will be greater if the two countries trade than if they are self-sufficient (do not trade). How much of this additional output each country gains from trade depends on the **terms of trade**—the rate at which imported and exported

TERMS OF TRADE

The amount of one good that must be given up to obtain a unit of a second good.

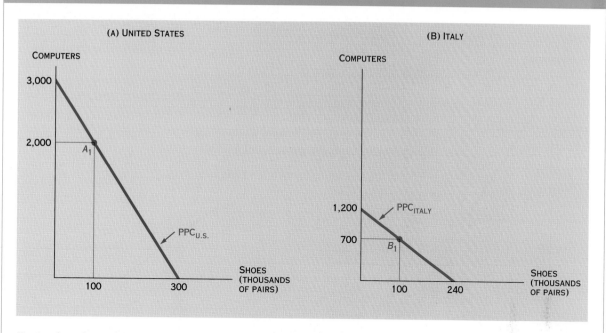

(A) UNITED STATES

COMPUTERS

3,000

2,000

A_1

PPC$_{U.S.}$

100   300

SHOES
(THOUSANDS
OF PAIRS)

(B) ITALY

COMPUTERS

1,200   PPC$_{ITALY}$

700   B_1

100   240

SHOES
(THOUSANDS
OF PAIRS)

Depicted are the production possibilities curves for the United States and Italy. In the absence of trade, each country is constrained to points along its production possibilities curve, such as A_1 and B_1.

FIGURE 37.2

TRADING POSSIBILITIES CURVE

A line showing the combinations of two goods a country may obtain by producing the good for which it has a comparative advantage and trading it for the other good.

goods are exchanged. This is determined by the relative price of these goods. For example, if the price of a computer is 150 times greater than the price of a pair of shoes, the terms of trade are 150 pairs of shoes for each computer.

The terms of trade are constrained by the opportunity cost in each country. Given the fact that the opportunity cost of producing 1 computer is 100 pairs of shoes in the United States and 200 pairs of shoes in Italy, the terms of trade must settle somewhere between 100 and 200 pairs of shoes per computer. If the terms of trade were less than 100 pairs of shoes per computer, the United States would refuse to export computers; if the terms of trade were more than 200 pairs of shoes per computer, Italy would refuse to export shoes. For concreteness, assume the terms of trade are 150 pairs of shoes per computer.[4]

Once the terms of trade are known, it is possible to construct a nation's **trading possibilities curve**, which indicates the combinations of the two goods

[4]Determination of the terms of trade depends on how prices are set. In the absence of government intervention, the price of each good—and therefore the terms of trade—is determined by world supply and demand for each good. For simplicity, we assume that neither country constitutes a large enough segment of the world market to affect prices.

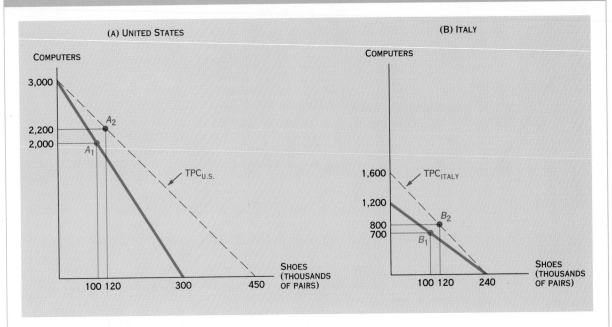

By specializing in the production of the good for which it has a comparative advantage and then trading for the other good, each country can move off its production possibilities curve. The options available from trade are depicted by the country's trading possibilities curve (TPC). For example, the United States can move from A_1 to A_2, gaining 200 computers and 20,000 pairs of shoes, while Italy moves from B_1 to B_2, gaining an additional 100 computers and an additional 20,000 pairs of shoes.

FIGURE 37.3

available to it through trade. For example, consider the options available to the United States if it specializes in producing computers (the good for which it has a comparative advantage). By devoting all its resources to the production of computers, it can produce 3,000 computers (and no shoes). If the U.S. trades 1 computer to Italy it ends up with 2,999 computers and 150 pairs of shoes. If it trades 1,000 computers it ends up with 2,000 computers and 150,000 pairs of shoes. These and other options are depicted on the trading possibilities curve in Figure 37.3(A).

Note that points on the trading possibilities curve lie *beyond* the production possibilities curve—trade enables a country to obtain additional output. Had the United States insisted on self-sufficiency it could have reached point A_1—corresponding to 2,000 computers and 100,000 pairs of shoes—but it could not have obtained more of one good without giving up some of the other. With trade, however, greater quantities of both goods become feasible. For example, with trade the United States can obtain 2,200 computers and 120,000 pairs of shoes (point A_2). Compared to point A_1, the United States gains 200 computers and 20,000 pairs of shoes.

Similarly, trade benefits Italy, bringing previously unattainable options within reach [see Figure 37.3(B)]. For instance, with trade Italy can move from point B_1 to point B_2, in the process gaining 100 computers and 20,000 pairs of shoes. As a consequence of trade, both countries obtain greater quantities of both goods. Thus, specialization and trade allow both countries to enjoy higher standards of living than would be possible in the absence of trade.

SOME QUALIFICATIONS

In illustrating the gains from trade, the preceding discussion made a number of simplifying assumptions. These do not alter the basic conclusion—that trade can be mutually advantageous—but they do have implications concerning the extent of trade and the magnitude of the gains from trade. To understand this we relax two of the preceding assumptions.

INCREASING COSTS   One simplifying assumption was that the costs of production are constant. In particular, the opportunity cost of one computer was assumed to be the same no matter how many computers a country produces. It was this assumption that caused the production possibilities curve to be a straight line. If the opportunity cost of producing a good increases with the amount produced (that is, if production possibilities curves have their traditional bowed shape), trade may, after some point, cease to be advantageous.

For example, if the cost of producing a pair of shoes rises in Italy with the number of shoes produced, beyond some point it may cost the United States more to import additional shoes than to produce them domestically (that is, in the United States). Once that point is reached, shoe imports will cease. Thus, increasing production costs may lead to *incomplete specialization*—the United States still produces extra computers, which it trades to Italy for shoes, but it also produces a portion of the shoes consumed in the United States. Similarly, rising computer costs in the United States may prompt Italy to produce computers as well as import them. In summary, the volume of trade is likely to be less when the opportunity cost of producing a good is increasing rather than constant.

TRANSACTION COSTS   The preceding discussion also ignored transaction costs, including the cost of transporting computers to Italy and shoes to the United States.[5] The presence of transaction costs alters the terms of trade. For example, after netting out transaction costs, the United States might receive only 140 pairs of shoes for each computer while Italy may have to give up 160 pairs of shoes to obtain a computer. The difference (20 pairs of shoes) reflects the costs of moving the goods between the two countries. Although transaction costs reduce the gains from trade, trade remains advantageous. Even with transaction costs, it costs the United States less to import shoes than to produce them in the United States and it costs Italy less to import computers than to produce them in Italy.

---

[5]See Chapter 2 for a review of transaction costs.

Limiting Trade

FREE TRADE
Trade that is free of artificial barriers that would restrict the movement of goods between countries.

Despite large potential gains from *unrestricted* or **free trade**, nations often erect barriers to impede trade. What are the major trade barriers? What are their consequences? And why do nations impose them?

Artificial Barriers to Trade

In contrast to natural barriers to trade, notably transaction costs, artificial barriers consist of government programs to obstruct the movement of goods across national borders. Sometimes a government limits exports in the belief that they would compromise national security. But, with this one exception, trade barriers are aimed at slowing or eliminating *imports*. Among the major barriers to imports are tariffs, import quotas, voluntary export restrictions, and antidumping laws.

TARIFFS

TARIFF (DUTY)
A tax levied on an imported product.

PROHIBITIVE TARIFF
A tariff set so high that it prevents the sale of a foreign product in the country imposing the tariff.

NONPROHIBITIVE TARIFF
A tariff that reduces but does not eliminate foreign sales in the country imposing the tariff.

A **tariff** (or **duty**) is a tax levied on an imported good. Because it increases the cost of selling the good, it reduces foreign supply. When the tariff is set high enough, it drives foreign producers from the country's market entirely. Such a tariff is called a **prohibitive tariff**. For example, during the 1988 presidential primaries, one candidate raised the prospect of slapping a tax on Hyundais to increase the price of this small Korean automobile to $48,000. At such a price, imports of the car would dry up completely.

More commonly, tariffs are **nonprohibitive**—that is, they reduce foreign supply but do not eliminate it. The effects of a nonprohibitive tariff are illustrated in Figure 37.4. $D_{U.S.}$ is the demand by U.S. consumers for the product in question and $S_{U.S.}$ is the supply of U.S. producers. In the absence of a tariff, the product sells at the world price of P_W.[6] At this price, U.S. consumers buy Q_1^c units of output, domestic (U.S.) producers sell Q_1^D units, and foreign producers make up the difference. That is, imports amount to $Q_1^c - Q_1^D$.

Now suppose the U.S. government levies a tariff of T dollars per unit on all imports. This raises the price for U.S. consumers to $P_W + T$, causing them to reduce their purchases to Q_2^c. Domestic producers respond to the higher price by boosting output to Q_2^D, with the government collecting $T \times (Q_2^c - Q_2^D)$ in taxes from foreign producers (represented by the shaded rectangle in Figure 37.4).

---

[6]The United States is assumed to be such a small part of the world market that it is a price taker. Although this assumption is not necessary, it simplifies the analysis.

At the world price of P_w, U.S. consumers buy Q_1^c output and domestic (U.S.) producers sell Q_1^p output. The difference ($Q_1^c - Q_1^p$) consists of imports. A tariff of T dollars per unit raises the U.S. price to $P_w + T$, reduces domestic consumption to Q_2^c, increases domestic production to Q_2^p, and shrinks imports to $Q_2^c - Q_2^p$. The shaded rectangle represents tariff revenues collected by the government.

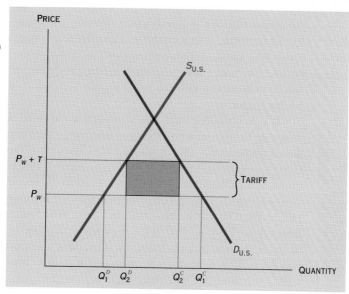

FIGURE 37.4

The tariff harms U.S. consumers, who now receive less output and must pay a higher price. It also hurts foreign producers, who lose sales in the United States without benefiting from the higher price there. (The increased price foreign producers receive is fully offset by the tariff they must pay.) On the other hand, the tariff benefits U.S. producers and workers in the protected industry. U.S. producers receive a higher price for their product and, because of reduced foreign selling, increase their output. With domestic production expanding, demand for U.S. workers in the industry rises, putting upward pressure on wages and employment in the industry.

To determine a tariff's net effect on the U.S. economy, it is necessary to compare the benefits of those gaining from the tariff with the costs of those losing. When that is done, the tariff must be judged a failure: losses exceed benefits. This is because the tariff, like other trade barriers, leads to a misallocation of resources within the United States. Too many resources are pulled into the protected industry (in response to artificially high prices there), leaving too few resources for other industries. In effect, resources are drawn away from industries in which the United States has a comparative advantage and diverted to industries in which the United States has a comparative disadvantage.

It is important to recognize that a tariff does not increase total output of the economy. Increased production in the protected industry comes at the expense of lower output in other industries—output that society values more highly. Overall, tariffs reduce the value of output produced by a country.

IMPORT QUOTAS

IMPORT QUOTA

A restriction setting a maximum limit on the amount of a product that may be legally imported into a country.

An **import quota** is a restriction limiting the quantity of a product that may be legally imported into a country. The effects of a quota are in many ways similar to those of a tariff: it reduces imports, increases domestic production, raises price, harms consumers, and benefits domestic producers in the protected industry. This can be understood with the aid of Figure 37.5, which examines the consequences of a sugar quota.

If U.S. consumers can buy sugar at a world price of 7 cents per pound, they will consume 11 million tons of sugar annually. Of that total, 3 million tons will be produced domestically and 8 million tons imported. Now consider what happens if Congress decides to protect the U.S. sugar industry by establishing an import quota of 2 million tons of sugar per year. With less imported sugar now available, U.S. consumers bid up the price of sugar, until the quantity of sugar available for sale in the United States (domestic sugar plus foreign sugar) equals the quantity demanded. That is, the price rises until the gap between domestic supply and demand narrows to 2 million tons. This occurs at a price of 20 cents per pound. At this price, U.S. consumers want to buy 8 million tons and U.S. producers want to sell 6 million tons. Once the 2 million tons of imports are included, the amount of sugar available in the United States coincides with the amount demanded.

THE EFFECTS OF A QUOTA

At the world price of 7 cents per pound, U.S. consumers purchase 11 million tons of sugar annually. Domestic production accounts for 3 million tons, imports for the remaining 8 million tons. An annual quota of 2 million tons causes the gap between domestic consumption and domestic production to shrink to 2 million tons, which occurs when the U.S. price rises to 20 cents per pound. Of the 8 million tons of sugar demanded at 20 cents per pound, 6 million tons are supplied domestically.

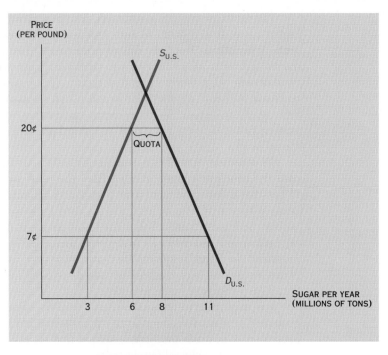

FIGURE 37.5

The U.S. sugar industry reaps the benefits of congressional intervention; consumers bear the costs. Sheltered from competition, sugar growers can sell twice as much output while receiving a premium of 13 cents per pound above the world price. Consumers receive less sugar despite paying more for it. As with a tariff, consumers lose more than producers gain; society is made worse off. Resources are drawn into the sugar industry to produce, at costs of up to 20 cents per pound, sugar that is available at 7 cents per pound. This means fewer resources are available to other industries to produce output that would be more valuable than the added sugar.

Despite the similarities with tariffs, quotas are in some ways even more damaging. First, they restrict imports to a given level no matter how strong demand is for the product. If domestic demand increases over time, quotas allow domestic prices to rise and the gap between domestic and world prices to widen. In contrast, with tariffs, increased demand leads to increased imports, sheltering consumers from higher prices. Second, tariffs have the advantage of raising revenue for the government. Both tariffs and quotas increase the price that foreign producers receive for selling in the domestic economy. With tariffs the price hike is taxed away; with quotas it accrues to foreign producers. In other words, a tariff generates revenues for the government, revenues that can be spent on the country's citizens, whereas a quota transfers these revenues to foreign producers.

VOLUNTARY EXPORT RESTRICTIONS

VOLUNTARY EXPORT RESTRICTION
An agreement by one country to limit exports to a second country.

A **voluntary export restriction** is, in essence, a quota by a different name. A foreign country promises not to export more than a specified volume of output to the domestic country. In other words, imports into the domestic country are limited to a prescribed amount. But this is exactly what a quota does. Therefore, the effects of a voluntary export restriction are identical to those of an import quota.

Voluntary export restrictions are voluntary in the sense that a holdup victim voluntarily parts with his money. Because it is not in the best interests of a nation to limit its exports, it will do so only reluctantly, as a means of heading off even more stringent measures by other nations. For example, Japan agreed to limit exports of automobiles to the United States not because it wanted to sell fewer automobiles there but because it wanted to avoid the more severe quotas Congress was proposing.

ANTIDUMPING LAWS

DUMPING
A practice in which a producer sells its product at a lower price in a foreign market than at home.

Dumping occurs when a company sells a good at a lower price in a foreign country than at home.[7] For example, companies in Japan have been accused of dumping computer chips in the United States and European companies of dumping steel. Antidumping laws are designed to halt this practice (for example, to force Japanese companies to raise the price of the computer chips they sell in the United States).

---

[7]Alternatively, dumping is sometimes defined as selling in a foreign market for *less than cost*.

As with tariffs and quotas, domestic producers benefit from the higher prices while consumers suffer.

Dumping may occur for several reasons. To begin with, the government of the companies engaged in dumping may subsidize their exports. For example, the Japanese government may defray the costs of chips exported to the United States. Japanese companies can then sell their chips for less in the United States because costs are lower there. In that event, the lower price in the United States is a gift to U.S. consumers from the Japanese government—U.S. consumers get their chips at less than cost, with the Japanese government (or more accurately Japanese taxpayers) footing the bill. Because the Japanese are paying for U.S. consumption, the standard of living in Japan falls while the standard of living in the United States rises. Although U.S. chip manufacturers are adversely affected, the United States as a whole benefits from Japanese subsidies.

An alternative reason for dumping is to create monopoly power. For instance, Japanese chip makers may be willing temporarily to sell at a loss in an attempt to drive American chip makers out of business—a practice known as *predatory pricing*. Once their American competitors are eliminated, the Japanese chip makers can then increase chip prices and earn monopoly profits. In that event, dumping would have a detrimental long-run effect on the U.S. economy.

But even if Japanese chip makers were so motivated, it is not clear that such a scheme would succeed. First, competition from non-American chip makers would prevent chip prices from soaring. Second, if prices rose sufficiently, U.S. producers would have an incentive to reenter the chip industry. In any event, most economists contend that dumping is not motivated by predatory pricing and that, as a consequence, antidumping laws are neither necessary nor desirable.

The Cost of Trade Barriers in the United States

By restricting trade, the United States government raises prices to consumers and reduces their standard of living. But by how much are consumers affected? The answer varies by product, depending on the amount of *protection* afforded a particular industry. It has been estimated that, because of trade barriers, U.S. consumers pay an additional $5 per sweater and an extra $3 per box of candy. Automobile prices have been inflated by more than $1,000. According to the Institute for International Economics, trade restrictions cost U.S. consumers more than $80 billion annually, or $310 per person.

PROTECTIONISM
Sheltering domestic industries from foreign competition through tariffs, quotas, or other programs that limit imports.

Another way to measure the cost of **protectionist** policies is in terms of the added costs to consumers per job created in the protected industry. For instance, in the textile and apparel industries—where the most jobs have been saved—consumers pay an additional $27 billion per year to preserve 640,000 jobs. That works out to approximately $42,000 per year for a job that pays less than half that amount. In some industries the cost per job saved is hundreds of thousands of dollars (see Table 37.7). If the government wishes to help workers in industries facing foreign competition, there are clearly less costly ways of providing relief.

THE COSTS OF SAVING JOBS IN PROTECTED INDUSTRIES

INDUSTRY	JOBS SAVED	TOTAL COST (MILLIONS OF DOLLARS)	COST PER JOB SAVED (DOLLARS)
Book manufacturing	5,000	$ 500	$ 100,000
Benzenoid chemicals	300	2,650	>1,000,000
Glassware	1,000	200	200,000
Rubber footwear	7,800	230	30,000
Nonrubber footwear	12,700	700	55,000
Ceramic tiles	850	116	135,000
Orange juice	2,200	525	240,000
Canned tuna	1,200	91	76,000
Textiles, apparel	640,000	27,000	42,000
Carbon steel	9,000	6,800	750,000
Automobiles	55,000	5,800	105,000
Maritime industries	11,000	3,000	270,000
Sugar	15,300	930	60,000
Dairy products	25,000	5,500	220,000

SOURCE: Adapted from Gary Clyde Hufbauer, Diane T. Berliner, and Kimberly Ann Elliott, *Trade Protection in the United States: 31 Case Studies* (Washington, D.C.: Institute for International Economics), Tables 1.1 and 1.2. Copyright © 1986 by the Institute for International Economics. Reprinted by permission.

TABLE 37.7

Explaining the Presence of Trade Barriers

If trade barriers reduce a country's standard of living, then why would a country impose them? Several explanations are relevant. We begin by analyzing some of the most frequently cited arguments for limiting imports. Some have merit, some do not. We follow with a discussion of the political factors that shape trade legislation.

TRADITIONAL ARGUMENTS FOR RESTRICTING TRADE

NATIONAL DEFENSE   Free trade increases a country's output but not necessarily its well-being. To dramatize this point, suppose the United States has a comparative advantage in the production of wheat and China a comparative advantage in producing military hardware. In that event, the total output of wheat and weapons is maximized when the United States specializes in the production of wheat, exporting wheat to China in return for military hardware. Yet even though specialization and trade lead to greater output for both countries, the United States, for strategic reasons, is likely to find this arrangement unacceptable. In the event of hostilities,

China might prove an unreliable supplier of weapons. Moreover, Chinese dominance in this industry would likely give it added political clout in the world. Therefore, most citizens would agree that it is in the best interests of the United States to produce its military hardware despite the fact that this policy reduces the output available to its citizens. A lower standard of living is considered a small price to pay for added national security.

Because national defense is generally accepted as a legitimate reason to protect an industry that does not have a comparative advantage, industries seeking relief from foreign competition often couch their requests in terms of national defense. Before agreeing to shelter an industry from foreign competition, the government must determine whether this industry truly is vital to national defense and whether the benefits of a stronger defense are worth the costs. If not, protection is legitimate only when it can be justified on other grounds.

INFANT INDUSTRY The infant-industry argument offers a second reason to protect a domestic industry. According to this argument, average costs of production typically are high during the transitional period in which an industry is established, but fall as the industry matures. That means an industry just starting in one country, say Mexico, may find it difficult to compete with other countries where the industry is well established and costs are lower. But if the Mexican industry were given an opportunity to mature, its costs might drop to the point where it could compete in foreign and domestic markets without government protection. Once established, the Mexican industry might have a comparative advantage. If the Mexican government believes this is likely to be the case, it has reason to provide temporary relief—either restricting imports of the good into Mexico or subsidizing the industry until it is strong enough to stand on its own.

Although this argument has logic, the assumptions on which it is based should be underscored. The first assumption is that the country has a comparative advantage in the production of the good that will be manifested only after the industry is mature. Without this eventual comparative advantage, the argument collapses. The risk then is that the government will shelter industries that will never have a comparative advantage and can never make it on their own.

Another assumption is that the government will provide only *temporary* relief, since the mature industry will be able to compete without government assistance. From a practical standpoint, history teaches that once an industry receives government relief, it is difficult to wean. It took almost 100 years to repeal an 1891 ban on the overseas printing of books written by U.S. authors and published in the United States; and the maritime industry, sheltered by the government since 1789, is still not ready to stand alone.

Finally, the infant-industry argument is premised on the assumption that a country is just entering an established market. For industrial countries, such as the United States, it is difficult to justify this assumption. Some industries, however, have devised creative ways of repackaging the infant-industry argument. For instance, U.S. automobile manufacturers convinced Congress that, even though theirs was a mature industry, they needed "breathing room" to become proficient in the small-car market, which was dominated by foreign producers. This was the reason the U.S. government pressured Japan into limiting automobile exports to the United States (see Exhibit 37.1, page 994).

RETALIATION   Some proponents of trade barriers argue that they support free trade in principle but that free trade is not an option. Foreign countries restrict our exports and, when they do, we must retaliate by limiting their exports to our country. If they won't play fair, why should we?

Critics of this argument point out that not only does retaliation harm the country that initially erected trade barriers, but it also harms the country that retaliates. Just as the benefits of trade accrue to both countries, the costs of every reduction in trade are borne by both countries. Some liken retaliation to the situation in which one passenger shoots a hole in a boat and a second passenger, to get even, adds a second hole.

There is, however, one case where retaliation could prove beneficial, and that is where the second country's retaliation proves so onerous that the first country agrees to roll back its trade barriers provided that the second country does likewise. In other words, retaliation could improve the bargaining position of the second country and lead to the eventual elimination of the trade barrier that triggered the retaliation. But this is a risky game to play. The first country may instead respond to the retaliation by erecting additional barriers, further harming both countries. In fact, historically retaliation often leads to trade wars, such as the one that deepened the Great Depression.

INCREASING EMPLOYMENT   Some advocate trade restrictions as a means of expanding a country's employment, and as Table 37.7 shows, trade restrictions have created jobs in protected industries. *But trade restrictions do not increase total employment in the country. Increased employment in protected industries comes at the expense of lower employment in other industries.*

A reduction in foreign cars entering the United States reduces maritime employment in San Francisco and other port cities and eliminates jobs at dealerships selling imported cars. Similarly, import restrictions that force U.S. computer makers to pay three times the world price for computer chips—in order to increase employment in the domestic chip industry—make U.S. computers more costly, thus reducing the number of computers purchased and dragging down employment in the computer industry. Beyond that, if the United States buys less from other countries they in turn have fewer dollars to buy U.S. products. As a consequence, U.S. exports fall, leading to lower employment in export industries. Some studies suggest that trade restrictions actually *reduce* total employment. One such study estimates that each $10 billion in imports costs the United States 179,000 jobs but that an equal volume of exports creates 193,000 jobs, for a net gain of 14,000 jobs.[8] In summary, import restrictions alter the distribution of jobs across industries, but they do not increase employment in the country.

LOW FOREIGN WAGES   Another bogus argument for restricting imports is that U.S. workers cannot compete with cheap foreign labor. Wages average more than $10 per hour in the United States but less than $1 per hour in many developing countries. Given wage differences of this magnitude, how can U.S. workers possibly compete? Unless the United States restricts imports, this argument continues,

---

[8]Richard Belous and Andrew Wyckoff, "Trade Has Job Winners Too," *Across the Board* (September 1987), pp. 53–55.

EXHIBIT 37.1

U. S. automobile producers suffered record losses in 1980. Misreading the market and failing to foresee higher gasoline prices, they continued to produce large cars at a time when consumers wanted smaller, more fuel-efficient vehicles. Because foreign companies were producing the type of vehicles consumers wanted, the import share of the U.S. automobile market zoomed. With the 1980 recession compounding their woes, U.S. automobile producers turned to Congress for relief. What they needed, said automotive executives, was a chance to restructure, time to design a more-efficient fleet of cars—General Motors' chairman suggested two or three years. Once that was accomplished, they assured Congress, automakers would be ready to go head-to-head with foreign producers without government protection.

Because the Japanese were the principal exporter of small cars, bills were introduced in Congress to limit the number of Japanese cars entering the United States. Facing prospects of severe import restrictions, the Japanese government reluctantly entered negotiations with the U.S. government to reduce the number of cars exported to the United States. On May 1, 1981, the two governments announced that Japan would "voluntarily" limit exports to the United States for the next three years. The cap for the first year would be 1.68 million cars, with caps for future years to be negotiated.

As the flow of cars from Japan slowed, waiting lists developed and consumers began offering dealers as much as $2,500 above list price to obtain Japanese cars. Soon the Japanese companies raised car prices and, as they did, their American counterparts followed suit. The U.S. International Trade Commission estimates that the voluntary export restrictions raised the average price of Japanese cars by $185 in 1981, $359 in 1982, $831 in 1983, and $1,300 in 1984. The corresponding increases in domestic car prices were $78, $170, $426, and $659. The commission estimates that, from May

wages in the United States will be driven down to foreign levels, thereby depressing the U.S. standard of living.

A major flaw in this argument is that it neglects productivity differences across countries. Compared to workers in less-developed countries, U.S. workers have more education and training, greater amounts of capital to work with, and more-advanced technologies. Therefore, U.S. workers can produce more output per hour. As long as their greater productivity offsets their higher wages, U.S. workers will not be at a competitive disadvantage.

A simple example illustrates this point. Suppose shoe workers in the United States are paid $8 per hour. If it takes a worker 2 hours to produce a pair of shoes, the labor cost per pair of shoes manufactured in the United States is $16 (see Table

1981 through 1984, U.S. consumers paid an additional $15.8 billion for new cars as a result of export restrictions. An alternative agency, the International Monetary Fund, puts the cost at $17 billion. Despite these studies, Japan was pressured to extend the export restrictions, which it did, although raising the export cap to 1.85 million cars in 1984 and to 2.3 million cars in 1986.

With less competition from Japan and a generally improving economy, profits of U.S. automobile companies soared to record levels in 1988. Chrysler became so profitable that it made its chairman, Lee Iacocca, the country's highest paid executive. The companies had downsized their fleets, dramatically increasing fuel efficiency, and car sales were strong. So in 1988, after seven years of export restrictions and the emergence of a leaner, more-efficient automobile industry in the United States, American automobile companies clearly had the "breathing room" they had requested.

Yet, rather than agree to the elimination of the export restrictions, executives at Ford and Chrysler petitioned for *tougher* restrictions, asking that the number of Japanese cars admitted to the United States be reduced by 26 percent, to 1.7 million vehicles. As a compromise, the 2.3 million cap was left in place. But in 1992, in response to new protectionist pressures, Japan agreed to limit annual exports to the United States to 1.65 million vehicles.

SOURCES: Adapted from Arthur Denzau, *Made in America* (St. Louis: Center for the Study of American Business, 1986); Art Pine, "Study Says Curb on Japan's Cars Lifts U.S. Prices," *The Wall Street Journal*, February 14, 1985, p. 3; Melinda Guiles and Gregory Witcher, "U.S. Auto Makers Are Unhappy," *The Wall Street Journal*, February 1, 1988, p. 34; Christopher Chipello, "Limit on Car Exports to U.S. Is Reduced By Japan but Big Three Aren't Satisfied," *The Wall Street Journal*, March 20, 1992, p. A2.

37.8, page 996). Now suppose workers in Thailand receive $1 per hour but require 16 hours to produce a pair of shoes. Then the labor cost per pair of shoes is also $16. Although wages are 8 times higher in the United States, U.S. productivity is also 8 times higher. Therefore, U.S. shoe workers are not at a competitive disadvantage compared to shoe workers in Thailand.

Of course, productivity differences vary by industry. In the aircraft industry, U.S. workers may be 20 times more productive; in the textile industry, they may be only twice as productive. If wages are 8 times higher in the United States for both industries, the United States and Thailand each gain if the United States exports aircraft to Thailand and imports textiles. Observe that higher textile wages in the United States are not the reason the United States imports textiles—wages in the

A HIGHER WAGE RATE DOES NOT IMPLY HIGHER PRODUCTION COSTS			
COUNTRY	HOURS OF LABOR PER PAIR OF SHOES	LABOR COST PER HOUR (WAGE RATE)	LABOR COST PER PAIR OF SHOES
United States	2	$8	$16
Thailand	16	1	16

The labor cost per pair of shoes is the same in the United States as in Thailand despite a higher wage rate in the United States ($8 versus $1). This is because U.S. workers are more productive, requiring just 2 hours to produce a pair of shoes, rather than 16.

TABLE 37.8

aircraft industry are also higher in the United States, yet the United States exports aircraft. The United States imports textiles because the U.S. productivity advantage in textiles is small whereas the U.S. productivity advantage in the aircraft industry is large. In other words, the United States' comparative advantage lies in the aircraft industry, Thailand's in the textile industry. To shelter U.S. textile workers from competition means forgoing the gains of trade and therefore reducing the standard of living in the United States, not raising it.

Cheap foreign labor has sometimes induced U.S. companies to move their operations to foreign soil, but such moves are not always a success. Unless the wage advantage of foreign workers offsets their productivity disadvantage, labor costs are no lower in foreign countries. Other disadvantages of foreign operations include greater transportation costs to U.S. markets and communications problems. For such reasons, some companies that left the United States in hope of paring costs have since returned (see Exhibit 37.2).

THE NEW THEORY OF MANAGED TRADE

Recently, certain economists have suggested another reason for government intervention in international markets based on cost considerations. Where large-scale production drives down the average cost of output, large producers will gain a cost advantage over small producers and ultimately drive the small producers out of business. In the limit, a single firm may produce all the industry's output for two or more countries. In this situation, the government may find it advantageous to support the domestic industry to make sure that the surviving firm is domestic.

Here the argument is not that the industry is essential for national defense or that the industry needs temporary relief until it matures. Rather, some other benefit accrues to the country that has the surviving firm. Think of it as a prize consisting of profits in excess of those available from alternative uses of the industry's resources. In other words, the surviving firm may be able to earn monopoly profits,

The Train Comes Home

Chesterfield Township, Michigan—When Lionel Trains shut down its sprawling plant here, fired all but five of its 350 factory workers and moved its manufacturing to Tijuana, Mexico, the toy-train maker thought that it was on to a no-lose proposition: 55-cent-an-hour wages. It wasn't. Quality, supply, labor and communications problems made the move a fiasco. Lionel couldn't fill two-thirds of its orders, and complaints poured in from dealers and customers. It wound up with big losses.

Last April, not quite three years later, the company completed its return to this pro-union industrial area 30 miles north of Detroit. It leased back the plant that it had sold and rehired many of its former workers. It's making money again. Gloats the township supervisor, James Pollard: "Here was the industry that left Michigan for the green grass of a foreign country. And it turned out that the grass was brown."

Lionel isn't the only company to find that the pastures of Mexico, Taiwan and other havens of low-cost labor aren't so verdant. While companies in the shoe, textile, clothing and electronics industries continue to go offshore, a handful of companies in industries ranging from high technology to sporting goods are taking another look at manufacturing in the U.S. And some longtime importers are concluding that increased automation and a weaker dollar enable them to manufacture products more cheaply here. Distance adds myriad headaches: Suppliers 10,000 miles away can't fill orders quickly; checking on a production run is tougher; and the long lag between orders and deliveries makes forecasting even dicier than usual.

Lionel dispatched only a few managers in Tijuana with the idea of hiring and training the rest locally. It quickly found that it couldn't, and it wound up spending thousands of dollars a month on air fare and housing to send down engineers. Lionel also didn't foresee the long waiting lists at the Tijuana telephone company; for a year, Lionel had to operate with only two phone lines. Nor did it realize that there were no Mexican subcontractors for important plating processes; it had to shuttle parts to California subcontractors and back. "It started to seem ridiculous," an engineering executive says.

Meanwhile, the problems were causing sales and public-relations nightmares at Michigan headquarters. Lionel could deliver only one-third of its orders, and it lost shelf space to competitors. But Lionel was determined not to lose its 90 percent share of the high-priced collector-train business, and it realized that Tijuana might never make those trains well. So it rehired fifty workers last fall to make them in Michigan. Soon after, the entire train line was back, too.

Note: Lionel Trains Inc., which makes toy trains, should not be confused with Lionel Corp., the giant retailer that filed for bankruptcy in 1991. Lionel Trains was still manufacturing trains in the United States in 1992, employing an estimated 400 workers.

SOURCE: Cynthia Mitchell, "Coming Home: Some Firms Resume Manufacturing in U.S.," *The Wall Street Journal*, October 14, 1986, pp. 1 and 31. Reprinted by permission of *The Wall Street Journal*; © Dow Jones & Company, 1986. All rights reserved.

EXHIBIT 37.2

and the government may be able to "share the prize" by taxing these profits. According to this argument, a country may be able to win more of these international prizes if it pursues a policy of *managed trade* (government intervention to promote certain strategic industries) rather than a policy of free trade.

But even if managed trade offers the potential for gains, there is the question of whether this potential will be realized. Is the government smart enough to pick which industries to support? And once the government starts targeting select industries, won't decisions be colored by political considerations (special-interest pressures)? Exhibit 37.3 (page 1000) examines these issues in detail.

THE POLITICS OF SPECIAL INTERESTS

If trade barriers were erected only where they benefit society (for example, for reasons of national defense), many industries would lose their protection from foreign competition. But, as a practical matter, trade restrictions are often based on political considerations rather than public interest. Even though society in general is harmed, trade restrictions benefit certain groups. For instance, steel workers, their companies, and steel-producing states (such as Pennsylvania) all gain from legislation that keeps foreign steel out of the United States. Because of these gains, they all lobby Congress for protective legislation.

Even though such legislation harms more people than it helps, it is unlikely to meet organized opposition. Consumers—who must pay the higher prices for cars, refrigerators, and other goods that use steel—are unlikely to associate these higher prices with protection for the steel industry. Therefore, they are unlikely to complain about this protection. Higher steel prices also reduce employment in other industries in the United States. According to one study, for each job created in the steel industry as a result of import restrictions, higher steel prices eliminate three jobs in steel-using industries.[9] But the three workers who lose their jobs or are never hired are probably unaware of the cause of their joblessness.

Moreover, those harmed by import restrictions—consumers who must pay the higher prices and workers in other industries who lose their jobs—are widely dispersed throughout the economy. Therefore, even if these consumers and workers are aware of the adverse effects of import restrictions, it is difficult for them to organize and fight such restrictions. In this event, politicians face intense pressure from the steel lobby to keep foreign steel out of the country but little pressure from other groups to let it in. Politicians also realize that by voting for such legislation they are likely to receive the support of a grateful steel industry during the next political campaign while losing few if any votes as a result of protectionist steel legislation (the treatment of steel imports is unlikely to be a high priority for anyone not associated with the steel industry). For such reasons, politicians stand to reap political benefits from the passage of special-interest trade legislation.

Politicians may also have a genuine concern for workers displaced by imports. Even though a more-open trade policy would benefit society as a whole, Congress may want to shield current steel workers from the pain and lost income associated

---

[9]Arthur Denzau, *How Import Restraints Reduce Employment* (St. Louis: Center for the Study of American Business, 1987).

with job loss. But there are less costly ways of accomplishing this than erecting import barriers. Workers who lose their jobs because of imports can be provided job training and placement services and given financial assistance until alternative employment is found. Indeed, various pieces of legislation, including the 1988 Trade Act, contain such provisions. The fact that Congress chooses to erect trade barriers in the face of such trade assistance suggests that political considerations remain a major force in crafting trade legislation.

A History of Tariffs and Other Trade Restrictions

The rate at which imports are taxed has varied widely over time in the United States (see Figure 37.6). The average tariff rate peaked at more than 60 percent fol-

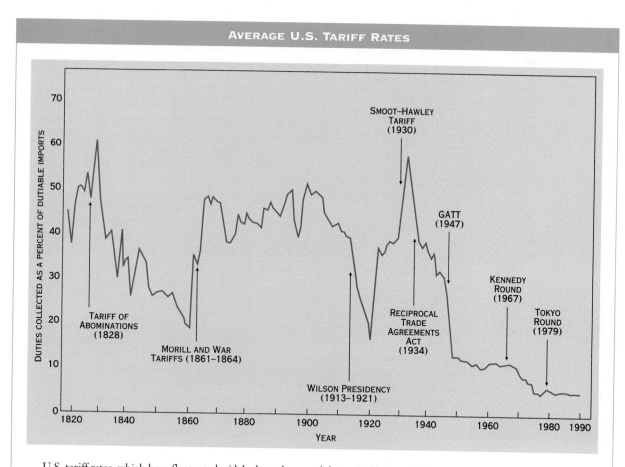

AVERAGE U.S. TARIFF RATES

U.S. tariff rates, which have fluctuated widely, have decreased dramatically since 1930.

SOURCE: U.S. Department of Commerce, *Historical Statistics of the United States* (1976) and *Statistical Abstract of the United States.*

FIGURE 37.6

Managed Trade

Economist Paul Krugman presents the theoretical case for managed trade with an example based on *game theory*.[10] Suppose two companies are capable of producing a certain size of large aircraft—Boeing, from the United States, and Airbus, from the European Community. Further suppose that, because of large startup costs, both companies will suffer losses if they share the market but that either firm, producing alone, will earn large profits. The possibilities are laid out in the first *payoff matrix*, which shows profits for Boeing and Airbus as a function of both firms' production decisions. For example, if both Boeing and Airbus produce aircraft, each will lose $5 billion. But if Boeing alone produces aircraft it will earn $100 billion while Airbus earns zero profit.

Assume that Boeing gets a jump on Airbus and commits itself to production. In that event, the profit-maximizing decision of Airbus is not to enter the market. (Given Boeing's decision to produce, Airbus loses $5 billion if it produces, compared to a zero loss if it does not produce.) This leaves the $100 billion prize to Boeing and the U.S. economy.

Because this outcome is unattractive to Europe, the government of the European Community has an incentive to intervene, for example, by committing a $10 billion subsidy to Airbus before Boeing begins production. Once the subsidy is included, the payoff matrix for Airbus improves (see case 2). Airbus will now produce aircraft regardless of what Boeing does. (Airbus earns $5 billion in profit if Boeing produces and $110 billion if Boeing does not produce.) In turn, knowledge that Airbus is committed to production deters Boeing from proceeding with its plans to produce. The $10 billion subsidy ends up generating $110 billion in profit for Airbus and, given a tax of 10 percent or more on profits, the additional taxes more than cover the cost of the subsidy. In this example, strategic planning by the European government succeeds in transferring the $100 billion prize from the United States to Europe.

Before concluding that the government should become more actively involved in trade policy, several caveats are in order, as Krugman freely acknowledges. First, the analysis assumes accurate information on the part of the government—the government knows what profits at Boeing and Airbus will be with and without government intervention. In reality, such information is not likely to be available. If the government tends to be overly optimistic about the benefits from intervention, it will intervene in cases where the subsidy exceeds the value of the prize, thereby reducing the country's output.

Beyond that, economies of scale (the cost advantages associated with large-scale production) are rarely so extensive that international markets can support only a single firm. Even if a government succeeds in deterring foreign firms from

EXHIBIT 37.3

entering a market, competition among domestic firms could dissipate the monopoly profits. Resources employed by domestic producers in an effort to win the prize increase costs in the industry and therefore reduce or eliminate profits. Again, it is possible that the costs of government intervention exceed the benefits.

Government intervention also raises the concern that decisions will be shaped by the influences of special-interest groups rather than by what is best for the country. At issue is whether government officials, operating in a political environment, are able to do a better job of allocating resources and directing trade than is the marketplace. Historically, such industries as textiles, sugar, and footwear have been favored because of their politi-

cal rather than economic significance. In part because of these concerns, Krugman concludes that even in the presence of economies of scale and imperfect competition:

> Free trade is not passé. . . . It is possible both to believe that comparative advantage is an incomplete model of trade and to believe that free trade is nevertheless the right policy. In fact, this is the position taken by most of the new trade theorists themselves.[11]

[10]Paul Krugman, "Is Free Trade Passé?" *Economic Perspectives* (Fall 1987), pp. 131–144. For an analysis of this article, see *The Economist*, "The Economics of Managed Trade," September 22, 1990, pp. 19–25.

[11]Krugman, same as 10, p. 143.

PAYOFF MATRIX (PROFITS IN BILLIONS OF DOLLARS)

CASE 1: NO SUBSIDY

AIRBUS

BOEING	PRODUCES	DOES NOT PRODUCE
PRODUCES	AIRBUS -5 BOEING -5	AIRBUS 0 BOEING 100
DOES NOT PRODUCE	AIRBUS 100 BOEING 0	AIRBUS 0 BOEING 0

CASE 2: $10 BILLION SUBSIDY TO AIRBUS

AIRBUS

BOEING	PRODUCES	DOES NOT PRODUCE
PRODUCES	AIRBUS 5 BOEING -5	AIRBUS 0 BOEING 100
DOES NOT PRODUCE	AIRBUS 110 BOEING 0	AIRBUS 0 BOEING 0

SOURCE: Krugman, same as fn. 10, p. 136.

lowing the Tariff of Abominations (in 1828) and then moved erratically lower until 1861 when, in an effort to finance the Civil War, it was again raised. Protectionist sentiment remained strong over the next 70 years except for a brief return to more-open trade during the Woodrow Wilson presidency. In 1930, Congress enacted the Smoot–Hawley Tariff, once again pushing the tariff rate above 60 percent. Foreign countries retaliated and U.S. exports plunged. Rather than expanding employment, as its sponsors had promised, the Smoot–Hawley Tariff contributed to the highest unemployment rate in U.S. history.

After being swept into office in 1932, President Franklin Roosevelt pressed Congress to reform trade policy. Congress responded by enacting the Reciprocal Trade Agreements Act of 1934, which gave the president the power to negotiate bilaterally with other countries to reduce tariff rates by as much as 50 percent. The next major development occurred in 1947, when the United States joined 22 other nations in establishing the **General Agreement on Tariffs and Trade** (GATT). With more than 100 nations presently agreeing to abide by its rules, GATT provides a mechanism for resolving trade disputes and negotiating a reduction in trade barriers. Of the various "rounds" of negotiations sponsored by GATT, the Kennedy Round and Tokyo Round were particularly successful in reducing tariff rates. Today the average U.S. tariff rate is close to 5 percent, as low as it has ever been in the country's history.

Although the United States and other countries have moved toward a policy of freer trade over the past 60 years, the decline in the tariff rate overstates the strength of that movement. Other forms of protection, including voluntary export restrictions and antidumping laws, have become more common in recent years.[12] Politicians continue to face pressure from special-interest groups, and much of the public remains ignorant of the costs of trade barriers. Even though the costs to society exceed the benefits, the benefits are more visible.

Another concern of various economists is that GATT may be weakening. The Uruguay Round of negotiations, which began in 1986, was scheduled to end in 1990. But because of bickering, especially over trade restrictions to protect European farmers, negotiations dragged on for years past the deadline. In addition, nations' increased reliance on voluntary export restrictions, red tape to impede imports, and other more subtle trade restraints is making it more difficult for the GATT system to uncover violations of international trade policy.

GATT

An international agreement promoting more-open trade policy and providing the machinery to settle trade disputes among participating nations.

FREE-TRADE AGREEMENTS

The trend in recent years has been for nations to negotiate a reduction in trade barriers either bilaterally, as Canada and the United States did with their 1988 free-trade pact, or as part of a regional agreement. For example, the twelve-nation *European Community (EC)* adopted changes that increased trade flows among member nations effective in 1992 while accelerating social, political, and economic integration. The EC also reached an agreement with the seven-member European Free

---

[12]According to the Institute for International Economics, nontariff trade restrictions reduce world trade by more than $330 billion per year.

FREE-TRADE
AGREEMENT
A pact that removes trade
restrictions among member
nations but leaves in place
restrictions against non-
member nations.

Trade Association (EFTA) that will allow goods to flow freely between the EC and the EFTA beginning in 1993.[13]

Economists are of mixed opinion as to whether such **free-trade agreements** help or hurt the world economy.[14] Removal of trade barriers increases trade among nations covered by a free-trade agreement, and where this leads to more efficient use of resources within the trading bloc the result is a higher level of output. On the other hand, part of the increased trade among member nations comes at the expense of nonmember nations. Where this leads to greater production of a good by a high-cost member of the trading bloc at the expense of a low-cost nonmember, the result is a reduction in world output. (If Spain substitutes high-cost French wheat for low-cost U.S. wheat, the EC promotes a less efficient use of resources.)

The ideal solution, of course, is to reduce trade barriers worldwide, not just in regional trading zones. But recent developments raise concerns about whether global agreements may be increasingly difficult to achieve. In that event, free-trade agreements may become even more prevalent. Consistent with this view, in August 1992 the United States, Canada, and Mexico hammered out terms to the *North American Free Trade Agreement*. The accord, to become effective January 1, 1994, subject to legislative approval, would phase out tariffs over 15 years and otherwise reduce impediments to trade among the three nations. As a result of this treaty, many economists predict that Mexico will soon overtake Japan and become the largest buyer of U.S. exports other than Canada. The United States is also considering free-trade agreements with other countries. Meanwhile, in Europe, the former Soviet republics are establishing ties with the EC and may eventually seek full membership. The fear of some observers is that trading blocs may erect new external barriers, creating "Fortress Europe" and similar arrangements elsewhere. Even proponents of free-trade agreements acknowledge that such developments would be detrimental to economic well-being.

Summary

1. Despite exporting less than 10 percent of its output, the United States, as the world's largest producer, plays a major role in world trade. One-third of all exports come from the United States, Germany, or Japan.

2. Most of the United States' trade is with other industrial countries, including Canada, its largest buyer. The United States is a leading exporter of capital goods and a major importer of petroleum.

---

[13]The EC consists of Belgium, Denmark, France, Germany, Greece, Ireland, Italy, Luxembourg, the Netherlands, Portugal, Spain, and the United Kingdom. Members of the EFTA are Austria, Finland, Iceland, Liechtenstein, Norway, Sweden, and Switzerland. The new nineteen-member organization, known as the European Economic Area, is the world's largest trading bloc.

[14]For the two sides of this debate, see Paul Krugman, "The Move Toward Free Trade Zones," and C. Fred Bergsten, "Commentary: The Move Toward Free Trade Zones," in *Federal Reserve Bank of Kansas City Economic Review* (November/December 1991), pp. 5–35.

3. Although countries sometimes trade to gain access to goods and resources not otherwise available to the country, most trade is based on the principle of comparative advantage. Even if two countries produce the same goods, each can benefit from specializing in the production of that good for which it has a comparative advantage (lower opportunity cost) and then trading this good to the other country. Specialization and trade lead to greater output of each good and therefore to a higher standard of living in each country.

4. Despite the potential gains from trade, nations often restrict imports. Among the major trade barriers are tariffs, import quotas, voluntary export restrictions, and antidumping laws. Each of these barriers reduces imports, leads to higher prices in the domestic country, expands domestic production in the protected industry, and pares domestic consumption of the good. A nonprohibitive tariff also generates revenue for the government.

5. Trade barriers lead to a misallocation of resources, causing a country to divert resources from industries where it enjoys a comparative advantage to industries where it is a relatively high-cost producer. In the United States, trade restrictions cost consumers tens of billions of dollars annually.

6. The national-defense and infant-industry arguments provide two potentially valid reasons for restricting trade. If a nation considers an industry vital for national defense, protection may be warranted despite the cost it imposes on consumers. Protection may also be justified where a nation's emerging (infant) industry is forced to compete with mature industries of other countries. If the industry ultimately will have a comparative advantage once it matures, temporary protection provides the industry time to establish itself and to reduce its costs to the point where it can compete without government assistance.

7. Trade restrictions have also been defended on the basis of increasing employment and sheltering workers from low-wage foreign labor, but these arguments are not valid. Although import restrictions save jobs in protected industries, they reduce employment in other industries—total employment does not increase. The low-wage argument ignores productivity differences across countries. When U.S. workers are more productive, they can compete with lower-paid foreign workers.

8. Some observers suggest that managed trade may be preferable to free trade. Where advantages of large-scale production are important, government policy may determine whether a domestic industry survives and whether the nation receives the economic profits going to the survivor. But even if this is possible in theory, many economists doubt that government can redirect trade in a manner that will actually benefit the nation.

9. Trade barriers often result from political pressure applied by groups that stand to gain from such barriers. Although the social costs of protection exceed its benefits, the costs are less visible and more widely dispersed throughout the country. Therefore, opposition to trade barriers is difficult to organize.

10. The average U.S. tariff rate has fallen from over 60 percent, following the Smoot–Hawley Tariff of 1930, to close to 5 percent today. Although this signals a move to a more-open trade policy, protectionism remains a powerful force. In fact, nontariff barriers have increased in recent years.

11. Free-trade agreements among two or more nations have become increasingly popular in recent years. These agreements may either promote beneficial new trade or divert trade from low-cost nonmember nations to high-cost member nations. As such, their effect on economic well-being is mixed.

trade deficit

prohibitive tariff

trade surplus

nonprohibitive tariff

absolute advantage

import quota

comparative advantage

voluntary export restriction

law of comparative advantage

dumping

terms of trade

protectionism

trading possibilities curve

General Agreement on

free trade

   Tariffs and Trade (GATT)

tariff (duty)

free-trade agreement

Study Questions and Problems

1. Explain why nations trade.

2. Would you expect the United States or Honduras to have an absolute advantage in producing precision machinery? Which is likely to have an absolute advantage in growing bananas? Explain your reasoning.

3. In Korea each unit of labor can produce 2 computers or 4 VCRs. In the United States each unit of labor can produce 3 computers or 5 VCRs. Both countries experience constant costs of production.
   a. Which country has an absolute advantage in producing computers?
   b. Which country has an absolute advantage in producing VCRs?
   c. Within Korea what is the opportunity cost of producing 100 VCRs?
   d. Within the United States what is the opportunity cost of producing 100 VCRs?
   e. Which country has a comparative advantage in producing VCRs?
   f. Which country should specialize in producing VCRs?
   g. Which country should specialize in producing computers?

4. In Canada each unit of a resource can produce either 1 bushel of wheat or 2 boxes of apples.
   a. Assuming that Canada has 1 million units of the resource, draw its production possibilities curve.
   b. If the terms of trade with the United States are 1 bushel of wheat for 3 boxes of apples, should Canada specialize in the production of apples or wheat?
   c. Draw the trading possibilities curve for Canada.

5. How does a sugar quota affect employment in (a) the domestic sugar industry and (b) the domestic candy industry? Justify your answers.

6. In what ways are quotas and nonprohibitive tariffs similar? In what ways are they different?

7. If trade restrictions harm more people than they benefit, why don't voters pressure Congress to remove them?

8. The following diagram shows the supply by U.S. producers and demand by U.S. consumers for wool socks. The world price is $4.

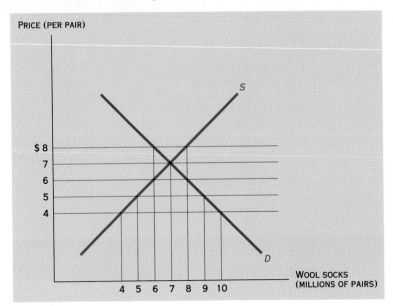

PRICE (PER PAIR)

$8
7
6
5
4

4 5 6 7 8 9 10

WOOL SOCKS
(MILLIONS OF PAIRS)

S

D

a. If there is free trade, how many pairs of wool socks will the United States produce and how many will it import?
b. If a quota of 2 million pairs is established, what will be the price of wool socks in the United States?
c. Given this quota, how many pairs of wool socks will the United States produce and how many will it import?
d. If the quota is replaced with a prohibitive tariff, what will happen to the price of wool socks in the United States?

9. An oil import fee has two things going for it: (a) it reduces U.S. dependence on foreign oil and (b) it increases employment in oil-producing states—and therefore in the country as a whole.

Evaluate this argument. Would taxing oil imports reduce the amount of foreign oil entering the United States? Would it expand total U.S. employment? Explain.

10. During the 1992 presidential campaign, Ross Perot criticized the North American Free Trade Agreement. According to Perot, the treaty will force U.S. companies to move their operations to Mexico to take advantage of lower labor costs there.

If you are running a factory in the United States at United States labor rates, and your identical twin can build a factory in Mexico and pay people a dollar an hour, have little or no health care, . . . there is no way to compete.

Assess Perot's argument.

(A) 100 PAIRS OF SHOES. (B) 100 PAIRS OF SHOES. (C) NO. BECAUSE THE OPPORTUNITY COST IS THE SAME FOR EACH COUNTRY, SPECIALIZATION AND TRADE WOULD NOT BOOST TOTAL OUTPUT OF THE TWO COUNTRIES.

YOUR TURN
Answers

Selected References

Baldwin, Robert. "Are Economists' Traditional Trade Policy Views Still Valid?" *Journal of Economic Literature* (June 1992), pp. 804–829. Analyzes the new theory of international trade.

Bhagwati, Jagdish. *Protectionism* (Cambridge, Mass.: MIT Press, 1988). Eloquent critique of trade restrictions.

Butler, Alison. "Trade Imbalances and Economic Theory: The Case for a U.S.–Japan Trade Deficit," *Federal Reserve Bank of St. Louis Review* (March/April 1991), pp. 16–31. Explains why one country may persistently run a trade deficit with certain countries and trade surpluses with others.

Federal Reserve Bank of Kansas City. *Policy Implications of Trade and Currency Zones*, 1991. Proceedings of a 1991 symposium on free-trade agreements.

Hufbauer, Gary and Kimberly Elliott. *Comparing the Costs of Protection: Europe, Japan, and the United States* (Washington, D.C.: Institute for International Economics, 1993). Estimates the costs of trade restrictions in major world markets.

Krugman, Paul, ed. *Strategic Trade Policy and the New International Economics* (Cambridge, Mass.: MIT Press, 1986). Presents the case for managed trade, arguing that government intervention in trade might under certain conditions benefit a country.

United States International Trade Commission. *International Economic Review*. Monthly publication of the government agency responsible for monitoring international trade; contains data and short articles on trade policy.

THE ACTUAL RATE OF
EXCHANGE IS LARGELY
GOVERNED BY THE
EXPECTED BEHAVIOR
OF THE COUNTRY'S
MONETARY AUTHORITY.

—DENNIS H. ROBERTSON, 1922

The International Financial System

WE HAVE LEARNED THAT TRADE—BE IT LOCAL, INTER-REGIONAL, OR INTERNATION-AL—EXTENDS THE PRINCIPLE OF SPECIALIZATION AND DIVI-SION OF LABOR AND THEREBY PROMOTES HIGHER LIVING STANDARDS. WE ALL BENEFIT FROM A THRIVING INTERNA-TIONAL ECONOMY. ONE OF THE KEY CONSIDERATIONS THAT DIFFERENTIATES INTER-NATIONAL TRADE FROM DOMESTIC TRADE IS THAT DIF-FERENT NATIONS HAVE DIF-FERENT CURRENCIES. IF YOU BUY A KODAK CAMERA MADE IN THE UNITED STATES, THE SELLER WANTS TO BE PAID IN U.S. CURRENCY—DOLLARS. IF YOU PURCHASE A NIKON CAM-ERA FROM JAPAN, THE SELL-ER WANTS TO BE PAID IN THE JAPANESE CURRENCY—YEN. BY THE SAME TOKEN, THE JAPANESE IMPORTER OF LUX-URY U.S. AUTOMOBILES MUST PAY IN DOLLARS.

IN CHAPTER 38, WE STUDY THE FINANCIAL ASPECTS OF INTERNATIONAL ECONOMICS. WE BEGIN BY LOOKING AT THE FOREIGN EXCHANGE MARKET AND ANALYZING THE CAUSES AND CONSEQUENCES OF CHANGING EXCHANGE RATES. THE DEBATE OVER FIXED VER-SUS FLOATING EXCHANGE RATES IS OUTLINED. WE THEN TURN TO A DISCUSSION OF THE INTERNATIONAL ECONOM-IC ACCOUNTS OF A NATION—ITS BALANCE OF PAYMENTS. THE LARGE INTERNATIONAL TRADE DEFICITS OF THE UNIT-ED STATES DURING THE PAST DECADE ARE ANALYZED. WE CONCLUDE THE CHAPTER WITH AN OVERVIEW OF THE INTERNATIONAL DEBT PROB-LEM OF THE LESS-DEVELOPED COUNTRIES (LDCS).

The Foreign Exchange Market

FOREIGN EXCHANGE MARKET

The market in which the currencies of different countries are bought and sold.

FOREIGN EXCHANGE RATE

The amount of another country's money that residents of a country can obtain in exchange for one unit of their own money; the price at which one country's currency may be traded for foreign currency.

CURRENCY DEPRECIATION

A decline in the international value of the currency; the currency buys fewer units of foreign currency.

The **foreign exchange market** is the market in which such national currencies as dollars, yen, deutsche marks, pesos, and lire are exchanged. The price at which such currencies are exchanged is the **foreign exchange rate**. Activity in the foreign exchange market has expanded enormously in recent decades as the result of rapid growth of merchandise trade, tourism, and especially international *capital flows*— acquisition of real and financial assets across national borders. Several major U.S. banks maintain inventories of *foreign exchange* in the form of foreign-denominated currencies held in branch or correspondent banks in foreign cities. Americans generally may obtain this foreign exchange from home town banks that, in turn, purchase it from large New York banks.

A foreign exchange rate exists between each pair of nations that engage in international commerce. A sample of dollar exchange rates for selected foreign currencies at several points in time is illustrated in Table 38.1, where each exchange rate is quoted as the number of units of foreign currency per U.S. dollar. Hence, the exchange rates listed indicate the *value of the U.S. dollar* measured in units of foreign currency. For example, at the end of 1991 the U.S. dollar was exchangeable for 125 Japanese yen and 5.18 French francs. With the exception of the U.S.–England exchange rate, this is the way exchange rates are conventionally quoted in this country. Note, however, that international currency values are reciprocal in nature. If the dollar is worth 125 yen, the yen is equivalent to $0.008 or eight-tenths of a penny. Likewise, if the dollar is worth £0.534, the British pound is valued at $1.87.

As Table 38.1 indicates, exchange rates vary considerably over time. At the end of 1991, for example, the U.S. dollar was worth fewer French francs, Japanese yen, and German deutsche marks than at the end of 1983. The dollar **depreciated**

FOREIGN EXCHANGE RATES WITH THE UNITED STATES FOR SELECTED NATIONS (END-OF-YEAR QUOTATIONS)							
			UNITS OF FOREIGN CURRENCY PER DOLLAR				
COUNTRY	CURRENCY UNIT	SYMBOL	1973	1978	1983	1991	
Austria	Schilling	S	19.9	13.7	19.3	10.7	
Canada	Dollar	$	1.00	1.19	1.24	1.16	
France	Franc	Fr	4.71	4.18	8.34	5.18	
Germany	Deutsche mark	DM	3.20	2.12	2.39	1.52	
Italy	Lira	L	608	830	1660	1151	
Japan	Yen	¥	280	195	232	125	
Mexico	Peso	$	12.5	22.7	144	4419	
Switzerland	Franc	SFr	3.24	1.62	2.18	1.36	
United Kingdom	Pound	£	0.425	0.517	0.637	0.534	

SOURCE: International Monetary Fund, *International Financial Statistics*, 1992.

TABLE 38.1

against the franc, yen, and deutsche mark—meaning that the value of the dollar declined. These foreign currencies **appreciated** (became worth more) against the dollar. On the other hand, the dollar *appreciated* against the Mexican peso in the same period. The peso *depreciated* vis-à-vis the dollar.[1]

Since the early 1970s, most major currencies have been **floating**—exchange rates have been allowed to change from day to day in the marketplace, sometimes by a substantial amount. Prior to the early 1970s, governments aggressively intervened in foreign exchange markets to **fix** or **peg** exchange rates at prearranged levels. The exchange rate is not a matter of indifference to the nations involved. In fact, important disputes have sometimes arisen as a result of the decisions of some nations to intervene to influence the level of the exchange rate. Before we examine the ramifications of changing exchange rates, however, let us analyze the factors that determine the level of the exchange rate at a given point in time and the forces that cause it to change over time.

CURRENCY APPRECIATION

An increase in the international value of the currency; the currency buys more units of foreign currency.

FLOATING EXCHANGE RATES

Exchange rates that are allowed to change continuously in response to market forces of supply and demand.

Exchange Rate Determination in a Regime of Freely Floating Rates

FIXED EXCHANGE RATES

A system in which governments intervene aggressively to keep exchange rates at certain levels rather than permitting them to float in response to market forces.

The foreign exchange market is a good example of a highly competitive market. There are many buyers and sellers, each relatively small compared to the total market. Total *daily* worldwide foreign exchange market transactions typically exceed $900 billion. In a system of *freely floating exchange rates*, governments abstain from intervention in the foreign exchange market and permit exchange rates to be driven entirely by the forces of the free market. Like prices in the wheat market and other auction markets, the impersonal forces of supply and demand determine the exchange rate. Today, even when governments occasionally intervene, the volume of such activity tends to be quite small relative to the amount of private activity.

Consider the determination of the U.S. exchange rate with Japan as illustrated in Figure 38.1 (page 1012). In the analysis we explain the value of the U.S. dollar. In the event we want to find the price of apples, we find out the number of units of money per apple. By the same token, we express the value of the U.S. dollar in terms of the number of units of foreign currency such as yen. The units on the horizontal axis are the quantity of dollars. The vertical axis expresses the value or price of the dollar. The supply and demand curves represent the flow of dollars supplied and demanded each period. In the figure, the supply and demand curves for dollars intersect to determine an equilibrium exchange rate of 130 yen per dollar.

What forces lie behind the supply and demand curves for dollars? The demand for dollars stems from Japanese buyers of American goods and services, U.S. financial assets such as stocks and bonds, and real assets such as land, office buildings, and factories. Because the Japanese buyers must pay for these American items with

---

[1]Because exchange rates are reciprocal in nature and can be quoted either in units of foreign currency per unit of domestic currency or units of domestic currency per unit of foreign currency, one is easily confused. To minimize confusion, think first in terms of the value of the currency in the *denominator* of the quotation. If the U.S.–Japan exchange rate moves from 120 yen/dollar to 130 yen/dollar, the dollar clearly appreciates—it becomes worth more yen. Hence, the yen depreciates against the dollar. If you are told that the U.S.–England exchange rate moves from $1.50/£ to $1.70/£, you can clearly see that the pound appreciates as it becomes worth more dollars. Hence, the dollar depreciates.

The foreign exchange market value of the U.S. dollar relative to the Japanese yen (measured as yen/$) is determined by the forces of supply and demand. In a free-exchange market, the exchange rate fluctuates each day in response to shifts in the supply and demand curves.

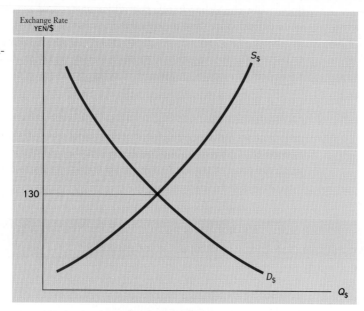

FIGURE 38.1

dollars, they demand U.S. dollars, selling their yen in exchange. The demand curve in Figure 38.1 is downward sloping because, *given all other factors*, a decline in the U.S. dollar makes everything purchased in America cheaper to potential Japanese buyers. For example, if the dollar were to depreciate from 200 yen to 120 yen, a $3 U.S. bushel of wheat would decline in price in Japan from 600 yen to 360 yen (ignoring transportation costs, and so forth).

The supply curve of dollars in Figure 38.1 comes from Americans seeking to purchase Japanese goods and services, financial assets, and real assets. Because Americans must pay for the Japanese transactions in yen, they must sell dollars to obtain yen and finance the transactions. The supply curve of dollars corresponds to a demand curve for yen.[2] The supply curve in Figure 38.1 slopes upward because, *given other factors*, an increase in the value of the dollar (measured in yen) reduces the price of Japanese goods, services, and assets in the United States. A Nikon camera selling for 100,000 yen in Tokyo costs an American $400 if the dollar exchanges for 250 yen but costs $800 if the dollar fetches only 125 yen. Since a stronger dollar

---

[2]One could draw a corresponding figure to accompany Figure 38.1, in which the exchange rate is expressed as $/Yen rather than Yen/$. The horizontal axis would be labeled as Q_{yen} and the supply and demand schedules would be in yen rather than in dollars. The $D_{¥}$ in such a figure would correspond to the $S_{\$}$ in our Figure 38.1—Americans selling dollars to buy yen to make payment in Japan. The $S_{¥}$ in this hypothetical figure would be related to the $D_{\$}$ in our Figure 38.1—Japanese selling yen to buy dollars to make payment in the United States. The equilibrium exchange rate in this hypothetical figure, given the equilibrium rate in Figure 38.1 of 130¥/$, would be $.00769/¥.

reduces the cost of Japanese items to Americans, we tend to respond to a higher dollar by supplying more dollars to finance enlarged purchases.[3]

Forces Causing Changes in Exchange Rates

Price changes in competitive markets are precipitated by shifts in supply and demand curves. Any factor that results in a shift in the supply or demand curve of Figure 38.1 produces a change in the U.S.–Japan exchange rate. Fundamental factors causing shifts in the supply and demand curves and thereby inducing changes in exchange rates include changes in relative price levels, income levels, and real interest rates among the countries involved. Also, changes in consumer preferences and development of new products for export markets can initiate changes in supply and demand curves in foreign exchange markets, thereby producing a change in exchange rates. Speculators' anticipations of forthcoming changes in these fundamental factors also influence current exchange rates. In the long run, these preferences, product development, and relative price level behavior in nations are powerful forces that influence the exchange rate. In the medium run, relative income levels of nations are important, and relative interest rate behavior seems to exert a powerful short-run influence on the exchange rate. Hour-to-hour and day-to-day exchange-rate movements are often precipitated by activity of foreign-exchange market speculators.

RELATIVE PRICE LEVEL BEHAVIOR AND EXCHANGE RATES

Assume the United States–Japan exchange rate is initially 130 yen/$, with supply and demand curves for dollars ($S_\$^1$ and $D_\$^1$) intersecting at A in Figure 38.2 (page 1014). Now assume the price level increases by 20 percent in Japan but remains constant in the United States. Clearly, American goods and services are now relatively more attractive to both Japanese and Americans at each and every exchange rate. The increased willingness of the Japanese to purchase American items shifts the demand curve for dollars from $D_\$^1$ to $D_\$^2$. This would move the equilibrium to B in the figure, indicating an appreciation of the dollar (depreciation of the yen). Also, because American goods now look relatively more attractive to Americans at each and every exchange rate, the willingness to import from Japan is reduced and the supply curve of dollars decreases—shifts leftward from $S_\$^1$ to $S_\$^2$. This indicates

[3]Technically, this assumes that American demand for Japanese products is relatively elastic with respect to the price in dollars. If, instead, we continue to purchase roughly the same amount of Japanese items in spite of a lower dollar price to Americans owing to a stronger dollar, we would actually need to supply fewer dollars at higher exchange rates. In the short run, the supply curve may be negatively sloped because people do not respond fully at once to a more favorable price. In the longer run, economists believe the supply curve is upward sloping as illustrated because American demand for imported goods and services is highly responsive to the price in dollars.

When prices rise faster in Japan than in the United States, the demand for dollars increases, the supply of dollars decreases, and the dollar appreciates (rises in value) against the yen.

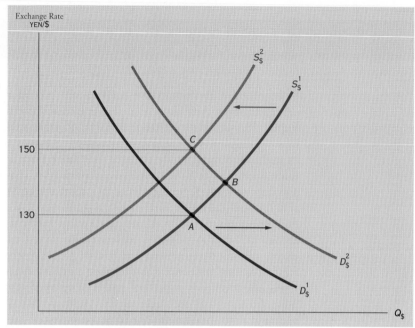

FIGURE 38.2

a further appreciation of the dollar, the new equilibrium being at *C* in the figure and the exchange rate reaching 150 yen per dollar.

The analysis suggests that countries with high inflation will experience depreciation of their currencies in the foreign exchange market. Indeed, the two countries depicted in Table 38.1 that exhibited the most rapid inflation from 1973 to 1991—Mexico and Italy—also experienced the most severe depreciation of their currencies against the dollar in that period. Mexico, which experienced extremely high inflation, saw the peso lose more than 99 percent of its value vis-à-vis the U.S. dollar in that period. Equivalently stated, the U.S. dollar appreciated more than a hundredfold against the Mexican peso.

PURCHASING POWER PARITY THEORY (PPP) Theory that the exchange rate between any two national currencies adjusts to reflect changes in the relative price levels in the two nations.

THE PURCHASING POWER PARITY THEORY (PPP) Building on the preceding analysis, the **purchasing power parity theory (PPP)** postulates that exchange rates adjust to offset different rates of inflation in two countries. If the U.S.–Japan exchange rate is initially in equilibrium at 150 yen/\$ and the U.S. price level then doubles relative to the price level in Japan, PPP theory predicts that the dollar will depreciate sufficiently to restore purchasing power parity. That is, PPP predicts the dollar will depreciate by 50 percent (that is, fall by half) to a level of 75 yen per dollar. If the dollar fell by less than 50 percent, Japanese products would look more attractive relative to American products—both to Japanese and to Americans—than was the case prior to the price level disturbance. American imports from Japan would increase and U.S. exports to Japan would decline, exerting downward pressure on the U.S. dollar until it had restored purchasing power parity by declining 50 percent.[4]

Under highly restrictive and very unrealistic conditions, PPP would always precisely hold. Suppose only two countries exist—the United States and Turkey. Suppose these nations produce one homogeneous product for export—wheat. Suppose wheat costs $3 per bushel in the United States and 3,000 lire per bushel in Turkey. Then the U.S.–Turkey exchange rate must be 1,000 lire per dollar. The wheat must cost the same to an American or a Turk whether purchased at home or abroad. Otherwise, one country's wheat industry would be forced out of business. If American wheat were to rise to $6 per bushel while Turkish wheat remains at 3,000 lire, the dollar would depreciate from 1,000 lire to 500 lire. This example reflects the fundamental intuition behind PPP theory.

Adapting this framework to the real world, we must recognize that many products are not homogeneous in nature. When the dollar falls and Toyotas become more expensive relative to Fords, Americans continue to purchase Toyotas (though presumably in reduced quantities) because of perceived quality differences and other reasons. Also, a nation's price level includes many nontradeable goods and services, whereas only tradeable items are strictly relevant to PPP. Prices of tradeable and nontradeable goods do not necessarily move together over time. In episodes of severe inflation, PPP theory seems to work well in accounting for exchange-rate movements. For example, the U.S. dollar depreciated sharply against the deutsche mark and yen in the late 1970s because the U.S. inflation rate considerably exceeded that of Germany and Japan. However, in the low-inflation environment of the 1980s, PPP pretty much collapsed as an explanation of exchange-rate movements. As an example, from 1980 to 1985, the U.S. dollar *appreciated* strongly against the yen and mark. PPP would have called for a modest *depreciation* of the dollar in that period inasmuch as U.S. inflation was slightly greater than that of Japan and Germany. Then, in 1985 through 1988, the dollar fell sharply, even though PPP would have called for a very modest decline. PPP clearly broke down in the 1980s, and you will understand why from the analysis that follows. Don't count PPP out yet, though! It is likely to stage a comeback the next time severe inflation rears its ugly head.

RELATIVE INCOME LEVELS AND EXCHANGE RATES

Assume output and income in the United States rise while in Germany they remain stagnant. American demand for goods and services, both domestically produced and imported, expands while German demand remains flat. As a result, the U.S.

---

[4]Hence, PPP implies that domestic inflation does not impair a nation's long-run competitive position in world markets if freely floating exchange rates prevail. The exchange rate is alleged to move precisely to compensate for inflation differences among nations, thus leaving each nation's products relatively unchanged in price in foreign markets. If—when U.S. prices double and an American Buick increases in price from $25,000 to $50,000—the dollar falls from 3 deutsche marks to 1.5 deutsche marks, the Buick continues to sell for 75,000 DM in Germany. Suppose in Germany, where the price level remains constant, a Mercedes-Benz sells for 90,000 DM. The decline in the U.S. dollar raises its price in the United States from $30,000 to $60,000—the same percentage price increase experienced by the Buick and other U.S. goods.

dollar tends to depreciate against the deutsche mark. Paradoxically, growth of domestic income leads to a weaker currency *if other factors are held constant.*[5] This principle is illustrated in Figure 38.3.

Initially, supply and demand curves for dollars are represented by $S_\$^1$ and $D_\$$, with equilibrium at A and the exchange rate at 1.60 deutsche marks per dollar. Then U.S. income growth induces Americans to purchase more imported goods as well as domestic goods. To purchase more German goods, Americans must sell more dollars for marks. The $S_\$$ curve shifts rightward to $S_\$^2$, moving the equilibrium to B. In Figure 38.3, the dollar depreciates to 1.40 deutsche marks. Because German income is constant, German demand for U.S. goods and services remains unchanged. Hence, the demand curve for dollars in the figure remains unchanged. The expansion in relative U.S. income causes a depreciation of the dollar and an

RELATIVE INCOME GROWTH LEADS TO CURRENCY DEPRECIATION

When other factors remain constant, an increase in U.S. income causes the dollar to depreciate. The increase in American income shifts the supply curve of dollars rightward as Americans seek to purchase more German goods.

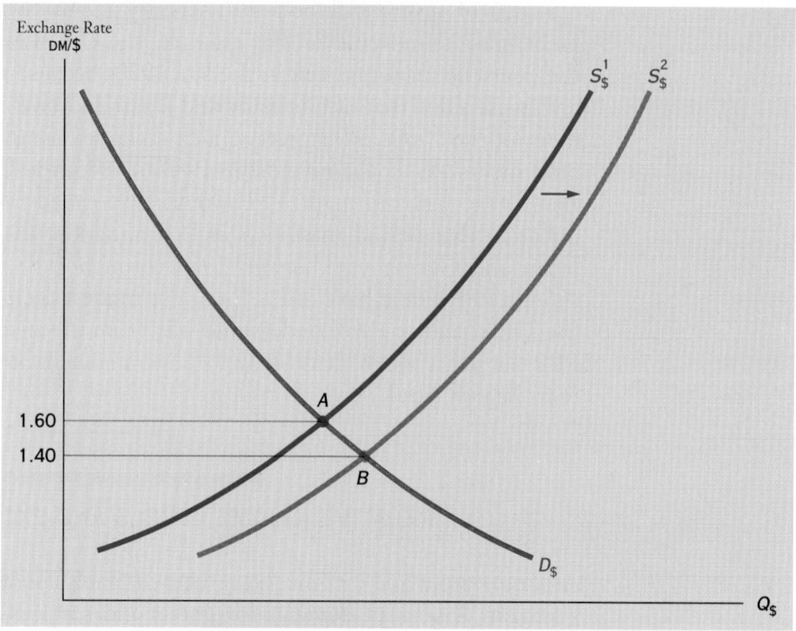

FIGURE 38.3

[5]However, we must qualify this point. Quite often, strong income growth leads to an increase in real interest rates as domestic demand for loans escalates and the central bank moves to tighten credit to restrain economic activity. As we shall see, higher real interest rates tend to cause currency *appreciation* by attracting foreign funds to purchase the high-yielding domestic securities. Hence, we can say that relative income growth leads to currency depreciation *unless* it also leads to higher relative real interest rates. Other things equal, higher income growth leads to currency depreciation—but in the real world other things are not always equal.

increase in the U.S. international trade deficit as imports into the United States expand.[6]

Between 1985 and 1988, the U.S. experienced a declining dollar accompanied by a burgeoning deficit in our trade balance (exports minus imports). This was partially attributable to the fact that U.S. income expanded more rapidly than the income of such major trading partners as Japan and Germany. During this period the Reagan Administration became quite concerned about the falling dollar and the huge trade deficit. Rather than deliberately introducing contractionary policies in the United States to reduce income and thereby help arrest the falling dollar, U.S. officials pleaded with Japan and European nations to stimulate their domestic economies. In terms of Figure 38.3, such measures would raise the demand curve for dollars and thereby strengthen the dollar in foreign exchange markets. At the same time, such measures would stimulate American exports, thereby reducing the American trade deficit.

RELATIVE REAL INTEREST RATES AND EXCHANGE RATES

In recent years, changes in relative interest rates among countries—especially changes in *real* (inflation-adjusted) interest rates—have played an increasingly important role in precipitating changes in exchange rates. There exists a huge pool of liquid funds (so-called "hot money") that has grown enormously in the past 20 years. These funds are owned by banks, other financial and nonfinancial firms, and wealthy individuals eager to invest such funds in the financial centers exhibiting the most attractive rates of return. As relative real rates of return among nations change, these funds are likely to be shifted from nation to nation.[7] To illustrate the effect of a change in real interest rates upon the U.S.-France exchange rate, consider Figure 38.4 (page 1018).

Suppose initially we are at A in Figure 38.4, the exchange rate being 5 francs per dollar. Suppose the American central bank—the Federal Reserve—tightens credit and raises interest rates (nominal and real) in the United States. To take advantage of more attractive yields here, French investors buy an increased amount of U.S. securities. This increases the demand for dollars to $D_\$^2$, which would move

---

[6]If German income expanded in line with U.S. income, the demand curve for dollars would shift rightward as Germans stepped up their purchases of American items. Hence, both the supply and demand curves in Figure 38.3 would increase over time (shifting rightward) and the exchange rate and the U.S. trade balance with Germany would remain approximately unchanged.

[7]Actually, a rational investor must consider the change in the exchange rate that is likely to occur while the funds are invested as well as the yield differential in deciding the most profitable country in which to invest. If a country is expected to experience significant depreciation of its currency in the exchange market because of domestic inflation or other reasons, it may have difficulty attracting investors (foreign or domestic) even if its yields are considerably higher than those in other nations. Would an American investor have done well buying Mexican securities yielding 30 percent in 1983 (see Table 38.1)? It is the differential between the yield available in country X and the expected annual net-percentage-exchange market depreciation of the currency of country X that the rational investor must focus on and compare with similar measures for countries Y and Z. If U.S. securities are yielding 2 percent more than German securities but the dollar is expected to depreciate against the deutsche mark at an annual rate of 2 percent, American and German investors are indifferent between U.S. and German securities.

An increase in American real interest rates increases the demand for dollars as foreigners seek to purchase American bonds and other interest-bearing assets. Also, the supply of dollars shifts leftward as Americans become less interested in foreign securities. Through these forces, higher American real interest rates cause the dollar to appreciate.

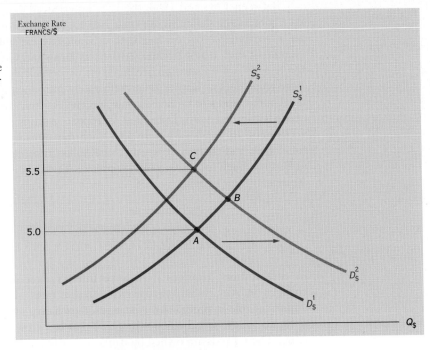

FIGURE 38.4

the equilibrium to *B* in the figure, causing the dollar to appreciate. Also, American investors become less inclined to purchase French securities. Hence, they offer fewer dollars for francs, and the supply curve in the figure decreases to $S_\$^2$. The new equilibrium is at *C*, the dollar having appreciated to 5.5 francs because of the increase in real American yields.[8] Higher real interest rates, given other factors, make for a strong currency in the foreign exchange market.

The volume of financial capital ("hot money") worldwide has expanded more rapidly in recent decades than has the volume of import and export activity. This may help to explain the increased responsiveness of exchange rates to real interest rate differentials. It may also help to account for the weakening of PPP as a factor in exchange-rate movements after the 1970s. The other factor accounting for the decline in PPP is the fact that inflation has been relatively subdued since the 1970s throughout the world. Since price levels among nations have not diverged as much

[8]If interest rates increase solely because of higher expected inflation, there is no increase in real interest rates and probably no additional net capital inflow and no appreciation of the dollar. The higher nominal rate of return is roughly offset by expected depreciation of the dollar. Much of the change in relative interest rates in countries exhibiting modest inflation in recent years has been real rather than nominal, however. When U.S. interest rates declined sharply in 1991 and 1992, most of the decline was reflected in lower real interest rates. This helped to account for a severe depreciation of the U.S. dollar.

in recent years as in the 1970s, other factors have naturally assumed increased relative importance in explaining exchange-rate movements.

SPECULATION AND EXCHANGE-RATE MOVEMENTS

FOREIGN-EXCHANGE MARKET SPECULATORS Individuals and firms that buy and sell foreign currencies with the intent of profiting from exchange-rate movements.

Intraday and day-to-day exchange-rate movements are often driven by speculative transactions. **Speculators** buy or sell foreign currencies solely to profit from exchange-rate changes. Speculators are often exporters, importers, and others who want foreign currencies for fundamental reasons but alter the *timing* of their foreign exchange transactions in expectation that the exchange rate will move in a certain direction. Suppose a U.S. exporter of mainframe computers receives payments denominated in French francs. If the exporter expects the franc to rise (appreciate) against the dollar in the next week, the exporter may wait to convert the francs to dollars. If so, this exporter is acting as a speculator.

Speculators essentially attempt to forecast movements in the factors that drive exchange rates and then act upon these forecasts. For example, if speculators believe the U.S. dollar will fall because of an impending increase in U.S. inflation not yet recognized by the market, the speculators sell dollars now, hoping to repurchase them later at a lower price. Likewise, if news is released indicating that U.S. real interest rates are likely to rise, speculators purchase dollars immediately in hopes of selling them after they appreciate. Each hour of the day, as relevant new information is released, speculators seize upon the information to forecast likely future exchange-rate movements and place their bets accordingly.

There is some disagreement about the effects of currency speculation on the stability of foreign exchange rates. Some economists believe such speculation destabilizes markets by causing sharp, disruptive exchange-rate movements not attributable to fundamental factors. Other economists point out that if speculators correctly forecast the direction of the fundamental factors driving exchange rates, they simply take actions that move the exchange rate in the direction it is bound to move in any event. If so, speculators are really serving to smooth exchange-rate movements. Nevertheless, central banks around the world have frequently intervened in foreign exchange markets in recent years in an attempt to prevent disruptive exchange-rate changes not believed to be justified by fundamental considerations. For example as the U.S. dollar depreciated to a 47-year low against the deutsche mark in August 1992, central banks purchased billions of dollars with foreign currencies in order to support the dollar and hold down the surging deutsche mark.

YOUR TURN

How Interest Rates Affect Exchange Rates

SUPPOSE THE GERMAN CENTRAL BANK (THE BUNDESBANK) SURPRISES FINANCIAL MARKETS BY SHARPLY RAISING ITS DISCOUNT RATE (THAT IS, THE INTEREST RATE IT CHARGES GERMAN COMMERCIAL BANKS). ANALYZE THE IMPACT OF THIS ANNOUNCEMENT ON THE U.S.–GERMAN EXCHANGE RATE, EXPRESSED AS DEUTSCHE MARKS PER DOLLAR.

AN ANALYSIS OF THE GYRATING DOLLAR, 1973–1992

The *dancing dollar* has experienced innumerable short-term movements in recent years. More significantly, there were three major sustained swings of the dollar between 1973 and 1992, as illustrated in Figure 38.5. These swings include the substantial depreciation of the dollar during the late 1970s, the sustained bull market in the dollar during the first half of the 1980s, and the sharp fall of the dollar between 1985 and 1988. Using our new framework of analysis, we now attempt to

GYRATIONS OF THE U.S. DOLLAR, 1973–1992

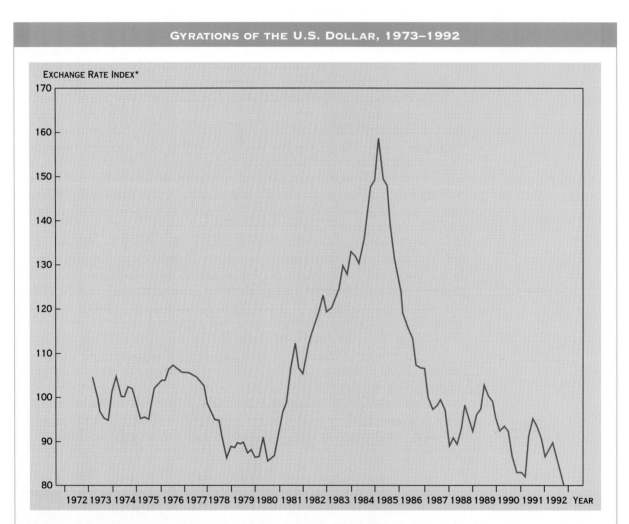

Relative to a currency index for ten of our trading partners, the U.S. dollar depreciated in the late 1970s. The dollar appreciated dramatically from late 1980 until early 1985, then fell again between 1985 and 1992. In the early 1990s, the dollar traded at levels similar to those experienced in 1979 and 1980.

*A multilateral trade-weighted value of the U.S. dollar against currencies of the G-10 countries (United Kingdom, Germany, Japan, France, Canada, Italy, the Netherlands, Belgium, Sweden, and Switzerland; March 1973 = 100).

SOURCE: Board of Governors of the Federal Reserve System.

FIGURE 38.5

account for these three major swings in exchange rates. (On the more recent decline of the dollar to new all-time lows, see Exhibit 38.2 on page 1026–1027.)

THE GREAT DEPRECIATION OF 1976–1979 The American inflation rate ratcheted upward from less than 2 percent in 1964 to double-digit levels by 1980. Several events in this period contributed to the massive increase in the underlying rate of inflation. These include the overheating of the U.S. economy associated with the escalation of the Vietnam War (1965–1969), two dramatic increases in the price of imported oil (1974 and 1979), and an excessively stimulative U.S. monetary policy in the late 1970s. By the late 1970s, money supply growth was surging and inflation was solidly in the double-digit range. Because inflation was more subdued in most other nations, PPP theory predicts that the dollar should have fallen—and it did! By the end of the decade of the 1970s, the dollar stood at roughly 1.8 German deutsche marks, 240 Japanese yen, and 1.60 Swiss francs—down sharply from 1970 quotations of 3.65 deutsche marks, 358 yen, and 4.30 francs, respectively. American real interest rates were low (usually negative) and falling as inflation escalated in the late 1970s. Also, U.S. income was rising strongly as we approached the peak of the business cycle at the end of the decade. It is clear that the three fundamental factors (relative inflation rates, income levels, and real interest rates) do an excellent job of tracking the depreciation of the U.S. dollar in the late 1970s.

THE BULL MARKET IN THE DOLLAR, 1980–1985 In the early 1980s, the United States experienced a dramatic increase in interest rates, which remained well above 10 percent for several years. At the same time, the U.S. inflation rate came down much faster than anyone had expected (12 percent in 1980 to about 4 percent by early 1983). As a result, real interest rates swung dramatically upward from the negative rates of the late 1970s to virtually unprecedented positive levels of 6 to 10 percent in the early 1980s. This increase in real interest rates helped to trigger a large net inflow of capital into U.S. financial markets. Part of the upsurge in real interest rates was probably due to the burgeoning federal budget deficits of the early 1980s. In addition, in early 1981, the first Reagan Administration inaugurated a pro-business agenda that contributed to the improving perception of America as an excellent environment in which to invest. Also contributing to the capital inflow was the deterioration of economic and political conditions in Latin America and the consequent emergence of the United States as a relatively *safe haven* in which to invest.

In its latter stages, the rising dollar was probably boosted to unrealistically high levels by the *bandwagon effect*, in which speculators sometimes contribute to excessive movements in exchange rates by purchasing currencies that have already appreciated strongly because of fundamental factors. By early 1985, the U.S. dollar had risen by more than 60 percent on average compared to its 1979–1980 levels. As a predictor of exchange rates, PPP collapsed in this period. Although the U.S. inflation rate was subdued in the 1982–1985 period, it remained higher than that of most of our trading partners. Hence, PPP called for a modest depreciation of the dollar. Also, because domestic income grew much faster in the United States than in other industrial countries between 1983 and 1985, this also should have depreciated the dollar. Instead, we got an enormous *rise* in the dollar—and must look to the massive net capital inflow caused by high real American interest rates for the explanation.

Many factors can motivate speculators to turn bullish or bearish on a particular currency in the foreign exchange market. It is interesting to note how the particular information deemed most crucial by such speculators changes over time.

In the late 1970s, U.S. inflation was raging and many questioned the extent to which the U.S. government was willing to pay the price to defeat it. Each month, foreign exchange speculators watched for the release of the official price indexes—the Consumer Price Index, the Producer Price Index, and the GDP deflator. In the 1970s, purchasing power parity theory (PPP) provided a fairly reliable model for exchange-rate movements. If the monthly price indexes revealed that inflation was running higher than expected, speculators would immediately sell dollars on the basis that import and export activity would ultimately produce a depreciation of the dollar.

During the 1980s, PPP broke down as a reliable tracker of exchange-rate movements. Capital flows based on real interest rate levels assumed a larger role in explaining exchange rates. In late 1979, the Fed moved to a policy of targeting money supply growth at relatively low rates, allowing interest rates to seek whatever levels were compatible with the modest growth of the money supply. Speculators turned their attention to the weekly money supply announcement that flashed across the ticker at 2:00 p.m. EST each Thursday. If the announced money supply exceeded market expectations, speculators anticipated a tightening of Fed policy to get back on the money target. This suggested that interest rates (nominal and real) would have to rise, thus inducing an inflow of capital and an appreciation of the dollar. Hence, speculators purchased dollars immediately upon the announcement, causing the dollar to firm up quickly. If the money supply announcement came in below expectations, speculators immediately sold dollars to take advantage of an expected easing of monetary policy and a resulting decline in U.S. interest rates and the U.S. dollar.

By the mid-1980s, the Fed had abandoned its experiment with monetarism and speculators had abandoned their fascination with the money supply. In this period (1983–1987) the U.S. trade deficit increased sharply—chiefly in response to the enormous 1981–1985 appreciation of the U.S. dollar and the faster growth of income in America relative to Europe and developing nations. After early 1985, the dollar began to depreciate in foreign exchange markets. However, in 1986 and 1987, the trade deficit continued to grow in spite of the falling dollar. Speculators focused attention on the monthly release of information revealing the most recent trade figures. If the trade deficit figure came in larger than expected, speculators would dump dollars in anticipation that a further depreciation in the dollar would be required in order to turn around our trade deficit. In January 1988, when the new figures showed an unexpectedly large decline in the trade deficit, the dollar rallied sharply as speculators turned bullish on the dollar en masse.

Based on your observation of the evening news and your reading of the daily newspaper, what chief indicators are the foreign exchange market speculators watching this year?

EXHIBIT

38.1

THE FALL IN THE DOLLAR, 1985–1988 The rapid depreciation of the dollar between 1985 and 1988 cannot be explained fully by the three fundamental factors. Inflation remained quite subdued in the United States, so PPP forces can only account for a very minor portion of the dollar's depreciation. Stronger income growth in the U.S. than in other nations helps to account partially for the falling dollar. Also, the yield differential favoring the United States, though still positive, declined. After 1986, the falling dollar seems to have been driven significantly by speculative forces responding to several seemingly intractable problems in the United States. The U.S. trade deficits increased rapidly after 1983 and the United States emerged for the first time in seventy years as a net debtor in global financial markets—our obligations to foreigners exceeding our assets abroad. A growing awareness of the lack of political will in this country to come to grips with the large structural budget deficit may have contributed to the speculative attack on the dollar. By late 1987 and early 1988, the second Reagan Administration became concerned that the dollar was falling too rapidly and perhaps too far. The United States arranged for international cooperation among central banks to support the dollar and limit its depreciation. In 1987, for example, governments collectively purchased approximately $100 billion of U.S. currency in foreign exchange markets to prevent additional weakness in the dollar.

Consequences of Exchange-Rate Changes

Changes in exchange rates may significantly affect a nation's standard of living and such key macroeconomic variables as the unemployment rate and the inflation rate. Moreover, changes in exchange rates may affect income distribution, helping certain groups in society while simultaneously impairing others. For these reasons, nations are sometimes reluctant to accept changes in exchange rates, even when they are dictated by the fundamental forces analyzed in this chapter. We now consider the consequences of currency appreciation and depreciation.

EFFECTS OF THE STRONG DOLLAR, 1980–1985

There were both positive and negative influences stemming from the sustained appreciation of the U.S. dollar. On the positive side, the rising dollar unleashed powerful disinflationary forces that helped to bring down the U.S. inflation rate from more than 12 percent in 1980 to less than 4 percent between 1983 and 1986. Appreciation of the dollar reduces the cost in dollars of imports into the United States. To the extent that imports enter into our price indexes, this directly reduces the U.S. price level. More important, it places increased pressure on U.S. manufacturing firms to hold down wages and prices in order to remain competitive in world markets. Concurrently, a strong dollar—by making foreign products look attractive to Americans and by raising the prices of American products abroad—redirects some of the demand for American products to products produced abroad. This effect is often considered disadvantageous because it worsens our trade deficit and increases our unemployment rate. A positive side effect, however, is that it helps to reduce U.S. inflation by reducing aggregate demand for American goods and services.

The masses of American consumers experience an improvement in their standard of living because of the availability of cheaper foreign-produced goods. The **U.S. terms of trade**—the ratio of the price of U.S. exports to the price of U.S. imports—improves as each unit of our exports pays for a larger amount of imported goods.[9] American tourists abroad benefit as the dollar purchases more units of foreign currencies. Those Americans engaged in import businesses reap an obvious gain as the American cost of foreign items declines.

On the other hand, there are many people—some domestic, some foreign—who suffer from a strong dollar. American losers are concentrated in the U.S. export- and import-competing industries. Examples include workers and firms in the auto, steel, textile, heavy machinery, computer, and agricultural sectors. It was estimated that more than a million American workers lost their jobs during 1983–1985 because of the strong dollar. This led to powerful sentiment in the United States for legislation restricting the free flow of imports into this country. In addition, some U.S. firms relocated production facilities from domestic to foreign locations to benefit from the greater purchasing power of the dollar abroad.

The strong dollar of 1980–1985 also had negative implications for foreign nations. To prevent their currencies from falling excessively against the dollar, many European nations maintained interest rates at higher levels than they normally would have preferred. As a result, economic activity in Europe was abnormally sluggish for several years following the worldwide recession of 1981–1983. Unemployment remained above 10 percent in some European nations until the late 1980s. Because OPEC requires that oil payments be made in dollars, the booming dollar boosted oil prices sharply for many oil-importing countries. This created an effect similar to (though somewhat milder than) the shocks administered by the OPEC oil price hikes of the 1970s. Finally, LDC debtor nations such as Brazil and Mexico, whose debts are denominated in dollars, found it more difficult to meet payments on their debts because of the high cost of the dollar.

TERMS OF TRADE
The ratio of the average price of a country's exports to the average price of its imports (both prices measured in units of domestic currency).

EFFECTS OF THE FALLING DOLLAR, 1985–1988

By raising the cost of imports, reducing the pressure on American industries to hold the line on wages and prices, and raising foreign (and American) demand for

---

[9]A nation's terms of trade are defined as the ratio of the price of its exports divided by the price of its imports, both measured in units of domestic currency. When the U.S. dollar appreciates, the dollar price of U.S. wheat in America stays the same while the dollar price of an imported Toyota falls. Fewer bushels of American wheat are needed to purchase one imported Toyota. This favorable change in the U.S. terms of trade associated with a rising dollar increases the overall American standard of living.

"You hate me when I'm strong and despise me when I'm weak."

By permission of Bill Mauldin and Wil-Jo Associates.

U.S. goods and services, a depreciation of the U.S. dollar tends to stimulate inflationary forces.[10]

U.S. export- and import-competing industries are stimulated by a falling dollar, though with a significant time lag. Beginning in 1988, U.S. exports began to increase strongly. This led to a welcome revival in the long-depressed U.S. manufacturing sector. By the early 1990s, the U.S. trade deficit was sharply lower than its 1986–1988 levels.

---

[10]It should be noted that the consequences of a rising dollar are not perfectly symmetrical with the effects of a falling dollar. As the dollar declined following early 1985, tending to place Japanese exporters at a disadvantage in selling to U.S. markets, many Japanese manufacturing firms reduced prices (in yen) to offset the rising cost of the yen to Americans. These Japanese firms were sometimes willing to reduce profit margins sharply to protect established markets. Hence, even though the dollar fell against the yen by roughly 50 percent from the second half of 1984 to the beginning of 1988, Japanese-made Hondas and Toyotas increased in price only by about 20 percent in U.S. markets. The halving of the value of the dollar against the yen would have doubled the U.S. price of these cars if the Japanese automobile manufacturers had neither implemented cost-cutting measures nor accepted lower profit margins on their cars.

EXHIBIT

38.2

The Falling Dollar of 1992— How It Played in Europe and the United States

In 1991 and 1992, a huge discrepancy developed between the level of short-term interest rates in Germany and the United States. Because the inflation rate in Germany was only about one percentage point higher than that in the United States, the differential in nominal interest rates was reflected in a similar differential in *real* rates.

U.S. short-term interest rates plunged first in response to the recession of 1990–1991, and then because of the anemic recovery that followed the recession and efforts by the Federal Reserve to ease credit conditions to bolster the flagging economy in 1991 and 1992. By the late summer of 1992, American short-term interest rates reached approximately 3 percent—the lowest levels in about 30 years. At the same time, German interest rates moved up from approximately 8 percent in 1990 to nearly 10 percent in September 1992. This occurred chiefly because of efforts by the Bundesbank (the German central bank) to stem incipient inflationary pressures resulting from the enormous costs associated with the unification of the two Germanies in 1990.

With German short-term interest rates three times as high as those in the United States, and with investors worldwide apprehensive about investing in American stocks and bonds, the incentive to move funds from New York to Frankfurt was irresistible. The dollar plunged during the spring and summer of 1992, reaching all-time lows against the German mark by August.

With a stagnant U.S. economy, and with record-breaking budget deficits in place, there was little the U.S. government was willing and able to do to halt the slide of the dollar. The Fed was reluctant to push up short-term rates because the economic recovery was already listless, the unemployment rate remaining above 7.5 percent in the summer of 1992. In late August, the Fed and 15 other central banks (mostly European) purchased dollars directly in the foreign exchange market in an effort to keep the dollar's decline orderly. Clearly, the Bush Administration—campaigning for re-election in November 1992—preferred an orderly decline in the dollar to having the Fed risk aborting the fledgling recov-

The masses of American consumers are hurt by the falling dollar as the array of cheap foreign autos, electronics goods, and other imports are stripped away. The increased cost of imports (and domestic goods) tends to reduce real wages and the standard of living of Americans. The decline in the dollar adversely affects the U.S. terms of trade as more bushels of U.S. wheat are required to pay for each Nikon camera from Japan. Hence, a net loss accrues to U.S. society. That is, the aggregate cost imposed on the masses of losers by the falling dollar exceeds the aggregate benefits accruing to the minority of individuals engaged in the sectors directly exposed to foreign competition.

ery by restricting credit and boosting interest rates. In a foreign exchange market involving transactions of $1 trillion ($1,000 billion) per day, however, economists are skeptical of governments' capacity to manage exchange rates through direct foreign exchange market intervention in the event speculative fervor arrives with a vengeance.

The flip side of the falling dollar was the booming deutsche mark. The perennially strong German currency, by tending to further appreciate, increased tensions within the European Community. European nations were confronted with the need to pursue restrictive monetary policies that push up interest rates to prevent currency depreciation in order to maintain their commitment to a fixed exchange rate against the German mark as per European Monetary System (EMS) agreements. In 1992, such measures meant risking further damage to weak European economies. Britain had agreed in 1990 to join the EMS and fix the pound against the German mark. Already ambivalent about her unification with Europe, British politicians would have preferred to see Germany ease credit and reduce interest rates to being forced to push up British rates in the midst of a national recession.

The situation demonstrates the awesome power of Germany—the nation with the premier currency—to influence economic policy throughout Europe and the world in the increasingly interwoven global economy. In 1992, politicians worldwide were frustrated with a Bundesbank mindset that places a uniquely high priority on preventing inflation. Countries most affected are those with relatively weak currencies—France, Italy, and Britain. The European Community is scheduled to adopt a common currency by the year 1999—essentially becoming a single economy. The restrictive monetary policies of the Bundesbank risked triggering a realignment of exchange rates within the twelve-nation EMS which, in turn, could place the scheduled adoption of a uniform currency before the turn of the century at risk.

How Changing Exchange Rates Alter the Terms of Trade

YOUR TURN

SUPPOSE, HYPOTHETICALLY, THAT THE DOLLAR DEPRECIATES AGAINST THE JAPANESE YEN FROM 200 YEN TO 100 YEN. SUPPOSE A NIKON CAMERA SELLS FOR ¥100,000 IN JAPAN AND A BUSHEL OF WHEAT SELLS FOR $2 IN THE UNITED STATES. DEMONSTRATE HOW THIS DEPRECIATION OF THE DOLLAR IMPAIRS THE U.S. TERMS OF TRADE BY CALCULATING THE NUMBER OF BUSHELS OF AMERICAN WHEAT THAT MUST BE YIELDED TO PURCHASE ONE JAPANESE CAMERA BEFORE AND AFTER THE DEPRECIATION OF THE DOLLAR.

Exchange-rate movements exert major effects—some good, some bad. In addition, highly variable exchange rates can increase risk and therefore discourage international economic activity. Therefore, it is not surprising that there is a fair amount of sentiment for governments to intervene to limit exchange-rate movements or to prevent them from changing at all.

WHY DO GOVERNMENTS INTERVENE IN FOREIGN EXCHANGE MARKETS?

In principle, governments may directly intervene in foreign exchange markets either to attempt to smooth excessive short-term changes in exchange rates or to attempt to push the rate in a direction perceived to be in the government's interest. If exchange rates are highly unstable, a case can be made for government activity to stabilize rates. Highly volatile exchange rates increase the risk of entering into international transactions and are therefore thought to inhibit the volume of trade. However, critics of government intervention doubt that governments know better than speculators what the *correct* exchange rate is at any point in time. Unless speculators are on average losing money, they are right most of the time. This means, on average, that speculators are purchasing currencies that are too weak and selling currencies that are too strong, thereby serving to stabilize movements in exchange rates.

Governments also intervene to influence exchange rates for other, more selfish reasons. We have analyzed how changes in exchange rates benefit some groups and harm others. Over the years, the Japanese government has frequently intervened to hold down the yen (that is, to support the U.S. dollar or keep it from declining). This activity can probably be explained by the political power of the electronics, automobile, and other Japanese export industries that prosper from strong sales in American markets. A strongly appreciating yen—though it benefits the great masses of Japanese consumers—reduces the state of prosperity in the powerful Japanese export industries. Apparently these industries have more political clout than the less-organized masses of Japanese consumers. In the colorful language of international finance, such politically motivated interventionist actions in foreign exchange markets by governments have earned the floating exchange-rate system the moniker *dirty float*.[11]

---

[11]These activities by the Japanese government might correctly be regarded by American manufacturing firms and workers as a form of trade restriction against U.S. products. If, by purchasing dollars (selling yen), the Japanese government keeps the dollar 5 percent higher than it would otherwise be, it is making American products artificially expensive in Japan and Japanese products artificially cheap in the United States by roughly 5 percent.

The experience with floating exchange rates since the early 1970s has not been as free of problems as early supporters of floating rates had expected. Exchange-rate fluctuations have been quite volatile at times—considerably more volatile than expected. For example, the dollar's decline in the late 1970s (and in 1992) was probably of greater magnitude than fundamental factors dictated, as was the dollar's appreciation in 1984 through early 1985. Contrary to the belief of many early advocates of floating rates, implementation of floating rates has not allowed countries to ignore external considerations and to set macroeconomic policy solely on the basis of domestic goals. As noted earlier, for instance, European nations kept interest rates high in spite of depressed economic activity between 1982 and 1985 to prevent their currencies from depreciating excessively against the dollar. And the United States did the same thing in the winter of 1987–1988 to guard against a feared additional decline in the dollar. Also, trade protectionist sentiment has been stronger in the United States in the past decade than at any time since the 1930s. Some economists and officials therefore advocate a return to the system of fixed exchange rates that prevailed from 1944 through 1973. In fact, many nations currently have fixed exchange rates with certain close trading partners.[12] For these reasons, a brief analysis of the workings of fixed exchange rates is pertinent.

THE BRETTON WOODS SYSTEM OF THE ADJUSTABLE PEG, 1944–1973

The *adjustable-peg* system was established at an international conference held at Bretton Woods, New Hampshire, in 1944. In the agreement, each nation's government or central bank was required to intervene in the foreign exchange market to *peg* the exchange rate at a specific level known as *parity* or *par value* for an indefinite period of time. For many years, the U.S.–England exchange rate parity was established at $2.80 per £.[13] The government of England kept the pound from depreciating below $2.80 by using its **international reserves** to purchase its own currency in the foreign exchange market. These reserves consisted primarily of the British central bank's holdings of gold and U.S. dollars. Figure 38.6 (page 1030) illustrates how this system functioned.

INTERNATIONAL RESERVES

A government's stock of foreign currencies and gold available to support the country's currency in the foreign exchange market.

---

[12]As of mid-1992, some twenty-five nations (mostly LDCs) have pegged their currencies to the dollar. Fourteen nations tied their currencies to the French franc; 44 nations pegged themselves to other currencies or baskets of currencies. A group of 12 members of the European Monetary System (EMS) fix their exchange rate with each other, allowing the whole bloc to float against the dollar, yen, and other independently floating currencies. The EMS members currently consist of Belgium, Denmark, France, Germany, Greece, Ireland, Italy, Luxembourg, the Netherlands, Portugal, Spain, and Britain.

[13]Technically, this parity was established by each nation defining the value of its currency unit in terms of gold. If the U.S. official gold price were $35/ounce and the British official price were £12.5/ounce, the par value would be established at $2.80/£ (because $35 and £12.5 are equivalent). If England were to raise its gold price to £14.6, it would devalue the pound and reduce the par value exchange rate to $2.40/£. This is precisely what England did in 1967.

In a system of fixed exchange rates (the *adjustable-peg system*), the government of each nation whose currency is tending to depreciate agrees to purchase its own currency with foreign currency. In the figure, if the demand for British sterling declines from $D_£^1$ to $D_£^2$, the British government must purchase CA units of sterling (£10 billion) each period to maintain the exchange rate at the specified parity or par value of $2.80/£.

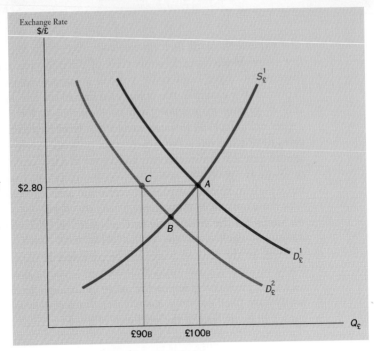

FIGURE 38.6

Suppose England manages initially to set the par value at exactly the intersection of $S_£^1$ and $D_£^1$ (that is, *$2.80/£*), exactly the level at which a free float would have established the exchange rate. No intervention is needed initially. However, the supply and demand curves do not remain fixed, but instead are constantly shifting about. Suppose the demand curve for sterling shifts down to $D_£^2$ because of a recession in America or a price level increase in England. In a free float, the pound would depreciate to a new equilibrium (point *B* in Figure 38.6). However, the British central bank is obligated to prevent this from happening. It can do this for a while by purchasing the excess supply of sterling each period (*CA* or £10 billion in the figure). Essentially, in purchasing the surplus sterling, the Bank of England shifts the demand curve back to $D_£^1$ to maintain the pound at $2.80.

As this British currency support operation continues, the British government's stock of international reserves decreases. At some point speculators anticipate that the government will run out of ammunition (gold and dollars) and will be forced to *devalue* the pound to a sustainable level—approximately in line with the intersection of $S_£^1$ and $D_£^2$ (that is, point *B*) in Figure 38.6. This is what happened in 1967, when England devalued the pound from $2.80 to $2.40, or by roughly 15 percent. When speculators foresee the likelihood of devaluation, they sell sterling in large quantities, shifting the $S_£$ schedule sharply rightward. This creates a much larger excess supply of sterling, forcing the government to give up the game. The pound is devalued—and the government now pegs the pound at the new, lower level for an indefinite period.

To avoid the preceding devaluation scenario in the first place, nations with chronically weak currencies (England, France, Italy) were tempted to try to move the equilibrium rate back to the original par values by measures that were highly destructive. These measures include such trade restrictions as quotas and tariffs and such domestic austerity programs as higher taxes, reduced government outlays, and higher interest rates fostered by the central bank. In terms of Figure 38.6, austerity programs in England would shift the $S_£$ schedule leftward by reducing British incomes and the demand for imports. By depressing the domestic price level, such measures would improve the competitive posture of British goods in world markets and shift the $D_£$ schedule rightward. A tariff imposed by Britain on imported items would reduce the willingness of British citizens to import, thus shifting the $S_£$ schedule leftward. Any of these destructive measures would help sustain the exchange rate at its par value.

CRITICISMS OF THE ADJUSTABLE-PEG EXCHANGE-RATE SYSTEM The chief criticism of the adjustable-peg system is that it forced countries with chronically weak currencies to implement policies that created high unemployment, slow growth, financial distress, and international trade restrictions. In many cases, monetary and fiscal policies were being set on the basis of international considerations rather than on domestic needs. Of course, when the British pound was weak, some other currency—the dollar, yen, or deutsche mark—must have been strong. The strong-currency nation could in principle have helped by boosting its own economy, thereby boosting demand for imports and strengthening the weak currency's position in the foreign exchange market. Unfortunately, the strong-currency nations tended to view the situation as strictly the problem of the weak-currency nation. Therefore, the burden of adjustment typically was placed entirely upon the weak-currency nation.

The fixed exchange-rate system of 1944–1973 was dubbed the "adjustable-peg system" because of the periodic realignments of the level at which the exchange rate was pegged. Critics of this system argue that it is eminently more sensible to let the exchange rate freely adjust to resolve a disequilibrium of the type illustrated in Figure 38.6 than to resort to such destructive measures as trade barriers and increased domestic unemployment in a largely futile effort to restore the equilibrium exchange rate to the glorified par value level. Typically such measures only *delayed* the exchange rate adjustment in any event. Nations with *overvalued currencies* (that is, exchange rates held above market equilibrium levels—such as England in the preceding example) clearly experience less agony through letting their currencies depreciate than by attempting to become competitive by pushing down the nation's entire structure of costs and prices via restrictive monetary and fiscal policies.[14]

---

[14]The ultimate example of this folly, in the eyes of most economists, was "Mr. Churchill's mistake" of 1925. During World War I (1914–1918), British prices had risen considerably faster than those in the United States and other nations. Exchange rates were floated between 1919 and 1925, and the pound depreciated sharply, as predicted by PPP theory. But in early 1925, Winston Churchill (the British Chancellor of the Exchequer) decided to return to the prewar parity of $4.86/£. This put England at a large competitive disadvantage and almost destroyed its export industries. For many years, the British unemployment rate never fell below 10 percent.

By the early 1970s, the divergence of inflation rates and other imbalances among nations had become quite substantial. The adjustable-peg system was no longer viable because the volume of international reserves held by weak-currency nations (including the United States) was insufficient to maintain fixed parities for long periods of time. Exchange rates were unpegged—set free—and have been floating ever since. The floating system now in place is not utopian; it does not solve all our international problems. But most economists believe that the floating system is better equipped to deal with the increasing volume of international economic activity and the shocks that from time to time hit the global economy than the adjustable-peg exchange rate system that preceded it. It is unlikely we will return to fixed exchange rates in the near future.

The Balance of Payments

BALANCE OF PAYMENTS
A statistical tabulation of a nation's transactions with other countries for a given period.

A nation's **balance of payments** is a statistical tabulation of all transactions between that nation and the rest of the world for a given year. Transactions that give rise to payments to the rest of the world are recorded as debits (–); transactions that generate receipts from the rest of the world are recorded as credits (+). The balance of payments includes transactions made by individuals, firms, and governments.

The overall balance of payments accounts include the *current account* and the *capital account*. Both accounts are influenced by government transactions as well as by transactions of private entities. Table 38.2 outlines the components of the U.S. balance of payments in 1991.

THE CURRENT ACCOUNT

BALANCE OF TRADE
The difference between the value of a nation's exports and imports of merchandise or goods; one component of the balance of payments.

The *current account* includes trade in currently produced goods and services, where *services* is broadly interpreted. The current account is dominated by the **balance of trade**, which is the net difference between merchandise exports and merchandise imports. Line 3 reveals that the United States ran a "balance of trade" deficit of approximately $74 billion in 1991. The U.S. trade deficit figure, released monthly by the Department of Commerce, has been one of the most eagerly observed economic statistics in recent years. Its release sometimes triggers large changes in foreign exchange rates as well as changes in prices in U.S. financial markets, including the stock market.

Several other items included in the current account are conceptually regarded as exports and imports of *services*, and are listed for 1991 in lines 4–6 of Table 38.2. An American tourist who buys a meal in London or pays a hotel bill in Paris contributes to our current account deficit in the same way as an American who buys an imported VCR. So does an American importer who utilizes foreign-owned ships to transport cargo. Foreigners make corresponding transactions in the United States, and line 4 indicates a $10.3 billion U.S. surplus on travel and transportation. U.S.

THE U.S. BALANCE OF PAYMENTS, 1991 (BILLIONS OF DOLLARS)

CURRENT ACCOUNT

1. Merchandise exports	+416.5
2. Merchandise imports	−490.1
3. Balance of trade	− 73.6
4. Net travel and transportation	+ 10.3
5. Net military transactions	− 5.3
6. Other services and net income from foreign investments	+ 40.3
7. Balance on goods and services	− 28.3
8. Unilateral transfers (net)	+ 19.7
9. Balance on current account	− 8.6

CAPITAL ACCOUNT

Private

10. Change in U.S. private assets abroad	− 77.1
11. Change in foreign assets in U.S.	+ 58.9
12. Net private capital flows	− 18.2

Government

13. Change in U.S. government assets abroad	+ 9.3
14. Change in foreign government assets in U.S.	+ 20.6
15. Net government capital flows	+ 29.9
16. Balance on capital account	+ 11.7
17. Statistical discrepancy (lines 9 + 16, with sign reversed)	− 3.1
18. **Total balance of payments**	**0**

SOURCE: Adapted from Department of Commerce, *Survey of Current Business*, June 1992.

TABLE 38.2

military activities abroad contribute to the deficit (line 5). Income flowing from past American investment abroad (plants, real estate, securities) is conceptually treated as payment for use of the services of U.S. capital. Of course, foreign nations have also accumulated vast assets in this country, from which they earn a rapidly growing income. In 1991, a net positive balance of $16.4 billion (not shown) from those income flows in favor of the United States is included in the surplus on line 6 of the table. When these net exports of U.S. services (lines 4, 5, 6) are added to our trade balance (line 3), we arrive at the "balance on goods and services." Line 7 indicates a deficit of $28.3 billion for 1991 on goods and services.

Finally, we consider "unilateral transfers." Income earners may send money to family and friends abroad. Charitable organizations send aid to famine-stricken regions of the world. The U.S. government provides foreign aid to low-income nations. In the five years prior to 1991, net unilateral transfers *from* the United States averaged more than $16 billion annually. In 1991, however, the United States collected huge one-time payments from foreign governments to help pay for the 1991 U.S. military action against Iraq, Operation Desert Storm. As a result, the

1991 figures indicate a highly atypical net unilateral transfer *to* the United States of $19.7 billion (line 8).

When net unilateral transfers are added to the balance on goods and services, we obtain the current account balance (line 9). The 1991 current account deficit was only $8.6 billion, a figure artificially reduced on a one-time basis in 1991 by the war in the Persian Gulf. In the six prior years (1985 through 1990), the U.S. current account deficit averaged $125 billion per year. This current account deficit reached a peak of $160 billion in 1987 and declined each year thereafter until 1992.

CAPITAL ACCOUNT

The *capital account* tallies up changes in foreign assets—securities, real estate, checking accounts, and the like—owned by Americans and subtracts changes in the stock of similar American assets owned by foreigners. These changes in net foreign assets, known as *capital flows*, may be attributable either to governments or to private parties. Private capital flows have traditionally dominated government capital flows. Table 38.2 indicates that foreign private investors purchased $58.9 billion of additional U.S. assets in 1991, whereas Americans purchased $77.1 billion of new foreign assets. This indicates a net private capital *outflow* of $18.2 billion (line 12). In addition, governments (U.S. and foreign) purchased (net) about $30 billion of U.S. assets (line 15). This activity is explained by the desire of governments in 1991 to reduce holdings of foreign currencies and increase holdings of dollars. Central banks (especially foreign) purchased dollars in exchange markets and typically placed the funds in U.S. checking accounts or U.S. government securities.

When private and government capital flows are combined, we obtain line 16—the net balance on capital account. Note that this item ($11.7 billion) fails to offset precisely the deficit balance on current account ($8.6 billion). In principle, this outcome is impossible because each event generating a credit (+) for the United States gives rise to a corresponding transaction generating a debit (–). For example, when a U.S. computer manufacturer (IBM) makes a $100 million shipment to Canada, "merchandise exports" rise $100 million (line 1). But the Canadian importer pays for the shipment by writing a check on its account in a U.S. bank (line 11 declines by $100 million) or perhaps by making payment to IBM's bank account in Toronto, in which case U.S. private assets abroad increase $100 million (line 10).

The failure of the capital account balance to offset the current account balance precisely is attributable to imperfections inherent in compiling the balance of payments. The Department of Commerce may have accurate data on the value of U.S. imports of Hyundais from South Korea, but the method of payment may not be known. In this event, imports are recorded as a debt item (line 2) but the corresponding credit item is simply recorded under "statistical discrepancy" (line 17). Hence, most of the *statistical discrepancy* derives from unrecorded capital movements. Note in Table 38.2 that the "total balance of payments" is precisely zero. In a trivial accounting sense, each nation's total balance of payments is zero.

If each nation's balance of payments is always zero, why worry? What's all the talk about a U.S. balance of payments problem? International payments imbalances imply problems with the *composition* of the overall international accounts. Hardship in certain sectors of the economy may be occurring. Alternatively, the composition may be unsustainable and problems may occur later when inevitable adjustments are made. For example, suppose a highly developed nation is temporarily enjoying an artificially high standard of living by purchasing and enjoying 5 percent more goods and services each year than it produces. Suppose it accomplishes this feat by running a $200 billion trade deficit—importing $200 billion more goods and services each year than it exports. It finances the trade deficit through net annual capital inflows of $200 billion. That is, foreigners are purchasing the nation's assets (on balance) and granting loans to it.

This may be fun while it lasts, but it seems unlikely that such a policy can be continued for 100 years. At some point, foreigners will grow wary of investing and lending additional funds. At this point, the nation in question will have to eliminate its trade deficit by bringing imports and exports into alignment. In fact, if the rest of the world not only refuses to loan new money but also decides to cash in some of its accumulated IOUs, the nation will have to run a trade surplus. It will have to reduce significantly its standard of living by purchasing and enjoying fewer goods than it produces (that is, by achieving a trade surplus and by using the proceeds to pay off some of the external debt).

The U.S. experienced large international deficits in its trade, goods and services, and current accounts in the past decade. The profile of these deficits is illustrated in Figure 38.7 (page 1036). These deficits increased in magnitude between 1981 and 1987, but declined steadily from 1987 through 1991.

THE UNITED STATES AS AN INTERNATIONAL DEBTOR

From approximately World War I until the mid-1980s, the United States was a net creditor in global markets. This means that the sum of all foreign investments accumulated by Americans—foreign stocks, bonds, real estate, and so forth—exceeded the corresponding stock of American assets owned by foreigners. As a result of the capital inflows of the 1980s and the trade deficits that accompanied them (Figure 38.7), the United States in 1984 became a net debtor for the first time in roughly seventy years. In fact, during the decade of the 1980s, the United States moved from being the largest creditor nation in the world to the largest debtor.

Thoughtful economists worry that this might be a lot like "enjoy now, pay later"—the quintessential "fool's paradise." If foreigners decide they have overinvested in American assets and begin to liquidate some of their IOUs, the United States will be forced to run trade surpluses. Hence, a potential scenario for the next decade could be just the reverse of the experience of the past ten years. We may be

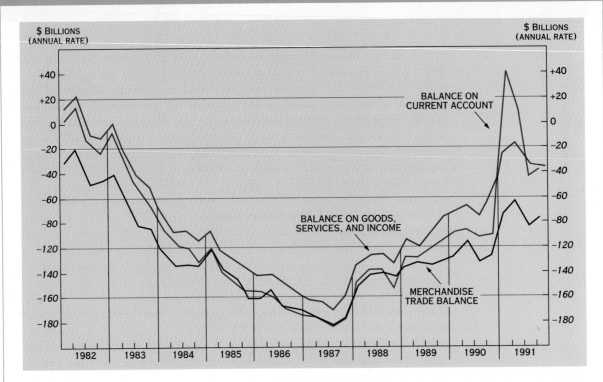

All measures of the American international trade deficit swung sharply into the red following 1981. After increasing for six consecutive years, the trade deficits began declining after mid-1987.

SOURCE: Council of Economic Advisors, 1992.

FIGURE 38.7

forced to tighten our belts and accept a lower standard of living. That is, we Americans may be forced to acquire *fewer* goods and services than we collectively produce, using the revenues from our trade surplus to pay off the foreigners who cash in their IOUs. If foreign willingness to hold American assets decreases precipitously, the dollar would depreciate sharply in foreign exchange markets. By stimulating U.S. exports and slowing imports, the falling dollar would be the chief mechanism through which the turnaround in our current account would occur. Unfortunately, a rapid fall of the dollar would cause domestic problems such as higher inflation.

The LDC Debt Crises

Less-developed countries (LDCs) typically have inadequate domestic savings with which to finance economic growth. Such nations as Brazil, Mexico, and Argentina rely on the export of raw materials and international borrowing to obtain funds for investment in infrastructure and plant and equipment. The United States, for example, was an international debtor nation during most of our history until World War I. We borrowed from the rest of the world to finance the expansion of railroads and other infrastructure. Hence, one normally expects such LDC nations as Brazil, Mexico, Argentina, and Peru to be net debtors. Developed nations regard the LDCs, which typically exhibit low wages and often are well endowed with natural resources, as attractive places to lend and invest.

Much of the LDC debt problem today can be traced to decisions made in the 1970s. In that decade, raw material prices rose sharply, boosting export revenues of the LDCs. Real interest rates in the United States and other creditor nations were low, significantly easing the burden of debtors. LDCs faced few problems in meeting interest payments. From the vantage point of the 1970s, LDC prosperity seemed easy to sustain. Given this environment, many LDCs—especially Latin American nations—sought a major expansion in credit, and the large American banks were eager to accommodate them. Some of these funds were used for legitimate investment projects; others were used to finance ventures of questionable merit.

The LDC debt crisis was triggered by a series of shocks in the first half of the decade of the 1980s. These shocks severely reduced the ability of many LDCs to meet the interest payments on their debts. First, a severe worldwide recession occurred between 1981 and 1983. This resulted in a major drop in LDC exports demanded by industrial nations. Also, prices of raw materials dropped sharply, ensuring a severe contraction in the revenues generated by LDC exports.

Second, real interest rates in developed countries (the lending nations) increased sharply and remained high for several years, especially in the United States. Recall that debtors come under increased pressure when real interest rates rise. Third, the U.S. dollar appreciated dramatically in foreign exchange markets between 1980 and 1985 (review Figure 38.5). Because many LDC debts are denominated in dollars, the increased cost of obtaining dollars tended to exacerbate the LDC debt problem.

In 1982, Mexico declared that it was unable to meet payments on its debt to the United States. In ensuing years, Argentina, Brazil, Peru, and the Philippines encountered similar problems. The interim *remedy* has been to postpone payments and *renegotiate* the loans on scaled-back terms. The enormous LDC debts and the difficulties in meeting payments continue to constitute a serious problem for many large American banks. Several of these banks have loans outstanding to LDCs in amounts equal to 200 percent or more of bank capital or net worth. This means in principle that wholesale default on the LDC debt could bankrupt several of our largest banks, perhaps touching off a major financial panic.

None of the parties involved would benefit from widespread default. The LDCs themselves would lose heavily, inasmuch as they would be sealed off from future credit. For this reason there is no choice but for the LDC nations, the U.S. government, and international financial institutions to achieve maximum cooperation to manage the debt crisis. In the past five years, several U.S. banks acknowledged the reduced prospects for full loan repayments by sharply increasing loan-loss reserve provisions. Although such provisions reduced bank earnings temporarily, they implicitly acknowledged an emerging political reality—that many of the loans will never be repaid in full and that banks will be forced to take losses resulting from their decisions to make the loans.

A fundamental solution to the debt crisis requires that the LDCs generate a healthy surplus in their international trade accounts and use the proceeds to work down the debts by meeting interest and amortization expenses. Two basic avenues can contribute to this result. First, the LDCs can attempt to bring about a real depreciation of their currencies in foreign exchange markets through austerity programs and other measures in order to boost export sales. Unfortunately, such measures typically involve reducing standards of living of the populace in the short run. The living standards in LDCs are already grim and have declined significantly in the past decade. Real wages in Mexico, for example, declined by roughly 50 percent in the decade of the 1980s. Second, the industrial nations can boost the export sales of the LDC nations by implementing stimulative macroeconomic measures to strengthen aggregate demand in the developed nations.

The LDC debt crisis eased somewhat after the mid-1980s as the dollar and U.S. interest rates declined and economic activity in the industrial nations strengthened. In the early 1990s, with the world economy in a state of stagnation, the situation continues to simmer. Many LDCs remain vulnerable to any further weakening of worldwide economic activity or major increase in interest rates in the creditor nations. The LDC debt crisis may be exacerbated by strong protectionist sentiment in the United States and Europe and by the desire of the U.S. to bring down its own trade deficit and reduce its role as an international debtor.

Summary

1. The foreign exchange market is the market in which the various national currencies are exchanged. The exchange rate is the price at which these currencies are exchanged. Exchange rates may be quoted as the number of units of foreign currency per unit of domestic currency or as units of domestic currency per unit of foreign currency. If the dollar is worth half of one pound sterling, the pound is worth two dollars.

2. Since the early 1970s, exchange rates have been unpegged and allowed to float in the market, although with occasional intervention by governments. Exchange rates change daily, sometimes by a significant amount. If a currency rises in value or becomes worth more units of foreign currency, it is said to *appreciate*. If a currency falls in value, it *depreciates*.

3. The fundamental economic forces that cause changes in exchange rates are changes in relative price levels, relative incomes, and relative real interest rates among countries. Given other factors, the U.S. dollar appreciates against the German mark if the U.S. price level rises more slowly than the German price level, if U.S. income expands more slowly than German income, and if U.S. real interest rates increase relative to those in Germany.

4. Speculators attempt to forecast the behavior of the fundamental determinants underlying exchange rates and act according to these forecasts. For example, if speculators anticipate an increase in the Federal Reserve discount rate, they will foresee higher U.S. yields and thus immediately purchase dollars with yen, deutsche marks, and other currencies. Speculative activity is responsible for a major portion of intraday exchange-rate movements. Interest rate movements are also reflected very quickly in exchange-rate changes. Relative income changes among nations influence exchange rates over a somewhat longer horizon and relative price level behavior is a long-run determinant of exchange rates.

5. The three fundamental determinants help to explain three major swings in the value of the U.S. dollar—the depreciation of 1976–1979, the rising dollar of 1980–1985, and the falling dollar of 1985–1988. The falling dollar of the 1970s is explained largely by the high U.S. inflation rate compared to that of other nations. Booming U.S. income and low real interest rates in the United States also explain the dollar's sustained depreciation. The soaring dollar of the 1980–1985 period was fueled principally by an enormous change in the net flow of capital in favor of the United States owing to sharply higher real interest rates here and the perception of this country as a favorable place to invest. The falling dollar of the late 1980s is not so clearly explained by fundamental factors. It is true that income expanded more rapidly at home than abroad and that the net real yield advantage here decreased. However, these factors are insufficient to account for the magnitude of the decline of the dollar. Speculation against the dollar accounts for much of the depreciation, especially after 1986.

6. A change in exchange rates has important implications for a nation's economy. When the dollar appreciates, domestic inflation is held down and the nation's terms of trade improve as each unit of our exports pays for more imports. However, exports are slowed, imports are stimulated, and real domestic income is redistributed from those whose livelihood depends on the prosperity of the manufacturing and agricultural sectors to the masses of consumers who benefit from cheap imports. A depreciation of the dollar has the opposite consequences. Domestic inflation is boosted and the terms of trade worsen. The trade balance is tilted in the direction of a smaller deficit or larger surplus as exports increase relative to imports. Workers and firms in the sectors exposed to foreign competition benefit, and the masses of consumers suffer a reduction in their real incomes because of higher prices of imports and, ultimately, domestic goods.

7. Governments sometimes intervene directly in foreign exchange markets to influence exchange rates intentionally. Hence, the system in place since the early 1970s has been a *managed float* and not a totally *free float*. Since governments sometimes intervene to manipulate the exchange rate deliberately in a direction perceived to be in that government's interest and contrary to the interest of other nations, the system has been dubbed the "dirty float."

8. From 1944 to 1973, world trade was based on a fixed exchange-rate system known as the "adjustable peg." Each nation agreed to support ("peg") its own currency when it tended to depreciate, through direct purchases of the currency in the foreign exchange market. The knowledge that exchange rates would be constant from week to week was thought to be beneficial to a thriving system of trade. Unfortunately, nations whose currencies were prone to depreciate were forced to bear the entire burden of the adjustment to the disequilibrium. Strong-currency nations typically refused to alter their policies. Weak-currency nations were forced either to implement restrictive trade measures or to attempt to force down their domestic price structure to regain competitiveness. Barring the correction of balance of payments deficits through these measures, nations could only throw in the towel and devalue, pegging their currency at a new, lower value relative to other nations.

9. A nation's balance of payments is an organized tabulation of its financial transactions with other nations. The *current account* summarizes all transactions in currently produced goods and services. The *capital account* tabulates capital movements across borders—changes in holdings of such assets as real estate, securities, and bank accounts between countries. Except for a statistical discrepancy owing to imperfection in data collection, the capital account and the current account sum to zero. That is, the overall balance of payments is always zero.

10. In the 1980s, the United States experienced burgeoning deficits in its international balance on merchandise trade, goods and services, and current accounts. This implies an equivalent offsetting change in the capital account—a massive net inflow of foreign capital. This reversed the experience of the previous seven decades, in which the United States exhibited persistent surpluses in current account and was a net exporter of capital to the rest of the world. This role reversal is basically attributable to a major increase in the desire to invest funds in the United States in the 1980s. This, in turn, is accounted for chiefly by the phenomenal increase in real interest rates in this country in the early 1980s.

Key Terms

foreign exchange market
foreign exchange rate
currency depreciation
currency appreciation
floating exchange rates
fixed exchange rates
purchasing power parity theory
  (PPP)

foreign-exchange market
  speculators
terms of trade
international reserves
balance of payments
balance of trade

1. What does it mean to say the U.S. dollar "depreciates" in foreign exchange markets? If the U.S. exchange rate with Italy moves from 1,200 lire per dollar to 1,400 lire per dollar, does the dollar appreciate or depreciate? What about the lira?

2. Focusing on the U.S.–Italy exchange rate, draw appropriate supply and demand curves and label them and the axes. Explain the reasons for the slopes of the supply and demand curves. What is the equilibrium exchange rate in your drawing?

3. Consider the U.S.–France exchange rate, expressed as francs per dollar. Analyze the effects of each of the following events on the value of the dollar, assuming other factors remain constant. Use the appropriate supply–demand framework.
    a. Income in France rises.
    b. The Fed raises U.S. interest rates.
    c. The U.S. price level rises 5 percent.
    d. A French company introduces a highly attractive new line of tennis shoes.
    e. The U.S. announces new tariffs on all French goods.
    f. A new "buy-American" ethic is promoted in this country.
    g. U.S. budget deficits are eliminated.

4. Explain the purchasing power parity theory of foreign exchange rates and the intuition underlying it. Why do you suppose PPP does a better job of tracking the U.S.–Mexico exchange rate in the past decade than the U.S.–Japan exchange rate?

5. Under what set of conditions would purchasing power parity exchange rates always precisely prevail? Explain.

6. Suppose you are employed by an investment bank as a foreign-exchange-rate analyst. The investment bank is involved in taking positions in various currencies. New U.S. inflation figures have been released, and they reveal that inflation is running lower than expected. What advice would you give your investment bank?

7. Explain the rationale underlying the following: "The policy of the Japanese central bank of supporting the dollar or holding down the yen through direct foreign exchange market transactions is equivalent to Japan placing a tariff on U.S. goods."

8. Explain why a depreciating or appreciating U.S. dollar affects the U.S. inflation rate.

9. Given that a strong dollar in foreign exchange markets holds down U.S. inflation and raises our standard of living, why would anyone oppose measures that cause the dollar to appreciate strongly?

10. Using a supply and demand framework, show how a government in a pegged exchange-rate system prevents the exchange rate from fluctuating. Why might the government at some point be unable to continue to do this?

11. Do you feel governments should intervene to *manage* the exchange rate or withdraw and permit a *free float*? Defend your answer.

12. What are the drawbacks of the Bretton Woods adjustable-peg exchange-rate system of 1944 through 1973? Why was it abandoned? Should we return to it in the 1990s?

13. In what sense can one say that the large U.S. trade deficits of the last 10 years were a "bad" thing? A "good" thing?

14. Outline the causes and consequences of the simmering LDC debt crises. What steps could the United States take to ease the burden of this debt and make it easier for the LDCs to meet their payments?

15. Why were European nations hostile toward the Bundesbank's (German central bank) policies of high interest rates in 1992?

YOUR TURN
Answers

How Interest Rates Affect Exchange Rates

THE ANNOUNCEMENT INDICATES TO THE WORLD FINANCIAL COMMUNITY THAT GERMAN SHORT-TERM INTEREST RATES WILL BE INCREASING. THIS WILL ULTIMATELY CAUSE THE DEUTSCHE MARK TO APPRECIATE (DOLLAR TO DEPRECIATE) AS NET DEMAND FOR GERMAN SECURITIES (AND DEUTSCHE MARKS) INCREASES. ALSO, THE ANNOUNCEMENT SIGNALS THE GERMAN INTENT TO KEEP INFLATION IN CHECK, WHICH IS BULLISH FOR THE DEUTSCHE MARK. FOR THESE REASONS, SPECULATORS WILL IMMEDIATELY BUY MARKS (SELL DOLLARS) UPON THE ANNOUNCEMENT. THE MARK WILL APPRECIATE AND THE DOLLAR WILL DEPRECIATE.

How Changing Exchange Rates Alter the Terms of Trade

WHEN THE EXCHANGE RATE IS 200 YEN/DOLLAR, THE NIKON CAMERA COSTS $500 IN THE UNITED STATES (100,000 YEN ÷ 200 YEN/$). BECAUSE WHEAT COSTS $2 PER BUSHEL IN THE U.S., 250 BUSHELS OF AMERICAN WHEAT ARE REQUIRED TO OBTAIN ONE JAPANESE CAMERA. AFTER THE DOLLAR DEPRECIATES TO 100 YEN, IT COSTS AN AMERICAN $1,000 TO PURCHASE THE CAMERA (100,000 YEN ÷ 100 YEN/$). WITH WHEAT AT $2 PER BUSHEL, THE U.S. MUST GIVE UP 500 BUSHELS OF WHEAT TO GET THE CAMERA. WHEN THE DOLLAR DEPRECIATES BY 50 PERCENT (FALLS BY HALF) ON THE FOREIGN EXCHANGE MARKET, WE MUST YIELD TWICE AS MANY UNITS OF OUR EXPORT GOODS FOR EACH IMPORTED GOOD WE PURCHASE. HENCE, A DEPRECIATION OF THE DOLLAR PRODUCES AN ADVERSE CHANGE IN THE U.S. TERMS OF TRADE.

Selected References

Bergsten, C. Fred. *Dilemmas of the Dollar*. (New York: M. E. Sharpe, 1990). This book analyzes U.S. international monetary policy and the role of the dollar in the international financial system.

Economic Report of the President. (Washington, D.C.: U.S. Government Printing Office, published annually). This document analyzes recent international financial developments as they pertain to the U.S. economy.

Kreinin, Mordechai E. *International Economics: A Policy Approach*, 6th ed. (Fort Worth: Harcourt Brace Jovanovich, 1991). This textbook in international economics amplifies the topics presented in this chapter. See especially chapters 2, 3, 4, and 7.

Krugman, Paul R., and Maurice Obstfeld. *International Economics: Theory and Policy* (New York: HarperCollins Publishers, 1991). Parts III and IV of this popular intermediate-level international trade book treat the topics sketched in this chapter in depth.

Lindert, Peter H. *International Economics*, 9th ed. (Homewood, Ill.: Richard D. Irwin, 1991). This international economics textbook covers all the issues analyzed in this chapter.

U.S. Department of Commerce, *Survey of Current Business*. This monthly publication contains detailed information on U.S. international economic transactions. Especially pertinent is the annual March issue, which discusses the previous year's international transactions in detail.

ONE THOUGHT EVER AT THE FORE——THAT IN THE
DIVINE SHIP, THE WORLD, BREASTING TIME
AND SPACE, ALL PEOPLES OF THE GLOBE
TOGETHER SAIL, SAIL THE SAME
VOYAGE, ARE BOUND TO THE SAME
DESTINATION.

——WALT WHITMAN

WE TRAVEL TOGETHER,
PASSENGERS ON A
LITTLE SPACESHIP,
DEPENDENT ON ITS
VULNERABLE RESERVES
OF AIR AND SOIL; ALL
COMMITTED FOR OUR
SAFETY TO ITS
SECURITY AND PEACE;
PRESERVED FROM
ANNIHILATION ONLY
BY THE CARE, THE
WORK, AND I WILL SAY
THE LOVE WE GIVE OUR
FRAGIL CRAFT. WE
CANNOT MAINTAIN
IT HALF FORTUNATE,
HALF MISERABLE,
HALF CONFIDENT, HALF
DESPAIRING, HALF SLAVE
TO THE ANCIENT ENEMIES OF
MAN. . . . NO CRAFT, NO CREW CAN
TRAVEL SAFELY WITH SUCH VAST
CONTRADICTIONS. ON THEIR RESOLUTION
DEPENDS THE SURVIVAL OF US ALL.

——ADLAI STEVENSON

The Economics of Less-Developed Countries

FROM OUR INDIVIDUAL POINTS OF VIEW, THE EARTH SEEMS LARGE. EVEN IN OUR OWN NEIGHBORHOODS THERE ARE PEOPLE WE DO NOT KNOW AND PLACES WE ARE NOT INVITED TO GO, SO PEOPLE AND PLACES IN OTHER COUNTRIES SEEM UNRELATED TO US. BUT FROM THE COSMIC VIEWPOINT EVOKED BY WHITMAN AND STEVENSON, THE WHOLE EARTH IS BEST THOUGHT OF AS A SPACESHIP AND THE EARTH'S WHOLE POPULATION AS FELLOW PASSENGERS. THE SPACESHIP METAPHOR EXPRESSES THE ESSENTIAL UNITY OF THE HUMAN RACE. THE EARTH SEEMS IMMENSE TO INDIVIDUALS, BUT IT IS UNIMAGINABLY SMALL IN RELATION TO THE WHOLE OF CREATION. AND HUMAN COMMUNITIES, EVEN THOSE THAT HAVE EXISTED FOR A FEW THOUSAND YEARS, ARE VERY RECENT EVENTS IN A UNIVERSE PERHAPS 15 BILLION YEARS OLD. IN LIGHT OF THE STUPENDOUS SIZE AND AGE OF THE UNIVERSE, OUR EARTH IS MINISCULE AND ALL OF HUMAN LIFE VERY RECENT AND FLEETING. WISDOM REQUIRES US TO BE SENSITIVE TO THE HUMAN CONDITION IN ALL SEGMENTS OF OUR SMALL PLANET-SPACESHIP.

The Division of the World into Developed and Less-Developed Countries

LESS-DEVELOPED

COUNTRIES (LDCS)

Countries in which living standards are low because modern technology generally has not been applied to production processes.

The economic principles discussed in this book are applicable everywhere; nevertheless most of their applications and factual content relate to the United States, which is one of about twenty-five economically *developed* countries. In these countries science-based technology is applied to production processes in all major sectors (agriculture, industry, and services) and, as a consequence, production per worker is high. The high output per worker is the fundamental reason why economic well-being is generally high in developed countries.

In contrast, most of the people on the earth today live in countries that have not yet applied technology to production processes in all sectors. In these **less-developed countries (LDCs)**, production per worker is generally low. Consequently, levels of economic well-being are low. Chapter 39 analyzes the economics of the LDCs.[1]

Classifying Countries by Levels of Output per Person

There were more than 170 countries in the world in 1990. About three-fourths of these had populations of more than 1 million. Table 39.1 (pages 1048–49) shows the World Bank's ranking of 108 of these countries from low to high per-capita production.[2] Data for 17 other countries are inadequate, so these countries (italicized in the table) are arranged alphabetically at the bottom of the World Bank's groupings. The "Other Economies" group is composed of 3 countries with populations over 1 million (Cuba, North Korea, and the former USSR) and all of the countries with populations less than 1 million. The table gives the five categories into which the World Bank classifies the countries: low-income, lower-middle-income, upper-middle-income, high-income, and other. There is wide agreement that all of the low-income and lower-middle-income countries and most of the upper-middle-income countries are LDCs. The high-income countries (with the possible exception of some high-income oil exporters) and some of the upper-middle income countries are developed countries.

Table 39.1 also gives the population of each country. In 1990, approximately three-quarters of the world's population lived in LDCs. This means that the economics discussed in this chapter is relevant for three-quarters of the human race.

The countries are ranked by level of per-capita production, not by total production, because we are interested in the economic well-being of people. Although

---

[1] The terms *industrialized* and *developing* are often used in place of *developed* and *less developed*.

[2] The World Bank (also known as the International Bank for Reconstruction and Development) is the major international institution involved in economic development. It is an important source of finance for development and for research into development problems. (Most statistical data used in this chapter are taken from its extremely valuable annual *World Development Report*.) The World Bank was created in 1944 at the same time as the International Monetary Fund. Both have their headquarters in Washington, D.C.

total production (GDP) in China or India is much larger than in Sweden or Denmark, the level of economic well-being is not nearly as high. Total production may be a good indicator of national power (China is probably a more *powerful* country than Sweden) but not of economic well-being.

Table 39.2 (page 1050) narrows our focus to 34 countries that together account for about three-fourths of the world's population.[3] As before, the countries are arranged in order from low to high per-capita incomes in 1990. While there is no universally acceptable criterion by which to classify a country as developed or less developed, there is widespread agreement with the classification of these thirty-four large countries as twenty-six LDCs and eight developed countries.

The figures in Table 39.2 show an enormous range in per-capita production, from Tanzania and Ethiopia at the *poor* extreme to Germany and Japan at the *rich* extreme. These production differences are an indication that the levels of economic well-being also show an enormous range.

Notice that the range of incomes *within* the LDC category is wider than the range within the developed-country category. That is, the differences in economic performance between say Ethiopia and Algeria, countries within the less-developed category, are much larger than the differences between say Spain and the United States, countries within the developed-country category.

The per-capita income figures used to arrange the countries from poor to rich are all expressed in U.S. dollars. In Chapter 10 you learned how GDP is measured in the United States. The per-capita income figure for the United States is found simply by dividing the 1990 U.S. GDP figure by the 1990 U.S. population. The figures for the other countries in Table 39.2 require an additional step. Because each country has its own currency, its per-capita GDP is first reckoned using its own currency. Then these figures must be converted into U.S. dollars before a country can be ranked in the table. For example, India's GDP is measured using the Indian currency, the rupee. Dividing this GDP figure by India's population gives India's per-capita GDP in rupees. But comparison with other countries requires all figures to be in the same currency units. India's per-capita GDP in rupees is converted into its dollar equivalent using the 1990 dollar–rupee exchange rate (about 18 rupees to the dollar). A similar procedure is used for all the other countries. (Each value in column two of Table 39.2 is obtained using market exchange rates.) To facilitate comparisons, column three sets the United States at 100 percent and lists all other countries relative to the United States. Thus, for example, the table shows Brazil's per-capita production to be 12.3 percent of U.S. per-capita production.

This standard comparison makes the gaps between a poor country like India and a rich country like the United States appear very large. Specifically, it appears that 1990 average incomes in the United States were about 62 times larger than in India ($21,790/$350 = 62)! We hope you suspect that there is something unrealistic about this. Imagine your parents offering to give you $350 to live on for the next year. This would be your entire income. Is it realistic to think that you could survive for a whole year on so little?

---

[3] Each of these 34 countries has a population in excess of 20 million. Only 6 countries with populations in excess of 20 million are not included here: Myanmar, North Korea, Sudan, the USSR, Vietnam, and Yugoslavia.

	POPULATION (MILLIONS) MID-1990	GDP PER CAPITA IN DOLLARS 1990		POPULATION (MILLIONS) MID-1990	GDP PER CAPITA IN DOLLARS 1990
LOW-INCOME ECONOMIES	**3,058.3**	**350**	Honduras	5.1	590
			Egypt, Arab Republic	52.1	600
Mozambique	15.7	80	*Afghanistan*	—	—
Tanzania	24.5	110	*Cambodia*	8.5	—
Ethiopia	51.2	120	*Liberia*	2.6	—
Somalia	7.8	120	*Myanmar*	41.6	—
Nepal	18.9	170	*Sudan*	25.1	—
Chad	5.7	190	*Vietnam*	66.3	—
Bhutan	1.4	190			
Lao PDR	4.1	200	**LOWER-MIDDLE-INCOME**	**629.1**	**1,530**
Malawi	8.5	200			
Bangladesh	106.7	210	Bolivia	7.2	630
Burundi	5.4	210	Zimbabwe	9.8	640
Zaire	37.3	220	Senegal	7.4	710
Uganda	16.3	220	Philippines	61.5	730
Madagascar	11.7	230	Côte d'Ivoire	11.9	750
Sierra Leone	4.1	240	Dominican Republic	7.1	830
Mali	8.5	270	Papua New Guinea	3.9	860
Nigeria	115.5	290	Guatemala	9.2	900
Niger	7.7	310	Morocco	25.1	950
Rwanda	7.1	310	Cameroon	11.7	960
Burkina Faso	9.0	330	Ecuador	10.3	980
India	849.5	350	Syrian Arab Republic	12.4	1,000
Benin	4.7	360	Congo	2.3	1,010
China	1,133.7	370	El Salvador	5.2	1,110
Haiti	6.5	370	Paraguay	4.3	1,110
Kenya	24.2	370	Peru	21.7	1,160
Pakistan	112.4	380	Jordan	3.2	1,240
Ghana	14.9	390	Colombia	32.3	1,260
Central African Republic	3.0	390	Thailand	55.8	1,420
Togo	3.6	410	Tunisia	8.1	1,440
Zambia	8.1	420	Jamaica	2.4	1,500
Guinea	5.7	440	Turkey	56.1	1,630
Sri Lanka	17.0	470	Romania	23.2	1,640
Mauritania	2.0	500	Poland	38.2	1,690
Lesotho	1.8	530	Panama	2.4	1,830
Indonesia	178.2	570	Costa Rica	2.8	1,900

TABLE 39.1

Measuring Gaps Using Purchasing-Power Exchange Rates

Research has shown that the exchange rates used for the preceding comparisons systematically underestimate the real production that takes place in the LDCs. The

	POPULATION (MILLIONS) MID-1990	GDP PER CAPITA IN DOLLARS 1990		POPULATION (MILLIONS) MID-1990	GDP PER CAPITA IN DOLLARS 1990
Chile	13.2	1,940	**OTHER ECONOMIES**	320.9	—
Botswana	1.3	2,040			
Algeria	25.1	2,060			
Bulgaria	8.8	2,250	**HIGH-INCOME ECONOMIES**	816.4	19,590
Mauritius	1.1	2,250			
Malaysia	17.9	2,320	Ireland	3.5	9,550
Argentina	32.3	2,370	Israel	4.7	10,920
Iran, Islamic Republic	55.8	2,490	Spain	39.0	11,020
Albania	3.3	—	Singapore	3.0	11,160
Angola	10.0	—	Hong Kong	5.8	11,490
Lebanon	—	—	New Zealand	3.4	12,680
Mongolia	2.1	—	Belgium	10.0	15,540
Namibia	1.8	—	United Kingdom	57.4	16,100
Nicaragua	3.9	—	Italy	57.7	16,830
Yemen, Republic	11.3	—	Australia	17.1	17,000
			Netherlands	14.9	17,320
UPPER-MIDDLE-INCOME	458.4	3,410	Austria	7.7	19,060
			France	56.4	19,490
Mexico	86.2	2,490	United Arab Emirates	1.6	19,860
South Africa	35.9	2,530	Canada	26.5	20,470
Venezuela	19.7	2,560	United States	250.0	21,790
Uruguay	3.1	2,560	Denmark	5.1	22,080
Brazil	150.4	2,680	Germany	79.5	22,320
Hungary	10.6	2,780	Norway	4.2	23,120
Yugoslavia	23.8	3,060	Sweden	8.6	23,660
Czechoslovakia	15.7	3,140	Japan	123.5	25,430
Gabon	1.1	3,330	Finland	5.0	26,040
Trinidad and Tobago	1.2	3,610	Switzerland	6.7	32,680
Portugal	10.4	4,900	*Kuwait*	2.1	—
Korea, Republic	42.8	5,400			
Greece	10.1	5,990	**WORLD**	5,283.9	4,200
Saudi Arabia	14.9	7,050			
Iraq	18.9	—			
Libya	4.5	—			
Oman	1.6	—			

SOURCE: World Bank, *World Development Report 1992.*

exchange rate of about 18 rupees per U.S. dollar turns out to be an unrealistic estimate of the real purchasing power of the rupee in India. In other words, 18 rupees in India actually purchase more than 1 dollar purchases in the United States. In fact, the evidence is that 18 rupees buy about three times more than 1 dollar purchases—that is, three times more than the exchange rate indicates.

Exchange rates are heavily influenced by the market prices of the goods that enter international trade, but not by the prices of goods and services that cannot

| | | | INTERNATIONAL | |
COUNTRIES	IN U.S. DOLLARS (USING MARKET-EXCHANGE RATE)	INDEX RELATIVE TO U.S. = 100	DOLLARS (USING PURCHASING-POWER EXCHANGE RATE)	INDEX RELATIVE TO U.S. = 100
LESS DEVELOPED				
Tanzania	$110	0.5	$540	2.5
Ethiopia	$120	0.6	$310	1.5
Bangladesh	$210	1.0	$1,050	4.9
Zaire	$220	1.0	$950	4.4
Nigeria	$290	1.3	$1,420	6.6
India	$350	1.6	$1,150	5.4
China	$370	1.7	$1,950	9.1
Kenya	$370	1.7	$1,120	5.2
Pakistan	$380	1.7	$1,770	8.3
Indonesia	$570	2.6	$2,350	11.0
Egypt	$600	2.8	$3,100	14.5
Philippines	$730	3.4	$2,320	10.9
Morocco	$950	4.4	$2,670	12.5
Peru	$1,160	5.3	$2,720	12.7
Colombia	$1,260	5.8	$4,950	23.2
Thailand	$1,420	6.5	$4,610	21.6
Turkey	$1,630	7.5	$5,020	23.5
Romania	$1,640	7.5	$6,780	31.7
Poland	$1,690	7.8	$4,530	21.2
Algeria	$2,060	9.5	$4,680	21.9
Argentina	$2,370	10.9	$4,680	21.9
Iran	$2,490	11.4	$4,360	20.4
Mexico	$2,490	11.4	$5,980	28.0
South Africa	$2,530	11.6	$5,500	25.7
Brazil	$2,680	12.3	$4,780	22.4
South Korea	$5,400	24.8	$7,190	33.7
DEVELOPED				
Spain	$11,020	50.6	$10,840	50.7
Britain	$16,100	73.9	$14,960	70.0
Italy	$16,830	77.2	$14,550	68.1
France	$19,490	89.4	$15,200	71.2
Canada	$20,470	93.9	$19,650	92.0
United States	$21,790	100.0	$21,360	100.0
Germany	$22,320	102.4	$16,290	76.3
Japan	$25,430	116.7	$16,950	79.4

PER-CAPITA PRODUCTION FOR SELECTED COUNTRIES, 1990

SOURCE: World Bank, *World Development Report 1992.*

TABLE 39.2

enter international trade (for example, haircuts and housing). Compared to goods traded internationally, nontradable goods and services are relatively low-priced and relatively abundant in LDCs.

Because the exchange-rate method of measuring income gaps leads to serious problems, a major effort has been made to obtain more realistic comparisons.[4] The result of this effort is **purchasing-power exchange rates** (PP), which take into account the purchasing power of a country's currency over the entire range of goods and services. These purchasing-power exchange rates are then used to express each country's 1990 per-capita GDP in "International dollars" shown in column four of Table 39.2. To facilitate comparisons, column five sets the United States at 100 percent and expresses all other countries relative to the United States. The table shows that India's per-capita GDP is 5.4 percent of U.S. per-capita GDP (about 1/19), not the 1.6 percent (about 1/62) derived earlier using market exchange rates. Such purchasing-power-based comparisons are the best available estimates of the real differences in per-capita GDP. (It is interesting to note that when the purchasing power of currencies is used to make the comparisons, Germany and Japan no longer display per-capita GDPs above that of the United States.)

Although the relative gaps between poor and rich countries are smaller using the PP exchange rates rather than the standard exchange rates, they are still quite large. The poorest countries in Africa and Asia have average incomes that are less than 5 percent of the U.S. level. The large developed countries of western Europe have per-capita production levels 10 to 15 times higher than the India–Bangladesh–Pakistan levels.

HOW THE GAPS EMERGED

How did these differences in living standards emerge? Why is per-capita production so much higher in developed countries? The short answer to these complex questions is that over the last 100–150 years the developed countries have experienced more rapid rates of growth in per-capita production than the LDCs.

Even small differences in rates of growth can result in wide gaps after only a century or so. To understand this we must first review the simple math of growth rates (sometimes called the simple math of *compound interest*). Table 39.3 gives the results of various annual rates of growth over selected time periods. For example, an initial sum of $1 million growing at 2 percent per year compounded once each year increases to $2.7 million after 50 years, $7.2 million after 100 years, and $52.5 million after 200 years. Also indicated for each growth rate is the *doubling time*: the number of years required for a quantity to double.[5] Anything growing at 2 percent per year doubles in only 35 years. For illustrative purposes, a growth rate of 7 percent is included; this rate has a doubling time of only 10 years. After 100 years, anything growing at 7 percent is 868 times larger than when it started. It is obvious that no economy can grow at 7 percent per year for very long. The basic point stressed here is that even *low* growth rates extended for a century or more lead to extremely large increases.

---

[4]The International Comparison Program of the U.N. began with detailed purchasing-power comparisons for just ten countries in 1970, but its coverage has grown over time. The detailed results for fifty-seven countries for 1985 have been extrapolated to many additional countries and to 1990.

[5]The so-called "Rule of 70" can be used to approximate the doubling time. When the number 70 is divided by a growth rate, the result is the approximate doubling time. For example, something growing at 3 percent doubles in just over 23 years (70/3 = 23.3).

CONSEQUENCES OF VARIOUS RATES OF GROWTH*					
YEAR	0%	1%	2%	3%	7%
0	1.0	1.0	1.0	1.0	1.0
10	1.0	1.1	1.2	1.3	2.0
50	1.0	1.6	2.7	4.4	29.5
100	1.0	2.7	7.2	19.2	867.7
200	1.0	7.3	52.5	369.4	752,931.6
Doubling times (years)		69.7	35.0	23.4	10.2

*The table indicates how much one unit grows when compounded at various growth rates for various lengths of time. One unit may be viewed as millions of dollars, thousands of people, and so forth.

TABLE 39.3

We can now use this information to explore the emergence of the gaps between rich countries and LDCs. It is clear that today's gap of, say, 12 to 1 between developed countries and LDCs could emerge after only 100 years from even small differences in growth rates. If two countries start at the same productivity level but the first does not grow at all and the second grows at 2 percent, the second will produce at a level 7.2 times higher after only 100 years. It is almost certain that 100 years ago the European countries that are developed today already had somewhat higher output per capita than the Asian countries that are less developed today. Assume the gap 100 years ago was already 2 to 1. If in the last 100 years the European countries grew at 1.8 percent while the Asian LDCs were stagnant, the 12 to 1 gap we now observe would emerge. We conclude that the current gaps between developed countries and LDCs are probably best understood as the consequence of a speeding up in growth rates in developed countries in the last century or so, causing them to move far ahead of the relatively stagnant LDCs.

The Industrial Revolution began in Britain about 200 years ago and then spread out from Britain to a number of other European countries, and to Europe's offshoots abroad—Canada, the United States, Australia, and New Zealand.[6] These countries—plus Japan with its spectacular economic performance over the past century—are today's developed countries. In contrast, the LDCs are those countries—containing about three-quarters of the world's current population—that have not fully applied science-based technology to production.[7]

---

[6]It is now recognized that we should speak of both an "industrial" and an "agricultural" revolution in Britain and other developed countries. Agricultural productivity increased as a consequence of increasing knowledge of plants, animals, fertilizers, and so forth.

[7]The classic treatment of these topics is Simon Kuznets, *Modern Economic Growth: Rate, Structure and Spread* (New Haven, Conn.: Yale University Press, 1966).

Characteristics of Less-Developed Countries

The major characteristic of LDCs—that which distinguishes them from the developed countries—is the low level of production and income per person. But money figures on per-capita production (and income) are inadequate to convey the level of economic well-being. For example, hundreds of millions of people in LDCs suffer from poor health and inadequate education.

One of the saddest facts about LDCs is their high **infant mortality rate**, defined as the number of babies who die before their first birthday per 1,000 live births. Table 39.4 (page 1054) shows the extremely high levels in many LDCs. Related to infant mortality is short *life expectancy*, measured as the number of years a newborn can expect to live given current patterns of mortality. In the poorest LDCs, life expectancies are in the range of 48 to 60 years; without exception the developed countries have life expectancies in excess of 75 years. Not shown in the table are improvements in these indices during recent decades. As bad as health conditions are in LDCs, they are better now than they used to be.

Relatively high infant mortality and short life expectancy are caused in part by unsafe water and inadequate food. Whereas most people living in developed countries take for granted clean drinking water and sanitary waste disposal, it has been estimated that one-fourth of the world's population lack such resources. The situation is particularly bad in rural areas of Africa and Asia, where perhaps four-fifths of the inhabitants lack access to clean water.[8]

It is not easy to summarize the food situation in the LDCs. Calorie supply as a percentage of essential calorie requirements is given for LDCs in Table 39.4. These figures cannot take into account either seasonal differences in food availability or, more importantly, unequal distribution of food to persons in LDCs. Thus, even when an LDC's figure is above 100 percent, it is certain that some inadequate nutrition exists. And, clearly, when an LDC's figure is near or below 100 percent, serious nutrition problems exist. This and other information support the conclusion that hundreds of millions of people have inadequate amounts of nutrients (calories, proteins, vitamins, and minerals) during all or part of the year.

Parents in LDCs have inadequate access to schooling for their children. Whereas in developed countries almost all the secondary school-age population is enrolled in secondary school, in most LDCs secondary enrollments are much lower (Table 39.4). Primary school-age enrollments in LDCs (not given) have increased dramatically in recent decades, but caution is appropriate when using these figures because they are unable to measure the quality of the educational services available. In many extremely poor LDCs the *teachers* in primary schools are themselves just primary school graduates with scant additional training. Unlike developed countries, most teachers in LDCs are not college graduates. In addition, the facilities and educational materials available to the students are often severely limited in both quantity and quality. So the educational services available to primary students may not be as adequate as the enrollment numbers seem to indicate.

---

[8]Lester R. Brown et. al., *State of the World 1986* (New York: Norton, 1986), pp. 167–168.

SOME INDICATORS OF ECONOMIC WELL-BEING FOR SELECTED COUNTRIES, 1990

COUNTRIES	INFANT MORTALITY (DEATHS PER 1,000 BIRTHS)	LIFE EXPECTANCY (YEARS)	CALORIES (% OF REQUIREMENTS)	SECONDARY ENROLLMENT (% OF AGE GROUP)	PER-CAPITA ENERGY CONSUMPTION (KG OF OIL EQUIVALENT/YEAR)
LESS DEVELOPED					
Tanzania	115	48	96	4	38
Ethiopia	132	48	71	15	20
Bangladesh	105	52	83	17	57
Zaire	94	52	98	24	71
Nigeria	98	52	90	19	138
India	92	59	100	43	231
China	29	70	111	44	598
Kenya	67	59	92	23	100
Pakistan	103	56	97	20	233
Indonesia	61	62	116	47	272
Egypt	66	60	132	81	598
Philippines	41	64	104	73	215
Morocco	67	62	118	36	247
Peru	69	63	93	67	509
Colombia	37	69	110	52	811
Thailand	27	66	105	28	352
Turkey	60	67	125	51	857
Romania	27	70		88	3,623
Poland	16	71		81	3,416
Algeria	67	65	112	61	1,956
Argentina	29	71	136	74	1,801
Iran	88	63	138	53	1,026
Mexico	39	70	135	53	1,300
South Africa	66	62	120		2,447
Brazil	57	66	111	39	915
South Korea	17	71	122	86	1,898
DEVELOPED					
Spain	8	76		105*	2,201
Britain	8	76		82	3,646
Italy	9	77		78	2,754
France	7	77		97	3,845
Canada	7	77		105*	10,009
United States	9	76			7,822
Germany	7	76		97	3,491
Japan	5	79		96	3,563

*Because the numerator of the expression includes some older students, this ratio can exceed 100 percent.
SOURCE: World Bank, *World Development Report 1992*. UNDP, *Human Development Report 1991*.

TABLE 39.4

Energy consumption per person is very low in LDCs. Table 39.4 gives the annual per-capita "oil-equivalent" energy consumption. Firewood and such traditional fuels as dung used in LDCs are not included in the totals because of measurement problems; however, their inclusion would not change the overall picture. The gap between developed countries and LDCs shown by these figures is staggering. In many LDCs there is a serious shortage of fuelwood, with hundreds of millions of persons depending on wood that is being cut faster than it can be replaced.[9] In the developed countries, the gargantuan energy appetite is a matter of grave economic and ecological concern. A large share of these energy needs are met by *exhaustible* fossil fuels that ultimately must be replaced by other energy sources. In addition, we now know that the carbon dioxide resulting from the combustion of fossil fuels exceeds the biosphere's ability to recycle, thus causing the *greenhouse effect* and consequent rise in atmospheric temperature. To the extent that increased productivity and incomes in LDCs are accompanied by increased use of exhaustible fossil fuels, as is highly likely, these problems will only increase. Clearly, the energy problems on Spaceship Earth require attention.

Population Growth is Rapid in LDCs

THE DEMOGRAPHIC TRANSITION

DEMOGRAPHIC TRANSITION

The transition from a society experiencing high birth and death rates to low birth and death rates; in the transition, the decline in birthrates lags the decline in death rates, leading to rapid population growth.

We now turn to perhaps the most important characteristic of LDCs—their rapid population growth. Before discussing LDC population problems in some detail, a little history is in order. Such population history is referred to as the **demographic transition**, and is illustrated in Figure 39.1. Until recent centuries, birth and death rates were high in all countries, with birthrates exceeding death rates by only a very small amount—so world population growth was very slow. For most of human history, zero population growth was the rule rather than the exception. In other words, Phase 1 in Figure 39.1 encompasses most of human history. The phase lasted for thousands of years, right up to recent times.

Today a number of developed countries are experiencing little or no population growth; in these countries birth and death rates are approximately equal with both at low levels. Such countries are already in Phase 3, having completed the demographic transition from a traditional society in which both birth and death rates are high and approximately equal (Phase 1) to a modern developed society in which both birth and death rates are low and approximately equal (Phase 3). For such developed countries, Phase 2 generally lasted a century or two, during which the gap between birth and death rates was probably not as large as shown in the figure.

The basic fact about the present world population is that most developed countries have completed the demographic transition from high birth and death rates to low birth and death rates, but most LDCs are only part way through the transition. LDC death rates have fallen, but LDC birthrates have not yet fallen sufficiently to

---

[9]Same as footnote 8, Ch. 5, "Reforesting the Earth."

In the first phase of development, both birthrates and death rates are high and population growth is very slow. In the second phase, the declining death rate precedes the declining birthrate, and population growth is rapid. In the final phase, the birthrate declines sufficiently to slow population growth dramatically. Economically advanced nations are in phase three; LDCs are in phase two.

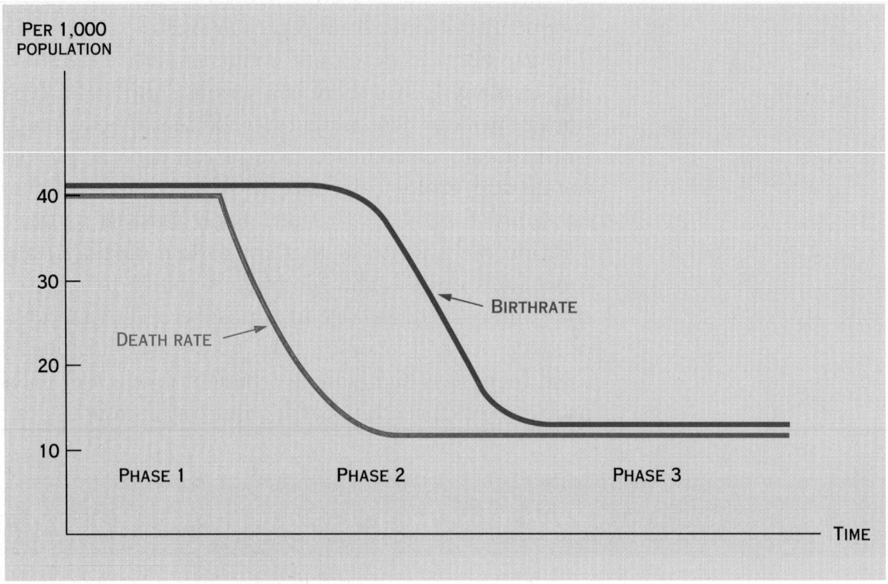

FIGURE 39.1

approximate the lower death rates—so population in most LDCs is growing rapidly. In terms of Figure 39.1, today's LDCs are still in Phase 2. Some LDCs (for example, those in sub-Saharan Africa) are in the early part of the phase, with birthrates still at traditionally high levels, while many other LDCs are in the latter part of the phase, with birthrates falling but remaining significantly above death rates.

Because the population cannot grow indefinitely on a finite planet, birthrates and death rates must eventually come into approximate equality. This means that for the world as a whole, and for each country, Phase 2 must be a temporary phase. How long it takes for LDCs to complete the demographic transition and move into Phase 3 is a matter of great importance.[10]

WHY POPULATION GROWS RAPIDLY IN LDCS

Table 39.5 (page 1057) reports prospective annual population growth rates for the period 1990–2000. In general, population growth is much more rapid in LDCs than in developed countries. Extremely high rates, in excess of 2.5 percent per year (leading to doubling in less than 30 years), are expected in Iran, Pakistan, and numerous

---

[10]It is useful to make clear why the low birth and death rates of Phase 3 are desirable. A long average life expectancy requires a low death rate. To the extent that societies prefer long lives over short lives, death rates must be low. But the finite nature of the planet requires essentially zero population growth. So birthrates must equal death rates, and must therefore also be low.

COUNTRIES	POPULATION (MILLIONS)		EXPECTED GROWTH RATE 1990–2000 (%)	BIRTH RATE (PER 1,000)	DEATH RATE (PER 1,000)	DEPENDENCY RATE
	1990	2000				
LESS DEVELOPED						
Tanzania	25	33	3.1	48	18	99
Ethiopia	51	71	3.4	51	18	99
Bangladesh	107	128	1.8	35	14	85
Zaire	37	50	3.0	45	14	96
Nigeria	115	153	2.8	43	14	96
India	850	1,006	1.7	30	11	70
China	1,134	1,294	1.3	22	7	49
Kenya	24	34	3.5	45	10	111
Pakistan	112	147	2.7	42	12	89
Indonesia	178	209	1.6	26	9	66
Egypt	52	62	1.8	31	10	77
Philippines	61	74	1.8	29	7	76
Morocco	25	32	2.4	35	9	80
Peru	22	27	2.0	30	8	72
Colombia	32	38	1.5	24	6	65
Thailand	56	64	1.4	22	7	58
Turkey	56	68	1.9	28	7	64
Romania	23	24	0.4	16	11	52
Poland	38	40	0.4	15	10	54
Algeria	25	33	2.8	36	8	90
Argentina	32	36	1.0	20	9	64
Iran	56	78	3.4	45	9	90
Mexico	86	103	1.8	27	5	69
South Africa	36	45	2.2	33	9	73
Brazil	150	178	1.7	27	7	66
South Korea	43	47	0.9	16	16	44
DEVELOPED						
Spain	39	40	0.2	11	9	49
Britain	57	59	0.2	13	11	53
Italy	58	58	0.1	10	9	46
France	56	59	0.4	13	10	51
Canada	27	29	0.8	14	7	47
United States	250	270	0.8	17	9	51
Germany	79	80	0.1	11	11	45
Japan	124	128	0.3	11	7	43

*Population for the year 1990 is actual; population for the year 2000 is projected. The final three columns reflect data for 1990.
SOURCE: World Bank, *World Development Report 1992*.

TABLE 39.5

African LDCs. The rates exceed 2 percent in eleven of the twenty-six LDCs. Only in relatively high-income Argentina, South Korea, Romania, Poland, Thailand, and in China (with its intrusive government population policy) is the rate less than 1.5

percent. With the exception of Romania and Poland, no LDC is expected to grow slower than 0.9 percent annually. In sharp contrast, none of the developed countries is expected to grow faster than 0.8 percent. These different population growth rates sharply distinguish developed from less-developed countries.

The population figures in Table 39.5 can be used to compute a striking fact. The expected *increase* in just the ten years from 1990 to 2000 in the total population of the twenty-six less-developed countries (648 million) is almost as large as the expected *total* population in the year 2000 of the eight developed countries (723 million)!

Population is growing rapidly in LDCs because births exceed deaths. Table 39.5 gives birthrates and death rates for 1990. In recent decades, with the introduction of modern medicine and improved transportation that reduce deaths from periodic famines, LDC death rates have fallen. Population is growing rapidly in LDCs at present because of the gap between the unchanged high birthrates and the now lower death rates (Phase 2).

Why are birthrates still high in LDCs? A few decades ago it was thought that parents in LDCs had more children than they wanted because of their lack of knowledge about contraceptives or because of limited availability of contraceptives. If it were indeed the case that the *actual* number of children exceeds the *desired* number of children, the increased provision of contraceptives would bring about a reduction of the population growth rate. For this reason, many early population-control programs focused on making contraceptives available. But we now know that a more fundamental reason exists. Parents may *desire* many children because children become productive at an early age or because having many children ensures that one or more survives into adulthood to be able to look after the parents in their old age. In the absence of anything like a social security system, in most traditional societies aged parents are looked after by their children. Thus, high fertility rates are *traditional*. For countless generations parents had to conceive and bear many children to ensure that some of the babies would survive high infant and child mortality and become adults. In summary, rapid population growth in LDCs occurs not because parents have more children than they want but because parents want a large number of children.

This is both good news and bad news. The good news is that if parents have many children in order to increase the probability that one or more become adults, the decrease in infant and child mortality seen in recent years will by itself eventually cause the desired (and actual) number of children to decrease as parents come to understand and act upon the knowledge that they do not need six or eight children to be sure of having one or two survive to become adults. The bad news is that it is harder to bring about the reductions in desired family size than it is to provide contraceptives.

CONSEQUENCES OF RAPID POPULATION GROWTH

DEPENDENCY RATE
The number of people not working per 100 workers in the population.

Rapid population growth has several important economic consequences. The first is that it causes a high **dependency rate**, defined as the number of nonworkers per 100 workers in the population. Table 39.5 shows the dependency rate based on the assumption that persons aged 15–64 are "workers" and persons aged 0–14 and above 64 are "nonworkers." The dependency rate is much higher for LDCs than for developed countries, because in a rapidly growing population a relatively large proportion of its members are young. (In LDCs the increased proportion of persons aged 0–14 more than makes up for the reduced proportion aged 64 and older.) The table shows that 100 workers in the poorest LDCs must support about twice as many dependents as do 100 workers in developed countries. The LDCs' low ratio of workers to total population in conjunction with the low output per worker causes the low output/population ratio (the low per-capita income) that characterizes LDCs.

A second economic consequence of rapid population growth is the existence of **population momentum**, which is defined as the tendency of a population to continue to increase even after the replacement level of fertility has been reached. The **replacement level of fertility** occurs when two parents replace themselves with two children. Most LDCs have fertility rates far above the replacement level: parents generally have more than two children. LDC populations are expected to grow rapidly for a long time to come because their fertility rates will be above replacement levels for a long time to come. But even if LDC fertility rates decreased immediately to the replacement level—so that beginning now all future couples would limit themselves to two children—the population would continue growing for a long time because of the disproportionately large number of youngsters (potential parents) already alive. Thus rapid population growth in the past guarantees some population growth in the future. Just as a fast-moving train does not stop immediately when its brakes are applied, a population does not stop growing immediately even when all couples decide to limit themselves to two children. Moving trains and rapidly growing populations have momentum.

In 1988, the World Bank estimated the magnitude of population momentum—the increase in population that would occur during the period from 1985 until population growth ceased—on the unrealistically optimistic assumption that the replacement level of fertility was reached in 1985. In fully 17 of the 25 countries the increase is at least 80 percent. This is a truly dismaying prospect. It means that even with the most optimistic scenario imaginable, LDCs will have to cope with much larger populations in the near future.

The third important economic consequence of rapid population growth is that it causes a rapid growth in the labor force. An increase in the labor/capital ratio slows down the growth of labor productivity—output per man-hour—which is the basic source of improved economic well-being.

The upshot of this discussion is that rapid population growth is a serious problem for LDCs and that a slowing down of the population growth rate would make a contribution to economic well-being.[11]

POPULATION MOMENTUM

The tendency of population to continue to increase even when the average couple bears two children; this phenomenon is attributable to the disproportionate number of youth in the population.

REPLACEMENT LEVEL OF FERTILITY

The fertility level that exactly "replaces" the parents—that is, two children per couple.

The Agricultural (Rural) Sector is Important in LDCs

The economic structure of the LDCs differs from the economic structure of the developed countries. By "structure," economists mean the relative importance of an

---

[11]While most of us can agree that birthrates must fall, there is now and perhaps will continue to be substantial disagreement about the morality, the legality, and the practicality of the various means capable of bringing this about (for example, various methods of contraception or abortion).

economy's major sectors (agriculture, industry, and services) in production and employment. The relative importance of sectors changes as per-capita income rises. We discuss the agricultural sector here because it illustrates the changes that occur and because an important point about agricultural development in LDCs can be made.

One of the most reliable characteristics of economic development is the inverse relationship between per-capita income and the relative importance of agriculture: the higher the level of per-capita income is, the smaller the relative importance of agriculture is. This is illustrated in Figure 39.2. This figure can be derived in two ways. We can use data for a given point in time from a large number of countries with incomes ranging from low to high (this is called cross-section data). These data show that the lower a country's per-capita income, the greater the percentage of its labor force in agriculture. In the poorest LDCs, more than 80 percent of the labor force is engaged in agriculture; in the richest developed countries, less than 10 percent is engaged in agriculture.

The fundamental reason for this is consumer demand. In countries where per-capita production and incomes are low, people spend large proportions of their low incomes on agricultural products. Thus, in poor countries agriculture accounts for large proportions of both production and consumption. International trade can modify the rigid link between a nation's production and consumption, but only infrequently can this cause the pattern to be broken.

The other way of deriving a figure such as 39.2 is to use data for a single country as it experiences economic development, that is, as its per-capita income increases from a low level to a high level over a period of time (this is called time-series data). As economic development occurs and per-capita production and

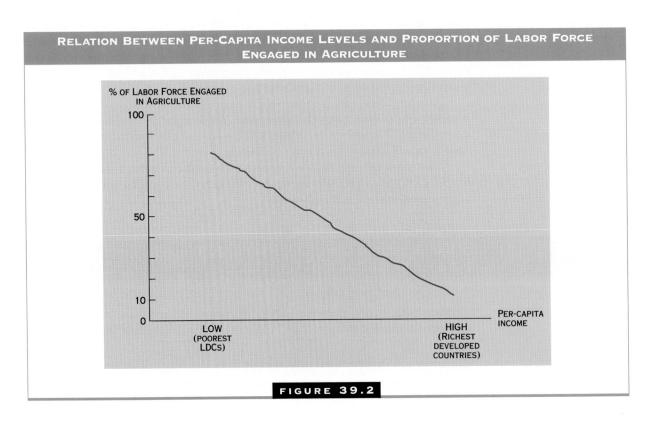

RELATION BETWEEN PER-CAPITA INCOME LEVELS AND PROPORTION OF LABOR FORCE ENGAGED IN AGRICULTURE

FIGURE 39.2

income increase within the country, the proportion of income spent on agricultural products decreases. This is reflected in a decreased proportion of a country's labor force and GDP in agriculture.[12] For example, in the United States in 1850, 50 percent of the labor force was engaged in agriculture. As per-capita production and incomes grew after 1850, the proportion engaged in agriculture decreased to its current low level. Note that these structural patterns refer to proportions, not absolute amounts. While the proportion of GDP accounted for by agriculture shrinks, the absolute amount of agricultural output increases. And while the proportion of the labor force in agriculture shrinks, for a long time the absolute number of workers in agriculture increases. As mentioned, in the United States the proportion of the labor force engaged in agriculture decreased from 1850 to the present, but the absolute number of people in agriculture (and the absolute number of farms) increased until about 1910. Only since then have both the proportion and the absolute numbers in agriculture declined. Today's LDCs are still in the pre-1910 U.S. phase: the proportion of the labor force in LDC agriculture will decrease as per-capita output grows, but the absolute numbers in agriculture will increase for a long time to come. This means that the kind of agricultural development that has been occurring in the United States (for the last 80 years) and in other developed countries—with decreasing numbers in agriculture accompanied by increasing average farm size—will not occur in LDCs in the near future. In the LDCs, increasing numbers of people will make their living in agriculture; the tendency will be for rural density (the population/land area ratio) to increase. This means that much of the agricultural research relevant to developed countries with lots of land and few workers is not relevant to LDCs with their prospective increases in rural densities.

Growth Theory for LDCs

CAUSES OF OUTWARD SHIFT OF THE PPC

The production possibilities curve (PPC) was used in Chapter 2 to illustrate certain economic principles; you should review this material at this time. You will recall that at a given moment in time (or a period of time short enough that changes in the quantity or quality of inputs are not significant) a country has a *given* amount of natural resources, capital, and labor, and a given level of technology. The PPC shows the maximum amounts of goods (output) that can be produced with these given inputs and technology. If the available inputs are not all employed, or are employed inefficiently, then actual production takes place at a point inside the PPC.

The PPC was also used to show that choices must be made. If a country is producing efficiently at a point on the PPC, it can achieve an increase in production of

---

[12]The corollary is that development is associated with increased proportions of a country's labor force and GDP in industry and services. This is the reason that economic development is sometimes referred to as "industrialization."

one good only by decreasing production of the other. One choice illustrated in Chapter 2 is particularly relevant here. If the two goods on the axes of the PPC are consumer goods and investment goods, the PPC shows that to increase the production of investment goods requires a decrease in the production of consumer goods. Current consumption is reduced to allow increased production of investment goods, more rapid economic growth and, consequently, higher *future* living standards and consumption. (As a practical matter, consumption in LDCs is often so low that it is quite difficult to reduce it further.) The increased production of investment goods causes an outward shift of the next period's PPC because there is an increased quantity of capital available for production in the next time period.

The PPC can also illustrate economic growth. If over time the quantity or quality of the inputs increases, or the level of technology increases, the PPC shifts outward. This means that more can be produced—the production possibilities have increased.

Note that an increase in GDP does not by itself mean that economic well-being has improved. We saw earlier that GDP per capita, not GDP by itself, is the appropriate indicator of economic well-being. If over a period of time both GDP and population increase by the same proportion, we can say that economic growth (measured by the outward shift of the PPC) has occurred but that economic well-being has not increased. For well-being to increase, GDP must grow more rapidly than population grows. This means that the outward shift of the PPC must be caused predominantly by increases in factors other than the quantity of labor—that is, by increases in the nonhuman inputs or increases in technology.

NATURAL RESOURCES

We now take a closer look at the increases in natural resources, capital, labor, and technology that will cause economic well-being in LDCs to improve. It is not possible here to deal adequately with natural resource issues in LDCs. Many LDCs clearly face critical problems with large populations in relation to their natural resource base.

There is a sense in which a country's natural resources are *fixed*. A country has a given surface area on which to catch sunlight, rainfall, and given mineral deposits. An *increase* in the natural resource input to production really means an increase in the proportion of the surface area used for economic production or an increase in the rate at which the fixed natural-resource deposits are depleted. In the short run an increased utilization of natural resources causes GDP to increase. But we must distinguish GDP increases sustainable over long periods of time from GDP increases not sustainable over long periods. To do this we must distinguish between *exhaustible* and *nonexhaustible* natural resources.

Coal and petroleum are exhaustible natural resources. An increase in the rate at which such resources are mined from geological deposits causes GDP to increase, but the resources cannot be mined forever. The depletion of exhaustible resources eventually requires finding alternative resources or reducing consumption. A critical problem for every society is achieving an optimal rate of depletion of exhaustible natural resources.

Forests and bodies of water are nonexhaustible natural resources, provided they are properly managed. Timber and fish are goods that can be harvested from such resources. If the harvest of timber or of fish does not exceed the regenerative powers of the forest or deplete the breeding population of fish, we obtain a sustainable flow of such goods. An important task for every society is to create a decision-making environment in which yields do not exceed sustainable levels.

In some densely populated LDCs it will be difficult to increase the rate of utilization of natural resources. For example, all available land may already be in use for agricultural production. But even when resources appear abundant, great caution must be exercised. The clearing of tropical forests to obtain land for raising crops or animals can easily led to soil erosion. And the destruction of tropical forests in LDCs influences global climate by reducing the biosphere's ability to recycle carbon dioxide.

CAPITAL

Recall that when economists speak of "capital" they mean such material objects as trucks, tractors, computers, roads, irrigation systems, and electricity-generation facilities. It is growth in this real capital that allows workers to be more productive and that supports higher levels of economic well-being. Research consistently shows a positive relationship between the investment/gross domestic product ratio (investment as a share of GDP) and the rate of growth of GDP. Recent research at the World Bank is summarized below.

It is important not to exaggerate the role of capital accumulation as a source of economic growth in LDCs. The rapid increase in Europe's production after World War II following the rebuilding of war-damaged capital caused just such an exaggeration. The productive capital of Europe had been very heavily damaged by the war. After the war this capital was restored in just a few years, partly by U.S. assistance through the Marshall Plan. GDP in Europe expanded quite rapidly, causing economists and others to place great emphasis on physical capital as a cause of growth and perhaps not enough emphasis on other essential inputs in the production process. Early foreign-aid programs to assist LDCs placed much emphasis on increasing the physical capital of LDCs, but GDP in LDCs did not rise rapidly as it had in Europe. Only later was it realized that reequipping workers in Europe who already had experience with capital was quite different from equipping workers in LDCs who had no previous industrial experience. Economists now pay increased attention to the human factor in the production process in LDCs.

LABOR

In most cases, an increase in the number of workers causes an increase in output. But if an increase in labor input is not accompanied by increases in other cooperating inputs (natural resources and capital), there will not be a proportional increase in output. Put more precisely, a 10 percent increase in labor input results in *less* than a 10 percent increase in output, other things equal. By itself, population (and labor force) growth leads to increases in GDP *and decreases in GDP per capita*. This, of course, is the primary reason why rapid population growth can be a serious problem. A famous economist once remarked that each new person (worker) in the economy comes with two hands—but not with a combine harvester or with farmland or other natural resources.

There is sometimes uninformed talk of "a shortage of labor" in LDCs. This reflects either an inappropriate focus on GDP rather than GDP per capita as the best indicator of economic well-being or a failure to recognize that an increase in labor, while leading to a GDP increase, leads to a *decrease* in GDP per capita. Developed countries are developed precisely because they exhibit high ratios of capital and other inputs per unit of labor—that is, because labor is in short supply relative to capital and other resources. To the extent that individual economic well-being is an appropriate goal, a small amount of labor relative to capital and other inputs is exactly what LDCs should strive for because this is what makes productivity and living standards high.

So far we have been talking about the quantity of labor. We must also talk about the quality of labor—because production is related to both the quantity and the quality of workers. Healthy, well-trained workers can produce more than unhealthy, poorly trained workers. In general, workers in developed countries are both healthier and better trained than workers in LDCs. Expenditures that increase the health and training of workers increase the productivity of the workers. Because expenditures of this sort have basically the same output-increasing impact as expenditures on physical capital, such expenditures on improving the health and training of workers are called "human-capital investments." In summary, increases in labor quality brought about by investments in improved health and education lead to increases in GDP per-capita. A major part of development efforts in LDCs must be directed toward increasing the quality of labor. Recent research at the World Bank showing that LDCs with more highly educated workers grow faster is reported below.

TECHNOLOGY

Along with natural resources, capital, and labor, the level of technology available at a given time determines the production possibilities of a country. The major contributing factor to economic development in recent centuries has been the application of science-based technology to production processes. The developed countries have applied modern technology to all or most of their production processes; the LDCs have not. The application of technology is the main reason why the developed countries are not still LDCs.

Because of the enormous backlog of *existing* technology, the LDCs are in the favorable position of being able to adopt existing technology rather than having to invent it. This is fortunate, because many of the LDCs are so small that it is unlikely they would be efficient producers of new technology. However, the possibility of being able to adopt existing technology should not be exaggerated. Much of the available technology is not suited to LDCs. For example, much of the agricultural technology developed for the large-farm environment of developed countries is not applicable in the crowded, small-farm environment of most LDCs. Thus it is necessary to adapt the existing technology to the requirements of the LDC. Another way of saying this is that the LDCs need *appropriate* technology, not necessarily the latest technology.

Each LDC must determine effective methods by which to obtain and implement appropriate technology. A variety of methods are available: sending capable students abroad to learn about improved technology, striking deals with multinational corporations whereby they invest in LDCs, implementing improved technology, transferring skills to LDC managers and workers, and establishing indigenous institutions capable of using basic science (probably produced almost exclusively in developed countries or larger LDCs) as a foundation for designing improved technology.

LDC Development Policies

We have seen that increasing the productivity of a country's labor force is the essence of its economic development. The preceding discussion of the major factors in economic growth leads to the conclusion that LDC governments must encourage the wise use of natural resources, the accumulation of both physical and human capital, and the adoption of improved technology. Here we mention certain other specific requirements: LDC governments must maintain law and order, must genuinely desire widespread increases in economic well-being, must carry out needed public investments, and must adopt appropriate domestic and international economic policies.

BASIC REQUIREMENTS

The most basic governmental function is to maintain law and order. An efficient economy requires at least minimal personal security. If the police, army, or bands of armed civilians routinely extort resources from others, the incentive to produce and invest is severely disrupted or eliminated. In some LDCs such minimum security does not exist. Where this is the case, the first developmental step is clear.

LDC governments must be committed to improving the economic well-being of all citizens, not just a few. This commitment is far from universal in LDCs. Some societies are run by elites (oligarchies) interested solely in self-aggrandizement. In such societies the governments do not use available resources to make the needed investments in social overhead capital such as education and public health. It is unrealistic to expect significant increases in the economic well-being of the poor majority in such societies so long as the government acts in this fashion. Another way of saying this is that existence of a responsive political system—one in which government officials are genuinely committed to the needs and interests of the masses—may be a necessary condition for economic development.

But even assuming an LDC's government maintains law and order and is committed to promoting widespread economic development, it is still essential that it make wise public investments and implement appropriate economic policies. Good intentions are not enough. Some LDC governments ostensibly committed to economic development adhere to policies that systematically stifle incentives to save, invest, and produce efficiently. The economic principles you have learned from this textbook—especially the microeconomics concerning the role of markets in coordinating the behavior of buyers and sellers—are frequently ignored by governments otherwise intent on economic development.

The ideal case is that an LDC's government has both good intentions and good policies. The worst case scenario is that an LDC's government has both bad intentions and bad policies. The intermediate cases are difficult to rank. Perhaps cases where bad intentions are accompanied by (inadvertent) good policies are better than cases of good intentions accompanied by bad policies.

PUBLIC INVESTMENTS

Many productive investments can be undertaken only by government authorities. When the benefits are widespread and payments cannot efficiently be collected from individual beneficiaries (for example, roads, education, public health, agricultural research and extension), public investment is required. These investments in *social overhead capital* must be financed out of the limited resources available to governments through taxation, and from internal and external borrowing. Careful analysis of the possible benefits and costs of potential public investment projects is required to obtain the greatest possible impact on economic development through available public resources. Choices must be made between additional investments in education, transportation, and so forth. Efficiency requires that, say, $10 million not be spent on a particular road project if the same expenditure on an education project would have a greater impact on development. Of course, an efficient use of government resources is easy to recommend, but difficult to achieve, even in developed countries!

APPROPRIATE ECONOMIC POLICIES

In addition to its own expenditures, LDC governments must put in place appropriate domestic and international economic policies. Economic life consists literally of millions of individual decisions about working, saving, investing, consuming, conceiving children, and so on. You have learned in earlier chapters how prices influence individual decisions and in turn how individual decisions influence prices. When actual prices accurately reflect the values of resources and goods, the decisions taken by individuals are appropriate from both individual and social perspectives. When actual prices do not reflect such values, private decisions cannot lead to socially optimal results. In short, appropriate government policy includes *getting prices right* and allowing private decision makers to act in light of those correct prices. Governments must ensure that their taxing and subsidy policies move prices in appropriate directions.

Appropriate *domestic economic policies* are crucial. For example, if governmental intervention keeps prices below equilibrium, shortages result. This often happens with food prices in LDCs. LDC governments often act to keep the price of food low; this increases consumption and reduces the incentive for LDC farmers to produce. (Incidentally, this is the opposite of what frequently happens in developed countries where government intervention keeps food prices *above* equilibrium, causing surpluses.)

Prices of such inputs as labor and capital influence the techniques used in production. LDC governments often act to keep the price of labor high and the price of capital low. Such price distortions result in the choice of production techniques that use too little labor and too much capital—exactly the opposite of the appropriate combination in LDCs, given that labor is quite plentiful in LDCs.

Appropriate *international economic policies* are also crucial. An overvalued exchange rate—putting too high a price on the LDC's own currency or, said the other way, putting too low a price on foreign currency—reduces the incentives for LDC exporters to export and increases the incentives to import. Eliminating the distortion caused by an overvalued exchange rate can simultaneously increase exports and reduce imports.

A case can be made that relative prices inside an LDC should reflect relative prices on the world market. Only in this way are the LDC's resources allocated according to comparative advantage. Following comparative advantage means that a country imports those goods and services that are cheaper on the world market than at home and exports to the world market those goods and services more valuable abroad than at home. Such policy instruments as taxes (including import tariffs), subsidies, and exchange rates influence relative prices directly; such instruments as import and export quotas influence relative prices indirectly.

In summary, both LDC domestic economic policy and LDC international economic policy should seek to reduce price distortions.

LDC POLICIES, INVESTMENT, AND EDUCATION AS DETERMINANTS OF GROWTH

In our discussion of growth theory for LDCs we made the point that increases in investment rates (to increase the quantity of capital per worker) and increases in the education level of workers would contribute to economic development. And we have just argued that eliminating distorted prices is important. Recent research at the World Bank shows the results of the interaction of policy distortion with investment rates and education levels in sixty-eight LDCs for the period 1965–1987. Table 39.6 (page 1068) shows the results of this research.

Each country was classified as having low or high policy "distortion," a low or high education level, and a low or high investment rate. Comparisons of average GDP growth rates of the countries in various categories are then possible. Table 39.6 shows the clear advantage of policies that result in low distortion of prices, high levels of education, and high investment rates. For example, comparing only the countries that have high education levels, those with low price distortion grew

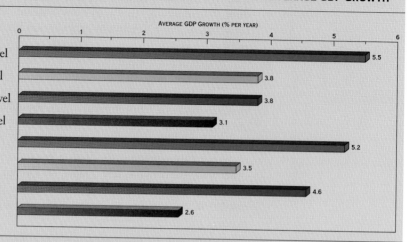

IMPACT OF POLICY DISTORTION, EDUCATION LEVEL, AND INVESTMENT RATE ON LDC GROWTH RATES (1965–1987)

LESS-DEVELOPED COUNTRIES WITH: **AVERAGE GDP GROWTH**

AVERAGE GDP GROWTH (% PER YEAR)

Less-developed countries with:	Average GDP Growth
Low distortion and high education level	5.5
Low distortion and low education level	3.8
High distortion and high education level	3.8
High distortion and low education level	3.1
Low distortion and high investment	5.2
Low distortion and low investment	3.5
High distortion and high investment	4.6
High distortion and low investment	2.6

Notes:
a. High-distortion LDCs have foreign exchange premiums above 30 percent. Low-distortion LDCs have premiums of 30 percent or less.
b. High-education LDCs average more than 3.5 years of education. Low-education LDCs average less than 3.5 years.
c. High-investment LDCs have investment to GDP ratios above the median. Low-investment LDCs have ratios below the median.
SOURCE: World Bank, *World Development Report 1991*, p. 47.

TABLE 39.6

at 5.5 percent, and those with high price distortion grew at 3.8 percent. For countries with low education levels, those with low price distortion grew at 3.8 percent and those with high price distortion grew at 3.1 percent.

Role of Developed Countries in the Development of LDCs

Finally, we return to the theme with which we began this chapter: All people are fellow passengers on Spaceship Earth. So how can those in the developed parts of the craft help those still in less-developed parts?

The theme of the development process underlying this chapter is that decisions made by the LDC's own government and by the LDC's private citizens are primary determinants of the LDC's economic performance. (Exhibit 39.1, page 1069, summarizes a competing theme of the development process.) While the main burden is therefore on the LDC itself, developed countries can do two things to help speed up the development process. Developed countries can help LDCs accumulate more rapidly the resources needed for economic development and can help LDCs achieve an efficient allocation of available resources in production by adhering to liberal international trade policies—that is, by abandoning all impediments to free trade.

E
X
H
I
B
I
T

Lenin's Exploitation Theory

There is another theory of economic development, one that views LDCs as victims of decisions made and actions taken by outsiders. This theory blames developed countries for the poverty of LDCs.

Briefly, the theory begins with Karl Marx's prediction that the impoverishment of the workers in capitalist countries will eventually lead to revolutions that will end private ownership of the means of production and establish socialist economies in place of capitalism. But the predicted overthrow of capitalism did not take place in the 70 years following Marx's prediction. Lenin explained the delay in the predicted revolutions in capitalist countries by arguing that developed capitalist countries had exploited LDCs. In effect, the conditions in developed countries that would otherwise have led to revolutions had been temporarily alleviated by developed countries enriching themselves by "ripping-off" LDCs, either through colonial exploitation or through international trade and investment linkages from which developed countries benefited most.

This Leninist theory links most or a large part of the poverty in today's LDCs to contacts with developed capitalist countries and to the LDCs' own capitalism (private ownership of natural resources, capital goods, and so forth).[13]

This theory leads to the policy prescription that LDCs must eliminate domestic capitalism and severely limit all international economic contacts with developed capitalist countries. This Leninist theory implies that, from the LDC perspective, help from developed countries should be limited to resource transfers to LDC governments. Private investment by developed countries in LDCs, in this view, should be prohibited by the LDCs.[14]

[13]These ideas are sometimes labeled "Marxism–Leninism," but this label inappropriately links Marx with Lenin. Whereas Lenin argued that economic development in LDCs was hindered by colonialism and other contacts with developed capitalist countries, Marx recognized the net beneficial impact on LDCs of such contacts. On this important topic, see Bill Warren, *Imperialism: Pioneer of Capitalism* (London: New Left Books, 1980).

[14]Citizens of both developed countries and LDCs must be sensitive to their possible biases. As citizens of a developed country, we are possibly biased against the Leninist view because it would make us uncomfortable to think that the economic success of the United States was causally linked to any lack of economic success in LDCs. On the other hand, citizens of LDCs may be attracted to the Leninist theory because it attributes their poverty to outsiders and not to defective political institutions and other factors inside their own societies.

39 . 1

DEVELOPED COUNTRIES AS SOURCES OF INVESTMENT FUNDS

Earlier we mentioned the great importance of LDC investment in human and physical capital to increase production. In most LDCs these investments are constrained by limits on the LDC's available savings. Developed countries can foster both public and private net transfers of resources to LDCs. When savings from developed countries can be transferred to LDCs, accumulation of human and physical capital in LDCs is speeded up.[15]

Private investment resources can flow to LDCs through direct investments by private firms, including investments by multinational corporations (firms with production facilities in more than one country). LDCs must negotiate good agreements with multinationals not only to obtain capital and technology, but to ensure development and training of LDC human resources. Private investment resources can also flow through loans to the LDC from private banks. (On this latter topic, see the discussion of the world debt problem in Chapter 38.)

Public investment resources can flow bilaterally (directly from the developed country to the LDC) or multilaterally (from developed countries to the World Bank and then from the World Bank to the LDC). Public resources are especially important in assisting LDC governments to provide the needed infrastructure: transportation, education, health, and agricultural research. These public resources for development are sometimes termed "foreign aid." In recent years U.S. foreign aid for economic development has been in the range of $10–$15 billion per year.[16]

DEVELOPED COUNTRIES AS LIBERAL TRADING PARTNERS

Finally, although it is less dramatic than contributing to the flow of resources and technology to LDCs, developed countries can contribute to an efficient allocation of all productive resources in both LDCs and developed countries by adhering to a liberal international trading regime. As resources and technology accumulate in LDCs, comparative advantage shifts. LDCs move beyond being exporters of primary products into labor-intensive manufactured goods, and later into a full range of manufactured goods. This means that LDCs will gain comparative advantage in sectors hitherto important in developed countries. For both LDCs and developed countries to achieve the benefits that come from an efficient worldwide allocation of resources, it is necessary that reallocations occur in developed countries. Some industries in developed countries must diminish or perhaps even disappear.

---

[15]In the absence of international economic contacts, a country's investment is limited by its own saving. But if a country can import more than it exports, it can invest more than it saves. It seems *natural* that a poor country should be enabled to invest more than it saves by becoming able to import more than it exports—that is, by running a trade deficit financed by savings transfers from other countries. Resources can be transferred from rich countries to LDCs to support higher investment in LDCs if LDCs run trade deficits and developed countries run trade surpluses. (Seen in this light, the United States trade deficit of recent years—a case of a developed country absorbing savings from the rest of the world—seems *unnatural*.)

[16]Many citizens of the United States appear to think that the United States gives a lot of economic aid to LDCs, and many think a reduction of foreign aid would make a substantial contribution to reducing the federal deficit. In reality, foreign economic aid represents less than 1 percent of federal expenditures, and its complete elimination would make only a minute contribution to solving the deficit problem. Foreign aid is an easy target because citizens of LDCs do not vote in U.S. elections. It is important that those who do vote and who are interested in promoting the economic development of LDCs have a correct understanding of the importance and the limited magnitude of U.S. foreign aid.

Although economic theory shows that the developed country as a whole gains from such reallocation, particular sectors may suffer losses. Steps taken in developed countries to facilitate such efficient reallocations simultaneously increase the economic well-being of developed countries and contribute importantly to economic development of LDCs.

Summary

1. Less-developed countries (LDCs) account for about three-fourths of the world's population. This proportion will increase in the decades ahead because of the more rapid population growth in LDCs.

2. Countries can be ranked according to production per person. The LDCs are countries in which production per person is low. Low production (economic output) per worker is the basic cause of low levels of economic well-being in LDCs.

3. When the gaps between developed countries and LDCs are measured using actual exchange rates, the gaps appear unrealistically large. Purchasing-power exchange rates show the gaps to be much smaller, but there still is a large difference between the economic well-being of rich and poor nations. The gaps between today's developed countries and LDCs emerged over the last two centuries as a consequence of the speeding up of growth rates in the now-developed countries.

4. The lower level of economic well-being in LDCs is characterized by high infant mortality, short life expectancy, unsafe water supplies, inadequate food for hundreds of millions of people, and inadequate access to decent housing, educational opportunities, and medical services. In recent decades, many LDCs have been successful in increasing the levels of economic well-being available to their populations, but rapid rates of per-capita output growth over extended periods of time are still needed to eliminate poverty.

5. An especially important characteristic of LDCs is rapid population growth, which is caused by the large gap between birth and death rates. The demographic transition from high birth and death rates to low birth and death rates is not yet complete in LDCs. Death rates have decreased in recent decades but birthrates are often still at high traditional levels. The population will continue to grow until birthrates decrease and again become equal to death rates.

6. Rapid population growth causes a high dependency rate (many dependents per each 100 workers). Past rapid growth ensures a large population increase in the future because of population momentum. Rapid population growth slows down the growth of worker productivity by slowing the accumulation of both human and nonhuman capital and by increasing the pressure on limited amounts of natural resources.

7. Agriculture is the dominant sector in LDCs. The lower a country's per-capita production, the greater the relative importance of agriculture. As per-capita production rises, the relative importance of agriculture shrinks. Because of the enormous size of agriculture and rapid growth of population, the absolute numbers of people in agriculture will rise in the years ahead, further complicating the problems of agricultural development.

8. Output per worker is a function of the quantities of nonhuman inputs available per worker and the level of technology. Development requires increased inputs per worker and improved technology.

9. LDC governments must intend to promote widespread economic development and must adopt economic policies that promote it. If either element is missing, growth will be

slow or nonexistent. Development problems are so serious that if the LDC's government is uninterested in development, the problems will not be tackled. But good intentions are not enough; good intentions accompanied by inappropriate economic policies stifle progress.

10. LDC governments need appropriate domestic economic policies and programs. Government must provide the social infrastructure for development and create an economic environment in which private sector decisions about childbearing, saving, investment, and production lead to increases in economic well-being.

11. LDC governments need appropriate international economic policies. These policies must foster appropriate specialization according to comparative advantage and create an environment that attracts useful direct foreign (multinational corporation) investment and foreign lending.

12. The United States and other developed countries can contribute to LDC development by public (government-to-government) resource transfers, but probably more importantly by adhering to liberal international economic policies that encourage efficient international specialization. This means that developed countries must be willing to restructure their own economies to accommodate more imports from and more exports to LDCs.

Key Terms

less-developed countries (LDCs)
purchasing-power exchange rates (PP)
infant mortality rate

demographic transition
dependency rate
population momentum
replacement level of fertility
exhaustible natural resources
nonexhaustible natural resources

Study Questions and Problems

1. Approximately what proportion of the human race lives in LDCs? Are there any large countries (with, say, more than 20 million citizens) that are difficult to classify as either developed or less-developed? If so, why?

2. Per-capita income comparisons using market exchange rates exaggerate the gaps between LDCs and developed countries. The richest countries appear 50–60 times better off than the poorest countries. Why does this happen? When purchasing-power exchange rates are used, how large does the gap between rich and poor appear? Why do the magnitudes of the gaps change so much when purchasing-power exchange rates are used?

3. Have the current income gaps between the rich and poor countries emerged because growth rates in rich countries speeded up, because growth rates in LDCs slowed down, or for some other reason? Discuss.

4. If GDP grows at 2 percent per year, how many years will it take for GDP to double? If population grows at 1 percent for 100 years, by how much will it expand?

5. Is population in LDCs growing fast because birthrates have risen or because death rates have fallen? What is the relationship between life expectancy and death rates? Why is the dependency rate high in LDCs?

6. Why is the agricultural sector so large in LDCs?

7. What is the distinction between exhaustible and nonexhaustible natural resources?

8. What historical experience after World War II caused the role of capital in the development process to be exaggerated?

9. What steps can developed countries take to help speed up development in LDCs?

10. What measures can LDCs themselves implement to bolster growth?

Selected References

Brown, Lester R. et. al. *State of the World 1986* (New York: Norton, 1986).

Hogendorn, Jan S. *Economic Development*, Second Edition (New York: HarperCollins, 1992).

Kuznets, Simon. *Modern Economic Growth: Rate, Structure and Spread* (New Haven, Conn.: Yale University Press, 1966).

Summers, Robert, and Alan Heston. "The Penn World Table (Mark 5): An Expanded Set of International Comparisons, 1950–1988," *Quarterly Journal of Economics*, May 1991, pp. 327–368.

United Nations Development Programme. *Human Development Report* (New York: Oxford University Press, published annually since 1990).

Warren, Bill. *Imperialism: Pioneer of Capitalism* (London: New Left Books, 1980).

World Bank. *World Development Report* (Washington, D.C.: World Bank, published annually).

LESS THAN 75 YEARS AFTER IT OFFICIALLY BEGAN, THE CONTEST BETWEEN CAPITALISM AND SOCIALISM IS OVER: CAPITALISM HAS WON. THE SOVIET UNION, CHINA, AND EASTERN EUROPE HAVE GIVEN US THE CLEAREST POSSIBLE PROOF THAT CAPITALISM ORGANIZES THE MATERIAL AFFAIRS OF HUMANKIND MORE SATISFACTORILY THAN SOCIALISM. . . . INDEED, IT IS DIFFICULT TO OBSERVE THE CHANGES TAKING PLACE IN THE WORLD TODAY AND NOT CONCLUDE THAT THE NOSE OF THE CAPITALIST CAMEL HAS BEEN PUSHED SO FAR UNDER THE SOCIALIST TENT THAT THE GREAT QUESTION NOW SEEMS HOW RAPID WILL BE THE TRANSFORMATION OF SOCIALISM INTO CAPITALISM, AND NOT THE OTHER WAY AROUND, AS THINGS LOOKED ONLY A HALF CENTURY AGO.

—ROBERT HEILBRONER[1]

[1]Robert Heilbroner, *The New Yorker* (January 23, 1989), p. 98.

Economic Systems—Transformation of Command Economies

EARLIER CHAPTERS HAVE DESCRIBED CAPITALIST ECONOMIES THAT USE MARKETS FOR COORDINATING ECONOMIC DECISIONS AND THAT RESORT TO ONLY LIMITED GOVERNMENT REGULATION OF PRIVATE ECONOMIC ACTIVITY. THIS FINAL CHAPTER TURNS TO THE MUCH MORE HIGHLY REGULATED COMMAND ECONOMIES IN WHICH ECONOMIC DECISIONS ARE COORDINATED BUREAUCRATICALLY. STARTING IN THE 1930S WITH STALIN'S DEVELOPMENT PUSH IN THE SOVIET UNION, SEVERAL COUNTRIES (CONTAINING NEARLY HALF THE WORLD'S PEOPLE TODAY) ADOPTED ELEMENTS OF THE COMMAND ECONOMY IN AN ATTEMPT TO APPLY MARXIAN SOCIALIST IDEOLOGY AND TO CATCH UP ECONOMICALLY WITH THE ADVANCED INDUSTRIAL COUNTRIES. BACKED BY STATE OWNERSHIP OF INDUSTRY, CENTRAL PLANNING WAS TO HAVE ANSWERED THE BASIC ECONOMIC QUESTIONS OF WHAT, HOW, AND FOR WHOM TO PRODUCE IN A WAY THAT PRESERVED AND EXPANDED SOCIALISM.

COMMAND ECONOMIES WERE BORN IN REVOLUTIONS CARRIED OUT BY COMMUNIST PARTIES WHOSE LATER RETENTION OF POWER WAS LARGELY BASED ON THEIR FIRM CONTROL OF THE ECONOMY. IN TURN, PARTY MONOPOLIZATION OF POLITICAL POWER PRECLUDED ANY OPPOSITION TO GOVERNMENT ECONOMIC PLANS. ALTHOUGH THE COMMAND ECONOMIES YIELDED HIGH GROWTH RATES FOR A WHILE, BY THE 1980S THERE WAS WIDESPREAD STAGNATION AND A GROWING RECOGNITION OF THE DISTANCE they had fallen behind their capitalist rivals. In a dramatic recent development, crises brought on by the failure of economic reform in command economies have led to new revolutions that cost communist parties their power. New, democratically elected governments are no longer interested in merely reforming the command economies. They are resolved to transform them into capitalist economies.

What are the prospects for the success of this transformation when nothing like it has ever been attempted before? And why was the *command economy* tried in the first place? Why did it fail? Why were the governments of the command economies unable to save their system through reforms? This chapter attempts to answer these questions.

Origins of the Command Economy

REVOLUTION IN BACKWARD AREAS

When communists led by Vladimir Lenin seized power in Russia in 1917, they violated Karl Marx's theory of historical progression.[2] According to this theory, the political situation would be ripe for revolution only after capitalists had fully developed the world's productive possibilities. Marx conceded that capitalists were capable of revolutionizing the instruments of production:

> The bourgeoisie [the capitalist class], during its rule of scarce one hundred years, has created more massive and more colossal productive forces than have all the preceding generations together . . . what earlier century had even a presentiment that such productive forces slumbered in the lap of social labor?[3]

Marx observed capitalists taking advantage of new technology and economies of scale by organizing groups of workers for mass production in factories. Eventually, capitalists were expected to create an industrial system yielding such abundance that economic scarcity would disappear. But, in Marx's view, capitalists would also create the instrument of their own destruction: a dissatisfied class of industrial workers, the **proletariat**, ready to revolt. Marx was certain that workers would come to see capitalism as a hindrance to economic progress.

As it turned out, some of the more backward countries, such as Russia, with little experience of capitalism were most ripe for revolution, while the advanced countries proved resistant. Marx greatly underestimated capitalism's capacity for reform and its ability to improve the well-being of workers. In 1949, communists led by Mao Tse-tung took power in China, another underdeveloped country.

In Russia (later the Soviet Union), the socialist experiment came to be equated with a full-blown command economy dominated politically by the Communist party. Without a large proletariat backing it, Lenin created an elite, centralized

PROLETARIAT
The working class under capitalism, consisting of people who own only their own labor (as opposed to the capitalist or bourgeoisie class of property and capital owners).

---

[2]The communists proceeded to build the Union of Soviet Socialist Republics (USSR) on the foundations of the former Russian Empire.

[3]Karl Marx and Friedrich Engels, *The Communist Manifesto*, (New York: International Press, [1848] 1948).

Communist party as a "dictatorship of the proletariat" to hold power until an actual proletariat arose. The party's strict control was aimed at developing the economy as rapidly as possible. Lenin's successor as Communist party leader, Joseph Stalin, expressed this sense of haste in speaking of overtaking his capitalist rivals in ten years: "Either we do it or they will crush us."[4] Thus, the backward conditions in the Soviet Union had as much to do with determining the shape of this **Stalinist growth model** as Marxist ideology. What Marxist ideology contributed to the socialist experiment was its critique of capitalism and its description of the ideal of future communism.

STALINIST GROWTH MODEL
Plan aimed at pursuit of rapid economic growth by collectivizing agriculture and concentrating investment spending on heavy industry.

THE ROLE OF MARXIAN IDEOLOGY

CRITIQUE OF CAPITALISM   There were three fundamental Marxian criticisms of capitalism: it exploited workers, it alienated workers, and it was inefficient. In Marx's model, all the means of production (factories, machines, and sources of raw materials) were owned and controlled by a capitalist class. With almost no chance of becoming capitalists themselves, workers were forced to hire themselves out. Unequal power in favor of capitalists meant that workers were paid less than the value of their labor. According to Marx, all value is derived from the labor content of goods. Therefore, the profit and interest earned by capitalist owners were not legitimate payments for factor services but an *unearned surplus* extracted from labor's share of output. What kept potentially restive workers under control was a threat of unemployment made credible by an "army of the unemployed"—joblessness maintained by successive rounds of job-destroying automation.

Marx argued that workers under capitalism would be alienated from their own human possibilities in being subject to market forces as well as decision making by capitalist owners. These owners organized their large factories for domination and control of the work force. A strict division of labor downgraded the skills and cheapened the labor of the mass of workers, while at the same time worker solidarity was suppressed by dividing workers into types (skilled/nonskilled, mental/manual) with different pay and status. People, who should obtain satisfaction from work, were forced to toil like machines.

Finally, Marx saw capitalism as inefficient and wasteful because of the business cycle and because of the chaotic nature of markets. The business cycle was attributed to underconsumption caused by workers lacking the income to purchase all their output. Crises during which goods went unsold and people went unemployed were endemic to the system and a tragic waste of resources. More recently, Marxists have argued that only high military spending has kept capitalist countries from total collapse.

Marx saw at least one advantage of the capitalist system: competition drove capitalists to search constantly for new technology, vastly increasing society's capability to produce (even though much of the new technology might be designed just to get rid of pesky workers or to gain better control over them). But, in general, Marxists view the market as chaotic. Not even large companies could be certain of

---

[4]Quoted in Gur Ofer, "Soviet Economic Growth: 1928–1985," *Journal of Economic Literature* (December 1987) p. 1,798.

selling what they produced, and workers could not be certain of their jobs. A big company might try to create and control markets through advertising and other forms of consumer manipulation (thereby denying consumer sovereignty), but competition from other giants could still cause it to fail. Socialists tend to view such battling for market control as wasteful rather than part of an innovative process with winners and losers. Instead of allowing the waste of resources on losing efforts, government planners should pick the winners before resources are committed as part of an **industrial policy**. Under capitalism such planning is done by monopolistic corporations (which act in the interest of private profit) rather than by the state agencies (which could act in the public interest).

SOCIALISM AND COMMUNISM   Why was *socialism* supposed to be better? Marx envisioned an eventual **communist utopia** that would take the productive forces created by the capitalists and, through redistribution and planning, enhance them. With the foundation of abundance created by capitalism, there would be the possibility of a new era without suffering and without economic classes. Given the Marxian scenario of capitalist exploitation, communists vowed to expropriate private property (especially land) and to prohibit the private hiring of workers. Social ownership of industry was expected to end worker alienation. Communism would then outproduce capitalism as capitalism had outproduced feudalism. All workers would do enjoyable work; no one would be relegated forever to menial labor!

There is very little, however, in Marx's writings or in the vast Marxist literature on what the actual organization of such a society might look like, although there was great emphasis on egalitarianism and social planning. Whereas capitalism stresses equality of opportunity, socialism stresses equality of income. The Marxist model also appears to rule out capitalist-style accumulation of wealth on the grounds that "unearned" income from private investment does not rightly belong to owners of the capital. In addition, social planning was seen as a more rational method than the market for coordinating production; it would also have the advantage of ending the business cycle and unemployment. Workers were to participate fully in decision making on "what" to produce, with social control over the division of labor. "How" and "for whom" were answered by a slogan: "from each according to his ability, to each according to his needs." This was not much to go on in setting up a real **socialist economy** in backward countries.

In addition, Stalin and his followers had to create, practically from scratch, another missing prerequisite of communism—the proletariat. Marxist ideology had stressed how people's attitudes were shaped by economic relations. Thus it was hoped that the socialist experience would quickly wipe out the old capitalist mentality. A new type of human, more concerned with the interest of society than with narrow self-interest, would result. (In reality, communist states resorted to massive political and cultural repression to ensure that people conformed to the Communist party line on how socialists should think and act.)

Because communist revolutions took place in backward areas, the expected contest between socialism and capitalism in handling abundance was not to be. Instead of the happy prospect of redistributing the productive resources inherited from capitalism, socialist planners had to undertake the careful allocation of painfully scarce resources. They had to show that socialist methods would be better at industrializing a poor nation than capitalist methods. Would socialist planners be able to do what Marx had claimed only capitalist entrepreneurs could do in fostering rapid technological change? In Marx's view "it was the special incentives of the

INDUSTRIAL POLICY
Targeting of certain sectors thought to be crucial for economic growth through government investment and other mechanisms.

COMMUNIST UTOPIA
The Marxian conception of an ideal society without economic classes and with all people realizing their full potential as creative human beings.

SOCIALIST ECONOMY
In Marx's conception, an intermediate stage of communism in which workers are paid according to their work; identified with the Stalinist growth model in the Soviet bloc and China.

capitalist marketplace that led to the large-scale application of scientific knowledge to industry."[5]

Lenin also understood the power of markets. In a temporary compromise of his anti-capitalist principles, he instituted the New Economic Policy (NEP) in the 1920s to combat widespread shortages. The NEP restored some markets, allowed private farming, and encouraged private enterprise in light industry and services. However, Stalin ended this experiment with markets in the 1930s, not because it did not work, but in order to begin a more socialist policy for industrialization. There was also the object of securing food supplies for the growing industrial work force. Peasants, who had been troublesome in this regard, were forced onto collective farms; those who had prospered under the NEP were sent to Siberia. Private property was expropriated, but not for some vague ideal of "social" ownership. Instead, the state was to own and control the means of production. Markets were abolished and almost all private economic activity prohibited. For coordinating production and distribution, Stalin resorted to central planning with the first in a series of five-year plans.

THE PUSH FOR GROWTH AND THE STALINIST GROWTH MODEL

The main objective of the Stalinist growth model as applied by the Soviet Union and other countries was to develop the national economy as quickly as possible in order to catch up with the leading capitalist countries. Allegedly, this model would demonstrate that socialist methods are better at industrializing poor nations than capitalist methods.

THE IDEAL OF CENTRAL PLANNING Central planning in the Stalinist growth model substituted coordination by central authorities for the coordination provided by the market in a capitalist system. For capital goods and other producer inputs, planners struck a so-called "material balance" to equate supply and demand (something done automatically by the *invisible hand* in a market economy) and to ensure that there were neither shortages nor waste of resources. Inputs of intermediate goods were then administratively allocated (see Figure 40.1). It was assumed that the planners could obtain the tremendous amount of detailed information necessary to make the system work. Enterprise managers were responsible for reporting faithfully on their capacity to produce and for meeting mandatory plan targets. Consumer needs were seen as simple and easily identifiable. Thus, they could be satisfied with mass-produced, standardized goods—one color toothbrush would do for all (just as Henry Ford once said, "Customers can have any color car they want, as long as it's black").

The Leninist concentration of political power in communist countries was instrumental in developing and maintaining centralized economic coordination. (In turn, of course, control of the economy greatly enhanced party power.) This centralized system was supposed to be better than the decentralized and democratic system of capitalism at defining and achieving clear growth goals. Time and effort would not be wasted on developing popular consent for tough economic measures.

---

[5]Quoted in Nathan Rosenberg, "Essay: Marx Wasn't all Wrong," *Scientific American* (December 1991), p. 158.

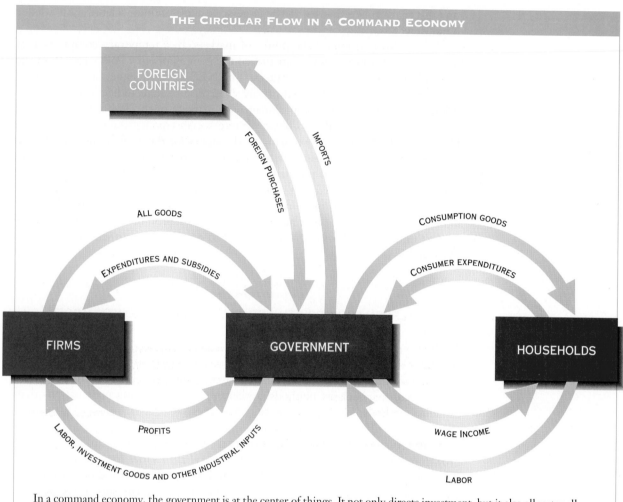

THE CIRCULAR FLOW IN A COMMAND ECONOMY

FOREIGN COUNTRIES

FOREIGN PURCHASES

IMPORTS

ALL GOODS

EXPENDITURES AND SUBSIDIES

CONSUMPTION GOODS

CONSUMER EXPENDITURES

FIRMS

GOVERNMENT

HOUSEHOLDS

PROFITS

LABOR, INVESTMENT GOODS AND OTHER INDUSTRIAL INPUTS

WAGE INCOME

LABOR

In a command economy, the government is at the center of things. It not only directs investment, but it also allocates all inputs for firms. It receives profits and dispenses subsidies. Households spend almost all their income at state stores and have their labor allocated according to the state plan. The government determines the nation's consumption/investment mix and sets wages and prices to balance household income and expenditures. Exports and imports are strictly controlled.

FIGURE 40.1

In particular, the lack of political opposition enabled the Communist parties to pursue two major unpopular elements of the Stalinist growth model: the collectivization of agriculture (which resulted in a disastrous famine in the Soviet Union during the 1930s) and the promotion of the capital goods industry over the production of consumer goods.

One important objective of central planning was to force society to save as much as possible and invest the funds according to central priorities. This was to be accomplished partly by holding down current consumption and partly by generating a surplus of funds from the agricultural sector. The surplus accruing from collectivized agriculture was to be obtained by paying farmers low prices and selling food at high prices. The payoff for the sacrifice of present consumption was to come in future abundance.

STALIN'S INDUSTRIAL POLICY   All investment was centrally controlled with funding through state budget grants or state bank loans at low rates. Stalinist *industrial policy* favored investments in heavy industry and large monopolistic enterprises. This policy was based on mistaken notions about what had been important to industrialization in the advanced countries. One misconception was that these countries were advanced because of their heavy industry (that is, the capital-intensive, producer-goods industry). Another was the notion that "the bigger, the better" policy was necessary to capture economies of scale. Thus, investment in agriculture went to large-scale, collectivized farms even though returns would have been higher in smaller private farms. Instead of the competition that was essential to the beneficial running of capitalist economies, the industrial policy produced a monopolistic structure in both industry and agriculture that enhanced top-down bureaucratic and party control of the economy.

It is ironic that Stalinist industrial policy produced in the command economy a result that Marx had predicted for competitive capitalism—an inevitable increase in business size and concentration. This tendency (which is often cited as something Marx was right about) was to have been an important element in the downfall of capitalism because it sharpened class differences and made revolution easy (there would not be that many capitalists left to overthrow). But what Marx and his followers did not realize was how important small and medium-sized firms would continue to be to the success of capitalism, especially when it came to innovation. The opportunity for workers to start their own firms and become capitalists reduced worker alienation and blunted their eagerness to revolt. As it turned out, the high degree of economic concentration under the Stalinist model led to many problems in command economies and made reform very difficult.

Marx himself had emphasized how vulnerable even large and seemingly secure companies under capitalism were to market forces. But enterprises under the Stalinist model were completely shielded from market forces; both sales and supplies were guaranteed by the state. In addition, a state monopoly in international trade protected enterprises from foreign competition. There were to be no failures and no layoffs of workers. In a real sense, socialist enterprises were "too big to fail." Despite this emphasis on large-scale enterprises, there were to be no monopoly problems. Communist managers would not use their power in a self-interested way to maximize profits but would follow the plan while minimizing costs. It was expected that the state, as owner, could effectively monitor and control its managers.

Besides ending unemployment and controlling monopolies, central planning was supposed to take care of other market failures typical of capitalism. Planners could supposedly "internalize" negative externalities, thereby preventing environmental problems. They could also ensure the proper production of public goods such as infrastructure and education.

COMPROMISES IN THE STALINIST GROWTH MODEL   No country that adopted the *Stalinist growth model*, including the Soviet Union itself, was ever able to put all its desired ideological and practical features into force. There remained a vestige of markets; not all goods were allocated administratively by the planners. Some consumer goods were delivered in-kind or were highly subsidized (including housing and medical care), but most items had to be purchased in state stores. People had a limited degree of "consumer choice" but not real "consumer sovereignty." *What* goods would be available in the stores was decided by central planners rather than by market forces of supply and demand. Similarly, workers had some choice of jobs, but this was limited by the state's attempts to allocate labor administratively according to the output plan. Controlled entry into education and training programs and compulsory assignment to first jobs for graduates helped this objective. Every able-bodied adult was to have a job.

Matching of supply and demand for individual goods was not to be trusted to the price system. In the case of intermediate goods, administrative allocation would create a balance. For consumer goods, prices had more of a role, but they were not free to move and seldom were set to balance supply and demand. Given Marxist labor-based value theory, prices were to reflect cost of production. In addition, prices were used to favor the consumption of some goods over others. Basic goods were sold below cost (subsidized) and luxury goods above cost (taxed).

Despite the prevalence of in-kind distribution and subsidies, the envisioned equal income distribution never was achieved. Material incentives, especially the profit motive, were scorned as bourgeois and unnecessary because the **moral incentive** of working for the future of communism (when there would be plenty of material goods) was sufficient reason for hard work now. Workers would compete for medals for being a model worker rather than striving for cash bonuses. But, almost from the beginning, it was found that some of the most important jobs would not get done without material incentives in the form of extra income. Later, special perquisites (including access to special shops having goods unavailable to ordinary citizens) were forthcoming for those with status in the Communist Party, the arts, and the professions. In fact, the ruling parties in both China and the Soviet Union waged ideological battles against leftists who demanded more egalitarianism. The argument was that the existing systems were socialist and not fully communist. Therefore, the proper distribution principle was "from each according to his ability, to each according to his work."

MORAL INCENTIVES
Promotion of desirable behavior by appealing to the individual's responsibility to society and by raising the individual's social stature within the community.

SUCCESS AND EMULATION

The Stalinist model of a command economy was quite successful for a time in mobilizing resources for growth. Stalin was able to build a formidable military machine for the defeat of Nazi Germany in World War II and to take communism to Eastern Europe. When, on a 1959 trip to the United States, Soviet leader Nikita Khrushchev declared, "We will bury you," the boast seemed plausible. There were notable successes in science and space, as well as enviable increases in the output of basic industrial materials. Many newly independent developing countries tended to look on the Soviet Union as a model for successful development. In China, centralized planning and state ownership were used to end widespread hunger and bring basic services to the people. By achieving a magnitude of forced saving consistent with the Stalinist growth model, China (under Mao's leadership) was able to devote 30 percent of its GDP to investment and to increase the share of industrial production in total output much faster than other very poor developing countries.

By the 1970s, however, growth in command economies began to fall short of the rosy projections. Stagnation continued into the mid-1980s with Soviet (and Eastern European) growth rates running less than two-thirds of the average for major capitalist economies. Output per capita in the Soviet Union was less than one-third that of the United States (see Table 40.1). The extra emphasis given to investment and military spending in Soviet plans meant that consumption per

INDICATORS OF LIVING STANDARDS IN EASTERN EUROPE, THE SOVIET UNION AND SELECTED WESTERN COUNTRIES

	PER CAPITA GDP, 1988 INDEX RELATIVE TO U.S. = 100		OTHER DATA, MID-1980S	
	USING MARKET EXCHANGE RATE	USING PURCHASING POWER PARITY EXCHANGE RATE	CARS PER 1,000 POP.	TELEPHONES PER 1,000 POP.
Bulgaria	25	26	127	248
Czechoslovakia	17	35	186	246
East Germany	36	43	214	233
Hungary	13	30	156	152
Poland	9	25	112	122
Romania	16	19	NA	111
USSR	25	31	46	124
Yugoslavia	14	24	129	146
Austria	85	62	355	525
Finland	107	70	343	617
Greece	27	32	143	413
Portugal	20	30	191	202
Spain	45	42	262	396
Turkey	7	20	20	91
West Germany	99	74	459	650
United States	100	100	565	789

SOURCE: Peter Murrell, "Symposium on Economic Transitions in the Soviet Union and Eastern Europe," *Journal of Economic Perspectives* (Fall 1991), p. 6.

TABLE 40.1

capita was even worse, close to only one-fourth of that in the United States. Soviet citizens complained about inadequate food, clothing, housing, and medical care. Per-capita output as well as life expectancy (69.5 years) and infant mortality (24 deaths per 1,000 births) put the Soviet Union in the category of less-developed countries. Slower growth made it very difficult for the Soviets to match the American increases in military spending in the early 1980s and to maintain their superpower status. It was ultimately clear that the Stalinist model had been a disastrous mistake.

Stagnation under the Stalinist Model

Why was there stagnation in the command economies? The fundamental reason was that the technological progress characteristic of capitalist economies was missing under the *Stalinist growth model*. The extra haste to grow and the means chosen to pursue growth were not conducive to innovation. The means—central planning—proved to be impossible in a complex modern economy. Equally important, however, was the fact that no one had an incentive to make central planning work effectively to serve consumers. In fact, it seemed the party and bureaucratic elite actually stood to gain from the system not working well. All sectors suffered from widespread shortages and inefficiency associated with state ownership and centralized planning. As Soviet leader Gorbachev recently said:

> If anyone is nostalgic about the economic system of the past, I can say this: By the early 1980s, the command system of economic management had shown that it had totally exhausted its potential, and the people did not gain the appropriate benefits from the enormous resources that were expended in the process of that command management.[6]

BORROWING FROM THE FUTURE

Much of the earlier growth, especially in the Soviet Union, had been illusory in that it was so unbalanced in favor of heavy industry. There were rapid increases in the output of steel and energy, but much of it was wasted. Meanwhile, as investment boomed, consumers waited for the promised future abundance. They, of course, had little choice in the matter; their apparent willingness to wait was not caused by a high value placed on future consumption, but rather reflected the planners' decisions. The real goal was not high future consumption, but as much output as possible of highly visible goods such as steel, energy, and military hardware. This would demonstrate the success of socialism and maintain Communist power. Steel and energy were desired for their own sake, not for their value as intermediate goods in the production of desirable final goods. The Soviet Union used twice as much steel and energy per unit of output as the advanced capitalist economies. Communist leaders ended up doing what Marx had accused capitalists of doing: producing goods not for use but merely for the sake of producing.

In trying to catch up to the capitalist countries quickly, extra costs were incurred and necessary expenditures delayed. Agriculture, consumer goods, services, and the infrastructure were all neglected in the haste to build a heavy industrial sector. An important reason for agricultural shortages and food rationing in the Soviet Union was the lack of adequate transportation and storage facilities and the subsequent high level of spoilage. In effect, the countries using the Stalinist growth model borrowed from the future in their impatience to industrialize and build a formidable military apparatus. Interest on the "loan" was paid in many ways. For example, roads, bridges, and other infrastructure were in a state of disrepair.

There are other ways in which the borrowing from the future has shown up. There is a tremendous "debt" to the environment, which has been severely damaged in command economies—the internalizing of externalities that was supposed to be possible under central planning did not happen. In a sense there is another "debt," caused by the hasty exploitation of natural resources—easily accessible resources were depleted too rapidly. There exist actual financial debts, too. Command economies have built up large international debts to capitalist countries.

NEGLECT OF AGRICULTURE

In agriculture, the Stalinist model called for collectivization (large-scale state farms and communes) and central planning in an attempt to ensure an adequate food

---

[6]Mikhail Gorbachev, interview in *U.S. News & World Report* (December 2, 1991), pp. 64–67.

supply for industrial workers, as well as to generate a surplus for investment in industry. But agriculture faltered badly as poor incentives and the inefficiency of bureaucratic planning overwhelmed the anticipated economies of scale.[7] The Soviet Union was not able to feed its own people, even though 20 percent of the population worked on farms. Although a surplus initially was extracted from agriculture, soon the government was forced to subsidize agriculture to keep food prices low in urban areas. That is, instead of paying low prices at the farm and selling at high prices in state food stores (thus generating surplus state revenue for use in industry), the state paid low prices and charged even lower prices (thus using up state revenues from elsewhere). The subsidy on bread was so high in the Soviet Union that farmers found it profitable to sell their grain at the state procurement price and use cheap bread from the state stores to feed their livestock.[8]

LACK OF TECHNOLOGICAL PROGRESS

There was a failure to shift, as the advanced capitalist countries have, from an "extensive" basis for growth to an "intensive" basis. Chapter 2 pointed out that economic growth (outward shift in the production possibilities curve) can occur by increasing resources (**extensive growth**) or by applying new technology, (**intensive growth**). The record shows that the Soviet Union and other countries following the Stalinist growth model were unable to develop and apply new technology consistently. And, because they ran into limits on increasing resource inputs, their growth rates faltered. In the Soviet Union, with its already high labor force participation rate and slow population growth, there was no choice but to rely on increasing labor productivity for growth. Increases in natural resources were also harder to come by, because any new supplies had to come from more inhospitable and costly areas.

The success in generating high levels of national saving for investment was one of the hallmarks of command economies. But central planners had great difficulty making the high investment work as a vehicle for rapid technological progress. Too much research and development tended to be carried out in centralized institutes separate from the producing enterprises, making it difficult to move innovations to the shop floor. Too much investment was also tied up in the old basic industries, where there had been economies of scale. Given that all decisions were made bureaucratically and that these previously favored industries would constitute powerful interests, this is not surprising. Central planning turned out to be very inflexible, especially when it came to reallocating investment from the older rust-belt industries to the promising newer industries.

EXTENSIVE GROWTH Economic growth attributable to increases in the quantity of such inputs as natural resources, labor, and capital goods.

INTENSIVE GROWTH Economic growth attributable to technological progress, which increases the productivity of inputs.

---

[7]Soviet poet Maxim Gorky eulogized collectivized agriculture in metaphors: "Twenty five million heads will form one wise, efficient head. This will decide in which region and on what soil it will be advantageous to sow only wheat, and where it will be best to sow only rye or barley. . . . The vision of a single head combining the 25 million others will transcend the narrow bounds of the province to absorb the entire country, and the new laborer on the land will see all the ugliness of his past, the senseless and useless way he habitually wasted his energies." Quoted in *Business in the USSR* (September 1991), p. 15.

[8]Not all command economies collectivized agriculture as extensively as the Soviet Union and China. Poland's agriculture remained almost entirely private. And even in the Soviet Union, farmers were allocated small private plots of land for feeding their own families (echoing the traditional practice of feudalism); plot output could be sold on a limited free market. With only about 3 percent of the Soviet Union's arable land, the peasants on their private plots produced about 25 percent of the country's total crop output and about 30 percent of the total milk and meat output. Marshall Goldman, *Gorbachev's Challenge: Economic Reform in the Age of High Technology* (New York: Norton, 1987) pp. 33–34.

In addition, investment without technological progress meant diminishing returns to additional capital accumulation. Therefore, investment had to increase continually or growth would fall even further. In fact, over the last three decades the ratio of investment to GDP has climbed from 17 to 26 percent, while productivity growth declined and was actually negative in the 1980s (that is, output per worker declined). Furthermore, continuing the high investment/GDP ratio from the early period of industrialization meant retaining also the low output of consumer goods typical of command economies.

PERVERSE INCENTIVES IN INDUSTRY

OVER-CENTRALIZATION OF PLANNING Excessive centralization of decision making and implementation through an inflexible bureaucracy not only repressed initiative by enterprise managers, but it also resulted in misallocation of inputs and outputs. The system bogged down under the sheer scale of the required detailed decision making. The former mathematics professor Konstantine Borovoy says there were several hundred thousand enterprises in all branches of the Soviet economy, and they turned out more than 12 million different commodities. In order to draft a well-balanced production plan, one would need about 30,000 years, even with the most advanced computers. In Stalin's day, when there were just a few priorities involving standardized goods and simple mass-production processes, it was possible to imagine that centralized planning could work. However, it is simply not suited to the modern economy.

PROBLEMS IN ENTERPRISE MANAGEMENT In theory, ownership of enterprises in the Stalinist system resided in "the whole people," but effective control was exercised by the state bureaucracy (within which enterprise managers were minor officials). Given the Communist Party's domination over the state, this meant that ownership rights and management prerogatives were actually held by the party hierarchy. Under capitalism, such merging of ownership and management is viewed as a good thing, but under communism it meant that managers paid too much attention to the wishes of higher bureaucrats and party officials and not enough to the needs of customers. For party officials themselves, top priority went to the maintenance of party power and the comfortable life-style available only to the party elite.

Managers were in strict control of their enterprises, but they were themselves strictly controlled by the party and the bureaucracy. Even so, proper control of enterprises in pursuit of the center's goals proved elusive in the Stalinist system. Being under the thumb of the bureaucracy, managers tended to exhibit a lack of responsibility and initiative. The fact that the targets were annual ones led to short-sightedness. Useful longer-run innovations in products or processes were not undertaken because this would have interfered with getting the immediate job done. Workers in command economies had little incentive to work hard, given that there were few goods available to buy and little chance of being fired for laziness. Soviet workers had a saying, "They pretend to pay us and we pretend to work."

A major problem in central planning was that the government plans were never complete enough to provide proper guidelines for production. Managerial performance was judged primarily on the fulfilling of annual targets for total quantity or total value of output. Managers knew how difficult it was to measure quality and how seldom they would be disciplined for poor quality. Judging managers simply on the basis of total value of output also meant that it was seldom in a manager's self-interest to reduce costs.

DISTORTED PRICES AND SHORTAGES Almost all prices in command economies were set by the central planners and bore little relationship to the scarcity values that would have been determined in free markets. One reason distortions developed was that there were just too many prices to set and essential adjustments were postponed.[9] Since prices were adjusted neither for changes in demand nor for short-run supply conditions, they failed to give appropriate signals to producers and consumers. In a market economy, deviations of market prices from average costs signal the opportunity for entry or the need for exit from the industry by profit-maximizing firms. In a command economy, bureaucratic price setting along with the lack of a real profit motive severely inhibited such responses.

Many prices ended up either too high or too low. One cause of high prices was that enterprises often deemphasized product quality in order to meet plan targets. Consumers then saw the price as too high given the quality. Excess goods piled up. But the most common problem in command economies was prices kept artificially low with little relationship to supply and demand. Many prices were below production costs, requiring government subsidies.

Other features besides the artificially low prices contributed to the predominance of shortages in command economies. Exhibit 40.1 points out the problem of having to order inputs far before they are needed. In addition, enterprises tended to have an unlimited demand for investment funds and other inputs, because with **soft budgets** there was no real penalty for failure of investment projects or for cost overruns. There was also no financial constraint on investment, because the funds were either free (government grants) or low cost (because of below-market interest rates at state banks). Paying for inputs in a command economy was not a problem, because enterprise managers could count on being provided with whatever funds were necessary to meet the output plan. That is, enterprises faced a *soft budget* constraint under which inputs were essentially free. The plan may have specified a spending limit, but it was always negotiable. Unprofitable firms were not allowed to fail; instead, their losses were covered with government subsidies.

Demand for inputs was also boosted by the information game that central planners and enterprise managers tended to play. The latter had an incentive to understate capacity in order to obtain a more easily achieved mandatory plan for output; bonuses were paid only for surpassing the plan. The planners naturally countered by assuming the enterprises could produce more than they said, and gave everyone a high target. Such planning left little slack to take care of the inevitable errors and breakdowns in production. A failure of one enterprise to meet its goal caused problems for other enterprises dependent on it for inputs. Managers would try to protect against such supply failures by asking for and hoarding extra inputs. Enterprises also tended to carry extra employees for the same reason; workers ended up

SOFT BUDGET
A flexible, almost unlimited budget enjoyed by enterprises; they can rely on the state for subsidies and tax breaks to bail out inefficient and unprofitable operations.

---

[9]There are reported to be 25 million individual items to be priced in the Soviet Union. That seems like a lot, but in the United States, there are 25 million trucking tariffs alone! Cited in William D. Nordhaus, "Soviet Economic Reforms: The Longest Road," [an allusion to socialism being the longest road from capitalism to capitalism] *Brookings Papers on Economic Activity* (1: 1990), p. 293.

Plan and Market

One of the main impediments to scientific technological progress lies in the existence of shortages. And these shortages are not primarily caused by too little being produced. Their main underlying cause rests in the lack of any real feedback between consumer and producer. In other words, shortages are generated by the working of the economic system.

The existing system itself gives rise to shortages where the consumer is simply an adjunct of the producer, where the consumer has no freedom of choice, but confronts a centralized distribution of products quite heedless of their quality. To support this statement I will present a hypothetical example. Let us suppose that the entire population's need for sugar is wholly and fully met. Nobody hoards bags of sugar at home. Now imagine a situation in which from 1st January of the following year the open sale of sugar is abolished and sugar is to be given out according to applications which must be made well in advance. It is difficult to estimate how much sugar a family requires to meet its various needs, which can include jam-making, providing for guests, as well as for unforeseen demands. Therefore every family will try to obtain the maximum quantity of sugar so as to meet in full whatever needs may arise. And if these applications are likely to be pruned then every claimant will consciously increase the quantity of sugar demanded to guarantee a supply for all eventualities. All these applications will be collected and totalled and in all probability the volume of sugar production will turn out to be quite insufficient. The applications will have to be reduced. A shortage of sugar will arise in the country, while in every home bags are being stored up and gradually everybody will accumulate enough sugar to last for many months to come.

I have introduced an intentionally simple example. But imagine a present-day enterprise: it must make applications for rolled steel and other materials long before the plan of production for the following year has been determined. Not yet knowing the details of its final plans, these applications are naturally exaggerated. Much is acquired that is not needed. So difficult is the existing bureaucratic method of passing on unneeded resources to another enterprise, that it is easier to leave the unneeded materials in the storehouse.

SOURCE: Reprinted from *The Challenge of Perestroika*, pp. 136–137, by Abel Aganbegyan (former advisor to Mikhail Gorbachev), Indiana University Press, 1988.

EXHIBIT 40.1

underemployed with very low measured productivity. Low prices for producer inputs and low wages encouraged these outcomes.

Many goods in short supply were either directly allocated or rationed by the planners. Others went to whomever was first in the queue or to whomever had the right "connections" with the official distributors. In the consumer goods sector, sales taxes could have been used to bring low retail prices up to market-clearing levels, but this was seldom done. For many goods, low prices were deliberately maintained as a subsidy for consumers. In addition, planners contributed to excess

Assume planners target the level of output for a consumer good at Q_0 and set the price at P_1. Given that the price is below the market-clearing level (P_0), there is a shortage ($Q_1 - Q_0$).

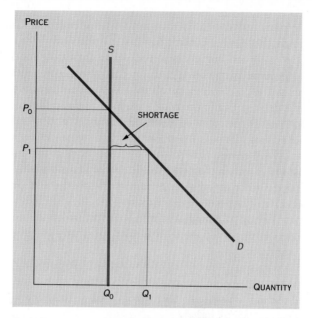

FIGURE 40.2

demand (shortages) by not maintaining an overall balance between total wages paid and the total value of available consumer goods. The widespread prevalence of product shortage caused by the combination of low planned output and high demand in consumer markets is illustrated in Figure 40.2. People had to spend hours each day standing in lines and searching for goods. Consumers would join a queue without even knowing what was being offered for sale, just to make sure they did not miss anything.

Attempting Reform in Command Economies

Reform in command economies has a long history, including retreats from the attempt to run the economy as "one vast corporation." The origin and necessity of the repressive features of the Stalinist growth model were also questioned. The political breaks from the Soviet Union by Yugoslavia and China led to experiments in worker management of enterprises in the former and to Mao's "cultural revolution" against the dominance of central officialdom in the latter. There was discussion in the Soviet Union and China as early as the 1950s about increasing the role of markets. But until recently, reform mainly involved efforts to make the command system work better either by tightening discipline or by decentralizing within the bureaucratic system. As the Chinese say about this record: "We relax control, and get chaos; we recentralize, and get inertia." Hungary, however, did go further by dropping mandatory plan targets in 1968 without causing chaos.

ELEMENTS OF COMMUNIST REFORM PROGRAMS

With new reform-minded communist leadership in China (Deng Xiaoping, 1978) and in the Soviet Union (Mikhail Gorbachev, 1985), more serious efforts were taken to loosen bureaucratic control and institute market-type decentralization. It had become increasingly evident that their economies would fall further behind unless drastic changes were made in the command system. Lagging productivity threatened not only the economic base of the military-industrial complex, but also the "perks" that the bureaucratic and party elite obtained from the system. Gorbachev's and Deng's intentions for this reform effort were to achieve greater efficiency and ensure that production met the needs of both industrial and household customers rather than just fulfilling the central plan. The burden of central planning was to be eased so managers and workers could begin to show more individual initiative. The resulting increased technological change would raise the standard of living. They had no intention, however, of letting the loosening of bureaucratic control over the economy lead to a loosening of the Communist Party's grip on political control.

Gorbachev's program of *perestroika* (restructuring) and Deng's **responsibility system** differed in many details, but they had some common elements. Besides redirecting investment away from heavy industry toward the consumer goods industry, they included:

1. greater reliance on material incentives to direct economic activity,
2. concessions to the private sector, and
3. increased enterprise autonomy in the state sector.

GREATER MATERIAL INCENTIVES In emphasizing material incentives, new reformers in command economies were seeking better ways of tying rewards to productivity in order to encourage more productive work. They justified this apparent violation of the communist egalitarian ideal by citing the motto said to be appropriate for the socialist stage of development: "To each according to his work." Arguing that the time had passed for merely *exhorting* people to work hard, Gorbachev called for a system of incentives to get "all workers to fully reveal their capability, work fruitfully and use resources most effectively." To achieve this,

> The system of pay and labor incentives must be arranged in a new way. It is particularly important that the actual pay of every worker be closely linked to his personal contribution to the end result, and that no limit be set on it. There is only one criteria of justice: whether or not it is earned.[10]

So the promise to workers was this: if you work harder, the rewards will be greater. However, long accustomed to a system that neither rewarded hard work nor penalized low effort, workers in the command economies were not likely to increase their effort until there were more goods in the shops. Enterprise profits were to play an important role in the new system of material incentives. Both managers and workers would be able to earn cash bonuses if profits increased.

---

[10]Secretary Gorbachev to the Communist Party Central Committee in 1987, quoted approvingly by the conservative American economist Paul Craig Roberts in *Business Week*, September 9, 1987.

RESPONSIBILITY SYSTEM
An arrangement designed to tie monetary rewards more closely to work actually performed. In Chinese agriculture, a system of family farming based on long-term leases of land.

MORE PRIVATE ECONOMIC ACTIVITY A movement toward a more private, market-oriented rural sector led the reform effort in China, where farmers had been forcibly collectivized into large communes. Although the incomes of commune members had depended on how well the commune did as a whole, a firm link between the individual farmer's remuneration and his output was never developed. The reforms accomplished this first by raising agricultural prices to encourage production and second by establishing a responsibility system. Rural families were allocated a portion of the collective land on 15-year leases (later increased to 50 years) for which they were responsible for profits and losses. Rather than assigning production quotas to the millions of new farm units, there was a switch to the market mechanism (higher prices) for assuring the nation's food supply. As a result of the Chinese agricultural reforms, farm output doubled and peasant income nearly tripled. Despite this example, the Soviet reform effort did not emphasize agriculture, in part because of the larger scale and higher degree of mechanization of Soviet agriculture.

New concessions were made to private enterprise and to markets in such nonagricultural sectors as small-scale consumer goods production and services, which had been neglected in the Soviet growth model. Only individual and family firms or cooperatives were contemplated because of a continued aversion to the hiring of outside workers. As in Chinese agriculture, the autonomy of small firms and cooperatives from the central plan and the opportunity to work for their own reward in the market promised increased production and efficiency.

The concessions to private activity were partly an official recognition of, and an attempt to bring under state control, a large existing *underground* or *secondary economy* that increasingly diverted people's efforts from the planned economy (but also provided a safety valve of sorts for the very inflexible planned sectors). But, especially in the Soviet Union, private enterprise continued to be highly circumscribed by bureaucratic and political interference.

INCREASED AUTONOMY FOR STATE ENTERPRISES It was in the state sector with its large, monopolistic enterprises where most of the problems for reform lay. China has been struggling the longest, trying to extend the responsibility system that worked so well in rural areas to state-owned industry. The Soviets tried a similar "self-finance" system in order to tighten enterprise budgets. Enterprise managers were to have greater autonomy—they could make decisions with minimal interference from central planners. Central planners would conduct long-term strategic planning, allowing state enterprise managers to use their own local information to answer the questions of *what* and *how*. Instead of having to fulfill the mandatory production targets of the state plan, enterprises were supposed to produce for the market.

Managers were told to use their new decision-making autonomy to maximize profits. Profit seeking was supposed to make managers more innovative and more attentive to costs and quality. Such a radical change in behavior and motivation came easily in agriculture and small business, where the family was a natural profit or income maximizer. Prospects for similar changes in behavior on the part of state enterprise managers accustomed to following the plan and depending on the bureaucracy for help are less encouraging.

Managers perhaps still thought it was in their best interest to satisfy the desires of those above them in the heirarchy rather than to pursue profits. They might have found it easier to make a profit by negotiating with bureaucrats rather than hunting for customers in the market. Under the old command system, important determinants of enterprise profits such as prices, taxes, and subsidies had not been uniform across enterprises. Managers had an incentive to claim special problems and obtain a special deal from the bureaucracy. And the tax system was such that the profits of successful enterprises were confiscated while the losses of unsuccessful ones were covered by subsidies. In order to put an end to such a perverse pattern of incentives, reforms were to include a system of uniform tax rates.

How were managers to be restrained from abusing their new autonomy? First, there was to be increased market "discipline" and the possibility of failure and bankruptcy. Under a self-finance or responsibility system, bad decisions that resulted in losses were no longer to be met with an unlimited safety net as in the days of soft budgets. Second, there was to be an increased decision-making role for the enterprise's workers, who were to be allowed to elect managers. At the same time, there was no longer to be an ironclad guarantee of full employment. A worker who risked losing a job could no longer think of an enterprise in trouble as "no concern of mine."

OPPOSITION TO REFORM: IDEOLOGY AND VESTED INTERESTS

Communist reform tended to be hesitant and incomplete partly because of ideology and fear of market problems. Ideological opposition to reform arose because it called into question the ideals of socialism embodied in the Stalinist growth model. Increased enterprise autonomy and dependence on markets deny to socialism the necessity of social planning. Concessions to private activity negate the interpretation of socialism as a system without private ownership. The turn toward material incentives seems to negate the moral thrust of Marxism. Many in the Soviet Union and China wished to see the move to markets slowed and the central political and economic control strengthened. In answer, reform advocates cited the example of Lenin's New Economic Policy, which used capitalistic methods to improve efficiency. Like Lenin, some reformers viewed the capitalistic backsliding as just a temporary retreat on the way to true socialism. While the Chinese have been more pragmatic in their approach to reform, the Soviets tended to emphasize the strengthening of socialism. As Gorbachev said to Soviet bloc leaders: "Some of you look to markets as a lifesaver for your economies," but "you should not think about lifesavers but about the ship, and the ship is socialism."[11]

MARKET PROBLEMS Fear of market-type problems also held back reform. Experience had shown that serious opposition to reform (and to the government) arose when some of the characteristics that Marxists complain about in market economies—inequality, inflation, and unemployment—began to appear. For governments undertaking a gradual reform, these problems made it very difficult to continue the process. There had always been inequality in command economies, of course, but under the reforms there were more instances of conspicuous wealth. Supposedly there was to be no limit to individual incomes as long as they were *earned*. There was, however, a tendency in communist countries to label the activities giving rise to wealth "money grubbing" and "speculation" and to stop them.

---

[11]Quoted in Robert Bazell, "Silicon Gulag," *New Republic* (June 6, 1988).

There was to be no "buying cheap and selling dear." Cuba's communist leader, Fidel Castro, abolished new farmers' markets on the basis that people were using them to get ahead financially.

By administratively setting most prices, the command economies avoided overt inflation, despite the prevalence of widespread shortages. There was instead repressed inflation (review Figure 40.2). But given the need to raise many formerly repressed prices to reflect supply and demand, inflation was likely to emerge with price reform. In addition, there was fear that the large, monopolistic enterprises created by the planners would use their new autonomy to raise prices. So far, however, it has been the unwinding of the subsidies to housing and food that has sparked the most vigorous and politically threatening opposition to reform. Poland's Solidarity trade union had been formed originally to protest such price increases.

Officially, command economies did not admit to unemployment, but restructuring under reform (and the continual restructuring that takes place under capitalism) meant that many more people would be "between jobs." Low profits and failing firms lead to layoffs. Workers, whose jobs were put at risk by reforms and who faced paying more for necessities, constituted one vested interest resisting change. The reforms violated the Stalinist social contract under which the workers traded political freedom for economic security (life-long employment, subsidized food). The trouble with this was that workers were paid regardless of effort and therefore also enjoyed freedom from hard work.

Also holding a vested interest in the command economy were the "captains of industry" in the big enterprises, government ministries, and planning bureaus. Many bureaucrats stood to lose their perks and even their jobs. State firms, especially in trade and services, faced new competition as the economy was decentralized. One of the dilemmas of reform was how to obtain the active participation of the very people who would lose a part of their power if the reform was successful. There was a long record of half-hearted reforms that looked good on paper but whose full implementation was blocked by the bureaucracy. The bureaucracy, with the backing of the Communist Party, had an interest in keeping the economy highly regulated.

A REGULATED MARKET? While the reformers' oft-stated intention was to rely more on markets under socialism, the emphasis was definitely on regulated markets. Direct state control was still the favored choice when it came to coordinating the economy. Regulation was to be relaxed only when and where it was proven not to work. This was far different from the usual position under capitalism that government interference in private activity should be undertaken only if there is some proven market failure that government has some prospect of overcoming. Under reformed socialism, the bureaucracy would no longer centrally plan the economy (and allocate inputs). Instead it would use "economic regulators" such as prices, subsidies, taxes, and credit for investment to control the economy. This reflected the authorities' intention to continue favoring certain activities over others regardless of market signals. Continued bureaucratic discretion over important economic variables meant that firms would still "look up" for direction, showing little independent initiative. For example, as long as tax rates remained variable, bureaucrats would still have the discretion to reduce rates to help out a faltering enterprise.

The primacy of regulation under the proposed reforms is shown by the type of price reform that was contemplated. It was realized that price reform was a vital part of any reform program. Prices had to be correct so that enterprise profits properly reflected enterprise efforts in cost-cutting and innovation. Prices were unlikely to be correct, however, if price setting by central authorities continued or if price-setting rules required that enterprises still keep prices equal to long-run average costs. Only prices that find their own level in real markets carry the necessary information about product demands and input scarcities that can be relied on to direct production decisions by the enterprises. Reformers nevertheless were reluctant to set prices free. They proposed making the necessary changes in prices administratively while maintaining the old state controls over prices. With the government taking direct responsibility for prices, they remained politically controversial. It is therefore not surprising that meaningful price reform was always put off.

THE POLITICS OF REFORM Communist reformers wanted to use markets for efficiency and innovation without giving up the leading role of the party. They thought there could be decentralization of economic decision making without decentralization of political power. There is a sense in which reform has to be "imposed" from above or it will not happen (new laws must be passed, etc.). But at the same time, reform needs support from below (for people to begin showing initiative). Also, without political change, people worry that the government will someday confiscate profits and expropriate private property. Soviet citizens remembered what happened after Lenin's New Economic Policy. The solution ultimately reached in Eastern Europe and then in the Soviet Union is the democratization of politics. In China, on the other hand, political reform lags behind economic reform and the party remains supreme.

The basis for party power (and socialism) in command economies is state ownership of the means of production. Communist reformers naturally did not want to give this up. But could markets function without private property? Some argued that markets could be made to work under state ownership by reducing central planning and giving state enterprises more autonomy (and leasing some state factories to private groups). More radical reformers were willing to see extensive **privatization** of state property. Political changes are making this possible.

PRIVATIZATION
Turning over of government activities or state assets to the private sector, that is, to individuals and privately owned firms.

PERESTROIKA—"TOO LITTLE, TOO LATE"

Although Gorbachev had risen through the ranks of the communist apparatus, he came to the conclusion that radical reform was needed in the Soviet Union. As he said in his resignation message (December 25, 1991), the nation was "suffocating under the shackles of the bureaucratic command system—doomed to cater to ideology." However, as most observers now say, his reform program was too little, too late. Gorbachev dragged his feet on the truly radical reforms that were necessary to get a new market-oriented system started. Nevertheless, the results were startling as democratization led to the collapse of communist power in the Soviet Union as well as in Eastern Europe. Economic crisis caused by the failure of the reforms was also important in the collapse. As Gorbachev went on to explain, the "old system fell apart even before the new system began to work."

Gorbachev had attempted to generate support for his reforms among the general population in order to get around the ideological opposition and counter the vested interests in the bureaucracy. A campaign of openness called *glasnost* encouraged people to learn about the repressive history of the Stalinist system and to criticize officials who blocked reform. In 1989, the first contested elections in the history of Soviet Union elections were held for seats in a new legislative body.

When the people in Eastern Europe got their chances to vote in 1989 and 1990, Communist parties lost. The "revolution" ended up a peaceful one as Gorbachev declined to use military force to help Communist parties stay in power. The end of communism in the Soviet Union came after the abortive August 1991 coup by conservatives. Accused of complicity, the Communist party was abolished, and the republics declared independence. With the party and the union disappearing beneath him, Gorbachev resigned. The baton of reform passed to the new republic leaders such as Boris Yeltsin of the Russian republic.

WHAT HAD BEEN MISSING FROM PERESTROIKA? It was fairly easy to reduce the scope of central planning, but not so easy to reduce the role of the bureaucracy in price-setting and input allocation. Meaningful price reform was always put off. The Soviets had planned to have a "market in means of production" in which state enterprises would make contracts specifying deliveries and setting prices for industrial inputs without the interference of the bureaucracy. The state was to obtain its goods through state orders, for which enterprises were to compete. Progress in this direction was frustrated, however, because the bureaucrats were able to maintain their control over Soviet enterprises by substituting large state orders for the old mandatory production targets, leaving little production for the market. So as central planning collapsed, there were no price signals to rely on.

Also missing from Gorbachev's program was any meaningful privatization. A new law on state enterprise allowed joint-stock companies and leasing of state factories, but not much had happened under it. Joint ventures with foreign firms were encouraged, but other than the new McDonald's restaurant in Moscow, very few were implemented. New private businesses were too often assumed to be engaged in illegal speculation; at one point, the KGB was given special authority to check on them. Leasing of land on a limited basis was made available to farmers, but Gorbachev and other party leaders were very reluctant to permit the private ownership of land.

In the summer of 1990, government economists drew up a 500-day plan for radical reform that would have freed most prices by January 1991. Gorbachev rejected the plan, however, siding with conservatives who opposed change.

ECONOMIC CRISIS IN THE SOVIET BLOC The economic crisis in the Soviet Union grew worse as Gorbachev delayed settling on a new reform plan. As the central planning system decayed, production fell (the drop in GDP in 1991 exceeded the decline experienced in any American recession since the 1930s). It was not just that there were no orders forthcoming. People were no longer willing to obey. Glasnost had undermined the ideological foundation of the system and the legitimacy of the government. The willingness to work had been based on faith that socialism was the better way. With the realization of how much worse workers in the command economies were living than in the capitalist countries, this was now seen as a lie.

Budget deficits in the Soviet Union soared to the equivalent of more than 20 percent of GDP. Tax collections fell along with production. More importantly, subsidies for food (and other basic consumer items) and subsidies to cover state enterprise losses expanded sharply. Enterprise autonomy was not used to pursue profits by cutting costs and enhancing product quality. Instead, enterprises raised wages, which meant they required even more government credits and subsidies. Managers were responding to the increased power of workers, who could now strike (and Soviet miners did) and who had a role in electing the managers. Autonomy was therefore a disaster for the budget. And, because the deficits were increasingly financed by printing money, inflation was becoming inevitable—it threatened to explode once prices were freed. In trying to get rid of their rapidly depreciating money, people cleared store shelves of everything.

So, while the economic crisis in the Soviet bloc helped bring to power new noncommunist governments, it also made the transition to a market economy more difficult as well as more urgent.

HIGH GROWTH IN REFORMED CHINA

Rather than glasnost and democratization, China's reformers have depended more on the direct benefits of reform (higher incomes, more goods) to build support for further reform. China had one of the highest growth rates in the world in the 1980s and early 1990s. However, the massive Chinese demonstrations in favor of democracy and freedom in 1989 showed that even improved living standards may still leave people dissatisfied.

Why did China's reform produce high growth instead of economic crisis as in the former Soviet Union and Eastern Europe? Besides the early changes in agriculture mentioned above, there has been much more private enterprise in China and more openness to the outside world. Higher farm income and looser controls greatly buoyed rural areas, private industry and trade. People were actually encouraged to become rich. In addition, exposure of state enterprises to market forces has been encouraged by a two-tier price system that allows the sale of production above plan quotas at market-determined prices. But state enterprises are still a drain on the budget because of their shoddy goods and inefficiency. In contrast, private industrial output has soared, cutting the proportion of output produced by the state sector from 74 percent in 1984 (see Table 40.2) to 45 percent in 1991. With respect to openness, China's use of free-trade zones and joint ventures with foreign firms has resulted in many new private enterprises. All in all, China's reform has been more "bottom-up" than "top-down," in contrast to Soviet reform.

Chinese communist leaders have avoided radical reform. During the spring of 1989, their indecisiveness on the future pace and scope of reform helped foster nationwide demonstrations. When these were finally brutally suppressed, including the well-known one in Tiananmen Square, it was evident that the hard-liners who favored continuing the political and cultural dominance of the Communist party were still in charge. Student demonstrations were also concerned with rising prices, inequality, and unemployment. The gradual nature of the reforms favored by the Chinese contributed to inequality. During the transition from the command economy, officials who allocated supplies of items that were still price-controlled were able to exact kickbacks and other favors. In addition, the Communist party elite and their families were likely to be better positioned than others to take advantage of the new opportunities for private enterprise. Students demanded action against such corruption and nepotism, asking for publication of the salaries and personal assets of government leaders and their children. They also asked for continued

IMPORTANCE OF STATE SECTOR AND PUBLIC CORPORATIONS

COUNTRIES	PERCENT OF TOTAL VALUE ADDED IN THE NATION
Communist Countries	
Czechoslovakia (1986)	97.0
East Germany (1982)	96.5
Soviet Union (1985)	96.0
Poland (1985)	81.7
China (1984)	73.6
Hungary (1984)	65.2
Noncommunist Countries	
France (1982)	16.5
Austria (1978–1979)	14.5
Italy (1982)	14.0
New Zealand (1987)	12.0
Turkey (1985)	11.2
West Germany (1982)	10.7
United Kingdom (1983)	10.7
Portugal (1976)	9.7
Australia (1978–1979)	9.4
Denmark (1974)	6.3
Greece (1979)	6.1
Spain (1979)	4.1
Netherlands (1971–1973)	3.6
United States (1983)	1.3

SOURCE: Branko Milanovic, "Privatization in Post-Communist Societies," *Communist Economies and Economic Transformation*, (Vol. 3, No. 1, 1991), p. 8.

TABLE 40.2

price controls on consumer goods. For a while after this, foreigners were wary of investing in China, but many have quietly returned and trade is booming.

Transformation to Capitalism

Hundreds of books have been written on the transition from capitalism to communism but not the other way around. There is no known recipe for unmaking an omelet.[12]

—*The Economist*

No blueprint existed for the transformation of command economies to capitalism. There were some telling examples of developing countries that, under the

---

[12]*The Economist* (March 24–30, 1990), p. 22.

tutelage of the International Monetary Fund (IMF), moved away from high state regulation of their economies and began to grow more rapidly. Asian countries had great success with policies geared to foreign markets. And Germany and Japan, whose capital stock was severely damaged in World War II, with market-oriented policies (and Marshall Plan funds), managed to become leaders among the industrial nations. All these examples indicate that it takes time, maybe five years, but that appropriate policies can raise growth rates and standards of living. In 1992, led by Russia, the republics of the former Soviet Union cautiously followed the pattern of reform undertaken in Eastern Europe. In both areas the problems were enormous, as the decline in output that began under communist reform continued, accompanied by high inflation and high unemployment.

As always when major adjustments in economic policy are contemplated, some argued for gradualism and others recommended something closer to "shock therapy." The gradualists, worried about the inevitability of a long and painful transition, wanted regulation to continue. Price controls were to be kept to prevent the old monopolies from abusing their power and to protect pensioners and others on fixed incomes. Subsidies were to be continued to help state enterprises prepare for market competition and to avoid excessive unemployment. Those in favor of a quicker transition, on the other hand, argued that a gradual approach would not work. Jokes were made about it: "One does not jump across a chasm in two steps," and "you cannot change traffic from driving on the left side to the right side gradually." More seriously, they argued for a comprehensive approach that would not leave so much decision making to the bureaucracy. The hope was that the more quickly enterprises were moved away from dependence on government protection the more quickly they would learn to operate in markets. It was generally recognized that higher unemployment and higher prices for necessities required a new "safety net," including unemployment insurance.

While there is no blueprint for transformation, several steps can be identified. There are negative steps required to overcome the legacies of the command system, such as extreme political centralization (and the intertwining, from top to bottom, of political power with control of the economy) and the high degree of industrial concentration. Democratization is taking care of the former; a long and difficult period of restructuring to bring in competition will be necessary for the latter. Of more immediate concern is the inflationary legacy of the communist reform period requiring macroeconomic stabilization. This will lay the foundation for more positive steps involving liberalization of economic activity and privatization of state enterprises.

MACROECONOMIC STABILIZATION

The basic stabilization problem in the reforming countries stemmed from their massive government budget deficits. These fed inflation that proved impossible to repress any longer with the old price controls. There finally was no alternative but to free prices to find their own level. Poland had freed prices quickly in the so-called "big bang" of January 1, 1990; and Russia followed suit on January 2, 1992. Other countries freed their prices in a less dramatic fashion. Without an end to the budget deficits, inflation represented a constant threat. Two items had to be attacked: massive military spending and excessive subsidies to industry and to consumers. The end of the cold war allowed a reduction in military spending. Ending subsidies to state enterprises was necessary anyway to end the soft budgets and force enterprises to respond to market forces. Part of the problem was the easy credit traditionally available to enterprises. Much of it was never repaid, showing up in government budgets as subsidies.

Consumer subsidies were implicit in the artificially low prices of necessities. The inflationary blowout provided an opportunity to get rid of these and other relative price distortions that had long plagued the system. Thus, it was a *corrective* inflation in the following sense: repressed prices found their own level, permitting distortions in relative prices to disappear. Before the inflation, people had stripped the store shelves clean in an effort to avoid holding worthless money. Afterwards, stores had goods again, but many cost more in real terms. It can be argued that people are not necessarily made worse off by the new higher prices for formerly subsidized goods. Previously, they had to wait in long lines to buy those goods with artificially low prices. The true price was probably close to the marketing-clearing level when the value of wasted time is taken into account. The main question was, would producers (both old and new) respond to the higher prices by stepping up production?

'IT WON'T WORK. FIRST WE'LL GET A DEFICIT, A RECESSION, INFLATION AND UNEMPLOYMENT, THEN EVERYONE WILL START QUIBBLING ABOUT THE CAPITAL GAINS TAX.'

OLIPHANT Copyright © 1990 UNIVERSAL PRESS SYNDICATE.
Reprinted with permission. All rights reserved.

Both Poland and Russia made currency convertibility and greater international trade an important part of their shock therapy. Convertibility means that the country's citizens can freely buy and sell foreign money (usually referred to as *currency* in this context). A commitment to maintain the value of the local currency relative to the dollar and other *hard currencies* helps limit the growth of the money supply and gives people confidence in the money. Currency convertibility, along with the removal of barriers to imports, lines up domestic prices with international prices. Opening up the economy to foreign goods quickly brings competition to bear on monopolistic state enterprises. All the former command economies in Eastern Europe were eager to integrate with Western Europe in this way and eventually join the European Community.

RESTRUCTURING INDUSTRY

Success of the transformation requires much more restructuring than was intended by Gorbachev in his *perestroika* program. Clearly, a deeper cut is needed in the government bureaucracy and the military–industrial complex than Gorbachev had contemplated. It means converting heavy industry to the production of consumer goods and orienting the economy toward exports. There is, however, a deeper problem that needs to be addressed that cannot be solved with a one-shot conversion of old production facilities. That is the need for flexibility. It was one of Gorbachev's intentions to achieve this, but his reforms never went far enough. To be able to serve well-informed consumers and be competitive internationally, workers, managers, and the capital they work with have to be able to adjust quickly to changing technical and demand conditions. The relatively unregulated firms in capitalist economies have learned to be more flexible; it was either learn or be swept aside in today's competitive world market. In contrast, firms in the command economies learned to work to the plan and to depend on the state for protection from consumers at home and abroad. The result was a very low adaptability to change.

There is reason to believe that much of the capital stock in the former command economies is of little value today. The Soviet Union claimed a capital stock equal to that of the United States, but the Soviet capital produced only half as much output as its capitalist counterpart. Much of the command economies' capital stock is old and obsolete, there having been no penalty under the old system for keeping high-cost facilities in place. Given the absence of incentives to minimize costs, even the relatively new factories were quite inefficient. In addition, the old capital was designed without regard to environmental considerations.[13]

LIBERALIZATION AND PRIVATIZATION

While much attention had been given to the privatization of large state enterprises, the development of new private business is crucial to the success of transformation.

---

[13]For example, nuclear power plants similar to the one that blew up at Chernobyl in 1986 were built all over Eastern Europe; they may all have to be shut down. Many other power plants and factories are probably not worth retrofitting with abatement equipment.

The price reform and the opening of foreign trade mentioned above are, of course, both very important to its growth. The higher prices of many items that were formerly in short supply provide an incentive for new production. Financing for the new businesses will have to be forthcoming. Significant foreign investment may be attracted, but primary reliance will have to rest on domestic savings. Freer capital markets with private banks will be helpful in encouraging the necessary saving and channeling of funds where they are most needed. Stock markets have even begun to operate.

Besides price reforms and financial system reform, a basic requirement for the development of private enterprise is a clear set of general rules under which all business can operate. For example, laws are needed to enforce contracts and protect private property. A nonconfiscatory tax system with uniform rates is also essential. Under the old command system there were no set rules; party bureaucrats could interfere whenever they wished. That complete discretion is largely gone. But, as in many nonsocialist countries, there still can be many obstacles to free enterprise. The key to growth is to limit government interference in the marketplace and ensure that it enhances competition rather than prevents it. The result of initial liberalization moves in the former command economies was the formation of thousands of new businesses, easing worries that there would not be any entrepreneurs in the former command economies.

With respect to the privatization of state assets, it has proved quite easy to find buyers for thousands of small units in the old state retail, transportation, and service networks. Entrepreneurs anticipate profits, given the neglect of these areas by the planners. Privatization of the large, run-down state enterprises is much more difficult. Governments originally expected high revenues from their sale, but the process was slowed by valuation problems. In addition, the domestic public, the nominal owners of state industry, did not have sufficient liquid funds to pay the expected price. While most of the governments welcomed foreign investment, they did not want to hold a fire sale of national assets to foreigners. Giving away shares in state enterprises to the public seemed to be one solution. Another involved the distribution of vouchers that people can use in subsequent share auctions (see Exhibit 40.2). Vouchers are being used today in Eastern Europe and Russia.

Prospects for the Former Command Economies

The socialist experiment appears to be over, and the "great experiment" to transform the former command economies into capitalist economies has begun. The command economy was to have been better than the capitalist economy, but it ended up worse. Central planning was supposed to give command economies the flexibility to apply new technology efficiently; instead, central planning proved highly inflexible and the industry it controlled proved very slow to innovate. Central planning could not coordinate an increasingly complex economy and it failed to satisfy new, more sophisticated consumer preferences. The end finally arrived when ill-conceived reforms created the worst of both worlds: an economic crisis in which enterprises were not following central commands but had not yet begun to respond to market signals.

EXHIBIT

40.2

The Free Market Comes to Mongolia

At the Institute of Economics in Ulan Bator, a group of Mongolians is trying to understand the intricacies of the stock market. "Where does client A get that 3,000 tugriks from?" barks an American instructor. After translation, the answer comes back: "It's additional capital." "If it's additional capital." "If it's additional, it isn't there," says the instructor.

Most things are not there in Mongolia. But the country, like other ex-communist strongholds, has become fascinated by the charms of the market economy. It can't wait to have a stock exchange.

The financially creative student is one of 214 brokers, managers, and dealers who will staff the stock exchange being installed in a Stalinist-looking building in Sukhebator Square. At the end of two months of study they hope to know their bulls from their bears. Privatization has come to Mongolia. Some 70% of state assets are to be sold off.

The problem is that few Mongolians have any money. Nearly half the population of about 2 million are pastoral nomads, living in large tents known as yurts. No one has much idea what the decrepit state-owned factories are worth. Because of this, Mongolia has devised what Naidansurengiin Zolzhargal, chairman-designate of the future stock exchange, calls "the great give-away policy."

Every Mongolian man, woman and child is getting a voucher. The voucher, like most symbols of the new Mongolia, bears a picture of Genghis Khan and has a nominal value of 10,000 tugriks (a lot of money in Mongolia, but worth only $100 on the black market). For this, the holders pay 200 tugriks, or nothing if they are very poor.

To the voucher are attached pink coupons, which can be torn off. With these the owner can take part in a small privatization, and buy a stake in a restaurant (if he can find one), a shop or a taxi, or in the sheep, cattle, and camels owned by a cooperative. Auctions are already

A SUCCESSFUL TRANSFORMATION?

Most of the countries in Eastern Europe, no longer under the dominance of the Soviet Union, have developed the political consensus and political authority necessary to begin the difficult process of transformation. The same is true for the newly developed independent republics of the former Soviet Union. They are essentially starting over again to create the legal foundation of what their people refer to as a "normal" system. The process of restructuring and privatization necessary for competitive discipline has started. There is hope that, after some very difficult years with severe economic dislocations and high unemployment, economic growth will take off as it has in other backward countries that have turned to markets. The question is whether this hope will be sufficient to sustain popular support for strong government policies.

taking place in Ulan Bator, where bidders pool their coupons to buy small businesses.

The voucher also has a blue coupon, with which the holder can acquire shares in state enterprises during the forthcoming "big privatization." The stock exchange will start by running a market in blue coupons, moving on to shares of privatized enterprises later.

Mr. Zolzhargal is 26, has gold-rimmed spectacles and wears striped shirts. It is tempting to think of him as Mongolia's first yuppie. He talks dreamily of turning Mongolia into a Hong Kong. He says the figure of 10,000 tugriks was arrived at by dividing the national value of state assets by the number of Mongolians. Most factories are operating at below 50% capacity. Pilfering is rife. An opposition politician says that, if the government does not hurry up, there will be nothing left to privatize.

On the other hand, some Mongolians have not entirely abandoned their communist beliefs. They say herdsmen need the state for marketing and distribution. Mr. Zolzhargal says this is nonsense. A herdsman has as shrewd an understanding of the market as a townsman. Mongolians fed themselves for thousands of years before communism. Today, though there are 12 times more livestock than people, meat is rationed.

Already, on the streets outside the Institute of Economics, a secondary market in pink coupons is growing up. "Only 1,000 tugriks," says one would-be seller, who has grasped at least one feature of the way markets can behave. "Next week, it will be worth 3,000." The appeal of the new Mongolia is that you can buy at the bottom (so far) of the market.

SOURCE: *The Economist*, October 19, 1991, p. 40.

Much depends on people's attitudes and willingness to see the process through in the former command economies. Many observers are quite pessimistic on this score. They cite, in the case of the Soviet Union, the seventy-plus years under communism during which people had been taught to let those who *know better* make decisions. They think people who have become used to obeying rather than taking initiative and to depending on the state for protection rather than looking out for their own welfare will not be able to survive under a market system, much less make it work. Others are much more optimistic. When the former Yugoslavian Communist leader-turned-dissident, Milovan Dijlas, was asked about the mentality that initiative is bad and that no one should live better than anyone else, he replied, "That will pass very quickly."[14] Once markets begin to operate, attitudes will change.

---

[14]From an interview in *Time* (February 19, 1990).

This may happen more quickly in Eastern Europe, where there is the memory of how markets worked and where the example of Western Europe is closer. But the problems experienced by East Germany, which received massive aid (as well as a liberalized legal system) from the former West Germany, show how difficult the adjustment to capitalism can be. What helps is that rewards are beginning to be based on technical and entrepreneurial skills rather than on influence within the state and party bureaucracy.

Summary

1. The command economy originated in countries that were in a hurry to catch up economically with the advanced capitalist countries. The Marxian utopian vision and critique of capitalism provided the ideological basis for this approach.

2. Building socialism in the backward countries came to mean a highly centralized political and economic system with state ownership of the means of production and central planning. This Stalinist growth model involved collectivization of agriculture and a concentration on heavy industry.

3. The main impetus behind the attempts at reform in the command economies was the slow growth in these countries and a recognition that they were falling further behind their capitalist rivals. The Stalinist growth model was no longer an attractive development alternative to capitalism.

4. Growth rates slowed in command economies partly because of the haste behind the growth effort and partly because of the means chosen. The centralized planning and state ownership led to inefficiency and, because technological progress lagged, the command economies failed to make the switch from an extensive mode of growth to an intensive one.

5. Agriculture did poorly in command economies because of poor incentives and the inefficiency of faraway planning. Expected surpluses from agriculture turned into costly food subsidies for urban workers. As demonstrated in China, successful reform of agriculture requires both ownership changes and higher prices.

6. The planning system contributed to slower growth in command economies through excessive centralization of decision making as well as overbureaucratization of their implementation. Central political control repressed initiative. Quality suffered as enterprise managers concentrated on annual quantity targets. Soft budgets and no layoffs meant there was no penalty for poor performance.

7. Centrally set prices in command economies generally differed from market-clearing levels; resource allocation therefore involved much bureaucratic involvement rather than relying on the "invisible hand" of the market.

8. Communist reforms attempted to increase efficiency in command economies with material incentives, enterprise autonomy, and tolerance of private economy activity. There was to be less central direction and more use of market forces to direct economic activity. But markets were to be highly regulated and the party was to retain its monopoly of political power. Failure of Soviet reforms created an economic crisis; China's reforms, relying more on private initiative, have yielded impressive economic growth.

9. Democratization meant the end of communist rule in Eastern Europe and the Soviet Union; in China the party retained control by force of arms. Where political change has come, new governments face the daunting task of transforming command economies into market economies.

10. Transformation of the command economies requires a long period of restructuring. This is made difficult by the poor quality of existing capital stock. Macroeconomic stabilization will lay the foundation for the necessary liberalization of economic activity and the privatization of state enterprises.

11. The success of the transformation of the former command economies depends on changes in the attitudes toward private market activity and individual initiative that were ingrained under communism.

Key Terms

proletariat	extensive growth
Stalinist growth model	intensive growth
industrial policy	soft budget
communist utopia	responsibility system
socialist economy	privatization
moral incentives	

Study Questions and Problems

1. Reform of agriculture in command economies may include the leasing of formerly collective land to individual farmers. What difference would it make for the amount of investment farmers are willing to undertake whether the lease is for 15 years or 50 years?

2. Why do producers generally operate in a buyers' market in capitalist countries instead of in the sellers' market that is so prevalent in the command economies?

3. Identify the tax or subsidy in the following situations:
   a. Potatoes have a fixed price of 1 ruble per kilogram, and the average cost of production is 1.75 rubles.
   b. The fixed price of vodka is 10.50 rubles per half liter and the average cost is 1.25 rubles.

4. In each of the following cases, indicate whether growth is extensive or intensive:
   a. The labor force increases by 10 percent.
   b. Investment causes the capital stock to rise by 5 percent.
   c. A new technique is discovered for producing steel pipe that cuts required materials.

5. What do you regard as the chief obstacles that the former command economies must overcome to achieve a successful transition to capitalism? Analyze.

6. "The fact that output is down while both inflation and unemployment are up in the former Soviet Union is evidence that the command economies should not have embarked upon their attempted transformation to capitalism." Do you agree or disagree? Defend your position.

Selected References

Carson, Richard L. "On the Decline of Socialism," *Comparative Economic Studies* (Fall, 1991), pp. 167–178. A lucid analysis of the downfall of communist economies.

Goldman, Marshall. *Gorbachev's Challenge: Economic Reform in the Age of High Technology* (New York: Norton, 1987). An early critique of communist reforms.

Gregory, Paul R., and Robert C. Stuart, *Comparative Economic Systems*, 4th ed. (Boston: Houghton Mifflin, 1992). A popular text on economic systems.

Kornai, Janos. *The Road to a Free Economy* (New York: Norton, 1990). An analysis of reform by a leading Hungarian economist.

Ofer, Gur. "Soviet Economic Growth: 1928–1985," *Journal of Economic Literature* (December 1987), pp. 1,767–1,833. Explains why the haste to grow under the Stalinist growth model ultimately led to slow growth.

Perkins, Dwight Heald. "Reforming China's Economic System," *Journal of Economic Literature* (June 1988), pp. 601–645. Discusses the early success of Chinese reforms.

Glossary

ABSOLUTE ADVANTAGE
The ability to produce a particular good using less resources than a second country (that is, a lower ratio of resources to output).

ACCOUNTING PROFIT
Total revenue minus accounting costs. (Because accountants and economists measure costs differently, accounting profit differs from economic profit.)

AFFIRMATIVE ACTION
A policy designed to increase the representation of women or minorities (for example, to increase their relative employment).

AGGREGATE DEMAND CURVE
The aggregate demand curve shows the quantity of the nation's output demanded at each possible price level.

AGGREGATE SUPPLY CURVE
The aggregate supply curve shows the quantity of the nation's output supplied at each possible price level.

ANTITRUST POLICY
Government laws and procedures designed to shape market structure and influence the behavior of firms.

ASSETS
Items that the firm owns and claims that the firm has upon entities external to the firm.

AUTOMATIC STABILIZER OR BUILT-IN STABILIZER
A feature of the economy that acts automatically to inhibit economic fluctuations without discretionary policy changes being implemented.

AUTONOMOUS CONSUMPTION
The portion of consumption that is independent of disposable income; consumer expenditures that would occur in the event that disposable income were zero.

AVERAGE COST PRICING
A regulatory procedure intended to equate price with average cost, and thereby limit the firm to normal profits.

AVERAGE PRODUCT OF LABOR
Total product divided by the quantity of labor, holding capital constant.

AVERAGE TAX RATE
The percentage of total income paid in taxes.

BALANCE OF PAYMENTS
A statistical tabulation of a nation's transactions with other countries for a given period.

BALANCE OF TRADE
The difference between the value of a nation's exports and imports of merchandise or goods; one component of the balance of payments.

BALANCE SHEET
A financial report listing a firm's assets and liabilities at a moment in time.

BANK ASSETS
Items a bank owns.

BANK BALANCE SHEET
A statement of a bank's assets, liabilities, and capital accounts (or net worth).

BANK INSOLVENCY
Condition in which value of bank liabilities exceeds value of assets, that is, capital accounts are negative.

BANK LIABILITIES
Items a bank owes; the debts of the bank.

BARTER
A system of exchange whereby goods and services are traded directly without the use of money.

BLACK MARKET
A market in which goods are bought and sold at prices above the legal maximum.

BOARD OF GOVERNORS (OF THE FEDERAL RESERVE SYSTEM)
Key seven-person board that dominates the decision-making process in conducting monetary policy.

BRACKET CREEP
The tendency for inflation to push individuals automatically into higher marginal- and average-tax rates in an unindexed income-tax system.

BREAK-EVEN INCOME
The level of income at which the government's subsidy disappears and beyond which the family must start paying income tax.

BREAK-EVEN INCOME LEVEL
Income level at which consumption equals income; income level at which saving is zero.

BUBBLE
An imaginary enclosure around one or more plants that becomes the basis for a firm's pollution-control requirements. In particular, a firm is allowed to exceed pollution-control standards at individual points in the bubble provided that these excesses are offset elsewhere within the same bubble.

BUDGET DEFICIT
The shortfall of federal receipts relative to expenditures, measured at an annual rate.

BUDGET LINE
A line indicating all combinations of two goods that can be purchased with an income, given the price of each good.

BUSINESS CYCLE
A pattern of irregular but repeated expansion and contraction of real output.

CAPITAL
Output such as machines, tools, and structures used to produce goods and services.

CAPITAL ACCOUNTS
The difference between a bank's assets and its liabilities; indicates owners' equity stake in the bank.

CAPITAL DEEPENING
Expansion in the average amount of capital goods per worker. An important source of productivity growth.

CAPITAL GOODS
Output used to produce other goods.

CAPTURE HYPOTHESIS
The claim that regulators promote the interests of the industry they regulate rather than protecting the public.

CARTEL
An organization of producers that determines price and output for its members in order to increase their profits.

CENTRAL BANK
Official agency that oversees the banking system and is responsible for the conduct of monetary policy.

CLASSICAL ECONOMICS
Viewpoint that dominated economic thinking before Keynes. It held that market prices would quickly adjust to boost the economy out of recession, and therefore government intervention in the macroeconomy was unnecessary.

CLOSED SHOP
A work arrangement that permits a company to hire only those workers who are currently members of a union.

COLLECTIVE BARGAINING
The process through which unions and management negotiate wages, fringe benefits, and nonmonetary terms of employment.

COMMAND ECONOMY
An economic system in which property is publicly owned and central authorities coordinate economic decisions.

COMMODITY CREDIT CORPORATION (CCC)
A government agency that purchases surplus commodities from farmers.

COMMON STOCK
A certificate of partial ownership of a corporation that gives its holder a vote in the selection of the firm's directors and a residual claim on the assets and profits of the firm.

COMMUNIST UTOPIA
The Marxian conception of an ideal society without economic classes and with all people realizing their full potential as creative human beings.

COMPARABLE WORTH
A doctrine that each job has an intrinsic value, independent of labor supply and demand, and that jobs with similar intrinsic values have similar (comparable) worth.

COMPARATIVE ADVANTAGE
The ability of one country to produce a particular good at a lower opportunity cost than a second country.

COMPENSATING WAGE DIFFERENTIAL
The wage premium a worker receives for a job with undesirable characteristics, to compensate for those characteristics.

COMPLEMENTARY GOODS
Goods that are consumed together. Two goods are complements when an increase in the price of one good reduces demand for the other.

COMPLEMENTARY INPUTS
Inputs that are complements in production: an increase in the price of one reduces demand for the other.

CONGLOMERATE MERGER
A merger between companies in unrelated markets.

CONSTANT-COST INDUSTRY
An industry in which input prices (and therefore cost curves) remain unchanged as the industry expands.

CONSTANT RETURNS TO SCALE
A situation in which long-run average cost does not change with the level of output.

CONSUMER EQUILIBRIUM
A situation in which the consumer is obtaining the maximum total utility consistent with a given income (budget); a consumer is in equilibrium when marginal utility per dollar is the same for each good and all income is spent.

CONSUMER GOODS
Output consumed directly, rather than used to produce other goods.

CONSUMER PRICE INDEX
The most widely quoted index of U.S. prices; based on the market basket of goods and services purchased by a typical household.

CONSUMER SOVEREIGNTY
The principle that consumers, through spending decisions, determine how much of each good is produced.

CONSUMER SURPLUS
The difference between the maximum amount a consumer is willing to pay for a given quantity of a good and the amount actually paid.

CONSUMPTION EXPENDITURES (C)
Household expenditures on all goods and services except housing; consists of household expenditures on durable goods, nondurables, and services.

CONSUMPTION FUNCTION
The relationship between consumer expenditures and disposable income, holding all other determinants of consumer spending constant.

CONVERGENCE PRINCIPLE
Tendency of industrial nations with relatively low living standards to grow more rapidly than more affluent nations, thereby reducing the gap in living standards.

COPYRIGHT
An exclusive right, granted by the government, to publish, copy, or sell a piece of music, art, or literature.

CORPORATE BOND
An IOU or evidence of debt issued by a corporation that carries a specified schedule of interest payments to be made to the bondholder (lender) and a date for redemption of the principal face value.

CORPORATION
A firm that takes the form of an independent legal entity with ownership divided into shares and each owner's liability limited to his or her investment in the firm.

COST–BENEFIT ANALYSIS
A framework for comparing the costs and benefits of a particular activity (for example, to determine the optimal level of that activity).

COST EFFECTIVE
Achieving a given objective (for example, the elimination of a certain volume of pollution) at the lowest cost possible.

COST–PUSH INFLATION
Inflation caused by leftward-shifting AS curve, usually triggered by wage hikes or price increases of other inputs (such as oil) that are caused by factors other than excess demand for these inputs.

CROWDING IN
The favorable effect of increased deficits upon investment spending owing to the stimulative effect of larger deficits upon aggregate demand, output, and the utilization rate of capital equipment.

CROWDING-IN EFFECT
The tendency for an expansionary fiscal policy to induce an *increase* in investment spending by stimulating sales growth and utilization rate of existing plant and equipment.

CROWDING OUT
The adverse effect of increased deficits on investment spending owing to the negative effect of higher interest rates associated with the larger deficits.

CROWDING-OUT EFFECT
The tendency for an expansionary fiscal policy to induce an offsetting reduction in investment expenditures by raising interest rates.

CRUDE QUANTITY THEORY
The proposition that velocity is constant in the short run and that aggregate demand (PY) and the price level vary proportionally with the money supply.

CURRENCY APPRECIATION
An increase in the international value of the currency; the currency buys more units of foreign currency.

CURRENCY DEPRECIATION
A decline in the international value of the currency; the currency buys fewer units of foreign currency.

CUSTOMER DISCRIMINATION
A preference of customers to be served by members of a particular group (for example, males).

CYCLICAL DEFICIT
The portion of the actual deficit attributable to a shortfall of actual GDP relative to full-employment GDP.

CYCLICAL UNEMPLOYMENT
Unemployment attributable to weak aggregate demand; the difference between the actual unemployment rate and the rate associated with full employment.

DECREASING-COST INDUSTRY
An industry in which input prices decrease as the industry expands.

DEFICIENCY PAYMENT
A supplemental payment that farmers receive for each unit of output they produce, equal to the difference between the target price and the market price. If the market price exceeds the target price, there is no deficiency payment.

DEFLATION
Period of time in which the nation's price level declines; period in which the value of the unit of currency rises.

DEMAND CURVE
A diagram showing the relationship between the price of a good and the quantity demanded per period of time, other things equal.

DEMAND–PULL INFLATION
Inflation caused by rightward-shifting AD curve, usually triggered by increasing money supply and government expenditures.

DEMAND SCHEDULE
A table showing the relationship between the price of a good and the quantity demanded per period of time, other things equal.

DEMOGRAPHIC TRANSITION
The transition from a society experiencing high birth and death rates to low birth and death rates; in the transition, the decline in birthrates lags the decline in death rates, leading to rapid population growth.

DEPENDENCY RATE
The number of people not working per 100 workers in the population.

DEPRECIATION
The value of the nation's capital equipment that is used up in a given period, normally one year; indicates how much investment is needed to keep the nation's capital stock intact.

DEPRESSION
A very severe and prolonged economic downturn.

DEREGULATION
The removal of government regulations.

DERIVED DEMAND
The demand for a resource; determined by (derived from) the demand for the product it produces.

DISCOUNT RATE
The interest rate charged on loans to financial institutions made by the Federal Reserve.

DISCOUNTS AND ADVANCES
Loans to banks and other depository institutions by the Federal Reserve.

DISECONOMIES OF SCALE
A situation in which long-run average cost rises with the level of output.

DISEQUILIBRIUM
A state of imbalance: a market is in disequilibrium when the quantity demanded does not coincide with the quantity supplied.

DISEQUILIBRIUM PRICE
Any price for which the quantity demanded differs from the quantity supplied.

DISPOSABLE INCOME (Y_d)
Income in the hands of individuals after deducting income taxes; income available to households to spend and save.

DUMPING
A practice in which a producer sells its product at a lower price in a foreign market than at home.

ECONOMIC GOOD
A good that is scarce. At a price of zero the amount of the good desired exceeds the quantity available.

ECONOMIC GROWTH
The ability of a country to produce greater levels of output—represented by an outward shift of its production possibilities curve.

ECONOMIC PROFIT
Total revenue minus the total cost of production (implicit as well as explicit).

ECONOMIC REGULATION
The regulation of specific industries, designed to influence such outcomes as price, service, and number of producers in an industry.

ECONOMIC RENT
The premium received by a resource in excess of its opportunity cost.

ECONOMIC RENT OF A WORKER
The return to a scarce natural talent: the difference between the wage received (because of that talent) and the wage available in the best alternative line of work.

ECONOMIC SYSTEM
An institutional arrangement for determining what goods are produced, how they are produced, and for whom.

ECONOMICS
The study of how scarce resources are allocated among competing uses.

ECONOMIES OF SCALE
A situation in which long-run average cost declines as the firm increases its level of output.

EFFICIENT PRODUCTION
Achieving maximum feasible output from a given amount of resources.

EFFLUENT FEE
A charge or tax levied on each unit of a pollutant emitted into the environment.

ELASTIC DEMAND
Demand is elastic when $E_d > 1$.

EMPLOYEE DISCRIMINATION
A preference of employees to work with members of the same group (for example, other males) and to avoid contact with different workers (for example, women).

ENTITLEMENT PROGRAM
A system for allocating oil to U.S. refiners that consisted of entitlement fees (taxes) on domestic oil and subsidies on imported oil. Once the entitlement fees and subsidies were taken into account, all refiners faced the same effective price for their oil.

ENTREPRENEUR
An individual who organizes resources for production, introduces new products or techniques of production, and reaps the rewards/bears the consequences of such endeavors.

EQUATION OF EXCHANGE
Equation which sets forth the relationship between the supply of money, velocity, the price level, and real output; $MV \equiv PY$.

EQUILIBRIUM
A state of balance; a market is in equilibrium when the quantity demanded equals the quantity supplied.

EQUILIBRIUM OUTPUT
The unique level of GDP at which aggregate demand equals output; the only output level at which there is no involuntary change in inventories, hence no signal to change production.

EQUILIBRIUM PRICE
The price for which the quantity demanded equals the quantity supplied.

EXCESS RESERVES
The amount by which the reserves of a financial institution exceed its required reserves.

EXPECTED LIFE (OF A RESOURCE)
Proven reserves divided by consumption.

EXPLICIT COSTS
Direct payments made to others for the resources they own.

EXTENSIVE GROWTH
Economic growth attributable to increases in the quantity of such inputs as natural resources, labor, and capital goods.

FALLACY OF COMPOSITION
Falsely concluding that what is true for the individual must be true for the group.

FEDERAL FUNDS MARKET
Market in which banks trade their excess reserve deposits (at the Fed) on a one-day basis.

FEDERAL FUNDS RATE
The interest rate on loans made among financial institutions in the federal funds market.

FEDERAL OPEN MARKET COMMITTEE (FOMC)
The committee responsible for determining the basic thrust of monetary policy and conducting open market operations; consists of the seven members of the Board of Governors and five of the twelve Federal Reserve Bank presidents.

FEDERAL RESERVE SYSTEM
The central bank of the United States; the organization responsible for conducting monetary policy by influencing the supply of money and credit and the level of interest rates.

FEDERAL RESERVE SYSTEM (THE FED)
The central bank of the United States; the organization responsible for conducting monetary policy by influencing the supply of money and credit and the level of interest rates.

FIAT MONEY
Money that attains its value by government decree; it has little value as a commodity. All U.S. currency and coins today are fiat money.

FISCAL POLICY
The deliberate manipulation of federal expenditures and taxes for the purpose of influencing economic activity.

FISHER EFFECT
The effect that higher expected inflation has in inducing higher interest rates.

FIXED COSTS
Costs that are independent of the level of production.

FIXED EXCHANGE RATES
A system in which governments intervene aggressively to keep exchange rates at certain levels rather than permitting them to float in response to market forces.

FLOATING EXCHANGE RATES
Exchange rates that are allowed to change continuously in response to market forces of supply and demand.

FOREIGN EXCHANGE MARKET
The market in which the currencies of different countries are bought and sold.

FOREIGN EXCHANGE MARKET SPECULATORS
Individuals and firms that buy and sell foreign currencies with the intent of profiting from exchange-rate movements.

FOREIGN EXCHANGE RATE
The amount of another country's money that residents of a country can obtain in exchange for one unit of their own money; the price at which one country's currency may be traded for foreign currency.

FRACTIONAL RESERVE BANKING
A system in which banks hold reserves equivalent to only a rather small fraction of deposit liabilities.

FREE GOOD
A good that is not scarce.

FREE TRADE
Trade that is free of artificial barriers that would restrict the movement of goods between countries.

FREE-TRADE AGREEMENT
A pact that removes trade restrictions among member nations but leaves in place restrictions against non-member nations.

FRICTIONAL UNEMPLOYMENT
Unemployment due to normal job search by individuals who have quit their jobs, are initially entering the labor force, or are reentering the labor force.

FULL-BODIED MONEY
A form of money whose value in exchange (as money) is equivalent to its value as a commodity.

GATT
An international agreement promoting more open trade policy and providing the machinery to settle trade disputes among participating nations.

GDP DEFLATOR
A price index constructed by taking a weighted average of prices of all goods and services that enter into the nation's gross domestic product; it reveals the change since the base year in the cost of purchasing the items that constitute the nation's GDP.

GENTLEMEN'S AGREEMENT
An informal understanding among members of a group to pursue practices that are in the best interests of the group.

GOVERNMENT PURCHASES
Federal, state, and local government spending on final goods and services, including costs of hiring government employees but excluding government transfer payments.

GOVERNMENT TRANSFER PAYMENTS
Expenditures by government for which no goods or services are concurrently received by the government.

GROSS DOMESTIC PRODUCT (GDP)
The aggregate money value of all final goods and services produced by the economy in a given period, typically one year.

GROSS INVESTMENT (I)
The total value of all investment goods produced in the economy during a specific time period, normally one year.

HERFINDAHL INDEX
A measure of market concentration obtained by squaring the market share of each firm in the industry and then summing these numbers.

HORIZONTAL MERGER
A merger between companies in the same market.

HOSTILE TAKEOVER
A merger accomplished by purchasing controlling interest directly from the stockholders of the target firm, against the wishes of its management.

HUMAN CAPITAL
The knowledge and skills acquired by workers, principally through education and training.

HYPOTHESIS
A proposition concerning a particular relationship or event—often part of a theory.

IMPACT LAG
The period that elapses between the point at which a new policy is implemented and when the policy begins to influence economic activity.

IMPLEMENTATION LAG
The period that elapses between the point at which a need for policy change is recognized and when the change in policy is implemented.

IMPLICIT COSTS
The opportunity costs of using resources already owned by the firm.

IMPLICIT TAX RATE
The amount by which the government reduces its subsidy in response to another dollar of earned income—that is, the change in subsidy divided by the change in earned income.

IMPORT QUOTA
A restriction limiting the amount of a foreign good that may enter a country legally.

INCOME EFFECT
The change in quantity demanded of a good that results from a change in purchasing power (when the price of the good changes).

INCOME EFFECT (FOR LABOR)
The change in the amount of labor supplied that can be attributed to a change in income. A higher income increases the demand for leisure, reducing the hours of work.

INCOME STATEMENT
A financial report showing the revenues, costs, and profits from the firm's activities over a specified period of time.

INCREASING-COST INDUSTRY
An industry in which input prices increase as the industry expands.

INDEPENDENT GOODS
Goods for which the cross elasticity of demand is zero.

INDEXATION
Widespread use of escalator clauses that tie wages, rents, and other prices directly to the nation's price index in order to reduce the redistributive effects of inflation.

INDIFFERENCE CURVE
A curve depicting all combinations of two goods among which an individual is indifferent—that is, all combinations that have the same total utility.

INDIFFERENCE MAP
A set of indifference curves.

INDIVIDUAL RETIREMENT ACCOUNT (IRA)
Voluntary, tax-deductible, self-managed retirement savings program authorized by legislation in the early 1980s to promote saving.

INDUSTRIALIZATION
Movement toward widespread application of technology and capital goods in production processes.

INDUSTRIAL POLICY
Targeting of certain sectors thought to be crucial for economic growth through government investment and other mechanisms.

INDUSTRY LONG-RUN SUPPLY CURVE
A curve indicating the relationship between the price of a good and the amount supplied by the industry after the entry of new firms to the industry or the exit of existing firms.

INDUSTRY SHORT-RUN SUPPLY CURVE

A curve indicating the relationship between the price of a good and the amount supplied by the industry in the short run. (In the short run the number of firms in the industry is fixed.)

INEFFICIENT PRODUCTION

Producing less than maximum output; occurs when resources are left idle or used ineffectively.

INELASTIC DEMAND

Demand is inelastic when $E_d < 1$.

INFERIOR GOOD

A good for which demand falls in response to a higher income.

INFLATION

A persistent and sustained increase in the general level of prices; a persistent decline in the value of the monetary unit (for example, the dollar).

INFLATION RATE

The rate at which a nation's average prices rise over time.

INFLATIONARY GAP

The amount by which equilibrium GDP exceeds the full-employment GDP level; occurs when aggregate expenditures are excessive relative to the capacity to produce goods and services.

IN-KIND TRANSFERS

Transfer payments that consist of goods and services rather than cash. Included are food, public housing, and medical care.

INNOVATION

The application of new technical knowledge to such economic processes as production and distribution.

INTENSIVE GROWTH

Economic growth attributable to technological progress, which increases the productivity of inputs.

INTEREST INCOME

The payments received by lenders for the use of their funds (expressed in dollars).

INTEREST RATE

The price paid for the use of lenders' funds (expressed in percentage terms).

INTERGENERATIONAL BURDEN

The costs imposed by the current generation upon future generations by bequeathing an inadequate capital stock.

INTERMEDIATE GOOD

A good that is used as an input in producing other goods and services.

INTERMEDIATE TARGET

A variable (such as the money supply or interest rates) the Fed attempts to control in the short run in order to influence such ultimate objectives as unemployment and inflation rates.

INTERNALIZE COSTS

To shift external costs from third parties back to those parties directly responsible for the costs.

INTERNATIONAL RESERVES

A government's stock of foreign currencies and gold available to support the country's currency in the foreign exchange market.

INTERNATIONAL TRADE

The exchange of goods or resources between countries.

INVENTION

The discovery of new knowledge.

ISOCOST LINE

A line showing all the combinations of capital and labor that can be purchased with a given amount of money.

ISOQUANT

A curve depicting the various input combinations that are capable of producing a given level of output when used efficiently.

KEYNESIANS

Economists who, like Keynes, believe that a capitalistic economy does not tend automatically toward a full-employment equilibrium; hence, activist monetary and fiscal policies are advocated.

KINKED DEMAND CURVE

The demand curve facing an oligopolist if rivals in the industry match the firm's price reductions but ignore its price increases.

LABOR

The physical and mental abilities of workers.

LABOR FORCE

Those individuals 16 years of age and over who are counted as either employed or unemployed.

LABOR FORCE PARTICIPATION RATE

The percentage of the working-age population that is in the labor force.

LAND

A country's natural resources.

LAW OF COMPARATIVE ADVANTAGE

Total output is maximized when countries specialize in the production of those goods for which they have a comparative advantage.

LAW OF DIMINISHING MARGINAL UTILITY

The proposition that marginal utility of a good eventually declines as consumption of the good increases.

LAW OF INCREASING COSTS

The hypothesis that the opportunity cost of a good rises as the quantity of the good produced increases.

LESS-DEVELOPED COUNTRIES (LDCS)

Countries in which living standards are low because modern technology generally has not been applied to production processes.

LIABILITIES
Debts of the firm or claims that outsiders have on the firm.

LIQUIDITY
The ease and willingness with which one may convert an asset into money when one needs cash. Savings accounts are highly liquid; land is not.

LOANABLE FUNDS MODEL
A model that explains interest rates in terms of the demand for and supply of lenders' funds. According to this model, the interest rate is the price paid for the use of these funds.

LONG RUN
A period of time long enough to change the quantities of all inputs.

LONG-RUN AVERAGE COST CURVE
A curve revealing the lowest cost per unit at which a firm can produce each level of output, given sufficient time to change all inputs.

LORENZ CURVE
A diagram illustrating the cumulative distribution of income by families.

LUXURY
A good for which the income elasticity of demand is greater than 1.

M-1
Demand deposits and other checkable accounts plus currency and coins in the hands of the public; the narrow medium of exchange or *transactions* measure of money.

MACROECONOMICS
The study of the aggregate economy.

MARGINAL ANALYSIS
An examination of what occurs when current conditions change.

MARGINAL COST PRICING
A regulatory procedure intended to equate price with marginal cost, and thereby promote efficient allocation of resources.

MARGINAL FACTOR COST
The increase in the total cost of an input associated with using an additional unit of the input.

MARGINAL PRODUCT OF LABOR
The increase in output associated with a one-unit increase in labor, holding capital constant.

MARGINAL PRODUCTIVITY THEORY OF INCOME DISTRIBUTION
The theory that income is distributed to factors of production according to each factor's marginal revenue product. In particular, the theory predicts that each input will be paid an amount equal to its marginal revenue product.

MARGINAL PROPENSITY TO CONSUME (MPC)
The ratio of the change in consumption to the change in disposable income that induces the change in consumption; the slope of the consumption function.

MARGINAL PROPENSITY TO SAVE (MPS)
The ratio of the change in saving to the change in disposable income that induces the change in saving; the slope of the saving function.

MARGINAL REVENUE
The increase in total revenue associated with a one-unit increase in output.

MARGINAL REVENUE PRODUCT OF LABOR
The increase in total revenue to a firm resulting from the hiring of an additional unit of labor.

MARGINAL TAX RATE
The percentage of an *additional* dollar of income paid in taxes.

MARGINAL UTILITY
The extra satisfaction (change in total utility) from consuming one more unit of a good.

MARKET
A mechanism through which buyers and sellers are brought together for the purpose of exchanging some good or resource.

MARKET CONCENTRATION RATIO
The percentage of industry sales attributable to the four largest firms in an industry.

MARKET DEMAND CURVE
A curve showing the relationship between the price of a good and the total quantity demanded by all consumers in the market (per period of time): obtained by summing the demand curves of individual consumers.

MARKET DEMAND FOR LABOR
The relationship between the wage rate and the total amount of labor demanded by all firms in the labor market (other things equal).

MARKET FAILURE
A situation in which unrestricted markets produce either more or less of a good than is socially optimal.

MARKET FOR POLLUTION RIGHTS
A market in which pollution rights are bought and sold, at prices determined by the supply of and demand for these permits.

MARKETING ORDER
A directive, enforced by the Department of Agriculture, limiting the quantity of a product that each producer may sell on the market.

MARKET PERIOD
A period of time during which the quantity supplied cannot be changed—represented by a perfectly inelastic supply curve.

MARKET STRUCTURE
The distinguishing characteristics of a market, including number of firms, the similarity of the products they sell, and the ease with which new firms can enter the market.

MARKET SUPPLY OF LABOR
The relationship between the wage rate and the total amount of labor supplied to the market (other things equal).

MEANS TEST

A requirement that a family's income not exceed a certain level; if it does the family is declared ineligible for that particular form of public assistance.

MICROECONOMICS

The study of the individual units that comprise the economy.

MINIMUM EFFICIENT SCALE

The level of output at which economies of scale end.

MIXED ECONOMY

An economic system that mixes pure capitalism and a command economy. Some resources are owned privately, others publicly. Some economic decisions are made in markets, others by central authorities.

MODEL

A formal presentation of a theory, often mathematical or graphical.

MONETARISM

The viewpoint that monetary instability is the dominant cause of output fluctuations and that money supply growth is the dominant cause of inflation.

MONETARISTS

Economists who share the view that money exerts a dominant effect on economic activity and that a capitalistic economy has an effective self-regulating mechanism. Activist policies are thought to hinder these corrective mechanisms and to destabilize economic activity, and are therefore rejected.

MONETARY AGGREGATES

The various measures of the nation's money supply, including M-1, M-2, M-3, and L.

MONETARY POLICY

The use of certain tools by the Federal Reserve System to alter the availability of credit, the level of interest rates, and the supply of money in order to influence economic activity.

MONEY

Anything widely accepted as payment for goods and services; any generally accepted medium of exchange.

MONEY MARKET MUTUAL FUNDS (MMMFs)

Institutions that pool funds of thousands of individuals to buy large blocks of safe, interest-bearing assets. These accounts are checkable and pay a yield that floats with yields in the market.

MONOPOLISTIC COMPETITION

A market structure characterized by a large number of firms selling distinct (differentiated) products and in which entry into and exit from the industry is easy.

MONOPOLY

An industry with only one seller. There are no good substitutes for the product of the monopolist.

MONOPOLY POWER

The ability of a firm to influence output price by changing the amount it sells. Any firm facing a downward-sloping demand curve has some monopoly power.

MONOPSONIST

The only buyer of a particular input.

MORAL INCENTIVES

Promotion of desirable behavior by appealing to the individual's responsibility to society and by raising the individual's social stature within the community.

MULTIPLIER

The ratio of the change in equilibrium output to the original change in spending (C, I, G, or net exports) that caused the change in output.

MUTUAL INTERDEPENDENCE

An interrelationship among producers. Firms, aware that their actions affect others in the industry, make decisions only after taking into account how rivals are likely to respond.

NATIONAL DEBT

The total stock of bonds and other federal government IOUs outstanding; the sum of past federal budget deficits minus the sum of past surpluses.

NATIONAL INCOME ACCOUNTING

The set of rules and procedures used to measure the total flow of output produced by a nation, together with the income generated by this production.

NATIONAL INCOME (NY)

The aggregate income received by the resource owners of land, labor, capital, and entrepreneurship; equal to GDP minus the sum of depreciation and indirect business taxes.

NATURAL MONOPOLY

An industry characterized by extensive economies of scale. The total cost of producing a given output is minimized when only one firm is in the industry.

NATURAL RATE OF UNEMPLOYMENT

The minimum sustainable unemployment rate below which inflation tends to accelerate; the percentage of the labor force either frictionally or structurally unemployed.

NATURAL UNEMPLOYMENT RATE HYPOTHESIS

View that there is no long-run trade-off between inflation and unemployment; that the nation's long-run Phillips Curve is a vertical line at the natural rate of unemployment.

NECESSITY

A good for which the income elasticity of demand is greater than 0 but less than 1.

NEGATIVE EXTERNALITIES

Uncompensated costs imposed on third parties as a result of consumption or production by other individuals or firms.

NEGATIVE INCOME TAX
A program in which families with low incomes would receive a negative tax (that is, subsidy). The subsidy would be reduced as the family's income from other sources increased.

NET DOMESTIC PRODUCT (NDP)
Gross domestic product minus a depreciation allowance for the value of capital goods wearing out during the period.

NET FARM INCOME
The total revenue generated by a nation's farms minus farm production costs.

NET INVESTMENT
The net addition to the nation's capital stock in a given period; gross investment minus depreciation.

NET WORTH
The difference between a firm's assets and its liabilities; net worth is the residual equity or claim of the owners of the firm.

NOMINAL GDP
The value of all final goods and services produced by a nation in a given year, measured in prices prevailing in that year.

NOMINAL INTEREST RATE
The interest rate measured in actual dollars borrowers must pay.

NONPROHIBITIVE TARIFF
A tariff that reduces but does not eliminate foreign sales in the country imposing the tariff.

NONRECOURSE LOAN
A government loan that, at the farmer's discretion, may be either repaid or canceled. To cancel, the farmer transfers ownership of the commodity to the government, keeping whatever funds have been borrowed.

NORMAL GOOD
A good for which demand increases in response to a higher income.

NORMATIVE ECONOMICS
Deals with value judgments.

OFFSETS
Reductions in pollution beyond the amount required of one firm (or plant) that are used to permit a second firm (or plant) in the same area to increase its pollution.

OKUN'S LAW
Rule of thumb that indicates that each 1 percent of unemployment above the natural rate is associated with a 2.5 percent gap between actual and potential GDP.

OLIGOPOLY
A market structure in which a small number of firms dominates the industry; other firms are kept out through barriers to entry.

OPEN MARKET OPERATIONS
Buying and selling of U.S. government securities by the Fed with a view toward influencing monetary and credit conditions.

OPEN SHOP
A work arrangement in which employees cannot be compelled to join a union, even if one has been chosen to represent the company's work force.

OPPORTUNITY COST
The best alternative to the option chosen.

OTHER THINGS (BEING) EQUAL
A condition in which only the specific variables under consideration change; all other variables remain constant.

OUTPUT GAP
The magnitude by which actual GDP falls short of potential GDP.

PARTNERSHIP
An unincorporated firm with two or more owners who have unlimited liability for the firm's debts.

PATENT
An exclusive right, granted by the government, to market a product or process for 17 years.

PAY GAP
The difference in pay between two groups, traditionally specified in percentage terms.

PERFECTLY ELASTIC DEMAND
A demand that is infinitely responsive to price—represented by a horizontal demand curve.

PERFECTLY ELASTIC SUPPLY
A supply that is infinitely responsive to price—represented by a horizontal supply curve.

PERFECTLY INELASTIC DEMAND
A demand that is totally unresponsive to price—represented by a vertical demand curve.

PERFECTLY INELASTIC SUPPLY
A supply that is totally unresponsive to price—represented by a vertical supply curve.

PHILLIPS CURVE
A graph illustrating the relationship between the unemployment rate and the rate of inflation.

POLICY INEFFECTIVENESS THEOREM
Proposition advocated by proponents of REM that only *surprise* or *unanticipated* policies have an effect on such real economic variables as output and employment.

POLLUTION RIGHT
A permit that entitles its bearer to emit one unit of a certain pollutant into the environment.

POPULATION MOMENTUM
The tendency of population to continue to increase even when the average couple bears two children; this phenomenon is attributable to the disproportionate number of youth in the population.

POSITIVE ECONOMICS
Involves statements based on fact.

POSITIVE EXTERNALITIES
Benefits received but not paid for by third parties as a result of production or consumption by others.

POSITIVE TIME PREFERENCE
A preference to consume now rather than wait.

POTENTIAL GDP
The hypothetical output level produced under conditions of full employment—when only frictional and structural unemployment exist.

POTENTIAL OUTPUT
The output level (real GDP) that would be produced if the actual unemployment rate were equal to the natural unemployment rate, that is, if the economy were at full employment.

POVERTY LINE
A level of income below which a family is classified as poor. The poverty line is based on the cost of those items deemed necessary to maintain a minimally acceptable standard of living.

PREDATORY PRICING
A practice whereby one or more firms temporarily reduce price in order to drive weaker firms from the industry and then raise price once these competitors have been eliminated.

PRESENT VALUE
The value now of one or a series of payments to be received in the future; often referred to as the *discounted present value* of future payments.

PRICE-CAP REGULATION
A form of regulation limiting the price a firm may charge (but not limiting allowable profits).

PRICE CEILING
The maximum legal price that may be charged for a good.

PRICE DISCRIMINATION
The practice of selling a good at different prices that are not attributable to differences in cost.

PRICE FLOOR
The minimum legal price that must be paid for a good.

PRICE INDEX
A weighted average of the prices of goods and services expressed in relation to a base year value of 100.

PRICE LEADERSHIP
A practice in certain oligopolistic industries whereby one firm initiates price changes and other firms in the industry follow its lead.

PRICE SUPPORT
A minimum price guaranteed by the government. The government preserves the minimum price by agreeing to buy any output offered at this price.

PRICE SYSTEM
A mechanism for coordinating economic decisions in which prices are determined in markets and used to allocate resources and output.

PRICE TAKER
An economic unit that has no control over price. The perfectly competitive firm is a price taker in the product market.

PRIME LOAN RATE
A benchmark bank loan rate that is widely publicized and used as a standard by which other bank loan rates are set.

PRIVATE BENEFITS
The benefits received by those consuming or producing a good.

PRIVATE COSTS
The costs incurred by those producing or consuming a good.

PRIVATIZATION
Transferring government activities or state assets to the private sector, that is, to individuals and privately owned firms.

PROCYCLICAL POLICY
A (misguided) policy that stimulates aggregate demand when economic activity is strong and reduces aggregate demand in periods of economic weakness; a policy that destabilizes economic activity.

PRODUCER PRICE INDEX
A price index based on a large sample of materials and goods purchased by firms; formerly known as the wholesale price index.

PRODUCTION FUNCTION
A relationship indicating the maximum amount of output that can be produced per period with various quantities of inputs and a given technology.

PRODUCTION POSSIBILITIES CURVE
A line revealing the maximum combinations of two goods that can be produced with a given quantity of resources, assuming that technology is fixed.

PRODUCTIVE EFFICIENCY
An industry's output is produced at the lowest cost possible.

PRODUCTIVITY
The amount of output produced per unit of input.

PRODUCTIVITY GROWTH
Expansion of output and real income per hour of work; the main source of rising living standards.

PRODUCT MARKET
A market in which a particular good or service is bought and sold.

PROGRESSIVE TAX
The fraction of income paid in tax rises as income rises.

PROHIBITIVE TARIFF
A tariff set so high that it prevents the sale of a foreign product in the country imposing the tariff.

PROLETARIAT
The working class under capitalism, consisting of people who own only their own labor (as opposed to the capitalist or bourgeoisie class of property and capital owners).

PROPORTIONAL TAX
The fraction of income paid in tax that remains constant at all income levels.

PROPRIETORSHIP
A firm owned by a single individual who has unlimited liability for the firm's debts.

PROTECTIONISM
Sheltering domestic industries from foreign competition through tariffs, quotas, or other programs that limit imports.

PROVEN RESERVES
The amount of a natural resource that has been discovered and that producers are willing to extract given current costs and prices.

PUBLIC ASSISTANCE/WELFARE
Transfer programs that are means-tested—that is, available only to low-income families.

PUBLIC CHOICE ANALYSIS
The application of basic economic principles to analyze government decision making.

PUBLIC GOOD
A good or service that cannot be provided for one person without being made available to others, and once provided for one person can be provided for others at no additional cost.

PUBLIC-INTEREST THEORY OF REGULATION
The theory that regulation is a response to market failure and therefore designed to benefit society.

PURCHASING POWER PARITY THEORY (PPP)
Theory that the exchange rate between any two national currencies adjusts to reflect changes in the relative price levels in the two nations.

PURE CAPITALISM
An economic system in which property is privately owned and markets rather than central authorities coordinate economic decisions.

PURE ECONOMIC RENT
The payment for using a resource that is fixed in supply.

QUANTITY DEMANDED
The amount of a good consumers choose to buy at a particular price.

QUANTITY SUPPLIED
The amount of a good firms choose to sell at a particular price.

RATE BASE
The value of a firm's capital, as determined by a regulatory commission.

RATE OF RETURN
The annual return received on a firm's capital (or rate base) expressed as a percentage of the firm's capital.

RATE-OF-RETURN REGULATION
A form of regulation limiting a firm to a prescribed rate of return on its capital (rate base).

RATIONAL BEHAVIOR
Acting in a manner consistent with a decision maker's objectives.

RATIONAL EXPECTATIONS MACROECONOMICS (REM) OR NEW CLASSICAL MACROECONOMICS
Modern school of economists that emphasizes the effectiveness of market forces pushing the economy toward full employment and views discretionary stabilization policies as being ineffective.

REAL DEFICIT
The actual deficit adjusted for the net balance sheet gain experienced by government because of inflation; actual deficit minus the inflation rate times the net federal debt outstanding.

REAL GDP
GDP adjusted for inflation; the value of gross domestic product in constant or base-year prices.

REAL INTEREST RATE
The nominal (actual) interest rate minus the expected rate of inflation.

RECESSION
A period of time in which a nation's real output declines for at least two consecutive quarters (six months).

RECESSIONARY GAP
The amount by which equilibrium GDP falls short of the full-employment GDP level; the amount of additional output required to generate full employment.

RECOGNITION LAG
The period that elapses between the point at which a change in policy is needed and when the need is recognized by policymakers.

REGRESSIVE TAX
The fraction of income paid in tax declines as income rises.

RENT SEEKING
The use of scarce resources in an attempt to secure a monopoly and therefore earn monopoly profits.

REPLACEMENT LEVEL OF FERTILITY
The fertility level that exactly "replaces" the parents—that is, two children per couple.

REQUIRED RESERVES
The minimum amount of reserves a financial institution is required to hold based on the institution's deposit liabilities and the percentage reserve requirement set by the Fed.

RESERVE REQUIREMENT
The percentage of a bank's deposit liabilities that by law it must hold in reserves—in cash or deposits with the Federal Reserve.

RESERVES
Cash holdings of a financial institution plus its deposit at the Federal Reserve.

RESOURCE (FACTOR) MARKET
A market in which a particular resource (factor of production) is bought and sold.

RESOURCES
Inputs (land, capital, and labor) used to produce goods and services.

RESPONSIBILITY SYSTEM
An arrangement designed to tie monetary rewards more closely to work actually performed. In Chinese agriculture, a system of family farming based on long-term leases of land.

RICARDIAN EQUIVALENCE THEOREM
Hypothesis that increased federal budget deficits induce an equivalent increase in private saving, thus leaving the gross pool of saving (government plus private) unaltered. If valid, most of the alleged adverse consequences of budget deficits are nonexistent.

RIGHT-TO-WORK LAWS
Legislation enacted by certain states to require open shops (that is, to outlaw compulsory union membership).

RISK OF DEFAULT
The probability that a borrower will fail to meet his or her interest obligations or repay the loan.

ROUNDABOUT PRODUCTION
The process of obtaining capital and using it to produce consumer goods rather than producing consumer goods directly, without capital.

RULE OF REASON
The doctrine that all monopolies are not illegal, only monopolies that have engaged in unreasonable behavior.

SAVING
The difference between disposable income and consumption expenditures.

SAY'S LAW
The view that production creates its own demand because it generates an equivalent amount of income with which the output may be purchased.

SCARCITY OF RESOURCES
Insufficient resources are available to produce all goods and services desired by consumers.

SCHUMPETER–GALBRAITH HYPOTHESIS
The claim that innovation occurs more rapidly when firms are large in size and comprise a substantial share of the market.

SCREENING HYPOTHESIS
The claim that employers make hiring decisions on the basis of a person's education but that education does not make a worker more productive.

SELF-CORRECTING MECHANISM
The forces in the economy that tend to push equilibrium output toward the full-employment output level in the absence of government implementation of monetary and fiscal policies.

SHORTAGE
The amount by which quantity demanded exceeds quantity supplied at a given price.

SHORT RUN
A period of time so short that the quantities of some inputs cannot be changed.

SHUTTING DOWN
Temporarily halting operations; producing no output in the current period. This limits the firm's loss to its fixed costs.

SIMPLE DEPOSIT EXPANSION MULTIPLIER
The maximum expansion of demand deposits per unit of additional reserves; the reciprocal of the reserve requirement for *DDO*.

SOCIAL BENEFITS
Private benefits plus external benefits.

SOCIAL COSTS
Private costs plus external costs.

SOCIAL INSURANCE
Transfer programs based on some criteria other than income (for example, retirement or unemployment).

SOCIALIST ECONOMY
In Marx's conception, an intermediate stage of communism in which workers are paid according to their work; identified with the Stalinist growth model in the Soviet bloc and China.

SOCIAL REGULATION
Broad-based regulations designed to improve the environment and to enhance health and safety.

SOFT BUDGET
A flexible, almost unlimited budget enjoyed by enterprises; they can rely on the state for subsidies and tax breaks to bail out inefficient and unprofitable operations.

SPECIAL-INTEREST THEORY OF REGULATION
The theory that regulation is designed to protect special-interest groups at the expense of the public.

SPECIALIZATION
An arrangement in which persons or countries concentrate on the production of a limited number of goods or activities, rather than becoming self-sufficient.

STAGFLATION
A situation in which sluggish or declining output is accompanied by strong inflation.

STALINIST GROWTH MODEL
Plan aimed at pursuit of rapid economic growth by collectivizing agriculture and concentrating investment spending on heavy industry.

STANDARD OF LIVING
The average output or real income per person; annual output divided by the population.

STRUCTURAL DEFICIT OR HIGH-EMPLOYMENT DEFICIT
The deficit that would prevail under conditions of full employment; depends on legislated programs and tax rates, not on economic activity.

STRUCTURAL UNEMPLOYMENT
The portion of unemployment accounted for by those out of work for long periods because their job skills do not match those required for available jobs; often caused by structural changes in the economy.

SUBSTITUTE GOODS
Goods that are substitutable in consumption. Two goods are substitutes when an increase in the price of one good increases demand for the other.

SUBSTITUTE INPUTS
Inputs that are substitutes in production: an increase in the price of one increases demand for the other.

SUBSTITUTION EFFECT
The change in quantity demanded of a good that results from a change in the price of the good relative to its substitutes.

SUBSTITUTION EFFECT (FOR LABOR)
The change in the amount of labor supplied that can be attributed to a change in the opportunity cost of leisure. By increasing the opportunity cost of leisure, a higher wage rate induces an individual to substitute work for leisure.

SUNK COST
A cost that has already been incurred and cannot be recovered.

SUPERIORITY HYPOTHESIS
The claim that large oligopolistic producers captured sizable market shares due to their superior efficiency (lower cost curves).

SUPPLY CURVE
A diagram showing the relationship between the price of a good and the quantity supplied per period of time, other things equal.

SUPPLY SCHEDULE
A table showing the relationship between the price of a good and the quantity supplied per period of time, other things equal.

SUPPLY-SIDE ECONOMICS
School of economics that emphasizes the importance of promoting policies to shift the aggregate supply curve rightward by implementing measures that boost the incentive to work, produce, save, and invest.

SURPLUS
The amount by which quantity supplied exceeds quantity demanded at a given price.

TARGET PRICE
A minimum price guaranteed by the government. If the market price falls below the target price, the government reimburses farmers for the difference.

TARIFF (DUTY)
A tax levied on an imported product.

TAX INCIDENCE
The distribution of the tax burden—that is, who ultimately pays the tax.

TECHNOLOGY
The body of knowledge encompassing techniques for transforming resources into output.

TERMS OF TRADE
The ratio of the average price of a country's exports to the average price of its imports (both prices measured in units of domestic currency).

THEORY
A formulation of underlying relationships in an attempt to explain certain pheomena.

THEORY OF OCCUPATIONAL CROWDING
A theory that the lower wages of women (or minority workers) result from their being denied entrance into certain high-paying occupations and, instead, their being crowded into other occupations, thereby depressing wages in those occupations.

TOTAL REVENUE
The price of a good times the quantity sold (TR = $P \times Q$).

TOTAL UTILITY
The total amount of satisfaction received from all the units consumed of a good.

TRADE DEFICIT
The amount by which a country's imports exceed its exports.

TRADE SURPLUS
The amount by which a country's exports exceed its imports.

TRADING POSSIBILITIES CURVE
A line showing the combinations of two goods a country may obtain by producing the good for which it has a comparative advantage and trading it for the other good.

TRANSACTION COSTS
The costs associated with the exchange of a good or resource.

TRANSACTIONS DEMAND FOR MONEY
Money held to finance a stream of expenditures that does not coincide precisely in time with the receipt of funds such as paychecks.

TREASURY BILL YIELD
The yield on safe, short-term government securities known as Treasury bills.

TRUST
A combination of companies acting in concert in order to increase control of an industry.

UNEMPLOYMENT RATE
Percentage of the labor force that is unemployed, that is, out of work and looking for work.

UNION SHOP
A work arrangement that requires employees to join a union within a certain period of time after they are hired.

UNIT ELASTIC DEMAND
DEMAND is unit elastic when $E_d = 1$.

VARIABLE COSTS
Costs that increase as the level of production rises.

VELOCITY
The number of times annually that an *average dollar* is spent on final goods and services; the ratio of the nominal GDP to the money supply.

VERTICAL MERGER
A merger between a company supplying an input and a company buying it.

VOLUNTARY EXPORT RESTRICTION
An agreement by one country to limit exports to a second country.

WEALTH EFFECT
The effect that a change in the nation's price level exerts on consumption, aggregate demand, and equilibrium output by changing the real value of such financial assets as money, savings accounts, and government bonds held by individuals.

WORKFARE
A program in which low-income individuals receive government support in return for agreeing to work.

Credits

The authors are indebted to the following publishers, (listed alphabetically) for permission to reprint from copyrighted material:

Peter Murrell, "Symposium on Economic Transitions in the Soviet Union and Eastern Europe," (Fall p. 6. Reprinted with permission from American Economic Association.

Murray L. Weidenbaum, adapted from Murray L. Weidenbaum, *Rendezvous with Reality: The American Economy After Reagan* (New York: Basic Books, 1988), p. 218. Reprinted with permission from HarperCollins Publishers.

R.A. Radford, "The Economic Organization of a P.O.W. Camp," *Economica*, 1945, pp. 189-201. Reprinted with permission of Basil Blackwater, publisher, and the author.

Data in IBM's stock from *The Wall Street Journal*, September 13, 1991. Reprinted by permission of *The Wall Street Journal*. © 1991, Dow Jones & Company, Inc. All rights reserved worldwide.

Eugene Carlson, "Video Stores Try Sharper Focus in Market Glut," *The Wall Street Journal*, July 2, 1990, p. B1. Reprinted by permission of *The Wall Street Journal*, © 1990, Dow Jones & Company, Inc. All rights reserved worldwide.

Dorothy Gaiter, "Pygmalion Story," *The Wall Street Journal*, July 24, 1991, pp. A1, A4. Reprinted by permission of *The Wall Street Journal*, © 1991, Dow Jones & Company, Inc. All rights reserved worldwide.

Margaret Warner, adapted from Margaret Warner, "Ruling to Drop Suit Against Cereal Firms Deals Blow to 'Shared Monopoly' Theory," *The Wall Street Journal*, September 11, 1981, p. 4. Reprinted by permission of *The Wall Street Journal*, © 1981, Dow Jones & Company, Inc. All right reserved worldwide. "FTC Drops 10-Year-Old Antitrust Suit Against the 3 Largest U.S. Cereal Makers." *The Wall Street Journal*, January 18, 1982. Reprinted by permission of *The Wall Street Journal*, © 1982, Dow Jones & Company, Inc. All rights reserved worldwide.

"25 Years of Stock Market History," copyright © 1991 and reprinted with permission of Dow Theory Forecasts, Inc.

"The Free Market Comes to Mongolia," *The Economist*, p. 40, October 19, 1991. © 1991 The Economist Newspaper Group, Inc. Reprinted with permission.

"Principles of Economics," *Forbes*, September 30, 1991. Source for earnings, *Forbes*, September 30, 1991, p. 113. Reprinted with permission.

F.M. Scherer and David Ross, "*Industrial Market Structure and Economic Performance*, 3rd ed., p. 84. Copyright © 1990 by Houghton Mifflin Company. Adapted with permission.

Earl Heady, John Pesek, William Brown and John Doll. "Crop Response Surfaces and Economic Optima in Fertilizer Use." Chapter 14, in Earl Heady and John Dillon, *Agricultural Production Functions*, (Table 14.11). Reprinted by permission. Copyright © 1961 by Iowa State University.

"Poland Weighs Giving Stakes in Business to All Adult Citizens," *The Kansas City Star*, June 28, 1991, p. A-1. Reprinted by permission. © 1991 *The Kansas City Star*, all rights reserved.

Scott Canon, "Talk Turns to Trash after Farm Failure," *The Kansas City Star*, August 11, 1991, p. A-8. Reprinted by permission, © 1991 *The Kansas City Star*, all rights reserved.

Angus Maddison, *Phases of Capitalist Development*, Oxford University Press, 1982, page 8. Reprinted by permission of Oxford University Press.

Milton Friedman and Anna Schwartz, *A Monetary History of the United States 1867-1960.* Copyright © 1953 by Milton Friedman and Princeton University Press. Reprinted by permission of Princeton University Press.

Marjorie Mandel, "Contaminated Fish May Be Mislabelled," *St. Louis Post Dispatch*, May 3, 1987, pp. 1-6. Copyright © 1987, Pulitzer Publishing Co. Reprinted by permission.

Orley Ashenfelter, "Union Relative Wage Exists" from *Econometric Contributions to Public Policy* by William Peterson and Richard Stone (New York: St. Martin's Press, 1979). Table 6, p. 33. Copyright © 1979 by St. Martin's Press, Incorporated. Reprinted with permission of St. Martin's Press, Incorporated.

Melinda Warren, *Regulation on the Rise: Analysis of the Federal Budget for 1992.* Tables A-2 and A-3. Reprinted with permission of Center for the Study of American Business, Washington University in St. Louis.

Photo Credits

Bio photo of James F. Ragan, Jr., Blaker Studio Royal, Manhattan, Kansas; bio photo of Lloyd B. Thomas, Jr., Creative Image Portrait Design, Pullman, Washington; Stock Boston (p. 5); The Bettmann Archives (p. 10); The Bettmann Archives (p. 72); Stephen P. Allen/Gamma Liaison (p. 75); Richards/Magnum Photos (p. 225); Wide World Photos (p. 297); The Bettmann Archives (p. 326); Wide World Photos (p. 467); Courtesy of Robert J. Barro (photo by Robert G. Gordon) (p. 510); Wide World Photos (p. 545); Courtesy of R. Solow (p. 574); Photo Researchers (p. 594); Jeff Share (p. 615); Courtesy of Joan V. Robinson (p. 697); Tony Freeman/Photo Edit (p. 744); © George Olson/Photo File (p. 760); Courtesy of The Walt Disney Company (p. 788); "Reprinted by permission of *The Wall Street Journal* © 1991, Dow Jones & Company, Inc., All Rights Reserved Worldwide." (p. 898) Part Openers II and IX, Chapter Openers 8, 9, 10, 11, 12, 13, 14, 35, 36, are provided courtesy of Linda Wooton Miller, © 1992. Part Opener VII and Chapter Openers 25, 26, 27, 28, 29 are provided courtesy of the Dallas Infomart. Part Openers I, III, IV, V, VI, VII, X and Chapter Openers 1, 2, 3, 4, 5, 6, 7, 15, 16, 17, 18, 19, 20, 21, 22, 23, 24, 30, 31, 32, 33, 34, 37, 38, 39, 40 are provided by Tony Stone Worldwide Photography, Chicago.

Subject/Name Index

Correlation, vs. causality, 12–13
Cosby, Bill, 75
Cost-benefit analysis, environment and, 919–921
Cost curves
   average and marginal, 621
   shifting, 627–629
   short-run, 620–621
Cost effective pollution reduction, 922–924
Cost of living, 209
Cost-push inflation, 486–487
Costs
   competitive factor markets and, 820–822
   economies of scale and, 624–627
   explicit, 608–609
   of farm programs, 964
   implicit, 609
   law of increasing, 42
   in long run, 622–627
   marginal, 652–656
   marginal factor, 812
   opportunity, 7, 41–42
   and production, 90–91, 607–633
   profit and, 608–611
   of regulation, 756–757
   in short run, 616–621
   total, 648–652
   of trade, 985
Cost schedules, 618, 619, 620
Council of Economic Advisors (CEA), 358, 542n
CPI. *See* Consumer price index
CPSC. *See* Consumer Product Safety Commission
Cramer, Gail L., 969r
Crandall, Robert W., 757n, 942r
Crash. *See* Stock market
Creditors, inflation and, 227
Credit unions, 377
Crime, and unemployment, 223
Cross elasticity
   of demand, 109, 121–122, 674, 727n
   of demand and supply, 123
Cross-media pollution, 932–933
Crowding-in effect, 309, 544–545
Crowding-out effect, 308, 543–545
   and investment, 360
Crown jewels, selling, 147
Crude quantity theory, 460–464
Cuba, 1093
Cuban Americans, 850
Currency, 67. *See also* Money
   appreciation of, 1011, 1015, 1016
   convertibility of, 1100
   depreciation of, 1010–1011, 1015, 1016
Current account, and balance of payments, 1032–1034, 1036
Current income, 294n
Curves. *See also* Aggregate supply-aggregate demand model; Cost curves; Slope
   demand, 25, 26, 27
   indifference, 598–605
   production possibilities, 40–46, 982–983

supply, 89–90
   trading possibilities, 983–985
Customer discrimination, 841
Cyclical deficits, 534, 535–537, 538, 539
Cyclical unemployment, 205–206
Czechoslovakia, 51, 53

D

Daniels, Larry, 922, 923
Danziger, Sheldon, 908r
Daub, Mervin, 18
Daymond, Thomas N., 839n
Death rates. *See* Birthrate
Deavors, Kenneth, 956n
Debt
   bonds as, 148
   corporate, 147
Debtors, inflation and, 227–228
Decertification, of unions, 795, 798
Decision making, 8–9
Decoupling, and farm programs, 966
Decreasing-cost industry, 661, 663–665
Deductions, 188
   tax, 179
Default risk, 865
Defense, 171
Deficiency payment, to farmers, 962–963
Deficient-demand unemployment, 205
Deficit. *See also* Budget deficits
   federal, 177
   in 1990s, 279–280
   real, 541
   trade, 975, 1035–1036
Deficit-spending units, 431
DeFina, Robert, 756n
Deflation, 227, 417, 487n
DeLorean, John, 643
Demand, 82. *See also* Supply
   agricultural expansion programs, 960–961
   consumer expectations and, 87
   cross elasticity of, 109
   elasticities of, 107–122, 126–129, 678, 950
   expected future growth of, 299–300
   income elasticity of, 109, 242n
   individual to market, 593
   for labor, 779–781
   law of, 82–83, 591–593
   for loanable funds, 431, 860–862
   marginal utility and, 587
   for monopolist, 677
   perfectly elastic, 113
   perfectly inelastic, 112–113
   price elasticity of, 109–119
   prices and, 85
   and quantity demanded, 87–88
   and resource markets, 67
   shift in, 95, 96
   supply and, 92–93, 97–98
   and supply elasticities, 107–133
   for union labor, 799–802
Demand curve, 25, 26, 27, 83. *See also* Aggregate demand curve
   aggregate, 262–263

income and, 84
income and substitution effects and, 592
indifference curves and, 603–604
kinked, 710–712
linear, 678n
market, 593
for monopolistically competitive firm, 699
for perfectly competitive firm, 646
and price elasticity of demand, 128–129
shifts in, 83–87
shift vs. movement in, 87–88
Demand-pull inflation, 485–486, 488–489
Demand schedule, 83
Demographics, and labor force, 481
Demographic transition, in LDCs, 1055–1056
Demsetz, Harold, 160r, 745n
Deng Xiaoping, 1090
Denison, Edward F., 561, 562, 578r
Denzau, Arthur, 995, 998n
Dependency rate, 1058–1059
Dependent variables, 25
Deposit accounts, 398
Deposit creation
   bank lending and, 385–386
   bank security purchases and, 386–387
Deposit multiplier, 390–392
Depository Institutions Deregulation and Monetary Control Act (DIDMCA) (1980), 382, 403n, 754n
   interest-bearing checkable accounts and, 460n
Deposits, 379–380. *See also* Banks and banking
   multiple expansion of, 387–391
Depreciation, 157–158, 248
   of dollar, 1021
   straight-line, 610
Depreciation allowances, 230n, 300
Depression, 196, 274
Deregulation, 754–755, 797–798
   of airline industry, 765. *See also* Airline industry
   of financial system, 377n
Derived demand, 781
   labor as, 819
Derthick, Martha, 764n
Devaluations, of U.S. dollar, 272–273
Developed countries, 1046. *See also* Less developed countries (LDCs)
   LDC investments by, 1069–1070
   as LDC trading partners, 1070–1071
   role of, with LDCs, 1068–1071
Developing countries, 1046n
   command economies, capitalism, and, 1097–1098
Differentiated products, 708
Dijlas, Milovan, 1103
Dillard, Dudley, 313r
Diminishing marginal utility
   consumer surplus and, 588
   law of, 583, 587
Diminishing returns
   law of, 613–616, 779

Direct payments, as farm policy, 962–963
Direct relationships, of variables, 27
Discomfort index, 480
Discounted present value, 149–153
Discount policy, of Federal Reserve System, 410
Discount rate, 400, 410–412, 428
    change in, 410–412
Discount retailing, 859
Discounts and advances, 407
Discount window, 410
Discouraged workers, 200–201
Discretionary monetary policy, monetarist view of, 468
Discrimination, 791
    and labor market outcomes, 831–857
    within occupations, 842–844
    racial inequality and, 806
    against women workers, 837–841
Diseconomies of scale, 625–627
Disequilibrium, 94
Disequilibrium price, 94
Disincentives, 904–905
Disinflation, 441n
    REM and, 514–515
    supply-side economics and, 360–361
Disintermediation, 382
Disney, Roy, 788
Disposable income, 250, 288–292
Dissavers, 430n
Distribution of income, 48, 362–363, 824–825, 875–876, 881–908
Diversification, 734–735
Divestment, 145
Dividends, 142, 148. See also Stocks
Doll, John, 821n, 823n
Dollar(s)
    analysis of (1973–1992), 1020–1023
    currencies pegged to, 1029n
    devaluations of, 272–273
    falling (1985–1988), 1023, 1024–1026
    falling (1992), 1026–1027
    income as flow of, 370
    and international trade, 1009
    real interest rates and, 1018
    strong (1980–1985), 1023–1024
Domestic economic policies, in LDCs, 1067
Donn, Clifford, 767n
Donohue, John, III, 847n, 856r
Dorsey, Stuart, 790n
Double taxation, 142, 183
Doyle, A. Conan, 9n
Drabenstott, Mark, 969r
Dr Pepper, 725
Drugs, FDA approval of, 757
Dukakis, Michael, 213
Dumping, 683, 989–990
Duncan, Greg J., 761n, 837n, 897n, 908r
Duopoly, 731
Du Pont, cross elasticities and, 123
Du Pont Case (1957), 740, 742
Durable goods, 242
    owned by households, 295
Duration, of unemployment, 203–204

Duty (tariff), 986–987
Dwyer, Paula, 676

E

Earl, Paul H., 217r
Earnings, 777–778. See also Labor market
    retained, 156
Earth Summit (1992), 934
Easterbrook, Gregg, 956n
Eastern Europe, 39. See also Russia; Soviet system; Soviet Union
    capitalism and, 51–54
    command economy in, 48, 49–51. See also Command economies
    living standards in, 1083
    prospects for, 1101–1104
    stabilization of former command economies in, 1098–1101
    Stalinist growth model in, 1082. See also Stalinist growth model
EC. See European Community
Economic regulation, 754
Economic "bads," 255
Economic analysis, public choice analysis as, 168
Economic Consequences of Mr. Churchill, 326
Economic Consequences of the Peace, 326
Economic decisions, 39–61
Economic growth, 44–45, 521. See also Stalinist growth model
    historical perspective on, 555–560
    importance of, 554–555
    in industrial nations, 551–578
    inflation and, 229
    of LDCs, 1036–1038
    measures of, 552–554
    policies to increase, 572–575
    sources of, 560–565
Economic instability, 75–76
Economic models, production possibilities curve, 40–46
Economic policies
    international, and LDCs, 1067
    in LDCs, 1066–1067
Economic profits, 609–610, 651n, 872
    and accounting profit, 610–612
    and long-run equilibrium, 659–665
Economic Recovery Tax Act (ERTA) (1981), 182n, 188, 189, 278
    depreciation tax allowances and, 300
    and supply-side economics, 355–358, 575
Economic regulation, 755
Economic rent, 870–871
    of worker, 786
Economics
    normative, 177
    research in, 16
    supply-side, 275, 276–277, 352–363
Economic security, expenditures for, 175
Economic systems, 46–48
    command economies, 46–48, 1075–1107
    market economy, 46–48
    pure capitalism, 46–48

Economic theory, 12. See also Keynesian economists; Monetarists; Supply-side economics; Theory
Economic uncertainty, 458
Economic variables, 236–237
Economic views, of aggregate supply curve, 346–347
Economic welfare, measure of, 256
Economic well-being, for LDCs, 1054. See also Less developed countries
Economies of scale, 624–627, 629
    mergers and, 145
    and monopoly, 675
    and perfect competition, 666–667
Economists
    disagreements among, 14–16
    functions of, 20
    Keynesian, 452. See also Keynes, John Maynard
    Monetarist, 452. See also Monetarists
Economy. See also Communism; Equilibrium; Federal Reserve System; Macroeconomics; Macroeconomy; Socialism
    aggregate, 195, 736
    business firms in, 135–161
    equilibrium output in simple, 300–304
    government role in, 163–192, 491–492
    international trade and, 971, 973–1007
    monetary policy and, 450–453
    in 1960s, 269
    in 1970s, 270–274
    in 1980s, 274–277
    in 1990s, 277–280
    performance of, 35–36
    and recession, 197
    socialist, 1078–1079
    underground, 254
Education. See also Unemployment
    and incomes of blacks, 846–847
    in LDCs, 1053, 1054, 1067–1068
    unemployment rates by, 851
    and wage differentials, 784–786, 787
Edwards, Corwin D., 685
EEOC. See Equal Employment Opportunity Commission
Efficiency, 75
    in production, 40–41, 874
    in resource allocation, 665–666
Effluent fees, 924, 932
EFTA. See European Free Trade Association
Egalitarianism, 171
Ehrenberg, Ronald, 217r, 809r, 833n
Eisenhower, Dwight, 270n
Eisner, Michael, 788
Eisner, Robert, 452, 541n, 549r
Elastic demand, 111
    and monopolistic competition, 698
Elasticity. See also Elasticity of demand
    categorizing, 111–113
    cross, 109, 121–122
    demand and supply, 107–133
    estimating, 128–129
    income, 109, 120–121
    of supply, 122–128

Hostile takeovers, 145
"Hot money," 1018
Households, 237–239, 240, 431n
  durable goods owned by, 295
  investment spending by, 316
Housing assistance, 901
Houthakker, H.S., 119
Hufbauer, Gary, 1007r
Huff, Darrell, 32n
Human capital, 563–564, 786–787, 861
  occupational choices of women and, 840
  pay gap and, 837
Humphrey-Hawkins Full-Employment
  Act (1978), 512, 517
Hungary, 51, 53, 1089
Hunt, Nelson Bunker, 888
Hurd, Richard, 810, 813n
Hurdle, Gloria, 763n
Hussein, Saddam, 280
Hutchinson, Harry D., 395r
Hyman, David N., 192n
Hyperinflation, 175n, 372–373
Hypothesis, 9

I
IBM, 150–151, 607
Ibrahim, Youssef, 715n
ICC. See Interstate Commerce Commis-
  sion
Ichniowski, Casey, 772n
Ideology, 15
Illiquidity. See Liquidity
IMF. See International Monetary Fund
Impact lag, 507
Imperfect information, regulation and,
  758–761
Implementation lag, 507
Implicit costs, 609
Implicit tax rate, 904
Import quotas, 988–989
Imports, 17, 316. See also Price level behavior
  quota on, 56
  restrictions on, 994–995
  U.S., 977, 978
Incentives, 8
  material, 1090
  perverse, 1086–1089
Income, 370. See also Flow-of-income
  approach; Gross domestic product
  (GDP); Macroeconomy; Wages
  break-even, 291, 904
  circular flow of, 67–70, 237–239
  and demand curve, 84
  determinants of, 560–561
  disposable, 250, 288–292
  distribution of, 48. See also Labor markets
  family patterns, 25, 26
  farm, 947–954
  functional distribution of, 875–876
  inequality of, 74–75, 882–890
  interest as, 859, 860–866
  measures of, 249–250
  median family, 882
  and monopoly, 689

national, 249
national accounting for, 237
personal, 249–250
profit as, 859, 872–874
proprietor's, 248
racial differences in, 845–849
redistribution of, 443
rents as, 247, 859, 866–871
security of, 171
supplemental security, 903
unemployment and loss of, 220–222
wealth and, 226–229
Income determination model, mathematics
  of, 336–338
Income distribution, 775
  international comparisons, of, 885–887
  marginal productivity theory of,
    824–825
  poverty and, 881–908
  supply-side economics and, 362–363
  utility and, 584–586
Income effect, 342–343, 591, 592
  for labor, 782, 783
Income elasticity of demand, 109,
  120–121, 242n
Income-expenditure model
  and aggregate demand curve, 347–349
  multiplier analysis and, 310
  taxes and, 320
Income levels, and exchange rates,
  1015–1017
Income statement, 156–158
Income support, for farmers, 956–957
Income taxes, 175, 176
  automatic stabilizer and, 308, 338, 339
  corporate, 183
  federal individual, 178–182
  indexation of, 357
  investment decisions and, 300
  and multiplier, 308
  negative, 903–905
  state, 182, 186
Increasing-cost industry, 661, 663
Independent goods, 122
Independent variables, 25
Indexation, 229
  of income taxes, 357
Indexes
  consumer price, 209
  Herfindahl, 730–733
  price, 209
  producer price, 209, 210
Indifference curves
  analysis of, 598–605
  inconsistent, 601
Indifference map, 599–600
Individual demand, 593
Individual income tax, 178–182
Individualism, and public choice theory,
  169
Individual retirement accounts (IRAs),
  182n, 278–279, 357–358, 430
Industrial concentration, Herfindahl Index
  and, 730–736
Industrial corporations, largest U.S., 136.
  See also Business firms

Industrialization, 555
Industrial nations, 1046n
  economic growth and productivity in,
    551–578
  living standards and productivity in,
    557–560
  productivity growth rate in, 564
Industrial organization, and antitrust policy, 725–749
Industrial policy, 1078
  of Stalin, 1081
Industrial pollution, 916. See also Pollution
Industrial production, and recession, 197
Industrial Revolution, 1052
Industry
  constant-cost, 661–663
  decreasing-cost, 663–665
  Eastern European restructuring of, 1100
  increasing-cost, 661, 663
  long-run supply for, 661–665
  perverse incentives in, 1086–1089
  short-run equilibrium for, 659
  short-run supply curve of, 657–658
  unemployment rates by, 851
Inefficient production, 40
Inelastic demand, 111
Inelastic supply, 123
  perfectly, 124
Infant industries, 992
Infant mortality rate, in LDCs, 1053, 1054
Inferior goods, 84, 120
Infinite geometric progression, multiplier
  and, 307
Inflation, 175, 194, 208–213, 219–220,
  225–231, 264, 484–487
  average annual rate, 484
  causes of, 485–487
  consequences of, 225–231
  in former command economies,
    1098–1099
  hyperinflation, 372–373
  income and wealth distribution and,
    226–229
  interest payments and, 541
  interest rates and, 433–435
  monetarists and, 465–466, 508
  and money growth, 462
  national debt explosion and, 546–547
  nature and history of U.S., 487–492
  in 1960s, 269
  in 1970s, 270–274
  in 1980s, 274–275
  and Phillips Curve, 473–495
  REM and, 512–513
  and resource allocation, 230–231
  stocks and bonds as hedge against,
    148–149
  theories of, 11
  and U.S. money growth, 463
  unemployment and, 474–476
Inflationary expectations, 862–864
Inflationary gap, 329–333, 349–350
  monetary and fiscal restraint and,
    332–333
Inflation rates, 10, 226
  bank status and, 405

Nonprice competition, 703
　oligopolies and, 708–709
　in video industry, 704
Nonprice methods, of allocation, 100
Nonprohibitive tariff, 986
Nonrecourse loan, 958
Nonrenewable natural resources, 934–935
Nonwage job characteristics, 787–791
Nonwhites, income differences and,
　845–849
Nordhaus, William, 256, 258r, 766n,
　1087n
Normal goods, 84, 120
Normal profit, 611
Normative economics, 15–16, 177
　and income distribution, 889
Norris-LaGuardia Act (1932), 794
North American Free Trade Agreement,
　1003
Nowotny, Kenneth, 774r, 774n
Nutrition assistance, 901

O

OASDI. *See* Old Age, Survivors, and Dis-
　ability Insurance
O'Brian, Bridget, 721n
Obstfeld, Maurice, 1042r
Occupational crowding theory, 840–841
Occupational Safety and Health Adminis-
　tration (OSHA), 752
Occupations, 778. *See also* Labor market
　discrimination within, 842–844
　distribution of women within, 837–841
　unemployment rates by, 851
Ofer, Gur, 1077n, 1107r
Off-budget activities, 540
Office of Management and Budget (OMB),
　public ownership and, 772
Offsets, 929
Oil, shortages of, 937–938. *See also*
　Resources
Oil-producing states, 383
Oil tanker spills, 165n
Oksanen, Ernest, 122n
Okun, Arthur M., 217r, 220, 232r, 472,
　494r, 890n, 908r
Okun's Law, 220
Old Age, Survivors, and Disability Insur-
　ance (OASDI), 901
Old-age insurance. *See* Social Security;
　Social Security Act
Oligarchies, in LDCs, 1065
Oligopoly, 642–644, 695, 696, 707–719
　barriers to entry and, 707
　evaluation of, 717–719
　interdependence and, 707–708
　models of, 709–717
Olsen, Randall, 897n
Olson, Kevin, 607
Olson, Mancur, 169n, 578r
OMB. *See* Office of Management and Bud-
　get
O'Neill, June, 844n, 857r
OPEC. *See* Organization of Petroleum
　Exporting Countries

Open market operations, 400, 408–410
Open shop, 795
Operating budget, 541
Operation Desert Storm, 1033–1034
Opportunity cost, 7, 41–42, 455
Optimal combination of output, 45–46
Organization of Petroleum Exporting
　Countries (OPEC), 271, 274, 478n,
　716
　as cartel, 644, 716
　and cost-push inflation, 486
　and oil price controls, 938
OSHA. *See* Occupational Safety and
　Health Administration
OTC. *See* Over-the-counter dealers
Other things (being) equal (*ceteris paribus*),
　12, 84, 89
Our Land and Land Policy, 870
Output. *See also* Economies of scale; Equi-
　librium output; Gross domestic prod-
　uct (GDP); Macroeconomy; Multipli-
　er; Profit(s); Profit maximization; Real
　GDP
　classifying countries by, 1046–1047
　equilibrium, 300–304
　European recession and, 320
　measures of, 249–250
　monopolistic restrictions on, 686
　optimal combination of, 45–46
　potential, 267
　production function and, 612
　real, 18
　real and projected, 557
　resources and, 560–561
　technology and, 43
　unemployment and loss of, 220–222
　variable inputs and, 634–638
Output gap, 221–222
Output tax, and pollution regulation,
　924–925, 931
Over-the-counter (OTC) dealers, 148

P

Pacific Rim nations, 558n
Paglin, Morton, 839n
Palmeri, Christopher, 75n
Panzar, John C., 729
Paper, commercial, 147
Paradox of value, 581, 589
Partnerships, 138, 139, 140, 141–142
　advantages and disadvantages of, 143
Patent, monopoly and, 675–676
Pay gap, 836–844
　by ethnicity, 849–850
　by race, 846–849
Payment. *See* Money
Payment-in-Kind (PIK) program, 959
Payoff matrix, 1000
Payroll tax, 182–183, 902
PCE deflator. *See* Personal consumption
　expenditures deflator
Peak phase, 196, 198
Pechman, Joseph A., 181n, 192r, 887n
Pegging interest rates, 416–418
Penoyer, Ronald, 753

Penson, John B., Jr., 969r
PepsiCo, acquisition by, 725, 727
Per capita GDP, 237
　real, 552
Per-capita income, and agricultural labor
　force, 1060
Per-capita production
　country classifications by, 1046–1047
　in LDCs, 1048–1049
　for selected countries, 1050
Perestroika (restructuring), 51, 1090,
　1094–1096
Perfect competition, 627, 641–671. *See also*
　Factor markets; Product markets
　evaluation of, 665–668
　labor and, 779
　labor market outcomes under, 813
　long-run equilibrium in, 659–665
Perfectly competitive firm, short-run sup-
　ply curve of, 657
Perfectly elastic demand, 113
Perfectly elastic supply, 124
Perfectly inelastic demand, 112–113
Perfectly inelastic supply, 124
Performance, payment for, 788–789
Perkins, Dwight Heald, 1107r
Perloff, Jeffrey, 723r, 749r
Permanent income, 294n
Per se doctrine, 740, 741
Persian Gulf crisis, 280, 1033–1034
Personal consumption expenditures (PCE)
　deflator, 211
Personal income, 249–250
Personal income tax
　exemptions and, 178–179
　progressive nature of, 180–181
Per-unit costs, 616–618
Pesek, John, 821n, 823n
Pet-food industry, 703
Petri, Peter, 39n
Phelps, Charles E., 118n
Phillips, A.W., 474
Phillips Curve, 471, 474–476
　inflation, unemployment, and, 473,
　474–495
　as policy choice menu, 482–484
　and REM, 513–516
　shifting, 479–482
　slope of, 475–476
　theoretical intuition underlying,
　476–478
PICs. *See* Private Industry Councils
Pierce, James L., 395r
PIK program. *See* Payment-in-Kind pro-
　gram
Plotnick, Robert, 908r
Poison pills, 147
Polachek, Solomon, 840n
Poland, 1100
　capitalism and, 51, 53
Polaroid, 644
Policy activists, and monetarists, 507–509
Policy ineffectiveness theorem, 512
Policymakers, and Phillips Curve, 482–484
Political business cycle, 508–509, 510
Politics, and trade barriers, 998–999

Productivity (continued)
  convergence with standard of living, 557–560
  cyclical pattern of, 568–569
  farm, 947–950
  in industrial nations, 551–578
  slowdown in U.S., 565–572
Productivity growth, 553
  in future, 572
  in industrial nations, 564
  of labor, 553–554
  and living standards, 554
  in United States, 562
Product markets 66, 727, 811
  circular flow in, 67–69, 70
  imperfectly competitive, 811–829
Products
  differentiated, 708
  heterogeneous, and oligopoly, 715
  homogeneous, 708
  variety of, 667–668
Profit(s), 8, 248, 608–611
  allocative function of, 611
  competitive factor markets and, 822–824
  economic, 609–610, 872
  as income, 859, 872–875
  regulation effect on, 764–766
  role of, 874
  short-run, 654
  sources of, 872–873
Profit margins, 345
Profit maximization
  marginal revenue and marginal cost, 652–656
  for monopolist, 678, 679
  in short run, 678–680
  total revenue and total cost, 648–652
Progress and Poverty, 870
Progressive tax, 176, 177
  income tax as, 180–181
Prohibitive tariff, 986
Proletariat, 1076
Propensity-to-consume relationship, 289, 290
Property rights
  assigning, 926
  Coase, Ronald, and, 927
Property taxes, 175–176, 187
Property values, rent controls and, 101
Proportional tax, 176
Proprietorships, 138, 139–141
  advantages and disadvantages of, 143
Proprietor's income, 248
Protectionism, 990, 991, 1029
Proven reserves, 935
Public assistance (welfare), 901, 902–903
Public choice
  analysis of, 168
  economists, 545
  theory of, 167–170
Public goods, 74, 166–167
Public interests, 73
Public-interest theory of regulation, 757–761
Public investments, in LDCs, 1066
Public ownership, 770–772

Public utilities. *See* Public ownership
Purchasing-power exchange rates, 1048–1052
Purchasing power parity (PPP) theory, 1014–1015, 1022
Pure capitalism, 46–48
Pure economic profit, 611
Pure economic rent, 866

Q

Quantity demanded, 82, 126
  demand and, 87–88
  and price, 83
Quantity supplied, 88, 124–125
Quantity theory of money, 460–464
Quasi-public goods, 167
Quintiles, 882, 883
Quirk, Paul J., 764n
Quotas, import, 56, 988–989

R

Race
  income differences by, 845–849
  unemployment rates by, 850
Rachlin, Howard, 595
Racial discrimination, legislation against, 847
Racial inequality, unions and, 806
Radford, R.A., 69n
Ragan, James F., 789n, 841n, 900n
Raiders, corporate, 144
Railroads, monopoly power of, 752
Raisian, John, 772n
R and D. *See* Research and development
Rankin, Robert, 789
Rate base, 769
Rate of exchange. *See* Exchange rate
Rate of return, 769
Rates
  Laffer Curve and, 31
  of inflation, 226
Rational behavior, 7–8
Rational expectations macroeconomics (REM), 347, 498, 509–518
  assumptions of, 510–511
  critique of, 516–518
  disinflation and, 514–515
  implications for macroeconomic policy, 511–513
  Phillips Curve and, 513–516
Rationing, nonprice, 100
Ratios. *See* type of ratio
Raw materials
  monopolistic control of, 674–675
  shortages of, 936–937
Ray, 29, 30
Reagan, Ronald, 185, 213, 274, 340, 400n, 542n
  antitrust activity under, 743–745
  economic growth and, 572
  labor unions and, 797
  regulation and, 754, 755
  supply-side economics and, 352–353, 355–358. *See also* Supply-side economics

Reagan Administration, 274–275
  discomfort index and, 480n
  dollar and, 1021
  EEOC and, 848
  fiscal policy of, 574
  interest rates and, 443
  and supply-side economics, 275, 276–277, 352–353, 355–358
  tax rates and, 180
Reaganomics, 188, 276–277
Real deficit, 541
Real GDP, 33, 196, 251, 253, 552
Real income, 343
Real interest rates, 226–227, 862–864
  and exchange rates, 1017–1019
  vs. nominal interest rates, 440–444
Real output (real GDP), 18, 19
  determinants of, 560–561
  nation's price level and, 264
Real wages, 33, 185
Recession, 153n, 196
  duration and severity of, 197
  economic activity during, 197
  European, 320
  1960–1992, 268
  in 1980s, 274
  in 1991, 201
  output during, 568–569
  productivity slowdown and, 570
Recessionary gap, 321–329, 331–332, 349–350
  removing, 328–329
  self-correcting mechanism and, 324–328
Reciprocal Trade Agreements Act (1934), 1002
Recognition lag, 506–507
Recycling, 925
Redistribution of income, 443
Rees, Albert, 809r
Reese, David A., 352n, 366r
Reform programs
  communist, 1090–1092
  opposition to, 1092–1094
  politics of, 1094
Regressive tax, 176, 177
  payroll tax as, 182–183
  sales tax as, 186
Regulated market, and command economies, 1093–1094
Regulation, 164, 751–774. *See also* Airline industry; Trucking industry
  of ATVs, 760
  bank, 398
  capture hypothesis and, 762
  costs and benefits for, 756–757
  and deregulation, 754–755
  economic, 754
  effects of, 763–767
  of energy resources, 107–108
  evolution of federal, 752–755
  monopoly and, 687–689
  of natural monopoly, 758, 767–770
  and pollution control, 922–924, 931–932
  price-cap, 769–770
  and productivity slowdown, 570
  public-interest theory of, 757–761

Waste disposal, and recycling, 925
Wealth, 370
  channel of, 451
  and consumer spending, 293, 294
  holding, 454–455
  income and, 226–229
  and inflationary gap, 330
Wealth effect, 295, 324, 325, 343
  economic views of, 349
Wealth of Nations, The, 71–73, 168
Weidenbaum, Murray L., 756n, 774r,
  916n, 919n, 920n, 937n
Weighted average, 252
Welch, Finis, 845n, 847n, 850n
Welfare, 898. *See also* Workfare
  economic, 256
  payments, 171
Wellington, Brent, 117
Wenders, John, 774n
Wheeler-Lea Act (1938), 739
White, Joseph, 676
Whiting, G.C., 15n
Whitman, Walt, 1044
Wholesale price index. *See* Producer price
  index (PPI)
Wilcox, James A., 423r
Wilder, Ronald, 719n
Williams, Jeffery, 922n
Willig, Robert D., 729

Wilson, Charles E., 78n
Wilson, Woodrow, 397, 1002
Wimmer, L.T., 15n
Winslow, Ron, 693n
Winston, Clifford, 625n, 763n, 765n,
  766n, 774r
Wise, Deborah, 625n
Witcher, Gregory, 995
Withholding tax, 178
Wolff, Edward N., 578r, 844n
Women
  income effect for, 783
  labor discrimination and, 831, 841–844
  labor force participation by, 481, 833,
    834–835
  in labor unions, 798
  occupational distribution of, 837–841
  pay gap of, 836–844
  unemployment rates of, 850, 851
Womer, Norman, 765n
Work, Clemens P., 676
Workers. *See also* Labor; Labor force
  economic rent of, 786
  increase in numbers, 569–570
  as proletariat, 1076
Workfare, 896, 898–899
World Bank, 1046
World economy. *See* International financial
  system; International trade

World War II. *See also* Velocity, changes in
  consumption after, 295
  POW camps in, 68–69
  price level behavior after, 489
  price level behavior before, 488–489
  productivity after, 567
  REM and price–level behavior after,
    516–517
Worrall, John, 790n
Write-offs, 300
Wyckoff, Andrew, 993n

Y

Yellen, Janet L., 549r
Yellow-dog contracts, 793
Yeltsin, Boris, 1095
Yield, 149n
Youngstown Steel, horizontal merger of,
  742–743
Yugoslavia, 1103

Z

Zellner, Wendy, 888
Zero-coupon bond, 149n
Zero-sum game, 54
Zolzhargal, Naidansurenglin, 1102

STUDY GUIDE

PRINCIPLES OF ECONOMICS

SECOND EDITION

ROGER C. TRENARY
KANSAS STATE UNIVERSITY

WITH THE ASSISTANCE OF

JAMES F. RAGAN, JR.
KANSAS STATE UNIVERSITY

AND

LLOYD B. THOMAS, JR.
KANSAS STATE UNIVERSITY

THE DRYDEN PRESS

HARCOURT BRACE JOVANOVICH COLLEGE PUBLISHERS

FORT WORTH   PHILADELPHIA   SAN DIEGO   NEW YORK   ORLANDO   AUSTIN   SAN ANTONIO
TORONTO   MONTREAL   LONDON   SYDNEY   TOKYO

TABLE OF CONTENTS

CHAPTER 1

Economics and Economic Thinking

Chapter 1 introduces you to economics and to the way economists look at the world. The problem of scarcity—*the* economic problem—is described, as are its causes and implications. Finally, this chapter discusses the way economists attempt to discover how an economy works and some of the errors commonly made in doing so. The ideas and principles in this chapter are found throughout the rest of this book. Good luck and enjoy!

CHAPTER OUTLINE

I. Resources and Output
   A. Resources (or Factors of Production)
      1. **Resources** are the inputs used to produce goods and services. Resources are important because the amount and the quality of the resources determine how much output the economy can produce.
      2. Kinds of Resources:
         a. **Land**: natural resources
         b. **Labor**: physical and mental abilities of workers
         c. **Capital**: machines and other output used to produce goods and services
         d. **Entrepreneurship**: ability to organize production and introduce new products and ideas
      3. Resources in any economy are limited or **scarce**—there are not enough resources to produce all the goods and services consumers want.
   B. **Economic Good**: A good (or service) that is scarce; that is, the amount that people want when the good is free exceeds the amount available. A good (or service) that is not scarce is called a **free good**.

II. The Study of Economics
   A. **Economics** is the study of how scarce resources are allocated among competing ends. Because resources are scarce, it is impossible for an economy to provide everything that people in the economy want. Because of scarcity, choices must be made.
   B. **Opportunity cost** is the best alternative to the option that is chosen. When a choice is made, one option is picked and other options are not picked. The best alternative that is not picked is the opportunity cost of the option that was picked.

III. Economic Thinking
   A. Rational Behavior
      1. Rational behavior involves acting in a manner consistent with a decision maker's objectives. If someone is rational, the person has a goal in mind and chooses the appropriate method for achieving that goal.

2. Goals:
a. The goal of consumers is maximum utility.
b. The goal of firms is maximum profit.
3. Decision makers make decisions by comparing the costs and benefits associated with each alternative.

B. **Marginal analysis** examines what happens if current conditions change. Decision makers choose by examining possible changes from the current situation. For example, when deciding whether to have one or two scoops of ice cream, consumers compare the benefit associated with the second scoop relative to the cost of the second scoop.

IV. Methodology of Economics: The **Scientific Method**
A. Step 1: Develop a **theory**. A theory is a formulation of underlying relationships in an attempt to explain certain phenomena.
B. Step 2: State a **hypothesis**. A hypothesis is a proposition or an "educated guess" about a particular relationship or event.
C. Step 3: Gather evidence or data to see whether your hypothesis is correct.
D. To clarify the analysis, economists often use models—formal mathematical or graphical presentations of a theory. Models allow economists to work out the full implications of a theory.

V. Avoiding Common Errors in Thinking
A. **Other Things (Being) Equal**: Most economic theories assume that all variables except those directly part of the theory are being held constant. If other things are actually changing, a particular hypothesis or theory is difficult to test.
B. **Correlation versus Causation**: The fact that two variables tend to move together does not mean that one of the variables is causing the other to change.
C. **Fallacy of Composition**: It is not true that what is true for an individual is necessarily true for a whole group of people acting in unison.

VI. Disagreements Among Economists
A. Economists disagree because (a) the evidence does not convincingly show that one theory is superior to another, (b) they are making different assumptions about what will occur in the future, and (c) they have different values and beliefs about what is good.
B. **Positive economics** involves statements about fact. At least in principle, positive economic statements can be shown to be true or false by looking at data. This is the primary focus of economics.
C. **Normative economics** involves statements about value judgments. Because the statements are based on values or opinions, they cannot be proven true or false.

VII. Branches of Economics
A. **Macroeconomics** is the study of the aggregate economy. Typical issues are: What determines the economy's total output or **Gross Domestic Product (GDP)**? What percent of the entire labor force in the country is unemployed? How fast have prices on average been rising (that is, What is the **rate of inflation**)?
B. **Microeconomics** is the study of the individual units making up the economy. Typical issues are: Why does the price of gasoline rise and fall? How do firms choose what output to produce and how much? What things influence whether a particular job will pay well or not?

HINTS AND HELP

1. Scarcity To grasp the balance of this Study Guide, and economics in general, it is important to understand that the fundamental problem is scarcity. Without scarcity, economics would not exist. It is the choices that scarcity forces on us that are the focus of the science of economics.

2. Theories and Models Theories and models are tools. They organize our thoughts and help us think more clearly *about the real world*. You do not have to choose between theory and reality. Theories help us understand reality.

3. Positive and Normative Economics In order to organize our thinking, it is important to distinguish between normative and positive economic statements. Positive economic statements are statements that, at least in principle, can be verified or rejected by looking at information from the real world. The statement "The average price of gasoline in the United States was $.25 in 1992" is a positive economic statement because its truth can be determined by observing the real world. It is a false statement because the average price of gasoline in 1992 was actually closer to $1.00.

Normative economic statements involve value judgments (or norms). Because they concern individual values, they are not verifiably true or false. The statement "The price of gasoline is too high" is a statement one person (for example, a consumer of gasoline) may believe but another person (for example, an oil rig worker) may not believe.

When individuals disagree about something in economics it often helps to determine whether the disagreement concerns positive or normative economics. If it is a dispute over positive economics, then the participants should focus on what information about the real world is needed to resolve the disagreement and whether the information is available. If the dispute is over normative economics, the participants might just as well agree just to disagree and leave it at that.

FILL IN THE BLANK

Capital

entrepreneur

economic goods

opportunity cost

hypothesis

Macroeconomics

Normative economics

scarcity

Correlation

fixed

1. _____ is the resource that an economy can produce.

2. The individual in an economy responsible for taking the risks associated with introducing a new product or idea is called a(n) _____.

3. The kind of goods that are scarce are _____.

4. "There is no such thing as a free lunch" because the use of resources in a particular way means that an alternative output cannot be produced. The lost alternative output is called the _____.

5. A _____ is a proposed relationship between variables, which can be tested by comparing the prediction to what happens in the real world.

6. _____ is the study of the aggregate economy.

7. _____ statements are based on people's values and thus cannot be proven true or false.

8. The fundamental economics problem is _____.

9. _____ measures how closely two variables tend to move together.

10. At any given moment, the quantity of resources in an economy is _____.

TRUE OR FALSE

_____ 1. To discover whether a theory is useful it must be tested by comparing its predictions to what goes on in the real world.

_____ 2. Scarcity occurs only when there is unemployment.

_____ 3. An example of marginal analysis is comparing the extra benefits and the extra costs associated with making a decision.

_____ 4. If a company owns a lumberyard, it can produce chairs at zero opportunity cost.

_____ 5. Theories can never be disproven.

_____ 6. The scientific method is used only in experiments performed in laboratories.

_____ 7. If a theory says that a higher price causes people to buy less of a good, the theory is correct only if every price increase is followed by a decrease in the amount that people buy.

_____ 8. What is true for one person acting alone is not necessarily true for all people acting together.

_____ 9. Positive economic statements can be proven true or false.

_____ 10. The decisions of individual firms are part of microeconomics.

MULTIPLE CHOICE

1. Which of the following is counted as capital?
   A. worker
   B. oil
   C. tool
   D. air

2. Because resources have many uses:
   A. the government must plan how resources are used.
   B. resources must be allocated.
   C. unemployment is impossible.
   D. consumers cannot decide what to do.

3. Which of the following is a free good?
   A. free public education
   B. sand in a desert
   C. national park
   D. carrot

4. Economic goods are:
   A. expensive.
   B. bought in stores.
   C. produced by firms.
   D. scarce.

5. People must make choices because there is:
   A. poverty.
   B. scarcity.
   C. inflation.
   D. unemployment.

6. Which of the following is an example of marginal analysis?
   A. Students compare the costs of an extra year of school and the extra income that is possible due to having the extra education.
   B. Consumers' expenditures are limited by their incomes.
   C. A firm will build a new factory only if the firm earns a profit.
   D. The government borrows money if it cannot collect enough in taxes to pay for its expenditures.

7. Historically, unemployment has tended to rise in years of extraordinary sunspot activity. Predicting higher unemployment because there are more sunspots is an example of:
   A. marginal analysis.
   B. the fallacy of composition.
   C. confusing correlation and causation.
   D. all things equal.

8. A hypothesis must:
   A. be mathematical.
   B. be testable.
   C. concern people.
   D. contain all aspects of the real world.

9. Which of the following is a part of microeconomics?
   A. explaining why the price of tomatoes has fallen
   B. explaining why unemployment is falling
   C. measuring how high prices are in the economy
   D. measuring how fast an economy's output is growing

10. When an individual believes that if she can make a profit in the market by knowing certain good news about a stock then everyone can make a profit on the stock by knowing the same information, she is making which of the following errors?
   A. violating the assumption of "all things equal"
   B. committing the fallacy of composition
   C. confusing correlation and causation
   D. confusing normative and positive economics

PROBLEMS

At the end of each of the following statements place an N if the statement is a *normative economic statement* or a P if the statement is a *positive economic statement*.

1. Poverty in the United States is too high. _____

2. When inflation is higher, the income distribution is less equal. _____

3. An economy that produces less output has higher unemployment. _____

4. Increases of the money supply are associated with inflation. _____

5. Environmental degradation is the most important issue the world faces in the 1990s. _____

Answers

TRUE OR FALSE

1. True. A theory is judged on the basis of how well it predicts events in the real world.

2. False. Scarcity is ever present because every economy faces the problem of not having enough resources to produce all the goods and services that people want.

3. True. Marginal analysis involves looking at changes from the current situation.

4. False. Opportunity costs exist even when a company owns its resources. The opportunity cost of making chairs is the next best alternative for the lumber—for example, making tables.

5. False. Theories can be refuted by showing that they are inconsistent with the real world.

6. False. The scientific method involves the development of theories and the collection of data to determine whether a theory is consistent with the real world. Although experiments are a means of collecting data, they are not the only means. In economics, data are collected directly from the real world by keeping track of how an economy behaves.

7. False. Theories have all-things-equal conditions associated with them. Only if "everything else is constant" does theory predict that price increases will result in less being bought.

8. True. Something can be true for one person but not true for everyone acting together. The belief that what is true for one is true for all is known as the fallacy of composition.

9. True. Positive economics deals with facts and statements that can be proven true or false by looking at the facts.

10. True. Microeconomics studies the individual decision makers in the economy, including firms.

MULTIPLE CHOICE

1. C. Capital is the resource produced by people. Tools are made by humans and are used to produce other output.

2. B. Because resources are scarce, they must be allocated. Some method must be devised for distributing the resources among their alternative uses.

3. B. If the amount that people want is less than what is available when the price is zero, the good is a free good. Because people would not buy bags of sand in a desert, sand is a free good.

4. D. The distinguishing characteristic of economic goods is that they are scarce.

5. B. Because of scarcity, people must make choices. Even if there were no poverty, unemployment, or inflation, choices would still be necessary.

6. A. Marginal analysis involves comparing the current situation with small changes from it. Deciding whether to go to school an extra year on the basis of extra benefits and extra costs involves this kind of reasoning.

7. C. Because two variables—sunspot activity and unemployment—tend to move together does not mean that one (sunspots) causes the other (unemployment).

8. B. A hypothesis is a proposition—a guess—about how some variables are related. To discover whether the hypothesis is true or false, it must be stated in such a way that it can be tested. Otherwise, the hypothesis is useless because its validity can never be determined.

9. A. Microeconomics focuses on the component parts of the economy—consumers, producers, and individual markets (like the market for tomatoes). Macroeconomics focuses on the aggregate economy.

10. B. The fallacy of composition is the error of believing that what is true for one person is true for all people. Although it is true that if one person knows some good information about a company she could make a profit, if everyone knows the information then no profit can be made because there will be no sellers of the company's stock until after the price has risen.

PROBLEMS

1. N (normative). Whether the poverty rate is too high, too low, or just right is a matter of opinion. Although it is possible to measure the poverty rate objectively by observing the real world, it is not possible to determine objectively whether the amount of poverty is excessive.

2. P (positive). By observing the distribution of income during periods of high and low inflation, it is possible to determine whether the distribution is less equal when inflation is high.

3. P (positive). Whether or not unemployment rises when production falls can be determined by also observing the amount of unemployment when production is high and when it is low.

4. P (positive). Because inflation rates and the money supply are observable, it is possible to see whether increases in the money supply are associated with more inflation.

5. N (normative). Whether environmental degradation is the most important issue for the world in the 1990s is a matter of opinion. Others might consider hunger and poverty or the development of new technologies more important.

CHAPTER 2

The Economic Decisions Facing a Country

Chapter 1 introduced some of the fundamental concepts in economics. Chapter 2 expands on that introduction. Using a simple but useful model called the production possibilities curve, the issues of scarcity, efficiency, unemployment, and economic growth are discussed. This chapter also discusses alternative economic systems and the gains that result from international specialization and trading.

CHAPTER OUTLINE

I. **Production Possibilities Curve**
   A. Assumptions:
      1. The quantities of each resource—land, labor, and capital—are fixed.
      2. The economy produces only two goods. Although this assumption is "unrealistic" because every economy produces many more than two goods, the assumption allows us to focus on fundamental principles. Nothing of importance is true for two goods that is not true for hundreds of goods.
      3. The economy's technology is fixed. **Technology** is the economy's "cookbook" of information about how to produce output from resources.
   B. The **production possibilities curve** is the line that contains all the maximum combinations of the two goods that the economy can produce with the resources and the technological information currently available. Because the economy's resources are scarce and the technological information is fixed, the economy can produce only combinations of the goods that are *on* or *inside* the production possibilities curve. Any combination of the two goods that is outside of the curve is unattainable.
   C. To be *on* the production possibilities curve requires that the economy be **efficient**—that is, an economy must be getting the greatest output possible from its resources. If an economy is producing a combination of goods *inside* its production possibilities curve, it is inefficient. **Inefficient production** means that the economy is leaving some resources unemployed or in some way is wasting them.
   D. Once an economy has become efficient and is producing a combination of goods on the production possibilities curve, trade-offs are necessary—more of one good can be produced only if less of the other good is produced. The amount of, say, tractors given up when more corn is produced is the opportunity cost of the corn. Because resources are usually specialized, the production possibilities curve exhibits **increasing opportunity costs**. As more of one good (corn) is produced, the amount of the other good (tractors) given up for each unit of the first good grows larger and larger. This gives the production possibilities curve its bowed shape. If resources are not specialized, each extra unit of corn requires the sac-

rifice of the same amount of tractors. This is called **constant costs**, and the production possibilities curve is a straight line.

    E.   An outward shift of an economy's production possibilities curve represents **economic growth**. Economic growth is caused by an increase in the economy's resources or by technological progress. An economy can produce economic growth by producing more **capital goods** or by devoting more resources to research for the discovery of new technologies. But producing more **consumption goods**—goods like shoes and cars, which people consume directly—does not cause economic growth. Economic growth then involves a trade-off. An economy can have fewer goods to enjoy now but have more in the future by using its resources now to produce the things that cause economic growth or it can consume more now but have a less advantageous production possibilities curve in the future.

II. Alternative Economic Systems

    A.   An **economic system** is an institutional arrangement for making the *what, how,* and *for whom* decisions. An economic system is characterized by (a) who owns the economy's resources and (b) how economic decisions are made.

    B.   Fundamental Economic Systems:

        1. **Pure capitalism** is characterized by private ownership of resources and by the use of **markets** to allocate resources and outputs. Markets are a system in which buyers and sellers together determine what quantities are exchanged and at what prices.

        2. A **command economy** is a system in which resources are collectively owned and allocation decisions are made by the government.

    C.   In reality, all modern economies are **mixed economies**. That is, some resources are owned privately and some publicly, and some economic choices are made through markets and some by central authorities.

III. How Basic Economic Decisions Are Made

    A.   Pure Capitalism:

        1. *What* Decision: Consumers decide what is produced through their spending decisions. This is called **consumer sovereignty**.

        2. *How* Decision: Individual firms choose what inputs are used to produce the output. Because firms attempt to maximize profit, they choose the least costly input combination.

        3. *For Whom* Decision: Goods and services are distributed on the basis of ability to pay. Ability to pay depends on the quantity and the quality of the resources the individual owns. Because resources are distributed unequally, so are goods and services.

    B.   Command Economy:

        1. The government determines what goods and services are produced, what combinations of inputs are used to produce the goods and services, and how the goods and services are distributed among the people in the economy.

        2. The advantages of a command economy are that the government can make the economy produce goods and services that would not otherwise be produced (for example, housing for the poor), and the distribution of the output can be made more equal.

        3. The Disadvantages of a Command Economy:

            a. Coordination: It is difficult for the government to give detailed instructions to the many producers needed to produce the output the economy produces.

            b. Efficiency: Because the firms in a command economy are not rewarded on the basis of profit, they have less incentive to minimize costs and are more likely to be wasteful.

            c. Quality and Variety of Output: Firms in command economies are less likely to respond to consumer desires for better quality and more varied goods because the managers of the firms are not rewarded for doing so.

            d. Use of Queues: Because prices are held to artificially low levels in order to make them affordable to all, shortages are frequent and rationing is often on the basis of first come, first served.

IV. **International Trade:** The exchange of goods and resources among countries
   A. Countries trade because each can enjoy a higher standard of living if it specializes and trades than if it does not. Because both participants gain from international trade, it is a **positive-sum game**. A **zero-sum game** is a game in which one participant gains only if the other participant loses.
   B. **Specialization** involves people or countries concentrating on the production of a limited number of goods and services rather than trying to produce everything they consume. **Comparative advantage**, the ability to produce a particular good at a lower opportunity cost, determines what goods a country specializes in.
   C. The amount of trading is influenced by such **transaction costs** as transportation costs and by such artificial impediments as **import quotas**.

HINTS AND HELP

1. The Production Possibilities Curve and Economic Models The production possibilities curve is an important economic model. As simple as it is, the production possibilities curve illustrates such fundamentally important issues as the costs of unemployment (an economy with unemployed resources is operating inside its production possibilities curve and is losing goods and services), opportunity costs (production of more of one good requires an economy to give up some of another good when operating on its production possibilities curve), and economic growth (increases in an economy's productive capacity require an economy to sacrifice consumption now in order to produce more of the things that cause economic growth—like capital goods and new technologies). Economists often use models like the production possibilities curve because the models allows them to discover the answers to important questions. Like any tool, the more familiar you are with it the better you will be using it.

FILL IN THE BLANKS

technology

efficient

constant

economic growth

capital

consumption

mixed

zero-sum

comparative advantage

import quota

1. The information that an economy possesses about how to produce output from inputs is called _____.

2. For an economy to be on its production possibilities curve, production must be _____.

3. A straight-line production possibilities curve exhibits _____ opportunity cost.

4. An outward shift of an economy's production possibilities curve is called _____.

5. The goods an economy can produce that cause economic growth are called _____ goods.

6. The goods an economy can produce that give people enjoyment but do not cause economic growth are called _____ goods.

7. Economic decisions are made both by the government and in markets in a(n) _____ economy.

8. If the amount that winners win in a game equals the amount losers lose, the game is called a(n) _____ game.

9. The good or service an individual or economy specializes in is determined by _____.

10. A(n) _____ fixes the quantity of a good that may be brought into a country.

TRUE OR FALSE

_____ 1. To be on its production possibilities curve, an economy must have full employment of resources.

_____ 2. If an economy can produce output with constant costs, its production possibilities curve is a straight line.

_____ 3. Economic growth is caused only by increases in the economy's resources.

_____ 4. Reducing unemployment causes economic growth.

_____ 5. A command economy primarily uses prices to coordinate economic decisions.

_____ 6. A mixed economy involves using both the market and the government to make economic choices.

_____ 7. One advantage of a command economy compared to a market economy is that it is more efficient.

_____ 8. In a positive-sum game, all participants in the game can win.

_____ 9. Specialization increases the self-sufficiency of economies.

_____ 10. An import quota places an upper limit on the price that foreign producers can charge for their product.

MULTIPLE CHOICE

1. A production possibilities curve shows the amount of output:
   A. an economy should produce.
   B. an economy could produce.
   C. consumers want to consume.
   D. producers want to produce.

2. An economy producing a bundle inside its production possibilities curve is experiencing:
   A. equilibrium.
   B. inflation.
   C. inefficient production.
   D. a deficit.

3. Which of the following is most likely to cause a production possibilities curve to shift outward?
   A. an increase in the education level of the population
   B. a reduction in the production of capital goods
   C. an increase in the production of consumption goods
   D. a decrease in the unemployment rate of the economy

4. When an economy is on its production possibilities curve, increasing the production of one good:
   A. shifts the production possibilities curve outward.
   B. shifts the production possibilities curve inward.
   C. reduces the unemployment rate.
   D. reduces the amount of the other good the economy can produce.

5. When an economy's resources are specialized, its production possibilities curve:
   A. does not exist.
   B. is a downward-sloping straight line.
   C. is bowed.
   D. is upward sloping.

6. An outward shift of an economy's production possibilities curve is called:
   A. lower unemployment.
   B. higher unemployment.
   C. increasing costs.
   D. economic growth.

7. The best bundle for an economy to produce on its production possibilities curve is:
   A. the bundle on the vertical axis.
   B. the bundle on the horizontal axis.
   C. the bundle in the middle of the production possibilities curve.
   D. something the production possibilities curve cannot determine.

8. Pure capitalism involves which of the following?
   A. private ownership of resources
   B. production by large firms
   C. large unemployment
   D. high inflation

9. Consumer sovereignty means that:
   A. output is determined by the election of government officials.
   B. prices are determined by consumers.
   C. firms tell consumers what to buy.
   D. consumers decide what goods and services will be produced.

10. Seven-foot-tall teachers who are able to jump well and who can consistently shoot a basketball into a basket ten feet above the ground play basketball rather than teach because of:
    A. market failure.
    B. comparative advantage.
    C. government regulations.
    D. increasing opportunity costs.

PROBLEMS

1. The following data are combinations of two goods—guns and butter—that the economy of the United States of Econ (USE) can produce.

POINT	GUNS	BUTTER (LBS)
A	0	5,000
B	700	4,000
C	500	4,500
D	500	3,000
E	1,000	0
F	900	2,500

(a) Plot the combinations of guns and butter on Figure 2.1. Label each point with its appropriate letter. Draw a production possibilities curve that has the typical "bowed" shaped and that goes through the most points. (*Hint*: The production possibilities curve will not go through all the points.)

FIGURE 2.1

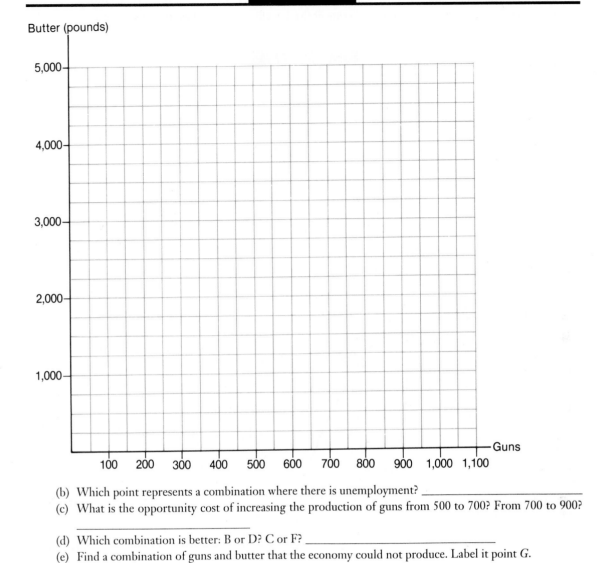

Butter (pounds)

(b) Which point represents a combination where there is unemployment? _____

(c) What is the opportunity cost of increasing the production of guns from 500 to 700? From 700 to 900?

_____

(d) Which combination is better: B or D? C or F? _____

(e) Find a combination of guns and butter that the economy could not produce. Label it point G.

2. Beginning with the production possibilities curve in Figure 2.2, draw the new production possibilities curve after there has been a technological improvement that benefits only the wheat industry.

FIGURE 2.2

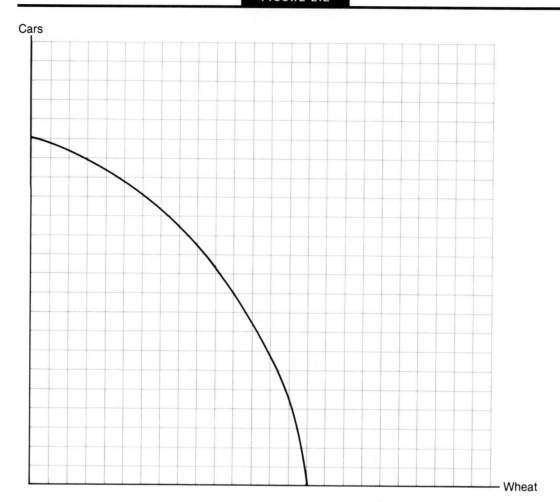

3. (a) Using the production possibilities curve in Figure 2.3, what is the opportunity cost of increasing the production of bolts from 50 to 60? From 60 to 70? _____

FIGURE 2.3

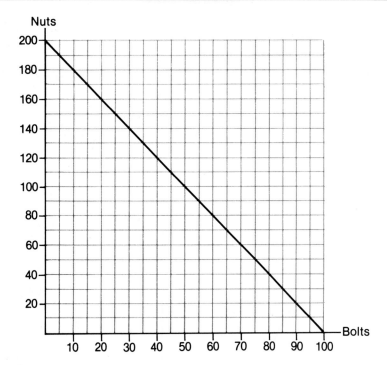

(b) What is different about the resources in the economies pictured in Figure 2.3 and Figure 2.1?

_____

_____

4. (a) The countries of Blue and Gold are identical in all respects except in terms of how each country allocates its resources. Their identical production possibilities curves are pictured below. Blue and Gold are currently producing at point A on their respective production possibilities curves. Which economy will probably experience greater economic growth in the future? Explain. _____

(b) If the slower growing of the two countries wants to grow as fast as the faster growing one, what does it need to do with its resources? Indicate this on the country's production possibilities curve in the graph below and designate the new point B. Also, indicate the opportunity cost of the decision to grow faster.

FIGURE 2.3A₁   **FIGURE 2.3A₂**

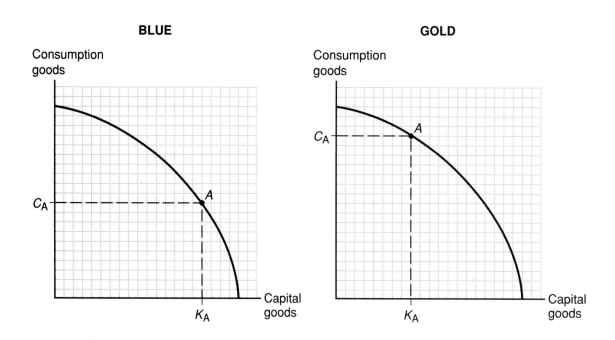

5. In the examples below, calculate the opportunity cost of producing each good in each economy and determine which economy has the comparative advantage in the production of each commodity?

(a) In Italy each unit of labor can produce 1 carrot or 4 cucumbers. In France each unit of labor produces 2 carrots or 4 cucumbers.

(b) A worker in Brazil can produce 5 pounds of coffee or 10 bushels of wheat, and a worker in Argentina can produce 2 pounds of coffee or 6 bushels of wheat.

(c) An hour of work in Germany can produce 3 cakes or 3 tires, and in Sweden an hour of work produces 2 cakes or 4 tires.

6. Assume an individual worker in Spain is able to produce 2 hats or 2 belts and there are 200 such workers in Spain. In Portugal, a individual worker can produce 1 hat or 4 belts. There are also 200 workers in Portugal.

(a) If Spain and Portugal initially do not trade and if half the workers in each country are in hat production and the other half are in belt production, how many hats and belts would each economy produce?

(b) Once Spain and Portugal agree to trade, which good does Spain specialize in and which good does Portugal specialize in? Explain.

(c) Assume Spain uses all of its 200 workers to produce the good for which it has a comparative advantage and Portugal does the same with its 200 workers. Then Spain sends half of its output to Portugal in exchange for half of Portugal's output. How many hats and belts do Spain and Portugal end up with?

TRUE OR FALSE

1. True. If an economy has unemployed resources, it is not producing all the output it could and is inside its production possibilities curve.

2. True. A straight-line production possibilities curve shows that each unit of one of the goods requires the sacrifice of a fixed number of units of the other good, which is what is meant by constant costs.

3. False. Economic growth can also be caused by an improvement in the economy's technology.

4. False. Lower unemployment moves an economy from a point inside its production possibilities curve, but does not cause the production possibilities curve to shift outward.

5. False. A command economy relies on central authorities (government) to make economic decisions.

6. True. A mixed economy is a mix of pure capitalism using markets and command using central authorities to make economic decisions.

7. False. Command economies typically are less efficient than market economies because producers have less incentive to maximize the output available from resources.

8. True. A positive sum-game is a game where the sum of the winnings and losses is positive. All individuals can be winners.

9. False. Specialization involves people and countries concentrating on the production of some good or service, which means they must rely upon other people and countries for more of the other goods and services they want.

10. False. An import quota places a numerical limitation on the amount of a good that can be imported.

MULTIPLE CHOICE

1. B. As its name indicates, the production possibilities curve shows the combinations of goods the economy could possibly produce.

2. C. If an economy is producing a combination of the goods inside its production possibilities curve, it is inefficient. Either there is unemployment or resources are being wasted.

3. A. Any increase in the economy's resources—like an improvement in the education level—shifts the production possibilities curve outward.

4. D. Because all the economy's resources are being used when an economy is on its production possibilities curve, increasing the production of one good requires that less of the other good be produced.

5. C. When resources are specialized, the production possibilities curve is bowed because specialized resources cause increasing opportunity costs.

6. D. An outward shift of the production possibilities curve means the economy's productive capacity has increased. This is called economic growth.

7. D. The production possibilities curve shows only the options available to the economy. The best combination must be determined by the economy when making the *what* choice.

8. A. Pure capitalism involves private ownership of resources and the use of markets to allocate resources.

9. D. Consumer sovereignty means that consumers determine what output an economy produces through their purchase decisions.

10. B. Many people can teach. Few are tall, able to jump well, and able to shoot basketballs consistently into baskets. Such individuals' comparative advantage lies in playing basketball.

PROBLEMS

1. (a) The correct production possibilities curve is drawn in Figure 2.4. The production possibilities curve goes through all the points but point D.

FIGURE 2.4

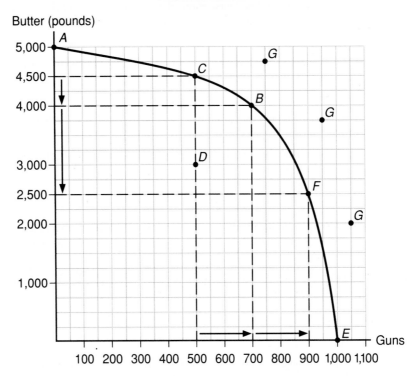

(b) Input combination D represents a situation of unemployment. When an economy experiences unemployment, it is producing a bundle inside its production possibilities curve.

(c) The opportunity cost of increasing gun production from 500 to 700 is the butter that is lost by doing so. In this case the loss is 500 pounds of butter. The opportunity cost of increasing gun production from 700 to 900 is 1,500 pounds of butter. This production possibilities curve exhibits increasing opportunity costs.

(d) Bundle B is better than bundle D because B contains more of both goods. It is not possible to determine whether bundle C or F is better. Both bundles are on the production possibilities curve, so there is no inefficiency. Which combination is better depends on the feelings of people in the economy, and that is not known here.

(e) Any point outside the production possibilities curve is impossible for this economy.

2. A technological advance that increased production in the wheat industry only would shift the production possibilities curve outward along the wheat axis but not along the car axis. This is shown below in Figure 2.5.

FIGURE 2.5

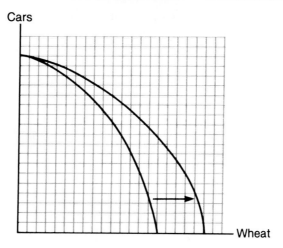

3. (a) The opportunity cost of increasing bolt production from 50 to 60 is 20 nuts; the opportunity cost of increasing bolt production from 60 to 70 is also 20 (shown below).

FIGURE 2.6

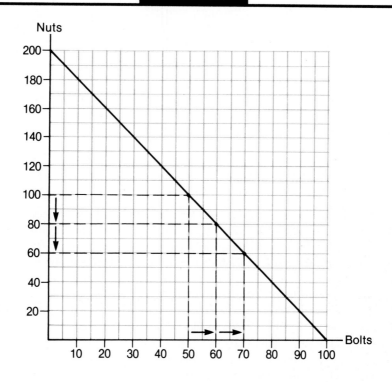

(b) The production possibilities curve in Figure 2.1 is "bowed" because resources are specialized. This results in a situation in which the production of more of one good means the sacrifice of increasing amounts of the other good. In Figure 2.3 resources are not specialized, so extra units of one good can be produced with exactly the same sacrifice of the other good. (Each 10 bolts produced requires the sacrifice of 20 nuts.)

4. (a) Blue will probably have faster economic growth because it is devoting more of its resources to the production of capital goods while Gold is using more of its resources to produce consumption goods. Capital goods are a source of economic growth while consumption goods are not.

(b) To grow as fast as Blue, Gold needs to produce as much capital as Blue is producing. This requires that it move from point A on its production possibilities curve to point B, which is the same as Blue's point A. The opportunity cost of such a move is the reduced production of consumption goods from C_A to C_B.

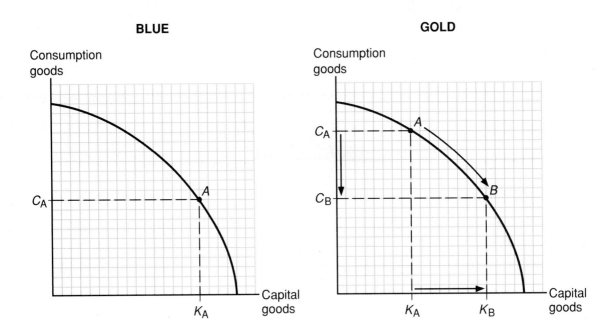

FIGURE 2.6A₁

FIGURE 2.6A₂

5. (a) In Italy the production of 1 more carrot costs 4 cucumbers because the production of 1 more carrot requires Italy to shift one unit of labor out of the cucumber industry into the carrot industry. In doing so, carrot production rises by 1 but cucumber production drops by 4. If instead one unit of labor is moved out of the carrot industry into the cucumber industry, cucumber production rises by 4 and carrot production drops by 1 which means each cucumber costs 1/4 carrot.

In France the production of 2 more carrots costs 4 cucumbers, so 1 carrot costs 2 cucumbers. And reversing the process means that 4 cucumbers cost 2 carrots so 1 cucumber costs 1/2 carrot.

Each extra carrot produced requires a smaller reduction in cucumber production in France than in Italy (2 versus 4) so France is said to have the comparative advantage in carrot production. Extra cucumbers "cost" fewer carrots (that is, have a smaller opportunity cost) in Italy than in France so Italy has the comparative advantage in cucumber production.

(b) A Brazilian worker moved out of the wheat industry into the coffee industry increases coffee production by 5 pounds and reduces wheat production by 10 bushels. Each pound of coffee thus costs 2 bushels of wheat. And the reverse is true: each bushel of wheat costs 1/2 pound of coffee.

A worker in Argentina moved out of wheat production into coffee production increases coffee output by 2 pounds and reduces wheat output by 6 bushels. One pound of coffee thus has an opportunity cost of 3 bushels of wheat, and a bushel of wheat costs 1/3 of a pound of coffee.

Because each pound of Brazilian coffee requires a sacrifice of fewer bushels of wheat than coffee from Argentina (2 bushels versus 3 bushels), Brazil has the comparative advantage in coffee production. Because each bushel of wheat produced in Argentina has an opportunity cost of 1/3 of a pound of coffee, and in Brazil each bushel has an opportunity cost of 1/2 of a pound of coffee, Argentina has the comparative advantage in wheat production.

(c) Each German cake involves the sacrifice of 1 tire, and each tire requires the sacrifice of 1 cake. In Sweden, the production of 2 more cakes involves the sacrifice of 4 tires, so 1 cake costs 2 tires. And because 4 more tires reduce cake output by 2, each tire costs 1/2 cake.

Germany has the comparative advantage in cake production because the opportunity cost of an extra cake in Germany is only 1 tire while in Sweden the opportunity cost is 2 tires. Because the opportunity cost of an additional tire in Sweden is 1/2 cake while in Germany it is 1 cake, Sweden has the comparative advantage in tire production.

6. (a) With 100 workers in hat production and the other 100 in belt production, Spain would produce 200 hats and 200 belts. In Portugal, 100 workers in the hat industry would produce 100 hats while 100 workers in the belt industry would produce 400 belts.

(b) Because each extra hat produced in Spain reduces belt production by 1 and each hat produced in Portugal lowers belt production by 4, Spain has the comparative advantage in hat production and will specialize in their production. Portugal has the comparative advantage in (and specializes in) belt production. An extra belt there reduces hat output by only 1/4 of a hat, and in Spain an additional belt costs 1 hat.

(c) Employing all its workers in hat production, Spain produces 400 hats. Portugal, employing all its workers producing belts, produces 800 belts. After each economy trades half its output for half of the other country's output, Spain and Portugal each end up with 200 hats and 400 belts. Notice that Spain ends up with the same number of hats and more belts when it trades with Portugal (than when it does not) and Portugal ends up with the same number of belts and more hats when it trades.

CHAPTER 3

The Price System

Chapter 2 described some of the important decisions every economy must make and introduced two ways to make those decisions—a market system and a command economy. Chapter 3 presents a more detailed picture of how the price system in a market economy works and notes some of its problems. Because the United States relies primarily on markets and prices for making economic decisions, this chapter is particularly important to understanding the economy in which you live.

CHAPTER OUTLINE

I. There are three groups of decision makers in a mixed economy such as the United States.
   A. **Consumers** earn income from their labor and from the other resources they own. With their incomes they buy goods and services or save. Another name for consumers is *households*, because most consumption decisions are made in the context of a family.
   B. **Firms** have the primary responsibility for producing the goods and services in the economy. They hire the resources—land, labor, and capital—and use them to produce output. Economists assume that the goal of all firms is to maximize profit.
   C. **Government** includes all the activities of local, state, and federal governments. These include the minimum government activity of law enforcement as well as the expanded activities of regulation of business and the production of some goods. Unlike consumers and firms, it is assumed the government does not have any single goal when it acts.

II. There are two kinds of markets in an economy.
   A. **Product markets** are where goods and services (outputs) are bought and sold.
   B. **Resource (or factor) markets** are where resources (factors of production) are bought and sold.

III. Money is an important part of an efficient market system. **Barter,** where goods are traded directly for other goods, is inefficient because of the time required to arrange trades. Money comes from both the government (coins and currency) and from private institutions (checking accounts).

IV. The **circular flow of income** shows the relationship between the market participants—consumers and firms—and the kinds of markets. It is called a "flow" because money, goods, services, and resources are continually moving through the markets. It is called "circular" because the dollars always return to the place where they began. For example, firms buy resources from households in the resource market. Dollars flow to the households and the resources flow to the firms. In turn, households buy goods and services from the firms in the product market. The dollars return to the firms in exchange for the output produced with the resources that the firms bought.

V. The Price System, the Invisible Hand, and Market Failure

A. The **price system** is a mechanism for coordinating economic decisions. Prices determined in the markets are used to allocate resources and output. Prices in the product market send signals to producers about the willingness of consumers to buy various goods and motivate the producers to adjust their production accordingly. Similarly, prices in the resource market signal resource owners where their resources are wanted the most. Also, resource prices induce firms to adjust their mix of inputs so that they use more of the more available inputs.

B. The "Invisible Hand," a phrase coined by Adam Smith, describes the belief that the decisions of consumers and producers result in the allocation of resources that is best for the economy even though consumers and producers are motivated only by their own self-interest. According to Smith, there is no conflict between what consumers and producers find to be best and what society finds to be best. The Invisible Hand says that the price system is the best way of achieving what is best for society.

C. As even its supporters concede, under certain circumstances the Invisible Hand breaks down—the private decisions of consumers and producers may be in conflict with society's best interests. This occurs when there is:

1. Lack of Competition: If firms are not forced to compete against each other in the market place, they have less incentive to offer consumers the goods the consumers want at the lowest prices or pay resource owners prices consistent with the resources' contributions to the output.

2. **Market Failure**: Market failure occurs when competitive markets fail to produce the output that is best for society. There are four major causes of market failure:

   a. Public goods are goods that people consume collectively, such as national defense or the light from a lighthouse. Because everyone—those who pay and those who do not pay—can consume public goods if they are produced, consumers have no incentive to pay for public goods.

   b. Externalities occur when one individual's actions have an impact on others who do not participate in the market. In this case, prices do not contain all the information that is necessary for the market to do what is best for society.

   c. Because people can influence market decisions only by making purchases, those with no income have no way to notify the market of what they want produced.

   d. Capitalist economies have historically experienced fluctuations in their incomes and price levels. Government intervention is often necessary to reduce the frequency and severity of the fluctuations.

HINTS AND HELP

1. Circular Flow Like the production possibilities curve, the circular flow of income is an economic model that illustrates an important economic principle. The circular flow shows that decisions in one part of the economy—the resource market—are related to decisions in other parts of the economy—the product market. As will be shown in more detail in Chapter 12, this interrelationship is the key to understanding why lower output in the economy generally leads to lower employment and to higher unemployment.

One key to remembering how the circular flow works is to keep in mind that dollars flow in the opposite direction that goods and resources flow.

2. Invisible Hand The Invisible Hand concept is important in economics. Many disputes about economics are debates about the extent to which the market can be counted on to provide the goods and services that are best for society without the involvement of the government. Although economists probably have a greater faith in the Invisible Hand than noneconomists, there are still many debates within the economics profession that rest on this question.

FILL IN THE BLANK

Consumers

resource

product

barter

price

market failure

government

Adam Smith

goods and services

public

1. _____ sell their resources in the circular flow of income.

2. Factors of production are sold in the _____ market.

3. Firms sell their output in the _____ market.

4. An economy without money is called a _____ economy.

5. A capitalistic economy coordinates economic decisions through the _____ system.

6. Externalities are one cause of _____.

7. The correction of market failure may require the involvement of _____.

8. The originator of the "Invisible Hand" concept was _____ _____.

9. In the circular flow, consumers give money to firms and receive in return _____.

10. Goods that are consumed by all members of a group, even those who do not pay, are called _____ goods.

TRUE OR FALSE

_____ 1. Money always is produced by the government.

_____ 2. In the circular flow of income, money flows only from households to firms.

_____ 3. Goods and services produced by households for their own consumption—as occurs when people mow their own lawns—do not enter the circular flow.

_____ 4. In the circular-flow-of-income model, the government is the only producer of output.

_____ 5. In the price system, firms are encouraged to use more of the inputs that are more abundant.

_____ 6. The *how* decision is influenced by decisions made in the resource market.

_____ 7. The market system uses self-interested individuals to determine what an economy produces.

_____ 8. A market system always produces the goods that are best for society.

_____ 9. Barter occurs when some money is not spent but is saved.

_____ 10. Resources are bought in the factor market.

MULTIPLE CHOICE

1. Which of the following transactions would take place in the product market?
   A. Joe pays taxes to the government.
   B. Mary hires an employee to type letters.
   C. Sue cuts her son's hair.
   D. Bill is paid for tutoring an economics student.

2. Which of the following transactions would take place in the resource market?
   A. Joe pays taxes to the government.
   B. Mary hires an employee to type letters.
   C. Sue cuts her son's hair.
   D. Bill is paid for tutoring an economics student.

3. Which of the following is an example of the principle of the Invisible Hand?
   A. A bakery sells me a birthday cake on my birthday.
   B. The government takes taxes out of my paycheck before I can spend the money.
   C. A pickpocket takes my wallet without my knowing it.
   D. I paint my house a color my neighbor dislikes.

4. In a market economy, producers are kept from using too much of an extremely scarce resource by:
   A. government regulations on how goods and services can be produced.
   B. rivals who keep track of how goods are being made and report any evidence of waste to authorities.
   C. high prices on extremely scarce resources.
   D. shortages of extremely scarce resources.

5. Which of the following is not one of the major economic decision makers?
   A. consumers
   B. resources
   C. government
   D. producers

6. Which of the following is an example of a barter transaction?
   A. Latoya trades a book for Bill's sweatshirt.
   B. Nancy buys a notebook at the bookstore.
   C. Biff buffs his own shoes.
   D. Jamie receives a paycheck for playing in a band.

7. The primary problem with barter is:
   A. the high inflation that occurs because of it.
   B. more trades made than are necessary.
   C. trades are too time-consuming to arrange.
   D. too much unemployment.

8. Which of the following is a public good?
   A. loaf of bread
   B. national defense
   C. health care
   D. college

9. Which of the following would cause the Invisible Hand to fail?
   A. selfish consumers
   B. greedy business owners
   C. the profit motive
   D. monopoly

10. Because the price system rewards each individual with income on the basis of the amount and the value of the resources he or she owns:
    A. production is inefficient.
    B. income is distributed unequally.
    C. the economy's output is reduced.
    D. unemployment is not a problem.

TRUE OR FALSE

1. False. While money is often produced by the government, money also is produced by private firms (banks) and occasionally by individuals (cigarettes in a POW camp).

2. False. In the circular flow, money also flows back to households when the firms buy the households' resources.

3. True. Because there is no sale involved, the transaction is not considered part of the product market.

4. False. In the circular-flow model, firms are the producers of output. Government is not even a part of the simple model.

5. True. The price system sets prices according to the relative scarcity of the item, with more abundant items having lower prices. Firms interested in maximizing profit have an incentive to use more of the more-abundant input in order to hold down their costs and increase their profit.

6. True. The *how* decision concerns how inputs are used to produce output. The prices of inputs, which are determined in the resource market, determine what inputs firms use.

7. True. A market system relies upon individual consumers motivated by a desire to maximize utility and individual firms motivated by a desire to maximize profits to determine what output is produced.

8. False. If there is no competition or if one of the other causes of market failure exists, the market fails to produce the best output for society.

9. False. Barter occurs when goods are traded directly for other goods.

10. True. The factor market is another name for the resource market. The name comes from the term "factors of production," another name for resources.

MULTIPLE CHOICE

1. D. The product market is where goods and services are traded for money. Bill's tutoring is a service that is being sold.

2. B. The resource market is the market where resources are exchanged for money. Hiring an employee is the purchase of a labor resource.

3. A. The idea of the Invisible Hand is that people making voluntary exchanges in the market place do what is most desirable from society's point of view.

4. C. Prices are the rationing device in a market economy. High prices induce profit-making firms to minimize their use of extremely scarce resources.

5. B. Resources are bought and sold, but the decisions about how resources are allocated are made by consumers, firms, and the government.

6. A. Barter occurs when goods are traded directly for other goods.

7. C. The primary problem with barter is that arranging trades consumes a large amount of time because it is difficult to find a trading partner.

8. B. Because national defense is provided collectively to all individuals, whether or not they pay for it, national defense is a public good.

9. D. The Invisible Hand works only if there is competition between producers. If no competition exists, consumers will not be best served by the market.

10. B. Because resources are distributed unequally, income is also distributed unequally in a price system, because an individual's income is determined by the amount and value of his or her resources.

CHAPTER 4

Supply and Demand

Chapter 3 showed that markets determine how resources and outputs are allocated in a capitalist economy. This chapter describes in detail how those markets work.

Supply and demand is the most important tool in economics. It is used to solve more problems and answer more questions than any other model you will study in this book. This is why Chapter 4 is one of the most important you will read. Learn this material and you will be well served throughout the rest of your course in economics.

CHAPTER OUTLINE

I. The theory of demand summarizes the behavior of consumers.
   A. The primary determinant of the **quantity demanded**—the number of units of a good that consumers choose to buy—is price. The relationship between price and quantity demanded is described in the law of demand.
      1. **Law of Demand**: The quantity demanded of a good and the price of the good vary inversely, assuming that everything else that influences consumers' decisions about how much to buy is being held constant.
      2. There are two reasons to expect that a lower price increases the quantity demanded:
         a. As the price of a good falls, the good becomes more attractive relative to its substitutes and more of it is bought.
         b. As the price of a good falls, the purchasing power of consumers' income increases. Consumers can use this extra purchasing power to buy more of many goods, including the good that has fallen in price.
      3. The law of demand can be presented two ways:
         a. A **demand schedule** is a table that shows how much of a good consumers choose to buy per time period at various prices, assuming that other things are equal.
         b. A **demand curve** is a diagram made of the price and quantity demanded combinations that are in the demand schedule. The demand curve is downward sloping.
   B. The amount of a good that consumers want to buy is influenced by factors other than the price. These "other factors" were held constant when the law of demand and the demand curve were being derived. But if they change, they cause the demand curve to shift. The "other factors" that cause the demand curve to shift are:
      1. Consumers' Income
         a. For most goods, as income rises consumers demand more of the good, which means the demand curve shifts to the right. Such goods are called **normal goods**.

      b. The demand for some goods responds to income changes in an unusual way. As income rises, people demand less of them. Goods that follow this pattern are called **inferior goods**.

   2. The Prices of **Substitute Goods**: The demand for beef depends on the price of chicken, because consumers can buy either beef or chicken for dinner. As the price of chicken rises, beef becomes more attractive to consumers and the demand for beef increases.

   3. The Prices of **Complementary Goods**: Some goods are consumed together—peanut butter and jelly, for example. How much peanut butter consumers buy depends not only on the price of peanut butter but also on the price of jelly, because consumers like to use the two together. If the price of jelly rises, it makes consuming jelly less attractive. But it also makes consuming peanut butter less attractive. So the higher price of jelly decreases the demand for peanut butter, its complement.

   4. The **number of potential consumers** influences demand in the obvious way: more consumers, more demand.

   5. **Tastes** also affect demand in an obvious way. As consumers begin to like a particular good more, demand increases.

   6. The **expectations of consumers** also influence demand. If consumers expect that the price of a good will be higher in the future than it is now, consumers attempt to buy more now and less in the future. The current demand for the good increases.

  C. A **Change in Demand** and a **Change in Quantity Demanded**

   1. The word "demand" refers to the entire demand schedule or demand curve. "Increase in demand" means that the entire demand curve has shifted to the right, so that at each and every price consumers want to buy a larger quantity than they did before. "Decrease in demand" means the demand curve has shifted to the left. A change in demand is caused only by those things that were held constant when the demand curve was drawn. The things that cause the demand curve to shift are the items numbered 1–6 under point B above. One of the things that does *not cause* a change in demand is a change in the price of the good.

   2. "Quantity demanded" refers to a particular quantity of the good as measured along the horizontal axis of the demand curve graph. As the price of a good falls, the amount of the good consumers want to buy—the quantity demanded—rises but there is *not* an increase in demand.

II. The theory of supply summarizes the behavior of producers.

  A. As with the quantity demanded, the first factor that economists look at to explain the **quantity supplied**—which is defined as the amount of a good producers choose to sell—is its price. The relationship between the quantity supplied and price is summarized in the law of supply.

   1. **Law of Supply**: The number of units of a good that producers choose to produce and sell is directly related to the price at which the producers can sell the good, assuming that other things are the same.

   2. A higher price increases the quantity supplied because existing producers can increase profit by selling more at the higher price and new producers are more willing to enter the industry.

   3. As with the law of demand, the law of supply can be presented two ways:

     a. A **supply schedule** is a table that shows the amount of a good per unit of time that producers want to sell at various prices, assuming that other things are equal.

     b. The **supply curve** is a diagram of the price and output combinations that are in the supply schedule. The supply curve is upward sloping.

  B. Factors other than the good's price influence how many units producers want to produce and sell. As these "other factors" change, the supply curve of the good shifts. The "other factors" that shift supply are:

   1. Costs of Production: Anything that makes it less expensive to produce makes the firm more willing to produce output and increase supply. Anything that makes it more expensive to produce output reduces supply. The major factors influencing the costs of production are:

     a. Input Prices: Higher input prices increase the costs of production and decrease supply.

     b. Taxes: Higher taxes also make it more expensive to produce and decrease supply.

     c. Technological Change: If a new technology is found that allows the product to be produced at a lower cost, supply increases.

2. Prices of Other Goods the Firm Could Produce: A producer often can produce different goods with the same inputs. This is the case with corn and soybeans. The amount of corn that is produced depends on the price of soybeans as well as the price of corn. As the price of soybeans rises, the production of soybeans becomes more attractive, which means that the production of corn becomes less attractive. The higher price of soybeans causes a decrease in the supply of corn.

3. Expectations of Producers: As long as a good is storable, producers can change the amount of a good they are willing to sell now if they expect the future price to change. For example, when producers expect the price to be higher in the future, they choose to sell less now and more in the future. This means a decrease in the current supply.

C. A **Change in Supply** and a **Change in Quantity Supplied**

1. The word "supply" refers to the entire supply schedule or the supply curve. If the supply curve shifts to the right, it is called an "increase in supply." If the supply curve shifts to the left, it is called a "decrease in supply." The factors that cause the supply curve to shift are the things that were held constant when the law of supply and the supply curve were derived. These are (a) costs of production, (b) prices of other goods the producer could produce, and (c) expectations of producers. One of the things that will *not* cause a change in supply is the price of the good.

2. "Quantity supplied" is the particular amount of the good that the producers choose to produce and sell as measured along the horizontal axis. As the price of the good changes, the number of units that producers choose to sell—the quantity supplied—changes, but there is *not* a change in supply.

III. The Determination of Price and Quantity

A. The price of a good and the quantity of the good that is actually bought and sold is determined by demand and supply *together* in the market. The market eventually is in **equilibrium** where the quantity demanded equals the quantity supplied. Such a situation is a state of rest where neither producers nor consumers have a reason to change what they are doing. The price that makes the quantity demanded equal to the quantity supplied is called the **equilibrium price**. Graphically, the equilibrium occurs where the demand and supply curves intersect.

B. If the price is not the equilibrium price, the price is a **disequilibrium price**. A **disequilibrium** occurs whenever the quantity supplied is not equal to the quantity demanded.

1. If the price is *below* the equilibrium price, the quantity demanded is greater than the quantity supplied. The difference between the two is called the **shortage**. When there is a shortage, prices begin to rise as some consumers unable to get the product bid up the price.

2. If the price is *above* the equilibrium price, the quantity supplied is greater than the quantity demanded. The amount by which the quantity supplied is greater than the quantity demanded is called the **surplus**. When there is a surplus, prices began to fall as producers attempt to dispose of their extra output.

IV. Changes in Equilibrium

A. The equilibrium price and the equilibrium quantity change if either the demand curve, the supply curve, or both curves shift.

B. Change in Demand

1. An increase in demand causes both the equilibrium price and the equilibrium quantity to rise.

2. A decrease in demand causes both the equilibrium price and the equilibrium quantity to fall.

C. Change in Supply

1. An increase in supply causes the equilibrium price to fall and the equilibrium quantity to rise.

2. A decrease in supply causes the equilibrium price to rise and the equilibrium quantity to fall.

D. Changes in Both Demand and Supply

1. If both demand and supply increase, the equilibrium quantity increases. What happens to the equilibrium price depends on whether the demand or the supply increase is larger.

2. If both demand and supply decrease, the equilibrium quantity decreases. Again, what happens to the equilibrium price depends on whether the demand or the supply decrease is larger.

3. If demand increases while supply decreases, the equilibrium price rises. In this case, it is the equilibrium quantity that depends on the relative size of the demand and supply shifts.

4. If demand decreases and supply increases, the equilibrium price falls. What happens to the equilibrium quantity depends on whether the demand or the supply curve shifts the more.

V. On occasion the government intervenes by placing restrictions on the price of a good or service. Price restrictions are of two varieties:

    A. A **price ceiling** places a maximum value (upper limit) on the price that can be charged.

        1. If the price ceiling is above the equilibrium price, it has no impact.

        2. If the price ceiling is below the equilibrium price, it creates a shortage. This requires that another rationing method be used to allocate the available output. Options include first-come first-served, government mandate, and seller's choice. When the government limits the legal price at which a good can be traded, **black markets** often develop. A black market involves trading a good at a price above the legal maximum.

    B. A **price floor** imposes a minimum value on the price that can be charged.

        1. If the price floor is below the equilibrium price, it has no impact.

        2. If the price floor is above the equilibrium price, it causes a surplus.

HINTS AND HELP

1. Use Common Sense Remember that supply and demand is a model that describes everyday behavior. While the curves may be unfamiliar to you, the behavior the curves describe is not. Supply and demand is about you!

    This is particularly important for demand. When trying to figure out a problem involving demand, put yourself in the situation described and ask how you would behave. Just use common sense and you usually will be correct. The supply and demand curves will help you understand how your intuition explains the behavior of prices and quantities.

2. Demand and Quantity Demanded If students began economics without having ever talked about economics, the distinction between demand and quantity demanded would be easy. But that is unfortunately not the case. Despite the fact that much of economics may seem new to you, you have been talking about economics for a long time. The reason this creates a problem is that economists sometimes use words differently than noneconomists. You are now being asked to speak the language of economists, and that means altering your use of certain expressions.

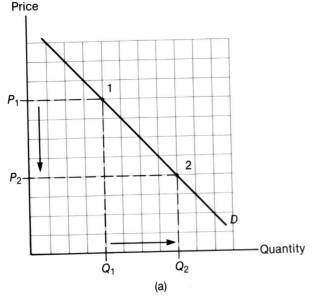

(a)

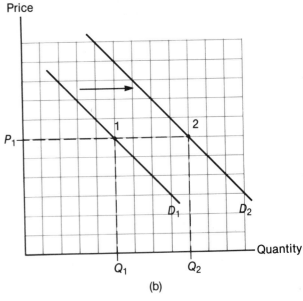

(b)

The figures on the preceding page clearly show two different events. In (a) price has fallen and the quantity demanded has risen, but the demand *curve* has not moved. In (b) the demand curve has shifted to the right, so that at the same old price of P_1, the quantity demanded has increased.

It is important to give these two events different names. If the two events were called by the same name, it would be difficult to know which event was being discussed. The event pictured in (b) is called *an increase in demand*. The word "demand" refers to the demand curve. The words "increase in" mean "shift to the right." If the demand curve moves to the left, it is called *a decrease in demand*. (The forces that cause the demand curve to move are discussed in the section "Shifts in Demand.")

The event pictured in (a) is called *an increase in the quantity demanded*. The habit that is difficult to break involves (a). Most people would describe the event in (a) by saying "The price fell and demand increased." But that is *wrong*. The phrase "demand increased" refers to a rightward shift of the demand curve. When the price falls, there is an increase in the *quantity demanded* but not an increase in demand.

3. Supply and Demand Are Alike   Although supply has less to do with a student's immediate life than does demand, learning supply is not so difficult. Many of the terms and rules that apply to demand also apply to supply. Also, even though most students are not producers, there is a certain common sense about supply too. If it becomes more expensive to produce a good, it is fairly easy to figure out that producers produce less of the good.

As with demand, it is important to keep in mind the difference between a movement along the supply curve and a shift of the curve, and to call each by its correct name. "An increase in supply" refers to the supply curve shifting to the right. ("Increase—to the right" and "decrease—to the left" works for both the demand and the supply curves.) If the price of the good changes, there is *not* a change in supply because the supply curve does not move. A decrease in the price of a good causes a decrease in the *quantity supplied*.

4. Price   The word "price" is another word that sometimes causes problems for students. Price refers to the number of dollars the buyer is required to give up to get *one* unit of the good. Price does not refer to the cost of producing the good nor the total amount of money that consumers spend on the good when more than one unit is bought.

FILL IN THE BLANK

normal

complements

shortage

surplus

price ceiling

price floor

black market

equilibrium

decrease in supply

quantity demanded

1. Consumers buy less of a good when their income falls if the good is a(n) _____ good.

2. Goods that consumers typically use together are _____.

3. When the price is below the equilibrium price there is a _____ _____.

4. When the quantity supplied is greater than the quantity demanded there is a _____.

5. A law that places a maximum on how high a price can be is called a _____.

6. There is a surplus when a _____ is placed above the equilibrium price.

7. The market where trades take place at illegal prices is called a _____ _____.

8. The price that makes the quantity demanded equal to the quantity supplied is called the _____ price.

9. A leftward shift of the supply curve is called a _____.

10. When the price of a good falls there is an increase in _____ _____.

TRUE OR FALSE

_____ 1. Disequilibrium means that the quantity supplied is not equal to the quantity demanded.

_____ 2. Black markets exist only when there are legal limits on the prices that can be charged.

_____ 3. The quantity demanded is greater than the quantity supplied when the price is above the equilibrium price.

_____ 4. A demand curve shows the amounts of a good that consumers choose to buy at various incomes.

_____ 5. If consumers buy more of a good at a higher price, the law of demand has been violated.

_____ 6. An increase in the price of a good results in an increase in the supply of that good, assuming other things are the same.

_____ 7. As incomes rise, consumers choose to buy more of a good if the good is a normal good.

_____ 8. Complementary goods are two goods that can do the same thing.

_____ 9. A price floor always causes the price of the good to rise.

_____ 10. If consumers begin to expect that the price of a good will be lower in the future than it is now, the price of the good falls now.

MULTIPLE CHOICE

1. A shortage occurs whenever:
   A. the price is below equilibrium.
   B. the price is above equilibrium.
   C. resources are unemployed.
   D. there is a price floor.

2. Which of the following causes the demand for hot dogs to increase?
   A. a decline in the price of hot dogs
   B. an increase in the price of hamburgers
   C. an increase in the price of hot dog buns
   D. a decrease in the wages of hot dog makers

3. A leftward shift of the demand curve is called:
   A. a decrease in price.
   B. a decrease in output.
   C. a decrease in demand.
   D. a decrease in income.

4. Compared to lower-income families, high-income families consume less of which of the following kinds of goods?
   A. substitute goods
   B. complementary goods
   C. normal goods
   D. inferior goods

5. A higher price of good X causes the demand for good Z to fall if goods X and Z are:
   A. complementary goods.
   B. substitute goods.
   C. inferior goods.
   D. in equilibrium.

6. If the price of a good is above the equilibrium price, which of the following occurs as the market moves to equilibrium?
   A. Demand increases.
   B. Supply decreases.
   C. The price falls.
   D. All the alternatives are correct.

7. If goods A and B are two alternative goods that a producer could produce with the same resources, which of the following causes an increase in the supply of good A?
   A. an increase in the price of good A
   B. a decrease in the price of good B
   C. an increase in the demand for good B
   D. an increase in the cost of producing good A

8. When the supply curve is a vertical line, which of the following is true?
   A. Changes in demand have no impact on the amount of the good producers sell.
   B. There is no equilibrium.
   C. The equilibrium price is the same regardless of demand.
   D. The law of demand does not hold.

9. Which of the following best explains why the equilibrium price of wool would fall at the same time the equilibrium quantity would rise?
   A. Consumers, but not producers, of wool expect a higher future price.
   B. Producers, but not consumers, of wool expect a lower future price.
   C. Abnormally cold weather increases the demand for wool sweaters.
   D. The cost of feeding sheep increased.

10. An increase in input prices means that:
    A. the amount of the good that consumers buy at the equilibrium price rises.
    B. the amount of the good that producers want to sell at any particular price is less than before.
    C. producers try to produce more to offset the higher costs.
    D. consumers decrease their demand for the good.

PROBLEMS

1. For each of the following events described, shift the curve or curves in the appropriate way in the figure that follows each question. Record for each event what has happened to demand, to supply, and to the equilibrium values of price and quantity. For example, in (a) the demand curve shifted to the right because the demand for a normal good increases when income rises. As a result, the answers are: demand has *increased*, supply has *not changed*, the equilibrium price has *increased*, and the equilibrium quantity has also *increased*.

   I = increase   D = decrease   NC = no change

EVENT	DEMAND	SUPPLY	EQUILIBRIUM PRICE	EQUILIBRIUM QUANTITY
(a) What happens in the movie market if movies are a normal good and consumers receive more income?	I	NC	I	I

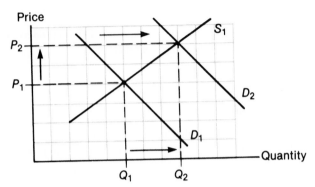

(b) What is the impact in the wooden yo-yo market if the price of wood increases?

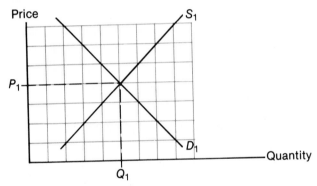

| (c) What happens in the market for big, gas-guzzling cars if the price of gasoline falls? | I | NC | I | I |

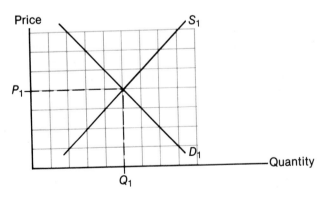

EVENT	DEMAND	SUPPLY	EQUILIBRIUM PRICE	EQUILIBRIUM QUANTITY
(d) What happens in the market for wood-burning stoves if there is a decrease in the price of electricity and natural gas?	D	NC	D	D

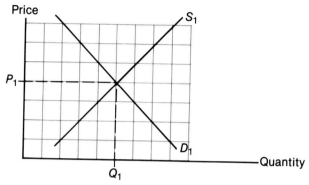

EVENT	DEMAND	SUPPLY	EQUILIBRIUM PRICE	EQUILIBRIUM QUANTITY
(e) What happens in the wheat market if scientists discover a higher-yielding strain of wheat?	NC	I	D	I

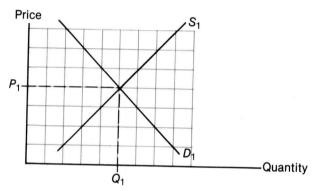

EVENT	DEMAND	SUPPLY	EQUILIBRIUM PRICE	EQUILIBRIUM QUANTITY
(f) What happens in the beef market if there is an increase in the price of chicken and an increase in the price of feed for cattle?	I	D	I	I, D, or NC

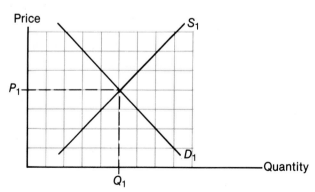

EVENT	DEMAND	SUPPLY	EQUILIBRIUM PRICE	EQUILIBRIUM QUANTITY
(g) What happens in the gold market if both consumers and producers begin to expect a lower future price of gold?	D	I	D	I, D, or NC

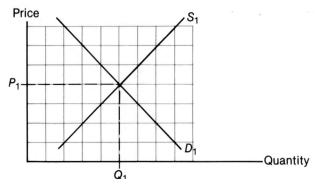

| (h) What happens in the market for potatoes, an inferior good, if incomes rise at the same time that a freeze kills some potato buds? | D | D | I, D, or NC | D |

2. (a) In Figure 4.1, show the impact of a price ceiling set at $300. What is the:
    quantity demanded? _____
    quantity supplied? _____
    price paid by consumers? _____
    quantity consumed by consumers? _____
    (b) In Figure 4.1, show the impact of a price ceiling set at $100. What is the:
    quantity demanded? _____
    quantity supplied? _____
    price paid by consumers? _____
    quantity consumed by consumers? _____

FIGURE 4.1

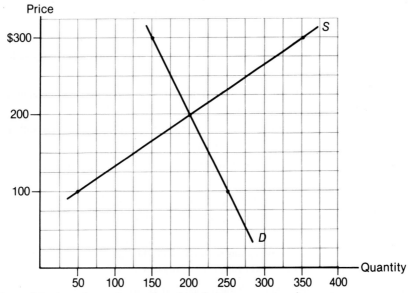

3. (a) In Figure 4.2, plot a demand curve based on the accompanying data.

PRICE	QUANTITY DEMANDED
$70	75
60	100
50	125
40	150
30	175
20	200

FIGURE 4.2

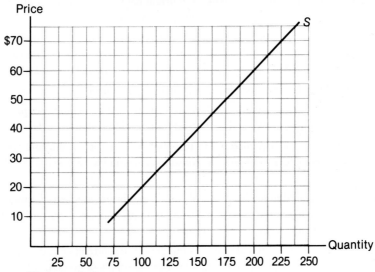

(b) What is the equilibrium price? _____

(c) What is the equilibrium quantity? _____

Answers

TRUE OR FALSE

1. True. An equilibrium occurs if the quantity demanded equals the quantity supplied. Otherwise, there is a disequilibrium.

2. True. A black market exists only when the market is not legally allowed to reach the equilibrium price because of price ceilings.

3. False. If the price is above the equilibrium price, the amount that producers choose to sell at that high price is greater than the amount that consumers choose to buy.

4. False. A demand schedule shows the relationship between the amount of a good consumers choose to buy and the price of the good.

5. False. The law of demand holds only when "other things are the same." If the demand curve shifts outward because the price of a substitute good has risen, consumers buy more of the good at a higher price—but "other things" have *not* stayed the same.

6. False. An increase in the price of a good causes an increase in the quantity supplied but not an increase in supply. An increase in supply refers to a rightward shift of the supply curve.

7. True. A normal good is a good that has the characteristic that as incomes rise the demand for the good rises.

8. False. Complementary goods are goods that are typically consumed together—like tennis balls and tennis rackets. Two goods that can do the same thing are called substitutes.

9. False. A price floor that is below the equilibrium price has no impact on the equilibrium price, and so does not cause the price of the good to rise.

10. True. If consumers begin to expect that the price of a good will fall, they decrease their demand for the good now. As a result, the equilibrium price now declines.

MULTIPLE CHOICE

1. A. A shortage occurs when the price is below equilibrium because at such a low price the amount that consumers want to buy is greater than the amount that producers want to sell.

2. B. Because most consumers treat hot dogs and hamburgers as substitutes, a higher price of hamburgers makes hamburgers less attractive and hot dogs more attractive to consumers. As a result, the demand curve for hot dogs shifts to the right, which is what is meant by an increase in the demand for hot dogs.

3. C. A leftward shift of the demand curve is called a decrease in demand.

4. D. Inferior goods are defined as goods with the characteristic that as income rises people demand less of the good. Higher-income families consume less of an inferior good than do poorer families.

5. A. A higher price of good X makes good X less attractive to consumers and causes consumers to buy less of good X. If good Z is a complement of good X, consumers buying less of good X also decrease their demand for good Z.

6. C. If the price is above equilibrium, the price falls until equilibrium is achieved, unless there is a price floor in place that limits the ability of the price to move. A fall in price causes the quantity demanded, but not demand, to rise and the quantity supplied, but not supply, to fall.

7. B. A decline in the price of good B makes producing good B less attractive and induces the firm to transfer resources into the production of good A, which increases the supply of good A.

8. A. A vertical supply curve means that regardless of where the demand curve is, the equilibrium quantity is the same.

9. **B.** If producers expect the price of wool to go lower, they sell more now before the price falls. This increases supply, which lowers price and increases the equilibrium quantity.

10. **B.** Higher input prices cause a decrease in supply. A decrease in supply means that the quantity supplied at each and every price is less than before.

PROBLEMS

1.

EVENT	DEMAND	SUPPLY	EQUILIBRIUM PRICE	EQUILIBRIUM QUANTITY
(b) What is the impact of the wooden yo-yo market if the price of wood increases?	NC	D	I	D

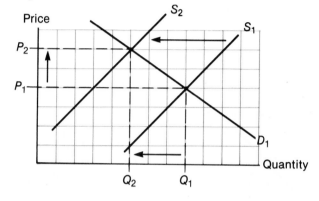

An increase in the price of an input decreases supply.

| (c) What happens in the market for big, gas-guzzling cars if the price of gasoline falls? | I | NC | I | I |

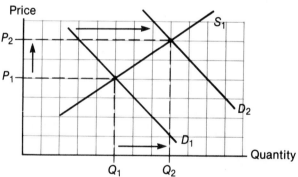

Gasoline is a complement to the consumption of large, gas-guzzling cars. A lower price of a good increases the demand for its complement.

EVENT	DEMAND	SUPPLY	EQUILIBRIUM PRICE	EQUILIBRIUM QUANTITY
(d) What happens in the market for wood-burning stoves if there is a decrease in the price of electricity and natural gas?	D	NC	D	D

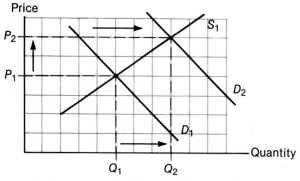

Electricity is a substitute for wood as a means of heating homes. As the price of electricity and natural gas falls, heating with wood and wood-burning stoves becomes less attractive. This causes a decrease in the demand for wood-burning stoves.

EVENT	DEMAND	SUPPLY	EQUILIBRIUM PRICE	EQUILIBRIUM QUANTITY
(e) What happens in the wheat market if scientists discover a higher-yielding strain of wheat?	NC	I	D	I

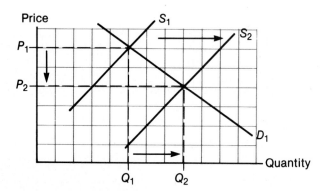

A new strain of wheat constitutes a technological advance in the production of wheat. This lowers the cost of producing wheat and increases the supply.

EVENT	DEMAND	SUPPLY	EQUILIBRIUM PRICE	EQUILIBRIUM QUANTITY
(f) What happens in the beef market if there is an increase in the price of chicken and an increase in the price of feed for cattle?	I	D	I	I, D, or NC

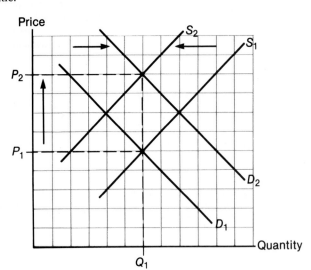

An increase in the price of chicken increases the demand for beef because chicken and beef are substitutes. The increase in the price of cattle feed increases the cost of raising cattle and decreases the supply. Although what happens to price is known, what happens to quantity depends on whether the increase in demand is larger than, smaller than, or equal to the decrease in supply.

EVENT	DEMAND	SUPPLY	EQUILIBRIUM PRICE	EQUILIBRIUM QUANTITY
(g) What happens in the gold market if if both consumers and producers begin to expect a lower future price of gold?	D	I	D	I, D, or NC

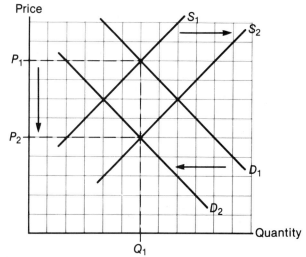

The expectation of lower prices by consumers decreases demand. If producers expect lower prices, supply increases. The price now falls—but what happens to quantity depends on which curve shifts more.

EVENT	DEMAND	SUPPLY	EQUILIBRIUM PRICE	EQUILIBRIUM QUANTITY
(h) What happens in the market for potatoes, an inferior good, if incomes rise at the same time that a freeze kills some potato buds?	D	D	I, D, or NC	D

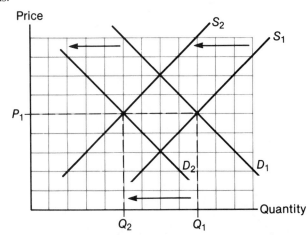

The demand for potatoes falls because people buy less of an inferior good as incomes rise. The supply of potatoes falls. The quantity falls but what happens to the price depends on which curve shifts more.

2. (a) A price ceiling set above the equilibrium price has no impact on a market because it is still possible for the market to achieve equilibrium. A price ceiling only means that the market price cannot go above the ceiling price. But it can go below the ceiling price.

   Referring to Figure 4.3, a price ceiling set at $300 results in a quantity demanded equal to **200**, a quantity supplied of **200**, a price paid by consumers equal to **$200**, and an amount actually consumed by consumers equal to **200**.

   (b) A price ceiling set below the equilibrium price increases the quantity demanded from 200 to **250** and decreases the quantity supplied from 200 to **50**. Consumers pay the ceiling price of **$100**, but consume only **50** units because that is all that is available for sale.

FIGURE 4.3

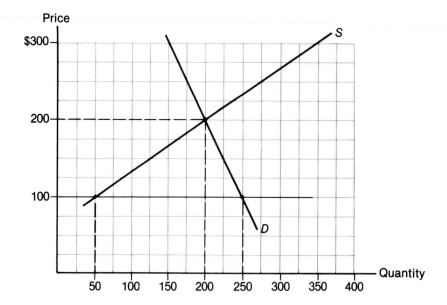

3.

FIGURE 4.4

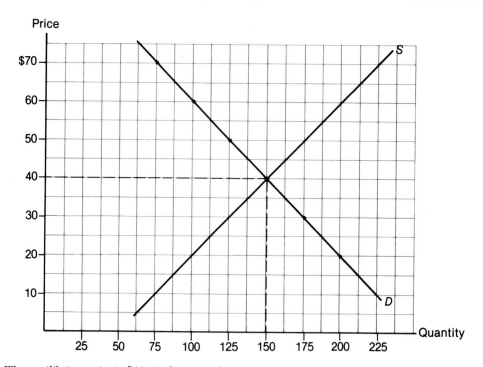

(a) The equilibrium price is **$40**. At that price the quantity demanded equals the quantity supplied.
(b) The equilibrium quantity is **150**.

CHAPTER 5

Demand and Supply Elasticities

Chapter 4 described the behavior of consumers and producers in a capitalist economy. Chapter 5 describes how economists measure and quantify such behavior. Elasticities are important measures of demand and supply that provide a means for classifying goods and services and for predicting the behavior of consumers and producers.

CHAPTER OUTLINE

I. Elasticities are various measures of how responsive market participants are to changes in the market. Demand elasticities measure how responsive consumers are to changes in price, income, and other factors. Supply elasticities measure the responsiveness of producers.

II. The **price elasticity of demand** (E_d) measures how responsive the quantity demanded of a good is to changes in the price of the good.
   A. The formula for calculating price elasticity of demand is:

$$E_d = \frac{\text{percentage change in the quantity demanded}}{\text{percentage change in price}}.$$

   The negative sign is dropped, so that price elasticity of demand is expressed as a positive number even though the formula always gives a negative number.
   B. Percentage changes are calculated using the midpoint formula. Instead of expressing the change as a percent of the beginning or the ending value, the change is expressed as a percent of the average of the beginning and ending values. For example, if price rises from $4 to $6, the percentage change would be the change in the price ($2) divided by the average of the beginning and ending price [($4 + $6)/2] = ($10/$2) = $5. The percentage change would be $2/$5 = 0.4 = 40%.
   C. Goods are categorized on the basis of the value of their price elasticity of the demand. The classifications are:
      1. Demand is **elastic** if $E_d > 1$.
      2. Demand is **inelastic** if $E_d = < 1$.
      3. Demand is **unit elastic** if $E_d = 1$.
   D. Price Elasticity of Demand and the Shape of the Demand Curve
      1. A typical downward-sloping, straight-line (that is, linear) demand curve has declining values of demand elasticity as price falls. The value for the elasticity of demand is high when price is high and low when price is low.

2. If the demand curve is vertical, demand is called **perfectly inelastic** because the quantity demanded does not change when price changes.

3. If the demand curve is horizontal, demand is called **perfectly elastic** because the amount that consumers want to buy falls to zero if price rises by the smallest amount above the equilibrium price. The responsiveness of consumers to price changes is at its greatest.

4. It is not possible to determine price elasticity of demand by looking at the slope of the demand curve. By changing the units of measure (for example, measuring meat in ounces or pounds) a demand curve can be made to look steep or flat. But changing the units of measure does not alter elasticity.

E. Price Elasticity of Demand and Total Revenue

1. **Total revenue** equals the price of a good times the number of units of the good that are sold. Considered from the point of view of sellers, total revenue is the number of dollars sellers collect from selling their output. Considered from the point of view of consumers, it measures the number of dollars consumers are spending on the good.

2. Total revenue responds differently to price changes depending on the value of the price elasticity of demand.

   a. If demand is elastic, total revenue rises when price falls and falls when price rises. Because consumers are quite responsive to price changes, the change in the quantity demanded more than offsets the impact of the price change.

   b. If demand is inelastic, total revenue falls when price falls and rises when price rises. Because consumers respond modestly when the price changes, the change in the quantity demanded is not large enough to offset the impact of the price change.

   c. If demand is unit elastic, total revenue stays the same whether the price rises or falls. The change in quantity demanded exactly offsets the change in price.

F. Whether a good has a low- or high-price elasticity of demand depends on the following factors:

1. Availability of Substitutes: The more and better the substitutes for a good, the greater is the price elasticity of demand.

2. Degree of Necessity: The more essential the good, the lower is the price elasticity of demand.

3. Share of Budget Spent on the Good: The smaller the portion of a consumer's budget spent on the good, the smaller is the price elasticity of demand.

4. Time Period: The more time consumers are given to adjust to a price change, the greater is the price elasticity of demand.

III. The **income elasticity of demand** (E_d^y) measures how consumers respond when their income changes.

A. The formula for calculating income elasticity of demand is:

$$E_d^y = \frac{\text{percentage change in the quantity demanded}}{\text{percentage change in income}}$$

B. Goods are classified on the basis of the value of the income elasticity of demand. The categories are:

1. A good is an **inferior** good if $E_d^y < 0$ (negative).

2. A good is a **normal** good if $E_d^y > 0$ (positive).

   a. A normal good is a **necessity** if $0 < E_d^y < 1$. If a good is a necessity, consumers spend a smaller and smaller percent of their incomes on the good as their incomes rise.

   b. A normal good is a **luxury** if $E_d^y > 1$. If a good is a luxury, consumers spend a larger and larger percent of their incomes on the good as their incomes rise.

IV. The **cross elasticity of demand** ($E_{1,2}$) measures how consumers respond when the price of another good changes.

A. The formula for calculating the cross elasticity of demand is:

$$E_{1,2} = \frac{\text{percentage change in the quantity demanded of good 1}}{\text{percentage change in price of good 2}}$$

B. Goods are classified on the basis of the value of the cross elasticity of demand. The categories are:
1. Goods 1 and 2 are **substitutes** if $E_{1,2} > 0$ (positive).
2. Goods 1 and 2 are **complements** if $E_{1,2} < 0$ (negative).
3. Goods 1 and 2 are **independent goods** if $E_{1,2} = 0$.

V. The **elasticity of supply** (E_s) measures how responsive the quantity supplied is to changes in the price of the good.
   A. The formula for calculating the elasticity of supply is:

$$E_s = \frac{\text{percentage change in the quantity supplied}}{\text{percentage change in price}}$$

   B. Goods are classified on the basis of the value of the elasticity of supply. The categories are:
   1. Supply is **elastic** if $E_s > 1$.
   2. Supply is **inelastic** if $E_s < 1$.
   3. Supply is **unit elastic** if $E_s = 1$.
   4. Supply is **perfectly inelastic** when the supply curve is vertical. The amount producers want to sell is the same regardless of the price.
   5. Supply is **perfectly elastic** when the supply curve is horizontal. The quantity supplied is infinitely responsive to price.

   C. The primary determinant of the price elasticity of supply is time. The more time producers have to respond to a price change, the greater the price elasticity of supply.
   1. **Market Period**: A time during which producers cannot change the quantity supplied. The supply curve is vertical.
   2. **Short Run**: A time during which the producers can change output by changing some inputs—but at least one input is fixed.
   3. **Long Run**: A time long enough for all inputs to be variable.

VI. Demand and supply elasticities influence how a tax is divided between consumers and producers. The study of who actually pays a tax is called **tax incidence**.
   A. Price Elasticity of Demand
   1. Given supply, the more elastic the demand the smaller the proportion of a unit tax passed on to consumers.
   2. Given supply, the less elastic the demand the greater the proportion of a unit tax passed on to consumers.
   B. Price Elasticity of Supply
   1. Given demand, the more elastic the supply the greater the proportion of a unit tax passed on to consumers.
   2. Given demand, the less elastic the supply the smaller the proportion of a unit tax passed on to consumers.

HINTS AND HELP

1. Formulas and More Formulas Although there are many formulas introduced in this chapter, remembering them is not as difficult as it may seem. First of all, the numerators are generally the same. All the demand elasticities —price, income, and cross—have the percentage change in the quantity demanded in their numerators. The supply elasticity has the percentage change in the quantity supplied in its numerator.

What is in the denominators is indicated by the name of the elasticity. Both the *price* elasticity of demand and the *price* elasticity of supply have the percentage change in *price* in the denominator. *Income* elasticity has the percentage change in *income*. The only difficult one is *cross* elasticity, which has the *price of another good*.

FILL IN THE BLANK

elastic

total revenue

inelastic

cross

income

inferior

vertical

market period

tax incidence

necessity

1. If the value of the price elasticity of demand is greater than 1, then demand is said to be _____.

2. Price times quantity sold (that is, $P \times Q$) is called _____ _____.

3. The percentage change in the price is greater than the percentage change in the quantity demanded if demand is _____.

4. To know if two goods are substitutes or complements, one would calculate the _____ elasticity of demand.

5. To know if a good is normal or inferior, one would calculate the _____ elasticity of demand.

6. If the income elasticity of demand is negative, the good is _____.

7. A perfectly inelastic demand curve is drawn as a _____ line.

8. The quantity supplied is fixed in the _____.

9. The study of how a tax burden is shared by the producers and consumers is called _____.

10. A good with an income elasticity of demand between 0 and 1 is called a _____.

TRUE OR FALSE

_____ 1. If the price elasticity of demand for a good is unit elastic, the percentage change in the quantity demanded equals the percentage change in income—forgetting about positive or negative values.

_____ 2. A typical linear demand curve (that is, neither vertical nor horizontal) has the same value of price elasticity of demand at each point on the demand curve.

_____ 3. The steeper a demand curve, the smaller the value of the price elasticity of demand.

_____ 4. A fall in price decreases total revenue if the price elasticity of demand is less than 1.

_____ 5. The more time consumers are given to adjust to a price change the lower is the value of the price elasticity of demand.

_____ 6. The income elasticity of demand for food is greater than 0 and less than 1. As economies grow and people in them become richer, people spend a smaller percent of their income on food.

_____ 7. If income elasticity of demand is less than 0, then demand is inelastic.

_____ 8. If two goods are substitutes, the value of the cross elasticity of demand is greater than zero.

_____ 9. A given increase in demand causes a larger increase in price in the short run than in the long run.

_____ 10. With a vertical supply curve, a tax is paid entirely by the consumers.

MULTIPLE CHOICE

1. The larger the price elasticity of demand:
   A. the steeper the demand curve.
   B. the higher the price.
   C. the more responsive consumers are to price changes.
   D. the flatter the demand curve.

2. If the value of price elasticity of demand is greater than 1, the good's demand is classified as:
   A. normal.
   B. complement.
   C. elastic.
   D. necessity.

3. If the value of price elasticity of demand is 2, it means that:
   A. the percentage change in the quantity demanded is twice as large as the percentage change in the price.
   B. the percentage change in the quantity demanded is one-half as large as the percentage change in the price.
   C. the percentage change in income is one-half as large the percentage change in the price.
   D. the percentage change in quantity demanded is twice as large as the percentage change in the price of another good.

4. When demand is elastic:
   A. profit is higher when the price is lower.
   B. profit is higher when the price is higher.
   C. total revenue is higher when the price is lower.
   D. total revenue is higher when the price is higher.

5. Total revenue is constant if demand is:
   A. unit elastic and the price falls.
   B. elastic and the price rises.
   C. inelastic and the price rises.
   D. inelastic and the price falls.

6. Price elasticity of demand is likely to be largest if:
   A. the good is a necessity.
   B. consumers spend a large part of their income on the good.
   C. the good has few substitutes.
   D. the price is low.

7. A good is a necessity if:
   A. the price elasticity of demand is less than 0.
   B. the price elasticity of demand is greater than 0.
   C. the cross elasticity of demand is less than 0.
   D. the income elasticity of demand is between 0 and 1.

8. If the cross elasticity of demand is negative, the good is:
   A. elastic.
   B. a substitute.
   C. a complement.
   D. an inferior good.

9. When a supply curve is vertical, the price elasticity of supply:
   A. equals 0.
   B. equals 1.
   C. is between 0 and 1.
   D. is very large.

10. If the demand curve is vertical:
    A. consumers pay no portion of a unit tax.
    B. consumers pay all of a unit tax.
    C. the government does not collect any of a tax.
    D. the producer pays all of a unit tax.

PROBLEMS

1. Figure 5.1 shows the demand curve for televisions in Ripple Creek, Montana. The price of televisions was initially $450. Because of the closing of the railroad into Ripple Creek, the price of televisions rose to $550.

FIGURE 5.1

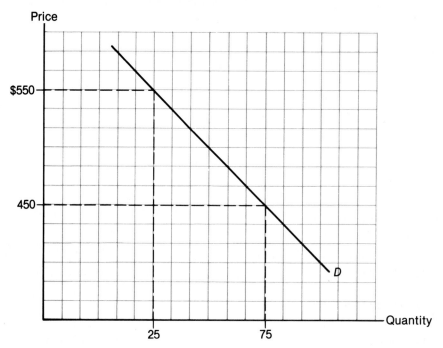

(a) What is the price elasticity of demand for televisions in Ripple Creek? _____

(b) How would the demand be classified on the basis of the value of the price elasticity of demand? _____

(c) What was the total revenue of television sellers before the price increase? _____
What was the total revenue after the price increase? _____

2. The following information has been gathered by following the spending behavior of the consumers in Bison, New York.

When average income is $25,000 and the price of tomatoes is $.55 per pound and the price of green peppers is $1.10 per pound, people buy 120 pounds of tomatoes and 45 pounds of green peppers in a week.
When average income is $15,000 and the price of tomatoes is $.55 per pound and the price of green peppers is $1.10 per pound, people buy 80 pounds of tomatoes and 55 pounds of green peppers in a week.
When average income is $25,000 and the price of tomatoes is $.55 per pound and the price of green peppers is $.90 per pound, people buy 180 pounds of tomatoes and 75 pounds of green peppers in a week.

(a) What is the income elasticity of demand for tomatoes? _____
On the basis of the value of the income elasticity of demand for tomatoes, how would you classify tomatoes? _____

(b) What is the income elasticity of demand for green peppers? _____
On the basis of the value of income elasticity of demand for green peppers, how would you classify green peppers? _____

(c) What is the cross elasticity of demand between tomatoes and green peppers? _____

   On the basis of the value of the cross elasticity of demand between tomatoes and green peppers, how would you classify tomatoes and green peppers? _____

3. Elasticity is often used to make predictions about changes in price or quantity demanded. Use the information provided in each of the situations described below to calculate the percentage change that is requested.

   (a) Price elasticity of demand for tickets to college football games is 0.4, and ticket prices rise by 10 percent. What is the predicted change in the percentage of tickets demanded? _____ percent

   (b) Income elasticity for dresses is 1.5, and income rises by 6 percent. By what percentage will the quantity demand increase? _____ percent

   (c) The cross elasticity of demand for softballs relative to the price of softball bats is –0.5. If the price of softball bats declines by 20 percent, the quantity demanded of softballs increases by _____ percent

   (d) The government increases the price it pays for wheat by 5 percent. The price elasticity of supply for wheat is 1. What is the predicted increase in the production of wheat? _____ percent

   (e) A flower shop just received an unexpected shipment of roses, so the store must increase the amount of roses it sells by 10 percent. By how much must the price of roses be lowered in order to increase the quantity demanded by 10 percent when the price elasticity equals 2? _____ percent

Answers

TRUE OR FALSE

1. False. The price elasticity of demand measures the relationship between quantity demanded and price. Unit elasticity means that the percentage change in quantity demanded equals the percentage change in price—forgetting about sign.

2. False. The price elasticity of demand changes as you move along a linear demand curve. The value of price elasticity falls as price falls.

3. False. The slope of a demand curve is influenced by the units of measure but the price elasticity of demand is not. The slope, then, is not a good indicator of price elasticity.

4. True. When price elasticity of demand is less than 1, the percentage change in quantity demanded is less than the percentage change in price. When price falls, the increase in the quantity purchased does not offset the lower price and total revenue decreases.

5. False. The more time consumers are given to adjust to a price change, the greater is the change in the quantity demanded and the larger is the price elasticity of demand.

6. True. The amount spent on any good that has an income elasticity of demand greater than 0 but less than 1 constitutes a smaller and smaller part of people's incomes because purchases of the good are growing more slowly than incomes.

7. False. If income elasticity of demand is less than 0, the good is an inferior good.

8. True. If the cross elasticity of demand is greater than 0, it means that the quantity demanded for good 1 rises when the price of good 2 rises. This is what happens when two goods are substitutes.

9. True. Because the supply curve is less elastic in the short run than in the long run, an increase in demand causes a larger increase in price in the short run than in the long run.

10. False. When supply is vertical, the entire tax is paid by the producers because a vertical supply curve means that producers continue to supply the same amount of the good regardless of price.

MULTIPLE CHOICE

1. C. The price elasticity of demand measures how responsive consumers are to price changes. The larger the elasticity, the greater is the change in quantity demanded for any given change in price.

2. C. On the basis of price elasticity of demand, goods are classified as elastic, inelastic, or unit elastic. A value greater than 1 puts the good in the elastic category.

3. A. Price elasticity of demand is the ratio of the percentage change in the quantity demanded divided by the percentage change in the price. If price elasticity of demand equals 2, the percentage change in the quantity demanded is twice as large as the percentage change in price.

4. C. When demand is elastic, total revenue rises as price falls because the quantity demanded increases more than enough to offset the lower price.

5. A. When demand is unit elastic, total revenue stays the same whether price rises or falls because the change in the quantity demanded exactly offsets the change in price.

6. B. Price elasticity of demand tends to be greater the larger the percentage of income spent on the good.

7. D. When income elasticity of demand is between 0 and 1, the good is classified as a necessity.

8. C. When cross elasticity of demand is negative, it means that the amount demanded of one good falls when the price of another good rises. This is what occurs when two goods are complements.

9. A. When a supply curve is vertical, the percentage change in the quantity supplied equals 0, which means the price elasticity of supply equals 0.

10. B. When the demand curve is vertical, consumers pay all of a tax because price rises by the amount of the tax.

PROBLEMS

1. (a) Price elasticity of demand equals:

$$E_d = \frac{(75 - 25)/(50)}{(\$550 - \$450)/(\$500)}$$

$$= \frac{50/50}{\$100/\$500}$$

$$= \frac{100\%}{20\%} = 5$$

Note that 50 is the average of the beginning and ending quantities and $500 is the average of the beginning and ending prices.

   (b) When price elasticity of demand is greater than 1, demand is **elastic**.

   (c) Total revenue initially was $450 × 75 = **$33,750**. Total revenue after the price change is $550 × 25 = **$13,750**.

2. (a) The income elasticity of demand of tomatoes is:

$$E_d^y = \frac{(80 - 120)/100}{(\$15,000 - \$25,000)/\$20,000)}$$

$$= \frac{-40/100}{-\$10,000/\$20,000}$$

$$= \frac{-40\%}{-50\%} = 0.8$$

Tomatoes are a **normal good** because the income elasticity is greater than 0 and a **necessity** because the income elasticity is less than 1.

(b) The income elasticity of demand of green peppers is:

$$E_d^y = \frac{(55-45)/50}{(\$15,000 - \$25,000)/\$20,000}$$

$$= \frac{10/50}{-\$10,000/\$20,000}$$

$$= \frac{20\%}{-50\%} = -\mathbf{0.4}$$

Green peppers would be classified as an **inferior good** because the income elasticity of demand is negative.

(c) The cross elasticity of demand of tomatoes and green peppers is:

$$E_{1,2} = \frac{(180-120)/150}{(\$.90 - \$1.10)/\$1.00}$$

$$= \frac{60/150}{-\$.20/\$1.00}$$

$$= \frac{40\%}{-20\%} = -\mathbf{2}$$

Because the cross elasticity of demand is negative, tomatoes and green peppers would be classified as **complements**.

3. (a) A price elasticity of 0.4 means that the percentage change in the quantity of football tickets demanded is 0.4 times as large as the percentage change in the price of football tickets. When price rises by 10 percent, quantity demanded **falls** by $0.4 \times 10\% = \mathbf{4\%}$. (Even though the negative sign is dropped from the formula for the price elasticity of demand, remember that price and quantity demanded move in opposite directions.)

(b) An income elasticity of 1.5 means that the percentage change in the quantity demanded is 1.5 times as large as the percentage change in income. A 6 percent increase in income means the quantity demanded of dresses increases by $1.5 \times 6\% = \mathbf{9\%}$.

(c) When the cross elasticity of demand for baseballs relative to the price of baseball bats equals –0.5, a 20 percent decrease in the price of bats increases the quantity of baseballs demanded by $-0.5 \times -20\% = \mathbf{+10\%}$.

(d) When the price elasticity of supply equals 1, the percentage change in quantity supplied equals the percentage change in price. Thus an increase in the price equal to 5 percent increases the quantity supplied by **5 percent**.

(e) A price elasticity of 2 means that the percentage change in the quantity demanded is twice the percentage change in the price. Turning this around, this means the percentage change in price is half the percentage change in the quantity demanded. To increase the quantity demanded by 10 percent, price must fall by $0.5 \times 10\% = \mathbf{5\%}$.

CHAPTER 6

Business Firms in the U.S. Economy

Chapter 4 described how consumers and producers interact in a market. Chapter 6 provides a detailed discussion of one market participant—producers. Forms of business organization are described and the advantages and disadvantages of each form are explained. Finally, the financial details of the largest and most important of these business organizations—the corporation—are explained.

CHAPTER OUTLINE

I. General Information about American Business
   A. Size Characteristics:
      1. There are about 20 million business firms in the United States.
      2. Most business firms are small.
      3. The largest firms are corporations.
   B. Business Failures:
      1. In the 1980s, about 1 percent of all businesses failed each year. This was almost double the rate in the 1970s.
      2. Approximately 10 new businesses are established for each business that fails.

II. Forms of Business Organization
   A. The characteristics of a **proprietorship** are:
      1. It is a firm owned and operated by an individual.
      2. Proprietorships are the most popular form of business organization. About 70 percent of all firms are proprietorships.
      3. Proprietorships are generally small firms with average sales of about $47,000 per year.
      4. Advantages of a Proprietorship:
         a. It is the easiest type of firm to start. No special legal document or agreement is required.
         b. The owner has complete control over all business operations.
         c. The profit is taxed once—as the personal income of the owner.
      5. Disadvantages of a Proprietorship:
         a. The owner is personally liable for all debts of the business.
         b. It is difficult for a proprietorship to raise large amounts of financial support.
   B. The characteristics of a **partnership** are:
      1. A partnership is a firm owned and operated by two or more people. It is similar to a proprietorship, except that there are two or more owners rather than one.

2. A partnership requires an agreement that outlines the responsibilities and rewards of each partner.

3. Partnerships are the least popular form of business organization, with only about 9 percent of all firms organized as partnerships.

4. Partnerships are larger than proprietorships, with average sales of almost $250,000 per year.

5. Partnerships are concentrated in such industries and occupations as law and medicine, where there are legal restrictions on forming a corporation.

6. Advantages of a Partnership:

    a. A partnership is easy to set up.

    b. Because more people are involved, a partnership has access to more financial resources.

    c. Because the partnership is larger and involves more people, more specialization in the management is possible.

    d. Profits are taxed once—as the personal income of the partners.

7. Disadvantages of a Partnership:

    a. Decision making is cumbersome because each partner must be consulted.

    b. Each partner is personally responsible for the liabilities of the partnership.

    c. The partnership must be reorganized whenever any partner leaves or dies.

C. The characteristics of a **corporation** are:

  1. A corporation is a fictitious, legal "person."

  2. The corporation sells **common stock**. Each share of stock represents part ownership of the corporation and gives its owner one vote in determining the corporation's decisions.

  3. A **board of directors** is elected by the stockholders to establish overall policy for the corporation and to hire managers who are responsible for the day-to-day operations of the business.

  4. Advantages of a Corporation:

    a. Each owner of a corporation—each common stockholder—has **limited liability**. That is, the stockholder is not liable for the business' liabilities. If a corporation fails, the most money a stockholder can lose is the amount the stockholder paid for the stock.

    b. Because it does not terminate with the death of any of its owners, the corporation can have an infinite life.

    c. Because of its infinite life, the corporation can raise large sums of money through stock and bond sales.

    d. The management of the corporation can be placed in the hands of professionals.

  5. Disadvantages of a Corporation:

    a. The corporation is more costly to establish than a partnership or proprietorship.

    b. The profits of the corporation are taxed twice. The corporation's profits are subject to a corporate income tax and then taxed again when the stockholders pay income taxes on any dividends received from the corporation.

    c. There may be a conflict between the goal of the owners—maximum profit—and the goals of the managers, who may be more interested in maximizing their personal power, income, or job security.

III. Corporate Takeovers

A. Corporations are taken over when the majority of a corporation's stock is purchased by an individual, group of individuals, or another corporation.

  1. A takeover bid is an attempt to take over a corporation.

  2. The object of the takeover bid is called the target firm.

  3. A takeover bid begins with a tender offer, which is an offer to buy a majority of the target firm's stock at a price that is usually above the market price of the stock.

  4. A takeover can be a friendly one, where the existing management agrees to the takeover. But the takeover can also be a **hostile takeover**, where the current managers resist the takeover attempt. Hostile takeovers have been most prevalent in the past decade.

  5. Existing management can resist a hostile takeover in a number of ways:

a. The management can sell a part of the firm's assets in order to raise funds to buy some of the company's stock, and to make the firm less attractive to buyers.

b. The management can engage in greenmail, which involves buying the stock the corporate raiders have accumulated, at a price far above the market value of the stock.

c. The management can issue poison pills, which are rights granted to existing stockholders if there is ever a hostile takeover. The poison pills make the firm less attractive as a takeover target.

B. Causes of the Recent Takeover Movement:

1. Less strict enforcement of antitrust laws has allowed more mergers to occur. Larger firms may be better able to compete in world markets with foreign firms because larger firms can take advantage of economies of scale that occur when costs can be reduced by large-scale operations.

2. New managers may be better able to take advantage of new ideas or new technologies because they have no ties to the old way of doing things.

3. If stock prices are low, it is often cheaper for new managers to get into a business by taking over an existing one rather than building a new firm from scratch.

C. Consequences of the Takeover Movement:

1. The major argument in favor of takeovers is that the threat of a hostile takeover keeps current management on its toes and forces it to act in the best interests of the stockholders. Although stockholders have legal control over a corporation, they rarely vote to remove managers even when they are unhappy with them. Instead, it is easier simply to sell the stock. If enough stockholders are unhappy with the policies of the current managers, the company's stock price will be low, making it an attractive takeover target.

2. Major Arguments Against Takeovers:

a. Managers are forced to keep current profits high to keep stockholders happy, even though such policies may not be to the long-run advantage of the business.

b. Takeovers are usually financed by borrowed funds. Firms that are taken over are left with a large debt and large interest payments.

c. New management often closes less-profitable operations, which causes economic dislocations for employees and for localities where such operations were located.

IV. The Financial Side of Corporations

A. A corporation issues three types of securities:

1. **Common stock** represents ownership of the corporation. Each share gives the owner a single vote. Owners of shares are periodically paid a **dividend** by the corporation. The amount of the dividend and when it will be paid are determined by the board of directors. Owners of stock can also benefit from the long-run growth of the firm if they can sell the stock for a price greater than they paid for it. The difference between the sale price and the purchase price is called a **capital gain**. Publicly held stock is bought and sold on a stock market.

2. **Preferred stock** differs from common stock in the following ways:

a. Owners of preferred stock have no vote in the affairs of the corporation.

b. The size of the dividend payment is fixed.

c. The dividend payment on preferred stock must be paid before any dividends on common stock are paid.

3. **Bonds** represent debts of the corporation. Owners of bonds have no part in the ownership of the firm. Bondholders are paid a fixed interest payment semiannually and a fixed payment, called the principal, when the bond matures. Interest on bonds is paid before dividends on either preferred stock or common stock. If the corporation is bankrupt, the bondholders must be paid their interest and principal in full before any money goes to the stockholders. Because the dollar payments to bondholders are fixed, the bondholders are more vulnerable to inflation than owners of common stock.

B. The market value of a security equals the present value of the expected future payments associated with the security. The present value of a specific sum of money to be paid in the future is the amount of money one would need to put away now at the current interest rate in order to accumulate that amount of money in the future. For example, if the current interest rate is 10 percent, $110 to be received in one year has a present value of $100. This follows from the fact that $100 now would grow to $110 in one year if invested at 10 percent interest. The higher the interest rate the lower the present value of a future sum of money because fewer dollars need to be set aside now to grow to that future sum of money. Calculating the present value of a payment to be received in the future is sometimes called discounting.

V. Simple Elements of Accounting

A. A **balance sheet** lists on its left side the value of the firm's **assets**, which are the things that the firm owns. On the right side of the balance sheet two things are listed. These are the firm's **liabilities**, that is, the amounts that the firm owes to others; and the firm's **net worth**, which is simply the difference between the value of the assets and the value of the liabilities. Because of the way net worth is calculated, the total value of the firm's assets—the left side of the balance sheet—must equal the sum of the total value of the liabilities and the value of the firm's net worth—the right side of the balance sheet.

B. An **income statement** shows the firm's revenues, costs, and profit. In general, profit equals revenues minus costs. Costs include all the expenses associated with the firm's output, including depreciation. **Depreciation** represents the value of the firm's capital that is consumed during the year.

HINTS AND HELP

1. Present Values   Understanding what the calculation of present value involves takes time, and learning how to do it takes some practice. Calculating present value means that you are trying to figure out what a *future* amount of money is worth *now*. This has nothing to do with the fact that inflation reduces the purchasing power of dollars. Even if there were no inflation, a dollar now is worth more than a dollar in the future because a dollar in your hand now can be lent out and earn interest. The present value calculation tells you how much money an investor must set aside today at the current interest rate in order to accumulate the future amount.

FILL IN THE BLANK

hostile	1. A takeover is _____ if the management of the firm being taken over resists.
dividend	2. The payment that the owners of common stock receive from the company is called a _____.
balance sheet	3. The net worth of a business can be found on the company's _____ _____.
depreciation	4. The value of the company's capital that is consumed in a year is called _____.
corporation	5. The owners of a _____ have limited liability.
board of directors	6. The _____ sets the overall direction of policy of a corporation.
common stock	7. The owners of a corporation are the people who own the company's _____.
preferred stock	8. The dividend is fixed for _____.
partnership	9. Two or more individuals can start a company and avoid double taxation by forming a _____.
proprietorship	10. The most popular form of business organization in the United States is the _____.

TRUE OR FALSE

_____ 1. Corporations are the only form of business organization that has limited liability.

_____ 2. Bondholders are hurt more by inflation than are owners of common stock.

_____ 3. A dollar today is worth less than a dollar to be received in one year.

_____ 4. Bondholders are paid interest before dividends are paid.

_____ 5. The dividend on preferred stock changes every year depending on how well the company does financially.

_____ 6. The net worth of a business is the value of its assets minus the value of its liabilities.

_____ 7. A firm's profit is calculated on its income statement.

_____ 8. Management and ownership are separate in a proprietorship.

_____ 9. Double taxation is a problem for all business organizations.

_____ 10. If a business has economies of scale, its profits are lower as it gets larger.

MULTIPLE CHOICE

1. An individual wants to start a business, avoid the problem of double taxation, and maintain maximum control over the business' operations. What kind of business organization should the individual form?
   A. a corporation
   B. a partnership
   C. a nonprofit organization
   D. a proprietorship

2. Someone beginning a risky business that requires a large amount of capital should form a:
   A. corporation.
   B. partnership.
   C. proprietorship.
   D. It does not matter which type of business is formed.

3. Which of the following is _not_ subject to double taxation?
   A. dividends paid on common stock
   B. dividends paid on preferred stock
   C. interest on bonds
   D. None of the above is correct because all are subject to double taxation

4. Which of the following is worth more _now_?
   A. $10 now
   B. $10 to be received in a year if the interest rate is 10 percent
   C. $10 to be received in a year if the interest rate is 5 percent
   D. $10 to be received in two years if the interest rate is 10 percent

5. A raider trying to take over a corporation would start with a:
   A. poison pill.
   B. tender offer.
   C. greenmail.
   D. dividend.

6. The owner of which of the following has the best chance of benefiting from the long-run growth of a corporation?
   A. bonds
   B. preferred stock
   C. common stock
   D. All the alternatives are correct.

7. The value of a business' assets are found on the:
   A. income statement.
   B. depreciation schedule.
   C. present value list.
   D. balance sheet.

8. A major problem associated with takeovers is:
   A. they may lower the firm's costs.
   B. they induce firms to focus excessively on short-run profits.
   C. weak management is often removed from office.
   D. the price of the firm's stock may increase.

9. Mergers lower costs of production when there:
   A. are capital gains.
   B. is double taxation.
   C. is limited liability.
   D. are economies of scale.

10. The present value of $100 available in two years, given an interest rate of 10 percent is:
   A. $(2)(\$100)/(1.10)$
   B. $\$100/(1.10)(2)$
   C. $\$100/(1.10)^2$
   D. $\$100/1.20$

PROBLEMS

1. This problem involves choosing a current amount of money or a future amount of money. Column A gives the amount of money you can have now. Column B gives the amount of money you can have in the future and when you can have it. Column C tells you the interest rate. Calculate the present value of the future amount and write it in column D. On the basis of your calculations, indicate whether you would rather have the current amount or the future amount by circling the amount of money in either column A or column B.

(A) CURRENT AMOUNT		(B) FUTURE AMOUNT	(C) INTEREST RATE	(D) PRESENT VALUE
(a)	$10,000	$ 10,500 in 1 year	10%	_____
(b)	1,000	1,500 in 1 year	5%	_____
(c)	95,000	100,000 in 1 year	10%	_____
(d)	95,000	100,000 in 1 year	5%	_____
(e)	2,400	2,600 in 2 years	5%	_____

2. You are Michael Jordan and it is time to renegotiate your contract. You are offered three alternatives. Assume the first payment is received today, year 2's payment is received a year from now, and so forth.

Contract 1: $2,000,000 in year 1, $1,000,000 in year 2, and $1,000,000 in year 3.

Contract 2: $1,500,000 per year for years 1, 2, and 3.

Contract 3: $1,100,000 in year 1, $1,000,000 in year 2, and $2,500,000 in year 3.

The interest rate is 10 percent. All other parts of the contracts are the same. Which contract do you choose?

Answers

TRUE OR FALSE

1. True. In partnerships and proprietorships the owners of the business are personally responsible for the company's liabilities.

2. True. Because the interest payments and the principal are fixed in terms of dollars, inflation reduces the purchasing power of those dollar payments. The dividends and the dollar value of common stock are not fixed.

3. False. Because a dollar today can earn interest and become a larger sum of money in the future, it is better to have a dollar today than a dollar in a year.

4. True. The interest on bonds must be paid before any dividends can be paid on stocks.

5. False. The dividend on preferred stock is fixed.

6. True. Assets minus liabilities equals net worth.

7. True. An income statement shows a firm's revenue, its costs, and its profit, which is the difference between revenue and costs.

8. False. In a proprietorship there is a single owner of the business who takes all the financial risks and makes all of the management decisions for the business.

9. False. Only the income of corporations is taxed twice. Owners of partnerships and proprietorships include any profits as part of their personal income.

10. False. Economies of scale occur when there are cost advantages associated with larger size. Profits should increase if a business has economies of scale and expands its size.

MULTIPLE CHOICE

1. D. A proprietorship gives the individual maximum control over a business and, because profits are taxed as the personal income of the owner, there is no double taxation.

2. A. A corporation has limited liability and can raise large amounts of funds through the sale of stock.

3. C. Interest on bonds is not subject to double taxation because a corporation can deduct the interest paid as a cost before any corporate taxes are calculated.

4. A. A dollar now is always worth more than a dollar in the future because the dollar can earn interest.

5. B. A tender offer is an offer to buy the majority of the stock in a corporation.

6. C. Because the dividends it pays are not fixed, common stock is most likely to benefit from the long-run growth of a corporation. The dividends paid on preferred stock and the interest paid on bonds are fixed.

7. D. A balance sheet lists the value of the firm's assets on one side and its liabilities and net worth on the other.

8. B. Firms often focus on short-run profits in order to keep the firm's stock price high and make the firm an unattractive target for takeover.

9. D. Economies of scale occur when larger size lowers the costs of production. Mergers that increase the size of a business operation lower costs when there are economies of scale.

10. C. The formula for calculating the present value of some amount of money is the amount of money divided by the quantity 1 plus the rate of interest raised to the power equal to the number of years until the money is available.

PROBLEMS

1. (a) $10,000 now is better than $10,500 in a year if the interest rate is 10 percent. The present value of the future money is: $\dfrac{\$10,500}{(1 + .10)} = \$9,545.45$.

    (b) $1,500 in a year if the interest rate is 5 percent is better than $1,000 now. The present value of the future money is: $\dfrac{\$1,500}{(1 + .05)} = \$1,428.57$.

    (c) $95,000 now is better than $100,000 in a year if the interest rate is 10 percent. The present value of the future money is: $\dfrac{\$100,000}{(1 + .10)} = \$90,909.10$.

    (d) $100,000 in a year if the interest rate is 5 percent is better than $95,000 now. The present value of the future money is: $\dfrac{\$100,000}{(1 + .05)} = \$95,238.10$.

    (e) $2,400 now is better than $2,600 in 2 years if the interest rate is 5 percent. The present value of the future money is:

$$\frac{\$2,600}{(1 + .05)(1 + .05)} = \frac{\$2,600}{(1 + .05)^2} = \$2,358.28.$$

2. The present values of the contracts are:

    Contract 1:

$$PV = \$2,000,000 + \frac{\$1,000,000}{(1 + .10)} + \frac{\$1,000,000}{(1 + .10)^2}$$

PV = $2,000,000 + $909,090.91 + $826,446.28 = $3,735,537.19

Contract 2:

$$PV = \$1,500,000 + \frac{\$1,500,000}{(1.10)} + \frac{\$1,500,000}{(1.10)^2}$$

PV = $1,500,000 + $1,363,636.36 + $1,239,669.42 = $4,103,305.78

Contract 3:

$$PV = \$1,100,000 + \frac{\$1,000,000}{(1.10)} + \frac{\$2,500,000}{(1.10)^2}$$

PV = $1,100,000 + $909,090.91 + $2,066,115.70 = $4,075,206.61

Contract 2 is the best contract.

CHAPTER 7

Government in the U.S. Economy— Spending and Taxation

After discussing the mechanics of markets in Chapter 4 and the characteristics of firms in a market economy in Chapter 6, Chapter 7 discusses the role of government. Reasons for and kinds of government spending are considered first. Next, the chapter focuses on taxes. It answers such questions as: What are the major sources of tax revenue? What kinds of taxes are there? Is our system of taxes fair?

CHAPTER OUTLINE

I. Rationale for Government Activity
   A. Promote competition through antitrust enforcement or regulation.
   B. Stabilize the macroeconomy to reduce unemployment and inflation.
   C. Redistribute income in order to reduce poverty.
   D. Correct for externalities (spillover effects).
      1. **Negative Externalities** (Negative Spillovers)
         a. Negative externalities are costs imposed on individuals other than the consumers or producers of a product; the costs are not reflected in market prices (for example, pollution).
         b. Negative externalities are a problem for the market because the producers do not pay the spillover costs, so they do not consider these costs in their production decisions; more of the good is produced than would be produced if all costs were considered.
         c. Solution: Reduce output to the socially optimum level through taxes, regulation, sale of pollution rights, or output restrictions.
      2. **Positive Externalities** (Positive Spillovers)
         a. Positive externalities are benefits received by people other than the consumers or the producers of the good; the benefits are transmitted outside of the market (for example, vaccinations that reduce the chances of others contracting the disease).
         b. Positive externalities are a problem because buyers of the good ignore them when they make purchases; less of the good is demanded and produced than would be the case if all the benefits were considered.
         c. Solution: Subsidize the production or purchase of the product or service.
   E. Provision of **Public Goods**
      1. Public goods have two characteristics:
         a. People cannot be excluded from consuming a public good once it is produced.
         b. There is little or no cost associated with providing a public good to additional consumers.

2. Examples: National defense, police protection.
3. People will not voluntarily pay for public goods because they know that if others pay for the good, they can have the good for nothing. This is called the "free rider" problem.
4. Solution: Government must compel payment by all people through taxes. *Note:* Not all goods the government provides are public goods.

II. **Public Choice Analysis:** Applies basic economic principles to the analysis of political actions
   A. Public choice theory states that people always attempt to maximize their own satisfaction. To understand the behavior of voters, politicians, and bureaucrats, it is necessary to apply the principle of self-interest to the political realm.
   B. Fundamental assumptions behind public choice theory are:
     1. Political decisions are ultimately the decisions of individuals.
     2. Self-interest is the primary motivation of people in both the private and public spheres.
     3. Exchanges occur in the political realm as in the private realm.
   C. Predictions arising from public choice theory are:
     1. Small groups with significant individual interests often succeed in the political arena at the expense of larger groups with smaller individual interests because members of the small group are more willing to devote resources to achieve their desired outcome.
     2. Rent seeking is prevalent. **Rent seeking**, the pursuit of government grants that convey economic benefits, is wasteful because it diverts resources from more constructive uses. These grants also typically increase prices paid by consumers.

III. Growth of the Government
   A. Causes:
     1. Urbanization of population means that individuals must rely upon the government for the provision of certain goods that rural populations can provide for themselves (for example, waste disposal).
     2. National defense needs have necessitated a large and expensive system of weapons and personnel.
     3. Government has taken over some of the responsibility of providing for retirement (Social Security), unemployment (unemployment insurance), income support (welfare), and health care (Medicare). This is called the **welfare state**.
   B. Kinds of Government Spending
     1. Government Purchases of Goods and Services: Use of resources by the government; called **exhaustive expenditures** because they use up economic resources, that is, reduce the resources available to the rest of the economy (for example, public schools, national defense).
     2. Transfer Payments: government redistribution of income; called **nonexhaustive expenditures** because the government itself is not using resources—although the government does determine who gets the increased purchasing power (for example, Social Security, welfare payments).
   C. Measuring the Size of Government
     1. Government Purchases measure the resources controlled by the government.
     2. Total government spending (purchases plus transfer payments) measures the degree to which the government influences the use of resources.
     3. Data:
       a. Developed economies tend to have a relatively larger government sector than less developed countries. U.S. government spending is a smaller percent of GDP than for most European countries.
       b. Income security and national defense are the two largest categories of spending for the federal government.
       c. Education and health and welfare are the two largest categories of spending for state and local governments.

IV. Taxes
   A. Purposes:
     1. Provide revenue for government spending.

2. Release resources from the private sector for government use.
   B. Classification and Definitions:
      1. **Progressive Tax**: A tax that takes a larger percentage of income as income rises.
      2. **Proportional Tax**: A tax that takes the same percentage of income at all income levels.
      3. **Regressive Tax**: A tax that takes a smaller percentage of income as income rises.
   C. **Tax Incidence**:
      1. The study of tax incidence involves discovering how the burden of the tax is distributed, that is, who actually pays the tax.
      2. The incidence of a tax is often difficult to determine because of tax shifting: passing on the burden of a tax to someone else. For example the property tax on apartments is passed on to tenants by raising rents.
   D. Is a tax fair or equitable? This is a normative question. The issues are:
      1. **Horizontal Equity**: People with the same ability to pay taxes should pay the same taxes.
      2. **Vertical Equity**: People with more ability to pay taxes should pay more taxes.

V. Federal Taxes
   A. **Individual Income Tax**:
      1. The tax is the primary source of revenue for the federal government.
      2. Calculation of tax liability:
         a. Calculate **adjusted gross income** by adding up income subject to taxation.
         b. Calculate **taxable income** by subtracting deductions and exemptions from adjusted gross income.
         c. The federal income tax is considered progressive because the **average tax rate** rises as income rises.
      3. The individual income tax is progressive because (a) the first few thousand dollars of income are not taxed because of exemptions and deductions, and (b) the **marginal tax rate** rises with income.
      4. The progressivity is reduced because people can itemize deductions and reduce their tax liability. The major legal tax loopholes include the nontaxability of interest on municipal bonds and the preferential treatment of homeowners.
   B. **Payroll Tax**:
      1. A payroll tax is a tax on wages. The payroll tax is the most rapidly rising source of federal revenue. An example is the Social Security tax.
      2. Social Security tax is regressive because only approximately the first $55,000 of wages are taxed and non-wage income is not taxed.
      3. The Social Security system suffered financial problems in the past 20 years because the birthrate fell, life expectancy rose, real-wage increases slowed, and benefits were expanded.
   C. **Corporate Income Tax**:
      1. The corporate income tax is a tax on the profits of corporations.
      2. Whether the corporate income tax is progressive or regressive depends on whether the tax is shifted onto consumers through higher prices, shifted onto employees through lower wages, or absorbed by the corporation. Economists disagree about the incidence of this tax.
      3. The corporate income tax results in **double taxation** because corporate income is taxed once as corporate income and once again by the individual income tax when the income is distributed to stockholders as dividend income.

VI. State and Local Taxes
   A. **Sales Tax**:
      1. The sales tax contributes one-third of total state revenues.
      2. The sales tax is regressive because higher-income families spend a smaller percentage of their income than lower-income families.
      3. **Excise taxes** are sales taxes that apply to only a few specific goods. Examples are the gasoline tax and the cigarette tax.
   B. **Property Tax**:
      1. This is the primary source of income for local governments.

2. Problems with Property Tax:
   a. The property tax is usually considered regressive because higher-income families spend a smaller percentage of income on housing than do lower-income families.
   b. Because property is not reassessed often, inequities occur.
   c. Localities with low property values must impose high tax rates to raise the same revenue as those localities with higher property values.

VII. Important Tax Legislation of the Past 15 Years
   A. The Economic Recovery Tax Act of 1981
      1. Significantly reduced marginal income-tax rates for the purpose of increasing the incentive to be productive.
      2. Reduced taxes on corporations.
      3. Resulted in large federal budget deficits because tax receipts were reduced while government spending was not.
   B. The Tax Reform Act of 1986
      1. Broadened the tax base—the income subject to taxation—while simultaneously reducing tax rates. The act was revenue neutral, that is, tax revenue neither increased nor decreased.
      2. Outcomes of Act:
         a. The act improved economic efficiency by eliminating many deductions and lowering tax rates, which reduced the incentive to undertake activities solely for tax benefits.
         b. By eliminating deductions, the act improved tax equity by reducing the ways in which taxes can be avoided.
         c. Because favorable tax treatment for capital gains was eliminated and because corporate taxes were increased, the implications for economic growth were negative.

HINTS AND HELP

1. Externalities (Spillovers)   Understanding the supply and demand diagrams for negative and positive externalities can be difficult. Remember that negative externalities are not considered when firms make production decisions. The supply curve is based upon the private costs of production. Where this supply curve intersects the demand curve determines the equilibrium output. (See point *A* in Figure 7.1.) When all costs—private plus nega-

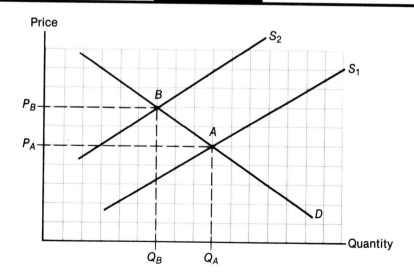

FIGURE 7.1

tive externalities—are considered, the supply curve is above and to the left of the market's supply curve. Where this supply curve intersects the demand curve determines the socially optimal output. (See point *B* in Figure 7.1.) Because this "social" supply curve is to the left of the market's, the socially optimal output is less than the market output. The market overproduces when there are negative externalities.

By similar reasoning, positive externalities are ignored by consumers. The demand curve measures only the private benefits. Where it intersects the supply curve determines the market output. When all benefits are considered society will want a greater amount of output than the consumers choose. The socially optimal output is then greater than the market output. The market underproduces when there are external benefits.

2. Progressive, Proportional, and Regressive   Whether a tax is progressive, proportional, or regressive depends on the *percent of income* paid in taxes as income rises, not the *dollars* paid in taxes as income rises. It is possible for a tax to be regressive even though the rich pay more dollars. When determining how to categorize any particular tax it is necessary to calculate the percentage of income paid in taxes in order to be sure.

3. Marginal and Average Tax Rates   Students in economics become aware very early that it is important to distinguish between an average and a marginal value. The *average tax rate* is (total taxes paid/total income). The *marginal tax rate* is (extra taxes paid/extra income).

FILL IN THE BLANK

private, external	1. The benefits associated with the consumption of a good that go to the buyers of the good are the _____ benefits; the benefits that go to the individuals other than the buyers or the producers are the _____ benefits.
public good	2. If consumers cannot be excluded from consuming a good and if extra units of the good can be produced at little or no cost, the good is a _____.
rent seeking	3. The pursuit of special government grants that provide economic benefits to their recipient is called _____.
regressive	4. If the percentage of income paid in taxes falls as income increases, the tax is _____.
incidence	5. Discovering who actually loses purchasing power when a tax is imposed involves discovering the _____ of the tax.
average tax rate marginal tax rate	6. Total taxes paid divided by income is the _____; the additional tax paid divided by additional income is the _____.
excise	7. A tax based on the amount of a particular good you buy is a(n) _____ tax.
fell fell	8. The Social Security system got into financial problems because the birthrate in the United States _____ and the rate of growth of real wages _____.
double taxation	9. Because corporate profits are taxed once by the corporate income tax and once again when distributed as dividends by the individual income tax, there is _____.
tax base	10. The Tax Reform Act of 1986 reduced the number of deductions and thus increased the _____ of the federal income tax.

TRUE OR FALSE

_____ 1. Transfer payments are a kind of exhaustive government spending.

_____ 2. Stabilizing the economy is considered to be one of the reasons for government involvement in the economy.

_____ 3. If a good creates external costs, a possible solution is to tax the producer of the good.

_____ 4. The urbanization of the population has resulted in a reduced role of the government in the economy.

_____ 5. Developed countries tend to spend proportionally more of their income on government activities than less developed countries.

_____ 6. Taxing higher income individuals more than the less affluent is an example of vertical equity.

_____ 7. A proportional income tax is a tax where all families pay the same amount of taxes.

_____ 8. The nontaxability of interest on municipal bonds tends to reduce the progressivity of the individual income tax.

_____ 9. The primary benefit of the Tax Reform Act of 1986 was that it increased the revenue of the federal government and reduced the deficit.

_____ 10. The Social Security tax is regressive because the tax is not imposed on wages above a specific amount.

MULTIPLE CHOICE

1. Social costs are:
   A. the costs of production that the firm pays.
   B. the costs that the consumer of the good pays.
   C. the sum of private and external costs.
   D. private costs less external costs.

2. External benefits are received by:
   A. the consumers of a product.
   B. the producers of a product.
   C. neither the consumer nor the producer of the product.
   D. the government.

3. Public goods are difficult for a market to produce because:
   A. they benefit a large number of people.
   B. people can refuse to pay for them and still receive them.
   C. there are many different inputs used.
   D. there are not many unemployed resources.

4. An exhaustive government expenditure:
   A. consumes resources.
   B. consumes tax dollars.
   C. produces economic growth.
   D. produces tax revenue.

5. The gasoline tax is an example of:
   A. an excise tax.
   B. a progressive tax.
   C. rent-seeking behavior.
   D. double taxation.

6. If two families that earn the same income pay substantially different amounts of taxes, the tax:
   A. is regressive.
   B. violates horizontal equity.
   C. violates vertical equity.
   D. involves tax shifting.

7. When a landlord raises the rent in response to a higher property tax, it is an example of:
   A. rent seeking.
   B. a transfer payment.
   C. using loopholes to reduce one's tax liability.
   D. tax shifting.

8. The progressivity of the individual income tax is reduced by:
   A. transfer payments.
   B. rising marginal tax rates.
   C. loopholes.
   D. double taxation.

9. Which of the following taxes is progressive?
   A. individual income tax
   B. Social Security tax
   C. excise tax
   D. sales tax

10. Use the following information to determine the nature of this tax.

INCOME EARNED	TAXES OWED
$40,000	$ 8,000
50,000	9,000
60,000	10,000

Based on this information, this tax is a:
A. progressive tax.
B. proportional tax.
C. regressive tax.
D. excise tax.

PROBLEMS

1.

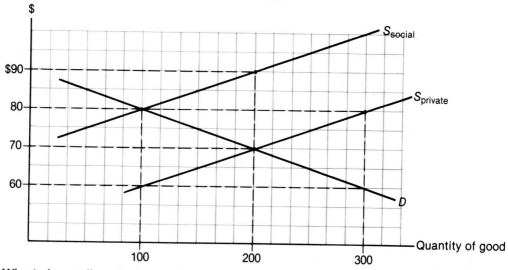

FIGURE 7.2

a. What is the socially optimal output? _____
b. What is the market output? _____
c. What is the private cost of producing the 200th unit of output? _____
d. What is the social cost of producing the 200th unit of output? _____
e. What is the external cost of producing the 200th unit of output? _____

2. The table below describes a tax. Use the information to answer the questions that follow.

INCOME	TAXES PAID	AVERAGE TAX RATE	MARGINAL TAX RATE
$ 0	$ 0		
10,000	500	_____	_____
15,000	1,000	_____	_____
20,000	2,000	_____	_____
25,000	3,500	_____	_____
30,000	5,500	_____	_____

a. Calculate the average tax rate for each level of income.
b. Calculate the marginal tax rate for each level of income.
c. Is this tax progressive, proportional, or regressive? _____

Answers

TRUE OR FALSE

1. False. Transfer payments are not an exhaustive government expenditure because no resources are used; the government merely transfers purchasing power from one group of individuals to another without using any real economic resources.

2. True. Because economies suffer periods of unemployment and inflation and do not seem capable of solving these problems quickly, most economists believe that the government has an important role to play in stabilizing the economy.

3. True. Because a producer ignores costs that it does not have to pay (that is, any external costs associated with its production), a possible solution is to impose a tax that increases the firm's costs as if it were taking into consideration the external costs.

4. False. Urbanization has added to the role of government because the government must perform certain functions for urban residents that are performed by rural residents for themselves (for example, refuse collection and disposal).

5. True. Partly because of the fact that developed countries are more urbanized, and partly because rich countries demand more government-provided goods and services than less developed ones (for example, public education, public parks), government spending is higher relative to GDP in developed countries than in less developed ones.

6. True. Vertical equity is the normative value that people who have different abilities to pay should be taxed differently. In particular, it is the belief that those with higher incomes should be required to pay a larger share of their incomes in taxes.

7. False. A proportional tax is a tax where all taxpayers pay the same percent of their income in taxes.

8. True. The interest on municipal bonds is not taxed by the federal government. Municipal bonds are purchased more often by higher-income individuals than lower-income individuals. Thus the average tax rate is reduced for upper income taxpayers relative to the rate for lower income taxpayers.

9. False. The Tax Reform Act of 1986 was revenue neutral, which means that it did not increase federal tax revenue above what it would have been if the legislation had not been enacted.

10. True. The Social Security tax is imposed only on wages to about $55,000. Any wages above that amount are not taxed. As a result, individuals who earn $55,000 pay about 7 percent of their wages, while those who earn $110,000 pay exactly the same dollars—which equals only 3.5 percent of their wages.

MULTIPLE CHOICE

1. C. Social costs are the sum of all costs associated with the production of a product. These are the private costs paid by the firm and the external costs imposed on others.

2. C. External benefits are benefits that go to neither the producer nor the consumer of a product. That is why they are not considered when the production decision is made. And that is why the market underproduces goods when external benefits exist.

3. B. A characteristic of public goods is that once they are produced people cannot be excluded from consuming them. Knowing this, consumers of public goods will not contribute to their production, believing that they can have the good without having paid for it. This is the "free rider" problem.

4. A. An exhaustive government expenditure is one that consumes (or exhausts) some of the economy's resources.

5. A. The gasoline tax is an excise tax because it is levied on the consumption of a particular good or service.

6. B. Horizontal equity is the principle that a fair tax is one where families with the same income pay the same taxes.

7. D. Tax shifting involves shifting to someone else—through higher prices or lower incomes—the true cost of paying a tax.

8. C. Loopholes are exemptions and deductions that reduce an individual's income tax liability. The higher one's income the more advantage there is to reducing one's taxable income. As a result, tax loopholes are used more frequently as income rises.

9. A. Because the first few thousand dollars of income are not taxed and because the marginal tax rates increase with income, the individual income tax is progressive.

10. C. The tax is regressive because as income rises the percentage of income paid in taxes falls. When income is $40,000 taxes owed equal 20 percent of income. When income is $50,000 taxes owed equal 18 percent. And when income equals $60,000 taxes owed equal about 16 percent of income.

PROBLEMS

1. a. **100 units**. The socially optimal output is determined by the intersection of the demand curve and the supply curve that measures *all* costs. The supply curve labeled "social" includes both the private costs and the external costs.

   b. **200 units**. The market output is determined by the intersection of the demand curve and the market's supply curve. Because the firms consider only the private costs when making production decisions, the supply curve labeled "private" determines the market output.

   c. **$70**. The private costs are read off the "private" supply curve. The dollar amount associated with 200 units of output is $70.

   d. **$90**. The social costs are read off the "social" supply curve. The dollar amount associated with 200 units of output is $90.

   e. **$20**. External costs equal social costs ($90) less private costs ($70), which is $20.

2. a. and b.

INCOME	TAXES PAID	AVERAGE TAX RATE	MARGINAL TAX RATE
$ 0	$ 0		
10,000	500	5%	5%
15,000	1,000	6.6%	10%
20,000	2,000	10%	20%
25,000	3,500	14%	30%
30,000	5,500	18.3%	40%

The marginal tax rate is calculated by dividing the additional taxes paid by the additional income. For example, when income rises from $25,000 to $30,000, the additional tax is $5,500 – $3,500 = $2,000 and the additional income is $5,000. The marginal tax rate is $2,000/$5,000 = 0.40 or 40%.

The average tax rate is calculated by dividing total taxes paid by total income. For example, when income is $20,000, the total taxes due are $2,000. The average tax rate is $2,000/$20,000 = 0.10 or 10%.

   c. The tax is **progressive**. As income rises, the average tax rate rises.

CHAPTER 8

Introduction to Macroeconomics: Fundamental Concepts

As the title indicates, this chapter is an introduction to **macroeconomics**, which is the study of the aggregate economy. Your introduction begins by explaining three important concepts in macroeconomics–the business cycle, unemployment, and inflation. This chapter discusses the nature and measurement of both unemployment and the nation's price indexes. The next chapter analyzes the economic consequences of unemployment and inflation.

CHAPTER OUTLINE

I. Business Cycle
   A. The **business cycle** refers to the repetitive swings in real gross domestic product (GDP) that have historically characterized an economy.
      1. **Real GDP** measures the value of an economy's output after the effect of inflation has been removed. Changes in real GDP indicate changes in an economy's output of goods and services.
      2. **Nominal GDP** is the value of an economy's output measured using current prices. Because prices change from year to year, nominal GDP can be a misleading indicator of annual production.
   B. Phases of the Business Cycle:
      1. Expansion: period during which output (real GDP) increases.
      2. Peak: point at which output achieves its maximum value.
      3. Contraction: period during which output falls.
         a. If output falls for six months or longer, the contraction is called a **recession**.
         b. A severe recession is termed a **depression**. There is no exact criterion for determining when a recession becomes a depression.
      4. Trough: point at which output reaches its lowest point.
   C. Stabilization Policies
      1. In order to reduce the size and frequency of the business cycle's fluctuations, the government often implements policies to stabilize demand for the nation's goods and services.
      2. Elements of Stabilization Policy:
         a. **Monetary policy** involves the manipulation of the money supply, credit, and interest rates. Monetary policy is controlled by the **Federal Reserve System**, which is the central bank in the United States.
         b. **Fiscal policy** concerns the manipulation of federal government expenditures and taxes by Congress and the president.

II. Unemployment
   A. Measurement
      1. Everyone 16 or older in the United States can be placed in one of three categories:
         a. If the individual has a job, the individual is employed.
         b. An individual is considered unemployed if the person has no job but has looked for one within the past four weeks. The **labor force** is made up of those people classified as employed plus those classified as unemployed.
         c. An individual who has no job and has not looked for one in the past month is considered to be not in the labor force.
      2. **Unemployment rate:** the percentage of the labor force classified as unemployed. The formula is:

$$\text{unemployment rate} = \frac{\text{number unemployed}}{\text{number in labor force}} \times 100$$

      3. There are reasons to question the validity of the government's reported unemployment rate:
         a. An individual is counted as employed regardless of the number of hours worked. People who are working fewer hours than they want to work are underemployed (that is, involuntarily working part time). The unemployment figures neglect this fact.
         b. Some individuals quit looking for work because they question their ability to find a job. These individuals are called discouraged workers. Such workers represent hidden unemployment; they are jobless but are not counted as unemployed by the government because they are not looking for work.
         c. Some individuals enter the labor force only after others in the family have become unemployed. These workers are called secondary workers. They tend to cause the reported unemployment rate to be higher than it would otherwise be.
      4. A second important gauge of the labor market is the **labor force participation rate**, which measures the percentage of the population 16 or older in the labor force. The formula is:

$$\text{labor force participation rate} = \frac{\text{number in labor force}}{\text{population, 16 or older}} \times 100$$

   B. Categories of Unemployment
      1. **Frictional unemployment** occurs when workers are temporarily between jobs. Some frictional unemployment is unavoidable because it takes time for those who are switching jobs or are just entering the labor force to find a new job. Frictional unemployment of a particular worker usually does not last long.
      2. **Structural unemployment** occurs when there is a mismatch between the skills desired by employers (for the available jobs) and the skills possessed by the unemployed. Structural unemployment occurs because of changes in technology and changes in the demand for particular types of goods and services, and because of lack of education and training.
      3. **Cyclical unemployment** is unemployment caused by the economy producing an output less than its potential (or full-employment) output. Cyclical unemployment is the kind of unemployment most closely linked to the swings in output during the business cycle.
      4. It is not simple to determine how much unemployment falls into each of the three categories. As an economy improves and output expands, cyclical unemployment declines. At the same time, it takes less time for workers to find new jobs, so frictional unemployment declines. Finally, employers are more willing to hire less-skilled workers, so structural unemployment falls too.
   C. The Natural Rate of Unemployment
      1. The **natural rate of unemployment** is the unemployment rate when the economy is at full employment. The natural rate can be defined in two ways:
         a. It is the unemployment rate when there is no cyclical unemployment (that is, when all unemployment is frictional or structural unemployment).
         b. It is the lowest unemployment rate that can be achieved without triggering an increase in the inflation rate. For this reason it is sometimes referred to as the nonaccelerating inflation rate of unemployment, or NAIRU.

2. The natural rate of unemployment is not constant over time.
    a. From the early 1960s to the early 1980s the natural rate rose in the United States because:
        i. The baby-boom generation entered the labor market. This increased both frictional and structural unemployment because young workers have above-average amounts of each.
        ii. Women, who typically experience above-average rates of frictional unemployment, increased their participation in the labor force.
        iii. Unemployment benefits improved. This reduced the personal cost of being unemployed and therefore increased the length of job searches and frictional unemployment.
    b. Since the early 1980s the natural rate has fallen.
        i. Young people have entered the labor force at slower rates because of the decline of the birth rate after the early 1960s.
        ii. The labor market skills of women have increased, and their frictional unemployment has decreased (because of lower labor market turnover).
    c. Government policies potentially can influence the natural rate of unemployment.
        i. Improved information about job openings could reduce frictional unemployment.
        ii. Government programs such as welfare and unemployment insurance could be reformed to provide a greater incentive to return to work quickly.
        iii. The minimum wage could be reduced, thereby increasing the quantity of unskilled workers demanded by employers.

III. Inflation
    A. **Inflation** is a persistent and sustained increase in the general level of prices.
    B. Price Index
        1. A **price index** is a measure of the average level of prices in a year relative to the average level of prices in another year, called the base year. How fast the index changes during a year measures the rate of inflation.
        2. A price index is calculated by comparing the cost of buying a basket of goods and services in the current year relative to the cost of buying the same basket in the base year.
        3. The value of the index is always 100 in the base year. If, for example, the index has a value of 150 in another year, then prices are 50 percent higher in that year than they were in the base year.
    C. Major Price Indexes in the United States
        1. The **Consumer Price Index (CPI)** measures the prices of goods and services consumers buy. This index is the one most relevant for evaluating the living standards of people in the economy. The CPI is published monthly and has a base period of 1982-1984.
        2. The **Producer Price Index (PPI)** measures the prices of goods producers buy–the raw materials and products that are used to produce the goods sold in stores. It is often used as a predictor of future changes in the CPI. The PPI is available monthly and has a base year of 1982.
        3. The **GDP Deflator** measures the prices of all the goods and services contained in GDP. Because it is the broadest price index, monitoring the most prices, most economists consider it the best gauge of inflation. It is available quarterly and has a base year of 1987.
    D. There are two major sources of upward bias in the price indexes.
        1. Price indexes do not account well for quality improvements. To the extent that price increases of goods and services are attributable to improvements in quality, the higher prices are not harmful—one pays a higher price but gets a better product. But a price index often incorrectly records the higher prices as inflation.
        2. A price index is biased because it repeatedly estimates the cost of buying a fixed basket of goods. In reality, the basket people purchase from year to year is not fixed. People typically substitute goods that have had smaller (or negative) price increases for goods that have had larger price increases. By ignoring this substitution on the part of consumers, the price index overestimates the increase in the "cost of living."

HINTS AND HELP

1. Frictional, Structural, and Cyclical Unemployment To recall the three kinds of unemployment, it helps to picture a situation typical of each. Frictional unemployment can be seen as a situation where there is a worker and there is a job, but it takes time for the two to find each other. An experienced computer programmer who quits one job to search for another may be temporarily between jobs. In that event, the person experiences frictional unemployment.

Structural unemployment can be pictured as a situation where there is a worker and a job but they will never match because the skills possessed by the unemployed do not match the skills required on the job.

Cyclical unemployment is a situation where there is a worker but there is no job. Because the economy is producing less output than it is capable of, fewer workers are needed to produce the output.

2. The Perfect Price Index? No price index can be a perfect measure of inflation. Every price index must hold constant the quantities of goods and services in the bundle it is tracking so that the only reason the cost of the bundle changes is because of changes in prices. (Remember that the bundle of goods and services is held constant. This is a favorite exam question.)

However, by holding the quantities constant, the index ignores the possibility of substitution on the part of consumers. Within the basket, consumers will expand purchases of goods whose prices have remained stable and reduce purchases of goods whose prices have increased sharply since the base year. By neglecting this consideration, the substitution bias is created.

FILL IN THE BLANK

real GDP

1. The business cycle refers to the swings in the economy's _____ _____.

peak

2. Output reaches its largest value at the _____ of the business cycle.

not in the labor force

3. If an individual is neither employed nor looking for a job, the individual is considered to be _____.

Cyclical

4. _____ unemployment is the kind of unemployment caused by an economy producing an output less than its potential output.

labor force

5. The sum of the employed and the unemployed equals the _____ _____.

16 or older

6. To determine employment statistics, the government surveys individuals who are of age _____.

GDP deflator

7. The price index that keeps track of the largest, most diverse set of prices is the _____.

base year

8. A price index compares prices now to prices in the _____ _____.

over

9. Price indexes generally _____ estimate the increase in the "cost of living."

Consumer

10. The price index that keeps track of the prices that are most important to individual families is the _____ Price Index.

TRUE OR FALSE

_____ 1. Nominal GDP is influenced by both prices and output.

_____ 2. A discouraged worker is counted as unemployed by the government.

_____ 3. The natural rate of unemployment can be increased or decreased through stabilization policy.

_____ 4. Inflation occurs any time the price of any product increases.

_____ 5. If unemployment is entirely frictional and structural, the economy is at full employment.

_____ 6. Everyone in the United States age 16 or older who is looking for a job is counted as unemployed by the government.

_____ 7. A price index with a value of 300 means that, on average, prices are three times higher than they were in the base year.

_____ 8. A depression is more severe than a recession.

_____ 9. Unemployment rises during the contraction phase of the business cycle.

_____ 10. When the labor force participation rate equals 50 percent, half the population 16 or older has a job.

MULTIPLE CHOICE

1. Fiscal and monetary policies make up what are called:
   A. stabilization policies.
   B. the Federal Reserve System.
   C. macroeconomics.
   D. supply-side economics.

2. When the actual unemployment rate is greater than the natural unemployment rate:
   A. the natural rate of unemployment rises.
   B. there is cyclical unemployment.
   C. the rate of inflation increases.
   D. the economy is at the trough of the business cycle.

3. Discouraged workers are part of:
   A. hidden unemployment.
   B. underemployment.
   C. secondary workers.
   D. the labor force.

4. The Federal Reserve System controls:
   A. the natural rate of unemployment.
   B. income tax rates.
   C. monetary policy.
   D. fiscal policy.

5. The kind of unemployment that is usually of the shortest duration is:
   A. natural unemployment.
   B. structural unemployment.
   C. frictional unemployment.
   D. cyclical unemployment.

6. Which of the following policies would be most effective in reducing structural unemployment?
   A. stabilization policies
   B. retraining programs
   C. unemployment benefits
   D. information about jobs

7. A recession ends at which phase of the business cycle?
   A. contraction
   B. trough
   C. expansion
   D. peak
8. Holding the composition of the basket of goods in the price index constant results in:
   A. downward bias.
   B. a substitution bias.
   C. quality bias.
   D. inflation.
9. Real gross domestic product equals nominal gross domestic product after the effects of which of the following have been removed from nominal GDP?
   A. inflation
   B. the business cycle
   C. natural unemployment rates
   D. the substitution bias
10. Which of the following caused the natural unemployment rate to rise during the 1970s?
   A. lower structural unemployment
   B. a larger percentage of the work force made up of young workers
   C. decreased labor force participation of women
   D. increased labor force participation of men

PROBLEMS

1. The leaders of Caines have discovered that they do not know exactly what the unemployment rate is in Caines. They have decided to institute a series of surveys to discover the number of workers in Caines, the number of unemployed, and the number not in the labor force. They have adopted the same rules for classifying people as employed, unemployed, and not in the labor force as the United States has. That is why you have been called in. As a student of the U.S. system, you have been hired as a consultant. It is your job to determine in which category each of the following individuals belongs. You should add a word or two explaining why you made that choice.

INDIVIDUAL	CATEGORY (EMPLOYED, UNEMPLOYED, NOT IN LABOR FORCE)	WHY
a. Sally Student works part time, attends school part time.	_____	_____
b. Joe Goofoff lives off checks from home, rarely goes to class, never looks for work.	_____	_____
c. Jane works part time but is looking for a full-time job.	_____	_____
d. Harry Happy plays tennis most days but calls an employment agency once a month to see if a tennis pro job is available.	_____	_____

2. Caines has now collected all the data on its population:
   Total population 16 or older: 100,000
   Working part time: 15,000
   Working full time: 25,000
   Unemployed: 10,000

a. How many people are in the labor force? _____
b. How many people are not in the labor force? _____
c. What is the unemployment rate? _____
d. What is the labor force participation rate? _____

3. The country of Caines has decided to start the Caines Price Index (or CPI). A survey has revealed that the typical consumer in Caines consumed the following bundle of goods in 1989:

GOOD	QUANTITY (Q1989)	1989 PRICES (P1989)	(P1989) (Q1989)
Chicken	24 pounds	$2/pound	_____
Shoes	6 pairs	$11/pair	_____
Shirts	9	$20/shirt	_____
Potatoes	48 pounds	$.75/pound	_____

a. How much did the bundle cost in 1989? _____

Assume the prices in 1993 are the following:

GOOD	1993 PRICES (P1993)	(P1993) (Q1989)
Chicken	$7/pound	_____
Shoes	$20/pair	_____
Shirts	$15/shirt	_____
Potatoes	$1.50/pound	_____

b. What does the bundle cost in 1993? _____
c. What is the CPI value for 1989? _____
d. What is the CPI value for 1993? _____

4. Calculate the percentage change in the average level of prices since the base year in each of the following cases:

	VALUE OF PRICE INDEX	PERCENTAGE CHANGE IN PRICES SINCE BASE YEAR
a.	150	_____
b.	200	_____
c.	90	_____
d.	100	_____
e.	500	_____

5. Calculate the annual percentage change in the price index–the rate of inflation.

	VALUE OF PRICE INDEX		RATE OF INFLATION
	1992	1993	
a.	100	110	_____
b.	200	220	_____
c.	200	160	_____
d.	125	75	_____
e.	300	310	_____

TRUE OR FALSE

1. True. Nominal GDP is the value of an economy's output at current prices. Because both output and prices can change from year to year, nominal GDP is influenced by both.

2. False. A discouraged worker–a worker who has stopped looking for work because the chances of finding a job are small–is considered to be not in the labor force by the government because he or she has not looked for a job in the past four weeks. Individuals not in the labor force are not counted among the unemployed.

3. False. Stabilization policy is designed to move the economy toward full employment. It influences the actual unemployment rate but does not change the unemployment rate associated with full employment.

4. False. Inflation is a rise in the general level of prices. If the prices of a few items are rising while other prices are falling, the general price level may not be rising.

5. True. An economy is at full employment when there is no cyclical unemployment, which means there is only frictional and structural unemployment.

6. False. If someone has a job and at the same time is looking for a new one, that person is considered employed.

7. True. Because the value of a price index in the base year is 100, a price index reading of 300 means prices are three times higher than they were in the base year.

8. True. A depression is a severe recession, although there is no exact definition of when a recession becomes a depression.

9. True. During a contraction the economy produces less output, which means fewer people are employed and unemployment rises.

10. False. When the labor force participation rate equals 50 percent, half the population 16 or older are in the labor force, but they could be either employed or unemployed.

MULTIPLE CHOICE

1. A. Fiscal and monetary policies constitute what are called stabilization policies, which are actions by the government to reduce swings in the economy's output.

2. B. When the actual unemployment rate is greater than the natural unemployment rate, the economy is not producing to its capacity and there is cyclical unemployment.

3. A. Because they are jobless but are not counted as such by the government, discouraged workers are part of hidden unemployment.

4. C. The Federal Reserve System controls monetary policy through its influence over the money supply, interest rates, and credit availability.

5. C. Frictional unemployment is usually short term because it occurs only because of the natural search process in which unemployed workers locate available jobs.

6. B. Retraining programs can provide the skills required for available jobs. The absence of these skills is a major cause of structural unemployment.

7. B. The trough is the point in the business cycle at which output ceases to decline.

8. B. Holding constant the bundle of goods in the price index means that the price index ignores the possibility of consumers substituting goods whose prices have declined or remained stable for goods whose prices have risen since the base year. Because consumers actually make such substitutions, the reported price index places too much weight on those products whose prices have risen the most since the base year.

9. A. Real gross domestic product removes the effect of inflation from nominal gross domestic product to create a more accurate measure of the amount of output the economy has produced.

10. B. Because young workers have high rates of frictional and structural unemployment, an increase in the portion of the labor force made up by them raises the natural rate of unemployment. This happened in the 1970s.

PROBLEMS

1. a. Sally Student is employed; anyone working for pay is considered employed even if attending school.
    b. Joe Goofoff is not in the labor force; he has no job and has not looked for one within the past month.
    c. Jane is employed; anyone working for pay is considered employed regardless of hours of work.
    d. Harry Happy is unemployed; he is not working but has looked for work within the past month.

2. a. The labor force is made up of all the people who are employed or are unemployed. The labor force equals $15,000 + 25,000 + 10,000 = \textbf{50,000}$.
    b. Individuals not in the labor force are all those over 16 who are not in the labor force. This equals $100,000 - 50,000 = \textbf{50,000}$.
    c. The unemployment rate is the percent of the labor force that is unemployed. The unemployment rate is $(10,000/50,000) \times 100 = \textbf{20\%}$.
    d. The labor force participation rate is the percent of the population in the labor force. It equals $(50,000/100,000) \times 100 = \textbf{50\%}$.

3. a. The cost of the bundle in 1989 is:

Chicken	(24 pounds)($2) = $48
Shoes	(6 pairs)($11) = $66
Shirts	(9)($20) = $180
Potatoes	(48 pounds)($.75) = $36
	$\Sigma(P^{1989}Q^{1989}) = \textbf{\$330}$

    b. The cost of the 1989 bundle at 1993 prices is:

Chicken	(24 pounds)($7) = $168
Shoes	(6 pairs)($20) = $120
Shirts	(9)($15) = $135
Potatoes	(48 pounds)($1.50) = $72
	$\Sigma(P^{1993}Q^{1989}) = \textbf{\$495}$

    c. The CPI value for 1989 is **100** because 1989 is the base year.
    d. The CPI value for 1993 is:

$$\frac{\Sigma(P^{1993}Q^{1989})}{\Sigma(P^{1989}Q^{1989})} \times 100 = \frac{\$495}{\$330} \times 100 = \textbf{150}$$

4. a. $(150 - 100)/100 = 50/100 = \textbf{50\%}$
    b. $(200 - 100)/100 = 100/100 = \textbf{100\%}$
    c. $(90 - 100)/100 = -10/100 = \textbf{--10\%}$
    d. $(100 - 100)/100 = 0/100 = \textbf{0\%}$
    e. $(500 - 100)/100 = 400/100 = \textbf{400\%}$

5. a. $(110 - 100)/100 = 10/100 = \textbf{10\%}$
    b. $(220 - 200)/200 = 20/200 = \textbf{10\%}$
    c. $(160 - 200)/200 = -40/200 = \textbf{--20\%}$
    d. $(75 - 125)/125 = -50/125 = \textbf{--40\%}$
    e. $(310 - 300)/300 = 10/300 = \textbf{3.3\%}$

CHAPTER 9

Unemployment and Inflation: Their Consequences

Chapter 8 introduced the concepts of unemployment and inflation, and explained how unemployment rates are measured and price indexes are constructed in the United States. Both inflation and unemployment are economic "evils" that plague all nations. In this chapter, we explore in depth the actual consequences of unemployment and inflation.

CHAPTER OUTLINE

I. Consequences of Unemployment
   A. Loss of Output and Income
      1. The most obvious consequence of unemployment is the associated loss of output.
         a. **Potential output (or potential GDP)** is the amount of output an economy produces when there is full employment.
         b. The **output gap** is the difference between potential output and actual output. When the output gap is positive—when actual output is less than potential output—the economy is not at full employment and there is cyclical unemployment.
      2. **Okun's law** estimates the relationship between the size of the output gap and the unemployment rate. The relationship is expressed in the equation:

$$\left(\frac{\text{Potential GDP} - \text{Actual GDP}}{\text{Actual GDP}} \right) \times 100 = 2.5 \, (U - 5.5\%)$$

Okun's law indicates that each 1 percent increase in the unemployment rate (U) above the natural rate of unemployment (assumed to be 5.5 percent in the equation) causes an output gap of 2.5 percent.
   B. Distribution of the Impact of Increased Unemployment
      1. The unemployment rate of blacks is typically double that of whites, so a 1 percent increase in the white unemployment rate is associated with a 2 percent rise in the black unemployment rate.
      2. Teenage unemployment rates are higher than the unemployment rates of older workers. Greater unemployment hits the young harder, and black teenagers are hit hardest.
   C. Other Consequences of Unemployment
      1. Social problems—crime, mental health problems, and the like—rise with unemployment.
      2. Unemployment reduces the tax base of states and localities and therefore reduces funds to support public services.

3. Because smaller output lowers profit, higher unemployment leads to less investment and leaves the economy with a lower capital stock. Because of unemployment, some workers fail to receive on-the-job training and do not acquire the skills that increase productivity. Together, these consequences leave potential GDP smaller because of the unemployment.

II. Consequences of Inflation
   A. Impact on the Distribution of Income and Wealth
      1. The effect of inflation depends on how well the inflation has been anticipated and the adaptation to the inflation.
         a. The **real interest rate**, which is the difference between the actual (nominal) interest rate and the rate of inflation, determines the financial outcome between lenders and borrowers. The higher the real interest rate, the greater the reward to lenders and the greater the cost to borrowers.
         b. The real interest rate is influenced by the rate of inflation and how nominal interest rates have been adjusted for the inflation.
            i. If inflation increases and the nominal interest rate does not rise by an equal amount, the real interest rate declines. Lenders lose and borrowers gain because of the inflation in this case. This is most likely to occur in the early stages of inflation when the inflation is unexpected.
            ii. If inflation increases and the nominal interest rate rises by an amount equal to the extra inflation, the real interest rate is not changed by the inflation and the relationship between lenders and borrowers is not influenced.
            iii. If interest rates rise by more than the additional inflation, real interest rates increase, to the benefit of lenders and the detriment of borrowers. This is most likely to occur when inflation is being reduced and during deflations, that is, periods of falling prices.
      2. **Indexation** refers to the practice of using escalator clauses in contracts in order to reduce the redistributive effects of inflation.
   B. Impact on Long-Term Economic Growth
      1. Many economists, including John Maynard Keynes, have argued that inflation stimulates economic growth because it is believed to increase profits and favor debtors. Because firms finance investment with profits and debt, investment and economic growth supposedly increase with economic growth.
      2. Most economists today believe that inflation harms economic growth.
         a. Inflation benefits debtors only if inflation is continually underestimated. But the experience during the last 50 years indicates that eventually markets and institutions adapt to inflation and the benefits to profits and debtors are eliminated.
         b. Higher inflation typically means more variable inflation. A less predictable environment makes long-term commitments such as investment in new factories and technologies riskier and less attractive.
         c. Because lenders are hurt by unexpected inflation, inflation makes bonds and other debt instruments used to finance investment less attractive to lenders. Funds instead flow into the purchase of assets like gold and real estate, which do not contribute to economic growth.
         d. Economies with inflation often find their governments alternating between restrictive, inflation-fighting policies and expansionary, employment-inducing policies. Unstable policies like this contribute to uncertainty and hinder investment.
   C. Impact on the Nation's Resource Allocation
      1. Inflation induces people to do things that are wasteful for the economy even though they may benefit the individual.
         a. Because inflation reduces the purchasing power of money, individuals make more frequent trips to the banks to reduce their holdings of cash. More severe inflation results in more extreme but similar actions to avoid the effects of the inflation. These evasive actions are called "shoe-leather" costs.
         b. Inflation makes long-term commitments more risky. Long-term contracts such as labor agreements and loans are avoided in order to escape the uncertainty. As a result, greater effort is devoted to the more frequent negotiations involved in making contracts. This is wasteful.

2. The extent of these inflation-induced inefficiencies is positively related to the amount of inflation. When inflation rates are high, these costs become quite significant.

HINTS AND HELP

1. Winners and Losers Who wins and who loses when there is inflation depends fundamentally on the extent to which the inflation is expected. If inflation is unexpected, lenders are hurt because they have signed contracts that permit the borrower to repay the loan with a bundle of dollars that has lost some of its purchasing power.

If the inflation is accurately anticipated, the lender can raise the interest rate enough to ensure that the bundle of money that is returned gives the lender a real return that is attractive and satisfactory.

FILL IN THE BLANK

potential

1. The output level that an economy produces at full employment is called _____ output.

output

2. When there is unemployment, the _____ gap is positive.

Okun's law

3. The functional relationship between the output gap and the unemployment rate is called _____.

twice

4. Typically, the unemployment rate for blacks is _____ as high as the unemployment rate for whites.

indexation

5. Automatically adjusting wages and other payments to changes in the price level is called _____.

deflation

6. A period of falling prices is called _____.

real

7. The _____ rate of interest is the nominal rate of interest minus the rate of inflation.

borrowers

8. Unexpected inflation typically benefits _____.

hinders

9. In the opinion of most economists today, inflation _____ economic growth.

individuals, society

10. "Shoe-leather" costs involve actions to avoid the effects of inflation that are beneficial to _____ but wasteful to _____.

TRUE OR FALSE

_____ 1. The cost of unemployment is spread evenly over society.

_____ 2. As an economy falls into a recession, its output gap grows.

_____ 3. The output gap and the unemployment rate are positively related.

_____ 4. Current unemployment can have no impact on future levels of potential output.

_____ 5. The relationship between lenders and borrowers is not changed by inflation if the nominal interest rate stays the same when inflation begins.

_____ 6. Lenders gain when the real rate of interest rises.

_____ 7. The indexation of Social Security payments means Social Security payments rise as the price level rises.

_____ 8. Higher inflation rates make long-term investment more attractive.

_____ 9. Evidence indicates that inflation induces the economy to be more efficient.

_____ 10. Stop-and-go macroeconomic policies are detrimental to economic growth.

MULTIPLE CHOICE

Use the following version of Okun's law to answer Questions 1 and 2.

$$\left(\frac{\text{Potential GDP} - \text{Actual GDP}}{\text{Actual GDP}}\right) \times 100 = 2\,(U - 5\%)$$

1. The natural unemployment rate equals:
   A. 2 percent.
   B. 5 percent.
   C. 10 percent.
   D. none of the above.

2. If the unemployment rate equals 5 percent, the output gap equals:
   A. 0 percent.
   B. 2 percent.
   C. 5 percent.
   D. 10 percent.

3. Inflation imposes a "tax" on:
   A. interest rates.
   B. all income.
   C. stocks and bonds.
   D. money.

4. Lenders lose when inflation is unexpected because:
   A. the nominal interest rate is not high enough to offset the impact of the higher prices in reducing the value of the principal lent.
   B. the real interest rate falls when inflation is unexpectedly higher.
   C. they are repaid with dollars that have less purchasing power and the interest rate has not increased sufficiently to offset it.
   D. All alternatives are correct.

5. A potential cost of inflation is:
   A. more frequent contract negotiations.
   B. excessive economic growth.
   C. increases in investment spending.
   D. greater economic efficiency.

6. Which of the following is an example of "shoe-leather" costs?
   A. increased production of shoes as individual incomes rise because of inflation
   B. effort devoted to writing, publishing, and reading books on avoiding damage of inflation
   C. increased tax revenue that governments receive caused by higher inflation
   D. extra cost of assets like gold and real estate caused by additional inflation

7. If the rate of inflation rose from 5 percent to 8 percent and the nominal rate of interest increased from 6 percent to 10 percent:
   A. lenders would lose.
   B. borrowers would lose.
   C. borrowers and lenders would come out even.
   D. there is insufficient information to know who loses.

8. Which of the following groups is most likely to suffer if unexpected inflation occurs?
   A. the government
   B. the elderly
   C. businesses
   D. the young

9. Unexpected deflation helps:
   A. lenders.
   B. borrowers.
   C. the government.
   D. everyone.

10. Lenders are most likely to gain from inflation when the inflation is:
   A. just beginning.
   B. starting to be reduced.
   C. completely and fully anticipated.
   D. reflected exactly in interest rates.

PROBLEMS

1. Each of the following describes a particular occurrence involving inflation and nominal interest rates. In the space provided, identify whether lenders, borrowers, or neither group would benefit from the situation described.

   a. Inflation rises from 4 percent to 6 percent and nominal interest rates rise from 7 percent to 8 percent.
   _____

   b. Inflation rises from 2 percent to 5 percent and nominal interest rates rise from 6 percent to 9 percent.
   _____

   c. Inflation falls from 10 percent to 6 percent while nominal interest rates fall from 12 percent to 10 percent. _____

   d. Inflation falls from 7 percent to 5 percent while nominal interest rates fall from 10 percent to 6 percent.
   _____

Answers

TRUE OR FALSE

1. False. Unemployment hits minorities, the less educated, and the young more than other groups.

2. True. As an economy falls into a recession, its output declines. As a result the gap between potential output and actual output—the output gap—grows.

3. True. Okun's law shows that for every 1 percent rise of the unemployment rate above the natural rate, the output gap grows by 2.5 percent.

4. False. Unemployment frequently reduces investment spending and the amount of on-the-job training received by the labor force. Both of these consequences would cause potential output in the future to be smaller.

5. False. The financial relationship between lenders and borrowers is determined by the real interest rate. If the nominal interest rate remains the same as inflation begins, the real interest rate falls, which benefits the borrower.

6. True. Lenders receive a higher reward for making a loan when the real interest rate rises.

7. True. Indexation links Social Security payments to the Consumer Price Index. As the price level rises, Social Security payments rise.

8. False. Higher inflation makes it difficult to predict future prices. This unpredictability makes long-term commitments more risky and less attractive.

9. False. Inflation creates inefficiencies as individuals devote more of their resources to avoiding the damage of inflation and fewer resources to the production of society's goods and services.

10. True. Stop-and-go economic policies create uncertainty about the future and make the long-term commitments that are necessary for growth less attractive.

MULTIPLE CHOICE

1. B. The natural rate of unemployment is the percentage in the parenthesis with U, the symbol for the actual unemployment rate. Only if the actual unemployment rate is above 5 percent is there a positive output gap.

2. A. If the actual unemployment rate (U) is 5 percent, U – 5 % equals 5% – 5% or zero. This makes the right-hand side of the equation zero, which makes the left-hand side zero. The output gap would equal 0 percent.

3. D. Inflation imposes a tax on money (checking accounts and currency) because inflation erodes the purchasing power of money and there is no way to offset this erosion except by holding less money.

4. D. Lenders lose when there is unexpected inflation because borrowers are able to pay back the loan with less valuable dollars. Because interest rates are not sufficiently increased when there is unexpected inflation to offset this impact, the real interest rate falls.

5. A. Because inflation creates uncertainties about the future, people frequently choose shorter-term contracts to avoid being caught in an unfavorable situation. Shorter contracts mean more frequent negotiations.

6. B. "Shoe-leather" costs refer to the waste of resources that occurs as individuals attempt to diminish the damage caused by inflation. Without inflation the book's author, the book publisher, and the reader would use their time and resources in pursuits that are more valuable to society.

7. B. Borrowers would lose because the rise in the interest rate exceeds the rise in the rate of inflation, which means that the real rate of interest has increased.

8. B. Because the elderly are typically lenders, they lose when there is unexpected inflation. The other groups are more likely to be borrowers.

9. A. Unexpected deflation helps lenders because they have their loans repaid with dollars more valuable than the dollars lent.

10. B. Lenders are more likely to gain when inflation is just being reduced for that is when it is most likely that the real interest rate rises (as inflation declines more than nominal interest rates).

PROBLEMS

1. a. **Borrowers gain**. The 2 percent higher inflation combined with a 1 percent higher interest rate means the real interest rate has fallen by 1 percent. This benefits borrowers.

   b. **Neither gains**. A 3 percent rise in inflation is matched by a 3 percent rise in nominal interest rates, which leaves real interest rates the same. Neither lenders nor borrowers benefit.

   c. **Lenders gain**. The 4 percent lower inflation rate is combined with a decline in the nominal interest rate of only 2 percent. This increases the real interest rate, benefiting lenders.

   d. **Borrowers gain**. The 2 percent fall in the inflation rate and the 4 percent fall in nominal interest rates lowers the real interest rate by 2 percent. This benefits borrowers.

CHAPTER 10

Measuring the Macroeconomy

Chapters 8 and 9 explained the measurement and consequences of unemployment and inflation. This chapter explores the measurement of another key gauge of an economy's performance: its output and income. National income accounting, the formal name given to defining and calculating an economy's output and income, was developed so that policymakers would have a better idea of how the economy was performing. Without this knowledge it would be difficult to know what problems exist and what policies are needed. This chapter also explains how these measures of the economy's output and income must be adjusted to gain a more accurate impression of how well people in the economy are living. Finally, real gross domestic product is described and calculated.

CHAPTER OUTLINE

I. Types of Variables
   A. A flow variable is a variable that is measured per time unit (for example, per week, per year). Gross domestic product is a flow variable. It is usually measured on an annual basis (that is, per year).
   B. A stock variable is a variable that is measured at a point in time. Population and assets are stock variables.

II. National Income Accounting
   A. **National income accounting** refers to the procedures for measuring an economy's aggregate output and income and their components.
   B. An economy's performance can be monitored by a flow-of-output approach or a flow-of-income approach.
      1. The flow-of-output approach measures the rate at which the economy is producing goods and services.
      2. The flow-of-income approach measures the rate at which income is being earned by resources owners.
      3. As the circular flow model shows, there is a tight relationship between the flow of output and the flow of income. As households sell the services of their factors of production to firms, they earn income. In turn, that income is spent to buy the output that the firms produce with these factors of production. The total value of the income earned equals the total value of the output sold.
      4. If the flow of output changes, it changes the flow of income in the same direction. If the flow of spending on output changes, it causes the flow of output and income to change. It is such changes in expenditures and incomes that create the economic fluctuations observed in the real world.

III. The Flow-of-Output Approach—**Gross Domestic Product (GDP)**
   A. The flow-of-output approach computes the value of the final goods and services that an economy produces in a year.

1. Final goods and services are those in the hands of their ultimate users; final goods and services are not processed further and resold.

2. The value of intermediate goods and services is not counted directly. **Intermediate goods** are used up in the production of other outputs that are sold. Intermediate goods are not included in GDP; to do so would let them be counted twice—once as an intermediate good and once again as part of the value of the final good produced from the intermediate good.

3. Gross domestic product (GDP) recently replaced gross national product (GNP) as the primary measure of the U.S. output. The difference between the two measures involves the output and income of resources owned by citizens of one country that is produced and earned in another country. GDP counts the output and income in the country where they are earned; GNP allocates the output and income to the country that owns the resources with which the output is produced.

B. There are four kinds or categories of final goods that make up GDP:

1. **Consumption goods (C)** is the largest category of final goods. It includes everything consumers buy except new homes, which are counted as part of investment. There are three kinds of consumption goods:
   a. durable goods
   b. nondurable goods
   c. services

2. **Gross investment (I)** is the value of all new *private* capital goods produced in one year. It is called "gross" because it includes the value of the capital goods bought to replace those that have worn out during the year. **Net investment** counts only the capital goods that represent a net addition to the economy's stock of capital goods. Net investment equals gross investment minus depreciation. Gross investment can be divided into two categories:
   a. **Fixed investment** includes the value of nonresidential structures (that is, factories and office buildings), durable equipment (that is, machines), and residential structures.
   b. **Inventory investment** is the change in the inventories of goods held by businesses. If a good has been produced but not sold by the end of the year, it is included in GDP as part of inventory investment.

3. **Government purchases (G)** measures the amount that governments—federal, state, and local—spend to provide their citizens with the goods and services the government provides.
   a. This category does not include **government transfer payments** because transfer payments do not represent a cost of producing any good or service.
   b. The government does not make a distinction between the production of investment goods and goods for consumption. Some of the things the government produces—highways and university buildings, for example—are actually investment goods.

4. **Net exports (X – M)** measures the difference between the value of domestically produced goods and services sold abroad and the value of the goods and services the United States buys from foreign producers. Because GDP is an output measure, U.S. exports are included because the United States produced them. By similar reasoning, U.S. imports are excluded because we did not produce them. The net exports of the United States were negative each year from 1982 to 1992.

IV. The Flow-of-Income Approach

A. Measuring the flow of income paid to resource owners is a second way to calculate GDP. Because the flow of dollars in the upper loop of the circular flow—the flow of output—equals the flow of dollars in the lower loop—the flow of income—these are alternative ways of arriving at the same number. The flow of income is also equal to the difference between the revenues of all firms and the amounts that the firms are spending on intermediate goods.

B. The kinds of income that make up the flow of income are:

1. Compensation to Employees: This includes the wages paid workers as well as the cost of fringe benefits and payroll taxes.

2. Interest: Only interest paid by private borrowers to lenders is counted. Interest paid by the government is considered a transfer payment.

3. Rent: This is the value of the amounts paid to property owners for the use of their property. Rent of apartments as well as land is included.

4. Proprietor's Income: This includes the salaries of the owners of the business as well as the profit of the business. Proprietorships and partnerships pay taxes on the business' profit as part of the owners' personal income tax.

5. Corporate Profit: This is the total profit earned by corporations. It includes the amount paid to the government in corporate income taxes, the amount of dividends paid to stockholders, and the part of the profit kept by the corporation (which is called retained earnings).

C. Although in principle the flow of income should exactly equal the flow of output, in practice it does not. There are two uses of a firm's receipts that are not income to anyone.

1. **Depreciation**: As mentioned earlier, depreciation is simply the value of the firm's capital that has been consumed in the year. While it is a cost to the firm, it is no one's income.

2. Indirect Business Taxes: When consumers pay for a product, often a part of what they pay is taxes on that product. These indirect taxes are, again, not part of anyone's income.

V. Other National Income Accounts

A. **Net Domestic Product (NDP)** is the same as GDP except that it includes net investment rather than gross investment. Net domestic product equals gross domestic product minus depreciation. Net domestic product is considered a better measure of an economy's output but, because of the uncertainty associated with the calculation of depreciation, gross domestic product is the measure more often used.

B. **National Income (NY)** subtracts from NDP the indirect business taxes paid by business. National income is the income actually paid to resources.

C. **Personal Income (PY)** is the income actually received by people in the economy. The retained earnings of corporations and the income taxes paid by corporations on their profits are never received by any individual in an economy. The amounts paid by employers and employees in Social Security taxes are also never received by the people who earned the income. These items are subtracted from national income. Added in are transfer payments—primarily Social Security payments, interest on government debt, and welfare payments—because these are income to people even though they are not earned.

D. **Disposable Income (Y_d)** is the income households have available to spend or save. It equals personal income minus income taxes.

VI. Nominal GDP and Real GDP

A. **Nominal GDP** measures the value of each year's output using the prices at which the output was sold in that year. Nominal GDP can change from one year to the next because of output changes or price changes.

B. **Real GDP** starts with nominal GDP and removes the effects of price changes. Real GDP changes only if the output of goods and services of an economy changes. It does not change when the price level changes.

C. The **GDP deflator** measures changes in the prices of all goods and services contained in GDP since the base year. Currently, the GDP deflator has a base year of 1987, which means the value of the index for 1987 is 100. If the GDP deflator value for 1993 is 130, it means that prices in 1993 are 30 percent higher than they were in 1987.

D. To calculate real GDP for 1993 use the formula:

$$\text{real 1993 GDP} = \frac{\text{nominal 1993 GDP}}{\text{GDP deflator value for 1993}} \times 100$$

The answer tells you what 1993 GDP would have been if the prices in 1993 had been the same as they were in 1987 (the base year).

VII. GDP and Economic Well-Being
   A. GDP does not measure all output produced in an economy. Generally, output is counted as part of GDP only if the output is sold in a market and if that market transaction is reported in some official way. Two examples of uncounted output are:
      1. Nonmarket Activity: Output produced for the consumption of the producer—such as mowing your own lawn—is output but does not show up in GDP because you do not pay yourself for doing your own work.
      2. Underground Economy: Illegal goods and services or legal goods and services sold but not reported in order to avoid taxation make up the underground economy.
   B. GDP is an imperfect measure of how well-off people are in an economy because it does not correctly account for items that influence one's economic well-being. Examples are:
      1. Leisure Time: Leisure time is obviously valuable to people but its value is not included in GDP. Exclusion of leisure time makes GDP an underestimate of true economic well-being.
      2. "Bads" in GDP: GDP makes no distinction between outputs people genuinely like and outputs that are required but not liked. Cleaning up a natural disaster or fighting a war are activities that add to GDP but are not liked. This factor makes GDP look larger than is justified in terms of economic well-being.
      3. Environmental Damage: Damage to the environment and other adverse events associated with the production of goods and services are not subtracted from the value of the output produced. For this reason GDP again overestimates well-being.
   C. Net economic welfare (NEW) is a measure of economic well-being constructed by economists William Nordhaus and James Tobin. It adjust GDP for some of the factors listed previously. For example, it adds to the official GDP a measure of the value of leisure time and subtracts from it an estimate of environmental damage.

HINTS AND HELP

1. Final versus Intermediate Goods   GDP directly measures only the value of final goods. Intermediate goods and services are not counted directly. For example, if GDP included the value of steel the economy produced as well as the value of the car produced from the steel, the steel would be counted twice—once as steel and again as part of the value of the car. By counting only final goods, intermediate goods are included but only indirectly as part of the value of the final goods.

To determine whether something is an intermediate good or a final good, ask: "Is this going to be used up in the production of something else that will be sold?" If the answer is "Yes," the good is an intermediate good and should not be included in GDP.

2. Investment versus Intermediate Goods   Intermediate goods and services are not included when calculating the value of GDP. Investment goods are a kind of final good and are counted directly in GDP. But investment goods and intermediate goods seem very much alike. Both are used to produce other goods.

The distinguishing characteristic of an intermediate good is that it becomes part of or is used up when producing the final good. Fertilizer is consumed when producing wheat. The same fertilizer cannot be used again. Steel becomes part of the automobile. Fertilizer and steel are intermediate goods, and their sales are not included directly in GDP.

Investment goods, although used to produce other goods and services, are not totally consumed during the production process. The farmer's tractor is used to produce wheat, but the tractor is still there after the wheat is grown and can be used again the following year. The tractor is an investment good, and the value of new tractors produced by an economy is included directly in GDP.

3. Personal Income, National Income, and All That   It may be difficult to keep straight all the different measures of national output and income. Some memorization is required, but there is a certain logic to what is included in each category.

Gross Domestic Product: Because it is *gross*, it includes gross investment. All final goods and services are included in GDP.

Net Domestic Product: Because it is *net*, it includes only net investment. Depreciation is removed from GDP to yield NDP.

National Income: This is the *nation's income*, so all income that has been earned is included. It would be equal to GDP, except that depreciation and indirect business taxes are in GDP but really do not represent any income earned by resources. Because depreciation has already been subtracted to arrive at NDP, subtracting indirect business taxes from NDP yields national income.

Personal Income: This is all the income that goes to *persons*. Because a corporation is not a person, any income not paid by the corporation to its stockholders (corporate taxes and retained earning) is subtracted, as well as any income that individuals must pay to the government first (Social Security taxes). Added, however, are transfer payments because they are income to their recipients.

Disposable Income: This is the income people have available to *dispose* of as they wish. It equals the income that people have received—personal income—less income taxes.

4. Real versus Nominal GDP   It is important to know whether nominal GDP has increased because of higher prices or higher output. To the extent it is caused by higher output, the country is better off. To the extent it is caused by higher prices, the country is not. The calculation of real GDP removes the impact of price level changes and reveals the changes in nominal GDP that are caused by higher output only.

Do not let the equation for calculating real GDP intimidate you; what the formula does is rather simple. The question the formula answers is: If prices in, say, 1993 had been the same as they were in the base year, what would 1993 GDP have been? If the GDP deflator value for 1993 is 125, it means that prices in 1993 are 25 percent higher than they were in the base year, 1987. If prices in 1993 had been the same as they were in 1987, 1993 GDP would be 25 percent lower. All the formula does is reduce 1993 GDP by that 25 percent.

FILL IN THE BLANK

stock	1. A _____ variable is one that is measured at a point in time.
Intermediate	2. _____ goods are processed to produce other goods and services that are sold.
consumption	3. The largest category of final goods and services included in GDP is _____ goods and services.
net investment	4. Gross investment after depreciation has been subtracted is called _____.
indirect business taxes	5. National income is gross domestic product less depreciation and _____.
disposable income	6. The amount of income that people have available to spend or save is called _____.
Nominal	7. _____ GDP changes because of either output or price changes.
GDP deflator	8. The _____ measures the behavior of the prices of the items contained in GDP.

underground 9. The production of illegal goods and services is part of the _____ _____ economy.

government purchases 10. The value of new roads and other investment goods produced by the government is counted as part of _____.

TRUE OR FALSE

_____ 1. Net investment can never be negative.

_____ 2. Exports are part of an economy's GDP.

_____ 3. Because it is not sold, the output of the government is ignored in GDP.

_____ 4. New houses are counted as part of investment.

_____ 5. Social Security benefits are not part of GDP but are part of personal income.

_____ 6. Only final goods and services are included in GDP.

_____ 7. Profit is not part of national income.

_____ 8. If I pay you to iron my shirts and you pay me to iron yours, GDP rises.

_____ 9. If a firm produces output that is not sold it is not included in GDP.

_____ 10. Disposable income is personal income less income taxes.

MULTIPLE CHOICE

1. The term "national income" refers to:
   A. the total income of the government.
   B. the income earned by resource owners.
   C. the value of the economy's intermediate goods.
   D. the value of the resources in an economy.

2. Which of the following is a flow variable?
   A. money supply
   B. land
   C. debt
   D. investment

3. If imports are greater than exports:
   A. GDP is negative.
   B. net investment is negative.
   C. GDP is less than $C + I + G$.
   D. national income is greater than GDP.

4. In the circular flow diagram, which of the following is correct?
   A. taxes equal government spending
   B. imports equal exports
   C. value of output of final goods equals the income earned
   D. profit equals zero

5. If a firm increases output by $1,000 on December 31, 1992, but the output is not sold until January 3, 1993:
   A. GDP in 1992 increased by $1,000.
   B. GDP in 1993 increased by $1,000.
   C. GDP in both 1992 and 1993 increased by $1,000.
   D. GDP in both 1992 and 1993 increased, so that the total increase in the two years totals $1,000.

6. If gross investment and depreciation each increase by $10,000:
   A. both GDP and NDP increase by $10,000.
   B. GDP increases by $10,000 but NDP does not change.
   C. NDP increases by $10,000 but GDP does not change.
   D. neither GDP nor NDP increases.

7. If the government spends $2,000,000,000 to replace highways destroyed in an earthquake in San Francisco, what is the impact on GDP?
   A. There is no impact on GDP because the expenditures are only replacing something that once was there.
   B. GDP rises by $2,000,000,000 because the new highways are newly produced final goods.
   C. GDP falls by $2,000,000,000 because spending $2,000,000,000 on the highways means $2,000,000,000 worth of other output must be sacrificed.
   D. There is insufficient information provided to answer the question.

8. GDP counts only final goods:
   A. to avoid counting the value of intermediate goods twice.
   B. because those are the only kind of goods that an economy actually produces.
   C. because these are the only goods that have a market price.
   D. because these are the only goods that a country actually consumes.

9. Leisure time:
   A. is included in GDP because it is something of value.
   B. is included in GDP because it is something the economy produces.
   C. is not included in GDP because it is an intermediate good.
   D. is not included in GDP because it is a nonmarket good.

10. Net Economic Welfare:
    A. adjusts GDP for changes in output.
    B. attempts to measure economic well-being.
    C. measures the purchasing power of transfer payments.
    D. is GDP less depreciation.

PROBLEMS

1. The following information has been gathered from the economy of Caines. Fill in the missing information by using the data available.

$$
\begin{aligned}
\text{Gross Domestic Product} &= \$700 \\
\text{income taxes} &= \$\ 50 \\
\text{corporate income taxes} &= \$\ 10 \\
\text{Social Security taxes} &= \$\ 30 \\
\text{transfer payments} &= \$\ 25 \\
\text{corporate retained earnings} &= \$\ 10 \\
\text{depreciation} &= \$\ 50 \\
\text{indirect business taxes} &= \$\ 25 \\
\text{National Income} &= \underline{\quad} \\
\text{Disposable Income} &= \underline{\quad} \\
\text{Personal Income} &= \underline{\quad} \\
\text{Net Domestic Product} &= \underline{\quad}
\end{aligned}
$$

2. a. Calculate real GDP for each year using the available information.

	1987	1988	1989	1990	1991	1992
Nominal GDP: (billions)	$3,800	$5,000	$5,700	$7,000	$9,000	$10,000
GDP Deflator: (base year: 1987)	100	125	150	175	200	250
Real GDP: (billions)	_____	_____	_____	_____	_____	_____

b. Plot the values for real GDP for each year in Figure 10.1.

FIGURE 10.1

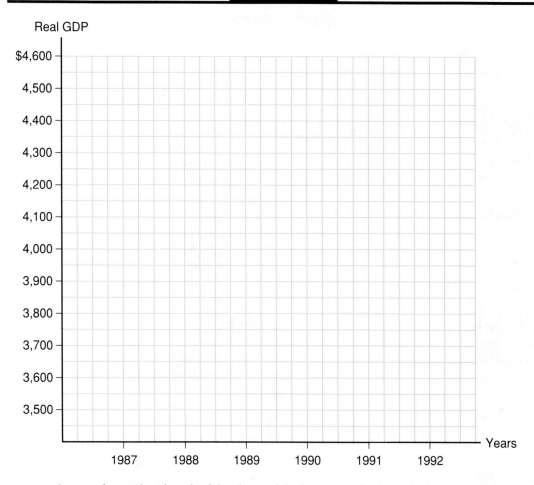

c. On your figure identify each of the phases of the business cycle: the peak, the contraction, the trough, and the expansion.

3. For each of the following, indicate whether the good is a consumption good or service (C), an investment good (I), a government purchase (G), an export (X), an import (M), or an intermediate good (T) by putting the appropriate letter next to the item:
   a. pair of glasses for student _____
   b. pair of goggles for soldier _____
   c. feed for pigs _____
   d. new post office building _____
   e. new copy machine for office _____
   f. tuition at private high school _____
   g. steel from Germany used in U.S. car _____
   h. U.S. wheat shipped to Russia _____
   i. new automobile bought by family _____
   j. gasoline used by taxi _____

Answers

TRUE OR FALSE

1. False. Net investment is gross investment less depreciation. If an economy consumes more capital (depreciation) than it produces (gross investment), net investment is negative.

2. True. The value of all the output a country produces is included in GDP, including that part of the output shipped to other countries.

3. False. Included in GDP is the amount that the government spends producing the goods and services it provides. It is called government purchases.

4. True. New houses are considered part of investment.

5. True. Because Social Security benefits are a transfer payment, they are not counted as part of government purchases. But they are added in when personal income is calculated because they are part of the income of individuals.

6. True. GDP includes only the value of final goods and services. Intermediate goods and services are not counted directly in GDP.

7. False. Profit is one of the kinds of income that make up national income.

8. True. Because nonmarket output is not included in GDP, ironing your own shirts adds nothing to GDP. But paying someone to iron your shirts is a market transaction and therefore is added to GDP.

9. False. Inventories include the value of goods that have been produced but not yet sold. Changes in inventories are part of private investment, which is part of the GDP.

10. True. Disposable income is the amount of income people have to spend or save. It equals the income that the people receive (personal income) less what must be paid in income taxes.

MULTIPLE CHOICE

1. B. National Income is the total of all income paid to resource owners in a year.

2. D. Investment is measured per time period, usually a year, which means it is a flow variable. The other variables are measured at a moment in time and are stock variables.

3. C. If imports (M) are greater than exports (X), net exports are negative. Because GDP equals $C + I + G + (X - M)$, if $(X - M)$ is negative, $C + I + G$ would be greater than GDP.

4. C. In the circular flow model, the upper loop—value of final goods produced—equals the lower loop—the total income earned by resource owners.

5. A. Output is counted in the year it is produced, not when it is sold. Thus, GDP in 1992 was increased by $1,000.

6. B. GDP includes the value of all investment goods a country produces. NDP includes only the value of the new machines that represent a net addition to the economy's capital.

7. B. The new highways are new output even though they are replacing highways that were destroyed. GDP rises.

8. A. Only final goods are included in GDP in order to avoid counting intermediate goods twice. The value of intermediate goods is counted indirectly in the value of the final goods.

9. D. Because leisure time is not bought, even though it has value, it is not included in GDP.

10. B. Net Economic Welfare adjusts GDP in various ways to more accurately measure economic well-being.

PROBLEMS

1. The national income accounts for the country of Caines are:

$$
\begin{array}{rcl}
\text{Gross Domestic Product} & = & \$700 \\
\text{minus depreciation} & = & \$\ 50 \\
\text{equals Net Domestic Product} & = & \textbf{\$650} \\
\text{minus indirect business taxes} & = & \$\ 25 \\
\text{equals National Income} & = & \textbf{\$625} \\
\text{minus corporate income taxes} & = & \$\ 10 \\
\text{minus corporate retained earnings} & = & \$\ 10 \\
\text{minus Social Security taxes} & = & \$\ 30 \\
\text{plus transfer payments} & = & \$\ 25 \\
\text{equals Personal Income} & = & \textbf{\$600} \\
\text{minus income taxes} & = & \$\ 50 \\
\text{equals Disposable Income} & = & \textbf{\$550}
\end{array}
$$

2. a.

$$1987\text{: } \frac{\$3,800}{100} \times 100 = \textbf{\$3,800}$$

$$1988\text{: } \frac{\$5,000}{125} \times 100 = \textbf{\$4,000}$$

$$1989\text{: } \frac{\$5,700}{150} \times 100 = \textbf{\$3,800}$$

$$1990\text{: } \frac{\$7,000}{175} \times 100 = \textbf{\$4,000}$$

$$1991\text{: } \frac{\$9,000}{200} \times 100 = \textbf{\$4,500}$$

$$1992\text{: } \frac{\$10,000}{250} \times 100 = \textbf{\$4,000}$$

b. See Figure 10.2.

FIGURE 10.2

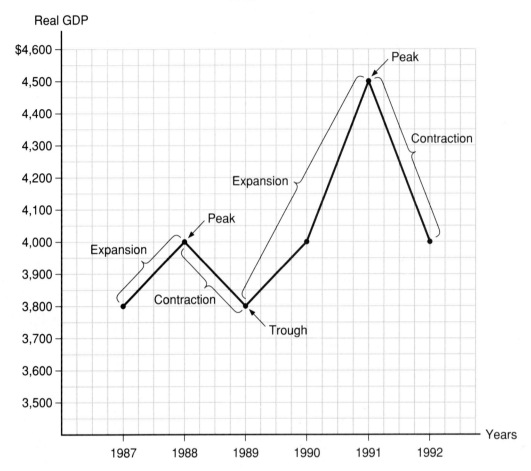

The peak of the business cycle is the point at which output reaches its maximum value. This occurs in 1988 and in 1991. A contraction occurs when real GDP falls. This occurs from 1988 to 1989 and from 1991 to 1992. A trough is when output reaches its low point. This occurred in 1989. An expansion is when real GDP grows. This occurs from 1987 to 1988 and from 1989 to 1991.

3. a. pair of glasses for student _____ *C* _____
    b. pair of goggles for soldier _____ *G* _____
    c. feed for pigs _____ *T* _____
    d. new post office building _____ *G* _____
    e. new copy machine for office _____ *I* _____
    f. tuition at private high school _____ *C* _____
    g. steel from Germany used in U.S. car _____ *M* _____
    h. U.S wheat shipped to Russia _____ *X* _____
    i. new automobile bought by family _____ *C* _____
    j. gasoline used by taxi _____ *T* _____

CHAPTER 11

The Aggregate Supply—Aggregate Demand Model of Macroeconomics: Introduction

Chapters 8, 9, and 10 have introduced and discussed the key measures of an economy's performance—unemployment, inflation, and gross domestic product. This chapter begins the presentation of the macroeconomic framework economists have developed to explain the behavior of an economy. This chapter introduces an important macroeconomic tool—aggregate supply and aggregate demand—and uses it to discuss macroeconomic issues that will be explained in detail in later chapters. The aggregate demand and aggregate supply curves are used to describe and explain the major economic events and policies occurring since 1960, including the supply-side policies of the Reagan and Bush administrations.

CHAPTER OUTLINE

I. Basic Aggregate Demand–Aggregate Supply Model
   A. An **aggregate demand curve** shows the relationship between an economy's price level and the amount of real output demanded, other things held constant. The aggregate demand curve is downward sloping because:
      1. A lower price level increases the purchasing power of each individual's money holdings, which increases the amount of output demanded.
      2. A lower price level makes U.S. goods more attractive to foreign buyers and increases the amount of U.S. output demanded.
      3. A lower price level reduces the demand for credit, lowering the interest rate and raising the demand for interest-sensitive goods.
   B. An **aggregate supply curve** shows the relationship between the economy's price level and the amount of output that firms in the economy would like to produce, other things held constant. It is upward sloping because, as the average level of prices rises, profits rise since many of the firms' costs are constant.
   C. The economy's equilibrium output and price level occur where the quantity of output demanded in the economy equals the amount of output firms want to produce. This is the price level and output associated with the intersection of the aggregate demand and aggregate supply curves.
   D. The equilibrium output and price level change when either the aggregate demand or aggregate supply curve shifts.
      1. Changes in equilibrium can have the following consequences:
         a. Inflation is caused by persistent increases in aggregate demand or decreases in aggregate supply.
         b. Increases in the economy's output and reductions in unemployment are caused by increases in aggregate demand or increases in aggregate supply.

      c. Decreases in the price level are caused by increases in aggregate supply or decreases in aggregate demand.

      d. Decreases in the economy's output and increases in unemployment are caused by decreases in aggregate demand or decreases in aggregate supply.

  2. Shifts in the aggregate demand curve are caused by changes in the demand for goods and services in the form of changes in consumption spending, investment spending, government spending, or net exports.

  3. Shifts in the aggregate supply curve are caused by changes in the prices of resources, the quantity of resources, and the economy's productivity. Productivity is the amount of output produced per unit of input.

E. Stabilization Policy

  1. The government sometimes attempts to influence the economy's output and rate of inflation by shifting the aggregate demand curve. These programs are called stabilization policies. There are two kinds of stabilization policies:

      a. Monetary policy involves the manipulation of the money supply, credit, and interest rates by the Federal Reserve in order to shift the aggregate demand curve.

      b. Fiscal policy involves the manipulation of the federal government's spending and taxes in order to shift the aggregate demand curve.

  2. Appropriate stabilization policies:

      a. In the Case of Unemployment

         i. Unemployment occurs when actual output is less than potential output, which means the actual unemployment rate exceeds the natural unemployment rate.

         ii. **Potential output (Y_F)** is the level of the real GDP that an economy must produce to have full employment.

         iii. When there is unemployment, the stabilization policies (monetary and fiscal policy) should be directed toward increasing aggregate demand.

      b. In the Case of Inflation

         i. When equilibrium output exceeds potential output, inflation develops.

         ii. Stabilization policies should be directed toward reducing aggregate demand.

  3. In reality, there are difficulties associated with using monetary and fiscal policies to achieve full employment without inflation.

      a. Policymakers do not know the exact shapes or locations of the aggregate demand or aggregate supply curves.

      b. Policymakers do not know what other factors might currently be shifting these curves.

      c. Policymakers do not know the level of real output associated with full employment.

II. Recent U.S. Economic History

A. The 1960s:

  1. The 1960s began with the United States in a recession. In 1964, a major income-tax cut shifted the aggregate demand curve outward and a sustained expansion of output occurred.

  2. In 1965, increases in government spending associated with the Vietnam War were financed by borrowing and not by higher taxes. This expansion in aggregate demand overheated the economy and increased the rate of inflation.

  3. By the end of the decade inflation had reached an unacceptable rate of 5 percent. A recession in 1969 did little to slow the inflation.

B. The 1970s:

  1. The decade began with an historically high rate of inflation. In August 1971, President Richard Nixon imposed wage and price controls with the goal of eliminating the expectations of inflation that were fueling actual inflation. Unfortunately, the wage–price freeze was not accompanied by decreases in aggregate demand, and therefore the inflationary pressures were not reduced.

  2. In 1973 and 1974, the United States simultaneously experienced high rates of unemployment and high rates of inflation, a situation known as **stagflation.**

a. The cause of the stagflation was a series of adverse supply shocks, that is, increases in input prices that shift the aggregate supply curve to the left. The sources of the supply shocks were oil price increases by OPEC and poor weather that increased the price of agricultural commodities.

b. When there are supply shocks, policymakers can attempt to reduce the inflation by reducing aggregate demand, but that increases unemployment even more. If aggregate demand is increased to reduce the unemployment, the already high inflation is increased. Policymakers find themselves in a no-win situation.

3. The U.S. emerged from the stagflation in 1975 and output rose through 1979.

C. The 1980s:

1. The 1980s began with a short recession combined with another OPEC oil price increase. Unhappiness with the economy was a major reason for the landslide election of Ronald Reagan in 1980. Policymakers, particularly the Federal Reserve, focused initially on inflation. A severe recession, the worst since the 1930s, followed a series of restrictive monetary policy actions that reduced aggregate demand. Inflation receded faster than most economists thought possible but unemployment rose above 10 percent.

2. By 1983, the economy began to come out of the recession. The economy entered an expansion that continued to the end of the decade. Inflation also stayed low, partly because of the reversal of some of the adverse supply shocks of the 1970s. Oil prices fell and the U.S. dollar rose (making foreign goods less expensive).

3. Regan's economic program of the 1980s was based on **supply-side economics**. This is the belief that large cuts in income tax rates raise saving and investment and shift the aggregate supply curve outward. But the large tax cuts without equal cuts in government spending resulted in large budget deficits. The desired increases in investment and productivity did not occur.

D. The 1990s:

1. The economic expansion of the 1980s continued into the first year of the 1990s with low unemployment and low inflation. However, large budget and trade deficits persisted.

2. The economic expansion of the 1980s ended in July 1990 as the United States entered a recession. The downturn was attributed primarily to a decline in consumer and business confidence.

3. The large budget deficits limited the ability to use fiscal policy, so monetary policy became the primary stabilization tool to end the recession.

HINTS AND HELP

1. Aggregate Demand and Aggregate Supply   The aggregate demand and aggregate supply models will be important tools in the next few chapters dealing with macroeconomics. They are analogous to the supply and demand models of Chapter 4, but with some subtle differences. One such difference concerns the explanation for the downward slope of the aggregate demand curve.

The aggregate demand curve is *not* downward sloping because a good is becoming less expensive relative to other goods—which is a major reason the demand curve for an individual good is downward sloping. In the aggregate, all prices are pictured as moving together.

Also, the aggregate demand curve does *not* slope downward because, with the lower prices, people's incomes can buy more—which is the other important reason an individual good's demand curve is downward sloping. In the aggregate, output prices and incomes change together. Lower prices mean proportionally smaller paychecks. A decline in the price level reduces the level of the nation's nominal income without increasing its real income.

Aggregate demand rises when all prices and incomes fall because (a) currency and other forms of money can buy more goods when prices are lower; (b) U.S. goods are cheaper to foreign buyers, whose incomes have not declined when the U.S. price level falls; and (c) interest rates fall, stimulating spending on goods sensitive to interest rates.

The aggregate supply curve is much like the supply curve for an individual firm or industry. It slopes upward because some of the firms' costs are fixed. As a result, a higher price level increases profits and generates more output.

FILL IN THE BLANK

price level

1. The aggregate demand curve shows how the amount of output demanded changes as the _____ changes.

money, savings accounts, ment bonds

2. The wealth effect is caused by the increase in the real value of and government- _____ as the price level falls, which in turn stimulates the quantity of output demanded.

rise, rise

3. Increases in aggregate demand cause the economy's price level to_____ _____ and its real output to _____.

supply

4. Changes in productivity cause the aggregate _____ _____ curve to shift.

intersect

5. Equilibrium for the economy occurs where the aggregate demand and aggregate supply curves _____.

tax cut

6. The economic expansion of the 1960s was spurred by a _____ _____ in the early years of the decade.

wage–price

7. In 1971, Richard Nixon attempted to reduce inflation by imposing a _____ freeze.

stagflation

8. When the inflation rate and the unemployment rate are both high, there is _____.

supply-side

9. The economic policies of the Reagan administration were based on _____ _____ economics.

supply shocks

10. The increases in the price of oil that occurred in the 1970s were examples of _____.

TRUE OR FALSE

_____ 1. Inflation is caused only by increases in aggregate demand.

_____ 2. Increases in the price level increase the amount of output firms in the economy want to produce, everything else the same.

_____ 3. Equilibrium output always equals potential output.

_____ 4. Stabilization policies must increase aggregate demand if they are to reduce unemployment.

_____ 5. Changes in government spending influence the economy by shifting aggregate demand.

_____ 6. Stagflation makes it easier for stabilization policies to achieve their goals.

_____ 7. During the decade of the 1980s the federal government typically had budget surpluses.

_____ 8. The 1960s were characterized by frequent periods of recession.

_____ 9. The supply-side theory asserts that personal income-tax cuts stimulate saving and investment.

_____ 10. Increases in the price of oil cause inflation by shifting the aggregate demand curve outward.

MULTIPLE CHOICE

1. A higher minimum wage would be expected to:
   A. lower the price level.
   B. shift the aggregate demand curve leftward.
   C. shift the aggregate supply curve leftward.
   D. shift the aggregate supply curve rightward.

2. One of the problems with stabilization policy is that policymakers:
   A. do not know the goals of policy.
   B. do not know what output level corresponds to full employment.
   C. prefer more inflation than the public wants.
   D. have little control over the level of taxes.

3. The inflation that began in the late 1960s was caused by higher:
   A. oil prices by OPEC.
   B. interest rates without raising borrowing.
   C. government spending without raising taxes.
   D. productivity without rasing wages.

4. The 1980s began with:
   A. two recessions, one small and one large.
   B. low inflation and low unemployment.
   C. a major tax increase.
   D. falling interest rates.

5. If the price level falls, the amount of real output demanded:
   A. falls because people have less income.
   B. falls because taxes rise.
   C. rises because taxes fall.
   D. rises because the purchasing power of money rises.

6. "Stagflation" is a term used to describe:
   A. the 1960s.
   B. the 1970s.
   C. the 1980s.
   D. the 1990s.

7. When the price level falls, assuming everything else is the same, firms want to produce:
   A. more output because costs are lower.
   B. more output because consumers buy more.
   C. less output because demand is lower.
   D. less output because output is less profitable since some costs do not fall.

8. Wage and price controls in the early 1970s:
   A. eliminated the source of inflation.
   B. eventually eliminated inflation but took some time to have an impact.
   C. did not eliminate inflation because the controls were circumvented by firms improving quality.
   D. did not eliminate the source of inflation because aggregate demand was allowed to continue rising through expansionary monetary policy.

9. To reduce inflation, policymakers would attempt to:
   A. decrease aggregate demand.
   B. decrease aggregate supply.
   C. increase aggregate demand.
   D. increase aggregate supply.

10. The ability to use fiscal policy in the 1990s was limited by:
    A. high inflation.
    B. high unemployment.
    C. large budget deficits.
    D. large trade surpluses.

PROBLEMS

1. a. Identify the equilibrium price level as P_1 and output level as Y_1 for the economy pictured in Figure 11.1.

FIGURE 11.1

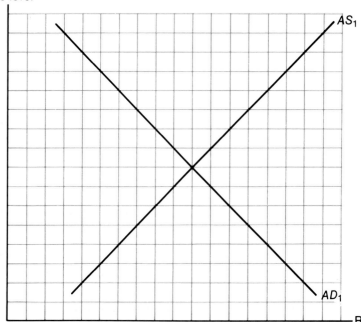

b. In Figure 11.1, show the effect on this economy of a decrease in the amount of investment spending. Identify the new equilibrium values for output and the price level as Y_2 and P_2.

c. What economic problem is the economy experiencing because of the decline in investment spending?

_____

d. In Figure 11.1, show how stabilization policies could be used to eliminate the economic problem. To achieve this, what should be done with the tools of fiscal and monetary policy? _____

2. a. The economy pictured in Figure 11.2 on the next page is initially in equilibrium at A, with a price level of P_1 and an output level of Y_1. Shift the appropriate curve so that this economy experiences stagflation. Label the new equilibrium as P_2 and Y_2.

b. In Figure 11.2, show what happens if stabilization policies are used to reduce the unemployment.

c. In Figure 11.2, show what happens if stabilization policies are used to reduce the inflation.

Answers

TRUE OR FALSE

1. False. Inflation also can be caused by reductions in aggregate supply. This is caused by adverse supply shocks.

2. True. Because some input prices are fixed, increases in prices make it profitable to expand output when prices rise.

FIGURE 11.2

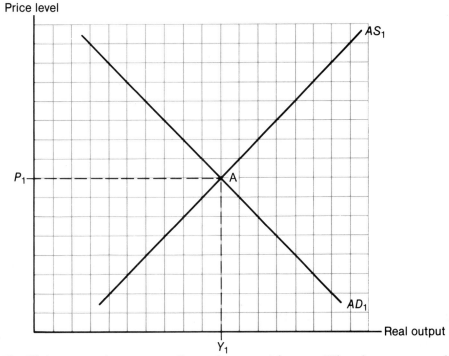

Price level

AS_1

P_1 — — — — — — — — — — — A

AD_1

Real output

Y_1

3. False. Equilibrium output is not necessarily equal to potential output. When they are not equal, economic problems—unemployment or inflation—result.

4. True. Stabilization policies influence the economy by changing aggregate demand. To reduce unemployment requires greater output. To do that means aggregate demand must increase.

5. True. As part of fiscal policy, government spending influences the economy by shifting aggregate demand.

6. False. Stagflation makes stabilization more difficult because it is impossible to reduce both unemployment and inflation by shifting the aggregate demand curve.

7. False. Budget deficits were large and growing during the 1980s.

8. False. In the 1960s, the economy experienced an uninterrupted period of economic expansion that ended with the emergence of a serious problem of inflation.

9. True. By lowering income tax rates, the supply-side theory asserts that people have a greater incentive to save and invest because they keep a larger part of any earnings they receive from such activities.

10. False. Increases in oil prices cause inflation by shifting the aggregate supply curve to the left because oil-price increases make it more expensive to produce output.

MULTIPLE CHOICE

1. C. By increasing the costs of production, a higher minimum wage would be expected to shift the aggregate supply curve leftward.

2. B. Policymakers do not know what output level or what unemployment rate corresponds to full employment in the economy.

3. C. Higher government spending associated with the Vietnam War occurred without higher taxes when the economy already was near full employment. This overstimulated the economy and led to inflation.

4. A. A short recession occurred in 1980 while a longer, deeper one occurred from 1981 to 1982.

5. D. As the price level falls, the purchasing power of money rises. The increased purchasing power induces individuals to demand more output.

6. B. The 1970s were characterized by stagflation primarily because of increases in the price of oil brought on by OPEC.

7. D. As the price level falls, it becomes less profitable for firms to produce output because some of the firms' costs are fixed and do not decline along with the price level.

8. D. Wage and price controls did not eliminate the inflationary pressure because the Federal Reserve continued to allow the money supply to grow at very high rates.

9. A. To reduce inflation, policymakers would attempt to reduce aggregate demand. Stabilization policy primarily affects aggregate demand. Inflation can be reduced using aggregate demand by shifting the curve to the left.

10. C. Already large budget deficits limited the ability to use fiscal policy to reduce unemployment in the early 1990s.

PROBLEMS

1. a. The equilibrium price level is P_1 and the equilibrium output level is Y_1 in Figure 11.3.

FIGURE 11.3

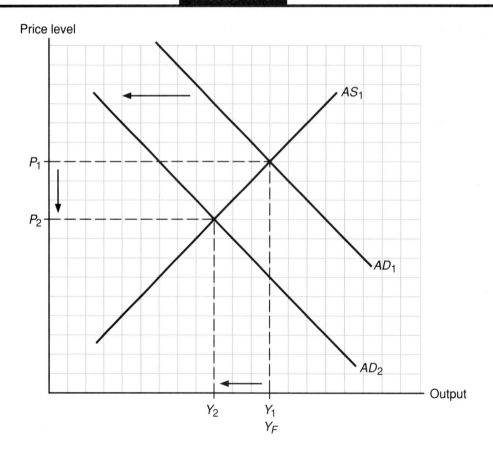

b. A decline in investment spending shifts the aggregate demand curve to the left because investment spending is part of aggregate demand. As a result, the price level declines to P_2 and the output level falls to Y_2.

c. The economy experiences an increase in **unemployment** because of the decline in investment spending because the economy's output level has declined.

d. Stabilization policy should attempt to shift the aggregate demand curve outward so the original equilibrium can be restored. This can be achieved by lowering taxes, increasing government spending, or increasing the money supply.

2. a. Stagflation is caused by a leftward shift of the aggregate supply curve. As a result the equilibrium price level rises to P_2 and the equilibrium output level falls to Y_2. The economy is at B and experiences inflation and higher unemployment simultaneously. That is the meaning of stagflation.

FIGURE 11.4

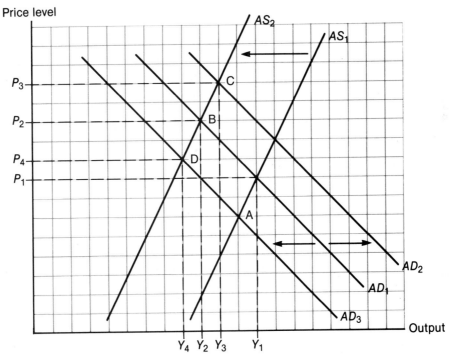

b. If stabilization policies are used to reduce unemployment, the aggregate demand curve shifts to the right to AD_2, increasing output to Y_3 but increasing the price level even more, to P_3. The economy is at C.

c. If stabilization policies are used to reduce inflation, the aggregate demand curve shifts to the left, reducing the price level to P_4 but also reducing output to Y_4 which means unemployment increases even more. The economy is at D.

CHAPTER 12

Aggregate Demand—
The Building Blocks

The determination of a nation's output is one of the most important topics in macroeconomics. Output and income are of paramount importance in our lives. For example, the level of output determines the unemployment rate and the inflation rate, two elements of great significance to our well-being.

As outlined in Chapter 11, changes in aggregate demand for goods and services typically initiate changes in output, income, unemployment, and the price level. The emphasis on aggregate demand was spurred by John Maynard Keynes, the great English economist and the author of most of the ideas in this chapter and the two that follow.

CHAPTER OUTLINE

I. Aggregate Demand
   A. In order to focus on aggregate demand, in this chapter it is assumed that the aggregate supply curve is horizontal. As a result, changes in aggregate demand cause changes in output but not in the price level.
   B. Aggregate demand has four components:
      1. Consumption demand (C) is the largest part of aggregate spending, making up about 69 percent of the total.
      2. Investment demand (I) is about 13 percent of total spending. It is made up primarily of the demand for new capital.
      3. Government demand (G) is the total amount the government purchases of goods and services, representing about 19 percent of total spending.
      4. Net exports ($X - M$) are the demand for U.S. goods on the part of foreigners less the demand for foreign goods on the part of U.S. buyers. Historically, net exports in the U.S. have been positive but small. In the 1980s, net exports became negative, equal to about –2 percent of GDP.

II. Consumption Spending
   A. John Maynard Keynes was the first economist to systematically describe the determinants of consumption spending. What follows is based on Keynes' analysis.
      1. The primary determinant of consumption spending is disposable income.
         a. **Disposable income** is income available for spending; it is personal income after income taxes have been paid.
         b. As disposable income rises, consumption spending rises. The increase in consumption because of an increase in disposable income is called induced consumption spending.

2. When people receive an increase in disposable income, they spend some and save some. The **marginal propensity to consume (MPC)** measures what percent of the extra disposable income consumers spend on goods and services. The formula for calculating the MPC is:

$$MPC = \frac{\Delta C}{\Delta Y_d}$$

For example, if an economy's disposable income rises by \$1,000 and its consumption spending rises by \$800, the MPC equals \$800/\$1,000 = 0.8.

3. There is a similar concept for saving. The **marginal propensity to save (MPS)** is the percent of extra disposable income that is saved. It equals $\Delta S / \Delta Y_d$. The MPC + MPS always equals 1.

4. Factors other than disposable income also influence consumption spending. The amount of consumption spending that is caused by factors other than income is called **autonomous consumption**. It can be calculated by finding what consumption spending would be if disposable income was zero.

5. The information about autonomous consumption and the MPC can be combined in an equation called the **consumption function**. If MPC equals 0.8 and autonomous consumption equals \$4,000, the consumption function is:

$$C = \$4,000 + 0.8(Y_d)$$

6. The information about consumption can be pictured on a figure that measures levels of disposable income on the horizontal axis and amounts of consumption spending on the vertical axis. Such a figure is called the income-expenditure diagram. The characteristics of this figure are:
   a. Where a 45° line crosses the consumption line, consumption equals income. This is called the **break-even level of income**. This is also the income level where saving equals zero.
   b. The slope of the consumption line equals the MPC.
   c. If consumption increases because of a change in something other than income—a change in autonomous consumption—the consumption line shifts upward.

7. The factors that determine autonomous consumption are:
   a. Wealth: The greater a family's wealth, the more it spends on consumer goods. If the value of a family's assets increases, they have no more income but they are "richer." Thus their consumption is expected to be higher.
   b. Expected Future Disposable Income: If a family expects a higher future income, its current consumption rises even though its current disposable income has not increased.
   c. Price Level: A lower price level means that the purchasing power of financial assets increases, and this boost in real wealth increases consumption. This is called the **wealth effect**.
   d. Expected Future Inflation Rate: Expectations of greater inflation have no certain impact on consumption. For some, it causes increases in consumption as they attempt to buy before prices rise. For others, inflation creates uncertainty and causes them to reduce consumption.
   e. Stock of Durable Goods: If consumers own few durable goods—as is true for most young families—consumption spending is higher.

III. Investment Spending
   A. Although consumption spending is the largest category of spending, investment spending is in some respects the most important because it is the most volatile. Changes in investment cause many of the swings in the economy.
   B. The primary determinants of investment spending are:
      1. Interest Rates: Many investment projects are financed by borrowing. Higher interest rates make borrowing less attractive and reduce investment. Even for businesses able to pay for the investment goods without borrowing, higher interest rates reduce investment because they make lending the funds a more attractive alternative to investment spending. The line showing the relationship between interest rates and investment spending is downward sloping.

2. Business Confidence: Businesses must be confident about the course of the economy in order to commit large amounts of spending to investment. As business expectations improve, the investment curve shifts to the right.

3. Capacity Utilization and Expected Growth of Demand: Because investment adds to the productive capacity of the firms, firms are willing to invest only if their existing capacity is being used and if they expect demand to grow. Increases in capacity utilization rates and increases in expected demand growth shift the investment line to the right.

4. Income Tax Provisions: Tax laws are often changed to make investment more attractive. An investment tax credit allows firms to reduce their tax liability by an amount equal to some percent of their spending on investment goods. A 10 percent tax credit reduces taxes by 10 percent of the amount spent on investment goods.

5. Stock Market Prices: If the price of a business' stock is high, the firm can more easily finance the purchase of new equipment by issuing more stock.

IV. Equilibrium Output.

A. **Equilibrium output** is the output level at which there is no tendency to change production; it is the output level that is sustainable. In an economy with no government and no international trade, the equilibrium output level can be found one of three ways. Equilibrium output occurs where:

1. Aggregate output equals aggregate expenditures ($Y = C + I$).
2. Saving equals investment ($S = I$).
3. Involuntary changes in inventories equal $0.

B. All three conditions lead to the same equilibrium output level.

C. Graphically, equilibrium output is found at the intersection of the aggregate expenditures ($C + I$) line and the 45° line in the income-expenditure diagram.

V. The Multiplier

A. The multiplier effect refers to what happens when an economy moves from one equilibrium level of output to another. It gets its name from the fact that when investment spending increases, equilibrium output increases by more than the increase in investment spending. The **multiplier** is the ratio of the increase in output to the initial increase in investment spending. For example, if a $20 increase in investment spending results in an increase in equilibrium output of $100, the multiplier is $100/$20 or 5.

B. The multiplier effect occurs because the increase in investment spending sets off a chain reaction of spending. As businesses buy machines, more output is produced and more income is earned. As a consequence, those with more income increase their consumption spending, which leads to further increases in output and income. In the end, output and income increase by much more than the initial increase in investment.

C. The formula for calculating the increase in equilibrium output is:

$$\Delta Y = \frac{1}{1 - \text{MPC}} (\Delta I)$$

The multiplier is 1/(1 – MPC) or 1/MPS. For example, when the MPC equals 0.8, the multiplier equals 1/(1 – .8) = 1/.2 = 5.

D. The larger the MPC the larger the multiplier effect. The larger the MPC, the more of any extra income that is spent on goods and services—and the larger, then, the extra output produced.

E. In the real world, the size of the multiplier effect is less than the one predicted by the formula. The formula implies that a $200 increase in investment increases output by $1,000 when the MPC equals 0.8. In reality, output increases by less than $1,000. The formula ignores:

1. Income Taxes: As income rises, the amount of taxes owed increases because taxes in the United States are linked to income. This reduces the amount of extra spending that additional income creates and reduces the total increase in output. This reduction in size of the multiplier is called an **automatic stabilizer** because it stabilizes the economy by reducing the magnitude of the swings in spending.

2. Effects on Investment Spending: As an economy expands, interest rates rise. The higher interest rates reduce investment spending. This is called the **crowding-out effect** and reduces the size of the multi-

plier effect because the reduction in investment offsets some of the extra spending. It is possible, though, that the economic expansion could *increase* investment spending if the expansion began when the economy was in a deep recession. In this case the economic expansion improves the economic outlook of businesses, which induces them to *increase* their investment spending. This is called **crowding in**.

3. Price Level Changes: The simple multiplier effect assumes that increases in demand are translated entirely into increases in output. In reality some of the extra demand increases prices, so the increase in output is smaller than the equation predicts.

HINTS AND HELP

1. The Marginal Propensity to Consume (MPC) The marginal propensity to consume plays an important role in Keynes' theory, and it is essential that you understand it. Despite its imposing name, it is a fairly simple concept. The MPC describes what a family or an economy does when it receives extra income. Yes, you have an MPC. To discover it, simply keep track from year to year of what happens to your disposable income and your consumption spending. The extra consumption spending divided by the extra disposable income is your MPC.

It is also important to understand what the MPC does *not* tell you. An MPC of 0.8 means only that 80 percent of any *extra* income is spent. It does *not* mean that 80 percent of *all* income is spent.

The same thing is true of the marginal propensity to save (MPS). It measures only the part of *additional* income that is saved. Because all increases in disposable income are either spent or saved, the MPC plus the MPS must sum to 1.

2. Induced and Autonomous Consumption Consumption spending can change for two reasons. The most obvious is that it can change because of a change in disposable income. In this case the change is called an induced change in consumption. Graphically, this appears as a movement *along* a consumption line.

The second way consumption can change is if something other than disposable income that influences consumption changes. These "other things" are wealth, expected future disposable income, the price level, expected future inflation, and the stock of consumer durables. The amount of consumption that is caused by these other factors is called autonomous consumption.

The word "autonomous" means independent. In this context, autonomous refers to consumption that is independent of income. To find the value of autonomous consumption, find what consumption spending would be if current disposable income were zero. A change in autonomous consumption appears as a *shift* of the consumption line.

3. Finding Equilibrium There are three equally valid ways to discover the equilibrium output level. They are:

a. Find the output level at which aggregate expenditures ($C + I$) equal aggregate output (Y). If aggregate spending does not equal aggregate output, firms adjust their production so that output equals spending.

b. Find the output level at which leakages (S) equal injections (I). If leakages are not equal to injections, goods are not being bought at the same rate they are being produced. Firms adjust production to make the rate at which output is being produced equal to the rate at which output is being bought.

c. Find the output level at which involuntary (that is, unwanted) changes in inventories are zero. If goods are either building up on or are disappearing from store shelves at a faster rate than businesses want, production is changed until the undesired changes in inventories end.

Having three methods to find equilibrium output means that if there is not enough information to find equilibrium one way, you can always use one of the other methods. Having more than one method also serves as a check. All three methods must lead to the same answer. If they do not, an error has been made.

Graphically, finding equilibrium involves one of two methods. Find the level of output where the $C + I$ line crosses the 45° line or find the output level where the saving line crosses the investment line.

4. The Multiplier The multiplier effect was one of Keynes' most significant discoveries. Keynes reasoned that increases in spending in any sector of the economy spill over to increase consumption spending. If firms demand more machinery, that increase in demand stimulates consumer spending because the people producing the machines have more income. The total increase in spending and output is greater than just the increase in investment spending that began the process.

Investment spending is not the only factor that sets off a multiplier effect. An increase in autonomous consumption causes a multiplier effect, as do increases in government spending and net exports.

FILL IN THE BLANK

autonomous

1. Consumption spending caused by factors other than disposable income is _____ consumption.

investment

2. The category of aggregate demand that is the most volatile is _____.

equilibrium

3. The output level where aggregate spending equals aggregate output is the _____ level of output.

rises

4. If businesses experience an increase in the rate of capacity utilization, investment spending _____.

demand

5. Keynes believed that changes in an economy's output were caused primarily by changes in aggregate _____.

aggregate expenditures $(C + I)$

6. Where the _____ line crosses the 45° line is where aggregate spending equals aggregate output.

investment, autonomous

7. A multiplier effect can be caused by a change in _____ or a change in _____ consumption.

MPC

8. In the consumption function, $C = \$300 + .9(Y_d)$, .9 is the _____.

upward

9. An increase in wealth causes the consumption line to shift _____.

larger than

10. The multiplier effect is given that name because the increase in equilibrium output that results from an increase in investment spending is _____ the increase in investment spending.

TRUE OR FALSE

_____ 1. In an economy without a government or international trade, equilibrium occurs when investment equals consumption.

_____ 2. The wealth effect associated with an increase in the price level works to reduce consumption.

_____ 3. It is assumed that as consumption spending rises, the marginal propensity to consume rises.

_____ 4. Keynes believed that both consumption and saving rise when income increases.

_____ 5. If the marginal propensity to consume is 0.9, people are consuming 90 percent of their income.

_____ 6. The multiplier effect refers to how investment spending changes when there is a change in interest rates.

_____ 7. Assume a family has been earning $30,000 per year steadily. If its income temporarily falls to $25,000, its consumption spending would be expected to temporarily fall by $5,000.

_____ 8. Assuming everything else is the same, investment spending varies inversely with the interest rate.

_____ 9. The marginal propensity to save equals 1 minus the marginal propensity to consume.

_____ 10. When price-level changes are taken into consideration, the size of the multiplier effect is reduced.

MULTIPLE CHOICE

1. The break-even level of income is the income level at which:
   A. unemployment equals zero.
   B. saving equals zero.
   C. consumption equals zero.
   D. the MPC equals zero.

2. If an individual's consumption spending increases because of an increase in the individual's income, it is an example of:
   A. an induced increase in consumption.
   B. an increase in autonomous consumption.
   C. the multiplier effect.
   D. the crowding-out effect.

3. The steeper the consumption line:
   A. the larger the autonomous consumption.
   B. the larger the MPS.
   C. the smaller the autonomous consumption.
   D. the larger the multiplier.

4. If MPS = 0.25, people:
   A. are spending 25 percent of their income.
   B. are saving 25 percent of their income.
   C. will save 25 percent of extra income they might receive.
   D. will spend 25 percent of extra income they might receive.

5. Which of the following does *not* cause an increase in autonomous consumption?
   A. an increase in wealth
   B. a fall in the price level
   C. an increase in disposable income
   D. the expectation of higher future income

6. If families begin to expect lower future incomes, they:
   A. increase investment spending.
   B. reduce consumption spending.
   C. decrease investment spending.
   D. reduce current saving.

7. Assume Bill and Sue each have a disposable income of $30,000. Further, assume Bill has wealth of $50,000 and Sue has wealth of $100,000. Because of Sue's greater wealth, which of the following is true?
   A. Sue spends a larger part of her income than Bill.
   B. Sue spends a smaller part of her income than Bill.
   C. Sue has a smaller MPC than Bill.
   D. Sue has a larger MPC than Bill.

8. Declining inventories of goods are an indication of which of the following?
   A. inflation
   B. total spending exceeds output
   C. government spending exceeds taxes
   D. rising unemployment

9. The formula for the simple multiplier is:
   A. 1/MPC.
   B. 1/(1 – MPC).
   C. 1/(1 + MPS).
   D. 1/(MPC + MPS).

10. When MPC = 0.9 and prices do not change, an increase in investment spending of $2,000 causes equilibrium output to:
   A. decrease by $2,000.
   B. increase by $2,000.
   C. increase by $5,000.
   D. increase by $20,000.

PROBLEMS

1. The information in the following table comes from the government of Caines, a small nation in the South Pacific. The data are disposable income, consumption, and saving in Caines.

DISPOSABLE INCOME (Y_d)	CONSUMPTION (C)	SAVING (S)
$ 0	$ 400	____
1,000	1,200	–$200
2,000	2,000	____
3,000	____	$200
4,000	3,600	____
5,000	____	600
6,000	5,200	800

Because of a computer malfunction, some of the data have been destroyed. Fill in the missing numbers.
   a. What is the marginal propensity to consume in Caines? _____
   b. What is the amount of autonomous consumption? _____
   c. What is Caines' break-even level of income? _____
   d. Plot the data in Figure 12.1 by drawing the consumption and saving lines. Identify the break-even level of income as Y_{d_1} and the amount of autonomous consumption as C_0.

2. a. The country of Caines has a business community but no government or international trade. The businesses are investing $400 per year. Use the following information to determine aggregate sales for each level of output and list it in column (5). Place a star (*) next to the equilibrium output.

OUTPUT OR INCOME (GDP)	CONSUMPTION (C)	INVESTMENT I_1	I_2	AGGREGATE EXPENDITURES ($C + I_1$)	($C + I_2$)
(1)	(2)	(3)	(4)	(5)	(6)
$ 0	$ 400	$400	____	____	____
1,000	1,200	400	____	____	____
2,000	2,000	400	____	____	____
3,000	2,800	400	____	____	____
4,000	3,600	400	____	____	____
5,000	4,400	400	____	____	____
6,000	5,200	400	____	____	____

   b. Assume business prospects improve in Caines. As a result, businesses decide to increase their investment to a constant $600. List this new amount of investment in column (4). Calculate the new amounts of aggregate expenditures in column (6) and place two stars (**) next to the new equilibrium level of output.
   c. What is the size of the multiplier in Caines? _____

FIGURE 12.1

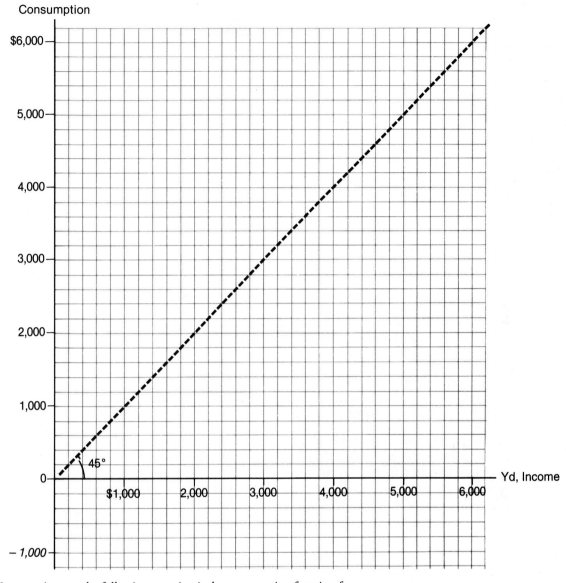

3. a. Assume the following equation is the consumption function for an economy.

$$C = \$3,000 + .5(Y_d)$$

Use the equation to fill in the missing values on the table below.

Y_d	C	Y_d	C
$ 0	_____	$6,000	_____
1,000	_____	7,000	_____
2,000	_____	8,000	_____
3,000	_____	9,000	_____
4,000	_____	10,000	_____
5,000	_____	11,000	_____
		12,000	_____

b. Plot the income and consumption combinations on Figure 12.2 below and label the line C.

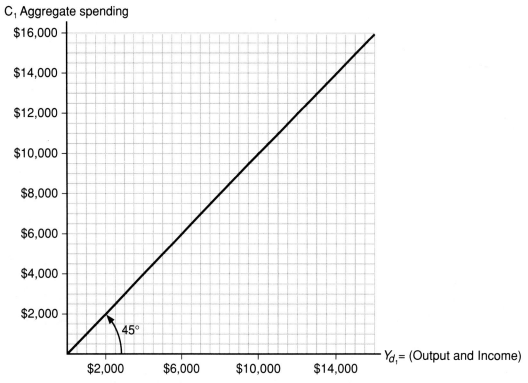

FIGURE 12.2

c. What is the break-even value of income? _____

d. Assume investment spending is $2,000. Draw the aggregate expenditures $(C + I)$ line in Figure 12.2 and label it $C + I_1$. What is the equilibrium value of output? _____

e. Assume investment spending rises from $2,000 to $4,000. Draw the new aggregate expenditures $(C + I)$ line in Figure 12.2 and label it $C + I_2$. What is the new value of equilibrium output? _____

4. Calculate the multiplier for each of the following MPCs.

	MPC	MULTIPLIER
a.	0.5	_____
b.	0.75	_____
c.	0.8	_____
d.	0.9	_____

Answers

TRUE OR FALSE

1. False. Equilibrium requires that investment equals saving.

2. True. A higher price level causes lower consumption spending through the wealth effect because it reduces the purchasing power of financial wealth. This causes autonomous consumption spending to decline.

3. False. The marginal propensity to consume is assumed to be a constant; it is assumed to be the same at all income levels.

4. True. Keynes believed that as people earned more income they would spend some of the extra income but that they would also save part of it. Increases in income would result in more spending and more saving.

5. False. The marginal propensity to consume only measures what people do with *extra* income. If the MPC equals 0.9, it only means that people spend 90 percent of any *additional* income they might receive.

6. False. The multiplier effect refers to how an increase in investment spending causes equilibrium output to increase by more than the increase in investment.

7. False. The decline in income is temporary. Because a family's consumption depends on expected future income as well as current income, the family does not reduce consumption in line with the temporary reduction in income.

8. True. The amount of investment spending declines as interest rates rise. The most obvious reason for this is that higher interest rates make it more expensive for firms that must borrow to finance investment spending.

9. True. The marginal propensity to consume plus the marginal propensity to save always sum to 1. If the MPC = .6, the MPS equals (1 − .6) = .4.

10. True. The multiplier effect is at its greatest when the price level remains constant. When the price level rises in response to increased aggregate demand, the increase in output is smaller.

MULTIPLE CHOICE

1. B. The break-even level of income is the income level at which all income is spent, that is, where saving equals zero.

2. A. Induced consumption is consumption caused by changes in disposable income.

3. D. The slope of the consumption line measures the MPC. The larger the MPC the steeper the consumption line. And the larger the MPC the larger the multiplier.

4. C. The MPS measures what percent or proportion of any additional income is saved.

5. C. Autonomous consumption is consumption caused by factors other than disposable income. Wealth, the price level, and expected future income are each factors other than disposable income that influence consumption spending.

6. B. People who expect lower future incomes tend to reduce their current consumption even though their current disposable income has not changed.

7. A. Wealth is one factor that influences consumption spending. As wealth increases, consumption spending increases even if disposable income has not changed. Sue spends more than Bill, even though their incomes are identical.

8. B. If inventories are declining, it is a sign that goods are being bought at a faster rate than they are being produced. Spending exceeds output.

9. B.

10. D. If the MPC equals 0.9, the multiplier equals 1/(1 − .9) = 1/.1 = 10. Because investment has increased by $2,000, equilibrium output increases by 10 x $2,000 or $20,000.

PROBLEMS

1. The blanks can be filled knowing that:

$$Y_d = C + S$$

DISPOSABLE INCOME (Y_d)	CONSUMPTION (C)	SAVING (S)
$ 0	$ 400	−$400
1,000	1,200	− 200
2,000	2,000	0
3,000	2,800	200
4,000	3,600	400
5,000	4,400	600
6,000	5,200	800

a. The marginal propensity to consume is:

$$\frac{\Delta C}{\Delta Y_d} = \frac{+\$800}{+\$1,000} = .8$$

b. The amount of autonomous consumption equals consumption spending when disposable income equals $0. In this example, consumption spending equals **$400** when disposable income equals $0, and that is the amount of autonomous consumption.

c. The break-even level of income is the income level where disposable income equals consumption spending or where saving equals $0. In this example, this occurs when income equals **$2,000**.

d. See Figure 12.3 on the next page.

2. a. and b.

OUTPUT OR INCOME (GDP)	CONSUMPTION (C)	INVESTMENT I_1	INVESTMENT I_2	AGGREGATE EXPENDITURES ($C + I_1$)	AGGREGATE EXPENDITURES ($C + I_2$)
(1)	(2)	(3)	(4)	(5)	(6)
$ 0	$ 400	$400	$600	$ 800	$1,000
1,000	1,200	400	600	1,600	1,800
2,000	2,000	400	600	2,400	2,600
3,000	2,800	400	600	3,200	3,400
4,000*	3,600	400	600	4,000*	4,200
5,000**	4,400	400	600	4,800	5,000**
6,000	5,200	400	600	5,600	5,800

Equilibrium output occurs where aggregate expenditures equal aggregate output. When Investment equals $400, equilibrium occurs when output is $4,000. When Investment is $600, equilibrium is **$5,000**.

c. The multiplier in Caines equals 1/(1 − .8) = 1/.2 = **5**.

3. a. To find the missing values it is necessary to substitute the various values of Y_d into the consumption equation and solve for the value of C. For example, when Y_d equal $4,000:

FIGURE 12.3

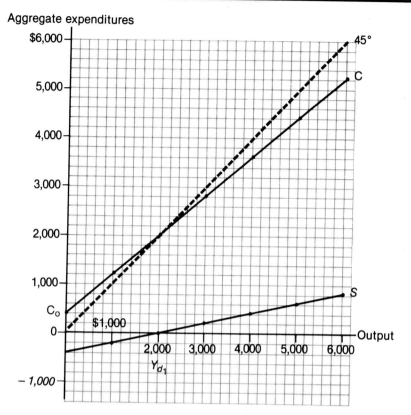

$C = \$3,000 + .5 \times \$4,000; \ C = \$3,000 + \$2,000; \ C = \$5,000$

The other values for C are in the table below.

Y_d	C
$ 0	$3,000
1,000	3,500
2,000	4,000
3,000	4,500
4,000	5,000
5,000	5,500
6,000	6,000
7,000	6,500
8,000	7,000
9,000	7,500
10,000	8,000
11,000	8,500
12,000	9,000

b. Figure 12.4 shows the plot of the consumption line using the data in the table above. It is line C.
c. The break-even level of income occurs where the C line crosses the 45° line. This occurs at an income level of **$6,000**.

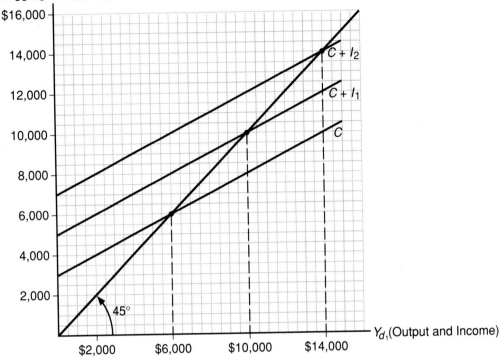

FIGURE 12.4

C_1 Aggregate spending

C + I_2

C + I_1

C

45°

Y_{d_1}(Output and Income)

d. Assuming I equals $2,000, the $C + I_1$ line is a line parallel to the C line but $2,000 above it. (See Figure 12.4.) The equilibrium level of income and output is where this line crosses the 45° line. This occurs when income is **$10,000**.

e. When investment spending increases from $2,000 to $4,000 the aggregate expenditures line shifts upward by $2,000. This is the $C + I_2$ line in Figure 12.4. The new value of equilibrium output is where this line crosses the 45° line, which is at **$14,000**.

4. The formula for the multiplier is:

$$\text{Multiplier} = \frac{1}{(1 - \text{MPC})}$$

a. $\dfrac{1}{1 - .5} = \dfrac{1}{.5} = 2$

b. $\dfrac{1}{1 - .75} = \dfrac{1}{.25} = 4$

c. $\dfrac{1}{1 - .8} = \dfrac{1}{.2} = 5$

d. $\dfrac{1}{1 - .9} = \dfrac{1}{.1} = 10$

CHAPTER 13

Macroeconomic Equilibrium in Models with Government and International Sectors

As described in Chapter 12, aggregate demand is the key determinant of aggregate output in an economy where there are only households and firms. Chapter 13 expands on that theme by adding government and international trade. But the conclusion remains the same—output depends on spending.

This chapter also discusses the conditions that lead to unemployment and inflation in an economy. Finally, there is a discussion of the role government should play in the economy when unemployment or inflation rises.

CHAPTER OUTLINE

I. Making the Model More Realistic
   A. Adding government to our simple model of the economy involves two adjustments:
      1. Government spending (G) is added as a component of total spending. Government spending is assumed to be constant, independent of output and income.
      2. Taxes (T) are added as an additional leakage. Taxes are assumed to be the same regardless of income. Taxes that do not change when income changes are called lump-sum taxes.
   B. Adding international trade, that is, net exports ($X - M$), also involves two adjustments:
      1. Exports (X) are added to the spending stream. They are assumed to be fixed.
      2. Imports (M) are another leakage from the spending stream. They are also assumed to be constant.
   C. Equilibrium output
      1. **Equilibrium output** is the level of output toward which the economy tends to settle.
      2. The equilibrium output can be found using any one of three ways. The equilibrium occurs at the output where:
         a. aggregate expenditures ($C + I + G + X - M$) = aggregate output (Y).
         b. leakages ($S + T + M$) = injections ($I + G + X$).
         c. involuntary changes in inventories = $0.
      3. Graphically the equilibrium occurs where the aggregate expenditures ($C + I + G + X - M$) line crosses the 45° line.
   D. The Multiplier in the More Realistic Model
      1. The multiplier does not change with the addition of the government sector because taxes are assumed to not vary with income. If the model includes an income tax, the multiplier is reduced. The model with an income tax is described in Appendix 13A.

2. Changes in government spending, investment, and net exports all create a multiplier effect on equilibrium output.
3. Tax changes influence the economy because they change the amount people have to spend from the income they have earned.
   a. If taxes are decreased, people have more disposable income. As with other increases in disposable income, consumption increases.
   b. The size of the increase in consumption spending depends on the size of the MPC. If the MPC is 0.8, a $1,000 tax cut increases consumption spending by (.8) x ($1,000) or $800.
   c. A multiplier effect follows from this also. With an MPC = 0.8, the $800 increase in consumption spending increases total spending and output by 5 x $800 or $4,000.
4. Transfer payments operate similarly to taxes. An increase in transfer payments of $1,000 increases disposable income by $1,000 which increases consumption spending by 0.8 x $1,000 = $800. The multiplier effect increases equilibrium output by 5 x $800 or $4,000.

II. Equilibrium Output versus Full Employment Output
A. **Potential** GDP (Y_F) is the output level associated with full employment. One of the key conclusions of Keynes' analysis of the economy was that there is no reason to believe that an economy automatically produces the amount of output required in order to be at full employment.
B. Recessionary Gap
   1. If the equilibrium output is less than potential GDP, the economy experiences unemployment because the economy is not producing enough output to have a fully employed labor force. The difference between potential GDP and the output the economy is actually producing is called the **recessionary gap**. This situation is often described as an "underemployment equilibrium."
   2. Some economists question whether an economy really can be in equilibrium when there is unemployment. These economists believe that an economy has a **self-correcting mechanism**. According to this view, unemployment reduces wages and prices. As a result, financial assets increase in value and, because of the wealth effect, consumption spending increases. This continues until the economy is pushed to full employment.
   3. Keynesians argue that wages and prices do not display the downward flexibility necessary for the self-correcting mechanism to work. This inflexibility is attributable to legal and contractual restrictions that inhibit flexibility.
   4. Rather than rely on the unlikely prospect of an economy eliminating a recessionary gap on its own, Keynesian economists suggest that the government must step in to eliminate the gap. The correct policies when an economy has a recessionary gap are higher government spending, lower taxes, or increases in the money supply to lower interest rates and increase investment spending. If the gap is $200 billion and the multiplier is 4, spending must be shifted upward by $50 billion to push the economy to full employment.
C. Inflationary Gap
   1. An **inflationary gap** occurs when equilibrium output exceeds potential GDP.
   2. The consensus among economists is that an economy eliminates an inflationary gap automatically. As prices rise, the purchasing power of financial assets declines. As a result, consumption and total spending decline and equilibrium output is reduced to the full-employment level.
   3. An inflationary gap may be eliminated more quickly through the use of stabilization policies. Total spending can be reduced by cutting government spending, raising taxes, or by reducing the money supply to raise interest rates and reduce investment spending. The extent of the policy actions required depends on the size of the gap and the size of the multiplier.
   4. A major debate in economics concerns the wisdom of attempting to prevent fluctuations in economic activity through stabilization policies. Keynesians believe that these active policies can stabilize the economy. Critics argue that attempts to stabilize the economy often create problems because of ignorance about how the economy operates.

III. Appendix 13A: Elementary Mathematics of Income Determination

A simple model of the economy can be presented and solved using simple algebra. Assuming no international trade, the relevant equations are:

equilibrium condition:	$Y = C + I + G$
consumption:	$C = a + bY_d$ (a: autonomous consumption; b: MPC)
investment:	$I = I_0$ (investment: fixed at I_0)
government:	$G = G_0$ (government spending: fixed at G_0)
disposable income:	$Y_d = Y - tY$ (t: proportional income tax rate)
consumption with taxes:	$C = a + bY(1 - t)$
equilibrium:	$Y = \dfrac{1}{1 - b(1 - t)}(a + I_0 + G_0)$
multiplier:	$\dfrac{1}{1 - b(1 - t)}$

(The larger the tax rate (t) the smaller the multiplier.)

HINTS AND HELP

1. Recessionary and Inflationary Gaps "Gaps" occur when the economy's equilibrium output does not equal the economy's potential output. It is fairly easy to keep the recessionary and inflationary gaps straight. If aggregate output is *less than* potential output, the economy is not producing enough goods and services to have full employment. Unemployment results. "Recession" is a word associated with unemployment, so "recessionary gap" should remind you of unemployment. The other gap—the one where equilibrium output is *greater than* potential output—is the inflationary gap.

An inflationary gap probably sounds a bit strange when it is first described. A natural question is: "How can an economy produce more output than its potential output?" The secret to understanding this curiosity is that potential output is not *maximum* output. Potential output means that the labor force is at full employment. But it also means that people are doing what they normally do in the labor force: people who want to work are working and those who don't are not. The people who are employed are working the number of hours they want to work. The economy can produce more output than its potential output if people work more hours than they normally would work (for example, work overtime hours) or if people work who normally would not.

2. Taxes and Transfer Payments The impact of taxes and transfer payments on aggregate spending is different from the impact of government spending. The difference occurs because people treat changes in taxes and transfer payments in the same way they treat changes in disposable income.

A decrease in taxes creates an increase in disposable income. When taxes fall, consumption increases but so does saving. It is only the increase in consumption that causes a multiplier effect. The size of the consumption increase equals the marginal propensity to consume times the change in taxes. If taxes are cut by $1,000 and the MPC equals 0.75, consumption increases by (.75) x ($1,000) = $750. A $1,000 increase in transfer payments also increases consumption spending by (.75) x ($1,000) = $750. On the other hand, a $1,000 increase in government purchases expands output in the first round by the full $1,000.

3. The Self-Correcting Mechanism An important issue in macroeconomics is whether an economy can be expected to eliminate its "gaps"—recessionary or inflationary—without any active involvement on the part of the government. If it can, there is little need for the government to be concerned or involved when gaps occur.

Keynes believed that an economy would have difficulty closing a recessionary gap. For an economy to automatically eliminate a recessionary gap requires that wages and prices fall, increasing the purchasing power of financial assets enough so that consumption increases sufficiently to push the economy to full employment. Not only do Keynesian economists doubt that wages and prices can fall easily, but they believe that the wealth effect is weak. To self-correct requires an unrealistically large price decline.

Rather than count on an unlikely self-correcting mechanism to solve unemployment, Keynesians believe that the government must play an active role in the solution.

Compared to Keynesians, monetarists believe that wages and prices are more likely to decline when there is high unemployment. They also believe that the wealth effect is stronger. To close a recessionary gap would require a smaller price decline than Keynesians believe would be necessary. This is one reason monetarists believe that government involvement is not needed as much as Keynesians believe it is.

FILL IN THE BLANKS

recessionary   1. If aggregate output is less than potential output, there is a _____ gap.

increasing   2. A recessionary gap can be eliminated by _____ government spending.

leakage   3. Taxes are a _____ in the circular flow of spending.

inflationary   4. Tax increases are a solution for an _____ gap.

fall   5. To eliminate a recessionary gap automatically requires that wages and prices _____.

reduced   6. When imports rise more than exports, aggregate expenditures are _____.

unemployment   7. When an economy has a recessionary gap it experiences the problem of _____.

Monetarist   8. _____ economists have less faith in the government's ability to adjust spending and taxes to achieve full employment and would be more likely to rely on the economy's self-correcting mechanism.

downward   9. Increases in the price level cause the $C + I + G + (X - M)$ line to shift _____.

lump-sum   10. Taxes that remain the same regardless of the level of income are called _____ taxes.

TRUE OR FALSE

_____   1. With the government and the international sector included, total spending equals $C + I + G + (X - M)$.

_____   2. Keynes believed that an economy could never be at full employment.

_____   3. The wealth effect refers to the idea that an economy automatically becomes wealthier when unemployment falls.

_____   4. An economy is more likely to self-correct a recessionary gap if wages and prices fall easily.

_____   5. A larger trade deficit reduces aggregate expenditures.

_____   6. When $C + I + G + X - M$ exceeds Y, there is an inflationary gap.

_____   7. According to Keynesian economists, an economy is more likely to self-correct an inflationary gap than a recessionary gap.

_____   8. One solution for a recessionary gap is lower taxes.

_____   9. Monetarists and Keynesians believe that the government must be actively involved in the economy to achieve full employment.

_____ 10. An economy with large government spending can never experience unemployment.

MULTIPLE CHOICE

1. An increase in transfer payments of $20,000, when the marginal propensity to consume equals 0.75, causes consumption spending to increase by:
   A. $30,000.
   B. $20,000.
   C. $15,000.
   D. $12,000.

2. An economy experiences unemployment when:
   A. there is an inflationary gap.
   B. total spending is less than output.
   C. there is no government spending.
   D. equilibrium output is less than potential output.

3. Greater government spending is one solution for:
   A. a recessionary gap.
   B. an inflationary gap.
   C. aggregate spending exceeding aggregate output.
   D. reducing the budget deficit.

4. A major reason for the existence of inflationary or deflationary gaps is that:
   A. governments cannot control their tax receipts.
   B. saving and investment decisions are made by separate groups.
   C. the marginal propensity to consume is variable.
   D. prices and wages are very flexible.

5. When prices are rising, the wealth effect should result in which of the following?
   A. rising consumption spending
   B. rising government spending
   C. falling consumption spending
   D. falling unemployment

6. If inventories are being accumulated involuntarily, then:
   A. $C + I + G + (X - M) > Y.$
   B. $C + S + X > Y.$
   C. $G + I + X < S + T + M.$
   D. $G + T < X + M.$

7. If the economy is in a severe recession, a Keynesian economist would recommend which of the following?
   A. lower Social Security payments to elderly
   B. higher taxes in order to balance the budget
   C. lower defense spending
   D. higher welfare payments

8. Which of the following actions is appropriate when there is an inflationary gap? (I) Higher taxes, (II) lower taxes, (III) higher government spending, (IV) lower government spending, (V) higher transfer payments, (VI) lower transfer payments.
   A. (I), (IV), (VI)
   B. (I), (III), (V)
   C. (II), (III), (V)
   D. (II), (VI), (V)

9. Because of the depression of the 1930s, Keynesian economists are convinced that:
   A. consumption does not vary with income.
   B. increases in government spending cause aggregate spending to decline.
   C. inflationary gaps are unavoidable.
   D. wages and prices do not fall sufficiently to eliminate a recessionary gap.

10. One dollar of government spending causes a greater increase in aggregate spending than a $1 tax cut because:
   A. government spending is an injection in the spending stream, and taxes are a leakage.
   B. government spending creates a multiplier effect, and tax changes do not.
   C. government spending is financed by borrowing and tax changes are not.
   D. government spending is entirely spending, and tax cuts are partly saved.

PROBLEMS

1. Figure 13.1 shows the current aggregate expenditure $(C + I + G + X - M)$ line in the economy of Caines. Use it to answer the following questions. Note: The MPC is 0.8.

FIGURE 13.1

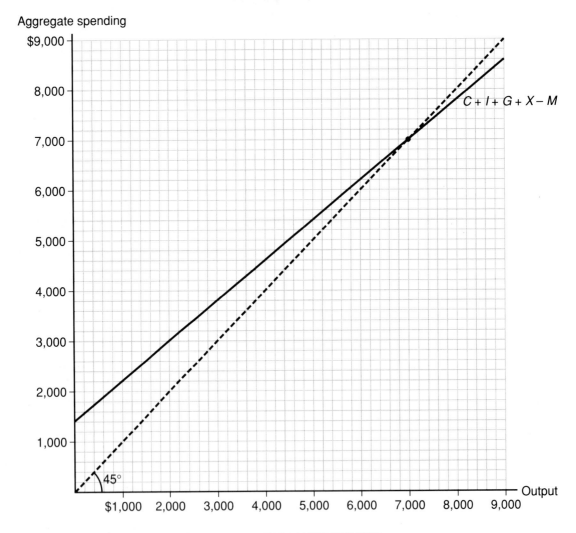

a. What is the equilibrium output level in Caines? _____

b. Potential output in Caines is $9,000. What kind of "gap" does Caines have? _____

c. Assuming prices in Caines remain the same, what change in government spending is needed in order to make equilibrium output equal to full-employment output? _____

d. Suppose policymakers in Caines do not want to change government spending; they prefer to change transfer payments. What change in transfer payments is needed to move equilibrium output so it equals full-employment output? _____

2. For each of the following, list the kind of "gap" that exists. Calculate the size of the gap, the change in government spending needed to eliminate the gap, and the change in taxes needed to eliminate the gap.

   a. equilibrium output = $20,000
      potential output   = $26,000.
      MPC   = 0.666 (2/3)
      kind of gap: _____
      size of gap: _____
      change in government spending: _____
      change in taxes: _____

   b. equilibrium output = $415,000
      potential output   = $400,000
      MPC   = 0.6
      kind of gap: _____
      size of gap: _____
      change in government spending: _____
      change in taxes: _____

   c. equilibrium output = $50,000
      potential output   = $60,000
      MPC   = 0.5
      kind of gap: _____
      size of gap: _____
      change in government spending: _____
      change in taxes: _____

3. Problem 3 relies on material in Appendix 13A.

   a. Use the following information to calculate the economy's equilibrium output:

$$G_0 = \$90,000$$
$$MPC = .8$$
$$I_0 = \$70,000$$
$$t = .25$$
$$a = \$40,000$$

   b. If potential output equals $600,000, does this economy have a recessionary gap, an inflationary gap, or neither? _____

   c. How much must government spending change to eliminate the gap? _____

Answers

TRUE OR FALSE

1. True. Total expenditures consist of consumption spending (C), investment spending (I), government spending (G), and net exports ($X - M$).

2. False. Keynes believed that an economy could achieve full employment but there was nothing that ensured it would occur all the time.

3. False. The wealth effect refers to the idea that changes in the price level change wealth, which causes consumption spending to change.

4. True. To eliminate a recessionary gap without government involvement requires that wages and prices fall so that wealth increases, boosting consumption expenditures.

5. True. A larger trade deficit occurs when imports rise or exports decline, which means $(X - M)$ decreases. This reduces aggregate expenditures.

6. False. When $C + I + G + X - M$ exceeds Y, inventories are falling and the economy is not in equilibrium. An inflationary gap occurs when the output level where $C + I + G + X - M = Y$ (that is, equilibrium output) exceeds potential output.

7. True. Keynesian economists believe that wages and prices rise more easily than they fall. An economy is more likely to eliminate an inflationary gap than a recessionary gap.

8. True. Lower taxes increase consumption spending, increase total spending, and raise output.

9. False. While Keynesians support an activist policy, monetarists question the ability of the government to consistently succeed with such a policy.

10. False. An economy with large government spending can experience unemployment if the total of all spending—consumption, investment, government, and net exports—results in an output less than potential output.

MULTIPLE CHOICE

1. C. Consumption increases by 0.75 times the $20,000 increase in transfer payments, or $15,000.

2. D. If the output the economy is producing is less than its potential output, unemployment occurs.

3. A. A recessionary gap occurs when an economy is producing less than its potential output. One way to increase the economy's output is to increase total spending by increasing government spending.

4. B. Because saving and investment decisions are made by separate groups, there is little reason to believe that injections always equal leakages at potential output.

5. C. As prices rise, the purchasing power of financial assets declines, which causes consumption spending to fall.

6. C. Inventories accumulate involuntarily if leakages $(S + T + M)$ exceed injections $(I + G + X)$.

7. D. Higher welfare payments would increase total spending and push output higher. The other policies would reduce aggregate spending.

8. A. When there is an inflationary gap, policies should be directed toward reducing aggregate expenditures. Higher taxes, lower government spending, and lower transfer payments each tend to reduce aggregate expenditures.

9. D. During the 1930s, unemployment remained at or above 10 percent for a decade. The self-correcting mechanism, which involves declines in wages and prices, did not seem to work.

10. D. One dollar of additional government spending is totally spent on goods and services, and a $1 tax cut is partly spent and partly saved, depending on the size of the MPC. The fact that part of the tax cut is saved reduces the increase in total spending.

PROBLEMS

1. a. Equilibrium output is **$7,000**. It is the output amount associated with the intersection of the $C + I + G + X - M$ line and the 45° line.

   b. Because equilibrium output is less than potential output, there is a **recessionary gap**. The gap is the difference between potential output and actual output, which is **$2,000**.

c. With a marginal propensity to consume of 0.8, the multiplier equals $1/(1 - .8) = 1/.2 = 5$. To eliminate a recessionary gap of $2,000 requires that government spending **increase** by $2,000/5 = **$400**.

d. Transfer payments must be increased by **$500**. If transfer payments are increased by $500, individuals spend $(.8) \times (\$500) = \$400$. With a multiplier of 5, the total increase in spending and output equals $2,000.

2. a. There is a **recessionary gap** equal to **$6,000**. The multiplier is $1/(1 - 2/3) = 1/1/3 = 3$, so government spending must increase by **$2,000** to eliminate the recessionary gap. Taxes must be changed by – **$3,000**. A $3,000 tax cut shifts consumption spending higher by $2,000 and also closes the gap.

b. The gap is an **inflationary gap** of **$15,000**. With an MPC = .6, the multiplier is $1/(- .6) = 1/.4 = 2.5$. To eliminate the inflationary gap requires that government spending be changed by – **$6,000** or that taxes be increased by **$10,000**.

c. The gap is a **recessionary gap** of **$10,000**. The multiplier is $1/(1 - .5) = 1/.5 = 2$ when the MPC is .5. To eliminate the $10,000 recessionary gap requires that government spending increase by **$5,000** or that taxes be changed by – **$10,000**.

3. a. The formula for equilibrium output is:

$$Y = \frac{1}{1 - b(1 - t)} (a + I_0 + G_0)$$

Substituting the values from the problem, the equation becomes:

$$Y = \frac{1}{1 - .8(1 - .25)} (\$40,000 + \$70,000 + \$90,000)$$

$$Y = \frac{1}{1 - .8(.75)} (\$200,000)$$

$$Y = \frac{1}{1 - .6} (\$200,000)$$

$$Y = \frac{1}{.4} (\$200,000)$$

$$Y = (2.5) \times (\$200,000)$$

$$Y = \mathbf{\$500,000}$$

b. If potential output equals $600,000, this economy has a **recessionary gap** of $100,000 and experiences unemployment.

c. With a multiplier of 2.5, government spending must increase by **$40,000** to increase output by 2.5 times $40,000 or by $100,000 and eliminate the $100,000 recessionary gap.

CHAPTER 14

The Model of Aggregate Supply— Aggregate Demand

Chapters 12 and 13 focused on the demand side of the economy. Chapter 14 emphasizes the supply side of the economy in macroeconomic analysis. While Keynesian economists believe that fluctuations in demand are the source of most economic problems, the supply side cannot be ignored because it influences how changes in demand are divided between changes in the price level and changes in real output.

Some economists have placed such emphasis on the aggregate supply curve that they have been called "supply-side economists." Their views and policies dominated the administrations of Ronald Reagan and George Bush. This chapter describes these policies and evaluates their successes.

CHAPTER OUTLINE

I. Equilibrium and Shifts of the Aggregate Demand and Aggregate Supply Curves
   A. Equilibrium occurs where aggregate demand equals aggregate supply, that is, at the intersection of the aggregate demand and aggregate supply curves.
   B. The aggregate demand curve shifts as such determinants of demand as wealth, monetary and fiscal policies, and exchange rates change.
   C. The aggregate supply curve shifts as such determinants of aggregate supply as the quantity of resources, productivity, technology, and input prices change.

II. Aggregate Demand Curve
   A. The explanation of the downward slope of the aggregate demand curve is different from the explanation for the downward-sloping demand curve for a specific good.
      1. A lower price level does not increase the quantity of output demanded because one good is becoming less expensive relative to other goods. Rather, it is assumed that the prices of all goods move together.
      2. A lower price level does not increase the quantity of output demanded because the lower prices are raising purchasing power. Instead, the lower prices are accompanied by lower nominal incomes, leaving real income the same.
   B. The aggregate demand curve is downward sloping because:
      1. a lower price level raises the purchasing power of financial assets, thereby boosting wealth and stimulating consumption spending. This is called the wealth effect.
      2. a decline in the price level lowers the amount that borrowers need to borrow to finance necessary expenditures, which reduces interest rates and increases expenditures on interest-sensitive items such as housing and automobiles.

3. a lower price level increases the quantity of goods that a given allocation of government funds is able to buy.

4. a lower price level makes U.S. goods less expensive relative to foreign goods, which increases U.S. exports and reduces U.S. imports.

III. Aggregate Supply Curve
   A. The explanation for the upward slope of the aggregate supply curve is not based upon a higher price of one output relative to other outputs, making it more profitable to produce. Because all prices are assumed to move together, relative prices do not change.
   B. The upward slope of the aggregate supply curve is caused by the fact that some input prices are fixed in the short run because of contractual commitments.
      1. A rising price level increases the profit margin and makes the production of more output profitable.
      2. The ability to expand output when the price level rises is influenced by how near the economy is to full employment. The closer to full employment, the more difficult it is to expand output. This appears as a steepening of the aggregate supply curve.
   C. In the long run, the supply curve is vertical because all input prices adjust to the higher demand and to the higher prices of output.
   D. There is a debate about the shape of the aggregate supply curve in the short run.
      1. Mainstream economists believe that there is considerable stickiness to input prices, allowing for significant short-run expansion of output when demand rises.
      2. Neoclassical economists believe that input prices are highly flexible in the short run because economic agents anticipate changes in the economic environment and adjust input prices accordingly. As a result, increases in demand lead to higher prices and little extra output in the short run.

IV. The Self-Correcting Mechanism
   A. The description of the wealth effect presented in Chapter 13 can be pictured using the aggregate demand curve.
      1. In the aggregate expenditure model in Chapter 13, the lower price level boosts consumption expenditures (through the wealth effect), government purchases, and net exports, shifting the aggregate expenditures ($C + I + G + X - M$) line upward, which increases the amount of output demanded.
      2. In the aggregate demand model of this chapter, the increase in consumption, government, and net export expenditures caused by a lower price level appears as a movement along the aggregate demand curve.
      3. **Keynesians** are skeptical of the strength of the wealth effect while **monetarists** believe the wealth effect is powerful.
   B. The self-correcting mechanism described in Chapter 13 can also be illustrated in the aggregate demand–aggregate supply model.
      1. An economy with a recessionary gap and unemployment would be able to eliminate the gap and the unemployment if its price level fell sufficiently. The recessionary gap would cause a decline in wages and other input prices. This appears as a rightward shift of the aggregate supply curve. As the price level falls, spending on goods increases, which appears as a movement along the aggregate demand curve, and increases the economy's output. This process would continue until the recessionary gap is eliminated.
      2. An economy with an inflationary gap would have the opposite experience. The inflationary gap would increase wages and other input prices, shifting the aggregate supply curve to the left. As the price level rose, consumption and other spending would fall and output would drop. This process would continue until the inflationary gap is eliminated.
   C. There is no agreement among economists on the reliability of the self-correcting mechanism:
      1. **Keynesians** believe that the aggregate demand curve is steep because the wealth effect is weak. To eliminate a recessionary gap would require a substantial decline in the price level. Such a large decline is not only unlikely because prices are inflexible downward, but it also would create other problems in the economy. Falling prices, for example, would hurt borrowers at the expense of lenders, creating financial problems for firms and home-buyers with fixed-rate mortgages.

2. **Monetarists** view the wealth effect as stronger than do the Keynesians. As a result, the aggregate demand curve is viewed as being flatter. To self-correct a recessionary gap requires a smaller decline in the price level. Combined with their greater belief in the flexibility of prices, the strong wealth effect causes monetarists to have greater faith in the ability of the economy to self-correct.

V. Supply-Side Economics
  A. **Supply-side economics** is the belief that government policies should focus on shifting the aggregate supply curve rather than shifting the aggregate demand curve as suggested by Keynesians. By shifting the aggregate supply curve rightward, output can increase without increasing prices.
    1. The aggregate supply curve shifts rightward if any of the following occurs:
      a. Input prices fall: Inputs include labor, capital, land, and materials.
      b. An increase in the economy's resources: The resources that an economy can increase most easily are labor and capital.
      c. An increase in the work effort of labor: This increases labor productivity.
      d. An improvement in technology: This also increases labor productivity.
    2. In a market economy, government policies can do little to change the prices of inputs. But the government can:
      a. influence the supply of capital by making saving and investment more attractive.
      b. increase the supply of labor and work effort by making work more financially rewarding.
      c. improve the technology by making research more profitable.
  B. President Reagan's economic program contained numerous proposals. Among them were:
    1. Reducing inflation to encourage investment.
    2. Promoting international trade to make markets more competitive.
    3. Reducing government regulations to allow businesses the greatest opportunity to be productive.
    4. Implementing the Economic Recovery Tax Act of 1981 (ERTA), the major focus of the Reagan program. This act changed taxes in the following ways:
      a. Individual tax rates were reduced by 25 percent over three years.
      b. A tax exemption was provided for families in which both husband and wife worked. This made it more attractive for both to enter the labor force.
      c. The income tax was indexed to eliminate bracket creep. **Bracket creep** is the tendency for inflation to move people into higher and higher tax brackets. Indexation involves adjusting tax brackets to offset inflation.
      d. Individuals were permitted to establish **Individual Retirement Accounts (IRAs)**, which allow earnings from savings to accumulate tax-free until withdrawn at retirement, in order to encourage saving.
      e. Corporate taxes and taxes on capital gains were reduced in order to increase the rate of return on investment and provide an incentive to increase investment.
      f. Tax credits were provided for research.
  C. Some supply-side economists who supported the Reagan economic program made assertions that proved false. These include:
    1. *The assertion that the income-tax cuts would increase tax revenue*
      a. This belief is based on the Laffer curve, named after Arthur Laffer. The Laffer curve begins with the noncontroversial proposition that the government collects no tax revenue if the tax rate is zero. As the tax rate increases, tax revenue initially rises. But eventually, as the tax rate continues to rise, tax revenue begins to fall—until it again reaches zero when the tax rate equals 100 percent.
      b. The controversial part of Laffer's argument was the assertion that the U.S. federal tax system in 1980 was beyond the peak of the Laffer curve. This meant that lower tax rates would *increase* tax revenue. Although this is possible in principle, it did not happen. The lower income-tax rates actually reduced income-tax receipts.
    2. *The assertion that budget deficits would induce people to save more*

a. Larger budget deficits would normally be expected to reduce the funds available to finance private investment, particularly when the deficits occur as the economy is at or near full employment. This was one of the reasons that the Reagan policies were opposed by many economists.

b. Some supply-side economists asserted that taxpayers would increase their saving as budget deficits increase. The extra saving is in anticipation of the higher taxes that will be necessary to pay the interest on the additional debt. This phenomenon is called the **Ricardian Equivalence Theorem**. If valid, the budget deficits do not reduce the funds available for private investment.

c. Evidence indicates that saving did not increase. As a result, the budget deficits required the United States to borrow more from foreigners.

3. *The assertion that inflation could be reduced without a period of higher unemployment*

a. Most economists believe that reducing inflation requires a period of higher unemployment. In order to reduce the inflation, stabilization policies must reduce aggregate demand. As a consequence, output falls and unemployment rises.

b. Extreme supply-siders asserted that large tax cuts would cause a dramatic increase in aggregate supply, counteracting the effect of the reduction in aggregate demand on output. As a result, prices would fall at the same time that unemployment declined, according to these supply-siders.

c. As a result of the restrictive monetary policies imposed by the Federal Reserve in the early 1980s, inflation did decline. But the United States also went through its most severe recession since the 1930s. Unemployment soared.

D. An evaluation of the 1980s supply-side policies reveals that, although some benefits occurred, supply-side policies were not as successful as their strongest supporters anticipated. The reasons for the disappointing result are:

1. The supply-side effects were exaggerated. The large reduction in the rate of inflation and the tax incentives that increased the rate of return on savings did not boost the nation's saving rate. Nor did the lower income-tax rates significantly increase hours of work.

2. The large budget deficits negated the favorable aspects of the program. The large budget deficits caused the Federal Reserve to follow restrictive monetary policies. Stimulative fiscal policies combined with tight monetary policies result in high interest rates that discourage investment spending and slow economic growth.

3. The supply-side policies increased the inequality in the distribution of income. Because supply-side policies focus on rewarding hard work and success, those who are most able benefit the most. Those less able to work, save, and invest—the poor—benefit less.

HINTS AND HELP

1. Aggregate Demand versus Aggregate Supply   One issue that divides economists is the importance of aggregate demand versus aggregate supply. Keynesian economists emphasize shifts of the aggregate demand curve to explain economic events. Supply-side economists, as their name implies, believe that shifts of the aggregate supply curve are more important, and have been neglected in the past.

These two groups also disagree about the way taxes influence the economy. As described in the previous chapter, Keynesians argue that tax changes shift the aggregate demand curve by changing the amount people have available to spend. Supply-siders believe that taxes influence the economy by changing the incentives to be productive, shifting aggregate supply.

FILL IN THE BLANK

vertical   1.   In the long run the aggregate supply curve is _____.

closer

2. As the economy gets _____ to full employment the aggregate supply curve becomes steeper, meaning it is more difficult to increase output.

supply, demand

3. The slope of the aggregate _____ curve determines how increases in aggregate _____ are divided between higher output and higher prices.

demand

4. The wealth effect influences the steepness of the aggregate _____ curve.

flat

5. Monetarists believe that the aggregate demand curve is relatively _____.

Bracket creep

6. _____ occurs when inflation increases the tax rates that people are required to pay.

supply-side

7. The economic policies of the Reagan administration were based on _____ _____ economics.

steep

8. Neoclassical economists believe that the aggregate supply curve is _____ because owners of inputs anticipate increases in the price level.

greater

9. The weaker the wealth effect the _____ the decline in wages and prices required to move the economy to full employment.

increase

10. The Ricardian Equivalence Theorem implies that larger budget deficits _____ private saving.

TRUE OR FALSE

_____ 1. The aggregate supply curve is upward sloping because wages are perfectly flexible.

_____ 2. When there is a recessionary gap, total output is greater than output at the full-employment level.

_____ 3. A recessionary gap is eliminated through the self-correcting mechanism by outward shifts of the aggregate demand curve.

_____ 4. When there is an inflationary gap, total spending must increase in order to achieve equilibrium at full employment.

_____ 5. Economists believe that the aggregate supply curve becomes steeper as the economy approaches full employment.

_____ 6. The major plank in Ronald Reagan's economic program was a cut in income-tax rates.

_____ 7. An improved technology increases aggregate supply.

_____ 8. Economists agree that the wealth effect is strong.

_____ 9. The self-correcting mechanism works better for an inflationary gap than for a recessionary gap.

_____ 10. Supply-side economists believe that increases in government spending are necessary to increase aggregate supply.

MULTIPLE CHOICE

1. Keynesians believe that an economy is unlikely to self-correct a(n) _____ gap because workers resist wage _____. Fill in the blanks with the appropriate words.

	First blank	Second blank
A.	recessionary	cuts
B.	recessionary	increases
C.	inflationary	cuts
D.	inflationary	increases

2. In general, supply-side policies focus on shifting the:
   A. production possibilities curve outward.
   B. production possibilities curve inward.
   C. aggregate demand curve rightward.
   D. aggregate demand curve leftward.

3. An increase in aggregate supply has which of the following effects?

	Output	Price level
A.	increase	increase
B.	increase	decrease
C.	decrease	increase
D.	decrease	decrease

4. Monetarists and Keynesians disagree on which of the following issues?
   A. whether a decline in the price level increases or decreases total spending
   B. whether an inflationary gap is possible
   C. whether an economy can ever have full employment
   D. whether the wealth effect is strong or weak

5. What is it called when inflation increases the percentage of income paid in income taxes?
   A. wealth effect
   B. recessionary gap
   C. bracket creep
   D. supply-side tax

6. If the Ricardian Equivalence Theorem is valid:
   A. budget deficits can be financed with increased saving by taxpayers.
   B. taxpayers pay their taxes entirely out of their saving.
   C. increases in government spending decrease investment spending.
   D. tax increases have no impact on the economy's ouput.

7. Individual Retirement Accounts (IRAs):
   A. reduced taxable income.
   B. provided an incentive to save.
   C. were available to all taxpayers when they were first introduced.
   D. All the alternatives are correct.

8. The Laffer curve shows that:
   A. budget deficits are impossible.
   B. tax cuts always increase tax revenue.
   C. tax cuts never increase tax revenue.
   D. tax cuts may increase tax revenue.

9. The supply-side policies of the Reagan administration had which of the following effects?
   A. reduced budget deficits
   B. increased tax revenues
   C. increased income inequalities
   D. increased trade surpluses

10. Critics of supply-side economics believe that:
    A. inflation is not a problem and policies should not be directed toward eliminating it.
    B. unemployment is eliminated easily through the economy's self-correcting mechanism.
    C. the claims made by supply-side economists were exaggerated.
    D. taxes have no impact on an economy's performance and thus should rarely be reduced.

PROBLEMS

1. Figure 14.1 pictures the equilibrium of an economy.
   a. What kind of "gap" does this economy have? _____
      Identify the size of the gap on the figure.
   b. Show how this economy could theoretically self-correct this gap by shifting the appropriate curve in the correct direction on the graph.
   c. Describe what happens to wages in the economy to achieve this self-correction. According to Keynesian economists, is this outcome likely? _____

FIGURE 14.1

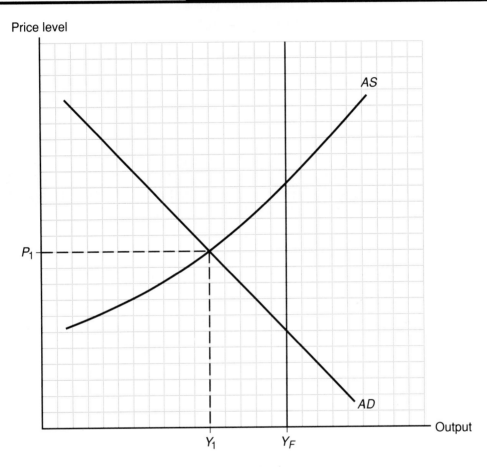

2. Figure 14.2 pictures the equilibrium of another economy.
   a. What kind of "gap" does this economy have? _____ Identify the size of the gap on the figure.
   b. Show how this economy would self-correct this gap by shifting the appropriate curve in the correct direction on the graph. Identify the equilibrium after the economy has self-corrected with P_2, Y_2.
   c. Describe what happens to wages in the economy to achieve this self-correction. _____ _____ According to Keynesian economists, is this outcome likely? _____

FIGURE 14.2

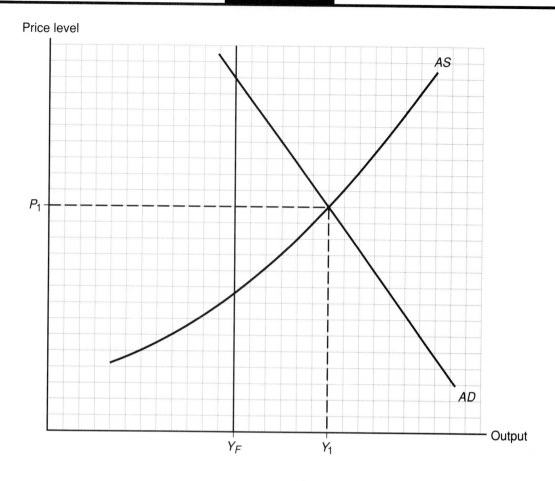

Price level — Output axis with curves AS, AD, P_1, Y_F, Y_1

TRUE OR FALSE

1. False. The aggregate supply curve is upward sloping because wages and other input prices are fixed in the short run, so that higher prices make it more profitable for firms to produce more.

2. False. When there is a recessionary gap, total output is less than output at the full-employment level of output.

3. False. The self-correcting mechanism eliminates a recessionary gap through increases in the aggregate supply curve, which cause output prices to fall and boost consumption spending because of the wealth effect.

4. False. To move equilibrium output so it equals full employment output requires that total expenditures be reduced.

5. True. As the economy approaches its capacity, it becomes more difficult to expand output. As a consequence, more of any increase in demand is reflected in higher prices and less is reflected in increases in output.

6. True. The Reagan economic program had as its centerpiece a major reduction in income-tax rates with the goal of stimulating increases in aggregate supply.

7. True. One thing that increases an economy's aggregate supply curve is an improvement in the economy's technology.

8. False. Monetarists believe that the wealth effect is strong, but Keynesians believe that it is weak.

9. True. Because prices are more flexible upward than downward, the self-correcting mechanism works better when there is an inflationary gap than when there is a recessionary gap.

10. False. Supply-side economists believe that tax cuts are the key to increasing aggregate supply.

MULTIPLE CHOICE

1. A. Keynesians believe an economy is unlikely to self-correct a recessionary gap because to do so requires wage cuts, which workers resist.

2. A. The intent of supply-side policies is to boost the economy's rate of growth, which appears as an outward shift of the production possibilities curve as well as a rightward shift of the aggregate supply curve.

3. B. An outward shift of the aggregate supply curve increases output while lowering the price level.

4. D. Monetarists believe that the wealth effect is strong; Keynesians believe it is weak.

5. C. Bracket creep occurs when inflation moves taxpayers into higher tax brackets.

6. A. The Richardian Equivalence Theorem holds that taxpayers save more when the government has a larger budget deficit. The extra borrowing by the government is offset by the extra saving by taxpayers.

7. D. Individual Retirement Accounts (IRAs) provided an incentive to save by allowing everyone to reduce their taxable income by putting some of their income into certain kinds of savings accounts.

8. D. The Laffer curve shows that it is possible, though not certain, for tax cuts to increase tax revenues.

9. C. The supply-side policies of the Reagan administration—by focusing tax cuts on those who work, save, and invest the most—tended to increase the incomes of the wealthy more than the incomes of the poor.

10. C. Critics of supply-side economics charge that supply-side economists exaggerated the benefits that were possible with such policies.

PROBLEMS

1. a. There is a **recessionary gap**. It is equal to $Y_F - Y_1$ in Figure 14.3.

    b. Self-correcting this gap requires that the aggregate supply (AS) curve shift to the right to AS_2. The new equilibrium is P_2, Y_2 which means prices are lower and output higher.

    c. To achieve the self-correction **wages must fall**. Keynesians doubt that this will happen easily because workers resist the necessary wage declines.

2. a. There is an **inflationary gap**. It is equal to $Y_1 - Y_F$ in Figure 14.4.

    b. Self-correcting this gap requires that the aggregate supply (AS) curve shift to the left to AS_2. The new equilibrium is P_2, Y_2, which means prices are higher and output lower.

    c. To achieve the self-correction **wages must rise**. This outcome is more likely because workers typically do not resist wage increases.

FIGURE 14.3

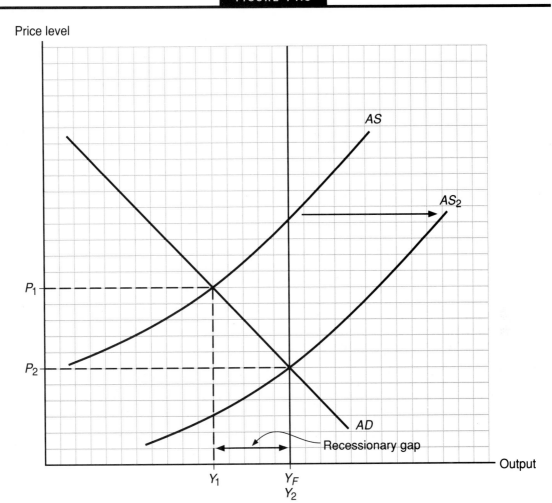

Price level

P_1

P_2

AS

AS_2

AD

Recessionary gap

Output

Y_1

Y_F
Y_2

FIGURE 14.4

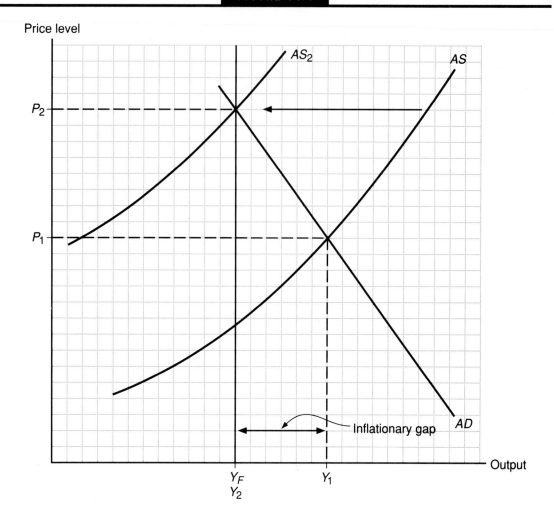

CHAPTER 15

Money, Banking, and the Creation of Bank Deposits

One of the more intriguing aspects of economics is money and banking. We are familiar with banks but do not always understand them. Chapter 15 answers many questions about money that are often posed. What exactly *is* money? Where does it come from? Why is money a part of all but the most primitive economies? What do banks do with deposits? And what role, if any, do banks have in supplying money?

Upon completion of this chapter you will be equipped to learn how the government, through the Federal Reserve, is able to influence the money supply—the topic of Chapter 16.

CHAPTER OUTLINE

I. Money
   A. The word *money* is often confused with the concepts of income (He makes a lot of money) and wealth (She has a lot of money).
   B. The most common, correct meaning of **money** is anything that is widely accepted for payment. This is known as the narrow definition of money. Officially, this is called the **M-1** definition. It includes:
      1. Currency not in the vaults of financial institutions (C^P)
      2. All checkable deposits (*DDO*). Checkable deposits are:
         a. demand deposits
         b. Negotiable Order of Withdrawal (NOW) accounts
         c. Automatic Transfer Service (ATS) accounts

II. The Functions of Money
   A. Medium of Exchange: Money is given in exchange for the goods and services that are bought. Without money, trades would be difficult to arrange because of the need for a coincidence of wants—each trader must want exactly what the other has. The M-1 definition is based on this function of money.
   B. Unit of Account: A unit of account is a yardstick—a common measure of value. Using one yardstick of value reduces to one the number of prices for each good.
   C. Store of Value: Money is one way to store purchasing power. There are alternatives to money for storing purchasing power. These alternatives differ in their **liquidity**—the ability to be turned into a medium of exchange quickly. The things included in M-1 are perfectly liquid because they are already a medium of exchange. Other definitions of money focus on the store of value function of money. They add to the items in M-1 other assets that are highly liquid. What is included or not included is somewhat arbitrary. Often the deciding issue is an empirical one: How well does the particular money supply definition

correlate with economic activity? These other definitions are designated M-2, M-3, and L. The various measures of the money supply are known as the **monetary aggregates**.

III. Evolution of Money
   A. Early money was **full-bodied money**. It was made of a valuable commodity, typically gold or silver, and had the same value both as a commodity and as money. That is, there was a dollar's worth of gold in a $1 gold coin.
   B. Today, coin and currency are **fiat money** or fiduciary money. They are valuable only because they are generally acceptable for goods and services. This kind of money is less expensive to produce but is subject to excessive issue.
   C. Goldsmiths, who held gold for safe keeping, issued gold certificates as receipts. These certificates soon circulated as money. This system was the forerunner of today's banks.

IV. Commercial Banks and the Supply of Money
   A. A **balance sheet** lists assets on one side of the ledger and the liabilities and net worth on the other. Because net worth is defined as the difference between assets and liabilities, the two sides of the balance sheet must sum to the same total. Net worth is also known as capital accounts.
   B. The **assets** of a bank include its earning assets such as loans and securities, its physical assets such as buildings and equipment, and its reserves.
   C. Reserves:
      1. The **reserves** of the bank are the cash it has in its vault and its deposits at the Federal Reserve. The Federal Reserve requires banks to keep reserves.
      2. **Required reserves** are the dollar amount of reserves a particular bank must hold.
      3. The required reserves are determined by multiplying the reserve requirement times the bank's deposits. The **reserve requirement** is the minimum, legally allowable ratio of reserves to deposits, a percentage.
      4. Any reserves a bank has above what it is required to hold are called the bank's **excess reserves**.
   D. The primary **liabilities** of a bank are its deposits. The major deposits are:
      1. The checkable deposits—demand deposits and other checkable deposits.
      2. Other kinds of deposits—savings accounts, certificates of deposit, and time deposits.
   E. The **capital account** is the book value of the business. The capital account protects the bank owners if the value of its assets declines. There is often a trade-off between the bank's safety and profitability. More risky assets are less likely to be repaid and threaten the bank's safety but offer potentially greater profit.
   F. **Bank insolvency** occurs when the value of the bank's assets declines enough so that the value of the bank's liabilities exceeds the value of its assets. It means that the net worth or the capital account is negative. In the 1980s, bank failures were very high because of high-risk investments coupled with poor business conditions in agriculture, oil, and Latin American countries.

V. The Creation of Money
   A. Banks are able to create money because they operate within a fractional reserve banking system. **Fractional reserve banking** means banks are required to hold reserves that are only a fraction of their deposits.
   B. A checking account deposit (*DDO*) is created when a bank makes a loan.
      1. The money that is lent is a new checking account for the borrower. The new checking account deposit is new money because checking account deposits are money.
      2. In return for the checking account, the borrower signs a loan agreement (an IOU) promising to repay the loan. On the bank's balance sheet, assets rise by the amount of the loan because the bank has a new loan agreement, and its liabilities rise by the amount of the loan because the borrower has that much in the newly created checking account deposit.
      3. The borrower soon writes a check to buy what the money was borrowed to buy. That check is deposited in another bank. The bank making the loan loses reserves (deposits at the Federal Reserve) equal to the size of the loan to the bank receiving the check.
   C. Deposits are also increased when a bank buys U.S. government securities, but the mechanics are different.

1. The bank buying the securities writes a check on its account at the Federal Reserve bank. When that check is deposited by the seller of the securities in its bank account, checking account balances (DDO) rise. This represents new money.
2. The bank that bought the securities loses reserves (deposits at the Federal Reserve) to the bank receiving the check.

D. The deposit-creating ability of banks is limited by the requirement that reserves be held against deposits. Because deposit creation eventually results in an equal loss of reserves to an individual bank, the size of a loan or a security purchase is limited to the amount of reserves a bank can afford to lose—the bank's excess reserves.

E. The expansion of deposits from that bank extends beyond the first bank that makes a loan or buys a security. The banks that receive the checks written on the deposits created by the first bank receive reserves from that bank. Only a part of these reserves must be held; the rest are excess reserves and form the basis of new loans. This process repeats itself until eventually there are no excess reserves remaining and no new loans are possible.

F. The ultimate increase in deposits due to the initial increase in the banks' excess reserves, called the induced change in deposits, can be calculated using the formula:

$$\Delta DDO = \frac{1}{\% RR_{DD}} \times (\Delta ER)$$

The term $1/\% RR_{DD}$ is the simple **deposit expansion multiplier**.

G. To calculate the total increase in deposits involves adding to the induced change in deposits any deposits created when the bank initially gained the excess reserves. For example, when cash is deposited in a bank, deposits are immediately created as the bank gains excess reserves. This increase in deposits would be added to the induced increase in deposits to yield the total increase in deposits.

H. In reality, the actual increase in deposits is lower than what the equation predicts because of two factors:
1. Banks deliberately hold some excess reserves. Because they do not make the largest possible loan each time, the increase in the money supply is smaller than the formula indicates.
2. Because individuals prefer to hold some money in the form of currency, they turn some of the extra deposits into cash. The cash withdrawal reduces the excess reserves of the banks and reduces the possible increase in deposits.

HINTS AND HELP

1. Money, Money, Money . . . It is unfortunately the case that people, including economists, often use the word "money" in many different ways. As discussed earlier, money is *not* the same thing as income and it is *not* the same thing as wealth. You should get into the habit of checking your use of the word "money." Make sure it is being used to describe the amount of currency outside the vaults of banks (C^P) and all checkable deposits (DDO). Using the right word eliminates much confusion and many mistakes.

2. Money Creation Undoubtedly one of the most fascinating parts of this course is money creation. Although banks are familiar to everyone, it is strange to picture them in the important role of money creation. What is most difficult for most students to believe is that banks can create money seemingly out of thin air. But they can.

One reason this is so difficult to accept is that it is easy to forget that checking accounts are money just as currency is. If the bank printed currency, everyone would accept that the bank created money. Creating a checking account is not so convincing. But checking accounts *are* money. And the ability to create checking accounts, which banks certainly have, is the ability to create money.

The reason banks have the power to create checkable deposits is that they are required to hold reserves equal to only a portion of their deposits. When someone deposits cash or a check that gives the bank reserves, the bank must hold only a portion of those reserves. The rest they can *afford* to lose. The reserves they can afford to lose are called the bank's excess reserves.

When a bank makes a loan, the bank is certain that it will lose reserves equal to the size of the loan. But the bank does not mind. In return for losing the reserves, the bank has gained an interest-earning asset—the loan. A side effect of this activity is that money is created.

3. Multiple Expansion   Deposit expansion does not stop with the first bank that makes a loan. As the bank that made the first loan loses deposits and reserves, a second bank gains them. Because, again, the second bank is required to hold only a portion of its new reserves, it now has excess reserves. It can repeat what the first bank did—make a loan and create a new checking account balance in the process.

Remember that the total increase in checking deposits has two parts. There is the multiple expansion because of the introduction of excess reserves, plus any increase in deposits that occurred when the excess reserves were added to the banking system.

FILL IN THE BLANK

liquidity

1. The ability of an asset to be turned quickly into a medium of exchange is called _____.

excess reserves

2. Total reserves minus required reserves are called _____.

reserves

3. The sum of a bank's cash in its vault and its deposits with the Federal Reserve is called _____ .

full-bodied or commodity

4. Money that is as valuable as a commodity as it is as money is called _____ _____ money.

fractional

5. Banks can create money if there is a _____ reserve banking system.

medium of exchange

6. The M-1 definition of money is based on the _____ function of money.

unit of account

7. The fact that all prices in the United States are quoted in dollars means dollars are a _____.

assets

8. Liabilities plus net worth equal _____ .

insolvent

9. When net worth is negative, the bank is _____.

money supply

10. When a bank makes a loan, the new demand deposits represent an increase in the _____.

TRUE OR FALSE

_____ 1. Paper money is valuable only if it is backed by gold or silver.

_____ 2. All money is issued by the government.

_____ 3. Currency and checking accounts are perfectly liquid.

_____ 4. M-2 is made up of mediums of exchange only.

_____ 5. The deposit of currency into a bank checking account has no immediate effect on the money supply.

_____ 6. Checking account balances are liabilities of banks.

_____ 7. Currency withdrawals remove reserves from the banking system.

_____ 8. In order to make a loan, a bank needs to have required reserves.

_____ 9. If the reserve requirement is 0.25, the simple deposit expansion multiplier is 0.75.

_____ 10. The reserve requirement requires banks to hold a certain amount of currency in their vaults.

MULTIPLE CHOICE

1. A medium of exchange solves the problem of:
   A. coincidence of wants.
   B. scarcity of resources.
   C. unemployment.
   D. a unit of account.

2. The largest monetary aggregate is:
   A. reserves.
   B. L.
   C. M-1.
   D. M-3.

3. Because there is a unit of account, consumers:
   A. must remember fewer prices.
   B. can easily store purchasing power.
   C. spend a larger amount of their income.
   D. hold more currency.

4. Which of the following is *not* a function of money?
   A. store of value
   B. unit of account
   C. standard of credit
   D. medium of exchange

5. Which of the following is *not* part of M-1?
   A. currency in the hands of individuals
   B. demand deposits
   C. currency in the vaults of banks
   D. Automatic Transfer Services

6. A bank is insolvent when:
   A. assets exceed net worth.
   B. liabilities exceed net worth.
   C. net worth exceeds capital accounts.
   D. liabilities exceed assets.

7. If there are excess reserves of $10,000 and the reserve requirement equals 10 percent, the maximum possible increase in deposits through the multiple expansion of deposits is:
   A. $9,000.
   B. $10,000.
   C. $25,000.
   D. $100,000.

8. When banks do not make the largest possible loan:
   A. there is more currency outside of the vaults of banks.
   B. the money supply expansion is smaller.
   C. the bank's required reserves are higher.
   D. deposits at the Federal Reserve are smaller.

9. Fiat or fiduciary money has which of the following characteristics?
   A. It is made out of valuable metals such as gold.
   B. It is issued only by banks and other financial institutions.
   C. It makes up half of the U.S. money supply.
   D. It is valuable only because it is accepted for goods and services.

10. Which of the following is fiat money?
    A. a car
    B. a $10 gold coin made from gold worth $10
    C. a savings bond
    D. a $10 bill

PROBLEMS

1. Listed below are four transactions. Record on the T-accounts the changes (+ or − and the dollar amount) in the bank's balance sheets due to the transactions. Also, list what has happened to the bank's total reserves, the bank's required reserves, the bank's excess reserves, and the money supply. Assume the reserve requirement (%RR_{DD}) is 0.2, or 20 percent.

   a. $10,000 in currency is deposited in a checking account balance.

ASSETS		LIABILITIES	
Cash	_____	DDO	_____
Deposit at Federal Reserve bank	_____		
Loans	_____	Net worth	_____

   Change in total reserves   _____
   Change in required reserves   _____
   Change in excess reserves   _____
   Change in M–1   _____

   b. A $100,000 loan is made by the bank.

ASSETS		LIABILITIES	
Cash	_____	DDO	_____
Deposit at Federal Reserve bank	_____		
Loans	_____	Net worth	_____

   Change in total reserves   _____
   Change in required reserves   _____
   Change in excess reserves   _____
   Change in M-1   _____

c. A $50,000 check is written by a depositor, the check is deposited in another bank, and the check is cleared.

ASSETS		LIABILITIES	
Cash	_____	DDO	_____
Deposit at Federal Reserve bank	_____		
Loans	_____	Net worth	_____

Change in total reserves _____
Change in required reserves _____
Change in excess reserves _____
Change in M-1 _____

d. A company that took out a $25,000 loan defaults on the loan.

ASSETS		LIABILITIES	
Cash	_____	DDO	_____
Deposit at Federal Reserve bank	_____		
Loans	_____	Net worth	_____

Change in total reserves _____
Change in required reserves _____
Change in excess reserves _____
Change in M-1 _____

2. This question concerns the multiple expansion of deposits. Use the information provided to fill in the missing value in each of the following cases.

	EXCESS RESERVES	RESERVE REQUIREMENT	MAXIMUM INDUCED CHANGE IN DEPOSITS
a.	$4,000	0.10	_____
b.	$5,000	0.20	_____
c.	$20,000	_____	$100,000
d.	_____	0.25	$100,000
e.	$25,000	_____	$ 75,000

Answers

TRUE OR FALSE

1. False. Money is valuable because it is generally accepted in exchange for goods and services. U.S. currency is not backed by gold or silver, yet it is still valuable.

2. False. Most of the money supply comes from banks and other financial institutions that issue checking accounts.

3. True. Liquidity refers to the ability of something to be turned into a medium of exchange. Because currency and checking accounts are mediums of exchange, they are perfectly liquid.

4. False. Although M-2 includes mediums of exchange, it also includes items that are not. The M-2 definition is based upon the store of value function and includes savings accounts and time deposits, which are not mediums of exchange, as well as currency and checking account balances.

5. True. When currency is deposited in a bank, the currency is no longer counted as part of the money supply. But at the same time there is an increase in checking account balances. The decrease in currency (C^P) offsets the increase in checking account balances (DDO), so there is no change in the money supply.

6. True. A checking account is a liability of a bank because it represents a potential claim on some of the bank's assets. The owner of the checking account can withdraw the funds or instruct the bank to transfer funds to someone else.

7. True. When currency is withdrawn from a bank, the bank gives up some of its vault cash. Since vault cash counts as reserves, the bank's reserves are reduced.

8. False. In order to make a loan, a bank needs to have reserves it can afford to lose—excess reserves.

9. False. The simple deposit expansion multiplier is 1 divided by the reserve requirement. If the reserve requirement equals 0.25, the deposit expansion multiplier equals 1/.25 = 4.

10. False. The reserve requirement requires a bank to hold a certain amount of reserves. What part of the reserves is held in the form of currency in the vault and what part is held in their account at the Federal Reserve is up to the bank.

MULTIPLE CHOICE

1. A. Coincidence of wants is the requirement that two people must be in exactly the opposite circumstance in terms of what they have and what they want. It is required in order to make a trade in a barter economy. That problem is eliminated when there is a medium of exchange.

2. B. L is the largest monetary aggregate. It includes all financial assets that are highly liquid and safe.

3. A. Because a unit of account is a common denominator of value, consumers need to remember fewer prices because all prices are quoted in terms of that one common denominator, such as dollars or pesos.

4. C. The three functions of money are as a medium of exchange, unit of account, and store of value.

5. C. Currency in the vaults of banks is not part of M-1; it is counted as part of the bank's reserves.

6. D. A bank is insolvent if its net worth is negative, which occurs when its liabilities exceed its assets.

7. D. The maximum possible increase in deposits depends on the simple deposit expansion multiplier, which in this case equals 1/.1 or 10. The maximum increase in deposits is 10 x $10,000 or $100,000.

8. B. The money supply expansion is smaller because banks are not making all the loans and creating all the money they otherwise could.

9. D. Fiat or fiduciary money is valuable because the government declares it to be money. It is typically made of inexpensive paper or metals such as zinc.

10. D. Fiat money is money that has value only because it has been declared to be money. A $10 bill is fiat money.

PROBLEMS

1. a. *Cash* + **$10,000**, *DDO* + **$10,000**
       Total reserves + **$10,000**

Required reserves + **$2,000**

Excess reserves + **$8,000**

M-1 no change

When the $10,000 in currency is deposited, the cash in the bank's vault rises by $10,000 and in exchange for the currency the checking account (*DDO*) of the depositor rises by an equal amount.

Because cash in the vault is not counted as part of M-1, once the currency is given to the bank the currency component of M-1 falls by $10,000. This is offset by an increase in *DDO* of $10,000.

b. *Loans* + **$100,000**, *DDO* + **$100,000**

Total reserves **no change**

Required Reserves + **$20,000**

Excess reserves – **$20,000**

M-1 + **$100,000**

The money supply rises because the money that the bank is lending is a new checking account (*DDO*) that is part of the money supply. The required reserves rise and excess reserves fall because the bank's deposits are larger.

Eventually, the new $100,000 *DDO* will be spent by the borrower. In the process of check clearing, this bank will lose $100,000 of reserves.

c. *Deposit at Federal Reserve bank* – **$50,000**, *DDO* – **$50,000**

Total reserves – **$50,000**

Required reserves – **$10,000**

Excess reserves – **$40,000**

M-1 no change

Check clearing requires the bank on which the check was written to transfer to the bank that received the check an amount of reserves equal to the size of the check. Because deposits are lower, the bank's required reserves are also lower.

The money supply does not change because, although this bank has lost deposits of $50,000, deposits in the other bank have risen by $50,000. The net change is zero.

d. *Loans* – **$25,000**, Net worth – **$25,000**

Total reserves **no change**

Required reserves **no change**

Excess reserves **no change**

M-1 no change

2. Each can be answered using the deposit expansion formula:

$$\Delta DDO = \frac{1}{\% RR_{DD}} \times (\Delta ER)$$

a. Maximum induced change in deposits = **$40,000**. The deposit expansion multiplier is 1/.1 = 10, which means that the maximum increase in deposits is 10 times the excess reserves or $40,000.

b. Maximum induced change in deposits = **$25,000**. The deposit expansion multiplier is 1/.2 = 5.

c. The deposit expansion multiplier is 5 because the maximum increase in the deposits is five times larger than the excess reserves. As calculated in answer b, the deposit expansion multiplier equals 5 when the reserve requirement is **0.2**.

d. The deposit expansion multiplier is 1/.25 = 4. Because the maximum increase in deposits is $100,000, the excess reserves must equal $100,000/4 = **$25,000**.

e. The deposit multiplier is 3 because the maximum increase in deposits is three times larger than the excess reserves. The reserve requirement can be found in the following way:

$$\frac{1}{\% RR_{DD}} = 3; 1 = 3 \times \% RR_{DD}; 33\tfrac{1}{3} = \% RR_{DD}$$

CHAPTER 16

The Federal Reserve System and Its Conduct of Monetary Policy

Chapter 15 described the money supply and explained the role of banks in creating money. Chapter 16 introduces the Federal Reserve System, the institution responsible for controlling the money supply in the United States. The primary tools of monetary policy are outlined, as is the organization of the Federal Reserve.

In the next two chapters the impact of money on interest rates and on economic activity is analyzed.

CHAPTER OUTLINE

I. The **Federal Reserve System (the Fed)** is the central bank of the United States. A **central bank** is a country's official agency for monitoring banks and conducting monetary policy. The functions of the Federal Reserve are to:
    A. Supervise and Regulate Banks
    B. Clear Checks
    C. Issue Currency
    D. Serve as the Bank and Agent of the U.S. Treasury
    E. Conduct Monetary Policy

II. Structure of the Federal Reserve System
    A. The **Board of Governors**:
        1. Seven-person board, each member appointed to a 14-year term by the President of the United States.
        2. One member appointed to a four-year term as chairman.
        3. The board sets the reserve requirement and the discount rate. The **discount rate** is the interest rate the Federal Reserve charges when it lends reserves to banks.
    B. The **Federal Open Market Committee (FOMC)**:
        1. This board consists of twelve people:
            a. Seven members of the Board of Governors
            b. The president of the New York Federal Reserve Bank
            c. Four other Federal Reserve bank presidents on a rotating basis
        2. The Federal Open Market Committee determines monetary policy.
    C. The District Federal Reserve Banks:
        1. The district banks are privately owned by the banks in the district.
        2. Administration of each bank is under the control of a board of directors.
    D. Member Banks: Not all banks are members of the Federal Reserve but all banks are subject to the reserve requirements set by the Federal Reserve.

E. The Federal Reserve System is independent of direct control by either the legislative or the executive branches of government because members are appointed for 14-year terms and because the Federal Reserve does not have to go to Congress for appropriations (it has its own sources of income). The Fed's income comes from interest on its large portfolio of securities.

   1. Arguments in Favor of Independence:
      a. The Federal Reserve is less likely to be influenced by political and other short-term issues. Long-run issues should dominate in the determination of monetary policy.
      b. The public does not understand monetary policy issues; thus a more democratic process would probably not result in effective policies.
      c. There is evidence that economies with more independent central banks experience less inflation.
   2. Arguments Against Independence:
      a. Monetary and fiscal policies must be coordinated.
      b. The Federal Reserve is not accountable to the public through the democratic process; it should be accountable.

III. The Balance Sheet of the Federal Reserve System
   A. Assets:
      1. Coins are held by the Federal Reserve banks until they are requested by the banks in their district. The coins are bought from the U.S. Treasury by crediting Treasury deposits at the Federal Reserve banks.
      2. When banks cannot meet their reserve requirement, they may borrow reserves from the Federal Reserve bank. The loans to banks, called **discounts and advances**, are an asset of the Federal Reserve banks.
      3. The largest asset of Federal Reserve banks is the U.S. government securities they own. When a Federal Reserve bank buys U.S. government securities, it pays for them by crediting the Federal Reserve deposit of the bank in which the seller of the securities maintains a checking account.
   B. Liabilities:
      1. All paper currency is issued by Federal Reserve banks. When a bank requests more currency, the Federal Reserve bank ships it to the bank and deducts that amount from the bank's deposit at the Federal Reserve.
      2. Deposits of banks, savings and loan institutions, and the U.S. Treasury are the second largest of the Federal Reserve's liabilities.
      3. The Federal Reserve banks have a positive net worth, so there is a capital account representing private banks' ownership equity in the Federal Reserve.

IV. Tools of the Federal Reserve
   A. Open Market Operations
      1. **Open market operations** involve the Federal Reserve buying and selling U.S. government securities. By buying and selling the securities, the Federal Reserve adds or subtracts reserves from the banks and thus influences the money supply. This occurs in the following way:
         a. When the Federal Reserve buys U.S. government securities, it pays for them by writing a check on itself.
         b. When the seller of the bonds deposits the check in its account, the money supply immediately rises because there now are additional checking account balances in private banks.
         c. The bank in which the check is deposited receives more in its account at the Federal Reserve bank when the check clears. This increases the reserves and excess reserves of the bank.
         d. When a bank has excess reserves, it can make loans and the money supply can rise.
         e. When the Federal Reserve sells U.S. government securities, everything is reversed. Banks lose reserves and the money supply falls.
      2. Open market operations are the most frequently used tool of the Federal Reserve to control bank lending and the money supply.
   B. Discount Policy
      1. Banks have the privilege of borrowing reserves if they find themselves with a reserve deficiency and no other source of funds. When reserves are borrowed, the Federal Reserve charges interest. The interest rate is called the discount rate.

2. Changes in the discount rate have two effects:
   a. The mechanical effect is to encourage or discourage the borrowing of reserves. A higher discount rate makes banks less willing to borrow reserves. Total reserves fall as does the money supply. A lower discount rate increases reserves and increases the money supply.
   b. A change in the discount rate can have an announcement effect. If a discount rate change occurs unexpectedly, people often see the change as an announcement by the Federal Reserve of a change in its policy intentions. A higher discount rate indicates a restrictive policy is coming; a lower rate indicates an easing in the future.

C. Changes in Reserve Requirements
1. Changes in the **reserve requirement**—the minimum, legal ratio of reserves to deposits that a bank must maintain—do not change the amount of reserves in the banking system. But they do have two effects that cause the money supply to change.
   a. A change in the reserve requirement changes the proportion of the reserves that must be held as required reserves. A lower reserve requirement immediately increases excess reserves.
   b. A change in the reserve requirement changes the deposit expansion multiplier and thus changes the amount of deposits a given amount of reserves can support. A lower reserve requirement increases the deposit expansion multiplier.
2. Reserve requirement changes represent the most powerful tool of the Federal Reserve and are rarely used.

V. Intermediate Targets of Monetary Policy
A. An **intermediate target of monetary policy** is a variable that the Federal Reserve attempts to control in the short run in order to influence the ultimate objectives of unemployment and inflation.
B. Intermediate targets are needed because of the many steps and lags between the tools of the Federal Reserve—open market operations, the discount rate, and the reserve requirement—and the ultimate policy goals of full employment and price stability. Intermediate targets are given that name to indicate their position intermediate in the linkage between the tools and the ultimate policy goals.
C. The Federal Reserve sets its policy in terms of the intermediate targets. Policy is changed as information is accumulated about how consistent the settings are for the intermediate targets with the ultimate policy goals.
D. The ideal intermediate target variable has three characteristics:
1. It must have a strong link with the ultimate policy goals.
2. The Federal Reserve must be able to dominate the movements in the target variable.
3. The target variable must be frequently and accurately measured.
E. There are disputes among economists over which variable should be employed as the intermediate target.
1. Monetarists believe that one of the monetary aggregates—M-1, M-2, M-3, or L—is best.
2. Keynesians believe that interest rates are best.
F. The Federal Reserve has used various intermediate targets in the past:
1. From World War II until the early 1950s, the Federal Reserve followed a rigid policy of *pegging* interest rates, that is, keeping them absolutely constant at low levels. Such actions result in a *procyclical* policy, stimulating the economy when it is already strong and restricting the economy when it weakens.
   a. When the economy is expanding, the demand for credit rises, pulling up interest rates. In order to prevent this and stay rigidly on its target, the Fed must expand reserves and the money supply, thus stimulating a strong economy.
   b. When the economy is contracting, the demand for credit falls, pulling down interest rates. To prevent this and stay on its rigid interest rate target, the Fed must reduce reserves and the money supply, which further restricts a weakening economy.
2. From the 1950s through the 1970s, the Fed targeted interest rates. These targets were flexible, that is, the Fed changed them periodically. This policy was less rigid than the policy of pegging interest rates.
3. In 1975, Congress passed legislation requiring the Federal Reserve to announce and attempt to hit annual money supply growth targets. The Federal Reserve often failed to adhere strictly to these tar-

gets, sometimes overshooting and sometimes undershooting them. Monetarists criticize this failure, while Keynesians defend the Fed's actions.

4. From 1979 until 1982, the Federal Reserve abandoned interest rate targets in favor of money supply growth targets. In this period, interest rates soared.

5. Since 1982, the Fed has returned to a targeting procedure that is essentially one of targeting interest rates. Money growth rates often have deviated from the Fed's announced targets.

G. The Federal Reserve cannot simultaneously hit a money supply target *and* an interest rate target. If it seeks to hit an interest rate target in the face of an uncertain economy, it must vary the money supply aggressively to do so. If the Fed seeks to hit a money supply target in the face of an uncertain economy, it must give up control over the interest rate. The Fed must make a choice between hitting money supply targets and hitting interest rate targets. Economists disagree about which variable should have priority.

HINTS AND HELP

1. **The Federal Reserve and the Money Supply**   The Federal Reserve controls the money supply indirectly. If the Federal Reserve wants to increase the money supply it does not print $20 bills and throw them out the windows of the Federal Reserve banks. Instead, it works through banks. By adding or subtracting reserves from the banking system, the Federal Reserve influences the ability of banks to make loans and thus their ability to create money. (Recall from Chapter 15 that banks create money when they make loans.) While this indirect system may seem inexact, in most situations the Federal Reserve has the ability to be fairly precise in its control of the money supply.

2. **Open Market Operation**   The key tool of the Federal Reserve for control of the money supply is open market operations. When purchases are made by the Federal Reserve, the reserves and thus the lending and deposit-creating ability of banks is increased. It is important to understand the mechanics of this tool.

The Federal Reserve pays for its purchases of U.S. securities, or anything else that it buys, by writing checks on itself. These checks are always accepted by banks because they represent new reserves for the banks. Being able to write a check on itself means, in essence, that the Federal Reserve can give itself more funds in its checking account any time it wants. It simply pays for its security purchases by creating new reserves—deposit entries of banks at the Fed.

One reason the Federal Reserve is organized as it is—twelve separate banks and an independent Board of Governors—is the belief that this enormous power must be decentralized and kept out of the hands of politicians who might be tempted to use this power for short-run political gain at the expense of long-run economic considerations.

FILL IN THE BLANKS

central bank

1. In most countries, control of the money supply is in the hands of a _____.

discount rate, reserve requirement

2. The tools of the Federal Reserve controlled by the Board of Governors are the _____ and the _____.

twelve

3. The United States is divided into _____ Federal Reserve districts.

U.S. government securities

4. The largest asset of the Federal Reserve System is its holdings of _____.

open market operations

5. The most frequently used tool of the Federal Reserve is _____.

discount rate

6. Changes in the _____ have an important impact on the amount of borrowed reserves.

interest rates	7. Keynesians prefer to use _____ as an intermediate target.
announcement effect	8. The _____ occurs when changes in the discount rate are interpreted to signal future Federal Reserve policies.
Federal Reserve, U.S. Treasury	9. Paper money comes from the _____; coins are issued by the _____.
pegging	10. A policy of adjusting the tools of monetary policy so that interest rates remain constant is called _____ interest rates.

TRUE OR FALSE

_____ 1. The Federal Reserve is considered independent because the Board of Governors appoints its own members.

_____ 2. The Federal Reserve has an unlimited ability to purchase assets such as U.S. government securities.

_____ 3. The Federal Open Market Committee has the greatest impact on monetary policy.

_____ 4. Only the presidents of the Federal Reserve banks sit on the Federal Open Market Committee.

_____ 5. Lowering the reserve requirement lowers the deposit expansion multiplier.

_____ 6. The Federal Reserve banks are privately owned.

_____ 7. The largest liability on the balance sheet of the Federal Reserve is the deposits of banks, savings and loan institutions, and the U.S. Treasury.

_____ 8. When the Federal Reserve buys U.S. government securities from a bond dealer, the money supply immediately increases.

_____ 9. Monetary policy influences the economy by changing the government's tax receipts.

_____ 10. Intermediate targets are necessary because there is a loose linkage between changes in the Federal Reserve tools and changes in its ultimate goals.

MULTIPLE CHOICE

1. If total deposits in a bank equal $200,000, total reserves are $25,000, and excess reserves equal $5,000, the reserve requirement is:
   A. 20%.
   B. 15%.
   C. 10%.
   D. 5%.

2. Open market operations refer to:
   A. the purchase and sale of U.S. government securities by the Federal Reserve.
   B. the lending of money by a bank.
   C. the lending of reserves by the Federal Reserve.
   D. the clearing of checks by the Federal Reserve.

3. Which of the following is an appropriate policy action by the Federal Reserve if there is inflation?
   A. lower discount rate
   B. higher tax rates
   C. open market sales
   D. lower reserve requirement

4. The independence of the Federal Reserve means that the Federal Reserve:
   A. appoints its own members.
   B. pays its employees any salary it wants.
   C. adjusts the tools of monetary policy without consulting Congress or the president.
   D. is not a branch of the government.

5. The members of the Federal Open Market Committee consist of:
   A. the members of the Board of Governors and five Federal Reserve bank presidents.
   B. all the Federal Reserve bank presidents and five U.S. senators.
   C. the secretary of the Treasury and the Board of Governors.
   D. the vice president and the Board of Governors.

6. The reserves in the banking system rise whenever:
   A. the discount rate is increased.
   B. banks make loans.
   C. currency is withdrawn from a bank.
   D. the Federal Reserve buys something.

7. An increase in the discount rate would "announce" which of the following?
   A. a future decrease in taxes
   B. a future open market sale by the Federal Reserve
   C. a future open market purchase by the Federal Reserve
   D. a future reduction in reserve requirements

8. M-2 would most likely be the intermediate target selected by:
   A. a monetarist.
   B. a Keynesian.
   C. a Marxist.
   D. a supply-side economist.

9. Monetary policy is most likely to be procyclical if the Federal Reserve:
   A. uses open market operations as the primary tool of monetary policy.
   B. sells U.S. government securities.
   C. uses the money supply as an intermediate target.
   D. pegs interest rates.

10. Evidence cited in the text indicates that the more independent an economy's central bank, the lower the:
    A. unemployment rate.
    B. rate of inflation.
    C. reserve requirement.
    D. discount rate.

PROBLEMS

1. Suppose the Federal Reserve buys $100,000 of U.S. government securities directly from Third Bank of Manhattan. Show the effect of the transaction on the balance sheet of the Federal Reserve and the Third Bank of Manhattan. Record only the changes (+ or – and the dollar amount). The reserve requirement is 0.10.

THIRD BANK OF MANHATTAN	
ASSETS	**LIABILITIES**
Cash in vault _____	*DDO* _____
Deposits at Fed. Res. bank _____	Net worth _____
Loans _____	
U.S. securities _____	

FEDERAL RESERVE BANK	
ASSETS	**LIABILITIES**
U.S. securities _____	Deposit of _____ Third Bank

What is the change in total reserves? _____

What is the change in excess reserves? _____

What is the immediate impact on the money supply? _____

2. Suppose the Federal Reserve buys $500,000 of U.S. government securities from a securities dealer. The dealer deposits the Federal Reserve's check in a checking account in the Third Bank of Manhattan and the check clears. Record the impact of the transactions on the balance sheets of the Third Bank of Manhattan and the Federal Reserve bank. Record only the changes (+ or – and the dollar amounts). Assume the reserve requirement is 0.10.

THIRD BANK OF MANHATTAN	
ASSETS	**LIABILITIES**
Cash in vault _____	*DDO* _____
Deposits at Fed. Res. bank _____	Net worth _____
Loans _____	
U.S. securities _____	

FEDERAL RESERVE BANK	
ASSETS	**LIABILITIES**
U.S. securities _____	Deposit of _____ Third Bank

What is the change in total reserves? _____

What is the change in excess reserves? _____

What is the immediate impact on the money supply? _____

3. The banks in Caines have the following collective balance sheet.

ASSETS		LIABILITIES	
Reserves	$ 40,000	*DDO*	$200,000
Loans	$190,000	Capital account	$ 30,000

a. If the reserve requirement is 0.2, how many excess reserves do the banks have? _____

b. If the reserve requirement is lowered to 0.1, what are the banks' excess reserves? _____

c. What is the maximum possible increase in deposits due to the lowering of the reserve requirement? _____

Answers

TRUE OR FALSE

1. False. The Federal Reserve is considered independent because members of the Board of Governors, who are appointed by the president, are appointed for 14-year terms and because the Federal Reserve has its own sources of income.

2. True. The Federal Reserve buys U.S. government securities and other assets by writing checks on itself. There is no limit on its ability to write checks.

3. True. The Federal Open Market Committee controls open market operations, which is the most frequently used tool of the Federal Reserve.

4. False. The seven members of the Board of Governors sit on the Federal Open Market Committee together with five of the twelve presidents of the Federal Reserve banks.

5. False. The deposit expansion multiplier is $1/\%RR_{DD}$. A lower value of $\%RR_{DD}$ makes the deposit expansion multiplier larger.

6. True. Each Federal Reserve bank is owned by the banks in its district. However, these banks do not control Fed policy.

7. False. The largest liability is Federal Reserve Notes.

8. True. The money supply increases immediately because the Federal Reserve pays for the U.S. government securities with a check that, when deposited in the account of the seller of the securities, increases checking account balances and increases the money supply.

9. False. Monetary policy influences the economy by changing the money supply, interest rates, and total spending.

10. True. Because of the loose linkage, the Federal Reserve needs an intermediate target to judge whether its policies are appropriate.

MULTIPLE CHOICE

1. C. If total reserves equal $25,000 and excess reserves equal $5,000, required reserves equal $20,000. The reserve requirement is $20,000/$200,000 = 0.10, or 10 percent.

2. A. Open market operations are purchases and sales of U.S. government securities by the Federal Reserve.

3. C. An open market sale removes reserves from the banks, which reduces their ability to make loans. This tends to reduce the excessive demand that is the source of the inflation.

4. C. The independence of the Federal Reserve refers to its ability to independently determine the thrust of monetary policy by adjusting its tools.

5. A. The seven members of the Board of Governors as well as five of the twelve Federal Reserve bank presidents are voting members of the Federal Open Market Committee.

6. D. The reserves in the banking system rise whenever the Federal Reserve buys something because the Federal Reserve pays for its purchase with checks written on the Federal Reserve that, when deposited, add to the reserves of the bank depositing the check.

7. B. An increase in the discount rate would announce a future tightening of monetary policy. That would be achieved through open market sales by the Federal Reserve with the intention of pulling reserves out of the bank system.

8. A. Monetarists believe that monetary aggregates such as M-2 are the best intermediate targets.

9. D. Pegging interest rates forces the Federal Reserve to increase the money supply when an economy is in an expansion and when interest rates are rising due to an increased demand for loans.

10. B. Evidence indicates that more independent central banks are able to implement the less popular policies that keep inflation rates low.

PROBLEMS

1. *Third Bank of Manhattan*
    Deposits at Federal Reserve bank **+$100,000**
    U.S. Securities *–$100,000*

    Federal Reserve
    U.S. Securities **+$100,000**, Deposits of Third Bank **+$100,000**

    The Federal Reserve pays Third Bank of Manhattan for the $100,000 of government securities the bank gives up (and the Federal Reserve bank receives) by placing $100,000 in Third Bank of Manhattan's account at the Federal Reserve bank. As a result, total reserves are higher by **+ $100,000**. Excess reserves are also higher by **+ $100,000**. Because Third Bank's *DDO* has not changed, the bank's required reserves have not changed. There is no immediate change in the money supply because there has been no change in the *DDO* in the bank.

2. *Third Bank of Manhattan*
    Deposits at Federal Reserve **+ $500,000**, *DDO* **+ $500,000**

    Federal Reserve
    U.S. Securities **+ $500,000**, Deposits of Third Bank **+ $500,000**

    When the securities dealer deposits the $500,000 check from the Federal Reserve, checking accounts (*DDO*) in Third Bank of Manhattan rise by that amount because the dealer has that much more in its account.

    When Third Bank of Manhattan sends the check to the Federal Reserve for payment, the Federal Reserve adds $500,000 to Third Bank's account in the Federal Reserve. As a result, reserves are higher by **+ $500,000**. Excess reserves are higher by **+ $450,000** because the bank's required reserves are higher by $50,000. The money supply increases by **+ $500,000** because *DDO* increases by that amount.

3. a. Excess reserves are **$0** because the banks are required to hold reserves equal to .2 × $200,000 = $40,000.
    b. Excess reserves equal **$20,000**; total reserves equal $40,000. The banks would be required to hold reserves equal to .1 × $200,000 = $20,000.
    c. The maximum increase in deposits is ten times $20,000, or **$200,000**. The deposit expansion multiplier is (1/.1) = 10 and the excess reserves are $20,000.

CHAPTER 17

Interest Rates

Chapter 17 provides an analysis of interest rates, one of the crucial variables in economics. Interest rates play a key role in the linkage by which the Federal Reserve influences economic activity. Demand for houses, automobiles and capital goods depends greatly on the level of interest rates. Interest rates in the United States, by influencing the foreign exchange rate, even help determine the cost of imported television sets and the cost of a vacation in Europe.

Chapter 17 describes the various interest rates that exist in the U.S. economy and provides a framework for understanding the forces that govern interest rates. The impact on interest rates of the business cycle, federal budget deficits, the Federal Reserve System, and expected inflation are all analyzed in this chapter. You will learn the distinction between nominal and real interest rates. You will emerge from a careful reading of this chapter with a much stronger understanding of interest rates.

CHAPTER OUTLINE

I. Meaning of Interest Rates
    A. The **interest rate** is the price paid for credit—the use of loanable funds. Even if inflation is zero, interest rates are positive for two reasons:
        1. Individuals prefer to consume now rather than later. To induce a saver to give up the use of funds for a period requires that he or she be paid for it. This is called "time preference."
        2. Businesses are willing to pay savers in order to increase their capital. Capital increases the productive capacity of the business and the economy. Paying savers for the use of their funds allows firms to buy and use capital, boosting productivity.
    B. There are many different interest rates, but they all usually move together. Some of the more important interest rates are:
        1. **Prime Loan Rate:** This is the interest rate banks usually charge their best customers. Other borrowers are charged a higher rate. A prime rate is set by each bank. It tends to follow the path of other interest rates.
        2. **Treasury Bill Rate:** The Treasury bill rate is the rate available on short-term debt of the U.S. government. Loans to the federal government are the safest of all loans, so this interest rate is often pictured as the minimum yield on securities.
        3. **Discount Rate:** The discount rate is the interest rate that the Federal Reserve charges banks when they borrow reserves. The discount rate is changed periodically by the Federal Reserve as part of monetary policy.
        4. **Federal Funds Rate:** Banks with excess reserves can lend those reserves to banks with reserve deficiencies. The market where these reserves are traded is called the **federal funds market** and the interest rate that is charged for borrowing the reserves is the federal funds rate.

5. Corporate Bond Rate: A bond is an IOU that promises to pay its owner a series of annual payments for a specified number of years, usually somewhere between 10 and 30 years. Not all corporations can borrow at the same interest rate. Less stable businesses are more risky and must offer a higher interest rate in order to attract funds.

6. Mortgage Rate: Buyers of homes typically borrow most of the money needed to pay for the house. The mortgage rate is the interest rate on these kinds of loans. Some rates on mortgages are fixed, and are called fixed-rate mortgages. Mortgages that have interest rates that can be changed periodically are called adjustable-rate mortgages.

II. The Loanable Funds Model

    A. The **loanable funds model** is used to explain the determination of interest rates. Because an interest rate is the price of borrowing, the interest rate depends on the quantity of funds available for loans—the supply of loanable funds—and the amount that people wish to borrow—the demand for loanable funds.

    B. The supply of loanable funds comes from two sources:

        1. Individuals, families, and businesses often spend less than their income (that is, save). These entities, called surplus units, make funds available in order to earn interest income. The amount people are willing to lend depends on the following factors:

           a. The Interest Rate: The higher the rate of interest, the more people are willing to lend and the greater is the quantity of loanable funds supplied.

           b. Taxes: Subsidies and tax reductions for saving shift the supply of loanable funds curve to the right. Individual Retirement Accounts (IRAs) were introduced in the 1980s to stimulate saving.

           c. Demographics: The young are net borrowers—they tend to spend more than their incomes. The middle-aged are net savers as they pay off their earlier debt and save for retirement. The retired are net dissavers—they are consuming their past savings. As the age distribution of the population shifts between these three groups, the supply of loanable funds changes.

        2. The Federal Reserve influences the supply of loanable funds through its impact on the reserves and the lending ability of banks.

    C. The demand for loanable funds is the amount of funds that individuals, businesses, and the government want to borrow to finance their current expenditures. The determinants are:

        1. The Interest Rate: The higher the interest rate the more expensive it is to borrow and the lower is the quantity of loanable funds demanded.

        2. The Federal Government's Budget Deficit: Budget deficits are financed by borrowing. A larger budget deficit causes an outward shift of the demand for loanable funds.

        3. Attitudes Toward Debt: As borrowing becomes more acceptable, the demand for loanable funds increases.

        4. Taxes: If borrowing is subsidized because borrowers are allowed to deduct the interest they pay from taxable income, the demand curve for loanable funds increases.

    D. Equilibrium in the Loanable Funds Market

        1. An increase in the demand for loanable funds increases interest rates and increases the quantity of loans.

        2. A decrease in the demand for loanable funds decreases interest rates and decreases the quantity of loans.

        3. An increase in the supply of loanable funds decreases interest rates and increases the quantity of loans.

        4. A decrease in the supply of loanable funds increases interest rates and decreases the quantity of loans.

III. Expected Inflation and Interest Rates

    A. A major factor influencing interest rates is the magnitude of expected inflation.

        1. If lenders expect the rate of inflation to rise, they are less willing to make loans.

           a. Because of inflation, the loans will be paid back with dollars that have less purchasing power than the dollars that were lent. As a result, granting of loans is less attractive.

           b. The expectation of higher inflation on the part of lenders results in a decrease in the supply of loanable funds.

        2. If borrowers expect the rate of inflation to rise, they find borrowing more attractive.

a. Because inflation erodes the purchasing power of dollars, borrowers will be able to repay with dollars that are less valuable than the dollars that they borrowed.

b. The expectation of higher inflation by borrowers increases the demand for loanable funds.

3. The decrease in the supply of loanable funds combined with the increase in the demand means interest rates rise. The tendency for interest rates to rise as expectations of inflation rise is called the **Fisher Effect**, named after Irving Fisher, the economist who discovered this relationship.

B. Evidence supporting the Fisher Effect is provided by both domestic (U.S.) and global data.

1. In the United States, interest rates and inflation rates were at historic highs at the beginning of the 1980s. As the decade progressed, the expectations of inflation subsided and interest rates fell.

2. Internationally, countries with the highest rates of inflation tend to be the countries with the highest interest rates.

IV. Other Factors Influencing Interest Rates

A. Business Cycles:

1. Interest rates vary systematically over the business cycle. As an economic expansion begins, businesses and consumers increase their demand for loans to finance larger expenditures (for example, investment goods, automobiles, and housing). This increase in the demand for loans raises interest rates.

2. As the economic expansion continues, interest rates continue to rise as expectations of inflation build. The Federal Reserve System, concerned about inflation, might reduce the supply of loanable funds and increase interest rates even more in order to reduce the inflation.

3. As the economy enters a recession, the demand for loanable funds declines as consumers and businesses reduce their spending. Interest rates decline. The downward push on interest rates is reinforced by declines in inflation expectations and by expansionary policies on the part of the Federal Reserve.

B. Federal Budget Deficits:

1. Larger budget deficits should cause interest rates to rise because they represent an increase in the demand for loanable funds.

2. Empirical evidence apparently does not consistently support the idea that larger budget deficits are associated with higher interest rates. Possible reasons for the failure of the data to confirm the expected positive relationship between deficits and interest rates are:

a. U.S. budget deficits have been small relative to the world's supply of loanable funds. The budget deficits have represented only a slight increase in the world's demand for loanable funds, and so the interest rate increase has been slight.

b. Individuals may save more when the government runs a budget deficit. Because budget deficits commit the government to paying interest on the additional IOUs it has issued, taxpayers may save more in anticipation of the increase in taxes that will eventually be required to pay the interest. But many economists doubt people actually behave this way.

C. Federal Reserve System:

1. By adding reserves to the banking system, the Federal Reserve increases the supply of loanable funds. When reserves are removed from the banks, the supply is reduced.

2. The Federal Reserve is given more credit or blame for movements in interest rates than is justified. Inflationary expectations and the business cycle often cause movements in interest rates that are falsely ascribed to the Federal Reserve.

V. Real versus Nominal Interest Rates:

A. The nominal interest rate is what people usually think of when they think of interest rates. It is the interest rate before it is adjusted for inflation.

B. Real Interest Rate

1. The **real interest rate** is the difference between the nominal interest rate and the expected rate of inflation.

a. It measures the real (purchasing power) cost to the borrower and the real return to the lender of a loan.

b. Because the expected rate of inflation is difficult to measure, it is difficult to estimate the real rate of interest.
2. The real rate of interest is determined by:
   a. the thriftiness of the population, the primary determinant of the supply of loanable funds.
   b. the productivity of capital, the primary determinant of the demand for loanable funds.
3. It is the real, not the nominal, rate of interest that has the greatest effect on the performance of an economy.
4. Real interest rates were apparently low, even negative, in the 1970s but were at historical highs in the early 1980s. Possible explanations for the high real rates in the 1980s are:
   a. An increase in the expected returns from investment. Because of lower tax rates, the return on capital increased and the demand for loanable funds increased.
   b. Large budget deficits increased the demand for loanable funds and increased interest rates.
   c. Because of high taxes, high interest rates before taxes were required in order to make after-tax real rates attractive.

HINTS AND HELP

1. The Interest Rate   Economists often refer to *the* interest rate as if there were only one. As this chapter discusses, there are in fact many interest rates—the Treasury bill rate, the mortgage rate, the corporate bond rate, and others. The reason economists talk about interest rates as if there were just one is that interest rates tend to move together. It usually is not necessary to keep track of each interest rate individually to know whether one particular interest rate is rising or falling. With few exceptions, if any interest rate is rising, then all interest rates are rising.

2. Real and Nominal Interest Rates   It is confusing when economists sometimes refer to an interest rate of 15 percent as low and an interest rate of 5 percent as high. Understanding the distinction between nominal and real interest rates will eliminate this confusion.

Real rates are more important than nominal rates when discussing the impact of interest rates—because the real rate measures the purchasing power cost of a loan. It is the real rate that influences the decisions of borrowers and lenders.

A high nominal interest rate can represent a low real rate if the expected rate of inflation is also high. If the nominal rate is 15 percent but people expect 12 percent inflation, the real rate is only 3 percent. If the nominal interest rate is 5 percent and expected inflation is 1 percent, the real rate is 4 percent. Thus, a 15 percent nominal rate may be more attractive to a potential borrower than a 5 percent nominal rate, after expectations of inflation are taken into consideration.

FILL IN THE BLANK

interest rate

federal funds rate

Treasury bill rate

demand

supply

Fisher Effect

fall

1. The price of borrowing loanable funds is the _____.
2. The interest rate that one bank charges another bank when excess reserves are lent is the _____.
3. The lowest interest rate is usually the _____.
4. The federal budget deficit is part of the _____ for loanable funds.
5. The Federal Reserve influences the _____ of loanable funds.
6. The _____ is the increase in interest rates caused by the expectation of greater inflation.
7. During a recession interest rates would be expected to _____.

demand

8. When borrowers expect that the rate of inflation will fall, the _____ _____ for loanable funds declines.

supply, increase

9. An open market purchase of U.S. government securities by the Federal Reserve causes the _____ of loanable funds to _____.

nominal, real

10. The _____ interest rate minus the expected rate of inflation equals the _____ interest rate.

TRUE OR FALSE

_____ **1.** As long as rates of inflation do not change, interest rates tend to remain the same over the business cycle.

_____ **2.** Real interest rates were high during the 1970s.

_____ **3.** According to the Fisher Effect, countries with the lowest nominal interest rates are the countries with the lowest inflation.

_____ **4.** The supply curve of loanable funds is upward sloping because people prefer to spend now rather than in the future.

_____ **5.** A bank's best customers are charged the prime rate when they borrow.

_____ **6.** There is abundant evidence indicating that larger budget deficits result in higher interest rates.

_____ **7.** The Federal Reserve has direct control over the discount rate.

_____ **8.** Interest-sensitive industries benefit from higher interest rates.

_____ **9.** The expectation of higher rates of inflation makes borrowing more attractive.

_____ **10.** Real interest rates have historically been highest when nominal interest rates have been highest.

MULTIPLE CHOICE

1. Because the demand for new homes is influenced by interest rates, the housing industry would be called:
A. interest sensitive.
B. highly stable.
C. immune to business cycles.
D. a declining industry.

2. The federal funds market is the market where:
A. U.S. government securities are bought and sold.
B. deposits at Federal Reserve banks are lent among banks.
C. savings accounts are created.
D. currency is introduced into the economy.

3. The idea that people prefer to have things now rather than wait for them is called:
A. productivity.
B. interest.
C. anticipation.
D. time preference.

4. If the Federal Reserve engages in an open market sale:
A. the demand for loanable funds curve shifts rightward, increasing interest rates.
B. the demand for loanable funds curve shifts leftward, decreasing interest rates.
C. the supply of loanable funds curve shifts rightward, decreasing interest rates.
D. the supply of loanable funds curve shifts leftward, increasing interest rates.

5. Loanable funds are provided by:
   A. the government.
   B. surplus units.
   C. deficit-spending units.
   D. sellers of bonds.

6. The Fisher Effect implies which of the following?
   A. Real interest rates fall as expectations of inflation fall.
   B. Real interest rates rise as expectations of inflation fall.
   C. Nominal interest rates fall as expectations of inflation fall.
   D. Nominal interest rates rise as expectations of inflation fall.

7. If the supply curve of loanable funds is horizontal:
   A. the Fisher Effect cannot occur.
   B. full employment is impossible.
   C. full employment is assured.
   D. larger budget deficits have no effect on interest rates.

8. If lenders expect lower inflation in the future:
   A. the demand curve for loanable funds shifts upward.
   B. the demand curve for loanable funds shifts rightward.
   C. the supply curve for loanable funds shifts leftward.
   D. the supply curve for loanable funds shifts rightward.

9. The equilibrium interest rate is the rate at which:
   A. the real rate of interest equals zero.
   B. the nominal rate of interest equals zero.
   C. the quantity of loans demanded equals the quantity of loans supplied.
   D. the increase in the money supply equals the budget deficit.

10. Assume the federal government has a larger budget deficit. If taxpayers increase their saving because of the larger budget deficit:
    A. the rise in interest rates is made greater.
    B. the rise in interest rates is made smaller.
    C. the fall in interest rates is made greater.
    D. the fall in interest rates is made smaller.

PROBLEMS

1. Fill in the missing values in the table.

	NOMINAL INTEREST RATES	EXPECTED RATE OF INFLATION	REAL INTEREST RATE
a.	10%	8%	_____
b.	7%	6%	_____
c.	10%	10%	_____
d.	5%	−5%	_____
e.	7%	9%	_____
f.	_____	5%	6%
g.	_____	10%	2%
h.	_____	−4%	5%

2. For each of the following events, indicate with a plus (+), a minus (–), or a zero (0) its impact on the demand for loanable funds, the supply of loanable funds, the equilibrium interest rate (i), and the equilibrium quantity of loanable funds (Q_{LF}).

EVENT	DEMAND FOR LOANABLE FUNDS	SUPPLY OF LOANABLE FUNDS	i	Q_{LF}
a. Larger budget deficit	_____	_____	_____	_____
b. Open market purchase by the Federal Reserve	_____	_____	_____	_____
c. A recession	_____	_____	_____	_____
d. Introduction of IRAs	_____	_____	_____	_____
e. Surplus units begin to expect higher inflation	_____	_____	_____	_____
f. Deficit-spending units begin to expect lower inflation	_____	_____	_____	_____
g. Businesses want to increase their spending on new capital	_____	_____	_____	_____

Answers

TRUE OR FALSE

1. False. Even if expectations of inflation do not change, interest rates change during the business cycle because of changes in the demand for loanable funds on the part of businesses and consumers.
2. False. During the 1970s, real interest rates were low and sometimes even negative.
3. True. According to the Fisher Effect, increased expectations of inflation raise nominal interest rates. Those countries with the lowest inflation should be the ones with the lowest nominal interest rates.
4. True. People must be paid in order to induce them to give up the use of funds, because they prefer to spend now.
5. True. The prime rate is reserved for the best, least risky borrowers. Other borrowers pay interest rates above the prime rate.
6. False. There is only mixed empirical evidence that higher budget deficits result in higher interest rates despite the logic of the argument.
7. True. The discount rate is one of the tools the Federal Reserve controls.
8. False. Higher interest rates reduce spending on interest-sensitive products like housing and investment goods.
9. True. Because borrowers can repay loans using dollars that have a lower purchasing power, the expectation of higher rates of inflation makes borrowing more attractive.
10. False. In the 1970s, nominal interest rates were very high but real interest rates were low.

MULTIPLE CHOICE

1. A. Interest-sensitive industries are industries that sell output frequently paid for with borrowed money. As interest rates change, the sales of these industries change.
2. B. The federal funds market is the market where reserves in the form of deposits at a Federal Reserve bank are lent and borrowed by banks.

3. D. Time preference refers to the desire of people to have things now rather than later.
4. D. An open market sale by the Federal Reserve removes reserves from the banking system, which reduces banks' ability to make loans. This appears as a leftward shift of the supply of loanable funds curve and increases interest rates.
5. B. Surplus units provide loanable funds by spending less than their income, thus yielding a surplus of funds.
6. C. The Fisher Effect says that nominal interest rates vary directly with expectations of inflation. As less inflation is expected, nominal interest rates fall.
7. D. If the supply curve of loanable funds is horizontal, outward shifts of the demand for loanable funds curve caused by budget deficits do not affect interest rates.
8. D. If lenders expect lower inflation, the supply curve shifts rightward as lenders are more willing to lend at each and every interest rate.
9. C. In the loanable funds model, equilibrium occurs when the quantity supplied of loanable funds equals the quantity demanded of loanable funds.
10. B. By itself, the larger budget deficit increases nominal interest rates by increasing the demand for loanable funds. If saving increases, the supply of loanable funds is increased and the increase in the interest rate is partially negated.

PROBLEMS

1. The answers may be determined using the following relationships:

$$\text{real interest rate} = \text{nominal interest rate} - \text{expected inflation}$$
$$\text{and}$$
$$\text{nominal interest rate} = \text{real interest rate} + \text{expected inflation}$$

a. $10\% - 8\% = \mathbf{2\%}$
b. $7\% - 6\% = \mathbf{1\%}$
c. $10\% - 10\% = \mathbf{0\%}$
d. $5\% - (-5\%) = \mathbf{10\%}$
e. $7\% - 9\% = \mathbf{-2\%}$
f. $5\% + 6\% = \mathbf{11\%}$
g. $10\% + 2\% = \mathbf{12\%}$
h. $(-4\%) + 5\% = \mathbf{1\%}$

2.

	EVENT	DEMAND FOR LOANABLE FUNDS	SUPPLY OF LOANABLE FUNDS	i	Q_{LF}
a.	Larger budget deficit	+	0	+	+
b.	Open market purchase by the Federal Reserve	0	+	−	+
c.	A recession	−	0	−	−
d.	Introduction of IRAs	0	+	−	+
e.	Surplus units begin to expect higher inflation	0	−	+	−
f.	Deficit-spending units begin to expect lower inflation	−	0	−	−
g.	Businesses want to increase their spending on new capital	+	0	+	+

CHAPTER 18

The Impact of the Fed and the Money Supply on Economic Activity

Chapters 15, 16 and 17 focused on banking, the mechanics of money creation, the tools and intermediate targets of Federal Reserve monetary policy, and the determinants of interest rates. The Federal Reserve is heavily involved in all of these issues. The focus on the Federal Reserve continues in this chapter, which looks at the link between money and economic activity. This issue has been among the most hotly debated issues in economics during the last fifty years, and it is still unresolved. The combatants are the Keynesians (followers of John Maynard Keynes) and the monetarists. This chapter does not resolve the debate, but it does analyze the major points of contention between monetarists and Keynesians. In the process, one of the most venerable concepts in macroeconomics—the equation of exchange—is introduced and discussed.

CHAPTER OUTLINE

I. Monetary Policy
    A. There are three channels through which Federal Reserve monetary policy influences the economy:
        1. Interest Rate Channel: An increase in the money supply lowers interest rates. In turn, the lower interest rates increase the kinds of spending that are sensitive to interest rates, such as investment and housing construction. The decline in U.S. interest rates also can trigger a decline in the value of the dollar, increasing net exports of American goods and services.
        2. Portfolio Adjustment Channel: An increase in the money supply causes an imbalance in portfolios. Because of the increase in money, people find themselves holding more money relative to other assets than they want to hold. This imbalance induces them to rearrange their portfolios by buying more of other assets, both financial and real. This stimulates economic activity.
        3. Wealth Channel: An increase in the money supply reduces interest rates, which causes certain kinds of wealth—bonds and stocks—to increase in price. This increase in wealth boosts consumption spending.
    B. Equation of Exchange
        1. The **equation of exchange** provides a framework for analyzing the impact of money and the Fed on the economy. The equation is:

$$M \times V = \sum P_i \ Y_i = P \times Y$$

        a. M is the supply of money, say M-1.
        b. V is **velocity**. It measures the average number of times a dollar is spent on GDP. It is calculated by dividing nominal GDP by the money supply.
        c. P is the average level of prices.

d. Y is the output of the economy. The right-hand side of the equation ($P \times Y$) measures GDP.

2. Because of the way V is calculated, the two sides of the equation must be equal. The total amount of money spent ($M \times V$) must equal the value of the goods bought ($P \times Y$).

3. The equation of exchange provides a framework for looking at the effects of money supply changes. For example, if the money supply rises, either velocity falls, nominal GDP rises, or some combination of the two occurs.

4. The impact of fiscal policy can also be analyzed. An expansionary fiscal policy either increases velocity or has no impact on GDP.

5. Monetarists and Keynesians differ in their views on velocity.
   a. Monetarists believe that velocity is predictable and stable so that changes in GDP mirror changes in the money supply. Fiscal policy is less predictable because its impact on velocity is uncertain.
   b. Keynesians accept that the money supply has an impact on GDP; but the impact is unpredictable because velocity is unstable. Fiscal policy is considered to have a more predictable relationship to GDP.

II. Velocity and Money Demand
   A. Velocity and money demand—the amount of money people choose to hold—are inversely related. The more money people hold, the slower they are spending each dollar, that is, the lower is velocity.
   B. There are three motives for holding money. They are:
      1. **Transactions demand**: This is money held to finance anticipated purchases. This is the most important motive for holding money.
      2. Precautionary demand: This is money held to protect against uncertainties.
      3. Speculative demand: This is money held in order to take advantage of potential investment opportunities.
   C. The determinants of money demand and velocity are:
      1. Frequency of Paydays
         a. The more often an individual receives a paycheck the easier it is to coordinate receipts and expenditures.
         b. The individual can make purchases using, on average, a smaller bundle of money, which means velocity is higher.
      2. Institutional Factors and the Payment Process
         a. Credit cards reduce the amount of money people must hold in order to make purchases.
         b. Making the same amount of purchases with less money means a higher value of velocity.
      3. Financial Technology and Money Substitutes
         a. New accounts and assets have been developed that pay interest, are highly liquid, and have little, if any, risk.
         b. Individuals and firms have increasingly used these assets as substitutes for money as a store of value. As a result, velocity has risen.
         c. An excellent example of an innovation is **money market mutual funds (MMMFs)**. These funds pool individuals' savings in accounts that pay competitive interest rates while allowing checks to be written on the balances.
      4. Interest Rates
         a. Money pays little interest (NOW and ATS accounts) or no interest (demand deposits and currency).
         b. As interest rates rise, individuals and firms reduce their money holdings in order to take advantage of the opportunity to earn income by purchasing bonds and other financial instruments. In such circumstances, velocity rises.
      5. Economic Uncertainty
         a. Money is seen by many as the safest and most liquid of assets.
         b. When people are worried about the future, they often increase their money holdings as a form of protection. The increase in money holdings reduces velocity.
   D. The major trends in velocity in the United States can be explained in terms of the preceding analysis:
      1. From 1880 to 1945, velocity fell.

a. During this period the U.S. price level fell, on average, and interest rates were low. Money was an attractive asset to hold.

b. Few substitutes for money were available.

c. During the 1930s and 1940s, money holdings increased (and velocity fell even further) because of the economic uncertainties associated with a depression and war.

2. From 1945 to the early 1980s, velocity rose.

a. During this period important substitutes for money were developed, interest rates rose, credit cards became popular, and the economy was much more stable.

b. Each of these factors tended to reduce money holdings and increase velocity.

3. Since 1981, velocity has declined.

a. The major development has been the introduction of interest-earning checking accounts, which reduced the cost of holding money.

b. The major recession in 1981–1982 and the decline in interest rates contributed to the lower velocity. People have decided to keep more of their wealth in checking accounts.

III. Crude Quantity Theory and Monetarism

A. Early economists believed in the **crude quantity theory**.

1. The theory starts with the equation of exchange and makes the assumptions that V and Y are fixed.

a. V is assumed to be fixed because it is believed that only the frequency of payments and other institutional factors influence money demand and velocity. Because these two factors change slowly, V can be pictured as constant most of the time.

b. Y is assumed to be fixed because the normal level of output is the output produced at full employment.

2. If V and Y are fixed, changes in the money supply (M) cause proportional changes in the price level (P). Data reveal that countries with higher money supply growth experience more inflation, although there is not the proportional relationship between money supply growth and changes in prices that the crude quantity theory asserts there should be.

3. Critics of the crude quantity theory make the following points:

a. Although excessive money growth can cause inflation, it is not the only possible source of inflation.

i. Total spending (MV) can change with fiscal policy as well as monetary policy. Increases in government spending or tax cuts can increase aggregate demand and cause inflation without increasing the money supply.

ii. Idle money balances can be transferred (lent) to those more likely to spend the funds. When this occurs, velocity and prices rise without an increase in the money supply.

b. It is inappropriate to treat Y as fixed. And because an economy is not usually at full employment, the effect of a money supply increase on the price level is not always predictable. The further an economy is from full employment, the greater the increase in output and the smaller the increase in prices.

B. Monetarism

1. Modern monetarists reject the assumptions of the crude quantity theory that V and Y are fixed.

2. Monetarists do believe that velocity is stable and predictable. Because of that, the relationship between monetary policy and GDP is more stable and more predictable than the relationship between fiscal policy and GDP.

3. Monetarists, believing that inflation is always a result of excessive money growth, point to the strong correlation between money growth and changes in the price level as evidence. Critics charge it is possible for money growth and prices to move together without money supply changes being the cause of the relationship. If the aggregate supply curve shifts to the left and the Federal Reserve increases the money supply in order to hold down unemployment, prices and money would both increase, but the fundamental cause of the association would be the shift of the aggregate supply curve.

4. Monetarists believe that the Federal Reserve should be required to keep the money supply rising at a constant rate year after year. It is their belief that attempting to stabilize the economy through discretionary monetary policy often creates new problems. Critics argue that although making the

correct policy moves is never easy, economists know enough to solve many economic problems through discretionary policy actions.

HINTS AND HELP

1. Monetarists and Keynesians A demanding part of learning a new subject is keeping track of what various theories say. This problem is of particular difficulty in economics because there are many different views about the sources of economic problems and their solutions.

   The most important debates in economics during the last 50 years have been between monetarists and Keynesians. The most frequent topic for debate has been the significance of monetary policy. As their names imply, monetarists (from the word "money") believe that the money supply is *the* key to understanding the behavior of the economy while Keynesians—followers of Keynes—assign the money supply importance but not overriding importance. The money supply is only one of many variables that cause the economy to move.

FILL IN THE BLANK

velocity (*V*)

transactions

velocity, output

money market

falls

10 percent

interest rate

equation of exchange

precautionary

speculative

1. Nominal GDP divided by the money supply equals _____.

2. Money held in order to purchase goods and services is called the _____ _____ demand for money.

3. The crude quantity theory assumes that _____ and _____ are constant.

4. Funds that pool the savings of individuals and allow them to earn competitive interest rates and write checks are called _____ _____ mutual funds.

5. If money demand rises (that is, people choose to hold more money), velocity _____.

6. The crude quantity theory argued that a 10 percent increase in the money supply would increase prices by _____.

7. Through the _____ channel, increases in the money supply reduce interest rates and increase investment spending.

8. The expression $MV = PY$ is called the _____.

9. Holding money in case of emergencies is called the _____ motive for holding money.

10. Holding money in order to take advantage of potential investment opportunities is called the _____ motive for holding money.

TRUE OR FALSE

_____ 1. Monetarists favor a policy of constant money supply growth.

_____ 2. The crude quantity theory says that the price level moves inversely with the money supply.

_____ 3. The equation of exchange assumes that *V* and *Y* are constant.

_____ 4. Velocity is the same whether the money supply is M-1 or M-2.

_____ 5. Velocity rises as interest rates rise.

_____ 6. The introduction of credit cards has tended to increase velocity.

_____ 7. Excessive money supply growth is the only cause of inflation, according to the crude quantity theory.

_____ 8. Reduced economic fluctuations since World War II have caused velocity to rise.

_____ 9. Monetarists assume that velocity is constant.

_____ 10. The behavior of velocity after 1980 differed from the behavior of velocity between 1945 and 1980.

MULTIPLE CHOICE

1. According to the crude quantity theory, a change in the money supply causes:
   A. an increase in velocity.
   B. a proportional rise in the price level.
   C. a rise in real GDP.
   D. a fall in real GDP.

2. Keynesians believe that a change in the money supply:
   A. has no effect on an economy's nominal GDP.
   B. is the only thing that influences an economy's nominal GDP.
   C. has an unpredictable effect on an economy's nominal GDP.
   D. has an important and predictable effect on an economy's nominal GDP.

3. When economic activity changes, monetarists immediately look to which of the following as a cause of the change?
   A. money supply
   B. stock market
   C. government spending
   D. tax rates

4. If the time between paychecks is increased, people:
   A. increase their spending.
   B. reduce their spending.
   C. increase their average money holdings.
   D. decrease their average money holdings.

5. During the Depression, velocity fell. Which of the following would account for the fall in velocity?
   A. Interest rates fell in the 1930s.
   B. There was great uncertainty about the course of the economy in the 1930s.
   C. Few money substitutes existed in the 1930s.
   D. All the alternatives are correct.

6. If velocity is fixed:
   A. the money supply has no effect on the economy.
   B. only changes in the money supply can cause changes in nominal GDP.
   C. fiscal policy can affect the economy independent of the money supply.
   D. the economy is always at full employment.

7. Evidence in the textbook indicates that in the United States.:
   A. the crude quantity theory has been verified.
   B. more rapid increases in the money supply have been associated with periods of higher inflation.
   C. the rate of growth of the money supply has little impact on the rate of inflation.
   D. most inflation has been caused by adverse supply shocks.

8. Monetarists believe that:
   A. V is more stable than the expenditure multiplier.
   B. the money supply is more stable than V.
   C. velocity is constant.
   D. real GDP is constant.

9. If a woman earns $60,000 per year, is paid once a month, and spends her income evenly over the year, her average money holdings are:
   A. $60,000.
   B. $30,000.
   C. $5,000.
   D. $2,500.

10. When criticizing monetarists, nonmonetarists argue that:
    A. the economy is normally at full employment.
    B. changes in the money supply influence prices and real GDP only.
    C. fiscal policy influences output but not prices.
    D. velocity is influenced greatly by interest rates.

PROBLEMS

1. Fill in the missing values in the table.

	M	V	P	Y
a.	$100		$10	400
b.	$200		$20	400
c.	$100		$ 8	100
d.	$200	8		100
e.	$ 50	5		250
f.		8	$40	20

2. The island of Caines has a new economist named Milton, a believer in the crude quantity theory. He has been called in for advice on the economy.

   Nominal GDP in Caines is $40,000. The output in Caines is 1,000 "Things." Each "Thing" is sold for a price of $40. The money supply is 800 $1 bills.
   a. What is velocity? _____
   b. Because Milton believes in the crude quantity theory, what does he believe about velocity and the economy's output? _____
   c. One-half the $1 bills in Caines are destroyed in a fire. What does Milton predict will happen in Caines?
   _____

Answers

TRUE OR FALSE

1. True. Monetarists believe that by strictly controlling the money supply it is possible to make the economy more stable.
2. False. The crude quantity theory asserts that the price level moves directly and proportionally to the money supply.

3. False. The equation of exchange says only that $M \times V = P \times Y$. The crude quantity theory goes further and assumes that V and Y are fixed.
4. False. Because M-2 is larger than M-1, the velocity for M-2 is smaller.
5. True. As interest rates rise, people want to hold less money so they make their purchases with smaller money balances.
6. True. Credit cards allow one to make purchases with fewer money balances, which means velocity is higher.
7. True. Because velocity and output are fixed in the equation of exchange according to the crude quantity theory, increases in the price level (inflation) occur only if the money supply rises.
8. True. Reduced fluctuations give people more confidence and induce them to hold less money. As a result, velocity increases.
9. False. Monetarists argue that velocity is not constant but is predictable and relatively stable.
10. True. After World War II, velocity rose. After 1980, velocity has fallen.

MULTIPLE CHOICE

1. B. Because V and Y are assumed to be fixed, a rise in the money supply causes a proportional rise in the price level.
2. C. Monetary policy is unpredictable because the behavior of velocity is unpredictable in the view of Keynesians.
3. A. Monetarists believe that the money supply is the key determinant of economic changes.
4. C. Average money holdings increase as the time between paychecks increases.
5. D. Falling interest rates, economic uncertainty, and the absence of money substitutes would each contribute to a decline in velocity.
6. B. If velocity (V) is fixed, $P \times Y$ (that is, nominal GDP) can change only if the money supply (M) changes.
7. B. As a general rule, decades in which money growth has been relatively high have been decades of relatively severe inflation. However, the relationship has not been proportional, as suggested by the crude quantity theory.
8. A. Monetarists believe that there is a more stable and predictable relationship between changes in the money supply and changes in nominal GDP than there is between changes in government spending or investment and changes in nominal GDP.
9. D. The individual's paycheck would be $60,000/12 = $5,000. If the money is spent evenly over the month, average holdings of money would be $5,000/2 = $2,500.
10. D. Nonmonetarists emphasize that increases in interest rates reduce money demand, thereby raising velocity.

PROBLEMS

1. a. $V = (P \times Y)/M = GDP/M = (\$10)(400)/\$100 = \$4,000/\$100 = \mathbf{40}$
    b. $V = (\$20)(400)/\$200 = \$8,000/\$200 = \mathbf{40}$
    c. $V = (\$8)(100)/\$100 = \$800/\$100 = \mathbf{8}$
    d. $P = (M \times V)/Y = (\$200)(8)/100 = \$1,600/100 = \mathbf{\$16}$
    e. $P = (\$50)(5)/250 = \$250/250 = \mathbf{\$1}$
    f. $M = (P \times Y)/V = (\$40)(20)/8 = \$800/8 = \mathbf{\$100}$

2. a. Velocity is $40,000/$800 = **50**.
    b. Milton, a believer in the crude quantity theory, believes that velocity and the economy's output are fixed.
    c. If one-half the money supply is destroyed, the price level will fall by one-half, with velocity and the level of real output remaining the same. The price level will fall to $20.

CHAPTER 19

Inflation and the Phillips Curve

The problems of unemployment and inflation are of foremost concern to most citizens. This chapter explores more deeply the relationship between these two economic ills. The inverse relationship between unemployment and inflation is described by the Phillips curve.

This chapter also discusses in detail the nature of inflation and its history in the United States. In the next chapter, the focus shifts to alternative viewpoints on how policymakers should conduct policy to best attain the goals of low inflation and low unemployment.

CHAPTER OUTLINE

I. The Phillips Curve
  A. The original study by economist A. W. Phillips concerned the relationship between the unemployment rate and the rate at which wages increased in Great Britain. He discovered an inverse relationship between the two variables. In years when unemployment was high, wages rose slowly or even declined.
  B. The modern **Phillips curve** focuses on the relationship between the rate of unemployment and the rate of inflation.
    1. Because wages and prices are closely related, the same inverse relationship was discovered.
    2. There appears to be a trade-off between these two important economic variables. In years when unemployment is high, the rate of inflation is low.
  C. Economists have offered various theoretical rationales for the downward slope of the Phillips curve.
    1. Bargaining Hypothesis:
      a. As output rises and unemployment falls, workers gain bargaining power at the expense of management because of the increased cost of a strike and increased profits earned by firms.
      b. The increased bargaining power of labor increases the rate at which wages and prices rise.
    2. Structural Explanation:
      a. As an economy approaches full employment, more sectors of the economy reach full capacity.
      b. As more of these bottlenecks form, the rate at which prices are rising increases.
    3. Aggregate Supply–Aggregate Demand Explanation:
      a. As the aggregate demand curve shifts to the right, the price level rises (inflation occurs) and output falls (unemployment falls).
      b. The Phillips curve relationship is the result of shifts of aggregate demand that historically have been larger than any shifts in the aggregate supply curve.

D. Shifting the Phillips Curve
   1. In the 1960s, the Phillips curve appeared to be a single, stable curve. It seemed possible to pick a desirable unemployment–inflation combination off the curve and remain there.
   2. In the 1970s, the Phillips curve appeared to shift significantly rightward. The inflation rate that accompanied any unemployment rate increased. The causes of this outward shift were:
      a. Rising Inflationary Expectations:
         i. As workers expected higher rates of inflation, they bargained for larger wage hikes in order to maintain the purchasing power of their income.
         ii. Because inflation rates rose in the late 1960s and 1970s, wage inflation associated with any given unemployment rate increased.
         iii. As a result, the rate of inflation associated with any unemployment rate increased.
      b. Demographic Changes:
         i. As more and more teenagers and females entered the labor force, frictional unemployment rose.
         ii. The amount of stimulus required to achieve any given rate of unemployment increased.
      c. Liberalization of Unemployment Benefits: Unemployment benefits were made more generous after the 1960s and increased frictional unemployment.
   3. In the 1980s, the Phillips curve appeared to shift leftward. The leftward shift was caused by:
      a. a decline in the proportion of the labor force constituted by young workers.
      b. a decline in inflationary expectations as inflation rates fell beginning in 1981.
E. Long-run Phillips Curve
   1. Although it appears that the Phillips curve offers policymakers a choice between unemployment or inflation, that choice is only temporary or short-run in nature.
      a. Assume an economy starts with the unemployment rate equal to the natural rate of unemployment.
      b. An expansionary policy can lower unemployment by raising the rate of inflation.
      c. Eventually, workers bargain for larger wage hikes to offset the higher inflation.
      d. The acceleration of wage hikes returns the unemployment rate to the natural rate of unemployment.
      e. In the long run, stimulating the economy results only in higher inflation.
   2. The **natural unemployment rate hypothesis** is the view that the long-run Phillips curve is a vertical line; there is no trade-off between unemployment and inflation in the long run.

II. Inflation
   A. Causes of Inflation:
      1. **Demand–pull inflation** is caused by persistent rightward shifts of the aggregate demand curve, typically attributable to expansionary monetary and fiscal policies.
      2. **Cost–push inflation** is caused by leftward shifts of the aggregate supply curve, usually caused by wage increases or price increases of other inputs.
         a. Cost–push inflation causes **stagflation**—the simultaneous worsening of unemployment and inflation.
         b. Cost-push inflation is unlikely to be sustained for long; to do so would require a continuous succession of unfavorable supply shocks.
   B. History of U.S. Inflation
      1. For the first 170 years of U.S. history, periods of inflation were followed by periods of **deflation** or falling prices. As a result, the price level was about the same in 1940 as in 1770.
         a. Inflation usually occurred during wars. The inflation was caused by increases in government spending and money supply growth associated with financing the war.
         b. After wars, government spending and the money supply decreased, which reduced prices and reversed the wartime inflation.
      2. Since World War II, inflation has been continual; deflation has been rare. The possible causes of this change in behavior of the price level are:
         a. The government has taken a greater role in the economy.
            i. The government has assumed responsibility for the economy, using monetary and fiscal policy to enhance the achievement of full employment.

ii. A system of government programs called **automatic stabilizers** has been built into the economic system. These reduce economic volatility yet require no discretionary actions by decision makers. Examples are transfer payments and the income tax.

iii. Because of the government's commitment to full employment, workers have become resistant to wage cuts during hard times. This creates a situation of "sticky wages and prices."

b. The labor movement and institutional changes made wages and prices less flexible on the downside.

i. Unions were protected by new legislation enacted in the 1930s.

ii. Deposit insurance eliminated bank runs as a source of economic downturns, and reduced the exposure of the economy to depressions.

iii. Minimum wage legislation and unemployment insurance made wages less flexible.

HINTS AND HELP

1. The Phillips Curve—the short and the long of it   The Phillips curve depicts the relationship between unemployment and inflation. It is important to keep in mind that the relationship is different in the short run than in the long run.

In the short run, less of one results in more of the other. This is what makes stabilization policy so difficult for those in charge. Attempts to reduce inflation (unemployment) lead to more unemployment (inflation). This trade-off between unemployment and inflation appears as the downward-sloping short-run Phillips curve.

In the long run, no such trade-off occurs. Unemployment always returns to the natural rate of unemployment in the long run, which means that more inflation simply leads to more inflation with no gains in terms of lower unemployment. The long-run Phillips curve appears as a vertical line.

FILL IN THE BLANK

unemployment,
wage increase

1. The original Phillips curve looked at the relationship between the rate of _____ and the rate of _____.

unemployment, inflation

2. The modern Phillips curve looks at the relationship between the rate of _____ and the rate of _____.

vertical

3. In the long run, the Phillips curve is _____.

shifts to right

4. As workers react to higher expected inflation and bargain for higher wages, the Phillips curve _____.

demand, supply

5. The negative slope of the short-run Phillips curve can be explained as the consequence of the aggregate _____ curve shifting more than the aggregate _____ curve shifts.

demand–pull

6. Inflation that occurs along with greater output is called _____ _____ inflation.

cost–push

7. Inflation that occurs along with rising unemployment is called _____ _____ inflation.

wars

8. During the first 170 years of U.S. history, periods of inflation occurred during _____.

fallen

9. Since World War II, the price level in the United States has rarely _____.

sticky downward   10. A greater commitment to full employment on the part of the government and legislation strengthening the bargaining power of workers have made U.S. wages and prices _____ in the last fifty years.

TRUE OR FALSE

_____   1. The *short-run* Phillips curve shows that it is impossible to push the unemployment rate below the natural rate of unemployment.

_____   2. The *long-run* Phillips curve shows that it is impossible to maintain the unemployment rate below the natural rate of unemployment.

_____   3. Decreasing the natural rate of unemployment shifts the long-run Phillips curve to the left.

_____   4. Originally, the downward-sloping short-run Phillips curve was thought to be stable.

_____   5. The short-run Phillips curve in the 1970s was to the left of the 1960s' Phillips curve.

_____   6. Prices have risen more or less continually in the United States since the beginning of the twentieth century.

_____   7. Automatic stabilizers have made price declines more likely.

_____   8. The kind of inflation that can last for a long time is demand–pull inflation.

_____   9. A possible cause of demand–pull inflation is rising oil prices.

_____   10. The price level in the United States in 1945 was approximately equal to the price level in 1800.

MULTIPLE CHOICE

1. The short-run Phillips curve shows that:
   A. output and employment are inversely related.
   B. output and employment are directly related.
   C. expected inflation and actual inflation are directly related.
   D. unemployment and inflation are inversely related.

2. The long-run Phillips curve shifts to the right if:
   A. investment spending rises.
   B. government spending rises.
   C. structural unemployment rises.
   D. the money supply rises.

3. The structural explanation of the Phillips curve is that:
   A. unskilled workers cause inflation rates to rise.
   B. shifts in the aggregate demand curve create the Phillips curve.
   C. increases in government spending make the economy less productive.
   D. bottlenecks form in more markets as an economy approaches full employment.

4. The Phillips curve shifted to the right in the 1970s because:
   A. workers began to expect higher inflation.
   B. fewer young workers entered the labor force.
   C. government spending decreased.
   D. the frictional unemployment rate fell.

5. The entry of the baby-boom generation into the labor force had which of the following effects?
   A. caused cost–push inflation
   B. caused demand–pull inflation
   C. shifted the Phillips curve to the right
   D. shifted the Phillips curve to the left

6. Cost–push inflation is caused by:
   A. increases in aggregate demand.
   B. decreases in aggregate demand.
   C. increases in aggregate supply.
   D. decreases in aggregate supply.

7. Considering both the long-run and the short-run Phillips curves, which of the following is correct for an economy that is initially at the natural unemployment rate?
   A. An increase in demand causes a larger decline in unemployment in the long run than in the short run.
   B. An increase in demand causes a smaller increase in prices in the long run than in the short run.
   C. An increase in demand causes unemployment to decrease, but only temporarily.
   D. An increase in demand causes the rate of inflation to increase, but only temporarily.

8. During recessions before World War II:
   A. unemployment fell.
   B. deflation occurred.
   C. there were sharp increases in government spending.
   D. the Phillips curve shifted rightward.

9. During the post-World War II recessions:
   A. unemployment fell.
   B. prices continued to rise.
   C. deflation was typical.
   D. the Phillips curve shifted rightward.

10. The idea that a negatively sloped Phillips curve exists because high unemployment makes employers become resistant to wage increases is called the:
    A. bargaining hypothesis.
    B. structural hypothesis.
    C. bottleneck theory.
    D. aggregate supply theory.

PROBLEMS

1. The Phillips curve for the country of Caines is pictured in Figure 19.1. The economy is at point A with inflation of 0 percent and unemployment of 6 percent.
   a. Assume a new administration is elected in Caines on the platform of lowering unemployment below 6 percent. Once in office it uses expansionary monetary and fiscal policies to lower unemployment to 4 percent. According to the Phillips curve, what inflation rate does Caines experience in the short run? _____

   b. Assume the expansionary policies are maintained as are the lower unemployment and higher inflation rates. Eventually, workers begin to expect the inflation and build it into their wage bargains. Draw a new short-run Phillips curve in Figure 19.1 that reflects the effect of the higher wage bargains.
   c. In Figure 19.1 draw the long-run Phillips curve for this economy. In the long run, what will be the unemployment rate and the inflation rate if the expansionary policies are maintained? Explain _____

FIGURE 19.1

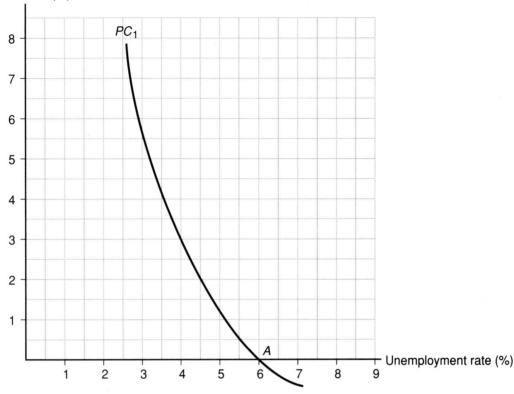

TRUE OR FALSE

1. False. The short-run Phillips curve shows that if unemployment is pushed below the natural rate of unemployment, the rate of inflation increases. The unemployment rate can *temporarily* be below the natural rate.

2. True. The long-run Phillips curve is vertical, which means that in the long run attempts to reduce unemployment below the natural rate of unemployment lead only to inflation. To permanently maintain the unemployment rate below the natural rate would lead to runaway inflation.

3. True. The long-run Phillips curve is vertical at the natural rate of unemployment. If the natural rate of unemployment falls, it would shift the long-run (vertical) Phillips curve to a lower value of unemployment, that is, to the left.

4. True. In the 1960s when the modern Phillips curve was first explored, all the observed combinations of unemployment and inflation rates seemed to fall along a single, negatively sloped Phillips curve.

5. False. The Phillips curve shifted to the right from the 1960s to the 1970s, meaning that the same level of inflation was associated with a higher rate of unemployment.

6. False. Prices have risen more or less continuously only since World War II. The price level fell during the Depression of the 1930s.

7. False. Automatic stabilizers, by reducing the severity of economic downturns, have made workers less likely to take pay cuts when there is unemployment; as a result, the price level is less flexible than it used to be.

8. True. Demand–pull inflation depends on increases in demand fueled by increases in government spending or the money supply. Both of these sources of demand–pull inflation can continue and generate persistent demand–pull inflation.

9. False. Rising oil prices are a possible cause of cost–push inflation. They shift the aggregate supply curve leftward.

10. True. Because periods of inflation were followed by periods of deflation, the price level in 1945 was approximately the same as the price level in 1800.

MULTIPLE CHOICE

1. D. The short-run Phillips curve shows that if unemployment is pushed lower, the rate of inflation rises.

2. C. The location of the long-run Phillips curve is determined by the natural unemployment rate. If structural unemployment rises, the natural unemployment rate rises, which shifts the long-run Phillips curve rightward.

3. D. The structural explanation of the Phillips curve argues that bottlenecks arise in more and more markets as the economy approaches full employment, which results in greater inflation.

4. A. The inflation that began to accelerate in the late 1960s created an expectation of higher inflation that resulted in larger wage increases in the 1970s. As a result, the Phillips curve shifted to the right, meaning the same unemployment rate was associated with a higher rate of inflation.

5. C. The entry of the baby-boom generation increased the amount of frictional and structural unemployment, which raised the natural rate of unemployment and shifted the Phillips curve to the right.

6. D. Decreases in aggregate supply cause higher prices; this is called cost–push inflation because the shift of the aggregate supply curve is caused by higher costs of inputs.

7. C. Because the short-run Phillips curve is downward sloping, an increase in demand decreases unemployment and increases inflation. In the long run, the unemployment rate returns to the natural rate, leaving the economy with a higher rate of inflation.

8. B. During recessions before World War II, deflation occurred. As a result, the price level exhibited no strong upward trend over the entire business cycle.

9. B. During post-World War II recessions, prices have continued to rise. As a result, the price level has had a strong upward trend in the last 50 years.

10. A. The bargaining hypothesis explains the downward slope of the Phillips curve as the result of large wage increases becoming more difficult to negotiate when the unemployment rate is high. This is partly caused by employers becoming more resistant to wage increases when unemployment is high.

PROBLEMS

1. a. Referring to the original short-run Phillips curve labeled PC_1 in Figure 19.2, reducing the unemployment rate to 4 percent causes the inflation rate to rise to **3 percent** in the short run.
    b. The new Phillips curve after workers begin to expect the inflation is to the right of the original one; it is PC_2 in Figure 19.2. The expectation of greater inflation causes the short-run Phillips curve to shift rightward.
    c. The long-run Phillips curve is the vertical line in Figure 19.2. In the long run, the economy's unemployment rate returns to the natural rate, which in this case is **6 percent**, and the inflation rate is 3 percent as determined by the expansionary policies.

FIGURE 19.2

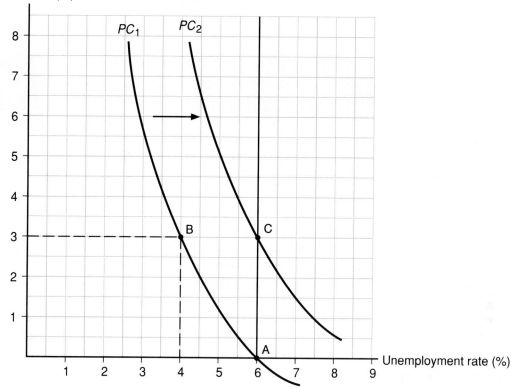

CHAPTER 20

Alternative Viewpoints on the Conduct of Stabilization Policies

Economics has always been an arena for debate, yet rarely has the discipline seen as many major disputes as exist today in macroeconomics. Thirty years ago the economics profession was overwhelmingly Keynesian in its outlook. But that near unanimity has been eroded in the intervening years as more and more economists have become dissatisfied with the failure of Keynesian theory and its policy prescriptions to be reflected in outstanding macroeconomic performance. Whether that dissatisfaction is justified is itself a matter of dispute.

Chapter 20 summarizes many issues that divide macroeconomists, outlines the positions of four major theories—classical, Keynesian, monetarist, and rational expectations—and highlights the areas in dispute.

CHAPTER OUTLINE

I. **Classical Economics**
  A. Classical economics asserts that the economy has a natural tendency to return to full employment. This belief rests on two mechanisms:
    1. **Say's law** asserts that "Supply creates its own demand." Firms can always produce the full-employment output and be confident that it will be bought.
      a. In a barter economy, production and offer for sale of one good ("supply") is exactly and simultaneously matched by the offer to buy ("demand") another good.
      b. In a money economy, people can sell their labor services or products without immediately demanding other goods. They can save, and this can cause complications for the macroeconomy.
    2. However, saving does not destroy the classical view, because the interest rate ensures that saving is equal to investment. In the classical world, if saving is greater than investment, the interest rate falls enough to bring the two into equality.
  B. Reinforcing the interest rate mechanism, wages and prices are also viewed as flexible, ensuring that the quantities demanded of labor and goods exactly match the quantities supplied of each.
  C. The flexibility of interest rates, wages, and prices guarantees that the economy always returns to full employment. Government intervention is not required to solve the problem of unemployment, in this view.

II. **Keynesians**
  A. Keynes questioned whether the world functions as the classical economists believed it did.
    1. Investment and Saving:
      a. Interest rates cannot be expected to keep saving and investment equal, as the classical theory asserts, because:

i. Saving and investment decisions are made by different groups of people.

ii. The interest rate does not significantly affect the saving decision.

iii. Technical factors sometimes limit the flexibility of interest rates.

b. Keynesians believe that saving is determined primarily by disposable income rather than by interest rates, and that investment depends on the volatile "animal spirits" of businesses.

2. Keynesians also doubt whether wages and prices can be as flexible downward as the classical theory implies. This is attributable to unions, minimum wage laws, and other impediments to flexible wages and prices.

B. Keynesians recommend a policy of active government involvement in the economy in order to maintain prosperity. In the immediate post-World War II period, industrialized nations generally followed Keynesian policy prescriptions. Keynesian economics was at its pinnacle in the United States in the mid-1960s.

C. Monetarists criticize the Keynesian approach to policy.

1. Early criticism concerned the importance of monetary policy versus fiscal policy. Monetarists favored monetary policy; Keynesians favored fiscal policy.

2. More recent criticism has focused on the use of active, discretionary policy. Monetarists believe that in the real world it is difficult to accurately manipulate policy tools to achieve full employment and price stability. Some of the problems are:

a. Ignorance of the location of the aggregate supply and aggregate demand curves.

b. Ignorance of the slopes of the curves.

c. Ignorance of how quickly the curves can be shifted by policy and by nonpolicy phenomena.

d. Ignorance of what output level or unemployment rate corresponds to full employment.

3. Monetarists cite several policy errors in the past:

a. In 1931 and after, the Federal Reserve followed restrictive policies that caused significant money supply declines and deepened the Depression.

b. In the 1940s, the Federal Reserve fueled inflation with large increases in the money supply.

c. In the late 1960s, the Federal Reserve again contributed to inflationary pressures by increasing the money supply too rapidly.

d. In 1981–1982, the Federal Reserve reduced money supply growth dramatically and caused unemployment to rise above 10 percent.

III. **Monetarism**

A. Monetarists assert that policymakers should follow a set of pre-determined rules rather than attempt to conduct discretionary policy actions to smooth economic fluctuations.

1. Such a policy would provide a more stable economic environment.

2. The rule that monetarists support is a stable monetary growth rule. The rule is based on the equation of exchange: $MV = PY$.

a. Choose a desired rate of inflation, presumed to be 0 percent.

b. Calculate the long-run % ΔY based on the expected growth rates of productivity and the labor force.

c. Estimate the expected % ΔV.

d. Calculate the % ΔM that is needed to achieve price stability, given these projections.

B. Monetarists believe that discretionary policies fail too often to be useful. They fail because:

1. Policymakers are ignorant of the economy. This knowledge is necessary in order to successfully implement policies.

2. Political considerations interfere with good economic policies.

3. Lags exist in policymaking.

a. There are three lags:

i. The **recognition lag** exists because it takes time for a problem to be discovered.

ii. The **implementation lag** exists because, once a problem is discovered, it takes time for a policy to be decided upon and implemented. The implementation lag associated with fiscal policy is longer than for monetary policy because of political considerations and the larger number of people involved in fiscal policy.

      iii. The **impact lag** is the time it takes for a policy to affect the economy. Monetary policy's impact lag is conceded to be longer than fiscal policy's.

    b. Lags create problems because, by delaying the policy's impacts, they create the risk that the policy will end up being counterproductive or perverse.

  C. Criticisms of the monetarists' "rules" proposition are that:

    1. The economy does not self-correct quickly.

    2. Velocity is unstable, so the appropriate growth rate for constant money growth must be changed frequently.

    3. A constant growth rule would result in more unemployment than Keynesians find acceptable.

IV. **Rational Expectations Macroeconomics (REM)**

  A. Assumptions:

    1. Economic agents form expectations rationally.

      a. Rational expectations mean that economic agents take all available information into account and use the information efficiently when forming expectations.

      b. Although these expectations may be incorrect, errors are random. Expectations are not consistently too low or too high.

      c. Rational expectations differ from adaptive expectations, which change gradually over time. With adaptive expectations, expectations can be consistently too low or too high.

    2. Economic agents have a sophisticated understanding of the economy and implicitly possess a model of how it behaves.

    3. Prices in the economy are flexible. Their flexibility ensures that markets are always in equilibrium.

  B. Implications:

    1. Expansionary macroeconomic policies are ineffective in boosting output and employment. This follows from the fact that the public can anticipate the implementation of economic stimulus by policymakers based on experience.

      a. During a recession an expansionary monetary or fiscal policy that shifts the aggregate demand curve rightward also raises wages and prices because workers and firms anticipate the increase in aggregate demand.

      b. The increase in wages shifts the aggregate supply curve leftward, negating the effect of the policy stimulus on output. Output remains unchanged, and all of the policy stimulus is dissipated in higher prices.

    2. The **policy ineffectiveness theorem** is the idea that anticipated changes in policy do not affect real economic variables such as output, real income, and employment. Only unexpected actions can have an impact. Furthermore, the public inevitably learns to anticipate government policy, in this view.

    3. Restrictive economic policies eliminate inflation with no increase in unemployment as long as the commitment to eliminating inflation is seen by economic agents as credible, that is, as long as the public believes the restrictive policies will be carried out.

    4. In the context of the Phillip curve, REM means that the short-run *and* the long-run Phillips curves are vertical. Anticipated reductions or increases in aggregate demand do not affect unemployment; they only influence the rate of inflation. There is no Phillips curve trade-off, even in the short run!

  C. Critics of REM argue that the theory is flawed because:

    1. Economic agents are not as knowledgeable about the economy as REM assumes.

    2. Economic agents are not as rational as REM assumes. Expectations of inflation do not adjust as quickly to changes in economic circumstances as REM assumes.

    3. Contracts reduce the ability of agents to adjust to new events and expectations.

HINTS AND HELP

1. Theories and Policies   It is often difficult to keep straight the key ideas of the various theories. The following table summarizes certain of these ideas.

	THEORIES			
ISSUES	CLASSICAL	KEYNESIAN	MONETARIST	REM
Stability of economy	Stable	Unstable	Stable	Stable
Flexibility of prices	Flexible	Inflexible downward	Relatively flexible	Flexible
Need for active policy	Not needed	Absolutely necessary	Not needed; cannot be done well consistently	Not needed; anticipated policies have no impact
Rules	No view	Discretionary policies preferable to any rule	Rules will outperform discretionary policies	Rules makes policies more predictable
Phillips curve:				
Short-run	No view	Downward sloping	Downward sloping	Vertical
Long-run	No view	Vertical	Vertical	Vertical

FILL IN THE BLANK

Say's law

interest rate

classical

barter

1930s

mid-1960s

aggregate demand

Monetarists

wages, prices

disposable income

1. "Supply creates its own demand" is called _____.

2. The _____ keeps savings equal to investment, in the classical theory.

3. Keynes criticized the _____ theory when he presented his theory.

4. Say's law is most likely to be true in a _____ economy.

5. The economic experience in the decade of the _____ seriously challenged the validity of the classical theory.

6. The _____ was the period of peak popularity for Keynesian economics.

7. Keynesian economics asserts that macroeconomic policy influences the _____ curve.

8. _____ believe that the Federal Reserve's errors in monetary policy were the primary cause of the Depression in the 1930s.

9. In the classical model, flexible _____ and _____ made it possible for the economy to return to full employment if there was unemployment.

10. Keynesians believe that _____ , not the interest rate, is the primary determinant of saving.

TRUE OR FALSE

_____ 1. Rational expectations macroeconomics asserts that people's expectations are always correct.

_____ 2. The implementation lag is shorter for monetary policy than for fiscal policy.

_____ 3. According to rational expectations macroeconomics, discretionary policy cannot influence output.

_____ 4. Keynesians believe that both fiscal and monetary policy affect the economy.

_____ 5. If the unemployment rate associated with full employment is unknown, the case for active policy-making is strengthened.

_____ 6. Monetarists believe that it is more important to set a rule for fiscal policy than for monetary policy in order to stabilize the economy.

_____ 7. Economists agree that the high correlation between the money supply and GDP proves that changes in the money supply are the primary cause of changes in GDP.

_____ 8. The recognition lag is the same for monetary and fiscal policy.

_____ 9. Rational expectations macroeconomics asserts that the Federal Reserve should follow a policy of expanding the money supply when there is rising unemployment and slowing its growth when there is accelerating inflation.

_____ 10. According to the REM model, a restrictive monetary policy has no impact on the rate of inflation.

MULTIPLE CHOICE

1. Which of the following best describes the views of Keynesians and monetarists on the topic of stabilization policy?
   A. Keynesians and monetarists agree that active discretionary policies are desirable.
   B. Keynesians and monetarists agree that active discretionary policies are not desirable.
   C. Keynesians believe that active policies are desirable; monetarists believe they are not desirable.
   D. Keynesians believe that active policies are not desirable; monetarists believe they are desirable.

2. The impact lag is the time it takes:
   A. to process information about the economy.
   B. for people in the economy to understand an economic problem.
   C. for policymakers to decide what to do.
   D. for the economy to respond to policy actions.

3. According to Keynesians, following the monetary rule proposed by monetarists would:
   A. increase the length of recessions.
   B. increase the chance of inflation.
   C. reduce the volatility of the business cycle.
   D. reduce the value of velocity.

4. Say's law is the idea that:
   A. lags in policy-making are long.
   B. aggregate demand always equals aggregate supply at full employment.
   C. the government's budget is always balanced.
   D. people's expectations are always rational.

5. Rational expectations macroeconomics asserts that an economic policy can influence the economy's output if the policy is:
   A. a fiscal policy.
   B. a monetary policy.
   C. expected.
   D. unexpected.

6. Keynesians believe that an economy is slow to achieve full employment on its own because:
   A. lags are long.
   B. velocity is not predictable.
   C. wages and prices are not flexible downward.
   D. expectations are rational.

7. Which lag is controlled by policymakers?
   A. impact lag
   B. implementation lag
   C. idea lag
   D. information lag

8. According to monetarists, which of the following is *not* considered a period during which there were monetary policy mistakes?
   A. the 1930s
   B. the early 1960s
   C. the early 1970s
   D. the 1940s

9. The optimum money supply growth rate rule depends on:
   A. the expected behavior of velocity.
   B. the desired rate of inflation.
   C. the anticipated long-run growth of real output.
   D. all of the above.

10. According to monetarists:
    A. monetary policy is not influenced by political considerations.
    B. fiscal policy is not influenced by political considerations.
    C. both monetary and fiscal policy are influenced by political considerations.
    D. neither monetary nor fiscal policy is influenced by political considerations.

PROBLEMS

1. Identify the theory (or theories) associated with each of the following ideas and concepts. Use the following symbols: C = Classical, K = Keynesian, M = Monetarism, REM = Rational Expectations Macroeconomics.

	IDEA	THEORY
a.	The economy requires active government policy-making in order to achieve full employment.	
b.	Monetary policy should follow a fixed growth rate rule.	
c.	The economy self-corrects relatively quickly.	
d.	Say's law ensures that aggregate demand equals aggregate supply at full employment.	
e.	Economic agents do not consistently make the same error.	
f.	Velocity is too unpredictable to allow a rule for monetary policy to result in full employment.	
g.	Expected macroeconomic policies have no impact on the economy's output or employment.	
h.	Lags in policy-making are too long to allow active policy-making to be consistently successful.	

2. Calculate the money growth rate that a monetarist would prescribe if given the information provided:

   a.

   expected change in velocity = –2%
   projected long-run growth in real output = +3%
   desired rate of inflation = 0%
   prescribed money growth rate = _____

b.

$$
\begin{aligned}
\text{expected change in velocity} &= +2\% \\
\text{projected long-run growth in real output} &= +1\% \\
\text{desired rate of inflation} &= +1\% \\
\text{prescribed money growth rate} &= \underline{\hspace{2cm}}
\end{aligned}
$$

c.

$$
\begin{aligned}
\text{expected change in velocity} &= 1\% \\
\text{projected long-run growth in real output} &= +3\% \\
\text{desired rate of inflation} &= 0\% \\
\text{prescribed money growth rate} &= \underline{\hspace{2cm}}
\end{aligned}
$$

Answers

TRUE OR FALSE

1. False. REM asserts that people's expectations can be wrong but that people do not make the same error repeatedly.
2. True. Because fewer people are involved in the policy-making, monetary policy can be implemented more quickly.
3. False. If the policy is unexpected, the policy action can influence output.
4. True. Keynesians believe both monetary and fiscal policy can shift aggregate demand and change the course of the economy.
5. False. If the unemployment rate associated with full employment is unknown, conducting successful policy is more difficult.
6. False. Monetarists believe that it is more important to set a rule for monetary policy because money has a greater impact on the economy than fiscal policy.
7. False. Keynesians believe that the high correlation between money and GDP could be due to factors other than money influencing GDP.
8. True. Both monetary and fiscal policymakers rely on the same sources of information, so the recognition lag is the same.
9. False. Because such a policy becomes predictable, rational expectations macroeconomics believes that eventually such a policy becomes ineffective.
10. False. A restrictive monetary policy reduces the rate of inflation, according to REM. A predictable restrictive policy has no impact on real values in the economy, such as employment and output.

MULTIPLE CHOICE

1. C. Keynesians favor active stabilization policies; monetarists, who believe that active policies are difficult to implement successfully, favor rules.
2. D. The time that expires between when a policy action is taken and when the economy responds is the impact lag.
3. A. The length of recessions would increase because, according to Keynesians, the economy does not self-correct rapidly and a monetary rule would reduce the ability of policymakers to combat recessions through active policy.
4. B. Say's law, "Supply creates its own demand," means that when output equals the full-employment output, aggregate demand automatically equals the output.

5. D. According to REM, only unexpected policy actions can influence such real variables as employment and output.

6. C. When prices and wages are not flexible downward, the economy is slow to self-correct.

7. B. The implementation lag is the time it takes to implement a policy action—which is under the control of policymakers.

8. B. The early 1960s was a period of rising output with low inflation.

9. D. The optimum money supply growth rule depends on all the other terms in the equation of exchange—velocity, inflation, and output growth.

10. C. According to monetarists, monetary and fiscal policies are influenced by political considerations.

PROBLEMS

1. a. K
   b. M, REM
   c. C, M, REM
   d. C
   e. REM
   f. K
   g. REM
   h. M

2. To determine the desired money growth rate, begin with the relationship:

$$\%\Delta M + \%\Delta V = \%\Delta P + \%\Delta Y$$

Moving the term $\%\Delta V$ to the right-hand side of the equation:

$$\%\Delta M = \%\Delta P + \%\Delta Y - \%\Delta V$$

Substituting in the values results in the following prescribed money growth rates:

a. $\%\Delta M = 0\% + 3\% - (-2\%)$

       $\%\Delta M = +5\%$

b. $\%\Delta M = 1\% + 1\% - 2\%$

       $\%\Delta M = 0\%$

c. $\%\Delta M = 0\% + 3\% - 1\%$

       $\%\Delta M = +2\%$

CHAPTER 21

The Economics of Federal Budget Deficits and the National Debt

The federal budget situation is constantly in the news. The historic turn of events since 1980, which has resulted in very large budget deficits and a rapidly escalating national debt, has focused public attention on these measures. As this chapter points out, many of the concerns expressed about the national debt are invalid. At the same time, the real consequences are subtle and not easily recognized by the public. For that reason, this chapter is one of the most timely and important in the book.

Chapter 21 begins with definitions and facts that are necessary to understand the key conceptual issues of this chapter. It indicates graphically the growth of the national debt relative to other variables in the U.S. economy. Legitimate and illegitimate concerns about the debt are discussed. Next comes an analysis of the deficit and the potential problems it poses. First among these problems is the potential impairment of the nation's long-run economic growth through the crowding out of investment expenditures. After analyzing other potential consequences of large deficits, the chapter concludes with a discussion of the proposal to impose special legislation to eliminate the budget deficit in the United States.

CHAPTER OUTLINE

I. The Economics of the National Debt
  A. Definitions and Facts
    1. The difference between annual federal revenue and expenditures is called a **budget surplus** (if the difference is positive) or a **budget deficit** (if the difference is negative). Deficits and surpluses are flow variables, typically expressed at annual rates. When the federal government has a budget deficit it borrows by issuing IOUs—bonds and securities—equal to the amount of the deficit.
    2. The **national debt**, a stock variable, is the sum of all federal government bonds and securities that are outstanding at a given time. The national debt rises when the federal government runs a budget deficit and issues bonds and other IOUs to raise funds.
    3. Gross and Net National Debt
      a. The gross national debt is the total of all outstanding federal debt securities.
      b. Net national debt is the gross national debt minus the amount that federal agencies have loaned to the U.S. Treasury.
    4. Trends in National Debt
      a. The national debt has increased more than 400 percent since the late 1970s. Until the 1970s, increases in the national debt were almost exclusively associated with periods of war and recession.

    b. The national debt, expressed as a ratio to GDP and to all other debt, declined from 1950 until the mid-1970s. Since then these ratios have been rising.

   5. The ownership of the gross national debt is divided among the following groups:

    a. Federal government agencies: 24 percent

    b. Federal Reserve System: 8 percent

    c. State and local governments: 10 percent

    d. U.S. banks and other companies: 38 percent

    e. U.S. individuals: 7 percent

    f. Foreign governments, business, and individuals: 13 percent

B. Fallacies About the National Debt

   1. "The national debt is a burden on future generations because the national debt must eventually be paid off."

    a. The national debt does not have to be paid off as long as securities can be refinanced or rolled over. Rolling over the debt means new securities are issued when old ones come due.

    b. Rolling over the debt is always possible because buying securities issued by the federal government is the safest choice possible for lenders, considering that the federal government has the power to impose taxes and print money.

   2. "The interest paid on the national debt is a drain on U.S. resources."

    a. To the extent the national debt is owed to U.S. individuals and businesses, the interest on the national debt is merely an income transfer program. U.S. taxpayers pay dollars to the government that are transferred to other U.S. entities.

    b. The interest paid on the foreign-held debt does represent a potential problem. However, foreign ownership is only 13 percent of the debt.

    c. Greater interest payments associated with a larger debt are potentially a problem if:

      i. the higher tax rates needed to pay the greater interest reduce incentives to engage in productive activities.

      ii. other government programs are reduced to pay the greater interest.

    d. Interest on the national debt has risen relative to GDP and relative to total government expenditures since 1980.

II. The Economics of Budget Deficits

A. Actual, Cyclical, and Structural Budget Deficits

   1. The **cyclical deficit** is the part of the actual budget deficit that exists because the economy is not at full employment. When output is below potential output, tax receipts are lower and expenditures are higher than they would be at full employment, which means the budget deficit is larger. Cyclical deficits automatically decrease as the economy moves toward full employment.

   2. The **structural deficit**, also called the high-employment deficit, is the deficit that exists if the economy is at full employment. The structural deficit can be eliminated only by tax hikes or spending cuts.

B. The economic impact of a budget deficit depends on whether the deficits are primarily cyclical or structural.

   1. Cyclical deficits are, in general, considered beneficial because they provide stimulus to the economy when it is weak. Attempts to eliminate cyclical deficits would require tax increases or reduced government spending when the economy weakens. Either policy would tend to push the economy deeper into recession.

   2. The structural deficit is the best measure of the impact of the budget on the economy. The large structural deficit in the United States since the early 1980s has been unprecedented.

   3. There are several measurement and conceptual issues that must be considered when evaluating the impact of budget deficits:

    a. Some government activities are financed with borrowed funds that are not considered part of the official budget totals. Including such off-budget activities would raise the reported deficit.

    b. State and local governments typically run surpluses. The total government deficit is smaller than the federal budget deficit because these surpluses offset a part of the federal budget deficit.

    c. The federal government does not distinguish between expenditures on capital assets—assets that will be used over several years—and current expenses, which are payments for items that are being used currently. The part of the deficit that is equal to the capital spending of the federal government should not be included in the reported deficit.

    d. When the government pays the interest on its debt, part of the interest payment is actually compensation for damage done to the principal by inflation and should not be included in the deficit.

        i. Inflation erodes the purchasing power of the money lent. When the inflation is known ahead of time, the interest rate increases to offset this impact.

        ii. The part of the interest payment that corresponds to the inflation adjustment should be counted as principal repayment and not as part of government spending and the deficit. The budget deficit after the inflation adjustment has been removed is called the **real deficit**.

C. The economic impact of the budget deficit depends on monetary policy. Both monetary and fiscal policy influence aggregate demand and can move the economy to full employment. But the mix of monetary and fiscal policies can have important consequences.

    1. Expansionary fiscal policy combined with restrictive monetary policy can achieve full employment, but interest rates will be high and investment low. As a consequence, long-run growth with be slowed. Also, the high interest rates raise the value of the U.S. dollar and make U.S. exports more expensive abroad.

    2. Restrictive fiscal policy combined with expansionary monetary policy can also achieve full employment, but with lower interest rates, higher investment, and greater long-run growth.

III. Legitimate Concerns About the Debt

  A. Crowding Out and Growth of Living Standards

    1. Large budget deficits can increase real interest rates, thereby reducing private investment. This is called **crowding out**. Because future generations will be left with a smaller stock of capital and thus a lower standard of living than would have been the case if there had been no deficit, future generations have an **intergenerational burden** imposed on them.

    2. Budget deficits do not always have this effect

      a. Cyclical deficits are less likely to cause crowding out than structural deficits. Cyclical deficits provide support to an economy operating at less than full employment.

      b. Structural deficits that occur when there is high unemployment also are unlikely to cause crowding out. To the extent that the structural deficits speed the recovery and cause investment spending to rebound, structural deficits may encourage investment. This is called **crowding in**.

      c. Structural deficits that occur when the economy is near full employment are most likely to cause crowding out. Slower growth can be avoided only in the event that the government borrowing is used to fund programs that increase economic growth, that is, capital expenditures.

  B. Debt Explosion and Inflation

    1. If the budget deficit to GDP ratio exceeds the growth rate of GDP, the budget deficit grows because the growth of interest expense exceeds the growth of tax revenue.

    2. To avoid the debt explosion scenario requires that the deficit to GDP ratio be kept below the 2.5 percent trend growth of U.S. real GDP.

    3. Because interest is an unavoidable expense, large current budget deficits make future budget deficits increasingly difficult to control.

    4. The exploding debt and the associated difficulty of financing the additional interest payments provide an incentive for the government to create inflation in order to reduce the real burden of the debt.

  C. Legislation to Control Budget Deficits

    1. Public-choice economists argue that deficits are a predictable outcome of a political process that allows politicians to vote for projects that benefit a limited constituency while spreading the cost across the entire population.

    2. To restrict such political activities, legislation has been proposed.

      a. A constitutional amendment to mandate balanced budgets would require tax increases or spending cuts during recessions. This action would reduce aggregate demand when the economy is already weak.

b. A constitutional amendment to require a balanced high-employment budget would avoid the need to raise taxes or cut spending during recessions.

c. A line-item veto would allow the president to veto specific parts of bills rather than the entire legislation.

d. Linking congressional salaries to the size of the budget deficit would provide the most direct incentive to control budgets.

HINTS AND HELP

1. National Debt—Truth and Fiction   As this chapter explains, many of the public's ideas about the national debt are mistaken. One of the mistakes people make when discussing the national debt is to suggest an analogy between family and government. It is often said that an individual cannot always be in debt and neither should a government. But the analogy is incorrect.

There are two significant ways in which the government is different from an individual. The government, unlike an individual, is not going to die. The U.S. government has lived for 200 years and could live *forever*. The same is not true for an individual. As long as a government, or an individual, is alive it can be in debt.

Unlike an individual, the government has the power to tax and print money. These powers make a loan to the federal government the safest loan that can be made. The government finds it relatively easy to borrow because of the safety factor.

Interestingly, although the public sometimes overstates the damage caused by deficits, it ignores some of the legitimate problems. Large deficits do threaten the long-run growth rate of the economy because of crowding out. Yet, because this is a problem of slow erosion rather than a sudden crisis, economists fear that the public will not recognize it until it is too late.

2. Structural and Cyclical Deficits   Keeping structural and cyclical deficits straight is important. Because a cyclical deficit disappears as the economy moves toward full employment, it is transitory and a much smaller problem. (The name "cyclical" comes from the term "business cycle." Similar to cyclical unemployment, the cyclical deficit occurs only when the economy's output is less than its potential output.)

Structural deficits cannot be eliminated so easily. To eliminate a structural deficit requires policy actions that few people, including politicians, find pleasant. Either taxes must be raised or government spending must be cut. Neither alternative is politically attractive.

FILL IN THE BLANK

natural unemployment rate	1. The unemployment rate when the economy is at full employment is called the _____.
cyclical, structural	2. The actual budget deficit can be divided into two parts: the _____ _____ deficit and the _____ deficit.
structural or high employment deficit	3. An estimate of what the government's deficit would be if the economy were operating at its capacity is the _____.
cyclical deficit	4. The part of the government's total budget deficit that automatically increases or decreases as the economy's output changes is called the _____ _____.
structural deficit (or surplus)	5. The correct measure of the fiscal stimulus of a budget is the _____ _____.
surplus	6. If government tax collections exceed expenditures, the government's budget is in _____.

real deficit	7. The deficit after the inflation adjustment has been removed is called the _____.
crowding out	8. Government borrowing that reduces private investment is called _____ _____.
net national debt	9. The _____ is the total debt of the federal government minus that part borrowed from federal agencies.
low	10. Restrictive fiscal policy combined with easy monetary policy causes _____ real interest rates.

TRUE OR FALSE

_____ 1. The reason the national debt is a burden on future generations is that it must be repaid.

_____ 2. The absolute size of the national debt today is smaller that it was at the end of World War II.

_____ 3. The interest on the national debt absorbed a larger part of the federal budget in the 1980s than in the 1950s, 1960s, and 1970s.

_____ 4. A federal budget deficit increases the national debt.

_____ 5. A fall in cyclical unemployment causes the structural deficit to fall.

_____ 6. The part of the actual deficit that varies with the economy's output is the cyclical deficit.

_____ 7. Including off-budget activities in the deficit calculation reduces the total government deficit.

_____ 8. An expansionary fiscal policy combined with tight monetary policy causes real interest rates to rise.

_____ 9. "Crowing out" refers to the fact that when the federal government collects a dollar of taxes, state and local governments cannot collect that same dollar in taxes.

_____ 10. Public-choice economics predicts that budget deficits rarely last long.

MULTIPLE CHOICE

1. The national debt explodes if the:
   A. national debt is larger than GDP.
   B. interest rate on the national debt is higher than the inflation rate.
   C. ratio of the deficit to GDP exceeds the growth rate of real GDP.
   D. ratio of the national debt to GDP exceeds the rate of inflation.

2. If the actual deficit is $200 billion and the structural deficit is $120 billion, the cyclical deficit is:
   A. $320 billion.
   B. $220 billion.
   C. $ 80 billion.
   D. –$ *80 billion.*

3. The national debt can be reduced only if:
   A. saving is increased.
   B. the economy is at full employment.
   C. there is a budget surplus.
   D. interest rates fall.

4. The interest on the national debt is primarily a transfer of income because:
   A. the interest is paid primarily to U.S. citizens.
   B. lending money to the federal government is the safest possible loan.
   C. the deficits are primarily cyclical.
   D. inflation is low.

5. When new bonds are issued to replace bonds that have come due, the government is:
   A. paying off the national debt.
   B. refinancing the debt.
   C. engaged in monetary policy.
   D. stabilizing the debt.

6. Automatic stabilizers:
   A. eliminate the structural deficit.
   B. are associated with the cyclical deficit.
   C. are part of monetary policy.
   D. are measured by the high-employment deficit.

7. The policy mix that is most appropriate for faster economic growth is:
   A. tight monetary and fiscal policies.
   B. easy monetary and fiscal policies.
   C. tight monetary policy and easy fiscal policy.
   D. easy monetary policy and tight fiscal policy.

8. The difference between the gross national debt and the net national debt is:
   A. the real national debt.
   B. the part of the national debt owed to foreign lenders.
   C. the part of the national debt owed to the Federal Reserve.
   D. the part of the national debt owed to federal agencies.

9. Crowding in is most likely to occur when:
   A. there is high unemployment.
   B. there is low unemployment.
   C. there is high inflation.
   D. the national debt is large.

10. A structural deficit can be eliminated only by:
    A. lowering taxes in order to stimulate spending.
    B. raising government spending.
    C. raising taxes or lowering government spending.
    D. lowering the rate of inflation.

PROBLEM

1. Assume Figure 21.1 presents three alternative budgets proposed by the Council of Economists for the government in the economy of Caines.
   a. Assume the economy is operating at 94 percent of capacity and the government has enacted budget B. What is the actual deficit? _____ What is the structural deficit? _____ What is the cyclical deficit? _____
   b. Under what circumstances will the government's actual budget exhibit neither a deficit nor a surplus?
   _____
   _____
   c. When the actual budget deficit with budget C is $140 million, what percentage of potential output is the economy producing? _____ How much of the budget deficit is cyclical? _____ How much of the budget deficit is structural? _____

d. Assume the government switches from budget B to budget C. Is such a budget shift expansionary, restrictive, or neutral? _____

FIGURE 21.1

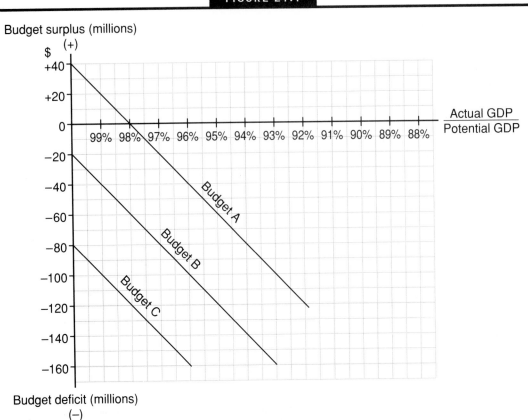

Budget surplus (millions)

Actual GDP
Potential GDP

Budget A

Budget B

Budget C

Budget deficit (millions)
(−)

Answers

TRUE OR FALSE

1. False. The national debt never has to be paid back. Future generations will not be burdened in this way.

2. False. The national debt is larger today than it was at the end of World War II, through the ratio of the national debt to GDP is smaller.

3. True. The interest on the national debt has risen as a percentage of federal expenditures since the 1950s.

4. True. A budget deficit increases the national debt because the deficit is financed by borrowing.

5. False. The structural deficit is the part of the deficit that is unaffected by the economy. It changes only when legislation results in changes in taxes or expenditures.

6. True. The cyclical deficit varies with the size of the gap between actual output and full employment output.

7. False. Off-budget activities are financed by borrowing, so adding them to the official budget deficit would make the deficit larger.

8. True. Budget deficits increase the demand for loanable funds. As a result, interest rates rise. When monetary policy is restrictive, the supply of loanable funds is reduced and interest rates rise further.

9. False. "Crowding out" refers to the idea that government borrowing reduces the funds available for private borrowing, thereby reducing investment.

10. False. Public-choice economics predicts budget deficits will be difficult to constrain because the budget-making process allows politicians to impose the costs of their favored projects on others.

MULTIPLE CHOICE

1. C. If the ratio of the deficit to GDP exceeds the growth rate of GDP, interest payments grow faster than tax revenue and the deficit expands.

2. C. The actual deficit minus the structural deficit equals the cyclical deficit. In this case, $200 billion minus $120 billion equals $80 billion.

3. C. Reducing the national debt requires that the government budget be in surplus so that some of the outstanding debt can be repaid.

4. A. Because U.S. citizens pay taxes and receive the bulk of the interest on the national debt, it is primarily an income transfer from taxpayers to bondholders.

5. B. When new bonds are issued to replace expiring bonds, the government is refinancing the debt.

6. B. The cyclical deficit is caused by increases in government spending and revenue reduction that occur automatically when unemployment rises. These are automatic stabilizers.

7. D. Easy monetary policy and tight fiscal policy each contribute to lower interest rates, greater investment, and faster economic growth.

8. D. The difference between the gross national debt and the net national debt is the part of the debt that the federal government owes itself.

9. A. Crowding in—a deficit that causes investment to rise—is most likely to occur when unemployment is high and investment spending is relatively low.

10. C. A structural deficit can be eliminated only through legislation that raises tax revenue or lowers government spending.

PROBLEM

1. a. When the economy is operating at 94 percent of capacity and the government has enacted budget B, the actual deficit is **$140 million**. The structural deficit, which can be found by finding the budget deficit when the economy's actual output is 100 percent of potential output, is **$20 million**. The cyclical deficit is thus **$120 million** because the structural deficit plus the cyclical deficit must equal the actual deficit.

   b. The actual deficit equals $0 when the government implements **budget A** and the economy is operating at **98 percent of potential**.

   c. The government has a budget deficit of $140 million with budget C when the economy is operating at **97 percent of potential**. In that case, the structural deficit is **$80 million** and the cyclical deficit is **$60 million**.

   d. A shift from budget B to budget C is **expansionary** because the structural deficit for C ($80 million) is larger than for B ($20 million). The structural deficit is the most accurate gauge of a budget's impact on the economy.

CHAPTER 22

Productivity Behavior and Economic Growth in Industrial Nations

Most of this book has focused on such immediate economic issues as the business cycle, unemployment, and inflation. While these issues are crucial, they are transitory. From the perspective of an entire lifetime, they are overwhelmed in importance by the growth rate of output and living standards. These latter considerations, not current unemployment and inflation rates, determine the well-being of our children and grandchildren.

Chapter 22 opens with a discussion of the meaning and measurement of economic growth, living standards, and productivity growth. The U.S. growth performance is analyzed in the context of the performance of a cross-section of industrial nations. We look at the tendency for living standards of industrial nations to converge toward the same level. The determinants of productivity growth are discussed, and the reasons for the sharp slowdown of productivity growth in the United States in the past 20 years are analyzed. Finally, the outlook for future growth is examined.

CHAPTER OUTLINE

I. The Meaning of Economic Growth
   A. **Economic growth** refers to the rate at which an economy's productive capacity expands. It can be pictured as an outward shift of the production possibilities curve or a rightward shift of the aggregate supply curve.
   B. Economic growth is commonly measured two ways:
      1. The rate of growth of real GDP over a long number of years is probably the best measure of an economy's economic and political power.
      2. The rate of growth of real GDP per capita over a long number of years measures the output available per person in the country. It is a measure of the **standard of living** in an economy—though it ignores such important factors as leisure time, the distribution of income, and the quality of the environment.
   C. The primary determinant of growth of standards of living is **productivity growth**—the rate of growth of output per hour of work. Although the growth rates of output per hour of work and output per person can diverge if the average work week and the labor force participation rates change, over long periods of time productivity growth and living standards move together very closely.
   D. Small differences in growth rates over long periods of time result in large differences in standards of living. Higher standards of living potentially provide the United States with the resources to eliminate poverty, provide medical care, and maintain its position as the leading economic power.
   E. Economic growth is a recent experience in human history. Only since the beginning of the eighteenth century has the world seen sustained increases in living standards. The widespread application of technology and capital to the production process, called **industrialization**, has been primarily responsible for modern economic growth.

II. International Comparisons
   A. All industrialized economies have grown significantly since 1870. U.S. productivity growth averaged about 1.9 percent per year. Generally, the industrialized countries that had the fastest rates of growth over this period were the economies that began with the lowest standards of living. This is called the **convergence principle** because of the effect of narrowing the international differences in standards of living.
   B. The primary cause of this convergence in standards of living is sharing of technologies. Technological advances are an important source of economic growth. Economies with lower standards of living can grow faster by gaining technological information from more advanced economies. These transfers of technological information are possible because:
      1. Improved communications make technology transfers more feasible.
      2. Improved levels of education in the industrial countries with lower standards of living make it possible for them to adopt the improved technologies.
   C. Because all industrial economies share in new technological information, countries are not rivals in technological innovation.
   D. The principle of convergence does not hold for all economies. Less-developed countries (LDCs) have not shared in new technologies because of low levels of education and because their economies are heavily concentrated in agriculture.

III. Sources of Economic Growth
   A. An economy's total output is equal to the hours of work performed in the economy multiplied by labor productivity. Everything that influences economic growth does so either by boosting hours worked per year or by stimulating productivity—output per hour of work.
      1. Hours of work are determined by:
         a. Size of the Labor Force.
         b. Average Hours of Work. Evidence indicates that increases in total hours of work have accounted for about a third of the U.S. economic growth since 1929.
      2. Improved labor productivity is caused by:
         a. Technological Change
            i. Technological change is linked to research and development (R and D) spending.
            ii. Evidence indicates that technological change accounts for about 40 percent of the improvements in labor productivity.
            iii. There are two components of technological change: **invention**, the discovery of new knowledge; and **innovation**, the application of such knowledge to production processes.
         b. Increased Capital Stock
            i. **Capital deepening**, which refers to increasing the amount of capital per worker, is the consequence of positive net investment. But capital deepening requires that an economy give up some current consumption in order to free resources to produce new machines and factories.
            ii. Increased capital per worker explains about 28 percent of the improvement in labor productivity in the United States in the last 50 years.
            iii. In recent years, net investment has slowed, as has the rate of growth in the amount of capital per worker.
         c. Increased Human Capital
            i. **Human capital** refers to the education, training, and skills of the labor force.
            ii. Increases in human capital account for about 21 percent of the recent increases in labor productivity.
         d. Other Factors:
            i. Attitudes and motivation of workers.
            ii. The transfer of workers out of agriculture—a low productivity industry—in the 1940s and 1950s raised average productivity.
            iii. Freer international trade resulted in greater specialization, thereby boosting productivity.

IV. Slowdown in American Productivity Growth
   A. Since the mid-1960s, U.S. productivity growth has slowed. Although the *level* of U.S. productivity is higher than other countries', the other countries' productivity levels are rising at a faster rate than ours. Even though some of this is caused by the convergence principle, the U.S. productivity slowdown is a serious concern.
   B. Causes of the Productivity Slowdown:
      1. Changes in the Composition of the Labor Force: More teenagers and women in the labor force from the mid-1960s to the early 1980s meant a less-experienced and therefore less-productive labor force. This factor cannot explain the continued slow productivity growth since 1982, because the influx of young workers has declined since then.
      2. Increasing Government Regulations: Firms were required to spend funds cleaning up the environment and making the workplace safer, which meant less spending for new capital goods.
      3. A Poor Saving and Investment Performance: The saving rate and net investment have fallen, slowing the rate of capital accumulation.
      4. Macroeconomic Conditions: From the late 1960s to the early 1980s recessions and inflation plagued the U.S. economy. Neither inflation nor high unemployment is good for investment.
      5. A Slowdown in Research and Development Spending: Research and development spending slowed during the 1970s, but returned to its earlier levels in the 1980s. Because of lags in the effect of R and D spending, the past slowdown in R and D spending may still be affecting U.S. economic growth.
      6. Supply Shocks of the 1970s: The large increases in the price of oil made energy-intensive capital obsolete and forced firms to devote more funds to the reduction of energy costs, which meant fewer funds allocated to raising labor productivity. Although declining oil prices in the past decade should have reversed this effect, productivity growth has remained sluggish.
      7. Shift to a Service Economy: The economy is increasingly oriented toward the production of services, an area where productivity improvements are more difficult to achieve. This shift slows overall productivity growth.
   C. The Outlook for Productivity Growth to the Year 2000
      1. Positive Factors: Several of the factors that contributed to the slowdown in productivity growth over the past 20 years have reversed themselves and are now contributing to faster productivity growth.
      2. Negative Factors: The U.S. still suffers from low saving, large budget deficits, low net investment, and low R and D spending, each of which slows productivity growth.
   D. Productivity Growth During the Business Cycle
      1. Productivity tends to fall during recessions. Firms are reluctant to let employees go, despite declining output, until the extent of the downturn is known. Hence, output per worker typically declines in the early portion of the cyclical downturn.
      2. Productivity rises during economic recovery because as output begins to grow, firms are reluctant to hire new workers until they know the extent of the upturn. Hence, output per worker typically rises during the early portion of the economic recovery.

V. Policies to Boost Economic Growth
   A. All economists believe that a more rapid expansion in a nation's capital stock is important for increasing the rate of economic growth. There is some disagreement on how to achieve that goal.
   B. Keynesians:
      1. Keynesians believe that investment requires an economy at or near full employment. The government must pursue active monetary and fiscal policies to achieve full employment.
      2. It is also important that the mix of policies be correct. Tight fiscal policy combined with easy monetary policy keeps interest rates low and stimulates investment. This is the opposite of the policies implemented in the 1980s.
      3. Some Keynesians favor a national sales tax to discourage consumption and encourage saving.

C. Supply-Siders:
1. Supply-siders believe that high tax rates discourage investment. High inflation in the 1970s coupled with progressive taxes moved individuals into higher and higher marginal tax brackets, inhibited investment spending, and slowed productivity growth.
2. Tax reform and tax cuts were enacted in the 1980s to provide incentives for increased investment.
3. Supply-siders argued that large tax cuts would not increase deficits because either government spending would be reduced or tax collections would actually increase as the Laffer curve implies is possible. The large budget deficits that actually occurred have brought both the supply-side policies and the Laffer analysis into question.

HINTS AND HELP

1. Productivity and the Long Run   To answer the question "How well-off will people be next year?" it is natural to focus on the short-run issues of unemployment and inflation. But if the question is "How well-off will people be in 50 or 100 years?" unemployment and inflation are much less important. Whether the unemployment or inflation rate is 4 percent or 10 percent in a particular year will not be significantly important. What will matter is what the rate of growth has been.

Economic growth is considered a long-run issue for two reasons. As already mentioned, over long periods of time the rate of economic growth is the overwhelming determinant of how fast standards of living improve. Secondly, the impact of small differences in growth rates does not show up except over long periods. The difference between a 2 percent and 3 percent growth rate does not seem to be critical in a given year. But over 50 years the economy that grows at a 3 percent rate will increase its standard of living by a factor of 4.4, whereas the economy that grows at 2 percent will increase its standard of living by a factor of only 2.7.

FILL IN THE BLANK

Capital deepening

per capita real GDP

economic growth

productivity growth

productivity, hours of work

less-developed countries

human capital

eighteenth

tax cuts

falls

1. _____ occurs when there is an increase in the amount of capital per worker.

2. The best measure of the standard of living in an economy is _____ _____.

3. An outward shift of an economy's production possibilities curve is called _____.

4. Long-term growth in living standards is predominantly determined by _____.

5. An economy's total output equals labor _____ times _____.

6. The convergence principle has not applied well to _____ _____.

7. The education and training of the labor force is called _____ _____.

8. Economic growth has been a sustained human experience only since the beginning of the _____ century.

9. The supply-side theory asserts that _____ are needed to encourage investment.

10. As an economy enters a recession, productivity typically _____.

TRUE OR FALSE

_____ 1. Transfers of human capital are the major cause of convergence.

_____ 2. The convergence principle refers to the convergence of total output across economies.

_____ 3. Productivity tends to fall as an economy enters a recession.

_____ 4. New technological information has been a minor factor in U.S. productivity growth.

_____ 5. In general, the shift to a service economy has increased the growth rate of labor productivity.

_____ 6. Higher oil prices encouraged firms to invest more in order to improve labor productivity.

_____ 7. The United States has the highest level of productivity in the world.

_____ 8. Because of the postwar baby boom in the 1940s and 1950s, the rate of growth of productivity slowed after the mid-1960s.

_____ 9. Any increase in output represents economic growth.

_____ 10. Agriculture is a high productivity industry.

MULTIPLE CHOICE

1. Convergence implies that the economies with the highest standards of living have the:
   A. highest rates of saving.
   B. slowest growth rate of per capita real GDP.
   C. lowest rates of unemployment.
   D. lowest rates of inflation.

2. Which of the following has not had a significant favorable impact on economic growth in the United States in the last 50 years?
   A. improved technology
   B. capital deepening
   C. higher inflation
   D. freer international trade

3. Saving and economic growth rates are positively related because:
   A. people who save more tend to work harder.
   B. the greater the amount of saving, the more resources the government allocates.
   C. economies that save more earn more interest and thus have more income.
   D. saving frees resources that can then be used to produce the capital goods that cause economic growth.

4. Keynesians believe which of the following is a significant determinant of the rate of economic growth?
   A. the mix of macroeconomic policies
   B. the rate of unemployment
   C. the real rate of interest
   D. All the alternatives are correct.

5. Some countries have not participated in convergence because of:
   A. excessive amounts of capital.
   B. a labor force too small for its stock of capital.
   C. inadequate levels of education.
   D. excessive income equality.

6. Keynesians doubt large tax cuts can significantly increase long-term economic growth because:
   A. taxes have no impact on people's decisions.
   B. the large deficits that result cause investment spending to fall.
   C. only monetary policy can have an impact on interest rates and investment spending.
   D. investment spending has no impact on economic growth.

7. Labor productivity is calculated as real GDP divided by:
   A. hours of work.
   B. total population.
   C. number of workers.
   D. total population over 16 years of age.

8. Labor productivity includes the impact of all factors that influence economic growth except:
   A. average hours of work and the size of the labor force.
   B. the unemployment rate and technology.
   C. innovation and invention.
   D. physical capital and human capital.

9. The cost of faster economic growth is:
   A. reduced consumption now.
   B. reduced consumption in the future.
   C. reduced capital now.
   D. higher inflation now.

10. Which of the following has *not* contributed to the productivity slowdown that began in the late 1960s?
   A. macroeconomic conditions
   B. government regulations
   C. lower saving rate
   D. increases in international trade

Answers

TRUE OR FALSE

1. False. Convergence is caused primarily by transfers of technological information.

2. False. The convergence principle refers to the fact that standards of living have grown closer over time.

3. True. As an economy enters a recession and output falls, firms hold onto workers until the depth of the recession is clearer. The falling output combined with about the same number of employees appears as a fall in productivity.

4. False. New technologies account for about 40 percent of the growth in productivity in the United States.

5. False. Because productivity in services is lower and more difficult to improve, increased relative importance of services has slowed labor productivity.

6. False. Higher oil prices encouraged firms to use less capital per worker in production processes. This slowed productivity growth in the 1970s and part of the 1980s.

7. True. Although the rate of growth of productivity in the United States is behind most industrialized countries, its *level* of productivity is the highest.

8. True. The entry of many young and inexperienced workers into the labor force in the 1970s, born during the postwar baby boom of the 1940s and 1950s, slowed U.S. productivity growth.

9. False. If the economy is moving from a point inside its production possibilities curve to a point on its production possibilities curve, output is growing but there is no economic growth. Economic growth implies an outward-shifting production possibilities curve.

10. False. Productivity in agriculture is below the productivity in the rest of the economy.

MULTIPLE CHOICE

1. B. Convergence means that the standards of living in industrialized countries appear to be heading toward the same level. To do that, countries with the highest standards of living must grow more slowly than those with lower standards of living.

2. C. Higher inflation has slowed economic growth in the last 50 years.

3. D. Greater saving by an economy means less consumption. As a consequence, there are more resources available to produce capital goods and other things that create economic growth.

4. D. Full employment (low unemployment), easy monetary and tight fiscal policies, and low real interest rates each encourage investment and economic growth, according to Keynesians.

5. C. Convergence relies on international transfers of technological information; but some countries do not have the educated labor force needed to use the technological information.

6. B. According to Keynesians, large tax cuts result in large deficits, which in turn raise interest rates and lower spending on capital goods.

7. A. Labor productivity measures output per hour of work.

8. A. Labor productivity includes the impact of everything that influences the economy's output except the quantity of labor resources, which is determined by the size of the labor force and the average hours of work.

9. A. Faster economic growth requires the economy to devote more resources to the production of the things that produce economic growth—education, capital, and technology. It requires that fewer resources be devoted to current consumption.

10. D. Greater international trade has, if anything, improved productivity by allowing for greater specialization.

CHAPTER 23

Demand and Utility

Chapter 4 introduced demand and showed how the interaction of demand and supply determine price and output in markets. Chapter 23 examines demand in more detail, explaining *why* consumers buy less of a good when its price rises. This explanation rests on the concept of *utility*, whose importance is emphasized throughout the chapter. Appendix 23A explains the downward-sloping demand curve using indifference curves and budget lines. It is a different method of arriving at the same conclusion.

CHAPTER OUTLINE

I. Marginal Utility Theory
   A. **Utility** is a measure of the satisfaction a consumer receives from consuming a good or service. Economists assume that whenever people make a choice, they choose the option that gives them the greatest amount of satisfaction or utility.
   B. Measuring Utility:
      1. **Total utility** is the total amount of satisfaction received from all units of a good that a consumer consumes.
      2. **Marginal utility** is the change in satisfaction (change in total utility) that results from consuming an extra unit of a good.
   C. Economists predict that marginal utility eventually declines as a consumer consumes more and more of a good. This is called the **law of diminishing marginal utility** because it is believed to be true for all goods.
   D. **Consumer Equilibrium**: A consumer receives the greatest possible satisfaction from the income available when two conditions are satisfied:
      1. The marginal utility per dollar spent is the same for all goods. When there are only two goods, this requirement is expressed in the equation:

$$\frac{MU_{good\ 1}}{P_{good\ 1}} = \frac{MU_{good\ 2}}{P_{good\ 2}}$$

      2. All income is spent.
   E. Demand Curves: There is an inverse relationship between the amount of a good a consumer chooses to buy and the good's price. Because of diminishing marginal utility, extra units of a good are bought only if the price falls (assuming the individual's income is constant).

F. **Consumer surplus** is the difference between the total amount of money a consumer is willing to pay in order to consume a particular quantity of a good and the amount of money the consumer actually pays to consume that quantity of the good.

G. **Paradox of Value**: Water, a good that is necessary for life, has a low price; diamonds, which are of little importance to life, have a high price. This seems to be a paradox. However, it can be explained when it is recognized that price is determined by the *marginal utility* of a good, not by its total utility. Because they are scarce, diamonds have a high marginal utility and therefore a high price. The low price of water means only that an extra unit of water increases total utility very little.

II. Deriving the Demand Curve a Different Way
A. When the price of a good falls, two things happen that change the amount of a good that a consumer buys. As the price falls, the purchasing power of the consumer's income increases, which in turn changes the amount of the good the consumer wants to buy. This is the **income effect**. At the same time, the lower price of the good makes that good cheaper relative to other goods. This is the **substitution effect**.

B. The shape of the demand curve can be determined from the income and substitution effects. For normal goods, both the income and substitution effects induce the consumer to buy more of a good when its price falls. For inferior goods, the income effect pushes the individual to buy less of a good while the substitution effect pushes in the opposite direction. As long as the substitution effect is stronger, the demand curve for an inferior good is downward sloping.

III. **Market Demand**
A. The market demand curve indicates the total quantity demanded by all consumers at each price.
B. It is derived by summing the individual demand curves. At each price, the quantities demanded by each consumer are summed and plotted.

IV. Appendix 23A: Indifference Curve Analysis
A. **Indifference curve**:
1. Definition: All the combinations of two goods that give the individual the same total utility.
2. Characteristics:
a. Downward sloping because the individual must be given more of one of the goods to offset the loss of some of the other good in order to keep utility constant.
b. Convex because the less of a good an individual has, the more of the other good the individual must be given in order to induce the individual to give up a unit of the first good.
c. Indifference curves that are farther from the origin are made up of bundles that give more utility because they contain more of the goods.
d. Indifference curves cannot intersect because that would mean that the same bundle provides two different amounts of total utility.

B. An **indifference map** is a set of indifference curves.

C. A **budget line** is all the combinations of the two goods that cost the same. The consumer can buy only bundles on or below the budget line.

D. **Consumer Equilibrium**: The bundle that maximizes the consumer's utility is the bundle on the budget line that is on the highest indifference curve. It is the bundle at the point of tangency between the budget line and an indifference curve.

E. Deriving a Demand Curve: If the price of a good is lowered, the budget line moves outward along that good's axis. The new budget line is tangent to a higher indifference curve. The bundle at the new tangency contains more of the good that has experienced the price decline.

HINTS AND HELP

1. Total Utility and Marginal Utility It is important to keep straight the difference between total utility and marginal utility. Total utility is the satisfaction that the individual receives from consuming *all* the units of the good that are consumed. Marginal utility is the *change* in utility that occurs when the *last* unit of the good is consumed. If total utility increases when the consumer consumes more, then marginal utility is positive because the consumption of the last unit added to total utility.

2. Diminishing Marginal Utility Economists believe that eventually marginal utility declines as more and more of a good is consumed. Diminishing marginal utility does not mean that the person is worse off having consumed the extra unit. As long as marginal utility is positive, the person is happier when more is consumed. Diminishing marginal utility just means that the *increases* in utility are getting smaller.

3. Consumer Equilibrium A consumer tries to derive the greatest amount of utility from the income available for spending on goods. To do this, the consumer must buy two goods so that the extra utility the consumer derives *per dollar spent* is the same for both goods when all the consumer's income is spent. To determine if this is the case, divide the marginal utility of the last unit that is bought of a good by the price of the good. This yields the marginal utility per dollar spent on that good. Do the same for the other good. The two should be equal if utility is being maximized.

FILL IN THE BLANK

total, marginal

1. Consumers maximize _____ utility by buying goods so that the _____ utility per dollar spent is the same for all goods.

one more unit of the good

2. Marginal utility equals the change in total utility as the consumer consumes _____.

declining

3. If marginal utility is negative, total utility is _____ as the individual consumes more of the good.

declines

4. The law of diminishing marginal utility says that eventually marginal utility _____ as more of a good is consumed.

$MU_1/P_1 = MU_2/P_2$

5. Given Goods 1 and 2, if a consumer is maximizing utility, then all the consumer's income is spent and the two goods are bought so that _____.

consumer surplus

6. The difference between the total benefit a consumer derives from consuming a good and the amount that the consumer spends buying the good is _____.

income

7. When the price of a good falls, the _____ effect causes the consumer to buy more only when the good is a normal good.

substitution

8. When the price of a good rises, the _____ effect induces the consumer to buy less of the good because the good has become more expensive relative to other goods.

indifference curve

9. (Appendix 23A) The line made up of all the bundles that give the individual the same amount of satisfaction is called the _____.

tangent

10. (Appendix 23A) The bundle that maximizes the consumer's utility is the bundle where the individual's budget line and one of the individual's indifference curves are _____.

TRUE OR FALSE

_____ 1. If the third unit of Good A has a higher marginal utility than the third unit of Good B, the consumer will buy the third unit of Good A before buying the third unit of Good B.

_____ 2. If marginal utility is diminishing, the consumer is worse off if more of the good is consumed.

_____ 3. According to economic theory, the demand curve of an inferior good is always downward sloping.

_____ 4. Consumers attempt to maximize marginal utility.

_____ 5. If each consumer's demand curve is downward sloping, the market demand curve is downward sloping.

_____ 6. Consumers buy the good with the lowest price.

_____ 7. Goods with lower prices yield less total utility than goods with higher prices.

_____ 8. When the price of a good rises, the marginal utility of the last unit of the good that is consumed rises.

_____ 9. (Appendix 23A) Indifference curves farther from the origin represent more preferred bundles.

_____ 10. (Appendix 23A) Budget lines are downward sloping.

MULTIPLE CHOICE

1. The law of diminishing marginal utility predicts that marginal utility declines as:
   A. consumption of the good increases.
   B. income falls.
   C. times goes by.
   D. price increases.

2. If total utility is rising, marginal utility is:
   A. rising.
   B. falling.
   C. positive.
   D. negative.

3. If Good X's price is twice as high as Good Y's, a consumer maximizing utility:
   A. buys twice as much of Good X as Good Y.
   B. buys twice as much of Good Y as Good X.
   C. buys Goods X and Y so that the marginal utility of Good X is twice as large as the marginal utility of Good Y.
   D. buys Goods X and Y so that the marginal utility of Good Y is twice as large as the marginal utility of Good X.

4. After a consumer maximizes utility, how much income is left?
   A. all income
   B. no income
   C. an amount equal to the price of one of the goods
   D. an amount equal to consumer surplus

5. Assume the price of videotapes increases. The decline in the amount bought because of the price increase means that the:
   A. total utility of videotapes increases.
   B. total utility of videotapes is unchanged.
   C. marginal utility of videotapes increases.
   D. marginal utility of videotapes is unchanged.

6. When the price of a good rises, the substitution effect:
   A. induces the person to buy more only if the good is a normal good.
   B. induces the person to buy less only if the good is a normal good.
   C. always induces the person to buy more of the good.
   D. always induces the person to buy less of the good.

7. When the price of a good rises, consumer surplus:
   A. rises.
   B. falls.
   C. rises only if the good is normal.
   D. rises only if the good is inferior.

8. The market demand curve:
   A. is obtained by adding the demand curves of different goods.
   B. shows the total quantity that consumers demand at each income.
   C. shows the total amount demanded by consumers at each price.
   D. is perfectly inelastic.

9. (Appendix 23A) Indifference curves:
   A. are downward sloping.
   B. do not intersect.
   C. are convex.
   D. have all the above characteristics.

10. (Appendix 23A) If a consumer buys a bundle for which the budget line and the indifference curve intersect:
    A. the individual is maximizing utility.
    B. the individual is spending more money than the individual has available.
    C. the individual is not spending all income.
    D. the individual is not maximizing utility.

PROBLEMS

1. The following table contains information about the utility Ben derives from donuts and pretzels.

DONUTS			PRETZELS		
QUANTITY	TOTAL UTILITY	MARGINAL UTILITY	QUANTITY	TOTAL UTILITY	MARGINAL UTILITY
1	20	_____	1	50	_____
2	50	_____	2	90	_____
3	70	_____	3	120	_____
4	85	_____	4	130	_____
5	90	_____	5	135	_____
6	92	_____	6	139	_____

   a. Calculate Ben's marginal utility for each donut and each pretzel.
   b. Which would Ben rather have: 4 donuts or 2 pretzels? _____ Explain why. _____
   c. Diminishing marginal utility first occurs for Ben with which unit of donuts? _____ _____ With which unit of pretzels? _____
   d. If the price of donuts is $1 each, the price of pretzels is $2 each, and Ben has $10 to spend, how many donuts and how many pretzels must Ben buy to maximize utility? _____

e. If the price of pretzels falls to $1 while the price of donuts stays at $1, and Ben's income stays at $10, how many donuts and how many pretzels does Ben buy if utility is maximized? _____

f. Using your answers to d. and e., draw Ben's demand curve for pretzels on Figure 23.1.

FIGURE 23.1

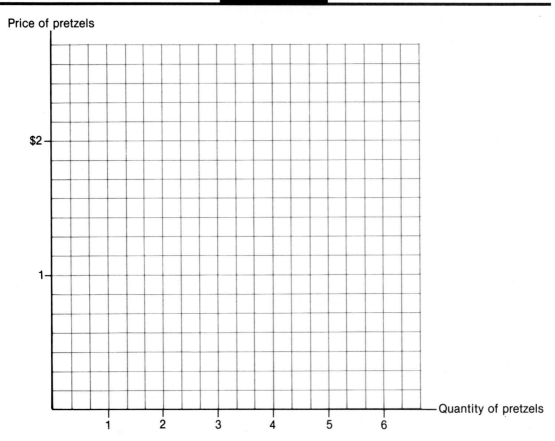

2. *(Problem 2 uses material from Appendix 23A.)*

Again derive Ben's demand for pretzels; this time use budget lines and indifference curves.

a. Using Figure 23.2 show Ben's budget line when the price of pretzels is $2, the price of donuts is $1, and Ben has $10 to spend.

FIGURE 23.2

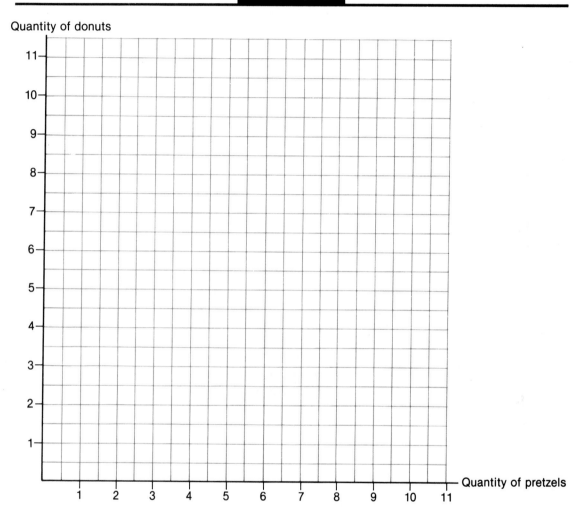

Quantity of donuts

Quantity of pretzels

b. Draw an indifference curve so that it is tangent to the budget line at the bundle made up of 4 donuts and 3 pretzels. Label this point *A*. (How do you know that this combination of donuts and pretzels is on the budget line? _____) Plot the price of pretzels and the quantity of pretzels demanded on Figure 23.3. Label it point *X*.

c. Draw Ben's budget line in Figure 23.2 after the price of pretzels has fallen to $1 while the price of donuts has stayed at $1, and he still has $10 to spend.

d. Draw an indifference curve tangent to this new budget line at the bundle made up of 5 donuts and 5 pretzels. Label this point *B*. Plot this price and quantity of pretzels demanded on Figure 23.3 Label it point *Y*.

FIGURE 23.3

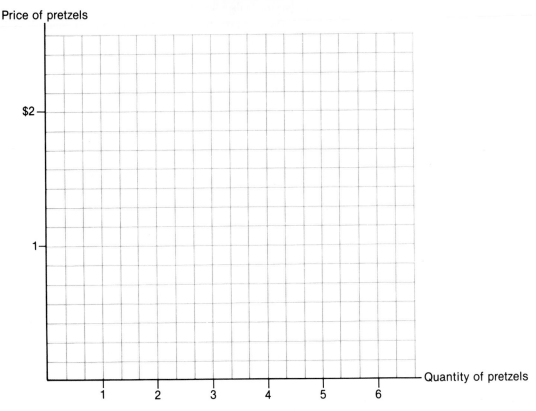

e. Draw Ben's demand curve for pretzels on Figure 23.3.

Answers

TRUE OR FALSE

1. False. Which unit is bought depends upon marginal utility *per dollar*. If the price of Good B is low enough relative to the price of Good A, B's third unit will be bought before A's third unit.

2. False. Marginal utility measures the change in total utility as the consumer consumes one more unit of the good. Diminishing marginal utility simply means that the changes in total utility are getting smaller and smaller. As long as total utility is increasing, the person is better off consuming more, even if the increases are getting smaller.

3. False. The demand curve for an inferior good can be upward sloping. When an inferior good's price falls, the substitution effect pushes the individual to buy more of the good but the income effect pushes in the opposite direction. If the income effect is stronger than the substitution effect, the demand curve is upward sloping.

4. False. Economists assume that consumers attempt to maximize *total* utility or satisfaction, not marginal utility.

5. True. The market demand curve is the sum of the individual demand curves. If each individual demand curve is downward sloping, the market demand curve must be downward sloping.

6. False. Consumers compare price and marginal utility. If the marginal utility divided by the price of one good is larger than the marginal utility divided by the price of the other good, the first good is bought even though its price is higher.

7. False. Price is an indicator of marginal utility, not total utility.

8. True. As the price of a good rises, people buy less of the good. Because of the law of diminishing marginal utility, the last unit consumed when the price is high has a higher marginal utility than when the price is lower.

9. True. Consumers prefer more goods to less. Because bundles farther from the origin contain more goods, they are preferred.

10. True. Budget lines are all the bundles that cost the same. If more of one good is bought, less of the other must be bought in order to keep the cost the same. This makes the budget line downward sloping.

MULTIPLE CHOICE

1. A. The assumption of diminishing marginal utility means that, as a consumer consumes more and more units of a good, eventually marginal utility becomes smaller and smaller.

2. C. When total utility is rising, the change in total utility must be positive when an extra unit of the good is consumed. This means that marginal utility must be positive. You cannot tell whether marginal utility is rising or falling without knowing *how much* total utility increases.

3. C. To maximize utility, a consumer buys goods so that each good's marginal utility divided by its price is equal. If the price of Good X is twice as high as the price of Good Y, then in equilibrium marginal utility of Good X must be twice as high.

4. B. To maximize utility, a consumer spends all income and has none left.

5. C. Because of the law of diminishing marginal utility, as less of a good is consumed marginal utility increases. By reducing the amount consumed, the higher price raises the marginal utility of videotapes.

6. D. The substitution effect always induces people to buy less of a good when its price rises. Because the good has become more expensive relative to other goods, consumers substitute other goods for it.

7. B. As the price of a good rises and the consumer buys less, the area between the demand curve and the price paid diminishes. Therefore, consumer surplus diminishes.

8. C. The market demand curve is constructed by summing the quantities that each individual demands at each price. It shows the total amount demanded by all consumers at each price.

9. D. Indifference curves slope downward, are convex, and cannot intersect.

10. D. If an individual is buying a bundle where the budget line and indifference curve intersect, the individual is not maximizing utility. To maximize utility the individual must buy a bundle where the budget line and indifference curve are tangent.

PROBLEMS

1. a.

DONUTS			PRETZELS		
QUANTITY	TOTAL UTILITY	MARGINAL UTILITY	QUANTITY	TOTAL UTILITY	MARGINAL UTILITY
1	20	20	1	50	50
2	50	30	2	90	40
3	70	20	3	120	30
4	85	15	4	130	10
5	90	5	5	135	5
6	92	2	6	139	4

Marginal utility is simply the change of utility that occurs when consumption of a good increases by one unit. For example, when Ben is consuming 2 donuts, his total utility is 50. When he consumes 3 units, total utility is 70. The increase in utility is 20, so marginal utility of the third donut is 20.

b. Ben would rather have **2 pretzels** than 4 donuts. Two pretzels yield a total utility of 90; 4 donuts yield a total utility of only 85.

c. Diminishing marginal utility first occurs when Ben consumes the **third donut**. The marginal utility of the second donut (30) was larger than the marginal utility of the first (20), so marginal utility was increasing. Diminishing marginal utility occurs with the **second pretzel** because the marginal utility of the second pretzel (40) was less than the marginal utility of the first (50).

d.

DONUTS			PRETZELS			
QUANTITY	MARGINAL UTILITY	MU/$1	QUANTITY	MARGINAL UTILITY	MU/$2	MU/$1
1	20	20/$1	1	50	25/$1	50/$1
2	30	30/$1	2	40	20/$1	40/$1
3	20	20/$1	3	30	15/$1	30/$1
4	15	15/$1	4	10	5/$1	10/$1
5	5	5/$1	5	5	2.5/$1	5/$1
6	2	2/$1	6	4	2/$1	4/$1

Ben must buy **4 donuts** and **3 pretzels**. To maximize utility requires that Ben spend all his income and buy a bundle where the marginal utility per dollar spent is the same for both goods. The bundle of 4 donuts and 3 pretzels costs $10 and the last donut and the last pretzel yielded a marginal utility per dollar of 15/$1. (*Hint*: To find the bundle that maximizes utility, check all the bundles that cost $10 and find the one where MU/$1 is the same for the last unit of each good.)

e. When the price of pretzels falls to $1, Ben maximizes utility by buying **5 donuts** and **5 pretzels**. That bundle costs $10, and the last donut and the last pretzel bought each have a marginal utility per dollar of 5/$1.

f.

FIGURE 23.4

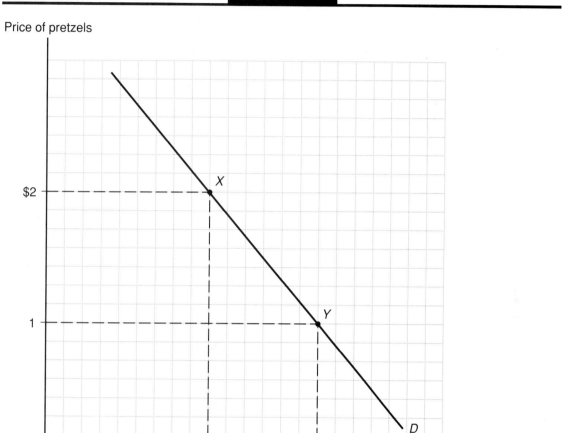

Price of pretzels

$2 ---- X

1 ---- Y

D

Quantity of pretzels

1 2 3 4 5 6

When the price of the pretzels was $2, Ben bought 3 pretzels. That combination is point X in Figure 23.4. When the price of pretzels was $1, Ben bought 5 pretzels. That is point Y on Figure 23.4. Connecting the two points gives Ben's demand curve for pretzels when the price of donuts is $1 and Ben has $10 to spend.

2. a. If Ben spent all his income on donuts, he could buy $10/$1 = 10 donuts. If he spent all his income on pretzels, he could buy $10/$2 = 5 pretzels. Ben's budget line then is a straight line from 10 donuts on the donut axis to 5 on the pretzel axis. This is shown in Figure 23.5 (on page 214).

  b. The indifference curve labeled I_1 is tangent to Ben's budget line at bundle A in Figure 23.5, which contains 4 donuts and 3 pretzels. This bundle is on the budget line because it costs $10 to buy that bundle. All bundles that cost $10 will be on the budget line. Point X in Figure 23.6 (on page 214) shows a price of $2 and a quantity demanded of 3.

  c. After the price of pretzels falls to $1, Ben can buy $10/$1 = 10 pretzels if he spends all his $10 on pretzels. He still can buy only 10 donuts if he buys nothing but donuts. His new budget line goes from 10 on the donut axis to 10 on the pretzel axis in Figure 23.5.

  d. Point B in Figure 23.5 is where indifference curve I_2 is tangent to Ben's new budget. This bundle contains 5 donuts and 5 pretzels. Point Y in Figure 23.6 shows the combination of a price of $1 and a quantity demanded of 5.

  e. Ben's demand curve for pretzels goes through points X and Y in Figure 23.6.

FIGURE 23.5

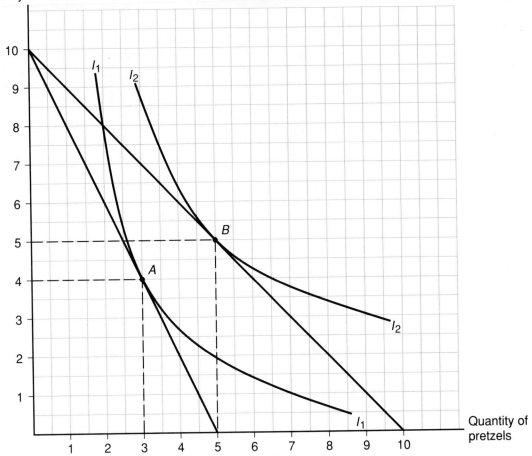

Quantity of donuts

I_1 I_2

B

A

I_2

I_1

Quantity of
pretzels

FIGURE 23.6

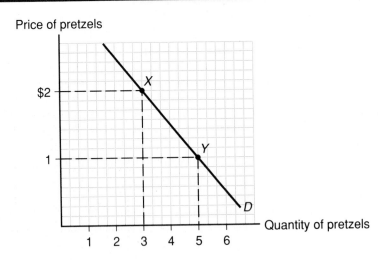

Price of pretzels

$2

X

1

Y

D

Quantity of pretzels

CHAPTER 24

Costs and Production

Chapter 23 looked behind the demand curve to describe the behavior of consumers that results in downward-sloping demand curves. Chapter 24 begins the study of firms. Every firm starts with information about how to produce output. With this technological know-how and information about the prices of inputs, the firm can construct its cost data. Costs play a critical role in determining how much output a firm produces and how much profit it earns.

Although all firms are assumed to have the goal of profit maximization, profit potential depends on the type of market in which a firm operates. Production decisions and profit potential for different markets are the focus of Chapters 25, 26, and 27.

CHAPTER OUTLINE

I. Profit, Cost, and Revenue
   A. Economists assume the owner of any business is motivated to maximize profit. This is the most reasonable motivation to assume because:
      1. Owners say that that is what they are trying to do.
      2. Models that use maximization of profit as the motivation for business decision makers predict more successfully than other models.
   B. Profit equals total revenue (TR) minus total cost (TC). If TC is greater than TR, profit is negative, which means the firm incurs a loss.
   C. Profit
      1. There are two ways to measure profit:
         a. **Economic profit** equals total revenue minus economic costs. Economic costs have two components:
            i. **Explicit costs** are direct payments to others for the resources they own.
            ii. **Implicit costs** are the opportunity costs of the resources the firm already owns.
         b. **Accounting profit** is total revenue minus accounting costs. Accounting costs differ from economic costs in the following ways:
            i. Accounting costs do not include the opportunity costs of resources owned by the firm.
            ii. Accountants base depreciation on historical costs rather than on current market value.
      2. Although there are advantages to each method of calculating profit, economists prefer economic profit because it is a more accurate measure of the success of a firm, primarily because it includes the opportunity costs of the firm's resources.

a. If economic profit is positive, the firm is earning a **pure economic profit** because the firm is more than able to cover the opportunity costs of the firm's resources.

b. If economic profit is negative, the firm is unable to cover its opportunity costs. The resources would earn more if employed elsewhere.

c. If economic profit equals zero, the firm is earning a **normal profit**. The resources would not earn more in any other use.

3. Profit plays an important role in an economy by indicating where resources can be most usefully employed. And profit provides an incentive for resource owners to respond to these signals.

II. Time Periods

A. The **short run** is a period of time so short that the quantities of some resources cannot be changed.

B. The **long run** is a period of time so long that the quantities of all resources can be changed.

III. Production in the Short Run

A. Definitions:

1. A **production function** is a relationship indicating the *maximum* amount of output that can be produced per time period with various quantities of inputs and a given technology:

a. It is typical to assume that there are only two inputs—labor (L) and capital (K).

b. Capital is usually assumed to be the input that is fixed in the short run.

2. **Average product of labor** measures output per worker. It is calculated as total output divided by the quantity of labor, holding the quantity of capital constant.

3. **Marginal product of labor** measures the increase in output associated with a one-unit change in labor, holding constant the quantity of capital.

B. Law of Diminishing Returns

1. All production functions are assumed to exhibit the **law of diminishing returns** in the short run. This means that, in a situation where at least one input is fixed, additional units of the variable input eventually cause output to increase by smaller and smaller amounts.

2. The reason the law of diminishing returns is assumed to be unavoidable is that the quantity of one of the inputs is fixed, and as the amount of the variable input is increased, each unit of the variable input has less and less of the fixed input with which to work.

IV. Costs in the Short Run

A. Definitions:

1. **Total fixed cost (TFC)** is cost that is the same regardless of the level of output produced.

2. **Total variable cost (TVC)** is the cost that varies as the level of output varies.

3. **Total cost (TC)** is the sum of total fixed cost and total variable cost.

4. **Average fixed cost (AFC)** equals total fixed cost per unit of output. It is calculated as TFC/q.

5. **Average variable cost (AVC)** equals total variable cost per unit of output. It is calculated as TVC/q.

6. **Average total cost (ATC)** equals average cost per unit of output. It is calculated as TC/q.

7. **Marginal cost (MC)** equals the increase in total variable cost associated with the production of an additional unit of output. It is calculated as ΔTVC/Δq because only variable cost changes when output changes.

B. The Behavior of Cost of the Short Run

1. Average fixed cost declines continuously as output increases because, referring to the equation TFC/q, the numerator is constant while the denominator rises continuously.

2. Marginal cost is pictured as falling initially, reaching a minimum, and then rising. Marginal cost depends on marginal product. As marginal product rises—as is typical with the first few units of labor hired—marginal cost falls. But, as the law of diminishing returns asserts, as the amount of labor employed increases, eventually the marginal product of labor falls, which means that marginal cost rises.

3. Average variable cost initially falls, reaches a minimum, and then rises. The output level at which AVC is at a minimum is larger than the output level at which MC reaches a minimum. The MC curve intersects the AVC curve at the minimum of the AVC curve.

4. The average total cost curve also initially falls, reaches a minimum, and then rises. For all levels of output, the ATC curve lies above the AVC curve. The output level at which ATC reaches its minimum is larger than the output level where the AVC curve reaches its minimum. As with the AVC curve, the MC curve intersects the ATC curve at the minimum of the ATC curve.

5. The relationship between the marginal cost curve and the average cost curve is the result of a mathematical rule. If the marginal value of any variable is less than its average value, the average value must fall. And if the marginal value is greater than the average value, the average value must rise.

V. Costs in the Long Run
A. In the long run all inputs are variable. As a result, all costs are variable. The **long-run average cost curve** shows the lowest average cost at which a firm can produce each level of output when there is sufficient time to change all inputs.
B. The shape of the long-run average cost curve depends on the cost characteristics of the industry.
   1. **Economies of scale** occur when long-run average cost declines as output increases. One reason this may occur is specialization. As output increases, it may be possible for the firm to use more specialized inputs that result in lower average costs.
   2. **Constant returns to scale** occur when long-run average cost remains the same as output expands.
   3. **Diseconomies of scale** occur when long-run average cost rises as output rises. This may occur because of the difficulty associated with controlling and coordinating production in very large operations.
   4. The long-run average cost curve is typically pictured as U-shaped. This assumes that initially there are economies of scale, then constant returns to scale, and finally diseconomies of scale. The output level where long-run average cost stops declining and economies of scale disappear is called the **minimum efficient scale**.
C. The cost curves shift if there is a change in input prices or a change in technology. Any change that makes production more costly shifts the cost curves upward. Any change that makes production less costly shifts the cost curves downward.

VI. Sunk Costs
A. A **sunk cost** is a cost that has been incurred and cannot be recovered.
B. Because the cost cannot be recovered, sunk costs should be ignored when decisions are made.

VII. Appendix 24A: The Optimal Combination of Variable Inputs
A. Isoquant
   1. An **isoquant** is made up of all the input combinations that produce exactly the same amount of output when the inputs are used efficiently.
   2. The characteristics of isoquants are:
      a. Downward sloping, because more of one input requires that less of the other input be used in order to keep output constant.
      b. Convex, because it becomes increasingly difficult to reduce the use of one input and keep output the same by using more of the other input.
      c. Isoquants do not intersect, for if they did it would mean that the same combination of inputs could produce two different amounts of output when used efficiently.
B. Isocost Line
   1. An **isocost line** is made up of all the input combinations that cost the same.
   2. The equation for an isocost line is:

$$(P_L \times L) + (P_K \times K) = \text{total cost}$$

C. Equilibrium: The Least-Cost Input Combination
   1. The least-cost input combination for producing any particular amount of output is the input combination where that isoquant is tangent to an isocost line.
   2. If the price of either input changes, the isocost lines change and the least-cost input combination changes.

HINTS AND HELP

1. The Law of Diminishing Returns   The law of diminishing returns is a term that is easily misunderstood. One reason for this is that in everyday use the phrase "diminishing returns" is used differently than in economics. It is common to hear people say, for example, "Studying economics has reached the point of diminishing returns, so I am going to stop." The implication is that more studying will add nothing to the understanding of economics. In other words, the marginal product of studying economics has reached zero or may even be negative.

But that is not what diminishing returns means to economists. Diminishing returns means only that the *additions* to output are getting smaller. Output is still rising but at a slower rate. There is nothing bad about diminishing returns. It is simply a fact of life, like gravity, that we must live with.

It is also important to be aware of the conditions under which the law of diminishing returns holds. Because diminishing returns occur only when there are fixed inputs, the law of diminishing returns is relevant only in the short run.

2. Drawing the Curves   Drawing average and marginal cost curves is relatively easy if done step by step.

Step 1. Draw a U-shaped curve and label it AVC. Mark the low point of the curve with a large dot.

FIGURE 24.1

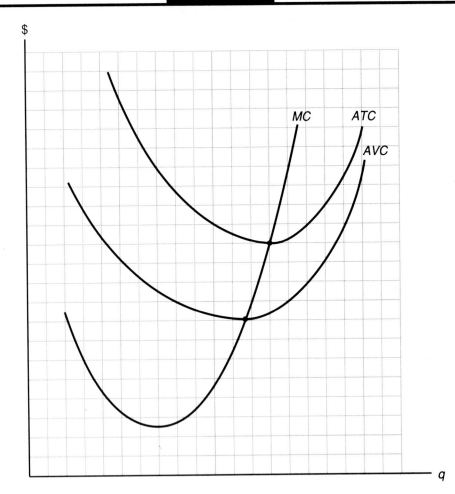

Step 2. Draw a second U-shaped curve. This curve should lie above the first U-shaped curve, and its minimum should be to the right of the minimum of the first curve. Mark the low point with a large dot. Label this second curve ATC. The two curves should move closer together as output grows because the vertical distance between the two curves equals average fixed cost (AFC). AFC declines continuously as output increases.

Step 3. Draw a third U-shaped curve. Initially, on its downward leg, this curve should be below and to the left of the other two curves. This curve should reach its minimum and then start rising, still below the other curves. The minimum point of this curve should be to the left of the minimums of the other curves. The rising leg of this curve should pass first through the minimum of the AVC curve and then the minimum of the ATC curve. After it passes through the minimum of the ATC curve, it will be above the other two curves. Label this curve MC.

Now it is your turn. In Figure 24.2 draw the AVC, ATC, and MC curves as outlined step by step. Start by drawing a U-shaped curve that has its minimum at the large dot on the figure. Label this curve AVC. Then follow steps 2 and 3.

FIGURE 24.2

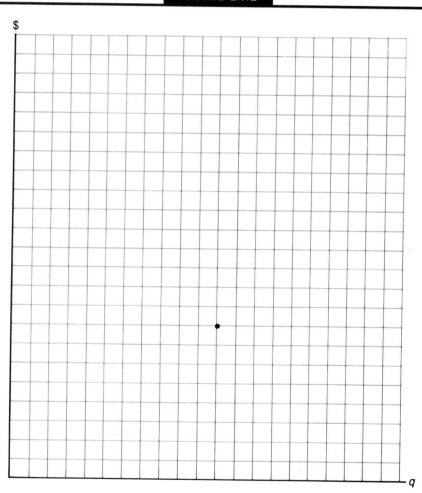

3. Product and Cost Calculations   The following relationships exist between the various cost concepts.

$$TC = TVC + TFC$$
$$ATC = TC/q$$
$$AVC = TVC/q$$
$$AFC = TFC/q$$
$$ATC = AVC + AFC$$
$$MC = \Delta TVC/\Delta q = \Delta TC/\Delta q$$

Undoubtedly all these cost concepts are mind boggling when first encountered. But there are hints to help you remember them.

Average Cost: All of the "average" costs are something divided by output (q). What the something is, is given in the name of the cost. For example, average *fixed* cost is total *fixed* cost divided by q. Average *variable* cost is total *variable* cost divided by q. And so on.

Marginal Cost: "Marginal" always refers to a change. Marginal cost equals the *change* in total variable cost divided by the *change* in output.

4. (Appendix 24A) Isoquants and Isocost Line   As you may have already noticed, there is a good deal of parallelism between the cost analysis in the appendix to this chapter and the material presented in the appendix to Chapter 23. The following are lists of similarities.

	DEMAND	COST
a.	Indifference curves: —All bundles of two goods that provide the same utility —Downward sloping —Convex	Isoquants: —All bundles of two inputs that produce the same output —Downward sloping —Convex
b.	Budget lines: —All bundles of two goods that cost the same —Downward sloping, straight lines	Isocost lines: —All bundles of two inputs that cost the same —Downward sloping, straight lines
c.	Equilibrium: —Indifference curve and budget line tangent	Equilibrium: —Isoquant and isocost line tangent

FILL IN THE BLANK

normal profit

1. If economic profit equals zero, the firm is earning a _____ _____.

long run

2. All inputs are variable in the _____.

Diseconomies of scale

3. _____ cause the long-run average cost curve to be upward sloping.

marginal, declines

4. The law of diminishing returns says that _____ product eventually _____.

accounting

5. The opportunity costs of the firm's resources are not included as part of _____ costs.

fixed

6. The law of diminishing returns applies only when the quantity of at least one input is _____.

explicit

7. An _____ cost involves a payment to others.

sunk costs

loss

pure economic

8. Costs that cannot be recovered and that should be ignored by firms when making decisions are called _____.

9. A negative profit is called a _____.

10. If total revenue is greater than economic costs, the firm is earning a _____ profit.

TRUE OR FALSE

_____ 1. Economic costs include only explicit costs.

_____ 2. Resources are attracted to industries that are earning pure economic profit.

_____ 3. Economies of scale cause long-run total cost to decline.

_____ 4. The short-run average total cost of producing any given level of output is never less than the long-run average cost of producing the same level of output.

_____ 5. The minimum efficient scale is the output at which long-run average cost stops declining.

_____ 6. Marginal product of labor eventually begins to decline as more and more workers are added because the additional workers are not as skilled as the other workers.

_____ 7. The short-run total cost curve is always upward sloping.

_____ 8. A technological change shifts only the long-run cost curves.

_____ 9. (Appendix 24A) A change in input prices causes the isoquant to change.

_____ 10. (Appendix 24A) The input combination for which the isoquant and isocost line are tangent represents the least costly way of producing a given output.

MULTIPLE CHOICE

1. If a farmer uses land that she owns to produce wheat:
   A. the farm earns a profit.
   B. the farm's explicit costs exceed its implicit costs.
   C. the farm's implicit costs exceed its explicit costs.
   D. the farm's economic costs exceed its explicit costs.

2. If firms in an industry are earning an amount less than their normal profit:
   A. resources are attracted to that industry.
   B. resources move away from that industry.
   C. the use of resources is not influenced.
   D. resources are unemployed.

3. The short run is:
   A. less than one year.
   B. when a firm is unable to change some of its inputs.
   C. when a firm is unable to change output.
   D. when a firm is unable to change its price.

4. The production function tells the firm:
   A. which input combination has the lowest total cost.
   B. which input combination produces a given output at the lowest possible cost.
   C. which output is the most profitable.
   D. the maximum output that can be produced from a given amount of inputs.

5. The law of diminishing returns says that, when all other inputs are fixed, additional units of labor eventually lead to a decline in:
   A. total product.
   B. marginal product.
   C. total cost.
   D. marginal cost.

6. The total fixed cost of a firm stays the same regardless of:
   A. the amount of output produced.
   B. the price of the fixed input.
   C. the amount of the fixed input employed.
   D. whether the firm is in the short run or the long run.

7. Which of the following declines continuously as output increases?
   A. total cost
   B. marginal cost
   C. average total cost
   D. average fixed cost

8. If the marginal value of some variable is above the average value of the variable:
   A. the marginal value must be rising.
   B. the marginal value must be falling.
   C. the average value must be rising.
   D. the average value must be falling.

9. The marginal cost curve crosses the:
   A. average total cost curve at the maximum of the average total cost curve.
   B. average variable cost curve at the minimum of the average variable cost curve.
   C. total cost curve at the minimum of the total cost curve.
   D. average fixed cost curve at the minimum of the average fixed cost curve.

10. (Appendix 24A) If two input combinations are on the same isoquant, the two input combinations:
    A. produce the same amount of output.
    B. cost the same.
    C. are on the same long-run average cost curve.
    D. have the same marginal cost.

PROBLEMS

1. a. Fill in the values for marginal product and average product on the following table.

LABOR	TOTAL PRODUCT	MARGINAL PRODUCT	AVERAGE PRODUCT
0	0	_____	_____
1	200	_____	_____
3	500	_____	_____
4	880	_____	_____
5	1,000	_____	_____
6	900	_____	_____

b. Plot the values for total product, marginal product, and average product on Figure 24.3.

FIGURE 24.3

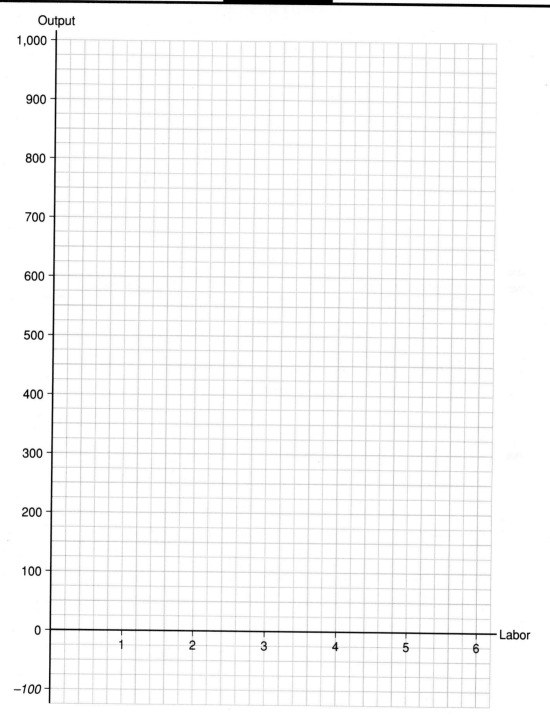

2. Fill in the missing values for the following table.

q	TFC	TVC	TC	AFC	AVC	ATC	MC
0	___						
1	___	$20	___	___	___	___	$10
2	___	___		___	___	___	
3	___	___	$113		___	___	
4	___	___	___	$20	___	___	$11
5	___	___	___		___	___	$16
6	___	$84	___	___		___	
7	___	___	___	___	$17	___	
8	___	___	___	___		___	$49
9	___	___	$314	___		___	
10	___	___	___	___	___	$40	

3. Figures 24.4 (a), (b), (c), and (d) are drawn incorrectly. Identify the error in each and explain why it is wrong.

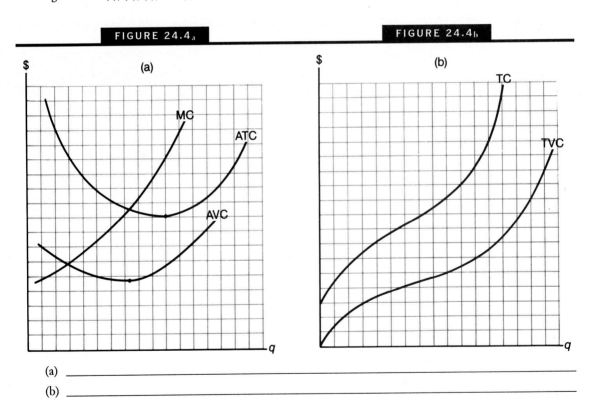

FIGURE 24.4a

$
(a)

MC

ATC

AVC

q

FIGURE 24.4b

$
(b)

TC

TVC

q

(a) _____

(b) _____

FIGURE 24.4 c   FIGURE 24.4 d

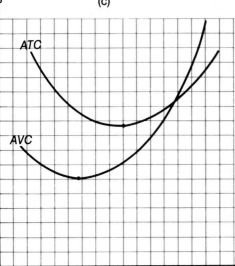

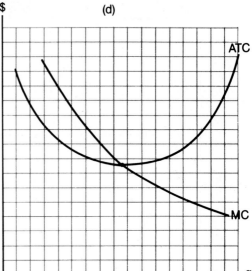

(c) _____

(d) _____

4. Use Figure 24.5 to answer the following questions.

FIGURE 24.5

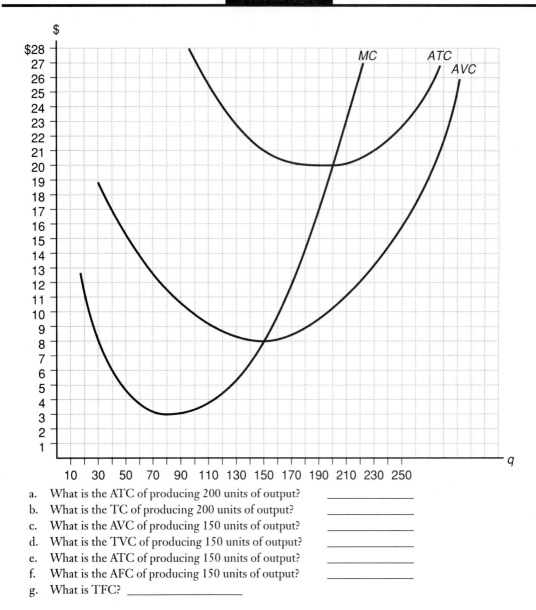

a. What is the ATC of producing 200 units of output? _____
b. What is the TC of producing 200 units of output? _____
c. What is the AVC of producing 150 units of output? _____
d. What is the TVC of producing 150 units of output? _____
e. What is the ATC of producing 150 units of output? _____
f. What is the AFC of producing 150 units of output? _____
g. What is TFC? _____

Answers

TRUE OR FALSE

1. False. Economic costs include both explicit costs and implicit costs.

2. True. Pure profits indicate that resources are earning more than they could earn in their best alternative use. Such a situation attracts new resources.

3. False. Economies of scale cause long-run *average* cost to decline.

4. True. Each point on a short-run average total cost curve lies on or above the long-run average cost curve. This means that the short-run average total cost of producing any given level of output is at least as high as the long-run average cost.

5. True. The minimum efficient scale is the output level where economies of scale end, which would be the output level where long-run average cost stops declining.

6. False. It is assumed that all workers are equally skilled. Diminishing marginal product occurs because, as workers are added, each worker has less and less of the fixed input to work with.

7. True. Because an increase in production adds to costs, total cost curves are always upward sloping.

8. False. Both the long-run and the short-run cost curves are derived assuming the technology if fixed. If technology changes, both the short-run and the long-run cost curves shift.

9. False. Isoquants are representations of a given technology. Input prices have no impact on technology.

10. True. All other points on the isoquant lie on higher isocost lines and therefore cost more to produce.

MULTIPLE CHOICE

1. D. The opportunity cost of the farmer's land is an implicit cost. Because economic costs equal explicit plus implicit costs, the economic costs exceed the explicit costs.

2. B. If firms in an industry are earning less than their normal profit, the resources can earn more in another use. As a result, the resources will leave the industry in order to receive higher returns elsewhere.

3. B. The short run is a period so short that the firm is unable to vary some of its inputs.

4. D. The production function tells the firm the maximum output that could be produced with various quantities of inputs, assuming that technology is fixed.

5. B. The law of diminishing returns says that marginal product eventually declines as units of labor are increased.

6. A. Total fixed cost does not vary with output.

7. D. Average fixed cost declines continuously as output increases.

8. C. If the marginal value is greater than the average value, it raises the average value.

9. B. The marginal cost curve intersects the average variable cost curve at the minimum of the average variable cost curve.

10. A. An isoquant contains all the input combinations that produce the same amount of output.

PROBLEMS

1. a.

LABOR	TOTAL PRODUCT	MARGINAL PRODUCT	AVERAGE PRODUCT
0	0		
1	200	200	200
2	500	300	250
3	750	250	250
4	880	130	220
5	1,000	120	200
6	900	−100	150

b. See Figure 24.6.

FIGURE 24.6

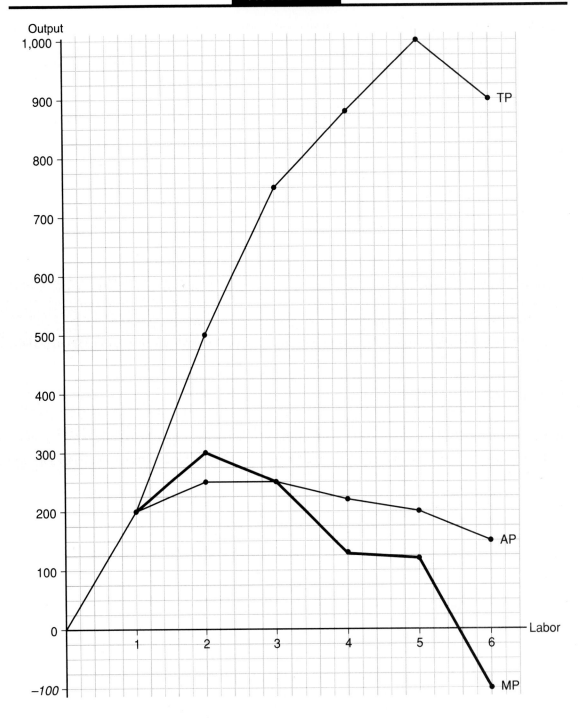

2. Fill in the missing values for the following table.

q	TFC	TVC	TC	AFC	AVC	ATC	MC
0	$80						
1	80	$ 20	$100	$80	$20	$100	$20
2	80	30	110	40	15	55	10
3	80	33	113	26.67	11	37.67	3
4	80	44	124	20	11	31	11
5	80	60	140	16	12	28	16
6	80	84	164	13.33	14	27.33	24
7	80	119	199	11.43	17	28.43	35
8	80	168	248	10	21	31	49
9	80	234	314	8.89	26	34.89	66
10	80	320	400	8	32	40	86

Hint: Start with AFC = $20 when output equals 4. That means total fixed cost (TFC) is $20 x 4 = $80. The entire first column can be filled with $80 because fixed cost is the same at each level of output.

Once total fixed cost is known, it is possible to calculate AFC by dividing TFC by the amount of output. This gives all the information for the AFC column.

To fill in the remaining blanks, work with the identities TC = TFC + TVC and ATC = AFC + AVC. Also remember that MC is the amount by which TC and TVC increase when one more unit of output is produced.

3. (a) shows the MC curve intersecting the AVC and ATC curves to the left of the minimums of the two average curves. The MC curve should intersect each average curve at the minimum value of the curve.

(b) shows the TC and TVC curves farther and farther apart as output grows. Because the vertical difference between the two curves represents TFC, which is constant, the distance between the two curves should be the same at each level of output.

(c) shows the ATC and AVC curves intersecting. But the ATC curve should always be above the AVC curve because the vertical distance between the two curves is AFC, which is always positive.

(d) shows a downward-sloping MC curve intersecting the minimum of the ATC curve. Instead, the MC curve should be upward sloping—MC intersects the ATC curve from below.

4. a. ATC for 200 = **$20**.
    b. TC for 200 = $20 x 200 = **$4,000**.
    c. AVC for 150 = **$8**.
    d. TVC for 150 = $8 x 150 = **$1,200**.
    e. ATC for 150 = **$21**.
    f. AFC for 150 = $21 – $8 = **$13**.
    g. TFC = $13 x 150 = **$1,950**.

CHAPTER 25

Perfect Competition

Given the background of the previous two chapters on demand and costs, it is time to consider production decisions of firms. How much output should the firm produce to maximize profit, and how much profit does the firm earn? The answers to these and other questions depend on the type of market in which the firm sells its product.

Chapter 25 considers production decisions in perfectly competitive markets in which the firm confronts a given, market-determined price and decides how much to produce given that price. The following two chapters examine markets in which firms have influence over price as well as output levels.

CHAPTER OUTLINE

I. The Structure of Markets
   A. **Market structure** refers to the distinguishable characteristics of a market.
   B. There are four important characteristics of a market:
      1. Number of Firms
         a. In perfectly competitive and monopolistically competitive markets there are many firms.
         b. In oligopoly there are only a few sellers.
         c. In monopoly there is one seller.
      2. Similarity of the Products They Sell
         a. In perfect competition all firms produce an identical (or homogeneous) product.
         b. In monopolistic competition each firm produces a slightly different product.
         c. In oligopolistic markets products can be either homogeneous or differentiated.
         d. In a monopoly the product is unique.
      3. Ease with Which New Firms Can Enter the Market
         a. In perfectly competitive and monopolistically competitive markets there is **free entry** (that is, firms can easily enter the industry). There is also **free exit** (that is, firms can easily exit).
         b. Oligopolistic and monopolistic markets have significant barriers to entry.
      4. The Firm's Influence Over Price
         a. A perfectly competitive firm has no control over price.
         b. A monopolist has the greatest control over price.
         c. Monopolistically competitive firms and oligopolies have some control over price.
   C. Market structure influences the output, price, and profits of the firms in the market.
II. **Perfect Competition**
   A. Assumptions:

1. The market contains a large number of buyers and sellers. No individual buyer or seller is large enough to have a noticeable impact on demand or supply.
2. The firms sell a homogeneous product, so buyers do not care who produced the product.
3. There is free entry and free exit.
4. Buyers and sellers have perfect information about prices and other market conditions.
   B. These assumptions imply that each firm in a perfectly competitive market is a **price taker**. The firm is able to sell as much as it wishes at the market price. But if it attempts to charge more than the market price it will find no buyers. The demand curve faced by a price taker is perfectly elastic.

III. Production in the Short Run.
   A. Profit Maximization Using Total Costs and Total Revenue
      1. The firm has the short-run cost curves—TC, TVC, ATC, AVC, MC—that were described in Chapter 24.
      2. Total revenue (TR) equals $P \times q$. Because P is fixed, the total revenue curve is a straight line from the origin, with a slope equal to the price.
      3. Profit (loss) equals the vertical distance between the TR and TC curves:
         a. If the TR curve is above the TC curve, the firm is earning a profit.
         b. If the TR curve is below the TC curve, the firm is suffering a loss.
         c. At the output where TR crosses TC, profit equals zero.
      4. Profit Maximization—Total Revenue and Total Cost
         a. When TR is greater than TC, the firm maximizes profit by producing the level of output for which TR – TC is greatest.
         b. When TR is less than TC for all levels of output, the firm cannot avoid a loss. Even so, the firm continues to produce provided that TR is greater than TVC.
         c. The firm **shuts down**—produces no output—only if TR is less than TVC at every output level. When the firm shuts down, its loss equals its fixed costs. If the firm were to produce when TR is less than TVC, the firm's loss would equal its fixed costs plus the part of TVC that the total revenue does not cover.
         d. The firm, then, makes two production decisions:
            i. Produce output only if $TR \geq TVC$.
            ii. If the firm is to produce, produce where TR – TC is greatest.
   B. Profit Maximization Using Marginal Revenue and Marginal Cost
      1. **Marginal revenue (MR)** is the increase in total revenue that the firm receives when it sells one more unit of output. Because the firm can always sell more units of the good without lowering the price, the extra revenue the firm gains equals the price of the good. That is, in perfectly competitive markets MR = P.
      2. If the firm produces any output, the firm should produce the output where MR = MC in order to maximize profit:
         a. If MR > MC, profit rises by producing more because the extra output increases revenue more than it increases cost.
         b. If MR < MC, profit rises by producing less because the reduction in output reduces cost more than it reduces revenue.
      3. The firm chooses to produce output only if $P \geq AVC$. If $P < AVC$, the firm would lose less by shutting down and limiting the loss to its fixed costs.
      4. Again, the firm has two production decisions:
         a. Produce output only if $P \geq AVC$.
         b. If production occurs, produce the output where MR = MC.
   C. **The Firm's Short-Run Supply Curve**
      1. A firm's supply curve shows the quantities of output the firm wants to produce at various prices.
      2. Because a perfectly competitive firm produces the output where MR = MC as long as $P \geq AVC$, the supply curve is that part of the MC curve on or above the AVC curve.

D. **The industry's short-run supply curve** is the horizontal sum of each firm's short-run supply curve.

E. The industry is in short-run equilibrium when:
1. The market demand curve intersects the market supply curve.
2. Each firm is producing its profit-maximizing level of output.

IV. Long-Run Equilibrium in Perfect Competition
   A. Long-run equilibrium requires that:
      1. No firm has an incentive to change its plant size, which means that the firm is producing its output at the lowest possible long-run average cost.
      2. No firm has an incentive to change its level of output, which means that MR (= P) = MC (that is, profit is maximized).
      3. No firm is earning a pure economic profit, so no firm has an incentive to enter the industry; no firm has a loss, so no firm has an incentive to leave. This can only happen if P = LRAC.
   B. Long-Run Equilibrium Output for the Firm
      1. The only output level where these conditions can be satisfied simultaneously is the output level at the minimum of LRAC curve.
      2. In long-run equilibrium, the following condition must hold for the firm:
         P = LRMC = LRAC = SRMC = SRAC.
   C. The Industry Long-Run Supply Curve
      1. The **long-run supply curve** is a curve made up of all the price and quantity combinations consistent with the preceding conditions. Its shape depends on what happens to input prices as industry output changes.
      2. There are three possible shapes to the long-run supply curve.
         a. In a **constant-cost industry**, input prices and cost curves remain the same as industry output changes. Because the average cost of production is the same in the long run regardless of how much output is produced, the long-run supply curve is perfectly elastic.
         b. In an **increasing-cost industry**, input prices increase as industry output expands, driving up the average cost of production. Because average cost is rising, firms are willing to produce more in the long run only if price increases. This means the long-run supply curve is upward sloping.
         c. As output expands in a **decreasing-cost industry**, input prices fall. This lowers the long-run average cost of production and therefore the price paid by consumers. The result is a downward-sloping supply curve in the long run.

V. Evaluation of Perfect Competition
   A. In Praise of Perfect Competition
      1. Because of the pressure of competition and the desire for maximum profit, firms have the incentive to produce output at the lowest possible cost. This is called **productive efficiency**.
      2. Price indicates the value consumers place on an extra unit of a product. If P > MC, consumers place a higher value on an extra unit than it costs to produce the extra unit. The extra unit should be produced. If P < MC, the cost of producing an extra unit is greater than the value consumers place on the extra unit. It should not be produced. Because perfect competition induces firms to produce where P = MC, all the units of the good that should be produced are produced and those that should not be produced are not. This is called an **efficient allocation of resources**.
      3. Perfect competition is consistent with maximum personal freedom. In perfect competition most decisions are made by individuals without government involvement.
   B. Possible Drawbacks:
      1. Substantial economies of scale mean that costs are minimized only with large-scale production. Perfect competition is not compatible with this situation because of the limited number of producers.
      2. Externalities result in an inefficient allocation of resources because price does not reflect the value to society of another unit of output or marginal cost does not reflect the cost to society of producing another unit of output. When externalities exist, perfect competition does not result in an efficient allocation of resources.

3. Other Considerations:
   a. When the distribution of resources under perfect competition is inequitable, the distribution of income will also be inequitable.
   b. Perfect competition may not sufficiently reward innovation because the payoff to new inventions will be eliminated quickly by the entry of new firms.
   c. Perfect competition may result in a boring set of alternatives because of the homogeneity of products.

HINTS AND HELP

1. The Horizontal Demand Curve   In a perfectly competitive market, no firm sees itself as having the power to influence price. Because few of us are producers, it may be difficult to understand what this means. But we are consumers, and consumers in a perfectly competitive world are in the same situation. No consumer sees his or her purchase decision as influencing the market price. What this means, for example, is that whether a consumer buys 1 package of cookies or 25 packages, the price charged for a bag of cookies will remain the same. It means that no consumer goes into a store and thinks, "Well, if I do not buy this bag of cookies today, the store will have to lower the price, and I'll be able to come back tomorrow and buy the bag of cookies at a lower price."

Producers think the same way. No grower of wheat thinks, "Well, if I grow 5,000 bushels rather than 500, the price of wheat will be lower." Each wheat producer is such a small part of the total wheat market that no individual grower's output decision influences the price at which wheat is sold.

It is possible to translate this behavior into a demand curve. The individual firm believes that it can sell all it can produce at the existing market price. If it offers to sell 1 bushel, the price buyers are willing to pay is the market price. If it offers to sell 10,000 bushels, again the price buyers are willing to pay is the market price. Because all quantities can be sold at the market price, the firm sees itself as facing a horizontal demand curve.

2. Shutting Down   Sometimes a firm cannot avoid a loss. The production decision in this case depends on whether the loss would be less if the firm operated or if it shut down.

If the firm shuts down, the firm's loss equals its fixed costs because the firm must pay those costs whether it produces or not.

The firm continues to produce if its loss is no greater than its fixed costs. This will happen as long as total revenue is equal to or exceeds its total variable cost. If total revenue exactly equals total variable cost, the firm's loss exactly equals its fixed costs—exactly what it would lose if it shut down. If total revenue is greater than its total variable cost, it can pay all its variable costs and have something left over to pay a part of its fixed costs. In that case, the loss is less if the firm operates than if it shuts down.

Remember: The question of whether the firm shuts down depends on whether the firm can cover its *variable* costs, not its fixed costs.

FILL IN THE BLANK

shuts down	1. If a firm's total revenue is less than its total variable cost, the firm _____.
free entry	2. If new firms can easily start up in an industry, there is _____ _____.
decreasing-cost	3. The industry long-run supply curve can be downward sloping only if the industry is a _____ industry.
productive efficiency	4. Producing output at the lowest possible cost is called _____ _____.

price	5. Because the firm faces a horizontal demand curve, marginal revenue equals _____.
supply	6. The perfectly competitive firm's short-run _____ curve is the same as the firm's marginal cost curve above average variable cost.
plant	7. In the short run, the firm's _____ size is fixed.
more	8. If price exceeds the marginal cost of the last unit produced, allocative efficiency requires that there be _____ output produced.
minimum	9. In long-run equilibrium, a perfectly competitive firms produces the output at the _____ of its long-run average cost curve.
unequal	10. Some criticize perfect competition because it may lead to an _____ _____ distribution of income.

TRUE OR FALSE

_____ 1. The demand curve faced by the perfectly competitive firm is upward sloping.

_____ 2. If firms in a market produce a homogeneous product, no firm can have an impact on the price of the product.

_____ 3. In long-run equilibrium, perfectly competitive firms must earn a pure profit.

_____ 4. A price taker is a firm that treats the market price as a constant.

_____ 5. If a perfectly competitive firm is producing a level of output where MR < MC, the firm is incurring a loss.

_____ 6. A firm shuts down when P < AFC.

_____ 7. A perfectly competitive firm never produces if the result is a loss.

_____ 8. The market supply curve is the horizontal summation of the firms' MC curves above average variable cost.

_____ 9. Perfect competition requires that there be a large number of buyers of the product.

_____ 10. Losses are the signal for resources to leave a competitive market.

MULTIPLE CHOICE

1. Which of the following markets is closest to a perfectly competitive market?
   A. lawn care
   B. automobile manufacturing
   C. steel production
   D. toothpaste

2. The demand curve faced by a perfectly competitive firm has an elasticity of:
   A. zero.
   B. 1.
   C. 2.
   D. infinity.

3. If a perfectly competitive firm produces in the short run, its profit-maximizing level of output will be at least as large as that corresponding to:
   A. the minimum of the MC curve.
   B. the minimum of the ATC curve.
   C. the minimum of the AVC curve.
   D. the minimum of the AFC curve.

4. Which of the following is true when a firm is in long-run equilibrium?
   A. P = LRAC
   B. P = SRMC
   C. MR = SRAC
   D. All the alternatives are correct.

5. Which of the following is true if price equals $15 and a profit-maximizing firm is producing 98 units of output in the short run?
   A. The average variable cost of producing 98 units is not more than $15.
   B. The marginal cost of producing the 98th unit is more than $15.
   C. The average total cost is less than $15.
   D. The average fixed cost of producing 98 units is not more than $15.

6. The largest possible loss a perfectly competitive firm experiences in the short run is:
   A. $0.
   B. equal to the firm's fixed cost.
   C. equal to the firm's variable cost.
   D. cannot be determined without knowing the price at which the product is sold.

7. The largest possible loss a perfectly competitive firm experiences in the long run is:
   A. $0.
   B. equal to the firm's fixed cost.
   C. equal to the firm's variable cost.
   D. cannot be determined without knowing the price at which the product is sold.

8. A perfectly competitive firm can increase its profit by producing more output if the firm is currently producing an output where:
   A. MR < MC.
   B. MC > AVC.
   C. P < ATC.
   D. P > MC.

9. Allocative efficiency requires that:
   A. P = MC.
   B. P = AVC.
   C. P = MR.
   D. P = ATC.

10. In a decreasing-cost industry:
    A. demand decreases as income increases.
    B. the demand curve is upward sloping.
    C. the industry long-run supply curve is downward sloping.
    D. firms can earn a pure economic profit in long-run equilibrium.

PROBLEMS

1. For each of the following characteristics, indicate which market structure(s) has the characteristic. Use the letters PC = perfect competition, MC = monopolistic competition, O = oligopoly, and M = monopoly.
   a. One producer _____
   b. Homogeneous product _____
   c. Barriers to entry _____
   d. Differentiated product _____
   e. No control over price _____
   f. Many producers _____
   g. Unique product _____
   h. Few producers _____
   i. Free entry _____

2. In Figure 25.1 draw the total revenue curve and the marginal revenue curve for a perfectly competitive firm when (a) price = $2 and (b) price = $5.

FIGURE 25.1

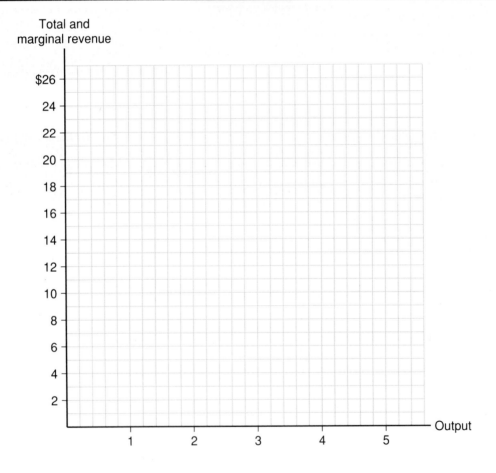

3. Use Figure 25.2, which shows a perfectly competitive firm's total cost and total variable cost curves as well as two total revenue curves, to answer the following questions.

   a. What is the firm's total fixed cost? _____

   b. What output should this firm produce if the price equals $2?_____What is the firm's total revenue? _____ What is the firm's total cost?_____What is the firm's total variable cost?_____ What is the firm's profit?_____ What would be the firm's profit if it shut down and produced nothing? _____

   c. What output should the firm produce if the price equals $4?_____ What is the firm's total revenue? _____ What is the firm's total cost?_____What is the firm's profit?_____

FIGURE 25.2

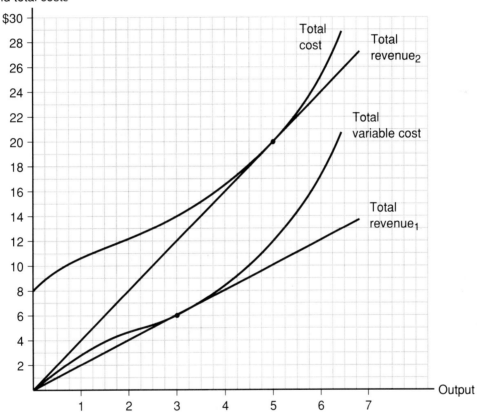

4. Use the following table to answer the following questions.
    a. What is the firm's total fixed cost?_____
    b. If the price of output is $3, what is the firm's profit if it produces?_____
        What output does the firm produce_____ Explain why._____
    c. If the price of output is $49, what output does the firm produce? _____
        Explain why._____ What is the firm's profit if it produces?
        _____

q	AVC	ATC	MC
0			
1	$20	$100	$20
2	15	55	10
3	11	37.67	3
4	11	31	11
5	12	16	16
6	14	27.33	24
7	17	28.43	35
8	21	31	49
9	26	34.89	66
10	32	40	86

5. Use Figure 25.3 to answer the following question.

FIGURE 25.3

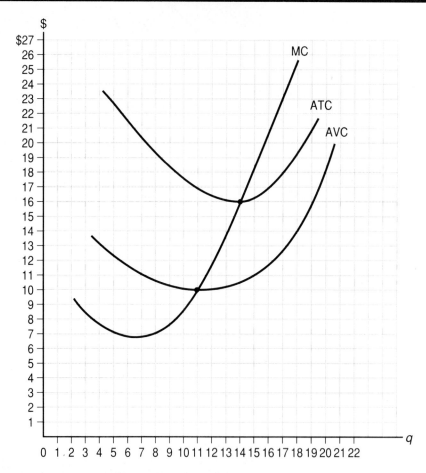

a. Draw the demand curve if the price equals $8. How much output should be produced to maximize profit. _____Explain. _____
b. Draw the demand curve if the price equals $10. How much output should be produced? _____.
c. Draw the demand curve if the price equals $16. How much output should be produced? _____ _____. What is the firm's profit? _____.
d. Draw the demand curve if the price equals $23. How much output should be produced? _____. Draw rectangles that correspond to the amount of total revenue, total cost, and profit.

Answers

TRUE OR FALSE

1. False. Because the firm is a price taker, it faces a horizontal demand curve.
2. False. Firms in some oligopolistic markets produce a homogeneous product yet have some control over price.
3. False. In long-run equilibrium, competitive firms must earn a normal profit. Pure profit would cause other firms to enter the industry, which would eventually eliminate the pure profit.
4. True.
5. False. The firm may still be earning a profit (if $P >$ ATC), but it is not earning the maximum possible profit.
6. False. A firm will shut down if $P <$ AVC.
7. False. A competitive firm still produces provided that total revenue covers total variable cost.
8. True.
9. True. Perfect competition requires that there be a large number of buyers and sellers.
10. True. Losses indicate that the resources can earn more in another use.

MULTIPLE CHOICE

1. A. The lawn care business is closest to perfect competition because the product is homogeneous, entry and exit are easy (buying a lawn mower is relatively cheap), and there are many producers.
2. D. The demand curve is horizontal. A horizontal demand curve has a price of elasticity of infinity.
3. C. The smallest output is the output corresponding to the minimum of the AVC curve.
4. D. In long-run equilibrium, P (= MR) = LRAC = LRMC = SRAC = SRMC.
5. A. If the average variable cost of producing 98 units of output were greater than $15 the firm would shut down.
6. B. Assuming that it maximizes profit, the largest loss a perfectly competitive firm would sustain in the short run is equal to the firm's fixed cost, because the firm can always shut down and lose only its fixed cost.
7. A. In the long run the largest loss is $0, because the firm in the long run can always move its resources to another industry.
8. D. If $P >$ MC, the production and sale of an extra unit of output adds more to total revenue (P) than it adds to total cost (MC), so profit rises.
9. A. Allocative efficiency requires that $P =$ MC. If that condition does not hold, it is possible to rearrange resources to make people better off.
10. C. The industry long-run supply curve is downward sloping because input prices and the long-run cost curves shift downward as industry output increases.

PROBLEMS

1. a. One producer: **M**
   b. Homogeneous product: **PC, possibly O**
   c. Barriers to entry: **O, M**
   d. Differentiated product: **MC, possibly O**
   e. No control over price: **PC**
   f. Many producers: **PC, MC**
   g. Unique product: **M**
   h. Few producers: **O**
   i. Free entry: **PC, MC**

2. a. When price = $2, total revenue equals $2 × q. When 1 unit of output is sold, q = 1 and total revenue is $2 × 1 or $2. When 2 units are sold, total revenue is $2 × 2 or $4, and so on. The total revenue curve is a straight line drawn from the origin with a slope equal to $2. (See line TR$_A$ in the figure below.)

      The marginal revenue curve is a horizontal line at $2. (See line labeled MR$_A$ below). Because the firm's sales do not affect the market price (remember: this firm is one of many sellers), it can sell additional units without lowering the market price. The additional revenue earned from each additional unit sold equals the price (that is, MR = P).

   b. With price = $5, total revenue is a line drawn from the origin with a slope equal to $5. As sales rise from 1 to 2 to 3 and so on, total revenue rises from $5 to $10 to $15, etc. This is the line labeled TR$_B$. The marginal revenue curve is again a horizontal line at $5 because P = MR = $5. This is line MR$_B$ below.

FIGURE 25.4

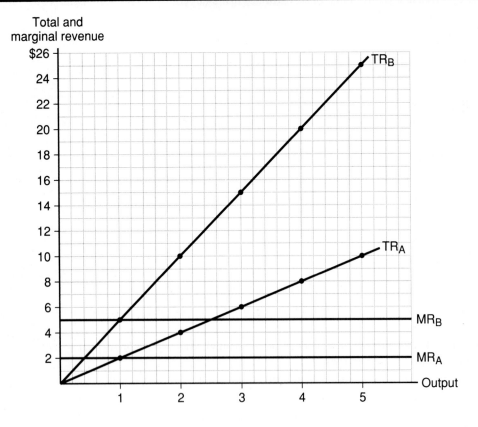

3. a. Total fixed cost equals total cost when output is zero. From the figure below, TFC = **$8**.
   b. When price equals $2, the firm faces the total revenue curve labeled Total Revenue$_1$. As can be seen in the figure below, at all output amounts except 3, total variable cost exceeds total revenue. At an output of 3 (see point A in the figure), total revenue equals total variable cost. That means 3 units of output is the only positive level of output the firm is willing to produce. Total revenue is **$6**, as can be read off the total revenue curve at point A. Total cost equals **$14** when output equals 3 (see point B in the figure). Profit equals $6 – $14 = **-$8**. If the firm produced no output its loss would equal its fixed cost of **-$8**. Therefore, the firm is equally well off producing **0 or 3 units of output**.
   c. If price equals $4 the firm faces the Total Revenue$_2$ curve in the figure below. Its best output is **5 units of output** because that is the only production level that results in no loss. At all other levels of output total cost exceeds total revenue. At 5 units of output, total revenue equals total cost equals **$20** (see point C in figure). Profit equals **$0**.

FIGURE 25.5

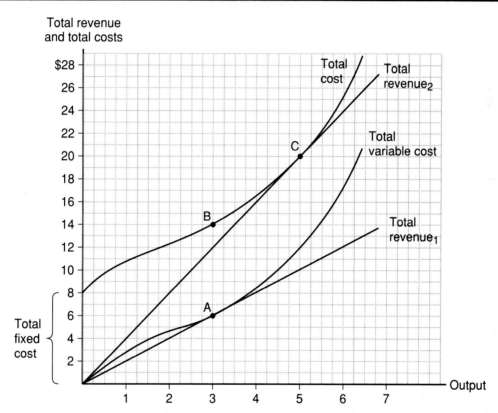

4. a. Total fixed cost equals **$80**. When output is 1 unit, total cost equals average total cost (ATC), which is $100, and total variable cost equals average variable cost, which equals $20. Because total fixed cost equals the difference between total cost and total variable cost, TFC = $100 – $20 = **$80**.
   b. If the price equals $3, the firm produces no output. The minimum value of AVC is $11. Because price is less than AVC for all levels of output, the firm shuts down.
   c. If the price equals $49, the firm produces 8 units of output because that is where MR (=P) = MC. The firm's total revenue equals $49 x 8 = $392. Total cost equals $31 x 8 = $248. Profit equals $392 – $248 = **$144**.

5. a. When the price is $8, the demand curve is the horizontal line drawn at $8 and labeled MR_1 in Figure 25.6. The firm produces **no output**. Because $P < AVC$, the firm's loss is less if it shuts down.

   b. When the price is $10, the demand curve is the horizontal line labeled MR_2. The firm produces **11** units of output because that is the output level at which $MR = MC$. Because $P = AVC$, the firm is willing to produce because it cannot reduce its loss by shutting down.

   c. When the price is $16, the demand curve is the horizontal line labeled MR_3. The firm produces **14** units of output. The firm's profit equals **$0** because $P = ATC$.

   d. When the price equals $23, the demand curve is the horizontal line labeled MR_4. The firm produces **17** units of output. The area of rectangle **ABC0** represents total revenue. The area of rectangle **EFC0** is the total cost. And the area of rectangle **ABFE** represents the firm's profit.

FIGURE 25.6

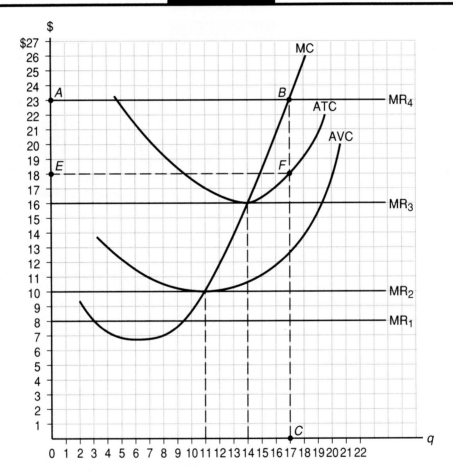

CHAPTER 26

Monopoly

The perfectly competitive market described in the previous chapter represents one extreme on the spectrum of market structures; monopoly represents the other extreme. Unlike the perfectly competitive firm that faces competition from numerous other firms that produce the same product, the monopolist operates alone in an industry. As the only seller of a product, the monopolist has the power to set product price and influence profit. This market power also leads the monopolist to do things that are not beneficial to society—which is an important reason why monopoly is rarely looked upon favorably by economists.

Other market structures—those between the extremes of perfect competition and monopoly—will be discussed in the chapter that follows.

CHAPTER OUTLINE

I. Meaning of Monopoly
   A. A **monopoly** is an industry with only one seller. The product that the monopoly sells has no good substitute.
   B. Because there is only one seller, there is no distinction between the firm and the market. Inasmuch as the monopoly firm is the only seller in the market, it faces the downward-sloping market demand curve.
   C. **Monopoly power** is the ability of a firm to influence the price of output. The ability to influence price depends on the degree to which there are good substitutes for the firm's product. The more good substitutes there are, the less is the firm's monopoly power.
   D. To maintain the firm's monopoly position there must be some restriction on other firms' entering the monopoly market. Some of the major barriers to entry are:
      1. Control of an Essential Raw Material: By limiting the access of others to a key ingredient in the production of some product, the monopolist can control production.
      2. Economies of Scale: If economies of scale occur over all output levels, one firm can produce the entire market output at a lower average cost than could more than one firm. In such a case, a monopoly will eventually evolve.
      3. Patents and Copyrights: A **patent** is a grant by the government that allows the developer of a new product the exclusive right to market a product for 17 years. A **copyright** is a right granted by the government to publish, copy, or sell a piece of music, art, or literature. Patents and copyrights are issued to encourage innovation and invention.
      4. Licensing and Other Government Restrictions: The government occasionally gives a producer the exclusive right to sell a service or product. Examples are the post office, television and radio licenses, and cable television franchises.

II. The Basic Monopoly Model
    A. Price and Marginal Revenue
        1. Because the monopolist faces a downward-sloping market demand curve, it must lower the price on all units it sells when it wishes to sell one more unit. As a result, marginal revenue (MR)—the increase in total revenue due to the sale of one more unit of output—is less than the price at which the extra unit is sold.
        2. The MR curve is below the demand curve.
    B. There is a relationship between the marginal revenue curve, the total revenue curve, and the elasticity of demand.
        1. When demand is elastic ($E_d > 1$), MR > 0 and total revenue (TR) rises as output is increased.
        2. When demand is inelastic ($E_d < 1$), MR < 0 and TR falls as output is increased.
        3. When demand has unitary elasticity ($E_d = 1$), MR = 0 and TR is constant.
    C. Profit Maximization—Short Run
        1. When the monopolist produces, it maximizes profit by choosing the output level for which MR = MC. The price that the monopolist charges is the price associated with that quantity of output on the demand curve.
        2. The monopolist does not charge the highest price anyone would pay. To do so would lower the firm's profit because it would reduce sales below the amount that maximizes profit.
        3. At the monopoly equilibrium, P > MC. Although MR = MC for the monopolist, P > MR and therefore P > MC.
        4. The monopolist always produces where MR is greater than zero because MC is always greater than zero. Thus, the monopolist's price and output choice are always in the elastic range of the demand curve.
        5. The monopolist does not necessarily earn a profit. If the demand curve is below the ATC curve at every level of output, there is no price that yields a profit.
        6. The monopoly shuts down under the same circumstances as a firm in a perfectly competitive market. If P < AVC for all possible levels of output, the firm does not produce.
    D. Profit Maximization—Long Run
        1. If the monopolist produces, it produces the output where MR = LRMC. The price for this level of output is given by the demand curve.
        2. If the demand curve is below the LRAC curve at all levels of output, there is no level of output where the monopolist can earn a profit. The monopolist will transfer its resources to more profitable industries.
        3. If the monopolist is earning pure profits in the long run, there must be barriers to entry in order for the monopolist to maintain its monopoly status. Otherwise, new firms would enter the industry.
        4. If the monopolist does not have a way to restrict entry, the monopolist may hold down its price and its profit in order to make entry into the industry less attractive or to forestall antitrust actions on the part of the government.

III. Price Discrimination
    A. **Price discrimination** is the practice of selling a good at different prices that are not the result of differences in costs.
    B. Price discrimination requires three conditions:
        1. The company must have some monopoly power, which means the firm must face a downward-sloping demand curve. Unless this occurs, it is impossible for the firm to set different prices.
        2. The company must be able to divide customers into at least two groups, each group having different price elasticities. If this condition did not hold, it would not be profitable to charge different prices. Price discrimination increases profit only if different groups of buyers have different price elasticities.
        3. The company must be able to prevent resale of its product. If the company could not prevent resale, customers in the lower-price market would buy the product and undersell the monopoly in the higher-price market.
    C. With price discrimination, profit maximization requires selecting the output level in each market for which MR = MC. This leads to a lower price in the market where demand is more elastic.

IV. An Evaluation of Monopoly
   A. The Evils of Monopoly
      1. The major criticism of monopoly is that it restricts output and raises price. Assuming that costs would be the same, an industry that switches from perfect competition to monopoly produces less output and charges a higher price.
      2. Inefficient Allocation of Resources: Because a monopolist produces an output where $P > MC$, there are units of the monopolist's product that would provide more benefit to consumers than they would cost to produce. Yet the monopolist does not produce them, for to do so would lower profit.
      3. Having a monopoly is valuable. Individuals devote resources to secure and protect a monopoly. These activities—called **rent seeking**—are wasteful from society's point of view, although they may be useful to the individual securing the monopoly.
      4. Monopolies are accused of being slow to introduce new technologies for fear of reducing their monopoly status.
      5. In general, monopolies lead to a less equal distribution of income.
   B. Potential Advantages of Monopoly
      1. If economies of scale occur throughout the entire range of production, one producer can produce the entire market output at a lower average cost than could many producers. This is called a **natural monopoly**. To take advantage of this technology, governments often allow a monopoly but regulate the price it may charge.
      2. The large profits of a monopoly position provide an incentive for people to invent. This is the rationale behind patents. Patents also reduce the expense an inventor would incur to hide the details of the invention and the expense rivals would incur attempting to discover them.

HINTS AND HELP

1. Price and Marginal Revenue   The relationship between price and marginal revenue for a monopoly is different than the relationship for a perfectly competitive firm because the monopolist faces a downward-sloping demand curve.

To understand the monopolist's situation, assume you are the marketing director for a monopoly. Your staff has developed the following information about the demand for your product:

QUANTITY	PRICE	TOTAL REVENUE
2	$40	$80
3	30	90
4	20	80

If you want to sell 2 units, the price must be $40. If you want to sell 3 units, the price must be $30. And so on.

If you want to expand sales from 2 units to 3 units, you must lower price from $40 to $30. The price at which the third unit is sold is $30. But the total revenue increases by only $10. The reason this happens is that the first two units, which otherwise would have sold for $40, must now be sold for $30. That is a loss of revenue of $20. When combined with the $30 gained from the third unit, the extra revenue coming from the sale of the third unit is $10.

It is even possible for the sale of more output to result in a decline in total revenue. This occurs in this example when sales expand from 3 to 4 units. The fourth unit is sold for $20 and the other three units are each sold for $10 less than they otherwise would have been. That decline in revenue of $30 combined with the $20 gained from the sale of the fourth unit results in a revenue loss of $10.

2. Drawing the Marginal Revenue Curve   Drawing the marginal revenue (MR) curve for any given straight-line demand curve is relatively simple. The following steps always work when the demand curve is a straight line.

Step 1: Extend the demand curve downward until it crosses the (horizontal) quantity axis. Mark the quantity value Q where the extended demand curve crosses the horizontal axis.

Step 2: Place a dot on the (horizontal) quantity axis at 1/2 Q.

Step 3: Extend the demand curve upward until it touches the (vertical) price axis. Mark the price where the extended demand curve crosses the vertical axis P.

Step 4: Draw a straight line starting at point P on the vertical axis through the point at 1/2 Q on the quantity axis. This is the MR curve for the demand curve.

FILL IN THE BLANK

higher

1. Compared to a perfectly competitive market, and assuming costs are the same, the price is _____ in a monopolistic market.

natural monopoly

2. An industry characterized by economies of scale over the entire range of output is a _____.

falling

3. If marginal revenue is negative, total revenue is _____.

one

4. When total revenue is at its maximum, the elasticity of demand equals _____.

substitutes

5. A monopolist is the only producer of a good without close _____.

rent seeking

6. Using resources in order to acquire or maintain a monopoly is called _____.

Monopoly power

7. _____ is the ability to influence the price of a product.

elastic

8. A monopolist always produces output in the _____ range of the demand curve.

barrier to entry

9. The control of the supply of uncut diamonds by the DeBeers Company is an example of a _____.

price discrimination

10. If price differences do not reflect cost differences, the monopoly is practicing _____.

TRUE OR FALSE

_____ 1. A monopoly can exist only in a market with economies of scale.

_____ 2. A monopolist can increase its profit if it is producing output where $P = MC$.

_____ 3. In long-run equilibrium, the monopolist produces output at the minimum of the long-run average cost curve.

_____ 4. A monopolist shuts down if $P < AVC$.

_____ 5. Marginal revenue equals 1 when the elasticity of demand equals 1.

_____ 6. A monopolist earning pure profit can exist in the long run only if there are barriers to entry.

_____ 7. In a monopoly market there is no difference between the market and the firm.

_____ 8. A patent establishes a monopoly.

_____ 9. Price discrimination has no impact on a monopolist's profit.

_____ 10. A monopoly may generate an increase in inventions and innovations.

MULTIPLE CHOICE

1. Which of the following is inconsistent with monopoly?
   A. economies of scale
   B. a large number of buyers
   C. a high value for cross price elasticity of demand for the good
   D. operating at a loss

2. If MR = MC = $25 and the firm does not shut down, the price a monopoly charges:
   A. is less than $25.
   B. is $25.
   C. is more than $25.
   D. cannot be determined with the available information.

3. Compared to a perfectly competitive industry and assuming costs stay the same, a monopoly produces:
   A. less output.
   B. the same output.
   C. more output.
   D. There is insufficient information to answer the question.

4. Which of the following is considered a problem associated with monopoly?
   A. Monopoly results in too few resources used in the industry.
   B. Monopoly makes the distribution of income less equal.
   C. Resources are wasted as individuals attempt to secure a monopoly.
   D. All the alternatives are correct.

5. Which of the following is true when a monopolist practices price discrimination compared to when it does not?
   A. All individuals pay more.
   B. No individual pays more.
   C. All individuals pay less.
   D. Some individuals pay less.

6. Which of the following is most likely to be a natural monopoly?
   A. a grocery store
   B. a physician
   C. a cable television franchise
   D. a movie theater

7. Price is greater than marginal revenue for a monopolist because the monopolist:
   A. always sells an amount of output corresponding to the inelastic part of the demand curve.
   B. does not have an incentive to minimize the costs of production.
   C. faces the market demand curve.
   D. earns pure profit.

8. At the output where marginal revenue equals zero:
   A. total revenue is at a maximum.
   B. profit is at a maximum.
   C. output is at a maximum.
   D. total cost is at a minimum.

9. If barriers to entry are weak:
   A. a monopolist may choose not to maximize profit in the short run.
   B. the firm's monopoly position will be eliminated in the short run.
   C. the monopolist cannot earn pure economic profit in the short run.
   D. All the alternatives are correct.

10. Which of the following is an example of price discrimination?
    A. a lower fee for renting a compact car than for renting a luxury car
    B. a lower price for an airplane trip if the passenger stays over a Saturday night
    C. a lower price for a smaller hotel room
    D. All the alternatives are correct.

PROBLEMS

1. a. Fill in the blanks for the following.

Q	P	TR	MR
0			
1	$500	_____	_____
2	450	_____	_____
3	400	_____	_____
4	350	_____	_____
5	300	_____	_____
6	250	_____	_____
7	200	_____	_____
8	150	_____	_____

b. Plot the demand curve, marginal revenue curve, and the total revenue curve in Figure 26.1.

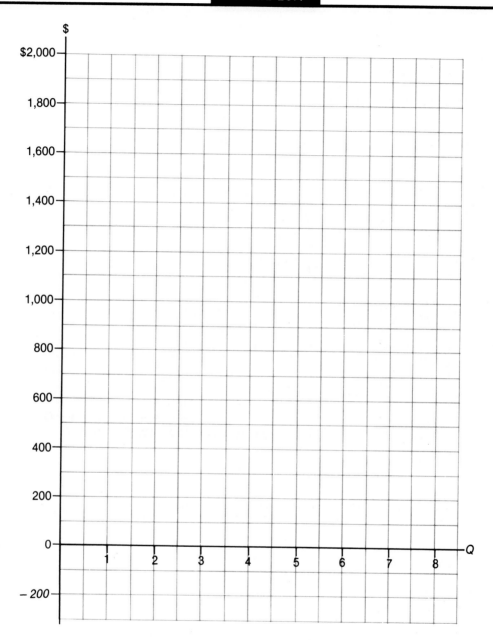

FIGURE 26.1

2. Use Figure 26.2 to answer the following questions.

FIGURE 26.2

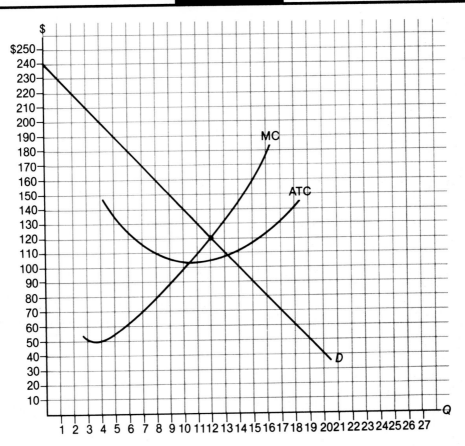

a. Draw the marginal revenue curve.
b. What is the profit-maximizing output? _____
c. What price does the monopolist charge? _____
d. Draw rectangles that correspond to total revenue, total cost, and profit of the firm.

3. In the Figure 26.3, draw the demand and marginal revenue curves so that the best the monopolist can do is earn a normal profit. Identify the monopolist's output and price.

FIGURE 26.3

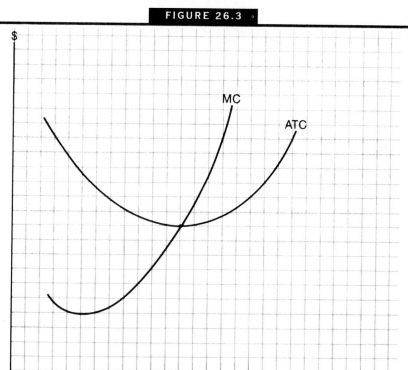

4. In the Figure 26.4, draw the demand and marginal revenue curves so that the monopolist shuts down.

FIGURE 26.4

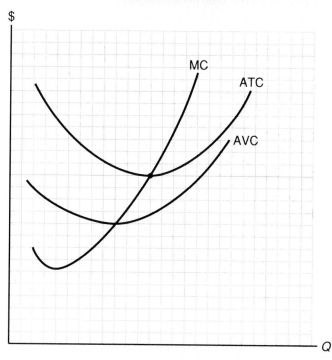

Answers

TRUE OR FALSE

1. False. Although economies of scale may lead to a monopoly, it is possible for a monopoly to develop in the absence of economies of scale.
2. True. Because $P > MR$ for a monopolist, if $P = MC$ then $MC > MR$. By reducing output, the monopolist can increase its profit.
3. False. Unlike the perfectly competitive firm, the monopolist need not produce the output for which long-run average cost is minimized.
4. True. If $P < AVC$ for all possible output, the monopolist would lose less by shutting down.
5. False. Marginal revenue equals zero when the elasticity of demand equals 1.
6. True. If there were no barriers to entry, new firms would enter the industry—attracted by the pure profit.
7. True. The monopoly firm supplies the entire market.
8. True. A patent gives its owner the exclusive right to some invention for 17 years.
9. False. Price discrimination is practiced because it increases the monopolist's profit.
10. True. By allowing the inventor and innovator a chance at having a monopoly, there may be greater incentive for such activities.

MULTIPLE CHOICE

1. C. A high cross price elasticity indicates that the good has close substitutes, which is inconsistent with a monopoly.
2. C. For a monopoly, price is greater than MR. Because MR = $25, the price at which the output is sold must be greater than $25.
3. A. Compared to a perfectly competitive firm, the monopoly produces less output. It is by restricting output that the monopolist is able to raise price and increase profit.
4. D.
5. D. Price discrimination results in some people paying more but some paying less than they would if the monopolist did not practice price discrimination.
6. C. A cable television franchise is most likely to be a natural monopoly because it is cheaper to provide cable television if there is only one set of wires connecting the homes for service.
7. C. The market demand curve is downward sloping, which means that the monopolist must lower the price in order to sell more units of output. Price is greater than marginal revenue for that reason.
8. A. Total revenue is at a maximum where marginal revenue equals zero.
9. A. To forestall the entry of new firms, a monopolist may hold down its price and profit and increase the amount of output that it produces in the short run.
10. B. Because it costs no more to fly on the airplane whether the individual stays over a Saturday night or not, the price difference does not reflect cost differences.

PROBLEMS

1. a.

Q	P	TR	MR
0			
1	$500	$ 500	$500
2	450	900	400
3	400	1,200	300
4	350	1,400	200
5	300	1,500	100
6	250	1,500	0
7	200	1,400	−100
8	150	1,200	−200

b. See Figure 26.5.

FIGURE 26.5

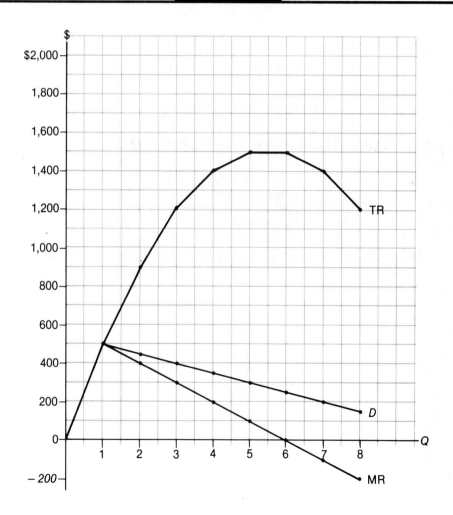

2. a. See Figure 26.6.

FIGURE 26.6

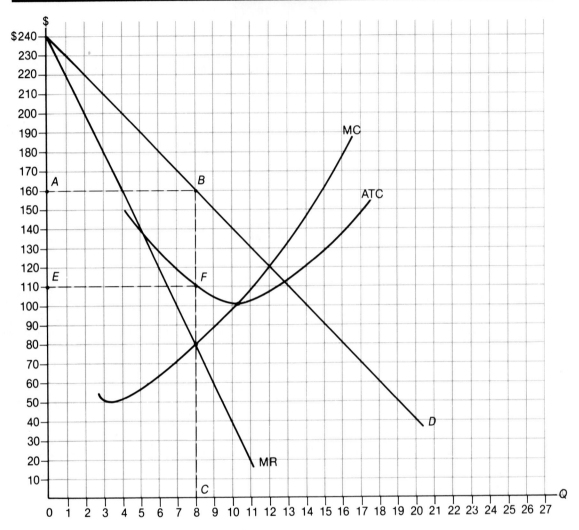

b. The profit-maximizing output is **8 units**.
c. The monopoly price is **$160**.
d. Total revenue is area **ABC0**. Total cost is area **EFC0**. Profit is area **ABFE**.

3. See Figure 26.7.

FIGURE 26.7

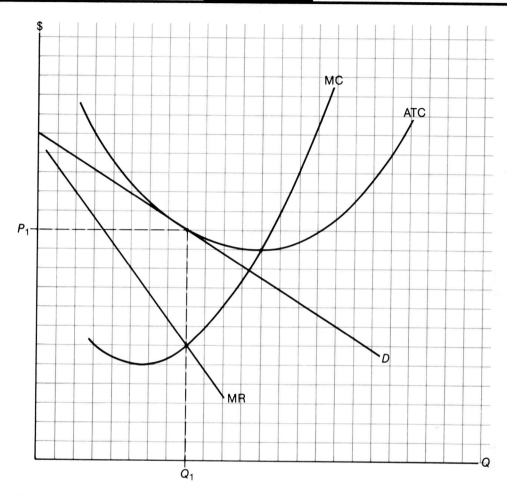

The trick here is first to draw the demand curve so that it just touches but does not intersect the ATC curve. (If the demand curve were above the ATC curve at any point, there would be some level of output that would earn the monopolist a pure profit.)

Once that is done, the MR curve must be drawn so that it crosses the MC curve directly below the point where the demand curve touches the ATC curve. Because the output where the demand curve crosses the ATC curve is the best output the firm can produce, that must be the output where MR = MC.

4.   See Figure 26.8.

FIGURE 26.8

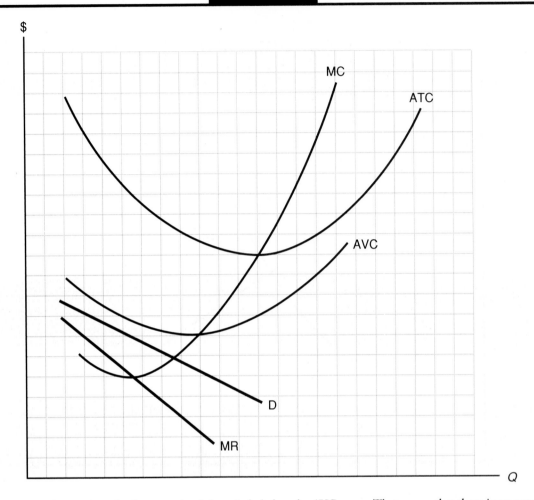

The demand curve must be drawn so that it is entirely below the AVC curve. That means that there is no output where total revenue is large enough to cover all the variable costs. In such a case the monopolist shuts down.

CHAPTER 27

Monopolistic Competition and Oligopoly

Perfect competition and monopoly represent the extremes of market structure. Some economists argue that few markets have either the large number of producers selling a homogeneous product that characterizes perfect competition or a single firm producing a unique product that defines monopoly.

The theory of monopolistic competition and the various oligopoly theories were developed to describe markets that are neither perfectly competitive nor monopolistic. These models explain why a firm has an incentive to differentiate its product from the products of other firms and why firms might work together when setting price. The two chapters that follow describe how the government limits the cooperation between firms when that cooperation is destructive to competition.

CHAPTER OUTLINE

I. Monopolistic Competition
   A. **Monopolistic competition** is a market structure that is a mixture of perfect competition and monopoly. The theory of monopolistic competition was developed by Joan Robinson and Edward Chamberlin.
   B. Characteristics:
      1. Product Differentiation
         a. **Product differentiation** occurs when each firm produces a product that is different from rival products. The differences can be real or imaginary.
         b. A differentiated product gives the producer some monopoly power, so firms have an incentive to create differences.
         c. The demand curve faced by the monopolistically competitive firm is downward sloping. If price increases, the firm does not lose all its customers. But there are many rivals selling similar products, so the demand curve is highly elastic.
      2. Number of Sellers: There are so many producers that each producer acts independently. Each firm ignores the behavior of its rivals.
      3. Free Entry and Exit: There are no significant barriers to entry, so new firms can easily enter the industry in the long run.
   C. Equilibrium in the Short Run
      1. The monopolistically competitive firm behaves like a monopoly. It finds the output where MR = MC and charges the price associated with that output on the demand curve.
      2. If price exceeds average total cost, the firm earns a profit. If price is less than the average total cost, the firm continues to operate as long as the firm can pay all its variable costs (that is, if $P \geq$ AVC). If $P <$ AVC, the firm shuts down.

D. Equilibrium in the Long Run
   1. In the long run, the monopolistically competitive firm earns only a normal profit.
      a. If the firm is incurring a loss, it leaves the industry. This means that the remaining firms have more customers to share. Graphically, the demand curve of each remaining firm shifts to the right until it is tangent to the long-run average cost curve.
      b. If the firm is earning a profit, new firms enter the industry. This means that each firm in the industry must share the existing customers with more firms. Graphically, the demand curve shifts to the left until it is tangent to the firm's long-run average cost curve.
   2. In the long run, MR = MC (the firm is maximizing profit) and P = LRAC (the firm is earning a normal profit).
E. Evaluating Monopolistic Competition
   1. Resource Allocation: Resources are not allocated efficiently because P > MC at the equilibrium. Society would benefit if more output were produced.
   2. Excess Capacity
      a. Production does not occur at the minimum of the long-run average cost curve. Each monopolistically competitive firm produces on the downward-sloping part of the long-run average cost curve. Firms do not take advantage of all the economies of scale. Fewer firms, each producing more, would produce the total market output at a lower average cost.
      b. However, more firms mean consumers have a wider range of options and can travel less to reach a seller.
   3. Nonprice Competition: A monopolistically competitive firm has the incentive to make its products distinctive. Doing so can shift its demand curve outward and increase its short-run profit. **Nonprice competition** includes any attempt to make a product more attractive to consumers, other than by lowering the price.
   4. Advertising is one form of nonprice competition.
      a. Advertising, Demand, and Cost
         i. Advertising is intended to shift the demand curve outward and increase the firm's sales, allowing it to take greater advantage of economies of scale.
         ii. Advertising also shifts the average total cost curve upward. The firm's short-run average cost can decline if the cost savings because of greater economies of scale offset the extra expense of the advertising.
      b. Benefits and Costs of Advertising
         i. Advertising is accused of being wasteful because it creates artificial product differences.
         ii. Advertising is defended as a means for the producer to provide information to customers about its product. In situations where advertising about prices has been restricted, the evidence is that prices are higher.

II. Oligopoly
A. **Oligopoly** is a market structure in which a few firms dominate the market because barriers to entry make it difficult for new producers to enter.
B. Characteristics:
   1. **Mutual Interdependence**: Because there are few firms, each firm is aware of its rivals and considers the expected behavior of its rivals when making decisions.
   2. Type of Product: Oligopolistic markets can produce homogeneous products (for example, steel) or differentiated products (for example, automobiles).
   3. Nonprice competition is more often used than price competition. It is easier for rivals to match price changes than it is to match product changes.

III. Oligopoly Models
A. Each oligopoly model is different because it makes different assumptions about the way an oligopolistic firm responds to its rivals.

B. **Kinked Demand Curve Model**
   1. The purpose of the model is to explain why oligopoly prices are more stable than prices in other markets.
   2. Assumptions:
      a. Each firm produces a differentiated product.
      b. The firm begins selling a particular quantity at a particular price.
      c. Response of rivals to price changes:
         i. The oligopoly firm assumes that its rivals will not follow a price increase. This makes the demand curve above the current price very elastic because the firm loses customers to its rivals if it raises price.
         ii. The firm assumes that its rivals will follow a price decrease. This makes the demand curve below the current price inelastic because the firm will be unable to attract buyers from other firms if it lowers price.
   3. Demand and Marginal Revenue
      a. The assumptions result in a demand curve with a kink at the current price and output combination.
      b. Because of the kink in the demand curve, the marginal revenue curve has a vertical gap at the current level of output.
   4. Equilibrium
      a. The oligopoly firm maximizes profit by producing all output for which $MR \geq MC$.
      b. Rising or falling costs have no impact on the equilibrium price or the amount of goods produced as long as the marginal cost curve stays in the gap of the marginal revenue curve.
      c. Because there are some cost changes that have no impact on the oligopolist's price, oligopoly prices are relatively stable.
   5. Evaluation
      a. The model is criticized because it does not explain how the original price and output are determined.
      b. There is little evidence that prices are more stable for oligopoly than for monopoly.
C. Game theory describes a situation where the price decision of one firm depends on the assumed response of the rival. Usually the payoff to each firm is higher if the firms cooperate than if they do not.
D. Collusion
   1. Collusion occurs when firms in a market coordinate their activities. The purpose of collusion is to increase the firms' profits. Collusion takes various forms:
      a. A **cartel** is an organization of producers designed to determine each firm's price and output collectively. Cartels are illegal in the United States, though legal in other countries.
      b. A **gentlemen's agreement** is an informal understanding among firms in an industry to pursue practices that are in the best interests of the group. It is less structured than a cartel.
   2. The survival of a collusive agreement depends on several factors:
      a. The Number of Firms: The more firms in the industry, the more likely it is that a firm will break the agreement. By operating outside the cartel, the firm can undersell its rivals and increase profits.
      b. Product Heterogeneity: The more heterogeneous the product that is sold in the market the more difficult it is to structure an agreement.
      c. Legal Barriers: Laws against collusion make collusion more difficult.
      d. Other Problems:
         i. If collusion succeeds in raising profits, new firms are attracted to the industry. The new firms either force the existing firms to share output or they operate outside the agreement.
         ii. Consumers more easily find substitutes for the industry's output the longer the collusive agreement lasts.
   3. Some industries are able to skirt the antitrust laws through price leadership. **Price leadership** is the practice of allowing one firm to initiate price changes with all other firms following the lead. The leader can be:
      a. The largest firm.

b. The low-cost producer.

c. The barometric firm—typically the firm that first recognizes changes in demand or costs.

IV. An Evaluation of Oligopoly

A. Most arguments in favor of or against monopoly can be made about oligopoly:

1. Advantage: economies of scale.

2. Disadvantage: $P > MC$, thus too little output is produced; output is not at the minimum long-run average cost.

B. **Schumpeter–Galbraith Hypothesis:**

1. This hypothesis argues that oligopolies facilitate the development and introduction of new technologies. Research is expensive, and only large firms can afford to spend the amounts of money needed when the outcome is uncertain.

2. Critics of this view argue that large firms are not flexible or creative enough for the development of new products.

HINTS AND HELP

1. Demand and Marginal Revenue in Monopolistic Competition Because a monopolistically competitive firm has monopoly power, the graphs for monopolistic competition are similar to those for monopoly. The demand curve is downward sloping, the marginal revenue curve is below the demand curve, production occurs where marginal revenue equals marginal cost, and so on.

The only difference is in the long run. Although it is possible for a monopoly to earn profit in the long run if it can maintain barriers to entry, a firm in a monopolistically competitive firm cannot earn economic profit. Entry into a monopolistically competitive market is easy. The entry of new firms shifts each firm's demand curve to the left because the firms must share the market with more and more producers. Equilibrium occurs when marginal revenue equals marginal cost and profit equals zero.

Drawing the curves of this situation requires that the demand curve be tangent to the long-run average cost curve at the same output level where the marginal revenue curve crosses the marginal cost curve. That is, the point of tangency must be directly above the point where the marginal revenue and marginal cost curves intersect. Notice that because the demand curve is downward sloping, it is tangent to the long-run average cost curve on its downward slope. Because output is not at the minimum of the long-run average cost curve, there is excess capacity.

2. Kinked Demand Curve In the kinked demand curve model, the firm faces two demand curves: one steep, one flat. Where they intersect is the current price and output. The construction of the marginal revenue curve is fairly easy. Follow the marginal revenue curve of the flatter demand curve until you get to the output level where the two demand curves intersect. Then take a vertical leap downward to the marginal revenue curve of the steeper demand curve and follow it.

FILL IN THE BLANK

oligopolistic	1. A(n) _____ market is made up of a few firms.
price leader	2. The firm that initiates price changes is called the _____.
match	3. The kinked demand curve model assumes that rivals _____ price decreases.
cartel	4. Firms jointly determine price and output when they are part of a _____.
left	5. The entry of new firms shifts the demand curve faced by a firm in monopolistic competition to the _____.

excess capacity	6. Because long-run equilibrium in monopolistic competition occurs on the downward-sloping part of the long-run average cost curve, the firm has _____.
mutual interdependence	7. When firms make decisions based on the expected behavior of their rivals, there is _____.
oligopoly	8. Game theory is an example of a(n) _____ model.
gap	9. When the demand curve has a kink in it, the marginal revenue curve has a(n) _____.
nonprice	10. Advertising is an example of _____ competition.

TRUE OR FALSE

_____ 1. A monopolistically competitive market is made up of a few firms.

_____ 2. It is difficult to be exact about outcomes in oligopolistic markets.

_____ 3. A firm in monopolistic competition cannot earn a profit in the long run.

_____ 4. Firms in monopolistic competition ignore the behavior of their rivals.

_____ 5. Firms in markets that are monopolistically competitive or oligopolistic have monopoly power.

_____ 6. A monopolistically competitive firm produces the output where $P = MC$.

_____ 7. All firms in oligopolistic markets collude.

_____ 8. The price leader is always the largest firm.

_____ 9. The success of Apple Computer Company supports the Schumpeter–Galbraith Hypothesis.

_____ 10. Oligopolies always earn pure economic profit.

MULTIPLE CHOICE

1. Which of the following is true in a monopolistically competitive market in long-run equilibrium?
   A. $MR = MC$ and $P = LRAC$
   B. $P = MR$ and $P = MC$
   C. $P = MC$ and $P = LRAC$
   D. $MR = MC$ and $P = MR$

2. The major difference between monopoly and monopolistic competition is:
   A. $P > MR$ for a monopolist, whereas $P = MR$ for a monopolistically competitive firm.
   B. A monopolist can earn pure profit in the long run, whereas a monopolistically competitive firm cannot.
   C. A monopolist produces the same output in both the short run and in the long run, whereas a monopolistically competitive firm produces less in the short run than in the long run.
   D. A monopolist has monopoly power, whereas a monopolistically competitive firm does not.

3. A monopolist and a monopolistically competitive firm are similar in which of the following ways?
   A. Both maximize profit by producing where $MR = MC$.
   B. Both use advertising to differentiate their product.
   C. Both produce at the minimum of the long-run average cost curve.
   D. Both earn zero profits in the long run.

4. One of the major differences between an oligopoly and a monopolistically competitive firm is:
   A. an oligopolistic firm cannot have a loss; a monopolistically competitive firm can.
   B. an oligopolistic firm produces an output where $P = MC$; a monopolistically competitive firm produces where $MR = MC$.
   C. an oligopolistic firm is aware of the behavior of its rivals; a monopolistically competitive firm ignores its rivals.
   D. an oligopolistic firm never shuts down; a monopolistically competitive firm may shut down.

5. The kinked demand curve model explains why:
   A. oligopolistic firms are large.
   B. collusion is difficult in oligopolistic markets.
   C. oligopoly prices are stable.
   D. consumers prefer to buy from producers in oligopolistic markets.

6. Price leadership is an example of:
   A. a cartel.
   B. monopolistic competition.
   C. pure profits.
   D. oligopolistic behavior.

7. Which of the following is *not* a characteristic of an oligopolistic market?
   A. few firms
   B. easy entry
   C. monopoly power
   D. mutual interdependence

8. An advantage of monopolistic competition over perfect competition is:
   A. prices are lower.
   B. consumers have more alternatives available.
   C. profits are lower in the long run.
   D. average cost of production is lower.

9. The evidence cited about advertising (in the textbook) supports which of the following statements?
   A. Where firms are not allowed to advertise their prices, prices are higher.
   B. Advertising has no impact on the demand for products and thus it is irrational to advertise.
   C. Advertising lowers the total cost of production.
   D. Advertising always increases profit.

10. Which of the following makes collusion more difficult?
    A. many producers
    B. laws against collusion
    C. differentiated products
    D. All the alternatives are correct.

PROBLEMS

1. Use Figure 27.1 to answer the following questions.
    a.   What output does the firm produce? _____
    b.   What is the price? _____
    c.   Diagrammatically identify the firm's total revenue, total cost, and profit (or loss).

FIGURE 27.1

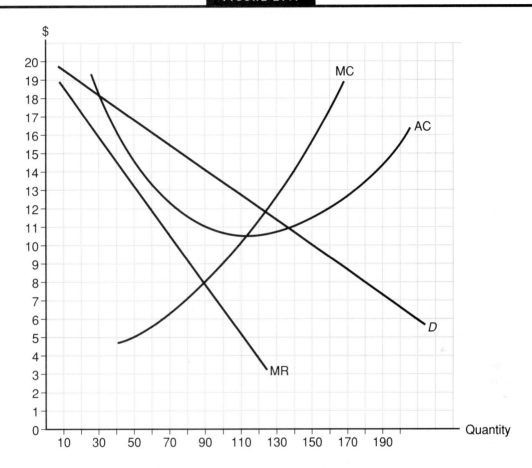

2. a. The current equilibrium is at point A. Identify the demand curve faced by a firm in the kinked demand curve model by darkening the appropriate part of the demand curves in Figure 27.2.

FIGURE 27.2

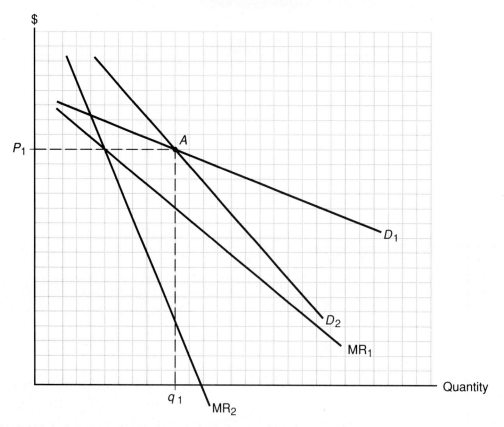

b. Identify the marginal revenue curve by darkening the appropriate lines.
c. Draw two marginal cost curves that result in the same price and output.

3. In Figure 27.3, draw the demand and marginal revenue curves of a monopolistically competitive firm in long-run equilibrium.

FIGURE 27.3

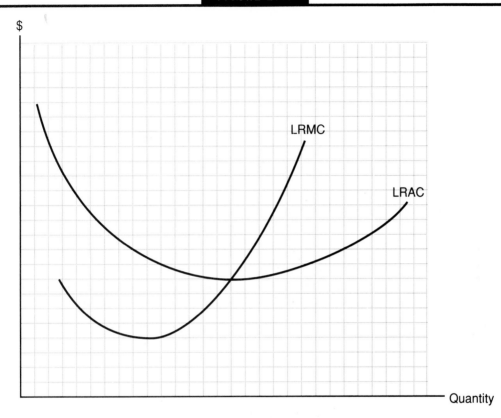

Answers

TRUE OR FALSE

1. False. A monopolistically competitive market contains many firms because entry is easy.

2. True. Because the outcome depends on how rivals respond to a firm's actions, it is difficult to be certain about outcomes in oligopolistic markets.

3. True. Profits are zero in the long run because new firms enter if there are pure profits.

4. True. Because there are many firms in the market, each firm ignores its rivals.

5. True. Firms in both kinds of markets face downward-sloping demand curves, which means they have some control over price.

6. False. A monopolistically competitive firm faces a downward-sloping demand curve. As a result, $P > MR$. To maximize profit, marginal revenue must equal marginal cost, so $P > MC$.

7. False. Although collusion in oligopolistic markets is possible, it is not automatic.

8. False. The price leader is not always the largest firm. It also may be the barometric firm or the low-cost producer.

9. False. Apple Computer Company was started in a garage and successfully evolved on its own, which is inconsistent with the Schumpeter-Galbraith Hypothesis that large firms are the source of innovations.

10. False. Just as with monopoly, there is nothing that ensures an oligopoly firm pure profit.

MULTIPLE CHOICE

1. A. In long-run equilibrium, the monopolistically competitive firm maximizes profit (MR = MC), yet profit is zero (P = LRAC).

2. B. Although a monopolist can have barriers to entry that limit the ability of rivals to enter the market in the long run, there is free entry in a monopolistically competitive market that results in zero economic profit in the long run.

3. A. Maximum profit occurs where MR = MC for all firms. The monopolist does not advertise to differentiate its product, because its product is unique.

4. C. Because there are few firms in the industry, an oligopolistic firm is aware of rivals' actions; a monopolistically competitive firm does not keep track of its many rivals.

5. C. The major conclusion of the kinked demand curve model is that it is possible for the firm's marginal cost curve to shift without influencing the price of the product.

6. D. Price leadership is a form of oligopolistic behavior.

7. B. Entry into an oligopolistic market is difficult, which explains why there are few producers.

8. B. Monopolistically competitive firms offer differentiated products, which means a wider range of alternatives is available than in a perfectly competitive market producing a homogeneous product.

9. A. The textbook cites evidence that prices of eyeglasses were higher in markets where advertising was prohibited.

10. D.

PROBLEMS

1. a. The firm produces **90** units of output.
    b. The price is **$14**.
    c. In Figure 27.4, total revenue is area **ABC0**, total cost is area **EFC0**, and profit is area **ABFE**.

FIGURE 27.4

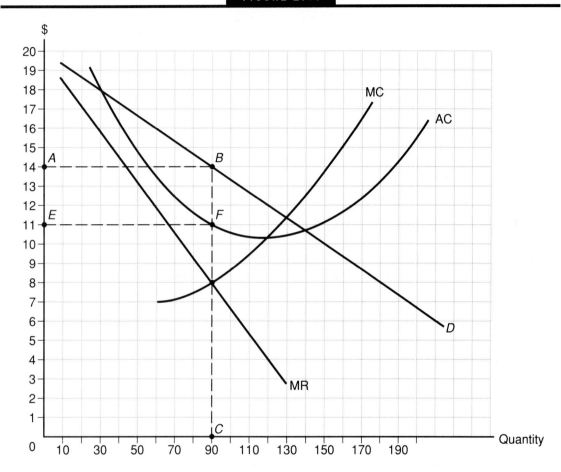

2. a. Because the firm assumes that its rivals will not follow a price increase, the firm believes it will lose customers to its rivals if it increases its price. That means the more elastic (flatter) D_1 demand curve is the relevant one at any price above the current price of P_1.

   On the other hand, the firm believes the other firms will lower price if it does. Thus it will not be able to gain customers from other producers at a lower price. In this case the less elastic (steeper) D_2 demand curve is the relevant one.

   b. The marginal revenue curve is constructed by using D_1's marginal revenue curve, MR_1, up to q_1 and then jumping down to D_2's marginal revenue curve, MR_2, for output beyond q_1.

   c. The marginal cost curves MC_1 and MC_2 both lie inside the gap of the MR curve. For each the price of P_1 and the output q_1 yield the largest possible profit.

FIGURE 27.5

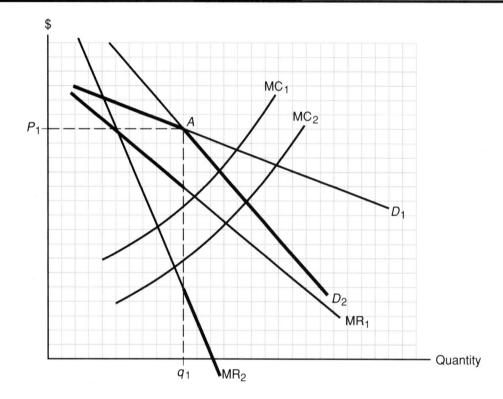

3. The demand curve must be drawn so that it is tangent to the LRAC curve. At this level of output, price equals long-run average cost, which means the firm is earning normal profit.

    The marginal revenue curve must be drawn so that it crosses the MC curve directly below the point where the demand and LRAC curves are tangent. That means that MR = MC at q_1 and that q_1 is the profit-maximizing level of output.

FIGURE 27.6

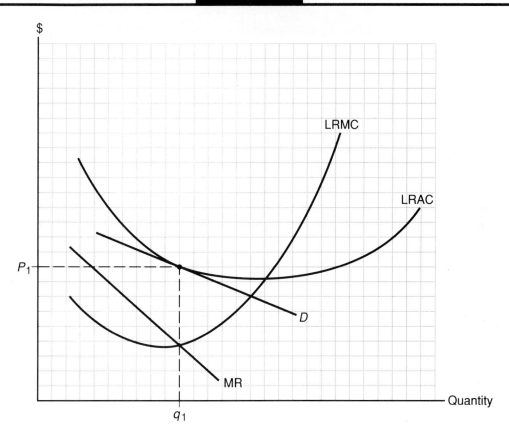

CHAPTER 28

Industrial Organization
and Antitrust Policy

Chapters 25–27 presented the major theories of market structure—perfect competition, monopoly, monopolistic competition, and oligopoly. As discussed in those chapters, in general perfect competition is the market structure that has the most desirable outcomes. But there is nothing natural or inherent about perfect competition. It is often necessary for the government to establish and protect competition.

This chapter begins by describing how competition (or its absence) is quantified. It then looks at major laws and court cases that make up government policy on market structure. The next chapter describes another dimension of government policy—regulation.

CHAPTER OUTLINE

I. Assessing the Extent of Competition
    A. Measures of Monopoly Power
        1. Market Concentration Ratio
            a. The **market concentration ratio** measures the percent of industry sales attributable to the four largest firms in the industry.
            b. It ranges in value from 0 (no concentration) to 100 (highest concentration).
            c. Problems with the Concentration Ratio
                i. It is difficult to define exactly which firms or products make up the appropriate market.
                ii. The measure ignores imports and thus overstates the concentration in markets where foreign producers account for a large part of sales.
                iii. The concentration ratio ignores the impact of potential competition on the behavior of firms. In **contestable markets**, where new firms can easily enter, the threat of competition can make a few firms behave as though they had many rivals. Yet the ratio would indicate high concentration.
                iv. Because the ratio is calculated using national sales, the index understates concentration in local or regional markets. Each of many sellers can have a near monopoly if the market is local (for example, newspapers), yet the concentration ratio has a small value.
                v. The ratio ignores how sales are divided among the four largest sellers.
        2. Herfindahl Index (HI)
            a. The **Herfindahl Index** is calculated by adding the squares of each firm's market share.
            b. The index ranges in value from 0 (little concentration) to 10,000 (a monopoly).

  c. The same criticisms made of the concentration ratio apply here except that this index does account for the distribution of sales among the four largest firms.

  d. The Justice Department has used the Herfindahl Index as a guide for approving or rejecting mergers.

 B. Concentration in the U.S. Economy

  1. Concentration in Manufacturing

   a. As measured by the value added of the 50 or 100 largest manufacturing companies, aggregate concentration has increased since 1947. This is misleading, however, in the sense that many of the largest companies are conglomerates that sell output in unrelated product markets. Hence a higher aggregate concentration ratio does not imply greater concentration in individual product markets.

   b. Concentration ratios for individual manufacturing industries do not reveal a long-run trend toward increased concentration. In fact, the average concentration ratio is lower today than at the turn of the century.

  2. Data for the aggregate economy do not reveal any increase in concentration.

II. Antitrust Policy

 A. **Antitrust policy** concerns laws and government procedures designed to shape the structure of markets and influence the behavior of firms.

 B. Major Antitrust Legislation

  1. The Sherman Act (1890)

   a. This act outlaws contracts, trusts, or conspiracies "in restraint of trade." A **trust** is a combination of companies acting together with specific intent to increase control of an industry.

   b. Another method used to eliminate competition is predatory pricing. **Predatory pricing** involves temporarily reducing price in order to drive weaker firms from a industry with the intent of raising the price once the competition has been eliminated.

   c. The Sherman Act was not a success because of the difficulty of interpreting key terms.

  2. The Clayton Act (1914) outlaws certain specific business practices. The practices outlawed are:

   a. Some forms of price discrimination.

   b. **Tying contracts**, where the sale of one product is dependent on the sale of a second good.

   c. Buying the stock of another company if the result is to reduce competition.

   d. **Interlocking directorates**, where the same individual serves on the boards of directors of two companies that compete in the same market.

  3. The Federal Trade Commission (FTC) Act (1914)

   a. This act prohibits "unfair methods of competition in commerce."

   b. It also creates the Federal Trade Commission to enforce the Clayton and FTC Acts.

    i. The commission is empowered to initiate lawsuits and issue "cease-and-desist orders" that instruct firms to halt practices the commission deems to be in violation of antitrust laws.

    ii. Beginning in 1938, with the passage of the Wheeler–Lea Act, the commission has the authority to halt false or deceptive business practices.

  4. The Robinson–Patman Act (1936)

   a. This act amends the Clayton Act, outlawing prices not justified on the basis of costs—if at least one seller is hurt. The act attempts to outlaw volume discounts available only to large stores.

   b. Economists are critical of the act because it protects less efficient producers and raises prices.

  5. The Celler–Kefauver Act (1950): This act strengthens restrictions against mergers by restricting purchases of a competitor's assets.

 C. Key Antitrust Rulings

  1. The Supreme Court has ruled on price fixing—agreements among companies on what prices will be. In the Addyston Pipe Case (1899) and Socony–Vacuum Case (1940), the court ruled that price fixing "per se" was illegal. In other words, there is never a justification for competitors' fixing prices.

2. Standards for Monopoly
   a. In the Standard Oil Case (1911), the Supreme Court ruled that Standard Oil was in violation of the Sherman Act. It found that monopoly per se is *not* illegal; it is illegal only if achieved through unreasonable business practices. This is known as the **rule of reason**.
   b. In the U.S. Steel Case (1920), the court ruled that the steel manufacturer was not in violation of the Sherman Act because it had not achieved dominance through unreasonable business practices.
   c. In the Alcoa Case (1945), the court overturned the rule of reason. The court said that any monopoly, regardless of how it is achieved, is illegal.
   d. The Berkey Photo versus Eastman Kodak Case (1979) returned the court to the rule of reason. It found that Eastman Kodak was not in violation of the Sherman Act simply because it was large. To be in violation, the court ruled, requires that a firm engage in improper behavior.
3. Mergers
   a. There are three types of mergers:
      i. A **horizontal merger** is a merger of companies in the same market.
      ii. A **vertical merger** is a merger of two companies, one of which produces an input for the product produced by the second firm.
      iii. A **conglomerate merger** is a merger between companies in unrelated markets.
   b. Laws have been enacted that restrict horizontal and vertical mergers. Conglomerate mergers have not been restricted.
   c. In the Du Pont Case (1957), the Supreme Court ruled that Du Pont's ownership of General Motors stock constituted an illegal vertical merger.
   d. In the Bethlehem Steel Case (1958), the court ruled that the proposed merger between Bethlehem Steel and Youngstown Steel was an illegal horizontal merger.
   e. In the Von's Grocery Case (1966), two groceries in the Los Angeles area were not allowed to merge because, although they were a small part of the market, the merger would contribute to reduced competition.
D. Enforcement
   1. Enforcement of antitrust laws is in the hands of two government agencies:
      a. The Federal Trade Commission.
      b. The Antitrust Division of the Justice Department.
   2. The two agencies have at times enforced the laws with different degrees of vigor.
      a. During the Reagan Administration the FTC dropped a case in which the cereal industry was accused of having a shared monopoly. A **shared monopoly** is a market where firms act to increase their joint profit even though there are no acts of price fixing or attempts to limit competition.
      b. The Reagan Administration emphasized the **superiority hypothesis** in its enforcement of antitrust laws. This hypothesis argues that companies with large market shares gained their dominance through superior efficiency rather than by taking advantage of monopoly power.
      c. The Bush Administration increased antitrust enforcement except in cases where the market is international in scope, as in banking.

FILL IN THE BLANK

tying contract

1. A _____ requires a firm to buy one product in order to buy a second.

Standard Oil

2. In the _____ case, the Supreme Court established the "rule of reason" for evaluating whether a monopoly exists.

Alcoa

3. In the _____ case, the Supreme Court reversed the "rule of reason" and ruled that monopoly per se is illegal.

Predatory pricing	4.	_____ involves a firm lowering its price with the intent of driving competitors from the market.
horizontal	5.	If two yo-yo makers merge, it would be a _____ merger.
vertical	6.	If a yo-yo manufacturer buys a string company, it would be a _____ merger.
conglomerate	7.	If a yo-yo manufacturer buys an apple orchard, it would be a _____ merger.
100	8.	The largest possible value of the concentration ratio is _____.
superiority hypothesis	9.	Large market shares are indicative of greater efficiency and lower costs according to the _____ .
shared monopoly	10.	The cereal industry was accused of being a _____ in a case that was eventually dropped.

TRUE OR FALSE

_____ 1. The concentration ratio is the same for a monopoly as it is when four large firms sell all the market output.

_____ 2. The Herfindahl Index ignores imports.

_____ 3. The theory of contestable markets says that potential rivals can limit the behavior of firms.

_____ 4. Evidence consistently shows that concentration in the U.S. economy has increased since the end of World War II.

_____ 5. Monopoly is always illegal.

_____ 6. A trust is similar to a cartel.

_____ 7. The Clayton Act outlaws specific business practices, such as tying contracts and interlocking directorates.

_____ 8. The Robinson–Patman Act has had the impact of lowering the prices of goods to consumers.

_____ 9. The Supreme Court has ruled that any attempt by competitors to fix prices is illegal.

_____ 10. Conglomerate mergers have been ruled to violate the Sherman Act.

MULTIPLE CHOICE

1. If there were 50 firms in a market, each firm selling 2 percent of the market output, the market concentration ratio would be:
   A. 4.
   B. 8.
   C. 50.
   D. 100.

2. If there were 50 firms in a market, each firm selling 2 percent of the market output, the Herfindahl Index would be:
   A. 8.
   B. 50.
   C. 100.
   D. 200.

3. The "rule of reason" is the idea that:
   A. a monopoly is illegal only if it is achieved using unreasonable business practices.
   B. a monopoly is illegal only if it earns an unreasonable profit.
   C. vertical mergers are reasonable but horizontal mergers are unreasonable.
   D. price discrimination is legal only if it is reasonable.

4. The Reagan Administration supported which of the following?
   A. the superiority hypothesis
   B. the shared monopoly theory
   C. the per se argument applied to monopolies
   D. the use of the concentration ratio as a test for acceptable mergers

5. Which of the following is a reason the concentration ratio may be misleading when applied to the automobile industry?
   A. Automobile prices are not constant over time.
   B. Automobile production is subject to significant economies of scale.
   C. Imports are a significant part of the automobile market.
   D. The automobile market is primarily a national market, not a highly localized one.

6. Which of the following is an advantage of the Herfindahl Index over the concentration ratio?
   A. The Herfindahl Index includes imports; the concentration ratio does not.
   B. The Herfindahl Index is measured on the basis of regional markets; the concentration ratio is based on national markets.
   C. The Herfindahl Index is calculated on the basis of profit; the concentration ratio is based on sales.
   D. The Herfindahl Index looks at all firms in the industry; the concentration ratio focuses on the four largest firms.

7. In which of the following cases would the government be least likely to oppose a merger?
   A. if the pre-merger Herfindahl Index was 2,500 and the post-merger index is 3,800
   B. if the pre-merger Herfindahl Index was 8,770 and the post-merger index is 9,200
   C. if the pre-merger Herfindahl Index was 9,990 and the post-merger index is 10,000
   D. if the pre-merger Herfindahl Index was 290 and the post-merger index is 400

8. Which of the following always reduces the degree of competition in a market?
   A. horizontal mergers
   B. conglomerate mergers
   C. manufacturing mergers
   D. vertical mergers

9. The major problem with the Sherman Act is it:
   A. is inexact in its definition of monopoly.
   B. is limited to manufacturing industries only.
   C. was declared unconstitutional by the Supreme Court.
   D. is primarily concerned with conglomerate mergers.

10. In which case did the Supreme Court rule that price fixing per se is illegal?
    A. Alcoa
    B. Addyston Pipe
    C. Du Pont
    D. Standard Oil

PROBLEMS

1. a. Calculate the concentration ratio and the Herfindahl Index for industries A, B, and C. The numbers are the percent of total market sales for each firm.

	INDUSTRY A	INDUSTRY B	INDUSTRY C
Firm 1	40%	60%	25%
Firm 2	30%	10%	25%
Firm 3	20%	10%	25%
Firm 4	5%	10%	25%
Firm 5	5%	10%	0%

   b. Rank the industries from most to least concentrated according to the concentration ratio. _____
   c. Rank the industries from most to least concentrated according to the Herfindahl Index. _____

Answers

TRUE OR FALSE

1. True. Because the concentration ratio focuses on the sales of the four largest firms, its value is the same whether one firm or four firms sell the entire market output.

2. True. Both the concentration ratio and the Herfindahl Index ignore imports, which critics say can result in an exaggerated measure of the extent of concentration when imports are significant.

3. True. When new firms can easily enter an industry, as they can in a contestable market, the threat of entry limits the exercise of monopoly power just as if the rivals actually existed.

4. False. Most evidence shows no increase in concentration.

5. False. According to current policy, the behavior of the monopolist must be considered before determining whether or not the monopoly is illegal.

6. True. Both a trust and a cartel attempt to coordinate the activities of the firms in a market in order to dominate the industry.

7. True. The Clayton Act outlaws specific business practices in order to overcome the imprecision of the earlier Sherman Act.

8. False. Because the Robinson–Patman Act makes it illegal to offer price concessions to some buyers unless they are made available to all buyers, it has had the impact of making price reductions more difficult.

9. True. Per se, price fixing is illegal.

10. False. Conglomerate mergers have never been found violative of the Sherman Act because they involve firms in unrelated industries.

MULTIPLE CHOICE

1. B. The market concentration ratio measures the percent of total market output sold by the four largest firms. The four largest firms would sell $4 \times 2\%$ or 8% of the market output, so the ratio would have a value of 8.

2. D. The Herfindahl Index is the sum of the squares of the market shares of each firm in the market. The Herfindahl Index would be $50 \times (2)^2 = 50 \times 4 = 200$.

3. A. The rule of reason says that monopoly is illegal only when achieved using unreasonable business practices.

4. A. The Reagan Administration prosecuted fewer antitrust cases because it believed that large market shares often reflect more efficient production, which is the claim of the superiority hypothesis.

5. C. The concentration ratio ignores imports.

6. D. The Herfindahl Index includes values for each firm; the concentration ratio totals the sale of the four largest firms.

7. D. A Herfindahl Index of 290 or 400 indicates an industry made up of many small firms. The proposed merger would have little impact on the degree of competition.

8. A. Because horizontal mergers reduce the number of firms in a market, the degree of competition is always reduced.

9. A. The Sherman Act had little impact on market structure because it is inexact in its terms.

10. B. In the Addyston Pipe Case the Supreme Court ruled that any price fixing is a violation of the Sherman Act.

PROBLEMS

1. a.

Industry A
Concentration ratio: $(40\%) + (30\%) + (20\%) + (5\%) = \mathbf{95}$
Herfindahl Index: $(40\%)^2 + (30\%)^2 + (20\%)^2 + (5\%)^2 + (5\%)^2 =$
$1{,}600 + 900 + 400 + 25 + 25 = \mathbf{2{,}950}$

Industry B
Concentration ratio: $(60\%) + (10\%) + (10\%) + (10\%) = \mathbf{90}$
Herfindahl Index: $(60\%)^2 + (10\%)^2 + (10\%)^2 + (10\%)^2 + (10\%)^2 =$
$3{,}600 + 100 + 100 + 100 + 100 = \mathbf{4{,}000}$

Industry C
Concentration ratio: $(25\%) + (25\%) + (25\%) + (25\%) = \mathbf{100}$
Herfindahl Index: $(25\%)^2 + (25\%)^2 + (25\%)^2 + (25\%)^2 =$
$625 + 625 + 625 + 625 = \mathbf{2{,}500}$

b. Ranking industries from most to least concentrated according to the concentration ratio: **C, A, B**

c. Ranking industries from most to least concentrated according to the Herfindahl Index: **B, A, C**

CHAPTER 29

Regulation

In addition to antitrust policy, government alters market outcomes through regulation. Some regulations benefit society at large; others benefit special-interest groups. Chapter 29 examines the rationale for government regulation, the evolution of regulation in the United States, and the economic effects of regulation. Special attention is paid to the regulation of natural monopolies.

CHAPTER OUTLINE

I. The Evolution of Federal Regulation
  A. The Interstate Commerce Commission (ICC) was the first federal regulatory agency. Established in 1887 to control entry into the railroad industry and to limit rates for rail transportation, the ICC was later given the power to regulate trucking and certain other forms of transportation.
  B. During the 1930s, more regulatory agencies were established.
    1. Until its abolition in 1984, the Civil Aeronautics Board (CAB) regulated air travel.
    2. The Federal Communications Commission (FCC) regulates the part of the communication industry that uses the airwaves—broadcasting, telephones, and telegraphs.
    3. The Securities and Exchange Commission (SEC) regulates the stock and bond markets.
  C. Beginning in the 1960s and continuing through the 1970s, there was a new wave of regulatory activity.
    1. In 1970, the Occupational Safety and Health Administration (OSHA) was established to regulate the workplace.
    2. In 1972, the Consumer Product Safety Commission (CPSC) was established to set safety standards for products.
    3. In 1970, the Environmental Protection Agency (EPA) was established to coordinate pollution standards.
  D. The Changing Nature of Regulation
    1. Early regulation focused on particular industries. Known as **economic regulation**, its intent is to change the market outcomes of price, output, and output quality.
    2. Recent regulation has focused on improving the well-being of all society. This is known as **social regulation**.
    3. A period of deregulation began in the late 1970s. **Deregulation** involves the removal of government regulations.
      a. The Carter Administration focused on reducing economic regulation.
      b. The Reagan Administration focused on reducing social regulation.

    c. The Bush Administration reversed the decline in social regulation, particularly by expanding environmental regulations.

  E. The Costs and Benefits of Regulation:

    1. The costs of regulation:

      a. The administrative costs of both the government agency and the businesses being regulated.

      b. The costs of complying with regulations, such as the addition of safety features or changes in the techniques of production. Where government regulations mandate that firms operate inefficiently, this is an added cost of compliance.

    2. Economically beneficial regulations create benefits in excess of their costs.

II. Reasons for Regulation

  A. There are two competing theories advanced to explain why the government imposes regulations:

    1. The public-interest theory

    2. The special-interest theory

  B. The **public-interest theory of regulation** argues that the government intervenes only to correct market failure—when the market fails to produce socially optimal outcomes. There are three causes of market failure:

    1. A natural monopoly is caused by a continually declining long-run average costs curve. One producer can produce the market output at a lower average cost than if more than one firm produces the output. The producer's price must be regulated to prevent the producer from exploiting its status as sole producer.

    2. Externalities exist when the actions of one group of market participants—producers or consumers— influence individuals who are not part of the market. An example is pollution. The government must regulate the market to ensure that these impacts are taken into consideration.

    3. Consumers may make incorrect choices when they possess imperfect information. For example, they may unknowingly buy unsafe products. There are two alternative policy actions in this situation:

      a. The government could provide information to consumers and let the consumers make choices based on the improved information. Consumers buy the extra safety if they believe the extra safety is worth the cost.

      b. The government could force unsafe products off the market.

        i. Supporters of this position argue that consumers are not able to evaluate the risks involved in unsafe products.

        ii. Opponents believe that taking less safe, less expensive products off the market disproportionately hurts the poor. Also, it forces firms to devote resources to government mandated characteristics rather than to characteristics that consumers prefer.

  C. The **special-interest theory of regulation** argues that regulations are made to benefit certain special interests at the expense of the general public.

    1. Regulations may be instituted to protect an industry from competition.

    2. Regulatory agencies may legitimatize activities that otherwise would be illegal, such as price fixing.

    3. According to the **capture hypothesis**, regulatory bodies that are intended to protect the public eventually promote the interests of the industry.

    4. Regulatory bodies avoid driving firms out of business. Prices are set in order to allow the least efficient to survive, which allows the more efficient to earn excessive profit.

    5. Workers and unions in regulated industries benefit because they share some of the high returns to the industry.

    6. Some consumers may benefit from the special-interest regulations, but at the expense of the majority of consumers.

    7. The regulators themselves have an interest in maintaining the regulations in order to maintain their incomes and power.

  D. The Effects of Regulation

    1. Evidence on prices supports the special-interest theory of regulation, as it appears prices are higher because of regulation.

2. Evidence on service is mixed. In some circumstances regulation has improved service, but in others regulation has reduced the services available.
3. Evidence on profits is also mixed. To the extent the regulations impose costs on firms, profits may fall. To the extent prices are set higher because of regulation, profits increase.
4. Labor productivity is probably lower because of regulation because regulation often restricts the introduction of new technologies and protects existing job classifications.
5. Union wages are probably easier to maintain under regulation than under deregulation.

III. Regulating Natural Monopoly
A. In industries characterized by significant economies of scale, one firm is granted a monopoly in order to lower the average cost of producing the output.
B. A regulatory commission is given the responsibility of setting the price the natural monopoly is allowed to charge. The regulatory body, in general, has three alternatives:
1. **Marginal cost pricing** sets the price at the point where the demand curve crosses the marginal cost curve.
   a. The advantage of this price is that it allows resources to be allocated efficiently.
   b. The disadvantage is that when price is less than average cost, the firm will not operate in the long run.
2. **Average cost pricing** sets the price at the point where the demand curve crosses the average cost curve.
   a. The advantage is that the firm earns a normal profit.
   b. The disadvantage is that resources are allocated inefficiently because $P > MC$ at the output produced.
3. Subsidies and access fees allow the price to be set at marginal cost and yet permit the firm to earn a normal profit. A subsidy is a direct grant from the government to the natural monopoly; an access fee requires customers to pay a price to use the firm's services.
C. Most regulatory commissions limit the profit the firm is allowed to earn by using rate-of-return regulation. **Rate-of-return regulation** limits a firm to a prescribed rate of return on its capital.
1. First, the government must determine the **rate base**—the value of the firm's capital according to the regulators. All the natural monopoly's capital may not be included if the commission believes that some of the capital is unnecessary.
2. Next, the government must set the allowable rate of return.
3. There are two potential problems with this approach:
   a. If the allowable rate of return is too high, the firm has an incentive to buy more capital than is efficient.
   b. By limiting the firm to only a normal profit, the business has no incentive to reduce costs because prices will be cut if costs are reduced.
D. An alternative to rate-of-return regulation is **price-cap regulation**. This places an upper limit on the price but allows the producer to receive higher profits if costs are reduced.
E. An alternative to regulation is public ownership of the natural monopoly. Evidence indicates that publicly owned firms are less efficient than private producers because of the impact of political factors on production decisions. This evidence has increased interest in **privatization**, which involves transferring the production of a good from the public sector to the private sector.

FILL IN THE BLANK

economic

1. Policies aimed at lowering the price or improving the quality of a product are known as _____ regulation.

capture hypothesis

2. Regulatory agencies cater to the preferences of the industries they are regulating, according to the _____.

deregulation

3. Reducing the number of regulatory bodies is called _____.

rate base

social

marginal

Price-cap

Interstate Commerce
Commission

Environmental Protection
Agency

privatization

4. The value of the firm's capital for the purpose of rate regulation is the
_____.

5. The Occupational Safety and Health Administration is an example of
_____ regulation.

6. Resources are allocated efficiently if rate regulators follow _____
_____ cost pricing.

7. _____ regulation places an upper limit on
the price a regulated firm can charge.

8. The _____ was the first regulatory agency
of the federal government.

9. Pollution standards are set by the _____ .
_____.

10. Hiring a firm to operate a prison rather than having the state administer the
prison is an example of _____.

TRUE OR FALSE

_____ 1. Evidence indicates that public provision of services like trash collection results in lower average costs than private provision of the services because there are no profits.

_____ 2. The elimination of the Occupational Safety and Health Administration (OSHA) was the first major step toward deregulation.

_____ 3. Regulation in the United States initially was economic regulation.

_____ 4. Evidence cited in the text argues that regulation has tended to increase the price of regulated products.

_____ 5. Social regulation tends to focus on individual industries and products.

_____ 6. The Reagan Administration supported increased social regulation but reduced economic regulation.

_____ 7. Everyone agrees that the solution to imperfect information is to provide consumers with the information necessary for them to make informed decisions.

_____ 8. Regulation is preferred to the unregulated market outcome whenever there is market failure.

_____ 9. An unregulated natural monopoly would never set its price equal to MC.

_____ 10. Regulators of public utilities determine the acceptable price of output by first deciding what wages are acceptable for workers at the utility.

MULTIPLE CHOICE

1. The fact that a regulated business resists the elimination of regulations is consistent with:
   A. the capture hypothesis.
   B. marginal cost pricing.
   C. economic regulation.
   D. privatization.

2. Which of the following agencies regulates the stock and bond markets?
   A. EPA
   B. SEC
   C. OSHA
   D. ICC

3. The Interstate Commerce Commission was formed to regulate:
   A. railroads.
   B. telegraph.
   C. trucking.
   D. all businesses engaging in interstate commerce.

4. A disadvantage of rate-of-return regulation is:
   A. firms have a reduced incentive to minimize costs.
   B. firms may acquire too much capital.
   C. firms may withhold new technologies.
   D. All the alternatives are correct.

5. Resources are allocated efficiently if the natural monopoly produces the output:
   A. at the minimum of the long-run average cost curve.
   B. where $MR = MC$.
   C. where $P = AC$.
   D. where $P = MC$.

6. Critics of minimum safety standards argue that they result in which of the following?
   A. lower wages
   B. higher costs of production
   C. higher prices of products
   D. All the alternatives are correct.

7. Which of the following is a reason for regulation according to the public-interest theory of regulation?
   A. externalities
   B. natural monopoly
   C. imperfect information
   D. All the alternatives are correct.

8. Average cost pricing requires producers to:
   A. allow new firms into the industry.
   B. produce more than the socially optimal output.
   C. earn only a normal profit.
   D. substitute labor for capital.

9. The Occupational Safety and Health Administration:
   A. sets minimum wages and maximum prices.
   B. regulates the prices charged by doctors and nurses.
   C. sets standards for workplace safety.
   D. regulates the size of the work force.

10. Which of the following industries does the FCC not regulate?
    A. newspapers
    B. television
    C. radio
    D. telephone

PROBLEMS

1. a. On Figure 29.1, identify with P_1 and Q_1 the price and output an unregulated monopoly would produce.
   b. On Figure 29.1, identify with P_2 and Q_2 the price and output the firm would produce if a regulator used average cost pricing.

c. On Figure 29.1, identify with P_3 and Q_3 the price and output the firm would produce if a regulator used marginal cost pricing.

FIGURE 29.1

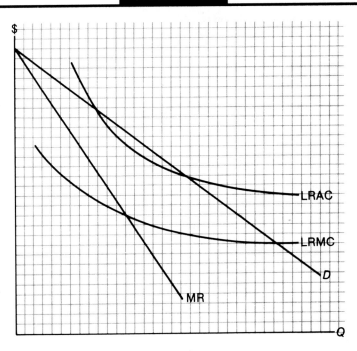

TRUE OR FALSE

1. False. Evidence indicates that public provision of services results in higher average costs.

2. False. It was the elimination of the Civil Aeronautics Board (CAB), which regulated the airline industry, that represented the first major step toward deregulation.

3. True. Early regulation was aimed at specific industries; for example, the Interstate Commerce Commission was created to regulate the railroad industry.

4. True. Either by increasing costs of production, which raises prices, or by allowing firms in an industry to raise prices above the competitive level in order to increase profit, regulation tends to increase prices.

5. False. Social regulation tends to cut across industry lines to focus on particular outcomes such as cleaner air or safer products.

6. False. The Reagan Administration supported reduced regulation of all kinds.

7. False. Some prefer that the government set minimum safety standards in lieu of information.

8. False. If the cost of the regulation is greater than the benefits produced, the regulation is not preferred even if there is market failure.

9. True. Because P > MR for a monopoly, it never voluntarily produces where P = MC.

10. False. Regulators first decide on an acceptable rate of return on the firm's capital. From that they determine what prices the utility can charge.

MULTIPLE CHOICE

1. A. The capture hypothesis states that regulators are eventually captured by the very industries the regulators are intended to regulate. As a result, regulated firms benefit from the regulations and resist their elimination.
2. B. The Securities and Exchange Commission (SEC) regulates the stock and bond markets.
3. A. Railroads were the initial focus of the ICC, with trucking added in the 1930s.
4. D. Each of the alternatives is a potential problem when the government regulates the rate of return a firm may earn.
5. D. Efficient allocation of resources requires that production occur where $P = MC$.
6. D. Safety standards in the workplace lower wages by requiring employers to substitute improved safety for wages, and safety standards for products impose additional costs on producers and result in higher prices.
7. D. Externalities, natural monopoly, and imperfect information are all sources of market failure and justifications for regulation of industry.
8. C. Average cost pricing sets price equal to average cost, so economic profit equals zero.
9. C. OSHA sets and enforces safety standards where people work.
10. A. The FCC only regulates industries that use the nation's airwaves.

PROBLEMS

1. a, b, and c; see Figure 29.2.

FIGURE 29.2

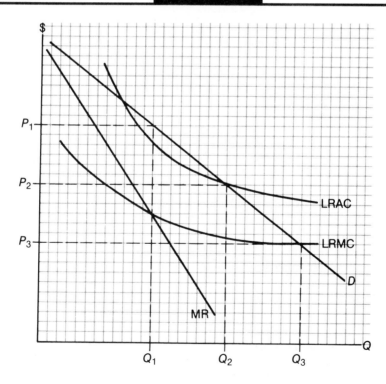

CHAPTER 30

The Labor Market—Why Are My Wages So Low (High)?

Firms produce output. But to do so they must hire inputs. Chapters 30-34 look at the input side of the economy from the perspective of both the firms buying the inputs and the resource owners selling them.

Chapter 30 starts the discussion by looking at the hiring decision in a competitive labor market where there are many firms and many workers. After explaining how wages are determined in this setting, the causes of wage differentials are discussed.

The chapter closes with a discussion of the impact of unions on the labor market. The union movement in the United States, major labor legislation, and the economic impact of unions are described.

CHAPTER OUTLINE

I. Wage Determination Under Perfect Competition
    A. Assumptions:
        1. No firm can influence the wage.
        2. No worker can influence the wage.
        3. All workers are equally skilled.
    B. The Firm's Demand for Labor
        1. **Marginal revenue product (MRP)** measures the increase in revenue received by the firm as a result of hiring an additional unit of labor. It is equal to the additional output the additional worker produces (MP_L) times the price of output (P).
        2. To maximize profit, the firm should hire an additional worker as long as the worker adds more to revenue than to costs—that is, as long as MRP ≥ wage.
        3. The firm's MRP curve is the firm's demand for labor curve. The marginal revenue product curve is downward sloping.
    C. The Market Demand for Labor
        1. The **market demand for labor** indicates the total amount of labor demanded, at each wage, by all the firms in the labor market.
        2. Because each firm's demand for labor curve is downward sloping, the market demand curve is downward sloping.
        3. The demand for labor is a **derived demand** because the amount of labor hired depends on the demand for the output labor produces.
    D. The Supply of Labor
        1. The Labor Supply of an Individual Worker

a. A wage increase has two effects on an individual's labor supply:
   i. The **substitution effect** of the wage increase induces the individual to supply more labor because the higher wage increases the opportunity cost of leisure (that is, not working).
   ii. The **income effect** of the wage increase induces the individual to supply less labor because, with the higher wage and higher income, the individual can afford to "buy" more leisure.
b. The shape of the individual's labor supply curve depends on whether the substitution or income effect is larger.
   i. If the substitution effect is greater than the income effect, the labor supply curve slopes upward.
   ii. If the substitution effect is less than the income effect, the labor supply curve slopes downward.
   iii. The individual's labor supply curve bends backward if at lower wages the substitution effect is larger while at higher wages the income effect is larger.
c. Empirical evidence indicates that the substitution effect is stronger than the income effect for females; data are inconclusive for males.

2. The **market supply of labor** is the sum of the individual labor supply curves. It is upward sloping for two reasons:
   a. A higher wage induces new workers to enter the labor force.
   b. Higher wages in one industry induce some workers to shift from other industries.
3. The supply curve that the individual firm faces is horizontal because the firm hires so little labor relative to the entire market that it can hire as many units of labor as it wishes without influencing the wage.

E. The equilibrium wage is the wage where the market demand curve for labor intersects the market supply curve of labor.

II. The Causes of Wage Differentials
   A. Skill Differences
      1. Innate skill differences cause wage differentials. The extra income earned because of scarce natural talent is an **economic rent of the worker**. The amount of the economic rent is the difference between the wage the individual earns due to the skill and the wage available in the next best occupation.
      2. Education and training also create wage differentials.
         a. The human capital theory says that the additional skills make the worker more productive and thus more valuable to the firm. **Human capital** is the knowledge and skills acquired by workers, principally through training.
         b. The **screening (credentialism) hypothesis** asserts that education does not make the workers more productive but merely gives the worker access to higher-paying jobs. To the employer, education is an indication of other attributes—motivation, ability—that make the worker valuable to the firm.
         c. Evidence indicates in most cases the extra income that additional education brings is worth the cost even when the opportunity cost of the individual's time is included (as it should be).
   B. Occupations offer a wide range of attributes, wage being one of them. Some occupations must offer a higher wage to offset other, less attractive characteristics. Wage differentials of this nature are called **compensating wage differentials**.
   C. Market imperfections and discrimination account for some differences in wages.
      1. If some individuals are excluded from an occupation, the wage in the occupation is higher and the wages in the occupations the individuals are allowed to enter are lower.
      2. The minimum-wage law raises the wages of certain low-skilled workers. On the other hand, the minimum wage results in lower employment of low-skilled workers.

III. Labor Unions
   A. A labor union is an organization of workers that negotiates collectively in order to increase the workers' bargaining power.

B. Early Labor Unions
   1. Unions existed in the United States as early as the eighteenth century. Citywide federations of unions first appeared in Philadelphia in 1827. National federations began soon after but were unsuccessful.
   2. In the nineteenth century, courts either ruled that unions were illegal conspiracies or issued injunctions prohibiting strikes and picketing, reasoning that they were restraints of trade.
   3. The courts approved "yellow-dog contracts," which required workers to agree not to join a union as a condition of employment.
C. Major Labor Legislation
   1. The Norris–LaGuardia Act (1932) limits the ability of courts to issue injunctions against unions and outlaws yellow-dog contracts.
   2. The National Labor Relations Act or Wagner Act (1935) is often called the Magna Carta of labor. Its major provisions are:
      a. Prohibits management from interfering in the workers' right to organize.
      b. Requires management to bargain in good faith with the union approved by the majority of the employees.
      c. Establishes the National Labor Relations Board (NLRB) to investigate accusations of unfair labor practices and to issue cease-and-desist orders. The NLRB also conducts worker elections for certifying a union.
   3. The Taft–Hartley Act (1947) reduces the power of unions. Its major provisions are:
      a. Permits the president to seek an injunction ordering workers back to work for 80 days if a strike threatens public health or safety.
      b. Requires unions to bargain with employers in good faith.
      c. Establishes procedures for decertifying a union.
      d. Outlaws closed shops. A **closed shop** permits the company to hire only workers who are members of a union.
      e. Permits states to pass **right-to-work laws** that outlaw union shops. A **union shop** is a work arrangement that requires employees to become members of a union once they are hired. In right-to-work states only open shops are legal. An **open shop** is a work arrangement under which employees cannot be compelled to join a union.
   4. The Landrum–Griffin Act (1959) requires secret ballots in union elections and restricts the power of union officers.
D. Unions in the U.S.
   1. Union membership doubled between 1930 and 1940 primarily because of favorable legislation of the 1930s.
   2. Since 1955, the percentage of the labor force that belongs to a union has declined. At the present time only 15 percent of workers belong to unions—the lowest percentage since the 1930s.
   3. The power of unions has diminished for various reasons.
      a. The favorable public opinion toward unions has switched to one of distrust.
      b. The public has elected more leaders who have less favorable attitudes toward unions.
      c. Management has become more sophisticated in its dealings with unions and is more willing to combat unions.
      d. Employment in highly unionized industries has declined while employment in nonunionized industries has expanded.
      e. Women, who are less likely to join unions, have become a larger share of the labor force.
E. The AFL–CIO is a federation of unions, formed in 1955 through the merger of the American Federation of Labor and the Congress of Industrial Organizations.
   1. The AFL was an association of craft unions—unions organized around a particular skill or craft.
   2. The CIO was made up of unions organized by industry, where all workers employed in a particular industry were members of the same union.

IV. How Unions Raise Wages of Their Members
   A. Increasing the demand for the good produced by the union increases the demand for union labor, which puts upward pressure on wages. Examples of this are:
      1. Campaigns to convince consumers to buy only union-made goods.
      2. Laws that require the purchase of goods or services provided by union members.
   B. Wages can be increased by restricting the supply of labor. This can be achieved by requiring workers to acquire licenses in order to enter a particular occupation (for example, barbers) or by apprenticeship programs. Such programs raise the wage but reduce the number employed.
   C. Through collective bargaining the union and the employer can agree to wage increases in order to avoid a strike. **Collective bargaining** is the process through which unions and management negotiate wages, fringe benefits, and nonmonetary terms of employment.
      1. Collective bargaining raises the wages of union workers by setting the wage above the equilibrium wage. As a consequence a surplus of labor is created.
      2. The ability of the union to raise wages through collective bargaining depends on the costs that the union can impose on the firm by striking. The cost of a strike to the employer depends on two factors:
         a. The degree to which the strike reduces the ability of the firm to produce. The firm may be able to continue producing during a strike if the firm can:
            i. Replace the striking workers with new workers.
            ii. Use current nonstriking employees to replace the striking workers.
            iii. Substitute capital for labor.
         b. The extent to which the firm is able to stockpile its output.
            i. If stockpiling is possible—as with most manufactured goods—the firm can continue selling its product during the strike.
            ii. If stockpiling is impossible—as with services—the firm will have no inventories to sell during a strike.
   D. Other Impacts of Unions
      1. The Impact of Unions on Nonunion Wages
         a. Some workers may receive higher wages due to unions because employers attempt to make union membership less attractive.
         b. Other workers may receive lower wages because union wages reduce employment in unionized occupations and increase the supply of labor in nonunionized occupations.
         c. The difference between the wages of union workers and nonunion workers—called the union wage premium—is estimated to be about 15 percent, although it varies from situation to situation.
      2. The Nonwage Impacts of Unions
         a. Unions have improved the fringe benefits received by all workers.
         b. Because of strikes and restrictive work practices, unions reduce output, though they sometimes force firms to be more efficient.
         c. Unions have fostered cooperation between workers and have provided an organized channel for communication between workers and employers.
         d. Unions probably have reduced income inequality by helping low-income workers more than high-income workers. Also, unions foster equality by treating workers in a nondiscriminatory way and protecting workers from discriminatory acts by employers.
         e. Unions have supported the passage of major social legislation on civil rights, child labor, worker safety, and plant closings.

HINTS AND HELP

1. Marginal Revenue Product (MRP) To measure the additional revenue that a worker adds requires two things. First, one must know how much extra output the additional worker produces. This is the worker's marginal product. Secondly, one must know the price at which the output is sold. The product of the two is marginal revenue product.

For example, if an additional worker produces 50 more units of output and the price of output is $.50, the marginal revenue product is $50 \times \$.50 = \$25$.

2. The Hiring Decision By now the production decision should be familiar: Produce a unit of output as long as the additional unit of output adds at least as much to revenue as it does to costs. That is, produce until the point where MR = MC.

The hiring decision follows the same reasoning, but from the perspective of inputs: Hire additional labor as long as the additional labor adds at least as much to revenue as it does to costs. Marginal revenue product (MRP) measures the extra revenue the additional unit of labor produces. In a competitive labor market, the cost of hiring an extra unit of labor is the wage. The hiring decision reduces to: Hire until MRP = W.

FILL IN THE BLANK

derived

1. Because the demand for labor depends on the demand for the output produced by the labor, it is a _____ demand.

horizontal

2. A perfectly competitive firm faces a _____ labor supply curve.

closed

3. There is a _____ shop if an employer can hire only workers who are members of a union.

open

4. Right-to-work laws allow only _____ shops.

screening hypothesis

5. The knowledge gained from college courses has little direct impact on an individual's productive capacity, according to the _____.

marginal revenue product

6. Labor's marginal product times the price of output equals _____ _____.

yellow-dog contract

7. A contract that requires a worker to agree not to join a union as a condition of employment is called a _____ .

reduced

8. The shift of jobs from manufacturing to the service sector has _____ union membership.

Collective bargaining

9. _____ is the process of contract negotiation between unions and management.

increase

10. The substitution effect of a wage increase causes an individual to _____ the hours of labor supplied.

TRUE OR FALSE

_____ 1. An upward-sloping labor supply curve exists when the income effect of a wage change is larger than the substitution effect.

_____ 2. The market labor supply curve can be upward sloping even if individual labor supply curves are not.

_____ 3. The labor demand curve of a firm in a perfectly competitive labor market is horizontal.

_____ 4. An increase in the price of output increases the demand for labor.

_____ 5. Evidence from the professional baseball market indicates that competition among baseball teams for players has had little impact on the salaries of baseball players.

_____ 6. Everything else the same, if a job has desirable nonwage characteristics, it probably pays a lower wage.

_____ 7. A minimum wage set below the equilibrium wage tends to lower the equilibrium wage.

_____ 8. The National Labor Relations Act gives workers the right to form unions and to strike without the interference of the courts.

_____ 9. The Taft–Hartley Act makes strikes longer than 80 days illegal.

_____ 10. The percentage of the labor force in the United States that belongs to unions has fallen since the mid-1950s.

MULTIPLE CHOICE

1. That fact that the average wage has increased at the same time that the average workweek has declined is consistent with:
   A. the substitution effect of a wage increase being greater than the income effect.
   B. the income effect of a wage increase being greater than the substitution effect.
   C. the income effect of a wage increase equal to the substitution effect.
   D. the income effect of a wage increase equaling zero.

2. Which of the following is perfectly elastic?
   A. the firm's demand for labor in a perfectly competitive labor market
   B. the market demand for labor in a perfectly competitive labor market
   C. the supply of labor to the firm in a perfectly competitive labor market
   D. the market supply of labor in a perfectly competitive labor market

3. Innate skill differences that create wage differentials create:
   A. a surplus of labor.
   B. a compensating wage differential.
   C. economic rent.
   D. human capital.

4. The marginal revenue product curve is downward sloping because:
   A. of the law of diminishing returns.
   B. the market demand curve for labor is downward sloping.
   C. the labor supply curve is upward sloping.
   D. the firm has no impact on the wage rate.

5. Which of the following causes an increase in the demand for labor?
   A. a fall in wages
   B. a fall in the productivity of labor
   C. an increase in the price of output
   D. an increase in the supply of labor

6. Which of the following is _not_ a part of the National Labor Relations Act?
   A. establishes the National Labor Relations Board
   B. requires unions to bargain in good faith with employers
   C. requires employers to bargain in good faith with unions
   D. establishes a procedure for certifying a union to represent workers

7. Which of the following is _not_ part of the Taft–Hartley Act?
   A. outlaws closed shops
   B. allows states to outlaw union shops
   C. establishes a union decertification procedure
   D. requires a secret ballot for union elections

8. Which of the following policies increases the wages *and* employment of union members?
   A. setting a wage above the equilibrium wage
   B. "buy union-made goods" campaigns
   C. occupational licensing
   D. an open shop

9. If an employer hires only college graduates yet provides all necessary training for the job, such behavior is an example of which of the following?
   A. the screening hypothesis
   B. the human capital theory
   C. a closed shop
   D. economic rent

10. Which of the following creates a backward-bending labor supply curve?
    A. workers entering occupations as the wage rises
    B. a compensating wage differential that offsets a nonwage aspect of the job
    C. a substitution effect that is initially larger than, then becomes smaller than, the income effect as the wage rises
    D. a minimum-wage law that has no effect after the wage reaches a certain level

PROBLEMS

1. a. Provide the missing values in the first five columns of the table. Ignore the MRP_2 column *for now.*

UNITS OF LABOR	OUTPUT	MARGINAL PRODUCT	PRICE	(MRP_1) MARGINAL REVENUE PRODUCT	(MRP_2) MARGINAL REVENUE PRODUCT
0	0				
1	50	_____	$20	_____	_____
2	90	_____	20	_____	_____
3	_____	_____	20	$600	_____
4	_____	20	20	_____	_____
5	_____	_____	20	$200	_____
6	155	_____	20	_____	_____

   b. Plot the firm's marginal revenue product curve on Figure 30.1.
   c. Draw the labor supply curve the firm faces if the wage is $400. How much labor does the firm hire? _____

   d. Draw the labor supply curve the firm faces if the wage is $100. How much labor does the firm hire? _____

   e. Assume the price of output falls to $10. Fill in the new values of the marginal revenue product in the MRP_2 column of the preceding table and plot it on Figure 30.1. How many units of labor are hired at a wage of $400? _____ How much at a wage of $100? _____

FIGURE 30.1

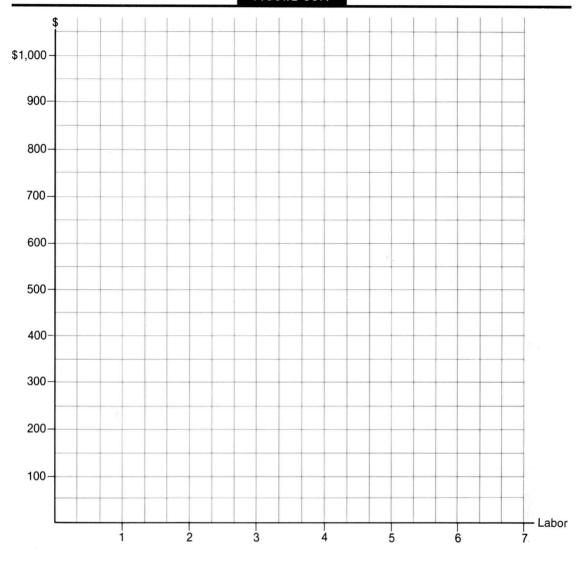

Answers

TRUE OR FALSE

1. False. An upward-sloping labor supply curve exists when the substitution effect is greater than the income effect.
2. True. The market supply curve includes the impact of new workers entering the labor force or entering that particular labor market. The entry of new workers can offset any reduction in hours of work by those already in the labor market.
3. False. The labor demand curve of a firm in a perfectly competitive labor market is downward sloping.
4. True. An increase in output price makes each worker's output more valuable. As a consequence, more labor is demanded.

5. False. The salaries of baseball players increased dramatically once they were allowed to negotiate with more than one team.

6. True. This is in keeping with the theory of compensating wage differentials.

7. False. A minimum wage set below the equilibrium wage has no effect on the equilibrium wage.

8. True. The National Labor Relations Act is often called the Magna Carta of labor because it established the right of workers to form unions and strike.

9. False. The Taft–Hartley Act permits the president to seek an 80–day injunction halting a strike if the strike endangers the public health or national security.

10. True. For a variety of reasons, the percentage of the labor force that is unionized has declined steadily since the mid-1950s.

MULTIPLE CHOICE

1. B. If the income effect is larger than the substitution effect, higher wages cause an individual to supply fewer hours of labor.

2. C. The firm can hire as much labor as it wishes without influencing the wage. This means the supply of labor curve is perfectly elastic.

3. C. Economic rent exists when an individual earns more in a particular occupation than could be earned in the next best occupation, which happens when skills are innate.

4. A. The marginal revenue product curve is downward sloping because the marginal product of labor declines, which is what the law of diminishing returns says happens.

5. C. The labor demand curve is derived by holding the price of output constant. If the price of output rises, labor becomes more profitable to hire and the labor demand curve shifts to the right.

6. B. The requirement that unions bargain in good faith with employers is contained in the Taft–Hartley Act.

7. D. Secret ballots for union elections are part of the Landrum–Griffin Act.

8. B. Increasing the demand for union-made products increases the demand for union labor, raises the amount hired, and increases the wage.

9. A. The screening hypothesis asserts that higher education raises earnings because it opens doors (screens) and not because it produces useful skills.

10. C. A worker has a backward-bending supply curve of labor if, as the wage rises, the substitution effect is initially larger than the income effect but eventually becomes smaller than the income effect.

PROBLEMS

1. a.

UNITS OF LABOR	OUTPUT	MARGINAL PRODUCT	PRICE	(MRP$_1$) MARGINAL REVENUE PRODUCT	(MRP$_2$) MARGINAL REVENUE PRODUCT
0	0				
1	50	50	$20	$1,000	$500
2	90	40	20	800	400
3	120	30	20	600	300
4	140	20	20	400	200
5	150	10	20	200	100
6	155	5	20	100	50

b. See Figure 30.2.

FIGURE 30.2

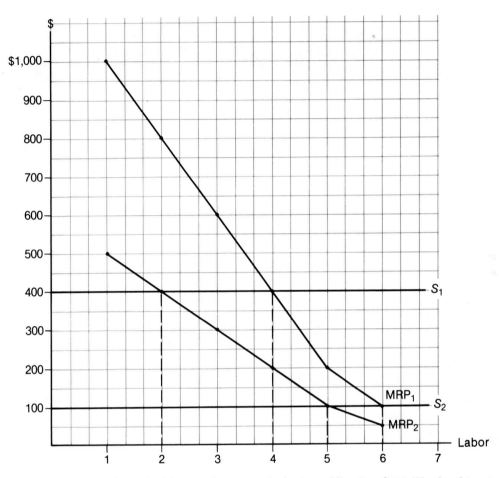

c. When the wage is $400, the labor supply curve is the horizontal line S_1 at $400. The firm hires **4** units of labor.

d. When the wage is $100, the labor supply curve is the horizontal line S_2 at $100. The firm hires **6** units of labor.

e. The values of marginal revenue product when the price of output is $10 are given in the MRP_2 column in the table drawn in Figure 30.2. When the wage is $400, **2** units of labor are hired. When the wage is $100, **5** units of labor are hired.

CHAPTER 31

Alternative Models of the Factor Market

Not all labor markets resemble the one described in Chapter 30. Some, called monopsonies, have a single buyer of labor as opposed to many buyers. Others are composed of firms that sell their output in noncompetitive output markets. Chapter 31 begins by exploring the labor market consequences of these two differences.

This chapter also discusses a more complicated input choice that firms often face: how to hire inputs when more than one input can be varied. Finally, the marginal productivity theory of income is described and evaluated.

CHAPTER OUTLINE

I. Monopsony in the Labor Market
   A. A **monopsonist** is the only buyer of an input (for example, labor).
   B. The Supply of Labor in Monopsony
      1. A monopsonist faces the upward-sloping labor market supply curve. To increase the amount of labor hired, the monopsonist must offer a higher wage.
      2. **Marginal factor cost (MFC)** measures the increase in total cost due to hiring an additional unit of labor (or any other factor of production).
      3. Marginal factor cost is greater than the wage paid the additional worker.
         a. The monopsonist pays all the workers the same wage.
         b. To hire an extra worker, the monopsonist must pay the additional worker a higher wage and the other workers must have their wages increased to the amount the additional worker receives.
         c. The total increase in costs—the MFC—equals the wage paid the additional worker plus the extra wages paid the other workers.
   C. Equilibrium
      1. The monopsonist hires workers as long as each additional worker adds at least as much to revenue as it adds to costs. Equilibrium occurs where MRP = MFC.
      2. The monopsonist pays the wage associated with the equilibrium amount of labor given by the labor supply curve.
      3. Compared to a competitive labor market, the monopsony equilibrium involves less labor employed and a lower wage paid.
   D. Unions and Minimum Wages in a Monopsonistic Market
      1. Unions or minimum-wage laws place a lower limit on wages.
      2. If the lower limit is above the wage the monopsonist was paying, the monopsonist is forced to raise its wage.

3. The lower limit on wages can induce the monopsonist to hire *more* workers. This is possible because the minimum or union wage makes a portion of the labor supply curve horizontal. As a consequence, MFC no longer increases over that range of employment and hiring more workers becomes profitable.

4. If the lower limit on wages is set too high it leads to lower employment, as is the case in competitive labor markets.

II. Factor Demand in Noncompetitive Product Markets

    A. If a firm sells its output in a competitive output market, marginal revenue equals price. Thus, marginal revenue product for the competitive firm (MRP_c) equals $MP_L \times MR = MP_L \times P$.

    B. If a firm sells its output in a noncompetitive output market, marginal revenue is less than price. Thus, marginal revenue product for the firm with monopoly power (MRP_m) equals $MP_L \times MR < MP_L \times P$.

        1. The MRP_m curve is below the MRP_c curve because $MR < P$.

        2. The MRP_m curve is steeper than the MRP_c curve because the decline in MP_L that occurs when additional labor is hired is reinforced by the decline in P and MR that occurs when a noncompetitive firm sells more output.

    C. Assuming the firm hires labor in a competitive labor market—which means that the firm treats the wage as a constant—the equilibrium amount of labor occurs where $MRP_m = W$.

        1. Because $MRP_m < MRP_c$, the firm selling output in a noncompetitive output market hires less labor than a firm selling its output in a perfectly competitive output market.

        2. This result is consistent with the fact that noncompetitive markets produce less output than competitive markets.

III. The General Rule for Hiring Inputs

    A. A rule for determining how much of an input to hire exists that can be applied to all possible input and output markets: Hire an input until its marginal revenue product (MRP) equals its marginal factor cost (MFC).

    B. The rules presented in previous market situations are special cases of this general rule:

        1. When the input market is competitive, MFC = W because the firm can hire labor without having an impact on the wage.

        2. When the output market is competitive, $MRP = MP_L \times P$.

IV. Shifts in Labor Demand

    A. A firm's labor demand curve is derived by assuming that certain things are held constant. If any of these things changes, the labor demand curve changes.

    B. There are two major factors that cause the labor demand curve to shift:

        1. When demand for the output produced by labor increases, demand for labor increases because it increases the marginal revenue associated with producing additional output.

        2. When marginal product of labor increases, labor becomes more attractive to hire and demand for labor increases. The marginal product of labor increases if:

            a. The workers invest in more human capital.

            b. Other inputs (for example, capital) are changed in a particular way.

                i. Two inputs are **substitute inputs** if an increase in the price of one increases the amount used of the other. Demand for labor increases if the price of a substitute input rises.

                ii. Two inputs are **complementary inputs** if an increase in the price of one decreases the amount used of the other. Demand for labor increases if the price of a complementary input falls.

V. Multiple Inputs

    A. Minimizing Costs When Factor Markets Are Competitive

        1. When more than one input is variable, the firm must decide what combination of inputs to use when producing the output.

        2. When two inputs, capital (K) and labor (L), can be bought in competitive input markets, the cost of producing any particular amount of the product is minimized when inputs are hired until:

$$\frac{MP_K}{P_K} = \frac{MP_L}{P_L}$$

For the last unit of each input hired, the marginal product per dollar spent for each unit must be the same.

B. Maximizing Profit When Factor Markets Are Competitive

1. To maximize profit when more than one input is variable and the inputs can be bought in competitive input markets, the firm must hire inputs so that:

$$\frac{MP_K}{P_K} = \frac{MP_L}{P_L} = \frac{1}{MR}$$

The ratio of each input's marginal product to its input price must equal 1/marginal revenue.

2. If the output is sold in a competitive market, the condition becomes:

$$\frac{MP_K}{P_K} = \frac{MP_L}{P_L} = \frac{1}{P}$$

C. If inputs are bought in noncompetitive input markets, the condition for minimizing cost is:

$$\frac{MP_K}{MFC_K} = \frac{MP_L}{MFC_L}$$

The profit-maximizing condition is:

$$\frac{MP_K}{MFC_K} = \frac{MP_L}{MFC_L} = \frac{1}{MR}$$

VI. The **Marginal Productivity Theory of Income Distribution**

A. In competitive input markets, each input is paid according to its marginal product because each firm maximizes profit by hiring so that the price of each input equals the input's marginal revenue product.

B. The distribution of income that results from this is criticized for two reasons:

1. Some say that paying inputs according to their marginal products results in an unfair distribution of income.

a. Some individuals own very productive inputs and earn very large incomes; others own many fewer productive inputs and earn much less income.

b. The response to this criticism is that the theory is intended to describe how the economy works and not to decide the best distribution of income. If desired, the distribution of income may be changed through government intervention.

2. Some say that labor markets are not as competitive as the marginal productivity theory assumes.

a. In monopsonistic markets, workers are paid less than their marginal revenue products. Unions also create market imperfections.

b. A response is that, although it is true that not all labor markets are competitive, the marginal productivity theory is accurate enough to provide a useful starting point for any discussion of income distribution.

HINTS AND HELP

1. Marginal Factor Cost   To understand the concept of marginal factor cost, assume you are the personnel director for a large coal mine hiring in a small town in Appalachia. The coal mine is the only employer in the area. You have conducted surveys and from them have constructed the supply curve of labor for the area. A portion of the information is reproduced as follows:

WAGE PER DAY	NUMBER OF WORKERS
$100	60
110	61
120	62

To hire 60 workers, you must offer a wage of $100 per day. The cost of hiring labor equals $100 × 60 = $6,000 per day. To hire 61 workers, you must offer a wage of $110 per day. In this case, labor cost equals $110 × 61 = $6,710. The cost of increasing employment from 60 to 61 (that is, the marginal factor cost of the sixty-first worker) is $710. The $710 has two parts to it. First, the sixty-first worker is paid $110. Secondly, the other 60 workers are paid an extra $10 per day, a total of $600.

A question that naturally comes to mind for many students is: Why doesn't the monopsonist coal mine pay only the sixty-first worker the wage of $110 per day while paying all the other workers $100? There are a couple of reasons it cannot. It may be impossible for the employer to identify the sixty-first employee. If hiring 61 workers turns out to be the most profitable option, the mine will post a sign saying it will hire people at $110 per day. Which of the workers who shows up is the one who will work only if the wage is $110 is not obvious.

Even if the employer could identify the sixty-first worker, once the other workers found out that the sixty-first worker was being paid a higher wage, each of the other workers could begin to claim that he or she also must be paid $110 to induce him or her to work. Although not actually true, it may be more expensive for the employer to battle the workers on this point than to pay everyone the same wage.

FILL IN THE BLANK

substitute

1. An increase in the price of a _____ input increases the demand for the other input.

monopsony

2. A market where there is one buyer of an input is a _____.

less

3. When a firm must offer a higher wage in order to hire more workers, the wage is _____ than the marginal factor cost.

price of output

4. The marginal revenue product for a firm that sells its output in a competitive output market equals the marginal product of labor times the _____ .

marginal revenue

5. The marginal revenue product for a firm that sells its output in a noncompetitive output market equals the marginal product of labor times _____ .

less

6. A monopolist hires _____ labor than if the output market were perfectly competitive.

equals

7. A monopolist hiring labor in a competitive labor market hires labor up to the point where MRP_m _____ the wage.

marginal revenue product

8. When input and output markets are competitive, each input is paid an amount equal to its _____ .

marginal factor cost

9. The amount by which total costs rise as additional labor is hired is the _____ .

$MRP_m = MFC$

10. A monopsonist selling output in a monopoly market hires labor until _____ = _____ .

TRUE OR FALSE

_____ 1. A monopsonist pays a lower wage than the wage that would be paid if the labor market were perfectly competitive.

_____ 2. A minimum wage imposed on a monopsonistic market always reduces the amount of labor hired.

_____ 3. Because it faces an upward-sloping labor supply curve, a monopsonist pays each worker a different wage.

_____ 4. A monopsonist always sells its output in a noncompetitive output market.

_____ 5. A monopolist hiring labor in a competitive input market pays a lower wage than a firm selling output in a perfectly competitive market.

_____ 6. All profit-maximizing firms hire labor up to the point where MRP = MFC.

_____ 7. Marginal revenue product for a monopoly is less than marginal revenue product for a firm in a competitive output market because the marginal product of labor is lower for a monopoly.

_____ 8. The marginal productivity theory of income distribution states that people earn what they deserve to earn.

_____ 9. When there is more than one variable input and the prices of the two inputs are equal, cost minimization requires that equal amounts of the two inputs be hired.

_____ 10. A lower price of a complementary input tends to increase the price of the other input.

MULTIPLE CHOICE

1. If a monopsonist hires the tenth worker for a wage of $10 and the tenth worker has a marginal revenue product of $10:
   A. the monopsonist's profit rises.
   B. the monopsonist's profit falls.
   C. the monopsonist's profit remains the same.
   D. the monopsonist has a loss.

2. The marginal revenue product curve of a monopolist is steeper than the marginal revenue product curve of a competitive firm because:
   A. marginal revenue declines as output is increased.
   B. the wage rate rises at a faster rate than marginal factor cost.
   C. the wage rate rises at a slower rate than marginal factor cost.
   D. the monopolist produces more output.

3. When a firm's rule for hiring inputs is $W = MP_L \times P$, the firm:
   A. sells output in a perfectly competitive product market and hires labor in a perfectly competitive labor market.
   B. sells output in a perfectly competitive product market and hires labor in a noncompetitive labor market.
   C. sells output in a noncompetitive product market and hires labor in a perfectly competitive labor market.
   D. sells output in a noncompetitive product market and hires labor in a noncompetitive labor market.

Use the following information to answer questions 4, 5, and 6.
A firm is hiring capital and labor. The price of labor is $10 and the price of capital is $20. Both input markets and output market are perfectly competitive.

4. If the marginal product of the last unit of labor hired is 30 and the marginal product of the last unit of capital hired is 40, which of the following is true?
   A. The firm is paying too much for its capital.
   B. The firm is hiring the cost-minimizing combination of capital and labor.
   C. The firm should hire more capital and less labor in order to minimize the cost of producing its output.
   D. The firm should hire more labor and less capital in order to minimize the cost of producing its output.

5. Assume the marginal product of labor is 20, the marginal product of capital is 40, and the price of output is $1. If the firm produces one more unit of output, total cost will rise by:
   A. $.50.
   B. $1.
   C. $2.
   D. $10.

6. Assume the same values for the marginal products of labor and capital as in question 5. Also assume an output price of $1. To maximize profit, this firm should:
   A. produce more output.
   B. produce less output.
   C. produce the same output.
   D. It is not possible to make a decision given the information provided.

7. Assume a monopsonist is paying a wage of $8 and has a marginal factor cost of $10. If marginal revenue product equals $9, the monopsonist can increase profit by:
   A. hiring more workers.
   B. hiring fewer workers.
   C. raising the wage.
   D. lowering the marginal revenue product.

8. Which of the following causes a decrease in the labor demand curve?
   A. an increase in the price of a complementary input
   B. an increase in the price of a substitute input
   C. an increase in the wage
   D. an increase in the price of output

9. For a profit-maximizing firm, the marginal products of the last units of each input hired are the same if the two inputs:
   A. have the same marginal product curve.
   B. are bought in competitive input markets.
   C. have the same marginal factor cost.
   D. have the same marginal revenue product.

10. Which of the following is true for a profit-maximizing monopsonist that sells output in a noncompetitive output market?
    A. $MP_L/P_L = 1/P$
    B. $MP_L/MFC_L = 1/MR$
    C. $MP_L/P_L = 1/MR$
    D. $MR/P_L = 1/P$

PROBLEMS

1. a. Provide the missing values for MFC_1 in the following table. Ignore the MFC_2 and the marginal revenue product columns *for now*.

WAGE	WORKERS	MARGINAL FACTOR COST (MFC₁)	MARGINAL FACTOR COST (MFC₂)	MARGINAL REVENUE PRODUCT
$1	1			$7
2	2			6
3	3			5
4	4			4
5	5			3
6	6			2
7	7			1

b. Plot the labor supply, the MFC₁ and the MRP curves in Figure 31.1.

FIGURE 31.1

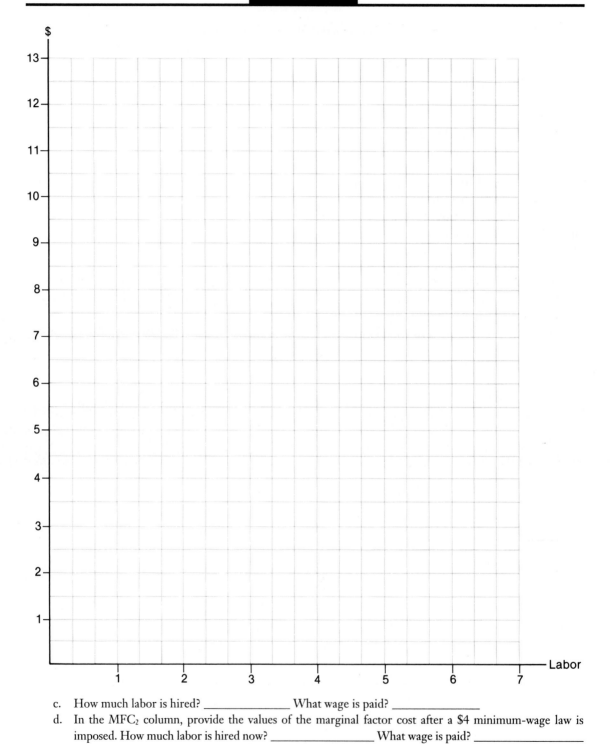

c. How much labor is hired? _____ What wage is paid? _____
d. In the MFC₂ column, provide the values of the marginal factor cost after a $4 minimum-wage law is imposed. How much labor is hired now? _____ What wage is paid? _____

TRUE OR FALSE

1. True. The market power of the monopsonist permits it to offer a lower wage than would exist if the labor market were perfectly competitive.

2. False. It is possible for a minimum wage imposed on a monopsony market to result in *more* labor being hired.

3. False. Even though it faces an upward-sloping labor supply curve, the monopsonist selects the wage–employment combination that maximizes profit and pays each worker it hires the same wage.

4. False. The output market of a monopsonist may be either competitive or noncompetitive.

5. False. A monopolist pays the same wage as other firms hiring labor in a competitive input market.

6. True. The hiring rule of MRP = MFC applies to all firms.

7. False. Marginal revenue product is lower for a monopoly than a firm selling output in a perfectly competitive market because marginal revenue is less than price.

8. False. The marginal productivity theory says that people are paid according to their marginal products. Whether that is what people deserve is a question the theory does not address.

9. False. The cost-minimizing combination of inputs depends on the marginal product schedule of inputs as well as on input prices. When input prices are the same, the firm hires more of the input whose marginal revenue product curve is greater (lies farther to the right).

10. True. If the price of a complementary input falls, the amount of it bought rises. Because it is a complementary input, the demand for the other input rises, which tends to cause an increase in the price of the other input.

MULTIPLE CHOICE

1. B. The monopsonist's profit falls because the increase in the monopsonist's costs caused by hiring the extra unit of labor (the MFC) is greater than the wage paid the last worker hired ($10) and greater than the extra revenue the last worker created ($10).

2. A. Because marginal revenue declines for a monopolist as output rises and marginal revenue remains constant for a competitive firm, marginal revenue product falls more quickly for a monopolist.

3. A. MRP = $MP_L \times P$ only if output is sold in a perfectly competitive product market, and MFC = W only if labor is hired in a perfectly competitive labor market.

4. D. The cost of producing output is minimized only when $MP_L/P_L = MP_K/P_K$. Because the ratio of marginal product divided by its price is greater for labor than for capital (30/$10 = 3/$1 > 40/$20 = 2/$1), costs can be lowered by substituting labor for capital.

5. A. For both capital and labor, MP/P = 2/$1. This means that an additional dollar spent on inputs will increase output by two units. Equivalently, an additional $.50 spent on inputs will increase output by one unit.

6. A. An additional dollar spent on inputs increases output by 2 units and increases total revenue by $2. Therefore, additional output increases profit.

7. B. By hiring 1 less worker, costs fall by $10 and revenue falls by $9, leaving the firm with more profit.

8. A. An increase in the price of a complementary input decreases the demand for the other input.

9. C. Costs are minimized if inputs are hired so that MP/MFC is the same for all inputs. Two inputs are hired so that their marginal products are the same only if their marginal factor costs are the same.

10. B. Profits are maximized when $MP_L/MFC_L = 1/MR$. Because the firm is a monopsonist, P_L cannot be substituted for MFC_L in the above formula.

PROBLEMS

1. a. See the following table:

WAGE	WORKERS	MARGINAL FACTOR COST (MFC₁)	MARGINAL FACTOR COST (MFC₂)	MARGINAL REVENUE PRODUCT
$1	1	$ 1	$ 4	$ 7
2	2	3	4	6
3	3	5	4	5
4	4	7	4	4
5	5	9	9	3
6	6	11	11	2
7	7	13	13	1

The marginal factor cost equals the extra cost due to hiring an extra worker. For example, two workers have a total cost of $4 ($2 × 2); three workers have a total cost of $9 ($3 × 3). The marginal factor cost of the third worker is $9 – $4 = $5.

  b. See Figure 31.2.

FIGURE 31.2

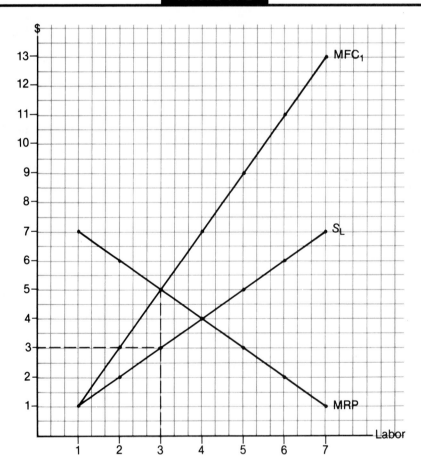

c. The firm hires labor up to the point where $MFC_1 = MRP$. This occurs at **3 workers** when $MFC_1 = MRP = \$5$. The wage is **\$3**, which is the lowest wage that must be paid in order to hire 3 workers.

d. For MFC_2, see the preceding table. Because no worker can be paid a wage less than \$4, the first 4 workers are each paid \$4 and the marginal factor cost of each worker is \$4. If the employer wants to hire the fifth worker, the wage must be increased to \$5—as is true when there is no minimum wage.

   The firm hires **4 workers** and pays a wage of **\$4**. With the \$4 minimum wage, $MFC_2 = MRP = \$4$ when 4 workers are hired.

CHAPTER 32

Discrimination and Differences in Labor Market Outcomes

Groups that participate in the labor market do not experience the same outcomes. Males and females, blacks, whites, and Hispanics earn different wages, work different jobs, and suffer unemployment at different rates. The causes of these differences are analyzed in Chapter 32. The roles of discrimination, human capital, and other factors are explored, as are current and proposed policies to eradicate labor market discrimination.

CHAPTER OUTLINE

I. Labor Force Participation
   A. Measuring Labor Force Participation
      1. The **labor force** is made up of all individuals 16 years of age or older who either have a job or are looking for one. Two groups comprise the labor force:
         a. The employed: those people who are working.
         b. The unemployed: those people who have no job but are looking for work.
      2. The **labor force participation rate** is the percentage of the population 16 and older who are in the labor force.
   B. Labor Force Participation by Gender
      1. Male labor participation rates have fallen in the twentieth century because:
         a. The percentage of the male population over the age of 65 has increased.
         b. The labor force participation rate of males over 65 has fallen dramatically.
      2. Females have lower labor force participation rates than males, but the difference between the two groups is declining. The causes of the rise in female labor force participation rates are:
         a. Lower birthrates, and thus fewer withdrawals from the labor force because of child care.
         b. Higher female wages, which have made working a more attractive option for females.
         c. A more positive attitude in society toward women who work.
         d. More time-saving devices in the home that make labor market participation easier.
         e. Increased availability of part-time employment.
II. Male–Female Pay Gap
   A. A **pay gap** is the difference in pay between two groups, usually expressed in percentage terms. The male–female pay gap based on annual earnings of full-time workers is about 30 percent. That is, average annual earnings of females are about 30 percent less than average annual earnings of males.
   B. The causes of the male–female pay gap are:

1. Women work fewer hours than men. More than 20 percent of the pay gap in average annual earnings is due to the fewer hours females work.
2. On average, men have more human capital than females.
   a. Males have more total work experience than females.
   b. Males have worked longer with their current employer than females.
   c. Males have received more on-the-job training than females.
   d. Males have slightly more formal education than females.
3. More females than males are employed in lower-paying jobs.
   a. This is true across broad occupational categories (for example, doctors versus nurses) and within occupations (lower-level accountant versus upper-level accountant).
   b. Within each job classification females typically earn 90 percent to 100 percent of what males earn in the same classification.
C. Possible causes of the concentration of females in some occupations are:
   1. Culture and Socialization: Females appear to place less emphasis on pay when making a job choice and to place more emphasis on helping others.
   2. Females have historically taken the primary responsibility for child rearing. This has restricted their job choices.
   3. Females have typically had shorter and more intermittent work lives. As a result, according to human capital theory, they have less incentive to make large investments in human capital because there is a shorter period to earn returns on the investment. For the same reason, females are less likely to enter occupations that place a premium on continuous work.
   4. The **theory of occupational crowding** asserts that females are concentrated in certain occupations because of discrimination.
      a. Employers give more training (human capital) to males than to females. As a consequence, males have more job alternatives than females.
      b. Artificial entrance requirements are constructed that discriminate against females.
      c. As a consequence of such discrimination, the supply of labor in male-intensive occupations is reduced, raising the wage, whereas the supply in the female-dominated occupations is increased, lowering the wage.
   5. Many who accept the occupational crowding theory support comparable worth as a solution. **Comparable worth** is the doctrine that each job has an intrinsic worth, independent of market forces. All jobs with the same intrinsic value have similar, or comparable, worth and should have similar pay.
      a. Opponents of comparable worth have the following criticisms:
         i. The evaluation of each job's intrinsic value is subjective.
         ii. Comparable worth ignores market factors. According to comparable worth, the pay should be the same regardless of the number of people in an occupation and regardless of the labor demand for such workers.
         iii. Comparable worth reduces the incentive for females to move to higher-paying occupations by removing the wage differential.
         iv. Increasing the pay in female occupations provides an incentive for employers to hire fewer females.
      b. Supporters of comparable worth make the following points:
         i. Market forces are already constrained by unions, laws, and other imperfections—so comparable worth would not be exceptional.
         ii. The market wage is not an accurate measure of a worker's value because female wages are artificially reduced through discrimination.
         iii. Fairness to women overrides any problems comparable worth may create in the labor market.
   6. Occupational crowding may be caused by employee discrimination.

a. **Employee discrimination** occurs when employees prefer to work with those having certain characteristics (for example, males) and demand extra pay if required to work with those having different characteristics (for example, females).

b. To avoid the added expense when workers are mixed, employers may segregate employees.

7. Occupational crowding also may be caused by customer discrimination.

a. **Customer discrimination** occurs when customers prefer output produced by members of a particular group (for example, males). The output of employees not having the characteristic desired by customers (for example, females) is less attractive to customers.

b. As a result of customer discrimination, employees without the desired characteristic sometimes avoid the occupation.

8. Within occupations, females earn less than males because a greater proportion of males are employed by higher-paying employers than are females. The higher-paying employers may hire proportionally more males because of discrimination or because males have more human capital.

D. The male–female pay gap based on average weekly earnings of full-time employees is approximately 26 percent. This gap is accounted for by the following factors:

1. About half the 26 percent pay gap in average weekly earnings is caused by males working more hours and by the greater human capital of males.

2. The other half is caused by occupational crowding and females employed by lower-paying employers.

E. The male–female pay gap has declined and will decline in the future as females accumulate more human capital relative to males through greater work experience.

III. Income Differences by Race

A. Nonwhites earn less than whites.

1. Nonwhite males earn about 25 percent less than white males.

2. Nonwhite females earn about 10 percent less than white females.

B. The causes of the racial pay gap are similar to those of the male–female pay gap.

1. Nonwhites typically have less human capital.

a. Nonwhites have less education and many have attended lower quality schools than whites.

b. Nonwhites are younger than whites and have lower labor force participation rates than whites—thus they have less job experience than whites.

c. Nonwhites have less job training than whites.

2. Nonwhites are more heavily concentrated in lower-paying jobs than are whites.

C. The white–black pay gap has declined.

1. The decline has been larger for females than for males.

2. The decline has been larger for young blacks, especially those with high education, than for older blacks.

D. Several factors have contributed to the decline of the racial pay gap.

1. More and better quality education for blacks has increased human capital among blacks.

2. Migration out of low-wage jobs in the rural South to higher-wage employment in the urban North has increased average earnings of blacks.

3. Government intervention in the labor market has reduced racial discrimination.

a. The **Equal Pay Act** (1963) requires employers to pay people without respect to race or gender. The law was not effective because employers could still refuse to hire blacks or hire them only for certain jobs.

b. The Civil Rights Act (1964) bans discrimination in both pay and employment. **Title VII of the Civil Rights Act** makes it illegal for an employer to hire, dismiss, or offer terms of employment on the basis of race, color, religion, gender, or national origin.

c. The Equal Employment Opportunity Commission (EEOC) administers both the Equal Pay Act and the Civil Rights Act. The commission can only seek voluntary compliance or encourage others to file lawsuits.

d. Executive Order 11246 (1965), signed by President Johnson, established the Office of Federal Contract Compliance Programs. This office requires that firms dealing with the federal government refrain from discrimination against women or minorities. If there is evidence of discrimination, the employer must file an affirmative-action plan. **Affirmative-action** plans are designed to increase the relative employment of women and minorities.

E. There is some reason to believe that the white–black pay gap is larger than data indicate. The labor force participation rate of blacks has declined at the same time that average income has increased. If the labor force "dropouts" had stayed in the labor force, the decline in the pay gap would have been smaller.

F. The pay gaps that exist between whites and other ethnic groups in general mirror educational differences. Those ethnic groups with pay equal to or above whites (for example, Chinese and Japanese) have more years of education than whites. Fluency in English, years in the United States, and place of education also influence the size of the pay gap.

IV. The Structure of Unemployment
   A. The **unemployment rate** measures the percentage of the labor force that is unemployed.
   B. Unemployment is not distributed evenly across groups.
      1. Blacks have about twice the unemployment rate of whites.
      2. Hispanic unemployment is 60 percent higher than that of whites.
      3. Recently, the unemployment rate of females has fallen below that of males. Before that time, females had a higher unemployment rate than males.
   C. The causes of the unemployment differences are similar to the causes of income differentials: education, occupation, and discrimination.
   D. The frequency and duration of unemployment also vary.
      1. Blacks have a higher frequency of unemployment than whites, and their periods of unemployment are longer.
      2. Females are unemployed more frequently than males, but their spells of unemployment are shorter.
   E. The female unemployment rate is now closer to the male unemployment rate than in the past for the following reasons:
      1. Women have accumulated additional human capital and thus are less vulnerable to layoffs.
      2. Women have a greater attachment to the labor market than in the past and thus less frequently experience unemployment associated with movement into and out of the labor force.
      3. Antidiscrimination laws have made females less vulnerable to discriminatory firing.
      4. Antidiscrimination laws that raise female wages have an ambiguous impact on female unemployment.
         a. By raising the wages of females relative to males, the laws have induced employers to substitute males for females and have increased female unemployment.
         b. By raising the demand for female employees, antidiscrimination laws can lower unemployment.
   F. During an economic downturn, the female unemployment rate rises more slowly than the male unemployment rate.
      1. Males are concentrated in cyclical industries where employment drops the most during an economic downturn.
      2. Females are more likely to drop out of the labor force when they become unemployed and thus not be counted as unemployed.

FILL IN THE BLANK

labor force   1. The _____ is made up of all individuals 16 or older who are employed or looking for a job.

labor force   2. The unemployment rate is the number of persons unemployed as a percentage of the _____ .

decreased, increased	3. In the last 50 years the labor force participation rate for males has _____ _____, whereas the rate for females has _____.
pay gap	4. The difference between the average earnings of two groups is called the _____.
decline	5. If women and men worked the same number of hours, the difference between the average earnings of males and females would _____.
occupational crowding	6. The theory of _____ asserts that females are denied access to certain high-paying occupations.
comparable worth	7. All jobs with the same intrinsic value—as revealed by an independent assessment—should be paid the same wage, according to the theory of _____.
Equal Pay Act	8. The _____ is legislation that requires "equal pay for equal work."
increased	9. Lower birth rates have _____ the labor force participation of females.
two	10. The unemployment rate for blacks is about _____ times the unemployment rate for whites.

TRUE OR FALSE

_____ 1. The labor force participation rate for males is greater than the rate for females.

_____ 2. The pay gap for women is about 50 percent and has remained at that level for decades.

_____ 3. The pay gap for blacks decreases with age.

_____ 4. If a worker expects to spend less time in the labor force, that person would be expected to invest more in human capital in order to earn as much as possible during the shorter working period.

_____ 5. If some occupations are open only to members of a particular group (for example, men), wages in other occupations are lower.

_____ 6. A policy of comparable worth provides incentives for more women to enter male-dominated occupations.

_____ 7. Only discrimination by employers can cause occupations to be segregated by gender.

_____ 8. The earnings of black females are closer to the earnings of white females than are the earnings of black males to white males.

_____ 9. Whites have the highest earnings of all racial or ethnic groups.

_____ 10. The Equal Employment Opportunity Commission can issue orders requiring employers to hire a certain number of minority workers if discrimination is uncovered.

MULTIPLE CHOICE

1. The labor force participation rate measures what percentage of the:
   A. population is employed.
   B. labor force is employed.
   C. population is employed or unemployed.
   D. unemployed are in the labor force.

2. Which of the following has contributed to the rise in the female labor force participation rate?
   A. higher wages for females
   B. occupational crowding
   C. higher fertility rates
   D. a larger pay gap

3. Which of the following contributes to the male–female pay gap?
   A. occupational crowding
   B. lower human capital for females
   C. fewer hours of work for females
   D. All the alternatives are correct.

4. Opponents of comparable worth argue that:
   A. wages have little impact on individual job choices.
   B. human capital has little impact on wages.
   C. differences in hours of work totally explain the pay gap between males and females.
   D. the evaluation of each job's "worth" is subjective.

5. Supporters of comparable worth argue that:
   A. the female pay gap is caused primarily by differences to human capital.
   B. wages determined in the labor market accurately reflect the relative productivity of workers.
   C. the government is unable to determine correct wages.
   D. fairness should be an important consideration in the determination of wages.

6. Which of the following is an example of customer discrimination?
   A. A customer refuses to buy poor quality products.
   B. A consumer buys pizza made only by Italians.
   C. A consumer buys only one unit of a good.
   D. A consumer buys the same goods each week.

7. Title VII of the Civil Rights Act:
   A. requires all firms to implement affirmative-action programs.
   B. applies only to firms that have contracts with the federal government.
   C. applies only to racial discrimination.
   D. outlaws racial discrimination in hiring and firing.

8. The reduction in the white-black pay gap is exaggerated because:
   A. only full-time workers are included.
   B. young workers are excluded.
   C. blacks have a much lower labor force participation rate.
   D. both males and females are included rather than just females.

9. When economic activity slows, females often:
   A. drop out of the labor force.
   B. enter the labor force.
   C. experience declining unemployment rates.
   D. switch to male-dominated occupations.

10. The Equal Pay Act, by raising the wages of females:
    A. reduces female unemployment.
    B. reduces the supply of female workers.
    C. reduces the demand for male workers.
    D. reduces the employment of females.

PROBLEMS

1. Provide the missing values in the following table.

	POPULATION (16 OR OLDER)	NUMBER EMPLOYED	NUMBER UNEMPLOYED	LABOR FORCE	UNEMPLOYMENT RATE	LABOR FORCE PARTICIPATION RATE
a.	1,000,000	400,000	100,000			
b.	300,000		33,333	100,000		
c.	5,000,000		600,000			60%
d.		150,000			25%	50%
e.	100,000		7,500		10%	

Answers

TRUE OR FALSE

1. True. Although the labor force participation rate of women has been rising lately, it is still less than the rate for men.

2. False. The pay gap for females is about 30 percent and has been declining in recent decades.

3. False. The pay gap for blacks is smaller for younger workers than for older workers.

4. False. The shorter time in the labor force reduces the time during which the worker can recoup the costs of human capital and thus makes investment in human capital less profitable.

5. True. Females, excluded from some occupations, shift the labor supply curves of the other occupations outward and lower the wage.

6. False. Implementing a policy of comparable worth reduces the wage differential between male- and female-dominated occupations and thus provides less incentive for females to switch occupations.

7. False. Employee or customer discrimination also can cause occupations to be segregated.

8. True. The pay gap is smaller for black females than for black males.

9. False. Certain groups—Chinese and Japanese—have higher average earnings than whites.

10. False. The EEOC has no enforcement powers.

MULTIPLE CHOICE

1. C. The labor force participation rate is the percentage of the population that is in the labor force (that is, either employed or unemployed).

2. A. Higher female wages have induced more females to enter the labor force.

3. D. Females work fewer hours, have less human capital, and are concentrated in lower-paying jobs than are males—each of which causes females to earn less than males.

4. D. Opponents of comparable worth assert that the evaluation of jobs, which is essential to a program of comparable worth, is a subjective process.

5. D. Supporters of comparable worth believe that fairness should be considered when wages are set.

6. B. Customer discrimination occurs when consumers prefer the output of workers having a particular characteristic.

7. D. Title VII of the Civil Rights Act makes it illegal to discriminate in hiring or firing on the basis of race, color, gender, religion, or national origin.

8. C. Because some black workers who otherwise would earn low wages have dropped out of the labor force, the decline in the pay gap is exaggerated.

9. A. Females are more likely to drop out of the labor market when they become unemployed. As a result, female unemployment rates do not rise as much as male unemployment rates when the economy slows.

10. D. By raising the wages of females relative to males, the Equal Pay Act makes females less attractive to hire and reduces their employment.

PROBLEMS

1. Filling in the blanks requires three equations:

$$\text{labor force} = \text{number employed} + \text{number unemployed}$$

$$\text{unemployment rate} = \frac{\text{number unemployed}}{\text{labor force}} \times 100$$

$$\text{labor force participation rate} = \frac{\text{labor force}}{\text{population (16 or older)}} \times 100$$

	POPULATION (16 OR OLDER)	NUMBER EMPLOYED	NUMBER UNEMPLOYED	LABOR FORCE	UNEMPLOYMENT RATE	LABOR FORCE PARTICIPATION RATE
a.	1,000,000	400,000	100,000	**500,000**	**20%**	**50%**
b.	300,000	**66,667**	33,333	100,000	**33%**	**33%**
c.	5,000,000	**2,400,000**	600,000	**3,000,000**	**20%**	60%
d.	**400,000**	150,000	**50,000**	**200,000**	25%	**50%**
e.	100,000	**67,500**	7,500	**75,000**	10%	**75%**

CHAPTER 33

Interest, Rent, and Profit

Wages and salaries—the focus of Chapters 30, 31, and 32—are the primary source of income for most people. But there are other kinds of income too—interest, rent, and profit.

Parties that lend funds to others receive interest. Land and other resources generate economic rent. And owners of businesses receive profit—the residual that remains after production costs are subtracted from total revenue. Chapter 33 explains how each type of nonwage income is determined and explores changes over time in the shares of income going to interest, rent, and profit.

CHAPTER OUTLINE

I. Interest
   A. Definitions:
      1. The **interest rate** is the price paid for the use of lenders' funds, expressed as a percentage.
      2. **Interest income** is the payment, expressed in dollars, received by lenders for the use of their funds.
   B. Interest rates are determined by means of the loanable funds model. The **loanable funds model** explains the determination of interest rates in terms of the supply of and the demand for loanable funds.
      1. The Demand for Loanable Funds
         a. The demand for loanable funds is the sum of the demands for loans by consumers, producers, and governments.
            i. Consumers demand loanable funds because of a **positive time preference**, which is a preference to consume now rather than later. Consumers also borrow to pay for the production of human capital.
            ii. Producers want to borrow because of **roundabout production**. Producing capital first and then using it to produce consumption goods takes more time than producing consumption goods immediately, without the capital. But because the capital is productive, its use generates a greater volume of consumption goods.
            iii. The government borrows whenever its expenditures exceed its revenues.
         b. The quantity of loanable funds demanded is inversely related to the interest rate, because the higher the rate of interest the more the borrower sacrifices to obtain the loan.
      2. The Supply of Loanable Funds
         a. The quantity of loanable funds supplied is the volume made available for loans by consumers, businesses, and government.

b. The quantity of loanable funds supplied varies directly with the interest rate, because lenders always have alternative uses for their funds.

3. The equilibrium interest rate is the interest rate that makes the quantity of loanable funds demanded equal to the quantity supplied.

4. Real versus Nominal Interest Rates

a. If lenders begin to expect higher inflation, they are less willing to make loans because they will be repaid with dollars that have less purchasing power. This appears as a leftward shift of the supply of loanable funds.

b. If borrowers begin to expect higher inflation, they are more willing to borrow because they will be able to repay the loan with dollars that are worth less than the dollars they borrow. This appears as a rightward shift of the demand for loanable funds.

c. The **nominal interest rate** is the interest rate measured in terms of the dollars the borrower actually pays. Expectations of higher inflation increase the nominal interest rate.

d. The **real interest rate** is the nominal interest rate minus the expected rate of inflation. If each 1 percent of expected inflation increases the nominal interest rate by exactly 1 percent, the real rate of interest does not depend on the expected rate of inflation.

C. The structure of interest rates refers to the array of interest rates that exists at any particular time. The factors that influence interest rates are:

1. The Length of the Loan

a. The interest rate on a long-term loan reflects the expected rates of interest between the time the loan is made and the time it is due. If short-term rates are expected to be higher in the future than they are now, the current long-term rate is above the current short-term rate.

b. Because making a long-term loan reduces the flexibility of lenders, long-term rates generally are above short-term rates.

2. The **risk of default** refers to the probability that a borrower will be unable to repay either the interest or the amount borrowed. The greater the default risk, the higher the interest rate.

3. Administrative costs are approximately the same regardless of the size of the loan, which means that administrative costs *per dollar* fall with the size of the loan. For that reason, larger loans tend to have lower interest rates.

D. Interest rates have a significant impact on the allocation of capital. As interest rates rise, only the more productive uses of capital can afford the higher rates.

E. **Usury laws** impose a legal ceiling on interest rates. If the equilibrium interest rate is above the legal limit set by a usury law, the following are expected:

1. A shortage of loanable funds.

2. Nonprice rationing to allocate the available funds. Favoritism, discrimination, and similar methods are possible.

3. Black market loans at rates above the legal limit.

4. The failure of loanable funds to flow to the most productive user.

II. Rents

A. **Pure economic rent** is the payment received by a resource whose supply is fixed.

B. The first theory of rent was developed by David Ricardo to explain land rents.

1. The supply curve of land is vertical under the assumption that the quantity of land is fixed.

2. The demand curve for land is downward sloping. The demand for land is a derived demand; it depends on the demand for the output produced on the land.

3. The rent on land depends entirely on the demand for land. Thus, a high rent on land derives from a high demand for the output produced on the land.

4. Because the supply of land is fixed, a tax on land has no impact on its supply. The tax is paid entirely by the landowner. At various times many economists (including John Stuart Mill and Henry George) have proposed taxing land heavily.

C. The theory of land rent can be expanded to other resources. Any resource earns economic rent when it is paid more than its opportunity cost.

III. Profit
    A. **Economic profit** is the residual after all implicit and explicit costs have been subtracted from total revenue.
    B. There are three sources of economic profit:
        1. If a firm has monopoly power it can increase the price it charges by reducing the output it produces. This increases the chance of earning a profit. Barriers to entry affect the firm's chance of earning economic profit in the long run.
        2. The future is uncertain. Firms adept (or lucky) at anticipating events that influence costs or demand earn more than other firms.
        3. Firms able through innovation to develop new products that appeal to consumers may earn an economic profit.
    C. Profit plays three important roles in an economy:
        1. Profit improves the allocation of resources by providing a signal as to where resources are most highly valued and an incentive for resource owners to move the resources to their most valuable use.
        2. Profit provides an incentive for resource owners to minimize the costs of production.
        3. Profit provides an incentive for firms and individuals to develop new products and new production techniques.

IV. The functional distribution of income charts the amount of income derived from wages, rent, interest, and profit.
    A. Government definitions of these various income categories do not correspond exactly to the definitions of economists.
    B. The major characteristics of the functional distribution of income in the United States as defined by the government are:
        1. The share of income going to profit is less than 10 percent.
        2. About 75 percent of all income is employee compensation. This has increased from about 55 percent in 1900.
        3. Rental income has fallen steadily as a percent of total income over the past 80 years.
        4. In the 1980s, interest was the fastest growing share of income.

FILL IN THE BLANK

interest income

1. The fastest growing share of income in the 1980s was _____ _____.

Economic rent

2. _____ was originally considered a payment that only land receives, but in fact all resources receive some.

vertical

3. A resource receives pure economic rent if its supply curve is _____ _____.

economic profit

4. When total revenue exceeds explicit and implicit costs, the difference is called _____.

75

5. Employee compensation accounts for about _____ percent of all income.

demand

6. Borrowers influence the _____ curve in the loanable funds market.

supply

7. Lenders influence the _____ curve in the loanable funds market.

real

roundabout

usury

8. The nominal interest rate less the expected rate of inflation equals the _____ rate of interest.

9. Producing capital in order to increase the future production of consumer goods is called _____ production.

10. The laws that place a legal limit on interest rates are _____ laws.

TRUE OR FALSE

_____ 1. The supply of loanable funds is perfectly inelastic (that is, the supply curve is vertical).

_____ 2. Individuals must be paid to postpone consumption.

_____ 3. Roundabout production is valuable only with physical capital.

_____ 4. Usury laws increase the role of noneconomic factors in the allocation of loanable funds.

_____ 5. Under most circumstances, long-term interest rates are below short-term interest rates.

_____ 6. Interest rates influence only the allocation of loanable funds and have no impact on the allocation of resources.

_____ 7. Only land earns economic rent.

_____ 8. Henry George's "single tax" was a tax on profit.

_____ 9. Accounting costs cause small loans to be charged a higher interest rate than large loans.

_____ 10. Profit is about 25 percent of total income.

MULTIPLE CHOICE

1. Pure economic rent exists only if:
   A. demand is perfectly elastic.
   B. demand is perfectly inelastic.
   C. supply is perfectly elastic.
   D. supply is perfectly inelastic.

2. Mary, a musician, muses: "I can't believe they pay me $10 an hour to teach piano; I'd do it for nothing!" On the basis of this information:
   A. Mary is earning no economic rent from teaching piano.
   B. Mary is earning no wages from teaching piano.
   C. All Mary's earnings from teaching piano are economic rent.
   D. All Mary's earnings from teaching piano are interest.

3. Which of the following is *not* a source of profit?
   A. monopoly power
   B. expected inflation
   C. uncertainty
   D. innovation

4. If lenders, but not borrowers, begin to expect a lower rate of inflation:
   A. the nominal interest rate and the total amount lent fall.
   B. the nominal interest rate and the total amount lent rise.
   C. the nominal interest rate rises and the total amount lent falls.
   D. the nominal interest rate falls and the total amount lent rises.

5. Wages are partly economic rent if:
   A. the individual is earning more than his or her opportunity cost.
   B. the individual is involved in agriculture.
   C. the wage paid is the equilibrium wage.
   D. the individual owns a parcel of land.

6. In which of these circumstances is the real interest rate highest?
   A. expected inflation rate = 5 percent, nominal interest rate = 7 percent
   B. expected inflation rate = 8 percent, nominal interest rate = 8 percent
   C. expected inflation rate = 1 percent, nominal interest rate = 5 percent
   D. expected inflation rate = 13 percent, nominal interest rate = 16 percent

7. Positive time preference refers to which of the following?
   A. The government prefers to pay its expenses with tax revenue rather than with borrowed funds.
   B. Firms can increase their productive capacity by buying capital.
   C. Consumers prefer to consume now rather than later.
   D. The market usually produces more in the future than it does now.

8. The interest rate compensates:
   A. firms for roundabout production.
   B. savers for postponing consumption.
   C. borrowers for unexpected inflation.
   D. consumers for purchases of human capital.

9. Which of the following promotes higher market interest rates?
   A. A company with outstanding debts announces it has lost a major lawsuit and is contemplating bankruptcy.
   B. The government announces that the rate of inflation is expected to be significantly higher in the future because of previously unforeseen government expenditures.
   C. The government outlaws all loans of less than ten years.
   D. All alternatives are correct.

10. Landowners pay all of a property tax if:
    A. the land is not fully employed.
    B. the supply curve of land is vertical.
    C. the demand curve for land is vertical.
    D. the demand curve for the output produced on the land is downward sloping.

Answers

TRUE OR FALSE

1. False. The loanable funds supply curve is upward sloping, not vertical. A higher interest rate increases the quantity of loanable funds supplied.

2. True. In general, consumers prefer to consume now rather than later. To postpone consumption requires compensation.

3. False. Roundabout production also applies to human capital. Using resources now to produce human capital makes it possible to produce even more output (and earn more income) in the future.

4. True. By placing an upper limit on interest rates, a usury law reduces the role of interest rates in the allocation of loanable funds and makes noneconomic factors of greater importance.

5. False. Normally, long-term rates are above short-term rates because lenders prefer the greater flexibility associated with a short-term loan.

6. False. By influencing the allocation of loanable funds, the interest rate influences the allocation of capital.

7. False. Any resource earning more than its opportunity cost earns economic rent.

8. False. The "single tax" was a tax on the pure economic rent of land.

9. True. Because accounting costs are approximately the same regardless of the size of the loan, the interest rate on small loans must be higher than on large loans to cover the costs.

10. False. Profit is less than 10 percent of total income.

MULTIPLE CHOICE

1. D. Pure economic rent exists only if the supply of the resource is perfectly inelastic (that is, the supply curve is vertical).

2. C. Because Mary would be willing to teach piano for nothing, all the income she earns is considered economic rent.

3. B. Profit is created by monopoly power, uncertainty, and innovation.

4. D. The supply curve of loanable funds shifts to the right, lowering the nominal rate of interest and increasing the total amount of funds loaned.

5. A. Economic rent is earned any time a resource is paid more than its opportunity cost.

6. C. The real rate of interest equals the nominal rate minus the expected rate of inflation.

7. C. Positive time preference refers to the preference that consumers have for consumption now over consumption in the future.

8. B. Because consumers prefer consumption now rather than later (that is, have a positive time preference), they must be compensated for postponing their consumption.

9. D. Greater risk of default, expectations of higher inflation, and longer-term loans each tend to cause interest rates to rise.

10. B. If the supply curve for land is vertical, the landowner pays all of a property tax because the tax has no impact on the amount of land supplied.

CHAPTER 34

Poverty and the Distribution of Income

The market system is often criticized because of the distribution of income it creates. Chapter 34 discusses how to measure the distribution of income, provides data on current and past distributions, and looks at what factors contribute to the distribution of income. Although no economist can prescribe the correct income distribution, this information contributes to an informed discussion of the issue.

Poverty, closely related to income distribution, is also defined and described. This chapter closes with an evaluation of current and proposed policies to alter the distribution of income and to reduce poverty.

CHAPTER OUTLINE

I. The Distribution of Income
   A. Measuring Income Inequality
      1. Data on families are ranked according to income and divided into five equal groups called quintiles. The first quintile contains the poorest 20 percent of all families; the last quintile contains the 20 percent of families with the highest incomes.
      2. The percent of total income earned by the families in each quintile is calculated.
      3. A **Lorenz curve** is a diagram illustrating the cumulative distribution of income.
         a. The Lorenz curve is constructed by plotting the percentage of total families and the percentage of total income received, beginning with the lowest-income quintile. Successive quintiles and their percentages are added until 100 percent of the families receive 100 percent of the income.
         b. If all families received identical incomes, the Lorenz curve would be a diagonal line.
         c. How far the actual Lorenz curve is from the diagonal indicates the degree of income inequality. The closer to the diagonal, the greater the income equality.
      4. Income Inequality Comparisons
         a. Income in the United States was more equally distributed in 1990 than in 1929. Almost all this decline in inequality had occurred by 1950.
         b. Inequality in the United States is greater than in Japan but less than in Honduras. Industrialized and centrally planned economies tend to have a greater degree of income equality than do less-developed and capitalistic economies.
   B. Why Incomes Differ
      1. An obvious cause of income inequality is differences in wage rates.
      2. Differences in the hours worked also contribute to income differences.
      3. Differences in the number of workers in a family contribute to income inequality.

4. Nonwage income—rent, interest, and profit—is less equally distributed than wage income because the source of the nonwage income—wealth—is highly concentrated.

C. The Effect of Taxation and Transfers on the Distribution of Income

   1. Because taxes overall are approximately proportional, the after-tax distribution of income is about the same as the pretax distribution.

   2. Most transfer payments have a **means test**: families are eligible only if their incomes are less than a certain level. Transfer payments tend to make the distribution of income more equal.

D. How Much Income Inequality Is Desirable?

   1. Complete income equality is probably not desirable.

     a. If all workers are guaranteed the same income, they have less incentive to perform well, to undertake unusual tasks, or take risks.

     b. It is less likely that resources are used efficiently if all incomes are the same because users of resources have less incentive to be efficient.

   2. Making no effort to improve the distribution of income also may be undesirable because it condemns to poverty many individuals—such as the very young, aged, and handicapped—who lack sufficient marketable skills.

   3. How income is redistributed has important impacts on the economy. There is a trade-off between greater incentives to be productive and greater equality.

   4. A distinction must be made between equality of opportunities—providing each person with the same chance to succeed—and equality of outcomes—ensuring that everyone has the same income.

II. Poverty

A. Definitions of Poverty

   1. Poverty can be defined in relative terms (for example, the 20 percent of the population with the lowest incomes). A relative poverty definition means that poverty can never be eliminated.

   2. An absolute definition of poverty sets a poverty line and classifies anyone below that line as poor. A **poverty line** is a level of income below which a family is classified as poor. It is based on the cost of buying the goods that constitute a minimally acceptable standard of living.

   3. The definition of poverty in the United States is an absolute definition.

     a. The first poverty line was established in 1964. It was set at three times the cost of buying the economy food plan, adjusted for family size. The poverty line is adjusted annually to reflect the change in the Consumer Price Index.

     b. Some believe the poverty line is too low (that is, fewer people are classified as poor than truly are poor) because extraordinary expenses make it difficult for some families with incomes above the poverty line to achieve a basic standard of living.

     c. Others believe that the poverty line is too high (that is, more families are classified as poor than truly are poor). Because in-kind transfers and the rental value of owner-occupied housing are not included in the income measure, some families have a higher standard of living than their incomes would indicate. **In-kind transfers** are payments in goods and services (for example, medical care and public housing) rather than dollars.

B. Who Are The Poor?

   1. There are about 34 million people, or 13.5 percent of the population, living below the poverty line in the United States. If taxes, in-kind transfers, and the imputed rent on home equity are included, the poverty rate falls to 9.8 percent.

   2. Characteristics of the Poor

     a. The poverty rate for blacks is about three times that for whites.

     b. Poverty is least likely in married-couple families and most likely in female-headed families.

     c. The poverty rate for children under 15 is over 20 percent, the highest of any age group, whereas the rate for those 65 and older is about 12 percent. The poverty rate for the elderly has declined greatly over the last 25 years, primarily because of increased social spending on the elderly.

3. Trends in Poverty
   a. From 1959 to 1969, the poverty rate fell from 22 percent to 12 percent because of strong economic growth.
   b. During the 1970s the poverty rate generally held constant.
   c. The poverty rate was higher in the 1980s. Contributing to the increase were:
      i. A severe recession at the beginning of the decade.
      ii. An increase in the incidence of female-headed households.
      iii. The slow growth of wages paid to low-skilled workers during the decade.
      iv. Reduced antipoverty spending.

C. Transfers and Poverty
   1. Some economists argue that transfer payments to the poor increase poverty because they:
      a. Reduce the incentive to work.
      b. Often caused families to break up; in the past, frequently only female-headed families were eligible for support.
   2. Other economists, conceding that these effects occur, argue nevertheless that transfer payments are valuable antipoverty tools.

D. Conflicting Views of Poverty
   1. Some hold the view that poverty is caused by the poor not taking full advantage of their labor market skills. To encourage participation in the labor market, governments have recently started workfare programs. **Workfare** requires low-income individuals to enter the labor market to be eligible for government support.
   2. Others hold that poverty is caused primarily by the inability of the poor to work because of poor health, disability, and similar factors. Workfare is of little value in these circumstances.

E. Evidence indicates that the majority of the poor are poor temporarily because of poor health, job loss, and the like. Another segment, however, is chronically poor.

III. Major Antipoverty Programs
   A. Employment and Training Programs
      1. The intent of training programs is to provide participants with sufficient employable skills with which to escape poverty. Most programs have failed because of insufficient training or training in inappropriate skills.
      2. The Job Training Partnership Act (JTPA), enacted in 1982, involves the participation of local firms to identify needed skills before training begins.
      3. The federal government can serve as the employer of last resort. But such programs, critics claim, are not productive or merely replace jobs elsewhere in the economy.

   B. Transfer Programs
      1. **Social insurance** refers to transfer programs based on some eligibility criteria other than income (for example, age or unemployment). The major social insurance programs are:
         a. Social Security and Medicare
            i. Old Age, Survivors, and Disability Insurance (OASDI) was established in 1935. Its primary beneficiaries are the retired over 62, disabled workers, and their spouses and children.
            ii. Medicare was established in 1965 to provide health care for the retired and disabled.
            iii. Both programs are financed by a payroll tax imposed equally on the employer and the employee. There is a maximum earnings level beyond which no additional taxes are owed.
            iv. Benefits are determined by Congress. Currently the monthly check and the maximum taxable earnings are adjusted annually for inflation. Because of the expected large increase in retirees as the postwar baby-boom generation grows old, future taxes may need to be increased.
         b. Unemployment insurance is paid to unemployed workers who satisfy state eligibility requirements. The program is financed by a state payroll tax on employers.

2. **Public assistance** (welfare) refers to means-tested transfer programs.
   a. Aid to Families with Dependent Children (AFDC) is a joint federal, state, and local program to aid low-income families. Support levels are set by the states, with the federal government paying just over half the cost. In the past this program was available only to female-headed households, which encouraged family breakups, but that requirement was dropped in 1988.
   b. Supplementary Social Income (SSI) is a federal payment to the low-income aged, the blind, and the disabled.
   c. In-kind benefits are noncash benefits. Examples include medicaid, public housing, and food stamps.

IV. Negative Income Tax
   A. A **negative income tax** program provides low-income families a cash payment that is inversely related to the family's income from other sources.
      1. The program sets a guaranteed annual income, which is the payment the family receives if it has no income.
      2. The program also sets an **implicit tax rate**, which is the rate at which benefits are reduced as income is earned. If the implicit tax rate is 66 percent, the family loses $.66 of benefits for every dollar earned.
      3. The **break-even income** is the level of earnings at which the payment from the government falls to zero. It equals the guaranteed annual income divided by the implicit tax rate.
   B. Those in favor of the negative income tax believe that it would be easier to administer and would provide more uniform benefits across states than does the current welfare system.
   C. The negative income tax creates work disincentives.
      1. By guaranteeing a minimum income, the incentive to work is reduced.
      2. By reducing benefits when income is earned, the effective wage is reduced. Reducing the implicit tax rate increases the incentive to work by increasing the effective wage but raises the break-even level of income.

FILL IN THE BLANK

Lorenz

1. The curvature of the _____ curve indicates the degree of income inequality.

means

2. A _____ test limits government benefits to those whose incomes are below a specified level.

in-kind

3. A(n) _____ transfer is the transfer of goods and services rather than money.

65 and older

4. In the past two decades, the poverty rate has declined most dramatically for the age group _____.

taxes

5. Because they are proportional overall, _____ have little impact on the distribution of income.

absolute

6. The U.S. government's definition of poverty is based on the concept of _____ poverty.

Workfare

7. _____ requires those receiving public assistance to enter the labor force.

social insurance

8. Transfer programs that pay people regardless of their incomes are called _____.

poverty line

9. The income level that divides the poor from the nonpoor is called the _____ .

break-even

10. The income level at which payments under a negative income-tax program fall to zero is called the _____ income.

TRUE OR FALSE

_____ 1. The distribution of income is little changed when taxes and transfer payments are considered.

_____ 2. The distribution of income is less equal today than it was 60 to 70 years ago.

_____ 3. Social Security is financed by an income tax.

_____ 4. Wealth is less equally distributed than is income.

_____ 5. In general, developed economies have greater income equality than less-developed economies.

_____ 6. Programs to reduce income inequality tend to increase output.

_____ 7. Evidence indicates that most of the poor are chronically poor.

_____ 8. Children under 15 have the highest poverty rate of all age groups.

_____ 9. Transfer payments to the poor may increase poverty.

_____ 10. Aid to Families with Dependent Children is the largest transfer program in the United States.

MULTIPLE CHOICE

1. If income is distributed evenly, the Lorenz curve is:
   A. vertical.
   B. horizontal.
   C. diagonal.
   D. broken.

2. Which of the following can be determined using a Lorenz curve?
   A. the number of families in the top quintile of the income distribution.
   B. the percentage of total income received by families in the top quintile of the income distribution.
   C. the average income in the economy
   D. the average income of families in the bottom quintile of the income distribution.

3. A progressive income tax makes the Lorenz curve:
   A. less curved.
   B. more downward sloping.
   C. shift downward.
   D. shift to the right.

4. The U.S. poverty line is based on:
   A. one-half the median family income adjusted for changed in taxes and transfer payments.
   B. the income that could be earned if one worker worked full time at the minimum wage.
   C. the income earned by the poorest 20 percent of families.
   D. three times the cost of buying the economy food plan adjusted for changes in the average level of prices.

5. Equality of outcomes means:
   A. all individuals receive the same income.
   B. all individuals receive the same education.
   C. all individuals have the same opportunity to attend school.
   D. all individuals have the same job.

6. Which of the following is an absolute of definition of poverty?
   A. half the average income
   B. the income earned by the poorest 10 percent of the families
   C. the cost of buying a particular bundle of goods
   D. All the alternatives are correct.

7. Which of the following is *not* an in-kind payment?
   A. public housing
   B. medicaid
   C. Social Security
   D. food stamps

8. Which of the following is social insurance?
   A. food stamps
   B. unemployment insurance
   C. public housing
   D. medicaid

9. Which of the following underlies the belief that the number counted as poor in the United States is exaggerated?
   A. Social Security is paid in cash.
   B. High medical expenses are owed by some.
   C. Some families have more than one worker.
   D. In-kind transfers are not counted as income.

10. The poverty rate is lower than average for families headed by someone with which of the following characteristics?
    A. female
    B. works less than full time
    C. nonwhite
    D. aged 65 or older

PROBLEMS

1. a. Provide the missing values in the following table.

QUINTILE	CUMULATIVE PERCENT OF FAMILIES	PERCENT OF TOTAL INCOME	CUMULATIVE PERCENT OF TOTAL INCOME
First	_____	5	_____
Second	_____	10	_____
Third	_____	15	_____
Fourth	_____	30	_____
Fifth	_____	40	_____

b. Draw a Lorenz curve in Figure 34.1 using data from the preceding table.

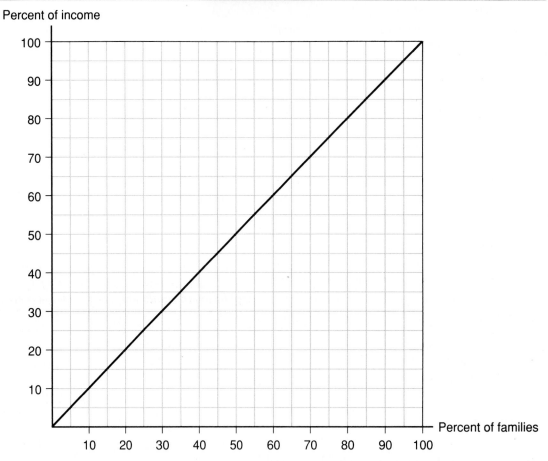

FIGURE 34.1

Percent of income

Percent of families

2. Assume a negative income tax is implemented with a guaranteed minimum income of $5,000 and an implicit tax rate of 50 percent. Provide the missing values in the following table.

EARNED INCOME	SUBSIDY	TOTAL INCOME
$ 0	_____	_____
1,000	_____	$5,500
2,000	_____	_____
3,000	$3,500	_____
4,000	_____	_____
5,000	_____	$7,500
6,000	_____	_____
7,000	_____	_____
8,000	$1,000	_____
9,000	_____	_____
10,000	_____	_____

3. The following are characteristics of alternative negative income-tax programs. Provide the missing values.

	GUARANTEED MINIMUM INCOME	IMPLICIT TAX RATE	BREAK-EVEN INCOME
a.	$ 5,000	50%	_____
b.	10,000	50	_____
c.	4,000	33	
d.	_____	25	$12,000
e.	6,000	_____	$18,000

Answers

TRUE OR FALSE

1. False. The consideration of taxes and transfer payments makes the distribution of income more equal.

2. False. Income is actually distributed more equally today than it was in the first half of this century.

3. False. Social Security is financed by a payroll tax—a tax on wages.

4. True. Wealth is much less equally distributed than income in the United States.

5. True. Developed economies typically have greater income equality than less-developed economies.

6. False. By imposing taxes on some so that income can be redistributed, the incentive to be productive is reduced.

7. False. Evidence indicates that most people in poverty are poor temporarily; only a small minority are chronically poor.

8. True. More than 20 percent of children under 15 live in poverty.

9. True. Because transfer programs may induce people to work less and may cause families to split, poverty rates may rise because of them.

10. False. The largest transfer program in the United States is Social Security, which transfers more than ten times as much to the elderly as Aid to Families with Dependent Children transfers to poor families.

MULTIPLE CHOICE

1. C. The Lorenz curve lies along the diagonal when income is distributed evenly.

2. B. The Lorenz curve reveals the *percentage* of income received by various quintiles of families.

3. A. A progressive income tax distributes incomes more equally and makes the Lorenz curve less curved.

4. D. The poverty line, first defined in 1964, was three times the economy food plan. Annually, the dollar amount is adjusted for changes in prices.

5. A. Equality of outcomes occurs when all individuals experience the same outcomes (that is, receive the same income).

6. C. An absolute definition of poverty is one stated in terms of the amount of money required to maintain some minimum standard of living.

7. C. Social Security is a money payment.

8. B. Because unemployment insurance is available regardless of income, it is social insurance.

9. D. In-kind transfers are not counted when measuring poverty, but they do improve standards of living.

10. D. Families headed by someone 65 or older have lower poverty rates than average.

PROBLEMS

1. a.

QUINTILE	CUMULATIVE PERCENT OF FAMILIES	PERCENT OF TOTAL INCOME	CUMULATIVE PERCENT OF TOTAL INCOME
First	20	5	5
Second	40	10	15
Third	60	15	30
Fourth	80	30	60
Fifth	100	40	100

b. See Figure 34.2.

FIGURE 34.2

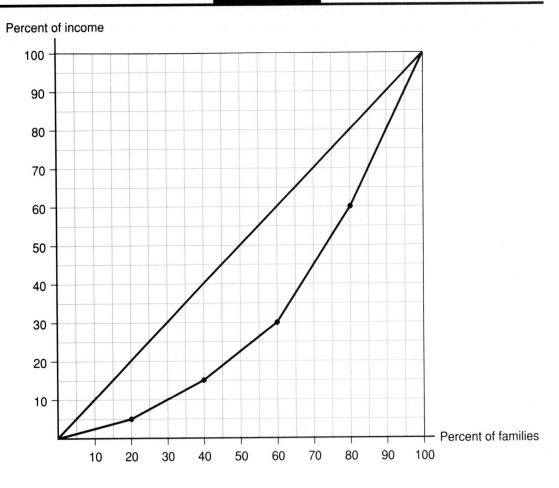

Percent of income

2. The subsidy equals $5,000 less 50 percent of earned income. For example, when earnings are $4,000, the subsidy is $5,000 – (.5 x $4,000) = $5,000 – $2,000 = $3,000. Total income is earned income plus the subsidy.

EARNED INCOME	SUBSIDY	TOTAL INCOME
$ 0	$5,000	$ 5,000
1,000	4,500	5,500
2,000	4,000	6,000
3,000	3,500	6,500
4,000	3,000	7,000
5,000	2,500	7,500
6,000	2,000	8,000
7,000	1,500	8,500
8,000	1,000	9,000
9,000	500	9,500
10,000	0	10,000

3. The missing values can be calculated using the formula:

$$\text{break-even income} = \frac{\text{guaranteed minimum income}}{\text{implicit tax rate}}$$

	GUARANTEED MINIMUM INCOME	IMPLICIT TAX RATE	BREAK-EVEN INCOME
a.	$ 5,000	50%	$10,000
b.	10,000	50	20,000
c.	4,000	33	12,000
d.	3,000	25	12,000
e.	6,000	33	18,000

CHAPTER 35

Externalities, the Environment, and Nonrenewable Natural Resources

In certain circumstances, markets fail to allocate resources optimally. Chapter 35 focuses on one of the major causes of this situation—externalities. External benefits and costs are defined and explained. This chapter also looks at the most common example of external costs—pollution—and at public policies designed to protect the environment. The chapter closes with an analysis of the economics of nonrenewable resources.

CHAPTER OUTLINE

I. Externalities (or Spillovers)
    A. **Externalities** occur when the actions of consumers or producers affect others who are not part of the market. They are a cause of market failure.
    B. External Benefits
        1. **External benefits (positive externalities)** are gains that third parties receive, without payment, as a result of the consumption or production of others.
        2. **Private benefits** are benefits received by those consuming or producing a good. The market demand curve is an indicator of private benefits because buyers of goods consider only the benefits they receive when making a purchase decision.
        3. **Social benefits** are private benefits plus external benefits.
        4. Because external benefits are ignored in the purchase decision, resources are underallocated to the production of goods that create external benefits. To correct for the underallocation of resources, subsidies can be given either to consumers or producers of the good in order to increase the equilibrium output.
    C. External Costs
        1. **External costs (negative externalities)** are injuries imposed on third parties, without compensation, as a result of the consumption or production decisions of others.
        2. **Private costs** are costs incurred by those producing or consuming the good. The market supply curve is based on private costs because those are the only costs the producer pays.
        3. **Social costs** are the sum of private costs and external costs.
        4. Because not all costs are considered when making the production decision, the market overallocates resources to the production of goods that create external costs. Also, the prices of the goods are too low for optimum allocation of resources.
        5. A solution is to increase the costs to producers through taxation or regulation. Shifting the external costs from third parties back to those directly responsible for the costs is **internalizing costs.**

II. The Environment
   A. Some Background
      1. Consumers, producers, and the government all create pollution.
      2. The Environmental Protection Agency (EPA) is responsible for monitoring the environment and for enforcing the major environmental laws.
      3. In general, pollution levels have declined since 1981. Because of the introduction of unleaded gasoline and catalytic converters, lead pollution has decreased by 85 percent.
      4. Ozone is the pollutant most often in violation of EPA standards.
      5. Pollution standards and compliance deadlines are set by Congress.
   B. Cost-Benefit Analysis
      1. **Cost-benefit analysis** is a framework for comparing the costs and benefits of a particular activity. It can be used to determine the optimum amounts of pollution control.
      2. The benefits of lower pollution include better health, improved recreation facilities, reduced crop damage, and additional wildlife. The marginal benefit of lower pollution declines as pollution is reduced.
      3. The cost of reduced pollution is the output that is sacrificed by deploying resources for environmental purposes. The marginal cost of pollution reduction rises because the pollution easiest to eliminate is eliminated first.
      4. The optimal amount of pollution control is the amount for which the marginal benefit of lower pollution equals the marginal cost.
         a. Until this point is reached, the benefit from an incremental reduction in pollution exceeds the cost.
         b. Beyond this point, the cost of a further reduction in pollution exceeds the benefit.
      5. The application of cost-benefit analysis to a particular activity is often hampered by imprecise estimates of the costs and benefits.
   C. Ways to Reduce Pollution
      1. Voluntary compliance appeals to the social conscience of individuals and firms that pollute. A major problem is that firms that comply experience higher costs than competitors that do not comply.
      2. Direct regulation involves the government mandating certain actions (for example, catalytic converters). Often direct regulation is not cost effective. A policy is **cost effective** when it is the least costly method of achieving a particular goal. One reason direct regulation is often not cost effective is that it is tied to current technologies.
      3. Effluent fees are a market-based strategy. An **effluent fee** is a tax or charge on each unit of pollution emitted into the environment.
         a. Such a policy makes pollution costly, provides an incentive to employ the optimum amount of pollution control, and encourages firms to seek a cost-effective method of reducing pollution.
         b. A difficulty connected with effluent fees is that they require continuous monitoring of pollution levels, which represents an added cost of the policy.
      4. An output tax is levied directly on the output produced by the polluting firm. Although this method does not require continuous monitoring of pollution, it provides no incentive for firms to adopt less-polluting methods of production.
      5. Subsidizing pollution control involves the government paying part of the cost of buying pollution-control equipment. Such a policy contains certain shortcomings.
         a. Unless the policy is compulsory, firms can avoid the cost of reducing pollution by not buying the subsidized equipment.
         b. The policy passes on to taxpayers the costs of reducing pollution rather than requiring the polluter and the consumers of the polluter's output to pay the costs of the pollution reduction.
         c. Subsidies may induce firms to buy excessive amounts of pollution-control devices rather than choosing more efficient methods of pollution control.
      6. If property rights are assigned to consumers, polluters can be sued for damages, which provides an incentive to reduce pollution. Problems include costly and time-consuming litigation and proving who the actual polluter is.

7. Firms could be sold pollution rights. A **pollution right** entitles its bearer to emit one unit of pollutant.
    a. By limiting the amount of pollution rights, pollution levels can be set at the optimal level.
    b. The sale of pollution rights yields revenue for the government.
    c. Firms have an incentive to reduce pollution in order to avoid the expense of buying pollution rights.
    d. Pollution is reduced in a cost-effective manner. The firm has an incentive to reduce pollution whenever this is less costly than buying a pollution right.
8. The EPA has adopted several variants of emissions trading.
    a. **Offsets** are pollution reductions by one firm in an area beyond the amount required of that firm, which can be used by another firm in the same area to exceed its pollution limit. Offsets can be bought by new firms entering the area or by existing firms attempting to expand. Offsets have many of the advantages of pollution rights.
    b. A **bubble** is a geographic area that contains more than one plant of a particular firm. Pollution by the firm within the bubble is limited, but how much pollution is emitted by each plant is determined by the firm.
    c. The 1990 amendments to the Clean Air Act allow utilities that reduce pollution below maximum assigned levels to sell sulphur dioxide allowances to other parties.
9. Currently the government relies primarily upon direct regulation, occasionally combined with subsidies.
10. Under certain circumstances, the private market may lead to optimal pollution control.
    a. Necessary conditions for a market-determined outcome to be optimal are:
        i. Clearly assigned property rights.
        ii. A small number of participants involved in the negotiations.
        iii. No negotiation costs.
    b. In markets satisfying these conditions, negotiations between the polluter and those suffering pollution concerning the use of resources and compensation for the damage done by pollution may result in optimal pollution control.
D. Some Complications With Pollution Control:
    1. Cross-media pollution occurs when one form of pollution is transformed into another form. Lower pollution in one form may be offset by higher pollution in another.
    2. When pollution crosses international boundaries, pollution regulation must be global.

III. Nonrenewable Natural Resources
    A. Estimating the Amounts of Nonrenewable Resources
        1. **Proven reserves** represent the amount of a natural resource that has been discovered and that producers are willing to extract, given current costs and prices. Proven reserves increase as:
            a. The price of the resource increases because certain sources of the resource previously not part of proven reserves (they were too expensive to extract) became economically viable at the higher price.
            b. The costs of extraction decline, which again makes previously unprofitable sources profitable.
            c. New sources of the resource are discovered.
        2. The **expected life of a resource** is the resource's proven reserves divided by its consumption. Estimates of expected life are misleading because:
            a. Price hikes increase the amount of proven reserves and increase expected life.
            b. Price hikes also decrease the rate of consumption and increase the expected life.
    B. Explaining the Shortages of Raw Materials
        1. Natural Gas
            a. Natural gas was in short supply during much of the 1970s, especially during the winter of 1976–1977, because of a price ceiling on natural gas prices in effect since 1954.
            b. The Natural Gas Policy Act of 1978 gradually lifted price controls for most natural gas. The Natural Gas Wellhead Decontrol Act of 1989 eliminated price controls for the remaining categories of natural gas.

2. Oil
    a. The Energy Policy and Conservation Act of 1975 established a series of price controls for domestically produced oil.
    b. To eliminate the cost advantage of refiners with access to price-controlled domestic oil, an **entitlement program** was instituted.
        i. Refiners with access to the cheaper, domestic oil were required to purchase entitlements giving them the right to buy the domestic oil.
        ii. Refiners that had to rely on more expensive foreign oil were given subsidies financed by the entitlement purchases.
        iii. The system of entitlements established a common price of oil in the United States paid by all refiners.
    c. The entitlement program effectively lowered the price of foreign oil and encouraged its importation and consumption. The reduced price of domestic oil discouraged its discovery. Imports of oil increased.
    d. Price controls on oil were abolished in 1981. U.S. consumption of imported oil fell, which contributed to the decline in power of OPEC.

HINTS AND HELP

1. You Have Seen This Before! Now is a good time to review the material on externalities in Chapter 7: "Government in the Economy—Taxation and Spending." It provides a useful supplement and introduction to this chapter.

2. Pollution by Any Other Name Smells Just as Bad Unfortunately, economists use different names for the concept of externalities. You should be aware of these names and recognize that they refer to the same thing.

external benefit = positive externality = positive spillover
external cost = negative externality = negative spillover

FILL IN THE BLANK

social

1. The sum of private and external costs equals _____ costs.

internalizes

2. A firm _____ costs when it is forced to include in its production decision what previously had been external costs.

effluent fee

3. A(n) _____ requires polluters to pay for each unit of pollution emitted.

entitlement

4. Under the _____ program, firms were given a subsidy if they imported oil.

proven reserves

5. The expected life of a resource is the resource's _____ divided by its rate of consumption.

bubble

6. If one of a firm's plants inside a _____ lowers its pollution, the other plants can increase theirs.

cost effective

7. Pollution is reduced at the lowest possible cost if the pollution reduction method is _____.

offset

8. A firm that reduces its pollution below its required level can sell its _____ to a new firm entering the area.

direct regulation

9. If the optimal amount of a pollutant is zero, _____ _____ is the best way of reducing the pollution.

output tax

10. Imposing a tax of $25 per ton of steel in order to reduce the pollution in the steel industry is an example of an _____.

TRUE OR FALSE

_____ 1. External costs cause a market to underallocate resources to that product.

_____ 2. Only producers benefit when pollution is ignored.

_____ 3. A clear assignment of property rights may be sufficient to reduce pollution to its optimal level.

_____ 4. Congress passes pollution-control legislation on the basis of cost-benefit analysis.

_____ 5. Cost-benefit analysis involves comparison of damage caused by pollution to the costs of reducing it.

_____ 6. Without further exploration, a higher price for a resource increases its proven reserves.

_____ 7. The demand curve indicates the private benefit associated with the consumption of a good or service.

_____ 8. Subsidizing the producer is a possible solution in a market where there are external benefits.

_____ 9. Effluent fees are likely to be cost effective.

_____ 10. Requiring all firms to reduce pollution to the same level is likely to be cost effective.

MULTIPLE CHOICE

1. External benefits create a problem for a market because:
   A. firms ignore them when making cost calculations.
   B. consumers ignore them when making purchase decisions.
   C. exporters ignore them when making exporting decisions.
   D. they cause the price of the good to rise above the equilibrium price.

2. External benefits cause which of the following?
   A. a shortage
   B. a surplus
   C. output less than socially optimal
   D. output greater than socially optimal

3. The market supply curve indicates:
   A. private benefits.
   B. private costs.
   C. external benefits.
   D. external costs.

4. Which of the following occurs because of internalization of external costs?
   A. The market produces the socially optimal output.
   B. Firms' costs of production decline.
   C. The market output increases.
   D. The demand for output increases.

5. Cost-benefit analysis asserts that, from an economic perspective, the optimal amount of pollution:
   A. is no pollution.
   B. occurs when the total benefit of pollution control equals the total cost of pollution control.
   C. occurs when the marginal benefit of pollution control equals the marginal cost of pollution control.
   D. occurs when the marginal cost of eliminating pollution equals zero.

6. The major problem associated with using voluntary compliance to reduce pollution is that:
   A. firms tend to devote too many resources to pollution control.
   B. firms have little knowledge of how to reduce their pollution.
   C. no single firm can affect the total amount of pollution.
   D. firms that reduce pollution experience a cost disadvantage relative to firms that do not.

7. Which of the following methods of pollution control requires continuous monitoring of pollution?
   A. voluntary compliance
   B. direct regulation
   C. output tax
   D. market for pollution rights

8. Which of the following is an example of cross-media pollution?
   A. Pollution emitted in Ohio damages the environment of New York.
   B. Solid-waste pollution is reduced but reintroduced into the environment when the waste is burned.
   C. Total air pollution is reduced even though some individual firms emit more pollution.
   D. Pollution by the government offsets reduced pollution by private firms.

9. Which of the following is a renewable resource?
   A. oil
   B. timber
   C. natural gas
   D. coal

10. Proven reserves are the total amount of a resource that are:
    A. known to exist.
    B. processed, stored, and ready for sale.
    C. economical to extract, given the current price of the resource.
    D. being consumed during a particular year.

PROBLEMS

1. Figure 35.1 presents the supply and demand curves for coal.
   a. What is the equilibrium price? _____ What is the equilibrium quantity? _____
   b. Assume that coal emits pollution that causes $6 of damage per ton of coal burned. Draw the supply curve in Figure 35.1 that includes the pollution damage. Label it S_2. What is the optimal amount of coal to burn? _____ What is the equilibrium price if coal producers are required to internalize pollution costs? _____ How much pollution damage still occurs at the optimal amount of output? _____

FIGURE 35.1

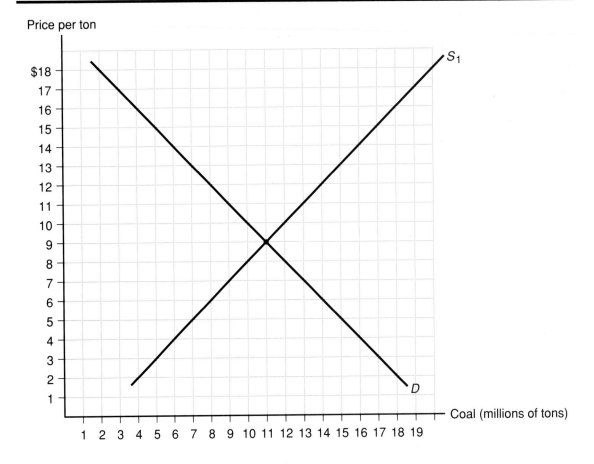

Price per ton

Coal (millions of tons)

Answers

TRUE OR FALSE

1. False. External costs result in overallocation of resources to the product because producers ignore certain costs.

2. False. Consumers of the product produced by the polluter benefit because they can buy the product at a lower price than would exist if the producer used a cleaner production process.

3. True. Where property rights are clearly assigned, few parties are involved in the negotiations, and negotiations have no cost, the parties involved in a pollution dispute may be able to negotiate a solution that is optimal.

4. False. Congress uses no formal analysis in deciding pollution-control legislation.

5. True. The benefits of reduced pollution are improved health, and so forth, because of pollution reduction. The costs are the expenses associated with controlling pollution. Cost-benefit analysis compares the two.

6. True. Proven reserves are based on the amount of the resource that is profitable to extract. A higher price makes previously unprofitable sources profitable, raising proven reserves.

7. True. The demand curve indicates the benefit received by the purchaser of a good or service, which is the private benefit.

8. True. Where external benefits exist, the market underproduces output. A solution is to subsidize the producer in order to expand output.

9. True. When pollution is taxed, producers have an incentive to discover the lowest cost alternative—a cost-effective pollution reduction method.

10. False. Because some firms probably can reduce pollution more easily than others, requiring all firms to reduce pollution to the same level is unlikely to be cost effective.

MULTIPLE CHOICE

1. B. Consumers consider only private benefits when making purchase decisions because they are benefits the consumers receive.

2. C. Resources are underallocated to markets that create external benefits.

3. B. Firms consider only private costs when making production decisions, so the market supply curve reflects only private costs.

4. A. By internalizing external costs, firms consider all costs and produce the socially optimal amount of output.

5. C. The optimal amount of pollution is achieved when any further pollution reduction costs more than the benefit achieved. This occurs when the marginal cost of pollution reduction equals its marginal benefit.

6. D. Because reducing pollution is costly, firms that do so have higher costs than those that do not.

7. D. Because fees are assessed on the basis of the volume of pollution produced, it is necessary to know continuously how much pollution is being emitted.

8. B. Cross-media pollution occurs when the reduction of pollution of one kind causes an increase in another kind.

9. B. Because more trees can be grown, timber is renewable.

10. C. Proven reserves are those reserves of a resource that producers are willing to extract at current market prices.

PROBLEMS

1. a. The equilibrium price is **$9** and the equilibrium quantity is **11 million tons.**
   b. The supply curve that includes the $6 pollution damage is S_2 drawn in Figure 35.2. It is $6 above the market supply curve, S_1. The optimal amount of coal is **8 million tons** and the price (if pollution costs are internalized) is **$12.** At the optimum, the total damage done by the pollution is $6 per ton × 8 million tons, or **$48 million.**

FIGURE 35.2

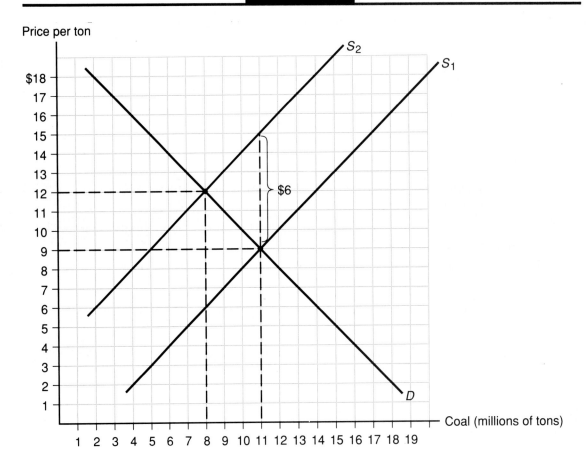

Price per ton

Coal (millions of tons)

CHAPTER 36

Economic Adjustment in Agriculture

Because agriculture provides the necessities of life, many consider it the most important industry. In the United States, agriculture has always played a substantial role in the economy. From the beginning of our history and until 1930, at least 25 percent of the population was involved in farming. Even today, with less than 2 percent of our population in farming, agricultural output accounts for a large fraction of our output.

Chapter 36 focuses on agriculture in the United States. Trends in agriculture are presented and explained. Because the government plays an important role in agriculture, rationales for government farm programs and their consequences are analyzed.

CHAPTER OUTLINE

I. Why Study Agriculture?
   A. Agriculture is a large industry, its output accounting for about one-sixth of total output in the United States.
   B. Agriculture is a highly competitive industry: there are many producers, and entry and exit are relatively easy.
   C. Government intervention in agriculture is great, so agriculture provides an example of the consequences of the impact of government actions on the workings of a market.

II. Economic Trends in Agriculture
   A. After accounting for inflation, net farm income has fallen more than 50 percent since 1945 and, as a percentage of national income, has fallen from about 7 percent in 1945 to 1 percent in 1991. **Net farm income** equals total revenue of farms minus farm production costs.
   B. The relative price of farm products has declined.
   C. Supply and Demand Explanation
      1. Productivity growth in agriculture has occurred at a rapid pace since World War II, greatly shifting the supply curve outward.
      2. Demand for agricultural products has increased slowly because food has a low income elasticity. As a result, the demand curve has shifted modestly.
      3. The combination of the shifts has increased farm output and lowered relative farm prices.
      4. The downward push on prices is enhanced because agricultural products have a low price elasticity. Increases in supply require substantial decreases in prices to reestablish equilibrium when demand is price inelastic.
      5. Inelastic demand combined with falling prices causes falling income because total revenue decreases as prices fall. Although improved productivity has lowered costs, revenue has fallen even more—resulting in lower net farm income.

D. Average Income of Farm Operators
   1. The decline in the farm population has been even greater than the decline in net farm income.
      a. Farm population has declined dramatically from 40 percent of the population in 1900 to 15 percent in 1950 and 1.8 percent in 1990.
      b. As a consequence of the decline in the farm population, average income *per farm* has increased.
   2. Off-farm income has increased as a share of total farm income and has contributed to the improved economic situation on the farm.
   3. Although incomes of farm families are volatile, in recent decades they have generally increased faster than incomes of nonfarm families. As a result, the average income of farm families is now at least as high as the average income of nonfarm families.
E. Good Times, Bad Times
   1. The 1970s were an exceptionally good time for U.S. agriculture.
      a. Rapid increases in living standards in many less-developed countries increased the demand for U.S. commodities.
      b. The falling value of the dollar made U.S. agricultural exports less expensive.
      c. Poor farm production outside of the United States contributed to demand for U.S. agricultural output.
      d. The value of U.S. farmland increased, and many farmers borrowed heavily to buy land.
   2. The early 1980s were a bad time for agriculture.
      a. A severe world recession reduced demand for U.S. agricultural output.
      b. The U.S. dollar appreciated in value, making U.S. exports less attractive to foreign buyers.
      c. Foreign agricultural output increased because of increases in foreign government subsidies. This reduced demand for U.S. crops and increased international competition.
      d. U.S. farmland prices fell, bankrupting many farmers who had borrowed heavily.

III. Should the Government Be in Agriculture?
   A. Reduction of Risk
      1. Argument for Government Involvement:
         a. Farming is an exceptionally risky business because of uncertain weather conditions, political events that influence demand and supply, and shifts in demand caused by erratic international sales.
         b. Shifts in supply cause large fluctuations in price because of inelastic demand.
         c. Consumers prefer price stability to price instability. Thus the government should attempt to stabilize farm prices.
      2. Argument Against Government Involvement:
         a. Private insurance is available to protect farmers from the uncertainties of weather and price fluctuations.
         b. Government involvement has discouraged farmers from obtaining private insurance.
   B. The Family Farm
      1. Argument for Government Involvement: The family farm is a unique life-style that should not be allowed to disappear.
      2. Argument Against Government Involvement:
         a. Low-income farmers should receive income support just as others with low incomes, but support should not go to all farmers.
         b. Family farms typically are less efficient than larger farms. Supporting family farms raises the cost of producing farm output.
   C. Income Support
      1. Argument for Government Involvement: Historically, farmers have had lower incomes and higher poverty rates than nonfarmers.
      2. Argument Against Government Involvement:
         a. Average income and poverty rates are no longer significantly different for farm families than for nonfarm families.
         b. Subsidies to agriculture aid all farmers—poor and nonpoor.

D. All agree that government involvement in agriculture is necessary when farming practices pollute the environment—an external cost.

IV. Government Farm Programs

    A. **Price supports** are minimum prices guaranteed by the government through a system in which the government buys any output offered at the support price.

        1. The mechanics of the price support system are:

            a. The **Commodity Credit Corporation (CCC)** makes a loan to a farmer equal to the support price times the size of the crop. The CCC is the government agency that purchases surplus commodities from farmers.

            b. The crop is the collateral for the loan.

            c. The loan is a **nonrecourse loan**: the farmer can choose to default on the loan, in which case the government accepts the collateral (that is, the crop) as full payment for the loan.

            d. Farmers choose to repay the loan only if the market price is above the support price. Otherwise farmers default.

        2. The effects of a price support program when the support price is above the equilibrium price are:

            a. The price of agricultural commodities increases.

            b. The quantity consumed decreases.

            c. The quantity produced increases beyond the socially optimal amount.

            d. Government-held surpluses are created, which are difficult to reduce and require tax dollars to buy and maintain.

    B. Supply restrictions attempt to increase the price of agricultural commodities without creating a surplus by reducing their supply. Two methods used to reduce supply are:

        1. Restricting the acreage farmers can plant.

            a. Under the Acreage Reduction Program, farmers must set aside a specified percentage of their land to be eligible for price supports.

            b. The Conservation Reserve Act pays farmers not to plant on highly erodible land.

            c. In 1983, the Payment-In-Kind (PIK) program gave farmers surplus commodities in exchange for not planting.

            d. Programs removing acreage from cultivation have not been highly successful in reducing supply because farmers remove the least productive acres and farm the remaining acres more intensively.

            e. Acreage restrictions cause farm suppliers—seed companies, equipment producers, and the like—to suffer because the farmers use less of their products.

        2. Marketing orders.

            a. **Marketing orders** are directives of the Department of Agriculture that limit the quantity of a product that each producer may sell on the market.

            b. Marketing orders are inefficient because they either force productive resources to be idle or require output to be destroyed or used in a less valuable way.

    C. Demand expansion aids farmers by increasing demand for their output, which increases price and quantity sold.

        1. Programs to increase domestic demand for food include food stamps, school lunch programs, and others. Because food consumption in the United States is already high, such programs have limited impact.

        2. Programs to increase international demand for U.S. commodities include export subsidies, loans to less-developed countries, and reductions in foreign trade barriers. Export subsidy programs often result in foreign buyers purchasing U.S. commodities at lower prices than U.S. consumers.

        3. The demand for U.S. commodities can be increased by discovering new uses for the commodities. Examples include producing ethanol from corn to fuel cars and using sunflowers for fuel and fiber.

    D. Direct payments

        1. The mechanics of the program are:

            a. The government establishes a target price. The **target price** is the minimum price guaranteed by the government.

b. Farmers produce and sell all their output in the market.

c. For each unit of output sold, the government pays the farmer the difference between the target price and the market price. The difference between the target price and the market price is called the **deficiency payment**.

2. When the target price is above the equilibrium price, the effects of the target price system are:

a. The quantity of the commodity produced and consumed increases.

b. The market price falls.

c. Taxes increase to pay for the deficiency payments.

d. The resources used to produce the commodity increase beyond the optimal amount.

V. Criticisms of U.S. Farm Policy

A. U.S. farm programs impose a high cost on the economy because of administrative costs, higher food prices for consumers, higher taxes, and an inefficient use of resources.

B. Because farm support is linked to the amount of output produced, larger farms with higher incomes and less poverty receive more support than smaller, poorer farms.

C. Because of increased international sales, the price elasticity of demand has increased. This reduces the extent to which prices fluctuate and causes policies that restrict supply to be less appropriate.

D. Government programs make farming more attractive by increasing farm revenue. This raises the prices of farm inputs, particularly land. It becomes more expensive for those without land to enter farming.

E. Government programs introduce instability into farming because of frequent policy shifts.

VI. Alternative Proposals

A. Decoupling eliminates the link between government payments and the level of production by making a fixed payment per farm or per acre. This reduces the incentive to expand production, reduces the waste of resources, and reduces surpluses.

B. Targeting allocates support only to the lowest-income farmers. Although such a program reduces the cost of farm supports, it encourages less-efficient producers to remain in business unless they are provided an economic incentive to leave.

HINTS AND HELP

1. Lower Net Farm Income, Higher per-Farm Income   Net farm income measures the difference between the total receipts of all farms and their total production costs. Net farm income has been on a downward trend for 50 years. Per-farm income is net farm income divided by the number of farms. Per-farm income has been on an upward trend for 50 years.

As the chapter describes, it is important to keep the two concepts clear. Declining net farm income means that farming has become a smaller and smaller part of the entire economy. Rising per-farm income means that those engaged in farming, on average, are enjoying a higher standard of living. The difference arises because people have been leaving farming at a faster rate than net farm income has been falling.

2. Support Prices, Target Prices, and Supply Restrictions   Support prices, target prices, and supply restrictions raise the price farmers receive for their output and increase farm income. But they do it in fundamentally different ways.

Support prices establish the government as a buyer of last resort. If the farmer cannot sell output at a price at or above the support price, the government, through a loan program, buys it. The government must pay for the surplus as well as the costs of storing it.

Target prices (or deficiency payments) pay the farmer the difference between the price received in the market when the farmer sells the output and the target price established by the government. The payment is called a deficiency payment; there is no surplus.

Supply restrictions shift the supply curve leftward. This increases the equilibrium price and reduces the equilibrium quantity. Because the demand for agricultural commodities is inelastic, the higher price increases total revenue.

FILL IN THE BLANK

inelastic   1. Increases in productivity result in a lower total revenue when demand is price _____.

more   2. Rapid technological advances in agriculture combined with a demand that has a low income elasticity means that over time the equilibrium price declines proportionally _____ than the equilibrium quantity rises.

fall   3. The rising value of the dollar in the 1980s caused U.S. agricultural exports to _____.

family farm   4. Some argue that the _____ is a life-style that should be maintained through government subsidies.

external costs   5. Pollution caused by the runoff of pesticides and fertilizers creates _____ that require government intervention to correct.

surplus commodities   6. The Commodity Credit Corporation buys _____.

price support   7. The government accumulates surpluses when the _____ is set above the equilibrium price.

nonrecourse   8. A _____ loan allows the borrower to repay the loan by forfeiting the collateral.

target   9. The _____ price program causes the market price of agricultural commodities to fall.

Targeting   10. _____ farm aid would limit government support to the poorest farmers only.

TRUE OR FALSE

_____ 1. Less than 2 percent of the population is engaged in farming.

_____ 2. In the past 50 years, net farm income and average farm income have fallen.

_____ 3. Average income of farm families has never been above average income of nonfarm families.

_____ 4. Because of increasing international sales, price elasticity of demand for U.S. agricultural commodities has increased.

_____ 5. Acreage restrictions have dramatically limited the supply of agricultural commodities.

_____ 6. Decoupling encourages excess production and results in surpluses.

_____ 7. Per-farm acreage in the United States has increased over the last 50 years.

_____ 8. Government programs that increase international purchases of U.S. commodities often result in U.S. citizens' paying more for U.S. commodities than foreign buyers pay.

_____ 9. More government support goes to large farms than to small farms.

_____ 10. The Payment-In-Kind program paid farmers with commodities rather than with cash.

MULTIPLE CHOICE

1. Net farm income is:
   A. total revenue of farmers.
   B. total revenue less the cost of intermediate goods.
   C. total revenue less the cost of labor.
   D. total revenue less the costs of production.

2. Which of the following is true because income elasticity of demand for most agricultural commodities is less than one?
   A. As income grows, the demand for agricultural commodities declines.
   B. As income grows, the demand for agricultural commodities grows more slowly than income.
   C. As income grows, the demand for agricultural commodities grows faster than income.
   D. As income grows, the demand for agricultural commodities grows faster than the rate at which agricultural productivity grows.

3. Which of the following best describes the demand for agricultural commodities in the United States?
   A. price elasticity of demand of 0.4 and income elasticity of 1.6
   B. price elasticity of demand of 0.4 and income elasticity of 0.2
   C. price elasticity of demand of 1.2 and income elasticity of 0.2
   D. price elasticity of demand of 1.2 and income elasticity of 1.6

4. The decline in the farm population is evidence that:
   A. nonfarm occupations were more attractive than farming.
   B. farm output is falling.
   C. farm output is rising.
   D. farming is inefficient.

5. In the 1970s, farmers earned exceptionally high incomes because:
   A. government payments were high.
   B. land prices were high.
   C. exports were high.
   D. input prices were low.

6. Which of the following is *not* a reason given for government support of agriculture?
   A. Farming has a high degree of risk.
   B. Imports threaten the survival of U.S. farmers.
   C. Farmers are poorer, on average, than nonfarmers.
   D. Maintaining the family farm is desirable for the entire economy.

7. Which of the following is *not* offered as a defense of the family farm?
   A. Family farms produce output at the lowest possible cost.
   B. Family farms are a unique aspect of American culture.
   C. Family farmers are poorer than the average American worker.
   D. Family farmers work hard and deserve a decent income.

8. If the support price is above the equilibrium price, farmers under the support price program:
   A. sell their output at the equilibrium price.
   B. default on their commodity loans.
   C. lower the price of output.
   D. produce less output.

9. The price support program lowers the:
   A. price of agricultural commodities to consumers.
   B. amount of agricultural commodities produced by farmers.
   C. amount of agricultural commodities consumers buy.
   D. incomes of farmers.

10. A marketing order:
    A. sets the minimum price at which farmers can sell their products.
    B. sets a minimum price consumers must pay for agricultural commodities.
    C. restricts the amount of an agricultural commodity that a farmer can sell.
    D. attempts to increase the demand for agricultural commodities through advertising and other marketing devices.

PROBLEMS

1. Figures 36.1 and 36.2 present the demand and supply curves for the corn market. Answer the following questions on the basis of the information given.

FIGURE 36.1

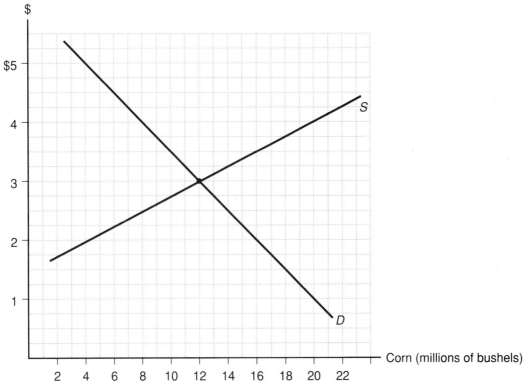

a. What is the equilibrium price of corn? _____ What is the equilibrium quantity? _____

b. Assume a price support program is established with the support price set at $4. What is the quantity produced? _____ What is the quantity consumed? _____ What is the surplus? _____ How much does the government spend to buy the surplus? _____ In Figure 36.1, draw a rectangle that measures the tax cost of the surplus.

FIGURE 36.2

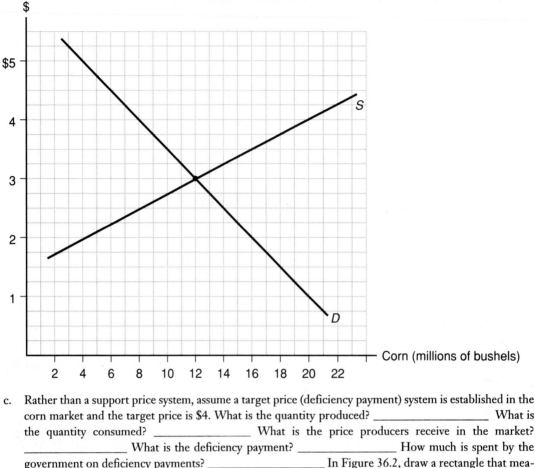

c. Rather than a support price system, assume a target price (deficiency payment) system is established in the corn market and the target price is $4. What is the quantity produced? _____ What is the quantity consumed? _____ What is the price producers receive in the market? _____ What is the deficiency payment? _____ How much is spent by the government on deficiency payments? _____ In Figure 36.2, draw a rectangle that measures that tax cost of the deficiency payments.

d. Assume a supply restriction program is established. In Figure 36.2, draw the supply curve that establishes $4 as the equilibrium price. Label it S_2. What is the quantity produced and consumed? _____ _____

Answers

TRUE OR FALSE

1. True. This is down significantly from 15 percent in 1950.

2. False. Although net farm income has fallen, average farm income has increased because the number of farmers has declined even more than net farm income.

3. False. In the mid-1970s and again more recently, average income for farm families has exceeded average income for nonfarm families.

4. True. Increasing international sales make the quantity sold increasingly responsive to price.

5. False. Acreage restrictions have not substantially limited supply, because farmers idle the least productive acres and farm the other acres more intensively.

6. False. Decoupling makes payments on a per-acre or per-farm basis. Farmers are not encouraged to increase production because payments are the same regardless of the amount produced.

7. True. Although the number of farms and farmers has fallen dramatically, the number of acres in cultivation has not, which means that the acres per farm have increased.

8. True. Increasing foreign purchases of U.S. commodities often requires export subsidies. That lowers the price below the price in the United States.

9. True. Because support is primarily based on output, large farms that produce more output receive more support.

10. True. The Payment-in-Kind program made payments using commodities rather than money.

MULTIPLE CHOICE

1. D. Net farm income is the revenue from all farm sales less the farmers' costs of production.

2. B. When income elasticity is less than one, purchases of the good rise more slowly than income.

3. B. Demand for agricultural commodities is price inelastic (price elasticity is less than one) and income inelastic (income elasticity between zero and one).

4. A. Farmers leave the farm when nonfarm alternatives become more attractive than farming.

5. C. Exports were exceptionally high during the 1970s, which caused farm income to be high.

6. B. The United States is a net exporter of agricultural commodities. Imports are not a threat to U.S. agriculture.

7. A. Small family farms tend to have a higher average cost than larger farms.

8. B. When the support price is above the equilibrium price, farmers are better off defaulting on their commodity loans, forfeiting their crop, and pocketing the additional amount from the commodity loan.

9. C. The price support program raises the price of agricultural commodities to consumers and reduces the quantity demanded.

10. C. A marketing order limits the amount of a commodity that each farmer can sell.

PROBLEMS

1. a. The equilibrium price is **$3**. The equilibrium quantity is **12 million bushels**.
   b. With a price support set at $4, the quantity produced is **20 million** bushels of corn; the quantity consumed is **8 million** bushels. The surplus is **12 million** bushels, the difference between the quantities produced and consumed. The cost to the government is $4 × 12 million = **$48 million**. The tax cost of the program is illustrated in Figure 36.3.

FIGURE 36.3

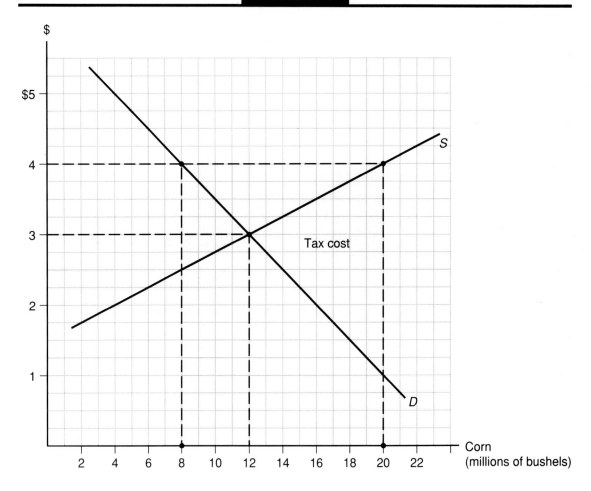

FIGURE 36.4

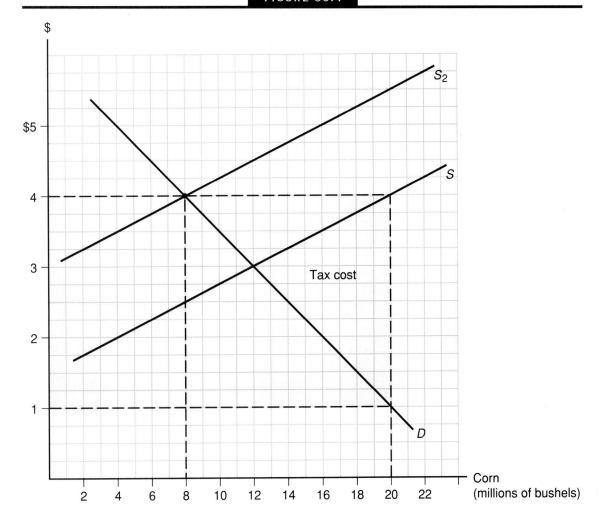

c. With a target price at $4, the quantity produced equals **20 million** bushels. The quantity consumed also equals **20 million** bushels because the growers sell all they produce. The market price is **$1**. The deficiency payment equals the target price less the market price or $4 − $1 = **$3**. The tax cost of the deficiency payments is $3 × 20 million or **$60 million**. This cost is illustrated in Figure 36.4.

d. See Figure 36.4 for supply curve S_2. The quantity produced and consumed is **8 million** bushels.

CHAPTER 37

International Trade

Every economy faces the problem of scarcity because of limited resources. One way to make more goods available in an economy is to trade with others. Yet international trade is viewed with suspicion by many.

Chapter 37 presents the economic arguments in favor of free trade. It also discusses how countries have restricted trade and analyzes the most frequent arguments favoring trade restrictions.

CHAPTER OUTLINE

I. Patterns of Trade
   A. The large industrialized countries dominate international trade.
   B. Countries differ greatly in the degree to which they rely upon international trade. The United States exports 7 percent of its GDP; Malaysia exports 70 percent of its GDP.
   C. The United States trades primarily with other industrialized economies.
   D. In recent years the U.S. has had a trade deficit. A **trade deficit** is the amount by which a country's imports exceed its exports. A **trade surplus** is the amount by which a country's exports exceed its imports.
   E. The primary exports of the United States are capital goods and industrial materials. Major imports to the United States include petroleum and automobiles.

II. Reasons for Trade
   A. By trading, a country gains access to goods and services that it cannot produce. For the United States, examples are bananas and a wide range of minerals. However, the United States produces a wider range of products than most economies and as a result is less dependent on other economies than most.
   B. Even when a country can produce a good, it may be advantageous to import the good from another country if the other country has lower production costs. **Absolute advantage** occurs when one country has the ability to produce a particular good using fewer resources than another country.
   C. Even if one country has the absolute advantage in the production of all goods relative to another country, it is still to the advantage of both countries to trade if one country has a comparative advantage in the production of a good. **Comparative advantage** is the ability to produce a particular good at a lower opportunity cost than another country.
   D. According to the **law of comparative advantage**, total output is maximized if each country specializes in the production of the goods for which it has a comparative advantage and then trades with the other country. Specialization increases total output because the relative costs of the goods differ by country.

E. The analysis of the gains from trading when comparative advantage exists can be modeled using production possibilities and trading possibilities curves.

  1. Production Possibilities

    a. Assuming a fixed amount of available labor, the economy's production possibilities curve is constructed using the amount of labor required per unit of each good. A production possibilities curve is constructed for each economy.

    b. When the amount of labor required to produce a good is the same for every unit produced, the production possibilities curve is a straight line.

  2. Trading Possibilities

    a. The **trading possibilities curve** is a line showing the combinations of two goods a country can obtain by producing the good for which it has a comparative advantage and trading with the other country for the other good.

    b. The slope of the trading possibilities curve equals the terms of trade. The **terms of trade** is the amount of one good that must be given up to obtain a unit of a second good.

    c. When the terms of trade are beneficial to both countries, the trading possibilities curve lies beyond the production possibilities curve, indicating that specialization and trading allows the country to consume a bundle that its economy could not produce.

F. Two factors influence the characteristics of the final outcome when there is specialization and trading, although they do not change the conclusion that both countries gain from trading:

  1. The production possibilities curves can exhibit increasing opportunity costs, as they normally do. In this case, specialization occurs but there is only partial specialization. The economy produces some units of the good it imports. As a result, the volume of trade is likely reduced.

  2. Transportation costs make trading with other countries more expensive and reduce the volume of trading.

III. Limiting Trade

A. **Free trade** is international trade free of any artificial barriers that limit the movement of goods between countries. Although free trade raises standards of living, countries often attempt to limit international trade.

B. **Protectionism** is sheltering domestic industries from foreign competition through one or more artificial barriers to trade.

  1. A **tariff** (or duty) is a tax on imported products.

    a. A **prohibitive tariff** is a tax so high that none of the good being taxed is imported.

    b. A **nonprohibitive tariff** is a tariff that reduces but does not totally eliminate imports of the product.

    c. A tariff on a product raises the price of the product and reduces the quantity imported.

    d. Costs and Benefits of Tariffs

      i. Costs: (1) Consumers receive less of the product and pay a higher price. (2) Foreign producers have lower sales.

      ii. Benefits: (1) Domestic producers in the protected industry sell more output at a higher price. (2) Workers in the protected industry have more jobs with higher pay because of the extra output.

      iii. The net impact of the tariff depends on a comparison of the costs and benefits. The costs of tariffs exceed the benefits because tariffs result in a misallocation of resources. Too many resources are employed in the protected industry; too few are employed in the rest of the economy. Employment gains in the protected industry are achieved at the expense of lower employment in other industries.

  2. An **import quota** sets a limit on the amount of a product that may be legally imported into a country.

    a. The effects of an import quota are similar to the effects of a tariff: a higher price, less consumption, lower imports, greater domestic production of the good with a quota.

b. Quotas are probably more damaging than tariffs.
   i. The quantity imported is fixed and cannot respond to changes in demand; the quantity imported changes with demand when there is a tariff.
   ii. Quotas yield no tax revenue; tariffs do. Under quotas, revenues from the higher price are transferred to the foreign producer.
3. A **voluntary export restriction** is an agreement by one country to limit exports to another country. It has the same effect as a quota. The agreement is usually reached as the result of a threat on the part of the importing country to impose a harsher trade restriction if no action is taken.
4. Antidumping laws make it illegal for foreign countries to engage in dumping. **Dumping** occurs when a producer sells its output at a lower price in a foreign market than at home. There are various reasons dumping occurs:
   a. A country may subsidize exports. As a result, citizens in the country importing the product are receiving a tax subsidy from the exporting country.
   b. Dumping may be an attempt to create a monopoly. By setting the price below average cost, the foreign producer may be able to drive competitors out of business. Once done, the foreign producer can raise prices and enjoy monopoly profits. The ability to do this is limited by the ability of domestic producers to reenter the industry once prices are increased and by the availability of the product from other countries.

IV. Explaining the Presence of Trade Barriers
   A. Traditional Arguments for Trade Restrictions
      1. National Defense
         a. The national defense argument asserts that some products and industries are of such vital importance during wartime that a country cannot rely upon imports for fear that the imports will be cut off during hostilities.
         b. This argument certainly is valid in some cases, but care must be taken to ensure that the lower standard of living imposed by import restrictions warrants the protectionism.
      2. Infant Industry
         a. The infant industry argument asserts that industries have higher costs when they are starting up. During this period the industry must be protected from lower-cost foreign competitors. Once established, the protection can be removed.
         b. The validity of this argument to any particular industry depends on the answers to the following questions:
            i. Does the country have or can it develop a comparative advantage in the production of the good? If not, the protection must be permanent in order for the industry to survive.
            ii. Will the protection be temporary? Most industries prefer protection to free trade and are reluctant to give up protection once it is given.
            iii. Is the industry new? Established industries in industrialized economies cannot claim to be infants.
      3. Retaliation
         a. Retaliation refers to trade restrictions imposed by one country in response to trade restrictions of a second country. Retaliation is worthwhile if it induces other countries to reduce their trade barriers.
         b. Retaliation is not worthwhile if the other countries maintain their barriers, as this lowers the standard of living in both countries. One country should not deny its citizens the benefits of free trade because others deny their citizens those benefits. Retaliation can also lead to an escalation of trade barriers, which can result in trade wars.
      4. Increasing Employment
         a. Trade restrictions are often imposed because it is argued that doing so increases employment.

b. Although trade restrictions increase employment in protected industries, they do not increase employment in total. Greater employment in the protected industry comes at the expense of employment in other industries.

    5. Low Foreign Wages

        a. Trade restrictions occasionally are imposed because it is believed that U.S. workers, earning high wages, cannot compete against foreign workers who earn low wages.

        b. Focusing on differences in wages ignores differences in productivity. Workers earning higher wages can compete against workers earning lower wages if their productivity is sufficiently higher. A wage five times as high is competitive if productivity is five times as high.

B. The New Theory of Managed Trade

    1. Where there are substantial economies of scale, government involvement may result in profit to domestic firms (and additional tax revenue for the government). This outcome is possible if government subsidies to or protection of a domestic producer drives foreign rivals out of business.

    2. While such an outcome is possible, the probability that the government can consistently identify industries that would lead to this result without falling prey to purely political manipulation is small.

C. The Politics of Special Interests

    1. Trade restrictions reduce standards of living but nevertheless are often imposed.

    2. Reasons protectionist legislation is enacted include:

        a. Individuals in protected industries who benefit from trade restrictions—owners and workers—are more likely to vote on the basis of the single issue of trade restrictions.

        b. Individuals harmed by trade restrictions—consumers—are less aware of the impacts of such restrictions, less well organized, and more widely dispersed than the beneficiaries.

        c. Politicians may be genuinely concerned about the workers hurt by free trade. But there are usually less expensive ways to aid the workers than trade restrictions.

V. History of Tariffs and Other Trade Restrictions

A. Tariffs have varied widely over time. Tariffs were highest in 1828, 1860–1900, and 1930.

B. Since the end of World War II, tariffs in the United States have declined because of the **General Agreement on Tariffs and Trade (GATT)**. This accord, agreed to by more than 100 nations, sets rules for tariffs and provides a mechanism for resolving trade disputes.

C. GATT has been weakened in recent years by the increasing use of:

    1. Such nontariff trade restrictions as voluntary export restrictions which subvert GATT's free-trade principles.

    2. **Free-trade agreements**, in which a few countries agree to remove trade barriers among themselves but maintain the trade restrictions against nonmembers.

HINTS AND HELP

1. Gains from Trading   It is difficult to fully appreciate the gains from trading. Graphs and simple numerical examples might appear deceiving, or at least unrealistic.

To appreciate the benefits of trading, ask what your standard of living would be if the only things you could consume were those things you produced. If you wanted a slice of bread, you must grow the wheat and harvest it. You must mill the wheat into flour. Of course, you must build the mill. To bake the bread, you must build the oven. And so on.

The point is obvious. It is *impossible* to enjoy the standard of living you now enjoy if you must produce all the goods yourself. The only way you can consume the bundle of goods you now consume is by relying on others. Each of us specializes in the production of some good or service and trades some of the output for the output of others.

This idea, which is so obvious to us on an individual level, is the principle behind international trade. It is impossible for the United States to enjoy the standard of living it now enjoys if it must produce everything itself. Only through international trade can the United States consume what it now consumes.

2. Comparative and Absolute Advantage   Determining when there is absolute advantage and when there is comparative advantage is simple when certain steps are followed. Absolute advantage depends on which economy can produce more output with a unit of input. To determine this, find the economy that can produce more of the good with a given amount of an input (or can produce the same amount of output with a smaller amount of an input).

Comparative advantage is determined by calculating the opportunity cost of each good in each country. For example, if country A must give up 2 cars to produce another boat and country B must give up 3 cars to obtain a boat, country A has the comparative advantage in the production of boats.

Once it has been determined that one country has a comparative advantage for producing one good, automatically the other country has the comparative advantage in production of the other good. Country B sacrifices 1/3 boat to produce an additional car; country A gives up 1/2 boat. Country B sacrifices fewer boats, and thus has a comparative advantage for producing cars.

FILL IN THE BLANK

deficit

1. A country has a trade _____ if its imports exceed its exports.

terms of trade

2. The number of units of a good one country gives up to obtain a unit of the other country's good is the _____.

comparative

3. Output is maximized if each country produces the product for which it has a(n) _____ advantage.

prohibitive

4. A tariff that eliminates all imports of a good is a(n) _____ _____ tariff.

dumping

5. Selling a product in a foreign country at a price below its domestic price is called _____.

infant industry

6. Providing a temporary tariff while firms are becoming established is favored by the _____ argument for trade restrictions.

import quota

7. A law that places a numerical limitation on the amount of a good that can be imported is a(n) _____.

voluntary export restrictions

8. Import quotas and _____ have identical impacts.

Protectionism

9. _____ is the use of artificial trade barriers to restrict trade.

increase, decrease

10. Trade barriers _____ employment in the protected industry and _____ employment in the other industries.

TRUE OR FALSE

_____ 1. Tariffs raise prices; import quotas do not.

_____ 2. Tariffs are less damaging than quotas.

_____ 3. A country always exports the product for which it has an absolute advantage.

_____ 4. Free trade benefits consumers but hurts those in the import-competing industry.

_____ 5. Free trade allows a country to consume a bundle outside its production possibilities curve.

_____ 6. Free trade involves a trade-off between a higher standard of living for consumers and the number of jobs in the economy.

_____ 7. The benefits of free trade are the result of increased resources.

_____ 8. In the United States today, tariffs are at historic lows.

_____ 9. The United States depends on imports for a greater proportion of its goods than do most industrialized countries.

_____ 10. The United States sells more of its output to Japan than to any other country.

MULTIPLE CHOICE

1. In the United States, exports exceed imports for which of the following goods?
   A. petroleum
   B. food
   C. automobiles
   D. shoes

2. The benefits from international trade occur:
   A. only when there are no transportation costs.
   B. only when opportunity costs do not increase.
   C. only when there is no unemployment.
   D. even when there are transportation costs, increasing opportunity costs, and unemployment.

3. The slope of the trading possibilities curve equals the:
   A. terms of trade.
   B. opportunity cost.
   C. relative amounts of resources in the two countries.
   D. absolute advantage.

4. The primary purpose of GATT is:
   A. raising tax revenue for the government.
   B. reducing trade barriers and resolving trade disputes.
   C. redistributing income from rich countries to poor countries.
   D. reducing the budget deficit and the national debt.

5. Comparative advantage depends on the:
   A. terms of trade.
   B. absolute advantage.
   C. amount of resources.
   D. opportunity costs.

6. The U.S. trade restriction on Japanese automobiles is an example of:
   A. a voluntary export restriction.
   B. a tariff.
   C. an antidumping law.
   D. a free-trade agreement.

7. Which of the following is a difficulty associated with imposing trade barriers to protect infant industries?
   A. It is difficult to identify which industries eventually develop a comparative advantage.
   B. Industries dislike giving up protection from foreign competition.
   C. Established industries seek protection with the argument that they are infant industries.
   D. All the alternatives are correct.

8. Retaliation:
   A. imposes trade barriers on all foreign producers.
   B. imposes trade barriers on only the smallest and weakest foreign producers.
   C. is intended to force others to reduce their trade barriers.
   D. is intended to improve the terms of trade.
9. Critics of managed trade assert that:
   A. the government is a better judge of opportunities in international trade than is private industry.
   B. in practice, the allocation of government subsidies often is determined by political rather than economic considerations.
   C. specialization is determined by absolute advantage rather than by comparative advantage.
   D. an economy's endowment of natural resources is responsible for the determination of comparative advantage.
10. A nonprohibitive tariff:
   A. has no impact on the volume of trading.
   B. applies only to a few goods.
   C. does not eliminate the importation of products.
   D. yields no revenue for the government.

PROBLEMS

1. The following table contains data on pairs of goods that can be produced by a single worker in the countries of Grant and Lee. For example, the information on the first pair of goods is that one worker in Grant can produce 3 books or 1 hammer and that one worker in Lee can produce 4 books or 2 hammers.

   Place the letter A in the space next to a good if the country has an absolute advantage in its production and place the letter C if the country has a comparative advantage.

	GRANT	LEE
a.	3 books _____ 1 hammer _____	4 books _____ 2 hammers _____
b.	10 shirts _____ 1 coat _____	8 shirts _____ 2 coats _____
c.	20 baseballs _____ 80 footballs _____	15 baseballs _____ 45 footballs _____
d.	1 VCR _____ 500 newspapers _____	2 VCRs _____ 600 newspapers _____
e.	25 apples _____ 50 bananas _____	20 apples _____ 30 bananas _____

2. A worker in Brazil can produce 10 pounds of tomatoes or 5 pounds of coffee. A worker in Canada can produce 9 pounds of tomatoes or 1 pound of coffee. Assume Brazil and Canada each have 1,000 workers.

   a. Construct Brazil's production possibilities curve in Figure 37.1 and Canada's production possibilities curve in Figure 37.2.

   b. Which good does Brazil export to Canada? _____

   c. Which good does Canada export to Brazil? _____

   d. Assume the terms of trade are 3 pounds of tomatoes for 1 pound of coffee. Construct each economy's trading possibilities curve in Figures 37.1 and 37.2.

FIGURE 37.1

Brazil

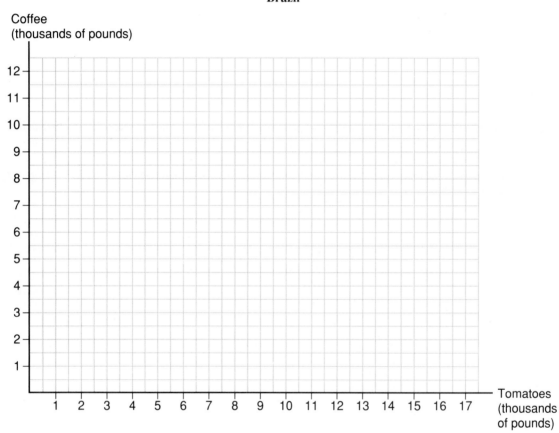

Coffee
(thousands of pounds)

Tomatoes
(thousands of pounds)

FIGURE 37.2

Canada

Coffee
(thousands of pounds)

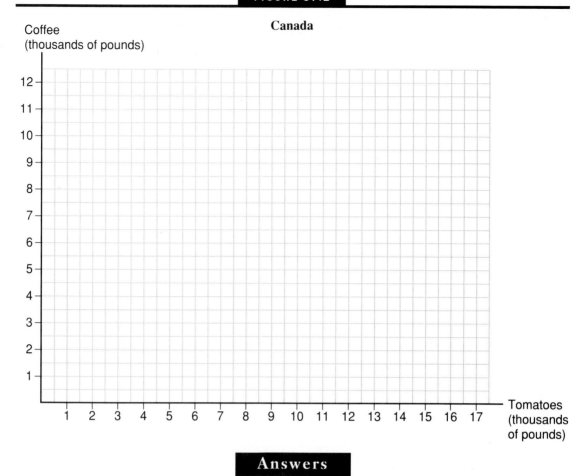

Tomatoes
(thousands
of pounds)

Answers

TRUE OR FALSE

1. False. Tariffs *and* import quotas raise the prices of imported products.

2. True. Tariffs generate tax revenue and allow the quantity imported to vary in response to demand; quotas do neither.

3. False. A country exports the product for which it has a comparative advantage. Although this may be a good for which it has an absolute advantage, it is not necessarily the case.

4. True. Free trade benefits consumers because it offers a wider range of products at lower prices. Domestic firms having to compete against foreign producers are hurt.

5. True. Specialization and trading allows each country participating in the trade to consume a bundle of goods it could not itself produce, that is, a bundle outside its production possibilities curve.

6. False. Free trade does not reduce the number of jobs in an economy; thus there is no trade-off between the standard of living and the number of jobs.

7. False. The benefits of free trade occur even though the resources in all trading countries remain the same.

8. True. Because of GATT, tariffs in the United States and around the world are at historic lows.

9. False. The United States is more self-sufficient than most industrialized countries.

10. False. The United States exports more to Canada than any other country.

MULTIPLE CHOICE

1. B. The United States exports more food than it imports.

2. D. There are benefits from international trade even when there are transportation costs, increasing opportunity costs, and unemployment.

3. A. The slope of the trading possibilities curve measures how much of one good must be traded for a unit of the other good, a concept named the terms of trade.

4. B. GATT is a forum for negotiating freer trade and resolving trade disputes.

5. D. Comparative advantage depends on which economy can produce a good at the lower opportunity cost.

6. A. The agreement between the United States and Japan to limit Japanese exports of automobiles to the United States is an example of a voluntary export restriction.

7. D. Tariffs imposed to protect infant industries create difficulties because it is not easy to know whether the industry will develop a comparative advantage, protected industries rarely agree to give up their protection, and established industries seek protection under the guise of being an infant industry.

8. C. Retaliation imposes trade barriers on another country's imports to induce that country to reduce its own trade barriers.

9. B. Critics of managed trade assert that, although it is conceivable that the government can develop internationally competitive industries with appropriate subsidies and protectionism, often such government decisions are dominated by political rather than economic considerations.

10. C. A nonprohibitive tariff reduces but does not eliminate imports.

PROBLEMS

1. Absolute advantage depends on the amount of output per worker, while comparative advantage depends on the opportunity cost of producing a good.

   In (a), both the number of books per worker and the number of hammers per worker are greater for Lee than for Grant. Therefore, Lee has an absolute advantage in the production of both goods.

   The opportunity cost of 1 hammer is 2 books for Lee but 3 books for Grant. Because of the lower opportunity cost, Lee has a comparative advantage in the production of hammers. But Grant has a comparative advantage in the production of books—the opportunity cost of 1 book is only 1/3 hammer for Grant compared to 1/2 hammer for Lee.

   Based on similar reasoning, answers for (b) through (e) can be derived. Those answers are presented in the accompanying table.

	GRANT	LEE
a.	3 books __C__ 1 hammer _____	4 books __A__ 2 hammers __A, C__
b.	10 shirts __A, C__ 1 coat _____	8 shirts _____ 2 coats __A, C__
c.	20 baseballs __A__ 80 footballs __A, C__	15 baseballs __C__ 45 footballs _____
d.	1 VCR _____ 500 newspapers __C__	2 VCRs __A, C__ 600 newspapers __A__
e.	25 apples __A__ 50 bananas __A, C__	20 apples __C__ 30 bananas _____

FIGURE 37.3

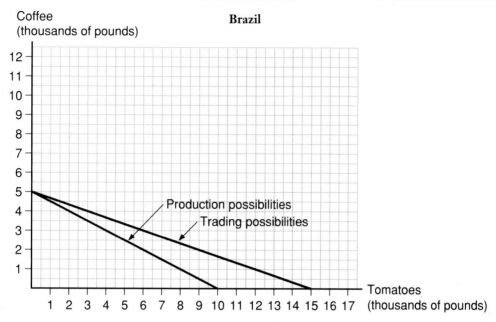

2. a. See Figures 37.3 and 37.4 for the production possibility curves for Brazil and Canada. To construct the production possibilities curves, calculate the maximum amount of each good an economy can produce. For example, Brazil can produce a maximum of 10 pounds of tomatoes per worker × 1,000 workers or 10,000 pounds of tomatoes. It can also produce a maximum of 5,000 pounds of coffee. The maximums are plotted on the tomato and coffee axes and connected with a straight line.

   b. Brazil exports coffee because the opportunity cost of producing 1 pound of coffee in Brazil is 2 pounds of tomatoes; it is 9 pounds of tomatoes in Canada.

   c. Canada exports tomatoes because the opportunity cost of producing 1 pound of tomatoes in Canada is 1/9 pound of coffee; the opportunity cost in Brazil is 1/2 pound of coffee.

   d. See Figures 37.3 and 37.4 for the trading possibilities curves. The trading possibilities curve is constructed by drawing a line with a slope equal to the terms of trade starting on the axis of the good in which the country has a comparative advantage. In this case the slope is 1 pound of coffee/3 pounds of tomatoes.

FIGURE 37.4

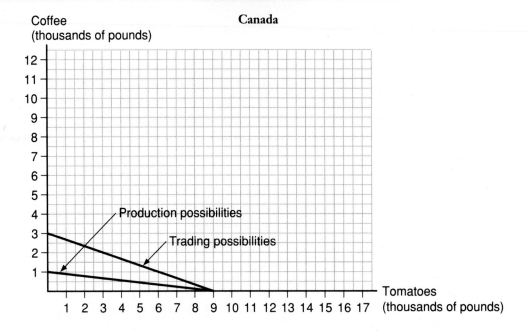

CHAPTER 38

The International Financial System

Chapter 37 explained the benefits that result from international trade. However, the trades described in that chapter—goods traded directly for goods—rarely occur. Instead, goods are almost always exchanged for money. International transactions are more complicated than domestic ones because there are two currencies involved: that of the buyer and that of the seller. The exchange rate is the number of units of foreign currency that can be purchased with one unit of domestic currency.

This chapter describes the mechanism of international currency transactions. It explains how foreign exchange rates are determined, the factors that cause exchange rates to change, and the consequences of exchange rate changes. The experience of the U.S. dollar since the mid-1970s is analyzed.

Chapter 38 includes a discussion of the balance of payments—the statistical tabulation of a nation's international transactions—and discusses the U.S. international trade deficits of the past decade. The chapter closes with an analysis of the debt crises of the less-developed countries.

CHAPTER OUTLINE

I. The Foreign Exchange Market
   A. The **foreign exchange market** is the market in which national currencies are bought and sold. The price at which one country's currency may be traded for another country's currency is the **foreign exchange rate**.
   B. Changes in Foreign Exchange Rates
      1. **Currency depreciation** occurs when a country's currency buys fewer units of another country's currency. **Currency appreciation** occurs when a country's currency buys more units of another country's currency.
      2. Currently, most countries have floating exchange rates. **Floating exchange rates** allow currency values to change continuously in the foreign exchange market. In the past, most countries had fixed exchange rates. **Fixed exchange rates** require each government to intervene in the foreign exchange market in order to hold the international value of its currency within a narrow range.

II. Determination of Exchange Rates in a Regime of Freely Floating Rates
   A. Equilibrium
      1. The demand for dollars depends on the foreign demand for U.S. goods and services, financial assets, and real assets. The demand curve is downward sloping because, everything else the same, a lower value of the dollar makes U.S. goods and services and assets less expensive to foreign buyers.

2. The supply of dollars depends on domestic demand for foreign goods, services, and assets. The supply curve is upward sloping because the higher the value of the dollar, the less expensive foreign goods, services, and assets are to U.S. buyers.

3. The equilibrium exchange rate is the rate at which the quantity of dollars demanded is equal to the quantity of dollars supplied.

B. The equilibrium exchange rate changes whenever the demand for or supply of dollars shifts. The forces that shift the supply and demand curves for dollars are:

1. Relative Prices

a. If the prices of U.S. goods and services rise faster than the prices of foreign goods and services, U.S. goods and services become less attractive. This reduces the demand for U.S. dollars, increases the supply, and reduces the value of the dollar (the dollar depreciates).

b. The **purchasing power parity (PPP) theory** asserts that the exchange rate between two currencies adjusts to completely reflect differences in price-level behavior in the two countries.

i. The purchasing power parity theory holds precisely in the unrealistic situation where two economies produce a single, homogeneous product for both domestic consumption and export.

ii. In reality, goods and services are not homogeneous and not all goods and services can be exported. As a result, actual exchange rate movements do not mirror purchasing power parity exchange rates.

2. Relative Income: If U.S. income rises at a faster rate than income in foreign countries, the demand for foreign products by U.S. consumers rises more rapidly than the demand for U.S. products by foreign consumers. This increases the supply of dollars and lowers the exchange rate value of the dollar.

3. Relative Real Interest Rates: If U.S. real interest rates increase relative to real interest rates in foreign economies, U.S. financial assets become more attractive. This increases the demand for dollars and increases the U.S. exchange rate. The dollar appreciates.

4. Speculation: Speculators buy and sell currencies to profit from exchange rate movements. If speculators believe the dollar will rise soon, they buy dollars now and sell them after the exchange rate moves. There is some disagreement about whether speculators increase or reduce exchange rate fluctuations.

III. U.S. Exchange Rate Movements, 1975–1992

A. From 1975 to 1979, the dollar fell as the U.S. rate of inflation accelerated. Low real rates of interest in the United States contributed to the low value of the dollar, as did a strong economic expansion.

B. From 1980 to 1985, the dollar rose. High real interest rates and lower inflation made U.S. assets and goods and services more attractive. A severe recession reduced the demand for foreign goods by U.S. consumers. Unstable political and economic conditions in some parts of the world made the stable climate in the United States attractive.

C. From 1985 to 1992, the dollar fell in value. Inflation was low in the United States, which is inconsistent with a falling value of the dollar. Stronger income growth and lower real interest rates explain some of the fall in the dollar's value. The fall in the dollar's value may have been partially in response to U.S. inability to reduce its budget and trade deficits.

IV. Consequences of Exchange-Rate Changes

A. Effects of the Strong Dollar, 1980–1985

1. The rising value of the dollar reduced the prices of imported goods and services, which pressured U.S. producers to hold down their prices and helped reduce the U.S. inflation rate.

2. U.S. consumers enjoyed higher living standards as foreign goods become less expensive.

3. U.S. firms that sold imported goods had greater sales.

4. U.S. exports declined, as did employment in those industries.

5. U.S. firms competing against imports found themselves at a cost disadvantage, losing sales and employment.

6. Other countries kept interest rates high in order to keep their currencies from falling even farther in value relative to the dollar. As a result, their economies experienced lower demand and higher unemployment than desired.

B. Effects of the Falling Dollar, 1985–1992
1. Imported goods and services became more expensive in the United States. U.S. firms producing goods and services similar to the imported products experienced an increase in demand, which allowed them to sell more at higher prices.
2. U.S. exports increased strongly as U.S. goods became less expensive to foreign buyers. After a period, the U.S. trade deficit declined.
3. U.S. consumers experienced lower standards of living because of the higher prices of imports (and of domestic goods).

V. Government Intervention in Foreign Exchange Markets
A. Governments intervene in foreign exchange markets by buying and selling currencies with the intent of influencing the exchange rate.
B. Governments occasionally intervene to attempt to stabilize exchange rate movements. But there is some question whether governments are capable of successfully doing this.
C. Governments also intervene to benefit certain industries or portions of their population. The Japanese have been known to intervene to hold down the value of the yen in order to keep their exports attractive in world markets. Such intervention has caused the floating rate system to be dubbed "the dirty float."

VI. Fixed Exchange Rates—The Bretton Woods System
A. The Bretton Woods System required countries to fix (or peg) their exchange rates at an agreed-upon parity or par value. Countries were allowed to change their parity value under certain conditions. Thus, the Bretton Woods System was an adjustable-peg system.
1. If the value of its currency was tending to depreciate, a government was required to increase the demand for its currency by buying it with its international reserves. **International reserves** are the government's stock of foreign currencies and gold available for use in the foreign exchange market.
2. To avoid using up international reserves, countries often imposed trade restrictions, currency controls, or restrictive macroeconomic policies to reduce the supply of their own currencies offered in the foreign exchange market.
B. Critics of the adjustable-peg system claim that it forced countries with weak currencies to follow policies that reduced aggregate demand, output, and employment.
C. The Bretton Woods System ended in 1973 when it became impossible for many countries to maintain their parity values because of large differences in inflation rates and insufficient foreign reserves.

VII. The Balance of Payments
A. The **balance of payments** is a statistical tabulation of a nation's transactions with other countries for a given period. The total balance of payments accounts include the current account and the capital account.
B. The current account is the difference between the value of the nation's exports and imports of goods and services.
1. The **balance of trade** measures the difference between the exports and imports of merchandise (that is, goods).
2. Also included in the current account is the difference between the exports and imports of services. These services include:
a. Purchases of services by U.S. citizens while traveling abroad.
b. U.S. military transactions.
c. Earnings from U.S.-owned assets overseas less earnings of foreign-owned assets in the United States.
3. The current account also includes any gifts or transfers by U.S. citizens to foreigners.
C. The capital account measures changes in foreign assets owned by U.S. citizens less the changes in U.S. assets owned by foreigners. The capital account includes changes in privately held assets and government-owned assets.

D. Because all transactions are not recorded or correctly accounted for, a statistical discrepancy is included to balance the accounts.

E. The total balance of payments must sum to zero.

F. The U.S. Trade Deficit

1. The United States had a trade deficit for most of the 1980s and very large ones after 1983.

2. Because a trade deficit must be offset by an inflow of capital (that is, a positive capital account), the trade deficit has led to the United States borrowing large sums from foreigners.

3. It is unlikely that such large foreign borrowing can continue for long periods. Eventually, the United States must reduce its foreign borrowing, which means the trade deficit must be reduced or eliminated.

VIII. The LDC Debt Crisis

A. Less-developed countries (LDCs) often borrow from foreign lenders because they lack the domestic savings with which to finance domestic investment.

B. The LDC debt crisis can be traced to the 1970s when raw material prices rose, increasing the export earnings of LDCs. At the same time, real interest rates were low. LDCs borrowed large sums.

C. In the 1980s, many LDCs were unable to repay their debts. Causes of the debt crisis include:

1. A severe worldwide recession reduced the demand for LDC exports, particularly raw materials.

2. Real interest rates rose, increasing the interest cost of the loans.

3. The value of the U.S. dollar increased during 1981–1985, making loans—many denominated in dollars—more difficult to repay.

D. There is uncertainty about the ability of many LDCs to repay loans. If the countries default, some U.S. banks will fail and the defaulting countries will lose the ability to borrow in the future.

E. A solution requires LDCs to increase their trade surpluses to repay their loans. To do so requires a depreciation of the LDCs' currencies, which lowers the standards of living of their citizens and increases exports to developed countries.

HINTS AND HELP

1. One Currency's Demand is Another Currency's Supply   In foreign exchange markets, demanding one currency involves simultaneously supplying another. For a U.S. wine importer to buy a bottle of French champagne, she must first exchange dollars for francs. Demanding francs simultaneously supplies dollars.

Remembering how the supply and demand curves shift is not difficult. One demand curve corresponds to the other supply curve. And the curves move in the same direction. If the *demand* for one currency *increases*, the *supply* of the other currency also *increases*. If the *supply* of one currency *decreases*, the *demand* for the other currency *decreases*. In the U.S.–Japan example, increased demand for dollars by the Japanese is accompanied by an increased supply of yen.

2. Calculating Exchange Rates   Calculating exchange rates is not as difficult as it may appear. Assume $1 costs 2 Swiss francs. To calculate how much 1 Swiss franc costs in dollars, divide both sides of the equation by 2:

$$\$1 = 2 \text{ Swiss francs}$$
$$\frac{\$1}{2} = \frac{2 \text{ Swiss francs}}{2}$$
$$\$.50 = 1 \text{ Swiss franc}$$

The procedure also works in reverse:

$$1 \text{ Swiss franc} = \$.50$$
$$\frac{1 \text{ Swiss franc}}{.50} = \frac{\$.50}{.50}$$
$$2 \text{ Swiss francs} = \$1$$

FILL IN THE BLANK

exchange rate

depreciates

floating

Purchasing power parity

appreciate

international reserves

fixed or pegged

balance of trade

zero

current account

1. The price of a currency is its foreign _____.

2. When one currency buys fewer units of another currency, the first currency's value _____.

3. When the value of a currency is permitted to change daily in the foreign exchange market, the country has a _____ exchange rate.

4. _____ theory asserts that exchange rate movements exactly reflect differences in the economies' rates of inflation.

5. If real interest rates in the United States rise, the dollar tends to _____.

6. A government increases the value of its currency by using its _____ _____ to buy its currency in the foreign exchange market.

7. When exchange rates are _____, governments are required to buy and sell their currency to keep its value in a narrow range.

8. The difference between the value of a country's exports of goods and its imports of goods is the _____.

9. The total balance of payments must equal _____.

10. The difference between exports and imports of all goods and services is the balance on _____.

TRUE OR FALSE

_____ 1. All international reserves are gold.

_____ 2. According to purchasing power parity theory, a dollar spent in Chicago should buy as much as a dollar, converted into francs at the market exchange rate, can buy in Paris.

_____ 3. Under the Bretton Woods System, a country with an overvalued currency lost international reserves.

_____ 4. A balance of trade deficit means imports of goods exceed exports of goods.

_____ 5. Currently, exchange rates of industrialized nations are predominantly floating exchange rates.

_____ 6. Higher rates of inflation in Germany should cause the German mark to appreciate, according to the purchasing power parity theory.

_____ 7. A depreciation of the dollar helps U.S. consumers.

_____ 8. An additional restaurant meal in Rome purchased by a U.S. citizen reduces the current account deficit.

_____ 9. The United States became a net international debtor in the 1980s.

_____ 10. The U.S. dollar rose in the period 1980–1985 because of high real interest rates in the United States.

MULTIPLE CHOICE

1. Which of the following is a capital account inflow to the United States?
   A. export of U.S.-produced machinery to a Japanese firm
   B. import of Japanese-produced machines by U.S. firms
   C. purchase of British steel by U.S. automobile company
   D. a new deposit in a savings account held by a citizen of Taiwan in a U.S. bank

2. The demand for the Japanese yen slopes downward because:
   A. Japan exports a large part of its output.
   B. Japan has trade restrictions on imports.
   C. Japanese goods cost foreign buyers less when the value of the yen declines.
   D. Japanese producers earn higher profits when the value of the yen rises.

3. Fixed exchange rates often force countries with overvalued currencies to:
   A. reduce domestic aggregate demand and income.
   B. cut taxes.
   C. cut interest rates.
   D. buy foreign assets.

4. Which of the following is most likely true when the quantity supplied of U.S. dollars exceeds the quantity demanded?
   A. The United States has a current account deficit.
   B. The United States is exporting capital.
   C. The dollar's exchange rate is too low.
   D. All alternatives are correct.

5. The purchasing power parity theory is most likely correct in which of the following circumstances?
   A. Countries consume and produce identical products.
   B. Countries do not trade.
   C. All transactions are barter.
   D. Exchange rates are fixed.

6. An increase in real interest rates in Great Britain causes:
   A. an increased supply of pounds.
   B. a decreased supply of dollars.
   C. an increased demand for pounds.
   D. a decreased demand for pounds.

7. Suppose U.S. prices increase 5 percent next year and Japanese prices remain constant. According to the purchasing power parity theory:
   A. the dollar will depreciate 5 percent against the yen.
   B. the dollar will appreciate 5 percent against the yen.
   C. the exchange rate will stay constant because it is fixed.
   D. Insufficient information is given to predict the outcome.

8. The burgeoning U.S. trade deficits of the middle 1980s were triggered mainly by:
   A. rising inflation in the United States.
   B. declining inflation in the United States.
   C. rising interest rates in Europe.
   D. capital inflows into the United States, which caused the dollar to appreciate.

9. Suppose the United States takes strong measures to reduce the federal budget deficit. The following reactions are likely to occur:
   A. U.S. interest rates rise and the dollar appreciates.
   B. U.S. interest rates rise and the dollar depreciates.
   C. U.S. interest rates fall and the dollar depreciates.
   D. U.S. interest rates fall and the dollar appreciates.

10. Which of the following would contribute toward an easing of the LDC debt crisis?
   A. Interest rates in the United States rise.
   B. The world economy expands strongly.
   C. A recession occurs in the United States.
   D. None of the above work to improve LDC conditions.

PROBLEMS

1. For each of the following, calculate the exchange rate that corresponds to the one provided. For example, when $1 costs 5 marks, 1 mark costs $.20.
   a. When $1 costs 4 francs, 1 franc costs _____.
   b. When $1 costs .5 British pound, 1 British pound costs _____.
   c. When $1 costs 100 yen, 1 yen costs _____.
   d. When 1 peso costs $.001, $1 costs _____.
   e. When 1 ruble costs $1.50, $1 costs _____.

2. Listed are ten events that influence the value of the dollar relative to the German mark. For each event indicate which curve (demand or supply) in the market for dollars shifts, the direction of the shift (increase or decrease), and the impact on the equilibrium value of the dollar (appreciate or depreciate).
   a. German automobiles become more popular in the United States. As a result, imports from Germany rise.
      Curve:_____ Shift:_____ Dollar:_____
   b. The United States experiences a rapid increase in its inflation rate while Germany has no inflation.
      Curve:_____ Shift:_____ Dollar:_____
   c. Real interest rates decline in Germany.
      Curve:_____ Shift:_____ Dollar:_____
   d. The U.S. imposes quotas on German steel, reducing the amount imported.
      Curve:_____ Shift:_____ Dollar:_____
   e. A recession hits Germany while U.S. output continues to grow. (Assume interest rates remain constant.)
      Curve:_____ Shift:_____ Dollar:_____
   f. The U.S. budget deficit falls dramatically, reducing real interest rates in the United States.
      Curve:_____ Shift:_____ Dollar:_____
   g. Many people begin to expect a major purchase of German-made rifles by the U.S. Army.
      Curve:_____ Shift:_____ Dollar:_____
   h. U.S. unemployment rises and income falls. (Assume interest rates remain constant.)
      Curve:_____ Shift:_____ Dollar:_____
   i. Germany agrees to reduce its tariff on U.S. wheat.
      Curve:_____ Shift:_____ Dollar:_____
   j. Speculators believe that Germany will soon experience inflation because of rapid growth of money supply.
      Curve:_____ Shift:_____ Dollar:_____

Answers

TRUE OR FALSE

1. False. International reserves include gold and foreign currencies held by a government.
2. True. According to purchasing power parity, exchange rates exactly reflect differences in the purchasing power of a currency.
3. True. A country with an overvalued currency was forced to purchase its currency with its international reserves in order to prevent its currency from depreciating.
4. True. A country has a balance of trade deficit when it imports more than it exports.
5. True. Currently, most developed countries allow the value of their currency to change daily in the foreign exchange market.
6. False. Purchasing power parity asserts that a currency's exchange rate *depreciates* when inflation escalates.
7. False. When the dollar depreciates, it buys fewer units of foreign currency. This means the price of foreign products rises in the United States, hurting consumers.
8. False. When an American spends money abroad, this is regarded as an import of a service. It increases the current account deficit.
9. True. By 1984, the stock of American assets owned by foreigners exceeded the stock of foreign assets owned by Americans. The United States became a net international debtor.
10. True. Because of rising budget deficits and other factors, U.S. real interest rates rose sharply in the early 1980s. This attracted foreign money and drove up the dollar.

MULTIPLE CHOICE

1. D. Capital inflows include increases in ownership of U.S. financial assets by citizens of foreign countries.
2. C. The quantity demanded of yen increases as the price of yen declines because foreign consumers demand a larger quantity of Japanese goods when the yen and, thus, the price of Japanese goods, fall.
3. A. By reducing aggregate demand and income, the demand for imports declines as does the supply of the economy's currency on the foreign exchange market. As a result, the value of the currency strengthens.
4. A. If the quantity supplied of U.S. dollars exceeds the quantity demanded, U.S. consumers are buying more goods and services overseas than foreign buyers are buying in the United States.
5. A. PPP theory is most likely to be confirmed when countries produce and export identical products.
6. C. Higher British real interest rates make pounds more attractive to foreigners, thereby increasing demand for pounds.
7. A. Because U.S. prices increase 5 percent faster than Japanese prices, PPP theory predicts a 5 percent depreciation in the U.S. dollar.
8. D. Extremely high U.S. real interest rates induced a large capital inflow in the United States. This caused the dollar to appreciate sharply during 1981–1985, which triggered the trade deficits.
9. C. If the U.S. budget deficit were sharply reduced, American interest rates would fall. This would reduce foreign demand for U.S. assets, increase U.S. demand for foreign assets, and cause the dollar to depreciate.
10. B. An expanding world economy would pull up the demand for the products produced for export by LDCs, thus generating expanding export earnings for the LDCs.

PROBLEMS

1. a. When $1 costs 4 francs, 1 franc costs $1/4 = **$.25**.
    b. When $1 costs .5 pound, 1 pound costs $1/.5 = **$2**.
    c. When $1 costs 100 yen, 1 yen costs $1/100 = **$.01**.
    d. When 1 peso costs $.001, $1 costs 1/.001 = **1,000 pesos**.
    e. When 1 ruble costs $1.50, $1 costs 1/1.5 = **.666 rubles**.

2. a. The **supply of dollars increases** and the dollar **depreciates** as people demand more marks in order to buy German cars.
    b. The **demand for dollars decreases** and the dollar **depreciates**. Inflation makes U.S. goods less attractive to German consumers, which reduces the demand for dollars. (Also, supply of dollars increases.)
    c. The **supply of dollars decreases** and the dollar **appreciates**. Lower German real interest rates reduce the attractiveness of making loans in Germany. U.S. lenders demand fewer marks and supply fewer dollars. (Also, demand for dollars increases.)
    d. The **supply of dollars decreases** and the dollar **appreciates**. A quota on German steel reduces the amount of steel imported. As a result, the demand for marks falls and the supply of dollars falls.
    e. The **demand for dollars decreases** and the dollar **depreciates**. A recession in Germany reduces the demand for U.S. goods, which reduces the demand for dollars.
    f. The **demand for dollars decreases** and the dollar **depreciates**. Lower real interest rates in the United States make it less attractive to make loans in the United States. German lenders thus demand fewer dollars.
    g. The **supply of dollar increases, the demand for dollars decreases**, and the dollar **depreciates**. Speculators, anticipating a fall in the value of the dollar because of increased imports, supply (sell) dollars to buy other currencies and demand (buy) fewer dollars. Each event causes the value of the dollar to fall.
    h. The **supply of dollars decreases** and the dollar **appreciates**. Higher unemployment and lower income in the United States reduce the demand for imported items and reduce the supply of dollars.
    i. The **demand for dollars increases** and the dollar **appreciates**. Lower German tariffs on U.S. wheat increase the demand for U.S. wheat and increase the demand for dollars.
    j. The **demand for dollars increases, the supply of dollars decreases**, and the dollar **appreciates**. Inflation in Germany reduces the value of the mark and increases the value of the dollar. Speculators demand (buy) more dollars and supply (sell) fewer dollars in anticipation of the higher value of the dollar. As a result, the dollar rises in value.

CHAPTER 39

Economics of
Less-Developed Countries

The economic problems in the United States that have until now dominated the discussion in this textbook pale in significance compared to the problems in most of the world. Three-fourths of the world's population live in less-developed countries—countries whose living standards are only a small fraction of those of the United States, Japan, and European countries. Although such issues as monetary policy, regulation of monopoly, and the environment are important to developed nations, most of the world's economies are preoccupied with trying to achieve a decent standard of living for their people.

Chapter 39 describes the economic circumstances in less-developed countries and explains the forces that distinguish developed from less-developed countries. This chapter pays special attention to the problem of population growth in LDCs. It outlines policies that less developed, as well as industrial nations can follow to increase the standards of living in LDCs.

CHAPTER OUTLINE

I. Classifying Countries
    A. Categories:
        1. Developed countries—of which there are about 25—have applied science-based technologies to all major sectors of the economy and, as a consequence, enjoy high production per worker and high living standards.
        2. **Less-developed countries (LDCs)** have low living standards because science-based technology generally has not been applied to production processes. Output per worker is very low.
    B. Classification:
        1. Countries are classified on the basis of output per capita.
        2. No exact criteria exist for dividing countries into "developed" and "less-developed" categories.
        3. There is more variation of per-capita income within the less-developed category than within the developed category.
    C. Measuring Per-Capita Income
        1. Using Foreign Exchange Rates
            a. Per-capita income is calculated for each country using its own currency. This per-capita income value is then converted to a value expressed using a common currency, usually the U.S. dollar, using actual foreign exchange rates.

b. This technique makes the gap in per-capita income between rich and poor countries appear unrealistically large because foreign exchange rates are inaccurate indicators of the relative purchasing powers of currencies.

    c. Foreign exchange rates tend to underestimate the purchasing power of currencies in LDCs because exchange rates measure the relative value of internationally traded goods only. Nontraded goods and services are relatively low priced in LDCs.

  2. Using Purchasing Power Exchange Rates

    a. Purchasing power exchange rates take account of all goods consumed in each economy—traded and nontraded.

    b. Using purchasing power exchange rates significantly reduces the measured gap in per-capita income between developed and less-developed countries. But the remaining gap is still enormous.

D. The gap in per-capita income between the developed and less-developed economies developed over the last 150–200 years because of a moderate rise in the rate of growth in developed economies.

II. Characteristics of Less-Developed Countries

A. Although income and production per capita are low in LDCs, there are other characteristics that also distinguish LDCs.

  1. Infant mortality rates are high. The **infant mortality rate** is the number of children who die before their first birthday per 1,000 births.

  2. Closely related to high infant mortality is short life expectancy. The average life ends after 45–50 years in LDCs, compared to more than 70 years in developed countries.

  3. Often water is unclean, waste disposal unsanitary, and food inadequate in LDCs.

  4. Schooling is limited. Elementary education is widely available, but secondary education is not. Teachers are often ill trained and poorly educated.

  5. Energy use is very low, corresponding to the low levels of production. Any future economic development and increase in energy consumption will add to pollution and natural resource depletion problems on the earth.

B. Rapid Population Growth

  1. Demographic Transition

    a. **Demographic transition** is the transition from a society experiencing high birth and death rates to low birth and death rates.

    b. Phases of Demographic Transition:

      i. *Phase 1* occurs when birth and death rates are high.

      ii. *Phase 2* occurs when death rates have declined but birthrates remain high. Because the decline in birthrates occurs after the decline in death rates, population growth is rapid.

      iii. *Phase 3* occurs when both death rates and birthrates are low.

  2. Population Growth in LDCs

    a. Currently, most LDCs are in *Phase 2* of the demographic transition.

    b. Birthrates remain high in LDCs primarily because parents often desire many children. Children are productive assets in an agrarian society and provide support in old age.

    c. Parents have not yet learned that, because of lower death rates, they need fewer births to provide the workers and old-age support desired.

  3. Consequences of Rapid Population Growth

    a. A High Dependency Rate

      i. The **dependency rate** is the number of nonworkers per 100 workers in the population. The number of nonworkers is measured by those individuals 14 or younger or 65 or older.

      ii. Typically, a worker in an LDC has twice as many nonworkers to support as a worker in a developed economy.

    b. Population Momentum

       i. **Population momentum** is the tendency of a population to continue to increase after the fertility rate has reached the replacement level. The **replacement level of fertility** is two children per couple, the fertility level that exactly replaces the parents.

      ii. Population momentum occurs because, when population growth is rapid, a large proportion of the population is at or below the childbearing age. As a result, even if each female has only two children, population continues to grow.

  c. Rapid population growth causes the labor force to grow rapidly. Because this slows the growth of the capital/labor ratio, growth of labor productivity (that is, output per hour of work) slows.

  C. A Large Agricultural Sector

    1. One of the most consistent indicators of development is the proportion of the population engaged in agriculture. The more highly developed a country, the smaller the proportion of the population that is engaged in agriculture.

    2. In most LDCs, 50 to 80 percent of the population is engaged in agriculture; in developed countries, the proportion is less than 10 percent.

    3. The large proportion of the labor force engaged in agriculture is a result of the large proportion of income spent on food in LDCs.

    4. The *number* of people engaged in agriculture continues to rise for a while after the *proportion* of people in farming begins to decline. As a result, the agricultural sector in LDCs must employ a larger and larger number of people in the future.

III. Growth Theory for Less-Developed Countries

  A. Economic Growth

    1. Economic growth is represented by an outward shift of the economy's production possibilities curve.

    2. For economic growth to raise standards of living, the outward shift of the production possibilities curve must be caused by something other than population growth.

  B. Causes of Economic Growth

    1. Natural Resources

      a. Increased use of natural resources causes economic growth.

      b. If the natural resource is exhaustible (for example, oil or coal), economic growth is not sustainable. If the natural resource is nonexhaustible (for example, timber and water), properly managed use of the resources can create sustained economic growth.

      c. Some LDCs have very limited amounts of unused land available or find that increased cultivation of land creates other serious problems.

    2. Capital

      a. Growth in physical capital—machines, tools, and the like—is important for increasing output per worker.

      b. To be most effective, the labor force must be trained to use the capital.

    3. Labor

      a. A larger labor force creates economic growth. But labor-force increases are subject to diminishing returns: a 10 percent increase in the labor force causes output to increase by less than 10 percent. As a result, output per worker falls.

      b. Because a greater labor force causes output to rise does not mean that LDCs have a shortage of labor, as some assert. Increasing standards of living require output to grow more rapidly than the labor force.

      c. Improving the quality of labor by adding to people's health and training also generates economic growth.

    4. Technology

      a. LDCs increase growth by adapting science-based technologies to production.

      b. The LDCs do not need to develop new technologies, as there are many already available. Unfortunately, many new technologies are developed in and for more-advanced economies and are inappropriate for LDCs.

IV. LDC Development Policies
  A. Basic Requirements:
    1. The government must provide minimal amounts of national and personal security.
    2. The government must be committed to helping all citizens, not just a few. Policies intended to help only the elite do not generate economic growth.
    3. The government must be committed to good economic policies—policies that lead to efficient resource allocation.
  B. Public Investments
    1. The government is responsible for providing such social overhead capital as roads, public health, and research.
    2. Government funds must be allocated so that projects with the greatest return receive the most funding.
  C. Appropriate Economic Policies
    1. Most economic decisions are made by individuals. It is the government's responsibility to set the appropriate environment for such decisions so that they result in the best allocation of resources.
    2. Domestic policies must allow output prices to accurately reflect resource costs and individual desires. Input prices must accurately reflect the scarcity of these inputs.
    3. International policies require that the country's exchange rate not be overvalued. An overvalued exchange rate encourages imports and discourages exports, and so discourages development of industries.
    4. To enhance international specialization, all countries—developed and less developed—should avoid tariffs, quotas, and subsidies that distort prices and misallocate resources.
    5. Studies comparing growth rates for various LDCs indicate that countries grow faster when investment is high, levels of education are high, and policies distorting prices are few.
  D. Role of Developed Countries
    1. Developed countries are a source of investment funds for physical and human capital for LDCs. Funds are available from private investors, governments, and international agencies.
    2. Developed countries also aid LDCs by providing open markets. Free international trade allows LDCs to take advantage of their comparative advantages and allows resources to be allocated efficiently.
    3. Lenin's exploitation theory argues that developed, capitalist countries grew rich by exploiting the resources of LDCs. If true, LDCs should avoid economic contacts with developed, capitalist economies and establish socialist economies. Mainstream economists reject Lenin's theory.

FILL IN THE BLANK

per-capita output	1. Countries are classified as developed or less developed on the basis of _____.
25	2. There are about _____ developed economies.
overestimate or exaggerate	3. Comparisons of per-capita income based on actual foreign exchange rates _____ the gap between developed and less-developed economies.
demographic transition	4. The change from high birth and death rates to low birth and death rates is called the _____.
dependency rate	5. The number of nonworkers per 100 workers is the _____ _____.
replacement	6. Two children per family is the _____ level of fertility.
living standards	7. Increases in population and the labor force cause economic growth but do not increase _____.

rapid   8. Most LDCs have _____ rates of population
                                   growth.

infant mortality   9. The number of babies who die before their first birthday per 1,000 live births
                                   is the _____ rate.

exploitation theory   10. According to Lenin's _____, LDCs are
                                   poor primarily because of their contacts with capitalist economies.

TRUE OR FALSE

_____   1. The majority of the world's population lives in less-developed countries.

_____   2. Purchasing power exchange rates include all products—traded and nontraded—in the calculation
             of relative purchasing power.

_____   3. The gap between developed and less-developed countries has existed for at least 500 years.

_____   4. The range of standards of living among LDCs is narrower than among developed countries.

_____   5. Death rates tend to fall before birthrates fall during demographic transition.

_____   6. Government economic policies that change market prices have historically tended to improve
             growth rates in LDCs.

_____   7. Because of diminishing returns in agriculture, additional agricultural workers lower per-capita
             output.

_____   8. Most production and consumption in LDCs involve agriculture and food.

_____   9. The economic gap between developed and less-developed countries resulted from a slowing of the
             LDCs' growth rates.

_____ 10. LDCs may simply copy all science-based technologies of developed countries in order to increase
             growth.

MULTIPLE CHOICE

1. More rapid economic development in LDCs will most likely cause:
   A. more rapid population growth.
   B. reduced literacy.
   C. increased environmental damage.
   D. greater inflation.

2. Which of the following does *not* contribute to faster economic growth?
   A. more education
   B. higher tariffs
   C. more investment
   D. fewer price distortions

3. Evidence indicates that families in LDCs have high birthrates because they:
   A. desire many children.
   B. have no access to birth control.
   C. do not want higher standards of living.
   D. receive subsidies from the government.

4. Developed countries can help LDCs by:
   A. lowering tariffs on products produced in LDCs.
   B. providing investment funds.
   C. training local managers.
   D. All alternatives are correct.

5. Which of the following is an example of social overhead capital?
   A. roads
   B. machines
   C. automobiles
   D. food

6. Population momentum is the increase in population:
   A. that occurs after the fertility rate falls to the replacement rate.
   B. caused by rising birthrates as income rises.
   C. caused by longer life expectancy in less-developed countries.
   D. caused by the absence of birth control.

7. Compared to developed countries, LDCs have:
   A. fewer workers per nonworker.
   B. a larger percentage of their population in agriculture.
   C. higher infant mortality.
   D. All alternatives are correct.

8. Population increases in LDCs:
   A. cause economic growth.
   B. reduce per-capital output.
   C. are caused primarily by falling death rates.
   D. All alternatives are correct.

9. The demographic transition:
   A. is complete in LDCs.
   B. lowers death rates before lowering birthrates.
   C. occurs only with the introduction of social security programs.
   D. has no impact on the population of LDCs.

10. After the demographic transition:
    A. birth and death rates are high.
    B. birth and death rates are low.
    C. birthrates are high and death rates are low.
    D. birthrates are low and death rates are high.

Answers

TRUE OR FALSE

1. True. About 75 percent of the world's population lives in LDCs.

2. True. Purchasing power exchange rates are considered more accurate because they include the value of both traded and nontraded goods and services.

3. False. The economic gap between developed and less-developed countries has existed for only 150–200 years.

4. False. The range of living standards is greater among the LDCs than among the developed economies.

5. True. Lower death rates caused by improved sanitary conditions, better health care, and better diets occur before birthrates fall. As a consequence, population grows.

6. False. Evidence indicates that policies that distort prices tend to lower rates of economic growth.

7. True. Because marginal product is less than average product, additional workers add less than the average to output. Output per worker declines.

8. True. More than one-half of all workers are engaged in agriculture, and more than one-half of all income is spent on food.

9. False. The gap developed because of an increase in the growth of (now) developed economies.

10. False. Not all science-based technologies used in developed countries are appropriate for LDCs because they have been developed for economies that are richer in human capital than are LDCs.

MULTIPLE CHOICE

1. C. Faster economic growth in LDCs will increase their demand for natural resources and contribute to damage to the environment.

2. B. Tariffs distort prices, which, evidence indicates, tends to inhibit economic growth.

3. A. Because children become workers for the family and provide support in old age, families in LDC's desire many children.

4. D. By lowering tariffs, developed countries increase income in LDCs. Investment funds and training increase the resources of an economy.

5. A. Social overhead capital provides widespread benefits that are not easily financed by charging the beneficiaries of the expenditure. Roads and other infrastructure are examples.

6. A. Population momentum occurs because there are a disproportionate number of females of childbearing age. Even after the fertility rate falls to the replacement rate, population keeps growing for a period.

7. D. LDCs tend to have a higher dependency rate, a larger agricultural sector, and higher infant mortality than developed countries.

8. D. Population increases, which are primarily caused by lower death rates, cause economic growth (though not increases in living standards) and tend to lower per-capita output.

9. B. Death rates fall before birthrates, which causes population to rise during the demographic transition.

10. B. The demographic transition involves a transition from high birth and death rates to low birth and death rates.

CHAPTER 40

Economic Systems—Transformation of Command Economies

Until very recently, much of the world's population lived in countries where the principles presented in this book did not apply. The ideas that the leaders of these communist countries followed were those of Karl Marx, not Adam Smith. The recent economic breakdowns in the Soviet Union and Eastern Europe have forced these countries to reevaluate their commitment to a command economy and search for an alternative economic organization.

Chapter 40 begins with a presentation of the ideas of Marx and how they were applied in the command economies of the Soviet Union and Eastern Europe. Next, it examines the forces that led to the recent economic collapse in the communist countries. This chapter closes with a description of the economic reforms in China, Russia, and Eastern Europe, and a summary of the steps needed for the transition to capitalism to be successful.

CHAPTER OUTLINE

I. Origins of the Command Economy
    A. Revolution in Less-Developed Areas
        1. Contrary to the predictions of Karl Marx, communism first appeared in less-developed countries.
            a. Marx predicted that the communist revolution would occur after capitalism had fully developed mass production.
            b. Capitalism, Marx believed, would create a class of dissatisfied industrial workers called the **proletariat.**
            c. In fact, Communist parties first took power in less-developed countries such as Russia and China.
        2. The fact that communism developed in less-developed economies explains the use of the **Stalinist growth model**, which aims at rapid economic growth by collectivizing agriculture and concentrating investment spending on heavy industry.
    B. Role of Marxian Ideology
        1. Marx's Critique of Capitalism
            a. Capitalism exploits labor because labor, which produces all value, does not receive all the value. Instead, wages are held to abnormally low levels by an "army of unemployed," which allows capitalists to extract an unearned surplus (profit) for their own use.
            b. Workers are alienated under capitalism because division of labor makes jobs routine, repetitive, and uninteresting.
            c. Capitalism is inefficient because of the business cycles and unemployment that are caused by the inability of workers to buy the output they produced.

        d. Capitalism does have the advantage of being highly productive. But the market system involves wasteful competition and bankruptcy. An **industrial policy** whereby the government targets certain parts of the economy for economic expansion through investment and other means improves the allocation of resources.

   2. Socialism and Communism

      a. Marx's Communist Utopia

         i. The ultimate goal for a Marxian economy is a **communist utopia**, which is an ideal society without economic classes and with all people realizing their full potential as creative human beings.

        ii. Marx did not describe in detail how such a society would work, although egalitarianism, absence of "unearned income," elimination of unemployment and business cycles, and worker participation in decision making were mentioned.

      b. Socialist Economy

         i. An intermediate stage between capitalism and the communist utopia was the **socialist economy** in which workers would be paid according to their work while the state would control the capital.

        ii. Because communism arose in less-developed countries, Communist Party leaders had to develop the highly productive economy that Marx envisioned would be developed by capitalism.

        iii. Lenin, under the New Economic Policy, allowed some markets in Russia to combat shortages. Stalin eliminated most markets in a drive toward industrialization and collective agriculture.

C. The Push for Growth and the Stalinist Growth Model

   1. The Ideal of Central Planning

      a. Central planning under socialism determines the allocation of resources, replacing the "invisible hand" of the market.

      b. Under Stalin, central planners primarily directed resources to heavy industry rather than consumer goods. Consumers were forced to save because they were offered only a limited range of goods and services to buy.

      c. Centralized political power restricted the ability of consumers to complain about the allocation of resources.

   2. Stalin's Industrial Policy

      a. Stalin's central planners favored large, industrial projects under the belief that such projects:

         i. created the abundance evident in capitalistic economies.

         ii. were needed to take advantage of scale economies.

         iii. internalize externalities.

         iv. provide the stability needed to avoid business cycles and unemployment.

      b. Central planners ignored the benefits of innovation and flexibility that small and medium-sized firms create.

   3. Compromises in the Stalin Growth Model

      a. Markets did not disappear under the Stalin growth model.

      b. All resources were not allocated through central planning.

      c. Material incentives were used rather than moral incentives. **Moral incentives** promote desirable behavior by appealing to the individual's responsibility to society and by raising the individual's social stature within the community.

D. Success and Emulation

   1. Russia and China were able to grow rapidly until the 1970s, and made dramatic achievements in science, space, and military equipment.

   2. During the 1970s and 1980s growth slowed, with standards of living stuck at less than a third of that in the United States.

II. Stagnation Under the Stalinist Model

A. Borrowing from the Future

   1. Rapid industrialization in the Soviet Union represented only an illusion of success.

a. Standards of living for consumers failed to improve dramatically because the industrialization was not undertaken to enable the economy eventually to produce more consumption goods.

b. Rather than consumption goods, industrialization produced such highly visible outputs as steel, energy, and military hardware in order to demonstrate the success of socialism.

2. Agriculture and infrastructure investment were neglected in the pursuit of rapid industrialization.

3. The environment incurred excessive damage as industrialization progressed.

B. Neglect of Agriculture

1. Collectivized agriculture failed as the result of inadequate incentives and an inefficient bureaucracy.

2. In an attempt to keep food prices low, farmers were paid low prices and consumers were further subsidized through even lower retail prices.

C. Lack of Technological Progress

1. Soviet economic growth relied on **extensive growth**, which is growth caused by increasing use of labor, capital, and natural resources, rather than **intensive growth**, which is growth attributable to improved technologies.

2. The failure to develop new technologies is related to the:

a. Inability to convert basic research to practical applications.

b. Excessive emphasis on heavy industry, where technological improvements were less likely.

3. Reliance on extensive growth made economic progress more difficult because of diminishing returns to investment in physical capital.

D. Perverse Incentives in Industry

1. Over-Centralization of Planning: As the variety of products expanded, it became impossible for central planners to keep track of all outputs and their input requirements. Waste and misallocation of resources resulted.

2. Problems in Enterprise Management

a. The political and economic domination of the Communist Party made managers more concerned with pleasing party officials than customers.

b. Plant managers were given little responsibility and showed little initiative, exhibited shortsightedness, and were unable to induce workers to work hard.

c. Instructions to managers were never complete enough to avoid waste or poor quality.

3. Distorted Prices and Shortages

a. Prices did not reflect scarcity values, as planners were unable to adjust prices to changing conditions.

b. The prices of poor quality goods were perceived as too high by consumers.

c. Most goods had prices that were too low relative to production costs. This was made possible by **soft budgets**, which were flexible, almost unlimited budgets for producers. Soft budgets allowed managers to avoid bankruptcy and failure.

d. Shortages of inputs occurred because inputs were hoarded in order to protect against unforeseen events.

e. Prices, deliberately kept low in order to subsidize consumers, created shortages. Contributing to shortages were payments to workers in excess of the value of the output that was available for purchase.

III. Attempting Reform in Command Economies

A. Reforms in the Soviet Union and China

1. The economic reforms in the Soviet Union started by Mikhail Gorbachev are named "perestroika." In China, the reforms of Deng Xiaoping are called the **responsibility system**. The responsibility system links monetary rewards more closely to the work performed. In China, this has led to a system of family farming based on long-term leases of land.

2. Each reform emphasizes less bureaucratic control and decentralized decision making.

B. Elements of Communist Reform Programs

1. Greater Material Incentives

a. Pay is increasingly linked to productivity.

      b. But workers have little incentive to earn higher pay without there being more goods available to buy.

  2. More Private Economic Activity

      a. Agricultural markets in China were freed. Soon, agricultural output doubled and peasant incomes tripled.

      b. In Russia, production of consumer products and services on a small scale has been allowed. Only individual, family, and cooperative organizations are allowed.

  3. Increased Autonomy for State Enterprises

      a. China and Russia have attempted to force managers to become efficient and responsible by instituting a "self-finance" system.

      b. Managers are encouraged to look to the market rather than bureaucrats for information and incentives.

      c. The market would also limit the power of managers by requiring businesses to close if they incur losses.

C. Opposition to Reform

  1. Market Problems

      a. Some worry about the problems of inequity, inflation, and unemployment that Marxists often cite as failings of capitalism.

      b. Central planners, who control the key levers in the economy, did not want to give up their power to a free market.

  2. A Regulated Market?

      a. Reformers often prefer a regulated market, where the government remains intimately involved in the determination of market outcomes. Only after it is shown that such interference does not work are free and open markets allowed.

      b. Price reforms, intended to make market prices accurately reflect relative scarcity, have left price-setting in the hands of bureaucrats. Because prices are not set in a free market, it is unlikely the goal of accurate prices has been achieved.

  3. The Politics of Reform

      a. Free markets function best when accompanied by political freedom. But the Communist Party did not want to give up its tightly held political control.

      b. State ownership of resources allowed Communist Party officials to maintain control over the economy. They resisted **privatization**, which would turn over government activities or state assets to the private sector.

D. Perestroika—Too Little, Too Late

  1. a. Gorbachev's economic reforms did not go far enough or fast enough to achieve success.

      b. His political reforms were more dramatic and successful.

  2. What Had Been Missing from Perestroika?

      a. Control over output and prices was never removed from the hands of bureaucrats and planners.

      b. Privatization did not occur in any meaningful way.

  3. Economic Crisis in the Soviet Bloc

      a. Production fell as central planners no longer organized production and workers stopped working.

      b. Budget deficits surged as tax receipts dropped and greater subsidies were required to avoid factory closings.

E. High Growth in Reformed China

  1. China in the 1980s enjoyed one of the highest growth rates in the world.

  2. Reform of agriculture increased productivity and incomes in rural areas.

  3. China has allowed more private development and greater contact with the outside world through international trade.

  4. Political reform has been limited.

IV. Transformation to Capitalism

  A. Little is known about how to transform a command economy into one that is capitalist.

1. Some reformers prefer "shock therapy," in which the transition period is short and market forces take over quickly.
2. Others prefer a gradual approach where central controls, subsidies, and regulations are removed slowly.

   B. Necessary Adjustments:
   1. Macroeconomic Stabilization
      a. Budget deficits must be reduced to eliminate the threat of inflation.
      b. Prices must be freed to eliminate shortages and reduce subsidies to consumers.
      c. Currency reform is needed to make the currency convertible into other currencies in order to facilitate international trade.
   2. Restructuring Industry
      a. Deeper cuts in the bureaucracy and military spending are necessary in order to produce more consumer goods.
      b. Production must be made more flexible so that the response to changes in demand and other conditions can be made more rapidly.
      c. Obsolete, inefficient capital must be replaced.
   3. Liberalization and Privatization
      a. New businesses must be encouraged to develop, financed by greater access to domestic and international funds.
      b. A legal system that protects private property, enforces contracts, and enumerates the powers of the government is needed to eliminate the threat of capricious acts by those in power.
      c. Privatization must continue.

   C. Prospects for the Former Command Economies
   1. It is clear that command economies in the form seen in the former Soviet Union and Eastern Europe have failed.
   2. Whether they can be transformed into capitalist economies depends on the willingness of their people to persevere through the transition.
      a. Some believe that the transition will fail because people have grown accustomed to taking orders rather than taking initiative.
      b. Others believe attitudes toward change will improve once markets begin to work.

FILL IN THE BLANK

labor

1. Marx believed that _____ produced all value and deserved to receive all income.

proletariat

2. According to Marx, the _____ is a class of dissatisfied workers created by capitalism.

Stalinist growth

3. Economic growth through investment in heavy industry characterizes the _____ model.

less-developed

4. Communist parties initially took control in _____ economies, contrary to Marx's predictions.

communist utopia

5. The ultimate goal for a Marxian economy is a _____ _____.

Extensive

6. _____ growth relies on more resources to create economic growth.

Intensive

7. _____ growth relies upon new technology to create economic growth.

soft budgets

Central planning

China

8. Managers of factories in the Soviet Union were able to avoid business failure and bankruptcy because of _____.

9. _____ allocates resources in socialist economies.

10. Agricultural reform in _____ resulted in a doubling of farm output.

TRUE OR FALSE

_____ 1. Marx believed that profit is justified by the productive power of capital.

_____ 2. Marx believed that capitalists create unemployment to keep wages low.

_____ 3. The communist revolutions in the Soviet Union and China occurred according to Marx's predictions.

_____ 4. The Stalinist growth model requires a large bureaucracy.

_____ 5. The Stalinist growth model initially devoted large amounts of resources to modernizing agriculture.

_____ 6. Marx praised capitalism for its ability to produce large amounts of output.

_____ 7. Managers in socialist enterprises were rewarded on the basis of the quality of their products.

_____ 8. The Stalinist growth model emphasizes extensive growth.

_____ 9. Part of the necessary reform in the former command economies is the need to lower prices on consumer goods.

_____ 10. Economic reforms in the former Soviet Union have been more successful than those in China.

MULTIPLE CHOICE

1. In Marxian economics the proletariat are:
   A. the owners of businesses.
   B. the managers of businesses.
   C. the workers.
   D. the bureaucracy.

2. The Stalinist growth model emphasizes which of the following for economic growth?
   A. new resources (particularly capital)
   B. new technologies
   C. lower unemployment
   D. improved efficiency

3. The responsibility system:
   A. places production decisions in the hands of the bureaucracy.
   B. was practiced primarily in the Soviet Union.
   C. rewards managers for work performed.
   D. keeps prices below costs of production.

4. A soft-budget constraint:
   A. links costs to profits.
   B. allows an enterprise to request additional funds if costs increase.
   C. forces managers to improve the quality of output.
   D. rewards producers who reduce costs.

5. An industrial policy involves:
   A. more resources directed toward heavy industry.
   B. the use of the invisible hand to allocate resources.
   C. the targeting of certain industries for government subsidies.
   D. the correction of externalities by industry rather than by the government.

6. In a communist utopia there are:
   A. no workers.
   B. no economic classes.
   C. no capital.
   D. no products.

7. An advantage of central planning is that it:
   A. responds quickly to changes in demand.
   B. requires a small bureaucracy.
   C. keeps enterprises small.
   D. can internalize externalities.

8. Intensive growth is produced by:
   A. population growth.
   B. development of natural resources.
   C. research and development.
   D. new capital.

9. Under central planning, a manager is most responsive to:
   A. bureaucrats.
   B. customers.
   C. exporters.
   D. importers.

10. Which of the following contributed to the failure of Gorbachev's perestroika?
    A. Workers' wages were kept too low.
    B. Privatization was insufficient.
    C. Demand for output was kept at a level below the economy's ability to produce.
    D. Bureaucratic control over the economy ended.

Answers

TRUE OR FALSE

1. False. Marx believed that profit is legitimately owed to workers because labor produces all value.

2. True. According to Marx, the "army of unemployed" keeps wages low in a capitalist economy.

3. False. Marx believed communist revolutions would occur initially in the most advanced capitalist economies, not in less-developed countries like the Soviet Union and China.

4. True. A large bureaucracy is required to process the information needed for central planning.

5. False. Agriculture was allotted few resources. Instead, resources went to industry.

6. True. Marx asserted that the capitalists' push for profit drove them to discover new technologies that were highly productive.

7. False. Managers were rewarded for fulfilling production quotas, which are expressed in terms of quantity, not quality.

8. True. The Stalinist growth model emphasizes the production of new capital to generate economic growth.

9. False. In general, prices on consumer goods were too low in the former Soviet Union. The prices do not reflect their true resource costs.

10. False. Economic reforms in China have gone farther and have been more successful than in the former Soviet Union.

MULTIPLE CHOICE

1. C. The proletariat, who were to lead the revolution, were the workers in the economy.

2. A. The Stalinist growth model primarily uses increases in resources (that is, extensive growth) to generate economic growth.

3. C. The responsibility system allows managers to make production decisions and rewards them on the basis of work performed.

4. B. A soft-budget constraint is a flexible budget constraint that allows managers to request more funds if costs rise.

5. C. An industrial policy directs government aid to certain industries that are believed to be of particular importance.

6. B. In the communist utopia there are no economic classes.

7. D. Central planning makes it possible for one decision maker to consider all consequences of an action.

8. C. Intensive growth is caused by new technologies created by research and development.

9. A. Because bureaucrats allocate resources, a manager is most responsive to their desires.

10. B. Privatization of the economy progressed at too slow a pace to allow for the development of extensive private markets.